An entirely new financial reporting system is not easy to grasp or apply. It should therefore not become a moving target. A stable platform is needed. Continuous changes in the standards are not conducive to a good, consistent and rigorous application of the standards.

The authors of this book should be commended for their efforts. The first book is always the most difficult to write. I am sure that many people will find it useful and that it will be of great help in preparing for and applying International GAAP.

September 2004 *Karel Van Hulle*

Preface

From January 2005 over 70 countries, including the entire European Union, will require the use of International Financial Reporting Standards by at least all listed companies. The world is on the threshold of having only two major financial reporting regimes, US GAAP and International GAAP, a statement that would have been considered astonishing even a decade ago, yet today seems not only obvious, but normal.

This represents an achievement by all concerned: the European Union whose leaders had the vision to set the agenda for a common financial reporting regime across the EU; the IASB's forerunner the IASC, who undertook the core standards programme that laid the groundwork for global acceptance of international standards; the many countries throughout the world whose standard-setters have contributed to the work of the IASC and the IASB; and the large number of governments who have recognised the value of a common financial reporting regime, and adopted it.

It is also an indication of the interdependence of the global economy. Investors are now easily able to make investments on a global scale, whether the investor is large or small. As a consequence, the objective of investors receiving internationally comparable financial reports has changed from being a theoretically desirable ideal to a practical necessity.

Nevertheless, a considerable task remains, and it is the responsibility of all who are involved with producing financial reports, and all who use them, as well as the standard-setters and regulators, to fulfil it. That task is to make financial reports produced under International GAAP of the highest quality, truly comparable and, consequently, as useful as possible for investors. Whilst a common approach by the market regulators is vital, regulation alone will not suffice. There has to be, in addition, an acceptance by preparers and auditors, fully supported by investors and the providers of finance, that international comparability and high quality is the responsibility of everyone involved in the reporting process. This means that all those involved with the development of IFRS into a global financial reporting framework bear a considerable responsibility to ensure that the development is evolutionary and not revolutionary. In particular, the need to ensure cross-border consistency in application, regulation and enforcement is paramount if this bold initiative is to succeed.

To an extent the most straightforward part is over. The most testing time for all concerned will start as financial reporting under IFRS moves from the theoretical to the real. To date, no substantial body of custom, practice or generally accepted ways of employing IFRS has had an opportunity to develop. Indeed, one of the challenges is to put in place a regime under which an International GAAP that is understood and commonly applied throughout the world, can develop. Paradoxically, it may be that this situation best illustrates the real meaning of GAAP in an IFRS context. A comprehensive set of International Financial Reporting Standards exists, but no GAAP as yet.

Therefore, in writing International GAAP, we have attempted to set out clearly the thinking behind each standard, the meaning of its detailed requirements, and the practical matters to be considered when applying it. We hope that it will be of value to all who need to understand and apply IFRS; and more widely, we hope it will contribute to developing an international consensus on the proper and consistent application of IFRS that alone can make it a success.

Finally, we are deeply indebted to many of our colleagues within the entire global organisation of Ernst & Young for their selfless assistance in the publication of this book. It has been a truly international effort with contributions from Ernst & Young staff in Australia, Belgium, China, Denmark, Finland, France, Germany, Hong Kong, Italy, Middle-East, Netherlands, Norway, Russia, Sweden, Switzerland, UK and the USA.

Our thanks go particularly to those who reviewed and edited drafts, most notably Richard Addison, Mauro Castelli, Tony Clifford, Macy Coffey, Dave Cook, Daniel van Cutsem, Anwaar Farooqi, Sven Hayn, Paul Hebditch, Eskild Jacobsen, Jean-Yves Jegourel, Trish LaValle, May Kassis-Morin, Ken Marshall, Eric Ohlund, Lars Pettersen, Ruth Picker, Nigel Reid, George Schleier, Denis Slepov, Eric Tarleton, Leo van der Tas, Dominique Thouvenin, Mira Tugnait, Päivi Virtanen and Ola Wahlquist. Within the Financial Reporting Group itself, our thanks go to everyone who directly and indirectly contributed to the book's creation, especially Charlotte Ashley, Denise Brand, Larissa Connor, Richard Crisp, George Goodwin, Machiel Klaarenbeek, Robert Overend, Margaret Pankhurst, Jo-Anne du Plessis and Nicola Stead.

As authors, however, we take responsibility for all the opinions expressed in the book, and the blame for all its faults.

October 2004

Mike Bonham
Matthew Curtis
Mike Davies
Pieter Dekker
Tim Denton
Richard Moore
Hedy Richards
Gregory Wilkinson-Riddle
Allister Wilson

List of chapters

Detailed contents

CHAPTER 4   FIRST-TIME ADOPTION

CHAPTER 5   CONSOLIDATED AND SEPARATE FINANCIAL STATEMENTS

CHAPTER 6   BUSINESS COMBINATIONS AND GOODWILL

CHAPTER 7   ASSOCIATES

CHAPTER 8   JOINT VENTURES

CHAPTER 9   FOREIGN EXCHANGE

CHAPTER 10   HYPERINFLATION

CHAPTER 11   INTANGIBLE ASSETS AND GOODWILL

CHAPTER 12   PROPERTY PLANT AND EQUIPMENT

CHAPTER 13 IMPAIRMENT OF FIXED ASSETS AND GOODWILL

CHAPTER 14   CAPITALISATION OF BORROWING COSTS

CHAPTER 15   FINANCIAL INSTRUMENTS: INTRODUCTION

CHAPTER 16   FINANCIAL INSTRUMENTS: RECOGNITION, DERECOGNITION AND OFFSET

CHAPTER 17   FINANCIAL INSTRUMENTS: FINANCIAL LIABILITIES
             AND EQUITY

CHAPTER 18   FINANCIAL INSTRUMENTS: MEASUREMENT

CHAPTER 19   FINANCIAL INSTRUMENTS: HEDGE ACCOUNTING

CHAPTER 20   FINANCIAL INSTRUMENTS: DISCLOSURES

CHAPTER 21   INVENTORIES

CHAPTER 22   CONSTRUCTION CONTRACTS

CHAPTER 23   LEASES

CHAPTER 24   INCOME TAXES

CHAPTER 25   PROVISIONS, CONTINGENT LIABILITIES AND CONTINGENT ASSETS

CHAPTER 26   REVENUE

CHAPTER 28   SEGMENT REPORTING

CHAPTER 29   SHARE-BASED PAYMENT

CHAPTER 30   EMPLOYEE BENEFITS

CHAPTER 31   EARNINGS PER SHARE

CHAPTER 32   CASH FLOW STATEMENTS

CHAPTER 33   RELATED PARTY DISCLOSURES

CHAPTER 34   EVENTS AFTER THE BALANCE SHEET DATE

CHAPTER 35   INTERIM REPORTING

CHAPTER 36 AGRICULTURE

Abbreviations

The following abbreviations are used in this book:

Professional and regulatory bodies:

AASB	Australian Accounting Standards Board
AICPA	American Institute of Certified Public Accountants
APB	Accounting Principles Board (of the AICPA, predecessor of the FASB)
ARC	Accounting Regulatory Committee of representatives of EU Member States
ASB	Accounting Standards Board in the UK
ASC	Accounting Standards Committee (the predecessor of the ASB)
CESR	Committee of European Securities Regulators
CICA	Canadian Institute of Chartered Accountants
EC	European Commission
EFRAG	European Financial Reporting Advisory Group
EITF	Emerging Issues Task Force in the US
EU	European Union
FAF	Financial Accounting Foundation
FASB	Financial Accounting Standards Board in the US
G4+1	The (now disbanded) group of four plus 1, actually with six members, that comprised an informal 'think tank' of standard setters from Australia, Canada, New Zealand, UK, and USA, plus the IASC
IASB	International Accounting Standards Board
IASC	International Accounting Standards Committee
ICAEW	Institute of Chartered Accountants in England and Wales
ICAS	Institute of Chartered Accountants of Scotland
IFRIC	International Financial Reporting Interpretations Committee of the IASB
IGC	Implementation Guidance Committee on IAS 39
IOSCO	International Organisation of Securities Commissions
JWG	Joint Working Group of Standard-setters

SAC   Standards Advisory Council

SEC   Securities and Exchange Commission (the US securities regulator)

SIC   Standing Interpretations Committee of the IASC (replaced by IFRIC)

Accounting related terms:

ADS   American Depositary Shares

AFS   Available-for-sale investment

ARB   Accounting Research Bulletins (issued by the AICPA)

ARS   Accounting Research Studies (issued by the APB)

CGU   Cash Generating Unit

CIS   Comprehensive Income Statement, as developed by the G4+1 group of accounting standard-setters, and published in June 1999 in the ASB Discussion Paper *Reporting Financial Performance: Proposals for Change*

CU   Currency Unit

CULS   Convertible Unsecured Loan Stock

E   Exposure Draft (of an IAS)

EBIT   Earnings Before Interest and Taxes

EBITDA   Earnings Before Interest, Taxes, Depreciation and Amortisation

ED   Exposure Draft

EPS   Earnings per Share

FAS   Financial Accounting Standards (issued by the FASB)

FC   Foreign currency

FIFO   First-In, First-Out basis of valuation

FRS   Financial Reporting Standard (issued by the ASB)

FTA   First-time Adoption

GAAP   Generally accepted accounting practice (as it applies to the UK and under IFRS), or generally accepted accounting principles (as it applies to the US)

HTM   Held-to-maturity investment

IAS   International Accounting Standard (issued by the IASC)

IFAC   International Federation of Accountants

IFRS   International Financial Reporting Standard (issued by the IASB)

IPO   Initial Public Offering

IPR&D   In-process Research and Development

IRR   Internal Rate of Return

JV   Joint Venture

LC	Local Currency
LIBOR	London Inter Bank Offered Rate
LIFO	Last-In, First-Out basis of valuation
NBV	Net Book Value
NRV	Net Realisable Value
PP&E	Property, Plant and Equipment
R&D	Research and development
SFAC	Statement of Financial Accounting Concepts (issued by the FASB as part of its conceptual framework project)
SFAS	Statement of Financial Accounting Standards (issued by the FASB)
SPE	Special Purpose Entity
SSAP	Statement of Standard Accounting Practice (issued by the ASC)
TSR	Total Shareholder Return
VIU	Value In Use
WACC	Weighted Average Cost of Capital

References to IFRSs, IASs, Interpretations and supporting documentation:

AG	Application Guidance
AV	Alternative View
B, BCZ	Basis for Conclusions
BC	Basis for Conclusions
DO	Dissenting Opinion
IE	Illustrative Examples
IG	Implementation Guidance
IN	Introduction

Authoritative literature

The content of this book takes into account all accounting standards and other relevant rules issued up to 8 October 2004. Consequently, it covers the IASB's *Framework for the Preparation and Presentation of Financial Statements* and following authoritative literature.

† The standards and interpretations marked with a dagger have been withdrawn or superseded.

IASB Framework

Framework for the Preparation and Presentation of Financial Statements

International Financial Reporting Standards

IFRS 1	First-time Adoption of International Financial Reporting Standards
IFRS 2	Share-based Payment
IFRS 3	Business Combinations
IFRS 4	Insurance Contracts
IFRS 5	Non-current Assets Held for Sale and Discontinued Operations

International Accounting Standards

	IAS 1	Presentation of Financial Statements
	IAS 2	Inventories
	IAS 7	Cash Flow Statements
	IAS 8	Accounting Policies, Changes in Accounting Estimates and Errors
	IAS 10	Events After the Balance Sheet Date
	IAS 11	Construction Contracts
	IAS 12	Income Taxes
	IAS 14	Segment Reporting
†	IAS 15	Information Reflecting the Effects of Changing Prices
	IAS 16	Property, Plant and Equipment
	IAS 17	Leases
	IAS 18	Revenue
	IAS 19	Employee Benefits
	IAS 20	Accounting for Government Grants and Disclosure of Government Assistance
	IAS 21	The Effects of Changes in Foreign Exchange Rates
†	IAS 22	Business Combinations

International Financial Reporting Interpretations Committee Interpretations

Standing Interpretations Committee Interpretations

IASB Exposure Drafts

IFRIC Exposure Drafts

Chapter 1   The development of International GAAP

1   THE EVOLUTION OF THE INTERNATIONAL ACCOUNTING STANDARDS BOARD

1.1   The Accountants International Study Group

Whilst many remarkable individuals have featured in the past 40 years' evolution of International GAAP, perhaps the single person that stands out as the visionary behind the formation of the International Accounting Standards Committee (IASC) is Lord Benson, former President of the Institute of Chartered Accountants in England and Wales (ICAEW) and Senior partner in Cooper Brothers & Co.[1] Lord Benson foresaw the importance of international accounting standards and, as President of the ICAEW, pioneered the practical steps that led to the creation, first, of the Accountants International Study Group in 1967 and, ultimately, of the International Accounting Standards Committee in 1973. Lord Benson was the first Chairman of the IASC, serving from 1973 to 1975.

The idea of the Accountants International Study Group was initiated by Lord Benson during his term as President of the ICAEW, when he unveiled his proposal publicly at the Annual Conference of the Canadian Institute of Chartered Accountants (CICA), held in August 1966. Following further discussions with the Presidents of the CICA and the American Institute of Certified Public Accountants (AICPA), the three institutes announced in January 1967 that agreement had been reached for the formation of the Study Group, with AICPA President Robert Trueblood appointed as its first Chairman.

It seems that the formation of the Group may well have been driven by Lord Benson's early conviction of the essential need for harmonised accounting and auditing rules and procedures. This first indication of Lord Benson's vision of the need for international harmonisation may be found in the Terms of Reference of the Study Group, which read as follows: 'To institute comparative studies as to accounting thought and practice in participating countries, to make reports from time to time, which, subject to the prior approval of the sponsoring Institutes, would be issued to members of those Institutes.[2] Thus, although Lord Benson was not necessarily advocating uniformity in accounting and auditing practice, he clearly did not believe that the UK, US and Canada should each be operating in their own technical vacuums without considering developments in the two other countries.

The Study Group lasted for ten years, being wound up in 1977. During its existence, it published 20 documents covering a wide range of accounting and auditing topics. These publications were, in effect, comparative studies of existing accepted practice, and the opinions expressed therein were termed 'conclusions'.

1.2   The International Accounting Standards Committee (IASC)

The origins of the IASC can be traced back to the 10th World Congress of Accountants, which was held in September 1972 in Sydney. It was here that Lord Benson – who had been asked to create an international accounting body based on the Accountants International Study Group – proposed the formation of a new body that would be responsible for the formulation of international accounting standards. Following further meetings between the Presidents of the AICPA, CICA, ICAEW and The Institute of Chartered Accountants of Scotland (ICAS) it was agreed to broaden the participation of countries in the formation of an international accounting body beyond the 'three nations' of the Study Group. Accordingly, invitations were extended to the accounting bodies in Australia, Canada, France, Germany, Japan, Mexico and the Netherlands to attend a meeting in London in March 1973.

This meeting led ultimately to the formation in June 1973 of the International Accounting Standards Committee as an independent private-sector body through an agreement made by professional accountancy bodies from Australia, Canada, France, Germany, Japan, Mexico, the Netherlands, the United Kingdom and Ireland and the United States of America. From 1983, the IASC's members included all the professional accountancy bodies that were members of the International Federation of Accountants (IFAC). At the time when the Board of the IASC was dissolved in 2001, there were 153 members in 112 countries.

The IASC was founded to formulate and publish, in the public interest, International Accounting Standards (IAS) to be observed in the presentation of published financial statements and to promote their worldwide acceptance and observance.[3] It was envisaged that IAS should be capable of worldwide acceptance and contribute to a significant improvement in the quality and comparability of corporate disclosure.[4]

Although the composition of the IASC Board changed over time, during the last part of its life the business of the IASC was conducted by a Board comprising representatives of accountancy bodies in thirteen countries (or combinations of countries) appointed by the Council of IFAC, and up to four other organisations with an interest in financial reporting. Each Board Member was permitted to nominate up to two representatives and a technical adviser to attend Board meetings. The IASC encouraged each Board Member to include in its delegation at least one person working in industry and one person who was directly involved in the work of the national standard setting body.[5] The Board also had a number of observer members (including representatives of the International Organisation of Securities Commissions (IOSCO), FASB, and the European Commission) who participated in the debate but did not vote. In 1998, the People's Republic of China became a member of IFAC and joined the IASC Board as an observer member. In 1999, IASC Board meetings were opened up to public observation.

The IASC Board established an international Consultative Group in 1981 that included representatives of international organisations of preparers and users of financial statements, stock exchanges and securities regulators. The Consultative Group met periodically to discuss the technical issues in IASC projects, the IASC's work programme and its strategy. This group played an important part in the IASC's due process for the setting of International Accounting Standards and in gaining acceptance for the resulting standards.

In 1995, the IASC established a high-level international Advisory Council, made up of outstanding individuals in senior positions from the accountancy profession, business and the other users of financial statements. The role of the Advisory Council was to promote generally the acceptability of International Accounting Standards and enhance the credibility of the IASC's work.

1.2.1 The formation of the Standing Interpretations Committee (SIC)

The IASC Board formed a Standing Interpretations Committee (SIC) in 1997 to consider, on a timely basis, accounting issues that were likely to receive divergent or unacceptable treatment in the absence of authoritative guidance. Its consideration was within the context of existing International Accounting Standards and the IASC *Framework*. In developing interpretations, the SIC consulted similar national committees that had been nominated for that purpose by Member Bodies. The SIC had up to twelve voting members from various countries, including individuals from the accountancy profession, preparer groups, user groups and accounting academics. The European Commission and the International Organisation of Securities Commissions (IOSCO) had observer seats. In 2000, SIC meetings were opened up to public observation.

The SIC considered the following criteria for taking issues on its agenda:

- the issue should involve an interpretation of an existing Standard within the context of the IASC Framework;
- the issue should have practical and widespread relevance;
- the issue should relate to a specific fact pattern; and
- significantly divergent interpretations must either be emerging or already exist in practice.

SIC interpretations were initially published in draft form for public comment (usually 60 days), and if no more than three of its voting members voted against an interpretation, the SIC asked the Board to approve the final interpretation for issue; as for International Accounting Standards, this required three-quarters of the Board to vote in favour. The SIC dealt with issues of reasonably widespread importance, not issues of concern to only a small number of businesses. The interpretations that were issued covered both mature issues, where there was unsatisfactory practice within the scope of existing International Accounting Standards, and emerging issues relating to topics not considered when the standards were developed.

1.2.2   *The IASC's comparability/improvements project*

When International Accounting Standards were first issued, they permitted several alternative accounting treatments. The principal reason for this was that the IASC viewed its initial function as prohibiting undesirable accounting practices, whilst acknowledging that there might be more than one acceptable solution to a specific accounting issue.

In 1993, the Board of the IASC completed a major project (known as the comparability/improvements project), which had set out to reduce many of the permitted alternative accounting options. This project took four years and culminated in the publication of a package of ten revised international standards, which became operative for accounting periods beginning on or after 1 January 1995. Unfortunately, this project was less successful than most had hoped it would be, and although the number of permitted alternative options was reduced, they were not eliminated; this meant that international standards still incorporated 'benchmark' treatments and 'allowed alternative' treatments. However, as discussed more fully below, the new International Accounting Standards Board (IASB) has, through its own Improvements Project, further eliminated a number of the alternative accounting treatments. Where an IAS retains alternative treatments, the IASB removed virtually all references to 'benchmark treatment' and 'allowed alternative treatment', instead using descriptive references, such as 'cost model' and 'revaluation model'.

1.3   The IASC/IOSCO agreement

An increasingly global marketplace brings with it an increasing interdependence of regulators. There must be strong links between regulators and the capacity to give effect to those links. Created in 1983, the International Organisation of Securities Commissions (IOSCO) is the world's primary forum of international cooperation for securities regulatory agencies. Its membership comprises national regulatory bodies that have day-to-day responsibility for securities regulation and the administration of securities laws in their countries. The objectives of the organisation's members are:

- to cooperate together to promote high standards of regulation in order to maintain just, efficient and sound markets;

- to exchange information on their respective experiences in order to promote the development of domestic markets;

- to unite their efforts to establish standards and an effective surveillance of international securities transactions; and

- to provide mutual assistance to promote the integrity of the markets by a rigorous application of the standards and by effective enforcement against offences.[6]

In 1989, IOSCO prepared a report entitled *International Equity Offers,* which noted that cross-border offerings would be facilitated by the development of internationally accepted accounting standards. Rather than attempt to develop those standards itself, IOSCO focused on the efforts of the IASC to provide acceptable international accounting standards for use in multinational securities offerings.

In 1993, IOSCO wrote to the IASC detailing the necessary components of a reasonably complete set of standards to create a comprehensive body of principles for enterprises undertaking cross-border securities offerings. In 1994, IOSCO completed a review of the then-current IASC standards and identified a number of issues that would have to be addressed, as well as standards that the IASC would have to improve, before IOSCO could consider recommending IASC standards for use in cross-border listings and offerings. IOSCO divided the issues into three categories:

- issues that required a solution prior to consideration by IOSCO of an endorsement of the IASC standards;

- issues that would not require resolution before IOSCO could consider endorsement, although individual jurisdictions might specify treatments that they would require if those issues were not addressed satisfactorily in the IASC standards; and

- areas where improvements could be made, but that the IASC did not need to address prior to consideration of the IASC standards by IOSCO.

In July 1995, the Board of the IASC and IOSCO's Technical Committee announced that an important milestone had been reached in the development of IAS. The Board had developed a work plan (to become known as 'the core standards work programme') that the Technical Committee agreed would result, upon successful completion, in IAS comprising a comprehensive core set of standards. Completion of comprehensive core standards that were acceptable to the Technical Committee would allow the Technical Committee to recommend the endorsement of IAS by IOSCO for cross-border capital raising and listing purposes in all global markets. IOSCO had already endorsed IAS 7 – *Cash Flow Statements* – and had indicated to the IASC that fourteen of the existing international standards did not require additional improvement, provided that the other core standards were successfully completed.[7]

Both the IASC and IOSCO agreed that there was a compelling need for high quality, comprehensive IAS. The goal of both bodies in reaching this agreement was that financial statements prepared in accordance with IAS could be used worldwide in cross border offerings and listings as an alternative to the use of national accounting standards.

The IASC Board worked extraordinarily hard over the ensuing four and a half years to fulfil its side of the IOSCO agreement. Board meetings were increased both in terms of frequency and duration, several new Steering Committees were formed and several major new projects were placed on the Board's agenda. The Board completed its revised core set of standards at its December 1998 meeting, at which IAS 39 – *Financial Instruments: Recognition and Measurement* – was approved for issue. As a result, the IOSCO review of these core standards began in 1999. In the meantime, IOSCO announced that it wished the issue of accounting for investment properties to be added to the list of core standards, and this matter was dealt with in a new standard, IAS 40 – *Investment Property* – which was approved for issue by the IASC Board at its March 2000 meeting.

So all that remained outstanding was for the IOSCO Technical Committee to announce the result of its assessment of the IASC core standards. However, at the time, many observers felt that the US Securities and Exchange Commission (SEC) was unlikely to allow IOSCO to endorse IASC standards unconditionally unless they corresponded closely to existing US standards. A more likely scenario was that some or all of the IASC standards would be accepted by the SEC only on the basis of additional disclosures and other conditions. Such an attitude was likely to have been reinforced by a FASB publication that claimed to have identified 255 differences between US GAAP and IASC standards.[8]

1.4 The SEC Concept Release on International Accounting Standards

Whilst the financial reporting world was waiting for IOSCO's Technical Committee to complete its assessment of the IASC's core standards and to declare its likely attitude towards recognising the new body of IAS without requiring reconciliation to national standards, the US Securities and Exchange Commission (SEC) appeared to pre-empt what was to come by publishing in February 2000 a 'Concept Release' on International Accounting Standards.[9]

The Concept Release set out the hurdles IAS would have to clear if they were to be deemed acceptable for US filing purposes. The document was mainly in the form of a series of questions apparently seeking opinions about, and experiences of, using, IAS. However, although it claimed to be seeking input to determine under what conditions the SEC 'should accept financial statements of foreign private issuers that are prepared using the standards promulgated by the International Accounting Standards Committee', in reality it discussed a number of other matters related to the financial reporting environment, such as auditing standards, audit quality assurance, regulation and enforcement.

There is little doubt that the SEC would argue that its Release was objective and fair-minded. Indeed, it started out in a noble enough manner: 'The globalisation of the securities markets has challenged securities regulators around the world to adapt to meet the needs of market participants while maintaining the current high levels of investor protection and market integrity'. This sentence contained two main statements; first, the challenge for securities regulators to adapt and, second, an assertion that, in general, levels of investor protection and market integrity are currently high.

However, what followed these encouraging statements was an elaborate exposition on why the SEC should not itself adapt in order to help realise the globalisation aim. Furthermore, it seemed to follow from the SEC's views about the need for changes (i.e. improvements) in what it called 'infrastructure support' that the SEC did not in fact believe that there are high levels of investor protection and market integrity outside the US.

Of course, the central issue at hand was essentially whether the SEC should accept financial statements prepared under IAS. Instead of responding directly to this question and looking for ways of adapting its own approach as a basis for embracing IAS, the SEC's view seemed to be that the world should adopt its philosophy of regulation. However, it made no suggestions as to how this should be done, or by whom. Although the SEC at one point stated that it was not focusing on differences between IAS and US GAAP, elsewhere it made it clear that differences between IAS and US GAAP were less than desirable, and clearly implied that the benchmark that IAS needed to meet was US GAAP.

Unfortunately, this posture led some commentators to the inescapable conclusion that the SEC was in favour of adaptation – but by everyone except the SEC. It seemed that countries that wished to adapt and progress in relation to IAS should do so separately and apart from the SEC.

The phase 'high quality' was a recurring theme throughout the Release. However, on occasion, it seemed to be used to the point of being overdone. This is because no one would disagree with the need for high quality accounting standards in the context of the global financial markets. The problem, though, was that the Release used the phase 'high quality' in a somewhat pejorative manner.

This was achieved by the implicit assumption within the Release that the US model meets the criteria for high quality, and that any other model, being different, by definition does not. The inference inevitably to be drawn by readers of the Release was that US standards are high quality standards; the US system of formulating and explaining standards is best; any standards that are different, or differently formulated and explained, are lesser quality standards; US standards give better investor protection than other standards; and regulation and enforcement of standards and the auditing profession is better in the US than anywhere else.

The SEC position centred on investor protection and the pre-eminence of US GAAP, and its regulatory and enforcement regime in delivering it. Therefore, the clear message was that companies must use US GAAP if they want to raise capital in the US – at least companies must produce a US GAAP reconciliation, which is tantamount to the same thing – or else investors will be at risk.

The Concept Release attracted numerous letters of response, many of which expressed views that were unsupportive of the general thrust of the document. Although there was never any follow-up to the Release by the SEC, it nevertheless appeared to set the scene for what was to come three months later in IOSCO's Assessment Report on IAS.

1.5   The IOSCO Assessment Report on International Accounting Standards

The IOSCO assessment should be seen in the context of the then situation regarding the acceptance of IAS by the international capital markets. The reality was that many of the world's stock exchanges – including, the European Union exchanges, Sydney and Zurich – already accepted IAS financial statements for cross-border listing purposes without reconciliation to national GAAP. The only significant exceptions were the exchanges in Canada and the USA. Consequently, a large part of the IOSCO effort was directed towards gaining the acceptance of the North American securities regulators.

In May 2000, IOSCO announced the completion of its assessment of the IASC's core standards through the publication by IOSCO's Technical Committee of a report that summarised its assessment work.[10] In view of the SEC Concept Release that had been issued three months earlier (see above), the outcome of the Technical Committee's assessment of the IASC's core standards was perhaps not unexpected. Nevertheless, its content was a great disappointment to many observers and those that had been involved in the core standards programme, who believed that the IASC Board had, in good faith, fulfilled all its obligations under the IOSCO agreement.

The report stated that IOSCO had assessed 30 IASC standards, including their related interpretations (termed 'the IASC 2000 standards'), and considered their suitability for use in cross-border offerings and listings. Although the report recommended that IOSCO members permit incoming multinational issuers to use the IASC 2000 standards to prepare their financial statements for cross-border offerings and listings, this recommendation was made subject to a significant proviso. The proviso was that each IOSCO member, in deciding how to implement the IASC 2000 standards in its jurisdiction, could choose to mandate one or more of the following 'supplemental treatments':

- *Reconciliation:* this would require reconciliation of the treatment specified in an IASC 2000 standard to another specified accounting treatment (which may be a host country national accounting treatment). This reconciliation would be expected to be presented in a footnote to the financial statements and would quantify the effect of applying the specified alternative accounting treatment.

- *Supplemental disclosure:* this would require supplemental disclosure, either in the form of:

  - more detailed footnote disclosure than an IASC 2000 standard requires; or

  - additional detail on the face of the primary financial statements (e.g. income statement or balance sheet line items) that would have to be presented.

- *Interpretation:* this would require a specific application of an IASC 2000 standard, either:

  - in cases where an IASC 2000 standard permits different approaches to an issue, generally with one approach identified as a 'benchmark' and another as an 'allowed alternative', specifying which approach (the 'benchmark' or 'allowed alternative') is accepted in a host jurisdiction; or

  - to clarify ambiguity or address silence in an IASC 2000 standard, by specifying a particular interpretation of the IASC 2000 standard that should be used in a host jurisdiction.

- If the specified treatment is not followed, it is expected that an IOSCO member will require reconciliation to the specified treatment.

In an Appendix running to more than 100 pages, the report identified numerous 'concerns' raised by IOSCO members during the assessment of the IASC 2000 standards. These 'concerns' included an analysis of outstanding substantive issues relating to the standards, specifying supplemental treatments that might be required in a particular jurisdiction to address each of these concerns.

The effect of this report by the Technical Committee of IOSCO was to negate the intention of the IASC/IOSCO agreement. Its impact was to perpetuate the existing position whereby a company faced the possibility of having to comply with more than one reporting regime in order to obtain a cross-border listing, thereby doing nothing to remove duplication, complication and expense.

Thus, the long-awaited 'endorsement' from IOSCO was, in fact, only a qualified acceptance of IAS that still allowed IOSCO members to request any supplemental treatment that they considered necessary. Whilst one could accept that different regulatory jurisdictions might require additional note disclosures in line with local circumstances, the imposition of any reconciliation requirement requiring different recognition and measurement rules was clearly contrary to any notion of accounting harmonisation. It therefore seemed that any such unconditional endorsement of IAS by IOSCO for cross-border capital raising and listing purposes in all global markets was a long way off, and would require substantial further effort by both sides.

1.6   The influence of the G4+1 Group of 'standard setters' on international accounting

The G4+1 Group of standard setters was an informal grouping of staff members of the accounting standard-setting bodies of Australia, Canada, New Zealand, the United Kingdom, the United States of America and the IASC. Although not an official standard-setting body in its own right, the G4+1 became influential through the publication of discussion papers that dealt with highly topical and usually controversial accounting issues. Examples include: accounting for leases, reporting financial performance and accounting for share-based payments. Although these papers did not reflect the official views of any of the standard-setting bodies represented, the Group was able, through its links with the major Anglo-Saxon standard setters, to set the agenda for the development of new global accounting standards.

Perhaps unfortunately, because of their rather privileged positions and self-referential 'membership' criteria (for example, membership of the Group required acceptance of a conceptual framework similar to that of other members), the Group was something of a closed shop. The result was that much of the output from the Group was predictable, not always of the highest quality and not necessarily informed by practical business considerations.

In any event, at a meeting of the G4+1 held in January 2001, the Group discussed whether its activities should continue given the imminent commencement of activities by the new International Accounting Standards Board (IASB), and agreed to disband and cancel its planned future activities with immediate effect.

1.7   Shaping IASC for the future

Few would disagree that since its formation in 1973, the IASC had achieved a great deal within the limitations of its structure. However, with the globalisation of the world's capital markets, the increasing complexity of business transactions and the growing pressure for a single set of internationally harmonised accounting standards, the IASC Board believed that structural changes were needed for it to anticipate and meet effectively the new challenges that it faced.

Consequently, the IASC Board saw the completion of its core standards programme as an appropriate moment to undertake a review of its strategy. As a result, in 1998 it appointed a Strategy Working Party to conduct a general review of the strategy of the IASC.

The Working Party published its proposals in December 1998 in a Discussion Paper entitled 'Shaping IASC for the future'.[11] The Working Party's proposals were fairly radical, but were framed within the rather nebulous notion of a 'partnership with national standard setters'.[12] The rationale behind this was that the IASC should enter into a partnership with national standard setters enabling the IASC to work with them to accelerate convergence between national standards and International Accounting Standards. However, in order to form this 'partnership', the Working Party proposed the abolition of the IASC Board structure and the establishment of a bicameral system in its place. Under this system, a disproportionate amount of power would be concentrated in a Standards Development Committee (SDC), comprising a small group of select full-time standard setters. It was also proposed that the SDC would replace the IASC's Steering Committee system, under which Standards had been developed. The Working Party's recommendations covered a number of other areas, including the IASC's system of due process, implementation, education, enforcement and funding.

Perhaps not surprisingly, the Working Party's proposals met with considerable opposition, both from within the IASC Board and outside. The principal criticisms of the proposals centred on the bicameral system and the concept of the SDC. One general perception was that the Discussion Paper was aimed at further entrenching the position of the G4+1 group of Anglo-Saxon accounting standard setters (see 1.6 above).[13]

However, many saw the biggest single failing of the Working Party's proposals to be that they did not address adequately the key issue of legitimacy among the IASC's constituencies. So, whilst there was agreement with the objectives identified by the Working Party, there was less support for the structure that was proposed in order to achieve them, since the proposed structure would not have ensured legitimacy. The Discussion Paper contained little elaboration on the details of the proposed 'partnership with national standard setters' and other key constituencies, with the result that their role under the proposed structure was unclear.

There was particular concern expressed also about the representation of users and preparers of accounts in any new standard setting structure. Ultimately, the long-term credibility of International Accounting Standards would depend on their acceptance by the preparer and user communities as well as the international capital markets. There therefore had to be full participation by all the key players in the marketplace in order to secure the future of IAS.

The IASC Board had a joint meeting on 30 June 1999 with the Strategy Working Party to discuss the comments received on the Discussion Paper. The discussion indicated that the proposed bicameral/SDC system should be abandoned in favour of a single Board structure. There was a general consensus that this single Board should comprise a blend of full and part-time members, although the overall size of the Board and precise proportion of full and part-timers was not agreed. The Strategy Working Party met again during July 1999 in order to develop a new proposal along the lines of its discussions with the IASC Board.

1.8 The new IASC structure

In November 1999, the IASC's Strategy Working Party presented its final report – *Recommendations on Shaping IASC for the Future* – to the IASC Board.[14] In fact, the report was delivered somewhat as a *fait accompli*, and it was clear to the members of the IASC Board that there was little room for discussion: they could either take it or leave it. It seemed to many observers that the process had become highly politicised, and that the influence of the US SEC could be detected in ensuring that the IASB would be constituted as closely as possible in the image of the FASB. Thus, although the Strategy Working Party had seemingly dealt with the objections raised concerning its original bi-cameral structure, a number of fundamental difficulties that many observers and commentators had raised had not been resolved.

From a European perspective, these difficulties surrounded the issue of legitimacy and political accountability. This is because many believed that the essential feature of any new model should be that it was seen to be legitimate. This was considered as vital in order to ensure maximum commitment from those constituencies who would have to implement, regulate and enforce the system. Legitimacy and enforcement are linked, because broader support from the key constituencies in setting the standards makes it significantly more likely that the standards will be applied and enforced, which in turn gives them credibility. However, there was a clear tension between this 'representative' model that was clearly preferred in Europe and elsewhere on the one hand, and the SEC/FASB 'expert' model on the other.

In any event, the Strategy Working Party's proposal was presented to the IASC Board as a non-negotiable agreement with the SEC. This meant that the Board, left with no room to manoeuvre, adopted unanimously the recommendations of the Strategy Working Party. These were then approved by the member bodies of the International Federation of Accountants, under whose patronage the IASC Board operated. The new structure adopted is outlined below.

1.8.1 The IASC Foundation

The governance of the IASC Organisation[15] is ultimately in the hands of the Trustees of the IASC Foundation. The Trustees were appointed during the second half of 2000 by a Nominating Committee that was set up for that sole purpose under the Chairmanship of the then US SEC Chairman, Mr. Arthur Levitt. There are nineteen Trustees from diverse career backgrounds, under the Chairmanship of

Mr. Paul A. Volcker, a Former Chairman of the US Federal Reserve Board. To ensure a broad international representation, there are six Trustees from North America, six from Europe, four from the Asia/Pacific region and three from any area, subject to establishing an overall geographical balance. The appointment of all subsequent Trustees to fill vacancies caused by routine retirement or other reasons is the responsibility of the existing Trustees. The appointment of the Trustees is normally for a term of three years, renewable once. However, to provide continuity, some of the initial Trustees will serve staggered terms so as to retire after four or five years.

The IASC Foundation Constitution provides that 'all Trustees shall be required to show a firm commitment to the IASC Foundation and the IASB as a high quality global standard-setter, to be financially knowledgeable, and to have an ability to meet the time commitment. Each Trustee shall have an understanding of, and be sensitive to, international issues relevant to the success of an international organisation responsible for the development of high quality global accounting standards for use in the world's capital markets and by other users.'[16]

The first act of the Board of Trustees was to appoint Sir David Tweedie (who had just completed a highly distinguished period of ten years as the Chairman of the UK's Accounting Standards Board) as the first Chairman of the new International Accounting Standards Board (IASB). Subsequently, in January 2001, the Trustees appointed the thirteen other members of the IASB. The Trustees are responsible also for appointing the members of the International Financial Reporting Interpretations Committee (IFRIC) and Standards Advisory Council (SAC). In addition, their duties include the following:[17]

- fundraising;
- reviewing annually the strategy of the IASC Foundation and the IASB and their effectiveness;
- approving annually the budget of the IASC Foundation and determining the basis for funding;
- reviewing broad strategic issues affecting accounting standards, promoting the IASC Foundation and its work and promoting the objective of rigorous application of International Accounting Standards and International Financial Reporting Standards (the Trustees are, however, excluded from involvement in technical matters relating to accounting standards);
- establishing and amending operating procedures for the IASB, IFRIC and the SAC;
- approving amendments to the Constitution after following a due process, including consultation with the SAC and publication of an Exposure Draft for public comment;
- exercising all powers of the IASC Foundation except for those expressly reserved to the IASB, IFRIC and the SAC; and
- publishing an annual report on the IASC's activities, including audited financial statements and priorities for the coming year.

With effect from 1 April 2001, the IASB assumed international accounting standard setting responsibilities from its predecessor body, the IASC.

The IASB structure has the following main features: the IASC Foundation is an independent organisation having two main bodies, the Trustees and the IASB, as well as a Standards Advisory Council and the International Financial Reporting Interpretations Committee. The IASC Foundation Trustees appoint the IASB Members, exercise oversight and raise the funds needed, whereas the IASB has sole responsibility for setting accounting standards.

Set out below is a graphical representation of the IASC Foundation structure:[18]

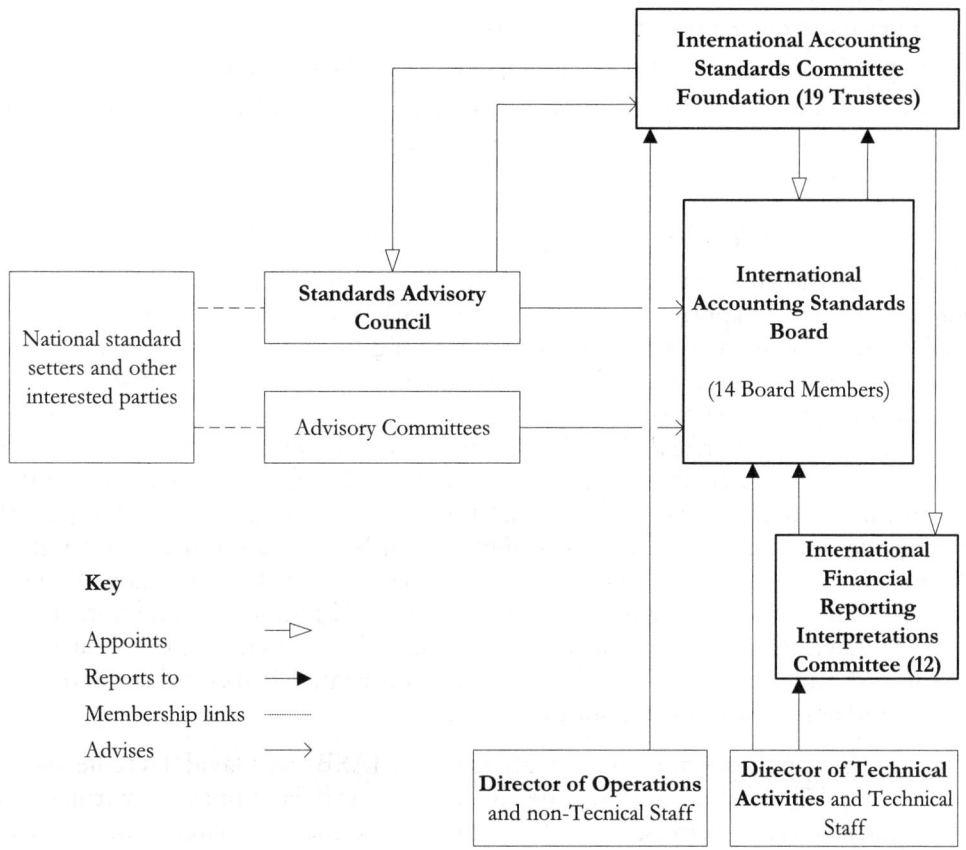

1.8.2 The IASC Foundation Constitution

The IASC Foundation Constitution was approved in its original form by the Board of the former International Accounting Standards Committee (IASC) in March 2000 and by the members of IASC at a meeting in Edinburgh on 24 May 2000. At its meeting in December 1999, the IASC Board had appointed a Nominating Committee to select the first Trustees. These Trustees were nominated on 22 May 2000 and took office on 24 May 2000 as a result of the approval of the Constitution. In execution of their duties under the Constitution, the Trustees formed the International Accounting

Standards Committee Foundation on 6 February 2001. The Foundation was formed as a not-for-profit corporation incorporated in the State of Delaware, USA, and is the parent entity of the IASB, which is based in London.

The Constitution sets out the basic structural and procedural framework for the various bodies of the IASC Organisation. Article 2 of the Constitution sets the objectives of the IASC Foundation as follows:[19]

(a)   to develop, in the public interest, a single set of high quality, understandable and enforceable global accounting standards that require high quality, transparent and comparable information in financial statements and other financial reporting to help participants in the world's capital markets and other users make economic decisions;

(b)   to promote the use and rigorous application of those standards; and

(c)   to bring about convergence of national accounting standards and International Accounting Standards and International Financial Reporting Standards to high quality solutions.

1.8.3   The International Accounting Standards Board (IASB)

As stated above, in accordance with Article 19 of the Constitution, the IASC Foundation Trustees appointed twelve of the IASB Members to full-time positions, including the Chairman and the Vice-Chairman, and two to part-time positions. To encourage cooperation among the new Board and national standard-setters, the Trustees appointed seven of the IASB Members as official liaisons to national bodies. These liaison IASB Members must maintain close contact with their respective national standard-setters and are responsible for coordinating agendas and ensuring that the IASB and national bodies are working toward the goal of convergence on a single set of high quality standards around the world. Countries with formal liaisons are Australia and New Zealand together, Canada, France, Germany, Japan, the United States, and the United Kingdom. In addition, IASB Members have frequent contacts with organisations such as the European Commission and the SEC, financial regulators and central banks, private industry, analysts, and academics throughout the world.

Following the appointment of the members of the IASB, Sir David Tweedie stated the following: 'The mission of the newly-created IASB is simple. In partnership with national standard setters, we will aim to increase the transparency of financial reporting by achieving a single, global method of accounting for transactions – whether in Stuttgart, Sydney, Seattle or Singapore. The potential benefit to the world economy by removing barriers to investment through applying uniform, high-quality standards is enormous.'[20]

The members of the IASB are not selected based on geographical representation. However, the Constitution stipulates that the Trustees shall ensure that the IASB is not dominated by any particular constituency or geographical interest. The foremost qualification for membership of the IASB is technical expertise. The IASB must comprise a group of people representing, within that group, the best available combination of technical skills and background experience of relevant international business and market conditions to contribute to the development of high quality, global accounting standards. No individual can be Trustee and IASB Member at the same time.

To achieve a balance of perspectives and experience, a minimum of five members of the IASB must have a background as practising auditors, a minimum of three a background in the preparation of financial statements, a minimum of three a background as users of financial statements, and at least one an academic background.[21]

The responsibilities of the IASB are listed in Article 32 of the Constitution. The primary role of the IASB is to have complete responsibility for all technical matters including the preparation and publication of International Financial Reporting Standards and Exposure Drafts, both of which shall include any dissenting opinions, and final approval of Interpretations by IFRIC. Decisions by the IASB require only a simple majority (i.e. eight out of fourteen votes) to be adopted. The IASB has full discretion over its technical agenda and over project assignments on technical matters. It must, however, consult the SAC on major projects, agenda decisions and work priorities.

The IASB (whose meetings are open to the public) met in technical session for the first time in April 2001. During this meeting, it approved a resolution to adopt the existing body of International Accounting Standards and Interpretations issued by the former IASC Board and the SIC. The IASB announced also that the IASC Foundation Trustees had agreed that the accounting standards issued by the IASB would be designated 'International Financial Reporting Standards (IFRS)'. The existing pronouncements will, however, continue to be designated 'International Accounting Standards (IAS)'.

1.8.4   The Standards Advisory Council (SAC)

The SAC provides a forum for participation by organisations and individuals with an interest in international financial reporting, who have diverse geographic and functional backgrounds, with the objective of (a) giving advice to the IASB on agenda decisions and priorities in the Board's work, (b) informing the IASB of the views of the SAC members on major standard setting projects and (c) giving other advice to the IASB or the Trustees.[22]

The SAC must be consulted by the IASB in advance of Board decisions on major projects and by the Trustees in advance of any proposed changes to the Constitution.[23]

In June 2001, the Trustees of the IASC Foundation announced the appointment of 49 SAC members. The members include chief financial and accounting officers from some of the world's largest corporations and international organisations, leading financial analysts and academics, regulators, accounting standard setters, and partners from leading accounting firms. The members of the SAC are drawn from six continents, 29 countries, and five international organisations. In addition, the European Commission, the US Securities and Exchange Commission, and the Financial Services Agency of Japan participate as observers.

The SAC (whose meetings are open to the public) normally meets three times a year under the chairmanship of the IASB Chairman. The SAC met for the first time with the IASB in July 2001.

1.8.5 The International Financial Reporting Interpretations Committee (IFRIC)

The SIC, which was formed in 1997 under the former IASC structure, continued to operate for approximately nine months under the new structure.

At its July 2001 meeting, the SAC discussed with the Board the Board's proposals to amend the mandate and operating procedures of the SIC. The IASB's proposal was to rename the committee as the International Financial Reporting Interpretations Committee (IFRIC) and to expand its mandate to enable the committee to address issues beyond interpretations of existing standards.

The result was that the SIC was reconstituted as IFRIC in December 2001, with the IASB's Director of Technical Activities appointed as its non-voting Chairman. IFRIC comprises twelve voting members, with the European Commission and IOSCO having observer status. [24]

IFRIC meets about every two months. All technical decisions are taken at sessions that are open to public observation. The Committee addresses issues of reasonably widespread importance, and not issues of concern to only a small set of enterprises. The interpretations cover both:

- newly identified financial reporting issues not specifically addressed in IFRSs; or
- issues where unsatisfactory or conflicting interpretations have developed, or seem likely to develop in the absence of authoritative guidance, with a view to reaching a consensus on the appropriate treatment.

The due process for each IFRIC project normally, but not necessarily, involves the following steps (the steps that are required under the terms of the IASC Foundation Constitution are indicated by an asterisk*): [25]

(a) the staff are asked to identify and review all the issues associated with the topic and to consider the application of the *Framework* to the issues;

(b) study of national accounting requirements and practice and an exchange of views about the issues with national standard-setters, including national committees that have responsibility for interpretations of national standards;

(c) publication of a draft interpretation for public comment if no more than three IFRIC members have voted against the proposal;*

(d) consideration of all comments received within the comment period on a draft interpretation;*

(e) approval by the IFRIC of an interpretation if no more than three IFRIC members have voted against the interpretation after considering public comments on the draft interpretation;* and

(f) approval of the interpretation by at least eight votes of the IASB.*

To date, the output from IFRIC has been somewhat limited, with the Committee taking more than two years to issue its first Interpretation. In reality, IFRIC has acted much more in the capacity of a Steering Committee of the IASB, as opposed to a conventional interpretations committee. Nevertheless, it does currently have approximately ten items under consideration, including some important issues such as service concession arrangements.

1.9 The IASC Foundation's Constitution review

1.9.1 The Constitution Committee

As part of the governance structure of the IASCF, the Constitution requires that the Trustees of the IASC Foundation should undertake a review of the entire structure of the IASC Foundation and its effectiveness. The Constitution specifies that this review should commence three years after the coming into force of the Constitution, with the objective of implementing any agreed changes five years after the coming into force of the Constitution (i.e. 6 February 2006).[26]

At a meeting on 4 November 2003, the Trustees discussed the need to consult interested parties on the full range of issues raised by the Constitution, and agreed on various aspects of the review, including the procedures for conducting the review, the extent of consultation, staffing, and the issues to be discussed. On 12 November 2003, the Trustees announced that they had initiated a review of the Foundation's constitutional arrangements that govern the operating procedures of the Foundation and the IASB. In launching this, the Trustees emphasised that they were willing to examine any aspect of the Constitution and would be consulting a wide range of organisations. To coordinate the process, the Trustees established an internal committee (the 'Constitution Committee'), chaired by Paul Volcker.

1.9.2 The Constitution Committee's initial consultation

As the first step of the review, comments were invited on a consultation paper that discussed the issues to be considered by the Trustees and posed some preliminary questions to those interested in participating in the review. The comment period closed on 11 February 2004 and attracted 70 letters. The Trustees received a number of hard-hitting comments on a wide range of matters, including the due process of the IASB and the Trustees' oversight of the Board. For example, the European Roundtable of Industrialists (ERT) stated that 'If we look at the Board's activities over the last two years, it seems to us that the due process has not worked very efficiently and that some problems have occurred with the Board's agenda though we have to acknowledge that the Board has no doubt had to suffer the pressure of the 2005 deadline for the use of IFRS in the EU. Nevertheless, we consider that it has conducted some projects too fast and it has added certain projects to the agenda without finishing others.' The ERT letter stated further that 'A proper governance and constant control process of the Trustees over the Board's work programme and activities should be implemented. Even an independent standard setter should be subject to a control procedure. ... In general the Trustees should ensure that the Board issues standards that are practicable and in the public interest but do not become an intellectual and theoretical end in themselves.'[27]

In a similar vein, the French Accounting Standard Setter (Conseil National de la Comptabilité) stated in its submission that 'The IASC Foundation objectives have not always been reached, due to a lack in transparency and dialogue in the due process. More consideration should be given by the Trustees in the processes followed. The IAS Board needs improvements in openness in order to reduce a lot of today's technical tensions and misunderstandings on many subjects.'[28]

1.9.3   The next steps for the Constitution review

On the basis of the comment letters received, the Constitution Committee determined the key issues to be taken forward and, on 22 March 2004, the Committee posted a paper – *Next Steps for the Constitution Review following initial consultation* – on the IASC Foundation Website. The paper noted that the Constitution Committee:

- had identified ten main issues for consideration, but had not yet reached conclusions on them;

- would be establishing a subcommittee of the Standards Advisory Council (SAC) to provide guidance on the Constitution Review; and

- would hold a series of public hearings to provide an additional opportunity for public comment.

The ten main issues for consideration were listed as follows:

1.   Whether the objectives of the IASC Foundation should expressly refer to the challenges facing small- and medium-sized entities (SMEs);

2.   The number of Trustees and their geographical and professional distribution;

3.   The oversight role of the Trustees;

4.   Funding of the IASC Foundation;

5.   The composition of the IASB;

6.   The appropriateness of the IASB's existing formal liaison relationships;

7.   Consultative arrangements of the IASB;

8.   Voting procedures of the IASB;

9.   Resources and effectiveness of IFRIC; and

10.   The composition, role, and effectiveness of the SAC.

On 7 May 2004, the Constitution Committee published a paper – *An Update on the Constitution Review and Information regarding Public Hearings* – outlining possible approaches to the ten issues identified by the Committee in the Constitution Review. These approaches were not formal recommendations but were meant to stimulate discussion at the public hearings.

The Constitution Committee then held the first three of four public hearings during June and July 2004 in New York, London and Tokyo. The Committee invited a broad range of organisations, including professional bodies, regulators, audit firms and industry organisations to the hearings and to discuss their views and suggestion on the ten issues and possible approaches Again, the Committee received challenging feedback from participants in the process. (The views of Ernst & Young on the IASC Foundation's Constitution are set out at 1.9.4 below.)

With the benefit of the input received in these first three public hearings, the Committee met on 22 September 2004 to reach some preliminary conclusions on the issues and possible approaches described in the 7 May paper. As a result, the Committee published a further paper on 28 September 2004 in order to bring participants in the Mexico City hearing (held on 6 October 2004) up to date with the Committee's thinking.[29]

The Committee then met again after the Mexico City hearing to finalise the recommendations to be presented to the full Trustees on 25 October in the form of a detailed report. The report also included a description of the philosophy that underpinned the Committee's analysis and the rationale for decisions taken. Once the Trustees have reached a common position on recommendations, they will publish a report with proposed constitutional changes for public comment.

The Trustees are only required to implement any constitutional changes by February 2006. On the other hand, given the strength of views expressed both at the public hearings and in the accompanying written submissions, it may well be that the Trustees will feel compelled to accelerate their timetable for effecting the necessary changes.

In the meantime, on 24 March 2004, the IASB announced that it had initiated an internal review of its own deliberative procedures alongside the Trustees' Constitution Review. In so doing, the IASB published a consultation paper – *Strengthening the IASB's deliberative processes* – which set out its preliminary findings and inviting public comment on improvements to its procedures that were already in progress.[30] Particular attention was given to the following matters:

- the accessibility and transparency of the IASB's deliberative process;
- the IASB's responsiveness to constituents' comments; and
- the extent of consultation before releasing proposals and Standards.

The deadline for comments was 25 June 2004. The IASC Foundation Trustees have stated that their Constitution Committee will review the IASB's conclusions on the deliberative process as part of its broader consideration of possible changes to the Constitution.

The Board received 50 comment letters on the consultation paper, and these were discussed at its September 2004 meeting. With the exception of five comments on the publication of near-final drafts, there was strong support for the steps proposed.

After considering further actions recommended by some respondents, the Board tentatively decided:[31]

- to continue to make observer notes available on its Website, with paragraph numbers corresponding to those in the Board's papers;
- to make all public meetings available, if possible, by Internet or audio;
- to publish near-final drafts of final documents only;

- to enhance the due process procedures as proposed and to explain its reasons when it decides not to undertake a non-mandatory step of its due process;

- to conduct field tests when appropriate;

- to distinguish clearly field tests, field visits and other means of obtaining input from constituents while an IFRS is being developed;

- to vary the length of comment periods, taking account of the complexity of the project and with sensitivity to the problems of translation; and

- to clarify the procedure for adding items to its agenda.

1.9.4   Ernst & Young's views on the IASC Foundation's Constitution[32]

Ernst & Young believes that the global acceptance and use of a single set of high quality accounting standards, throughout the capital markets of the world, is highly desirable. A single set of global accounting standards will improve the comparability and overall transparency of corporate financial reporting, thereby enhancing the confidence of investors and increasing the efficiency of capital allocation.

In our view, the Foundation has made enormous progress towards this goal over the past three years, building on the foundations established by its predecessor body. A comprehensive 'stable platform' of generally high quality International Financial Reporting Standards has now been promulgated, and nearly 100 countries are committed to adopt IFRS directly, or to align their national standards with IFRS, from 2005 or later.

We therefore agree that this is a good moment to assess and, where necessary, revise the structures and processes of the IASC Foundation in order to ensure it is well equipped to meet the current and future expectations of its constituents. To assess the constitutional amendments that are required, we believe that this Review needs to consider the extent to which the existing governance and operational processes should change to address the challenges of the next phase in the development and use of international standards.

The need to develop a core set of high quality standards in time for the adoption of IFRS by companies in Europe and elsewhere in 2005 has placed immense pressure on the IASB. In these circumstances, it was perhaps inevitable that the IASB would have some difficulty in always observing the desired level of due process.

However, in our view, the Board and Trustees have compounded this problem by giving insufficient consideration to the coherence and practicality of the IASB's agenda. As a consequence, there is now a growing concern that the IASB's processes have not been sufficiently rigorous or transparent.

Underlying the views of many constituents lies a concern that the Board has given priority to accounting theory and, in some cases, convergence with US GAAP over other equally important aspects of standard-setting, such as the inherent complexity and change management implications of the standards developed by the IASB.

With investors in mind, there are concerns as to whether the financial statements prepared on the basis of the new standards will be well understood by users and, importantly, whether the resulting financial statements can be audited appropriately. As more standards based on the Board's 'asset/liability fair value model' are developed, even greater difficulty will be experienced by preparers of financial statements in establishing — and by auditors in evaluating — relevant and/or reliable 'fair values' for assets and liabilities.

In many cases, other than those for which there are deep and active markets, what is informally described as a 'mark-to-market' basis, which suggests relevance and reliability, is in reality a 'mark-to-model' basis that is hypothetical and not likely to be supported by a market transaction. There is also growing concern that, although based on principles, IASB standards increasingly include detailed rules.

Although members of the Board frequently emphasise the need for professional judgment to be used in the application of its standards, the standards often are drafted in a manner that appears to de-emphasize the use of judgment and also, in some cases, may appear driven by a desire to achieve short-term convergence with US GAAP. We foresee that these concerns and difficulties could increase substantially as widespread first-time adoption of IFRS and application of the new and revised IFRS occurs in 2005.

Therefore, in our view, to maintain its standing as the global standard setter, the Foundation's structures and processes should be revised to achieve several specific objectives, namely:

- the oversight exercised by the Trustees should ensure that the IASB's procedures meet, and are seen to meet, the reasonable expectations of constituents regarding due process;

- the Board's members, as well as its operating processes, must demonstrate that due consideration is given to the practicality of proposed standards and interpretations;

- the IASB's 'asset/liability fair value model' should be subjected to public debate in order to decide whether to refresh the Board's mandate, place boundaries around the use of the model, or move to an alternative model;

- convergence between US GAAP and IFRS should be viewed by the Board as an important objective, primarily as a longer-term objective to be achieved through new standards and integrated interpretation mechanisms, and not as a short-term objective based on the elimination of detailed differences; and finally

- the Foundation should seek to broaden and deepen its relationships with legislators and securities regulators as well as national standard-setters to maintain its position as the global standard-setter and issuer of IFRS interpretations.

We support the overall direction of the Constitution Committee's thinking on the ten issues identified for further consideration, although several of the Committee's proposals, in our opinion, do not go far enough to ensure that the required structural and operational changes are carried out. In particular:

- as to the composition of the Trustees, the current, largely geographical, representation model for Trustees should be replaced by an arrangement under which a nominating committee of international organisations of preparers, users, auditors, academics and regulators is responsible for nominating Trustees;

- the Trustees should exercise oversight over the Board, in particular, over the setting and prioritisation of the IASB's work program. In general, we also believe that the IASB should have less discretion over its due process and should be required to explain publicly its reasons for not carrying out any of the due process elements listed in the *Preface*;

- as to the Board itself, proposed changes to the Constitution indicate that the foremost qualification for Board membership should be 'professional competence and practical experience'. We strongly believe that Board members' practical experience should be 'recent and relevant'. To achieve that criterion, we believe the proportion of part time members should be allowed to increase significantly; and the geographical interests of IASB members should be widened; and

- the Constitution should place greater emphasis on the need for expanded dialogue with national standard setters, legislators and securities regulators. This will be needed to promote convergence of national with international standards and discourage the emergence of national variations in the interpretation and application of IFRS.

2   THE IASB'S TECHNICAL AGENDA

2.1   An initial agenda of twenty-five technical projects

In contemplation of the handover of its functions to the new IASB, the Board of the former International Accounting Standards Committee approved a public Statement at its December 2000 meeting.[33] The purpose of the Statement was to comment on the IASC Board's current work-in-progress and record some of the thinking of the Board resulting from its work on agenda items in progress and other discussions.

In the light of this, and after consultation with the SAC, national accounting standard setters, regulators and other interested parties, the IASB determined an initial agenda of nine technical projects. These were divided into three broad categories:

- Projects intended to provide leadership and promote convergence, which comprised the following:
  - Accounting for insurance contracts
  - Business combinations
  - Reporting financial performance
  - Accounting for share based payments;

- Projects intended to provide for easier application of International Financial Reporting Standards, which comprised the following:
  - Guidance on first-time application of IFRSs
  - Activities of financial institutions: disclosure and presentation; and
- Projects intended to improve existing standards, which comprised the following:
  - Preface to IFRSs
  - Improvements to existing IASs (see 2.2 below)
  - Amendments to IAS 39 – *Financial Instruments: Recognition and Measurement.*

In addition to these, sixteen other issues were adopted as 'partner projects' by one or more of the IASB's national standard setting partners. The IASB announced that it would be working with these partners, or at least monitoring their efforts, in order to ensure that any differences between national standard setters or with the IASB would be identified and resolved as quickly as possible. These issues comprised the following:

- accounting measurement;
- accounting by extractive industries;
- accounting for financial instruments (i.e. the comprehensive full fair value project);
- accounting for leases;
- accounting by small and medium entities and emerging economies;
- accounting for taxes on income (i.e. dealing with issues of convergence between IAS 12 and certain national standards such as FRS 19);
- business combinations;
- consolidation policy;
- definitions of elements of financial statements;
- derecognition issues, other than those addressed in IAS 39;
- employee benefits (dealing with issues of convergence between IAS 19 and certain national standards such as FRS 17);
- impairment of assets;
- intangible assets;
- liabilities and revenue recognition;
- Management's Discussion and Analysis (an area not currently dealt with in the IASC literature);
- revaluation of certain assets.

More than three years later, virtually all of these projects are still work-in-progress and at various stages of development. It is for this reason that the IASB has attracted substantial criticism for the way that it has allowed its agenda to lengthen without appropriate public consultation or proper prioritisation. Whilst we acknowledge both that the Board has set itself some highly ambitious targets, and that it cannot be expected to achieve everything in three or four years, we nevertheless believe that it has failed properly to prioritise its projects according to the needs of preparers and users. As a result, it is trying to do too much too quickly, without appropriate prioritisation and without allowing sufficient time for full consideration of the practical implications and economic impact of its proposals.

2.2   The Improvements Project

In April 2001, the IASB announced the launch of its 'Improvements Project' and called for suggestions as to how existing standards could be improved. The objective of the project was to add clarity and consistency to the requirements of existing IASs issued by the former IASC Board. The specific topics that were addressed came from information already provided to the IASB by sources such as IOSCO, national standard setters, the SIC, major accounting firms and other commentators. The issues addressed were those identified as narrow issues of substance whose resolution could improve the quality of an IAS and/or increase convergence of national and international standards. The Board wished to address these issues immediately, so that companies adopting IAS for the first time would not be faced with significant additional change thereafter.

An Improvements Sub-Committee comprising four Board members was established to consider all the suggestions made for improvement and to make recommendations to the full Board. In May 2002, the Board issued an Exposure Draft proposing amendments to thirteen standards and the withdrawal of one (IAS 15 – *Information reflecting the effect of changing prices*). Eventually, in December 2003, the Board issued the thirteen revised standards in final form, together with 'consequential amendments' to a further seventeen standards. In fact, many of the 'consequential amendments' were somewhat more in the form of substantive change (for example, the definition of 'joint control' in IAS 31) – again raising questions about the Board's due process. The Improvements Project eliminated some of the alternative accounting treatments in these 'improved' standards. Where an IAS retains alternative treatments, the IASB removed virtually all references to 'benchmark treatment' and 'allowed alternative treatment', instead using descriptive references, such as 'cost model' and 'revaluation model'.

Introducing the revised standards, Sir David Tweedie commented as follows: 'The Improvements Project has raised the quality and enhanced the consistency of international accounting standards. The Board has devoted much time and resources during its first two years of operation to ensuring that we have a solid base on which we can build. From this improved set of standards, we shall move forward on the many complex issues facing accounting today and pursue our longer-term goal of global convergence.'[34]

In reality, the improvements project took more time than originally envisaged (almost three years) to complete, with the result that the Board was not able to devote sufficient time either to dealing with fundamental issues such as measurement, revenue recognition, performance reporting and accounting for common control transactions, or to resolving crucial industry issues such as those relating to the insurance and extractive industries. Consequently, the 2005 landmark will be reached with significant gaps in the IASB's authoritative literature, which will, on occasion, require preparers and their auditors to exercise a considerable degree of judgement in determining the appropriate accounting.

2.3   Convergence with US GAAP

2.3.1   *The Norwalk Agreement*

The co-operation between the IASC/IASB and national standard setters had, in the past, been occurring at a mostly informal level for many years through a variety of bodies such as the G4+1 and the Joint Working Group of Standard Setters.[35] However, in 2002 the co-operation specifically between the IASB and FASB was placed on a more formal footing.

On 29 October 2002, the IASB and FASB issued a memorandum of understanding that marked a significant step towards the two Boards formalising their commitment to the convergence of IFRS and US GAAP.[36] This agreement was reached at a joint meeting held at the FASB's offices in Norwalk, Connecticut, USA on 18 September 2002, where the two Boards each acknowledged their commitment to the development of high-quality, compatible accounting standards that could be used for both domestic and cross-border financial reporting. At that meeting, both Boards pledged to use their best efforts to (a) make their existing financial reporting standards fully compatible as soon as is practicable and (b) to coordinate their future work programs to ensure that once achieved, compatibility is maintained.[37]

To achieve compatibility, the two Boards agreed, as a matter of high priority, to:

- undertake a short-term project aimed at removing a variety of individual differences between US GAAP and IFRS;

- remove other differences between IFRSs and US GAAP that will remain at 1 January 2005, through coordination of their future work programs; that is, through the mutual undertaking of discrete, substantial projects that both Boards would address concurrently;

- continue progress on the joint projects that they are currently undertaking; and,

- encourage their respective interpretative bodies to coordinate their activities.[38]

The Boards agreed to commit the necessary resources to complete such a major undertaking and to start deliberating differences identified for resolution in the short-term project with the objective of achieving compatibility by identifying common, high-quality solutions. Both Boards agreed also to use their best efforts to issue an exposure draft of proposed changes to US GAAP or IFRSs that reflected common solutions to some, and perhaps all, of the differences identified for inclusion in the short-term project during 2003.[39]

2.3.2 *What does convergence mean in practice?*

Significant progress has already been made towards global convergence with the commitment of a significant number of countries around the globe to adopt IFRSs directly or to align their national standards with IFRS from 2005 or later. However, the world's largest capital market – the US – has not yet committed to adopt IFRS. Consequently, from 2005 onwards convergence will largely be an IFRS-US GAAP issue, and it is therefore encouraging that the IASB and FASB have committed to joint working arrangements on all major projects with the aim of achieving convergence of IFRS and US GAAP in the long term.

The first real evidence of 'convergence' can be found in IFRS 5 – *Non-current Assets Held for Sale and Discontinued Operations* – which was published in April 2004. However, it is highly debatable whether IFRS 5 heralds the 'development of high-quality, compatible accounting standards'. IFRS 5 is virtually identical to the equivalent US standard, SFAS 144 – *Accounting for the Impairment or Disposal of Long-Lived Assets*. Unfortunately, though, SFAS 144 is not generally regarded as a 'high quality' standard, and IFRS 5 cannot be seen as being a superior solution to the standard that it superseded, IAS 35 – *Discontinuing Operations*.

Part of the difficulty arises from the fact that the FASB has its own governance arrangements that are based on the US GAAP preparer and user communities and regulatory and legal environments. In the light of the joint working arrangements that have now been agreed by the IASB and the FASB, it is particularly important that an appropriate balance is maintained between the respective interests of users of IFRSs and users of US GAAP as convergence between IFRS and US GAAP is sought.

There is a real concern amongst the IASB's constituency that IFRS/US GAAP convergence means the adoption of US GAAP into IFRS through the back door – as evidenced by the IFRS 5 example. The underlying problem is that IFRS and US GAAP are two fundamentally different systems of financial reporting. US GAAP is a highly detailed rules-based system that places emphasis on the legal form of transactions and arrangements over their economic substance. In contrast, IFRSs have traditionally been principles-based and substantially less detailed, with much greater emphasis placed on economic reality and the exercise of judgment. However, our concern is that, although based on principles, recently issued IFRSs increasingly include detailed rules. Although members of the IASB frequently emphasise the need for professional judgment to be used in the application of IFRSs, the standards often are drafted in a manner that appears to de-emphasise the use of judgment and, in some cases, may appear driven by a desire to achieve short-term convergence with US GAAP.

We, on the other hand, see convergence as a long-term issue and we increasingly believe that IFRS and US GAAP convergence should progress towards new standards and integrated interpretation mechanisms rather than the elimination of detailed differences between existing IFRS and US GAAP.

2.3.3 US GAAP convergence and the SEC reconciliation requirement for foreign private issuers

A significant proportion of the world's largest companies outside the US are listed on the New York Stock Exchange and NASDAQ and are therefore subject to SEC regulation. For those that file a Form 20-F, there is a requirement to provide reconciliations from National GAAP to US GAAP for both income and equity.

Consequently, the Norwalk Agreement was warmly welcomed around the world – particularly by those SEC-registered foreign private issuer companies that are currently required to provide US GAAP reconciliations, who saw this as a means of removing the reconciliation requirement. In addition, a European Commission statement welcomed the IASB/FASB commitment to achieving real convergence between their respective accounting standards by 2005, when listed EU companies would be required to apply IFRS. The EU statement made the point that the announcement heralded a major step towards a global system of accounting standards and hoped that it would, in particular, help the SEC to accept financial statements prepared by EU companies in accordance with IFRS, without reconciliation to US GAAP, for the purposes of listing on the US markets.

There was therefore the widespread hope that the IASB/FASB short-term convergence project would obviate the necessity for foreign private issuer companies reporting under IFRS to prepare US GAAP reconciliations beyond 2005. However, the present disposition of the SEC is that this will still take some time to achieve. In response to a question asked of him in August 2004 at the 2004 Annual Meeting of the American Accounting Association, Mr Donald Nicolaisen, Chief Accountant of the SEC, suggested that the reconciliation requirement could be removed by the end of the current decade. This would seem to suggest that the removal of the reconciliation is increasingly becoming a political issue, rather than a technical one. Many would argue that, given the IASB's completion of its improvements project – which resulted in 30 new and amended IASs – and the publication of six new IFRSs, that there is no objective reason for the SEC not to recognise IFRS in 2005. In our view, the removal or retention of the reconciliation is a matter of equivalence, not convergence. Global convergence around new accounting solutions is a long-term objective; whether or not the reconciliation is removed in the short-term is therefore not a matter of convergence – it is an issue of mutual recognition on the basis of equivalence. However, it seems that the unconditional acceptance of IFRS by the SEC will still involve a long process of political negotiation.

2.3.4 Adoption by the US Financial Reporting System of a Principles-Based Accounting System[40]

The recent spate of major corporate accounting scandals in the US (such as Waste Management and Enron) suggested to many that the US system of corporate governance and financial reporting was in need of improvement. To many it appeared that, at least in some cases, the checks-and-balances within the US financial reporting system-ranging from management to auditors, audit committees, boards of directors, analysts, rating agencies, corporate counsel, standard setters, regulators, banks and the investors themselves-failed to prevent or detect large-scale fraud in major corporations that were carried out over extended periods of time.

The US Congress responded by passing the Sarbanes-Oxley Act of 2002[41] ('the Act'), the most significant piece of US securities legislation since the 1930s. Much of the Act may be viewed as a legislative attempt to align better the incentives of management, auditors and other professionals with those of investors. For example, with respect to corporate management, the Act increased penalties for violations of securities laws and required certification of financial results by key corporate officers.

In summary, the Act called for improvement in the checks and balances that govern the production of financial information provided to investors. However, the question arose as to whether these actions addressed fully the causes of the recent corporate scandals. Many questioned whether the accounting standards themselves might have played some role in facilitating or even encouraging the behaviour of some of the individuals involved. More generally, many asked whether technical compliance with US accounting standards necessarily results in financial reporting that fairly reflects the underlying economic reality of reporting entities.

Amongst these concerns, there was a growing sense that the standard setting process in the US may have become overly rules-based. Three of the more significant and commonly-accepted shortcomings of rules-based standards are that they:

- contain numerous 'bright-line' tests, which ultimately can be misused by financial engineers as a roadmap to comply with the letter, but not the spirit, of standards;

- contain numerous exceptions to the principles purportedly underlying the standards, resulting in inconsistencies in accounting treatment of transactions and events with similar economic substance; and

- further a need and demand for voluminously detailed implementation guidance on the application of the standard, creating complexity in, and uncertainty about, the application of the standard.

Accordingly, Section 108(d) of the Act called upon the staff of the US Securities and Exchange Commission to conduct a study on the adoption by the US financial reporting system of a principles-based accounting system and for the SEC to submit a report thereon to the US Congress by 30 July 2003. The Act mandated that the study should include: (i) the extent to which principles-based accounting and financial reporting exists in the US; (ii) the length of time required for change from a rules-based to a principles-based financial reporting system; (iii) the feasibility of and proposed methods by which a principles-based system may be implemented; and (iv) a thorough economic analysis of the implementation of a principles-based system. The SEC staff submitted its study to the US Congress during July 2003.

The study asserts that imperfections exist when standards are established on either a rules-based or a principles-only basis. Principles-only standards may present enforcement difficulties because they provide little guidance or structure for exercising professional judgment by preparers and auditors. Rules-based standards often provide a vehicle for circumventing the intention of the standard. As a result, the SEC staff recommended that those involved in the standard-setting process should develop standards more consistently on a principles-based or 'objectives-oriented' basis. According to the study, such standards should have the following characteristics:

- be based on an improved and consistently applied conceptual framework;

- clearly state the accounting objective of the standard;

- provide sufficient detail and structure so that the standard can be 'operationalised' and applied on a consistent basis;

- minimise exceptions from the standard; and

- avoid use of percentage tests ('bright-lines') that allow financial engineers to achieve technical compliance with the standard while evading the intent of the standard.

According to the SEC staff, neither US GAAP nor IFRS, as currently drafted, are representative of the optimal type of principles-based standards. In their view, an optimal standard involves a concise statement of substantive accounting principle where the accounting objective has been included at an appropriate level of specificity as an integral part of the standard and where few, if any, exceptions or conceptual inconsistencies are included in the standard. Further, such a standard should provide an appropriate amount of implementation guidance given the nature of the class of transactions or events and should be devoid of 'bright-line' tests. Finally, such a standard should be consistent with, and derive from, a coherent conceptual framework of financial reporting.

The SEC staff refers to this system as 'objectives-oriented' standard setting, and distinguishes it from a principles-only approach, which they believe typically provides insufficient guidance to make the standards reliably operational. The assertion is that objectives-oriented standards explicitly charge management with the responsibility for capturing within the company's financial reports the economic substance of transactions and events – not abstractly, but as defined specifically and framed by the substantive objectives built into each pertinent standard. In turn, auditors would be held responsible for reporting whether management has fulfilled that responsibility. Accordingly, it is considered that objectives-oriented standards place greater emphasis on the responsibility of both management and auditors to ensure that the financial reporting captures the objectives of the standard than is the case with either rules-based standards or principles-only standards. Further, if properly constructed, the SEC staff believes that objectives-oriented standards may require less use of judgment than either rules-based or principles-only standards, and thus, may serve better to facilitate consistency and compliance with the intention of the standards.

However, as noted in the study, a move towards more objectives-oriented standards will require a change in behaviour of standard setters, preparers, auditors and investors, including the ways in which standards are interpreted and applied and professional judgment is exercised.[42] In our view, it could well take several years for the necessary changes in behaviour, attitude and expertise to take root – particularly given the legal and regulatory frameworks in the US. In any event, the first step must be for the FASB and IASB to develop jointly an agreed conceptual framework to be used as the foundation for the preparation of truly globally accepted objectives-oriented standards. It is for this reason that we believe that IFRS and US GAAP convergence should involve the development of new standards based on a sound conceptual framework, rather than the elimination of detailed differences between existing IFRS and US GAAP.

2.4   The IASB's current agenda

The IASB has several projects in progress at the moment. These cover a wide range of topics, some of which could potentially have a fundamental impact on financial reporting under IFRS. In addition, it has identified other topics that it may place on its agenda as resources permit.

The IASB's current agenda includes the following:

- various issues relating to accounting for financial instruments, such as cash flow hedge accounting of forecast intragroup transactions;
- financial guarantee contracts and credit insurance;
- business combinations *phase II* – application of the purchase method;
- reporting comprehensive income;
- exploration for, and evaluation of, mineral resources;
- insurance contracts *phase II*;
- revenue and related liabilities;
- consolidation (including special purpose entities);
- various convergence projects, including:
    - provisions, contingent liabilities and contingent assets;
    - income taxes;
    - employment benefits; and
    - government grants;
- accounting standards for small and medium-sized entities.

In addition, the IASB has embarked on active research, in collaboration with others, on the following topics:

- financial instruments;
- joint ventures;
- leases; and
- measurement.

The intention is that, when the preparatory work on these research projects is concluded, they will be moved to the IASB's main agenda.

Furthermore, in response to the criticism that the IASB has received regarding its consultative procedures, the Board has announced the formation of three new advisory groups. The IASB has stated that it is establishing these groups to bring together expertise from a broad range of perspectives on three critical projects – insurance contracts, financial instruments and performance reporting. In selecting the advisory groups' membership, the IASB has sought a balance of geographical and professional backgrounds in these three complex and controversial areas.[43]

The insurance advisory group will bring members' experience with national insurance accounting systems to an international setting. Insurance accounting varies widely by jurisdiction, and there is broad agreement that financial statement users would benefit from a single, cohesive and international standard. The Board hopes that the advisory group members will help it to establish whether it can draw on aspects of existing national standards, and from them produce a high quality international solution. If not, the Board will look to the group for assistance in developing new approaches.

The financial instruments advisory group will take a fresh look at the existing accounting requirements in an effort to improve, simplify and, ultimately, replace IAS 39.

The performance reporting advisory group will bring together a group of users, preparers, auditors, regulators, academics and standard setters to see whether the IASB could improve the existing financial reporting statements.

Building on the advice of these groups, the IASB expects to produce discussion papers on the insurance and performance reporting projects and any potential overhaul of IAS 39. In this way, the Board hopes to encourage people and organisations with a wide range of perspectives around the world to join the debate on the IASB's projects. In due course Exposure Drafts will follow, but that may well be several years into the future.

2.5   Changed format of new IFRSs

When the new IASB took office on 1 April 2001, it announced that the IASC Foundation Trustees had agreed that the accounting standards issued by the IASB would be designated 'International Financial Reporting Standards (IFRS)', whilst the existing standards would continue to be designated 'International Accounting Standards (IAS)'. Presumably, this change was made in order to enable the Board to distinguish between the new standards issued by them, and those that they had inherited from the former IASC Board.

In addition, the new IFRSs issued by the IASB have adopted an entirely new format. In future, all IFRSs will incorporate some or all of the following components:

- An introduction to the IFRS
- The text of the IFRS itself
- Appendices that form part of the standards:
  - Defined terms
  - Application Guidance
  - Amendments to other IFRSs
- Statement of approval of the IFRS by the Board

- Basis for Conclusions, that does not form part of the IFRS
- Dissenting opinions of Board Members
- Illustrative examples, that do not form part of the IFRS
- Implementation Guidance, that does not form part of the IFRS.

In our view, this new format represents a substantial improvement over the old style IASs. However, there are those that express the concern that principles-based standards will be turned into rules-based standards through the imposition of extensive mandatory application guidance.

It should be noted also that the EU's process of adopting an IFRS applies only to the IFRS itself and those appendices that the IASB designates as forming part of the standard. This means that all appendices that do not form part of the standard, including the basis for conclusions, illustrative examples and implementation guidance do not form part of 'adopted' IFRS in the EU.

3 FINANCIAL REPORTING IN COMPLIANCE WITH INTERNATIONAL FINANCIAL REPORTING STANDARDS

3.1 Statement of compliance with IFRS

Although IFRS, in themselves, do not have the force of law, they have become internationally accepted and are applied by a growing number of companies. More importantly, though, 2005 is a watershed year for IFRS with a significant number of countries adopting IFRS as their principal financial reporting regime – either directly (for example, by the 25 Member States in the European Union), or by aligning their national standards with IFRS (for example, Australia and South Africa).

The main document setting out the basis on which financial statements should be presented under IAS, and the required contents of those financial statements, is IAS 1 – *Presentation of Financial Statements*.[44] An entity whose financial statements comply with IFRS 'shall make an explicit and unreserved statement of such compliance in the notes'.[45] IAS compliance involves compliance with all the recognition, measurement and disclosure provisions of the standards and interpretations. For this reason, IAS 1 states that 'financial statements shall not be described as complying with IFRSs unless they comply with all the requirements of IFRSs'.[46] The IASB has therefore established unambiguously the principle that full application of its standards and related interpretations is a necessary prerequisite for a company to assert that its financial statements comply with International Financial Reporting Standards.

3.2 Fair presentation and compliance with IFRS

Paragraph 13 of IAS 1 requires that 'financial statements shall present fairly the financial position, financial performance and cash flows of an entity.' It goes on to state that fair presentation requires the faithful representation of the effects of transactions, other events and conditions in accordance with the definitions and recognition criteria for assets, liabilities, income and expenses set out in the

Framework. The application of IFRSs, with additional disclosure when necessary, is presumed to result in financial statements that achieve a fair presentation.[47]

IAS 1 states that in virtually all circumstances, a fair presentation is achieved by compliance with applicable IFRSs.[48] A fair presentation under IFRS also requires an entity:

(a) to select and apply accounting policies in accordance with IAS 8 – *Accounting Policies, Changes in Accounting Estimates and Errors.* IAS 8 sets out a hierarchy of authoritative guidance that management considers in the absence of a Standard or an Interpretation that specifically applies to an item;

(b) to present information, including accounting policies, in a manner that provides relevant, reliable, comparable and understandable information; and

(c) to provide additional disclosures when compliance with the specific requirements in IFRSs is insufficient to enable users to understand the impact of particular transactions, other events and conditions on the entity's financial position and financial performance.[49]

3.3 The fair presentation override

IAS 1 makes it clear that inappropriate accounting policies are not rectified either by disclosure of the accounting policies used or by notes or explanatory material.[50] For this reason, the standard was required to cater for those situations where compliance with a standard or interpretation would distort fair presentation. Consequently, the standard provides that in the extremely rare circumstances in which management concludes that compliance with a requirement in a Standard or an Interpretation would be so misleading that it would conflict with the objective of financial statements set out in the *Framework*, the entity shall depart from that requirement if the relevant regulatory framework requires, or otherwise does not prohibit, such a departure.[51]

When an entity applies the override in these circumstances, it must disclose the following:[52]

(a) that management has concluded that the financial statements present fairly the entity's financial position, financial performance and cash flows;

(b) that it has complied with applicable Standards and Interpretations, except that it has departed from a particular requirement to achieve a fair presentation;

(c) the title of the Standard or Interpretation from which the entity has departed, the nature of the departure, including the treatment that the Standard or Interpretation would require, the reason why that treatment would be so misleading in the circumstances that it would conflict with the objective of financial statements set out in the *Framework*, and the treatment adopted; and

(d) for each period presented, the financial impact of the departure on each item in the financial statements that would have been reported in complying with the requirement.

When an entity has departed from a requirement of a Standard or an Interpretation in a prior period, and that departure affects the amounts recognised in the financial statements for the current period, the standard requires it to make the disclosures set out in (c) and (d) above.[53]

It is worth noting that the fair presentation override is a requirement (not an option) of IAS 1 to be applied in the extremely rare circumstances in which management concludes that compliance with a requirement in a Standard or an Interpretation would be so misleading that it would conflict with the objective of financial statements set out in the *Framework*.

However, at the same time, the IASB has introduced a somewhat contradictory twist to the application of the override. As stated above, the override can be applied only if 'the relevant regulatory framework requires, or otherwise does not prohibit' its use. This means that the Board has built into IAS 1 the possibility of regulatory intervention in its application. Paragraph 21 of IAS 1 provides for the situation where 'the relevant regulatory framework' prohibits departure from a requirement in a particular standard or interpretation. In such cases, the standard requires an entity, to the maximum extent possible, to reduce the perceived misleading aspects of compliance by disclosing:[54]

(a)   the title of the Standard or Interpretation in question, the nature of the requirement, and the reason why management has concluded that complying with that requirement is so misleading in the circumstances that it conflicts with the objective of financial statements set out in the *Framework*; and

(b)   for each period presented, the adjustments to each item in the financial statements that management has concluded would be necessary to achieve a fair presentation.

This seems to contradict the clear statement in paragraph 16 of IAS 1 that 'inappropriate accounting policies are not rectified either by disclosure of the accounting policies used or by notes or explanatory material'.[55] It seems also to create the unwelcome precedent of a standard formally giving regulators the ability to determine how standards should be applied.

The detailed requirements of IAS 1 are discussed in Chapter 3 of this book.

4 THE MOVE TO IFRS IN THE EUROPEAN UNION

4.1 Historical differences in European accounting

European accounting is the product of disparate social, economic and political factors, which have resulted in a number of deep-rooted differences in financial reporting practice throughout the region. The factors that have caused these differences include a variety of legal and tax systems, the perceived objectives of financial reporting and the significance of different sources of finance.

In contrast to IFRS and US GAAP, there is no broad-based statement of generally accepted theoretical principles that underpins financial reporting in the European Union (EU). Clearly, though, it is not the lack of a conceptual framework that has caused the European differences in financial reporting practices. European accounting has evolved over many centuries, and the differences that exist throughout Europe have been shaped by the conditions in each European country.

Until recently, the principal mechanism employed by the European Union to reduce these differences has been through the adoption of Directives under its company law harmonisation programme. These Directives are not laws that apply directly to companies, but instructions to Member States to alter, if necessary, their own national legislation to ensure compliance with the provisions of the Directive. In most cases, the Directives lay down minimum requirements only, so that there is nothing to prevent a Member State having supplementary requirements of a more stringent nature, provided that these are not incompatible with the Directives.

The most significant Directives in the area of financial reporting are the Fourth and Seventh, which were adopted into national legislation by most EU countries during the 1980s.[56] The principal objective of the Fourth Directive was to achieve harmonisation in respect of formats, valuation rules and note disclosure, whilst the Seventh established a requirement for EU companies to prepare consolidated accounts on a common basis.

However, in negotiating the Fourth and Seventh Directives with the EU Member States, the Commission found that the deep-rooted differences in European accounting could be reconciled only through compromise. For example, in the case of the Fourth Directive, this involved a compromise between the German and French desire for certainty and precision in accounts (as reflected in the compulsory charts of accounts in France and the mandatory formats for the balance sheet and profit and loss account in Germany), and the Anglo-Saxon/Dutch desire for a more pragmatic approach requiring the accounts taken as a whole to present a true and fair view; and in the case of the Seventh Directive, a compromise between the economic and legal concepts of a group.

4.2 Harmonisation achieved by the Fourth and Seventh Directives

Historically, the objectives of financial reporting have varied in different countries, and this fact is reflected in the relative importance given to the various parties who have an interest in accounting information. For example, financial reporting in certain countries has developed on the basis of considering shareholders as being the most important party entitled to receive financial information. This approach arose from the situation where businesses had obtained a substantial proportion of their funds from the public generally and where responsibility for the conduct of the operations of the business was divorced from ownership. Investors required regular reports to assess the performance achieved by management and future prospects, and annual accounts ensured that the stewardship function was being exercised properly.

On the other hand, in other countries financial reporting has evolved from the premise that accounts were provided largely for the tax authorities and other government bodies interested in national economic planning. The assessment of liabilities to tax had to be based on standard rules regarding the recognition of income, deduction of expenses and valuation of assets; in this way, all businesses would be subject to tax on the same basis. In Belgium, France, Germany, Greece, Italy, Luxembourg and Portugal, accounts have been used mainly to measure taxable profits. Although in Germany Company Law has been the principal authority for financial reporting measurement practices, it has historically been based on principles of historical cost and tax-based depreciation.

These contrasting attitudes to the purpose of financial reporting have adversely affected harmonisation of accounting law and practice in the EU. This being the case, it is probable that the harmonisation programme under the Directives has been only partially successful. This is clearly evidenced by the fact that harmonisation has not been achieved in the areas of recognition and measurement – both of which are fundamental to achieving comparability in financial reporting. Nevertheless, it is clear also that the Fourth and Seventh Directives have provided a base level for harmonisation of financial reporting in the EU, and have undoubtedly led to improvements in the quality and comparability of company accounts throughout the Union over the last twenty years. They have contributed also to improving the conditions for cross-border business and have allowed the mutual recognition of accounts for the purposes of quotation on securities exchanges throughout the EU. Moreover, a further important contribution of the Directives is in the area of creditor protection through the public availability of financial information. In contrast to the US, where only SEC registrant companies are required to publish financial statements, all limited liability companies in the EU are required to produce and publish financial information.

4.3 The European Commission's 1995 Communication on international harmonisation

In 1995, the European Commission issued a Communication (i.e. policy statement)[57] stating that, while EU legislation has considerably improved the quality of financial reporting in the Union, the Directives do not provide answers to all the problems facing preparers and users of accounts and accounting standard setters. In the Commission's view, the most urgent problem to be addressed concerns European companies with an 'international vocation' (the so-called 'global players') and the need to facilitate the access of such European global players to the international capital markets. The accounts prepared by those companies in accordance with their national legislation (based on the Accounting Directives) are not acceptable for international capital market purposes. These companies are therefore obliged to prepare two sets of accounts, one set which is in conformity with the Accounting Directives and another set required by the international capital markets.

The Commission examined several possible approaches to dealing with the issue of 'upgrading' EU accounting legislation. After careful consideration, the Commission suggested that a closer cooperation between the EU and the IASC, with the objective of ultimately adopting International Accounting Standards at the EU level, was the preferred solution. Referring to the 1995 agreement between IOSCO and the IASC to produce a core set of international accounting standards which would be endorsed by IOSCO (see 1.3 above), the Commission concluded that 'rather than amend the existing Directives, the proposal is to improve the present situation by associating the EU with the efforts undertaken by IASC and IOSCO towards a broader international harmonisation of accounting standards'.

This policy statement of the Commission paved the way to the acceptance of IAS by the EU. Unfortunately, the Commission could not anticipate in 1995 that the ultimate endorsement of IAS by IOSCO in May 2000 would only be a qualified acceptance of the standards. As it turned out, one of the main objectives of the Commission in moving towards IAS (access of European companies to international capital markets without having to provide reconciliations to any National GAAP) was only partly achieved.

4.4 The European Commission's Financial Services Action Plan

Meanwhile, certain EU Member States set about making it easier for their multinational companies to gain access to the international capital markets. In February 1998, new legislation was enacted in Germany to the effect that International Accounting Standards (or indeed other 'internationally recognised accounting principles' such as US GAAP) could be used in the consolidated financial statements of listed groups instead of German law and accounting principles. There was an added proviso that the financial statements must also be 'consistent with' the EU Accounting Directives.

Similar amended legislation was enacted in France in April 1998, allowing French companies whose securities were traded on a regulated market to use IAS or another body of international standards as the sole basis for their consolidated accounts. A number of other European countries (including Italy, Austria, Luxembourg, Belgium and Spain) followed suit. At the time, these were revolutionary changes, and demonstrated the influence of Anglo-American accounting philosophies, at least on those companies that wished either to seek access to the international capital markets, or to achieve greater transparency in their financial reporting. It also raised the stakes for the European Commission, emphasising the need for the Commission to deliver on the strategy set out in its 1995 Communication.

As part of its strategy to embrace IAS, and in response to its growing use by EU multinational companies, the Commission carried out an ongoing examination of the conformity between the Accounting Directives and IASs and SIC Interpretations.[58] Generally, these comparisons concluded that (with the exception of IAS 39 – see below) there are few conflicts between the Accounting Directives and IAS. Those minor conflicts that did exist would be addressed by the Commission in the context of the modernisation of the Accounting Directives that took place during the next two years or so. The Commission's programme of modernising the Accounting Directives not only removed existing conflicts between IAS and the Directives, but also ensured that all the options then available under IAS would be available to EU companies.

In May 1999, the Commission issued its Financial Services Action Plan.[59] The plan confirmed the Commission's position that comparable, transparent and reliable financial information is fundamental to an efficient and integrated EU capital market, and that International Accounting Standards seemed the most appropriate benchmark for a single set of financial reporting requirements which would be the catalyst for the development of a single EU capital market.

This initiative was given further impetus by the summit of the European Heads of Government held in Lisbon in March 2000, where it was agreed that a single European capital market should be developed as a matter of priority. It was acknowledged further that the adoption of a single financial reporting framework for the European Union was a vital element in that process. The summit conclusions stressed the need to accelerate completion of the internal market for financial services and set a deadline of 2005 to implement the Commission's Financial Services Action Plan.

Following this lead by the European Heads of Government, the Commission announced in June 2000 that it would present proposals to:

- introduce the requirement that all listed EU companies report in accordance with IAS by 2005; and

- modernise the EU Accounting Directives to reduce potential conflicts with IAS and bring the Directives into line with modern accounting developments.[60]

Meanwhile, EU companies reporting at the time under IAS faced an immediate problem with respect to IAS 39 – *Financial instruments: recognition and measurement.* IAS 39 requires that certain financial instruments are valued at fair value and that, in some cases, the changes in fair value are recorded in the profit and loss account. These requirements meant that there was a significant conflict between an IAS and the Accounting Directives, with the result that EU companies would not be able to continue to apply IAS unless significant amendments were made to the Directives. Consequently, because IAS 39 became operative for financial statements covering financial years beginning on or after 1 January 2001, there arose an urgent need to amend the Directives in order to allow the application of IAS 39 by EU companies.

Accordingly, the Commission put forward a proposal to amend the Fourth and Seventh Directives in order to enable EU companies to comply with IAS 39, and therefore prepare their financial statements in conformity with IAS. This was eventually approved by the Council and by the European Parliament in May 2001 in the form of a Directive (the 'Fair Value' Directive) that amended the Fourth, Seventh and Bank Accounts Directives.[61]

Although the Commission wanted to provide more flexibility in the Fair Value Directive in order to anticipate future developments in accounting for financial instruments, the EU Member States insisted on including certain restrictions in the Directive in order to make it as close as possible to the then current version of IAS 39 as possible. Unfortunately, as a result, these restrictions mean that the IASB's extension of the fair value provisions in IAS 39 (the 'full fair value option') has created new conflicts with the Fourth Directive, which will in all probability have to be addressed through further amendments to the Directive.

4.5   The European Commission's Regulation on the application of IAS in the European Union

On 13 February 2001, the European Commission published a draft EU Regulation[62] that would require publicly traded EU incorporated companies[63] to prepare, by 2005 at the latest, their consolidated accounts under IAS 'adopted' (see below) for application within the EU. This was adopted unanimously by the Council, and on 12 March 2002, by a vote of 492 for, 5 against, and 29 abstentions, the European Parliament endorsed this proposal. This was adopted as Regulation No. 1606/2002 of the European Parliament and of the Council on 19 July 2002.[64]

An EU Regulation has direct effect on companies, without the need for national legislation. However, the Regulation also provides an option for Member States to permit or require the application of adopted IAS in the preparation of annual (unconsolidated) accounts and to permit or require the application of adopted IAS by unlisted companies. This means that Member States can require the uniform application of adopted IAS to important sectors such as banking or insurance, regardless of whether or not companies are listed.

The Regulation established also the basic rules for the creation of an endorsement mechanism for the adoption of IAS, the timetable for implementation and a review clause to permit an assessment of the overall approach proposed. The endorsement mechanism is discussed below.

Internal Market Commissioner, Frits Bolkestein, commented as follows on the adoption of the Regulation by the Council: 'I am delighted that the IAS Regulation has been adopted in a single reading and am grateful for the positive attitude of both the Parliament and the Council. I believe IAS are the best standards that exist. Applying them throughout the EU will put an end to the current Tower of Babel in financial reporting. It will help protect us against malpractice. It will mean investors and other stakeholders will be able to compare like with like. It will help European firms to compete on equal terms when raising capital on world markets. What is more, during my recent visit to the US, I saw hopeful signs that the US will now work with us towards full convergence of our accounting standards.'

The Regulation provides the facility for individual Member States, at their option, to defer the application of the Regulation until 2007 for those companies publicly traded both in the Community and on a regulated third-country market which are already applying 'another set of internationally accepted standards' (essentially, US GAAP) as the primary basis for their consolidated accounts as well as for companies which have only publicly traded debt securities.[65] However, the Regulation states that it is nonetheless crucial that by 2007 at the latest IAS are applied by all Community companies publicly traded on a Community regulated market.[66]

To date, Denmark, Finland, Germany, Poland and Sweden have announced that they will allow this transitional provision to be applied by companies whose debt securities only are traded on a regulated market, with Austria, Belgium, France and Luxembourg likely to do so as well. However, only Germany has announced formally that it will provide the transitional relief to companies currently reporting under US GAAP, although Austria and Belgium are likely to do so as well.[67]

There are currently approximately 7,000 companies listed on EU regulated markets that will be subject to the proposed Regulation. Only about 275 of these companies applied IAS prior to 2005.

4.6   The EU endorsement mechanism

The Regulation defines the EU endorsement mechanism, which was already foreseen in the Commission's June 2000 Communication. The Commission took the view that an endorsement mechanism is needed to provide the necessary public oversight. The Commission considered also that it was not appropriate, politically or legally, to delegate accounting standard setting unconditionally and irrevocably to a private organisation over which the EU has no influence. In addition, the endorsement mechanism has the responsibility of examining whether the standards adopted by the IASB conform with EU public policy concerns.

The role of the endorsement mechanism is not to reformulate or replace IFRS, but to oversee the adoption of new standards and interpretations, intervening only when these contain material deficiencies or have failed to cater for features specific to the EU economic or legal environments. The central task of this mechanism is to confirm that IFRS provide a suitable basis for financial reporting by listed EU companies. The mechanism is based on a two-tier structure, combining a regulatory level with an expert level, to assist the Commission in its endorsement role.

The recitals to the Regulation state that the endorsement mechanism should act expeditiously on proposed international accounting standards and also be a means to deliberate, reflect and exchange information on international accounting standards among the main parties concerned, in particular national accounting standard setters, supervisors in the fields of securities, banking and insurance, central banks including the ECB, the accounting profession and users and preparers of accounts. The mechanism should be a means to foster common understanding of adopted international accounting standards in the Community.[68]

There are three criteria set out in the Regulation on the application of IAS in the EU with which any individual IAS must comply if it is to be adopted:[69]

- the standard should not be contrary to the principle of true and fair in conformity with the Accounting Directives;
- the standard should be conducive to the European public good; and
- the standard should meet basic criteria as to the quality of information required for financial statements to be useful to users.

These criteria, although wide, are fundamentally reasonable and cannot be considered overly difficult or burdensome in view of the substantial power the EU is effectively vesting in the IASB, a body not accountable to the EU electorate in any manner. It is important to note that whilst a standard or interpretation can only be adopted if all three criteria are met, this does not mean that if all three criteria are met that a standard or interpretation must necessarily be adopted. However, if a standard or interpretation is not adopted, EU companies are free to apply it, except in those cases where such application would be in conflict with binding EU law.

4.6.1 Regulatory level of the endorsement mechanism

An Accounting Regulatory Committee (ARC) has been formed, composed of representatives of the Member States and chaired by a representative of the Commission. The ARC operates on the basis of appropriate institutional arrangements and under existing comitology rules that will ensure full transparency and accountability towards the Council and the European Parliament.

Under these rules, the Commission presents to the ARC a report that is required to identify the standard and examine both its conformity with the conditions set out in the Regulation and its suitability as a basis for financial reporting in the EU. The ARC must decide, on the basis of qualified majority voting, whether to recommend to the European Commission that it should adopt or reject a standard for application in the EU. The same procedure applies to the adoption of amendments to previously adopted Standards and Interpretations.

4.6.2 The European Financial Reporting Advisory Group (EFRAG)

The European Financial Reporting Advisory Group (EFRAG) was established as a private-sector initiative by ten key constituents (EFRAG's 'Founding Fathers') interested in financial reporting in Europe, including the European Federation of Accountants (FEE), the Union des Confédérations de l'Industrie et des Employeurs d'Europe (UNICE), the European Banking Federation (EBF), and the Comité Européen des Assurances (CEA).

EFRAG is a two-tier organisation, comprising:

- a group of eleven highly qualified experts (the EFRAG Technical Expert Group), to carry out the technical work; and
- a Supervisory Board of European Organisations (the EFRAG Supervisory Board), to guarantee representation of the full European interest and to enhance the legitimacy and credibility of EFRAG.

The manner in which EFRAG fits into the EC comitology framework of endorsement of IAS is shown diagrammatically below:[70]

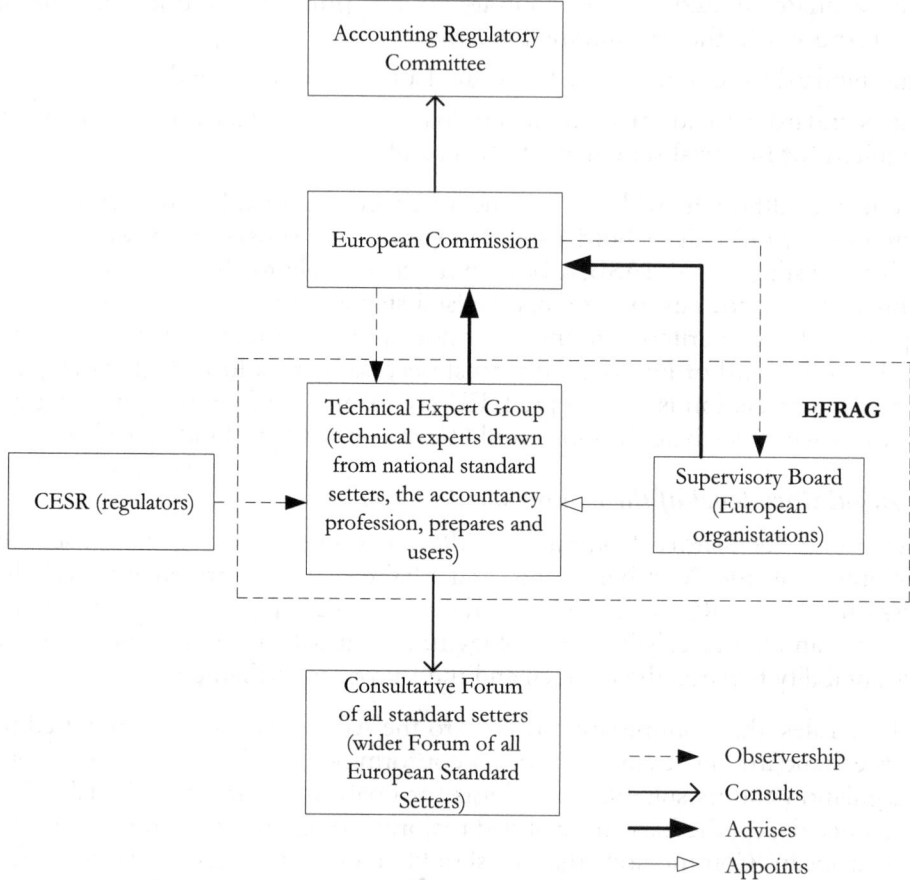

The principal aim of EFRAG is to provide proactive input into the work of the IASB. EFRAG will advise the Commission on the technical assessment of IFRSs and Interpretations, for application in the EU. The technical work of EFRAG will be carried out by the Technical Expert Group on the basis of a wide consultation process. National standard setters of Europe have access to EFRAG through a number of routes. In common with other consultative organisations, they receive regular updates of EFRAG agenda items and decisions. Additionally, they comprise EFRAG's Consultative Forum, meeting at least twice a year to engage in technical debate on matters arising from the EFRAG agenda.

The Technical Expert Group was set up by EFRAG on 26 June 2001. Its role is to provide the private sector support and expertise needed to assess the standards and interpretations developed by the IASB on a timely basis. It also has the responsibility to provide input into the IASB standard setting process at all stages of a particular project, and particularly in the early phases. The Technical Expert Group will ensure that EU users and preparers are involved in the preparatory discussions of the standards at the international level, and in the technical assessment of the standards, before their adoption by the EU. The meetings of the Technical Expert Group are open to public observation.

The Technical Expert Group provides advice to the Commission on the adoption of existing IAS for their use in the EU, and it advises the Commission also on whether or not an amendment to the Directives is recommended in the light of international accounting developments. However, the Technical Expert Group has a somewhat uneasy voting arrangement: EFRAG cannot recommend non-endorsement of a standard unless there is a two third's majority vote against the standard. This means that a majority of the Group's members can be against endorsement, yet EFRAG would not be able to recommend non-endorsement unless that majority is at least two-thirds. As the Group comprises eleven members, including the Chairman, this means that at least eight must vote against a particular IFRS or Interpretation in order to be able to recommend non-endorsement.

This uneasy arrangement manifested itself in EFRAG's letter of adoption of the amended IAS 39 – *Financial Instruments: Recognition and Measurement* – sent to the Commission on 8 July 2004. In voting on the adoption of IAS 39, five members of the Group voted to support endorsement and six members voted to oppose endorsement. As a result, EFRAG's endorsement advice to the Commission read as follows: 'We have decided only to issue a positive endorsement advice if there is a majority supporting endorsement ... EFRAG cannot recommend non-endorsement of a standard unless there is a two third's majority vote against the standard and EFRAG does not support endorsement unless there is majority in favour. Therefore, EFRAG does not issue any advice whether to endorse IAS 39 or not.'[71]

In addition, a special sub-committee of EFRAG has been established in close co-operation with the European Insurers Association (CEA) to deal with insurance matters. Insurance has priority in Europe, given the fact that there is no comprehensive IFRS on accounting for insurance contracts yet, even though listed insurance undertakings will have to apply adopted IAS from the financial year 2005 onwards, in line with other listed companies.

4.7 Enforcement and regulation in an integrated European capital market

The European Commission has set an ambitious agenda for the European Union to become the world's most competitive economy by 2010. However, progress with European capital market integration – a vital ingredient of this agenda – so far has been slow. Nevertheless, the economic gains to be derived from an integrated pan-European financial and capital market are considerable. European companies will have greater access to a deep and liquid market at lower costs of capital; and European consumers will enjoy wider investment choice and increasing net returns on their investments. The macroeconomic benefits could be substantial also, as increased investment implies stronger job creation and GDP growth.

However, the basic structures needed for an integrated market are not yet in place. In Europe, trans-national companies have to report to regulators in twenty-five member states. They face a wide variety of different rules and regulations and investors have to negotiate fragmented markets that frustrate cross-border trading. Taken together with the differences in regulation, enforcement, taxation, legal systems and bankruptcy laws, this gives a situation that Baron Alexandre Lamfalussy described as 'a remarkable cocktail of Kafkaesque inefficiency that serves no-one – neither consumers, nor investors, nor SMEs, nor large companies, nor governments.'

By contrast, the US capital markets provide clear evidence that efficiencies are forced upon businesses once their performances are easily comparable; without these pressures, inefficiency can go unnoticed. Globalisation of competition will punish less efficient businesses that cannot be price-competitive, and their revenues will reduce. Businesses enjoying semi-protected markets for their services, under less than transparent financing arrangements, will not be able to enjoy that shelter indefinitely.

Consequently, the greatest challenge facing Europe in delivering an efficient single capital market is the task of efficient regulation and enforcement. The absence of an effective and coordinated enforcement mechanism severely limits the credibility of any financial reporting regime. Clearly, the adoption of IFRS in Europe will improve the functioning of the securities markets only when it is properly and rigorously enforced. This means that the supervisors of the European capital markets have a crucial role to play in ensuring that companies comply with financial reporting requirements. In our view, this can be achieved only through the establishment of an efficient and lean Europe-wide regulatory system. This implies the co-operative development and implementation of a common EU approach to regulation that would establish a level playing field for EU financial reporting, maintained by rigorous enforcement that will prevent regulatory arbitrage.

In introducing the IAS Regulation, the European Commission stated that one of its key actions would be the development of an enforcement infrastructure that will ensure the rigorous application of IAS by listed companies in the EU. The focus of this initiative will be on disseminating implementation guidance, encouraging high quality auditing, and reinforcing coordinated regulatory oversight. A coordinating body has been set up, as described below.

4.7.1   *The Committee of European Securities Regulators (CESR)*

The Committee of European Securities Regulators (CESR) was established by the European Commission Decision of June 2001.[72] This decision was taken in the light of the recommendation of the Report of the Committee of Wise Men on the Regulation of European Securities Markets (the Lamfalussy Report) as endorsed by the European Council and the European Parliament.[73] CESR is an independent Committee whose members comprise senior representatives from national public authorities competent in the field of securities. CESR has set out its own operational arrangements in its Charter.[74]

The CESR Chair and Vice-Chair are elected from among the Members for a period of two years. The Committee meets at least four times a year. CESR works with the support of a secretariat headed by a Secretary General. A representative of the European Commission is entitled to participate actively in all discussions held by CESR.

CESR submits an Annual Report to the European Commission, which is also sent to the European Parliament and the Council. The Chair of CESR reports regularly to the European Parliament and maintains strong links with the European Securities Committee.

The main roles of CESR are to:

- improve coordination among European Securities Regulators;
- act as an advisory group to assist the European Commission, in particular in its preparation of draft implementing measures to support the legislative framework for the regulation of Europe's securities markets; and
- work to ensure more consistent and timely day-to-day implementation of the European legislative framework in the Member States.

In doing so, CESR advises the European Commission on securities policy issues relating to Europe's securities markets and responds to mandates given by the European Commission. To foster common and uniform implementation of EU securities law, CESR may issue guidelines, recommendations and standards.

CESR is also developing effective operational network mechanisms to enhance day-to-day consistent supervision and enforcement within the single market for financial services. Having agreed a Multilateral Memorandum of Understanding, CESR has made a significant contribution to greater surveillance and enforcement of securities activities. CESR-Pol a permanent group of senior enforcement officials, is responsible for ensuring this task functions smoothly. As regards financial reporting, CESR-Fin coordinates the work of CESR members in the area of endorsement and enforcement of IFRS and other financial disclosure requirements in the European Union. CESR-Fin's Work Plan, which was approved by CESR in January 2002, includes the development of principles, guidelines and standards in the areas of:

- definition of enforcement;
- selection techniques;
- powers to be attributed to the enforcers; and
- cross border listings and offerings.

4.7.2 CESR Standard No. 1

During the seventh meeting of CESR held in Paris in March 2003, the first CESR standard on *Financial Information: Enforcement of standards on financial information in Europe*, was approved.[75] The standard represents a significant part of CESR's contribution to the task of developing and implementing a common approach to the enforcement of IFRS in Europe.

The standard sets down 21 principles on which, in CESR's view, harmonisation of the institutional oversight systems in Europe may be achieved. In particular, a definition of enforcement of standards on financial information, its scope, the selection techniques applicable by the enforcers and the responsibility of the different parties involved are outlined.

The standard states that for financial information other than prospectuses, ex-post enforcement is the normal procedure, whilst for prospectuses ex-ante approval is the normal procedure. Enforcement of all financial information should normally be achieved by selecting a number of issuers and documents to be examined. The preferred models for selecting financial information for enforcement purposes are mixed models whereby a risk-based approach is combined with a rotation and/or a sampling approach.[76]

Where a material misstatement in the financial information is detected, enforcers are required to take appropriate actions to achieve an appropriate disclosure and where relevant, public correction of misstatement.[77] Enforcers should periodically report to the public on their activities providing, as a minimum, information on the enforcement policies adopted and decisions taken in individual cases including accounting and disclosure matters.[78]

4.7.3   CESR Recommendation on communication of the impact of IFRS

In December 2003, CESR published a recommendation for regulators on how listed EU companies can effectively manage the communication of the financial impact of transitioning to IFRS in 2005.[79] CESR considers it essential that the transition must be monitored carefully by regulators to ensure that every company continues to meet its reporting requirements and that investors are able to understand the effect of the new reporting standards on the financial position of listed companies. CESR has identified four milestones in the transition process, as follows:

(a)   the publication of the 2003 annual report (including the 2003 financial statements);

(b)   the publication of the 2004 annual report (including the 2004 financial statements);

(c)   the 2005 interim financial reports (half-yearly and quarterly financial reports); and

(d)   the 2005 annual financial statements.

CESR's advice to its members (Europe's securities regulators) following consultation during October and November 2003, attempts to blend the needs of listed companies and investors by proposing that listed companies implement a phased transition process. This will facilitate listed companies in their assessment of the financial consequences and enable appropriate planning for the application of the international accounting standards whilst also ensuring investors are provided with financial information that is easy to interpret.

4.7.4 CESR Standard No. 2

In April 2004, CESR issued a standard on the organisation of greater co-ordination of enforcement activities by supervisors of financial information in Europe.[80] The standard's aim is further to contribute to the creation within Europe of robust and consistent enforcement of IFRS. The key principles introduced by Standard no. 2 include:

- discussion of enforcement decisions and experiences within a formalised structure;

- the principle that all supervisors should take into account existing decisions taken by EU National Enforcers; and

- the development of a database as a practical reference tool that sets out decisions taken by EU National Enforcers to provide a record of previous decisions reached in particular cases.

5 THE ADOPTION OF IFRS IN OTHER COUNTRIES

A comprehensive 'stable platform' of generally high quality International Financial Reporting Standards has now been promulgated, and nearly 100 countries are committed to adopt IFRS directly, or to align their national standards with IFRS, from 2005 or later. Although the European Union, comprising twenty-five Member States, will almost certainly be the IASB's most significant constituency, there are also a number of other economically developed countries that will be adopting IFRS as their primary system of GAAP. Set out below is a brief summary of the basis on which some of these countries have adopted IFRS.

5.1 Australia

The Australian Financial Reporting Council (FRC) is a statutory body established under the *Australian Securities and Investments Commission Act 2001, as amended by the Corporate Law Economic Reform Program (Audit Reform and Corporate Disclosure) Act 2004.* The FRC is responsible for providing broad oversight of the process for setting accounting and auditing standards as well as monitoring the effectiveness of auditor independence requirements in Australia and providing the Australian Government with reports and advice on these matters. It comprises key stakeholders from the business community, the professional accounting bodies, governments and regulatory agencies.

In July 2002, the Chairman of the FRC announced that the FRC had formalised its support for the adoption by Australia of international accounting standards by 1 January 2005. In accordance with this strategic directive, the Australian Accounting Standards Board (AASB) issued Australian equivalents to IFRSs on 15 July 2004. The issuing of the Australian equivalents to international standards achieves the FRC's strategic directive of ensuring that for-profit entities applying AASB standards for reporting periods beginning on or after 1 January 2005 will also be complying with IASB standards.

In adopting the IASB's standards, the AASB's overall approach is to adopt the content and wording of the standards. Words are only being changed where there is a need to accommodate the Australian legislative environment. In addition, subject to due process, the AASB sometimes permits only one of a number of optional treatments available in IASB standards and sometimes requires additional disclosures, particularly where these are already required under existing AASB standards.

In some cases, existing AASB standards contain helpful commentary that is not included in the equivalent IASB standards. The AASB has retained this commentary as guidance that is not part of the standards where it is considered to be of benefit to users of AASB standards, and provided it does not contradict the content of Australian equivalents to IASB standards. Such guidance may, for example, deal with situations that are commonly encountered in the Australian environment but which are not catered for in the IASB standards.

The AASB plans to continue to work to maintain consistency with the IASB's standards in order that the FRC's strategic directive continues to be met.

5.2   China and Hong Kong

5.2.1   China

The developments in IFRS have been playing an important role in the development of accounting standards and practices in China. The Ministry of Finance (the "MOF") is responsible for the promulgation of accounting standards. In 1993, the MOF started a work programme to develop a set of *Accounting Standards for Business Enterprises*. To date, sixteen accounting standards have been published, as well as several exposure drafts covering a number of topics.

The overall approach is to converge, as far as is practicable, with international practices and, in particular, with IFRS. Many of the accounting standards published to date are similar to the corresponding IFRSs. For instance, the requirements set out in the local accounting standards on revenue, construction contracts, post balance sheet date events, cash flow statements are very similar to those in IAS 18, IAS 11, IAS 10 and IAS 7, respectively. However, there are accounting standards that do not have an IFRS equivalent, and the requirements contained therein may not be in line entirely with international practices. Notable examples are the accounting standards on non-monetary transactions and on debt restructuring, the accounting treatments of which are based on carrying value instead of fair value.

The MOF also promulgated the *Accounting System for Business Enterprises*, which codifies the accounting practices introduced by the accounting standards into a single volume of accounting rules.

The publication of the accounting standards and the *Accounting System for Business Enterprises* are important milestones in the convergence process. Prior to their publication, the local accounting regulations and practices were primarily tax-driven, with virtually no provisions, for example, for impairment testing. Thus, whilst there are still some historic differences between local and international practices, the convergence process is closing the gap, particularly during the last few years where significant progress has been made.

5.2.2   *Hong Kong*

The Hong Kong Institute of Certified Public Accountants ("HKICPA"), formerly the Hong Kong Society of Accountants, a statutory body established under the Professional Accountants Ordinance, is the principal source of accounting principles in Hong Kong. These include a series of Hong Kong Financial Reporting Standards ("HKFRS"), accounting standards referred to as Statements of Standard Accounting Practice ("SSAPs") and Interpretations issued by the HKICPA. The term "Hong Kong Financial Reporting Standards" is deemed to include all of the foregoing. While HKFRS have no direct legal force, they derive their authority from the HKICPA, which may take disciplinary action against any of its members responsible, as preparer or as auditor, for financial statements that do not follow the requirements of the pronouncements.

In 2001, the HKICPA Council mandated a strategy of achieving convergence of its accounting standards with International Financial Reporting Standards ("IFRS") issued by the IASB. Today the overwhelming majority of extant HKFRS are based on their equivalent IFRS, IAS and Interpretations promulgated by the IASB. The HKICPA Council supports the integration of its standard setting process with that of the IASB.

As of October 2004, IFRSs 1 to 5 had been adopted as HKFRS 1 to 5 and, with effect from 1 January 2005, all the existing SSAPs and Interpretations for which there are equivalent IAS and SIC Interpretations will be replaced by Hong Kong Accounting Standards and Hong Kong Accounting Standards Interpretations with numbers corresponding to the equivalent IAS and SIC Interpretations, respectively. There will be 31 such standards and 11 such Interpretations.

Although the HKICPA Council has a policy to achieve convergence of HKFRSs with IFRSs, the HKICPA Council may consider it appropriate to include additional disclosure requirements in a HKFRS or, in some exceptional cases, to deviate from an IFRS. Each HKFRS issued by Council contains information about the extent of compliance with the equivalent IFRS. Where the requirements of a HKFRS and an IFRS differ, the HKFRS should be followed by entities reporting within the area of application of the HKFRSs. However, such situations are relatively few.

HKFRS are considered to be strongly persuasive in interpreting the legal requirement that financial statements should give a true and fair view. HKFRSs set out recognition, measurement, presentation and disclosure requirements dealing with transactions and events that are important in general purpose financial statements. They may also set out such requirements for transactions and events that arise mainly in specific industries. HKFRSs are based on a Framework, adopted from IFRS, which addresses the concepts underlying the information presented in general purpose financial statements. The objective of the Framework is to facilitate the consistent and logical formulation of HKFRSs. The Framework also provides a basis for the use of judgement in resolving accounting issues.

HKFRSs are designed to apply to the general purpose financial statements and other financial reporting of all profit-oriented entities. Profit-oriented entities include those engaged in commercial, industrial, financial and similar activities, whether organised in corporate or in other forms. They include organisations such as mutual insurance companies and other mutual cooperative entities that provide dividends or other economic benefits directly and proportionately to their owners, members or participants. Although HKFRSs are not designed to apply to not-for-profit activities in the private sector, public sector or government, entities with such activities may find them appropriate.

5.3   Norway

Norway is not a member of the EU. However, as a member of the European Economic Agreement (EEA), Norway is obligated to adopt the EU Regulation requiring all entities in the EU listed on a regulated market to their prepare consolidated accounts in accordance with IFRS by 2005 ('the mandatory scope'). Clearly, this puts a constraint on the development of Norwegian financial reporting in the future.

Financial reporting in Norway is regulated by legislation. The Norwegian Accounting Act of 1998 does not contain detailed rules and may best be characterised as a legal framework. This legal framework, as opposed to a set of detailed rules, leaves room for the exercise of professional judgment. The concept of 'good accounting practice' (GAP) plays a fundamental role in the framework. A basic principle set out in the legislation is that financial reports should be prepared in accordance with GAP. Underlying the GAP concept are accounting principles and concepts developed in a transaction based historical cost model.

The legal framework approach assumes an active standard setting body. Norsk RegnskapsStiftelse (NRS, 'The Norwegian Accounting Standards Board' (NASB)) is the standard setting body in Norway. Today, in addition to the NASB accounting standards, pronouncements made by the Oslo Stock Exchange are considered authoritative GAP literature. Similarly, pronouncements made by the Norwegian Institute of Public Accountants (DnR) are generally considered to have impact on Norwegian GAP.

Norwegian GAP has traditionally drawn on the accounting standards issued by the FASB in the US, the ASB in the UK, and the IASB in its standard setting process. The leading role of US GAAP in international accounting practice has greatly influenced Norwegian GAP. However, the increased importance of the IFRS in the international accounting harmonisation process led to a shift in the Norwegian approach in the mid-nineties. In the preamble of the Accounting Act 1998, the Parliament assumes that harmonisation towards IFRS should be regarded an objective in accounting standard setting. The international harmonisation process led the NASB to adopt a strategy in 2001 where harmonization with IFRS was the primary objective.

In any event, though, as a result of the EU Regulation and the EEA, listed Norwegian companies will be required to adopt full IFRS in their consolidated accounts by 2005, and the enforcement mechanism assumed under the Regulation applies to Norway as well. However, it has not yet been determined whether IFRS reporting will be allowed or required for other than listed companies and whether IFRS-reporting will be allowed or required in the separate accounts. In the report of the Accounting Act Committee of 2002, which was commissioned to assess the demand for changes in the current accounting legislation to meet the requirements of the EU Regulation, it was proposed that other than listed companies should be allowed, but not required, to apply IFRS in their consolidated accounts by 2005. However, the report recommended also that neither listed nor unlisted companies should be allowed to apply IFRS in the separate accounts. Nevertheless, in spite of this recommendation, a government bill on the subject was released in June 2004, suggesting that the application of IFRS in the separate accounts of companies should be permitted.

The report of the Accounting Act Committee also proposed changes in the Accounting Act that would allow accounting policies that are permissible under IFRS to be adopted under Norwegian GAP as well (with the exception of the revaluation alternative under IAS 16). Thus, even though a two-tier system of both IFRS and Norwegian GAP will most likely will apply in Norway from 2005, Norwegian GAP is intended to allow companies applying it to adopt IFRS accounting policies even though these companies are not applying IFRS *per se.*

The harmonisation of Norwegian GAP with IFRS outside the mandatory scope of the EU Regulation creates difficult challenges, both conceptually and in practice. The Norwegian legal framework and Norwegian GAP are focused on revenue and expense recognition and the main objective is to provide a framework for meaningful income measurement, as opposed to the emphasis on asset and liability recognition under IFRS.

The NASB will in the future not only develop accounting standards dealing with Norwegian GAP, but will also issue recommendations or guidelines on the interpretation of IFRS on issues specific to Norwegian companies. For instance, there may be issues relating to the oil and gas, hydroelectric power generating and shipping industries that may specific to Norwegian companies. The NASB has so far issued one document dealing with the interpretation of IFRS: in an exposure draft dealing the public and private pension arrangements in Norway in the context of IFRS, the NASB discusses guidelines for the application of IAS 19.

5.4   South Africa

In 1994 the South African standard setting body, the Accounting Practices Board, made the decision to base future accounting standards on international standards. As a result, the South African standards that were issued were generally the same as the equivalent international standards, but with a few minor differences. These differences mainly related to certain additional disclosures that were included in the South African standards, and in addition, the South African standards did not incorporate the allowed alternative method for a change in accounting policy. Some of the international standards were issued in South Africa after they were issued internationally, meaning that some standards had different effective dates. For example, IAS 41 – *Agriculture* – was issued in South Africa with an unchanged effective date, whereas South Africa did not have an accounting standard dealing with business combinations until years beginning on or after 1 January 2000, although IAS 22 – *Business Combinations* – had been initially issued in 1993.

In 2003, the Accounting Standards Board decided to remove the remaining differences, as far as possible, between international standards and South African standards. As a result, in the first half of 2004 all international standards in issue at that time were adopted in South Africa. Consequently, the standards have a dual number, namely an international and South African number (for example IFRS 1/AC 138) to reflect the fact that the Accounting Practices Board has approved them for use in South Africa.

Whilst this harmonisation process has left some historic differences in effective dates, which are included by way of footnote in the accounting standards, for IFRSs issued since the end of 2003 there are none. In addition, South Africa has issued its own interpretation on one issue, dealing with an additional tax payable when dividends are declared, as a result of the IASB deciding not to issue an opinion on an issue that was considered to be specific to South Africa.

The South African securities exchange, the Johannesburg Stock Exchange, revised its listing requirements in 2003, and with effect from periods beginning on or after 1 January 2005 listed companies will be required to prepare financial statements under IFRS.

The Companies Act, together with its related Fourth Schedule that governs the disclosure requirements for South African companies, and the stock exchange's listing requirements have certain disclosure requirements that are additional to those contained in IFRS.

5.5   Switzerland

In Switzerland, Swiss GAAP Financial Reporting Standards (FER) came into life in the mid 1980s to address the need for a Swiss set of financial accounting standards that presented a true and fair view of the state of affairs of companies (as opposed to the generally conservative tax- or creditor-oriented financial statements prepared under statutory rules applicable to all companies). Swiss GAAP FER had (and has) as one of its goals to 'embrace the concepts of IAS' and to not conflict with IAS, but rather, to allow further alternatives than those included under IAS. In the early years, Swiss GAAP FER allowed many alternative treatments and implementation was very diverse. As time passed, many alternative treatments were abandoned and Swiss GAAP FER today can be viewed as a fairly complete set of standards with more flexibility and less required disclosure than IAS. It is now targeted at small and medium-sized enterprises.

However, International Accounting Standards have played a very significant role since the beginning of the 1990s, when consolidated accounts became required for the first time. Because the local Swiss accounting standards and practices in those days were primarily tax-driven and creditor-oriented, global companies were forced to look to a set of accounting standards more accepted on the world stage. As a result, many of the large Swiss multinational companies implemented IAS for their consolidated accounts. Over time, the importance of IAS (and US GAAP) grew, and by the mid-nineties, virtually all large listed companies were applying either IAS or US GAAP. The majority of these currently apply IFRS. The Swiss Exchange (SWX) requires the adoption of either IFRS or US GAAP for all registrants on the main exchange with effect from 2005, whilst for those companies not listed on the main exchange, Swiss GAAP FER provides a minimum standard (although IAS or US GAAP are also allowed).

6   WHAT CONSTITUTES INTERNATIONAL GAAP?

6.1   Generally accepted practice

It is clear that 2005 is a watershed year for IFRS with a significant number of countries adopting it as their principal financial reporting regime. However, to date, no substantial body of custom, practice or generally accepted ways of employing IFRS has had an opportunity to develop. Indeed, one of the challenges is to put in place a regime under which an 'International GAAP' that is understood and commonly applied throughout the world, can develop. Paradoxically, it may be that this situation best illustrates the real meaning of GAAP in an IFRS context. A comprehensive set of International Financial Reporting Standards exists, but no GAAP as yet.

So what else has to happen before 'International GAAP' can be said to have emerged? The extra element, which only time, practical application, and the inevitable disputes and compromises can supply, is generally accepted practice. It will only be after a number of years of full implementation by a representative cross-section of businesses in a number of countries, that a consensus will emerge over the way that in practice, and in the context of real commercial transactions, IFRS is actually to be applied.

The term 'generally accepted' does not necessarily imply that there must exist a large number of actual applications of a particular accounting practice. For example, new areas of accounting that have not yet been generally applied may be accepted as part of GAAP. Similarly, alternative accounting treatments for similar items may both be generally accepted.

It is our view that in the developing context of IFRS, 'generally accepted' will refer to accounting practices that are regarded as permissible by the accounting profession and regulators internationally – which means a broad consensus will come to exist between users, preparers, auditors, regulators and the markets, across what are currently regarded as national boundaries.

In general, any accounting practice which is legitimate in the circumstances under which it has been applied has come to be regarded as GAAP. The decision as to whether or not a particular practice is permissible or legitimate is normally governed by one or more of the following factors, which may therefore be expected to apply to the emergence of 'International GAAP':

- Is the practice addressed in accounting standards or other official pronouncements?
- Is the practice addressed in accounting standards that deal with similar and related issues?
- If the practice is not addressed in accounting standards, is it dealt with in the standards of another country that could reasonably be considered to offer authoritative guidance?
- Is the practice consistent with the needs of users and the objectives of financial reporting?
- Does the practice have authoritative support in the accounting literature?
- Is the practice consistent with the underlying conceptual framework document?
- Does the practice meet basic criteria as to the quality of information required for financial statements to be useful to users?
- Does the practice fairly reflect the economic substance of the transaction involved?
- Is the practice consistent with the fundamental concept of 'fair presentation'?
- Are other companies in similar situations generally applying the practice?

In an IFRS context, these factors build on the requirements set out in paragraphs 10 to 12 of IAS 8, which state that, in the absence of a Standard or an Interpretation that specifically applies to a transaction, other event or condition, management is required to use its judgement in developing and applying an accounting policy that results in information that is:

(a)   relevant to the economic decision-making needs of users; and

(b)   reliable, in that the financial statements:

(i)   represent faithfully the financial position, financial performance and cash flows of the entity;

(ii)   reflect the economic substance of transactions, other events and conditions, and not merely the legal form;

(iii)   are neutral, i.e. free from bias;

(iv)   are prudent; and

(v)   are complete in all material respects.[81]

In support of this primary requirement, the standard gives guidance on how management should apply this judgement. This guidance comes in two 'strengths' – certain things which management is required to consider, and others which it 'may' consider, as follows.

In making this judgement, management *shall* refer to, and consider the applicability of, the following sources in descending order:

(a)   the requirements and guidance in standards and interpretations dealing with similar and related issues; and

(b)   the definitions, recognition criteria and measurement concepts for assets, liabilities, income and expenses in the Framework;[82] and

in making this judgement, management *may also* consider the most recent pronouncements of other standard-setting bodies that use a similar conceptual framework to develop accounting standards, other accounting literature and accepted industry practices, to the extent that these do not conflict with the sources in (a) and (b) above.[83]

6.2   Practical interpretations of IFRS

Relatively speaking, IFRS financial reporting is still in its infancy. However, in 2005 IFRS becomes the global standard for financial reporting outside North America virtually overnight, therefore significant questions of interpretation will inevitably arise. Many of these will be issues of precedent and will have cross-border implications. The biggest challenge facing regulators is to ensure that national variations in the interpretation and application of IFRS do not emerge. Although IFRIC does exist as the IASB's interpretations arm, IFRIC is neither able to, nor can it be expected to, deal with issues of interpretation that will arise on a day-to-day basis. IFRIC took more than two years to issue its first interpretation, and it is fruitless for companies to expect either IFRIC or the IASB to provide immediate answers to every practical issue as it arises.

In reality, the day-to-day issues of interpretation will be decided, initially, by company management and their auditors. Thereafter, Regulators may become influential to a greater or lesser extent. However, the role of IFRIC and the IASB will principally be to monitor the practical application of standards and, if deemed necessary, issue an interpretation or amend a standard in response to what they consider to be the development of divergent or unacceptable treatments or inappropriate practices.

This means that all those involved with the development of IFRS into a global financial reporting framework bear a considerable responsibility to ensure that the development is evolutionary and not revolutionary. For the EU in particular, the need to ensure cross-border consistency in application, regulation and enforcement is paramount if this bold initiative is to succeed. Consequently, one of the interesting aspects of financial reporting during the next decade will be to observe how the process of acceptance and implementation of IFRS across the world generally, and the EU in particular, develops. Put simply, it will be interesting to watch the emergence of 'International GAAP'.

6.3   Who 'owns' International GAAP?

The adoption of IFRS in the European Union as the single financial reporting framework for listed companies will mean that it has become a major force in world accounting. Its adoption by thousands of EU companies, including some of the largest companies in the world, will inevitably ensure its prominence. Combine this with other countries such as Australia, China and Switzerland, and it will not be long before the question of the 'ownership' of International GAAP arises, and who, therefore, is the ultimate authority when the inevitable differences of opinion and judgements occur.

This issue has a number of practical implications for companies applying IFRS, for example:

- What happens in cases where different (and potentially conflicting) interpretations of the same standard are given by different regulators?

- There is uncertainty surrounding the legal issue of who has jurisdiction in cases of conflict between two parties on the question of the conformity of a specific set of financial statements with IFRS. For example, what are the roles of the national courts, the European Court of Justice, National Regulators, the IASB, IFRIC etc.?

However there is a possibility of an even greater level of uncertainty being created as the custom and practice that are an essential part of any GAAP, begin to accrue. Hitherto, all standard setting bodies have been given their legitimacy by, and have operated within, national legislative frameworks; by contrast, the IASB is a private sector body, with no political accountability. In theory at least, all it does is set the standards; issues of compliance and enforcement are outside its frame of reference. As International GAAP develops there will no longer be a supreme legislative body that can decide, for all concerned with applying International GAAP, what does and does not constitute conformity with it. Moreover, pronouncements, rulings, and interpretations issued by others outside the IASB setup, will inevitably become part of International GAAP.

Therefore, it seems that it is only a matter of time before the ultimate ownership and authority of International GAAP is tested. Paradoxically it may be that the more successful International GAAP becomes as a global financial reporting system, the more its interpretation, integrity and meaning will be disputed.

7 CONCLUSION

The European Commission's regulation that all EU companies listed on a regulated market should prepare their consolidated accounts in accordance with IFRS means that the much-talked-about notion of harmonised financial reporting under a single set of accounting standards is now a practical reality. Clearly, Europe's decision has encouraged several other countries to adopt a similar path. However, for companies, the requirement to adopt IFRS is not merely a technical exercise involving the reordering of information and rearrangement of the financial statements. Conversion to IFRS will often challenge fundamentally a company's existing business model. It will provide a unique opportunity for the company to re-examine and re-engineer the way it looks at itself through its internal management reporting. It will affect the way the company presents itself to investors and other users of its financial statements.

It is vital that company managements recognise the far-reaching impact that IFRS will have on their businesses. Failure to do so could place their companies at a competitive disadvantage. The adoption of IFRS is not simply a matter of choosing different accounting policies; it involves the adoption of an entirely different system of performance measurement and communication with the markets. There will be substantially increased levels of transparency for many companies – for example, through expanded segmental disclosures and the recognition of derivatives on balance sheets at fair value. In addition, IFRS conversion presents management with an opportunity to reconsider the business reporting model, for example:

- how key performance indicators are determined and used in the business;
- how transactions are executed;
- how company performance is communicated to, and evaluated by, the markets and how the market evaluates the company against its competitors;
- how financial data is made more accessible to the markets more frequently;
- how the company's finance function is organised;
- how executives are compensated; and
- how performance-related remuneration for employees is determined.

Changing accounting standards may not sound strategic, but it will change fundamentally the way that businesses are run, the way that success is measured and the information and records that companies need to maintain. For many companies in Europe and elsewhere, this change is huge. This is because, by embracing International GAAP, Europe and the rest of the world are embracing also a vision for financial reporting that is not necessarily particularly widely known or understood. It is a vision that considers fair value measurement to be paramount, and rejects historical costs, accruals and the realisation principle as irrelevant. Moreover, it is a vision that regards the determination of taxable income or realised profits as having no place in financial reporting.

This vision is based on an approach to company financial reporting that has been developed over the past several years by a group of Anglo-Saxon accounting standard setters, and has now been adopted by the International Accounting Standards Board. This approach is based on a balance sheet oriented, fair value model, where the emphasis is on measuring the fair values of companies' assets and liabilities. Inevitably, the approach entails that many 'fair values' will be determined largely on the basis of financial models. This means that the accounting process will in future be focused extensively on the recognition, derecognition and measurement at the 'mark-to-model' fair value of companies' assets and liabilities, rather than fair values based on actual market prices. As a consequence, the measurement of income will rely heavily on changes in the fair value of net assets. Income will be reported in a single statement of financial performance that will aggregate all accrual-based income with all value changes, whether realised or unrealised. The implications of this fair value approach for reported earnings are enormous; for example, will it any longer be possible to maintain any form of linkage between financial reporting and the determination of tax liabilities?

For many companies, the impact of IFRS on investor relations will be considerable. Not only will the increased transparency provide the markets with substantially more insight into European companies, but businesses will also have to rethink the ways in which they measure performance and communicate with the markets. This is because the adoption of IFRS will have a fundamental impact on a number of important areas of financial reporting, for example:

- structured financial products are often entered into on the basis of a specific accounting treatment. If that treatment is no longer permitted, material liabilities not currently shown on the balance sheet might have to be included;

- IFRS will necessitate the redefinition of the scope of the group consolidation so as to include material subsidiaries or special purpose entities currently not consolidated. Conversely, entities currently consolidated under national GAAP may have to be de-consolidated for IFRS reporting purposes;

- moves are afoot to require the capitalisation on balance sheet at fair value of leases currently held off balance sheet. Again this could have a significant impact on both the balance sheet and income statement;

- the requirement under IFRS to include on the balance sheet the company's net pension liability or asset at fair value may have a material impact on the equity of companies with under-funded pension obligations. Companies will be required to have annual actuarial valuations of their pension liabilities on the basis prescribed by IFRS, and many will face the likelihood of large amounts of equity being wiped off their balance sheets on adoption of the employee benefits standard alone. Even for those companies that have adequately funded pension liabilities, the adoption of the fair value approach to employee benefit accounting is likely to cause significant volatility in reported earnings; and

- the requirement for companies to record a charge in the income statement for the value of share options granted to employees, calculated on the basis of the fair value of the options on the date that they are granted, could have a significant impact on company earnings and cause earnings volatility.

Clearly, therefore, company management will have to learn how to deal with volatility in reported performance. The examples listed above show that the adoption of the IASB's new financial reporting regime – with all its growing emphasis on fair values – will inevitably introduce significant volatility in the balance sheet and, more importantly, in earnings. This increases substantially the challenge for company management of providing to the markets a coherent articulation of their company's performance.

From the users' perspective, analysts will perhaps for the first time have truly transparent and comparable data about all companies within a particular industry on a pan-European and, in some cases, global basis. Companies will be benchmarked against their cross-border competitors and key performance indicators will be compared. As a result, companies presently operating in less than transparent and semi-protected financial reporting environments will soon have no place to hide.

Ultimately, the most important challenge in financial reporting during the next decade will be to ensure International GAAP delivers financial reporting that investors and markets can trust. This puts a great burden of responsibility upon all involved – securities regulators, national governments, the EC, the IASB, EFRAG, CESR, professional accountants, providers of finance, legal advisors and company managements – to work actively and selflessly towards this goal.

References

1 Henry Alexander Benson was a Chartered Accountant who was born and educated in South Africa. He served on the Council of the ICAEW between 1956 and 1975, and as President in 1966-67. He was advisor to the Governor of the Bank of England from 1975 to 1983 and served as Chairman, Royal Commission on Legal Services 1976 to 1979. In his Obituary published in *The Times* on 7 March 1995 it was stated that 'Few men outside Whitehall can have had more influence on public affairs in post-war Britain than Henry Benson. As senior partner in the firm of Coopers & Lybrand, he built up an international reputation as one of the most formidable accountants of his time.' Lord Benson died on 5 March 1995, aged 85.

2 Foreword to *Accounting and Auditing Approaches to Inventories in Three Nations: Stock in Trade and Work in Progress in Canada,* *the United Kingdom and the United States: a survey,* Accountants International Study Group, Institute of Chartered Accountants in England and Wales, January 1968.

3 IASC, *Preface to Statements of International Accounting Standards,* para. 2.

4 IASC, *Shaping IASC for the future: A Discussion Paper issued for comment by the Strategy Working Party of the International Accounting Standards Committee,* IASC, 7 December 1998, para. 2.

5 At the time of its dissolution on 1 April 2001, the IASC Board members were: Australia, Canada, France, Germany, India, Japan, Malaysia, Mexico, Netherlands, Nordic Federation of Public Accountants, South Africa, United Kingdom, United States of America and representatives of the International Council of Investment Associations (ICIA), the Federation of Swiss Industrial Holding Companies and the

International Association of Financial Executives Institutes (IAFEI). The Indian delegation included a representative from Sri Lanka and the South African delegation included a representative from Zimbabwe. Representatives of the European Commission, the United States Financial Accounting Standards Board (FASB), the International Organisation of Securities Commissions (IOSCO), and the People's Republic of China attended Board meetings as observers.

6 IOSCO Annual Report 2003.

7 IASC Board and IOSCO Technical Committee, *Joint Press Release*, Paris, July 9, 1995.

8 *The IASC-U.S. Comparison Project: A Report on the Similarities and Differences between IASC Standards and U.S. GAAP*, FASB, November 1996.

9 U.S. Securities And Exchange Commission, *SEC Concept Release: International Accounting Standards*, Release Nos. 33-7801, 34-42430; International Series No. 1215 Washington, 18 February 2000.

10 IOSCO, Report of the Technical Committee of the International Organisation of Securities Commissions, *IASC Standards – Assessment Report*, May 2000.

11 IASC, *Shaping IASC for the future: A Discussion Paper issued for comment by the Strategy Working Party of the International Accounting Standards Committee*, IASC, 7 December 1998, para. 2.

12 IASC, *Shaping IASC for the future: A Discussion Paper issued for comment by the Strategy Working Party of the International Accounting Standards Committee*, para. 115 *et seq*.

13 The G4+1 was an informal grouping of staff members of the standard-setting bodies of Australia, Canada, New Zealand, the United Kingdom, the United States of America and the IASC. From time to time, the G4+1 published position papers on accounting topics of current interest. These papers did not necessarily reflect the official views of any of the standard-setting bodies represented. At a meeting of the G4+1 held in January 2001, the Group discussed whether its activities should continue given the imminent commencement of activities by the new International Accounting Standards Board (IASB) and agreed to disband and cancel its planned future activities.

14 Report of the IASC's Strategy Working Party, *Recommendations on shaping IASC for the future*, November 1999.

15 The IASC Foundation Constitution refers to the 'IASC' as the overall 'Organisation'.

16 IASC Foundation Constitution, Article 6.

17 IASC Foundation Constitution, Articles 14 and 16.

18 The IASC Foundation structure is depicted in this way on the IASB website, www.iasb.org.

19 IASC Foundation Constitution, Article 2.

20 IASC Foundation Press Release, 25 January 2001.

21 IASC Foundation Constitution, Article 22.

22 IASC Foundation Constitution, Article 38.

23 IASC Foundation Constitution, Article 40.

24 See the IASC Foundation Constitution, Articles 34 to 37.

25 Preface to Statements of International Accounting Standards, para. 19.

26 IASC Foundation Constitution, Article 18(b).

27 European Roundtable of Industrialists, comment letter to the IASC Foundation on *Identifying issues for the IASC Foundation Constitution Review*, 9 February 2004.

28 Conseil National de la Comptabilite comment letter to the IASC Foundation on *Identifying issues for the IASC Foundation Constitution Review*, 11 February 2004.

29 IASC Foundation Constitution Committee, *An Update on the Constitution Review for the Public Hearing in Mexico City*, 28 September 2004.

30 IASB, *Strengthening the IASB's deliberative processes*, 24 March 2004.

31 IASB, *Update*, September 2004.

32 Based on the opening remarks made by Mr James S Turley, Chairman of Ernst & Young Global at the IASC Foundation Public Hearing on 29 June 2004.

33 Statement by the Board of the International Accounting Standards Committee, December 2000.

34 IASB Press Release, *International Accounting Standards Board issues wide-ranging improvements to Standards*, 18 December 2003.

35 The Joint Working Group of Standard Setters comprised representatives from the IASC, the FASB and eight other international bodies. The purpose of the Group was develop an integrated and harmonised standard on financial instruments – a task that they were unable to complete.

36 FASB and IASB joint Press Release, *FASB and IASB Agree to Work Together toward Convergence of Global Accounting Standards*, London, 29 October 2002.

37 Memorandum of Understanding – the Norwalk Agreement.

38 Memorandum of Understanding – the Norwalk Agreement.

39 Memorandum of Understanding – the Norwalk Agreement.

40 This section is summarised from a report prepared by the staff of the U.S. Securities and Exchange Commission: *Study Pursuant to Section 108(d) of the Sarbanes-Oxley Act of 2002 on the Adoption by the United States Financial Reporting System of a Principles-Based Accounting System*, 25 July 2003. See also *FASB Response to SEC Study on the Adoption of a Principles-Based Accounting System*, July 2004, which concurs with the proposals set out in the SEC staff study.

41 The Sarbanes-Oxley Act of 2002, Pub. L. No. 107-204, 2002.

42 SEC staff, *Study Pursuant to Section 108(d) of the Sarbanes-Oxley Act of 2002 on the Adoption by the United States Financial Reporting System of a Principles-Based Accounting System*, 25 July 2003. See also *FASB Response to SEC Study on the Adoption of a Principles-Based Accounting System*, Section III., para. I.

43 This was announced in *The Chairman's page – a personal view by Sir David Tweedie*, in *Insight*, July 2004.

44 IAS 1, *Presentation of financial statements*, IASC Foundation, Revised 2004.

45 IAS 1, para. 14.

46 IAS 1, para. 14.

47 IAS 1, para. 13.

48 IAS 1, para. 15.

49 IAS 1, para. 15.

50 IAS 1, para. 16.

51 IAS 1, para. 17.

52 IAS 1, para. 18.

53 IAS 1, para. 19.

54 IAS 1, para. 21.

55 IAS 1, para. 16.

56 Fourth Council Directive 78/660/EEC of 25 July 1978 based on Article 54 (3) (g) of the Treaty on the annual accounts of certain types of companies; Seventh Council Directive 83/349/EEC of 13 June 1983 based on the Article 54 (3) (g) of the Treaty on consolidated accounts.

57 Communication from the European Commission, *Accounting harmonisation: a new strategy vis-à-vis international harmonisation*, 1995.

58 See for example, European Commission, *Examination of the conformity between International Accounting Standards applicable to accounting periods beginning before 1 July 1999 and the European Accounting Directives*, February 2000; European Commission, *Examination of the Conformity between SIC-1 to SIC-25 and the European Accounting Directives*, February 2001. The full set of these comparisons may be found on the EC website: http://europa.eu.int/comm/internal_market/en/company/account/index.htm

59 European Commission, COM(1999) 232 final of 11.05.1999, *Financial Services: Implementing the Framework for Financial Markets : Action Plan*, May 1999.

60 European Commission, *EU Financial Reporting Strategy: the way forward*, June 2000.

61 European Union, *Directive of the European Parliament and of the Council amending Directives 78/660/EEC, 83/349/EEC and 86/635/EEC as regards the valuation rules for the annual accounts and consolidated accounts of certain types of companies as well as of banks and other financial institutions*, PE-CONS 3624/01, Brussels, 22 May 2001.

62 European Commission, *Proposal for a Regulation of the Parliament and of the Council on the Application of International Accounting Standards*, COM(2001) 80, February 2001.

63 This means those with their securities admitted to trading on a regulated market within the meaning of Article 1(13) of Council Directive 93/22/EEC (on investment services in the securities field) or those offered to the public in view of their admission to such trading under Council Directive 80/390/EEC (co-ordinating the requirements for the drawing up, scrutiny and distribution of the listing particulars to be published for the admission of securities to official stock exchange listing).

64 European Union, *Regulation of the European Parliament and of the Council on the application of international accounting standards*, Regulation No. 1606/2002, 19 July 2002.

65 EU IAS Regulation, Article 9.

66 EU IAS Regulation, Recital 17.

67 See 'Planned use of options in the IAS Regulation' on the Europa website:

http://europa.eu.int/comm/internal_market/
accounting/ias_en.htm#options

68 EU IAS Regulation, Recital 11.

69 EU IAS Regulation, Article 3.

70 As depicted on the EFRAG website, www.efrag.org.

71 EFRAG, letter to Dr. Alexander Schaub, Director General, Internal Market, European Commission, *Adoption of the amended IAS 39 Financial Instruments: Recognition and Measurement.*

72 Commission of the European Communities, *Establishing the Committee of European Securities Regulators*, Commission Decision of 6 June 2001.

73 The Lamfalussy Report, *Final Report of the Committee of Wise Men on The Regulation of European Securities Markets,* Brussels, 15 February 2001.

74 The Committee of European Securities Regulators, *Charter of the Committee of European Securities Regulators.* The Charter took effect on 11 September 2001.

75 The Committee of European Securities Regulators, Standard No. 1 on Financial Information: *Enforcement of standards on financial information in Europe*, CESR/03-073, 12 March 2003.

76 CESR Standard No.1, Principles 11 to 13.

77 CESR Standard No.1, Principle 16.

78 CESR Standard No.1, Principle 21.

79 The Committee of European Securities Regulators, *Recommendation for additional guidance regarding the implementation of International Financial Reporting Standards (IFRS)*, 30 December 2003.

80 The Committee of European Securities Regulators, Standard No. 2, *Co-ordination of Enforcement Activities*, CESR/03-317c, 22 April 2004.

81 IAS 8 (Revised 2003), *Accounting Policies, Changes in Accounting Estimates and Errors,* IASCF, December 2003, para, 10.

82 IAS 8, para. 11.

83 IAS 8, para. 12.

Chapter 2   The quest for a conceptual framework

1   INTRODUCTION

1.1   What is a conceptual framework?

In general terms, a conceptual framework is a statement of generally accepted theoretical principles which form the frame of reference for a particular field of enquiry. In terms of financial reporting, these theoretical principles provide the basis for both the development of new reporting practices and the evaluation of existing ones. Since the financial reporting process is concerned with the provision of information that is useful in making business and economic decisions, a conceptual framework will form the theoretical basis for determining which events should be accounted for, how they should be measured and how they should be communicated to the user. Therefore, although it is theoretical in nature, a conceptual framework for financial reporting has a highly practical end in view.

1.2   Why is a conceptual framework necessary?

A conceptual framework for financial reporting should therefore be a theory of accounting against which practical problems can be tested objectively, the utility of which is decided by the adequacy of the practical solutions it provides. However, the various standard-setting bodies around the world initially often attempted to resolve practical accounting and reporting problems through the development of accounting standards, without such an accepted theoretical frame of reference. The end result was that standard-setters determined the form and content of external financial reports, without resolving such fundamental issues as:

- what are the objectives of these reports?
- who are the users of these reports?
- what are the informational needs of these users?
- what types of report will best satisfy their needs?

Consequently, standards were often produced on a haphazard and 'fire-fighting' basis with the danger of mutual inconsistencies. On the other hand, if an agreed framework were to exist, the role of the standard-setters would be changed from that of fireman to that of architect, by being able to design external financial reports on the basis of the needs of the user.

Perhaps the word 'agreed' is the key qualification in this argument. The IASB's conceptual framework was clearly derived from the FASB framework, which was developed much earlier. Not surprisingly therefore, the IASB framework (although substantially less detailed) has many aspects in common with the FASB equivalent. The resulting underlying similarity between the FASB and IASB conceptual frameworks is explained within this chapter. However, whilst there is now a degree of fundamental similarity between the conceptual frameworks of the main global standard setting bodies, the way these principles are translated into detailed rules within the accounting standards issued by each can result in very different financial reports.

Furthermore, the existence of a given conceptual framework can be used as a lever to alter the basis of actual financial reporting towards the type of measurement base chosen in that framework – the full implications of which may not be understood by accountants generally. At times, also, standard-setters adopt strategies that are absent from their frameworks – the current policy of the IASB towards the use of fair values in asset and liability valuation is a case in point.

Equally, experience of the last thirty years shows that, in the absence of an agreed conceptual framework, the same theoretical issues are revisited on numerous occasions by different standard-setting working parties. This inevitably sometimes resulted in the development of standards that were inconsistent with each other, or which were founded on incompatible concepts. For example, inconsistencies and conflicts have existed between substance versus form; matching versus prudence; and whether earnings should be determined through balance sheet measurements or by matching costs and revenue. Some standard-setters have permitted two or more methods of accounting for the same set of circumstances, whilst others permitted certain accounting practices to be followed on an arbitrary and unspecified basis. These ambiguities perhaps illustrate the difficulty involved in determining what is 'true and fair'.

There have also been differences in the tactics adopted by standard setters concerning how the tenets of a conceptual framework become practically realised in actual financial reports. There are significant differences between the tactics adopted by the FASB on the one hand, and the IASB on the other. In the US the FASB, in spite of its pioneering work on a conceptual framework, has also produced a large number of highly detailed accounting rules. Clearly, the proliferation of accounting standards in the US stems from many factors, including legal and regulatory; however, a more satisfactory conceptual framework might reduce the need for such a large number of highly detailed standards, since more emphasis could be placed on general principles rather than specific rules. Indeed this change of emphasis has been specifically considered by the US authorities following the reporting problems that led to the creation of the Sarbanes-Oxley act and the setting up of the Public Company Accounting Oversight Board in the USA. It is also true that the more 'general principles' based IASB approach to standard setting does not imply its framework is more satisfactory than the FASB's; rather that the legal and statutory context within which non-US businesses habitually work is quite different from that of the USA.

However, standard-setters must also contend with the larger political and economic context into which financial reporting fits. While the European Union's decision to require listed entities to apply adopted IFRS has brought credibility to IFRS as a set of standards, greatly assisting the speed with which they have been accepted elsewhere in the world, it inevitably brings an extra dimension to the decisions made by the IASB. Standard-setters' best bulwark against undue interference in the standard-setting process is the capital markets' need for financial reporting that is a sound basis for decision making, which in turn implies consistency, practicality and understandability. While it is probable that these characteristics are more likely to be achieved using a sound theoretical foundation, the converse also applies: namely that the framework must result in standards that account appropriately for actual business practice. Otherwise how, for example, is an industry to be persuaded that a particular accounting treatment perceived as adversely affecting its economic interests is better than one which does not?[1]

An agreed framework is therefore not the panacea for all accounting problems. Nor does it obviate the need for judgement to be exercised in the process of resolving accounting issues. What it can provide is a framework within which those judgements can be made. Indeed this is happening, as the principles expressed in the IASB's *Framework for the Preparation and Presentation of Financial Statements* are frequently referred to in IFRSs and during the process of their derivation. Unfortunately there is clear evidence also of the IASB issuing standards that contravene its own conceptual framework. For example IAS 38 requires the capitalisation of goodwill as an asset, despite the fact that goodwill does not meet the definition of an asset in the IASB's conceptual framework. Similarly IAS 12 requires recognition of deferred tax liabilities that do not meet the liability definition under the framework.

1.3   Accounting and the globalisation of economic activity

A further dimension to any consideration of the development of a conceptual framework must be the economic background to this process. Globalisation – the global interdependence, cultural homogeneity, integration of ownership and use, and depersonalisation of economic assets – is a term now frequently used, when even a few years ago it was relatively rare. The process of globalisation has been happening for centuries if not millennia – arguably since the first empires started to spread their core cultural and economic systems. However, it has now become obvious that since the 1960s the huge growth in telecommunications; the ease, speed and low cost of physical travel; the economic growth experienced by many countries throughout the world together with the spread of the 'western' business culture, has resulted in globalisation on an unprecedented scale.

Obviously, financial reporting has not been insulated from this process. As discussed below, during the last fifty years the development of a conceptual framework has increasingly preoccupied standard-setting bodies. To start with these were mainly single-country attempts, the first modern work being undertaken in the US. Some time later the UK's standard setting body together with those from other countries in the guise of the 'G4 plus 1 – a 'think-tank' that consisted of staff from the standard setters of the USA, UK, Canada, Australia, New Zealand and the then IASC – contributed considerably to the development process, culminating as can now be seen in the creation of the IASB and in the IASB's own framework as the theoretical basis of IFRS.

Reflecting economic globalisation, the world now finds itself with only two principal sets of accounting standards: IFRS and US GAAP, a state of affairs that seemed unlikely even 10 years ago. With the benefit of hindsight it seems obvious that globalisation would require harmonisation of financial reporting; nevertheless the speed with which it has occurred has been remarkable, greatly assisted by the European Union's decision to harmonise financial reporting for listed EU entities. Furthermore, the integration process has not stopped, as in September 2002 the FASB and the IASB signed the Norwalk Agreement that commits both standard setters to further converge and harmonise their respective regimes.

These developments illustrate the paradoxical nature of the search for a conceptual framework. The idea of a framework is to have a set of principles that guide the detailed requirements of individual standards, yet those principles are influenced by practical global economic and political reality. Ultimately, economic forces and the needs of the capital markets for useful information will be the context in which standard-setters operate. Arguably, their frameworks, or even as seems possible now, their framework, will always be as much practice into theory, as the reverse.

2   THE DEVELOPMENT OF A US CONCEPTUAL FRAMEWORK

2.1   Accounting Research Studies

The Accounting Principles Board (APB) of the American Institute of Certified Public Accountants (AICPA) was formed in 1959 to replace the former Committee on Accounting Procedure and the Committee on Terminology. During its existence, the Committee on Accounting Procedure had issued a series of Accounting Research Bulletins (ARBs). In 1953, the first 42 ARBs (eight of which dealt solely with terminology) were revised and restated as a consolidated ARB No. 43 and Accounting Terminology Bulletin No. 1; thereafter, a further eight ARBs were issued. The ARBs were supposedly aimed at the development of generally accepted accounting principles; however, the Committee met with considerable criticism over its failure to deal with contemporary accounting issues (such as leasing and business combinations), which could not be solved from precedents and required the development of accounting principles through pure accounting research.

As a direct response to this, the President of the AICPA set up the Special Committee on Research Program in 1957; in 1958 the Committee recommended the formation of the APB, and the appointment of a director of research with a permanent research staff. The Special Committee also recommended that 'an immediate project of the accounting research staff should be a study of the basic postulates underlying accounting principles generally, and the preparation of a brief statement thereof. There should be also a study of the broad principles of accounting. ... The results of these, as adopted by the [Accounting Principles] Board, should serve as the foundation for the entire body of future pronouncements by the Institute on accounting matters, to which each new release should be related.'[2]

This, therefore, was probably the first mandate given by a professional body for the development of a conceptual framework. The AICPA appointed Maurice Moonitz as its first Director of Accounting Research; Moonitz started work on the postulates study, and appointed Robert Sprouse to work with him on the study of broad accounting principles. The products of the research were contained in Accounting Research Study No. 1 – *The Basic Postulates of Accounting*[3] – and Accounting Research Study No. 3 – *A Tentative Set of Broad Accounting Principles for Business Enterprises* – which were published in 1961 and 1962 respectively.[4]

These studies, however, caused a storm of controversy. Instead of establishing a sound foundation of accounting theory through rigorous argument based on deductive reasoning, Moonitz and Sprouse attempted to persuade the accounting profession to accept a new system of financial reporting based on current values. Furthermore, the realisation principle was discarded on the basis of the assertion that 'profit is attributable to the whole process of business activity, not just to the moment of sale'.[5] This was reflected, for example, in the statement that 'inventories which are readily saleable at known prices with negligible costs of disposal, or with known or readily predictable costs of disposal, should be measured at net realizable value'.[6]

However, the criticism which was levelled at these studies appeared to be based more on the fear of the unknown, rather than on any intellectual shortcomings. Consequently, they were viewed as being too radically different from contemporary generally accepted accounting practice to be accepted, and were rejected by the APB. This resulted in the commissioning of Grady's Accounting Research Study No. 7 – *Inventory of Generally Accepted Accounting Principles for Business Enterprises* – which was published in 1965 and which catalogued the various accounting methods which had been approved by ARBs, APB Opinions or some other precedent.

In all, 15 Accounting Research Studies were published during the life of the APB. However, following the rejection of ARS Nos. 1 and 3, the studies tended to be carried out on an ad hoc basis and without the support of a common foundation. Furthermore, the recommendations contained in the research studies appeared to have been largely ignored in the drafting of the 31 Opinions which the APB issued between 1962 and 1973. Consequently, generally accepted accounting principles in the US were continuing to be formulated without the benefit of research or the foundation of an agreed theoretical framework and, for all intents and purposes, the APB slowly resorted to the position of its predecessor, the Committee on Accounting Procedure.

2.2   APB Statement No. 4

In 1965 the APB made a further attempt to provide a basis for guiding the future development of accounting by establishing a committee to carry out a study which could be used as a basis for understanding the broad fundamentals of accounting. In 1970, the APB approved Statement No. 4 – *Basic Concepts and Accounting Principles Underlying Financial Statements of Business Enterprises.*[7] The statement contained a description of (1) the environment of financial accounting, (2) the objectives of financial statements, (3) the basic features and basic elements of financial accounting and (4) a summary of existing generally accepted accounting principles.

Therefore, it was (on its own admission)[8] a descriptive statement, not prescriptive. For example, assets and liabilities were defined as economic resources and obligations 'that are recognised and measured in conformity with generally accepted accounting principles',[9] which meant that the definitions failed to provide a theoretical basis for the development of generally accepted principles. As a result APB No. 4 was deficient as a theory of accounting and did not respond to the problems which were facing the profession at the time and which had been brought about by the inconsistencies and inadequacies of financial reporting practice.

2.3   The Wheat and Trueblood Committees

In 1971, in response to continued criticism from both within the profession and from the SEC about its inability to establish sound accounting principles, the AICPA announced the formation of two study groups: the *Study Group on Establishment of Accounting Principles*, to be chaired by Francis Wheat, and the *Study Group on Objectives of Financial Statements*, to be chaired by Robert Trueblood. The Wheat Committee published its report in 1972, resulting in the establishment of the Financial Accounting Standards Board (FASB) in 1973 as the successor to the APB. This had the effect of taking the responsibility for setting accounting standards away from the accounting profession and placing it in the hands of an independent body in the private sector. The FASB comprises seven members appointed by the Financial Accounting Foundation (FAF), and is funded by the sale of publications and from contributions made to the FAF. The Board of Trustees of the FAF is appointed by its eight sponsoring organisations, which include, inter alia, the American Accounting Association, the AICPA and two organisations which represent government.

The study carried out by the Trueblood Committee represents the next significant step in the attempt to develop a conceptual framework. In setting the terms of reference of the study group, the Board of Directors of the AICPA stated that the main purpose of the study was 'to refine the objectives of financial statements'.[10] They went on to suggest that APB Statement No. 4 would be a logical starting point for the study, whilst at the same time noting that APB 4 'contains objectives in terms of what is considered acceptable today rather than in terms of what is needed and what is attainable to meet these needs'.[11] The study group was asked to consider at least the following questions:

- Who needs financial statements?
- What information do they need?
- How much of the needed information can be provided by accounting?
- What framework is required to provide the needed information?[12]

The Trueblood Report[13] was published in October 1973 and developed twelve objectives of financial statements. The principal objective was stated in the following terms: 'the basic objective of financial statements is to provide information useful for making economic decisions'.[14] Having established its twelve objectives of financial statements, the report then discussed seven qualitative characteristics which information contained in financial statements should possess in order to satisfy the needs of users.[15] As will be seen below, the Trueblood Report's objectives of financial statements formed the basis for the development of the FASB's first concepts statement, whilst the qualitative characteristics identified were amongst those discussed in the second concepts statement.

2.4   The FASB conceptual framework

The Trueblood Committee was at work on its report when the FASB came into existence. Consequently, the Trueblood Report was effectively passed on to the FASB for consideration, thus signalling the beginnings of the FASB's Conceptual Framework Project. The FASB duly considered the report and in June 1974 published a Discussion Memorandum – *Conceptual Framework for Accounting and Reporting: Consideration of the Report of the Study Group on the Objectives of Financial Statements* – which asked for comments on the issues raised.[16] A public hearing was held during September 1974, and in December 1976 the FASB published its *Tentative Conclusions on Objectives of Financial Statements of Business Enterprises*. In December 1976 the FASB also published a paper – *Scope and Implications of the Conceptual Framework Project* – which summarised its aims for the project, the expected benefits to be derived and the main areas which were expected to be covered.[17]

Following the criticism and eventual replacement of first the Committee on Accounting Procedure, followed by the APB, the FASB was seen by many commentators to be the last opportunity of keeping accounting standard-setting in the private sector. The FASB was clearly aware that accounting standards had to regain the credibility of public opinion which had been lost as a result of the many perceived abuses of financial reporting during the 1960s. The FASB referred to this lack of public confidence, and the possible consequences thereof, as follows: 'skepticism about financial reporting has adverse effects on businesses, on business leaders, and on the public at large. One of these effects is the risk of imposition of government reporting and other regulatory requirements that are not justified – requirements that are not in the public interest because the perceived benefits do not exist or are more than offset by costly interference with the orderly operation of the economy. Skepticism creates adverse public opinion, which may be the antecedent of unjustified government regulation. Every company, every industry stands to suffer because of skepticism about financial reporting.'[18] The FASB, therefore, saw its conceptual framework project as the means of enhancing the credibility of financial statements in the eyes of the public.

The FASB also recognised that although there had been many attempts by individuals and organisations (such as the American Accounting Association) to develop a theory of accounting, none of these individual theories had become universally accepted or relied on in practice. They therefore expressed a need for a *'constitution*, a coherent system of interrelated objectives and fundamentals that can lead to consistent standards and that prescribes the nature, function, and limits of financial accounting and financial statements'.[19] The conceptual framework was expected to:

(a)   guide the body responsible for establishing standards;

(b)   provide a frame of reference for resolving accounting questions in the absence of a specific promulgated standard;

(c)   determine bounds for judgement in preparing financial statements;

(d)   increase financial statement users' understanding of and confidence in financial statements; and

(e)   enhance comparability.[20]

To date the FASB has issued seven concepts statements, of which one (SFAC No. 4) deals with the objectives of financial reporting by non-business organisations and is beyond the scope of this book, whilst another (SFAC No. 3) dealt with elements of financial statements by business enterprises, and was superseded by SFAC No. 6, which expanded the scope of SFAC No. 3 to encompass not-for-profit organisations. The remaining five are discussed in the sections which follow.

2.5   The objectives of financial reporting

The first phase of the FASB's conceptual framework project was to develop a statement of the objectives of financial reporting. Clearly, some pioneering work in this area had been done by the Trueblood Committee (see 2.3 above), and this formed the basis of the FASB's first concepts statement. Nevertheless, it was not until 1978 that the FASB finally published this statement.

SFAC No. 1 – *Objectives of Financial Reporting by Business Enterprises* – starts off by making the point that financial reporting includes not only financial statements, but also incorporates other means of communicating financial and non-financial information; this may be achieved, for example, through the medium of stock exchange documents, news releases, management forecasts etc.[21] Having said this, the statement stresses that 'financial reporting is not an end in itself but is intended to provide information that is useful in making business and economic decisions'.[22] This, however, is no new revelation; it is the type of broad generalisation that has characterised numerous previous attempts at establishing a conceptual framework. On the other hand, what it does do is raise all the same issues which the Trueblood Committee had been asked to consider seven years previously, such as: For whom is this information intended? What types of 'business and economic decisions' do they make? What information do they need to enable them to make these decisions? What framework is required to provide this needed information?

The statement details an extensive list of potential users, distinguishing between those with a direct interest and those with an indirect interest in the information provided by financial reporting.[23] The groups of user which have a direct interest include owners, management, creditors and employees; whilst user groups such as financial analysts and advisers, journalists, regulatory authorities and trade unions are deemed to have an indirect interest, since they advise or represent those who have a direct interest. However, having identified this wide range of users, the statement focuses on the information needs of investors and creditors. These are encompassed in the first of three primary objectives identified in the statement: 'financial reporting should provide information that is useful to present and potential investors and creditors and other users in making rational investment, credit, and similar decisions'.[24]

This objective leads to the first of the two most significant and far-reaching conclusions in the statement, namely that 'financial reporting should provide information to help investors, creditors, and others assess the amounts, timing, and uncertainty of prospective net cash inflows to the related enterprise'.[25] The statement articulated its reasoning behind this conclusion as follows: 'Potential users of financial information most directly concerned with a particular business enterprise are generally interested in its ability to generate favourable cash flows, because their decisions relate to amounts, timing, and uncertainties of expected cash flows. To investors, lenders, suppliers, and employees, a business enterprise is a source of cash in the form of dividends or interest and perhaps appreciated market prices, repayment of borrowing, payment for goods or services, or salaries and wages. They invest cash, goods, or services in an enterprise and expect to obtain sufficient cash in return to make the investment worthwhile. They are directly concerned with the ability of the enterprise to generate favourable cash flows and may also be concerned with how the market's perception of that ability affects the relative prices of its securities. To customers, a business enterprise is a source of goods or services, but only by obtaining sufficient cash to pay for the resources it uses and to meet its other obligations can the enterprise provide those goods or services. To managers, the cash flows of a business enterprise are a significant part of their management responsibilities, including their accountability to directors and owners. Many, if not most, of their decisions have cash flow consequences for the enterprise. Thus, investors, creditors, employees, customers, and managers significantly share a common interest in an enterprise's ability to generate favourable cash flows. Other potential users of financial information share the same interest, derived from investors, creditors, employees, customers, or managers whom they advise or represent or derived from an interest in how those groups (and especially stockholders) are faring.'[26]

In reaching this conclusion, the FASB was aware of the fact that it might precipitate an adverse reaction leading to the possible rejection of the statement through what might have been seen as an objective which would ultimately result in companies being required to present cash flow, management forecast or current value information. The FASB pre-empted this potential adverse reaction by stating that 'the objective focuses on the purpose for which information provided should be useful ... rather than the kinds of information that may be useful for that purpose. The objective neither requires nor prohibits "cash flow information", "current value information", "management forecast information", or any other specific information. Conclusions about "current value information" and "management forecast information" are beyond the scope of this Statement. Paragraphs 42-44 [of SFAC No. 1] note that information about cash receipts and disbursements is not usually considered to be the most useful information for the purposes described in this objective.'[27]

However, in examining this objective, it is important to take cognisance of empirical research which has been conducted in this area. In 1979, Chang and Most investigated the views of individual investors, institutional investors and financial analysts in the USA, UK and New Zealand as part of a study into the importance of financial statements for investment decisions.[28] Their study included an investigation into the investment objectives of individual and institutional investors, and reached the conclusion that 'the most important investment objective for both individual and institutional investors is long-term capital gains. This, and a combination of dividend income and capital gains, are considerably more important than short-term capital gains. It would appear that prediction of short-term cash flows would not be one of the more important investor uses of financial statements, and this calls in question the conventional assumption that a principal objective of financial statements is to assist users to predict future cash flows in terms of timing, as distinct from amount and relative uncertainty.'[29] On the other hand, it is, of course, possible that institutional investors are much more influenced by short-term expectations today than they were over twenty years ago; consequently, the findings of Chang and Most may no longer be valid.

The second fundamental conclusion reached in SFAC No. 1 which has far-reaching implications for the future development of accounting standards is concerned with the primary focus of financial reporting. During the early stages of the development of accounting rules in the first half of this century, the primary focus of financial statements was based on the principle of 'stewardship'. This arose from the fact that the management of an enterprise were primarily seen to be accountable to the owners for safeguarding the assets which had been entrusted to them, leading to a balance sheet emphasis in financial reporting. However, the focus has gradually shifted away from the notion of the balance sheet reporting on the custodianship of assets, to an earnings emphasis based on the principle that the income statement should present 'decision-useful' information. This is encapsulated in the statement in SFAC No. 1 that 'the primary focus of financial reporting is information about an enterprise's performance provided by measures of earnings and its components. Investors, creditors, and others who are concerned with assessing the prospects for enterprise net cash inflows are especially interested in that information.'[30]

SFAC No. 1 still recognises the fact that financial reporting should provide information about how the management of an enterprise has discharged its stewardship responsibility.[31] However, it goes on to say that 'earnings information is commonly the focus for assessing management's stewardship or accountability. Management, owners, and others emphasize enterprise performance or profitability in describing how management has discharged its stewardship accountability.[32]

In other words, the statement is asserting that the measurement of earnings in the income statement should take precedence over the measurement of assets and liabilities in the balance sheet. This is an important principle which should have had an important impact on the principles laid down in the development of future accounting standards. However, as will be seen below, the FASB's subsequent concepts statements have essentially avoided the issue of how to determine net income. Furthermore, more recent statements issued by the FASB tend to suggest an uncertainty as to whether an earnings or balance sheet approach should be followed (for example, SFAS 109 – *Accounting for Income Taxes* – would appear to view the balance sheet as the primary statement).

This tension between income statement and balance sheet primacy has swayed towards the balance sheet, at least as far as recent IASB standards indicate. As is more fully described at 3 below, the IASB's conceptual framework adopts a balance sheet approach to recognition, whereby all the elements of financial statements are defined in terms of assets and liabilities, with the consequence that income recognition is a function of increases and decreases in net assets rather than the completion of acts of performance.

Consequently, despite the focus of the capital markets on performance measurement, the conceptual underpinning for financial reporting adopted by the FASB and the IASB appears to be focusing principally on the recognition and derecognition of assets and liabilities.

2.6　The qualitative characteristics of accounting information

The FASB's second Concepts Statement – *Qualitative Characteristics of Accounting Information* – examines the characteristics that make accounting information useful to the users of that information. The statement views these characteristics as 'a hierarchy of accounting qualities', which then form the basis for selecting and evaluating information for inclusion in financial reports. The hierarchy is represented in Figure 1 below:[33]

Figure 1

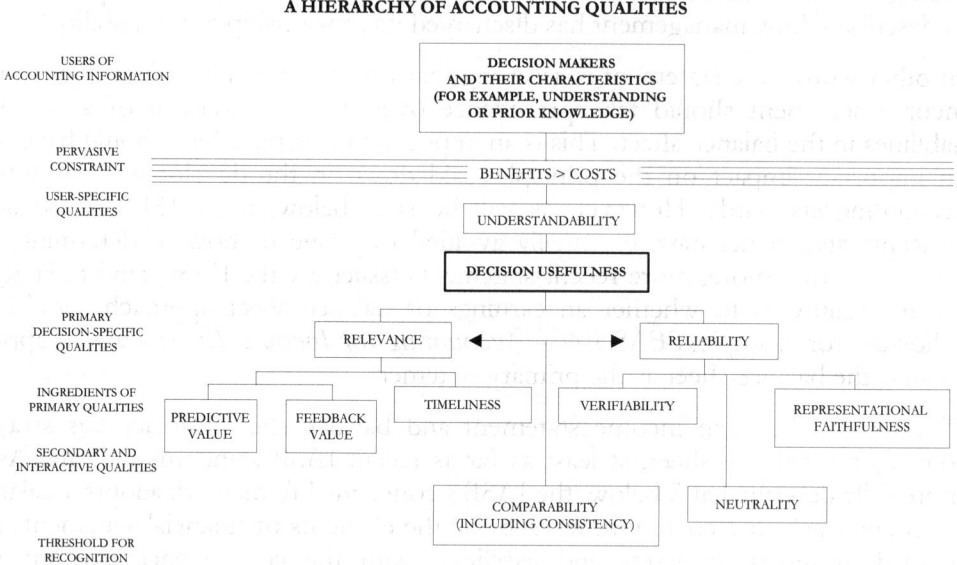

2.6.1   The decision-makers

The decision-makers (users) appear at the top of the hierarchy against the background of their own specific characteristics. Whilst usefulness for decision-making is the most important quality that accounting information should possess, each decision-maker has to judge what information is useful for a specific decision. This judgement would be based on such factors as the nature of the decision to be made, the information already in the individual's possession or available from other sources, the decision-making process employed and the decision maker's capacity to process all the information obtained.

2.6.2   The cost/benefit constraint

Since information should be provided only if the benefits to be derived from that information outweigh the costs of providing it, the cost/benefit constraint pervades the hierarchy. However, the application of this constraint may cause a certain amount of difficulty, since the costs of providing financial information are normally borne by the enterprise (and ultimately passed on to its customers), whilst the users reap the benefits. For this reason, the normal forces of demand and supply will not prevail in the market of financial information, since the external user will almost always view the benefits of additional information as outweighing the costs.

2.6.3 *Understandability*

The hierarchy depicts understandability as being the key quality for accounting information to achieve 'decision usefulness'. SFAC No. 1 stated that the information provided by financial reporting 'should be comprehensible to those who have a reasonable understanding of business and economic activities and are willing to study the information with reasonable diligence'.[34] Information, whilst it may be relevant, will be wasted if it is provided in a form which cannot be understood by the users for whom it was intended. SFAC No. 1 elaborated on the relationship between useful information and understandability as follows: 'financial information is a tool and, like most tools, cannot be of much direct help to those who are unable or unwilling to use it or who misuse it. Its use can be learned, however, and financial reporting should provide information that can be used by all – nonprofessionals as well as professionals – who are willing to learn to use it properly. Efforts may be needed to increase the understandability of financial information. Cost-benefit considerations may indicate that information understood or used by only a few should not be provided. Conversely, financial reporting should not exclude relevant information merely because it is difficult for some to understand or because some investors or creditors choose not to use it.'[35]

2.6.4 *Relevance and reliability*

The qualities that distinguish 'better' (more useful) information from 'inferior' (less useful) information are primarily the qualities of relevance and reliability, with some other characteristics that those qualities imply. SFAC No. 2 identifies relevance and reliability as 'the two primary qualities that make accounting information useful for decision making. Subject to constraints imposed by cost and materiality, increased relevance and increased reliability are the characteristics that make information a more desirable commodity – that is, one useful in making decisions.'[36] However, this was not new – the qualitative characteristics of relevance and reliability had been discussed in several preceding studies (such as the Trueblood and Corporate Reports). What was new (and probably the most significant aspect of SFAC No. 2), was the explicit recognition of the fact that 'reliability and relevance often impinge on each other'.[37] Consequently, whenever accounting standards are set, decisions have to be made concerning the relative importance of these two characteristics, often resulting in trade-offs being made between them.

In today's context, where standard-setting bodies seem intent on replacing the historical cost system by an income and measurement system based on fair values, deciding the relative weight to be attributed to relevance and to reliability when presenting information is increasingly pertinent. However, one matter that is easily overlooked in the debate is that reliability is, in our view, a necessary precondition for relevance. If markets and users generally consider information is not reliable, it will certainly not be considered relevant. Consequently, fair values attributed to assets that do not have readily available market prices, may be subjective to a degree that is not always understood.

A   Relevance

The statement defines relevant accounting information as being information which is 'capable of making a difference in a decision by helping users to form predictions about the outcomes of past, present, and future events or to confirm or correct prior expectations'.[38] The statement further describes 'timeliness' as an 'ancillary aspect of relevance. If information is not available when it is needed or becomes available only so long after the reported events that it has no value for future action, it lacks relevance and is of little or no use'.[39] Therefore, in the context of financial reporting, the characteristic of timeliness means that information must be made available to users before it loses its capacity to influence their decisions. However, while timeliness alone cannot make information relevant, a lack of timeliness can result in information losing a degree of relevance which it once had.[40] On the other hand, in many instances there also has to be a trade-off between timeliness and reliability, since generally the more timely the information the less reliable it is.

The hierarchy identifies 'predictive value' and 'feedback value' as the other components of relevance on the basis that 'information can make a difference to decisions by improving decision makers' capacities to predict or by confirming or correcting their earlier expectations'.[41] Predictive value is defined as 'the quality of information that helps users to increase the likelihood of correctly forecasting the outcome of past or present events',[42] whilst feedback value is defined as 'the quality of information that enables users to confirm or correct prior expectations'.[43] Clearly, however, in saying that accounting information has predictive value, it is not suggesting that it is itself a prediction.

B   Reliability

Reliability is the second of the primary qualities, and is ascribed three attributes in the hierarchy. The statement asserts that the 'reliability of a measure rests on the faithfulness with which it represents what it purports to represent, coupled with an assurance for the user, which comes through verification, that it has that representational quality'.[44] This definition gives rise to the three subsidiary qualities of 'representational faithfulness', 'verifiability', and 'neutrality'. Representational faithfulness is an unnecessary piece of jargon introduced into accounting terminology by SFAC No. 2; what it essentially means is that information included in financial reports should represent what it purports to represent. In other words, financial reporting should be truthful. For example, if a group's consolidated balance sheet discloses cash and bank balances, users would be justified in assuming that, in the absence of any statement to the contrary, the financial statements were truthful, and that these represented cash resources freely available to the group; however, if the reality of the situation was that the cash resources were situated in countries which had severe exchange control restrictions, and were, therefore, not available to the group, some might hold the view that the financial statements were not entirely 'representationally faithful'.

It should be noted, however, that there are degrees of representational faithfulness. Because the financial reporting process involves allocations, estimations and subjective judgements, it cannot produce an 'exact' result; consequently, the trade-off between relevance and reliability will often apply, resulting in the presentation of information which is assigned a high degree of relevance, but which sacrifices representational faithfulness. An example of where this might apply is in fair value accounting for an acquisition, where fair values have to be assigned to the separable net assets acquired.

Reliable information should also be verifiable and neutral so that neither measurement nor measurer bias results in the information being presented in such a way that it unjustifiably influences the particular decision being made. Verifiability is a quality of representational faithfulness in that it excludes the possibility of measurement bias, whilst neutrality implies the provision of all relevant and reliable information – irrespective of the effects that the information will have on the entity or a particular user group. This entire aspect has recently come to prominence with the issuance by the IASB of the exposure draft *Proposed amendments to IAS 39 Financial instruments: Recognition and Measurement, the Fair Value Option*. In this ED, the IASB effectively acknowledges the tension the criteria relevant and reliable, and envisages introducing a verifiability test, in addition, under certain circumstances. This aspect is discussed further in section 5.3 below.

2.6.5 Comparability

The hierarchy lists comparability as an additional quality that financial information should possess in order to achieve relevance and reliability. The quality of comparability includes the fundamental accounting concept of consistency, since the usefulness of information is greatly enhanced if it is prepared on a consistent basis from one period to the next, and can be compared with corresponding information of the same enterprise for some other period, or with similar information about some other enterprise.

2.6.6 Materiality

All the qualitative criteria discussed in SFAC No. 2 are subject to a materiality threshold, since only material information will have an impact on the decision-making process. However, the statement provides no quantitative guidelines for materiality, and it will be a matter of judgement for the providers of information to determine whether or not an item of information has crossed the materiality threshold for recognition. Materiality is closely related to the characteristic of relevance, since both are defined in terms of what influences or makes a difference to an investor or other decision-maker. On the other hand, the two concepts can be distinguished; a decision by management not to disclose certain information may be made because users have no interest in that kind of information (i.e. it is not relevant to their specific needs), or because the amounts involved are too small to make a difference to the users' decisions (i.e. they are not material).

However, if the preparers of financial statements are to decide on what to include in their reporting package, they must have a clear understanding of the users of their reports and their specific information and decision-making needs. In so doing, they should be aware of the types of information likely to influence their decisions (i.e. relevance) as well as the associated magnitude of this information (i.e.

materiality). Consequently, financial reporting will focus generally on information which is regarded as relevant, and specifically on that which is material. The principal difficulty with this, however, is that the materiality thresholds of users vary from class to class and amongst individual users in the same class.

There is an element of rationalisation of practice, rather than revelation of principle, about the entire relevance-reliability-materiality discussion, which has also pervaded many subsequent conceptual framework attempts. It is becoming increasingly noticeable that new accounting standards are seemingly heavily biased towards relevance at the expense of reliability. For example, in introducing fair value accounting for most financial assets in IAS 39 – *Financial Instruments: Recognition and Measurement*, the IASB has effectively codified the assumption that 'fair value can be reliably determined for most financial assets classified as available for sale or held for trading'.[45] Under the standard, the reliability of measurement presumption can only be rebutted under very limited circumstances, with the result that the fair value measurement attribute has to be applied even in circumstances where it might be deemed to produce relatively unreliable results.

The standard setters rationalise this by asserting (perhaps rather pejoratively) that it is better to have financial statements that are approximately right rather than precisely wrong. By this they imply that historical cost information is *ipso facto* irrelevant, and it is preferable to have financial statements that are prepared on a fair value basis that are, in the view of the standard setters, considerably more relevant, if not as reliable. Consequently, as the use of fair values is introduced more and more into the measurement of assets and liabilities, the context of the trade-off between relevance and reliability has changed considerably. As mentioned above in 2.6.4, this entire aspect has recently come to prominence with the issuance by the IASB of the exposure draft *Proposed amendments to IAS 39 Financial instruments: Recognition and Measurement, the Fair Value Option*. In this ED, the IASB seeks to keep its relevant and reliable criteria unchanged, but to restrict in certain circumstances the use of fair values (that meet these criteria) unless a further verifiability test is passed. This is symptomatic of the current circumstances where standard setters frequently use the term 'fair value' unhampered both by the fact that there is no general agreement about exactly what 'fair value' means in the context of many categories of asset, and in the IASB's case that the term does not appear at all in its own Framework document. This matter and the FASB's recent exposure draft on fair value measurements is discussed at 5.3 below.

2.6.7 Conservatism

SFAC No. 2 includes an interesting discussion on the convention of 'conservatism' (i.e. prudence).[46] In so doing, it draws a distinction between the 'deliberate, consistent understatement of net assets and profits',[47] and the practice of ensuring that 'uncertainties and risks inherent in business situations are adequately considered'.[48] The statement recognised the fact that, in the eyes of bankers and other lenders, deliberate understatement of assets was desirable, since it increased their margin of safety on assets pledged as security for debts. On the other hand, it was also recognised that consistent understatement was difficult to maintain over a period of any length, and that understated assets would clearly lead to overstated income in later periods when the assets were ultimately realised. Consequently, unwarranted and deliberate conservatism in financial reporting would lead to a contravention of certain of the qualitative characteristics, such as neutrality and representational faithfulness.

2.7 The elements of financial statements

SFAC No. 6 – *Elements of Financial Statements* – was issued in 1985 as a replacement to SFAC No. 3 – *Elements of Financial Statements of Business Enterprises* – having expanded its scope to encompass non-profit organisations. The statement defines ten 'elements' of financial statements that are directly related to the measurement of performance and financial status of an entity. However, the elements are very much interrelated, as six of them are arithmetically derived from the definitions of assets and liabilities.

2.7.1 Assets

Assets are defined as being 'probable future economic benefits obtained or controlled by a particular entity as a result of past transactions or events'.[49] However, the statement then goes on to say that the kinds of items that qualify as assets under this definition are also commonly called 'economic resources'. They are the scarce means that are useful for carrying out economic activities, such as consumption, production and exchange.[50] The common characteristic possessed by all assets is 'service potential' or 'future economic benefit' which eventually results in net cash inflows to the enterprise.[51]

The adequacy of this definition, which is used almost unchanged in the IASB's own conceptual framework, is discussed in more detail at 5 below. It does however represent a major shift from the implied definition of an asset under historical cost accounting. Under historical cost accounting a non-monetary asset is no more than a deferred cost; a cost which has been incurred before the balance sheet date and, in terms of the accruals concept, relates to future periods beyond the balance sheet date, thereby justifying it being carried forward as an asset. This applies to all non-monetary assets that are recognised in an historical cost balance sheet – whether they be tangible fixed assets, stock, prepayments or deferred development expenditure. Consequently, there are certain occasions when items will be recognised as assets under the traditional historical cost system, but which will not fit the SFAC No. 6 definition of an asset. For example the spreading of certain pension-related expenses over the service lives of employees is prohibited by this definition because an unexpensed pension cost, if carried forward in the balance sheet, would fail to conform to the 'economic resource with future benefits' definition of an asset.

The selection of this definition has also embedded a deep-rooted problem within the FASB's conceptual framework project. First, as far as SFAC No. 6 is concerned, since most of the elements defined in the statement are derived from the definition of an asset, any inadequacy in this definition inevitably affects the validity of the definitions of other elements. Second, in identifying the elements of financial statements before addressing the fundamental issues of how they are to be measured and on what basis of capital maintenance profit is to be determined, the FASB seriously limited its ability to address the issues of recognition and measurement properly. The result of this is that SFAC No. 5 – *Recognition and Measurement in Financial Statements of Business Enterprises* – has serious shortcomings (see 2.8 below).

2.7.2 Liabilities

Liabilities are defined as 'probable future sacrifices of economic benefits arising from present obligations of a particular entity to transfer assets or provide services to other entities in the future as a result of past transactions or events'.[52] The statement goes on to say that a liability has three essential characteristics:

(a)   it embodies a present duty or responsibility to one or more other entities that entails settlement by probable future transfer or use of assets at a specified or determinable date, on occurrence of a specified event, or on demand;

(b)   the duty or responsibility obligates the entity, leaving it little or no discretion to avoid the future sacrifice; and

(c)   the transaction or other event obligating the entity has already happened.[53]

Thus, in terms of this definition, liabilities represent the amounts of obligations – giving rise to a problem similar to that outlined above in respect of the definition of assets. There are certain items which have traditionally been recognised as liabilities, but which do not meet the statement's definition. This is because they are deferred credits awaiting recognition in the profit and loss account, or are 'voluntary' liabilities such as provisions for refurbishing components of assets, rather than obligations to other entities. This has led to quite tortuous methods of accounting for what are straightforward matters under traditional historic cost accounting.

2.7.3 Equity

Equity is defined as 'the residual interest in the assets of an entity that remains after deducting its liabilities'.[54] This is a somewhat tautological definition arising from the accounting equation that assets minus liabilities equals equity. Equity is, in fact, the sum of the equity investments made by the entity's owners, and the entity's earnings retained from its profit-making activities. Because of the way in which the definitions of the various elements are interrelated, it might appear to some that the FASB have taken the easy route in defining equity as net assets, rather than in terms of capital contributions plus retained earnings; a possible explanation for this might be that it enabled the FASB to define income in terms of changes in equity. Interestingly, and underlining the fundamental similarity of many of the framework attempts, the IASB's framework document (see section 5 below) has taken exactly this route to defining equity.

2.7.4 Investments by owners

Investments by owners are defined as being 'increases in equity of a particular business enterprise resulting from transfers to it from other entities of something valuable to obtain or increase ownership interests (or equity) in it'.[55] The statement goes on to say that although investments by owners are most commonly made in the form of assets, the investments can also be represented by services, or the settlement or conversion of liabilities of the enterprise.[56]

2.7.5 *Distributions to owners*

Distributions to owners are defined as 'decreases in equity of a particular business enterprise resulting from transferring assets, rendering services, or incurring liabilities by the enterprise to owners'.[57] Distributions to owners, therefore, incorporate all forms of capital distributions which result in a decrease in net assets.

2.7.6 *Comprehensive income*

Comprehensive income is defined as 'the change in equity of a business enterprise during a period from transactions and other events and circumstances from nonowner sources. It includes all changes in equity during a period except those resulting from investments by owners and distributions to owners.'[58] On its own, the term 'comprehensive income' is somewhat meaningless; for example, how does it tie in with the statement in SFAC No. 1[59] that 'the primary focus of financial reporting is information about an enterprise's performance provided by measures of earnings and its components'? Clearly, the FASB was keeping its options open by not defining earnings; in fact, it explained (in a footnote to SFAC No. 6) that whilst 'comprehensive income' is the term used in the statement for the concept that was called 'earnings' in SFAC No. 1, SFAC No. 5 had described earnings for a period as excluding certain cumulative accounting adjustments and other non-owner changes in equity that are included in comprehensive income for a period.[60]

The FASB issued a standard on this topic in June 1997, SFAS 130 – *Reporting Comprehensive Income*, however a generally accepted standard based on the concept continues to elude standard-setters. The IASB in 2003 decided to postpone its project to produce an exposure draft on the topic, and at the IASB/FASB joint meeting in April 2004 the joint boards gave every impression that the difficulties of defining and accounting for comprehensive income continue to remain formidable.

2.7.7 *Revenues, expenses, gains and losses*

SFAC No. 6 identifies the remaining four elements as those which constitute the basic components of 'comprehensive income':

Revenues, which are 'inflows or other enhancements of assets of an entity or settlements of its liabilities (or a combination of both) from delivering or producing goods, rendering services, or other activities that constitute the entity's ongoing major central operations'.[61]

Expenses, which are 'outflows or other using up of assets or incurrences of liabilities (or a combination of both) from delivering or producing goods, rendering services, or carrying out other activities that constitute the entity's ongoing major or central operations'.[62]

Gains, which are 'increases in equity (net assets) from peripheral or incidental transactions of an entity and from all other transactions and other events and circumstances affecting the entity except those that result from revenues or investments by owners'.[63]

Losses, which are 'decreases in equity (net assets) from peripheral or incidental transactions of an entity and from all other transactions and other events and circumstances affecting the entity except those that result from expenses or distributions to owners'.[64]

Therefore, comprehensive income equals revenues minus expenses plus gains minus losses; however, although the statement states that revenues, expenses, gains and losses can be combined in various ways to obtain various measures of enterprise performance,[65] it fails to define net income.

The difficulty surrounding the FASB's definitions of the ten elements is that they are so interrelated, that in attempting to piece them together into a meaningful accounting framework, one gets caught up in a tautology of terms which all lead back to the definitions of assets and liabilities. Essentially, what the FASB is saying is that assets minus liabilities equals equity and comprehensive income equals changes in equity (excluding transactions with owners), therefore comprehensive income equals the change in net assets. Consequently, the definition of comprehensive income would incorporate items such as capital contributions from non-owners, government grants for capital expenditure and unrealised holding gains. This is all very well, provided that the issues of measurement and capital maintenance have already been settled. However, this is clearly not the case, with the result that the FASB is either restricting itself in the future development of different accounting models for different purposes, or it might have to develop different definitions of the elements of financial statements as different models are developed.

In fact it now seems that the FASB and IASB, have concluded that the definitions of the elements of financial statements are, indeed, deficient and require reconsideration. This view is confirmed by the IASB announcement in July 2001 that it has placed the definitions of the elements of financial statements on its agenda of technical projects. Further confirmation is provided by the decision taken at the April 2004 FASB/IASB joint board meeting to begin work on a new conceptual framework project.

2.8   Recognition and measurement

Throughout the framework project, the FASB had avoided dealing with certain fundamental issues on the basis that they were the 'subject of another project'.[66] The result was the publication in December 1984 of SFAC No. 5 – *Recognition and Measurement in Financial Statements of Business Enterprises* – which attempted to deal with all the previously unresolved issues. However, the statement was somewhat inconclusive – possibly as a consequence of both its self-imposed restrictions discussed above, and the need to reach compromises in order to complete this phase of the project. The statement tends to describe practices current at the time, rather than indicate preferences or propose improvements; for example, in dealing with the issue of measurement attributes, the statement merely states that 'items currently reported in financial statements are measured by different attributes, depending on the nature of the item and the relevance and reliability of the attribute measured'.[67] Then, instead of either prescribing a particular measurement attribute, or discussing the circumstances under which particular attributes should apply, the statement discusses five different attributes which 'are used in present practice' – historical cost, current cost, current market value, net realisable value and present value of future cash flows – and concludes that 'the use of different attributes will continue'.[68] Furthermore, the statement fails to prescribe a particular concept of capital maintenance that should be adopted by an entity, although the FASB bases its discussions on the concept of financial capital maintenance.[69]

The statement defines recognition as 'the process of formally recording or incorporating an item into the financial statements of an entity as an asset, liability, revenue, expense, or the like'.[70] It goes on to discuss four 'fundamental recognition criteria' which any item should meet in order for it to be recognised in the financial statements of an entity. These criteria, which are subject to a cost-benefit constraint and a materiality threshold, are described as follows:

Definitions – the item meets the definition of an element of financial statements.

Measurability – the item has a relevant attribute measurable with sufficient reliability.

Relevance – the information about the item is capable of making a difference in user decisions.

Reliability – the information is representationally faithful, verifiable and neutral.[71]

Although it was probably worth setting out these criteria, they are no more than an encapsulation of certain criteria contained in Concepts Statements 2 and 6.

SFAC No. 5 does make some progress in distinguishing between comprehensive income, earnings and net income. It states that the concept of earnings is similar to net income in present practice, and that a statement of earnings will be much like a present income statement, although 'earnings' does not include the cumulative effect of certain accounting adjustments of earlier periods that are recognised in the current period.[72] However, the statement goes on to say that the FASB 'expects the concept of earnings to be subject to the process of gradual change or evolution that has characterised the development of net income'.[73] Whilst many would agree with the principle that gradual change is the best approach towards gaining general acceptance, one of the problems with SFAC No. 5 is that the FASB does not indicate what it considers to be the desirable direction for this gradual change to follow. Furthermore, the FASB seems to be saying that concepts will evolve as accounting standards are developed – instead of the other way around.

In an evaluation of the FASB's conceptual framework, Professor David Solomons (who, incidentally, was the principal author of SFAC No. 2) took a distinctly critical view of this 'evolutionary' view of the emergence of concepts, stating the following:

'These appeals to evolution should be seen as what they are – a cop-out. If all that is needed to improve our accounting model is reliance on evolution … why was an expensive and protracted conceptual framework project necessary in the first place? … And, for that matter, if progress is simply a matter of waiting for evolution, who needs the FASB?'[74] Professor Solomons came to the following conclusions about SFAC No. 5: 'Under a rigorous grading system I would give Concepts Statement No. 5 an F and require the board to take the course over again – that is, to scrap the statement and start afresh.'[75] This led Solomons to conclude ultimately that 'my judgment of the project as a whole must be that it has failed'.[76]

Interestingly, the FASB's own special report on its conceptual framework makes the point that although SFAC No. 5's name implies that it gives conceptual guidance on recognition and measurement, its conceptual contributions to financial reporting are not really in those areas.[77] The report goes on to say that 'as a result of compromises necessary to issue it, much of Concepts Statement 5 merely describes present practice and some of the reasons that have been used to support or explain it but provides little or no conceptual basis for analyzing and attempting to resolve the controversial issues of recognition and measurement about which accountants have disagreed for years.'[78] The concluding sentence of the FASB's report sums up elegantly the views that have long been expressed by critics of SFAC No. 5: 'Concepts Statement 5 does make some noteworthy conceptual contributions— they are just not on recognition and measurement.'[79]

2.9   Using cash flow information in accounting measurements (discounting)

In February 2000 the FASB issued a new Statement of Financial Accounting Concepts, SFAC 7 – *Using cash flow information and present value in accounting measurements*. The finalised statement resulted from drafts published in 1999 and 1997. The purpose of the statement is to provide a framework for using future cash flows as the basis for accounting measurement. It aims to provide general principles governing the use of present value, especially when the amounts of future cash flows and/or their timing are uncertain. The proposals are limited to issues of measurement and do not address recognition questions.

Present values are used to incorporate the time value of money in a measurement. In their simplest form, present value techniques capture the amount that an entity demands (or that others demand from it) for money that it will receive (or pay) in the future.[80] The FASB's objective of using present value in an accounting measurement is to capture, to the extent that it is possible, the economic difference between sets of estimated future cash flows, taking into account their uncertainty as well as their timing differences. Normal discounting distinguishes between a cash flow of €1,000 due in one day and a cash flow of €1,000 due in ten years, although both have an undiscounted measurement of €1,000. SFAC 7 seeks to distinguish additionally between cash flows based upon their different risks. For example to distinguish between two identical inflows due in (say) five years time, but which have different risks attached to them because of the relative uncertainties of their being received. Consequently, SFAC 7 postulates that a present value measurement which incorporates the uncertainty in estimated future cash flows always provides more relevant information than a measurement based on the undiscounted sum of those cash flows or a discounted measurement that ignores uncertainty.[81]

Any combination of cash flows and interest rates could be used to compute a present value, at least in the broadest sense of the term. However, present value is not an end in itself. Simply applying an arbitrary interest rate to a series of cash flows provides limited information to financial statement users, and may mislead rather than assist. To provide relevant information in financial reporting, present value must represent some observable measurement attribute of assets or liabilities. The statement identifies the following characteristics of a present value measurement which would capture fully the economic differences between various future cash flows:

- An estimate of the future cash flow;

- Expectations about possible variations in amount or timing of those cash flows;

- The time value of money, represented by the risk free rate of interest;

- The price for bearing the uncertainty inherent in the asset or liability;

- Other, sometimes unidentifiable, factors including illiquidity and market imperfections.[82]

SFAC 7 selects fair value as the sole measurement attribute that incorporates all the above aspects, and rejects the possible alternatives of value in use, effective settlement and cost-accumulation as being less satisfactory. The FASB holds that each of the rejected measurement attributes (a) adds factors that are not contemplated in the price of a market transaction for the asset or liability in question, (b) inserts assumptions made by the entity's management in the place of those the market would make, and/or (c) excludes factors that would be contemplated in the price of a market transaction. Consequently fair value represents a price and, as such, provides an unambiguous objective for the development of the cash flows and interest rates used in present value measurement.[83]

The statement sets out the following four general principles that, it considers, govern any application of present value techniques in measuring assets:

- To the extent possible, estimated cash flows and interest rates should reflect assumptions about all future events and uncertainties that would be considered in deciding whether to acquire an asset or group of assets in an arm's-length transaction for cash.

- Interest rates used to discount cash flows should reflect assumptions that are consistent with those inherent in the estimated cash flows. Otherwise, the effect of some assumptions will be double counted or ignored. For example, an interest rate of 12 per cent might be applied to contractual cash flows of a loan. That rate reflects expectations about future defaults from loans with particular characteristics. That same 12 per cent rate should not be used to discount expected cash flows because those cash flows already reflect assumptions about future defaults.

- Estimated cash flows and interest rates should be free from both bias and factors unrelated to the asset or group of assets in question. For example, deliberately understating estimated net cash flows to enhance the apparent future profitability of an asset introduces a bias into the measurement.

- Estimated cash flows or interest rates should reflect the range of possible outcomes rather than a single most likely, minimum, or maximum possible amount.[84]

The stance adopted by SFAC 7 on the measurement of liabilities is consistent with its conclusion on assets. Thus fair value is the single measurement objective when present value is to be used in measuring liabilities, although the statement is not particularly specific as to how fair value is to be determined, stating that the measurement of liabilities 'may require different techniques in arriving at fair value'. However it does state that the objective of using present value techniques to estimate the fair value of a liability is to estimate the value of assets required currently to (a) settle the liability or (b) transfer the liability to an entity of comparable credit standing.[85] The difficulty of defining and identifying fair value remains a problem for any conceptual framework that relies upon the notion, and is further discussed at 5 below in relation to the IASB's framework.

The most significant element of SFAC 7 as concerns liabilities, centres around the incorporation of the entity's own credit standing into the measurement. Fair value in settlement as described above implies that the credit standing of the entity must be taken into account in arriving at the fair value of its liabilities. Accordingly, the fair value in settlement of an entity's liability should assume settlement with an entity of comparable, rather than superior, credit standing. Consequently, as the entity's credit standing affects the interest rate at which it borrows in the market place, it therefore affects the fair value of its liabilities.

This view entails the FASB adopting a quite complex form of discounting in SFAC 7, to facilitate which it has defined for its purposes a number of terms that are not necessarily used in their normal everyday sense. Instead of discounting the best estimate of any future cash flow (i.e. the most likely amount), the statement insists that the 'expected' cash flows should be discounted. The 'expected' cash flow to be used is defined as the sum of probability-weighted amounts in a range of possible estimated amounts.[86] Therefore, SFAC 7 requires the estimation of the likelihood of a range of outcomes (for example, for the repayment of a debt); the probability weighting of each; the calculation of each probability weighted amount; their summation and finally the calculation of the present value of that derived total. The statement does not define the rate to be used in any discounting but appears to indicate that a risk free rate is often the appropriate rate to use.

The statement implies a number of practical results, which many will find odd. For instance the fair valuation of warranty obligations, if not calculated on a cost accumulation (incremental) basis, could result in the liability being overstated. It is probable that the market's rate for performing warranty work would involve overhead costs not incurred by the entity itself, which would incur only incremental costs. This could result in the understatement of current profits and the overstatement of subsequent ones, as the extra cost factored into the (market price based) fair value warranty obligations and charged as an expense at the time of sale, was subsequently written back (usually referred to as 'unwound').

The inclusion of the credit standing of entities in the calculations can produce unwanted results. The lower the credit rating of a business, the higher the interest rate it will have to pay. Therefore, after discounting, the obligation of a low credit rated firm (using the higher discount rate its higher borrowing rate implies) will produce a lower net present value than that of a firm with an identical obligation and a better credit rating. This produces the extraordinary result whereby a poorer credit-rated, less safe firm, shows a significantly lower liability than a higher rated, safer firm – despite the fact that both have an identical settlement payment to make. Nevertheless, this is the position that the IASB (following the lead of the G4+1[87]) has taken in its standard on the recognition and measurement of financial instruments, IAS 39. This standard allows that, in determining the fair value of its liabilities, an entity should take account of its own credit risk.[88]

All in all, SFAC 7 comes across as no more than an overview of the issues surrounding the use of present values in accounting measurement. In spite of choosing fair values as the sole allowable measurement base, it leaves the door open to a fairly wide range of discounting practices, which can be applied as and when the FASB so decides. It is unfortunate that the statement contains no explanation in plain English of what its practical ramifications are and where, if it were to be adopted, financial reporting would be heading. It is therefore possible that the FASB has deliberately adopted a SFAC that will seemingly provide conceptual support for the introduction of an ever widening variety of discounting practices into US financial reporting, and further extend the notion of fair value. In view of the manner in which the IASB has followed the FASB's lead throughout its own conceptual framework project (see 3 below); the avowed strategy of the IASB of convergence with US GAAP; and the recently issued FASB exposure draft – *Proposed statement of accounting standards Fair Value Measurements* – that owes much to SFAC 7; that concepts statement may have wide ranging implications for financial reporting in the EU in the future and is discussed at 5.3 below.

2.10   Concluding remarks on the FASB conceptual framework

In order to be able to assess the success or failure of the FASB's conceptual framework project, one must refer back to the originally perceived benefits of the project and evaluate whether or not any of them has been achieved (see 2.4 above). Perhaps the acid test may be found in analysing the extent to which the FASB has used the framework in the development of accounting standards. Possibly the best example of where the framework has been used as the basis for an accounting standard is in the development of SFAS 95 – *Statement of Cash Flows*; however, this is clearly the exception. An analysis of the Appendices headed 'Basis for Conclusions' in the more recently issued SFASs, reveals few references to the fact that the members of the FASB have used the concepts statements to guide their thinking – and where reference is made it is generally to broad objectives or qualitative characteristics. On the other hand, it might be argued that the concepts statements have guided the thinking of FASB members without it being expressly stated. However, if this were the case, why is it that the FASB has, for example, issued a statement on reporting comprehensive income (SFAS 130) that seemingly lacks any conceptual integrity and is in conflict with the framework? The same might be said of the standard on deferred tax (SFAS 109) that similarly lacks any discernible conceptual underpinning.

The weakness of the FASB's conceptual framework project may be attributed to a number of factors; however, the most significant reason will probably be shown to be the Board's failure to deal with the fundamental issues of recognition and measurement. To a certain extent, the FASB has fallen into the same trap as the AICPA did in APB Statement No. 4, in that SFAC No. 5 is a descriptive rather than a prescriptive statement; a statement of accounting concepts should provide a frame of reference for the formulation of financial reporting practice, and not be a description of what current reporting practices are. In the words of Professor Stephen Zeff, 'the FASB's conceptual framework failed to fulfil expectations that it might constitute a powerful intellectual force for improving financial reporting'.[89]

Underlying the entire issue of developing a conceptual framework is the unspoken yet pervasive view of the project's authors that the logical structure for the framework should be a highly deductive one whereby the entire schema follows from a number of definitional assertions. To the practically minded accountant it seems the problem of (for instance) ensuring worthless research and development expenditure is not carried forward, is one of determining whether the expenditure in question is likely to result in profitable sales in the future. By contrast, this precise problem is cited in the FASB special report as a prime reason for adopting a definition that excludes all deferred charges. This desire for an entirely deductive system amounts to a view of what accounting is that may not coincide with reality. Accounting is an activity born out of the needs of society (principally the needs of industrialised nations) that responds to those needs as and when conditions alter. The fact that the framework project has not obviously impinged upon the thinking behind a number of standards seems to be evidence for this view. It may not be a fault that accounting lacks a set of principles that accurately and inescapably predict the future in the way that scientific laws do; rather it may be a necessary attribute of accounting continuing to be useful to society.

This is not to say that the FASB's project has been ineffective; it contains some outstanding work, particularly in the area of qualitative characteristics, and has fundamentally influenced the thinking and output of other standard setters, most notably the IASC and its successor the IASB. As discussed below, the definitions adopted in the conceptual framework of the IASB are taken essentially unchanged from the FASB's concept statements. Thus, intentionally or not, the FASB's framework project has created a global language and definitional structure used by the only two standard-setting bodies currently involved with global-scale financial reporting.

However, both for the FASB and for the IASB, if the deductive model is to be maintained, a way must be found to address the fundamental issues of recognition and measurement that does not involve both attempting to maintain the truth of the framework's definitions while quietly compromising them when events require it. As discussed in 5 below, the IASB and the FASB have recently set up a new Framework project and it is to be hoped that the opportunity will be taken both to acknowledge and address the inconsistencies and difficulties that currently exist.

3   THE IASB'S CONCEPTUAL FRAMEWORK

3.1   Introduction

In May 1988, the Board of the IASC (before it was reconstituted as the IASB) issued an exposure draft – *Framework for the Preparation and Presentation of Financial Statements* – which set out its understanding of 'the conceptual framework that underlies the preparation and presentation of financial statements'.[90] This was converted without major change into a final statement in September 1989, although it is stressed within the statement that it will be revised from time to time in the light of the Board's experience in working with it.[91] The statement is not an accounting standard and does not override any specific IAS;[92] it therefore has much the same status as the FASB's concepts statements.

In April 2001 the newly constituted IASB formally adopted the framework and it is the most recently published version of it that is referred to in this section. The *Framework* is a short document at 35 pages and just over 100 numbered paragraphs, and clearly is derived from the FASB's first six concepts statements. It is therefore open to the same criticisms and contains the same flaws as the FASB's framework, which are discussed at 2.4 to 2.10 above.

3.2   The contents of the IASB's Framework

The Framework sets out in its introduction that its purpose is to:

'(a)   assist the Board of IASC in the development of future International Accounting Standards and in its review of existing International Accounting Standards;

(b)   assist the Board of IASC in promoting harmonisation of regulations, accounting standards and procedures relating to the presentation of financial statements by providing a basis for reducing the number of alternative accounting treatments permitted by International Accounting Standards;

(c)   assist national standard-setting bodies in developing national standards;

(d)   assist preparers of financial statements in applying International Accounting Standards and in dealing with topics that have yet to form the subject of an International Accounting Standard;

(e)   assist auditors in forming an opinion as to whether financial statements conform with International Accounting Standards;

(f)   assist users of financial statements in interpreting the information contained in financial statements prepared in conformity with International Accounting Standards; and

(g)   provide those who are interested in the work of IASC with information about its approach to the formulation of International Accounting Standards.[93]

The Board accepts that there may be conflicts between the Framework and the provisions of individual standards, but states that these are expected to diminish over time as standards are reviewed or replaced.

Perhaps inevitably the reporting status quo seems to be taken as read by the Framework; as evidenced, for example, by the statement in the introduction to the effect that financial statements normally include a balance sheet, a profit and loss statement, a statement of changes in financial position and notes.[94] The document is then devoted to applying its discussion to this traditional financial reporting package, without, for example, following or apparently considering the possibility of an entirely new package.

Following the Introduction, the IASB's *Framework* is divided into the following seven major sections that are discussed below:

- The objective of financial statements
- Underlying assumptions
- Qualitative characteristics of financial statements
- The elements of financial statements
- Recognition of the elements of financial statements
- Measurement of the elements of financial statements
- Concepts of capital and capital maintenance

3.2.1   The objective and underlying assumptions of financial statements

The objective of financial statements set out in the IASB's Framework will be quite familiar to readers of the FASB equivalent:

> 'to provide information about the financial position, performance and changes in financial position of an enterprise that is useful to a wide range of users in making economic decisions.'[95]

Users are listed in the Introduction as investors, employees, lenders, suppliers and trade creditors, customers, governments and their agencies, and the public – a list that excludes nobody – however, it has to be admitted that the needs of all these groups cannot be met. Therefore financial statements that meet the needs of investors who 'are providers of risk capital' are stated to satisfy also 'most of the needs of other users that financial statements can satisfy'.[96] Perhaps it may be indicative of the derivative nature of the Framework that the phrase 'that financial statements can satisfy' is used. If an examination of a subject starts with preconceptions of what can and cannot be done, it is unlikely that much in the way of new insights or approaches will emerge. In any event, the investor's perspective is chosen as the one most likely to be useful in the preparation of what will remain general purpose financial statements.

The remainder of this part of the Framework contains a range of assertions, also quite familiar, covering how users need to know about the performance, financial position, cash generation, and liquidity and solvency of an entity, including changes in them.

The Framework sets out two 'underlying assumptions': the accruals basis of accounting and the going concern basis. Accruals is described as follows, significantly omitting matching from the concept:

> 'effects of transactions and other events are recognised when they occur (and not as cash or its equivalent is received or paid) and they are recorded in the accounting records and reported in the financial statements of the periods to which they relate'.[97]

Later on in the Framework, in the section on recognition, the point is specifically made that 'the application of the matching concept under this framework does not allow the recognition of items in the balance sheet which do not meet the definition of assets and liabilities'.[98] Equally significantly, prudence is not an underlying assumption of the Framework, but is relegated to being a subsidiary quality of reliability.

The going concern assumption is quite conventionally stated as follows:

> 'financial statements are normally prepared on the assumption that an enterprise is a going concern and will continue in operation for the foreseeable future. Hence, it is assumed that the enterprise has neither the intention nor the need to liquidate or curtail materially the scale of its operations'[99]

3.2.2 *The qualitative characteristics of financial statements*

A *Understandability*

The qualitative characteristics advanced in the document are also taken directly from the FASB conceptual framework project. The familiar list of understandability, relevance, reliability and comparability is advanced. One of the factors that all framework attempts have paid lip-service to is understandability, that is dealt with in its entirety in the IASB's Framework as follows:

> 'An essential quality of the information provided in financial statements is that it is readily understandable by users. For this purpose, users are assumed to have a reasonable knowledge of business and economic activities and accounting and a willingness to study the information with reasonable diligence. However, information about complex matters that should be included in the financial statements because of its relevance to the economic decision-making needs of users should not be excluded merely on the grounds that it may be too difficult for certain users to understand.'[100]

The Framework has advanced as an essential quality in the above paragraph that the 'information provided in financial statements ... is readily understandable by users'; however, this is significantly different from financial statements actually *being* understood. The paragraph goes on to specify the required capabilities of users as having 'a reasonable knowledge of business and economic activities and accounting and a willingness to study the information with reasonable diligence'. This assertion, whilst similar to those in other frameworks, avoids the understandability problem in two ways.

First the phrase 'reasonable knowledge ... of accounting' is entirely open-ended. It is highly unlikely that this could possibly be interpreted to mean 'a complete technical understanding of all the nuances involved with the intricacies of the many accounting rules and regulations', for example. In which case it is clear that much of what the IASB promulgates is not, in this sense, understandable.

Second, the capabilities required would probably reduce the 'allowable' users to a small set of professional analysts, accountants, academics, and the odd graduate of the subject. When this constituency is contrasted with the many types of people who actually own shares; the extremely diverse individual capabilities of even this 'providers of risk capital' user group; and with the very wide definition of users in the Framework; it becomes apparent that the issue of understandability remains considerable and cannot comfortably be defined away in the manner attempted.

B   Relevance

Relevance is the second principal qualitative characteristic put forward. The Framework asserts that 'Information has the quality of relevance when it influences the economic decisions of users by helping them evaluate past, present or future events or confirming, or correcting, their past evaluations'[101] The predictive value of relevant information is emphasised. Not that financial statements should be predictions in the sense of forecasts, but that the information they contain should be relevant to predictions that users might make for themselves about the 'ability of the enterprise to take advantage of opportunities and its ability to react to adverse situations'[102]

Materiality is discussed as a subsection of relevance, in terms of providing a threshold point below which relevance does not exist. Information is stated to be material 'if its omission or misstatement could influence the economic decisions of users taken on the basis of the financial statements'.[103] The important question, however, is against which yardstick information should be judged to be material or immaterial, and for whom, but the Framework provides no further discussion of or guidance about, identifying material items. In practice materiality is both a qualitative as well as a quantitative concept, mere small size would not necessarily make an item immaterial. Thus in this matter the Framework seems more superficial than would be expected.

C   *Reliability*

Reliability is the third primary qualitative characteristic. Information is reliable if 'it is free from material error and bias and can be depended upon by users to represent faithfully that which it either purports to represent or could reasonably be expected to represent.'[104] Faithful representation is used by the Framework as a term that can explain and clarify the notion of reliability. It states that 'Most financial information is subject to some risk of being less than a faithful representation of that which it purports to portray'.[105] This is a considerable admission and either is an overstatement of the case (i.e. there is no material risk in most cases) or if considered true, calls into question why the IASB has accepted it as a satisfactory state of affairs. More importantly, 'faithful representation' assumes satisfactory answers exist to fundamental questions. In particular, answers about what a given item in a set of financial statements might 'purport to represent'. Fundamentally this is taking as solved and understood the entire set of difficulties that the accounting profession and the many framework attempts have, and are still, grappling with.

Substance over form, neutrality, prudence and completeness are cited as four other characteristics that along with representational faithfulness, contribute to the principal qualitative characteristic of reliability. Substance over form is well understood in some jurisdictions, but not in others. In the USA, for example, it is not considered a useful concept, whereas in the UK and certain other countries throughout the world, it is clearly understood and applied. Essentially, substance over form relies upon accepting the possibility that the economic reality of a transaction can be disguised by its legal form. This doctrine means that any transactions structured to give a legal form that does not reflect the underlying economic reality, should be accounted for in accordance with that economic reality rather than the legal form. Thus a sale of a property would not be considered to result in an immediate profit to an entity if the entity simultaneously entered into a leasing agreement that had all the characteristics of a secured loan on that property. This is a key concept in the Framework that in our view is of great importance to the reliability and utility of financial statements if applied wisely in accounting standards.

The Framework defines neutrality as freedom from bias. Prudence (conservatism) is dealt with slightly more fully. Prudence is characterised as follows:

> 'Prudence is the inclusion of a degree of caution in the exercise of the judgements needed in making the estimates required under conditions of uncertainty, such that assets or income are not overstated and liabilities or expenses are not understated. However, the exercise of prudence does not allow, for example, the creation of hidden reserves or excessive provisions, the deliberate understatement of assets or income, or the deliberate overstatement of liabilities or expenses, because the financial statements would not be neutral and, therefore, not have the quality of reliability.'[106]

This statement is of considerable importance in the understanding of the IASB's deliberate move towards financial statements based on fair values. Prudence is characterised here as (a) to be exercised only when uncertainty exists, and (b) not to include 'income smoothing' – characterised as overstatement of provisions or liabilities or understatement of assets. Under an historical cost system this is not what prudence means. Rather it means the necessary caution, once thought fundamental to financial reporting, whereby profit is not taken until it is earned. Under the prudence concept, revenue and profits are not anticipated but are recognised by inclusion in the profit and loss account only when realised in the form of cash or of other assets the ultimate cash realisation of which can be assessed with reasonable certainty. On the other hand, provision is made for all known liabilities whether the amount of these is known with certainty or is a best estimate in the light of the information available. Obviously therefore, if fair values are to be used in financial statements, the original meaning of the prudence concept has to be changed.

Completeness, the fourth sub-characteristic of reliability, means 'the financial statements must be complete within the bounds of materiality and cost'.[107]

D   *Comparability*

Comparability is the fourth principal qualitative characteristic in the Framework, which is an uncontroversial characteristic shared by all conceptual frameworks. Additionally, the IASB includes in the discussion the importance of disclosing accounting policies as an essential part of comparability:

> 'An important implication of the qualitative characteristic of comparability is that users be informed of the accounting policies employed in the preparation of the financial statements, any changes in those policies and the effects of such changes. Users need to be able to identify differences between the accounting policies for like transactions and other events used by the same enterprise from period to period and by different enterprises.'[108]

The point is made however, that comparability does not extend to preventing the improvement of accounting standards. Comparability also entails the provision of comparative figures for the corresponding preceding accounting periods.

There follows a discussion under the heading 'Timeliness' that recognises that there is an element of conflict between two of the principal qualitative characteristics: relevance and reliability:

> 'To provide information on a timely basis it may often be necessary to report before all aspects of a transaction or other event are known, thus impairing reliability. Conversely, if reporting is delayed until all aspects are known, the information may be highly reliable but of little use to users who have had to make decisions in the interim.'[109]

The Framework indicates that this conflict is to be resolved by considering 'how best to satisfy the economic decision-making needs of users'[110] although how these are to be identified in any particular case is not discussed. The first point to make is that the conflict between relevance and reliability is an entirely self-inflicted problem, caused by the downgrading of the prudence concept as explained above, because the IASB wishes to incorporate fair values (that are inherently less reliable than realised profits) into financial statements. Secondly, the advice that this conflict should be resolved by determining 'how best to satisfy the economic decision-making needs of users' is utterly vacuous. It is unclear what this can mean in practice, and how it can assist a preparer, other than by a circular appeal to produce relevant and reliable financial statements. Probably in recognition of this difficulty, paragraph 45 of the Framework acknowledges that a 'trade-off between qualitative characteristics is often necessary' and that their relative importance 'is a matter of professional judgement'.

3.2.3 *The elements of financial statements*

A   *Assets*

The section of the Framework that deals with the elements of financial statements is also derived from its FASB equivalent. Assets are defined as:

'(a)   An asset is a resource controlled by the enterprise as a result of past events and from which future economic benefits are expected to flow to the enterprise.'[111]

The definition of an assets used by the Framework is adopted wholesale from the FASB conceptual framework project, with one important difference. Under SFAC 6 the discussion is in the context of benefits 'obtained or controlled', while the Framework definition refers solely to resources 'controlled' by the enterprise. This is a fundamental difference – for example goodwill falls within the definition of an asset under the FASB concepts, but falls outside the definition under the IASB's framework, as it fails to meet the 'controlled' requirement. The problem the IASB's Framework therefore has, is that it fails to include within its asset definition an asset that all accountants in practice, and the IASB itself, acknowledge *is* an asset. The same problem occurred in the UK's framework project (see 4.6 below for a further discussion of this point).

This definition also has to contend with the problem that future economic benefits may not materialise. Consequently, for an item to be recognised as an asset it must be 'probable that any future economic benefit associated with the item will flow to … the enterprise'.[112] The question therefore arises: what is a future economic benefit? Future economic benefits are obviously other items of property, near cash such as debtors, or cash itself. The logical problem in the absence of any other meaning being given to the phrase 'future economic benefits' is that the asset definition is completely circular. It has no explanatory power, but is precisely logically equivalent to: 'an asset is a resource controlled by the enterprise from which assets are expected to be gained by the enterprise in the future'.

Thus both the FASB and the IASB have a flawed definition at the heart of their conceptual frameworks. If the definition of assets is flawed the entire logical structure derived from it is too, including all the remaining definitions of the elements of financial statements that depend upon the asset definition.

Disregarding the logical objections, what the IASB seems to be driving at in its definition is that an asset is not the physical item, but the cash inflows that it will generate in the future. This approach is inextricably linked to the concept of value in use. The value in use of an asset is the present value of the cash flows that will be derived from the asset through its use in the business. Thus the IASB seems to be saying that an asset is the right to these cash flows, which is why it is necessary to include the notion of control within the definition of an asset.

The notion of control possibly introduces an unwanted side-effect of the Framework's asset definition. There are various expenditures, such as those incurred in staff training or developing market share that, judging by the IASB's accounting standards, the Board does not want to allow into the balance sheet, even though they bring future benefits. It is not clear from the Framework on what grounds they are excluded.

Paragraph 50 makes it clear that because something meets the definition of an asset or liability, it does not imply it will necessarily be included ('recognised') in the balance sheet. That is, meeting the definition is a necessary but not a sufficient condition for inclusion in the financial statements. The IASB's recognition criteria are discussed in the following section. Once again, and importantly, the Framework emphasises that:

> 'In assessing whether an item meets the definition of an asset, liability or equity, attention needs to be given to its underlying substance and economic reality and not merely its legal form.'[113]

The emphasis on substance over form is a key practical difference between the FASB conceptual framework and that of the IASB. It is potentially immensely powerful and of great importance to users, in that it requires preparers to produce financial statements that clearly report on the underlying economic reality of the transactions an entity has undertaken. There is another concept fundamental to the IASB's approach that is included in this paragraph of the Framework, even though it appears only as part of an illustration of the substance over form approach:

> 'Thus, for example, in the case of finance leases, the substance and economic reality are that the lessee acquires the economic benefits of the use of the leased asset for the major part of its useful life in return for entering into an obligation to pay for that right an amount approximating to the fair value of the asset and the related finance charge.'[114]

Thus the term 'fair value' appears for the first time in the Framework. The meaning that can be ascribed to this term is discussed at 5.3 below. However, in view of the importance and wide use of this term throughout the IASB's later standards, it is an omission of some magnitude that it is not defined or discussed at all in the Framework.

B   Liabilities

In the IASB's Framework a liability is defined as:

> 'a present obligation of the enterprise arising from past events, the settlement of which is expected to result in an outflow from the enterprise of resources embodying economic benefits.'[115]

The 'present obligation arising from a past event' definition of a liability is also adopted from the FASB equivalent, with the same consequences for recognising provisions which, if based solely on the basis of a management decision, will not qualify under this definition. For example, IAS 37 – *Provisions, Contingent Liabilities and Contingent Assets* – relies heavily on this definition to severely restrict the circumstances under which provisions can be recognised. This is because provisions are not seen as a separate element of financial statements and, instead, are defined as being a subset of liabilities (see Chapter 25). The concept of the 'constructive obligation' used in IAS 37 as a sub-set of the term present obligation, is not referred to in the Framework.

Assets and liabilities are therefore characterised as rights and obligations – rights to receive future economic benefits in the form of cash inflows and obligations to transfer out economic benefits in the form of cash outflows. The remaining definitions are derived from these definitions of assets and liabilities.

C   Equity

Equity is defined as follows:

> 'Equity is the residual interest in the assets of the enterprise after deducting all its liabilities.'[116]

Again the wording is similar to that used in SFAC 6. The logic of the definition is identical, and follows from the equation that assets minus liabilities equals equity.

D   Income and expenses

Income and expenses definitions rely directly upon the balance sheet approach outlined above., and are defined in terms of the changes to assets and liabilities as follows:

> 'Income is increases in economic benefits during the accounting period in the form of inflows or enhancements of assets or decreases of liabilities that result in increases in equity, other than those relating to contributions from equity participants.
>
> Expenses are decreases in economic benefits during the accounting period in the form of outflows or depletions of assets or incurrences of liabilities that result in decreases in equity, other than those relating to distributions to equity participants.'[117]

Although income and expenses are defined in terms of balance sheet recognition criteria in the same manner as adopted by the FASB, the Framework has adopted a simpler approach as it uses a single element to cover what SFAC 6 describes separately as revenues and gains (see 2.7.7 above). The distinction is that the US definitions differentiate between gains arising from central operations and those which do not, whereas the Framework uses a single definition for both.

Similarly, the definition of expenses embraces both expenses and losses as the terms are used in SFAC 6 (see 2.7.7 above). Realisation is not mentioned at all in the Framework as a criterion for income recognition, thus in principle the IASB's conceptual framework sanctions the recognition of fair value based unrealised revaluations as income.

3.2.4 *Recognition of the elements of financial statements*

The recognition criteria adopted in the Framework are also entirely familiar from other conceptual framework projects. Thus an asset will be recognised if 'it is probable that the future economic benefits will flow to the enterprise and the asset has a cost or value that can be measured reliably'.[118] A liability is recognised 'when it is probable that an outflow of resources embodying economic benefits will result from the settlement of a present obligation and the amount at which the settlement will take place can be measured reliably.'[119] Just as with its US equivalents, the recognition criteria for income and expenses are derived by deduction from these definitions.

The balance sheet approach to income and expense recognition is absolutely explicit in the Framework, as demonstrated by paragraph 92:

> 'Income is recognised in the income statement when an increase in future economic benefits related to an increase in an asset or a decrease of a liability has arisen that can be measured reliably. This means, in effect, that recognition of income occurs simultaneously with the recognition of increases in assets or decreases in liabilities'

Paragraph 94 contains similar wording relating to expense recognition.

3.2.5 *Measurement of the elements of financial statements*

This is the third stage of the IASB's process of inclusion of an item into the financial statements. First there is definition (e.g. of an asset); if an item meets the definition, then comes recognition; if an item can be recognised (i.e. it is probable that economic benefits will come to the enterprise and that cost or value can be measured reliably) the final stage is measurement.

Measurement is defined as:

> 'the process of determining the monetary amounts at which the elements of the financial statements are to be recognised and carried in the balance sheet and income statement. This involves the selection of the particular basis of measurement'[120]

The 'basis of measurement' actually refers to the type of accounting conceptual basis that could be used. The Framework lists four possibilities: historical cost; current cost; realisable value; and present value. Present value meaning assets are carried at the present value of their expected future cash flows, while liabilities are carried at the present value of the amount that will be required to settle the liability in the future. In spite of its frequent use in the IASB's standards, fair value is not mentioned at all in the Framework, and therefore not as a measurement basis. In its current standards the IASB defines fair value as 'the amount for which an asset could be exchanged between knowledgeable, willing parties in an arm's length transaction'. The recognition and measurement of fair values is crucial to performance measurement under the system the IASB is developing, and this topic is fully discussed in Chapter 26. The definition and meaning of fair value is further discussed at 5.3 below.

There is no further discussion of which might be preferable. The subject is dealt with in its entirety in a solely descriptive manner in three paragraphs, and ends with the statement that historical cost is most commonly adopted. No recommendations are made about which might be considered the most satisfactory.

3.2.6 *Concepts of capital and capital maintenance*

Finally, there is a short section dealing with concepts of capital maintenance. This summarises the concepts of physical and financial capital maintenance as follows:

> 'Under a financial concept of capital, such as invested money or invested purchasing power, capital is synonymous with the net assets or equity of the enterprise. Under a physical concept of capital, such as operating capability, capital is regarded as the productive capacity of the enterprise based on, for example, units of output per day.'[121]

No attempt is made to examine or discuss the adequacy of each concept or how their use might contribute to improving financial reporting. Even recommending one or the other is avoided by the customary and in effect empty formula of 'selection of the appropriate concept of capital by an enterprise should be based on the needs of the users of its financial statements'.[122]

This final section ends with the entirely unsupported assertion that the Framework is applicable to any chosen accounting model, in that it is 'applicable to a range of accounting models and provides guidance on preparing and presenting the financial statements constructed under the [any] chosen model.'[123] This is unlikely to be the case, as for example, even a brief reading of 4 above shows that there are a number of alternative conceptual framework possibilities to which the notions of definition and recognition outlined in the IASB's Framework would have no obvious application or relevance. Finally the Framework ends on a rather open ended note as follows:

> 'At the present time, it is not the intention of the Board of IASC to prescribe a particular model other than in exceptional circumstances, such as for those enterprises reporting in the currency of a hyperinflationary economy. This intention will, however, be reviewed in the light of world developments'[124]

3.3 Assessment of the IASB's Framework

There is no really fundamental difference between the IASB and FASB conceptual frameworks. The IASB document clearly derives from the original FASB work embodied in its concepts statements (see 2 above) and in truth the IASB's Framework is little more than a synopsis of the FASB conceptual statements. It is perhaps unfortunate, and certainly was a lost opportunity at the time, that the IASB did not taken the chance presented by the publication of a conceptual framework document to explore more fundamentally the questions posed by such an endeavour. A conceptual framework should be more than an *ex post facto* justification of an already chosen approach, in our view.

The balance sheet approach taken by the IASB views the accounting process differently from how it has been viewed traditionally. Traditionally, assets and liabilities have not formed the natural starting point for devising recognition rules. In practice, the traditional building blocks of accounting are transactions, to which are applied criteria for revenue and expense recognition. The balance sheet being a result of this process not the starting point, with there being no intention of it capturing all aspects of a company's value.

A general concern about IASB's approach is that it does not adequately acknowledge the legal and business context in which accounting is practised and the constraints thereby placed on it. The objective of financial statements is said to be to provide information about the financial position, performance and changes in financial position of an enterprise that is useful to a wide range of users in making economic decisions; but this definition is then immediately narrowed down to the providers of risk capital – shareholders. As it is explicit in the Framework's definitional structure that future cash generation is the key to asset recognition and thus income recognition, the objective of financial statements, therefore, becomes to predict future cash flows. This objective is suspect in as much as it is either not always true, or only trivially true. If a shareholder takes the view that she wishes to invest in property, even if that property is never realised, the proponents of the 'future cash flow' objective would still claim the objective holds because at some point the investor would want to realise the investment, even if that point is several lifetimes away.

This 'predict future cash flows' tenet is the fundamental assumption in an established branch of academic thought. As an aid to academic thought and research it is a helpful simplification. As the basis for regulatory endeavour, however, it is not necessarily entirely appropriate. Accounts do not, in fact, exist solely to predict cash flows for investment decisions; they form a report by the stewards of an enterprise to its owners, and they sit within a legal and social context that cannot simply be ignored. There is a degree of conflict between the needs of regulators and analysts that is ignored by the 'meet the needs of investors and you meet the needs of everyone else' assumption in the objectives of the Framework. Regulators, as is from time to time unhappily illustrated when businesses fail, are far more interested in the proper stewardship of assets that currently exist than in predicting future cash flows.

Financial statements also fulfil a variety of other roles, including the identification of profits available for dividend; a starting point for the assessment of taxation; a reference point that can be used for conditions in contracts with lenders and other parties; the calculation of executive directors' performance bonuses; and so on.

Undoubtedly, how accounting is actually done in the world is, in fact, transactions based. Arguably even though equivalent frameworks elsewhere in the world also suggest a balance sheet approach, these documents do not correspond to the reality of the accounting process in those countries either. If the (equivalent) approach in the FASB's concepts were actually applied in the US, for example, the extensive literature on revenue recognition in that country would be redundant. The question therefore arises why the IASB has adopted a set of criteria that do not fit the practice of accounting they attempt to govern.

An answer to this question might be that the IASB wants fundamentally to change the basis of financial reporting to a full balance sheet oriented, fair-value based system of reporting. This intention was inherent in many of the publications of the G4+1 – effectively the standard setters' think-tank until disbanded in 2001. An examination of the notion of fair value in itself is curiously absent from any of the conceptual literature of the IASB and it is far from clear exactly what is meant by the term in most practical business contexts. The definition provided in IFRS 1: 'the amount for which an asset could be exchanged, or a liability settled, between knowledgeable, willing parties in an arm's length transaction', has little practical meaning outside the listed securities and financial markets.

These real difficulties are reflected both in the unease of the business community and also implicitly by the IASB itself. In April 2004, UNICE (a group representing European industry) and Nippon Keidanren (the Japan Business Federation) jointly wrote to the IASB to express their concerns about the fair value approach the Board is increasingly embracing, in the following terms:

> 'We strongly oppose the IASB's further consideration of the 'full fair value concept' without further research on the needs of users and preparers, and the economic consequences of this fundamental change in concepts because of its inherent theoretical and practical problems.'

The two industry groups further expressed concern about the control exerted by the IASC foundation over the IASB, which is indicative of the disquiet that the somewhat didactic approach of the IASB to preparers has caused:

> 'The IASB must improve its governance structure and the process of developing standards in order to be recognised as a genuine legitimate international institution. In particular, a structure should be created to ensure that in the study of standards by the IASB, the opinions of capital markets are properly considered'

The IASB itself, perhaps recognising the inadequacy of its conceptual document and the absence of a theoretical underpinning for its fair value agenda, at its April meeting jointly decided with the FASB to set up a staff team to work on a new conceptual framework. The expressed intention is that an identical framework for the IASB and the FASB will result, and a work programme for it will be discussed at the September 2004 meeting of the IASB. This cooperation is one of the outcomes of the joint agreement between the IASB and the FASB, the 'Norwalk Agreement' outlined below at 5.1. This project may well bring a global GAAP somewhat nearer to becoming a reality, but we hope the opportunity will not be lost to involve preparers, users and market regulators in the exercise, in the hope that the outcome will have practical use, and widespread support from business worldwide.

4   OTHER FRAMEWORK ENDEAVOURS

For those concerned with understanding the process by which the IASB has arrived at many of its standards, or with making a contribution to the development of future IFRSs through Exposure Draft responses, an understanding of how the profession has moved from uncritical use of historical cost in the 1960s to a mix of cost and fair value today, is valuable. The IASB and many national equivalents developed their views in response to the appearance of practical financial reporting problems that caused users and others to require change. In the past this imperative triggered fundamental work by a number of accounting bodies and standard setters from different nations, and their contributions to the development of financial reporting are outlined below. This work taken together, has contributed consciously or not to the development of the IASB's own framework, and the thinking that underlies it.

4.1   The Corporate Report

The first real attempt by the accounting profession in Europe to develop a conceptual framework is to be found in a discussion paper issued by the UK accounting profession in 1975 by the then-styled Accounting Standards Steering Committee and entitled *The Corporate Report.*[125]

The discussion paper dealt with 'the fundamental aims of published financial reports and the means by which these aims can be achieved'[126] and used the term 'corporate report' to mean 'the comprehensive package of information of all kinds which most completely describes an organisation's economic activity'.[127] It was suggested that this 'comprehensive package' should include more than the 'basic financial statements' (i.e. the balance sheet, profit and loss account and funds statement), and should incorporate additional narrative and descriptive statements.[128] The discussion paper centred around three main elements: 'the types of organisation which should be expected to publish regular financial information; the main users of such information and their needs; and the form of report which will best meet those needs'.[129]

The discussion paper followed the basic approach that corporate reports should seek to satisfy, as far as possible, the information needs of users.[130] The Committee argued that every economic entity of significant size has an implicit responsibility to report publicly, and concluded that general purpose reports designed for general purpose use are the primary means by which this public accountability is fulfilled. Users were defined 'as those having a reasonable right to information concerning the reporting entity',[131] a right which arises from the entity's public accountability.

The paper identified seven user groups[132] as having a reasonable right to information, and discussed the basis of the rights of each group and their information needs. Not surprisingly, the Committee identified a considerable overlap of interest between each of the user groups, including items such as 'evaluating the performance of the entity', 'estimating the future prospects of the entity', 'evaluating managerial performance', 'assessing the liquidity of the entity, its present or future requirements for additional fixed or working capital, and its ability to raise long and short term finance'.[133]

On this basis the Committee concluded that 'the fundamental objective of corporate reports is to communicate economic measurements of and information about the resources and performance of the reporting entity useful to those having reasonable rights to such information'.[134] They went on to say that in order to fulfil this objective and be useful, corporate reports should be relevant, understandable, reliable, complete, objective, timely and comparable[135] (these qualitative characteristics identified were similar to those discussed in the Trueblood Report).

The discussion paper then reviewed the conventional thinking on the aim of published reports together with the then-existing features of published financial statements of UK companies. The Committee also conducted a survey of corporate objectives amongst the chairmen of 300 of the largest UK listed companies, and concluded that 'distributable profit can no longer be regarded as the sole or premier indicator of performance'.[136] Consequently, it was suggested that there was a need for additional indicators of performance in the corporate reports of all entities.[137]

Part II of the study considered the 'measurement and method' of achieving the above aims. Since the Committee had concluded that current reporting practices did not fully satisfy the needs of users, it was suggested that the following additional statements should be published in the corporate report: a statement of value added, an employment report, a statement of money exchanges with government, a statement of transactions in foreign currency, a statement of future prospects and a statement of corporate objectives.[138] In addition, the Committee recommended further study into methods of social accounting as well as the disaggregation of certain financial information.[139]

Finally, the Committee discussed the concepts and measurements employed in the 'basic financial statements'. In considering the purpose of profit measurement, it concluded that income statements 'should be concerned with the measurement of performance although they may also be used in the measurement of capital maintenance and income distributability'.[140] It was, however, recognised that this dual purpose of income statements often gave rise to conflict in the application of accounting concepts – particularly the fundamental concepts of prudence and matching. Various measurement bases were then discussed in the context of the inadequacies of the historical cost system. The Committee stated that 'the usefulness of financial statements in fulfilling user needs is restricted at the present time because of the defects of the basis of measurement generally used. Historical cost accounting fails, in times of rapidly changing prices and values, to ensure that sufficient provision is made for capital maintenance.'[141]

The committee then briefly surveyed several bases of measurement, including historical cost, current purchasing power (CPP) and various current value bases such as replacement cost and net realisable value. The conclusion reached was that no one system of measurement is capable of satisfying the user needs identified in the study, and that, therefore, research should be undertaken into the feasibility of multi-column reporting, as well as into the development of a standardised system of current value accounting.[142]

It is probable that the business community were concerned about the possibility of their reporting responsibility being extended through the development of the Committee's concept of public accountability. Although this aspect of the Corporate Report has largely been absent from all further conceptual framework documents, arguably it was a far-sighted approach. The rise of public interest in, and of academic research into, alternative reports such as environmental reports by businesses, may indicate that the public accountability aspect of corporate reporting will have to become more formally recognised as integral to company financial reporting. Indeed, this is the case already with the prominence now being attached to corporate governance disclosures by a number of listing authorities.

4.2   Financial reporting in times of high inflation

Through most of the 1970s and early 1980s, inflation was an intractable problem in the UK and in certain other countries, with rates of inflation well above 10% common, and on occasion over 20%. Inflation poses insoluble problems for historical cost based financial statements because the buying-power of a monetary unit from one accounting period to the next is so different. Outlining the findings of a UK Government committee set up to consider this problem provides a useful way of considering the alternative systems of accounting that have been put forward, as opposed to the more evolutionary nature of the FASB's approach.

The UK Government announced the creation of an Inflation Accounting Committee, subsequently referred to as the Sandilands Committee after its chairman, 'to consider whether, and if so how, company accounts should allow for changes (including relative changes) in costs and prices'.[143] The Sandilands Report is dealt with here in some detail, as it was, and remains, the most comprehensive summary of the many different approaches that have been taken by academic and professional accountants, prompted by a variety of economic conditions, to solving the problems that have surrounded the development of a conceptual framework.

The Sandilands Report followed a similar approach to that of the Corporate Report to the extent that it focused on the information needs of users. The report stated that 'the requirements of users of accounts should be the fundamental consideration in deciding the information to be disclosed in company accounts'.[144]

The report proposed the development of a system of accounting for inflation that would evolve towards a system of current cost accounting, the essential features of which are:

(a)   money is the unit of measurement (as opposed to the 'current purchasing power' basis of expressing financial information in terms of a unit of measurement of constant value when prices change);

(b)   assets and liabilities should be shown in the balance sheet at their 'value to the business'; and

(c)   operating profit (to be known as 'current cost profit') would be calculated after charging the 'value to the business' of the assets consumed during the period, thereby excluding holding gains and showing them separately.[145]

4.2.1 *Current Purchasing Power accounting*

In formulating its system of current cost accounting, the Committee examined three alternative accounting systems which had been developed in an attempt to overcome the deficiencies of historical cost accounting. The first of these systems studied was a 'current purchasing power' (CPP) method of inflation accounting, whereby supplementary information would be given in addition to the historical cost financial statements. The main features of which were:

(a) companies would continue to keep their records and present their basic annual accounts in historical pounds, i.e. in terms of the value of the pound at the time of each transaction or revaluation;

(b) in addition, all listed companies should present to their shareholders a supplementary statement in terms of the value of the pound at the end of the period to which the accounts relate;

(c) the conversion of the figures in the basic accounts into the figures in the supplementary statement should be by means of a general index of the purchasing power of the pound;[146] and

(d) the directors would be required to provide in a note to the supplementary statement an explanation of the basis on which it has been prepared and it is desirable that directors should comment on the significance of the figures.[147]

The Committee concluded that the CPP method 'does not remedy the main deficiencies of historic cost accounting during a time of changing costs and prices and we do not recommend it as the best long-term solution to the problem of accounting for inflation'.[148] Numerous arguments were put forward to support this conclusion, for example:

- since, during a period of changing prices, historical cost figures expressed in terms of monetary units do not show the 'value to the business' of assets, a CPP supplementary statement will show the historic cost figures restated in units of current purchasing power, not the 'value to the business' of assets.[149] Thus, a major deficiency of historical cost accounts would not be overcome;

- since companies were required to express their CPP supplementary statements in terms of the current purchasing power of the pound at the closing balance sheet date, the unit of measurement in the supplementary statement would change from year to year. This was likely to cause confusion, compounded by the fact that companies which had different accounting dates would be preparing supplementary statements in terms of different units, resulting in a lack of comparability;[150] and

- since a unit of measurement with an absolute value through time is unattainable, there is no advantage in preparing financial statements in CPP units rather than in units of money.[151]

4.2.2   Value accounting

The Committee then examined three forms of 'value accounting' – a term used to describe a wide range of different accounting systems which measure net assets by reference to their 'value' rather than their cost. The three value accounting systems examined were: replacement cost accounting; present value accounting; and continuously contemporary accounting.

A   Replacement cost accounting based on current entry values

'Replacement cost' is the price which will have to be paid to replace an asset used or given up in exchange for another asset. Consequently, the basic principle underlying replacement cost accounting is that, since a business has to replace its assets over time in order to continue in operational existence, charges for the consumption or exchange of an asset should be based on the cost of replacing it. Consequently, assets are valued at the balance sheet date by reference to the price which would have to be paid at that date to purchase a similar asset in a similar condition – i.e. the replacement cost of the assets. This system, therefore, adopts a method of income determination that reflects changes in capital both at the point of realisation of assets and, before realisation, while holding assets.

The pioneers of an income and value model based on replacement costs (entry values) were Edwards and Bell,[152] who attempted to interpret accounting concepts in terms of economic concepts. Their theory abandoned both the realisation principle and the idea of the 'unitary income statement' which does not separate operating profit from holding gains. They introduced a new concept of 'business profit', which was made up of current operating profit of the current period, realised holding gains of the same period and unrealised holding gains.

A major disadvantage of the replacement cost model is difficulty and subjectivity involved in assigning replacement costs; for example, are replacement costs based on identical or equivalent replacement, and how is technological obsolescence dealt with? However, this disadvantage is far outweighed by the usefulness of the information provided by the system in the form of meaningful balance sheet values and a segregated business profit figure. The Sandilands Committee concluded that the replacement cost accounting system 'comes close to meeting the dominant requirements of users of accounts and the Committee's own proposals have many similarities with certain forms of this system of accounting'.[153]

B   Present value accounting

Present value accounting is based on the economic concept of income, and values an asset on the basis of the present value of the cash flows that are expected to be derived from that asset. In order to maintain the capital of the entity, an amount at least equal to the original investment should be reinvested, whilst the remaining cash flows are treated as realised. For example, if the discounted net present value of all expected future cash flows of an entity are €100,000 at the beginning of the year and €115,000 at the end of the year, and if the net cash flows arising during the year were €10,000, then the profit for the year will be €25,000, since this amount could be distributed whilst maintaining the original capital base of €100,000.

Whilst this approach might have some degree of theoretical soundness, the Sandilands Committee considered it to be totally impracticable. The Committee believed that issues such as risk, the determination of discount rates, changes in interest rates and the uncertainty of future cash flows presented virtually insurmountable problems. The Sandilands Committee therefore rejected present value accounting on the grounds that use of economic value as the basis of valuation of an asset would not meet the needs of users, as it would only be in comparatively few cases that this would represent the value of an asset to a business.[154]

C   Continuously Contemporary Accounting (CoCoA)

The current value income model based on exit prices or realisable market values was first advocated by MacNeal in a book published by him in 1939 which dealt, inter alia, with the ethical issue of 'truth' in accounting.[155] MacNeal maintained that financial statements could only present the 'truth' if assets were stated at their current value and the profit and losses accruing from the changes in these values are included in income, and classified as either realised or unrealised. MacNeal did, however, concede that under certain circumstances the use of net realisable values was not appropriate, and that in such cases current replacement costs should be used.

The system known as continuously contemporary accounting (CoCoA) was formally introduced by Chambers in a book published in 1966,[156] and the case for exit value accounting was further developed by Sterling.[157] Chambers' theory is based on the premise that entities must be able to choose between alternative courses of action and, because resources are limited, they need to know what resources are available to enable them to engage in exchanges. Consequently, Chambers asserts that this capacity to engage in exchanges is measured by the opportunity cost of holding assets in their existing form, and that this opportunity cost is represented by the current cash equivalent of assets – which Chambers defines as being their current sales value. Initially, Chambers did not apply this principle rigorously and proposed that stocks should be valued at current replacement cost. However, he subsequently amended his view and advocated that exit values should be applied to the valuation of all assets. A difference in the theories of Chambers and Sterling is, for example, that Chambers believed that net realisable values should be based on the assumption that assets are realised in an orderly manner based on sensible adaptations to changing circumstances; Sterling, on the other hand, believed that net realisable values should be based on immediate liquidation prices.

The capital maintenance concept adopted by CoCoA is based on the preservation of the purchasing power of shareholders' equity (using the monetary unit as the unit of measurement, and not the current purchasing power unit used in CPP accounting). Consequently, since all assets (both monetary and non-monetary) are measured at net realisable value, income is defined as the difference between opening and closing equity after maintaining the purchasing power or cash equivalent of such equity. Income for the year, therefore, will comprise (1) the net profit/loss on business operations, (2) the accrued profit/loss arising from the change in the current cash equivalent of assets and (3) the effect on the capital of the entity brought about by the change in the purchasing power of money.

However, despite the widespread publication of his theories, Chambers failed to gain any measure of support for CoCoA outside academic circles.

There is no doubt that there are some compelling theoretical arguments for the presentation of financial statements based on net realisable values; for example, they provide useful information in the assessment of liquidity and financial flexibility. However, net realisable value is unlikely to reflect an asset's 'value to the business', since, for instance, an item of plant might have negligible net realisable value but substantial use value. Therefore, whilst the disclosure of net realisable values might provide useful supplementary information, the arguments in favour of CoCoA as the primary basis of accounting are unconvincing. CoCoA was rejected by the Sandilands Committee on the basis that, as a whole, it did not satisfy the information needs of users which they had identified.[158] It is, however, noteworthy that in its discussion document – *Making Corporate Reports Valuable* – the Research Committee of the ICAS advocated a reporting system based on net realisable values[159] (see 4.4 below).

4.2.3   Cash flow accounting

Finally the Sandilands Committee considered cash flow accounting. The principal proponents of cash flow reporting were Lee[160] and Lawson,[161] although there are several other advocates of various approaches to cash flow reporting. Lee's system of cash flow reporting relied heavily on exit value theory and aimed to report both actual and potential cash flows. Assets are classified according to their realisability, based on Chambers' principle of orderly liquidation. If a sale price does not exist, assets are to be accounted for as having a zero cash equivalent.[162] Lee suggested the following four asset classifications for his statement of financial position:

1.   realised assets (e.g. bank balances);

2.   readily-realisable assets (i.e. assets which have a ready market and sale price, such as listed securities, debtors and stocks of finished goods);

3.   non-readily-realisable assets (i.e. assets which do have a market and sale price, but which would not be quickly realised because of the limited nature of the market, such as certain items of plant and work-in-progress); and

4.   not-realisable assets (i.e. assets which have no known sales price and no market, and would therefore be ascribed a zero value, such as highly specialised or obsolete plant).[163]

Liabilities are classified according to maturity, in line with conventional accounting practice.

Lee proposed that, in addition to a 'statement of financial position', the cash flow reporting system should present a 'statement of realised cash flow', a 'statement of realisable earnings' and a 'statement of changes in financial position'.[164] The statement of realised cash flow would report an entity's actual cash inflows and outflows during a particular period; it is noteworthy that the information contained in this statement would be broadly equivalent to that which would be presented in a statement of cash flows under IAS 7 (see Chapter 32). The statement of realisable earnings would report periodic profit similar to that provided by a net realisable value accounting system, except that it is described in terms of realised and realisable cash flows. The statement would provide an analysis of realised earnings (derived from the entity's operating cash flow), and unrealised earnings (which represent potential cash flows that have accrued during the period as a result of changes in the realisable values of assets, net of the changes in liabilities). The statement of changes in financial position was effectively a conventional funds statement presented on an exit value basis.

Although there are a number of practical accounting and disclosure problems in cash flow reporting, it does have considerable merit. Furthermore, a number of the problems are not unique to cash flow reporting, with equivalent issues remaining unsolved in historical cost accounting. However, one difficulty which does exist is caused by the artificial 12 month reporting period and the necessity to measure 'profitability' over that period and from one period to the next. The principal reason for the development of the accrual basis of accounting was that financial statements prepared on a cash basis (which was probably the oldest form of presentation) provided distorted profit figures from one period to the next.

Although the Sandilands Committee stated that there was 'much of value in the cash flow accounting principle',[165] it was felt that cash flow accounting would rekindle all the 'old difficulties of assessing the profit or loss for the year when the accounting system does not match revenues against costs incurred in their generation'.[166] The Committee therefore concluded that the abandonment of the existing concept of the profit and loss account in favour of a cash flow statement would result in the information needs of users not being met. Clearly, however, the Committee had not considered the possibility of the presentation of a 'statement of realisable earnings' as advocated by Lee, which would provide a more stable basis for reporting profit than the statement of receipts and payments the Committee apparently envisaged. Lee, however, recognised the problems created by the traditional 12 month reporting period, and suggested that a solution might be found in the use of multi-period aggregates for analysis purposes.

4.2.4   Current cost accounting (CCA)

The Sandilands Committee recommended the development of a system of current cost accounting that used the monetary unit as the unit of measurement and dealt with the effects of specific price changes (as opposed to changes in the general purchasing power of money) on individual businesses. The Committee recommended that the balance sheet should present the 'value to the business' of the company's assets, which was equated with the amount of the loss which would be suffered by an entity if the asset were to be lost or destroyed. Whilst it was stated that the 'value to the business' of an asset might, under certain circumstances, be its net realisable value or economic value, it would normally be based on its replacement cost. Because the Committee recommended that financial statements be drawn up in terms of the monetary unit, no adjustment would be made for monetary items.[167] However, it is arguable that current cost accounting does not produce a balance sheet which seeks to be a statement of values of the resources of the company; it simply updates the costs at which they are recorded. This distinction can be illustrated by looking at the financial statements of an oil and gas exploration company. Even on a current cost basis, the carrying value of its principal assets is still based on the (backward-looking) cost of exploration expenditure incurred, not the (forward-looking) value of the oil and gas it has found.

Under the Sandilands system, an entity's 'current cost profit' for a period would be calculated by charging against income 'the value to the business' of assets consumed during the year. In simple terms, therefore, the current cost profit could be derived from the historical cost profit by means of an adjustment to depreciation and a cost of sales adjustment. The Committee also recommended the presentation of a summary statement of total gains or losses for the period, which would present the entity's total gains/losses in terms of three classifications: operating gains/losses (i.e. current cost profit/loss), extraordinary gains/losses and holding gains/losses. An interesting observation regarding these two statements recommended by the Committee is that each is based on a different capital maintenance concept. The calculation of current cost profit was based on the concept of physical capital maintenance, whilst the summary statement of total gains was concerned with the maintenance of financial capital. However, because the calculation of current cost profit subsequently received greater prominence than the summary of total gains, it is generally thought that the Sandilands proposals were based on the concept of physical capital maintenance.[168]

The Committee recommended that current cost accounting should replace historical cost accounting, and that its proposals should be incorporated in an accounting standard. Its recommendations met with little support which was attributed at the time to the fact that there was considerable objection to the replacement of historical cost accounting by a new untested system; the proposals were considered too complicated; and the profit figure was considered misleading without adjustment for monetary items.

Subsequently a further UK study *The Hyde Guidelines* recommended that three adjustments should be made to the historical cost results: in addition to the depreciation and cost of sales adjustments proposed by Sandilands, it was recommended that a 'gearing adjustment' be made as an interim solution to dealing with monetary items in inflation-adjusted financial statements. Since no account of the existence of borrowings was taken in calculating current cost operating profit, the implication was that operating capability had to be maintained entirely out of the generation of revenues. However, the reality is clearly that this could be financed partly by borrowings; consequently, the gearing adjustment was designed to take account of the extent to which fixed assets and working capital were financed by borrowings.

Following these efforts a standard, SSAP 16,[169] was issued in the UK in 1980 that:

(a)   introduced a fourth adjustment, called the 'monetary working capital adjustment', which effectively extended the cost of sales adjustment (which allowed for increases in the investment needed to maintain stocks when prices were increasing) to the other working capital items. Consequently, the monetary working capital adjustment represented an estimate of the extra investment in debtors, creditors and liquid resources required to maintain operations when prices were increasing;

(b) proposed the presentation of a current cost balance sheet, in which fixed assets and stock would be measured on a current cost basis; and

(c) proposed that listed companies disclose current cost earnings per share.[170]

SSAP 16 perpetuated the concept of current cost operating profit based on the maintenance of physical capital, which had been extended to monetary working capital through the monetary working capital adjustment. The associated gearing adjustment probably arose as a result of the need to compromise with critics of the entire process in order to find an acceptable solution – as opposed to having any theoretically sound justification.

It is worthy of note, given our view that ultimately any accounting theoretical framework is subject to the rigorous test of whether it is applicable and useful in practice, that SSAP 16 suffered a very low level of compliance until it was eventually withdrawn.

It might be argued that the activities described in this section provide evidence for the view that accounting standard setting is a process of establishing convention in response to the needs of the times. The high inflation rates of the late 1970s and early 1980s drove both practitioners and academics to undertake various studies and produce a number of recommendations. Since inflation has ceased to be a concern, interest in this problem has noticeably waned.

4.3 Canada: The Stamp Report

In 1980, Professor Edward Stamp produced a research study primarily for the Canadian Institute of Chartered Accountants which was 'intended to provide a Canadian solution to the problem of improving the quality of corporate financial reporting standards'.[171] Stamp adopted a similar approach to that of other studies (such as the Corporate Report and Trueblood) by looking at users, their needs, their rights to information and the qualitative characteristics of that information. Stamp identified a more detailed list of users (15 in all) than did, for example, the Corporate or Sandilands Reports.

Stamp developed a set of 20 qualitative criteria which could be used as yardsticks whereby standard-setters, as well as the preparers and users of published financial statements, can decide whether or not the financial statements are meeting the objectives of financial reporting and the needs of users. An interesting rider to this aspect of Stamp's study was that he subsequently used his list of qualitative criteria as the basis of an empirical study of the relative importance of each of the criteria.[172] Stamp supplied each member of the UK's standard setting body (the ASC at that time) with a copy of chapter 7 of his CICA research study in which the significance and meaning of each of the 20 criteria were discussed. He also gave them each a questionnaire in which they were asked to rank the 20 criteria in order of importance.[173] Although the ranking revealed 'relevance' as the most important criterion and 'conservatism' as the least important, this in itself was not the most significant aspect of Stamp's study. The real significance was that he demonstrated it would be possible to establish rankings of characteristics of accounting information for each category of user.

In his CICA research study, Stamp also devoted a considerable amount of effort towards discussing certain fundamental conceptual issues such as problems of allocation, income measurement, capital maintenance, the proprietary versus the entity theory, and the question of which attribute accounting should measure.[174] These issues are all fundamental to the development of a conceptual framework for financial reporting; yet they have not been unequivocally resolved by the conceptual frameworks of the two most influential global standard setting bodies – the FASB and the IASB.

4.4 Discussion document: 'Making Corporate Reports Valuable'

4.4.1 Background

This discussion document, which was issued in 1988, was the product of a major research project undertaken by the Research Committee of the Institute of Chartered Accountants of Scotland, and included a David Tweedie (now Sir David Tweedie, Chairman of the IASB) among its project members. The reason why this paper was so refreshing was principally because the research committee started from the basis of a 'clean sheet'. In other words, the members were able to ignore existing laws, accounting rules, terminology and all other constraints in order to try and achieve what they believed to be the best result. The Committee started off by explaining what motivated it to reconsider the nature of corporate reporting. The reasons which were given included the following basic conclusions:

- all financial reports ought to reflect economic reality;
- the information which investors need is the same in kind, but not in volume, as the information which managements need to run their entities;
- some of the information that management has but does not normally communicate comes out into the open when management wants something – such as additional capital or to be able to defend a hostile take-over bid;
- present-day financial reports are deficient in that they are based on legal form rather than economic substance, on cost rather than value, on the past rather than the future, and on 'profit' rather than 'wealth';
- there is no consistent conceptual basis underlying the production of either the profit and loss account or the balance sheet, and some of the concepts used appear to defy normal understanding of financial affairs;
- corporate reports are not made public sufficiently speedily; and
- the audit report is insufficiently informative and is often incomprehensible to non-auditors.[175]

The Committee then discussed various bases for applying values to assets, focusing on historical cost, current replacement cost, current net realisable values and economic values. Having discussed what it saw as the deficiencies of historical cost and economic value, the Committee noted that current replacement cost and net realisable value both met its criteria of economic reality and 'additivity' (i.e. the total number in a statement should not mean something different in kind from its constituent numbers). Nevertheless, the Committee expressed a preference for net realisable value as the basis for applying values to assets, 'principally because it is value-based whereas replacement cost is cost-based',[176] and it was felt that 'value rather than cost is important in assessing financial wealth'.[177]

4.4.2 The proposed information package

The Committee proposed what was then an entirely new information package, using net realisable values as the basis of valuation. In order to present the financial wealth of an entity, the Committee proposed that the following four basic statements should replace the existing financial statements:

(a) *Assets and Liabilities Statement*, which would present the assets and liabilities of the entity at the reporting date, each stated at its net realisable value. Net realisable values would normally be determined according to the principle of orderly disposal, unless the entity is in financial trouble, in which case 'a more appropriate method' (such as break-up values) should be used;[178]

(b) *Operations Statement*, which calculates the financial wealth added to the entity by trading and by its operations generally. It differs from the present form of profit and loss account in that:

    (i) there would be no depreciation charge,

    (ii) the stock would be accounted for at net realisable value, and

    (iii) the only exceptional or extraordinary items would be those arising out of unusual events of a revenue nature; exceptional or extraordinary gains or losses on fixed assets would be dealt with in the Statement of Changes in Financial Wealth outlined at (c) below;[179]

(c) *Statement of Changes in Financial Wealth*, which shows the change in the worth of the business for the period under consideration, such change being split into its main components with an indication of how each of these arose. The Committee proposed that the change in wealth would be measured in terms of year-end pounds, although 'in times of significant inflation it may be helpful if investors can be given an indication of the real change in financial wealth over the period concerned by applying the retail price index';[180] and

(d) *Distributions Statement*, which reflects the distributable change in financial wealth for the period plus any surpluses retained from previous periods, less dividends paid and proposed. In times of rising prices the 'real value' of capital should be maintained by an inflation adjustment which should be shown in the distributions statement and might be computed by applying the retail price index to the value of shareholders' contributed capital as at the start of the period. The paper went on to say that entities wishing to maintain their operating capability in physical terms could make a further appropriation to maintain the asset portfolio or to provide for the replacement of the services which these assets have been supplying.[181]

In addition to the four basic statements and information relating to corporate objectives and future financial plans, the Committee suggested the inclusion of the following additional information in the reporting package:

(a)   a cash flow statement;

(b)   segmental information;[182]

(c)   information on related parties;

(d)   information on accounting areas subject to uncertainty, for example management's view on the margin of error in accounting estimates;

(e)   a statement on relative innovation which would illustrate the stance that the company is adopting in relation to innovation;

(f)   information on effectiveness and lead-time of research and development;

(g)   information on the economic environment within which the entity operates, including an analysis of facts such as market share, market strength, market size, the activities of competitors etc.;

(h)   comparative operational statistics contrasting the reporting firm with its competitors;[183]

(i)   information on staff resources; and

(j)   information on ownership, management and their responsibilities.

4.4.3   Conclusion

This was one of the boldest, most innovative and refreshing discussion documents ever to be published by a professional accounting body anywhere in the world. Of course it had flaws and can be criticised for either failing to address or inadequately addressing certain issues; however, it should be seen for what it was – a document designed to stimulate discussion, experimentation and further research. Although there was always the danger that the document would be regarded as too revolutionary in its approach, and be dismissed as being an amusing intellectual exercise, it is now clear that the IASB's agenda of accounting change and development draws heavily on MCRV. For example the list of supplementary information above no longer looks innovative – solely because so much of its suggested contents now appears in the financial reports of companies.

4.5   The Solomons Report

In May 1987, the Research Board of the ICAEW announced that it had decided to sponsor a project to address the need for guidelines for decisions in financial reporting. Professor David Solomons, a recently retired academic who in his lifetime was president of both the American Accounting Association and the British Accounting Association, agreed to carry out the study.

Solomons followed an approach to the subject that was almost identical to that taken by the FASB (see 2 above), perhaps not surprisingly considering that he acted as consultant to the FASB on its conceptual framework project and was principal author of SFAC No. 2. He started by examining the purposes of financial reporting, identifying users and how their needs were at present being met. His report then discussed the elements of financial statements and decided upon the asset and liability, rather than the revenue and expense, approach to financial accounting.[184]

Solomons' principal argument against the revenue and expense view of income determination was that it 'opens the door to all kinds of income smoothing'[185] and that it 'threatens the integrity of the balance sheet and its value as a useful financial statement. Its value is maximized if it can be seen as a statement of financial position; but it can only be that if all the items in it are truly assets, liabilities, and equity, and not other bits left over from the profit and loss account, and if all such items that are capable of being recognised are included in it.'[186] This attitude of Solomons has obviously been influential in the thinking of the IASB subsequently.

Solomons then set about defining the elements of financial statements on much the same basis as was done in SFAC No. 6 (see 2.4 above). Assets are defined as 'resources or rights incontestably controlled by an entity at the accounting date that are expected to yield it future economic benefits',[187] whilst liabilities are defined as 'obligations of an entity at the accounting date to make future transfers of assets or services (sometimes uncertain as to timing and amount) to other entities'.[188] As with the FASB concepts all the other elements are then derived from these basic definitions; for example, owners' equity comprises net assets and income is the change in net assets.[189]

The Report focused attention on the issues of recognition and measurement and the choice of an accounting model for use in preparing general purpose financial statements. In view of the fact that Solomons' guidelines are based on the asset and liability view, it is not surprising that his recognition criteria concentrate on these two elements. Consequently, under Solomons' approach, an item should only be recognised in financial statements if:

'(a) it conforms to the definition of an asset or liability or of one of the sub-elements derived therefrom; and

(b) its magnitude as specified by the accounting model being used can be measured and verified with reasonable certainty; and

(c) the magnitude so arrived at is material in amount'.[190]

These recognition criteria obviously influenced the recognition criteria adopted by the IASB in its own framework, as discussed at 5 below.

Solomons, having rejected the historical cost model generally in use at the time, set about devising an improved model for general purpose financial reporting, and listed the following five criteria that such an improved model should possess:

(a) the balance sheet should be a true and fair statement of an entity's financial condition, showing all its assets and liabilities that satisfy the above recognition criteria and conform with the asset and liability definitions;

(b) the entity's assets and liabilities should be carried in the balance sheet at their value to a going concern at the balance sheet date;

(c) profits or losses should mean increases or decreases of real financial capital as compared with the amount at the beginning of the year;

(d)   the results shown by the financial statements should be measured consistently and should therefore be comparable from year to year, both in periods of fluctuating prices and stable prices; and

(e)   all the information given by the financial statements should be verifiable and cost-effective.[191]

(In a subsequent posthumous publication entitled *Commentary: criteria for choosing an accounting model*[192] the number of criteria is expanded to seven, the extra two being essentially clarifications of the meanings of the original five.)

Solomons then attempted to prove that the model which best satisfies these requirements rests on two concepts: value to the business (as espoused by the Corporate Report and Sandilands Committee) and the maintenance of real financial capital. Although these may have some intellectual appeal, it is difficult to see whether either of them has any practical meaning. Solomons identified an asset's value to the business as being the loss that the business would suffer if it were deprived of the asset. He argued that since if deprived of an asset, the business would normally seek to replace it, replacement cost would determine value to the business.

However, Solomons recognised that circumstances exist where an asset's value to the business might be less than its replacement cost; for example, in the circumstances where a plant asset is technologically inferior to an equivalent new asset, the current cost of replacing the services rendered by the existing asset should be used. Furthermore, where an asset would not be replaced by a business if it were lost, its value to the business would be its recoverable amount, which is the higher of the asset's present value and its net realisable value. Therefore, Solomons' final formula for 'value to the business' is that it is equal to 'current cost or recoverable amount, if that is lower'.[193] It is interesting to note that this approach is almost identical to the criteria specified in IAS 36 – *Impairment of assets* – for identifying if an asset is impaired (see Chapter 13).

In the case of liabilities, the Solomons' equivalent to an asset's deprival value is a liability's relief value. In other words, liabilities would be valued at the amount that the entity 'could currently raise by the issue of a precisely similar debt security or the cost of discharging the liability by the most economical means, whichever is the higher'.[194] The view advanced in the late 1990s by the G4+1, is very similar to the Solomons approach and is clearly still influential in the thinking of the IASB today.

As mentioned above, Solomons' model is based on the maintenance of real financial capital, with income being defined in terms of the change in net worth. He took the view that because of the uncertainty surrounding the measurement and verification of intangible assets, the changes in such assets cannot be recognised in financial statements; consequently, income will only include changes in recognised tangible assets minus changes in recognised liabilities.[195] This view seems untenable today in view of the important role intangibles play in business and commerce, and provides another interesting example of the influence that business practice has on accounting theory, as at the time Solomons wrote, his views on the recognition of intangibles were not considered obviously flawed.

Solomons recommended a 'current-cost-constant-purchasing-power model' that recognised both changes in the general level of prices and changes in specific prices, and was based on the maintenance of real financial capital, not operating capacity.[196] The following pro forma profit and loss account illustrates how Solomons' version of real income is derived:[197]

Pro forma profit and loss account as proposed by Solomons

		€
Sales revenue		×××
Current cost (or lower recoverable amount) of goods sold		×××
		×××
Depreciation at current cost	×××	
Other expenses	×××	
		×××
Current operating profit		×××
Add:		
Holding gains less losses on non-monetary assets (net of inflation)	×××	
Purchasing power gains on monetary liabilities less purchasing power losses on monetary assets	×××	
		×××
Real income		×××

However it is the views expressed by Solomons on pensions that seem extraordinarily prescient and influential to the present day reader. For example he recommended if all or most of the assets of a pension plan can be freely moved back to the employer from the plan by a vote of the trustees, then the affairs of the plan should be consolidated with those of the employer. This approach is based on the view that a pension fund is, in effect, an off balance sheet vehicle set up to meet a company's future obligations. Solomons' proposal was extremely close to the approach adopted by the IASB in IAS 19 (Revised) – *Employee Benefits*, which is discussed in Chapter 30.

On the subject of goodwill, Solomons states that non-purchased goodwill should not be recognised; his reason for this being that 'determining the value of goodwill where it is not the subject of a purchase and sale transaction and in the presence of a highly imperfect market is too subjective to yield a reliable measure for the purpose of recognition'.[198] What he is saying is that since non-purchased goodwill does not have an historical cost, it is not possible to update an unknown cost in order to determine its current cost. The same argument applies to all internally generated intangibles, such as brand names. This remains a considerable problem for standard setters, in view of the commercial importance of intangible assets, and is a major stumbling block to the adoption of a full fair-value based system of accounting, which the IASB is clearly moving towards, as discussed at 5 below.

4.6   The UK's conceptual framework

The United Kingdom's conceptual framework document is interesting as it was the most recently published and also because the then Chairman of the UK's Accounting Standards Board, Sir David Tweedie, is currently Chairman of the IASB. The finalised version of the UK's Accounting Standards Board's *Statement of Principles for Financial Reporting* was published in December 1999 and the abbreviation 'SoP' is used hereafter.[199] The SoP is now somewhat redundant in the context of EU reporting under IFRS, and is therefore very briefly outlined below; although in view of the involvement of Sir David Tweedie, and its relatively recent publication, it may subsequently be seen as indicative of the new IASB/FASB framework project's outcome.

The SoP comprised a compendium of eight 'chapters', with titles that owe much to the US and IASC's framework projects:

1.   The objective of financial statements

2.   The reporting entity

3.   The qualitative characteristics of financial information

4.   The elements of financial statements

5.   Recognition in financial statements

6.   Measurement in financial statements

7.   Presentation of financial information

8.   Accounting for interests in other entities.

The ASB acknowledged that, in drafting the SoP it was drawing heavily on the work of previous projects in other countries, notably the FASB concept statements discussed at 2 above and the IASC Framework discussed at 3 above. The objectives ascribed to financial statements are therefore quite familiar.[200]

As in the IASB's Framework, the investor's perspective is deemed to represent the user's needs. Having established this generalisation, the SoP then goes on to assert that investors need information about the generation and use of cash in order to assess the entity's: liquidity and solvency; the relationship between profits and cash flows; the implications that financial performance has for future cash flows; and other aspects of financial adaptability.[201] Therefore, the academic stance that predicting future cash flows is the objective of reporting is endorsed.

The SoP also selects relevance and reliability as the two primary characteristics of accounting information, and again recognises that they are sometimes in conflict, so as to require a trade-off between them. In this case the choice is to be resolved as follows:

> 'if a choice exists between relevant and reliable approaches that are mutually exclusive, the approach chosen needs to be the one that results in the relevance of the information provided being maximised.'[202]

Therefore, the SoP takes the view that relevance takes priority over reliability and states that relevant information has the ability to 'influence the economic decisions of users and is provided in time to influence those decisions'.[203] This assertion of the priority of relevance over reliability is a substantial departure from the traditional view of prudence (conservatism), and may be a guide to what will emerge from the IASB/FASB project in 2005. However it is a departure that is not altogether surprising, given the move towards fair value accounting that is predicated on the view that fair values are more relevant than cost, even if they are somewhat unreliable. This view chooses to overlook that fact that users find information relevant only if it is reliable, and there is a threshold of reliability below which relevance ceases.

Thereafter the discussion of qualitative characteristics follows closely the IASB's Framework discussed above, including the unsatisfactory defining away of the problem of understandability.

Seven elements of financial statements are defined: Assets, Liabilities, Ownership Interest, Gains, Losses, Contributions from Owners, Distributions to Owners. The definitions and their deductive structure closely follow the IASB's Framework, starting with a near-identical asset definition. A definitional refinement is added however, namely that for a future economic benefit to be an asset it must also be 'controlled independently of the business as a whole'.[204] This new concept of independence from the business as a whole is only illustrated, not defined, although examples are given: 'market share, superior management or good labour relations … cannot be controlled independently of the business as a whole'.[205] In this way, the SoP intends to prevent certain types of expenditure from being deferred and carried forward in the balance sheet as an asset. A problem that is shared by all FASB-based 'future cash flow' asset definition.

Revenue recognition (which is not characterised as such) is referred to as follows:

> 'In a transaction involving the provision of services or goods for a net gain, the recognition criteria described above [i.e. the asset/liability criteria above] will be met on the occurrence of the critical event in the operating cycle involved'.[206]

By including this paragraph, the UK framework document seems to be fending off any potential criticism of its asset/liability approach to revenue recognition. In defending the approach that gains and losses are merely increases and decreases in net assets, other than those resulting from transactions with shareholders, the ASB is attempting to assert that both an asset/liability approach and a critical event approach to revenue recognition end up with the same answer. What the above paragraph is saying is that a net gain that is recognised on the basis of the critical event approach will necessarily result in an increase in net assets, with the result that the asset/liability recognition criteria will also be met.

However, while this is so, the converse is not. The implication is that irrespective of whether one follows a balance sheet approach to income recognition or a transactions-based income statement approach, one will always get to the same end-result. This is patently not true. Just because all revenue recognised under an income statement based transactions system will satisfy the asset/liability recognition criteria, it does not follow that the reverse will apply. Revenue recognition criteria are more demanding than those for recognising assets and liabilities, since in our view they should embody the concept of the revenue having been earned, based on performance by the reporting company. The issue of revenue recognition is discussed in detail in Chapter 26.

The SoP settles for a traditional approach to the statements that should be included in financial reports. However its discussion of how to account for investments in other entities acknowledges a difficulty inherent in the both the UK's and IASB's framework documents. This difficulty is that the definition of assets excludes goodwill (because goodwill cannot meet the 'controlled' part of the definition), therefore this creates a particular problem for the presentation of group accounts. This difficulty is acknowledged in the SoP that seeks to justify the departure from the principle as follows:

> 'Purchased goodwill ... is not an asset in itself ... [but] if the parent's investment is to be fully reflected in the group's financial statements and the parent is to be held accountable for its investment ... purchased goodwill needs to be recognised as if it were an asset'.[207]

Perhaps this admission puts this entire conceptual framework project into perspective. It is to be hoped that the decision by the IASB and the FASB in April 2004 to cooperate on a new framework document will result in such anomalies being resolved.

4.7   Conclusion

It can be seen that much of the academic and professionally sponsored research described above has been influential in shaping the underlying thinking in, and the practical requirements of, the IASB's accounting standards. Equally it is clear that much of this research has been influenced by the economic reality of the periods in which it took place. For example, inflation is no longer the preoccupation either of the profession or of economists, yet it was the phenomenon that drove much of the work described above. Somewhat paradoxically, historical cost accounting with its inherent simplicity, certainty and understandability, although easily dismissed as inadequate in inflationary times, becomes increasingly viable in the current almost deflationary environment. It is one of those historical 'what-if' questions, but whether the IASB would be moving towards a full fair-value system if the current low-inflationary economic environment has existed for the last 40 years is an interesting moot point.

5　THE PATH TO A GLOBAL FRAMEWORK

5.1　The IASB/FASB new framework project

The IASB and the FASB have a stated policy to work towards the convergence of International GAAP and US GAAP. This has been happening at a mostly informal level for many years through a variety of bodies such as the G4+1 and the Joint Working Group. However, as described in Chapter 1, in September 2002 at a formal meeting between the IASB and the FASB, held at Norwalk, Connecticut, USA, this cooperation was placed on a more formal footing. Consequently in April 2004 at a joint meeting the FASB and the IASB agreed that their underlying conceptual frameworks should be revisited and if possible an agreed single conceptual framework produced. The September 2004 meeting of the IASB is expected to discuss the project as a prelude to starting work soon thereafter. Certainly the decision by both bodies to work on a new conceptual framework is an opportunity to develop a practical and consistent conceptual framework as a basis for a widely acceptable global GAAP.

5.2　The IASB's measurement project

In 2002 the IASB initiated a project on 'Measurement', the Canadian Accounting Standards Board agreed to undertake the preliminary work and a report was produced in April 2004 for consideration at the 'Liaison meeting' between the IASB and various national standard setters. It is the policy of the IASB – partly because in the event of IFRS becoming widely accepted it could effectively remove the need for national bodies – to involve national standard setters in such non-core projects. The liaison meetings give a formality to what is in reality only a voluntary relationship between the IASB and the national bodies.

'Measurement' in this context essentially refers to whether actual cost, or fair value, or some other method is best to use in considering the values at which assets are to be recognised and carried (i.e. capitalised) in the balance sheet. The measurement objectives research project report was summarised in the information given to observers at the April 2004 meeting. Perhaps better than any other single publication emanating from the IASB, it illustrates the wide gulf that is developing between the perceptions of the IASB and its 'satellites' on the one hand, and real business accounting on the other. The paper is lengthy and posits a number of entirely unnecessary and often barely distinguishable, possible alternative measurement methods (referred to as 'bases').

The alternative measurement bases identified by the Canadian report are as follows:

Historical cost; reproduction cost (replacing an asset with an identical one); replacement cost (replacing an asset with one of an equivalent productive capacity); net realisable value (selling price less costs to sell); value in use (VIU is defined as present value of expected future cash flows, as in IAS 36); fair value (amount at which an asset could be exchanged between knowledgeable and willing parties in an arms length transaction); deprival value (loss suffered if deprived of the asset, being the lower of replacement cost or recoverable amount – itself the higher of VIU and net realisable value).

A number of these suggested alternatives are not in fact alternatives, as most of them rely upon others for their meaning. More worryingly though, for the practical purpose of improving the financial statements of real companies undertaking real work, the report's discussion seems irrelevant. Particularly compared with the many more pressing matters that, for example, a reading of the comment letters on suggested new standards clearly points to.

This apparent lack of relevance to accounting practice is illustrated best by the report's recommendation that if a business buys an asset (e.g. a new machine for production purposes) it should not be recognised at cost, but at fair value. This means that 'market evidence' would be considered and that evidence would over-ride the price actually paid by the business. How might this apply to an oil refinery or to a car factory? It would seem to imply that an asset with no or little 'market' value (in the sense that a second hand one has a readily identifiable market price) would have a fair value much lower than its cost. Thus a loss would be immediately realised on investing in new plant and machinery. Under this regime, an imaginary amount to be paid by a business that did not want and could not use the asset, would be more relevant than the actual price paid by one that did.

The report abounds with unsupported assertions that bear no relation to the practical world of business that accounting exists to describe. For example it asserts that if fair value is not available because there is no market, a mathematical model that best estimates what the fair value would be if there were a market would be the next most preferable alternative. So 'mark to model' can be substituted for mark to market, and is seemingly considered by the authors of the report as more relevant and reliable than the actual purchase price of the asset.

In general terms, the paper wishes to exclude 'entity specific' considerations from asset valuations. This of course does not sit easily with needs of investors, the primary user group in the IASB's Framework, who need precisely that to make discriminating investment decisions.

It seems that a number of established national standard setters have expressed considerable reservation about the Canadian/IASB measurement paper, so the ultimate influence it will have remains an open question. Nevertheless, the fact that such a report can surface at all for serious consideration, gives a warning to practically orientated accountants and business people everywhere of the ease with which accounting standard setters can lose touch with their *raison d'etre*.

5.3   Measurement under a fair value-based system

'Fair value' is a term that immediately inspires a degree of confidence, as the term draws much from the linguistic power, understood by all English speakers, of the words 'value' and 'fair', both of which carry very deep-seated, positive, essentially good, connotations. Quite whether the accounting outcomes of the technical term 'fair value' will actually reflect the linguistic undertones of its component words is a an open question.

Fundamentally, under any balance sheet-orientated recognition and measurement system, changes in asset and liability values drive performance measurement, as fully discussed in Chapter 26. If that system selects fair values to arrive at the balance sheet valuations, it follows that *when* a fair valued asset is to be recognised and *how* it is to be measured (i.e. quantified), are central to the reported result. The current IASB definition of fair value as incorporated in its standards (though the term is absent from the IASB's Framework) is 'the amount for which an asset could be exchanged between knowledgeable, willing parties in an arm's length transaction'.

This definition seems to be set in the context of a market transaction, but does not actually require it. In fact a reading the standards themselves indicates that often a fair value is envisaged being arrived at that is not based on a transaction, but on a model or specialist opinion of some kind. Thus, while market prices are one aspect of identifying a fair value, it is not generally understood that the term is increasingly being coined to describe measurement by other means also. The IASB's measurement project, discussed above, is a recent example of this drift.

In this general context, the meanings of the criteria 'relevant and reliable' become critical. It is an intuitive use of 'fair value' to describe (say) a quoted investment carried in the balance sheet at market value. However, if the same term is used to describe the valuation of a share option charged as an expense to the income statement, derived by applying a model unintelligible to all but a professional mathematician, the term 'fair value' seems rather less apposite. Therefore what represents relevant and reliable information in the mark-to-model sense of fair value, constitutes a problem for standard setters, regulators and users.

The IASB itself has recently had to address this issue in the area of financial instruments, as demonstrated by it by issuing the exposure draft *Proposed amendments to IAS 39 Financial instruments: Recognition and Measurement, the Fair Value Option*. In this ED, the IASB explicitly acknowledges that in certain cases the relevant and reliable criteria are insufficient, and proposes to introduce a verifiability test, in addition. The reasons advanced for this move are:

- entities might apply the fair value option to financial assets or financial liabilities whose fair value is not verifiable. If so, because the valuation of these financial assets and financial liabilities is subjective, entities might determine their fair value in a way that inappropriately affects profit or loss;

- use of the option might increase, rather than decrease volatility in profit or loss, for example if an entity applied the option to only one part of a matched position; and

- if an entity applied the fair value option to financial liabilities, it might result in the entity recognising gains or losses in profit or loss for changes in its own creditworthiness.[208]

The IASB's 'fix' for the revenue recognition problem they identify (i.e. recording 'gains' in the income statement that result from the drop market value of an entity's own debt) is that a fair value gain must pass a verifiability test that is a further hurdle to be surmounted after passing the existing relevant and reliable criteria. Unfortunately, the position adopted by the IASB in the ED implies that there are financial instruments that its standards require to be held at fair value that are not verifiable.

More significant, in context of a discussion of conceptual frameworks, is the underlying assumption that the price at which two willing third parties trade an entity's debt is a suitable basis to measure such debt in the entity's financial statements. In our view this assumption needs specifically justifying.

While the necessity for issuing this exposure draft illustrates the conflict between relevance and reliability – perhaps too aptly for proponents of those recognition criteria – it also throws into relief the problem of defining what fair value means. This point has been recently addressed by the FASB, that in June 2004 issued an exposure draft – *Proposed Statement of Accounting Standards Fair Value Measurements* – that if adopted as a standard would provide guidance on the measurement of fair values under US GAAP. The proposed standard acknowledges that it owes much to SFAC 7, discussed at 2.9 above. The proposed FASB statement defines fair value differently from the definition in the IASB's standards, as 'the price at which an asset or liability could be exchanged in a current transaction between knowledgeable unrelated willing parties'.[209]

It explicitly deals with the problem of fair values that do not result from market prices, by proposing a valuation hierarchy that divides into three 'levels'. Level 1 is fair values derived from quoted market prices for identical assets or liabilities from an active market to which an entity has immediate access. Level 2 is where there are market prices available for similar (as opposed to identical) assets or liabilities.[210]

Level 3 however is a different matter, and it is described thus:

'If quoted prices for identical or similar assets or liabilities are not available, or differences between similar assets or liabilities are not objectively determinable, fair value shall be estimated using multiple valuation techniques consistent with the market approach, income approach, and cost approach whenever the information necessary to apply those techniques is available without undue cost or effort.'[211]

It is our view that the quite different methods used in level 3 to determine fair value in reality indicate that something entirely different in nature is being described by the term than when it is used in the context of levels 1 and 2. Conventionally, both in normal language and in academic work, this would be recognised by choosing a different term to describe level 3 valuations (for instance 'calculated value') and it is not clear why such an obvious and helpful way of resolving the problem, and assisting users, should not be adopted by standard setters.

The FASB acknowledges that the proposed statement represents only the initial phase of the project. It states that in subsequent phases other issues will be addressed including issues relating to the relevance and reliability of fair value measurements. It is perhaps symptomatic of the inadequacy of the current conceptual frameworks that a standard setter can contemplate introducing a standard, yet simultaneously acknowledge there are issues of relevance and reliability to resolve.

In conclusion, the two major standard-setting regimes, the IASB and the FASB, are both using the term fair value ever more frequently. Their definitions are not identical, and the practical meaning ascribed to the term differs radically, even in the context of the FASB exposure draft, depending upon the existence or otherwise of market prices. Therefore we hope that, in view of their increasing reliance on the concept, the IASB and the FASB, will take the chance offered by their new conceptual framework project to make their use of the term consistent and transparent, and the meaning of the term discrete.

6   CONCLUSION

This chapter provides an outline of the immense amount of energy that has been expended (both on the part of individuals and by specifically constituted committees) in attempting to establish an agreed conceptual framework for financial reporting. It has also highlighted the irreconcilable differences and logical difficulties that exist in the various accounting theories that have been developed over the years.

The existence of such framework documents might have raised the prospect of a degree of rigour and consistency being applied to accounting standards issued by the various standard-setting bodies; whereas in practice, these documents have been used to prevent practices disliked by the standard setters, and have been conveniently ignored when a standard is required that conflicts with them. Inconsistencies of this nature are probably inevitable whilst matters that are fundamental to their resolution remain unresolved. Since Edwards and Bell and Maurice Moonitz (see 4.2.2A and 2.1 above respectively) published their work in the early 1960s, there has been controversy over, and disagreement about, the valuation basis to be used in financial reporting. These disagreements have been over whether current values should to be used in place of historical costs at all, and if so what type of current value system is to be used. Further disagreement surrounds the way current values are to be determined even if a given system is selected.

What has emerged is the adoption of a particular balance sheet orientated model by the IASB and the FASB. It seems likely that this model has been adopted because it supports the use of fair values, the goal towards which it appears the IASB wants to move financial reporting. We can understand the superficial attraction of stating all assets and liabilities at 'fair value' but there are important issues about what this means in practice to resolve. Most obviously, the enduring underlying difficulties and disagreements, referred to above, have not been removed by the common adoption of the words 'fair value' if each standard setter means something different by the term, and preparers cannot understand it.

At the same time, it is clear that many users do not understand the asset/liability fair value model either, and that many of those that do are not convinced about its appropriateness as the basis for historical financial statements. In addition, preparers are experiencing difficulty in establishing relevant and/or reliable fair values for assets and liabilities other than those for which there are deep and active markets. Much of what is published by the standard setters seems to carry a presumption that a fair value, however determined, will always be relevant. This is not obviously the case, particularly where fair values are not based upon observable market prices, or where markets do not exist for the item concerned.

In many cases what is described as a 'mark-to-market' basis, with all the relevance and reliability the term implies, is in reality a 'mark-to-model' basis, which is actually hypothetical. We agree that financial reports should be relevant and reliable, but these terms as used in the current literature seem in danger of being confused. In our view reliability is a necessary condition for information to be relevant, and information needs to pass a reliability threshold before it can be considered relevant at all. Hence we consider it is important that reliability is given due weight under a fair value system in cases where observable market prices are not available.

This issue is of such fundamental importance in our view, that a way needs to be found of subjecting the IASB's asset/liability fair value model to the specific scrutiny and debate that, as demonstrated in this chapter, it has so far avoided. This exercise could then have the effect of either refreshing the Board's mandate; or placing boundaries on the use of the fair value model; or possibly allowing a move to an alternative.

At the global level, reporting harmonisation is being led by the EU where all listed EU companies will apply adopted IFRS from January 2005 in the preparation of their consolidated accounts. This is an important development in European accounting that we strongly support, and that we hope will contribute to the development of an eventual global GAAP. However, we consider that the IASB should be sensitive to the concerns of preparers and regulators throughout its intended global constituency, and be sure that it gives sufficient consideration to the coherence and practicality of its agenda in relation to this timetable.

There is a danger that practical aspects such as the coherence of standards effective at any point in time, the complexity and change management implications of the standards the Board has developed, and the understandability of financial statements prepared on the basis of them, will be overlooked by the IASB. We strongly support the strategic goal of global convergence of accounting standards; however, the IASB's priority must be to put in place a coherent, high quality set of international accounting standards that are supported by the preparers that will apply them, that result in reports understood by the users that will read them, and are based on a conceptual framework that receives general support from all involved with business endeavour.

References

1 For a full discussion on the politicisation of accounting see: David Solomons, 'The Politicization of Accounting', *Journal of Accountancy*, November 1978, p. 71.

2 Maurice Moonitz, *The Basic Postulates of Accounting*, Accounting Research Study No. 1, AICPA, 1961, Preface.

3 The basic postulates of accounting.

4 Robert T. Sprouse and Maurice Moonitz, *A Tentative Set of Broad Accounting Principles for Business Enterprises*, Accounting Research Study No. 3, AICPA, 1962.

5 A Tentative Set of Broad Accounting Principles for Business Enterprises, p. 14.

6 A Tentative Set of Broad Accounting Principles for Business Enterprises, p. 27.

7 APB Statement No. 4, *Basic Concepts and Accounting Principles Underlying Financial Statements of Business Enterprises*, AICPA, October 1970.

8 APB Statement No. 4, para. 3.

9 APB Statement No. 4, para. 132.

10 Report of the Study Group on the Objectives of Financial Statements, *Objectives of Financial Statements*, AICPA, October 1973, p. 65.

11 *Objectives of Financial Statements*, AICPA

12 *Objectives of Financial Statements*, AICPA

13 Objectives of Financial Statements, AICPA.

14 *Objectives of Financial Statements*, AICPA p. 13.

15 *Objectives of Financial Statements, AICPA* pp. 57-60.

16 FASB Discussion Memorandum, *Conceptual Framework for Accounting and Reporting: Consideration of the Report of the Study Group on the Objectives of Financial Statements*, FASB, June 6, 1974.

17 FASB, Scope and Implications of the Conceptual Framework Project, FASB, December 2, 1976.

18 FASB, Scope and Implications of the Conceptual Framework Project, p. 5.

19 FASB, Scope and Implications of the Conceptual Framework Project, p. 2.

20 FASB, Scope and Implications of the Conceptual Framework Project, pp. 5 and 6.

21 SFAC No. 1, *Objectives of Financial Reporting by Business Enterprises*, FASB, November 1978, para. 7.

22 SFAC No. 1, para. 9.

23 SFAC No. 1, para. 24.

24 SFAC No. 1, para. 34.

25 SFAC No. 1, para. 37.

26 SFAC No. 1, para. 24.

27 SFAC No. 1, footnote 6.

28 Lucia S. Chang and Kenneth S. Most, *Financial Statements and Investment Decisions*, Miami: Florida International University, 1979.

29 *Financial Statements and Investment Decisions*, p. 33.

30 SFAC No. 1, para. 43.

31 SFAC No. 1, para. 50.

32 SFAC No. 1, para. 51.

33 SFAC No. 2, *Qualitative Characteristics of Accounting Information*, FASB, May 1980, Figure 1.

34 SFAC No. 1, para. 34.

35 SFAC No. 2, para. 36.

36 SFAC No. 2, p. x.

37 SFAC No. 2, para. 90.

38 SFAC No. 2, p. xi.

39 SFAC No. 2, para. 56.

40 SFAC No. 2.

41 SFAC No. 2, para. 51.

42 SFAC No. 2, p. xvi.

43 SFAC No. 2.

44 SFAC No. 2, para. 59.

45 IAS 39 (1998), *Financial Instruments: Recognition and Measurement*, IASC, December 1998, para. 70.

46 SFAC No. 2, paras. 91-97.

47 SFAC No. 2, para. 93.

48 SFAC No. 2, para. 95.

49 SFAC No. 6, *Elements of Financial Statements*, a replacement of FASB Concepts Statement No. 3, FASB, December 1985, para. 25.

50 SFAC No. 6, para. 27.

51 SFAC No. 6, para. 28.

52 SFAC No. 6, para. 35.

53 SFAC No. 6, para. 36.

54 SFAC No. 6, para. 49.

55 SFAC No. 6, para. 66.

56 SFAC No. 6.

57 SFAC No. 6, para. 67.

58 SFAC No. 6, para. 70.

59 SFAC No. 1, para. 43.

60 SFAC No. 6, p. 1, footnote 1.

61 SFAC No. 6, para. 78.

62 SFAC No. 6, para. 80.

63 SFAC No. 6, para. 82.

64 SFAC No. 6, para. 83.

65 SFAC No. 6, para. 77.

66 See, for example, SFAC No. 3, *Elements of Financial Statements of Business Enterprises*, FASB, December 1980, para. 58.

67 SFAC No. 5, *Recognition and Measurement in Financial Statements of Business Enterprises*, FASB, December 1984, para. 66.

68 SFAC No. 5, paras. 66-70.

69 SFAC No. 5, paras. 45-48.

70 SFAC No. 5, para. 58.

71 SFAC No. 5, para. 63.

72 SFAC No. 5, paras. 33 and 34.

73 SFAC No. 5, para. 35.

74 David Solomons, 'The FASB's Conceptual Framework: An evaluation', *Journal of Accountancy*, June 1986, pp. 114-124, at p. 122.

75 The FASB's Conceptual Framework: An evaluation, p. 124.

76 The FASB's Conceptual Framework: An evaluation.

77 Reed K. Storey and Sylvia Storey, *Special Report: The Framework of Financial Accounting Concepts and Standards*, FASB, January 1998, p. 158.

78 *Ibid.*

79 *Ibid.*, p. 160.

80 Statement of Financial Accounting Concepts 7, *Using Cash Flow Information and Present Value in Accounting Measurements*, FASB, February 2000, para. 19.

81 SFAC No. 7, *Using Cash Flow Information and Present Value in Accounting Measurements*, FASB, February 2000, para. 21.

82 SFAC No. 7, para. 23.

83 SFAC No. 7, paras. 31 and 37

84 SFAC No. 7, para. 41.

85 SFAC No. 7, para. 75.

86 SFAC No. 7, Glossary of terms.

87 Draft standard *Financial Instruments and similar items*, JWG, December 2000, paras. 118-121.

88 IAS 39, *Financial Instruments: Recognition and Measurement,* IASB, December 2003 (amended March 2004), para. BC89.

89 Stephen A. Zeff, *Accounting Horizons*, 'A Perspective on the U.S. Public/Private-Sector Approach to the Regulation of Financial Reporting', Vol. 9 No. 1, March 1995, p. 60.

90 Exposure Draft, *Framework for the Preparation and Presentation of Financial Statements*, IASC, May 1988.

91 *Framework for the Preparation and Presentation of Financial Statements*, IASB, September 1989, para. 4.

92 Framework, para. 2.

93 Framework, para. 1

94 Framework, para. 12.

95 Framework, paras. 22-23.

96 Framework, para. 11.

97 Framework, para. 22.

98 Framework, para. 95.

99 Framework, para. 23.

100 Framework, para. 25.

101 Framework, para. 26

102 Framework, para. 27

103 Framework, para. 30

104 Framework, para. 31

105 Framework, para. 33

106 Framework, para. 37

107 Framework, para. 38

108 Framework, para. 40

109 Framework, para. 43

110 Framework, para. 43

111 Framework, para. 25.

112 Framework, para. 83.

113 Framework, para. 51.

114 Framework, para. 51.

115 Framework, para. 25.

116 Framework, para. 25.

117 Framework, para. 70.

118 Framework, para. 88.

119 Framework, para. 91.

120 Framework, para. 99.

121 Framework, para. 102.

122 Framework, para. 103.

123 Framework, para. 110.

124 Framework, para. 110.

125 *The Corporate Report*, A discussion paper published for comment by the Accounting Standards Steering Committee, London, 1975.

126 The Corporate Report, para. 0.1.

127 The Corporate Report, para. 0.2.

128 The committee's recommended package of information which should be contained in the annual corporate reports of business enterprises is listed in Appendix 2 of the discussion paper.

129 The Corporate Report, para. 0.3.

130 The Corporate Report, para. 1.1.

131 The Corporate Report, para. 1.8.

132 The Corporate Report, para. 1.9. The seven user groups identified were: (a) the equity investor group, (b) the loan creditor group, (c) the employee group, (d) the analyst-adviser group, (e) the business contact group, (f) the government and (g) the public.

133 The Corporate Report, paras. 2.1-2.40.

134 The Corporate Report, para. 3.2.

135 The Corporate Report, para. 3.3.

136 The Corporate Report, para. 4.30.

137 The Corporate Report, para. 4.40.

138 The Corporate Report, para. 6.56.

139 The Corporate Report, paras. 6.56 and 6.57.

140 The Corporate Report, para. 7.4.

141 The Corporate Report, para. 7.15.

142 The Corporate Report, paras. 7.40 and 7.43.

143 Report of the Inflation Accounting Committee, *Inflation Accounting*, Cmnd. 6225, London: HMSO, 1975, (the Sandilands Report), p. iv.

144 Inflation Accounting, para. 144.

145 Inflation Accounting, Chapter 12.

146 SSAP 7 (Provisional) *Accounting for the changes in the purchasing power of money*, May 1974 recommended that the RPI should be used for this purpose.

147 SSAP 7, para. 12.

148 The Sandilands Report, para. 20.

149 The Sandilands Report, para. 422.

150 The Sandilands Report, paras. 411 and 412.

151 The Sandilands Report, para. 415.

152 Edwards and Bell have made significant contributions in the areas of income determination and value measurement – however, it is beyond the scope of this book to provide a detailed analysis of their theories. Their case for income and value measurement based on replacement costs may be found in their classic work: E. O. Edwards and P. W. Bell, *The Theory and Measurement of Business Income*, University of California Press, 1961.

153 The Sandilands Report, para. 453.

154 The Sandilands Report, para. 499.

155 Kenneth MacNeal, *Truth in Accounting*, Philadelphia: University of Pennsylvania Press, 1939.

156 R. J. Chambers, *Accounting, Evaluation and Economic Behaviour*, Prentice-Hall, 1966.

157 R. R. Sterling, *Theory of the Measurement of Enterprise Income*, University of Kansas Press, 1970.

158 The Sandilands Report, para. 510.

159 The Institute of Chartered Accountants of Scotland, *Making Corporate Reports Valuable*, London: Kogan Page, 1988, paras. 6.20-6.23.

160 Lee has published numerous papers on the subject of cash flow accounting, the ideas of which have been drawn together in his book:

161 Lawson has published widely on the subject of cash flow accounting — see, for example: G. H. Lawson, 'Cash-flow Accounting', *The Accountant*, October 28th, 1971, pp. 586-589; G. H. Lawson, 'The Measurement of Corporate Profitability on a Cash-flow Basis', *The International Journal of Accounting Education and Research*, Vol. 16, No. 1, pp. 11-46.

162 Tom Lee, *op. cit.*, p. 51.

163 Tom Lee, *op. cit.*, pp. 51-52.

164 Lee presents a quantified example of his proposed cash flow reporting system, *Ibid.*, pp. 57-72.

165 The Sandilands Report, para. 518.

166 The Sandilands Report, para. 517.

167 The Sandilands Report, para. 537.

168 For a detailed discussion of the capital maintenance concepts which apply in the Sandilands proposals, see: H. C. Edey, 'Sandilands and the Logic of Current Cost', *Accounting and Business Research*, Volume 9, No. 35, Summer 1979, pp. 191-200.

169 SSAP 16, *Current cost accounting*, March 1980.

170 SSAP 16, para. 9.

171 Edward Stamp, *Corporate Reporting: Its Future Evolution*, a research study published by the Canadian Institute of Chartered Accountants, 1980, (the Stamp Report), Ch. 1, para. 3.

172 Edward Stamp, 'First steps towards a British conceptual framework', *Accountancy*, March 1982, pp. 123-130.

173 Stamp's qualitative criteria were ranked (from most important to least important) by the ASC members as follows (*Ibid.*, Figure 2, p. 126): relevance, clarity, substance over form, timeliness, comparability, materiality, freedom from bias, objectivity, rationality, full disclosure, consistency, isomorphism, verifiability, cost/benefit effectiveness, non-arbitrariness, data availability, flexibility, uniformity, precision, conservatism.

174 The Stamp Report, Chapter 2.

175 Making Corporate Reports Valuable, paras. 1.1-1.20, *passim*.

176 Making Corporate Reports Valuable, para. 6.36.

177 Making Corporate Reports Valuable,

178 ICAS, *Making Corporate Reports Valuable*, paras. 7.12-7.20, *passim*.

179 Making Corporate Reports Valuable, para. 7.21.

180 Making Corporate Reports Valuable, paras. 7.23-7.26, *passim*.

181 Making Corporate Reports Valuable, paras. 7.27-7.32, *passim*.

182 Making Corporate Reports Valuable, para. 7.39.

183 Making Corporate Reports Valuable, para. 5.44.

184 David Solomons, *Guidelines for Financial Reporting Standards*, A Paper Prepared for The

Tom Lee, *Cash Flow Accounting*, Wokingham, Van Nostrand Reinhold (UK), 1984.

Research Board of the Institute of Chartered
Accountants in England and Wales and
addressed to the Accounting Standards
Committee, ICAEW, 1989, (the Solomons
Report), p. 17.

185 Guidelines for Financial Reporting Standards,
p. 18.

186 Guidelines for Financial Reporting Standards,

187 Guidelines for Financial Reporting Standards,
p. 20.

188 Guidelines for Financial Reporting Standards,
p. 21.

189 Guidelines for Financial Reporting Standards,
pp. 23-28.

190 Guidelines for Financial Reporting Standards,
p. 43.

191 Guidelines for Financial Reporting Standards,
pp. 51-52.

192 Accounting Horizons, vol. 9 no. 1, pages 42-51.

193 Guidelines for Financial Reporting Standards,
p. 53.

194 Guidelines for Financial Reporting Standards,

195 Guidelines for Financial Reporting Standards,
p. 54.

196 Guidelines for Financial Reporting Standards,
p. 55.

197 Guidelines for Financial Reporting Standards,
p. 56.

198 Guidelines for Financial Reporting Standards,
p. 69.

199 Statement of Principles for Financial Reporting,
ASB, December 1999.

200 Statement of Principles for Financial Reporting
Chapter 1, Principles.

201 Statement of Principles for Financial Reporting
para. 1.18

202 Statement of Principles for Financial Reporting
Chapter 3, Principles.

203 Statement of Principles for Financial Reporting
Chapter 3, Principles.

204 Statement of Principles for Financial Reporting
para. 4.21.

205 Statement of Principles for Financial Reporting
para. 4.21.

206 Statement of Principles for Financial Reporting
Chapter 5, Principles.

207 Statement of Principles for Financial Reporting
para. 8.13.

208 Exposure Draft, *Amendments to IAS 39
Financial Instruments: Recognition and
Measurement – The Fair Value Option*, IASB,
April 2004.

209 Exposure draft, Proposed statement of financial
accounting standards, Fair Value Measurement,
FASB, June 2004. para. 4.

210 Proposed statement of financial accounting
standards, Fair Value Measurement, paras. 14
and 19.

211 Proposed statement of financial accounting
standards, Fair Value Measurement, para. 21.

Chapter 3

Presentation of financial statements and accounting policies

1 INTRODUCTION

There is no single standard dealing with the form, content and structure of financial statements and the accounting policies to be applied in their preparation. Of course, all international accounting standards specify some required disclosures and many mention the level of prominence required (such as on the face of a primary statement rather than in the notes). The subject of just what financial statements are, their purpose, contents and presentation is addressed principally by three standards.

IAS 1 – *Presentation of Financial Statements*[1] – is the main standard dealing with the overall requirements for the presentation of financial statements, including their purpose, form, content and structure. IAS 8 – *Accounting Policies, Changes in Accounting Estimates and Errors*[2] – deals with the requirements for the selection and application of accounting policies. It also deals with the requirements as to when changes in accounting policies should be made, and how such changes should be accounted for and disclosed. This chapter deals with the requirements of IAS 1 and IAS 8, including the requirements of the latter dealing with changes in accounting estimates and errors. Also discussed in this chapter are the requirements of IFRS 5 – *Non-current Assets Held for Sale and Discontinued Operations*.[3] This standard principally deals with the classification and presentation of non-current assets held for sale in the balance sheet, and the presentation of discontinued operations in the income statement, although it also sets out the measurement requirements for such items.

1.1   IAS 1

1.1.1   *Background to IAS 1*

In August 1997, the IASC issued IAS 1 (revised) – *Presentation of Financial Statements* – which consolidated and replaced IAS 1 – *Disclosure of Accounting Policies* (originally published in 1974), IAS 5 – *Information to be Disclosed in Financial Statements* (originally published in 1974), and IAS 13 – *Presentation of Current Assets and Current Liabilities* (originally published in 1979). In December 2003 the standard was updated as part of the IASB's improvements project and some further revisions were made in March 2004 by IFRS 5. This version of IAS 1 applies to periods beginning on or after 1 January 2005. Earlier application is encouraged and if it is applied early that fact should be disclosed.[4] IFRS 1 – *First-time Adoption of International Financial Reporting Standards* – has no specific requirements in relation to the application of IAS 1.

The Board's main objectives in updating IAS 1 were (without reconsidering the fundamental approach to the presentation of financial statements):

(a)   to provide a framework within which an entity assesses how to present fairly the effects of transactions and other events, and assesses whether the result of complying with a requirement in a standard or an interpretation would be so misleading that it would not give a fair presentation;

(b)   to base the criteria for classifying liabilities as current or non-current solely on the conditions existing at the balance sheet date;

(c)   to prohibit the presentation of items of income and expense as 'extraordinary items';

(d)   to specify disclosures about the judgements management has made in the process of applying the entity's accounting policies, apart from those involving estimations, that have the most significant effect on the amounts recognised in the financial statements; and

(e)   to specify disclosures about key sources of estimation uncertainty at the balance sheet date that have a significant risk of causing a material adjustment to the carrying amounts of assets and liabilities within the next financial year.[5]

Items (b) to (e) above represent some of the main changes from the previous version of IAS 1.[6] Others identified by the standard include:

- whilst retaining the 'fair presentation override', emphasising the presumption that compliance with IFRS will achieve a fair presentation;[7]

- allowing a 'relevant regulatory framework' to prohibit the fair presentation override, even if the entity believes it is necessary;[8]

- removing the requirement to present the results of operating activities on the face of the income statement;[9]

- including a definition of the term 'material';[10]

- reallocating the guidance of various topics between IAS 1 and IAS 8;[11] and

- modifying the requirements for the display in the primary statements of minority interests.[12]

For readers approaching the topic from an EU background, IAS 1 can best be described as the IASB's version of the EU Fourth Directive. It deals with the components of financial statements, fair presentation, fundamental accounting concepts, disclosure of accounting policies, the structure and content of financial statements and the statement of changes in equity.

1.1.2   Objective and scope of IAS 1

IAS 1 applies to what it calls 'general purpose financial statements', that is those intended to meet the needs of users who are not in a position to demand reports tailored to meet their particular information needs, and it should be applied to all such financial statements prepared in accordance with International Financial Reporting Standards.[13] Although International Financial Reporting Standards (IFRSs) is probably a self explanatory phrase, both IAS 1 and IAS 8 define it as 'Standards and Interpretations adopted by the International Accounting Standards Board (IASB). They comprise:

(a)   International Financial Reporting Standards;

(b)   International Accounting Standards; and

(c)   Interpretations originated by the International Financial Reporting Interpretations Committee (IFRIC) or the former Standing Interpretations Committee (SIC).'[14]

An important point here is that implementation guidance for standards issued by the IASB does not form part of those standards, and therefore does not contain requirements for financial statements.[15] Accordingly, the often voluminous implementation guidance accompanying standards is not, strictly speaking, part of 'IFRS'. We would generally be surprised, though, at entities not following such guidance without valid reason.

General purpose financial statements include those that are presented separately or within another public document such as an annual report or a prospectus. The standard applies equally to all entities and whether or not they need to prepare consolidated financial statements or separate financial statements, as defined in IAS 27 – *Consolidated and Separate Financial Statements* (discussed in Chapter 5).[16] IAS 1 does not apply to the structure and content of condensed interim financial statements prepared in accordance with IAS 34 – *Interim Financial Reporting*[17] (discussed in Chapter 35), although its provisions relating to fair presentation, compliance with IFRS and fundamental accounting principles do apply to interims.[18] These provisions of IAS 1 are discussed at 4.1 below.

The objective of the standard is to prescribe the basis for presentation of general purpose financial statements, and by doing so to ensure comparability both with the entity's financial statements of previous periods and with the financial statements of other entities. To achieve this objective, the standard sets out overall requirements for the presentation of financial statements, guidelines for their structure and minimum requirements for their content. The recognition, measurement and disclosure of specific transactions and other events are dealt with in other standards and in interpretations.[19]

IAS 1 is primarily directed at profit oriented entities (including public sector business entities), and this is reflected in the terminology it uses and its requirements. It acknowledges that entities with not-for-profit activities in the private sector, public sector or government may want to apply the standard and that such entities may need to amend the descriptions used for particular line items in the financial statements and for the financial statements themselves.[20] Furthermore, IAS 1 is a general standard that doesn't address issues specific to particular industries. It does observe, though, that entities without equity (such as some mutual funds) or whose share capital is not equity (such as some co-operative entities) may need to adapt the presentation of members' or unit holders' interests.[21] The standard also cross refers to the more specific requirements of IAS 30 – *Disclosures in the Financial Statements of Banks and Similar Financial Institutions*, which are considered consistent with IAS 1.[22]

1.2 IAS 8

1.2.1 Background to IAS 8

IAS 8 has a long history, and the evolution of its title alone says much about the changing focus of the standard. In October 1976 the IASC issued its eighth exposure draft, E8 – *The Treatment in the Income Statement of Unusual Items and Changes in Accounting Estimates and Accounting Policies*. This led, in February 1978 to the publication of IAS 8 – *Unusual and Prior Period Items and Changes in Accounting Policies*.

July 1992 saw the publication of E46 – *Extraordinary Items, Fundamental Errors and Changes in Accounting Policies* which resulted in December 1993 with a revised version of the standard: IAS 8 (Revised 1993) – *Net Profit or Loss for the period, Fundamental Errors and Changes in Accounting Policies*.

In December 2003, the IASB's improvements project revised the standard again and re-titled it IAS 8 – *Accounting Policies, Changes in Accounting Estimates and Errors*. This revision also superseded the following two interpretations:

(a) SIC-2 – *Consistency – Capitalisation of Borrowing Costs*; and

(b) SIC-18 – *Consistency – Alternative Methods*.[23]

This version applies to periods beginning on or after 1 January 2005. Earlier application is encouraged and if it is applied early that fact should be disclosed.[24] IFRS 1 has no specific requirements in relation to the application of IAS 1.

The Board's main objectives in updating IAS 8 were:

(a) to remove the allowed alternative to retrospective application of voluntary changes in accounting policies and retrospective restatement to correct prior period errors;

(b) to eliminate the concept of a fundamental error;

(c) to articulate the hierarchy of guidance to which management refers, whose applicability it considers when selecting accounting policies in the absence of standards and interpretations that specifically apply;

(d)   to define material omissions or misstatements, and describe how to apply the concept of materiality when applying accounting policies and correcting errors; and

(e)   to incorporate the consensus in SIC-2 and in SIC-18.[25]

The above represent some of the main changes from the previous version of IAS 8.[26] Others identified by the standard include:

- more detailed guidance on materiality;[27]

- more detailed guidance on the impracticability of restatement of prior periods for changes in accounting policies and the correction of errors;[28]

- a requirement (rather than just encouragement) to disclose an impending change in accounting policy due to a new standard or interpretation;[29]

- a definition of a change in accounting estimate;[30]

- some further disclosure requirements;[31] and

- reallocating the guidance of various topics between IAS 1 and IAS 8.[32]

1.2.2   Objective and scope of IAS 8

IAS 8 applies to selecting and applying accounting policies, and accounting for changes in accounting policies, changes in accounting estimates and corrections of prior period errors.[33] Its objective is to prescribe the criteria for selecting and changing accounting policies, together with the accounting treatment and disclosure of changes in accounting policies, changes in accounting estimates and corrections of errors. The standard's intention is to enhance the relevance and reliability of an entity's financial statements, and the comparability of those financial statements over time and with the financial statements of other entities.[34]

Two particular issues which one might expect to be dealt with regarding the above are discussed in other standards and cross-referred to by IAS 8:

- disclosure requirements for accounting policies, except those for changes in accounting policies, are dealt with in IAS 1;[35] and

- accounting and disclosure requirements regarding the tax effects of corrections of prior period errors and of retrospective adjustments made to apply changes in accounting policies are dealt with in IAS 12 – *Income Taxes* (discussed in Chapter 24).[36]

1.3   IFRS 5

1.3.1   Background to IFRS 5

The IASC issued IAS 35 – *Discontinuing Operations* – in June 1998, which was concerned with the presentation and disclosures relating to *discontinuing* operations. It contained no recognition or measurement rules of its own. In March 2004 IAS 35 was replaced by IFRS 5 – *Non-current Assets Held for Sale and Discontinued Operations.*[37]

IFRS 5 was developed as part of the IASB's convergence project and arises from the IASB's consideration of FASB Statement No. 144 – *Accounting for the Impairment or Disposal of Long-Lived Assets* (SFAS 144), which was issued in 2001.[38] SFAS 144 addresses three areas:

(a)   the impairment of long-lived assets to be held and used;

(b)   the classification, measurement and presentation of assets held for sale; and

(c)   the classification and presentation of discontinued operations.

The IASB concluded that there were extensive differences between IFRSs and US GAAP as regards (a) above, which it did not think capable of resolution in a relatively short time. However, convergence on the other two areas was thought to be worth pursuing within the context of the short-term convergence project.[39] Accordingly, IFRS 5 was published, which achieves substantial convergence with the requirements of SFAS 144 relating to assets held for sale, the timing of the classification of operations as discontinued and the presentation of such operations.[40] However, there are still differences between the two. In particular, the definition of a discontinued operation in IFRS 5 is narrower. The IASB used a different definition to the one contained in SFAS 144 on the grounds that the size of the operation which would meet SFAS 144's definition was too small and that this was causing practical problems. Accordingly, the IASB 'intends to work with the FASB to arrive at a converged definition within a relatively short time'.[41]

1.3.2   Objective and scope of IFRS 5

The objective of IFRS 5 is to specify the accounting for assets held for sale, and the presentation and disclosure of discontinued operations. In particular, the standard requires that non-current assets (and, in a 'disposal group', liabilities and current assets, discussed at 5.1.1 below) meeting its criteria to be classified as held for sale:

(a)   be measured at the lower of carrying amount and fair value less costs to sell, with depreciation on them ceasing; and

(b)   be presented separately on the face of the balance sheet with the results of discontinued operations presented separately in the income statement.[42]

The classification and presentation requirements apply to all recognised non-current assets and disposal groups, while there are certain exceptions to the measurement provisions of the standard.[43] These issues are discussed further at 5 below.

1.3.3   Effective date and transitional provisions

IFRS 5 is mandatory for annual periods beginning on or after 1 January 2005, with earlier application encouraged. If it is applied for a period beginning before 1 January 2005, that fact should be disclosed.[44]

A   Transitional arrangements for entities already reporting under IFRS

The standard should be applied prospectively to non-current assets (or disposal groups) that meet the criteria to be classified as held for sale and operations that meet the criteria to be classified as discontinued after the effective date of the IFRS. The requirements may be applied to all non-current assets (or disposal groups) that meet the criteria to be classified as held for sale and operations that meet the criteria to be classified as discontinued after any date before the effective date of the IFRS, provided the valuations and other information needed to apply the standard were obtained at the time those criteria were originally met.[45]

B First-time adoption issues

IFRS 1 requires an entity with a date of transition to IFRS before 1 January 2005 to apply the transitional provisions of IFRS 5 described above. For an entity with a date of transition to IFRSs on or after 1 January 2005 IFRS 5 is required to be applied retrospectively.[46]

2 THE PURPOSE AND COMPOSITION OF FINANCIAL STATEMENTS

What financial statements are and what they are for are clearly important basic questions for any body of accounting literature, and answering them is the main purpose of IAS 1.

2.1 The purpose of financial statements

IAS 1 describes financial statements as a structured representation of the financial position and financial performance of an entity. It states that the objective of general purpose financial statements is to provide information about the financial position, financial performance and cash flows of an entity that is useful to a wide range of users in making economic decisions. A focus on assisting decision making by the users of financial statements is seeking (at least in part) a forward looking or predictive quality. This is reflected by some requirements of accounting standards (for example, the disclosure of discontinued operations (discussed at 3.2.3 below), and the use of profit from continuing operations as the control number in calculating diluted earnings per share (discussed at 6.3.1 in Chapter 31)) and also the desire of some entities to present performance measures excluding what they see as unusual, infrequent or just historic items (discussed at 3.2.4 below).

IAS 1 also acknowledges a second important role of financial statements. That is, that they also show the results of management's stewardship of the resources entrusted to it. To meet this objective, IAS 1 requires financial statements provide information about an entity's:

(a) assets;
(b) liabilities;
(c) equity;
(d) income and expenses, including gains and losses;
(e) other changes in equity; and
(f) cash flows.

The standard observes that this information, along with other information in the notes, assists users of financial statements in predicting the entity's future cash flows and, in particular, their timing and certainty.[47]

2.2   Frequency of reporting and period covered

IAS 1 requires that financial statements be presented 'at least annually'. Whilst this drafting isn't exactly precise, it does not seem to mean that financial statements must never be more than a year apart (which is perhaps the most natural meaning of the phrase). This is because the standard goes on to mention that an entity's balance sheet date may change, and that the annual financial statements are therefore presented for a period *longer* or shorter than one year. When this is the case, IAS 1 requires disclosure of, in addition to the period covered by the financial statements:

(a)   the reason for using a longer or shorter period; and

(b)   the fact that comparative amounts for the income statement, statement of changes in equity, cash flow statement and related notes are not entirely comparable.[48]

Some entities, particularly in the retail sector, traditionally present financial statements for a 52-week period. IAS 1 does not preclude this practice. Whilst it notes that normally financial statements are consistently prepared covering a one-year period, it states that a 52-week period is unlikely to produce materially different results.[49]

2.3   The components of financial statements

A complete set of financial statements under IAS 1 comprises:

(a)   a balance sheet;

(b)   an income statement;

(c)   a statement of changes in equity showing either:

(i)   all changes in equity, or

(ii)   changes in equity other than those arising from transactions with equity holders acting in their capacity as such;

(d)   a cash flow statement; and

(e)   notes, comprising a summary of significant accounting policies and other explanatory notes.[50] The standard explains that notes contain information in addition to that presented in the balance sheet, income statement, statement of changes in equity and cash flow statement, and provide narrative descriptions or disaggregations of items disclosed in those statements and information about items that do not qualify for recognition in those statements.[51]

In addition to information about the reporting period, IAS 1 also requires information about the preceding period. Comparative information is discussed at 2.4 below.

Financial statements are usually published as part of a larger annual report, with the accompanying discussions and analyses often being more voluminous than the financial statements themselves. IAS 1 acknowledges this, but makes clear that such reports and statements (including financial reviews, environmental reports and value added statements) presented outside financial statements are outside the scope of IFRSs.[52]

Notwithstanding that this type of information is not within the scope of IFRSs, IAS 1 devotes two paragraphs to discussing what this information may comprise, observing that:

- a financial review by management may describe and explain the main features of the entity's financial performance and financial position and the principal uncertainties it faces and that it may include a review of:
  - (a) the main factors and influences determining financial performance, including changes in the environment in which the entity operates, the entity's response to those changes and their effect, and the entity's policy for investment to maintain and enhance financial performance, including its dividend policy;
  - (b) the entity's sources of funding and its targeted ratio of liabilities to equity; and
  - (c) the entity's resources not recognised in the balance sheet in accordance with IFRS.[53]
- reports and statements such as environmental reports and value added statements may be presented, particularly in industries in which environmental factors are significant and when employees are regarded as an important user group.[54]

It strikes us as strange that an accounting standard would concern itself with a discussion of matters outside its scope in this way. However, discursive reports accompanying financial statements are not just common (indeed, required by most markets) but also clearly useful, so perhaps the IASB's discussion is attempting to encourage and support their preparation.

2.4   Comparative information

IAS 1 requires that, except when a standard or an interpretation permits or requires otherwise, comparative information shall be disclosed in respect of the previous period for all amounts reported in the financial statements. Comparative information is also required for narrative and descriptive information when it is relevant to an understanding of the current period's financial statements.[55]

The standard illustrates the current year relevance of the previous year's narratives with a legal dispute, the outcome of which is was uncertain at the last balance sheet date and is yet to be resolved (the disclosure of contingent liabilities is discussed in Chapter 25). It observes that users benefit from information that the uncertainty existed at the last balance sheet date, and about the steps that have been taken during the period to resolve the uncertainty.[56]

Another example would be the required disclosure of material items, which would include items commonly called exceptional items, although that expression is not used by the standard (see 3.2.4 below). IAS 1 requires that the nature and amount of such items be disclosed separately.[57] Often a simple caption or line item heading will be sufficient to convey the 'nature' of material items. Sometimes, though a more extensive description in the notes may be needed to do this. In that case, the same information is likely to be relevant the following year.

As noted at 1.1.2 above, one of the objectives of IAS 1 is to ensure the comparability of financial statements with previous periods. The standard notes that enhancing the inter-period comparability of information assists users in making economic decisions, especially by allowing the assessment of trends in financial information for predictive purposes.[58] Requiring the presentation of comparatives allows such a comparison to be made within one set of financial statements. For a comparison to be meaningful, the amounts for prior periods need to be reclassified whenever the presentation or classification of items in the financial statements is amended. When this is the case, disclosure is required of the nature, amount and reasons for the reclassification.[59]

The standard acknowledges, though, that in some circumstances it is impracticable to reclassify comparative information for a particular prior period to achieve comparability with the current period. For these purposes, reclassification is impracticable when it cannot be done after making every reasonable effort to do so.[60] An example given by the standard is that data may not have been collected in the prior period(s) in a way that allows reclassification, and it may not be practicable to recreate the information.[61] When it proves impracticable to reclassify comparative data, IAS 1 requires disclosure of the reason for this and also the nature of the adjustments that would have been made if the amounts had been reclassified.[62]

As well as reclassification to reflect current period classifications as required by IAS 1, a change to comparatives as they were originally reported could be necessary:

(a)   following a change in accounting policy (discussed at 4.4 below);

(b)   to correct an error discovered in previous financial statements (discussed at 4.6 below); or

(c)   in relation to non-current assets held for sale, disposal groups and discontinued operations (discussed at 5.3 below).

2.5   Identification of the financial statements and accompanying information

2.5.1   Identification of financial statements

It is commonly the case that financial statements will form only part of a larger annual report or other document. As IFRSs only apply to financial statements, it is important that the financial statements are clearly identified so that users of the report can distinguish information that is prepared using IFRSs from other information that may be useful but is not the subject of those requirements.[63]

As well as requiring that the financial statements be clearly distinguished, IAS 1 also requires that each component of the financial statements be identified clearly. Furthermore, the following information is required to be displayed prominently, and repeated when it is necessary for a proper understanding of the information presented:

(a) the name of the reporting entity or other means of identification, and any change in that information from the preceding balance sheet date;

(b) whether the financial statements cover the individual entity or a group of entities;

(c) the balance sheet date or the period covered by the financial statements, whichever is appropriate to that component of the financial statements;

(d) the presentation currency, as defined in IAS 21 – *The Effects of Changes in Foreign Exchange Rates* (discussed in Chapter 9); and

(e) the level of rounding used in presenting amounts in the financial statements.[64]

These requirements are normally met by the use of page headings and abbreviated column headings on each page of the financial statements. The standard notes that judgement is required in determining the best way of presenting such information. For example, when the financial statements are presented electronically, separate pages are not always used; the above items then need to be presented frequently enough to ensure a proper understanding of the information included in the financial statements.[65] IAS 1 considers that financial statements are often made more understandable by presenting information in thousands or millions of units of the presentation currency. It considers this acceptable as long as the level of rounding in presentation is disclosed and material information is not omitted.[66]

2.5.2 Statement of compliance with IFRS

As well as identifying which particular part of any larger document constitutes the financial statements, IAS 1 also requires that financial statements complying with IFRSs make an explicit and unreserved statement of such compliance in the notes.[67] As this statement itself is required for full compliance, its absence would render the whole financial statements non-compliant, even if there was otherwise full compliance. In a curious twist, the standard goes on to say that financial statements 'shall not be described as complying with IFRSs unless they comply with all the requirements of IFRSs'.[68] It is one thing for a standard setter to say what is necessary to comply with its rules. However, it is quite another thing to try and prescribe what an entity (which is, by definition, *not* complying with its rules) may or may not say.

3   THE STRUCTURE OF FINANCIAL STATEMENTS

As noted at 2.3 above, a complete set of financial statements under IAS 1 comprises:

(a)   a balance sheet;

(b)   an income statement;

(c)   a statement of changes in equity showing either:

   (i)   all changes in equity, or

   (ii)   changes in equity other than those arising from transactions with equity holders acting in their capacity as equity holders;

(d)   a cash flow statement; and

(e)   notes, comprising a summary of significant accounting policies and other explanatory notes.

The standard adopts a generally permissive stance, by setting out minimum levels of required items to be shown in each statement (sometimes specifically on the face of the statement, and sometimes either on the face or in the notes) whilst allowing great flexibility of order and layout.[69] The standard notes that sometimes it uses the term 'disclosure' in a broad sense, encompassing items presented on the face of the balance sheet, income statement, statement of changes in equity and cash flow statement, as well as in the notes. Other standards and interpretations also require 'disclosures'. IAS 1 makes clear that unless specified to the contrary in IAS 1, or in another standard or interpretation, such disclosures can be made either on the face of the balance sheet, income statement, statement of changes in equity or cash flow statement (whichever is relevant), or in the notes.[70]

In addition to the requirements of IAS 1, IAS 30 specifies additional requirements for those entities within its scope that IAS 1 considers consistent with its requirements.[71] The industry specific nature of these requirements puts them outside the scope of this book.

IAS 1 observes that cash flow information provides users of financial statements with a basis to assess the ability of the entity to generate cash and cash equivalents and the needs of the entity to utilise those cash flows. Requirements for the presentation of the cash flow statement and related disclosures are set out IAS 7 – *Cash Flow Statements*.[72] Cash flow statements are discussed in Chapter 32, each of the other primary statements listed above is discussed in the following sections.

3.1   The balance sheet

3.1.1   *The distinction between current/non-current assets and liabilities*

In most situations (but see the exception discussed below, and the treatment of non-current assets held for sale discussed at 3.1.2 below) IAS 1 requires balance sheets to distinguish current assets and liabilities from non-current ones.[73] The standard uses the term 'non-current' to include tangible, intangible and financial assets of a long-term nature. It does not prohibit the use of alternative descriptions as long as the meaning is clear.[74] A common alternative description seen in practice is the term fixed assets.

The standard explains the requirement to present current and non-current items separately by observing that when an entity supplies goods or services within a clearly identifiable operating cycle, separate classification of current and non-current assets and liabilities on the face of the balance sheet will provide useful information by distinguishing the net assets that are continuously circulating as working capital from those used in long-term operations. Furthermore, the analysis will also highlight assets that are expected to be realised within the current operating cycle, and liabilities that are due for settlement within the same period.[75] The distinction between current and non-current items therefore depends on the length of the entity's operating cycle. The standard states that the operating cycle of an entity is the time between the acquisition of assets for processing and their realisation in cash or cash equivalents. However, when the entity's normal operating cycle is not clearly identifiable, its duration is assumed to be twelve months.[76]

Once assets have been classified as non-current they should not be reclassified as current assets until they meet the criteria to be classified as held for sale in accordance with IFRS 5 (see 5.1 below). Assets of a class that an entity would normally regard as non-current that are acquired exclusively with a view to resale also should not be classified as current unless they meet those criteria.[77]

The basic requirement of the standard is that current and non-current assets, and current and non-current liabilities, should be presented as separate classifications on the face of its balance sheet.[78] The standard defines current assets and current liabilities (discussed at 3.1.3 and 3.1.4 below), with the non-current category being the residual.[79] Example 3.2 at 3.1.7 below provides an illustration of a balance sheet presenting this classification.

An exception to this requirement is when a presentation based on liquidity provides information that is reliable and is more relevant. When that exception applies, all assets and liabilities are required to be presented broadly in order of liquidity.[80] The reason for this exception given by the standard is that some entities (such as financial institutions) do not supply goods or services within a clearly identifiable operating cycle, and for these entities a presentation of assets and liabilities in increasing or decreasing order of liquidity provides information that is reliable and is more relevant than a current/non-current presentation.[81]

The standard also makes clear that an entity is permitted to present some of its assets and liabilities using a current/non-current classification and others in order of liquidity when this provides information that is reliable and is more relevant. It goes on to observe that the need for a mixed basis of presentation might arise when an entity has diverse operations.[82]

Whichever method of presentation is adopted, IAS 1 requires for each asset and liability line item that combines amounts expected to be recovered or settled:

(a)   no more than twelve months after the balance sheet date; and

(b)   more than twelve months after the balance sheet date;

disclosure of the amount expected to be recovered or settled after more than twelve months.[83]

The standard explains this requirement by noting that information about expected dates of realisation of assets and liabilities is useful in assessing the liquidity and solvency of an entity. In this vein, IAS 1 contains a reminder that IAS 32 – *Financial Instruments: Disclosure and Presentation* requires disclosure of the maturity dates of financial assets (including trade and other receivables) and financial liabilities (including trade and other payables) – see Chapter 20. Similarly, IAS 1 views information on the expected date of recovery and settlement of non-monetary assets and liabilities such as inventories and provisions as also useful, whether or not assets and liabilities are classified as current or non-current. An example of this given by the standard is that an entity should disclose the amount of inventories that are expected to be recovered more than twelve months after the balance sheet date.[84]

3.1.2   *Non-current assets and disposal groups held for sale*

The general requirement to classify balance sheet items as current or non-current (or present them broadly in order of liquidity) is overlaid with further requirements by IFRS 5 regarding non-current assets held for sale and disposal groups (discussed at 5 below). IFRS 5's aim is that entities should present and disclose information that enables users of the financial statements to evaluate the financial effects of disposals of non-current assets (or disposal groups).[85] In pursuit of this aim, IFRS 5 requires:

•   non-current assets classified as held for sale and the assets of a disposal group classified as held for sale to be presented separately from other assets in the balance sheet; and

•   the liabilities of a disposal group classified as held for sale to be presented separately from other liabilities in the balance sheet.

These assets and liabilities should not be offset and presented as a single amount. In addition:

(a)   major classes of assets and liabilities classified as held for sale should generally be separately disclosed either on the face of the balance sheet or in the notes (see 3.1.6 below). However, this is not necessary for a disposal group if it is a subsidiary that met the criteria to be classified as held for sale on acquisition; and

(b)   any cumulative income or expense recognised directly in equity relating to a non-current asset (or disposal group) classified as held for sale should be presented separately.[86]

The requirement in (b) was included in response to comments made to the IASB during the development of the standard. The Board describes the development as follows. 'Respondents to ED 4 noted that the separate presentation within equity of amounts relating to assets and disposal groups classified as held for sale (such as, for example, unrealised gains and losses on available-for-sale assets and foreign currency translation adjustments) would also provide useful information. The Board agreed and has added such a requirement to the IFRS.'[87] On that basis, it might be considered that any minority interest relating to non-current assets (or disposal groups) held for sale should also be presented separately as it would seem to represent equally useful information about amounts within equity.

IFRS 5 is silent as to whether the information specified in (b) above should be on the face of the balance sheet or in a note. However, the implementation guidance to IFRS 5 shows a caption called 'Amounts recognised directly in equity in relation to non-current assets held for sale' and illustrates the requirements as follows.

Example 3.1:　　*Presenting non-current assets or disposal groups classified as held for sale*[88]

At the end of 2005, an entity decides to dispose of part of its assets (and directly associated liabilities). The disposal, which meets the criteria to be classified as held for sale, takes the form of two disposal groups, as follows:

	Carrying amount after classification as held for sale	
	Disposal group I	Disposal group II
	€	€
Property, plant and equipment	4,900	1,700
AFS financial asset	1,400*	-
Liabilities	(2,400)	(900)
Net carrying amount of disposal group	3,900	800

*　An amount of €400 relating to these assets has been recognised directly in equity.

The presentation in the entity's balance sheet of the disposal groups classified as held for sale can be shown as follows:

	2005 €	2004 €
ASSETS		
Non-current assets	×	×
AAA	×	×
BBB	×	×
CCC	×	×
	×	×
Current assets		
DDD	×	×
EEE	×	×
	×	×
Non-current assets classified as held for sale	8,000	–
Total assets	×	×
EQUITY AND LIABILITIES		
Equity attributable to equity holders of the parent		
FFF	×	×
GGG	×	×
Amounts recognised directly in equity relating to non-current assets held for sale	400	–
	×	×
Minority interest	×	×
Total equity	×	×
Non-current liabilities		
HHH	×	×
III	×	×
JJJ	×	×
	×	×
Current liabilities		
KKK	×	×
LLL	×	×
MMM	×	×
	×	×
Liabilities directly associated with non-current assets classified as held for sale	3,300	–
	×	×
Total liabilities	×	×
Total equity and liabilities	×	×

The presentation requirements for assets (or disposal groups) classified as held for sale at the end of the reporting period do not apply retrospectively. The comparative balance sheets for any previous periods are therefore not re-presented.

The treatment of comparatives when the classification as held for sale commences or ceases is discussed at 5.3 below.

3.1.3 Current assets

IAS 1 requires an asset to be classified as current when it satisfies any of the following criteria, with all other assets classified as non-current. The criteria are:

(a)   it is expected to be realised in, or is intended for sale or consumption in, the entity's normal operating cycle (discussed at 3.1.1 above);

(b)   it is held primarily for the purpose of being traded;

(c)   it is expected to be realised within twelve months after the balance sheet date; or

(d)   it is cash or a cash equivalent (as defined in IAS 7, discussed in Chapter 32) unless it is restricted from being exchanged or used to settle a liability for at least twelve months after the balance sheet date.[89]

As an exception to this, deferred tax assets are never allowed to be classified as current.[90]

Current assets include assets (such as inventories and trade receivables) that are sold, consumed or realised as part of the normal operating cycle even when they are not expected to be realised within twelve months after the balance sheet date. Current assets also include assets held primarily for the purpose of being traded (financial assets within this category would be classified as held for trading in accordance with IAS 39 – *Financial Instruments: Recognition and Measurement*, discussed in Chapter 15 at 7.1.1) and the current portion of non-current financial assets.[91]

3.1.4 Current liabilities

IAS 1 requires a liability to be classified as current when it satisfies any of the following criteria, with all other liabilities classified as non-current. The criteria are:

(a)   it is expected to be settled in the entity's normal operating cycle (discussed at 3.1.1 above);

(b)   it is held primarily for the purpose of being traded;

(c)   it is due to be settled within twelve months after the balance sheet date; or

(d)   the entity does not have an unconditional right to defer settlement of the liability for at least twelve months after the balance sheet date.[92]

As an exception to this, deferred tax liabilities are never allowed to be classified as current.[93]

The standard notes that some current liabilities, such as trade payables and some accruals for employee and other operating costs, are part of the working capital used in the entity's normal operating cycle. Such operating items are classified as current liabilities even if they are due to be settled more than twelve months after the balance sheet date.[94]

However, neither IAS 19 – *Employee Benefits* – nor IAS 1 specifies where in the balance sheet an asset or liability in respect of a defined benefit plan should be presented, nor whether such balances should be shown separately on the face of the balance sheet or only in the notes – this is left to the judgement of the reporting entity (see 3.1.5 below). When the format of balance sheet distinguishes current assets and liabilities from non-current ones, the question arises as to whether this split needs also to be made for defined benefit plan balances. IAS 19 does not specify whether such a split should be made, on the grounds that it may sometimes be arbitrary.[95]

Some current liabilities are not settled as part of the normal operating cycle, but are due for settlement within twelve months after the balance sheet date or held primarily for the purpose of being traded. Examples given by the standard are financial liabilities classified as held for trading in accordance with IAS 39, bank overdrafts, and the current portion of non-current financial liabilities, dividends payable, income taxes and other non-trade payables. Financial liabilities that provide financing on a long-term basis (i.e. are not part of the working capital used in the entity's normal operating cycle) and are not due for settlement within twelve months after the balance sheet date are non-current liabilities.[96]

The assessment of a liability as current or non-current is applied very strictly in IAS 1. In particular, a liability should be classified as current:

(a)   when it is due to be settled within twelve months after the balance sheet date, even if:

    (i)   the original term was for a period longer than twelve months; and

    (ii)   an agreement to refinance, or to reschedule payments, on a long-term basis is completed after the balance sheet date and before the financial statements are authorised for issue (although disclosure of the post balance sheet refinancing would be required);[97] or

(b)   when an entity breaches an undertaking under a long-term loan agreement on or before the balance sheet date with the effect that the liability becomes payable on demand. This is the case even if the lender has agreed, after the balance sheet date and before the authorisation of the financial statements for issue, not to demand payment as a consequence of the breach (although the post balance sheet agreement would be disclosed). The meaning of the term 'authorised for issue' is discussed in Chapter 34 at 2.1. The standard explains that the liability should be classified as current because, at the balance sheet date, the entity does not have an unconditional right to defer its settlement for at least twelve months after that date.[98] However, the liability would be classified as non-current if the lender agreed by the balance sheet date to provide a period of grace ending at least twelve months after the balance sheet date, within which the entity can rectify the breach and during which the lender cannot demand immediate repayment.[99]

The key point here is that for a liability to be classified as non-current requires that the entity has *at the balance sheet date* an unconditional right to defer its settlement for at least twelve months after the balance sheet date. Accordingly, the standard explains that liabilities would be non-current if an entity expects, and has the discretion, to refinance or roll over an obligation for at least twelve months after the balance sheet date under an existing loan facility, even if it would otherwise be due within a shorter period. However, when refinancing or rolling over the obligation is not at the discretion of the entity the obligation is classified as current.[100]

3.1.5   Information required on the face of the balance sheet

IAS 1 does not contain a prescriptive format or order for the balance sheet.[101] Rather, it contains two mechanisms which require certain information to be shown on the face of the balance sheet. First, it contains a list of specific items for which this is required, on the basis that they are sufficiently different in nature or function to warrant separate presentation.[102] Second, it stipulates that additional line items, headings and subtotals should be presented on the face of the balance sheet when such presentation is relevant to an understanding of the entity's financial position.[103] Clearly this is a highly judgemental decision for entities to make when preparing a balance sheet, and allows a wide variety of possible presentations. The judgement as to whether additional items should be presented separately is based on an assessment of:

(a)   the nature and liquidity of assets;

(b)   the function of assets within the entity; and

(c)   the amounts, nature and timing of liabilities.[104]

IAS 1 indicates that the use of different measurement bases for different classes of assets suggests that their nature or function differs and, therefore, that they should be presented as separate line items. For example, different classes of property, plant and equipment can be carried at cost or revalued amounts in accordance with IAS 16 – *Property, Plant and Equipment*.[105]

As a minimum, the face of the balance sheet should include line items that present the following amounts:

(a)   property, plant and equipment;

(b)   investment property;

(c)   intangible assets;

(d)   financial assets (excluding amounts shown under (e), (h) and (i));

(e)   investments accounted for using the equity method;

(f)   biological assets;

(g)   inventories;

(h)   trade and other receivables;

(i)   cash and cash equivalents;

(j)   trade and other payables;

(k)   provisions;

(l)   financial liabilities (excluding amounts shown under (j) and (k));

(m)   liabilities and assets for current tax, as defined in IAS 12;

(n)   deferred tax liabilities and deferred tax assets, as defined in IAS 12;

(o)   minority interest, presented within equity;

(p)   issued capital and reserves attributable to equity holders of the parent;

(q)   the total of assets classified as held for sale and assets included in disposal groups classified as held for sale in accordance with IFRS 5; and

(r)   liabilities included in disposal groups classified as held for sale in accordance with IFRS 5.

Those items covered by (q) and (r) should be excluded from all other captions.[106]

The standard notes that items (a) to (p) above represents a list of items that are sufficiently different in nature or function to warrant separate presentation on the face of the balance sheet ((q) and (r) were introduced by IFRS 5, presumably for the same reason). In addition:

(a)   line items should be included when the size, nature or function of an item or aggregation of similar items is such that separate presentation is relevant to an understanding of the entity's financial position; and

(b)   the descriptions used and the ordering of items or aggregation of similar items may be amended according to the nature of the entity and its transactions, to provide information that is relevant to an understanding of the entity's financial position. For example, a bank amends the above descriptions to apply the more specific requirements in IAS 30.[107]

3.1.6   *Information required either on the face of the balance sheet or in the notes*

IAS 1 requires further sub-classifications of the line items shown on the face of the balance sheet to be presented either on the face of the balance sheet or in the notes. The requirements for these further sub-classifications are approached by the standard in a similar manner to those for line items on the face of the balance sheet. There is a prescriptive list of items required (see below) and also a more general requirement that the sub-classifications should be made in a manner appropriate to the entity's operations.[108] The standard notes that the detail provided in sub-classifications depends on the requirements of IFRSs (as numerous disclosures are required by other standards) and on the size, nature and function of the amounts involved.[109]

Aside of the specific requirements, deciding what level of detailed disclosure is necessary is clearly a judgemental exercise. As is the case for items on the face of the balance sheet, IAS 1 requires that the judgement as to whether additional items should be presented separately should be based on an assessment of:

(a)   the nature and liquidity of assets;

(b)   the function of assets within the entity; and

(c)   the amounts, nature and timing of liabilities.[110]

The disclosures will also vary for each item, examples given by the standard are:

(a)   items of property, plant and equipment are disaggregated into classes in accordance with IAS 16;

(b)   receivables are disaggregated into amounts receivable from trade customers, receivables from related parties, prepayments and other amounts;

(c) inventories are sub-classified, in accordance with IAS 2 – *Inventories*, into classifications such as merchandise, production supplies, materials, work in progress and finished goods;

(d) provisions are disaggregated into provisions for employee benefits and other items; and

(e) equity capital and reserves are disaggregated into various classes, such as paid-in capital, share premium and reserves.[111]

The list in IAS 1 of specific items to be shown either on the face of the balance sheet or the notes is as follows:

(a) for each class of share capital:

    (i) the number of shares authorised;

    (ii) the number of shares issued and fully paid, and issued but not fully paid;

    (iii) par value per share, or that the shares have no par value;

    (iv) a reconciliation of the number of shares outstanding at the beginning and at the end of the period;

    (v) the rights, preferences and restrictions attaching to that class including restrictions on the distribution of dividends and the repayment of capital;

    (vi) shares in the entity held by the entity or by its subsidiaries or associates; and

    (vii) shares reserved for issue under options and contracts for the sale of shares, including the terms and amounts; and

(b) a description of the nature and purpose of each reserve within equity.[112]

An entity without share capital (such as a partnership or trust) should disclose information equivalent to that required by (a) above, showing changes during the period in each category of equity interest, and the rights, preferences and restrictions attaching to each category of equity interest.[113]

3.1.7 Illustrative balance sheets

The implementation guidance accompanying IAS 1 provides an illustration of a balance sheet presented to distinguish current and non-current items. It makes clear that other formats may be equally appropriate, as long as the distinction is clear.[114] As discussed at 3.1.2 above, IFRS 5 provides further guidance relating to the presentation of non-current assets and disposal groups held for sale.

Example 3.2:   Illustrative balance sheet[115]

XYZ GROUP – BALANCE SHEET AS AT 31 DECEMBER 2005
(in thousands of Euros)

	2005	2004
ASSETS		
Non-current assets		
Property, plant and equipment	×	×
Goodwill	×	×
Other intangible assets	×	×
Investments in associates	×	×
Available-for-sale investments	×	×
	×	×
Current assets		
Inventories	×	×
Trade receivables	×	×
Other current assets	×	×
Cash and cash equivalents	×	×
	×	×
Total assets	×	×
EQUITY AND LIABILITIES		
Equity attributable to equity holders of the parent		
Share capital	×	×
Other reserves	×	×
Retained earnings	×	×
	×	×
Minority interest	×	×
Total equity	×	×
Non-current liabilities		
Long-term borrowings	×	×
Deferred tax	×	×
Long-term provisions	×	×
Total non-current liabilities	×	×
Current liabilities		
Trade and other payables	×	×
Short-term borrowings	×	×
Current portion of long-term borrowings	×	×
Current tax payable	×	×
Short-term provisions	×	×
Total current liabilities	×	×
Total liabilities	×	×
Total equity and liabilities	×	×

3.2 The income statement

IAS 1 adopts an essentially permissive approach to the format of the income statement. It observes that, because the effects of an entity's various activities, transactions and other events differ in frequency, potential for gain or loss and predictability, disclosing the components of financial performance assists in an understanding of the financial performance achieved and in making projections of future results.[116] In other words, some analysis of the make-up of net profit is needed, but a wide variety of presentations would all be acceptable. The general rule is that income and expense items are not offset unless certain criteria are met, this is discussed at 4.1.5 B below.

As is the case for the balance sheet, IAS 1 sets out certain items which must appear on the face of the income statement and other required disclosures which may be made either on the face or in the notes.

3.2.1 Information required on the face of the income statement

As for the balance sheet, IAS 1 requires certain specific items to appear on the face of the income statement then supplements this with a more general requirement that additional line items, headings and subtotals should be presented on the face of the statement when such presentation is relevant to an understanding of the entity's financial performance.[117] The standard explains that additional line items should be included on the face of the income statement, and the descriptions used and the ordering of items are amended when this is necessary to explain the elements of financial performance. Factors to be considered would include materiality and the nature and function of the components of income and expenses. An example of this is that a bank should amend the descriptions to apply the more specific requirements in IAS 30.[118]

As a minimum, the face of the income statement should include line items that present the following amounts (although as noted above, the order and description of the items should be amended as necessary):

(a) revenue;

(b) finance costs;

(c) share of the profit or loss of associates and joint ventures accounted for using the equity method;

(d) tax expense;

(e) a single amount comprising the total of (i) the post-tax profit or loss of discontinued operations and (ii) the post-tax gain or loss recognised on the measurement to fair value less costs to sell or on the disposal of the assets or disposal group(s) constituting the discontinued operation;

(f) profit or loss;[119] and

(g) the following as allocations of profit or loss for the period:

    (i) profit or loss attributable to minority interest; and

    (ii) profit or loss attributable to equity holders of the parent.[120]

As discussed in the next section, an analysis of expenses is required based either on their nature or their function. IAS 1 encourages, but does not require this to be shown on the face of the income statement.[121]

The standard also requires the disclosure of the amount of dividends recognised as distributions to equity holders during the period, and the related amount per share. This may be shown either on the face of the income statement or the statement of changes in equity, or in the notes.[122]

The improved version of IAS 1 omits the requirement in the previous version to disclose the results of operating activities as a line item on the face of the income statement. The reason given for this in the Basis for Conclusions to the standard is that 'Operating activities' are not defined in the standard, and the Board decided not to require disclosure of an undefined item.[123]

The Basis for Conclusions to IAS 1 goes on to state that 'The Board recognises that an entity may elect to disclose the results of operating activities, or a similar line item, even though this term is not defined. In such cases, the Board notes that the entity should ensure the amount disclosed is representative of activities that would normally be considered to be 'operating'.

In the Board's view, it would be misleading and would impair the comparability of financial statements if items of an operating nature were excluded from the results of operating activities, even if that had been industry practice. For example, it would be inappropriate to exclude items clearly related to operations (such as inventory write-downs and restructuring and relocation expenses) because they occur irregularly or infrequently or are unusual in amount. Similarly, it would be inappropriate to exclude items on the grounds that they do not involve cash flows, such as depreciation and amortisation expenses.'[124]

Whilst we agree with the sentiments in the second paragraph, in our view it is regrettable that the IASB has approached this issue by presenting its opinions *outside* of IFRS about something not required by IFRS but which it thinks some entities may choose to do. As it has, though, we question how the authority of this 'guidance' will be viewed. However, in our view the general requirement for a fair presentation (discussed at 4.1.1 below) would seem to prohibit the exclusion from any voluntarily presented 'operating' result of items which reasonable users of the financial statements would generally consider to be 'operating' in nature.

The implementation guidance accompanying the standard provides illustrative examples of an income statement (see 3.2.2 below).

3.2.2   *Classification of expenses by nature or function*

IAS 1 states that components of financial performance may differ in terms of frequency, potential for gain or loss and predictability, and requires that expenses should be sub-classified to highlight this.[125] To achieve this, the standard requires the presentation of an analysis of expenses using a classification based on either the nature of expenses or their function within the entity, whichever provides information that is reliable and more relevant.[126] It is because each method of presentation has merit for different types of entities, that the standard requires management to select the most relevant and reliable presentation. As noted at 3.2.1 above IAS 1 encourages, but does not require the chosen analysis to be shown on the face of the income statement.[127] This means that entities are permitted to disclose the classification on the face on a mixed basis, as long as the required classification is provided in the notes.

The standard also notes that the choice between the function of expense method and the nature of expense method will depend on historical and industry factors and the nature of the entity. Both methods provide an indication of those costs that might vary, directly or indirectly, with the level of sales or production of the entity. However, because information on the nature of expenses is useful in predicting future cash flows, additional disclosure is required when the function of expense classification is used (see B below).[128]

A   *Analysis of expenses by nature*

For some entities, 'more reliable and relevant information' may be achieved by aggregating expenses for display in the income statement according to their nature (for example, depreciation, purchases of materials, transport costs, employee benefits and advertising costs), and not reallocating them among various functions within the entity. IAS 1 observes that this method may be simple to apply because no allocations of expenses to functional classifications are necessary. The standard illustrates a classification using the nature of expense method is as follows:

Example 3.3:   *Example of classification of expenses by nature*[129]

Revenue		×
Other income		×
Changes in inventories of finished goods and work in progress	×	
Raw materials and consumables used	×	
Employee benefits costs	×	
Depreciation and amortisation expense	×	
Other expenses	×	
Total expenses		(×)
Profit		×

The implementation guidance accompanying the standard provides a further example of an income statement analysing expenses by nature. Whilst very similar to the above, it is expanded to show further captions as follows:[130]

XYZ GROUP – INCOME STATEMENT FOR THE YEAR ENDED 31 DECEMBER 2005

(in thousands of Euro)

	2005	2004
Revenue	×	×
Other income	×	×
Changes in inventories of finished goods and work in progress	(×)	×
Work performed by the entity and capitalised	×	×
Raw material and consumables used	(×)	(×)
Employee benefits expense	(×)	(×)
Depreciation and amortisation expense	(×)	(×)
Impairment of property, plant and equipment	(×)	(×)
Other expenses	(×)	(×)
Finance costs	(×)	(×)
Share of profit of associates	×	×
Profit before tax	×	×
Income tax expense	(×)	(×)
Profit for the period	×	×
Attributable to:		
Equity holders of the parent	×	×
Minority interest	×	×
	×	×

The guidance observes that in an income statement in which expenses are classified by nature, an impairment of property, plant and equipment is shown as a separate line item. By contrast, if expenses are classified by function, the impairment is included in the function(s) to which it relates. The guidance also notes that the line item relating to associates means the share of associates' profit attributable to equity holders of the associates, i.e. it is after tax and minority interests in the associates.

B   Analysis of expenses by function

For some entities, 'more reliable and relevant information' may achieved by aggregating expenses for display in the income statement according to their function for example, as part of cost of sales, the costs of distribution or administrative activities. Under this method, IAS 1 requires as a minimum, disclosure of cost of sales separately from other expenses (although it does not specify whether this should be on the face of the statement or in the notes). The standard observes that this method can provide more relevant information to users than the classification of expenses by nature, but that allocating costs to functions may require arbitrary allocations and involve considerable judgement. Examples of classification using the function of expense method given by the standard are as follows:

Example 3.4:   *Example of classification by function[131]*

Revenue	×
Cost of sales	(×)
Gross profit	×
Other income	×
Distribution costs	(×)
Administrative expenses	(×)
Other expenses	(×)
Profit	×

The implementation guidance accompanying the standard provides a further example of an income statement analysing expenses by nature. Whilst very similar to the above, it is expanded to show further captions as follows.[132]

XYZ GROUP – INCOME STATEMENT FOR THE YEAR ENDED 31 DECEMBER 2005

(illustrating the classification of expenses by function)
(in thousands of Euros)

	2005	2004
Revenue	×	×
Cost of sales	(×)	(×)
Gross profit	×	×
Other income	×	×
Distribution costs	(×)	(×)
Administrative expenses	(×)	(×)
Other expenses	(×)	(×)
Finance costs	(×)	(×)
Share of profit of associates	×	×
Profit before tax	×	×
Income tax expense	(×)	(×)
Profit for the period	×	×
Attributable to:		
Equity holders of the parent	×	×
Minority interest	×	×
	×	×

The guidance notes that the line item relating to associates means the share of associates' profit attributable to equity holders of the associates, i.e. it is after tax and minority interests in the associates.

Entities classifying expenses by function are required by IAS 1 to disclose additional information on the nature of expenses, and this must include depreciation and amortisation expense and employee benefits expense.[133] This requirement of IAS 1 strikes us as unnecessary as the disclosure of these items (broken down into their components) is specifically required by IAS 16, IAS 19 and IAS 38.

3.2.3 Discontinued operations

As discussed at B below, IFRS 5 requires the presentation of a single amount on the face of the income statement relating to discontinued operations, with further analysis either on the face of the income statement or in the notes.

A   Definition of a discontinued operation

IFRS 5 defines a discontinued operation as 'a component of an entity that either has been disposed of, or is classified as held for sale, and

(a)   represents a separate major line of business or geographical area of operations;

(b)   is part of a single co-ordinated plan to dispose of a separate major line of business or geographical area of operations; or

(c)   is a subsidiary acquired exclusively with a view to resale.'[134]

Classification as held for sale is discussed at 5.1 below. For the purposes of the above definition, a 'component of an entity' is also defined by the standard as comprising 'operations and cash flows that can be clearly distinguished, operationally and for financial reporting purposes, from the rest of the entity. In other words, a component of an entity will have been a cash-generating unit or a group of cash-generating units while being held for use.'[135] IFRS 5 defines cash generating unit in the same way as IAS 36, that is as 'the smallest identifiable group of assets that generates cash inflows that are largely independent of the cash inflows from other assets or groups of assets.'[136] Cash generating units are discussed in Chapter 13.

It seems highly unlikely that this definition of a discontinued operation would ever be met by a single non-current asset. Accordingly, a discontinued operation will also be a 'disposal group' which is a group of assets to be disposed of, by sale or otherwise, together as a group in a single transaction, and liabilities directly associated with those assets that will be transferred in the transaction (discussed at 5.1.1 below). In our view, the definition of a discontinued operation is somewhat vague, and in particular much will depend on the interpretation of 'a separate major line of business or geographical area of business'. We think this will inevitably mean different things to different people, and that comparability in financial reporting will suffer as a result. However, it is only an interim measure. The IASB used this definition in preference to the one contained in SFAS 144, on the grounds that the size of the operation which would meet SFAS 144's definition was too small and that this was causing practical problems. Accordingly, the IASB 'intends to work with the FASB to arrive at a converged definition within a relatively short time'.[137]

As discussed at 5.1 below, IFRS 5 stipulates that a non-current asset (or disposal group) that is to be abandoned should not be classified as held for sale. This includes non-current assets (or disposal groups) that are to be used to the end of their economic life and non-current assets (or disposal groups) that are to be closed rather than sold. However, if the disposal group to be abandoned meets the criteria above for being a discontinued operation the standard requires it to be treated as such in the income statement and relevant notes 'at the date on which it ceases to be used'.[138] In other words, the treatment as discontinued in the income statement only starts in the period when abandonment actually occurs (see Example 3.5 below).

A non-current asset that has been temporarily taken out of use should not be accounted for as if it had been abandoned.[139] Accordingly it would not be disclosed as a discontinued operation. The standard illustrates a discontinued operation arising from abandonment with the following example.

Example 3.5:   Discontinued operation arising from abandonment[140]

In October 2005 an entity decides to abandon all of its cotton mills, which constitute a major line of business. All work stops at the cotton mills during the year ended 31 December 2006. In the financial statements for the year ended 31 December 2005, results and cash flows of the cotton mills are treated as continuing operations. In the financial statements for the year ended 31 December 2006, the results and cash flows of the cotton mills are treated as discontinued operations and the entity makes the disclosures required (see B below).

B   *Presentation of discontinued operations*

IFRS 5 requires the presentation of a single amount on the face of the income statement comprising:

(a)   the post-tax profit or loss of discontinued operations; and

(b)   the post-tax gain or loss recognised on the measurement to fair value less costs to sell or on the disposal of the assets or disposal group(s) constituting the discontinued operation.[141]

This single amount should be further analysed (either on the face of the income statement or in the notes) into:

(a)   the revenue, expenses and pre-tax profit or loss of discontinued operations;

(b)   the gain or loss recognised on the measurement to fair value less costs to sell or on the disposal of the assets or disposal group(s) constituting the discontinued operation; and

(c)   separately for each of (a) and (b) the related income tax expense as required IAS 12 (see Chapter 24).

The analysis is not required for disposal groups that are newly acquired subsidiaries that meet the criteria to be classified as held for sale on acquisition (see 5.2.2 below).[142]

If the required analysis is presented on the face of the income statement it should be presented in a section identified as relating to discontinued operations, i.e. separately from continuing operations. One possibility would be a columnar approach. The standard also makes clear that any gain or loss on the remeasurement of a non-current asset (or disposal group) classified as held for sale that does not meet the definition of a discontinued operation should not be included within these amounts for discontinued operations, but be included in profit or loss from continuing operations.[143]

IFRS 5 requires that these disclosures be re-presented for prior periods presented in the financial statements so that the disclosures relate to all operations that have been discontinued by the balance sheet date for the latest period presented.[144] Accordingly, adjustments to the comparative information as originally reported will be necessary for those disposal groups categorised as discontinued operations. Comparative information relating to discontinued operations is discussed further at 5.3 below.

The implementation guidance accompanying IFRS 5 provides the following illustration of the presentation of discontinued operations.

Example 3.6:   *Presenting discontinued operations*[145]

XYZ GROUP – INCOME STATEMENT FOR THE YEAR ENDED31 DECEMBER 2005
(illustrating the classification of expenses by function)

(in thousands of Euros)

	2005	2004
Continuing operations		
Revenue	×	×
Cost of sales	(×)	(×)
Gross profit	×	×
Other income	×	×
Distribution costs	(×)	(×)
Administrative expenses	(×)	(×)
Other expenses	(×)	(×)
Finance costs	(×)	(×)
Share of profit of associates	×	×
Profit before tax	×	×
Income tax expense	(×)	(×)
Profit for the period from continuing operations	×	×
Discontinued operations		
Profit for the period from discontinued operations*	×	×
Profit for the period	×	×
Attributable to:		
Equity holders of the parent	×	×
Minority interest	×	×
	×	×

*   The required analysis would be given in the notes.

Adjustments in the current period to amounts previously presented in discontinued operations that are directly related to the disposal of a discontinued operation in a prior period should be classified separately in discontinued operations. The nature and amount of the adjustments should be disclosed. Examples given by the standard of circumstances in which these adjustments may arise include the following:

(a)   the resolution of uncertainties that arise from the terms of the disposal transaction, such as the resolution of purchase price adjustments and indemnification issues with the purchaser;

(b)   the resolution of uncertainties that arise from and are directly related to the operations of the component before its disposal, such as environmental and product warranty obligations retained by the seller; and

(c)   the settlement of employee benefit plan obligations, provided that the settlement is directly related to the disposal transaction.[146]

In addition, IFRS 5 requires disclosure of the net cash flows attributable to the operating, investing and financing activities of discontinued operations. The standard allows that these disclosures may be presented either in the notes or on the face of the financial statements. It isn't readily clear what 'on the face of the financial statements' is intended to mean, but it seems likely that this data would be presented on the face of the cash flow statement. These disclosures are not required for disposal groups that are newly acquired subsidiaries that meet the criteria to be classified as held for sale on acquisition (see 5.2.2 below).[147]

3.2.4   *Material, exceptional and extraordinary items*

A   *Exceptional or material items*

IAS 1 does not use the phrase exceptional items. However, it does require that when items of income and expense are material, their nature and amount should be disclosed separately.[148] Materiality is discussed at 4.1.5 A below. The standard goes on to suggest that circumstances that would give rise to the separate disclosure of items of income and expense include:

(a)   write-downs of inventories to net realisable value or of property, plant and equipment to recoverable amount, as well as reversals of such write-downs;

(b)   restructurings of the activities of an entity and reversals of any provisions for the costs of restructuring;

(c)   disposals of items of property, plant and equipment;

(d)   disposals of investments;

(e)   discontinued operations;

(f)   litigation settlements; and

(g)   other reversals of provisions.[149]

IAS 1 is silent as to whether this disclosure is required on the face of the income statement or in the notes. Given the permissive approach taken to the format of the income statement discussed above, the level of prominence given to such items is left to the judgement of the entity concerned.

B   *Ordinary activities and extraordinary items*

There is a certain amount of tension (or at least of ongoing evolution) in the IFRS literature concerning results from ordinary activities, and in particular the categorisation of certain items as falling outwith them – that is extraordinary items.

The IASB's *Framework* seems to consider the distinction a useful one, and states 'Income and expenses may be presented in the income statement in different ways so as to provide information that is relevant for economic decision-making. For example, it is common practice to distinguish between those items of income and expenses that arise in the course of the ordinary activities of the enterprise and those that do not. This distinction is made on the basis that the source of an item is relevant in evaluating the ability of the enterprise to generate cash and cash equivalents in the future; for example, incidental activities such as the disposal of a long-term investment are unlikely to recur on a regular basis. When distinguishing between items in this way consideration needs to be given to the nature of the enterprise and its operations. Items that arise from the ordinary activities of one enterprise may be unusual in respect of another.'[150] This was reflected in the requirement in IAS 8 to present this distinction on the face of the income statement supported by a definition of ordinary activities and extraordinary items.[151]

The IASB's improvements project took a different view of the ordinary/extraordinary distinction, perhaps due to a feeling that it was being abused. The 'improved' IAS 1 and IAS 8 prohibit entities making this distinction, IAS 1 now stating that an entity 'shall not present any items of income and expense as extraordinary items, either on the face of the income statement or in the notes.'[152] Also, definitions of ordinary activities and extraordinary items have been removed. The IASB explains its decision to eliminate the concept of extraordinary items as follows 'The Board decided that items treated as extraordinary result from the normal business risks faced by an entity and do not warrant presentation in a separate component of the income statement. The nature or function of a transaction or other event, rather than its frequency, should determine its presentation within the income statement. Items currently classified as 'extraordinary' are only a subset of the items of income and expense that may warrant disclosure to assist users in predicting an entity's future performance.'[153]

We do not expect that the changes will have any real impact on the prominence given to items in the income statement and the earnings measures which entities choose to focus on when discussing their performance. This is because the whole approach to the content and layout of the income statement is permissive. Certain items must be shown on the face, yet the order of them and their captions are left to the judgement of the entity. Furthermore, additional items can (indeed, must) be introduced where necessary. Against that backdrop banning extraordinary items seems to us like mere semantics.

3.3 The statement of changes in equity

The net assets of an entity (its equity) can change for various reasons, principally income and expenses reported in the income statement and the introduction by or return of capital to shareholders, although in addition some items of income and expense are required to bypass the income statement.

IAS 1 requires all items of income and expense recognised in a period to be included in profit or loss unless another standard or an interpretation requires otherwise (discussed at 4.1.6 below).[154] Other standards require some gains and losses (such as revaluation increases and decreases, particular foreign exchange differences, gains or losses on remeasuring available-for-sale financial assets, and related amounts of current tax and deferred tax) to be recognised directly as changes in equity. The standard asserts that, because it is important to consider all items of income and expense in assessing changes in an entity's financial position between two balance sheet dates, the presentation of a statement of changes in equity is required that highlights an entity's total income and expenses, including those that are recognised directly in equity.[155] Accordingly, IAS 1 requires the presentation of a statement of changes in equity showing on the face of the statement:

(a) profit or loss for the period;

(b) each item of income and expense for the period that, as required by other standards or by interpretations, is recognised directly in equity, and the total of these items;

(c) total income and expense for the period (calculated as the sum of (a) and (b)), showing separately the total amounts attributable to equity holders of the parent and to minority interest; and

(d) for each component of equity, the effects of changes in accounting policies and corrections of errors recognised in accordance with IAS 8 (discussed at 4.4 and 4.6 below).[156]

Items (a) to (c) above reflect the focus of the IASB on the balance sheet – whereby any changes in net assets (aside of those arising from transactions with shareholders) are gains and losses, regarded as performance. In this vein, IAS 1 observes that changes in an entity's equity between two balance sheet dates reflect the increase or decrease in its net assets during the period. Except for changes resulting from transactions with equity holders acting in their capacity as equity holders (such as equity contributions, reacquisitions of the entity's own equity instruments and dividends) and transaction costs directly related to such transactions, the overall change in equity during a period represents the total amount of income and expenses, including gains and losses, generated by the entity's activities during that period (whether those items of income and expenses are recognised in profit or loss or directly as changes in equity).[157]

After taking account of total gains and losses in this way, any other changes in equity will result from either:

- the restatement of prior periods; or
- transactions with owners in their capacity as such.

Point (d) above reflects the first of these. IAS 8 requires retrospective adjustments to effect changes in accounting policies, to the extent practicable, except when the transitional provisions in another standard or an interpretation require otherwise. IAS 8 also requires that restatements to correct errors are made retrospectively, to the extent practicable. Retrospective adjustments and retrospective restatements should be made to the balance of retained earnings, except when a standard or an interpretation requires retrospective adjustment of another component of equity. Point (d) above therefore requires disclosure in the statement of changes in equity of the total adjustment to each component of equity resulting, separately, from changes in accounting policies and from corrections of errors. These adjustments should be disclosed for each prior period and the beginning of the period.[158]

At this point, entities have a choice as regards the second bullet above. IAS 1 requires the presentation either on the face of the statement of changes in equity or in the notes of:

(a)   the amounts of transactions with equity holders acting in their capacity as equity holders, showing separately distributions to equity holders (although, as noted at 3.2.1 above, distributions may be presented on the face of the income statement);

(b)   the balance of retained earnings (i.e. accumulated profit or loss) at the beginning of the period and at the balance sheet date, and the changes during the period; and

(c)   a reconciliation between the carrying amount of each class of contributed equity and each reserve at the beginning and the end of the period, separately disclosing each change.[159]

The standard notes that the above requirements may be met in various ways. One example would be a columnar format that reconciles the opening and closing balances of each element within equity on the face of the statement. An alternative would be to present the items set out (a) to (c) above in the notes.[160] In other words, the statement of changes in equity could be left as a kind of 'performance statement' excluding transactions with owners, or it could be presented as a combined statement of all changes in equity.

The implementation guidance accompanying the IAS 1 provides two illustrations of how its requirements could be met reflecting the two choices described above.

First, the full reconciliation of each component of equity in a columnar format is illustrated as follows.

Example 3.7: *Combined statement of all changes in equity.*[161]

XYZ GROUP – STATEMENT OF CHANGES IN EQUITY FOR THE YEAR ENDED 31 DECEMBER 2005

(in thousands of Euros)

	Attributable to equity holders of the parent					Minority interest	Total equity
	Share capital	Other reserves*	Trans-lation reserve	Retained earnings	Total	Minority interest	Total equity
Balance at 31 December 2003	×	×	(×)	×	×	×	×
Changes in accounting policy				(×)	(×)	(×)	(×)
Restated balance	×	×	(×)	×	×	×	×
Changes in equity for 2004							
Gain on property revaluation		×			×	×	×
Available-for-sale investments:							
Valuation gains/(losses) taken to equity		(×)			(×)		(×)
Transferred to profit or loss on sale		(×)			(×)		(×)
Cash flow hedges:							
Gains/(losses) taken to equity		×			×	×	×
Transferred to profit or loss for the period		×			×	×	×
Transferred to initial carrying amount of hedged items		(×)			(×)		(×)
Exchange differences on translating foreign operations			(×)		(×)	(×)	(×)
Tax on items taken directly to or transferred from equity		(×)	×		(×)	(×)	(×)
Net income recognised directly in equity		×	(×)		×	×	×
Profit for the period				×	×	×	×
Total recognised income and expense for the period		×	(×)	×	×	×	×
Dividends				(×)	(×)	(×)	(×)
Issue of share capital	×				×		×
Equity share options issued		×			×		×
Balance at 31 December 2004 carried forward	×	×	(×)	×	×	×	×

XYZ GROUP – STATEMENT OF CHANGES IN EQUITY FOR THE YEAR ENDED 31 DECEMBER 2005 (continued)

(in thousands of Euros)

	Share capital	Other reserves*	Trans- lation reserve	Retained earnings	Total	Minority interest	Total equity
Balance at 31 December 2004 brought forward	×	×	(×)	×	×	×	×
Changes in equity for 2005							
Loss on property revaluation		(×)			(×)	(×)	(×)
Available-for-sale investments:							
Valuation gains/(losses) taken to equity		(×)			(×)		(×)
Transferred to profit or loss on sale		×			×		×
Cash flow hedges:							
Gains/(losses) taken to equity		×			×	×	×
Transferred to profit or loss for the period		(×)			(×)	(×)	(×)
Transferred to initial carrying amount of hedged items		(×)			(×)		(×)
Exchange differences on translating foreign operations			(×)		(×)	(×)	(×)
Tax on items taken directly to or transferred from equity		×	×		×	×	×
Net income recognised directly in equity		(×)	(×)		(×)	(×)	(×)
Profit for the period				×	×	×	×
Total recognised income and expense for the period		(×)	(×)	×	×	×	×
Dividends				(×)	(×)	(×)	(×)
Issue of share capital	×				×		×
Balance at 31 December 2005	×	×	(×)	×	×	×	×

*   Other reserves are analysed into their components, if material.

Second, the guidance illustrates a statement of recognised income and expense as follows.

Example 3.8:   Statement of recognised income and expense[162]

XYZ GROUP – STATEMENT OF RECOGNISED INCOME AND EXPENSE FOR THE YEAR ENDED 31 DECEMBER 2005

(in thousands of Euro)

	2005	2004
Gain/(loss) on revaluation of properties	(×)	×
Available-for-sale investments:		
Valuation gains/(losses) taken to equity	(×)	(×)
Transferred to profit or loss on sale	×	(×)
Cash flow hedges:		
Gains/(losses) taken to equity	×	×
Transferred to profit or loss for the period	(×)	×
Transferred to the initial carrying amount of hedged items	(×)	(×)
Exchange differences on translation of foreign operations	(×)	(×)
Tax on items taken directly to or transferred from equity	×	(×)
Net income recognised directly in equity	(×)	×
Profit for the period	×	×
Total recognised income and expense for the period	×	×
Attributable to:		
Equity holders of the parent	×	×
Minority interest	×	×
	×	×
Effect of changes in accounting policy:		
Equity holders of the parent		(×)
Minority interest		(×)
		(×)

This example illustrates an approach that presents changes in equity representing income and expense in a separate component of the financial statements. Under this approach, a reconciliation of opening and closing balances of share capital, reserves and accumulated profit would be given in the notes.

As discussed in Chapter 30 at 10.2.1, the IASB are proposing to change IAS 19 to allow entities choosing to recognise actuarial gains and losses immediately to do so outside of profit and loss. In that case, the proposals would require a statement of recognised income and expense as illustrated in Example 3.8 above.

3.4   The notes to the financial statements

IAS 1 requires the presentation of notes to the financial statements that:

(a)   present information about the basis of preparation of the financial statements and the specific accounting policies used (see 6.1 below);

(b)   disclose the information required by IFRSs that is not presented on the face of the balance sheet, income statement, statement of changes in equity or cash flow statement; and

(c)   provide additional information that is not presented on the face of the balance sheet, income statement, statement of changes in equity or cash flow statement, but is relevant to an understanding of any of them.[163]

An example of information under (c) relates to service concession agreements. SIC-29 sets out some detailed requirements for the type of disclosures required for such arrangements to satisfy the requirement of IAS 1. This is discussed in Chapter 27.

The notes should, as far as practicable, be presented in a systematic manner. Each item on the face of the balance sheet, income statement, statement of changes in equity and cash flow statement should be cross-referenced to any related information in the notes.[164]

The notes are normally be presented in the following order, which is intended to assist users in understanding the financial statements and comparing them with financial statements of other entities:

(a)   a statement of compliance with IFRSs (see 6.1 below);

(b)   a summary of significant accounting policies applied (see 6.1 below);

(c)   supporting information for items presented on the face of the balance sheet, income statement, statement of changes in equity and cash flow statement, in the order in which each statement and each line item is presented; and

(d)   other disclosures, including:

(i)   contingent liabilities (discussed in Chapter 25) and unrecognised contractual commitments; and

(ii)   non-financial disclosures, e.g. the entity's financial risk management objectives and policies (discussed in Chapter 20).[165]

However, the standard allows that notes providing information about the basis of preparation of the financial statements and specific accounting policies may be presented as a separate component of the financial statements.[166]

Although the above represents the normal arrangement of the notes, in some circumstances it may be necessary or desirable to vary the ordering of specific items within the notes. An example given by the standard is that information on changes in fair value recognised in profit or loss may be combined with information on maturities of financial instruments, although the former disclosures relate to the income statement and the latter relate to the balance sheet. Nevertheless, a systematic structure for the notes should be retained as far as practicable.[167]

4   ACCOUNTING POLICIES

The selection and application of accounting policies is obviously crucial in the preparation of financial statements. As a general premise, the whole purpose of accounting standards is to specify required accounting policies, presentation and disclosure. However, judgement will always remain; many standards may allow choices to accommodate different views, and no body of accounting literature could hope to prescribe precise treatments for all possible situations.

In the broadest sense, accounting policies are discussed by both IAS 1 and IAS 8. Whilst, as its title suggest, IAS 8 deals explicitly with accounting policies, IAS 1 deals with what one might describe as overarching or general principles.

4.1   General principles

IAS 1 deals with some general principles relating to accounting policies, with IAS 8 discussing the detail of selection and application of individual accounting policies and their disclosure.

The general principles discussed by IAS 1 can be described as follows:

- fair presentation and compliance with accounting standards;
- going concern;
- the accrual basis of accounting;
- consistency;
- materiality and aggregation;
- offsetting; and
- profit or loss for the period.

These are discussed in the sections that follow.

4.1.1   Fair presentation

A   Fair presentation and compliance with IFRS

Consistent with its objective and statement of the purpose of financial statements, IAS 1 requires that financial statements present fairly the financial position, financial performance and cash flows of an entity. Fair presentation for these purposes requires the faithful representation of the effects of transactions, other events and conditions in accordance with the definitions and recognition criteria for assets, liabilities, income and expenses set out in the Framework (discussed in Chapter 2).

The main premise of the standard is that application of IFRSs, with additional disclosure when necessary, is presumed to result in financial statements that achieve a fair presentation.[168] As noted at 1.1.2 above, an important point here is that implementation guidance for standards issued by the IASB does not form part of those standards, and therefore does not contain requirements for financial statements.[169] Accordingly, the often voluminous implementation guidance accompanying standards is not, strictly speaking, part of 'IFRS'. We would generally be surprised, though, at entities not following such guidance without valid reason.

The presumption that application of IFRS (with any necessary additional disclosure) results in a fair presentation is potentially rebuttable, as discussed at B below.

To reflect this presumption, as discussed at 2.3.3 above, the standard requires an explicit and unreserved statement of compliance to be included in the notes. A fair presentation also requires an entity to:

(a)   select and apply accounting policies in accordance with IAS 8, which also sets out a hierarchy of authoritative guidance that should be considered in the absence of a standard or an interpretation that specifically applies to an item;

(b)   present information, including accounting policies, in a manner that provides relevant, reliable, comparable and understandable information; and

(c)   provide additional disclosures when compliance with the specific requirements in IFRSs is insufficient to enable users to understand the impact of particular transactions, other events and conditions on the entity's financial position and financial performance.[170]

However, the standard makes clear that inappropriate accounting policies are not rectified either by disclosure of the accounting policies used or by notes or explanatory material.[171] We support this position, however the IASB has (admittedly only in rare situations) essentially delegated standard setting to the authors of 'relevant regulatory frameworks' in this regard. As discussed at B below, it is possible that a rare circumstance arises where departure from a provision of IFRS is needed to achieve fair presentation. This is only allowed by IAS 1, however, if permitted by such a regulatory framework. If it is not, then it seems the fairest presentation politically possible for the IASB is indeed achieved through additional disclosure in the face of inappropriate accounting policies.

B   The fair presentation override

The presumption that the application of IFRSs, with additional disclosure when necessary, results in financial statements that achieve a fair presentation is a rebutabble one, although the standard makes clear that in virtually all situations a fair presentation is achieved through compliance.[172]

The standard observes that an item of information would conflict with the objective of financial statements when it does not represent faithfully the transactions, other events and conditions that it either purports to represent or could reasonably be expected to represent and, consequently, it would be likely to influence economic decisions made by users of financial statements. When assessing whether complying with a specific requirement in a standard or an interpretation would be so misleading that it would conflict with the objective of financial statements, IAS 1 requires consideration of:

(a)   why the objective of financial statements is not achieved in the particular circumstances; and

(b)   how the entity's circumstances differ from those of other entities that comply with the requirement. If other entities in similar circumstances comply with the requirement, there is a rebuttable presumption that the entity's compliance with the requirement would not be so misleading that it would conflict with the objective of financial statements.[173]

In the extremely rare circumstances in which management concludes that compliance with a requirement in a standard or an interpretation would be so misleading that it would conflict with the objective of financial statements, IAS 1 requires departure from that requirement. However, this is only permitted if the 'relevant regulatory framework requires, or otherwise does not prohibit, such a departure', which is discussed further below.[174]

When the relevant regulatory framework allows a departure, an entity should make it and also disclose:

(a)   that management has concluded that the financial statements present fairly the entity's financial position, financial performance and cash flows;

(b)   that it has complied with applicable standards and interpretations, except that it has departed from a particular requirement to achieve a fair presentation;

(c)   the title of the standard or interpretation from which the entity has departed, the nature of the departure, including:

　　(i)   the treatment that the standard or interpretation would require,

　　(ii)   the reason why that treatment would be so misleading in the circumstances that it would conflict with the objective of financial statements set out in the Framework; and

　　(iii)   the treatment adopted;

(d)   for each period presented, the financial impact of the departure on each item in the financial statements that would have been reported in complying with the requirement; and

(e)   when there has been a departure from a requirement of a standard or an interpretation in a prior period, and that departure affects the amounts recognised in the financial statements for the current period, the disclosures set out in (c) and (d) above.[175]

Regarding (e) above, the standard explains that the requirement could apply, for example, when an entity departed in a prior period from a requirement in a standard or an interpretation for the measurement of assets or liabilities and that departure affects the measurement of changes in assets and liabilities recognised in the current period's financial statements.[176]

When the relevant regulatory framework does not allow a departure from IFRS, IAS 1 accepts that, notwithstanding the failure to achieve fair presentation, that it should not be made. Although intended to occur only in extremely rare circumstances, this is a very important provision of the standard as it allows a 'relevant regulatory framework' to override a requirement of IFRS which is specifically necessary to achieve a fair presentation. In that light, it is perhaps surprising that there is no definition or discussion in the standard of just what a relevant regulatory framework may be.

Deferring to regulators in this way strikes us as political expediency. The most likely explanation for it in our view is that the relevant regulatory framework is most likely to be the source of the original requirement for an entity to comply with IFRS in the first place. On that basis, the Board may well have taken the view that overall compliance with IFRS in that jurisdiction would be enhanced by allowing the regulator to ban the fair presentation override.

When a departure otherwise required by IAS 1 is not allowed by the relevant regulatory framework, the standard requires that the perceived misleading aspects of compliance are reduced, to the maximum extent possible, by the disclosure of:

(a)   the title of the standard or interpretation in question, the nature of the requirement, and the reason why management has concluded that complying with that requirement is so misleading in the circumstances that it conflicts with the objective of financial statements set out in the Framework; and

(b)   for each period presented, the adjustments to each item in the financial statements that management has concluded would be necessary to achieve a fair presentation.[177]

Overall, this strikes us as a fairly uncomfortable compromise, as it involves:

- the entity stating publicly that it considers its financial statements fail to achieve a fair presentation;

- the IASB essentially allowing unspecified regulators to overrule it; and

- an accounting standard that contradicts itself.

However, the rule is reasonably clear and in our view such a circumstance will indeed be a rare one.

4.1.2   *Going concern*

When preparing financial statements, IAS 1 requires management to make an assessment of an entity's ability to continue as a going concern. This term is not defined, but its meaning is implicit in the requirement of the standard that financial statements should be prepared on a going concern basis unless management either intends to liquidate the entity or to cease trading, or has no realistic alternative but to do so. The standard goes on to require that when management is aware, in making its assessment, of material uncertainties related to events or conditions that may cast significant doubt upon the entity's ability to continue as a going concern, those uncertainties shall be disclosed. When financial statements are not prepared on a going concern basis, that fact should be disclosed, together with the basis on which the financial statements are prepared and the reason why the entity is not regarded as a going concern.[178]

In assessing whether the going concern assumption is appropriate, the standard requires that all available information about the future, which is at least, but is not limited to, twelve months from the balance sheet date should be taken into account. The degree of consideration required will depend on the facts in each case. When an entity has a history of profitable operations and ready access to financial resources, a conclusion that the going concern basis of accounting is appropriate may be reached without detailed analysis. In other cases, management may need to consider a wide range of factors relating to current and expected profitability, debt repayment schedules and potential sources of replacement financing before it can satisfy itself that the going concern basis is appropriate.[179]

There is no guidance in the standard concerning what impact there should be on the financial statements if it is determined that the going concern basis is not appropriate. Accordingly, entities will need to consider carefully their individual circumstances to arrive at an appropriate basis.

4.1.3   *The accrual basis of accounting*

IAS 1 requires that financial statements be prepared, except for cash flow information, using the accrual basis of accounting.[180] No definition of this is given by the standard, but an explanation is presented that 'When the accrual basis of accounting is used, items are recognised as assets, liabilities, equity, income and expenses (the elements of financial statements) when they satisfy the definitions and recognition criteria for those elements in the Framework.'[181]

The Framework itself is a little more helpful, explaining the accruals basis as follows. 'Under this basis, the effects of transactions and other events are recognised when they occur (and not as cash or its equivalent is received or paid) and they are recorded in the accounting records and reported in the financial statements of the periods to which they relate. Financial statements prepared on the accrual basis inform users not only of past transactions involving the payment and receipt of cash but also of obligations to pay cash in the future and of resources that represent cash to be received in the future. Hence, they provide the type of information about past transactions and other events that is most useful to users in making economic decisions.'[182]

The requirements of the framework are discussed in more detail in Chapter 2.

4.1.4   *Consistency*

As noted at 1.1.2 and 1.2.2 above, one of the objectives of both IAS 1 and IAS 8 is to ensure the comparability of financial statements with those of previous periods. To this end, each standard addresses the principle of consistency.

IAS 1 requires that the 'presentation and classification' of items in the financial statements be retained from one period to the next unless:

(a)   it is apparent, following a significant change in the nature of the entity's operations or a review of its financial statements, that another presentation or classification would be more appropriate having regard to the criteria for the selection and application of accounting policies in IAS 8 (see 4.3 below); or

(b)   a standard or an interpretation requires a change in presentation.[183]

The standard goes on to amplify this by explaining that a significant acquisition or disposal, or a review of the presentation of the financial statements, might suggest that the financial statements need to be presented differently. An entity should change the presentation of its financial statements only if the changed presentation provides information that is reliable and is more relevant to users of the financial statements and the revised structure is likely to continue, so that comparability is not impaired. When making such changes in presentation, an entity will need to reclassify its comparative information as discussed at 2.4 above.[184]

IAS 8 addresses consistency of accounting policies and observes that users of financial statements need to be able to compare the financial statements of an entity over time to identify trends in its financial position, financial performance and cash flows. For this reason, the same accounting policies need to be applied within each period and from one period to the next unless a change in accounting policy meets certain criteria (changes in accounting policy are discussed at 4.4 below).[185] Accordingly, the standard requires that accounting policies be selected and applied consistently for similar transactions, other events and conditions, unless a standard or an interpretation specifically requires or permits categorisation of items for which different policies may be appropriate. If a standard or an interpretation requires or permits such categorisation, an appropriate accounting policy should be selected and applied consistently to each category.[186]

4.1.5   Materiality, aggregation and offset

A   Materiality and aggregation

Financial statements result from processing large numbers of transactions or other events that are aggregated into classes according to their nature or function. The final stage in the process of aggregation and classification is the presentation of condensed and classified data, which form line items on the face of the balance sheet, income statement, statement of changes in equity and cash flow statement, or in the notes.[187] The extent of aggregation versus detailed analysis is clearly a judgemental one, with either extreme eroding the usefulness of the information.

IAS 1 resolves this issue with the concept of materiality, by requiring:

- each material class of similar items to be presented separately in the financial statements; and

- items of a dissimilar nature or function to be presented separately unless they are immaterial.[188]

Materiality is defined by both IAS 1 and IAS 8 as follows. 'Omissions or misstatements of items are material if they could, individually or collectively, influence the economic decisions of users taken on the basis of the financial statements. Materiality depends on the size and nature of the omission or misstatement judged in the surrounding circumstances. The size or nature of the item, or a combination of both, could be the determining factor.'[189] At a general level, applying the concept of materiality means that a specific disclosure requirement in a standard or an interpretation need not be satisfied if the information is not material.[190]

IAS 1 and IAS 8 go on to observe that assessing whether an omission or misstatement could influence economic decisions of users, and so be material, requires consideration of the characteristics of those users. For these purposes users are assumed to have a reasonable knowledge of business and economic activities and accounting and a willingness to study the information with reasonable diligence. Therefore, the assessment of materiality needs to take into account how users with such attributes could reasonably be expected to be influenced in making economic decisions.[191]

Regarding the presentation of financial statements, IAS 1 requires that if a line item is not individually material, it should be aggregated with other items either on the face of those statements or in the notes. The standard also states that an item that is not sufficiently material to warrant separate presentation on the face of those statements may nevertheless be sufficiently material for it to be presented separately in the notes.[192]

B   Offset

IAS 1 considers it important that assets and liabilities, and income and expenses, are reported separately. This is because offsetting in the income statement or the balance sheet, except when offsetting reflects the substance of the transaction or other event, detracts from the ability of users both to understand the transactions, other events and conditions that have occurred and to assess the entity's future cash flows. It clarifies, though, that measuring assets net of valuation allowances – for example, obsolescence allowances on inventories and doubtful debts allowances on receivables – is not offsetting.[193]

Accordingly, IAS 1 requires that assets and liabilities, and income and expenses, should not be offset unless required or permitted by a standard or an interpretation.[194]

Just what constitutes offsetting, particularly given the rider noted above of 'reflecting the substance of the transaction' is not always obvious. IAS 1 expands on its meaning as follows. It notes that:

(a)   IAS 18 – *Revenue* – defines revenue and requires it to be measured at the fair value of the consideration received or receivable, taking into account the amount of any trade discounts and volume rebates allowed by the entity – in other words a notional 'gross' turnover and a discount should not be shown separately, but should be offset;

(b)   entities can undertake, in the course of their ordinary activities, other transactions that do not generate revenue but are incidental to the main revenue-generating activities. The results of such transactions should be presented, when this presentation reflects the substance of the transaction or other event, by netting any income with related expenses arising on the same transaction. For example:

(i)   gains and losses on the disposal of non-current assets, including investments and operating assets, should be reported by deducting from the proceeds on disposal the carrying amount of the asset and related selling expenses; and

(ii)   expenditure related to a provision that is recognised in accordance with IAS 37 – *Provisions, Contingent Liabilities and Contingent Assets* – and reimbursed under a contractual arrangement with a third party (for example, a supplier's warranty agreement) may be netted against the related reimbursement;[195] and

(c)   gains and losses arising from a group of similar transactions should be reported on a net basis, for example, foreign exchange gains and losses or gains and losses arising on financial instruments held for trading. However, such gains and losses should be reported separately if they are material.[196]

4.1.6   Profit or loss for the period

The final provision of IAS 1 which we term a general principle is a very important one. It is that, unless a standard or an interpretation requires otherwise, all items of income and expense recognised in a period should be included in profit or loss.[197]

Income and expense are not defined by the standard, but they are defined by the Framework as follows:

(a)   income is increases in economic benefits during the accounting period in the form of inflows or enhancements of assets or decreases of liabilities that result in increases in equity, other than those relating to contributions from equity participants; and

(b)   expenses are decreases in economic benefits during the accounting period in the form of outflows or depletions of assets or incurrences of liabilities that result in decreases in equity, other than those relating to distributions to equity participants.[198]

This clearly indicates to us that the terms do not have what many would consider their natural meaning, as they encompass all gains and losses (for example, capital appreciation in a non-current asset like property). As discussed in Chapter 2, how to present financial performance, including all gains and losses, is currently being debated by the Board and key to this is the meaning of an income statement. As things stand now, there is a somewhat awkward compromise with various gains and losses either required or permitted to bypass the income statement and be reported directly in equity.

IAS 1 notes that normally, all items of income and expense recognised in a period are included in profit or loss, and that this includes the effects of changes in accounting estimates. However, circumstances may exist when particular items may be excluded from profit or loss for the current period. IAS 8 deals with two such circumstances: the correction of errors and the effect of changes in accounting policies (discussed at 4.4 and 4.6 below).[199] Other standards deal with items that may meet the Framework's definitions of income or expense but are usually excluded from profit or loss. Examples include revaluation surpluses (discussed in Chapter 12), particular gains and losses arising on translating the financial statements of a foreign operation (discussed in Chapter 9) and gains or losses on remeasuring available-for-sale financial assets (discussed in Chapter 18).[200]

4.2   The distinction between accounting policies and accounting estimates

IAS 8 defines accounting policies as 'the specific principles, bases, conventions, rules and practices applied by an entity in preparing and presenting financial statements'.[201] In particular, IAS 8 considers a change in 'measurement basis' to be a change in accounting policy (rather than a change in estimate).[202] Although not a defined term, IAS 1 (when requiring disclosure of them) gives examples of measurement bases as follows:

- historical cost;
- current cost;
- net realisable value;
- fair value; and
- recoverable amount.[203]

'Accounting estimates' is not a term defined directly by the standards. However, it is indirectly defined by the definition in IAS 8 of a change in an accounting estimate as follows. A change in accounting estimate is an adjustment of the carrying amount of an asset or a liability, or the amount of the periodic consumption of an asset, that results from the assessment of the present status of, and expected future benefits and obligations associated with, assets and liabilities. Changes in accounting estimates result from new information or new developments and, accordingly, are not corrections of errors.[204] Examples given by the IASB are estimates of bad debts and the estimated useful life of, or the expected pattern of consumption of the future economic benefits embodied in, a depreciable asset.[205]

The standard also notes that corrections of errors should be distinguished from changes in accounting estimates. Accounting estimates by their nature are approximations that may need revision as additional information becomes known. For example, the gain or loss recognised on the outcome of a contingency is not the correction of an error.[206]

The distinction between an accounting policy and an accounting estimate is particularly important because a very different treatment is required when there are changes in accounting policies or accounting estimates (discussed at 4.4 and 4.5 below). When it is difficult to distinguish a change in an accounting policy from a change in an accounting estimate, IAS 8 requires the change to be treated as a change in an accounting estimate.[207]

4.3   The selection and application of accounting policies

Entities complying with IFRS (which is a defined term, discussed at 1.1.2 above) do not have a free hand in selecting accounting policies, indeed the very purpose of a body of accounting literature is to confine such choices.

IFRS set out accounting policies that the IASB has concluded result in financial statements containing relevant and reliable information about the transactions, other events and conditions to which they apply.[208]

To this end, IAS 8's starting point is that when a standard or an interpretation specifically applies to a transaction, other event or condition, the accounting policy or policies applied to that item should be determined by applying the standard or interpretation and considering any relevant implementation guidance issued by the IASB for the standard or interpretation.[209] This draws out the distinction that IFRS must be *applied* whereas implementation guidance (which, as discussed at 1.1.2 above, is not part of IFRS) must be *considered*. As noted earlier, though, we would generally be surprised at entities not following such guidance without good reason.

Those policies need not be applied when the effect of applying them is immaterial. However, it is inappropriate to make, or leave uncorrected, immaterial departures from IFRSs to achieve a particular presentation of an entity's financial position, financial performance or cash flows.[210] The concept of materiality is discussed at 4.1.5 above.

There will be circumstances where a particular event, transaction or other condition is not specifically addressed by IFRS. When this is the case, IAS 8 sets out a hierarchy of guidance to be considered in the selection of an accounting policy.

The primary requirement of the standard is that management should use its judgement in developing and applying an accounting policy that results in information that is:

(a)   relevant to the economic decision-making needs of users; and

(b)   reliable, in that the financial statements:

   (i)   represent faithfully the financial position, financial performance and cash flows of the entity;

   (ii)   reflect the economic substance of transactions, other events and conditions, and not merely the legal form;

   (iii)   are neutral, i.e. free from bias;

   (iv)   are prudent; and

   (v)   are complete in all material respects.[211]

There is, in our view, clearly a tension between (b) (iii) and (b) (iv) above. Prudence and neutrality are not defined or otherwise discussed by IAS 8. However, the Framework discusses them and goes some way to addressing this tension as follows. 'To be reliable, the information contained in financial statements must be neutral, that is, free from bias. Financial statements are not neutral if, by the selection or presentation of information, they influence the making of a decision or judgement in order to achieve a predetermined result or outcome.

The preparers of financial statements do, however, have to contend with the uncertainties that inevitably surround many events and circumstances, such as the collectability of doubtful receivables, the probable useful life of plant and equipment and the number of warranty claims that may occur. Such uncertainties are recognised by the disclosure of their nature and extent and by the exercise of prudence in the preparation of the financial statements. Prudence is the inclusion of a degree of caution in the exercise of the judgements needed in making the estimates required under conditions of uncertainty, such that assets or income are not overstated and liabilities or expenses are not understated. However, the exercise of prudence does not allow, for example, the creation of hidden reserves or excessive provisions, the deliberate understatement of assets or income, or the deliberate overstatement of liabilities or expenses, because the financial statements would not be neutral and, therefore, not have the quality of reliability.'[212]

In support of this primary requirement, the standard gives guidance on how management should apply this judgement. This guidance comes in two 'strengths' – certain things which management is required to consider, and others which it 'may' consider, as follows.

In making this judgement, management *should* refer to, and consider the applicability of, the following sources in descending order:

(a) the requirements and guidance in standards and interpretations dealing with similar and related issues; and

(b) the definitions, recognition criteria and measurement concepts for assets, liabilities, income and expenses in the Framework;[213] and

in making this judgement, management *may* also consider the most recent pronouncements of other standard-setting bodies that use a similar conceptual framework to develop accounting standards, other accounting literature and accepted industry practices, to the extent that these do not conflict with the sources in (a) and (b) above.[214]

4.4 Changes in accounting policies

As discussed at 4.1.4 above, consistency of accounting policies and presentation is a basic principle in both IAS 1 and IAS 8. Accordingly, IAS 8 only permits a change in accounting policies if the change:

(a) is required by a standard or an interpretation; or

(b) results in the financial statements providing reliable and more relevant information about the effects of transactions, other events or conditions on the entity's financial position, financial performance or cash flows.[215]

IAS 8 addresses changes of accounting policy arising from three sources:

(a) the initial application (including early application) of a standard or interpretation containing specific transitional provisions;

(b) the initial application of a standard or interpretation which does not contain specific transitional provisions; and

(c) voluntary changes in accounting policy.

Policy changes under (a) should be accounted for in accordance with the specific transitional provisions of that standard or interpretation.

A change of accounting policy under (b) or (c) should be applied retrospectively, that is applied to transactions, other events and conditions as if it had always been applied.[216] The standard goes on to explain that retrospective application requires adjustment of the opening balance of each affected component of equity for the earliest prior period presented and the other comparative amounts disclosed for each prior period presented as if the new accounting policy had always been applied.[217] The standard observes that the amount of the resulting adjustment relating to periods before those presented in the financial statements (which is made to the opening balance of each affected component of equity of the earliest prior period presented) will usually be made to retained earnings. However, it goes on to note that the adjustment may be made to another component of equity (for example, to comply with a standard or an interpretation). IAS 8 also makes clear that any other information about prior periods, such as historical summaries of financial data, should be also adjusted.[218]

Frequently it will be straightforward to apply a change in accounting policy retrospectively. However, the standard accepts that sometimes it may be impractical to do so. Accordingly, retrospective application of a change in accounting policy is not required to the extent that it is impracticable to determine either the period-specific effects or the cumulative effect of the change.[219] This is discussed further at 4.7 below. As noted at 4.3 above, in the absence of a specifically applicable standard or an interpretation an entity may apply an accounting policy from the most recent pronouncements of another standard-setting body that use a similar conceptual framework. The standard makes clear that a change in accounting policy reflecting a change in such a pronouncement is a voluntary change in accounting policy which should be accounted for and disclosed as such.[220]

Perhaps unnecessarily, the standard clarifies that the following are not changes in accounting policy:

- the application of an accounting policy for transactions, other events or conditions that differ in substance from those previously occurring; and

- the application of a new accounting policy for transactions, other events or conditions that did not occur previously or were immaterial.[221]

More importantly, the standard requires that a change to a policy of revaluing intangible assets or property plant and equipment in accordance with IAS 38 – *Intangible Assets* – and IAS 16 respectively is not to be accounted for under IAS 8 as a change in accounting policy. Rather, the change should be dealt with as revaluations in accordance with the relevant standards (discussed in Chapter 11 and Chapter 12).[222] What this means is that it is not necessary to restate prior periods for the carrying value and depreciation charge of the assets concerned. Aside of this particular exception, the standard makes clear that a change in measurement basis is a change in an accounting policy, and is not a change in an accounting estimate. However, when it is difficult to distinguish a change in an accounting policy from a change in an accounting estimate, the standard requires it to be treated as a change in an accounting estimate, discussed in 4.5 below.[223]

The implementation guidance accompanying the standard provides an illustration of the retrospective application of a change in accounting policy as follows.

Example 3.9:   Change in accounting policy with retrospective application[224]

During 2005, Gamma Co changed its accounting policy for the treatment of borrowing costs that are directly attributable to the acquisition of a hydro-electric power station under construction for use by Gamma. In previous periods, Gamma had capitalised such costs. Gamma has now decided to treat these costs as an expense, rather than capitalise them. Management judges that the new policy is preferable because it results in a more transparent treatment of finance costs and is consistent with local industry practice, making Gamma's financial statements more comparable.

Gamma capitalised borrowing costs incurred of €2,600 during 2004 and €5,200 in periods before 2004. All borrowing costs incurred in previous years in respect of the acquisition of the power station were capitalised.

Gamma's accounting records for 2005 show profit before interest and income taxes of €30,000; interest expense of €3,000 (which relates only to 2005); and income taxes of €8,100.

Gamma has not yet recognised any depreciation on the power station because it is not yet in use.

In 2004, Gamma reported:

	€
Profit before interest and income taxes	18,000
Interest expense	–
Profit before income taxes	18,000
Income taxes	(5,400)
Profit	12,600

The 2004 opening retained earnings was €20,000 and closing retained earnings was €32,600.

Gamma's tax rate was 30 per cent for 2005, 2004 and prior periods.

Gamma had €10,000 of share capital throughout, and no other components of equity except for retained earnings. Its shares are not publicly traded and it does not disclose earnings per share.

Gamma Co
Extract from the Income Statement

	2005	(restated) 2004
	€	€
Profit before interest and income taxes	30,000	18,000
Interest expense	(3,000)	(2,600)
Profit before income taxes	27,000	15,400
Income taxes	(8,100)	(4,620)
Profit	18,900	10,780

Gamma Co
Statement of Changes in Equity

	Share capital €	(restated) Retained earnings €	Total €
Balance at 31 December 2003 as previously reported	10,000	20,000	30,000
Change in accounting policy for the capitalisation of interest (net of income taxes of €1,560) (Note 1)	–	(3,640)	(3,640)
Balance at 31 December 2003 as restated	10,000	16,360	26,360
Profit for the year ended 31 December 2004 (restated)	–	10,780	10,780
Balance at 31 December 2004	10,000	27,140	37,140
Profit for the year ended 31 December 2005	–	18,900	18,900
Balance at 31 December 2005	10,000	46,040	56,040

Extracts from the Notes

1   During 2005, Gamma changed its accounting policy for the treatment of borrowing costs related to a hydro-electric power station under construction for use by Gamma. Previously, Gamma capitalised such costs. They are now written off as expenses as incurred. Management judges that this policy provides reliable and more relevant information because it results in a more transparent treatment of finance costs and is consistent with local industry practice, making Gamma's financial statements more comparable. This change in accounting policy has been accounted for retrospectively, and the comparative statements for 2004 have been restated. The effect of the change on 2004 is tabulated below. Opening retained earnings for 2004 have been reduced by €3,640, which is the amount of the adjustment relating to periods prior to 2004.

Effect on 2004	€
(Increase) in interest expense	(2,600)
Decrease in income tax expense	780
(Decrease) in profit	(1,820)

Effect on periods prior to 2004	
(Decrease) in profit (€5,200 interest expense less tax of €1,560)	(3,640)
(Decrease) in assets in the course of construction and in retained earnings at 31 December 2004	(5,460)

4.5 Changes in accounting estimates

The making of estimates is a fundamental feature of financial reporting reflecting the uncertainties inherent in business activities. IAS 8 notes that the use of reasonable estimates is an essential part of the preparation of financial statements and it does not undermine their reliability. Examples of estimates given by the standard are:

- bad debts;
- inventory obsolescence;
- the fair value of financial assets or financial liabilities;
- the useful lives of, or expected pattern of consumption of the future economic benefits embodied in, depreciable assets; and
- warranty obligations.[225]

Of course there are many others, some of the more subjective relating to share-based payments and post-retirement benefits.

Estimates will need revision as changes occur in the circumstances on which they are based or as a result of new information or more experience. The standard observes that, by its nature, the revision of an estimate does not relate to prior periods and is not the correction of an error.[226] Accordingly, IAS 8 requires that changes in estimate be accounted for prospectively;[227] defined as recognising the effect of the change in the accounting estimate in the current and future periods affected by the change.[228] The standard goes on to explain that this will mean (as appropriate):

- adjusting the carrying amount of an asset, liability or item of equity in the balance sheet in the period of change; and
- recognising the change by including it in profit and loss in:
  - the period of change, if it affects that period only (for example, a change in estimate of bad debts); or
  - the period of change and future periods, if it affects both (for example, a change in estimated useful life of a depreciable asset or the expected pattern of consumption of the economic benefits embodied in it).[229]

4.6 Correction of errors

Errors can arise in respect of the recognition, measurement, presentation or disclosure of elements of financial statements. IAS 8 states that financial statements do not comply with IFRS if they contain errors that are:

(a)   material; or

(b)   immaterial but are made intentionally to achieve a particular presentation of an entities financial position, financial performance or cash flows.[230]

The concept in (b) is a little curious. As discussed at 4.1.5 above, an error is material if it could influence the economic decisions of users taken on the basis of the financial statements. We find it difficult to imagine a scenario where an entity would deliberately seek to misstate its financial statements to achieve a particular presentation of its financial position, performance or cash flows but only in such a way that *did not* influence the decisions of users. In any event, and perhaps somewhat unnecessarily, IAS 8 notes that potential current period errors detected before the financial statements are authorised for issue should be corrected in those financial statements. This requirement is phrased so as to apply to all potential errors, not just material ones.[231] The standard notes that corrections of errors are distinguished from changes in accounting estimates. Accounting estimates by their nature are approximations that may need revision as additional information becomes known. For example, the gain or loss recognised on the outcome of a contingency is not the correction of an error.[232]

As with all things, financial reporting is not immune to error and sometimes financial statements can be published which, whether by accident or design, contain errors. IAS 8 defines prior period errors as omissions from, and misstatements in, an entity's financial statements for one or more prior periods (including the effects of mathematical mistakes, mistakes in applying accounting policies, oversights or misinterpretations of facts, and fraud) arising from a failure to use, or misuse of, reliable information that:

(a)   was available when financial statements for those periods were authorised for issue; and

(b)   could reasonably be expected to have been obtained and taken into account in the preparation and presentation of those financial statements.[233]

When it is discovered that material prior period errors have occurred, IAS 8 requires that they be corrected in the first set of financial statements prepared after their discovery.[234] The correction should be excluded from profit or loss for the period in which the error is discovered. Rather, any information presented about prior periods (including any historical summaries of financial data) should be restated as far back as practicable.[235] This should be done by:

(a)   restating the comparative amounts for the prior period(s) presented in which the error occurred; or

(b)   if the error occurred before the earliest prior period presented, restating the opening balances of assets, liabilities and equity for the earliest prior period presented.[236]

This process is described by the standard as retrospective restatement, which it also defines as correcting the recognition, measurement and disclosure of amounts of elements of financial statements as if a prior period error had never occurred.[237]

The implementation guidance accompanying the standard provides an example of the retrospective restatement of errors as follows.

Example 3.10: *Retrospective restatement of errors*[238]

During 2005, Beta Co discovered that some products that had been sold during 2004 were incorrectly included in inventory at 31 December 2004 at €6,500.

Beta's accounting records for 2005 show sales of €104,000, cost of goods sold of €86,500 (including €6,500 for the error in opening inventory), and income taxes of €5,250.

In 2004, Beta reported:

	€
Sales	73,500
Cost of goods sold	(53,500)
Profit before income taxes	20,000
Income taxes	(6,000)
Profit	14,000

The 2004 opening retained earnings was €20,000 and closing retained earnings was €34,000.

Beta's income tax rate was 30 per cent for 2005 and 2004. It had no other income or expenses.

Beta had €5,000 of share capital throughout, and no other components of equity except for retained earnings. Its shares are not publicly traded and it does not disclose earnings per share.

Beta Co
Extract from the Income Statement

	2005 €	(restated) 2004 €
Sales	104,000	73,500
Cost of goods sold	(80,000)	(60,000)
Profit before income taxes	24,000	13,500
Income taxes	(7,200)	(4,050)
Profit	16,800	9,450

Beta Co
Statement of Changes in Equity

	Share capital €	Retained earnings €	Total €
Balance at 31 December 2003	5,000	20,000	25,000
Profit for the year ended 31 December 2004 as restated	–	9,450	9,450
Balance at 31 December 2004	5,000	29,450	34,450
Profit for the year ended 31 December 2005	–	16,800	16,800
Balance at 31 December 2005	5,000	46,250	51,250

Extracts from the Notes

1. Some products that had been sold in 2004 were incorrectly included in inventory at 31 December 2004 at €6,500. The financial statements of 2004 have been restated to correct this error. The effect of the restatement on those financial statements is summarised below. There is no effect in 2005.

	Effect on 2004 €
(Increase) in cost of goods sold	(6,500)
Decrease in income tax expense	1,950
(Decrease) in profit	(4,550)
(Decrease) in inventory	(6,500)
Decrease in income tax payable	1,950
(Decrease) in equity	(4,550)

As is the case for the retrospective application of a change in accounting policy, retrospective restatement for the correction of prior period material errors is not required to the extent that it is impracticable to determine either the period-specific effects or the cumulative effect of the error.[239] This is discussed further at 4.7 below.

4.7   Impracticability of restatement

As noted at 4.4 and 4.6 above, IAS 8 does not require the restatement of prior periods following a change in accounting policy or the correction of material errors if such a restatement is impracticable.

The standard devotes a considerable amount of guidance to discussing what 'impracticable' means for these purposes.

The standard states that applying a requirement is impracticable when an entity cannot apply it after making every reasonable effort to do so. It goes on to note that, for a particular prior period, it is impracticable to apply a change in an accounting policy retrospectively or to make a retrospective restatement to correct an error if:

(a)   the effects of the retrospective application or retrospective restatement are not determinable;

(b)   the retrospective application or retrospective restatement requires assumptions about what management's intent would have been in that period; or

(c)   the retrospective application or retrospective restatement requires significant estimates of amounts and it is impossible to distinguish objectively information about those estimates that:

(i)   provides evidence of circumstances that existed on the date(s) as at which those amounts are to be recognised, measured or disclosed; and

(ii)   would have been available when the financial statements for that prior period were authorised for issue,

from other information.[240]

An example of a scenario covered by (a) above given by the standard is that in some circumstances it may impracticable to adjust comparative information for one or more prior periods to achieve comparability with the current period because data may not have been collected in the prior period(s) in a way that allows either retrospective application of a new accounting policy (or its prospective application to prior periods) or retrospective restatement to correct a prior period error, and it may be impracticable to recreate the information.[241]

IAS 8 observes that it is frequently necessary to make estimates in applying an accounting policy and that estimation is inherently subjective, and that estimates may be developed after the balance sheet date. Developing estimates is potentially more difficult when retrospectively applying an accounting policy or making a retrospective restatement to correct a prior period error, because of the longer period of time that might have passed since the affected transaction, other event or condition occurred.

However, the objective of estimates related to prior periods remains the same as for estimates made in the current period, namely, for the estimate to reflect the circumstances that existed when the transaction, other event or condition occurred.[242] Hindsight should not be used when applying a new accounting policy to, or correcting amounts for, a prior period, either in making assumptions about what management's intentions would have been in a prior period or estimating the amounts recognised, measured or disclosed in a prior period. For example, if an entity corrects a prior period error in measuring financial assets previously classified as held-to-maturity investments in accordance with IAS 39, it should not change their basis of measurement for that period if management decided later not to hold them to maturity. In addition, if an entity corrects a prior period error in calculating its liability for employees' accumulated sick leave in accordance with IAS 19, it would disregard information about an unusually severe influenza season during the next period that became available after the financial statements for the prior period were authorised for issue. However, the fact that significant estimates are frequently required when amending comparative information presented for prior periods does not prevent reliable adjustment or correction of the comparative information.[243]

Therefore, retrospectively applying a new accounting policy or correcting a prior period error requires distinguishing information that:

(a)   provides evidence of circumstances that existed on the date(s) as at which the transaction, other event or condition occurred; and

(b)   would have been available when the financial statements for that prior period were authorised for issue,

from other information. The standard states that for some types of estimates (e.g. an estimate of fair value not based on an observable price or observable inputs), it is impracticable to distinguish these types of information. When retrospective application or retrospective restatement would require making a significant estimate for which it is impossible to distinguish these two types of information, it is impracticable to apply the new accounting policy or correct the prior period error retrospectively.[244]

IAS 8 addresses the impracticability of restatement separately (although similarly) for changes in accounting policy and the correction of material errors.

A   *Impracticability of restatement for a change in accounting policy.*

When retrospective application of a change in accounting policy is required, the change in policy should be applied retrospectively except to the extent that it is impracticable to determine either the period-specific effects or the cumulative effect of the change.[245] When an entity applies a new accounting policy retrospectively, the standard requires it to be applied to comparative information for prior periods as far back as is practicable. Retrospective application to a prior period is not practicable for these purposes unless it is practicable to determine the cumulative effect on the amounts in both the opening and closing balance sheets for that period.[246]

When it is impracticable to determine the period-specific effects of changing an accounting policy on comparative information for one or more prior periods presented, the new accounting policy should be applied to the carrying amounts of assets and liabilities as at the beginning of the earliest period for which retrospective application is practicable and a corresponding adjustment to the opening balance of each affected component of equity for that period should be made. The standard notes that this may be the current period.[247]

When it is impracticable to determine the cumulative effect, at the beginning of the current period, of applying a new accounting policy to all prior periods, the standard requires an adjustment to the comparative information to apply the new accounting policy prospectively from the earliest date practicable.[248] Prospective application is defined by the standard as applying the new accounting policy to transactions, other events and conditions occurring after the date as at which the policy is changed.[249] This means that the portion of the cumulative adjustment to assets, liabilities and equity arising before that date is disregarded. Changing an accounting policy is permitted by IAS 8 even if it is impracticable to apply the policy prospectively for any prior period.[250]

The implementation guidance accompanying the standard illustrates the prospective application of a change in accounting policy as follows.

Example 3.11:   Prospective application of a change in accounting policy when retrospective application is not practicable[251]

During 2005, Delta Co changed its accounting policy for depreciating property, plant and equipment, so as to apply much more fully a components approach, whilst at the same time adopting the revaluation model.

In years before 2005, Delta's asset records were not sufficiently detailed to apply a components approach fully. At the end of 2004, management commissioned an engineering survey, which provided information on the components held and their fair values, useful lives, estimated residual values and depreciable amounts at the beginning of 2005. However, the survey did not provide a sufficient basis for reliably estimating the cost of those components that had not previously been accounted for separately, and the existing records before the survey did not permit this information to be reconstructed.

Delta's management considered how to account for each of the two aspects of the accounting change. They determined that it was not practicable to account for the change to a fuller components approach retrospectively, or to account for that change prospectively from any earlier date than the start of 2005. Also, the change from a cost model to a revaluation model is required to be accounted for prospectively (see 4.4 above). Therefore, management concluded that it should apply Delta's new policy prospectively from the start of 2005.

Additional information:

Delta's tax rate is 30 per cent.

	€
Property, plant and equipment at the end of 2004:	
Cost	25,000
Depreciation	(14,000)
Net book value	11,000
Prospective depreciation expense for 2005 (old basis)	1,500
Some results of the engineering survey:	
Valuation	17,000
Estimated residual value	3,000
Average remaining asset life (years)	7
Depreciation expense on existing property, plant and equipment for 2005 (new basis)	2,000

Extract from the Notes

1   From the start of 2005, Delta changed its accounting policy for depreciating property, plant and equipment, so as to apply much more fully a components approach, whilst at the same time adopting the revaluation model. Management takes the view that this policy provides reliable and more relevant information because it deals more accurately with the components of property, plant and equipment and is based on up-to-date values. The policy has been applied prospectively from the start of 2005 because it was not practicable to estimate the effects of applying the policy either retrospectively, or prospectively from any earlier date. Accordingly, the adoption of the new policy has no effect on prior years. The effect on the current year is to increase the carrying amount of property, plant and equipment at the start of the year by €6,000; increase the opening deferred tax provision by €1,800; create a revaluation reserve at the start of the year of €4,200; increase depreciation expense by €500; and reduce tax expense by €150.

B   Impracticability of restatement for a material error

IAS 8 requires that a prior period error should be corrected by retrospective restatement except to the extent that it is impracticable to determine either the period-specific effects or the cumulative effect of the error.[252]

When it is impracticable to determine the period-specific effects of an error on comparative information for one or more prior periods presented, the opening balances of assets, liabilities and equity should be restated for the earliest period for which retrospective restatement is practicable (which the standard notes may be the current period).[253]

When it is impracticable to determine the cumulative effect, at the beginning of the current period, of an error on all prior periods, the comparative information should be restated to correct the error prospectively from the earliest date practicable.[254] The standard explains that this will mean disregarding the portion of the cumulative restatement of assets, liabilities and equity arising before that date.[255]

5   NON-CURRENT ASSETS (AND DISPOSAL GROUPS) HELD FOR SALE AND DISCONTINUED ACTIVITIES

5.1   Classification of non-current assets (and disposal groups) held for sale

IFRS 5 frequently refers to current assets and non-current assets. It provides a definition of each term as follows:

A current asset is 'an asset that satisfies any of the following criteria:

(a)   it is expected to be realised in, or is intended for sale or consumption in, the entity's normal operating cycle;

(b)   it is held primarily for the purpose of being traded;

(c)   it is expected to be realised within twelve months after the balance sheet date; or

(d)   it is cash or a cash equivalent asset unless it is restricted from being exchanged or used to settle a liability for at least twelve months after the balance sheet date.

A non-current asset is 'an asset that does not meet the definition of a current asset'.[256]

These definitions are essentially the same as those in IAS 1 (discussed at 3.1.1 above). There is one minor difference, in that the IAS 1 definition of a current asset makes explicit that 'cash or a cash equivalent' should have the meaning defined in IAS 7. However, we do not think this is intended to produce a difference in practice.

5.1.1   The concept of a disposal group

As its title suggests, IFRS 5 addresses the accounting treatment of non-current assets held for sale, that is assets whose carrying amount will be recovered principally through sale rather than continuing use in the business.[257] However, the standard also applies to certain liabilities and current assets where they form part of a 'disposal group'.

The standard observes that sometimes an entity will dispose of a group of assets, possibly with some directly associated liabilities, together in a single transaction.[258] A common example would be the disposal of a subsidiary. For these circumstances, IFRS 5 introduces the concept of a disposal group, which it defines as 'a group of assets to be disposed of, by sale or otherwise, together as a group in a single transaction, and liabilities directly associated with those assets that will be transferred in the transaction. The group includes goodwill acquired in a business combination if the group is a cash-generating unit to which goodwill has been allocated in accordance with the requirements of paragraphs 80-87 of IAS 36 *Impairment of Assets* (as revised in 2004) or if it is an operation within such a cash-generating unit.'[259]

The use of the phrase 'together in a single transaction' seems to indicate that the only liabilities that can be included in the group are those assumed by the purchaser. Accordingly, any borrowings of the entity which are to be repaid out of the sales proceeds would be excluded from the disposal group.

The standard goes on to explain that a disposal group:

- may be a group of cash-generating units, a single cash-generating unit, or part of a cash-generating unit. However, once the cash flows from an asset or group of assets are expected to arise principally from sale rather than continuing use, they become less dependent on cash flows arising from other assets, and a disposal group that was part of a cash-generating unit becomes a separate cash-generating unit; and

- may include any assets and any liabilities of the entity, including current assets, current liabilities and assets excluded from the measurement requirements of this IFRS (see 5.2 below).[260]

Discontinued operations are discussed at 3.2.3 above. As noted there, it seems highly unlikely that the definition of a discontinued operation would ever be met by a single non-current asset. Accordingly, a discontinued operation will also be disposal group.

5.1.2   Classification as held for sale

IFRS 5 requires a non-current asset (or disposal group) to be classified as held for sale if its carrying amount will be recovered principally through a sale transaction rather than through continuing use.[261] For these purposes, sale transactions include exchanges of non-current assets for other non-current assets when the exchange has commercial substance in accordance with IAS 16 (discussed in Chapter 12).[262] For assets classified according to a liquidity presentation (see 3.1.1 above), non-current assets are taken to be assets that include amounts expected to be recovered more than twelve months after the balance sheet date.[263]

Determining whether (and when) an asset stops being recovered through use and becomes recoverable through sale is clearly the critical distinction, and much of the standard is devoted to explaining how to make the determination.

For an asset (or disposal group) to be classified as held for sale:

(a)   it must be available for immediate sale in its present condition, subject only to terms that are usual and customary for sales of such assets (or disposal groups);

(b)   its sale must be highly probable.[264] and

(c)   it must genuinely be sold, not abandoned.[265]

These criteria are discussed further below. If an asset (or disposal group) has been classified as held for sale, but these criteria cease to be met, an entity should cease to classify the asset (or disposal group) as held for sale.[266] Changes in plan are discussed at 5.2.4 below.

Slightly different criteria apply when an entity acquires a non-current asset (or disposal group) exclusively with a view to its subsequent disposal. In that case it should only classify the non-current asset (or disposal group) as held for sale at the acquisition date if:

- the 'one-year requirement' is met subject to the exception to it (this is part of being 'highly probable', discussed at B below); and

- it is highly probable that any other criteria in (a) and (b) above that are not met at that date will be met within a short period following the acquisition (usually within three months).[267]

The standard also makes clear that the criteria in (a) and (b) above must be met at the balance sheet date for a non-current asset (or disposal group) to be classified as held for sale in those financial statements when issued. However, if those criteria are met after the balance sheet date but before the authorisation of the financial statements for issue, the standard requires certain additional disclosure (discussed at 6.4 below).[268]

A   Meaning of available for immediate sale

To qualify for classification as held for sale, a non-current asset (or disposal group) must be available for immediate sale in its present condition subject only to terms that are usual and customary for sales of such assets (or disposal groups). This is taken to mean that an entity currently has the intention and ability to transfer the asset (or disposal group) to a buyer in its present condition. The standard illustrates this concept with the following examples.

Example 3.12:   Non-current assets and disposal groups available for immediate sale[269]

1   Disposal of a headquarters building

An entity is committed to a plan to sell its headquarters building and has initiated actions to locate a buyer.

(a)   The entity intends to transfer the building to a buyer after it vacates the building. The time necessary to vacate the building is usual and customary for sales of such assets. The criterion of being available for immediate sale would therefore be met at the plan commitment date.

(b)   The entity will continue to use the building until construction of a new headquarters building is completed. The entity does not intend to transfer the existing building to a buyer until after construction of the new building is completed (and it vacates the existing building). The delay in the timing of the transfer of the existing building imposed by the entity (seller) demonstrates that the building is not available for immediate sale. The criterion would not be met until construction of the new building is completed, even if a firm purchase commitment for the future transfer of the existing building is obtained earlier.

2   Sale of a manufacturing facility

An entity is committed to a plan to sell a manufacturing facility and has initiated actions to locate a buyer. At the plan commitment date, there is a backlog of uncompleted customer orders.

(a)   The entity intends to sell the manufacturing facility with its operations. Any uncompleted customer orders at the sale date will be transferred to the buyer. The transfer of uncompleted customer orders at the sale date will not affect the timing of the transfer of the facility. The criterion of being available for immediate sale would therefore be met at the plan commitment date.

(b)   The entity intends to sell the manufacturing facility, but without its operations. The entity does not intend to transfer the facility to a buyer until after it ceases all operations of the facility and eliminates the backlog of uncompleted customer orders. The delay in the timing of the transfer of the facility imposed by the entity (seller) demonstrates that the facility is not available for immediate sale. The criterion would not be met until the operations of the facility cease, even if a firm purchase commitment for the future transfer of the facility were obtained earlier.

3   Land and buildings acquired through foreclosure

An entity acquires through foreclosure a property comprising land and buildings that it intends to sell.

(a)   The entity does not intend to transfer the property to a buyer until after it completes renovations to increase the property's sales value. The delay in the timing of the transfer of the property imposed by the entity (seller) demonstrates that the property is not available for immediate sale. The criterion of being available for immediate sale would therefore not be met until the renovations are completed.

(b)   After the renovations are completed and the property is classified as held for sale but before a firm purchase commitment is obtained, the entity becomes aware of environmental damage requiring remediation. The entity still intends to sell the property. However, the entity does not have the ability to transfer the property to a buyer until after the remediation is completed. The delay in the timing of the transfer of the property imposed by others *before* a firm purchase commitment is obtained demonstrates that the property is not available for immediate sale (different requirements could apply if this happened *after* a firm commitment is obtained, as illustrated in scenario (b) of Example 3.13 below). The criterion would not continue to be met. The property would be reclassified as held and used in accordance with the requirements discussed at 5.2.4 below.

B   *Meaning of highly probable*

Many observers may consider the meaning of 'highly probable' to be reasonably self-evident, albeit highly judgemental. However, IFRS 5 provides extensive discussion of the topic. As a first step, the term is defined by the standard as meaning 'significantly more likely than probable'. This is supplemented by a second definition – probable is defined as 'more likely than not'.[270] Substituting the latter into the former leads to a definition of highly probable as meaning 'significantly more likely than more likely than not'. This is reassuringly close to (but, a little surprisingly, not the same as) the meaning given to the term in IAS 39 which observes that 'The term "highly probable" indicates a much greater likelihood of happening than the term "more likely than not"'.[271]

In the particular context of classification as held for sale, the IASB evidently did not consider that 'significantly more likely than more likely than not' was an adequate definition of the phrase, so the standard goes on to elaborate as follows.

For the sale to be highly probable:

- the appropriate level of management must be committed to a plan to sell the asset (or disposal group);

- an active programme to locate a buyer and complete the plan must have been initiated;

- the asset (or disposal group) must be actively marketed for sale at a price that is reasonable in relation to its current fair value;

- the sale should be expected to qualify for recognition as a completed sale within one year from the date of classification (although in certain circumstances this period may be extended as discussed below); and

- actions required to complete the plan should indicate that it is unlikely that significant changes to the plan will be made or that the plan will be withdrawn.[272]

The basic rule above that for qualification as held for sale the sale should be expected to qualify for recognition as a completed sale within one year from the date of classification (the 'one-year rule') is treated quite strictly by the standard. In particular, that criterion would not be met if:

(a)   an entity that is a commercial leasing and finance company is holding for sale or lease equipment that has recently ceased to be leased and the ultimate form of a future transaction (sale or lease) has not yet been determined.

(b)   an entity is committed to a plan to 'sell' a property that is in use, and the transfer of the property will be accounted for as a sale and finance leaseback.[273]

In (a), the entity does not yet know whether the asset will be sold at all and hence may not presume that it will be sold within a year. In (b), whilst in legal form the asset has been sold it will not be *recognised* as sold in the financial statements.

As indicated above, the standard contains an exception to the one-year rule. It states that events or circumstances may extend the period to complete the sale beyond one year. Such an extension would not preclude an asset (or disposal group) from being classified as held for sale if the delay is caused by events or circumstances beyond the entity's control and there is sufficient evidence that the entity remains committed to its plan to sell the asset (or disposal group). This will be the case when the following criteria are met:[274]

(a)   at the date an entity commits itself to a plan to sell a non-current asset (or disposal group) it reasonably expects that others (not a buyer) will impose conditions on the transfer of the asset (or disposal group) that will extend the period required to complete the sale; and:

    (i)   actions necessary to respond to those conditions cannot be initiated until after a firm purchase commitment is obtained; and

    (ii)   a firm purchase commitment is highly probable within one year;

(b)   an entity obtains a firm purchase commitment and, as a result, a buyer or others unexpectedly impose conditions on the transfer of a non-current asset (or disposal group) previously classified as held for sale that will extend the period required to complete the sale; and:

    (i)   timely actions necessary to respond to the conditions have been taken; and

    (ii)   a favourable resolution of the delaying factors is expected;

(c)   during the initial one-year period, circumstances arise that were previously considered unlikely and, as a result, a non-current asset (or disposal group) previously classified as held for sale is not sold by the end of that period; and

    (i)   during the initial one-year period the entity took action necessary to respond to the change in circumstances;

    (ii)   the non-current asset (or disposal group) is being actively marketed at a price that is reasonable, given the change in circumstances; and

    (iii)   the non-current asset (or disposal group) remains available for immediate sale and the sale is highly probable.[275]

Firm purchase commitment is a defined term in IFRS 5, meaning an agreement with an unrelated party, binding on both parties and usually legally enforceable, that:

- specifies all significant terms, including the price and timing of the transactions; and

- includes a disincentive for non-performance that is sufficiently large to make performance highly probable.[276]

The word 'binding' in this definition seems to envisage an agreement still being subject to contingencies. The standard provides an example where a 'firm purchase commitment' exists but is subject to regulatory approval (see scenario (a) in Example 3.13 below). In our view, to be 'binding' in this sense a contingent agreement should be only subject to contingencies outside the control of both parties.

The standard illustrates each of these exceptions to the one-year rule with the following examples.

Example 3.13:   Exceptions to the 'one-year rule'.

Scenario illustrating (a) above[277]

An entity in the power generating industry is committed to a plan to sell a disposal group that represents a significant portion of its regulated operations. The sale requires regulatory approval, which could extend the period required to complete the sale beyond one year. Actions necessary to obtain that approval cannot be initiated until after a buyer is known and a firm purchase commitment is obtained. However, a firm purchase commitment is highly probable within one year. In that situation, the conditions for an exception to the one-year requirement would be met.

Scenario illustrating (b) above[278]

An entity is committed to a plan to sell a manufacturing facility in its present condition and classifies the facility as held for sale at that date. After a firm purchase commitment is obtained, the buyer's inspection of the property identifies environmental damage not previously known to exist. The entity is required by the buyer to make good the damage, which will extend the period required to complete the sale beyond one year. However, the entity has initiated actions to make good the damage, and satisfactory rectification of the damage is highly probable. In that situation, the conditions for an exception to the one-year requirement would be met.

Scenario illustrating (c) above[279]

An entity is committed to a plan to sell a non-current asset and classifies the asset as held for sale at that date.

(a) During the initial one-year period, the market conditions that existed at the date the asset was classified initially as held for sale deteriorate and, as a result, the asset is not sold by the end of that period. During that period, the entity actively solicited but did not receive any reasonable offers to purchase the asset and, in response, reduced the price. The asset continues to be actively marketed at a price that is reasonable given the change in market conditions, and the criteria regarding availability for immediate sale which is highly probable are therefore met. In that situation, the conditions for an exception to the one-year requirement would be met. At the end of the initial one-year period, the asset would continue to be classified as held for sale.

(b) During the following one-year period, market conditions deteriorate further, and the asset is not sold by the end of that period. The entity believes that the market conditions will improve and has not further reduced the price of the asset. The asset continues to be held for sale, but at a price in excess of its current fair value. In that situation, the absence of a price reduction demonstrates that the asset is not available for immediate sale. In addition, to meet the condition that a sale be highly probable also requires an asset to be marketed at a price that is reasonable in relation to its current fair value. Therefore, the conditions for an exception to the one-year requirement would not be met. The asset would be reclassified as held and used in accordance with the requirements discussed at 5.2.4 below.

C   *Abandonment*

IFRS 5 stipulates that a non-current asset (or disposal group) that is to be abandoned should not be classified as held for sale. This includes non-current assets (or disposal groups) that are to be used to the end of their economic life and non-current assets (or disposal groups) that are to be closed rather than sold. The standard explains that this is because its carrying amount will be recovered principally through continuing use.[280]

If the disposal group to be abandoned meets the criteria for being a discontinued operation the standard requires it to be treated as such in the income statement and relevant notes.[281] This is discussed at 3.2.3 A above. However, a non-current asset that has been temporarily taken out of use should not be accounted for as if it had been abandoned.[282] An example given by the standard is of a manufacturing plant that ceases to be used because demand for its product has declined but which is maintained in workable condition and is expected to be brought back into use if demand picks up. The plant is not regarded as abandoned.[283] However, in these circumstances an impairment loss may need to be recognised in accordance with IAS 36 (discussed in Chapter 13).

5.2   Measurement of non-current assets (and disposal groups) held for sale

5.2.1   *Scope of the measurement requirements*

IFRS 5's classification and presentation requirements apply to all recognised non-current assets (which is defined in the same way as in IAS 1, discussed at 3.1.1 above) and disposal groups. However, the measurement provisions of the standard do not apply to the following assets (which remain covered by the standards listed) either as individual assets or as part of a disposal group:[284]

(a)   deferred tax assets, dealt with in IAS 12);

(b)   assets arising from employee benefits, dealt with in IAS 19);

(c)   financial assets within the scope of IAS 39;

(d)   non-current assets that are accounted for in accordance with the fair value model in IAS 40 – *Investment Property*;

(e)   non-current assets that are measured at fair value less estimated point-of-sale costs in accordance with IAS 41 – *Agriculture;* and

(f)   contractual rights under insurance contracts as defined in IFRS 4 – *Insurance Contracts.*

5.2.2   *Measurement of non-current assets and disposal groups held for sale*

A   *Measurement on initial classification as held for sale*

IFRS 5 requires that immediately before the initial classification of an asset (or disposal group) as held for sale, the carrying amount of the asset (or all the assets and liabilities in the group) should be measured in accordance with applicable IFRSs.[285] In other words, an entity should apply its usual accounting policies up until the criteria for classification as held for sale are met.

Thereafter a non-current asset (or disposal group) classified as held for sale should be measured at the lower of its carrying amount and fair value less costs to sell.[286] Fair value is defined as 'the amount for which an asset could be exchanged, or a liability settled, between knowledgeable, willing parties in an arm's length transaction'. Costs to sell are defined as 'the incremental costs directly attributable to the disposal of an asset (or disposal group), excluding finance costs and income tax expense'.[287] When the sale is expected to occur beyond one year, the costs to sell should be measured at their present value. Any increase in the present value of the costs to sell that arises from the passage of time should be presented in profit or loss as a financing cost.[288] There is no similar requirement to present that element of an increase in fair value which also relates to just the passage of time as finance income.

For disposal groups, the standard adopts a portfolio approach. It requires that if a non-current asset within the scope of its measurement requirements is part of a disposal group, the measurement requirements should apply to the group as a whole, so that the group is measured at the lower of its carrying amount and fair value less costs to sell.[289] It will still be necessary to apportion any write down to the underlying assets of the disposal group, but no element is apportioned to items outside the scope of the standard's measurement provisions. This is discussed further at 5.2.3 below.

If a newly acquired asset (or disposal group) meets the criteria to be classified as held for sale (which, as discussed at 5.1.2 above are subtly different for assets acquired exclusively with a view to subsequent disposal), applying the above requirements will result in the asset (or disposal group) being measured on initial recognition at the lower of its carrying amount had it not been so classified (for example, cost) and fair value less costs to sell. This means that, if the asset (or disposal group) is acquired as part of a business combination, it will be measured at fair value less costs to sell.[290]

The implementation guidance accompanying the standard provides the following illustration of a subsidiary acquired with a view to sale.

Example 3.14:   *Measuring and presenting subsidiaries acquired with a view to sale and classified as held for sale*[291]

Entity A acquires an entity H, which is a holding company with two subsidiaries, S1 and S2. S2 is acquired exclusively with a view to sale and meets the criteria to be classified as held for sale. Accordingly, S2 is also a discontinued operation (see 3.2.3 above).

The estimated fair value less costs to sell of S2 is €135. A accounts for S2 as follows:

- initially, A measures the identifiable liabilities of S2 at fair value, say at €40;

- initially, A measures the acquired assets as the fair value less costs to sell of S2 (€135) plus the fair value of the identifiable liabilities (€40), i.e. at €175;

- at the balance sheet date, A remeasures the disposal group at the lower of its cost and fair value less costs to sell, say at €130. The liabilities are remeasured in accordance with applicable IFRSs, say at €35. The total assets are measured at €130 + €35, i.e. at €165;

- at the balance sheet date, A presents the assets and liabilities separately from other assets and liabilities in its consolidated financial statements as illustrated in Example 3.1 at 3.1.2 above; and

- in the income statement, A presents the total of the post-tax profit or loss of S2 and the post-tax gain or loss recognised on the subsequent remeasurement of S2, which equals the remeasurement of the disposal group from €135 to €130.

Further analysis of the assets and liabilities or of the change in value of the disposal group is not required.

B   Subsequent remeasurement

While a non-current asset is classified as held for sale or while it is part of a disposal group classified as held for sale it should not be depreciated or amortised. Interest and other expenses attributable to the liabilities of a disposal group classified as held for sale should continue to be recognised.[292]

On subsequent remeasurement of a disposal group, the standard requires that the carrying amounts of any assets and liabilities that are not within the scope of its measurement requirements, be remeasured in accordance with applicable IFRSs before the fair value less costs to sell of the disposal group is remeasured.[293]

5.2.3   Impairments and reversals of impairment

The requirement to measure a non-current asset or disposal group held for sale at the lower of carrying amount less costs to sell may give rise to a write down in value (impairment loss) and possibly its subsequent reversal. As noted above, the first step is to account for any items outwith the scope of the standard in the normal way. After that, any excess of carrying value over fair value less costs to sell should be recognised as an impairment.[294]

Any subsequent increase in fair value less costs to sell of an asset up to the cumulative impairment loss previously recognised either in accordance with IFRS 5 or in accordance with IAS 36 – *Impairment of Assets* – should be recognised as a gain.[295] In the case of a disposal group, any subsequent increase in fair value less costs to sell should be recognised:

(a)   to the extent that it has not been recognised under another standard in relation to those assets outside the scope of IFRS 5's measurement requirements; but

(b)   not in excess of the cumulative amount of losses previously recognised under IFRS 5 or before that under IAS 36 in respect of the non-current assets in the group which are within the scope of the measurement rules of IFRS 5.[296]

Any impairment loss (or any subsequent gain) recognised for a disposal group should be allocated to the non-current assets in the group that are within the scope of the measurement requirements of IFRS 5. The order of allocation should be:

*   first, to reduce the carrying amount of any goodwill in the group; and

*   then, to the other assets of the group pro rata on the basis of the carrying amount of each asset in the group.[297]

This is illustrated by the standard with the following example.

Example 3.15:   Allocation of impairment loss to the components of a disposal group[298]

An entity plans to dispose of a group of its assets (as an asset sale). The assets form a disposal group, and are measured as follows:

	Carrying amount at the reporting date before classification as held for sale €	Carrying amount as remeasured immediately before classification as held for sale €
Goodwill	1,500	1,500
Property, plant and equipment (carried at revalued amounts)	4,600	4,000
Property, plant and equipment (carried at cost)	5,700	5,700
Inventory	2,400	2,200
Available for sale financial assets	1,800	1,500
Total	16,000	14,900

The entity recognises the loss of €1,100 (€16,000-€14,900) immediately before classifying the disposal group as held for sale. The entity estimates that fair value less costs to sell of the disposal group amounts to €13,000. Because an entity measures a disposal group classified as held for sale at the lower of its carrying amount and fair value less costs to sell, the entity recognises an impairment loss of €1,900 (€14,900-€13,000) when the group is initially classified as held for sale. The impairment loss is allocated to non-current assets to which the measurement requirements of the

IFRS are applicable. Therefore, no impairment loss is allocated to inventory and AFS financial assets. The loss is allocated to the other assets in the order of allocation described above.

The allocation can be illustrated as follows:

First, the impairment loss reduces any amount of goodwill. Then, the residual loss is allocated to other assets pro rata based on the carrying amounts of those assets.

	Carrying amount as remeasured immediately before classification as held for sale €	Allocated impairment loss €	Carrying amount after allocation of impairment loss €
Goodwill	1,500	(1,500)	–
Property, plant and equipment (carried at revalued amounts)	4,000	(165)	3,835
Property, plant and equipment (carried at cost)	5,700	(235)	5,465
Inventory	2,200	–	2,200
AFS financial assets	1,500	–	1,500
Total	14,900	(1,900)	13,000

In the first table of this example, it isn't particularly clear what the meaning and purpose of the left hand column is. The fact that some of the figures are different in each column, seems to indicate that the column header 'Carrying amount at the reporting date before classification as held for sale' is referring to the opening balance sheet at the beginning of the period in which the classification is made. As noted at 5.2.2 A above, an entity is required to remeasure the assets as normal under the relevant standards immediately before classifying them as held for sale. This would mean the difference of €1,100 reflects routine accounting entries (such as depreciation and revaluation) from the start of the period to the date of classification as held to sale. Also worthy of note is that the example does not say where the entity recognises the loss of €1,100. Given that the disposal group contains available for sale financial assets, some of this amount would probably be recorded in equity rather than the income statement. Similarly, movements in property plant and equipment held at revalued amounts may fall to be recorded directly in equity.

The standard contains a reminder that requirements relating to derecognition are set out in IAS 16 for property, plant and equipment (discussed in Chapter 12), and IAS 38 for intangible assets (discussed in Chapter 11) and notes that a gain or loss not previously recognised by the date of the sale of a non-current asset (or disposal group) should be recognised at the date of derecognition.[299]

5.2.4 Changes to a plan of sale

An asset (or disposal group) should cease to be classified as held for sale if the criteria discussed in 5.1.2 are no longer met.[300]

If an individual asset or liability is removed from a disposal group classified as held for sale, the remaining assets and liabilities of the disposal group to be sold should only continue to be measured as a group if the group still meets these criteria.

Otherwise, the remaining non-current assets of the group that individually meet the criteria should be measured individually at the lower of their carrying amounts and fair values less costs to sell at that date. Any that do not meet the criteria should cease to be classified as held for sale.[301]

A non-current asset that ceases to be classified as held for sale (or ceases to be included in a disposal group classified as held for sale) should be measured at the lower of:

(a)   its carrying amount before the asset (or disposal group) was classified as held for sale, adjusted for any depreciation, amortisation or revaluations that would have been recognised had the asset (or disposal group) not been classified as held for sale; and

(b)   its recoverable amount at the date of the subsequent decision not to sell.

Regarding (b) above, the standard notes that if the non-current asset is part of a cash-generating unit, its recoverable amount is the carrying amount that would have been recognised after the allocation of any impairment loss arising on that cash-generating unit in accordance with IAS 36.[302] Recoverable amount is defined as the higher of:

- an asset's fair value less costs to sell; and

- its value in use.

Value in use is defined as 'the present value of estimated future cash flows expected to arise from the continuing use of an asset and from its disposal at the end of its useful life'.[303]

Any required adjustment to the carrying amount of a non-current asset that ceases to be classified as held for sale should be included

- in income from continuing operations in the period in which the criteria are no longer met (unless the asset had been revalued in accordance with IAS 16 or IAS 38 before classification as held for sale, in which case the adjustment should be treated as a revaluation increase or decrease); and

- in the same income statement caption used to present any gain or loss recognised in relation to remeasuring non-current assets (or disposal groups) held for sale but not meeting the definition of a discontinued operation.[304]

5.3   Comparative information

As discussed at 2.4 above, IAS 1 requires the presentation of comparative information. IFRS 5 deals with the particular requirements for non-current assets held for sale (and disposal groups) and discontinued operations. However, in our view, the way it does so is somewhat muddled.

Entities will need to consider whether any (and if so what) changes are necessary to comparative information as previously reported whenever:

- non-current assets or disposal groups first become classified as such; and

- that classification ceases.

This will need to be considered in terms of both the income statement and balance sheet and separately (for the income statement) for those components falling to be treated as discontinued operations.

5.3.1 Treatment of comparative information on initial classification as held for sale

A The income statement

For non-current assets and disposal groups not qualifying as discontinued operations there are no special requirements relating to income statement presentation, accordingly no restatement of comparative amounts would be relevant.

When a component of an entity becomes classified as a discontinued operation, separate presentation of the total of its results for the period and any gain or loss on remeasurement is required on the face of the income statement (see 3.2.3 above). IFRS 5 requires that these disclosures be re-presented for prior periods presented in the financial statements so that the disclosures relate to all operations that have been discontinued by the balance sheet date for the latest period presented.[305] Accordingly, adjustments to the comparative information as originally reported will be necessary for those disposal groups categorised as discontinued operations.

B The balance sheet

IFRS 5 states that 'An entity shall not reclassify or re-present amounts presented for non-current assets or for the assets and liabilities of disposal groups classified as held for sale in the balance sheets for prior periods to reflect the classification in the balance sheet for the latest period presented.'[306] The exact meaning of this is imprecise, and would be clarified if the sentence contained some punctuation. In particular, it is unclear whether the prohibition is aimed at the commencement or cessation of the held for sale classification or both. The implementation guidance accompanying the standard contains an example of a disposal group becoming classified as held for sale (see Example 3.1 at 3.1.2 above), and states that the presentation requirements for assets (or disposal groups) classified as held for sale at the end of the reporting period do not apply retrospectively. The comparative balance sheets for any previous periods are therefore not re-presented.[307] In our view, comparatives should not be re-presented when the classification as held for sale ceases.

The standard has no separate requirements relating to the balance sheet for a disposal group also qualifying as a discontinued operation.

5.3.2 Treatment of comparative information on the cessation of classification as held for sale

A   General requirements

As discussed at 5.2.4 above, when a non-current asset ceases to be classified as held for sale the measurement basis for it reverts to what it would have been if it hadn't been so classified at all (or recoverable amount if lower). Typically this would require a 'catch-up' depreciation charge as depreciation would not have been accounted for while it was held for sale. The standard explicitly requires this to be a current year charge.[308] This seems to indicate that for non-current assets and disposal groups ceasing to be so classified the *measurement* of items in comparative information (income statement and balance sheet) should not be revisited. This requirement applies equally to discontinued operations. However, as discussed at B below, this is not the case for associates and joint ventures.

Regarding the treatment of discontinued operations in the income statement, the standard states that if an entity ceases to classify a component as held for sale, the results of operations of the component previously presented in discontinued operations should be reclassified and included in income from continuing operations for all periods presented. The amounts for prior periods should be described as having been re-presented.[309]

As discussed at 5.3.1 B above, the amounts presented for non-current assets or for the assets and liabilities of disposal groups classified as held for sale in the comparative balance sheet should not be reclassified or re-presented.

B   The treatment of associates and joint ventures

Somewhat perplexingly, both IAS 28 – *Investments in Associates* and IAS 31 – *Interests in Joint Ventures* require a different approach to that discussed above. When an investment in an associate or an interest in a jointly controlled entity previously classified as held for sale (and hence accounted for in accordance with IFRS 5) ceases to be so classified they are required to be accounted for using the equity method or proportionate consolidation (as appropriate) *as from the date of classification as held for sale.*[310] Both standards also state that financial statements for the periods since classification as held for sale should be amended accordingly.

6   DISCLOSURE REQUIREMENTS

6.1   Disclosures relating to accounting policies

6.1.1   *Disclosure of accounting policies*

A   Summary of significant accounting policies

IAS 1 makes the valid observation that it is important for users to be informed of the measurement basis or bases used in the financial statements (for example, historical cost, current cost, net realisable value, fair value or recoverable amount) because the basis on which the financial statements are prepared significantly affects their analysis.[311]

Accordingly, the standard requires disclosure in a summary of significant accounting policies of:

(a)   the measurement basis (or bases) used in preparing the financial statements; and

(b)   the other accounting policies used that are relevant to an understanding of the financial statements.[312]

When more than one measurement basis is used in the financial statements, for example when particular classes of assets are revalued, it is sufficient to provide an indication of the categories of assets and liabilities to which each measurement basis is applied.[313]

It is clearly necessary to apply judgement when deciding on the level of detail required in a summary of accounting policies. However, the general tone of IAS 1 suggests a quite detailed analysis is necessary. Of particular note, is that the decision as to whether to disclose a policy should not just be a function of the magnitude of the sums involved. The standard states that an accounting policy may be significant because of the nature of the entity's operations even if amounts for current and prior periods are not material. It is also appropriate to disclose each significant accounting policy that is not specifically required by IFRSs, but is selected and applied in accordance with IAS 8 (discussed at 4.3 above).[314]

In deciding whether a particular accounting policy should be disclosed, IAS 1 requires consideration of whether disclosure would assist users in understanding how transactions, other events and conditions are reflected in the reported financial performance and financial position. Disclosure of particular accounting policies is especially useful to users when those policies are selected from alternatives allowed in standards and interpretations. An example is disclosure of whether a venturer recognises its interest in a jointly controlled entity using proportionate consolidation or the equity method (discussed in Chapter 8). Some standards specifically require disclosure of particular accounting policies, including choices made by management between different policies they allow. For example:

- IAS 16 requires disclosure of the measurement bases used for classes of property, plant and equipment (discussed in Chapter 12); and

- IAS 23 – *Borrowing Costs* – requires disclosure of whether borrowing costs are recognised immediately as an expense or capitalised as part of the cost of qualifying assets.[315]

Each entity is required to consider the nature of its operations and the policies that the users of its financial statements would expect to be disclosed for that type of entity. For example:

- an entity subject to income taxes would be expected to disclose its accounting policies for income taxes, including those applicable to deferred tax liabilities and assets;

- when an entity has significant foreign operations or transactions in foreign currencies, disclosure of accounting policies for the recognition of foreign exchange gains and losses would be expected; and

- when business combinations have occurred, the policies used for measuring goodwill and minority interest should be disclosed.[316]

B   Judgements made in applying accounting policies

The process of applying an entity's accounting policies, requires various judgements, apart from those involving estimations, that can significantly affect the amounts recognised in the financial statements. For example, judgements are required in determining:

(a)   whether financial assets are held-to-maturity investments;

(b)   when substantially all the significant risks and rewards of ownership of financial assets and lease assets are transferred to other entities;

(c)   whether, in substance, particular sales of goods are financing arrangements and therefore do not give rise to revenue; and

(d)   whether the substance of the relationship between the entity and a special purpose entity indicates that the special purpose entity is controlled by the entity.[317]

IAS 1 requires disclosure, in the summary of significant accounting policies or other notes, of the judgements (apart from those involving estimations, see 6.2.1 below) management has made in the process of applying the entity's accounting policies that have the most significant effect on the amounts recognised in the financial statements.[318]

Some of these disclosures are required by other standards. For example:

- IAS 27 requires an entity to disclose the reasons why the entity's ownership interest does not constitute control, in respect of an investee that is not a subsidiary even though more than half of its voting or potential voting power is owned directly or indirectly through subsidiaries; and

- IAS 40 requires disclosure of the criteria developed by the entity to distinguish investment property from owner-occupied property and from property held for sale in the ordinary course of business, when classification of the property is difficult.[319]

6.1.2 Disclosure of changes in accounting policies

IAS 8 distinguishes between accounting policy changes made pursuant to the initial application of a standard or interpretation from voluntary changes in accounting policy (discussed at 4.4 above). It sets out different disclosure requirements for each, as set out in A and B below. Also, if a standard or interpretation is in issue but is not yet effective and has not been applied certain disclosures of its likely impact are required. These are set out in C below.

A   *Accounting policy changes pursuant to the initial application of a standard or interpretation*

When initial application of a standard or an interpretation has an effect on the current period or any prior period, would have such an effect except that it is impracticable to determine the amount of the adjustment, or might have an effect on future periods, an entity should disclose:

(a)   the title of the standard or interpretation;

(b)   when applicable, that the change in accounting policy is made in accordance with its transitional provisions;

(c)   the nature of the change in accounting policy;

(d)   when applicable, a description of the transitional provisions;

(e)   when applicable, the transitional provisions that might have an effect on future periods;

(f)   for the current period and each prior period presented, to the extent practicable, the amount of the adjustment:

   (i)   for each financial statement line item affected; and

   (ii)   if IAS 33 – *Earnings per Share* – applies to the entity, for basic and diluted earnings per share;

(g)   the amount of the adjustment relating to periods before those presented, to the extent practicable; and

(h)   if retrospective application required by IAS 8 is impracticable for a particular prior period, or for periods before those presented, the circumstances that led to the existence of that condition and a description of how and from when the change in accounting policy has been applied.

Impracticability of restatement is discussed at 4.7 above. Financial statements of subsequent periods need not repeat these disclosures.[320]

B   *Voluntary changes in accounting policy*

When a voluntary change in accounting policy has an effect on the current period or any prior period, would have an effect on that period except that it is impracticable to determine the amount of the adjustment, or might have an effect on future periods, an entity should disclose:

(a)   the nature of the change in accounting policy;

(b)   the reasons why applying the new accounting policy provides reliable and more relevant information;

(c)   for the current period and each prior period presented, to the extent practicable, the amount of the adjustment:

   (i)   for each financial statement line item affected; and

   (ii)   if IAS 33 applies to the entity, for basic and diluted earnings per share;

(d)   the amount of the adjustment relating to periods before those presented, to the extent practicable; and

(e)   if retrospective application is impracticable for a particular prior period, or for periods before those presented, the circumstances that led to the existence of that condition and a description of how and from when the change in accounting policy has been applied.

Financial statements of subsequent periods need not repeat these disclosures.[321]

Impracticability of restatement is discussed at 4.7 above. Example 3.11 therein illustrates the above disclosure requirements.

C   *Future impact of a new standard or interpretation*

When an entity has not applied a new standard or interpretation that has been issued but is not yet effective, it should disclose:

(a)   that fact; and

(b)   known or reasonably estimable information relevant to assessing the possible impact that application of the new standard or interpretation will have on the financial statements in the period of initial application.[322]

In producing the above disclosure, the standard requires that an entity should consider disclosing:

(a)   the title of the new standard or interpretation;

(b)   the nature of the impending change or changes in accounting policy;

(c)   the date by which application of the standard or interpretation is required;

(d)   the date as at which it plans to apply the standard or interpretation initially; and

(e)   either:

   (i)   a discussion of the impact that initial application of the standard or interpretation is expected to have on the entity's financial statements; or

   (ii)   if that impact is not known or reasonably estimable, a statement to that effect.[323]

6.2   Disclosure of estimation uncertainty and changes in estimates

6.2.1   *Key sources of estimation uncertainty*

Determining the carrying amounts of some assets and liabilities requires estimation of the effects of uncertain future events on those assets and liabilities at the balance sheet date. Examples given by IAS 1 are that, in the absence of recently observed market prices used to measure them, the following assets and liabilities require future-oriented estimates to measure them:

- the recoverable amount of classes of property, plant and equipment;
- the effect of technological obsolescence on inventories;
- provisions subject to the future outcome of litigation in progress; and
- long-term employee benefit liabilities such as pension obligations.

These estimates involve assumptions about such items as the risk adjustment to cash flows or discount rates used, future changes in salaries and future changes in prices affecting other costs.[324]

In light of this, IAS 1 requires disclosure in the notes of information about the key assumptions concerning the future, and other key sources of estimation uncertainty at the balance sheet date, that have a significant risk of causing a material adjustment to the carrying amounts of assets and liabilities within the next financial year. In respect of those assets and liabilities, the notes must include details of:

(a)   their nature; and

(b)   their carrying amount as at the balance sheet date.[325]

IAS 1 goes on to observe that these key assumptions and other key sources of estimation uncertainty relate to the estimates that require management's most difficult, subjective or complex judgements. As the number of variables and assumptions affecting the possible future resolution of the uncertainties increases, those judgements become more subjective and complex, and the potential for a consequential material adjustment to the carrying amounts of assets and liabilities normally increases accordingly.[326]

The disclosures are required to be presented in a manner that helps users of financial statements to understand the judgements management makes about the future and about other key sources of estimation uncertainty. The nature and extent of the information provided will vary according to the nature of the assumption and other circumstances. Examples given by the standard of the types of disclosures to be made are:

(a)   the nature of the assumption or other estimation uncertainty;

(b)   the sensitivity of carrying amounts to the methods, assumptions and estimates underlying their calculation, including the reasons for the sensitivity;

(c) the expected resolution of an uncertainty and the range of reasonably possible outcomes within the next financial year in respect of the carrying amounts of the assets and liabilities affected; and

(d) an explanation of changes made to past assumptions concerning those assets and liabilities, if the uncertainty remains unresolved.[327]

The disclosure of some of these key assumptions is required by other standards. IAS 1 notes the following examples:

- IAS 37 requires disclosure, in specified circumstances, of major assumptions concerning future events affecting classes of provisions;

- IAS 32 requires disclosure of significant assumptions applied in estimating fair values of financial assets and financial liabilities that are carried at fair value; and

- IAS 16 requires disclosure of significant assumptions applied in estimating fair values of revalued items of property, plant and equipment.[328]

Other examples would include:

- IAS 19 requires disclosure of actuarial assumptions;

- IFRS 2 requires disclosure, in certain circumstances, of: the option pricing model used, and the method used and the assumptions made to incorporate the effects of early exercise; and

- IAS 36 requires disclosure, in certain circumstances, of each key assumption on which management has based its cash flow projections.

These key assumptions and other key sources of estimation uncertainty are not required to be disclosed for assets and liabilities with a significant risk that their carrying amounts might change materially within the next financial year if, at the balance sheet date, they are measured at fair value based on recently observed market prices. This is because, whilst their fair values might change materially within the next financial year those changes would not arise from assumptions or other sources of estimation uncertainty at the balance sheet date.[329] Also, it is not necessary to disclose budget information or forecasts in making the disclosures.[330] Furthermore, the disclosures of particular judgements management made in the process of applying the entity's accounting policies (discussed at 6.1.1 B above) do not relate to the disclosures of key sources of estimation uncertainty.[331]

When it is impracticable to disclose the extent of the possible effects of a key assumption or another key source of estimation uncertainty at the balance sheet date, the entity should disclose that it is reasonably possible, based on existing knowledge, that outcomes within the next financial year that are different from assumptions could require a material adjustment to the carrying amount of the asset or liability affected. In all cases, the entity should disclose the nature and carrying amount of the specific asset or liability (or class of assets or liabilities) affected by the assumption.[332]

In our view, these new requirements of IAS 1 (introduced as part of the IASB's improvements project) represent potentially highly onerous disclosures. The extensive judgements required in deciding the level of detail to be given leads us to expect that, once the requirement comes into force in 2005, practice will be mixed. The Basis for

Conclusions to the standard reveals that the Board was aware that the requirement could potentially require quite extensive disclosures and explains its attempt to limit this as follows. 'The revised Standard limits the scope of the disclosures to items that have a significant risk of causing a material adjustment to the carrying amounts of assets and liabilities *within the next financial year.* The longer the future period to which the disclosures relate, the greater the range of items that would qualify for disclosure, and the less specific the disclosures that could be made about particular assets or liabilities. A period longer than the next financial year might obscure the most relevant information with other disclosures.'[333]

6.2.2   Changes in accounting estimates

IAS 8 requires disclosure of the nature and amount of a change in an accounting estimate that has an effect in the current period or is expected to have an effect in future periods, except for the disclosure of the effect on future periods when it is impracticable to estimate that effect.[334] If the amount of the effect in future periods is not disclosed because estimating it is impracticable, that fact should be disclosed.[335]

6.3   Disclosure of prior period errors

When correction has been made for a material prior period error, IAS 8 requires disclosure of the following:

(a)   the nature of the prior period error;

(b)   for each prior period presented, to the extent practicable, the amount of the correction:

    (i)   for each financial statement line item affected; and

    (ii)   if IAS 33 applies to the entity, for basic and diluted earnings per share;

(c)   the amount of the correction at the beginning of the earliest prior period presented; and

(d)   if retrospective restatement is impracticable for a particular prior period, the circumstances that led to the existence of that condition and a description of how and from when the error has been corrected.

Financial statements of subsequent periods need not repeat these disclosures.[336]

Example 3.10 at 4.6 above illustrates these disclosure requirements.

6.4   Disclosures relating to non-current assets held for resale

As discussed at 3.1.2 and 3.2.3 above, IFRS 5 sets out detailed requirements for the prominent presentation of amounts relating to non-current assets held for resale, disposal groups and discontinued operations. In addition, disclosure is required in the notes in the period in which a non-current asset (or disposal group) has been either classified as held for sale or sold of:

(a)   a description of the non-current asset (or disposal group);

(b)   a description of the facts and circumstances of the sale, or leading to the expected disposal, and the expected manner and timing of that disposal;

(c)   the gain or loss recognised as a result of measuring the non-current asset (or disposal group) at fair value less costs to sell (discussed at 5 above) and, if not separately presented on the face of the income statement, the caption in the income statement that includes that gain or loss; and

(d)   if applicable, the segment in which the non-current asset (or disposal group) is presented in accordance with IAS 14 – *Segment Reporting* (discussed in Chapter 28).[337]

If a non-current asset (or disposal group) meets the criteria to be classified as held for sale after the balance sheet date but before the financial statements are authorised for issue, the information specified in (a), (b) and (d) above should also be disclosed in the notes.[338]

Further, should:

- a non-current asset (or disposal group) cease to be classified as held for sale; or

- an individual asset or liability be removed from a disposal group,

IFRS 5 requires disclosure, in the period of the decision to change the plan to sell the non-current asset (or disposal group), a description of the facts and circumstances leading to the decision and the effect of the decision on the results of operations for the period and any prior periods presented.[339]

6.5   Other disclosures

6.5.1   IAS 1

IAS 1 also requires disclosure:

(a)   in the notes of:

(i)   the amount of dividends proposed or declared before the financial statements were authorised for issue but not recognised as a distribution to equity holders during the period, and the related amount per share; and

(ii)   the amount of any cumulative preference dividends not recognised;[340]

(b)   either on the face of the income statement or the statement of changes in equity, or in the notes, the amount of dividends recognised as distributions to equity holders during the period, and the related amount per share;[341]

(c)   in accordance with IAS 10 – *Events after the Balance Sheet Date* – the following non-adjusting events in respect of loans classified as current liabilities, if they occur between the balance sheet date and the date the financial statements are authorised for issue:

(i)   refinancing on a long-term basis;

(ii)   rectification of a breach of a long-term loan agreement; and

(iii)   the receipt from the lender of a period of grace to rectify a breach of a long-term loan agreement ending at least twelve months after the balance sheet date;[342]

(d)   the following, if not disclosed elsewhere in information published with the financial statements:

(i)   the domicile and legal form of the entity, its country of incorporation and the address of its registered office (or principal place of business, if different from the registered office);

(ii)   a description of the nature of the entity's operations and its principal activities; and

(iii) the name of the parent and the ultimate parent of the group.[343]

7   FUTURE DEVELOPMENTS

The IASB is currently pursuing a project which they term 'reporting comprehensive income'. Although the project began as a consideration of the presentation of gains and losses, its has evolved to have a much wider scope. The current intention of the IASB is to pursue the project jointly with the FASB. At a joint meeting of the two Boards it was decided to divide the project into two segments. The Boards expect to pursue both segments at the same time, although they expect that the issues in Segment A will be resolved first.

Segment A includes:

•   whether to require a single statement of comprehensive income that includes a subtotal similar to the concept of 'net income from continuing operations' or 'profit and loss';

•   the required primary financial statements;

•   the number of years required to be presented in comparative financial statements and related disclosures in the notes to the financial statements; and

•   considering whether the direct method should be required for the presentation of the statement of cash flows.

Segment B includes:

•   considering whether there is value in the notion of 'recycling' items between the subtotals of net income and other comprehensive income and, if so, the basis for the types of transactions and events that should be recycled and when recycling should occur;

•   developing consistent principles for disaggregating information on each of the required financial statements; and

•   defining the totals and subtotals to be reported on each of the required financial statements (for example, categories such as business and financing).[344]

8   CONCLUSION

IAS 1 and IAS 8 deal with overlapping issues and together run to over 180 detailed paragraphs, along with extensive further material in appendices. In our view their usefulness could be greatly enhanced by combining them in one standard and reducing repetition. Notwithstanding this and the occasional lack of clarity, they provide a workable backbone for IFRS. Some of the new requirements introduced by the improvements project, such as the disclosure of key sources of estimation uncertainty, are potentially onerous. Time will tell how entities reporting under IFRS will address this once the rules come into force.

The removal of the requirement to present the results of operating activities in the income statement is, in our view, a retrograde step. The reason given by the Board is that, because operating activities is not defined, it 'decided not to require disclosure of an undefined term.' It would have been preferable, in our view, to develop a robust definition of operating activities. Furthermore, it is regrettable that the IASB (expecting that some entities will voluntarily present the results of operating activities) has presented its opinions as to just what such an item should and not include in the Basis for Conclusions to the standard. Giving such 'guidance' *outside* of IFRS about something not actually required by IFRS but which the Board thinks may be given voluntarily strikes us as a recipe for confusion.

In our view, IFRS 5 is not particularly well drafted nor well conceived. The definition of a discontinued operation is vague, and in particular the meaning of 'a separate major line of business' will inevitably mean different things to different people. The requirement not to depreciate assets which are still actively used (for periods which could exceed a year) introduces a conflict with how assets which are not intended to be sold are treated – although the requirements for impairment and the use of current price residuals may limit the practical impact of this on the balance sheet. Also, the portfolio approach to measuring disposal groups conflicts with the general requirements for separate determination used elsewhere in IFRS and sits particularly awkwardly with the components approach of IAS 16.

References

1 IAS 1, *Presentation of Financial Statements*, IASB, December 2003 (amended March 2004).

2 IAS 8, *Accounting Policies, Changes in Accounting Estimates and Errors*, IASB, December 2003 (amended March 2004).

3 IFRS 5, *Non-current Assets Held for Sale and Discontinued Operations*, IASB, March 2004.

4 IAS 1, para. 127.

5 IAS 1, paras. IN3-IN4.

6 IAS 1, paras. IN10-IN13.

7 IAS 1, para. IN6.

8 IAS 1, para. IN7.

9 IAS 1, para. IN13.

10 IAS 1, para. IN17.

11 IAS 1, paras. IN15-IN16.

12 IAS 1, paras. IN18-IN19.

13 IAS 1, paras. 2-3.

14 IAS 1, para. 11 and IAS 8, para. 5.

15 IAS 8, para. 9.

16 IAS 27, *Consolidated and Separate Financial Statements*, IASB, December 2003 (amended March 2004).

17 IAS 34, *Interim Financial Reporting*, IASB, March 2004.
18 IAS 1, para. 3.
19 IAS 1, para. 1.
20 IAS 1, para. 5.
21 IAS 1, para. 6.
22 IAS 1, para. 4.
23 IAS 8, para. 56.
24 IAS 8, para. 54.
25 IAS 8, para. IN3.
26 IAS 8, paras. IN7-IN9, IN12 and IN16.
27 IAS 8, para. IN7.
28 IAS 8, paras. IN10-IN11.
29 IAS 8, para. IN14.
30 IAS 8, para. IN17.
31 IAS 8, para. IN14.
32 IAS 8, paras. IN6 and IN15.
33 IAS 8, para. 3.
34 IAS 8, para. 1.
35 IAS 8, para. 2.
36 IAS 8, para. 4.
37 IFRS 5, para. 45.
38 IFRS 5, paras. IN2-IN3.
39 IFRS 5, para. IN4.
40 IFRS 5, para. IN5.
41 IFRS 5, paras. BC67-BC71.
42 IFRS 5, para. 1.
43 IFRS 5, paras. 2 and 5.
44 IFRS 5, para. 44.
45 IFRS 5, para. 43.
46 IFRS 1, *First-time Adoption of International Financial Reporting Standards*, IASB, June 2003 (amended March 2004), para. 34B.
47 IAS 1, para. 7.
48 IAS 1, para. 49.
49 IAS 1, para. 50.
50 IAS 1, para. 8.
51 IAS 1, para. 11.
52 IAS 1, para. 10.
53 IAS 1, para. 9.
54 IAS 1, para. 10.
55 IAS 1, para. 36.
56 IAS 1, para. 37.
57 IAS 1, para. 86.
58 IAS 1, para. 40.
59 IAS 1, para. 38.
60 IAS 1, para. 11.
61 IAS 1, para. 40.
62 IAS 1, para. 39.
63 IAS 1, paras. 44-45.
64 IAS 1, para. 46.
65 IAS 1, para. 47.
66 IAS 1, para. 48.
67 IAS 1, para. 14.
68 IAS 1, para. 14.
69 IAS 1, para. 42.
70 IAS 1, para. 43.
71 IAS 1, para. 4.
72 IAS 1, para. 102.
73 IAS 1, para. 51.
74 IAS 1, para. 58.
75 IAS 1, para. 53.
76 IAS 1, paras. 59 and 61.
77 IFRS 5, para. 3.
78 IAS 1, para. 51.
79 IAS 1, paras. 57 and 60.
80 IAS 1, para. 51.
81 IAS 1, para. 54.
82 IAS 1, para. 55.
83 IAS 1, para. 52.
84 IAS 1, para. 56.
85 IFRS 5, para. 30.
86 IFRS 5, paras. 38-39.
87 IFRS 5, para. BC58.
88 IFRS 5, Implementation Guidance, Example 12.
89 IAS 1, para. 57.
90 IAS 1, para. 70.
91 IAS 1, para. 59.
92 IAS 1, para. 60.
93 IAS 1, para. 70.
94 IAS 1, para. 61.
95 IAS 19 (amended 2004), *Employee Benefits*, IASB, 2004, para. 118 and Basis for Conclusions, para. 81.
96 IAS 1, para. 62.
97 IAS 1, paras. 63 and 67.
98 IAS 1, paras. 65 and 67.
99 IAS 1, para. 66.
100 IAS 1, para. 64.
101 IAS 1, para. 71.
102 IAS 1, paras. 68 and 71.
103 IAS 1, para. 69.
104 IAS 1, para. 72.
105 IAS 1, para. 73.
106 IAS 1, paras. 68 and 68A.
107 IAS 1, para. 71.
108 IAS 1, para. 74.
109 IAS 1, para. 75.
110 IAS 1, paras. 72 and 75.
111 IAS 1, para. 75.
112 IAS 1, para. 76.
113 IAS 1, para. 77.
114 IAS 1, para. IG2.
115 IAS 1, para. IG4.
116 IAS 1, para. 84.
117 IAS 1, para. 83.
118 IAS 1, para. 84.
119 IAS 1, para. 81.
120 IAS 1, para. 82.
121 IAS 1, para. 89.
122 IAS 1, para. 95.
123 IAS 1, para. BC12.
124 IAS 1, para. BC13.
125 IAS 1, para. 90.
126 IAS 1, para. 88.
127 IAS 1, para. 89.

128 IAS 1, para. 94.
129 IAS 1, para. 91.
130 IAS 1, para. IG4.
131 IAS 1, para. 92.
132 IAS 1, para. IG4.
133 IAS 1, para. 93.
134 IFRS 5, para. 32 and Appendix A.
135 IFRS 5, para. 31 and Appendix A.
136 IFRS 5, Appendix A.
137 IFRS 5, paras. BC67-BC71.
138 IFRS 5, para. 13.
139 IFRS 5, para. 14.
140 IFRS 5, Implementation Guidance, Example 9.
141 IFRS 5, para. 33(a).
142 IFRS 5, para. 33(b).
143 IFRS 5, para. 37.
144 IFRS 5, para. 34.
145 IFRS 5, Implementation Guidance, Example 11.
146 IFRS 5, para. 35.
147 IFRS 5, para. 33(c).
148 IAS 1, para. 86.
149 IAS 1, para. 87.
150 *Framework for the Preparation and Presentation of Financial Statements*, IASB, September 1989, para. 72.
151 IAS 8 (revised 1993), *Net Profit or Loss for the period, Fundamental Errors and Changes in Accounting Policies*, IASC, December 1993, paras. 6 and 10-15.
152 IAS 1, para. 85.
153 IAS 1, para. BC17.
154 IAS 1, paras. 78 and 99.
155 IAS 1, para. 99.
156 IAS 1, para. 96.
157 IAS 1, para. 98.
158 IAS 1, para. 100.
159 IAS 1, para. 97.
160 IAS 1, para. 101.
161 IAS 1, para. IG4.
162 IAS 1, para. IG4.
163 IAS 1, para. 103.
164 IAS 1, para. 104.
165 IAS 1, para. 105.
166 IAS 1, para. 107.
167 IAS 1, para. 106.
168 IAS 1, para. 13.
169 IAS 8, para. 9.
170 IAS 1, para. 15.
171 IAS 1, para. 16.
172 IAS 1, para. 15.
173 IAS 1, para. 22.
174 IAS 1, para. 17.
175 IAS 1, paras. 18-19.
176 IAS 1, para. 20.
177 IAS 1, para. 21.
178 IAS 1, para. 23.
179 IAS 1, para. 24.
180 IAS 1, para. 25.

181 IAS 1, para. 26.
182 Framework, para. 22.
183 IAS 1, para. 27.
184 IAS 1, para. 28.
185 IAS 8, para. 15.
186 IAS 8, para. 13.
187 IAS 1, para. 30.
188 IAS 1, para. 29.
189 IAS 1, para. 11 and IAS 8, para. 5.
190 IAS 1, para. 31.
191 IAS 8, paras. 6 and 12.
192 IAS 1, para. 30.
193 IAS 1, para. 33.
194 IAS 1, para. 32.
195 IAS 1, para. 34.
196 IAS 1, para. 35.
197 IAS 1, para. 78.
198 Framework, para. 70.
199 IAS 1, para. 79.
200 IAS 1, para. 80.
201 IAS 8, para. 5.
202 IAS 8, para. 35.
203 IAS 1, para. 109.
204 IAS 8, para. 5.
205 IAS 8, para. 38.
206 IAS 8, para. 48.
207 IAS 8, para. 35.
208 IAS 8, para. 8.
209 IAS 8, para. 7.
210 IAS 8, para. 8.
211 IAS 8, para. 10.
212 Framework, paras. 36-37.
213 IAS 8, para. 11.
214 IAS 8, para. 12.
215 IAS 8, para. 14.
216 IAS 8, paras. 5 and 19-20.
217 IAS 8, para. 22.
218 IAS 8, para. 26.
219 IAS 8, para. 23.
220 IAS 8, para. 21.
221 IAS 8, para. 16.
222 IAS 8, paras. 17-18.
223 IAS 8, para. 35.
224 IAS 8, Implementation Guidance, Example 2.
225 IAS 8, paras. 32-33.
226 IAS 8, para. 34.
227 IAS 8, para. 36.
228 IAS 8, para. 5.
229 IAS 8, paras. 36- 38.
230 IAS 8, para. 41.
231 IAS 8, para. 41.
232 IAS 8, para. 48.
233 IAS 8, para. 5.
234 IAS 8, para. 42.
235 IAS 8, para. 46.
236 IAS 8, para. 42.
237 IAS 8, para. 5.
238 IAS 8, Implementation Guidance, Example 1.

239 IAS 8, para. 43.
240 IAS 8, para. 5.
241 IAS 8, para. 50.
242 IAS 8, para. 51.
243 IAS 8, para. 53.
244 IAS 8, para. 52.
245 IAS 8, para. 23.
246 IAS 8, para. 26.
247 IAS 8, para. 24.
248 IAS 8, para. 25.
249 IAS 8, para. 5.
250 IAS 8, para. 27.
251 IAS 8, Implementation Guidance, Example 3.
252 IAS 8, para. 43.
253 IAS 8, para. 44.
254 IAS 8, para. 45.
255 IAS 8, para. 47.
256 IFRS 5, Appendix A.
257 IFRS 5, para. 6.
258 IFRS 5, para. 4.
259 IFRS 5, Appendix A.
260 IFRS 5, para. 4.
261 IFRS 5, para. 6.
262 IFRS 5, para. 10.
263 IFRS 5, para. 2.
264 IFRS 5, para. 7.
265 IFRS 5, para. 13.
266 IFRS 5, para. 26.
267 IFRS 5, para. 11.
268 IFRS 5, para. 12.
269 IFRS 5, Implementation Guidance, Examples 1-3.
270 IFRS 5, Appendix A.
271 IAS 39, *Financial Instruments: Recognition and Measurement*, IASB, December 2003 (amended March 2004), para. F.3.7.
272 IFRS 5, para. 8.
273 IFRS 5, Implementation Guidance, Example 4.
274 IFRS 5, para. 9.
275 IFRS 5, Appendix B.
276 IFRS 5, Appendix A.
277 IFRS 5, Implementation Guidance, Example 5.
278 IFRS 5, Implementation Guidance, Example 6.
279 IFRS 5, Implementation Guidance, Example 7.
280 IFRS 5, para. 13.
281 IFRS 5, para. 13.
282 IFRS 5, para. 14.
283 IFRS 5, Implementation Guidance, Example 8.
284 IFRS 5, paras. 2 and 5.
285 IFRS 5, para. 18.
286 IFRS 5, para. 15.
287 IFRS 5, Appendix A.
288 IFRS 5, para. 17.
289 IFRS 5, para. 4.
290 IFRS 5, para. 16.
291 IFRS 5, Implementation Guidance, Example 13.
292 IFRS 5, para. 25.
293 IFRS 5, para. 19.
294 IFRS 5, para. 20.
295 IFRS 5, para. 21.
296 IFRS 5, para. 22.
297 IFRS 5, para. 23.
298 IFRS 5, Implementation Guidance, Example 10.
299 IFRS 5, para. 24.
300 IFRS 5, para. 26.
301 IFRS 5, para. 29.
302 IFRS 5, para. 27.
303 IFRS 5, Appendix A.
304 IFRS 5, paras. 28 and 37.
305 IFRS 5, para. 34.
306 IFRS 5, para. 40.
307 IFRS 5, Implementation Guidance, Example 13.
308 IFRS 5, para. 28.
309 IFRS 5, para. 36.
310 IAS 28, *Investments in Associates*, IASB, December 2003 (amended March 2004), para. 15 and IAS 31, para. 43.
311 IAS 1, para. 109.
312 IAS 1, para. 108.
313 IAS 1, para. 109.
314 IAS 1, para. 112.
315 IAS 1, para. 110.
316 IAS 1, para. 111.
317 IAS 1, para. 114.
318 IAS 1, para. 113.
319 IAS 1, para. 115.
320 IAS 8, para. 28.
321 IAS 8, para. 29.
322 IAS 8, para. 30.
323 IAS 8, para. 31.
324 IAS 1, para. 117.
325 IAS 1, para. 116.
326 IAS 1, para. 118.
327 IAS 1, para. 120.
328 IAS 1, para. 124.
329 IAS 1, para. 119.
330 IAS 1, para. 121.
331 IAS 1, para. 123.
332 IAS 1, para. 122.
333 IAS 1, para. BC37.
334 IAS 8, para. 39.
335 IAS 8, para. 40.
336 IAS 8, para. 49.
337 IFRS 5, para. 41.
338 IFRS 5, para. 12.
339 IFRS 5, para. 42.
340 IAS 1, para. 125.
341 IAS 1, para. 95.
342 IAS 1, para. 67.
343 IAS 1, para. 126.
344 *IASB Update,* IASB, April 2004, page 5.

Chapter 4 First-time adoption

1 INTRODUCTION

1.1 Background

IFRS 1 – *First-time Adoption of International Financial Reporting Standards* – is a unique standard. It owes its existence primarily to the 2005 adoption of IFRS by EU companies whose securities are traded on a EU regulated market.[1] Also, following the EU's lead, entities in many other jurisdictions will be required by their governments to adopt IFRS from 2005 or later. It is the radically different nature of IFRS compared with many national GAAPs that has necessitated IFRS 1.

Although entities are frequently required to adopt new accounting standards under their national GAAP, adopting IFRS, an entirely different basis of accounting, poses a distinct set of problems:

- the sheer magnitude of the effort involved in adopting a large number of new accounting standards;
- the requirements of individual standards will often differ significantly from those under an entity's previous GAAP;
- information may need to be collected that was not required under the previous GAAP; and
- practical experience of applying a principles-based system of financial reporting standards such as IFRS does not exist in many entities.

1.2 Development of IFRS 1

1.2.1 SIC-8

In 1997 the former IASC Board asked its Standing Interpretations Committee to address the issue of how first-time adopters should account for the transition to IFRS. This resulted, in July 1998, in the adoption of SIC-8 – *First-Time Application of IASs as the Primary Basis of Accounting*. SIC-8 required that 'in the period when IASs are applied in full for the first time as the primary accounting basis, the financial statements of an enterprise should be prepared and presented as if the financial statements had always been prepared in accordance with the Standards and Interpretations effective for the period of first-time application'.[2] It became clear shortly after SIC-8 was issued that, although theoretically sound, the approach taken by the interpretation could give rise to substantial practical difficulties for entities adopting IFRS for the first time. For example, it would have required all prior business combinations to be restated on an IFRS basis, which would have been wholly impracticable.

1.2.2   The need for IFRS 1

The spotlight was placed firmly on first-time adoption of IFRS when the European Commission proposed to require all publicly traded EU incorporated companies to prepare their consolidated accounts under IFRS, by 2005 at the latest. After the IASB had been made aware of the considerable practical difficulties surrounding first-time application under SIC-8, it announced that it would undertake a separate project on this subject. Consequently, in July 2002, the IASB published ED 1 – *First-time Application of International Financial Reporting Standards.*[3] The Board made significant changes to the exposure draft before finalising it in June 2003 as IFRS 1 – *First-time Adoption of International Financial Reporting Standards.*

In the introduction to the standard, the IASB cites the following reasons for replacing SIC-8 by IFRS 1:[4]

- SIC-8 required full retrospective application that could cause costs that exceeded the likely benefits for users of financial statements;

- although SIC-8 did not require retrospective application when this would be impracticable, it did not define 'impracticable' leaving it unclear whether it should be interpreted as a high hurdle or a low hurdle;

- 'SIC-8 could require a first-time adopter to apply two different versions of a Standard if a new version were introduced during the periods covered by its first financial statements prepared under IASs and the new version prohibited retrospective application';

- 'SIC-8 did not state clearly whether a first-time adopter should use hindsight in applying recognition and measurement decisions retrospectively'; and

- 'there was some doubt about how SIC-8 interacted with specific transitional provisions in individual Standards'.

IFRS 1 offers many significant improvements over SIC-8, but it also has a number of weaknesses. First, given the IASB's worldwide constituency, IFRS 1 had to be written in a way that completely ignores a first-time adopter's previous GAAP. One of the IASB's aims in developing IFRS 1 was 'to find solutions that will be appropriate for any entity, in any part of the world, regardless of whether adoption occurs in 2005 or at a different time'.[5] Consequently, first-time adoption exemptions are made available to all first-time adopters, even those first-time adopters whose previous GAAP was very close to IFRS. A first-time adopter will be able to make considerable adjustments to its opening IFRS balance sheet, using the available exemptions in IFRS 1, even if the difference between its previous

GAAP and IFRS was only minor. It may even be required to make considerable adjustments due to the exemptions and exceptions.

Secondly, in its basis for conclusions, the IASB notes that ideally a regime for the first-time adoption of IFRS would achieve comparability between the financial statements of an entity over time, between different first-time adopters, and between first-time adopters and entities already applying IFRS.[6] SIC-8 gave priority to ensuring comparability between a first-time adopter and entities already adopting IFRS. Inevitably there are tensions between these objectives, and IFRS 1 gives priority to achieving 'comparability over time within a first-time adopter's first IFRS financial statements and between different entities adopting IFRS for the first time at a given date; achieving comparability between first-time adopters and entities that already apply IFRS is a secondary objective'.[7]

The detailed requirements of the standard are discussed below. The practical application of the standard is illustrated by worked examples throughout this chapter, by comprehensive extracts from the financial statements of three companies applying IFRS 1 and by a discussion of practical issues at 3 below.

2 REQUIREMENTS OF IFRS 1

2.1 Objective

The underlying principle in IFRS 1 is that a first-time adopter should prepare financial statements as if it had always applied IFRS, but there are a number of exemptions and exceptions that allow or require a first-time adopter to deviate from the general rule. The objective of IFRS 1 is to ensure that an entity's first IFRS financial statements and its first IFRS interim financial statements contain high quality financial information that:[8]

(a) is transparent for users and comparable over all periods presented;

(b) provides a suitable starting point for accounting under IFRS; and

(c) can be generated at a cost that does not exceed the benefits to users.

2.2 Scope and definitions

2.2.1 What counts as first-time adoption?

Clearly, given the differing regimes between first-time adopters and entities already using IFRS, what counts as first-time adoption is a question of some importance. The standard defines an entity's first IFRS financial statements as being the first annual financial statements in which an entity adopts IFRS by an 'explicit and unreserved statement' of compliance with IFRS in those financial statements.[9] The decisive factor is whether or not the entity made that explicit and unreserved statement. Even if an entity departed from certain IFRS (whether recognition, measurement or disclosure) in its previous financial statements but still made an explicit and unreserved statement of compliance, that entity is *not* considered to be a first-time adopter. Accordingly, such an entity is not allowed to apply IFRS 1 in accounting for changes in its accounting policies. Instead, it is required to apply IAS 8 – *Accounting Policies, Changes in Accounting Estimates and Errors* – in making any corrections or changes.

IFRS 1 states that an entity's first IFRS financial statements will be subject to IFRS 1 even if it presented its most recent previous financial statements in conformity with IFRS in all respects except that they did not contain an explicit and unreserved statement.[10] An entity's financial statements are considered its first IFRS financial statements, and thus fall within the scope of IFRS 1, when it:

'(a)   presented its most recent previous financial statements:

   (i)   under national requirements that are not consistent with IFRSs in all respects;

   (ii)   in conformity with IFRSs in all respects, except that the financial statements did not contain an explicit and unreserved statement that they complied with IFRS;

   (iii)   containing an explicit statement of compliance with some, but not all, IFRSs;

   (iv)   under national requirements inconsistent with IFRSs, using some individual IFRSs to account for items for which national requirements did not exist; or

   (v)   under national requirements, with a reconciliation of some amounts to the amounts determined under IFRSs;

(b)   prepared financial statements under IFRSs for internal use only, without making them available to the entity's owners or any other external users;

(c)   prepared a reporting package under IFRSs for consolidation purposes without preparing a complete set of financial statements as defined in IAS 1 *Presentation of Financial Statements*; or

(d)   did not present financial statements for previous periods'.[11]

Therefore, an entity whose most recent previous financial statements contained an explicit and unreserved statement of compliance with IFRS can never be considered a first-time adopter. This is the case even in the following circumstances:

(a)   the entity issued financial statements claiming to comply both with national GAAP and IFRS, and subsequently drops the national GAAP compliance claim; or

(b)   the auditors issued a qualified audit report on the IFRS financial statements; or

(c)   the entity stops presenting a separate set of financial statements under national requirements.[12]

The IASB could have introduced special rules that would have required an entity that significantly departed from IFRS to apply IFRS 1. However, the IASB considered that such rules would lead to 'complexity and uncertainty'.[13] In addition, this would have given entities applying 'IFRS-lite' (i.e. entities not applying IFRS rigorously in all respects) an option to side step the requirements of IAS 8.[14]

It is clear that the scope of IFRS 1 is very much rule-based, which, as the example below illustrates, can lead to different answers in similar situations and sometimes to counterintuitive answers.

Example 4.1:   Scope of application of IFRS 1

Entity A applied IFRS in its previous financial statements, but stated that it 'applied IFRS except for SIC-12 – *Consolidation – Special Purpose Entities*'.

Entity A is a first-time adopter because its financial statements did not contain an unreserved statement of compliance with IFRS. It is irrelevant as to whether or not the auditors' report was qualified.

Entity B applied IFRS in its previous financial statements and stated that the 'financial statements are prepared in conformity with IFRS'. Despite that statement, B had not applied SIC-12.

Entity B is not a first-time adopter because its financial statements contained an unreserved statement of compliance with IFRS. Even if the auditors had qualified their report, the entity would still not be a first-time adopter.

Example 4.2:   Entity applying national GAAP and IFRS

Entity C prepares two sets of financial statements, one set of financial statements based on its national GAAP and the other set based on IFRS. The IFRS financial statements contained an explicit and unreserved statement of compliance with IFRS and were made available externally. From 2005 onwards, C stops presenting financial statements based on its national GAAP.

Entity C is not a first-time adopter because it already published financial statements that contained an explicit and unreserved statement of compliance with IFRS.

An entity that is not a first-time adopter cannot apply IFRS 1 to changes in its accounting policies. Instead, such an entity should apply:

* the requirements of IAS 8; and
* specific transitional requirements in other IFRS.[15]

2.2.2   When should IFRS 1 be applied?

An entity that presents its first IFRS financial statements is a first-time adopter[16] and should apply IFRS 1 in preparing those financial statements.[17] It should also apply the standard in each interim financial report that it presents under IAS 34 – *Interim Financial Reporting* – for a part of the period covered by its first IFRS financial statements.[18] However, a first-time adopter that only issues a 'trading statement' at its interim reporting dates, which is not described as complying with IAS 34 or IFRS, is not required to apply IAS 34.[19] Therefore, IFRS 1 does not apply to such interim reports.

2.2.3   First-time adoption timeline

IFRS 1 defines the following terms in connection with the transition to IFRS:[20]

Date of transition to IFRS: The beginning of the earliest period for which an entity presents full comparative information under IFRS in its first IFRS financial statements.

Reporting date: The end of the latest period covered by financial statements or by an interim financial report.

First IFRS financial statements: The first annual financial statements in which an entity adopts International Financial Reporting Standards, by an explicit and unreserved statement of compliance with IFRS.

First IFRS reporting period: The reporting period ending on the reporting date of an entity's first IFRS financial statements.

Opening IFRS balance sheet: An entity's balance sheet (published or unpublished) at the date of transition to IFRS.

International Financial Reporting Standards: Standards and Interpretations adopted by the International Accounting Standards Board (IASB). They comprise:

(a)   International Financial Reporting Standards;

(b)   International Accounting Standards; and

(c)   Interpretations originated by the International Financial Reporting Interpretations Committee (IFRIC) or the former Standing Interpretations Committee (SIC).

Previous GAAP: The basis of accounting that a first-time adopter used immediately before adopting IFRS.

An entity's first IFRS financial statements must include at least one comparative period, but an entity may elect or be required to provide more than one comparative period.[21] The beginning of the earliest comparative period for which the entity presents full comparative information under IFRS will be treated as its date of transition to IFRS. The diagram below shows how for an entity with a December year-end the above terms are related:

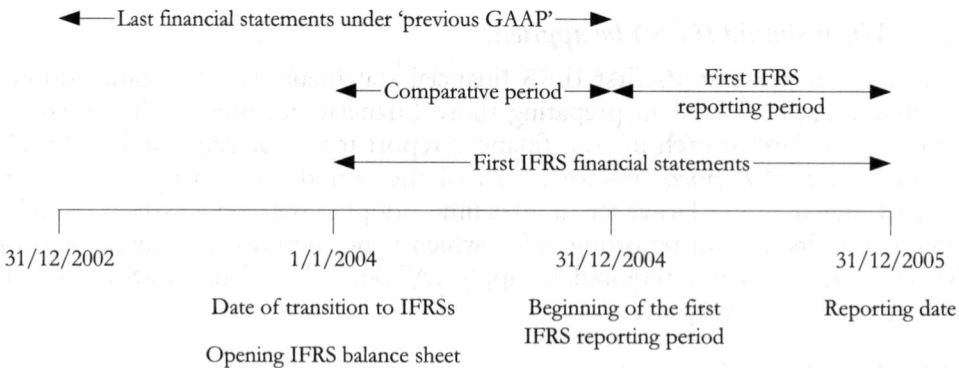

The diagram above also illustrates that there is a period of overlap, for the financial year 2004, which is reported first under the entity's previous GAAP and then as a comparative period under IFRS. The following examples illustrate how an entity should determine its date of transition to IFRS.

Example 4.3:   *Determining the date of transition to IFRS*

Entity D's year-end is 31 December and it presents financial statements that include one comparative period. D is required to produce IFRS financial statements for the first accounting period starting on or after 1 January 2005.

D's first reporting date under IFRS is 31 December 2005. Its date of transition to IFRS is 1 January 2004, which is the beginning of the first comparative period included in its IFRS financial statements.

Entity E's year-end is 31 July and it presents financial statements that include two comparative periods. E is required to produce IFRS financial statements for the first accounting period starting on or after 1 January 2005.

E's first reporting date under IFRS is 31 July 2006. Its date of transition to IFRS is 1 August 2003, which is the beginning of the first comparative period included in its IFRS financial statements.

IFRS 1 does not specifically address how these requirements apply to an entity whose current or comparative financial period is not exactly equal to one year. In the case of an entity with a 52-week financial reporting cycle, IAS 1 considers 52-week financial periods to be acceptable because they 'are unlikely to be materially different from those that would be presented for one year'.[22] Consequently, it is generally not considered to be a problem if the current or comparative period in an entity's first IFRS financial statements only covers a 52-week period. However, when an entity's current or comparative period is considerably longer or shorter than one year, it needs to consider the requirements of IFRS 1 carefully.

2.2.4 Fair value and deemed cost

Some exemptions in IFRS 1 refer to 'fair value' and 'deemed cost', and the standard defines these terms. These definitions are important to the practical application of IFRS 1 and an understanding of the exemptions it contains:[23]

Deemed cost: An amount used as a surrogate for cost or depreciated cost at a given date. Subsequent depreciation or amortisation assumes that the entity had initially recognised the asset or liability at the given date and that its cost was equal to the deemed cost.

Fair value: The amount for which an asset could be exchanged, or a liability settled, between knowledgeable, willing parties in an arm's length transaction.

In determining the fair value of items, a first-time adopter should use the guidance in IFRS 3 – *Business Combinations* (see Chapter 6) unless 'another IFRS contains more specific guidance on the determination of fair values for the asset or liability in question'. The fair values determined by a first-time adopter should reflect the conditions that existed at the date for which they were determined,[24] i.e. the first-time adopter should not apply hindsight in measuring the fair value at an earlier date (see Chapter 6 at 2.3.3 D).

2.3   Recognition and measurement principles

2.3.1   *Opening IFRS balance sheet and accounting policies*

At the date of transition to IFRS (i.e. 1 January 2004 for an entity presenting one year of comparative figures and reporting at 31 December 2005) an entity should prepare an opening IFRS balance sheet that is the starting point for its accounting under IFRS. This opening balance sheet does not have to be published in the first IFRS financial statements.[25] However, it is required for, and integral to an equity reconciliation that has to be presented in an entity's first IFRS financial statements (see 2.10.2 below).

The requirement to prepare an opening IFRS balance sheet and 'reset the clock' at that date poses a number of challenges for first-time adopters. Even a first-time adopter that already applies a standard that is directly based on IFRS may need to restate items in its opening IFRS balance sheet. This happens, for example, in the case of an entity applying a pensions standard that is based on IAS 19 – *Employee Benefits* – before an entity's date of transition to IFRS (see 2.7.1 below).

With the exception of financial instruments and insurance contracts (see 2.6.1 below), IFRS 1 requires a first-time adopter to use the same accounting policies in its opening IFRS balance sheet and all periods presented in its first IFRS financial statements. However, this will not happen quite so straightforwardly, since to achieve this, the entity should comply with each IFRS effective at the reporting date for its first IFRS financial statements, and should take into account a number of exemptions from other IFRS and exceptions to retrospective application of other IFRS allowed by IFRS 1 (see 2.3.3 below).[26] In other words, the fundamental principle of IFRS 1 is to require full retrospective application of the standards in force at an entity's reporting date, but with limited exceptions. The IASB initially entertained a suggestion to restrict retrospective application of IFRS to a limited 'look back' period of three to five years – to avoid the cost of investigating very old transactions – but concluded that this approach could lead to the omission of material assets or liabilities from an entity's opening IFRS balance sheet.[27] The diagram shows how the process of selecting IFRS accounting policies operates.

The requirement to apply the same accounting policies to all periods also prohibits a first-time adopter from applying previous versions of standards that were effective at earlier dates.[28] The IASB believes that this:

- enhances comparability because the first IFRS financial statements are prepared on a consistent basis over time;
- gives users comparative information that is based on IFRS that are superior to superseded versions of those standards; and
- avoids unnecessary costs.[29]

For similar reasons, IFRS 1 also permits an entity to apply a new IFRS that is not yet mandatory if that standard allows early application.[30] Users of financial statements should be aware that, depending on an entity's reporting date, it may or may not have the option to choose which version of a particular standard it may apply, as can be seen in the example below.

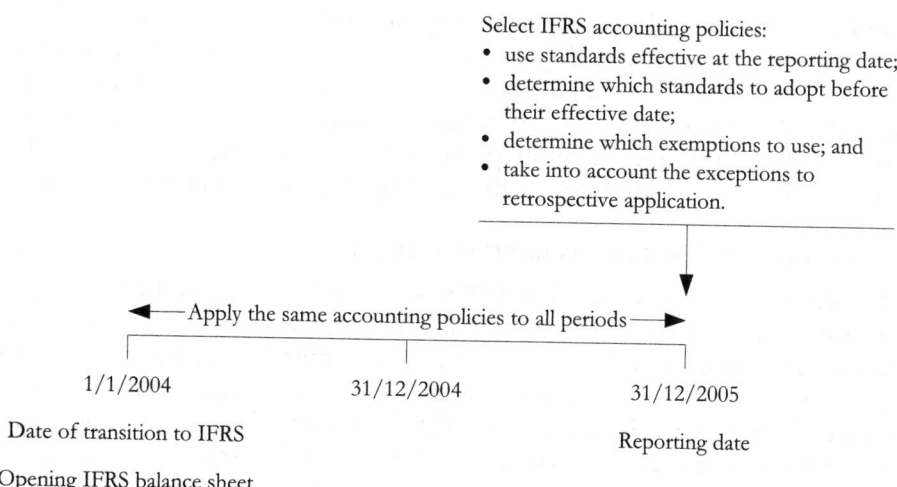

Select IFRS accounting policies:
- use standards effective at the reporting date;
- determine which standards to adopt before their effective date;
- determine which exemptions to use; and
- take into account the exceptions to retrospective application.

Apply the same accounting policies to all periods

| 1/1/2004 | 31/12/2004 | 31/12/2005 |

Date of transition to IFRS   Reporting date

Opening IFRS balance sheet

Example 4.4: *Prohibition from applying superseded IFRS*

Entity F's date of transition to IFRS is 1 January 2003 and its first reporting date under IFRS is 31 December 2005. Should F apply IAS 35 – *Discontinuing Operations* – in its first comparative period or should it apply IFRS 5 – *Non-current Assets Held for Sale and Discontinued Operations* – to all periods presented?

IFRS 1 prohibits F from applying IAS 35 in its first IFRS financial statements because IFRS 5, which is effective for financial periods starting on or after 1 January 2005, is effective at its first IFRS reporting date.

Entity G's date of transition to IFRS is 1 January 2003 and its first reporting date under IFRS is 31 December 2004. Should G apply IAS 21 – *The Effects of Changes in Foreign Exchange Rates (revised 1993)* – or IAS 21 – *The Effects of Changes in Foreign Exchange Rates (revised 2003)* – to all periods presented?

IFRS 1 allows G to apply IAS 21 (revised 1993), which is effective at 31 December 2004. IFRS 1 also allows G to apply IAS 21 (revised 2003) because although it is only mandatory for periods starting on or after 1 January 2005 that standard also permits early application. However, IFRS 1 prohibits an entity from applying IAS 21 (revised 1993) to 2003 and IAS 21 (revised 2003) to 2004.

Apart from when the exceptions at 2.3.3 below apply, an entity should in preparing its opening IFRS balance sheet:

'(a) recognise all assets and liabilities whose recognition is required by IFRSs;

(b) not recognise items as assets or liabilities if IFRSs do not permit such recognition;

(c) reclassify items that it recognised under previous GAAP as one type of asset, liability or component of equity, but are a different type of asset, liability or component of equity under IFRSs; and

(d) apply IFRSs in measuring all recognised assets and liabilities.'[31]

Any change in accounting policies on adoption of IFRS may cause changes in the amounts previously recorded as a result of events and transactions that occurred before the date of transition. These adjustments should be recognised at the date of transition to IFRS in either retained earnings or another category of equity, if this is appropriate.[32] For example, an entity that applies the IAS 16 – *Property, Plant and Equipment* – revaluation model (see Chapter 12 at 2.4.1) in its first IFRS financial statements would recognise the difference between cost and the revalued amount of property, plant and equipment in a revaluation reserve. Conversely, an entity that had applied a revaluation model under its previous GAAP, but decided to apply the cost model under IAS 16 would reallocate the revaluation reserves to retained earnings.

2.3.2 Transitional provisions in other standards

The transitional provisions in other IFRS only apply to entities that already report under IFRS. For a first-time adopter, the requirements in IFRS 1 override the transitional provisions in other IFRS.[33] There are limited exceptions to this general rule relating to (1) insurance contracts and (2) assets classified as held for sale and discontinued operations. In these cases IFRS 1 specifically requires application of the transitional rules in the relevant IFRS (see 2.7.4 and 2.8.2 below). It is important to note that the transition rules for first-time adopters and entities that already report under IFRS may differ significantly.

When it issues a new IFRS, the IASB will consider whether a first-time adopter should apply that IFRS retrospectively or prospectively. In the limited number of cases that the IASB considers prospective application more appropriate it will amend IFRS 1.[34] Furthermore, the IASB also amended IFRS 1 to introduce a special first-time adoption regime for IAS 32 – *Financial Instruments: Disclosure and Presentation* , IAS 39 – *Financial Instruments: Recognition and Measurement* – and IFRS 4 – *Insurance Contracts* (see 2.6.1 below).

The IASB's desire to ensure that IFRS 1 comprises all first-time adoption rules has meant that IFRS 1 has been amended by all the standards that the Board has subsequently issued as well as by IFRIC 1 – *Changes in Existing Decommissioning, Restoration and Similar Liabilities*. The complexity involved in this strategy may eventually overwhelm its practical application but for 2005 at least it is manageable.

2.3.3 Departures from full retrospective application of IFRS

The IASB's *Framework* recognises the necessity to balance the cost and benefit of information as a constraint that may limit the provision of relevant and reliable information in financial reporting.[35] In developing IFRS 1 the IASB specifically considered this cost-benefit constraint, which resulted in a number exceptions from the general principle of retrospective application. It is worthwhile noting that the IASB 'expects that most first-time adopters will begin planning on a timely basis for the transition to IFRSs. Accordingly, in balancing benefits and costs, the Board took as its benchmark an entity that plans the transition well in advance and can collect most information needed for its opening IFRS balance sheet at, or very soon after, the date of transition to IFRSs.'[36]

IFRS 1 establishes two types of departure from the principle of full retrospective application of standards in force at the date of transition to IFRS:[37]

- it allows a number of optional exemptions from some of the requirements of other IFRS;[38] and

- it requires a number of mandatory exceptions from the requirement for the retrospective application of other IFRS.[39]

A   *Optional exemptions from the requirements of other IFRS*

IFRS 1 grants limited *exemptions* from the general requirement of full retrospective application of the standards in force at an entity's reporting date 'where the cost of complying with them would be likely to exceed the benefits to users of financial statements'.[40] The standard establishes exemptions in relation to:[41]

(a)   business combinations (see 2.4 below);

(b)   the use of fair value or revaluation as deemed cost of property, plant and equipment, investment properties and certain intangible assets (see 2.5 below);

(c)   financial instruments:

- restatement of comparative information (see 2.6.1 below);

- designation of previously recognised financial instruments (see 2.6.2 below);

- compound financial instruments (see 2.6.3 below);

(d)   employee benefits (see 2.7.1 below);

(e)   cumulative translation differences (see 2.7.2 below);

(f)   share-based payment transactions (see 2.7.3 below);

(g)   insurance contracts (see 2.7.4 below); and

(h)   assets and liabilities of subsidiaries, associates and joint ventures (see 2.7.5 below). Some commentators have argued that this is not really an exemption, because it is not optional and actually requires a parent to use the IFRS measurements already used in a subsidiary's separate IFRS financial statements.

It is specifically prohibited under IFRS 1 to apply these exemptions by analogy to other items.[42]

Application of these exemptions is entirely optional, i.e. a first-time adopter can pick and choose the exemptions that it wants to apply. Importantly, the IASB did not establish a hierarchy of exemptions. Therefore, when an item is covered by more than one exemption, a first-time adopter has a free choice in determining the order in which it applies the exemptions.

Example 4.5:   *Order of application of exemptions*

Entity H acquired a building in a business combination. If H applied the business combinations exemption it would have to value the building at €120. However, if it used fair value as the deemed cost of the building it would have to value it at €150. Which value should H use?

H can choose whether it wants to value the building at €120 or €150 in its opening IFRS balance sheet. The fact that H uses the business combinations exemption does not prohibit it from applying the 'fair value as deemed cost' exemption in relation to the same assets.

B   *Exceptions to retrospective application of other IFRS*

In addition to the optional *exemptions* discussed above, IFRS 1 also defines a number of mandatory *exceptions* that prohibit 'retrospective application of IFRSs in some areas, particularly where retrospective application would require judgements by management about past conditions after the outcome of a particular transaction is already known'.[43] The mandatory *exceptions* in the standard cover the following situations:[44]

(a)   financial instruments:

  •   derecognition of financial assets and financial liabilities(see 2.6.4 below);

  •   hedge accounting(see 2.6.5 below);

(b)   estimates (see 2.8.1 below); and

(c)   assets classified as held for sale and discontinued operations (see 2.8.2 below).

The reasoning behind these exceptions is that retrospective application of IFRS in these situations could easily result in an unacceptable use of hindsight and lead to arbitrary or biased restatements, which would be neither relevant nor reliable.

2.4   Business combinations exemption

The business combinations exemption in IFRS 1 is probably the single most important exemption in the standard, as it permits a first-time adopter not to restate business combinations prior to its date of transition to IFRS. The detailed guidance on the application of the business combinations exemption is contained in a separate appendix to IFRS 1 and is described below.[45]

2.4.1   *Option to restate business combinations retrospectively*

A first-time adopter must account for business combinations after its date of transition to IFRS under IFRS 3 (see Chapter 6). However, it may elect not to apply IFRS 3 to any business combination before that date, but may do so if it so chooses. However, if a first-time adopter restates any business combination prior to its date of transition to comply with IFRS 3 it must also restate all subsequent business combinations under IFRS 3 and apply both IAS 36 (revised 2004) – *Impairment of Assets* – and IAS 38 (revised 2004) – *Intangible Assets* – from that date onwards.[46] In other words, as shown on the time line below, a first-time adopter is allowed to choose any date in the past and account for business combinations going forward under IFRS 3 without having to restate business combinations prior to the earliest IFRS 3 restatement.

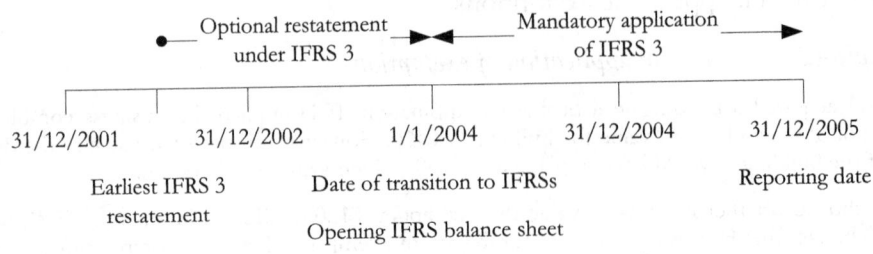

This exemption for past business combinations applies also to past acquisitions of associates and interests in joint ventures. However, it is important to note that the date selected for the first restatement of business combinations should also be applied to the restatement of acquisitions of associates and interests in joint ventures.[47]

The extract below shows a first-time adopter that opted not to restate business combinations before its date of transition to IFRS (IAS 22 being the relevant standard at that time).

Extract 4.1: Belgacom SA (2003)

Note 2. Significant accounting policies [extract]

Basis of preparation [extract]

… The Group furthermore elected to apply the exemption possibility granted by IFRS 1 in respect of business combinations and therefore did not apply International Accounting Standard 22 ("*IAS 22, Business combinations*") to business combinations that occurred prior to the transition date of 1 January 2001.

Originally, the IASB proposed not to permit restatement of business combinations prior to the date of transition to IFRS as this 'could require an entity to recreate data that it did not capture at the date of a past business combination and make subjective estimates about conditions that existed at that date. These factors could reduce the relevance and reliability of the entity's first IFRS financial statements.'[48] However, the IASB considered that – especially where the information is more likely to be available – it would be conceptually preferable to restate business combinations as the 'effects of business combination accounting can last for many years' and 'previous GAAP may differ significantly from IFRS'.[49] Therefore, the IASB concluded that although it could not require restatement of business combinations for cost-benefit reasons, it should at least permit restatement on condition that all subsequent business combinations are also restated.[50]

It is remarkable that availability of reliable contemporaneous information necessary for the application of IFRS 3 is not an explicit condition for retrospective application of IFRS 3 by first-time adopters; especially because this is a condition that existing IFRS-reporting entities need to meet.[51] Nevertheless, a first-time adopter should not restate its business combinations before the date of transition when this would require the use of hindsight, even though this is not specifically prohibited.

2.4.2 Classification of business combinations

IFRS mandates that business combinations should be accounted for as acquisitions or reverse acquisitions. An entity's previous GAAP may be based on a different definition of, for example, a business combination, an acquisition, a merger and a reverse acquisition. An important benefit of the business combinations exemption is that a first-time adopter will not have to determine the classification of past business combinations in accordance with IFRS 3.[52] For example, a transaction that was accounted for as a merger or uniting of interests using the pooling-of-interests method under an entity's previous GAAP will not have to be reclassified and accounted for under the IFRS 3 purchase method. However, an entity may still elect to do so if it so wishes – subject, of course, to the conditions set out under 2.4.1 above.

The business combinations exemption applies only to 'business combinations that the entity recognised before the date of transition to IFRSs'.[53] Consequently, the business combinations exemption does not apply to a transaction that IFRS considers to be an acquisition of an asset. First-time adopters will therefore have to consider whether past transactions would qualify as business combinations under IFRS, which are defined as 'the bringing together of separate entities or businesses into one reporting entity'.[54] A business is defined as follows:[55]

> 'An integrated set of activities and assets conducted and managed for the purpose of providing:
>
> (a)   a return to investors; or
>
> (b)   lower costs or other economic benefits directly and proportionately to policyholders or participants. A business generally consists of inputs, processes applied to those inputs, and resulting outputs that are, or will be, used to generate revenues. If goodwill is present in a transferred set of activities and assets, the transferred set shall be presumed to be a business.'

Furthermore, IFRS 3 states that 'if an entity obtains control of one or more other entities that are not businesses, the bringing together of those entities is not a business combination.'[56] Therefore, it is possible that under some national GAAPs, transactions that are not business combinations (e.g. asset purchases) may have been accounted for as if they were business combinations. A first-time adopter will need to restate any transactions that it accounted for as a business combination under its previous GAAP, but which are not business combinations under IFRS.

Example 4.6:   Acquisition of an asset

Entity J acquired a holding company that held a single asset at the time of acquisition. That holding company had no employees and the asset itself was not in use at the date of acquisition. J accounted for the transaction under its previous GAAP using the purchase method, which resulted in goodwill. Can J apply the business combinations exemption to the acquisition of the asset?

If J concludes that the asset is not a business, as defined in IFRS 3, it will not be able to apply the business combinations exemption to the acquisition of the asset.

2.4.3   Recognition and measurement of assets and liabilities

A   Derecognition of assets and liabilities

A first-time adopter should exclude from its opening IFRS balance sheet any items it recognised under its previous GAAP that do not qualify for recognition as an asset or liability under IFRS. If the first-time adopter previously recognised an intangible asset, as part of a business combination, that does not qualify for recognition as an asset under IAS 38, it should reclassify that item and the related deferred tax and minority interests as part of goodwill (unless it previously deducted goodwill directly from equity under its previous GAAP) (see 2.4.4 below). All other changes resulting from derecognition of such assets and liabilities should be accounted for as adjustments of retained earnings.[57]

B   Recognition of assets and liabilities

In its opening IFRS balance sheet, a first-time adopter should recognise all assets and liabilities that were acquired or assumed in a past business combination, with the exception of:

- certain financial assets and liabilities that were derecognised and that fall under the derecognition exception (see 2.6.4 below); and

- assets (including goodwill) and liabilities that were not recognised in the acquirer's consolidated balance sheet under its previous GAAP that would not qualify for recognition under IFRS in the separate balance sheet of the acquiree (see Example 4.11 below).[58]

The change resulting from the recognition of such assets and liabilities should be accounted for as an adjustment of retained earnings or another category of equity, if appropriate. However, if the change results from the recognition of an intangible asset that was previously subsumed in goodwill, it should be accounted for as an adjustment of that goodwill (see 2.4.4 A below).[59]

The following examples, which are based on the guidance on implementation of IFRS 1, illustrates how a first-time adopter would apply these requirements to an unrecognised finance lease (further examples can be found at 2.4.3 E below).

Example 4.7:   *Finance lease not capitalised under previous GAAP*[60]

Background

Parent L's date of transition to IFRSs is 1 January 2004. Parent L acquired subsidiary M on 15 January 2001 and did not capitalise subsidiary M's finance leases. If subsidiary M prepared separate financial statements under IFRSs, it would recognise finance lease obligations of 300 and leased assets of 250 at 1 January 2004.

Application of requirements

In its consolidated opening IFRS balance sheet, parent L recognises finance lease obligations of 300 and leased assets of 250, and charges 50 to retained earnings.

Example 4.8:   *Restructuring provision*[61]

Background

Entity D's first IFRS financial statements have a reporting date of 31 December 2005 and include comparative information for 2004 only. It chooses not to restate previous business combinations for IFRS 3. On 1 July 2003, entity D acquired 100 per cent of subsidiary E. Under its previous GAAP, entity D recognised an (undiscounted) restructuring provision of 100 that would not have qualified as an identifiable liability under IFRS 3. The recognition of this restructuring provision increased goodwill by 100. At 31 December 2003 (date of transition to IFRSs), entity D:

(a) had paid restructuring costs of 60; and

(b) estimated that it would pay further costs of 40 in 2004, and that the effects of discounting were immaterial. At 31 December 2003, those further costs did not qualify for recognition as a provision under IAS 37.

Application of requirements

In its opening IFRS balance sheet, entity D:

(a)   does not recognise a restructuring provision.

(b)   does not adjust the amount assigned to goodwill. However, entity D tests the goodwill for impairment under IAS 36, and recognises any resulting impairment loss.

(c)   as a result of (a) and (b), reports retained earnings in its opening IFRS balance sheet that are higher by 40 (before income taxes, and before recognising any impairment loss) than in the balance sheet at the same date under previous GAAP.

C   Subsequent measurement under IFRS not based on cost

IFRS requires subsequent measurement of some assets and liabilities on a basis other than original cost, such as fair value. When a first-time adopter does not apply IFRS 3 retrospectively to a business combination, such assets and liabilities must be measured on that other basis in its opening IFRS balance sheet. Any change in the carrying amount of those assets and liabilities should be accounted for as an adjustment of retained earnings, or other appropriate category of equity, rather than as an adjustment of goodwill.[62]

Example 4.9:   Items not measured at original cost

Entity K acquired in a business combination a trading portfolio of equity securities and a number of investment properties. Under its previous GAAP, K initially measured these assets at cost (i.e. their fair value at the date of acquisition).

Upon adoption of IFRS, K measures the trading portfolio of equity securities and the investment properties (under the IAS 40 – *Investment Properties* – fair value model) at fair value in its opening IFRS balance sheet. The resulting adjustment to these assets at the date of transition is reflected in retained earnings.

D   Subsequent measurement on a cost basis under IFRS

For assets and liabilities that are accounted for on a cost basis under IFRS, the standard stipulates that 'immediately after the business combination, the carrying amount under previous GAAP, of assets acquired and liabilities assumed in that business combination shall be their deemed cost under IFRSs at that date. If IFRSs require a cost-based measurement of those assets and liabilities at a later date, that deemed cost shall be the basis for cost-based depreciation or amortisation from the date of the business combination.'[63]

The standard does not specifically define 'immediately after a business combination', but it is commonly understood that this takes account of the completion of purchase accounting. In other words, a first-time adopter would not use the provisionally determined fair values of assets acquired and liabilities assumed.

This cost basis, being based on previous GAAP, might be considered as inconsistent with the requirements of IFRS for assets and liabilities that were *not* acquired in a business combination. However, the IASB did not identify any situations in which 'it would not be acceptable to bring forward cost-based measurements made under previous GAAP'.[64]

Example 4.10:   Items measured on a cost basis

Entity L acquired in a business combination, property, plant and equipment, inventory and accounts receivable. Under its previous GAAP, L initially measured these assets at cost (i.e. their fair value at the date of acquisition).

Upon adoption of IFRS, L determines that its accounting policy for these assets under its previous GAAP complied with the requirements of IFRS. Therefore, property, plant and equipment, inventory and accounts receivable are not adjusted, but recognised in the opening IFRS balance sheet at the carrying amount under the previous GAAP.

E   Measurement of items not recognised under previous GAAP

An asset acquired or a liability assumed in a past business combination may not have been recognised under the entity's previous GAAP. However, this does not mean that such items have a deemed cost of zero in the opening IFRS balance sheet. Instead, the acquirer recognises and measures those items in its opening IFRS balance sheet on the basis that IFRS would require in the balance sheet of the acquiree.[65] The change resulting from the recognition of such assets and liabilities should be accounted for as an adjustment of retained earnings or another category of equity, if appropriate. The IASB included this requirement to avoid 'an unjustifiable departure from the principle that the opening IFRS balance sheet should include all assets and liabilities'.[66]

Intangible assets acquired as part of a business combination that were not recognised under a first-time adopter's previous GAAP, will rarely be recognised in the opening IFRS balance sheet because either (1) they cannot be capitalised in the acquiree's own balance sheet or (2) capitalisation would require the use of hindsight which is not permitted under IAS 38 (see 2.9.5 below).

Example 4.11:   Items not recognised under previous GAAP

Entity K acquired Entity L but did not capitalise L's finance leases and internally generated customer lists under its previous GAAP.

Upon first-time adoption of IFRS, K recognises the finance leases in its opening IFRS balance sheet using the amounts that L would recognise in its IFRS balance sheet. The resulting adjustment to the net assets at the date of transition is reflected in retained earnings; goodwill is not restated to reflect the net assets that would have been recognised at the date of acquisition (see 2.4.4 below). However, K does not recognise the customer lists in its opening IFRS balance sheet, because L is not permitted to capitalise internally generated customer lists. Any value that might have been attributable to the customer lists would remain subsumed in goodwill in K's opening IFRS balance sheet.

Entity M acquired Entity N but did not recognise N's brand name as a separate intangible asset under its previous GAAP.

Upon first-time adoption of IFRS, M will not recognise N's brand name in its opening IFRS balance sheet because N would not have been permitted under IAS 38 to recognise it as an asset in its own separate balance sheet. Again, any value that might have been attributable to the brand name would remain subsumed in goodwill in M's opening IFRS balance sheet.

F   Summary of recognition and measurement requirements

The following diagram summarises the recognition and measurement rules – that are discussed above – for assets acquired and liabilities assumed in a business combination that is accounted for under the business combinations exemption.

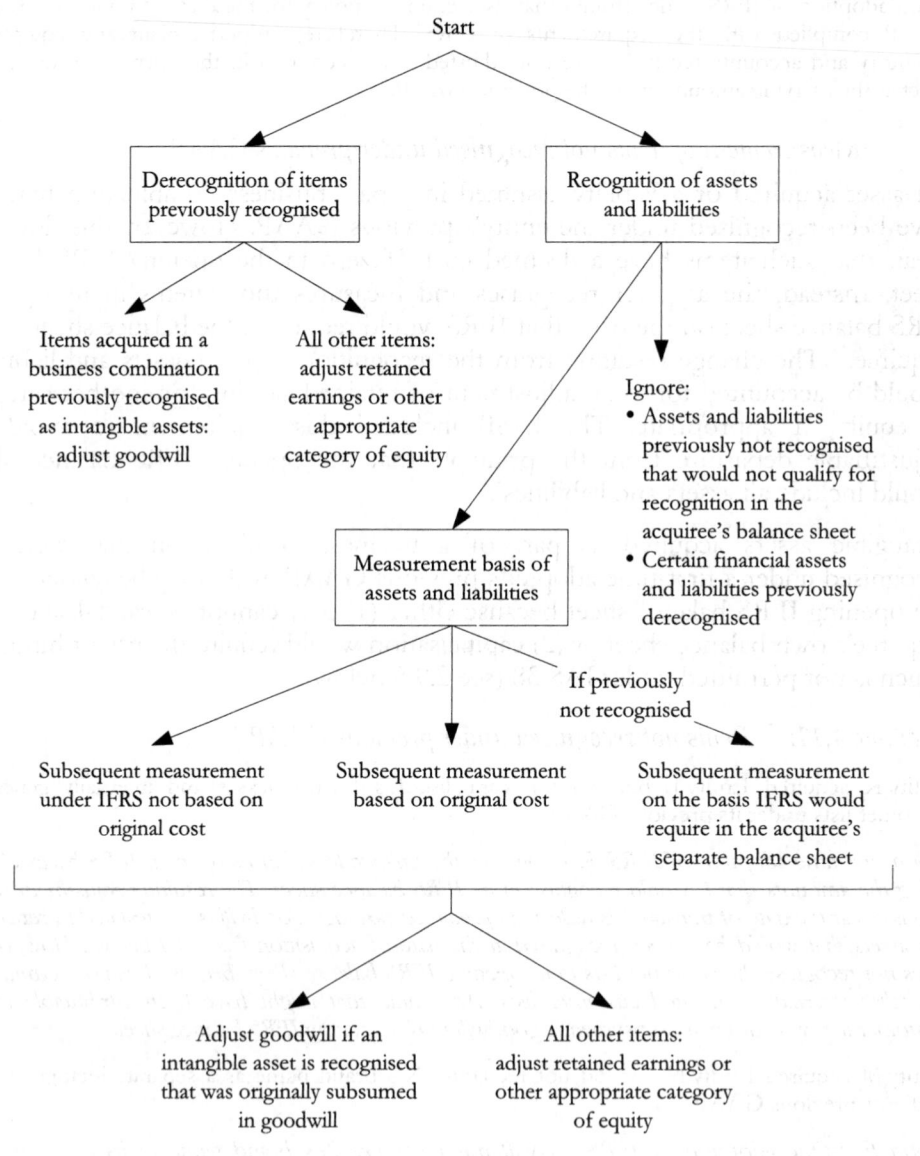

The guidance on implementation of IFRS 1 contains the following example that illustrates many of the requirements discussed above.[67]

Example 4.12:   Business combination example

Background

Entity B's first IFRS financial statements have a reporting date of 31 December 2005 and include comparative information for 2004 only. On 1 July 2001, entity B acquired 100 per cent of subsidiary C. Under its previous GAAP, entity B:

(a)   classified the business combination as an acquisition by entity B;

(b)   measured the assets acquired and liabilities assumed at the following amounts under previous GAAP at 31 December 2003 (date of transition to IFRSs):

    (i)   identifiable assets less liabilities for which IFRSs require cost-based measurement at a date after the business combination: 200 (with a tax base of 150 and an applicable tax rate of 30 per cent);

    (ii)   pension liability (for which the present value of the defined benefit obligation measured under IAS 19 is 130 and the fair value of plan assets is 100): nil (because entity B used a pay-as-you-go cash method of accounting for pensions under its previous GAAP). The tax base of the pension liability is also nil;

    (iii) goodwill: 180;

(c)   did not, at the date of acquisition, recognise deferred tax arising from temporary differences associated with the identifiable assets acquired and liabilities assumed.

Application of requirements

In its opening (consolidated) IFRS balance sheet, entity B:

(a)   classifies the business combination as an acquisition by entity B even if the business combination would have qualified under IAS 22 as a reverse acquisition by subsidiary C or a uniting of interests;

(b)   does not adjust the accumulated amortisation of goodwill. Entity B tests the goodwill for impairment under IAS 36 and recognises any resulting impairment loss, based on conditions that existed at the date of transition to IFRSs. If no impairment exists, the carrying amount of the goodwill remains at 180;

(c)   for those net identifiable assets acquired for which IFRSs require cost-based measurement at a date after the business combination, treats their carrying amount under previous GAAP immediately after the business combination as their deemed cost at that date;

(d)   does not restate the accumulated depreciation and amortisation of the net identifiable assets in (c) above, unless the depreciation methods and rates under previous GAAP result in amounts that differ materially from those required under IFRSs (for example, if they were adopted solely for tax purposes and do not reflect a reasonable estimate of the asset's useful life under IFRSs). If no such restatement is made, the carrying amount of those assets in the opening IFRS balance sheet equals their carrying amount under previous GAAP at the date of transition to IFRSs (200);

(e)   if there is any indication that identifiable assets are impaired, tests those assets for impairment, based on conditions that existed at the date of transition to IFRSs (see IAS 36);

(f)   recognises the pension liability, and measures it, at the present value of the defined benefit obligation (130) less the fair value of the plan assets (100), giving a carrying amount of 30, with a corresponding debit of 30 to retained earnings. However, if subsidiary C had already adopted IFRSs in an earlier period, entity B would measure the pension liability at the same amount as in subsidiary C's separate financial statements;

(g) recognises a net deferred tax liability of 6 (20 at 30 per cent) arising from:

   (i)   the taxable temporary difference of 50 (200 less 150) associated with the identifiable assets acquired and non-pension liabilities assumed, less

   (ii) the deductible temporary difference of 30 (30 less nil) associated with the pension liability.

The entity recognises the resulting increase in the deferred tax liability as a deduction from retained earnings. If a taxable temporary difference arises from the initial recognition of the goodwill, entity B does not recognise the resulting deferred tax liability.

2.4.4   Restatement of goodwill

A   Mandatory adjustments of goodwill

Under the business combinations exemption, a first-time adopter takes the carrying amount of goodwill under its previous GAAP at the date of transition to IFRS as a starting point and only adjusts it as follows:[68]

*   A first-time adopter increases goodwill at the date of transition by an amount equal to the carrying amount of an item that it recognised as an intangible asset acquired in a business combination under its previous GAAP (less any related deferred tax and minority interests), but which does not meet the recognition criteria under IFRS. That is, the first-time adopter accounts for the change in classification prospectively and does not, for example, reverse the cumulative amortisation on the item that it recognised as an intangible asset under its previous GAAP;

*   If a first-time adopter is required to recognise an intangible asset under IFRS that was subsumed in goodwill under its previous GAAP, it decreases goodwill accordingly and adjusts deferred tax and minority interests;

*   'A contingency affecting the amount of the purchase consideration for a past business combination may have been resolved before the date of transition to IFRS. If a reliable estimate of the contingent adjustment can be made and its payment is probable, the first-time adopter shall adjust the goodwill by that amount. Similarly, the first-time adopter shall adjust the carrying amount of goodwill if a previously recognised contingent adjustment can no longer be measured reliably or its payment is no longer probable';[69] and

*   'Regardless of whether there is any indication that the goodwill may be impaired, the first-time adopter shall apply IAS 36 *Impairment of Assets* in testing the goodwill for impairment at the date of transition to IFRS and in recognising any resulting impairment loss in retained earnings (or, if so required by IAS 36, in revaluation surplus). The impairment test shall be based on conditions at the date of transition to IFRS.'[70]

    The estimates used to determine whether a first-time adopter recognises an impairment loss or provision at the date of transition to IFRS should be consistent with estimates made for the same date under previous GAAP (after adjustments to reflect any difference in accounting policies), unless there is objective evidence that those estimates were in error.[71] If a first-time adopter needs to make estimates for that date that were not necessary under its previous GAAP, such estimates and assumptions should not reflect conditions that arose after the date of transition to IFRS.[72]

If a first-time adopter's opening IFRS balance sheet reflects impairment losses, it recognises any later reversal of those impairment losses in the income statement unless IAS 36 requires that reversal to be treated as a revaluation. This applies to both impairment losses recognised under previous GAAP and additional impairment losses recognised on transition to IFRS.[73]

Under IFRS 1, assets acquired and liabilities assumed in a business combination prior to the date of transition to IFRS are not necessarily valued on a basis that is consistent with IFRS 3. This can lead to 'double counting' in the carrying amount of assets and goodwill as is illustrated in the example below.

Example 4.13:   Impairment testing of goodwill on first-time adoption

Entity P acquired a business before its date of transition to IFRS. The cost of acquisition was €530 and P allocated the purchase price as follows:

	€
Properties, at carry-over cost	450
Liabilities, at amortised cost	(180)
Goodwill	260
Purchase price	530

The goodwill under P's previous GAAP relates entirely to the properties that had a fair value at date of acquisition that was significantly in excess of their value on a carry-over cost basis. In P's opening IFRS balance sheet the same assets, liabilities and goodwill are valued as follows:

	€
Properties, at fair value	750
Liabilities, at amortised cost	(200)
Provisional IFRS goodwill (before impairment test)	260
Total carrying amount	810

P used the option to measure the properties at fair value at its date of transition in its opening IFRS balance sheet. However, IFRS 1 does not permit goodwill to be adjusted to reflect the extent to which the increase in fair value relates to the time of the acquisition. The total carrying amount of the acquired net assets including goodwill of €810 may now exceed the recoverable amount. When P tests the 'provisional IFRS goodwill' for impairment on first-time adoption of IFRS, the recoverable amount of the business is determined to be €600. Accordingly, it will have to recognise an impairment of goodwill of €210 and disclose this impairment under IFRS 1.

In some cases the write-off will completely eliminate the goodwill and thereby any 'double counting'. However, in this particular case the remaining goodwill of €50 in truth represents goodwill that was internally generated between the date of acquisition and the date of transition to IFRS.

The IASB accepted that IFRS 1 'does not prevent the implicit recognition of internally generated goodwill that arose after the date of the business combination. However, the Board concluded that an attempt to exclude such internally generated goodwill would be costly and lead to arbitrary results.'[74]

B   Prohibition of other adjustments of goodwill

The IASB concluded that 'to avoid costs that would exceed the likely benefits to users', IFRS 1 should prohibit 'restatement of goodwill for most other adjustments reflected in the opening IFRS balance sheet, unless a first-time adopter elects to apply IFRS 3 retrospectively'.[75] Therefore, a first-time adopter electing not to apply IFRS 3 retrospectively is not permitted to make any adjustments to goodwill other than those described at 2.4.4 A above. For example, such a first-time adopter should not restate the carrying amount of goodwill:[76]

'(i)   to exclude in-process research and development acquired in that business combination (unless the related intangible asset would qualify for recognition under IAS 38 in the balance sheet of the acquiree);

(ii)   to adjust previous amortisation of goodwill;

(iii)   to reverse adjustments to goodwill that IFRS 3 would not permit, but were made under previous GAAP because of adjustments to assets and liabilities between the date of the business combination and the date of transition to IFRS.'

Although IFRS 1 specifically prohibits other adjustments of goodwill, differences between the goodwill amount in the opening IFRS balance sheet and that in the financial statements under previous GAAP may arise because:

(a)   goodwill may have to be restated as a result of a retrospective application of IAS 21 (see 2.4.5 below);

(b)   goodwill in relation to previously unconsolidated subsidiaries will have to be recognised (see 2.4.6 below); and

(c)   goodwill in relation to transactions that do not qualify as business combinations under IFRS must be derecognised (see 2.4.2 above).

Example 4.14:   Adjusting goodwill

Entity R acquired Entity S but under its previous GAAP it did not recognise the following items:

- S's customer lists which had a fair value of ¥1,100 at the date of the acquisition and ¥1,500 at the date of transition to IFRS; and

- Deferred tax liabilities related to the fair value adjustment of S's property, plant and equipment, which amounted to ¥9,500 at the date of the acquisition and ¥7,800 at the date of transition to IFRS.

What adjustment should R make to goodwill to account for the customer lists and deferred tax liabilities at its date of transition to IFRS?

As explained at 2.4.3 E above, R cannot recognise the customer lists when it uses the business combinations exemption. Accordingly, R cannot adjust goodwill for the customer lists.

R must recognise the deferred tax liability at its date of transition under IAS 12 – Income Taxes – because there is no exemption from recognising deferred taxation under IFRS 1. However, R is not permitted to adjust goodwill for the deferred tax liability that would have been recognised at the date of acquisition. Instead, R should recognise the change in deferred tax in retained earnings or other category of equity, if appropriate.

C   Derecognition of negative goodwill

IFRS 3 specifically requires derecognition of negative goodwill (which IFRS 3 calls 'excess of acquirer's interest in the net fair value of acquiree's identifiable assets, liabilities and contingent liabilities over cost') with a corresponding adjustment to the opening balance of retained earnings on adoption of the standard (see Chapter 6 at 4.1.2).[77] Although IFRS 1 does not specifically address accounting for negative goodwill recognised under a previous GAAP, negative goodwill should be derecognised by a first-time adopter because it is not permitted 'to recognise items or liabilities if IFRS do not permit such recognition'.[78] Negative goodwill clearly does not meet the definition of a liability under the IASB's *Framework* and its recognition is not permitted under IFRS 3.

D   Goodwill previously deducted from equity

If a first-time adopter deducted goodwill from equity under its previous GAAP then 'it shall not recognise that goodwill in its opening IFRS balance sheet. Furthermore, it shall not transfer that goodwill to the income statement if it disposes of the subsidiary or if the investment in the subsidiary becomes impaired.'[79] Effectively, under IFRS such goodwill ceases to exist. The prohibition to reinstate goodwill that was deducted from equity may have a significant impact on first-time adopters that hedge their foreign net investments.

Example 4.15:   Goodwill related to foreign net investments

Entity T, which uses the euro (€) as its functional currency, acquired a subsidiary in the United States whose functional currency is the US dollar ($). The goodwill on the acquisition of $2,100 was deducted from equity, but under its previous GAAP Entity T hedged the currency exposure on the goodwill because it would be required to recognise the goodwill as an expense upon disposal of the subsidiary.

IFRS 1 does not permit reinstatement of goodwill deducted from equity nor does it permit transfer of goodwill to the income statement upon disposal of the investment of the subsidiary. Under IFRS, goodwill deducted from equity ceases to exist and T can no longer hedge the currency exposure on that goodwill.

If a first-time adopter deducted goodwill from equity under its previous GAAP then 'adjustments resulting from the subsequent resolution of a contingency affecting the purchase consideration shall be recognised in retained earnings'.[80] Effectively, the adjustment is being accounted for in the same way as the original goodwill that arose on the acquisition, rather than having to be adjusted against capitalised goodwill under IFRS 3. This requirement could affect, for example, the way a first-time adopter accounts for earn-out clauses relating to business combinations prior to its date of transition to IFRS.

Example 4.16:   Earn-out clause in acquisition

Entity U acquired a business before its date of transition to IFRS and agreed to make an initial payment to the vendor together with further payments based on a multiple of future profits of the acquiree. The fair value of the earn-out is contingent on future profits and could not be determined reliably at the date of transition to IFRS. Under U's previous GAAP any goodwill was written off against equity as incurred.

After its date of transition to IFRS, U will account for the earn-out as a change in purchase consideration and recognise it in retained earnings.

2.4.5   Currency adjustments to goodwill

IAS 21 – *The Effects of Changes in Foreign Exchange Rates* – requires that 'any goodwill arising on the acquisition of a foreign operation and any fair value adjustments to the carrying amounts of assets and liabilities arising on the acquisition of that foreign operation shall be treated as assets and liabilities of the foreign operation'.[81] For a first-time adopter it may be impracticable, especially after a corporate restructuring, to determine retrospectively the currency in which goodwill and fair value adjustments should be expressed. Consequently, under IFRS 1, a first-time adopter need not apply this requirement of IAS 21 'retrospectively to fair value adjustments and goodwill arising in business combinations that occurred before the date of transition to IFRSs'.[82] If IAS 21 is not applied retrospectively a first-time adopter should treat such fair value adjustments and goodwill 'as assets and liabilities of the entity rather than as assets and liabilities of the acquiree. Therefore, those goodwill and fair value adjustments either are already expressed in the entity's functional currency or are non-monetary foreign currency items, which are reported using the exchange rate applied under previous GAAP.'[83]

If a first-time adopter chooses not to take the exemption, it must apply IAS 21 retrospectively to fair value adjustments and goodwill arising in either:

'(a)   all business combinations that occurred before the date of transition to IFRSs; or

(b)   all business combinations that the entity elects to restate to comply with IFRS 3.'[84]

The decision to treat goodwill and fair value adjustments as either items denominated in the parent's or the acquiree's functional currency will also affect the extent to which the net investment in those foreign subsidiaries can be hedged (see also 2.4.4 D).

Despite this exemption, there are a number of significant practical issues relating to currency adjustments to goodwill that are discussed at 3.5 below. It should also be noted that the above exemption is different from the 'cumulative translation differences' exemption, which is discussed at 2.7.2 below.

2.4.6 *Previously unconsolidated subsidiaries*

Under its previous GAAP a first-time adopter may not have consolidated a subsidiary acquired in a past business combination. In that case a first-time adopter applying the business combinations exemption should 'adjust the carrying amounts of the subsidiary's assets and liabilities to the amounts that IFRSs would require in the subsidiary's balance sheet. The deemed cost of goodwill equals the difference at the date of transition to IFRSs between:

(i) the parent's interest in those adjusted carrying amounts; and

(ii) the cost in the parent's separate financial statements of its investment in the subsidiary.'[85]

The cost of a subsidiary in the parent's separate financial statements should be determined under the cost method of accounting under IAS 27 (see Chapter 5 at 7.2.1). Thus, a first-time adopter does not have to calculate what the goodwill would have been at the date of the original acquisition. The deemed cost of goodwill will, however, be capitalised as an asset in the opening IFRS balance sheet. The guidance on the implementation of IFRS 1 contains the following example that illustrates this.[86]

Example 4.17: Subsidiary not consolidated under previous GAAP

Background

Parent J's date of transition to IFRSs is 1 January 2004. Under its previous GAAP, parent J did not consolidate its 75 per cent subsidiary K, acquired in a business combination on 15 July 2001. On 1 January 2004:

(a) the cost of parent J's investment in subsidiary K is 180.

(b) under IFRSs, subsidiary K would measure its assets at 500 and its liabilities (including deferred tax under IAS 12) at 300. On this basis, subsidiary K's net assets are 200 under IFRSs.

Application of requirements

Parent J consolidates subsidiary K. The consolidated balance sheet at 1 January 2004 includes:

(a) subsidiary K's assets at 500 and liabilities at 300;

(b) minority interests of 50 (25 per cent of [500-300]); and

(c) goodwill of 30 (cost of 180 less 75 per cent of [500-300]). Parent J tests the goodwill for impairment under IAS 36 and recognises any resulting impairment loss, based on conditions that existed at the date of transition to IFRSs.

If the original acquisition cost is lower than the net asset value at the date of transition to IFRS, the difference is taken to retained earnings.

Slightly different rules apply to all other subsidiaries (i.e. those not acquired in a business combination) that an entity did not consolidate under its previous GAAP, the main difference being that goodwill should not be recognised in relation to those subsidiaries (see 2.9.3 below).

It should be noted that in calculating the deemed cost of the goodwill, the first-time adopter is required to compare the historical cost of the investment to its share of the carrying amount of the net assets determined on a different date. In the case of a highly profitable subsidiary this could give rise to the following anomaly:

Example 4.18:   Calculation of deemed goodwill

Parent L acquired subsidiary M before the date of transition for $500. The net assets of M would have been $220 under IFRS at the date of acquisition. M makes on average an annual net profit of $60, which it does not distribute to L.

At the date of transition to IFRS, the cost of L's investment in M is still $500. However, the net assets of M have increased to $460. Therefore, under IFRS 1 the deemed cost of goodwill is $40.

The deemed goodwill is much lower than the goodwill that was paid at the date of acquisition because M did not distribute its profits. In fact, if M had distributed a dividend to its parent just before the date of transition, the deemed goodwill would have been significantly higher.

2.4.7   *Previously consolidated entities that are not subsidiaries*

A first-time adopter may have consolidated an investment under its previous GAAP that does not meet the definition of a subsidiary under IFRS. In this case the entity should first determine the appropriate classification of the investment under IFRS and then apply the first-time adoption rules in IFRS 1. Generally such previously consolidated investments should be accounted for as either:

- *an associate:* First-time adopters applying the business combinations exemption (see 2.4) should also apply that exemption to past acquisitions of investments in associates. If the business combinations exemption is not applicable or the entity did not acquire the investment in the associate, IAS 28 – *Investments in Associates* – should be applied retrospectively;

- *a joint venture:* First-time adopters applying the business combinations exemption (see 2.4) should also apply that exemption to past acquisitions of investments in joint ventures. If the business combinations exemption is not applicable or the entity did not acquire the investment in the joint venture, IAS 31 – *Interests in Joint Ventures* – should be applied retrospectively;

- *an investment under IAS 39* (see 2.6.2 below); or

- *an executory contract* or *service concession arrangement:* There are no first-time adoption exemptions that apply; therefore, IFRS should be applied retrospectively.

2.4.8   *Measurement of deferred taxation and minority interests*

Deferred taxation is calculated based on the difference between the carrying amount of assets and liabilities and their respective tax base. Therefore, deferred taxation should be calculated after all assets acquired and liabilities assumed have been adjusted under IFRS 1.[87]

Minority interest is defined in IAS 27 – *Consolidated and Separate Financial Statements* – as 'that portion of the profit or loss and net assets of a subsidiary attributable to equity interests that are not owned, directly or indirectly through subsidiaries, by the parent'.[88] Minority interests related to subsidiaries acquired in a business combination should be calculated after all assets acquired, liabilities assumed and deferred taxation have been adjusted under IFRS 1.[89]

Any resulting change in the carrying amount of deferred taxation and minority interests should be recognised by adjusting retained earnings (or, if appropriate, another category of equity), unless they relate to adjustments to intangible assets that are adjusted against goodwill.

Example 4.19: *Restatement of intangible assets, deferred tax and minority interests*[90]

Entity V's first IFRS financial statements have a reporting date of 31 December 2005 and include comparative information for 2004 only. On 1 July 2001, V acquired 75% of subsidiary W. Under its previous GAAP, V assigned an initial carrying amount of 200 to intangible assets that would not have qualified for recognition under IAS 38. The tax base of the intangible assets was nil, giving rise to a deferred tax liability (at 30%) of 60. V measured minority interests as the minority's share of the fair value of the identifiable net assets acquired (the allowed alternative treatment in IAS 22 – *Business Combinations*). Goodwill arising on the acquisition was capitalised as an asset in V's consolidated financial statements.

On 1 January 2004 (the date of transition to IFRS), the carrying amount of the intangible assets under previous GAAP was 160, and the carrying amount of the related deferred tax liability was 48 (30% of 160).

Under IFRS 1, V reclassifies intangible assets that do not qualify for recognition as separate assets under IAS 38, together with the related deferred tax liability of 48 and minority interests, as part of goodwill (see 2.4.4 A above). The related minority interests amount to 28 (25% of 112 (160 minus 48)). V makes the following adjustment in its opening IFRS balance sheet:

Goodwill	84	
Deferred tax liability	48	
Minority interests	28	
Intangible assets		160

V tests the goodwill for impairment under IAS 36 and recognises any resulting impairment loss, based on conditions that existed at the date of transition to IFRS.

2.5 Fair value or revaluation as deemed cost exemption

2.5.1 Background

IFRS 1 requires full retrospective application of standards extant at a first-time adopter's first IFRS reporting date. Therefore, in the absence of the deemed cost exemption, the requirements of IAS 16, IAS 38 and IAS 40 would have to be applied as if the first-time adopter had always applied these standards. This could be quite onerous because:

- these items are long-lived which means that accounting records for the period of acquisition may not be available anymore. In the case of formerly state-owned businesses, the required accounting records possibly never even existed;

- the entity may have revalued the items in the past as a matter of accounting policy or because this was required under national law; or

- even if the items were carried at depreciated cost, the accounting policy for recognition and depreciation may not have been IFRS compliant.

Given the significance of property, plant and equipment in particular in the balance sheet of most first-time adopters (and the sheer number of transactions affecting property, plant and equipment), restatement is not only extremely difficult but would often also involve undue cost and effort. Nevertheless, a first-time adopter needs a cost basis for the assets in its opening IFRS balance sheet. Therefore, the IASB decided to introduce the notion of a 'deemed cost' that is not the 'true' IFRS compliant cost basis of an asset, but a surrogate that is deemed to be a suitable starting point.

In its deliberations on IFRS 1, the IASB noted that 'reconstructed cost data might be less relevant to users, and less reliable, than current fair value data. ... Therefore, the IFRS permits an entity to use fair value as deemed cost in some cases without any need to demonstrate undue cost or effort.'[91]

2.5.2   Scope of 'fair value or revaluation as deemed cost' exemption

To deal with the problem of restatement of long-lived assets upon first-time adoption of IFRS, the standard permits a first-time adopter – for the categories of assets listed below – to measure an item in its opening IFRS balance sheet using an amount that is based on its deemed cost:[92]

- property, plant and equipment;[93]
- investment property, if an entity elects to use the cost model in IAS 40 – *Investment Property*. The fact that the exemption can only be applied to investment property accounted for under the cost model will not pose any problems in practice as the fair value model under IAS 40 requires an entity to measure its investment property at fair value at its date of transition to IFRS;[94] and
- intangible assets that meet:
  - the recognition criteria in IAS 38 (including reliable measurement of original cost); and
  - the criteria in IAS 38 for revaluation (including the existence of an active market).[95]

A first-time adopter cannot use a deemed cost approach for any other assets or liabilities.[96]

The use of fair value or revaluation as deemed cost for intangible assets will be very limited in practice because of the very restrictive definition of an active market in IAS 38 (see Chapter 11 at 2.3.2 A).[97] It is therefore unlikely that a first-time adopter will be able to apply this exemption to any intangible assets.

It is important to note that the deemed cost exemption in IFRS 1 does not take classes or categories of assets as its unit of measure, but refers to 'an item of property, plant and equipment'.[98] The same exemption is available for investment property and intangible assets. IAS 16 does not 'prescribe the unit of measure for recognition, i.e. what constitutes an item of property, plant and equipment. Thus, judgement is required in applying the recognition criteria to an entity's specific circumstances' (see Chapter 12 at 2.2.2).[99] A first-time adopter can therefore apply the deemed cost exemption to only some of its assets, for example, it could apply the exemption only to:

- a selection of properties;

- part of a factory; or

- some of the assets leased under a single finance lease.

The IASB argued that it is not necessary to restrict application of the exemption to classes of assets to prevent selective revaluations, because 'IAS 36 *Impairment of Assets* requires an impairment test if there is any indication that an asset is impaired. Thus, if an entity uses fair value as deemed cost for assets whose fair value is above cost, it cannot ignore indications that the recoverable amount of other assets may have fallen below their carrying amount. Therefore, the IFRS does not restrict the use of fair value as deemed cost to entire classes of asset.'[100] Nevertheless, it seems doubtful that the quality of financial information would benefit from a revaluation of a haphazard selection of items of property, plant and equipment. Therefore, a first-time adopter should exercise judgment in selecting the items it believes appropriate to apply the exemption to.

2.5.3 Determining deemed cost

The deemed cost that a first-time adopter uses is either:

(1) the fair value of the item at the date of transition to IFRS (see 2.2.4 above);[101]

(2) a revaluation under its previous GAAP at or before the date of transition to IFRS, if the revaluation was, at the date of the revaluation, broadly comparable to:[102]

'(a) fair value; or

(b) cost or depreciated cost under IFRS, adjusted to reflect, for example, changes in a general or specific price index'; or

(3) the deemed cost under its previous GAAP that was established by measuring items at their fair value at one particular date because of an event such as a privatisation or initial public offering.[103]

The revaluations referred to in (2) above need only be 'broadly comparable to fair value or reflect an index applied to a cost that is broadly comparable to cost determined under IFRSs'.[104] It appears that in the interest of practicality the IASB is allowing a good deal of flexibility in this matter. The IASB explains in the basis for conclusions that 'it may not always be clear whether a previous revaluation was intended as a measure of fair value or differs materially from fair value. The flexibility in this area permits a cost-effective solution for the unique problem of transition to IFRS. It allows a first-time adopter to establish a deemed cost using a measurement that is already available and is a reasonable starting point for a cost-based measurement'.[105]

If the deemed cost of an asset was determined before the date of transition to IFRSs then an IFRS accounting policy needs to be applied to that deemed cost in the intervening period to determine what the carrying amount of the asset is in the opening IFRS balance sheet, as is illustrated in the example below.

Example 4.20: Deemed cost of property, plant and equipment

Entity X used to revalue items of property, plant and equipment to fair value under its previous GAAP, but changed its accounting policy on 1 January 1999 when it adopted a different accounting policy. Under that accounting policy, X did not depreciate the asset and only recognised the maintenance costs as an expense. X's date of transition to IFRS is 1 January 2003.

In its balance sheet under previous GAAP the carrying amount of the asset is £80 at the date of transition to IFRS, which is equal to the last revaluation. X can use the last revalued amount as the deemed cost of the asset on 1 January 1999. However, X will need to apply IAS 16 to the period after 1 January 1999 because the accounting policy under previous GAAP is not permitted under IFRS. Assuming that the economic life of the asset is 40 years and a residual value of nil, X would account for the asset at £72 in its opening IFRS balance sheet, which represents the deemed cost minus 4 years of depreciation.

In summary, at its date of transition to IFRS, a first-time adopter is allowed under IFRS 1 to measure property, plant and equipment, investment properties and intangible assets at an amount based on either:

- historical cost determined in accordance with IAS 16, IAS 38 and IAS 40;

- fair value at the date of transition to IFRS;

- a revalued amount that is equal to:

  - fair value at the date of revaluation;

  - cost adjusted for changes in a general or specific index; or

  - an event-driven fair value, for example, at the date of an initial public offering or privatisation; or

- in the case of an item acquired in a business combination:

  - carrying amount under previous GAAP immediately after acquisition; or

  - if the item was not recognised under previous GAAP, the carrying amount on the basis that IFRS would require in the separate balance sheet of the acquiree.

The fact that IFRS 1 offers so many different bases for valuation does not disturb the IASB as it reasons that 'cost is generally equivalent to fair value at the date of acquisition. Therefore, the use of fair value as the deemed cost of an asset means that an entity will report the same cost data as if it had acquired an asset with the same remaining service potential at the date of transition to IFRSs. If there is any lack of comparability, it arises from the aggregation of costs incurred at different dates, rather than from the targeted use of fair value as deemed cost for some assets. The Board regarded this approach as justified to solve the unique problem of introducing IFRSs in a cost-effective way without damaging transparency.'[106] Although this is valid, it still means that an individual first-time adopter can greatly influence its future reported performance by carefully selecting a first-time adoption policy for the valuation of its assets. Users of the financial statements of a first-time adopter should therefore be mindful that historical trends under the previous GAAP might no longer be present in an entity's IFRS financial statements.

2.6 Financial instruments

2.6.1 Exemption from the requirement to restate comparative information

The IASB issued the revised IAS 32 and the revised IAS 39 in December 2003; and the amendment to IAS 39 – *Fair Value Hedge Accounting for a Portfolio Hedge of Interest Rate Risk* – in March 2004. To allow entities adopting IFRS for the first time before 1 January 2006 sufficient time to comply with the requirements of those standards, the IASB decided not to require them to prepare comparative information under IAS 32, IAS 39 and IFRS 4 (see 2.7.4).[107] The fact that the IASB did not use the defined terms 'date of transition' or 'reporting date' in drafting the exemption, is generally interpreted as meaning that the IASB intended the exemption to apply to entities whose first IFRS reporting period started before 1 January 2006.

A first-time adopter that chooses to present comparative information that does not comply with IAS 32, IAS 39 and IFRS 4 in its first year of transition should:

- apply its previous GAAP in the comparative period to financial instruments that are within the scope of IAS 32 or IAS 39 and to insurance contracts with the scope of IFRS 4. In other words, this exemption also affects the application of certain aspects of other standards. For example, it overrides the requirements of IAS 1 on the balance sheet presentation of financial instruments and insurance contracts and IAS 18 – *Revenue* – on the application of the effective interest method; and

- make certain additional disclosures (see 2.10.1 A).[108]

A first-time adopter that does not present comparative information under IAS 32, IAS 39 and IFRS 4 should use *'the beginning of the first IFRS reporting period'* (e.g. 1 January 2005 for an entity reporting at 31 December 2005) as the relevant date for the application of the first-time adoption rules in IFRS 1, and not the *date of transition to IFRS*, for the purpose of these standards only.[109]

In applying this exemption a first-time adopter should be aware of the following:

- the wording of the standard does not explicitly require the exemption to be applied to IAS 32, IAS 39 and IFRS 4 as a package. Even though the transitional provisions in both IAS 32 and IAS 39 that require the standards to be adopted simultaneously do not apply to first-time adopters, the IASB clearly intended both standards to be adopted simultaneously. In any case, the many cross-references between the two standards make it virtually impossible to adopt one of the standards without the other. Therefore, we believe that the exemption applies to IAS 32 and IAS 39 as a package. However, there do not seem to be any convincing reasons for prohibiting a first-time adopter from separately applying the exemption to IFRS 4;

- a first-time adopter that presents two comparative periods under IFRS will not be permitted to restate the most recent comparative financial period because the exemption must be applied as of the beginning of the first IFRS reporting period (e.g. an entity reporting at 31 December 2005 would not be allowed to restate 2004 unless it also restated 2003);

- the exemption only covers items that are within the scope of IAS 32, IAS 39 and IFRS 4. The comparative information relating to all other items must be restated under IFRS; and

- a first-time adopter not applying IAS 39 would need to apply its previous GAAP in accounting for hedges.

2.6.2 *Designation of previously recognised financial instruments*

IAS 39 permits a financial instrument to be designated on initial recognition as:

- a *financial asset or financial liability at fair value through profit or loss*, which is a financial instrument that is either classified as *held for trading* or is designated as such on initial recognition;[110] or

- an *available-for-sale financial asset*, which is a financial asset designated as 'available for sale', or which is not specifically classified as 'loans and receivables', 'held-to-maturity investments' or 'at fair value through profit or loss'.[111]

A first-time adopter is allowed to designate a financial instrument at the date of transition to IFRS (or the beginning of the first IFRS reporting period, if comparatives are not restated) as a 'financial asset or financial liability at fair value through profit or loss' or as available-for-sale.[112] This exemption that allows retrospective designation by first-time adopters is based on the transitional rule applied by entities that already report under IFRS.[113] Therefore, if upon initial application of IAS 39 the investment is classified as:[114]

- *at fair value through profit or loss*, the pre-IAS 39 revaluation gain that had been recognised in equity is reclassified into retained earnings on initial application of IAS 39;

- *available for sale*, then the pre-IAS 39 revaluation gain is recognised in a separate component of equity. Subsequently, the entity recognises gains and losses on the available-for-sale financial asset in that separate component of equity until the investment is impaired, sold, collected or otherwise disposed of. On subsequent derecognition or impairment of the available-for-sale financial asset, the first-time adopter transfers to profit or loss the cumulative gain or loss remaining in equity.

A first-time adopter that applies this exemption needs to make certain additional disclosures (see 2.10.2 B below).[115]

Retrospective designation of financial instruments as available-for-sale financial assets 'requires a first-time adopter to recognise the cumulative fair value changes in a separate component of equity in the opening IFRS balance sheet [or the balance sheet at the beginning of its first IFRS reporting period, if comparatives are not restated], and transfer those fair value changes to the income statement on subsequent disposal or impairment of the asset'.[116] The IASB recognised that this could give rise to a selective approach, whereby first-time adopters would only designate financial instruments with cumulative gains as available-for-sale, but it noted that a first-time adopter could achieve similar results by selectively disposing of some financial assets before the date of transition to IFRS.[117] Therefore, IFRS 1 does not impose any additional restrictions on first-time adopters regarding the designation of financial instruments as available-for-sale financial assets.

2.6.3 *Compound financial instruments*

IAS 32 requires compound financial instruments (such as a convertible bond) to be split at inception into separate equity and liability components. If the liability component is no longer outstanding, a full retrospective application of IAS 32 would involve identifying two components, one representing the original equity component and the other representing the cumulative interest on the liability component, both of which are accounted for in equity (see Chapter 17 at 8.1.2). A first-time adopter does not need to make this allocation if the liability component is no longer outstanding at the date of transition to IFRS (or the beginning of the first IFRS reporting period, if comparatives are not restated).[118] For example, in the case of a convertible bond that has been converted into equity, it is not necessary to make this split.

A first-time adopter applying this exemption can therefore avoid the possibly complex allocation process that would be involved. However, where the compound instrument is still outstanding at the date of transition to IFRS (or the beginning of the first IFRS reporting period, if comparatives are not restated), then a split will need to be made (see Chapter 17).[119] In practice this exemption is of limited value because the number of different compound financial instruments outstanding at the date of transition to IFRS (or the beginning of the first IFRS reporting period, if comparatives are not restated) is bound to be limited.

2.6.4 *Derecognition of financial assets and financial liabilities*

A first-time adopter should apply the derecognition requirements in IAS 39 prospectively to transactions occurring on or after 1 January 2004. Therefore, if a first-time adopter derecognised non-derivative financial assets or non-derivative financial liabilities under its previous GAAP as a result of a transaction that occurred before 1 January 2004, it should not recognise those assets and liabilities under IFRS (unless they qualify for recognition as a result of a later transaction or event).[120] Though this seems similar to the transitional rules that apply to existing IFRS reporting entities, first-time adopters do not have to apply IAS 39 (revised 2000) to transactions before 1 January 2004. A first-time adopter that wants to apply the derecognition requirements in IAS 39 retrospectively from a date of the entity's choosing can only do so 'provided that the information needed to apply IAS 39 to financial assets and financial liabilities derecognised as a result of past transactions was obtained at the time of initially accounting for those transactions'.[121] This will effectively ban most first-time adopters from restating transactions before 1 January 2004.

A first-time adopter that derecognised non-derivative financial assets and liabilities under its previous GAAP before 1 January 2004 will not have to recognise these items under IFRS even if they meet the IAS 39 recognition criteria. However, a first-time adopter is not exempt from:

- SIC-12 – *Consolidation* – *Special Purpose Entities* – which requires consolidation of all SPEs; and

- the requirement under IAS 39 to measure all derivatives at fair value.

Therefore, not all previously derecognised items will remain off-balance sheet upon adoption of IFRS.

2.6.5 Hedge accounting

Hedge accounting is dealt with comprehensively in Chapter 19. The discussion of first-time adoption issues relating to hedge accounting below can also be found in Chapter 19 at 7.3.3 to 7.3.5. Detailed worked examples illustrating the first-time adoption requirements in IFRS 1 can be found in Chapter 19 at 7.3.6.

A   Prohibition on retrospective application

IFRS 1 explains that entities are prohibited from applying retrospectively some of the hedge accounting provisions of IAS 39.[122] In the basis for conclusions, it is explained that:

> '... it is unlikely that most entities would have adopted IAS 39's criteria for (a) documenting hedges at their inception and (b) testing the hedges for effectiveness, even if they intended to continue the same hedging strategies after adopting IAS 39. Furthermore, retrospective designation of hedges (or retrospective reversal of their designation) could lead to selective designation of some hedges to report a particular result.[123] To overcome these problems, the transitional requirements in [the previous version of] IAS 39 require an entity already applying IFRS to apply the hedging requirements prospectively when it adopts IAS 39. As the same problems arise for a first-time adopter, the IFRS requires prospective application by a first-time adopter.'[124]

Unfortunately, there is only a limited amount of guidance in IFRS 1 regarding hedge accounting and therefore it is not entirely clear what applying these requirements of IAS 39 'prospectively' actually involves, especially insofar as the opening IFRS balance sheet is concerned. However, the basis for conclusions continues:

> 'ED 1 included a redrafted version of the transitional provisions in IAS 39 and related Questions and Answers (Q&As) developed by the IAS 39 Implementation Guidance Committee. The Board confirmed in the Basis for Conclusions published with ED 1 that it did not intend the redrafting to create substantive changes. However, in the light of responses to ED 1, the Board decided in finalising IFRS 1 that the redrafting would not make it easier for first-time adopters and others to understand and apply the transition provisions and Q&As. However, the project to improve IAS 32 and IAS 39 resulted in certain amendments to the transition requirements. In

addition, this project incorporated selected other Q&As (ie not on transition) into IAS 39. The Board therefore took this opportunity to consolidate all the guidance for first-time adopters in one place, by incorporating the Q&As on transition into IFRS 1.'[125]

This indicates that the transitional provisions set out in the previous version of IAS 39 and IGC Q&As, ED 1 and IFRS 1 are intended to be broadly consistent. Consequently, the fact that all three sources are expressed in different ways can be useful in interpreting this aspect of IFRS 1. These documents are referred to at B below where they assist in understanding the requirements set out in IFRS 1.

B   *Hedge accounting: opening IFRS balance sheet*

I   *Measurement of derivatives and elimination of deferred gains and losses*

Under its previous GAAP an entity's accounting policies might have included a number of accounting treatments for derivatives that formed part of a hedge relationship. For example, accounting policies might have included those where the derivative was:

- not explicitly recognised as an asset or liability (e.g. in the case of a forward contract used to hedge an expected but uncontracted future transaction);

- recognised as an asset or liability but at an amount different from its fair value (e.g. a purchased option recognised at its original cost, perhaps less amortisation; or an interest rate swap accounted for by accruing the periodic interest payments and receipts); or

- subsumed within the accounting for another asset or liability (e.g. a foreign currency denominated monetary item and a matching forward contract or swap accounted for as a 'synthetic' functional currency denominated monetary item).

Whatever the previous accounting treatment, a first-time adopter should isolate and separately account for all derivatives in its opening IFRS balance sheet as assets or liabilities measured at fair value.[126]

The implementation guidance explains that all derivatives, other than those that are designated and effective hedging instruments, are classified as held for trading. Accordingly, the difference between the previous carrying amount of a derivative (which may have been zero) and its fair value should be recognised as an adjustment of the balance of retained earnings at the beginning of the financial year in which IFRS 1 is initially applied (other than for a derivative that is a designated and effective hedging instrument).[127]

Hedge accounting policies under an entity's previous GAAP might also have included one or both of the following accounting treatments:

- derivatives were measured at fair value but, to the extent they were regarded as hedging future transactions, the gain (or loss) arising was reported as a liability (or asset) such as deferred (or accrued) income;

- realised gains or losses arising on the termination of a previously unrecognised derivative used in a hedge relationship (such as an interest rate swap hedging a borrowing) were included in the balance sheet as deferred or accrued income and amortised over the remaining term of the hedged exposure.

In all cases an entity is required to eliminate deferred gains and losses arising on derivatives 'that were reported under previous GAAP as if they were assets or liabilities.'[128] Essentially this is because deferred gains and losses do not meet the definition of assets or liabilities under the IASB's *Framework*. In contrast to adjustments made to restate derivatives at fair value, the implementation guidance does not specify in general terms how to deal with adjustments to eliminate deferred gains or losses.

The requirement to eliminate deferred gains and losses does not appear to extend to those that have been included in the carrying amount of other assets or liabilities that will continue to be recognised under IFRS. For example, under an entity's previous GAAP, the carrying amount of non-financial assets such as inventories or property, plant and equipment might have included the equivalent of a basis adjustment (i.e. hedging gains or losses were considered an integral part of the asset's cost). In fact carrying forward this treatment into an entity's first set of IFRS financial statements would be consistent with the transitional provisions of the revised IAS 39 (see Chapter 19 at 7.2). Of course entities should also consider any other provisions of IFRS 1 that apply to those hedged items.

The way in which an entity accounts for these adjustments will, to a large extent, dictate how its existing hedge relationships will be reflected in its ongoing IFRS financial statements. Particularly, an entity's future results will be different depending on whether the adjustments are taken to retained earnings or to a separate component of equity – in the latter case they would be recycled to profit or loss at a later date but would not in the former. Similarly, its future results would be affected if the carrying amount of related assets or liabilities are changed to reflect these adjustments (as opposed to the adjustments being made to retained earnings).

For short-term hedges (e.g. of sales and inventory purchases) these effects are likely to work their way out of the IFRS financial statements relatively quickly. However for other hedges (e.g. of long term borrowings) an entity's results may be affected for many years. The question of which hedge relationships should be reflected in an entity's opening IFRS balance sheet is dealt with at II to IV below.

II   *Hedge relationships reflected in the opening IFRS balance sheet*

The standard states that a first-time adopter *should not* reflect a hedging relationship in its opening IFRS balance sheet (or the balance sheet at the beginning of its first IFRS reporting period, if comparatives are not restated) if that hedging relationship is of a type that *does not* qualify for hedge accounting under IAS 39. As examples of this it cites many hedging relationships where the hedging instrument is a cash instrument or written option; where the hedged item is a net position; or where the hedge covers interest risk in a held-to-maturity investment.[129]

However, if an entity had designated a net position as a hedged item under its previous GAAP, the IASB decided that an individual item within that net position *may* be designated as a hedged item under IFRS, provided that it does so no later than the date of transition to IFRS (or the beginning of the first IFRS reporting period, if comparatives are not restated).[130] In other words, such designation could allow the hedge relationship to be reflected in the opening IFRS balance sheet (or the balance sheet at the beginning of its first IFRS reporting period, if comparatives are not restated).

Further, a first-time adopter is not permitted to designate hedges retrospectively in relation to transactions entered into before the date of transition to IFRS (or the beginning of the first IFRS reporting period, if comparatives are not restated).[131] This would appear to prevent an entity from reflecting hedge relationships in its opening balance sheet that it did not identify as such under its previous GAAP.

It might seem to follow that a hedge relationship designated under an entity's previous GAAP *should* be reflected in its opening IFRS balance sheet (or the balance sheet at the beginning of its first IFRS reporting period, if comparatives are not restated) if that hedging relationship *is* of a type that *does* qualify for hedge accounting under IAS 39. In fact, if an entity was allowed not to reflect such a hedge in its opening IFRS balance sheet (or the balance sheet at the beginning of its first IFRS reporting period, if comparatives are not restated) this would effectively allow the retrospective reversal of the hedge designation. As noted at I above, this is something the IASB has sought to avoid.[132] However, while such a 'principle' seems to be implied by the implementation guidance (see III and IV below), the IASB has not actually articulated it in these terms.

There are, perhaps, a number of reasons for the IASB's reticence. For example, under an entity's previous GAAP, it might not have been clear whether a derivative instrument was actually designated as a hedge. Further, even if it were clear that a derivative had previously been designated as a hedge, the hedged item might not have been identified with sufficiently specificity to allow the effects of the hedge to be reflected in the opening IFRS balance sheet and/or, thereafter, to be 'unwound' at the appropriate time.

III   *Reflecting cash flow hedges in the opening IFRS balance sheet*

The implementation guidance to IFRS 1 explains that a first-time adopter may, under its previous GAAP, have deferred gains and losses on a cash flow hedge of a forecast transaction. If, at the date of transition to IFRS (or the beginning of the first IFRS reporting period, if comparatives are not restated) the hedged forecast transaction is not highly probable, but is expected to occur, the entire deferred gain or loss should be recognised in equity.[133] To be consistent, this would be included in the same component of equity an entity would use to record future gains and losses on cash flow hedges.

This raises the question of how to deal with such a hedge if, at the date of transition to IFRS (or the beginning of the first IFRS reporting period, if comparatives are not restated), the forecast transaction *was* highly probable. It would make no sense if the former was required to be reflected in the opening IFRS balance sheet, but the latter (which is clearly a 'better' hedge) was not. Therefore, it must follow that a cash flow hedge should be reflected in the opening IFRS balance sheet in the way set out above if the hedged item is a forecast transaction that is highly probable. Similarly, it follows that a cash flow hedge of the variability in cash flows attributable to a particular risk associated with a recognised asset or liability (such as all or some future interest payments on variable rate debt) should also be reflected in the opening balance sheet.

If, at the date of transition to IFRS (or the beginning of the first IFRS reporting period, if comparatives are not restated), the forecast transaction was *not* expected to occur, this would be a relationship of a type that does not qualify for hedge accounting under IAS 39. Therefore the hedging relationship should not be reflected in the opening IFRS balance sheet. In fact ED 1 was explicit on this point.[134]

There are various ways in which gains or losses might have been deferred under an entity's previous GAAP. ED 1 explained that, in this context, deferral included:

- treating deferred gains as if they were liabilities and deferred losses as if they were assets; and
- not recognising changes in the fair value of the hedging instrument.[135]

Even though this explanation was not incorporated into IFRS 1, at a conceptual level there is scarce reason why it should not apply under the standard. However, it is possible to read parts of the implementation guidance as preventing this treatment if the hedge has not been designated in an effective hedge under IAS 39 by the date of transition (or the beginning of the first IFRS reporting period, if comparatives are not restated). The following example highlights this issue.

Example 4.21:   Unrecognised gains and losses on existing cash flow hedge

Company T has the euro as its functional currency. In September 2003 it entered into a forward currency contract to sell dollars for euros in twelve months to hedge dollar denominated sales it forecasts are highly probable to occur in September 2004. T will apply IAS 39 from 1 January 2004, its date of transition to IFRS. The historical cost of the forward contract is €nil and at the date of transition it had a positive fair value of €100.

Case 1: Gains and losses deferred

Under T's previous GAAP, until the sales occurred the forward contract was recognised in the balance sheet at its fair value and the resulting gain or loss was deferred in the balance sheet as a liability or asset. When the sale occurred any deferred gain or loss was recognised in profit or loss as an offset to the revenue recognised on the hedged sales.

Case 2: Gains and losses unrecognised

Under T's previous GAAP the contract was not recognised in the balance sheet. When the sale occurred any unrecognised gain or loss was recognised in profit or loss as an offset to the revenue recognised on the hedged sales.

In Case 1 the relationship can clearly be reflected in T's opening IFRS balance sheet whether or not it is designated as an effective hedge in accordance with IAS 39 at the date of transition: there is no restriction on transferring the deferred gain to a separate component of equity and there is no adjustment to the carrying amount of the forward contract.

Case 2 is slightly more problematical. As noted at I above, the implementation guidance explains that the difference between the previous carrying amount of a derivative and its fair value should be recognised as an adjustment of the balance of retained earnings (other than for a derivative that is a designated and effective hedging instrument).[136] Read literally, if T had not designated the relationship as an effective hedge in accordance with IAS 39 at the date of transition, this implementation guidance could prevent the relationship from being reflected in T's opening IFRS balance sheet. This is because the adjustment to the carrying amount of the forward would be recorded in retained earnings rather than a separate component of equity.

Such an interpretation would allow T to choose not to designate (in accordance with IAS 39) certain cash flow hedges, say those that are in a loss position, until one day after its date of transition, thereby allowing associated hedging losses to bypass profit or loss completely. Notwithstanding this, some have suggested the literal interpretation is appropriate. However, this would effectively result in the retrospective de-designation of hedges to achieve a desired result, thereby breaching this general principle of IFRS 1. Arguably this general principle of the standard should take precedence over the implementation guidance.

IV   Reflecting fair value hedges in the opening IFRS balance sheet

The implementation guidance to IFRS 1 explains that a first-time adopter may, under its previous GAAP, have deferred or not recognised gains and losses on a fair value hedge of a hedged item that is not measured at fair value. For such a fair value hedge, the entity should adjust the carrying amount of the hedged item at the date of transition to IFRS (or the beginning of the first IFRS reporting period, if comparatives are not restated). The adjustment, which is essentially the effective part of the hedge that was not recognised in the carrying amount of the hedged item under the previous GAAP, should be calculated as the lower of:

(a) that portion of the cumulative change in the fair value of the hedged item that reflects the designated hedged risk and was not recognised under previous GAAP; and

(b) that portion of the cumulative change in the fair value of the hedging instrument that reflects the designated hedged risk and, under previous GAAP, was either (i) not recognised or (ii) deferred in the balance sheet as an asset or liability.[137]

The is consistent with the requirement in the previous version of IAS 39 (and the proposals in ED 1) under which any balance sheet positions in fair value hedges of existing assets and liabilities would be accounted for in the opening balance sheet in (broadly) the same manner as above.[138]

Available-for-sale assets are measured at fair value so the guidance above would not appear to apply to fair value hedges of such instruments. However, it would be logical to apply an equivalent adjustment to the cost or amortised cost of such assets.

C   *Hedge accounting: subsequent treatment*

The implementation guidance explains that hedge accounting can be applied prospectively only from the date the hedge relationship is fully designated and documented. Therefore, if the hedging instrument is still held at the date of transition to IFRS (or the beginning of the first IFRS reporting period, if comparatives are not restated) the designation and documentation of a hedge relationship must be completed on or before that date if the hedge relationship is to qualify for hedge accounting on an ongoing basis from that date.[139]

An entity may, before the date of transition to IFRS (or the beginning of the first IFRS reporting period, if comparatives are not restated), have designated a transaction as a hedge that does not meet the conditions for hedge accounting in IAS 39. In these cases it should following the general requirements in IAS 39 for discontinuing hedge accounting – these are dealt with in Chapter 19 at 4.1.3 for fair value hedges and in Chapter 19 at 4.2.3 for cash flow hedges.[140]

For cash flow hedges, any net cumulative gain or loss that was reclassified to equity on initial application of IAS 39 (see 2.6.5 B III above) should remain in equity until:

(a)   the forecast transaction subsequently results in the recognition of a non-financial asset or non-financial liability;

(b)   the forecast transaction affects profit or loss; or

(c)   subsequently circumstances change and the forecast transaction is no longer expected to occur, in which case any related net cumulative gain or loss that had been recognised directly in equity is recognised in profit or loss.[141]

The requirements above do little more than reiterate the general requirements of IAS 39, i.e. that hedge accounting can only be applied prospectively if the qualifying conditions are met, and entities should experience few interpretative problems in dealing with this aspect of the hedge accounting requirements.

2.6.6 *Derivatives, embedded derivatives and transaction costs*

At the date of transition to IFRS (or the beginning of the first IFRS reporting period, if comparatives are not restated), IAS 39 requires a first-time adopter to measure all derivatives at fair value and to eliminate deferred gains and losses arising 'on derivatives that were reported under previous GAAP as if they were assets or liabilities'.[142]

A   *Derivatives*

All derivatives, except for those that are designated and effective hedging instruments, are classified as held for trading under IAS 39. Therefore, the difference between their fair value and their previous carrying amount should be recognised as an adjustment to retained earnings at the beginning of the financial year in which IAS 39 is initially applied (other than for a derivative that is a designated and effective hedging instrument).[143]

B   Embedded derivatives

IAS 39 requires an entity to account separately for some embedded derivatives at fair value (see Chapter 15 at 5). Under US GAAP, the transitional provisions of SFAS 133 – *Accounting for Derivative Instruments and Hedging Activities* – exempt an entity from having to account for some pre-existing embedded derivatives separately. The IASB considered this and the fact that full retrospective accounting for embedded derivatives might be costly, but concluded 'that the failure to measure embedded derivatives at fair value would diminish the relevance and reliability of an entity's first IFRS financial statements'.[144] A first-time adopter will therefore have to consider all contracts existing at its date of transition to IFRS (or the beginning of the first IFRS reporting period, if comparatives are not restated) and decide whether or not they contain embedded derivatives. Any embedded derivatives that are identified and have to be accounted for separately should be recognised as assets or liabilities, and be measured at their fair value.

C   Transaction costs

To determine the amortised cost of a financial asset or liability using the effective interest rate method, a first-time adopter needs to establish the transaction costs incurred when the instrument was originated. Despite arguments by some commentators that this might involve undue cost or effort, the IASB concluded that 'the unamortised portion of transaction costs at the date of transition to IFRSs [or the beginning of the first IFRS reporting period, if comparatives are not restated] is unlikely to be material for most financial assets and financial liabilities' and therefore presumably do not require restatement.[145] The IASB presumes that 'even when the unamortised portion is material, reasonable estimates should be possible'.[146]

2.7   Other exemptions

As discussed at 2.3.3 A above, IFRS 1 establishes exemptions from the requirements of other IFRS. Those exemptions not already dealt with above are discussed at 2.7.1 to 2.7.5 below.

2.7.1   Employee benefits

Under IAS 19 an entity is allowed to use a 'corridor' approach that leaves some actuarial gains and losses on defined benefit plans unrecognised.[147] To calculate the net cumulative unrecognised gains or losses at the date of transition to IFRS, a first-time adopter would need to determine actuarial gains or losses for each year since inception of each defined benefit plan. It is obvious that a full retrospective application of IAS 19 would be costly (if not impossible to achieve) and not benefit users of the financial statements.[148] Therefore, the IASB introduced an exemption that allows a first-time adopter 'to recognise all cumulative actuarial gains and losses at the date of transition to IFRS, even if it uses the corridor approach for later actuarial gains and losses'. If a first-time adopter uses this exemption it will have to apply the exemption to all its defined benefit plans.[149] In the extract below an entity discloses that it used the employee benefits exemption in IFRS 1.

Extract 4.2: N.V. Bekaert S.A. (2003)

Notes to the consolidated financial statements [extract]

1. Summary of significant accounting policies [extract]

Defined benefit plans [extract]

In accordance with IFRS 1 "First-Time Adoption of International Financial Reporting Standards" (§ 20), the Group has opted to recognise all cumulative actuarial gains and losses at the date of transition to IFRS (being 1 January 2002) as an adjustment to equity.

A   Full actuarial valuations

An entity's first IFRS financial statements may reflect its defined benefit liabilities at three different dates, that is, the reporting date, the end of the comparative period and the date of transition to IFRS. An entity that presents two comparative periods would have to calculate its defined benefits liabilities at four different dates. Clearly, it is quite costly to require a first-time adopter to perform three, or possibly even four, actuarial valuations. However, the IASB decided against permitting 'an entity to use a single actuarial valuation, based, for example, on assumptions valid at the reporting date, with service costs and interest costs based on those assumptions for each of the periods presented'.[150] The IASB's main objection to such an exemption was that it 'would conflict with the objective of providing understandable, relevant, reliable and comparable information for users'.[151] Nevertheless, the IASB agreed to the compromise position that if an entity obtains a full actuarial valuation at one or two dates, it is allowed to roll forward (or roll back) to another date but only as long as the roll forward (or roll back) reflects material transactions and other material events between those dates (including changes in market prices and interest rates).[152]

B   Actuarial assumptions

A first-time adopter's actuarial assumptions at its date of transition to IFRS should be consistent with the ones it used for the same date under its previous GAAP, unless there is objective evidence that those assumptions were in error (see 2.8.1 below). The impact of any later revisions to those assumptions is an actuarial gain or loss of the period in which the entity makes the revisions.[153] If a first-time adopter needs 'to make actuarial assumptions at the date of transition to IFRSs that were not necessary under its previous GAAP' these actuarial assumptions should 'not reflect conditions that arose after the date of transition to IFRS. In particular, discount rates and the fair value of plan assets at the date of transition to IFRSs reflect market conditions at that date. Similarly, the entity's actuarial assumptions at the date of transition to IFRSs about future employee turnover rates do not reflect a significant increase in estimated employee turnover rates as a result of a curtailment of the pension plan that occurred after the date of transition to IFRSs'.[154]

C   Unrecognised past service costs

It is worth mentioning that the employee benefits exemption only applies to unrecognised actuarial gains or losses, it does not apply to 'unrecognised past service costs' that relate to unvested benefits. The IASB decided that an exemption for past service cost was not justified because a full retrospective application of

IAS 19 to unrecognised past service costs 'is less onerous than the retrospective application of the corridor for actuarial gains and losses because it does not require the recreation of data since the inception of the plan'.[155] A first-time adopter therefore needs to look at periods before its date of transition to IFRS to determine the amount of unrecognised past service costs that relate to unvested benefits in accordance with IAS 19.

2.7.2 Cumulative translation differences

Exchange differences arising on a monetary item that forms part of a reporting entity's net investment in a foreign operation are recognised in a separate component of equity under IAS 21.[156] IAS 21 and IAS 39 require that, on disposal of a foreign operation, the cumulative amount of the exchange differences deferred in the separate component of equity relating to that foreign operation (which includes, for example, the cumulative translation difference for that foreign operation, the exchange differences arising on certain translations to a different presentation currency and any gains and losses on related hedges) should be recognised in profit or loss when the gain or loss on disposal is recognised.[157]

Full retrospective application of IAS 21 would require a first-time adopter to restate all financial statements of its foreign operations to IFRS from their date of inception or later acquisition onwards, and then determine the cumulative translation differences arising in relation to each of these foreign operations. The costs of this restatement are likely to exceed the benefits to users of financial statements. For this reason 'a first-time adopter need not comply with these requirements for cumulative translation differences that existed at the date of transition to IFRSs. If a first-time adopter uses this exemption:

(a)   the cumulative translation differences for all foreign operations are deemed to be zero at the date of transition to IFRSs; and

(b)   the gain or loss on a subsequent disposal of any foreign operation shall exclude translation differences that arose before the date of transition to IFRS and shall include later translation differences.'[158]

As discussed in Chapter 19 at 8.3.2, IFRS 1 is unfortunately not entirely whether the exemption extends to similar gains and losses arising on related hedges. Therefore, entities will need to apply judgement in determining how and when the cumulative gains and losses on net investment hedges are reset to zero.

2.7.3 Share-based payment transactions

IFRS 2 – *Share-based Payment* – applies to accounting for the acquisition of goods or services in equity-settled share-based payment transactions, cash-settled share-based payment transactions and transactions in which the entity has the option to chose between settlement in cash or equity. The transitional rules for first-time adopters are based on the transitional rules for existing IFRS reporting entities. However, the IASB added the following exemptions for first-time adopters:[159]

• a first-time adopter is not required to apply IFRS 2 to equity instruments that were granted after 7 November 2002 but that vested before the date of transition to IFRS; and

- a first-time adopter is not required to apply IFRS 2 to liabilities arising from cash-settled share-based payment transactions if those liabilities were settled before 1 January 2005 or before the date of transition to IFRS.

The IFRS 1 exemption for share-based payment transactions contains the following options that a first-time adopter may elect to apply:

(a)   only if a first-time adopter 'has disclosed publicly the fair value of those equity instruments, determined at the measurement date, as defined in IFRS 2' is it encouraged but not required to apply IFRS 2 to:[160]

   (i)   equity instruments that were granted on or before 7 November 2002;

   (ii)   equity instruments that were granted after 7 November 2002 but vested before the later of (1) the date of transition to IFRS and (2) 1 January 2005.

Many first-time adopters will not have published the fair value of equity instruments granted and are, therefore, not allowed to apply IFRS 2 retrospectively to those share-based transactions;

(b)   for all grants of equity instruments to which IFRS 2 has not been applied a first-time adopter shall nevertheless disclose the information required by paragraphs 44 and 45 of IFRS 2;[161] and

(c)   if a first-time adopter modifies the terms or conditions of a grant of equity instruments to which IFRS 2 has not been applied, the entity is not required to apply paragraphs 26-29 of IFRS 2 if the modification occurred before the later of (1) the date of transition to IFRS and (2) 1 January 2005.[162]

Furthermore, if share-based payments give rise to liabilities, a first-time adopter is:[163]

(d)   'encouraged, but not required, to apply IFRS 2 to liabilities arising from share-based payment transactions that were settled before the date of transition to IFRS';

(e)   'also encouraged, but not required, to apply IFRS 2 to liabilities that were settled before 1 January 2005' and

(f)   'for liabilities to which IFRS 2 is applied … not required to restate comparative information to the extent that the information relates to a period or date that is earlier than 7 November 2002'.

IFRS 1 allows a first-time adopter to pick and choose from these options as it sees fit, i.e. it does not encourage or require a first-time adopter to make logical use of the options. However, the qualitative characteristics of financial statements as set out in the *Framework* would seem to dictate that a first-time adopter should not apply the above exemptions in a random fashion.[164]

2.7.4   Insurance contracts

A first-time adopter may apply the transitional provisions in IFRS 4. That standard limits an insurer to changing 'its accounting policies for insurance contracts if, and only if, the change makes the financial statements more relevant to the economic decision-making needs of users and no less reliable, or more reliable and no less relevant to those needs. An insurer shall judge relevance and reliability by the criteria in IAS 8.'[165] As discussed at 2.6.1 above, an entity adopting IFRS for the first time before 1 January 2006 is not required to prepare comparative information under IAS 32, IAS 39 and IFRS 4.[166] Instead, a first-time adopter that chooses to present comparative information that does not comply with IAS 32, IAS 39 and IFRS 4 in its first year of transition should:

- apply its previous GAAP in the comparative period to financial instruments that are within the scope of IAS 32, IAS 39 and IFRS 4; and

- make certain additional disclosures (see 2.10.1 A below).[167]

2.7.5 Assets and liabilities of subsidiaries, associates and joint ventures

A   Subsidiary becomes a first-time adopter later than its parent

Within groups, some subsidiaries, associates and joint ventures may have a different date of transition to IFRS than the parent/investor (for example, national legislation required IFRS after, or prohibited IFRS at, the date of transition to IFRS of the parent/investor). This could result in permanent differences between the IFRS figures in a subsidiary's own financial statements and those it reports to its parent. In turn this could force a subsidiary to keep two parallel sets of accounting records based on different dates of transition to IFRS.[168] To mitigate this difficulty, the IASB introduced a special exemption regarding the assets and liabilities of subsidiaries, associates and joint ventures.

If a subsidiary becomes a first-time adopter later that its parent, it should in its financial statements measure its assets and liabilities at either:

'(a)   the carrying amounts that would be included in the parent's consolidated financial statements, based on the parent's date of transition to IFRSs, if no adjustments were made for consolidation procedures and for the effects of the business combination in which the parent acquired the subsidiary; or

(b)   the carrying amounts required by the rest of this IFRS [IFRS 1], based on the subsidiary's date of transition to IFRSs. These carrying amounts could differ from those described in (a):

    (i)   when the exemptions in this IFRS result in measurements that depend on the date of transition to IFRSs.

    (ii)   when the accounting policies used in the subsidiary's financial statements differ from those in the consolidated financial statements. For example, the subsidiary may use as its accounting policy the cost model in IAS 16 *Property, Plant and Equipment*, whereas the group may use the revaluation model.'[169]

A similar election is available to an associate or joint venture that becomes a first-time adopter later than an entity that has significant influence or joint control over it.[170] The following example, which is taken from the guidance on implementation of IFRS 1, illustrates how an entity should apply these requirements.

Example 4.22:   Parent adopts IFRSs before subsidiary[171]

Background

Parent N presents its (consolidated) first IFRS financial statements in 2005. Its foreign subsidiary O, wholly owned by parent N since formation, prepares information under IFRSs for internal consolidation purposes from that date, but subsidiary O will not present its first IFRS financial statements until 2007.

Application of requirements

If subsidiary O applies paragraph 24(a) of the IFRS, the carrying amounts of its assets and liabilities are the same in both its opening IFRS balance sheet at 1 January 2006 and parent N's consolidated balance sheet (except for adjustments for consolidation procedures) and are based on parent N's date of transition to IFRSs.

Alternatively, subsidiary O may, under paragraph 24(b) of the IFRS, measure all its assets or liabilities based on its own date of transition to IFRSs (1 January 2006). However, the fact that subsidiary O becomes a first-time adopter in 2007 does not change the carrying amounts of its assets and liabilities in parent N's consolidated financial statements.

Under option (b) a subsidiary would prepare its own IFRS financial statements, completely ignoring the IFRS reports that its parent uses in preparing its consolidated financial statements. Under option (a) the numbers in a subsidiary's IFRS financial statements will be as close to those used by its parent as possible. However, differences other than those arising from consolidation procedures and business combinations will still exist in many cases, for example:

- a subsidiary may have hedged an exposure by entering into a transaction with a fellow subsidiary, such transaction could qualify for hedge accounting in the subsidiary's own financial statements but not in the parent's consolidated financial statements; or

- a pension plan may have to be classified as a defined contribution plan from the subsidiary's point of view, but is accounted for as a defined benefit plan in the parent's consolidated financial statements.

The IASB seems content with the fact that the exemption 'will ease some practical problems', though it will rarely succeed in achieving more than a moderate reduction of the number of reconciling differences between a subsidiary's own reporting and the numbers used by its parent.[172]

Application of option (a) would be more difficult when a parent and its subsidiary (joint venture or associate) have different financial years. In that case, IFRS 1 would seem to require the IFRS information for the subsidiary (joint venture or associate) to be based on the parent's date of transition to IFRS, which may not even coincide with an interim reporting date of the subsidiary (joint venture or associate).

A subsidiary may become a first-time adopter later than its parent, because it previously prepared a reporting package under IFRS for consolidation purposes but did not present a full set of financial statements under IFRS. The above election may be 'relevant not only when a subsidiary's reporting package complies fully with the recognition and measurement requirements of IFRSs, but also when it is adjusted centrally for matters such as post-balance sheet events review and central allocation of pension costs'.[173] Adjustments made centrally to an unpublished reporting package are not considered to be corrections of errors for the purposes of the disclosure requirements in IFRS 1. However, a subsidiary is not permitted to ignore misstatements that are immaterial to the consolidated financial statements of its parent but material to its own financial statements.

If a subsidiary was acquired after the parent's date of transition to IFRS, it seems that the subsidiary cannot apply option (a) because 'the carrying amounts that would be included in the parent's consolidated financial statements, based on the parent's date of transition to IFRS' would not exist.[174]

The exemption is also available to associates and joint ventures. This means that in many cases an associate or joint venture that wants to apply option (a) will need to choose which shareholder it considers its 'parent' for IFRS 1 purposes and determine its IFRS carrying amount of its assets and liabilities by reference to that parent's date of transition to IFRS.

B   Parent becomes a first-time adopter later than its subsidiary

If an entity becomes a first-time adopter later that its subsidiary, associate or joint venture the entity should 'in its consolidated financial statements, measure the assets and liabilities of the subsidiary (or associate or joint venture) at the same carrying amounts as in the financial statements of the subsidiary (or associate or joint venture), after adjusting for consolidation and equity accounting adjustments and for the effects of the business combination in which the entity acquired the subsidiary'.[175]

Whereas a subsidiary can choose to prepare its first IFRS financial statements by reference to its own date of transition to IFRS or that of its parent, the parent itself must use the IFRS measurements already used in the subsidiary's separate financial statements, except to adjust for consolidation procedures and for the effects of the business combination in which the parent acquired the subsidiary.[176]

The following example, which is taken from the guidance on implementation of IFRS 1, illustrates how an entity should apply these requirements.

Example 4.23:   Subsidiary adopts IFRSs before parent[177]

Background

Parent P presents its (consolidated) first IFRS financial statements in 2007. Its foreign subsidiary Q, wholly owned by parent P since formation, presented its first IFRS financial statements in 2005. Until 2007, subsidiary Q prepared information for internal consolidation purposes under parent P's previous GAAP.

Application of requirements

The carrying amounts of subsidiary Q's assets and liabilities at 1 January 2006 are the same in both parent P's (consolidated) opening IFRS balance sheet and subsidiary Q's separate financial statements (except for adjustments for consolidation procedures) and are based on subsidiary Q's date of transition to IFRSs. The fact that parent P becomes a first-time adopter in 2007 does not change those carrying amounts.

C   *Implementation guidance on accounting for assets and liabilities of subsidiaries, associates and joint ventures*

When an entity applies the rules discussed under A and B above, these do not override the requirements:

'(a)   to apply Appendix B of the IFRS to assets acquired, and liabilities assumed, in a business combination that occurred before the acquirer's date of transition to IFRSs. However, the acquirer applies paragraph 25 to new assets acquired, and liabilities assumed, by the acquiree after that business combination and still held at the acquirer's date of transition to IFRSs.

(b)   to apply the rest of the IFRS in measuring all assets and liabilities for which paragraphs 24 and 25 are not relevant.

(c)   to give all disclosures required by the IFRS as of the first-time adopter's own date of transition to IFRSs.'[178]

D   *Adoption of IFRS on different dates in separate and consolidated financial statements*

If a parent adopts IFRS in its 'separate financial statements earlier or later than for its consolidated financial statements, it shall measure its assets and liabilities at the same amounts in both financial statements, except for consolidation adjustments'.[179] An entity that prepares both separate and consolidated IFRS financial statements is required to prepare them using the same date of transition to IFRS for both, which greatly improves comparability. Although it might seem natural to use the earliest date of transition, the standard does not specifically require this.

2.8   Other exceptions to retrospective application of other IFRSs

As discussed at 2.3.3 B above, IFRS 1 specifically prohibits retrospective application of IFRS in a number of situations. The exceptions that have not been covered at 2.6.4 and 2.6.5 above are discussed below.

2.8.1   *Estimates*

IFRS 1 requires an entity to use estimates under IFRS that are consistent with the estimates made for the same date under its previous GAAP – after adjusting for any difference in accounting policy – unless there is objective evidence that those estimates were in error.[180] IAS 8 defines prior period errors as:

'omissions from, and misstatements in, the entity's financial statements for one or more prior periods arising from a failure to use, or misuse of, reliable information that:

(a)   was available when financial statements for those periods were authorised for issue; and

(b)   could reasonably be expected to have been obtained and taken into account in the preparation and presentation of those financial statements.

Such errors include the effects of mathematical mistakes, mistakes in applying accounting policies, oversights or misinterpretations of facts, and fraud.'[181]

Under IFRS 1 an entity cannot apply hindsight and make 'better' estimates when it prepares its first IFRS financial statements. It also means that an entity is not allowed to take account of any subsequent events that provide evidence of conditions that existed at that date, but that came to light after the date of its previous GAAP financial statements were finalised. The IASB considers that although 'some of those events might qualify as adjusting events under IAS 10 *Events After the Balance Sheet Date* ... if the entity made those estimates on a basis consistent with IFRSs ... it would be more helpful to users – and more consistent with IAS 8 *Accounting Policies, Changes in Accounting Estimates and Errors* – to recognise the revision of those estimates as income or expense in the period when the entity made the revision, rather than in preparing the opening IFRS balance sheet'.[182] Effectively, the IASB wishes to prevent entities using hindsight to 'clean up' their balance sheets by direct write-offs to equity as part of the opening IFRS balance sheet exercise.

The requirement that an entity should use estimates consistent with those made under its previous GAAP applies both to estimates made in respect to the date of transition to IFRS and to those in respect of the end of any comparative period.[183] IFRS 1 provides the following guidance on how an entity should put this requirement into practice:

- When an entity receives information after the relevant date about estimates that it had made under previous GAAP, it treats this information in the same way as a non-adjusting event after the balance sheet date under IAS 10.[184] An entity can be in one of the following two positions:

  - its previous GAAP accounting policy was consistent with IFRS, in which case the adjustment is reflected in the period in which the revision is made;[185] or

  - its previous GAAP accounting policy was not consistent with IFRS, in which case it will need to adjust the estimate for the difference in accounting policies.[186]

  In both situations, if an entity later adjusts those estimates, it accounts for those estimates as events of the period in which it makes the revisions;[187]

- When an entity needs to make estimates under IFRS at the relevant date that were not required under its previous GAAP, those estimates should be consistent with IAS 10 and reflect conditions that existed at the relevant date. This means, for example, that estimates of market prices, interest rates or foreign exchange rates should reflect market conditions at that date;[188] and

- IFRS 1 does not override the requirements in other IFRS that base classifications or measurements on circumstances existing at a particular date, such as for example:

  - the distinction between finance leases and operating leases;

  - the restrictions in IAS 38 that prohibit capitalisation of expenditure on an internally generated intangible asset if the asset did not qualify for recognition when the expenditure was incurred; and

  - the distinction between financial liabilities and equity instruments (see IAS 32).[189]

The flowchart below shows the decision-making process that an entity needs to apply in dealing with estimates under its previous GAAP.

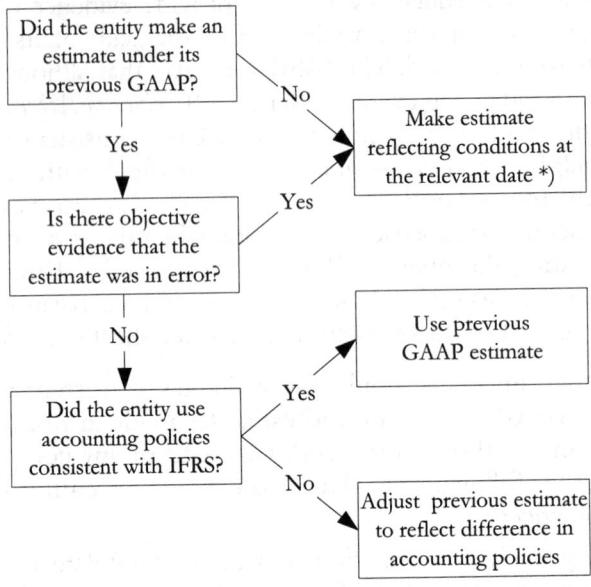

*) the relevant date is the date to which the estimate relates

The example below illustrates how an entity should deal with estimates under its previous GAAP.

Example 4.24:   Application of IFRS 1 to estimates

Entity A previously accounted for its pension plan on a cash basis. However, under IAS 19 – *Employee Benefits* – the plan is classified as a defined benefit plan and actuarial estimates are required.

A will need to make estimates under IFRS at the relevant date that reflect conditions that existed at the relevant date. This means, for example, that it needs to use a discount rate that would have been used at that time, ignoring any developments after that date.

Entity B accounted for inventories at the lower of cost and net realisable value under it previous GAAP. B's accounting policy is consistent with the requirements of IAS 2 – *Inventories*. Under previous GAAP, the goods were accounted for at a price of £1.25/kg. Due to changes in market circumstances, B ultimately could only sell the goods in the following period for £0.80/kg.

Assuming that B's estimate of the net realisable value was not in error, it will account for the goods at £1.25/kg upon transition to IFRS and makes no adjustments because the estimate was not in error and its accounting policy was consistent with IFRS. The effect of selling the goods for £0.80/kg will be reflected in the period in which they were sold.

Entity C accounted for a provision of $125,000 in connection with a court case. C's accounting policy was consistent with the requirements of IAS 37 – *Provisions, Contingent Liabilities and Contingent Assets* – except for the fact that C did not discount the provision for the time value of money. The discounted value of the provision would have been $90,000. The case was settled for $190,000 several months after the date of C's IFRS opening balance sheet.

In its opening IFRS balance sheet C will measure the provision at $90,000. IFRS 1 does not permit an entity to adjust the estimate itself, unless it was in error, but does require an adjustment to reflect the difference in accounting policies.

2.8.2 Assets classified as held for sale and discontinued operations

The transitional rules for existing IFRS reporting entities in IFRS 5 – *Non-current Assets Held for Sale and Discontinued Operations* – require prospective application for financial periods starting on or after 1 January 2005. However, early adoption of IFRS 5 – after any date before its effective date – is permitted, 'provided the valuations and other information needed to apply the IFRS were obtained at the time those criteria were originally met'. These transitional rules have been extended to apply to first-time adopters whose date of transition to IFRS is before 1 January 2005.[190] By contrast, first-time adopters whose date of transition to IFRS is on or after 1 January 2005 will need to apply IFRS 5 retrospectively.[191]

2.9 Additional IFRS 1 implementation guidance

Accounting areas that have not been covered above, but for which IFRS 1 provides specific implementation guidance, are discussed at 2.9.1 to 2.9.7 below.

2.9.1 Property, plant and equipment

A   Depreciation method and rate

If a first-time adopter's depreciation methods and rates under its previous GAAP are acceptable under IFRS then it accounts for any change in estimated useful life or depreciation pattern prospectively from when it makes that change in estimate (see 2.8.1 above). However, if the depreciation methods and rates are not acceptable under IFRS and the difference has a material impact on the financial statements, a first-time adopter should adjust the accumulated depreciation in its opening IFRS balance sheet retrospectively.[192] If a restatement would be too onerous, a first-time adopter could opt instead to use fair value as the deemed cost.

B   Use of fair value or revaluation as deemed cost

As discussed at 2.5 above, a first-time adopter may elect to use fair value or a revaluation as the deemed cost of an item of property, plant and equipment. When a first-time adopter uses a fair value or a revaluation as the deemed cost of an item of property, plant and equipment it will need to start depreciating the item 'from the date for which the entity established the fair value measurement or revaluation' and not from its date of transition to IFRS (see Example 4.20 at 2.5.3 above).[193]

C   Revaluation model

A first-time adopter that chooses to account for some or all classes of property, plant and equipment under the revaluation model needs to present the cumulative revaluation surplus as a separate component of equity. However, IFRS 1 requires that 'the revaluation surplus at the date of transition to IFRS is based on a comparison of the carrying amount of the asset at that date with its cost or deemed cost'.[194] If revaluations under previous GAAP did not satisfy the criteria in IFRS 1, a first-time adopter measures the revalued assets in its opening balance sheet on one of the following bases:[195]

(a)   cost (or deemed cost) less any accumulated depreciation and any accumulated impairment losses under the cost model in IAS 16;

(b)   deemed cost, being the fair value at the date of transition to IFRS; or

(c)   revalued amount, if the entity adopts the revaluation model in IAS 16 as its accounting policy under IFRSs for all items of property, plant and equipment in the same class.

A first-time adopter that uses fair value as the deemed cost for those classes of property, plant and equipment would be required to reset the cumulative revaluation surplus to zero.

D   Decommissioning provisions

Under IAS 16 the cost of an item of property, plant and equipment includes 'the initial estimate of the costs of dismantling and removing the item and restoring the site on which it is located, the obligation for which an entity incurs either when the item is acquired or as a consequence of having used the item during a particular period for purposes other than to produce inventories during that period'.[196] Therefore, a first-time adopter needs to ensure that cost includes an item representing the decommissioning provision as determined under IAS 37 – *Provisions, Contingent Liabilities and Contingent Assets.*[197]

The entity applies IAS 16 in determining the resulting amount included in the cost of the asset, before depreciation and impairment losses. Items such as depreciation and impairment losses cause differences between the carrying amount of the liability and the amount included in the carrying amount of the asset. An entity accounts for changes in decommissioning provisions in accordance with IFRIC 1 – *Changes in Existing Decommissioning, Restoration and Similar Liabilities*, but IFRS 1 provides an exemption for changes that occurred before the date of transition to IFRS and prescribes an alternative treatment.[198]

Example 4.25:   Decommissioning component in property, plant and equipment

Entity D's date of transition to IFRS is 1 January 2004 and its first IFRS reporting date is 31 December 2005. D built a factory that was completed and ready for use on 1 January 1999. Under its previous GAAP, D accrued a decommissioning provision over the expected life of the plant. The facts can be summarised as follows:

Cost of the plant	€1,400
Residual value	€200
Economic life	20 years
Original estimate of decommissioning cost in year 20	€175
Revised estimate at 2001 of decommissioning cost in year 20	€300
Discount rate applicable to decommissioning liability (the discount rate is assumed to be constant)	5.65%
Discounted value of decommissioning liability on 1 January 1999	€100
Discounted value of revised decommissioning liability on 1 January 2004	€131

If D applies the exemption from full retrospective application, what are the carrying amounts of the factory and the decommissioning liability in D's opening IFRS balance sheet?

The tables below shows how D accounts for the decommissioning liability and the factory under its previous GAAP, under IFRS 1 using the exemption and under IFRS 1 applying IFRIC 1 retrospectively.

	Decommissioning liability		
	Previous GAAP	*Exemption IFRS*	*Retrospective application IFRS*
1 January 1999	–	100	58
Decommissioning costs €175 ÷ 20 years × 2 =	17.5		
Decommissioning costs €100 × $(1.0565^2 - 1) =$		12	
Decommissioning costs €58 × $(1.0565^2 - 1) =$			7
1 January 2001	17.5	112	65
Revised estimate of decommissioning provision	12.5		47
1 January 2001	30	112	112
Decommissioning costs €300 ÷ 20 years × 3 =	45		
Decommissioning costs €112 × $(1.0565^3 - 1) =$		19	
Decommissioning costs €112 × $(1.0565^3 - 1) =$			19
1 January 2004	75	131	131
Decommissioning costs €300 ÷ 20 years × 2 =	30		
Decommissioning costs €131 × $(1.0565^2 - 1) =$		16	
Decommissioning costs €131 × $(1.0565^2 - 1) =$			16
31 December 2005	105	147	147

In calculating the decommissioning provision, it makes no difference whether D goes back in time and tracks the history of the decommissioning provision or whether it just calculates the decommissioning provision at its date of transition to IFRS. This is not the case for the calculation of the related asset, as can be seen below.

	Factory		
	Previous GAAP	*Exemption IFRS*	*Retrospective application IFRS*
1 January 1999	1,400	1,500	1,458
Depreciation (€1,400 − €200) ÷ 20 years × 2 =	(120)		
Depreciation (€1,500 − €200) ÷ 20 years × 2 =		(130)	
Depreciation (€1,458 − €200) ÷ 20 years × 2 =			(126)
1 January 2001			1,332
Revised estimate of decommissioning provision			47
1 January 2001			1,379
Depreciation (€1,400 − €200) ÷ 20 years × 3 =	(180)		
Depreciation (€1,500 − €200) ÷ 20 years × 3 =		(195)	
Depreciation (€1,379 − €200) ÷ 18 years × 3 =			(197)
1 January 2004	1,100	1,175	1,182
Depreciation (€1,400 − €200) ÷ 20 years × 2 =	(120)		
Depreciation (€1,500 − €200) ÷ 20 years × 2 =		(130)	
Depreciation (€1,379 − €200) ÷ 18 years × 2 =			(131)
31 December 2005	980	1,045	1,051

As can be seen above, a full retrospective application of IFRIC 1 would require an entity to go back in time and account for each revision of the decommissioning provision in accordance with IFRIC 1. In the case of a long-lived asset there could be a significant number of revisions that a first-time adopter would need to account for. It should also be noted that despite the significant revision of the commissioning costs, the impact on the carrying amount of the factory is quite modest.

At its date of transition to IFRS (1 January 2004), D makes the following adjustments:

- the decommissioning liability is increased by €56 to reflect the difference in accounting policy, irrespective of whether D applies the exemption or not; and

- if D applies the exemption it increases the carrying amount of the factory by €75. Whereas if D applies IFRIC 1 retrospectively, the carrying amount of the factory would increase by €82.

It is important to note that in both cases the decommissioning component of the factory will be significantly lower than the decommissioning liability itself.

From the above example it is clear that the exemption reduces the amount of effort required restating items of property, plant and equipment with a decommissioning component. In many cases the difference between the two methods will be insignificant, except where an entity had to make major adjustments to the estimate of the decommissioning costs near the end of the life of the related assets.

2.9.2 Leases

IFRS 1 requires a first-time adopter to classify leases as operating or finance leases based on the circumstances existing at the inception of the lease and not those existing at the date of transition to IFRS.[199] However, if 'at any time the lessee and the lessor agree to change the provisions of the lease, other than by renewing the lease, in a manner that would have resulted in a different classification of the lease ... if the changed terms had been in effect at the inception of the lease, the revised agreement is regarded as a new agreement over its term'.[200] In other words, an entity classifies the lease based on the lease terms that are in force at its date of transition to IFRS, the lease classification is not based on lease terms that are no longer in force.

A first-time adopter should apply SIC-15 – *Operating Leases – Incentives (amended 2003)* – retrospectively to all leases.[201]

2.9.3 Subsidiaries and Special Purpose Entities

A first-time adopter should consolidate all subsidiaries and Special Purpose Entities, except when IAS 27 requires otherwise.[202] If a first-time adopter did not consolidate a subsidiary under its previous GAAP, it should in its opening IFRS balance sheet measure the subsidiary's assets and liabilities at either:[203]

- the same carrying amounts as in the separate IFRS financial statements of the subsidiary, after adjusting for consolidation procedures and for the effects of the business combination in which it acquired the subsidiary;[204] or

- if the subsidiary has not adopted IFRS, the carrying amounts that IFRS would require in the subsidiary's separate balance sheet.

If the parent acquired the subsidiary in a business combination it should recognise goodwill as explained at 2.4.6 above. If the parent created the subsidiary it should not recognise goodwill.[205] The adjustment of the carrying amounts of assets and liabilities of a first-time adopter's subsidiaries may affect minority interests and deferred tax.[206]

2.9.4 *Hyperinflation*

The IASB decided not to exempt first-time adopters from retrospective application of IAS 29 – *Financial Reporting in Hyperinflationary Economies*. Although the cost of restating financial statements for the effects of hyperinflation in periods before the date of transition to IFRS might exceed the benefits, particularly if the currency is no longer hyperinflationary, the IASB concluded that a full retrospective 'restatement should be required, because hyperinflation can make unadjusted financial statements meaningless or misleading'.[207]

In preparing its opening IFRS balance sheet a first-time adopter should apply 'IAS 29 to any periods during which the economy of the functional currency or presentation currency was hyperinflationary'.[208] To make the restatement process less onerous, a first-time adopter may want to consider using fair value as deemed cost for long-lived assets such as property, plant and equipment, investment properties and certain intangible assets (see 2.5 above).[209] If a first-time adopter applies the exemption to use fair value or a revaluation as deemed cost, 'it applies IAS 29 to periods after the date for which the revalued amount or fair value was determined'.[210]

2.9.5 *Intangible assets*

In its opening IFRS balance sheet a first-time adopter:

'(a) excludes all intangible assets and other intangible items that do not meet the criteria for recognition under IAS 38 at the date of transition to IFRSs; and

(b) includes all intangible assets that meet the recognition criteria in IAS 38 at that date, except for intangible assets acquired in a business combination that were not recognised in the acquirer's consolidated balance sheet under previous GAAP and also would not qualify for recognition under IAS 38 in the separate balance sheet of the acquiree'.[211]

An intangible asset is only capable of capitalisation under IAS 38 if it is probable that the future economic benefits attributable to the asset will flow to the entity and the cost of the asset can be measured reliably.[212] The standard imposes a number of additional criteria that further restrict capitalisation of internally generated intangible assets. An important restriction is the prohibition from using hindsight to conclude retrospectively that recognition criteria are met.[213] Therefore, a first-time adopter is only permitted to capitalise the costs of internally generated intangible assets when it:[214]

'(a) concludes, based on an assessment made and documented at the date of that conclusion, that it is probable that future economic benefits from the asset will flow to the entity; and

(b) has a reliable system for accumulating the costs of internally generated intangible assets when, or shortly after, they are incurred.'

In other words, it is not permitted under IFRS 1 to reconstruct retrospectively the costs of intangible assets. If an internally generated intangible asset qualifies for recognition at the date of transition to IFRS, a first-time adopter recognises the asset in its opening IFRS balance sheet even if it had recognised the related expenditure as an expense under its previous GAAP.[215] However, first-time adopters that did not capitalise internally generated intangible assets are unlikely to have the type of documentation and systems required by IFRS 1 and will therefore not be able to capitalise these items in their opening IFRS balance sheet. Furthermore, if the asset does not qualify 'for recognition under IAS 38 until a later date, its cost is the sum of the expenditure incurred from that later date'.[216] Nonetheless, going forward first-time adopters will need to implement the internal systems and procedures that enable them to determine whether or not any future internally generated intangible assets should be capitalised (for example, in the case of development costs). Capitalisation of separately acquired intangible assets will generally be easier because contemporaneous documentation that was prepared to support the investment decisions often exists.[217]

If a first-time adopter's 'amortisation methods and rates under previous GAAP would be acceptable under IFRSs, the entity does not restate the accumulated amortisation in its opening IFRS balance sheet. Instead, the entity accounts for any change in estimated useful life or amortisation pattern prospectively from the period when it makes that change in estimate ... However, in some cases, an entity's amortisation methods and rates under previous GAAP may differ from those that would be acceptable under IFRSs ... If those differences have a material effect on the financial statements, the entity adjusts the accumulated amortisation in its opening IFRS balance sheet retrospectively so that it complies with IFRSs'.[218]

2.9.6   *Revenue recognition*

If a first-time adopter 'has received amounts that do not yet qualify for recognition as revenue under IAS 18 (for example, the proceeds of a sale that does not qualify for revenue recognition), [it] recognises the amounts received as a liability in its opening IFRS balance sheet and measures that liability at the amount received'.[219] It is therefore possible that revenue that was already recognised under a first-time adopter's previous GAAP, will need to be deferred in its opening IFRS balance sheet and recognised again (this time under IFRS) as revenue at a later date.

2.9.7   *Borrowing costs*

If on first-time adoption of IFRS an entity 'adopts a policy of capitalising borrowing costs ... or not capitalising them ... The entity applies that policy consistently in its opening IFRS balance sheet and in all periods presented in its first IFRS financial statements'.[220] It is therefore not possible to capitalise borrowing costs prospectively from the date of transition. Instead, a first-time adopter that applies IAS 23's allowed alternative treatment to capitalise borrowing costs, should apply that treatment retrospectively, even for periods before the effective date of the standard.[221] However, if the entity established a deemed cost for an asset, it does not capitalise borrowing costs incurred before the date of the measurement that established the deemed cost.

2.10 Presentation and disclosure

As a general principle, IFRS 1 does not exempt a first-time adopter from any of the presentation and disclosure requirements in other IFRSs, with one noteworthy exception relating to comparative information under IAS 32, IAS 39 and IFRS 4 (see 2.10.1 A below).[222]

If an entity adopts IFRS 1 early, i.e. in its first IFRS financial statements for a period beginning before 1 January 2004, it should disclose the fact that it applies IFRS 1 and not SIC-8.[223]

Extract 4.3: Belgacom SA (2003)

Note 2. Significant accounting policies [extract]

Basis of preparation [extract]

… As first-time adopter of IFRS, the Group elected to apply IFRS 1 (*"IFRS 1, First-time adoption of IFRS"*) instead of Standing Interpretations Committee 8 (*"SIC 8, First-time application of IASs as the primary basis of accounting"*) of the International Auditing Standards Board ("IASB").

2.10.1 Comparative information

IAS 1 requires (except where a standard or interpretation permits or requires otherwise) comparative information 'in respect of the previous period for all amounts reported in the financial statements' and 'for narrative and descriptive information when it is relevant to an understanding of the current period's financial statements'.[224] Accordingly, an entity's first IFRS financial statements should include at least one year of comparative information under IFRS.[225] It is however not required to present its opening IFRS balance sheet in its first IFRS financial statements, although it is integral to the equity reconciliation at the date of transition that has to be presented in the entity's first IFRS financial statements (see 2.10.2 below).[226] The IASB does not require a first-time adopter to present more than one comparative period under IFRS because 'such a requirement would impose costs out of proportion to the benefits to users, and increase the risk that preparers might need to make arbitrary assumptions in applying hindsight'.[227]

A   Exemption from the requirement to restate comparative information for IAS 32, IAS 39 and IFRS 4

As discussed at 2.6.1 above, an entity adopting IFRS for the first time before 1 January 2006 may elect to present comparative information that does not comply with IAS 32, IAS 39 and IFRS 4, in which case it needs to:[228]

- disclose that the comparative information does not comply with IAS 32, IAS 39 and IFRS 4, but that it has been prepared on the basis of its previous GAAP;

- disclose the nature, but not the amount, of the main adjustments that would make the information comply with IAS 32, IAS 39 and IFRS 4; and

- treat any adjustment between the balance sheet at the comparative period's reporting date and the start of the first IFRS reporting period as arising from a change in accounting policy. This difference is accounted for as an 'adjustment to the opening balance of each affected component of equity' at the start of the first IFRS reporting period.[229] The entity is required to make the disclosures prescribed by paragraphs 28(a)-(e) and (f)(i) of IAS 8 (see Chapter 3 at 6.1.2 A).[230]

Originally IFRS 1 also required first-time adopters to prepare comparative information that complied with IAS 32 and IAS 39 because this improved 'comparability within the first IFRS financial statements' and because the IASB believed that this should not be a problem for entities that planned the adoption of IFRS in a timely manner.[231] Unfortunately, the less-than-timely publication of the revised IAS 32 and IAS 39 obliged the IASB to exempt entities adopting IFRS before 1 January 2006 from applying these standards in preparing comparative information.

B   Historical summaries

Normally IFRS requires comparative information that is prepared on the same basis as information relating to the current reporting period. However, when an entity presents 'historical summaries of selected data for periods before the first period for which they present full comparative information under IFRS', the standard does not 'require such summaries to comply with the recognition and measurement requirements of IFRS'.[232] The extract below shows an entity that makes use of the exemption that allows it not to have to restate certain comparative historical data.

Extract 4.4: Huhtamäki Oyj (2003)

Accounting principles for consolidated accounts [extract]

Per share data

Comparison figures (1999-2001) adjusted for the 3:1 bonus issue in August 2002

		FAS				IFRS	
		1999	2000	2001	2002	2002	2003
Earnings per share	EUR	0.60	0.65	0.74	0.88	0.86	0.38
Earnings per share (diluted)						0.86	0.38
Dividend, nominal	EUR	0.26	0.28	0.31	0.38	0.38	(1) 0.38
Dividend/earnings per share	%	43.3	43.1	41.9	43.2	44.2	(1) 100.0
Dividend yield	%	3.1	3.9	3.5	4.0	4.0	(1) 4.1
Shareholders' equity per share	EUR	7.61	8.20	8.64	8.79	8.26	7.85
Share price at December 31	EUR	8.40	7.10	8.88	9.55	9.55	9.35
Average number of shares adjusted for share issue		111,856,128	125,903,852	117,117,696	100,769,970	100,769,970	96,292,220
Number of shares adjusted for share issue at year end		125,903,852	125,903,852	101,215,792	97,547,792	97,547,792	96,161,703
P/E ratio		14.0	10.9	12.0	10.9	11.1	24.6
Market capitalization at December 31	EUR million	1,057.6	893.9	898.3	931.6	931.6	899.1

(1) 2003: Board's proposal

As an entity is only allowed to apply IFRS 1 in its first IFRS financial statements, a literal reading of IFRS 1 would seem to suggest that the above exemption is not available to an entity that prepares its second IFRS financial statements. In practice this is not likely to cause a significant problem because this type of information is generally presented outside the financial statements where it is not covered by the requirements of IFRS.

If an entity presents comparative information under its previous GAAP in addition to the comparative information required by IFRS it should:[233]

'(a) label the previous GAAP information prominently as not being prepared under IFRSs; and

(b) disclose the nature of the main adjustments that would make it comply with IFRSs. An entity need not quantify those adjustments.'

Although IFRS 1 does not specifically require disclosure of this information when the historical summary is part of the financial statements, such disclosure would be of benefit to users of such historical summaries.

Extracts 4.5 and 4.6 (at 2.10.2 below) illustrate how first-time adopters disclose the nature of the differences between their previous GAAP and IFRS.

2.10.2 Explanation of transition to IFRS

A first-time adopter is required to explain how the transition from its previous GAAP to IFRS affected its reported financial position, financial performance and cash flows.[234] The IASB decided 'that such disclosures are essential ... because they help users understand the effect and implications of the transition to IFRS and how they need to change their analytical models to make the best use of information presented using IFRS'.[235]

As indicated at 2.3.3 A above, IFRS 1 offers a wide range of exemptions that a first-time adopter may elect to apply. However, somewhat curiously, the standard does not explicitly require an entity to disclose which exemptions it has applied and how it applied them. In the case of, for example, the exemptions relating to employee benefits and cumulative translation differences it will be rather obvious whether or not an entity has chosen to apply the exemption. In other cases, users will have to rely on a first-time adopter disclosing those transitional accounting policies that are 'relevant to an understanding of the financial statements'.[236]

Extract 4.5: Huhtamäki Oyj (2003)

Accounting principles for consolidated accounts [extract]

In 2003 the group adopted all IFRS standards and the adoption was done according to the IFRS 1 – First-Time Adoption of the IFRS standard using January 1, 2002 as the transition date. The effect of adopting IFRS is summarised in the bridge calculations provided with the current year financial statements. Comparative figures for 2002 have been restated accordingly.

Transition to IFRS reporting [extract]

The transition to IFRS reporting has resulted in a number of changes in the reported financial statements, notes thereto and accounting principles compared to what has been presented previously.

Until the adoption of IFRS, Huhtamaki's financial statements were based on Finnish Accounting Standards (FAS). The following explanatory notes and financial statements describe the differences between IFRS and FAS reporting for the financial year 2002 as well as for the IFRS opening balance sheet as of Jan 1, 2002. The comparison figures are presented in accordance with FAS, and are identical to the full year information disclosed previously.

Effects of the transition have also been explained in a document published on October 16, 2003. That document includes quarterly comparisons as well.

The following notes related to IFRS transition should be read in conjunction with the preceding. Accounting principles for consolidated accounts. which describes the IFRS treatment applied by the group.

1) Segment reporting

Geographical regions – Europe, Americas and Asia-Oceania-Africa – have been defined as the primary segments for IFRS segment reporting. The Foodservice and Consumer Goods business segments are secondary segments. Goodwill and the related amortization expense have been allocated to geographical regions as well as to business segments in accordance with allocation principles and reporting requirements in IAS 14.

Restatement of business segments

Closer review of secondary segment characteristics has led to restatement of the majority of Fresh Foods rigid products as well as the majority of Molded Fiber products from Foodservice to Consumer Goods.

2) Intangible assets

Increases in intangible assets derive from reclassification of land use rights and certain software from tangible to intangible assets in the opening IFRS balance sheet.

Impairment An impairment loss for certain unusable software licenses has been booked in the opening balance sheet as a result of impairment testing.

In accordance with the First-Time Adoption standard all goodwill has been tested for impairment at the date of transition to IFRS. This testing has not resulted in any impairment losses in the opening IFRS balance sheet.

3) Tangible assets

Leases

In accordance with the criteria for finance leases in IAS 17 Leases, a number of lease contracts have been classified as finance leases in IFRS.

Assets financed with leasing contracts that are defined as finance leases under IAS 17 have been capitalized and are depreciated at the rates stated in Huhtamaki's policy on tangible assets.

Impairment

An impairment loss has been recognized in the opening IFRS balance sheet for a production line in the Americas where the carrying amount exceeded the recoverable amount. In addition the changes in tangible assets include reclassifications from tangible to intangible assets (see note 2) and reversal of previously capitalized FX gains/losses. Revaluations in certain property values that had been recognized in FAS have been reversed from the IFRS balance sheet.

4) Investments

Financial instruments – available-for-sale assets

Publicly traded shares are recognized at fair value, which is based on quoted market prices at the balance sheet date. In FAS reporting these instruments have been recognized at historical cost.

5) Inventory

Changes in inventory arise from adjustments to obsolete inventory reserves as well as from reclassification of major spare parts from inventory to tangible assets.

6) Interest bearing receivables

The differences in interest bearing receivables are attributed to reclassification of leased assets under finance leases from tangible assets to interest bearing receivables as of the transition date (see note 3).

7) Other receivables

Changes in other receivables arise from movements in employee benefit assets, deferred tax assets, bad debt reserves and due to offsetting.

Offsetting

Under IAS 1 Presentation of Financials Statements, assets and liabilities or income and expenses should not be offset unless offsetting is specifically allowed in another standard. Therefore in the IFRS balance sheet certain insurance contracts are recognized on both sides of the balance sheet instead of using offsetting under FAS. Also, employee benefit plans within a country that previously had been netted to one side of the balance sheet are now shown separately plan-by- plan either in assets or in liabilities.

Deferred taxes

In FAS reporting deferred taxes have been recognized for fewer items than what is required in IFRS. This has caused many changes to deferred taxes during the transition.

Employee benefits

Employee benefit plans were reported in accordance with local conditions and practices in FAS reporting. In the transition to IFRS all plans have been studied and defined benefit plans have been recalculated in accordance with IAS 19 Employee Benefits.

8) Cash and cash equivalents

Treasury shares

The company purchased its own shares during Q4 2002 and Q1 2003. In IFRS financial statements these treasury shares are deducted from equity at the transaction date. In FAS reporting purchased shares have been reported in marketable securities and as a separate component of equity until the shares are invalidated.

9) Minority interest

IFRS adjustments are also incorporated into accounts of subsidiaries that are partially owned by external parties. This has resulted in changes that affect the equity of such subsidiaries. Accordingly the Group's minority interest account has been adjusted by such changes.

The preference shares in a German subsidiary, which have been reported as minority interest in FAS reporting, have been reclassified as debt in the IFRS opening balance sheet. These shares amounting to EUR 64 million were converted into an equal amount of external debt in December 2002.

10) Interest bearing liabilities

The change is attributed to loans payable from finance leases (see note 3) as well as from reclassification of preferred shares from minority interest to debt (see note 9).

11) Other liabilities

Movements in pension and other employee benefit liabilities, deferred tax liabilities and offsetting (see note 7) resulted in a change in other liabilities.

Extract 4.6: Belgacom SA (2003)

Note 40. First-time adoption of IFRS [extract]

This note provides a reconciliation of net equity at 1 January 2001 and at 31 December 2002 as well as net income for the year ended 2002 from the previously published consolidated financial statements, prepared in accordance with Belgian GAAP, to the accompanying consolidated financial statements prepared in accordance with IFRS, as well as a summary of the significant adjustments under IFRS.

The Group chose to comply with IFRS 1 instead of SIC 8 for its first-time adoption of IFRS. In adopting IFRS 1, the Group elected not to restate any business combinations that occurred prior to the transition date of 1 January 2001.

Accounting principles under IFRS differ in various areas from Belgian GAAP. The significant differences between IFRS and Belgian GAAP affecting net income and shareholders' equity of the Group for the years 2001 and 2002 are detailed below.

Pensions and other post-employment benefits
Under IFRS, the Group's liability for pensions and other post-employment benefits is recorded on the balance sheet since some of these benefits are granted to employees in the framework of a defined benefit plan while others are considered a constructive obligation. In the Belgian GAAP financial statements, the pension benefits are recorded on a cash basis and the related liability is shown as an off balance sheet commitment in accordance with an advice issued by the Belgian Commission for Accounting Rules ("Commissie voor Boekhoudkundige Normen/Commission des Normes Comptables") to the Group on 16 July 1993. In the Belgian GAAP financial statements, the liability for the constructive obligation in respect of other post-employment benefits for retirees is recognized since 2002.

Depreciation of intangible assets and property, plant and equipment
Under IFRS, the Group's acquisitions of intangible assets and property, plant and equipment are amortized/depreciated as of the moment they are ready for their intended use. Under Belgian GAAP, such assets are depreciated for a full year in their year of acquisition, until 2002.

Investments available for sale
Under IFRS, financial assets classified as available for sale are remeasured to fair value through the shareholders' equity. Under Belgian GAAP, these financial assets are carried at historical cost (possibly with the recording of impairment losses).

Derivatives
Under IFRS, the Group's derivatives are recorded at fair value in the balance sheet. Under Belgian GAAP, derivatives are disclosed as off balance sheet rights and commitments and accounted for on an accrual basis.

Fair value hedges
Financial assets and liabilities involved in fair value hedges are remeasured at fair value under IFRS (to the extent of the risk being hedged) while they are recorded at cost under Belgian GAAP.

Business combination
Under IFRS, the gain on the partial sale of Ben Nederland Group shares to a special purpose entity on 28 November 2001 was not recognized until the special purpose entity sold the shares to T-Mobile on 25 September 2002 (see note 5.4). Under Belgian GAAP, the gain on this partial sale was recognized on 28 November 2001.

Dividends
Under IFRS, dividends proposed at balance sheet date are recorded as a liability only when the annual meeting of shareholders has approved their distribution (i.e. after balance sheet date). Under Belgian GAAP, proposed dividends are recorded as a liability at the balance sheet date.

Provisions
Under IFRS, a provision for accumulating non-vesting illness days is recognized. In the Belgian GAAP financial statements, the liability for the constructive obligation in respect of such illness days is not recognized.

Deferred taxes
Under IFRS, deferred taxes are recognized on the aforementioned differences in accounting principles between IFRS and Belgian GAAP, and on all temporary differences and on tax carry-forward losses that are deemed recoverable in the foreseeable future. In the Belgian GAAP financial statements, deferred tax assets on tax carry-forward losses that are deemed recoverable in the foreseeable future, are recognized since 2002.

Minority interests
Minority interests represent the share of minority shareholders in differences between Belgian GAAP and IFRS in respect of subsidiaries where the Group holds less than 100% participating interests.

If a first-time adopter did not present financial statements for previous periods this fact should be disclosed.[237] In that case an explanation of how the transition to IFRS affected the entity's reported financial position, financial performance and cash flows cannot be presented, because a relevant comparison under the entity's previous GAAP does not exist.

A   Reconciliations

A first-time adopter is required to present:

- reconciliations of its equity reported under previous GAAP to its equity under IFRS at:[238]
  - the date of transition to IFRS; and
  - the end of the latest period presented in the entity's most recent annual financial statements under previous GAAP;
- a reconciliation of the profit or loss reported under previous GAAP for the latest period in the entity's most recent annual financial statements to its profit or loss under IFRS for the same period; and[239]
- an explanation of the material adjustments to the cash flow statement, if it presented one under its previous GAAP.[240]

First-time adopters should not apply the requirements of IAS 8 relating to the disclosure of changes in accounting policies because that standard 'does not deal with changes in accounting policies that occur when an entity first adopts IFRS'.[241]

The example below illustrates how these requirements apply to an entity whose first reporting date is 31 December 2005 and date of transition to IFRS is 1 January 2004.

Example 4.26:   Reconciliations to be presented in first IFRS financial statements

Entity E's date of transition to IFRS is 1 January 2004 and its reporting date is 31 December 2005. Which primary financial statements and reconciliations should E present in its first IFRS financial statements?

	1 January 2004	*31 December 2004*	*31 December 2005*
Balance sheet		●	●
Reconciliation of equity	●	●	
For the period ending			
Income statement		●	●
Cash flow statement		●	●
Statement of changes in equity		●	●
Reconciliation of profit or loss		●	
Explanation of material adjustments to cash flow statement		●	

These reconciliations should be sufficiently detailed 'to enable users to understand the material adjustments to the balance sheet and income statement'[242] and the entity should 'distinguish the correction of ... errors from changes in accounting policies'.[243] While the standard does not prescribe a layout for these reconciliations, the Implementation Guidance contains an example of a reconciliation of equity and profit or loss that contains a line-by-line reconciliation of both balance sheet and income statement.[244] Such as presentation may be particularly appropriate when a first-time adopter needs to make transitional adjustments that affect a significant number of line items in the primary financial statements. If the adjustments are less pervasive a straightforward reconciliation of the equity and profit or loss figures may be able to provide an equally effective explanation of how the adoption of

IFRS affects the reported financial position, financial performance and cash flows. The extracts below show how a first-time adopter might present the reconciliations required by IFRS 1.

Extract 4.7: Huhtamäki Oyj (2003)

Transition to IFRS reporting [extract]

...

IFRS 2002 comparison

Income statement

EUR million	Item	IFRS 2002	FAS 2002	Diff.
Net sales		2,238.7	2,238.7	0.0
EBITDA		324.3	326.8	-2.5
Operating profit (EBITA)		215.3	217.8	-2.5
EBIT		172.6	175.1	-2.5
% of net sales		7.7	7.8	–
Net financial items		-48.8	-45.0	-3.8
Income from associated companies		1.0	1.0	0.0
Profit before tax		124.8	131.1	-6.3
Taxes		-34.0	-35.0	1.0
Minority interest		-3.5	-7.8	4.3
Net income		87.3	88.3	-1.0
EPS basic		0.86	0.88	–
EPS basic ba		1.29	1.30	–
EPS diluted		0.86		–

Balance sheet EUR million		IFRS Dec 31/02	FAS Dec 31/02	Diff.
Assets				
Intangible assets	2	652.5	651.3	1.2
Tangible assets	3	927.3	939.4	-12.1
Investments	4	5.8	6.5	-0.7
Inventory	5	284.9	285.6	-0.7
Interest bearing receivables	6	39.0	9.2	29.8
Other receivables	7	584.9	519.8	65.1
Cash and cash equivalents	8	19.7	53.7	-34.0
		2,514.1	**2,465.5**	**48.6**
Equity and liabilities				
Shareholders' equity		805.5	857.7	-52.2
Minority interest	9	14.9	14.7	0.2
Interest bearing liabilities	10	915.7	913.2	2.5
Other liabilities	11	778.0	679.9	98.1
		2,514.1	**2,465.5**	**48.6**

Key financial ratios		IFRS 2002	FAS 2002	
ROE,	%	10.7	10.5	
ROI,	%	10.1	10.0	
ROE before amortization,	%	15.7	15.1	
ROI before amortization,	%	12.4	12.4	

	IFRS Dec 31/02	FAS Dec 31/02
Net debt	857.0	850.2
Gearing	1.04	0.97

Regions (item 1) EBITA	IFRS 2002	FAS 2002	Diff.	EBIT	IFRS 2002
Europe	98.6	99.2	-0.6		81.1
Americas	62.9	63.6	-0.7		44.1
Asia, Oceania, Africa	31.6	31.9	-0.3		25.4
Unallocated corporate net	22.2	23.1	-0.9		22.2
Total	**215.3**	**217.8**	**-2.5**	**Total**	**172.6**

Business segments (item 1) Net sales	IFRS 2002	FAS 2002	Diff.		
Consumer Goods	1,485.8	1,268.8	217.0		
Foodservice	752.9	969.9	-217.0		
Total	**2,238.7**	**2,238.7**	**0.0**		

EBITA	IFRS 2002	FAS 2002	Diff.	EBIT	IFRS 2002
Consumer Goods	122.4	99.1	23.3		92.5
Foodservice	70.7	95.6	-24.9		57.9
Unallocated corporate net	22.2	23.1	-0.9		22.2
Total	**215.3**	**217.8**	**-2.5**	**Total**	**172.6**

Net income reconciliation

EUR million	2002
Net Income (FAS)	88.3
Effect of adopting	
IAS 12 Income taxes	0.9
IAS 19 Employee benefits	-0.1
IAS 39 Financial Instruments	-1.0
Other IFRS movements (inventories, provisions etc.)	-0.8
Total IFRS restatement	-1.0
Net income (IFRS)	**87.3**

Equity reconciliation

EUR million	Jan 1/02	Dec 31/02
Equity according to FAS	874.6	857.7
Effect of Adopting		
IAS 12 Income taxes	16.3	21.0
IAS 17 Leases	19.3	15.2
IAS 19 Employee benefits	-32.8	-31.9
IAS 32 Treasury shares	–	-34.1
IAS 36 Impairment:		
Intangible assets	-4.9	-4.9
Tangible assets	-3.7	-3.1
IAS 39 Financial Instruments	-3.9	-17.8
Other IFRS movements (inventories, provisions etc.)	-2.0	3.4
Total IFRS restatement	-11.7	-52.2
Equity according to IFRS	862.9	805.5

Extract 4.8: Belgacom SA (2003)

Note 40. First-time adoption of IFRS [extract]

...

Equity reconciliation between Belgian GAAP and IFRS at the transition date, 1 January 2001:

(in EUR millions – as of 1 January 2001)	
Shareholders' equity under Belgian GAAP	**2,626**
Pensions and other post-employment benefits	-1,124
Depreciation and amortization of intangible assets and property, plant and equipment	214
Remeasurement to fair value of financial instruments	2
Dividends 2001 paid in 2002	231
Provisions	-42
Other adjustments	-5
Deferred taxes	423
Minority interests	-17
Shareholders' equity under IFRS	**2,307**

Equity reconciliation between Belgian GAAP and IFRS at 31 December 2002, being the last period published under Belgian GAAP:

(in EUR millions – as of 31 December 2002)	
Shareholders' equity under Belgian GAAP	**2,900**
Pensions and other post-employment benefits	-612
Depreciation and amortization of intangible assets and property, plant and equipment	313
Remeasurement of financial instruments	21
Dividends 2002 paid in 2003	280
Provisions	-40
Other adjustments	2
Deferred taxes	142
Minority interests	-27
Shareholders' equity under IFRS	**2,978**

Net income reconciliation for the year 2002, being the latest period published under Belgian GAAP:

(in EUR millions – year ended 31 December 2002)	
Net income under Belgian GAAP	**911**
Pensions and other post-employment benefits	264
Depreciation and amortization of intangible assets and property, plant and equipment	25
Remeasurement of financial instruments	-14
Business combinations	200
Provisions	-11
Other adjustments	-2
Deferred taxes	-228
Minority interests	-2
Net income under IFRS	**1,142**

If a first-time adopter recognised or reversed any impairment losses it should disclose the information that IAS 36 would have required 'if the entity had recognised those impairment losses or reversals in the period beginning with the date of transition to IFRS' (see Chapter 13 at 4).[245] The purpose of this disclosure requirement is that while 'there is inevitably subjectivity about impairment losses [the] disclosure provides transparency about impairment losses recognised on transition to IFRS. These losses might otherwise receive less attention than impairment losses recognised in earlier or later periods'.[246]

B   *Designation of financial assets and financial liabilities*

IAS 39 permits a financial instrument to be designated on initial recognition as a:

- *financial asset or financial liability at fair value through profit or loss*, which is a financial instrument that is either classified as *held for trading* or is designated as such on initial recognition; or

- *available-for-sale financial asset*, which is a financial asset designated as 'available for sale' or that are not specifically classified as 'loans and receivables', 'held-to-maturity investments' or 'at fair value through profit or loss'.

If a first-time adopter designates a previously recognised financial asset or financial liability as a 'financial asset or financial liability at fair value through profit or loss' or as available-for-sale (see 2.6.2 above), it should disclose for each category:[247]

- the fair value of any financial assets or financial liabilities designated into it; and

- the classification and carrying amount in the previous financial statements.

C   *Use of fair value as deemed cost*

If a first-time adopter uses 'fair value in its opening IFRS balance sheet as deemed cost for an item of property, plant and equipment, an investment property or an intangible asset' (see 2.5 above), it should disclose for each line item in the opening IFRS balance sheet:[248]

- the aggregate of those fair values; and

- the aggregate adjustment to the carrying amounts reported under previous GAAP.

2.10.3 Interim financial reports

If a first-time adopter presents an interim financial report under IAS 34 for part of the period covered by its first IFRS financial statements, that report should:[249]

(a)   include reconciliations of:

- its equity under previous GAAP at the end of that comparable interim period to its equity under IFRS at that date; and

- its profit or loss under previous GAAP for that comparable interim period, both on a current and year-to-date basis, to its profit or loss under IFRS for that period; and

(b)   include the reconciliations described at 2.10.2 A above or a cross-reference to another published document that includes these reconciliations.

For an entity presenting annual financial statements under IFRS it is not compulsory to prepare interim financial reports under IAS 34. Therefore, the above requirements only apply to first-time adopters that prepare interim reports under IAS 34 on a voluntary basis or that are required to do so by a regulator or other party.[250] However, even if an entity does not present interim financial reports prepared in accordance with IAS 34, the accounting policies applied in preparing its interim financial statements should still be IFRS compliant.

Example 4.27:   Reconciliations to be presented in IFRS half-year reports

As in Example 4.26 at 2.10.2 A above, Entity E's date of transition to IFRS is 1 January 2004, its reporting date is 31 December 2005 and it publishes a half-year report as of 30 June under IAS 34. Which primary financial statements and reconciliations should E in its first IFRS half-year report?

	1 January 2004	*30 June 2004*	*31 December 2004*	*30 June 2005*
Balance sheet			●	●
Reconciliation of equity	● *	●	● *	
For the period ending				
Income statement		●		●
Cash flow statement		●		●
Statement of changes in equity		●		●
Reconciliation of profit or loss		●	● *	
Explanation of material adjustments to cash flow statement			● *	

*   Additional reconciliations required under paragraph 39 of IFRS 1.

The IAS 34 requirements regarding the disclosure of primary financial statements in interim reports are discussed in Chapter 35.

As can be seen from the table in Example 4.27, the additional reconciliations and explanations required under (b) above would be presented out of context, i.e. without the balance sheet, income statement and cash flow statement that they relate to. For this reason a first-time adopter may want either (1) to include the primary financial statements to which these reconciliations relate or (2) to refer to another document that includes these reconciliations.

Example 4.28: **Reconciliations to be presented in first IFRS financial statement and interim reports**[251]

Entity F's date of transition to IFRS is 1 January 2004, its reporting date is 31 December 2005 and it publishes quarterly reports under IAS 34. Which reconciliations should F present in its 2005 interim reports and in its first IFRS financial statements?

	Reconciliation of equity	Reconciliation of profit or loss	Explanation of material adjustments to cash flow statement
First quarter			
1 January 2004	o		
31 March 2004 – 3 months ending	●	●	
31 December 2004	o	o	o
Second quarter			
1 January 2004	o		
30 June 2004 – 3 months ending		●	
– 6 months ending	●	●	
31 December 2004	o	o	o
Third quarter			
1 January 2004	o		
30 September 2004 – 3 months ending		●	
– 9 months ending	●	●	
31 December 2004	o	o	o
First IFRS financial statements			
1 January 2004	●		
31 December 2004	●	●	●

● Mandatory disclosures required to be included in the interim report.

o Instead of including these reconciliations, the entity may include a cross-reference to another published document that includes these reconciliations.

Interim financial reports under IAS 34 contain considerably less detail than annual financial statements because they 'are based on the assumption that users of the interim financial report also have access to the most recent annual financial statements'.[252] Therefore, a first-time adopter will have to ensure that its first interim financial report contains sufficient information about events or transactions that are material to an understanding of the current interim period. Hence it may be necessary for a first-time adopter to include in its first IFRS interim report significantly more information that it would normally include in an interim report; alternatively it could include a cross-reference to another published document that includes such information.[253]

2.11   Effective date

IFRS 1 is mandatory for an entity's first IFRS financial statements for a period beginning on or after 1 January 2004, although early application is encouraged. If an entity applies IFRS 1 early, it should disclose this fact (see 2.10 above).[254]

3   PRACTICAL ISSUES

3.1   First-time adopters presenting two comparative periods

3.1.1   General

Some first-time adopters are required to present two comparative periods in the their financial statements. The diagram below illustrates the key dates for a first-time adopter that presents full comparative information under IFRS with a 31 December 2005 reporting date.

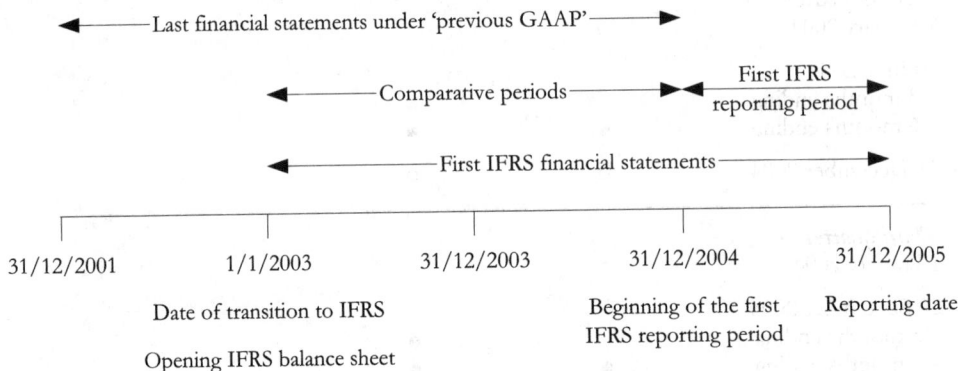

As can be seen above, the financial years 2003 and 2004 are initially reported under the entity's previous GAAP and then as comparative periods in the first IFRS financial statements. The exemptions under IFRS 1 also apply to a first-time adopter that presents two comparative periods, however, it is important to note the following:

- the exemption from the requirement to restate comparative information for financial instruments that are within the scope of IAS 32, IAS 39 and IFRS 4 would apply from the beginning of first IFRS reporting, i.e. the two comparative periods would not be restated to IFRS (see 2.6.1 above);[255]

- when a first-time adopter applies IAS 39, it should apply the derecognition requirements in IAS 39 prospectively to transactions occurring on or after 1 January 2004. This date does not change if the entity presents an additional comparative period (see 2.6.4 above);[256]

- in relation to the IFRS 2 transitional rules, a change in the date of transition to IFRS may affect the exemptions regarding the restatement of liabilities arising from share-based payment transactions that were settled before the date of transition to IFRS (see 2.7.3 above); and

- the exception from retrospective application of IFRS 5 also applies to a first-time adopter that discloses two comparative periods. Retrospective application is effectively only required for first-time reporting dates on or after 31 December 2007, as compared with 31 December 2006 for entities that only present one comparative period (see 2.8.2 above).

It is worthwhile to note that IAS 1 only requires disclosure of one comparative period. Therefore, an entity that voluntarily presented two comparative periods under its previous GAAP could decide to present only one comparative period in its first IFRS financial statements and thereby move its date of transition back one year.

3.1.2 SEC registrants

The US Securities and Exchange Commission (SEC) have published proposed amendments to Form 20-F that change the filing requirements for foreign private issuers that are first-time adopters of IFRS.[257] The proposed amendments would apply to foreign private issuers:

- that have not previously published financial statements under IFRS; and
- that publish IFRS financial statements for the first time for any financial year beginning no later than 1 January 2007.

However, the proposed accommodation would not be available to an entity adopting a set of accounting standards that includes deviations from the standards promulgated by the IASB and the IASC. The accommodation would only be available to a company that is able to state unreservedly and explicitly that its general-purpose financial statements comply with IFRS, and whose audited financial statements are not subject to any qualification relating to the application of IFRS. The proposed amendments would 'permit eligible foreign private issuers for their first year of reporting under IFRS to file two years rather than three years of statements of income, changes in shareholders' equity and cash flows prepared in accordance with IFRS, with appropriate related disclosure. The accommodation would retain current requirements regarding the reconciliation of financial statement items to generally accepted accounting principles (GAAP) as used in the United States (US GAAP), but modify the form in which the reconciliations are presented in the first filing that includes IFRS financial statements.'[258]

Foreign private issuers relying on the accommodation would be required to provide US GAAP reconciliations for the two financial years presented under IFRS. However, to ensure that all filings contain three years of financial information prepared on a consistent basis, the SEC is proposing that first-time adopters taking advantage of the accommodation present audited condensed income statements and audited condensed balance sheets for the three most recent financial years under US GAAP.

First-time adopters that rely on the accommodation will not be required to include any financial statements, discussions or other financial information based on their previous GAAP. If first-time adopters do include such information, they should disclose that the filing contains financial information based on their previous GAAP, which is not comparable to financial information based on IFRS.

In addition, the proposed accommodation would only require entities to provide selected historical financial data based on IFRS for the two most recent financial years. Selected historical financial data based on US GAAP would continue to be required for the five most recent financial years. Although the SEC does not intend to prohibit entities from including selected financial data based on previous GAAP in their annual reports, side-by-side presentation of data prepared under IFRS and data prepared under previous GAAP is discouraged.

Where a narrative discussion of its financial condition is provided, the accommodation requires management to focus on the financial statements prepared under IFRS and the reconciliation to US GAAP for the past two financial years. In addition, management should explain any differences between IFRS and US GAAP that are not otherwise discussed in the reconciliation necessary for an understanding of the financial statements as a whole. An entity should not include any discussion relating to the financial statements prepared under its previous GAAP unless it has elected to include such financial information.

IFRS 1 requires a first-time adopter to present a reconciliation from its previous GAAP to IFRS in the notes to its financial statements and allows certain exceptions from full retrospective application of IFRS in deriving the relevant data. Under the SEC's proposal, any issuer relying on any of the elective or mandatory exceptions from IFRS that are contained within IFRS 1 will have to disclose the following additional information:

- a detailed discussion of each exception used and the circumstances that gave rise to its use;
- the items or class of items to which each exception was applied;
- a description of what accounting principles were used and how they were applied;
- an explanation of the significance of each exception to the entity's financial condition and to the changes in its financial condition and results of operations;
- where material, the line items in the financial statements that were affected by the exceptions from IFRS;
- where material, qualitative disclosure of the impact on the financial condition, changes in the entity's financial condition, and results of operations that the alternatives would have had; and
- when relying on a mandatory exception, a description of the exception and a statement that the entity complied with it.

If adopted in their current form, the amendments to Form 20-F would permit first-time adopters for their first year of reporting under IFRS to file two years rather than three years of statements of income, changes in shareholders' equity and cash flows. However, in exchange for that accommodation a first-time adopter would need to provide a considerable amount of additional disclosure. Consequently, first-time adopters that are SEC registrants need to consider carefully the costs and benefits before deciding whether or not to use the accommodation.

3.2   Income taxes

IFRS 1 requires full retrospective application of IAS 12 – *Income Taxes*. A first-time adopter needs to apply IAS 12 to 'temporary differences between the carrying amount of the assets and liabilities in its opening IFRS balance sheet and their tax bases'.[259] This poses several problems that may not be immediately obvious at first sight. First of all, IAS 12 does not require an entity to account for all temporary differences. For example, an entity is not required under IAS 12 to recognise deferred tax for temporary differences relating to:

- the initial recognition of goodwill; and[260]

- the initial recognition of an asset or liability in a transaction that is not a business combination and that affected neither accounting profit nor taxable profit.[261]

Secondly, a change in deferred tax should be accounted for in equity, instead of income, when the tax relates to an item that was originally accounted for in equity. Thirdly, IAS 12 requires that goodwill be adjusted when deferred tax assets that did not satisfy the criteria in IFRS 3 for separate recognition when a business combination was initially accounted are subsequently realised.[262]

Therefore, full retrospective application of IAS 12 requires a first-time adopter to establish the history of the items that give rise to temporary differences because, depending on the type of transaction, it may not be necessary to account for deferred tax, or changes in the deferred tax may need to be accounted for in equity.

3.3   Property, plant and equipment

IAS 16 requires a 'parts approach' to the recognition of property, plant and equipment. Thus a large item such as an aircraft is recognised as a series of 'parts' that may have different useful lives. An engine of an aircraft may be a part. IAS 16 does not prescribe the physical unit of measure (the 'part') for recognition or what constitutes an item of property, plant and equipment. Instead the standard relies on judgement 'in applying the recognition criteria to an entity's specific circumstances'.[263] However, the standard does require an entity to:

- apply a very restrictive definition of maintenance costs (or costs of day-to-day servicing) which it describes as 'primarily the costs of labour and consumables, and may include the cost of small parts. The purpose of these expenditures is often described as for the 'repairs and maintenance' of the item of property, plant and equipment';[264]

- derecognise the carrying amount of the parts that are replaced; and[265]

- depreciate separately each part of an item of property, plant and equipment with a cost that is significant in relation to the total cost of the item.[266]

Based on this, it is reasonable to surmise that parts can be relatively small units. Therefore, it is possible that even though a first-time adopter's depreciation methods and rates are acceptable under IFRS, it may have to restate property, plant and equipment because its unit of measure was based on physical units significantly larger than IAS 16's parts.

3.4   Functional currency

Under IAS 21 an entity is required to record a foreign currency transaction 'on initial recognition in the functional currency, by applying to the foreign currency amount the spot exchange rate between the functional currency and the foreign currency at the date of the transaction'.[267] The standard defines an entity's functional currency as 'the currency of the primary economic environment in which the entity operates' and contains detailed guidance on determining the functional currency.[268]

Many national GAAPs do not specifically define the concept of functional currency, or they may contain guidance on identifying the functional currency that differs from that in IAS 21. Consequently, a first-time adopter that measured transactions in a currency that was not its functional currency will need to restate its financial statements. Full retrospective application of IAS 21 is extremely onerous as it affects measurement of all non-monetary items in a first-time adopter's opening IFRS balance sheet. The exemption that allows a first-time adopter to reset the cumulative exchange differences in equity to zero cannot be applied to assets or liabilities (see 2.7.2 above). Therefore, a restatement cannot be avoided because IFRS 1 does not contain an exemption that would allow a first-time adopter to use a currency other than the functional currency in determining the cost of assets and liabilities. The only possible mitigation would be if a first-time adopter chose to use fair value or a revaluation as deemed cost for property, plant and equipment.

3.5   Currency adjustments to goodwill

Under IFRS 1, a first-time adopter need not apply this requirement of IAS 21 retrospectively to fair value adjustments and goodwill arising in business combinations that occurred before the date of transition to IFRS. However, in practice that exemption may be of limited use for a number of reasons.

First, the exemption permits 'goodwill and fair value adjustments' to be treated as assets and liabilities of the entity rather than as assets and liabilities of the acquiree. Implicit in the exemption is the requirement to treat goodwill and fair value adjustments consistently. However, the IASB apparently did not consider that many first-time adopters, under their previous GAAP, will have treated fair value adjustments as assets or liabilities of the acquiree, while at the same time treating goodwill as an asset of the acquirer. As the exemption under IFRS 1 did not foresee this particular situation, those first-time adopters will need to restate either their goodwill or fair value adjustments. In many cases restatement of goodwill is less onerous than restatement of fair value adjustments.

Secondly, the paragraphs in IFRS 1 that introduce the exemption were drafted at a later date than the rest of the Appendix that they form part of. Instead of referring to 'first-time adopter' these paragraphs refer to 'entity'. Nevertheless, it is clear from the context that 'entity' should be read as 'first-time adopter'. This means that the exemption only permits goodwill and fair value adjustments to be treated as assets of the first-time adopter (i.e. ultimate parent). In practice, however, many groups have treated goodwill (and fair value adjustments) as an asset of an intermediate parent. Where the intermediate parent has a functional currency that is different from that of the ultimate parent or the acquiree, it will be necessary to restate goodwill (and fair value adjustments).

3.6 Disclosure of IFRS information in annual financial statements before the reporting date

3.6.1 CESR recommendation

An entity that has a date of transition of 1 January 2004 will still report under its previous GAAP at 31 December 2004. It may well wish to give some indication in its 2004 financial statements of the effect of the transition to IFRS. Indeed its financial statements would be enhanced for users if such information were to be provided. In December 2003, the Committee of European Securities Regulators (CESR) published a recommendation that encourages European listed companies 'to provide markets with appropriate and useful information during the transition phase from local accounting standards to International Financial Reporting Standards', which a first-time adopter may want to follow.[269]

In drawing up its recommendation, CESR identified four milestones – which it considers 'to be the most natural moments at which reporting on the transition would take place, but [which] are not intended to create compulsory reporting deadlines'.[270] The four milestones are discussed below.

A   Publication of 2003 financial statements

CESR encourages list companies 'to describe their plan and degree of achievement in their move towards IAS/IFRS when they publish their financial statements for the year 2003. This description could usefully cover the general policies to address the operational and control issues as well as the risks and uncertainties associated with the transition as they affect the business.'[271] An entity may also want to include narrative information about the main differences between its current GAAP and IFRS that it knows about with sufficient certainty.[272]

B   Publication of 2004 financial statements

CESR encourages an entity to disclose the following information on the impact of the change to IFRS in its 2004 financial statements as soon as it can quantify the impact in a sufficiently reliable manner:[273]

- a reconciliation of shareholders' equity at the date of transition from previously used GAAP to IFRS, which may take the form of a three-column table presenting a summarised opening balance sheet under previous GAAP, the effect of the transition to IFRSs and the corresponding IFRS figures. In addition, an explanatory note should be included in the financial statements which explains the effect on each line item presented;

- a reconciliation of shareholders' equity at the end of the reporting period from previous GAAP to IFRS under the same format and with the same level of information;

- a reconciliation of the profit and loss account from previous GAAP to IFRS under the same format and with the same level of information; and

- an explanation of the main adjustments to the cash flow statement.

An entity should make every effort to ensure that the information it publishes is accurate, so as to avoid potentially embarrassing later corrections of the quantified information.[274] It may therefore be more sensible in some cases to disclose the information outlined under A above in the 2004 financial statements.[275]

C   2005 interim information

If an entity intends to present its 2005 interim information under IFRS, it should disclose the information under B above before the publication of that interim information, in order to 'have a clear and valid starting point for the preparation and presentation of the interim IAS/IFRS figures'.[276]

The CESR recommendation should be read in the context of applicable European and national legislation and market practices. Therefore, the recommendation does not require an entity to produce interim financial reports if it is not required to do so already.[277] CESR recommends that 'where the issuer is required to, or chooses to, present half-yearly and quarterly financial information, it is preferred that such information is prepared on the basis of the accounting framework to be applied at year end, i.e. the IAS/IFRS framework. In this approach, the issuer will then have the possibility to adopt one of the following alternative methods for the presentation of the interim information:

- either to fully comply with IAS 34 requirements,

- or to present interim financial data as required by the national reporting rules and prepared on the basis of IAS/IFRS recognition and measurement principles which will be applicable at year end.'[278]

It is considered best practice for an entity that decides to adopt IFRS in its 2005 interim financial report 'to provide comparative figures for the same period in 2004 using accounting policies identical to those applied for 2005 (where permitted by the accounting standards themselves)'.[279] The entity should provide a detailed explanation of the restatements of previously published data in the notes to the interim financial statements.[280] However, if an entity is required by national rules to publish financial information on three successive periods, CESR considers it acceptable not to restate the first period. Instead the entity could present the comparative information using a 'bridge approach'. Under the 'bridge approach' the entity would need to present financial information for the bridge period under both IFRS and its previous GAAP.[281] The table below illustrates how this approach would apply in an entity's interim report for the first quarter of 2005.

Bridge			
First quarter 2005 under IFRS	First quarter 2004 under IFRS (restated)	First quarter 2004 under previous GAAP (as published)	First quarter 2003 under previous GAAP (as published)

It should be noted that the 'bridge approach' will probably only be useful if the layouts of the primary financial statements under IFRS and the previous GAAP are reasonably similar.

D   2005 annual financial statements

As discussed at 2.10.2 above, IFRS 1 requires a first-time adopter to explain how the transition from its previous GAAP to IFRS affected its reported financial position, financial performance and cash flows. Although IFRS 1 requires comparative information for the preceding period(s) to be prepared under IFRS, it does not prohibit an entity from presenting previously published information again. Therefore, if such information is considered to be useful, it can be presented again by the entity.[282]

CESR considers the 'bridge approach' discussed at C above, to be equally acceptable for the annual financial statements.[283] Therefore, if an entity is required by national rules to publish financial information on three successive periods, it could also use the bridge approach and not restate the first period of comparative figures, as shown below.

	Bridge		
2005 under IFRS	2004 under IFRS (restated)	2004 under previous GAAP (as published)	2003 under previous GAAP (as published)

As noted above, the 'bridge approach' will really only be useful if the layouts of the primary financial statements under IFRS and the previous GAAP are reasonably similar.

3.6.2   IFRS guidance

Although IFRS 1 provides detailed rules on disclosures to be made in an entity's first IFRS financial statements and in interim reports covering part of its first IFRS reporting period, it does not provide any guidance on presenting a reconciliation to IFRS in financial reports before the start of the first IFRS reporting period. An entity wishing to disclose the impact of IFRS in its last financial statements under its previous GAAP cannot claim that this information was prepared and presented in accordance with IFRS because it does not disclose all information required in full IFRS financial statements and it does not disclose comparative information.

As the extract below illustrates, in practice, some entities get around this problem by disclosing pro forma IFRS information and stating that the pro forma information does not comply with IFRS.

Extract 4.9: ARINSO International SA (2003)

2003 IFRS Consolidated Financial Information [extract]

1. OPENING BALANCE AT JANUARY 1, 2003 [extract]

In 2003, ARINSO decided to anticipate the adoption of the International Financial Reporting Standards (earlier called International Accounting Standards (IAS)). These standards will become mandatory in 2005 for the consolidated financial statements of all companies listed on stock exchanges within the European Union.

As of 2004 ARINSO will publish quarterly reports in full compliance with IFRS. In order to have comparable figures as requested by IFRS, the 2003 financial statements were already prepared on an IFRS basis. In 2003, the impact of the IFRS conversion on the quarterly figures was published in our press releases.

The main differences between Belgian Generally Accepted Accounting Principles (GAAP) and IFRS as well as a reconciliation of the equity to IFRS at the date of conversion are presented hereunder.

3. IFRS VALUATION RULES [extract]

3.2 Adoption of the IFRS

The IFRS standards will be adopted for the first time in the consolidated financial statements for the year ended December 31, 2004. The standard for the first time application of the IFRS, published by the IASB in June 2003, was utilized in the pro forma consolidated IFRS balance sheet, income statement and cash flow statement published for the year ended December 31, 2003.

The information related to accounting year 2003 was converted from Belgian GAAP to IFRS in view of the comparison of information next year. The 2004 annual report will include all necessary comparable information.

Free translation of the Statutory Auditor's Report submitted to the shareholders, originally prepared in Dutch, on the restatement of the consolidated balance sheet, the profit and loss account and cash flow statement from accounting principles generally accepted in Belgium into IFRS [extract]

The financial statements provided, which do not include all notes to the financial statements in accordance with IFRS, have been prepared under the responsibility of the company's management, and do not comply with IFRS.

---

4 CONCLUSION

It was always clear that a first-time adoption standard driven by the desire to avoid undue cost and effort would have to include exemptions that would permit first-time adopters to apply IFRS in a practical manner. The objectives that the IASB sets out in the standard are:

> to ensure that an entity's first IFRS financial statements and its first IFRS interim financial statements contain high quality financial information that:[284]
>
> (a)   is transparent for users and comparable over all periods presented;
>
> (b)   provides a suitable starting point for accounting under IFRS; and
>
> (c)   can be generated at a cost that does not exceed the benefits to users.

It seems unavoidable that these objectives will be subject to practical reality. Inevitably, the range of options available in IFRS 1 means that similar entities may produce dissimilar IFRS financial statements. For example, the first-time adoption rules on hedge accounting, derecognition and estimates will result in financial statements that still owe much to the first-time adopter's previous GAAP. Nevertheless, the effect of these exemptions and exceptions will most likely fade quickly.

In the long run only the effect of the business combinations and 'fair value or revaluation as deemed cost' exemptions will be enduring. However, even the impact of those exemptions will be relatively insignificant compared with, for example, the huge effect an acquisition has on the comparability of financial statements from one period to another.

IFRS 1 may not quite meet the lofty goals set by the IASB, but five or ten years from now this will be long forgotten. In the meantime, for first-time adopters, IFRS 1 represents a marked improvement over the theoretically pure but practically unworkable SIC-8. It is therefore no surprise to see that many first-time adopters are applying IFRS 1 early. Still, some first-time adopters of IFRS will have concerns about, for example, the complexity of the first-time adoption exemption for share-based payments. Others will complain about the unfairness of a business combination exemption that does not allow an adjustment of goodwill for items other than intangible assets, contingencies and impairments.

Overall the IASB is to be complemented for taking a practical approach to first-time adoption. It has steered a reasonable course between practicality and theoretical perfection that most preparers will, with effort, be able to follow.

References

1 Regulation (EC) No 1606/2002 of the European Parliament and of the Council of 19 July 2002 on the application of international accounting standards, article 4 defines these companies as follows: 'For each financial year starting on or after 1 January 2005, companies governed by the law of a Member State shall prepare their consolidated accounts in conformity with the international accounting standards adopted in accordance with the procedure laid down in Article 6(2) if, at their balance sheet date, their securities are admitted to trading on a regulated market of any Member State within the meaning of Article 1(13) of Council Directive 93/22/EEC of 10 May 1993 on investment services in the securities field.'

2 SIC-8, *First-Time Application of IASs as the Primary Basis of Accounting*, SIC, July 1998, para. 3.

3 ED 1, *First-time Application of International Financial Reporting Standards*, IASB, July 2002.

4 IFRS 1, *First-time Adoption of International Financial Reporting Standards*, IASB, June 2003 (amended March 2004), para. IN1.

5 IFRS 1, para. BC3.

6 IFRS 1, para. BC9.

7 IFRS 1, para. BC10.

8 IFRS 1, para. 1.

9 IFRS 1, para. 3 and Appendix A.

10 IFRS 1, para. 3.

11 IFRS 1, para. 3.

12 IFRS 1, para. 4.

13 IFRS 1, para. BC5.

14 IFRS 1, para. BC6.

15 IFRS 1, para. 5.

16 IFRS 1, Appendix A.

17 IFRS 1, para. 2.

18 IFRS 1, para. 2.

19 IAS 34, *Interim Financial Reporting*, IASB, February 1998 (amended March 2004), para. 3.
20 IFRS 1, Appendix A.
21 IFRS 1, para. 36.
22 IAS 1, *Presentation of Financial Statements*, IASB, December 2003 (amended March 2004), para. 50.
23 IFRS 1, Appendix A.
24 IFRS 1, para. 14.
25 IFRS 1, para. 6.
26 IFRS 1, para. 7.
27 IFRS 1, paras. BC17-BC18.
28 IFRS 1, para. 8.
29 IFRS 1, para. BC11.
30 IFRS 1, para. 8.
31 IFRS 1, para. 10.
32 IFRS 1, para. 11.
33 IFRS 1, para. 9.
34 IFRS 1, para. BC14.
35 *Framework for the Preparation and Presentation of Financial Statements* (Framework), IASB, September 1989, para. 44.
36 IFRS 1, para. BC27.
37 IFRS 1, para. 12.
38 IFRS 1, para. 13.
39 IFRS 1, para. 26.
40 IFRS 1, para. IN4.
41 IFRS 1, paras. 13 and 36A.
42 IFRS 1, para. 13.
43 IFRS 1, para. IN4.
44 IFRS 1, para. 26.
45 IFRS 1, para. 15 and Appendix B.
46 IFRS 1, para. B1.
47 IFRS 1, para. B3.
48 IFRS 1, para. BC32.
49 IFRS 1, paras. BC33-BC34.
50 IFRS 1, para. BC34.
51 IFRS 3, *Business Combinations*, IASB, March 2004, para. 85.
52 IFRS 1, para. B2(a).
53 IFRS 1, para. 15.
54 IFRS 3, Appendix A.
55 IFRS 3, Appendix A.
56 IFRS 3, para. 4.
57 IFRS 1, para. B2(c).
58 IFRS 1, para. B2(b).
59 IFRS 1, para. B2(b).
60 IFRS 1, IG Example 7.
61 IFRS 1, IG Example 3.
62 IFRS 1, para. B2(d).
63 IFRS 1, para. B2(e).
64 IFRS 1, para. BC36.
65 IFRS 1, para. B2(f).
66 IFRS 1, para. BC35.
67 IFRS 1, IG Example 2.
68 IFRS 1, para. B2(g).
69 IFRS 1, para. B2(g).
70 IFRS 1, para. B2(g).
71 IFRS 1, para. IG40.
72 IFRS 1, para. IG41.
73 IFRS 1, para. IG43.
74 IFRS 1, para. BC39.
75 IFRS 1, para. BC38.
76 IFRS 1, para. B2(h).
77 IFRS 3, para. 81.
78 IFRS 1, para. 10.
79 IFRS 1, para. B2(i).
80 IFRS 1, para. B2(i).
81 IAS 21, *The Effects of Changes in Foreign Exchange Rates*, IASB, December 2003, para. 47.
82 IFRS 1, paras. B1A and IG21A.
83 IFRS 1, para. B1A.
84 IFRS 1, para. B1B.
85 IFRS 1, para. B2(j).
86 IFRS 1, IG Example 6.
87 IFRS 1, para. B2(k).
88 IAS 27, *Consolidated and Separate Financial Statements*, IASB, December 2003 (amended March 2004), para. 4.
89 IFRS 1, para. B2(k).
90 IFRS 1, IG Example 4.
91 IFRS 1, para. BC42.
92 IFRS 1, paras. 16-17.
93 IFRS 1, para. 16.
94 IFRS 1, para. 18.
95 IFRS 1, para. 18.
96 IFRS 1, para. 18.
97 IFRS 1, para. IG50.
98 IFRS 1, para. 16.
99 IAS 16, *Property, Plant and Equipment*, IASB, December 2003 (amended March 2004), para. 9.
100 IFRS 1, para. BC45.
101 IFRS 1, para. 16.
102 IFRS 1, para. 17.
103 IFRS 1, para. 19.
104 IFRS 1, para. BC47.
105 IFRS 1, para. BC47.
106 IFRS 1, para. BC43.
107 IFRS 1, para. BC89A.
108 IFRS 1, para. 36A.
109 IFRS 1, para. 36A.
110 IAS 39, *Financial Instruments: Recognition and Measurement*, IASB, December 2003 (amended March 2004), para. 9.
111 IAS 39, para. 9.
112 IFRS 1, para. 25A.
113 IFRS 1, para. BC63A.
114 IFRS 1, para. IG59.
115 IFRS 1, para. 43A.
116 IFRS 1, para. BC81.
117 IFRS 1, paras. BC81-BC82.
118 IFRS 1, para. 23.
119 IFRS 1, paras. IG35-IG36.
120 IFRS 1, para. 27.
121 IFRS 1, para. 27A.
122 IFRS 1, para. 26(c).

123 IFRS 1, para. BC75.
124 IFRS 1, para. BC76.
125 IFRS 1, para. BC77.
126 IFRS 1, para. 28.
127 IFRS 1, para. IG58A.
128 IFRS 1, para. 28.
129 IFRS 1, para. 29.
130 IFRS 1, para. 29.
131 IFRS 1, para. 30.
132 IFRS 1, para. BC75.
133 IFRS 1, para. IG60B.
134 ED 1, para. C3(c)(i).
135 ED 1, para. C4.
136 IFRS 1, para. IG58A.
137 IFRS 1, para. IG60A.
138 IAS 39, *Financial Instruments: Recognition and Measurement*, IASB, December 1998 (amended 2000), para. 172(e) and ED 1, para. C3(b).
139 IFRS 1, paras. IG60 and IG60B.
140 IFRS 1, para. 30.
141 IFRS 1, para. IG60B.
142 IFRS 1, para. 28.
143 IFRS 1, para. IG58A.
144 IFRS 1, paras. BC65-BC66.
145 IFRS 1, para. BC73.
146 IFRS 1, para. BC73.
147 IFRS 1, para. 20.
148 IFRS 1, para. BC48.
149 IFRS 1, paras. 20 and IG18.
150 IFRS 1, paras. BC50-BC51.
151 IFRS 1, para. BC51.
152 IFRS 1, paras. BC51 and IG21.
153 IFRS 1, para. IG19.
154 IFRS 1, para. IG20.
155 IFRS 1, para. BC52.
156 IAS 21, paras. 32 and 39 and IFRS 1, para. 21.
157 IAS 21, para. 48 and IFRS 1, para. 21.
158 IFRS 1, para. 22.
159 IFRS 1, para. BC63B.
160 IFRS 1, para. 25B.
161 IFRS 1, para. 25B.
162 IFRS 1, para. 25B.
163 IFRS 1, para. 25C.
164 Framework, paras. 25-28.
165 IFRS 1, para. 25D and IFRS 4, para. 22.
166 IFRS 1, para. BC89A.
167 IFRS 1, para. 36A.
168 IFRS 1, para. BC59.
169 IFRS 1, para. 24.
170 IFRS 1, para. 24.
171 IFRS 1, IG Example 8.
172 IFRS 1, para. BC62.
173 IFRS 1, para. IG31.
174 IFRS 1, para. 24.
175 IFRS 1, para. 25.
176 IFRS 1, para. BC63.
177 IFRS 1, IG Example 9.
178 IFRS 1, para. IG30.

179 IFRS 1, para. 25.
180 IFRS 1, para. 31.
181 IAS 8, *Accounting Policies, Changes in Accounting Estimates and Errors*, IASB, December 2003 (amended March 2004), para. 5.
182 IFRS 1, para. BC84.
183 IFRS 1, para. 34.
184 IFRS 1, paras. 32 and IG2.
185 IFRS 1, para. IG3.
186 IFRS 1, para. IG3.
187 IFRS 1, para. IG3.
188 IFRS 1, paras. 33 and IG3.
189 IFRS 1, para. IG4.
190 IFRS 1, para. 34A.
191 IFRS 1, para. 34B.
192 IFRS 1, para. IG7.
193 IFRS 1, paras. IG8-IG9.
194 IFRS 1, para. IG10.
195 IFRS 1, para. IG11.
196 IAS 16, para. 16.
197 IFRS 1, para. IG13.
198 IFRS 1, paras. 25E and IG201-IG203.
199 IFRS 1, para. IG14.
200 IAS 17, *Leases*, IASB, December 2003 (amended March 2004), para. 13.
201 IFRS 1, para. IG16.
202 IFRS 1, para. IG26.
203 IFRS 1, para. IG27.
204 IFRS 1, para. 25.
205 IFRS 1, para. IG27.
206 IFRS 1, para. IG28.
207 IFRS 1, para. BC67.
208 IFRS 1, para. IG32.
209 IFRS 1, para. IG33.
210 IFRS 1, para. IG34.
211 IFRS 1, para. IG44.
212 IAS 38, *Intangible Assets*, IASB, March 2004, para. 21.
213 IAS 38, para. 71.
214 IFRS 1, para. IG46.
215 IFRS 1, para. IG47.
216 IFRS 1, para. IG47.
217 IFRS 1, para. IG48.
218 IFRS 1, para. IG51.
219 IFRS 1, para. IG17.
220 IFRS 1, para. IG23.
221 IFRS 1, para. IG25.
222 IFRS 1, para. 35.
223 IFRS 1, para. 47.
224 IAS 1, para. 36.
225 IFRS 1, para. 36.
226 IFRS 1, para. 6.
227 IFRS 1, para. BC86.
228 IFRS 1, para. 36A.
229 IAS 8, para. 24.
230 IAS 8, para. 28.
231 IFRS 1, para. BC89.
232 IFRS 1, para. 37.

233 IFRS 1, para. 37.
234 IFRS 1, para. 38.
235 IFRS 1, para. BC91.
236 IAS 1, para. 108.
237 IFRS 1, para. 43.
238 IFRS 1, para. 39.
239 IFRS 1, para. 39.
240 IFRS 1, para. 40.
241 IFRS 1, para. 42.
242 IFRS 1, para. 40.
243 IFRS 1, para. 41.
244 IFRS 1, para. IG63.
245 IFRS 1, para. 39.
246 IFRS 1, para. BC94.
247 IFRS 1, para. 43A.
248 IFRS 1, para. 44.
249 IFRS 1, para. 45.
250 IFRS 1, para. IG37.
251 IFRS 1, IG Example 10.
252 IFRS 1, para. 46.
253 IFRS 1, para. 46.
254 IFRS 1, para. 47.
255 IFRS 1, para. 36A.
256 IFRS 1, para. 27.
257 Release No. 33-8397, *First-Time Application of International Financial Reporting Standards*, Securities and Exchange Commission (SEC), 11 March 2004.
258 Release No. 33-8397.
259 IFRS 1, para. IG5.
260 IAS 12, *Income Taxes*, IASB, October 1996 (amended March 2004), para. 15.
261 IAS 12, paras. 15 and 24.
262 IAS 12, para. 68.
263 IAS 16, para. 9.
264 IAS 16, para. 12.
265 IAS 16, para. 13.
266 IAS 16, para. 43.
267 IAS 21, para. 21.
268 IAS 21, paras. 8-14.
269 *European Regulation on the Application of IFRS in 2005 – Recommendation for Additional Guidance Regarding the Transition to IFRS*, Committee of European Securities Regulators (CESR), December 2003.
270 CESR, para. 13.
271 CESR, para. 17.
272 CESR, para. 18.
273 CESR, pars. 22 and 25.
274 CESR, para. 23.
275 CESR, para. 24.
276 CESR, para. 26.
277 CESR, para. 27.
278 CESR, para. 30.
279 CESR, para. 32.
280 CESR, para. 34.
281 CESR, paras. 35-37.
282 CESR, para. 38.
283 CESR, paras. 39-41.
284 IFRS 1, para. 1.

Chapter 5

Consolidated and separate financial statements

1 THE CONCEPT OF A GROUP

1.1 Background

It is a commercial practice of long standing for an entity to conduct its business not only directly but also through strategic investments in other entities. IFRS, and most national GAAPs, broadly distinguish three types of such strategic investment:

- entities controlled by the reporting entity (subsidiaries);
- entities jointly controlled by the reporting entity and one or more third parties (joint ventures);[1] and
- entities that, while not controlled or jointly controlled by the reporting entity, are subject to significant influence by it (associates).

This raises the question of how such strategic investments should be accounted for. There is a consensus that it is not adequate to account for such entities merely by recording income received from them, and that some mechanism is required to reflect their activities directly in the financial statements of reporting entities that hold them. Under IFRS:

- an entity and its subsidiaries are collectively referred to as a 'group', and accounted for in accordance with IAS 27 – *Consolidated and Separate Financial Statements*[2] – using consolidated financial statements (which are addressed in the remainder of this Chapter);
- associates are accounted for in accordance with IAS 28 – *Investments in Associates* – using equity accounting (which is addressed in Chapter 7); and

- joint ventures are accounted for in accordance with IAS 31 – *Interests in Joint Ventures* – using a variety of methods, depending on their structure (see Chapter 8).

IFRS also acknowledges that entities may wish (or be obliged by local legal requirements) to present additional financial statements in which such strategic investments are accounted for on some other basis, such as cost or valuation. Whilst IFRS does not require the preparation of such additional financial statements (referred to as 'separate financial statements'), it does prescribe the accounting treatment to be followed where they are prepared and stated to be in compliance with IFRS.[3] Separate financial statements are discussed further at 7 below.

1.2   The objectives of consolidated financial statements

Consolidated financial statements are designed to extend the reporting entity so as to embrace other entities which are subject to its control. They involve treating the net assets and activities of subsidiaries held by a reporting entity as if they were part of the holding entity's own net assets and activities; the overall aim is to present the results and state of affairs of the reporting entity and its subsidiaries (referred to as a group) as if they were those of a single entity.

As noted above, the standard dealing with this topic under IFRS is IAS 27, which requires a parent (i.e. an entity with one or more subsidiaries)[4] to present consolidated financial statements in which all subsidiaries are included.[5]

1.3   What is a subsidiary?

The definition of a subsidiary is fundamental to any discussion of consolidated financial statements, since this determines the scope and extent of the reporting entity which is the subject of the consolidated financial statements. When the concept of consolidated financial statements was originally introduced in the first half of the last century, the question of whether or not an entity was a subsidiary was generally determined by legal ownership. In other words, any entity in which the reporting entity held more than half the equity would be regarded as subject to the reporting entity's control (and therefore a subsidiary), whereas any entity in which the reporting entity held half or less of the equity would be regarded as not subject to the reporting entity's control (and therefore a not subsidiary).

However, this 'ownership' model proved increasingly inadequate, particularly with the growth of 'off-balance sheet' financing from the 1970s onwards. It proved relatively easy for a reporting entity to set up another entity in which it had little or no legal ownership interest, but which it effectively controlled (for example, because the shares were owned by parties who could be expected to act in accordance with the reporting entity's wishes). It became common for companies to use such entities as vehicles for making borrowings that did not appear in the consolidated financial statements, because the borrowing entity, although controlled by the reporting entity, did not meet the definition of a subsidiary under the ownership model.

As a result, there emerged a new concept: the question of whether or not an entity is a subsidiary for consolidation purposes should be determined not by legal ownership, but by the existence of economic control. The first major codification of an 'economic control' model for consolidated financial statements was in the EU Seventh Company Law Directive in 1983.

However, the concept of economic control in the Seventh Directive was widely drawn. For example, the Directive allowed (but did not require) consolidation of an entity by a shareholder that in practice appointed the majority of the board, even if it did not have the majority of the voting rights. This was to cater with the situation where, due to the wide dispersal of the majority of shareholdings, a significant minority shareholder can exercise *de facto* control. The Directive also permitted, but did not require, a further extension of the 'economic control' model to so-called 'horizontal' groups – i.e. entities with no shareholding relationship but under common control (e.g. because they are owned by the same individual). IAS 27 does not require consolidation of 'horizontal' groups, or of entities over which there is *de facto* control.

The consolidation model in IAS 27 is based primarily on the legal and contractual rights of shareholders, rather than on a pure 'ownership' model or 'economic control' model. However, aspects of an 'economic control' model are also in evidence, particularly in the SIC interpretation SIC-12 – *Consolidation – Special Purpose Entities*[6] (see 3 below).

1.4   Consolidating partly owned subsidiaries

Various alternative ways of looking at a group become relevant when there are subsidiary companies which are not wholly owned by the holding entity. The particular matters which are affected are:

- the elimination of the effects of intragroup transactions;

- the calculation and treatment of minority interests, i.e. the interests of shareholders other than the controlling shareholder. (The term 'minority' is strictly a legacy from the 'ownership' model of consolidation. Under a 'legal and contractual' model or an 'economic control' model it is quite possible for the 'minority' shareholders to own more than half the shares in a subsidiary); and

- the treatment of changes in stake in the subsidiary.

There are two widely accepted concepts, referred to respectively as the entity concept and the proprietary concept, although the latter has a number of further variants.

1.4.1 The entity concept

The entity concept focuses on the existence of the group as an economic unit, rather than looking at it only through the eyes of the dominant shareholder group. It concentrates on the resources controlled by the entity, and regards the identity of owners with claims on these resources as being of secondary importance. It therefore makes no distinction between the treatment given to different classes of shareholders, whether majority or minority, and all transactions between the shareholders are regarded as internal to the group.

1.4.2 The proprietary (parent entity) concept

The proprietary concept emphasises ownership through a controlling shareholding interest, and regards the consolidated financial statements as being principally for the information of the shareholders of the holding entity. Its primary concern is not to present financial statements which are relevant to the minority shareholders. This is achieved either by treating the minority shareholders as 'outsiders' and reflecting their interests as quasi-liabilities or by leaving them out of the group financial statements entirely, thereby consolidating only the parent's percentage interest in the assets and liabilities of the subsidiary (the 'proportionate consolidation' method). The proprietary concept is sometimes referred to as the 'parent entity' concept, and there is a variant of it known as the 'parent entity extension' concept, which leans more towards the entity concept described above.

IFRS (IAS 27 together with IFRS 3 – *Business Combinations*, discussed in Chapter 6) currently requires the 'parent entity extension' concept, whereby the separable net assets (i.e. other than goodwill) of the group are reported without regard to the underlying ownership (as in the entity concept), whilst goodwill is recognised only to the extent of the controlling shareholder's interest (as in the proprietary concept). However, the IASB has agreed in principle to move to requiring an approach more akin to the entity concept as part of Phase II of its business combinations project, whereby goodwill would be calculated for an acquired business as a whole and allocated between the controlling shareholder and any minority. Moreover, any subsequent increases or decreases (not resulting in loss of control) in the parent's ownership interest would be treated as movements within equity.[7]

It will become apparent from the discussion in 1.4.3 and following below that the current approach of IFRS actually contains elements of each of these different concepts rather than following any one on a consistent basis.

1.4.3　Comparison between the different concepts of a group

The distinction between the different methods in practice can best be illustrated by an example:

Example 5.1:　Comparison between the different concepts of a group

Assume that entity A buys 75% of entity B for €1,200 when entity B has total net assets with a fair value of €1,000 and a carrying amount of €800. Under the various concepts described above, the consolidated balance sheet of entity A would incorporate the effects of the acquisition calculated as follows:

	Entity concept €	Proprietary concept €	Parent coy. extension concept €
Net assets of B	1,000	950	1,000
Goodwill	600	450	450
	1,600	1,400	1,450
Investor interest	1,200	1,200	1,200
Minority interest	400	200	250
	1,600	1,400	1,450

Entity concept

Both the separable net assets and goodwill are reported in the balance sheet at the full amount of their fair value as determined by the transaction involving the majority shareholder. These amounts are then apportioned between the majority and minority shareholders.

Proprietary concept

The proprietary concept leaves the minority interest unaffected by the transaction of the majority shareholder. It is shown simply as their proportionate share of the carrying values of the net assets of the entity. This means that the goodwill is stated at a figure which represents the difference between the cost of the 75% investment (€1,200) and 75% of the fair value of the assets (€750). Perhaps more disturbingly, the assets are carried on a mixed basis which represents 75% of their fair value and 25% of their book value.

This feature is eliminated if proportionate consolidation is adopted, since the minority interest is disregarded altogether, being set against the assets and liabilities of the subsidiary on a line by line basis, so that only the majority investor's share of the subsidiary's assets is consolidated. This would result in the consolidation of assets of €750 and goodwill of €450, representing the total of the investment of €1,200. However, IFRS does not allow proportionate consolidation for subsidiaries, although it is one of the permitted treatments for certain types of joint venture (see Chapter 8).

Parent entity extension concept

The mixed basis for the carrying amount of separable net assets is also avoided in the parent entity extension concept, which includes the separable net assets at the whole amount of their fair value and apportions that between the majority and minority interests, but includes goodwill only as it relates to the majority investor.

A   Intragroup transactions

The different concepts are also relevant to the calculation of the adjustments made to eliminate the effects of intragroup transactions (i.e. those between entities within the same group). If entity A in Example 5.1 sold an item of stock to entity B for a profit of €100, and entity B still held the stock at the year end, it would be necessary to make an adjustment on consolidation to eliminate what was an unrealised profit from the group point of view.

Under the proprietary concept, the minority shareholders are regarded as outsiders, and therefore there is a case for saying that 25% of the profit *has* been realised; this would be done by limiting the write-down of stock to €75, all of which is taken off the balance on the group profit and loss account.

Under the proportionate consolidation method, only 75% of the stock would appear in the consolidated balance sheet in the first place, so the adjustment would simply be to deduct €75 from both the group profit and loss account and from the stock.

Under the entity concept, as it is the parent which has made the sale, the whole write-down of stock of €100 would be charged against the group profit and loss account, with no amount attributed to the minority interest. This is the approach adopted in IAS 27.

A further possible approach is the separate entities approach,[8] whereby the adjustment is effected by apportioning the €100 between the group profit and loss account and the minority interest in the ratio 75:25.

B   Loss-making subsidiaries

A further practical situation where differences between the concepts emerge is when the partly-owned subsidiary makes losses which put it into overall deficit. Under the entity concept, the consolidated financial statements would continue to account for these losses and apportion them between the majority and minority interests in proportion to their holdings, even if this created a debit balance for the minority interest in the balance sheet.

A proprietary concept would not normally permit the minority interest to be shown as a debit balance, because it could not usually be regarded as a recoverable asset from the point of view of the majority interest, which is the orientation of the financial statements under the proprietary concept. This is the approach adopted in IAS 27 (see 6.7.2 below).

1.5   Other issues

The composition of a group may change, either through entities joining or leaving the group, or by the parent's increasing or decreasing its stake in existing subsidiaries. Currently IFRS does not address many of these issues, which will be dealt with in the IASB's Business Combinations (Phase II) project. Some aspects of accounting for an increase in stake in an existing subsidiary are discussed in Chapter 6.

There are some situations where it is considered unnecessary for a parent to prepare consolidated financial statements, particularly where the parent is itself a subsidiary of another entity. The exemptions given by IAS 27 are dealt with at 4 below.

2 DEVELOPMENT OF IAS 27

IAS 27 was originally issued in 1988 and has since been subject to various amendments, most significantly in December 2003 as part of the IASB's improvements project, when the previous version of IAS 27 was withdrawn and superseded by a substantially revised version, which must be applied for accounting periods beginning on or after 1 January 2005. Entities are encouraged to adopt the revised version of IAS 27 for earlier periods, but must disclose that they have done so.[9]

The main changes made by the current version of IAS 27 to previous IFRS (other than the incorporation into IAS 27 of requirements previously contained in other pronouncements) were to:[10]

- include specific provisions relating to the separate financial statements (if prepared) not only of entities with subsidiaries, but also of entities with associates or joint ventures, with a consequent change in the title of the standard;

- prohibit the previously allowed use of equity accounting for investments in subsidiaries in separate financial statements;

- revise the exemptions from preparation of consolidated financial statements;

- reinforce the (already existing) requirement for venture capital organisations and similar entities to consolidate subsidiaries;

- remove the previous exemption from consolidation in respect of a subsidiary subject to severe-long term restrictions (unless those restrictions amount to a loss of control);

- require the financial statements of members of a group used for consolidation purposes to use consistent accounting policies; and

- require minority interests to be shown as a component of equity.

Since its publication in December 2003, IAS 27 has been further amended, notably by IFRS 3 and IFRS 5 – *Non-current Assets Held for Sale and Discontinued Operations*.[11] As a result, the previous requirements regarding investments that are intended to be held on a temporary basis have been removed from IAS 27. Such investments will now generally be accounted for under IFRS 5[12] (see Chapter 3).

3   DEFINITION OF SUBSIDIARY

As indicated at 1.3 above, the definition of 'subsidiary' is fundamental to any discussion of consolidated financial statements. The question is also relevant to the subject of off-balance sheet financing, because frequently this definition determines whether the group balance sheet should include the accounts of an entity which holds certain assets and liabilities which management may not wish to include in the consolidated financial statements.

IAS 27 uses the following definition of subsidiary and related terms.

A *parent* is an entity with one or more subsidiaries.[13]

A *subsidiary* is an entity, including an unincorporated entity such as a partnership, that is controlled by another entity (known as the parent).[14]

A *group* is a parent and all its subsidiaries.[15]

Control is the power to govern the financial and operating policies of an entity so as to obtain benefits from its activities.[16]

3.1   Control

As can be seen, the definition of control effectively underpins the definition of parent and subsidiary, and IAS 27 therefore elaborates on it further.

3.1.1   *Primary indicators of control*

IAS 27 states that control is presumed to exist if the parent owns, directly or indirectly through subsidiaries, more than half of the voting power of an entity unless, in exceptional circumstances, it can be clearly demonstrated that such ownership does not constitute control. Control is also considered to exist even when the parent does not own a majority of the voting rights when there is:

(a)   power over more than half of the voting rights by virtue of an agreement with other investors;

(b)   power to govern the financial and operating policies of the entity under a statute or an agreement;

(c)   power to appoint or remove the majority of the members of the board of directors or equivalent governing body and control of the entity is by that board or body; or

(d)   power to cast the majority of votes at meetings of the board of directors or equivalent governing body and control of the entity is by that board or body.[17]

IAS 27 does not elaborate on the situations in which it might be 'clearly demonstrated' that ownership of more than half the voting power does not constitute control. The most obvious, and common, example will be where, by virtue of one or more of (a) to (d) above, an entity is a subsidiary of another shareholder owning half or less of the voting power.

More complex situations may arise where minority shareholders have rights of veto or approval over certain issues. In such situations, it may be helpful to have regard to the analysis, for the purposes of US GAAP, in EITF 96-16.[18] Broadly, EITF 96-16 draws a distinction between minority rights that essentially exist to protect the minority from potentially damaging actions by the majority shareholders (which would not normally impact on the control exercised by majority shareholders) and minority rights that result in active participation in day-to-day decisions of the entity (which may result in a rebuttal of the presumption that the majority shareholder has control). In some cases, the effect might be that the entity is in fact a joint venture between the majority and minority shareholder which should be accounted for in accordance with IAS 31 (see Chapter 8). However, minority rights giving rise only to *de facto* control, as opposed to a legal or contractual right to control, will not necessarily amount to control for the purposes of IAS 27.

The implementation guidance to IAS 27 notes that it is inherent in the definition of control than an entity cannot be controlled by more than one party (although it might be jointly controlled by more than one party). Accordingly, when two or more entities each hold significant voting rights (whether actual rights or potential rights – see 3.1.2 below), the factors in (a) to (d) above should be reassessed into order to determine which entity (if any) actually has control.[19]

IAS 27 emphasises that the reference to 'power' in the definition of 'control' above means the ability to do or affect something. Consequently, an entity has control over another entity when it currently has the ability to exercise that power, regardless of whether control is actively demonstrated or is passive in nature.[20] Passive control may be exercised over another entity through potential voting rights (see 3.1.2 below).

3.1.2 Potential voting rights

An entity may own share warrants, share call options, debt or equity instruments that are convertible into ordinary shares, or other similar instruments that have the potential, if exercised or converted, to give the entity voting power or reduce another party's voting power over the financial and operating policies of another entity (potential voting rights).[21]

IAS 27 requires an entity to consider the existence and effect of potential voting rights that are currently exercisable or convertible, including potential voting rights held by another entity (see B below), when assessing whether an entity has the power to govern the financial and operating policies of another entity.[22] As will discussed further at B below, IAS 27 takes a very strict and, some might argue, rather form-based approach to determining what potential voting rights should be taken into account for this purpose.

A   Interaction with IAS 28 and IAS 31

IAS 28 and IAS 31 also require the existence and effect of potential voting rights to be taken into account in assessing whether an entity has, respectively, significant influence over, or joint control of, another entity. Accordingly, the guidance in IAS 27 on this issue, summarised below, is also relevant to IAS 28 and IAS 31.[23]

However, IAS 27 notes that its guidance may be less relevant to IAS 31, since the issue of whether or not an entity is a joint venture depends primarily on the contractual relationship between the parties[24] (which would not typically be affected by the existence of potential voting rights).

B   What rights are 'currently exercisable'?

Potential voting rights are not currently exercisable or convertible when they cannot be exercised or converted until a future date or until the occurrence of a future event.[25] The effect of this requirement is illustrated by Example 5.2 below.

Example 5.2:   Potential voting rights (1)

An entity (A) holds 40% of another entity (B), together with loan notes in B convertible, at A's option, into further shares in B which, if issued, would give A a 60% interest in B. A can require conversion of its loan notes into shares at any time on or after the fifth anniversary of their issue.

Until that fifth anniversary occurs, A cannot exercise its conversion rights. They are therefore ignored, such that B would not (absent other circumstances) be a subsidiary of A. Once the fifth anniversary has occurred, A can exercise its option to convert and is therefore regarded as having the majority of the voting rights of B, such that B would (absent exceptional circumstances) become a subsidiary of A for the purposes of IAS 27.

The implementation guidance indicates that potential voting rights include not only those actually held by an entity (as in Example 5.2 above), but also those to which the entity currently has the right of access, as illustrated by Example 5.3 below.[26]

Example 5.3:   Potential voting rights (2)

Entities A, B and C own 25%, 35% and 40% respectively of the ordinary shares that carry voting rights at a general meeting of shareholders of entity D. B and C also have share warrants that are exercisable at any time at a fixed price and provide potential voting rights. A has a call option to purchase these share warrants at any time for a nominal amount. If the call option is exercised, A would have the potential to increase its ownership interest, and thereby its voting rights, in D to 51% and dilute B's and C's interests to 23% and 26% respectively.

Although the share warrants are not owned by A, they are considered in assessing control because they are currently exercisable by B and C. Normally, if an action (e.g. purchase or exercise of another right) is required before an entity has ownership of a potential voting right, the potential voting right is not regarded as held by the entity. However, the share warrants are, in substance, held by A, because the terms of the call option are designed to ensure A's position. The combination of the call option and share warrants gives A the power to set the operating and financial policies of D, because A could currently exercise the option and share warrants.

Example 5.3 also illustrates the requirement of IAS 27 that the reporting entity must have regard not only to its own potential voting rights in an investee, but also to those of other shareholders. A potential practical issue here is that, in some more secretive jurisdictions, it might be difficult to obtain information about the potential voting power of other shareholders.

C   Management intention and ability to exercise potential ownership rights

IAS 27 adds some further points of clarification. In assessing whether potential voting rights contribute to control, an entity must examine all facts and circumstances (including the terms of exercise of the potential voting rights and any other contractual arrangements whether considered individually or in combination) that affect potential voting rights, except the intention of management and the financial ability to exercise or convert.[27]

The implementation guidance expands on this point at some length, but in the process adds some confusion. On the one hand, it gives some illustrative examples (the substance of which is reproduced as Examples 5.4 to 5.6 below) which suggest that this requirement is to be interpreted very strictly.[28]

Example 5.4:   Potential voting rights (3)

Entities A and B own 80% and 20% respectively of the ordinary shares that carry voting rights at a general meeting of shareholders of entity C. A sells one half of its interest to D and buys call options from D that are exercisable at any time at a premium to the market price when issued and, if exercised, would return to A its original 80% ownership interest and voting rights. Although the options are out of the money, they are currently exercisable and give A the power to continue to set the operating and financial policies of C, because A could exercise its options now. The existence of the potential voting rights is considered, and it is determined (absent other special circumstances) that A controls C.

Example 5.5:   Potential voting rights (4)

Entities A, B and C each own one third of the ordinary shares that carry voting rights at a general meeting of shareholders of entity D. A, B and C each have the right to appoint two directors to the board of D. A also owns call options that are exercisable at a fixed price at any time and, if exercised, would give it all the voting rights in D. The management of A does not intend to exercise the call options, even if B and C do not vote in the same manner as A. The existence of the potential voting rights is considered and it is determined (absent other special circumstances) that A controls D. The intention of A's management does not influence the assessment.

Example 5.6:   Potential voting rights (5)

Entities A and B own 55% and 45% respectively of the ordinary shares that carry voting rights at a general meeting of shareholders of Entity C. B also holds debt instruments that are convertible into ordinary shares of C. The debt can be converted, on payment of a substantial exercise price in comparison with B's net assets, at any time and, if converted, would require B to borrow additional funds to make the payment. If the debt were to be converted, B would hold 70% of the voting rights and A's interest would reduce to 30%. Although the debt instruments are convertible at a substantial price, they are currently convertible and the conversion feature gives B the power to set the operating and financial policies of C. The existence of the potential voting rights, as well as the other factors described at 4.1.1 below, is considered and it is determined (absent other special circumstances) that that B, not A, controls C. The financial ability of B to pay the conversion price does not influence the assessment.

On the other hand, the guidance states, somewhat contradictorily, that potential voting rights should be ignored where they lack economic substance '(e.g. where the exercise price is set in a manner that precludes exercise in any feasible scenario)'.[29] The use of the word 'feasible' is rather curious, but may have been used in deliberate distinction from the more expected 'foreseeable' – in other words exercise has to be impossible rather than merely highly unlikely. However, this is somewhat contradicted by Example 5.6 above, which stresses that B's financial inability to exercise its conversion rights is irrelevant, and by the overall emphasis on the importance of there being a currently exercisable right.

This almost casual reference to economic substance in the implementation guidance together with the requirement in the main body of IAS 27 (and IAS 28) to examine 'all facts and circumstances' surrounding potential voting rights is no doubt in part an attempt to prevent potential abuses by the use of contrived agreements to deconsolidate loss-making or highly-geared subsidiaries.

However, in our view, the IASB has been so preoccupied by an understandable anxiety to prevent deconsolidation of subsidiaries through contrived sales (as in Example 5.4 above) that it has, particularly through the explicit prohibition on having regard to 'the intention of management and the financial ability to exercise or convert', created the real risk of entities achieving deconsolidation through contrived option arrangements, as illustrated in Example 5.7 below.

Example 5.7:   Potential voting rights (6)

A parent (P) wishes to deconsolidate its loss-making subsidiary (S). It grants immediately exercisable options at an uneconomically high price to a friendly third party (F) which, if exercised, would give F ownership of more than half of the voting power of S. It is known by all concerned that F has no intention of actually exercising its options, and that it would not be in its financial interest to do so. Yet IAS 27 appears to require H to ignore these very pertinent facts in its assessment of whether or not S should continue to be treated as a subsidiary of H.

However, this is not the end of the matter. It might well be that H would continue to be regarded as the parent on the basis that it had an (unwritten) agreement with F that F would never actually exercise its options, thus falling within condition (a) in 3.1.1 above. Moreover, the provisions of SIC–12 could well be relevant (see 3.2 below). Most importantly perhaps, F would be unlikely to enter into such a transaction if it were subject to IAS 27 or a broadly comparable national standard.

Whilst fully exercisable potential voting rights may give rise to situations where an entity becomes (or ceases to be) a subsidiary, the proportion of the entity that is accounted for depends on the actual ownership interests at each reporting date (see 6.2 below).

3.2   Special Purpose Entities

Like many national standard setters before it, the IASB (strictly, its predecessor the IASC) has had to address the issue of an entity conducting its affairs through a vehicle that, though not meeting the definition of a subsidiary, is still controlled by the entity. In principle, there should be less need for such guidance under IFRS (which defines a subsidiary simply as a controlled entity) as compared to other national GAAPs where subsidiary is defined by reference to a number of more specific, or more legally framed, indicators (so that further guidance is required in order to establish an over-riding control test).

In practice, however, the off-balance sheet industry proved no less active under IFRS than elsewhere, so that the SIC felt compelled to issue SIC–12. This requires an entity to consolidate a 'special purpose entity' ('SPE') when the substance of the relationship between them indicates that the entity controls the SPE.[30]

3.2.1 Definition of SPE

SIC-12 is in fact careful *not* to define an SPE, so as to minimise the possibility of avoiding its requirements through exploitation of a loophole in the drafting. Instead an SPE is described as an entity 'created to accomplish a narrow and well-defined objective (e.g. to effect a lease, research and development activities or a securitisation of financial assets)'. An SPE may take the form of a corporation, trust, partnership or unincorporated entity. SPEs are often created with legal arrangements that impose strict and sometimes permanent limits on the decision-making powers of their governing board, trustee or management over the operations of the SPE that cannot be modified, other than perhaps by the creator or sponsor of the SPE (i.e. they operate on 'autopilot').[31]

This description is extremely wide and could, in our view, encompass not only a separate legal entity, but also an economic entity represented by a parcel of 'ring fenced' assets and liabilities within a larger legal entity, such as a cell in a protected cell entity (see Chapter 8 at 2.5), or a portfolio of securitised assets and the related borrowings.

The sponsor (or entity on whose behalf the SPE was created) frequently transfers assets to the SPE, obtains the right to use assets held by the SPE or performs services for the SPE, while other parties ('capital providers') may provide the funding to the SPE. An entity that engages in transactions with an SPE (frequently the creator or sponsor) may in substance control the SPE.[32] A beneficial interest in an SPE may, for example, take the form of a debt instrument, an equity instrument, a participation right, a residual interest or a lease. Some beneficial interests may simply provide the holder with a fixed or stated rate of return, while others give the holder rights or access to other future economic benefits of the SPE's activities. In most cases, the creator or sponsor (or the entity on whose behalf the SPE was created) retains a significant beneficial interest in the SPE's activities, even though it may own little or none of the SPE's equity.[33]

A   Post-employment benefit plans and equity compensation plans

Neither a post-employment benefit plan nor an equity compensation plan is an SPE for the purposes of SIC-12.[34] However, in June 2004 IFRIC issued an exposure draft D7 – *Scope of SIC–12 Consolidation–Special Purpose Entities* – which proposes the amendment of SIC–12 so as to:

(a)   remove the exemption for equity compensation plans; and

(b)   refine the scope of the exemption for post-employment benefit plans to include other long-term employee benefit plans with plan assets that are required to be included in the measurement of a defined benefit liability or a liability for other long-term employee benefits under IAS 19 – *Employee Benefits*.[35]

The accounting for such equity compensation plans and post-employment plans is dealt with in Chapters 29 and 30 respectively.

3.2.2 *Determining whether an entity is an SPE*

SIC-12 notes that control of an SPE may arise through the predetermination of its activities so that it operates on 'autopilot', or otherwise. It emphasises those provisions of IAS 27 that indicate that an entity has control over another entity, even though it owns one half or less (or even none) of the voting power in that other entity[36] (see 3.1 above).

In particular, SIC–12 points out that, under IAS 27, control of an entity comprises the ability to control the entity's decision making with a view to obtaining benefits from the entity. The ability to control decision-making alone is not sufficient to establish control for accounting purposes, but must be accompanied by the objective of obtaining benefits from the entity's activities.[37]

These reminders are doubtless made in the context that the first line of defence for those seeking to establish an off-balance sheet SPE tends to be to argue that some third party (such as a charitable trust) owns all the voting rights. However, if the trust (as is typically the case) does not obtain any real benefit from the SPE, this indicates that it is not the SPE's parent for accounting purposes.

SIC-12 states that determining whether or not an entity controls an SPE is a matter of judgement on the facts of each case. However, one or more of the circumstances set out in (a) to (d) below may indicate that an entity controls an SPE:[38]

(a)   In substance, the activities of the SPE are being conducted on behalf of the entity according to its specific business needs so that the entity obtains benefits from the SPE's operation. This is particularly likely to be the case where the SPE was directly or indirectly created by the reporting entity. Examples are where the SPE:

   (i)   is principally engaged in providing a source of long-term capital to an entity or funding to support an entity's ongoing major or central operations; or

   (ii)   provides a supply of goods or services that is consistent with an entity's ongoing major or central operations which, without the existence of the SPE, would have to be provided by the entity itself.

   However, economic dependence of an entity on the reporting entity (such as may arise from the relationship of a supplier to a significant customer) does not, by itself, lead to control.

(b)   In substance, the entity has the decision-making powers (including those coming into existence after the formation of the SPE) to obtain the majority of the benefits of the activities of the SPE or, by setting up an 'autopilot' mechanism, the entity has delegated these decision-making powers. Examples of such powers are:

   (i)   power unilaterally to dissolve an SPE; or

   (ii)   power to change, or veto proposed changes to, the SPE's charter or bylaws.

(c)   In substance, the entity has the rights to obtain the majority of the benefits of the SPE and therefore may be exposed to risks incident to the activities of the SPE. These rights may arise through a statute, contract, agreement, or trust deed, or any other scheme, arrangement or device. Such rights to benefits in the SPE may be indicators of control when they are specified in favour of an entity that is engaged in transactions with an SPE and that entity stands to gain those benefits from the financial performance of the SPE. Examples are:

(i)   rights to a majority of any economic benefits distributed by an entity in the form of future net cash flows, earnings, net assets, or other economic benefits; or

(ii)   rights to majority residual interests in scheduled residual distributions or in a liquidation of the SPE.

(d)   In substance, the entity retains the majority of the residual or ownership risks related to the SPE or its assets in order to obtain benefits from its activities. Frequently, the reporting entity guarantees a return or credit protection directly or indirectly through the SPE to outside investors who provide substantially all of the capital to the SPE. As a result of the guarantee, the entity retains residual or ownership risks and the investors are, in substance, only lenders because their exposure to gains and losses is limited. Examples are:

(i)   the capital providers do not have a significant interest in the underlying net assets of the SPE;

(ii)   the capital providers do not have rights to the future economic benefits of the SPE;

(iii)   the capital providers are not substantively exposed to the inherent risks of the underlying net assets or operations of the SPE; or

(iv)   in substance, the capital providers receive mainly consideration equivalent to a lender's return through a debt or equity interest.

A   Securitisation transactions

SPEs are most common, but not unique, to the financial services sector, where they are used as vehicles for securitisation of financial assets such as mortgages or credit card receivables. The effect of SIC-12, combined with the derecognition provisions of IAS 39 – *Financial Instruments: Recognition and Measurement* – may be that:

- a securitisation transaction qualifies as a sale of the financial asset concerned (which is thus, in principle, derecognised, or removed from the financial statements); but

- the 'buyer' is an SPE, so that the asset is immediately re-recognised through consolidation of the SPE.

This is discussed further in Chapter 16 at 4.

3.3   Possible future developments

The IASB is undertaking a project on consolidation that is intended to lead to a new IFRS replacing IAS 27 with significant changes to the criteria for consolidation. This is discussed further at 10 below.

4   REQUIREMENT TO PREPARE CONSOLIDATED FINANCIAL STATEMENTS

IAS 27 requires a parent to prepare consolidated financial statements – i.e. financial statements of a group presented as those of a single economic entity,[39] unless it avails itself the exemption discussed in 4.1 below.[40] The consolidated financial statements of a parent that is an investor in an associate must also comply with IAS 28 (see Chapter 7), and the consolidated financial statements of a parent that is a venturer in a jointly controlled entity must also comply with IAS 31 (see Chapter 8).[41]

4.1   Exemption from preparing consolidated financial statements

A parent need not present consolidated financial statements if and only if:[42]

(a)   the parent is itself a wholly-owned subsidiary, or is a partially-owned subsidiary of another entity and its other owners, including those not otherwise entitled to vote, have been informed about, and do not object to, the parent not presenting consolidated financial statements;

(b)   the parent's debt or equity instruments are not traded in a public market (a domestic or foreign stock exchange or an over-the-counter market, including local and regional markets);

(c)   the parent did not file, nor is it in the process of filing, its financial statements with a securities commission or other regulatory organisation for the purpose of issuing any class of instruments in a public market; and

(d)   the ultimate or any intermediate parent of the parent produces consolidated financial statements available for public use that comply with International Financial Reporting Standards.

Where an entity avails itself of this exemption, it may, but is not required, to prepare separate financial statements (see 7 below) as its only financial statements.[43] If separate financial statements are prepared, however, they must comply with the provisions of IAS 27 for such statements.[44]

The conditions for exemption from preparing consolidated financial statements, although mostly self-explanatory, raise a number of detailed issues of interpretation as follows.

4.1.1 Condition (a) – consent of minority shareholders

IAS 27 requires that, where the parent is itself a partly-owned subsidiary, any minority shareholders are actively informed of the parent's intention not to prepare consolidated financial statements. The minority do not have to give explicit consent – the absence of dissent is sufficient. Interestingly, however, IAS 27 sets no limit on when the minority can register any objection. Thus, in principle, it would be open to a minority to object to a parent's election not to prepare consolidated financial statements not merely at the eleventh hour before the accounts are printed but even after they have been issued. Parents that are partly-owned subsidiaries and wish to take the exemption from preparing consolidated financial statements might therefore be well-advised to obtain explicit written consent from minority shareholders in advance.

IAS 27 also requires all minority owners 'including those not otherwise entitled to vote' to be informed of the parent's intention not to prepare consolidated financial statements. Thus, for example, any the holders of any non-voting preference shares must be notified of, and consent (or not object) to, the entity's intention to take the exemption.

As drafted, the requirement to inform the minority where the parent 'is a partially-owned subsidiary of another entity' is slightly ambiguous, as illustrated by Examples 5.8 and 5.9 below.

Example 5.8:   Minority consent for not preparing consolidated financial statements (1)

A parent wishing to claim the exemption (P) is owned 60% by entity A and 40% by entity B. Entity A and entity B are both wholly-owned by entity C. In this case, in our view, P would not be obliged inform its minority shareholder B of any intention not to prepare consolidated financial statements since, although it is a partly-owned subsidiary of B, it is a wholly-owned subsidiary of C (and therefore satisfies condition (a) without regard to its immediate owners).

Example 5.9:   Minority consent for not preparing consolidated financial statements (2)

The facts are as in Example 5.8 above, except that A and B were both owned by an individual (Mr X). P is not a wholly-owned subsidiary of any other entity, and therefore the rules applicable to partly-owned subsidiaries apply. Thus, it appears that in such a case IAS 27 requires P to inform C of any intention not to prepare consolidated financial statements.

4.1.2 Condition (b) – securities not traded in a public market

The potential source of confusion here is what exactly constitutes a 'public market'. It is clear that, where quoted prices are available for any of the parent's securities on a generally recognised stock exchange, it cannot avoid the requirement to prepare consolidated financial statements. However, what is the position of a parent with securities for which there are no quoted prices but which are occasionally traded, for example on a matched bargain basis, through an exchange (as opposed to by private treaty between individual buyers and sellers)?

It is clear from the Basis for Conclusions for IAS 27 that the IASB regarded conditions (b) and (c) above as linked, in other words that an entity would fall within (c) before falling within (b).[45] It will be seen that condition (c) refers to the filing of financial statements with a securities commission or regulator as a precursor to public listing of securities. In our view, therefore, it may reasonably be inferred that any security that is traded in circumstances where it is necessary to have filed financial statements with a securities commission or regulator should be regarded as 'traded in a public market' for the purposes of condition (b).

4.1.3 Condition (c) – no filing of financial statements for the purpose of listing securities

The difficulties here arise from the less than clear drafting.

Firstly, it is not clear whether the 'financial statements' referred to are only those prepared under IFRS or include those prepared in pursuance of local requirements. In our view, the phrase is intended to mean any financial statements filed in connection with the public trading of securities. This is because the Basis for Conclusions for IAS 27 makes clear the IASB's view that 'that the information needs of users of financial statements of entities whose debt or equity instruments are traded in a public market are best served when investments in subsidiaries, jointly controlled entities and associates are accounted for in accordance with IAS 27, IAS 28 and IAS 31. The Board therefore decided that the exemption from preparing such consolidated financial statements should not be available to such entities or to entities in the process of issuing instruments in a public market.'[46] In other words, the key test is that the entity's securities are, or are about to be, publicly traded.

Secondly, IAS 27 allows an exemption from preparing consolidated financial statements only to an entity that 'did' not file financial statements in connection with the public trading of securities, without any reference to the period to which those financial statements relate. Thus, if read literally, IAS 27 would deny the exemption to any parent that has ever had publicly traded securities, which would include those hundreds of previously listed entities that are now wholly-owned subsidiaries as a result of takeover activity or group reorganisations. This, we suggest, is a nonsense that the IASB cannot have intended. On the other hand, the use of the word 'did' means that, again if read literally, IAS 27 cannot be referring to already filed financial statements for the current period, since an entity that had already prepared its financial statements for the current period would have no reason to be considering IAS 27 in respect of that period. In our view, condition (c) makes sense only if 'did' is regarded as a drafting slip for 'does'. In other words, the test is whether the entity currently has, or shortly will have, an ongoing obligation to file financial statements with a regulator in connection with the public trading of any of its securities.

4.1.4 Condition (d) – IFRS financial statements of parent's parent publicly available

A possible issue here might be whether the exemption can be claimed only where a parent of the parent prepares consolidated financial statements under IFRS that are publicly available through some form of national or regional public filing requirement, or whether it also applies where those consolidated financial statements are available on request.

The disclosure requirements in respect of entities that have taken advantage of the exemption from preparing consolidated financial statements make it clear that either route is acceptable, provided that the source for obtaining the consolidated financial statements of the relevant parent of the parent is disclosed (see 8.2 below).

5. SCOPE OF CONSOLIDATED FINANCIAL STATEMENTS

Consolidated financial statements must include all subsidiaries of the parent, including SPEs (see 3.2 above). However, if on acquisition a subsidiary meets the criteria to be classified as held for sale in accordance with IFRS 5, it is accounted for in accordance with IFRS 5[47] (see Chapter 3 at 5.1). The exemption in the previous version of IAS 27 from consolidating certain subsidiaries held for sale is no longer available.

5.1 Venture capital organisations and similar entities

IAS 27 specifically notes that a subsidiary is not excluded from consolidation simply because the investor is a venture capital organisation, mutual fund, unit trust or similar entity.[48] The intention here is to emphasise that, although certain associates and joint ventures held by such investors are exempt from the general requirements of IAS 28 and IAS 31 (see Chapters 7 and 8), there is no such exemption for investments in subsidiaries under IAS 27.

A number of commentators on the exposure draft of the improved IAS 27 expressed the view that it was inconsistent to allow venture capitalists and similar entities to use fair value accounting for their portfolio investments in associates and joint ventures, but not for their investments in subsidiaries. The IASB rejects this view at some length in the Basis for Conclusions by drawing a clear distinction, in its mind, between investments in controlled entities (i.e. subsidiaries) and those in uncontrolled entities. Essentially, the IASB sees the fact that a subsidiary is controlled as more significant than the fact that it may be held as part of a portfolio of investments, and believes that a consistent accounting approach (i.e. consolidation) should be applied to all controlled entities by all investors, irrespective of their industry, or the strategy for holding the investment.[49]

5.2   Subsidiaries with dissimilar activities

A subsidiary cannot be excluded from consolidation because its business activities are dissimilar from those of the other entities within the group. Instead, relevant information is provided by consolidating such subsidiaries and disclosing additional information in the consolidated financial statements about the different business activities of subsidiaries. IAS 27 clarifies that the disclosures required by IAS 14 – *Segment Reporting* (see Chapter 28) help to explain the significance of different business activities within the group.[50]

5.3   Subsidiaries subject to restrictions

It is noted in the introduction to IAS 27 that an entity is not permitted to exclude from consolidation an entity that it continues to control simply because that entity is operating under severe long-term restrictions that significantly impair its ability to transfer funds to the parent. Control must be lost for exclusion to occur.[51]

In fact, such a requirement does not appear explicitly in the main body of IAS 27, but it is broadly consistent with the fact that the standard notes that a parent loses control when it loses the power to govern the financial and operating policies of an investee so as to obtain benefit from its activities. The loss of control can occur with or without a change in absolute or relative ownership levels. It could occur, for example, when a subsidiary becomes subject to the control of a government, court, administrator or regulator. It could also occur as a result of a contractual agreement.[52]

However, there is a certain lack of clarity as to the IASB's precise intentions here. On the one hand, the previous paragraph suggests that control of a subsidiary is lost (other than through disposal or reduction of ownership) only when a third party actively manages the subsidiary. However, the basic definition of a subsidiary is an entity that is subject to control, defined as the power to govern the financial and operating policies of an entity 'so as to obtain benefits from its activities'. If an investor is unable through exchange controls or other restrictions to obtain any benefits from another entity – even an entity that it owns and manages on a day-to-day basis – is there not an argument that, since the investor is unable 'to obtain benefits from its activities', the investor does not have control of the entity as defined by IAS 27?

Perhaps the distinction that the IASB is intending to draw is between:

- restrictions, that 'significantly impair' the ability of a subsidiary to transfer funds to its parent (which do not result in a loss of control as defined in IAS 27), such as
  - exchange controls, or
  - in the case of a US-registered subsidiary, filing for protection from creditors under Chapter 11 of the United States Bankruptcy Code (and similar arrangements in other jurisdictions), and
- restrictions which completely prevent such transfers (which do result in a loss of control as defined in IAS 27).

6   CONSOLIDATION PROCEDURES

It is beyond the scope of this Chapter to discuss the detailed mechanics of the consolidation process, for which reference should be made to the various specialised texts which give a full exposition of this subject. The analysis below essentially deals only with those areas where IAS 27 prescribes one of a number of possible treatments.

6.1   Basic principles

In preparing consolidated financial statements, an entity first combines the financial statements of the parent and its subsidiaries on a 'line-by-line' basis by adding together like items of assets, liabilities, equity, income and expenses. In order that the consolidated financial statements present financial information about the group as that of a single economic entity, the following adjustments are made:

(a)   the carrying amount of the parent's investment in each subsidiary and the parent's portion of equity of each subsidiary are eliminated. Any difference (representing either goodwill if positive or, if negative, the excess of the acquirer's interest in the net fair value of the acquiree's identifiable assets, liabilities and contingent liabilities over cost) is accounted for in accordance with IFRS 3 (see Chapter 6);

(b)   minority interests (see below) in the profit or loss of consolidated subsidiaries for the reporting period are identified; and

(c)   minority interests in the net assets of consolidated subsidiaries are identified separately from the parent shareholders' equity in them. Minority interests in the net assets consist of:

(i)   the amount of those minority interests at the date of the original combination calculated in accordance with IFRS 3; and

(ii)   the minority's share of changes in equity since the date of the combination.[53]

Minority interest is that portion of the profit or loss and net assets of a subsidiary attributable to equity interests that are not owned, directly or indirectly through subsidiaries, by the parent.[54] The accounting treatment for minority interests is discussed in more detail at 6.7 below.

6.2   Proportion consolidated

As discussed at 3.1.2 above, IAS 27 requires that, where an investor has currently exercisable contingent rights over shares (such as options or conversion rights) in another entity, those rights should be taken into account in determining whether or not the investor controls that other entity.

However, when potential voting rights exist, the proportions of profit or loss and changes in equity allocated to the parent and minority interests are determined on the basis of present ownership interests and do not reflect the possible exercise or conversion of potential voting rights.[55] These provisions are equally applicable to determining what share of an associate or joint venture should be accounted for under, respectively IAS 28 and IAS 31.[56]

The basic principle is illustrated by Example 5.10 below.

Example 5.10:   Potential voting rights (7)

Entities A and B hold 40% and 60% respectively of the equity of Entity C. A also holds a currently exercisable option over one third of B's shares, which, if exercised, would give A a 60% interest in B. This would, absent exceptional circumstances, lead to the conclusion that C was a subsidiary of A. However, in preparing its consolidated financial statements, A would attribute 60% of the results and net assets of C to minority interests.

However, simply to allocate the proportions of profit or loss and changes in equity on the basis of present legal ownership interests might not always be appropriate. This treatment would be appropriate if the options in Example 5.10 above contained one or more of the following features:

- the option price has not yet been determined;
- the option price is based on expected the future results or net assets of the subsidiary at the date of exercise; or
- it has been agreed between A and B that, prior to the exercise of the option, all retained profits may be freely distributed to the existing shareholders according to their current shareholdings.

If, on the other hand, the option price is fixed (or determinable) and it is agreed between the parties that no dividends will be paid to the existing shareholders, it may well be more appropriate to include the minority interests at an amount equivalent to the exercise price under the option.

Accordingly, the implementation guidance to IAS 27 clarifies that in determining the level of present ownership interest, an entity should have regard to the eventual exercise of potential rights and other derivatives that give the entity access to the economic benefits at present.[57] An option with terms such as those in the previous paragraph would, in our view, be such a derivative.

6.2.1   Interaction with IAS 39

Interests in subsidiaries, associates or joint ventures are normally accounted for in accordance with, respectively, IAS 27, IAS 28 and IAS 31, while derivatives over such interests are normally accounted for in accordance with IAS 39 (see Chapter 15 at 3.1). Where, however, the effect of a derivative is taken into account in determining not merely the existence of control (or of significant influence or joint control) but also the share of the investment to be accounted for, it ceases to be within the scope of IAS 39.[58] This is entirely appropriate, since, if IAS 39 continued to be applied, there would clearly be an element of double counting by an entity that accounted both for changes in the fair value of such a derivative under IAS 39 and for the effective interest created by the derivative in the underlying investment under IAS 27, IAS 28 or IAS 31.

6.3 Intragroup eliminations

IAS 27 requires intragroup balances, transactions, income, expenses and dividends to be eliminated in full.[59] Profits and losses resulting from intragroup transactions that are recognised in assets, such as inventory and fixed assets, are eliminated in full.[60]

However, intragroup losses may indicate an impairment that requires recognition in the consolidated financial statements.[61] For example, if one member of a group sells a property to another at a price intended to replicate an arm's-length price which is lower than the carrying value of the asset, the transfer may well indicate that the property is no longer part of a larger cash-generating unit whose value in use is not sensitive to the shortfall in the individual asset's fair value. The property may now be impaired from the perspective of the consolidated financial statements (see Chapter 13).

Moreover, intragroup transactions, although eliminated, may, under IAS 12 – *Income Taxes*, give rise to a tax charge or credit in the consolidated financial statements if they result in a change in the tax base of the item that is the subject of the transaction.[62] This is discussed in Chapter 24 at 5.4.

6.4 Non-coterminous accounting periods

It is implicit in the objective of consolidated financial statements (i.e. that they should be prepared as if the group were a single entity) that the financial statements of the various members of the group incorporated in the consolidated financial statements should cover the same accounting period.

Accordingly, IAS 27 requires the financial statements of the parent and its subsidiaries used in the preparation of the consolidated financial statements to be prepared as at the same reporting date. When the reporting dates of the parent and a subsidiary are different, the subsidiary prepares, for consolidation purposes, additional financial statements as of the same date as the financial statements of the parent unless it is impracticable to do so.[63] IAS 27 does not clarify what is meant by 'impracticable' in this context, but it may reasonably be assumed that the IASB intended the same meaning as in IAS 1 – *Presentation of Financial Statements*, i.e. that the entity cannot comply with the requirement after making every effort to do so[64] (see Chapter 3 at 2.4).

When the financial statements of a subsidiary used in the preparation of consolidated financial statements are prepared as of a reporting date different from that of the parent, adjustments must be made for the effects of significant transactions or events that occur between that date and the date of the parent's financial statements. In any case, the difference between the reporting date of the subsidiary and that of the parent must be no more than three months. The length of the reporting periods and any difference in the reporting dates must be the same from period to period.[65] This implies that where a subsidiary previously consolidated on the basis of non-coterminous financial statements is consolidated using coterminous financial statements, it is necessary to restate comparative information so that financial information in respect of the subsidiary is included in the consolidated financial statements for an equivalent period in each period presented.

IAS 27 requires merely that a non-coterminous accounting period of a subsidiary used for consolidation purposes ends within three months of that of the parent. It is not necessary (as in some current national GAAPs) for such a period to end before that of the parent.

6.5 Consistent accounting policies

The objective that consolidated financial statements should be prepared as if the group were a single entity also implies that the financial statements being aggregated in the consolidation process have been compiled on a consistent basis and, therefore, that uniform accounting policies have been adopted by all the members of the group. Of course, local reporting requirements for each subsidiary might dictate that different policies must be used for domestic purposes. Where this occurs it is necessary to ensure that appropriate adjustments are made in the course of the consolidation process to eliminate the effects of such differences.

IAS 27 requires consolidated financial statements to be prepared using uniform accounting policies for like transactions and other events in similar circumstances.[66] Accordingly, if a member of the group uses accounting policies other than those adopted in the consolidated financial statements for like transactions and events in similar circumstances, appropriate adjustments must be made to its financial statements in preparing the consolidated financial statements.[67]

6.6 Date of commencement and cessation of consolidation

It is inherent in the definition of a subsidiary (i.e. an entity controlled by the parent) that it should be consolidated from the date on which the parent first achieves control to the date on which control is lost. The determination of the date of acquisition (i.e. the date on which control is first obtained) is discussed in IFRS 3 (see Chapter 6 at 2.3).

IAS 27 notes that the income and expenses of a subsidiary are included from the date of acquisition until the date on which the parent ceases to control the subsidiary.[68] This also applies to a subsidiary held for sale accounted for under IFRS 5 (see Chapter 3 at 5.1).

When a subsidiary is disposed of, a gain or loss on disposal is recognised in the income statement comprising the difference between any proceeds on disposal of the subsidiary and its carrying amount (i.e. net assets and recognised goodwill) as at the date of disposal, including the cumulative amount of any exchange differences relating to the subsidiary that have previously been recognised in equity in accordance with IAS 21 – *The Effects of Foreign Exchange Rates*[69] (see Chapter 9 at 2.7.3 and 6.6.1 below).

6.6.1 Cumulative exchange gains and losses

IAS 27 requires cumulative foreign exchange differences relating to subsidiaries to be 'recycled' in the income statement only on a disposal of the investment in the subsidiary. IAS 21 clarifies that disposal of a foreign operation may occur through sale, liquidation, repayment of share capital, abandonment or receipt of a dividend out of pre-acquisition profits (see 7.2.1 below). When a partial disposal occurs, only the proportionate share of the related accumulated exchange difference is included in profit or loss.

IAS 21 further clarifies that a write-down of a foreign operation does not constitute a partial disposal, and accordingly no part of the deferred foreign exchange gain or loss is recognised in profit or loss at the time of the such a write-down,[70] unless of course the write-down is consequent upon an event of 'disposal' as described in the previous paragraph. Moreover, it is implicit in the requirement of IFRS 5 for separate disclosure of cumulative gains and losses recognised in equity relating to a disposal group (see Chapter 3 at 3.1.2) that the classification of a subsidiary as held for sale under IFRS 5 does not give rise to recycling of foreign exchange differences.

However, the IASB may be proposing significant changes in this area as part of its Business Combinations (Phase II) project (see B below)

A   *Other cumulative gains and losses previously recognised in equity*

IAS 27 does not specifically address the accounting treatment, on disposal of a subsidiary, of other cumulative gains and losses previously accounted for in equity relating to assets and liabilities of the disposed subsidiary that would, if those assets and liabilities had been disposed of separately, been recycled in profit or loss. These could include:

- accumulated hedging gains and losses accounted for under IAS 39 (see Chapter 19); and

- any other amounts previously recognised in equity that would have been recognised in profit or loss if the group had directly disposed of the assets to which they relate, such as gains or losses on available-for-sale financial assets accounted for under IAS 39 (see Chapter 18 at 3.2).

IAS 39 does not specifically address this issue either. However, it would appear that recycling is appropriate, since the disposal of a subsidiary does give rise to the derecognition of the separate assets and liabilities of that subsidiary just as if they had been disposed of separately. Moreover, the IASB's discussions on possible amendments to IAS 27 (see B below) appear to assume that it is clear that such gains and losses should be recycled on disposal of a subsidiary.

B   Possible future developments

As part of its Business Combinations (Phase II) project, the IASB has tentatively agreed to amend IAS 21 and IAS 39 so as to require that, when control of a subsidiary is lost, the following gains or losses previously recognised in equity, should be recognised in profit or loss:

- foreign exchange differences recognised in equity under IAS 21;

- accumulated hedging gains and losses recognised in equity under IAS 39 (see Chapter 19); and

- any other amounts previously recognised in equity that would have been recognised in profit or loss if the group had directly disposed of the assets to which they relate, such as gains or losses on available-for-sale financial assets accounted for under IAS 39 (see Chapter 18 at 3.2).

The IASB intends to require that the entire amount of such gains and losses should be 'recycled' on a loss of control, even if the reporting entity still has an investment in its former subsidiary (including an investment accounted for as an associate or joint venture). The IASB notes that 'this is the only approach that is consistent with the Board's previous conclusion that any remaining investment should be recognised at its fair value when control of the former subsidiary is lost'[71] – this point is illustrated by the discussion at 6.6.2 A below.

6.6.2   *Group investment ceasing to be subsidiary*

Where an investment ceases to be a subsidiary, and does not become either an associate as defined in IAS 28 (see Chapter 7) or a joint venture as defined in IAS 31 (see Chapter 8), it must be accounted for in accordance with IAS 39.[72]

The measurement rules in IAS 39 are complex and discussed in detail in Chapter 18. In brief, however, they will entail the former subsidiary being recorded initially at 'cost' (which is deemed to be its carrying amount on the date that it ceases to be a subsidiary)[73] and then classified as either a 'financial asset at fair value through profit or loss' or an 'available-for-sale' financial asset. In either case, the investment will be measured at fair value – what differs is whether the gains and losses arising on revaluation are accounted for in the income statement or in equity.

A   Cumulative exchange differences on former subsidiaries

As noted above, IAS 27 requires the cost of an investment formerly a subsidiary to be treated as its 'carrying amount', which excludes, in the case of a foreign subsidiary, the cumulative amount of any exchange differences relating to the subsidiary that have previously been recognised in equity in accordance with IAS 21. This begs the question of how such differences are to be dealt with. The question is only one of time – it is clearly a fundamental principle of IAS 21, IAS 27 and IAS 39 that such differences must at some point be recognised in the income statement.

In our view, the provisions of IAS 21 summarised in 6.6.1 above indicate that cumulative foreign exchange differences are 'recycled' only when the reporting entity's interest in the relevant investment is disposed of, not when its status changes (e.g. because of changes in the relative voting powers of the owners of the investment). However, this does create the slight anomaly in the case of a former subsidiary which is to be accounted for as 'at fair value through profit or loss' that some part of the gains or losses related to that subsidiary will have been accounted for in equity, and not in profit or loss, until ultimate disposal of the investment.

However, as noted at 6.6.1 B above, the IASB may be proposing significant changes in this area as part of its Business Combinations (Phase II) project.

6.7　Minority interests

IAS 27 requires minority interests to be presented in the consolidated balance sheet within equity, separately from the parent shareholders' equity. Minority interests in the profit or loss of the group must also be separately disclosed.[74] The profit or loss is attributed to the parent shareholders and minority interests (see also 6.1 above). Because the interest of parent shareholders and minority interests are both equity, the amount attributed to minority interests is not income or expense.[75]

This requirement caused one member of the IASB (Tatsumi Yamada) to dissent from the improved version of IAS 27. The main grounds for Mr Yamada's dissent were a concern that this presentation effectively pre-empts the outcome of the IASB's broader debate as to whether to require the entity model or the parent company model (see 1.4 above) for consolidated financial statements, and should not therefore be mandated until that debate has been concluded.[76]

6.7.1　*Interaction with IAS 32*

Notwithstanding the requirement of IAS 27 to treat minority interests as equity, there are some circumstances – essentially where the minority have a claim on the group more akin to that of a creditor than that of an equity shareholder – where minority interests are required to be classified as financial liabilities (and payments to them as interest expense) by IAS 32 – *Financial Instruments: Disclosure and Presentation.* This is discussed further in Chapter 17 at 3.6.

6.7.2　*Loss-making subsidiaries*

Where losses attributable to the minority in a consolidated subsidiary exceed the minority interest in the subsidiary's equity, the excess, and any further losses applicable to the minority, are allocated against the majority interest except to the extent that the minority has a binding obligation, and is able, to make an additional investment to cover the losses. If the subsidiary subsequently reports profits, such profits are allocated to the majority interest until the minority's share of losses previously absorbed by the majority has been recovered.[77]

This treatment, sometimes referred to as 'waterline accounting', is illustrated by Example 5.11 below.

Example 5.11:   Minority interest in loss-making subsidiary ('waterline accounting')

The reporting entity (P) sets up a subsidiary (S) with another party (M). P owns 70%, and M 30%, of the equity, and the terms of the arrangement are such that S is a subsidiary of P (rather than a joint venture of P and M), and M has no obligation to make additional investment to cover any losses.

The initial investment of the parties is €700,000 by P and €300,000 by M. Further finance is provided by way of a bank loan. The first five years' results of S are as follows.

Year	Profit/(loss) (€)	Shareholders' equity (€)
0		1,000,000
1	(700,000)	300,000
2	(800,000)	(500,000)
3	400,000	(100,000)
4	500,000	400,000
5	750,000	1,150,000

The allocation of each year's result between P and M would be as follows.

Year	Profit/(loss) (€)	P's share of result (€)	P's share of net equity (€)	M's share of result (€)	M's share of net equity (€)
0			700,000		300,000
1	(700,000)	(490,000)	210,000	(210,000)	90,000
2	(800,000)	(710,000)	(500,000)	(90,000)	–
3	400,000	400,000	(100,000)	–	–
4	500,000	380,000	280,000	120,000	120,000
5	750,000	525,000	805,000	225,000	345,000

In year 1 the loss does not reduce shareholders' equity to zero, and is therefore allocated 70/30 according the relative shareholdings of P and M. By year 2 the cumulative losses of €1,500,000 are greater than P's and M's initial investment, so that the share of the loss allocated to M is restricted to the amount needed to write its investment down to zero, with the balance of the loss being borne by P. In year 3, the profit is insufficient to return the shareholders' equity of S to more than zero, so that P takes credit for the full profit. At the end of year 4, shareholders' equity, though less than P's and M's initial investment, is €400,000, of which M's 30% share is €120,000. Accordingly, M's share of the year 4 profit is restricted to €120,000. In year 5, P and M once more participate in the result according to their relative shareholdings.

6.7.3   Cumulative preference shares held by minority interests

If a subsidiary has outstanding cumulative preference shares that are held by minority interests and classified as equity, the parent is required to compute its share of profits or losses after adjusting for the dividends on such shares, whether or not dividends have been declared.[78]

7 SEPARATE FINANCIAL STATEMENTS

7.1 What are 'separate financial statements'?

IAS 27 defines 'separate financial statements' as those presented by a parent, an investor in an associate or a venturer in a jointly controlled entity, in which the investments are accounted for on the basis of the direct equity interest rather than on the basis of the reported results and net assets of the investees.[79] It follows from this definition that the financial statements of an entity that does not have a subsidiary, associate or joint venture are not 'separate financial statements'.[80]

As noted in 4 above, the consolidated financial statements of a parent that is an investor in an associate must also comply with IAS 28 and the consolidated financial statements of a parent that is a venturer in a jointly controlled entity must also comply with IAS 31. Any other financial statements prepared by such a parent are separate financial statements.[81] There is no requirement for such a parent to prepare separate financial statements, or for any separate financial statements that are voluntarily prepared to be appended to, or accompany, the consolidated financial statements.[82]

The IASB takes the view that the needs of users of financial statements are fully met by requiring entities to consolidate subsidiaries, equity account for associates, and proportionately consolidate or equity account for jointly controlled entities. However, it is recognised that entities with subsidiaries, associates or joint ventures may wish, or may be required by local law, to present financial statements in which their investments are accounted for simply as equity investments.[83]

Accordingly, IFRS does not require the preparation of separate financial statements. However, where an investor with subsidiaries, associates or joint ventures does prepare separate financial statements purporting to comply with IFRS, they must be prepared in accordance with IAS 27.[84]

7.1.1 Practical implications

As noted above, IAS 27:

(a) requires consolidated financial statements of a parent that is also an investor in an associate or a venturer in a jointly controlled entity to comply with IAS 28 and/or IAS 31;

(b) defines separate financial statements as those presented by a parent, an investor in an associate or a venturer in a jointly controlled entity, in which the investments are accounted for on the basis of the direct equity interest rather than on the basis of the reported results and net assets of the investees.

This has the effect that a parent cannot prepare financial statements in purported compliance with IFRS in which subsidiaries are consolidated, but associates and joint ventures are not accounted for under, respectively, IAS 28 and IAS 31 but on some other basis (e.g. at cost). Financial statements prepared such a basis would be neither consolidated financial statements (because of the failure to apply IAS 28 and IAS 31) nor separate financial statements (because of the failure to account for subsidiaries on the basis of the direct equity interest).

Moreover, 'separate financial statements' as defined in IAS 27 are not, other than by coincidence, equivalent to what is meant in some jurisdictions by terms such as 'single entity accounts', 'solus accounts', 'parent entity accounts', 'entity-only accounts', 'stand-alone accounts', which are used to refer to the accounts of an entity other than its consolidated accounts.

The main difference arises from the fact that, in some national GAAPs, investors that have no subsidiaries (and therefore do not prepare consolidated accounts), but do have associates or joint ventures, are not required to account for their share of the profits and net assets of associates or joint ventures in their 'single entity accounts'.

By contrast, as discussed further in Chapters 7 and 8, IFRS may well require an investor in an associate, or a venturer jointly controlled entity, to account for its share of the net assets and profits of its investee even though it is not preparing consolidated financial statements. Such non-consolidated financial statements prepared by an investor in an associate or a venturer in a jointly controlled entity include the investment in the associate or joint venture on the basis of the reported results and net assets of the investment, and are thus *not* 'separate financial statements' as defined in IAS 27 (see definition above).

7.2   Requirements for separate financial statements

In separate financial statements, investments in subsidiaries, associates and joint ventures that are classified as held for sale (or included in a disposal group that is classified as held for sale) in accordance with IFRS 5 are accounted for in accordance with IFRS 5 (see Chapter 3 at 5.1).[85]

All other investments are accounted for either at cost (see 7.2.1 below) or in accordance with IAS 39 (see 7.2.2 below). The previously allowed use of equity accounting in separate financial statements is no longer permitted. Each 'category' of investments must be accounted for consistently.[86] While 'category' is not defined, we take this to mean, for example, that, while all subsidiaries must be accounted for at cost or in accordance with IAS 39, it would be permissible (if perhaps rather strange) to account for all subsidiaries at cost and all associates under IAS 39.

Where an investment in a subsidiary, associate or jointly controlled entity is accounted for in accordance with IAS 39 in the consolidated financial statements, it must also be accounted for in accordance with IAS 39 in the separate financial statements.[87] In fact, following the amendments to IAS 27 by IFRS 3 and IFRS 5, there appear to be no circumstances in which an investment in a *subsidiary* (as opposed to an investment formerly treated as a subsidiary) is accounted for in accordance with IAS 39 in consolidated financial statements. The circumstances in which investments in associates or jointly controlled entities are accounted for in accordance with IAS 39 in consolidated financial statements are discussed in, respectively, Chapter 7 at 2.1 and Chapter 8 at 2.1.

Whilst IAS 27 does not say so explicitly, it seems clear that not only must such investments be accounted for in accordance with IAS 39 in both the consolidated and separate financial statements, but they must also follow the same accounting model in IAS 39. In other words, the same investment cannot be treated as a 'financial asset at fair value through profit or loss' in one set of financial statements and as an 'available-for-sale financial asset' in the other.

7.2.1 Cost method

IAS 27 describes the cost method as 'a method of accounting for an investment whereby the investment is recognised at cost. The investor recognises income from the investment only to the extent that the investor receives distributions from accumulated profits of the investee arising after the date of acquisition. Distributions received in excess of such profits are regarded as a recovery of investment and are recognised as a reduction of the cost of the investment.'[88]

This raises the following issues of interpretation:

- the meaning of 'cost' (see A below); and

- the meaning of 'profits ... arising after the date of acquisition' in the context of the treatment of dividend income (see B below).

A   Cost of investment

IAS 27 does not define what is meant by 'cost'. As discussed further in Chapter 3 at 4.3, IAS 8 – *Accounting Policies, Changes in Estimates and Errors* – requires that, in the absence of specific guidance in IFRS, management should first refer to the requirements and guidance in IFRS dealing with similar and related issues. The obvious point of reference would be IAS 32 and IAS 39. Investments in subsidiaries, associates and joint ventures, while outside the scope of IAS 32 and IAS 39, are clearly financial assets (and therefore financial instruments) as defined in those standards.

IAS 39 requires financial assets to be initially recognised at fair value together with directly attributable transaction costs (see Chapter 18 at 2). This is also consistent with the approach required by IFRS for the initial recognition and measurement of non-monetary assets such as PPE and intangible assets.

I   Investments acquired for shares or other equity instruments

A transaction in which an investment in a subsidiary, associate or joint venture is acquired in exchange for an issue of shares or other equity instruments is not specifically addressed under IFRS, since it falls outside the scope of both IAS 39 (see above) and IFRS 2 – *Share-based Payment* (see Chapter 29 at 2.2.3).

Moreover, IFRS has no general requirements for accounting of the issue of equity instruments. Rather, consistent with the position taken by the *Framework* that equity is a residual rather than an item 'in its own right', the amount of an equity instrument is normally measured by reference to the item (expense or asset) in consideration for which the equity is issued, as determined in accordance with IFRS applicable to that other item. Again, however, we believe that it would be appropriate, by analogy with

IFRS on related areas, to account for such a transaction at the fair value of the investment acquired (together with directly attributable acquisition costs).

In some jurisdictions, local law may permit investments acquired for an issue of shares to be recorded at a notional value (for example, the nominal value of the shares issued). In our view, this is not an appropriate measure of cost under IFRS.

B   'Pre-acquisition' profits

As noted above, IAS 27 requires distributions received in excess of profits arising after the date of acquisition (sometimes referred to as dividends out of 'pre-acquisition' profits) to be regarded as a recovery of the investment and therefore accounted for as a reduction of the cost of the investment.

The underlying principle is clear – namely that if an investor receives income in the form of a dividend of 'pre-acquisition' profits, in reality that 'income' is no more than a return of some part of the initial investment. However, the drafting of IAS 27 creates potential difficulties by referring specifically to distributions in excess of post-acquisition *profits*, since situations arise under IFRS where:

- expenses are recognised in the income statement, with a corresponding credit to equity (such that the expense does not represent a reduction in the investor's initial investment); or

- income is recognised directly in equity (such that there is an increase in the investor's initial investment, but no corresponding increase in accumulated profits).

In either case, the investee may be in a position to make distributions that are in excess of its post-acquisition profits, at least as recognised in the income statement, without any economic reduction in the investor's investment.

For example, if an investee enters into an equity-settled share-based payment transaction as defined in IFRS 2, IFRS 2 requires the investee to account for the transaction by recording a charge in the income statement with a corresponding credit to equity (see Chapter 29 at 4). In some jurisdictions, the credit will be made to a component of equity comprising part of the entity's distributable reserves, so that the accounting entry will have no overall effect on either the profits available for distribution or the net worth of the investee.

Moreover, if the investee receives tax relief on the share-based payment transaction, IAS 12 may require some element of that tax relief to be credited directly to equity (see Chapter 24 at 6.3). In some jurisdictions, such tax relief will increase distributable profits. Thus, the increase in the investee's post-acquisition distributable reserves may exceed its post-acquisition reported profits.

Another example might be where the investee has adopted a policy of revaluing PPE under IAS 16 – *Property, Plant and Equipment* (see Chapter 12 at 2.4.1). Under IAS 16 any gains on revaluation are recorded in equity and never subsequently recycled through the income statement. In some jurisdictions, however, the revaluation gains may become realised (and hence available for distribution) as the assets to which they relate are sold or consumed in the business. Some of these realised gains may relate to revaluation gains that have arisen since the acquisition of the subsidiary. Thus, again, the increase in the investee's post-acquisition distributable reserves may exceed its post-acquisition reported profits.

If the investee were to pay a dividend equivalent to the post-acquisition increase in its distributable reserves in such cases, it would not in any sense represent a return of the investor's initial investment. However, IAS 27 as drafted requires any excess over reported profits to be treated as such. In our view, entities must adopt some pragmatism in applying the cost method. We suggest that it remains within the spirit and intention of IAS 27 for an investor to treat dividends representing a post-acquisition increase in the net assets of an investee (other than one arising from further investment by the investor) as income whether or not that increase was accounted for as a profit by the investee.

Equally, it would, in our view, be inappropriate for a parent to regard as income a dividend paid out of a post-acquisition reported profit of a subsidiary that in fact represents the 'recycling' of a pre-acquisition gain previously recognised in equity. This means that gains and losses held in equity as at the date of acquisition and reflected in the acquiree's fair value must be taken into account in calculating the accumulated pre- and post-acquisition profits.

The accounting treatment currently applied under some national GAAPs is to treat all dividends from an investment as income and then, as a separate exercise, to determine whether or not the investment has been impaired as a result. Even where dividends are received out of 'pre-acquisition' profits, it might be possible to conclude that the investment is not impaired because it is worth at least its carrying amount, for example as the result of a post-acquisition increase in the goodwill of the investment, which is not recognised in its financial statements under IFRS.

IAS 27 does not permit this treatment, but requires all dividends of 'pre-acquisition' profits to be treated as a reduction in the cost of investment. This approach is arguably not consistent with the treatment of goodwill under IFRS 3, which effectively, albeit not explicitly, permits reductions in the value of acquired goodwill to be offset by new goodwill arising after the acquisition.[89]

7.2.2   IAS 39 method

The measurement rules in IAS 39 are complex and discussed in detail in Chapter 18. In brief, however, they will entail the subsidiary being recorded initially at cost and then classified as either a 'financial asset at fair value through profit or loss' or an 'available-for-sale financial asset'. In either case, the investment will be measured at fair value. However, the gains and losses arising on periodic remeasurement are accounted for:

- in the case of a financial asset at fair value through profit or loss, in the income statement; and

- in the case of an available-for-sale financial asset, in equity.

8   DISCLOSURE

8.1   Consolidated financial statements

The following disclosures are required in consolidated financial statements:[90]

(a)   the nature of the relationship between the parent and a subsidiary when the parent does not own, directly or indirectly through subsidiaries, more than half of the voting power;

(b)   the reasons why the ownership, directly or indirectly through subsidiaries, of more than half of the voting or potential voting power of an investee does not constitute control;

(c)   where the reporting date or period of the financial statements of a subsidiary used to prepare consolidated financial statements is different from the reporting date or period of the parent:

(i)   the reporting date of that subsidiary's financial statements; and

(ii)   the reason for using a different reporting date or period; and

(d)   the nature and extent of any significant restrictions (e.g. resulting from borrowing arrangements or regulatory requirements) on the ability of subsidiaries to transfer funds to the parent in the form of cash dividends or to repay loans or advances.

8.2   Separate financial statements prepared by parent electing not to prepare consolidated financial statements

When separate financial statements are prepared for a parent that, in accordance with the exemption discussed at 4 above, elects not to prepare consolidated financial statements, those separate financial statements shall disclose:[91]

(a)   the fact that the financial statements are separate financial statements;

(b)   that the exemption from consolidation has been used;

(c)   the name and country of incorporation or residence of the entity whose consolidated financial statements that comply with International Financial Reporting Standards have been produced for public use and the address where those consolidated financial statements are obtainable;

(d)   a list of significant investments in subsidiaries, jointly controlled entities and associates, including for each such investment its:

(i)   name;

(ii)   country of incorporation or residence; and

(iii)   proportion of ownership interest and, if different, proportion of voting power held; and

(e)   a description of the method used to account for the investments listed under (d).

These disclosures are given only where the parent has taken advantage of the exemption from preparing consolidated financial statements. Where the parent has not taken advantage of the exemption, and also prepares separate financial statements, it gives the disclosures in 8.3 below in respect of those separate financial statements.

8.3 Separate financial statements prepared by an entity other than a parent electing not to prepare consolidated financial statements

As drafted, IAS 27 requires these disclosures to be given by:

- a parent preparing separate financial statements in addition to consolidated financial statements (i.e. whether or not it is required to prepare consolidated financial statements – the disclosures in 8.2 apply only when the parent has actually taken advantage of the exemption, not merely when it is eligible to do so), and

- an entity (not being a parent) that is an investor in an associate or a venturer in joint venture in respect of any separate financial statements that it prepares, i.e. whether:

  (i)   as its only financial statements (if permitted by IAS 28 or IAS 31), or

  (ii)   in addition to financial statements in which the results and net assets of associates or joint ventures are included.

  However, the relevance of certain of these disclosures to financial statements falling within (i) above is not immediately obvious – see 8.3.1 below.

Where an entity is both a parent and either an investor in an associate or a venturer in a joint venture, it should follow the disclosure requirements governing parents – in other words, it complies with the disclosures in 8.2 above if electing not to prepare consolidated financial statements and otherwise with the disclosures below.

Separate financial statements prepared by an entity other than a parent electing not to prepare consolidated financial must disclose:[92]

(a)   the fact that the statements are separate financial statements and the reasons why those statements are prepared if not required by law;

(b)   a list of significant investments in subsidiaries, jointly controlled entities and associates, including for including for each such investment its:

  (i)   name;

  (ii)   country of incorporation or residence; and

  (iii) proportion of ownership interest and, if different, proportion of voting power held; and

(c)   a description of the method used to account for the investments listed under (b).

The separate financial statements must also identify the financial statements prepared in accordance with the requirements of paragraph 9 of IAS 27 (requirement to prepare consolidated financial statements), IAS 28 and IAS 31 to which they relate.[93] In other words, they must draw attention to the fact that the entity also prepares consolidated financial statements or, as the case may be, financial statements in which the results and net assets of associates or joint ventures are included.

8.3.1 Entities with no subsidiaries but exempt from applying IAS 28 or IAS 31

Entities which have no subsidiaries, but which have investments in associates or jointly controlled entities are permitted by IAS 28 and IAS 31 to prepare separate financial statements as their only financial statements if they satisfy criteria broadly similar to those in 4 above (see Chapter 7 at 2.3 and Chapter 8 at 2.3).

As drafted IAS 27 requires such entities make the disclosures above, even though some of them are nonsensical – in particular the requirement to identify the 'full' financial statements (which, under the exemptions in IAS 28 and IAS 31, are not required to be prepared) to which the separate financial statements relate. It would be far more relevant for entities with no subsidiaries that qualify for the exemptions in IAS 28 and IAS 31 to be required to make disclosures equivalent to those in 8.2 above. On the face of it, this appears to be a drafting error by the IASB.

9   TRANSITIONAL AND FIRST FIRST-TIME ADOPTION ISSUES

As noted at 2 above, IAS 27 must be applied for accounting periods beginning on or after 1 January 2005. Entities are encouraged to adopt the revised version of IAS 27 for earlier periods, but must disclose that they have done so.[94]

There are no transitional provisions, so that an existing IFRS user must apply the revised version of IAS 27 with full retrospective effect. The main differences from the current version of IAS 27 (which may give rise to retrospective restatement of prior periods under IAS 8) are summarised at 2 above.

For first-time adopters of IFRS, IFRS 1 – *First-time Adoption of International Financial Reporting Standards*, together with its implementation guidance, identifies a number of issues in relation to IAS 27, as discussed below.

A first-time adopter that is a parent must consolidate all subsidiaries that it controls, unless IAS 27 'requires' otherwise.[95] Despite this wording, we presume that it is acceptable for a first-time adopter to avail itself of the exemption in IAS 27 from preparing consolidated financial statements (see 4 above), even though the use of this exemption is merely permitted, and not 'required', by IAS 27.

9.1 Subsidiaries consolidated for the first time on first-time adoption

First-time adoption of IFRS may result in the consolidation for the first time of a subsidiary not consolidated under previous GAAP, either because the subsidiary was not regarded as such under previous GAAP, or because the parent did not prepare consolidated financial statements under previous GAAP. In that case, the first time adopter should recognise the assets and liabilities of that subsidiary in its consolidated financial statements at the date of transition at either:

(a)   if the subsidiary prepares financial statements in accordance with IFRS, the amounts at which they are recorded in the subsidiary's financial statements; or

(b)   if the subsidiary does not prepare financial statements in accordance with IFRS, the amounts at which they would be recorded if it did so,

in either case after adjusting for consolidation procedures and for the effects of the business combination in which the subsidiary was acquired.[96]

If the newly-consolidated subsidiary was acquired in a business combination before the date of the parent's transition to IFRS, it calculates goodwill as the difference between the carrying amount determined under either (a) or (b) above and the cost in the parent's separate financial statements of its investment in the subsidiary.[97] 'Goodwill' calculated on this basis is no more than a pragmatic 'plug' in order to facilitate the consolidation process and does not represent the true goodwill that might have been recorded if IFRS had been applied at the date of the original business combination. IFRS 1 provides further guidance on this, which is discussed in Chapter 6 at 4.2.

If the parent did not acquire the subsidiary, but established it, it does not recognise goodwill.[98] Any difference between the carrying amount of the subsidiary and the separable net assets as determined in (a) or (b) above would be treated as an adjustment to equity, representing the accumulated profits or losses that would have been recognised had the subsidiary been consolidated *ab initio*.

9.2 Subsidiaries consolidated under previous GAAP

IFRS 1 contains extensive exemptions from the requirement to apply the provisions of IFRS 3 to subsidiaries already consolidated under previous GAAP. These are discussed in more detail in Chapter 4 at 2.4 and Chapter 6 at 4.2.

IFRS 1 reminds first-time adopters that adjustments to the assets and liabilities of consolidated subsidiaries may well require consequential adjustments to minority interests and deferred tax.[99]

9.3   Parents and subsidiaries and with different dates of adoption of IFRS

IFRS 1 contains quite extensive guidance on the approach to be adopted where a parent adopts IFRS before its subsidiary (see 9.3.1 below) and where a subsidiary adopts IFRS before its parent (see 9.3.2 below). These provisions also apply when IFRS is adopted at different dates by:

- an investor in an associate and the associate; or

- a venturer in a jointly controlled entity and the jointly controlled entity.[100]

In the discussion that follows 'parent' should be therefore read as including an investor in an associate or a venturer in a jointly controlled entity, and 'subsidiary' as including an associate or a jointly controlled entity. Additionally, references to consolidation adjustments should be read as including similar adjustments made when applying equity accounting (see Chapter 7) or proportionate consolidation (see Chapter 8).

IFRS 1 also addresses the requirements for a parent that adopts IFRS at different dates for the purposes of its consolidated and its separate financial statements (see 9.3.3 below).

More discussion of these aspects of first-time adoption may be found in Chapter 4 at 2.7.5.

9.3.1   *Subsidiary adopting IFRS after parent*

If a subsidiary becomes a first-time adopter later than its parent, IFRS 1 allows the subsidiary, in its financial statements, to measure its assets and liabilities at either:

(a)   the carrying amounts that would be included in the parent's consolidated financial statements, based on the parent's date of transition to IFRS, if no adjustments were made for consolidation procedures and for the effects of the business combination in which the parent acquired the subsidiary; or

(b)   the carrying amounts otherwise required by IFRS 1 (see Chapter 4), based on the subsidiary's date of transition to IFRS. These carrying amounts could differ from those in (a) above when:

   (i)   the exemptions in IFRS 1 result in measurements that depend on the date of transition to IFRS (see Chapter 4); or

   (ii)   the accounting policies used in the subsidiary's financial statements differ from those in the consolidated financial statements. For example, in accounting for PPE, the subsidiary may use the cost model in IAS 16, whereas the group may use the revaluation model.[101]

Example 5.12 illustrates the effect of these provisions.[102]

Example 5.12:   Subsidiary adopting IFRS after parent

A parent (P) presents its first consolidated IFRS financial statements in 2005. Its foreign subsidiary (S), wholly-owned since its formation, prepares information under IFRS for internal consolidation purposes from that date, but S does not present its (separate) first IFRS financial statements until the year ended 31 December 2007.

If S adopts alternative (a) above, the carrying amounts of its assets and liabilities are the same in both S's (separate) opening IFRS balance sheet at 1 January 2006 and P's consolidated balance sheet (except for adjustments for consolidation procedures) and are based on P's date of transition to IFRS.

Alternatively, S may, under alternative (b) above, measure all its assets or liabilities based on its own date of transition to IFRS (1 January 2006). However, the fact that S becomes a first-time adopter in 2007 does not change the carrying amounts of S's assets and liabilities in P's consolidated financial statements.

For the purposes of the reconciliation disclosures required by a first-time adopter (see Chapter 4 at 2.10.2 A), a subsidiary cannot ignore previous misstatements that are material to its own financial statements, even if they are not material to the consolidated financial statements of its parent.[103]

A   Subsidiaries preparing consolidation reporting packs under IFRS

A subsidiary may have prepared a reporting pack for consolidation purposes either in full compliance with IFRS, or in compliance with IFRS but subject to central adjustments. In either case, the subsidiary is not regarded as having adopted IFRS – it does so only when it first presents full financial statements with an explicit and unreserved statement of compliance with IFRS as required by IFRS 1 (see Chapter 4 at 2.2.1). For the purposes of the reconciliation disclosures required by a first-time adopter (see Chapter 4 at 2.10.2 A), central adjustments made to consolidation packs, such as post-balance sheet events and the allocation of pension costs, are not regarded as corrections of errors.[104]

9.3.2   Parent adopting IFRS after its subsidiary

If a parent becomes a first-time adopter later than its subsidiary, IFRS 1 requires the parent, in its consolidated financial statements, to measure the assets and liabilities of the subsidiary at the same carrying amounts as in the separate financial statements of the subsidiary, after adjusting for consolidation adjustments and for the effects of the business combination in which the entity acquired the subsidiary.[105]

Example 5.13 illustrates the effect of these provisions.[106]

Example 5.13:   Parent adopting IFRS after subsidiary

A parent (P) presents its first consolidated IFRS financial statements in 2007. Its foreign subsidiary S, wholly-owned by P since formation, presented its first (separate) IFRS financial statements in the year ended 31 December 2005. Until 2007, S prepares information for internal consolidation purposes under parent P's previous GAAP.

The carrying amounts of S's assets and liabilities at 1 January 2006 are the same in both parent P's (consolidated) opening IFRS balance sheet and S's separate financial statements (except for adjustments for consolidation procedures) and are based on S's date of transition to IFRSs (1 January 2004). The fact that P becomes a first-time adopter in 2007 does not change those carrying amounts.

IFRS 1 does not elaborate on exactly what constitute 'consolidation adjustments' but in our view it would encompass adjustments required in order to harmonise S's accounting policies with those of P as well as purely 'mechanical' consolidation adjustments such as the elimination of intragroup balances, profits and losses.

9.3.3   Parent adopting IFRS at different dates in consolidated and separate financial statements

If a parent becomes a first-time adopter for its separate financial statements earlier or later than for its consolidated financial statements, it must measure its assets and liabilities at the same amounts in both financial statements, except for consolidation adjustments.[107] As drafted, the requirement is merely that the 'same' basis be used, without being explicit as to which set of financial statements should be used as the benchmark. However, it seems clear from the context that the IASB intends that the measurement basis used in whichever set of financial statements first comply with IFRS must also be used when IFRS are subsequently adopted in the other set.

9.3.4   Interaction with other requirements of IFRS 1

The implementation guidance to IFRS 1 clarifies that the provisions summarised in 9.3.1 to 9.3.3 above do not override the following requirements of IFRS 1:[108]

- the business combinations exemption in Appendix B to IFRS 1 (see Chapter 4 at 2.4) applies in respect of assets and liabilities of a subsidiary acquired and assumed in a business combination that occurred before the parent's date of transition to IFRS. The rules summarised in 9.3.2 above (parent adopting IFRS after subsidiary) apply only to assets and liabilities acquired and assumed by the subsidiary after the business combination and still held and owed by it at the parent's date of transition to IFRS;

- the requirements in IFRS 1 other than the provisions summarised in 9.3.1 to 9.3.3 above apply in full to assets and liabilities to which those provisions are not relevant; and

- a first-time adopter must give all the disclosures required by IFRS 1 as of its own date of transition to IFRS.

10 POSSIBLE FUTURE DEVELOPMENTS

The IASB is engaged on two projects that will affect the accounting treatment of subsidiaries:

- Business Combinations (Phase II), and
- Consolidation.

10.1 Business Combinations (Phase II)

This is principally discussed in Chapter 6 at 5.2. However, as noted at 1.4 above, one of the proposed changes is to treat minority shareholders as part of the equity of the consolidated group such that *inter alia*:

- consolidated goodwill would include the minority's share of goodwill,
- the minority would bear their proportionate share of losses even if this reduced their interest below zero, and
- transactions between the majority and minority shareholders (not resulting in a loss of control over the subsidiary) would be treated as equity transactions not giving rise to a profit or loss.[109]

10.2 Consolidation

The ultimate aim of the consolidation project is to issue a new IFRS to replace IAS 27.[110] Like IAS 27, the new IFRS will require consolidation to be based on control. However, it is likely that there will be significant changes to the criteria giving rise to a presumption of control.

The IASB has tentatively agreed that the concept of control should require satisfaction three criteria:

- *power criterion* (the ability to set strategic direction and to direct operating policy and strategy) – see 10.2.1 below
- *benefit criterion* (the ability to access benefits) – see 10.2.2 below, and
- the *link* (the ability to use power so as to increase protect or maintain benefits) – see 10.2.3 below.

10.2.1 Power criterion

The main substantive change proposed is that there should be a rebuttable presumption that certain individuals and entities are in effect agents of the reporting entity (A), such that any shareholdings of those individuals and entities in another entity (B) should be treated as shareholdings of A in determining whether A controls B. The individuals and entities concerned are:

- related parties of A as defined in IAS 24 – *Related Party Disclosures* (see Chapter 33);
- an entity which received its interest in the investee as a contribution or loan from A;

- an entity that cannot sell, transfer or encumber its interests in the investee without the consent of A;

- senior employees of A;

- an entity that has a close business relationship ('like the relationship between a professional service provider and one of its significant clients') with A; and

- an entity with the same board of directors as A.

The IASB proposes to refine the treatment of currently exercisable potential voting rights (see 3.1.2 above) so as to clarify that, where one entity (A) currently holds the majority of the voting rights of an investee and another entity (B) holds currently exercisable potential voting rights, the investee should be treated as:

- controlled by A if exercise of B's potential voting rights would not remove A's control of the investee, or would remove A's control but not give B control the investee, but

- controlled by B if exercise of B's potential voting rights would give B control of the investee.

10.2.2 Benefit criterion

The IASB has tentatively agreed that benefit may flow from an investee other than directly as a result of ownership interest (i.e. through profits and other increases in the value of the investment), for example in the form of synergistic benefits, access to technology, or the exclusion of competitors from patents held by the investee.

10.2.3 The 'link'

The 'link' criterion is simply a way of ensuring that the interests of controllers are distinguished from the powers of fiduciaries or agents. The issue is that in some sectors (for example fund management) owners may entrust nearly all key management decisions to agents. Whilst such agents often have *de facto* control of the entities under their management, such control is exercised for the benefit of owners, not that of the agents themselves. Thus, entities under the control of such agents would generally be treated as controlled by their owners (who appointed the agents in first place). In some cases, however, the boundaries are blurred – for example where an agent is remunerated not by a fixed fee but by a participation in the results of an entity under its control. The IASB intends to develop examples giving further guidance.

10.2.4 Special purpose entities (SPEs)

The new consolidation standard will also deal with SPEs (see 3.2 above). The IASB is still at a relatively early stage of its deliberations on SPEs, although it is intended that consolidation will be based on control. An issue that appears to be causing some difficulty for the IASB is that of 'autopilot' entities (i.e. those whose activities are largely predetermined). Such entities (which are often components of financial products devised by banks and similar financial institutions for their clients) present a problem in terms of the IASB's proposed new consolidation model, in that the SPE's operating policies may be determined by the bank, but the SPE operates for the benefit of the client. Such an arrangement breaks the 'link' (see 10.2.3 above) between power and benefits, implying that the SPE is not a subsidiary of either the bank or the client – a somewhat counter-intuitive outcome, suggesting perhaps that further refinements to the new model are required.

References

1 A joint venture need not take the form of a separate entity (see Chapter 8).
2 IAS 27, *Consolidated and Separate Financial Statements*, IASB, December 2003 (amended March 2004), para. 1.
3 IAS 27, para. 3.
4 IAS 27, para. 4.
5 IAS 27, paras. 9 and 12.
6 SIC-12, *Consolidation – Special Purpose Entities*, SIC, November 1998 (amended December 2003).
7 *Project Update: Business Combinations (Phase II) – Application of the Purchase Method*, IASB, January 2004.
8 R. M. Wilkins, *Group Accounts*, Second edition, London: ICAEW, 1979, p.170.
9 IAS 27, para. 43.
10 IAS 27, paras. IN1-IN14.
11 IFRS 3, *Business Combinations*, IASB, March 2004; IFRS 5 – *Non-current Assets Held for Sale and Discontinued Operations*, IASB, March 2004.
12 IFRS 3, para. 36.
13 IAS 27, para. 4.
14 IAS 27, para. 4.
15 IAS 27, para. 4.
16 IAS 27, para. 4.
17 IAS 27, para. 13.
18 EITF 96-16, *Investor's Accounting for an Investee When the Investor Has a Majority of the Voting Interest but the Minority Shareholder or Shareholders Have Certain Approval or Veto Rights*, EITF, July 1998.
19 IAS 27, para. IG4.
20 IAS 27, para. IG2.
21 IAS 27, para. 14.
22 IAS 27, paras. 14 and IG1-IG4.
23 IAS 27, paras. 14 and IG1.
24 IAS 27, para. IG3.
25 IAS 27, para. 14.
26 IAS 27, para. IG8 (Example 3).
27 IAS 27, para. 15.
28 IAS 27, para. IG8 (Examples 1, 4 and 5).
29 IAS 27, para. IG2.
30 SIC-12, para. 8.
31 SIC-12, para. 1.
32 SIC-12, para. 2.
33 SIC-12, para. 3.
34 SIC-12, para. 6.
35 IFRIC D7, *Scope of SIC-12 Consolidation – Special Purpose Entities*, IFRIC, June 2004, para. 6.
36 SIC-12, para. 9.
37 SIC-12, para. 13.
38 SIC-12, para. 10 and Appendix.
39 IAS 27, para. 4.
40 IAS 27, para. 10.
41 IAS 27, para. 5.
42 IAS 27, para. 10
, 43, IFRS 2, *Share-based Payment*, IASB, February 2004, para. 8.
44 IAS 27, para. 11.
45 IAS 27, para. BC10.
46 IAS 27, para. BC10.
47 IFRS 3, para. 36.
48 IAS 27, para. 19.
49 IAS 27, paras. BC16-BC22.
50 IAS 27, para. 20.
51 IAS 27, para. IN9.
52 IAS 27, para. 21.
53 IAS 27, para. 22.
54 IAS 27, para. 4.
55 IAS 27, para. 23.
56 IAS 27, paras. IG1-IG8
57 IAS 27, para. IG6.
58 IAS 27, para. IG7.
59 IAS 27, para. 24.
60 IAS 27, para. 25.
61 IAS 27, para. 25.
62 IAS 27, para. 25.
63 IAS 27, para. 26.
64 IAS 1, *Presentation of Financial Statements*, IASB, December 2003 (amended March 2004), para. 11.
65 IAS 27, para. 27.
66 IAS 27, para. 28.
67 IAS 27, para. 29.
68 IAS 27, para. 30.

69 IAS 27, para. 30.
70 IAS 21, *The Effects of Changes in Foreign Exchange Rates*, IASB, December 2003, para. 49.
71 *IASB Update*, IASB, April 2004.
72 IAS 27, para. 31.
73 IAS 27, para. 32.
74 IAS 27, para. 33.
75 IAS 27, para. 34.
76 IAS 27, paras. DO1-DO3.
77 IAS 27, para. 35.
78 IAS 27, para. 36.
79 IAS 27, para. 4.
80 IAS 27, para. 7.
81 IAS 27, paras. 5-6.
82 IAS 27, paras. 6 and 38.
83 IAS 27, paras. IN13 and BC10.
84 IAS 27, para. 38.
85 IAS 27, para. 37.
86 IAS 27, para. 37.
87 IAS 27, para. 39.
88 IAS 27, para. 4.
89 IFRS 3, para. BC140.
90 IAS 27, para. 40.
91 IAS 27, para. 41.
92 IAS 27, para. 42.
93 IAS 27, para. 42.
94 IAS 27, para. 43.
95 IFRS 1, *First-time Adoption of International Financial Reporting Standards*, IASB, June 2003, (amended March 2004), para. IG26.
96 IFRS 1, para. IG27(a).
97 IFRS 1, paras. B2(j) and IG27(b).
98 IFRS 1, para. IG27(c).
99 IFRS 1, paras. B2(k) and IG28.
100 IFRS 1, paras. 24-25.
101 IFRS 1, para. 24.
102 IFRS 1, para. IG29 (IG Example 8).
103 IFRS 1, para. IG31
104 IFRS 1, para. IG31.
105 IFRS 1, para. 25.
106 IFRS 1, para. IG29 (IG Example 9).
107 IFRS 1, para. 25.
108 IFRS 1, para. IG30.
109 IASB project summary, *Business Combinations (Phase II) – Application of the Purchase Method*, IASB, January 2004.
110 IASB project summary *Consolidation (including special purpose entities)*, IASB, 20 August 2004 version.

Chapter 6 Business combinations and goodwill

1 INTRODUCTION

1.1 Background

A business combination is defined by the IASB as 'the bringing together of separate entities or businesses into one reporting entity'.[1] This applies not only when an entity becomes a subsidiary of a parent but also where an entity purchases a business comprising the net assets, including any goodwill, of another entity.[2]

In accounting terms there have traditionally been two distinctly different forms of reporting the effects of a business combination; the purchase method of accounting (or acquisition accounting) and the pooling of interests method (or merger accounting).

The two methods of accounting look at business combinations through quite different eyes. An acquisition is seen as the absorption of the target into the clutches of the predator; there is continuity only of the acquiring entity, in the sense that only the post-acquisition results of the target are reported as earnings of the acquiring entity, and the comparative figures remain those of the acquiring entity. In contrast, a uniting of interests is seen as the pooling together of two formerly distinct shareholder groups, and in order to present continuity of both entities there is retrospective restatement to show the enlarged entity as if the two entities had always been together, by combining the results of both entities pre- and post-combination and also by restatement of the comparatives. The difficulty for accountants, however, has been how to translate this difference in philosophy into criteria which permit particular transactions to be categorised as being of one type or the other.

The other main issues facing accountants have been in relation to accounting for an acquisition. In order to do so, the acquiring entity has to determine the cost of its acquisition and then allocate that cost between the identifiable assets and liabilities of the target. Depending on what items are included within this allocation process and what values are placed on them, this will invariably result in a difference that has to accounted for. Where the amounts allocated to the assets and liabilities are less than the overall cost, the difference is accounted for as goodwill. Over the years there have been different views on how goodwill should be accounted for, but the general method has been to deal with it as an asset. The question then has been: should it be amortised over its economic life (whatever that may be thought to be) or should it not be amortised at all, but subjected to some form of impairment test? Where the cost has been less than the values allocated to the identifiable assets and liabilities, then this has traditionally been treated as negative goodwill. The issue has then been how such a credit should be released to the income statement.

1.2   Development of an international standard

1.2.1   IAS 22

Until recently, the relevant international standard was IAS 22 – *Business Combinations*. The original standard was issued in November 1983, but had been revised and amended on a number of occasions since then.[3]

The main accounting requirements of IAS 22 can be summarised as follows.

A   Scope

IAS 22 applied in accounting for business combinations, irrespective of the particular structure adopted for the combination, although it excluded from its scope:

(a)   transactions among entities under common control; and

(b)   interests in joint ventures and the financial statements of joint ventures.[4]

B   General approach

IAS 22 required business combinations to be classified as either acquisitions or uniting of interests and contained both general definitions and additional guidance for each classification. A uniting of interests was a business combination in which it was not possible to identify an acquirer. Instead of a dominant party emerging, the shareholder groups of the combining entities join in a substantially equal arrangement to share control over effectively the whole of their net assets and operations and share mutually in the risks and benefits of the combined entity. Furthermore, the managements of the combining entities participated in the management of the combined entity. Under those circumstances, a business combination was accounted for as a uniting of interests.

Nevertheless, the standard was clear that it would be possible to identify an acquirer in virtually all cases and hence uniting of interests was expected to occur only in exceptional circumstances. It also recognised that occasionally an entity obtained ownership of the shares of another entity but as part of the exchange transaction issued enough voting shares, as consideration, such that control of the combined entity passed to the owners of the entity whose shares had been acquired.[5] However, the standard was then silent as to how its requirements should be applied in practice to such reverse acquisitions.

C   *Accounting for a uniting of interests*

Under IAS 22, a uniting of interests was accounted for using the pooling of interests accounting method. This method required that the financial statement items of the combining entities for the period in which the combination occurred and for any comparative periods presented were to be included as if they had been combined from the beginning of the earliest period presented. Thus the pre- and post-combination results of both entities were included in the income statements. Also, the existing carrying values of the assets and liabilities of the separate entities were combined in the balance sheets; no fair value adjustments were made. Any difference between (1) the amount recorded as share capital issued plus any additional consideration in the form of cash or other assets and (2) the amount recorded for the share capital acquired was adjusted against equity; there was no recognition of any new goodwill or negative goodwill. Expenses related to effecting the uniting of interests were recognised as expenses in the period in which they were incurred.[6]

D   *Accounting for acquisitions*

If a business combination did not meet the uniting of interests criteria, it had to be accounted for as an acquisition by applying the purchase method of accounting.[7]

Under IAS 22, the application of the purchase method meant that as from the date of acquisition (the date on which control of the acquiree was effectively transferred to the acquirer) the acquirer:

(a)   incorporated the results of operations of the acquiree in its own income statement; and

(b)   recognised in its own balance sheet the identifiable assets and liabilities of the acquiree and any goodwill or negative goodwill on the acquisition.[8]

The acquisition was to be accounted for at cost, being the amount of cash or cash equivalents, or the fair value of the other purchase consideration given, as determined at the 'date of exchange', plus any costs directly attributable to the acquisition. Guidance was given as to how to determine the fair values of the consideration and what costs could be included.[9] IAS 22 recognised that the acquisition agreement may provide for adjustments to the purchase consideration contingent on one or more future events, and required that, at the date of acquisition, any contingent purchase consideration that was probable and could be measured reliably was to be recognised in the cost of the acquisition. The cost of the acquisition was to be adjusted when the contingency was resolved.[10]

The identifiable assets and liabilities of the acquiree that existed at the date of acquisition were to be recognised separately at the date of acquisition if, and only if:

(a)   it is probable that any associated future economic benefits will flow to, or resources embodying economic benefits will flow from, the acquirer; and

(b)   a reliable measure is available of their cost or fair value.

The assets and liabilities could include items that were not previously recognised by the acquiree.[11] The liabilities to be recognised at the date of acquisition were not to include any that resulted from the acquirer's intentions or actions, except for reorganisation provisions that were an integral part of the acquirer's plan of acquisition, that related to the acquiree's business only, and that came into existence as a direct consequence of the acquisition. Even then such reorganisation provisions could only be included provided certain criteria were met. Liabilities could also not be recognised for future losses or other costs expected to be incurred as a result of the acquisition, whether they related to the acquirer or the acquiree.[12]

Where an acquirer purchased less than 100% of the acquiree so that a minority interest had a stake in the identifiable assets and liabilities, IAS 22 included a benchmark and an allowed alternative treatment for the initial measurement of the identifiable net assets acquired in a business combination, and therefore for the initial measurement of any minority interests. The benchmark treatment required identifiable assets and liabilities to be recognised at the sum of:

(a)   the aggregate of the acquirer's share in their fair values plus

(b)   the minority's proportion of their pre-acquisition carrying amounts, i.e. book values.

The allowed alternative treatment required the identifiable assets and liabilities to be valued at their respective fair values as at the date of acquisition.[13]

The standard included general guidelines for determining the fair values of the identifiable assets and liabilities acquired.[14] However, if the fair value of an intangible asset could not be measured by reference to an active market (as defined in IAS 38), its value was limited such that it did not create or increase negative goodwill.[15]

IAS 22 required that any excess of the cost of the acquisition over the acquirer's interest in the fair value of the identifiable net assets of the acquiree was to be described as goodwill and recognised as an asset. This was to be amortised over its useful life, using a straight-line method unless there was persuasive evidence that another method was appropriate. There was a rebuttable presumption that the useful life of goodwill did not exceed twenty years. An impairment test for such goodwill was required only if there were indicators of impairment. However, if the goodwill was being amortised over a longer period than twenty years, an annual impairment test was required.[16]

Any excess of the acquirer's interest in the fair value of the identifiable net assets over the cost of the acquisition was accounted for as negative goodwill as follows:

(a)   to the extent that it related to expectations of future losses and expenses identified in the acquirer's acquisition plan, it was required to be carried forward and recognised as income in the same period in which the future losses and expenses were recognised;

(b)   to the extent that it did not relate to expectations of future losses and expenses identified in the acquirer's acquisition plan, it was required to be recognised as income as follows:

    (i)   for the amount of negative goodwill not exceeding the aggregate fair value of acquired identifiable non-monetary assets, on a systematic basis over the remaining weighted average useful life of the identifiable depreciable assets;

    (ii)   for any remaining excess, immediately.[17]

Where an acquisition involved more than one exchange transaction, IAS 22 required that each significant transaction was to be treated separately for the purpose of determining the fair values of the identifiable assets and liabilities acquired and for determining the amount of any goodwill or negative goodwill on that transaction. The acquirer was required to compare the costs of the individual investments with the fair values of the identifiable assets and liabilities acquired at each significant step.[18]

After the date of an acquisition, additional information may become available about the identifiable assets and liabilities acquired. The additional evidence may necessitate either recognition of a previously unrecognised asset or liability or an adjustment to the fair values assigned at the date of acquisition. IAS 22 generally required that the amount assigned to goodwill or negative goodwill should also be adjusted to the extent that:

(a)   the adjustment did not increase the carrying amount of goodwill above its recoverable amount; and

(b)   such adjustment was made by the end of the first annual accounting period commencing after acquisition.

If these conditions were not met the adjustments to the identifiable assets and liabilities were to be recognised as income or expense.[19] However, the standard included two exceptions to this requirement relating to previously unrecognised deferred tax assets of the acquiree[20] and the reversal of any reorganisation provisions.[21]

1.2.2   SICs 9, 22 and 28

The SIC issued 3 interpretations relating to IAS 22.

It was recognised that the standard did not provide explicit guidance on the interaction between the definitions and the additional guidance for classifying a business combination as either an acquisition or a uniting of interests.[22] Accordingly, the SIC considered this issue, as well as whether a business combination might be classified as neither, and in January 2000 issued an interpretation, SIC-9 – *Business Combinations – Classification either as Acquisitions or Unitings of Interests.*

SIC-9 confirmed that all business combinations under IAS 22 were either an acquisition or a uniting of interests.[23] It also stated that a business combination should be accounted for as an acquisition, unless an acquirer could not be identified. It took the view that in virtually all business combinations an acquirer could be identified.[24]

In July 2000, the SIC issued SIC-22 – *Business Combinations – Subsequent Adjustment of Fair Values and Goodwill Initially Reported* – which considered the following issues:[25]

(a)   whether an adjustment to the initial fair values of identifiable assets and liabilities acquired should include the effects of depreciation and other changes which would have resulted if the adjusted fair values had been applied from the date of acquisition;

(b)   whether a related adjustment of goodwill or negative goodwill should include the effect of amortisation of the adjusted amount assigned to goodwill or negative goodwill from the date of acquisition; and

(c)   how the adjustments to identifiable assets and liabilities acquired, and to goodwill or negative goodwill, should be presented.

The SIC concluded that such adjustments to the identifiable assets and liabilities should be calculated as if the adjusted fair values had been applied from the date of acquisition. They were to include both the effect of the change to the fair values initially assigned, and the effect of depreciation and other changes which would have resulted if the adjusted fair values had been applied from the date of acquisition.[26] The carrying amount of goodwill or negative goodwill was also to be calculated as if the adjusted fair values had been applied from the date of acquisition, with goodwill amortisation or recognition of negative goodwill also being adjusted from the date of acquisition. However, the adjustment to goodwill was not to increase the carrying amount above its recoverable amount.[27] The adjustments to depreciation and amortisation, impairment charges and other amounts were to be included in the net profit or loss in the respective classification of income or expense.[28]

Finally, in December 2001, the SIC issued SIC-28 – *Business Combinations – "Date of Exchange" and Fair Value of Equity Instruments*. This principally dealt with the meaning of the term 'date of exchange' since IAS 22 was not entirely clear as to its meaning, and when it was appropriate to consider other evidence and valuation methods in addition to a published price at the date of exchange of a quoted equity instrument.[29] The SIC concluded that when an acquisition was achieved in one exchange transaction, the date of exchange 'should be the date of acquisition'[30] and that the fair value of shares issued should be the published price at that date except in rare circumstances. Another price should be used only if the published price was an unreliable indicator of the fair value. This would only be the case when it had been affected by an undue price fluctuation or a narrowness of the market.[31]

1.2.3   IASB's project

In 2001 the IASB began a project to review IAS 22 as part of its initial agenda, with the objective of improving the quality of, and seeking international convergence on, the accounting for business combinations. The project on business combinations has two phases.

As part of phase I, the IASB published in December 2002 ED 3 – *Business Combinations*, together with an exposure draft of proposed related amendments to IAS 38 – *Intangible Assets* – and IAS 36 – *Impairment of Assets*.[32] The Board's intention in developing an IFRS as part of the first phase of the project was not to reconsider all of the requirements in IAS 22. Instead, the Board's primary focus was on:

(a) the method of accounting for business combinations;

(b) the initial measurement of the identifiable assets acquired and liabilities and contingent liabilities assumed in a business combination;

(c) the recognition of liabilities for terminating or reducing the activities of an acquiree;

(d) the treatment of any excess of the acquirer's interest in the fair value of identifiable net assets acquired in a business combination over the cost of the combination; and

(e) the accounting for goodwill and intangible assets acquired in a business combination.[33]

There are three aspects to phase II of the project:[34]

- issues related to the application of the purchase method. This is being conducted as a joint project with the FASB;

- the accounting for business combinations in which separate entities or operations of entities are brought together to form a joint venture, including possible applications for 'fresh start' accounting. 'Fresh-start' accounting derives from the view that a new entity emerges as a result of a business combination. Therefore, the assets and liabilities of each of the combining entities, including assets and liabilities not previously recognised, are recorded by the new entity at their fair values; and

- the accounting for business combinations excluded from phase I, i.e.:

  - business combination involving entities (or operations of entities) under common control;

  - business combinations involving two or more mutual entities (such as mutual insurance companies or mutual cooperative entities); and

  - business combinations in which separate entities are brought together to form a reporting entity by contract only without the obtaining of an ownership interest (for example, business combinations in which separate entities are brought together by contract to form a dual listed company).

1.2.4   IFRS 3

The first phase of the IASB's project has resulted in the Board issuing, simultaneously in March 2004, IFRS 3 – *Business Combinations* – and revised versions of IAS 36 and IAS 38. The requirements of IFRS 3 are principally dealt with at 2 below. The requirements of IAS 36 relating specifically to the impairment of goodwill are dealt with at 3 below; the general requirements of IAS 36 are covered in Chapter 13. The specific requirements of IAS 38 relating to intangible assets acquired as part of a business combination are dealt with at 2.3.3 B below; the other requirements of IAS 38 are covered in Chapter 11.

A   Reasons for revising IAS 22

The IASB's reasons for revising IAS 22 are set out in the introduction to IFRS 3.

As indicated at 1.2.1 B above, IAS 22 permitted business combinations to be accounted for using one of two methods: the pooling of interests method or the purchase method. Although IAS 22 restricted the use of the pooling of interests method to business combinations classified as unitings of interests, the IASB has stated that 'analysts and other users of financial statements indicated that permitting two methods of accounting for substantially similar transactions impaired the comparability of financial statements. Others argued that requiring more than one method of accounting for such transactions created incentives for structuring those transactions to achieve a desired accounting result, particularly given that the two methods produce quite different results.'[35]

The IASB goes on to say that 'these factors, combined with the prohibition of the pooling of interests method in Australia, Canada and the United States, prompted the International Accounting Standards Board to examine whether, given that few combinations were understood to be accounted for in accordance with IAS 22 using the pooling of interests method, it would be advantageous for international standards to converge with those in Australia and North America by also prohibiting the method'.[36]

It is also noted that 'accounting for business combinations varied across jurisdictions in other respects as well. These included the accounting for goodwill and intangible assets acquired in a business combination, the treatment of any excess of the acquirer's interest in the fair values of identifiable net assets acquired over the cost of the business combination, and the recognition of liabilities for terminating or reducing the activities of an acquiree.'[37]

As indicated at 1.2.1 D above, where an acquirer purchased less than 100% of the acquiree, IAS 22 contained an option in respect of how the purchase method could be applied. The IASB 'believes that permitting similar transactions to be accounted for in dissimilar ways impairs the usefulness of the information provided to users of financial statements, because both comparability and reliability are diminished'.[38]

The IASB has stated therefore that IFRS 3 'has been issued to improve the quality of, and seek international convergence on, the accounting for business combinations' including those areas that were the primary focus of phase I of the project (see 1.2.3 above).[39]

B   Main changes from IAS 22

The main changes from IAS 22 as described by the IASB are set out below.

I   Method of accounting

IFRS 3 requires all business combinations within its scope to be accounted for using the purchase method, whereas IAS 22 permitted business combinations to be accounted for using one of two methods: the pooling of interests method for combinations classified as unitings of interests and the purchase method for combinations classified as acquisitions.[40]

II   *Recognising the identifiable assets acquired and liabilities and contingent liabilities assumed*

IFRS 3 changes the requirements in IAS 22 for separately recognising the identifiable assets acquired and liabilities and contingent liabilities assumed as part of allocating the cost of a business combination.

The standard clarifies the criteria for separately recognising intangible assets of the acquiree as part of allocating the cost of a combination, such that more intangible assets will now be recognised separately from goodwill. IAS 22 required an intangible asset to be recognised if, and only if, it was probable that the future economic benefits attributable to the asset would flow to the entity, and its cost could be measured reliably. The probability recognition criterion is not included in IFRS 3 because it is always considered to be satisfied for intangible assets acquired in business combinations.[41] The effect of probability is reflected in the fair value measurement of the intangible asset.[42] Additionally, the standard includes guidance clarifying that the fair value of an intangible asset acquired in a business combination can normally be measured with sufficient reliability to qualify for recognition separately from goodwill. If an intangible asset acquired in a business combination has a finite useful life, there is a rebuttable presumption that its fair value can be measured reliably.[43] IFRS 3 also provides a large list of examples of items that meet the definition of an intangible asset and are therefore to be recognised separately from goodwill (see 2.3.3 below).

IFRS 3 restricts the recognition of restructuring or reorganisation provisions as part of allocating the cost of the combination such that they can only be made when the acquiree has, at the acquisition date, an existing liability for restructuring recognised in accordance with IAS 37 – *Provisions, Contingent Liabilities and Contingent Assets.* IAS 22 required an acquirer to recognise as part of allocating the cost of a business combination a provision for terminating or reducing the activities of the acquiree that was not a liability of the acquiree at the acquisition date, provided the acquirer satisfied specified criteria.[44]

IFRS 3 requires an acquirer to recognise separately the acquiree's contingent liabilities (as defined in IAS 37) at the acquisition date as part of allocating the cost of a business combination, provided their fair values can be measured reliably. Such contingent liabilities were, in accordance with IAS 22, subsumed within the amount recognised as goodwill or negative goodwill.[45]

III   *Measuring the identifiable assets acquired and liabilities and contingent liabilities assumed*

Where an acquirer purchases less than 100% of the acquiree so that a minority interest has a stake in the identifiable assets and liabilities, IAS 22 included a benchmark and an allowed alternative treatment for the initial measurement of the identifiable net assets acquired in a business combination, and therefore for the initial measurement of any minority interests (see 1.2.1 D above). IFRS 3 requires the acquiree's identifiable assets, liabilities and contingent liabilities recognised as part of allocating the cost of the combination to be measured initially by the acquirer at their fair values at the acquisition date. Therefore, any minority interest in the acquiree is stated at the minority's proportion of the net fair values of those items. This is consistent with IAS 22's allowed alternative treatment.[46]

IV   *Subsequent accounting for goodwill*

IFRS 3 requires goodwill acquired in a business combination to be measured after initial recognition at cost less any accumulated impairment losses. Therefore, the goodwill is not amortised and instead must be tested for impairment annually, or more frequently if events or changes in circumstances indicate that it might be impaired. IAS 22 required acquired goodwill to be systematically amortised over its useful life, and included a rebuttable presumption that its useful life could not exceed twenty years from initial recognition.[47]

V   *Excess of acquirer's interest in the net fair value of acquiree's identifiable assets,*
        liabilities and contingent liabilities over cost

IFRS 3 requires the acquirer to reassess the identification and measurement of the acquiree's identifiable assets, liabilities and contingent liabilities and the measurement of the cost of the combination if, at the acquisition date, the acquirer's interest in the net fair value of those items exceeds the cost of the combination. Any excess remaining after that reassessment must be recognised by the acquirer immediately in profit or loss.[48] As indicated at 1.2.1 D above, IAS 22 required such 'negative goodwill', to be recognised in income depending on whether it related to identifiable expected future losses and expenses which did not represent liabilities at the date of the acquisition and the extent of any identifiable acquired depreciable/amortisable assets.

1.2.5   Future developments

As indicated at 1.2.3 above, the IASB is considering a number of other issues relating to business combinations in phase II of its project.

In April 2004, the IASB issued an exposure draft of proposed amendments to IFRS 3 to remove the scope exceptions for combinations by contract alone or involving mutual entities (see 2.2.2 below). This is only an interim solution and proposes that in applying the purchase method of accounting, the acquirer measures the cost of such combinations in such a way that no goodwill would be recognised in the former type of combination and that goodwill would only be recognised in the latter situation to the extent that consideration was given by the acquirer in exchange for control of the acquiree. This is discussed further at 5.1 below.

The IASB expects to issue another exposure draft in the final quarter of 2004 dealing with a number of issues arising in respect of the application of the purchase method. This is discussed further at 5.2 below. Having issued that exposure draft, the IASB is then expected to consider the other aspects of phase II of its project.

2   BUSINESS COMBINATIONS

IFRS 3 does not have an effective date in the sense that it is applicable for accounting periods commencing on or after a certain date. Instead, the standard applies to the accounting for business combinations for which the agreement date is on or after 31 March 2004 (the date of issue of the standard). It also applies to the accounting for:

(a)   goodwill arising from a business combination for which the agreement date is on or after 31 March 2004; or

(b)   any excess of the acquirer's interest in the net fair value of the acquiree's identifiable assets, liabilities and contingent liabilities over the cost of a business combination for which the agreement date is on or after 31 March 2004.[49]

The 'agreement date' is defined as 'the date that a substantive agreement between the combining parties is reached and, in the case of publicly listed entities, announced to the public. In the case of a hostile takeover, the earliest date that a substantive agreement between the combining parties is reached is the date that a sufficient number of the acquiree's owners have accepted the acquirer's offer for the acquirer to obtain control of the acquiree.'[50] However, no further elaboration is given as to what a 'substantive agreement' might mean in other situations.

It is unclear why the Board has used the term 'agreement date' for the purpose of determining which business combinations have to be accounted for under the new requirements of IFRS 3, rather than the 'acquisition date', i.e. the date on which the acquirer effectively obtains control of the acquiree, which is the date from which the standard requires a business combination to be accounted for under the purchase method (see 2.3 below). The implication, however, is that where the acquisition date for a business combination is on or after 31 March 2004, it does not necessarily mean that it has to be accounted for under IFRS 3. If the circumstances are such that there was a substantive agreement between the parties at a date prior to 31 March 2004, then the acquirer would not be required to account for the business combination under IFRS 3.

As far as previously recognised goodwill, negative goodwill and intangibles in respect of business combinations for which the agreement date was before 31 March 2004 is concerned, the standard has transitional provisions that are to be applied from the beginning of the first annual period beginning on or after 31 March 2004.[51] These are discussed at 4.1 below.

Entities, however, are permitted to apply the requirements of the standard to goodwill existing at or acquired after, and to business combinations occurring from, any date before the effective dates outlined above, provided certain conditions are met.[52] This is discussed at 4.1.5 below.

The above discussion does not apply to first-time adopters. They must account for business combinations after their date of transition to IFRS under IFRS 3. However, IFRS 1 provides an exemption that permits a first-time adopter not to restate business combinations prior to its date of transition to IFRS. This is discussed at 4.2 below.

2.1   Objective of IFRS 3

IFRS 3 states that its objective 'is to specify the financial reporting by an entity when it undertakes a business combination. In particular, it specifies that all business combinations should be accounted for by applying the purchase method. Therefore, the acquirer recognises the acquiree's identifiable assets, liabilities and contingent liabilities at their fair values at the acquisition date, and also recognises goodwill, which is subsequently tested for impairment rather than amortised.'[53]

2.2   Scope of IFRS 3

Entities are required to apply the provisions of IFRS 3 when accounting for all business combinations, except for those that are specifically excluded as set out at 2.2.2 below.[54] These types of business combination that are excluded are being dealt with in phase II of the IASB's project on business combinations.

2.2.1   *Identifying a business combination*

IFRS 3 defines a business combination as 'the bringing together of separate entities or businesses into one reporting entity'.[55] The standard then goes on to say that 'the result of nearly all business combinations is that one entity, the acquirer, obtains control of one or more other businesses, the acquiree'.[56]

For this purpose, IFRS 3 defines a 'business' as 'an integrated set of activities and assets conducted and managed for the purpose of providing:

(a)   a return to investors; or

(b)   lower costs or other economic benefits directly and proportionately to policyholders or participants'.[57]

It goes on to say that 'a business generally consists of inputs, processes applied to those inputs, and resulting outputs that are, or will be, used to generate revenues. If goodwill is present in a transferred set of activities and assets, the transferred set shall be presumed to be a business.'[58]

If an entity obtains control of one or more other entities that are not businesses, the bringing together of those entities is not a business combination.[59] Thus, it would seem that the requirements of IFRS 3 do not apply. However, the standard states that 'when an entity acquires a group of assets or net assets that does not constitute a business, it shall allocate the cost of the group between the individual identifiable assets and liabilities in the group based on their relative fair values at the date of acquisition'.[60] Thus existing book values or values in the acquisition agreement may not be appropriate, and no goodwill can be recognised in such an asset deal.

In some situations, there may be difficulties in determining whether or not an acquisition of a group of assets constitutes a business, and judgement will be required to be exercised based on the particular circumstances.

IFRS 3 indicates that a business combination may be structured in a variety of ways for legal, taxation or other reasons. It may involve the purchase by an entity of the equity of another entity, the purchase of all the net assets of another entity, the assumption of the liabilities of another entity, or the purchase of some of the net assets of another entity that together form one or more businesses. It may be effected by the issue of equity instruments, the transfer of cash, cash equivalents or other assets, or a combination thereof. The transaction may be between the shareholders of the combining entities or between one entity and the shareholders of another entity. It may involve the establishment of a new entity to control the combining entities or net assets transferred, or the restructuring of one or more of the combining entities.[61] Whatever the legal structure, if it is a 'business combination' then the requirements of IFRS 3 apply (unless it is specifically excluded by the standard).

The standard notes that a business combination may result in a parent-subsidiary relationship in which the acquirer is the parent and the acquiree a subsidiary of the acquirer. In such circumstances, the acquirer applies IFRS 3 in its consolidated financial statements. It includes its interest in the acquiree in any separate financial statements it issues as an investment in a subsidiary under IAS 27 – *Consolidated and Separate Financial Statements* (see Chapter 5 at 7.2).[62]

As indicated above, a business combination may involve the purchase of the net assets, including any goodwill, of another entity rather than the purchase of the equity of the other entity. The standard notes that such a combination does not result in a parent-subsidiary relationship.[63] Nevertheless, the acquirer (even if it is a single entity) will account for such a business combination under the standard in its individual or separate financial statements and consequently in any consolidated financial statements.

The standard emphasises that, included within the definition of a business combination, and therefore the scope of IFRS 3, are business combinations in which one entity obtains control of another entity but for which the date of obtaining control (i.e. the acquisition date) does not coincide with the date or dates of acquiring an ownership interest (i.e. the date or dates of exchange). This situation may arise, for example, when an investee enters into share buy-back arrangements with some of its investors and, as a result, control of the investee changes.[64] Although not explicitly discussed in the standard, it would seem that the accounting for such a business combination would be done in a similar manner to that for business combinations achieved in stages (see 2.3.7 below).

2.2.2 Exclusions

The standard excludes the following types of business combinations from its scope:[65]

(a)   business combinations in which separate entities or businesses are brought together to form a joint venture.

(b)   business combinations involving entities or businesses under common control.

(c)   business combinations involving two or more mutual entities.

(d)   business combinations in which separate entities or businesses are brought together to form a reporting entity by contract alone without the obtaining of an ownership interest (for example, combinations in which separate entities are brought together by contract alone to form a dual listed corporation).

These exclusions are only intended to be a temporary measure while the IASB considers the issues relating to such combinations under phase II of its business combinations project. As discussed at 5.1 below, in April 2004, the IASB issued an exposure draft of proposed amendments to IFRS 3 to remove the scope exclusions (c) and (d) above. The intention being that by the time entities apply IFRS 3, it will already have been revised with these exclusions removed from the standard.

For the purposes of exclusion (b) above, a business combination involving entities or businesses under common control 'is a business combination in which all of the combining entities or businesses are ultimately controlled by the same party or parties both before and after the business combination, and that control is not transitory'.[66] This will include transactions between entities within a group.

The extent of minority interests in each of the combining entities before and after the business combination is not relevant to determining whether the combination involves entities under common control.[67] This is because a partially-owned subsidiary is nevertheless under the control of the parent entity. Therefore transactions involving partially-owned subsidiaries would be outside the scope of the standard. Similarly, the fact that one of the combining entities is a subsidiary that has been excluded from the consolidated financial statements of the group in accordance with IAS 27 is not relevant to determining whether a combination involves entities under common control.[68]

The exclusion is not, however, restricted to transactions between entities within a group. The standard notes that an entity can be controlled by an individual, or by a group of individuals acting together under a contractual arrangement, and that individual or group of individuals may not be subject to the financial reporting requirements of IFRSs.[69] Thus a transaction that results in a new parent entity, or a transaction involving entities controlled by the same individual, would be outwith the scope of the standard. It is not necessary for combining entities to be included as part of the same consolidated financial statements for a business combination to be regarded as one involving entities under common control.[70]

A group of individuals shall be regarded as controlling an entity when, as a result of contractual arrangements, they collectively have the power to govern its financial and operating policies so as to obtain benefits from its activities. Therefore, a business combination is outside the scope of IFRS 3 when the same group of individuals has, as a result of contractual arrangements, ultimate collective power to govern the financial and operating policies of each of the combining entities so as to obtain benefits from their activities, and that ultimate collective power is not transitory.[71]

The inclusion of the condition that the 'control is not transitory' is intended to deal with concerns expressed by some commentators that business combinations between parties acting at arm's length could be structured through the use of 'grooming' transactions so that, for a brief period immediately before the combination, the combining entities or businesses are under common control. In this way, it might have been possible for combinations that would otherwise be accounted for in accordance with IFRS 3 using the purchase method to be accounted for using some other method.[72]

As discussed in 5.3 below, the IASB is considering as part of phase II of its project, the treatment of business combinations involving entities or businesses under common control. In the meantime, IFRS 3 only prescribes the purchase method for combinations that are within its scope and does not describe any other methods; it does not address at all the methods of accounting that may be appropriate when a business combination involves entities under common control.

As discussed further in Chapter 3 at 4.3, IAS 8 – *Accounting Policies, Changes in Accounting Estimates and Errors* – requires that in the absence of specific guidance in IFRS, management shall use its judgement in developing and applying an accounting policy that is relevant and reliable.[73] In making that judgement, in the absence of IFRS dealing with similar or related issues or guidance within the IASB *Framework*, management may also consider the most recent pronouncements of other standard-setting bodies that use a similar conceptual framework to develop accounting standards.[74] Since several such bodies have issued guidance and some allow or require the pooling of interests method in accounting for business combinations involving entities under common control. Accordingly, we consider that the pooling of interests method is still available to such combinations until such time as the IASB publishes its conclusions and there may be other approaches (including the purchase method) that will be considered to give a fair presentation in particular circumstances.

2.3   Purchase method of accounting

All business combinations (apart from those excluded from the scope of the standard) shall be accounted for by applying the purchase method.[75]

The purchase method views a business combination from the perspective of the combining entity that is identified as the acquirer. The acquirer purchases net assets and recognises the assets acquired and the liabilities and contingent liabilities assumed, including those not previously recognised by the acquiree. The measurement of the acquirer's assets and liabilities is not affected by the transaction, nor are any additional assets or liabilities of the acquirer recognised as a result of the transaction, because they are not the subjects of the transaction.[76] For example, if as a result of the business combination the acquirer is able to recognise a previously unrecognised tax asset of its own, this is not included as part of the accounting for the business combination and thus impact on the calculation of goodwill; the recognition of such an asset will be accounted for as income.

Application of the purchase method starts from the acquisition date, which is the date on which the acquirer effectively obtains control of the acquiree. Because control is the power to govern the financial and operating policies of an entity or business so as to obtain benefits from its activities, it is not necessary for a transaction to be closed or finalised at law before the acquirer obtains control. All pertinent facts and circumstances surrounding a business combination shall be considered in assessing when the acquirer has obtained control.[77]

Applying the purchase method involves the following steps:[78]

(a)   identifying an acquirer;

(b)   measuring the cost of the business combination; and

(c)   allocating, at the acquisition date, the cost of the business combination to the assets acquired and liabilities and contingent liabilities assumed.

These steps are discussed below.

2.3.1   *Identifying the acquirer*

Since the purchase method views a business combination from the acquirer's perspective, it assumes that one of the parties to the transaction can be identified as the acquirer.[79]

IFRS 3 therefore requires that an acquirer shall be identified for all business combinations. The acquirer is the combining entity that obtains control of the other combining entities or businesses.[80]

Control is defined as 'the power to govern the financial and operating policies of an entity or business so as to obtain benefits from its activities'.[81] The standard states that 'a combining entity shall be presumed to have obtained control of another combining entity when it acquires more than one-half of that other entity's voting rights, unless it can be demonstrated that such ownership does not constitute control. Even if one of the combining entities does not acquire more than one-half of the voting rights of another combining entity, it might have obtained control of that other entity if, as a result of the combination, it obtains:

(a)   power over more than one-half of the voting rights of the other entity by virtue of an agreement with other investors; or

(b)   power to govern the financial and operating policies of the other entity under a statute or an agreement; or

(c)   power to appoint or remove the majority of the members of the board of directors or equivalent governing body of the other entity; or

(d)   power to cast the majority of votes at meetings of the board of directors or equivalent governing body of the other entity.[82]

These provisions about 'control' are equivalent to those in IAS 27 with respect to the identification of subsidiaries for the purposes of consolidation. (See Chapter 5 at 3.1)

The standard notes that although sometimes it may be difficult to identify an acquirer, there are usually indications that one exists. For example:

(a)   if the fair value of one of the combining entities is significantly greater than that of the other combining entity, the entity with the greater fair value is likely to be the acquirer;

(b)   if the business combination is effected through an exchange of voting ordinary equity instruments for cash or other assets, the entity giving up cash or other assets is likely to be the acquirer; and

(c)   if the business combination results in the management of one of the combining entities being able to dominate the selection of the management team of the resulting combined entity, the entity whose management is able so to dominate is likely to be the acquirer.[83]

In a business combination effected through an exchange of equity interests, the standard takes the view that the entity that issues the equity interests is normally the acquirer. However, it emphasises that all pertinent facts and circumstances shall be considered to determine which of the combining entities has the power to govern the financial and operating policies of the other entity (or entities) so as to obtain benefits from its (or their) activities. The standard recognises that in some business combinations, commonly referred to as reverse acquisitions, the acquirer is the entity whose equity interests have been acquired and the issuing entity is the acquiree. This might be the case when, for example, a private entity arranges to have itself 'acquired' by a smaller public entity as a means of obtaining a stock exchange listing[84] and, as part of the agreement, the directors of the public entity resign and are replaced with directors appointed by the private entity and its former owners.[85] Although legally the issuing public entity is regarded as the parent and the private entity is regarded as the subsidiary, the legal subsidiary is the acquirer if it has the power to govern the financial and operating policies of the legal parent so as to obtain benefits from its activities. Guidance on the accounting for reverse acquisitions is now provided in Appendix B to IFRS 3 (see 2.3.8 below).[86]

Occasionally, a new entity is formed to issue equity instruments to effect a business combination between, for example, two other entities. In that situation, IFRS 3 requires that one of the combining entities that existed before the combination to be identified as the acquirer on the basis of the evidence available;[87] the new entity formed to effect the combination cannot be the acquirer.[88]

Similarly, when a business combination involves more than two combining entities, one of the combining entities that existed before the combination shall be identified as the acquirer on the basis of the evidence available. Determining the acquirer in such cases shall include a consideration of, amongst other things, which of the combining entities initiated the combination and whether the assets or revenues of one of the combining entities significantly exceed those of the others.[89]

2.3.2   *Cost of a business combination*

Having identified the acquirer, the next step is for the acquirer to measure the cost of the business combination. IFRS 3 requires this to be the aggregate of:

(a)   the fair values, at the date of exchange, of assets given, liabilities incurred or assumed, and equity instruments issued by the acquirer, in exchange for control of the acquiree; plus

(b)   any costs directly attributable to the business combination.[90]

It should be noted that these requirements are essentially the same as those in IAS 22 and SIC-28, without reconsideration, but the IASB will be reconsidering these requirements as part of the second phase of its project.[91]

A   Date of exchange

When a business combination is achieved in a single exchange transaction, the date of exchange coincides with the acquisition date (see 2.3 above). However, a business combination may involve more than one exchange transaction, for example when it is achieved in stages by successive share purchases. When this occurs:

(a)   the cost of the combination is the aggregate cost of the individual transactions; and

(b)   the date of exchange is the date of each exchange transaction (i.e. the date that each individual investment is recognised in the financial statements of the acquirer), whereas the acquisition date is the date on which the acquirer obtains control of the acquiree.[92]

The accounting for business combinations achieved in stages is discussed at 2.3.7 below.

B   Assets given and liabilities incurred or assumed by the acquirer

Assets given and liabilities incurred or assumed by the acquirer in exchange for control of the acquiree are required by paragraph 24 of the standard to be measured at their fair values at the date of exchange. Fair value is defined as 'the amount for which an asset could be exchanged, or a liability settled, between knowledgeable, willing parties in an arm's length transaction'.[93] The standard gives no guidance as to how such fair values might be arrived at, other than to say that when settlement of all or any part of the cost of a business combination is deferred, the fair value of that deferred component shall be determined by discounting the amounts payable to their present value at the date of exchange, taking into account any premium or discount likely to be incurred in settlement.[94] No guidance is given as to what an appropriate discount rate would be. However, IAS 39 – *Financial Instruments: Recognition and Measurement* – would suggest using a rate currently charged by others for similar debt instruments (i.e. similar remaining maturity, cash flow pattern, currency, credit risk, collateral and interest basis).[95] Where the assets given as consideration or the liabilities incurred or assumed by the acquirer are financial assets or financial liabilities under IAS 39, then it would seem appropriate that the guidance in determining the fair values of such financial instruments should be followed (see Chapter 18 at 4).

The cost of a business combination includes liabilities incurred or assumed by the acquirer in exchange for control of the acquiree. IFRS 3 now states explicitly that future losses or other costs expected to be incurred as a result of a combination are not liabilities incurred or assumed by the acquirer in exchange for control of the acquiree, and are not, therefore, included as part of the cost of the combination.[96] The very restricted circumstances in which future losses or other costs may be recognised as part of the liabilities of the acquired entity are described at 2.3.3 A below.

C   Equity instruments issued by the acquirer

Where equity instruments issued by the acquirer are given as consideration, IFRS 3 states that the published price at the date of exchange of a quoted equity instrument provides the best evidence of the instrument's fair value and shall be used, except in rare circumstances. Other evidence and valuation methods shall be considered only in the rare circumstances when the acquirer can demonstrate that the published price at the date of exchange is an unreliable indicator of fair value, and that the other evidence and valuation methods provide a more reliable measure of the equity instrument's fair value. The standard takes the view that the published price at the date of exchange is an unreliable indicator only when it has been affected by the thinness of the market.[97] The fact that the price may have been affected by an undue price fluctuation is no longer considered by the IASB to be a justification for not using the published price at the date of exchange.[98] Also, the Basis for Conclusions indicates that 'estimates of premiums for large, and discounts for small, blocks of equity instruments issued in comparison to that exchanged in observable transactions are not considered'.[99]

If the published price at the date of exchange is an unreliable indicator or if a published price does not exist for equity instruments issued by the acquirer, the standard states that the fair value of those instruments could, for example, be estimated by reference to their proportional interest in the fair value of the acquirer or by reference to the proportional interest in the fair value of the acquiree obtained, whichever is the more clearly evident. The fair value at the date of exchange of monetary assets given to equity holders of the acquiree as an alternative to equity instruments may also provide evidence of the total fair value given by the acquirer in exchange for control of the acquiree. In any event, the standard requires that all aspects of the combination, including significant factors influencing the negotiations, shall be considered. Reference is also made to the further guidance on determining the fair value of equity instruments (held as investments) set out in IAS 39 (see Chapter 18 at 4).[100]

D   Costs directly attributable to the business combination

The cost of a business combination includes any costs directly attributable to the combination, such as professional fees paid to accountants, legal advisers, valuers and other consultants to effect the combination. General administrative costs, including the costs of maintaining an acquisitions department, and other costs that cannot be directly attributed to the particular combination being accounted for are not included in the cost of the combination: they are recognised as an expense when incurred.[101]

IFRS 3 now requires that the costs of arranging and issuing financial liabilities are an integral part of the liability issue transaction, even when the liabilities are issued to effect a business combination, rather than costs directly attributable to the combination. Therefore, entities shall not include such costs in the cost of a business combination. In accordance with IAS 39, such costs shall be included in the initial measurement of the liability (see Chapter 18 at 2.3).[102]

Similarly, the costs of issuing equity instruments are an integral part of the equity issue transaction, even when the equity instruments are issued to effect a business combination, rather than costs directly attributable to the combination. Therefore, entities shall not include such costs in the cost of a business combination. In accordance with IAS 32 – *Financial Instruments: Disclosure and Presentation*, such costs reduce the proceeds from the equity issue.[103] While these requirements will affect the amount at which the entity's liabilities and equity are recorded in the consolidated financial statements, they do not affect the measurement of goodwill in the business combination.

Where professional advisors may be providing advice on all aspects of the business combination, including the arranging and issuing of financial liabilities and/or issuing equity instruments, it will be necessary for some allocation of the fees payable to be made, possibly by obtaining a breakdown from the relevant advisor.

E   Contingent consideration

IFRS 3 recognises that the terms of a business combination agreement may provide for an adjustment to the cost of the combination contingent on future events, such as a specified level of profit being maintained or achieved in future periods, or on the market price of the instruments issued being maintained.[104]

Where this is the case, IFRS 3 requires that the acquirer shall include the amount of that adjustment in the cost of the combination at the acquisition date if the adjustment is probable and can be measured reliably.[105] If the future events do not occur or the estimate needs to be revised, the cost of the business combination shall be adjusted accordingly.[106]

The standard states that 'it is usually possible to estimate the amount of any such adjustment at the time of initially accounting for the combination without impairing the reliability of the information, even though some uncertainty exists'.[107] This is more likely to be the case in those situations where the contingent consideration is based on the acquiree maintaining a level of profits which it is currently earning (either for a particular period or as an average over a set period) or achieving profits which it is currently budgeting.

However, when a business combination agreement provides for such an adjustment, that adjustment is not included in the cost of the combination at the time of initially accounting for the combination if it either is not probable or cannot be measured reliably. If that adjustment subsequently becomes probable and can be measured reliably, the additional consideration shall be treated as an adjustment to the cost of the combination.[108]

Any subsequent adjustments in respect of such contingent consideration will consequently be reflected in the carrying amount of goodwill. However, if an impairment loss has already been recognised in respect of the goodwill (see 3 below), this is likely to require a further impairment loss to be recognised.

The standard also recognises that in some circumstances, the acquirer may be required to make a subsequent payment to the seller as compensation for a reduction in the value of the assets given, equity instruments issued or liabilities incurred or assumed by the acquirer in exchange for control of the acquiree. For example, the acquirer may guarantee the market price of equity or debt instruments issued as part of the cost of the business combination and is required to issue additional equity or debt instruments to restore the originally determined cost. In such cases, no increase in the cost of the business combination is recognised. In the case of equity instruments, the fair value of the additional payment is offset by an equal reduction in the value attributed to the instruments initially issued.[109] Thus, it would appear that any increase reflected in equity for the extra equity instruments issued is offset by a corresponding debit to equity. In the case of debt instruments, the additional payment is regarded as a reduction in the premium or an increase in the discount on the initial issue.[110] Thus, the extra payment will be taken to the income statement as part of an increased interest expense over the period of the debt instrument.

2.3.3 Allocating the cost to the assets acquired and liabilities and contingent liabilities assumed

Having determined the cost of the business combination, the next stage is to allocate that cost to the assets acquired and liabilities and contingent liabilities assumed.

IFRS 3 requires that the acquirer shall, at the acquisition date, allocate the cost of a business combination by recognising the acquiree's identifiable assets, liabilities and contingent liabilities that satisfy the recognition criteria in paragraph 37 of the standard at their fair values at that date, except for non-current assets (or disposal groups) that are classified as held for sale in accordance with IFRS 5 – *Non-current Assets Held for Sale and Discontinued Operations*, which shall be recognised at fair value less costs to sell. Any difference between the cost of the business combination and the acquirer's interest in the net fair value of the identifiable assets, liabilities and contingent liabilities so recognised is accounted for as goodwill or 'negative goodwill' (see 2.3.4 and 2.3.5 below respectively).[111]

Paragraph 37 of IFRS 3 states that the acquirer shall recognise separately the acquiree's identifiable assets, liabilities and contingent liabilities at the acquisition date only if they satisfy the following criteria at that date:

(a) in the case of an asset other than an intangible asset, it is probable that any associated future economic benefits will flow to the acquirer, and its fair value can be measured reliably;

(b) in the case of a liability other than a contingent liability, it is probable that an outflow of resources embodying economic benefits will be required to settle the obligation, and its fair value can be measured reliably;

(c) in the case of an intangible asset or a contingent liability, its fair value can be measured reliably.[112]

It can be seen that the recognition criteria for intangible assets and contingent liabilities are different from those of other assets and liabilities. In the case of intangible assets, the IASB has taken the view that the probability recognition criterion is always considered to be satisfied for such assets acquired in a business combination. In developing the standard, the Board observed that the fair value of an intangible asset reflects market expectations about the probability that the future economic benefits associated with the intangible asset will flow to the acquirer. In other words, the effect of probability is reflected in the fair value measurement of an intangible asset. The IASB notes that this highlights a general inconsistency between the recognition criteria for assets and liabilities in its *Framework* (see Chapter 2 at 3.2.4) and the fair value measurements required in a business combination, but has concluded that the role of probability as a criterion for recognition in the *Framework* should be considered more generally as part of a forthcoming Concepts project.[113] The allocation of the cost of the business combination to intangible assets is discussed further at 2.3.3 B below.

Similarly, in the case of contingent liabilities, the IASB takes the view that although a contingent liability of the acquiree is not recognised by the acquiree before the business combination, that contingent liability has a fair value, the amount of which reflects market expectations about any uncertainty surrounding the possibility that an outflow of resources embodying economic benefits will be required to settle the possible or present obligation. Again, the IASB notes that this highlights an inconsistency between the recognition criteria applying to liabilities and contingent liabilities in IAS 37 (see Chapter 25 at 3) and the *Framework* and the fair value measurement cost of a business combination, and that the role of probability should be considered more generally as part of a forthcoming Concepts project.[114] The allocation of the cost of the business combination to contingent liabilities is discussed further at 2.3.3 C below.

The recognition criteria in paragraph 37 of the standard set out above makes no reference to contingent assets of the acquiree. We believe that, consistent with the treatment of contingent liabilities, an acquirer should recognise an acquiree's contingent assets at their fair value as part of allocating the cost of the business combination provided their fair values can be measured reliably. We see no conceptual justification to only include contingent liabilities but not contingent assets in the cost allocation process of a business combination, as both are likely to have had an impact on the purchase price and the contingent asset is as much an asset as the contingent liability is a liability. Arguably, a contingent asset that has not been recognised as an asset by the acquiree on the basis that the inflow of benefits is not virtually certain (see Chapter 25 at 3.2.2), but it is probable that the benefits will arise, then it is covered by criterion (a) above. The IASB has indicated that it is considering whether contingent assets should be recognised separately as part of the second phase of its business combinations project.[115]

The allocation of the cost of the business combination to the assets acquired and liabilities and contingent liabilities assumed is critical to the reporting of the post-acquisition performance relating to the business combination. As indicated in the standard, the acquirer's income statement shall incorporate the acquiree's profits and losses after the acquisition date by including the acquiree's income and expenses based on that allocation. For example, depreciation expense included after the acquisition date in the acquirer's income statement that relates to the acquiree's depreciable assets shall be based on the fair values of those depreciable assets at the acquisition date, i.e. their cost to the acquirer.[116] However, of more importance, is the fact that the subsequent accounting for the items that are being recognised separately will in most cases be different from that required for goodwill. For example, the requirement to recognise intangible assets with finite useful lives separately (rather than subsuming them within goodwill), will mean that the values attributed will be amortised over that useful life (see Chapter 11 at 2.4 and 2.5) whereas the goodwill will not be amortised, but subjected to an impairment test (see 3 below).

Further explanation as to how the recognition requirements for other assets and liabilities, principally liabilities, are to be applied is given in the standard. This is discussed at 2.3.3 A below.

Guidance on determining the fair values of the acquiree's identifiable assets, liabilities and contingent liabilities for the purpose of allocating the cost of a business combination is discussed at 2.3.3 D below.

Since the acquirer recognises the acquiree's identifiable assets, liabilities and contingent liabilities that satisfy the recognition criteria in paragraph 37 at their fair values at the acquisition date, any minority interest in the acquiree is stated at the minority's proportion of the net fair value of those items.[117]

A   *Acquiree's identifiable assets and liabilities*

As indicated above, further explanation about how the recognition requirements for other assets and liabilities, principally liabilities, are to be applied is given in the standard.

Firstly, IFRS 3 makes it clear that the acquirer, when allocating the cost of the combination, shall not recognise liabilities for future losses or other costs expected to be incurred as a result of the business combination.[118]

Secondly, the standard severely restricts the ability of an acquirer to recognise a liability for reorganisation or restructuring costs resulting from the business combination. The standard states that 'the acquirer shall recognise liabilities for terminating or reducing the activities of the acquiree as part of allocating the cost of the combination only when the acquiree has, at the acquisition date, an existing liability for restructuring recognised in accordance with IAS 37'.[119] The requirements for the recognition of restructuring provisions under IAS 37 are discussed in Chapter 25 at 5.1.

The Basis for Conclusions accompanying IFRS 3 considers a number of ways that it might be thought possible to get around this requirement, for example, by the acquiree, on instructions of the acquirer, entering into obligations to restructure the business before the formal transfer of control.[120] It indicates that 'if the acquirer can compel the acquiree to incur obligations, then it is likely that the acquirer already controls the acquiree, given that control is the power to govern the financial and operating policies of an entity so as to obtain benefits from its activities'.[121] In that situation, the date of acquisition would be date the acquirer effectively obtained control, and at that time the acquiree would not have had an existing liability under IAS 37. However, the Basis for Conclusions does state that 'if, alternatively, the acquirer suggests that negotiations cannot proceed until the acquiree arranges, for example, to restructure its workforce, and the acquiree takes the steps necessary to satisfy the recognition criteria for restructuring provisions in IAS 37, then those obligations are pre-combination obligations of the acquiree and, in the Board's view, should be recognised as part of allocating the cost of the combination'.[122] In that situation, the acquiree has a liability for the restructuring irrespective of whether the business combination takes place or not, and is taking the risk that having made that commitment the acquirer may not complete the acquisition.

The IASB also considered the situation whereby the acquiree and the acquirer could agree for the acquiree to take the steps necessary to satisfy the recognition requirements of the standard, but to make the execution of the plan conditional on the acquiree being acquired in a business combination.[123] However, the standard clarifies that an acquiree's restructuring plan whose execution is conditional upon its being acquired in a business combination is not, immediately before the business combination, a present obligation of the acquiree.[124] The reason being that even if the main features of the plan were announced to those that would be affected by it, the entity has not raised the 'valid expectation' that it will be carried out since it is conditional on the entity being acquired in a business combination.[125] Nor is it a contingent liability of the acquiree immediately before the combination because it is not a possible obligation arising from a past event whose existence will be confirmed only by the occurrence or non-occurrence of one or more uncertain future events not wholly within the control of the acquiree.[126] The reason being that the uncertain future event (i.e. being acquired in a business combination) is generally within the acquiree's control.[127] Therefore, an acquirer shall not recognise a liability for such restructuring plans as part of allocating the cost of the combination.[128]

Thirdly, IFRS 3 states that a payment that an entity is contractually required to make, for example, to its employees or suppliers in the event that it is acquired in a business combination is a present obligation of the entity that is regarded as a contingent liability until it becomes probable that a business combination will take place. The contractual obligation is recognised as a liability by that entity in accordance with IAS 37 when a business combination becomes probable and the liability can be measured reliably. Therefore, when the business combination is effected, that liability of the acquiree is recognised by the acquirer as part of allocating the cost of the combination.[129]

Lastly, the standard states that the identifiable assets and liabilities that are recognised in accordance with paragraph 36 of the standard include all of the acquiree's assets and liabilities that the acquirer purchases or assumes, including all of its financial assets and financial liabilities. They might also include assets and liabilities not previously recognised in the acquiree's financial statements, e.g. because they did not qualify for recognition before the acquisition. For example, a tax benefit arising from the acquiree's tax losses that was not recognised by the acquiree before the business combination qualifies for recognition as an identifiable asset in accordance with paragraph 36 if it is probable that the acquirer will have future taxable profits against which the unrecognised tax benefit can be applied.[130]

B   Acquiree's intangible assets

As indicated at 2.3.3 above, the allocation of the cost of the business combination includes the separate recognition of the acquiree's intangible assets. This is irrespective of whether the asset had been recognised by the acquiree before the business combination.[131] IFRS 3 requires the acquirer to recognise separately an intangible asset of the acquiree at the acquisition date only if:

- it meets the definition of an intangible asset in IAS 38; and
- its fair value can be measured reliably.[132]

IAS 38 includes equivalent requirements, and also emphasises that the probability recognition criterion in paragraph 21(a) of IAS 38 (see Chapter 11 at 2.2) is always considered to be satisfied for intangible asset acquired in a business combination; the effect of probability being taken into account in the determination of fair value.[133]

IFRS 3 refers to the guidance provided within IAS 38 on determining whether the fair value of an intangible asset acquired in a business combination can be measured reliably.[134]

I   What is an intangible asset?

IAS 38 defines an 'intangible asset' as 'an identifiable non-monetary asset without physical substance'.[135] Thus to meet the definition of an intangible asset, a non-monetary asset without physical substance must be identifiable. IFRS 3 states that in accordance with IAS 38, an asset meets the identifiability criterion in the definition of an intangible asset only if it:

(a)   is separable, i.e. capable of being separated or divided from the entity and sold, transferred, licensed, rented or exchanged, either individually or together with a related contract, asset or liability; or

(b)   arises from contractual or other legal rights, regardless of whether those rights are transferable or separable from the entity or from other rights and obligations.[136]

Both IFRS 3 and IAS 38 explicitly refer to the fact that this means that the acquirer recognises as an asset separately from goodwill an in-process research and development project of the acquiree (if the project meets the definition of an intangible asset and its fair value can be measured reliably).[137] This is discussed further below. IFRS 3 gives guidance in an Illustrative Example that provides a large list of examples of items acquired in a business combination that meet the definition of an intangible asset and are therefore to be recognised separately from goodwill, provided that their fair values can be measured reliably, whilst noting that they are not intended to be an exhaustive list of items acquired in a business combination that meet the definition of an intangible asset.[138] A non-monetary asset without physical substance acquired in a business combination might meet the identifiability criterion for identification as an intangible asset but not be included in the guidance.

The guidance designates the assets listed with symbols to identify those that meet part (a) of the definition and those that meet part (b) of the definition, whilst noting that those designated as meeting part (b) might also be separable. However, it emphasises that separability is not a necessary condition for an asset to meet the contractual-legal criterion.

The table below summarises the items included in the Illustrative Example that the IASB regard as meeting the definition of an intangible asset and are therefore to be recognised separately from goodwill, provided that their fair values can be measured reliably. Reference should be made to the Illustrative Example for any further explanation about some of these items.

Intangible assets arising from contractual or other legal rights (regardless of being separable)	Other intangible assets that are separable
Marketing-related	
– Trademarks, trade names, service marks, collective marks and certification marks – Internet domain names – Trade dress (unique colour, shape or package design) – Newspaper mastheads – Non-competition agreements	
Customer-related	
– Order or production backlogs – Customer contracts and the related customer relationships	– Customer lists – Non-contractual customer relationships
Artistic-related	
– Plays, operas and ballets – Books, magazines, newspapers and other literary works – Musical works such as compositions, song lyrics and advertising jingles – Pictures and photographs – Video and audiovisual material, including films, music videos and television programmes	
Contract-based	
– Licensing, royalty and standstill agreements – Advertising, construction, management, service or supply contracts – Lease agreements – Construction permits – Franchise agreements – Operating and broadcasting rights – Use rights such as drilling, water, air, mineral, timber-cutting and route authorities – Servicing contracts such as mortgage servicing contracts – Employment contracts that are beneficial contracts from the perspective of the employer because the pricing of those contracts is below their current market value	
Technology-based	
– Patented technology – Computer software and mask works – Trade secrets such as secret formulas, processes or recipes	– Unpatented technology – Databases

It can be seen from the table that customer relationships can potentially fall under either category. Where relationships are established with customers through contracts, those customer relationships arise from contractual rights, regardless of whether a contract exists, or there is any backlog of orders, at the date of acquisition. In such cases, it does not matter that the relationship is separable. It would only be if the relationship did not arise from a contract that the recognition depends on the separability criterion.

It is clear from the table above that the IASB envisages a wide range of items meeting the definition of an intangible asset, and therefore potentially being recognised separately from goodwill. Whether they are recognised separately or not will depend on whether their fair values can be measured reliably.

II   Can fair value be measured reliably?

IFRS 3 itself provides no guidance on whether the fair value of an intangible asset can be measured reliably. Instead, it refers to the guidance contained in IAS 38.[139]

IAS 38 states that the fair value of intangible assets acquired in business combinations can normally be measured with sufficient reliability to be recognised separately from goodwill.[140] As indicated earlier, IAS 38 indicates that the fair value of an intangible asset reflects market expectations about the probability that the future economic benefits embodied in the asset will flow to the entity. In other words, the effect of probability is reflected in the fair value measurement of the intangible asset.[141]

When, for the estimates used to measure an intangible asset's fair value, there is a range of possible outcomes with different probabilities, that uncertainty is factored into the measurement of the asset's fair value, rather than demonstrating an inability to measure fair value reliably.

If an intangible asset acquired in a business combination has a finite useful life, there is a rebuttable presumption in IAS 38 that its fair value can be measured reliably.[142]

In developing its proposals, the IASB had originally concluded that, except for an assembled workforce, sufficient information could reasonably be expected to exist to measure reliably the fair value of all intangible assets. However, after considering respondents' comments and the experiences of field visit and round-table participants, it concluded that, in some instances, there might not be sufficient information to measure reliably the fair value of an intangible asset separately from goodwill, notwithstanding that the asset is 'identifiable'.[143]

IAS 38 therefore states that 'the only circumstances in which it might not be possible to measure reliably the fair value of an intangible asset acquired in a business combination are when the intangible asset arises from legal or other contractual rights and either:

(a)   is not separable; or

(b)   is separable, but there is no history or evidence of exchange transactions for the same or similar assets, and otherwise estimating fair value would be dependent on immeasurable variables.[144]

It is clear that the IASB envisages that most intangible assets will be accounted for separately from goodwill and it remains to be seen how practice develops with respect to this question of when it may not be possible to measure reliably the fair value of intangible assets. Possibly as an anti-avoidance measure, the IASB has introduced a specific disclosure requirement to give a description of each intangible asset that was not recognised separately from goodwill and an explanation of why the intangible asset's fair value could not be measured reliably (see item (h) at 2.3.9 A below).

The IASB has recognised that an intangible asset acquired in a business combination might be separable, but only together with a related tangible or intangible asset. For example, a magazine's publishing title might not be able to be sold separately from a related subscriber database, or a trademark for natural spring water might relate to a particular spring and could not be sold separately from the spring. In such cases IAS 38 requires the acquirer to recognise the group of assets as a single asset separately from goodwill if the individual fair values of the assets in the group are not reliably measurable.[145] In practice, where the other asset is a tangible asset it is likely that its fair value can be determined.

IAS 38 notes that the terms 'brand' and 'brand name' are often used as synonyms for trademarks and other marks. However, the former are regarded as general marketing terms that are typically used to refer to a group of complementary assets such as a trademark (or service mark) and its related trade name, formulas, recipes and technological expertise. Accordingly, IAS 38 requires the acquirer to recognise as a single asset a group of complementary intangible assets comprising a brand if the individual fair values of the complementary assets are not reliably measurable. If the individual fair values of the complementary assets are reliably measurable, an acquirer may nevertheless still recognise them as a single asset provided the individual assets have similar useful lives.[146] Guidance on the determination of asset lives of intangible assets is discussed in Chapter 11 at 2.4.

III   *In-process research or development project expenditure*

As indicated earlier, both IFRS 3 and IAS 38 explicitly refer to the fact that the acquirer recognises as an asset separately from goodwill an in-process research and development project of the acquiree (if the project meets the definition of an intangible asset and its fair value can be measured reliably).[147] It is worth considering further the meaning of the words in parentheses.

An intangible asset meets the identifiability criterion under IAS 38 when it:

'(a)   is separable, i.e. is capable of being separated or divided from the entity and sold, transferred, licensed, rented or exchanged, either individually or together with a related contract, asset or liability; or

(b)   arises from contractual or other legal rights, regardless of whether those rights are transferable or separable from the entity or from other rights and obligations'.[148]

In-process research and development projects, whether or not recognised by the acquiree, are protected by legal rights and are on occasion bought and sold by entities without there being a business acquisition. Therefore, they are intangible assets as defined by IAS 38. Moreover, because they are separable and there is evidence of exchange transactions, the standard assumes that the fair value can be measured reliably. In addition, under IFRS 3 the probability criterion for recognition of an intangible asset is deemed to be met as long as its fair value can be measured reliably.

Therefore, the recognition of in-process research and development as an asset on acquisition applies different criteria to those that are required for internal projects. The research costs of internal projects may under no circumstances be capitalised.[149] Before capitalising development expenditure, entities must meet a series of exacting requirements. They must demonstrate the intangible assets' technical feasibility, their ability to complete the assets and use them or sell them and must be able to measure reliably the attributable expenditure.[150] The probable future economic benefits must be assessed using the principles in IAS 36 which means that they have to be calculated as the net present value of the cash flows generated by the asset or, if it can only generate cash flows in conjunction with other assets, of the cash-generating unit of which it is a part.[151] This process is described further in Chapter 13.

What this means is that entities will be required to recognise on acquisition some research and development expenditure that they would not have been able to recognise if it had been an internal project. The IASB was aware of this inconsistency but concluded that this did not provide a basis for subsuming in-process research and development within goodwill. It has considered the alternative (a reconsideration of the conditions for recognition of research and development costs) as being outwith the scope of the business combinations project.[152]

Although the amount attributed to the project is accounted for as an asset, IAS 38 goes on to require that any subsequent expenditure incurred after the acquisition of the project shall be accounted for in accordance with paragraphs 54-62 of IAS 38.[153] These requirements are discussed in Chapter 11 at 2.2.6.

In summary, this means that the subsequent expenditure is:

(a)   recognised as an expense when incurred if it is research expenditure;

(b)   recognised as an expense when incurred if it is development expenditure that does not satisfy the criteria for recognition as an intangible asset in paragraph 57; and

(c)   added to the carrying amount of the acquired in-process research or development project if it is development expenditure that satisfies the recognition criteria in paragraph 57.[154]

The inference is that the in-process research and development expenditure recognised as an asset on acquisition that never progresses to the stage of satisfying the recognition criteria for an internal project will ultimately be impaired, although it may be that this impairment will not arise until the entity is satisfied that the project will not continue. However, since it is an intangible asset not yet available for use, it will need to be tested for impairment annually by comparing its carrying amount with its recoverable amount.[155] Any impairment loss will be reflected in the entity's income statement as a post–acquisition event.

C   *Acquiree's contingent liabilities*

As indicated at 2.3.3 above, the allocation of the cost of the business combination includes the separate recognition of the acquiree's contingent liabilities, if its fair value can be measured reliably, despite the fact that the acquiree has not recognised any liability for that contingency and that the recognition as a liability by the acquirer in accounting for the business combination is inconsistent with the recognition criteria in IAS 37. As indicated earlier, the IASB takes the view that the fair value of a contingent liability reflects market expectations about any uncertainty surrounding the possibility that an outflow of resources embodying economic benefits will be required to settle the possible or present obligation.

Since the recognition of this liability is not what would be required by IAS 37, IFRS 3 therefore includes requirements for the subsequent measurement of such liabilities. Accordingly, after their initial recognition, the acquirer shall measure contingent liabilities that are recognised separately in accordance with paragraph 36 of the standard at the higher of:

(a)   the amount that would be recognised in accordance with IAS 37, and

(b)   the amount initially recognised less, when appropriate, cumulative amortisation recognised in accordance with IAS 18.[156]

In developing the requirements the IASB had originally proposed that the amount should be remeasured at fair value, with any changes recognised in profit or loss until settled or the uncertain future event resolved. However, in considering respondents' comments, the IASB noted that the proposal was inconsistent with the accounting for financial guarantees and commitments to provide loans at below-market interest rates under IAS 39 (see Chapter 18 at 9.2 and Chapter 15 at 3.4) and so decided to amend its proposals for consistency with IAS 39.[157]

The implications of part (a) of the requirement are clear. If the acquiree has to recognise a provision in respect of the former contingent liability, and the best estimate of this liability is higher than the original fair value attributed by the acquirer, then the greater liability should now be recognised by the acquirer with the difference taken to the income statement. It would now be a provision to be measured and recognised in accordance with IAS 37. What is less clear is part (b) of the requirement. The reference to 'amortisation recognised in accordance with IAS 18' might relate to the recognition of income in respect of those loan commitments that are contingent liabilities of the acquiree, but have been recognised at fair value at date of acquisition. The implication of the requirement would appear to mean that the amount of the liability cannot be reduced below its originally attributed fair value except in restrictive circumstances. It would also seem to imply that the liability could not be derecognised even if the contingency were resolved without an outflow of economic benefits or the item has been settled at a lower amount, which clearly could not have been what was intended.

We consider that it is important to bear in mind that the contingent liabilities have not been recognised by the acquiree because they are either:

- possible obligations, as it has yet to be confirmed whether the entity has a present obligation that could lead to an outflow of resources embodying economic benefits; or

- present obligations that do not meet the recognition criteria in IAS 37 (because either it is not probable that an outflow of resources embodying economic benefits will be required to settle the obligation, or a sufficiently reliable estimate of the amount of the obligation cannot be made).[158]

In many instances, therefore, these contingent liabilities will never become liabilities under IAS 37 or be settled (in cash or other resources) by the entities. Therefore, it must be acceptable to write back the contingent liability if the uncertainty is resolved (whether by payment or otherwise) and it is clear that there is no remaining obligation on the part of the entity.

Despite the fact that the requirement for subsequent measurement discussed above was introduced for consistency with IAS 39, the standard makes it clear that the requirement does not apply to contracts accounted for in accordance with IAS 39. However, loan commitments excluded from the scope of IAS 39 (other than those that are commitments to provide loans at below-market interest rates) will fall within the requirements of IFRS 3. Such loan commitments are to be regarded as contingent liabilities of the acquiree if, at the acquisition date, it is not probable that an outflow of resources embodying economic benefits will be required to settle the obligation or if the amount of the obligation cannot be measured with sufficient reliability. As with other contingent liabilities of the acquiree, such a loan commitment is recognised separately as part of allocating the cost of a combination only if its fair value can be measured reliably.[159]

IFRS 3 notes that contingent liabilities recognised separately as part of allocating the cost of a business combination are excluded from the scope of IAS 37. Nevertheless, the acquirer has to disclose for those contingent liabilities the information required to be disclosed by IAS 37 for each class of provision (see Chapter 25 at 6.1).[160]

If the fair value of a contingent liability cannot be measured reliably then the standard notes that this will impact on the amount recognised as goodwill or 'negative goodwill' (see 2.3.4 and 2.3.5 below). In that case, the acquirer shall disclose the information about that contingent liability required to be disclosed by IAS 37 (see Chapter 25 at 6.2).[161]

D   *Determining the fair values of the acquiree's identifiable assets, liabilities and contingent liabilities*

As indicated earlier, IFRS 3 requires an acquirer to recognise the acquiree's identifiable assets, liabilities and contingent liabilities that satisfy the relevant recognition criteria at their fair values at the acquisition date (except for non-current assets (or disposal groups) that are classified as held for sale in accordance with IFRS 5 which shall be recognised at fair value less costs to sell). Fair value is defined as 'the amount for which an asset could be exchanged, or a liability settled, between knowledgeable, willing parties in an arm's length transaction'.[162] Appendix B to IFRS 3, which is an integral part of the standard, gives guidance on the measures that should be used in determining the fair values of various items. It also notes that if the guidance for a particular item does not refer to the use of present value techniques, such techniques may be used in estimating the fair value of that item.[163] In addition, IAS 38 contains specific guidance on measuring the fair values of intangible assets. The guidance for particular items is discussed below.

I   Financial instruments

Financial instruments traded in an active market should be valued at their current market values. For financial instruments not traded in an active market estimated values should be used taking into consideration features such as price-earnings ratios, dividend yields and expected growth rates of comparable instruments of entities with similar characteristics.[164] This guidance reflects the fact that its origin comes from IAS 22, which only referred to 'securities' rather than financial instruments. For other types of financial instruments that are not traded on an active market, fair values may need to be estimated using present value techniques. Further guidance on the fair values of financial instruments is discussed in Chapter 18 at 4.

II   Receivables, beneficial contracts and other identifiable assets

Receivables, beneficial contracts and other identifiable assets should be valued based on the present values of the amounts to be received, determined at appropriate current interest rates, less allowances for uncollectibility and collection costs, if necessary. However, discounting is not required for short-term receivables, beneficial contracts and other identifiable assets when the difference between the nominal and discounted amounts is not material.[165]

III   Inventories

Finished goods and merchandise should be valued using selling prices less the costs of disposal and a reasonable profit allowance for the selling effort of the acquirer based on profit for similar finished goods and merchandise. Work in progress should be valued using selling prices of finished goods less the sum of the costs to complete, the costs of disposal and a reasonable profit allowance for the completing and selling effort based on profit for similar finished goods. Raw materials should be valued using current replacement costs.[166]

IV   Land and buildings

These should be valued using market values.[167] Like plant and equipment below, these will probably need to be determined by appraisal. Also, in our view if there is no market-based evidence of fair value because of the specialised nature of the property, the fair value may need to be estimated using an income or a depreciated replacement cost approach.

V   Plant and equipment

Again, these should be valued using market values, normally determined by appraisal. If there is no market-based evidence of fair value because of the specialised nature of the item of plant and equipment and the item is rarely sold, except as part of a continuing business, an acquirer may need to estimate fair value using an income or a depreciated replacement cost approach.[168]

VI   Intangible assets

Intangible assets should be valued by reference to an active market as defined in IAS 38 (see Chapter 11 at 2.3.2 A).[169] IAS 38 states that 'quoted market prices in an active market provide the most reliable estimate of the fair value of an intangible asset'. It goes on to say that 'the appropriate market price is usually the current bid price. If current bid prices are unavailable, the price of the most recent similar transaction may provide a basis from which to estimate fair value, provided that there has not been a significant change in economic circumstances between the transaction date and the date at which the asset's fair value is estimated.'[170]

However, IAS 38 also notes that it is uncommon for an active market to exist for intangible assets and that such a market cannot exist for brands, newspaper mastheads, music and publishing rights, patents or trademarks,[171] i.e. many of the intangible assets that IFRS 3 and IAS 38 require an acquirer to recognise as part of the allocation process. Accordingly, if no active market exists, the intangible assets should be valued on a basis that reflects the amounts the acquirer would have paid for the assets in arm's length transactions between knowledgeable willing parties, based on the best information available.[172] In determining this amount, an entity considers the outcome of recent transactions for similar assets.[173]

IAS 38 acknowledges that entities that are regularly involved in the purchase and sale of unique intangible assets may have developed techniques for estimating their fair values indirectly. Accordingly, it allows these techniques to be used for initial measurement of an intangible asset acquired in a business combination if their objective is to estimate fair value and if they reflect current transactions and practices in the industry to which the asset belongs. These techniques include, when appropriate:

(a)   applying multiples reflecting current market transactions to indicators that drive the profitability of the asset (such as revenue, market shares and operating profit) or to the royalty stream that could be obtained from licensing the intangible asset to another party in an arm's length transaction (as in the 'relief from royalty' approach); or

(b)   discounting estimated future net cash flows from the asset.[174]

VII   Defined benefit plans

Net employee benefit assets or liabilities for defined benefit plans should be valued using the present value of the defined benefit obligation less the fair value of any plan assets. However, an asset is recognised only to the extent that it is probable it will be available to the acquirer in the form of refunds from the plan or a reduction in future contributions.[175] In computing the present value of the obligation, IAS 19 – *Employee Benefits* – states that any items such as actuarial gains and losses (whether or not within the 10% corridor allowed by IAS 19), past service costs and amounts not yet recognised by the acquiree under the transitional provisions of IAS 19 at the date of the acquisition should be included.[176] This means that there are no exemptions for the acquirer from recognising the full defined benefit obligation on acquisition.

VIII   Tax assets and liabilities

Tax assets and liabilities should be valued using the amount of the tax benefit arising from tax losses or the taxes payable in respect of profit or loss in accordance with IAS 12 – *Income Taxes*, assessed from the perspective of the combined entity. The tax asset or liability is determined after allowing for the tax effect of restating identifiable assets, liabilities and contingent liabilities to their fair values and is not discounted.[177] The deferred tax consequences of business combinations are discussed further in Chapter 24 at 6.2.

IX   Payables

Accounts and notes payable, long-term debt, liabilities, accruals and other claims payable should be valued using the present values of amounts to be disbursed in settling the liabilities determined at appropriate current interest rates. However, discounting is not required for short-term liabilities when the difference between the nominal and discounted amounts is not material.[178]

X   Onerous contracts and other identifiable liabilities

Onerous contracts and other identifiable liabilities of the acquiree the acquirer shall use the present values of amounts to be disbursed in settling the obligations determined at appropriate current interest rates.[179]

XI   Contingent liabilities

Contingent liabilities of the acquiree should be valued using the amounts that a third party would charge to assume those contingent liabilities. Such an amount shall reflect all expectations about possible cash flows and not the single most likely or the expected maximum or minimum cash flow.[180] This is especially relevant given that many contingent liabilities are so defined as it is not probable that an outflow of resources embodying economic benefits will be required to settle the obligation[181] – even though the minimum cash flow may be zero, a third party would still charge a sum to assume the contingent liability.

2.3.4   Goodwill

IFRS 3 now defines 'goodwill' in terms of its nature, rather than in terms of its measurement.[182] It is defined as 'future economic benefits arising from assets that are not capable of being individually identified and separately recognised'.[183]

Accordingly, the standard requires that an acquirer shall, at the acquisition date, recognise goodwill acquired in a business combination as an asset. However, rather than attributing a fair value to the goodwill directly, the standard requires that the initial measurement of goodwill is its cost, being the excess of the cost of the business combination (as determined in 2.3.2 above) over the acquirer's interest in the net fair value of the identifiable assets, liabilities and contingent liabilities recognised in accordance with the standard (as determined in 2.3.3 above).[184]

IFRS 3 thus considers goodwill acquired in a business combination to represent a payment made by the acquirer in anticipation of future economic benefits from assets that are not capable of being individually identified and separately recognised.[185]

Since goodwill is measured as the residual cost of the business combination after recognising the acquiree's identifiable assets, liabilities and contingent liabilities, then to the extent that the acquiree's identifiable assets, liabilities or contingent liabilities do not satisfy the criteria in IFRS 3 for separate recognition at the acquisition date (see 2.3.3 above), there is a resulting effect on the amount recognised as goodwill.[186]

The IASB in developing the standard observed that 'when goodwill is measured as a residual it could comprise the following components:

(a)   the fair value of the "going concern" element of the acquiree. The going concern element represents the ability of the acquiree to earn a higher rate of return on an assembled collection of net assets than would be expected from those net assets operating separately. That value stems from the synergies of the net assets of the acquiree, as well as from other benefits such as factors related to market imperfections, including the ability to earn monopoly profits and barriers to market entry.

(b)   the fair value of the expected synergies and other benefits from combining the acquiree's net assets with those of the acquirer. Those synergies and other benefits are unique to each business combination, and different combinations produce different synergies and, hence, different values.

(c)   overpayments by the acquirer.

(d)   errors in measuring and recognising the fair value of either the cost of the business combination or the acquiree's identifiable assets, liabilities or contingent liabilities, or a requirement in an accounting standard to measure those identifiable items at an amount that is not fair value.'[187]

The Board regards components (a) and (b) as being 'core goodwill' and conceptually part of goodwill that should be recognised as an asset, whereas components (c) and (d) are not. However, it took the view that it would not be feasible to determine the amount attributable to each component and, since the residual amount is likely to consist primarily of core goodwill, concluded it should be recognised as an asset.[188] Any overpayment logically would be exposed by the impairment test now required in the subsequent accounting for goodwill discussed at 3 below.

2.3.5   *Excess of acquirer's interest in the net fair value of acquiree's identifiable assets, liabilities and contingent liabilities over cost*

IFRS 3 recognises that in some business combinations, the acquirer's interest in the net fair value of the acquiree's identifiable assets, liabilities and contingent liabilities exceeds the cost of the combination. Traditionally, that excess has been commonly referred to as 'negative goodwill' (although IFRS 3 does not use this term).

Where such an excess arises, IFRS 3 requires the acquirer to reassess the identification and measurement of the acquiree's identifiable assets, liabilities and contingent liabilities and the measurement of the cost of the combination.[189] This is because the existence of this excess might indicate that:

(a)   the values attributed to the acquiree's identifiable assets have been overstated;

(b)   identifiable liabilities and/or contingent liabilities of the acquiree have been omitted or the values attributed to those items have been understated; or

(c)   the values assigned to the items comprising the cost of the business combination have been understated.[190]

The IASB considers that the excess cannot come about because there is an expectation of future losses and expenses. Instead, it considers that the expectation of such losses and expenses will depress the fair value of the acquiree's identifiable assets, liabilities and contingent liabilities.[191] As future losses and restructuring expenses are expressly prohibited from recognition as liabilities of the acquiree (see 2.3.3 A above), there would appear to be many occasions where the acquirer will have to perform an impairment exercise of the assets or cash generating assets that it has acquired in order to reflect their fair values.

Having undertaken that reassessment, the standard then requires that any excess remaining after that reassessment shall be recognised immediately in profit or loss.[192]

The standard notes that a gain recognised in accordance with the above requirement could comprise one or more of the following components:

(a)   errors in measuring the fair value of either the cost of the combination or the acquiree's identifiable assets, liabilities or contingent liabilities, notwithstanding the reassessment. Possible future costs arising in respect of the acquiree that have not been reflected correctly in the fair value of the acquiree's identifiable assets, liabilities or contingent liabilities are a potential cause of such errors.

(b)   a requirement in an accounting standard to measure identifiable net assets acquired at an amount that is not fair value, but is treated as though it is fair value for the purpose of allocating the cost of the combination. For example, the guidance in Appendix B to the standard (see 2.3.3 D above) on determining the fair values of the acquiree's identifiable assets and liabilities requires the amount assigned to tax assets and liabilities to be undiscounted.

(c)   a bargain purchase.[193] This might occur, for example, when the seller of a business wishes to exit from that business for other than economic reasons and is prepared to accept less than its fair value as consideration;[194] this is particularly common if there is a distressed or 'fire' sale.

In developing the standard, the IASB considered whether the appropriate treatment for these components should be to recognise it as a reduction in the values attributed to the identifiable net asset, as a separate liability or immediately in profit or loss. However, the Board rejected the first two treatments and decided that the immediate recognition of a gain was the most faithful treatment of the part of the excess arising from a bargain purchase and that it would not be feasible to identify separately the amounts that are attributable to components (a) and (b) above.[195]

2.3.6 *Subsequent adjustments to fair values*

The initial accounting for a business combination under IFRS 3 involves identifying and determining the fair values to be assigned to the acquiree's identifiable assets, liabilities and contingent liabilities and the cost of the combination.[196]

The fact that the fair value process is inevitably, to some degree, a rationalisation of the price paid after the event means that an accounting issue arises: how much hindsight can the acquirer impute into the values assigned, or must the allocation be based solely on the information which it had at the time when it was making the bid? There is a theoretical argument for the latter, which is that if the acquirer was unaware of a particular matter, such as the fact that there was a deficiency in the pension fund of the target, then it cannot have influenced the acquisition price and thus should not feature in any allocation of that price.

Whatever the merits of that view in theory, however, it cannot be used in practice. If the acquirer was only able to assign values to items that it knew about at the time of the acquisition, the exercise would in many cases be completely impossible, because most acquisitions are not primarily based on an assessment of the value of the assets and liabilities of the target entity, but on an assessment of future earnings and cash flows. It is therefore necessary to allow the acquirer a reasonable period of time in which to investigate the assets and liabilities that have been acquired and make a reasoned allocation of values to them. The remaining question is, how much time should be allowed?

IFRS 3 effectively requires the acquirer to complete the allocation of the cost of the business combination to the acquiree's assets, liabilities and contingent liabilities within a period of twelve months of the acquisition date.[197] The important practical point for an acquirer is that it will have to demonstrate that any subsequent adjustments were in fact made by this date and not at its subsequent period end date.

If the initial accounting for a business combination can be determined only provisionally by the end of the period in which the combination is effected because either the fair values to be assigned to the acquiree's identifiable assets, liabilities or contingent liabilities or the cost of the combination can be determined only provisionally, the acquirer shall account for the combination using those provisional values.[198] It should be noted that IFRS 3 requires disclosure of the fact that it has only been determined provisionally, with an explanation as to why that has been case (see 2.3.9 below).

A   *Adjustments upon completion of initial accounting*

Where as a result of completing the initial accounting within twelve months from the acquisition date adjustments to the provisional values have been found to be necessary, IFRS 3 requires them to be recognised from the acquisition date. This means, therefore, that:

(a)   the carrying amount of an identifiable asset, liability or contingent liability that is recognised or adjusted as a result of completing the initial accounting shall be calculated as if its fair value at the acquisition date had been recognised from that date;

(b)   goodwill or any gain recognised in accordance with paragraph 56 of the standard shall be adjusted from the acquisition date by an amount equal to the adjustment to the fair value at the acquisition date of the identifiable asset, liability or contingent liability being recognised or adjusted; and

(c)   comparative information presented for the periods before the initial accounting for the combination is complete shall be presented as if the initial accounting had been completed from the acquisition date. This includes any additional depreciation, amortisation or other profit or loss effect recognised as a result of completing the initial accounting.[199]

These requirements are illustrated in the following example, which is based on Example 7 included within the Illustrative Examples accompanying IFRS 3. The deferred tax implications have been ignored.

Example 6.1

Entity A prepares financial statements for annual periods ending on 31 December and does not prepare interim financial statements. The entity acquired another entity on 30 September 2004. Entity A sought an independent appraisal for an item of property, plant and equipment acquired in the combination. However, the appraisal was not finalised by the time the entity completed its 2004 annual financial statements. Entity A recognised in its 2004 annual financial statements a provisional fair value for the asset of €30,000, and a provisional value for acquired goodwill of €100,000. The item of property, plant and equipment had a remaining useful life at the acquisition date of five years.

Six months after the acquisition date, the entity received the independent appraisal, which estimated the asset's fair value at the acquisition date at €40,000.

In preparing its 2005 financial statements, Entity A is required to recognise any adjustments to provisional values as a result of completing the initial accounting from the acquisition date.

Part (a) of the requirement means that an adjustment is made to the carrying amount of the item of property, plant and equipment. That adjustment is measured as the fair value adjustment at the acquisition date of €10,000, less the additional depreciation that would have been recognised had the asset's fair value at the acquisition date been recognised from that date (€500 for three months' depreciation to 31 December 2004), i.e. an increase of €9,500. Part (b) requires the carrying amount of goodwill to be adjusted for the increase in value of the asset at the acquisition date of €10,000. Part (c) requires the 2004 comparative information to be restated to reflect these adjustments. Accordingly, the 2004 balance sheet is restated by increasing the carrying amount of property, plant and equipment by €9,500, reducing goodwill by €10,000 and retained earnings by €500. The 2004 income statement is restated to include additional depreciation of €500.

Entity A will disclose in its 2004 financial statements that the initial accounting for the business combination has been determined only provisionally, and explain why this is the case. In its 2005 financial statements it will disclose the amounts and explanations of the adjustments to the provisional values recognised during the current reporting period. Therefore, Entity A will disclose that:

•   the fair value of the item of property, plant and equipment at the acquisition date has been increased by €10,000 with a corresponding decrease in goodwill; and

•   the 2004 comparative information is restated to reflect this adjustment, including additional depreciation of €500 relating to the year ended 31 December 2004.

Although IFRS 3 allows this period of hindsight to be used, it is important that any adjustments to the provisional allocation reflect conditions as they existed at the date of the acquisition, rather than being affected by subsequent events; the objective is to determine the fair values of the items at the date of acquisition. There is a parallel to be drawn here with the accounting treatment of events after the balance sheet date; only those events which provide further evidence of conditions as they existed at the acquisition date should be taken into account.

B   *Adjustments after the initial accounting is complete*

With three exceptions (see C below), after the initial accounting is complete, IFRS 3 only allows adjustments to the initial accounting for a business combination to be made to correct an error in accordance with IAS 8 (see Chapter 3 at 4.6).[200] This would probably be the case only if the original allocation was based on a complete misinterpretation of the facts which were available at the time; it would not apply simply because new information had come to light which changed the acquiring management's view of the value of the item in question.

Adjustments to the initial accounting for a business combination after it is complete are not made for the effect of changes in estimates. In accordance with IAS 8, the effect of a change in estimates are recognised in the current and future periods (see Chapter 3 at 4.5).[201]

Where it is determined that an error has been made, IFRS 3 notes that IAS 8 requires an entity to account for an error correction retrospectively, and to present financial statements as if the error had never occurred by restating the comparative information for the prior period(s) in which the error occurred.[202] The accounting is similar to that outlined above for adjustments upon completion of initial accounting. The only difference being there is no time limit as to when such adjustments may be required.

These requirements are illustrated in Examples 6.2 and 6.3 below, which are based on Examples 8 and 9 included within the Illustrative Examples accompanying IFRS 3. The deferred tax implications have been ignored.

Example 6.2:   *Error resulting in an increase in identifiable assets leading to a decrease in goodwill*

Entity A prepares financial statements for annual periods ending on 31 December and does not prepare interim financial statements. The entity acquired another entity on 30 September 2004. As part of the initial accounting for that combination, Entity A recognised goodwill of €100,000 in its 2004 financial statements. No impairment was recognised for this goodwill, so the carrying amount of goodwill at 31 December 2004 was €100,000.

During 2005, Entity A becomes aware of an error relating to the amount initially allocated to property, plant and equipment assets acquired in the business combination. In particular, €20,000 of the €100,000 initially allocated to goodwill should have been allocated to property, plant and equipment assets that had a remaining useful life at the acquisition date of five years, with an assumed residual value of nil.

In preparing its 2005 financial statements, Entity A is required to account for the correction of the error retrospectively, and for the financial statements to be presented as if the error had never occurred by correcting the error in the comparative information for the prior period in which it occurred.

Therefore, in the 2005 financial statements, an adjustment is made to the carrying amount of property, plant and equipment assets at 31 December 2004. The adjustment is measured as the fair value adjustment at the acquisition date of €20,000 less the amount that would have been recognised as depreciation of the fair value adjustment (€1,000 for three months' depreciation to 31 December 2004); i.e. property, plant and equipment is increased by €19,000. The carrying amount of goodwill is also adjusted for the reduction in its value at the acquisition date of €20,000. Accordingly, retained earnings at 31 December 2004 are reduced by €1,000. The 2004 income statement is restated to include additional depreciation of €1,000.

In accordance with IAS 8, Entity A will disclose in its 2005 financial statements the nature of the error and that, as a result of correcting that error, an adjustment was made to the carrying amount of property, plant and equipment. It will also disclose that:

- the fair value of property, plant and equipment assets at the acquisition date has been increased by €20,000 with a corresponding decrease in goodwill; and

- the 2004 comparative information is restated to reflect this adjustment, including additional depreciation of €1,000 for the year ended 31 December 2004.

Example 6.3:   Error resulting in a decrease in identifiable assets leading to an increase in goodwill

This example assumes the same facts as in Example 6.2 above, except that the amount initially allocated to property, plant and equipment assets is decreased by €20,000 to correct the error, rather than increased by €20,000. This example also assumes that Entity A determines that the recoverable amount of the additional goodwill is only €17,000 at 31 December 2004.

Therefore, in the 2005 financial statements, an adjustment is made to the carrying amount of property, plant and equipment assets at 31 December 2004. The adjustment is measured as the fair value adjustment at the acquisition date of €20,000 less the amount that should not have been recognised as depreciation of the fair value adjustment (€1,000 for three months' depreciation to 31 December 2004); i.e. property, plant and equipment is reduced by €19,000. The carrying amount of goodwill is increased by €17,000, being the increase in value at the acquisition date of €20,000 less a €3,000 impairment loss to reflect that the carrying amount of the adjustment exceeds its recoverable amount. Accordingly, retained earnings at 31 December 2004 are reduced by €2,000. The 2004 income statement is restated to reflect these adjustments; i.e. it includes the €3,000 impairment loss but excludes the €1,000 depreciation.

C   Recognition of deferred tax assets after the initial accounting is complete

IFRS 3 makes three exceptions to this requirement of only allowing adjustments for errors once the initial accounting is complete. The first two relate to adjustments to the cost of a business combination that was contingent on future events (see 2.3.2 E above). The other exception relates to the recognition of deferred tax assets. It should be noted that this exception was carried forward from IAS 22 without reconsideration by the IASB, and will be reconsidered as part of phase II of its business combinations project (as are the other two exceptions).

If the potential benefit of the acquiree's income tax loss carry-forwards or other deferred tax assets did not satisfy the criteria in paragraph 37 of IFRS 3 for separate recognition when a business combination is initially accounted for but is subsequently realised, IFRS 3 states that the acquirer shall recognise that benefit as income in accordance with IAS 12. However, in addition, the acquirer shall:

(a)   reduce the carrying amount of goodwill to the amount that would have been recognised if the deferred tax asset had been recognised as an identifiable asset from the acquisition date; and

(b)   recognise the reduction in the carrying amount of the goodwill as an expense.

The standard goes on to say that this procedure shall not result in the creation of an excess as described in paragraph 56 of the standard (see 2.3.5 above), nor shall it increase the amount of any gain previously recognised in accordance with paragraph 56.[203]

This issue is discussed further in Chapter 24 at 6.2.2 B.

2.3.7   *Business combinations achieved in stages*

So far, this chapter has discussed the application of the purchase method of accounting in the context of business combinations that result from a single exchange transaction. However, in practice some subsidiaries are acquired in a series of steps which can take place over an extended period, during which the underlying value of the subsidiary is likely to change, both because of the trading profits (or losses) which it retains and because of other movements in the fair values of its assets and liabilities. The accounting problems which this creates are therefore how to establish the cost of the business combination, the fair values of the net assets acquired, and therefore the amount of goodwill arising. It also has implications for the impact of the business combination on the post-acquisition reserves in the consolidated financial statements of the acquirer.

IFRS 3 recognises that a business combination may involve more than one exchange transaction, for example when it occurs in stages by successive share purchases. It should be noted that the requirements of the standard have principally been carried forward from IAS 22 and they will be reconsidered as part of the second phase of the business combinations project.[204]

Where a business combination does involve more than one exchange transaction, the standard requires that each exchange transaction shall be treated separately by the acquirer; i.e. by using the cost of the transaction and fair value information at the date of each exchange transaction, to determine the amount of any goodwill associated with that transaction. This results in a step-by-step comparison of the cost of the individual investments with the acquirer's interest in the fair values of the acquiree's identifiable assets, liabilities and contingent liabilities at each step.[205] (It has to be said that this actually contradicts the requirement of paragraph 36 of the standard (see 2.3.3 above) which is to allocate the cost of the business combination (this is the same under both requirements) to the acquiree's identifiable assets, liabilities and contingent liabilities at their fair values at the date of acquisition (i.e. the date that it obtains control), with any difference between the cost and the acquirer's interest in those net fair values being accounted for as goodwill or a gain in profit or loss. This is because the methodology in paragraph 36 would otherwise result in the share of reserves and asset revaluation reserves relating to the interest in the associate being rolled into the calculation of goodwill, as can be seen in the following examples.)

Where a subsidiary has been acquired by successive share purchases, then theoretically the standard would require separate comparisons, even if the shares were purchased over a short period of time. However, it may that in such a situation that the fair values of the acquiree's identifiable assets, liabilities and contingent liabilities at the date of acquisition could be used, as long as the values are unlikely to have been materially different during the period the shares were being purchased.

The standard notes that when a business combination involves more than one exchange transaction, the fair values of the acquiree's identifiable assets, liabilities and contingent liabilities may be different at the date of each exchange transaction.[206] This is likely to be the case where the transactions have taken place over an extended period. The standard states that because:

(a)   the acquiree's identifiable assets, liabilities and contingent liabilities are notionally restated to their fair values at the date of each exchange transaction to determine the amount of any goodwill associated with each transaction; and

(b)   the acquiree's identifiable assets, liabilities and contingent liabilities must then be recognised by the acquirer at their fair values at the acquisition date,

any adjustment to those fair values relating to previously held interests of the acquirer is a revaluation and shall be accounted for as such. However, it goes on to say that because this revaluation arises on the initial recognition by the acquirer of the acquiree's assets, liabilities and contingent liabilities, it does not signify that the acquirer has elected to apply an accounting policy of revaluing those items after initial recognition in accordance with, for example, IAS 16.[207]

Before qualifying as a business combination, a transaction may qualify as an investment in an associate and be accounted for in accordance with IAS 28 using the equity method. If so, the fair values of the investee's identifiable net assets at the date of each earlier exchange transaction will have been determined previously in applying the equity method to the investment (see Chapter 7 at 3.2).[208]

These requirements are illustrated in the following examples which are based on Example 6 included within the Illustrative Examples accompanying IFRS 3, except that in Example 6.4 below the acquirer has reflected the changes in value of its original investment in equity rather than in profit or loss.

Example 6.4:   *Business combination achieved in stages – original investment treated as an available-for-sale investment under IAS 39*

Investor acquires a 20 per cent ownership interest in Investee (a service company) on 1 January 2004 for £3,500,000 cash. At that date, the fair value of Investee's identifiable assets is £10,000,000, and the carrying amount of those assets is £8,000,000. Investee has no liabilities or contingent liabilities at that date. The following shows Investee's balance sheet at 1 January 2004 together with the fair values of the identifiable assets:

Investee's balance sheet at 1 January 2004	Carrying amounts £'000	Fair values £'000
Cash and receivables	2,000	2,000
Land	6,000	8,000
	8,000	10,000
Issued equity: 1,000,000 ordinary shares	5,000	
Retained earnings	3,000	
	8,000	

During the year ended 31 December 2004, Investee reports a profit of £6,000,000 but does not pay any dividends. In addition, the fair value of Investee's land increases by £3,000,000 to £11,000,000. However, the amount recognised by Investee in respect of the land remains unchanged at £6,000,000. The following shows Investee's balance sheet at 31 December 2004 together with the fair values of the identifiable assets:

Investee's balance sheet at 31 December 2004	Carrying amounts £'000	Fair values £'000
Cash and receivables	8,000	8,000
Land	6,000	11,000
	14,000	19,000
Issued equity: 1,000,000 ordinary shares	5,000	
Retained earnings	9,000	
	14,000	

On 1 January 2005, Investor acquires a further 60 per cent ownership interest in Investee for £22,000,000 cash, thereby obtaining control. Before obtaining control, Investor does not have significant influence over Investee, and accounts for its initial 20 per cent investment at fair value with changes in value taken to equity. Investee's ordinary shares have a quoted market price at 31 December 2004 of £30 per share.

Throughout the period 1 January 2004 to 1 January 2005, Investor's issued equity was £30,000,000. Investor's only asset apart from its investment in Investee is cash.

Accounting for the initial investment before obtaining control

Investor's initial 20 per cent investment in Investee is measured at its cost of £3,500,000. However, Investee's 1,000,000 ordinary shares have a quoted market price at 31 December 2004 of £30 per share. Therefore, the carrying amount of Investor's initial 20 per cent investment is remeasured in Investor's financial statements to £6,000,000 at 31 December 2004, with the £2,500,000 increase recognised in equity. Therefore, Investor's balance sheet at 31 December 2004, before the acquisition of the additional 60 per cent ownership interest, is as follows:

Investor's balance sheet at 31 December 2004	£'000
Cash	26,500
Investment in Investee	6,000
	32,500
Issued equity	30,000
Gain on available-for-sale investment	2,500
	32,500

Accounting for the business combination

Paragraph 25 of IFRS 3 (see 2.3.2 A above) states that when a business combination involves more than one exchange transaction, the cost of the combination is the aggregate cost of the individual transactions, with the cost of each individual transaction determined at the date of each exchange transaction, i.e. the date that each individual investment is recognised in the acquirer's financial statements). This means that for this example, the cost to Investor of the business combination is the aggregate of the cost of the initial 20 per cent ownership interest (£3,500,000) plus the cost of the subsequent 60 per cent ownership interest (£22,000,000), irrespective of the fact that the carrying amount of the initial 20 per cent interest has changed.

In addition, and in accordance with paragraph 58 of IFRS 3, each transaction must be treated separately to determine the goodwill on that transaction, using cost and fair value information at the date of each exchange transaction. Therefore, Investor recognises the following amounts for goodwill in its consolidated financial statements:

	£'000	Goodwill £'000
Acquisition of 20% interest on 1 January 2004		
Cost	3,500	
Share of fair values at that date (20% × £10,000,000)	2,000	
		1,500
Acquisition of 60% interest on 1 January 2005		
Cost	22,000	
Share of fair values at that date (60% × £19,000,000)	11,400	
		10,600
		12,100

The following shows Investor's consolidation worksheet immediately after the acquisition of the additional 60 per cent ownership interest in Investee, together with consolidation adjustments and associated explanations:

	Investor	Investee	Consolidation adjustments		Consolidated
			Dr	Cr	
	£'000	£'000	£'000	£'000	£'000
Cash and receivables	4,500	8,000			12,500
Investment in investee	28,000	–		2,500 (2)	–
				3,500 (3)	
				22,000 (4)	
Land		6,000	5,000 (1)		11,000 (a)
Goodwill			1,500 (3)		12,100 (b)
			10,600 (4)		
	32,500	14,000			35,600
Issued equity	30,000	5,000	1,000 (3)		30,000 (c)
			3,000 (4)		
			1,000 (5)		
Asset revaluation surplus			400 (3)	5,000 (1)	600 (d)
			3,000 (4)		
			1,000 (5)		
Gain on available-for-sale investment	2,500		2,500 (2)		
Retained earnings		9,000	600 (3)		1,200 (e)
			5,400 (4)		
			1,800 (5)		
Minority interest				3,800 (5)	3,800 (a)
	32,500	14,000			35,600

Consolidation Adjustments

			£'000	£'000
(1)	Land		5,000	
	Asset revaluation surplus			5,000

To recognise Investee's identifiable assets at fair values at the acquisition date

			£'000	£'000
(2)	Gain on available-for-sale investment		2,500	
	Investment in Investee			2,500

To restate the initial 20 per cent investment in Investee to cost

	£'000	£'000
(3) Issued equity [20% × 5,000,000]	1,000	
Asset revaluation surplus [20% × 2,000,000]	400	
Retained earnings [20% × 3,000,000]	600	
Goodwill	1,500	
Investment in investee		3,500

To recognise goodwill on the initial 20 per cent investment in Investee and record the elimination of that investment against associated equity balances

	£'000	£'000
(4) Issued equity [60% × 5,000,000]	3,000	
Asset revaluation surplus [60% × 5,000,000]	3,000	
Retained earnings [60% × 9,000,000]	5,400	
Goodwill	10,600	
Investment in investee		22,000

To recognise goodwill on the subsequent 60 per cent investment in Investee and record elimination of that investment against associated equity balances

	£'000	£'000
(5) Issued equity [20% × 5,000,000]	1,000	
Asset revaluation surplus [20% × 5,000,000]	1,000	
Retained earnings [20% × 9,000,000]	1,800	
Minority interest (in issued equity)		1,000
Minority interest (in asset revaluation surplus)		1,000
Minority interest (in retained earnings)		1,800

To recognise the minority interest in the Investee

Notes

The above consolidation adjustments result in:

(a) Investee's identifiable net assets being stated at their full fair values at the date Investor obtains control of Investee, i.e. £19,000,000. This means that the 20 per cent minority interest in Investee also is stated at the minority's 20 per cent share of the fair values of Investee's identifiable net assets.

(b) goodwill being recognised from the acquisition date at an amount based on treating each exchange transaction separately and using cost and fair value information at the date of each exchange transaction.

(c) issued equity of £30,000,000 comprising the issued equity of Investor of £30,000,000.

(d) an asset revaluation surplus of £600,000. This amount reflects that part of the increase in the fair value of Investee's identifiable net assets after the acquisition of the initial 20 per cent interest that is attributable to that initial 20 per cent interest [20% × £3,000,000].

(e) a retained earnings balance of £1,200,000. This amount reflects the changes in Investee's retained earnings after Investor acquired its initial 20 per cent interest that is attributable to that 20 per cent interest [20% × £6,000,000].

Therefore, the effect of applying the requirements in IFRS 3 to business combinations involving successive share purchases for which the investment was previously accounted for at fair value with changes in value taken to equity is to cause:

- changes in the fair value of previously held ownership interests to be reversed (so that the carrying amounts of those ownership interests are restated to cost).

- changes in the investee's retained earnings and other equity balances after each exchange transaction to be included in the post-combination consolidated financial statements to the extent that they relate to the previously held ownership interests.

Theses changes will need to be reflected in the statement of changes in equity.

As noted earlier, these requirements contradict the requirements of paragraph 36 of the standard. If that paragraph had been applied literally, the goodwill would have been £10,300,000, being the total cost of investment of £25,500,000 less £15,200,000 (being Investor's interest of 80% of the fair value of Investee's assets of £19,000,000 at the date of acquisition). The difference of £1,800,000 between this figure and goodwill as calculated above on each exchange transaction is the asset revaluation surplus of £600,000 ((d) above) and the share of reserves of £1,200,000 ((e) above), both of which would be subsumed within goodwill calculated solely as at the date that Investee became a subsidiary.

If the investor in the above example had accounted for its original investment of 20% as an associate using the equity method under IAS 28, then the accounting would have been as follows:

Example 6.5: *Business combination achieved in stages – original investment treated as an associate under IAS 28*

This example uses the same facts as in Example 6.4 above, except that Investor does have significant influence over Investee following its initial 20 per cent investment.

Accounting for the initial investment before obtaining control

Investor's initial 20 per cent investment in Investee is included in Investor's consolidated financial statements under the equity method (see Chapter 7 at 3). Accordingly, it is initially recognised at its cost of £3,500,000 and adjusted thereafter for its share of the profits of Investee after the date of acquisition of £1,200,000 (being 20% × £6,000,000). Investor's policy for property, plant and equipment is to use the cost model under IAS 16 (see Chapter 12 at 2.4), therefore in applying the equity method it does not include its share of the increased value of the land held by Investee. IAS 28 requires that on the acquisition of an associate, any difference between the cost of the acquisition and its share of the fair values of the associate's identifiable assets, liabilities and contingent liabilities is accounted for under IFRS 3, although any goodwill is included within the carrying amount of the investment in the associate. Accordingly, Investor has already calculated the goodwill of £1,500,000 arising on its original investment of 20%. Therefore, Investor's consolidated balance sheet at 31 December 2004, before the acquisition of the additional 60 per cent ownership interest, is as follows:

Investor's consolidated balance sheet at 31 December 2004	£'000
Cash	26,500
Investment in associate	4,700
	31,200
Issued equity	30,000
Retained earnings	1,200
	31,200

In its separate financial statements, Investor includes its investment in the associate at its cost of £3,500,000.

Accounting for the business combination

As in Example 6.4, the cost of the combination is the aggregate cost of the individual transactions, with the cost of each individual transaction determined at the date of each exchange transaction, i.e. the date that each individual investment is recognised in the acquirer's financial statements), and each transaction must be treated separately to determine the goodwill on that transaction, using cost and fair value information at the date of each exchange transaction. Therefore, Investor recognises the following amounts for goodwill in its consolidated financial statements:

	£'000	Goodwill £'000
Acquisition of 20% interest on 1 January 2004		
Cost	3,500	
Share of fair values at that date (20% × £10,000,000)	2,000	
		1,500
Acquisition of 60% interest on 1 January 2005		
Cost	22,000	
Share of fair values at that date (60% × £19,000,000)	11,400	
		10,600
		12,100

As indicated above, Investor will have already calculated the goodwill arising on its original investment, but not recognised it separately.

The following shows Investor's consolidation worksheet immediately after the acquisition of the additional 60 per cent ownership interest in Investee, together with consolidation adjustments and associated explanations.

	Investor £'000	Investee £'000	Consolidation adjustments Dr £'000	Consolidation adjustments Cr £'000	Consolidated £'000
Cash and receivables	4,500	8,000			12,500
Investment in investee	25,500	–		3,500 (3) 22,000 (4)	–
Land		6,000	5,000 (1)		11,000 (a)
Goodwill			1,500 (3) 10,600 (4)		12,100 (b)
	30,000	14,000			35,600
Issued equity	30,000	5,000	1,000 (3) 3,000 (4) 1,000 (5)		30,000 (c)
Asset revaluation surplus			400 (3) 3,000 (4) 1,000 (5)	5,000 (1)	600 (d)
Retained earnings		9,000	600 (3) 5,400 (4) 1,800 (5)		1,200 (e)
Minority interest				3,800 (5)	3,800 (a)
	30,000	14,000			35,600

The consolidation adjustments are exactly the same as in Example 6.4, except that there was no need for adjustment (2) since the investment of 20% was already included at cost.

The notes in Example 6.4 also apply to this example. The only difference is that the retained earnings balance has already been reflected in the consolidated balance sheet of Investor at 31 December 2004.

Therefore, the effect of applying the requirements in IFRS 3 to business combinations involving successive share purchases for which the investment was previously accounted for under the equity method is to cause changes in the investee's equity balances after each exchange transaction that result from changes in fair values to be included in the post-combination consolidated financial statements to the extent that they relate to the previously held ownership interests (and have not already been recognised).

In this example, the £600,000 asset revaluation surplus will be recognised in the statement of changes in equity in Investor's consolidated financial statements for 2005.

Overall, therefore, the effect of applying IFRS 3 to any business combination involving successive share purchases is to cause:

- any changes in the carrying amount of previously held ownership interests to be reversed (so that the carrying amounts of those ownership interests are restated to cost).

- changes in the investee's retained earnings and other equity balances after each exchange transaction to be included in the post-combination consolidated financial statements to the extent that they relate to the previously held ownership interests.

Consequently, the consolidated financial statements immediately after Investor acquires the additional 60 per cent ownership interest and obtains control of Investee would be the same irrespective of the method used to account for the initial 20 per cent investment in Investee before obtaining control.

As indicated earlier, the standard states that the adjustment to those fair values relating to previously held interests of the acquirer is a revaluation and shall be accounted for as such.[209] However, the standard is silent as to whether any such revaluation gain (or loss) can be recycled into profit or loss at a later date. IAS 27 also does not make any reference to such items being taken into account in calculating the gain or loss on disposal of a subsidiary (see Chapter 5 at 6.6). Although in the above examples, the revaluation gain arose on land, in practice, any revaluation gain or loss is likely to arise on various assets or liabilities of the acquiree. In many cases, the revaluation amounts are likely to arise on items such as intangible assets and property, plant and equipment, where under the relevant standard for such items, revaluations gains and losses are not recycled upon disposal of the related asset. Accordingly, we believe that any revaluation amount recognised as a result of a business combination involving successive share purchases should not normally be recycled into profit or loss, either on disposal of the underlying assets or the business concerned. However, where the revaluation amounts relate specifically to items where the relevant accounting standard would require recycling, such as available-for-sale investments under IAS 39, then there may be a case for treating these gains no differently from any other subsequent gains or losses for such items that are taken to equity. Similarly, if the revaluation surplus in equity relates directly to an identifiable fixed asset, whether intangible or an item of property, plant and equipment, it may be transferred directly to retained earnings when the asset is derecognised, in whole on disposal or in part on depreciation or amortisation.[210] If, as may well be the case, the revaluation relates to fair value adjustments on a bundle of assets and liabilities, the reserve will only be transferred to retained earnings on derecognition of the interest in the subsidiary.

In situations such as that illustrated in Example 6.5 above, where the equity method of accounting has been applied to the original investments, the requirements of IFRS 3 do not appear to create any additional practical difficulties over and above those that arose when the acquirer had to originally allocate the cost of the associate to the fair values of the acquiree's assets, liabilities and contingent liabilities. The main practical difficulty will be where equity accounting has not been applied to earlier stages of the business combination, such as in Example 6.4 above. In that case, the acquirer has to calculate goodwill based on fair values at the time of that original acquisition, yet will not have had to carry out such an exercise at that time. This situation is similar in many ways to that considered by the IASB in relation to the transitional provisions of IFRS 3 where it was decided that applying the standard retrospectively would be problematic, particularly in relation to the role of hindsight, and may even be impossible because the information needed may not exist or may no longer be obtainable. As discussed at 4.1.5 below the IASB only allows retrospective application of the standard where valuations and other information was obtained at the time the business combinations were initially accounted for. Where entities are contemplating making initial investments in other entities with a view to possibly obtaining a controlling stake in the entity in the future, they should consider carrying out a fair value exercise at that time, albeit that it may have to be done on a broad brush basis due to the lack of detailed information.

A   Acquisitions of minority interests

The requirements discussed above deal only with those situations where there have been earlier exchange transactions prior to the one that has resulted in a business combination, such as the acquisition of a subsidiary, whereby the acquirer now has control over that business. However, the standard is silent on how later exchange transactions should be accounted for, such as the acquisition of some or all of the minority interest in a subsidiary.

Example 6.6:   Acquisition of minority interest

Following on from Example 6.4 above, during the year ended 31 December 2005, Investee, now an 80% subsidiary of Investor, reports a profit of £8,000,000 but does not pay any dividends. In addition, the fair value of Investee's land increases by a further £4,000,000 to £15,000,000. However, the amount recognised by Investee in respect of the land remains unchanged at £6,000,000. The following shows Investee's balance sheet at 31 December 2005 together with the fair values of the identifiable assets:

Investee's balance sheet at 31 December 2005	Carrying amounts £'000	Fair values £'000
Cash and receivables	16,000	16,000
Land	6,000	15,000
	22,000	31,000
Issued equity: 1,000,000 ordinary shares	5,000	
Retained earnings	17,000	
	22,000	

Investor's issued equity remains at £30,000,000 and has not reported any profits for the year ended 31 December 2005.

The following shows Investor's consolidation worksheet as at 31 December 2005, together with consolidation adjustments and associated explanations:

	Investor £'000	Investee £'000	Consolidation adjustments Dr £'000	Consolidation adjustments Cr £'000	Consolidated £'000
Cash and receivables	4,500	16,000			20,500
Investment in investee	28,000	–		2,500 (2) 3,500 (3) 22,000 (4)	–
Land		6,000	5,000 (1)		11,000 (a)
Goodwill			1,500 (3) 10,600 (4)		12,100 (b)
	32,500	22,000			43,600
Issued equity	30,000	5,000	1,000 (3) 3,000 (4) 1,000 (5)		30,000 (c)
Asset revaluation surplus			400 (3) 3,000 (4) 1,000 (5)	5,000 (1)	600 (d)
Gain on available-for-sale investment	2,500		2,500 (2)		
Retained earnings		17,000	600 (3) 5,400 (4) 1,800 (5) 1,600 (5)		7,600 (e)
Minority interest				5,400 (5)	5,400 (a)
	32,500	22,000			43,600

Consolidation Adjustments

The consolidation adjustments are the same as in Example 6.4, except that consolidation adjustment (5) reflects an additional adjustment of:

		£'000	£'000
(5)	Retained earnings [20% × 8,000,000]	1,600	
	Minority interest (in retained earnings)		1,600
	To recognise the minority interest in Investee's results for 2005		

Notes

The consolidation adjustments result in:

(a) Investee's identifiable net assets being stated at their full fair values at the date Investor obtains control of Investee, i.e. £19,000,000, plus the profits for the year of £8,000,000. This means that the 20 per cent minority interest in Investee is stated at the minority's 20 per cent share of £27,000,000.

(e) a retained earnings balance of £7,600,000, being the £1,200,000 as in Example 6.4 together with £6,400,000 being Investor's 80% share of Investee's profits of £8,000,000.

Notes (b), (c) and (d) in Example 6.4 also apply to this example.

On 1 January 2006, Investor acquires the remaining 20 per cent ownership interest in Investee for £6,500,000 cash. How should this be accounted for?

(i) Full application of IFRS 3

One method would be to adopt the same treatment in IFRS 3, i.e. by using the cost of the transaction and fair value information at the date of this exchange transaction to determine the amount of any goodwill associated with this transaction. In this case the share of fair values at 1 January 2006 is £6,200,000 (being 20% of £31,000,000), thus resulting in additional goodwill of £300,000. However, in order to achieve this it would be necessary to include an adjustment to reflect the increase in the fair value of Investee's land. If the land were to be included in the consolidated financial statements at its full fair value of £15,000,000 at 1 January 2006, this would result in a further asset revaluation surplus of £3,200,000, being 80% of £4,000,000. The £800,000 attributable to the minority interest's share is eliminated as part of the calculation of goodwill relating to the acquisition of the minority interest. However, one drawback with this method is that this revaluation does not arise on the initial recognition by the acquirer of the acquiree's assets, and in this example may signify that Investor has elected to apply an accounting policy of revaluing those items after initial recognition which it may not want to do. Another difficulty with this method is that it could involve assets and liabilities being included at fair values, which would fall foul of other IFRSs, e.g. certain internally generated intangibles.

(ii) Partial step-up (US GAAP)

A second method would be to adopt a similar approach to that in IFRS 3, but restricting the use of fair values for the purpose of determining the amount of any goodwill associated with that particular transaction. However, no adjustments are made to incorporate any revaluations in respect of the interest in the subsidiary that was already held. This is the treatment that would be required by US GAAP.[211] In this case, Investor would still recognise goodwill of £300,000 but, in order to do so, it would need to reflect the land at £11,800,000. This would effectively represent £8,800,000 (being 80% of £11,000,000, the fair value at the date Investee became a subsidiary) and £3,000,000 (being 20% of £15,000,000, the fair value at the date of acquiring the minority interest). Although this method may result in a more meaningful figure for the goodwill arising on this transaction, it suffers from the same drawbacks as method (i) above, and also results in a 'mixed basis' of accounting for the other assets/liabilities of the acquiree.

(iii) Parent entity extension method (See Chapter 5 at 1.4.2)

A third method would be to treat the difference between the cost of the additional interest in the subsidiary and the minority interest's share of the assets and liabilities reflected in the consolidated balance sheet at the date of the acquisition of the minority interest as being goodwill. The assets and liabilities of the subsidiary would not be remeasured to reflect their fair values at the date of the transaction. In this case, Investor would recognise additional goodwill of £1,100,000 being the difference between the cost of £6,500,000 and £5,400,000 (the minority interest's 20% share in the net assets of Investee). Although this method avoids the drawbacks of methods (i) and (ii) above (and the practical difficulties of determining the fair values of the assets and liabilities of the subsidiary at the date of acquisition of the additional interest), it does result in a figure for goodwill for that particular transaction that is not based on fair values at the date of that transaction.

(iv) Entity concept method (See Chapter 5 at 1.4.1)

A fourth method would be to treat the difference between the cost of the additional interest in the subsidiary and the minority interest's share of the assets and liabilities reflected in the consolidated balance sheet at the date of the acquisition of the minority interest as being a transaction between owners. In this case, Investor would recognise the £1,100,000 as an equity transaction. This method is supported by the fact IAS 27 requires minority interests to be presented in the consolidated balance sheet within equity, separately from the parent shareholders' equity (see Chapter 5 at 6.7). The drawback with this method is that the entity concept on which it is based, is not that which is presently used under IFRS 3 for determining goodwill. As indicated below, this is the method that the IASB has agreed as part of phase II of its business combinations project.

It is clear from the above example that all of these methods have drawbacks and that none of them are ideal. However, on balance, we believe that using method (iii) is preferable, particularly as the goodwill in any case will be subject to an impairment test (see 3 below). In our view, method (iv) is acceptable, but only if an entity follows the 'entity concept' consistently, with any disposals of less that a controlling interest in a subsidiary by a parent to a minority shareholder also being recorded as an equity transaction. For the reasons set out above, we do not believe that methods (i) and (ii) are acceptable under IFRS.

This is an area that the Board will be dealing with as part of phase II of its business combinations project (see 5.2 below). It has agreed that after a parent obtains control of a subsidiary, subsequent increases in the ownership interest in the subsidiary should be accounted for as an equity transaction. Accordingly, any premium or discount on subsequent purchases from minority shareholders should be recognised directly in equity. However, this reflects the IASB's proposed 'full goodwill' approach whereby all of the goodwill of the acquiree (including that attributable to minority interests) is recognised at the date of the original business combination.

2.3.8 Reverse acquisitions

As discussed at 2.3.1 above, in some business combinations, commonly referred to as reverse acquisitions, the acquirer is the entity whose equity interests have been acquired and the issuing entity is the acquiree. This might be the case when, for example, a private entity arranges to have itself 'acquired' by a smaller public entity as a means of obtaining a stock exchange listing. Although legally the issuing public entity is regarded as the parent and the private entity is regarded as the subsidiary, the legal subsidiary is the acquirer if it has the power to govern the financial and operating policies of the legal parent so as to obtain benefits from its activities.

Appendix B to IFRS 3, which is an integral part of the standard, gives guidance on the accounting for reverse acquisitions. It notes that reverse acquisition accounting determines the allocation of the cost of the business combination as at the acquisition date and does not apply to transactions after the combination.[212]

A   *Cost of the business combination*

When equity instruments are issued as part of the cost of the business combination, paragraph 24 of the standard requires the cost of the combination to include the fair value of those equity instruments at the date of exchange (see 2.3.2 above). Paragraph 27 notes that, in the absence of a reliable published price, the fair value of the equity instruments can be estimated by reference to the fair value of the acquirer or the fair value of the acquiree, whichever is more clearly evident (see 2.3.2 C above).[213]

In a reverse acquisition, the cost of the business combination is deemed to have been incurred by the legal subsidiary (i.e. the acquirer for accounting purposes) in the form of equity instruments issued to the owners of the legal parent (i.e. the acquiree for accounting purposes). If the published price of the equity instruments of the legal subsidiary is used to determine the cost of the combination, a calculation shall be made to determine the number of equity instruments the legal subsidiary would have had to issue to provide the same percentage ownership interest of the combined entity to the owners of the legal parent as they have in the combined entity as a result of the reverse acquisition. The fair value of the number of equity instruments so calculated shall be used as the cost of the combination.[214]

On the other hand, if the fair value of the equity instruments of the legal subsidiary is not otherwise clearly evident, the total fair value of all the issued equity instruments of the legal parent before the business combination shall be used as the basis for determining the cost of the combination.[215]

The following example illustrates the application of this guidance. It is based on Example 5 within the Illustrative Examples accompanying IFRS 3.

Example 6.7:   *Reverse acquisition – calculating the cost of the business combination using the fair value of the equity shares of the legal subsidiary*

Entity A, the entity issuing equity instruments and therefore the legal parent, is acquired in a reverse acquisition by Entity B, the legal subsidiary, on 30 September 2004. The accounting for any income tax effects is ignored.

Balance sheets of Entity A and Entity B immediately before the business combination

	Entity A €	Entity B €
Current assets	500	700
Non-current assets	1,300	3,000
	1,800	3,700
Current liabilities	300	600
Non-current liabilities	400	1,100
	700	1,700
Owner's equity		
Issued equity		
100 ordinary shares	300	
60 Ordinary shares		600
Retained earnings	800	1,400
	1,100	2,000

Other information

(a) On 30 September 2004, Entity A issues 2½ shares in exchange for each ordinary share of Entity B. All of Entity B's shareholders exchange their shares in Entity B. Therefore, Entity A issues 150 ordinary shares in exchange for all 60 ordinary shares of Entity B.

(b) The fair value of each ordinary share of Entity B at 30 September 2004 is €40. The quoted market price of Entity A's ordinary shares at that date is €12.

(c) The fair values of Entity A's identifiable assets and liabilities at 30 September 2004 are the same as their carrying amounts, with the exception of non-current assets. The fair value of Entity A's non-current assets at 30 September 2004 is €1,500.

Calculating the cost of the business combination

As a result of the issue of 150 ordinary shares by Entity A, Entity B's shareholders own 60 per cent of the issued shares of the combined entity (i.e. 150 shares out of 250 issued shares). The remaining 40 per cent are owned by Entity A's shareholders. If the business combination had taken place in the form of Entity B issuing additional ordinary shares to Entity A's shareholders in exchange for their ordinary shares in Entity A, Entity B would have had to issue 40 shares for the ratio of ownership interest in the combined entity to be the same. Entity B's shareholders would then own 60 out of the 100 issued shares of Entity B and therefore 60 per cent of the combined entity.

As a result, the cost of the business combination is €1,600 (i.e. 40 shares each with a fair value of €40).

In the above example, the fair value of the ordinary shares was evident. However, in those situations where a private entity arranges to have itself 'acquired' by a smaller public entity as a means of obtaining a stock exchange listing, it may be that this will not be the case. In which case, the fair value of the shares of the legal parent should be used.

Example 6.8:   *Reverse acquisition – calculating the cost of the business combination using the fair value of the shares of the legal parent*

If in the above example, the fair value of the ordinary shares of Entity B was not clearly evident, the total fair value of all the issued equity instruments of the Entity A before the business combination would be used as the basis for determining the cost of the combination.

The total fair value of all of Entity A's share before the business combination was €1,200 (i.e. 100 shares each with a fair value of €12). Since Entity B is treated as having acquired a 100% interest in Entity A, then the cost of the business combination would be €1,200.

B   Preparation and presentation of consolidated financial statements

Since the legal parent is the acquiree for accounting purposes, the consolidated financial statements prepared following a reverse acquisition reflect the fair values of the assets, liabilities and contingent liabilities of the legal parent, not those of the legal subsidiary. Therefore, the cost of the business combination (as determined under 2.3.8 A above) is allocated by measuring the identifiable assets, liabilities and contingent liabilities of the legal parent that satisfy the recognition criteria in paragraph 37 of the standard at their fair values at the acquisition date (see 2.3.3 above). Any excess of the cost of the combination over the acquirer's interest in the net fair value of those items is then accounted for as goodwill (see 2.3.4 above). Any excess of the acquirer's interest in the net fair value of those items over the cost of the combination is accounted for as an immediate gain in profit or loss (after having reassessed the fair value of those items and the measurement of the cost of the business combination) (see 2.3.5 above).[216]

Example 6.9:   *Reverse acquisition – allocating the cost of the business combination to the assets acquired and liabilities and contingent liabilities assumed*

Using the facts in Example 6.7 above, the acquirer, Entity B, has to allocate the cost of the business combination of €1,600 to the net fair value of Entity A's identifiable assets and liabilities. This results in goodwill of €300, measured as follows:

	€	€
Cost of the business combination		1,600
Net fair value of Entity A's identifiable assets and liabilities:		
Current assets	500	
Non-current assets	1,500	
Current liabilities	(300)	
Non-current liabilities	(400)	
		1,300
Goodwill		300

If the cost of the business combination had been determined as in Example 6.8 above, i.e. €1,200, then no goodwill would have arisen and, assuming no adjustments were required as a result of the re-assessment of that cost or of the net fair values of Entity A's net assets, a gain of €100 would be recognised immediately in profit or loss.

Although the accounting for the reverse acquisition reflects the legal subsidiary as being the acquirer, the consolidated financial statements prepared following a reverse acquisition are issued under the name of the legal parent. Consequently they have to be described in the notes as a continuation of the financial statements of the legal subsidiary, since it is the acquirer for accounting purposes. Because such consolidated financial statements represent a continuation of the financial statements of the legal subsidiary:

(a) the assets and liabilities of the legal subsidiary are recognised and measured in those consolidated financial statements at their pre-combination carrying amounts; i.e. no fair value adjustments are made to the assets and liabilities of the legal subsidiary;

(b) the retained earnings and other equity balances recognised in those consolidated financial statements are the retained earnings and other equity balances of the legal subsidiary immediately before the business combination, not those of the legal parent;

(c) the amount recognised as issued equity instruments in those consolidated financial statements shall be determined by adding to the issued equity of the legal subsidiary immediately before the business combination the cost of the combination determined as discussed at 2.3.8 A above. However, the equity structure appearing in those consolidated financial statements (i.e. the number and type of equity instruments issued) shall reflect the equity structure of the legal parent, including the equity instruments issued by the legal parent to effect the combination;

(d) the comparative information presented in those consolidated financial statements is that of the legal subsidiary, not that originally presented in the previous financial statements of the legal parent;[217] and

(e) the income statement for the current period reflects that of the legal subsidiary for the full period together with the post-acquisition results of the legal parent (based on the attributed fair values).

Continuing with Example 6.7 above, this results in the following consolidated balance sheet.

Example 6.10:   Reverse acquisition – consolidated balance sheet

Using the facts in Example 6.7 above, this results in the following consolidated balance sheet at the date of the business combination (the intermediate columns for Entity B and Entity A are included to show the workings):

	Entity B Book values €	Entity A Fair values €	Consolidated €
Current assets	700	500	1,200
Non-current assets	3,000	1,500	4,500
Goodwill		300	300
	3,700	2,300	6,000
Current liabilities	600	300	900
Non-current liabilities	1,100	400	1,500
	1,700	700	2,400
Owner's equity			
Issued equity			
250 ordinary shares	600	1,600	2,200
Retained earnings	1,400	–	1,400
	2,000	1,600	3,600

It should be noted that reverse acquisition accounting applies only in the consolidated financial statements. Therefore, in the legal parent's separate financial statements, if any, the investment in the legal subsidiary is accounted for in accordance with the requirements in IAS 27 on accounting for investments in an investor's separate financial statements.[218]

Example 6.11:   Reverse acquisition – legal parent's balance sheet in separate financial statements

Using the facts in Example 6.7 above, the balance sheet of Entity A, the legal parent, in its separate financial statements immediately following the business combination will be as follows:

	Entity A €
Current assets	500
Non-current assets	1,300
Investment in subsidiary (Entity B)	1,800
	3,600
Current liabilities	300
Non-current liabilities	400
	700
Owner's equity	
Issued equity	
250 ordinary shares	2,100
Retained earnings	800
	2,900

The investment in the subsidiary is included at its cost of €1,800, being the fair value of the shares issued by Entity A (150 × €12). It can be seen that the issued equity is different from that in the consolidated financial statements and its non-current assets remain at their carrying amounts before the business combination.

C   Minority interest

In some reverse acquisitions, some of the owners of the legal subsidiary do not exchange their equity instruments for equity instruments of the legal parent. Although reverse acquisition accounting regards the entity in which those owners hold equity instruments (the legal subsidiary) as having acquired another entity (the legal parent), those owners are required to be treated as a minority interest in the consolidated financial statements prepared after the reverse acquisition. This is because the owners of the legal subsidiary that do not exchange their equity instruments for equity instruments of the legal parent have an interest only in the results and net assets of the legal subsidiary, and not in the results and net assets of the combined entity. Conversely, all of the owners of the legal parent, notwithstanding that the legal parent is regarded as the acquiree, have an interest in the results and net assets of the combined entity.[219]

Because the assets and liabilities of the legal subsidiary are recognised and measured in the consolidated financial statements at their pre-combination carrying amounts, the minority interest shall reflect the minority shareholders' proportionate interest in the pre-combination carrying amounts of the legal subsidiary's net assets.[220]

These requirements are illustrated in the following example.

Example 6.12:   Reverse acquisition – minority interest

This example uses the same facts in Example 6.7 above, except that in this case only 56 of Entity B's ordinary shares are tendered for exchange rather than all 60. Because Entity A issues 2½ shares in exchange for each ordinary share of Entity B, Entity A issues only 140 (rather than 150) shares. As a result, Entity B's shareholders own 58.3 per cent of the issued shares of the combined entity (i.e. 140 shares out of 240 issued shares).

As in Example 6.7 above, the cost of the business combination is calculated by assuming that the combination had taken place in the form of Entity B issuing additional ordinary shares to the shareholders of Entity A in exchange for their ordinary shares in Entity A. In calculating the number of shares that would have to be issued by Entity B, the minority interest is ignored. The majority shareholders own 56 shares of Entity B. For this to represent a 58.3 per cent ownership interest, Entity B would have had to issue an additional 40 shares. The majority shareholders would then own 56 out of the 96 issued shares of Entity B and therefore 58.3 per cent of the combined entity.

As a result, the cost of the business combination is €1,600 (i.e. 40 shares each with a fair value of €40). This is the same amount as when all 60 of Entity B's ordinary shares are tendered for exchange (see Example 6.7 above). The cost of the combination does not change simply because some of Entity B's shareholders do not participate in the exchange.

The minority interest is represented by the 4 shares of the total 60 shares of Entity B that are not exchanged for shares of Entity A. Therefore, the minority interest is 6.7 per cent. The minority interest reflects the minority shareholders' proportionate interest in the pre-combination carrying amounts of the net assets of the legal subsidiary. Therefore, the consolidated balance sheet is adjusted to show a minority interest of 6.7 per cent of the pre-combination carrying amounts of Entity B's net assets (i.e. €134 or 6.7 per cent of €2,000).

The consolidated balance sheet at 30 September 2004 (the date of the business combination) reflecting the minority interest is as follows (the intermediate columns for Entity B, minority interest and Entity A are included to show the workings):

	Entity B Book values	Minority interest	Entity A Fair values	Consolidated
	€	€	€	€
Current assets	700		500	1,200
Non-current assets	3,000		1,500	4,500
Goodwill			300	300
	3,700		2,300	6,000
Current liabilities	600		300	900
Non-current liabilities	1,100		400	1,500
	1,700		700	2,400
Owner's equity				
Issued equity				
240 ordinary shares	600	(40)	1,600	2,160
Retained earnings	1,400	(84)	–	1,306
Minority interest	–	134	–	134
	2,000	–	1,600	3,600

D   Earnings per share

As indicated at 2.3.8 B above the equity structure appearing in the consolidated financial statements prepared following a reverse acquisition reflects the equity structure of the legal parent, including the equity instruments issued by the legal parent to effect the business combination.[221]

Where the legal parent is required by IAS 33 – *Earnings per Share* – to disclose earnings per share information (see Chapter 31), then for the purpose of calculating the weighted average number of ordinary shares outstanding (the denominator) during the period in which the reverse acquisition occurs:

(a)   the number of ordinary shares outstanding from the beginning of that period to the acquisition date shall be deemed to be the number of ordinary shares issued by the legal parent to the owners of the legal subsidiary (rather than the actual number of shares of the legal parent during that period); and

(b)   the number of ordinary shares outstanding from the acquisition date to the end of that period shall be the actual number of ordinary shares of the legal parent outstanding during that period.[222]

The basic earnings per share disclosed for each comparative period before the acquisition date that is presented in the consolidated financial statements following a reverse acquisition shall be calculated by dividing the profit or loss of the legal subsidiary attributable to ordinary shareholders in each of those periods by the number of ordinary shares issued by the legal parent to the owners of the legal subsidiary in the reverse acquisition.[223]

The calculations outlined above assume that there were no changes in the number of the legal subsidiary's issued ordinary shares during the comparative periods and during the period from the beginning of the period in which the reverse acquisition occurred to the acquisition date. The calculation of earnings per share shall be appropriately adjusted to take into account the effect of a change in the number of the legal subsidiary's issued ordinary shares during those periods.[224]

These requirements are illustrated in the following example.

Example 6.13:   Reverse acquisition – earnings per share

This example uses the same facts in Example 6.7 above. Assume that Entity B's profit for the annual period ending 31 December 2003 was €600, and that the consolidated profit for the annual period ending 31 December 2004 is €800. Assume also that there was no change in the number of ordinary shares issued by Entity B during the annual period ending 31 December 2003 and during the period from 1 January 2004 to the date of the reverse acquisition (30 September 2004).

Earnings per share for the annual period ending 31 December 2004 is calculated as follows:

Number of shares deemed to be outstanding for the period from 1 January 2004 to the acquisition date (30 September 2004), being. the number of ordinary shares issued by Entity A in the reverse acquisition	150
Number of shares outstanding from the acquisition date to 31 December 2004	250
Weighted average number of share outstanding $(150 \times 9/12) + (250 \times 3/12)$	175
Earnings per share €800/175	€4.57

The restated earnings per share for the annual period ending 31 December 2003 is €4.00 (being €600/150, i.e. the profit of Entity B for that period divided by the number of ordinary shares issued by Entity A in the reverse acquisition). Any earnings per share information for that period disclosed by either Entity A or Entity B is irrelevant.

2.3.9   Disclosure requirements relating to business combinations

In developing the disclosure requirements of IFRS 3, the IASB identified three disclosure objectives that should be met.[225] Accordingly the standards sets out three principles of disclosure dealing with these objectives, and supplements them with specific disclosure requirements. The first two principles relate to business combinations generally, while the third deals with goodwill. The disclosure requirements of the standard relating to goodwill are discussed at 3.9 below; the other requirements relating to business combinations generally are dealt with below.

A   Nature and financial effect of business combinations

The first disclosure principle is that an acquirer shall disclose information that enables users of its financial statements to evaluate the nature and financial effect of business combinations that were effected:

(a)   during the period, or

(b)   after the balance sheet date but before the financial statements are authorised for issue.[226]

I   *Business combinations during the period*

To give effect to this principle, the acquirer is required to disclose the following information for *each* business combination that was effected during the period:

(a)   the names and descriptions of the combining entities or businesses;

(b)   the acquisition date;

(c)   the percentage of voting equity instruments acquired;

(d)   the cost of the combination and a description of the components of that cost, including any costs directly attributable to the combination.

When equity instruments are issued or issuable as part of the cost, the following shall also be disclosed:

(i)   the number of equity instruments issued or issuable; and

(ii)   the fair value of those instruments and the basis for determining that fair value.

If a published price does not exist for the instruments at the date of exchange, the significant assumptions used to determine fair value shall be disclosed.

If a published price exists at the date of exchange but was not used as the basis for determining the cost of the combination, that fact shall be disclosed together with:

- the reasons the published price was not used;

- the method and significant assumptions used to attribute a value to the equity instruments; and

- the aggregate amount of the difference between the value attributed to, and the published price of, the equity instruments;

(e)   details of any operations the entity has decided to dispose of as a result of the combination;

(f)   the amounts recognised at the acquisition date for each class of the acquiree's assets, liabilities and contingent liabilities, and, unless disclosure would be impracticable, the carrying amounts of each of those classes, determined in accordance with IFRSs, immediately before the combination.

If such disclosure about the carrying amounts would be impracticable, that fact shall be disclosed, together with an explanation of why this is the case;

(g)   the amount of any excess recognised in profit or loss in accordance with paragraph 56 of the standard (see 2.3.5 above), and the line item in the income statement in which the excess is recognised;

(h)   a description of the factors that contributed to a cost that results in the recognition of goodwill, including a description of each intangible asset that was not recognised separately from goodwill and an explanation of why the intangible asset's fair value could not be measured reliably – or a description of the nature of any excess recognised in profit or loss in accordance with paragraph 56 of the standard; and

(i)   the amount of the acquiree's profit or loss since the acquisition date included in the acquirer's profit or loss for the period, unless disclosure would be impracticable.

If such disclosure would be impracticable, that fact shall be disclosed, together with an explanation of why this is the case.[227]

The above information is required to be disclosed for each material business combination. For business combinations effected during the reporting period that are individually immaterial, the standard requires that the above information is disclosed in aggregate.[228]

If the initial accounting for a business combination that was effected during the period was determined only provisionally (see 2.3.6 above), that fact shall also be disclosed together with an explanation of why this is the case.[229]

To give effect to the principle, the acquirer shall disclose the following information, unless such disclosure would be impracticable:

(a)   the revenue of the combined entity for the period as though the acquisition date for all business combinations effected during the period had been the beginning of that period; and

(b)   the profit or loss of the combined entity for the period as though the acquisition date for all business combinations effected during the period had been the beginning of the period.

If disclosure of this information would be impracticable, that fact shall be disclosed, together with an explanation of why this is the case.[230]

A number of the requirements allow the information not to be disclosed if disclosure would be impracticable. Whether an entity is justified to omit the disclosure on these grounds will depend on the particular circumstances. As discussed in Chapter 3 at 2.4 and 4.7, IAS 1 and IAS 8 both regard a requirement as being impracticable when the entity cannot apply it after making every reasonable effort to do so.

II   Business combinations effected after the balance sheet date

To give effect to the principle set out above, the acquirer shall disclose the information under items (a) to (i) above for each business combination effected after the balance sheet date but before the financial statements are authorised for issue, unless such disclosure would be impracticable. If disclosure of any of that information would be impracticable, that fact shall be disclosed, together with an explanation of why this is the case.[231]

B   Effects of gains, losses, error corrections and other adjustments recognised in the current period relating to business combinations

The second disclosure principle is that an acquirer shall disclose information that enables users of its financial statements to evaluate the financial effects of gains, losses, error corrections and other adjustments recognised in the current period that relate to business combinations that were effected in the current or in previous periods.[232]

To give effect to this principle, the acquirer is required to disclose the following information:

(a)   the amount and an explanation of any gain or loss recognised in the current period that:

    (i)   relates to the identifiable assets acquired or liabilities or contingent liabilities assumed in a business combination that was effected in the current or a previous period; and

    (ii) is of such size, nature or incidence that disclosure is relevant to an understanding of the combined entity's financial performance;

(b)   if the initial accounting for a business combination that was effected in the immediately preceding period was determined only provisionally at the end of that period, the amounts and explanations of the adjustments to the provisional values recognised during the current period (see 2.3.6 A above); and

(c)   the information about error corrections required to be disclosed by IAS 8 for any of the acquiree's identifiable assets, liabilities or contingent liabilities, or changes in the values assigned to those items, that the acquirer recognises during the current period (see 2.3.6 B above).[233]

Item (a) has been included as an aid in meeting the objective of the second disclosure principle,[234] but doesn't really add anything to the requirement within IAS 1 to disclose the nature and amount of items of income and expenditure when they are material (see Chapter 3 at 3.2.4). Similarly, item (c) merely appears to repeat the requirements of IAS 8 (see Chapter 3 at 6.3).

C   *Other necessary information*

The standard includes a catch-all disclosure requirement, that if in any situation the information required to be disclosed set out above does not satisfy the objectives of the disclosure principles, the entity shall disclose such additional information as is necessary to meet those objectives.[235] Possible disclosures under this requirement could be information relating to the cost of a business combination that is contingent on future events and any adjustments made thereto (see 2.3.2 E above).

In addition to the disclosures required by IFRS 3 discussed above, IAS 7 – *Cash Flow Statements* – requires disclosures in respect of acquisitions of subsidiaries and other business units (see Chapter 32 at 2.4.2).[236]

3 GOODWILL

The initial recognition and measurement of the goodwill acquired in a business combination as an asset was discussed at 2.3.4 above. The main issue relating to such goodwill is then how it should be subsequently accounted for. The requirements of IFRS 3 in this respect are straightforward; but that is only because the detailed requirements in relation to the subsequent accounting for goodwill are dealt with in IAS 36.

3.1 Subsequent accounting for goodwill

IFRS 3 requires that, after initial recognition, the acquirer shall measure goodwill acquired in a business combination at cost less any accumulated impairment losses.[237]

Goodwill acquired in a business combination is not to be amortised (as was the treatment under IAS 22). Instead, the acquirer has to test it for impairment annually, or more frequently if events or changes in circumstances indicate that it might be impaired, in accordance with IAS 36.[238] The requirements of IAS 36 relating specifically to the impairment of goodwill are dealt with below; the general requirements of IAS 36 are covered in Chapter 13.

3.2 Allocation of goodwill to cash-generating units

As indicated at 2.3.4 above, IFRS 3 considers goodwill acquired in a business combination to represent a payment made by an acquirer in anticipation of future economic benefits from assets that are not capable of being individually identified and separately recognised. Thus, an impairment test cannot be carried out on goodwill alone, since it does not generate cash flows independently of other assets. Therefore to test goodwill for impairment necessitates its allocation to a cash-generating unit (CGU) of the acquirer or to a group of CGUs. The concept of a CGU is discussed in Chapter 13 at 3.3.2.

IAS 36 requires that, for the purpose of impairment testing, goodwill acquired in a business combination is, from the acquisition date, to be allocated to each of the acquirer's CGUs or to a group of CGUs, that are expected to benefit from the synergies of the combination. This is irrespective of whether other assets or liabilities of the acquiree are assigned to those CGUs or group of CGUs. The standard recognises that goodwill sometimes cannot be allocated on a non-arbitrary basis to an individual CGU, so permits it to be allocated to a group of CGUs. However, each CGU or group of CGUs to which the goodwill is so allocated shall:

(a) represent the lowest level within the entity at which the goodwill is monitored for internal management purposes; and

(b) not be larger than a segment based on either the entity's primary or the entity's secondary reporting format determined in accordance with IAS 14.[239]

All CGUs or group of CGUs to which goodwill has been allocated have to be tested for impairment on an annual basis.

The standard takes the view that applying the above requirements results in goodwill being tested for impairment at a level that reflects the way an entity manages its operations and with which the goodwill would naturally be associated. Therefore, the development of additional reporting systems is typically not necessary.[240] It would only be if an entity did not monitor goodwill at or below the segment level that it would be necessary to develop new or additional reporting systems in order to comply with the standard.[241]

It can be seen from (b) above that the segment level is based on either the entity's primary or secondary reporting under IAS 14 (see Chapter 28 at 2.3). This is to ensure that entities that are managed on a matrix basis are able to test goodwill for impairment at the level of internal reporting that reflects the way they manage their operations.[242]

IAS 36 emphasises that a CGU to which goodwill is allocated for the purpose of impairment testing may not coincide with the level at which goodwill is allocated in accordance with IAS 21 for the purpose of measuring foreign currency gains and losses (see Chapter 9 at 3.3.4).[243] In many cases the allocation under IAS 21 will be at a lower level. This will apply not only on the acquisition of a multinational operation but could also apply on the acquisition of a single operation where the goodwill is allocated to a larger cash generating unit under IAS 36 that is made up of businesses with different functional currencies. However, IAS 36 clarifies that the entity is not required to test the goodwill for impairment at that same level unless it also monitors the goodwill at that level for internal management purposes.[244]

3.3   Goodwill initially unallocated to cash-generating units

As discussed at 2.3.6 above, the initial accounting for a business combination may only been determined provisionally by the end of the period in which the combination is effected. IAS 36 recognises that in such circumstances, it might also not be possible to complete the initial allocation of the goodwill to a CGU (or group of CGUs) for impairment purposes before the end of the annual period in which the combination is effected.[245]

Where this is the case, IAS 36 does not require a provisional allocation to be made, but the goodwill (or a portion thereof) is left unallocated for that period. However, the standard requires disclosure of the amount of the unallocated goodwill together with an explanation as to why that is the case (see 3.9 below).

The initial allocation has to be completed before the end of the first annual period beginning after the acquisition date.[246] It should be noted that this period differs from that required by IFRS 3 for finalisation of the allocation of the cost of the business combination (and hence the initial measurement of goodwill), which is twelve months after the acquisition date. The reason for this is that the IASB's view is that acquirers should be allowed a longer period to complete the goodwill allocation, because that allocation might not be able to be performed until after the initial allocating is complete.[247] However, where an entity was to change its annual reporting date, it could mean that it is in fact a shorter period.

Example 6.14

Entity A prepares its financial statements for annual periods ending on 31 December. It acquired Entity B on 30 September 2004. In accounting for this business combination in its financial statements for the year ended 31 December 2004, Entity A has only been able to determine the fair values to be assigned to Entity B's assets, liabilities and contingent liabilities on a provisional basis and has not allocated the resulting provisional amount of goodwill arising on the acquisition to any CGU (or group of CGUs). During 2005, Entity A changes its annual reporting date to June and is preparing its financial statements as at its new period end of 30 June 2005. IFRS 3 does not require the fair values assigned to Entity B's net assets (and therefore the initial amount of goodwill) to be finalised by that period end, since Entity A has until 30 September 2005 to finalise the values. However, IAS 36 would appear to require the allocation of the goodwill to CGUs for impairment purposes be completed by the date of those financial statements since these are for the first annual period beginning after the acquisition date, despite the fact that the initial accounting under IFRS 3 is not yet complete.

3.4 Testing cash-generating units with goodwill for impairment

IAS 36 requires a CGU (or group of CGUs) to which goodwill has been allocated to be tested for impairment annually by comparing the carrying amount of the CGU (or group of CGUs), including the goodwill, with its recoverable amount.[248] The requirements of the standard in relation to the timing of such an annual impairment test are discussed at 3.4.2 below. However, this annual impairment test is not a substitute for management being aware of events occurring or circumstances changing between annual tests indicating a possible impairment of goodwill.[249] IAS 36 requires an entity to assess at each reporting date whether there is an indication that a CGU may be impaired.[250] So, whenever there is an indication that a CGU (or group of CGUs) to which goodwill has been allocated may be impaired (see Chapter 13 at 3.2 for a discussion of what constitutes an indication of impairment), it shall be tested for impairment by comparing the carrying amount of the CGU (or group of CGUs), including the goodwill, with its recoverable amount.[251]

The determination of what is the carrying amount of a CGU is discussed in Chapter 13 at 3.3.2. The measurement of the recoverable amount of a CGU is discussed at 3.3 of that Chapter. If the recoverable amount of the CGU (or group of CGUs) exceeds the carrying amount of the CGU (or group of CGUs), including the goodwill, the CGU (or group of CGUs), and the goodwill allocated to that CGU (or group of CGUs), are not regarded as being impaired. If the carrying amount of the CGU (or group of CGUs), including the goodwill, exceeds the recoverable amount of the CGU (or group of CGUs), then an impairment loss has to be recognised in accordance with paragraph 104 of the standard (see 3.5 below).[252]

3.4.1 Minority interest

Under IFRS 3, goodwill recognised in a business combination only represents the goodwill acquired by a parent based on the parent's ownership interest, rather than the amount of goodwill controlled by the parent as a result of the business combination (see 2.3.4 above). Therefore, goodwill attributable to a minority interest is not recognised in the parent's consolidated financial statements (as noted at 2.3.3 above, the minority interest is stated at the minority's proportion of the net fair value of the acquiree). Accordingly, if there is a minority interest in a CGU to which goodwill has been allocated, the carrying amount of that CGU comprises:

(a)   both the parent's interest and the minority interest in the identifiable net assets of the CGU; and

(b)   the parent's interest in goodwill.

However, part of the recoverable amount of the CGU determined in accordance with IAS 36 is attributable to the minority interest in goodwill.[253]

Consequently, to enable a like-for-like comparison, for the purpose of impairment testing a non-wholly-owned CGU with goodwill, IAS 36 requires the carrying amount of that CGU to be notionally adjusted, before being compared with its recoverable amount. This is accomplished by grossing up the carrying amount of goodwill allocated to the CGU to include the goodwill attributable to the minority interest. This notionally adjusted carrying amount is then compared with the recoverable amount of the CGU to determine whether the CGU (including the goodwill) is impaired. If it is, the entity allocates the impairment loss in accordance with paragraph 104 of the standard first to reduce the carrying amount of goodwill allocated to the CGU (see 3.5 below).[254]

However, because goodwill is recognised only to the extent of the parent's ownership interest, any impairment loss relating to the goodwill is apportioned between that attributable to the parent and that attributable to the minority interest, with only the former being recognised as a goodwill impairment loss.[255]

If the total impairment loss relating to goodwill is less than the amount by which the notionally adjusted carrying amount of the CGU exceeds its recoverable amount, paragraph 104 of the standard requires the remaining excess to be allocated to the other assets of the CGU pro rata on the basis of the carrying amount of each asset in the CGU.[256]

These requirements are illustrated in the following example which is based on Example 7 included within the Illustrative Examples accompanying IAS 36. In the examples, tax effects are ignored.

Example 6.15:   Impairment testing of a CGU with goodwill and minority interests

Entity X acquires an 80 per cent ownership interest in Entity Y for €1,600 on 1 January 2005. At that date, Entity Y's identifiable net assets have a fair value of €1,500. Entity Y has no contingent liabilities. Therefore, Entity X recognises in its consolidated financial statements:

(a)   goodwill of €400, being the difference between the cost of the business combination of €1,600 and Entity X's 80 per cent interest in Entity Y's identifiable net assets;

(b)   Entity Y's identifiable net assets at their fair value of €1,500; and

(c)   a minority interest of €300, being the 20 per cent interest in Entity Y's identifiable net assets held by parties outside Entity X.

The assets of Entity Y together are the smallest group of assets that generate cash inflows that are largely independent of the cash inflows from other assets or groups of assets. Therefore Entity Y is a CGU. Because this CGU includes goodwill within its carrying amount, it must be tested for impairment annually, or more frequently if there is an indication that it may be impaired (see paragraph 90 of IAS 36).

At the end of 2005, the carrying amount of Entity Y's identifiable assets have reduced to €1,350 and Entity X determines that the recoverable amount of CGU Y is €1,000.

Testing CGU Y for Impairment

A portion of CGU Y's recoverable amount of €1,000 is attributable to the unrecognised minority interest in goodwill. Therefore, in accordance with paragraph 92 of IAS 36, the carrying amount of CGU Y must be notionally adjusted to include goodwill attributable to the minority interest, before being compared with the recoverable amount of €1,000. Testing CGU Y for impairment at the end of 2005 gives rise to an impairment loss of €850 calculated as follows:

	Goodwill €	Identifiable net assets €	Total €
Carrying amount	400	1,350	1,750
Unrecognised minority interest*	100	–	100
Notionally adjusted carrying amount	500	1,350	1,850
Recoverable amount			1,000
Impairment loss			850

*   Goodwill attributable to Entity X's 80% interest in Entity Y at the acquisition date is €400. Therefore, goodwill notionally attributable to the 20% minority interest in Entity Y at the acquisition date is €100, being €400 × 20/80.

In accordance with paragraph 104 of IAS 36, the impairment loss of €850 is allocated to the assets in the CGU by first reducing the carrying amount of goodwill to zero.

Therefore, €500 of the €850 impairment loss for the CGU is allocated to the goodwill. However, because the goodwill is recognised only to the extent of Entity X's 80 per cent ownership interest in Entity Y, Entity X recognises only 80 per cent of that goodwill impairment loss (i.e. €400).

The remaining impairment loss of €350 is recognised by reducing the carrying amounts of Entity Y's identifiable assets.

This allocation of the impairment loss results in the following carrying amounts for CGU Y in the financial statements of Entity X at the end of 2005.

	Goodwill €	Identifiable net assets €	Total €
Carrying amount	400	1,350	1,750
Impairment loss	(400)	(350)	(750)
Carrying amount after impairment loss	–	1,000	1,000

Of the impairment loss of €350 relating to Entity Y's identifiable assets, €70 (i.e. 20% thereof) would be attributed to the minority interest.

It can be seen from the above example that in that situation the total carrying amount of the identifiable net assets and the goodwill has been reduced to the recoverable amount of €1,000. In fact the same result would have been achieved by just comparing the recoverable amount of €1,000 with the carrying amount of €1,750. However, what if the recoverable amount of the CGU had been greater than the carrying amount of the identifiable net assets prior to recognising the impairment loss?

Example 6.16:   Impairment testing of a CGU with goodwill and minority interests

This example is based on the same facts as Example 6.15 above, except that at the end of 2005, Entity X determines that the recoverable amount of CGU Y is €1,400.

Testing CGU Y for impairment

In this case, testing CGU Y for impairment at the end of 2005 gives rise to an impairment loss of €450 calculated as follows:

	Goodwill €	Identifiable net assets €	Total €
Carrying amount	400	1,350	1,750
Unrecognised minority interest	100	–	100
Notionally adjusted carrying amount	500	1,350	1,850
Recoverable amount			1,400
Impairment loss			450

As in Example 6.15 the impairment loss of €450 is allocated to the assets in the CGU by first reducing the carrying amount of goodwill.

Therefore, all of the €450 impairment loss for the CGU is allocated to the goodwill. However, because the goodwill is recognised only to the extent of Entity X's 80 per cent ownership interest in Entity Y, Entity X recognises only 80 per cent of that goodwill impairment loss (i.e. €360).

This allocation of the impairment loss results in the following carrying amounts for CGU Y in the financial statements of Entity X at the end of 2005.

	Goodwill €	Identifiable net assets €	Total €
Carrying amount	400	1,350	1,750
Impairment loss	(360)	–	(360)
Carrying amount after impairment loss	40	1,350	1,390

Of the impairment loss of €360, none of it is attributable to the minority interest since it all relates to the majority shareholder's goodwill.

It can be seen from the above example that in this situation the total carrying amount of the identifiable net assets and the goodwill has not been reduced to the recoverable amount of €1,400, but is actually less than the recoverable amount. This is because the recoverable amount of goodwill relating to the minority interest (20% of [€500 – €450]) is not recognised in the consolidated financial statements. If a direct comparison of the recoverable amount of €1,400 with the carrying amount of €1,750 was made, an impairment loss of €350 would have been recognised against goodwill. However, this would have meant that the goodwill would only have been reduced to €50, which would be overstated by €10 being the recoverable amount that is actually attributable to the minority interest.

3.4.2   *Timing of impairment tests*

As indicated at 3.4 above, IAS 36 requires a CGU or a group of CGUs to which goodwill has been allocated to be tested for impairment annually. It might be thought that this means that the impairment test has to be carried out at the end of the reporting period. However, the standard permits the annual impairment test to be performed at any time during an annual period, provided the test is performed at the same time every year. Indeed, different CGUs may be tested for impairment at different times.

However, if some or all of the goodwill allocated to a CGU (or group of CGUs) was acquired in a business combination during the current annual period, that unit shall be tested for impairment before the end of the current annual period.[257]

The reason for this last requirement is that the IASB 'observed that acquirers can sometimes "overpay" for an acquiree, resulting in the amount initially recognised for the business combination and the resulting goodwill exceeding the recoverable amount of the investment. The Board concluded that the users of an entity's financial statements are provided with representationally faithful, and therefore useful, information about a business combination if such an impairment loss is recognised by the acquirer in the annual period in which the business combination occurs.'[258] The Board was concerned that without this requirement it might be possible for entities to delay recognising such an impairment loss until the annual period after the business combination if the standard included only a requirement to impairment test CGUs (or groups of CGUs) to which goodwill has been allocated on an annual basis at any time during a period.[259]

It has to be said that the wording of the requirement may not achieve that result, since the goodwill may not have been allocated to a CGU in the period in which the business combination occurs (see 3.3 above). Consider the following example.

Example 6.17

Entity A prepares its financial statements for annual periods ending on 31 December. It carries out its annual impairment tests for all the CGUs to which it has allocated goodwill at the end of September. On 30 October 2004 Entity A acquires Entity B. In accounting for this business combination in its financial statements for the year ended 31 December 2004, Entity A has only been able to determine the fair values to be assigned to Entity B's assets, liabilities and contingent liabilities on a provisional basis and has not allocated the resulting provisional amount of goodwill arising on the acquisition to any CGU (or group of CGUs).

During 2005, as permitted by IFRS 3, Entity A does not finalise the fair values assigned to Entity B's net assets (and therefore the initial amount of goodwill) until 30 October 2005. Also, IAS 36 only requires Entity A to allocate the goodwill to CGUs by the end of the financial year. It does this in December.

In this case, at the time of carrying out its annual impairment tests at 30 September 2005, Entity A has not yet allocated the goodwill relating to Entity B. When it does allocate the goodwill in December, the requirement to perform an impairment test for the CGUs to which this goodwill is allocated does not seem to be applicable since the goodwill does not relate to a business combination during the current annual period. It actually relates to a business combination in the previous period; it is just that it has only been allocated for impairment purposes in the current period. Nevertheless we believe that Entity A should perform an updated impairment test for the CGUs to which this goodwill is allocated for the purposes of its financial statements ended 31 December 2005 since this would seem to be the intention of the IASB. Not to do so, would mean that the impairment of this goodwill would not be tested until September 2006, nearly 2 years after the business combination.

3.4.3   Sequence of impairment tests

At the time of impairment testing a CGU to which goodwill has been allocated, there may be an indication of an impairment of an asset within the unit containing the goodwill. In such circumstances, IAS 36 requires the entity to test the asset for impairment first, and recognise any impairment loss for that asset before testing for impairment the CGU containing the goodwill. Similarly, there may be an indication of an impairment of a CGU within a group of CGUs containing the goodwill. In such circumstances, the standard requires the entity to test the CGU for impairment first, and recognise any impairment loss for that CGU, before testing for impairment the group of CGUs to which the goodwill is allocated.[260]

3.4.4   Carry-forward of a previous impairment test calculation

IAS 36 permits the most recent detailed calculation of the recoverable amount of a CGU (or group of CGUs) to which goodwill has been allocated to be carried forward from a preceding period for use in the current period's impairment provided all of the following criteria are met:

(a)   the assets and liabilities making up the CGU (or group of CGUs) have not changed significantly since the most recent recoverable amount calculation;

(b)   the most recent recoverable amount calculation resulted in an amount that exceeded the carrying amount of the CGU (or group of CGUs) by a substantial margin; and

(c)   based on an analysis of events that have occurred and circumstances that have changed since the most recent recoverable amount calculation, the likelihood that a current recoverable amount determination would be less than the current carrying amount of the CGU (or group of CGUs) is remote.[261]

The Basis for Conclusions accompanying IAS 36 indicates that the reason for this dispensation is to reduce the costs of applying the impairment test, without compromising its integrity.[262] However, clearly it is a matter of considerable judgement as to whether each of the criteria is actually met.

3.5 Impairment loss for a cash-generating unit to which goodwill has been allocated

As indicated at 3.4 above, if the carrying amount of the CGU (or group of CGUs), including the goodwill, exceeds the recoverable amount of the CGU (or group of CGUs), then an impairment loss has to be recognised in accordance with paragraph 104 of the standard.[263]

That paragraph requires that the impairment loss is allocated to reduce the carrying amount of the assets of the CGU (or group of CGUs) in the following order:

(a)   first, to reduce the carrying amount of the allocated goodwill; and

(b)   then, to the other assets of the CGU (or group of CGUs) on a pro rata basis.

This is illustrated in Examples 6.15 and 6.16 at 3.4.1 above.

The impairment loss for goodwill is recognised in accordance with paragraph 60 of the standard, which is to recognise it immediately in profit or loss.[264] The recognition of the impairment loss under (b) above is discussed in detail in Chapter 13 at 3.3.2.

3.6 Reversing an impairment loss for goodwill

Once an impairment loss has been recognised for goodwill, IAS 36 prohibits its reversal in a subsequent period.[265] The standard justifies this on the grounds that any reversal 'is likely to be an increase in internally generated goodwill, rather than a reversal of the impairment loss recognised for the acquired goodwill', and IAS 38 prohibits the recognition of internally generated goodwill.[266]

3.7 Disposal of operation within a cash-generating unit to which goodwill has been allocated

If goodwill has been allocated to a CGU (or a group of CGUs) and the entity disposes of an operation within that CGU, IAS 36 requires that the goodwill associated with the operation disposed of is included in the carrying amount of the operation when determining the gain or loss on disposal. For that purpose, the standard requires that the amount to be included is measured on the basis of the relative values of the operation disposed of and the portion of the CGU retained, unless the entity can demonstrate that some other method better reflects the goodwill associated with the operation disposed of.[267]

Example 6.18:   Goodwill attributable to the disposal of an operation based on relative values

An entity sells for €100 an operation that was part of a CGU to which goodwill of €60 has been allocated. The goodwill allocated to the CGU cannot be identified or associated with an asset group at a level lower than that CGU, except arbitrarily. The recoverable amount of the portion of the CGU retained is €300. Because the goodwill allocated to the CGU cannot be non-arbitrarily identified or associated with an asset group at a level lower than that CGU, the goodwill associated with the operation disposed of is measured on the basis of the relative values of the operation disposed of and the portion of the CGU retained. Therefore, 25 per cent of the goodwill allocated to the CGU, i.e. €15 is included in the carrying amount of the operation that is sold.

The standard refers to the 'relative values' of the parts without specifying how these are to be calculated. It is more plausible that the recoverable amount of the part that it has retained is its value in use, rather than its fair value less costs to sell, which means that the value in use of the part retained may have to be calculated as part of the allocation exercise on disposal (see Chapter 13 at 3.3.2 for a discussion of the calculation of the value in use).

In addition, the value of the part disposed of is clearly based on its fair value less costs to sell, the only appropriate basis of valuation of something held for sale. It will not necessarily follow at all, for example, that the business disposed of generated 25% of the net cash flows of the combined CGU. Therefore, the method advocated by the standard to be applied in most circumstances will most likely be based on a mismatch in the valuation bases used on the different parts of the business, reflecting the purchaser's assessment of the value of the part disposed of at the point of sale rather than that of the vendor at purchase.

The standard allows the use of some other method if it better reflects the goodwill associated with the part disposed of. The IASB had in mind a scenario in which an entity buys a business, integrates it with an existing CGU that does not include any goodwill in its carrying amount and immediately sells a loss-making part of the combined CGU. It is accepted that in these circumstances it may be reasonable to conclude that no part of the carrying amount of the goodwill has been disposed of.[268] The loss-making business being disposed of could, of course, have been owned by the entity before the acquisition or it could be part of the acquired business.

Where the operation disposed of is a foreign operation for the purposes of IAS 21, another possibility might be to use the goodwill allocated to that foreign operation for the purpose of measuring foreign currency gains and losses (see Chapter 9 at 3.3.4), particularly as the exchange gains and losses on that amount of goodwill will also be taken to profit or loss on disposal of that foreign operation (see Chapter 9 at 2.7.3). Even then, this might only be a better method if there has been no previous impairments recognised in respect of goodwill allocated to the CGU including that foreign operation since it was acquired.

One has to bear in mind that any basis of allocation of goodwill on disposal other than that recommended by the standard could be an indication that goodwill should have been allocated on a different basis on acquisition, i.e. there may have been some basis of allocating goodwill within the CGU/CGU group that was not arbitrary.

3.8   Changes in composition of cash-generating units

If an entity reorganises its reporting structure in a way that changes the composition of one or more CGUs to which goodwill has been allocated, IAS 36 requires that the goodwill shall be reallocated to the units affected. For this purpose, the standard requires that this reallocation is performed using a relative value approach similar to that discussed at 3.7 above when an entity disposes of an operation within a CGU, unless the entity can demonstrate that some other method better reflects the goodwill associated with the reorganised units.[269]

Example 6.19:   *Reallocation of goodwill to CGUs based on relative values*

Goodwill of €160 had previously been allocated to CGU A. The goodwill allocated to A cannot be identified or associated with an asset group at a level lower than A, except arbitrarily. A is to be divided and integrated into three other CGUs, B, C and D. Because the goodwill allocated to A cannot be non-arbitrarily identified or associated with an asset group at a level lower than A, it is reallocated to CGUs B, C and D on the basis of the relative values of the three portions of A before those portions are integrated with B, C and D. The recoverable amounts of these portions of A before integration with the other CGUs are €200, €300 and €500 respectively. Accordingly, the amounts of goodwill reallocated to CGUs B, C and D are €32, €48 and €80 respectively.

Again, the standard gives no indication as to what other methods might be that better reflect the goodwill associated with the reorganised units.

In this situation as well, it would appear that it will often be necessary in practice to assess the value in use of all of the CGUs to which the goodwill is to be allocated.

In practice, situations may be considerably more complex than Examples 6.18 and 6.19 above. Elements of both may arise following an acquisition whereby there are disposals of acquired businesses, reorganisations and integrations. The entity may sell some parts of its acquired business immediately but may also use the acquisition in order to replace part of its existing capacity, disposing of existing elements. In addition, groups frequently undertake reorganisations of their statutory entities. It is often the case that CGUs do not correspond to these individual entities and the reorganisations may be undertaken for taxation reasons so the ownership structure within a group may not correspond to its CGUs. This makes it clear how important it is that entities identify their CGUs and the allocation of goodwill to them, so that they already have a basis for making any necessary allocations when an impairment issue arises or there is a disposal.

3.9   Disclosure requirements relating to goodwill

As indicated at 2.3.9 above, in developing the disclosure requirements of IFRS 3 in respect of business combinations, the IASB identified three disclosure objectives that should be met.[270] Accordingly the standard sets out three principles of disclosure dealing with these objectives, and supplements them with specific disclosure requirements. The third principle relates to goodwill, and is that 'an entity shall disclose information that enables users of its financial statements to evaluate changes in the carrying amount of goodwill during the period'.[271]

To give effect to this principle, the entity is required to disclose a reconciliation of the carrying amount of goodwill at the beginning and end of the period, showing separately:

(a)   the gross amount and accumulated impairment losses at the beginning of the period;

(b)   additional goodwill recognised during the period (except goodwill included in a disposal group that, on acquisition, meets the criteria to be classified as held for sale in accordance with IFRS 5 – see Chapter 3 at 5.1);

(c)   adjustments resulting from the subsequent recognition of deferred tax assets during the period (see 2.3.6 C above) ;

(d)   goodwill included in a disposal group classified as held for sale in accordance with IFRS 5 and goodwill derecognised during the period without having previously been included in a disposal group classified as held for sale;

(e)   impairment losses recognised during the period in accordance with IAS 36;

(f)   net exchange differences arising during the period in accordance with IAS 21 (see Chapter 9 at 3.3.4);

(g)   any other changes in the carrying amount during the period; and

(h)   the gross amount and accumulated impairment losses at the end of the period.[272]

As with the other disclosure requirements relating to business combinations dealt with at 2.3.9 above, IFRS 3 includes a catch-all disclosure requirement, that if in any situation the information required to be disclosed set out above does not satisfy the objectives of the disclosure principle, the entity shall disclose such additional information as is necessary to meet those objectives.[273]

IFRS 3 emphasises that in addition to the information required by (e) above, the entity also discloses information about the recoverable amount and impairment of goodwill in accordance with IAS 36.[274] These requirements are dealt with in Chapter 13 at 4.2.

As discussed at 3.3 above, a portion of the goodwill acquired in a business combination during the period may not been allocated to a CGU (or group of CGUs) at the reporting date. If that is the case, IAS 36 requires that the amount of the unallocated goodwill to be disclosed together with the reasons why that amount remains unallocated.[275]

4   TRANSITIONAL ARRANGEMENTS AND FIRST-TIME ADOPTION ISSUES

4.1   Transitional arrangements for entities already reporting under IFRS

As discussed at 2 above, IFRS 3 does not have an effective date in the sense that it is applicable for accounting periods commencing on or after a certain date. Instead, the standard applies to the accounting for business combinations for which the agreement date is on or after 31 March 2004 (the date of issue of the standard). It also applies to the accounting for:

(a)   goodwill arising from a business combination for which the agreement date is on or after 31 March 2004; or

(b)   any excess of the acquirer's interest in the net fair value of the acquiree's identifiable assets, liabilities and contingent liabilities over the cost of a business combination for which the agreement date is on or after 31 March 2004.[276]

Although the IASB observed that requiring the standard to be applied retrospectively to all business combinations might improve the comparability of financial information, it considered that such an approach would be problematic for the following reasons:

(a)   it is likely to be impossible for many business combinations because the information needed may not exist or may no longer be obtainable.

(b)   it requires the determination of estimates that would have been made at a prior date, and therefore raises problems in relation to the role of hindsight—in particular, whether the benefit of hindsight should be included or excluded from those estimates and, if excluded, how the effect of hindsight can be separated from the other factors existing at the date for which the estimates are required.

The IASB therefore concluded that the problems associated with applying the standard retrospectively, on balance, outweigh the benefit of improved comparability of financial information.[277]

As far as previously recognised goodwill, negative goodwill and intangibles in respect of business combinations for which the agreement date was before 31 March 2004 is concerned, the standard has transitional provisions that are to be applied from the beginning of the first annual period beginning on or after 31 March 2004.[278] These are discussed at 4.1.1, 4.1.2 and 4.1.3 below. The standard also deals with the implications for equity accounted investments. These are discussed at 4.1.4 below.

Entities, however, are permitted to apply the requirements of the standard to goodwill existing at or acquired after, and to business combinations occurring from, any date before the effective dates outlined above, provided certain conditions are met.[279] This is discussed at 4.1.5 below.

4.1.1   Previously recognised goodwill

The first issue addressed by IFRS 3 is whether goodwill acquired in a business combination for which the agreement date was before the date the standard is first applied should continue to be accounted for after that date in accordance with the requirements in IAS 22 (i.e. amortised and impairment tested), or in accordance with the requirements in IFRS 3 (i.e. impairment tested only).[280] The IASB concluded that non-amortisation of goodwill in conjunction with testing for impairment is the most representationally faithful method of accounting for goodwill and therefore should be applied in all circumstances, including to goodwill acquired in a business combination for which the agreement date was before the date the standard is first applied. The Board also concluded that if amortisation of such goodwill were to continue after the date the standard is first applied, financial statements would suffer the same lack of comparability that persuaded the Board to reject a mixed approach to accounting for goodwill, i.e. allowing entities a choice between amortisation and impairment testing.[281]

Accordingly, IFRS 3 requires that an entity shall apply the standard prospectively, from the beginning of the first annual period beginning on or after 31 March 2004, to goodwill acquired in a business combination for which the agreement date was before 31 March 2004, and to goodwill arising from an interest in a jointly controlled entity obtained before 31 March 2004 and accounted for by applying proportionate consolidation (see Chapter 8 at 3.3.3). Therefore, an entity shall:

(a)   from the beginning of the first annual period beginning on or after 31 March 2004, discontinue amortising such goodwill;

(b)   at the beginning of the first annual period beginning on or after 31 March 2004, eliminate the carrying amount of the related accumulated amortisation with a corresponding decrease in goodwill; and

(c)   from the beginning of the first annual period beginning on or after 31 March 2004, test the goodwill for impairment in accordance with IAS 36 (as revised in 2004).[282]

It should be noted that this transitional provision will not necessarily overcome the IASB's concerns about the lack of comparability in the first year of applying the standard.

Example 6.20:   Transitional provisions relating to previously recognised goodwill

Entity A is preparing its financial statements for the year ended 31 December 2004. It is not applying the limited retrospective provisions of the standard (see 4.1.5 below). During the year, it acquires Entity B giving rise to goodwill. The agreement date for this business combination was 30 June 2004. Since the agreement date for this business combination is after 31 March 2004, it has to be accounted for under the standard; therefore this goodwill will not be amortised, but will be subject to an impairment test (assuming it has been allocated to a CGU or group of CGUs). However, any existing goodwill recognised in Entity A's balance sheet at 1 January 2004, and on any business combination during the current year where the agreement date is before 31 March 2004 will be amortised this year. It will only be for the 31 December 2005 financial statements that there will be no amortisation of goodwill, since it is only from the beginning of that period that Entity A will discontinue amortising that goodwill.

Where an entity applies the limited retrospective application provisions discussed at 4.1.5 below, the references to 31 March 2004 above shall be replaced by the earlier date chosen by the entity.[283]

The second issue addressed by the standard relates to any previously recognised goodwill that has been deducted from equity. Where an entity previously recognised goodwill as a deduction from equity, it shall not recognise that goodwill in profit or loss when it disposes of all or part of the business to which that goodwill relates or when a CGU (or group of CGUs) to which the goodwill relates becomes impaired.[284]

4.1.2   Previously recognised negative goodwill

The issue addressed by IFRS 3 with respect to the carrying amount of negative goodwill arising from a business combination for which the agreement date was before the date the standard is first applied was whether it should:

(a)   continue to be accounted for after the date IFRS 3 is first applied in accordance with the requirements in IAS 22, i.e. deferred and recognised in profit or loss in future periods by matching the excess against the related future losses and/or expenses; or

(b)   be derecognised on the date IFRS 3 is first applied with a corresponding adjustment to the opening balance of retained earnings.[285]

The IASB concluded that the carrying amount of such negative goodwill was likely to comprise a number of components, most of which do not satisfy the definition of a liability and therefore for those components they should not be recognised as deferred credits after the date the standard is first applied. The one component that the IASB did consider as a liability was any unrecognised contingent liabilities of the acquiree at the acquisition date. However, due to a number of practical difficulties in determining how much of any negative goodwill related to the unresolved contingent liability, it was concluded that the full carrying amount of negative goodwill should be derecognised.[286]

Accordingly, IFRS 3 requires that the carrying amount of negative goodwill at the beginning of the first annual period beginning on or after 31 March 2004 that arose from either:

(a) a business combination for which the agreement date was before 31 March 2004; or

(b) an interest in a jointly controlled entity obtained before 31 March 2004 and accounted for by applying proportionate consolidation

shall be derecognised at the beginning of that period, with a corresponding adjustment to the opening balance of retained earnings.[287]

Where an entity applies the limited retrospective application provisions discussed at 4.1.5 below, the references to 31 March 2004 above shall be replaced by the earlier date chosen by the entity.

4.1.3 *Previously recognised intangible assets*

The standard clarifies the criteria for recognising intangible assets separately from goodwill (see 2.3.3 B above). The issue addressed by the IASB is whether entities should be required to apply those criteria to reassess:

(a) the carrying amount of intangible assets acquired in business combinations for which the agreement date was before the date IFRS 3 is applied and reclassify as goodwill any that do not meet the criteria for separate recognition; and

(b) the carrying amount of goodwill acquired in such business combinations and reclassify as an identifiable intangible asset any component of the goodwill that meets the criteria for separate recognition.[288]

Although the IASB noted that determining whether a recognised intangible asset meets the criteria for recognition separately from goodwill would be fairly straightforward, and that requiring reclassification as goodwill if the criteria are not met would improve the comparability of financial statements, it recognised that identifying and reclassifying intangible assets that meet those criteria but were previously subsumed in goodwill would be problematic for the same reasons that it would be problematic to require retrospective application of the requirements in the standard to all past business combinations.[289] As a result, the IASB concluded that the standard should require the criteria for recognising intangible assets separately from goodwill to be applied only to reassess the carrying amounts of existing recognised intangible assets, but should not require the criteria to be applied to reassess the existing carrying amount of goodwill.[290]

Accordingly, IFRS 3 requires that the carrying amount of an item classified as an intangible asset that either:

(a)   was acquired in a business combination for which the agreement date was before 31 March 2004; or

(b)   arises from an interest in a jointly controlled entity obtained before 31 March 2004 and accounted for by applying proportionate consolidation

shall be reclassified as goodwill at the beginning of the first annual period beginning on or after 31 March 2004, if that intangible asset does not at that date meet the identifiability criterion in IAS 38 (as revised in 2004).[291]

Where an entity applies the limited retrospective application provisions discussed at 4.1.5 below, the references to 31 March 2004 above shall be replaced by the earlier date chosen by the entity.

4.1.4   Equity accounted investments

IFRS 3 also deals with the treatment of goodwill and 'negative goodwill' that may be included in the carrying amount of investments accounted for under the equity method (see Chapters 7 and 8). Effectively the transitional provisions in this regard are to mirror the requirements for such items when they arise as separate items in a business combination discussed above.[292]

Accordingly, for investments accounted for by applying the equity method and acquired on or after 31 March 2004, an entity is required to apply the provisions of the standard in the accounting for:

(a)   any acquired goodwill included in the carrying amount of that investment. Therefore, amortisation of that notional goodwill shall not be included in the determination of the entity's share of the investee's profits or losses.

(b)   any excess included in the carrying amount of the investment of the entity's interest in the net fair value of the investee's identifiable assets, liabilities and contingent liabilities over the cost of the investment. Therefore, an entity shall include that excess as income in the determination of the entity's share of the investee's profits or losses in the period in which the investment is acquired.[293]

For investments accounted for by applying the equity method and acquired before 31 March 2004:

(a)   an entity shall apply the standard on a prospective basis, from the beginning of the first annual period beginning on or after 31 March 2004, to any acquired goodwill included in the carrying amount of that investment. Therefore, an entity shall, from that date, discontinue including the amortisation of that goodwill in the determination of the entity's share of the investee's profits or losses.

(b)   an entity shall derecognise any negative goodwill included in the carrying amount of that investment at the beginning of the first annual period beginning on or after 31 March 2004, with a corresponding adjustment to the opening balance of retained earnings.[294]

Where an entity applies the limited retrospective application provisions discussed at 4.1.5 below, the references to 31 March 2004 above shall be replaced by the earlier date chosen by the entity.

4.1.5 Limited retrospective application

As discussed at 4.1 above, although the IASB observed that requiring the standard to be applied retrospectively to all business combinations might improve the comparability of financial information, it concluded that the problems associated with applying the standard retrospectively, on balance, outweigh the benefit of improved comparability of financial information.

The IASB then considered whether retrospective application of the standard to business combinations for which the agreement date is before 31 March 2004 (the date of issue of the standard) should nonetheless be permitted. In ED 3, it had originally proposed that retrospective application of the standard would be prohibited. However, some respondents to ED 3 were concerned that prohibiting retrospective application of the standard would not be consistent with the option provided to first-time adopters in IFRS 1 – *First-time Adoption of International Financial Reporting Standards* (see 4.2 below). IFRS 1 permits a first-time adopter to restate a past business combination to comply with IFRSs, provided it also restates all later business combinations. In considering this issue, the IASB observed that IFRS preparers that are also US registrants would have the necessary information to apply the equivalent US standards. The availability of that information would make application of IFRS 3 and the revised versions of IAS 36 and IAS 38 practicable from at least the same date as applying the US standards. The IASB also noted that the issue of any new or revised standard reflects its opinion that the application of that standard results in more useful information for users of the financial statements and, on that basis, a case exists for permitting, and indeed encouraging, entities to apply a new or revised standard before its effective date.[295]

The IASB ultimately concluded that if it were practicable for an entity to apply the standard from any date before its effective dates, users of the entity's financial statements would be provided with more useful information than was previously the case under IAS 22, and that the benefit of providing users with more useful information about an entity's financial position and performance by allowing limited retrospective application of the standard outweighs the disadvantages of potentially diminished comparability.[296]

Accordingly, an entity is permitted to apply the requirements of IFRS 3 to goodwill existing at or acquired after, and to business combinations occurring from, any date before the effective dates outlined in paragraphs 78-84 of the standard, provided:

(a) the valuations and other information needed to apply the standard to past business combinations were obtained at the time those combinations were initially accounted for; and

(b)   the entity also applies IAS 36 (as revised in 2004) and IAS 38 (as revised in 2004) prospectively from that same date, and the valuations and other information needed to apply those standards from that date were previously obtained by the entity so that there is no need to determine estimates that would need to have been made at a prior date.[297]

It can be seen that the provision does not permit full retrospective application of IFRS 3 for all business combinations; it only permits it for those that satisfy conditions (a) and (b) above.

Although the reason for the provision was to permit retrospective application of the standard to business combinations for which the agreement date is before 31 March 2004, it also allows an entity to apply IFRS 3 to 'goodwill existing at or acquired after ... any date before' 31 March 2004. Accordingly, as illustrated and explained in the following example, we believe that an entity can stop amortising such goodwill from an earlier date than that mentioned at 4.1.1 above, without having to restate the business combinations that resulted in that goodwill.

Example 6.21:   Application of limited retrospective provisions to previously recognised goodwill

This example is based on the same facts as Example 6.20 above, except that Entity A wishes to invoke the limited retrospective provisions of the standard to the existing goodwill recognised in its balance sheet at 1 January 2004, and discontinue amortising that goodwill from that date, thus overcoming the lack of comparability of the treatment of goodwill in the year ended 31 December 2004. Can it do so?

It is unclear as to what goodwill the provision in the standard is referring. One view is that it is only intended to deal with that relating to equity accounted investments (see 4.1.4 above), in which case the retrospective application of the standard for business combinations is only permitted if the accounting for those combinations is completely restated in accordance with the standard. On this basis, Entity A could not discontinue amortising the goodwill from 1 January 2004.

However, we believe that it can be read to refer to previously recognised goodwill, and therefore entities can stop amortising such goodwill from an earlier date than that mentioned at 4.1.1 above, without having to restate the business combinations that resulted in that goodwill. Indeed, the Basis for Conclusions in discussing the agreed transitional provision in respect of previously recognised goodwill includes the phrase 'or from an earlier date if the entity elects to apply paragraph 85 of the IFRS'.[298] Nevertheless, if an entity does wish to stop amortising goodwill from an earlier date, it is subject to the following conditions:

(i)   all business combinations for which the agreement date was on or after that earlier date must be accounted for in accordance with IFRS 3, and both conditions (a) and (b) are met in respect of those combinations; and

(ii)   IAS 36 and IAS 38 are applied from that date onwards, provided condition (b) is met. Thus an annual impairment test will be required for the financial year ending after that date.

On this basis, if Entity A did not have any business combinations during the first quarter of 2004, it could discontinue amortising its existing goodwill from 1 January 2004, as long as it met condition (ii) above. However, if Entity A did have a business combination for which the agreement date was, say, 31 January 2004, it could only do so if it also accounted for that business combination fully under IFRS 3.

4.2   First-time adoption issues

As discussed in Chapter 4 at 2.4, IFRS 1 provides an exemption from full retrospective application of IFRS 3 on transition to IFRS for first-time adopters. The exemption permits a first-time adopter not to restate business combinations prior to its date of transition to IFRS. The detailed requirements on the application of the exemption are contained in Appendix B to IFRS 1,[299] with examples illustrating its effect given in the implementation guidance to IFRS 1,[300] and are discussed below.

4.2.1   *Option to restate business combinations retrospectively*

A first-time adopter must account for business combinations after its date of transition to IFRS under IFRS 3. Thus, any business combinations during the comparative periods presented by an entity will need to be restated in accordance with the standard. However, it may elect not to apply IFRS 3 to any business combination before that date, but may do so if it so chooses. However, if a first-time adopter restates any business combination prior to its date of transition to comply with IFRS 3 it must also restate all subsequent business combinations under IFRS 3 and apply both IAS 36 and IAS 38 from that date onwards.[301] In other words, as shown on the time line below, a first-time adopter is allowed to choose any date in the past and account for business combinations going forward under IFRS 3 without having to restate business combinations prior to the earliest IFRS 3 restatement.

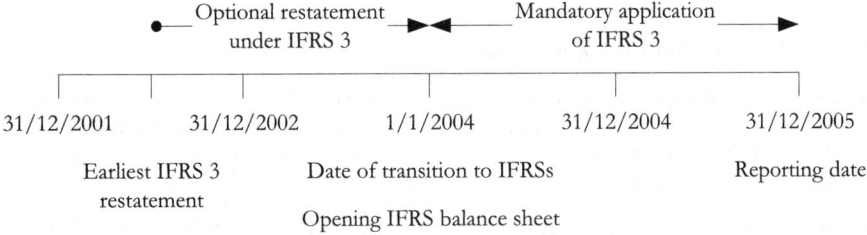

This exemption for past business combinations applies also to past acquisitions of associates and interests in joint ventures. However, it is important to note that the date selected for the first restatement of business combinations should also be applied to the restatement of acquisitions of associates and interests in joint ventures.[302]

Originally, the IASB proposed not to permit restatement of business combinations prior to the date of transition to IFRS as this 'could require an entity to recreate data that it did not capture at the date of a past business combination and make subjective estimates about conditions that existed at that date. These factors could reduce the relevance and reliability of the entity's first IFRS financial statements.'[303] However, the IASB considered that – especially where the information is more likely to be available – it would be conceptually preferable to restate business combinations as the 'effects of business combination accounting can last for many years' and 'previous GAAP may differ significantly from IFRS'.[304] Therefore, the IASB concluded that although it could not require restatement of business combinations for cost-benefit reasons, it should at least permit restatement on condition that all subsequent business combinations are also restated.[305]

4.2.2   Classification of business combinations

Considerable differences between IFRS and an entity's previous GAAP may exist in the definition of, for example, a business combination, an acquisition, a merger and a reverse acquisition. An important benefit of the business combinations exemption is that a first-time adopter will not have to determine the classification of business combinations in accordance with IFRS 3.[306] For example, a transaction that was accounted as a merger or uniting of interests using the pooling-of-interests method under an entity's previous GAAP will not have to reclassified and accounted for under the IFRS 3 purchase method.

The business combinations exemption only applies to 'business combinations that the entity recognised before the date of transition to IFRSs'.[307] Consequently, the business combinations exemption does not apply to a transaction that IFRS considers to be an acquisition of an asset. First-time adopters will therefore have to consider whether past transactions would qualify as business combinations under IFRS 3 (see 2.2.1 above).

Under some national GAAPs, transactions that are not business combinations (e.g. asset purchases) may have been accounted for as if they were business combinations. A first-time adopter will need to restate any transactions that it accounted for as a business combination under its previous GAAP, but which are not business combinations under IFRS 3.

Example 6.22:   Acquisition of an asset

Entity J acquired a holding company that held a single asset at the time of acquisition. That holding company had no employees and the asset itself was not in use at the date of acquisition. J accounted for the transaction under its previous GAAP using the purchase method, which resulted in goodwill. Can J apply the business combinations exemption to the acquisition of the asset?

If J concludes that the asset is not a business, as defined in IFRS 3, it will not be able to apply the business combination exemption to the acquisition of the asset.

4.2.3   Recognition and measurement of assets and liabilities

A   Derecognition of assets and liabilities

A first-time adopter should exclude from its opening IFRS balance sheet any items it recognised under its previous GAAP that do not qualify for recognition as an asset or liability under IFRS. If the first-time adopter previously recognised an intangible asset as part of a business combination that does not qualify for recognition as an asset under IAS 38, it should reclassify that item and the related deferred tax and minority interests as part of goodwill (unless it previously deducted goodwill directly from equity under its previous GAAP) (see 4.2.4 below). All other changes resulting from derecognition of such assets and liabilities should be accounted for as adjustments of retained earnings.[308]

B   Recognition of assets and liabilities

In its opening IFRS balance sheet, a first-time adopter should recognise all assets and liabilities that were acquired or assumed in a past business combination, with the exception of:

- certain financial assets and liabilities that were derecognised and that fall under the derecognition exception (see Chapter 4 at 2.6.4); and

- assets (including goodwill) and liabilities that were not recognised in the acquirer's consolidated balance sheet under its previous GAAP that would not qualify for recognition under IFRS in the separate balance sheet of the acquiree (see Example 6.27 below).[309]

The change resulting from the recognition of such assets and liabilities should be accounted for as an adjustment of retained earnings or another category of equity, if appropriate. However, if the change results from the recognition of an intangible asset that was previously subsumed in goodwill, it should be accounted for as an adjustment of that goodwill (see 4.2.4 A below).[310] As indicated at E below, the recognition of such intangibles will be rare.

The following examples, which are based on the guidance on implementation of IFRS 1, illustrates how a first-time adopter would apply these requirements to an unrecognised finance lease (further examples can be found at E below).

Example 6.23:   Finance lease not capitalised under previous GAAP[311]

Background

Parent L's date of transition to IFRSs is 1 January 2004. Parent L acquired subsidiary M on 15 January 2001 and did not capitalise subsidiary M's finance leases. If subsidiary M prepared separate financial statements under IFRSs, it would recognise finance lease obligations of 300 and leased assets of 250 at 1 January 2004.

Application of requirements

In its consolidated opening IFRS balance sheet, parent L recognises finance lease obligations of 300 and leased assets of 250, and charges 50 to retained earnings.

Example 6.24:   Restructuring provision[312]

Background

Entity D's first IFRS financial statements have a reporting date of 31 December 2005 and include comparative information for 2004 only. It chooses not to restate previous business combinations for IFRS 3. On 1 July 2003, entity D acquired 100 per cent of subsidiary E. Under its previous GAAP, entity D recognised an (undiscounted) restructuring provision of 100 that would not have qualified as an identifiable liability under IFRS 3. The recognition of this restructuring provision increased goodwill by 100. At 31 December 2003 (date of transition to IFRSs), entity D:

(a)   had paid restructuring costs of 60; and

(b)   estimated that it would pay further costs of 40 in 2004, and that the effects of discounting were immaterial. At 31 December 2003, those further costs did not qualify for recognition as a provision under IAS 37.

Application of requirements

In its opening IFRS balance sheet, entity D:

(a) does not recognise a restructuring provision.

(b) does not adjust the amount assigned to goodwill. However, entity D tests the goodwill for impairment under IAS 36, and recognises any resulting impairment loss.

(c) as a result of (a) and (b), reports retained earnings in its opening IFRS balance sheet that are higher by 40 (before income taxes, and before recognising any impairment loss) than in the balance sheet at the same date under previous GAAP.

C   Subsequent measurement under IFRS not based on cost

IFRS requires subsequent measurement of some assets and liabilities on a basis other than original cost, such as fair value. When a first-time adopter does not apply IFRS 3 retrospectively to a business combination, such assets and liabilities must be measured on that other basis in its opening IFRS balance sheet. Any change in the carrying amount of those assets and liabilities should be accounted for as an adjustment of retained earnings, or other appropriate category of equity, rather than as an adjustment of goodwill.[313]

Example 6.25:   Items not measured at original cost

Entity K acquired in a business combination a trading portfolio of equity securities and a number of investment properties. Under its previous GAAP, K initially measured these assets at cost (i.e. their fair value at the date of acquisition).

Upon adoption of IFRS, K measures the trading portfolio of equity securities and the investment properties (under the IAS 40 – *Investment Properties* – fair value model) at fair value on the date of transition in its opening IFRS balance sheet. The resulting adjustment to these assets at the date of transition is reflected in retained earnings.

D   Subsequent measurement on a cost basis under IFRS

For assets and liabilities that are accounted for on a cost basis under IFRS, IFRS 1 stipulates that 'immediately after the business combination, the carrying amount under previous GAAP, of assets acquired and liabilities assumed in that business combination shall be their deemed cost under IFRSs at that date. If IFRSs require a cost-based measurement of those assets and liabilities at a later date, that deemed cost shall be the basis for cost-based depreciation or amortisation from the date of the business combination.'[314]

IFRS 1 does not specifically define 'immediately after a business combination', but it is commonly understood that this takes account of the completion of purchase accounting. In other words, a first-time adopter would not use the provisionally determined fair values of assets acquired and liabilities assumed.

This cost basis, being based on previous GAAP, might be considered as inconsistent with the requirements of IFRS for assets and liabilities that were *not* acquired in a business combination. However, the IASB did not any identify any situations in which 'it would not be acceptable to bring forward cost-based measurements made under previous GAAP'.[315]

Example 6.26:   Items measured on a cost basis

Entity L acquired in a business combination, property, plant and equipment, inventory and accounts receivable. Under its previous GAAP, L initially measured these assets at cost (i.e. their fair value at the date of acquisition).

Upon adoption of IFRS, L determines that its accounting policy for these assets under its previous GAAP complied with the requirements of IFRS. Therefore, property, plant and equipment, inventory and accounts receivable are not adjusted, but recognised in the opening IFRS balance sheet at the carrying amount under the previous GAAP.

E   Measurement of items not recognised under previous GAAP

An asset acquired or a liability assumed in a past business combination may not have been recognised under the entity's previous GAAP. However, this does not mean that such items have a deemed cost of zero in the opening IFRS balance sheet. Instead, the acquirer recognises and measures those items in its opening IFRS balance sheet on the basis that IFRS would require in the balance sheet of the acquiree.[316] The change resulting from the recognition of such assets and liabilities should be accounted for as an adjustment of retained earnings or another category of equity, if appropriate. The IASB included this requirement to avoid 'an unjustifiable departure from the principle that the opening IFRS balance sheet should include all assets and liabilities'.[317]

Intangible assets acquired as part of a business combination that were not recognised under a first-time adopter's previous GAAP, will rarely be recognised in the opening IFRS balance sheet because either (1) they cannot be capitalised in the acquiree's own balance sheet or (2) capitalisation would require the use of hindsight which is not permitted under IAS 38 (see Chapter 4 at 2.9.5).

Example 6.27:   Items not recognised under previous GAAP

Entity K acquired Entity L but did not capitalise L's finance leases and internally generated customer lists under its previous GAAP.

Upon first-time adoption of IFRS, K recognises the finance leases in its opening IFRS balance sheet using the amounts that L would recognise in its IFRS balance sheet. The resulting adjustment to the net assets at the date of transition is reflected in retained earnings; goodwill is not restated to reflect the net assets that would have been recognised at the date of acquisition (see 4.2.4 below). However, K does not recognise the customer lists in its opening IFRS balance sheet, because L is not permitted to capitalise internally generated customer lists. Any value that might have been attributable to the customer lists would remain subsumed in goodwill in K's opening IFRS balance sheet.

Entity M acquired Entity N but did not recognise N's brand name as a separate intangible asset under its previous GAAP.

Upon first-time adoption of IFRS, M will not recognise N's brand name in its opening IFRS balance sheet because N would not have been permitted under IAS 38 to recognise it as an asset in its own separate balance sheet. Again, any value that might have been attributable to the brand name would remain subsumed in goodwill in M's opening IFRS balance sheet.

F   *Summary of recognition and measurement requirements*

The following diagram summarises the recognition and measurement rules – that are discussed above – for assets acquired and liabilities assumed in a business combination that is accounted for under the business combinations exemption.

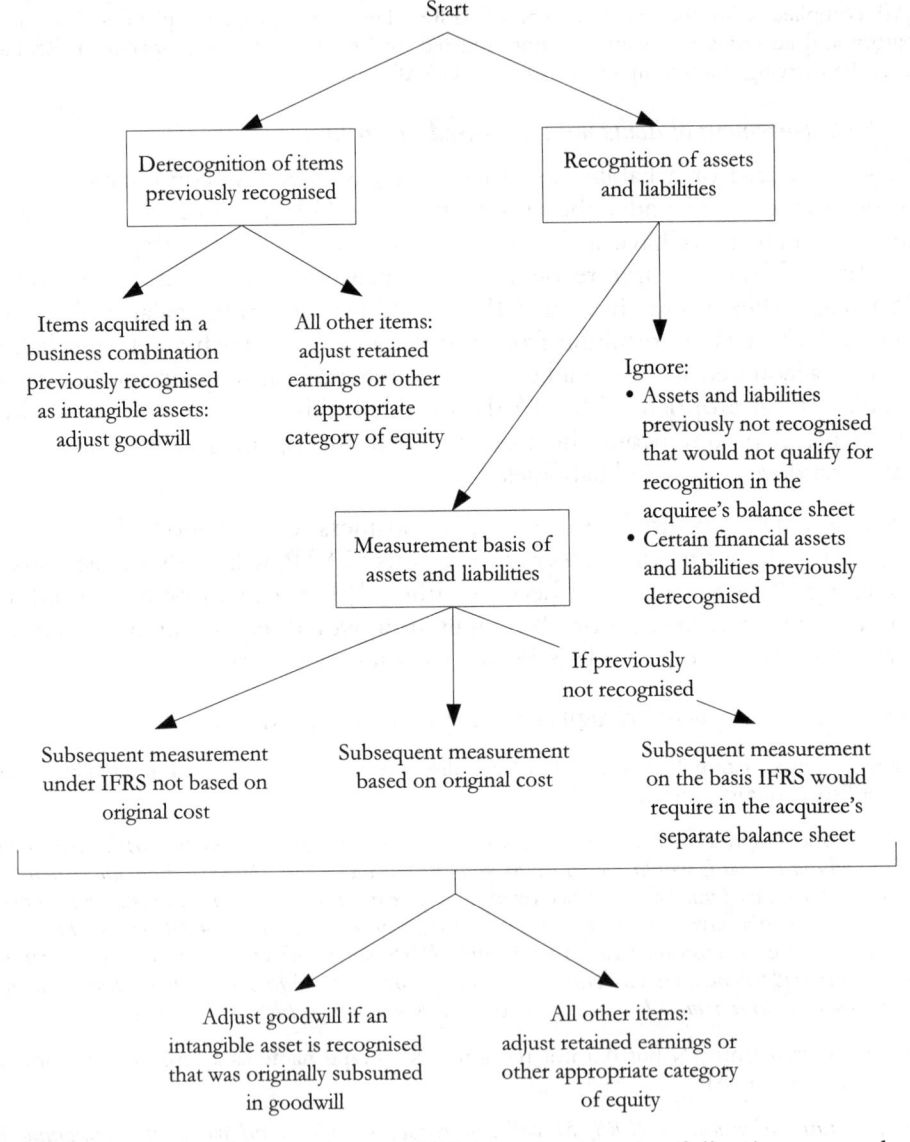

The guidance on implementation of IFRS 1 contains the following example that illustrates many of the requirements discussed above.[318]

Example 6.28:   Business combination example

Background

Entity B's first IFRS financial statements have a reporting date of 31 December 2005 and include comparative information for 2004 only. On 1 July 2001, entity B acquired 100 per cent of subsidiary C. Under its previous GAAP, entity B:

(a)   classified the business combination as an acquisition by entity B;

(b)   measured the assets acquired and liabilities assumed at the following amounts under previous GAAP at 31 December 2003 (date of transition to IFRSs):

   (i)   identifiable assets less liabilities for which IFRSs require cost-based measurement at a date after the business combination: 200 (with a tax base of 150 and an applicable tax rate of 30 per cent);

   (ii)   pension liability (for which the present value of the defined benefit obligation measured under IAS 19 is 130 and the fair value of plan assets is 100): nil (because entity B used a pay-as-you-go cash method of accounting for pensions under its previous GAAP). The tax base of the pension liability is also nil;

   (iii)   goodwill: 180;

(c)   did not, at the date of acquisition, recognise deferred tax arising from temporary differences associated with the identifiable assets acquired and liabilities assumed.

Application of requirements

In its opening (consolidated) IFRS balance sheet, entity B:

(a)   classifies the business combination as an acquisition by entity B even if the business combination would have qualified under IAS 22 as a reverse acquisition by subsidiary C or a uniting of interests;

(b)   does not adjust the accumulated amortisation of goodwill. Entity B tests the goodwill for impairment under IAS 36 and recognises any resulting impairment loss, based on conditions that existed at the date of transition to IFRSs. If no impairment exists, the carrying amount of the goodwill remains at 180;

(c)   for those net identifiable assets acquired for which IFRSs require cost-based measurement at a date after the business combination, treats their carrying amount under previous GAAP immediately after the business combination as their deemed cost at that date;

(d)   does not restate the accumulated depreciation and amortisation of the net identifiable assets in (c) above, unless the depreciation methods and rates under previous GAAP result in amounts that differ materially from those required under IFRSs (for example, if they were adopted solely for tax purposes and do not reflect a reasonable estimate of the asset's useful life under IFRSs). If no such restatement is made, the carrying amount of those assets in the opening IFRS balance sheet equals their carrying amount under previous GAAP at the date of transition to IFRSs (200);

(e)   if there is any indication that identifiable assets are impaired, tests those assets for impairment, based on conditions that existed at the date of transition to IFRSs (see IAS 36);

(f)   recognises the pension liability, and measures it, at the present value of the defined benefit obligation (130) less the fair value of the plan assets (100), giving a carrying amount of 30, with a corresponding debit of 30 to retained earnings. However, if subsidiary C had already adopted IFRSs in an earlier period, entity B would measure the pension liability at the same amount as in subsidiary C's separate financial statements;

(g)   recognises a net deferred tax liability of 6 (20 at 30 per cent) arising from:

   (i)   the taxable temporary difference of 50 (200 less 150) associated with the identifiable assets acquired and non-pension liabilities assumed, less

   (ii)   the deductible temporary difference of 30 (30 less nil) associated with the pension liability.

The entity recognises the resulting increase in the deferred tax liability as a deduction from retained earnings. If a taxable temporary difference arises from the initial recognition of the goodwill, entity B does not recognise the resulting deferred tax liability.

4.2.4 Restatement of goodwill

A   Mandatory adjustments of goodwill

Under the business combinations exemption, a first-time adopter takes the carrying amount of goodwill under its previous GAAP at the date of transition to IFRS as a starting point and only adjusts it as follows:[319]

- a first-time adopter increases goodwill by an amount equal to the carrying amount of an item that it recognised as an intangible asset under its previous GAAP (less any related deferred tax and minority interests), but which does not meet the recognition criteria under IFRS. That is, the first-time adopter accounts for the change in classification prospectively and does not, for example, reverse the cumulative amortisation on the item that it recognised as an intangible asset under its previous GAAP;

- if a first-time adopter is required to recognise an intangible asset under IFRS that was subsumed in goodwill under its previous GAAP, it decreases goodwill accordingly and adjusts deferred tax and minority interests;

- a contingency affecting the amount of the purchase consideration for a past business combination may have been resolved before the date of transition to IFRS. If a reliable estimate of the contingent adjustment can be made and its payment is probable, the first-time adopter shall adjust the goodwill by that amount. Similarly, the first-time adopter shall adjust the carrying amount of goodwill if a previously recognised contingent adjustment can no longer be measured reliably or its payment is no longer probable;[320] and

- regardless of whether there is any indication that the goodwill may be impaired, the first-time adopter shall apply IAS 36 in testing the goodwill for impairment at the date of transition to IFRS and in recognising any resulting impairment loss in retained earnings (or, if so required by IAS 36, in revaluation surplus). The impairment test shall be based on conditions at the date of transition to IFRS.[321]

Example 6.29:   Restatement of goodwill[322]

Entity V's first IFRS financial statements have a reporting date of 31 December 2005 and include comparative information for 2004 only. On 1 July 2001, V acquired 75% of subsidiary W. Under its previous GAAP, V assigned an initial carrying amount of 200 to intangible assets that would not have qualified for recognition under IAS 38. The tax base of the intangible assets was nil, giving rise to a deferred tax liability (at 30%) of 60. V measured minority interests at the minority's share of the fair value of the identifiable net assets acquired (the allowed alternative treatment in IAS 22). Goodwill arising on the acquisition was capitalised as an asset in V's consolidated financial statements.

On 1 January 2004 (the date of transition to IFRS), the carrying amount of the intangible assets under previous GAAP was 160, and the carrying amount of the related deferred tax liability was 48 (30% of 160).

Under IFRS 1, V reclassifies intangible assets that do not qualify for recognition as separate assets under IAS 38, together with the related deferred tax liability of 48 and minority interests, as part of goodwill. The related minority interests amount to 28 (25% of 112 (160 minus 48)). V makes the following adjustment in its opening IFRS balance sheet:

Goodwill	84	
Deferred tax liability	48	
Minority interests	28	
Intangible assets		160

V tests the goodwill for impairment under IAS 36 and recognises any resulting impairment loss, based on conditions that existed at the date of transition to IFRS.

The main implication for first-time adopters will clearly be the requirement to carry out an impairment test of goodwill at the date of transition to IFRS. The requirements of IAS 36 relating specifically to the impairment of goodwill are dealt with at 3 above. The estimates used to determine whether a first-time adopter recognises an impairment loss or provision at the date of transition to IFRS should be consistent with estimates made for the same date under previous GAAP (after adjustments to reflect any difference in accounting policies), unless there is objective evidence that those estimates were in error.[323] If a first-time adopter needs to make estimates for that date that were not necessary under its previous GAAP, such estimates and assumptions should not reflect conditions that arose after the date of transition to IFRS.[324]

If a first-time adopter's opening IFRS balance sheet reflects impairment losses, it recognises any later reversal of those impairment losses in the income statement unless IAS 36 requires that reversal to be treated as a revaluation. This applies to both impairment losses recognised under previous GAAP and additional impairment losses recognised on transition to IFRS.[325]

Under IFRS 1, assets acquired and liabilities assumed in a business combination prior to the date of transition to IFRS are not necessarily valued on a basis that is consistent with IFRS 3. This can lead to 'double counting' in the carrying amount of assets and goodwill as is illustrated in the example below.

Example 6.30:   Impairment testing of goodwill on first-time adoption

Entity P acquired a business before its date of transition to IFRS. The cost of acquisition was €530 and P allocated the purchase price as follows:

	€
Properties, at carry-over cost	450
Liabilities, at amortised cost	(180)
Goodwill	260
Purchase price	530

The goodwill under P's previous GAAP relates entirely to the properties that had a fair value at date of acquisition that was significantly in excess of their value on a carry-over cost basis. In P's opening IFRS balance sheet the same assets, liabilities and goodwill are valued as follows:

	€
Properties, at fair value	750
Liabilities, at amortised cost	(200)
Provisional IFRS goodwill (before impairment test)	260
Total carrying amount	810

P used the option to measure the properties at fair value at its date of transition in its opening IFRS balance sheet. However, IFRS 1 does not permit goodwill to be adjusted to reflect the extent to which the increase in fair value relates to the time of the acquisition. The total carrying amount of the acquired net assets including goodwill of €810 may now exceed the recoverable amount. When P tests the 'provisional IFRS goodwill' for impairment on first-time adoption of IFRS, the recoverable amount of the business is determined to be €600. Accordingly, it will have to recognise an impairment of goodwill of €210 and disclose this impairment under IFRS 1.

In some cases the write-off will completely eliminate the goodwill and thereby any 'double counting'. However, in this particular case the remaining goodwill of €50 in truth represents goodwill that was internally generated between the date of acquisition and the date of transition to IFRS.

The IASB accepted that IFRS 1 'does not prevent the implicit recognition of internally generated goodwill that arose after the date of the business combination. However, the Board concluded that an attempt to exclude such internally generated goodwill would be costly and lead to arbitrary results.'[326]

B   Prohibition of other adjustments of goodwill

The IASB concluded that 'to avoid costs that would exceed the likely benefits to users', IFRS 1 should prohibit 'restatement of goodwill for most other adjustments reflected in the opening IFRS balance sheet, unless a first-time adopter elects to apply IFRS 3 retrospectively'.[327] Therefore, a first-time adopter electing not to apply IFRS 3 retrospectively is not permitted to make any adjustments to goodwill other than those described at 4.2.4 A above. For example, a first-time adopter should not restate the carrying amount of goodwill:[328]

'(i)   to exclude in-process research and development acquired in that business combination (unless the related intangible asset would qualify for recognition under IAS 38 in the balance sheet of the acquiree);

(ii)   to adjust previous amortisation of goodwill;

(iii) to reverse adjustments to goodwill that IFRS 3 would not permit, but were made under previous GAAP because of adjustments to assets and liabilities between the date of the business combination and the date of transition to IFRS'.

Although IFRS 1 specifically prohibits other adjustments of goodwill, differences between the goodwill amount in the opening IFRS balance sheet and that in the financial statements under previous GAAP may arise because:

(a) goodwill may have been restated as a result of a retrospective application of IAS 21 (see Chapter 9 at 4.2.2);

(b) goodwill in relation to previously unconsolidated subsidiaries will have to be recognised (see 4.2.5 below); and

(c) goodwill in relation to transactions that do not qualify as business combinations under IFRS must be derecognised (see 4.2.2 above).

Example 6.31: Adjusting goodwill

Entity R acquired Entity S but under its previous GAAP it did not recognise the following items:

- S's customer lists which had a fair value of ¥1,100 at the date of the acquisition and ¥1,500 at the date of transition to IFRS; and

- Deferred tax liabilities related to the fair value adjustment of S's property, plant and equipment, which amounted to ¥9,500 at the date of the acquisition and ¥7,800 at the date of transition to IFRS.

What adjustment should R make to goodwill to account for the customer lists and deferred tax liabilities at its date of transition to IFRS?

As explained at 4.2.3 E above, R cannot recognise the customer lists when it uses the business combinations exemption. Accordingly, R cannot adjust goodwill for the customer lists.

R must recognise the deferred tax liability at its date of transition under IAS 12 – *Income Taxes* – because there is no exemption from recognising deferred taxation under IFRS 1. However, R is not permitted to adjust goodwill for the deferred tax liability that would have been recognised at the date of acquisition. Instead, R should recognise the change in deferred tax in retained earnings or other category of equity, if appropriate.

C   Derecognition of negative goodwill

IFRS 3 specifically requires derecognition of negative goodwill with a corresponding adjustment to the opening balance of retained earnings on adoption of the standard by entities already reporting under IFRS (see 4.1.2 above). Although IFRS 1 does not specifically address accounting for negative goodwill recognised under a previous GAAP, negative goodwill should be derecognised by a first-time adopter because it is not permitted 'to recognise items or liabilities if IFRS do not permit such recognition'.[329] Negative goodwill clearly does not meet the definition of a liability under the IASB's *Framework* and its recognition is not permitted under IFRS 3.

D   Goodwill previously deducted from equity

If a first-time adopter deducted goodwill from equity under its previous GAAP then 'it shall not recognise that goodwill in its opening IFRS balance sheet. Furthermore, it shall not transfer that goodwill to the income statement if it disposes of the subsidiary or if the investment in the subsidiary becomes impaired.'[330] Effectively, under IFRS such goodwill ceases to exist.

Example 6.32:   Goodwill deducted from equity and treatment of related intangible assets[331]

Entity H acquired a subsidiary before the date of transition to IFRS. Under its previous GAAP, H:

(a)   recognised goodwill as an immediate deduction from equity;

(b)   recognised an intangible asset of the subsidiary that does not qualify for recognition as an asset under IAS 38; and

(c)   did not recognise an intangible asset of the subsidiary that would qualify under IAS 38 for recognition as an asset in the financial statements of the subsidiary. The subsidiary held the asset at the date of its acquisition by H.

In its opening IFRS balance sheet, H:

(a)   does not recognise the goodwill, as it did not recognise the goodwill as an asset under previous GAAP;

(b)   does not recognise the intangible asset that does not qualify for recognition as an asset under IAS 38. Because H deducted goodwill from equity under its previous GAAP, the elimination of this intangible asset reduces retained earnings (see 4.2.3 A above); and

(c)   recognises the intangible asset that qualifies under IAS 38 for recognition as an asset in the financial statements of the subsidiary, even though the amount assigned to it under previous GAAP in H's consolidated financial statements was nil (see 4.2.3 E above)). The recognition criteria in IAS 38 include the availability of a reliable measurement of cost and H measures the asset at cost less accumulated depreciation and less any impairment losses identified under IAS 36 (see Chapter 4 at 2.9.5). Because H deducted goodwill from equity under its previous GAAP, the recognition of this intangible asset increases retained earnings. However, if this intangible asset had been subsumed in goodwill recognised as an asset under previous GAAP, H would have decreased the carrying amount of that goodwill accordingly (and, if applicable, adjusted deferred tax and minority interests) (see 4.2.4 A above).

If a first-time adopter deducted goodwill from equity under its previous GAAP then 'adjustments resulting from the subsequent resolution of a contingency affecting the purchase consideration shall be recognised in retained earnings'.[332] Effectively, the adjustment is being accounted for in the same way as the original goodwill that arose on the acquisition, rather than having to be adjusted against capitalised goodwill under IFRS 3. This requirement could affect, for example, the way a first-time adopter accounts for earn-out clauses relating to business combinations prior to its date of transition to IFRS.

Example 6.33:   Earn-out clause in acquisition

Entity U acquired a business before its date of transition to IFRS and agreed to make an initial payment to the vendor together with further payments based on a multiple of future profits of the acquiree. The fair value of the earn-out is contingent on future profits and could not be determined reliably at the date of transition to IFRS. Under U's previous GAAP any goodwill was written off against equity as incurred.

After its date of transition to IFRS, U will account for the earn-out as a change in purchase consideration and recognise it in retained earnings.

4.2.5 *Previously unconsolidated subsidiaries*

Under its previous GAAP a first-time adopter may not have consolidated a subsidiary acquired in a past business combination. In that case a first-time adopter applying the business combinations exemption should 'adjust the carrying amounts of the subsidiary's assets and liabilities to the amounts that IFRSs would require in the subsidiary's balance sheet. The deemed cost of goodwill equals the difference at the date of transition to IFRSs between:

(i)   the parent's interest in those adjusted carrying amounts; and

(ii)   the cost in the parent's separate financial statements of its investment in the subsidiary.'[333]

The cost of a subsidiary in the parent's separate financial statements should be determined under the cost method of accounting under IAS 27 (see Chapter 5 at 7.2.1). Thus, a first-time adopter does not have to calculate what the goodwill would have been at the date of the original acquisition. The deemed cost of goodwill will, however, be capitalised as an asset in the opening IFRS balance sheet. The guidance on the implementation of IFRS 1 contains the following example that illustrates this.[334]

Example 6.34:   Subsidiary not consolidated under previous GAAP

Background

Parent J's date of transition to IFRSs is 1 January 2004. Under its previous GAAP, parent J did not consolidate its 75 per cent subsidiary K, acquired in a business combination on 15 July 2001. On 1 January 2004:

(a)   the cost of parent J's investment in subsidiary K is 180.

(b)   under IFRSs, subsidiary K would measure its assets at 500 and its liabilities (including deferred tax under IAS 12) at 300. On this basis, subsidiary K's net assets are 200 under IFRSs.

Application of requirements

Parent J consolidates subsidiary K. The consolidated balance sheet at 1 January 2004 includes:

(a)   subsidiary K's assets at 500 and liabilities at 300;

(b)   minority interests of 50 (25 per cent of [500-300]); and

(c)   goodwill of 30 (cost of 180 less 75 per cent of [500-300]). Parent J tests the goodwill for impairment under IAS 36 and recognises any resulting impairment loss, based on conditions that existed at the date of transition to IFRSs.

If the original acquisition cost is lower than the net asset value at the date of transition to IFRS, the difference is taken to retained earnings.

Slightly different rules apply to all other subsidiaries (i.e. those not acquired in a business combination) that an entity did not consolidate under its previous GAAP, the main difference being that goodwill should not be recognised in relation to those subsidiaries (see Chapter 4 at 2.9.3).

It should be noted that in calculating the deemed cost of the goodwill, the first-time adopter is required to compare the historical cost of the investment to its share of the carrying amount of the net assets determined on a different date. In the case of a highly profitable subsidiary this could give rise to the following anomaly:

Example 6.35:   Calculation of deemed goodwill

Parent L acquired subsidiary M before the date of transition for $500. The net assets of M would have been $220 under IFRS at the date of acquisition. M makes on average an annual net profit of $60, which it does not distribute to L.

At the date of transition to IFRS, the cost of L's investment in M is still $500. However, the net assets of M have increased to $460. Therefore, under IFRS 1 the deemed cost of goodwill is $40.

The deemed goodwill is much lower than the goodwill that was paid at the date of acquisition because M did not distribute its profits. In fact, if M had distributed a dividend to its parent just before the date of transition, the deemed goodwill would have been significantly higher.

5   FUTURE DEVELOPMENTS

As indicated at 1.2.5 above, the IASB is considering a number of other issues relating to business combinations in phase II of its project.

In April 2004, the IASB issued an exposure draft of proposed amendments to IFRS 3 relating to its application to combinations by contract alone or involving mutual entities (see 2.2.2 above). This is discussed at 5.1 below.

As far as the part of the project dealing with a number of issues arising in respect of the application of the purchase method is concerned, this is being conducted as a joint project with the FASB. The IASB and the FASB have agreed to develop jointly a common, cohesive exposure draft on accounting for business combinations that will incorporate the decisions reached in their joint project and the guidance in their existing business combinations standards that will not be changed by the joint project. The IASB expects to issue the exposure draft in the final quarter of 2004. This is discussed at 5.2 below.

Having issued that exposure draft, the IASB will then consider the other aspects of phase II of its project. These are discussed at 5.3 below.

5.1   Combinations by contract alone or involving mutual entities

The exposure draft issued in April 2004 proposes:

(a)   to remove from IFRS 3 the scope exclusions for business combinations involving two or more mutual entities and business combinations in which separate entities are brought together to form a reporting entity by contract alone without the obtaining of an ownership interest (see 2.2.1 above);[335]

(b)   to require the acquirer to measure the cost of a business combination as:

   (i)   the aggregate of the following amounts when the combination is one in which the acquirer and acquiree are both mutual entities:

   •   the net fair value of the acquiree's identifiable assets, liabilities and contingent liabilities; and

   •   the fair value, at the date of exchange, of any assets given, liabilities incurred or assumed, or equity instruments issued by the acquirer in exchange for control of the acquiree.[336]

Therefore, goodwill would be recognised in the accounting for such transactions only to the extent of any consideration given by the acquirer in exchange for control of the acquiree.

(ii)　the net fair value of the acquiree's identifiable assets, liabilities and contingent liabilities when the combination is one in which separate entities or businesses are brought together to form a reporting entity by contract alone without the obtaining of an ownership interest.[337] Therefore, no goodwill would arise in the accounting for such transactions; and

(c)　to require the cost of such business combinations to exclude any costs directly attributable to the combination, such as professional fees paid to accountants, legal advisers, valuers and other consultants to effect the combination. Such costs would be recognised as an expense in profit or loss in the period in which they are incurred.[338]

ED 3 had not originally proposed to exclude such business combinations from the scope of IFRS 3, but to delay its application to the accounting for such transactions. The IASB had recognised that there were complications in applying the purchase method to such business combinations, and until those issues were resolved as part of the second phase of its project, IAS 22 should continue to apply to such transactions. However, during its redeliberations of these proposals, the IASB observed that continuing to apply IAS 22 to such transactions would result in them being classified either as unitings of interests or as acquisitions. If such a transaction were classified as a uniting of interests, IAS 22 would require it to be accounted for by applying the pooling of interests method. However, this would have been inconsistent with the Board's view that there are no circumstances in which the pooling of interests method provides information superior to that provided by the purchase method. The Board was also troubled by the fact that if such a transaction were classified as an acquisition, IAS 22 would require it to be accounted for by applying the purchase method, but a version of the purchase method different from that now contained in IFRS 3. Consequently, the IASB decided that such combinations should be within the scope of IFRS 3, but until it developed guidance on applying the purchase method to such transactions as part of the second phase of the project, as an interim measure it would measure the cost of such business combinations in such a way as to limit the amount of goodwill.[339] Since it would have been inappropriate to include this interim solution within IFRS 3 without first exposing it for public comment, the IASB decided to issue the standard including the scope exclusion for such business combinations, but with the intention of issuing this exposure draft shortly thereafter.[340] This enabled the IASB to meet its 31 March 2004 deadline for the issue of IFRS 3.

The exposure draft also proposes that no amendments be made to the transitional and effective date requirements in IFRS 3 (see 4.1 above). This would mean that:

(a)　entities would not be required to apply the revised version of IFRS 3 arising from this exposure draft to the accounting for any business combinations for which the agreement date is before 31 March 2004. This would include combinations in which the acquirer and acquiree are both mutual entities or in which separate entities or businesses are brought together to form a reporting entity by contract alone without the obtaining of an ownership interest;

(b)   entities would be permitted to apply the revised version of IFRS 3 arising from this exposure draft from any date before 31 March 2004, provided:

  (i)   the valuations and other information needed to apply the IFRS to past business combinations were obtained at the time those combinations were initially accounted for; and

  (ii)   the entity also applies IAS 36 and IAS 38 (both as revised in 2004) prospectively from that same date, and the valuations and other information needed to apply those standards from that date were previously obtained by the entity so that there is no need to determine estimates that would need to have been made at a prior date.

Therefore, entities that elect to apply the revised version of IFRS 3 from any date before 31 March 2004 would be required to apply that revised version to any combination in which the acquirer and acquiree are both mutual entities or in which separate entities or businesses are brought together to form a reporting entity by contract alone without the obtaining of an ownership interest, and for which the agreement date is after the date selected but before 31 March 2004; and

(c)   entities would be required to apply the revised version of IFRS 3 arising from this exposure draft to the accounting for all business combinations for which the agreement date is 31 March 2004 or later, including combinations addressed by this exposure draft.[341]

5.2   Application of the purchase method

As noted at 5 above, the IASB expects to issue an exposure draft in the final quarter of 2004 as part of the project that is being conducted as a joint project with the FASB. The IASB expects that the guidance in its exposure draft and the FASB's equivalent exposure draft will differ only to the extent of differing decisions reached in phase I and the joint project, and inherited differences that originate from other standards.

The IASB intends to post on its website a text of IFRS 3 accompanied by comments indicating how the standard would be amended by the tentative decisions reached by the IASB in the joint project, but at the time of writing this has not been done.[342]

At its meeting in July 2004 the IASB reviewed all the decisions it has made in this project together with an overview of the issues for which the IASB and FASB have reached different conclusions in phases I and II of their Business Combinations projects.[343]

5.2.1   Summary of decisions

The IASB considered a summary of its decisions up to and including its June 2004 meeting and decided to proceed with the decisions package for the purpose of drafting the Exposure Draft.[344] However, as noted in 5.2.2 below, some of these decisions were revised at the July meeting.

The summary of decisions was presented in the Observer Notes available for the July meeting,[345] and the main decisions contained therein relating to the application of the purchase method under IFRS 3 are set out below.

A   Working principle

The accounting for a business combination is to be based on the assumption that the transaction is an arm's-length transaction in which independent and willing parties exchange equal values, and, accordingly, absent evidence to the contrary, the consideration given by the acquirer is representative of the fair value of the acquirer's interest in the business acquired.

The total amount to be recognised by the acquirer should be the fair value of the business over which it obtains control. Assuming an exchange of equal values, the IASB had decided that there should be a rebuttable presumption that the consideration given by the acquirer provides the best basis for measuring the fair value of the business acquired. However, as noted at 5.2.2 B below, it has now decided to remove this rebuttable presumption and adopt the FASB's guidance.

Where the acquirer obtains control of all or substantially all of the ownership interest of the business acquired, the fair value of the consideration given generally is more clearly evident than the fair value of the business acquired. Therefore, absent evidence to the contrary, the fair value of the consideration given is used to determine the fair value of the business acquired.

In a business combination in which the acquirer obtains control of less than a 100% ownership interest of the business acquired, the consideration given by the acquirer normally provides the best basis for measuring the fair value of the business acquired. However, if the consideration given by the acquirer does not provide the best basis for measuring the fair value of the business acquired, the fair value of the business acquired should be measured directly using valuation techniques. In such cases, the objective of the valuation techniques is to measure the fair value of the consideration that market participants would have given to purchase a 100% ownership interest in the business acquired.

In a business combination, the acquirer obtains control over, and therefore is responsible for, the net assets acquired. The assets acquired and liabilities assumed are to be recognised on the date control is obtained, and measured at their fair values at that date. If the fair value of the business acquired exceeds the net fair value of the recognised identifiable assets acquired and liabilities assumed, that excess amount (which is the implied fair value of total goodwill) is recognised as an asset.

In those rare circumstances in which the business combination is not an exchange of equal values such that there is a difference between the fair value of the acquirer's interest in the business acquired and the consideration given for that interest:

(a)   any excess of the consideration given over the fair value of the acquirer's interest in the business acquired (i.e. any overpayment) should be recognised in profit or loss at the date of acquisition. As noted at 5.2.2 A below this is an issue where the FASB has reached a different conclusion.

(b)   any excess of the fair value of the acquirer's interest in the business acquired over the fair value of the consideration given for that interest should be recognised as a reduction in the total amount of goodwill (including goodwill attributable to minority interests) until the goodwill is reduced to zero. Any excess remaining after the total goodwill has been reduced to zero should be recognised immediately in profit or loss at the date of acquisition.

B   Scope

In relation to the definition of a business (see 2.2.1 above) the IASB had decided that it should be clarified in the application guidance that an entity (a) might not yet have outputs used to generate revenues, but (b) might nevertheless be a business, and had agreed on factors to be taken into account in assessing whether an entity without outputs is a business. However, as noted at 5.2.2 C below, the IASB has now decided to include the more detailed guidance of the FASB.

Paragraph 4 of IFRS 3 is to be amended to clarify that when an entity acquires a group of assets that is not a business, it should (a) identify and separately recognise all identifiable assets acquired and liabilities assumed, including those assets that meet the definition of, and recognition criteria for, intangible assets in IAS 38 and (b) allocate the cost of the group between the individual identifiable assets and liabilities on the basis of their relative fair values at the date of acquisition.

The IASB has tentatively decided that the Exposure Draft should propose that business combinations involving two or more mutual entities or business combinations in which separate entities are brought together by contract alone should be accounted for in accordance with the proposals in the Phase II project. In addition, before publishing its Exposure Draft of revised IFRS 3, the Board will consider the issues that the FASB considered in respect of mutual entities to the extent that those issues have not already been dealt with by the IASB. The Board also agreed to explore whether there might be issues unique to combinations in which separate entities are brought together by contract alone that justify an accounting treatment different from that provided in this project for other combinations.

C   *Treatment of contingencies in a business combination*

I   *Contingent assets and liabilities*

The IASB has decided that the definitions of contingent assets and contingent liabilities in IAS 37 should be replaced with the following definitions:

'A contingent asset is a conditional right that arises from past events from which future economic benefits may flow based on the occurrence or non-occurrence of one or more uncertain future events not wholly within the control of the entity.'

'A contingent liability is a conditional obligation that arises from past events that may require an outflow of resources embodying economic benefits based on the occurrence or non-occurrence of one or more uncertain future events not wholly within the control of the entity.'

Since contingent assets are conditional rights they do not meet the definition of an asset. Consequently, the acquirer does not recognise separately from goodwill contingent assets of the acquiree. However, the acquirer is to recognise as an asset separately from goodwill any *unconditional* right accompanying a contingent asset at the acquisition date if that unconditional right meets the definition of an asset, is identifiable (e.g. it meets the definition of a financial asset in IAS 39 or it satisfies the 'identifiable' criterion in IAS 38), and its fair value can be measured reliably. The fair value of such an unconditional right is to reflect the likelihood of the occurrence and the amount of the contingency.

Similarly, since contingent liabilities are conditional obligations they do not meet the definition of a liability. Consequently, the acquirer does not recognise separately from goodwill contingent liabilities of the acquiree. However, the acquirer recognises as a liability separately from goodwill any *unconditional* obligation accompanying a contingent liability at the acquisition date if that unconditional obligation meets the definition of a liability, and its fair value can be measured reliably. The fair value of such an unconditional obligation is to reflect the likelihood of the occurrence and the amount of the contingency.

Present obligations that fail to qualify for recognition under IAS 37 and are therefore at present defined as contingent liabilities (see Chapter 25 at 3.2.1), will no longer satisfy the definition of a contingent liability. However, such obligations, whilst not recognised under IAS 37, will qualify as liabilities to be considered for recognition in a business combination.

II   Contingent consideration given by the acquirer

The fair value of contingent consideration is to be included in determining the fair value at the acquisition date of the total consideration given.

After initial recognition, the acquirer should account for obligations for consideration contingent on future events as follows:

(a)   obligations that take the form of financial instruments classified as equity shall not be remeasured. Classification as either liability or equity would depend on the application of IAS 32;

(b)   obligations that take the form of financial instruments classified as liabilities and within the scope of IAS 39 shall be accounted for in accordance with IAS 39;

(c)   obligations that take the form of financial instruments excluded from the scope of IAS 39 shall be measured at fair value, with changes in fair value recognised in profit or loss; and

(d)   obligations that take the form of an unconditional obligation accompanying a contingent liability shall be accounted for in accordance with IAS 37.

Changes after initial recognition in the measurement of obligations for contingent consideration shall not be treated as adjustments to the accounting for a business combination. Consequently, there will be no adjustments to the goodwill originally recognised on the business combination.

D   Issues related to the exchange transaction and consideration given

The fair value at the acquisition date of the consideration given in a business combination is to exclude any costs directly attributable to the business combination that are not given in exchange for the business acquired. Such costs shall be recognised as an expense in profit and loss in the period in which they are incurred. This includes, for example, professional fees paid to accountants, legal advisers, valuers and other consultants to effect the combination.

Equity instruments issued as consideration in a business combination are to be measured at their fair value at the acquisition date.

In some cases, the consideration given by the acquirer includes a business or a non-monetary asset transferred to the acquiree in exchange for equity instruments issued by the acquiree. Such a business combination is to be accounted for at fair value, i.e. measured by direct measurement of the fair value of the business acquired or based on the fair value of the consideration given, whichever is more clearly evident of the fair value of the business acquired. However, the business or non-monetary asset transferred to the acquiree is not to be regarded by the acquirer as part of the business acquired. This is because the acquirer controls the business or non-monetary asset transferred both before and after the business combination. Therefore, the full amount of any profit or loss arising on the transfer to the acquiree of the business or non-monetary asset should be eliminated in the consolidated financial statements. This decision is not to be viewed as pre-empting its future consideration of 'fresh start' accounting issues as part of future phases of the IASB's business combinations project (see 5.3 below).

The IASB has also considered the accounting treatment of share-based payment awards of the acquiree that are replaced by the acquirer in a business combination. This issue and the IASB's tentative conclusions are dealt with in Chapter 29 at 10.1.

E   *Determining which identifiable assets and liabilities should be included in the business combination accounting*

An assessment is to be performed by the acquirer to ensure that the business combination accounting deals only with the consideration given and the assets acquired and liabilities assumed as part of the business combination. The assessment is to focus on transactions entered into by the parties to the combination (the acquirer, the business acquired, and their owners, directors, managers, and their agents) and past events affecting those parties. The purpose of the assessment is to determine whether transactions were arranged or events occurred that result in economic benefits that are to be derived primarily by the acquirer or combined entity (including favourable accounting effects).

If a transaction or event relates to benefits to be derived primarily by the acquirer or combined entity, assets and liabilities arising from such transactions and events are not to be considered part of the business combination and, therefore, shall be accounted for separately from the business combination accounting. For example, if a compensation arrangement with employees provides remuneration for the employees' pre-combination services, any associated liability at the acquisition date arises from a transaction for which the benefits are received by the acquiree. Therefore, the liability is assumed as part of the business combination and included in the accounting for the business combination. However, if the compensation arrangement provides remuneration for services to be provided by the employees after the acquisition date, any associated liability at the acquisition date arises from a transaction for which the benefits are to be received primarily by the acquirer. Therefore, any liability assumed is for post-combination expenses of the combined entity that are excluded from the business combination accounting.

The IASB has decided that the following factors, which are neither mutually exclusive nor individually conclusive, are to be considered in assessing whether the benefits derived from a transaction or event are to be received primarily by the acquirer (including achieving favourable accounting effects):

(a)   the timing of the transaction or obligating event. If a transaction or obligating event occurs during the negotiations of a business combination by parties to the combination, particularly by parties that have a continuing involvement and interest in the combined entity, it may provide evidence that the transaction was entered into in contemplation of the business combination for the purpose of providing future benefits to the combined entity. For example, continuing management might enter into a transaction to shift post-combination expenses of the acquirer into the business combination accounting;

(b)   the reason for the transaction. If a transaction or obligating event is entered into primarily for the purposes of recognising post-combination expenses of the acquiring entity as if they were liabilities assumed as part of the business combination that usually indicates that the transaction was entered into in contemplation of the business combination for the purpose of providing future benefits to the combined entity or achieving favourable accounting results; and

(c)   who initiated the transaction. If a transaction or obligating event is initiated by the acquirer it may indicate that the transaction was entered into in contemplation of the business combination for the purpose of providing future benefits to the combined entity or achieving favourable accounting results.

F   *General principle of measuring the fair value of acquired assets and assumed liabilities – Fair value hierarchy*

For the purpose of estimating the fair values of assets acquired and liabilities assumed, the acquirer is to apply the fair value hierarchy below. The fair value hierarchy reflects the general principle that fair value is reflective of the interaction of knowledgeable, unrelated, willing parties. It emphasises that market prices, when available, are the best evidence of fair value.

•   Level 1

        The estimate of fair value shall be determined by reference to observable prices of market transactions at or near the measurement date for *identical* assets or liabilities whenever that information is available. 'Market' refers to the markets to which the entity has reasonable access. Prices of market transactions near the measurement date, rather than at the measurement date, can be used to the extent that there were no changes in market conditions between the date of the observable transaction and the measurement date.

•   Level 2

        If observable prices of market transactions at or near the measurement date for identical assets or liabilities are not available, the estimate of fair value shall be determined by adjusting observable prices of market transactions at or near the measurement date for *similar* assets or liabilities. A similar asset or liability is one that is reasonably comparable, for example, one having similar patterns of cash flows that can be expected to respond similarly to those of the item being measured to changes in economic conditions. Generally, when an asset or liability is sufficiently similar to the asset or liability for which fair value is being estimated, adjustments for any differences are objectively determinable. For example, similar assets could be identical in all respects except for location. If the only difference between two assets were the location, the fair value would equal the observable price of an identical item in a different location plus costs to ship the item to the identical location as the asset for which fair value is being estimated.

- Level 3

  If observable prices of market transactions at or near the measurement date for identical or similar assets or liabilities are not available, the estimate of fair value shall be determined using other valuation techniques.

  There are multiple valuation techniques that can broadly be characterised as variations of the market, income and cost approaches to valuation. It is preferable to measure fair value by applying multiple valuation techniques if sufficient information necessary for their application is available without undue cost and effort. Valuation techniques are to be applied in a manner consistent with the objective of estimating fair value. That is, their application shall incorporate assumptions that marketplace participants would use based on facts or information known or knowable as of the measurement date whenever such information is available without undue cost and effort.

  If information about assumptions that marketplace participants would make is not available without undue cost and effort, as a practical expedient an entity may use as inputs its own assumptions. However, for any valuation technique, market inputs shall be maximised and use of internal estimates and assumptions shall be minimised. For example, if an entity is aware of unique advantages or disadvantages that it possesses, such as favourable labour rates, or superior processing or manufacturing technologies, it shall consider the impact of such unique advantages or disadvantages on the valuation process or model and adjust its entity-specific assumptions if those assumptions result in a value that is inconsistent with the objective of measuring fair value.

  The IASB recognises that additional guidance may need to be developed, but that this should be done as part of a broader consideration of fair value measurement issues.

After the Boards agreed to adopt the same wording of the fair value hierarchy, the FASB later agreed to make amendments to the fair value hierarchy to reflect decisions made by it as part of its Fair Value Measurements project and include that revised hierarchy in its phase II Exposure Draft. In the interests of convergence the IASB is to expose the same fair value hierarchy as the FASB. Therefore, at a future meeting the IASB will consider the issues that resulted in the changes to the hierarchy made by the FASB.

G   *Application guidance for recording and measuring specific types of acquired assets and assumed liabilities*

I   *Applying Level 2 of the hierarchy*

Generally, the fair value of individual items acquired in a business combination would be determined by focusing on their location and condition on the date of the business combination, and assessing the amounts for which they could be exchanged, given those characteristics, between willing buyers and sellers absent a business combination.

II   Tax assets and liabilities and post-employment benefits

The scope of the project excludes issues related to the initial recognition and measurement of the income tax assets acquired and income tax liabilities assumed and assets and liabilities arising from post-employment benefits of the acquiree. Those items, while recorded as part of the business combination, are not subsumed in the working principle and would not be measured at fair value. The recognition and measurement principles in IAS 12 are to continue to apply to those income tax assets and liabilities. The recognition and measurement principles in IAS 19 would continue to apply to assets and liabilities arising from post-employment benefits.

As far as the recognition and measurement of deferred tax assets are concerned, if the potential benefit of the income tax loss carry-forwards or other deferred tax assets acquired as part of the business combination did not satisfy the criteria for separate recognition when a business combination is initially accounted for but is subsequently realised, the acquirer is to recognise that benefit as income in accordance with IAS 12. However, if the benefit of such income tax loss carry-forwards or other deferred tax assets acquired is realised within twelve months of the acquisition date, there is to be a rebuttable presumption that the subsequent recognition of the benefits acquired is an adjustment to complete the initial accounting for the business combination. Therefore the acquirer shall reduce the carrying amount of goodwill, rather than recognise income in accordance with IAS 12. The presumption is to be rebutted if the recognition of the deferred tax benefit results from a discrete event or circumstance that occurred after the acquisition date.

Assets acquired and liabilities assumed as part of the business combination arising from the acquiree's post-employment benefit plans are to be measured in accordance with IAS 19 at the acquisition date, i.e. these assets and liabilities shall be measured based on the actuarial assumptions of the acquirer at the date of acquisition. Any changes to the terms of the benefit plan contemplated by the acquirer are not part of the measurement of the post-employment benefit obligation at the date of acquisition.

III   Measurement when the occurrence of a business combination affects the fair value of a liability

The fair value of a liability assumed as part of a business combination is to reflect the credit risk applicable to that liability. The credit rating of that liability will impound the extent to which marketplace participants believe it has been altered by the business combination. The determination of the fair value of the liability assumed should, therefore, be based on prices observed in recent market transactions for liabilities with a credit risk similar to that of the liability assumed at the acquisition date. If market prices are not observable, the fair value of liabilities assumed should be estimated using valuation techniques. These techniques should incorporate the appropriate discount rate relevant to the credit risk applicable to the liability at the acquisition date.

IV   Acquired receivables (including loans)

Loans and receivables acquired as part of a business combination are to be measured at their fair values at the acquisition date. Therefore, an acquirer shall not establish a separate allowance for uncollectible amounts when recognising such loans and receivables.

V   Assets held for disposal

At the acquisition date, the acquirer is to recognise any non-current asset (or disposal group) acquired, that satisfies the recognition criteria and is classified as held for sale in accordance with IFRS 5, at its fair value at the acquisition date less costs to sell.

VI   Recognition and measurement of operating leases acquired in a business combination

Leases acquired in a business combination are to be classified as operating leases or finance leases in accordance with their classification by the acquiree at inception. After the business combination, they should be accounted for in accordance with IAS 17. Assets and liabilities arising because an acquiree's operating leases are favourable or unfavourable are be recognised at their fair values at the acquisition date. Such assets and liabilities are to be presented as a single net amount for each lease.

H   Recognition criteria for identifiable assets acquired and liabilities assumed in a business combination

The probability recognition criterion (see 2.3.3 above) is not to be included in the draft IFRS for identifiable assets acquired and liabilities assumed, because the acquirer is required to recognise those items at their fair values at the acquisition date. Similar to existing requirements for intangible assets, the fair value reflects market expectations about the probability that future economic benefits associated with the assets acquired and liabilities assumed will flow to or from the acquirer. In other words, the effect of probability is reflected in the fair value measurement of the identifiable assets acquired and liabilities assumed.

The reliable measurement criterion is to be retained for all identifiable assets acquired and liabilities assumed in a business combination. The IFRS arising from phase II should include the following guidance:

- except in extremely rare cases, an acquirer would be able to measure the fair values of identifiable assets acquired and liabilities assumed in a business combination;

- when there is a range of possible outcomes with different probabilities, that uncertainty enters into the measurement of the fair value of an asset or a liability rather than demonstrates an inability to measure reliably; and

- valuation methods or techniques should deal with uncertainty about the amount and timing of the future cash flows. Expectations about possible variations in the amount or timing of those cash flows and the price for bearing the uncertainty inherent in an asset or a liability enter into determining the fair value of the asset or liability.

I   Goodwill

I   Recognition and measurement of goodwill in the acquisition of less than a 100% ownership interest

The full goodwill method is to be used to recognise goodwill in the acquisition of less than a 100% controlling interest in the business acquired. Under the full goodwill method, all of the goodwill of the acquiree (including goodwill attributable to minority interests), not just the acquirer's share, is recognised.

When an acquirer purchases less than a 100% ownership interest in the business acquired, the business combination is to be accounted for by inferring the fair value of the business acquired from the consideration given, provided any control premium paid by the acquirer is identifiable and measurable with sufficient reliability.

If the control premium paid by the acquirer cannot be measured with sufficient reliability, the fair value of the business acquired is to be measured directly using valuation techniques. In such cases, the objective of the valuation techniques should be to measure the fair value of the consideration that market participants would have paid to purchase a 100% ownership interest in the business acquired.

Application guidance is to be provided explaining that there may be several ways to estimate the fair value of the business acquired, based primarily on the consideration paid. For example:

(a)   by inference (gross-up) from the consideration paid for the controlling interest; or

(b)   by adding the amount for the consideration paid for the controlling interest to the fair value of the minority shares outstanding if, for example, the value of those minority shares is observable from prices for publicly-traded shares.

II   Allocating goodwill to the controlling and minority interests when the business combination is an exchange of equal values

The goodwill allocated to the controlling interest is to be measured as the difference, at the acquisition, between the fair value of the ownership interest acquired and the controlling interest's share of the fair value of the identifiable net assets acquired. The remainder of the goodwill should be allocated to the minority interests. The fair value of the ownership interest acquired should be measured as:

(a)   the fair value of the consideration given by the acquirer on the acquisition date; plus

(b)   the fair value on the acquisition date of the acquirer's previous investment in the acquiree.

III   *Allocation of goodwill impairment losses between the controlling and the minority interest*

If an entity has one or more partially owned subsidiaries, goodwill impairment losses are to be allocated on a pro rata basis using the relative carrying values of goodwill.

For example, if the partially-owned subsidiary is part of a larger CGU, the portion of the impairment loss allocated to that subsidiary would be determined by multiplying the goodwill impairment loss for the unit by the carrying value of the goodwill assigned to that subsidiary, divided by the carrying value of the goodwill assigned to the CGU as a whole. The amount of the impairment loss allocated to the partially-owned subsidiary would then be allocated to the controlling and minority interests based on the relative carrying values of goodwill allocated to those interests.

IV   *Expected synergies and other benefits from combining the businesses of the acquiree and the acquirer*

The fair value of the expected synergies and other benefits from combining the businesses of the acquiree and the acquirer is to be included in the measurement of the fair value of the acquiree and therefore the measurement of the full amount of goodwill. The fair value of those synergies and other benefits should be estimated using assumptions that are not contrary to those that marketplace participants would use.

V   *Goodwill and a bargain purchase should not be recognised at the same time*

If an acquired business does not include any goodwill, any excess of the fair value of the acquirer's interest in the identifiable net assets acquired over the consideration given for that interest should be recognised as a gain in profit or loss. No gain attributable to minority interests arises in such a business combination.

J   *Accounting for business combinations achieved in stages*

A business combination may involve more than one exchange transaction, for example, when it occurs in stages by successive share purchases (often referred to as a 'step acquisition'). If an acquirer obtains control of an acquiree in a step acquisition, the carrying amount of its previous investment in the acquiree should be increased to its fair value on the acquisition date, with any gain or loss on remeasurement recognised in profit or loss for the period. If the previous investment was classified as an available-for-sale financial asset, the cumulative gains or losses previously recognised in equity in respect of that asset should be recognised in profit or loss for the period.

If an acquirer obtains control of an acquiree but the date of obtaining control (the acquisition date) does not coincide with the date or dates of acquiring an ownership interest (the date or dates of exchange transactions), such business combinations shall be accounted for in the same way as business combinations achieved in stages.

A related issue that has been considered by the IASB as part of this project is that changes in ownership interests in a subsidiary after control is obtained that do not result in a loss of control should be accounted for as transactions with equity holders in their capacity as equity holders. Therefore where there is a subsequent increase in the ownership interest in a subsidiary, the carrying amount of the minority interest should be adjusted to reflect the change in its interest in the subsidiary's net assets. The difference between the amount by which the minority interest is so adjusted and the consideration paid, if any, is to be recognised directly in equity and attributed to equity holders of the parent. No goodwill is recognised on such a transaction.

K   Transitional provisions for revised IFRS 3

The revised IFRS 3 resulting from the exposure draft is to be effective for annual reporting periods beginning on or after 1 January 2006, with early application encouraged. It is to be required to be applied prospectively. Therefore, it would apply to business combinations for which the agreement date is after the effective date of the revised standard. In addition, the revised IFRS 3 is to preclude retrospective application to, or adjustments of amounts recognised in, combinations occurring before a revised IFRS 3 is issued.

As discussed at 2.3.6 above, IFRS 3 presently provides that adjustments relating to the initial accounting for a business combination that arise after that accounting is complete should be recognised as a correction of an error, except for:

(a)   adjustments to the cost of the combination that are contingent on future events; and

(b)   adjustments to the carrying amount of goodwill for the subsequent recognition of deferred tax benefits.

After the effective date of the revised IFRS 3, entities are to continue to apply the requirements in the current version of IFRS 3 when dealing with adjustments to the cost of a combination that are contingent on future events (and recognised after the effective date of the revised IFRS 3) if the business combination was effected before the effective date of the revised IFRS 3.

However, entities should no longer adjust the accounting for the business combinations effected before the effective date of the revised IFRS 3 for the subsequent recognition of acquired deferred tax assets, unless a rebuttable presumption applies. This presumption is that if the acquired deferred tax asset is realised within twelve months of the acquisition date, the subsequent recognition of the acquired benefits should be regarded as relating to conditions that existed at the acquisition date, and should therefore be accounted for as an adjustment to complete the initial accounting for the business combination.

After the effective date of the revised IFRS 3, entities are to retrospectively derecognise stand-alone contingent liabilities (i.e. contingent liabilities that are not accompanied by associated unconditional obligations) arising from business combinations effected before the effective date of the revised IFRS 3 that still appear in the entity's balance sheet. Therefore, goodwill or any gain recognised in a prior period relating to a bargain purchase are to be adjusted retrospectively by an amount equal to the fair value at the acquisition date of the standalone contingent liabilities. For example, an entity should reduce the carrying amount of goodwill to the amount that would have been recognised if the standalone contingent liability had not been recognised as an identifiable liability from the acquisition date. Any subsequent changes in the measurement of the contingent liability should be derecognised against the opening balance of retained earnings.

5.2.2 Issues on which the IASB and FASB have reached different conclusions

A   Treatment of an overpayment

The issue the IASB considered is whether, in a business combination that is not an exchange of equal values, an excess of the consideration paid over the fair value of the acquirer's interest in the business acquired (i.e. any overpayment) should be recognised in profit or loss at the acquisition date (see 5.2.1 A above).

The FASB had previously observed the difficulty of identifying and measuring the amount of any such overpayments and decided to retain the decision reflected in SFAS 141 – *Business Combinations* – that any overpayment should be subsumed in goodwill. In contrast, the IASB previously decided that any overpayment should be recognised in profit or loss at the acquisition date.

In considering the issue the IASB noted that conceptually any overpayment should be recognised in profit or loss at the acquisition date. However, it agreed with the FASB that in some circumstances it might be difficult to estimate the overpayment reliably. The IASB decided to ask the FASB to reconsider this issue with the objective of achieving a decision converged with the IASB's view. The IASB also decided that if the FASB is unable to modify its decision, the Boards should expose the FASB's decision. In either case, the Boards, in the Invitation to Comment, will seek views on the reliability of identifying and measuring any overpayment.[346]

B   Rebuttable presumption that consideration provides the best evidence of the fair value of the business acquired

The IASB had previously decided to adopt a rebuttable presumption that the fair value of the consideration given by the acquirer for its interest in the business provides the best basis for measuring the fair value of that business, even if the acquirer does not obtain control of all the ownership interests in the business. The FASB did not adopt an equivalent presumption. It had previously decided that the fair value of the total consideration exchanged is generally more clearly evident when the business combination involves the purchase of all the acquiree's ownership interests and normally provides the best basis for measuring the fair value of the business acquired in a purchase of less than 100 per cent ownership interest. At the July meeting the IASB decided to remove the rebuttable presumption and adopt the FASB's wording.[347]

C   *Application guidance on the definition of a business*

The definition of a business is not a convergence issue because the Boards decided to adopt the same definition. However, the extent of application guidance provided by each Board differs. The FASB decided to include more detailed application guidance than the IASB. However, the Boards had also previously decided that their Exposure Drafts for this joint project should as far as possible use identical style and wording. Therefore, the IASB considered whether it should adopt the more detailed application guidance of the FASB.

Recently, the FASB decided to clarify the definition of a business as follows:

- the definition of a business was clarified to emphasise that the assessment is based on the current capability of the acquired set;
- revised the description of inputs, processes applied to inputs, and outputs and clarified that the first two of those three elements are required in order for an acquired set of activities and assets to be regarded as a business (and affirmed that outputs are not required). However, the FASB noted that it is not essential that the set should have all forms of inputs or all forms of processes applied to those inputs that are or will be used to create outputs;
- eliminated the requirement to assess whether a missing element is minor and the related guidance and examples;
- clarified that the determination of whether a particular set of assets and activities is a business is based on whether the set is capable of being conducted and managed as a business by any willing acquirer; and
- added application guidance stating that an acquired set of activities and assets would be presumed to be a business if the going concern element of goodwill is present in the set.

The IASB observed that the FASB had addressed the IASB's concerns about the FASB's previous version of the definition and accompanying application guidance. The IASB also concluded that the FASB's revised application guidance could be useful in making a judgement whether the acquired set of activities and assets represent a business. Therefore, the IASB decided to include the FASB's revised application guidance in the IFRS.[348]

5.3   Other aspects of phase II of the IASB's project

Having issued the exposure draft discussed at 5.2 above, the IASB is expected to consider the other aspects of phase II of its project. These relate to the remaining scope exclusions from IFRS 3 (assuming the standard is revised following the exposure draft discussed at 5.1 above), being:

(a)   business combinations in which separate entities or businesses are brought together to form a joint venture; and

(b)   business combinations involving entities or businesses under common control.

At this stage, there are no details as to what any proposals about these issues might be, other than the fact that the accounting for business combinations in which separate entities or operations of entities are brought together to form a joint venture will include possible applications for 'fresh start' accounting. 'Fresh-start' accounting derives from the view that a new entity emerges as a result of a business combination. Therefore, the assets and liabilities of each of the combining entities, including assets and liabilities not previously recognised, are recorded by the new entity at their fair values, rather than just those of the acquiree.

6   CONCLUSION

The IASB clearly saw business combinations and goodwill as an area of considerable divergence across jurisdictions and one that was to be given priority in its initial agenda, but in splitting its project into two phases recognised that it would be a major task to deal with all of the issues.

The first phase of the project has resulted in the publication in March 2004 of IFRS 3, together with revised versions of IAS 36 and IAS 38, which has introduced a number of significant changes in accounting for business combinations and goodwill from that required by the previous standard, IAS 22.

Although we generally support the elimination of the use of the pooling of interests method of accounting for business combinations classified as unitings of interests under IAS 22 and agree that an acquirer can be identified in almost all business combinations, we believe that that there can be situations where either an acquirer cannot be identified or by the very nature of the transaction there is no acquirer. In our view such instances include combinations in which separate entities are brought together by contract alone without the obtaining of an ownership interest (for example, dual-listed corporations). Although IFRS 3 has initially exempted such transactions from its scope, the proposal in the exposure draft issued a mere 29 days after the publication of IFRS 3 to remove that scope exemption and require a 'modified purchase method' to be used will not help identify the acquirer. In the absence of guidance on the identification of the acquirer, the application of the exposure draft will require arbitrary decisions to be taken as to which entity is the acquirer. We believe that in such situations the exemptions should remain, thus allowing entities to use the pooling of interests under the IAS 8 hierarchy until a more suitable accounting approach is developed in phase II of the IASB's project.

One of the major implications of IFRS 3 will be the need for acquirers to recognise, separate from goodwill, the identifiable intangible assets of the acquiree and to attribute a fair value to them, assuming that the value can be measured reliably. The guidance for valuing intangibles is effectively contained in IAS 38, but in our view more detailed guidance is required. The fact that for most of the intangible assets that need to be valued there will be no quoted market price, means that entities have to determine the value 'based on the best information available'. Unless an entity has developed valuation techniques in valuing such assets, in many cases specialists may be needed to assist in determining the appropriate fair values.

The other major change brought about by IFRS 3 is in the treatment of goodwill, whereby it is no longer amortised but is subject to an annual impairment test under IAS 36 (see Chapter 13). Although we agree with the IASB's view that annual impairment testing of goodwill may better reflect the value of purchased goodwill as an asset, we consider that the cost of performing such a test, rather than systematic amortisation, may outweigh the benefits derived from it.

However, it should be recognised that IFRS 3 is not the last word on accounting for business combinations. As indicated at 5 above, the IASB is considering a number of other issues relating to business combinations in phase II of its project. As outlined at 5.2 above, the IASB expects to issue an exposure draft dealing with a number of issues related to the application of the purchase method under IFRS 3 in the final quarter of 2004 as part of the project that is being conducted as a joint project with the FASB. This is expected to lead a revised IFRS 3 that is to be effective for annual reporting periods beginning on or after 1 January 2006. Once that exposure draft has been issued, it is expected that the IASB will then proceed to consider the other parts of the phase II project.

References

1 IFRS 3, *Business Combinations*, IASB, March 2004, Appendix A.
2 IFRS 3, paras. 6-7.
3 See the introductory pages of IAS 22, *Business Combinations*, IASC, September 1998 (superseded March 2004), for a summary of the changes.
4 IAS 22, paras. 1-7.
5 IAS 22, paras. 8-16.
6 IAS 22, paras. 77-83.
7 IAS 22, paras. 17-18.
8 IAS 22, paras. 19-20.
9 IAS 22, paras. 21-25.
10 IAS 22, paras. 65-70.
11 IAS 22, paras. 26-28.
12 IAS 22, paras. 29-31.
13 IAS 22, paras. 32-35.
14 IAS 22, para. 39.
15 IAS 22, para. 40.
16 IAS 22, paras. 41-58.
17 IAS 22, para. 61-64.
18 IAS 22, paras. 36-38.
19 IAS 22, paras. 71-74.
20 IAS 22, paras. 84-85.
21 IAS 22, paras. 75-76.
22 SIC-9, *Business Combinations – Classification either as Acquisitions or Unitings of Interests*, SIC, January 2000 (superseded March 2004), para. 1.
23 SIC-9, para. 7.
24 SIC-9, para. 4.
25 SIC-22, *Business Combinations – Subsequent Adjustment of Fair Values and Goodwill Initially Reported*, SIC, July 2000 (superseded March 2004), para. 3.
26 SIC-22, para. 5.
27 SIC-22, para. 6.
28 SIC-22, para. 7.
29 SIC-28, *Business Combinations – "Date of Exchange" and Fair Value of Equity Instruments*, SIC, December 2001 (superseded March 2004), paras. 1-3.
30 SIC-28, para. 5.
31 SIC-28, para. 6.
32 IFRS 3, para. BC2.
33 IFRS 3, para. BC3.
34 Project Summary, *Business Combinations (Phase II) – Application of the Purchase Method*, IASB, 26 January 2004, pp. 1 and 2.
35 IFRS 3, para. IN2.

36 IFRS 3, para. IN3.
37 IFRS 3, para. IN4.
38 IFRS 3, para. IN5.
39 IFRS 3, para. IN6.
40 IFRS 3, para. IN9.
41 IFRS 3, para. IN13.
42 IFRS 3, para. BC96.
43 IFRS 3, para. IN13.
44 IFRS 3, para. IN11.
45 IFRS 3, para. IN12.
46 IFRS 3, para. IN14.
47 IFRS 3, para. IN15.
48 IFRS 3, para. IN16.
49 IFRS 3, para. 78.
50 IFRS 3, Appendix A.
51 IFRS 3, paras. 79-84.
52 IFRS 3, para. 85.
53 IFRS 3, para. 1.
54 IFRS 3, para. 2.
55 IFRS 3, para. 4.
56 IFRS 3, para. 4.
57 IFRS 3, Appendix A.
58 IFRS 3, Appendix A.
59 IFRS 3, para. 4.
60 IFRS 3, para. 4.
61 IFRS 3, para. 5.
62 IFRS 3, para. 6.
63 IFRS 3, para. 7.
64 IFRS 3, para. 8.
65 IFRS 3, para. 3.
66 IFRS 3, para. 10.
67 IFRS 3, para. 13.
68 IFRS 3, para. 13.
69 IFRS 3, para. 12.
70 IFRS 3, para. 12.
71 IFRS 3, para. 11.
72 IFRS 3, para. BC28.
73 IAS 8, *Accounting Policies, Changes in Accounting Estimates and Errors*, IASB, December 2003 (as amended March 2004), para. 10.
74 IAS 8, paras. 11-12.
75 IFRS 3, para. 14.
76 IFRS 3, para. 15.
77 IFRS 3, para. 39.
78 IFRS 3, para. 16.
79 IFRS 3, para. 18.
80 IFRS 3, para. 17.
81 IFRS 3, Appendix A.
82 IFRS 3, para. 19.
83 IFRS 3, para. 20.
84 IFRS 3, para. 21.
85 IFRS 3, para. BC59.
86 IFRS 3, para. 21.
87 IFRS 3, para. 22.
88 IFRS 3, para. BC66.
89 IFRS 3, para. 23.
90 IFRS 3, para. 24.
91 IFRS 3, para. BC67.
92 IFRS 3, para. 25.
93 IFRS 3, Appendix A.
94 IFRS 3, para. 26.
95 IAS 39, *Financial Instruments: Recognition and Measurement*, IASB, December 2003 (as amended March 2004), para. AG77.
96 IFRS 3, para. 28.
97 IFRS 3, para. 27.
98 IFRS 3, para. BC69.
99 IFRS 3, para. BC68.
100 IFRS 3, para. 27.
101 IFRS 3, para. 29.
102 IFRS 3, para. 30.
103 IFRS 3, para. 31.
104 IFRS 3, para. 33.
105 IFRS 3, para. 32.
106 IFRS 3, para. 33.
107 IFRS 3, para. 33.
108 IFRS 3, para. 34.
109 IFRS 3, para. 35.
110 IFRS 3, para. 35.
111 IFRS 3, para. 36.
112 IFRS 3, para. 37.
113 IFRS 3, paras. BC95-BC96.
114 IFRS 3, paras. BC111-BC112.
115 IFRS 3, para. BC117.
116 IFRS 3, para. 38.
117 IFRS 3, para. 40.
118 IFRS 3, para. 41.
119 IFRS 3, para. 41.
120 IFRS 3, paras. BC83-87.
121 IFRS 3, para. BC85.
122 IFRS 3, para. BC85.
123 IFRS 3, paras. BC108-BC110.
124 IFRS 3, para. 43.
125 IFRS 3, para. BC109.
126 IFRS 3, para. 43.
127 IFRS 3, para. BC109.
128 IFRS 3, para. 43.
129 IFRS 3, para. 42.
130 IFRS 3, para. 44.
131 IAS 38, *Intangible Assets*, IASB, March 2004, para. 34.
132 IFRS 3, para. 45.
133 IAS 38, paras. 33-34.
134 IFRS 3, para. 45.
135 IAS 38, para. 8.
136 IFRS 3, para. 46 and IAS 38, para. 12.
137 IFRS 3, para. 45 and IAS 38, para. 34.

138 IFRS 3, Illustrative Examples, *Examples of items acquired in a business combination that meet the definition of an intangible asset.*

139 IFRS 3, para. 45.

140 IAS 38, para. 35.

141 IAS 38, para. 33.

142 IAS 38, para. 35.

143 IFRS 3, paras. BC97-BC101.

144 IAS 38, para. 38.

145 IAS 38, para. 36.

146 IAS 38, para. 37.

147 IFRS 3, para. 45 and IAS 38, para. 34.

148 IAS 38, para. 12.

149 IAS 38, para. 54.

150 IAS 38, para. 57.

151 IAS 38, para. 60.

152 IFRS 3, BC106.

153 IAS 38, para. 42.

154 IAS 38, para. 43.

155 IAS 36, *Impairment of Assets*, IASB, March 2004, para. 10.

156 IFRS 3, para. 48.

157 IFRS 3, paras. BC114-BC115.

158 IAS 37, *Provisions, Contingent Liabilities and Contingent Assets*, IASB, September 1998 (amended March 2004), para. 13.

159 IFRS 3, para. 49.

160 IFRS 3, para. 50.

161 IFRS 3, para. 47.

162 IFRS 3, Appendix A.

163 IFRS 3, para. B17.

164 IFRS 3, para. B16.

165 IFRS 3, para. B16.

166 IFRS 3, para. B16.

167 IFRS 3, para. B16.

168 IFRS 3, para. B16.

169 IFRS 3, para. B16.

170 IAS 38, para. 39.

171 IAS 38, para. 78.

172 IFRS 3, para. B16 and IAS 38, para. 40.

173 IAS 38, para. 40.

174 IAS 38, para. 41.

175 IFRS 3, para. B16.

176 IAS 19, *Employee Benefits*, IASB, February 1998 (amended March 2004), para. 108.

177 IFRS 3, para. B16.

178 IFRS 3, para. B16.

179 IFRS 3, para. B16.

180 IFRS 3, para. B16.

181 IAS 37, para. 13.

182 IFRS 3, para. BC129.

183 IFRS 3, Appendix A.

184 IFRS 3, para. 51.

185 IFRS 3, para. 52.

186 IFRS 3, para. 53.

187 IFRS 3, para. BC130.

188 IFRS 3, paras. BC131-BC135.

189 IFRS 3, para. 56.

190 IFRS 3, para. BC146.

191 IFRS 3, para. BC149.

192 IFRS 3, para. 56.

193 IFRS 3, para. 57.

194 IFRS 3, para. BC148.

195 IFRS 3, paras. BC148-BC156.

196 IFRS 3, para. 61.

197 IFRS 3, para. 62.

198 IFRS 3, para. 62.

199 IFRS 3, para. 62.

200 IFRS 3, para. 63.

201 IFRS 3, para. 63.

202 IFRS 3, para. 64.

203 IFRS 3, para. 65.

204 IFRS 3, para. BC157.

205 IFRS 3, para. 58.

206 IFRS 3, para. 59.

207 IFRS 3, para. 59.

208 IFRS 3, para. 60.

209 IFRS 3, para. 59.

210 IAS 16, *Property, Plant and Equipment*, IASB, December 2003 (amended March 2004), para. 41 and IAS 38, para. 87.

211 SFAS 141, *Business Combinations*, FASB, June 2001, para. 14 and Appendix A.

212 IFRS 3, paras. B1-B3.

213 IFRS 3, para. B4.

214 IFRS 3, para. B5.

215 IFRS 3, para. B6.

216 IFRS 3, para. B9.

217 IFRS 3, para. B7.

218 IFRS 3, para. B8.

219 IFRS 3, para. B10.

220 IFRS 3, para. B11.

221 IFRS 3, para. B12.

222 IFRS 3, para. B13.

223 IFRS 3, para. B14.

224 IFRS 3, para. B15.

225 IFRS 3, para. BC170.

226 IFRS 3, para. 66.

227 IFRS 3, para. 67.

228 IFRS 3, para. 68.

229 IFRS 3, para. 69.

230 IFRS 3, para. 70.

231 IFRS 3, para. 71.

232 IFRS 3, para. 72.

233 IFRS 3, para. 73.

234 IFRS 3, para. BC175.

235 IFRS 3, para. 77.

236 IAS 7, *Cash Flow Statements*, IASB, December 1992 (amended March 2004), paras. 39-42.
237 IFRS 3, para. 54.
238 IFRS 3, para. 55.
239 IAS 36, paras. 80-81.
240 IAS 36, para. 82.
241 IAS 36, para. BC140.
242 IAS 36, paras. BC143-BC144.
243 IAS 36, para. 83.
244 IAS 36, para. 83.
245 IAS 36, para. 85.
246 IAS 36, para. 84.
247 IAS 36, para. BC152.
248 IAS 36, para. 90.
249 IAS 36, para. BC162.
250 IAS 36, para. 9.
251 IAS 36, para. 90.
252 IAS 36, para. 90.
253 IAS 36, para. 91.
254 IAS 36, para. 92.
255 IAS 36, para. 93.
256 IAS 36, para. 94.
257 IAS 36, para. 96.
258 IAS 36, para. BC172.
259 IAS 36, para. BC173.
260 IAS 36, paras. 97-98.
261 IAS 36, para. 99.
262 IAS 36, para. BC177.
263 IAS 36, para. 90.
264 IAS 36, para. 104.
265 IAS 36, para. 124.
266 IAS 36, para. 125.
267 IAS 36, para. 86.
268 IAS 36, para. BC156.
269 IAS 36, para. 87.
270 IFRS 3, para. BC170.
271 IFRS 3, para. 74.
272 IFRS 3, para. 75.
273 IFRS 3, para. 77.
274 IFRS 3, para. 76.
275 IAS 36, para. 133.
276 IFRS 3, para. 78.
277 IFRS 3, para. BC180.
278 IFRS 3, paras. 79-84.
279 IFRS 3, para. 85.
280 IFRS 3, para. BC185.
281 IFRS 3, para. BC186.
282 IFRS 3, para. 79.
283 IFRS 3, para. BC187.
284 IFRS 3, para. 80.
285 IFRS 3, para. BC189.
286 IFRS 3, paras. BC190-BC195.
287 IFRS 3, para. 81.
288 IFRS 3, para. BC196.
289 IFRS 3, para. BC197.
290 IFRS 3, para. BC198.
291 IFRS 3, para. 82.
292 IFRS 3, paras. BC200-BC204.
293 IFRS 3, para. 83.
294 IFRS 3, para. 84.
295 IFRS 3, paras. BC181-BC183.
296 IFRS 3, para. BC183.
297 IFRS 3, para. 85.
298 IFRS 3, para. BC187.
299 IFRS 1, *First-time Adoption of International Financial Reporting Standards*, IASB, June 2003 (amended March 2004), para. 15 and Appendix B.
300 IFRS 1, para. IG22.
301 IFRS 1, para. B1.
302 IFRS 1, para. B3.
303 IFRS 1, para. BC32.
304 IFRS 1, paras. BC33-BC34.
305 IFRS 1, para. BC34.
306 IFRS 1, para. B2(a).
307 IFRS 1, para. 15.
308 IFRS 1, para. B2(c).
309 IFRS 1, para. B2(b).
310 IFRS 1, para. B2(b).
311 IFRS 1, IG Example 7.
312 IFRS 1, IG Example 3.
313 IFRS 1, para. B2(d).
314 IFRS 1, para. B2(e).
315 IFRS 1, para. BC36.
316 IFRS 1, para. B2(f).
317 IFRS 1, para. BC35.
318 IFRS 1, IG Example 2.
319 IFRS 1, para. B2(g).
320 IFRS 1, para. B2(g).
321 IFRS 1, para. B2(g).
322 IFRS 1, IG Example 4.
323 IFRS 1, para. IG40.
324 IFRS 1, para. IG41.
325 IFRS 1, para. IG43.
326 IFRS 1, para. BC39.
327 IFRS 1, para. BC38.
328 IFRS 1, para. B2(h).
329 IFRS 1, para. 10.
330 IFRS 1, para. B2(i).
331 IFRS 1, IG Example 5.
332 IFRS 1, para. B2(i).
333 IFRS 1, para. B2(j).
334 IFRS 1, IG Example 6.
335 Exposure Draft, *Amendments to IFRS 3 Business Combinations – Combinations by Contract Alone or Involving Mutual Entities*, IASB, April 2004, proposed para. 3.
336 Exposure Draft, proposed para. 31A.
337 Exposure Draft, proposed para. 31A.

338 Exposure Draft, proposed para. 31B.
339 Exposure Draft, paras. BC5-BC9.
340 Exposure Draft, paras. BC10.
341 Exposure Draft, Background, para. 6.
342 *IASB Insight*, IASB, July 2004, p. 10.
343 *IASB Update*, IASB, July 2004, p. 1.
344 *IASB Update*, July 2004, p. 2.
345 See Section 3 of the Observer Notes relating to
    the Business Combinations Phase II project for
    the IASB meeting in July 2004.
346 *IASB Update*, July 2004, p. 1.
347 *IASB Update*, July 2004, p. 1.
348 *IASB Update*, July 2004, pp. 1-2.

Chapter 7   Associates

1   INTRODUCTION

1.1   The origins of equity accounting

As noted in the introduction to Chapter 5, an entity may conduct its business not only directly but also through strategic investments in other entities. IFRS, and most national GAAPs, broadly distinguish three types of such strategic investment:

- entities controlled by the reporting entity (subsidiaries – see Chapter 5);

- entities jointly controlled by the reporting entity and one or more third parties (joint ventures – see Chapter 8); and

- entities that, while not controlled or jointly controlled by the reporting entity, are subject to significant influence by it (associates – the subject of this Chapter).

In the early days of consolidated financial statements, investments in entities which did not satisfy the criteria for classification as subsidiaries were carried at cost, and the revenue from them was recognised only on the basis of dividends received. However, during the 1960s it was recognised that there was a case for an intermediate form of accounting, since there was a growing tendency for groups to conduct part of their activities by taking substantial minority stakes in other entities and exercising a degree of influence over their business which, although falling short of complete control, was nevertheless significant. Mere recognition of dividends was seen to be an inadequate measure of the results of this activity (and one which could be manipulated by the investor, where it could influence the investee's distribution policy). Moreover, since it was unlikely that the investee would fully distribute its earnings, the cost of the investment would give an increasingly unrealistic indication of its underlying value.

This intermediate form of accounting, equity accounting, was first used by the Royal Dutch Shell group in 1964. It involves a modified form of consolidation of the results and assets of investees in the investor's financial statements when the investor exercises 'significant influence', but not control, over the management of the investee.

The essence of equity accounting is that, rather than full scale consolidation on a line-by-line basis, it requires incorporation of the investor's share of net assets of the investee in one line in the investor's consolidated balance sheet and the share of its results at only one level of the income statement (although some national standards require equity accounting at more than one level of the income statement).

Another form of 'intermediate consolidation' used by some entities, particularly in certain industries, was proportional consolidation (now referred to under IFRS as 'proportionate' consolidation). As its name implies, this involves including the results and assets and liabilities of an investment on a line-by-line basis, but only to the extent of the investor's share, rather than, as under normal consolidation, in full with credit given for any minority interest. However, under IFRS, proportionate consolidation can be adopted only for certain types of joint venture (see Chapter 8).

1.2   Development of IAS 28

Under IFRS accounting for associates is dealt with principally by IAS 28 – *Investments in Associates.* This was originally issued in November 1988 and has since been subject to a number of amendments, most significantly in December 2003 as part of the IASB's improvements project, when the previous version of IAS 28 was withdrawn and replaced by a significantly revised version, which must be applied for accounting periods beginning on or after 1 January 2005. Entities are encouraged to adopt the new version of IAS 28 for earlier periods, but must disclose that they have done so.[1] IAS 28 has been subject to further amendment by IFRSs issued since December 2003.

The main changes made by the current version of IAS 28 to previous IFRS (other than the incorporation into IAS 28 of requirements previously contained in other pronouncements) were to:[2]

- not require equity accounting for associates held by venture capital organisations and similar financial institutions;

- require, subject to various exemptions, an investor that does not prepare consolidated accounts to equity account for associates;

- prohibit the use of equity accounting for associates in the separate financial statements of the investor (there is no contradiction between this and the previous bullet point due to the strict technical meaning of the term 'separate financial statements' in IFRS – see 2.4 below);

- remove from IAS 28 the requirements regarding investments held with a view to their disposal within twelve months, which are now generally accounted for under IFRS 5 – *Non-current Assets Held for Sale and Discontinued Operations;*[3]

- remove the exemption from equity accounting for associates subject to long-term restrictions impairing their ability to transfer funds to the investor;

- require the financial statements of an associate used for equity accounting to be prepared using accounting policies consistent with those of the investor;

- restrict the use of non-coterminous financial statements of associates to those prepared to a date within three months of the investor's period end; and

- require an investor, in accounting for loss-making associates, to consider the impact not merely on its investment in the equity of the associate but on the totality of its investment in the associate, including preference shares and certain long-term debt.

1.3   Other applicable IFRS

In addition to IAS 28, the following pronouncements are relevant to accounting for associates:

- IAS 27 – *Consolidated and Separate Financial Statements;*[4]
- IFRS 5 – *Non-current Assets Held for Sale and Discontinued Operations;*
- IAS 1 – *Presentation of Financial Statements;*[5]
- IFRS 1 – *First-time Adoption of International Financial Reporting Standards;*[6] and
- IAS 39 – *Financial Instruments: Recognition and Measurement.*[7]

2   SCOPE OF IAS 28

2.1   General

IAS 28 must be applied in accounting for investments in associates (see 2.2 below). However, it does not apply to investments in associates held by:

(a)   venture capital organisations, or

(b)   mutual funds, unit trusts and similar entities including investment-linked insurance funds

that upon initial recognition are designated as at fair value through profit or loss or are classified as held for trading and accounted for in accordance with IAS 39. Such investments are measured at fair value in accordance with IAS 39, with changes in fair value recognised in profit or loss in the period of the change[8] (see Chapter 18). This exemption is discussed further at 2.1.1 below.

In addition the requirements of IAS 28 relating to the equity method of accounting (see 3 below) are applied by an venturer with an interest in a jointly controlled entity within the scope of IAS 31 – *Interests in Joint Ventures* (see Chapter 8) which elects (as permitted by IAS 31) to account for that interest using the equity method.[9]

2.1.1   *Exemption for venture capital organisations and similar entities*

The exemption for venture capital organisations and other similar financial institutions raises a number of questions of interpretation. The first is exactly what entities comprise those described in (a) and (b) in 2.1 above, since they are not defined in IAS 28 – a deliberate decision by the IASB given the difficulty of crafting a definition.[10] The experience of similar exemptions in some national GAAPs has been that it can be difficult to limit precisely the entities to which they apply. The IASB no doubt hopes that preparers and their auditors can be relied upon not to abuse the scope of the exemption without the need for further intervention.

As discussed more fully in Chapter 5 at 5.1, IAS 27 does not exempt venture capital organisations and other similar financial institutions from consolidating investments in subsidiaries, a source of some controversy during the exposure period of the IASB's improvements project standard (which included the revised versions of IAS 27 and IAS 28).

A   Application of IAS 39 to associates exempt from IAS 28

As noted above, venture capital organisations and other similar financial institutions which use the exemption in IAS 28 for their investments in associates are required to apply IAS 39 to those investments. The exemption is available only where the associates are either (as defined under IAS 39) held for trading, or, if not, are designated upon initial recognition as investments to be accounted for 'at fair value through profit or loss' under IAS 39. Designation at a later date is not possible. Whilst IAS 28 does not say so explicitly, we consider that such designation is irrevocable, as there is no provision in IAS 39 for investments that have been designated in this way to be subsequently de-designated.

IAS 28 does not explicitly require venture capital organisations and other similar financial institutions consistently to designate all their associates (other than those defined as held for trading) as 'at fair value through profit or loss' under IAS 39. However, such entities need to balance the free choice apparently given by IAS 28 with the requirement of IAS 8 – *Accounting Policies, Changes in Accounting Estimates and Errors* – for the adoption of consistent accounting policies for similar transactions. The freedom of choice may have been given so as to allow such entities to apply IAS 39 to their own portfolio investments but to apply IAS 28 to any strategic investments in similar entities which act as an extension of their own business.

The recognition, measurement and disclosure requirements of IAS 39 for items classified as held for trading or designated as at fair value through profit or loss are discussed in Chapters 15, 18 and 20.

2.2   Definition of 'associate' and related terms

An *associate* is an entity, including an unincorporated entity such as a partnership, over which the investor has significant influence and that is neither a subsidiary nor an interest in a joint venture (see below).[11]

A *subsidiary* is an entity, including an unincorporated entity such as a partnership, that is controlled by another entity (known as the parent). *Control* is the power to govern the financial and operating policies of an entity so as to obtain benefits from its activities.[12] The definitions of 'subsidiary' and 'control' are the same as those in IAS 27 and are discussed is more detail in Chapter 5 at 3.

IAS 28 does not define *joint venture*, but the definition in IAS 31 is presumably intended to apply, namely a contractual arrangement whereby two or more parties undertake an economic activity that is subject to joint control.[13] *Joint control* is defined by IAS 28, albeit in the same terms as IAS 31, as contractually agreed sharing of control over an economic activity, which exists only when the strategic financial and operating decisions relating to the activity require the unanimous consent of the parties sharing control (the venturers).[14] The definitions of joint venture and joint control are discussed in more detail in Chapter 8 at 2.2.

Significant influence is the power to participate in the financial and operating policy decisions of the investee but is not control or joint control over those policies,[15] and is discussed further at 2.2.1 below.

2.2.1 Significant influence

Under IAS 28, a holding of 20% or more of the voting power of the investee is presumed to give rise to significant influence, unless it can be clearly demonstrated that this is not the case. Conversely, a holding of less than 20% of the voting power is presumed not to give rise to significant influence, unless it can be clearly demonstrated that there is in fact significant influence. The existence of a substantial or majority interest of another investor does not necessarily preclude the investor from having significant influence.[16] In calculating the interest of a group, account should be taken of shares held directly by the parent and those held indirectly through subsidiaries – holdings by other associates or joint ventures of the group are ignored.[17]

IAS 28 states that the exercise of significant influence will usually be evidenced in one or more of the following ways:

(a)   representation on the board of directors or equivalent governing body of the investee;

(b)   participation in policy-making processes, including participation in decisions about dividends and other distributions;

(c)   material transactions between the investor and the investee;

(d)   interchange of managerial personnel; or

(e)   provision of essential technical information.[18]

An entity loses significant influence over an investee when it loses the power to participate in the financial and operating policy decisions of that investee. The loss of significant influence can occur with or without a change in absolute or relative ownership levels. It could occur, for example, when an associate becomes subject to the control of a government, court, administrator or regulator. It could also occur as a result of a contractual agreement.[19]

Many of the factors relevant in assessing whether or not significant influence exists over another entity are also relevant to an assessment of whether control exists. Accordingly much of the implementation guidance to IAS 27 (discussed in Chapter 5 at 3.1) is also relevant to associates accounted for under IAS 28.[20]

In particular, IAS 27 notes that the reference to 'power' in the definition of 'significant influence' above means the ability to do or affect something. Consequently, an entity has significant influence over another entity when it currently has the ability to exercise that power, regardless of whether significant influence is actively demonstrated or is passive in nature.[21] Passive significant influence may be exercised over another entity through potential voting rights (see A below).

A   Potential voting rights

An entity may own share warrants, share call options, debt or equity instruments that are convertible into ordinary shares, or other similar instruments that have the potential, if exercised or converted, to give the entity voting power or reduce another party's voting power over the financial and operating policies of another entity (potential voting rights).[22]

IAS 27 requires an entity to consider the existence and effect of potential voting rights that are currently exercisable or convertible, including potential voting rights held by another entity, when assessing whether an entity has significant influence over the financial and operating policies of another entity.[23]

Potential voting rights are not currently exercisable or convertible when they cannot be exercised or converted until a future date or until the occurrence of a future event.[24]

IAS 28 adds some further points of clarification. In assessing whether potential voting rights contribute to significant influence, an entity must examine all facts and circumstances (including the terms of exercise of the potential voting rights and any other contractual arrangements whether considered individually or in combination) that affect potential voting rights, except the intention of management and the financial ability to exercise or convert.[25]

The implementation guidance in IAS 27 elaborates on the above requirements in some detail, and reference should be made to the further discussion in Chapter 5 at 3.1.2.

B   Long-term restrictions over associate's ability to transfer funds to investor

Previous versions of IAS 28 contained an exemption from applying the equity method for an associate when severe long-term restrictions impaired an associate's ability to transfer funds to the investor. This exemption no longer applies. The IASB indicates that it removed the exemption because such restrictions may not in fact affect the investor's significant influence over the associate. Whilst an investor should, when assessing its ability to exercise significant influence over an entity, consider restrictions on the transfer of funds from the associate to the investor, such restrictions do not in themselves preclude the exercise of significant influence.[26]

2.3 Requirement to apply the equity method

An investment in an associate must be accounted for using the equity method (see 3 below), except when:[27]

(a) the investment is classified as held for sale in accordance with IFRS 5 (in which case it is accounted for under IFRS 5[28] – see Chapter 3 at 5.1);

(b) the reporting entity is a parent (i.e. an entity with one or more subsidiaries)[29] exempt from preparing consolidated financial statements under IAS 27 (see Chapter 5 at 4.1); or

(c) all of the following apply:

    (i) the investor is a wholly-owned subsidiary, or is a partially-owned subsidiary of another entity and its other owners, including those not otherwise entitled to vote, have been informed about, and do not object to, the investor not applying the equity method;

    (ii) the investor's debt or equity instruments are not traded in a public market (a domestic or foreign stock exchange or an over-the-counter market, including local and regional markets);

    (iii) the investor did not file, nor is it in the process of filing, its financial statements with a securities commission or other regulatory organisation, for the purpose of issuing any class of instruments in a public market; and

    (iv) the ultimate or any intermediate parent of the investor produces consolidated financial statements available for public use that comply with International Financial Reporting Standards.

Exemption (c) above will apply only where the investor in an associate is not also a parent. If it is a parent, it must look to the similar exemption from preparation of consolidated financial statements in IAS 27 (see Chapter 5 at 4). In fact, however, the conditions (i) to (iv) in (c) above are identical to the criteria that must be satisfied by a parent in order to be exempt from preparing consolidated financial statements under IAS 27. Further discussion of the meaning and interpretation of these conditions may be found in Chapter 5 at 4.1.

The exemption in (c) above is available to only entities that are themselves either wholly-owned subsidiaries or whose minority shareholders consent to the presentation of financial statements that do not include associates using the equity method. Some of these 'intermediate' entities will not be exempt, for example if none of their parent companies prepares consolidated financial statements in accordance with IFRS. A typical example is that of an entity that is a subsidiary of a US group that prepares consolidated accounts in accordance with US GAAP only. In addition, any entity that has publicly traded debt or equity, or is in the process of obtaining a listing for such instruments, will not satisfy the criteria for exemption.

The effect of the above requirements is that a reporting entity that has associates, but no subsidiaries, and does not meet all the criteria above, is required to apply equity accounting for its associates in its own (non-consolidated) financial statements (not to be confused with its 'separate financial statements' – see 2.4 below). This may be a significant change from many national GAAPs, where equity accounting for associates is required (or indeed permitted) only in consolidated financial statements.

As drafted, IAS 28 *requires*, rather than merely permitting, an investor that meets the criteria in (b) or (c) above not to apply equity accounting. By contrast, the equivalent exemptions in IAS 27 (see Chapter 5 at 4) and IAS 31 (see Chapter 8 at 2.3) are drafted so as to be permissive rather than compulsory. We take the view that this was an unintentional drafting error, and that the exemption from equity accounting in IAS 28 is intended to be optional, not compulsory.

2.4   Separate financial statements

Separate financial statements are defined by IAS 28, consistent with IAS 27, as those presented by a parent, an investor in an associate or a venturer in a jointly controlled entity, in which the investments are accounted for on the basis of the direct equity interest rather than on the basis of the reported results and net assets of the investees.[30] The detailed IFRS requirements for separate financial statements are set out in IAS 27[31] and are discussed more fully in Chapter 5 at 7.

It follows from the definition of separate financial statements above that financial statements (including non-consolidated financial statements) in which the equity method is applied are not separate financial statements; neither are the financial statements of an entity that does not have a subsidiary, associate or venturer's interest in a joint venture.[32]

Separate financial statements are any financial statements presented in addition to:

- consolidated financial statements;
- financial statements in which investments are accounted for using the equity method; and
- financial statements in which venturers' interests in joint ventures are proportionately consolidated.

There is no requirement for any entity to prepare separate financial statements, or for any separate financial statements that are voluntarily prepared to be appended to, or accompany, the 'main' financial statements.[33]

An entity may present separate financial statements as its only financial statements if it satisfies the conditions for exemption from:[34]

- preparing consolidated financial statements under paragraph 10 of IAS 27 (see Chapter 5 at 4.1);
- equity accounting for associates under paragraph 13(c) of IAS 28 (see (c) under 2.3 above); and
- proportionately consolidating (or equity accounting for) jointly controlled entities under paragraph 2 of IAS 31 (see Chapter 8 at 2.4).

As drafted, this exemption makes a curious distinction between an entity with associates and one with jointly controlled entities only.

An entity with associates may prepare separate financial statements as its only financial statements only if it satisfies the exemption in 'paragraph 13(c)' of IAS 28. In other words, if an entity has associates, but is exempt from equity accounting for all of them under paragraph 13(a) – i.e. because they are all accounted for under IFRS 5 – it may apparently not present separate financial statements as its only financial statements. However, an entity with jointly controlled entities may prepare separate financial statements as its only financial statements if it satisfies the exemption in 'paragraph 2' of IAS 31, which includes jointly controlled entities accounted for under IFRS 5.

In our view, it can be assumed that this inconsistency was unintentional, but it is less obvious as to which exemption is correct and which incorrect. On balance, our view is that it is the exemption in relation to joint ventures which is incorrect. In other words, the IASB intended to give the exemption only to 'non-public interest' companies and should have referred to 'paragraph 2(c)' of IAS 31.

3   APPLICATION OF THE EQUITY METHOD

3.1   Overview

IAS 28 defines the equity method as 'a method of accounting whereby the investment is initially recorded at cost and adjusted thereafter for the post acquisition change in the investor's share of net assets of the investee. The profit or loss of the investor includes the investor's share of the results of operations of the investee.'[35] Distributions received from an investee reduce the carrying amount of the investment. Adjustments to the carrying amount may also be necessary for changes in the investor's proportionate interest in the investee arising from changes in the investee's equity that have not been recognised in the investee's profit or loss. Such changes include those arising from the revaluation of property, plant and equipment and from foreign exchange translation differences. The investor's share of any such changes is recognised directly in equity of the investor.[36]

IAS 28 explains that equity accounting is necessary because to recognise income simply on the basis of distributions received may not be an adequate measure of the income earned by an investor on an investment in an associate, since distributions received may bear little relation to the performance of the associate. Through its significant influence over the associate, the investor has an interest in the associate's performance and, as a result, the return on its investment. The investor accounts for this interest by extending the scope of its financial statements so as to include its share of profits or losses of such an associate. As a result, application of the equity method provides more informative reporting of the net assets and profit or loss of the investor.[37]

3.2   Similarities of equity accounting and consolidation

IAS 28 notes that many procedures appropriate for the application of the equity method, and described in more detail in 3.3 to 3.8 below, are similar to the consolidation procedures described in IAS 27 (see Chapter 5 at 6). Furthermore the concepts underlying the procedures used in accounting for the acquisition of a subsidiary are also adopted in accounting for the acquisition of an investment in an associate.[38]

In particular, on acquisition of an investment in an associate, any difference between the cost of the investment and the investor's share of the net fair value of the associate's identifiable assets, liabilities and contingent liabilities is accounted for in accordance with IFRS 3 – *Business Combinations* (see Chapter 6 at 2.3.3). This has the effect that:

- Goodwill relating to an associate is included in the carrying amount of the investment (and not as a separate item, as would be the case in respect of goodwill relating to the acquisition of a subsidiary). Amortisation of that goodwill is not permitted and is therefore not included in the determination of the investor's share of the associate's profits or losses.

- Any excess of the investor's share of the net fair value of the associate's identifiable assets, liabilities and contingent liabilities over the cost of the investment is excluded from the carrying amount of the investment and is instead included as income in the determination of the investor's share of the associate's profit or loss in the period in which the investment is acquired.

IAS 28 states that appropriate adjustments to the investor's share of the associate's profits or losses after acquisition are also made to account, for example, for depreciation of the depreciable assets based on their fair values at the acquisition date. Similarly, appropriate adjustments to the investor's share of the associate's profits or losses after acquisition are made for impairment losses recognised by the associate, such as for goodwill or property, plant and equipment.[39]

However, an investor will not necessarily simply recognise impairment losses in respect of an associate equivalent to its share of the impairment losses recognised by the associate itself (even after fair value and other consolidation adjustments). This is discussed further at 4 below.

Moreover, it may be necessary to make adjustments for transactions between the investor and its associates (see 3.4 below).

3.3   Share accounted for

3.3.1   Contingent voting rights

As noted at 2.2.1 A above, an entity is required to consider currently exercisable potential voting rights in determining whether it has significant influence over an investee such that the investee is an associate. However, when applying the equity method, the investor determines its share of the profit or loss of the investee, and of changes in the investee's equity, by reference to its current ownership interest and does not reflect the possible exercise or conversion of potential voting rights.[40]

However, the implementation guidance on potential voting rights in IAS 27, which applies also to IAS 28, recognises that in some rare cases potential voting rights actually give rise to present access to the economic benefits inherent in those rights. An example might be a presently exercisable option over shares in the investee at a fixed price combined with the right to veto any distribution by the investee before the option is exercised. In these rare cases, it might be appropriate to equity account for the share that would be held if the option were exercised. This is discussed further in Chapter 5 at 6.2.

3.3.2   Where the reporting entity or the associate is a group

As noted at 2.2.1 above, a group's share in an associate is the aggregate of the holdings in that associate by the parent and its subsidiaries. The holdings of the group's other associates or joint ventures are ignored for this purpose. When an associate itself has subsidiaries, associates, or joint ventures, the profits or losses and net assets taken into account in applying the equity method are those recognised in the associate's financial statements (including the associate's share of the profits or losses and net assets of its associates and joint ventures), but after any adjustments necessary to give effect to uniform accounting policies[41] (see 3.6 below).

3.3.3   Cumulative preference shares held by parties other than the investor

If an associate has outstanding cumulative preference shares that are held by parties other than the investor and classified as equity, the investor computes its share of profits or losses after adjusting for the dividends on such shares, whether or not the dividends have been declared.[42]

3.4   Transactions between the reporting entity and associates

IAS 28 requires profits and losses resulting from what it refers to as 'upstream' and 'downstream' transactions between an investor (including its consolidated subsidiaries) and an associate to be recognised in the investor's financial statements only to the extent of unrelated investors' interests in the associate. 'Upstream' transactions are, for example, sales of assets from an associate to the investor. 'Downstream' transactions are, for example, sales of assets from the investor to an associate. The investor's share in the associate's profits and losses resulting from these transactions is eliminated.[43]

IAS 28 is not entirely clear as to how this very generally expressed requirement translates into accounting entries, but we suggest that an appropriate approach might be to proceed as follows.

- In the profit and loss account, the adjustment should be taken against either the investor's profit or the share of the associate's profit, according to whether the investor or the associate recorded the profit on the transaction.

- In the balance sheet, the adjustment should be made against the asset which was the subject of the transaction if it is held by the investor or against the carrying amount for the associate if the asset is held by the associate.

This is consistent with the approach required by SIC–13 in dealing with the related area of the contribution of assets by venturers to joint ventures (see Chapter 8 at 3.4.3).

Examples 7.1 and 7.2 below illustrate our interpretation of this treatment. Both examples deal with the reporting entity H and its 40% associate A. The journal entries are based on the premise that H's financial statements are initially prepared as a simple aggregation of H and the relevant share of its associates. The entries below would then be applied to the numbers at that stage of the process.

Example 7.1:   Elimination of profit on sale by investor to associate

On 1 December 2005 H sells inventory costing £750,000 to A for £1 million. On 10 January 2006, A sells the inventory to a third party for £1.2 million. What adjustments are made in the group accounts of H at 31 December 2005 and 31 December 2006?

In the year ended 31 December 2005, H has recorded turnover of £1 million and cost of sales of £0.75 million. However since, at the balance sheet date, the inventory is still held by A, only 60% of this transaction is regarded by IAS 28 as having taken place (in effect with the other shareholders of A). This is reflected by the consolidation entry:

	£	£
Turnover	400,000	
Cost of sales		300,000
Investment in A		100,000

This effectively defers recognition of 40% the sale and offsets the deferred profit against the carrying amount of H's investment in A.

During 2006, when the inventory is sold on by A, this deferred profit can be released to the group profit and loss account, reflected by the following accounting entry.

	£	£
Opening reserves	100,000	
Cost of sales	300,000	
Turnover		400,000

Opening reserves are adjusted because the financial statement working papers (if prepared as assumed above) will already include this profit in opening reserves, since it forms part of H's opening reserves.

Example 7.2: *Elimination of profit on sale by associate to reporting entity*

This is the mirror image of the transaction in Example 7.1 above. On 1 December 2005 A sells inventory costing £750,000 to H for £1 million. On 10 January 2006, H sells the inventory to a third party for £1.2 million. What adjustments are made in the group accounts of H at 31 December 2005 and 31 December 2006?

H's share of the profit of A as included on the financial statement working papers at 31 December 2005 will include a profit of £250,000 (£1,000,000 − £750,000), 40% of which (£100,000) is regarded by IAS 28 as unrealised by H, and is therefore deferred and offset against closing inventory:

	£	£
Share of A's result (income statement)	100,000	
Inventory		100,000

In the following period when the stock is sold H's single entity accounts will record a profit of £200,000, which must be increased on consolidation by the £100,000 deferred from the previous period. The entry is:

	£	£
Opening reserves	100,000	
Share of A's result (income statement)		100,000

Again, opening reserves are adjusted because the financial statement working papers (if prepared as assumed above) will already include this profit in opening reserves, this time, however, as part of H's share of the opening reserves of A.

A slightly counter-intuitive consequence of this treatment is that at the end of 2005 the investment in A in H's consolidated balance sheet will have increased by £100,000 more than the share of profit of associates as reported in the group income statement (and in 2006 by £100,000 less). This is because the balance sheet adjustment at the end of 2005 is made against inventory rather than the carrying value of the investment in A, which could be seen as reflecting the fact that A has, indeed, made a profit. It might therefore be necessary to indicate in the notes to the financial statements that part of the profit made by A is regarded as unrealised by the group in 2001 and has therefore been deferred until 2006 by offsetting it against inventory.

It may be that a transaction between an associate and its investor indicates an impairment of the asset that is the subject of the transaction. IAS 28 does not specifically address this issue. However, IAS 31 indicates that where a transaction between a venturer and a joint venture indicates an impairment of the asset that is the subject of the transaction, the venturer should recognise the full impairment loss and not merely its share.[44] In our view, this treatment should also be adopted when a transaction between and an investor its associate indicates an impairment of the investor's asset. Further discussion, and examples, of this treatment may be found in Chapter 8 at 3.4.2.

3.4.1 *Loans etc. between the reporting entity and associates*

IAS 28's requirement to eliminate partially unrealised profits or losses on transactions with associates is expressed in terms of transactions involving the transfer of assets. In our view, the requirement for partial elimination of profits does not apply to items such as interest paid on loans between associates and the reporting entity, since such loans do not involve the transfer of assets giving rise to gains or losses. Moreover, they are not normally regarded as part of the investor's share of the net assets of the associate, but as separate transactions, except in the case of loss-making associates, where interests in long-term loans may be required to be accounted for as if they were part of the reporting entity's equity investment in determining the carrying value of the associate against which losses may be offset (see 3.7 below).

3.4.2   Cash flow statement

In the cash flow statement (whether in the consolidated or separate financial statements) no adjustment is made in respect of the cash flows relating to transactions with associates, whereas in consolidated cash flow statements cash flows between members of the group are eliminated in the same way as intragroup transactions are eliminated in the profit and loss account and balance sheet.

3.4.3   *Contributions of non-monetary assets to an associate*

It is fairly common for an entity to create or change its interest in an associate by contributing some of the entity's existing non-monetary assets to that associate. This raises a number of issues as to how such transactions should be accounted for, in particular whether they should be accounted for at book value or fair value. There is no explicit guidance on this issue in IFRS as regards the formation of associates. However, the SIC considered the issue in connection with the contribution of assets to joint ventures, and contributions of non-monetary assets are also addressed by IAS 16 – *Property, Plant and Equipment* – and IAS 38 – *Intangible Assets* (see Chapter 8 at 3.4.3). In our view, it would be appropriate to consider this guidance when accounting for contributions of assets to associates.

3.5   Non-coterminous accounting periods

In applying the equity method, the investor should use the most recent financial statements of the associate. Where the reporting dates of the investor and the associate are different, IAS 28 requires the associate to prepare, for the use of the investor, financial statements as of the same date as those of the investor unless it is impracticable to do so.[45]

When the financial statements of an associate used in applying the equity method are prepared as of a different reporting date from that of the investor, adjustments must be made for the effects of significant transactions or events that occur between that date and the date of the investor's financial statements. In no case can the difference between the reporting date of the associate and that of the investor be no than three months, and the length of the reporting periods and any difference in the reporting dates must be the same from period to period.[46] This implies that where an associate previously equity accounted for on the basis of non-coterminous financial statements is equity accounted for using coterminous financial statements, it is necessary to restate comparative information so that financial information in respect of the associate is included in the investor's financial statements for an equivalent period in each period presented.

IAS 28 requires merely that a non-coterminous accounting period of an associate used for equity accounting purposes ends within three months of that of the investor. It is not necessary for such a non-coterminous period to end before that of the investor.

3.6 Consistent accounting policies

IAS 28 requires the investor's financial statements to be prepared using uniform accounting policies for like transactions and events in similar circumstances.[47] If an associate uses accounting policies different from those of the investor for like transactions and events in similar circumstances, adjustments must be made to conform the associate's accounting policies to those of the investor when the associate's financial statements are used by the investor in applying the equity method.[48]

In practice, this may be easier said than done, since an investor's influence over an associate, although significant, may still not be sufficient to secure access to the relevant underlying information in sufficient detail to make such adjustments with certainty.

3.7 Loss-making associates

An investor in an associate should recognise its share of the losses of an associate until its share of losses equals or exceeds its interest in the associate, at which point the investor discontinues recognising its share of further losses. For this purpose, the investor's interest in an associate is the carrying amount of the investment in the associate under the equity method together with any long-term interests that, in substance, form part of the investor's net investment in the associate. For example, an item for which settlement is neither planned nor likely to occur in the foreseeable future is, in substance, an extension of the entity's investment in that associate.

Such items include:
* preference shares; or
* long-term receivables or loans (unless supported by adequate collateral),

but do not include:
* trade receivables
* trade payables; or
* any long-term receivables for which adequate collateral exists, such as secured loans

Once the investor's share of losses recognised under the equity method has reduced the investor's investment in ordinary shares to zero, its share of any further losses is applied so as to reduce the other components of the investor's interest in an associate in the reverse order of their seniority (i.e. priority in liquidation).[49]

Once the investor's interest is reduced to zero, additional losses are provided for, and a liability is recognised, only to the extent that the investor has incurred legal or constructive obligations or made payments on behalf of the associate. If the associate subsequently reports profits, the investor resumes recognising its share of those profits only after its share of the profits equals the share of losses not recognised.[50] Whilst IAS 28 does not say so explicitly, it is presumably envisaged that, when profits begin to be recognised again, they are applied to write back the various components of the investor's interest in the associate (see previous paragraph) in the reverse order to that in which they were written down (i.e. in order of their priority in a liquidation).

The method of accounting, sometimes referred to as 'waterline accounting', is broadly equivalent to the requirements of IAS 27 for the attribution of losses of partially-owned subsidiaries to the minority shareholders. An example of 'waterline accounting' may be found as Example 5.11 in Chapter 5 at 6.7.2. An investor in an associate would account for its share of the associate's losses in the same way that the losses of entity S in that example are allocated to the minority shareholder M.

In addition to the recognition of losses arising from application of the equity method, an investor in an associate must consider the additional requirements of IAS 28 in respect of impairment losses (see 4 below).

3.8   Date of commencement and cessation of equity accounting

Under the general requirements for equity accounting discussed at 2.3 above, an investor will begin equity accounting for an associate from the date on which it has significant influence over it (and is not otherwise exempt from equity accounting for it).

Where an investor has not been equity accounting for an associate on the basis that it is classified as held for sale under IFRS 5 (see 2.3 above), and the investment ceases to be so classified, the investor must apply equity accounting retrospectively as from the date on which the investment was originally classified as held for sale. The financial statements of any prior periods since that classification must be restated.[51]

An investor ceases to account for an investment using the equity method on the date that it ceases to have significant influence over it. If the investment becomes a subsidiary or joint venture, it will be accounted for in accordance with, respectively, IAS 27 (see Chapter 5) or IAS 31 (see Chapter 8). Otherwise it will be accounted for in accordance with IAS 39.[52]

The measurement rules in IAS 39 are complex and discussed in detail in Chapter 18. In brief, however, they will entail the former associate being recorded initially at 'cost' (which is deemed to be its carrying amount on the date that it ceases to be an associate)[53] and then classified as either a 'financial asset at fair value through profit or loss' or an 'available-for-sale' financial asset. In either case, the investment will be measured at fair value – what differs is whether the gains and losses arising on revaluation are accounted for in the income statement or in equity.

A   Possible future developments

The IASB has decided in principle to amend IAS 28 so as to require an investment in a former associate to be measured, as at the date on which significant influence is lost, at fair value (rather than at a deemed cost equal to carrying value, as currently required by IAS 28).[54]

3.8.1   Cumulative exchange differences on associates

IAS 27 (see Chapter 5 at 6.5) specifically reinforces the requirement of IAS 21 – *The Effects of Foreign Exchange Rates* (see Chapter 9 at 2.7.3) that, when an investment in a foreign operation is disposed of, the gain or loss on disposal should include the 'recycling' of the cumulative exchange gains and losses that have, in accordance with IAS 21, been recognised in equity in respect of that operation. Whilst there is no such explicit reinforcement of IAS 21 in IAS 28, it seems clear that the same principle should apply on disposal of an associate.

IAS 21 clarifies that disposal of a foreign operation may occur through sale, liquidation, repayment of share capital, abandonment or receipt of a dividend out of pre-acquisition profits. When a partial disposal occurs, only the proportionate share of the related accumulated exchange difference is included in profit or loss. IAS 21 further clarifies that a write-down of a foreign operation does not constitute a partial disposal, and accordingly no part of the deferred foreign exchange gain or loss is recognised in profit or loss at the time of the such a write-down,[55] unless of course the write-down is consequent upon an event of 'disposal' as just described.

This begs the further question of the appropriate treatment of any cumulative exchange gains and losses on a former associate which becomes subject to IAS 39 as described above. The issues here are very similar to those arising in respect of a former subsidiary which becomes subject to IAS 39, which are discussed in Chapter 5 at 6.6.2 A.

However, the IASB may be proposing significant changes in this area as part of its Business Combinations (Phase II) project (see B below).

A   Other cumulative gains and losses previously recognised in equity

Like IAS 27, IAS 28 does not specifically address the accounting treatment, on disposal of an associate, of the investor's share of other cumulative gains and losses previously accounted for in equity relating to assets and liabilities of the disposed associate that would, if those assets and liabilities had been disposed of separately by the associate, been recycled in profit or loss. These could include:

- accumulated hedging gains and losses accounted for under IAS 39 (see Chapter 19), and

- any other amounts previously recognised in equity that would have been recognised in profit or loss if the associate had directly disposed of the assets to which they relate, such as gains or losses on available-for-sale financial assets accounted for under IAS 39 (see Chapter 18 at 3.2).

IAS 39 does not specifically address this issue either. However, it would appear that recycling is appropriate, since the disposal of an associate does give rise to the derecognition of the investor's share of the separate assets and liabilities of that associate just as if they had been disposed of separately. Moreover, the IASB's discussions on possible amendments to IAS 28 (see B below) appear to assume that it is clear that such gains and losses should be recycled on disposal of an associate.

B   Possible future developments

As part of its Business Combinations Phase II project the IASB has tentatively agreed to amend IAS 21 and IAS 39 so as to require that, when an investor's interest in an associate is reduced (but the investee remains an associate), there should be should be recognised in profit or loss:

- foreign exchange differences recognised in equity under IAS 21,

- accumulated hedging gains and losses recognised in equity under IAS 39 (see Chapter 19), and

- any other amounts previously recognised in equity that would have been recognised in profit or loss if the associate had directly disposed of the assets to which they relate, such as gains or losses on available-for-sale financial assets accounted for under IAS 39 (see Chapter 18 at 3.2),

in each case proportionate to the interest disposed of.

However, where an investor's interest in an associate is reduced such that the investee ceases to be an associate, the IASB intends to require that the entire amount of such gains and losses should be 'recycled' on a loss of significant influence, even if the reporting entity still retains an investment in its former associate.[56]

3.9   Income taxes

Income taxes arising from investments in associates are accounted for in accordance with IAS 12 – *Income Taxes*. This will often lead to full provision for deferred tax on temporary differences relating to associates (see Chapter 24 at 4.2.5).

4   IMPAIRMENT LOSSES

4.1   General

As well as applying the equity method as summarised in 3 above, including the recognition of losses (see 3.7 above), IAS 28 requires an investor to apply the requirements of IAS 39 (which are discussed below and in Chapter 18 at 6) in order to determine whether it is necessary to recognise any additional impairment loss with respect to the investor's net investment in the associate.[57] Whilst IAS 39 is used to determine whether it is necessary to recognise any further impairment, the amount of any impairment is calculated in accordance with IAS 36 – *Impairment of Assets*[58] (see Chapter 13 and below).

The investor must also apply IAS 39 in order to determine whether it is necessary to recognise any additional impairment loss with respect to that part of the investor's interest in the associate that does not comprise its net investment in the associate. This would include, for example, trade receivables and payables, and collateralised long-term receivables (see 3.7 above). In this case, however, the impairment is calculated in accordance with IAS 39, and not IAS 36.[59]

The requirement of IAS 28 to apply both IAS 36 and IAS 39 perhaps indicates ambivalence on the part of the IASB about whether associates are similar to subsidiaries (in which case information about goodwill and the cash generating units to which it is attributed ought to be available) or are, in fact, a type of financial asset.

IAS 28 requires the recoverable amount of an investment in an associate to be assessed individually, unless the associate does not generate cash inflows from continuing use that are largely independent of those from other assets of the entity.[60]

4.2   Goodwill

As discussed at 3.2 above, goodwill arising on the acquisition of an associate is not separately recognised, but is included in the carrying value of an associate. Accordingly such goodwill, unlike that separately recognised, is not separately tested for impairment on an annual basis under IAS 36.

Instead, whenever application of the requirements in IAS 39 indicates that the investment may be impaired (see below), the entire carrying amount of the investment is tested under IAS 36 for impairment, by comparing its recoverable amount (the higher of value in use and fair value less costs to sell) with its carrying amount. In determining the value in use of the investment, an entity estimates:

- its share of the present value of the estimated future cash flows expected to be generated by the associate, including the cash flows from the operations of the associate and the proceeds on the ultimate disposal of the investment; or

- the present value of the estimated future cash flows expected to arise from dividends to be received from the investment and from its ultimate disposal.

IAS 28 notes that, under 'appropriate assumptions', both methods give the same result.[61] In effect, IAS 28 requires the investor to regard its investment in an associate as a single cash-generating unit, rather than 'drilling down' into the separate cash-generating units determined by the associate itself for the purposes of its own financial statements. The IASB does not explain why it adopted this approach, although we imagine that it may have been for the very practical reason that an investor's influence over an associate, although significant, may still not be sufficient to secure access to the relevant underlying information. Furthermore, the standard requires the investment as a whole to be reviewed for impairment as if it were a financial asset.

IAS 39 states that financial assets are not impaired unless there is 'objective evidence' that one or more events occurring after the initial recognition of the asset ('loss events') have had an impact on the estimated future cash flows of the financial asset or group of financial assets that can be reliably estimated.

Such 'objective evidence' that a financial asset or group of assets is impaired includes observable data that comes to the attention of the holder of the asset about the following loss events:

(a)   significant financial difficulty of the issuer or obligor;

(b)   a breach of contract, such as a default or delinquency in interest or principal payments;

(c)   the lender, for economic or legal reasons relating to the borrower's financial difficulty, granting to the borrower a concession that the lender would not otherwise consider;

(d)   it becoming probable that the borrower will enter bankruptcy or other financial reorganisation;

(e)   the disappearance of an active market for that financial asset because of financial difficulties; or

(f)   observable data indicating that there is a measurable decrease in the estimated future cash flows from a group of financial assets since the initial recognition of those assets, although the decrease cannot yet be identified with the individual financial assets in the group, including:

　　　(i)   adverse changes in the payment status of borrowers in the group (e.g. an increased number of delayed payments or an increased number of credit card borrowers who have reached their credit limit and are paying the minimum monthly amount); or

　　　(ii)   national or local economic conditions that correlate with defaults on the assets in the group (e.g. an increase in the unemployment rate in the geographical area of the borrowers, a decrease in property prices for mortgages in the relevant area, a decrease in oil prices for loan assets to oil producers, or adverse changes in industry conditions that affect the borrowers in the group).[62]

Many of these considerations can only be applied with difficulty to an investment in an associate.

We consider that the only practical way in which entities can assess whether interests in associates need to be tested for impairment is by focusing on the cash flow assumptions in the two bullets above, on which the value in use is to be based. IAS 28 appears to allow entities to estimate the present value of all cash flows that it expects to receive from the associate, no matter when it expects to get them. Only in these circumstances could any entity expect the present value of its share of the cash flows generated by the associate and the dividends it expects to receive (in both cases aggregated with the proceeds of ultimate disposal) to be equal to one another. This is consistent with impairment reviews of financial assets under IAS 39.

It is important to note that these cash flows are not estimated in accordance with IAS 36. IAS 36 imposes a restricted time horizon on cash flow estimates based on the entity's own budgets and forecasts, which can only cover a maximum period of five years. Cash flow projections beyond this are extrapolated using a steady or declining growth rate. A longer period or a higher rate may be justified only in specific circumstances.[63] Other aspects of the impairment review, such as selection of the discount rate, will be conducted in accordance with IAS 36 (see Chapter 13 for a description of impairment reviews under IAS 36).

Moreover, in contrast to the requirement in IAS 36 for continuous annual testing of goodwill relating to subsidiaries, an entity will have to test its associate for impairment only if an event has occurred that indicates that it will not recover its carrying value. The most common of these events, trading losses, will (subject to the requirement to adopt 'waterline accounting' – see 3.7 above) have automatically been taken into account in determining the carrying value of the investment, leaving only the remaining net carrying amount (i.e. after deducting the share of trading losses) to be assessed for impairment.

The requirements of IAS 28 with respect to impairment also mean that, even where the associate reports under IFRS and itself complies with IAS 36, the associate (particularly where it is itself a larger group) may be allocating goodwill for impairment purposes at a lower level of cash-generating unit (or group of cash-generating units) than the investor. This has the effect that any impairment charge recognised in respect of an associate may not simply be its share of any impairment charge recognised by the associate itself, even when the associate complies with IFRS.

5 PRESENTATION AND DISCLOSURE

5.1 Presentation

In the balance sheet, investments in associates accounted for using the equity method are classified as non-current assets,[64] within financial assets.[65]

In the income statement, the aggregate of the investor's share of the profit or loss of associates and joint ventures accounted for using the equity method must be shown.[66] However, there is no requirement as to where in the income statement this should be shown, and different approaches are therefore seen in practice.

Nokia includes its share of the (post-tax) results of associates after operating profit, but before pre-tax profit.

Extract 7.1: Nokia Corporation (2003)

Consolidated profit and loss accounts, IAS [extract]

Financial year ended Dec. 31	Notes	**2003 EURm**	2002 EURm	2001 EURm
Net sales		**29,455**	30,016	31,191
Cost of sales		**-17,237**	-18,278	-19,787
Research and development expenses		**-3,760**	-3,052	-2,985
Selling, general and administrative expenses	6,7	**-3,363**	-3,239	-3,523
Customer finance impairment charges, net of reversals	7	**226**	-279	-714
Impairment of goodwill	7	**-151**	-182	-518
Amortization of goodwill	9	**-159**	-206	-302
Operating profit	2,3,4,5,6,7,9	**5,011**	4,780	3,362
Share of results of associated companies	32	**-18**	-19	-12
Financial income and expenses	10	**352**	156	125
Profit before tax and minority interests		**5,345**	4,917	3,475

By contrast, Nestlé includes its share of the post-tax results of associates as the final item in its profit and loss account.

Extract 7.2: Nestlé S.A. (2003)

Consolidated income statement

For the year ended 31st December 2003 [extract]

In millions of CHF	Notes	**2003**	2002
Profit before taxes	4	**8,307**	9,684
Taxes	5	**(2,307)**	(2,295)
Net profit of consolidated companies		**6,000**	7,389
Share of profit attributable to minority interests		**(380)**	(329)
Share of results of associates	6	**593**	504
Net profit		**6,213**	7,564

The investor's share of items recognised directly in the equity of the associate is recognised directly in the investor's equity and separately disclosed on the face of the statement of changes in equity required by IAS 1.[67]

5.2   Disclosures

IAS 28 requires the following disclosures:

(a)   the investor's share of the profits of associates accounted for using the equity method;[68]

(b)   the carrying amount of investments in associates accounted for using the equity method;[69]

(c)   the investor's share of any discontinued operations of associates accounted for using the equity method;[70]

(d)   the fair value of investments in associates for which there are published price quotations;[71]

(e)   summarised financial information of associates, including the aggregated amounts of assets, liabilities, revenues and profit or loss;[72]

(f)   if applicable, the reasons why the presumption that an investor does not have significant influence is overcome if the investor holds, directly or indirectly through subsidiaries, less than 20% of the voting or potential voting power of the investee but concludes that it has significant influence;[73]

(g)   the reasons why the presumption that an investor has significant influence is overcome if the investor holds, directly or indirectly through subsidiaries, 20% or more of the voting or potential voting power of the investee but concludes that it does not have significant influence;[74]

(h)   the reporting date of the financial statements of an associate, when such financial statements are used in applying the equity method and are as of a reporting date or for a period that is different from that of the investor, and the reason for using a different reporting date or different period;[75]

(i) the nature and extent of any significant restrictions (e.g. resulting from borrowing arrangements or regulatory requirements) on the ability of associates to transfer funds to the investor in the form of cash dividends, or repayment of loans or advances;[76]

(j) the unrecognised share of losses of an associate, both for the period and cumulatively, if an investor has discontinued recognition of its share of losses of an associate;[77]

(k) the fact that an associate is not accounted for using the equity method in accordance with the exemptions summarised at 2.3 above;[78] and

(l) summarised financial information of associates, either individually or in groups, that are not accounted for using the equity method, including the amounts of total assets, total liabilities, revenues and profit or loss.[79]

Some of these disclosures can be seen in the financial statements of Anglo Gold.

Extract 7.3: AngloGold Limited (2003)

Notes to the group financial statements [extract]

19. Investments in associates

The group has the following associated undertakings:

– A 53.03% (2002: 53.03%) interest in Rand Refinery Limited, which is involved in the refining of bullion and by-products which are sourced inter alia from South Africa and foreign gold producing mining companies. The interest in Rand Refinery Limited has been consolidated from 31 December 2003 as AngloGold controls the financial and operating policies of this company. Prior to this date, Rand Refinery was equity accounted. The year-end of Rand Refinery Limited is 30 September. The results were equity accounted for 2003 and are based on the result for the 12 months ended 30 September 2003.

– A 26.6% (2002: 25.0%) interest in Oro Group (Proprietary) Limited which is involved in the manufacture and wholesale of jewellery. The year end of Oro Group (Proprietary) Limited is 31 March. Equity accounting is based on the results for the twelve months ended 30 September 2003.

2002	2003	Figures in million	2003	2002
SA Rands			**US Dollars**	
		Carrying value of associates consists of:		
84	**84**	Unlisted shares at cost	**10**	10
67	**81**	Share of retained earnings brought forward	**8**	6
37	**12**	Profit after taxation (note 6)	**2**	4
(19)	**(9)**	Dividends	**(1)**	(2)
		Rand Refinery Limited became a subsidiary		
–	**(116)**	with effect from 31 December 2003	**(17)**	–
(4)	**(5)**	Amortisation of goodwill (note 33)	**(1)**	–
–	**–**	Translation	**6**	1
165	**47**	Carrying value	**7**	19
165	**47**	Directors' valuation of unlisted associates	**7**	19
		The carrying value of the investment can be summarised as follows:		
84	**55**	Investment at cost	**7**	10
81	**(8)**	Share of retained earnings	**–**	9
165	**47**		**7**	19

		The group's effective share of certain balance sheet items of its associates is as follows:		
88	13	Non-current assets	2	10
145	47	Current assts	7	17
233	60	Total assets	9	27
32	24	Non-current liabilities	4	4
73	22	Current liabilities	3	8
105	46	Total equity and liabilities	7	12
128	14	Net assets	2	15
		Reconciliation of the carrying value of investments in associates with net assets:		
128	14	Net assets	2	15
37	33	Goodwill	5	4
165	47	Carrying value	7	19

5.2.1   IAS 37 – *Provisions, Contingent Liabilities and Contingent Assets*

In accordance with IAS 37 an investor must disclose:

- its share of the contingent liabilities of an associate incurred jointly with other investors; and

- those contingent liabilities that arise because the investor is severally liable for all or part of the liabilities of the associate.[80]

6   TRANSITIONAL AND FIRST-TIME ADOPTION ISSUES

6.1   General

As noted at 1.2 above, IAS 28 must be applied for accounting periods beginning on or after 1 January 2005. Entities are encouraged to adopt the revised version of IAS 28 for earlier periods, but must disclose that they have done so.[81]

There are no transitional provisions. An existing IFRS user must therefore apply the revised version of IAS 28 with full retrospective effect. The main differences from the current version of IAS 28 (which may give rise to retrospective restatement of prior periods under IAS 8) are summarised at 1.2 above.

There are no specific first-time adoption provisions in IAS 28, and IFRS 1 highlights no issues specific to IAS 28.

This means that a first-time adopter of IFRS is required to apply IAS 28 as if it had always done so. For some first-time adopters, this may mean application of the equity method for the first time. For the majority of first time adopters, however, we anticipate that the issue is that they are already applying the equity method under national GAAP, and will now need to identify the potentially significant differences between the methodology of the equity method under their predecessor GAAP and under IAS 28.

In particular there may be differences between:

- the criteria used to determine which investments are associates;
- the elimination of transactions between investors and associates;
- the treatment of loss-making associates;
- the permitted interval between the reporting dates of an investor and an associate with non-coterminous year-ends; and
- the treatment of investments in entities formerly classified as associates.

6.1.1 *Transition impairment review*

A first-time adopter of IFRS is required by IFRS 1 to apply an impairment test in accordance with IAS 36 to any goodwill recognised at the date of transition to IFRS, regardless of whether there is any indication of impairment[82] (see Chapter 4 at 2.4). This raises the question of whether the carrying amount of associates which include an element of goodwill should be similarly subject to a mandatory impairment review on transition.

Some might argue that, as goodwill arising on associates is not recognised as such under IFRS, it is not 'goodwill' but 'investment in associate' and therefore not subject to the requirements of IFRS 1 with respect to 'goodwill'.

The, in our view more convincing, counter-argument is that IAS 28 clearly indicates that the goodwill relating to an associate is indeed goodwill (see in particular 3.2 and 4.1 above) – in other words, it is merely an issue of presentation and not classification. Moreover:

- IFRS 1 notes that its provisions with regard to past business combinations apply also to past acquisitions of investments in associates (see Chapter 4 at 2.4); and
- IFRS 3 in its transitional provisions, treats goodwill included in the carrying amount of investments in associates in the same way as goodwill separately recognised (see Chapter 6 at 4.1.4).

This leads to the conclusion that a transition impairment review must be undertaken for investments in associates whose carrying value includes an element of goodwill. This impairment review will, however, to be carried on the basis required by IAS 28 as described in 4.1 above.

6.2   Investor and associate with different dates of first-time adoption of IFRS

IFRS 1 addresses in some detail the accounting treatment to be adopted when an investor in an associate adopts IFRS for the first time before its associate and where an associate adopts IFRS for the first time before its investor. This is discussed in Chapter 5 at 9.3.

References

1 IAS 28, *Investments in associates*, IASB, December 2003 (amended March 2004), para. 41.
2 IAS 28, paras. IN1-IN15.
3 IFRS 5, *Non-current Assets Held for Sale and Discontinued Operations*, IASB, March 2004.
4 IAS 27, *Consolidated and Separate Financial Statements*, IASB, December 2003 (amended March 2004).
5 IAS 1, *Presentation of Financial Statements*, IASB, December 2003 (amended March 2004).
6 IFRS 1, *First-time Adoption of International Financial Reporting Standards*, IASB, June 2003 (amended March 2004).
7 IAS 39, Financial Instruments: Recognition and Measurement, IASB, December 2003 (amended March 2004).
8 IAS 28, para. 1.
9 IAS 31, *Interests in Joint Ventures*, IASB, December 2003 (amended March 2004), para. 38.
10 IAS 28, para. BC12.
11 IAS 28, para. 2.
12 IAS 28, para. 2.
13 IAS 31, para. 3.
14 IAS 28, para. 2.
15 IAS 28, para. 2.
16 IAS 28, para. 6.
17 IAS 28, para. 21.
18 IAS 28, para. 7.
19 IAS 28, para. 10.
20 IAS 27, paras. 14 and IG1.
21 IAS 27, para. IG2.
22 IAS 28, para. 8.
23 IAS 28, para. 8 and IAS 27, paras. IG1-IG4.
24 IAS 28, para. 8.
25 IAS 28, para. 9.
26 IAS 28, para. BC15.
27 IAS 28, para. 13.
28 IAS 28, para. 14.
29 IAS 27, para. 4.
30 IAS 28, para. 2.
31 IAS 28, para. 35.
32 IAS 28, para. 3.
33 IAS 28, paras. 4 and 36.
34 IAS 28, para. 5.
35 IAS 28, para. 2.
36 IAS 28, para. 11.
37 IAS 28, para. 17.
38 IAS 28, para. 20.
39 IAS 28, para. 23.
40 IAS 28, para. 12.
41 IAS 28, para. 21.
42 IAS 28, para. 28.
43 IAS 28, para. 22.
44 There is a similar provision in IAS 27 (see Chapter 5 at 6.2).
45 IAS 28, para. 24.
46 IAS 28, para. 25.
47 IAS 28, para. 26.
48 IAS 28, para. 27.
49 IAS 28, para. 29.
50 IAS 28, para. 30.
51 IAS 28, para. 15.
52 IAS 28, para. 18.
53 IAS 28, para. 19.
54 *IASB Update*, IASB, April 2004.
55 IAS 21, *The Effects of Changes in Foreign Exchange Rates*, IASB, December 2003, para. 49.
56 *IASB Update*, IASB, April 2004.
57 IAS 28, para. 31.
58 IAS 28, para. 33.
59 IAS 28, para. 32.
60 IAS 28, para. 34.
61 IAS 28, para. 33.
62 IAS 39, para. 59.
63 IAS 36, *Impairment of Assets*, IASB, March 2004, para. 33.
64 IAS 28, para. 38.
65 IAS 1, para. 68(d).
66 IAS 1, para. 81(c).
67 IAS 1, para. 96 and IAS 28, para. 39.
68 IAS 28, para. 38.
69 IAS 28, para. 38.
70 IAS 28, para. 38.
71 IAS 28, para. 37.
72 IAS 28, para. 37.
73 IAS 28, para. 37.
74 IAS 28, para. 37.
75 IAS 28, para. 37.
76 IAS 28, para. 37.
77 IAS 28, para. 37.
78 IAS 28, para. 37.
79 IAS 28, para. 37.
80 IAS 28, para. 40.
81 IAS 28, para. 41.
82 IFRS 1, para. B2(g)(iii).

Chapter 8   Joint ventures

1   INTRODUCTION

1.1   The nature of joint ventures

As noted in the introduction to Chapter 5, an entity may conduct its business not only directly but also through strategic investments in other entities. IFRS, and most national GAAPs, broadly distinguish three types of such strategic investment:

- entities controlled by the reporting entity (subsidiaries – see Chapter 5);

- entities jointly controlled by the reporting entity and one or more third parties (joint ventures, the subject of this Chapter); and

- entities that, while not controlled or jointly controlled by the reporting entity, are subject to significant influence by it (associates – see Chapter 7).

There is a key distinction, both for the purposes of IFRS and commercially, between, on the one hand, subsidiaries and associates and, on the other hand, joint ventures. An interest in a subsidiary or an associate normally entails the acquisition or formation of a separate legal or economic entity. By contrast, a joint venture is essentially created by a legal or contractual relationship between the parties to the venture. Whilst many joint ventures do result in the creation of a separate legal entity to house the activities that are the subject of the venture, this is not a critical feature, and indeed many joint ventures result from direct joint ownership and control of assets, as opposed to joint ownership and control of an entity that in turn owns the assets.

Accounting for interests in joint ventures under IFRS is dealt with in IAS 31 – *Interests in Joint Ventures*. This is somewhat more complex than its 'sister' standards IAS 27 – *Consolidated and Separate Financial Statements* and IAS 28 – *Investments in Associates* (which are discussed, respectively, in Chapters 5 and 7) in two respects.

Firstly, it distinguishes between three types of joint venture (jointly controlled operations, jointly controlled assets, and jointly controlled entities) and prescribes different accounting treatments for each. Secondly, it allows two rather different accounting treatments (proportionate consolidation and equity accounting) for accounting for jointly controlled entities.

This choice of accounting treatment is somewhat unusual, given the IASB's efforts during its improvements project to eliminate alternative accounting treatments within IFRS, but must be seen against the following background. Joint ventures comprise a major part – sometimes all – of the activities of entities in some sectors (particularly extractive industries, property and construction). Over the years, these sectors have developed generally accepted 'industry GAAPs' that result in similar arrangements being accounted for differently in different sectors. Any attempt to standardise the accounting at this stage could have led to industry opposition so strong as to have seriously impeded the harmonisation programme.

The IASB itself is still in the process of debating the merits of equity accounting and proportionate consolidation, not merely in the context of accounting for interests in joint ventures but also more generally. To have prescribed one or other method in IAS 31 could have been seen as pre-empting the outcome of those discussions. However, the IASB does intend to move to abolish the choice of accounting treatment for jointly controlled entities in the relatively near future.

1.2   Development of IAS 31

Under IFRS accounting for joint ventures is dealt with principally by IAS 31. This was originally issued in November 1990 and has since been subject to a number of amendments, most notably in December 2003 as part of the IASB's improvements project, when the previous version of IAS 31 was withdrawn and replaced by a significantly revised version, which must be applied for accounting periods beginning on or after 1 January 2005. Entities are encouraged to adopt the new version of IAS 31 for earlier periods, but must disclose that they have done so.[1]

IAS 31 has been subject to further amendment by IFRSs issued since December 2003.

The main changes made by the current version of IAS 31 to previous IFRS (other than the incorporation into IAS 31 of requirements previously contained in other pronouncements) were to:[2]

- not require proportionate consolidation or equity accounting for jointly controlled entities held by venture capital organisations and similar financial institutions;

- require, but subject to various exemptions, a venturer that does not prepare consolidated financial statements to proportionately consolidate or equity account for jointly controlled entities;

- prohibit the use of proportionate consolidation or equity accounting for jointly controlled entities in the separate financial statements of the venturer (there is no contradiction between this and the previous bullet point due to the strict technical meaning of the term 'separate financial statements' in IFRS – see 2.4 below);

- remove from IAS 31 the requirements regarding investments held with a view to their disposal within twelve months. Such investments will now generally be accounted for under IFRS 5 – *Non-current Assets Held for Sale and Discontinued Operations;*[3]

- remove the exemption from proportionate consolidation or equity accounting for joint ventures subject to long-term restrictions that significantly impair their ability to transfer funds to the venturer.

The SIC has issued an interpretation of IAS 31, SIC-13 – *Jointly Controlled Entities–Non-monetary Contributions by Venturers.*[4]

1.3   Other applicable IFRS

In addition to IAS 31, the following pronouncements are relevant to accounting for joint ventures:

- IAS 27 – *Consolidated and Separate Financial Statements;*[5]
- IAS 28 – *Investments in Associates;*[6]
- IFRS 5 – *Non-current Assets Held for Sale and Discontinued Operations;*
- IFRS 1 – *First-time Adoption of International Financial Reporting Standards;*[7]
- IAS 1 – *Presentation of Financial Statements;*[8] and
- IAS 39 – *Financial Instruments: Recognition and Measurement.*[9]

2   SCOPE OF IAS 31

2.1   General

IAS 31 must be applied in accounting for interests in joint ventures (see 2.2 below) and the reporting of joint venture assets, liabilities, income and expenses in the financial statements of venturers and investors, regardless of the structures or forms under which the joint venture activities take place.

However, IAS 31 does not apply to venturers' interests (see 2.2.1 below) in jointly controlled entities (see 3.3.1 below) held by:

(a) venture capital organisations, or

(b) mutual funds, unit trusts and similar entities including investment-linked insurance funds

that upon initial recognition are designated as at fair value through profit or loss or are classified as held for trading and accounted for in accordance with IAS 39. Such investments are measured at fair value in accordance with IAS 39, with changes in fair value recognised in profit or loss in the period of the change.[10]

The exemption for venture capital organisations and other similar financial institutions raises the question of exactly what entities comprise those described in (a) and (b), since they are not defined. Essentially the same issues arise in respect of the equivalent exemption in IAS 28 for investments in associates held by such entities, which is discussed in Chapter 7 at 2.1.1.

2.2   Definition of 'joint venture' and related terms

A *joint venture* is a contractual arrangement whereby two or more parties undertake an economic activity that is subject to joint control.[11]

Joint control is the contractually agreed sharing of control over an economic activity, and exists only when the strategic financial and operating decisions relating to the activity require the unanimous consent of the parties sharing control (the venturers).[12]

An *investor* in a joint venture is a party to a joint venture and does not have joint control over that joint venture.[13]

A *venturer* is a party to a joint venture and has joint control over that joint venture.[14]

2.2.1   'Venturer' versus 'investor'

The definitions of 'investor' and 'venturer' above draw a distinction between participants in a joint venture who also participate in the joint control of that venture and more passive investors, as illustrated by Example 8.1

Example 8.1:   'Venturer' versus 'investor'

A, B and C establish a fourth entity D, of which A owns 40%, B 11% and C 49%. A and B enter into a contractual arrangement whereby any financial and operating decisions taken by A and B relating to the activity of D require the unanimous consent of A and B. In the jurisdiction where D is incorporated a simple majority of shareholders only is required for all major decisions. IAS 31 would regard A and B as being 'venturers', and C as an 'investor', in D.

The interest of an 'investor' in a jointly controlled entity is either:

(a)   where the investor has significant influence over the entity, an associate within the scope of IAS 28 (see Chapter 7); or

(b)   otherwise, a financial asset within the scope of IAS 39 (see Chapter 18).[15]

2.2.2   Joint control

As noted in 1.1 above, joint ventures take many different forms and structures. However, IAS 31 identifies three broad types:

- jointly controlled operations (see 3.1 below);
- jointly controlled assets (see 3.2 below); and
- jointly controlled entities (see 3.3 below).

Under IAS 31, the following characteristics are common to all joint ventures:

(a)   two or more venturers are bound by a contractual arrangement (see A below); and

(b)   the contractual arrangement establishes joint control.[16]

A   Contractual arrangement

IAS 31 emphasises that it is the existence of a contractual arrangement that distinguishes interests that involve joint control from investments in associates in which the investor has significant influence[17] (i.e. the power to participate in the financial and operating policy decisions of the investee but not amounting to control or joint control over those policies).[18]

Activities that have no contractual arrangement to establish joint control are not joint ventures for the purposes of IAS 31.[19] In other words, if two entities A and B set up a third entity C in which A and B each hold 50% of the equity, C will not, by virtue of the relative shareholdings *alone*, be a joint venture of A and B for the purposes of IAS 31. There needs to be an agreement for unanimous decision making on key matters – although this might automatically flow from the general provisions of corporate law in the jurisdiction concerned.

A contractual arrangement between venturers may be evidenced in a number of ways. There might be a separate contract between the venturers or minutes of discussions between them. In some cases, the arrangement is incorporated in the articles or other by-laws of the joint venture. Whatever its form, the contractual arrangement is usually in writing and deals with such matters as:

(a)   the activity, duration and reporting obligations of the joint venture;

(b)   the appointment of the board of directors or equivalent governing body of the joint venture and the voting rights of the venturers;

(c)   capital contributions by the venturers; and

(d)   the sharing by the venturers of the output, income, expenses or results of the joint venture.[20]

The effect of a contractual arrangement is to establish joint control over the joint venture, ensuring that no single venturer is in a position to control the activity unilaterally.[21]

A contractual arrangement may identify one venturer as the operator or manager of the joint venture. The operator does not control the joint venture but acts within the financial and operating policies agreed by the venturers in accordance with the contractual arrangement and delegated to the operator. If the operator does have the power to govern (i.e. not merely to execute) the financial and operating policies of the economic activity, the operator controls the venture and the venture is a subsidiary of the operator and not a joint venture.[22]

B   Legal and other restrictions on investee

IAS 31 notes that joint control may be precluded when an investee is in legal reorganisation or in bankruptcy, or operates under severe long-term restrictions on its ability to transfer funds to the venturer. However, if joint control continues, these events are not enough in themselves to justify not accounting for the investee as a joint venture in accordance with IAS 31.[23] This issue is discussed further (in the context of loss of control over subsidiaries) in Chapter 5 at 5.3.

C   Potential voting rights

An entity may own share warrants, share call options, debt or equity instruments that are convertible into ordinary shares, or other similar instruments that have the potential, if exercised or converted, to give the entity voting power or reduce another party's voting power over the financial and operating policies of another entity (potential voting rights).

Potential voting rights are not directly addressed in IAS 31. However, the application guidance on potential voting rights in IAS 27 indicates that it may also be relevant to the determination of joint control under IAS 31, while at the same time acknowledging that a contractual arrangement giving rise to joint control will tend to over-ride relative ownership interests (see Chapter 5 at 3.1.2). This is an issue that will need to be addressed in the light of individual facts and circumstances.

2.3   Requirement to apply IAS 31 to jointly controlled entities

There are no exemptions from applying IAS 31 to jointly controlled operations (see 3.1 below) or jointly controlled assets (see 3.2 below).

However, a venturer with an interest in a jointly controlled entity need not account for its interest using proportionate consolidation or equity accounting (see 3.3 below) if:[24]

(a)   the interest is classified as held for sale in accordance with IFRS 5 (in which case it is accounted for under IFRS 5[25] – see Chapter 3 at 5.1);

(b)   the venturer is a parent exempt from preparing consolidated financial statements under IAS 27 (see Chapter 5 at 4.1); or

(c)   all of the following apply:

    (i)   the venturer is a wholly-owned subsidiary, or is a partially-owned subsidiary of another entity and its other owners, including those not otherwise entitled to vote, have been informed about, and do not object to, the investor not applying proportionate consolidation or the equity method;

    (ii)   the venturer's debt or equity instruments are not traded in a public market (a domestic or foreign stock exchange or an over-the-counter market, including local and regional markets);

    (iii)   the venturer did not file, nor is it in the process of filing, its financial statements with a securities commission or other regulatory organisation, for the purpose of issuing any class of instruments in a public market; and

    (iv)   the ultimate or any intermediate parent of the venturer produces consolidated financial statements available for public use that comply with International Financial Reporting Standards.

Conditions (i) to (iv) in (c) above are identical to the criteria that must be satisfied by:

- a parent in order to be exempt from preparing consolidated financial statements under IAS 27, or

- an investor in an associate that is not a parent in order to be exempt from equity accounting for its investment under IAS 28.

Further discussion of the meaning and interpretation of these conditions may be found in Chapter 5 at 4.1 and Chapter 7 at 2.3.

Essentially, exemption (c) is only available to entities that are themselves either wholly-owned subsidiaries or whose minority shareholders approve the presentation of financial statements that do not include jointly controlled entities using proportionate consolidation or the equity method. Some of these 'intermediate' entities will not be exempt, for example if none of their parents prepares consolidated financial statements in accordance with IFRS. A typical example is that of an entity that is a subsidiary of a US group that prepares consolidated accounts in accordance with US GAAP only. In addition, any entity that has publicly traded debt or equity, or is in the process of obtaining a listing for such instruments, will not meet the exemptions.

The effect of the above requirements is that a reporting entity that has jointly controlled entities, but no subsidiaries, and does not meet all the criteria in (c), is required to apply proportionate consolidation or equity accounting to its jointly controlled entities in its own (non-consolidated) financial statements (not to be confused with its 'separate financial statements' – see 2.4 below). This may be a significant change from many national GAAPs, where proportionate consolidation or equity accounting for jointly controlled entities is required (or indeed permitted) only in consolidated financial statements.

2.4   Separate financial statements

Separate financial statements are defined by IAS 31, consistent with IAS 27, as those presented by a parent, an investor in an associate or a venturer in a jointly controlled entity, in which the investments are accounted for on the basis of the direct equity interest rather than on the basis of the reported results and net assets of the investees.[26] The detailed IFRS requirements for separate financial statements are set out in IAS 27 and are discussed more fully in Chapter 5 at 7.[27]

It follows from the definition of separate financial statements above that financial statements (including non-consolidated financial statements) in which proportionate consolidation or the equity method is applied are not separate financial statements; neither are the financial statements of an entity that does not have a subsidiary, associate or venturer's interest in a joint venture.[28]

Separate financial statements are any financial statements presented in addition to:

- consolidated financial statements;
- financial statements in which investments are accounted for using the equity method; and
- financial statements in which venturers' interests in joint ventures are proportionately consolidated.

There is no requirement for an entity to prepare separate financial statements, or for any separate financial statements that are voluntarily prepared to be appended to, or accompany, the 'main' financial statements.[29]

An entity may present separate financial statements as its only financial statements if it satisfies the conditions for exemption from:[30]

- preparing consolidated financial statements under paragraph 10 of IAS 27 (see Chapter 5 at 4.1);

- equity accounting for associates under paragraph 13(c) of IAS 28 (see Chapter 7 at 2.3); and

- proportionately consolidating (or equity accounting for) jointly controlled entities under paragraph 2 of IAS 31 (see above).

As drafted this exemption makes a curious distinction between an entity with associates only and one with jointly controlled entities only.

An entity with associates may prepare separate financial statements as its only financial statements only if it satisfies the exemption in 'paragraph 13(c)' of IAS 28. In other words, if an entity has associates, but is exempt from equity accounting for all of them under paragraph 13(a) – i.e. because they are all accounted for under IFRS 5 – it may apparently not present separate financial statements as its only financial statements. However, an entity with jointly controlled entities may prepare separate financial statements as its only financial statements if it satisfies the exemption in 'paragraph 2' of IAS 31, which includes jointly controlled entities accounted for under IFRS 5.

It can safely be assumed that this inconsistency was unintentional, but it is less obvious as to which exemption is correct and which incorrect. On balance, our view is that it is the exemption in relation to joint ventures which is incorrect. In other words, the IASB intended to give the exemption only to 'non-public interest' companies and should have referred to 'paragraph 2(c)' of IAS 31.

2.5 'Pseudo' joint ventures

Some entities may have certain general characteristics of joint ventures, but not in fact be joint ventures. A particular example is the protected cell entity.

Example 8.2:   Is it a joint venture? – protected cell entity

Some jurisdictions permit the formation of so called 'protected cell' entities. Essentially these are entities which have a number of 'cells', with the assets and liabilities of each cell being completely ring-fenced – in other words the creditors of a particular cell have recourse only to the assets of that cell. In addition to the cells, each one of which has its own capital, there is a so-called 'core', whose shareholders may manage the activities of the cells on behalf of their owners. Diagrammatically, the structure can be portrayed as follows:

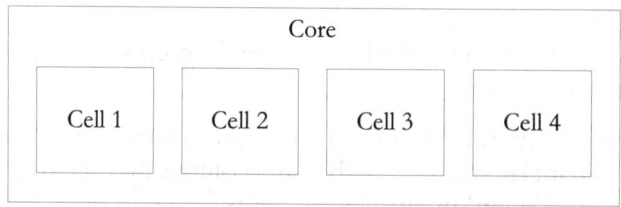

An original intention of this structure was to allow a fund-manager (who would hold the core shares) to run a number of independent funds (whose investors would hold the shares in the particular cell(s) concerned), with the incorporation of a single legal entity, as compared to the traditional position where each managed fund, and the management company, would be a separate legal entity, with all the attendant administrative costs and burdens.

Such a structure may give the superficial appearance of being a joint activity, but this is not the case. In most cases, it is extremely unlikely to be appropriate for an entity to regard an investment in a cell as a joint venture (or an associate). This is because the 'ring-fencing' of the assets and liabilities of each cell means that there is a direct linkage between the reporting entity and one or more particular cells, rather than that the reporting entity has some share of the profits or losses of the cell entity as a whole. The most likely conclusion is that each cell is a special purpose entity (SPE) of another entity (see Chapter 5 at 3.2).

3 ACCOUNTING REQUIREMENTS

3.1 Jointly Controlled Operations

A jointly controlled operation is one which involves the use of assets and other resources of the venturers, rather than the establishment of a corporation, partnership of other entity, or a financial structure, separate from the venturers themselves. Each venturer uses its own property, plant and equipment and carries its own inventories. It also incurs its own expenses and liabilities and raises its own finance, which represent its own obligations. The joint venture activities may be carried out by the venturer's employees alongside similar activities of the venturer. The joint venture agreement usually provides the basis for sharing among the venturers the revenue sales of the joint product and any common expenses incurred.[31]

An example of a jointly controlled operation might be that two or more venturers combine their operations, resources and expertise in order jointly to manufacture, market and distribute a particular product, such as an aircraft, with each venturer undertaking different parts of the manufacturing process. Each venturer bears its own costs and takes a share of the revenue from the sale of the aircraft, such share being determined in accordance with the contractual arrangement.[32]

In respect of its interest in a jointly controlled operation, IAS 31 requires a venturer to recognise in its financial statements:

- the assets that it controls and the liabilities that it incurs; and

- the expenses that it incurs and its share of the income that it earns from the sale of goods or services by the joint venture.[33]

IAS 31 notes that, because the assets, liabilities, income and expenses are already recognised in the financial statements of the venturer, no adjustments or other consolidation procedures are required in respect of these items when the venturer presents consolidated financial statements. Separate accounting records may not be required, nor financial statements prepared, for the joint venture itself, although the venturers may prepare management accounts so that they may assess the performance of the joint venture.[34]

3.2   Jointly Controlled Assets

Some joint ventures involve the joint control, and often the joint ownership, of one or more assets contributed to, or acquired for, and dedicated to the purposes of, the joint venture. The assets are used to obtain benefits for the venturers, who may each take a share of the output from the assets and bear an agreed share of the expenses incurred. Such ventures do not involve the establishment of an entity or financial structure separate from the venturers themselves, so that each venturer has control over its share of future economic benefits through its share in the jointly controlled asset.[35]

IAS 31 notes that joint ventures of this type are particularly common in extractive industries. For example, a number of oil companies may jointly control and operate an oil pipeline. Each venturer uses the pipeline to transport its own product in return for which it bears an agreed proportion of the operating expenses of the pipeline. Another example of a jointly controlled asset could be that two entities jointly control a property, each taking a share of the rents received and bearing a share of the expenses.[36]

In respect of its interest in jointly controlled assets, IAS 31 requires a venturer to recognise in its financial statements:

- its share of the jointly controlled assets, classified according to the nature of the assets (i.e. a share in a jointly controlled pipeline should be shown within plant, property and equipment rather than as an investment);
- any liabilities which it has incurred;
- its share of any liabilities incurred jointly with the other venturers;
- any income from the sale or use of its share of the output of the joint venture;
- its share of any expenses incurred by the joint venture; and
- any expenses which it has incurred in respect of its interest in the joint venture (e.g. those relating to financing the venturer's interest in the assets and selling its share of the output).[37]

The IASB believes that this treatment reflects the substance and economic reality and, usually, the legal form of the joint venture.[38] As in the case of jointly controlled operations (see 3.1 above), no adjustments or other consolidation procedures are required when the venturer presents consolidated financial statements, because the relevant assets, liabilities, income and expenses are already recognised in the financial statements of the venturer.[39]

IAS 31 notes that the accounting records of the joint venture itself may be limited to a record of the expenses incurred in common by the venturers, and ultimately borne by them according to their agreed shares. Financial statements may not be prepared for the joint venture, although the venturers may prepare management accounts so that they may assess the performance of the joint venture.[40]

3.3   Jointly controlled entities

3.3.1   *Definition*

In contrast to a jointly controlled operation or jointly controlled asset, a jointly controlled entity is a joint venture which involves the establishment of a corporation, partnership or other entity in which each venturer has an interest. The entity operates in the same way as any other entity, except that a contractual arrangement between the venturers establishes joint control over the economic activity of the entity.[41]

A jointly controlled entity controls the assets of the joint venture, incurs liabilities and expenses and earns income. It may enter into contracts in its own name and raise finance for the purposes of the joint venture activity. IAS 31 notes that 'each venturer is entitled to a share of the results of the jointly controlled entity, although some jointly controlled entities also involve a sharing of output.'[42]

IAS 31's reference to the fact that a venturer's interest in a jointly controlled entity may be in its 'output' rather than its results, suggests that, once a separate legal entity is involved, one is dealing with a jointly controlled entity and not a jointly controlled asset, even if the economic substance appears very similar. Example 8.3 illustrates the point.

Example 8.3   Jointly controlled asset or jointly controlled entity?

If three entities – A, B and C – each own one-third of a pipeline (and enter into a contractual agreement giving each party joint control), the venture is a jointly controlled asset. If, however, A, B and C each own one-third of a fourth entity D which holds the pipeline (and enter into a contractual agreement giving each party joint control), the venture is now a jointly controlled entity.

This suggests that a venturer's share of the output of an asset may be accounted for differently depending on whether the share in the asset is held directly or through a separate legal entity, particularly when it is borne in mind that IAS 31 gives an exemption in respect of accounting for a jointly controlled entity (see 2.3 above), but not in respect of a jointly controlled asset.

However, it could be said that these different outcomes are no different to the fact that, if a company owns a property, it shows a property in its separate financial statements whereas, if it incorporates a subsidiary to hold the property, it shows an investment in subsidiary in its separate financial statements.

IAS 31 goes on to say that many jointly controlled entities are similar in substance to jointly controlled operations or jointly controlled assets. For example, the venturers may transfer a jointly controlled asset, such as an oil pipeline, into a jointly controlled entity, for tax or other reasons. Similarly, the venturers may contribute into a jointly controlled entity assets which will be operated jointly. Some jointly controlled operations also involve the establishment of a jointly controlled entity to deal with particular aspects of the activity, for example, the design, marketing, distribution or after-sales service of the product.[43]

This emphasises the fact that, whilst the economic substance of a jointly controlled asset and a jointly controlled entity may in fact be similar, the difference in form does matter in determining the accounting treatment. This is articulated in paragraph 32 of the standard (which deals with proportionate consolidation – see 3.3.3 below), as follows:

> 'when recognising an interest in a jointly controlled entity, it is essential that a venturer reflects the substance and economic reality of the arrangement, rather than the joint venture's particular structure or form. In a jointly controlled entity, a venturer has control over its share of future economic benefits through its share of the assets and liabilities of the venture. This substance and economic reality are reflected in the consolidated financial statements of the venturer when the venturer recognises its interests in the assets, liabilities, income and expenses of the jointly controlled entity by using one of the two reporting formats for proportionate consolidation described [below].'

This indicates that, in the IASB's view, the substance of a joint venture is determined by its legal form and that, once joint ventures are enveloped in a separate legal entity, they become jointly controlled entities under IAS 31.

IAS 31 notes that a common example of a jointly controlled entity is when two entities combine their activities in a particular line of business by transferring the relevant assets and liabilities into a jointly controlled entity. Another example might be that an entity, in order to commence a business in a foreign country in conjunction with the government or other agency in that country, establishes a separate entity which is jointly controlled by the entity and the government or a government agency.[44]

IAS 31 adds that another feature of a jointly controlled entity is that it maintains its own accounting records and prepares and presents financial statements in the same way as other entities in conformity with IFRS.[45] This again reinforces the message that the classification of items as jointly controlled entities is, in fact, rather form-based. Whether or not an entity keeps its own books is arguably more a reflection of local legal requirements than of the economic substance of its activities.

IAS 31 notes that each venturer usually contributes cash or other resources to the jointly controlled entity. These contributions are included in the accounting records of the venturer and recognised in its separate financial statements as an investment in the jointly controlled entity.[46]

3.3.2   Accounting treatment – summary

IAS 31 permits two methods of accounting for jointly controlled entities:

- the preferred treatment, proportionate consolidation (see 3.3.3 below), using one of two permitted formats; and
- as a somewhat grudgingly allowed alternative treatment, equity accounting (see 3.3.4 below).[47]

Subject to the exemption discussed at 2.3 above, the venturer must apply whichever method it selects irrespective of whether it also has investments in subsidiaries or whether it describes its financial statements as 'consolidated financial statements'.[48] This is intended to emphasise that proportionate consolidation (or equity accounting) for jointly controlled entities may be required even by an entity that is not preparing consolidated financial statements.

A   Difference between allowed treatments

In many cases the essential difference between the two methods is simply one of presentation – i.e. whether items are shown on a 'line-by-line' basis (in the case of proportionate consolidation) or a 'one line' basis (in the case of equity accounting). However, this is not always the case. Most importantly, the treatment of a loss-making jointly controlled entity may differ significantly under each method. Where proportionate consolidation is used, the venturer will simply pick up its share of all losses as they arise. Where equity accounting is used, however, the reporting entity will apply 'waterline accounting' (see Chapter 7 at 3.8), so that the carrying amount of its interest in the joint venture never falls below zero, except to the extent that the investor has incurred legal or constructive obligations or made payments on behalf of the joint venture. Of course, it is in the nature of joint ventures that a venturer in a joint venture is more likely to have such legal or constructive obligations than an investor in an associate, which may mean that in some cases there is no difference between equity accounting for, and proportionate consolidation of, loss-making jointly controlled entities.

B   Consistency of treatment

As drafted, IAS 31 requires a venturer to apply either proportionate consolidation or equity accounting to its interest in 'a' jointly controlled entity.[49] This could be interpreted as suggesting that the venturer can make the choice of accounting treatment for each jointly controlled entity individually.

However, the disclosure provisions of IAS 31 (see 4.2.2 below) require a venturer to disclose 'the' method used to account for 'its interests in jointly controlled entities'.[50] In our view, this, together with:

- the use of similar wording in another disclosure requirement in IAS 31; and

- the overall requirement of IAS 1 for the use of consistent accounting policies for similar transactions (see Chapter 3 at 4.1.4),

clearly indicates that the IASB expects a venturer to account for all jointly controlled entities on a consistent basis.

3.3.3   Proportionate consolidation

IAS 31 defines proportionate consolidation as 'a method of accounting whereby a venturer's share of each of the assets, liabilities, income and expenses of a jointly controlled entity is combined line by line with similar items in the venturer's financial statements or reported as separate line items in the venturer's financial statements.'[51]

As noted in the discussion at 3.3.1 above, IAS 31 asserts that this method of accounting is necessary in order to capture the substance and economic reality of a venturer's interest in a jointly controlled entity.[52]

The application of proportionate consolidation means that the balance sheet of the venturer includes its share of the assets that it controls jointly and its share of the liabilities for which it is jointly responsible. The income statement of the venturer includes its share of the income and expenses of the jointly controlled entity.[53] In effect, the end result is equivalent to accounting for a partly-owned subsidiary, but excluding net assets attributable to the minority interest. IAS 31 notes that the procedures for consolidation of subsidiaries set out in IAS 27 (see Chapter 5 at 6) will generally be appropriate for the proportionate consolidation of joint ventures.[54]

Proportionate consolidation should be carried out using one of two permitted formats.

- Format A

    The jointly controlled entity is consolidated on an aggregated line-by-line basis (i.e. the venturer combines its share of the assets, liabilities, income and expenditure of the jointly controlled entity within the similar items in its own financial statements).

- Format B

    The venturer includes separate line items for its share of the total assets, liabilities, income and expenditure of the jointly controlled entity in its own consolidated accounts. Thus for example the item 'debtors' in the venturer's own financial statements would include a sub-heading 'share of debtors of joint ventures'.

The difference between the formats is clearly one of presentation only. Both formats result in the reporting of identical amounts of profit or loss and of each major classification of assets, liabilities, income and expenses.[55]

IAS 31 states that, whatever format is used to give effect to proportionate consolidation, it is inappropriate to offset any assets or liabilities by the deduction of other liabilities or assets or any income or expenses by the deduction of other expenses or income, unless a legal right of set-off exists and the offsetting represents the expectation as to the realisation of the asset or the settlement of the liability.[56] It is not entirely clear what IAS 31 means by this. We take it to mean that, whereas a balance between two members of a group would always be eliminated in consolidated financial statements as a matter of general consolidation practice (i.e. regardless of whether or not the balances are as a matter of law offsettable and intended to be settled net), a balance between a venturer and a joint venture is eliminated only where there exists a legal right of set-off, and an intention to settle net.

Proportionate consolidation of a jointly controlled entity should cease on the date that the venturer ceases to have joint control over the entity. This may occur either when the venturer disposes of its interest or when such external restrictions are placed on the jointly controlled entity that the venturer no longer has joint control.[57] See also 3.3.6 below.

Under proportionate consolidation, the venturer simply accounts for its share of the jointly controlled entity. It does not, for example, treat the interests of any passive investors (see 2.2 above) as some form of minority interest.

3.3.4   *Equity method*

The equity method is defined as in IAS 28, namely as a method of accounting whereby an interest in a jointly controlled entity is initially recorded at cost and adjusted thereafter for the post-acquisition change in the venturer's share of net assets of the jointly controlled entity. The profit or loss of the venturer includes the venturer's share of the profit or loss of the jointly controlled entity.[58]

Where a venturer accounts for its interest in jointly controlled entities using equity accounting, it follows the requirements of IAS 28 with regard to the application of the equity method[59] (see Chapter 7 at 3).

IAS 31 states that the use of the equity method is supported by:

(a)   those who argue that it is inappropriate to combine controlled items with jointly controlled items; and

(b)   those who believe that venturers have significant influence, rather than joint control, in a jointly controlled entity.[60]

Both these arguments are somewhat difficult to understand, at least as expressed here. The objection raised by the argument in (a) would be met by following the 'Format B' model of proportionate consolidation, whereby the share of jointly controlled entity's assets, liabilities, income and expenditure is shown alongside, but not aggregated with, those of the venturer (see 3.3.3 above).

The argument in (b) above makes little sense at all, since, as a matter of definition in IAS 28 and IAS 31, it is impossible for an entity over which the investor has only 'significant influence' to be a 'jointly controlled entity'. In effect, such an argument implies a belief that the definitions of 'significant influence' and 'joint control' are themselves wrong, and it therefore surprising that the IASB should permit an accounting treatment based on such a premise.

Rather curiously, IAS 31 does not acknowledge the real conceptual objection to proportionate consolidation, which is that in many cases 'joint control' is not the same as having an interest in part of the individual assets and liabilities; rather, it is a share in the venture as a whole. Indeed, those who hold this view often consider that there are circumstances in which it is appropriate to use equity accounting and others where proportionate consolidation may better represent the entity's interests in the underlying venture, so that it is not appropriate to prescribe a single accounting treatment for all joint ventures.

The IASB does not recommend the use of the equity method because, in its view, proportionate consolidation better reflects the substance and economic reality of a venturer's interest in a jointly controlled entity, that is to say, control over the venturer's share of the future economic benefits. Nevertheless, IAS 31 permits the use of the equity method, as an alternative treatment, when recognising interests in jointly controlled entities.[61]

As noted in 1.1 above, the choice of accounting treatment permitted by IAS 31 in all probability owes as much to 'political' as to technical considerations.

A venturer that applies the equity method to its interest in a jointly controlled entity discontinues this accounting treatment from the date on which it ceases to have joint control over the entity, unless the entity becomes an associate under IAS 28, in which case the equity method is continued, but pursuant to IAS 28 rather than IAS 31.[62] See also 3.3.6 below.

3.3.5   *Jointly controlled entity previously accounted for under IFRS 5*

Where an investor has not been proportionately consolidating, or equity accounting for, an interest in a jointly controlled entity on the basis that it is classified as held for sale under IFRS 5 (see 2.3 above), and the investment ceases to be so classified, the investor must apply proportionate consolidation or equity accounting retrospectively as from the date on which the investment was originally classified as held for sale. The financial statements of any prior periods since that classification must be restated.[63]

3.3.6   *Jointly controlled entity ceasing to be jointly controlled entity*

If a jointly controlled entity becomes a subsidiary, it should be accounted for, from the date that it does so, in accordance with IAS 27 (see Chapter 5). If a jointly controlled entity becomes an associate, it should be accounted for, from the date that it does so, in accordance with IAS 28 (see Chapter 7).[64]

Unlike IAS 27 and IAS 28, IAS 31 does not specifically provide any guidance on the treatment of an interest a jointly controlled entity that ceases to be so, and becomes neither a subsidiary nor an associate, but an investment. However, the clear inference is that:

- a former jointly controlled entity that has been accounted for using proportionate consolidation should be accounted for under the requirements of IAS 27 in respect of former subsidiaries that become investments (see Chapter 5 at 6.6.2); and

- a former jointly controlled entity that has been accounted for using equity accounting should be accounted for under the requirements of IAS 28 in respect of former associates that become investments (see Chapter 7 at 3.8).

In effect, the former jointly controlled entity will ultimately be accounted for in accordance with IAS 39. The measurement rules in IAS 39 are complex and discussed in detail in Chapter 18. In brief, however, they will entail the former jointly controlled entity being recorded initially at cost (being its carrying amount on that date that it ceases to be a jointly controlled entity) and then classified as either a 'financial asset at fair value through profit or loss' or an 'available-for-sale' financial asset. In either case, the investment will be measured at fair value — what differs is whether the gains and losses arising on revaluation are accounted for in the income statement or in equity.

The IASB has decided in principle to amend IAS 31 so as to require an investment in a former joint venture to be measured, as at the date on which joint control is lost, at fair value (rather than at a deemed cost equal to carrying value, as suggested above by analogy with IAS 27 and IAS 28). [65]

A   Cumulative exchange differences on jointly controlled entities

IAS 27 (see Chapter 5 at 6.5) specifically reinforces the requirement of IAS 21 – *The Effects of Foreign Exchange Rates* (see Chapter 9 at 2.7.3) that, when an investment in a foreign operation is disposed of, the gain or loss on disposal should include the 'recycling' of the cumulative exchange gains and losses that have, in accordance with IAS 21, been recognised in equity in respect of that operation. Whilst there is no such explicit reinforcement of IAS 21 in IAS 31, it seems clear that the same principle should apply on disposal of a jointly controlled entity.

IAS 21 clarifies that disposal of a foreign operation may occur through sale, liquidation, repayment of share capital, abandonment or receipt of a dividend out of pre-acquisition profits. When a partial disposal occurs, only the proportionate share of the related accumulated exchange difference is included in profit or loss. IAS 21 further clarifies that a write-down of a foreign operation does not constitute a partial disposal, and accordingly no part of the deferred foreign exchange gain or loss is recognised in profit or loss at the time of the such a write-down,[66] unless of course the write-down is consequent upon an event of 'disposal' as just described.

This begs the further question as to the appropriate treatment of any cumulative exchange gains and losses on a former jointly controlled entity which becomes subject to IAS 39, as described above. The issues here are very similar to those arising in respect of a former subsidiary which becomes subject to IAS 39, which are discussed in Chapter 5 at 6.6.2 A.

However, the IASB may be proposing significant changes in this area as part of its Business Combinations (Phase II) project (see C below).

B   Other cumulative gains and losses previously recognised in equity

Like IAS 27, IAS 31 does not specifically address the accounting treatment, on disposal of a jointly controlled entity, of the venturer's share of other cumulative gains and losses previously accounted for in equity relating to assets and liabilities of the disposed associate that would, if those assets and liabilities had been disposed of separately by the jointly controlled entity, been recycled in profit or loss. These could include:

- accumulated hedging gains and losses accounted for under IAS 39 (see Chapter 19), and

- any other amounts previously recognised in equity that would have been recognised in profit or loss if the jointly controlled entity had directly disposed of the assets to which they relate, such as gains or losses on available-for-sale financial assets accounted for under IAS 39 (see Chapter 18 at 3.2).

IAS 39 does not specifically address this issue either. However, it would appear that recycling is appropriate, since the disposal of a jointly controlled entity does give rise to the derecognition of the venturer's share of the separate assets and liabilities of that jointly controlled entity just as if they had been disposed of separately. Moreover, the IASB's discussions on possible amendments to IAS 31 (see C below) appear to assume that it is clear that such gains and losses should be recycled on disposal of a jointly controlled entity.

C   Possible future developments

As part of its Business Combinations Phase II project the IASB has tentatively agreed to amend IAS 21 and IAS 39 so as to require that, when an investor's interest in a joint venture is reduced (but the investor retains joint control over the joint venture), there should be should be recognised in profit or loss:

- foreign exchange differences recognised in equity or under IAS 21,

- accumulated hedging gains and losses recognised in equity under IAS 39 (see Chapter 19), and

- any other amounts previously recognised in equity that would have been recognised in profit or loss if the jointly controlled entity had directly disposed of the assets to which they relate, such as gains or losses on available-for-sale financial assets accounted for under IAS 39 (see Chapter 18 at 3.2),

in each case proportionate to the interest disposed of.

However, where an investor's interest in a joint venture is reduced such that the investee ceases to be a joint venture, the IASB intends to require that the entire amount of such gains and losses should be 'recycled' on a loss of control, even if the reporting entity still retains an investment in its former joint venture.[67]

3.4   Transactions between a venturer and a joint venture

3.4.1   *Background*

It is common for venturers to transact with the joint venture, in particular on the formation of the venture. Typical transactions include:

- The venturers contribute cash to the venture in proportion to their agreed relative shares. The venture then uses some or all of the cash to acquire assets from the venturers for use in the venture.

- The venturers contribute other assets (or a mixture of cash and other assets) to the joint venture with fair values, as agreed between the venturers, in proportion to the venturers' agreed relative shares in the venture.

- The venturers contribute other assets to the joint venture with fair values, as agreed between the venturers, not in proportion to the venturers' agreed relative shares. Cash 'equalisation' payments are then made between the venturers so that the overall financial position of the venturer does correspond to their agreed relative shares in the venture.

A further complication is that some of these assets that are the subject of such transactions may be intangible assets not recognised under IFRS in the financial statements of the contributing venturers (e.g. internally generated brands and know-how).

IAS 31, together with SIC–13, provides broad overall principles as to the treatment of such transactions, but no specific indication of the accounting entries required to give effect to those principles. Moreover, SIC–13 applies strictly only to transactions involving the transfer of assets to jointly controlled entities (and not to other types of joint venture).

3.4.2 IAS 31 requirements

When a venturer contributes or sells assets to a joint venture, IAS 31 requires that the recognition of any gain or loss should reflect the substance of the transaction. While the assets are retained by the joint venture, and provided that the venturer has transferred the significant risks and rewards of ownership, the venturer should recognise only that portion of the gain or loss which is attributable to the interests of the other venturers. However, the venturer should recognise the full amount of any loss when the contribution or sale provides evidence of a reduction in the net realisable value of current assets or an impairment loss. Where non-monetary assets are contributed to a jointly controlled entity, the additional guidance in SIC–13 must also be considered (see A below).[68]

When a venturer purchases assets from a joint venture, the venturer must not recognise its share of the profits of the joint venture from the transaction until it resells the assets to an independent party. A venturer recognises its share of the losses resulting from these transactions in the same way as profits, except that (as in the case of sales to the joint venture) losses should be recognised immediately when they represent a reduction in the net realisable value of current assets or an impairment loss.[69]

The venturer should assess whether a transaction between itself and a joint venture provides evidence of impairment of any asset transferred in accordance with IAS 36 – *Impairment of Assets*,[70] which is discussed in Chapter 13 at 4.

The effect of these requirements is illustrated in Examples 8.4 to 8.7 below. It should be noted that these requirements appear to apply to all transactions with joint ventures, irrespective of whether the venturer has availed itself of IAS 31's exemption from proportionate consolidation or equity accounting for joint ventures (see 2.3 above). They also appear to apply to the separate financial statements of a venturer.

Example 8.4:   *Sale of asset from venturer to joint venture at a profit*

Two entities A and B establish a joint venture involving the creation of a jointly controlled entity C in which A and B each hold 50%. A and B each contribute €5 million in cash to the joint venture in exchange for equity shares. C then uses €8 million of its €10 million cash to acquire from A a property recorded in the financial statements of A at €6 million. It is agreed that €8 million is the fair market value of the property. How should A account for these transactions?

The required accounting entry if A accounts for its interest in C using proportionate consolidation is:

	€m	€m
Cash[1]	3	
Share of cash of C[2]	1	
Share of property of C[3]	3	
Property[4]		6
Gain on disposal[5]		1

1   €8m received from C less €5m contributed to C.

2   50% of C's cash of €2m [€10m received from A and B less €8m paid to A]

3   50% of €8m (carrying value in books of C), less €1m (share of profit eliminated – see note 5). In effect, this treatment represents that A still holds 50% of the property at its original carrying value to A (50% of €6m = €3m).

4   Derecognition of A's original property.

5   Gain on sale of property €2m (€8m received from C less €6m carrying value = €2m), less 50% eliminated (so as to reflect only profit attributable to interest of other venturer B) = €1m.

If A accounted for C using equity accounting the accounting would be identical, except that it would show simply 'Investment in C' of €4 million rather than the €1m share of C's cash and €3m share of C's property.

Example 8.5:   *Sale of asset from venturer to joint venture at a loss*

Two entities A and B establish a joint venture involving the creation of a jointly controlled entity C in which A and B each hold 50%. A and B each contribute €5 million in cash to the joint venture in exchange for equity shares. C then uses €8 million of its €10 million cash to acquire from A a property recorded in the financial statements of A at €10 million. €8m is agreed to be the fair market value of the property. How should A account for these transactions?

The required accounting entry if A accounts for its interest in C using proportionate consolidation is:

	€m	€m
Cash[1]	3	
Share of cash of C[2]	1	
Share of property of C[3]	4	
Loss on disposal[4]	2	
Property[5]		10

1   €8m received from C less €5m contributed to C.

2   50% of C's cash €2m (€10m from A and B – €8m to A)

3   50% of €8m (carrying value in books of C), not adjusted since the transaction indicated an impairment of A's asset.

4   Loss on sale of property €2m (€8m received from C less €10m carrying value = €2m) not adjusted since the transaction indicated an impairment of the property. In effect, it is the result that would have been obtained if A had recognised an impairment charge immediately prior to the sale and then recognised no gain or loss on the sale.

5   Derecognition of A's original property.

If A accounted for C using equity accounting the accounting would be identical, except that it would show simply 'Investment in C' of €5 million rather than the €1m share of C's cash and €4m share of C's property.

Example 8.6: *Sale of asset from joint venture to venturer at a profit*

Two entities A and B establish a joint venture involving the creation of a jointly controlled entity C in which A and B each hold 50%. A and B each contribute €5 million in cash to the joint venture in exchange for equity shares. C then uses €8 million of its €10 million cash to acquire a property from an independent third party D. The property is later sold to A for €12 million, which is agreed to be its market value. How should A account for these transactions?

The required accounting entry if A accounts for its interest in C using proportionate consolidation is:

	€m	€m
Property[1]	10	
Share of cash of C[2]	7	
Cash[3]		17

1 €12m paid to C less elimination of A's share of the profit made by C €2m (50% of [€12m sales proceeds less €8m cost to C]).

2 50% of C's cash €14m (€10m from A and B – €8m to D + €12 from A).

3 €5m equity contributed to C plus €12m consideration paid for property

If A accounted for C using equity accounting the accounting would be identical, except that it would show 'Investment in C' of €7 million rather than the €7m share of C's cash.

Example 8.7: *Sale of asset from joint venture to venturer at a loss*

Two entities A and B establish a joint venture involving the creation of a jointly controlled entity C in which A and B each hold 50%. A and B each contribute €5 million in cash to the joint venture in exchange for equity shares. C then uses €8 million of its €10 million cash to acquire a property from an independent third party D. The property is then sold to A for €7 million, which is agreed to be its market value. How should A account for these transactions?

The required accounting entry if A accounts for its interest in C using proportionate consolidation is:

	€m	€m
Property[1]	7.0	
Share of cash of C[2]	4.5	
Share of loss of C[3]	0.5	
Cash[4]		12.0

1 €7m paid to C not adjusted since the transaction indicated an impairment of C's asset.

2 50% of C's cash €9m (€10m from A and B – €8m to D + €7 received from A).

3 Loss in C's books is €1m (€8m cost of property less €7m proceeds of sale). A recognises its 50% share because the transaction indicates an impairment of the asset. In effect, it is the result that would have been obtained if C had recognised an impairment charge immediately prior to the sale and then recognised no gain or loss on the sale.

4 €5m equity contributed to C plus €7m consideration for property.

If A accounted for C using equity accounting the accounting would be identical, except that it would show 'Investment in C' of €4.5 million rather than the €4.5m share of C's cash.

It may be that transactions occur between a venturer and a joint venture in assets, such as inventories, which are destined for onward sale in the normal course of business by the buying party. The accounting adjustments required are essentially as the same as those for similar transactions between an investor and its associate, examples of which are given in Chapter 7 at 3.4.

3.4.3   *Non-monetary contributions to joint ventures*

SIC-13 – *Jointly Controlled Entities – Non-Monetary Contributions by Venturers* provides guidance on the application of these general principles to the specific situation of a transfer of non-monetary assets to a jointly controlled entity in exchange for equity. This states that the venturer should recognise in its income statement the portion of any gain or loss arising on the transfer attributable to the other venturers unless:

- significant risks and rewards of ownership of the contributed non-monetary asset(s) have not been transferred to the jointly controlled entity; or

- the gain or loss on the non-monetary contribution cannot be measured reliably; or

- the contribution lacks commercial substance, as that term is described in IAS 16 – *Property, Plant and Equipment* (see A below and Chapter 12 at 2.3.2).[71]

If any of the above conditions applies, the gain or loss arising would be considered 'unrealised' (and therefore not recognised in the income statement), unless in addition to receiving an equity interest in the entity, a venturer receives monetary or non-monetary assets, in which case an 'appropriate portion' of the gain or loss on the transaction should be recognised by the venturer. SIC-13 does not elaborate on what would constitute an appropriate portion of the gain or loss in such circumstances.[72]

Where the venturer accounts for the jointly controlled entity using proportionate consolidation, any unrealised gains or losses should be eliminated against the venturer's share of the underlying assets of the entity. Where equity accounting is used, the elimination should be against the carrying value of the investment in the entity. Unrealised gains or losses should not be accounted for as deferred income or expenditure.[73] Where 'unrealised' losses are eliminated in this way, the effect will be to apply what is sometimes referred to as 'asset swap' accounting. In other words, the carrying value of the investment in the jointly controlled entity will be the same as the carrying value of the non-monetary assets transferred in exchange for it, subject of course to any necessary provision for impairment uncovered by the transaction.

A   'Commercial substance'

As noted above, SIC–13 requires that a transaction should not be treated as realised when, inter alia, it lacks commercial substance as described in IAS 16. IAS 16 states that an exchange of assets has 'commercial substance' when:

(a)   either:

(i)   the configuration (risk, timing and amount) of the cash flows of the asset received differs from the configuration of the cash flows of the asset transferred; or

(ii)   the entity-specific value of the portion of the entity's operations affected by the transaction changes as a result of the exchange; and

(b)   the difference in (i) or (ii) above is significant relative to the fair value of the assets exchanged.[74]

IAS 16's 'commercial substance' test is designed to enable an entity to measure, with reasonable objectivity, whether the asset that it has acquired in a non-monetary exchange is different to the asset it has given up.

The first stage is to determine the cash flows both of the asset given up and of the asset acquired (the latter being, of course, the interest in the jointly controlled entity). This determination may be sufficient by itself to satisfy (a) above, as it may be obvious that there are significant differences in the configuration of the cash flows. The type of income may have changed. For example, if the entity contributed a non-monetary asset such as a property or intangible asset to the jointly controlled entity, the reporting entity may now be receiving a rental or royalty stream from the jointly controlled entity, whereas previously the asset contributed to the cash flows of the cash-generating unit of which it was a part.

However, determining the cash flows may not result in a clear-cut conclusion, in which case the entity-specific value will have to be calculated. This is not the same as a value in use calculation under IAS 36, in that the entity is allowed to use a discount rate based on its own assessment of the risks specific to the operations, not those that reflect current market assessments[75] and post-tax cash flows.[76] The transaction will have commercial substance if these entity-specific values are not only different to one another but also significant compared to the fair values of the assets exchanged.

The calculation may not be highly sensitive to the discount rate as the same rate is used to calculate the entity-specific value of both the asset surrendered and the entity's interest in the jointly controlled entity. However, if the entity considers that a high discount rate is appropriate, this will have an impact on whether or not the difference is significant relative to the fair value of the assets exchanged. It is also necessary to consider the significance of:

(a)   the requirement above that the entity should 'recognise in its income statement the portion of any gain or loss arising on the transfer attributable to the other venturers';

(b)   the general requirements of IAS 31 in respect of transactions between venturers and their joint ventures; and

(c)   the general requirement of IFRS 3 to recognise assets acquired in a business combination at fair value (see Chapter 6).

As a result, we consider that it is likely that transactions entered into with genuine commercial purposes in mind are likely to pass the 'commercial substance' tests outlined above. However, these rules are designed to prevent the recognition of gains where an entity enters into an artificial transaction with the intention of manufacturing a gain by attributing inflated values to the assets exchanged.[77]

B   Applying SIC–13 in practice

SIC–13 does not give an example of the accounting treatment that it envisages when a gain is treated as 'realised'. However, we believe that the intended approach is that set out in Example 8.8 below. In essence, this approach reflects the fact that the reporting entity has:

(a)   acquired an interest in a jointly controlled entity that must be accounted for at fair value under IFRS 3; but

(b)   is required to restrict any gain arising as a result of the exchange relating to its own assets to the extent that the gain is attributable to the other party to the joint venture. This leads to an adjustment of the carrying amount of the assets of the joint venture (as in Example 8.4 at 3.4.2 above).

Example 8.8:   Contribution of non-monetary assets to form joint venture

A and B are two major pharmaceutical companies, which agree to form a joint venture (JV Co) in respect of a particular part of each of their businesses. A will own 40% of the joint venture, and B 60%. The parties agree that the total value of the new business is £250m.

A's contribution to the venture is one of its subsidiaries, in respect of which A's consolidated balance sheet reflects separable net assets of £50 million and goodwill of £10 million. The fair value of the separable net assets of the subsidiary contributed by A is considered to be £80 million. The implicit fair value of the business contributed is £100 million (40% of the total fair value of £250m).

B also contributes a subsidiary, in respect of which B's consolidated balance sheet reflects separable net assets of £85 million and goodwill of £15 million. The fair value of the separable net assets is considered to be £120m. The implicit fair value of the business contributed is £150 million (60% of total fair value of £250m).

The book and fair values of the businesses contributed by A and B can therefore be summarised as follows:

(in £m)	A		B	
	Book value	Fair value	Book value	Fair value
Separable net assets	50	80	85	120
Goodwill	10	20	15	30
Total	60	100	100	150

How should A apply SIC–13 in accounting for account for the set-up of the joint venture?

The general principles of IFRS 3 require that A should account at fair value for the acquisition of its 40% interest in the new venture. However, as noted above, any gain or loss recognised by A must reflect only the extent to which it has disposed of the assets to the other partners in the venture (i.e. in this case, 60% – the extent to which A's former subsidiary is effectively transferred to B through B's 60% interest in the new venture).

This gives rise to the following accounting entry.

	£m	£m
Share of net assets of JV Co[1]	68	
Goodwill[2]	16	
Net assets and goodwill contributed to JV Co[3]		60
Gain on disposal[4]		24

1   40% of fair value of separable net assets of new entity £80m (40% of [£80m+£120m] as in table above) less elimination of 40% of gain on disposal £12m (40% of £30m, being the difference between the book value [£50m] and fair value [£80m] of A's separable net assets, as in table above, contributed to JV Co) = £68m.

    This is equivalent to, and perhaps more easily calculated as, 40% of [book value of A's separable net assets + fair value of B's separable net assets], i.e. 40% × [£50m+£120m] = £68m.

    If A adopted proportionate consolidation, this £68m would naturally be allocated to the relevant balance sheet headings.

2   Fair value of consideration given £100m (as in table above) less fair value of 40% share of separable net assets of JV Co acquired £80m (see note 1) = £20m, less elimination of 40% gain on disposal £4m (40% of £10m, being the difference between the book value [£10m] and fair value [£20m] of A's goodwill, as in table above, contributed to JV Co) = £16m.

    This is equivalent to, and perhaps more easily calculated as, 40% of [book value of A's goodwill + fair value of B's goodwill], i.e. 40% × [£10m+£30m] = £16m.

3   Previous carrying amount of net assets contributed by A, now deconsolidated. In reality there would be a number of entries to deconsolidate these on a line-by-line basis.

4   Fair value of business acquired £100m (as in table above) less book value of assets disposed of £60m (as in table above) = £40m, less 40% of gain eliminated (£16m) = £24m. The £16m eliminated reduces A's share of JV Co's separable net assets by £12m (see note 1) and its share of JV Co's goodwill by £4m (see note 2).

As noted in the introductory remarks above, it is common when joint ventures are set up in this way for the fair value of the assets contributed not to be exactly in proportion to the fair values venturers' agreed relative shares. Cash 'equalisation' payments are then made between the venturers so that the overall financial position of the venturer does correspond to their agreed relative shares in the venture. Our suggested treatment of such payments in the context of a transaction within the scope of SIC–13 is illustrated in Example 8.9 below.

Example 8.9:   *Contribution of non-monetary assets to form joint venture with cash equalisation payment between venturers*

Suppose that the transaction in Example 8.8 was varied so that A is to have only a 36% interest in JV Co. However, as shown by the introductory table in Example 8.8, A is contributing a business worth 40% of the total fair value of JV Co. Accordingly, B makes good the shortfall by making a cash payment to A equivalent to 4% of the fair value of JV Co, i.e. £10 million (4% of £250 million).

This would require A to make the following accounting entries.

	£m	£m
Share of net assets of JV Co[1]	61.2	
Cash (equalisation payment from B)	10.0	
Goodwill[2]	14.4	
Separable net assets and goodwill contributed to JV Co[3]		60.0
Gain on disposal[4]		25.6

1   36% of fair value of separable net assets of new entity £72m (36% of [£80m+£120m] as in table above) less elimination of 36% of gain on disposal £10.8m (36% of £30m, being the difference between the book value [£50m] and fair value [£80m] of A's separable net assets, as in table above, contributed to JV Co) = £61.2m.

   This is equivalent to, and perhaps more easily calculated as, 36% of [book value of A's separable net assets + fair value of B's separable net assets], i.e. 36% × [£50m+£120m] = £61.2m.

   If A adopted proportionate consolidation, this £61.2m would naturally be allocated to the relevant balance sheet headings.

2   Fair value of consideration given £100m (as in table above), less cash equalisation payment received £10m = £90m less fair value of 36% share of separable net assets of JV Co acquired £72m (see note 1) = £18m, less elimination of 36% gain on disposal £3.6m (36% of £10m, being the difference between the book value [£10m] and fair value [£20m] of A's goodwill, as in table above, contributed to JV Co) = £14.4m.

   This is equivalent to, and perhaps more easily calculated as, 36% of [book value of A's goodwill + fair value of B's goodwill], i.e. 36% × [£10m+£30m] = £14.4m.

3   Previous carrying amount of net assets (excluding goodwill) contributed by A, now deconsolidated. In reality there would be a number of entries to deconsolidate these on a line-by-line basis.

4   Fair value of business acquired £90m (36% of £250m) plus cash equalisation payment £10m = £100m, less book value of assets disposed of £60m (as in table above) = £40m, less 36% of gain eliminated (£14.4m) = £25.6m. The £14.4m eliminated reduces A's share of JV Co's separable net assets by £10.8m (see note 1) and its share of JV Co's goodwill by £3.6m (see note 2).

I   *'Artificial' transactions*

A concern with transactions such as this is that it is the relative, rather than the absolute, value of the transaction that is of concern to the parties. In other words, in Example 8.8 above, it could be argued that the only clear inference that can be drawn is that A and B have agreed that the ratio of the fair values of the businesses they have each contributed is 40:60, rather than that the business as a whole is worth £250 million. Thus it might be open to A and B, without altering the substance of the transaction, to assert that the value of the combined operations is £500 million (with a view to enlarging their balance sheets) or £200 million, (with a view to increasing future profitability).

Another way in which the valuation of the transaction might be distorted is through disaggregation of the consideration. Suppose that the £60 million net assets contributed by A in Example 8.8 above comprised:

	£m
Cash	12
Other net current assets	13
Fixed assets and stock	25
Goodwill	10
	60

Further suppose that, for tax reasons, the transaction was structured such that A was issued with 4% of the shares of JV Co in exchange for the cash and 36% in exchange for the remaining assets. This could lead to the suggestion that, as there can be no doubt as to the fair value of the cash, A's entire investment must be worth £120 million (i.e. £12 million × 40/4). Testing transactions for their commercial substance will require entities to focus on the fair value of the transaction as a whole and not to follow the strict legal form.

Of course, once cash equalisation payments are introduced, as in Example 8.9 above, the transaction terms provide evidence as to both the relative and absolute fair values of the assets contributed by each party.

II   Accounts of JV Co

In the accounts of the JV Co itself (assuming that these are subject to IFRS), the acquisition of the former businesses of both A and B will be accounted for at fair value as a business combination under IFRS 3. This means that the amounts taken up in the accounts of A and B may bear little relation to either party's share of the net assets of the joint venture as reported in underlying financial statements of the investee. For example, A's share of any depreciation charge recorded by JV Co must be based on the carrying amount of A's share of JV Co's PPE, not as recorded in JV Co's books (i.e. at fair value) but as recorded in A's books, which will be based on book value as regards PPE contributed by A and a fair value as regards PPE contributed by B.

Accordingly it may be necessary for both A and B to keep a 'memorandum' set of books for consolidation purposes reflecting their share of assets originally their own at book value, those originally of the other party at fair value. In practice, however, this may be easier said than done, and a fairly broad brush approach may be needed.

3.4.4   Loans etc. between the reporting entity and joint ventures

IAS 31's requirement to eliminate partially unrealised profits or losses on transactions with joint ventures is expressed in terms of transactions involving the transfer of assets. This raises the question of whether this requirement is generally intended to items such as interest paid on loans between joint ventures and the reporting entity.

Where a jointly controlled entity is accounted for using proportionate consolidation, we believe that the requirement for partial elimination of profits is generally intended to be extended to loans and related items, but subject to the general restrictions on offset that IAS 31 requires when proportionate consolidation is adopted (see 3.3.3 above).

Where a jointly controlled entity is accounted for using equity accounting, however, we do not believe that the requirement for partial elimination of profits is generally intended to be extended to loans and related items, since such loans do not involve the transfer of assets giving rise to gains or losses. Moreover, they are not normally regarded as part of the investor's share of the net assets of the investee, but as separate transactions, except in the case of loss-making investees, where interests in long-term loans may be required to be accounted for as if they were part of the reporting entity's equity investment in determining the carrying value of the joint venture against which losses may be offset (see Chapter 7 at 3.7).

3.5 Income Taxes

Income taxes arising from interests in joint ventures are accounted for in accordance with IAS 12 – *Income Taxes*. In cases where joint control does not give joint control over the distribution policy of the joint venture, the venturer may be required to provide in full for deferred tax on temporary differences relating to joint ventures.

Some might question whether the lack of joint control over distribution policy suggests that in fact the venturer does not exert joint control sufficient for the investment to be treated as a joint venture under IAS 31. However, IAS 12 notes that a joint venture agreement will 'usually' give joint control over distribution policy, but does not appear to regard it as an essential feature of such an agreement.[78] This is discussed further in Chapter 24 at 4.2.5.

3.6 Operators of joint ventures

One or more venturers may act as the operator or manager of a joint venture. Operators are usually paid a management fee for such duties. The fees are accounted for by the joint venture as an expense. IAS 31 requires the operators or managers of a joint venture to account for any such fees in accordance with IAS 18 – *Revenue* (see Chapter 26).[79]

4   PRESENTATION AND DISCLOSURE

4.1   Presentation

In the income statement, the aggregate of the investor's share of the profit or loss of associates and joint ventures accounted for using the equity method must be shown.[80]

4.2   Disclosure

4.2.1   *Interests in joint ventures*

A venturer should disclose a listing and description of interests in significant joint ventures and the proportion of ownership interest held in jointly controlled entities.

A venturer which reports its interests in jointly controlled entities using the line-by-line reporting format for proportionate consolidation or the equity method should disclose the aggregate amounts of each of:

- current assets;
- long-term assets;
- current liabilities;
- long-term liabilities;
- income; and
- expenses.

related to its interests in joint ventures.[81] An example of this disclosure is found in the financial statements of Anglo Gold.

Extract 8.1: AngloGold Limited (2003)

Notes to the group financial statements [extract]

21. **Interest in joint ventures**[(1)]

The group's effective share of income, expenses, assets, liabilities and cash flows of joint ventures, which are included in the consolidated financial statements, are as follows:

2002	2003	Figures in million	2003	2002
SA Rands			US Dollars	
		Income statement		
3,271	**2,356**	Gold income	**312**	312
(2,149)	**(1,608)**	Cost of sales	**(213)**	(205)
1,122	**748**	Operating profit	**99**	107
10	**1**	Financial income	**–**	1
(94)	**(60)**	Finance costs	**(8)**	(9)
1,038	**689**	Profit on ordinary activities before taxation	**91**	99
		Balance sheet		
4,366	**3,321**	Non-current assets	**498**	509
1,218	**1,320**	Current assets	**198**	142
5,584	**4,641**	Total assets	**696**	651
3,500	**2,561**	Shareholders' equity	**384**	408
		Non-current liabilities		
746	**380**	Interest bearing borrowings	**57**	87
60	**80**	Provisions	**12**	7
317	**360**	Derivatives	**54**	37
		Current liabilities		
172	**400**	Interest-bearing borrowings	**60**	20
789	**860**	Other	**129**	92
5,584	**4,641**	Total equity and liabilities	**696**	651
		Cash flow statement		
1,573	**680**	Cash flows from operating activities	**90**	150
(178)	**(295)**	Cash flows from investing activities	**(39)**	(17)
(1,258)	**(574)**	Cash flows form financing activities	**(76)**	(120)
137	**(189)**	Net increase in cash and cash equivalents	**(25)**	13

(1)   Where the presentation or classification of an item has been amended, comparative amounts have been reclassified to ensure comparability with the current period. The amendments have been made to provide the users of the financial statements with additional information.

4.2.2   *Accounting policy for jointly controlled entities*

A venturer must disclose the method that it uses to recognise its interests in jointly controlled entities[82] (i.e. proportionate consolidation or the equity method – see 3.3 above).

4.2.3   *Contingencies and commitments*

IAS 31 requires a venturer to disclose the aggregate amount of the following contingent liabilities, unless the probability of loss is remote, separately from the amount of other contingent liabilities:

- any contingent liabilities that the venturer has incurred in relation to its interests in joint ventures and its share in each of the contingent liabilities that have been incurred jointly with other venturers;

- its share of the contingent liabilities of the joint ventures themselves for which it is contingently liable; and

- those contingent liabilities that arise because the venturer is contingently liable for the liabilities of the other venturers of a joint venture.[83]

A venturer must also disclose the aggregate amount of the following commitments in respect of its interests in joint ventures separately from other commitments:

- any capital commitments of the venturer in relation to its interests in joint ventures and its share in the capital commitments that have been incurred jointly with other venturers; and

- its share of the capital commitments of the joint ventures themselves.[84]

5   TRANSITIONAL AND FIRST-TIME ADOPTION ISSUES

5.1   General

As noted at 1.2 above, IAS 31 must be applied for accounting periods beginning on or after 1 January 2005. Entities are encouraged to adopt the revised version of IAS 31 for earlier periods, but must disclose that they have done so.[85]

There are no transitional provisions. Accordingly, an existing IFRS user must apply the revised version of IAS 31 with full retrospective effect. The main differences from the current version of IAS 31 (which may give rise to retrospective restatement of prior periods under IAS 8) are summarised at 1.2 above.

There are no specific first-time adoption provisions in IAS 31, and IFRS 1 highlights no issues specific to IAS 31.

This means that a first-time adopter of IFRS is required to apply IAS 31 as if it had always done so. For some first-time adopters, this may mean application of proportionate consolidation or the equity method for the first time. For the majority of first time adopters, however, we anticipate that the issue is that they are already applying proportionate consolidation or the equity method under national

GAAP, and will now need to identify the, potentially significant, differences between the methodology under their predecessor GAAP and under IAS 31.

In particular there may be differences between:

- the criteria used to determine what interests are joint ventures;
- the elimination of transactions between venturers and joint ventures;
- the treatment of loss-making jointly controlled entities;
- the permitted interval between the reporting dates of a venturer and a joint venture with non-coterminous year-ends; and
- the treatment of investments in entities formerly classified as joint ventures.

The requirements for 'jointly controlled operations' and 'jointly controlled assets' may result in assets that were previously derecognised under predecessor GAAP and reclassified as investments in joint ventures being re-recognised, so as to reflect the requirement of IAS 31 to treat assets used in such joint ventures as assets of the venturers themselves rather than of the venture.

5.1.1 Transition impairment review

A first-time adopter of IFRS is required by IFRS 1 to apply an impairment test in accordance with IAS 36 to any goodwill recognised at the date of transition to IFRS, regardless of whether there is any indication of impairment[86] (see Chapter 4 at 2.4). This raises the question of whether the carrying amount of joint ventures which include an element of goodwill should be similarly subject to a mandatory impairment review on transition.

IFRS 1 notes that its provisions with regard to past business combinations apply also to past acquisitions of investments in joint ventures (see Chapter 4 at 2.4). Moreover, IFRS 3, in its transitional provisions, treats goodwill included in the carrying amount of investments in joint ventures in the same way as goodwill separately recognised (see Chapter 6 at 4.1.4). This leads to the conclusion that a transition impairment review must be undertaken for investments in joint ventures whose carrying value includes an element of goodwill.

5.2 Venturer and joint venture with different dates of first-time adoption of IFRS

IFRS 1 addresses in some detail the accounting treatment to be adopted when a venturer in a joint venture adopts IFRS for the first time before the joint venture and vice-versa. This is discussed in Chapter 5 at 9.3.

References

1 IAS 31, *Interests in Joint Ventures*, IASB, December 2003 (amended March 2004), para. 58.
2 IAS 31, paras. IN1-IN10.
3 IFRS 5, *Non-current Assets Held for Sale and Discontinued Operations*, IASB, March 2004.
4 SIC-13, *Jointly Controlled Entities-Non-monetary Contributions by Venturers*, SIC, November 1998 (superseded December 2003).
5 IAS 27, *Consolidated and Separate Financial Statements*, IASB, December 2003 (amended March 2004).
6 IAS 28, *Investments in Associates*, IASB, December 2003 (amended March 2004).
7 IFRS 1, *First-time Adoption of International Financial Reporting Standards*, IASB, June 2003 (amended March 2004).
8 IAS 1, *Presentation of Financial Statements*, IASB, December 2003 (amended March 2004).
9 IAS 39, *Financial Instruments: Recognition and Measurement*, IASB, December 2003 (amended March 2004).
10 IAS 31, para. 1.
11 IAS 31, para. 3.
12 IAS 31, para. 3.
13 IAS 31, para. 3.
14 IAS 31, para. 3.
15 IAS 31, para. 51.
16 IAS 31, para. 7.
17 IAS 31, para. 9.
18 IAS 31, para. 3.
19 IAS 28, para. 9.
20 IAS 31, para. 10.
21 IAS 31, para. 11.
22 IAS 31, para. 12.
23 IAS 31, para. 8.
24 IAS 31, para. 2.
25 IAS 31, para. 42.
26 IAS 31, para. 3.
27 IAS 31, para. 46.
28 IAS 31, para. 4.
29 IAS 31, paras. 5 and 47.
30 IAS 31, para. 6.
31 IAS 31, para. 13.
32 IAS 31, para. 14.
33 IAS 31, para. 15.
34 IAS 31, paras. 16-17.
35 IAS 31, paras. 18-19.
36 IAS 31, para. 20.
37 IAS 31, paras. 21-22.
38 IAS 31, para. 23.
39 IAS 31, para. 22.
40 IAS 31, para. 23.
41 IAS 31, para. 24.
42 IAS 31, para. 25.
43 IAS 31, para. 27.
44 IAS 31, para. 26.
45 IAS 31, para. 28.
46 IAS 31, para. 29.
47 IAS 31, paras. 30 and 38.
48 IAS 31, paras. 31 and 39.
49 IAS 31, paras. 30 and 38.
50 IAS 31, para. 57.
51 IAS 31, para. 3.
52 IAS 31, para. 32.
53 IAS 31, para. 33.
54 IAS 31, para. 33.
55 IAS 31, para. 34.
56 IAS 31, para. 35.
57 IAS 31, paras. 36-37.
58 IAS 31, para. 3.
59 IAS 31, para. 40.
60 IAS 31, para. 40.
61 IAS 31, para. 40.
62 IAS 31, para. 41.
63 IAS 31, para. 43.
64 IAS 31, para. 45.
65 *IASB Update*, IASB, April 2004.
66 IAS 21, *The Effects of Changes in Foreign Exchange Rates*, IASB, December 2003, para. 49.
67 *IASB Update*, IASB, April 2004.
68 IAS 31, para. 48.
69 IAS 31, para. 49.
70 IAS 31, para. 51.
71 SIC-13, paras. 5-6.
72 SIC-13, para. 6.
73 SIC-13, para. 7.
74 IAS 16, *Property, Plant and Equipment*, IASB, December 2003 (amended March 2004), para. 25.
75 IAS 16, para. BC22.
76 IAS 16, para. 25.
77 IAS 16, para. BC23.
78 IAS 12, *Income Taxes*, IASB, October 1996 (amended March 2004), para. 43.
79 IAS 31, paras. 52-53
80 IAS 1, para. 81(c).
81 IAS 31, para. 56.
82 IAS 31, para. 57.
83 IAS 31, para. 54.
84 IAS 31, para. 55.
85 IAS 31, para. 58.
86 IFRS 1, para. B2(g)(iii).

Chapter 9   Foreign exchange

1   INTRODUCTION

1.1   Background

An entity can engage in foreign currency activities in two ways. It may enter directly into transactions which are denominated in foreign currencies, the results of which need to be translated into the currency in which the company measures its results and financial position. Alternatively, it may conduct foreign operations through a foreign entity, such as a subsidiary, associate or joint venture which keeps its accounting records in terms of its own currency. In this case it will need to translate the financial statements of the foreign entity for the purposes of inclusion in the consolidated financial statements.

Before an international standard was developed, there were four distinct methods which could be used in the translation process:

(a) *current rate method* – all assets and liabilities are translated at the current rate of exchange, i.e. the exchange rate at the balance sheet date;

(b) *temporal method* – assets and liabilities carried at current prices (e.g. cash, receivables, payables, and investments at market value) are translated at the current rate of exchange. Assets and liabilities carried at past prices (e.g. property, investments at cost, prepayments) are translated at the rate of exchange in effect at the dates to which the prices pertain;

(c) *current/non-current method* – all current assets and current liabilities are translated at the current rate of exchange. Non-current assets and liabilities are translated at historical rates, i.e. the exchange rate in effect at the time the asset was acquired or the liability incurred; and

(d) *monetary/non-monetary method* – monetary assets and liabilities, i.e. items which represent the right to receive or the obligation to pay a fixed amount of money, are translated at the current rate of exchange. Non-monetary assets and liabilities are translated at the historical rate.

There was no consensus internationally on the best theoretical approach to adopt. In essence, the arguments surround the choice of exchange rates to be used in the translation process and the subsequent treatment of the exchange differences which arise.

1.2   Development of an international standard

1.2.1   IAS 21

The principal international standard dealing with this topic is IAS 21 – *The Effects of Changes in Foreign Exchange Rates*. The original standard was issued by the IASC in July 1983. Equivalent standards in the UK, US and Canada had recently been issued following a long period of consultation between the ASC, the FASB and the CICA. The reason for the consultation was that it was considered that there was a need for international harmonisation in this field. The FASB had issued an earlier standard, SFAS 8,[1] in 1975 based on using the temporal method of translation. However, following the implementation of that standard it gradually became evident that when consolidated accounts are drawn up in a relatively weak currency, the temporal method produces results which do not seem to make commercial and economic sense. As a result the FASB decided to review SFAS 8. In Canada, the CICA, which had published its standard on foreign currencies in 1978,[2] advocating the use of the temporal method, suspended it in 1979 pending further study.

IAS 21 followed the same general approach as its international counterparts in that it was based on a closing rate/net investment concept and an approach to translation which is related to the cash flow consequences of exchange movements. Exchange differences which give rise to cash flows, i.e. those resulting from business transactions, were to be reported as part of the profit or loss for the period. Other exchange differences which do not give rise to cash flows, because they result from retranslations of the holding company's long-term investment in the foreign subsidiary, were reported as reserve movements.

The standard therefore required that the procedures to be adopted when accounting for foreign operations should be considered in two stages, namely the preparation of the financial statements of the individual company and the preparation of the consolidated financial statements. The method used to translate the financial statements of a foreign operation for inclusion in consolidated accounts depended on the way in which it was financed and operated in relation to the reporting entity. For this purpose, foreign operations were classified as either 'foreign entities' or 'foreign operations that are integral to the operations of the reporting enterprise'.[3] In the former case, the closing rate method of translation was used[4] and in the latter case the temporal method was used.[5] Although a revised version of IAS 21 was published in December 1993, it followed the same general approach as its predecessor.

IAS 21 has subsequently been revised as a result of the IASB's improvements project (see 1.2.3 below).

1.2.2 SIC pronouncements

The SIC issued four interpretations of IAS 21; SIC-7 – *Introduction of the Euro*, SIC-11 – *Foreign Exchange – Capitalisation of Losses Resulting from Severe Currency Devaluations*, SIC-19 – *Reporting Currency – Measurement and Presentation of Financial Statements under IAS 21 and IAS 29*, and SIC-30 – *Reporting Currency – Translation from Measurement Currency to Presentation Currency.*

SIC-7 deals with the application of IAS 21 to the changeover from the national currencies of participating Member States of the European Union to the euro and is covered at 3.5 below.

SIC-11 dealt with particular conditions that had to be met to allow exchange differences on liabilities that arose directly on the recent acquisition of an asset invoiced in a foreign currency to be included in the carrying amount of the related asset.[6] This has now been superseded as a result of the IASB's improvements project.

SIC-19 and SIC-30 dealt with issues that IAS 21 expressly stated that it did not deal with. IAS 21 used the term 'reporting currency' as being the currency used in presenting the financial statements of an entity. The standard did not specify the currency in which an entity presented its financial statements, although it noted that an entity would normally use the currency in which it was domiciled.[7] However, the choice of reporting currency established that all other currencies were treated as foreign currencies for the purposes of IAS 21 and therefore would affect the financial statements.

This was then considered by the SIC in SIC-19 which made a distinction between an entity's 'measurement currency', i.e. the currency for measuring items in its financial statements and its 'presentation currency', i.e. the currency used for presenting the financial statements. This effectively introduced the functional currency concept used in other countries national standards into IAS literature.

SIC-19 stated that the measurement currency should provide information about the entity that is useful and reflects the economic substance of the underlying events and circumstances relevant to that entity. If a particular currency is used to a significant extent in, or has a significant impact on, the entity, that currency may be an appropriate currency to be used as the measurement currency.[8]

Although an entity would normally present its financial statements in the same currency as the measurement currency, SIC-19 confirmed that it could choose to present its financial statements in a different currency, but gave no further guidance as to how this should be done. It merely stated that the translation method applied by an entity should not lead to reporting in a manner that is inconsistent with the measurement of items in the financial statements.[9]

This particular aspect was then addressed in SIC-30. It also dealt with what disclosures should be made in such circumstances as well as when an entity displays additional information in a currency as a convenience to certain users.

SIC-19 and SIC-30 have now been superseded since many of their requirements have now been incorporated in the revised version of IAS 21 issued by the IASB as part of its improvement project.

1.2.3   IAS 21 (Revised 2003)

In December 2003, the IASB issued a revised version of IAS 21 – *The Effects of Changes in Foreign Exchange Rates* to replace the earlier version issued by the IASC. The revised standard should be applied for annual periods beginning on or after 1 January 2005, although earlier application is encouraged. As indicated at 1.2.2 above, the standard also replaces SIC-11, SIC-19 and SIC-30.[10]

A   Reasons for revising IAS 21

The IASB developed this revised IAS 21 as part of its project on Improvements to International Accounting Standards. The project was undertaken in the light of queries and criticisms raised in relation to the standards by securities regulators, professional accountants and other interested parties. The objectives of the project were to reduce or eliminate alternatives, redundancies and conflicts within the standards, to deal with some convergence issues and to make other improvements.[11]

For IAS 21 the Board's main objective was to provide additional guidance on the translation method and on determining the functional and presentation currencies. The Board did not reconsider the fundamental approach to accounting for the effects of changes in foreign exchange rates contained in IAS 21.[12]

B   Main changes from the IASC's version of IAS 21

The main changes from the previous version of IAS 21 are set out below.

I   Scope

The standard excludes from its scope foreign currency derivatives that are within the scope of IAS 39 – *Financial Instruments: Recognition and Measurement.* Similarly, all material on hedge accounting has now been moved to IAS 39.[13]

II   Definitions

The notion of 'reporting currency' has been replaced with two notions:

- functional currency, i.e. the currency of the primary economic environment in which the entity operates. The term 'functional currency' is used in place of 'measurement currency' (the term used in SIC-19) because it is the more commonly used term, but with essentially the same meaning; and
- presentation currency, i.e. the currency in which financial statements are presented.[14]

III   *Functional currency*

When a reporting entity prepares financial statements, the standard requires each individual entity included in the reporting entity – whether it is a stand-alone entity, an entity with foreign operations (such as a parent) or a foreign operation (such as a subsidiary or branch) – to determine its functional currency and measure its results and financial position in that currency. The new material on functional currency incorporates some of the guidance previously included in SIC-19 on how to determine a measurement currency. However, the standard gives greater emphasis than SIC-19 gave to the currency of the economy that determines the pricing of transactions, as opposed to the currency in which transactions are denominated.[15]

As a result of these changes and the incorporation of guidance previously in SIC-19:

- an entity (whether a stand-alone entity or a foreign operation) does not have a free choice of functional currency,[16] although as discussed at 2.5 and 3.1 below the determination of the entity's functional currency will be based on management's judgement of all the circumstances; and

- an entity cannot avoid restatement in accordance with IAS 29 – *Financial Reporting in Hyperinflationary Economies* by, for example, adopting a stable currency (such as the functional currency of its parent) as its functional currency.[17]

The standard revises the requirements in the previous version of IAS 21 for distinguishing between foreign operations that are integral to the operations of the reporting entity (referred to below as 'integral foreign operations') and foreign entities. The requirements are now among the indicators of an entity's functional currency. As a result:

- there is no distinction between integral foreign operations and foreign entities. Rather, an entity that was previously classified as an integral foreign operation will have the same functional currency as the reporting entity; and

- only one translation method is used for foreign operations – namely that described in the previous version of IAS 21 as applying to foreign entities, i.e. the closing rate method.[18]

The standard replaces the previous requirement for accounting for a change in the classification of a foreign operation (which is now redundant) with a requirement that a change in functional currency is accounted for prospectively.[19]

IV   *Use of a presentation currency other than the functional currency – translation to the presentation currency*

The standard permits an entity to present its financial statements in any currency (or currencies).[20] An entity is required to translate its results and financial position from its functional currency into a presentation currency (or currencies) using the method required for translating a foreign operation for inclusion in the reporting entity's financial statements. Under this method, assets and liabilities are translated at the closing rate, and income and expenses are translated at the exchange rates at the dates of the transactions (or at the average rate for the period when this is a reasonable approximation).[21]

The translation of comparative amounts depends on whether or not the entity's functional currency is the currency of a hyperinflationary economy and, if it is, whether or not the comparative amounts are being translated into another hyperinflationary currency or not. This applies when translating the financial statements of a foreign operation for inclusion in the financial statements of the reporting entity, and when translating the financial statements of an entity into a different presentation currency.[22]

These requirements are based on those introduced by SIC-30 except for the translation of comparatives for an entity whose functional currency is the currency of a hyperinflationary economy, and which are being translated into a presentation currency of a nonhyperinflationary economy. In such a case, SIC-30 required the comparatives to be restated from those shown in the prior year financial statements for both the effects of inflation and for changes in exchange rates. Under IAS 21 no adjustment is made to the comparatives.[23]

V   *Goodwill and fair value adjustments*

The standard requires goodwill and fair value adjustments to assets and liabilities that arise on the acquisition of a foreign entity to be treated as part of the assets and liabilities of the acquired entity and translated at the closing rate.[24] The previous version allowed these items to be translated at historical rates.[25] For entities affected by this change in requirement, the transitional arrangements on implementation of the new standard are discussed at 4 below.

2   REQUIREMENTS OF IAS 21

IAS 21 is mandatory for annual periods beginning on or after 1 January 2005, although earlier application is encouraged. If an entity applies it for an earlier period, it shall disclose that fact.[26]

Apart from its requirements relating to goodwill and fair value adjustments, all changes resulting from the application of the standard shall be accounted for in accordance with the requirements of IAS 8 – *Accounting Policies, Changes in Accounting Estimates and Errors* (see Chapter 3 at 4.4),[27] i.e. by retrospective application of the new requirements. The transitional arrangements relating to goodwill and fair value adjustments for entities already reporting under IFRS, and the specific arrangements for first time adopters under IFRS 1, are discussed at 4 below.

2.1   Objective of the standard

As indicated at 1.1 above, an entity may carry on foreign activities in two ways. It may have transactions in foreign currencies or it may have foreign operations. In addition, an entity may present its financial statements in a foreign currency. IAS 21 does not set out what the objective of foreign currency translation should be, but just states that the objective of the standard is 'to prescribe how to include foreign currency transactions and foreign operations in the financial statements of an entity and how to translate financial statements into a presentation currency'.[28]

It also indicates that the principal issues to be addressed are 'which exchange rate(s) to use and how to report the effects of changes in exchange rates in the financial statements'.[29]

2.2 Scope

IAS 21 shall be applied:[30]

(a) in accounting for transactions and balances in foreign currencies, except for those derivative transactions and balances that are within the scope of IAS 39;

(b) in translating the results and financial position of foreign operations that are included in the financial statements of the entity by consolidation, proportionate consolidation or the equity method; and

(c) in translating an entity's results and financial position into a presentation currency.

The standard explains that IAS 39 applies to many foreign currency derivatives and, accordingly, these are excluded from the scope of this standard. However, it goes on to say that those foreign currency derivatives that are not within the scope of IAS 39 (e.g. some foreign currency derivatives that are embedded in other contracts) are within the scope of IAS 21. In addition, it also states that IAS 21 applies when an entity translates amounts relating to derivatives from its functional currency to its presentation currency.[31]

IAS 21 also does not apply to hedge accounting for foreign currency items, including the hedging of a net investment in a foreign operation.[32] This is dealt with in IAS 39, which has detailed rules on hedging (see Chapter 19).

The standard explains that its requirements are applicable to an entity's statements that are to be described as complying with International Financial Reporting Standards. They do not apply to translations of financial information into a foreign currency that do not meet these requirements, although the standard does specify information to be disclosed in respect of such 'convenience translations'.[33]

IAS 21 does not apply to the presentation in a cash flow statement of cash flows arising from transactions in a foreign currency, or to the translation of cash flows of a foreign operation.[34] These are dealt with in IAS 7 – *Cash Flow Statements* (see Chapter 32 at 2.5.2).

2.3 Definitions of terms

The definitions of terms which are contained in IAS 21 are as follows:[35]

Closing rate is the spot exchange rate at the balance sheet date.

Exchange difference is the difference resulting from translating a given number of units of one currency into another currency at different exchange rates.

Exchange rate is the ratio of exchange for two currencies.

Fair value is the amount for which an asset could be exchanged, or a liability settled, between knowledgeable, willing parties in an arm's length transaction.

Foreign currency is a currency other than the functional currency of the entity.

Foreign operation is an entity that is a subsidiary, associate, joint venture or branch of a reporting entity, the activities of which are based or conducted in a country or currency other than those of the reporting entity.

Functional currency is the currency of the primary economic environment in which the entity operates.

A *group* is a parent and all its subsidiaries.

Monetary items are units of currency held and assets and liabilities to be received or paid in a fixed or determinable number of units of currency.

Net investment in a foreign operation is the amount of the reporting entity's interest in the net assets of that operation.

Presentation currency is the currency in which the financial statements are presented.

Spot exchange rate is the exchange rate for immediate delivery.

The terms 'functional currency', 'monetary items' and 'net investment in a foreign operation' are elaborated on further within the standard. These are discussed at 2.5, 3.2.4 and 3.4.1 below.

2.4 Summary of the approach required by the standard

In preparing financial statements, each entity – whether a stand-alone entity, an entity with foreign operations (such as a parent) or a foreign operation (such as a subsidiary or branch) – determines its functional currency.[36] This is discussed at 2.5 below. In the case of group financial statements, it should be emphasised that there is not a 'group' functional currency; each entity included within the group financial statements, be it the parent, subsidiary, associate, joint venture or branch, has its own functional currency. Where an entity enters into a transaction denominated in a currency other than its functional currency, then it translates those foreign currency items into its functional currency and reports the effects of such translation in accordance with the provisions of IAS 21 discussed at 2.6 below.[37]

Many reporting entities comprise a number of individual entities (e.g. a group is made up of a parent and one or more subsidiaries). Various types of entities, whether members of a group or otherwise, may have investments in associates or joint ventures. They may also have branches. It is necessary for the results and financial position of each individual entity included in the reporting entity to be translated into the currency in which the reporting entity presents its financial statements (if this presentation currency is different from the individual entity's functional currency). The results and financial position of any individual entity within the reporting entity whose functional currency differs from the presentation currency are translated in accordance with the provisions of IAS 21 discussed at 2.7

below.[38] Since IAS 21 permits the presentation currency of a reporting entity to be any currency (or currencies), this translation process will also apply to the parent's figures if its functional currency is different from the presentation currency.

The standard also permits a stand-alone entity preparing financial statements or an entity preparing separate financial statements in accordance with IAS 27 – *Consolidated and Separate Financial Statements* – to present its financial statements in any currency (or currencies). If the entity's presentation currency differs from its functional currency, its results and financial position are also translated into the presentation currency in accordance with the provisions of IAS 21 discussed at 2.7 below.[39]

2.5   Determination of an entity's functional currency

As indicated at 2.3 above, functional currency is defined as the currency of 'the primary economic environment in which the entity operates'. This will normally be the one in which it primarily generates and expends cash.[40]

IAS 21 sets out a number of factors or indicators that any entity should or may need to consider in determining its functional currency. When the factors or indicators are mixed and the functional currency is not obvious, the standard requires management to use its judgement to determine the functional currency that most faithfully represents the economic effects of the underlying transactions, events and conditions. As part of this approach, management gives priority to the following primary indicators before considering the other indicators set out in the standard, which are designed to provide additional supporting evidence to determine an entity's functional currency.[41]

The primary factors that IAS 21 requires an entity to consider in determining its functional currency are as follows:[42]

(a)   the currency:

    (i)   that mainly influences sales prices for goods and services (this will often be the currency in which sales prices for its goods and services are denominated and settled); and

    (ii)   of the country whose competitive forces and regulations mainly determine the sales prices of its goods and services;

(b)   the currency that mainly influences labour, material and other costs of providing goods or services (this will often be the currency in which such costs are denominated and settled).

Where the functional currency of the entity is not obvious from the above, then the standard indicates that the following factors may also provide evidence of an entity's functional currency:[43]

(a)   the currency in which funds from financing activities (i.e. issuing debt and equity instruments) are generated;

(b)   the currency in which receipts from operating activities are usually retained.

The standard also says that the following additional factors are considered in determining the functional currency of a foreign operation, and whether its functional currency is the same as that of the reporting entity (the reporting entity, in this context, being the entity that has the foreign operation as its subsidiary, branch, associate or joint venture):[44]

(a) whether the activities of the foreign operation are carried out as an extension of the reporting entity, rather than being carried out with a significant degree of autonomy. An example of the former is when the foreign operation only sells goods imported from the reporting entity and remits the proceeds to it. An example of the latter is when the operation accumulates cash and other monetary items, incurs expenses, generates income and arranges borrowings, all substantially in its local currency;

(b) whether transactions with the reporting entity are a high or a low proportion of the foreign operation's activities;

(c) whether cash flows from the activities of the foreign operation directly affect the cash flows of the reporting entity and are readily available for remittance to it;

(d) whether cash flows from the activities of the foreign operation are sufficient to service existing and normally expected debt obligations without funds being made available by the reporting entity.

Although the standard says that these factors 'are' considered in determining the functional currency of a foreign operation, this contradicts the requirement in the standard that management gives priority to the primary indicators before considering the other indicators. If it is obvious from the primary indicators what the entity's functional currency is, then there is no need to consider any of the other factors.

Since an entity's functional currency reflects the underlying transactions, events and conditions that are relevant to it, once it is determined, IAS 21 requires that the functional currency is not changed unless there is a change in those underlying transactions, events and conditions.[45] The implication of this is that management of an entity cannot decree what the functional currency is – it is a matter of fact, albeit subjectively determined fact based on management's judgement of all the circumstances.

2.6 Reporting foreign currency transactions in the functional currency of an entity

As indicated at 1.1 above, an entity may carry on foreign activities in two ways. It may have transactions in foreign currencies or it may have foreign operations. Where an entity enters into a transaction denominated in a currency other than its functional currency then it will have to translate those foreign currency items into its functional currency and report the effects of such translation.

The general requirements of IAS 21 are as follows.

2.6.1   Initial recognition

A foreign currency transaction is a transaction that is denominated or requires settlement in a foreign currency, including transactions arising when an entity:[46]

(a)   buys or sells goods or services whose price is denominated in a foreign currency;

(b)   borrows or lends funds when the amounts payable or receivable are denominated in a foreign currency; or

(c)   otherwise acquires or disposes of assets, or incurs or settles liabilities, denominated in a foreign currency.

On initial recognition, foreign currency transactions shall be translated into the functional currency using the exchange rate between the foreign currency and the functional currency on the date of the transaction.[47] The date of a transaction is the date on which it first qualifies for recognition in accordance with IFRS. For convenience, an average rate for a week or month may be used for all foreign currency transactions occurring during that period, if the exchange rate does not fluctuate significantly.[48]

2.6.2   Reporting at subsequent balance sheet dates

At each balance sheet date:[49]

(a)   foreign currency monetary items shall be translated using the closing rate;

(b)   non-monetary items that are measured at historical cost denominated in a foreign currency shall be translated using the historical exchange rate; and

(c)   non-monetary items that are measured at fair value in a foreign currency shall be translated using the exchange rate as at the date that the fair value was determined.

2.6.3   Treatment of exchange differences

A   Monetary items

The general rule in IAS 21 is that exchange differences on the settlement or retranslation of monetary items shall be recognised in profit or loss in the period in which they arise.[50]

As the standard explains 'when monetary items arise from a foreign currency transaction and there is a change in the exchange rate between the transaction date and the date of settlement, an exchange difference results. When the transaction is settled within the same accounting period as that in which it occurred, all the exchange difference is recognised in that period. However, when the transaction is settled in a subsequent accounting period, the exchange difference recognised in each period up to the date of settlement is determined by the change in exchange rates during each period.'[51]

The above general requirements can be illustrated in the following examples:

Example 9.1:   Reporting a foreign currency transaction in the functional currency

A French entity purchases plant and equipment on credit from a Canadian supplier for C$328,000 in January 2006 when the exchange rate is €1=C$1.64. The entity records the asset at a cost of €200,000. At the French entity's year end at 31 March 2006 the account has not yet been settled. The closing rate is €1=C$1.61. The amount payable would be retranslated at €203,727 in the balance sheet and an exchange loss of €3,727 would be reported as part of the profit or loss for the period. The cost of the asset would remain as €200,000.

Example 9.2:   Reporting a foreign currency transaction in the functional currency

A UK entity sells goods to a German entity for €87,000 on 28 February 2005 when the exchange rate is £1=€1.45. It receives payment on 31 March 2005 when the exchange rate is £1=€1.50. On 28 February the UK entity will record a sale and corresponding receivable of £60,000. When payment is received on 31 March the actual amount received is only £58,000. The loss on exchange of £2,000 would be reported as part of the profit or loss for the period.

IAS 21 does not specify where any exchange differences on monetary items should be presented in the income statement. As indicated at 2.9.1 below, we recommend that entities in disclosing the amount of such exchange differences should indicate the line item(s) in which they are included.

However, there are situations where this will not be the case. The first exception to the general rule identified in IAS 21 relates to exchange differences arising on a monetary item that, in substance, forms part of an entity's net investment in a foreign operation (see 3.4.1 below). In this situation the exchange differences shall be recognised initially in a separate component of equity until the disposal of the investment (see 2.7.3 below). However, this treatment only applies in the financial statements that include the foreign operation and the reporting entity (i.e. financial statements in which the foreign operation is consolidated, proportionately consolidated or accounted for using the equity method). It does not apply to the reporting entity's separate financial statements or the financial statements of the foreign operation; the exchange differences will be recognised in profit or loss in the period in which they arise in the financial statements of the entity that has the foreign currency exposure.[52] This is discussed further at 3.4.1 below.

The next exception relates to hedge accounting. As noted at 2.2 above, IAS 39 applies to hedge accounting for foreign currency items. The application of hedge accounting requires an entity to account for some exchange differences differently from the treatment of exchange differences required by IAS 21. For example, IAS 39 requires that exchange differences on monetary items that qualify as hedging instruments in a cash flow hedge or a hedge of a net investment in a foreign operation are reported initially in equity to the extent the hedge is effective (see Chapter 19).

Although the general rule in IAS 21 suggests that all exchange differences on monetary items should be taken to the income statement (other than the specific exclusions discussed above), IAS 23 – *Borrowing Costs* – allows exchange differences arising from foreign currency borrowings to be capitalised, but only to the extent that they are regarded as an adjustment to interest costs (see Chapter 14).[53]

B   Non-monetary items

When non-monetary items that are measured at fair value in a foreign currency are translated using the exchange rate as at the date that the fair value was determined, any gain or loss will include an element relating to the change on exchange rates. In this situation, the exchange differences are recognised as part of the gain or loss arising on the fair value re-measurement.

When a gain or loss on a non-monetary item is recognised directly in equity, any exchange component of that gain or loss shall be recognised directly in equity.[54] For example, IAS 16 – *Property, Plant and Equipment* – requires some gains and losses arising on a revaluation of property, plant and equipment to be recognised directly in equity (see Chapter 12 at 2.4.1). When such an asset is measured in a foreign currency, the revalued amount has to be translated using the rate at the date the value is determined, resulting in an exchange difference that is also recognised in equity.[55]

Conversely, when a gain or loss on a non-monetary item is recognised in profit or loss, any exchange component of that gain or loss shall be recognised in profit or loss.[56] For example, financial instruments that are measured at fair value through profit or loss in accordance with IAS 39 (see Chapter 18 at 3.2).

2.6.4   Change in functional currency

As indicated at 2.5 above, IAS 21 requires management to use its judgment to determine the entity's functional currency such that it most faithfully represents the economic effects of the underlying transactions, events and conditions that are relevant to the entity. Accordingly, once the functional currency is determined, the standard only allows it to be changed if there is a change to those underlying transactions, events and conditions. For example, a change in the currency that mainly influences the sales prices of goods and services may lead to a change in an entity's functional currency.[57]

When there is a change in an entity's functional currency, the entity shall apply the translation procedures applicable to the new functional currency prospectively from the date of the change.[58]

In other words, an entity translates all items into the new functional currency using the exchange rate at the date of the change. The resulting translated amounts for non-monetary items are treated as their historical cost. Exchange differences arising from the translation of a foreign operation previously classified in equity are not recognised in profit or loss until the disposal of the operation (see 2.7.3 below).[59]

Example 9.3:   Change in functional currency

The management of Entity A has considered the functional currency of the entity to be the euro. However, as a result of change in circumstances affecting the operations of the entity, management determines that on 1 January 2005 the functional currency of the entity is now the US dollar. The exchange rate at that date is €1=US$1.20. The balance sheet of Entity A at 1 January 2005 in its old functional currency is as follows:

	€
Property, plant and equipment	200,000
Current assets	
Inventories	10,000
Receivables	20,000
Cash	5,000
	35,000
Current liabilities	
Payables	15,000
Taxation	3,000
	18,000
Net current assets	17,000
	217,000
Long-term loans	120,000
	97,000
Share capital	50,000
Retained profits	47,000
	97,000

Included within the balance sheet at 1 January 2005 are the following items:

- Equipment with a cost of €33,000 and a net book value of €16,500. This equipment was originally purchased for £20,000 in 2001 and has been translated at the rate ruling at the date of purchase of £1=€1.65.
- Inventories with a cost of €6,000. These were purchased for US$6,000 and have been translated at the rate ruling at the date of purchase of €1=US$1.00.
- Payables of €5,000 representing the US$6,000 due in respect of the above inventories, translated at the rate ruling at 1 January 2005.
- Long-term loans of €15,000 representing the outstanding balance of £10,000 on a loan originally taken out to finance the acquisition of the above equipment, translated at £1=€1.50, the rate ruling at 1 January 2005.

Entity A applies the translational procedures applicable to its new functional currency prospectively from the date of change. Accordingly, all items in its balance sheet at 1 January 2005 are translated at the rate of €1=US$1.20 giving rise to the following amounts:

	$
Property, plant and equipment	240,000
Current assets	
Inventories	12,000
Receivables	24,000
Cash	6,000
	42,000
Current liabilities	
Payables	18,000
Taxation	3,600
	21,600
Net current assets	20,400
	260,400
Long-term loans	144,000
	116,400
Share capital	60,000
Retained profits	56,400
	116,400

As far as the equipment that was originally purchased for £20,000 is concerned, the cost and net book value in terms of Entity A's new functional currency are US$39,600 and US$19,800 respectively, being €33,000 and €16,500 translated at €1=US$1.20. Entity A does not go back and translate the £20,000 cost at whatever the £ sterling/US dollar exchange rate was at the date of purchase and calculate a revised net book value on that basis.

Similarly, the inventories purchased in US dollars are included at $7,200, being €6,000 translated at €1=US$1.20. This is despite the fact that Entity A knows that the original cost was $6,000.

As far as the payables in respect of the inventories are concerned, these are included at $6,000, being €5,000 translated at €1=US$1.20. This represents the original amount payable in US dollars. However, this is as it should be since the original payable had been translated into euros at the rate ruling at 1 January 2005 and has just been translated back into US dollars at the same rate. The impact of the change in functional currency is that whereas Entity A had recorded an exchange gain of €1,000 while the functional currency was the euro, no further exchange difference will be recorded in respect of this amount payable. Exchange differences will now arise from 1 January 2005 on those payables denominated in euros, whereas no such differences would have arisen on such items prior to that date.

Similarly, the £10,000 amount outstanding on the loan will be included at $18,000, being €15,000 translated at €1=US$1.20. This is equivalent to the translation of the £10,000 at a rate of £1=US$1.80, being the direct exchange rate between the two currencies at 1 January 2005. In this case, whereas previously exchange gains and losses would have been recognised on this loan balance based on movements of the £/€ exchange rate, as from 1 January 2005 the exchange gains and losses will be recognised based on the £/$ exchange rate.

2.7 Use of a presentation currency other than the functional currency

As indicated at 2.4 above, an entity may present its financial statements in any currency (or currencies). If the presentation currency differs from the entity's functional currency, it needs to translate its results and financial position into the presentation currency. For example, when a group contains individual entities with different functional currencies, the results and financial position of each entity are expressed in a common currency so that consolidated financial statements may be presented.[60]

The requirements of IAS 21 in respect of this translation process are discussed below. The procedures to be adopted apply not only to the inclusion of foreign subsidiaries in consolidated financial statements but also to the incorporation of the results of associates and joint ventures.[61] They also apply when the results of a foreign branch are to be incorporated into the financial statements of an individual entity or a stand-alone entity preparing financial statements or when an entity preparing separate financial statements in accordance with IAS 27 presents its financial statements in a currency other than its functional currency.

2.7.1   Translation to the presentation currency

Under IAS 21, the method of translation depends on whether the entity's functional currency is that of a hyperinflationary economy or not, and if it is, whether it is being translated into a presentation currency which is that of a hyperinflationary economy or not. A hyperinflationary economy is defined in IAS 29 (see Chapter 10 at 2.3.1). The requirements of IAS 21 discussed below can be summarised as follows:

	Presentation currency	
	Non–hyperinflationary	**Hyperinflationary**
Non-hyperinflationary functional currency		
Assets/liabilities		
– current period	Closing rate (current B/S date)	Closing rate (current B/S date)
– comparative period	Closing rate (comparative B/S date)	Closing rate (comparative B/S date)
Equity items		
– current period	Not specified	Not specified
– comparative period	Not specified	Not specified
Income/expenses (including those recognised directly in equity)		
– current period	Actual rates (or appropriate average for current period)	Actual rates (or appropriate average for current period)
– comparative period	Actual rates (or appropriate average for comparative period)	Actual rates (or appropriate average for comparative period)
Exchange differences	Separate component of equity	Separate component of equity
Hyperinflationary functional currency		
Assets/liabilities		
– current period	Closing rate (current B/S date)	Closing rate (current B/S date)
– comparative period	Closing rate (comparative B/S date)	Closing rate (current B/S date)
Equity items		
– current period	Closing rate (current B/S date)	Closing rate (current B/S date)
– comparative period	Closing rate (comparative B/S date)	Closing rate (current B/S date)
Income/expenses (including those recognised directly in equity)		
– current period	Closing rate (current B/S date)	Closing rate (current B/S date)
– comparative period	Closing rate (comparative B/S date)	Closing rate (current B/S date)
Exchange differences	Not specified	Not applicable

A   *Functional currency is not that of a hyperinflationary economy*

The results and financial position of an entity whose functional currency is not the currency of a hyperinflationary economy shall be translated into a different presentation currency using the following procedures:[62]

(a)   assets and liabilities for each balance sheet presented (i.e. including comparatives) shall be translated at the closing rate at the date of that balance sheet;

(b)   income and expenses for each income statement (i.e. including comparatives) shall be translated at exchange rates at the dates of the transactions; and

(c)   all resulting exchange differences shall be recognised as a separate component of equity.

For practical reasons, the reporting entity may use a rate that approximates the actual exchange rate, e.g. an average rate for the period, to translate income and expense items. However, if exchange rates fluctuate significantly, the use of the average rate for a period is inappropriate.[63]

The translational process above makes no reference to the translation of equity items. The treatment of such items is discussed at 3.3.3 below.

IAS 21 indicates that the exchange differences referred to in item (c) above result from:[64]

• translating income and expenses at the exchange rates at the dates of the transactions and assets and liabilities at the closing rate. Such exchange differences arise both on income and expense items recognised in profit or loss and on those recognised directly in equity; and

• translating the opening net assets at a closing rate that differs from the previous closing rate.

This is not in fact completely accurate since if the entity has had any transactions with equity holders that have resulted in a change in the net assets during the period there are likely to be further exchange differences that need to be recognised to the extent that the closing rate differs from the rate used to translate the transaction. This will particularly be the case where a parent has subscribed for further equity shares in a subsidiary.

The reason why these exchange differences are not recognised in profit or loss is because the changes in exchange rates have little or no direct effect on the present and future cash flows from operations.[65]

The application of these procedures is illustrated in the following example.

Example 9.4: *Translation of a non-hyperinflationary functional currency to a non-hyperinflationary presentation currency*

An Australian entity owns 100% of the share capital of a foreign entity which was set up a number of years ago when the exchange rate was A$1=FC2. It is consolidating the financial statements of the subsidiary in its consolidated financial statements for the year ended 31 December 2005. The exchange rate at the year-end is A$1=FC4 (2004: A$1=FC3). For the purposes of illustration, it is assumed that exchange rates have not fluctuated significantly and the appropriate weighted average rate for the year was A$1=FC3.5, and that the currency of the foreign entity is not that of a hyperinflationary economy. The income statement of the subsidiary for that year and its balance sheet at the beginning and end of the year in its functional currency and translated into Australian dollars are as follows:

Income statement

	FC	A$
Sales	35,000	10,000
Cost of sales	(33,190)	(9,483)
Depreciation	(500)	(143)
Interest	(350)	(100)
Profit before taxation	960	274
Taxation	(460)	(131)
Profit after taxation	500	143

Balance sheets	2004 FC	2005 FC	2004 A$	2005 A$
Property, plant and equipment	6,000	5,500	2,000	1,375
Current assets				
Inventories	2,700	3,000	900	750
Receivables	4,800	4,000	1,600	1,000
Cash	200	600	67	150
	7,700	7,600	2,567	1,900
Current liabilities				
Payables	4,530	3,840	1,510	960
Taxation	870	460	290	115
	5,400	4,300	1,800	1,075
Net current assets	2,300	3,300	767	825
	8,300	8,800	2,767	2,200
Long-term loans	3,600	3,600	1,200	900
	4,700	5,200	1,567	1,300
Share capital	1,000	1,000	500	500
Retained profits*	3,700	4,200	1,500	1,643
Exchange reserve*			(433)	(843)
	4,700	5,200	1,567	2,600

* The opening balances for 2004 in A$ have been assumed and represent cumulative amounts since the foreign entity was set up.

The movement of A$(410) in the exchange reserve included as a separate component of equity is made up as follows:

(i) the exchange loss of A$392 on the opening net investment in the subsidiary, calculated as follows:

Opening net assets at opening rate	– FC4,700 at FC3=A$1 =	A$1,567
Opening net assets at closing rate	– FC4,700 at FC4=A$1 =	A$1,175
Exchange loss on net assets		A$392

(ii) the exchange loss of A$18, being the difference between the income account translated at an average rate, i.e. £143, and at the closing rate, i.e. £125.

When the exchange differences relate to a foreign operation that is consolidated but not wholly-owned, accumulated exchange differences arising from translation and attributable to minority interests are allocated to, and recognised as part of, minority interest in the consolidated balance sheet.[66]

The IASB had considered an alternative translation method, which would have been to translate all amounts (including comparatives) at the most recent closing rate. This was considered to have several advantages: it is simple to apply; it doesn't generate any new gains and losses; and it does not change ratios such as return on assets. Supporters of this method believed that the process of merely expressing amounts in a different currency should preserve the same relationships among amounts as measured in the functional currency.[67] These views were probably based more on the IASB's proposals for allowing an entity to present its financial statements in a currency other than its functional currency, rather than the translation of foreign operations for inclusion in consolidated financial statements. Such an approach does have theoretical appeal. However, the major drawback is that it would require the comparatives to be restated from those previously reported.

The IASB rejected this alternative and decided to require the method that the previous version of IAS 21 required for translation the financial statements of a foreign operation.[68] It is asserted that this method results in the same amounts in the presentation currency regardless of whether the financial statements of a foreign operation are first translated into the functional currency of another group entity and then into the presentation currency or translated directly into the presentation currency.[69] We agree that it will result in the same amounts for the balance sheet, regardless of whether the translation process is a single or two-stage process. However, it does not necessarily hold true for income and expense items particularly if an average rate is used, although any difference is likely to be insignificant.

The IASB states that the method chosen avoids the need to decide the currency in which to express the financial statements of a multinational group before they are translated into the presentation currency. In addition, it produces the same amounts in the presentation currency for a stand-alone entity as for an identical subsidiary of a parent whose functional currency is the presentation currency.[70] For example, if a Swiss entity with the Swiss franc as its functional currency wishes to present its financial statements in euros, the translated amounts in euros should be the same as those for an identical entity with the Swiss franc as its functional currency that are included within the consolidated financial statements of its parent that presents its financial statements in euros.

B   *Functional currency is that of a hyperinflationary economy*

The results and financial position of an entity whose functional currency is the currency of a hyperinflationary economy shall be translated into a different presentation currency using the following procedures:[71]

(a)   all amounts (i.e. assets, liabilities, equity items, income and expenses, including comparatives) shall be translated at the closing rate at the date of the most recent balance sheet, except that

(b)   when amounts are translated into the currency of a non-hyperinflationary economy, comparative amounts shall be those that were presented as current year amounts in the relevant prior year financial statements (i.e. not adjusted for subsequent changes in the price level or subsequent changes in exchange rates).

When an entity's functional currency is the currency of a hyperinflationary economy, the entity shall restate its financial statements in accordance with IAS 29 before applying the translation method set out above, except for comparative amounts that are translated into a currency of a non-hyperinflationary economy (see (b) above).[72]

When the economy ceases to be hyperinflationary and the entity no longer restates its financial statements in accordance with IAS 29, it shall use as the historical costs for translation into the presentation currency the amounts restated to the price level at the date the entity ceased restating its financial statements.[73]

Example 9.5:   Translation of a hyperinflationary functional currency to a non-hyperinflationary presentation currency

Using the same basic facts as Example 9.4 above, but assuming that the functional currency of the subsidiary is that of a hyperinflationary economy, the income account of the subsidiary for that year and its balance sheet at the beginning and end of the year in its functional currency and translated into Australian dollars are as shown below. For the purposes of illustration, any adjustments resulting from the restatement in accordance with IAS 29 have been ignored. See Chapter 10 for a discussion of such adjustments.

Income statement

	FC	A$		
Sales	35,000	8,750		
Cost of sales	(33,190)	(8,298)		
Depreciation	(500)	(125)		
Interest	(350)	(75)		
Profit before taxation	960	240		
Taxation	(460)	(115)		
Profit after taxation	500	125		

Balance sheets	2004 FC	2005 FC	2004 A$	2005 A$
Property, plant and equipment	6,000	5,500	2,000	1,375
Current assets				
Inventories	2,700	3,000	900	750
Receivables	4,800	4,000	1,600	1,000
Cash	200	600	67	150
	7,700	7,600	2,567	1,900
Current liabilities				
Payables	4,530	3,840	1,510	960
Taxation	870	460	290	115
	5,400	4,300	1,800	1,075
Net current assets	2,300	3,300	767	825
	8,300	8,800	2,767	2,200
Long-term loans	3,600	3,600	1,200	900
	4,700	5,200	1,567	1,300

Share capital	1,000	1,000	333	250
Retained profits*	3,700	4,200	1,234	1,050
	4,700	5,200	1,567	1,300

The movement in retained profits is as follows:

	A$
Balance brought forward	1,234
Profit for year	125
Exchange difference	(309)
	1,050

The exchange loss of A$309 represents the reduction in retained profits due the movements in exchange, calculated as follows:

Opening balance at opening rate	– FC3,700 at FC3=A$1 =	A$1,234
Opening balance at closing rate	– FC3,700 at FC4=A$1 =	A$925
Exchange loss		A$(309)

It is unclear what should happen to such an exchange difference (and also the movement in share capital caused by the change in exchange rates) since paragraph 42 of IAS 21 makes no reference any possible exchange differences arising from this process. However, in the absence of any requirement to take them to a separate component of equity (as in Example 9.4 above) or to the income statement, it would seem that they are to be included as movements in the equity balances to which they relate.

2.7.2 Translation of a foreign operation

In addition to the procedures discussed at 2.7.1 above, IAS 21 has additional provisions that apply when the results and financial position of a foreign operation are translated into a presentation currency so that the foreign operation can be included in the financial statements of the reporting entity by consolidation, proportionate consolidation or the equity method.[74]

A   Exchange differences on intragroup balances

The standard states that 'the incorporation of the results and financial position of a foreign operation with those of the reporting entity follows normal consolidation procedures, such as the elimination of intragroup balances and intragroup transactions of a subsidiary'.[75] However, an intragroup monetary asset (or liability), whether short-term or long-term, cannot be eliminated against the corresponding intragroup liability (or asset) without the entity with the currency exposure recognising an exchange difference on the intragroup balance. As indicated at 2.6.3 A above this will be reflected in that entity's profit or loss for the period. Except as indicated below, IAS 21 requires this exchange difference to continue to be included in profit or loss in the consolidated financial statements. This is because the monetary item represents a commitment to convert one currency into another and exposes the reporting entity to a gain or loss through currency fluctuations. However, where the exchange difference arises on an intragroup balance that, in substance, forms part of an entity's net investment in a foreign operation (see 3.4.1 below), then the exchange difference is not to be taken to profit or loss in the consolidated financial statements, but is classified as equity until the disposal of the foreign operation (see 2.7.3 below).[76]

B   *Non-coterminous period ends*

IAS 21 recognises that in preparing consolidated financial statements it may be that a foreign operation is consolidated on the basis of financial statements made up to a different date from that of the reporting entity (see Chapter 5 at 6.4). In such a case, the standard initially states that the assets and liabilities of the foreign operation are to be translated at the exchange rate at the balance sheet date of the foreign operation rather than that at the date of the consolidated financial statements. However, it then goes on to say that adjustments are made for significant changes in exchange rates up to the balance sheet date of the reporting entity in accordance with IAS 27. The same approach is used in applying the equity method to associates and joint ventures and in applying proportionate consolidation to joint ventures in accordance with IAS 28 and IAS 31 (see Chapters 7 and 8 respectively).[77]

The rationale for this approach is not explained in IAS 21. The initial treatment is that required by SFAS 52 and the reason given in that standard is that this presents the functional currency performance of the subsidiary during the subsidiary's financial year and its position at the end of that period in terms of the parent company's reporting (presentation) currency.[78] The subsidiary may have entered into transactions in other currencies, including the functional currency of the parent, and monetary items in these currencies will have been translated using rates ruling at the subsidiary's balance sheet date. The income statement of the subsidiary will reflect the economic consequences of carrying out these transactions during the period ended on that date. In order that the effects of these transactions in the subsidiary's financial statements are not distorted, the financial statements should be translated using the closing rate at the subsidiary's balance sheet date.

However, an alternative argument could be advanced for using the closing rate ruling at the parent's balance sheet date. All subsidiaries within a group should normally prepare financial statements up to the same date as the parent entity so that the parent can prepare consolidated financial statements that present fairly the financial performance and financial position about the group as that of a single entity. The use of financial statements of a subsidiary made up to a date earlier than that of the parent is only an administrative convenience and a surrogate for financial statements made up to the proper date. Arguably, therefore the closing rate that should be used is that which would have been used if the financial statements were made up to the proper date, i.e. that ruling at the date of the balance sheet date of the parent. Another reason for using this rate is that there may be subsidiaries that have the same functional currency as the subsidiary with the non-coterminous year end that do make up their financial statements to the same date as the parent company and therefore in order to be consistent with them the same rate should be used.

C   Goodwill and fair value adjustments

As indicated at 1.2.3 B above, the previous version of IAS 21 allowed these items to be translated at historical rates.[79] In revising the standard, the IASB decided that the treatment of such items depends on whether they are part of:[80]

(a)   the assets and liabilities of the acquired entity (which would imply translating them at the closing rate); or

(b)   the assets and liabilities of the parent (which would imply translating them at the historical rate).

In the case of fair value adjustments these clearly relate to the acquired entity. However, in the case of goodwill there were different views expressed by commentators.

Example 9.6:   Translation of goodwill

A UK company acquires all of the share capital of an Australian company on 30 June 2005 at a cost of A$3m. The fair value of the net assets of the Australian company at that date was A$2.1m. In the consolidated financial statements at 31 December 2005 the goodwill is recognised as an asset in accordance with IFRS 3. The relevant exchange rates at 30 June 2005 and 31 December 2005 are £1=A$2.61 and £1=A$2.43 respectively. At what amount should the goodwill on consolidation be included in the balance sheet?

	A$	(i) £	(ii) £
Goodwill	900,000	344,828	370,370

(i)   This method regards goodwill as being an asset of the parent and therefore translated at the historical rate. Supporters of this view believe that, in economic terms, the goodwill is an asset of the parent because it is part of the acquisition price paid by the parent, particularly in situations where the parent acquires a multinational operation comprising businesses with many different functional currencies.[81]

(ii)   This method regards goodwill as being part of the parent's net investment in the acquired entity and therefore translated at the closing rate. Supporters of this view believe that goodwill should be treated no differently from other assets of the acquired entity, in particular intangible assets, because a significant part of the goodwill is likely to comprise intangible assets that do not qualify for separate recognition; the goodwill arises only because of the investment in the foreign entity and has no existence apart from that entity; and the cash flows that support the continued recognition of the goodwill are generated in the entity's functional currency.[82]

The IASB was persuaded by the arguments set out in (ii) above.[83] Accordingly, IAS 21 requires that any goodwill arising on the acquisition of a foreign operation and any fair value adjustments to the carrying amounts of assets and liabilities arising on the acquisition of that foreign operation shall be treated as assets and liabilities of the foreign operation. Thus they shall be expressed in the functional currency of the foreign operation and shall be translated at the closing rate in accordance with the requirements discussed at 2.7.1 above.[84] For entities affected by this change in requirement, the transitional arrangements on implementation of the new standard are discussed at 4 below.

2.7.3   Disposal of a foreign operation

As discussed at 2.7.1 above, all resulting exchange differences on the translation of a foreign operation to a different presentation currency are to be recognised within a separate component of equity.

On the disposal of a foreign operation, IAS 21 requires that the cumulative amount of the exchange differences deferred in the separate component of equity relating to that foreign operation shall be recognised in profit or loss when the gain or loss on disposal is recognised.[85] As indicated at 2.7.2 A above, these will include exchange differences arising on an intragroup balance that, in substance, forms part of an entity's net investment in a foreign operation.

Example 9.7:   Disposal of a foreign operation

A German entity has a Swiss subsidiary which was set up on 1 January 2002 with a share capital of CHF200,000 when the exchange rate was €1=CHF1.55. The subsidiary is included at its original cost of €129,032. The profits of the subsidiary, all of which have been retained by the subsidiary, for each of the three years ended 31 December 2004 were CHF40,000, CHF50,000 and CHF60,000 respectively, so that the net assets at 31 December 2004 are CHF350,000. In the consolidated financial statements the results of the subsidiary have been translated at the respective average rates of €1=CHF1.60, €1=CHF1.68 and €1=CHF1.70 and the net assets at the respective closing rates of €1=CHF1.71, €1=CHF1.65 and €1=CHF1.66. All exchange differences have been taken to a separate exchange reserve. The consolidated reserves have therefore included the following amounts in respect of the subsidiary:

	Retained profit €	Exchange reserve €
1 January 2002	–	–
Movement during 2002	25,000	(13,681)
31 December 2002	25,000	(13,681)
Movement during 2003	29,762	5,645
31 December 2003	54,762	(8,036)
Movement during 2004	35,294	(209)
31 December 2004	90,056	(8,245)

The net assets at 31 December 2004 of CHF350,000 are included in the consolidated financial statements at €210,843.

On 1 January 2005 the subsidiary is sold for CHF400,000 (€240,964), thus resulting in a gain on disposal in the parent entity's books of €111,932, i.e. €240,964 less €129,032.

In the consolidated financial statements for 2005, IAS 21 requires the cumulative exchange losses of €8,245 to be recognised in the profit or loss for that year. Indeed, IAS 27 requires them to be included as part of the gain on disposal which is reduced to €21,876, being €30,121 (the difference between the proceeds of €240,964 and net asset value of €210,843 at the date of disposal) together with the cumulative exchange losses of €8,245.[86]

This gain on disposal of €21,876 represents the parent's profit of €111,932 less the cumulative profits already taken in the group income statement of €90,056.

The treatment in IAS 21 is to be adopted not only when an entity sells an interest in a foreign entity, but also when it disposes of its interest through liquidation, repayment of share capital, or abandonment of that entity. It also applies for partial disposals, in which case, only the proportionate share of the related accumulated exchange differences is included in the gain or loss. The payment of a dividend, however, is part of a disposal only when it constitutes a return of the investment, e.g. when the dividend is paid out of pre-acquisition profits. A write-down of the carrying amount of a foreign operation does not constitute a partial disposal, therefore no deferred exchange difference should be recognised in income at the time of the write-down.[87] Similarly, it is implicit in the requirement of IFRS 5 for separate disclosure of cumulative gains and losses recognised in equity relating to a disposal group (see Chapter 3 at 3.1.2) that the classification of a foreign operation as held for sale under IFRS 5 does not give rise to recycling of foreign exchange differences at that time.

In our view, the requirement to recycle such exchange differences applies not only on the disposal of a direct interest in a foreign operation, but also on the disposal of an indirect interest. For example, on the disposal of a US subsidiary by a US intermediate holding company within a group headed by a UK parent, any exchange differences deferred in the separate component of equity relating to the US subsidiary should be recognised in profit or loss on its disposal.

It should be noted, however, that the IASB may be proposing changes in this area as part of Phase II of its business combinations project. It has tentatively agreed to amend IAS 21 so as to require that any foreign exchange differences previously recognised in equity should be 'recycled' on a loss of control of a subsidiary, even if the reporting entity still has an investment in its former subsidiary (including an investment accounted for as an associate or joint venture). The IASB notes that 'this is the only approach that is consistent with the Board's previous conclusion that any remaining investment should be recognised at its fair value when control of the former subsidiary is lost'.

The Board has also decided that IAS 21 should be amended to require that on a loss of significant influence over an associate, or joint control over a joint venture, the investor should recognise in profit or loss the entire amount of accumulated foreign exchange differences that relate to the investment in that foreign operation, even if the investor retains an investment in the former investee.[88]

2.8 Tax effects of all exchange differences

IAS 21 merely states that 'gains and losses on foreign currency transactions and exchange differences arising on translating the results and financial position of an entity (including a foreign operation) into a different currency may have tax effects' and that IAS 12 – *Income Taxes* – applies to these tax effects.[89] The requirements of IAS 12 are discussed in Chapter 24.

2.9   Disclosure requirements

2.9.1   *Exchange differences*

IAS 21 requires the amount of exchange differences recognised in profit or loss (except for those arising on financial instruments measured at fair value through profit or loss in accordance with IAS 39) to be disclosed.[90] Since IAS 21 does not specify where such exchange differences are presented in the income statement, we recommend that entities in disclosing the amount of such exchange differences indicate the line item(s) in which they are included.

The standard also requires the net exchange differences classified in a separate component of equity, and a reconciliation of the amount of such exchange differences at the beginning and end of the period, to be disclosed.[91]

2.9.2   *Presentation and functional currency*

When the presentation currency is different from the functional currency, that fact shall be stated, together with disclosure of the functional currency and the reason for using a different presentation currency.[92] For this purpose, in the case of a group, the references to 'functional currency' are to that of the parent.[93]

When there is a change in the functional currency of either the reporting entity or a significant foreign operation, that fact and the reason for the change in functional currency shall be disclosed.[94]

2.9.3   *Convenience translations of financial statements or other financial information*

Paragraph 55 of IAS 21 indicates that when an entity presents its financial statements in a currency that is different from its functional currency, it shall describe the financial statements as complying with IFRS only if they comply with all the requirements of each applicable standard and interpretation of those standards, including the translation method set out in IAS 21 (see 2.7.1 above).[95]

However, the standard recognises that an entity sometimes presents its financial statements or other financial information in a currency that is not its functional currency without meeting the above requirements. Examples noted by IAS 21 are where an entity converts into another currency only selected items from its financial statements or where an entity whose functional currency is not the currency of a hyperinflationary economy converts the financial statements into another currency by translating all items at the most recent closing rate. Such conversions are not in accordance with IFRS; nevertheless IAS 21 requires disclosures to be made.[96]

The standard requires that when an entity displays its financial statements or other financial information in a currency that is different from either its functional currency or its presentation currency and the requirements of paragraph 55 are not met, it shall:[97]

(a)   clearly identify the information as supplementary information to distinguish it from the information that complies with IFRS;

(b) disclose the currency in which the supplementary information is displayed; and

(c) disclose the entity's functional currency and the method of translation used to determine the supplementary information.

For the purpose of these requirements, in the case of a group, the references to 'functional currency' are to that of the parent.[98]

3 PRACTICAL ISSUES

3.1 Determination of functional currency

As indicated earlier, an entity is required to determine its functional currency using the guidance discussed at 2.5 above. For some entities that determination may be relatively straightforward. However, for many entities, particularly entities within a group, this may not be the case. As indicated earlier, when the factors or indicators set out at 2.5 above are mixed and the functional currency is not obvious, the standard requires management to use its judgement to determine the functional currency that most faithfully represents the economic effects of the underlying transactions, events and conditions.

Since the determination of an entity's functional currency is critical to the translation process under IAS 21, we believe that an entity should clearly document its decision about its functional currency, setting out the factors taken into account in making that determination, particularly where it is not obvious from the primary factors set out in paragraph 9 of the standard. We would recommend that the ultimate parent entity of a group should do this for each entity within the group and agree that determination with the local management of those entities, particularly where those entities are presenting financial statements in accordance with IFRS. Although the determination of functional currency is a judgemental issue, it would be expected that within the group the same determination would be made as to the functional currency of a particular entity. If local management has come up with a different analysis of the facts from that of the parent, it should be discussed to ensure that both parties have considered all the relevant facts and circumstances and a final determination made.

By documenting the decision about the functional currency of each entity, and the factors taken into account in making that determination, the reporting entity will be better placed in the future to determine whether a change in the underlying transactions, events and conditions relating to that entity warrant a change in its functional currency.

3.2 Reporting foreign currency transactions in the functional currency of an entity

3.2.1 Date of transaction

As indicated at 2.6.1 above, the date of a transaction is the date on which it first qualifies for recognition in accordance with IFRS. Although this sounds relatively straightforward, the following example illustrates the difficulty that can sometimes arise in determining the transaction date:

Example 9.8:   Establishing the transaction date

A Belgian entity buys an item of inventory from a Canadian supplier. The dates relating to the transaction, and the relevant exchange rates, are as follows:

Date	Event	€1=C$
14 April 2005	Goods are ordered	1.50
5 May 2005	Goods are shipped from Canada and invoice dated that day	1.53
7 May 2005	Invoice is received	1.51
10 May 2005	Goods are received	1.54
14 May 2005	Invoice is recorded	1.56
7 June 2005	Invoice is paid	1.60

IAS 2 – *Inventories* – does not make any reference to the date of initial recognition of inventory. However, IAS 39 deals with the initial recognition of financial liabilities. It requires the financial liability to be recognised when, and only when, the entity becomes a party to the contractual provisions of the instrument.[99] In discussing firm commitments to purchase goods, it indicates that an entity placing the order does not recognise the liability at the time of the commitment, but delays recognition until the ordered goods have been shipped or delivered,[100] i.e. the date that the risks and rewards of ownership have passed.

Accordingly, it is unlikely that the date the goods are ordered should be used as the date of the transaction.

If the goods are shipped free on board (f.o.b.) then as the risks and rewards of ownership pass on shipment then this date should be used.

If, however, the goods are not shipped f.o.b. then the risks and rewards of ownership normally pass on delivery and therefore the date the goods are received should be treated as the date of the transaction.

The dates on which the invoice is received and is recorded are irrelevant to when the risks and rewards of ownership pass and therefore should not in principle be considered to be the date of the transaction. In practice, it may be acceptable that as a matter of administrative convenience that the exchange rate at the date the invoice is recorded is used, particularly if there is no undue delay in processing the invoice. If this is done then care should be taken to ensure that the exchange rate used is not significantly different from that ruling on the 'true' date of the transaction.

It is clear from IAS 21 that the date the invoice is paid is not the date of the transaction because if it were then no exchange differences would arise on unsettled transactions.

The above example illustrated that the date that a transaction is recorded in an entity's books and records is not necessarily the same as the date at which it qualifies for recognition under IFRS. Other situations where this is likely to arise is where an entity is recording a transaction that relates to a period, rather than one being recognised at a single point in time, as illustrated below:

Example 9.9:   *Establishing the transaction date*

On 30 September 2005 Company A, whose functional currency is the euro, acquires a US dollar bond for US$8,000. The bond carries fixed interest of 5% per annum paid quarterly, i.e. US$100 per quarter. The exchange rate at that date is US$1 to €1.50.

On 31 December 2005, the US dollar has appreciated and the exchange rate is US$1 to €2.00. Interest received on the bond on 31 December 2005 is US$100 (= €200).

Although the interest may only be being recorded at that date, the rate at 31 December 2005 is not the spot rate ruling at the date of the transaction. Since the interest has accrued over the 3-month period, it should be translated at the spot rates applicable to the accrual of interest during the 3-month period. Accordingly, a weighted average rate for the 3-month period should be used. Assuming that the appropriate average rate is US$1 to €1.75 the interest income is €175 (= US$100 × 1.75).

Accordingly, there is also an exchange gain on the interest receivable of €25 (= US$100 × [2.00 – 1.75]) to be reflected in the income statement. The journal entry for recording the receipt of the interest on 31 December 2005 is therefore as follows:

	€	€
Cash	200	
Interest income (income statement)		175
Exchange gain (income statement)		25

3.2.2   Use of average rate

As indicated at 2.6.1 above, rather than using the actual rate ruling at the date of the transaction 'an average rate for a week or month may be used for all foreign currency transactions occurring during that period', if the exchange rate does not fluctuate significantly.[101] For entities which engage in a large number of foreign currency transactions it will be more convenient for them to use an average rate rather than using the exact rate for each transaction. If an average rate is to be used, what guidance can be given in choosing and using such a rate?

(a)   Length of period

As an average rate should only be used as an approximation of actual rates then care has to be taken that significant fluctuations in the day-to-day exchange rates do not arise in the period selected. For this reason the period chosen should not be too long. We believe that the maximum length of period should be one month and where there is volatility of exchange rates it will be better to set rates on a more frequent basis, say, a weekly basis, especially where the value of transactions is significant.

(b)   Estimate of average rate

The estimation of the appropriate average rate will depend on whether the rate is to be applied to transactions which have already occurred or to transactions which will occur after setting the rate. Obviously, if the transactions have already occurred then the average rate used should relate to the period during which those transactions occurred; e.g. purchase transactions for the previous week should be translated using the average rate for that week, not an average rate for the week the invoices are being recorded.

If rate is being set for the following period the rate selected should be a reasonable estimate of the expected exchange rate during that period. This could be done by using the closing rate at the end of the previous period or by using the actual average rate for the previous period. We would suggest that the former be used. Whatever means is used to estimate the average rate, the actual rates during the period should be monitored and if there is a significant move in the exchange rate away from the average rate then the rate being applied should be revised.

(c)   Application of average rate

We believe that average rates should only be used as a matter of convenience where there are a large number of transactions. Even where an average rate is used, we recommend that the actual rate should be used for large one-off transactions such as the purchase of a fixed asset or an overseas investment or taking out a foreign loan. Where the number of foreign currency transactions is small it will probably not be worthwhile setting and monitoring average rates and therefore actual rates should be used.

3.2.3   Dual rates or suspension of rates

One practical difficulty in translating foreign currency amounts is where there is more than one exchange rate for that particular currency depending on the nature of the transaction. In some cases the difference between the exchange rates can be small and therefore it probably does not matter which rate is actually used. However, in other situations the difference can be quite significant. In these circumstances, what rate should be used? IAS 21 states that 'when several exchange rates are available, the rate used is that at which the future cash flows represented by the transaction or balance could have been settled if those cash flows had occurred at the measurement date'.[102] Companies should therefore look at the nature of the transaction and apply the appropriate exchange rate.

Another practical difficulty which could arise is where for some reason exchangeability between two currencies is temporarily lacking at the transaction date or at the subsequent balance sheet date. In this case, IAS 21 requires that the rate to be used is 'the first subsequent rate at which exchanges could be made'.[103]

3.2.4   Monetary or non-monetary?

As indicated in 2.6.2 above, IAS 21 generally requires that monetary items denominated in foreign currencies be retranslated using closing rates at each balance sheet date and non-monetary items should not be retranslated. Monetary items are defined as 'units of currency held and assets and liabilities to be received or paid in a fixed or determinable number of units of currency'.[104] The standard elaborates further on this by stating that 'the essential feature of a monetary item is a right to receive (or an obligation to deliver) a fixed or determinable number of units of currency'. Examples given by IAS 21 are pensions and other employee benefits to be paid in cash; provisions that are to be settled in cash; and cash dividends that are recognised as a liability.[105] More obvious examples are cash and bank balances; trade receivables and payables; and loan receivables and payables. IAS 39 also indicates that where a foreign currency bond is held as an available-for-sale financial asset, then it should first be accounted for at amortised cost in the underlying currency, thus effectively treating that amount as if it was a monetary item. This is discussed further in Chapter 18 at 7.1. This suggests that foreign currency bonds that are classified as held-to-maturity investments under IAS 39 are monetary items.

IAS 21 also states that 'a contract to receive (or deliver) a variable number of the entity's own equity instruments or a variable amount of assets in which the fair value to be received (or delivered) equals a fixed or determinable number of units of currency is a monetary item'.[106] No examples of such contracts are given in IAS 21. However, it would seem to embrace those contracts settled in the entity's own equity shares that under IAS 32 would be presented as financial assets or liabilities (see Chapter 17 at 3.3.2 A

Conversely, the essential feature of a non-monetary item is the absence of a right to receive (or an obligation to deliver) a fixed or determinable number of units of currency. Examples given by the standard are amounts prepaid for goods and services (e.g. prepaid rent); goodwill; intangible assets; inventories; property, plant and equipment; and provisions that are to be settled by the delivery of a non-monetary asset.[107] IAS 39 also indicates that equity instruments that are held as available-for-sale financial assets are non-monetary items.[108] This suggests that equity investments in subsidiaries, associates or joint ventures are non-monetary items.

Even with this guidance there will clearly be a number of situations where the distinction may not be altogether clear.

A   Deposits or progress payments paid against fixed assets or inventories

Entities may be required to pay deposits or progress payments when acquiring fixed assets or inventories from foreign suppliers. The question then arises as to whether such payments should be retranslated as monetary items or not.

Example 9.10:   Deposits or progress payments

A Dutch entity contracts to purchase an item of plant and machinery for US$10,000 on the following terms:

Payable on signing contract (1 August 2005)	– 10%
Payable on delivery (19 December 2005)	– 40%
Payable on installation (7 January 2006)	– 50%

At 31 December 2005 the entity has paid the first two amounts on the due dates when the respective exchange rates were €1=US$1.25 and €1=US$1.20. The closing rate at its balance sheet date, 31 December 2005, is €1=US$1.15.

		(i)	(ii)
		€	€
First payment	– US$1,000	800	870
Second payment	– US$4,000	3,333	3,478
		4,133	4,348

(i) If the payments made are regarded as prepayments or as progress payments then the amounts should be treated as non-monetary items and included in the balance sheet at €4,133. This would appear to be consistent with SFAS 52 which in defining 'transaction date' states: 'A long-term commitment may have more than one transaction date (for example, the due date of each progress payment under a construction contract is an anticipated transaction date).'[109]

(ii) If the payments made are regarded as deposits, and are refundable, then the amounts could possibly be treated as monetary items and included in the balance sheet at €4,348 and an exchange gain of €215 recorded in the income statement. A variant of this would be to only treat the first payment as a deposit until the second payment is made, since once delivery is made it is less likely that the asset will be returned and a refund sought from the supplier.

In practice, it will often be necessary to consider the terms of the contract to ascertain the nature of the payments made in order to determine the appropriate accounting treatment.

B   Investments in preference shares

Entities may invest in preference shares of other entities. Whether or nor such shares are monetary items or not will depend on the rights attaching to the shares. As noted at 3.2.4 above, IAS 39 indicates that equity instruments that are held as available-for-sale financial assets are non-monetary items.[110] Thus, it appears that if the terms of the preference shares are such that they are classified by the issuer as equity, rather than as a financial liability, then they are non-monetary items. However, if the terms of the preference shares are such that they are classified by the issuer as a financial liability (e.g. a preference share that provides for mandatory redemption by the issue for a fixed or determinable amount at a fixed or determinable future date), then it would appear that they should be treated as monetary items. Indeed, IAS 39 would allow such an instrument to be classified within loans and receivables by the holder provided the definition in IAS 39 is otherwise met (see Chapter 15 at 7.3). However, even where an investment in such redeemable preference shares is not classified within loans and receivables, but as a held-to-maturity investment or as an available-for-sale financial asset, then it would seem that it should be treated as a monetary item (in the latter case, to the extent that it would be measured at amortised cost, similar to an investment in a bond as discussed at 3.2.4 above).

C   Foreign currency share capital

Entities may issue share capital denominated in a currency that is not its functional currency or, due to changes in circumstances that result in a re-determination of its functional currency, find that its share capital is no longer denominated in its functional currency. Neither IAS 21 nor IAS 39 addresses the treatment of translation of share capital denominated in a currency other than the functional currency. In theory two treatments are possible: the foreign currency share capital (and any related share premium or additional paid-in capital) could be maintained at a fixed amount by being translated at a historical rate of exchange, or it could be retranslated annually at the closing rate as if it were a monetary amount. In the latter case a second question would arise: whether to take the difference arising on translation to the income statement or deal with it within equity.

Where the shares denominated in a foreign currency are ordinary shares, or are otherwise irredeemable and classified as equity instruments, it would seem to be more appropriate to use a historical exchange rate. This is because the effect of rate changes is not expected to have an impact on the entity's cash flows. Such capital items are included within the examples of non-monetary items listed in SFAS 52 as accounts to be remeasured using historical exchange rates when the temporal method is being applied.[111] This is also the treatment required by the equivalent Canadian standard.[112]

Where such share capital is retranslated at closing rate, we do not believe that it is appropriate for the exchange differences to be taken to the income statement, since they do not affect the cash flows of the entity; the exchange differences should be taken to equity. Consequently, whether such share capital is maintained at a historical rate, or is dealt with in this way, the treatment has no impact on the overall equity of the entity.

Where the shares are not classified as equity instruments, but as financial liabilities, under IAS 39, e.g. preference shares that provide for mandatory redemption by the issue for a fixed or determinable amount at a fixed or determinable future date, then, as with investments in such shares discussed at 3.2.4 B above, they should be treated as monetary items and translated at closing rate. Any exchange differences will be taken to profit or loss, unless the shares form part of a hedging relationship and IAS 39 would account for the exchange differences differently (see Chapter 19).

D   Deferred tax

One of the examples of a monetary item included within the exposure draft that preceded IAS 21 was deferred tax.[113] However, this has been dropped from the list of examples in the final standard. No explanation is given in IAS 21 as to why this is the case. Nevertheless, IAS 12 suggests that any deferred foreign tax assets or liabilities are monetary items since it states that 'where exchange differences on deferred foreign tax liabilities or assets are recognised in the income statement, such differences may be classified as deferred tax expense (income) if that presentation is considered to be the most useful to financial statement users'.[114]

3.2.5   Books and records not kept in functional currency

Occasionally, an entity may keep its underlying books and records in a currency that is not its functional currency under IAS 21. For example, it could record its transactions in terms of the local currency of the country in which it is located, possibly as a result of local requirements.

When an entity keeps its books and records in a currency other than its functional currency, then IAS 21 requires that at the time the entity prepares its financial statements all amounts are translated into the functional currency in accordance with paragraphs 20-26 of the standard,[115] i.e. those discussed at 2.6.1, 2.6.2 and 3.2.1 to 3.2.4 above. The standard goes on to say that 'this produces the same amounts in the functional currency as would have occurred had the items been recorded initially in the functional currency. For example, monetary items are translated into the functional currency using the closing rate, and non-monetary items that are measured on a historical cost basis are translated using the exchange rate at the date of the transaction that resulted in their recognition.'[116] This presupposes that the initial recording of transactions in foreign currencies (including the entity's functional currency), and any subsequent retranslation of the resulting balance sheet items, have been translated into the recording currency in accordance with those paragraphs. For example, all foreign currency monetary items have been translated into the recording currency at the closing rate at the balance sheet date. It is only if this has been done that the subsequent translation of those monetary items to the functional currency using the closing rate between the recording currency and the functional currency will result in the same amounts that would have occurred if the foreign currency amounts had been translated directly into the functional currency at their respective closing rates. However, if the foreign currency monetary items have been retained at their original historical rate in the books and records, then the subsequent translation of those monetary items to the functional currency using the closing rate between the recording currency and the functional currency will *not* result in the same amounts that would have occurred if the foreign currency amounts had been translated directly into the functional currency at their respective closing rates.

Accordingly, when an entity keeps its books and records in a currency other than its functional currency, it will be necessary to obtain an understanding about the underlying translation process before applying these requirements of the standard to ensure that the resulting amounts are the same amounts in the functional currency as would have occurred had the items been recorded initially in the functional currency.

As indicated above, IAS 21 only refers to the translation into the functional currency in accordance with paragraphs 20-26 of the standard. These paragraphs do not include those relating to the treatment of exchange differences arising from that translation process. However, we believe that any resulting exchange differences should be recognised as discussed at 2.6.3 above.

3.3   Translation to a different presentation currency

3.3.1   *Dual rates or suspension of rates*

The problems of dual rates and suspension of rates in relation to the translation of foreign currency transactions and balances into an entity's functional currency and the related requirements of IAS 21 dealing with such issues have already been discussed in 3.2.3 above. However, the standard makes no reference to them in the context of translating the results and financial position of an entity into a different presentation currency, particularly where the results and financial position of a foreign operation are being translated for inclusion in the financial statements of the reporting entity by consolidation, proportionate consolidation or the equity method.

Where the problem is one of suspension of rates, then we believe that the requirement in IAS 21 relating to transactions and balances should be followed; i.e. the rate to be used is 'the first subsequent rate at which exchanges could be made'.[117] However, the requirement in IAS 21 relating to dual rates is not entirely relevant in this context. Again, guidance can be sought from SFAS 52 which states that the rate to be used to translate foreign financial statements should be, in the absence of unusual circumstances, the rate applicable to dividend remittances.[118] The reason for this is that the use of that rate is more meaningful than any other rate because cash flows to the parent company from the foreign entity can be converted only at that rate, and realisation of a net investment in the foreign entity will ultimately be in the form of cash flows from that entity.[119]

3.3.2 Calculation of average rate

As indicated at 2.7.1 A above, when translating the results of an entity whose functional currency is not that of a hyperinflationary economy, for practical reasons, the reporting entity may use a rate that approximates the actual exchange rate, e.g. an average rate for the period, to translate income and expense items.[120]

The standard does not give any guidance on the factors that should be taken into account in determining what may be an appropriate average rate for the period – it merely says that 'if exchange rates fluctuate significantly, the use of the average rate for the period is inappropriate'.[121] What methods are, therefore, available to entities to use in calculating an appropriate average rate? Possible methods might be:

(a) mid-year rate;

(b) average of opening and closing rates;

(c) average of month end/quarter end rates;

(d) average of monthly average rates;

(e) monthly/quarterly results at month end/quarter end rates; or

(f) monthly/quarterly results at monthly/quarterly averages.

Example 9.11: *Calculation of average rate*

A Spanish entity has a foreign subsidiary and is preparing its consolidated accounts for the year ended 30 April 2006. It intends to use an average rate for translating the results of the subsidiary. The relevant exchange rates for €1=FC are as follows:

Month	Month end	Average for month	Average for quarter	Average for year
April 2005	1.67			
May 2005	1.63	1.67		
June 2005	1.67	1.64		
July 2005	1.64	1.65	1.65	
August 2005	1.67	1.64		
September 2005	1.70	1.63		
October 2005	1.67	1.68	1.65	
November 2005	1.65	1.70		
December 2005	1.66	1.66		
January 2006	1.64	1.67	1.68	
February 2006	1.60	1.65		
March 2006	1.61	1.63		
April 2006	1.61	1.62	1.63	1.65

Average of month end rates – 1.65

Average of quarter end rates – 1.64

The results of the subsidiary for each of the 12 months to 30 April 2006 and the translation thereof under each of the above methods (using monthly figures where appropriate) are shown below:

Method (a)	FC31,050 @ 1.67= €18,593
Method (b)	FC31,050 @ 1.64= €18,933
Method (c) – monthly	FC31,050 @ 1.65= €18,818
Method (c) – quarterly	FC31,050 @ 1.64= €18,933
Method (d)	FC31,050 @ 1.65= €18,818

Month	FC	(e) quarterly €	(e) monthly €	(f) quarterly €	(f) monthly €
May 2005	1,000		613		599
June 2005	1,100		659		671
July 2005	1,200	2,012	732	2,000	727
August 2005	1,300		778		793
September 2005	1,300		765		798
October 2005	1,350	2,365	808	2,394	804
November 2005	1,400		848		824
December 2005	1,400		843		843
January 2006	2,000	2,927	1,220	2,857	1,198
February 2006	5,000		3,125		3,030
March 2006	10,000		6,211		6,135
April 2006	4,000	11,801	2,484	11,656	2,469
Total	31,050	19,105	19,086	18,907	18,891

It can be seen that by far the simplest methods to use are the methods (a) to (d).

In our view methods (a) and (b) should not normally be used as it is unlikely in times of volatile exchange rates that they will give appropriate weighting to the exchange rates which have been in existence throughout the period in question. They are only likely to give an acceptable answer if the exchange rate has been static or steadily increasing or decreasing throughout the period.

Method (c) based on quarter end rates has similar drawbacks and therefore should not normally be used.

Method (c) based on month end rates and method (d) are better than the previous methods as they do take into account more exchange rates which have applied throughout the year, with method (d) being preferable, as this will have taken account of daily exchange rates. Average monthly rates for most major currencies are likely to be given in publications issued by the government, banks and other sources and therefore it is unnecessary for entities to calculate their own. The work involved in calculating an average for the year, therefore, is not very onerous. Method (d) will normally give reasonable and acceptable results when there are no seasonal variations in items of income and expenditure.

Where there are seasonal variations in items of income and expenditure then this may not be the case. In these situations appropriate exchange rates should be applied to the appropriate items. This can be done by using either of methods (e) or (f) preferably using figures and rates for each month. Where such a method is being used care should be taken to ensure that the periodic accounts are accurate and that cut-off procedures have been adequate, otherwise significant items may be translated at the wrong average rate.

Where there are significant one-off items of income and expenses then it is likely that actual rates at the date of the transaction should be used to translate such items.

3.3.3   *Translation of equity items*

The method of translation of the results and financial position of an entity whose functional currency is not the currency of a hyperinflationary economy is discussed at 2.7.1 A above. The translation process makes no reference to the translation of equity items. The exposure draft that preceded the standard had proposed that '… equity items other than those resulting from income and expense recognised in the period … shall be translated at the closing rate'. However, the IASB decided not to specify in the standard the translation rate for equity items,[122] but no explanation has been given in the Basis of Conclusions about this matter.

So how should entities deal with the translation of equity items?

A   *Share capital*

Where an entity is presenting its financial statements in a currency other than its functional currency, it would seem more appropriate that its share capital (whether they are ordinary shares, or are otherwise irredeemable and classified as equity instruments) should be translated at historical rates of exchange. As noted at 3.2.4 C above, such capital items are included within the examples of non-monetary items listed in SFAS 52 as accounts to be remeasured using historical exchange rates when the temporal method is being applied.[123] This is also the treatment required by the equivalent Canadian standard.[124] Translation at a historical rate would imply using the rate ruling at the date of the issue of the shares. However, where a subsidiary is presenting its financial statements in the currency of its parent, it may be that the more appropriate historical rate for share capital that was in issue at the date it became a subsidiary would be that ruling at the date it became a subsidiary of the parent, rather than at earlier dates of issue.

Where such share capital is retranslated at closing rate, we do not believe that it is appropriate for the exchange differences to be taken to the separate component of equity required by IAS 21 (since to do so could result in them being recycled to the income statement upon disposal of part of the entity's operations in the future), but should either be taken to retained earnings or some other reserve. Consequently, whether such share capital is maintained at a historical rate, or is dealt with in this way, the treatment has no impact on the overall equity of the entity.

B   *Other equity balances resulting from transactions with equity holders*

In addition to share capital, an entity may have other equity balances resulting from the issue of shares, such as a share premium account. Like share capital, the translation of such balances could be done at either historical rates or at closing rate. However, we believe that whichever method is adopted is consistent with the treatment used for share capital. Again, where exchange differences arise through using the closing rate, we believe that it is not appropriate for them to be taken to the separate component of equity required by IAS 21.

A similar approach should be adopted where an entity has acquired its own equity shares and has deducted those 'treasury shares' from equity as required by IAS 32 (see Chapter 17 at 6).

C   *Other equity balances resulting from income and expenses being taken direct to equity*

Although IAS 21 makes no reference to equity items in its translation process, the standard does suggest, however, that income and expenses that are recognised directly in equity will have been translated at the exchange rates ruling at the dates of the transaction, since it is only by doing so, and translating the period end assets and liabilities at closing rates, that exchange differences will arise on such items so that they get recognised within the separate component of equity.[125] Examples of such items of income and expense are certain revaluation gains and losses on property, plant and equipment under IAS 16 (see Chapter 12 at 2.4.1) and on certain intangible assets under IAS 38 (see Chapter 11 at 2.3.2), gains and losses on available-for-sale financial assets under IAS 39 (see Chapter 18 at 3.2), gains and losses on cash flow hedges under IAS 39 (see Chapter 19 at 4.2.1), and any amounts of current and deferred tax taken to equity under IAS 12 (see Chapter 24 at 6.1). This would suggest that where these gains and losses are taken to a separate reserve or component of equity, then any period-end balance should represent the cumulative translated amounts of such gains and losses. However, as IAS 21 is silent on the matter it would seem that it would be acceptable to translate these equity balances at closing rate, as long as the exchange differences arising are not taken to the separate component of equity required by IAS 21. The differences would have to be taken to retained earnings or some other reserve, effectively as a transfer between the reserves. Consequently, whether such balances are maintained at the original translated rates, or are translated at closing rates, the treatment has no impact on the overall equity of the entity.

3.3.4   Goodwill

As discussed at 2.7.2 C above, IAS 21 requires that any goodwill arising on the acquisition of a foreign operation shall be expressed in the functional currency of the foreign operation and shall be translated at the closing rate in accordance with the requirements discussed at 2.7.1 above.[126] Clearly, if an entity acquires a single foreign entity this will be a straightforward exercise. Where, however, the acquisition is of a multinational operation comprising a number of businesses with different functional currencies this will not be the case. The goodwill needs to be allocated to the level of each functional currency of the acquired operation. However, the standard gives no guidance on how this should be done.

It would seem that the most appropriate basis would be to effectively calculate the goodwill relating to each different functional currency operation. This could be done by allocating the cost of the acquisition to the different functional currency operations on the basis of the relative economic values of those businesses and then deducting the fair values that have been attributed to the net assets of those businesses as part of the fair value exercise in accounting for the business combination (see Chapter 6 at 2.3.3). An alternative approach might be to allocate the goodwill on the basis of the relative fair values of the net assets of the businesses.

The Basis of Conclusions issued by the IASB notes that the level to which goodwill is allocated for foreign currency translation purpose may be different from the level at which the goodwill is tested for impairment under IAS 36 (see Chapter 6 at 3).[127] In many cases the allocation under IAS 21 will be at a lower level. This will apply not only on the acquisition of a multinational operation but could also apply on the acquisition of a single operation where the goodwill is allocated to a larger cash generating unit under IAS 36 that is made up of businesses with different functional currencies.

As a consequence of this different level of allocation one particular difficulty that entities are likely to face is how to deal with an impairment loss that is recognised in respect of goodwill under IAS 36. If the impairment loss relates to a larger cash generating unit made up of businesses with different functional currencies, again some allocation of this impairment loss will be required to determine the amount of the remaining carrying amount of goodwill in each of the functional currencies for the purposes of translation under IAS 21.

3.4 Intragroup transactions

The standard states that 'the incorporation of the results and financial position of a foreign operation with those of the reporting entity follows normal consolidation procedures, such as the elimination of intragroup balances and intragroup transactions of a subsidiary'.[128] On this basis, there is a tendency sometimes to assume that exchange differences on intragroup balances should not impact on the reported profit or loss for the group in the consolidated financial statements. However, as discussed at 2.7.2 A above, that is not the case. The general requirement of IAS 21 is that exchange differences arising on intragroup balances continue to be reflected in profit or loss in the consolidated financial statements, effectively treating them in the same way as exchange differences on monetary items resulting from transactions with third parties.

Nevertheless, the standard makes an exception to this requirement where the exchange difference arises on an intragroup balance that, in substance, forms part of an entity's net investment in a foreign operation. In that case, the exchange difference is not to be taken to profit or loss in the consolidated financial statements, but is classified as equity until the disposal of the foreign operation (see 2.7.3 above).[129]

3.4.1 Monetary items included as part of the net investment in a foreign operation

The 'net investment in a foreign operation' is defined as being 'the amount of the reporting entity's interest in the net assets of that operation'.[130] The standard elaborates on this by stating that 'an entity may have a monetary item that is receivable from or payable to a foreign operation. An item for which settlement is neither planned nor likely to occur in the foreseeable future is, in substance, a part of the entity's net investment in that foreign operation'. Such monetary items may include long-term receivables or loans. They do not include trade receivables or trade payables.[131]

It can be seen from the above that this treatment for the exchange differences should be applied where settlement is neither planned nor likely to occur in the foreseeable future. Unfortunately, the term 'foreseeable future' is not defined and no specific time period is implied.

It could be argued that if it is planned or intended to repay the intragroup amount at any time while the entity is part of the group then the exchange differences should be taken to the income statement. On this view, the amount should be considered as part of the net investment if it will be repaid only when the reporting entity disinvests from the foreign operation. However, it is recognised that in most circumstances this would be unrealistic and therefore a shorter time span should be considered.

One particular area of difficulty will be if the intragroup amount is in the form of a loan with a specified term for repayment. By having a specified term, this might suggest that settlement is planned, and even if this not due to be until 20 years time, would mean that the loan is not part of the net investment in the foreign operation, and the exchange differences on the loan during that period should be recorded in the consolidated income statement.

Although the standard states that trade receivables and payables are not included, we do not believe that it necessarily precludes deferred trading balances from being included. Such balances could arise from the purchase and sale of goods and services, together with interest payments and dividend payments which have not been paid for in cash but are accumulated in the inter-company account.

In our view, such balances can be included as part of the net investment in the foreign operation, but only if cash settlement is not made or planned to be made in the foreseeable future. If a subsidiary makes payment for purchases from its parent, but is continually indebted to the parent as a result of new purchases, then in these circumstances, as individual transactions are settled, no part of the inter-company balance should be regarded as part of the net investment in the subsidiary. Accordingly, such exchange differences should be taken to the consolidated income account.

When a monetary item is considered to form part of a reporting entity's net investment in a foreign operation and is denominated in the functional currency of the reporting entity, an exchange difference will be recognised in profit or loss for the period when it arises in the foreign operation's individual financial statements.

Similarly, if such an item is denominated in the functional currency of the foreign operation, an exchange difference will be recognised in profit or loss for the period when it arises in the reporting entity's separate financial statements. Such exchange differences are only reclassified to the separate component of equity in the financial statements that include the foreign operation and the reporting entity (i.e. financial statements in which the foreign operation is consolidated, proportionately consolidated or accounted for using the equity method).[132]

Example 9.12: Monetary item in functional currency of either the reporting entity or the foreign operation

A UK entity has a Belgian subsidiary. On the last day of its financial year, 31 March 2004, the UK entity lends the subsidiary £1,000,000. Settlement of the loan is neither planned nor likely to occur in the foreseeable future, so the UK entity regards the loan as part of its net investment in the Belgian subsidiary. The exchange rate at 31 March 2004 was £1=€1.40. Since the loan was made on the last day of the year there are no exchange differences to recognise for that year. At 31 March 2005, the loan has not been repaid and is still regarded as part of the net investment in the Belgian subsidiary. The relevant exchange rate at that date was £1=€1.50. The average exchange rate for the year ended 31 March 2005 was £1=€1.45.

In the UK entity's separate financial statements no exchange difference is recognised since the loan is denominated in its functional currency of sterling. In the Belgian subsidiary's financial statements, the liability to the parent is translated into the subsidiary's functional currency of euros at the closing rate at €1,500,000, giving rise to an exchange loss of €100,000, i.e. €1,500,000 less €1,400,000 (£1,000,000 @ £1=€1.40). This exchange loss is reflected in the Belgian subsidiary's profit or loss for that year. In the UK entity's consolidated financial statements, this exchange loss included in the subsidiary's profit or loss for the year will be translated at the average rate for the year, giving rise a loss of £68,966 (€100,000@ £1=€1.45). This will be taken to the separate component of equity together with an exchange gain of £2,299, being the difference between the amount included in the Belgian subsidiary's income statement translated at average rate, i.e. £68,966, and at the closing rate, i.e. £66,667 (€100,000@ £1=€1.50). The overall exchange loss taken to equity is £66,667. This represents the exchange loss on the increased net investment of €1,400,000 in the subsidiary made at 31 March 2004, i.e. £1,000,000 (€1,400,000 @ £1=€1.40) less £933,333 (€1,400,000 @ £1=€1.50).

If, on the other hand, the loan made to the Belgian subsidiary had been denominated in the equivalent amount of euros at 31 March 2004, i.e. €1,400,000, the treatment would have been as follows.

In the UK entity's separate financial statements, the amount receivable from the Belgian subsidiary would be translated at the closing rate at £933,333 (€1,400,000 @ £1=€1.50), giving rise to an exchange loss of £66,667, i.e. £1,000,000 (€1,400,000 @ £1=€1.40) less £933,333, which is included in its profit or loss for the year. In the Belgian subsidiary's financial statements, no exchange difference is recognised since the loan is denominated in its functional currency of euros. In the UK entity's consolidated financial statements, the exchange loss included in its profit or loss for the year in its separate financial statements will be taken to the separate component of equity. As before, this represents the exchange loss on the increased net investment of €1,400,000 in the subsidiary made at 31 March 2004, i.e. £1,000,000 (€1,400,000 @ £1=€1.40) less £933,333 (€1,400,000 @ £1=€1.40).

In most situations, such an intragroup balance will be denominated in the functional currency of either the reporting entity or the foreign operation. However, IAS 21 indicates that this will not always be the case, and a monetary item that forms part of the reporting entity's net investment in a foreign operation may be denominated in a currency other than the functional currency of either the reporting entity or the foreign operation. In this situation, IAS 21 requires that the exchange differences that arise on translating the monetary item into the functional currencies of the reporting entity and the foreign operation are not reclassified to the separate component of equity in the financial statements that include the foreign operation and the reporting entity (i.e. they remain recognised in profit or loss).[133]

Example 9.13:   Monetary item in functional currency that is not that of either the reporting entity or the foreign operation

Suppose in Example 9.12 above, the loan made to the Belgian subsidiary had been denominated in the equivalent amount of US dollars at 31 March 2004. The relevant exchange rates at that date were £1=US$1.54, €1=US$1.10 and £1=€1.40. The loan would therefore have been $1,540,000, which is equivalent to £1,000,000 (US$1,540,000 @ £1=$1.54) and €1,400,000 (US$1,540,000 @ €1=US$1.10). The relevant exchange rates at 31 March 2005 were £1=US$1.80, €1=US$1.20 and £1=€1.50. The average exchange rates for the year ended 31 March 2005 were £1=US$1.656, €1=US$1.15 and £1=€1.45.

In the UK entity's separate financial statements, the amount receivable from the Belgian subsidiary would be translated at the closing rate at £855,555 (US$1,540,000 @ £1=$1.80), giving rise to an exchange loss of £144,445, i.e. £1,000,000 less £855,555. In the Belgian subsidiary's financial statements, the liability to the parent is translated into the subsidiary's functional currency of euros at the closing rate at €1,283,333 (US$1,540,000 @ €1=US$1.20), giving rise to an exchange gain of €116,667, i.e. €1,400,000 less €1,283,333. This exchange gain is reflected in the Belgian subsidiary's profit or loss for that year. In the UK entity's consolidated financial statements, this exchange gain included in the subsidiary's profit or loss for the year will be translated at the average rate for the year, giving rise a translated gain of £80,460 (€116,667@ £1=€1.45). This gain of £80,460 together with the exchange loss of £144,445 in the parent's profit or loss are not reclassified as part of the separate component of equity, but remain in the consolidated profit or loss for the year, i.e. a net loss of £63,985. The gain recognised by the Belgian subsidiary of €116,667 will give rise to an exchange loss of £2,682, being the difference between the amount included in the Belgian subsidiary's income statement translated at average rate, i.e. £80,460, and at the closing rate, i.e. £77,778 (€116,667@ £1=€1.50). This loss of £2,682 will be taken to the separate component of equity. The liability included in the Belgian subsidiary's balance sheet at €1,283,333 will be translated at the closing exchange rate of £1=€1.50, giving rise to a liability of £855,555 which will be eliminated against the receivable included in the UK entity's balance sheet.

The example above illustrates that the overall impact of this requirement in such a situation as this, is that it makes no difference as to whether the intragroup loan is regarded as forming part of the net investment in the foreign operation; the accounting is the same as it would have been if the intragroup loan had not been so regarded.

It is emphasised that the exception for exchange differences on monetary items forming part of the net investment in a foreign operation applies only in the consolidated financial statements. In the individual financial statements of the entity with the currency exposure the exchange differences have to be reflected in that entity's profit or loss for the period. It is unclear why this should be the case since the standard does not acknowledge that this represents a change from the previous version of IAS 21 nor is there is a discussion of the matter within the Basis of Conclusions issued along with the revised standard.

We see no reason why such exchange differences should have to be taken to the income statement. Our understanding of the rationale of why such exchange differences are not taken to profit or loss in the consolidated financial statements but to equity is that, since the monetary item forms part of the net investment in the foreign operation, the exchange differences should be treated in the same way as the exchange differences on the net assets of the foreign operation. The stated reason within the standard as to why those exchange differences are not recognised in profit or loss is because the changes in exchange rates have little or no direct effect on the present and future cash flows from operations.[134] On that basis, the same would hold true for the separate financial statements of the reporting entity. Indeed, since the item is considered to be, in substance, part of the net investment, in our view it would have been more appropriate to treat it as such, and therefore consider it to be a 'non-monetary item' under the standard. Thus, either no exchange differences would have been recognised or they would have been reflected in equity.

A   Monetary items becoming part of the net investment in a foreign operation

It may happen that a parent will decide that its subsidiary requires to be refinanced and instead of investing more equity capital in the subsidiary decides that an existing inter-company account, which has previously been regarded as a normal monetary item, should become a long-term deferred trading balance and no repayment of such amount will be requested within the foreseeable future. How should the parent treat the exchange differences relating to the inter-company account in the consolidated financial statements in the year it was so designated?

Example 9.14:   Monetary item becoming part of the net investment in a foreign operation

A UK entity has a wholly owned Canadian subsidiary whose net assets at 31 December 2004 were C$2,000,000. These net assets were arrived at after taking account of a liability to the UK parent of £250,000. Using the closing exchange rate of £1=C$2.35 this liability was included in the Canadian company's balance sheet at that date at C$587,500. On 30 June 2005, when the exchange rate was £1=C$2.45, the parent decided that in order to refinance the Canadian subsidiary it would regard the liability of £250,000 as a long-term liability which would not be called for repayment in the foreseeable future. Consequently, the parent thereafter regarded the loan as being part of its net investment in the subsidiary. In the year ended 31 December 2005 the Canadian company made no profit or loss other than any exchange difference to be recognised on its liability to its parent. The relevant exchange rate at that date was £1=C$2.56. The average exchange rate for the year ended 31 December 2005 was £1=C$2.50.

The financial statements of the subsidiary in C$ and translated using the closing rate are as follows:

Balance sheet	31 December 2005		31 December 2004	
	C$	£	C$	£
Assets	2,587,500	1,010,742	2,587,500	1,101,064
Amount due to parent	640,000	250,000	587,500	250,000
Net assets	1,947,500	760,742	2,000,000	851,064

Income statement	
Exchange difference	(52,500)

The normal treatment would be for this exchange loss to be translated at the average rate and included in the consolidated profit and loss account as £21,000. As the net investment was C$2,000,000 then there would have been an exchange loss taken to equity of £69,814, i.e. £851,064 less £781,250 (C$2,000,000 @ £1=C$2.56), together with an exchange gain of £492, being the difference between the income statement translated at average rate, i.e. £21,000, and at the closing rate, i.e. £20,508.

However, the parent now regards the amount due as being part of the net investment in the subsidiary. The question then arises as to when this should be regarded as having happened and how the exchange difference on it should be calculated. No guidance is given in IAS 21.

One treatment would be to regard the 'capital injection' as having taken place at the beginning of the accounting period and, therefore, the net investment increased at that date to C$2,587,500. The exchange loss on this amount is £90,322, i.e. £1,101,064 less £1,010,742, and this amount should be taken to equity. The effect of this would be that all of the exchange loss included in the subsidiary's income statement would be taken to equity on consolidation. This has the merit of treating all of the exchange loss for this year consistently in the same way.

An alternative treatment would be to regard the 'capital injection' as having occurred when it was decided to redesignate the inter-company account and to take the exchange difference arising on the account up to that date to the income statement. Only the exchange difference arising thereafter would be taken to equity. At 30 June 2005 the subsidiary would have translated the inter-company account as C$612,500 (£250,000 @ £1=C$2.45) and therefore the exchange loss up to that date was C$25,000. Translated at the average rate this amount would be included in the consolidated income statement as £10,000, with only an exchange gain of £234 taken to equity, being the difference between the income statement translated at average rate, i.e. £10,000, and at the closing rate, i.e. £9,766. Accordingly, £11,000 (£21,000 less £10,000) offset by a reduction in the exchange gain on the translation of the income statement of £258 (£492 less £234) would be taken to equity.

This amount represents the exchange loss on the 'capital injection' of C$612,500. Translated at the closing rate this amounts to £239,258 which is £10,742 less than the original £250,000. This treatment has the merit of treating the inter-company account up to the date of redesignation consistently with previous years and taking the same exchange difference to reserves which would have been taken if a capital injection had taken place at 30 June 2004. For these reasons we believe that this treatment is preferable to the former treatment although both treatments are acceptable.

Suppose, instead of the inter-company account being £250,000, it was denominated in dollars at C$587,500. In this case the parent would be exposed to the exchange risk; what would be the position?

The subsidiary's net assets at both 31 December 2004 and 2005 would be:

Assets	C$2,587,500
Amount due to parent	587,500
Net assets	C$2,000,000

As the inter-company account is expressed in Canadian dollars, there will be no exchange difference thereon in the subsidiary's income statement.

There will, however, be an exchange loss in the parent as follows:

C$587,500	@ 2.35 =	£250,000
	@ 2.56 =	£229,492
		£20,508

Again, in the consolidated financial statements as the inter-company account is now regarded as part of the equity investment some or all of this amount should be taken to equity. If the treatment adopted is to regard this as happening at the beginning of the period, then all of the exchange loss would be taken to equity. This gives the same result as when the account was expressed in sterling.

If the alternative treatment were adopted then the position would be:

C$587,500 @ 2.35 = £250,000
@ 2.45 = £239,796
£10,204

@ 2.45 = £239,796
@ 2.56 = £229,492
£10,304

The exchange loss up to 30 June 2005 of £10,204 would be taken to the consolidated income statement and the exchange loss thereafter of £10,304 would be taken to equity. This is different from when the account was expressed in sterling because the 'capital injection' in this case is C$587,500 whereas before it was effectively C$612,500.

B   Monetary items ceasing to be part of the net investment in a foreign operation

The previous section dealt with the situation where a monetary item is now considered to form part of the net investment in a foreign operation. However, what happens where a monetary item that was considered to be part of the net investment in a foreign operation is no longer the case, either because the circumstances have changed such that it is now planned or is likely to be settled in the foreseeable future or indeed that the monetary item is in fact settled?

Where the circumstances have changed such that the monetary item is now planned or is likely to be settled in the foreseeable future, then similar issues to those discussed at 3.4.1 A above apply; i.e. are the exchange differences on the intragroup balance to be taken to the income statement only from the date of change or from the beginning of the financial year? However, in this situation consideration also needs to be given as to the treatment of the cumulative exchange differences on the monetary item that had been taken to equity in prior years.

As indicated at 3.4 above, the treatment of these exchange differences was to classify them as equity until the disposal of the foreign operation (see 2.7.3 above).[135] Accordingly, the exchange differences should remain in the separate component of equity.

However, where the intragroup balance is actually settled in cash it appears that the cumulative exchange differences that relate to the amount repaid should be recognised in profit or loss at the time of the repayment. This is because the requirement to recycle the exchange differences applies when an entity disposes of its investment through the repayment of share capital (see 2.7.3 above) and the repayment of the intragroup balance is akin to the repayment of share capital.

3.4.2   *Other intragroup transactions*

As indicated in 3.4 above, exchange differences on intragroup transactions should normally be treated in the same way as if they arose on transactions with third parties. However, there are two further problem areas that arise when preparing the consolidated financial statements.

A   Dividends

The first area relates to dividends payable by a foreign subsidiary to its parent.

If a subsidiary pays a dividend to the parent during the year the parent should record the dividend at the rate ruling when the dividend was declared. An exchange difference will arise in the parent's own financial statements if the exchange rate moves between the declaration date and the date the dividend is actually received. This exchange difference requires to be taken to the income statement and will remain there on consolidation.

The same will apply if the subsidiary declares a dividend to its parent on the last day of its financial year and this is recorded at the year-end in both entities' financial statements. There is no problem in that year as both the intragroup balances and the dividends will eliminate on consolidation with no exchange differences arising. However, as the dividend will not be received until the following year an exchange difference will arise in the parent's financial statements in that year if exchange rates have moved in the meantime. Again, this exchange difference should remain in the consolidated income statement as it is no different from any other exchange difference arising on intragroup balances resulting from other types of intragroup transactions. It should not be taken to equity.

It may seem odd that the consolidated results can be affected by exchange differences on inter-company dividends. However, once the dividend has been declared, the parent now effectively has a functional currency exposure to assets that were previously regarded as part of the net investment. In order to minimise the effect of exchange rate movements entities should, therefore, arrange for inter-company dividends to be paid on the same day the dividend is declared, or as soon after the dividend is declared as possible.

B   Unrealised profits on intragroup transactions

The other problem area is the elimination of unrealised profits resulting from intragroup transactions when one of the parties to the transaction is a foreign subsidiary.

Example 9.15:   Unrealised profits on intragroup transaction

An Italian parent has a wholly owned Swiss subsidiary. On 30 November 2005 the subsidiary sold goods to the parent for CHF1,000. The cost of the goods to the subsidiary was CHF700. The goods were recorded by the parent at €685 based on the exchange rate ruling on 30 November 2005 of €1=CHF1.46. All of the goods are unsold by the year-end, 31 December 2005. The exchange rate at that date was €1=CHF1.52. How should the intragroup profit be eliminated?

IAS 21 contains no specific guidance on this matter. However, SFAS 52 requires the rate ruling at the date of the transaction to be used.[136]

The profit shown by the subsidiary is CHF300 which translated at the rate ruling on the transaction of €1=CHF1.46 equals €205. Consequently, the goods will be included in the balance sheet at:

Per parent company balance sheet	€685
Less unrealised profit eliminated	205
	€480

It can be seen that the resulting figure for inventory is equivalent to the original euro cost translated at the rate ruling on the date of the transaction. Whereas if the subsidiary still held the inventory it would be included at €461 (CHF700 @ €1=CHF1.52).

If in the above example the goods had been sold by the Italian parent to the Swiss subsidiary then we believe the amount to be eliminated is the amount of profit shown in the Italian entity's financial statements. Again, this will not necessarily result in the goods being carried in the consolidated financial statements at their original cost to the group.

3.5 Introduction of the euro

From 1 January 1999, the effective start of Economic and Monetary Union (EMU), the euro became a currency in its own right and the conversion rates between the euro and the national currencies of those countries who were going to participate in the first phase were irrevocably fixed, such that the risk of subsequent exchange differences related to these currencies was eliminated from that date on.

In October 1997, the SIC issued SIC-7 which deals with the application of IAS 21 to the changeover from the national currencies of participating Member States of the European Union to the euro. Consequential amendments have been made to this interpretation as a result of the IASB's revised version of IAS 21.

Although the Interpretation is no longer relevant with respect to the national currencies of those countries that participated in the first phase, SIC-7 makes it clear that the same rationale applies to the fixing of exchange rates when countries join EMU at later stages.[137]

Under SIC-7, the requirements of IAS 21 regarding the translation of foreign currency transactions and financial statements of foreign operations should be strictly applied to the changeover.[138]

This means that, in particular:

(a) foreign currency monetary assets and liabilities resulting from transactions shall continue to be translated into the functional currency at the closing rate. Any resultant exchange differences shall be recognised as income or expense immediately, except that an entity shall continue to apply its existing accounting policy for exchange gains and losses related to hedges of the currency risk of a forecast transaction.[139]

The effective start of the EMU after the balance sheet date does not change the application of these requirements at the balance sheet date; in accordance with IAS 10 it is not relevant whether or not the closing rate can fluctuate after the balance sheet date.[140]

Like IAS 21, the Interpretation does not address how foreign currency hedges should be accounted for. The effective start of EMU, of itself, does not justify a change to an entity's established accounting policy related to hedges of forecast transactions because the changeover does not affect the economic rationale of such hedges. Therefore, the changeover should not alter the accounting policy where gains and losses on financial instruments used as hedges of forecast transactions are initially recognised in equity and matched with the related income or expense in a future period.[141]

(b)   cumulative exchange differences relating to the translation of financial statements of foreign operations shall continue to be classified as equity and shall be recognised as income or expense only on the disposal of the net investment in the foreign operation.[142]

The fact that the cumulative amount of exchange differences will be fixed under EMU does not justify immediate recognition as income or expenses since the wording and the rationale of IAS 21 clearly preclude such a treatment.[143]

4   TRANSITIONAL ARRANGEMENTS AND FIRST-TIME ADOPTION ISSUES

4.1   Transitional arrangements for entities already reporting under IFRS

As indicated at 2 above, most changes resulting from the application of the standard shall be accounted for in accordance with the requirements of IAS 8 (see Chapter 3 at 4.4),[144] i.e. by retrospective application of the new requirements. However, in a change from the proposals in the exposure draft that preceded the standard, the IASB has made an exception from this requirement in respect of the new requirements for goodwill and fair value adjustments.

The standard requires that an entity shall apply the requirements for goodwill and fair value adjustments (i.e. expressed in the functional currency of the acquired entity and therefore translated at closing rate) prospectively to all acquisitions occurring after the beginning of the financial reporting period in which IAS 21 is first applied. However, retrospective application of the new requirements to earlier acquisitions is permitted.[145] The standard goes on to say that 'for an acquisition of a foreign operation treated prospectively but which occurred before the date on which this Standard is first applied, the entity shall not restate prior years and accordingly may, when appropriate, treat goodwill and fair value adjustments arising on that acquisition as assets and liabilities of the entity rather than as assets and liabilities of the foreign operation. Therefore, those goodwill and fair value adjustments either are already expressed in the entity's functional currency or are non-monetary foreign currency items, which are reported using the exchange rate at the date of the acquisition.'[146] Accordingly, those entities that used the option allowed under the previous version of the standard to translate goodwill and fair value adjustments in respect of earlier acquisitions at historical rates can continue to do so. It is unclear why this transitional arrangement is included in the standard since the Basis of Conclusions issued with the standard makes no reference to it, but it was presumably based on comments that entities may have had difficulty in restating old transactions.

4.2   First-time adoption issues

As discussed in Chapter 4 at 2.4.5 and 2.7.2, IFRS 1 provides 2 optional exemptions from full retrospective application of IAS 21 on transition to IFRS for first time adopters.

4.2.1   *Cumulative translation differences*

The first exemption relates to the requirements in IAS 21:[147]

(a)   to recognise some translation differences (principally those resulting from the process of translating the results and financial position of an entity whose functional currency is not that the currency of a hyperinflationary economy into a different presentation currency) as a separate component of equity (see 2.7.1 above); and

(b)   on disposal of a foreign operation, to transfer the cumulative translation differences included within that separate component of equity relating to that operation to the income statement as part of the gain or loss on disposal (see 2.7.3 above).

Under its previous GAAP, an entity may never have recorded such exchange differences as a separate component of equity. Clearly, it could be extremely onerous for an entity to compile such information. Even if under its previous GAAP, an entity did recognise such exchange differences as a separate component of equity, these might be affected by adjustments made on transition to IFRS to the recognised net assets of the foreign operation. Also, an entity might not have the information to determine how much of that separate component of equity related to individual foreign operations to make the necessary transfer on the disposal of a particular operation. Accordingly, the IASB considered that it would be more transparent and comparable to exempt an entity from the requirement to identify the cumulative translation differences at the date of transition to IFRS.[148]

Therefore, under IFRS 1, a first time adopter need not comply with these requirements for the cumulative exchange differences that existed at the date of transition to IFRS. Instead, it shall deem the cumulative translation differences for foreign operations to be zero at the date of transition and the gain or loss on a subsequent disposal shall exclude translation differences that arose before the date of transition and only include later translation differences.[149]

If a first time adopter chooses to use this exemption, it should apply it to all foreign operations at the date of transition to IFRS. If that entity has an existing separate component of equity relating to such translation differences at the date of transition then it should it transfer this reserve to retained earnings at that date.

Since there is no requirement to justify the use of the exemption on grounds of impracticality or undue cost or effort, an entity that already has a separate component of equity and the necessary information to determine how much of it relates to each foreign operation in accordance with IAS 21 (or can do so without much effort) is still able to use the exemption. Accordingly, an entity that has cumulative exchange losses in respect of foreign operations, may consider it advantageous to use the exemption so as to avoid having to recognise these losses in the event of the foreign operation being sold at some time in the future.

4.2.2   *Goodwill and fair value adjustments*

As a result of the transitional arrangement introduced in IAS 21 discussed at 4.1 above, a similar transitional arrangement was included with IFRS 1. Accordingly, a first time adopter need not apply the requirements of IAS 21 retrospectively to fair value adjustments and goodwill arising on business combinations that occurred before the date of transition to IFRS. If IAS 21 is not applied retrospectively a first-time adopter should treat such fair value adjustments and goodwill 'as assets and liabilities of the entity rather than as assets and liabilities of the acquiree. Therefore, those goodwill and fair value adjustments either are already expressed in the entity's functional currency or are non-monetary foreign currency items, which are reported using the exchange rate applied under previous GAAP.'[150]

If a first-time adopter chooses not to take the exemption, it must apply the requirements of IAS 21 retrospectively to fair value adjustments and goodwill arising in either:[151]

(a)   all business combinations that occurred before the date of transition to IFRS; or

(b)   all business combinations that the entity elects to restate to comply with IFRS 3, as permitted by IFRS 1 (see Chapter 6 at 4.2.1).

However, in practice the exemption may be of limited use for a number of reasons.

First, the exemption permits 'goodwill and fair value adjustments' to be treated as assets and liabilities of the entity rather than as assets and liabilities of the acquiree. Implicit in the exemption is the requirement to treat goodwill and fair value adjustments consistently. However, the IASB apparently did not consider that many first-time adopters, under their previous GAAP, will have treated fair value adjustments as assets or liabilities of the acquiree, while at the same time treating goodwill as an asset of the acquirer. As the exemption under IFRS 1 did not foresee this particular situation, those first-time adopters will need to restate either their goodwill or fair value adjustments. In many cases restatement of goodwill is less onerous than restatement of fair value adjustments.

Secondly, the paragraphs in IFRS 1 that introduce the exemption were drafted at a later date than the rest of the Appendix that they form part of. Instead of referring to 'first-time adopter' these paragraphs refer to 'entity'. Nevertheless, it is clear from the context that 'entity' should be read as 'first-time adopter'. This means that the exemption only permits goodwill and fair value adjustments to be treated as assets of the first-time adopter (i.e. ultimate parent). In practice, however, many groups have treated goodwill (and fair value adjustments) as an asset of an intermediate parent. Where the intermediate parent has a functional currency that is different from that of the ultimate parent or the acquiree, it will be necessary to restate goodwill (and fair value adjustments).

4.2.3 Other practical issues

These are the only exemptions allowed by IFRS 1 in relation to the requirements of IAS 21.

Companies will need to confirm whether all entities included within the financial statements are accounted for in the appropriate functional currency.

One other difficulty that an entity may face in preparing its opening IFRS balance sheet is that the guidance in IAS 21 in relation to the determination of the functional currency of each of the entities within the group (see 2.5 above) may mean that there has been a change in the functional currency of an entity from that which had been used under its previous GAAP. This will need to be accounted for by restating the assets and liabilities of the entity at the date of transition to IFRS, rather than prospectively from the date of transition as would be the case on an ongoing basis under IAS 21 (as discussed at 2.6.4 above). The translation of monetary items, or non-monetary assets included at valuation at the balance sheet date, are unlikely to cause much of a problem. Since these are likely to have been translated into the 'old' functional currency at a closing rate, the retranslation into the IAS 21 functional currency will be done at the exchange rate for those currencies at the date of transition. The principal difficulty relates to non-monetary items that are measured on the basis of historical cost, particularly property, plant and machinery, since these will need to be re-measured in terms of the IAS 21 functional currency at the rates of exchange applying at the date of acquisition of the assets concerned, and recalculating cumulative depreciation or amortisation charges accordingly. It may be that to circumvent this difficulty an entity should consider using the option in IFRS 1 whereby the fair value of such assets at the date of transition is treated as being the deemed cost of those assets (see Chapter 4 at 2.5).

Some of the practical issues discussed at 3 above may have to be considered in accounting for foreign exchange in the periods after the date of transition in preparing the first IFRS financial statements, including the comparatives.

5   CONCLUSION

The issues relating to the accounting for foreign currency activities, whether through having transactions in another currency or through foreign operations, generally come down to two choices – the exchange rate to be used in the translation process and the subsequent treatment of the exchange differences that arise. The changes made by the IASB to IAS 21 in December 2003 have, in general, resulted in a better standard, and the revised version provides a workable basis for dealing with these issues.

The accounting for transactions in a currency other than the functional currency of an entity required by the standard is basically the same as that in the original standard, and as such, is well understood and doesn't give rise to too many difficulties. The critical issue will be the determination of an entity's functional currency, since it is by reference to that currency that transactions and balances will be regarded as being 'foreign' and thus give rise to foreign exchange differences. The other main issue is that for certain items, the distinction as to whether it is a monetary item or not may not be clear cut; the importance being that it is only monetary items that are translated at closing rates and thus result in exchange differences being taken to profit or loss.

As far as the translation of foreign operations is concerned, the standard deals with this as part of the process of an entity presenting its financial statements in a currency other than its functional currency or the functional currencies of the individual entities included in consolidated financial statements. However, for most situations, this translation process is effectively based on that in the previous version of the standard for translating foreign operations in consolidated financial statements, i.e. assets and liabilities translated at closing rates, income and expenses at actual rates (or an appropriate average rate), and resulting exchange differences taken to equity to be recycled to profit or loss upon disposal of the operation. Again, this process is well understood and shouldn't give rise to too many difficulties that are not addressed by the standard. The main area that is not addressed is the translation of equity items where the IASB has deliberately remained silent.

One aspect of the revised standard that we consider has been given inadequate attention by the IASB is that relating to monetary items forming part of the net investment in a foreign operation (see 3.4.1 above). As before, the standard allows exchange differences on such monetary items to be taken to equity in the consolidated financial statements. However, such a treatment can no longer be adopted in the separate financial statements of the entity with the foreign currency exposure; it has to take the exchange differences to its income statement, despite the fact that these are not expected to have any impact of the entity's cash flows. In addition, where the monetary item is denominated in a currency that is not the functional currency of either entity, the exchange differences reflected in the individual entities' financial statements also remain in the consolidated financial statements, thus treating the item like any other intragroup balance. These changes introduced by the IASB have not been acknowledged as changes in the standard, and the Basis for Conclusions does not discuss the issue. As a result, it is unclear what the rationale is for the revised requirements.

References

1 SFAS 8, *Accounting for the translation of foreign currency transactions and foreign currency financial statements*, FASB, October 1975.
2 CICA Handbook, Section 1650, *Translation of foreign currency transactions and foreign currency financial statements.*
3 IAS 21 (revised 1993), *The Effects of Changes in Foreign Exchange Rates*, IASC, Revised 1993, para. 23.
4 IAS 21 (revised 1993), paras. 30-31.
5 IAS 21 (revised 1993), paras. 27-29.
6 IAS 21 (revised 1993), para. 21.
7 IAS 21 (revised 1993), para. 4.
8 SIC-19, *Reporting Currency – Measurement and Presentation of Financial Statements under IAS 21 and IAS 29*, SIC, November 2000, para. 5.
9 SIC-19, para. 9.
10 IAS 21, *The Effects of Changes in Foreign Exchange Rates,* IASB, December 2003, para. IN1.
11 IAS 21, para. IN2.
12 IAS 21, para. IN3.
13 IAS 21, para. IN5.
14 IAS 21, para. IN6.
15 IAS 21, para. IN7.
16 IAS 21, para. IN8.
17 IAS 21, para. IN8.
18 IAS 21, para. IN9.
19 IAS 21, para. IN11.
20 IAS 21, para. IN12.
21 IAS 21, para. IN13.
22 IAS 21, para. IN14.
23 IAS 21, paras. BC15-BC23.
24 IAS 21, para. IN15.
25 IAS 21 (revised 1993), para. 33.
26 IAS 21, para. 58.
27 IAS 21, paras. 59-60.
28 IAS 21, para. 1.
29 IAS 21, para. 2.
30 IAS 21, para. 3.
31 IAS 21, para. 4.
32 IAS 21, para. 5.
33 IAS 21, para. 6.
34 IAS 21, para. 7.
35 IAS 21, para. 8.
36 IAS 21, para. 17.
37 IAS 21, para. 17.
38 IAS 21, para. 18.
39 IAS 21, para. 19.
40 IAS 21, para. 9.
41 IAS 21, para. 12.
42 IAS 21, para. 9.
43 IAS 21, para. 10.
44 IAS 21, para. 11.
45 IAS 21, para. 13.
46 IAS 21, para. 20.
47 IAS 21, para. 21.
48 IAS 21, para. 22.
49 IAS 21, para. 23.
50 IAS 21, para. 28.
51 IAS 21, para. 29.
52 IAS 21, para. 32.
53 IAS 23, *Borrowing Costs*, IASC, December 1993 (amended December 2003), para. 5.
54 IAS 21, para. 30.
55 IAS 21, para. 31.
56 IAS 21, para. 30.
57 IAS 21, para. 36.
58 IAS 21, para. 35.
59 IAS 21, para. 37.
60 IAS 21, para. 38.
61 IAS 21, para. 44.
62 IAS 21, para. 39.
63 IAS 21, para. 40.
64 IAS 21, para. 41.
65 IAS 21, para. 41.
66 IAS 21, para. 41.
67 IAS 21, para. BC17.
68 IAS 21, para. BC20.
69 IAS 21, para. BC18.
70 IAS 21, para. BC19.
71 IAS 21, para. 42.
72 IAS 21, para. 43.
73 IAS 21, para. 43.
74 IAS 21, para. 44.
75 IAS 21, para. 45.
76 IAS 21, para. 45.
77 IAS 21, para. 46.
78 SFAS 52, *Foreign Currency Translation*, FASB, December 1981, para. 139.
79 IAS 21 (revised 1993), para. 33.
80 IAS 21, para. BC27.
81 IAS 21, para. BC30.
82 IAS 21, para. BC31.
83 IAS 21, para. BC32.
84 IAS 21, para. 47.
85 IAS 21, para. 48.
86 IAS 27, *Consolidated and Separate Financial Statements*, IASB, December 2003 (amended March 2004), para. 30.
87 IAS 21, para. 49.
88 *IASB Update*, IASB, April 2004, p. 2.
89 IAS 21, para. 50.
90 IAS 21, para. 52.
91 IAS 21, para. 52.
92 IAS 21, para. 53.
93 IAS 21, para. 51.
94 IAS 21, para. 54.
95 IAS 21, para. 55.

96 IAS 21, para. 56.
97 IAS 21, para. 57.
98 IAS 21, para. 51.
99 IAS 39, *Financial Instruments: Recognition and Measurement*, IASB, December 2003 (amended March 2004), para. 14.
100 IAS 39, para. AG35.
101 IAS 21, para. 22.
102 IAS 21, para. 26.
103 IAS 21, para. 26.
104 IAS 21, para. 8.
105 IAS 21, para. 16.
106 IAS 21, para. 16.
107 IAS 21, para. 16.
108 IAS 39, para. AG83.
109 SFAS 52, para. 162.
110 IAS 39, para. AG83.
111 SFAS 52, para. 48
112 CICA 1650, para. 63.
113 Exposure Draft of Revised IAS 21, IASB, May 2002, para. 14.
114 IAS 12, *Income Taxes*, IASB October 1996 (amended March 2004), para. 78.
115 IAS 21, para. 34.
116 IAS 21, para. 34.
117 IAS 21, para. 26.
118 SFAS 52, para. 27.
119 SFAS 52, para. 138.
120 IAS 21, para. 40.
121 IAS 21, para. 40.
122 *IASB Update*, IASB, February 2003, p.5.
123 SFAS 52, para. 48
124 CICA 1650, para. 63.
125 IAS 21, para. 41.
126 IAS 21, para. 47.
127 IAS 21, para. BC32.
128 IAS 21, para. 45.
129 IAS 21, para. 45.
130 IAS 21, para. 8.
131 IAS 21, para. 15.
132 IAS 21, paras. 32-33.
133 IAS 21, para. 33.
134 IAS 21, para. 41.
135 IAS 21, para. 45.
136 SFAS 52, para. 25.
137 SIC-7, *Introduction of the Euro*, SIC, May 1998 (amended December 2003), para. 3.
138 SIC-7, para. 3.
139 SIC-7, para. 4.
140 SIC-7, para. 5.
141 SIC-7, para. 6.
142 SIC-7, para. 4.
143 SIC-7, para. 7.
144 IAS 21, para. 60.
145 IAS 21, para. 59.
146 IAS 21, para. 59.
147 IFRS 1, *First-time Adoption of International Financial Reporting Standards*, IASB, June 2003 (amended March 2004), para. 21.
148 IFRS 1, paras. BC54-BC55.
149 IFRS 1, para. 22.
150 IFRS 1, para. B1A.
151 IFRS 1, para. B1B.

Chapter 10   Hyperinflation

1   INTRODUCTION

Accounting standards generally and the historical cost basis of accounting, assume that the value of money – the unit of measurement – is constant over time, which normally is an acceptable practical assumption. However, when the effect of inflation on the value of money is no longer negligible, the usefulness of historical cost based financial reporting is often significantly reduced. High rates of inflation give rise to a number of problems for entities that prepare their financial statements on a historical cost basis, for example:

- historical cost figures expressed in terms of monetary units do not show the 'value to the business' of assets;

- holding gains on non-monetary assets that are reported as operating profits do not represent real economic gains;

- financial information presented for the current period is not comparable with that presented for the prior periods; and

- 'real' capital can be reduced because profits reported do not take account of the higher replacement costs of resources used in the period. Therefore, if in calculating profit 'return on capital' is not distinguished properly from 'return of capital', the erosion of 'real' capital may go unnoticed in the financial statements. This is the underlying point in the concept of capital maintenance.

Rates of inflation well in excess of 10% during most of the 1970s and early 1980s in most of the world brought these and other shortcomings of historical cost based financial reporting in an inflationary environment to prominence. Though methods of inflation accounting were extensively debated, interest in the subject dissipated quickly in the late 1980s when inflation all but disappeared in the US and Western Europe. Moreover, the discussions about inflation accounting and concepts of capital maintenance, undeservingly, have left little traces in modern accounting standards. The IASB's *Framework* pays lip service to the existence of different concepts of capital maintenance but is ultimately based on the financial capital maintenance concept (see Chapter 3 at 3.2.6). Under this concept the capital of the entity will be maintained if the amount of gains during a period is at least equal to the amount of losses in that period. The IASB's Framework describes the concept of physical capital maintenance under which 'a profit is earned only if the physical productive capacity (or operating capability) of the enterprise (or the resources or funds needed to achieve that capacity) at the end of the period exceeds the physical productive capacity at the beginning of the period, after excluding any distributions to, and contributions from, owners during the period'.[1] However, the IASB did not really develop the physical capital maintenance concept in its Framework or any of its standards.[2] The financial capital maintenance concept on which International Financial Reporting Standards are based is only satisfactory under conditions of stable prices.

1.1   Hyperinflationary economies

From a Western European perspective it is easy to overlook that there are countries where inflation is still a major economic concern. In some of these countries, inflation has reached such levels – hyperinflation – that (1) the local currency is no longer a useful measure of value in the economy and (2) the general population may no longer prefer to hold its wealth in the local currency. Instead, they hold their wealth in a stable foreign currency or non-monetary assets. Under US accounting standards hyperinflation is deemed to exist when the cumulative rate of inflation over a three-year period exceeds 100%. As discussed at 2.3.1 below, there are several additional criteria that need to be taken into account under IFRS to determine whether hyperinflation exists.[3] Countries that are generally considered hyperinflationary, because they have recently had three-year cumulative inflation of 100% or more, include:[4]

Angola	Romania	Uzbekistan
Belarus	Serbia/Montenegro	Zimbabwe
Dem. Rep. of Congo	Suriname	
Myanmar	Turkey	

Information on inflation rates in various countries is available in *International Financial Statistics*, published monthly by the International Monetary Fund.

1.2   Adjustment approaches

The historical cost based financial reporting problems reach such a magnitude under hyperinflationary circumstances that financial reporting in the hyperinflationary currency is all but meaningless. Therefore, a solution is needed to allow meaningful financial reporting by entities that operate in hyperinflationary economies. Two solutions to accounting for hyperinflation that have traditionally been applied can be summarised as follows:

- *Restatement approach* – Financial information recorded in the hyperinflationary currency is adjusted by applying a general price index and expressed in the measuring unit (the hyperinflationary currency) current at the balance sheet date.

- *Stable foreign currency* – The entity uses a relatively stable currency, for example the presentation currency of its parent, as the currency in which it measures items in its financial statements. If the transactions of the operation are not recorded initially in that stable currency, then they are remeasured into the stable currency by applying the temporal method of translation (see Chapter 9 at 1.1 and 1.2.1).

The relevant international standard, IAS 29 – *Financial Reporting in Hyperinflationary Economies*, only permits the restatement approach. Entities operating in a hyperinflationary economy are prohibited under IFRS from selecting a stable currency as their unit of accounting if that currency is not its functional currency under IAS 21 – *The Effects of Changes in Foreign Exchange Rates*, i.e. 'the currency of the primary economic environment in which the entity operates' (see Chapter 9 at 2.5).[5]

2   REQUIREMENTS OF IAS 29

2.1   History

The (then) IASC adopted IAS 29 in April 1989 and has only addressed the subject of hyperinflation since to clarify the provisions of the standard. This is not surprising as memories of high inflation rapidly receded from the collective memory of most of the IASC's more influential constituents in the 1990s.

In February 2000, SIC-19 – *Reporting Currency – Measurement and Presentation of Financial Statements under IAS 21 and IAS 29* – was adopted, which provided rules on the selection of a measurement currency. Before the adoption of SIC-19 it was possible for entities operating in hyperinflationary economies to use any measurement currency of their liking, which allowed them to avoid using a hyperinflationary measurement currency and thereby to sidestep the requirements of IAS 29. As a result of the IASB's Improvements Project, the rules in SIC-19 have now been incorporated in IAS 21, which specifically prohibits an entity from avoiding 'restatement in accordance with IAS 29 by, for example, adopting as its functional currency a currency other than the functional currency determined in accordance with this Standard'.[6]

In March 2004, IFRIC issued Draft Interpretation D5 – *Applying IAS 29 Financial Reporting Hyperinflationary Economies for the First Time* – which proposes specific guidance to facilitate the first time application of IAS 29.[7]

The IFRS literature defines the following currency related notions:

- *Functional currency* is defined in IAS 21 as the currency of the primary economic environment in which the entity operates;[8]
- *Measurement currency* was defined in SIC-19 as the currency in which the entity measures the items in the financial statements.[9] This notion has now been replaced by functional currency which is more commonly used and, according to the IASB, has 'essentially the same meaning';[10]

- *Presentation currency* is defined in IAS 21 as the currency in which the financial statements are presented;[11]

- *Reporting currency* was defined in IAS 21 (revised 1993) as the currency used in presenting the financial statements.[12] The standard did not specify the currency in which an entity presented its financial statements, although it noted that an entity would normally use the currency in which it was domiciled.[13] However, the choice of reporting currency established that all other currencies were treated as foreign currencies for the purposes of IAS 21 (revised 1993) and therefore would affect the financial statements. IAS 21 (revised 2003) replaces the notion of 'reporting currency' with two notions 'functional currency' and 'presentation currency'.[14]

2.2   Objective

The underlying premise of IAS 29 is that 'reporting of operating results and financial position in the local [hyperinflationary] currency without restatement is not useful'.[15] The standard's approach is therefore to require that:

(a)   'the financial statements of an entity whose functional currency is the currency of a hyperinflationary economy, whether they are based on a historical cost approach or a current cost approach, shall be stated in terms of the measuring unit current at the balance sheet date';[16]

(b)   'the corresponding figures for the previous period required by IAS 1 – *Presentation of Financial Statements* – and any information in respect of earlier periods shall also be stated in terms of the measuring unit current at the balance sheet date';[17] and

(c)   'the gain or loss on the net monetary position should be included in net income and separately disclosed'.[18]

IAS 29 requires 'balance sheet amounts not already expressed in terms of the measuring unit current at the balance sheet date' to be restated in terms of the measuring unit current at the balance sheet date, by applying a general price index.[19] The example below gives an outline of how this would apply to the balance sheet of an entity (for a detailed discussion of IAS 29 and restatement process see 2.4 below):

Example 10.1:   Accounting for hyperinflation under IAS 29

Assuming Entity A operates in a hyperinflationary economy, it would be required under IAS 29 to restate all non-monetary items in its balance sheet to the measuring unit at balance sheet date by applying a general price index.

Entity A	Before restatement (HC)	Historical general price index	Year-end general price index	After restatement (HC)
Fixed assets	225	150	600	900
Inventory	250	500	600	300
Cash	100			100
Total assets	575			1,300
Accounts payable	180			180
Long-term debt	250			250
Equity *)	145			870
	575			1,300

*) The restatement of equity is not illustrated here, but discussed at 2.4.2 G below.

The simplified example above already raises a number of questions, such as:

• which balance sheet items are monetary and which are non-monetary?

• how does the entity select the appropriate general price index?

• what was the general price index when specific assets were acquired?

The standard provides guidance on the restatement to the measuring unit current at the balance sheet date, but concedes that 'the consistent application of these [inflation accounting] procedures and judgements from period to period is more important than the precise accuracy of the resulting amounts included in the restated financial statements'.[20] The requirements of the standard look deceptively straightforward but actually represent a considerable challenge to entities. These difficulties and other aspects of the practical application of the IAS 29 method of accounting for hyperinflation are discussed at 2.4.2 and 4 below.

Apart from the more technical reservations that exist about IAS 29, the concept of restating financial information to the measuring units current at the balance sheet date could have been articulated more clearly. Given the choice between (1) restating financial information for hyperinflation after the balance sheet date or (2) financial statements expressed in a stable foreign currency, some users might prefer the latter. Nevertheless, even when translated to a stable foreign currency, difficulties remain because of the complexities of the economic phenomenon of hyperinflation. Additionally, expressing financial statements of entities operating in hyperinflationary economies in a stable currency might give users a false sense of security.

2.3   Scope

IAS 29 should be applied by all entities whose functional currency is the currency of a hyperinflationary economy because 'money loses purchasing power at such a rate that comparison of amounts from transactions and other events that have occurred at different times, even within the same accounting period, is misleading'.[21] The standard should be applied both by entities in their stand-alone reporting as well as by parents that include such entities in their consolidated financial statements. Financial statements of entities whose functional currency is that of a hyperinflationary economy first have to be restated under IAS 29 and then, if their parent has a different functional currency, translated under IAS 21 before they can be incorporated within the consolidated financial statements of the parent entity.

Almost all entities operating in hyperinflationary economies will be subject to the accounting regime of IAS 29, unless they can legitimately argue that the local hyperinflationary currency is not their functional currency as defined by IAS 21 (see Chapter 9 at 2.5).

2.3.1   Definition of hyperinflation

Determining whether an economy is hyperinflationary in accordance with IAS 29 requires judgement. The standard does not establish an absolute rate at which hyperinflation is deemed to arise. Instead, it considers the following characteristics of the economic environment of a country to be strong indicators of the existence of hyperinflation:

'(a)   the general population prefers to keep its wealth in non-monetary assets or in a relatively stable foreign currency. Amounts of local currency held are immediately invested to maintain purchasing power;

(b)   the general population regards monetary amounts not in terms of the local currency but in terms of a relatively stable foreign currency. Prices may be quoted in that currency;

(c)   sales and purchases on credit take place at prices that compensate for the expected loss of purchasing power during the credit period, even if the period is short;

(d)   interest rates, wages and prices are linked to a price index; and

(e)   the cumulative inflation rate over three years is approaching, or exceeds, 100%'.[22]

The above list is not exhaustive and there may be other indicators that an economy is hyperinflationary, such as the existence of price controls and restrictive exchange controls. In determining whether an economy is hyperinflationary, condition (e) is quantitatively measurable while the other indicators require reliance on more qualitative, often anecdotal, evidence. For the purposes of testing condition (e), reference should be made to authoritative sources such as the International Monetary Fund's *International Financial Statistics Book*, though too-mechanical an application of the 100% criterion is not necessarily advisable. Despite the fact that

IAS 29 expresses a preference 'that all enterprises that report in the currency of the same hyperinflationary economy apply this Standard from the same date',[23] that is in practice an unrealistic wish given the way it defines hyperinflation. In any event, once an entity has identified the existence of hyperinflation, it should apply IAS 29 from the beginning of the reporting period in which it identified the existence of hyperinflation.[24]

Identifying when a currency becomes hyperinflationary, and as importantly when it ceases to be so, is not easy in practice. The consideration of trends, and the application of common sense, is important in this judgement, as are considerations of consistency of measurement and of presentation.

2.4 The IAS 29 restatement process

Restatement of financial statements in accordance with IAS 29 can be seen as a process comprising the following steps:

(a) selection of a general price index (see 2.4.1 below);

(b) analysis and restatement of assets and liabilities on the basis of this index (see 2.4.2 below);

(c) restatement of the income statement on the basis of this index (see 2.4.3 below);

(d) calculation of the gain or loss on the net monetary position on the basis of this index (see 2.4.4 below);

(e) restatement of the cash flow statement on the basis of this index (see 2.4.5 below); and

(f) restatement of the corresponding figures on the basis of this index (see 2.4.6 below).

These steps are discussed below.

2.4.1 Selection of a general price index

The standard requires entities to use 'a general price index that reflects changes in general purchasing power', preferably the same price index should be used by all entities in the same hyperinflationary currency (see 4.1 below).[25]

Sometimes the general price index chosen by the entity is not available for all periods for which the restatement of long-lived assets is required. In that case, the entity will need to make an estimate of the price index based, for example, on 'the movements in the exchange rate between the functional currency and a relatively stable foreign currency' (see 4.2 below).[26]

2.4.2   *Analysis and restatement of balance sheet items*

A broad outline of the process to restate assets and liabilities in accordance with the requirements of IAS 29 is shown in the diagram below:

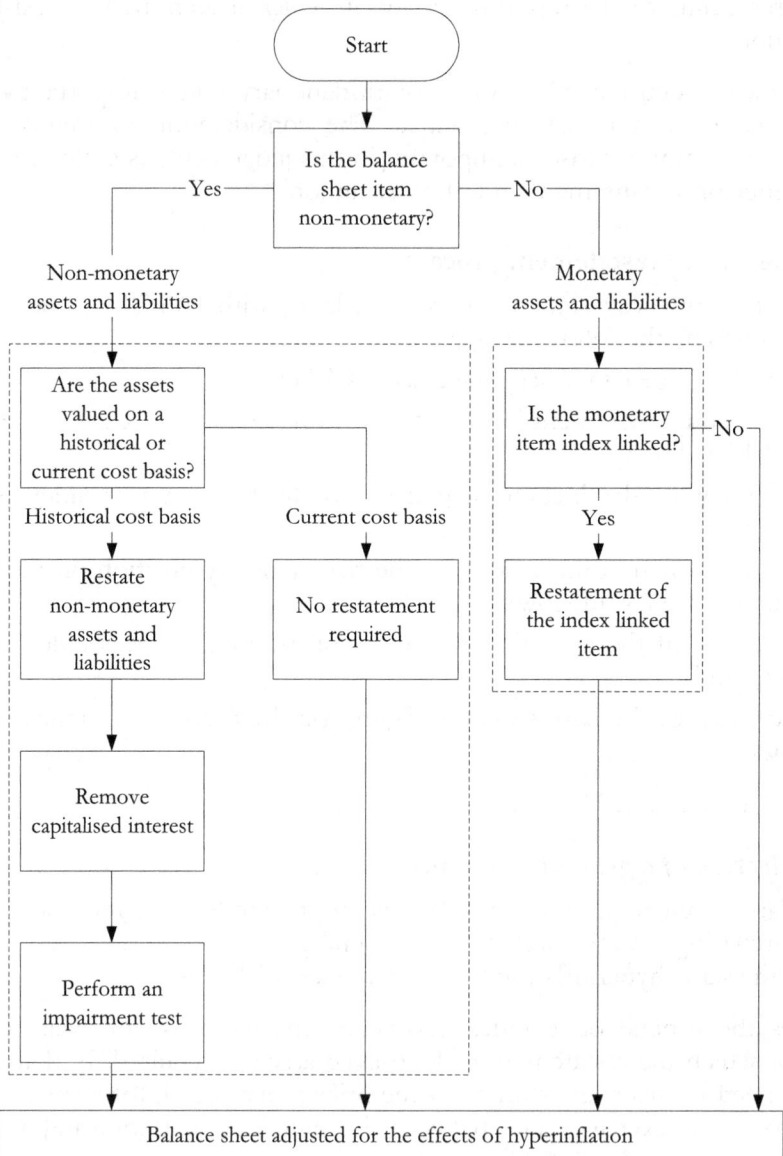

In many hyperinflationary economies, national legislation may require entities to adjust historical cost based financial information in a way that is not in accordance with IAS 29 (for example, national legislation may require entities to adjust the carrying amount of tangible fixed assets by applying a multiplier). Though financial information adjusted in accordance with national legislation is sometimes described as 'current cost' information, it will often not meet the definition of current cost in accordance with the IASB's Framework (see C below).[27] Where this is the case, entities must first determine the real historical cost basis of assets and liabilities before applying the requirements of IAS 29.

The above flowchart does not show the restatement of investees and subsidiaries (see E below), deferred taxation (see F below) and equity (see G below).

A   *Monetary or non-monetary*

The first question to be addressed in the restatement of the balance sheet is which items are monetary and which are not. This is because monetary items normally need not be restated as they are already expressed in the measurement unit current at the balance sheet date. Most balance sheet items are readily classified as either monetary or non-monetary as is shown in the table below:

Monetary items	Non-monetary items
Assets	**Assets**
Cash and cash equivalents	Property, plant and equipment
Debt securities	Intangible assets
Loans	Investments in equity securities
Trade and other receivables	Assets held for sale
	Inventories
	Construction contract work-in-progress
	Prepaid costs
	Investment properties
Liabilities	**Liabilities**
Trade and other payables	Warranty provision
Borrowings	
Other liabilities	
Tax payable	

Classification of items as either monetary or non-monetary is not always straightforward. Monetary items are defined in IAS 29 as 'money held and items to be received or paid in money'.[28] However, IAS 21 expands somewhat on this definition by defining monetary items as 'units of currency held and assets and liabilities to be received or paid in a fixed or determinable number of units of currency'.[29] The standard elaborates further on this by stating that 'the essential feature of a monetary item is a right to receive (or an obligation to deliver) a fixed or determinable number of units of currency'. Examples given by IAS 21 are pensions and other employee benefits to be paid in cash; provisions that are to be settled in cash; and cash dividends that are recognised as a liability.[30] More obvious examples are cash and bank balances; trade receivables and payables; and loan receivables and payables. IAS 39 also indicates that where a foreign currency bond is held as an available-for-sale financial asset, then it should first be accounted for at amortised cost in the underlying currency, thus effectively treating that amount as if it was a monetary item. This suggests that foreign currency bonds that are classified as held-to-maturity investments under IAS 39 are monetary items.

IAS 21 also states that 'a contract to receive (or deliver) a variable number of the entity's own equity instruments or a variable amount of assets in which the fair value to be received (or delivered) equals a fixed or determinable number of units of currency is a monetary item."[31] No examples of such contracts are given in IAS 21. However, it would seem to embrace those contracts settled in the entity's own equity shares that under IAS 32 would be presented as financial assets or liabilities.

Conversely, the essential feature of a non-monetary item is the absence of a right to receive (or an obligation to deliver) a fixed or determinable number of units of currency. Examples given by the standard are amounts prepaid for goods and services (e.g. prepaid rent); goodwill; intangible assets; inventories; property, plant and equipment; and provisions that are to be settled by the delivery of a non-monetary asset.[32] IAS 39 also indicates that equity instruments that are held as available-for-sale financial assets are non-monetary items.[33] This suggests that equity investments in subsidiaries, associates or joint ventures are non-monetary items.

Even with this guidance there will clearly be a number of situations where the distinction may not be altogether clear (see also Chapter 9 at 3.2.4). Certain assets and liabilities may require careful analysis before they can be classified, and even then their classification is not entirely satisfactory. Examples of items that are not easily classified as either monetary or non-monetary include:

(a) *provisions for liabilities:* these can be monetary, non-monetary or partly monetary. For example, a warranty provision would be:

   (i) entirely monetary when customers only have a right to return the product and obtain a cash refund equal to the amount they originally paid;

   (ii) non-monetary when customers have the right to have any defective product replaced; and

   (iii) partly monetary if customers can choose between a refund and a replacement of the defect product.

   Obviously, classification as either monetary or non-monetary is not very satisfactory in (iii) above. In the spirit of the IAS 29 requirements, part of the provision should be treated as a non-monetary item and the remainder as a monetary item;

(b) *deferred tax assets and liabilities:* characterising these as monetary or non-monetary is fraught with difficulties, which are explained in F below;

(c) *associates and joint ventures:* these are most likely to be at least partly monetary, depending on the degree to which they themselves hold monetary items or non-monetary items. Whatever the case may be, IAS 29 provides separate rules on restatement of investees that do not rely on the distinction between monetary and non-monetary (see E below);

(d) *deposits or progress payments paid or received:* if the payments made are regarded as prepayments or as progress payments then the amounts should be treated as non-monetary items. However, if the payments made are regarded as deposits, and are refundable, then the amounts should probably be treated as monetary items; and

(e) *index-linked assets and liabilities:* interest rates, lease payments, wages and prices that are linked to a price index are particularly difficult to classify.

In summary, the practical application of the monetary/non-monetary distinction is beset with difficulties and, after the classification of the more obvious items, judgement on the part of preparers of financial statements is required.[34] Further examples of problem areas in the application of the monetary/non-monetary distinction are discussed in Chapter 9 at 3.2.4.

B   Monetary items

Generally, monetary items need not be restated to reflect the effect of inflation. However, monetary assets and liabilities linked by agreement to changes in prices – such as index-linked bonds and loans – should be adjusted in accordance with the underlying agreement to show the repayment obligation in accordance with the terms of the agreement at the balance sheet date.[35] This adjustment should be offset against the gain or loss on the net monetary position (see 2.4.4 below). This type of restatement is in fact not an inflation accounting adjustment, but rather a gain or loss on a financial instrument. Accounting for inflation linked bonds and loans under IAS 39 may well lead to incomprehensible financial reporting. Depending on the specific wording of the inflation adjustment clause, such contracts may give rise to embedded derivatives and gains or losses will have to be recorded either in income or equity depending on how the instrument is classified for IAS 39 purposes (see Chapter 15 at 5.1.10).

C   Non-monetary items carried at current cost

Non-monetary items carried at current cost 'are not restated because they are already expressed in terms of the measuring unit current at the balance sheet date'.[36] Current cost is not defined by the standard, but the Framework provides the following definition: 'Assets are carried at the amount of cash or cash equivalents that would have to be paid if the same or an equivalent asset was acquired currently. Liabilities are carried at the undiscounted amount of cash or cash equivalents that would be required to settle the obligation currently'.[37] For the purposes of restating historical cost financial statements, IAS 29 expands this definition by including net realisable value and market value into the concept of 'amounts current at the balance sheet date'.[38] In the same way, non-monetary items valued at fair value are included in IAS 29's current cost concept.

It is important to note that revalued amounts, at which some non-monetary items are measured, are not necessarily equal to current cost and need to be restated from the date of their revaluation.[39]

D   Non-monetary items carried at historical cost

Non-monetary items carried at historical cost, or cost less depreciation, are stated at amounts that were current at the date of their acquisition. The restated cost, or cost less depreciation, of those items is calculated as follows:

$$\begin{array}{l}\text{net book value}\\ \quad\text{restated for}\\ \text{hyperinflation}\end{array} = \text{historical cost} \times \frac{\text{general price index at the balance sheet date}}{\text{general price index at the date of acquisition}}$$

Application of this formula to 'property, plant and equipment, investments, inventories of raw materials and merchandise, goodwill, patents, trademarks and similar assets'[40] appears to be straightforward, but does require detailed records of their acquisition dates and accurate price indices at those dates. It should be noted though that IAS 29 permits certain approximations as long as the procedures and judgements are consistent from period to period.[41] Where sufficiently detailed records are not available or capable of estimation, IAS 29 suggests that it may be necessary to obtain 'an independent professional assessment of the value of the items as the basis for their restatement' in the first period of application of the standard.[42]

Example 10.2:   Restatement of property, plant and equipment

The table below illustrates how the restatement of a non-monetary item (for example, property, plant and equipment) would be calculated in accordance with the requirements of IAS 29.

Net book value of property, plant and equipment	Historical movements	Conversion factor	Restated for hyperinflation	
Opening balance, 1 January	510	2.40	1,224	(a)
– Additions (May)	360	1.80	648	(b)
– Disposals (March)	(120)	2.10	(252)	(c)
– Depreciation	(200)	2.24	(448)	(d)
Closing balance, 31 December	550		1,172	(e)

(a) The opening balance is restated by adjusting the historical balance for the increase in the price index between the opening balance sheet date and closing balance sheet date;

(b) The additions are restated for the increase in the price index from May to December;

(c) The disposals are restated for the increase in the price index between the opening balance sheet date and closing balance sheet date;

(d) Depreciation has been recalculated using the cost balance restated for hyperinflation as a starting point. The alternative approach, to restate the depreciation charge by applying the appropriate conversion factor, is easier to apply but may not be as accurate when there is a significant level of additions and disposals during the reporting period;

(e) The closing balance is in practice determined by adding up items (a)-(d). Alternatively, the entity could calculate the closing balance by restating the acquisition cost of the individual assets for the change in the price index during the period of ownership.

The calculations described under (a)-(e) all require estimates regarding the general price index at given dates and are sometimes based on averages or best estimates of the actual date of the transaction.

Inventories of finished and partly finished goods should be restated from the dates on which the costs of purchase and of conversion were incurred.[43] This means that the individual components of finished goods should be restated from their respective purchase dates. Similarly, if assembly takes place in several distinct phases, the cost of each of those phases should be restated from the date that the cost was incurred.

When an entity purchases an asset and payment is deferred beyond normal credit terms, it would normally recognise the present value of the cash payment as its cost.[44] IAS 29 provides relief by allowing that when it is impracticable to determine the amount of interest, such assets are restated from the payment date and not the date of purchase.[45]

In order to arrive at the restated cost of the non-monetary items, the provisional restated cost needs to be adjusted as follows:

$$\text{restated costs} = \begin{array}{c}\text{net book value}\\\text{restated for}\\\text{hyperinflation}\end{array} - \begin{array}{c}\text{borrowing costs that}\\\text{compensate for inflation}\\\text{capitalised under IAS 23}\end{array} - \begin{array}{c}\text{adjustment to}\\\text{recoverable}\\\text{amount}\end{array}$$

Capitalisation of all borrowing costs (see Chapter 14) is not considered appropriate under IAS 29 because of the risk of double counting because the entity would both 'restate the capital expenditure financed by borrowing and … capitalise that part of the borrowing costs that compensates for the inflation during the same period'.[46] Full application of the allowed alternative treatment under IAS 23, which requires capitalisation of borrowing costs, is therefore allowed when an entity falls within the scope of IAS 29. Instead, an entity applying IAS 29 is only permitted to capitalise borrowing costs to the extent that they do not compensate for inflation. Unfortunately, the standard does not provide any guidance on how an entity should go about determining the component of borrowing costs that compensates for the effects of inflation.

It is possible that an IAS 29 inflation adjustment based on the general price index leads to non-monetary assets being stated above their net realisable value. Therefore, IAS 29 requires that 'the restated amount of a non-monetary item is reduced, in accordance with appropriate International Financial Reporting Standards, when it exceeds the amount recoverable from the item's future use (including sale or other disposal)'.[47] This requirement should be taken to mean that any overstatement of assets should generally be calculated in accordance with IAS 36 – *Impairment of Assets*.

Example 10.3:   Borrowing costs and net realisable value adjustments

After the entity has restated the historical cost based carrying amount of property, plant and equipment by applying the general price index, it needs to adjust the net book value restated for hyperinflation as follows:

Net book value restated for hyperinflation		1,725
Borrowing costs capitalised at historical cost under IAS 23	42	
Borrowing costs that compensated for inflation	(30)	
Borrowing costs permitted to be capitalised under IAS 29	12	
Borrowing costs that compensated for inflation	(30)	
Relevant conversion factor for the borrowing costs	2.10 ×	
	(63)	(a)
Net book value restated for hyperinflation and after adjustment of capitalised borrowing costs		1,662
Net book value restated for hyperinflation and after adjustment of capitalised borrowing costs	1,662	
Amount recoverable from the item's future use	1,750	
	(88)	
Adjustment to lower recoverable amount	–	(b)
Carrying amount restated under IAS 29		1,662

(a) The borrowing costs capitalised in the original historical cost financial statements are reversed, as they are not permitted under IAS 29;

(b) To the extent that the 'net book value restated for hyperinflation and after adjustment of capitalised borrowing costs' exceeds the 'amount recoverable from the item's future use', the restated amount should be reduced to the lower 'amount recoverable from the item's future use'.

E   Restatement of investees and subsidiaries

IAS 29 provides separate rules for the restatement of investees (i.e. associates and joint ventures) that are accounted for under the equity method. If the investee itself operates in the same currency, the entity should restate the balance sheet and income statement of the investee in accordance with the requirements of IAS 29 in order to calculate its share of the investee's net assets and results of operations. If the restated financial statements of the investee are expressed in a foreign currency – that is either hyperinflationary or a non-hyperinflationary – they should be translated at the closing rate.[48] IAS 21 contains a similar provision that requires that all current year amounts related to an entity (i.e. investee), whose functional currency is the currency of a hyperinflationary economy, should be translated at the closing rate at the date of the most recent balance sheet (see Chapter 9 at 2.7.1 B).[49]

If a parent that reports in the currency of a hyperinflationary economy has a subsidiary that also reports in the currency of a hyperinflationary economy, then the financial statements of that subsidiary must first be 'restated by applying a general price index of the country in whose currency it reports before they are included in the consolidated financial statements issued by its parent'.[50] IAS 21 further clarifies that all current year amounts related to an entity (i.e. subsidiary), whose functional currency is the currency of a hyperinflationary economy, should be translated at the closing rate at the date of the most recent balance sheet (see Chapter 9 at 2.7.1 B).[51]

If a parent that reports in the currency of a hyperinflationary economy has a subsidiary that reports in a currency that is not hyperinflationary, the financial statements of that subsidiary should be translated in accordance with paragraph 39 of IAS 21 (see Chapter 9 at 2.7.1 A).[52]

Finally, IAS 29 requires that when 'financial statements with different reporting dates are consolidated, all items, whether non-monetary or monetary, ... be restated into the measuring unit current at the date of the consolidated financial statements'.[53]

F   Calculation of deferred taxation

Determining whether deferred tax assets and liabilities are monetary or non-monetary is extremely difficult because:

- deferred taxation could be seen as a valuation adjustment that is either monetary or non-monetary depending on the asset or liability it relates to; and

- on the other hand it could also be argued that any deferred taxation payable or receivable in the very near future is almost identical to current tax payable and receivable. Therefore, at least the short-term portion of deferred taxation, if payable or receivable, could be treated as if it were monetary.

In any event, the debate as to whether deferred taxation is monetary or non-monetary is for practical purposes settled by the requirement of IAS 12 – *Income Taxes* – to calculate deferred taxation based on the difference between the carrying amount and the tax base of assets and liabilities at balance sheet date. Therefore, irrespective of the monetary/non-monetary distinction, deferred taxation needs to be recalculated at balance sheet date.

IAS 29 refers to IAS 12 for guidance on the calculation of deferred taxation by entities operating in hyperinflationary economies.[54] IAS 12 recognises that IAS 29 restatements of assets and liabilities may give rise to temporary differences when equivalent adjustments are not allowed for tax purposes.[55] Where IAS 29 adjustments give rise to temporary differences, IAS 12 requires the following accounting treatment:

'(1)   the deferred taxation is charged in the income statement; and

(2)   if, in addition to the restatement, the non-monetary assets are also revalued, the deferred tax relating to the revaluation is charged to equity and the deferred tax relating to the restatement is charged in the income statement'.[56]

For example, deferred taxation arising on *revaluation* of property, plant and equipment should be recognised in equity, just as it would be if the entity were not operating in a hyperinflationary economy. On the other hand, *restatement* in accordance with IAS 29 of property, plant and equipment that is measured at historical cost should be recognised in the income statement. Thus the treatment of deferred taxation related to non-monetary assets valued at historical cost and those that are revalued, is consistent with the general requirements of IAS 12.

G   *Restatement of equity and first-time application of IAS 29*

At the beginning of the first period when an entity applies IAS 29, because the economy in which it is operating has become hyperinflationary, it should restate the components of owners' equity as follows:

- 'the components of owners' equity, except retained earnings and any revaluation surplus, are restated by applying a general price index from the dates the components were contributed or otherwise arose';[57]

- 'any revaluation surplus that arose in previous periods is eliminated';[58] and

- 'restated retained earnings are derived from all the other amounts in the restated balance sheet'.[59]

'At the end of the first period and in subsequent periods, all components of owners' equity are restated by applying a general price index from the beginning of the period or the date of contribution, if later'.[60] It seems anomalous that the restatement of a historical cost balance sheet for hyperinflationary conditions may possibly result in an increase in retained earnings. However, this may well be the effect of the transfer of revaluation reserve to retained earnings implicit in the second bullet point above.

Though IAS 29 provides guidance on the restatement of assets, liabilities and individual components of shareholders' equity, it should be noted that national laws and regulations with which the entity needs to comply might not permit such revaluations. This can mean that IAS 29 may require restatement of distributable reserves, but that from a legal point of view those same reserves remain unchanged. That is, it is possible that 'restated retained earnings' under IAS 29 will not all be legally distributable.

Example 10.4:   Restatement of equity

The table below shows the effect of a hypothetical IAS 29 restatement on individual components of equity. Issued share capital and share premium increase by applying the general price index, the revaluation reserve is eliminated as required, and retained earnings is the balancing figure derived from all other amounts in the restated balance sheet.

	Amounts before restatement	Amounts after IAS 29 restatement	Components of equity under national law
Issued capital	1,500	3,150	1,500
Revaluation reserve	800	–	800
Retained earnings	350	1,600	350
Total equity	2,650	4,750	2,650

A user of the financial statements of the entity might get the impression, based on the information restated in accordance with IAS 29, that distributable reserves have increased from 350 to 1,600. However, if national law does not permit revaluation of assets, liabilities and components of equity then distributable reserves remain unchanged.

Users of financial statements restated under IAS 29 may for that reason be misled about the extent to which components of equity are distributable. Entities reporting under IAS 29 should therefore disclose the extent to which components of equity are distributable where this is not obvious from the financial statements. In our view it is important for entities to give supplementary information in the circumstances where the IAS 29 adjustments have produced large apparently distributable reserves that are in fact not distributable.

Because of its global constituency, the IASB's standards cannot deal with specific national legal requirements relating to a legal entity's equity. Therefore, instead of prescribing an accounting treatment for individual components of equity, we consider that the IASB would be better advised to recognise the wide variety in national legislation, and prescribe disclosure requirements that ensure users of financial statements are not misled.

2.4.3 Restatement of the income statement

IAS 29 requires that all items in historical cost based income statements be expressed in terms of the measuring unit current at the balance sheet date.[61] The standard contains a similar requirement for current cost based income statements, because the underlying transactions or events are recorded at current cost at the time they occurred rather than in the measuring unit current at the balance sheet date.[62] Therefore, all amounts in the income statement need to be restated as follows:

$$\frac{\text{restated}}{\text{amount}} = \frac{\text{amount before}}{\text{restatement}} \times \frac{\text{general price index at the balance sheet date}}{\substack{\text{general price index when the underlying} \\ \text{income or expenses were initially recorded}}}$$

Actually performing the above calculation on a real set of financial statements is often difficult because:

(a) entities would need to keep a very detailed record of when they entered into transactions and when they incurred expenses; and

(b) if exchange rates fluctuate significantly, the use of the average rate for a period is inappropriate. However, for practical reasons, a rate that approximates the actual rate at the date of the transaction is often used. For example, an average rate for a week or a month might be used for all transactions in each foreign currency occurring during that period. However, it must be stressed that if exchange rates fluctuate significantly, the use of the average rate for a period is inappropriate.[63]

Example 9.5 illustrates how an entity might, for example, restate its revenue to the measuring unit current at the balance sheet date. A similar calculation would work well for other items in the income statement, with the exception of:

(a) depreciation and amortisation charges which are often easier to restate by using the cost balance restated for hyperinflation as a starting point;

(b) deferred taxation which should be based on the temporary differences between the carrying amount and tax base of assets and liabilities, the restated carrying amount of balance sheet items, and the underlying tax base of those items; and

(c) the net monetary gain or loss which results from the IAS 29 restatements (see 2.4.4 below).

Example 10.5:   *Restatement of historical cost income statement*

An entity would restate its revenue for the period ending 31 December 2004, when the general price index was 2,880, as shown in the table below.

	General price index	Conversion factor	Revenue before restatement	Restated revenue
31 January 2004	1,315	(2,880÷1,315) = 2.19	40	87.6
28 February 2004	1,345	(2,880÷1,345) = 2.14	35	74.9
31 March 2004	1,371	etc. = 2.10	45	94.5
30 April 2004	1,490	1.93	45	87.0
31 May 2004	1,600	1.80	65	117.0
30 June 2004	1,846	1.56	70	109.2
31 July 2004	1,923	1.50	70	104.8
31 August 2004	2,071	1.39	65	90.4
30 September 2004	2,163	1.33	75	99.9
31 October 2004	2,511	1.15	75	86.0
30 November 2004	2,599	1.11	80	88.6
31 December 2004	2,880	1.00	80	80.0
			745	1,119.9

A similar calculation can be made for other items in the income statement. Inevitably, in practice there is some approximation because of the assumptions that the entity is required to make, for example:

(a) the use of weighted averages rather than more detailed calculations; and

(b) assumptions as to the timing of the underlying transactions (e.g. the calculation above assumes the revenues for the month are earned on the final day of the month, which is not realistic).

2.4.4   Calculation of the gain or loss on the net monetary position

In theory, hyperinflation only affects the value of money and monetary items and does not affect the value as distinct from the price of non-monetary items. Therefore, any gain or loss because of hyperinflation will be the gain or loss on the net monetary position of the entity. By arranging the items in an ordinary balance sheet, it can be shown that the monetary position minus the non-monetary position is always equal to zero:

	Total	Monetary items	Non-monetary items
Monetary assets	280	280	
Non-monetary assets	170		170
Monetary liabilities	(200)	(200)	
Non-monetary liabilities	(110)		(110)
Assets minus liabilities	140		
Shareholders' equity	(140)		(140)
Net position	0	80	(80)

Theoretically, the gain or loss on the net monetary position can be calculated by applying the general price index to the entity's monetary assets and liabilities. This would require the entity to determine its net monetary position on a daily basis, which would be entirely impracticable given the difficulties in making the monetary/non-monetary distinction (see 2.4.2 A above). The standard therefore allows the gain or loss on the net monetary position to 'be estimated by applying the change in a general price index to the weighted average for the period of the difference between monetary assets and monetary liabilities'.[64] Due care should be exercised in estimating the gain or loss on the net monetary position, as a calculation based on averages for the period (or monthly averages) can be unreliable if addressed without accurate consideration of the pattern of hyperinflation and the volatility of the net monetary position.

However, as shown in the above table, any restatement of the non-monetary items must be met by an equal restatement of the monetary items. Therefore, in preparing financial statements it is more practical to assume that the gain or loss on the net monetary position is exactly the reverse of the restatement of the non-monetary items. A stand-alone calculation of the net gain or loss can serve, however, as a check on the reasonableness of the restatement of the non-monetary items.

The gain or loss on the net monetary position should be included in net income and disclosed separately. It may be helpful to present it together with items that are also associated with the net monetary position such as 'interest income and expense, and foreign exchange differences related to invested or borrowed funds'.[65]

2.4.5 *Restatement of the cash flow statement*

The standard also requires that all items in the cash flow statement be expressed in terms of the measuring unit current at the balance sheet date.[66] This is a most difficult requirement to fulfil in practice.

An understanding of the complication inherent in this requirement of IAS 29 becomes apparent when the restatement of a cash flow is actually contemplated. IAS 7 – *Cash Flow Statements* – requires the following information to be presented:[67]

(a) cash flows from operating activities, which are the principal revenue-producing activities of the entity and other activities that are not investing or financing activities;

(b) cash flows from investing activities, which are the acquisition and disposal of long-term assets and other investments not included in cash equivalents; and

(c) cash flows from financing activities, which are activities that result in changes in the size and composition of the equity capital and borrowings of the entity.

In effect IAS 29 requires restatement of most items in a cash flow statement, implying that therefore the actual cash flows at the time of the transactions will be different from the numbers presented in the cash flow statement itself. However, not all items are restated using the same method and many of the restatements are based on estimates. For example, items in the income statement are to be restated using an estimate of the general price index at the time that the revenues were earned and the costs incurred. Unavoidably this will give rise to some inconsistencies. Similarly, the restatement of balance sheet items will give rise to discrepancies because some items are not easily classified as either monetary or non-monetary. This raises the question how an entity should classify the monetary gain or loss relating to a balance sheet item in its cash flow statement.

It is not clear from IAS 29 how a monetary gain or loss should be presented in the cash flow statements. In practice different approaches have been adopted such as:

(a)   presenting the effect of inflation on operating, investing and financing cash flows separately for each of these activities and present the net monetary gain or loss as a reconciling item in the cash and cash equivalents reconciliation;

(b)   presenting the monetary gain or loss on cash and cash equivalents and the effect of inflation on operating, investing and financing cash flows as one number; and

(c)   attributing the effect of inflation on operating, investing and financing cash flows to the underlying item and presenting the monetary gain or loss on cash and cash equivalents separately.

Irrespective of the method chosen, users of cash flow statements of prepared in the currency of a hyperinflationary economy should be mindful of the fact that figures presented in the cash flow statement may have been restated in accordance with IAS 29 and may differ from the actual underlying cash flows.

2.4.6   Restatement of the corresponding figures

The standard requires that all financial information be presented in terms of the measurement unit current at the balance sheet date, therefore:

•   'corresponding figures for the previous reporting period, whether they were based on a historical cost approach or a current cost approach, are restated by applying a general price index';[68] and

•   'information that is disclosed in respect of earlier periods is also expressed in terms of the measuring unit current at the end of the reporting period'.[69]

2.5   Interim reporting

Appendix B to IAS 34 – *Interim Financial Reporting* – requires that 'interim financial reports in hyperinflationary economies are prepared by the same principles as at financial year end'. This means that the financial statements must be stated in terms of the measuring unit current at the end of the interim period and that the gain or loss on the net monetary position is included in net income.[70] The comparative financial information reported for prior periods must also be restated to the current measuring unit.[71] An entity that reports quarterly information must restate the comparative balance sheets and income statements each quarter.

In restating its financial information an entity is not allowed to 'annualise the recognition of the gain or loss' on the net monetary position or to 'use an estimated annual inflation rate in preparing an interim financial report in a hyperinflationary economy'.[72]

2.6 Economies becoming hyperinflationary

When the functional currency of an entity becomes hyperinflationary it must start applying IAS 29. The standard requires that the financial statements and any information in respect of earlier periods 'should be stated in terms of the measuring unit current at the balance sheet date'.[73] The standard does not explicitly state:[74]

(a) whether restatement should be fully retrospective, i.e. items should be restated from the their date of acquisition; or

(b) whether restatements should be prospective from the date that the economy became hyperinflationary.

IFRIC considered that the wording of paragraph 4 of IAS 29 was not sufficiently clear and that there was therefore 'uncertainty whether the opening balance sheet at the beginning of the reporting period should be restated to reflect changes in prices before that date' (see at 5.1.1 below).[75] This means that until IFRIC D5 is issued in its final form, both interpretations seem to be permitted under IAS 29.

What is less clear is how an entity (a parent), which does not operate in a hyperinflationary economy, should account for the restatement of an entity (a subsidiary) that operates in an economy that became hyperinflationary in the current reporting period when incorporating it within its consolidated financial statements. This issue has been clarified by paragraph 42(b) of IAS 21 (as revised in 2003) which specifically prohibits restatement of comparative figures when the reporting currency is not hyperinflationary. This means that when the financial statements of a hyperinflationary subsidiary are translated into the non-hyperinflationary reporting currency of the parent, the comparative amounts are not adjusted.

2.7 Economies ceasing to be hyperinflationary

When an economy ceases to be hyperinflationary, entities should discontinue preparation and presentation of financial statements in accordance with IAS 29. The amounts expressed in the measuring unit current at the end of the previous reporting period will be treated as the deemed cost of the items in the balance sheet.[76]

Determining when a currency stops becoming hyperinflationary is not easy in practice. It is important to review trends, not just at the balance sheet date but also subsequently. In addition, consistency demands that the financial statements do not unnecessarily 'yo-yo' in and out of a hyperinflationary presentation, where a more careful judgement would have avoided it.

It is possible or even likely that an economy becomes hyperinflationary sometime during an entity's financial year. Therefore, it would be reasonable and sensible that as soon as an entity determines that it is operating in hyperinflation it starts preparing its interim reports using the principles underlying IAS 29. The standard should be applied from the beginning of the reporting period in which the existence of hyperinflation is identified.[77] Equally, it is possible that an economy ceases to be hyperinflationary during the year. The standard is silent on the question whether an entity can stop applying the requirements of IAS 29 during one of its interim periods. In practice, an amalgamation of interim periods during which IAS 29 was applied with those where it was not, may result in financial statements that are extremely difficult to interpret. Therefore, we believe that entities should only stop applying the standard from the beginning of the first annual period commencing after the economy ceased to be hyperinflationary.

2.8   Translation to a different presentation currency

If an entity, whose functional currency is hyperinflationary, wants to translate its financial statements into a different presentation currency it must first restate its financial statements in accordance with IAS 29 and then apply the following procedures under IAS 21:

'(a)   all amounts (i.e. assets, liabilities, equity items, income and expenses, including comparatives) shall be translated at the closing rate at the date of the most recent balance sheet, except that

(b)   when amounts are translated into the currency of a non-hyperinflationary economy, comparative amounts shall be those that were presented as current year amounts in the relevant prior year financial statements (i.e. not adjusted for subsequent changes in the price level or subsequent changes in exchange rates).'[78]

In other words, when an entity that applies IAS 29 translates its financial statements into a non-hyperinflationary presentation currency the comparative information should not be restated under IAS 29, instead IAS 21 should be applied (i.e. the comparative amounts should be those that were presented as current year amounts in the prior period). For a more detailed discussion of these requirements reference is made to Chapter 9 at 2.7.1 B.

When the economy ceases to be hyperinflationary – and restatement in accordance with IAS 29 is no longer required – an entity uses the amounts restated to the price level at the date it ceased restating its financial statements as the historical costs for translation into the presentation currency.[79]

2.9   Disclosures

IAS 29 requires that entities should disclose the following information when they apply the provisions of the standard:

'(a)   the fact that the financial statements and the corresponding figures for previous periods have been restated for the changes in the general purchasing power of the functional currency and, as a result, are stated in terms of the measuring unit current at the balance sheet date;

(b)   whether the financial statements are based on a historical cost approach or a current cost approach; and

(c)   the identity and level of the price index at the balance sheet date and the movement in the index during the current and the previous reporting period'.[80]

It should be noted that disclosure of financial information that is restated under IAS 29 as a supplement to unrestated financial information is not permitted.[81] This is to prevent entities from giving the historical cost based financial information greater prominence than the information that is restated under IAS 29. The standard also discourages separate presentation of unrestated financial information, but does not explicitly prohibit it.[82] However, such financial statements would not be in accordance with IFRS.

Koç Holding discloses that they operate in a hyperinflationary economy and make the appropriate disclosures:

Extract 10.1: Koç Holding A.Ş. (2002)

NOTES TO THE CONSOLIDATED FINANCIAL STATEMENTS

31 DECEMBER 2002

(Amounts expressed in billions of Turkish Lira (TL) in terms of the purchasing power of TL at 31 December 2002 unless otherwise indicated)

NOTE 2 - BASIS OF PREPARATION OF FINANCIAL STATEMENTS

a) Turkish lira financial statements [extract]

...

These consolidated financial statements are based on the statutory records, which are maintained under the historical cost convention (except for the statutory revaluation of property, plant and equipment as discussed in Note 15), with adjustments and reclassifications including restatement for changes in the general purchasing power of the Turkish Lira, for the purpose of fair presentation in accordance with IFRS.

...

The restatement for the changes in the general purchasing power of the Turkish Lira at 31 December 2002 is based on IAS 29 ("Financial Reporting in Hyperinflationary Economies"). IAS 29 requires that financial statements prepared in the currency of a hyperinflationary economy be stated in terms of the measuring unit current at the balance sheet date, and that corresponding figures for previous periods be restated in the same terms. One characteristic that necessitates the application of IAS 29 is a cumulative three-year inflation rate approaching or exceeding 100%. The restatement was calculated by means of conversion factors derived from the Turkish nationwide wholesale price index ("WPI") published by the State Institute of Statistics ("SIS"). Such indices and conversion factors used to restate the financial statements at 31 December are given below:

Dates	Index	Conversion factors
31 December 2002	**6,478.8**	**1.000**
31 December 2001	4,951.7	1.308
31 December 2000	2,626.0	2.467

The main procedures for the above-mentioned restatement are as follows:

- Financial statements prepared in the currency of a hyperinflationary economy are stated in terms of the measuring unit current at the balance sheet date, and corresponding figures for previous periods are restated in the same terms.

- Monetary assets and liabilities that are carried at amounts current at the balance sheet date are not restated because they are already expressed in terms of the monetary unit current at the balance sheet date.

- Non-monetary assets and liabilities that are not carried at amounts current at the balance sheet date and components of shareholders' equity are restated by applying the relevant monthly conversion factors.

- Comparative financial statements are restated using general inflation indices at the currency purchasing power at the latest balance sheet date.

- All items in the statements of loss and income are restated by applying the relevant (monthly, yearly average, year-end) conversion factors.

- The effect of inflation on the net monetary asset position of Koç Holding, the Subsidiaries and Joint Ventures operating in hyperinflationary economies is included in the statements of loss and income as loss on net monetary position.

The result of the Group's foreign undertakings are translated into Turkish Lira at the average rate for the year, except for foreign joint-venture reporting in the currency of a hyperinflationary economy for which closing rates are applied to local currency amounts. The assets and liabilities of Group's foreign undertakings are translated into Turkish Lira at the closing rate for the year. Exchange differences arising on retranslating of the opening net assets of foreign undertakings and differences between the average and year-end rates are included in the translation reserve.

3   TRANSITIONAL ARRANGEMENTS AND FIRST-TIME ADOPTION ISSUES

The requirements of IAS 29 must be observed initially in the following circumstances:

- Upon the introduction of IAS 29 in 1990 existing IFRS reporting entities had to transition to IAS 29 (see 3.1 below);

- First-time IFRS adopters that operate in hyperinflationary economies need to apply IAS 29 immediately (see 3.2 below); and

- When economies become hyperinflationary existing IFRS reporting entities must start applying IAS 29 (see 2.6 above).

3.1   Transition

IAS 29 became effective 'for financial statements covering periods beginning on or after 1 January 1990' and did not provide for a transitional regime for existing IFRS reporting companies.[83]

3.2   First-time adoption of IFRS

IFRS 1 – *First-time Adoption of International Financial Reporting Standards* – requires full retrospective application of IAS 29 'to any periods during which the economy of the functional currency or presentation currency was hyperinflationary'.[84] However, the option to use the fair value of an item of property, plant and equipment at the date of transition to IFRS (see Chapter 4 at 2.5), which is also available to entities operating in hyperinflationary economies, may be the practical way of reducing the burden of complying with the standard's requirements.[85]

The implementation guidance to IFRS 1 states that 'if an entity elects to use the exemptions in paragraphs 16-19 of the IFRS, it applies IAS 29 to periods after the date for which the revalued amount or fair value was determined.'[86] The basis for conclusions to IFRS 1 makes clear that the IASB expects that items not covered by the IFRS 1 exemptions to be restated under IAS 29.[87]

4 PRACTICAL PROBLEMS

4.1 Selecting a general price index

Selecting an appropriate general price index is fraught with difficulties in many cases. IAS 29 requires entities to use 'a general price index that reflects changes in general purchasing power'.[88] It is generally accepted practice to use a Consumer Price Index (CPI) for this purpose, unless that index is clearly flawed. National statistical offices in most countries issue several price indices that potentially could be used for the purposes of IAS 29. Important characteristics of a good general price index include the following:

- a wide range of goods and services should be included in the price index;

- continuity and consistency of measurement techniques and underlying assumptions;

- free from bias;

- frequently updated; and

- available for a long period.

The entity should use the above criteria to choose the most reliable and most readily available general price index and use that index consistently. It is important that the index selected is representative of the real position of the hyperinflationary currency concerned.

4.2 General price index not available for all periods

IAS 29 requires an entity to make an estimate of the price index if the general price index is not available for all periods for which the restatement of long-lived assets is required. The entity could base the estimate, for example, on 'the movements in the exchange rate between the functional currency and a relatively stable foreign currency'.[89] It should be noted that this method is only acceptable if the currency of the hyperinflationary economy is freely exchangeable, i.e. not subject to currency controls and 'official' exchange rates. Entities could use a similar approach when they cannot find a general price index that meets its minimum criteria for reliability (e.g. because the national statistical office in the hyperinflationary economy may be subject to significant political bias). However, this would only be acceptable if all available general price indices are fatally flawed.

4.3   Inventories

To restate the balance sheet under IAS 29 an entity needs to exercise judgement and make assumptions regarding:

- whether balance sheet items are monetary or non-monetary in nature;
- the date of acquisition of items; and
- the level of the general price index at the date of acquisition.

Given the large number of transactions affecting an entity's inventory position, it is often a challenge to determine the date of acquisition of inventory. Therefore, entities commonly approximate the ageing of inventories by basing it on inventory turnover. In a similar vain the level of the general price index at the date of acquisition is often determined at the average level for the month because an up-to-date price index is not available for each day of the month. Determining the appropriate level of the general price index can be particularly challenging when the price index is updated relatively infrequently and the entity's business is highly seasonal.

IAS 29 requires restatement of inventory by applying a general price index, which could result in an overvaluation when the price of inventory items increases at a different rate from the general price index. At the end of each period it is therefore essential to ensure that items of inventory are not valued in excess of their net realisable value.

4.4   Investees accounted for under the equity method

IAS 29 requires restatement of such investees that also operate in hyperinflationary economies 'in accordance with this Standard in order to calculate the investor's share of its net assets and results of operations'.[90] The standard specifically requires that the balance sheet and income statement of an investee to be restated in accordance with IAS 29 in order to calculate the investor's share of the net assets and results of operations, i.e. the standard does not permit the investment in the investee to be treated as a single indivisible item for the purposes of the IAS 29 restatement.

Restating the financial statements of an associate before application of the equity method will often be difficult because the investor may not have access to the detailed information required. The fact that the investor can exercise significant influence or has joint control over an investee often does not mean that the investor has completely unrestricted access to the investee's books and records at all times.

4.5 Restatement of interest and exchange differences

A common question is whether an entity should restate exchange differences under IAS 29, because the standard considers that 'foreign exchange differences related to invested or borrowed funds ... are also associated with the net monetary position'.[91] Nevertheless, the standard requires that 'all items in the income statement are expressed in terms of the measuring unit current at the balance sheet date. Therefore all amounts need to be restated by applying the change in the general price index from the dates when the items of income and expenses were initially recorded in the financial statements'.[92] Interest and exchange differences should therefore be restated for the effect of inflation as all the other items in the income statement and be presented on a gross basis though 'it may be helpful if they are presented together with the gain or loss on net monetary position in the income statement'.[93]

5 FUTURE DEVELOPMENTS

5.1 IFRIC D5

In March 2004, IFRIC issued Draft Interpretation D5 – *Applying IAS 29 Financial Reporting Hyperinflationary Economies for the First Time*, which proposes specific guidance to facilitate the first time application of IAS 29. IFRIC D5 is best described as an omnibus interpretation and it deals with a number of practical problems that entities applying IAS 29 for the first time might experience.

5.1.1 *Retrospective application*

IFRIC considered that the wording of paragraph 4 of IAS 29 was not sufficiently clear and that there was therefore 'uncertainty whether the opening balance sheet at the beginning of the reporting period should be restated to reflect changes in prices before that date'.[94] IFRIC D5 proposes to clarify this issue by requiring that when an entity identifies the existence of hyperinflation it should apply IAS 29 as if it had always applied that standard. The entity's balance sheet at the beginning of the earliest period presented should be 'restated to reflect the effect of inflation from the date the assets were acquired and the liabilities were incurred until the balance sheet date of the current reporting period'.[95] Once an entity has restated its financial statements for the first time 'all corresponding figures in the financial statements for a subsequent reporting period, including deferred tax items, are restated by applying the change in the measuring unit for that subsequent reporting period only to the restated financial statements for the previous reporting period' (see also 2.2 above).[96]

In July 2004, IFRIC discussed the comments received in response to IFRIC D5. IFRIC members observed that respondents who disagreed or expressed concerns 'did not believe that restating financial information provides useful information; others cited costs versus benefits as their primary objection'. Alternative approaches discussed during the meeting were the 'stable/hard currency approach' and requiring 'restatement from the beginning of the year the entity identifies the existence of hyperinflation'. However, IFRIC observed that an amendment along those lines would require direct action by the IASB Board.[97]

5.1.2 Deferred taxation

IFRIC was asked 'for guidance on measuring deferred tax items in the opening balance sheet for the first year an entity identifies the existence of hyperinflation', because it was not sufficiently clear how an entity should restate its comparative deferred tax items.[98] IFRIC D5 proposes that deferred tax figures in the opening balance sheet for the reporting period should be determined as follows (see also 2.4.2 F above):[99]

(a)   the entity remeasures the deferred tax items in accordance with IAS 12 after it has restated the nominal carrying amounts of its non-monetary items at the date of the opening balance sheet of the current reporting period by applying the measuring unit at that date;

(b)   the deferred tax items remeasured in accordance with item (a) above are restated for the change in the measuring unit from the date of the opening balance sheet of the current reporting period up to the balance sheet date; and

(c)   the entity applies the approach in items (a) and (b) above to the restatement of deferred tax items in the opening balance sheet of any comparative periods presented in the restated financial statements for the first year the entity applies IAS 29. For the purpose of this Interpretation, 'the opening balance sheet of the current reporting period' in items (a) and (b) is read as 'the opening balance sheet of the comparative period.

5.1.3 Unavailability of information relating to property, plant and equipment

IFRIC D5 puts forward two exemptions from the requirements of IAS 29 in the rare circumstances where:[100]

- detailed records of the acquisition dates of property, plant and equipment are not available or cannot be estimated, in which case the entity uses an independent professional assessment of the fair value of items of property, plant and equipment as the basis of their restatement;

- a general price index is not available, in which case it is permitted to use an estimated basis, e.g. based on the movements in the exchange rate between the entity's functional currency and a relatively stable foreign currency.

It should be noted though that the above exemptions are virtually identical to those that are already available under IAS 29 (see also 2.4.1 and 2.4.2 D above).[101]

References

1 *Framework for the Preparation and Presentation of Financial Statements* (Framework), IASB, September 1989, para. 104.

2 IAS 29, *Financial Reporting in Hyperinflationary Economies*, IASB, July 1989 (amended December 2003), para. 6.

3 It should be noted that the definition of hyperinflation used in financial reporting does not have a solid theoretical basis. In fact, economists researching hyperinflation often use Cagan's definition which defines hyperinflation as consumer price increases of more than 50% per month. International Monetary Fund, *World Economic Outlook – Fiscal Policy and Macroeconomic Stability*, May 2001. Cagan, Phillip. *op. cit.*, 'The Monetary Dynamics of Hyperinflation.' In Studies in the Quantity Theory of Money, ed. by Milton Friedman, pp. 25-117. Chicago: University of Chicago Press.

4 Based on information published by the International Monetary Fund, *International Financial Statistics Book*, Volume LVI, Number 9, September 2003. Countries that have a three-year cumulative inflation rate in excess of 70% are Argentina, Ghana, Tajikistan, Venezuela and Zambia. There may be additional countries with cumulative inflation of 100% or more, because the cited source does not include countries that have not reported data.

5 IAS 21, *The Effects of Changes in Foreign Exchange Rates*, IASB, December 2003, paras. 8-14.

6 IAS 21, para. 14.

7 *IFRIC D5, Applying IAS 29 Financial Reporting in Hyperinflationary Economies for the first time*, IFRIC, March 2004.

8 IAS 21, para. 8.

9 SIC-19, *Reporting Currency – Measurement and Presentation of Financial Statements under IAS 21 and IAS 29*, SIC, November 2000 (superseded December 2003).

10 IAS 21, para. IN6.

11 IAS 21, para. 8.

12 IAS 21 (revised 1993), *The Effects of Changes in Foreign Exchange Rates*, IASB, December 1993, para. 7.

13 IAS 21 (revised 1993), para. 4.

14 IAS 21, para. IN6.

15 IAS 29, para. 2.

16 IAS 29, para. 8.

17 IAS 29, para. 8.

18 IAS 29, para. 9.

19 IAS 29, para. 11.

20 IAS 29, para. 10.

21 IAS 29, paras. 1-2.

22 IAS 29, para. 3.

23 IAS 29, para. 4.

24 IAS 29, para. 4.

25 IAS 29, para. 37.

26 IAS 29, para. 17.

27 Framework, para. 100(b).

28 IAS 29, para. 12.

29 IAS 21, para. 8.

30 IAS 21, para. 16.

31 IAS 21, para. 16.

32 IAS 21, para. 16.

33 IAS 39, para. AG83.

34 *IFRIC Update*, IFRIC, October 2003. IFRIC concluded in its October 2003 meeting that 'it is not clear how an entity should restate items that are neither monetary nor non-monetary in nature, e.g. deferred tax assets and deferred tax liabilities'.

35 IAS 29, para. 13.

36 IAS 29, para. 29.

37 Framework, para. 100(b).

38 IAS 29, para. 14.

39 IAS 29, para. 18.

40 IAS 29, para. 15.

41 IAS 29, para. 10.

42 IAS 29, para. 15.

43 IAS 29, para. 16.

44 IAS 16, *Property, Plant and Equipment*, IASB, December 2003 (amended March 2004), para. 23.

45 IAS 29, para. 22.

46 IAS 29, para. 21.

47 IAS 29, para. 19.

48 IAS 29, para. 20.

49 IAS 21, para. 42.

50 IAS 29, para. 35.

51 IAS 21, para. 42.

52 IAS 29, para. 35.

53 IAS 29, para. 36.

54 IAS 29, para. 32.

55 IAS 12, *Income Taxes*, IASB, October 1996 (amended March 2004), Appendix A, para. 18.

56 IAS 12, Appendix A, para. 18.

57 IAS 29, para. 24.

58 IAS 29, para. 24.

59 IAS 29, para. 24.

60 IAS 29, para. 25.

61 IAS 29, para. 26.

62 IAS 29, para. 30.

63 IAS 21, para. 22.

64 IAS 29, paras. 27 and 31.

65 IAS 29, para. 28.

66 IAS 29, para. 33.

67 IAS 7, *Cash Flow Statements*, IASB, December 1992 (amended March 2004), paras. 6 and 10.
68 IAS 29, para. 34.
69 IAS 29, para. 34.
70 IAS 34, *Interim Financial Reporting*, IASB, February 1998 (amended March 2004), Appendix B, para. 33.
71 IAS 34, Appendix B, para. 32.
72 IAS 34, Appendix B, para. 34.
73 IAS 29, para. 8.
74 IAS 29, paras. 11-36.
75 IFRIC D5, para. BC2.
76 IAS 29, para. 38.
77 IAS 29, para. 4.
78 IAS 21, para. 42.
79 IAS 21, para. 43.
80 IAS 29, para. 39.
81 IAS 29, para. 7.
82 IAS 29, para. 7.
83 IAS 29, para. 41.
84 IFRS 1, *First-time Adoption of International Financial Reporting Standards*, IASB, June 2003 (amended March 2004), para. IG32.
85 IFRS 1, para. IG33.
86 IFRS 1, para. IG34.
87 IFRS 1, para. BC67.
88 IAS 29, para. 37.
89 IAS 29, para. 17.
90 IAS 29, para. 20.
91 IAS 29, para. 28.
92 IAS 29, para. 26.
93 IAS 29, para. 28.
94 IFRIC D5, para. BC2.
95 IFRIC D5, para. 3.
96 IFRIC D5, para. 5.
97 *IFRIC Update*, IFRIC, July 2004.
98 IFRIC D5, para. BC9.
99 IFRIC D5, para. 4.
100 IFRIC D5, para. 6.
101 IAS 29, paras. 16-17.

Chapter 11   Intangible assets and goodwill

1   INTRODUCTION

1.1   The incidence of intangible assets

Economic, commercial and marketing imperatives in the more developed world economies, particularly over the last twenty years, have driven many businesses to invest substantial sums in ways that were not previously commonplace. It is not unusual for the premium paid to acquire a business to be greater than the balance sheet value of net assets acquired. The commercial importance of brands that are attractive to consumers, and the cost and uncertainty of attempting to develop them from scratch, has partly fuelled this trend. Equally, businesses that own successful brands spend large sums in maintaining consumer awareness of, and loyalty to them.

There has also emerged over the last fifteen years or so the requirement to consider how to reflect in financial statements expenditure on a relatively new type of asset, based on software and related expenditure for computerised sales and marketing systems and website development. As with goodwill and brands, this type of expenditure was not unknown before. It is the commercial imperative brought about by much higher levels of spending on these items, and larger numbers of businesses incurring it, that has forced the topic into prominence.

These relatively high levels of expenditure on intangible aspects of commerce have inevitably resulted in companies wanting to account for it in various different ways. As the incidence and magnitude of such expenditure increased, it became necessary for the IASB, and the accounting profession generally, to develop common rules for its recognition and treatment in financial statements.

1.2 Background to accounting for intangible assets

1.2.1 *Development of IAS 9, IAS 22, IAS 38 and SIC-32*

The main debate surrounding the accounting treatment of expenditure on intangibles has centred on whether such expenditure should be written off immediately as incurred, or whether it should be capitalised in the balance sheet as a type of asset. A secondary consideration, if the decision to write off the expenditure was taken, was the manner of any write-off. For example was goodwill to be written off directly to reserves, rather than through the profit and loss account? If expenditure on intangibles was to be capitalised, there were a number of matters to be considered further. For example, could expenditure on creating a new brand from scratch (i.e. an internally developed intangible) be capitalised? Over what period would such expenditure be written off, if at all? Could such assets be revalued and if so, on what basis would they be valued?

The situation by the early 1990s was that there were well-established ways of accounting for goodwill (IAS 22 (revised 1993) – *Accounting for Business Combinations)* and for research and development costs (IAS 9 (revised 1993) – *Accounting for Research and Development Activities*). At that time there was relatively little incidence of 'traditional' intangibles such as patents and licenses, though 'new' intangibles such as brands were appearing on an increasing number of entity balance sheets. There were no specific rules governing expenditure on intangibles such as brands, and the most common method of accounting for goodwill (writing it off directly against reserves) began to seem inappropriate for the large goodwill figures being generated by acquisitions.

This unsatisfactory situation was resolved by the (then) IASC standardising the basis on which goodwill arising on acquisitions, and any other types of intangible asset, were to be treated by entities reporting under International Accounting Standards. This led in September 1998 to the adoption of IAS 22 (revised 1998) and IAS 38 (1998) – *Intangible Assets*. Under these standards there were now definite criteria that had to be met before any expenditure could be considered to have given rise to an intangible asset and definite requirements governing the amortisation and revaluation of such assets.

The accounting treatment of software related expenditure is not quite so clear under IAS. There is an inherent difficulty in deciding if such expenditures should be recognised as intangible assets or expenses. This is particularly so in relation to the costs of developing web-based marketing and information systems. The late 1990s saw very large sums spent on the operation and development of websites and this led to the issue of SIC-32 (amended 2003) – *Intangible Assets – Web Site Costs* – that is discussed at 2.2.6 D below.

1.2.2 *IFRS 3 and IAS 38 (as revised in 2004)*

In 2001 the IASB began a project to review its prescribed accounting for business combinations, which it is pursuing in two phases. Obviously therefore, this project will affect the accounting treatment of intangible assets and goodwill.[1] As part of the first phase, the IASB published in December 2002 ED 3 – *Business*

Combinations, together with an exposure draft of proposed related amendments to IAS 38 and IAS 36 – *Impairment of Assets*.[2] The IASB's intention in the first phase was not wholesale change to the existing provisions; rather it was to clarify the following matters:

(a) the treatment of any excess of the acquirer's interest in the fair value of identifiable net assets acquired in a business combination over the cost of the combination;[3]

(b) the accounting for goodwill and intangible assets acquired in a business combination;[4]

(c) the notion of 'identifiability' as it relates to intangible assets;[5]

(d) the useful life and amortisation of intangible assets;[6] and

(e) the accounting for in-process research and development projects acquired in business combinations.[7]

The first phase of the project has resulted in the IASB issuing in March 2004 IFRS 3 – *Business Combinations* – and revised versions of IAS 36 and IAS 38. The requirements of IFRS 3 are principally dealt with in Chapter 6 at 2; the requirements of IAS 36 relating specifically to the impairment of goodwill are dealt with in Chapter 6 at 3; and the general requirements of IAS 36 are covered in Chapter 13. The specific requirements of IAS 38 relating to intangible assets are dealt with at 2 below; while the requirements relating to intangible assets acquired as part of a business combination are covered both at 2.2.2 below and in Chapter 6 at 2.3.3 B.

Phase 2 of the IASB's business combinations project and other developments regarding purchase accounting are discussed in Chapter 6 at 5.

2 THE REQUIREMENTS OF IAS 38

2.1 Scope and definitions

2.1.1 Scope

This chapter discusses IAS 38 as revised in March 2004, which is effective for periods beginning on or after 1 January 2005. The objective of IAS 38 is to prescribe the accounting treatment for all intangible assets that are not specifically dealt with in another standard.[8] Hence, IAS 38 does not apply to accounting for:[9]

(a) intangible assets that are within the scope of another standard;

(b) financial assets, as defined in IAS 39 – *Financial Instruments: Recognition and Measurement*, and

(c) mineral rights and expenditure on the exploration for, or development and extraction of, minerals, oil, natural gas and similar non-regenerative resources.

Specific intangible assets that are beyond the scope of IAS 38 include:[10]

(a) intangible assets held by an entity for sale in the ordinary course of business, to which IAS 2 – *Inventories* – or IAS 11 – *Construction Contracts* – applies (see Chapters 21 and 22);

(b)   deferred tax assets (see Chapter 24);

(c)   leases that are within the scope of IAS 17 – *Leases* – (see Chapter 23). However, an entity that leases an intangible asset under a finance lease should apply IAS 38 after initial recognition to account for the underlying asset.[11] Leases that are outside the scope of IAS 17 such as 'licensing agreements for such items as motion picture films, video recordings, plays, manuscripts, patents and copyrights'[12] are within the scope of IAS 38;[13]

(d)   assets arising from employee benefits (see Chapter 30);

(e)   financial assets as defined in IAS 39. The recognition and measurement of some financial assets are covered by IAS 27 – *Consolidated and Separate Financial Statements*, IAS 28 – *Investments in Associates* – and IAS 31 – *Interests in Joint Ventures* (see Chapters 5, 7, 8 and 15 to 20);

(f)   goodwill acquired in a business combination (see Chapter 6);

(g)   deferred acquisition costs and intangible assets, arising from an insurer's contractual rights under insurance contracts within the scope of IFRS 4 – *Insurance Contracts*; and

(h)   non-current intangible assets classified as held for sale, or included in a disposal group that is classified as held for sale, in accordance with IFRS 5 – *Non-current Assets Held for Sale and Discontinued Operations* (see Chapter 3).

IAS 38 states that insurance contracts and expenditure on the exploration for, or development and extraction of, oil, gas and mineral deposits in extractive industries are also excluded from its scope. Activities or transactions in these areas are so specialised that they give rise to accounting issues that need to be dealt with in a different way. However, the standard does apply 'to other intangible assets used (such as computer software), and other expenditure incurred (such as start-up costs), in extractive industries or by insurers'.[14]

Finally, the standard makes it clear that it does apply to expenditure on advertising, training, start-up and research and development activities.[15]

2.1.2   What is an intangible asset

IAS 38 defines an asset as 'a resource controlled by an entity as a result of past events; and from which future economic benefits are expected to flow to the entity'.[16] Intangible assets form a sub-section of this group and are further defined as 'identifiable non-monetary assets without physical substance'.[17] It is important to note that the revised IAS 38 no longer requires that an intangible asset is 'held for use in the production or supply of goods or services, for rental to others, or for administrative services', because the IASB considers that 'the purpose for which an entity holds an item with these characteristics is not relevant to its classification as an intangible asset, and that all such items should be within the scope of the Standard'.[18] However, there is one caveat, intangible assets held for resale that are accounted for under IAS 2 or IAS 11 are specifically excluded from the scope of IAS 38.

Businesses frequently incur expenditure on all sorts of intangible resources such as scientific or technical knowledge, design and implementation of new processes or systems, licences, intellectual property, market knowledge, trademarks, brand names and publishing titles. Examples that fall under these headings are computer software, patents, copyrights, motion picture films, customer lists, and many others.[19]

However, although these items are covered by the standard, not all of them will meet the standard's definition of an intangible asset, which requires identifiability, control and the existence of future economic benefits. If they do not meet the definition they will be expensed when incurred, unless they have arisen in the context of an acquisition, where they will form part of the calculation of goodwill.[20]

A   Identifiability

An intangible asset needs to be identifiable to distinguish it from goodwill, which is defined in IFRS 3 as the 'future economic benefits arising from assets that are not capable of being individually identified and separately recognised.'[21] For example, the future economic benefits may result from synergy between the identifiable assets acquired or from assets that, individually, do not qualify for recognition in the financial statements but for which the acquirer is prepared to make a payment in the business combination.[22] An intangible asset meets the identifiability criterion under IAS 38 when it:[23]

'(a)   is separable, i.e. is capable of being separated or divided from the entity and sold, transferred, licensed, rented or exchanged, either individually or together with a related contract, asset or liability; or

(b)   arises from contractual or other legal rights, regardless of whether those rights are transferable or separable from the entity or from other rights and obligations.'

B   Control

Control is defined as the power to obtain the future economic benefits generated by the resource and the ability to deny access to those benefits to others. While these are normally legal rights, control may also be demonstrated in the absence of legal enforceability by factors such as market and technical knowledge.[24] Although legal enforceability of a right is not a necessary condition for control, because an entity may be able to control the future economic benefits in some other way, it will be more difficult to demonstrate control in its absence.[25]

An entity usually has insufficient control over the future economic benefits arising from a team of skilled workers, or specific management or technical talent for these items to meet the definition of an intangible asset.[26]

Therefore, if an entity acquires a pharmaceutical organisation, it is most unlikely that it will be able to recognise as an intangible asset the acquiree's team of research chemists. By contrast, a football club may pay a certain amount to a player's previous club in connection with the transfer of the player's registration, which enables the club to negotiate a playing contract with the footballer that covers a number of seasons. This may give the entity sufficient control to enable it to recognise the payment as an intangible asset. In this case, of course, this is a stand-alone payment and not part of a business combination; when an entity makes a separate acquisition it is much more likely that it can demonstrate that its purchase meets the definition of an asset (see 2.2.1 below).

Similarly, an entity 'may have a portfolio of customers or a market share and expect that, because of its efforts in building customer relationships and loyalty, the customers will continue to trade with the entity. However, in the absence of legal rights to protect or control the relationship or loyalty of customers, the entity usually has insufficient control over these items to meet the definition of intangible assets.'[27] Nevertheless, exchange transactions involving non-contractual customer relationships may provide evidence that the entity is able to control the expected future economic benefits even in the absence of legal control. In the rare situations where this is the case, those customer relationships could meet the definition of an intangible asset.[28]

C   *Future economic benefits*

Future economic benefits include not only future revenues from the sale of products or services but also cost savings. For example, the use of intellectual property in a production process that may reduce future production costs rather than increase future revenues.[29]

2.1.3   *Tangible and intangible assets*

Before the advent of IAS 38 many entities used to account for assets without physical substance in the same way as property, plant and equipment. Indeed, many intangible assets are 'contained in or on a physical substance such as a compact disc (in the case of computer software), legal documentation (in the case of a licence or patent) or film'.[30] An entity therefore needs to exercise judgement in determining whether an 'asset that incorporates both intangible and tangible elements should be treated under IAS 16 – *Property, Plant and Equipment* – or as an intangible asset' under IAS 38, for example:[31]

- software that is embedded in computer-controlled equipment that cannot operate without that specific software is an integral part of the related hardware and is treated as property, plant and equipment;

- application software that is being used on a computer is generally easily replaced and is not an integral part of the related hardware, whereas the operating system normally is;

- a database that is stored on a compact disc is considered to be an intangible asset because the value of the physical medium is wholly insignificant compared to that of the data collection; and

- research and development expenditure may result in an asset with physical substance (e.g. a prototype), but as the physical element is secondary to its intangible component.[32]

It is worthwhile noting that the 'parts approach' in IAS 16 requires an entity to account for significant parts of an asset separately because they have a different economic life or are often replaced (see Chapter 12). This raises 'boundary' problems between IAS 16 and IAS 38 when software and similar expenditure is involved. We believe that where IAS 16 requires an entity to identify parts of an asset and account for them separately, the entity needs to evaluate whether any intangible-type part is actually integral to the larger asset or whether it is really a separate asset in its own right. The intangible part is more likely to be an asset in its own right if it was developed separately or if it can be used independently of the item of property, plant and equipment that it apparently forms part of.

2.2 Recognition and measurement

Recognition of intangible assets under IAS 38 is based on a general recognition principle that 'applies to costs incurred initially to acquire or internally generate an intangible asset and those incurred subsequently to add to, replace part of, or service it'.[33] An item that meets the definition of an intangible asset should only be recognised if:

'(a) it is probable that the expected future economic benefits that are attributable to the asset will flow to the entity; and

(b) the cost of the asset can be measured reliably.'[34]

In measuring the probability of expected future economic benefits, the entity should use 'reasonable and supportable assumptions that represent management's best estimate of the set of economic conditions that will exist over the useful life of the asset'.[35] In making the above judgement the entity should assess the degree of certainty attached to the flow of future economic benefits at the time of initial recognition, giving greater weight to external evidence.[36]

Upon initial recognition an intangible asset should be measured at cost.[37] The standard defines this as 'the amount of cash or cash equivalents paid or the fair value of other consideration given to acquire an asset at the time of its acquisition or construction, or, when applicable, the amount attributed to that asset when initially recognised in accordance with the specific requirements of other IFRSs, e.g. IFRS 2 – *Share-based Payment*.'[38] The components of the cost of an internally generated intangible asset are discussed in more detail at 2.2.7 below.

Although IAS 38 is based on a general recognition principle that applies to both initial acquisition and subsequent expenditures, the hurdle for the recognition of subsequent expenditure as an addition to an intangible asset is set higher. The standard argues that 'the nature of intangible assets is such that, in many cases, there are no additions to such an asset or replacements of part of it. Accordingly, most subsequent expenditures are likely to maintain the expected future economic benefits embodied in an existing intangible asset rather than meet the definition of an intangible asset and the recognition criteria in this Standard. In addition, it is often difficult to attribute subsequent expenditure directly to a particular intangible asset rather than to the business as a whole.'

The standard therefore presumes that only rarely will subsequent expenditure-expenditure incurred after the initial recognition of an acquired intangible asset or after completion of an internally generated intangible asset be recognised in the carrying amount of an asset.[39] The capitalisation of subsequent expenditure on brands, mastheads, publishing titles, customer lists and similar items is expressly forbidden.[40] This is because the standard argues that such items cannot be distinguished from the business of which they are a part.[41] Thus, at best such expenditure creates internally generated goodwill.

The guidance in IAS 38 on the recognition and initial measurement of intangible assets takes account of the way in which an entity obtained the asset. Separate rules recognition and initial measurement exist for intangible assets depending on whether they were:

- acquired separately (see 2.2.1 below);
- acquired as part of a business combination (see 2.2.2 below);
- acquired by way of government grant (see 2.2.3 below);
- obtained in an exchange of assets (see 2.2.4 below); and
- generated internally (see 2.2.6 below).

2.2.1   *Separate acquisition*

A   *Recognition and components of cost*

IAS 38 assumes that the price paid to acquire an intangible asset separately, usually reflects expectations about the probability that future economic benefits, embodied in the asset will flow to the entity. In other words, the effect of probability is reflected in the cost of the asset.[42] Therefore, when an entity separately acquires an intangible asset the standard:

- considers future economic benefits to be probable;[43] and
- assumes that the cost of a separately acquired intangible asset can usually be measured reliably, especially in the case of a monetary purchase consideration.[44]

Separately acquired intangible assets should, therefore, normally be recognised. In its basis for conclusions on IAS 38, the IASB observed that 'this highlights a general inconsistency between the recognition criteria for assets and liabilities in the *Framework* (which states that an item meeting the definition of an element should be recognised only if it is probable that any future economic benefits associated with the item will flow to or from the entity, and the item can be measured reliably) and the fair value measurements required in, for example, a business combination. However, the Board concluded that the role of probability as a criterion for recognition in the *Framework* should be considered more generally as part of a forthcoming Concepts project.'[45]

An entity that subcontracts the development of intangible assets (e.g. research and development) to other parties, must exercise judgement in determining whether it is acquiring an intangible asset or whether it is obtaining goods and services that are being used to develop an intangible asset. That is, it cannot capitalise costs by claiming they are external and that the entity is therefore ipso facto acquiring the intangible asset.

The cost of a separately acquired intangible asset comprises:[46]

- its purchase price, including import duties and non-refundable purchase taxes, after deducting trade discounts and rebates; and

- any directly attributable cost of preparing the asset for its intended use, for example:[47]

  - costs of employee benefits arising directly from bringing the asset to its working condition;

  - professional fees arising directly from bringing the asset to its working condition; and

  - costs of testing whether the asset is functioning properly.

Capitalisation of expenditure ceases when the asset is in the condition necessary for it to be capable of operating in the manner intended by management.[48] This may well be before the date on which it is brought into use.

If 'payment for an intangible asset is deferred beyond normal credit terms, its cost is the cash price equivalent. The difference between this amount and the total payments is recognised as interest expense over the period of credit'.[49]

B Costs to be expensed

The following types of expenditure are not considered to be part of the cost of a separately acquired intangible asset:[50]

- costs of introducing a new product or service, including costs of advertising and promotional activities;

- costs of conducting business in a new location or with a new class of customer, including costs of staff training;

- administration and other general overhead costs;

- costs incurred in using or redeploying an intangible asset;

- costs incurred while an asset capable of operating in the manner intended by management has yet to be brought into use; and

- initial operating losses, such as those incurred while demand for the assets output builds up.

C Incidental operations

In September 2000, the (then) IASC issued draft interpretation SIC-D26 – *Property, Plant and Equipment – Results of Incidental Operations*, which proposed that an entity should recognise the results of incidental operations in profit or loss for the period. However, the IASB decided that it would be better to address this issue as part of its improvements project. It was therefore only in December 2003 that the IASB issued guidance on accounting for the results of incidental operations as part of IAS 16.[51] Identical guidance on accounting for the results of incidental operations is incorporated in IAS 38, which was issued several months later in March 2004.

When an entity engages in operations in connection with the development of an intangible asset that are 'not necessary to bring the asset to the condition necessary for it to be capable of operating in the manner intended by management', the entity should recognise the income and related expenses of incidental operations 'immediately in profit or loss … in their respective classifications of income and expense'.[52] Such incidental operations can occur before or during the development activities. The example below illustrates these requirements.

Example 11.1:   Incidental operations

Entity A is pioneering a new process for the production of a certain type of chemical. Entity A will be able to patent the new production process. During the development phase, A is selling quantities of the chemical that are produced as a by-product of the development activities that are taking place. The expenditure incurred comprises labour, raw materials, assembly costs, costs of equipment and professional fees.

The revenues and costs associated with the production and sale of the chemical are accounted for in profit or loss for the period, while the development costs that meet the strict recognition criteria of IAS 38 are recognised as an intangible asset. Development costs that fail the IAS 38 recognition test are also expensed.

As the above example suggests, identifying the revenue from incidental operations will often be much easier than allocating costs to incidental operations. Furthermore, it will often be challenging to determine when exactly a project moves from the development phase into its start-up phase.

2.2.2   Acquisition as part of a business combination

Chapter 6 at 2.3.3 discusses in detail the requirements regarding recognition and initial measurement of assets acquired and liabilities and contingent liabilities assumed in a business combination. A summary of requirements regarding intangible assets acquired in a business combination is provided at A to C below. However, it is worth noting that the effect of phase 1 of the IASB's business combinations project is to extend the range of intangible assets that should be recognised following a business combination, rather than being subsumed within goodwill. The illustrative examples in IFRS 3 state that, for example, the following types of intangible assets should be recognised separately if they meet the criteria in IAS 38: trademarks, trade names, internet domain names, non-competition agreements, customer lists, non-contractual customer relationships, films, music videos, television programmes, franchise agreements, unpatented technology and databases.[53]

A   Recognition of intangible assets acquired in a business combination

At the acquisition date, an acquirer should separately recognise, under IFRS 3, an intangible asset of the acquiree if:[54]

- it meets the definition of an intangible asset in IAS 38; and
- its fair value can be measured reliably.

For such item to be recognised as an intangible asset, it must also be probable that the expected future benefits that are attributable to the asset will flow to the entity.[55]

An acquirer should recognise an intangible asset acquired in a business combination at cost, which is its fair value at the acquisition date (see Chapter 6 at 2.3.3).[56] The standard indicates that the fair value of an intangible asset reflects market expectations about the probability that the future economic benefits embodied in the asset will flow to the entity. In other words, the effect of probability is reflected in the fair value measurement of the intangible asset. Therefore, in the case of intangible assets acquired in a business combination, the probability recognition criterion is always considered to be satisfied.[57]

An acquirer should recognise 'at the acquisition date separately from goodwill an intangible asset of the acquiree if the asset's fair value can be measured reliably, irrespective of whether the asset had been recognised by the acquiree before the business combination'.[58]

In developing the IAS 38 the IASB originally took the position that sufficient information should exist to measure reliably the fair value of intangible assets that have an underlying contractual or legal basis, or that are capable of being separated from the entity.[59] During its field visits and round-table discussions with auditors, preparers, accounting standard-setters and regulators the IASB was presented with numerous examples of acquired intangible assets whose fair value could not be measured reliably.[60] This includes many permits allocated by governments. It is often a feature of these assets that the entity has legal rights, they are clearly valuable but they cannot legally be bought and sold. Presumably if an airline were to buy a smaller competitor and then close its business, retaining only its landing slots, it might be able to establish reliably what it had paid for them. Prices on a 'grey' market of dubious legality may not be a good basis for establishing fair value. However, the Board remained concerned that 'failing the recognition criterion of reliability of measurement might be inappropriately used by entities as a basis for not recognising intangible assets separately from goodwill'.[61] Therefore, the standard is quite restrictive and states that 'the only circumstances in which it might not be possible to measure reliably the fair value of an intangible asset acquired in a business combination are when the intangible asset arises from legal or other contractual rights and either:

(a) is not separable; or

(b) is separable, but there is no history or evidence of exchange transactions for the same or similar assets, and otherwise estimating fair value would be dependent on immeasurable variables.'[62]

The IASB recognised that an intangible asset acquired in a business combination might be separable, but only together with a related tangible or intangible asset. For example, a magazine's publishing title might not be able to be sold separately from a related subscriber database. Therefore, IAS 38 requires the acquirer to recognise the group of assets as a single asset, separately from goodwill, if the individual fair values of the assets in the group are not reliably measurable.[63] This is to prevent an entity from having to allocate cash flows on an arbitrary basis between individual items in a group of assets.[64]

The standard notes that the terms 'brand' and 'brand name' are often used as synonyms for trademarks and other marks. However, the former are regarded as general marketing terms that are typically used to refer to a group of complementary assets such as a trademark (or service mark) and its related trade name, formulas, recipes and technological expertise. Accordingly, IAS 38 requires the acquirer to recognise a group of complementary intangible assets as a single asset comprising a brand if the individual fair values of the complementary assets are not reliably measurable. If the individual fair values of the complementary assets are reliably measurable, an acquirer may recognise them as a single asset provided the individual assets have similar useful lives.[65]

B   *Measuring fair value of intangible assets acquired in a business combination*

IAS 38 presumes that the fair value of intangible assets acquired in business combinations can normally be measured with sufficient reliability to be recognised separately from goodwill. When there is a range of possible outcomes with different probabilities for the estimates used to measure an intangible asset's fair value, that 'uncertainty enters into the measurement of the asset's fair value, rather than demonstrating an inability to measure fair value reliably'. If an intangible asset acquired in a business combination has a finite useful life, there is a rebuttable presumption in the standard that its fair value can be measured reliably.[66] This demonstrates the change to the way in which goodwill and intangible assets have been classified and distinguished in accounting standards. A characteristic of goodwill used to be the acquiring entity's ability to earn superprofits from an acquired business. Now, if that acquired business has a finite life, e.g. it is based on a contract or a franchise, this 'goodwill' must presumably now be defined as an intangible asset, because it arises from contractual rights and has a finite life, even though it is clearly not separable.

The standard states that quoted market prices in an active market provide the most reliable estimate of the fair value of an intangible asset.[67] It goes on to say that 'the appropriate market price is usually the current bid price. If current bid prices are unavailable, the price of the most recent similar transaction may provide a basis from which to estimate fair value, provided that there has not been a significant change in economic circumstances between the transaction date and the date at which the asset's fair value is estimated.'[68]

As the standard itself notes, it is uncommon for an active market to exist for intangible assets. The value of many intangible assets such as brands, newspaper mastheads, music and film publishing rights, patents or trademarks depends on the fact that they are unique, i.e. an active market cannot exist for many of the intangible assets that IFRS 3 and IAS 38 require an acquirer to recognise as part of the allocation process.[69] Accordingly, if no active market exists, the intangible assets should be valued on a basis that reflects the amounts the acquirer would have paid for the assets in arm's length transactions between knowledgeable willing parties, based on the best information available.[70] In determining this amount, an entity should consider recent transactions for similar assets.[71]

IAS 38 acknowledges that entities that are regularly involved in the purchase and sale of unique intangible assets may have developed techniques for estimating their fair values indirectly. Therefore, it allows these techniques to be used for initial measurement of an intangible asset acquired in a business combination if their objective is to estimate fair value and if they reflect current transactions and practices in the industry to which the asset belongs. These techniques include, when appropriate:[72]

(a) applying multiples reflecting current market transactions to indicators that drive the profitability of the asset (such as revenue, market shares and operating profit) or to the royalty stream that could be obtained from licensing the intangible asset to another party in an arm's length transaction (as in the 'relief from royalty' approach); or

(b) discounting estimated future net cash flows from the asset.

Newspaper and magazine titles frequently change hands based on multiples of revenue. Here, of course, it may be a challenge (if the acquisition is of another publishing entity) to establish the boundaries between the intangible titles and goodwill arising on the acquired entity as a whole.

C   In-process research and development

The term 'in-process research and development' (IPR&D) identifies those identifiable intangible assets resulting from research and development activities that are acquired in a business combination. The acquirer should recognise IPR&D separately from goodwill 'if the project meets the definition of an intangible asset and its fair value can be measured reliably. An acquiree's in-process research and development project meets the definition of an intangible asset when it:

(a) meets the definition of an asset; and

(b) is identifiable, i.e. is separable or arises from contractual or other legal rights.'[73]

Although the amount attributed to the project upon acquisition is accounted for as an asset, IAS 38 goes on to require that any subsequent expenditure incurred after the acquisition of the project should be accounted for in accordance with the rules on expenditure incurred in the research phase and development phase of internally generated intangible assets (see at 2.2.6 below).[74] In summary, this means that the subsequent expenditure is accounted for as follows:

- research expenditure is recognised as an expense when incurred;

- development expenditure that does not satisfy the criteria for recognition as an intangible asset is recognised as an expense when incurred (see at 2.2.6 below); and

- development expenditure that satisfies the recognition criteria is capitalised as part of the acquired in-process research or development project (see at 2.2.6 below).[75]

Critics of the above approach have pointed out in the past that 'applying the same criteria to all intangible assets acquired in a business combination to assess whether they should be recognised separately from goodwill results in treating some IPR&D

projects acquired in business combinations differently from similar projects started internally'.[76] The IASB acknowledges this criticism but decided not to address the issue when it revised IAS 38. Until the Board finds time to address this issue, users of financial statements will have to live with the problem that research and development expenditure is being accounted for differently depending on whether a project is acquired or started internally.[77]

The implication is that the in-process research and development expenditure recognised as an asset on acquisition that never progresses to the stage of satisfying the recognition criteria for an internal project will ultimately be impaired, although it may be that this impairment will not arise until the entity is satisfied that the project will not continue. However, since it is an intangible asset not yet available for use, it will need to be tested for impairment annually by comparing its carrying amount with its recoverable amount.[78] Any impairment loss will be reflected in the entity's income statement as a post-acquisition event. Hence accounting for IPR&D under IFRS is significantly different from US GAAP, which requires it to be expensed at the acquisition date.

2.2.3 Acquisition by way of government grant

An intangible asset may sometimes 'be acquired free of charge, or for nominal consideration, by way of a government grant'.[79] Examples of intangible assets that governments frequently allocate to entities include airport-landing rights, licences to operate radio or television stations, import licences or quotas or rights to access other restricted resources.[80]

Government grants should be accounted for under IAS 20 – *Government Grants and Disclosure of Government Assistance*, which permits initial recognition of intangible assets received at either:[81]

- fair value; or
- a nominal amount plus any expenditure that is directly attributable to preparing the asset for its intended use.

The accounting policy for intangible assets acquired by way of government grant should be applied consistently to all intangible assets acquired in this manner.

It is not possible to measure reliably the fair value of all of the permits allocated by governments because they may have been allocated for nil consideration, may not be transferable and may only be bought and sold as part of a business. Some of the issues surrounding the fair values of airline landing slots were considered under 2.2.A above. On the other hand, other allocated permits such as milk quotas are freely traded and therefore do have a fair value.

A   Future developments: Emission rights

Several governments either have, or are in the process of developing, schemes to encourage reduced emissions of pollutants, in particular of greenhouse gases. Some schemes are based on a cap and trade model whereby participants are allocated emission rights or allowances equal to a cap (i.e. target level of emissions) and are permitted to trade those allowances.

Because there is presently no guidance on the accounting for such schemes and because no consensus has emerged among market participants on what the accounting treatment should be, the IFRIC concluded that an interpretation should be issued to explain how IFRS should be applied to such schemes.

Accordingly, in May 2003 the IFRIC issued IFRIC D1 – *Emission Rights*, which addresses accounting for emission rights that arise from a 'cap and trade' scheme. However, the draft interpretation does not provide a concise definition of 'cap and trade' schemes. Instead it provides a list of characteristics that are generally, which include:[82]

- rights to emit pollutant at a specified level are allocated to entities participating in the scheme;

- the scheme operates for defined compliance periods;

- participants in the scheme are free to buy and sell emission rights;

- if at the end of the compliance period a participants' actual emissions exceeded its emission rights, the participant will incur a penalty;

- in some schemes emission rights may be carried forward to future periods; and

- the scheme may provide for brokers – who are not themselves participants – to buy and sell emission rights.

IFRIC D1 deals with accounting for a 'cap and trade' scheme by entities that participate in them. It does not address accounting by entities that are not yet subject to a scheme (even if they expect to be subject to one in the future) and brokers that are not themselves participants.[83] The provisions of the draft interpretation may also be relevant to similar types of schemes, such as 'renewable energy certificates' schemes that are described in the Appendix to the draft interpretation.[84] The draft interpretation provides guidance on accounting for the following elements that an emission rights scheme gives rise to:[85]

(a)   *an asset for emission rights held (allowances)* – 'Allowances, whether allocated by government or purchased, are intangible assets that shall be accounted for under IAS 38 *Intangible Assets*. Allowances that are allocated for less than fair value shall be measured initially at their fair value. Allowances shall not be amortised but may be impaired';[86]

(b)   *a government grant* – The difference between the amount paid and fair value is a government grant that should be accounted for under IAS 20. The grant is initially recognised as deferred income in the balance sheet and subsequently recognised as income on a systematic basis over the compliance period for which the allowances were allocated;[87]

(c)   *a liability for the obligation to deliver allowances equal to emissions that have been made* – This liability is a provision that falls within the scope of IAS 37 – *Provisions, Contingent Liabilities and Contingent Assets.* The liability is settled by delivering allowances, incurring a penalty or a combination of both. The liability should be measured at the best estimate of the expenditure required to settle the present obligation at the balance sheet date:

- this will normally be the present market price of the number of allowances required to cover emissions made up to the balance sheet date; or

- if the participant's best estimate is that some or all of the obligation will be settled by incurring a cash penalty, it shall measure that part of its obligation at the cost of the penalty rather than at the market price of the relevant number of allowances.[88]

Items (a) to (c) above should not be presented as a net asset or liability.[89] As the draft interpretation notes 'the existence of an emission rights scheme may cause certain assets to become impaired if the cash flows expected to be generated by those assets are reduced as a result of the scheme.'[90]

In March 2004, the IFRIC decided to suspend work on IFRIC D1 in the light of the Board's plans to amend IAS 20 by adopting the accounting model for government grants contained in IAS 41 – *Agriculture*.[91] However, in September 2004, the IFRIC noted it was unlikely that the Board would issue a final amended IAS 20 for at least another year and hence that the IFRIC would be unable to finalise IFRIC D1 until that time. Given that the EU Emissions Trading Scheme starts at the beginning of 2005, and given the potential for diversity of accounting for that scheme, the IFRIC reconsidered whether it should finalise its original proposals. The view of the majority of IFRIC members present was that IFRIC D1 should be finalised in substantially its present form and issued in the final quarter of 2004.[92]

2.2.4   Exchanges of assets

Asset exchanges are transactions that have preoccupied standard-setters for a number of years. For example, an entity might swap certain intangible assets that it does not require or is no longer allowed to use for those of a counterparty that has other surplus assets. It is not uncommon for airlines and newspaper chains to exchange landing slots and newspaper titles, respectively, to meet demands of competition authorities. The question arises whether such transactions give rise to a profit, in the circumstances where the outgoing asset is valued at less than the incoming one. Equally, it is possible that a transaction could be arranged with no real commercial substance, solely to boost apparent profits.

Three separate international accounting standards contain virtually identical guidance on accounting for exchanges of assets: IAS 16 (see Chapter 12), IAS 40 – *Investment Property* (also see Chapter 12) and IAS 38 (which is discussed below).

A   Measurement of assets exchanged

IAS 38 requires all acquisitions of intangible assets in exchange for non-monetary assets, or a combination of monetary and non-monetary assets, to be measured at fair value. The cost of such an intangible asset is measured at fair value unless:[93]

(a)   the exchange transaction lacks commercial substance; or

(b)   the fair value of neither the asset received nor the asset given up is reliably measurable.

The acquired asset is measured in this way even if an entity cannot immediately derecognise the asset given up. If an entity is able to determine reliably the fair value of either the asset received or the asset given up, then the fair value of the asset given up is used to measure cost unless the fair value of the asset received is more clearly evident.[94] If the fair value of neither the asset given up, nor the asset received can be measured reliably the cost is measured at the carrying amount of the asset given up.[95]

B   Commercial substance

The commercial substance test was put in place to prevent gains in income being recognised when the transaction had no 'discernable effect on the entity's economics'.[96] The commercial substance of an exchange is to be determined by forecasting and comparing the future cash flows budgeted to be generated by the incoming and outgoing assets. For commercial substance to be present, there must be a significant difference between the two forecasts. The standard sets out this requirement as follows:[97]

> 'An entity determines whether an exchange transaction has commercial substance by considering the extent to which its future cash flows are expected to change as a result of the transaction. An exchange transaction has commercial substance if:
>
> (a)   the configuration (i.e. risk, timing and amount) of the cash flows of the asset received differs from the configuration of the cash flows of the asset transferred; or
>
> (b)   the entity-specific value of the portion of the entity's operations affected by the transaction changes as a result of the exchange; and
>
> (c)   the difference in (a) or (b) is significant relative to the fair value of the assets exchanged.'

IAS 38 defines the 'entity-specific value' of an intangible asset as 'the present value of the cash flows an entity expects to arise from the continuing use of an asset and from its disposal at the end of its useful life or expects to incur when settling a liability'.[98] In determining whether an exchange transaction has commercial substance, the entity-specific value of the portion of the entity's operations affected by the transaction should reflect post-tax cash flows.[99] This is somewhat different from the calculation of an asset's value in use under IAS 36 (see Chapter 13), which uses a pre-tax discount rate based on the entity's own risks rather than the rate that the market would apply to a similar asset.

It should be noted that the above commercial substance test introduces a prediction of future cash flows element into the determination of the carrying amount of some intangible assets. The standard states that 'the fair value of an intangible asset for which comparable market transactions do not exist is reliably measurable if (a) the variability in the range of reasonable fair value estimates is not significant for that asset or (b) the probabilities of the various estimates within the range can be reasonably assessed and used in estimating fair value.'[100] The standard allows an entity to forego the effort of performing these detailed calculations when the outcome would be clear in advance[101] – perhaps if it is obvious that there is no 'commercial substance' in this very restricted sense.

2.2.5   *Internally generated goodwill*

IAS 38 explicitly prohibits the recognition of internally generated goodwill as an asset, because internally generated goodwill 'is not an identifiable resource ... controlled by the entity that can be measured reliably at cost'.[102] It therefore does not meet the definition of an intangible asset under the standard or that of an asset under the IASB's *Framework*. The standard maintains that the difference between the market value of an entity and the carrying amount of its identifiable net assets at any time may capture a range of factors that affect the value of the entity, but that such differences do not represent the cost of intangible assets controlled by the entity.[103]

2.2.6   *Internally generated intangible assets*

The IASB recognises that in determining whether an internally generated intangible asset qualifies for recognition may be difficult because of problems in:[104]

'(a)   identifying whether and when there is an identifiable asset that will generate expected future economic benefits; and

(b)   determining the cost of the asset reliably. In some cases, the cost of generating an intangible asset internally cannot be distinguished from the cost of maintaining or enhancing the entity's internally generated goodwill or of running day-to-day operations.'

To address these problems, IAS 38 requires that in addition to 'complying with the general requirements for the recognition and initial measurement of an intangible asset, an entity applies the requirements and guidance in paragraphs 52-67 to all internally generated intangible assets.'[105] Those paragraphs contain detailed guidance on accounting for intangible assets in the research phase (see A below), the development phase (see B below) and on components of cost of an internally generated intangible asset (see 2.2.7 below).

The standard defines research and development as follows:

Research is original and planned investigation undertaken with the prospect of gaining new scientific or technical knowledge and understanding.[106]

The standard gives the following examples of research activities:[107]

'(a)   activities aimed at obtaining new knowledge;

(b)   the search for, evaluation and final selection of, applications of research findings or other knowledge;

(c)   the search for alternatives for materials, devices, products, processes, systems or services; and

(d)   the formulation, design, evaluation and final selection of possible alternatives for new or improved materials, devices, products, processes, systems or services.'

Development is the application of research findings or other knowledge to a plan or design for the production of new or substantially improved materials, devices, products, processes, systems or services before the start of commercial production or use.[108]

The standard gives the following examples of development activities:[109]

'(a)   the design, construction and testing of pre-production or pre-use prototypes and models;

(b)   the design of tools, jigs, moulds and dies involving new technology;

(c)   the design, construction and operation of a pilot plant that is not of a scale economically feasible for commercial production; and

(d)   the design, construction and testing of a chosen alternative for new or improved materials, devices, products, processes, systems or services.'

A   Research phase

An entity cannot recognise an intangible asset arising from research or from the research phase of an internal project. Instead, any expenditure on research or the research phase of an internal project should be expensed as incurred because the entity cannot demonstrate that an intangible asset exists that will generate probable future economic benefits.[110]

B   Development phase

An intangible asset arising from development or from the development phase of an internal project should be recognised as an internally generated intangible 'if, and only if, an entity can demonstrate all of the following:

'(a)   the technical feasibility of completing the intangible asset so that it will be available for use or sale.

(b)   its intention to complete the intangible asset and use or sell it.

(c)   its ability to use or sell the intangible asset.

(d)   how the intangible asset will generate probable future economic benefits. Among other things, the entity can demonstrate the existence of a market for the output of the intangible asset or the intangible asset itself or, if it is to be used internally, the usefulness of the intangible asset.

(e)   the availability of adequate technical, financial and other resources to complete the development and to use or sell the intangible asset.

(f)   its ability to measure reliably the expenditure attributable to the intangible asset during its development.'[111]

The standard requires recognition of an intangible asset in the development phase because the development phase of a project is further advanced than the research phase and an entity may be able to demonstrate that the asset will generate probable future economic benefits.[112]

It may be challenging to obtain objective evidence on each of the above conditions because:

*   condition (b) relies on management intent;

*   conditions (c), (e) and (f) are entity-specific, i.e. whether development expenditure meets any of these conditions depends both on the development activity itself and the entity; and

*   condition (d) above is more restrictive than is immediately apparent because the entity needs to assess the probable future economic benefits using the principles in IAS 36, i.e. using discounted cash flows. If the asset will generate economic benefits only in conjunction with other assets, the entity should apply the concept of cash-generating units.[113] The requirements of the IAS 36 are discussed in Chapter 13.

IAS 38 indicates that evidence may be available in the form of:

*   a business plan showing the technical, financial and other resources needed and the entity's ability to secure those resources;[114]

*   a lender's indication of its willingness to fund the plan can evidence the availability of external finance;[115] and

*   'an entity's costing systems can often measure reliably the cost of generating an intangible asset internally, such as salary and other expenditure incurred in securing copyrights or licences or developing computer software.'[116]

In any case, an entity should maintain books and records that allow it to prove that it either meets or fails the conditions set out by IAS 38.

The standard explains that 'although the terms "research" and "development" are defined, the terms "research phase" and "development phase" have a broader meaning for the purpose of this Standard.'[117] This means that the research phase may include activities that do not necessarily meet the definition of 'research'. The research phase may cover the whole period in which research is taking place, regardless of the fact that activities that would otherwise characterise the development phase are taking place at the same time. As a result, if an entity cannot distinguish the research phase from the development phase of an internal project to create an intangible asset, the entity treats the expenditure on that project as if it were incurred in the research phase only.[118] It also means that the development phase may include activities that do not necessarily meet the definition of 'development'. The example below explains how an entity would apply these rules in practice.

Example 11.2:   *Research phase and development phase under IAS 38*

Entity K is working on a project to create a database containing satellite and aerial imagines of the earth, which it intends to sell to customers. K has identified the following stages in its project:

(a) Research stage – gaining the technical knowledge necessary to determine whether the project is feasible from a technological point of view;

(b) Development stage – developing the required database software and acquiring the required data to populate the database; and

(c) Production stage – after the commercial launch of the service, updating and managing the database.

The above can be summarised as follows:

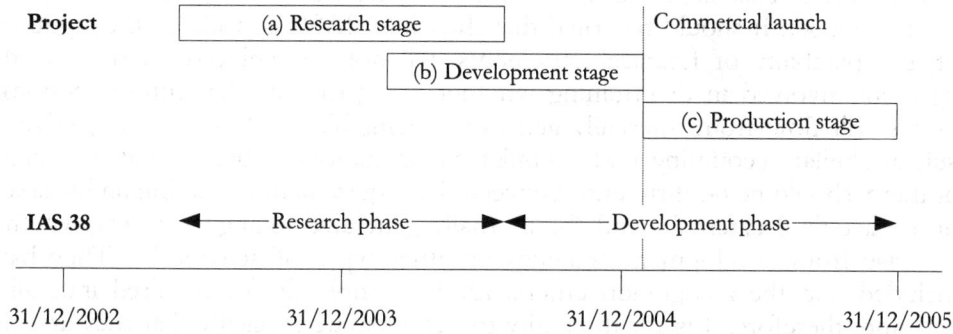

The activities in the research stage described under (a) meet the definition of research under IAS 38 and would be accounted for as part of the research phase of the project.

The activities in the development stage described under (b) meet the definition of development under IAS 38. However, because the development activities cannot be distinguished from the research activities taking place at the same time, the initial development activities are accounted for as if they were incurred in the research phase. Only once it becomes possible to identify the development activities properly, can the expenditure incurred be accounted for as part of the development phase.

After the commercial launch of the service, K continues to update and maintain the internally generated intangible asset, which involves adding, replacing and reorganising of data. Updating and maintaining the database is a routine process that does not involve any major innovation or new techniques. Therefore, the activities in the production stage do not meet the definition of 'research' or 'development'.

Under IAS 38, K should treat the production stage activities as part of the development phase, as the standard acknowledges that 'development phase' has a broader meaning than 'development'. This does not necessarily mean that K can capitalise the expenditure incurred in the production stage because it needs pass the double hurdle of:

- the presumption in paragraph 20 of IAS 38 that 'there are no additions to such an asset or replacements of part of it' (see 2.2 above); and

- the six criteria for recognition of development costs (see above).

As the above example illustrates, the guidance in IAS 38 seems to take a somewhat out of date view as to how internally generated intangible assets are created and managed in practice, as well what types of internally generated intangible assets there can be. It stresses research and development, but it is quite clear that the standard applies to intangible assets that are created for use by the entity itself. It therefore ignores the everyday reality of software companies, television production companies, newspapers and data vendors that produce intangible assets in an industrial-scale routine process. Many of the intangible assets produced in routine processes – i.e. software, television programmes, newspaper content and databases – meet the recognition criteria in the standard, but no specific guidance is available that could help an entity in dealing with the practical problems that arise when accounting for them.

On the one hand the standard requires recognition of an intangible asset arising from development (or the development phase of an internal project), while on the other hand it imposes stringent conditions that restrict recognition. For an entity that wants to recognise development expenditure as an intangible asset these tests create a sensible balance, ensuring that the entity does not recognise unrecoverable costs as an asset. It should be noted that the (then) IASC considered the argument that 'comparability of financial statements will not be achieved ... because the judgement involved in determining whether it is probable that future economic benefits will flow from internally generated intangible assets is too subjective to result in similar accounting under similar circumstances',[119] but ultimately decided that there 'should be no difference between the requirement for (a) intangible assets that are acquired externally and (b) internally generated intangible assets, whether they arise from development activities or other types of activities'.[120] They have concluded that the recognition criteria are met implicitly for acquired intangible assets and, therefore, it is for the entity to demonstrate explicitly that they are met in the case of the internally generated assets.

The extract below shows a typical accounting policy for research and development under IFRS.

Extract 11.1: Danisco A/S (2003)

Accounting policies [extract]
Research and development costs

Research and development costs include costs, salaries and depreciation directly or indirectly attributable to corporate R&D.

Research costs are recognised in the profit and loss account in the year in which they are incurred.

Clearly defined and identifiable development projects in which the technical degree of exploitation, adequate resources and potential market or development possibility in the undertaking are recognisable, and where it is the intention to produce, market or execute the project, are capitalised when a correlation exists between the costs incurred and future benefits.

The extract below, illustrates some of the difficulty in applying the IAS 38 recognition criteria for development costs in the pharmaceutical industry. Typically, technical and economic feasibility are established very late in the development phase, which means that usually only a small proportion of the development costs is capitalised (see 3.2 below).

Extract 11.2: Merck KgaA (2003)

[22] Research and development [extract]

The breakdown of research and development by business sectors and regions is disclosed under 'Segment Reporting'. In addition to the costs of research departments and process development, this item also includes the cost of purchased services and the cost of clinical trials. The costs of research and development are expensed in full in the period in which they are incurred. Development expenses in the Pharmaceuticals business sector cannot be capitalized since the high level of risk up to the time that pharmaceutical products are marketed means that the requirements of IAS 38 are not satisfied in full. Costs incurred after regulatory approval are insignificant. In the same way, the risks involved until products are marketed means that development expenses in the Chemicals business sector and Laboratory Distribution cannot be capitalized. Refunds are eliminated against research costs for research and development of EUR 8.6 million (previous year: EUR 13.0 million).

C Internally generated brands, mastheads, publishing titles and customer lists

IAS 38 considers internally generated brands, mastheads, publishing titles, customer lists and items similar in substance to be indistinguishable from the cost of developing a business as a whole.[121] In addition, the (then) IASC believed 'that internally generated intangible items of this kind would rarely, and perhaps never, meet the recognition criteria in IAS 38. However, to avoid any misunderstanding, IASC decided to set out this conclusion in the form of an explicit prohibition.'[122] Therefore, the standard prohibits recognition of such items as an intangible asset.[123]

D Website costs

In May 2001, the IASB issued SIC-32 (amended 2003) – *Intangible Assets – Web Site Costs* – in reaction to the vary large sums that were being spend at the time on the operation and development of websites. An entity's own website that arises from development and is for internal or external access is an internally generated intangible asset that is subject to the requirements of IAS 38.[124] SIC-32 clarifies how IAS 38 applies to accounting for costs in relation to websites, but does not apply to items that are accounted for under another standard, such as IAS 2, IAS 11, IAS 16 or IAS 17.[125]

The interpretation recognises that 'a web site designed for external access may be used for various purposes such as to promote and advertise an enterprise's own products and services, provide electronic services, and sell products and services. A web site designed for internal access may be used to store company policies and customer details, and search relevant information.'[126]

Under SIC-32, a website arising from development should be recognised as an intangible asset if it meets – in addition to complying with the general recognition requirements for intangible assets – the six conditions for the recognition of development costs (see 2.2.6 B).[127] The interpretations deems that an entity is 'not able to demonstrate how a web site developed solely or primarily for promoting and advertising its own products and services will generate probable future economic benefits, and consequently all expenditure on developing such a web site should be recognised as an expense when incurred'.[128]

The following stages of a website's development are identified by the interpretation:[129]

(a)   *planning* includes undertaking feasibility studies, defining objectives and specifications, evaluating alternatives and selecting preferences. Expenditure incurred in this stage is similar in nature to the research phase and should be recognised as an expense when it is incurred;

(b)   *application and infrastructure development* includes obtaining a domain name, purchasing and developing hardware and operating software, installing developed applications and stress testing. Provided it meets the recognition criteria for website costs, expenditure incurred in this stage – that can be directly attributed, or allocated on a reasonable and consistent basis, to preparing the website for its intended use – should be included in the cost of a website recognised as an intangible asset;

(c)   *graphical design development* includes designing the appearance of web pages. Expenditure incurred at this stage should be accounted for in the same way as expenditure incurred in the 'application and infrastructure development' stage described under (b) above;

(d)   *content development* includes creating, purchasing, preparing and uploading information, either textual or graphical in nature, on the website before the completion of the website's development. Expenditure incurred in this stage should be recognised as an expense when incurred to the extent that content is developed to advertise and promote an entity's own products and services;

(e)   in the *operating stage*, which starts after completion of the development of a website, an entity 'maintains and enhances the applications, infrastructure, graphical design and content of the website'.[130] Expenditure incurred in this stage should be recognised as an expense when it is incurred unless it meets the recognition criteria.

In making the above assessments, the entity should evaluate the nature of each activity for which expenditure is incurred, the website's stage of development and the additional guidance provided in the Appendix to SIC-32.[131]

A website that is recognised as an intangible asset should be measured after initial recognition by applying the cost model or the revaluation model. The IASB requires an entity to be prudent by stating that 'the best estimate of a web site's useful life should be short.'[132]

2.2.7   Cost of an internally generated intangible asset

As discussed at 2.2 above, upon initial recognition an intangible asset should be measured at cost, which the standard defines as 'the amount of cash or cash equivalents paid or the fair value of other consideration given to acquire an asset at the time of its acquisition or construction, or, when applicable, the amount attributed to that asset when initially recognised in accordance with the specific requirements of other IFRSs, e.g. IFRS 2 *Share-based Payment.*'[133]

The cost of an internally generated intangible asset is the sum of the expenditure incurred from the date when the intangible asset first meets the recognition criteria of the standard,[134] that is:

(a)   it is probable that the expected future economic benefits that are attributable to the asset will flow to the entity, using reasonable and supportable assumptions that represent management's best estimate of the set of economic conditions that will exist over the useful life of the asset;

(b)   the cost of the asset can be measured reliably;[135]

(c)   the asset meets the detailed conditions for recognition of development phase costs as an asset from paragraph 57 of the standard (see 2.2.6 B above); and

(d)   the expenditure on the asset was not initially recognised as an expense, because IAS 38 does not permit recognition of past expenses as an intangible asset at a later date.[136]

The following example, which is taken from IAS 38, illustrates how these above rules should be applied in practice.[137]

Example 11.3:   Recognition of internally generated intangible assets

An entity is developing a new production process. During 2005, expenditure incurred was €1,000, of which €900 was incurred before 1 December 2005 and €100 was incurred between 1 December 2005 and 31 December 2005. The entity is able to demonstrate that, at 1 December 2005, the production process met the criteria for recognition as an intangible asset. The recoverable amount of the know-how embodied in the process (including future cash outflows to complete the process before it is available for use) is estimated to be €500.

At the end of 2005, the production process is recognised as an intangible asset at a cost of €100 (expenditure incurred since the date when the recognition criteria were met, i.e. 1 December 2005). The €900 expenditure incurred before 1 December 2005 is recognised as an expense because the recognition criteria were not met until 1 December 2005. This expenditure does not form part of the cost of the production process recognised in the balance sheet.

During 2006, expenditure incurred is €2,000. At the end of 2006, the recoverable amount of the know-how embodied in the process (including future cash outflows to complete the process before it is available for use) is estimated to be €1,900.

At the end of 2006, the cost of the production process is €2,100 (€100 expenditure recognised at the end of 2005 plus €2,000 expenditure recognised in 2006). The entity recognises an impairment loss of €200 to adjust the carrying amount of the process before impairment loss (€2,100) to its recoverable amount (€1,900). This impairment loss will be reversed in a subsequent period if the requirements for the reversal of an impairment loss in IAS 36 are met.

The cost of an internally generated intangible asset comprises all directly attributable costs necessary to create, produce, and prepare the asset to be capable of operating in the manner intended by management.[138] Examples of directly attributable costs are:[139]

• costs of materials and services used or consumed in generating the intangible asset;

• costs of employee benefits arising from the generation of the intangible asset;

• fees to register a legal right;

- amortisation of patents and licences that are used to generate the intangible asset; and

- borrowing costs that meet the criteria under IAS 23 – *Borrowing Costs* – for recognition as an element of cost.

Indirect costs and general overheads, even if they can be allocated on a reasonable and consistent basis, can no longer be recognised as part of the cost of the asset, as was possible under the previous version of IAS 38 which specifically permitted this. The standard also specifically prohibits recognition of the following items as a component of cost:[140]

- selling, administrative and other general overhead expenditure unless this expenditure can be directly attributed to preparing the asset for use;

- identified inefficiencies and initial operating losses incurred before the asset achieves planned performance; and

- expenditure on training staff to operate the asset.

2.2.8 Recognition of an expense

Unless expenditure is in connection with an intangible item that the standard requires to be recognised, and of an allowable nature, it should be expensed. The only exception is in connection with a business combination, where the costs associated with an intangible that cannot be recognised will form part of the carrying amount of goodwill.[141]

Some of the costs that may not be capitalised in connection with specific projects were identified in 2.2.7 above. Sometimes expenditure is incurred to provide future economic benefits to an entity, but no intangible asset or other asset is acquired or created that can be recognised. In these cases, the expenditure is recognised as an expense when it is incurred.[142] Examples of expenditures that are recognised as an expense when incurred:[143]

(a) start-up costs, unless they are allowed as part of the cost of an asset under IAS 16. Start-up costs may consist of establishment costs such as legal and secretarial costs incurred in establishing a legal entity, expenditure to open a new facility or business or expenditures for starting new operations or launching new products or processes;

(b) training costs;

(c) advertising and promotional activities; and

(d) relocation or reorganisation costs.

The standard does not preclude an entity recognising a prepayment as an asset when payment for the delivery of goods or services has been made in advance of the delivery of goods or the rendering of services.[144]

2.3   Measurement after recognition

IAS 38, in common with a number of other international standards, provides an entity the option to choose between two alternative treatments that may be summarised as follows:[145]

- the *cost model*, which requires measurement at cost less any accumulated amortisation and any accumulated impairment losses (see 2.3.1 below); and

- the *revaluation model*, which requires measurement at a revalued amount less any subsequent accumulated amortisation and any subsequent accumulated impairment losses (see 2.3.2 below).

An entity needs to apply either the cost model or the revaluation model to an entire class of intangible assets, which is defined as 'a grouping of assets of a similar nature and use in an entity's operations'.[146] Examples of separate classes of intangible asset include:[147]

(a)   brand names;

(b)   mastheads and publishing titles;

(c)   computer software;

(d)   licences and franchises;

(e)   copyrights, patents and other industrial property rights, service and operating rights;

(f)   recipes, formulae, models, designs and prototypes; and

(g)   intangible assets under development.

The standard requires simultaneous revaluation of an entire class of intangible assets 'to avoid selective revaluation of assets and the reporting of amounts in the financial statements representing a mixture of costs and values as at different dates'.[148]

2.3.1   Cost model

Under the cost model, after initial recognition the carrying amount of an intangible asset is 'its cost less any accumulated amortisation and any accumulated impairment losses'.[149] The rules on amortisation of intangible assets are discussed at 2.4 and 2.5 below; impairment is discussed at 2.6 below.

2.3.2   Revaluation model

Under the revaluation model, after initial recognition an intangible asset should be carried at a revalued amount, which is its fair value at the date of the revaluation less any subsequent accumulated amortisation and any subsequent accumulated impairment losses.[150] An entity can only elect to apply the revaluation model if the fair value can be determined by reference to an active market for the intangible asset.[151] To prevent an entity from circumventing the recognition rules of the standard, the revaluation model does not allow:[152]

- the revaluation of intangible assets that have not previously been recognised as assets; or

- the initial recognition of intangible assets at amounts other than cost.

However, it is permitted to apply the revaluation model to the whole of an intangible asset even if only part of its cost is recognised as an asset because it did not meet the criteria for recognition until part of the way through the process.[153] These rules are designed to prevent an entity from recognising at a 'revalued' amount an intangible asset that was never recorded because its costs were expensed as they did not at the time meet the recognition rules. However, they would prohibit the revaluation of quotas and permits allocated by governments and similar bodies. These are amongst the few intangible assets that do have an active market. It is not, therefore, surprising that assets received by way of government grant are permitted to be revalued. The revaluation model may also be applied to 'an intangible asset that was received by way of a government grant and recognised at a nominal amount'.[154]

The example below illustrates how this would work in practice.

Example 11.4:   Application of revaluation model to intangible assets that are partially recognised or received by way of government grant

Entity C spent ¥1,200 in preparing its application for a number of taxi licenses, which it expensed because of the uncertain outcome of the process. C was granted a number of freely transferable taxi licenses and paid a nominal registration fee of ¥50, which it recognised as an asset. There is an active and liquid market in these taxi licenses.

C can apply the revaluation model under IAS 38 to these taxi licenses, because it previously recognised the license (even if it only recognised part of the costs as an asset) and there is an active market in these licenses.

Entity D obtained a number of freely transferable taxi licenses free of charge, which it recognised at a nominal amount as permitted under IAS 20. There is an active and liquid market in these taxi licenses.

D can apply the revaluation model under IAS 38 to these taxi licenses, because it previously recognised the license (even if it only recognised it at a nominal amount) and there is an active market in these licenses.

A   Active market

As mentioned above, an entity can only elect to apply the revaluation model if the fair value can be determined by reference to an active market for the intangible asset.[155] IAS 38 defines an active market as one in which all the following conditions exist:[156]

'(a)   the items traded in the market are homogeneous;

(b)   willing buyers and sellers can normally be found at any time; and

(c)   prices are available to the public.'

The standard concedes that 'it is uncommon for an active market with the characteristics described [above] to exist for an intangible asset, although this may happen. For example, in some jurisdictions, an active market may exist for freely transferable taxi licences, fishing licences or production quotas.'[157] However, under IAS 38 an active market as defined cannot exist for any type of intangible asset that is somehow unique or entity-specific. For example, 'an active market cannot exist for brands, newspaper mastheads, music and film publishing rights, patents or trademarks, because each such asset is unique'.[158] In other words, 'homogeneous' in the definition of an active market is to be interpreted as meaning 'identical' or 'virtually identical', it is not enough for intangible assets merely to be very similar in use or function.

Even if the intangible assets traded are homogenous, the standard does not consider there to be an active market if intangible assets are bought and sold, contracts are negotiated between individual buyers and sellers but transactions are relatively infrequent.[159] Hence, even if a market price exists for *one* intangible asset, the standard may not consider this to be sufficient evidence of the fair value of another.[160] Finally, if prices are not available to the public, this is taken as evidence that an active market does *not* exist.[161]

B   Frequency of revaluations

IAS 38 requires revaluation to be made 'with such regularity that at the balance sheet date the carrying amount of the asset does not differ materially from its fair value'.[162] The standard lets the frequency of revaluations depend on volatility of the fair values of the underlying intangible assets, though it does admit that 'some intangible assets may experience significant and volatile movements in fair value, thus necessitating annual revaluation. Such frequent revaluations are unnecessary for intangible assets with only insignificant movements in fair value.'[163] Nevertheless, considering the narrow definition of an 'active market' and the definition of 'material' in IAS 1 – *Presentation of Financial Statements*, an entity should err on the side of caution and revalue frequently because there is normally no excuse for ignoring price information that the standard requires to be available to the public.

C   Accounting for revaluations

Increases in an intangible asset's carrying amount as a result of a revaluation should be credited directly to equity under the heading of revaluation surplus, unless the revaluation reverses a revaluation decrease of the same asset that was previously recognised in profit or loss.[164] Conversely, decreases in an intangible asset's carrying amount as a result of a revaluation should be recognised in profit or loss, unless the revaluation reverses a revaluation increase, in which case the decrease should first be debited directly to equity to extinguish the revaluation surplus in respect of the asset.[165] The example below illustrates how this works.

Example 11.5:   Accounting for upward and downward revaluations

Entity E acquired an intangible asset that it accounts for under the revaluation model. The fair value of the asset changes as follows:

	£
Acquisition	530
A	550
B	520
C	510
D	555

The diagram below summarises this information (the impact of amortisation on the carrying amount and revaluation surplus has been ignored in this example for the sake of simplicity).

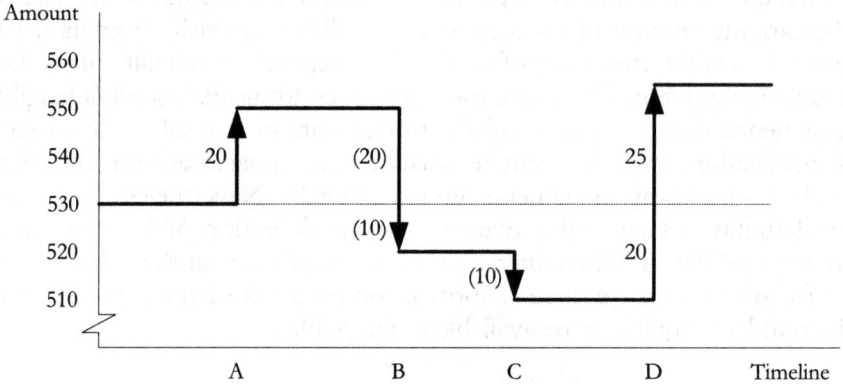

The table below shows how entity E should account for the upward and downward revaluations.

	Value of asset	Cumulative revaluation reserve	Revaluation recognised in equity	Revaluation recognised in profit or loss
	£	£	£	£
Acquisition	530	–	–	–
A	550	20	20	–
B	520	–	(20)	(10)
C	510	–	–	(10)
D	555	25	25	20

The upward revaluation at A is accounted for in equity. The downward revaluation at B first reduces the revaluation reserve to nil and the excess of £10 is recognised as a loss in income. The second downward revaluation at C is recognised as a loss in income. The upward revaluation at D first reverses the cumulative loss recognised in income and the excess is accounted for in the revaluation reserve.

In the example above the impact of amortisation on the carrying amount of the assets and the revaluation surplus was ignored for the sake of simplicity. However, IAS 38 requires the 'cumulative revaluation surplus included in equity to be transferred directly to retained earnings when the surplus is realised', which happens either (1) on the retirement or disposal of the asset or (2) as the asset is used by the entity.[166] In the latter case, the 'amount of the surplus realised is the difference between amortisation based on the revalued carrying amount of the asset and amortisation that would have been recognised based on the asset's historical cost'.[167] In practice this means two things:

- an entity applying the revaluation model would need to track both the historical cost and revalued amount of an asset to determine how much of the revaluation surplus has been realised; and

- any revaluation surplus is amortised over the life of the related asset. Therefore, in the case of a significant downward revaluation there is a smaller revaluation surplus available against which the downward revaluation can be offset.

The transfer from revaluation surplus to retained earnings is not made through the income statement.[168]

If an intangible asset is revalued, the standard allows an entity to account for the accumulated amortisation at the date of revaluation by either:[169]

(a) restating it proportionately with the change in the gross carrying amount of the asset so that the carrying amount of the asset after revaluation equals its revalued amount; or

(b) eliminating it against the gross carrying amount of the asset and the net amount restated to the revalued amount of the asset.

Example 11.6:   Restatement of accumulated amortisation after a revaluation

Entity F revalued an intangible asset from its carrying amount of £120 to its fair value of £150. The proportionate restatement approach (in the middle column) leads to grossing up of both gross carrying amount and the accumulated amortisation. The elimination approach (in the right-hand column) results in elimination of the accumulated amortisation.

	Before revaluation	*After revaluation*	
		Proportionate restatement	*Eliminating amortisation*
	£	£	£
Gross carrying amount	300	375	150
Accumulated amortisation	(180)	(225)	–
Net carrying amount	120	150	150

D   No active market

The standard requires an entity to apply the revaluation model to entire classes of intangible assets, but if an 'intangible asset in a class of revalued intangible assets cannot be revalued because there is no active market for this asset, the asset shall be carried at its cost less any accumulated amortisation and impairment losses'.[170]

Similarly, if the fair value of a previously revalued intangible asset 'can no longer be determined by reference to an active market, the carrying amount of the asset shall be its revalued amount at the date of the last revaluation by reference to the active market less any subsequent accumulated amortisation and any subsequent accumulated impairment losses'.[171] The IASB believes that, should this occur, it 'may indicate that the asset may be impaired and that it needs to be tested in accordance with IAS 36 *Impairment of Assets*'.[172]

If an entity is able again to determine the fair value of an asset, for which it 'froze' the revalued amount, 'by reference to an active market at a subsequent measurement date, the revaluation model is applied from that date'.[173]

2.4   Assessing the useful life of an intangible asset

IAS 38 defines the useful life of an intangible asset as:

'(a)   the period over which an asset is expected to be available for use by an entity; or

(b)   the number of production or similar units expected to be obtained from the asset by an entity.'[174]

Thus in some cases the useful life of an intangible asset should be expressed as a number of production or similar units rather than a period of time.

The standard requires an entity to assess 'whether the useful life of an intangible asset is finite or indefinite'.[175] The standard explains that the term 'indefinite' does not mean 'infinite'.[176] The standard requires 'an intangible asset to be regarded by an entity as having an indefinite useful life when, based on an analysis of all of the relevant factors, there is no foreseeable limit to the period over which the asset is expected to generate net cash inflows for the entity'.[177] If an entity concludes that the useful life of an intangible asset is finite, it assesses the length of the useful life or the number of production unit (or similar units) constituting that useful life.[178]

The previous version of IAS 38 prescribed a presumptive maximum useful life for intangible assets of 20 years.[179] However, the IASB observed that 'some intangible assets are based on legal rights that are conveyed in perpetuity rather than for finite terms. ... The Board concluded that if the cash flows are expected to continue for a finite period, the useful life of the asset is limited to that finite period. However, if the cash flows are expected to continue indefinitely, the useful life is indefinite.'[180] The IASB decided to remove the presumptive maximum useful life for intangible assets, because it is 'inconsistent with the view that the amortisation period for an intangible asset should, to be representationally faithful, reflect its useful life and, by extension, the cash flow streams associated with the asset'.[181]

This means that under IAS 38 it is now possible to account for intangible assets without amortising them at all. However, an important underlying assumption in making the assessment of the useful life of an intangible asset is that it 'reflects only that level of future maintenance expenditure required to maintain the asset at its standard of performance assessed at the time of estimating the asset's useful life, and the entity's ability and intention to reach such a level. A conclusion that the useful life of an intangible asset is indefinite should not depend on planned future expenditure in excess of that required to maintain the asset at that standard of performance.'[182]

The standard identifies a number of factors that may affect the useful life of an intangible asset:[183]

'(a) the expected usage of the asset by the entity and whether the asset could be managed efficiently by another management team;

(b) typical product life cycles for the asset and public information on estimates of useful lives of similar assets that are used in a similar way;

(c) technical, technological, commercial or other types of obsolescence;

(d) the stability of the industry in which the asset operates and changes in the market demand for the products or services output from the asset;

(e) expected actions by competitors or potential competitors;

(f) the level of maintenance expenditure required to obtain the expected future economic benefits from the asset and the entity's ability and intention to reach such a level;

(g) the period of control over the asset and legal or similar limits on the use of the asset, such as the expiry dates of related leases; and

(h) whether the useful life of the asset is dependent on the useful life of other assets of the entity.'

Further guidance is provided by IAS 38 in the form of Illustrative Examples (which are reproduced in the example below) that demonstrate how an entity would go about determining the useful life for different intangible assets and the subsequent accounting for those assets based on the useful life determinations.[184]

Example 11.7:   Assessing the useful life of an intangible asset[185]

Acquired customer list

A direct-mail marketing company acquires a customer list and expects that it will be able to derive benefit from the information on the list for at least one year, but no more than three years.

The customer list would be amortised over management's best estimate of its useful life, say 18 months. Although the direct-mail marketing company may intend to add customer names and other information to the list in the future, the expected benefits of the acquired customer list relate only to the customers on that list at the date it was acquired. The customer list also would be reviewed for impairment in accordance with IAS 36 *Impairment of Assets* by assessing at each reporting date whether there is any indication that the customer list may be impaired.

An acquired patent that expires in 15 years

The product protected by the patented technology is expected to be a source of net cash inflows for at least 15 years. The entity has a commitment from a third party to purchase that patent in five years for 60 per cent of the fair value of the patent at the date it was acquired, and the entity intends to sell the patent in five years.

The patent would be amortised over its five-year useful life to the entity, with a residual value equal to the present value of 60 per cent of the patent's fair value at the date it was acquired. The patent would also be reviewed for impairment in accordance with IAS 36 by assessing at each reporting date whether there is any indication that it may be impaired.

An acquired copyright that has a remaining legal life of 50 years

An analysis of consumer habits and market trends provides evidence that the copyrighted material will generate net cash inflows for only 30 more years.

The copyright would be amortised over its 30-year estimated useful life. The copyright also would be reviewed for impairment in accordance with IAS 36 by assessing at each reporting date whether there is any indication that it may be impaired.

An acquired broadcasting licence that expires in five years

The broadcasting licence is renewable every 10 years if the entity provides at least an average level of service to its customers and complies with the relevant legislative requirements. The licence may be renewed indefinitely at little cost and has been renewed twice before the most recent acquisition. The acquiring entity intends to renew the licence indefinitely and evidence supports its ability to do so. Historically, there has been no compelling challenge to the licence renewal. The technology used in broadcasting is not expected to be replaced by another technology at any time in the foreseeable future. Therefore, the licence is expected to contribute to the entity's net cash inflows indefinitely.

The broadcasting licence would be treated as having an indefinite useful life because it is expected to contribute to the entity's net cash inflows indefinitely. Therefore, the licence would not be amortised until its useful life is determined to be finite. The licence would be tested for impairment in accordance with IAS 36 annually and whenever there is an indication that it may be impaired.

The broadcasting licence in the example above

The licensing authority subsequently decides that it will no longer renew broadcasting licences, but rather will auction the licences. At the time the licensing authority's decision is made, the entity's broadcasting licence has three years until it expires. The entity expects that the licence will continue to contribute to net cash inflows until the licence expires.

Because the broadcasting licence can no longer be renewed, its useful life is no longer indefinite. Thus, the acquired licence would be amortised over its remaining three-year useful life and immediately tested for impairment in accordance with IAS 36.

An acquired airline route authority between two European cities that expires in three years

The route authority may be renewed every five years, and the acquiring entity intends to comply with the applicable rules and regulations surrounding renewal. Route authority renewals are routinely granted at a minimal cost and historically have been renewed when the airline has complied with the applicable rules and regulations. The acquiring entity expects to provide service indefinitely between the two cities from its hub airports and expects that the related supporting infrastructure (airport gates, slots, and terminal facility leases) will remain in place at those airports for as long as it has the route authority. An analysis of demand and cash flows supports those assumptions.

Because the facts and circumstances support the acquiring entity's ability to continue providing air service indefinitely between the two cities, the intangible asset related to the route authority is treated as having an indefinite useful life. Therefore, the route authority would not be amortised until its useful life is determined to be finite. It would be tested for impairment in accordance with IAS 36 annually and whenever there is an indication that it may be impaired.

An acquired trademark used to identify and distinguish a leading consumer product that has been a market-share leader for the past eight years

The trademark has a remaining legal life of five years but is renewable every 10 years at little cost. The acquiring entity intends to renew the trademark continuously and evidence supports its ability to do so. An analysis of (1) product life cycle studies, (2) market, competitive and environmental trends, and (3) brand extension opportunities provides evidence that the trademarked product will generate net cash inflows for the acquiring entity for an indefinite period.

The trademark would be treated as having an indefinite useful life because it is expected to contribute to net cash inflows indefinitely. Therefore, the trademark would not be amortised until its useful life is determined to be finite. It would be tested for impairment in accordance with IAS 36 annually and whenever there is an indication that it may be impaired.

A trademark acquired 10 years ago that distinguishes a leading consumer product

The trademark was regarded as having an indefinite useful life when it was acquired because the trademarked product was expected to generate net cash inflows indefinitely. However, unexpected competition has recently entered the market and will reduce future sales of the product. Management estimates that net cash inflows generated by the product will be 20 per cent less for the foreseeable future. However, management expects that the product will continue to generate net cash inflows indefinitely at those reduced amounts.

As a result of the projected decrease in future net cash inflows, the entity determines that the estimated recoverable amount of the trademark is less than its carrying amount, and an impairment loss is recognised. Because it is still regarded as having an indefinite useful life, the trademark would continue not to be amortised but would be tested for impairment in accordance with IAS 36 annually and whenever there is an indication that it may be impaired.

A trademark for a line of products acquired several years ago in a business combination

At the time of the business combination the acquiree had been producing the line of products for 35 years with many new models developed under the trademark. At the acquisition date the acquirer expected to continue producing the line, and an analysis of various economic factors indicated there was no limit to the period the trademark would contribute to net cash inflows. Consequently, the trademark was not amortised by the acquirer. However, management has recently decided that production of the product line will be discontinued over the next four years.

Because the useful life of the acquired trademark is no longer regarded as indefinite, the carrying amount of the trademark would be tested for impairment in accordance with IAS 36 and amortised over its remaining four-year useful life.

The standard explicitly warns against both:

- overestimating the useful life of an intangible asset. For example, 'given the history of rapid changes in technology, computer software and many other intangible assets are susceptible to technological obsolescence. Therefore, it is likely that their useful life is short.';[186] and

- underestimating the useful life. For example, 'the useful life of an intangible asset may be very long or even indefinite. Uncertainty justifies estimating the useful life of an intangible asset on a prudent basis, but it does not justify choosing a life that is unrealistically short.'[187]

It may be clear from the above discussion that despite the fairly detailed guidance in the standard an entity will need to exercise judgement in estimating the useful life of intangible assets.

2.4.1   *Useful life of contractual or other legal rights*

The standard requires an entity to take account of both economic and legal factors influencing the useful life of an intangible asset that arises from contractual or other legal rights, and determine the useful life as the shorter of:[188]

- the period of the contractual or other legal rights; and
- the period (determined by economic factors) over which the entity expects to obtain economic benefits from the asset.

If the contractual or other legal rights are conveyed for a limited term that can be renewed, the useful life of the intangible asset should include the renewal period only if there is evidence to support renewal by the entity without significant cost.[189] The existence of the following factors may indicate that an entity is able to renew the contractual or other legal rights without significant cost:

'(a)   there is evidence, possibly based on experience, that the contractual or other legal rights will be renewed. If renewal is contingent upon the consent of a third party, this includes evidence that the third party will give its consent;

(b)   there is evidence that any conditions necessary to obtain renewal will be satisfied; and

(c)   the cost to the entity of renewal is not significant when compared with the future economic benefits expected to flow to the entity from renewal.'[190]

'If the cost of renewal is significant when compared with the future economic benefits expected to flow to the entity from renewal' then the renewal cost is treated as the cost to acquire a new intangible asset at the renewal date.[191] An entity needs to exercise judgement in making this assessment.

2.5   Intangible assets with a finite useful life

2.5.1   *Amortisation period and method*

Amortisation is the systematic allocation of the depreciable amount of an intangible asset over its useful life. The depreciable amount is the cost of an asset, or other amount substituted for cost (e.g. revaluation), less its residual value.[192] The depreciable amount of an intangible asset with a finite useful life should be allocated on a systematic basis over its useful life in the following manner:

- amortisation should begin when the asset is available for use, i.e. when it is in the location and condition necessary for it to be capable of operating in the manner intended by management. Therefore, even if an entity is not using the asset, it should still be amortised because it is available for use,[193] although there may be exceptions from this general rule (see at 2.5.2 below);
- amortisation should cease at the earlier of:[194]
    - the date that the asset is classified as held for sale, or included in a disposal group that is classified as held for sale, in accordance with IFRS 5; and
    - the date that the asset is derecognised;

- the amortisation method should reflect the pattern of consumption of the economic benefits that the intangible asset provides. If that pattern cannot be reliably determined, a straight-line basis should be used.

Although a variety of amortisation methods can be used to allocate the depreciable amount of an asset on a systematic basis over its useful life (such as the straight-line method, the diminishing balance method and the unit of production method), there 'is rarely, if ever, persuasive evidence to support an amortisation method for intangible assets with finite useful lives that results in a lower amount of accumulated amortisation than under the straight-line method'.[195]

The amortisation charge for each period should be recognised in profit or loss unless IFRS specifically permits or requires it to be capitalised as part of the carrying amount of another asset (e.g. inventory or work in progress).[196]

2.5.2 *Review of amortisation period and amortisation method*

An entity should review the amortisation period and the amortisation method for an intangible asset with a finite useful life at least at each financial year-end. If the expected useful life of the asset has changed, the amortisation period should be changed accordingly.[197] An entity may, for example, consider its previous estimate of the useful life of an intangible asset inappropriate upon recognition of an impairment loss on the asset.[198]

If the expected pattern of consumption of the future economic benefits embodied in the asset has changed, the amortisation method should be changed to reflect the changed pattern.[199] The standard provides two examples of when this might happen:

- if it becomes apparent that a diminishing balance method of amortisation is appropriate rather than a straight-line method;[200] and

- if use of the rights represented by a licence is deferred pending action on other components of the business plan. In this case, economic benefits that flow from the asset may not be received until later periods.[201] This implies that circumstances may exist in which it is appropriate not to recognise an amortisation charge in relation to an intangible asset, because the entity may not be ready to use the intangible asset (e.g. as happens in the case of telecommunication companies that have acquired Universal Mobile Telecommunications System (UMTS) licenses, but that have not completed the physical network to use the license. Note that an entity must perform an impairment test at least annually for any intangible asset that has not yet been brought into use: see 2.6 below).

Both changes in the amortisation period and the amortisation method should be accounted for as changes in accounting estimates in accordance with IAS 8 – *Accounting Policies, Changes in Accounting Estimates and Errors,*[202] which requires such changes to be recognised prospectively.[203]

2.5.3   *Residual value*

The residual value of an intangible asset is the estimated amount that an entity would currently obtain from disposal of the asset, after deducting the estimated costs of disposal, if the asset were already of the age and in the condition expected at the end of its useful life.[204]

The residual value of an intangible asset with a finite useful life must be assumed to be zero unless there is a commitment by a third party to purchase the asset at the end of its useful life *or* there is an active market for the asset from which to determine its residual value and it is probable that such a market will exist at the end of the asset's useful life.[205] Given the very restrictive definition of 'active market' (see 2.3.2 A above) it seems highly unlikely that – in the absence of a commitment by a third party to buy the asset – an entity will ever be able to prove that the residual value is other than zero. A residual value other than zero implies that the entity intends to dispose of the asset before the end of its useful life.[206]

An entity's estimate of the residual value of an intangible asset 'is based on the amount recoverable from disposal using prices prevailing at the date of the estimate for the sale of a similar asset that has reached the end of its useful life and has operated under conditions similar to those in which the asset will be used'.[207] Contrary to what was required by the previous version of IAS 38, the standard now requires a review of the residual value at each financial year-end. This review can result in an upward or downward revision of the estimated residual value and thereby affect the depreciable amount of the asset; that change to depreciation should be accounted for as a change in an accounting estimate in accordance with IAS 8.[208]

The standard does not permit negative amortisation in the event that the residual value of an intangible asset increases to an amount greater than the asset's carrying amount. Instead, the asset's amortisation charge would be 'zero unless and until its residual value subsequently decreases to an amount below the asset's carrying amount'.[209]

2.6   Intangible assets with an indefinite useful life

IAS 38 prohibits amortisation of an intangible asset with an indefinite useful life.[210] Instead, such an intangible asset should be tested for impairment under IAS 36 by comparing 'its recoverable amount with its carrying amount:

(a)   annually, and

(b)   whenever there is an indication that the intangible asset may be impaired.'[211]

In other words, intangible assets with an indefinite useful life should be tested for impairment annually, irrespective of whether there exists an impairment trigger that warrants impairment testing (see Chapter 13).

An entity should review the 'useful life of an intangible asset that is not being amortised ... each period to determine whether events and circumstances continue to support an indefinite useful life assessment for that asset'. If the events and circumstances do not support an indefinite useful life, the change from indefinite to finite should be accounted for under IAS 8,[212] which requires such changes to be recognised prospectively.[213] Furthermore, reassessing the useful life of an intangible asset as finite rather than indefinite is an indicator that the asset may be impaired.[214]

2.7   Impairment losses

An impairment loss is the amount by which the carrying amount of an asset exceeds its recoverable amount.[215] An entity applies IAS 36 in determining whether an intangible asset is impaired (see Chapter 13 at 3.3).[216]

It is important to note that IAS 36 requires an entity to perform an annual test on every intangible asset that has an indefinite useful life and every intangible asset that is not yet available for use (see Chapter 13 at 3.4.1).[217] The previous version of IAS 38 also required an annual impairment test of intangible assets that had a useful life of over twenty years, irrespective of whether there were any indications of impairment. In its deliberations on the revised IAS 38, the IASB concluded that it 'could see no conceptual reason for requiring the recoverable amounts of some identifiable assets being amortised over very long periods to be determined more regularly than for other identifiable assets being amortised or depreciated over similar periods. ... Consequently, the Board decided to remove the requirement in the previous version of IAS 38 for the recoverable amount of such an intangible asset to be measured at least at each financial year-end.'[218] This reduces the administrative burden for entities somewhat, because the recoverable amount of such intangible assets only needs to be calculated under IAS 36 if there is an impairment indicator.

2.8   Retirements and disposals

An intangible asset should be derecognised on disposal or when no future economic benefits are expected from its use or disposal.[219] Although gains or losses on disposal should not be accounted for as revenue, an entity should apply the criteria for recognising revenue in IAS 18 – *Revenue* – in determining the date of disposal of an intangible asset. In the case of a disposal by a sale and leaseback, an entity should apply IAS 17.[220]

The gain or loss on derecognition, which is determined as the difference between the net disposal proceeds and the carrying amount of the asset, should be accounted for in profit or loss unless IAS 17 requires otherwise on a sale and leaseback. Gains on disposal should not be presented as revenue, because they are incidental to the main revenue-generating activities.[221]

The consideration receivable on disposal of an intangible asset is recognised initially at its fair value. This means that, if payment for the intangible asset is deferred, the consideration received is recognised initially at the cash price equivalent. The difference between the nominal amount and the cash price equivalent is recognised as interest using the effective interest method under IAS 18.[222]

The standard requires an entity to recognise in the carrying amount of an asset the cost of a replacement for part of an intangible asset and to derecognise the carrying amount of the replaced part. 'If it is not practicable for an entity to determine the carrying amount of the replaced part, it may use the cost of the replacement as an indication of what the cost of the replaced part was at the time it was acquired or internally generated.'[223] However, as noted by the standard, the nature of intangible assets is such that that, in many cases, there are no additions or replacements, so this should be an unlikely event.[224]

'Amortisation of an intangible asset with a finite useful life does not cease when the intangible asset is no longer used, unless the asset has been fully depreciated or is classified as held for sale (or included in a disposal group that is classified as held for sale) in accordance with IFRS 5.'[225]

2.9   Disclosure

IAS 38 contains a clear and well laid out disclosure section that is easy to use and understand. The main requirements are set out below, but it should be noted that the disclosure requirements of IFRS 5 are included in Chapter 3 and that the disclosure requirements of IAS 36 are included in Chapter 13.

2.9.1   *General disclosures*

A class of intangible assets is defined as a grouping of assets of a similar nature and use in an entity's operations. The standard provides examples of classes of assets (see 2.3 above), which may be 'disaggregated (aggregated) into smaller (larger) classes if this results in more relevant information for the users of the financial statements'.[226] Although, separate information is required for internally generated intangible assets and other intangible assets, these categories are not considered to be separate classes when they are of a similar nature and use in an entity's operations. For each class of intangible assets – distinguishing between internally generated intangible assets and other intangible assets – the following should be disclosed in the financial statements:[227]

'(a)   whether the useful lives are indefinite or finite and, if finite, the useful lives or the amortisation rates used;

(b)   the amortisation methods used for intangible assets with finite useful lives;

(c)   the gross carrying amount and any accumulated amortisation (aggregated with accumulated impairment losses) at the beginning and end of the period;

(d)   the line item(s) of the income statement in which any amortisation of intangible assets is included;

(e)   a reconciliation of the carrying amount at the beginning and end of the period showing:

(i)   additions, indicating separately those from internal development, those acquired separately, and those acquired through business combinations;

(ii)   assets classified as held for sale or included in a disposal group classified as held for sale in accordance with IFRS 5 and other disposals;

(iii) increases or decreases during the period resulting from revaluations under paragraphs 75, 85 and 86 and from impairment losses recognised or reversed directly in equity in accordance with IAS 36 *Impairment of Assets* (if any);

(iv) impairment losses recognised in profit or loss during the period in accordance with IAS 36 (if any);

(v) impairment losses reversed in profit or loss during the period in accordance with IAS 36 (if any);

(vi) any amortisation recognised during the period;

(vii) net exchange differences arising on the translation of the financial statements into the presentation currency, and on the translation of a foreign operation into the presentation currency of the entity; and

(viii) other changes in the carrying amount during the period.'

The standard permits an entity to present the reconciliation required under (e) above either for the net carrying amount or separately for (1) the gross carrying amount and (2) the accumulated amortisation and impairments (see Extract 11.3 below).

An entity may want to consider separate disclosure of intangible assets acquired by way of government grant or obtained in an exchange of assets, even though disclosure is not specifically required under (e)(i) above.

Under the previous version of IAS 38 it was not required to provide comparative information for the reconciliation in (e) above, because the standard offered a specific exemption from the requirement in IAS 1 to disclose 'comparative information … in respect of the previous period for all amounts reported in the financial statements'.[228] The current version of IAS 38 does not contain this exemption, making it thereby necessary to include comparative information for the reconciliation in (e) above.

The extract below provides a typical example of a goodwill and intangible assets reconciliation under IFRS.

Extract 11.3: Bayer AG (2003)

Notes to the Consolidated Financial Statements of the Bayer Group [extract]
[18] Intangible assets [extract]
Changes in intangible assets in 2003 were as follows:

	Acquired concessions, industrial property rights, similar rights and assets, and licenses thereunder	Acquired goodwill	Advance payments	Total
		(€ million)		
Gross carrying amounts, Dec. 31, 2002	7,923	3,306	58	11,287
Exchange differences	(553)	(291)	(10)	(854)
Changes in scope of consolidation	42	1	–	43
Acquisitions	–	52	–	52
Capital expenditures	217	–	78	295
Retirements	(192)	(48)	(43)	(283)
Subsequent adjustments relating to the Aventis Crop Science acquisition	(112)	(375)	–	(487)
Transfers	58	14	(23)	49
Gross carrying amounts, Dec. 31, 2003	7,383	2,659	60	10,102
Accumulated amortization and write-downs, Dec. 31, 2002	1,966	442	–	2,408
Exchange differences	(231)	(48)	–	(279)
Changes in scope of consolidation	6	–	–	6
Amortization and write-downs in 2003	1,334	366	49	1,749
of which write-downs	*[578]*	*[167]*	*[49]*	*[794]*
Write-backs	–	–	–	–
Retirements	(184)	(18)	(43)	(245)
Transfers	(32)	(19)	–	(51)
Accumulated amortization and write-downs Dec. 31, 2003	2,859	723	6	3,588
Net carrying amounts, Dec. 31, 2003	4,524	1,936	54	6,514
Net carrying amounts, Dec. 31, 2002	5,957	2,864	58	8,879

Any impairment of intangibles is to be disclosed in accordance with IAS 36, which is discussed in Chapter 13 at 4,[229] while any changes in useful life, amortisation method or residual value estimates should be disclosed in accordance with the provisions of IAS 8.[230]

There are a number of additional disclosure requirements, some of which only apply in certain circumstances:[231]

'(a)   for an intangible asset assessed as having an indefinite useful life, the carrying amount of that asset and the reasons supporting the assessment of an indefinite useful life. In giving these reasons, the entity shall describe the factor(s) that played a significant role in determining that the asset has an indefinite useful life.

(b) a description, the carrying amount and remaining amortisation period of any individual intangible asset that is material to the entity's financial statements.

(c) for intangible assets acquired by way of a government grant and initially recognised at fair value (see paragraph 44):

    (i) the fair value initially recognised for these assets;

    (ii) their carrying amount; and

    (iii) whether they are measured after recognition under the cost model or the revaluation model.

(d) the existence and carrying amounts of intangible assets whose title is restricted and the carrying amounts of intangible assets pledged as security for liabilities.

(e) the amount of contractual commitments for the acquisition of intangible assets.'

In describing the factors (as required under (a) above) that played a significant role in determining that the useful life of an intangible asset is indefinite, an entity considers the list of factors in paragraph 90 of IAS 38 (see 2.4 above).[232]

Finally, an entity is encouraged to disclose the following information:[233]

'(a) a description of any fully amortised intangible asset that is still in use; and

(b) a brief description of significant intangible assets controlled by the entity but not recognised as assets because they did not meet the recognition criteria in this Standard or because they were acquired or generated before the version of IAS 38 *Intangible Assets* issued in 1998 was effective.'

2.9.2 Balance sheet presentation

IAS 1 does not use the term fixed assets, which is used in accounting standards under many other GAAPs. Instead it draws a distinction between current and non-current assets. IAS 1 uses the term 'non-current' to include tangible, intangible and financial assets of a long-term nature, although it 'does not prohibit the use of alternative descriptions as long as the meaning is clear'.[234] Although most intangible assets are non-current, an intangible asset may meet the definition of a current asset (i.e. it has an economic life of less than 12 months) when it is acquired and should be classified accordingly.

IAS 1 requires intangible assets to be shown as a separate category of asset on the face of the balance sheet.[235] Intangible assets will, therefore, normally appear as a separate category of asset in the balance sheet at a suitable point within non-current assets, or at a point in an undifferentiated balance sheet that reflects their relative liquidity – that is the time over which they are to be amortised or sold. An entity that holds a wide variety of different intangible assets may need to present these in separate line items on the face of the balance sheet if such presentation is relevant to an understanding of the entity's financial position.[236]

While the balance sheet figure for intangible assets may include goodwill, the relevant standards require more detailed disclosures of the constituent elements of the balance sheet figure to be included in the notes to the financial statements.

The extract below shows how GN Store Nord discloses no less than seven different types of intangible asset on the face of its balance sheet.

Extract 11.4: GN Store Nord A/S (2003)		
BALANCE SHEET – ASSETS [extract]		
	Consolidated	
(DKK millions)	**2003**	**2002**
Non-current assets		
Goodwill	2,776	3,578
Development projects, developed in-house	347	339
Software, acquired	1	–
Software, developed in-house	99	101
Patents and rights	89	99
Telecommunications systems	50	58
Other intangible assets	282	360
Total intangible assets	**3,644**	**4,535**

In many cases though, entities may be able to aggregate the intangible assets into slightly broader categories in order to reduce the number of lines items on the face of their balance sheets.

2.9.3   Disclosures under the revaluation model

IAS 38 requires an entity, which accounts for intangible assets at revalued amounts, to disclose the following:[237]

'(a)   by class of intangible assets:

(i)   the effective date of the revaluation;

(ii)   the carrying amount of revalued intangible assets; and

(iii)   the carrying amount that would have been recognised had the revalued class of intangible assets been measured after recognition using the cost model in paragraph 74 (see 2.3.1 above);

(b)   the amount of the revaluation surplus that relates to intangible assets at the beginning and end of the period, indicating the changes during the period and any restrictions on the distribution of the balance to shareholders; and

(c)   the methods and significant assumptions applied in estimating the assets' fair values.'

Classes of revalued assets should only be aggregated for disclosure purposes to the extent that this does not result 'in the combination of a class of intangible assets that includes amounts measured under both the cost and revaluation models'.[238]

2.9.4   Research and development expenditure

An entity should disclose the aggregate total amount of all expenditure that is directly attributable to research or development activities that is recognised as an expense during the period.[239]

3   PRACTICAL ISSUES

3.1   Regulatory assets

In many countries the provision of utilities (e.g. water, natural gas or electricity) to consumers is regulated by the national government. Regulations differ between countries but often regulators operate a cost-plus system under which a utility is allowed to make a fixed return on investment. Similarly, a regulator may allow a utility to recoup its investments by increasing the prices over a defined period.

Consequently, the future price that a utility is allowed to charge its customer may be influenced by past costs levels and investment levels. Under many national GAAPs accounting practices have been developed that allow an entity to account for the effects of regulation by recognising a 'regulatory' asset (or liability) that reflects the increase (or decrease) in future prices approved by the regulator. Such 'regulatory assets' may have been classified as intangible assets under national GAAPs.

Most 'regulatory assets' do not meet the definition of an intangible asset under IFRS, because they are not 'a resource controlled by an entity as a result of past events; and from which future economic benefits are expected to flow to the entity'.[240] The right to charge a higher price to customers can only result in economic benefits as a result of future sales to those customers. The economic benefits from sales to customers should be recognised in accordance with IAS 18, which requires delivery of the goods or services to the customers.

Many would argue that 'regulatory assets' are better described as past costs, which the regulator allows the entity to recover through higher sales prices in the future. Instead of arguing that 'regulatory assets' result from the right to charge a higher price in the future, they would argue that these debits are 'regulatory losses' resulting from a price cap imposed by the regulator in the past.

It is also worth considering the situation when the opposite occurs and the entity is required by its regulator to reduce prices in the subsequent period. In most circumstances this would not be a provision under IAS 37; it is not a 'present obligation of the enterprise arising from past events, the settlement of which is expected to result in an outflow from the enterprise of resources embodying economic benefits'[241] – it means that the entity will charge less, and receive less from individual customers in the subsequent periods. This reinforces the argument that the regulatory asset should not be carried forward, whether as an intangible asset or as a prepayment.

3.2   Research and development in the pharmaceutical industry

Entities in the pharmaceutical industry consider research and development to be of primary importance to their business. Consequently, these entities spend a considerable amount on research and development every year. Therefore, one would expect pharmaceutical companies to carry internally generated development intangible assets on their balance sheets. However, a review of the financial statements of pharmaceutical company reveals that they consider the uncertainties in the development of pharmaceuticals to be too great to permit capitalisation of development costs. Extracts 11.5 and 11.6 and the extracts below illustrate this.

Extract 11.5: Bayer AG (2003)

Notes to the Consolidated Financial Statements of the Bayer Group [extract]
Accounting policies [extract]

Research and development expenses

According to IAS 38 (Intangible Assets), research costs cannot be capitalized; development costs can only be capitalized if specific conditions are fulfilled. Development costs must be capitalized if it is sufficiently certain that the future economic benefits to the company will cover not only the usual production, selling and administrative costs but also the development costs themselves. There are also several other criteria relating to the development project and the product or process being developed, all of which have to be met to justify asset recognition. As in previous years, these conditions are not satisfied.

Extract 11.6: Syngenta AG (2003)

1. Basis of preparation of the consolidated financial statements [extract]

Research and development

Research and development expenses are fully charged to the income statement when incurred. Syngenta considers that the regulatory and other uncertainties inherent in the development of its key new products preclude it from capitalizing development costs.

Costs of purchasing patent rights are capitalized as intangible assets. Costs of applying for patents for internally developed products, costs of defending existing patents, and costs of challenging patents held by third parties where these are considered invalid, are considered part of development expense and expensed as incurred.

It is clear that highly successful pharmaceutical companies generally have concluded that their development costs do not meet the recognition criteria in IAS 38 (see 2.2.6 B above). These companies have thereby defined what is 'generally acceptable accounting practice' (GAAP) in their industry.

One of the problems of course is that in the case of true 'development' activities in the pharmaceutical industry the technical and economic feasibility are typically established very late in the development phase, which means that only a small proportion of the development costs can ever be capitalised. In particular, many drugs require approval by a regulator such as the US Food and Drug Administration (FDA) before they can be put on the market and until that time the entity may be uncertain of their success. After approval, of course, there is little in the way of spend other than on advertising and entities are precluded from capitalising this as part of the asset.

Nevertheless, there is an inconsistency at the heart of IAS 38 that results in a different treatment of acquired versus internally generated intangible assets. Intangible assets acquired in a separate transaction or business combinations must be recognised while future economic benefits are deemed to be probable, whereas internally developed intangible assets can only be recognised when they meet the strict (and somewhat subjective) recognition criteria in IAS 38.

4 TRANSITION AND FIRST-TIME ADOPTION

4.1 Transitional arrangements for entities already reporting under IFRS

An entity should apply IAS 38 (as revised in 2004) to 'the accounting for intangible assets acquired in business combinations for which the agreement date is on or after 31 March 2004'.[242] The agreement date for a business combination is defined by the standard as 'the date that a substantive agreement between the combining parties is reached and, in the case of publicly listed entities, announced to the public. In the case of a hostile takeover, the earliest date that a substantive agreement between the combining parties is reached is the date that a sufficient number of the acquiree's owners have accepted the acquirer's offer for the acquirer to obtain control of the acquiree.'[243]

An entity should apply IAS 38 (as revised in 2004) to 'the accounting for all other intangible assets prospectively from the beginning of the first annual period beginning on or after 31 March 2004'.[244] The entity should not adjust the carrying amount of intangible assets recognised at that date, but should reassess the useful lives of such intangible assets. The change in the assessment of the useful life of an asset should be accounted for as a change in an accounting estimate in accordance with IAS 8, which requires such changes to be recognised prospectively.[245]

Early adoption of IAS 38 (as revised in 2004) is encouraged, but 'if an entity applies this Standard before those effective dates, it also shall apply IFRS 3 and IAS 36 *Impairment of Assets* (as revised in 2004) at the same time'.[246]

4.1.1 Early adoption of IFRS 3

If an entity applies IFRS 3 early, it should also apply IAS 38 (as revised in 2004) prospectively from the same date. The entity should not adjust the carrying amount of intangible assets recognised at that date, but should reassess the useful lives of such intangible assets. The change in the assessment of the useful life of an asset should be accounted for as a change in an accounting estimate in accordance with IAS 8, which requires such changes to be recognised prospectively.[247]

4.1.2 Exchanges of similar assets

IAS 38 (as revised in 2004) should be applied prospectively to exchanges of assets: 'if an exchange of assets was measured before the effective date of this Standard on the basis of the carrying amount of the asset given up, the entity does not restate the carrying amount of the asset acquired to reflect its fair value at the acquisition date'.[248] Therefore, an entity that already reports under IFRS is not required to restate prior exchanges of assets in accordance with the revised rules in IAS 38.

4.2   First-time adoption

4.2.1   *Retrospective application of IAS 38*

An intangible asset is only capable of capitalisation under IAS 38 if it is probable that the future economic benefits attributable to the asset will flow to the entity and the cost of the asset can be measured reliably.[249] The standard imposes a number of additional criteria that further restrict capitalisation of internally generated intangible assets. An important restriction is the prohibition from using hindsight to conclude retrospectively that the recognition criteria are met.[250] Therefore, if a first-time adopter is only permitted to capitalise the costs of internally generated intangible assets when it:[251]

'(a)   concludes, based on an assessment made and documented at the date of that conclusion, that it is probable that future economic benefits from the asset will flow to the entity; and

(b)   has a reliable system for accumulating the costs of internally generated intangible assets when, or shortly after, they are incurred.'

In other words, it is not permitted under IFRS 1 to retrospectively reconstruct the costs of intangible assets. First-time adopters that did not capitalise internally generated intangible assets will often not have the type of documentation and systems required by IFRS 1 and will therefore not be able to capitalise these items in their opening IFRS balance sheet, unless they had anticipated its requirements and established their intangible assets contemporaneously. However, going forward they will need to implement internal systems and procedures that enable them to determine whether any future internally generated intangible assets should be capitalised or not. Capitalisation of separately acquired intangible assets will generally be easier because contemporaneous documentation that was prepared to support the investment decisions often exists.[252]

4.2.2   *Using fair value or revaluation as deemed cost*

To deal with the problem of restatement of long-lived intangible assets upon first-time adoption of IFRS, IFRS 1 permits a first-time adopter to measure an intangible asset in its opening IFRS balance sheet at an amount that is based on its deemed cost. By using deemed cost – which is a surrogate for cost or depreciated cost at a given date – for an intangible asset a first-time adopter can avoid a potentially onerous exercise to reconstruct the true historical cost of that asset.[253] A first-time adopter is allowed to measure an intangible asset in its opening IFRS balance sheet at deemed cost if it meets:[254]

* the recognition criteria in IAS 38 (including reliable measurement of original cost); and

* the criteria in IAS 38 for revaluation (including the existence of an active market).

The use of fair value or revaluation as deemed cost for intangible assets will be very limited in practice, because of the very restrictive definition of an active market in

IAS 38 (see 2.3.2 A above).[255] It is therefore unlikely that a first-time adopter will be able to apply this exemption to any intangible assets.[256]

It is important to note that the deemed cost exemption in IFRS 1 does not take classes or categories assets as its unit of measure, but refers to items that are smaller than a class or category.[257] The IASB argued that it is not necessary to restrict application of the exemption to classes of assets to prevent selective revaluations, because 'IAS 36 *Impairment of Assets* requires an impairment test if there is any indication that an asset is impaired. Thus, if an entity uses fair value as deemed cost for assets whose fair value is above cost, it cannot ignore indications that the recoverable amount of other assets may have fallen below their carrying amount. Therefore, the IFRS does not restrict the use of fair value as deemed cost to entire classes of asset.'[258] Nevertheless, it seems doubtful that the quality of financial information would benefit from a revaluation of a haphazard selection of intangible assets. Therefore, a first-time adopter should exercise judgment in selecting the items that it wants the exemption to apply to.

In summary, at its date of transition to IFRS a first-time adopter is allowed under IFRS 1 to value intangible assets at either:

- historical cost determined in accordance with IAS 38;
- fair value at the date of transition to IFRS;
- a revalued amount that is equal to:
  - fair value at the date of revaluation;
  - cost adjusted for changes in a general or specific index; or
  - an event-driven fair value, for example, at the date of an initial public offering or privatisation; or
- in the case of an item acquired in a business combination:
  - carrying amount under previous GAAP immediately after acquisition; or
  - if the item was not recognised under previous GAAP, the carrying amount on the basis that IFRS would require in the separate balance sheet of the acquiree.

The fact that IFRS 1 offers seven different bases for valuation does not disturb the IASB as it reasons that 'cost is generally equivalent to fair value at the date of acquisition. Therefore, the use of fair value as the deemed cost of an asset means that an entity will report the same cost data as if it had acquired an asset with the same remaining service potential at the date of transition to IFRS. If there is any lack of comparability, it arises from the aggregation of costs incurred at different dates, rather than from the targeted use of fair value as deemed cost for some assets. The Board regarded this approach as justified to solve the unique problem of introducing IFRS in a cost-effective way without damaging transparency.'[259] Users of the financial statements of a first-time adopter should therefore be mindful that historical trends under the previous GAAP might no longer be present in an entity's IFRS financial statements.

5   CONCLUSION

Throughout the last decade there has been a gradual shift in the emphasis of what financial statements are meant to portray, from a transactions-based, performance-orientated model in which the profit and loss account is the most important statement towards a balance sheet-orientated model based on fair values.

This approach has not made the treatment of intangible assets in the balance sheet at the conceptual level any easier. The IASB has promulgated standards that have greatly reduced the scope for creative accounting as far as intangibles are concerned, as well as producing standards that are as unambiguously drafted as may reasonably be expected. It is also true that, in spite of the considerable effort put into its conceptual framework, the IASB has not come up with a conceptually integrated or logically consistent treatment of intangible assets.

The virtual prohibition on the recognition of many internally generated intangibles, is a tacit admission of the limits of our ability to deal with such items, rather than a deductive consequence of the reasons offered in the standards themselves. Thus it appears accounting for intangible assets is at the stage of having a workable but imperfect set of rules which falls well short of consistency.

If the move towards an accounting model based on recording the entire balance sheet at fair values continues, the challenge will be to find an acceptable, logically consistent method that can value all intangibles that have worth, without arbitrarily scoping out those that present too many difficulties.

References

1 IAS 38, *Intangible Assets*, IASB, March 2004, para. IN2.
2 IAS 38, para. IN3.
3 IAS 38, para. IN3.
4 IAS 38, para. IN3.
5 IAS 38, para. BC2.
6 IAS 38, para. BC2.
7 IAS 38, para. BC2.
8 IAS 38, para. 1.
9 IAS 38, para. 2.
10 IAS 38, para. 3.
11 IAS 38, para. 6.
12 IAS 17, *Leases*, IASB, December 2003 (amended March 2004), para. 2.
13 IAS 38, para. 6.
14 IAS 38, para. 7.
15 IAS 38, para. 5.
16 IAS 38, para. 8.
17 IAS 38, para. 8.
18 IAS 38, paras. BC4-BC5.
19 IAS 38, para. 9.
20 IAS 38, para. 10.
21 IFRS 3, *Business Combinations*, IASB, March 2004, Appendix A.
22 IAS 38, para. 11.
23 IAS 38, para. 12.
24 IAS 38, paras. 13-14.
25 IAS 38, para. 13.
26 IAS 38, para. 15.
27 IAS 38, para. 16.
28 IAS 38, para. 16.
29 IAS 38, para. 17.
30 IAS 38, para. 4.
31 IAS 38, para. 4.
32 IAS 38, para. 5.
33 IAS 38, para. 18.
34 IAS 38, para. 21.
35 IAS 38, para. 22.
36 IAS 38, para. 23.
37 IAS 38, para. 24.
38 IAS 38, para. 8.
39 IAS 38, para. 20.
40 IAS 38, para. 20.
41 IAS 38, paras. 63-64.
42 IAS 38, para. 25.

43 IAS 38, para. 25.
44 IAS 38, para. 26.
45 IAS 38, para. BC18.
46 IAS 38, para. 27.
47 IAS 38, para. 28.
48 IAS 38, para. 30.
49 IAS 38, para. 32.
50 IAS 38, paras. 29-30.
51 IAS 16, *Property, Plant and Equipment*, IASB, December 2003 (amended March 2004), para. 21.
52 IAS 38, para. 31.
53 IFRS 3, Illustrative Examples.
54 IFRS 3, para. 45.
55 IAS 38, para. 21.
56 IAS 38, para. 33.
57 IAS 38, para. 33.
58 IAS 38, para. 34.
59 IAS 38, para. BC19.
60 IAS 38, para. BC21.
61 IAS 38, para. BC23.
62 IAS 38, para. 38.
63 IAS 38, para. 36.
64 IAS 38, para. BC25.
65 IAS 38, para. 37.
66 IAS 38, para. 35.
67 IAS 38, para. 39.
68 IAS 38, para. 39.
69 IAS 38, para. 78.
70 IAS 38, para. 40.
71 IAS 38, para. 40.
72 IAS 38, para. 41.
73 IAS 38, para. 34.
74 IAS 38, para. 42.
75 IAS 38, para. 43.
76 IAS 38, para. BC82.
77 IAS 38, para. BC88.
78 IAS 36, *Impairment of Assets*, IASB, March 2004, para. 10.
79 IAS 38, para. 44.
80 IAS 38, para. 44.
81 IAS 20, *Accounting for Government Grants and Disclosure of Government Assistance*, IASB, April 1983 (amended December 2003), para. 23.
82 IFRIC D1, *Emission Rights*, IFRIC, May 2003, para. 1.
83 IFRIC D1, para. 2.
84 IFRIC D1, para. 3.
85 IFRIC D1, para. 5.
86 IFRIC D1, para. 6.
87 IFRIC D1, para. 7.
88 IFRIC D1, para. 8.
89 IFRIC D1, para. 5.
90 IFRIC D1, para. 9.
91 *IFRIC Update*, IFRIC, March 2004, p.1.
92 *IFRIC Update*, IFRIC, September 2004, p.1.
93 IAS 38, para. 45.
94 IAS 38, para. 47.
95 IAS 38, para. 45.
96 IAS 16, para. BC21.
97 IAS 38, para. 46.
98 IAS 38, para. 8.
99 IAS 38, para. 46.
100 IAS 38, para. 47.
101 IAS 38, para. 46.
102 IAS 38, paras. 48-49.
103 IAS 38, para. 50.
104 IAS 38, para. 51.
105 IAS 38, para. 51.
106 IAS 38 ,para. 8.
107 IAS 38, para. 56.
108 IAS 38 ,para. 8.
109 IAS 38, para. 59.
110 IAS 38, paras. 54-55.
111 IAS 38, para. 57.
112 IAS 38, para. 58.
113 IAS 38, para. 60.
114 IAS 38, para. 61.
115 IAS 38, para. 61.
116 IAS 38, para. 62.
117 IAS 38, para. 52.
118 IAS 38, para. 53.
119 IAS 38, para. BCZ38.
120 IAS 38, para. BCZ40.
121 IAS 38, para. 64.
122 IAS 38, para. BCZ45.
123 IAS 38, para. 63.
124 SIC-32, *Intangible Assets – Web Site Costs*, SIC, March 2002 (amended March 2004), para. 7.
125 SIC-32, paras. 5-6.
126 SIC-32, para. 1.
127 SIC-32, para. 8.
128 SIC-32, para. 8.
129 SIC-32, paras. 2 and 9.
130 SIC-32, para. 3.
131 SIC-32, para. 9.
132 SIC-32, para. 10.
133 IAS 38, para. 8.
134 IAS 38, para. 65.
135 IAS 38, paras. 21-22.
136 IAS 38, para. 71.
137 IAS 38, Example Illustrating paragraph 65.
138 IAS 38, para. 66.
139 IAS 38, para. 66.
140 IAS 38, para. 67.
141 IAS 38, para. 68.
142 IAS 38, para. 69.
143 IAS 38, para. 69.
144 IAS 38, para. 70.
145 IAS 38, para. 72.
146 IAS 38, para. 73.
147 IAS 38, para. 119.
148 IAS 38, para. 73.
149 IAS 38, para. 74.
150 IAS 38, para. 75.
151 IAS 38, paras. 72 and 75.

152 IAS 38, para. 76.
153 IAS 38, para. 77.
154 IAS 38, para. 77.
155 IAS 38, paras. 72 and 75.
156 IAS 38, para. 8.
157 IAS 38, para. 78.
158 IAS 38, para. 78.
159 IAS 38, para. 78.
160 IAS 38, para. 78.
161 IAS 38, para. 78.
162 IAS 38, para. 75.
163 IAS 38, para. 79.
164 IAS 38, para. 85.
165 IAS 38, para. 86.
166 IAS 38, para. 87.
167 IAS 38, para. 87.
168 IAS 38, para. 87.
169 IAS 38, para. 80.
170 IAS 38, para. 81.
171 IAS 38, para. 82.
172 IAS 38, para. 83.
173 IAS 38, para. 84.
174 IAS 38, para. 8.
175 IAS 38, para. 88.
176 IAS 38, para. 91.
177 IAS 38, para. 88.
178 IAS 38, para. 88.
179 IAS 38, para. BC63.
180 IAS 38, para. BC62.
181 IAS 38, para. BC63.
182 IAS 38, para. 91.
183 IAS 38, para. 90.
184 IAS 38, para. 89 and Illustrative Examples.
185 IAS 38, para. 89 and Illustrative Examples.
186 IAS 38, para. 92.
187 IAS 38, para. 93.
188 IAS 38, paras. 94-95.
189 IAS 38, para. 94.
190 IAS 38, para. 96.
191 IAS 38, para. 96.
192 IAS 38, para. 8.
193 IAS 38, para. 97.
194 IAS 38, para. 97.
195 IAS 38, para. 98.
196 IAS 38, paras. 97 and 99.
197 IAS 38, para. 104.
198 IAS 38, para.105.
199 IAS 38, para. 104.
200 IAS 38, para. 106.
201 IAS 38, para. 106.
202 IAS 38, para. 104.
203 IAS 8, *Accounting Policies, Changes in Accounting Estimates and Errors*, IASB, December 2003 (amended March 2004), para. 36.
204 IAS 38, para. 8.
205 IAS 38, para. 100.
206 IAS 38, para. 101.
207 IAS 38, para. 102.
208 IAS 38, para. 102.
209 IAS 38, para. 103.
210 IAS 38, para. 107.
211 IAS 38, para. 108.
212 IAS 38, para. 109.
213 IAS 8, para. 36.
214 IAS 38, para. 110
215 IAS 38, para. 8.
216 IAS 38, para. 111.
217 IAS 36, para. 10.
218 IAS 38, para. BC55.
219 IAS 38, para. 112.
220 IAS 38, para. 114.
221 IAS 38, para. 113.
222 IAS 38, para. 116.
223 IAS 38, para. 115.
224 IAS 38, para. 20.
225 IAS 38, para. 117.
226 IAS 38, para. 119.
227 IAS 38, para. 118.
228 IAS 1, *Presentation of Financial Statements*, IASB, December 2003 (amended March 2004), para. 36.
229 IAS 38, para. 120.
230 IAS 38, para. 121.
231 IAS 38, para. 122.
232 IAS 38, para. 123.
233 IAS 38, para. 128.
234 IAS 1, para. 58.
235 IAS 1, para. 68.
236 IAS 1, para. 69.
237 IAS 38, para. 124.
238 IAS 38, para. 125.
239 IAS 38, paras. 126-127.
240 IAS 38, para. 8.
241 IAS 37, *Provisions, Contingent Liabilities and Contingent Assets*, IASB, September 1998 (amended March 2004), para. 10.
242 IAS 38, para. 130.
243 IAS 38, para. 8.
244 IAS 38, para. 130.
245 IAS 8, para. 36.
246 IAS 38, para. 132.
247 IAS 38, para. 130.
248 IAS 38, para. 131.
249 IAS 38, para. 8.
250 IAS 38, para. 71.
251 IFRS 1, *First-time Adoption of International Financial Reporting Standards*, IASB, June 2003 (amended March 2004), para. IG46.
252 IFRS 1, para. IG48.
253 IFRS 1, Appendix A.
254 IFRS 1, paras. 16-17.
255 IAS 38, para. 8.
256 IAS 38, para. 78.
257 IFRS 1, para. 16.
258 IFRS 1, para. BC45.
259 IFRS 1, para. BC43.

Chapter 12   Property plant and equipment

1   INTRODUCTION

One fundamental problem in financial reporting is how to account annually for performance when many of the expenditures an entity incurs in the current period also contribute to future accounting periods. Expenditure on property plant and equipment (hereafter abbreviated to PP&E, but also known as fixed assets in many jurisdictions) is the paradigm example of this difficulty. The accounting conventions permitted by the IASB to solve it are the subject of this chapter, although the underlying broad principles involved are one of the first that accountants and business people learn in their business life. The cost of an item of PP&E is capitalised when acquired (i.e. recorded in the balance sheet as an asset); then subsequently a proportion of the cost is charged each year to the profit and loss account (i.e. the cost is spread out over the future accounting periods expected to benefit). Ideally, at the end of the item's working life the cost remaining in the balance sheet should be equal to the disposal proceeds of the item, or be zero if there are none.

Common prudence (or relevance, reliability and representational faithfulness in IASB parlance) dictates that during the life of the item any uncharged cost remaining in the balance sheet should be written down if it is not fully recoverable. Finally, when an item of PP&E is sold or scrapped, the difference between the written down value and any proceeds is recorded as the gain or loss on disposal.

There are inevitably some detailed rules required to apply these principles in practice, such as precisely when PP&E should initially be recognised, and how its cost should be measured. Additionally, not every type of expenditure is obviously PP&E or not, and if a policy of revaluation is adopted, how should the PP&E be accounted for? Thus, although the basic principle is commonly understood, as in most other areas of financial reporting, the development of more detailed requirements has necessitated an accounting standard.

Under IFRS the main standard is IAS 16 – *Property, Plant and Equipment.* Impairment is covered by IAS 36 – *Impairment of Assets* – and dealt with as a separate topic in Chapter 13. Impairment is a major consideration in accounting for PP&E, as this procedure is intended to ensure PP&E costs that are not fully recoverable are immediately written down to a level that is. In addition, there is a separate standard, IAS 40 – *Investment Property* – that deals with that particular category of PP&E. Finally, IFRS 5 – *Non-current Assets Held for Sale and Discontinued Operations* – deals with the accounting required when items of PP&E are held for sale.

IAS 16 was revised in 1998 and became operative for annual financial statements covering periods beginning on or after 1 July 1999. Further revisions were made in late 2003 and early 2004, as a result of the IASB's Improvements project and the publication of other new IFRSs. The most recent version of IAS 16 as at March 2004, effective for periods beginning on or after 1 January 2005, is discussed in this chapter. IAS 40 originally became operative for annual financial statements covering periods beginning on or after 1 January 2001; but it too was revised in late 2003 as part of the Improvements project. Similarly, it is the version published by the IASB as at March 2004, effective for periods beginning on or after 1 January 2005, that is discussed here.

2   THE REQUIREMENTS OF IAS 16

2.1   Introduction

IAS 16 as revised at March 2004, effective for periods beginning on or after 1 January 2005, is the version discussed by this chapter. One of the objectives of the IASB's Improvements project was to reduce the number of alternative treatments allowed by then existing IAS. However, in IAS 16 there remain two very different alternative accounting treatments that may be chosen to account for PP&E: items may be carried at either cost less depreciation, or at their fair value. Other than this, IAS 16 is a fairly straightforward standard that attempts to delineate the boundaries of what may, and may not, be considered part of the cost of an item of PP&E. The standard as revised, also reflects the IASB's fair value agenda for the valuation of assets. Thus, to an extent it forms a bridge between the way that PP&E has been accounted for traditionally (cost less depreciation) and – by allowing PP&E to be carried at fair value – the IASB's fair value agenda for the future.

2.2   Scope, definition and recognition

All PP&E is within the scope of IAS 16 except as follows:

- when another standard requires or permits a different accounting treatment (e.g. IAS 40 for investment properties);
- PP&E classified as held for sale in accordance with IFRS 5;
- biological assets related to agricultural activity (covered by IAS 41); and
- mineral rights and mineral reserves such as oil, gas, and similar 'non-regenerative' resources.[1]

Note that although the standard scopes out biological assets and mineral resources, it includes any PP&E used in developing or maintaining such resources. Therefore exploration PP&E is included in the scope of the standard, as is agricultural PP&E. Similarly, although investment property is subject to IAS 40, while such property is in the course of construction or development for future use as investment property, the IAS 16 does apply. However existing investment property being redeveloped for the same continuing use in the future remains subject to IAS 40 during its redevelopment.[2]

Other standards may require an item of PP&E to be recognised on a different basis to IAS 16. For example IAS 17 – *Leases* – has its own rules regarding recognition and measurement; see Chapter 23 for a description of how an item of PP&E held under a finance lease is recognised and measured. However, once an item of PP&E has been recognised under IAS 17, its treatment thereafter is in accordance with IAS 16.[3]

2.2.1 *Definitions*

IAS 16 defines the main terms it uses throughout the standard as follows:

Carrying amount is the amount at which an asset is recognised after deducting any accumulated depreciation and accumulated impairment losses.

Cost is the amount of cash or cash equivalents paid or the fair value of other consideration given to acquire an asset at the time of its acquisition or construction or, where applicable, the amount attributed to that asset when initially recognised in accordance with the specific requirements of other IFRSs, e.g. IFRS 2 – *Share-based Payment*.

Depreciable amount is the cost of an asset, or other amount substituted for cost, less its residual value.

Depreciation is the systematic allocation of the depreciable amount of an asset over its useful life.

Entity-specific value is the present value of the cash flows an entity expects to arise from the continuing use of an asset and from its disposal at the end of its useful life or expects to incur when settling a liability.

Fair value is the amount for which an asset could be exchanged between knowledgeable, willing parties in an arm's length transaction.

An *impairment loss* is the amount by which the carrying amount of an asset exceeds its recoverable amount.

Property, plant and equipment are tangible items that:

(a) are held for use in the production or supply of goods or services, for rental to others, or for administrative purposes; and

(b) are expected to be used during more than one period.

Recoverable amount is the higher of an asset's net selling price and its value in use.

The *residual value* of an asset is the estimated amount that an entity would currently obtain from disposal of the asset, after deducting the estimated costs of disposal, if the asset were already of the age and in the condition expected at the end of its useful life.

Useful life is:

(a) the period over which an asset is expected to be available for use by an entity; or

(b) the number of production or similar units expected to be obtained from the asset by an entity.[4]

These definitions are discussed in the relevant sections below.

2.2.2 Recognition

An item of PP&E should be recognised, i.e. its cost included in the balance sheet as an asset, only if its cost can be measured reliably and it is probable that future economic benefits associated with the item will flow to the entity.[5] This requirement for recognition is directly taken from the IASB's Framework, which is discussed in some detail in Chapter 2. It follows from the Framework's characterisation of an asset as future economic benefits, rather than the item of property itself, that to be recognised the economic benefits must be forthcoming, or at least probable.

Major spare parts, for example, qualify as property, plant and equipment, while smaller spares would be carried as inventory. However if a set of spares can only be used on one item of PP&E, then they should be accounted for as PP&E.[6]

Some types of business may have a very large number of minor fixed assets such as spare parts, tools, pallets and returnable containers, which nevertheless are used in more than one accounting period. There are practical problems in recording them on an asset-by-asset basis in an asset register; they are difficult to control and frequently lost. The main consequence is that it becomes very difficult to provide depreciation on them. The standard notes that there are issues concerning what actually constitutes a single item of PP&E to be individually recognised. The 'unit of measurement for recognition' is not prescribed and entities have to apply judgement in defining PP&E in their individual circumstances. The standard suggests that some parts such as tools, moulds and dies should be aggregated and the standard applied to the aggregate amount (presumably without having to identify the individual assets).[7] Most companies have a minimum value for capitalising assets.

The standard acknowledges that there may be expenditures forced upon an entity by legislation that require it to buy 'assets' that do not meet the recognition criteria because the expenditure does not directly increase the expected future benefits expected to flow from the asset.[8] Examples would be safety or environmental protection equipment. IAS 16 explains that these expenditures do qualify for recognition as they allow future benefits in excess of those that would flow if the expenditure had not been made; for example a plant might have to be closed down if the expenditures were not made.

In our view this approach is sensible (even if it is indicative of a deficiency in the recognition criteria) and has no more significance, and is in the same category as, the cost of fitting guards to machinery at original manufacture.

An entity may voluntarily invest in environmental equipment even though it is not required by law to do so. We consider that the entity should expense those investments in environmental and safety equipment as incurred, unless either it can demonstrate that the equipment is likely to increase the economic life of the related assets or that it can demonstrate all of the following:

- the entity can prove that a constructive obligation exists to invest in environmental and safety equipment (e.g. it is standard practice in the industry, environmental groups are likely to raise issues or employees demand certain equipment to be present);

- the expenditure is directly related to improvement of the asset's environmental and safety standards; and

- the expenditure is not related to repairs and maintenance or forms part of period costs or operational costs.

Whenever safety and environmental assets are capitalised, the standard requires the resulting carrying amount of the asset and any related asset to be reviewed in accordance with IAS 36 (see Chapter 13).[9]

A   Initial costs and subsequent costs

IAS 16 makes no distinction in principle between the initial costs of acquiring an asset and any subsequent expenditure upon it. In both cases any and all expenditure has to meet the recognition rules, and be expensed in the profit and loss account if it does not. IAS 16 states:

> 'An entity evaluates under this recognition principle all its property, plant and equipment costs at the time they are incurred. These costs include costs incurred initially to acquire or construct an item of property, plant and equipment and costs incurred subsequently to add to, replace part of, or service it.'[10]

The standard draws a distinction between servicing and more major expenditure. Day-to-day servicing, by which it means the repairs and maintenance of PP&E which largely comprises labour costs and minor parts, should be recognised in the income statement as incurred.[11] However, if the expenditure involves replacing a significant part of the asset, this part should be recognised, i.e. capitalised as part of the fixed asset, if the recognition criteria are met. The carrying amount of the part that has been replaced should be derecognised as described in 2.6 below.

IAS 16 identifies two particular types of parts of assets. The first is an item that requires replacement at regular intervals during the life of the asset. For example a furnace may require relining after a specified number of hours of use, or aircraft interiors such as seats and galleys may require replacement several times during the life of the airframe. There may also be less frequently recurring replacements, such as replacing the interior walls of a building. The standard proposes that under the recognition principle described above, an entity recognises in the carrying amount of an item of property, plant and equipment the cost of replacing part of such an item when that cost is incurred while derecognising the carrying amount of the parts that have been replaced.[12]

IAS 16 does not state that these expenditures necessarily qualify for recognition. Some of its examples, such as aircraft engines that require regular replacement, are clearly best treated as separate assets as they have a useful life different from that of the asset of which they are part. With others, such as interior walls, it is less clear why they meet the recognition criteria. However, replacing internal walls or similar expenditure may extend the useful life of a building while upgrading machinery may increase its capacity, improve the quality of its output or reduce operating costs. Hence, this type of expenditure may give rise to future economic benefits. Accounting for parts of assets is discussed in greater detail in 2.8.1 below.

The standard also allows a separate part to be recognised if an entity is required to perform regular major inspections for faults, regardless of whether any physical parts of the asset are replaced.

The reason for this approach is to maintain a degree of consistency with IAS 37 – *Provisions, Contingent Liabilities and Contingent Assets* – which forbids an entity from making provisions that are not obligations. Therefore an entity is prohibited by IAS 37 to make a provision to overhaul (say) an aircraft engine by providing a quarter of the cost for four years and then utilising the provision when the engine is overhauled in year 4. This had been a common practice in the airline and oil refining industries, although it had never been universally applied in either sector; some companies accounted for the expenditure when incurred, others capitalised the cost and depreciated it over the period until the next major overhaul. IAS 37 proposed that the entity's results could be largely insulated from the effects of any change in the policy of providing for repair costs over time by adjusting the asset's carrying value and depreciation charge.[13] IAS 16 now applies the same recognition criteria to the cost of major inspections. Inspection costs are added to the asset's cost and any amount remaining from the previous inspection is derecognised. This process of recognition and derecognition should take place regardless of whether the cost of the previous inspection was identified (and considered a separate part) when the asset was originally acquired or constructed. Therefore, if the element relating to the inspection had previously been identified, it would have been depreciated between that time and the current overhaul. However, if it had not been previously identified, the recognition and derecognition rules still apply; but the standard allows the estimated cost of a future similar inspection to be used as an indication of the cost of the existing inspection component that must be derecognised.[14] This appears to allow the entity to reconstruct the carrying amount of the previous inspection (i.e. to estimate the net depreciated carrying value of the previous inspection that will be derecognised) rather than simply using a depreciated replacement cost approach.

2.3 Measurement at recognition

IAS 16 draws a distinction between measurement at recognition (i.e. the initial recognition of an item of PP&E on acquisition) and measurement after recognition (i.e. the subsequent treatment of the item). Measurement after recognition is discussed at 2.4 below.

The standard states that 'An item of property, plant and equipment that qualifies for recognition as an asset shall be measured at its cost.'[15] Therefore the question arises of what may be included in the cost of an item, and the standard contains considerable guidance on this matter, under the heading 'Elements of cost'.

2.3.1 Elements of cost and cost measurement

IAS 16 sets out as follows what may be included within the cost of an item of PP&E on its initial recognition.

'The cost of an item of property, plant and equipment comprises:

(a) its purchase price, including import duties and non-refundable purchase taxes, after deducting trade discounts and rebates.

(b) any costs directly attributable to bringing the asset to the location and condition necessary for it to be capable of operating in the manner intended by management.

(c) the initial estimate of the costs of dismantling and removing the item and restoring the site on which it is located, the obligation for which an entity incurs either when the item is acquired or as a consequence of having used the item during a particular period for purposes other than to produce inventories during that period.'[16] The costs of obligations to dismantle, remove or restore an asset that is used to produce inventories are dealt with in accordance with IAS 2 – *Inventories* – as dealt with in Chapter 21.[17]

Note that all site restoration costs and other environmental restoration and similar costs must be estimated and capitalised at initial recognition, in order that such costs can be recovered over the life of the item of PP&E, even if the expenditure will only be incurred at the end of the item's life. The obligations are calculated in accordance with IAS 37.[18]

A common instance of (c) above is dilapidation obligations in lease agreements, under which a lessee is obliged to return premises to the landlord in an agreed condition. Arguably, a provision is required whenever the 'damage' is incurred. Therefore, if a retailer rents two adjoining premises and knocks them into one, it probably has an obligation to make good the party wall at the end of the lease term and should immediately provide for the costs of so doing. The 'other side' of the provision entry is an asset that will be amortised over the lease term – notwithstanding that some of the costs of modifying the premises may also have been capitalised as assets.

'Directly attributable' costs are the key issue in the measurement of cost. The standard gives examples of types of expenditure that are, and are not, considered to be directly attributable. The following examples are given of those types of expenditure that are considered to be directly attributable, and hence may be included in cost at initial recognition:

(a)   costs of employee benefits (as defined in IAS 19 – *Employee Benefits*) arising directly from the construction or acquisition of the item of property, plant and equipment. This means that the labour costs of an entity's own employees (e.g. site workers, in-house architects and surveyors) arising directly from the construction, or acquisition, of the specific item of PP&E may be recognised;

(b)   costs of site preparation;

(c)   initial delivery and handling costs;

(d)   installation and assembly costs;

(e)   costs of testing whether the asset is functioning properly, after deducting the net proceeds from selling any items produced while bringing the asset to that location and condition (such as samples produced when testing equipment); and

(f)   professional fees.[19]

Borrowing costs, if directly attributable to the item, may be included. This aspect is the subject of IAS 23 – *Borrowing Costs* – and is discussed separately in Chapter 14.[20] Administration and other general overhead costs are not costs of an item of PP&E.[21] This means that employee costs not related to a specific asset, such as site selection activities, and general management time do not qualify for capitalisation. Nor are entities allowed to recognise so-called 'start up costs' as part of the item of PP&E. These include costs related to opening a new facility, introducing a new product or service (including costs of advertising and promotional activities), conducting business in a new territory or with a new class of customer (including costs of staff training), and similar items.[22] These costs should be accounted for in the same way as similar costs incurred as part of the entity's on-going activities.

Once an item of PP&E is in the location and condition necessary for it to be capable of operating in the manner intended by management, which will usually be the date of practical completion of the physical asset, cost recognition ceases. IAS 16 therefore prohibits the recognition of relocation and reorganisation costs, costs incurred during the run up to full use once an item is ready to be used, and any initial operating losses.[23] An entity is not precluded from continuing to capitalise costs during an initial commissioning period that is necessary for running in machinery or testing equipment. By contrast no further costs should be capitalised if the asset is fully operational but is not yet achieving its targeted profitability because demand is still building up, for example in a new hotel or bookstore. In this case, the asset is clearly in the location and condition necessary for it to be capable of operating in the manner intended by management.

While constructing an asset, an entity may enter into incidental operations that are not themselves necessary to bring the asset itself into the location and condition necessary for it to be capable of operating in the manner intended by management, for example by renting space for another purpose. In the event of any revenue being earned during the construction period it should be credited to income and the related costs (which, of course may not be recognised as an asset) must be classified as an expense. IAS 16 does not allow the income and expense to be netted against one another.[24] It is our view that any revenue gained from the sale of output manufactured in the commissioning period should also be included in income, and not deducted from the cost of the item of PP&E.

If an asset is self-built by the entity, the same general principles apply as for an acquired asset. If the same type of asset is made for resale by the business, it should be recognised at cost of production, without including any profit element – this allows self-constructed assets to include attributable overheads in accordance with IAS 2 (see Chapter 21). Abnormal amounts of wasted resources, whether labour, materials or other resources may not be included in the cost of self-built assets. IAS 23 – discussed in Chapter 14 – contains criteria relating to the recognition of any interest as a component of a self-built item of PP&E.[25]

IAS 16 specifically eliminates the capitalisation of 'hidden' credit charges as part of the cost of an item of property, plant and equipment, so the cost of an item of PP&E is its 'cash price equivalent' at the recognition date. This means that if payment is made in some other manner, the cost to be capitalised is the normal cash price. Thus, if the payment terms are extended beyond 'normal' credit terms, the cost to be recognised must be the cash price equivalent; and any difference must be treated as an interest expense.[26] Assets partly paid for by government grants, and those held under finance leases are discussed in Chapters 27 and 23, respectively.

A   Accounting for changes in decommissioning and restoration costs

IAS 16 is unclear about the extent to which an item's carrying amount should be affected by changes in the estimated amount of dismantling and site restoration costs that occur *after* the estimate made upon initial measurement. This issue is the subject of IFRIC 1 – *Changes in Existing Decommissioning, Restoration and Similar Liabilities* – issued in final form in May 2004.

IFRIC 1 applies to any decommissioning or similar liability that has been both included as part of an asset measured in accordance with IAS 16 and measured as a liability in accordance with IAS 37.[27] It deals with the impact of events that change the measurement of an existing liability. Such events include a change in the estimated cash flows, the discount rate and the unwinding of the discount.[28]

IFRIC differentiates between the treatment under the cost and valuation models (these models are dealt with in 2.4 below).

If the asset is carried at cost, changes in the liability are added to, or deducted from, the cost of the asset. This deduction may not exceed the carrying amount of the asset and any excess over the carrying value is taken immediately to profit or loss. If the change in estimate results in an addition to the carrying value, the entity is required to consider whether this is an indication of impairment of the asset as a whole and test for impairment in accordance with IAS 36 (see Chapter 13).[29]

If the related asset is carried at valuation and changes in the estimated liability alter the valuation surplus (i.e. the re-estimation takes place independently of the valuation of the asset), then a decrease in the liability is credited directly to the revaluation surplus in equity, unless it reverses a revaluation deficit on the asset that was previously recognised in profit or loss, in which case it may be taken to the income statement. Similarly, an increase in the liability is taken straight to the profit or loss, unless there is a revaluation surplus existing in respect of that asset.[30]

If the liability decreases and the deduction exceeds the amount that the asset would have been carried at under the cost model (e.g. its depreciated historical cost), the amount by which the asset is reduced is capped at this amount. Any excess is taken immediately to the income statement.[31] This means that the maximum amount by which an asset can be reduced is the same whether it is carried at cost or valuation.

This change in the revalued amount must be assessed against the requirements in IAS 16 regarding revalued assets, particularly that they must be carried at an amount that does not differ materially from fair value (see 2.4.1 below for the standard's rules regarding revaluations of assets). Such an adjustment is an indication that the carrying amount may differ from fair value and the asset may have to be revalued. Any such revaluation must, of course, take account of the adjustment of the estimated liability. If a revaluation is necessary, all assets of the same class must be revalued.[32]

Any changes in estimate taken to equity must be disclosed on the face of the statement of changes in equity in accordance with IAS 1 (see Chapter 3).[33] Depreciation of the 'decommissioning asset' and any changes thereto are covered by 2.4.2C below. The unwinding of the discount must be recognised in profit or loss as a finance cost as it occurs. The allowed alternative treatment of capitalisation under IAS 23 is not permitted.[34]

IFRIC 1 applies to annual periods beginning on or after 1 September 2004. Earlier application is encouraged. If an entity applies the Interpretation for a period beginning before 1 September 2004, it must disclose that it has done so.[35]

Any changes in measurement as a result of implementing the Interpretation are changes in accounting policies to be accounted for in accordance with IAS 8. If an entity applies this Interpretation for a period beginning before 1 January 2005, it must follow the requirements of the previous version of IAS 8, which was entitled *Net Profit or Loss for the Period, Fundamental Errors and Changes in Accounting Policies*, unless the entity is applying the revised version of IAS 8 as at that earlier period[36]

2.3.2 Exchanges of assets

Asset exchanges are transactions that have preoccupied standard setters for a number of years. For example, an entity might swap a facility it does not require in an area, for one it does in another – the opposite being the case for the counterparty. Such exchanges are not uncommon in the hotel, retail and leisure businesses, particularly after an acquisition, for example. Indeed, governmental or EU competition rules may even require such exchanges in certain cases. The question arises whether such transactions give rise to a profit, in the circumstances where the carrying value of the outgoing facility is less than the incoming one. This can occur when carrying values are less than market values. Equally, it is possible that a transaction could be arranged with no real commercial substance, solely to boost apparent profits.

After its revision in 2003 as part of the IASB's Improvements project, the treatment of asset exchanges was simplified – to an extent. IAS 16 now requires all acquisitions of PP&E in exchange for non-monetary assets, or a combination of monetary and non-monetary assets, to be measured at fair value, subject to the following conditions:

> 'The cost of such an item of property, plant and equipment is measured at fair value unless (a) the exchange transaction lacks commercial substance or (b) the fair value of neither the asset received nor the asset given up is reliably measurable. The acquired item is measured in this way even if an entity cannot immediately derecognise the asset given up.'[37]

If the fair value of neither the asset given up nor the asset received can be measured reliably, the cost of the asset is measured at the carrying amount of the asset given up[38] and there is no gain on the transaction. That is, if at least one of the two fair values can be measured reliably, that value is used for measuring the exchange transaction; if not then the exchange is measured at the carrying value of the asset the entity no longer owns. However, this relatively understandable requirement (leaving aside how straightforward determining a reliable fair value will actually be) is qualified by a 'commercial substance' test.[39] The commercial substance test was put in place to prevent gains in income being recognised when the transaction had no discernable effect on the entity's economics.[40] The commercial substance of an exchange is to be determined by forecasting and comparing the future cash flows budgeted to be generated by the incoming and outgoing assets. For commercial substance to be present, there must be a significant difference between the two forecasts. The standard sets out this requirement as follows:

> 'An entity determines whether an exchange transaction has commercial substance by considering the extent to which its future cash flows are expected to change as a result of the transaction. An exchange transaction has commercial substance if:
>
> (a)   the configuration (risk, timing and amount) of the cash flows of the asset received differs from the configuration of the cash flows of the asset transferred; or
>
> (b)   the entity-specific value of the portion of the entity's operations affected by the transaction changes as a result of the exchange; and
>
> (c)   the difference in (a) or (b) is significant relative to the fair value of the assets exchanged.'[41]

As set out in the definitions of the standard, see 2.2.1 above, entity-specific value is the net present value of the future predicted cash flows from continuing use and disposal of the asset – note that post-tax cash flows should be used for this calculation. The standard contains no guidance on the discount rate to be used for this exercise, nor on any of the other parameters involved, but it does suggest that the result of these analyses might be clear without having to perform detailed calculations.[42]

The IASB has concluded that the recognition of income from an exchange of assets does not depend on whether the assets exchanged are dissimilar.[43] However, care will have to be taken to ensure that the transaction has commercial substance as defined in the standard if an entity receives a similar item of property, plant and equipment in exchange for a similar asset of its own. Commercial substance may be difficult to demonstrate if the entity is exchanging a piece of land for a similar one in a similar location. However, in the latter case, the risk, timing and amount of cash flows could differ if one asset were available for sale and the entity intended to sell it whereas the previous asset could not be realised by sale or only sold in a much longer timescale. It is feasible that such a transaction could meet conditions (a) and (c) above. Similarly, it would be unusual if the entity-specific values of similar assets differed enough in any arm's length exchange transaction to meet condition (c). However, many exchanges are more likely to pass the 'commercial substance' test, for example:

- exchanging an interest in an investment property for one that the entity uses for its own purposes. The entity has exchanged a rental stream and instead has an asset that contributes to the cash flows of the cash-generating unit of which it is a part; or
- exchanging a property for a stake in a jointly controlled entity. The entity will now receive a rental or royalty stream from an asset that was previously part of a cash-generating unit

In both of these cases it is possible that the risk, timing and amount of the cash flows of the asset received would differ from the configuration of the cash flows of the asset transferred.

In the context of asset exchanges, the standard contains guidance on the reliable determination of fair values in the circumstances where market values do not exist:

'The fair value of an asset for which comparable market transactions do not exist is reliably measurable if (a) the variability in the range of reasonable fair value estimates is not significant for that asset or (b) the probabilities of the various estimates within the range can be reasonably assessed and used in estimating fair value. If an entity is able to determine reliably the fair value of either the asset received or the asset given up, then the fair value of the asset given up is used to measure the cost of the asset received unless the fair value of the asset received is more clearly evident.'[44]

No guidance is given on how to assemble a 'range of reasonable fair value estimates'. IAS 16 itself permits the estimation of the fair value using income or depreciated replacement cost bases (see 2.8.3C below) but the latter hardly seems relevant to an exchange transaction. Another way would be to base fair value on the 'entity-specific value' – i.e. on the discounted budgeted cash flows of the entity. This is a technique used for valuing investment properties in thin markets (see 3.3.2 below). However, if the fair value *is* the entity-specific value, how can the difference between it and the fair value be significant?

The term 'commercial substance' is used by the standard in a particular sense only, as in practice commercial substance can exist (in the sense that an entity has a good reason for the exchange) even if forecast cash flows are similar. If it is not possible to demonstrate that the transaction has commercial substance as defined by the standard, assets received in exchange transactions will be recorded at the carrying value of the asset given up.

If the transaction passes the 'commercial substance' test then IAS 16 requires the exchanged asset to be recorded at its fair value. As discussed in 2.6 below, the standard requires gains or losses on items that have been derecognised to be included in profit or loss in the period of derecognition but does not allow gains on derecognition to be classified as revenue,[45] It gives no further indication regarding their classification in the income statement

2.3.3 Assets held under finance leases

The cost of assets held under finance leases is determined for in accordance with IAS 17,[46] as described in Chapter 23.

2.3.4 Assets acquired with the assistance of government grants

The carrying amount of an item of PP&E may be reduced by government grants in accordance with IAS 20 – *Accounting for Government Grants and Disclosure of Government Assistance*.[47] The requirements of this standard are discussed in Chapter 27.

2.4 Measurement after recognition

IAS 16 allows one of two alternatives to be chosen as the accounting policy for measurement of PP&E after initial recognition. The choice made must be applied to an entire class of PP&E, but all classes are not required to have the same policy.[48]

The first alternative is the 'cost model' (in fact the traditional way PP&E has been accounted for) whereby the item is carried at cost less accumulated depreciation and less any impairment losses.[49] The requirements of IAS 16 concerning depreciation are dealt with at 2.4.2 below. The second alternative, the revaluation model, is discussed below at 2.4.1.

2.4.1 Revaluation model

If the revaluation model is adopted, land and buildings are to be carried at fair value less subsequent accumulated depreciation or impairment losses.[50] 'Fair value' will usually be the market value of the asset. In the case of land and buildings this will be 'determined from market based evidence', in the actual phrase used, which is normally to be determined by professional valuers, though there is no requirement for a professional external valuation or even for a professionally qualified valuer to perform the appraisal. The fair value of other items of PP&E is usually their appraised market value.[51] Although market value is not discussed further, fair value is defined (see 2.2.1 above) as the amount at which an asset could be exchanged between knowledgeable, willing parties in an arm's length transaction.

If there is no market-based evidence of fair value because of the specialised nature of the items, or because they are rarely sold, a depreciated replacement cost approach or an 'income' approach is to be used.[52] Neither of these terms is explained further. These valuation issues are discussed further at 2.8.3 below.

Valuation frequency is not laid down precisely by IAS 16, which states that revaluations are to be made with sufficient regularity to ensure that the carrying amount does not differ materially from the fair value at the balance sheet date.[53] When the fair value of a revalued asset differs materially from its carrying amount, a further revaluation is necessary. The standard suggests that some items of property, plant and equipment have frequent and volatile changes in fair value and these should be revalued annually. This is true of property assets in many jurisdictions but even in such circumstances there may be much quieter periods with little movement in values. If there are only insignificant movements it may only be necessary to perform valuations at three or five year intervals.[54]

If the revaluation model is adopted, IAS 16 specifies that all items within a class of assets are to be revalued simultaneously to prevent selective revaluations. A class of PP&E is a grouping of assets of a similar nature and use in an entity's operations. This is not a precise definition. The following are examples of separate classes of asset given in IAS 16:

(i)   land;

(ii)   land and buildings;

(iii)   machinery

(iv)   ships;

(v)   aircraft;

(vi)   motor vehicles;

(vii)   furniture and fixtures; and

(viii) office equipment.[55]

These are very broad categories of asset and it is possible for them to be classified further into groupings of assets of a similar nature and use. Office buildings and factories or hotels and fitness centres, could be separate classes of asset. If the entity used the same type of asset in two different geographical locations, e.g. clothing manufacturing facilities for similar products or products with similar markets, say footwear in Sri Lanka and knitwear in Guatemala, it is likely that these would be seen as part of the same class of asset. However, if the entity manufactured pharmaceuticals and clothing, both in European facilities, then arguably these could be assets with a sufficiently different nature and use to be a separate class. Ultimately it must be a matter of judgement in the context of individual entities.

IAS 16 does permit a rolling valuation of a class of assets, whereby the class is revalued over an (undefined) short period of time, 'provided the valuations are kept up to date'.[56] This final condition makes it difficult to see how rolling valuations can be performed unless the value of the assets changes very little (in which case the standard states that valuations need only be performed every three to five years), or if a large change is revealed, then presumably a wholesale revaluation is required.

A   Accounting for valuation surpluses and deficits

Increases in a valuation should be credited to a revaluation surplus within equity. If a revaluation increase reverses a decrease that was recognised as an expense, it may be credited to income. Decreases in valuation should be charged to the income statement, except to the extent that they reverse an existing revaluation surplus on the same asset.[57] This means that it is not possible to carry a negative revaluation reserve in respect of any asset.

IAS 16 generally retains a model in which the revalued amount substitutes for cost in both balance sheet and income statement and there is no recycling of amounts taken directly to equity. This is unlike the treatment subsequently adopted by the IASB in relation to available for sale financial assets, in which gains and losses initially taken to equity on remeasurement to fair value are taken to income when the asset is derecognised (see Chapter 18 at 3.2). Different rules apply to impairment losses. An impairment loss on a revalued asset is first used to reduce the revaluation surplus for that asset. Only when the impairment loss exceeds the amount in the revaluation surplus for that same asset is any further impairment loss recognised in profit or loss (see Chapter 13 at 3.3.3).[58] The revaluation surplus included in equity may be transferred directly to retained earnings when the surplus is realised and all of it may be transferred when the asset is disposed of. However, the difference between depreciation based on the revalued carrying amount of the asset and depreciation based on its original cost may be transferred as the asset is used by the entity. This is illustrated in Example 12.1 below. This provision recognises that any depreciation on the revalued part of an asset's carrying value has been realised by being charged to income. Thus a transfer can be made of an equivalent amount from the revaluation surplus in equity to retained profits. However any transfer is made directly from revaluation surplus to retained earnings and not through the income statement.[59]

Example 12.1:   Effect of depreciation on the revaluation reserve

On 1 January 2000 an entity acquires an asset for €1,000. The asset has an economic life of ten years and is depreciated on a straight-line basis. The residual value is assumed to be €nil. At 31 December 2004 (when the depreciated cost would have been €600) the asset is valued at €900. The entity accounts for the revaluation by crediting €300 to the revaluation reserve. At 31 December 2004 the economic life of the asset is considered to be the remainder of its original life, i.e. six years, and its residual value is still considered to be €nil. In the year ended 31 December 2005 and in later years, the depreciation charged to the profit and loss account is €150.

The usual treatment thereafter for each of the remaining 6 years of the asset's life, is to transfer €50 p.a. from the revaluation reserve to retained earnings. This avoids the revaluation reserve being maintained indefinitely even after the asset ceases to exist, which does not seem sensible. The transfer is to equity and not to the profit and loss account for the year.

The effect on taxation, both current and deferred, of a policy of revaluing assets is dealt with in Chapter 24.

B   Adopting a policy of revaluation

Although the initial adoption of a policy of revaluation is a change in accounting policy, it is not dealt with as a prior year adjustment in accordance with IAS 8, but instead is treated as a revaluation during the year.[60]

2.4.2   Depreciation

IAS 16 links its recognition concept of a 'part' of an asset, discussed at 2.2.2 above, with the analysis of assets for the purpose of depreciation. Each part of an asset with a cost that is significant in relation to the total cost of the item must be separately depreciated,[61] which means that the initial cost must be allocated between the significant parts by the entity. The standard's example is again that of the airframe and engines of an aircraft.[62]

However, because parts are identified by their significant cost rather than their effect on depreciation, they may have the same useful lives and depreciation method and the standard allows them to be grouped for depreciation purposes.[63] It also identifies other circumstances in which the significant parts do not correspond to the depreciable components within the asset. The remainder of an asset that has not been separately identified into parts may consist of other parts that are individually not significant and the entity may need to use approximation techniques to calculate an appropriate depreciation method for all of these parts.[64] The standard also allows an entity to depreciate separately parts that are not significant in relation to the whole.[65]

This means that this new method of analysing assets, by parts and by significant parts which are identified by cost, is not intended to affect the depreciation charge based on components of an asset with different useful lives or depreciation methods.

The depreciation charge is recognised in the profit and loss account unless it forms part of the cost of another asset, e.g. as part of the cost of finished manufactured goods held in inventory in accordance with IAS 2.[66]

Accounting for parts of assets is discussed further at 2.6 and 2.8.1 below.

A   Depreciable amount, useful life and residual values

As noted in 2.2.1 above, the depreciable amount of an item of PP&E is its cost or valuation less its estimated residual value. The standard states that an entity must review the residual values of all its items of PP&E, and therefore all parts of them, at least at each financial year-end. If the estimated residual value differs from previous estimates, changes must be accounted for prospectively as a change in accounting estimate in accordance with IAS 8.[67] Although not expressly stated, this passage in the standard applies only to material differences.

This requirement of IAS 16 has been modified as a result of the Improvements project revisions, and now constitutes an important point for entities' attention. As the definition (see 2.2.1 above) implies, the residual value of an item of PP&E today, is to be calculated by taking the price such an asset would fetch today, but assuming that it was already in the condition it will be in at the end of its useful life. Therefore an element of continuous updating of one component of an asset's carrying value has been introduced into IAS 16.

As any change in the residual value directly affects the depreciable amount, it may also affect the depreciation charge. This is because the depreciable amount (i.e. the amount actually charged to the profit and loss account over the life of the asset) is calculated by deducting the residual value from the cost or valuation of the asset, although for these purposes the residual value is capped at the asset's carrying amount.[68] Although many items of PP&E have a negligible residual value because they are kept for significantly all of their useful lives, there are a number of types of asset where this requirement could have a significant effect, and conceivably cause noticeable volatility in the depreciation charge. The residual values, and hence depreciation charges, of ships, aircraft, hotels and other assets of this nature, could potentially be affected by this requirement.

In addition, the standard requires year-end reviews of an asset's useful life, and, if expectations differ from previous estimates, the depreciation charge should be adjusted prospectively.[69] Factors that may affect the useful life are discussed at C below.

The new requirement concerning the residual values of assets highlights how important it is that residual values are considered and reviewed in conjunction with the review of useful lives. The useful life is the period over which the entity expects to use the asset, not the asset's economic life. Residual values are of no relevance if the entity intends to keep the asset until it is of no use to anyone else. If an entity points to the prices fetched in the market by a type of asset that it holds, it must also demonstrate an intention to dispose of it before the end of its economic life.

B   *Depreciation charge*

The standard requires the depreciable amount of an asset to be allocated on a systematic basis over its useful life.[70]

The standard makes it clear that depreciation must be charged on all items of PP&E, including those carried under the revaluation model, even if the fair value of the asset at the year-end is higher than the carrying amount,[71] as long as the residual value of the item is lower than the carrying amount. If the residual value exceeds the carrying amount, no depreciation is charged until the residual value once again decreases to less than the carrying amount.[72] IAS 16 makes it clear that the repair and maintenance of an asset does not of itself negate the need to depreciate it.[73] This is discussed further below.

There is no requirement in IAS 16 for an automatic impairment review if no depreciation is charged.

C   *Useful lives*

The judgement that entities must make is how long the useful life of an item of PP&E will be. IAS 16 provides the following guidance about the factors to be considered when estimating the useful life of an asset:

'(a)   expected usage of the asset. Usage is assessed by reference to the asset's expected capacity or physical output.

(b)   expected physical wear and tear, which depends on operational factors such as the number of shifts for which the asset is to be used and the repair and maintenance programme, and the care and maintenance of the asset while idle.

(c)   technical or commercial obsolescence arising from changes or improvements in production, or from a change in the market demand for the product or service output of the asset.

(d)   legal or similar limits on the use of the asset, such as the expiry dates of related leases.[74]

The initial assessment of the useful life of the asset will take account of the expected routine spending on repairs and expenditure necessary for it to achieve that life. Although (b) above implies an item of plant and machinery, care and maintenance programmes are relevant to assessing the useful lives of many other types of asset. For example, an entity may assess the useful life of a railway engine at thirty-five years on the assumption that it has a major overhaul every seven years. Without this expenditure, the life of the engine would be much less certain and could be much shorter. Maintenance necessary to support the fabric of a building and its service potential will also be taken into account in assessing its useful life. Eventually, it will always become uneconomic for the entity to continue to maintain the asset so, while the expenditure may lengthen the useful life, it cannot make it indefinite. However, as the maintenance spend may affect the residual value, it may indirectly reduce the depreciable amount to zero.

The useful life of an asset is defined in terms of its use to the business, not its economic life, so it is quite possible that an asset's useful life will be shorter than its economic life. Many entities have a policy of disposing of assets when they still have a residual value, which means that another user will benefit from the asset.[75] This is particularly common with property and motor vehicles where there are effective second-hand markets but less usual for plant and machinery. The standard requires the land and the building element of property to be accounted for as separate components. Land, which usually has an unlimited life, is not depreciated, while buildings are depreciable assets. IAS 16 states that the useful life of a building is not affected by an increase in the value of the land on which it stands.[76]

There are two circumstances in which depreciation may be applied to land. In those instances in which land does have a finite life it will be either used for extractive purposes (a quarry or mine) or for some purpose such as landfill; it will be depreciated in an appropriate manner (but it is highly unlikely that there will be any issue regarding separating the interest in land from any building element). However, such land may include an element for site dismantlement or restoration (see 2.3.1 above), in which case this element will have to be depreciated over an appropriate period. The standard describes this as 'the period of benefits obtained by incurring these costs';[77] this will often be the estimated useful life of the site for its purpose and function. So, for example, an entity engaged in landfill on a new site may make a provision for restoring it as soon as it starts preparation by removing the overburden. It will depreciate this 'restoration asset' over the landfill site's estimated useful life. If the land does not have a finite useful life the restoration asset will be depreciated on an appropriate basis.

If the estimated costs are revised in accordance with IFRIC 1, the adjusted depreciable amount of the asset is depreciated over its useful life. Therefore, once the related asset has reached the end of its useful life, all subsequent changes in the liability shall be recognised in profit or loss as they occur, whether the entity applies the cost or revaluation model.[78]

D   *When depreciation starts*

The standard is clear on when deprecation should start and finish, and sets out the requirements succinctly as follows:

- depreciation of an asset begins when it is available for use, which is defined by the standard when it is in the location and condition necessary for it to be capable of operating in the manner intended by management. This is the point at which capitalisation of costs relating to the asset cease;

- depreciation of an asset ceases at the earlier of the date that the asset is classified as held for sale (or included in a disposal group that is classified as held for sale) in accordance with IFRS 5 and the date that the asset is derecognised.

Therefore, an entity does not stop depreciating an asset because it has become idle or has been retired from active use (unless, of course, the asset is fully depreciated). If the entity is using a usage method of depreciation the charge can be zero while there is no production.[79] Of course, a prolonged period in which there is no production may raise questions as to whether the asset is impaired: an asset becoming idle is a specific example of an indication of impairment in IAS 36 (see Chapter 13).[80]

Assets held for sale under IFRS 5 are discussed below at 2.6.1.

E   *Depreciation methods*

The standard is not prescriptive about methods of depreciation, mentioning straight line, reducing balance and sum of the units as possibilities. The overriding requirement is that the depreciation charge reflects the pattern of consumption of the benefits the asset brings over its useful life, and is applied consistently from period to period.[81] IAS 16 contains an explicit requirement for the depreciation method to be reviewed at least at each period end to determine if there has been a significant change in the pattern of consumption of an asset's benefits. This would be unusual; it would mean, for example, concluding that the unit of production method was no longer appropriate and changing to a straight line or diminishing balance method. Nevertheless, if there has been such a change the depreciation method should be changed to reflect it. The consequent depreciation adjustment should be made prospectively, that is the asset's depreciable amount should be written off over current and future periods. See 2.8.6 below for a discussion of depreciation methods in practice.

2.5 Impairment

All items of PP&E accounted for under IAS 16 are subject to the impairment requirements of IAS 36. Impairment is separately discussed in Chapter 13.[82]

2.5.1 Compensation for impairment

The question has arisen about the treatment of any compensation an entity may be due to receive, as a result of an asset being impaired. For example an asset might be insured, so repayment from an insurance company following a fire might be expected. IAS 16 states that these two events – the impairment and any compensation – are 'separate economic events' and should be accounted for separately as follows:

- impairments of PP&E are recognised in accordance with IAS 36 (see Chapter 13);

- derecognition of items retired or disposed of should be recognised in accordance with IAS 16 (derecognition is discussed below); and

- compensation from third parties for PP&E that is impaired lost or given up is included in profit and loss when it becomes receivable.[83]

Therefore any compensation is accounted for separately from any impairment, the question as to when 'compensation becomes receivable' is not discussed further in the standard. In our view the normal asset recognition criteria should be applied in determining this date.

2.6 Derecognition and disposal

Derecognition (i.e. removal of the carrying amount of the item from the financial statements of the entity) occurs when an item of PP&E is either disposed of, or when no further economic benefits are expected to flow from its use or disposal.[84] The actual date of disposal is to be determined in accordance with the criteria in IAS 18 for the recognition of revenue from the sale of goods[85] (revenue recognition is discussed in Chapter 26). All gains and losses on derecognition must be included in profit and loss for the period when the item is derecognised, unless another standard applies – for example under IAS 17 a sale and leaseback transaction might not give rise to a gain. Gains are not to be classified as revenue.[86] Gains and losses are to be calculated as the difference between any net disposal proceeds and the carrying value of the item of PP&E[87] – this means that any revaluation surplus relating to the asset disposed of is transferred directly to equity when the asset is derecognised and not reflected in profit or loss.[88]

Replacement of 'parts' or components of an asset requires derecognition of the carrying value of the original part, even if that part was not being separately depreciated. Under these circumstances the standard allows the cost of a replacement part to be a guide to the original cost of the replaced part, if that cannot be determined.[89]

Any consideration received on the disposal of an item should be recognised at its fair value. If deferred credit terms are given, the consideration for the sale is the cash price equivalent, and any surplus is treated as interest revenue using the effective yield method as required by IAS 18 (see Chapter 26).[90]

2.6.1 IFRS 5 – Non-current assets held for sale and discontinued operations

The IASB published IFRS 5 in March 2005, and it is has gone some way to removing uncertainty about the way PP&E held for sale and no longer being used, should be treated in an entity's financial statements. IFRS 5 introduces a new category of asset: 'held for sale' and PP&E within this category is outside the scope of IAS 16, although IAS 16 requires certain disclosures about assets held for sale to be made, as set out at 2.7 below.

IFRS 5 requires that an item of PP&E should be classified as held for sale if its carrying amount will be recovered principally though a sale transaction rather then continuing use, though continuing use is not in itself precluded for assets classified as held for sale.[91] An asset can also be part of a 'disposal group' (that is a group of assets that are to be disposed of together) in which case the group can be treated as a whole. Once this classification has been made, depreciation ceases (even if the asset is still being used); but the assets must be carried at the lower of their previous carrying amount and fair value less costs to sell. For assets to be classified as held for sale, they must be available for immediate sale in their present condition, and the sale must be highly probable.[92]

Additionally, the sale should be completed within one year from the date of classification as held for sale, management at an 'appropriate level' must be committed to the plan, and an active programme of marketing the assets must have been started.[93]

The requirements of IFRS 5 are further discussed in Chapter 3.

2.7 IAS 16 disclosure requirements

IAS 16 contains a clear and well laid out disclosure section that is easy to use and understand. The main requirements are set out below, but note that the disclosure requirements of IAS 36 are included in Chapter 13.

2.7.1 General disclosures

For each class of property plant and equipment the following should be disclosed in the financial statements:

(a) the measurement bases used for determining the gross carrying amount (for example, cost, fair value). When more than one basis has been used, the gross carrying amount for that basis in each category should be disclosed (however the standard requires that if revaluation is adopted the entire class of assets must be revalued);

(b) the depreciation methods used;

(c) the useful lives or the depreciation rates used;

(d)   the gross carrying amount and the accumulated depreciation (aggregated with accumulated impairment losses) at the beginning and end of the period;

(e)   a reconciliation of the carrying amount at the beginning and end of the period showing:

  (i)   additions;

  (ii)   disposals,

  (iii) assets classified as held for sale, or included in a disposal group held for sale;

  (iv)   acquisitions through business combinations;

  (v)   increases or decreases during the period resulting from revaluations and from impairment losses recognised or reversed directly in equity under IAS 36, Impairment of Assets (if any);

  (vi)   impairment losses recognised in the income statement during the period under IAS 36 (if any);

  (vii) impairment losses reversed in the income statement during the period under IAS 36 (if any);

  (viii) depreciation for the period;

  (ix)   the net exchange differences arising on the translation of the financial statements from the functional currency into a different presentation currency, including the translation of a foreign operation into the presentation currency of the reporting entity; and

  (x)   other changes.

Under the previous version of IAS 16 it was not required to provide comparative information for the reconciliation in (e) above, because the standard offered a specific exemption from the requirement in IAS 1 to disclose 'comparative information ... in respect of the previous period for all amounts reported in the financial statements'.[94] The current version of IAS 16 does not contain this exemption, making it thereby necessary to include comparative information for the reconciliation in (e) above.

Extract 12.1 below shows a comprehensive disclosure of accounting policies and PPE movement and reconciliation note (although in this case only for a single year), in this instance from Bayer AG.

Extract 12.1: Bayer AG (2003)

Basic principles of the Group financial statements [extract]

Property, plant and equipment

Property, plant and equipment is carried at the cost of acquisition or construction. Assets subject to depletion are depreciated over their estimated useful lives. Write-downs are made for any declines in value that go beyond the depletion reflected in depreciation. In compliance with IAS 36 (Impairment of Assets), such write-downs are measured by comparing the carrying amounts to the discounted cash flows expected to be generated by the respective assets. Where it is not possible to estimate the impairment loss for an individual asset, the loss is assessed on the basis of the discounted cash flow for the cash-generating unit to which the asset belongs. Assets are written back if the reasons for previous years' write-downs no longer apply.

The cost of construction of self-constructed property, plant and equipment comprises the direct cost of materials, direct manufacturing expenses, appropriate allocations of material and manufacturing overheads, and an appropriate share of the depreciation and write-downs of assets used in construction. It includes the shares of expenses for company pension plans and discretionary employee benefits that are attributable to construction.

If the construction phase of property, plant or equipment extends over a long period, the interest incurred on borrowed capital up to the date of completion is capitalised as part of the cost of acquisition or construction.

Expenses for the repair of property, plant and equipment are normally charged against income, but they are capitalized if they result in an enlargement or substantial improvement of the respective assets.

Property, plant and equipment is depreciated by the straight-line method, except where the declining-balance method is more appropriate in light of the actual utilization pattern. Depreciation for 2003 has been allocated to the cost of goods sold, selling expenses, research and development expenses or general administration expenses.

When assets are closed down, sold, or abandoned, the difference between the net proceeds and the net carrying amount of the asset is recognized as a gain or loss in other operating income or expenses, respectively.

The following depreciation periods, based on the estimated useful lives of the respective assets, are applied throughout the Group:

Buildings	20 to 50 years
Outdoor infrastructure	10 to 20 years
Plant installations	6 to 20 years
Machinery and apparatus	6 to 12 years
Laboratory and research facilities	3 to 5 years
Storage tanks and pipelines	10 to 20 years
Vehicles	5 to 8 years
Computer equipment	3 to 5 years
Furniture and fixtures	4 to 10 years

In accordance with IAS 17 (Leases), assets leased on terms equivalent to financing a purchase by a long-terms loan (finance leases) are capitalised at the lower of their fair value or the present value of the minimum lease payments at the date of addition. The leased assets are depreciated over their estimated useful lives except where subsequent transfer of title is uncertain, in which case they are depreciated over their estimated useful lives or the respective lease terms, whichever are shorter. The future lease payments are recorded as financial obligations.

19   Property, plant and equipment

Changes in property, plant and equipment in 2003 were as follows:

	Land and buildings	Machinery and technical equipment	Furniture, fixtures and other equipment	Construction in progress and advance payments to vendors and contractors	Total
			(€ million)		
Gross carrying amounts, Dec. 31, 2002	8,061	18,590	2,245	1,309	30,205
Exchange differences	(445)	(997)	(103)	(63)	(1,608)
Changes in scope of consolidation	8	143	–	66	217
Acquisitions	–	–	–	–	–
Capital expenditures	87	390	170	797	1,444
Retirements	(228)	(911)	(312)	(37)	(1,488)
Subsequent adjustments relating to the Aventis CropScience acquisition	61	110	–	–	171
Transfers	354	690	94	(1,187)	(49)
Gross carrying amounts, Dec. 31 2003	7,898	18,015	2,094	885	28,892

Accumulated depreciation and write-downs Dec 31 2002	4,052	12,176	1,540	1	17,769
Exchange differences	(158)	(566)	(70)	–	(794)
Changes in scope of consolidation	–	–	–	–	–
Depreciation and write-downs in 2003	617	2,046	312	33	3,008
of which write-downs	368	885	42	33	1,328
Write-backs	–	–	–	–	–
Retirements	(113)	(690)	(263)	(13)	(1,079)
Transfers	142	(141)	51	(1)	51
Accumulated depreciation and write-downs, Dec. 31, 2003	4,540	12,825	1,570	20	18,955
Net carrying amounts, Dec. 31, 2003	3,358	5,190	524	865	9,937
Net carrying amounts, Dec. 31, 2002	4,009	6,414	705	1,308	12,436

The exchange differences are as defined for intangible assets.

In connection with the acquisition of Aventis CropScience Holding S.A., France, in fiscal 2002, the carrying amounts of acquired and identifiable assets have been adjusted in accordance with IAS 22 (Business Combinations) to reflect material evidence obtained after December 31, 2002 which altered the allocation of the purchase price to intangible assets, property, plant and equipment.

Capitalised property, plant and equipment includes assets with a total net value of €344 million (2002: €504 million) held under finance leases. The gross carrying amounts of these assets total €937 million (2002: €1,106 million). These assets are mainly machinery and technical equipment with a carrying amount of €230 million (gross amount: €745 million) and buildings with a carrying amount of €102 million (gross amount: €139 million). In the case of buildings, either the present value of the minimum lease payments covers substantially all of the cost of acquisition, or title passes to the lessee on expiration of the lease.

Also included are products leased to other parties under operating leases with a carrying amount of €183 million (2002: €232 million). The gross carrying amount of these assets was €452 million (2002: €500 million); their depreciation in 2003 amounted to €72 million (2002: €83 million). However, if under the relevant agreements the lessee is to be regarded as the economic owner of the assets and the lease therefore constitutes a finance lease as defined in IAS 17 (Leases), a receivable is recognized in the balance sheet in the amount of the discounted future lease payments.

IAS 16 also requires the disclosure of the following information which is useful to gain a fuller understanding of the entire position of the entity's holdings of and its commitments to purchase property plant and equipment:

(a) the existence and amounts of restrictions on title, and property, plant and equipment pledged as security for liabilities;

(b) the amount of expenditures recognised in the carrying amount of property, plant and equipment in the course of construction;

(c) the amount of contractual commitments for the acquisition of property, plant and equipment; and

(d) if it is not disclosed separately on the face of the income statement, the amount of compensation from third parties for items of property, plant and equipment that were impaired, lost or given up that is included in profit or loss.[95]

In addition there is a reminder in the standard that, in accordance with IAS 8, any changes in accounting estimate (e.g. depreciation methods, useful lives, residual values) that have a material effect on the current or future periods must be disclosed.[96]

Extract 12.2 below from Deutsche Börse AG shows in a single note disclosures relating to all that entity's non-current assets, PPE, intangible assets and financial assets. It includes an example of disclosure of expenditure on assets in the course of construction.

Extract 12.2: Deutsche Börse AG (2003)

Consolidated Balance Sheet Disclosures [extract]

17   Statement of changes in noncurrent assets

Historical costs

	Balance as at 1 Jan. 2003 €m	Additions €m	Revalu- ations €m	Reclassi- fications €m	Disposals €m	Decon- solidation €m	Balance as at 31 Dec. 2003 €m
Intangible assets							
Software	681.2	52.1	0	107.9	27.9	-0.1	813.2
Goodwill	1,341.0	0	0	0	0	0	1,341.0
Payments on account	110.4	9.1	0	-107.9	0.5	0	11.1
	2,132.6	**61.2**	**0**	**0**	**28.4**	**-0.1**	**2,165.3**
Property, plant and equipment							
Land and buildings	27.7	23.8	0	82.2	0	0	133.7
Leasehold improvements	27.8	24.1	0	34.7	0	0	86.6
Computer hardware, operating and office equipment	214.8	31.3	0	2.0	22.4	-0.1	225.6
Payments on account and construction in progress	192.6	23.6	0	-161.5	0	0	54.7
	462.9	**102.8**	**0**	**-42.6**	**22.4**	**-0.1**	**500.6**
Financial assets							
Investments in associates:							
carried at equity	33.1	0	1.1	0	0	0	34.2
carried at cost	0.7	0	0	0	0.6	0	0.1
Other equity investments	14.9	13.3	0	0	0	0	28.2
Noncurrent receivables and securities from banking business	335.8	63.7	0	0	5.0	0	394.5
Other noncurrent financial instruments	11.1	0	0	0	0	0	11.1
Other noncurrent loans	262.6	0.2	0	0	262.0	0	0.8
Investment property	10.7	2.5	0	42.6	0	0	55.8
	668.9	**79.7**	**1.1**	**42.6**	**267.6**	**0**	**524.7**
Total	**3,264.4**	**243.7**	**1.1**	**0**	**318.4**	**-0.2**	**3,190.6**

Cumulative depreciation and amortization

	Balance as at 1 Jan. 2003 € m	Additions € m	Impair- ment losses € m	Disposals € m	Decon- solidation € m	Balance as at 31 Dec. 2003 € m
Intangible assets						
Software	343.8	139.4	5.8	27.3	-0.1	461.6
Goodwill	92.4	65.2	10.0	0	0	167.6
Payments on account	0	0	0	0	0	0
	436.2	**204.6**	**15.8**	**27.3**	**-0.1**	**629.2**
Property, plant and equipment						
Land and buildings	0	1.2	0	0	0	1.2
Leasehold improvements	7.4	7.7	0	0	0	15.1
Computer hardware, operating and office equipment	134.6	42.1	0	20.9	-0.1	155.7
Payments on account and construction in progress	0	0	0	0	0	0
	142.0	**51.0**	**0**	**20.9**	**-0.1**	**172.0**
Financial assets						
Investments in associates:						
carried at equity	23.5	0.2	0	0	0	23.7
carried at cost	0	0.1	0	0.1	0	0
Other equity investments	2.1	0	0	0	0	2.1
Noncurrent receivables and securities from banking business	0	10.0	0	0	0	10.0
Other noncurrent financial instruments	3.0	0	0	1.4[1]	0	1.6
Other noncurrent loans	1.2	0	0	1.2	0	0
Investment property	0	1.8	0	0	0	1.8
	29.8	**12.1**	**0**	**2.7**	**0**	**39.2**
Total	**608.0**	**267.7**	**15.8**	**50.9**	**-0.2**	**840.4**

(1) Appreciation not recognized in the income statement

	Carrying amount as at 31 Dec. 2003 € m	as at 31 Dec. 2002 € m
Intangible assets		
Software	351.6	337.4
Goodwill	1,173.4	1,248.6
Payments on account	11.1	110.4
	1,536.1	**1,696.4**
Property, plant and equipment		
Land and buildings	132.5	27.7
Leasehold improvements	71.5	20.4
Computer hardware, operating and office equipment	69.9	80.2
Payments on account and construction in progress	54.7	192.6
	328.6	**320.9**

Financial assets		
Investments in associates:		
carried at equity	10.5	9.6
carried at cost	0.1	0.7
Other equity investments	26.1	12.8
Noncurrent receivables and securities from		
banking business	384.5	335.8
Other noncurrent financial instruments	9.5	8.1
Other noncurrent loans	0.8	261.4
Investment property	54.0	10.7
	485.5	**639.1**
Total	**2,350.2**	**2,656.4**

2.7.2   *Extra disclosures for revalued assets*

The IASB has gone to some lengths in IAS 16 to ensure that if the revaluation model is adopted, users of the financial statements should have enough information to clearly see its effects. The extra requirements if the revaluation basis is adopted are:

(a)   the effective date of the revaluation;

(b)   whether an independent valuer was involved;

(c)   the methods and significant assumptions applied in estimating the items' fair values;

(d)   the extent to which the items' fair values were determined directly by reference to observable prices in an active market or recent market transactions on arm's length terms or were estimated using other valuation techniques;

(e)   for each revalued class of property, plant and equipment, the carrying amount that would have been recognised had the assets been carried under the cost model; and

(f)   the revaluation surplus, indicating the change for the period and any restrictions on the distribution of the balance to shareholders.[97]

In particular the requirement under (e) is quite onerous for entities, as it entails their keeping asset register information in some detail in order to meet it.

Extract 12.3 below from Jardine Matheson Holdings Limited shows disclosures relating to PPE held at a valuation.

Extract 12.3: Jardine Matheson Holdings Limited (2003)

Notes to the Financial Statements [extract]

9   Tangible Assets

	Freehold properties US$m	Leasehold properties US$m	Leasehold improve- ments US$m	Plant machinery US$m	Furniture, equipment & motor vehicles US$m	Total US$m
2003						
Net book value at 1st January						
– as previously reported	552	373	191	143	152	1,411
– change in accounting policy	(1)	(35)	–	–	–	(36)
– as restated	551	338	191	143	152	1,375
Exchange differences	49	4	2	3	3	61
Fair value adjustments*	1	4	–	–	–	5
New subsidiary undertakings	37	84	8	16	7	152
Additions	75	2	40	35	57	209
Disposals	(71)	–	(12)	(8)	(14)	(105)
Depreciation charge	(5)	(10)	(56)	(39)	(49)	(159)
Impairment charge	(3)	–	–	–	–	(3)
Net revaluation surplus/(deficit)	(13)	3	–	–	–	(10)
Transfer to investment properties	–	(4)	–	–	–	(4)
Net book value at 31st December	**621**	**421**	**173**	**150**	**156**	**1,521**
Cost or valuation	626	472	504	426	524	2,552
Depreciation and impairment	(5)	(51)	(331)	(276)	(368)	(1,031)
	621	**421**	**173**	**150**	**156**	**1,521**
2002						
Net book value at 1st January						
– as previously reported	488	325	222	182	175	1,392
– change in accounting policy	(1)	(32)	–	–	–	(33)
– as restated	487	293	222	182	175	1,359
Exchange differences	35	5	5	10	4	59
New subsidiary undertakings	39	38	1	10	9	97
Additions	79	–	51	43	50	223
Disposals	(72)	(9)	(32)	(62)	(25)	(200)
Depreciation charge	(3)	(6)	(54)	(40)	(59)	(162)
Impairment charge	(1)	–	(2)	–	(2)	(5)
Net revaluation surplus/(deficit)	(13)	17	–	–	–	4
Net book value at 31st December	**551**	**338**	**191**	**143**	**152**	**1,375**
Cost or valuation	555	373	500	392	499	2,319
Depreciation and impairment	(4)	(35)	(309)	(249)	(347)	(944)
	551	**338**	**191**	**143**	**152**	**1,375**

* In respect of acquisition of Jardine Cycle & Carriage in 2002 (refer note 8).

The Group's freehold properties and the building component of leasehold properties were revalued at 31st December 2002 by independent professionally qualified valuers. The Directors have reviewed the carrying value at 31st December 2003 and, as a result, deficits on individual properties below depreciated cost of US$1 million (2002: US$4 million) and impairment losses of US$3 million (2002: US$1 million) have been charged to the consolidated profit and loss account. A net deficit of US$9 million (2002: net surplus of US$8 million) has been taken directly to property revaluation reserves. The amounts attributable to the Group, after tax and outside interests, are US$1 million, US$3 million and US$10 million respectively.

Freehold properties include a hotel property under development of US$103 million (2002: US$32 million), which is stated net of a grant of US$33 million (2002: US$29 million).

Certain of the land and buildings are pledged as security for borrowings (refer note 22).

If the freehold properties and the building component of leasehold properties had been included in the financial statements at cost less depreciation, the carrying value would have been US$962 million (2002: US$814 million).

2.7.3 Other disclosures

The standard emphasises that entities are also required to disclose information about impairment in accordance with IAS 36, in addition to the disclosures on this matter required by IAS 16.

Extract 12.4 below from Merck KGaA shows their policy concerning write-downs in addition to the numerical disclosures.

Extract 12.4: Merck KGaA (2003)

Notes to the Balance Sheet [extract]

2   Property, plant, and equipment

EUR million	Land, land rights, and buildings including building on third-party land	Plant and machinery	Other facilities, operating and office equipment	Construction in progress and advance payments to vendors and contractors	Total
Accumulated acquisition cost as of Jan. 1, 2003	1,279.4	1,986.3	683.9	240.4	**4,190.0**
Currency translation	-59.3	-79.1	-23.0	-5.3	**-166.7**
Changes in companies consolidated	-1.6	-0.8	1.3	–	**-1.1**
Additions	20.4	49.8	38.8	171.8	**280.8**
Disposals	-16.8	-41.4	-43.4	-10.0	**-111.6**
Transfers	40.0	74.7	19.9	-141.4	**-6.8**
Accumulated acquisition cost as of Dec. 31, 2003	1,262.1	1,989.5	677.5	255.5	**4,184.6**

Accumulated depreciation, amortization and write-downs as of Jan. 1, 2003	-445.0	-1,178.9	-421.4	-11.0	**-2,056.3**
Currency translation	14.7	47.6	13.4	0.2	**75.9**
Changes in companies consolidated	1.6	2.5	-0.9	–	**3.2**
Depreciation and write-downs	-57.6	-146.3	-65.1	-0.9	**-269.9**
Disposals	9.6	33.8	38.0	0.3	**81.7**
Transfers	-3.2	7.0	-2.7	-	**1.1**
Write-ups	–	–	0.1	–	**0.1**
Accumulated depreciation, amortization and write-downs as of Dec. 31, 2003	-479.9	-1,234.3	-438.6	-11.4	**-2,164.2**
Net carrying amount as of Dec. 31, 2003	782.2	755.2	238.9	244.1	**2,020.4**

Property, plant, and equipment is carried at acquisition or manufacturing cost, less depreciation and write-downs. Subsequent acquisition costs are capitalized. The manufacturing cost of self-constructed property, plant, and equipment is calculated on the basis of the directly attributable unit costs as well as an appropriate share of overheads, including depreciation and write-downs. Financing costs are not capitalized. In the case of acquisitions denominated in foreign currencies, subsequent exchange rate movements do not affect recognition of the asset at the original acquisition or manufacturing cost.

In accordance with IAS 20, acquisition or manufacturing costs are reduced by the amount of government grants or subsidies in those cases where such grants or subsidies have been paid for the acquisition or manufacture of assets (investment grants). Grants related to income that will no longer be offset by future expenses are taken to income. Total government grants and subsidies during the fiscal year amounted to EUR 3.8 million (previous year: EUR 3.8 million).

Property, plant, and equipment is written down by straight-line depreciation over the useful life of the asset concerned. The useful life applied to production buildings is a maximum of 33 years. Administration buildings are depreciated over a maximum of 40 years. For technical equipment the depreciation period is between 8 and 20 years, and 4 to 10 years for other facilities, operating and office equipment. Special write-downs are charged where required in accordance with IAS 36, and these are subsequently reversed if the original grounds for the write-down no longer apply. In the year under review, special write-downs in the amount of EUR 38.1 million (previous year: EUR 16.7 million) were charged on property, plant, and equipment. This includes the write off in full of EUR 18.1 million relating to buildings and technical equipment in connection with planned restructuring programs in France (Pharmaceuticals business sector). These are part of the total expenses for restructuring costs in France that are shown under exceptional items. The remaining impairment losses mainly relate to production facilities in the Chemicals business sector. These are reported in the income statement under other operating expenses.

Where assets are rented or leased and economic ownership lies with the respective Group company (finance leases), they are recognised as assets at the present value of the lease payments or at a lower fair value in accordance with IAS 17 (revised 1997) and written down over the useful life of the asset. The corresponding payment obligations from future lease payments are recorded as liabilities. The total value of capitalised leased assets amounts to EUR 20.0 million and the corresponding obligations amount to EUR 9.9 million (please refer to the explanatory notes, section (13) 'Financial obligations').

EUR million	Dec,31 .2003	Dec.31, 2002
Capitalized leased land	**2.1**	2.1
Capitalized leased buildings	**16.5**	17.1
Capitalized leased facilities	**0.8**	3.0
Capitalized leased vehicles	**0.6**	1.4
	20.0	23.6

The standard encourages but does not require entities to disclose other additional information such as the carrying amount of any idle assets, the gross amount of any fully depreciated assets in use, and any held for disposal. For any property plant and equipment held at cost less depreciation, the disclosure of its fair value is also encouraged if it is materially different from the carrying amount.[98]

2.8   Practical issues

2.8.1   Accounting for parts of assets

When IAS 16 was revised in 2003, one of the main areas of change was to the recognition criteria. The standard no longer has different conditions for the initial recognition of assets and for subsequent expenditure. The IASB explained that the previous criteria for subsequent recognition did not align with the asset recognition principles in the Framework; in addition, it was difficult to distinguish between maintenance and enhancement expenditure.[99] The standard now has a single set of recognition criteria, which means that subsequent expenditure must also meet these criteria before it is recognised.

IAS 16's new requirement is that parts of an asset are to be identified so that the cost of replacing a part may be recognised (i.e. capitalised as part of the asset) and the previous part derecognised. 'Parts' are distinguished from day-to-day servicing but they are not otherwise identified and defined; moreover, the unit of measurement to which the standard applies (i.e. what comprises an item of PP&E) is not itself defined.

Previously, IAS 16 (Revised 1998) required assets to be separated into components if they had different useful lives or provided benefits to the entity in a different pattern. This was for depreciation purposes, as these separate components might need to be depreciated using different rates and methods. Therefore the 'components' approach was for depreciation purposes, unlike the 'parts' approach, which is a recognition and derecognition concept.

IAS 16 has replaced 'components' for depreciation purposes with 'significant parts' of an asset that will be depreciated separately.[100] These are parts that have a cost that is significant in relation to the total cost of the asset. The revised standard even uses the same example of an aircraft and its engines, demonstrating that in some cases a 'significant part' is the same as a 'component'. However because parts are identified by their cost they may not individually be the same as components. More than one part may have the same useful life or depreciation method, which suggests that they together form a component; on the other hand, a part may not be significant and therefore may not be depreciated separately, as the standard also allows.[101]

An entity will have to identify the significant parts of the asset on initial recognition in order for it to depreciate the asset properly. There is no requirement to identify all parts. IAS 16 requires entities to derecognise an existing part regardless of whether it has been depreciated separately and allows them to estimate the carrying value of the part that has been replaced:

'If it is not practicable for an entity to determine the carrying amount of the replaced part, it may use the cost of the replacement as an indication of what the cost of the replaced part was at the time it was acquired or constructed.'[102]

As a consequence, an entity may not actually identify the parts of an asset until it incurs the replacement expenditure, as in the following example.

Example 12.2: Recognition and derecognition of parts

An entity buys a piece of machinery with an estimated useful life of ten years for €10 million. The asset contains two identical pumps, which are assumed to have the same useful life as the machine of which they are a part. After seven years one of the pumps fails and is replaced at a cost of €200,000. The entity had not identified the pumps as separate parts and does not know the original cost. It uses the cost of the replacement part to estimate the carrying value of the original pump. With the help of the supplier, it estimates that the cost would have been approximately €170,000 and that this would have a remaining carrying value after seven year's depreciation of €51,000. Accordingly it derecognises €51,000 and capitalises the cost of the replacement.

It may be that the entity has no better information than the cost of the replacement part, in which case it appears that the entity is permitted to use a depreciated replacement cost basis to calculate the amount derecognised in respect of the original asset.

2.8.2 Useful economic life

One of the critical assumptions on which the depreciation charge depends is the useful economic life of the asset. The useful economic life is the period over which the present owner will benefit and not the total potential life of the asset; the two will often not be the same. For example, an entity may have a policy of replacing all of its motor vehicles after three years, so this will be their estimated useful life for depreciation purposes. The entity will depreciate them over this period down to the estimated residual value. The residual values of motor vehicles are often easy to obtain and the entity will be able to reassess these residuals in line with the requirements of the standard.

The effects of technological change are often underestimated. It affects many assets, not only high technology plant and equipment such as computer systems. For example, many offices that have been purpose-built can become obsolete long before their fabric has physically deteriorated, for reasons such as the difficulty of introducing computer network infrastructures, or air conditioning.

As explained above, the standard requires asset lives to be estimated on a realistic basis and reviewed at the end of each reporting period. The effects of changes in estimated life are to be recognised prospectively, over the remaining life of the asset. In practice, many entities have previously tended to use quite a 'broad brush' approach to estimating asset lives, often based on perceived norms (for example, 50 years for freehold buildings) rather than a close analysis of their own expectations. The requirements of IAS 16 will necessitate more attention being paid to asset lives and residual values.

2.8.3   The meaning of fair value

A   Fair value or market value

Prior to 1998, IAS 16 required the fair value of land and buildings to be 'market value for existing use'. This was changed in IAS 16 (revised 1998), under which the fair value of these assets was normally market value, without this being modified in any way. The current standard does not define the appropriate valuation bases at all but instead describes processes. For land and buildings, which are almost the only assets ever revalued, fair value should be 'based on market-based evidence' (although income or depreciated replacement cost approaches are permitted if no such evidence is available).[103] The standard no longer implies that fair value and market value are synonymous.

These changes appear to allow a broader meaning of the term 'fair value', rather than bringing increasing clarity into its meaning. The term certainly encompasses two different valuation bases: market value in existing use, an entry value for property in continuing use in the business which is based on the concept of net current replacement cost, and open market value, which is an exit value and based on the amount that a property that is surplus to requirements could reach when sold. Both of these bases are market derived, yet they can differ for a variety of reasons. A property may have a higher value on the open market if it could be redeployed to a more valuable use. On the other hand, the present owner may enjoy some benefits that could not be passed on in a sale, such as planning consents that are personal to the present occupier.

The IASB has deliberately not narrowed the definition of fair value for the purpose of financial statements. It notes that it is taking part in research activities with national standard-setters on revaluations of PP&E, which is intended to promote international convergence of standards. One such area is in identifying the preferred measurement attribute for revaluations, which could lead to proposals to amend IAS 16.[104]

In the mean time, IAS 16 requires detailed disclosures regarding the methods and significant assumptions applied in estimating the items' fair values.[105] This means that the basis or bases that an entity has applied in valuing its assets will have to be disclosed in the accounts, including the extent to which it has applied either or both of the bases described above.

B   Other methods of calculating fair value: income approaches

IAS 16 allows other methods of deriving the fair value of assets in the absence of market-based evidence. If there is no market-based evidence because of the specialised nature of the asset and because it is rarely sold except as part of a continuing business, the entity is allowed to base fair value on an income or a depreciated replacement cost ('DRC') approach.[106]

The standard does not define what it means by an income approach. There are a number of techniques that may be utilised. The valuation may be based on transactions in an active market for dissimilar assets as adjusted to reflect the differences, or on transactions on less active markets if they have been adjusted to take account of subsequent changes in economic conditions. Both of these are allowed methods of calculating the fair value of investment property (see 3.3.2 below). Presumably income approaches could include use of discounted cash flow projections based on estimated future cash flows that will be generated by the asset. Care would have to be taken as the asset may not generate income by itself, being instead part of a cash generating unit (see Chapter 13); obviously, cash flows generated by other assets are not relevant to the valuation of the asset in question. Other methods that are encountered in practice include valuation methods based on factors such as notional rentals or multiples reflecting current transactions of indicators such as revenue or profits, which may be relevant for certain assets.

An entity must disclose the extent to which it has determined fair value using a valuation technique that is not based on observable process in an active market or recent market transactions.[107]

C   *Other methods of calculating fair value: depreciated replacement cost*

IAS 16 states that the alternative basis for valuing assets when they are rarely sold except as pat of a continuing business is a depreciated replacement cost ('DRC') approach.[108] The basis underlying DRC is that the asset is so specialised that there is no market value for it. There are three main subsets of such assets: (i) those that are only ever sold as part of a business; (ii) assets primarily used to provide services to the public (whether on a paying or non-paying basis); and (iii) assets that are so specialised by nature of their size or location or similar features that there is no market for them.

Examples of specialised properties include:

* oil refineries and chemical works where, usually, the buildings are no more than housings or cladding for highly specialised plant;

* power stations and dock installations where the building and site engineering works are related directly to the business of the owner, it being highly unlikely that they would have a value to anyone other than a company acquiring the undertaking;

* schools, colleges, universities and research establishments where there is no competing market demand from other organisations using these types of property in the locality;

* hospitals, other specialised health care premises and leisure centres where there is no competing market demand from other organisations wishing to use these types of property in the locality; and

* museums, libraries, and other similar premises provided by the public sector.

In addition, there may be no market-based evidence for properties of such specialised construction, arrangement, size or specification that it is unlikely that there would be a single purchaser. The same may be the case even for standard properties in geographical areas remote from main business centres (perhaps originally located there for operational or business reasons that no longer exist).

This could occur if the buildings were of such an abnormal size for the district that no market for them would exist.

DRC is considered to be the aggregate amount of the value of the land for the existing use or a notional replacement site in the same locality, and the gross replacement cost of the buildings and other site works, from which appropriate deductions may then be made to allow for the age, condition, economic or functional obsolescence and environmental factors. The objective of DRC is to make a realistic estimate of the current cost of constructing an asset that has the same service potential as the existing asset.

DRC is inevitably a rather unsatisfactory valuation basis at the theoretical level. It is represented as a valuation of property, but in circumstances where, by definition, the asset has no market value. As a consequence increases in the cost of replacing assets will be reported as gains in equity.

Moreover, a DRC valuation is often likely to give a higher valuation than one using market-based evidence. For this reason, it is necessary to ensure that the property really is so specialised that such evidence cannot be obtained. It is also necessary to be satisfied that the potential profitability of the business is adequate to support the value derived on a DRC basis, and the requirements of IAS 36 should be considered (see Chapter 13).

DRC approaches are often applied also to the valuation of plant and machinery (as distinct from property assets) where there is rarely a market from which to derive a fair value.

2.8.4 Reversals of downward valuations

IAS 16 says that revaluation gains are only taken to the income statement if they are the reversal of losses previously recognised there.[109] If the revalued asset is being depreciated, it is questionable whether the full amount of any reversal may be taken to the income statement or whether it should take account of the depreciation that would have been charged on the previously higher book value. This is required by IAS 36 when impairment losses are reversed, that standard stating:

> 'The increased carrying amount of an asset other than goodwill attributable to a reversal of an impairment loss shall not exceed the carrying amount that would have been determined for the asset in prior years'.[110]

The following example demonstrates a way in which this could be applied:

Example 12.3:   Reversal of a downward valuation

An asset has a cost of £1,000,000 and a life of 10 years. At the end of year 3, when the asset's NBV is £700,000, it is written down to £350,000. This write down below historical cost is taken through the profit and loss account.

The entity will now depreciate its asset by £50,000 per annum, so as to write off the carrying value of £350,000 over the remaining 7 years.

At the end of year 6, the asset is revalued to £500,000. The effect on the entity's fixed asset is as follows:

Fixed assets *Valuation*	£000
At the beginning of the year	350
Surplus on revaluation	150
At the end of the year	500
Depreciation at beginning of the year*	100
Charge for the year	50
Depreciation written back on revaluation	(150)
At the end of the year	–
Net book value at the end of the year	500
Net book value at the beginning of the year	250

*   Two year's depreciation (years 4 and 5) at £50,000 per annum. The asset will be written off over the remaining four years at £125,000 per annum.

The total credit is £300,000. £100,000 represents depreciation that would otherwise have been charged to the profit and loss account in years 4 and 5. This will be taken to the revaluation surplus in equity.

In the example the amount of the revaluation that is credited to the revaluation surplus in equity represents the difference between the net book value on a historical cost basis (£400,000) and on a revalued basis (£500,000).

Of course this is an extreme example. Most assets that are subject to a policy of revaluation would not show such marked changes in value and it would be expected that there would be valuation movements in the intervening years rather than dramatic losses and gains in years 3 and 6. However, we consider that in principle this is the way in which downward valuations should be effected.

There may be major practical difficulties for any entity that finds itself in the position of reversing revaluation deficits on depreciating assets, although whether in practice this eventuality often occurs is open to doubt. If it were to occur though, the business would need to continue to maintain asset registers on the original, pre-write down basis.

2.8.5 Depreciation of infrastructure assets

In some jurisdictions, infrastructure assets such as electricity distribution networks have been dealt with on a renewals accounting basis. Renewals accounting means the level of annual expenditure required to maintain the operating capacity of the infrastructure asset is treated as the depreciation charged for the period and is deducted from the carrying amount of the asset (as part of accumulated depreciation). Actual expenditure is capitalised (as part of the cost of the asset) as incurred. IAS 16 makes no mention of renewals accounting, which does not appear to be allowable under the standard.

2.8.6 Depreciation methods

There is little discussion of depreciation methods in IAS 16 which simply says that 'the depreciation method shall reflect the pattern in which the asset's future economic benefits are expected to be consumed by the entity'.[111] The standard mentions only three depreciation methods, straight line and diminishing (reducing) balance, and units of production. The straight line and reducing balance methods are well known and understood. It may be appropriate to use other methods with particular assets, and for reference purposes, some are illustrated below.

A   Double declining balance

This method is sometimes applied in the US, where it has corresponded to tax allowances on assets. The method involves determining the asset's depreciation on a straight-line basis over its useful life. This annual amount is multiplied by an appropriate factor (it does not have to be doubled) to give the first year's charge and depreciation at the same percentage rate is charged on the reducing balance in subsequent years.

Example 12.4:   Double declining balance depreciation

An asset costs €6,000 and has a life of ten years, which means that, calculated on the straight-line basis, the annual depreciation charge would be €600. On the double declining balance method (assuming a factor of two), the depreciation charge for the first year would be €1,200 and depreciation would continue to be charged at 20% on the reducing balance thereafter.

B   Sum of the digits

This is another form of the reducing balance method, but one that is based on the estimated life of the asset and which can therefore easily be applied if the asset has a residual value. If an asset has an estimated useful life of four years then the digits 1, 2, 3, and 4 are added together, giving a total of 10. Depreciation of four-tenths, three-tenths and so on, of the cost of the asset, less any residual value, will be charged in the respective years. The method is sometimes called the 'rule of 78', 78 being the sum of the digits 1 to 12.

Example 12.5:   Sum of the digits depreciation

An asset costs €10,000 and is expected to be sold for €2,000 after four years. Depreciation is to be provided over four years using the sum of the digits method.

		€
Year 1	Cost	10,000
	Depreciation at 4/10 of €8,000	3,200
	Net book value	6,800
Year 2	Depreciation at 3/10 of €8,000	2,400
	Net book value	4,400
Year 3	Depreciation at 2/10 of €8,000	1,600
	Net book value	2,800
Year 4	Depreciation at 1/10 of €8,000	800
	Net book value	2,000

C   Unit of production method

Under this method, the asset is written off in line with its estimated total output. By relating depreciation to the proportion of productive capacity utilised to date, it reflects the fact that the useful economic life of certain assets, principally machinery, is more closely linked to its usage and output than to time. This method is normally used in extractive industries, for example, to amortise the costs of development of productive oil and gas facilities.

The essence of choosing a fair depreciation method is to reflect the consumption of economic benefits provided by the asset concerned. In most cases the straight-line basis will give perfectly acceptable results, and the vast majority of entities use this method. Where there are instances, such as the extraction of a known proportion of a mineral resource, or the use of a certain amount of the total available number of working hours of a machine, it may be that a unit of production method will give fairer results.

2.8.7   Tangible or intangible assets – the issue of new technology costs

IAS 38's restrictions on capitalising certain internally-generated intangible assets has focused attention on the treatment of many internal costs. In practice, items such as computer software purchased by entities are frequently capitalised as part of a tangible asset, for example as part of an accounting or communications infrastructure. Equally, internally written software may be capitalised as part of a tangible production facility, and so on. Judgement must be exercised in deciding whether such items are to be accounted for under IAS 16 or IAS 38 – *Intangible Assets* – and this distinction becomes increasingly important if the two standards would prescribe differing treatments in any particular case. IAS 16 does not refer to this type of asset; but IAS 38 does. That standard states, in paragraph 4, that an entity needs to exercise judgment in determining whether an asset that incorporates both intangible and tangible elements should be treated under IAS 16 or as an intangible asset under IAS 38, for example:

- computer software that is embedded in computer-controlled equipment that cannot operate without that specific software is an integral part of the related hardware and is treated as property, plant and equipment;

- application software that is being used on a computer is generally easily replaced and is not an integral part of the related hardware, whereas the operating system normally is; and

- a database that is stored on a compact disc is considered to be an intangible asset because the value of the physical medium is wholly insignificant compared to that of the data collection.

It is worthwhile noting that as the 'parts approach' in IAS 16 requires an entity to account for significant parts of an asset separately, this raises 'boundary' problems between IAS 16 and IAS 38 when software and similar expenditure is involved. We believe that where IAS 16 requires an entity to identify significant parts of an asset and account for them separately, the entity needs to evaluate whether any software-type intangible part is actually integral to the larger asset or whether it is really a separate asset in its own right. The intangible part is more likely to be an asset in its own right if it was developed separately or if it can be used independently of the item of property, plant and equipment that it apparently forms part of.

3 INVESTMENT PROPERTY

3.1 Introduction

IAS 40 is a rare example of the particular commercial characteristics of an industry resulting in special treatment of a certain category of its property plant and equipment (investment properties), even though the assets themselves are not intrinsically different. The standard originally came into force for all accounting periods beginning on or after 1 January 2001. It has been revised as part of the IASB's improvements project in 2003 to expand the definition of investment property to include some interests held under operating leases. The revised standard applies to annual periods beginning on or after 1 January 2005 and earlier application is encouraged. If an entity applies the standard for a period beginning before 1 January 2005 it must disclose that fact.[112]

The standard represents a major conceptual shift, as it is the first international standard to introduce the possibility of applying a full fair value model when accounting for non-financial assets. Under this option the asset is not depreciated, and all valuation changes (i.e. fair value changes) from one period to the next are treated as gains and losses and reported in the income statement. Consequently, the fair value option of IAS 40 entails that the income statement will contain a mixture of realised gains and losses (for example rental income and maintenance costs) and unrealised ones, as the fair value gains and losses are not separately presented in a special part of the income statement. This contrasts with the revaluation approach allowed under IAS 16 (see 2.4.1 above) where increases above cost, and their reversals, are recognised as revaluation surpluses and deficits directly in equity.

IAS 40 also allows investment property to be accounted for more conventionally, by being carried at cost less depreciation, under the cost model set out in IAS 16.

The exposure draft that preceded IAS 40 allowed only a fair value approach to the treatment of investment property and the Board appears to have relaxed its proposals in allowing the alternative treatment solely for pragmatic reasons. In Appendix B, when discussing the background to the standard, it states:

> '... the Board believes that it is impracticable, at this stage, to require a fair value model for all investment property. At the same time, the Board believes that it is desirable to permit a fair value model. This evolutionary step forward will allow preparers and users to gain greater experience working with a fair value model and will allow time for certain property markets to achieve greater maturity'.[113]

The treatment under the fair value model is in stark contrast to the treatment of properties held as inventory, even though the latter are more liquid assets. However, it is argued that this is entirely reasonable and that it is more important to use fair value accounting for investment properties than for assets that will be held for a short time. This, it is proposed, is because cost-based measurements become increasingly irrelevant and the aggregation of costs incurred over a long period is of 'questionable relevance'.[114]

3.2   Definition

An investment property is defined in IAS 40 as a:

> 'property (land or a building - or part of a building - or both) held (by the owner or by the lessee under a finance lease) to earn rentals or for capital appreciation or both, rather than for:
>
> (a)   use in the production or supply of goods or services or for administrative purposes; or
>
> (b)   sale in the ordinary course of business.'[115]

3.2.1   *Property interests held under operating leases*

Until both IAS 17 and IAS 40 were amended in 2003, it was not possible for an interest in property held under an operating lease to be classified as an investment property. This was of great significance to the UK property industry, where long leasehold interests in property are common, and to other jurisdictions such as Hong Kong where there are no freehold interests. As such interests are often acquired for an up-front premium – i.e. the purchase is in many respects identical to that of a freehold interest – amortisation of the prepayment would have effectively forced the companies to depreciate assets that had not previously been depreciated.

Following the Improvements project revisions to IAS 40, investment property companies are allowed to treat interests held under operating leases as investment properties – providing that they would otherwise meet the standard's investment property definition and that the fair value model is applied. This classification alternative is available on a property-by-property basis so that the entity need not classify all property interests held under operating leases as investment properties. However, it is only available to entities that use the fair value model for all of their investment properties, whether owned, held under finance leases or under operating leases. These leasehold interests are subject to the same disclosure requirements as other investment properties (see 3.6.2 below).[116]

IAS 17 requires leases to be separated into land and building components, subject to this being possible or the land element being material (see Chapter 23). If the interest is to be an investment property carried at fair value in accordance with IAS 40, there is no requirement to separate the land and buildings elements of the lease.[117]

3.2.2 Identifying investment property

What primarily distinguishes investment property from other types of property interest is that its cash flows (from rental or sale) are largely independent of those from other assets held by the entity. By contrast, property used by an entity for administrative purposes or for the production or supply of goods or services do not generate cash flows themselves but only do so in conjunction with other assets.[118]

However, even with this distinction it is often not easy to distinguish investment property from other forms of ownership to which the standard may not be applied. The standard therefore gives guidance to help determine whether an asset is an investment property or not.

A   Leases of land

Land is an investment property if it is either held for long-term capital appreciation or for a currently undetermined future use. This is in contrast with land that is held for sale in the short term in the ordinary course of business. If the entity has not concluded that it will use the land for its own purposes as occupied property or for short-term sale in the ordinary course of business, it is deemed to be held for capital appreciation and must be classified as an investment property.[119]

B   Buildings leased to others

Buildings leased out under one or more operating leases are investment properties, whether they are owned by the reporting entity or held under finance leases. This will also apply if the building is currently vacant while tenants are being sought.[120]

Property that is leased to another entity under a finance lease is not an investment property but is accounted for under IAS 17 (see Chapter 23).[121]

C   Property held for trading or being constructed for resale

Property held for trading purposes or being constructed for resale is not investment property. This includes property held in the following circumstances:

(a)   property intended for sale in the ordinary course of business, including property in the process of construction or development. This includes property acquired exclusively for sale in the near future or for development and resale. These are accounted for as inventory under IAS 2 (see Chapter 21); and

(b)   property being built or redeveloped under a construction contract for third parties. These are covered by IAS 11 – *Construction Contracts* – which is discussed in Chapter 22.[122]

IAS 16 makes it clear that investment property in the course of construction must be accounted for under IAS 16 until it is completed (see E below).

D   Owner occupation

Owner-occupied property is property held for use in the production or supply of goods or services or for administrative purposes.[123] Owner-occupied property is specifically excluded from being treated as investment property, and is subject to the provisions of IAS 16. This includes:

(a)   property that is going to be owner-occupied in the future (whether or not it has first to be redeveloped);

(b)   property occupied by employees, whether or not they pay rent at market rates; and

(c)   owner-occupied property awaiting disposal.[124]

Note that the treatment in the consolidated accounts does not necessarily determine the treatment by individual group entities. It may be the case that a property is held by one group company for occupation by another group company. This will be owner-occupied from the perspective of the group as a whole but classified as an investment property in the accounts of the individual entity that owns it.[125] This classification in the subsidiary's financial statements will apply even if the rental is not at arm's length and the subsidiary is not in a position to benefit from capital appreciation. The IASB has concluded that it is more significant that the property itself will still generate largely independent cash flows.

E   Property in the course of construction and redevelopment

IAS 16 applies to property that is being constructed or developed for future use as investment property until construction or development is complete, at which time the property becomes investment property. This relaxation of the approach in the standard is primarily because fair values of incomplete investment properties are difficult to obtain.[126] However, it also has the effect that IAS 16's rules regarding the recognition of costs apply during the construction period (see 2.3 above).

IAS 40 does apply to existing investment property that is currently being redeveloped for continued future use as investment property.[127] While this means that entities will not have to reclassify such investment properties when they are being redeveloped, they will still have to revalue them to fair value if they are applying that model.

F   Properties with dual uses

If a property has both investment property and non-investment property uses, providing the parts of the property could be sold or leased under a finance lease separately, they should be accounted for separately. In the event that no separation is possible, only if an insignificant proportion is used for non-investment property purposes may the property be treated as an investment property.[128]

G   *Provision of services*

If the owner supplies ancillary services to the user of the investment property, the property will not qualify as an investment property unless the value of these services is an insignificant component of the arrangement as a whole.

Security and maintenance services are described by the standard as being insignificant.[129] It becomes more difficult to make the analysis when the building itself is used to generate the revenues. The crucial issue is the extent to which the owner retains significant exposure to the risks of running a business.[130]

The standard uses the example of a hotel. An owner-managed hotel, for example, would be precluded from being an investment property as the services provided to guests are a significant component of the commercial arrangements. However, many owners transfer some of the responsibilities under management contracts. These may simply comprise outsourcing the day-to-day running of the hotel or could result in the owner being, in effect, a passive investor who has transferred all responsibilities under a management contract. This situation can arise where a financial institution takes ownership of the property but does not participate at all in running the hotel, although it will probably participate in the results by receiving contingent rents that may be linked to turnover.

The standard admits that this distinction can require judgements to be made, and specifies that businesses should develop consistent criteria for use in such instances that reflect the spirit of the provisions described above. These criteria must be disclosed in cases where classification is difficult.[131]

3.2.3   *Recognition*

An investment property should be recognised as an asset when it is probable that the future economic benefits that are associated with the investment property will flow to the entity and its cost can be measured reliably.[132]

Like IAS 16, IAS 40 now has a single set of recognition criteria for any costs incurred, whether initially or subsequently. This means that all investment property costs, whether on initial recognition or thereafter (e.g. to add to or replace part of a property) must meet the recognition criteria at the point at which the expenditure is incurred if they are to be capitalised.[133]

The standard expands on this point. Day-to-day servicing, by which it means the repairs and maintenance of the property which largely comprises labour costs and minor parts, should be recognised in the income statement as incurred.[134] However, larger parts of the building may have been replaced – the standard cites interior walls that are replacements of the original walls. In this case, the cost of replacing the part will be recognised, while the carrying amount of the original part is derecognised.[135] The inference is that by restoring the asset to its originally assessed standard of performance, the new part will meet the recognition criteria and future economic benefits will flow to the entity once the old part is replaced. The inference is also that replacement is needed for the total asset to be operative. This being the case, the new walls will therefore meet the recognition criteria and the cost will therefore be capitalised.

Other than interior walls (also quoted in IAS 16 as an example of an item that might require infrequent but recurring replacement, see 2.2.2 above) parts that might have to be replaced include elements such as lifts, escalators, air conditioning equipment and the like.

Like IAS 16, IAS 40 does not explicitly require an analysis of investment properties into parts. The IAS 16 analysis is required for the purposes of recognition and derecognition of all expenditure after the asset has initially been recognised and (if the parts are significant) for depreciation of those parts (see 2.6 above). Some of this is not relevant to assets held under the fair value model that are not depreciated and the standard expects the necessary adjustments to the carrying value of the asset as a whole to be made via the revaluation mechanism (see 3.3.2 below). However, entities that adopt the cost model are obliged to account for them after initial recognition in accordance with the requirements of IAS 16. This is discussed further at 3.3.3 below.

3.2.4   Initial measurement

IAS 40 requires an investment property to be measured initially at cost including transaction costs.[136] If a property is purchased, cost means purchase price and any directly attributable expenditure such as professional fees, and property transfer taxes.[137]

Self-constructed investment property during construction is subject to IAS 16. Once it is completed it becomes investment property to which IAS 40 applies.[138] This means that only those elements of cost that are allowed by IAS 16 may be capitalised and that capitalisation ceases when the asset has reached the condition necessary for it to be capable of operating in the manner intended by management (see also 2.3.1 above).[139] Abnormal wastage of resources in constructing it is not part of the cost of an investment property. IAS 40 also specifies that start up costs (unless necessary to bring the property into working condition) and operating losses before the investment property achieves the planned occupancy level are not to be capitalised.[140] It therefore prohibits the practice of capitalising costs until a particular level of occupation or rental income is achieved; this point would be reached well past the date at which the asset would be *capable* of operating in the manner intended by management, which is the date of its physical completion. This forestalls an argument, advanced in the past, that the asset being constructed was not simply the physical structure of the building but a fully tenanted investment property, and its cost correspondingly included not simply the construction period but also the letting period.

If payment for the property is deferred, the cost to be recognised is the cash price equivalent. Any difference between the cash price and the total payment to be made is recognised as interest over the credit period.[141]

3.2.5 *Initial measurement of property held under finance or operating leases*

The same rules apply to property acquired under finance leases and to operating leases where the property interests otherwise meet the definition as investment properties.

At the commencement of the lease term, the entity recognises the property asset and related liability in its balance sheet in accordance with IAS 17, at amounts equal at the inception of the lease to the fair value of the leased item or, if lower, at the present value of the minimum lease payments (see Chapter 23).[142] If the interest is held under an operating lease, then it must be recorded at the present value of the minimum lease payments. The entity's initial direct costs are added to the asset[143] – these might include similar costs to those described in 3.2.4 above such as professional fees for legal services.

If the entity pays a premium for the lease, this is part of the minimum lease payments and is included in the cost of the asset, but, of course, it reduces the amount of the liability.[144] In practice a lessee may pay a large up-front payment to acquire its interest and there will be no liability at all to the lessor.

The standard stresses that the property interest whose fair value is to be determined is the leasehold interest and not the underlying property. Guidance on fair values of property interests, which is also relevant for fair values used for initial recognition under the cost model, is described at 3.3.2 below.[145]

3.2.6 *Initial measurement of assets acquired in exchange transactions*

IAS 40 applies the same requirements for accounting for investment properties acquired in transactions in exchange for non-monetary assets, or a combination or monetary and non-monetary assets, as does IAS 16.[146] These provisions are discussed in detail at 2.3.2 above.

3.3 Measurement after initial recognition

Once recognised, IAS 40 allows one of two methods of accounting for investment property to be chosen: the 'fair value model' or the 'cost model'. The standard does not identify a preferred alternative. As explained above, IAS 40 is the first standard in which a full fair value model has been introduced for non-monetary assets.

The entity has to choose to use one model or the other, and to use it for all its investment property (unless the entity is an insurer or similar, in which case there are exemptions that are described briefly below at 3.3.1).[147] The standard discourages changes from the fair value model to the cost model, stating that it is highly unlikely that this will result in a more appropriate presentation, which is a requirement of IAS 8 for any change in accounting policy.[148]

All entities, regardless of which measurement option is chosen, are required to determine the fair value of investment properties. Entities that apply the fair value model will use them for measurement purposes while they need to be disclosed under the cost model. Use of an independent valuer with a recognised qualification and recent experience is encouraged but not required.[149]

3.3.1 Measurement by insurers and similar entities

The only exception to the requirement that an entity adopt either the fair value or the cost model is in respect of insurance companies and similar entities. They may hold investment properties whose return is directly linked to the return paid on specific liabilities. These entities are permitted to choose either the fair value or the cost model for these properties without it affecting the choice available for other investment properties that they hold. All properties within a fund must be held on the same basis and transfers between funds are to be made at fair value.[150]

3.3.2 The fair value model

Under this model all investment property is included in the balance sheet at its fair value at the balance sheet date, and all changes in the fair value from one balance sheet to the next are included in the profit and loss account for the period.[151] The entity must use the fair value model if it wishes to classify interests held under operating leases as investment properties.[152]

The standard defines fair value as 'the amount for which an asset could be exchanged between knowledgeable, willing parties in an arm's length transaction'.[153] Fair value specifically excludes an estimated price inflated or deflated by special terms or circumstances such as atypical financing, sale and leaseback arrangements or special considerations or concessions granted by anyone associated with the sale.[154] Transaction costs are not deducted.[155]

Paragraphs 38 to 52 contain a substantial amount of guidance on the methodology of revaluations in practice, necessitated by the number of jurisdictions to which the standard may apply. Fair value reflects market conditions as at the balance sheet date and is a valuation as at a specific moment in time. It assumes simultaneous exchange and completion, to avoid the variations in price that might otherwise take place.[156] The fair value of the property reflects rental income from tenants and, if appropriate, outflows such as rental payments. It is further assumed that the valuation is based on assumptions that would be considered to be reasonable and supportable by willing and knowledgeable parties.[157] The buyer and seller must be 'knowledgeable', which means that they are reasonably informed about the property and the market at the date of the transaction. Neither is under any compulsion to buy or sell; the buyer will not pay more than a knowledgeable, willing buyer and the seller is not a forced seller.[158] The transaction is presumed to be at arm's length between unrelated parties.[159]

The standard states that the best evidence of fair value will be given by actual transactions in similar property in a similar location and condition.[160] However, it allows the fair value to be estimated by using other information when market values are not available. This means that gains and losses may be recorded in the income statement where there is no market value for the property and its fair value has been constructed from a variety of other sources.

The other information that an entity may draw on includes:

(a)   transactions in an active market for dissimilar property (e.g. property of a different nature, condition or location, or subject to a different type of lease), as adjusted to reflect the differences;

(b)   transactions on less active markets if they have been adjusted to take account of subsequent changes in economic conditions; or

(c)   discounted cash flow projections based on estimated future cash flows (as long as these are reliable). These should be supported by existing leases and current market rents for similar properties in the same location and condition. The discount rate should reflect current market assessments of the uncertainty and timing of the cash flows.[161]

The technique suggested in (c) above is not dissimilar to a valuation using property yields (a basis on which properties are bought and sold) except that yields already assume rental growth that would have to be separately factored into a discounted cash flow calculation. Future capital expenditure that will enhance the benefits may not be taken into account in determining the fair value, nor may the income that will arise from the expenditure.[162]

The standard notes that the fair value of a leased asset at acquisition is zero. This, of course, means as at the commencement of the lease as defined by IAS 17, which is before any lease payments are due or any other accounting entries are required to be made (see Chapter 23). This applies regardless of whether the asset is brought in at fair value (as is usually the case with a finance lease) or at the present value of the minimum lease payments (for an interest under an operating lease). Remeasuring an interest in a lease to fair value will not give rise to a gain or loss unless the fair value model is applied at some time after initial measurement.[163]

As these various bases may result in a range of valuations, the entity must consider the underlying reasons for the variation in order to arrive at the most reliable estimate, within a range of 'reasonable' estimates of fair value.[164] The fair value will not be reliably determinable on a continuing basis if the range is too wide and the probabilities of various outcomes too difficult to assess.[165]

Fair value is based on a hypothetical transaction. It is not the same as value in use as defined in IAS 36. In particular, it does not take account of additional value derived from holding a portfolio of assets, synergies between the investment properties and other assets or legal rights or tax benefits or burdens pertaining to the current owner.[166] Fair value is also not the same as net realisable value. It is a valuation as a specific point in time rather than at a time at which the entity may realistically have expected to sell the property. It assumes circumstances that rarely apply in practice such as simultaneous exchange (i.e. contractual commitment) and completion.[167]

An entity must also take care not to double count assets and liabilities and the standard describes a number of specific situations where this might otherwise happen.

A   Assets and liabilities subsumed within fair value

Fixtures and fittings such as lifts or air conditioning units are usually reflected within the fair value of the investment property rather than being accounted for separately.[168] In other cases, additional assets may be necessary in order that the property can be used for its specific purposes. The standard refers to furniture within a property that is being let as furnished offices, and argues that this should not be recognised as a separate asset if it has been included in the fair value of the investment property.[169]

The entity may have other assets that have not been included within the valuation, in which case these will be separately recognised and accounted for in accordance with IAS 16.

B   Prepaid or accrued operating lease income

Prepaid or accrued operating lease income should be treated as separate assets and liabilities and not subsumed within the fair value of the asset.[170]

This applies to straightforward differences between the recognition of income and the receipt of cash and to lease incentives. For example, when an entity offers an initial rent-free period to the lessee, it will recognise an asset and amortise it over the lease term, thereby spreading the reduction in rental income over the duration of the lease. In this case revenue will be recognised in advance of lease income cash receipts. This is the treatment required by SIC-15 – *Operating Leases – Incentives* – that is described in Chapter 23. The fair value of the property excludes factors that are specific to the entity, such as this particular incentive, but will reflect market conditions at the balance sheet date, which will include assumptions regarding rental income and the general level of incentives being granted for such properties.

C   The fair value of properties held under a lease

The standard points out that the fair value of a lease interest takes account of all rental payments, including contingent rents, that an entity is expected to make. If the entity obtains a property valuation on a net basis, the recognised lease liability is to be added back to arrive at the fair value of the investment property for the purposes of the financial statements.

3.3.3   Inability to determine fair value

It is a rebuttable presumption that an entity can determine the fair value of a property reliably on a continuing basis, that is, on each subsequent occasion in which it records the investment property in its financial statements. The standard stresses that it is only in exceptional cases that the entity will be able to conclude, when it first recognises a particular investment property, that it will not be able to determine its fair value in the future. Additionally, entities are strongly discouraged from arguing that there is no fair value. It would only be an acceptable argument if there were infrequent market transactions and either that the entity was unable to construct a fair value using the alternative measures allowed by the standard or that the range of fair value estimates was too great to establish a reliable value. In such cases, the property should be treated under the cost model of IAS 16 and assumed to have a nil residual value.[171] This means that it has to be carried at cost and the building and its component parts depreciated over their useful lives. In these circumstances IAS 16's revaluation model under which assets may be revalued to fair value, is specifically ruled out. If this situation occurs, the cost model of IAS 16 should continue to be applied until disposal. Even if an entity is 'compelled' to carry an individual property at cost, all other investment property must be carried at fair value.[172]

In addition, once a property is initially recognised at its fair value, it must always be so recognised until disposed of or reclassified for owner-occupation or development, even if comparable market transactions become less frequent or market prices become less easily available.[173] This is to prevent a switch to the cost model if there is a property price collapse when there would be few transactions and the fair value could become uncomfortably low.

3.3.4   *The cost model*

The cost model requires that all investment property be measured after initial recognition under the cost model treatment of IAS 16, as explained above at 2.2. This means that the asset must be recognised at cost and depreciated systematically over its useful life.[174] The property has to be analysed into appropriate significant parts, each of which will have to be depreciated separately, as described in 2.4.2 above. The entity will recognise other parts and derecognise the replaced part as described in 2.2.2A and 2.6 above. The revaluation model of IAS 16 is not available.

If an entity adopts the cost model the fair value of its investment properties has to be disclosed (see 3.6.5 below). Entities may have limited internal resources and need to obtain professional assistance in order to meet the disclosure requirement. In the past, such entities may have chosen the cost model in part to avoid the cost of an annual valuation. This benefit of using the cost model may no longer be so evident. Investment properties that meet the criteria to be classified as held for sale, or that are included within a disposal group classified as held for sale, are measured in accordance with IFRS 5.[175] This means that it will be held at the lower of carrying amount and fair value less costs to sell and so depreciation of the asset will cease: see Chapter 3 and also 2.6.1 above.

3.4   Transfer of assets into or from investment property

The standard specifies the circumstances in which a property becomes, or ceases to be, an investment property. There must be a change in use, evidenced by:

(a)   the commencement or end of owner-occupation;

(b)   the commencement of development with a view to sale, at which point an investment property would be transferred to inventories. The standard allows a transfer to inventory only when there is a change of use evidenced by the start of a development with a view to subsequent sale;

(c)   entering into an operating lease to another party; or

(d)   the end of construction or development, when a property in the course of construction or development is transferred to investment property.[176] IAS 16 covers properties in the course of construction.

However, some changes in status do not result in transfers:

(a)   If an entity decides to dispose of an investment property, rather than develop it, it may not be transferred to inventory but remains as an investment property until disposal.

(b)   An existing investment property that is being redeveloped for continued future use as an investment property by the entity also must remain classified as an investment property.[177]

The transfers to and from the status of investment property are accounted for as follows:

- *Transfers to inventory or owner occupation*: the cost for subsequent accounting under IAS 16 or IAS 2 should be its fair value at the date the use changed;[178]

- *Transfers from owner occupation*: IAS 16 will be applied up to time the use changed. At that date any difference between the IAS 16 carrying amount and the fair value is to be treated in the same way as a revaluation under IAS 16.[179]

Up until the time that an owner occupied property becomes an investment property carried at fair value, depreciation under IAS 16 continues and any impairment losses up to that date of change of use must be recognised in accordance with IAS 36. The differences between the carrying value under IAS 16 and the fair value is accounted for in the same way as a revaluation under IAS 16. If the owner occupied property had not previously been revalued, the transfer does not imply that the entity has now chosen a policy of revaluation for other property in the same class. The treatment depends on whether it is a decrease or increase in value and whether the asset had previously been revalued or impaired in value (as described above at 2.4.1);[180]

- *Transfers from inventory*: the difference between the inventory carrying amount and the fair value at the date of change of use is to be recognised in the profit and loss account for the period. The standard points out that the treatment of transfers is consistent with the treatment of sales of inventories[181]

- *Transfers from self constructed property*: the difference between the previous carrying amount and the fair value at the date of change of use must be recognised in the profit and loss account for the period[182]

When the business uses the cost model for investment property, transfers between investment property, inventory and owner occupation do not change the carrying amount of the property transferred.[183]

3.4.1 *Transfers of investment property held under operating leases*

An entity applying the fair value model may have classified interests held under operating leases as investment properties as if they were held under finance leases. In these circumstances, neither IAS 17 nor IAS 40 requires the entity to separate the land value from the value of the buildings. IAS 17 allows this treatment to continue if the property interest ceases to be classified as an investment property to the lessee and gives two examples:

(a)   the lessee occupies the property, in which case it is transferred to owner-occupied property at fair value at the date of change of use; or

(b)   the lessee grants a sublease over substantially all of its property interest to an unrelated third party. It will treat the sublease as a finance lease to the third party even though the interest may well be accounted for as an operating lease by that party.[184]

Therefore, on transfer the treatment of interests held under operating leases mirrors that of other ownership interests.

3.5   Disposal of investment property

IAS 40 requires that an investment property should be removed from the balance sheet ('derecognised') under the following circumstances:

* when it is sold;

* when it becomes the subject of a finance lease (the owner becoming the lessor);

* when it becomes the subject of a sale and leaseback deal (the original owner becoming the lessee); or

* when it is withdrawn from use and no further economic benefits are expected to arise.[185]

These derecognition rules also apply to a part of the investment property that has been replaced, which is discussed below.

IAS 18 – *Revenue* – applies on a sale.[186] IAS 18 allows that while revenue would normally be recognised when legal title passes, in some jurisdictions the risks and rewards of ownership may pass to the buyer before legal title is passed. In such cases, provided that the seller has no further substantial acts to complete under the contract, it may be appropriate to recognise revenue. An example in IAS 18 of a 'substantial act' is the completion of construction.[187] Another common example of a substantial act that to be completed before recognition of a sale would be if shareholder approval were required.

IAS 17 applies on disposal by a finance lease or by sale and leaseback.[188]

Gains and losses are calculated based on the difference between the net disposal proceeds and the carrying amount of the asset. This is recognised in the income statement unless it is a sale and leaseback and IAS 17 requires a different treatment.[189] IAS 17 only allows the immediate recognition of profits and losses on a sale and operating leaseback if the transaction is established at fair value; no gains would be recognised if the transaction resulted in a finance leaseback. Refer to Chapter 23 for a discussion of sale and leaseback under IAS 17.

The proceeds of sale are recognised at their fair value. If the sale proceeds are deferred, (deferral is not defined but it must mean beyond normal credit terms) the consideration recognised on the disposal will be the cash price equivalent. Any difference between the total payments received and the cash equivalent will be treated as interest receivable under IAS 18 and accounted for on a time-proportionate basis that also takes account of the effective yield on the outstanding amount.[190]

If an entity retains any liabilities after disposing of an investment property these are measured and accounted for in accordance with IAS 37 or another relevant standard.[191]

3.5.1 Disposal of replaced parts

When an entity that applies the fair value model capitalises a replacement part, the question arises of how to deal with the original part. The basic principle in IAS 40 is that the entity derecognises the carrying value of the replaced part. However the problem arises that even if the cost of the part may be known, its carrying value – at fair value – is usually by no means clear. It is also possible that the fair value may already reflect the loss in value of the part to be replaced, because the valuation reflected the fact that an acquirer would reduce the price accordingly.

As all fair value changes are taken to the income statement, the standard concludes that it is not necessary to identify separately the elements that relate to replacements from other fair value movements. Therefore, if it is not practical to identify the amount by which fair value should be reduced for the part replaced, the cost of the replacement is added to the carrying amount of the asset and the fair value of the investment property as a whole is reassessed. The standard notes that this is the treatment that would be applied to additions that did not involve replacing any existing part of the property.

If the investment property is carried under the cost model, then the entity should derecognise the carrying amount of the original part. A replaced part may not have been depreciated separately, in which case the standard allows the entity to use the cost of the replacement as an indication of an appropriate carrying value.[192] This does not mean that the entity has to apply depreciated replacement cost, rather that it can use the cost of the replacement to reconstruct a suitable net present value for the original part. This is described in 2.8.1 and Example 12.2 above.

3.5.2 Compensation from third parties

IAS 40 applies the same rules as IAS 16 to the treatment of compensation from third parties if property has been impaired, lost or given up. It stresses that each element is a separate event that has to be accounted for separately.

Impairment of investment property will be automatically recorded if the fair value model is used but if the property is accounted for using the cost model then it is to be calculated in accordance with IAS 36. If the entity no longer owns the asset, e.g. because it has been destroyed or subject to a compulsory purchase order, it will be derecognised as described in 3.5 above. Compensation (e.g. from an insurance company) is recognised in income when it is receivable. The cost of any replacement asset is accounted for wholly on its own merits according to the recognition rules covered in 3.2.3 above.[193]

3.6 The disclosure requirements of IAS 40

3.6.1 Introduction

As discussed earlier in the chapter, IAS 40 heralds a major practical step towards what we consider to be the long-term aim of the IASB, namely full fair value based financial statements. If revaluation of investment property under IAS 40 is adopted, all revaluation changes go through the income statement (i.e. the profit and loss account). Thus businesses with investment property reporting under IFRS will show profits that include realised and unrealised profits, trading transactions and revaluations.

For businesses that adopt the revaluation option in IAS 40, it will be a major change in the way such items are reported. It will focus attention on the judgmental and subjective aspects of property revaluations, because they will be reported in the income statement rather than directly to equity. If a counter-intuitive failure were to occur (for instance a company that had reported large profits soon afterwards ran out of cash) this type of income statement easily could be discredited. Possibly as a consequence of these considerations, the disclosures under IAS 40 require significant amounts of information to be disclosed about the judgements involved and the cash-related performance of the investment property, as set out below.

3.6.2 Disclosures under both fair value and cost models

Whatever model is chosen, fair value or cost, IAS 40 requires all companies to disclose the fair value of their investment property. Therefore the following disclosures are required in both instances:

(a) whether it applies the cost model or the fair value model;

(b) if it applies the fair value model, whether, and in what circumstances, property interests held under operating leases are classified and accounted for as investment property.

(c) when classification is difficult (see paragraph 14), the criteria it uses to distinguish investment property from owner occupied property and from property held for sale in the ordinary course of business.

(d) the methods and significant assumptions applied in determining the fair value of investment property, including a statement whether the determination of fair value was supported by market evidence or was more heavily based on other factors (which the entity shall disclose) because of the nature of the property and lack of comparable market data.

(e)   the extent to which the fair value of investment property (as measured or disclosed in the financial statements) is based on a valuation by an independent valuer who holds a recognised and relevant professional qualification and has recent experience in the location and category of the investment property being valued. If there has been no such valuation, that fact shall be disclosed.

(f)   the amounts recognised in profit or loss for:

    (i)   rental income from investment property;

    (ii)   direct operating expenses (including repairs and maintenance) arising from investment property that generated rental income during the period; and

    (iii)   direct operating expenses (including repairs and maintenance) arising from investment property that did not generate rental income during the period.

    (iv)   the cumulative change in fair value recognised in profit or loss on sale of an investment property from a pool of assets in which the cost model is used into a pool in which the fair value model is used (see 3.4 above).

(g)   the existence and amounts of restrictions on the realisability of investment property or the remittance of income and proceeds of disposal.

(h)   contractual obligations to purchase, construct or develop investment property or for repairs, maintenance or enhancements.[194]

Hongkong Land Holdings Ltd discloses in its accounting policy the basis on which property interests held under operating leases are classified and accounted for as investment property.

Extract 12.5: Hongkong Land Holdings Ltd (2003)

Principal Accounting Policies [extract]

d.   Properties

i)   Investment properties

Investment properties are properties held for long-term rental yields. Investment properties are carried in the balance sheet at fair value, representing open market value determined annually by independent valuers. Changes in fair values are recorded in the consolidated profit and loss account. In accordance with IAS 40 (revised 2003), leasehold properties held for long-term rental yields are classified as investment properties and carried at fair value. This is a change in accounting policy as in previous years these properties were carried at depreciated cost. The comparative figures for 2002 have been restated to reflect the change in policy. The effect of the change has been to decrease profit attributable to shareholders for the year ended 31st December 2002 and 2003 by US$739.8 million and US$671.3 million respectively, and to increase shareholders' funds at 1st January 2002 and 2003 by US$4,789.1 million and US$4,050.2 million respectively.

3.6.3 Additional disclosures for the fair value model

A reconciliation of the carrying amounts of investment property at the start and finish of the period must be given showing the following:

(a) additions, disclosing separately those additions resulting from acquisitions and those resulting from subsequent expenditure recognised in the carrying amount of an asset;

(b) additions resulting from acquisitions through business combinations;

(c) disposals;

(d) net gains or losses from fair value adjustments;

(e) the net exchange differences arising on the translation of the financial statements into a different presentation currency, and on translation of a foreign operation into the presentation currency of the reporting entity;

(f) transfers to and from inventories and owner-occupied property; and

(g) other changes.[195]

When a valuation obtained for investment property is adjusted significantly for the purpose of the financial statements, for example to avoid double-counting of assets or liabilities that are recognised as separate assets and liabilities as described in paragraph 50 (see 3.3.2 above), the entity shall disclose a reconciliation between the valuation obtained and the adjusted valuation included in the financial statements, showing separately the aggregate amount of any recognised lease obligations that have been added back, and any other significant adjustments.[196]

Hongkong Land Holdings Ltd describes the basis of valuation of its investment properties as follows:

Extract 12.6: Hongkong Land Holdings Ltd (2003)

Notes to the Financial Statements [extract]

8   Tangible assets [extract]

The Group's investment properties were revalued at 31st December 2003 by Jones Lang LaSalle Ltd on an open market value basis calculated on the net income allowing for reversionary potential on a current use basis and as a result, a deficit of US$824.3 million (2002: US$987.7 million) has been charged to the consolidated profit and loss account.

All the Group's investment properties are held under leases with unexpired lease term of more than 20 years except for The Hong Kong Club Building, which is held under a sub-lease. Details concerning all of the Group's investment properties are set out on page 51.

It discloses its net gains or losses from fair value adjustments on the face of the income statement as follows.

Extract 12.7: Hongkong Land Holdings Ltd (2003)

Consolidated Profit and Loss Account [extract]

For the year ended 31st December 2003

	Note	2003 US$m	Restated 2002 US$m
Revenue	1	**383.7**	396.6
Cost of sales		**(100.5)**	(84.2)
Gross profit		**283.2**	312.4
Other income		**0.3**	0.5
Administrative and other expenses		**(27.9)**	(29.6)
		255.6	283.3
Decrease in fair value of investment properties		**(824.3)**	(987.7)
Asset impairments and disposals	2	**10.2**	(25.3)
Operating loss	3	**(558.5)**	(729.7)
Net financing charges	4	**(64.5)**	(64.8)
Share of results of joint ventures	5	**(5.3)**	(4.1)
Loss before tax		**(628.3)**	(798.6)
Tax	6	**60.0**	119.6
Loss for the year		**(568.3)**	(679.0)

3.6.4   *Extra disclosures where fair value cannot be reliably determined*

If fair value cannot be reliably measured and the asset is accounted for under the provisions of the cost model of IAS 16, the reconciliations described under 3.6.3 above should separately disclose the amounts for such investment property. In addition to this the following should be disclosed:

(a)   a description of the investment property;

(b)   an explanation of why fair value cannot be determined reliably;

(c)   if possible, the range of estimates within which fair value is highly likely to lie; and

(d)   on disposal of investment property not carried at fair value:

(i)   the fact that the entity has disposed of investment property not carried at fair value;

(ii)   the carrying amount of that investment property at the time of sale; and

(iii) the amount of gain or loss recognised.[197]

3.6.5 Additional disclosures for the cost model

In the event that investment property is carried at cost less depreciation, the following disclosures are required by IAS 40:

(a)   the depreciation methods used;

(b)   the useful lives or the depreciation rates used;

(c)   the gross carrying amount and the accumulated depreciation (aggregated with accumulated impairment losses) at the beginning and end of the period;

(d)   a reconciliation of the carrying amount of investment property at the beginning and end of the period, showing the following:

      (i)   additions, disclosing separately those additions resulting from acquisitions and those resulting from subsequent expenditure recognised as an asset;

      (ii)   additions resulting from acquisitions through business combinations;

      (iii)   disposals;

      (iv)   depreciation;

      (v)   the amount of impairment losses recognised, and the amount of impairment losses reversed, during the period in accordance with IAS 36;

      (vi)   the net exchange differences arising on the translation of the financial statements into a different presentation currency, and on translation of a foreign operation into the presentation currency of the reporting entity;

      (vii)   transfers to and from inventories and owner-occupied property; and

      (viii)   other changes; and

(e)   the fair value of investment property.

      In the exceptional cases when an entity cannot determine the fair value of the investment property reliably (see 3.3.3 above), it shall disclose:

      (i)   a description of the investment property;

      (ii)   an explanation of why fair value cannot be determined reliably; and

      (iii)   if possible, the range of estimates within which fair value is highly likely to lie.[198]

4   TRANSITIONAL PROVISIONS AND FIRST-TIME ADOPTION OF IAS 16 AND IAS 40

4.1   First-time adoption of IAS 16 and IAS 40

For first time adopters of IFRS, the main difficulty with the general approach of IFRS 1 – *First-time Adoption of International Financial Reporting Standards* – is that it requires full retrospective application of IAS 16. This means one of the two bases permitted by the standard, cost or fair value, in each case as adjusted for depreciation and impairment, as appropriate, which will involve identification of the significant parts of assets. This would be extremely difficult to achieve in many cases, as the original cost of many long-lived items of PP&E might be very costly, if not impossible to determine. Therefore the IASB decided to permit the use of 'deemed cost' in place of actual cost in the opening IFRS balance sheet. Under IFRS 1, deemed cost can be:

(1)   the fair value of the item at the date of transition to IFRS;[199]

(2)   a revaluation under its previous GAAP at or before the date of transition to IFRS, if the revaluation was at the date of the revaluation broadly comparable to:[200]

    '(a)   fair value; or

    (b)   cost or depreciated cost under IFRS, adjusted to reflect, for example, changes in a general or specific price index'; or

(3)   the deemed cost under its previous GAAP that was established by measuring items at their fair value at one particular date because of an event such as a privatisation or initial public offering.[201]

In addition, if the asset was acquired as part of a business combination, deemed cost can be the carrying amount under the previous GAAP immediately after acquisition, or, if the item was not recognised under a previous GAAP, the carrying amount on the basis that IFRS would require in the separate balance sheet of the acquiree.

Note that these alternatives are freely available to the entity, although obviously it will need to take its future IFRS accounting policy into account. This means that an entity that has previously carried its properties at fair value may use that fair value as deemed cost as at the date of transition to IFRS and thereafter apply the cost model.

This alternative is also available for investment properties, which could enable an entity to change from a valuation model under its previous GAAP to the cost model under IAS 40. This might be an attractive option for entities with only a few properties that meet the IAS 40 definition, especially if the residual values of its properties were so high that there was little depreciable amount. By adopting a new policy under IFRS, the entity would be exposed in the short term to a small amount of depreciation rather than the risk of taking valuation changes to the income statement.

In addition, an entity is permitted to bring forward assets on different bases, so, for example, it could bring into its IFRS accounts some assets of the same class at cost and others at a deemed cost based on a valuation under previous GAAP undertaken several years before.

Entities will have to ensure that they have adequately identified the significant parts of the asset at transition and that they have been depreciated on an appropriate basis. The same rules regarding deemed cost are available to significant parts.

These provisions are a sensible compromise by the IASB and will enable many of the initial difficulties in the area of PP&E on adoption of IFRS by EU listed companies in 2005 to be overcome. A full explanation of the provisions of IFRS 1 for first time application of IAS 16 and IAS 40 is set out in Chapter 4 at 2.5.

4.2 First-time adoption of IFRIC 1

A first-time adopter is not required to restate the carrying amount included in an asset in respect of decommissioning that occurred before the date of transition to IFRSs, e.g. those changes in respect of estimated cash outflows, discount rate and unwinding discount that are described in 2.3.1A above. Instead, the exemption allows the entity to estimate the liability by calculating it at the transition date in accordance with IAS 37 and adjusting this amount by discounting it at its best estimate of the historical risk-adjusted discount rate(s) that would have applied over the intervening period. Accumulated depreciation as at the transition date is then based on the current estimate of the useful life of the asset, using the depreciation policy adopted by the entity under IFRSs.[202]

4.3 The transitional provisions of IAS 40

The only transitional provision in IAS 40 is in relation to property interests held under operating leases that may, for the first time, be classified as investment properties. The entity should adjust the opening balance of retained earnings for the period in which the standard is first adopted.[203] This will include the transfer of any amount held in revaluation surplus for investment property to retained profits.[204] The transitional arrangements for the fair value model differ from the treatment required under IAS 8.[205]

If, however, the business has previously published fair value information about its property interests held under operating leases, and the fair value has been calculated in accordance with the standard's definition and guidance, it is encouraged but not required to adjust any comparative figures for earlier periods.[206] Presumably this is on the basis that the information is available, so it would enhance the financial statements to use it throughout. If the entity has not previously disclosed such information about the fair value of its investment property, comparative information should not be restated and that fact disclosed.[207]

If an entity chooses to adopt the cost model for its investment properties it may have to reclassify any existing revaluation surplus. IAS 8 would apply and the reclassification be effected by way of a prior year adjustment.[208]

The standard's modified requirements regarding investment properties acquired in an exchange transaction may only be applied prospectively to future transactions, i.e. there is no adjustment to the carrying value of assets that the entity has already acquired by way of asset exchange.[209]

5 CONCLUSION

The current state of accounting for PP&E under IFRS combines a spectrum of treatments from the cost model of IAS 16, through that standard's revaluation model, to a quite radical new approach to the income statement exemplified by the fair value model of IAS 40. In principle, accounting for PP&E is straightforward, the essential purpose is to allocate expenditure which provides enduring benefits against the revenues of the periods that use those benefits. This objective is increasingly difficult to achieve for a number of reasons.

First the meaning of 'PP&E' is deeply rooted in the manufacturing tradition and the conventional model still works well for machinery assets that wear out reasonably predictably. However the position is complicated by two factors: the first is the appearance of new types of asset, such as customer lists, brands, websites, and their generally ephemeral nature. The second has been a complicating factor for decades – the way to account for revaluations of assets.

Revaluations pose a number of accounting questions; for example, how to treat the revaluation surplus, whether depreciation is necessary if assets are carried at a valuation and more fundamentally, what a balance sheet is meant to be. The surreptitious 'stretching' by the IASB of the meaning of fair value from a market price-based concept to include a mark-to-model valuation (if a market price is not available) will only add further complexity. Although, at the conceptual level let alone practically, these problems remain unsolved, it is almost certain that fair value based accounting, with all valuation changes going through a single income statement, is the ultimate aim of the IASB.

If IAS 40 is the harbinger of a wholesale shift to fair values in the balance sheet, and of an undifferentiated income statement in which realised profits and unrealised gains are not distinguished, it is inevitable that the volatility of asset values will vastly increase. To avoid the possibility of financial reporting being discredited during the periodically inevitable times of low asset valuations, users will have to be educated about both what mark-to-model asset valuations really are, and about the cash implications of a fair value based 'profit'.

References

1 IAS 16, *Property Plant and Equipment*, IASB, December 2003 (amended March 2004), paras. 2-3.
2 IAS 16, para. 5.
3 IAS 16, para. 4.
4 IAS 16, para. 6.
5 IAS 16, para. 7.
6 IAS 16, para. 8.
7 IAS 16, para. 9.
8 IAS 16, para. 11.
9 IAS 16, para. 11.
10 IAS 16, para. 10.
11 IAS 16, para. 12.
12 IAS 16, para. 13.

13 IAS 37, *Provisions, Contingent Liabilities and Contingent Assets*, IASB, September 1998 (amended March 2004), Appendix C, Examples 11A and 11B.

14 IAS 16, para. 14.

15 IAS 16, para. 15.

16 IAS 16, para. 16.

17 IAS 16, para. 18.

18 IAS 16, para. 18.

19 IAS 16, para. 17.

20 IAS 16, para. 22.

21 IAS 16, para. 17.

22 IAS 16, para. 19.

23 IAS 16, para. 20.

24 IAS 16, para. 21.

25 IAS 16, para. 22.

26 IAS 16, para. 23.

27 IFRIC 1, *Changes in Existing Decommissioning, Restoration and Similar Liabilities*, IFRIC, May 2004, para. 2.

28 IFRIC 1, para. 3.

29 IFRIC 1, para. 5.

30 IFRIC 1, para. 6.

31 IFRIC 1, para. 7.

32 IFRIC 1, para. 7.

33 IFRIC 1, para. 6.

34 IFRIC 1, para. 8.

35 IFRIC 1, para. 9.

36 IFRIC 1, para. 10.

37 IAS 16, para. 24.

38 IAS 16, para. 24.

39 IAS 16, para. 24.

40 IAS 16, para. BC21.

41 IAS 16, para. 25.

42 IAS 16, para. 25.

43 IAS 16, para. BC19.

44 IAS 16, para. 26.

45 IAS 16, para. 68.

46 IAS 16, para. 27.

47 IAS 16, para. 28.

48 IAS 16, para. 29.

49 IAS 16, para. 30.

50 IAS 16, para. 31.

51 IAS 16, para. 32.

52 IAS 16, para. 33.

53 IAS 16, para. 31.

54 IAS 16, para. 34.

55 IAS 16, para. 37.

56 IAS 16, para. 38.

57 IAS 16, paras. 39-40.

58 IAS 36, *Impairment of assets*, IASB, March 2004, para. 61.

59 IAS 16, para. 41.

60 IAS 8, *Accounting Policies, Changes in Accounting Estimates and Errors*, IASB, December 2003 (amended March 2004), para. 17.

61 IAS 16, para. 43.

62 IAS 16, para. 44.

63 IAS 16, para. 45.

64 IAS 16, para. 46.

65 IAS 16, para. 47.

66 IAS 16, paras. 48-49.

67 IAS 16, para. 51.

68 IAS 16, paras. 53-54.

69 IAS 16, para. 51.

70 IAS 16, para. 50.

71 IAS 16, para. 52.

72 IAS 16, para. 54.

73 IAS 16, para. 52.

74 IAS 16, para. 56.

75 IAS 16, para. 57.

76 IAS 16, para. 58.

77 IAS 36, para. 12(f).

78 IAS 36, para. 12(f).

79 IAS 16, para. 55.

80 IFRIC 1, para. 7.

81 IAS 16, paras. 60-62.

82 IAS 16, para. 63.

83 IAS 16, paras. 65-66.

84 IAS 16, para. 67.

85 IAS 16, para. 69.

86 IAS 16, para. 68.

87 IAS 16, para. 71.

88 IAS 16, para. 41.

89 IAS 16, para. 70.

90 IAS 16, para. 72.

91 IFRS 5, *Non-current Assets Held for Sale and Discontinued Operations*, IASB, March 2004, para. 6.

92 IFRS 5, para. 7.

93 IFRS 5, para. 8.

94 IAS 1, *Presentation of Financial Statements*, IASB, December 2003 (amended March 2004), para. 36.

95 IAS 16, para. 74.

96 IAS 16, para. 76.

97 IAS 16, para. 77.

98 IAS 16, para. 79.

99 IAS 16, para. BC5.

100 IAS 16, paras. 43-44.

101 IAS 16, para. 46.

102 IAS 16, para. 70.

103 IAS 16, para. 32.

104 IAS 16, para. BC25.

105 IAS 16, para. 77(c).

106 IAS 16, para. 33.

107 IAS 16, para. 77(d).

108 IAS 16, para. 33.

109 IAS 16, para. 39.

110 IAS 36, para. 117.

111 IAS 16, para. 60.

112 IAS 40, *Investment Property*, IASB, December 2003 (amended March 2004), para. 85.

113 IAS 40, para. B4.

114 IAS 40, para. B33.

115 IAS 40, para. 5.

116 IAS 40, para. 6.
117 IAS 17, *Leases*, IASB, December 2003 (amended March 2004), para. 18
118 IAS 40, para. 7.
119 IAS 40, para. 8.
120 IAS 40, para. 8.
121 IAS 40, para. 9.
122 IAS 40, para. 9
123 IAS 40, para. 5
124 IAS 40, para. 9.
125 IAS 40, para. 15.
126 IAS 40, paras. B16-B18.
127 IAS 40, para. 9.
128 IAS 40, para. 10.
129 IAS 40, para. 11.
130 IAS 40, paras. 12-13.
131 IAS 40, para. 14.
132 IAS 40, para. 16.
133 IAS 40, para. 17.
134 IAS 40, para. 18.
135 IAS 40, para. 19.
136 IAS 40, para. 20.
137 IAS 40, para. 21.
138 IAS 40, para. 22.
139 IAS 16, para. 16(b).
140 IAS 40, para. 23.
141 IAS 40, para. 24.
142 IAS 40, para. 25.
143 IAS 17, para. 20.
144 IAS 40, para. 26.
145 IAS 40, para. 26.
146 IAS 40, para. 29.
147 IAS 40, para. 30.
148 IAS 40, para. 31.
149 IAS 40, para. 32.
150 IAS 40, paras. 32A-32C.
151 IAS 40, paras. 33-35.
152 IAS 40, para. 34.
153 IAS 40, para. 5.
154 IAS 40, para. 36.
155 IAS 40, para. 37.
156 IAS 40, paras. 38-39.
157 IAS 40, para. 40.
158 IAS 40, paras. 42-43.
159 IAS 40, para. 44.
160 IAS 40, para. 45.
161 IAS 40, para. 46.
162 IAS 40, para. 51.
163 IAS 40, para. 41.
164 IAS 40, para. 47.
165 IAS 40, para. 48.
166 IAS 40, para. 49.
167 IAS 40, para. 39.
168 IAS 40, para. 50.
169 IAS 40, para. 50.
170 IAS 40, para. 50.
171 IAS 40, para. 53.
172 IAS 40, para. 54.
173 IAS 40, para. 55.
174 IAS 40, para. 56.
175 IAS 40, para. 56.
176 IAS 40, para. 57.
177 IAS 40, para. 58.
178 IAS 40, para. 60.
179 IAS 40, para. 61.
180 IAS 40, para. 62.
181 IAS 40, paras. 63-64.
182 IAS 40, para. 65.
183 IAS 40, para. 59.
184 IAS 17, para. 19
185 IAS 40, paras. 66-67.
186 IAS 40, para. 67.
187 IAS 18, *Revenue*, IASB, December 1993 (amended March 2004), Appendix, para. 9.
188 IAS 40, para. 67.
189 IAS 40, para. 69.
190 IAS 40, para. 70.
191 IAS 40, para. 71.
192 IAS 40, para. 68.
193 IAS 40, para. 72.
194 IAS 40, para. 75.
195 IAS 40, para. 76.
196 IAS 40, para. 77.
197 IAS 40, para. 78.
198 IAS 40, para. 79.
199 IFRS 1, *First-time Adoption of International Financial Reporting Standards*, IASB, June 2003 (amended March 2004), para. 16.
200 IFRS 1, para. 17.
201 IFRS 1, para. 19.
202 IFRS 1, para. 25E.
203 IAS 40, para. 80.
204 IAS 40, para. 82.
205 IAS 40, para. 81.
206 IAS 40, para. 80.
207 IAS 40, para. 80.
208 IAS 40, para. 83.
209 IAS 40, para. 84.

Chapter 13   Impairment of fixed assets and goodwill

1   INTRODUCTION

Impairment, as a procedure, is an essential element in the IASB's strategy of moving financial reporting from historical cost to a fair value basis, as discussed in Chapter 2. When prudence (conservatism) ceases to be an underlying principle and is replaced by fair values – often arrived at after the application of a valuation model, rather than resulting from observable market prices – there has to be a control mechanism to prevent unduly optimistic valuations. In a fair value world, the impairment test performs this necessary function. Under a reporting system that increasingly relies on fair values, the impairment test is the 'new prudence'. Notwithstanding these strategic considerations, under IFRS the relevant standard, IAS 36 – *Impairment of Assets* – applies to most assets held by an entity regardless of the valuation basis used.

In principle an asset is impaired when an entity will not be able to recover that asset's balance sheet carrying value, either through using it or selling it. The (then) IASC introduced IAS 36 in 1998 and it applied to periods beginning on or after 1 July 1999. At the time the point was made that writing down impaired assets is not in principle a new requirement, and prudence apart, in many jurisdictions provisions for diminution in value are required to be made for assets if a reduction in value is expected to be permanent.

However, prior to IAS 36 there was little detailed guidance to support this broad principle, though the principle was either explicit or implicit in a number of standards. The position now is that the impairment provisions of IFRS are explicit and a broad summary of the standard is that, if circumstances arise which indicate assets might be impaired, a review should be undertaken of their cash generating abilities either through use or sale. This review will produce an amount which should be compared with the assets' carrying value, and if the carrying value is higher, the difference must be written off as an impairment adjustment in the income statement. The provisions within the standard that set out exactly how this is to be done, and how the figures involved are to be calculated, are detailed and quite complex. Therefore, as a preliminary introduction to the detail, the following section explains the theory underlying the type of impairment review adopted by the IASB in IAS 36.

2   THE THEORY BEHIND THE IMPAIRMENT REVIEW

The purpose of the review is to ensure that intangible and tangible assets, and goodwill are not carried at a figure greater than their *recoverable amount*. This recoverable amount is compared with the carrying value of the asset to determine if the asset is impaired. The definition of recoverable amount, therefore, is key. It is defined as the higher of *fair value less costs to sell* (FV) and *value in use* (VIU); the underlying concept being that an asset should not be carried at more than the amount it will raise, either from selling it now or from using it in the future.

Fair value less costs to sell essentially means what the asset could be sold for, having deducted *costs of disposal* (incrementally incurred direct selling costs). *Value in use* is defined in terms of discounted future cash flows, as the present value of the cash flows expected from the future use and eventual sale of the asset at the end of its useful life. As the recoverable amount is to be expressed as a present value, not in actual terms, discounting is a central feature of the impairment test.

Diagrammatically, this comparison between carrying value and recoverable amount, and the definition of recoverable amount, can be portrayed as follows:

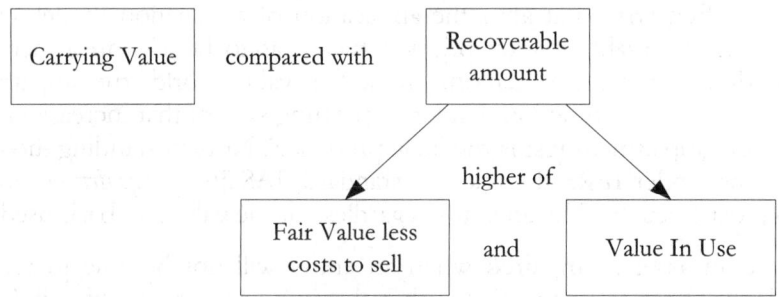

It may not always be necessary to identify both VIU and FV, as if either of VIU or FV is higher than the carrying amount then there is no impairment and no write-down is necessary. Thus, if FV is greater than the carrying amount then no further consideration need be given to VIU, or to the need for an impairment write down. The more complex issues arise when the FV is not greater than the carrying value, and so a VIU calculation is necessary. Typically for property plant and equipment used in manufacturing, this will be the case.

Although an impairment review might theoretically be conducted by looking at individual assets, this is likely to be a rare occurrence. It may not be possible to obtain reliable FV estimates for all assets and some, such as goodwill or certain intangible assets, may not have a separate FV at all. Even if FVs can be obtained for individual items of property plant and equipment, estimates of VIUs usually cannot be. This is because the cash flows necessary for the VIU calculation are not usually generated by single assets, but by groups of assets being used together.

Often, therefore, the impairment review cannot be done at the level of the individual asset and it must be done at what might be termed an operating unit level. IAS 36 uses the term *cash generating unit* (CGU) for the smallest identifiable group of assets that together have cash inflows that are largely independent of the cash inflows from other assets and that therefore can be the subject of a VIU calculation. CGU basically means a part of the business that generates income and which is largely independent other parts of the business. This focus on the CGU is fundamental, as it has the effect of making the review essentially a business-value test, in as much as the assets of a business unit cannot usually be carried at an amount greater than the value of that business unit.

As it would be unduly onerous for all fixed assets and goodwill to be reviewed for impairment every year, IAS 36 in the main requires property plant and equipment to be reviewed only if there is some indication that impairment may have occurred. If there are indications that the carrying amount of an asset may not be recoverable, a review for impairment should be carried out. The 'indications' of impairment may relate to either the assets themselves or to the economic environment in which they are operated. IAS 36 gives examples of indications of impairment, but makes it clear this is not an exhaustive list, and states explicitly that the entity may identify other indications that an asset is impaired, that would equally trigger an impairment review.[1]

The following section discusses in detail the individual provisions of IAS 36.

3   THE REQUIREMENTS OF IAS 36

3.1   Scope and definitions

IAS 36 – *Impairment of Assets* – was originally published in April 1998. A revised version of the standard was published in 2003 and amended variously in 2004, principally because of scope changes, as a result of the publication of IFRS 3 – *Business Combinations*, IFRS 4 – *Insurance Contracts*, IFRS 5 – *Non-current Assets Held for Sale and Discontinued Operations* – and as a result of the improvements project to existing standards, including IAS 38 – *Intangible Assets* – completed by the IASB in December 2003. For those already applying IFRS the implementation date of IAS 36 (revised) IAS 38 (revised) and IFRS 3 is 31 March 2004, and it applies as follows:

(a)   to goodwill and intangible assets acquired in business combinations for which the agreement date is on or after 31 March 2004; and

(b)   to all other assets prospectively from the beginning of the first annual period beginning on or after 31 March 2004.[2]

However if IFRS 3 is adopted early then IAS 36 and IAS 38 as revised must also be applied prospectively from that date.

The specific inclusion of business combinations within the scope of the standard represents a considerable extension of the application of the methodology – this is because under IFRS 3 goodwill is not to be systematically depreciated, but instead subject to an annual impairment test – however the basic methodology of the original standard remains unchanged. In this chapter it is the revised and amended version of IAS 36 that is referred to. The standard is a general impairment standard and its provisions are referred to in other standards, for example IAS 16, IAS 38 and IFRS 3, where impairment is to be considered.

The objective of the standard is to ensure that assets are not carried at more than their recoverable amount (the principles underlying the term recoverable amount and other terms are explained in 2 above). If the carrying amount is higher than the amount estimated to be able to be recovered by use or sale of the asset, then the business should recognise an impairment loss.[3]

The standard has a general application to all assets, but the following are outside its scope: inventories, assets arising from construction contracts, deferred tax assets, assets arising from employee benefits, financial assets that are included in the scope of IAS 39, investment property that is measured at fair value, biological assets under IAS 41, deferred acquisition costs and intangible assets arising from an insurer's contractual rights under insurance contracts within the scope of IFRS 4, and non-current assets (or disposal groups) classified as held for sale in accordance with IFRS 5.[4] This, the standard states, is because these issues are subject to specific recognition and measurement rules.[5] The effect of these exclusions is to reduce the scope of IAS 36 considerably, however, it does not exempt investment properties not carried at fair value, oil and mineral exploration costs or an entity's own shares held by a share trust. Investments in subsidiaries, joint ventures and associates in the separate financial statements of the parent are within its scope.[6]

The standard does apply to assets carried at valuation under IAS 16 – *Property, Plant and Equipment.* It is explained that there are two reasons for this. First, the only difference between fair value based on market value and fair value less costs to sell is the costs of disposal. Therefore, if these are not negligible, the entity may have to consider the asset's value in use. Second, in the absence of market values, the entity may have constructed a fair value using a technique acceptable under IAS 16 (see Chapter 12), in which case it would be quite possible for the asset to be impaired.[7] A specific example of a situation in which this might happen is if the asset is valued using depreciated replacement cost, a valuation method that often gives a higher valuation than one using market-based evidence.

The key definitions used in IAS 36 are:

'An *active market* is a market in which all the following conditions exist:

(a)   the items traded within the market are homogeneous;

(b)   willing buyers and sellers can normally be found at any time; and

(c)   prices are available to the public.

The *agreement date* for a business combination is the date that a substantive agreement between the combining parties is reached and, in the case of publicly listed entities, announced to the public. In the case of a hostile takeover, the earliest date that a substantive agreement between the combining parties is reached is the date that a sufficient number of the acquiree's owners have accepted the acquirer's offer for the acquirer to obtain control of the acquiree.

Carrying amount is the amount at which an asset is recognised after deducting any accumulated depreciation (amortisation) and accumulated impairment losses thereon.

A *cash-generating unit* is the smallest identifiable group of assets that generates cash inflows that are largely independent of the cash inflows from other assets or groups of assets.

Corporate assets are assets other than goodwill that contribute to the future cash flows of both the cash-generating unit under review and other cash-generating units.

Costs of disposal are incremental costs directly attributable to the disposal of an asset or cash-generating unit, excluding finance costs and income tax expense.

Depreciable amount is the cost of an asset, or other amount substituted for cost in the financial statements, less its residual value.

Depreciation (Amortisation) is the systematic allocation of the depreciable amount of an asset over its useful life.

Fair value less costs to sell is the amount obtainable from the sale of an asset or cash-generating unit in an arm's length transaction between knowledgeable, willing parties, less the costs of disposal.

An *impairment loss* is the amount by which the carrying amount of an asset or a cash-generating unit exceeds its recoverable amount.

The *recoverable amount* of an asset or a cash-generating unit is the higher of its fair value less costs to sell and its value in use.

Useful life is either:

(a) the period of time over which an asset is expected to be used by the entity; or

(b) the number of production or similar units expected to be obtained from the asset by the entity.

Value in use is the present value of the future cash flows expected to be derived from an asset or cash-generating unit.[8]

These definitions will be referred to when discussing the provisions of the standard in the remainder of the chapter.

3.2   When an impairment test is required

There is an important distinction in IAS 36 between (a) assessing whether there are indications of impairment, and (b) actually carrying out an impairment test. The standard has two different general requirements governing when an impairment test should be carried out:

- For all intangible assets with an indefinite life and goodwill (which as a result of the provisions of IFRS 3 will not be subject to systematic annual depreciation) the standard requires that an annual impairment test must be performed. The impairment test may be performed at any time in the annual reporting period, but it must be performed at the same time every year.[9]

- For all other classes of assets within the scope of IAS 36, the entity is required to assess at each balance sheet date whether there are any 'indications of impairment'. Only if indications of impairment are present will the impairment test itself have to be carried out.[10]

In addition, the carrying amount of an intangible asset that has not yet been brought into use must be tested at least annually. This, the standard argues, is because intangible assets are intrinsically subject to greater uncertainty before they are brought into use.[11]

The particular requirements of IAS 36 concerning the impairment testing of intangible assets with an indefinite life and goodwill are discussed separately at 3.4 below, however the methodology used is identical for all types of assets.

If indications of impairment exist, then an impairment test that estimates the asset's recoverable amount must be performed, using the method required by the standard unless there was sufficient headroom in a previous impairment calculation that would not have been eroded by subsequent events or the asset or CGU is not sensitive to a particular indicator; these exceptions are discussed further below.[12]

Normally however, if there are indications of impairment an impairment test (i.e. a formal estimate of the asset's recoverable amount as set out in the standard) must be undertaken.[13] Consequently the identification of indications of impairment becomes a crucial stage in the process.

IAS 36 lists examples of indications of impairment. The standard states that the examples represent the minimum indications that should be considered by the entity, and that the list is not exhaustive.[14] They are divided into external and internal indications as follows:

External sources of information

(a)   a decline in an asset's market value during the period that is significantly more than would be expected from normal use.

(b)   significant adverse changes that have taken place during the period, or will take place in the near future, in the technological, market, economic or legal environment in which the entity operates or in the market to which an asset is dedicated.

(c)   an increase in the period in market interest rates or other market rates of return on investments if these increases are likely to affect the discount rate used in calculating an asset's value in use and decrease the asset's recoverable amount materially.

(d)   the carrying amount of the net assets of the entity exceeds its market capitalisation.

Internal sources of information:

(e)   evidence of obsolescence or physical damage of an asset.

(f)   significant changes in the extent to which, or manner in which, an asset is used or is expected to be used, that have taken place in the period or soon thereafter and that will have an adverse effect on it. These changes include the asset becoming idle, plans to dispose of an asset sooner than expected, reassessing its useful life as finite rather than indefinite or plans to restructure the operation to which the asset belongs.

(g)   internal reports that indicates that the economic performance of an asset is, or will be, worse than expected.[15]

The standard amplifies and explains what is relevant evidence from internal reporting that indicates that an asset may be impaired as follows:

(a)   cash flows for acquiring the asset, or subsequent cash needs for operating or maintaining it, are significantly higher than originally budgeted;

(b)   operating profit or loss or actual net cash flows are significantly worse than those budgeted;

(c)   a significant decline in budgeted net cash flows or operating profit, or a significant increase in budgeted loss; or

(d)   operating losses or net cash outflows for the asset, if current period amounts are aggregated with budgeted amounts for the future.[16]

The presence of indicators or impairment will not necessarily mean that the entity has to calculate the recoverable amount of the asset in accordance with IAS 36. A previous calculation may have shown that an asset's recoverable amount was significantly greater than its carrying amount and it may be clear that subsequent events have been insufficient to eliminate this headroom. Similarly, previous analysis may show that an asset's recoverable amount is not sensitive to one or more of these indicators.[17]

There are two particularly significant elements in this list of indications. The first is the inclusion of market capitalisation as an external indication of impairment. Market capitalisation is, potentially, a powerful indicator as, if it shows a lower figure than the book value of shareholders' funds, it inescapably suggests the market considers that the business is overvalued. However, the market may have taken account of factors other than the return that the entity is generating on its assets (for example, the entity may have a high level of debt that it is unable to service fully) and a market capitalisation below shareholders' funds will not necessarily be reflected in an equivalent impairment loss. In these circumstances, entities will have to review their assets and CGUs for impairment but it is possible that not all assets or CGUs are sensitive to market capitalisation as an indicator. The second significant element is an explicit reference in (b), (c) and (d) above to internal evidence that future performance will be worse than expected. Thus IAS 36 requires that an impairment review should be undertaken if performance is or will be significantly below that previously budgeted. In particular, there may be indicators of impairment even if the asset is profitable in the current period if budgeted results for the future indicate that there will be losses or net cash outflows when these are aggregated with the current period results.

Some of the indicators are aimed at individual fixed assets rather than the CGU of which they are a part, for example a decline in the market value of an asset or evidence that it is obsolete or damaged. However, they may also imply that a wider review of the business or CGU is required. For example, if there is a property slump, and the market value of the entity's new head office falls below its carrying value this would constitute an indicator of impairment and trigger a review. At the level of the individual asset, as FV is below carrying amount this might indicate that a write-down is necessary. However, the building's recoverable amount may have to be considered in the context of a CGU of which it is a part and if it is, the recoverable amount will be based on VIU, not FV. This is an example of a situation where it may not be necessary to re-estimate an asset's recoverable amount because it may be obvious that the CGU has suffered no impairment. In short, it may be irrelevant to the recoverable amount of the CGU that it contains a head office whose market value has fallen.

The inclusion of interest rates as an indicator of impairment could imply that assets are judged to be impaired if they are no longer expected to earn a market rate of return, even though they may generate the same cash flows as before. However, it may well be that an upward movement in general interest rates will not give rise to a write-down in assets because they may not affect the rate of return expected from the asset itself. The standard indicates that this may be another instance where the asset's recoverable amount is not sensitive to a particular indicator.

An entity is not required to make a formal estimate of an asset's recoverable amount if the discount rate used in calculating the asset's VIU is unlikely to be affected by the increase in market rates. The discount rate used in a VIU calculation should be based on the rate specific for the asset, and if the asset has a long remaining useful life this may not be materially affected by increases in short-term rates. Previous sensitivity analyses of the recoverable amount may show that it is unlikely that there will be a material decrease because future cash flows are also likely to increase to compensate. Consequently, the potential decrease in recoverable amount may simply be unlikely to be material.[18]

If there are indications that the asset is impaired, it may also be necessary to examine the remaining useful life of the asset, its residual value and the depreciation method used, as these may also need to be adjusted even if no impairment loss is recognised.[19]

3.3 The impairment test

The standard requires the carrying amount to be compared with the recoverable amount. The recoverable amount is the higher of *value in use* (VIU) and *fair value less costs to sell* (FV), both terms are defined in 3.1 above.[20]

Estimating the VIU of an asset involves estimating the future cash inflows and outflows that will be derived from the use of the asset and from its ultimate disposal, and discounting them at an appropriate rate.[21] There are complex issues involved in determining the cash flows and choosing a discount rate and often there is no agreed methodology to follow (refer to 3.3.2 below for a discussion of some of these difficulties). However, broadly the requirement means that the recoverable amount is the higher of the net sale proceeds and the discounted future cash flows, where a discounting rate is used that is reasonable for the type of business and risks involved. If either the FV or the VIU is higher than the carrying amount, no further action is necessary as the asset is not impaired.[22] It may be possible to estimate the net selling price even in the absence of an active market but if it cannot be estimated satisfactorily then the value of an asset must be based on its VIU.[23] The practical point to emphasise is that if the FV is greater than the asset's carrying value, no VIU calculation is necessary.

The standard describes other circumstances in which it may be appropriate to use an asset's FV, rather than VIU, as the measure of an asset's recoverable amount In some cases there may be no significant difference between FV and VIU, in which case the asset's FV may be used as its recoverable amount.[24] This would be the case for example, if management were intending to dispose of the asset, as apart from its disposal proceeds there would be few if any cash flows from further use. Therefore there would be no significant difference between the asset's FV and VIU. The asset may also be held for sale as defined by IFRS 5, by which stage it will be outside the scope IAS 36, although it should be noted that IFRS 5 also requires such assets to be measured at the lower of carrying value and fair value less costs to sell (see Chapter 3).

The basic requirement of IAS 36 is that recoverable amount is calculated for an individual asset, unless that asset does not generate cash inflows that are largely independent of those from other assets or groups of assets. In this case, recoverable amount is determined for the CGU to which the asset belongs unless either:

(a) the asset's FV is higher than its carrying amount; or

(b) the asset's VIU can be estimated to be close to its FV and its FV can be determined.[25]

If either of (a) or (b) apply, then even if the asset generates cash flows in conjunction with other assets, and it would normally be necessary to calculate the VIU of the cash generating unit to which it belongs, it may in some circumstances be appropriate to base the recoverable amount of the asset on its FV. If for example, the CGU to which the asset belongs has been impaired, the asset's own carrying value could be based on its FV. Or if an asset is held for resale it would be carried at its estimated FV even though it only generates operating cash flows in conjunction with other assets.

IAS 36 allows the use of estimates, averages and computational shortcuts to provide a reasonable approximation of FV or VIU.[26]

3.3.1 Fair value less costs to sell

The standard goes into considerable detail regarding the estimation of an asset's FV. The best evidence is the sales price of the asset in question, based on a binding sale agreement negotiated at arm's length, less incremental costs directly attributable to the sale.[27] If there is no binding sale agreement for the asset in question, but there is an active market for assets of this type, net realisable value may be estimated from current or recent bid prices. If there are no current bid prices, the price may be estimated from the most recent transaction provided there has been no significant change in economic circumstances in the intervening period.[28]

There are few active markets for tangible and intangible assets, given that this requires a market in which all of the items traded are homogeneous, has a constant supply of willing buyers and sellers and prices are available to the public. Consequently, most estimates of fair value will be based on estimates of the market price of the asset in an arm's length transaction. This will involve consideration of the outcome of recent transactions for similar assets in the same industry. The entity will use the best information it has available at the balance sheet date to construct the price payable in an arm's length transaction between knowledgeable, willing parties.[29]

FV does not reflect a forced sale unless the management is compelled to sell immediately.[30] In all cases, FV should take account of estimated disposal costs. These include legal costs, stamp duty and other transaction taxes, costs of moving the asset and direct incremental costs. Business reorganisation costs and employee termination costs (as defined in IAS 19 – *Employee Benefits* – see Chapter 22) may not be treated as costs of disposal.[31]

If the disposal of an asset would entail the buyer assuming a liability, then this liability should be deducted from the FV in arriving at the relevant amount for determining the recoverable amount.[32] The obligation must also be taken into account in calculating the carrying value of the asset to enable a meaningful comparison.

3.3.2 Determining value in use (VIU)

IAS 36 requires the following elements to be reflected in the VIU calculation:

'(a)   an estimate of the future cash flows the entity expects to derive from the asset;

(b)   expectations about possible variations in the amount or timing of those future cash flows;

(c)   the time value of money, represented by the current market risk-free rate of interest;

(d)   the price for bearing the uncertainty inherent in the asset; and

(e)   other factors, such as illiquidity, that market participants would reflect in pricing the future cash flows the entity expects to derive from the asset.'[33]

The calculation requires the entity to estimate the future cash flows and discount them at an appropriate rate.[34] It also requires uncertainty as to the timing of cash flows or the market's assessment of risk in those assets ((d) and (e) above) to be taken into account either by adjusting the cash flows or the discount rate. The intention is that the VIU is to be the expected present value of those future cash flows.

If possible, recoverable amount is calculated for individual assets.[35]

If an impairment review has to be carried out then it will frequently be necessary to calculate the VIU of the CGU of which it is a part. This is because:

- if a single asset appears to be impaired, it will usually be necessary to calculate its VIU, as it is rarely the case that it can be assumed that this is similar to its FV; and

- it is unlikely that the asset generates sufficiently independent cash flows.[36]

Where a CGU is being reviewed for impairment, this will involve calculation of the VIU of the CGU as a whole unless a reliable estimate of the CGU's FV can be made. In general, the FVs of CGUs are far less reliable because they are far less homogeneous than individual assets and bought and sold far less often. If no such FV is identifiable, or if it is below the total of the CGU's net assets, VIU will have to be calculated.

VIU calculations at the level of the CGU will thus be required when:

- goodwill is suspected of being impaired;

- a CGU itself is suspected of being impaired (and no satisfactory FV is available); or

- intangible assets or other fixed assets are suspected of being impaired, individual future cash flows cannot be identified for them, and either no reliable FV is available or the FV is below carrying amount.

The standard contains detailed requirements concerning the data to be assembled to calculate VIU that can best be explained and set out as a series of steps. These are set out in 1 to 5 below and also contain a discussion of the practicalities and difficulties in determining the VIU of an asset. These steps are:

Step 1: Dividing the entity into cash-generating units (CGUs)

Step 2: Identifying the carrying amount of CGU assets

Step 3: Estimating the future pre-tax cash flows of the CGU under review

Step 4: Identifying an appropriate discount rate and discounting the future cash flows

Step 5: Comparing carrying value with VIU and recognising impairment losses

Although this process describes the determination of the VIU of a CGU, steps 2 to 5 are the same as those that would be applied to an individual asset if it generated cash flows independently of other assets.

Step 1   Dividing the entity into cash-generating units (CGUs)

If a VIU is required, one of the early tasks will be to identify the individual assets affected and if those assets do not have individually identifiable cash flows, divide the entity into CGUs i.e. groups of assets as defined in 3.1 above. The group of assets that is considered together should be as small as is reasonably practicable, i.e. the entity should be divided into as many CGUs as possible – an entity must identify the lowest aggregation of assets that generate largely independent cash inflows.[37]

Example 13.1:   Identification of CGUs and largely independent cash flows

An entity obtains a contract to deliver mail to all users within a region, for a price that depends solely on the weight of the item, regardless of the distance between sender and recipient. It makes a significant loss in deliveries to outlying regions. Because of the entity's service obligations, the CGU is the whole region covered by its mail services.

That said, the division should not go beyond the level at which each income stream is capable of being separately monitored and not beyond the point at which it would become necessary to start allocating direct costs between CGUs. For example, it may be difficult to identify a level below an individual factory as a CGU but of course an individual factory may or may not be a CGU.

The existence of a degree of flexibility over what constitutes a CGU is obvious. Indeed, the standard acknowledges that the identification of CGUs involves judgement.[38] The key guidance offered by the standard is that CGU selection will be influenced by 'how management monitors the entity's operations (such as by product lines, businesses, individual locations, districts or regional areas) or how management makes decisions about continuing or disposing of the entity's assets and operations'.[39] In the same way that the reporting of segmental information ultimately has to be left to the discretion of the entity, so too does the division of the entity into CGUs. The standard identifies in Example 1 in its accompanying section of illustrative examples, a number of scenarios that give an indication of how CGUs should be identified. These examples include the following:

Example 13.2:   Identification of cash-generating units

A   Retail Store Chain

A retail store chain M owns store X, five other stores in the same city as X (although in different neighbourhoods) and 20 other stores in other cities. All stores are managed in the same way as X. X and four other stores were purchased five years ago and goodwill was recognised. X makes all its retail purchases through M's purchasing centre. Pricing, marketing, advertising and human resources policies (except for hiring X's cashiers and sales staff) are decided by M.

In identifying X's cash-generating unit, an entity considers whether, for example:

• internal management reporting is organised to measure performance on a store-by-store basis; and

• the business is run on a store-by-store profit basis or on a region/city basis.

All M's stores are in different neighbourhoods and probably have different customer bases. So, although X is managed at a corporate level, X generates cash inflows that are largely independent of those of M's other stores. Therefore, it is likely that X is a cash-generating unit.

B   *Magazine Titles*

A publisher owns 150 magazine titles of which 70 were purchased and 80 were self-created. The price paid for a purchased magazine title is recognised as an intangible asset. The costs of creating magazine titles and maintaining the existing titles are recognised as an expense when incurred. Cash inflows from direct sales and advertising are identifiable for each magazine title. Titles are managed by customer segments. The level of advertising income for a magazine title depends on the range of titles in the customer segment to which the magazine title relates. Management has a policy to abandon old titles before the end of their economic lives and replace them immediately with new titles for the same customer segment. However, it is likely that the recoverable amount of an individual magazine title can be assessed. Even though the level of advertising income for a title is influenced, to a certain extent, by the other titles in the customer segment, cash inflows from direct sales and advertising are identifiable for each title. In addition, although titles are managed by customer segments, decisions to abandon titles are made on an individual title basis. Therefore, it is likely that individual magazine titles generate cash inflows that are largely independent of each other and that each magazine title is a separate cash-generating unit.[40]

Examples A and B above illustrate a very important point. In both cases, management may consider that the primary way in which they monitor their business is on a regional or segmental basis; but crucially, cash flows are monitored at the level of an individual store or title and closure decisions are made at this level. Another point of significance in deciding whether the CGU is at an individual level is whether the consumer will seek another of the same brand if one is closed. However, in other cases it may be that the entity is capable of monitoring individual cash flows from assets but this is not the most relevant feature in determining the composition of its CGUs.

Example 13.3:   Identification of cash-generating units – grouping of assets

A tour operator's hotels

A tour operator owns three hotels of a similar class near the beach at a large holiday resort. These hotels are advertised as alternatives in the operator's brochure, at the same price. Holidaymakers are frequently transferred from one to another and there is a central booking system for independent travellers. In this case, it may be that they can be regarded as offering genuinely substitutable products by a sufficiently high proportion of potential guests and can be grouped together as a single cash-generating unit. Effectively, the hotels are being run as a single hotel on three sites. The entity will have to bear in mind that disposal decisions may still be made on a hotel-by-hotel basis and have to weight this appropriately in its determination of its CGUs.

The standard allows reasonable approximations and one way in which entities may apply this in practice is through groupings of assets that are separate CGUs but could only have an immaterial effect if taken singly. Retail outlets may be grouped on a geographical basis (e.g. all of the retail outlets in a city centre owned by a branded clothes retailer) because they are all subject to the same economic circumstances and individually will have an immaterial effect. However, the entity will still have to scrutinise the individual CGUs to ensure that those that it intends to sell or that have significantly underperformed the others with which they are grouped are identified and dealt with individually.

In practice different entities will inevitably have varying approaches to determining their CGUs. There is judgement to be exercised in determining an income stream and in determining whether it is largely independent of other streams. Given this, therefore, entities may tend towards larger rather than smaller CGUs, to keep the complexity of the process within reasonable bounds.

The standard stresses the significance of an active market for the output of an asset in identifying a CGU. If there is an active market for the output produced by an asset or group of assets, the assets concerned are identified as a cash-generating unit, even if some or all of the output is used internally. If the cash inflows generated by the asset or CGU are based on internal transfer pricing, the best estimate of an external arm's length transaction price should be used in estimating the future cash flows to determine the asset's or CGU's VIU[41]

The reason given for this rule is that the existence of an active market means that the assets or CGU could generate cash flows independently from the rest of the business by selling on the active market.[42] The following example based on Example 1 in IAS 36's accompanying section of illustrative examples, illustrates the point.

Example 13.4:   Identification of cash-generating units – internally-used products

Plant for an Intermediate Step in a Production Process

A significant raw material used for plant Y's final production is an intermediate product bought from plant X of the same entity. X's products are sold to Y at a transfer price that passes all margins to X. Sixty per cent of X's final production is sold to Y and the remaining 40 per cent is sold to customers outside of the entity. Y sells 80 per cent of its products to customers outside of the entity

If X can sell its products in an active market and generate cash inflows that are largely independent of the cash inflows from Y, it is likely that X is a CGU even though part of its production is used by Y. Therefore, its cash inflows can be regarded as largely independent. It is likely that Y is also a separate cash-generating unit. However, internal transfer prices do not reflect market prices for X's output. Therefore, in determining value in use of both X and Y, the entity adjusts financial budgets/forecasts to reflect management's best estimate of future prices that could be achieved in arm's length transactions for those of X's products that are used internally.

If, on the other hand, there is no active market, it is likely that the recoverable amount of each plant cannot be assessed independently of the recoverable amount of the other plant. The majority of X's production is used internally and could not be sold in an active market. Cash inflows of X depend on demand for Y's products. Therefore, X cannot be considered to generate cash inflows that are largely independent of those of Y. In addition, the two plants are managed together. As a consequence, it is likely that X and Y together are the smallest group of assets that generates cash inflows that are largely independent.[43]

An active market is defined by the standard as one in which the items traded are homogeneous, willing buyers and sellers are normally available at any time and prices are available to the public. This applies to many metals, energy products (various grades of oil product, natural gas) and other commodities that are freely traded.

IAS 36 also requires that the identification of cash generating units shall be consistent from period to period unless the change is justified; if changes are made disclosures are required.[44]

Assets held for resale cannot be subsumed within a larger CGU and their impairment or otherwise should be judged solely by the cash flows expected to be generated by sale. Once they are classified as held for sale they will be accounted for in accordance with IFRS 5 and carried at an amount that may not exceed their FV (see Chapter 3 for a further discussion of IFRS 5's requirements).

Step 2   Identifying the carrying amount of CGU assets

The recoverable amount of a CGU is determined in the same way as for an individual asset and its carrying amount must be determined on a basis that is consistent with the way in which its recoverable amount is determined.[45]

The carrying amount of a CGU includes only those assets that can be attributed directly, or allocated on a reasonable and consistent basis. These must be the assets that will generate the future cash inflows used in determining the CGU's value in use. It does not include the carrying amount of any recognised liability, unless the recoverable amount of the cash-generating unit cannot be determined without taking it into account. Both FV and VIU of a CGU are determined excluding cash flows that relate to assets that are not part of the cash-generating unit and liabilities that have been recognised[46]

The standard emphasises the importance of completeness in the allocation of assets to CGUs. Every asset used in generating the cash flow being tested must be included in the CGU; otherwise an impaired CGU might appear to be unimpaired, as its carrying value would be understated by having missed out assets.[47]

There are exceptions allowed to the rule that recognised liabilities are not included in arriving at the CGU's carrying value or VIU. Paragraph 78 makes it clear that if the disposal of an asset would entail the buyer assuming a liability, then this liability should be deducted from the CGU's carrying amount and VIU in order to perform a meaningful comparison.[48]

The second exception occurs if it is only practicable to determine the recoverable amount of a CGU after taking into account assets and liabilities such as, receivables, or other financial assets, trade payables, pensions and other provisions.[49] Essentially this seems to mean that if the cash flows of a CGU or its FV can only be sensibly determined taking into account these sorts of items, then the entity should include them. In many cases in practice, particularly in the case of large CGUs, this is likely to be the case.

Other assets such as goodwill and corporate assets may not be able to be attributed on a reasonable and consistent basis and the standard has separate rules regarding their treatment. Goodwill is dealt with separately at 3.4 below in detail, and also in Chapter 6 in relation to business combinations.

I   Corporate assets

An entity may have assets that are inherently incapable of generating cash flows independently, such as headquarters buildings or central IT facilities. IAS 36 characterises this type of asset as 'corporate assets' and they are defined in 3.1 above. Paragraph 100 points out that 'the distinctive characteristics of corporate assets are that they do not generate cash inflows independently of other assets or groups of assets and their carrying amount cannot be fully attributed to the cash-generating unit under review.[50] As the definition makes clear, the characteristic of a corporate asset is that it contributes to more than one CGU.

This lack of cash flow generation by corporate assets presents a problem in the event of those assets showing indications of impairment. It also raises a question of what those indications might actually be, in the absence of cash flows directly relating to this type of asset. Some, but not all, of these assets may have relatively easily determinable FVs. However, while this is usually true of a headquarters building, the same could not be said for a central IT facility. We have already noted in 3.2 above that a decline in market value of itself may not trigger a need for an impairment review, if it is obvious that the CGUs of which corporate assets are a part are not showing any indications of impairment – unless, of course, management has decided to dispose of the asset. Therefore, it is most likely that a corporate asset will show indications of impairment if the CGU or group of CGUs it relates to are showing indications of it. It is this type of eventuality that requires rules for allocating the carrying values of corporate assets to individual CGUs or to groups of CGUs.

Therefore it is necessary, if there are indications of impairment of a corporate asset and its VIU needs to be determined, for the corporate asset's carrying value to be allocated to CGUs. This allocation allows the recoverable amount of all of the assets involved, both CGU and corporate ones, to be considered.[51]

The standard sets out the procedure as follows. If possible, the corporate assets are to be allocated to individual CGUs on a 'reasonable and consistent basis'. This is not expanded and affords some flexibility although obviously consistency is vital – the same criteria must be applied at all times. This means that if a the carrying value of a corporate asset can be allocated on a reasonable and consistent basis between individual CGUs, each CGU has its impairment test done separately and its carrying value includes its share of the corporate asset. If the corporate asset's carrying value cannot be allocated to an individual CGU, there are two steps. First the individual CGU is impairment tested and any impairment written off. Then as a second step a group of CGUs is identified to which, as a group, all or part of the carrying value of the corporate asset can be allocated. This group must include the individual CGU that was the subject of the first test. Finally, all CGUs in this group have to be tested to determine if the group's carrying value (including the allocation of the corporate asset's carrying value) is in excess of the group's VIU.[52] If it is not sufficient, the impairment loss will be allocated pro-rata to all assets in the group of CGUs and the allocated portion of the corporate asset, as described under 3.3.3 below.

In IAS 36's accompanying section of illustrative examples, Example 8 has a fully worked example of the allocation and calculation of VIU involving corporate assets.[53] The table below is included in it, and serves to illustrate the allocation of the corporate asset to CGUs:

Example 13.5: Allocation of corporate assets

An entity comprises three CGUs and a headquarters building. The carrying amount of the headquarter building of 150 is allocated to the carrying amount of each individual cash-generating unit. A weighted allocation basis is used because the estimated remaining useful life of A's cash-generating unit is 10 years, whereas the estimated remaining useful lives of B and C's cash-generating units are 20 years.

Schedule 1. Calculation of a weighted allocation of the carrying amount of the headquarter building

End of 20X0	A	B	C	Total
Carrying amount	100	150	200	450
Useful life	10 years	20 years	20 years	
Weighting based on useful life	1	2	2	
Carrying amount after weighting	100	300	400	800
Pro-rata allocation of the building	(100/800)= 12%	(300/800)= 38%	(400/800)= 50%	100%
Allocation of the carrying amount of the building (based on pro-rata above)	19	56	75	(150)
Carrying amount (after allocation of the building)	119	206	275	600

The allocation need not be made on carrying value or financial measures such as turnover – employee numbers or a time basis might be a valid basis in certain circumstances.

One effect of this pro-rata process is that the amount of the head office allocated to each CGU will change as the useful lives and carrying values change. In the above example, the allocation of the head office to CGU A will be redistributed to CGUs B and C as A's remaining life shortens. The entity will have to ensure that B and C can support an increased head office allocation. Similar effects will be observed if the sizes of any other factor on which the allocation to the CGUs is made change relative to one another.

Step 3   Estimating the future pre-tax cash flows of the CGU under review

This step need be performed only if the CGU concerned either has no identifiable FV, or a FV that is lower than its carrying value, and it shows indications of impairment. In order to calculate the VIU the entity needs to estimate the future cash flows that it will derive from its use and consider possible variations in their amount or timing.[54] In estimating future cash flows the entity should:

'(a)   base cash flow projections on reasonable and supportable assumptions that represent management's best estimate of the range of economic conditions that will exist over the remaining useful life of the asset. Greater weight shall be given to external evidence.

(b)   base cash flow projections on the most recent financial budgets/forecasts approved by management, but shall exclude any estimated future cash inflows or outflows expected to arise from future restructurings or from improving or enhancing the asset's performance. Projections based on these budgets/forecasts shall cover a maximum period of five years, unless a longer period can be justified.

(c)   estimate cash flow projections beyond the period covered by the most recent budgets/forecasts by extrapolating the projections based on the budgets/forecasts using a steady or declining growth rate for subsequent years, unless an increasing rate can be justified. This growth rate shall not exceed the long-term average growth rate for the products, industries, or country or countries in which the entity operates, or for the market in which the asset is used, unless a higher rate can be justified.'[55]

The standard describes the responsibilities of management towards the estimation of cash flows in some detail. Management are required to ensure that the assumptions on which its current cash flow projections are based are consistent with past actual outcomes by examining the causes of differences between past cash flow projections and actual cash flows. They can, of course, take account of the effects of subsequent events or circumstances that did not exist when those actual cash flows were generated.[56]

IAS 36 states that the cash flows should be based on the most recent budgets and forecasts for a maximum of five years because reliable forecasts are rarely available for a longer period. If management is confident that its projections are reliable and can demonstrate this from past experience, it may use a longer period.[57] In using budgets and forecasts, management is required to consider whether these really are the best estimate of economic conditions that will exist over the remaining useful life of the asset.[58] Cash flows for the period beyond that covered by the forecasts or budgets assume a steady, declining or even negative rate of growth. An increase in the rate may be used if it is supported by objective information.[59]

Therefore only in exceptional circumstances should a higher growth rate be used, or should the period before a steady or declining growth rate is assumed extend to more than five years. This five year rule is based on general economic theory that postulates above-average growth rates will only be achievable in the short-term, because such above-average growth will lead to competitors entering the market. This increased competition will, over a period of time, lead to a reduction of the growth rate, towards the average for the economy as a whole. IAS 36 suggests that entities will find it difficult to exceed the average historical growth rate for the products, countries or markets over the long term, say twenty years.[60]

This stage of the impairment review really illustrates the point that it is not only fixed assets that are being assessed. The future cash flow to be forecast is *all* cash flows – receipts from sales, purchases, administrative expenses, etc. It is akin to a free cash flow valuation of a business with the resulting valuation then being compared to the carrying value of the assets in the CGU.

The cash flow forecast should include three elements:

- cash inflows from the continuing use of the asset;

- the cash outflows necessary to generate these cash inflows, including cash outflows to prepare the asset for use, that can either be directly attributed, or allocated on a reasonable and consistent basis; and

- the net cash flows, if any, that the entity may receive or pay for the disposal of the asset at the end of its useful life.[61]

Cash flows can be estimated by taking into account general price changes caused by inflation, or on the basis of stable prices. If inflation is built into the cash flow then the discount rate selected must also be adjusted to remove the inflationary effect.[62] Generally entities will use whichever method is most convenient to them that is consistent with the method they use in their budgets and forecasts and it is, of course, fundamental that cash flows and discount rate are both estimated on a consistent basis.

To avoid the danger of double counting, the future cash flows exclude those relating to financial assets, including receivables and liabilities such as payables, pensions and provisions.[63]

Projections in the cash flow should include costs of day-to-day servicing and as well as overheads that can be reasonably attributed to the use of the asset.[64] Whilst a part-completed asset must have the costs to complete it included in the cash flow,[65] the general rule is that future cash flows should be forecast for CGUs or assets in their current condition. Forecasts should not include estimated future cash inflows or outflows that are expected to arise from improving or enhancing the asset's performance.[66]

While the restriction on enhanced performance may be understandable, it adds an element of unreality that is hard to reconcile with other assumptions made in the VIU process. For example, the underlying forecast cash flows that the standard makes the foundation of the procedure will obviously be based on the business as it is actually expected to develop in the future, growth, improvements and all. Producing a special forecast based on unrealistic assumptions, even for this limited purpose, may be difficult.

Nevertheless, paragraph 48 explicitly states that improvements to the current performance of an asset may not be included in the estimates of future cash flows until the expenditure that provides those improvements is incurred. The treatment of such expenditure is illustrated in Appendix A Example 6.[67] What this means is that if the asset is impaired and if the entity is making the future expenditure to reverse that impairment, the asset will still be written down. Subsequently the impairment can be reversed, to the degree appropriate, after the expenditure has taken place.

This restriction may stop optimistic forecasts, but an assumption of new capital investment is in practice intrinsic to the VIU test. What has to be assessed is the future cash flows of a productive unit, such as a factory or hotel. The cash flows, out into the far future, will include the sales of product, cost of sales, administrative expenses, etc. They must necessarily include capital expenditure as well, at least to the extent required to keep the CGU functioning as forecast. This is explicitly acknowledged as follows:

> 'Estimates of future cash flows include future cash outflows necessary to maintain the level of economic benefits expected to arise from the asset in its current condition. When a cash-generating unit consists of assets with different estimated useful lives, all of which are essential to the ongoing operation of the unit, the replacement of assets with shorter lives is considered to be part of the day-to-day servicing of the unit when estimating the future cash flows associated with the unit. Similarly, when a single asset consists of components with different estimated useful lives, the replacement of components with shorter lives is considered to be part of the day-to-day servicing of the asset when estimating the future cash flows generated by the asset.'[68]

Accordingly, *some* capital expenditure cash flows must be built into the forecast cash flows. Whilst improving capital expenditure may not be recognised, routine or replacement capital expenditure necessary to maintain the function of the asset or assets in the CGU has to be included. This distinction may not be easy to draw in practice.

The standard contains similar rules with regard to any future restructuring that may affect the VIU of the asset or CGU. The prohibition on including the results of restructuring applies only to those plans to which the entity is not committed. Again, this is because of the general rule that the cash flows must be based on the asset in its current condition and therefore future events that may change that condition are not to be taken into account.[69] When an entity becomes committed to a restructuring (as set out in IAS 37 – *Provisions, Contingent Assets and Contingent Liabilities* – see Chapter 25) IAS 36 then allows an entity's estimates of future cash inflows and outflows to reflect the cost savings and other benefits from the restructuring (based on the most recent financial budgets/forecasts approved by management).[70] Treatment of such a future restructuring is illustrated in the standard's accompanying section of illustrative examples by Example 5. The standard specifically points out that the increase in cash inflows as a result of such a restructuring may not be taken into account until after the cash flows associated with the restructuring have occurred.[71] Entities will sometimes be required to recognise impairment losses that will be reversed once the expenditure has been incurred and the restructuring completed.

The expected future cash flows of the CGU being assessed for impairment should not include cash inflows or outflows from financing activities or tax receipts or payments. This is because the discount rate used and the future cash flows are themselves to be determined on a pre-tax basis.[72]

The inclusion of the disposal proceeds and costs at the end of the useful life of the asset should be based on current prices and costs for similar assets, adjusted if necessary for price level changes if the entity has chosen to include this factor in its forecasts and selection of a discount rate. The entity must take care that its estimate is based on a proper assessment of the amount that would be received in an arm's length transaction.[73]

Foreign currency cash flows should first be estimated in the currency in which they will be generated and then discounted using a discount rate appropriate for that currency. An entity should translate the present value calculated in the foreign currency using the spot exchange rate at the date of the value in use calculation.[74] Significantly, this could well be a different rate from that used to translate the foreign currency assets, goodwill and liabilities of a subsidiary at the period end. For example, a non-monetary asset such as an item of property, plant and equipment may be carried at an amount based on exchange rates on the date on which it was acquired but generates foreign currency cash flows. In order to determine its carrying amount if there are indicators of impairment, IAS 21 – *The Effects of Changes in Foreign Exchange Rates* – states that the recoverable amount will be calculated in accordance with IAS 36, and the cash flows translated at the exchange rate at the date when that value was determined.[75] IAS 21 notes that this may be the rate at the balance sheet date. The VIU is then compared to the carrying value and the item is then carried forward at the lower of these two values. Similarly, different rates may be used if the impairment review is of goodwill or an intangible asset with indefinite life, where the review need not be carried out at the year-end.

Finally, although probably inherent in their identification, the forecast cash flows of the CGU have to be allocated to different periods for the purpose of the discounting step, discussed next.

Step 4   Identifying an appropriate discount rate and discounting the future cash flows

When the future cash flows have been estimated and allocated to different periods, the present value of these cash flows should then be calculated by discounting them. The standard expresses this as follows:

> 'The discount rate (rates) shall be a pre-tax rate (rates) that reflect(s) current market assessments of:
>
> (a)   the time value of money; and
>
> (b)   the risks specific to the asset for which the future cash flow estimates have not been adjusted.'[76]

What this means is that the discount rate to be applied should be an estimate of the rate that the market would expect on an equally risky investment. The standard states:

> 'A rate that reflects current market assessments of the time value of money and the risks specific to the asset is the return that investors would require if they were to choose an investment that would generate cash flows of amounts, timing and risk profile equivalent to those that the entity expects to derive from the asset.'

Therefore, if at all possible, the rate is to be obtained from market transactions or market rates. It should be the rate implicit in current market transactions for similar assets or the weighted average cost of capital (WACC) of a listed entity that has a single asset (or a portfolio of assets) with similar service potential and risks to the asset under review.[77] Even if such a listed entity could be found, care would have to be taken in using its WACC as the standard specifies that the discount rate is independent of the entity's capital structure and the way it financed the purchase of the asset (see below). The effect of gearing and its effect on calculating an appropriate WACC are discussed further in Example 13.6.

It is only in rare cases (e.g. property assets) that such market rates can be obtained. In the event of an asset-specific rate not being available from the market, 'surrogates' should be used which are set out in Appendix A of IAS 36. The discount rate that 'investors would require if they were to choose an investment that would generate cash flows of amounts, timing and risk profile equivalent to those that the entity expects to derive from the asset' will not be easy to determine in many cases, but what guidance IAS 36 provides is as follows:

'As a starting point, the enterprise may take into account the following rates:

(a)   the enterprise's weighted average cost of capital determined using techniques such as the Capital Asset Pricing Model;

(b)   the enterprise's incremental borrowing rate; and

(c)   other market borrowing rates.'[78]

Appendix A also gives the following guidelines for selecting the appropriate discount rate:

- it should be adjusted to reflect the specific risks associated with the projected cash flows (such as country, currency, price and cash flow risks) and to exclude risks that are not relevant;[79]

- to avoid double counting, the discount rate does not reflect risks for which future cash flow estimates have been adjusted;[80]

- the discount rate is independent of the entity's capital structure and the way it financed the purchase of the asset.[81]

- if the basis for the rate is post-tax (such as a weighted average cost of capital), it is adjusted to reflect a pre-tax rate;[82] and

- normally the entity uses a single discount rate for the estimation of an asset's VIU but it should use separate discount rates for different future periods if the VIU is sensitive to different risks or the terms structure of interest rates.[83]

Under IAS 36, therefore, assets are judged to be impaired if they are no longer expected to earn a current market rate of return. However, we have already seen that the IASB argues that the discount rate specific for the asset may not be sensitive to increases in short-term rates – this is discussed in 3.2 above.[84]

It is suggested that the incremental borrowing rate of the business is relevant to the selection of a discount rate. This could only be a starting point as the appropriate discount rate should be independent of the entity's capital structure or the way in which it financed the purchase of the asset. The incremental borrowing rate must be used with extreme caution as it might, for example, include an element of default risk for the entity as a whole, which is not relevant in assessing the return expected from the assets.

It is likely that in practice an estimate of the appropriate discount rate will have to be made using the concept of the WACC. Since most VIU calculations are done in the context of a CGU, and only rarely is there likely to be a market in similar CGUs, it is unlikely the discount rate can be calculated in any other way.

The appropriate way to calculate WACC is an extremely technical subject, and one about which there is much academic literature and no general agreement. The selection of the rate is obviously a crucial part of the impairment testing process and in practice it will probably not be possible to obtain a theoretically perfect rate. The objective, therefore, must be to obtain a rate which is sensible and justifiable. There are probably a number of acceptable methods of arriving at the appropriate rate and one method is set out below. While this illustration may appear to be quite complex, it has been written at a fairly general level. In practice, the calculation of the appropriate discount rate may be extremely complex and specialist advice may be needed.[85]

Example 13.6: Calculating a discount rate

This example is based on determining the WACC for a listed company with a similar risk profile to the CGU in question. Because it is highly unlikely that such a company will exist, it will usually have to be simulated by looking at a hypothetical company with a similar risk profile.

The following three elements need to be estimated for the hypothetical listed company with a similar risk profile:

- gearing, i.e. the ratio of market value of debt to market value of equity
- cost of debt; and
- cost of equity.

Gearing can best be obtained by reviewing quoted companies operating predominantly in the same industry as the CGU and identifying an average level of gearing for such companies. The companies need to be quoted so that the market value of equity can be readily determined.

Where companies in the sector typically have quoted debt, the cost of such debt can be determined directly. In order to calculate the cost of debt for bank loans and borrowings more generally, one method is to take the rate implicit in fixed interest government bonds – with a period to maturity similar to the expected life of the assets being reviewed for impairment – and to add to this rate a bank's margin, i.e. the commercial premium that would be added to the bond rate by a bank lending to the hypothetical listed company. In some cases, the margin being charged on existing borrowings to the company in question will provide evidence to help with establishing the bank's margin. Obviously, the appropriateness of this will depend upon the extent to which the risks facing the CGU being tested are similar to the risks facing the company or group as a whole.

If goodwill or intangible assets with an indefinite life were being included in a CGU reviewed for impairment (see 3.4 below) the appropriate gilt-edged bond rate to use might have to be adjusted towards that for irredeemable bonds. The additional bank's margin to add would be a matter for judgement but would vary according to the ease with which the sector under review was generally able to obtain bank finance and, as noted above, there might be evidence from the borrowings actually in place of the likely margin that would be chargeable. Sectors that invest significantly in tangible assets such as properties that are readily available as security for borrowings, would require a lower margin than other sectors where such security could not be found so easily.

Cost of equity is the hardest component of the cost of capital to determine. One technique referred to in the standard, frequently used in practice and written up in numerous textbooks is the 'Capital Asset Pricing Model' (CAPM). The theory underlying this model is that the cost of equity is equal to the risk-free rate plus a multiple, known as the beta, of the market risk premium. The risk-free rate is the same as that used to determine the nominal cost of debt and described above as being obtainable from government bond yields with an appropriate period to redemption. The market risk premium is the premium that investors require for investing in equities rather than government bonds. There are also reasons why this rate may be loaded in certain cases, for instance to take account of specific risks in the CGU in question that are not reflected in its market sector generally. Loadings are typically made when determining the cost of equity for a small company. The beta for a quoted company is a number that is greater or less than one according to whether market movements generally are reflected in a proportionately greater (beta more than one) or smaller (beta less than one) movement in the particular stock in question. Most betas fall into the range 0.4 to 1.5.

Various bodies, such as The London Business School, publish betas on a regular basis both for individual stocks and for industry sectors in general. Published betas are levered, i.e. they reflect the level of gearing in the company or sector concerned.

The cost of equity for the hypothetical company having a similar risk profile to the CGU is:

Cost of equity = risk-free rate + (levered beta × market risk premium)

Having determined the component costs of debt and equity and the appropriate level of gearing, the WACC for the hypothetical company having a similar risk profile to the CGU in question is:

$$WACC = (1 - t) \times D \times \frac{g}{(1 + g)} + E \times \left[1 - \frac{g}{(1 + g)} \right]$$

where:
D is the cost of debt;
E is the cost of equity
g is the gearing level (i.e. the ratio of debt to equity) for the sector; and
t is the rate of tax relief available on the debt servicing payments.

IAS 36 requires that the forecast cash flows are before tax and finance costs, though it is more common in discounted cash flow valuations to use cash flows after tax. However, as pre-tax cash flows are being used, the standard requires a pre-tax discount rate to be used.[86] This will theoretically involve discounting higher future cash flows (before deduction of tax) with a higher discount rate. This higher discount rate is the post-tax rate adjusted to reflect the specific amount and timing of the future tax flows, which, in principle, will be the rate of return that, after deduction of tax, gives the required post-tax rate of return. In other words, the pre-tax discount rate is the rate that gives the same present value when discounting the pre-tax cash flows as the post-tax cash flows discounted at the post-tax rate of return.[87]

In practice, for most purposes a simple grossing-up calculation will suffice. Once the WACC has been calculated, the pre-tax WACC can be calculated by applying the fraction 1/(1-t). Thus, if the WACC comes out at, say, 12% the pre-tax WACC will be 12% divided by 0.7 (assuming a corporation tax rate of 30% to be the appropriate rate in the context of the reporting entity), which would give a pre-tax rate of 17.1%.

However, the pre-tax discount rate is not always the post-tax rate grossed up by a standard rate of tax. It also depends on the timing of future tax cash flows and the useful life of the asset; these tax flows can be scheduled and an iterative process used to calculate the pre-tax discount rate.[88] The timing of tax cash flows can be extremely important if the CGU has tax losses that mean that there will be no payment of tax for a number of years, perhaps not until after the five year time horizon covered by budgets and forecasts. The effect of the tax cash flows on the VIU will have to be estimated and it may be necessary to consult a valuations expert on these more complex matters.

The selection of discount rates leaves considerable room for judgement in the absence of more specific guidance, and it is likely that many very different approaches will be applied in practice, even though this may not always be evident from the financial statements. However, once the discount rate has been chosen the future cash flows are discounted in order to produce a present value figure representing the VIU of the CGU or individual asset that is the subject of the impairment test. The final step in the impairment review can now be taken.

Step 5 Comparing carrying value with VIU and recognising impairment losses

If the carrying value of an individual asset or of a CGU is less than (or equal to) its calculated VIU, there is no impairment. On the other hand, if the carrying value of the CGU is greater than its VIU, an impairment write-down should be recognised. IAS 36 has rules on the allocation of impairment losses, depending upon whether an individual asset, an individual CGU, or a group of CGUs with goodwill or corporate assets allocated to the group as a whole, is involved. These aspects are discussed below.

3.3.3 Recognition of impairment losses

If the VIU calculation has produced an impairment loss, then IAS 36 sets out how such losses should be recognised. There are three cases involved, an impairment loss on an individual asset, an impairment loss on an individual CGU and an impairment loss on a group of CGUs. The latter may occur where there are corporate assets (see 3.3.1 Step 2 above) or goodwill (see 3.4 below) that have been allocated to a group of CGUs rather than to individual ones.

A Impairment losses on individual assets

For individual assets IAS 36 states:

> 'If, and only if, the recoverable amount of an asset is less than its carrying amount, the carrying amount of the asset shall be reduced to its recoverable amount. That reduction is an impairment loss.[89]
>
> An impairment loss shall be recognised immediately in profit or loss, unless the asset is carried at revalued amount in accordance with another Standard (for example, in accordance with the revaluation model in IAS 16 Property, Plant and Equipment). Any impairment loss of a revalued asset shall be treated as a revaluation decrease in accordance with that other Standard'[90]

If there is an impairment loss on a non-revalued asset it is recognised in profit or loss. However, an impairment loss on a revalued asset is first used to reduce the revaluation surplus for that asset. Only when the impairment loss exceeds the amount in the revaluation surplus for that same asset is any further impairment loss recognised in the profit and loss.[91] IAS 36 does not state a particular position in the income statement for impairment losses to be shown. Neither does it address whether any amounts written off a fixed asset should be treated as (i) a deduction from the gross amount (cost or valuation) or (ii) as an increase in cumulative depreciation, in the reconciliation required by IAS 16 between the carrying amounts at the beginning and end of the year.[92] If the asset is carried at cost, we consider that it is more appropriate to carry an impairment write down within cumulative depreciation. If the asset is held at valuation then there is less of an issue and the impairment will be reflected in the revalued carrying amount.

An impairment loss greater than the carrying value of the asset does not give rise to a liability unless another standard requires it, presumably as this would be tantamount to providing for future losses.[93] An impairment loss will reduce the depreciable amount of an asset and the revised amount will be written off prospectively over the remaining life.[94] However, an entity ought also to review the useful life and residual value of its impaired asset, as both of these may need to be revised. The circumstances that give rise to impairments frequently impact these as well. Finally, an impairment loss will have implications for any deferred tax calculation involving the asset and in the standard's accompanying section of illustrative examples Example 3, on which the following is based, illustrates the possible effects.

Example 13.7:   Recognition of an impairment loss creates a deferred tax asset

An entity has an asset with a carrying amount of €2,000 whose recoverable amount is €1300. The tax rate is 30% and the tax base of the asset is €1500. Impairment losses are not deductible for tax purposes. The effect of the impairment loss is as follows:

	Before impairment €	Effect of impairment €	After impairment €
Carrying amount	2,000	(700)	1,300
Tax base	1,500	–	1,500
Taxable (deductible) temporary difference	500	(700)	(200)
Deferred tax liability (asset) at 30%	150	(210)	(60)

The entity will recognise the deferred tax asset to the extent that it is probable that there will be available taxable profits against which the deductible temporary difference can be utilised.

B Impairment losses and CGUs

Impairment losses in a CGU can occur in two ways:

(i) an impairment loss is incurred in a CGU on its own, and that CGU may or may not have corporate assets or goodwill included in its carrying value;

(ii) an impairment loss is identified that must be allocated across a group of CGUs because a corporate asset or goodwill is involved whose carrying value could only be allocated to a group of CGUs as a whole, rather than to individual ones (the allocation of corporate assets to CGUs is discussed in 3.3.1 Step 2 above, and goodwill is discussed at 3.4 below).

The relevant paragraphs from the standard deal with both instances but are readily understandable only if the above distinction is appreciated. The standard lays down that impairment losses in CGUs should be recognised to reduce the carrying amount of the assets of the unit (group of units) in the following order:

(a) first, to reduce the carrying amount of any goodwill allocated to the CGU or group of units.; and

(b) if the goodwill has been written off, to reduce the other assets of the CGU (or group of CGUs) pro rata to their carrying amount.[95]

Note that if there are indicators of impairment in connection with a CGU to which goodwill has been allocated, this should be tested and any necessary impairment loss taken, prior to performing an impairment test for goodwill (see 3.4.2A below).[96] These impairment losses and consequent reductions in carrying values are treated in exactly the same way as those for individual assets, in accordance with paragraph 60 of IAS 36, as explained above.

The important point is to be clear about the order set out above. This requires any goodwill to be written down first, and thereafter if an impairment loss remains, the other assets in the CGU or group of CGUs are written down pro-rata to their carrying values. This pro-rating is in two stages if a group of CGUs is involved:

(i) the loss is eliminated against goodwill (which by definition in this instance is unallocated to individual CGUs in the group);

(ii) any remaining loss is pro-rated between the carrying values of the individual CGUs in the group; and

(iii) within each individual CGU the loss is again pro-rated between the individual assets' carrying values.

Unless it is possible to estimate the recoverable amount of each individual asset within a CGU, it is necessary to allocate impairment losses in such a way that the revised carrying amount of these assets correspond with the requirements of the standard. Therefore, the entity does not reduce the carrying amount of an asset below the highest of its FV or VIU (if these can be established), or zero. The amount of the impairment loss that would otherwise have been allocated to the asset is then allocated pro rata to the other assets of the CGU or CGU group.[97] The standard argues that this arbitrary allocation to individual assets when their recoverable amount cannot be individually assessed is appropriate because all assets of a CGU 'work together'.[98]

If corporate assets are allocated to a CGU or group of CGUs, then any remaining loss at (ii) above (i.e. after allocation to goodwill) is pro-rated against the allocated share of the corporate asset and the other assets in the CGU.

This process, then, writes down the carrying value attributed or allocated to a CGU until the carrying value of the net assets is not more than the computed VIU. As is recognised in paragraph 105 of IAS 36, set out above, it is logically possible, after all assets and goodwill are either written off or down to their FV, for the carrying value of the CGU to be higher than the computed VIU. There is no suggestion that the net assets should be reduced any further because at this point the FV would be the relevant impairment figure. The remaining amount will only be recognised as a liability if that is a requirement of another standard.[99]

IAS 36 includes in the standard's accompanying section of illustrative examples Example 2 which illustrates the calculation, recognition and allocation of an impairment loss across CGUs.

However, the standard stresses that no impairment loss should be reflected against an individual asset if the CGU to which it belongs has not been impaired, even if its carrying value exceeds its FV. This is expanded in the following example, based on that in paragraph 107 of the standard:

Example13.8:   Individually impaired assets within CGUs

A machine has suffered physical damage but is still working, although not as well as before it was damaged. The machine's FV is less than its carrying amount. The machine does not generate independent cash inflows. The smallest identifiable group of assets that includes the machine and generates cash inflows that are largely independent of the cash inflows from other assets is the production line to which the machine belongs. The recoverable amount of the production line shows that the production line taken as a whole is not impaired.

Assumption 1: budgets/forecasts approved by management reflect no commitment of management to replace the machine.

The recoverable amount of the machine alone cannot be estimated because the its VIU may be different from its FV (because the entity is going to continue to use it) and can be determined only for the CGU to which it belongs (the production line).

As the production line is not impaired, no impairment loss is recognised for the machine. Nevertheless, the entity may need to reassess the depreciation period or the depreciation method for the machine. Perhaps a shorter depreciation period or a faster depreciation method is required to reflect the expected remaining useful life of the machine or the pattern in which economic benefits are expected to be consumed by the entity.

Assumption 2: budgets/forecasts approved by management reflect a commitment of management to replace the machine and sell it in the near future.

Cash flows from continuing use of the machine until its disposal are estimated to be negligible. The machine's VIU can be estimated to be close to its FV. Therefore, the recoverable amount of the machine can be determined and no consideration is given to the CGU (the production line) to which it belongs. As the machine's carrying amount exceeds its FV, an impairment loss is recognised to write it down to FV.[100]

Note that it is assumed that the asset is still useable (otherwise it would not be contributing to the cash flows of the CGU and would have to be written off) and not held for sale as defined by IFRS 5, whose requirements are discussed further in Chapter 3.

Once the impairment write-down has been made, henceforth the entity will theoretically be able to make the rate of return on its assets which the providers of its capital are looking to see on their funds invested. This is the rate implicit in the calculation that forms the basis of the discount rate chosen for the impairment calculations. An implication of the standard therefore, but not one that we have seen much evidence of in those jurisdictions that have been operating similar impairment standards so far, is that no entities should be reporting materially sub-standard returns on an ongoing basis – at least not those in which an impairment review has been triggered by an 'indicator of impairment'.

The fact that in reality entities continue to report sub-market returns in jurisdictions where similar impairment rules apply, has implications for the practical efficacy of impairment as the check and balance against undue optimism about asset values in the IASB's intended fair-value based accounting future. Whether impairment as a system will actually be the effective safeguard it is intended to be in a fair-value future, is far from obvious. As noted in the introduction to this chapter, impairment in a fair-value world takes on the role of prudence (conservatism) under historical cost systems. The effectiveness of this 'new prudence' is only a theoretical hope so far, whether it turns out to be a sensible alternative to traditional prudence is an open question. Particularly as it must be remembered that the appearance of an 'indicator of impairment' is required before an impairment review is required at all.

3.4   Impairment of intangible assets with an indefinite life and goodwill

With the publication of IFRS 3 came a change to the treatment of goodwill previously required by IFRS. Hitherto, entities were required to systematically depreciate goodwill, with a very strong presumption that its useful life would not exceed twenty years. As a result of the IASB's strategy of converging towards US GAAP, this position has changed considerably.

Under IFRS 3 that will be effective from 1 January 2005, goodwill may not be systematically depreciated; instead it is required to be subject to an annual impairment review.[101] As a consequence of the change to the treatment of goodwill, the revised IAS 38 now allows that intangible assets may also have indefinite useful lives. IAS 38 makes a distinction between intangible assets with finite useful lives and those with indefinite useful lives. The former must be depreciated systematically over their useful lives; however intangible assets with an indefinite useful life may not be systematically depreciated, but must also be subject to an annual impairment test.[102]

An objective observer would probably be less than convinced that the changes to IFRS to accommodate convergence with US GAAP, described above, were an unquestioned improvement. The rather unconvincing record of impairment testing, which has not produced consistent effects, must mean that there is a degree of risk involved with the change. Certainly, volatility must accompany it. These considerations make it probable that if an impairment becomes necessary it is highly likely to involve a very considerable portion of the intangible asset or goodwill sum involved – all of which will be reported in profit and loss immediately.

The impairment tests required for goodwill and intangible assets with an indefinite life must be performed annually, but not necessarily at the period end balance sheet date. This is in contrast to the impairment tests for other assets described in 3.2 and 3.3 above that are required only if there are indications of impairment, but which must be performed at the period end. The detailed requirements of IAS 36 concerning goodwill and intangible assets with an indefinite life are discussed below; however the assumption is made that the reader is conversant with the previously described impairment test procedures.

3.4.1 Impairment of intangible assets with an indefinite useful life

IAS 38 makes the point that 'indefinite' does not mean 'infinite', and unforeseeable factors may affect the entity's ability and intention to maintain the asset at its standard of performance assessed at the time of estimating the asset's useful life.[103] An intangible asset with an indefinite useful life needs to be impairment tested annually, and at the same time each year but not necessarily the year-end, even though it is not subject to systematic depreciation.[104] However intangible assets with an indefinite useful life are not exempted from the normal requirements of IAS 36, so if there are any indications of impairment, an impairment test must be performed at the period end as set out in the standard and described in 3.1 to 3.3 above. This is in addition to the annual test unless, of course, that test indicated that there was sufficient headroom.

The requirements of IAS 36 can be summarised as follows:

1. All intangible assets with indefinite useful lives must be tested for impairment at least once per year and at the same time each year.[105]

2. Any intangible asset with an indefinite useful life recognised during the reporting period must be tested for impairment before the end of the period.[106]

3. Any intangible asset (regardless of whether it has an indefinite useful life or not) *that is not yet available for use* recognised during the reporting period must be impairment tested before the end of the period.[107]

4. If an intangible asset that has an indefinite useful life or is not yet available for use can only be tested for impairment as part of a CGU, then that CGU must be tested for impairment at least annually.[108]

The reason given for the annual requirement to test any intangible asset not yet ready for use is as follows:

> 'The ability of an intangible asset to generate sufficient future economic benefits to recover its carrying amount is usually subject to greater uncertainty before the asset is available for use than after it is available for use. Therefore, this Standard requires an entity to test for impairment, at least annually, the carrying amount of an intangible asset that is not yet available for use.'[109]

This will obviously have a major impact on any entity that capitalises development expenditure in accordance with IAS 38 where the period of development may straddle more than one accounting period.

A   Measuring the recoverable amount of an intangible asset with an indefinite useful life

An intangible asset with an indefinite useful life may generate cash flows as an individual asset, in which case the impairment testing procedure as set out in 3.2 and 3.3 above for a single asset applies. Additionally an intangible asset may form part of the assets within a CGU, in which case the procedures relevant to testing a CGU as set out above apply. In particular IAS 36 makes it clear that if an intangible asset with an indefinite useful life, or any intangible asset not yet ready for use, is included in the assets of a CGU, then that CGU has to be tested for impairment annually.[110]

However, IAS 36 allows a concession that only applies to those intangible assets with an indefinite useful life that form part of a CGU. It allows the most recent detailed calculation of such an asset's recoverable amount made in a preceding period to be used in the impairment test in the current period if all of the following criteria are met:

(a)   if the intangible asset is part of a CGU and the assets and liabilities making up that unit have not changed significantly since the most recent recoverable amount calculation;

(b)   that calculation of the asset's recoverable amount exceeded its carrying amount by a substantial margin; and

(c)   the likelihood that an updated calculation of the recoverable amount would be less than the asset's carrying amount is remote, based on an analysis of events and circumstances since the most recent calculation of the recoverable amount.[111]

Thus if there was sufficient headroom on the last calculation and little has changed in the CGU to which the asset belongs, it can be revisited and re-used rather than having to be entirely restarted from scratch, which considerably reduces the work involved in the annual test. The impairment test cannot be rolled forward forever, of course, and an entity will have to take a cautious approach to estimating when circumstances have changed sufficiently to require a new test.

Impairment losses experienced on intangible assets with an indefinite useful life are recognised exactly as set out above in 3.3.2, either as an individual asset or as part of a CGU, depending upon whether the intangible concerned is part of a CGU or not. There is an important distinction concerning the allocation of losses in a CGU between the treatment of goodwill and intangible assets with an indefinite useful life. As set out above in 3.3.2, if goodwill forms part of the assets of a CGU, any impairment loss first reduces the goodwill and thereafter the remaining assets are reduced pro-rata. However, if an intangible asset is part of a CGU that is impaired, there is no requirement to write down the intangible before the other assets in the CGU, rather all are written down pro-rata.

3.4.2 Impairment of goodwill

This topic is dealt with in detail in Chapter 6.

Under IFRS, only goodwill acquired in a business combination can be recognised. Inherently, goodwill cannot produce cash flows independently of other groups of assets; therefore to test it for impairment necessitates its allocation to CGUs (or groups of CGUs).

The standard does not require goodwill to be allocated between every CGU that is identified by the business. Rather it allows goodwill to be allocated to groups of CGUs, as it does corporate assets. In fact the only requirement is that goodwill is allocated to groups of CGUs that together are not larger than the 'lowest level within the entity at which the goodwill is monitored for internal management purposes' with the only proviso being that such groups should 'not be larger than a segment based on either the entity's primary or ... secondary reporting format determined in accordance with IAS 14 – *Segment Reporting*.'[112] The allocation of goodwill to CGUs and the provisions of IAS 36 concerning the minority interest's proportion of goodwill are dealt with in Chapter 6. That chapter also deals with IAS 36's requirements concerning the allocation and reallocation of goodwill following disposals or group reorganisations. Matters that affect the entity's CGUs arising from goodwill impairment testing are dealt with below.

Impairment losses on goodwill must be recognised immediately in the income statement. The losses first reduce the carrying value of the goodwill, and thereafter reduce the other assets in the CGU or group of CGUs pro-rata, as explained in more detail in 3.3.2 above.

A   Timing of the goodwill impairment test and testing of CGUs

The standard requires impairment testing for goodwill as follows:

1. All CGUs or groups of CGUs to which goodwill has been allocated must be tested for impairment at least once per year and at the same time each year. Different CGUs may be tested at different times.

2. If goodwill has been allocated during the current period, the CGU or CGU group must be tested before the end of the period (not necessarily at the end of the period).[113]

The standard makes it clear that if indications of impairment necessitate an impairment test for an individual CGU or one that is part of a group to which goodwill has been allocated, this test must be performed and any impairment loss recognised first. The impairment review is carried out on the CGU or CGU group excluding goodwill.[114] Similarly, if there are any indications of impairment with respect to the assets within a CGU, to a CGU itself or a CGU group to which goodwill has been allocated at the time of year as the goodwill impairment test is performed, these tests are carried out first and any impairment recognised. The test on the CGU or CGU group containing the goodwill must only be performed after the individual test.[115] Therefore, the entity may have to carry out an impairment test on an individual asset or CGU at a time other than at the end of its annual period.

CGUs to which goodwill has been allocated may also need to be reviewed at the end of the period if there has been an indicator of impairment even if they have been included in the goodwill test as at an earlier date.

Example 13.9:   Timing of the goodwill impairment test

An entity that prepares its financial statements to December reviews its goodwill for impairment in September. Goodwill is allocated to CGUs A, B and C and any allocation at a lower level would be arbitrary. At the time of the September 2006 impairment review, an indicator of impairment is noted in CGU A. The entity is required to test CGU A for impairment in September 2006 and provide for an impairment loss, if necessary, before testing the group of CGUs with regard to the allocated goodwill.

3.5   The reversal of impairment losses

IAS 36 does not permit an impairment loss on goodwill to be reversed under any circumstances.[116] The standard justifies this on the grounds that such a reversal would probably be an increase in internally generated goodwill, rather than a reversal of the impairment loss recognised for the acquired goodwill, and that internally generated goodwill is prohibited by IAS 38.[117]

Example 13.10:   Impairment of goodwill

Company A has a CGU that has a carrying value of $2,000,000 at 31 December 2005. This carrying value comprises $500,000 relating to goodwill and $1,500,000 relating to net tangible assets.

In 2006, as a result of losses, net tangible assets have decreased to $1,400,000 reducing the total carrying value of the unit to $1,900,000. Changes in the regulatory framework surrounding its business mean that the income-generating unit has a VIU of $1,600,000 and has thus suffered an impairment loss of $300,000. This is charged to the profit and loss account. The carrying value of goodwill is reduced to $200,000.

In 2007 the company develops a new product with the result that the VIU of the income-generating unit rises to $1,700,000. Net tangible assets have remained at $1,400,000. Despite the VIU of the business unit now being $1,700,000 compared to its carrying value of $1,600,000, it is not possible to reverse $100,000 of the prior year's impairment loss of $300,000 since the reason for the increase in value of the business unit (the launch of the new product) is not the same as the reason for the original impairment loss (the change in the regulatory environment in which the business operates).

For all other assets, including intangible assets with an indefinite life, IAS 36 requires entities to assess at each reporting date whether there is any indication that an impairment loss may no longer exist or may have decreased. If there is any such indication, the entity has to recalculate the recoverable amount of the asset.[118]

Therefore if there are indications that a previously recognised impairment loss has disappeared or reduced, it is necessary to determine again the recoverable amount (i.e. the higher of FV or VIU) so that the reversal can be quantified. The standard sets out examples of what it notes are in effect 'reverse indications' of impairment.[119] These are the reverse of those set out in paragraph 12 of the standard as indications of impairment (see 3.2 above) and are, as in paragraph 12, in two categories:

External sources of information:

(a)   a significant increase in the asset's market value.

(b)   significant changes during the period or expected in the near future in the entity's technological, market, economic or legal environment that will have a favourable effect.

(c)   decreases in market interest rates or other market rates of return on investments and those decreases are likely to affect the discount rate used in calculating the asset's value in use and increase the asset's recoverable amount materially.

Internal sources of information:

(d)   significant changes during the period or expected in the near future that will affect the extent to which, or manner in which, the asset is used. These changes include costs incurred during the period to improve or enhance the asset's performance or restructure the operation to which the asset belongs.

(e)   evidence from internal reporting that the economic performance of the asset is, or will be, better than expected[120]

Compared with paragraph 12, there are two notable omissions from this list of 'reverse indicators', one external and one internal.

The external indication not included is the mirror of the impairment indicator 'the carrying amount of the net assets of the reporting entity is more than its market capitalisation'. No explanation is provided about why, if a market capitalisation below shareholders' funds is an indication of impairment, its reversal should not be an indication of a reversal. The internal omission from the list of 'reverse indicators' is that evidence of obsolescence or physical deterioration has been reversed. Once again no reason is given but it may be that the standard-setters have assumed that no such reversal could take place without the entity incurring costs to improve or enhance the performance of the asset or the CGU so that this is, in effect, covered by indicator (d) above.

The standard also reminds preparers that a reversal, like an impairment, is evidence that depreciation method or residual value of the asset should be reviewed and may need to be adjusted, whether or not the impairment loss is reversed.[121]

A further stricture is that impairment losses should be reversed only if there has been a change in the estimates used to determine the impairment loss, e.g. a change in cash flows or discount rate (for VIU) or a change in FV. IAS 36 does not allow the mere passage of time (the 'unwinding' of the discount will increase the present value of future cash flows as they become closer) to trigger the reversal of an impairment. In other words the 'service potential' of the asset must genuinely improve if a reversal is to be recognised.[122] However, this inability to recognise the rise in value can give rise to some illogical effects, as demonstrated by the following example:

Example 13.11: Double counted losses

At the end of 2004, an entity with a single CGU is carrying out an impairment review. The discounted forecast cash flows for years 2006 and onwards would be just enough to support the carrying value of the firm's assets. However, 2005 is forecast to produce a loss and net cash outflow. The discounted value of this amount is accordingly written off the carrying value of the fixed assets in 2004 as an impairment loss. It is then suffered again in 2005 (at a slightly higher amount being now undiscounted) as the actual loss. Once that loss is past, the future cash flows are sufficient to support the original unimpaired value of the fixed assets. Nevertheless, the assets cannot be written back up through the profit and loss account to counter the double counting effect as the increase in value does not derive from a change in economic conditions or in the expected use of an asset. The entity will only 'benefit' as the assets are amortised.

If, on the other hand, the revival in cash flows is the result of expenditure by the entity to improve or enhance the performance of the asset or the CGU or on a restructuring of the CGU, there may be an obvious improvement in the service potential and the entity may be able to reverse some or all of the impairment write down.

In the event of an individual asset's impairment being reversed, the reversal may not raise the carrying value above the figure it would have stood at taking into account depreciation, if no impairment had originally been recognised.[123] Any increase above this figure would really be a revaluation, which would have to be accounted for in accordance with the standard relevant to the asset concerned.[124]

Example 13.12: Reversal of impairment losses

In 2004 an entity acquires an asset with a useful life of 10 years for $100. The asset generates net cash inflows that are largely independent of the cash inflows of other assets or groups of assets. At the end of 2006, when the carrying amount is $70, the entity recognises that there has been an impairment loss of $20. The entity writes the asset down to $50. As the useful life is not affected, the entity commences amortisation at $7 per annum to amortise the carrying value over the remaining useful life.

Two years later in 2008, the asset's carrying value is $36. Thanks to improvements in technology, the entity is able to increase the asset's VIU to $55 by spending $12 on parts that improve and enhance its performance.

The carrying value of the asset after the expenditure is $48. However, its depreciated historical cost (before charging depreciation for 2009) is $50. Therefore, the entity reverses an impairment loss of $2 and writes the asset back up to $50. Amortisation in 2009 and thereafter to the end of the asset's useful life is once again $10 per annum.

The reversal of the impairment loss of $2 represents the difference between the impairment loss of $20 and the cost of the expenditure of $12, to which has been added the reduction in the amortisation charge for two years based on the lower carrying amount ($10 – $7).

The Standard includes an illustration of the reversal of an impairment loss in the standard's accompanying section of illustrative examples, in Example 4.

All reversals are to be recognised in the income statement immediately, except for revalued assets which are dealt with below.[125]

If an impairment loss is reversed against an asset, its depreciation or amortisation is adjusted to allocate its revised carrying amount less residual value over its remaining useful life.[126]

A   Reversals of impairments – revalued assets

If an asset is recognised at a revalued amount under another IAS any reversal of an impairment loss should be treated as a revaluation increase under that other international standard. Thus a reversal of an impairment loss on a revalued asset is credited directly to equity under the heading revaluation surplus. However, to the extent that an impairment loss on the same revalued asset was previously recognised as an expense in the income statement, a reversal of that impairment loss is recognised as income in the income statement.[127]

As with assets carried at cost, after a reversal of an impairment loss is recognised on a revalued asset, the depreciation charge should be adjusted in future periods to allocate the asset's revised carrying amount, less any residual value, on a systematic basis over its remaining useful life.[128]

B   Reversals of impairments – cash-generating units

Where an entity recognises a reversal of an impairment loss on a CGU, the increase in the carrying amount of the assets of the unit should be allocated by increasing the carrying amount of the assets other than goodwill in the unit on a pro-rata basis. However, the carrying amount of an individual asset should not be increased above the lower of its recoverable amount and the carrying amount that would have resulted had no impairment loss been recognised in prior years. Any 'surplus' reversal is to be allocated to the remaining assets pro-rata, always remembering that goodwill, if allocated to an individual CGU, may not be increased under any circumstances.[129]

4 DISCLOSURES REQUIRED BY IAS 36

4.1 Introduction

This section sets out the principal disclosures required in financial statements complied under IAS for impairment as set out in IAS 36. Any disclosures required relating to impairment by other standards are dealt with in the chapter concerned. Disclosures that may be required by other authorities such as national statutes or listing authorities are not included.

4.2 IAS 36 disclosures

The disclosures required fall into two broad categories:

(i) disclosures concerning any actual impairment losses or reversals made in the period, that are obviously only required if such a loss or reversal has occurred, regardless of the type of asset involved; and

(ii) yearly disclosures concerning the annual impairment tests required for goodwill and intangible assets with an indefinite useful life, that are required regardless of whether an impairment adjustment to these types of assets has occurred or not.

4.2.1 *Disclosures required for impairment adjustments*

IAS 36 defines a class of assets as 'a grouping of assets of similar nature and use in the entity's operations'.[130] For each class of assets the entity must disclose:

'(a) the amount of impairment losses recognised in profit or loss during the period and the line item(s) of the income statement in which those impairment losses are included.

(b) the amount of reversals of impairment losses recognised in profit or loss during the period and the line item(s) of the income statement in which those impairment losses are reversed.

(c) the amount of impairment losses on revalued assets recognised directly in equity during the period.

(d) the amount of reversals of impairment losses on revalued assets recognised directly in equity during the period.'[131]

These disclosures can be made as an integral part of the other disclosures, for example the property plant and equipment note reconciling the opening and closing values (as set out in Chapter 12 at 2.7) may contain the required information.[132]

Additionally, IAS 36 links disclosure of impairments with segment disclosures. Thus, if a business is subject to IAS 14 then any impairments or reversals must be disclosed by primary reportable segment as follows:

(a) the amount of impairment losses recognised in profit or loss and directly in equity during the period.

(b) the amount of reversals of impairment losses recognised in profit or loss and directly in equity during the period.[133]

A   Material impairments

If an impairment loss for an individual asset or an individual cash-generating unit is recognised or reversed during the period and is material to the financial statements of the reporting entity as a whole, the following disclosures are required:

(a)   the events and circumstances that led to the recognition or reversal of the impairment loss;

(b)   the amount of the impairment loss recognised or reversed;

(c)   for an individual asset:

    (i)   the nature of the asset; and

    (ii)   the reportable segment [if the entity is subject to IAS 14] to which the asset belongs, based on the entity's primary format;

(d)   for a cash-generating unit:

    (i)   a description of the cash-generating unit (such as whether it is a product line, a plant, a business operation, a geographical area, a reportable segment as defined in IAS 14);

    (ii)   the amount of the impairment loss recognised or reversed by class of assets and [if the entity is subject to IAS 14] by reportable segment based on the entity's primary format; and

    (iii)   if the aggregation of assets for identifying the cash-generating unit has changed since the previous estimate of the cash-generating unit's recoverable amount (if any), a description of the current and former way of aggregating assets and the reasons for changing the way the cash-generating unit is identified;

(e)   whether the recoverable amount of the asset or cash-generating unit is its fair value less costs to sell (FV) or its value in use (VIU);

(f)   if recoverable amount is FV, the basis used to determine FV (such as whether FV was determined by reference to an active market); and

(g)   if recoverable amount is VIU, the discount rate used in the current estimate and previous estimate (if any) of VIU.[134]

It is logically possible for impairment adjustments *in aggregate* to be material, yet no single one material in itself – in which case the previous requirement that relates to individual assets or CGUs could theoretically be circumvented. Therefore the following 'catch all' requirement is added:

'An entity shall disclose the following information for the aggregate impairment losses and the aggregate reversals of impairment losses recognised during the period for which no information is disclosed in accordance with paragraph 130:

(a)   the main classes of assets affected by impairment losses and the main classes of assets affected by reversals of impairment losses.

(b)   the main events and circumstances that led to the recognition of these impairment losses and reversals of impairment losses.'[135]

If there are any cases of impairment adjustments where intangible asset with an indefinite useful life and goodwill are not involved, IAS 36 encourages the disclosure of key assumptions made in the recoverable amount calculations used to determine any impairments recognised in the period.[136] However, as set out below, if there is any impairment of a CGU containing intangible assets with an indefinite useful life or goodwill, this type of disclosure is a requirement.

4.2.2 Annual impairment disclosures required for goodwill and intangible assets with an indefinite useful life.

Paragraph 84 of IAS 36 accepts that following a business combination it may not have been possible to allocate all the goodwill to individual CGUs or groups of CGUs. In this case such allocation must have been completed by the end of the following period. In these circumstances the standard requires that the amount of any such unallocated goodwill be disclosed, together with the reasons why it has not been allocated.[137]

The annual disclosures are intended to provide the user with information about the types of estimates that have been used in arriving at the recoverable amounts of goodwill and intangible assets with an indefinite useful life, that are included in the assets of the entity at the period end. They are divided into two broad categories:

(i) those concerning individual CGUs or group of CGUs in which the carrying amount of goodwill or of intangible assets with an indefinite useful life is 'significant' in comparison with the entity's total carrying amount of these items. In this category disclosures are to be made separately for each significant CGU or group of CGUs; and

(ii) those concerning CGUs or groups of CGUs in which the carrying amount of goodwill or of intangible asset with an indefinite useful life is *not* 'significant' individually in comparison with the entity's total carrying amount of these items. In this case the disclosures can be made in aggregate.

No definition of 'significant' is given; but in our view it must be taken to mean significant in relation to any or all of asset values, shareholders funds, and to profit for the year if a write off were to be required.

For each cash-generating unit or group of units for which the carrying amount of goodwill or intangible assets with indefinite useful lives allocated to that unit or group of units is significant, the following disclosures are required every year:

'(a) the carrying amount of goodwill allocated to the unit (group of units).

(b) the carrying amount of intangible assets with indefinite useful lives allocated to the unit (group of units).

(c) the basis on which the unit's (group of units') recoverable amount has been determined (i.e. value in use or fair value less costs to sell).

(d) if the unit's (group of units') recoverable amount is based on value in use:

  (i) a description of each key assumption on which management has based its cash flow projections for the period covered by the most recent budgets/forecasts. Key assumptions are those to which the unit's (group of units') recoverable amount is most sensitive.

(ii)   a description of management's approach to determining the value(s) assigned to each key assumption, whether those value(s) reflect past experience or, if appropriate, are consistent with external sources of information, and, if not, how and why they differ from past experience or external sources of information.

(iii)   the period over which management has projected cash flows based on financial budgets/forecasts approved by management and, when a period greater than five years is used for a cash-generating unit (group of units), an explanation of why that longer period is justified.

(iv)   the growth rate used to extrapolate cash flow projections beyond the period covered by the most recent budgets/forecasts, and the justification for using any growth rate that exceeds the long-term average growth rate for the products, industries, or country or countries in which the entity operates, or for the market to which the unit (group of units) is dedicated.

(v)   the discount rate(s) applied to the cash flow projections.

(e)   if the unit's (group of units') recoverable amount is based on fair value less costs to sell, the methodology used to determine fair value less costs to sell. If fair value less costs to sell is not determined using an observable market price for the unit (group of units), the following information shall also be disclosed:

(i)   a description of each key assumption on which management has based its determination of fair value less costs to sell. Key assumptions are those to which the unit's (group of units') recoverable amount is most sensitive.

(ii)   a description of management's approach to determining the value(s) assigned to each key assumption, whether those value(s) reflect past experience or, if appropriate, are consistent with external sources of information, and, if not, how and why they differ from past experience or external sources of information.

(f)   if a reasonably possible change in a key assumption on which management has based its determination of the unit's (group of units') recoverable amount would cause the unit's (group of units') carrying amount to exceed its recoverable amount:

(i)   the amount by which the unit's (group of units') recoverable amount exceeds its carrying amount.

(ii)   the value assigned to the key assumption.

(iii)   the amount by which the value assigned to the key assumption must change, after incorporating any consequential effects of that change on the other variables used to measure recoverable amount, in order for the unit's (group of units') recoverable amount to be equal to its carrying amount.[138]

As set out above, there are separate disclosure requirements for those CGUs or groups of CGUs that taken individually do not have significant amounts of goodwill or of intangible assets with an indefinite useful life within their carrying values. First, an aggregate disclosure has to be made of the not significant amounts of goodwill or of intangible assets with an indefinite useful life, as follows:

'If some or all of the carrying amount of goodwill or intangible assets with indefinite useful lives is allocated across multiple cash-generating units (groups of units), and the amount so allocated to each unit (group of units) is not significant in comparison with the entity's total carrying amount of goodwill or intangible assets with indefinite useful lives, that fact shall be disclosed, together with the aggregate carrying amount of goodwill or intangible assets with indefinite useful lives allocated to those units (groups of units).'[139]

Secondly, if in aggregate these amounts are significant in relation to the entirety of the carrying amount of the entity's goodwill or intangible assets with an indefinite useful life, the following is required to be disclosed:

'In addition, if the recoverable amounts of any of those units (groups of units) are based on the same key assumption(s) and the aggregate carrying amount of goodwill or intangible assets with indefinite useful lives allocated to them is significant in comparison with the entity's total carrying amount of goodwill or intangible assets with indefinite useful lives, an entity shall disclose that fact, together with:

(a) the aggregate carrying amount of goodwill allocated to those units (groups of units).

(b) the aggregate carrying amount of intangible assets with indefinite useful lives allocated to those units (groups of units).

(c) a description of the key assumption(s).

(d) a description of management's approach to determining the value(s) assigned to the key assumption(s), whether those value(s) reflect past experience or, if appropriate, are consistent with external sources of information, and, if not, how and why they differ from past experience or external sources of information.

(e) if a reasonably possible change in the key assumption(s) would cause the aggregate of the units' (groups of units') carrying amounts to exceed the aggregate of their recoverable amounts:

(i) the amount by which the aggregate of the units' (groups of units') recoverable amounts exceeds the aggregate of their carrying amounts.

(ii) the value(s) assigned to the key assumption(s).

(iii) the amount by which the value(s) assigned to the key assumption(s) must change, after incorporating any consequential effects of the change on the other variables used to measure recoverable amount, in order for the aggregate of the units' (groups of units') recoverable amounts to be equal to the aggregate of their carrying amounts.'[140]

Example 9 in Appendix B of IAS 36, reproduced below, gives an indication of the types of assumptions and other relevant information the IASB envisages being disclosed under this requirement. Such detailed items as follows are envisaged by the IASB for disclosure: budgeted gross margins, average gross margins, expected efficiency improvements., whether values assigned to key assumptions reflect past experience, what improvements management believes are reasonably achievable each year, forecast exchange rates during the budget period, forecast consumer price indices during the budget period for raw materials, market share and anticipated growth in market share. It remains to be seen whether in reality such sensitive information will be provided by entities in anything other than a generalised format.

Example 13.13: Disclosures relating to impairment tests for goodwill and intangible assets

Entity M includes the following disclosure in the notes to its financial statements for the year ending 31 December 20X3.

Impairment Tests for Goodwill and Intangible Assets with Indefinite Lives

Goodwill has been allocated for impairment testing purposes to three individual cash-generating units—two in Europe (units A and B) and one in North America (unit C)—and to one group of cash generating units (comprising operation XYZ) in Asia. The carrying amount of goodwill allocated to unit C and operation XYZ is significant in comparison with the total carrying amount of goodwill, but the carrying amount of goodwill allocated to each of units A and B is not. Nevertheless, the recoverable amounts of units A and B are based on some of the same key assumptions, and the aggregate carrying amount of goodwill allocated to those units is significant.

Operation XYZ

The recoverable amount of operation XYZ has been determined based on a value in use calculation. That calculation uses cash flow projections based on financial budgets approved by management covering a five-year period, and a discount rate of 8.4 per cent. Cash flows beyond that five-year period have been extrapolated using a steady 6.3 per cent growth rate. This growth rate does not exceed the long-term average growth rate for the market in which XYZ operates. Management believes that any reasonably possible change in the key assumptions on which XYZ's recoverable amount is based would not cause XYZ's carrying amount to exceed its recoverable amount.

Unit C

The recoverable amount of unit C has also been determined based on a value in use calculation. That calculation uses cash flow projections based on financial budgets approved by management covering a five-year period, and a discount rate of 9.2 per cent. C's cash flows beyond the five-year period are extrapolated using a steady 12 per cent growth rate. This growth rate exceeds by 4 percentage points the long-term average growth rate for the market in which C operates. However, C benefits from the protection of a 10-year patent on its primary product, granted in December 20X2. Management believes that a 12 per cent growth rate is reasonable in the light of that patent. Management also believes that any reasonably possible change in the key assumptions on which C's recoverable amount is based would not cause C's carrying amount to exceed its recoverable amount.

Units A and B

The recoverable amounts of units A and B have been determined on the basis of value in use calculations. Those units produce complementary products, and their recoverable amounts are based on some of the same key assumptions. Both value in use calculations use cash flow projections based on financial budgets approved by management covering a four-year period, and a discount rate of 7.9 per cent. Both sets of cash flows beyond the four-year period are extrapolated using a steady 5 per cent growth rate. This growth rate does not exceed the long-term average growth rate for the market in which A and B operate. Cash flow projections during the budget period for both A and B are also based on the same expected gross margins during the budget period and the same raw materials price inflation during the budget period. Management believes that any reasonably possible change in any of these key assumptions would not cause the aggregate carrying amount of A and B to exceed the aggregate recoverable amount of those units.

	Operation XYZ	**Unit C**	**Units A and B (in aggregate)**
Carrying amount of goodwill	CU1,200	CU3,000	CU800
Carrying amount of brand name with indefinite useful life	–	CU1,000	–

Key assumptions used in value in use calculations *

Key assumption	**Budgeted gross margins**	**5-year US government bond rate**	**Budgeted gross margins**
Basis for determining value(s) assigned to key assumption	Average gross margins achieved in period immediately before the budget period, increased for expected efficiency improvements.	Yield on 5-year US government bonds at the beginning of the budget period.	Average gross margins achieved in period immediately before the budget period, increased for expected efficiency
	Values assigned to key assumption reflect past experience, except for efficiency improvements. Management believes improvements of 5% per year are reasonably achievable	Value assigned to key assumption is consistent with external sources of information.	Values assigned to key assumption reflect past experience, except for efficiency improvements. Management believes improvements of 5% per year are reasonably achievable

* The key assumptions shown in this table for units A and B are only those that are used in the recoverable amount calculations for both units

Key assumption	Japanese yen/US dollar exchange rate during the budget period	Raw materials price inflation	Raw materials price inflation
Basis for determining value(s) assigned to key assumption	Average market forward exchange rate over the budget period.	Forecast consumer price indices during the budget period for North American countries from which raw materials are purchased.	Forecast consumer price indices during the budget period for European countries from which raw materials are purchased
	Value assigned to key assumption is consistent with external sources of information.	Value assigned to key assumption is consistent with external sources of information	Value assigned to key assumption is consistent with external sources of information.

Key assumption	Budgeted market share	Budgeted market share
Basis for determining value(s) assigned to key assumption	Average market share in period immediately before the budget period.	Average market share in period immediately before the budget period, increased each year for anticipated growth in market share.
	Value assigned to key assumption reflects past experience. No change in market share expected as a result of ongoing product quality improvements coupled with anticipated increase in competition	Management believes market share growth of 6% per year is reasonably achievable due to increased advertising expenditure, the benefits from the protection of the 10year patent on C's primary product, and the expected synergies to be achieved from operating C as part of M's North American segment

5   EFFECTIVE DATE, TRANSITIONAL PROVISIONS AND FIRST-TIME ADOPTION

5.1   Transitional provisions and effective date

The transitional arrangements and effective date depend on whether an entity elects to apply IFRS 3 from any date earlier than that required by that standard. IFRS 3 requires prospective application, from the beginning of the first annual period beginning on or after 31 March 2004. Any entity that elects to apply IFRS 3 to earlier business combinations must also apply IAS 36 prospectively from that same date.[141] Otherwise, an entity is required to apply IAS 36:

(a)   to goodwill and intangible assets acquired in business combinations for which the agreement date is on or after 31 March 2004; and

(b)   to all other assets prospectively from the beginning of the first annual period beginning on or after 31 March 2004.[142]

5.2   First-time adoption

As far as goodwill is concerned, first time adopters of IFRS are required by IFRS 1 to subject all goodwill carried in the balance sheet at the date of transition to an impairment test, regardless of whether there are any indications of impairment.

> 'Regardless of whether there is any indication that the goodwill may be impaired, the first-time adopter shall apply IAS 36 *Impairment of Assets* in testing the goodwill for impairment at the date of transition to IFRS and in recognising any resulting impairment loss in retained earnings (or, if so required by IAS 36, in revaluation surplus). The impairment test shall be based on conditions at the date of transition to IFRS.'[143]

For other assets, first time adopters have the benefit of a number of exemptions from the requirement for full restatement of the opening IFRS balance sheet. Given the significance of property, plant and equipment in particular in the balance sheet of most first-time adopters (and the sheer number of transactions affecting property, plant and equipment) restatement is not only extremely important but will often also involve undue cost and effort. Still, a first-time adopter needs a cost basis for the assets in its opening IFRS balance sheet. Therefore, the IASB decided to introduce the notion of a 'deemed cost' that is not the 'true' IFRS compliant cost basis of an asset, but a surrogate that is deemed to be a suitable starting point.

The IASB argued that it is not necessary to restrict application of the exemption to classes of assets to prevent selective revaluations, because 'IAS 36 *Impairment of Assets* requires an impairment test if there is any indication that an asset is impaired. Thus, if an entity uses fair value as deemed cost for assets whose fair value is above cost, it cannot ignore indications that the recoverable amount of other assets may have fallen below their carrying amount. Therefore, IFRS 1 does not restrict the use of fair value as deemed cost to entire classes of asset.'[144] Nevertheless, it seems doubtful that the quality of financial information would benefit from a revaluation

If a first-time adopter recognised or reversed any impairment losses in preparing its opening IFRS balance sheet at the date of transition, it should disclose the information that IAS 36 would have required 'if the entity had recognised those impairment losses or reversals in the period beginning with the date of transition to IFRS'.[145] The purpose of this disclosure requirement is that while, as the IASB acknowledges, there is inevitably subjectivity about impairment losses, 'this disclosure provides transparency about impairment losses recognised on transition to IFRS. These losses might otherwise receive less attention than impairment losses recognised in earlier or later periods'.[146] Chapter 4 deals with first-time adoption and IFRS 1 in detail.

6   CONCLUSION

Two developments are placing increased emphasis on the part to be played by impairment within financial reporting under International GAAP. First, the new regime under which goodwill is not amortised means that impairment tests will have to be applied at least annually by all entities that record goodwill in their consolidated accounts. Additionally, those entities that are adopting IFRSs for the first time in 2005 will have to apply an impairment test to all goodwill carried forward at transition. Second, the policy of the IASB to extend fair value based accounting, especially fair values that are based on models and not on observable market transactions, will also increase the importance of testing for impairment.

Notwithstanding this central role, IAS 36 is not an easy standard for entities to apply in practice. To take discount rates as a case in point, an entity is required to arrive at an estimate of the rate that the market would expect on an equally risky investment.[147] This information is not readily obtainable. The standard allows a number of different methods to be used to estimate this rate; yet it gives little concrete guidance and allows as a starting point discount rates that are unlikely to be relevant, such as an entity's incremental borrowing rate. It is possible that the standard setters have attempted to deflect academic criticism by not specifying how a discount rate should be chosen; but this vagueness has left many entities unsure about how to proceed.

As a consequence, it becomes difficult to be convinced that the comparability requirement underlying IFRS will be met in practice, as entities will interpret the standard's requirements in differing ways. Moreover, because assets (other than goodwill) or CGUs are only tested for impairment if there are indicators of impairment, there will be comparability issues even within entities. There may be no indicators of impairment with regard to some assets or CGUs even though they are actually earning a sub-market rate of return, at least in the short term.

It is difficult to see how these issues can be resolved in the continuing absence of a clear underlying theoretical basis underpinning the carrying value of assets and liabilities. In the short term, it is likely that many entities will consult valuations experts in order to apply IAS 36. In the longer term it remains to be seen if the IASB will give entities the standard on impairment that they deserve, which is one that contains an unambiguous, comparable and useable impairment test.

References

1 IAS 36, *Impairment of assets*, IASB, March 2004, para. 13
2 IAS 36, paras. 138-139.
3 IAS 36, para. 1
4 IAS 36, para. 2.
5 IAS 36, para. 3.
6 IAS 36, para. 4.
7 IAS 36, para. 5.
8 IAS 36, para. 6.
9 IAS 36, para. 10.
10 IAS 36, paras. 8-9.
11 IAS 36, para. 11.
12 IAS 36, para. 15.
13 IAS 36, para. 9.
14 IAS 36, para. 13.
15 IAS 36, para. 12.
16 IAS 36, para. 14.
17 IAS 36, para. 15.
18 IAS 36, para. 16.
19 IAS 36, para. 17.
20 IAS 36, para. 18.
21 IAS 36, para. 31.
22 IAS 36, para. 19.
23 IAS 36, para. 20.
24 IAS 36, para. 21.
25 IAS 36, para. 22.
26 IAS 36, para. 23.
27 IAS 36, para. 25.
28 IAS 36, para. 26.
29 IAS 36, para. 27.
30 IAS 36, para. 27.
31 IAS 36, para. 28.
32 IAS 36, para. 29.
33 IAS 36, para. 30.
34 IAS 36, para. 31.
35 IAS 36, para. 66.
36 IAS 36, para. 67.
37 IAS 36, paras. 6 and 68.
38 IAS 36, para. 68.
39 IAS 36, para. 69.
40 IAS 36, Illustrative Examples, Example 1.
41 IAS 36, para. 70.
42 IAS 36, para. 71.
43 IAS 36, Illustrative Examples, Example 1.
44 IAS 36, paras. 72-73.
45 IAS 36, paras. 74-75.
46 IAS 36, para. 76.
47 IAS 36, para. 77.
48 IAS 36, para. 78.
49 IAS 36, para. 79.
50 IAS 36, para. 100
51 IAS 36, para. 101
52 IAS 36, para. 102

53 IAS 36, para. 103, Illustrative Examples, Example 8
54 IAS 36, para. 30.
55 IAS 36, para. 33.
56 IAS 36, para. 34.
57 IAS 36, para. 35.
58 IAS 36, para. 38.
59 IAS 36, para. 36.
60 IAS 36, para. 37.
61 IAS 36, para. 39.
62 IAS 36, para. 40.
63 IAS 36, para. 43.
64 IAS 36, para. 41.
65 IAS 36, para. 42.
66 IAS 36, para. 44.
67 IAS 36, para. 48.
68 IAS 36, para. 49.
69 IAS 36, paras. 44-45.
70 IAS 36, paras. 46-47.
71 IAS 36, para. 48.
72 IAS 36, paras. 50-51.
73 IAS 36, para. 52-53.
74 IAS 36, para. 54.
75 IAS 21, *The Effects of Changes in Foreign Exchange Rates* , IASB, December 2003, para. 25.
76 IAS 36, para. 55.
77 IAS 36, para. 56.
78 IAS 36, Appendix A, para. A17.
79 IAS 36, Appendix A, para. A18.
80 IAS 36, Appendix A, para. A18.
81 IAS 36, Appendix A, para. A19.
82 IAS 36, Appendix A, para. A20.
83 IAS 36, Appendix A, para. A21.
84 IAS 36, para. 16.
85 One source of reference which may prove useful is a Digest issued by the Corporate Finance Faculty of the ICAEW – *The Cost of Capital*, Simon Pallett, ICAEW, 1999.
86 IAS 36, para. 55.
87 IAS 36, para. BCZ85.
88 IAS 36, para. BCZ85.
89 IAS 36, para. 59.
90 IAS 36, para. 60.
91 IAS 36, para. 61.
92 IAS 16, *Property, Plant and Equipment*, IASB, December 2003, (amended March 2004), para. 73(d).
93 IAS 36, para. 62.
94 IAS 36, para. 63.
95 IAS 36, para. 104.
96 IAS 36, para. 88.
97 IAS 36, para. 105.
98 IAS 36, para. 106.
99 IAS 36, para. 108.
100 IAS 36, para. 107.

101 IFRS 3, *Business Combinations*, IASB, March 2004, paras. 54-55.
102 IAS 38, paras. 89, and 107-108.
103 IAS 38, *Intangible Assets*, IASB, March 2004, para. 91.
104 IAS 38, para. 108.
105 IAS 36, para. 10.
106 IAS 36, para. 10.
107 IAS 36, paras. 10-11.
108 IAS 36, para. 89.
109 IAS 36, para. 11.
110 IAS 36, para. 89.
111 IAS 36, para. 24.
112 IAS 36, para. 80.
113 IAS 36, para. 96.
114 IAS 36, para. 88.
115 IAS 36, paras. 97-98.
116 IAS 36, para. 124.
117 IAS 36, para. 125
118 IAS 36, para. 110.
119 IAS 36, para. 112.
120 IAS 36, para. 111.
121 IAS 36, para. 113.
122 IAS 36, paras. 114-116.
123 IAS 36, para. 117.
124 IAS 36, para. 118.
125 IAS 36, para. 119.
126 IAS 36, para. 121.
127 IAS 36, paras. 119-120.
128 IAS 36, para. 121.
129 IAS 36, paras. 122-123.
130 IAS 36, para. 127.
131 IAS 36, para. 126.
132 IAS 36, para. 128.
133 IAS 36, para. 129.
134 IAS 36, para. 130.
135 IAS 36, para. 131.
136 IAS 36, para. 132.
137 IAS 36, para. 133.
138 IAS 36, para. 134.
139 IAS 36, para. 135.
140 IAS 36, para. 135.
141 IAS 36, para. 138
142 IAS 36, para. 139.
143 IFRS 1, *First-time Adoption of International Financial Reporting Standards*, IASB, June 2003, (amended March 2004), para. B2(g).
144 IFRS 1, para. BC45.
145 IFRS 1, para. 39.
146 IFRS 1, para. BC94.
147 IAS 36, para. 55.

Chapter 14   Capitalisation of borrowing costs

1   INTRODUCTION

A point of contention in determining the initial measurement of an asset is whether or not finance costs incurred during the period of its construction should be capitalised. There have always been a number of strong arguments in favour of the capitalisation of directly attributable finance costs. It is argued that they are just as much a cost as any other directly attributable cost, that expensing finance costs distorts the choice between purchasing and constructing the asset, that capitalising the costs leads to a carrying value that is far more akin to the market value of the asset and that the accounts are more likely to represent the true success or failure of the project. However, some proponents of this view have noted that there is a cost to all entities of constructing assets whether or not they have taken out borrowings for the purpose. If capitalisation were to become mandatory, in theory notional interest should also be capitalised. No standard-setter has yet taken this step.

In March 1984, the (then) IASC published IAS 23 – *Capitalisation of Borrowing Costs*. Under this original version of IAS 23, capitalisation was optional, but certain rules were laid down if a policy of capitalisation were to be adopted.[1] A revised version of IAS 23 – *Borrowing Costs* – was issued in 1993, which took a different approach. The IASC did not go so far as to ban the capitalisation of borrowing costs. Under the revised IAS 23 the benchmark treatment for borrowing costs is that they should be recognised as an expense in the period in which they are incurred regardless of how the borrowings are applied.[2] However, the revised IAS 23 incorporates capitalisation of borrowing costs as an allowed alternative treatment.

2   THE REQUIREMENTS OF IAS 23

2.1   Scope and definitions

2.1.1   Scope

IAS 23 deals with the treatment of borrowing costs in general, rather than focusing on capitalising borrowing costs as part of the carrying value of assets.

The standard does not deal with the actual or imputed costs of equity, including preferred capital that is not classified as a liability.[3] This means that any distributions or other payments made in respect of equity instruments, as defined by IAS 32 – *Financial Instruments: Disclosure and Presentation* – are not within the scope of IAS 23; conversely, interest and dividends payable on instruments classified as financial liabilities would appear to be within the scope of the standard. See Chapter 17 regarding the classification of instruments as debt or equity.

2.1.2   Qualifying assets

IAS 23 defines a qualifying asset as 'an asset that necessarily takes a substantial period of time to get ready for its intended use or sale'.[4] Examples of qualifying assets in the standard are inventories that require a substantial period of time to bring them to a saleable condition, manufacturing plants, power generation facilities and investment properties. Stocks that are routinely manufactured, or otherwise produced in large quantities on a repetitive basis over a short period of time, and assets that are ready for their intended use or sale when acquired are not qualifying assets.[5] Construction contracts, by contrast, would appear to be capable of being qualifying assets.

In the case of equity accounted investments, the IASC considered whether or not the investor should look through to the investee's activities when applying the proposed revised Standard. However, it decided that this could involve an element of double-counting, since the investee itself would apply the Standard.[6] Accordingly, IAS 23 states that 'other investments' should not be qualifying assets.[7]

2.1.3   Borrowing costs

Borrowing costs are interest and other costs incurred by an entity in connection with the borrowing of funds.[8]

Borrowing costs include:

(a)   interest on bank overdrafts and short-term and long-term borrowings;

(b)   amortisation of discounts or premiums relating to borrowings;

(c)   amortisation of ancillary costs incurred in connection with the arrangement of borrowings;

(d)   finance charges in respect of finance leases recognised in accordance with IAS 17, Leases; and

(e)   exchange differences arising from foreign currency borrowings to the extent that they are regarded as an adjustment to interest costs.[9]

The recognition and measurement of finance costs is not a matter for IAS 23 and this is an area that has changed considerably since the standard was issued in 1984. This is discussed further at 3.1 below.

2.2 Accounting policies

2.2.1 Borrowing costs treated as an expense

The standard's benchmark treatment is that borrowing costs should be treated as an expense in the period in which they are incurred, regardless of how the borrowings have been applied.[10]

2.2.2 Capitalisation of borrowing costs

Borrowing costs are treated as an expense unless they meet the criteria for capitalisation. If an entity adopts the allowed alternative treatment, borrowing costs should be capitalised if they are directly attributable to the acquisition, construction or production of a qualifying asset.[11] These borrowing costs are included in the cost of the asset; all other borrowing costs are recognised as an expense in the period in which they are incurred.[12]

Some questioned whether an entity could choose to capitalise borrowing costs for certain qualifying assets and not for others or whether it had to select a policy to apply to all qualifying assets. In other words, is a policy of 'selective' capitalisation permitted under IFRS? This issue was referred to the IASC's Standing Interpretations Committee (SIC), which confirmed in SIC-2 – *Capitalisation of Borrowing Costs* – that an entity must choose one or other treatment as an accounting policy and apply it consistently.

As a result, if an entity adopts a policy of capitalising borrowing costs, that treatment must be applied consistently to all borrowing costs that are directly attributable to the acquisition, construction or production of all qualifying assets of the entity. An entity should continue to capitalise such borrowing costs even if the carrying amount of the asset exceeds its recoverable amount. However, the carrying amount of the asset should be written down to recognise impairment losses in such cases.[13]

2.3 Capitalisation of borrowing costs

2.3.1 Directly attributable borrowing costs

In determining which borrowing costs satisfy the 'directly attributable' criterion, the standard starts from the premise that directly attributable borrowing costs are those that would have been avoided if the expenditure on the qualifying asset had not been made.[14]

The standard notes that the borrowing costs that are directly related can be readily identified if an entity borrows funds specifically for the purpose.[15] In this case, the borrowing costs eligible for capitalisation are the actual borrowing costs incurred during the period.[16] However, as entities frequently borrow funds in advance of expenditure on qualifying assets, any investment income on the temporary investment of those borrowings should be deducted and only the net amount capitalised.[17]

2.3.2 *Capitalisation rate*

IAS 23 concedes that there may be practical difficulties in identifying a direct relationship between particular borrowings and a qualifying asset and in determining the borrowings that could otherwise have been avoided. This could happen if the financing activity of an entity is co-ordinated centrally, by which the standard presumably means that the entity borrows to meet its requirements as a whole and the construction is being financed out of general borrowings. Other circumstances that may cause difficulties are identified:

- an entity has a group treasury function that uses a range of debt instruments to borrow funds at varying rates of interest and lends those funds on various bases to other entities in the group; or

- loans are denominated in, or linked to, foreign currency, or the group operates in highly inflationary economies.

In any event, the standard makes allowance for the problems that arise in practice and concedes that the determination of attributable borrowing costs may be difficult and require the exercise of judgement.[18]

If funds are borrowed generally and used for the purpose of obtaining a qualifying asset, the amount of borrowing costs eligible for capitalisation should be determined by applying a capitalisation rate to the expenditures on that asset. The capitalisation rate should be the weighted average of the borrowing costs applicable to the borrowings of the entity that are outstanding during the period, other than borrowings made specifically for the purpose of obtaining a qualifying asset. The amount of borrowing costs capitalised during a period should not exceed the amount of borrowing costs incurred during that period.[19] Of course, where funds are borrowed generally, there is no question of reducing the amount of borrowing costs capitalised by interest income earned. The standard allows that the average carrying amount of the asset during a period, including borrowing costs previously capitalised, is normally a reasonable approximation of the expenditures to which the capitalisation rate is applied in that period.[20]

In some circumstances all borrowings made by the group can be taken into account in determining the weighted average of the borrowing costs. In other circumstances only those borrowings made by individual subsidiaries may be taken into account.[21] Presumably this will be largely determined by the extent to which borrowings are made centrally (and, perhaps, expenses met in the same way) and passed through to individual group companies via intercompany accounts and intra-group loans.

The capitalisation rate is discussed further at 3.2 below.

2.3.3 Impairment and capitalisation of borrowing costs

SIC-2 clearly states that when an entity has elected the allowed alternative in IAS 23, it continues to capitalise borrowing costs that are directly attributable to the acquisition, construction or production of a qualifying asset as part of the carrying amount of the asset, even if the capitalisation causes the carrying amount of the asset to exceed its recoverable amount.[22]

In the event that the carrying amount of the qualifying asset exceeds its recoverable amount or net realisable value, the asset must be written down in accordance with the relevant international standard. This also applies to the asset's expected ultimate cost if the asset is incomplete.[23] The expected ultimate cost must include costs to complete and the estimated capitalised interest thereon.

IAS 36 – *Impairment of assets* – will apply unless the asset is outside its scope because the asset's carrying value is covered by another, more specific standard. The following assets are outside the scope of IAS 36: inventories, assets arising from construction contracts, deferred tax assets, assets arising from employee benefits, financial assets that are included in the scope of IAS 39, investment property that is measured at fair value, biological assets under IAS 41, deferred acquisition costs and intangible assets arising from an insurer's contractual rights under insurance contracts within the scope of IFRS 4 and non-current assets (or disposal groups) classified as held for sale in accordance with IFRS 5.[24] Impairment is fully discussed in Chapter 13.

2.4 Commencement, suspension and cessation of capitalisation

2.4.1 Commencement of capitalisation

IAS 23 requires that capitalisation should commence when:

(a) expenditures for the asset are being incurred;

(b) borrowing costs are being incurred; and

(c) activities that are necessary to prepare the asset for its intended use or sale are in progress.[25]

The standard makes it explicit that only those expenditures on a qualifying asset that have resulted in payments of cash, transfers of other assets or the assumption of interest-bearing liabilities, may be included in determining borrowing costs. Such expenditures must be reduced by any progress payments and grants received in connection with the asset.[26]

The activities necessary to prepare an asset for its intended use or sale extend to more than the physical construction of the asset. Necessary activities can start before the commencement of physical construction and include, for example, technical and administrative work such as obtaining permits. However, interest may not be capitalised during a period in which there are no activities that change the asset's condition. For example, borrowing costs incurred while land is under development are capitalised during the period in which activities related to the development are being undertaken. However, borrowing costs incurred while land acquired for building purposes is held without any associated development activity do not qualify for capitalisation.[27] A house-builder or property developer may not capitalise borrowing costs on its 'land bank'.

2.4.2 Suspension of capitalisation

IAS 23 states that capitalisation should be suspended during extended periods in which active development is interrupted. However, the standard distinguishes between extended periods of interruption (when capitalisation would be suspended) and periods of temporary delay that are a necessary part of preparing the asset for its intended purpose (when capitalisation is not normally suspended). Capitalisation continues during periods when stock is undergoing slow transformation – the example is given of stocks taking an extended time to mature (presumably such products as scotch whisky or cognac). A bridge construction delayed by temporary adverse weather conditions, where such conditions are common in the region, would also not be a cause for suspension of capitalisation.[28]

2.4.3 Cessation of capitalisation

The standard requires capitalisation to cease when substantially all the activities necessary to prepare the qualifying asset for its intended use or sale are complete.[29] An asset is normally ready for its intended use or sale when the physical construction of the asset is complete even though routine administrative work might still continue. If minor modifications, such as the decoration of a property to the purchaser's specification, are all that are outstanding, this indicates that substantially all the activities are complete.[30]

Furthermore, when the construction of a qualifying asset is completed in parts and each part is capable of being used while construction continues on other parts, capitalisation should cease when substantially all the activities necessary to prepare that part for its intended use or sale are completed.[31] An example of this might be a business park comprising several buildings, each of which is capable of being fully utilised while construction continues on other parts.[32]

2.5   Disclosure requirements of IAS 23

Under the IAS 23 benchmark treatment the entity should disclose that it expenses all borrowing costs immediately.[33]

Under the IAS 23 allowed alternative treatment the following disclosures are required to be made:

(a)   that the entity capitalises borrowing costs in accordance with the allowed alternative treatment;

(b)   the amount of borrowing costs capitalised during the period; and

(c)   the capitalisation rate used to determine the amount of borrowing costs eligible for capitalisation.[34]

3   PRACTICAL ISSUES

3.1   Borrowing costs

At the time that IAS 23 was first implemented in 1984 there was little guidance on the measurement and accounting treatment of finance costs. Even after its revision in 1993, the standard predates the accounting rules now in IAS 32 and IAS 39 – *Financial Instruments: Recognition and Measurement.*[35] In addition, in the twenty years since the standard was originally issued, financial instruments have become considerably more complex.

The standard lists various interest and other costs that may comprise part of borrowing costs, together with finance charges in respect of finance leases recognised in accordance with IAS 17. Certain exchange differences may also be capitalised; their treatment is addressed at 3.1.2 below, whilst some of the other issues are discussed in 3.1.3. The treatment of lease liabilities is addressed further in Chapter 23.

3.1.2   *Exchange differences as a borrowing cost*

Borrowings in one currency may have been used to finance a development the costs of which are incurred primarily in another currency, e.g. a US dollar loan financing a rouble development. This may have been done on the basis that, over the period of the development, the cost, after allowing for exchange differences, was expected to be less than the interest cost of an equivalent rouble loan.

IAS 23 defines borrowing costs as including exchange differences arising from foreign currency borrowings to the extent that they are regarded as an adjustment to interest costs.[36] The standard does not expand on this point. We consider that, as exchange rate movements are largely a function of differential interest rates, in most circumstances the foreign exchange differences on directly attributable borrowings will be an adjustment to interest costs that can meet the definition of borrowing costs. However, care will have to be taken if there is a sudden fluctuation in exchange rates that cannot be attributed to changes in interest rates. In such cases we believe that a practical approach is to cap the exchange differences taken as borrowing costs at the amount of borrowing costs on functional currency equivalent borrowings.

3.1.3   *Other finance costs*

Borrowing costs as identified by the standard may include interest on bank overdrafts and short-term and long-term borrowings, amortisation of discounts or premiums relating to borrowings, amortisation of ancillary costs incurred in connection with the arrangement of borrowings.

These are the costs that an entity will encounter if it has financed its development through straightforward loan from banks or similar types of organisation. In general, such financial liabilities will be accounted for at amortised cost and the finance costs calculated in accordance with IAS 39 using the effective interest method, as follows.

The *amortised cost* of a financial liability is the amount at which it was measured at initial recognition minus principal repayments, plus or minus the cumulative amortisation of any difference between that initial amount and the maturity amount. The *effective interest method* calculates amortisation using the effective interest rate of a financial instrument and allocates the interest expense over the relevant period. The *effective interest rate* is the rate that exactly discounts estimated future cash payments over the expected life of the instrument or, when appropriate, a shorter period, to the instrument's net carrying amount.[37] This is further discussed in Chapter 18 at 5.

The borrowing costs eligible for capitalisation are those that are recognised as an expense in the period using the effective interest rate.

However IAS 23 does not address many of the ways in which an entity may finance its operations or other finance costs that it may incur. The standard does not, for example, address any of the following:

- the many derivative financial instruments such interest rate swaps, floors, caps and collars that are commonly used to manage interest rate risk on borrowings;

- gains and losses on derecognition of borrowings, for example early settlement of directly attributable borrowings that have been renegotiated prior to completion of an asset in the course of construction; and

- dividends payable on shares classified as financial liabilities (such as certain redeemable preference shares) that have been recognised as an expense in profit or loss.

These are simply a few of the most commonly encountered examples – the list is very far from exhaustive.

We consider that IAS 23 does not preclude the classification of costs other than those that it identifies as borrowing costs that may be eligible for capitalisation. However, they must meet the basic criterion in the standard, i.e. that they are costs that are directly attributable to the acquisition, construction or production or a qualifying asset. In addition, as in the case of exchange differences (see 3.1.2 above), capitalisation of such costs should be permitted only 'to the extent that they are regarded as an adjustment to interest costs'.

A   Derivative financial instruments

The most straightforward and most commonly encountered derivative financial instrument used to manage interest rate risk is a floating to fixed interest rate swap, as in the following example.

Example 14.1:   Interest rate swaps

Entity A has borrowed €4 million for five years at a floating interest rate to fund the construction of a building. In order to hedge the cash flow interest rate risk arising from these borrowings, A has entered into a matching pay-fixed receive-floating interest rate swap based on the same underlying nominal sum and duration as the borrowing that effectively converts the interest rates on the borrowings to fixed rate. The net effect of the periodic cash settlements under the instrument is as if A had borrowed €4 million at a fixed rate of interest.

Prior to IAS 39, entities simply recognised, on an accruals basis, each periodic cash settlement in profit or loss. Although these instruments are not addressed in IAS 23, there is no doubt that the net costs of such 'synthetic' fixed rate debt would have been treated as a borrowing cost and therefore eligible for capitalisation if it met the criteria in the standard.

IAS 39 has complicated the situation considerably by completely changing the basis on which such instruments are recognised and measured. Briefly, a derivative financial instrument is classified as by IAS 39 as held for trading and recognised initially at its fair value with changes in the fair value being taken to profit or loss (see Chapter 15 at 7.1.1) unless it is a designated effective hedging instrument (see Chapter 19), in which case the entity may be eligible to apply hedge accounting. IAS 39 describes hedge accounting as 'recognising the offsetting effects on net profit or loss of changes in the fair values of hedging instruments and related items being hedged';[38] this is achieved by taking fair value changes on hedging instruments to equity and recycling the effective element to income to match the gain or loss on the hedged item. Those elements of the changes in value of designated effective hedging instruments that are not effective in offsetting the changes in fair value of the item being hedged (e.g. changes in the counterparties' creditworthiness) are always taken to the income statement. See Chapter 19 at 4 and 5 regarding how to account for effective hedges and the conditions that these instruments must meet.

However, the net effect on income of an interest rate swap such as the above (a 'cash flow swap' in IAS 39 parlance because it is a hedge of the exposure to variability in cash flows) is very similar to the accruals accounting treatment under which the cash flows on the borrowing and the swap were recognised in income (see Chapter 19 at 4.2).

The consequence of this is that not all derivative financial instruments that are directly attributable to the acquisition, construction or production or a qualifying asset will be accounted for in the same way. If the instrument does not meet the conditions for hedge accounting then the effects on income will be different to those if it does and they will also be dissimilar from year to year.

The question arises as to whether the borrowing costs of the entity should be based on the amount that is recognised in the income statement, regardless of the treatment of the derivative, or whether (as with exchange differences) it should be based on the cost to the entity of its borrowings. We consider that the latter is the more appropriate interpretation, so that the costs eligible for capitalisation should not differ depending on whether or not hedge accounting has been applied.

B   *Gains or losses on termination of derivative financial instruments*

If an entity terminates an interest rate swap, for example, before the end of the term of the instrument, it will usually either have to make or will receive a payment depending on the fair value of the instrument at that time. This fair value is, of course, based on expected future interest rates; in other words it is an estimated prepayment of the future cash flows under the instrument. Again the accounting under IAS 39 will differ depending on whether the instrument has been designated as a hedge or not; in the former case, the entity will usually continue to account for the cumulative gain or loss on the instrument as if the hedge were still in place (see Chapter 19 at 4.2).

In considering whether such gains or losses are borrowing costs, therefore, there is an argument that only that element that applies to the period of construction of the asset is eligible for capitalisation as part of the asset. This will obviously be easier to calculate if hedge accounting continues to be applied and in this case, as a matter of practicalities, the amount taken to income should be reflected in borrowing costs.

C   Gains and losses on derecognition of borrowings

If an entity repays borrowings early, in whole or in part, then it may recognise a gain or loss on the early settlement. Once again, the gain or loss is a function of relative interest rates and how the interest rate of the instrument differs from current and anticipated future interest rates. Exactly the same issues arise as in the above example: to what extent should the gain or loss be treated as a borrowing cost? We consider that the same argument applies and only that element that applies to the period of construction of the asset is eligible for capitalisation as part of the asset.

D   Dividends payable on shares classified as financial liabilities

An entity might finance its operations in whole or in part by the issue of preference shares and in some circumstances these will be classified as financial liabilities (see Chapter 17 at 3.2.1). It is feasible that an entity might issue redeemable preference shares that are redeemable at the option of the holder (and are classified as financial liabilities) that have been issued to fund the development of a qualifying asset. In this case the dividends would meet the definition of borrowing costs. This would not apply to irredeemable shares as they could never be directly attributable.

3.2   Borrowings and capitalisation rate

IAS 23 requires that the borrowing costs capitalised are to be those costs that would have been avoided if the expenditure on the qualifying asset had not been made. If a project has been financed from the entity's general borrowings, the standard imposes a detailed calculation method as indicated at 2.3.2 above.

The standard acknowledges that determining general borrowings will not always be straightforward. It will be necessary to exercise judgement to meet the main objective – a reasonable measure of the directly attributable finance costs.[39]

The following example illustrates the practical application of the method of calculating the amount of finance costs to be capitalised:

Example 14.3: Calculation of capitalisation rate

On 1 April 2005 a company engages in the development of a property, which is expected to take five years to complete, at a cost of £6,000,000. The balance sheets at 31 December 2004 and 31 December 2005, prior to capitalisation of interest, are as follows:

	31 December 2004 €	31 December 2005 €
Development property	–	1,200,000
Other assets	6,000,000	6,800,000
	6,000,000	8,000,000
Loans		
5.5% debenture stock	2,500,000	2,500,000
Bank loan at 6% p.a.	–	2,000,000
Bank loan at 7% p.a.	1,000,000	1,000,000
	3,500,000	5,500,000
Shareholders' equity	2,500,000	2,500,000

The bank loan at 6% was taken out on 31 March 2005 and the total interest charge for the year ended 31 December 2005 was as follows:

	€
€2,500,000 × 5.5%	137,500
€2,000,000 × 6% × 9/12	90,000
€1,000,000 × 7%	70,000
	297,500

Expenditure was incurred on the development as follows:

	€
1 April 2005	600,000
1 July 2005	400,000
1 October 2005	200,000
	1,200,000

(a) If the bank loan at 6% p.a. is a new borrowing taken out specifically to finance the development, then the amount of interest to be capitalised is:

	€
£600,000 × 6% × 9/12	27,000
£400,000 × 6% × 6/12	12,000
£200,000 × 6% × 3/12	3,000
	42,000

(b) If all the borrowings would have been avoided but for the development then the amount of interest to be capitalised is:

$$\frac{\text{Total interest expense for period}}{\text{Weighted average total borrowings}} \times \text{Development expenditure}$$

i.e.:

$$\frac{297{,}500}{3{,}500{,}000 + (2{,}000{,}000 \times 9/12)} = 5.95\%$$

	€
€600,000 × 5.95% × 9/12	26,775
€400,000 × 5.95% × 6/12	11,900
€200,000 × 5.95% × 3/12	2,975
	41,650

If the 5.5% debenture stock were irredeemable then it would be excluded from the above calculation as it could no longer be a borrowing that could have been avoided. The calculation would be done using the figures for the bank loans and their related interest costs only.

Note that the company's share capital will not be taken into account and outstanding borrowings are presumed to finance the acquisition or construction of qualifying assets.

3.3   Accrued costs

IAS 23 states that expenditures on qualifying assets include only those that have resulted in the payments of cash, transfers of other assets or the assumption of interest-bearing liabilities.[40] Therefore, costs of a qualifying asset that have only been accrued but have not yet been paid in cash should be excluded from the amount on which interest is capitalised, as by definition no interest can have been incurred on an accrued payment. It should be noted that the effect of applying this principle is often merely to delay the capitalisation of interest since the costs will be included once they have been paid in cash. In most cases it is unlikely that the effect will be material as the time between accrual and payment of the cost will not be that great. However, the effect is potentially material where a significant part of the amount capitalised relates to costs that have been financed interest-free by third parties for a long period. An example of this is retention money that is not generally payable until the asset is completed.

3.4 Assets carried in the balance sheet below cost

An asset may be recognised in the financial statements during the period of production on a basis other than cost, i.e. it may have been written down below cost as a result of being impaired. As discussed in 2.3.2 above, an asset may be impaired when its expected ultimate cost, including costs to complete and the estimated capitalised interest thereon, exceed its estimated recoverable amount or net realisable value.

The question then arises whether the calculation of interest to be capitalised should be based on the asset's cost or its carrying amount. In this case, cost should be used, as this is the amount that the company or group has had to finance. This is consistent with SIC-2 (see 2.2.2 above).

3.5 Group financial statements

3.5.1 *Borrowings in one company and development in another*

A question which often arises in practice is whether it is appropriate to capitalise interest in the group financial statements on borrowings that appear in the financial statements of a different group company from that carrying out the development. Based on the underlying philosophy of IAS 23, capitalisation in such circumstances would only be appropriate if the amount capitalised fairly reflected the interest cost of the group on borrowings from third parties which could theoretically have been avoided if the expenditure on the qualifying asset were not made.

Although it may be appropriate to capitalise interest in the group financial statements, the company carrying out the development should not capitalise any interest in its own financial statements as it has no borrowings. If, however, the company has intra-group borrowings then interest on such borrowings may be capitalised.

3.5.2 *Qualifying assets held by joint ventures*

A number of sectors carry out developments through the medium of joint ventures– this is particularly common with property developments. In such cases, the joint venture may be financed principally by equity and the joint venture partners may have financed their participating interests by borrowings. It is not appropriate to capitalise interest in the joint venture on the borrowings of the partners as the interest charge is not a cost of the joint venture. Neither would it be appropriate to capitalise interest in the individual (as opposed to group) financial statements of the venturers because the qualifying asset does not belong to them. The investing entities have an investment as an asset, which is excluded by IAS 23 from being a qualifying asset (see 2.1.2 above).

3.6   Change of accounting policy

IAS 23 allows two different treatments of borrowing costs and this raises the possibility of a change in accounting policy.

Under IAS 8, a change in policy that is not mandated by a standard may only be made where it results in the financial statements providing reliable and more relevant information about the effects of transactions, other events or conditions on the entity's financial position, financial performance or cash flows.[41] It must be remembered that the benchmark treatment in IAS 23 is that borrowing costs be written off as incurred. Thus a business that has previously not capitalised interest, if it wishes to do so subsequently, must have extremely good reasons which explain why the new policy of capitalisation is more reliable and relevant. In deciding upon a new policy the entity is permitted to look to accepted industry practices and this may provide a basis for a change in policy with retrospective application.[42] It is clear that this can apply at initial adoption of IAS 23 (e.g. on transition to IFRS, see 4 below). However, IAS 8's rules on applying changes in accounting policy permit a change in the absence of a standard or interpretation that specifically applies if the new policy is based on the most recent pronouncements of other standard-setting bodies that use a similar conceptual framework.[43] Therefore, it appears that a change is possible because US GAAP requires capitalisation of borrowing costs in certain circumstances.[44]

4   TRANSITION AND FIRST-TIME ADOPTION

IAS 23 (revised 1993) became operative for financial statements covering periods beginning on or after 1 January 1995.[45]

Under IFRS 1 an entity that chooses to apply the allowed alternative treatment in IAS 23, and capitalise borrowing costs, should apply IAS 23 fully retrospectively from its date of transition.[46]

In theory, the adjustment should be made in respect of all assets still held which would have satisfied the criteria adopted for capitalisation. However, this can create considerable difficulty in the case of fixed assets that were produced many years ago; accordingly, some compromises may have to be made in calculating the prior year adjustment. Nevertheless it should be possible to produce a materially accurate figure.

5 CONCLUSION

The IASB has in effect adopted a holding position on the issue of capitalisation of borrowing costs, by neither banning it nor making it compulsory. The capitalisation of finance costs is an important part of the wider issue of accounting for interest effects, about which there is no international consensus. The decision on whether or not to capitalise interest requires a discussion of the nature of finance costs and how they fit within the structure of financial reporting by a company to its stakeholders – in short, whether or not the capitalisation of finance costs is a conceptually sound basis of accounting.

At the conceptual level, there is a valid argument for measuring the cost of financing the acquisition of qualifying assets on the basis of the entity's cost of capital, including imputed interest on equity capital as well as interest on borrowings. At the same time it must be recognised that the capitalisation of the cost of equity capital does not conform to the historical cost accounting framework, under which the cost of a resource is measured by reference to historical exchange prices. Nevertheless, to permit the capitalisation of interest only on borrowed capital is an incomplete approach.

Conversely, it may be argued that the capitalisation of borrowing costs into most types of property development is an entirely logical and appropriate policy. Interest is a development cost and is no different in this respect to the concrete and bricks. The IASB will, therefore, need to decide whether or not the arguments in favour of capitalisation of borrowing costs outweigh the disadvantages of allowing an accounting practice which is essentially arbitrary. The only way to do this is to conduct a proper debate on the issue of accounting for interest effects, which would encompass both the capitalisation of all types of finance costs as well as discounting. This debate may have to wait until the IASB has addressed other issues connected with the carrying values of assets and in particular whether they should be carried in the balance sheet at historical cost or whether fair value will be mandated.

References

1 IAS 23 (1984), *Capitalisation of Borrowing Costs*, IASC, March 1984, paras. 21-27.
2 IAS 23, *Borrowing Costs*, IASB, December 1993 (amended December 2003), para. 8.
3 IAS 23, para. 3.
4 IAS 23, para. 4.
5 IAS 23, para. 6.
6 IASC, *Insight*, October 1991, p. 10.
7 IAS 23, para. 6.
8 IAS 23, para. 4.
9 IAS 23, para. 5.
10 IAS 23, paras. 7-8.
11 IAS 23, paras. 10-11.
12 IAS 23, para. 12.
13 SIC-2, *Consistency – Capitalisation of Borrowing Costs*, SIC, December 1997 (superseded December 2003), para. 3 and IAS 23, para. 19.
14 IAS 23, para. 13.
15 IAS 23, para. 13.
16 IAS 23, para. 15.
17 IAS 23, paras. 15-16.
18 IAS 23, para. 14.

19 IAS 23, para. 17.

20 IAS 23, para. 21.

21 IAS 23, para. 18.

22 SIC-2, para. 3.

23 IAS 23, para. 19.

24 IAS 36, *Impairment of assets*, IASB, March 2004, para. 2.

25 IAS 23, para. 20.

26 IAS 23, para. 21.

27 IAS 23, para. 22.

28 IAS 23, paras. 23-24.

29 IAS 23, para. 25.

30 IAS 23, para. 26.

31 IAS 23, para. 27.

32 IAS 23, para. 28.

33 IAS 23, para. 9.

34 IAS 23, para. 29.

35 IAS 32, *Financial Instruments: Disclosure and Presentation*, IASB, December 2003 (amended March 2004); IAS 39, *Financial Instruments: Recognition and Measurement*, IASB, December 2003 (amended March 2004).

36 IAS 23, para. 5(e).

37 IAS 39, para. 9.

38 IAS 39, para. 85.

39 IAS 23, para. 14.

40 IAS 23, para. 21.

41 IAS 8, *Accounting policies, changes in accounting estimates and errors*, IASB, December 2003 (amended March 2004), para. 14.

42 IAS 8, para. 12.

43 IAS 8, para. 21.

44 FAS 34, *Capitalization of Interest Cost*, FASB, October 1979, paras. 6-8.

45 IAS 23, para. 31.

46 IFRS 1, *First-time Adoption of International Financial Reporting Standards*, IASB, June 2003 (amended March 2004), paras. 7 and 9.

Chapter 15 Financial instruments: Introduction

1 INTRODUCTION

1.1 Accounting for financial instruments – the challenge

The development of increasingly sophisticated financial markets, which permit companies to trade in newly devised contracts and thereby transform their risk profile, is perhaps the single factor in business life that poses the most searching challenge to traditional financial reporting practices. The IASC, in its newsletter of December 1996, commented on the issue in these terms:

'At the roots of the need for change in accounting for financial instruments are fundamental changes in international financial markets. ... An enterprise can substantially change its financial risk profile instantaneously, requiring careful and continuous monitoring. ... Alternatively, an enterprise may use derivatives as speculative tools to multiply the effects of changes in interest, foreign exchange or security or commodity prices, thus multiplying the gains if prices move advantageously or, alternatively, multiplying the losses if they move adversely. ... Accounting for financial instruments has not kept pace with information needs of financial market participants.

'Existing accounting practices are founded on principles developed when the primary focus of accounting was on manufacturing companies that combine inputs (materials, labour, plant and equipment, and various types of overheads) and transform them into outputs (goods or services) for sale. Accounting for these revenue-generating processes is concerned primarily with accruing costs to be matched with revenues. A key point in this process is the point of revenue realisation – the point at which a company is considered to have transformed its inputs into cash or claims to cash (i.e. financial instruments).

'These traditional realisation and cost-based measurement concepts are not adequate for the recognition and measurement of financial instruments. Recognising this, many countries have moved part way to embrace fair value accounting for some financial instruments. ...'[1]

This lays down the challenge very clearly. Do we need a new approach to financial reporting if we are to cope with the specific characteristics of financial instruments? And indeed, does the intellectual theory behind this new approach in turn imply that we should now abandon traditional accounting methods for other areas of business activity as well? The IASC felt able to distinguish the two issues, but some of the thinking behind the developments in accounting for financial instruments has had a profound effect on work of the IASC and IASB in other areas. This has manifested itself through the IASB placing a growing emphasis on the development of its balance sheet-focused fair value model in subjects such as insurance contracts, agriculture, investment property and revenue recognition.

1.2   Publication of the original IAS 32

At the time the newsletter referred to above was issued, the IASC had been conducting a project on financial instruments for several years, initially in conjunction with the Canadian Institute of Chartered Accountants (CICA). Two attempts were made to deal comprehensively with the issue, in two successive exposure drafts (E40 in 1991 and E48 in 1994). However, the IASC then decided to lower its sights and converted E48 into a standard dealing with presentation (debt and equity classification and offset) and disclosure issues alone and the original version of IAS 32 – *Financial Instruments: Disclosure and Presentation*[2] was published in March 1995.

1.3   Evolution of a 'full fair value' accounting model

In March 1997 – two years after the publication of IAS 32 – the IASC/CICA Steering Committee published a Discussion Paper[3] dealing extensively with the measurement and recognition issues and making proposals for a comprehensive standard on financial assets and liabilities. In concept, its main proposals were straightforward: all financial assets and liabilities should be recognised as soon as the reporting entity becomes a party to the contractual provisions that they entail;[4] thereafter they should be stated at fair value in the balance sheet;[5] and all movements in fair value thereafter should be reported in income.[6] The Discussion Paper also took a very restrictive view of hedge accounting. With two minor exceptions, it proposed that no special treatment should be accorded to financial instruments that are designated as hedges of other exposures; they should all still be carried at fair value and gains or losses reported in income.

However, later in 1997 the IASC recognised that completion of such a comprehensive standard to meet the IOSCO deadline (see Chapter 1) was not a realistic possibility and therefore committed to completing an interim international standard on recognition and measurement in 1998. Also in 1997, the IASC decided that they should join with national standard setters to develop an integrated and harmonised standard on financial instruments, building on their own Discussion Paper, existing and emerging national standards, and the best thinking and research on the subject world-wide. Thus, the Joint Working Group of standard setters (JWG) was established to perform this task. The JWG comprised representatives from the IASC, the US FASB and eight other international bodies. December 2000 saw the culmination of their work with the publication by each constituent member of its proposals in the form of a Draft Standard.[7]

Perhaps not surprisingly the JWG proposals built on the theoretical approach of the IASC/CICA Discussion Paper. With only minor exceptions, all financial instruments would be recorded at fair value with corresponding gains and losses reported in income. This meant, for example, that the reported amount of an entity's own debt would reflect its fair value and thus take account of changes in the entity's credit risk. Likewise, even changes in the value of debt and other instruments used to hedge foreign currency net investments would be reported in income (although the basic method of accounting for foreign net investments was not altered). A corollary of this was that hedge accounting would no longer be allowed.

1.4 Publication of the original IAS 39

Following the decision in 1997, the IASC issued an exposure draft, E62,[8] in May 1998 and in December 1998 approved for publication the original version of IAS 39 – *Financial Instruments: Recognition and Measurement,*[9] its interim standard dealing with recognition and measurement of financial instruments, including rules on hedging. It was finally published in March 1999.

The origins of IAS 39 can be found in US GAAP and at a high level there are only limited differences between the two systems. Consequently, it adopted a 'mixed attribute' model, i.e. some financial instruments are measured by reference to their historical cost and some by reference to their fair value. The main ideas embodied in IAS 39 were:

- derivatives (including some embedded within other contracts) were measured at fair value;
- many financial assets were also measured at fair value;
- non-derivative liabilities were measured at amortised cost;
- hedging rules were established such that:
  - the methods of hedge accounting were defined in a way that severely curtailed existing practices in many countries;
  - hedges were tested for effectiveness; and
  - ineffectiveness was reported in income; and
- certain fair value gains and losses could be reported initially in equity before being recycled into income at a later date.

The standard had a long lead-time – although issued in 1999, adoption was only mandatory for periods commencing in 2001. At the time, some held the view (or at least the hope) that IAS 39 would never actually be implemented, and that by 2001 a 'full fair value' standard (along the lines of the JWG proposals) would have replaced it. However, this was not to be.

By dealing with most aspects of virtually all financial instruments, it was the longest, and by far the most complex, standard issued by the IASC. Because of this, and perhaps also as it became clear that a 'full fair value' standard would not be available in 2001, the IASC saw a need to help preparers, auditors and users to understand the practical implications of IAS 39. In March 2000, a process was established whereby an IAS 39 Implementation Guidance Committee (IGC) published guidance, developed to be consistent with the standard, in the form of Questions and Answers (Q&A).[10] In all, over 200 final Q&A were published under the authority of the IASC.

1.5 IASB 'improvements' project and EU adoption

In spite of the efforts that had been made in producing the implementation guidance, in 2001 the new IASB inherited a standard that many companies already reporting under IAS were experiencing great difficulty in implementing. Because of this, a project designed to clarify the application of IAS 39 based on issues identified by constituents and the IGC was included on the IASB's initial technical agenda.[11]

The project was subsequently expanded to incorporate IAS 32 and the IGC Q&A, and in June 2002 an Exposure Draft containing proposals to improve IAS 32 and IAS 39 was published.[12] In what can now be seen as the start of a trend of dissent, two (out of fourteen) members formally opposed the proposals.

The Exposure Draft was launched in an atmosphere of growing awareness of IFRS, not least by the thousands of companies that would adopt these standards for the first time in the forthcoming few years. One of the biggest concerns was the extent to which IAS 39 would allow entities to account for their risk management and hedging strategies in a manner that reflected the actual hedging practices adopted. This was especially true in the retail banking sector where entities normally manage their risk on a net basis using sophisticated techniques to balance the various exposures that exist in an entity (often referred to as 'macro-hedging'). In due course the IASB was to receive over 170 comment letters,[13] many of them critical both of the original standards and the proposed revisions.

Constituents also started to exert pressure on the IASB in other ways. With the European Union requiring all listed EU companies to apply IFRS in their consolidated accounts with effect from 2005, the EU became the IASB's most important constituency. As a result, the European Commission's 'endorsement mechanism' (see Chapter 1) provided a potentially powerful lever for the exertion of pressure on the IASB to take note of the concerns of preparers, users and auditors, the ultimate sanction being non-adoption of a standard. Various groups, particularly financial institutions, used this opportunity to ensure that the IASB entered into a constructive dialogue with their constituents and addressed their concerns – particularly with respect to fundamental issues such as derecognition, loan loss provisioning, macro-hedging and effectiveness testing. Accordingly, the IASB's revision of IASs 32 and 39 was conducted in a political, as well as a technical, arena and the non-adoption of IAS 39 became a real possibility. One of the most high profile illustrations of political pressure being exerted on the IASB was a letter written by French President Jacques Chirac to EC President Romano Prodi. In his letter, President Chirac expressed general reservations about IFRS, including concerns that the increasing use of fair values would lead to excessive volatility in the economy and that IASs 32 and 39 could have adverse consequences for financial stability in the EU.

As a result of the pressure, political and otherwise, publication of the revised standards was significantly delayed as the IASB took steps to demonstrate the due process it was following in the development of these standards. The most visible of these was a series of nine 'roundtable' discussions with constituents during March 2003; they were conducted in Brussels and London and over 100 organisations and individuals took part. In addition, the Board made the welcome move of entering into a formal dialogue with the financial institutions, with the result that regular meetings were held between IASB members and staff and representatives of European banks and insurers; discussions were also held with the Standards Advisory Council and liaison standard setters.[14]

The IASB's principal aim in all of this was to educate and inform constituents as to why it considered its standards to be appropriate. It certainly did not appear to intend to make any fundamental changes to the standards and, as a result, there was scepticism expressed in some quarters as to whether the Board really was conducting due process or simply going through the motions. In the meantime, the threat of eventual non-adoption of IASs 32 and 39 by the European Commission suddenly became greater, as the EC adopted all existing IASs and SICs, with the exception of these two standards and related interpretations.[15] Accordingly, the IASB was introduced to both the political reality of standard setting and the need to listen to its constituents and, without shifting significantly its overall position on amendments, started to warm to the possibility of developing compromise solutions.

The most tangible sign of progress came in August 2003, when the IASB published an Exposure Draft[16] of proposed amendments to the revised version of IAS 39 (which was at the time unpublished) dealing with macro-hedging issues for banks. However, it is telling that five (out of fourteen) IASB members voted against its publication,[17] suggesting that the IASB was only reluctantly conceding any ground in what was becoming a bruising experience on all sides.

The dialogue continued and, in December 2003, provisional final versions of IAS 32 and IAS 39[18] were published. Amendments to IAS 39, dealing principally with macro-hedging matters, followed in March 2004.[19] Certain members of the IASB continued to object – one opposed the publication of IAS 32, three were against IAS 39 and one against the macro-hedging proposals.[20] Unfortunately, the proposed amendments did not deal with all of the banks' major concerns, particularly with regard to the impact of cash flow hedging on equity volatility and the hedging of core deposits in the case of those banks that operate in a predominantly fixed interest environment. At the same time, insurers were expressing concern about the asset/liability mis-match that would result from the application of IAS 39 to their businesses. This mis-match meant that IAS 39 would require certain financial assets to be stated in the balance sheet at fair value, whilst the related insurance liabilities would be on some other basis.

In what was almost certainly an attempt to reduce the scope for confrontations of this nature in the future, concurrently with the publication of the macro-hedging amendments, the IASB announced plans to establish an international working party to assist it in developing its long-term replacement for IAS 39, which it conceded may take several years to complete. However, in a public show of conciliation, it also acknowledged that it would be willing to revise IAS 39 in the short term in the light of any solutions arising from the working party's discussions.[21] This followed a separate invitation in February 2004 to regulators and participants in the European financial services sector to form a high level consultative group to advise the IASB on matters relating to financial instrument accounting.[22]

At present it is still not clear whether IAS 32 and IAS 39 will be adopted for use within the European Union and, if so, in what form. Under pressure from the European Central Bank (likely to be a very powerful force in the adoption process), the IASB published in April 2004 further proposed amendments to IAS 39 (see 9.1 below).[23] These proposals would limit an entity's ability to measure instruments at fair value with associated gains and losses recorded in profit or loss (i.e., the full fair value option) and this is proving unpopular with many banks and insurers. On a different front, proposals are being considered for another macro-hedging methodology[24] and other proposed changes to the standards are still being debated.

1.6   Conclusion

It is clear that the subject of accounting for financial instruments is likely to remain an extremely difficult area, both in the short term and for a number of years. Perhaps surprisingly, there seems to be a high degree of consensus among the major standard setters and their representatives on the former Joint Working Group that fair valuing all financial instruments can be the only ultimate solution (although there is less agreement on what fair value actually means). This is still a controversial view that is meeting with considerable resistance. Standard setters in this area appear to have moved considerably ahead of current practice, since the proposed solution has not yet commanded acceptance in any country. This is a bold step since the traditional role of accounting standard setters has been to codify accepted best practice rather than, as now, to invent new practice.

The arguments for fair value accounting seem cogent, and they have been assembled very persuasively in the IASC Discussion Paper and JWG Draft Standard. But they are nonetheless revolutionary; by the IASC's own admission, they would require the adoption of a new capital maintenance concept ('current-market-rate-of-return') for measuring financial instruments[25] and this would simply introduce a new inconsistency, unless it was applied to the measurement of other items in the financial statements as well. That would have been an even more radical proposal at the time, but with items such as investment properties and certain biological assets now being recorded at fair value, it now seems slightly less drastic. Although elegant, and in spite of the IASB's continued move towards the use of fair values in other aspects of accounting, the proposals do not sit well with widespread perceptions of the role and meaning of financial statements.

In the meantime, companies have to get to grips with the revised version of IAS 39, the basic principles of which are expected to be in place for a 'considerable period'.[26] Potentially this will not be easy, especially for those preparing to adopt IFRS for the first time in 2005, and only time will tell whether the IASB has met one of its main aims in revising IAS 32 and IAS 39, that is of easing implementation. However, it is reasonably clear that the current versions of these standards are, in many respects, better as a result of the further deliberations, even if many financial institutions remain to be convinced.

1.7 How financial instruments are dealt with in Chapters 15 to 20

Putting these broader ramifications to one side, the subject matter of this and the next five chapters is the recognition, measurement, presentation and disclosure of financial instruments. More specifically, these chapters address the requirements of the revised versions of IAS 32 and IAS 39.

The main text of IAS 32 is supplemented by application guidance (which is an integral part of the standard)[27] and by illustrative examples (which accompany, but are not part of, the standard).[28] Similarly, the main text of IAS 39 is supplemented by application guidance (which is an integral part of the standard)[29] and by implementation guidance and an illustrative example (both of which accompany, but are not part of, the standard).[30]

The objective of IAS 32 is to enhance financial statement users' understanding of the significance of financial instruments to an entity's financial position, performance and cash flows[31] whilst for IAS 39 it is to establish principles for recognising and measuring financial assets, financial liabilities and some contracts to buy or sell non-financial items.[32]

The chapters dealing with financial instruments are structured as follows:

Chapter 15 – *Introduction*, covers the following:
- key definitions;
- scope and exceptions;
- the defining characteristics of derivatives;
- derivatives embedded within other contracts;
- linked and separate transactions and 'synthetic' instruments; and
- classification of financial assets and financial liabilities.

Chapter 16 – *Recognition, derecognition and offset*, covers the following:

- recognition;
- derecognition of financial assets;
- derecognition of financial liabilities; and
- offset.

Chapter 17 – *Classification of debt and equity*, covers the following:

- the classification of financial instruments by their issuer as financial liabilities or equity;
- compound financial instruments (i.e. those containing both a liability and an equity component from the issuer's perspective);
- accounting for interest, dividends gains and losses;
- treasury shares (i.e. shares legally owned by their issuer); and
- contracts over own equity instruments.

Chapter 18 – *Measurement*, covers the following

- initial measurement;
- subsequent measurement and recognition of gains and losses;
- fair value measurement considerations;
- amortised cost and the effective interest method;
- impairment of financial assets; and
- the effect of foreign currencies.

Chapter 19 – *Hedge accounting*, covers the following

- hedging instruments and hedged items;
- types of hedging relationships;
- accounting for effective hedges;
- qualifying conditions for hedge accounting; and
- portfolio (or macro) hedging.

Chapter 20 – *Disclosure*, covers the following

- narrative disclosures, including risk management and hedging;
- numerical disclosures; and
- presentation of financial instruments and related transactions, gains and losses in the financial statements.

Consequently, IAS 32 is largely dealt with in Chapters 15, 17 and 20 and IAS 39 in Chapters 15, 16, 18 and 19.

2 WHAT IS A FINANCIAL INSTRUMENT?

2.1 Definitions

The main terms used are defined as follows:

A *financial instrument* is any contract that gives rise to a financial asset of one entity and a financial liability or equity instrument of another entity.

A *financial asset* is any asset that is:

(a) cash;

(b) an equity instrument of another entity;

(c) a contractual right:

    (i) to receive cash or another financial asset from another entity; or

    (ii) to exchange financial assets or financial liabilities with another entity under conditions that are potentially favourable to the entity; or

(d) a contract that will or may be settled in the entity's own equity instruments and is:

    (i) a non-derivative for which the entity is or may be obliged to receive a variable number of the entity's own equity instruments; or

    (ii) a derivative that will or may be settled other than by the exchange of a fixed amount of cash or another financial asset for a fixed number of the entity's own equity instruments. For this purpose the entity's own equity instruments do not include instruments that are themselves contracts for the future receipt or delivery of the entity's own equity instruments.

A *financial liability* is any liability that is:

(a) a contractual obligation:

    (i) to deliver cash or another financial asset to another entity; or

    (ii) to exchange financial assets or financial liabilities with another entity under conditions that are potentially unfavourable to the entity; or

(b) a contract that will or may be settled in the entity's own equity instruments and is:

    (i) a non-derivative for which the entity is or may be obliged to deliver a variable number of the entity's own equity instruments; or

    (ii) a derivative that will or may be settled other than by the exchange of a fixed amount of cash or another financial asset for a fixed number of the entity's own equity instruments. For this purpose the entity's own equity instruments do not include instruments that are themselves contracts for the future receipt or delivery of the entity's own equity instruments.

An *equity instrument* is any contract that evidences a residual interest in the assets of an entity after deducting all of its liabilities.[33]

These definitions are taken from the December 2003 version of IAS 32 and were amended from those used previously to reflect the IASB's thinking on contracts involving own shares. Essentially, part (d) was added to the definition of financial asset and part (b) to the definition of financial liability – previously such contracts were dealt with on a more piecemeal basis. These parts are not at all easy to apply and can lead to some rather counter-intuitive accounting. The implications of these particular changes are considered further in Chapter 17.

For the purpose of these definitions, 'entity' includes individuals, partnerships, incorporated bodies, trusts and government agencies.[34]

2.2   Applying the definitions

2.2.1   *The need for a contract*

The terms 'contract' and 'contractual' are important to the definitions and refer to 'an agreement between two or more parties that has clear economic consequences that the parties have little, if any, discretion to avoid, usually because the agreement is enforceable at law.' Such contracts may take a variety of forms and need not be in writing.[35]

A contractual right or contractual obligation to receive, deliver or exchange financial instruments is itself a financial instrument. A chain of contractual rights or contractual obligations meets the definition of a financial instrument if it will ultimately lead to the receipt or payment of cash or to the acquisition or issue of an equity instrument.[36] Therefore it can be seen that the definitions are iterative, but not circular.

Assets and liabilities relating to income taxes that arise as a result of statutory requirements imposed by governments are not financial liabilities or financial assets because they are not contractual.[37] This is convenient because accounting for income taxes is dealt with in more detail (and not necessarily consistently with IAS 39) in another standard, IAS 12 – *Income Taxes* (see Chapter 24).

Similarly, constructive obligations as defined in IAS 37 – *Provisions, Contingent Liabilities and Contingent Assets* (see Chapter 25 at 3.1.1) do not arise from contracts and are therefore not financial liabilities.[38]

2.2.2   *Simple examples*

The application guidance to IAS 32 explains that currency (or cash) is a financial asset 'because it represents the medium of exchange and is therefore the basis on which all transactions are measured and recognised in financial statements'. A deposit of cash with a bank or similar financial institution is a financial asset because it represents the contractual right of the depositor to obtain cash from the institution or to draw a cheque or similar instrument against the balance in favour of a creditor in payment of a financial liability.[39]

The following common financial instruments give rise to financial assets representing a contractual right to receive cash in the future and corresponding financial liabilities representing a contractual obligation to deliver cash in the future:

(a)   trade accounts receivable and payable;

(b)   notes receivable and payable;

(c)   loans receivable and payable; and

(d)   bonds receivable and payable.

In each case, one party's contractual right to receive (or obligation to pay) cash is matched by the other party's corresponding obligation to pay (or right to receive).[40]

Another type of financial instrument is one for which the economic benefit to be received or given up is a financial asset other than cash. For example, a note payable in government bonds gives the holder the contractual right to receive, and the issuer the contractual obligation to deliver, government bonds, not cash. The bonds are financial assets because they represent obligations of the issuing government to pay cash. The note is, therefore, a financial asset of the note holder and a financial liability of the note issuer.[41]

Perpetual debt instruments (such as perpetual bonds, debentures and capital notes) normally provide the holder with the contractual right to receive payments on account of interest at fixed dates extending indefinitely, either with no right to receive a return of principal or a right to a return of principal under terms that make it very unlikely or very far in the future. For example, an entity may issue a financial instrument requiring it to make annual payments in perpetuity equal to a stated interest rate of 8% applied to a stated par or principal amount of $1,000. Assuming 8% is the market rate of interest for the instrument when issued, the issuer assumes a contractual obligation to make a stream of future interest payments having a net present value (or fair value) of $1,000 on initial recognition. The holder and issuer of the instrument have a financial asset and a financial liability, respectively.[42]

2.2.3   *Contingent rights and obligations*

The ability to exercise a contractual right or the requirement to satisfy a contractual obligation may be absolute (as in the examples at 2.2.2 above), or it may be contingent on the occurrence of a future event. A contingent right or obligation, e.g. to receive or deliver cash, meets the definition of a financial asset or a financial liability.[43]

For example, a financial guarantee is a contractual right of the lender to receive cash from the guarantor, and a corresponding contractual obligation of the guarantor to pay the lender, if the borrower defaults. The contractual right and obligation exist because of a past transaction or event (the assumption of the guarantee), even though the lender's ability to exercise its right and the requirement for the guarantor to perform under its obligation are both contingent on a future act of default by the borrower.[44]

However, even though contingent rights and obligations can meet the definition of a financial instrument, they are not always recognised in the financial statements as such. For example, the contingent rights and obligations may be insurance contracts within the scope of IFRS 4 – *Insurance Contracts* (see 3.3 below) or may otherwise be excluded from the scope of IAS 39 (see 3 below).[45]

2.2.4 Leases

In accordance with the accounting model in IAS 17 – *Leases* – a finance lease is regarded as primarily an entitlement to receive, and an obligation to make, a stream of payments that are substantially the same as blended payments of principal and interest under a loan agreement. The lessor accounts for its investment in the amount receivable under the lease contract rather than the leased asset itself.[46] The lessee accounts for its obligation to the lessor (in addition to the leased asset).

An operating lease, on the other hand, is regarded as primarily an uncompleted contract committing the lessor to provide the use of an asset in future periods in exchange for consideration similar to a fee for a service. The lessor continues to account for the leased asset itself rather than any amount receivable in the future under the contract.[47]

Accordingly, a finance lease arrangement is regarded as a financial instrument and an operating lease is not regarded as a financial instrument (except as regards individual payments currently due and payable).[48]

2.2.5 Non-financial assets and liabilities and contracts thereon

Physical assets (such as inventories, property, plant and equipment), leased assets and intangible assets (such as patents and trademarks) are not financial assets. Control of such physical and intangible assets creates an opportunity to generate an inflow of cash or another financial asset, but it does not give rise to a present right to receive cash or another financial asset.[49] For example, whilst gold bullion is highly liquid (and perhaps more liquid than many financial instruments), it gives no contractual right to receive cash or another financial asset, so is therefore a commodity, not a financial asset.[50]

Assets such as prepaid expenses, for which the future economic benefit is the receipt of goods or services rather than the right to receive cash or another financial asset, are not financial assets. Similarly, items such as deferred revenue and most warranty obligations are not financial liabilities because the outflow of economic benefits associated with them is the delivery of goods and services rather than a contractual obligation to pay cash or another financial asset.[51]

Contracts to buy or sell non-financial items do not meet the definition of a financial instrument because the contractual right of one party to receive a non-financial asset or service and the corresponding obligation of the other party do not establish a present right or obligation of either party to receive, deliver or exchange a financial asset. For example, contracts that provide for settlement only by the receipt or delivery of a non-financial item (e.g. an option, futures or forward contract on silver and many similar commodity contracts) are not financial instruments. However, as set out at 3.8 below, certain contracts to buy or sell non-financial items are included within the scope of IAS 32 and IAS 39, essentially where they exhibit similar characteristics to financial instruments.[52]

Where payment on a contract involving the receipt or delivery of physical assets is deferred past the date of transfer of the asset, a financial instrument does arise at that date. In other words, the sale or purchase of goods on trade credit gives rise to a financial asset (a trade receivable) and a financial liability (a trade payable) when the goods are transferred.[53]

Some contracts are commodity-linked, but do not involve settlement through the physical receipt or delivery of a commodity. For example, the principal amount of a bond may be calculated by applying the market price of oil prevailing at the maturity of the bond to a fixed quantity of oil. Such a contract does constitute a financial instrument.[54]

Financial instruments also include contracts that give rise to a non-financial asset or non-financial liability in addition to a financial asset or financial liability. Such arrangements often give one party an option to exchange a financial asset for a non-financial asset. For example, an oil-linked bond may give the holder the right to receive a stream of fixed periodic interest payments and a fixed amount of cash on maturity, with the option to exchange the principal amount for a fixed quantity of oil. The desirability of exercising this option will vary over time depending on the fair value of oil relative to the exchange ratio of cash for oil (the exchange price) inherent in the bond, but the intentions of the bondholder do not affect the substance of the component assets. The financial asset of the holder and the financial liability of the issuer make the bond a financial instrument, regardless of the other types of assets and liabilities also created.[55]

2.2.6 Equity instruments

Examples of equity instruments include non-puttable ordinary shares, some types of preference shares and warrants or written call options that allow the holder to subscribe for or purchase a fixed number of non-puttable ordinary shares in the issuing entity, in exchange for a fixed amount of cash or another financial asset.[56] The definition of equity instruments is considered in more detail in Chapter 17.

2.2.7 Derivative financial instruments

As well as primary instruments such as receivables, payables and equity instruments, financial instruments also include derivatives such as financial options, futures and forwards, interest rate swaps and currency swaps. Derivatives effectively transfer the risks inherent in an underlying primary instrument between the contracting parties without any need to transfer the underlying instruments themselves (either at inception of the contract or even, where cash settled, on termination).[57]

There are important accounting consequences for financial instruments that are considered to be derivatives, and the defining characteristics of derivatives are covered in more detail at 4 below. As noted at 2.2.5 above, certain derivative contracts on non-financial items are included within the scope of IAS 32 and

IAS 39, even though they are not, strictly, financial instruments as defined. These contracts are covered in more detail at 3.8 below.

On inception, the terms of a derivative financial instrument generally give one party a contractual right (or obligation) to exchange financial assets or financial liabilities with another party under conditions that are potentially favourable (or unfavourable). Some instruments embody both a right and an obligation to make an exchange and, as prices in financial markets change, those terms may become either favourable or unfavourable.[58]

A put or call option to exchange financial assets or financial liabilities gives the holder a right to obtain potential future economic benefits associated with changes in the fair value of the underlying instrument. Conversely, the writer of an option assumes an obligation to forgo such economic benefits or bear potential losses associated with the underlying instrument. The contractual right (or obligation) of the holder (or writer) meets the definition of a financial asset (or liability). The financial instrument underlying an option contract may be any financial asset, including shares in other entities and interest-bearing instruments. An option may require the writer to issue a debt instrument, rather than transfer a financial asset, but the instrument underlying the option would constitute a financial asset of the holder if the option were exercised. The option-holder's right (or writer's obligation) to exchange the financial asset under potentially favourable (or unfavourable) conditions is distinct from the underlying financial asset to be exchanged upon exercise of the option. The nature of the holder's right and of the writer's obligation (which characterises such contracts as a financial instrument) are not affected by the likelihood that the option will be exercised.[59]

Another common type of derivative is a forward contract. For example, consider a contract in which two parties (the seller and the purchaser) promise in six months' time to exchange $1,000 cash (the purchaser will pay cash) for $1,000 face amount of fixed rate government bonds (the seller will deliver the bonds). During those six months, both parties have a contractual right and a contractual obligation to exchange financial instruments (cash in exchange for bonds). If the market price of the government bonds rises above $1,000, the conditions will be favourable to the purchaser and unfavourable to the seller, and vice versa if the market price falls below $1,000. The purchaser has a contractual right (a financial asset) similar to the right under a call option held and a contractual obligation (a financial liability) similar to the obligation under a put option written. The seller has a contractual right (a financial asset) similar to the right under a put option held and a contractual obligation (a financial liability) similar to the obligation under a call option written. As with options, these contractual rights and obligations constitute financial assets and financial liabilities separate and distinct from the underlying financial instruments (the bonds and cash to be exchanged). Both parties to a forward contract have an obligation to perform at the agreed time, whereas performance under an option contract occurs only if and when the holder of the option chooses to exercise it.[60]

Many other types of derivative embody a right or obligation to make a future exchange, including interest rate and currency swaps, interest rate caps, collars and floors, loan commitments, note issuance facilities and letters of credit. An interest rate swap contract may be viewed as a variation of a forward contract in which the parties agree to make a series of future exchanges of cash amounts, one amount calculated with reference to a floating interest rate and the other with reference to a fixed interest rate. Futures contracts are another variation of forward contracts, differing primarily in that the contracts are standardised and traded on an exchange.[61]

3 SCOPE

Both IAS 32 and IAS 39 apply to the financial statements of all entities that are prepared in accordance with International Financial Reporting Standards.[62] In other words there are no exclusions from the presentation, recognition, measurement, or even the disclosure requirements, of these standards, even for entities that do not have publicly traded securities or those that are subsidiaries of other entities.

The standards do not, however, apply to all of an entity's financial instruments, some of which are excluded from their scope, for example insurance contracts. Conversely, certain contracts over non-financial items that behave in a similar way to financial instruments but do not actually fall within the definition – essentially some commodity contracts – are included within the scope of the standards. These exceptions are considered in more detail below.

3.1 Subsidiaries, associates, joint ventures and similar investments

Most interests in subsidiaries, associates, and joint ventures that are consolidated, proportionately consolidated or equity accounted in consolidated financial statements are outside the scope of IAS 32 and IAS 39.[63] However, such instruments should be accounted for in accordance with IAS 39 and disclosed in accordance with IAS 32 in the following situations:

- in separate financial statements of the parent or investor if they are neither recorded at cost nor accounted for in accordance with IFRS 5 – *Non-current Assets Held for Sale and Discontinued Operations* (see Chapter 5 at 7);[64] and

- when investments in associates or joint ventures held by venture capital organisations, mutual funds, unit trusts or similar entities are classified as 'at fair value through profit or loss' on initial recognition (see Chapter 7 at 2.1, Chapter 8 at 2.1 and 7.1.2 below).[65]

Under the previous version of IAS 39, the extent to which derivatives on interests in subsidiaries, associates or joint ventures, were within its scope was unclear – in fact the issue had been considered by IFRIC, but no conclusion was reached, essentially because the improvements project was under way.[66] The revised versions of IAS 32 and IAS 39 now apply to most such derivatives, irrespective of how the investment is otherwise accounted for.

However, the requirements of IAS 39 do not apply to such derivatives if they meet the definition of an equity instrument of the entity.[67] For example, a written call option issued by a subsidiary that can only be settled by the subsidiary issuing a fixed number of its shares to the holder in exchange for a fixed amount of cash might meet the definition of equity (see 3.5 below and Chapter 17 at 3.3). Further, IAS 39 does not apply to instruments containing potential voting rights that, in substance, currently give access to the economic benefits associated with an ownership interest where that ownership interest is consolidated, proportionately consolidated or equity accounted (see Chapter 5 at 6.2, Chapter 7 at 2.1.1 A and Chapter 8 at 2.2.2 C).[68]

Sometimes strategic equity investments are made in entities that that are not controlled by the reporting entity. These are often made with the intention of establishing or maintaining a long-term operating relationship with the investee. Unless they are equity accounted as associates or proportionately consolidated or equity accounted as joint ventures, these investments are covered by IAS 39.[69]

3.2   Leases

Whilst all rights and obligations under leases to which IAS 17 applies (see Chapter 23) are within the scope of IAS 32, they are only within the scope of IAS 39 to the following extent:

- lease receivables and payables are subject to IAS 39's derecognition provisions (see Chapter 16 at 4 and 5 respectively);

- lease receivables are subject to IAS 39's impairment provisions (see Chapter 18 at 6); and

- the relevant provisions of IAS 39 apply to derivatives embedded within leases (see 5 below).

Otherwise IAS 17, not IAS 39 is applicable.[70] Previously, it was unclear whether the derecognition and impairment provisions of IAS 39 should apply.

3.3   Insurance contracts (including financial guarantees and weather derivatives)

Although insurance contracts often satisfy the definition of a financial instrument, in general they have not, historically, been accounted for as such. In fact the IASB, and before it the IASC, has been conducting a project on accounting for insurance contracts for a number of years and the first standard on the topic, IFRS 4 was published in March 2004. A number of amendments were made to IAS 32 and IAS 39 by IFRS 4[71] and this subsection deals with IAS 32 and IAS 39 as amended. Comparisons are made to the standards as they existed before the December 2003 revisions.

An insurance contract is defined in IFRS 4 as one 'under which one party (the insurer) accepts significant insurance risk from another party (the policyholder) by agreeing to compensate the policyholder if a specified uncertain future event (the insured event) adversely affects the policyholder.'[72] In many cases it will be quite clear whether a contract is an insurance contract or not, although this will not always be the case and IFRS 4 contains ten pages of guidance on this definition.[73] As was the case under the previous standards, insurance contracts as defined are outside the scope of IAS 32 and IAS 39[74] – in many cases the new definition will not amend significantly the scope of the revised standards compared to the previous versions, but there will inevitably be some changes at the margins.

IAS 39 does, however, apply to derivatives that are embedded in insurance contracts or in contracts containing discretionary participation features (see 3.3.4 below) if the derivative itself is not within the scope of IFRS 4.[75] IAS 32 applies to derivatives embedded in insurance contracts if IAS 39 requires them to be accounted for separately[76] and to derivatives embedded in contracts containing discretionary participation features[77] (seemingly whether or not they are required to be separately accounted for under IAS 39).

The application guidance makes it clear that insurers' financial instruments, other than those that are within the scope of IFRS 4, should be accounted for under IAS 39.[78]

3.3.1 *Financial guarantees and credit insurance*

Under the original version of IAS 39, financial guarantee contracts, including letters of credit, that provided for payments to be made if a debtor failed to make payments when due were outside of its scope.[79]

Under the revised standards, there is no specific exemption for financial guarantee contracts, although they will often meet the definition of an insurance contract and therefore be outside the scope of IAS 39. This will normally be the case for those contracts that require the issuer to make specified payments to reimburse the holder for a loss it incurs because a specified debtor fails to make payment when due under the terms (original or modified) of a debt instrument, provided the contract transfers significant risk to the issuer.[80]

Although used extensively, the term 'debt instrument' is not defined in IAS 32, IAS 39 or IFRS 4. It will typically include trade debts, overdrafts and other borrowings including mortgage loans and certain debt securities. Using the analysis at 2.2.4 above, there is no reason why, in this context, it should not also include lease payments – even for operating leases, individual payments currently due and payable are recognised as financial (debt) instruments. Accordingly, we believe a guarantee of a lessor's receipts under an operating lease can also meet the definition of an insurance contract.

Other financial guarantee contracts can require payments to be made in response to changes in a specified interest rate, financial instrument price, commodity price, foreign exchange rate, index of prices or rates, credit rating or credit index, or other underlying variables and these are within the scope of IAS 39 (provided, in the case of an underlying that is a non-financial variable, the variable is not specific to a party to the contract).[81]

Therefore a financial guarantee contract that requires payments if the credit rating of a debtor falls below a particular level is accounted for as a financial instrument under IAS 39 because it does not necessarily reimburse the holder for a loss it incurs – payments may be made under the contract even if the debtor does not default.[82] However, a financial guarantee contract that requires payments based on a non-financial variable that is specific to a party to the contract will normally meet the definition of an insurance contract and therefore be outside the scope of IAS 39. For example, if a guarantee of the residual value of a specific car exposes the guarantor to the risk of changes in the car's physical condition, the change in that residual value is specific to the owner of the car[83] and accordingly could meet the definition of an insurance contract.

The application guidance emphasises that whilst financial guarantee contracts may have various legal forms (such as financial guarantees, letters of credit, credit default contracts or insurance contracts) their accounting treatment does not depend on their legal form.[84]

In the case of insurance contracts that are financial guarantees entered into or retained on transferring to another party financial assets or financial liabilities within the scope of IAS 39 (see Chapter 16 at 4 and 5), the issuer should apply IAS 39 to the contract.[85]

As regards financial guarantees given in connection with the sale of goods, these are dealt with under IAS 18 – *Revenue*. The guarantee is likely to affect how and when the associated revenue is accounted for (see Chapter 26).[86]

In July 2004, the IASB published an exposure draft of proposed amendments to IAS 39 (and IFRS 4) proposing accounting requirements to be applied by issuers of financial guarantees. Further details are provided at 9.2 below.

3.3.2 Intra-group guarantees

No specific guidance is given in respect of intra-group guarantees, for example where a parent guarantees the borrowings of a subsidiary. For the purposes of the parent's consolidated financial statements, such guarantees are normally considered an integral part of the terms of the borrowing (see Chapter 17 at 3.6) and therefore should not be accounted for independently of the borrowing.[87] However, in the parent's separate financial statements the guarantee should be accounted for as a standalone instrument, although it will normally meet the definition of an insurance contract.

3.3.3 Weather derivatives

Some contracts require a payment based on climatic variables (often referred to as 'weather derivatives') or on geological or other physical variables. Previously such contracts were excluded from the scope of IAS 39;[88] now they are within its scope unless they meet the definition of an insurance contract.[89] Generic or standardised contracts will rarely meet the definition of insurance contracts because the variable is unlikely to be specific to either party to the contract.[90] This is illustrated in the following example.

Example 15.1:   Rainfall contract

Company E has contracted to lease a stall at an open-air event from which it plans to sells goods to people attending the event. The event will be held at a village approximately 100 km from Capital City.

Because E is concerned that poor weather may deter people from attending the event, it enters into a contract with Financial Institution K, the terms of which are that in return for a premium paid by E on inception of the contract, K will pay a fixed amount of money to E if, during the day of the event, it rains for more than three hours at the meteorological station in the centre of Capital City.

The non-financial variable in the contract, i.e. rainfall at the meteorological station, is not specific to E. Particularly, E will only suffer loss as a result of rainfall at the village, not at Capital City. Also, because the potential payment to be received is for a fixed amount, it might not be possible to demonstrate that E has suffered a loss for which it has been compensated. Therefore, E should account for the contract as a financial instrument under IAS 39.

3.3.4   Contracts with discretionary participation features

Certain financial instruments (normally taking the form of life insurance policies) contain what are called discretionary participation features – essentially rights of the holder to receive benefits whose amount or timing is, contractually, at the discretion of the issuer – and these are dealt with under IFRS 4.[91] Accordingly, IAS 39 and the parts of IAS 32 dealing with the distinction between financial liabilities and equity instruments (see Chapter 17) do not apply to such contracts, although the disclosure requirements of IAS 32 do apply.[92]

3.4   Loan commitments

Loan commitments are described in the revised standard as 'firm commitments to provide credit under pre-specified terms and conditions.'[93] The term can include arrangements such as offers to individuals in respect of a residential mortgage loan as well as committed borrowing facilities granted to a corporate entity.

In the previous version of IAS 39, loan commitments were dealt with no differently to other financial instruments and, in most cases, they meet the definition of a derivative financial instrument (see 2.2.7 above and 4 below). Accordingly, they were potentially subject to fair value accounting, although the IGC did take some steps to ameliorate this.[94]

To many, including the IASB, this seemed somewhat counter-intuitive, not least because the resulting assets or liabilities were normally recorded at amortised cost, and in developing the revised version of IAS 39 a pragmatic decision was taken to simplify the accounting for holders and issuers of many loan commitments.[95] Accordingly, loan commitments that cannot be settled net may now be excluded from most of the scope of IAS 39. They are, however, subject to its derecognition provisions[96] (see Chapter 16 at 5) and are included within the scope of IAS 32.[97]

The standard contains only limited guidance on what 'net settlement' means in this context. Clearly a fixed interest rate loan commitment that gives the lender and/or the borrower an explicit right to settle the value of the contract (taking into account changes in interest rates etc.) in cash would be considered a form of net settlement. The IASB also sees a past practice of selling the assets resulting from loan commitments shortly after origination as achieving net settlement and, accordingly, IAS 39 is applied in full to all such commitments within the same class.[98] However, paying out a loan in instalments (for example, a mortgage construction loan where instalments are paid out in line with the progress of construction) is not regarded as net settlement.[99]

As a matter of fact, most loan commitments could be settled net if both parties agreed, essentially by renegotiating the terms of the contract. We do not believe the IASB intended the possibility of such renegotiations to be considered in determining whether or not the commitment may be settled net. Of more relevance is the question of whether one party has the practical ability to settle net, e.g. because the terms of the contract allow net settlement or by the use of some market mechanism.

In addition, many loan commitments allow the lender to withdraw the borrowing facility in the event that there is a significant decline in the borrower's credit risk evidenced, perhaps, by the borrower breaching conventional covenants specified in the agreement. Again, we do not believe the IASB intended such terms, which are common in most facility agreements, to be considered as allowing net settlement and preventing this exception being used.

No guidance is given on what is meant by a class in this context (although the basis for conclusions makes it clear that an entity can have more than one).[100] Therefore, an assessment will need to be made based on individual circumstances.

Example 15.2:   Classes of loan commitment

A banking group has two main operating subsidiaries, one in country A and the other in country B. Although they share common functions (management and information systems etc.) the two subsidiaries' operations are clearly distinct.

Both subsidiaries originate similar loans under loan commitments. In country A there is an active and liquid market for the assets resulting from loan commitments issued in that country. The subsidiary operating in that country has a past practice of disposing of such assets in this market shortly after origination. There is no such market in country B.

The fact that one subsidiary has a past practice of settling its loan commitments net (as the term is used in the standard) would not normally mean that the loan commitments issued in country B are required to be classified as at fair value through profit or loss.

The above example is relatively straightforward – in some circumstances it may be more difficult to define the class. However, there is no reason why an individual entity (say a subsidiary of a group) cannot have two or more classes of loan commitment, e.g. where they result in the origination of different types of asset that are clearly managed separately.

Notwithstanding this permitted exclusion, an entity can choose to account for any loan commitment under IAS 39 by designating it as a financial liability 'at fair value through profit or loss' on inception of the contract (see 7.1.2 below). This may be appropriate if the associated risk exposures are managed on a fair value basis.[101]

An issuer of loan commitments is required to apply IAS 37 if they are not subject to the requirements of IAS 39.[102] Particularly, a provision should be established if a loan commitment becomes an onerous contract as defined in that standard (see Chapter 25 at 5.3). Any associated entitlement to fees should be accounted for in accordance with IAS 18 (see Chapter 26). No accounting requirements are specified for holders of loan commitments, but they will normally be accounted for as executory contracts – essentially, this means that fees payable will be recognised as an expense in a manner that is appropriate to the terms of the commitment. Any resulting borrowing will obviously be accounted for as a financial liability under IAS 32 and IAS 39.

Where loan commitments are issued at below-market interest rates, often no cash consideration is received, and the IASB was concerned that liabilities resulting from such commitments might not be recognised in the balance sheet.[103] Therefore, such commitments should now be recognised and measured initially at their (negative) fair value and, subsequently, at the higher of:

- the amount recognised under IAS 37 (see Chapter 25); and
- the amount initially recognised less, where appropriate, cumulative amortisation recognised in accordance with IAS 18 (see Chapter 26).[104]

The debit entry on initial recognition will be an expense unless the commitment was issued in connection with an arrangement that allows it to be recognised as an asset. In practice, it is unlikely that an entity will grant such a commitment without some prospect of economic return, but that does not mean an asset should always be recognised. (A similar situation is considered in Chapter 18 at 2.2).

Although much of the discussion of loan commitments has focused on *options* to provide credit,[105] we believe it is entirely appropriate to apply the exclusion to non-optional commitments to provide credit, provided the necessary conditions above are met.

It should be recognised that the exclusion is only available for contracts to provide credit. Normally, therefore, it will be applicable only where there is a commitment to lend funds, and certainly not for all contracts that may result in the subsequent recognition of an asset or liability that is accounted for at amortised cost. Consider, for example, a contract between entities A and B that gives B the right to sell to A a transferable (but unquoted) debt security issued by entity C that B currently owns. Even if, on subsequent acquisition, A will classify the debt security within loans and receivables (see 7.3 below), the contract would not generally be considered a loan commitment as it does not involve A providing credit to B.

3.5 Equity instruments

Financial instruments, including options and warrants, that are issued by the reporting entity and meet the definition of equity instruments in IAS 32 (see 2.1 above and Chapter 17) are outside the scope of IAS 39. However, the holder of such an instrument should apply IAS 39 unless it meets the exception at 3.1 above.[106]

Equity instruments are within the scope of IAS 32 from the point of view of the issuer and the holder.[107]

3.6 Business combinations

Neither IAS 32, nor IAS 39, applies to contracts for contingent consideration in business combinations. In the revised standards it was made clear that this exclusion only applies to the acquiror,[108] not the vendor, a recommendation that had earlier been made by IFRIC.[109] This exception is perfectly sensible as the accounting for such contracts from the point of view of the acquiror is dealt with more specifically in other standards, particularly IFRS 3 – *Business Combinations* – and its predecessor IAS 22 – *Business Combinations* (see Chapter 6).

IAS 39 does not go on to explain whether the vendor should be accounting for the contract in accordance with its provisions. This is a somewhat grey area that has, in the past, been considered by IFRIC. They decided to take it no further because 'it is not pervasive in practice' and, a little unconvincingly, because the accounting for contingent consideration from the purchaser's (not vendor's) perspective is being considered in the IASB's business combinations phase II project. They did add that 'one of the questions to consider is whether IAS 37 ... or IAS 39 ... applies'.[110] Whichever standard is used the fundamental question remains: when, and on what basis, should an uncertain amount to be received in the future be recognised as an asset?

Finally, IAS 39 does not apply to contracts between an acquirer and a vendor in a business combination to buy or sell an acquiree at a future date.[111]

3.7 Employee benefit plans and share-based payment

Employers' rights and obligations under employee benefit plans, which are dealt with under IAS 19 – *Employee Benefits* – are excluded from the scope of IAS 32 and IAS 39.[112] Similarly, most financial instruments, contracts and obligations under share-based payment transactions, which are dealt with under IFRS 2 – *Share-based Payment* – are also excluded.

However, IAS 32 and IAS 39 do apply to contracts to buy or sell non-financial items in share-based transactions that can be settled net (as that term is used in this context) unless they are considered to be 'normal' sales and purchases (see 3.8 below).[113] For example, a contract to purchase a fixed quantity of oil in exchange for issuing of a fixed number of shares that could be settled net would be excluded from the scope of IAS 32 and IAS 39 only if it qualified as a 'normal' purchase.

In addition, IAS 32 applies to treasury shares (see Chapter 17 at 6) that are purchased, sold, issued or cancelled in connection with employee share option plans, employee share purchase plans, and all other share-based payment arrangements.[114]

3.8 Contracts to buy or sell non-financial items

As set out at 2.2.5 above, contracts to buy or sell non-financial items do not generally meet the definition of a financial instrument. However, many such contracts are standardised in form and traded on organised markets in much the same way as some derivative financial instruments. The application guidance explains that a commodity futures contract, for example, may be bought and sold readily for cash because it is listed for trading on an exchange and may change hands many times.[115] In fact, this is not strictly true because such contracts are bilateral agreements that cannot be transferred in this way. Rather, the contract would normally be 'closed out' (rather than sold) by entering into an offsetting agreement with the original counterparty or with the exchange on which it is traded.

The ability to buy or sell such a contract for cash, the ease with which it may be bought or sold (or, more correctly, closed out), and the possibility of negotiating a cash settlement of the obligation to receive or deliver the commodity, do not alter the fundamental character of the contract in a way that creates a financial instrument. The buying and selling parties are, in effect, trading the underlying commodity. However, the IASB is of the view that there are many circumstances where they should be accounted for as if they were financial instruments.[116]

Accordingly, the provisions of IAS 32 and IAS 39 are to be applied to those contracts to buy or sell non-financial items that can be settled net in cash or another financial instrument or by exchanging financial instruments, effectively as if the contracts were financial instruments. This is unless they were entered into and continue to be held for the purpose of the receipt or delivery of the non-financial item in accordance with the entity's expected purchase, sale or usage requirements (a 'normal' purchase or sale).[117]

3.8.1 Contracts that may be settled net

There are various ways in which a contract to buy or sell a non-financial item can be settled net, including when:

(a) the terms of the contract permit either party to settle it net;

(b) the ability to settle the contract net is not explicit in its terms, but the entity has a practice of settling similar contracts net (whether with the counterparty, by entering into offsetting contracts or by selling the contract before its exercise or lapse);

(c) for similar contracts, the entity has a practice of taking delivery of the underlying and selling it within a short period after delivery for the purpose of generating a profit from short-term fluctuations in price or dealer's margin; and

(d) the non-financial item that is the subject of the contract is readily convertible to cash.

The IASB views the practice of settling net or taking delivery of the underlying and selling it within a short period after delivery as an indication that the contracts are not 'normal' purchases or sales. Therefore, contracts to which (b) or (c) apply cannot be subject to the normal purchase or sale exception. Other contracts that can be settled net are evaluated to determine whether this exception can actually apply.[118]

Example 15.3:   Copper forward

Company XYZ enters into a fixed-price forward contract to purchase 1,000 kg of copper in accordance with its expected usage requirements. The contract permits XYZ to take physical delivery of the copper at the end of twelve months, or to pay or receive a net settlement in cash, based on the change in fair value of copper.

The contract is a derivative instrument because there is no initial net investment, the contract is based on the price of copper, and it is to be settled at a future date. However, if XYZ intends to settle the contract by taking delivery and has no history for similar contracts of settling net in cash, or of taking delivery of the copper and selling it within a short period after delivery for the purpose of generating a profit from short-term fluctuations in price or dealer's margin, the contract is accounted for as an executory contract rather than as a derivative.[119]

Like loan commitments, as a matter of fact most contracts could be settled net if both parties agreed to renegotiate terms. Again we do not believe the IASB intended the possibility of such renegotiations to be considered in determining whether or not such contracts may be settled net. Of more relevance is the question of whether one party has the practical ability to settle net, e.g. in accordance with the terms of the contract or by the use of some market mechanism.

3.8.2   Similar contracts

The reference to 'similar contracts' in both (b) and (c) at 3.8.1 above is proving to be particularly troublesome.

For example, it is common for entities in, say, the energy sector to have a trading arm that is managed completely separately from their other operations. These trading operations commonly trade in contracts on non-financial assets, the terms of which are similar, if not identical, to those used by the entity's other operations for the purpose of physical supply. Accordingly, a literal reading of the standard might suggest that the normal purchase or sale exemption is unavailable to any entity that has a trading operation. A more generous interpretation might suggest that contracts should be 'similar' as to their purpose within the business (e.g. for trading or for physical supply) not just as to their contractual terms.

Even for entities without trading operations, the reference to similar contracts can cause problems. For example, some entities find it necessary to close out normal sale or purchase contracts, e.g. because they become surplus to requirements. It is possible to argue that such actions might taint an entity's ability to consider contracts as normal sales or purchases. There are no explicit tainting rules as there are for held-to-maturity investments (see 7.2.3 below), but should a similar regime be applied?

Many entities are actively addressing these issues and some are working within industry groups to try and form a common view. However, a widely accepted consensus has yet to emerge.

3.8.3 Written options that can be settled net

The IASB does not believe that a written option to buy or sell a non-financial item that can be settled net can be entered into for the purpose of receipt or delivery in accordance with the entity's expected sale or usage requirements. Accordingly, IAS 32 and IAS 39 apply to any such contracts falling within (a) and (d) above.[120]

Example 15.4:   Put option on office building

Company XYZ owns an office building. It enters into a put option with an investor, which expires in five years and permits it to put the building to the investor for £150 million. The current value of the building is £175 million. The option, if exercised, may be settled through physical delivery or net cash, at XYZ's option.

XYZ's accounting depends on its intention and past practice for settlement. Although the contract meets the definition of a derivative, XYZ does not account for it as a derivative if it intends to settle the contract by delivering the building in the event of exercise and there is no past practice of settling net.

The investor, however, cannot conclude that the option was entered into to meet its expected purchase, sale, or usage requirements – the contract may be settled net and is a written option. Regardless of past practices, its intention does not affect whether settlement is by delivery or in cash. Accordingly, the contract is accounted for as a derivative. As noted at 4 and 7.1 below, this will involve remeasuring the derivative to its fair value each reporting period with any associated gains and losses recognised in profit or loss.

However, if the contract were a forward contract rather than an option, it required physical delivery and the investor had no past practice of settling net (either in cash or by way of taking delivery and subsequently selling within a short period), the contract would not be accounted for as a derivative.[121]

3.8.4 Comparison with previous version of IAS 32 and IAS 39

The previous versions of IAS 32 and IAS 39 required certain commodity-based contracts to be accounted for as if they were financial instruments. However, those standards were not entirely consistent; they provided much less guidance in respect of what constituted 'net settlement'; and there was also a requirement for formal designation of such contracts where the normal sale, purchase or usage exception was to be taken.[122]

Accordingly, it is quite possible for contracts that were previously accounted for as executory contracts to be accounted for as financial instruments under the revised standards (and, to a lesser extent, vice versa). The meaning of similar contracts (see 3.8.2 above) is likely to be the greatest influence on the extent of any change in scope.

It is also worth noting that IAS 2 – *Inventories* – was revised at the same time as IAS 32 and IAS 39. As a result, certain commodities are now measured at net realisable value or fair value less costs to sell with associated gains and losses recognised in profit or loss.[123] This can reduce accounting inconsistencies between commodity-contracts within the scope of IAS 39 and the commodities themselves. IAS 2 is dealt with in Chapter 21.

3.8.5   *Disclosure of contracts not accounted for as financial instruments*

Although IAS 32 was not developed to apply to commodity or other contracts that do not satisfy the definition of, or fall to be accounted for as, financial instruments, entities may regard it as appropriate to apply the relevant disclosure requirements to such contracts.[124] These requirements are considered in Chapter 20.

4   DERIVATIVES

The question of whether an instrument is a derivative or not is an important one for accounting purposes. As noted at 7.1 below, derivatives are normally recorded on the balance sheet at fair value with any changes in value reported in profit or loss (although there are some exceptions, e.g. derivatives that are designated in certain effective hedge relationships).

For many financial instruments, it will be reasonably clear whether or not they are derivatives, but there will be more marginal cases. Accordingly, the term derivative is formally defined within IAS 39 – it is a financial instrument, or other contract within the scope of IAS 39 (see 3.8 above), with all of the following characteristics:

(a)   its value changes in response to the change in a specified interest rate, financial instrument price, commodity price, foreign exchange rate, index of prices or rates, a credit rating or credit index, or similar underlying (provided in the case of a non-financial variable that it is not specific to a party to the contract);

(b)   it requires no initial net investment, or one that is smaller than would be required for other types of contracts that would be expected to have a similar response to changes in market factors; and

(c)   it is settled at a future date.[125]

This definition has been subject to only limited revision and the three defining characteristics are considered further below.

4.1   Changes in value in response to changes in underlying

A derivative usually has a notional amount, such as an amount of currency, number of shares or units of weight or volume, but does not require the holder or writer to invest or receive the notional amount at inception. However, this is not always the case: a derivative could require a fixed payment or payment of an amount that can change (but not proportionally with a change in the underlying) as a result of some future event that is unrelated to a notional amount. For example, a contract that requires a fixed payment of €1,000 if six-month LIBOR increases by 100 basis points is a derivative, but does not have a specified notional amount.[126] A further example is shown below.

Example 15.5:   Derivative containing no notional amount

XYZ enters into a contract that requires payment of $1,000 if ABC's share price increases by $5 or more during a six-month period; XYZ will receive $1,000 if the share price decreases by $5 or more during the same six-month period; no payment will be made if the price swing is less than $5 up or down.

The settlement amount changes with an underlying, ABC's share price, although there is no notional amount to determine the settlement amount. Instead, there is a payment provision that is based on changes in the underlying. Provided all the other characteristics of a derivative are present, which they are in this case, such an instrument is a derivative.[127]

A contract to pay a royalty in exchange for the use of certain property that is not exchange traded, and where the payment is based on the volume of related sales or service revenues, is not accounted for as a derivative. Guidance on accounting for royalty agreements is included in IAS 18 (see Chapter 26).[128] However, derivatives that are based on sales volume are not excluded from the scope of IAS 39, as set out in the next example.

Example 15.6:   Derivative containing two underlyings

Company XYZ, whose functional currency is the US dollar, sells products in France denominated in euros. XYZ enters into a contract with an investment bank to convert euros to US dollars at a fixed exchange rate. The contract requires XYZ to remit euros based on its sales volume in France in exchange for US dollars at a fixed exchange rate of 1.00.

The contract has two underlying variables, the foreign exchange rate and the volume of sales, no initial net investment, and a payment provision. Therefore it is a derivative.[129]

The definition of a derivative (see 4 above) refers to non-financial variables that are not specific to one party to the contract. This is in the context of determining whether or not the financial instrument is an insurance contract (see 3.3 above). Such variables might include an index of earthquake losses in a particular region or an index of temperatures in a particular city. Non-financial variables that are specific to a party to a contract can include the occurrence or non-occurrence of a fire that damages or destroys an asset of a party to the contract. A change in the fair value of a non-financial asset is specific to the owner if the fair value reflects not only changes in market prices for such assets (a financial variable) but also the condition of the specific non-financial asset held (a non-financial variable). An example of such a contract is included at 3.3.1 above.[130]

4.2   Initial net investment

As set out at 4 above, one of the key characteristics of a derivative is that it has no initial net investment, or one that is smaller than would be required for other types of contracts that would be expected to have a similar response to changes in market factors.[131] The revised standard does not use quite the same words as previously[132] although the meaning is substantially the same.

An option contract meets the definition because the premium is less than the investment that would be required to obtain the underlying financial instrument to which the option is linked.[133]

The implementation guidance previously suggested that the purchase of a deep in the money call option would fail to satisfy the original 'little net investment' test if the premium paid was equal *or close to* the amount required to invest in the underlying instrument.[134] A strict reading of the standard would suggest that unless the premium was at least equal (as opposed to close) to the amount required to invest in the underlying, such a contract would now be deemed to exhibit the 'no or smaller net investment' characteristic. However, the implementation guidance on which Example 15.10 below is based explains that a contract is not a derivative if the initial net investment *approximates* the amount that an entity otherwise would be required to invest.[135] This may seem a somewhat esoteric analysis, but it illustrates the problems in defining the boundaries between different classes of instrument in a mixed attribute model.

Currency swaps sometimes require an exchange of different currencies of equal value at inception as in the following example.

Example 15.7:   Currency swap – initial exchange of principal

Company A and Company B enter into a five year fixed-for-fixed currency swap on euros and US dollars. The current spot exchange rate is €1 per US$. The five-year interest rate in the US is 8%, while the five-year interest rate in Europe is 6%. On initiation of the swap, A pays €2,000 to B, which in return pays US$2,000 to A. During the swap's life, A and B make periodic interest payments to each other without netting. B pays 6% per year on the €2,000 it has received (€120 per year), while A pays 8% per year on the US$2,000 it has received (US$160 per year). On termination of the swap, the two parties again exchange the original principal amounts.

The currency swap is a derivative financial instrument since the contract involves a zero initial *net* investment (only an exchange of one currency for another of equal fair values), it has an underlying, and it will be settled at a future date.[136]

The following examples illustrate how to assess the initial net investment characteristic in various prepaid derivatives – these can provide guidance when assessing whether what appears to be a non-derivative instrument is actually a derivative.

Example 15.8:   Prepaid interest rate swap (prepaid fixed leg)

Company S enters into a €1,000 notional amount five year pay-fixed, receive-variable interest rate swap. The interest rate of the variable part of the swap resets on a quarterly basis to three month LIBOR. The interest rate of the fixed part of the swap is 10% per annum. At inception of the swap S prepays its fixed obligation of €500 (€1,000 × 10% × 5 years), discounted using market interest rates, while retaining the right to receive the LIBOR based interest payments on the €1,000 over the life of the swap.

The initial net investment in the swap is significantly less than the notional amount on which the variable payments under the variable leg will be calculated and therefore requires an initial net investment that is smaller than would be required for other types of contracts that would be expected to have a similar response to changes in market conditions, such as a variable rate bond. It therefore exhibits characteristic (b) at 4 above. Even though S has no future performance obligation, the ultimate settlement of the contract is at a future date and its value changes in response to changes in LIBOR. Accordingly, it is a derivative.[137]

Example 15.9: Prepaid interest rate swap (prepaid floating leg)

Instead of the transactions in Example 15.8, Company S enters into a €1,000 notional amount five-year pay-variable, receive-fixed interest rate swap. The variable leg of the swap resets on a quarterly basis to three month LIBOR. The fixed interest payments under the swap are calculated as 10% of the notional amount, i.e. €100 per year. By agreement with the counterparty, S prepays and discharges its obligation under the variable leg of the swap at inception by paying a fixed amount determined according to current market rates, while retaining the right to receive the fixed interest payments of €100 per year.

The cash inflows under the contract are equivalent to those of a financial instrument with a fixed annuity stream since S knows it will receive €100 per year over the life of the swap. Therefore, all else being equal, the initial investment in the contract should equal that of other financial instruments consisting of fixed annuities. Thus, the initial net investment in the pay-variable, receive-fixed interest rate swap is equal to the investment required in a non-derivative contract that has a similar response to changes in market conditions. For this reason, the instrument does not exhibit characteristic (b) above and is not a derivative.[138]

Example 15.10: Prepaid forward purchase of shares

Company S also enters into a forward contract to purchase 100 shares in T in one year. The current share price is £50 per share and the one year forward price £55. S is required to prepay the forward contract at inception with a £5,000 payment.

The initial investment in the forward contract of £5,000 is less than the notional amount applied to the underlying, 100 shares at the forward price of £55 per share, i.e. £5,500. However, the initial net investment approximates the investment that would be required for other types of contracts that would be expected to have a similar response to changes in market factors because T's shares could be purchased at inception for the same price of £50. Accordingly, the prepaid forward does not exhibit characteristic (b) above and is not a derivative.[139]

The conclusions in Examples 15.8 and 15.9 above are fundamentally different for what, on the face of it, appear to be very similar transactions. The key difference is that in Example 15.8 all possible cash flow variances are eliminated and, consequently, the resulting cash flows exhibit the characteristics of a simple non-derivative instrument, i.e. an amortising loan.

Many derivative instruments, such as futures contracts and exchange traded written options, require margin payments. The margin payment is not part of the initial net investment in a derivative, but is a form of collateral for the counterparty or clearing-house and may take the form of cash, securities, or other specified assets, typically liquid assets. They are separate assets that are accounted for separately.[140]

4.3   Future settlement

The third characteristic is that settlement takes place at a future date. Sometimes, a contract will require gross cash settlement. However, as illustrated in the next example, it makes no difference whether the future settlements are gross or net.

Example 15.11:   Interest rate swap – gross or net settlement

Company ABC is considering entering into an interest rate swap with a counterparty, XYZ. The proposed terms are that ABC pays a fixed rate of 8% and receives a variable amount based on three month LIBOR, reset on a quarterly basis; the fixed and variable amounts are determined based on a €1,000 notional amount; ABC and XYZ do not exchange the notional amount and ABC pays or receives a net cash amount each quarter based on the difference between 8% and three month LIBOR. Alternatively, settlement may be on a gross basis.

The contract meets the definition of a derivative regardless of whether there is net or gross settlement because its value changes in response to changes in an underlying variable (LIBOR), there is no initial net investment and settlements occur at future dates – it makes no difference whether ABC and XYZ actually make the interest payments to each other (gross settlement) or settle on a net basis.[141]

The definition of a derivative also includes contracts that are settled gross by delivery of the underlying item, e.g. a forward contract to purchase a fixed rate debt instrument. An entity may have a contract to buy or sell a non-financial item that can be settled net, e.g. a contract to buy or sell a commodity at a fixed price at a future date; if that contract is within the scope of IAS 39 (see 3.8 above) the question of whether or not it is a derivative will be assessed in the same way as a financial instrument that may be settled gross.[142]

Expiry of an option at its maturity is a form of settlement even though there is no additional exchange of consideration. Therefore, even if an option is not expected to be exercised, e.g. because it is significantly 'out of the money', it can still be a derivative.[143] Such an option will have some value, albeit quite small, because it still offers the opportunity for gain if it becomes 'in the money' before expiry even if such a possibility is remote – the more remote the possibility, the lower its value.

4.4   Common examples of derivatives

The following table provides examples of contracts that normally qualify as derivatives. The list is not exhaustive – any contract that has an underlying may be a derivative. Moreover, as set out at 3 above, even if an instrument meets the definition of a derivative, it may not fall within the scope of IAS 39.

Type of contract	*Main pricing-settlement underlying variable*
Interest rate swap	Interest rates
Currency swap (foreign exchange swap)	Currency rates
Commodity swap	Commodity prices
Equity swap	Equity prices (equity of another entity)
Credit swap	Credit rating, credit index, or credit price
Total return swap	Total fair value of the reference asset and interest rates
Purchased or written treasury bond option (call or put)	Interest rates
Purchased or written currency option (call or put)	Currency rates
Purchased or written commodity option (call or put)	Commodity prices
Purchased or written stock option (call or put)	Equity prices (equity of another entity)
Interest rate futures linked to government debt (treasury futures)	Interest rates
Currency futures	Currency rates
Commodity futures	Commodity prices
Interest rate forward linked to government debt (treasury forward)	Interest rates
Currency forward	Currency rates
Commodity forward	Commodity prices
Equity forward	Equity prices (equity of another entity)[144]

4.5   In-substance derivatives

The implementation guidance explains that the accounting should follow the substance of arrangements. In particular, non-derivative transactions should be aggregated and treated as a derivative when, in substance, the transactions result in a derivative. Indicators of this would include:

- they are entered into at the same time and in contemplation of one another;

- they have the same counterparty;

- they relate to the same risk; and

- there is no apparent economic need or substantive business purpose for structuring the transactions separately that could not also have been accomplished in a single transaction.[145]

The application of this guidance is illustrated in the following example.

Example 15.12: In-substance derivative – offsetting loans

Company A makes a five-year fixed rate loan to Company B, while at the same time B makes a five-year variable rate loan for the same amount to A. There are no transfers of principal at inception of the two loans, since A and B have a netting agreement.

The combined contractual effect of the loans is the equivalent of an interest rate swap arrangement, i.e. there is an underlying variable, no initial net investment, and future settlement. This meets the definition of a derivative.

This would be the case even if there was no netting agreement, because the definition of a derivative instrument does not require net settlement (see Example 15.11 at 4.3 above).[146]

4.6   Regular way contracts

A regular way purchase or sale is a purchase or sale of a financial asset under a contract whose terms require delivery of the asset within the time frame established generally by regulation or convention in the marketplace concerned.[147] Such contracts give rise to a fixed price commitment between trade date and settlement date that meets the definition of a derivative. However, because of the short duration of the commitments, they are not accounted for as a derivative but in accordance with special accounting rules. These requirements are discussed in Chapter 16 at 3.1.[148]

5   EMBEDDED DERIVATIVES

An embedded derivative is a component of a hybrid or combined instrument that also includes a non-derivative host contract; it has the effect that some of the cash flows of the combined instrument vary in a similar way to a stand-alone derivative. In other words, it causes some or all of the cash flows that otherwise would be required by the contract to be modified according to a specified interest rate, financial instrument price, commodity price, foreign exchange rate, index of prices or rates, credit rating or credit index, or other underlying variable (provided in the case of a non-financial variable that the variable is not specific to a party to the contract).[149]

The concept of embedded derivatives is one of the most difficult for many preparers and users of financial statements to understand, a fact that even the IASB has acknowledged.[150] Some may regard it as a little unfortunate, therefore, that in revising IAS 39 the IASB's main response was to allow the greater use of fair value accounting for financial instruments containing embedded derivatives, rather than to ease the existing requirements (although there was one principle exception – see 5.1.9 below).

The IASB believes that entities should not be able to circumvent the accounting requirements for derivatives merely by embedding a derivative in a non-derivative financial instrument or other contract, e.g. a commodity forward in a debt instrument, and this is provided as a rationale for the requirements on embedded derivatives. In other words, they are chiefly an anti-abuse measure designed to require 'derivative accounting' to those derivatives that are 'hidden' in other contracts.[151]

Common examples of contracts that can contain embedded derivatives include non-derivative financial instruments (especially debt instruments), leases, insurance contracts as well as contracts for the supply of goods or services. In fact, they may occur in all sorts of unsuspected locations.

In the basis for conclusions to IAS 39, the IASB asserts that, in principle, *all* embedded derivatives ought to be accounted for separately, but explains that, as a practical expedient, they need not be where they are regarded as 'closely related' to their host contracts. In those cases, it is believed less likely that the derivative was embedded to achieve a desired accounting result.[152]

Accordingly, only where the following conditions are met should an embedded derivative be separated from the host contract and accounted for separately:

(a)   the economic characteristics and risks of the embedded derivative are not closely related to those of the host contract;

(b)   a separate instrument with the same terms as the embedded derivative would meet the definition of a derivative; and

(c)   the hybrid (combined) instrument is not measured at fair value with changes in fair value recognised in profit or loss.[153]

If any of these conditions are not met, the embedded derivative should not be accounted for separately.[154] The process is similar, although not identical, to that applied when separating the equity element of a compound instrument under IAS 32 (see Chapter 17 at 4).

The accounting treatment for a separated embedded derivative (examples of which are included throughout this section) is the same as for a standalone derivative. As noted at 4 above, and 7.1 below, such an instrument (actually, in this case, a component of an instrument) will normally be recorded on the balance sheet at fair value with all changes in value being recognised in profit or loss (although there are some exceptions, e.g. derivatives that are designated in certain effective hedge relationships).

A derivative that is attached to a financial instrument but is contractually transferable independently of that instrument, or has a different counterparty from that instrument, is not an embedded derivative, but a separate financial instrument.[155]

Where an entity is unable to measure an embedded derivative that is required to be separated from its host, either on acquisition or subsequently, the entire contract is treated as held for trading.[156] Even if the embedded derivative's fair value cannot be determined reliably on the basis of its terms and conditions (for example if it is based on an unquoted equity instrument – see Chapter 18 at 4.4), if the fair values of both the hybrid instrument and host can be determined, it may be determined indirectly as the difference between the two.[157]

5.1   The meaning of 'closely related'

The standard does not define what is meant by 'closely related'. Instead, it illustrates what was intended by providing a series of situations where the embedded derivative is, or is not, regarded as closely related to the host. Making this determination can prove very challenging, not least because the illustrations do not always seem to be consistent with each other. This guidance is considered in the remainder of this subsection.

Where a host contract has no stated or predetermined maturity and represents a residual interest in the net assets of an entity, its economic characteristics and risks are those of an equity instrument – therefore, an embedded derivative would need to possess equity characteristics related to the same entity to be regarded as closely related. More commonly, if the host is not an equity instrument and meets the definition of a financial instrument, then its economic characteristics and risks are those of a debt instrument.[158] The application of these principles is considered at 5.1.1 to 5.1.9 below.

5.1.1   Puttable instruments

An example of a hybrid contract is a financial instrument that gives the holder a right to put it back to the issuer in exchange for an amount that varies on the basis of the change in an equity or commodity index (a 'puttable instrument'). As noted at 5.1 above, the host is deemed to be a debt instrument and the embedded derivative, the indexed principal payment, cannot be regarded as closely related to the debt instrument. Because the principal payment can increase and decrease, the embedded derivative is a non-option derivative whose value is indexed to the underlying variable (see 5.2 below).[159]

In the case of a puttable instrument that can be put back at any time for cash equal to a proportionate share of the net asset value of an entity (such as units of an open-ended mutual fund or some unit-linked investment products), the effect of separating an embedded derivative and accounting for each component will be to measure the combined instrument at the redemption amount that is payable at the balance sheet date if the holder were to exercise its right to put the instrument back to the issuer.[160]

These instruments were brought into focus by a SIC project. The SIC's conclusions, which were consistent with the treatment described in the previous paragraph, resulted in the publication of a draft interpretation.[161] However, this was never finalised and the issue was subsequently absorbed into the 'improvements' project. The accounting treatment noted above, which is considered in more detail in Chapter 17 at 3.2.2, is controversial because it means that under IFRS a unit trust or similar vehicle is effectively required to account for such instruments at fair value with all changes reported in profit or loss and, as a result, it may report no equity and no profit.

In theory, there is no reason why a similar treatment should not apply to the holder of such an instrument. This would mean that all changes in the fair value of an entity's investment in a unit trust would be recognised in profit or loss, even if it were classified as available-for-sale. However, this seems entirely wrong. To the extent that anyone has a residual interest in the net assets of a unit trust, it is the unit-holders. Consequently, a more intuitive view of the investment would be as an equity instrument host with an embedded put option, exercisable at net asset value. Further, because net asset value will approximate fair value, the embedded derivative would have little or no value.

The original SIC project dealt only with the accounting from the point of view of the issuer and, in discussing puttable instruments that vary on the basis of the change in an equity or commodity index, paragraph AG31 of IAS 39 refers only to the treatment by the issuer of such an instrument. This suggests that a different analysis is permissible when viewing the instrument from the perspective of the holder. Further support for this can be found in the definition of loans and receivables: as noted at 7.3 below, an interest in a pool of assets that are not loans or receivables (such as a mutual fund) is not considered to be a loan or receivable.[162] This also suggests the host might validly be considered an equity instrument from the point of view of the holder.

Therefore, we suspect that many entities will continue accounting for unit trust and similar investments as available-for-sale equity investments whilst recognising fair value gains and losses in equity.

5.1.2 Callable equity instruments

An equity instrument containing an embedded call option enabling the issuer to reacquire that equity instrument at a specified price is not closely related to the host equity instrument from the perspective of the holder.[163]

From the issuer's perspective, the call option is an equity instrument provided it meets the conditions for that classification under IAS 32, in which case it is excluded from the scope of IAS 39.[164] This reaffirms an important point – if a financial instrument (including its embedded features) satisfies the definition of an equity instrument from the point of view of the issuer, it cannot contain an embedded derivative requiring separation for accounting purposes.

The potential effect of this guidance is illustrated below.

Example 15.13: Callable preference share

Company J issues preference shares for their par value of $1,000. The shares carry the right to a discretionary 8% cumulative annual dividend and are redeemable at the sole option of Company J on the fifth anniversary of issue and each fifth anniversary thereafter. The redemption amount is the par value of the shares plus any unpaid dividends. Although it is not foreseen that J will choose not to pay these dividends, from J's perspective the shares are presented as equity (see Chapter 17 at 3.2.1).

On issuance, Company R acquires the preference shares and classifies them as available-for-sale assets (rather than at fair value through profit or loss, the only other possible classification for an investment in an equity instrument). Therefore R accounts for J's embedded call (redemption) option separately as an embedded derivative. The embedded option will have a fair value that, from R's perspective, can only be negative because it is a written option. The host instrument will be equivalent to an 8% perpetual preference share with no call (or redemption) option and will have an initial fair value in excess of the $1,000 purchase price of the hybrid.

If there is no significant change in J's credit risk or the risk of J choosing not to exercise its discretion to pay dividends, a fall in interest rates will cause the value of the host instrument to increase. This results from the present value of the expected dividend payments, discounted at the lower interest rate, being higher. However, as the possible redemption date approaches, the value of the hybrid instrument as a whole should not significantly exceed the par value of the shares because J can always choose to settle the combined instrument at that par value.

Therefore, if the fair value of the host investment increases because of falls in interest rates, the negative fair value of the embedded option will also increase, especially as the redemption date approaches. Chapter 18 explains how different types of financial instrument are accounted for under IAS 39, but in simple terms, increases in the fair value of an available for sale asset are recognised and recorded in equity, whereas changes in the fair value of a derivative (including an embedded derivative) are recorded in profit or loss. In this case any such gains and losses arising on the same instrument (which in very broad terms will offset) cannot be offset in the financial statements, creating a potentially significant mismatch.

If R had designated the shares at fair value through profit or loss, it would not have accounted separately for the embedded derivative.

5.1.3   Term extension and similar call, put and prepayment options in debt instruments

The application guidance explains that a call, put or prepayment option embedded in a host debt instrument (or insurance contract) is closely related to the host instrument if, on each exercise date, the option's exercise price is approximately equal to the debt instrument's amortised cost (or carrying amount of the host insurance contract); otherwise it is not regarded as closely related.[165]

It also says that an option or automatic provision to extend the remaining term to maturity of a debt instrument is not closely related to the host unless, at the time of the extension, there is a concurrent adjustment to the approximate current market rate of interest.[166]

Taken in isolation the above two paragraphs appear reasonably straightforward to apply. However, in some situations, they appear contradictory as set out in the following example.

Example 15.14: Extension and prepayment options

Company Z borrows €1,000 from Bank A on which it is required to pay €50 per annum interest. Under the terms of the borrowing agreement, Z is required to repay €1,000 in three year's time unless, at repayment date, it exercises an option to extend the term of the borrowing for a further two years. If this option is exercised €50 interest per annum is payable for the additional term.

Company Z also borrows €1,000 from Bank B on which it is required to pay €50 per annum interest. Under the terms of this borrowing agreement, Z is required to repay €1,000 in five year's time unless, at the end of three years, it exercises an option to redeem the borrowing for €1,000.

It can be seen that in all practical respects these two instruments are identical – the only difference is the way in which the terms of the embedded options are expressed. In the first case the guidance suggests that the (term extension) option is not closely related to the debt as there is no concurrent adjustment to market interest rates. However, in the second case the (prepayment) option *is* considered closely related provided the amortised cost of the liability would be approximately €1,000, the exercise price of the settlement option, at the end of year three (which it should be).

For put, call and prepayment options, there is a further complication that the determination as to whether or not the option is closely related depends on the amortised cost of the instrument. It is not clear whether this reference is to the amortised cost of the host instrument on the assumption that the option is separated or the amortised cost of the entire instrument on the assumption that the option is not separated – as can be seen in Chapter 18 at 5.2, the existence of such options can affect that amortised cost, especially for a portfolio of instruments. Entities are left to apply their own judgment to assess which appears the most appropriate in the specific circumstances.

From the perspective of the issuer of a convertible debt instrument with an embedded call or put option feature, the assessment of whether the call or put option is closely related to the host debt instrument is made before separating the equity element under IAS 32.[167] This provides a specific relaxation from the general guidance on prepayment options above because, for accounting purposes, separate accounting for the equity component results in a discount on recognition of the liability component (see Chapter 17 at 4.3) which means that the amortised cost and exercise price are unlikely to approximate each other for much of the term of the instrument.

An embedded prepayment option in an interest-only or principal-only strip is regarded as closely related to the host contract provided the host contract (i) initially resulted from separating the right to receive contractual cash flows of a financial instrument that, in and of itself, did not contain an embedded derivative, and (ii) does not contain any terms not present in the original host debt contract.[168] Again this is a specific relaxation from the general guidance on prepayment options above.

If an entity issues a debt instrument and the holder writes a call option on the debt instrument to a third party, the issuer regards the call option as extending the term to maturity of the debt instrument provided it can be required to participate in or facilitate the remarketing of the debt instrument as a result of the call option being exercised.[169] Such a component is presumably considered to represent part of a hybrid financial instrument contract rather than a separate instrument in its own right (see 5 above).

5.1.4 Commodity and equity linked interest and principal payments

Equity-indexed or commodity-indexed interest or principal payments embedded in a host debt instrument or insurance contract, i.e. where the amount of interest or principal is indexed to the value of an equity instrument or commodity (e.g. gold), are not closely related to the host debt instrument because the risks inherent in the embedded derivative are dissimilar to those of the host.[170] An example of such an instrument is given in Example 15.20 at 7.2.1 below.

5.1.5 Convertible and exchangeable debt instruments

An equity conversion feature embedded in a convertible debt instrument is not closely related to the host debt instrument from the perspective of the holder of the instrument (from the issuer's perspective, the equity conversion option is generally an equity instrument and excluded from the scope of IAS 39 – see Chapter 17 at 4.3).[171]

In some instances, venture capital entities provide subordinated loans on terms that they are entitled to receive shares if and when the borrowing entity lists its shares on a stock exchange, as illustrated in the following example.

Example 15.15: Equity kicker

A venture capital investor, Company V, provides a subordinated loan to Company A and agrees that, in addition to interest and repayment of principal, if A lists its shares on a stock exchange, V will be entitled to receive shares in A free of charge or at a very low price (an 'equity kicker'). As a result of this feature, interest on the loan is lower than it would otherwise be. The loan is not measured at fair value with changes in fair value recognised in profit or loss.

The economic characteristics and risks of an equity return are not closely related to those of the host debt instrument. The equity kicker meets the definition of a derivative because it has a value that changes in response to the change in the price of A's shares, requires only a relatively small initial net investment, and is settled at a future date. It does not matter that the right to receive shares is contingent upon the borrower's future listing.[172]

Similarly, the derivative embedded in a bond that is convertible (or exchangeable) into equity shares of a third party will not be closely related to the host debt instrument – in this case, both from the point of view of the holder and of the issuer.

5.1.6   Credit linked notes

Credit derivatives are sometimes embedded in a host debt instrument whereby one party (the 'beneficiary') transfers the credit risk of a particular reference asset, which it may not own, to another party (the 'guarantor'). Such credit derivatives allow the guarantor to assume the credit risk associated with the reference asset without directly owning it.

Although the economic characteristics of a debt instrument include credit risk, in general the embedded derivative will be a credit derivative linked to the credit standing of an entity other than the issuer, and is therefore not regarded as closely related to the host debt instrument.[173]

5.1.7   Interest rate indices

Many debt instruments contain embedded interest rate indices that can change the amount of interest that would otherwise be paid or received. One of the simplest examples would be a floating rate loan whereby interest is paid quarterly based on three month LIBOR. More complex examples might include the following:

- inverse floater – coupons are paid at a fixed rate minus LIBOR;
- levered inverse floater – as above but a multiplier greater than 1.0 is applied to the resulting coupon;
- delevered floater – coupons lag overall movements in a specified rate, e.g. coupons equal a proportion of the ten-year constantly maturity treasuries rate plus a fixed premium; or
- range floater – interest is paid at a fixed rate but only for each day in a given period that LIBOR is within a stated range.[174]

In such cases the embedded derivative is closely related to the host debt instrument (or insurance contract) unless:

(a)   the combined instrument can be settled in such a way that the holder would not recover substantially all of its recognised investment; or

(b)   the embedded derivative could at least double the holder's initial rate of return on the host contract and could result in a rate of return that is at least twice what the market return would be for a contract with the same terms as the host contract.[175]

If a holder is permitted, but not required, to settle the combined instrument in a manner such that it does not recover substantially all of its recognised investment, e.g. puttable debt, the first condition is not satisfied and the embedded derivative is not separated.[176]

To meet the second condition, the embedded derivative must be able to double the initial return *and* result in a rate of return that is at least twice what would be expected for a similar contract at the time it takes effect. If it meets only one, but not the other part of this condition, the derivative is regarded as closely related to the host. Therefore, the derivative embedded in a simple variable rate loan would be considered closely related to the host as it would not meet the second part.

5.1.8   Floors and caps

An embedded floor or cap on the interest rate on a debt instrument (or insurance contract) is closely related to the host debt instrument, provided the cap is at or above the market rate of interest, and the floor is at or below the market rate of interest, when the instrument is issued, and the cap or floor is not leveraged in relation to the host instrument.

Similarly, a contract to purchase or sell an asset (e.g. a commodity) that establishes a cap and a floor on the price to be paid or received for the asset are closely related to the host contract if both the cap and floor were out of the money at inception and are not leveraged.[177]

We do not believe it is necessary for both a cap *and* a floor to be present to be considered closely related. For example, a cap (or floor) on the coupon paid on a debt instrument without a corresponding floor (or cap) could be regarded as closely related to the host provided it was above (or below) the market rate of interest on origination.

5.1.9   Foreign currency derivatives

A monetary item denominated in a currency other than an entity's functional currency is accounted for under IAS 21 – *The Effects of Changes in Foreign Exchange Rates* – with foreign currency gains and losses recognised in profit or loss. For this reason, the embedded foreign currency derivative is considered closely related to the host and is not separated. This also applies where the embedded derivative in a host debt instrument provides a stream either of principal or of interest payments denominated in a foreign currency (e.g. a dual currency bond).[178]

An embedded foreign currency derivative in a contract that is not a financial instrument (or is a financial instrument that is an insurance contract), such as a contract for the purchase or sale of a non-financial item where the price is denominated in a foreign currency, is closely related to the host contract provided it is not leveraged, does not contain an option feature and requires payments denominated in one of the following currencies:

(i)   the functional currency of any substantial party to the contract;

(ii)   the currency in which the price of the related good or service that is acquired or delivered is routinely denominated in commercial transactions around the world (such as the US dollar for crude oil transactions); or

(iii)   a currency that is commonly used in contracts to purchase or sell non-financial items in the economic environment in which the transaction takes place (e.g. a relatively stable and liquid currency that is commonly used in local business transactions or external trade).

Therefore, in such cases the embedded foreign currency derivative is not accounted for separately from the host contract.[179]

As noted at 2.2.4 above, a finance lease payable or receivable is accounted for as a financial instrument and an operating lease as an executory contract. Therefore, a finance lease denominated in a foreign currency will not generally be considered to contain an embedded foreign currency derivative requiring separation (because the payable or receivable is a monetary item within the scope of IAS 21). However, an operating lease denominated in a foreign currency may contain a foreign currency embedded derivative requiring separation.

For the purposes of (ii) above, the currency must be used for similar transactions all around the world, not just in one local area. For example, if cross-border transactions in natural gas in North America are routinely denominated in US dollars and such transactions are routinely denominated in euros in Europe, neither the US dollar nor the euro is a currency in which the good or service is routinely denominated in international commerce.[180] Accordingly, the number of items to which this will apply will be limited – in practice it will be mainly commodities that are traded in, say, US dollars throughout much of the world, although one notable exception might be wide-bodied aircraft where it appears that Boeing and Airbus, the two major manufacturers, routinely denominate sales in US dollars.

The addition of (iii) above represents the only substantive change to the embedded derivative requirements in the revised version of IAS 39 and will be welcomed by many, especially those operating in small or developing economies.

The application of the guidance above is illustrated in the examples below.

Example 15.16:   Oil contract denominated in Swiss francs

A Norwegian company agrees to sell oil to a company in France. The oil contract is denominated in Swiss francs, although oil contracts are routinely denominated in US dollars in international commerce and Norwegian Krone are commonly used in contracts to purchase or sell non-financial items in Norway. Neither company carries out any significant activities in Swiss francs.

The Norwegian company should regard the supply contract as a host contract with an embedded foreign currency forward to purchase Swiss francs. The French company should regard it as a host contract with an embedded foreign currency forward to sell Swiss francs.[181]

Example 15.17:   Oil contract, denominated in US dollars and containing a leveraged foreign exchange payment

Company A, whose functional currency is the euro, enters into a contract with Company B, whose functional currency is the Norwegian Krone, to purchase oil in six months for US$1,000. The host oil contract will be settled by making and taking delivery in the normal course of business and is not accounted for as a financial instrument because it qualifies as a normal sale or purchase contract (see 3.8 above). The oil contract includes a leveraged foreign exchange provision whereby the parties, in addition to the provision of, and payment for, oil will exchange an amount equal to the fluctuation in the exchange rate of the US dollar and Norwegian Krone applied to a notional amount of US$100,000.

The payment of US$1,000 under the host oil contract can be viewed as a foreign currency derivative because the dollar is neither Company A nor B's functional currency. However, it would not be separated as the US dollar is the currency in which crude oil transactions are routinely denominated in international commerce.

The leveraged foreign exchange provision is in addition to the required payment for the oil transaction. It is unrelated to the host oil contract and is therefore separated and accounted for as an embedded derivative.[182]

In practice, all but the simplest contracts will contain other terms and features that can often make it much more difficult to isolate the precise terms of the embedded foreign currency derivative (and the host). For example, a clause may allow a purchaser to terminate the contract in return for making a specified compensation payment to the supplier – the standard offers little guidance as to whether such a feature should be included within the terms of the host, of the embedded foreign currency derivative or, possibly, of both. Other problematic terms can include options to defer the specified delivery date and options to order additional goods or services. Where an embedded foreign currency derivative is separated from a supply contract it is important to consider whether the host (which will be denominated in a different currency to the original hybrid contract) is an onerous contract under IAS 37.

5.1.10 Leases and inflation-linked contracts

With regard to a contract that is a lease, an embedded derivative is closely related to the host if it is:

(i)   an inflation-related index such as an index of lease payments to a consumer price index (provided that the lease is not leveraged and the index relates to inflation in the entity's own economic environment); or

(ii)   contingent rentals based on related sales or on variable interest rates.[183]

The guidance does not make it clear whether or not this guidance is intended to apply to operating leases, to finance leases or to both – in the absence of evidence to the contrary we believe it is appropriate to apply it to both types.

Apart from (i) above, there is no reference in the guidance to contracts containing payments that are linked to inflation. Many other types of contracts contain inflation-linked payments and it would appear sensible to apply the guidance in respect of leases to these contracts. Consider, for example, a long-term agreement to supply services under which payments increase by reference to a general price index and are not leveraged in any way. In cases such as this, the embedded inflation-linked derivative would normally be considered closely related to the host provided the index related to a measure of inflation in an appropriate economic environment, such as the one in which the services were being supplied.

For some entities (and governments) it is quite common to issue inflation linked debt instruments, i.e. where interest and/or principal payments are linked to, say, a consumer price index. If the guidance above is accepted as applying to finance leases, it should also apply to debt instruments because finance leases result in assets and liabilities that are, in substance, no different to debt instruments (see 2.2.4 above). Further, in much finance theory, either real (applied to current prices) or nominal (applied to inflation adjusted prices) interest rates are used, suggesting a strong link between inflation and interest rates. Finally, a government or central bank will generally raise short-term interest rates as inflation rises and reduce rates as inflation recedes, which also suggests a close relationship between the two.

Therefore, it would normally be appropriate to treat the embedded derivative in inflation-linked debt as equivalent to an interest rate index and apply the guidance at 5.1.7 to determine whether the index is regarded as closely related to the debt. Typically, the index will be closely related to the debt where it is based on inflation in an economic environment in which the bond is issued/denominated and is not significantly leveraged in relation to the debt.

5.1.11 Insurance contracts

As noted at 5.1.1 to 5.1.10 above, much of the application guidance dealing with a 'closely related' determination applies to insurance contracts as it does to any other contract. IFRS 4 also added two further illustrations to IAS 39 that deal primarily with insurance contracts.

A unit-linking feature embedded in a host financial instrument, or host insurance contract, is closely related to the host if the unit-denominated payments are measured at current unit values that reflect the fair values of the assets of the fund. A unit-linking feature is a contractual term that requires payments denominated in units of an internal or external investment fund.[184]

A derivative embedded in an insurance contract is closely related to the host if the embedded derivative and host are so interdependent that the embedded derivative cannot be measured separately, i.e. without considering the host contract.[185]

5.2 Identifying the terms of embedded derivatives and host contracts

The IASB has provided only limited guidance on determining the terms of a separated embedded derivative and host contract. Accordingly, entities may find this aspect of the embedded derivative requirements particularly difficult to implement. In addition to the guidance set out below, Examples 15.13 and 15.16 above also identify the terms of an embedded derivative requiring separation.

5.2.1 Embedded non-option derivatives

IAS 39 does not define the term 'non-option derivative' but suggests that it includes forwards, swaps and similar contracts. An embedded derivative of this type should be separated from its host contract on the basis of its stated or implied substantive terms, so as to result in it having a fair value of zero at initial recognition.[186]

The IASB has provided implementation guidance on separating non-option derivatives in the situation where the host is a debt instrument. It is explained that, in the absence of implied or stated terms, judgement will be necessary to identify the terms of the host (e.g. whether it should be a fixed rate, variable rate or zero coupon instrument) and the embedded derivative. However, an embedded derivative that is not already clearly present in the hybrid should not be separated, i.e. a cash flow that does not exist cannot be created.[187]

For example, if a five year debt instrument has fixed annual interest payments of £40 and a principal payment at maturity of £1,000 multiplied by the change in an equity price index, it would be inappropriate to identify a floating rate host and an embedded equity swap that has an offsetting floating rate leg. The host should be a fixed rate debt instrument that pays £40 annually because there are no floating interest rate cash flows in the hybrid instrument.[188]

Further, as noted above, the terms of the embedded derivative should be determined so that is has a fair value of zero on inception of the hybrid instrument. It is explained that if an embedded non-option derivative could be separated on other terms, a single hybrid instrument could be decomposed into an infinite variety of combinations of host debt instruments and embedded derivatives. This might be achieved, for example, by separating embedded derivatives with terms that create leverage, asymmetry or some other risk exposure not already present in the hybrid instrument.[189]

Finally, it is explained that the terms of the embedded derivative should be identified based on the conditions existing when the financial instrument was issued.[190]

5.2.2   *Embedded option-based derivative*

As for non-option derivatives, IAS 39 does not define the term 'option-based derivative' but suggests that it includes puts, calls, caps, floors and swaptions. An embedded derivative of this type should be separated from its host contract on the basis of the stated terms of the option feature.[191]

The implementation guidance explains that the economic nature of an option-based derivative is fundamentally different from a non-option derivative and depends critically on the strike price (or strike rate) specified for the option feature in the hybrid instrument. Therefore, the separation of such a derivative should be based on the stated terms of the option feature documented in the hybrid instrument. Consequently, in contrast to the position for non-option derivatives (see 5.2.1 above), an embedded option-based derivative would not normally have a fair value of zero.[192]

In fact, if the terms of an embedded option-based derivative were identified so as to result in it having a fair value of zero, the strike price generally would have to be determined so as to result in the option being infinitely out of the money. This would imply a zero probability of the option feature being exercised. However, since the probability of the option feature in a hybrid instrument being exercised generally is not zero, this would be inconsistent with the likely economic behaviour of the hybrid.[193]

Similarly, if the terms were identified so as to achieve an intrinsic value of zero, the strike price would equal the price of the underlying at initial recognition. In this case, the fair value of the option would consist only of time value. However, this also would be inconsistent with the likely economic behaviour of the hybrid, including the probability of the option feature being exercised, unless the agreed strike price was indeed equal to the price of the underlying at initial recognition.[194]

5.2.3   *Nature of a financial instrument host*

Consistent with the 'closely related' assessment (see 5.1 above), it is suggested that, where a financial instrument contains an embedded derivative, the host should be considered as a debt instrument 'if the hybrid instrument has a stated maturity, i.e. it does not meet the definition of an equity instrument.'[195]

The implementation guidance illustrates this by way of an example, the substance of which is reproduced below.

Example 15.18:   Equity linked debt

Company A purchases a five-year 'debt' instrument issued by Company B with a principal of £1,000, indexed to Company C's share price. At maturity, A will receive the principal plus or minus the change in the fair value of 100 of C's shares and no interest payments are made before maturity. On the date of acquisition, the purchase price is £1,000 and C's share price is £10. A classifies the instrument as available-for-sale.

The instrument is a hybrid instrument with an embedded derivative because of the equity-indexed principal and the host is a debt instrument (see above). The embedded non-option derivative (a forward contract on shares of C) is separated so as to have an initial fair value of zero.[196]

The implementation guidance states that the host is accounted for as a zero coupon debt with interest imputed on the £1,000 over five years using the applicable market interest rate at initial recognition.[197] However, this exposes a flaw in the fact pattern. If the purchase price of the hybrid instrument at inception really did represent its fair value, the initial carrying amount of the host would be £1,000. As the host is a zero coupon debt with a principal payment of £1,000, there can be no interest imputed over the term of the instrument. To be a more realistic example, the fact pattern would have to be amended. For example, the hybrid instrument could have carried a coupon, or the purchase price could have been less than £1,000. As it stands, the example illustrates a financial product that no rational investor should purchase.

A financial instrument can give rise to a residual interest in the net assets of an entity, even though IAS 32 prevents the issuing entity from classifying the instrument as equity. Where such an instrument contains an embedded derivative that requires separation, it may be appropriate to classify the host as equity rather than debt. This will commonly be the case for an investment in a unit trust (see 5.1.1 above).

Host contracts that are financial instruments should be accounted for under IAS 39. Otherwise, they are accounted for in accordance with other appropriate standards. This doesn't necessarily mean that the embedded derivative and host should be presented separately (or together) on the face of the financial statements (see Chapter 20 at 6.3.1).[198]

5.3 Multiple embedded derivatives

Generally, multiple embedded derivatives in a single instrument should be treated as a single compound embedded derivative. However, embedded derivatives that are classified as equity are accounted for separately from those classified as assets or liabilities (see Chapter 17 at 4). In addition, derivatives embedded in a single instrument that relate to different risk exposures and are readily separable and independent of each other should be accounted for separately from each other.[199]

For example, if a debt instrument has a principal amount related to an equity index and that amount doubles if the equity index exceeds a certain level, it is not appropriate to separate both a forward and an option on the equity index because those derivative features relate to the same risk exposure. Instead, the forward and option elements are treated as a single compound embedded derivative. For the same reason, an embedded floor or cap on interest rates should not be separated into a series of 'floorlets' or 'caplets'.[200]

In addition, if a single hybrid contains both a put option and a written call option on the hybrid instrument that require separation, e.g. callable debt with a put to the holder, those options are treated as a single embedded derivative because they are not independent of each other. Furthermore, if an investor holds callable convertible debt for which separation of the call option is required, it is not appropriate to separate an equity conversion option and a written call option on the debt instrument separately because the two embedded derivative features should not be valued independently of each other.[201]

On the other hand, if a hybrid debt instrument contains, for example, two options that give the holder a right to choose both the interest rate index on which interest payments are determined and the currency in which the principal is repaid, those two options may qualify for separation as two separate embedded derivatives since they relate to different risk exposures and are readily separable and independent of each other.[202]

5.4   Updating the 'closely related' assessment

It is clear that, on initial recognition, a contract should be reviewed to assess whether it contains (an) embedded derivative(s) requiring separation. However, the standard is silent on whether this initial assessment should be revisited throughout the life of the contract.

Consider, for example, an entity that enters into a purchase contract denominated in US dollars. If, at the time the contract is entered into, US dollars are commonly used in the economic environment in which the transaction takes place, the contract will not contain an embedded foreign currency derivative requiring separation. Subsequently, however, the economic environment may change such that transactions are now commonly denominated in euros, but not in US dollars. Countries joining the European Union may encounter just such a scenario.

Clearly, in this situation, an embedded foreign currency derivative would be separated from any new US dollar denominated purchase contracts (assuming they would not otherwise be considered closely related). However, should the entity separately account for derivatives embedded within its existing US dollar denominated contracts that were outstanding prior to the change in the market?

Conversely, the entity may have identified, and separately accounted for, embedded foreign currency derivatives in contracts denominated in euros that were entered into before the economic environment changed. Does the change in economic circumstances mean that the embedded derivative should now be considered closely related and not separately accounted for as a derivative?

Even if assessments are updated, it is not clear on what basis an embedded derivative should be subsequently separated. For example, should it reflect market conditions that existed at the date of the reassessment, or at the start of the contract? The difference in amount between these two approaches could be significant for long-dated contracts and may result in an immediate profit or loss reflecting the cumulative fair value of the embedded derivative up to the date it is recognised. Similarly, it is not clear how an entity would account for an embedded derivative that was initially accounted for separately but which was subsequently determined to be closely related.

In practice, there appear to be differing views on this issue. Therefore, without further guidance from IFRIC or the IASB, it is quite possible that inconsistent practice will develop.

6   LINKED AND SEPARATE TRANSACTIONS AND 'SYNTHETIC' INSTRUMENTS

As noted at 5 above, a derivative that is attached to a financial instrument, but is contractually transferable independently of that instrument, or has a different counterparty from that instrument, is not an embedded derivative, but a separate financial instrument.[203] This is also the case where a synthetic instrument is created by using derivatives to 'alter' the nature of a non-derivative instrument, as illustrated in the following example:

Example 15.19: Investment in synthetic fixed-rate debt

Company A acquires a five-year floating rate debt instrument issued by Company B. At the same time, it enters into a five-year pay-variable, receive-fixed interest rate swap with Bank C. A considers the combination of the two instruments to be a synthetic fixed rate bond and, since it has the positive intent and ability to hold them to maturity, wants to classify them as a held-to-maturity investment (see 7.2 below).

Embedded derivatives are terms and conditions that are *included in* non-derivative host contracts and it is generally inappropriate to treat two or more separate financial instruments as a single combined, or synthetic, instrument. Each of the financial instruments has its own terms and conditions and may be transferred or settled separately. Therefore, the debt instrument and the swap must be classified separately.[204]

It is asserted that these transactions differ from those discussed at 4.5 above because those had no substance apart from the resulting interest rate swap.[205] Although some might argue that the only substance of the two transactions above is the resulting synthetic fixed rate debt instrument, this interpretation is clearly not allowed under the standard.

Interestingly, the guidance doesn't deal with a much more common situation whereby a company both borrows from, and transacts a related derivative with, the same counterparty – typically the borrowing will be floating rate and the derivative a perfectly matched pay-fixed, receive-floating interest rate swap. Such transactions can offer cheaper funding than conventional fixed rate borrowings (in a perfect market this should not be true, but anecdotal evidence suggests it often is).

In fact the subject of linking transactions for accounting purposes is a difficult one, especially in the context of financial instruments. The IASB's *Framework* specifies that transactions should be reported in accordance with their substance and economic reality and not merely their legal form[206] and linking transactions can be seen as dealing with the question of how to interpret this principle.

The revised versions of IAS 32 and IAS 39 deal with the subject in a piecemeal way. For example, in addition to the synthetic instrument illustration above:

- two or more non-derivative contracts that are, 'in substance', no more than a single derivative are treated as a single derivative (see 4.5 above);

- derivatives that are 'attached' to a non-derivative financial instrument may sometimes be regarded as part of a single combined instrument (see 5.1.3 above);

- in classifying an instrument in consolidated financial statements as equity or a financial liability, all terms and conditions agreed between members of the group and holders of the instrument are considered (see Chapter 17 at 3.6); and

- determining the appropriate accounting treatment for a transaction that involves the transfer of some or all rights associated with financial assets without the sale of the assets themselves inevitably involves linking separate contracts to assess whether the transaction results in derecognition of the assets. For example, there might be one contract defining the continued ownership of the asset and another obliging the owner to transfer the rights associated with the asset to a third party (see Chapter 16 at 4).

IFRIC has been considering the subject of linkage since 2002 and has, in the past, made certain recommendations to the IASB. In fact, the requirement to take account of linked terms when classifying instruments as debt or equity in consolidated financial statements was introduced into IAS 32 following IFRIC's deliberations. In spite of agreeing proposed indicators for when transactions should be linked, and proposed guidance on accounting for linked transactions, these have never been published as an interpretation or standard.[207]

Consequently, in considering the borrowing and swap situation above we are left principally with the guidance in IAS 39. It is likely that the swap and the loan have their own terms and conditions and may be transferred or settled independently of each other. Therefore, the principles in Example 15.19 above would suggest separate accounting for the two instruments. Applying the guidance at 4.5 above would also suggest separate accounting in most cases. Even though the instruments are transacted with the same counterparty, there will normally be a substantive business purpose for transacting the instruments separately, namely the fact that it leads to cheaper funding.

It seems clear that in situations involving two separate legal contracts the IASB has set the bar very high and, in most cases, the two instruments will be regarded as separate for accounting purposes. However, in rare situations the linkage between those contracts (normally itself contractual) may be such that for accounting purposes those contracts cannot be regarded as existing independently of each other.

7   CLASSIFICATION OF FINANCIAL INSTRUMENTS

The accounting treatment for a particular financial instrument (e.g. whether it is carried at historical cost or fair value and whether any remeasurement gains are reported immediately in profit or loss or initially in equity) depends on its classification.

Four types of financial asset and, effectively, two types of financial liability are defined as follows:

- *Financial assets or liabilities at fair value through profit or loss* – financial instruments that are either classified as *held for trading*, or are designated as such on initial recognition.

- *Held-to-maturity investments* – financial assets with fixed or determinable payments and fixed maturity, other than loans and receivables, for which there is a positive intention and ability to hold to maturity and which have not been designated 'at fair value through profit or loss' or as 'available-for-sale'.

- *Loans and receivables* – financial assets with fixed or determinable payments that are not quoted in an active market, do not qualify as 'trading' assets and have not been designated 'at fair value through profit or loss' or as 'available-for-sale'.

- *Available-for-sale financial assets* – financial assets that are designated as 'available-for-sale' or are not classified as 'loans and receivables', 'held-to-maturity investments' or 'at fair value through profit or loss'.[208]

- *Other financial liabilities* are not explicitly defined but are those that are not held for trading or designated 'at fair value through profit or loss'.

These definitions and key changes from their equivalents in the previous version of the standard, are covered in more detail below.

7.1 Assets and liabilities at fair value through profit or loss

This is a new category that was introduced in the revised version of IAS 39. It will come as no surprise that the basic accounting requirements for all instruments included in the category are that they are recorded on the balance sheet at fair value and any changes in value are reported in profit or loss (see Chapter 18 at 3).

It incorporates (with some changes) the previous 'held for trading' category (see 7.1.1). More significantly, it also allows financial instruments to be designated, with only very limited restrictions, into this category (see 7.1.2).

The IASB's stated objective in creating this category (the 'fair value option') was to simplify the application of IAS 39 by mitigating some of the anomalies that result from its mixed model approach. For example, it eliminates:

- the need for hedge accounting for hedges of fair value exposures when there are natural offsets, and thereby eliminates the related burden of designating, tracking and analysing hedge effectiveness;

- the burden of separating embedded derivatives; and

- problems arising from a mixed measurement model where financial assets are measured at fair value and related financial liabilities are measured at amortised cost.

In particular, it eliminates volatility in profit or loss and equity that results when matched positions of financial assets and financial liabilities are not measured consistently. It also de-emphasises interpretive issues around what constitutes trading. However, it is also clear that this moves the accounting closer to a 'full fair value model' as described at 1.3 above. In fact, by using this option for all financial instruments, entities may voluntarily adopt such a model in full, although it is unlikely that many will do so.[209]

The IASB makes it clear that this new category only encompasses, and is not the same as, the former held for trading category and that trading instruments are not a separate class.[210] In practice, however, it is likely that the two terms (trading and at fair value through profit or loss) will become synonymous, not least because of the length of the formal description.

7.1.1 Assets and liabilities held for trading

Assets and liabilities held for trading are defined as those that are:

- acquired or incurred principally for the purpose of sale or repurchase in the near term;

- part of a portfolio of identified financial instruments that are managed together and for which there is evidence of a recent actual pattern of short-term profit-taking; or

- derivatives (except for designated effective hedging instruments – see Chapter 19).[211]

It is explained that trading generally reflects active and frequent buying and selling, and financial instruments held for trading generally are used with the objective of generating a profit from short-term fluctuations in price or dealer's margin.[212] This is obviously not always true because, for example, many derivatives will be held for hedging or risk management purposes yet by default they are included in this category (unless the entity chooses to designate them as hedges and is successful in achieving hedge accounting as set out in Chapter 19).

In addition to derivatives that are not accounted for as hedging instruments, financial liabilities held for trading include:

(a)   obligations to deliver financial assets borrowed by a short seller (i.e. an entity that sells financial assets it has borrowed and does not yet own);

(b)   financial liabilities that are incurred with an intention to repurchase them in the near term, such as quoted debt instruments that the issuer may buy back in the near term depending on changes in fair value; and

(c)   financial liabilities that are part of a portfolio of identified financial instruments that are managed together and for which there is evidence of a recent pattern of short-term profit-taking.[213]

This represents a change from the previous version of IAS 39 under which only liabilities within (a) would be included in the trading category. The IASB believed that the previous version of IAS 39 permitted cherry picking of unrealised gains or losses on liabilities within (b) and (c) and was keen to reduce the scope for this.[214] However, as before, the fact that a liability is used to fund trading activities does not in itself make that liability one that is held for trading.[215]

The term 'portfolio' is not explicitly defined in IAS 39, but the context in which it is used suggests that a portfolio is a group of financial assets or financial liabilities that are managed as part of that group. If there is evidence of a recent actual pattern of short-term profit taking on financial instruments included in such a portfolio, those financial instruments qualify as held for trading even though an individual financial instrument may, in fact, be held for a longer period of time.[216] Previously where an entity's intention was to hold an asset for a long period of time there was a prohibition on including it in within the trading category[217] but now if the asset is part of a 'trading' portfolio (as described above) it *must* be included in this category.

7.1.2 Instruments designated 'at fair value through profit or loss'

Virtually any financial asset or financial liability within the scope of IAS 39 (and some that need not be – see 3.4 above) may be designated as a financial asset or financial liability at fair value through profit or loss. Aside from when the revised version of IAS 39 is first adopted (see 8 below) this option is available only when the instrument is initially recognised.

The only situation where the fair value option is not currently available is for investments in equity instruments that do not have a quoted market price in an active market, and whose fair value cannot be reliably measured (see Chapter 18 at 4.4). Such instruments cannot be designated at fair value through profit or loss, although theoretically they could be classified as trading.[218] Developments in this might result in amendments to IAS 39 that restrict the use of this category – these are covered at 9.1 below.

The option can be applied only to whole instruments, not to portions of an instrument, such as a component of a debt instrument that is associated with interest rate risk but not with credit risk.[219]

During the improvements project some had expressed concern that entities could use the option to recognise, selectively, changes in fair value in profit or loss. This argument was rejected by the IASB, noting that the requirement to designate irrevocably on initial recognition results in an entity being unable to 'cherry pick' in this way because it will not be known at the time the option is made whether the fair value of the instrument will increase or decrease.[220] However, a one-time designation opportunity does arise on initial adoption of the standard (see 8.2 and 8.3 below).

Venture capital organisations, mutual funds, unit trusts and similar entities are permitted not to equity account for investments in associates or equity account or proportionately consolidate investments in joint ventures. However, if they choose not to, such investments must be designated at fair value through profit or loss on initial recognition, or classified as held for trading, and accounted for in accordance with IAS 39.[221]

7.2 Held-to-maturity investments

As noted at 7 above, the held-to-maturity category comprises financial assets with fixed or determinable payments and fixed maturity, other than loans and receivables, for which there is a positive intention and ability to hold to maturity and which have not been designated at fair value through profit or loss or as available-for-sale.[222]

This category is viewed as an exception to be used only in limited circumstances.[223] Consequently, its use is restricted by a number of detailed conditions, largely designed to test whether there is a genuine intention and ability to hold such investments to maturity. To further restrict the use of this category, hedge accounting cannot be used if interest rate or prepayment risk associated with held-to-maturity investments is hedged,[224] for example by using a pay-fixed, receive-floating rate interest rate swap to hedge an investment that pays a fixed rate of interest (see Chapter 19). In revising IAS 39, the definition of such investments and related restrictions were left largely unchanged.

In theory investments are not *designated* as held-to-maturity – they *must* be included in this category if they meet the appropriate conditions. However, because it is relatively easy for an entity to selectively fail any of the conditions, in practice it is effectively a voluntary classification.

7.2.1 Instruments that may be classified as held-to-maturity

Only assets with fixed or determinable payments and fixed maturity can be included in this category (see 7 and 7.2 above). Most equity instruments cannot be held-to-maturity investments either because they have an indefinite life (such as ordinary shares) or because the amounts the holder may receive can vary in a manner that is not predetermined (such as share options, warrants, and rights). A debt instrument with a variable interest rate generally can satisfy this condition.[225]

A perpetual debt instrument on which interest payments are made for an indefinite period cannot be classified as a held-to-maturity investment because there is no maturity date.[226] However, there is no reason why a perpetual debt instrument with fixed or determinable payments for a limited period cannot be classified as held-to-maturity. In effect, the instrument matures at the date of the last contractual payment and the amount invested is recovered through fixed or determinable payments and the rights in liquidation have no fair value (see Example 18.24 in Chapter 18 at 5.4).

A financial asset that is callable by the issuer satisfies the criteria for a held-to-maturity investment if the holder intends, and is able, to hold it until it is called, or until maturity, and if the holder would recover substantially all of its carrying amount. The call option, if exercised, simply accelerates the investment's maturity. However, if the investment is callable on a basis that the holder would not recover substantially all of its carrying amount, it cannot be classified as held-to-maturity. Any premium paid and capitalised transaction costs should be considered in determining whether the carrying amount would be substantially recovered.[227]

A financial asset that is puttable (the holder has the right to require the issuer to repay or redeem the instrument before maturity) cannot be classified as a held-to-maturity investment. Paying for a put feature is considered inconsistent with expressing an intention of holding such an instrument to maturity.[228] The previous version of IAS 39 entertained the possibility ('with great care') of classifying such an instrument as held-to-maturity.[229]

The reference to 'fixed or determinable payments and fixed maturity' in the definition means a contractual arrangement that defines the amounts and dates of payments to the holder, such as interest and principal payments. The likelihood of default is not a consideration in qualifying for this category, provided there is an intention and ability, considering the credit condition existing at the acquisition date, to hold the investment to maturity. Even if there is a significant risk of non-payment of interest and principal, for example a bond with a very low credit rating, the contractual payments on the bond may well be fixed or determinable.[230]

Where a combined instrument contains a host contract and an embedded derivative (see 5 above), the host may be classified as held-to-maturity if it has fixed or determinable payments and no other conditions are breached. This is illustrated in the following examples.

Example 15.20:   Note with index-linked principal

Company A purchases a five-year interest free equity-index-linked note, with an original issue price of €10, for its market price of €12. At maturity, the note requires payment of the original issue price of €10 plus a supplemental redemption amount that depends on whether a specified stock price index exceeds a predetermined level at the maturity date. If the stock index does not exceed the predetermined level, no supplemental redemption amount is paid. If it does, the supplemental redemption amount equals the product of €1.15 and the difference between the level of the stock index at maturity and original issuance divided by the level at original issuance. A has the positive intention and ability to hold the note to maturity.

The note can be classified as a held-to-maturity investment because it has a fixed payment of €10 and fixed maturity and there is the positive intention and ability to hold it to maturity. However, the equity index feature is a call option not closely related to the debt host which must be separated as an embedded derivative (see 5.1.4 above). The purchase price (initial fair value) of €12 is allocated between the host debt instrument and the embedded derivative – the latter will have a non-zero fair value because it is an option-based derivative.[231]

Example 15.21:   Note with index-linked interest

Subsequently, A purchases a note with a fixed payment at a fixed maturity date and interest payments that are indexed to the price of a commodity or equity. There is an intention and ability to hold the note to maturity.

Again the note can be classified as a held-to-maturity investment because it has a fixed payment and fixed maturity. However, the commodity-indexed or equity-indexed interest payments result in an embedded derivative that is separated and accounted for as a derivative.[232]

It is possible for the terms of the embedded derivative to breach other conditions for classifying the host as held-to-maturity. For example, an investment in a convertible bond that can be converted *before* maturity generally cannot be classified as a held-to-maturity investment. The embedded conversion feature allows the investor to settle the host investment before maturity and, as noted above, paying for such a conversion feature would be inconsistent with an intention to hold the host to maturity.[233]

7.2.2   Positive intention and ability to hold to maturity

An entity should assess its intention and ability to hold these instruments to maturity when they are initially acquired and also at each balance sheet date.[234]

If any one of the following criteria is met, a positive intention to hold an investment to maturity is deemed not to exist (and the asset cannot be classified as such):

- the intention to hold the investment is for only an undefined period;

- the holder stands ready to sell the financial asset in response to changes in market interest rates or risks, liquidity needs, changes in the availability of and the yield on alternative investments, changes in financing sources and terms, or changes in foreign currency risk (although this does not apply to situations that are non-recurring and could not have been reasonably anticipated); or

- the issuer has a right to settle the financial asset at an amount significantly below its amortised cost.[235]

Further, an investor is deemed not to have a demonstrated ability to hold an investment to maturity if:

- it does not have the financial resources available to continue to finance the investment until maturity; or

- it is subject to an existing legal or other constraint that could frustrate its intention to hold the financial asset to maturity (although as noted at 7.2.1 above, an issuer's call option does not necessarily frustrate this intention).[236]

The intention and ability to hold debt instruments to maturity is not necessarily constrained if those instruments have been pledged as collateral or are subject to a repurchase or securities lending agreements. However, an entity would not have the positive intention and ability to hold the debt instruments until maturity if it did not expect to be able to maintain or recover access to the instruments.[237]

The standard also suggest that circumstances other than those described above can indicate that an entity does not have a positive intention or ability to hold an investment to maturity.[238]

7.2.3   The tainting provisions

When an entity's actions cast doubt on its intention or ability to hold such investments to maturity, the use of amortised cost for held-to-maturity assets is precluded for 'a reasonable period of time'.[239] Consequently, no investment should be classified as held-to-maturity if, during either the current financial year or the two preceding financial years, the reporting entity has sold or reclassified more than an insignificant (in relation to the total) amount of such investments before maturity other than by those effected:

(a)   close enough to maturity or call date (e.g. less than three months before maturity) so that changes in the market rate of interest did not have a significant effect on the investment's fair value;

(b)   after substantially all of the investment's original principal had been collected through scheduled payments or prepayments; or

(c)   due to an isolated non-recurring event that is beyond the holder's control and could not have been reasonably anticipated by the holder.[240]

Therefore, if an entity makes any 'not insignificant' sale or reclassification of a held-to-maturity investment that does not fall within (a) to (c) above, the entire remaining portfolio of such investments will have to be reclassified as available-for-sale (see 7.4 and 7.5 below) and will be remeasured to fair value for at least the following two financial years. The nature of this 'punishment' is unique within accounting standards and has become known as the 'tainting' or, by rugby followers, the 'sin-bin' provisions.

The guidance to the previous version of IAS 39 explained that conditions (a) and (b) relate to situations in which an entity is expected to be indifferent whether to hold or sell a financial asset because movements in interest rates after substantially all of the original principal has been collected or when the instrument is close to maturity will not have a significant impact on its fair value. Accordingly, such a sale should not affect reported income and no price volatility would be expected during the remaining period to maturity.[241]

It went on to say that if a financial asset is sold less than three months prior to maturity, that would generally qualify for this exception because the impact on the instrument's fair value of a difference between the stated interest rate and the market rate would generally be small for an instrument that matures in three months relative to an instrument that matures in several years. If sold after 90% or more of its original principal has been collected through scheduled payments or prepayments, condition (b) would generally be met. However, if only, say, 10% of the original principal has been collected, then that condition is clearly not met.[242]

The implementation guidance makes it clear that condition (c) does not extend to an unsolicited tender offer on economically favourable terms.[243]

The conditions must be applied to all held-to-maturity investments in aggregate and not to separate sub-categories of such assets (e.g. US dollar and euro denominated investments).[244] In consolidated financial statements they must be applied to all investments classified as held-to-maturity in those financial statements, even if they are held by different entities within the group, in different countries or in different legal or economic environments.[245]

A 'disaster scenario' that is only remotely possible, such as a run on a bank or a similar situation affecting an insurer, is not anticipated in deciding whether there is positive intention and ability to hold an investment to maturity.[246] The standard also explains that sales before maturity may satisfy condition (c) above – and therefore not trigger the tainting provisions – if they are attributable to:

- a significant deterioration in the issuer's creditworthiness (see below);

- a change in tax law that eliminates or significantly reduces the tax-exempt status of interest on the held-to-maturity investment, but not a change in tax law that revises the marginal tax rates applicable to interest income;

- a major business combination or major disposition, such as the sale of a segment, that necessitates the sale or transfer of held-to-maturity investments to maintain the holder's existing interest rate risk position or credit risk policy. Although the business combination itself is an event within the holder's control, the changes to its investment portfolio to maintain its interest rate risk position or credit risk policy may be consequential rather than anticipated;

- a change in statutory or regulatory requirements significantly modifying either what constitutes a permissible investment or the maximum level of particular types of investments, thereby causing disposal of a held-to-maturity investment;

- a significant increase in the industry's regulatory capital requirements that causes a downsizing by selling held-to-maturity investments; or

- a significant increase in the risk weights of held-to-maturity investments used for regulatory risk-based capital purposes.[247]

A sale following a downgrade in a credit rating by an external rating agency would not necessarily raise a question about the entity's intention to hold other investments to maturity if the downgrade provides evidence of a significant deterioration in the issuer's creditworthiness judged by reference to the credit rating at initial recognition.[248] However, the rating downgrade must not have been reasonably anticipated when the investment was classified as held to maturity. A credit downgrade of a notch within a class or from one rating class to the immediately lower rating class could often be regarded as reasonably anticipated.[249]

Similarly, where internal ratings are used for assessing exposures, changes in those ratings may help to identify issuers for which there has been a significant deterioration in creditworthiness, provided the approach to assigning ratings and changes therein give a consistent, reliable and objective measure of the credit quality of the issuers.[250]

If there is evidence that a financial asset is impaired (see Chapter 18 at 6), for example a rating downgrade in combination with other information, the deterioration in creditworthiness is often regarded as significant.[251]

Sales of held-to-maturity investments in response to an unanticipated significant increase by the regulator in the *industry's* capital requirements may not necessarily raise a question about the intention to hold other investments to maturity. However, in some countries, regulators may set *entity-specific* capital requirements based on an assessment of the risk in that particular entity. Therefore sales that are due to a significant increase in entity-specific capital requirements imposed by regulators *will* raise doubt over the intention to hold other financial assets to maturity unless it can be demonstrated that the sales fulfil condition (c) above. In other words, they should result from an increase in capital requirements which is an isolated non-recurring event that is beyond the entity's control and could not have been reasonably anticipated.[252]

A change in management is not identified as an exception and the guidance explains that sales in response to such a change would call into question the intention to hold investments to maturity.[253]

Example 15.22: Change of management

A company has a portfolio of financial assets that is classified as held-to-maturity. In the current period, at the direction of the board of directors, the senior management team has been replaced. The new management wishes to sell a portion of the held-to-maturity financial assets in order to carry out an expansion strategy designated and approved by the board.

Although the previous management team had been in place since the company's formation and had never before undergone a major restructuring, the sale nevertheless calls into question the company's intention to hold remaining held-to-maturity financial assets to maturity.[254]

7.3 Loans and receivables

At noted at 7 above, the loans and receivables category comprises financial assets with fixed or determinable payments that are not quoted in an active market, do not qualify as 'trading' assets and have not been designated at fair value through profit or loss or as available-for-sale.[255]

This category replaces 'originated loans and receivables' in the previous version of IAS 39. Although there are some differences between the two, for most entities both comprise mainly trade receivables, other debtors and bank deposits; for banks and similar financial institutions both constitute a significant proportion (possibly more or less than previously) of their non-trading assets, in particular loans and advances to customers.[256]

Previously, to be included in this category, a loan asset had to be originated by the entity (either directly or by way of a syndication/participation arrangement). Purchased, as opposed to originated, loans and receivables were classified as held-to-maturity, available-for-sale, or held for trading, as appropriate.[257] However, in developing the revised version of IAS 39 the IASB took account of respondents' concerns that:

(a)   some entities typically manage purchased and originated loans together; and

(b)   there are systems problems associated with segregating purchased and originated loans because any distinction between them is likely to be made only for accounting purposes.

It therefore decided to remove the requirement that loans and receivables must be originated so that if an entity purchases a portfolio of loans they may be included within this category.[258]

In response to this relaxation, the IASB decided that an asset with terms such that the holder may not recover substantially all of its initial investment (other than because of credit deterioration), for example a fixed rate interest-only strip created in a securitisation and subject to prepayment risk, should not be classified within loans and receivables. The IASB believes such instruments should be recorded at fair value,[259] perhaps because their value can be more volatile than other loans and receivables.

As noted above, instruments 'quoted in an active market' are prohibited from being included within this category and must therefore be included in one of the other three categories of financial asset.[260] Previously there was no such restriction. The

IASB considered that an unrestricted ability to record an asset at amortised cost (as is the case for loans and receivables) should not apply to liquid assets. For those instruments, amortised cost accounting should only be available where there is a positive intention and ability to hold the investment to maturity.[261] Accordingly, it is likely that many originated investments in bonds are likely to be classified as available-for-sale under the revised standard. The meaning of 'quoted in an active market' is considered in more detail in Chapter 18 at 4 and 4.1.

Provided there is no intention to sell the instrument immediately or in the short term, where a bank makes a term deposit with a central or other bank it is classified within loans and receivables even if the proof of deposit is negotiable, i.e. the deposit is capable of being sold. If there was such an intention to sell, the deposit would be a trading asset.[262]

Instruments that have the legal form of equities, such as preference shares, but which under IAS 32 would be classified as liabilities in the financial statements of the issuer and have fixed or determinable payments and fixed maturity (see Chapter 17) can potentially be classified within loans and receivables, provided the instrument is not quoted in an active market. However if, under IAS 32, it would be classified as an equity instrument in the financial statements of the issuer, it could not be classified within loans and receivables by the holder.[263]

The standard explains that an interest acquired in a pool of assets that are not loans or receivables (for example, an interest in a mutual fund or a similar fund) is not a loan or receivable.[264] We believe this was added to clarify the treatment of investments in mutual funds, unit trusts and similar funds – this issue is dealt with in more detail at 5.1.1 above.

The principal difference between loans and receivables and held-to-maturity investments is that loans and receivables are not subject to the tainting provisions (see 7.2.3 above). Consequently, loans and receivables that are not held for trading may be measured at amortised cost even if an entity does not have the positive intention and ability to hold the loan asset until maturity.[265] Financial assets that do not meet the definition of loans and receivables, e.g. because they are quoted in an active market, may be classified as held-to-maturity investments if they meet the relevant conditions.[266]

On initial recognition a financial asset that would otherwise be classified as a loan or receivable may now be designated at fair value through profit or loss or as available-for-sale (see 7.1.2 above and 7.4 below respectively).[267]

7.4   Available-for-sale assets

Previously, a financial asset was classified as available-for-sale if it did not properly belong in one of the three other categories of financial assets – held for trading, held-to-maturity and loans and receivables.[268] The ability to designate instruments within certain categories means that available-for-sale is no longer quite the 'default' classification that it was.

In practice, the only type of asset that would be designated into this category on initial recognition is one that would otherwise be classified within loans and receivables (see 7.3 above).

The main interpretative issue an entity is likely to experience in respect of this classification is whether a portfolio of investments can properly be regarded as available-for-sale rather than trading. The implementation guidance provides the following example to assist in making this judgment.

Example 15.23: Portfolio balancing

Company A has an investment portfolio of debt and equity instruments. The documented portfolio management guidelines specify that the equity exposure of the portfolio should be limited to between 30% and 50% of total portfolio value. The investment manager of the portfolio is authorised to balance the portfolio within the designated guidelines by buying and selling equity and debt instruments. The instruments should be classified as trading or available-for-sale depending on Company A's intent and past practice.

If the portfolio manager is authorised to buy and sell instruments to balance the risks in a portfolio, but there is no intention to trade and there is no past practice of trading for short-term profit, the instruments can be classified as available-for-sale. If instruments are bought and sold to generate short-term profits, the financial instruments in the portfolio should be classified as held for trading.[269]

7.5 Reclassifications

The revised version of IAS 39 has limited the scope for reclassifying assets and liabilities between the different categories considered in this section.

To impose discipline on an entity's ability to designate items at fair value through profit or loss, financial instruments cannot be reclassified into or out of this category subsequent to initial recognition.[270] Previously there was only a prohibition on reclassifying instruments out of the trading category and it was possible to reclassify assets as trading if there was a recent pattern of short-term profit taking within the portfolio in which they were held.[271]

Accordingly, if an entity starts to trade (as set out at 7.1.1 above) a portfolio of available-for-sale investments, say, all newly acquired investments will be classified as trading, but the legacy investments will continue to be classified as available-for-sale. Under the previous version of IAS 39 they would all have become trading assets. Whilst we see no reason for the IASB to prohibit reclassifications in these circumstances, there seems no scope to justify reclassification under the revised standard. Fortunately, this situation should not arise too frequently. Further, if the portfolio is genuinely being traded, only a limited amount of time need pass before most of the legacy instruments are disposed of and replaced with new instruments that are classified as trading.

Taken at face value, the prohibition on reclassifying instruments into or out of 'at fair value through profit or loss' prevents an entity from (a) designating a derivative as a hedging instrument if it was previously classified as trading, and (b) revoking the designation of an effective hedge involving a derivative. However, the parts of

IAS 39 dealing with hedge accounting (see Chapter 19) are clear that these are not regarded as prohibited reclassifications.

Otherwise, the only reclassifications permitted are between held-to-maturity investments and available-for-sale assets. An investment will be reclassified as available-for-sale if, as a result of a change in intention or ability, it fails to meet the requirements for classification as held-to-maturity.[272] If the tainting provisions (see 7.2.3 above) are triggered, any remaining held-to-maturity investments should also be reclassified as available-for-sale.[273] Similarly if, as a result of a change in intention or ability or because the tainting period has passed, it becomes appropriate to regard an available-for-sale asset as held-to-maturity, it should be reclassified accordingly.[274] Accounting for reclassifications is dealt with in Chapter 18 at 3.3.

8   EFFECTIVE DATE, TRANSITIONAL PROVISIONS AND FIRST-TIME ADOPTION

8.1   Effective date

The revised versions of both IAS 32 and IAS 39 must be applied for annual periods beginning on or after 1 January 2005. Entities are 'permitted' (rather than 'encouraged', as in the case of other recently issued standards) to adopt the standard in earlier periods, but must disclose that they have done so. They must also adopt both IAS 32 and IAS 39 at the same time and must adopt IAS 39 as amended in March 2004, not as originally issued.[275]

8.2   Transitional provisions

In general, both standards should be applied retrospectively and the opening balance of retained earnings for the earliest period presented and all other comparative amounts should be adjusted as if the standards had always been in use.[276] However, there are some exceptions to this general rule within IAS 39 and those relating to the topics covered in this chapter are dealt with below.

In terms of the classification of financial instruments, when the revised version of IAS 39 is first applied, previously recognised financial assets or financial liabilities may be designated at fair value through profit or loss, or as available-for-sale, despite the normal requirement to make such designation upon initial recognition (see 7.1.2 and 7.4 above).[277]

These requirements are illustrated in the following example.

Example 15.24:   Transitional requirements

Prior to its adoption of the revised version of IAS 39, Bank B had entered into the following transactions.

(a) Portfolios of unquoted loans had been acquired in the secondary market. Because B had not originated these loans itself they had to be classified as trading, held-to-maturity or available-for-sale. In fact some were classified within each of these three categories.

(b) B had participated in various original debt issues. A number of the resulting loan assets that were quoted in active markets had been classified as originated loans and receivables.

(c) Included in a portfolio of identified financial instruments that are managed together for which there is recent evidence of short-term profit taking were various liabilities. Some of these were actively issued and repurchased, some were not, but all were held at amortised cost because they could not be classified as trading under the previous version of IAS 39.

(d) A number of loan commitments had been made by B. They did not qualify as regular way transactions (see Chapter 16 at 3.1) and, because they were derivatives as defined, they were accounted for as trading instruments. The commitments could not be settled net and the resulting assets were not regularly sold shortly after origination.

How will these instruments be classified on transition to the new version of IAS 39?

(a) The loans previously classified as held-to-maturity and available-for-sale will be loans and receivables as defined in the new standard and this will be their default classification. However, B may also choose to designate any of these loans as available-for-sale or at fair value through profit or loss. The loans classified as trading under the previous standard will continue to meet the trading definition and there is no scope for reclassifying them into another category.

(b) These investments cannot qualify as loans and receivables under the new standard because they are quoted in active markets. They will not qualify as trading instruments (or they would almost certainly have done so previously) but they may be designated at fair value through profit or loss. If B has a positive intention and ability to hold them to maturity they may be classified as held-to-maturity. Otherwise they will be classified as available-for-sale.

(c) These liabilities will now be treated as trading instruments, either because they are actively issued and repurchased or because they are managed as part of a 'trading' portfolio.

(d) B is permitted not to apply IAS 39 to the loan commitments – instead it would apply IAS 18 and IAS 37. Alternatively, B may continue its existing treatment in part or in full by designating any or all of the commitments at fair value through profit or loss.

In each case the revised classification will be applied retrospectively from the beginning of the earliest accounting period presented or, if later, from initial recognition.

Unusually, it is acknowledged in IAS 39 that restatement may be impracticable. Where this is the case, disclosure should be made of this fact together with an indication of the extent to which the information was restated.[278] This situation is dealt with in more detail in Chapter 3 at 4.4 and 4.6.

8.3   First-time adoption

IFRS 1 – *First-time Adoption of International Financial Reporting Standards* – is dealt with comprehensively in Chapter 4 and the particular aspects of that standard applying to financial instruments are principally covered at 2.6 of that chapter. The aspects related to the topics covered in this chapter are summarised below. Further similar sections are included in Chapters 16 to 20.

8.3.1   Exemption from the requirement to restate comparatives

The IASB issued the revised versions of IAS 32 and IAS 39 in December 2003; and the amendment to IAS 39 – *Fair Value Hedge Accounting for a Portfolio Hedge of Interest Rate Risk* – in March 2004. To allow entities adopting IFRS for the first time before 1 January 2006 sufficient time to comply with the requirements of those standards, the IASB decided not to require them to prepare comparative information under IAS 32 and IAS 39.[279] Instead, a first-time adopter that chooses to present comparative information that does not comply with IAS 32 and IAS 39 in its first year of transition should:

- apply its previous GAAP in the comparative information to financial instruments that are within the scope of IAS 32 and IAS 39. In other words, this exemption also affects the application of certain aspects of other standards. For example, it overrides the requirements of IAS 1 – *Presentation of Financial Statements* – on the balance sheet presentation of financial instruments; and

- make certain additional disclosures (see below).[280]

(A similar exemption applies to insurance contracts within the scope of IFRS 4.)

A first-time adopter that does not present comparative information under IAS 32 and IAS 39 should use *the beginning of the first IFRS reporting period* (e.g. 1 January 2005 for an entity reporting at 31 December 2005) as the relevant date for the application of the first-time adoption rules in IFRS 1, and not the *date of transition to IFRS*, for the purpose of these standards only.[281]

In applying this exemption, a first-time adopter should be aware of the following:

- the wording of the standard does not explicitly require the exemption to be applied to IAS 32 and IAS 39 as a package. However, even though the transitional provisions in both IAS 32 and IAS 39 that require the standards to be adopted simultaneously do not apply to first-time adopters, the IASB clearly intended both standards to be adopted simultaneously. In any case, the many cross-references between the two standards make it virtually impossible to adopt one of the standards without the other. Therefore, we believe that the exemption applies to IAS 32 and IAS 39 as a package;

- a first-time adopter that presents two comparative periods under IFRS will not be permitted to restate the most recent comparative financial period because the exemption must be applied as of the beginning of the first IFRS reporting period (e.g. an entity reporting at 31 December 2005 would not be allowed to restate 2004 unless it also restated 2003); and

- the exemption only covers items that are within the scope of IAS 32 and IAS 39 (and IFRS 4). The comparative information relating to all other items must be restated under IFRS,

Where an entity makes this election, it needs to:[282]

- disclose that the comparative information does not comply with IAS 32 and IAS 39, but that it has been prepared on the basis of its previous GAAP;

- disclose the nature, but not the amount, of the main adjustments that would make the information comply with IAS 32 and IAS 39; and

- treat any adjustment between the balance sheet at the comparative period's reporting date and the start of the first IFRS reporting period as arising from a change in accounting policy. This difference is accounted for as an adjustment to the opening balance of each affected component of equity at the start of the first IFRS reporting period.[283] The entity is required to make related disclosures (see Chapter 4 at 2.10.1 A and Chapter 20 at 7.3.1).[284]

Originally, IFRS 1 also required first-time adopters to prepare comparative information that complied with IAS 32 and IAS 39 because this improved 'comparability within the first IFRS financial statements' and because the IASB believed that this should not be a problem for entities that planned the adoption of IFRS in a timely manner.[285] Unfortunately, the less-than-timely publication of the revised versions of IAS 32 and IAS 39 obliged the IASB to exempt entities adopting IFRS before 1 January 2006 from applying these standards in preparing comparative information.

8.3.2　Classification of financial instruments

A　Derivatives and embedded derivatives

Except for those that are designated and effective hedging instruments, all derivatives (including those that are embedded in other contracts and are required by IAS 39 to be accounted for separately) should be classified as held for trading with effect from the date of transition to IFRS (or the beginning of the first IFRS reporting period, if comparatives are not restated).[286]

Under US GAAP, an entity was not required to account for some pre-existing embedded derivatives separately. The IASB considered this, and the fact that full retrospective accounting for embedded derivatives might be costly, but concluded 'that the failure to measure embedded derivatives at fair value would diminish the relevance and reliability of an entity's first IFRS financial statements'. Therefore, a first-time adopter should review all contracts existing at its date of transition to IFRS (or the beginning of the first IFRS reporting period, if comparatives are not restated) to determine whether they contain embedded derivatives requiring separation.[287]

On first-time adoption, an entity should make an assessment of whether the terms of an embedded derivative were closely related to the host at the date it first satisfied the recognition criteria in IAS 39.[288] This will normally be on inception of the hybrid contract. However, it is less clear whether this assessment should be updated, either on a continuous basis or at the date of transition, to take account of subsequent changes that might affect this assessment. This issue is considered in further detail at 5.4 above.

B   *Other financial assets and liabilities at fair value through profit or loss*

Similar to the transitional provision set out at 8.2 above, a first-time adopter is allowed to designate a non-derivative financial instrument at the date of transition to IFRS (or the beginning of the first IFRS reporting period, if comparatives are not restated) at fair value through profit or loss, even though the general requirement in IAS 39 is to make such a designation on initial recognition of the instrument.[289] Where advantage of this exemption is taken, certain additional disclosures are required which are set out in Chapter 4 at 2.10.2 B and Chapter 20 at 7.3.2.

Other non-derivative financial instruments are included within this category if, and only if:

- they were acquired or incurred principally for the purpose of selling or repurchasing it in the near term; or

- at the date of transition to IFRS (or the beginning of the first IFRS reporting period, if comparatives are not restated) were part of a portfolio of identified financial instruments that were managed together and for which there was evidence of a recent actual pattern of short-term profit taking.[290]

C   *Held-to-maturity investments*

The classification of investments as held-to-maturity relies, effectively, on a designation made by the entity reflecting its intention and ability to hold the investment to maturity (see 7.2 above). It is explained that sales or transfers of an entity's held-to-maturity investments before the date of transition to IFRS (or the beginning of the first IFRS reporting period, if comparatives are not restated) do not trigger the 'tainting' provisions (see 7.2.3 above) and therefore do not prevent an entity using this classification on first-time adoption.[291]

D   *Loans and receivables*

In assessing whether or not a financial asset can meet the definition of loans and receivables at the date of transition to IFRS (or the beginning of the first IFRS reporting period, if comparatives are not restated) the circumstances that existed when it first met the recognition criteria in IAS 39 (see Chapter 16 at 3) should be considered.[292]

E   *Available-for-sale assets*

As for financial instruments at fair value through profit or loss, a first-time adopter is allowed to designate a non-derivative financial asset at the date of transition to IFRS (or the beginning of the first IFRS reporting period, if comparatives are not restated) as available-for-sale even though the general requirement in IAS 39 is to make such a designation on initial recognition of the instrument.[293] Where advantage of this exemption is taken, certain additional disclosures are required which are set out in Chapter 4 at 2.10.2 B and Chapter 20 at 7.3.2.

In addition to those financial assets that are designated as available-for-sale, this category includes those assets that are not in any of the other categories above.[294]

9 FUTURE DEVELOPMENTS

As noted at 1.5 above, the IASB acknowledged that it would be willing to revise IAS 39 in the short term and has published a number of exposure drafts of proposed amendments to IAS 39. Two of these proposals, dealing with the topics covered in this chapter, are summarised below.

9.1 The fair value option

As noted at 7.1 above, the ability of entities to designate virtually any financial instrument at fair value through profit or loss (the 'fair value option') was introduced in the December 2003 revision of IAS 39 after it had originally been proposed in the June 2002 exposure draft. Of the respondents to the exposure draft who commented on the fair value option, a substantial majority agreed with it and this included a majority of each type of respondent except for banking, securities and insurance regulators.[295]

After considering these comments, the IASB decided to retain the fair value option but to require additional disclosure when the option is used for a financial liability (see Chapter 20 at 5.4).[296] However, after further discussions with some constituents on the fair value option, the IASB became aware that some, especially prudential supervisors of banks, securities companies and insurers, were concerned that the fair value option might be used inappropriately. In particular, these regulators were concerned that:

- entities might apply the fair value option to financial assets or liabilities whose fair value is not verifiable. If so, because the valuation of these financial assets and financial liabilities is subjective, entities might determine their fair value in a way that inappropriately affects profit or loss;

- use of the option might increase, rather than decrease, volatility in profit or loss, for example if an entity applied the option to only one part of a matched position; and

- if an entity applied the fair value option to financial liabilities, it might result in the entity recognising gains or losses in profit or loss for changes in its own creditworthiness.[297]

Because of the political influence exercised in Europe by these regulators, particularly the European Central Bank, the IASB decided to propose amendments to IAS 39 limiting the use of the fair value option. Accordingly, an exposure draft was published in April 2004 proposing that the fair value option be limited to the following instruments:

(i) financial assets or liabilities that contain one or more embedded derivatives, whether or not they are required to be separated;

(ii) financial liabilities whose cash flows are contractually linked to the performance of assets that are measured at fair value. This condition is met only if the contract specifies the assets to whose performance the cash flows on the liability are linked;

(iii)   a financial asset, liability or portfolio of such instruments where the exposure to changes in their fair value is substantially offset by an exposure to changes in the fair value of another financial asset, liability or portfolio of such instruments, including a derivative or portfolio of derivatives;

Many have questioned the meaning of 'substantially offset' in this context. It is likely the IASB meant it to be less onerous than the 'highly effective' test applied to determine whether hedge accounting can be used (see Chapter 19) but even this is not entirely clear.

(iv)   financial assets other than those that meet the definition of loans and receivables; and

(v)   financial assets and liabilities that IAS 39 or another international standard allows or requires to be designated at fair value through profit or loss.[298]

In the case of (ii) and (iii), to designate instruments as at fair value through profit or loss, the offsetting exposure should be identified. Further, the related instrument must also be measured at fair value through profit or loss, either by designation or (when the definition is met) by classification as held for trading.[299]

The use of the fair value option would also be restricted to instruments whose fair value is 'verifiable'.[300] This means that the variability in the range of reasonable fair value estimates made in accordance with IAS 39 should be low. This will be the case if, for example, the fair value estimate is based on:

• observable current market transactions in the same instrument (i.e. without modification or repackaging);

• a valuation technique whose variables include primarily observable market data and that is calibrated periodically to observable current market transactions in the same instrument (without modification or repackaging) or to other observable current market data; or

• a valuation technique that is commonly used by market participants to price the instrument and has been demonstrated to provide realistic estimates of prices obtained in actual market transactions.[301]

We consider these proposals to be a retrograde step in relation to in the move towards the most meaningful accounting framework for financial instruments. In particular, we have concerns about introducing the notions of 'verifiability' and 'substantially offset', both of which should in our view be rejected by the Board. These proposals are also proving unpopular with entities planning to make use of the fair value option and even the IASB was not entirely convinced by them (three Board members formally objected to the exposure draft).[302]

9.2   Financial guarantees

In July 2004, the IASB issued an exposure draft proposing amendments to IAS 39 (and IFRS 4) that would specify the accounting requirements for many financial guarantee contracts that are currently within the scope of IFRS 4 (see 3.3.1).[303] The proposals would require the issuer of such a financial guarantee contract to measure the contract:

- initially at fair value. If the financial guarantee contract was issued in a stand-alone arm's length transaction to an unrelated party, its fair value at inception is likely to equal the premium received, unless there is evidence to the contrary; and

- subsequently at the higher of:

  - the amount determined in accordance with IAS 37; and

  - the amount initially recognised less, when appropriate, cumulative amortisation recognised in accordance with IAS 18.[304]

These requirements would be mandatory for accounting periods commencing 1 January 2006, although earlier adoption would be encouraged.[305]

References

1 *IASC Update*, IASC, December 1996.

2 IAS 32 (1995), *Financial Instruments: Disclosure and Presentation*, IASC, March 1995.

3 Discussion Paper, *Accounting for Financial Assets and Financial Liabilities*, IASC, March 1997.

4 Discussion Paper, Chapter 3, para. 3.1.

5 Discussion Paper, Chapter 4, para. 2.1 and Chapter 5, para. 3.1.

6 Discussion Paper, Chapter 6, para. 5.1.

7 Draft Standard, *Financial Instruments and Similar Items*, JWG, December 2000.

8 E62, *Financial Instruments: Recognition and Measurement*, IASC, June 1998.

9 IAS 39 (1998), *Financial Instruments: Recognition and Measurement*, IASC, December 1998.

10 *IAS 39 Implementation Guidance*, IASC, May 2000 and subsequently, Introduction.

11 *Press Release*, IASB, 31 July 2001.

12 Exposure Draft, *Amendments to IAS 32, Financial Instruments: Disclosure and Presentation, and IAS 39, Financial Instruments: Recognition and Measurement*, IASB, June 2002.

13 *Press Release*, IASB, 17 December 2003.

14 *Press Release*, IASB, 17 December 2003.

15 *Press Release*, European Commission, 29 September 2003.

16 Exposure Draft, Amendments to IAS 39 Financial Instruments: Recognition and Measurement, *Fair Value Hedge Accounting for a Portfolio Hedge of Interest Rate Risk*, IASB, August 2003.

17 ED, para. AV1.

18 IAS 32, *Financial Instruments: Disclosure and Presentation*, IASB, December 2003 (amended March 2004); IAS 39, *Financial Instruments: Recognition and Measurement*, IASB, December 2003 (amended March 2004).

19 Amendment to IAS 39, Financial Instruments: Recognition and Measurement, *Fair Value Hedge Accounting for a Portfolio Hedge of Interest Rate Risk*, IASB, March 2004.

20 IAS 32, para. DO1; IAS 39, para. DO1 and Amendment to IAS 39, para. DO1.

21 *Press Release*, IASB, 31 March 2004.

22 *Press Release*, IASB, 10 February 2004.

23 Exposure Draft, *Amendments to IAS 39 Financial Instruments: Recognition and Measurement – The Fair Value Option*, IASB, April 2004.

24 *Press Release*, IASB, 21 April 2004.

25 Discussion Paper, *Accounting for Financial Assets and Financial Liabilities*, IASC, March 1997, Chapter 6, para. 2.4.
26 IAS 39, para. BC14.
27 IAS 32, Application Guidance, para. before para. AG1.
28 IAS 32, Illustrative Examples, para. after main heading.
29 IAS 39, Application Guidance, para. before para. AG1.
30 IAS 39, Guidance on Implementing, para. before main heading Section A; Illustrative Example, para. after main heading.
31 IAS 32, para. 1.
32 IAS 39, para. 1.
33 IAS 32, para. 11.
34 IAS 32, para. 14.
35 IAS 32, para. 13.
36 IAS 32, para. AG7.
37 IAS 32, para. AG12.
38 IAS 32, para. AG12.
39 IAS 32, para. AG3.
40 IAS 32, para. AG4.
41 IAS 32, para. AG5.
42 IAS 32, para. AG6.
43 IAS 32, para. AG8.
44 IAS 32, para. AG8.
45 IAS 32, para. AG8.
46 IAS 32, para. AG9.
47 IAS 32, para. AG9.
48 IAS 32, para. AG9.
49 IAS 32, para. AG10.
50 IAS 39, para. B.1.
51 IAS 32, para. AG11.
52 IAS 32, para. AG20.
53 IAS 32, para. AG21.
54 IAS 32, para. AG22.
55 IAS 32, para. AG23.
56 IAS 32, para. AG13.
57 IAS 32, paras. AG15-AG16.
58 IAS 32, para. AG16.
59 IAS 32, para. AG17.
60 IAS 32, para. AG18.
61 IAS 32, para. AG19.
62 IAS 32, para. 4 and IAS 39, para. 2.
63 IAS 32, para. 4(a) and IAS 39, para. 2(a).
64 IAS 27, *Consolidated and Separate Financial Statements*, IASB, December 2003 (amended March 2004), paras. 37-38; IAS 28, *Investments in Associates*, IASB, December 2003, para. 35; IAS 31, *Interests in Joint Ventures*, IASB, December 2003 (amended March 2004), para. 46; IAS 32, para. 4(a) and IAS 39, para. 2(a).
65 IAS 28, para. 1; IAS 31, para. 1; IAS 32, para. 4(a) and IAS 39, para. 2(a).
66 *IFRIC Update*, IASB, August 2002.
67 IAS 32, para. 4(a) and IAS 39, para. 2(a).
68 IAS 27, para. IG7.
69 IAS 39, para. AG3.
70 IAS 39, para. 2(b).
71 IFRS 4, *Insurance Contracts*, IASB, March 2004, Appendix C, paras. 1-8.
72 IFRS 4, Appendix A, Defined terms.
73 IFRS 4, Appendix B, Definition of an insurance contract.
74 IAS 32, para. 4(d) and IAS 39, para. 2(e).
75 IAS 39, para. 2(e).
76 IAS 32, para. 4(d).
77 IAS 32, para. 4(e).
78 IAS 39, para. AG1.
79 IAS 39 (2000), *Financial Instruments: Recognition and Measurement*, IASB, December 1998 to October 2000, para. 1(f); IGC Q&A 1-1, Q&A 1-2, Q&A 1-5-a, and Q&A 1-5-b.
80 IAS 39, para. 3.
81 IAS 39, para. 3.
82 IAS 39, para. AG4A(a).
83 IAS 39, para. AG12A.
84 IAS 39, para. AG4A.
85 IAS 39, paras. 2(e) and AG4A(b).
86 IAS 39, para. AG4A(d).
87 IAS 32, para. AG29.
88 IAS 39 (2000), para. 1(h).
89 IAS 39, para. AG1.
90 IFRS 4, paras. B18(l) and B19(g).
91 IFRS 4, para. 2(b) and Appendix A, Defined terms.
92 IAS 32, para. 4(e) and IAS 39, para. 2(e).
93 IAS 39, para. BC15.
94 IGC Q&A 30-1 explained that in certain circumstances loan commitments may fall to be treated as 'regular way' transactions.
95 IAS 39, para. BC16.
96 IAS 39, para. 2(h).
97 IAS 32, para. 5.
98 IAS 39, paras. 4 and BC18-BC19.
99 IAS 39, para. 2(h).
100 IAS 39, para. BC19.
101 IAS 39, paras. 4 and BC17.
102 IAS 39, para. 2(h).
103 IAS 39, para. BC20.
104 IAS 39, para. 2(h).
105 IAS 39, para. BC15.
106 IAS 39, para. 2(d).
107 IAS 32, para. 5.
108 IAS 32, para. 4(c) and IAS 39, para. 2(f).
109 *IFRIC Update*, IASB, August 2002.
110 *IFRIC Update*, IASB, August 2002.
111 IAS 39, para. 2(g).
112 IAS 32, para. 4(b) and IAS 39, para. 2(c).
113 IAS 32, para. 4(f) and IAS 39, para. 2(i).
114 IAS 32, para. 4(f)(ii).
115 IAS 32, para. AG20.
116 IAS 32, para. AG20.
117 IAS 32, para. 8 and IAS 39, para. 5.
118 IAS 32, para. 9 and IAS 39, paras. 6 and BC24.

119 IAS 39, para. A.1.
120 IAS 32, para. 10 and IAS 39, paras. 7 and BC24.
121 IAS 39, para. A.2.
122 IAS 39, para. BC24; IAS 32 (2000), para. 5 and IAS 39 (2000), paras. 6-7 and 14.
123 IAS 2, *Inventories*, IASB, December 2003, para. 3.
124 IAS 32, para. AG24.
125 IAS 39, para. 9.
126 IAS 39, para. AG9.
127 IGC Q&A 10-6.
128 IAS 39, para. AG2.
129 IAS 39, para. B.8.
130 IAS 39, para. AG12A.
131 IAS 39, para. 9.
132 IAS 39 (2000), para. 10 and IGC Q&A 10-10.
133 IAS 39, para. AG11.
134 IGC Q&A 10-10.
135 IAS 39, para. B.9.
136 IAS 39, para. AG11 and IGC Q&A 10-3.
137 IAS 39, para. B.4.
138 IAS 39, para. B.5.
139 IAS 39, para. B.9.
140 IAS 39, para. B.10.
141 IAS 39, para. B.3.
142 IAS 39, para. AG10.
143 IAS 39, para. B.7.
144 IAS 39, para. B.2.
145 IAS 39, para. B.6.
146 IAS 39, para. B.6.
147 IAS 39, para. 9.
148 IAS 39, para. AG12.
149 IAS 39, para. 10.
150 IAS 39, para. BC76.
151 IAS 39, para. BC37.
152 IAS 39, para. BC37.
153 IAS 39, para. 11.
154 IAS 39, paras. 11 and AG33.
155 IAS 39, para. 10.
156 IAS 39, para. 12.
157 IAS 39, para. 13.
158 IAS 39, para. AG27.
159 IAS 39, paras. AG30(a) and AG31.
160 IAS 39, para. AG32.
161 SIC D-34, *Financial Instrument – Instruments or Rights Redeemable by the Holder*, IASB, September 2001.
162 IAS 39, para. 9.
163 IAS 39, para. AG30(b).
164 IAS 39, para. AG30(b).
165 IAS 39, para. AG30(g).
166 IAS 39, para. AG30(c).
167 IAS 39, para. AG30(g).
168 IAS 39, para. AG33(e).
169 IAS 39, para. AG30(c).
170 IAS 39, paras. AG30(d)-(e).
171 IAS 39, paras. AG30(f) and C.3.
172 IAS 39, para. C.4.
173 IAS 39, para. AG30(h).
174 Based on examples in Statement 133, *Accounting for Derivative Instruments and Hedging Activities*, FASB, June 1998, paras. 178-181.
175 IAS 39, para. AG33(a).
176 IAS 39, para. C.10.
177 IAS 39, para. AG33(b).
178 IAS 39, para. AG33(c).
179 IAS 39, para. AG33(d).
180 IAS 39, para. C.9.
181 IAS 39, para. C.7.
182 IAS 39, para. C.8.
183 IAS 39, para. AG33(f).
184 IAS 39, para. AG33(g).
185 IAS 39, para. AG33(h).
186 IAS 39, para. AG28.
187 IAS 39, para. C.1.
188 IAS 39, para. C.1.
189 IAS 39, para. C.1.
190 IAS 39, para. C.1.
191 IAS 39, para. AG28.
192 IAS 39, para. C.2.
193 IAS 39, para. C.2.
194 IAS 39, para. C.2.
195 IAS 39, para. C.5.
196 IAS 39, para. C.5.
197 IAS 39, para. C.5.
198 IAS 39, para. 11.
199 IAS 39, para. AG29.
200 IGC Q&A 23-8.
201 IGC Q&A 23-8.
202 IGC Q&A 23-8.
203 IAS 39, para. 10.
204 IAS 39, para. C.6.
205 IAS 39, para. C.6.
206 *Framework for the Preparation and Presentation of Financial Statements*, IASB, September 1989, para. 35 and 51.
207 *IFRIC Update*, IASB, April 2002, July 2002 and February 2003 and *IASB Update*, IASB, October 2002.
208 IAS 39, para. 9.
209 IAS 39, paras. BC71-BC79.
210 IAS 39, para. BC81.
211 IAS 39, para. 9.
212 IAS 39, para. AG14.
213 IAS 39, para. AG15.
214 IAS 39, para. BC82.
215 IAS 39, para. AG15.
216 IAS 39, para. B.11.
217 IGC Q&A 10-15.
218 IAS 39, para. 9.
219 IAS 39, paras. BC85-BC86.
220 IAS 39, para. BC73.
221 IAS 28, para. 1 and IAS 31, para. 1.
222 IAS 39, para. 9.
223 IAS 39, para. AG20.
224 IAS 39, para. 79.

225 IAS 39, para. AG17.
226 IAS 39, para. AG17.
227 IAS 39, para. AG18.
228 IAS 39, para. AG19.
229 IAS 39 (2000), para. 82 and IGC Q&A 83-3.
230 IAS 39, para. AG17.
231 IAS 39, para. B.13.
232 IAS 39, para. B.14.
233 IAS 39, para. C.3.
234 IAS 39, para. AG25.
235 IAS 39, para. AG16.
236 IAS 39, para. AG23.
237 IAS 39, para. B.18.
238 IAS 39, para. AG24.
239 IAS 39, para. AG20.
240 IAS 39, para. 9.
241 IGC Q&A 83-1.
242 IGC Q&A 83-1.
243 IAS 39, para. B.19.
244 IAS 39, para. B.20.
245 IAS 39, para. B.21.
246 IAS 39, para. AG21.
247 IAS 39, para. AG22.
248 IAS 39, para. AG22.
249 IAS 39, para. B.15.
250 IAS 39, para. AG22.
251 IAS 39, paras. AG22 and B.15.
252 IAS 39, para. B.17.
253 IAS 39, para. B.16.
254 IAS 39, para. B.16.
255 IAS 39, para. 9.
256 IAS 39, para. AG26.
257 IAS 39 (2000), paras. 10 and 19-20.
258 IAS 39, para. BC28.
259 IAS 39, paras. 9 and BC29.
260 IAS 39, para. 9.
261 IAS 39, paras. BC26-BC27.
262 IAS 39, para. B.23.
263 IAS 39, para. B.22.
264 IAS 39, para. 9.
265 IAS 39, para. BC25.
266 IAS 39, para. AG26.
267 IAS 39, para. 9.
268 IAS 39 (2000), para. 21.
269 IAS 39, para. B.12.
270 IAS 39, paras. 50 and BC73.
271 IAS 39 (2000), para. 107 and IGC Q&A 107-1
     and Q&A 107-2.
272 IAS 39, para. 51.
273 IAS 39, para. 52.
274 IAS 39, para. 54.
275 IAS 32, para. 96 and IAS 39, para. 103.
276 IAS 32, para. 97 and IAS 39, para. 104.
277 IAS 39, para. 105.
278 IAS 39, para. 104.
279 IFRS 1, *First-time Adoption of International
     Financial Reporting Standards*, IASB, June 2003
     (amended March 2004), para. BC89A.
280 IFRS 1, para. 36A.
281 IFRS 1, para. 36A.
282 IFRS 1, para. 36A.
283 IAS 8, *Accounting Policies, Changes in
     Accounting Estimates and Errors*, IASB,
     December 2003, (amended March 2004),
     para. 24.
284 IAS 8, para. 28.
285 IFRS 1, para. BC89.
286 IFRS 1, para. IG56(c).
287 IFRS 1, paras. BC65-BC66.
288 IFRS 1, para. IG56(c).
289 IFRS 1, para. 25A.
290 IFRS 1, para. IG56(d).
291 IFRS 1, para. IG56(a).
292 IFRS 1, para. IG56(b).
293 IFRS 1, para. 25A.
294 IFRS 1, para. IG56(e).
295 Exposure Draft (ED), *Amendments to IAS 39
     Financial Instruments: Recognition and
     Measurement – The Fair Value Option*,
     para. BC3.
296 ED, para. BC4.
297 ED, para. BC9.
298 ED, para. 9.
299 ED, para. 9.
300 ED, para. 9.
301 ED, para. 48B.
302 ED, para. AV1.
303 Exposure Draft, Amendments to IAS 39,
     Financial Instruments: Recognition and
     Measurement and IFRS 4.
304 ED, para. IN3.
305 ED, para. IN10.

Chapter 16   Financial instruments: Recognition, derecognition and offset

1   INTRODUCTION

1.1   Background

This chapter deals with the question of when financial instruments should be included – or, to use the formal language of IFRS, 'recognised' – in financial statements. The IASB, and other national standards setters, have found this question particularly difficult to answer in the context of financial instruments. In part, this is because it is in the nature of financial instruments that there may be more separation than is usual in the case of other assets and liabilities between legal and 'economic' ownership. To take a very simple case, if an entity buys a quoted share in the financial markets it may be entitled to all the benefits, and exposed to all the risks, inherent in owning that share somewhat earlier than the date on which it is registered as the legal owner.

The question of recognition raises the reciprocal question of derecognition – i.e. at what point should an item already recognised in financial statements cease to be included? To use the example of a traded equity share once more, if an entity sells a quoted share in the financial markets it may cease to be entitled to all the benefits, and exposed to all the risks, inherent in owning that share somewhat earlier than the date on which it ceases to be registered as the legal owner. However, the question of derecognition goes much further than this, as it encroaches on what is commonly referred to as 'off-balance sheet' finance (see 1.2 below).

Related to recognition and derecognition is the question of offset – i.e. when, or whether, an entity may offset any of its financial assets against any of its financial liabilities. At first sight, the answer to this seems rather obvious, given the general prohibition on offsetting in IAS 1 – *Presentation of Financial Statements* (see Chapter 3 at 4.1.5). However, in the context of financial instruments, the question is more subtle. In effect, the issue is whether certain assets and liabilities, although legally separate, should be regarded as a single item from an economic perspective and reported as such in financial statements. A simple example might be where an entity has accounts in debit and in credit with the same bank.

1.2   Off-balance sheet finance

In order to understand the rationale for the requirements of IFRS for the derecognition of financial assets and financial liabilities, it is necessary to appreciate the fact that those requirements, and those in equivalent national standards, have their origins in the response by financial regulators to the growing use of off-balance sheet finance from the early 1980s onwards.

'Off-balance sheet' transactions can be difficult to define, and this poses the first problem in discussing the subject. The term implies that certain things belong on the balance sheet and that those which escape the net are deviations from this norm. The practical effect of off-balance sheet transactions is that the financial statements do not fully present the underlying activities of the reporting entity. This is generally for one of two reasons. The items in question may be included in the balance sheet but presented 'net' rather than 'gross' – for example, by netting off loans received against the assets they finance. Alternatively, the items might be excluded from the balance sheet altogether on the basis that they do not represent present assets and liabilities. Examples include operating lease commitments and certain contingent liabilities.

The result in all cases will be that the balance sheet may suggest less exposure to assets and liabilities than really exists, with a consequential flattering effect on certain ratios, such as gearing and return on assets employed. There is usually an income statement dimension to be considered as well, perhaps because assets taken off-balance sheet purport to have been sold (with a possible profit effect), and also more generally because the presentation of off-balance sheet activity influences the timing or disclosure of associated revenue items. In particular, the presence or absence of items in the balance sheet usually affects whether the finance cost implicit in a transaction is reported as such or rolled up within another item of income or expense.

Depending on their roles, different people react differently to the term 'off-balance sheet finance'. To an accounting standard setter, or other financial regulator, the expression carries the connotation of devious accounting, intended to mislead the reader of financial statements. Off-balance sheet transactions are those which are designed to allow an entity to avoid reflecting certain aspects of its activities in its financial statements. The term is therefore pejorative and carries the slightly self-righteous inference that those who indulge in such transactions are up to no good and need to be stopped.

However, there is also room for a more honourable use of the term 'off-balance sheet finance'. Entities may wish, for sound commercial reasons, to engage in transactions which share with other parties the risks and benefits associated with certain assets and liabilities. Increasingly sophisticated financial markets allow businesses to protect themselves from selected risks, or to take limited ownership interests which carry the entitlement to restricted rewards of particular assets.

In theory, it should be possible to determine what items belong in the balance sheet by reference to general principles such as those in the IASB's *Framework* and similar concepts statements. In practice, however, such principles on their own have proved a less than adequate response to the increasingly ingenious and aggressive structures being developed for what would generally be regarded as the less honourable forms of off-balance sheet finance. Accordingly, standard-setters throughout the world, including the IASB, have developed increasingly detailed rules to deal with the issue. This 'anti-avoidance' aspect of the derecognition rules helps to explain why, rather unusually for IFRS, IAS 39 considers not only the economic position of the entity at the reporting date, but also prior transactions which gave rise to that position and the reporting entity's motives in undertaking them. This is discussed further at 4.1.1 below.

2   DEVELOPMENT OF IFRS

2.1   General

Under IFRS:

- the recognition and derecognition of financial assets and financial liabilities is addressed in IAS 39 – *Financial Instruments: Recognition and Measurement*[1] (see 4 and 5 below);

- the offset of financial assets and financial liabilities is addressed in IAS 32 – *Financial Instruments: Disclosure and Presentation*[2] (see 6 below).

The provisions of SIC–12 – *Consolidation – Special Purpose Entities*[3] are also very relevant to certain aspects of the recognition and derecognition of financial assets and financial liabilities. Since SIC–12 is issued as an interpretation of IAS 27 – *Consolidated and Separate Financial Statements*, it is discussed principally in Chapter 5 at 3.2, but is also referred to at various points below.

IAS 32 was originally issued in March 1995 and IAS 39 in December 1998, with each standard subject to some amendment following its initial publication. However, in December 2003, the then current versions of both standards were superseded by revised versions. These new versions of IAS 32 and IAS 39 must be applied for annual periods beginning on or after 1 January 2005. Entities are 'permitted' (rather than 'encouraged', as in the case of other recently issued standards) to adopt both standards in earlier periods, but must disclose that they have done so. They must also adopt IAS 39 as amended in March 2004, not as originally issued, and must adopt both IAS 32 and IAS 39 (as amended) at the same time.[4]

The main text of IAS 32 is supplemented by application guidance (which is an integral part of the standard)[5] and by illustrative examples (which accompany, but are not part of, the standard).[6] Similarly, the main text of IAS 39 is supplemented by application guidance (which is an integral part of the standard)[7] and by implementation guidance and an illustrative example (both of which accompany, but are not part of, the standard).[8]

The new versions of IAS 32 and IAS 39 make no significant changes to the criteria in the previous versions for the offset of financial assets and financial liabilities, the recognition of financial assets and liabilities, or the derecognition of financial liabilities. However, the new version of IAS 39 has made significant changes to the criteria for the derecognition of financial assets (see 2.1.1 below).

2.1.1   Derecognition of assets – a mixed accounting model

Underlying these changes was the fact that the approach in the original version of IAS 39 was more than a little confusing. In part, this was because it drew on elements of different, and ultimately incompatible, concepts. To take a simple example, suppose that an entity has €100 of receivables, with an expected bad debt risk of €2. It sells these to a bank for their agreed net present value of €96. The entity also agrees with the bank that it will indemnify the bank if it fails to collect the full €100 by the due date for payment, but only up to a maximum of €10.

One analysis (sometimes referred to as a 'risks and rewards' approach) might be that the expected bad and slow payment risk was €2. In effect, the entity retains this entire risk through its €10 guarantee, and should therefore continue to recognise the entire €100 asset. An alternative analysis (sometimes referred to as a 'components' or 'control' approach) would be that either:

(a)   the entire risks and rewards associated with €90 of the receivables; or

(b)   the rewards, but not the risks, of the whole portfolio

have been passed to the bank and that, accordingly, either:

- at least €90 of the receivables should be considered for derecognition, or

- the whole portfolio should be derecognised and a liability recognised for the guarantee.[9]

In its 2002 exposure draft of proposed amendments to IAS 32 and IAS 39 (see Chapter 15 at 1.5), the IASB proposed that derecognition should be based on the single concept of 'continuing involvement'. However, this proposal did not find favour with many respondents to the exposure draft, including those who acknowledged the inconsistencies identified by the IASB in the original version of IAS 39. In the light of such comment from respondents, IAS 39 still retains elements of a number of derecognition concepts, but seeks to avoid conflict between them by requiring various factors to be considered in a specific order.

The main changes made by the revised IAS 39 to the derecognition provisions for assets (which are discussed in detail at 4 below) were:

- to clarify that an asset should be separated into components only in defined circumstances and otherwise regarded as a whole, and

- to require the question of derecognition to be determined by considering, in order:

    - whether the asset has been 'transferred' to another party; and

    - if so, whether the entity has also transferred substantially all the risks and rewards of the asset.

    If the asset, and substantially all its associated risks and rewards, have been transferred it is derecognised.

    Otherwise, the entity then determines whether or not it has retained control of the asset. If control has been retained the asset continues to be recognised. If control has not been retained, the asset is recognised only to the extent of the entity's 'continuing involvement' (see 4.8.3 below) in the asset.[10]

2.2 Definitions

The following definitions in IAS 32 and IAS 39 are generally relevant to the discussion in this chapter.

A *financial instrument* is any contract that gives rise to a financial asset of one entity and a financial liability or equity instrument of another entity.[11]

A *financial asset* is any asset that is:

(a) cash;

(b) an equity instrument of another entity;

(c) a contractual right:

    (i) to receive cash or another financial asset from another entity; or

    (ii) to exchange financial assets or financial liabilities with another entity under conditions that are potentially favourable to the entity; or

(d) a contract that will or may be settled in the entity's own equity instruments and is:

    (i) a non-derivative for which the entity is or may be obliged to receive a variable number of the entity's own equity instruments; or

    (ii) a derivative that will or may be settled other than by the exchange of a fixed amount of cash or another financial asset for a fixed number of the entity's own equity instruments. For this purpose the entity's own equity instruments do not include instruments that are themselves contracts for the future receipt or delivery of the entity's own equity instruments.[12]

A *financial liability* is any liability that is:

(a)   a contractual obligation:

    (i)   to deliver cash or another financial asset to another entity; or

    (ii) to exchange financial assets or financial liabilities with another entity under conditions that are potentially unfavourable to the entity; or

(b)   a contract that will or may be settled in the entity's own equity instruments and is:

    (i)   a non-derivative for which the entity is or may be obliged to deliver a variable number of the entity's own equity instruments; or

    (ii) a derivative that will or may be settled other than by the exchange of a fixed amount of cash or another financial asset for a fixed number of the entity's own equity instruments. For this purpose the entity's own equity instruments do not include instruments that are themselves contracts for the future receipt or delivery of the entity's own equity instruments.[13]

An *equity instrument* is any contract that evidences a residual interest in the assets of an entity after deducting all of its liabilities.[14]

A *derivative* is a financial instrument or other contract within the scope of IAS 39 (see Chapter 15 at 3) with all three of the following characteristics:

*   its value changes in response to the change in a specified interest rate, financial instrument price, commodity price, foreign exchange rate, index of prices or rates, credit rating or credit index, or other variable (sometimes called the 'underlying');

*   it requires no initial net investment or an initial net investment that is smaller than would be required for other types of contracts that would be expected to have a similar response to changes in market factors; and

*   it is settled at a future date.[15]

Fair value is the amount for which an asset could be exchanged, or a liability settled, between knowledgeable, willing parties in an arm's length transaction.[16]

3   RECOGNITION

IAS 39 provides that an entity must recognise a financial asset or a financial liability on its balance sheet when, and only when, the entity becomes a party to the contractual provisions of the instrument.[17] The specific application of this general rule to the particular case of 'regular way' purchases of financial assets is discussed further at 3.1 below. IAS 39 gives the following examples of the more general application of this principle.

A   Receivables and payables

Unconditional receivables and payables are recognised as assets or liabilities when the entity becomes a party to the contract and, as a consequence, has a legal right to receive or a legal obligation to pay cash.[18]

B   Firm commitments

Generally under IFRS, assets to be acquired and liabilities to be incurred as a result of a firm commitment to purchase or sell goods or services are generally not recognised until at least one of the parties has performed under the agreement. For example, an entity that receives a firm order for goods or services does not recognise an asset (and the entity that places the order does not recognise a liability) at the time of the commitment, but delays recognition until the ordered goods or services have been shipped, delivered or rendered.[19]

However, IAS 39 supplies numerous exceptions to this general rule. For example, if a firm commitment to buy or sell non-financial items is within the scope of IAS 39 (see Chapter 15 at 3), its net fair value is recognised as an asset or liability on the commitment date (see C below). In addition, if a previously unrecognised firm commitment is designated as a hedged item in a fair value hedge, any change in the net fair value attributable to the hedged risk is recognised as an asset or liability after the inception of the hedge (see Chapter 19 at 4.1).[20] Another exception, not noted in IAS 39, is the treatment of a gross-settled forward purchase of, or written put option over, an entity's own shares which may require a liability to be recognised on entering into the contract (see Chapter 17 at 3.3.3 and 7).

This highlights the fundamental difference between the recognition criteria in IAS 39 and those in most other standards. Broadly speaking, under IAS 39 recognition is triggered by entering into a legal agreement, whereas under most other standards it is triggered by performance under the agreement – even though a strict application of the definitions of 'asset' and 'liability' in the IASB's *Framework* might suggest that recognition should in all cases flow from entering into, rather than performing under, a contractual agreement.

The Basis for Conclusions in IAS 39 touches on this in explaining the rationale for IAS 39's allowed treatment of hedges of firm commitments (see Chapter 19 at 3.3). The IASB argues that a firm commitment to buy or sell, say, inventory or PPE is in fact recognised when it is entered into, but at its historical cost of zero.[21] In other words, the difference (in the IASB's view) is not so much that commitments in respect of financial instruments are recognised at inception and others not, but rather that commitments in respect of financial instruments are measured at fair value, and others at historical cost.

Whatever the conceptual rationale, one suspects that the true underlying reason for the difference is simply one of practicality – or at least perceived practicality. In other words, whilst the IASB's *Framework* might in theory require all firm commitments to be recognised immediately they are entered into, the types of commitment accounted for under IAS 39 are often easier to measure than those in the scope of other IFRS. Moreover many commitments accounted for under IAS 39 can be traded, and the risks associated with them laid off, with third parties, as if they were assets or liabilities in their own right. For example, a forward contract to buy government bonds can be more objectively and reliably measured, (and more readily transferred to a third party) than a contract to buy an item of PPE or a block of wood.

C   Forward contracts

A forward contract is a contract which obliges one party to the contract to buy, and the other party to sell, the asset that is the subject of the contract for a fixed price at a future date.

A forward contract within the scope of IAS 39 (see Chapter 15 at 3) is recognised as an asset or a liability at commitment date, rather than on settlement. When an entity becomes a party to a forward contract, the fair values of the right and obligation are often equal, so that the net fair value of the forward is zero. If the net fair value of the right and obligation is not zero, the contract is recognised as an asset or liability.[22]

D   Option contracts

An option contract is a contract which gives one party to the contract the right, but not the obligation, to buy from, or sell to, the other party to the contract the asset that is the subject of the contract for a fixed price at a future date (or during a longer period ending on a future date). An option giving the right to buy an asset is referred to as a 'call' option and one giving the right to sell as a 'put' option. An option is referred to as a 'bought' or 'purchased' option from the perspective of the party with the right to buy or sell (the 'holder') and as a 'written' option from the perspective of the party with the potential obligation to buy or sell. An option is referred to as 'in the money' when it would be in the holder's interest to exercise it and as 'out of the money' when it would not be in the holder's interest to exercise it.

Under IAS 39 an option is:

* 'deeply in the money' when it is so far in the money that it is highly unlikely to go out of the money before expiry,[23] and

* 'deeply out of the money' when it is so far out of the money that it is highly unlikely to become in the money before expiry.[24]

IAS 39 does not elaborate on what it means by 'highly unlikely' in this context, although the Implementation Guidance clarifies that 'highly probable' (in the context of a 'highly probable forecast transaction' subject to a hedge) indicates a much greater likelihood of happening than the term 'more likely than not'.[25] Perhaps the IASB will issue further guidance as to whether 'highly unlikely' indicates a lesser or greater probability of occurrence than 'not highly probable'!

Option contracts that are within the scope of IAS 39 (see Chapter 15 at 3) are recognised as assets or liabilities when the holder or writer becomes a party to the contract.[26]

E   Planned future transactions

Planned future transactions, no matter how likely, are not assets and liabilities because the entity has not become a party to a contract. They are therefore not recognised under IAS 39.[27] However, transactions that have been entered into as a hedge of certain 'highly probable' future transactions are recognised under IAS 39 – this raises the issue of the accounting treatment of any gains or losses arising on such hedging transactions (see Chapter 19 at 4.1 and 4.2).

3.1   'Regular way' transactions

A *regular way purchase or sale* is defined as a purchase or sale of a financial asset under a contract whose terms require delivery of the asset within the time frame established generally by regulation or convention in the marketplace concerned.[28] A contract that can be settled by net settlement (i.e. payment or receipt of cash or other financial assets equivalent to the change in value of the contract) is not a regular way transaction, but a derivative accounted for in accordance with the requirements of IAS 39 in respect of derivatives (see Chapter 18 at 3.1).[29]

Many financial markets provide a mechanism whereby all transactions in certain financial instruments (particularly quoted equities and bonds) entered into on a particular date are settled a fixed number of days after that date. The date on which the agreement is entered into is called the 'trade date' and the date on which it is settled by delivery of the assets that are the subject of the agreement is called the 'settlement date'.[30] Among other benefits, this system allows each market participant to settle all its transactions with a single net transfer of cash or other financial assets to or from a central clearing house, or a particular counterparty, rather than having to settle each transaction individually with each counterparty.

One effect of this system is that, while legal title to the assets that are the subject of the transaction passes only on or after settlement date, the buyer is effectively exposed to the risks and rewards of ownership of the assets from trade date. For example, suppose that an entity enters into a contract to purchase a financial asset but, before settlement date, decides that it no longer requires that asset and therefore enters into a second contract to sell the asset immediately it is received. The price of the second contract will be influenced, *inter alia*, by movements in the market value of the asset between the trade date of the first contract and that of the second, just as if the entity had actually owned the asset in that period.

Absent any special provisions, the accounting analysis for such transactions under IAS 39 would be that, between trade date and settlement date, an entity has a forward contract to purchase an asset (see C under 3 above) which, in common with all derivatives, should be recorded at fair value, with all changes in fair value recognised in profit or loss (see Chapter 18 at 3.1), unless the special rules for hedge accounting apply (see Chapter 19). This would not only be somewhat onerous but would also have the effect, in the case of an asset to be accounted for at amortised cost or as available-for-sale, that changes in its fair value between trade date and settlement date would be recognised in profit or loss, notwithstanding that any changes in fair value after settlement date would either not be recognised at all (in the case of an asset accounted for at amortised cost) or recognised in equity (in the case of an asset accounted for as available-for-sale).

To avoid this, IAS 39 permits assets subject to regular way transactions to be recognised, or derecognised, either as at the trade date ('trade date accounting') or as at the settlement date ('settlement date accounting').[31] Whichever method is used is applied consistently to each of the four main categories of financial asset identified by IAS 39[32] – i.e. at fair value through profit or loss, held-to-maturity, loans and receivables and available-for-sale (see Chapter 15 at 7).

3.1.1 Trade date accounting

As noted above, the trade date is the date on which an entity commits itself to purchase or sell an asset. Trade date accounting requires:

(a)   in respect of an asset to be bought: recognition on the trade date of the asset and the liability to pay for it; and

(b)   in respect of an asset to be sold: derecognition on the trade date of the asset, together with recognition of any gain or loss on disposal and the recognition of a receivable from the buyer for payment.

IAS 39 notes that, generally, interest does not start to accrue on the asset and corresponding liability until the settlement date when title passes.[33] However, this is in fact not necessarily the case – see 3.1.2 A below.

3.1.2 Settlement date accounting

As noted above, the settlement date is the date that an asset is delivered to or by an entity. Settlement date accounting requires:

(a)   in respect of an asset to be bought, the recognition of the asset on the settlement date. Any change in the fair value of the asset to be received during the period between the trade date and the settlement date is accounted for in the same way as the acquired asset (see Chapter 18 at 3). In other words:

- for assets carried at cost or amortised cost, the change in value is not recognised;

- for assets classified as financial assets at fair value through profit or loss, the change in value is recognised in profit or loss; and

- for available-for-sale assets, the change in value is recognised in equity; and

(b)   in respect of an asset to be sold, derecognition of the asset, recognition of any gain or loss on disposal and the recognition of a receivable from the buyer for payment on the settlement date.[34] A change in the fair value of the asset between trade date and settlement date is not recorded in the financial statements, even if the entity applies settlement date accounting, because the seller's right to changes in the fair value ceases on the trade date.[35]

A   Current market practice – 'due date' accounting

In fact, the IAS 39's version of 'settlement date accounting' differs from what is often understood by the term in the financial markets. A common current practice among entities not subject to IAS 39 is to recognise and derecognise assets subject to regular way transactions at the due date for settlement, as opposed to the actual settlement date (which is often delayed beyond the due date due to unforeseen circumstances). This treatment is reinforced by the fact that interest on unsettled transactions in practice usually accrues from the due date, rather than the settlement date as stated by IAS 39.

3.1.3 Illustrative examples

Examples 16.1 and 16.2 below (which are based on those in the implementation guidance appended to IAS 39)[36] illustrate the application of trade date and settlement date accounting to the various categories of financial asset identified by IAS 39. The accounting treatment for these categories of asset is discussed in more detail in Chapter 18.

Example 16.1:   Trade date and settlement date accounting – regular way purchase

On 29 December 2005 (trade date), an entity commits itself to purchase a financial asset for €1,000 (including transaction costs), which is its fair value on trade date. On 31 December 2005 (financial year-end) and on 4 January 2006 (settlement date) the fair value of the asset is €1,002 and €1,003, respectively. The accounting entries required to be recorded for the transaction will depend on how it is classified and whether trade date or settlement date accounting is used, as shown in the tables below.

A   *Financial asset accounted for at amortised cost*

	Trade date accounting			*Settlement date accounting*		
		€	€		€	€
29 December 2005						
	Financial asset	1,000				
	Liability to counterparty		1,000			
	To record liability to purchase asset					
31 December 2005						
	No accounting entries					
4 January 2006						
	Liability to counterparty	1,000		Financial asset	1,000	
	Cash		1,000	Cash		1,000
	Settlement of liability			*To record purchase of asset*		

B   *Financial asset accounted for at fair value through profit or loss*

	Trade date accounting			*Settlement date accounting*		
		€	€		€	€
29 December 2005						
	Financial asset	1,000				
	Liability to counterparty		1,000			
	To record liability to purchase asset					
31 December 2006						
	Financial Asset	2		Receivable	2	
	Income statement		2	Income statement		2
	To record change in fair value of asset			*To record change in fair value of contract*		

4 January 2006

Liability to counterparty	1,000		Financial asset	1,003	
Cash		1,000	Cash		1,000
Financial asset	1		Receivable		2
Income statement		1	Income statement		1

To record settlement of liability and change in fair value of asset | To record change in fair value, and settlement, of contract

C   Financial asset accounted for as available-for-sale

Trade date accounting			Settlement date accounting		
	€	€		€	€

29 December 2005

Financial asset	1,000				
Liability to counterparty		1,000			

To record liability to purchase asset

31 December 2006

Financial Asset	2		Receivable	2	
Equity		2	Equity		2

To record change in fair value of asset | To record change in fair value of contract

4 January 2006

Liability to counterparty	1,000		Financial asset	1,003	
Cash		1,000	Cash		1,000
Financial asset	1		Receivable		2
Equity		1	Equity		1

To record settlement of liability and change in fair value of asset | To record change in fair value, and settlement, of contract

Example 16.2:   Trade date and settlement date accounting – regular way sale

On 29 December 2005 (trade date) an entity enters into a contract to sell a financial asset for its then current fair value of €1,010. The asset was acquired one year earlier for €1,000 and its amortised cost is €1,000. On 31 December 2005 (financial year-end), the fair value of the asset is €1,012. On 4 January 2006 (settlement date), the fair value is €1,013. The amounts to be recorded will depend on how the asset is classified and whether trade date or settlement date accounting is used as shown in the tables below (any interest that might have accrued on the asset is disregarded).

A change in the fair value of a financial asset that is sold on a regular way basis is not recorded in the financial statements between trade date and settlement date, even if the entity applies settlement date accounting, because the seller's right to changes in the fair value ceases on the trade date.

A   ***Financial asset accounted for at amortised cost***

	Trade date accounting			Settlement date accounting		
		€	€		€	€
Before 29 December 2005 (cumulative net entries)						
Financial asset	1,000			Financial asset	1,000	
Cash		1,000		Cash		1,000

29 December 2005

		€	€
Receivable from counterparty	1,010		
Financial asset		1,000	
Income statement		10	

To record disposal of asset

4 January 2006

	Trade date accounting			Settlement date accounting		
Cash	1,010			Cash	1,010	
Receivable from counterparty		1,010		Financial asset		1,000
				Income statement		10
	To record settlement of sale contract			*To record disposal of asset*		

B   ***Financial asset accounted for at fair value through profit or loss***

	Trade date accounting			Settlement date accounting		
		€	€		€	€
Before 29 December 2005 (cumulative net entries)						
Financial asset	1,010			Financial asset	1,010	
Cash		1,000		Cash		1,000
Income statement		10		Income statement		10

29 December 2005

		€	€
Receivable from counterparty	1,010		
Financial asset		1,010	

To record disposal of asset

4 January 2006

	Trade date accounting			Settlement date accounting		
Cash	1,010			Cash	1,010	
Receivable from counterparty		1,010		Financial asset		1,010
	To record settlement of sale contract			*To record disposal of asset*		

C   Financial asset accounted for at as available-for-sale

Trade date accounting			*Settlement date accounting*		
	€	€		€	€

Before 29 December 2005 (cumulative net entries)

Financial asset	1,010		Financial asset	1,010	
Cash		1,000	Cash		1,000
Equity		10	Equity		10

29 December 2005

Receivable from counterparty	1,010		
Financial asset		1,010	
* Equity	10		
Income statement		10	

To record disposal of asset

4 January 2006

Cash	1,010		Cash	1,010	
Receivable from counterparty		1,010	Financial asset		1,010
*			Equity	10	
			Income statement		10

To record settlement of sale contract   *To record disposal of asset*

* The transfers between equity and retained earnings represent the 'recycling' of cumulative gains and losses required by IAS 39 on disposal of an available-for-sale asset (see Chapter 18 at 3.2). Disposal is regarded as occurring on trade date when trade date accounting applies and on settlement date when settlement date accounting applies.

A   Exchanges of non-cash financial assets

The implementation guidance to IAS 39 addresses the situation in which an entity enters into a regular way transaction whereby it commits to sell a non-cash financial asset in exchange for another non-cash financial asset. This raises the question of whether, if the entity applies settlement date accounting, it should recognise any change in the fair value of the financial asset to be received arising between trade date and settlement date. A further issue is that the asset being sold may be in a category of asset to which trade date accounting is applied, while the asset being bought may be in a category of asset to which settlement date accounting is applied.

The implementation guidance essentially requires the buying and selling legs of the transaction to be accounted for independently, as illustrated by Example 16.3.[37]

Example 16.3:   *Trade date and settlement date accounting – exchange of non-cash financial assets*

On 29 December 2005 (trade date), an entity enters into a contract to sell Note Receivable A, which is carried at amortised cost, in exchange for Bond B, which will be classified as held for trading and measured at fair value. Both assets have a fair value of €1,010 on 29 December, while the amortised cost of Note Receivable A is €1,000. The entity uses settlement date accounting for loans and receivables and trade date accounting for assets held for trading. On 31 December 2005 (financial year-end), the fair value of Note Receivable A is €1,012 and the fair value of Bond B is €1,009. On 4 January 2006, the fair value of Note Receivable A is €1,013 and the fair value of Bond B is €1,007. The following entries are made:

	€	€
29 December 2005		
Bond B	1,010	
Liability to counterparty		1,010
To record purchase of Bond B (trade date accounting)		
31 December 2005		
Loss on Bond B (income statement)	1	
Bond B		1
To record change in fair value of Bond B		
4 January 2006		
Liability to counterparty	1,010	
Note Receivable A		1,000
Gain on disposal (income statement)		10
To record disposal of receivable A (settlement date accounting)		
Loss on Bond B (income statement)	2	
Bond B		2
To record change in fair value of Bond B		

The simultaneous recognition, between 29 December and 4 January, both of the asset being bought and the asset being given in consideration for it may seem counter-intuitive. However, it is no different from the accounting treatment of any purchase of goods for credit which results, in the period between delivery of, and payment for, the goods, in the simultaneous recognition of the liability to pay the supplier and the cash that will be used to do so.

3.2   Treatment by transferee of transfers of financial assets not qualifying for derecognition by transferor

IAS 39 adds that, where an asset is transferred from one party to another in circumstances where the transferor does not derecognise the asset, the transferee should not recognise the asset.[38] Instead, the transferee derecognises the cash or other consideration paid and recognises a receivable from the transferor. If the transferor has both a right and an obligation to reacquire control of the entire transferred asset for a fixed amount (such as under a repurchase agreement – see 4.7 below), the transferee may account for its receivable as a loan or receivable.[39]

Underlying this requirement appears to be a concern that more than one party cannot satisfy the criteria in IAS 39 for recognition of the same financial asset at the same time. In fact, however, such concern is misplaced, since it is easy for the same assets to be simultaneously recognised by more than one entity – for example if the transferor adopts settlement date accounting and the transferee trade date accounting (see 3.1 above).

4 DERECOGNITION – FINANCIAL ASSETS

4.1 Summary

4.1.1 Background

As discussed at 1.2 above, the requirements of IAS 39 for the derecognition of financial assets are primarily designed to deal with the accounting challenges posed by various types of off-balance sheet finance. As a result, the real focus of many of the rules for the derecognition of assets is in fact the recognition of liabilities. The starting point for most of the transactions discussed below is that the reporting entity receives cash or other consideration in return for a transfer or 'sale' of all or part of a financial asset. This raises the question of whether such consideration should be treated as income or as a liability. IAS 39 effectively answers that question by determining whether the financial asset to which the consideration relates should be derecognised (such that the proceeds are treated as income) or should continue to be recognised (such that the proceeds are treated as a liability).

This underlying objective of the derecognition criteria helps to explain why, rather unusually for IFRS, IAS 39 considers not only the economic position of the entity at the reporting date, but also prior transactions which gave rise to that position and the reporting entity's motives in undertaking them. For example, if, at a reporting date, an entity has two identical forward contracts for the purchase of a financial asset, the accounting treatment of the contracts may vary significantly if one contract relates to the purchase of an asset previously owned by the entity and the other does not.

This is because the derecognition rules of IAS 39 (like those of some other national standards) are based on the premise that, if a transfer of an asset leaves the transferor's economic exposure to the transferred asset much as if the transfer had never taken place, the financial statements should represent that the transferor still holds the asset. Thus, if an entity sells (say) a listed bond subject to a forward contract to repurchase the bond from the buyer at a fixed price, IAS 39 argues that the entity is exposed to the risks and rewards of that bond as if it had never sold it, but had simply borrowed an amount equivalent to the original sales proceeds secured on the bond. IAS 39 therefore concludes that the bond should not be removed from the balance sheet and the sale proceeds should be accounted for as a liability (in effect the obligation to repurchase the bond under the forward contract – see 4.7 below).

By contrast, if the entity were to enter into a second identical forward contract over another bond (i.e. one not previously owned by the entity), IAS 39 would simply require it to be accounted for as a derivative at fair value (see Chapter 18). This might seem a rather counter-intuitive outcome of a framework that purports to report economically equivalent transactions in a consistent and objective manner. However, the IASB would argue that the two transactions are not economically equivalent: they are distinguished by the fact that entering into the forward contract over the originally owned asset gave rise to a cash inflow (i.e. the 'sales' proceeds from the counterparty), whereas entering into the second contract did not. This reinforces the point that the real focus of IAS 39 is to determine the appropriate accounting treatment for that cash inflow and that of not the previously owned bond *per se*.

4.1.2 Decision tree

The provisions of IAS 39 concerning the derecognition of financial assets are complex, but are summarised in the flowchart overleaf.[40] It may be helpful to refer to this while reading the discussion that follows.

It will be seen that the process presupposes that the reporting entity has correctly consolidated all its subsidiaries in accordance with IAS 27 (see Chapter 5). This will include any entities identified as special purpose entities (SPEs) – see A below.

It is clearly highly significant from an accounting perspective whether an entity to which a financial asset or liability is transferred is a subsidiary or a consolidated SPE of the transferor. A financial asset (or financial liability) transferred from an entity to its subsidiary or SPE (on whatever terms) will continue to be recognised in the entity's consolidated financial statements through the normal elimination of intragroup transactions required by the consolidation procedures set out in IAS 27 (see Chapter 5 at 6.3). Thus, the criteria in 4.2 to 4.6 are irrelevant to the treatment, in an entity's consolidated financial statements, of any transfer of a financial asset by the entity to a subsidiary or SPE. However, the criteria may be relevant to any onward transfer by the SPE, and to the entity's separate financial statements (see Chapter 5 at 7), if prepared.

The subsequent steps towards determining whether derecognition is appropriate are discussed in 4.2 to 4.6 below. Some examples of how these criteria might be applied to some common transactions in financial assets are given in 4.7 below. The accounting consequences of the derecognition of a financial asset are discussed at 4.8 below.

A Special purpose entities (SPEs)

As discussed more fully in Chapter 5 at 3.2, the IASB (or strictly, its predecessor the IASC), like many national standard setters before it, has had to address the issue of an entity conducting its affairs through a vehicle that, though not meeting the definition of a subsidiary, is still controlled by the entity. Under IFRS such an entity is referred to as an SPE. SPEs are the subject of SIC-12, which requires an entity to consolidate an SPE when the substance of the relationship between them indicates that the entity controls the SPE.[41] SPEs are commonly used in transactions such as securitisations and debt sub-participations (see 4.4.3 below).

Figure 1:   *Flowchart*

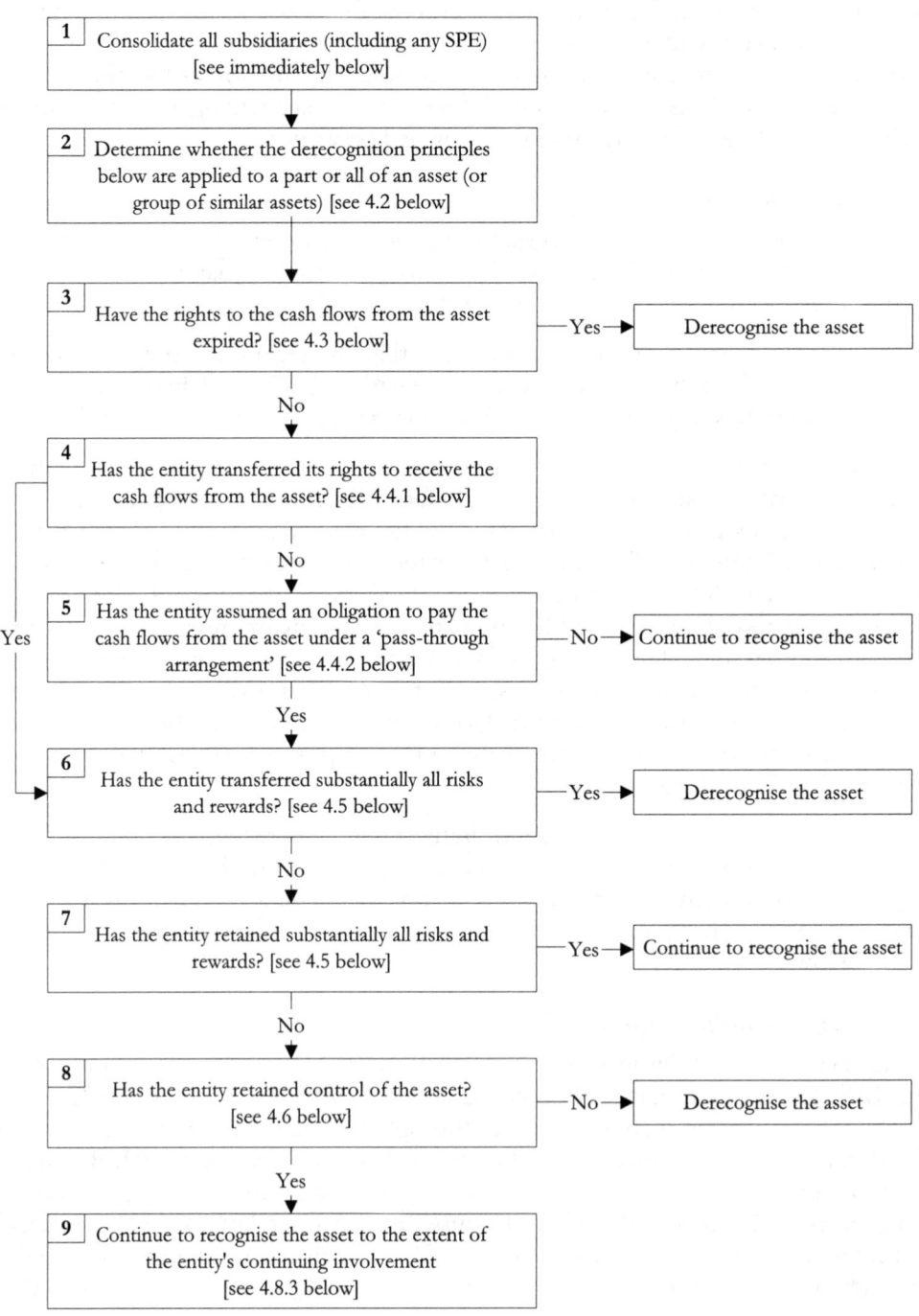

4.1.3   *Importance of applying tests in sequence*

As noted at 2.1.1 above, the derecognition rules in IAS 39 are based on several different accounting concepts, in particular a 'risks and rewards' model and a 'control' model, which may lead to opposite conclusions.

For example, an entity (A) might have a portfolio of listed securities for which there is a deep liquid market. It might enter into a contract with a third party counterparty (B) on the following terms. A sells the portfolio to B for €10 million, agreeing to repurchase it in two years' time for €10 million plus interest at market rates on €10 million less dividends on the shares.

The nature of the portfolio is such that B is able to sell it to third parties (since it will easily be able to reacquire the necessary shares to deliver back to A under the repurchase agreement). This indicates that B has control over the portfolio and therefore, since the same asset cannot be controlled by more than one party, that A does not. Thus, under a 'control' model of derecognition, A would derecognise the portfolio.

However, the nature of the repurchase agreement is also such that A is exposed to all the economic risks and rewards of the portfolio as if it had never been sold to B (since the repurchase price effectively returns to A all dividends paid on the portfolio, and all movements in its market value, during its period of ownership by B). Thus, under a 'risks and rewards' model of derecognition, A would continue to recognise the portfolio.

IAS 39 seeks to avoid the potential conflict between those accounting models by the practically effective, if intellectually rather crude, requirement to consider them in the strict sequence in the flowchart in 4.1.2 above – i.e. the 'risks and rewards' model first and the 'control' model second. Thus, as will be seen from the discussion below (particularly at 4.7 and 4.8), if an entity (A) transfers an asset to a third party (B) on terms that B is free to sell or pledge the asset:

- if A retains substantially all the risks and rewards of the asset (i.e. the answer to Box 7 in the flowchart in 'Yes'), B's right to sell or pledge is irrelevant and the asset continues to be recognised by A, but

- if A has neither transferred nor retained substantially all the risks and rewards of the asset (i.e. the answer to Box 7 in the flowchart is 'No'), B's right to sell or pledge is highly relevant, indicating a loss of control over the asset by A (i.e. the answer to Box 8 in the flowchart is 'No'), such that A derecognises the asset.

In other words, depending on the reporting entity's position in the decision tree at 4.1.2 above, the fact that B has the right to sell the sell or pledge the asset is either irrelevant or leads directly to derecognition of the asset by A. It is therefore crucial that the various asset derecognition tests in IAS 39 are applied in the order required by IAS 39.

4.2   Are the derecognition principles applied to all or part of an asset?

The discussion in this section relates to Box 2 in the flowchart at 4.1.2 above.

IAS 39 requires an entity, before evaluating whether, and to what extent, derecognition is appropriate under the provisions discussed at 4.3 and following below, to determine whether those provisions should be applied to the whole, or a part only, of a financial asset (or a part of a group of similar financial assets).

It is important to remember throughout the discussion in 4.3 that these are criteria for determining at what level the derecognition rules should be applied, not for determining whether the conditions in those rules have been satisfied.

The derecognition provisions must be applied to a part of a financial asset (or a part of a group of similar financial assets) if, and only if, the part being considered for derecognition meets one of the three conditions set out in (a) to (c) below:

(a)   The part comprises only specifically identified cash flows from a financial asset (or a group of similar financial assets).

For example, if an entity enters into an interest rate strip whereby the counterparty obtains the right to the interest cash flows, but not the principal cash flows, from a debt instrument, the derecognition provisions are applied to the interest cash flows.

(b)   The part comprises only a fully proportionate (pro rata) share of the cash flows from a financial asset (or a group of similar financial assets).

For example, if an entity enters into an arrangement in which the counterparty obtains the rights to 90% of all cash flows of a debt instrument, the derecognition provisions are applied to 90% of those cash flows. If there is more than one counterparty, it is not necessary for each counterparty to have a proportionate share of the cash flows provided that the transferring entity has a fully proportionate share. In other words, the test in this case would be whether the reporting entity has retained a 10% proportionate share of the total cash flows.

(c)   The part comprises only a fully proportionate (pro rata) share of specifically identified cash flows from a financial asset (or a group of similar financial assets).

For example, if an entity enters into an arrangement whereby the counterparty obtains the rights to a 90% share of interest cash flows from a financial asset, the derecognition provisions are applied to 90% of those interest cash flows. If there is more than one counterparty, it is not necessary for each counterparty to have a proportionate share of the specifically identified cash flows provided that the transferring entity has a fully proportionate share. In other words, the test is ultimately whether the reporting entity has retained a 10% proportionate share of the interest cash flows.

If none of the criteria in (a) to (c) above is met, the derecognition provisions are applied to the financial asset in its entirety (or to the group of similar financial assets in their entirety).

For example, if an entity transfers the rights to the first or the last 90% of cash collections from a financial asset (or a group of financial assets), or the rights to 90% of the cash flows from a group of receivables, but provides a guarantee to compensate the buyer for any credit losses up to 8% of the principal amount of the receivables, the derecognition provisions are applied to the financial asset (or a group of similar financial assets) in its entirety.[42]

The various examples above illustrate that the tests in (a) to (c) are to be applied very strictly. It is essential that the entity transfers 100%, or a lower fixed proportion, of a definable cash flow. In the arrangement in the previous paragraph, the transferor provides a guarantee the effect of which is that the transferor may have to return some part of the consideration it has already received. This has the effect that the derecognition provisions must be applied to the asset in its entirety and not just to the proportion of cash flows transferred. If the guarantee had not been given, the arrangement would have satisfied condition (b) above, and the derecognition provisions would have been applied only to the 90% of cash flows transferred.

4.2.1 Credit enhancement through transferor's waiver of right to future cash flows

IAS 39 gives an illustrative example, the substance of which is reproduced as Example 16.18 at 4.8.4 D below, of the accounting treatment of a transaction in which 90% of the cash flows of a portfolio of loans are sold. All cash collections are allocated 90:10 to the transferee and transferor respectively, but subject to any losses on the loans being fully allocated to the transferor until its 10% retained interest in the portfolio is reduced to zero, and only then allocated to the transferee. IAS 39 indicates that in this case it is appropriate to apply the derecognition criteria to the 90% sold, rather than the portfolio as whole.

At first sight, this seems inconsistent with the position in the scenario just discussed, where application of the derecognition criteria to the 90% transferred is precluded by the transferor's having given a guarantee to the transferee. Is not the arrangement in Example 16.18 below (whereby the transferor may have to cede some of its right to receive future cash flows to the transferee) a guarantee in all but name?

Whilst IAS 39 does not expand on this explicitly, the reasoning must be that the two transactions are distinguished as follows:

(a)   the transaction in Example 16.18 may result in the transferor losing the right to receive a future cash inflow, whereas a guarantee arrangement may give rise to an obligation to return a past cash inflow;

(b)   the transaction in Example 16.18 gives the transferee a greater chance of recovering its full 90% share, but does not guarantee that it will do so. For example, if only 85% of the portfolio is recovered, the transferor is under no obligation to make up the shortfall.

It may be worth reminding readers that we are here addressing the issue of whether or not the derecognition criteria should be applied to all or part of an asset, not whether derecognition is actually achieved. In many cases an asset transferred subject to a guarantee would not satisfy the derecognition criteria, since the guarantee would mean that the transferor had not transferred substantially all the risks of the asset. For derecognition to be possible, the scope of the guarantee would need to be restricted so that some significant risks are passed to the transferee.

4.2.2   *Transfer of asset (or part of asset) for only part of its life*

The examples given in IAS 39 implicitly appear have in mind the transfer of a tranche of cash flows from the date of transfer for the remainder of the life of an instrument. This raises the question of the appropriate accounting treatment where (for example) an entity with a loan receivable repayable in 10 years' time enters into a transaction whereby all the interest flows for the next 5 years only (or those for years 6 to 10) are transferred to a third party. In our view, there is no reason why such a transaction could not be considered for partial derecognition.

4.2.3   *'Financial asset' includes whole or part of a financial asset in 4.3 to 4.8 below*

In the derecognition provisions in IAS 39, and the discussion in 4.3. to 4.8 below, the term 'financial asset' is used to refer to either the whole, or a part, of a financial asset (or a part of a group of similar financial assets).[43] It is therefore important to remember throughout the following discussion that a reference to an asset being derecognised 'in its entirety' does not necessarily mean that 100% of the asset is derecognised. It may mean, for example, that there has been full derecognition of, say, 80% of the asset to which the derecognition rules have applied separately (in accordance the criteria above).

4.3   Have the contractual rights to cash flows from the asset expired?

The discussion in this section refers to Box 3 in the flowchart at 4.1.2 above.

The first step in determining whether derecognition of a financial asset is appropriate is to establish whether the contractual rights to the cash flows from that asset have expired. If they have, the asset is derecognised. Examples might be:

- a loan receivable is repaid;
- the holder of a perpetual debt, whose terms provide for ten annual 'interest' payments that, in effect, provide both interest and a return of capital, receives the final payment of interest; or
- a purchased option expires unexercised.

If the cash flows from the financial asset have not expired, it is derecognised when, and only when, the entity 'transfers' the asset within the specified meaning of the term in IAS 39 (see 4.4 below), and the transfer has the effect that the entity has either:

- transferred substantially all the risks and rewards of the asset (see 4.5 below); or
- neither transferred nor retained substantially all the risks and rewards of the asset (see 4.5 below), and has not retained control of the asset (see 4.6 below).[44]

4.4   Has the entity 'transferred' the asset?

An entity is regarded by IAS 39 as 'transferring' a financial asset if, and only if, it either:

(a)   transfers the contractual rights to receive the cash flows of the financial asset (see 4.4.1 below); or

(b)   retains the contractual rights to receive the cash flows of the financial asset, but assumes a contractual obligation to pay the cash flows on to one or more recipients in an arrangement that meets the conditions in 4.4.2 below[45] (a so-called 'pass-through arrangement')

> This might be the case where the entity is a special purpose entity or trust, and issues to investors beneficial interests in financial assets that it owns and provides servicing of those assets,[46] as typically happens in securitisation transactions (see 4.4.3 below).

4.4.1   *Transfers of contractual rights to receive cash flows*

The discussion in this section refers to Box 4 in the flowchart at 4.1.2 above.

IAS 39 does not define what it means by the phrase 'transfers the contractual rights to receive the cash flows of the financial asset' in (a) above, possibly on the assumption that this is self-evident. However, this is far from the case, since the phrase raises a number of questions of interpretation.

This has become a real issue in connection with securitisations and other transactions using 'pass through arrangements' (see 4.4.2 and 4.4.3 below). It will be seen, by reference to the decision tree in 4.1.2 above, that a reporting entity seeking to derecognise a financial asset subject to such an arrangement must determine (in order):

(a)   whether or not it has transferred the contractual rights to receive the cash flows of the financial asset (if so, it derecognises the asset, if not, it considers (b) below); then

(b)   whether or not the transaction satisfies the requirements for 'pass-through arrangements'.

Following the publication of the June 2002 exposure draft of proposed changes to IAS 32 and IAS 39 (see Chapter 15 at 1.5), it was assumed that the analysis for most securitisations and similar transactions would be that they do not satisfy (a) above, but do satisfy (b), allowing derecognition of the assets concerned. However, as discussed further at 4.4.2 and 4.4.3 D below, it now appears that many securitisations and similar transactions will not in fact satisfy the tests for 'pass through arrangements' in the final form in which they appear in IAS 39.

This has the effect that a financial asset subject to a transaction involving a 'pass through arrangement' that fails the tests in 4.4.2 below can be derecognised under IAS 39 only if it can be shown that contractual rights to receive the cash flows of the asset have been 'transferred' – i.e. the transaction meets test (a) above. This has created a strong incentive for entities that enter into such transactions to argue that they have transferred the cash flows relating to the financial assets concerned.

This raises a number of questions. The first is whether it is a 'legal' or 'economic' test – in other words:

- is it sufficient that the cash flows have been transferred as a matter of law; or

- does the transfer have to satisfy certain minimum, and objectively determinable, economic criteria?

If it is a legal test, further issues are raised. The requirement to transfer 'the contractual rights to receive cash flows' suggests that it is necessary for the transfer to have the effect that the transferee has a direct legal claim on those cash flows. On this interpretation, if a bank securitises (see 4.4.3 below) the future cash flows from a portfolio of credit cards, it has arguably 'transferred' them for the purposes of IAS 39 if and only if the finance provider could, directly and in its own name, sue the credit card account holder for default. In many jurisdictions, this would simply not be possible without either:

- a tri-partite agreement between the bank, the finance provider and the cardholder, or

- a clause in the standard terms and conditions of the credit card allowing such transfer at the sole discretion of the bank without the express consent of the cardholder, allowing transfer to be affected by a subsequent bi-partite agreement between the bank and the finance provider.

4.4.2 Retention of rights to receive cash flows subject to obligation to pay over to others ('pass-through arrangement')

The discussion in this section refers to Box 5 in the flowchart at 4.1.2 above.

It is common in certain securitisation and debt sub-participation transactions (see 4.4.3 below) for an entity to enter into an arrangement whereby it continues to collect cash receipts from a financial asset (or more typically a pool of financial assets), but is obliged to pass on those receipts to a third party that has provided finance in connection with the financial asset.

Under IAS 39, an arrangement whereby the reporting entity retains the contractual rights to receive the cash flows of a financial asset (the 'original asset'), but assumes a contractual obligation to pay the cash flows to one or more recipients (the 'eventual recipients') is regarded as a transfer of the original asset if, and only if, all of the following three conditions are met:

(a)   the entity has no obligation to pay amounts to the eventual recipients unless it collects equivalent amounts from the original asset. Short-term advances by the entity with the right of full recovery of the amount lent plus accrued interest at market rates do not violate this condition (see 4.4.3 A and B below);

(b)   the entity is prohibited by the terms of the transfer contract from selling or pledging the original asset other than as security to the eventual recipients for the obligation to pay them cash flows; and

(c)   the entity has an obligation to remit any cash flows it collects on behalf of the eventual recipients without material delay. In addition, the entity is not entitled to reinvest such cash flows, except in cash or cash equivalents as defined in IAS 7 – *Cash Flow Statements* (see Chapter 32 at 2.2.1) during the short settlement period from the collection date to the date of required remittance to the eventual recipients, with any interest earned on such investments being passed to the eventual recipients.[47]

See also the further discussion at 4.4.3 D below.

These conditions first appeared in paragraph 41 of the June 2002 exposure draft of proposed amendments to IAS 32 and IAS 39 (see Chapter 15 at 1.5), where they were referred to as a 'pass-through arrangement'. Whilst this term does not actually appear in the revised version of IAS 39 it has become part of the language of the financial markets to refer to such transactions as 'pass-through arrangements'. However, it should be noted that condition (c) above is slightly more onerous than that in the June 2002 exposure draft in that:

• the exposure draft proposed merely a prohibition on investment for the benefit of the transferor, but

• IAS 39 not only prohibits investment for the benefit of the transferor, but also restricts any investment made for the benefit of the transferee to cash or cash equivalents. This means that many current securitisation arrangements will fail the pass-through test – see 4.4.3 D below.

IAS 39 notes that an entity that is required to consider the impact of these conditions on a transaction is likely to be either:

• the originator of the financial asset in a securitisation transaction (see 4.4.3 below); or

• a group that includes a consolidated special purpose entity that has acquired the financial asset and passes on cash flows to unrelated third party investors.[48]

Indeed, conditions (a) to (c) above, although applicable to any transaction to which they are relevant, have clearly been framed in the context of securitisation transactions (see 4.4.3 below).

4.4.3   *Securitisations*

Securitisation is a process whereby finance can be raised from external investors by enabling them to invest in parcels of specific financial assets. The first main type of assets to be securitised was domestic mortgage loans, but the technique is regularly extended to other assets, such as credit card receivables, other consumer loans, or lease receivables. Securitisations are a complex area of financial reporting beyond the scope of a general text such as this to discuss in detail. However, it may assist understanding of the IASB's thinking to consider a 'generic' example of such a transaction.

A typical securitisation transaction involving a portfolio of mortgage loans would operate as follows. The entity which has initially advanced the loans in question (the 'originator') will sell them to another entity set up for the purpose (the 'issuer'). The issuer will typically be a subsidiary or SPE of the originator (and therefore consolidated – see 4.1.2 above) and its equity share capital will be small. The issuer will finance its purchase of these loans by issuing loan notes on interest terms which will be related to the rate of interest receivable on the mortgages. The originator will continue to administer the loans as before, for which it will receive a service fee.

The structure might therefore be as shown in this diagram:

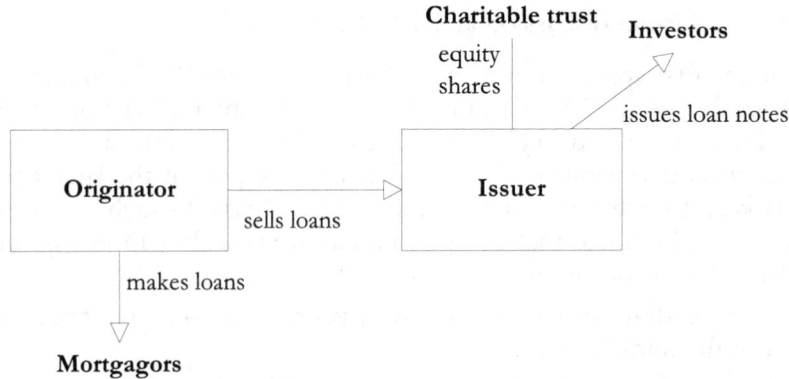

Potential investors in the mortgage-backed loan notes will want to be assured that their investment is relatively risk-free, and the issue will normally be supported by obtaining a high rating from a credit rating agency. This may be achieved by use of a range of credit enhancement techniques which will add to the security already inherent in the quality of the mortgage portfolio. Such techniques can include the following:

- limited recourse to the originator in the event that the income from the mortgages falls short of the interest payable to the investors under the loan notes and other expenses. This may be made available in a number of ways; for example, by the provision of subordinated loan finance from the originator to the issuer; by the deferral of part of the consideration for the sale of the mortgages; or by the provision of a guarantee (see A below);

- the provision of loan facilities to meet temporary shortfalls as a result of slow payments of mortgage interest (see B below); or

- insurance against default on the mortgages (see C below).

The overall effect of the arrangement is that outside investors have been brought in to finance a particular portion of the originator's activities. These investors have first call on the income from the mortgages which back their investment. The originator is left with only the residual interest in the differential between the rates paid on the notes and earned on the mortgages, net of expenses; generally, this profit element is extracted by adjustments to the service fee or through the mechanism of interest rate swaps. It has thus limited its upside interest in the mortgages, while its remaining downside risk on the whole arrangement will depend on the extent to which it has assumed obligations under the credit enhancement measures.

A   Recourse to originator

The conditions in 4.4.2 clearly have the effect that an arrangement that provides for direct recourse to the originator does not meet the definition of a 'transfer' in IAS 39 and therefore does not qualify to be considered for derecognition. Direct recourse would include an arrangement whereby part of the consideration for the financial asset transferred was deferred depending on the performance of the asset, as illustrated by Example 16.4 below.

Example 16.4:   Securitisation with deferred consideration

An originator wishes to securitise 90% of a particular portfolio of its credit card receivables. Outside investors agree to pay for 85% of the receivables immediately (with no further recourse to the originator in the event that less than 85% recovery is achieved), with the further 5% to be paid to the extent that the receivables are recovered. Under such an arrangement, IAS 39 would regard 85% of the portfolio at most as having been transferred (subject to the other conditions in 4.4.1 above having been met). This is entirely appropriate, since the originator clearly remains exposed to all the risks associated with recoveries in the range 85%-90% of the portfolio.

In our view, however, certain techniques for providing indirect recourse do not breach the conditions for transfer. These include:

(i)   the originator waiving its right to receive cash flows on any retained portion of the portfolio to the extent of any losses suffered by the investors (but providing no other guarantee – see 4.2.1 above; or

(ii)   the provision of certain types of insurance (see C below).

B   Short-term loan facilities

Under IAS 39 (see 4.4.2 above) it is permissible to enhance a securitised asset with the provision of loan facilities to meet temporary shortfalls as a result of slow payments from the asset, but only where the loans are:

- made on a 'short-term' basis;
- repayable irrespective of whether the slow payments are eventually received; and
- bear interest at market rates.

The purpose of these restrictions is to ensure that IAS 39 allows derecognition of assets subject to such facilities only where the facilities are providing a short-term cash flow benefit to the investor, and not when they effectively transfer slow payment risk back to the originator (as would be the case if the originator made significant interest-free loans to the investor).

C   Insurance protection

The conditions for 'transfer' are not, in our view, breached by the originator purchasing an insurance contract for the benefit of investors in the event of a shortfall in cash collections from the securitised assets, provided that the investors' only recourse is to the insurance policy. In other words, the originator cannot give a guarantee to investors to make good any shortfalls should the insurer become insolvent, nor can the originator provide any support to the insurer through a guarantee arrangement or a reinsurance contract.

D   Treatment of collection proceeds

Securitisation contracts rarely require any amount received on the securitised assets to be immediately transferred to investors. This is for the obvious practical reason that it would be administratively inefficient, in the case of a securitisation of credit card receivables for example, to transfer the relevant portion of each individual, and relatively small, cash flow received from the hundreds, if not thousands, of cards in the portfolio. Instead, it is usual for transfers to be made in bulk on a periodic basis (e.g. weekly or monthly). This raises the question of what happens to the cash in the period between receipt by the issuer and onward transfer to the investors.

IAS 39 requires cash flows from transferred financial assets for which derecognition is sought to be:

- passed to the eventual recipients 'without material delay', and

- invested only in cash or cash equivalents as defined in IAS 7 entirely for the benefit of the investors (see condition (c) in 4.4.2 above).

These requirements mean that many securitisation arrangements may well fail to satisfy the 'pass through' test in 4.4.2 above, as explained below.

Suppose that a credit card issuer wishes to raise 5-year finance secured on its portfolio of credit card receivables. The assets concerned are essentially short term (being in most cases settled in full within 4 to 8 weeks), whereas the term of the borrowings secured on them is longer. In practice, what generally happens is that at the start of the securitisation a 'pool' of balances is transferred to the issuer. The cash receipts from that 'pool' are used to pay interest on the borrowings, and to fund new advances on cards in the 'pool' or to purchase other balances. Such an arrangement appears to breach the requirement of the 'pass through' tests:

(a)   to pass on cash receipts without material delay (since only the amount of cash receipts necessary to pay the interest on the borrowings is passed on, with the balance being reinvested until the principal of the borrowings falls due); and

(b)   only to invest in cash or cash equivalents as defined in IAS 7 (since the cash not required to pay interest on the borrowings is invested in further credit card receivables, which are not cash or cash equivalents as defined in IAS 7).

Any arrangement that provides for even a small tranche of the interest from such short-term deposits to be retained by or for the benefit of the originator will not satisfy the criteria for transfer under IAS 39. Moreover, IAS 39 requires that the reporting entity 'is not entitled' to invest the cash other than as described in condition (c) in 4.4.2 above. Thus, it appears that the criteria for transfer are not satisfied merely where the entity does not in fact invest the cash in any other way – it must be contractually prohibited from doing so. In practice, this is often achieved by having the funds paid into a trustee bank account that can be used only for the benefit of the providers of finance.

The strict requirements of IAS 39 in respect of cash received from assets subject to a 'pass-through arrangement' raise the related, but broader, issue of the appropriate treatment, under IAS 39, of client money (see 4.4.5 below).

4.4.4   'Empty' SPEs

If an entity enters into a transaction whereby:

- the entity transfers an asset to an SPE, and

- the SPE transfers the asset to noteholders on terms that satisfy the 'pass through' derecognition criteria in IAS 39 discussed at 4.4.2 and 4.4.3 above,

the overall effect will be that the individual financial statements of the SPE will not include either the transferred asset or the finance raised from noteholders. This may well mean that the financial statements show nothing apart from the relatively small amount of equity of the entity and any related assets.

This, at first sight, rather strange result is perfectly consistent with SIC 12's analysis that the SPE is no more than an extension of the originating entity rather than an economic entity in its own right. Nevertheless, investors in loan notes issued by the SPE may be disturbed by the lack of any acknowledgement in the SPE's financial statements of its liability to them!

4.4.5   Client money

A number of financial institutions and other entities hold money on behalf of clients. The terms on which such money is held can vary widely. In the case of normal deposits with a bank, the bank is free to use the client's money for any purpose, with the client being protected by the solvency margin requirements imposed by the regulatory authorities. By contrast there are cases (e.g. in the case of certain monies held by legal advisers on behalf of their clients in some jurisdictions) where funds held on behalf of clients must be kept in a bank account completely separate from that of the depositary entity itself, with all interest earned on the account being for the benefit of clients. There are also intermediate situations where, for example:

- funds are required to be segregated in separate bank accounts but the depositary entity is allowed to retain some or all of the interest on the client accounts, or

- client funds are allowed to be commingled with those of the depositary entity, but some or all income on the funds must be passed on to clients.

This raises the question of how client monies should be accounted for in the financial statements under IFRS, and whether, in the absence of specific guidance the rules for the treatment of funds received under a 'pass-through arrangement' (see 4.4.3 D above) should be applied.

In our view, the types of arrangement to deal with client money are so varied that it is impossible to generalise as to the appropriate treatment. However, the analysis for the two extreme cases seems relatively straightforward. In the case of a bank deposit (or any arrangement where the entity may freely use client cash for its own benefit), the general recognition criteria of IAS 39 indicate that an asset and a liability should be recognised. Conversely, where the entity is required to hold funds held on behalf of clients in a bank account completely separate from that of the entity itself, with all interest earned on the account being for the benefit of clients, it is hard to see how such funds meet the general definition of an asset under the *Framework*. The entity controls such funds, but can derive no economic benefits from them. This might lead to the conclusion that such funds (and the related liability to the clients) should not be recognised in the financial statements. It is, however, important to have regard to the fact that the entity may be assuming significant risks in connection with such funds – i.e. it will be fully liable for any loss or misappropriation of them. This might lead to the opposite conclusion that recognition of the funds is appropriate, with a corresponding liability to the client. It might also be relevant to any analysis to consider the status of the funds in the event of the insolvency of either the reporting entity or the client.

The intermediate cases may be harder to deal with but in general the appropriate analysis is likely to be that the depositary entity enjoys sufficient use of the client money that it should be recognised as an asset with a corresponding liability due to the client.

4.5   Has the entity transferred or retained substantially all the risks and rewards of ownership?

The discussion in this section refers to Boxes 6 and 7 in the flowchart at 4.1.2 above.

Once an entity has established that it has transferred a financial asset (see 4.4 above), IAS 39 then requires it to evaluate the extent to which it retains the risks and rewards of ownership of the financial asset.[49]

If the entity transfers substantially all the risks and rewards of ownership of the financial asset, the entity must derecognise the financial asset and recognise separately as assets or liabilities any rights and obligations created or retained in the transfer.[50] Examples of such transactions are given at 4.5.1, 4.7 and 4.8 below. If an entity determines that, as a result of the transfer, it has transferred substantially all the risks and rewards of ownership of the transferred asset, it does not recognise the transferred asset again in a future period, unless it reacquires the transferred asset in a new transaction.[51]

If the entity retains substantially all the risks and rewards of ownership of the financial asset, the entity continues to recognise the financial asset.[52] Examples of such transactions are given at 4.5.2, 4.7 and 4.8 below.

If the entity neither transfers nor retains substantially all the risks and rewards of ownership of the financial asset (see 4.5.3 below), the entity determines whether it has retained control of the financial asset[53] (see 4.6 below).

IAS 39 clarifies that the transfer of risks and rewards should be evaluated by comparing the entity's exposure, before and after the transfer, to the variability in the amounts and timing of the net cash flows of the transferred asset.[54] Often it will be obvious whether the entity has transferred or retained substantially all risks and rewards of ownership. In other cases, it will be necessary to determine this by computing and comparing the entity's exposure to the variability in the present value (discounted at an appropriate current market interest rate) of the future net cash flows before and after the transfer. All reasonably possible variability in net cash flows is considered, with greater weight being given to those outcomes that are more likely to occur.[55]

4.5.1   *Transfers resulting in transfer of substantially all risks and rewards*

An entity has transferred substantially all the risks and rewards of ownership of a financial asset if its exposure to the variability in the amounts and timing of the net cash flows of the transferred asset is no longer significant in relation to the total such variability. IAS 39 gives the following examples of transactions that transfer substantially all the risks and rewards of ownership:

- an unconditional sale of a financial asset;

- a sale of a financial asset together with an option to repurchase the financial asset at its fair value at the time of repurchase (since this does not expose the entity to any risk of loss or give any opportunity for profit);

- a sale of a financial asset together with a put or call option that is deeply out of the money (i.e. an option that is so far out of the money it is highly unlikely to go into the money before expiry); or

- the sale of a fully proportionate share of the cash flows from a larger financial asset in an arrangement, such as a loan sub-participation, that satisfies the criteria for a 'transfer' in 4.4.2 above.[56]

Such transactions are discussed in more detail at 4.7 below.

It is important to note that, in order for derecognition to be achieved, it is necessary that the entity's exposure to the variability in the amounts and timing of the net cash flows of the transferred asset is considered not in isolation, but 'in relation to the total such variability' (see above). Thus derecognition is not achieved simply because the entity's remaining exposure to the risks or rewards of an asset is small in absolute terms.

4.5.2   *Transfers resulting in retention of substantially all risks and rewards*

An entity has retained substantially all the risks and rewards of ownership of a financial asset if its exposure to the variability in the present value of the future net cash flows from the financial asset does not change significantly as a result of the transfer. IAS 39 gives the following examples of transactions in which an entity has retained substantially all the risks and rewards of ownership:

- a sale and repurchase transaction where the repurchase price is a fixed price or the sale price plus a lender's return;

- a securities lending agreement;

- a sale of a financial asset together with a total return swap that transfers the market risk exposure back to the entity;

- a sale of a financial asset together with a deeply in the money put or call option (i.e. an option that is so far in the money that it is highly unlikely to go out of the money before expiry). It will be in the holder's interest to exercise such an option, so that the asset will almost certainly revert to the transferor; and

- a sale of short-term receivables in which the entity guarantees to compensate the transferee for credit losses that are likely to occur.[57]

Such transactions are discussed in more detail at 4.7 below.

4.5.3 *Transfers resulting in neither transfer nor retention of substantially all risks and rewards*

IAS 39 gives the following examples of transactions in which an entity has neither transferred nor retained substantially all the risks and rewards of ownership:

- a sale of a financial asset together with a put or call option that is neither deeply in the money nor deeply out of the money.[58] The effect of such an option is that the transferor will have either (in the case of purchased call option) capped its exposure to a loss in value of the asset but have potentially unlimited access to increases in value or (in the case of a written put option) capped its potential access to increases in value in the asset but assumed potential exposure to a total loss in value of the asset; and

- a sale of 90% of a loan portfolio with significant transfer of prepayment risk, but retention of a 10% interest, with losses allocated first to that 10% retained interest.[59]

Such transactions are discussed in more detail at 4.7 below.

4.6   Has the entity retained control of the asset?

The discussion in this section relates to Boxes 8 and 9 of the flowchart at 4.1.2 above.

If the transferring entity has neither transferred nor retained substantially all the risks and rewards of a transferred financial asset, IAS 39 requires the entity to determine whether or not it has retained control of the financial asset. If the entity has not retained control, it must derecognise the financial asset and recognise separately as assets or liabilities any rights and obligations created or retained in the transfer. If the entity has retained control, it must continue to recognise the financial asset to the extent of its continuing involvement in the financial asset (see 4.8.3 below).[60]

IAS 39 requires the question of whether the entity has retained control of the transferred asset to be determined by the transferee's ability to sell the asset. If the transferee:

- has the practical ability to sell the asset in its entirety to an unrelated third party, and

- is able to exercise that ability unilaterally and without needing to impose additional restrictions on the transfer,

the entity has not retained control (see 4.6.1 below).

In all other cases, the entity has retained control.[61]

4.6.1 Transferee's 'practical ability' to sell the asset

IAS 39 clarifies that, in order for the transferee to have the practical ability to sell a transferred asset, the asset must be traded in an active market, on the basis that the transferee must have the ability to repurchase the transferred asset in the market if it needs to return the asset to the entity. For example, if a transferred asset is sold subject to an option that allows the entity to repurchase it:

- the transferee may (subject to the further considerations discussed below) have the practical ability to sell the asset if it can readily obtain the transferred asset in the market if the option is exercised, but

- the transferee does not have the practical ability to sell the transferred asset if it cannot readily obtain the transferred asset in the market if the option is exercised.[62]

Moreover, the transferee has the practical ability to sell the transferred asset only if the transferee can sell the transferred asset in its entirety to an unrelated third party and is able to exercise that ability unilaterally and without imposing additional restrictions on the transfer. IAS 39 requires that to be determined by considering what the transferee is able to do in practice, rather than by reference to any contractual rights or prohibitions. For example, the standard notes that a contractual right to dispose of the transferred asset has little practical effect if there is no market for the transferred asset.[63]

IAS 39 goes on to point out that an ability to dispose of the transferred asset also has little practical effect if it cannot be exercised freely. Accordingly, the transferee's ability to dispose of the transferred asset must be a unilateral ability independent of the actions of others. In other words, the transferee must be able to dispose of the transferred asset without needing to attach conditions to the transfer (e.g. conditions about how a loan asset is serviced, or an option giving the transferee the right to repurchase the asset).[64]

For example, the entity might sell a financial asset to a transferee subject to the transferee having the benefit of an option to put the asset back to the entity or a performance guarantee from the entity. IAS 39 argues that such an option or guarantee might be so valuable to the transferee that the transferee would not, in practice, sell the transferred asset to a third party without attaching a similar option or other restrictive conditions. Instead, the transferee would hold the transferred asset so as to obtain payments under the guarantee or put option. Under these circumstances IAS 39 regards the transferor as having retained control of the transferred asset.[65]

However, IAS 39 notes that the fact that the transferee is simply unlikely to sell the transferred asset does not, of itself, mean that the transferor has retained control of the transferred asset.[66]

4.7 Practical application of the derecognition criteria

IAS 39 gives a number of practical examples of the application of the derecognition criteria in IAS 39, which are discussed below. In some cases, it has to be said that the guidance in IAS 39 is less than satisfactory, amounting to little more than repetition of the standard.

In order to provide a link with the flowchart at 4.1.2 above we have used the following convention:

'Box 6, Yes'   the transaction would result in the answer 'Yes' at Box 6 in the flowchart

'Box 7, No'   the transaction would result in the answer 'No' at Box 7 in the flowchart

4.7.1   *Repurchase agreements ('repos') and securities lending*

A   Agreements to return the same asset

If a financial asset is:

*   sold under an agreement to repurchase it at a fixed price or at the sale price plus a lender's return, or

*   loaned under an agreement to return it to the transferor,

the asset is not derecognised, because the transferor retains substantially all the risks and rewards of ownership[67] (Figure 1, Box 7, Yes). The accounting treatment of such transactions is discussed in Example 16.12 at 4.8.2 below.

I   Transferee's right to pledge

If the transferee obtains the right to sell or pledge an asset that is the subject of such a transaction, the transferor reclassifies the asset on its balance sheet, for example, as a loaned asset or repurchase receivable.[68]

It appears that this accounting treatment is required merely where the transferee has the 'right' to sell or pledge the asset. This contrasts with the requirements for determining whether an asset subject to a transaction in which the entity neither transfers nor retains substantially all the risks and rewards associated with the asset (Figure 1, Box 7, No) nevertheless qualifies for derecognition because the transferee has control (Figure 1, Box 8, Yes). In order for the transferee to be regarded as having control for the purposes of Box 8, any rights of the transferee to sell or pledge as asset must have economic substance – see 4.6 above.

The accounting treatment of such transactions is discussed in Example 16.12 at 4.8.2 below.

B   *Agreements with right to return the same or substantially the same asset*

If a financial asset is:

- sold under an agreement to repurchase the same or substantially the same asset at a fixed price or at the sale price plus a lender's return, or

- loaned under an agreement to return the same or substantially the same asset to the transferor,

the asset is not derecognised because the transferor retains substantially all the risks and rewards of ownership[69] (Figure 1, Box 7, Yes). The accounting treatment of such transactions is discussed in Example 16.12 at 4.8.2 below.

C   *Agreements with right of substitution*

If a financial asset is the subject of:

- a repurchase agreement at a fixed repurchase price or a price equal to the sale price plus a lender's return, or

- a similar securities lending transaction

that provides the transferee with a right to substitute assets that are similar and of equal fair value to the transferred asset at the repurchase date, the asset sold or lent is not derecognised because the transferor retains substantially all the risks and rewards of ownership[70] (Figure 1, Box 7, Yes). The accounting treatment of such transactions is discussed at 4.8.1 below.

D   *Net cash-settled forward repurchase*

IAS 39 gives some guidance on the treatment of net cash-settled options over transferred assets (see 4.7.2 E below), which in passing refers to net cash-settled forward contracts. This guidance says that that key factor remains whether or not the entity has transferred substantially all the risks and rewards of the transferred asset.[71] This suggests that an asset sold subject to a fixed price net-settled forward contract to reacquire it should not be derecognised (see A to C above) until the contract is settled (Figure 1, Box 7, Yes).

The accounting treatment of such transactions is discussed in Example 16.12 at 4.8.2 below.

E   *Agreement to repurchase at fair value*

A transfer of a financial asset subject only to a forward repurchase agreement with a repurchase price equal to the fair value of the financial asset at the time of repurchase results in derecognition because of the transfer of substantially all the risks and rewards of ownership[72] (Figure 1, Box 6, Yes). The accounting treatment of such transactions is discussed at 4.8.1 below.

F Right of first refusal to repurchase at fair value

If an entity sells a financial asset and retains only a right of first refusal to repurchase the transferred asset at fair value if the transferee subsequently sells it, the entity derecognises the asset because it has transferred substantially all the risks and rewards of ownership[73] (Figure 1, Box 6, Yes).

IAS 39 does not address the treatment of a financial asset sold with a right of first refusal to repurchase the transferred asset at a predetermined value that might well be lower or higher than fair value (e.g. an amount estimated, at the time at which the original transaction was entered into, as the future market value of the asset). One analysis might be that, since the transferee is under no obligation to put the asset up for sale, derecognition is still appropriate. Another analysis might be that, if the asset can ultimately only be realised by onward sale, the arrangement is nearer in substance to a transferor's call option (see 4.7.2 below).

G Wash sale

A 'wash sale' is the repurchase of a financial asset shortly after it has been sold. Such a repurchase does not preclude derecognition provided that the original transaction met the derecognition requirements. However, if an agreement to sell a financial asset is entered into concurrently with an agreement to repurchase the same asset at a fixed price or the sale price plus a lender's return, then the asset is not derecognised.[74] Such a transaction would be equivalent to those in A to D above.

4.7.2 Transfers subject to put and call options

Some of the technical 'jargon' used to describe option contracts is explained at D under 3 above.

A Deeply in the money put and call options

If a transferred financial asset can be called back by the transferor, and the call option is deeply in the money, the transfer does not qualify for derecognition because the transferor has retained substantially all the risks and rewards of ownership (Figure 1, Box 7, Yes).

Similarly, if the financial asset can be put back by the transferee, and the put option is deeply in the money, the transfer does not qualify for derecognition because the transferor has retained substantially all the risks and rewards of ownership[75] (Figure 1, Box 7, Yes).

The accounting treatment for such transactions would be similar to that for 'repos' as set out in Example 16.12 at 4.8.2 below.

If transferred assets continue to be recognised because of a transferor's call option or transferee's put option, but the option subsequently lapses unexercised, the asset and any associated liability would then be derecognised.

B *Deeply out of the money put and call options*

A financial asset that is transferred subject only to a transferee's deeply out of the money put option, or a transferor's deeply out of the money call option, is derecognised. This is because the transferor has transferred substantially all the risks and rewards of ownership[76] (Figure 1, Box 7, Yes).

C *Options that are neither deeply out of the money nor deeply in the money*

Where a financial asset is transferred subject to an option (whether a transferor's call option or a transferee's put option) that is neither deeply in the money nor deeply out of the money, the result is that the entity neither transfers nor retains substantially all the risks and rewards associated with the asset[77] (Figure 1, Box 7, No). It is therefore necessary to determine whether or not the transferor has retained control of the asset under the criteria summarised in 4.6 above.

The accounting treatment for such transactions would be similar to that for 'repos' as set out in Example 16.12 at 4.8.2 below.

If a transferred asset continues to be recognised because of a transferor's call option or transferee's put option, but the option subsequently lapses unexercised, the asset and any associated liability would then be derecognised.

I *Assets readily obtainable in the market*

If the transferor has a call option over a transferred financial asset that is readily obtainable in the market, IAS 39 considers that control of the asset has passed to the transferee (Figure 1, Box 8, No – see 4.6 above).[78] This would presumably also be the conclusion where the transferee had a put option over a transferred financial asset that is readily obtainable in the market, although IAS 39 does not specifically address this.

II *Assets not readily obtainable in the market*

If the transferor has a call option over a transferred financial asset that is not readily obtainable in the market, IAS 39 considers that control of the asset remains with the transferor (Figure 1, Box 8, Yes – see 4.6 above). Accordingly, derecognition is precluded to the extent of the amount of the asset that is subject to the call option.[79]

If the transferee has a put option over a transferred financial asset that is not readily obtainable in the market, IAS 39 requires the transferee's likely economic behaviour to be assessed – in effect to determine whether the option gives the transferee the practical ability to sell the transferred asset (see 4.6.1 above).

If the put option is sufficiently valuable to prevent the transferee from selling the asset, the transferor is considered to retain control of the asset and should account for the asset to the extent of its continuing involvement[80] (Figure 1, Box 9). The accounting treatment required is discussed at 4.8.3 below.

If the put option is not sufficiently valuable to prevent the transferee from selling the asset, the transferor is considered to have ceded control of the asset, and should derecognise it[81] (Figure 1, Box 8, No).

The requirements above beg two questions. First the question of whether or not a put option is sufficiently valuable to prevent the transferee from selling the asset is not a matter of objective fact, but rather a function of the transferee's appetite for risk, its need for liquidity and so forth. It is not clear how the transferor can readily assess these factors.

Second, IAS 39 is not explicit as to the accounting consequences (if any) of an option that was considered at the time of the original transfer to be deeply out of the money subsequently becoming neither deeply in the money nor deeply out of the money, or even deeply in the money, (or any other of the possible permutations). This is discussed further at I below.

D   Option to put or call at fair value

A transfer of a financial asset subject only to a put or call option with an exercise price equal to the fair value of the financial asset at the time of repurchase results in derecognition because of the transfer of substantially all the risks and rewards of ownership[82] (Figure 1, Box 6, Yes).

E   Net cash-settled options

Where transfer of a financial asset is subject to a put or call option that will be settled net in cash, IAS 39 requires the entity the entity to evaluate the transfer so as to determine whether it has retained or transferred substantially all the risks and rewards of ownership.[83] IAS 39 comments that 'if the entity has not retained substantially all the risks and rewards of ownership of the transferred asset, it determines whether it has retained control of the transferred asset' – which is simply a repetition of the basic principles of the standard adding no clarification specific to this type of transaction.

F   Removal of accounts provision

A 'removal of accounts provision' is an unconditional repurchase (i.e. call) option that gives an entity the right to reclaim transferred assets subject to some restrictions. Provided that such an option results in the entity neither retaining nor transferring substantially all the risks and rewards of ownership, IAS 39 allows derecognition, except to the extent of the amount subject to repurchase (assuming that the transferee cannot sell the assets).

For example, if an entity transfers loan receivables with a carrying amounts of €100,000 for proceeds of €100,000, subject only to the right to call back any individual loan(s) up to a maximum of €10,000, €90,000 of the loans would qualify for derecognition.[84]

G   Clean-up call options

A 'clean-up call' option is an option held by an entity that services transferred assets (and may be the transferor of those assets) to purchase remaining transferred assets when the cost of servicing the assets exceeds the entity's participation in their benefits. If such a clean-up call results in the entity neither retaining nor transferring substantially all the risks and rewards of ownership, and the transferee cannot sell the assets, IAS 39 precludes derecognition only to the extent of the amount of assets subject to the call option.[85]

H   Same (or nearly the same) price put and call options

IAS 39 does not specifically address the transfer of an asset subject to both a transferee's option to put, and a transferor's option to call, the asset at a fixed price rather than at fair value (as discussed in D above). Assuming that:

- both options can be exercised simultaneously, and

- both the transferor and transferee behave rationally,

it will clearly be in the interest of either the transferor or the transferee to exercise its option, so that the asset will be reacquired by the transferor. This indicates that the transferor has retained substantially all the risks and rewards of ownership.

However, if the two options were exercisable on different dates or at different prices the effects of each option would need to be considered carefully.

I   Changes in probability of exercise of options after initial transfer of asset

As noted at C above, IAS 39 is not explicit as to the accounting consequences (if any) of an option that was considered at the time of the original transfer to be deeply out of the money subsequently becoming neither deeply in the money nor deeply out of the money, or even deeply in the money, (or any other of the possible permutations). This is explored further in Examples 16.5 to 16.7 below.

Example 16.5   Financial asset transferred subject only to deeply out of the money call option

On 1 January 2005 an entity transferred a financial asset to a counterparty, subject only to a call option to repurchase the asset at any time up to 31 December 2009. At 1 January 2005 the option was considered deeply out of the money and the asset was accordingly derecognised (see B above).

At 31 December 2008 market conditions have changed considerably and the option is now deeply in the money. What is the accounting consequence of this change?

There are no accounting consequences since, as noted at 4.5 above, IAS 39 (paragraph AG41) specifies that an asset previously derecognised because substantially all the risks and rewards associated with the asset have been transferred (as would be the analysis for an asset transferred subject only to a deeply out of the money call – see B above) is not re-recognised in a future period unless it is reacquired. Instead the increase in the fair value of the option would be captured in the financial statements as a gain under the normal requirement of

IAS 39 to account for derivatives at fair value with changes in value reflected in profit or loss (see Chapter 18).

However, if the market changes were not demonstrably beyond any reasonable expectation as at 1 January 2005, there might be an argument (given the definition of a deeply out of the money option as an option that is 'highly unlikely' to go in the money before expiry – see 3 above) that the fact that the option is now not merely in the money, but deeply in the money, indicates that the original assessment that that option was deeply out of the money was in fact an accounting error requiring correction under IAS 8 – *Accounting Policies, Changes in Accounting Estimates and Errors* (see Chapter 3),

Example 16.6   Financial asset transferred subject only to deeply in the money call option

On 1 January 2005 an entity transferred a financial asset to a counterparty, subject only to a call option to repurchase the asset at any time up to 31 December 2009. At 1 January 2005 the option was considered deeply in the money and the asset was accordingly not derecognised (see A above).

At 31 December 2008 market conditions have changed considerably and the option is now deeply out of the money. What is the accounting consequence of this change?

This is the mirror image of the fact pattern in Example 16.5. However, whereas IAS 39 makes it clear that an asset previously derecognised is not re-recognised, there is no comparable provision that an asset that previously did not qualify for derecognition on the origination of a particular transaction may not later be derecognised as a result of a subsequent change in the assessed likely impact of the transaction.

In our view, however, the original assessment as to whether or not the asset should be derecognised should not be subsequently revisited, unless (in exceptional circumstances) the original assessment was an accounting error within the scope of IAS 8. Thus, in Example 16.6 above the asset would not be derecognised. However, the fall in the value of the option indicates an impairment of the asset which might need to be reflected in the financial statements under the normal requirements of IAS 39 (see Chapter 18 at 6).

Example 16.7   Financial asset transferred subject to call option neither deeply in the money nor deeply out of the money

On 1 January 2005 an entity transferred a financial asset (an equity share) to a counterparty, subject only to a call option to repurchase the asset at any time up to 31 December 2009. At 1 January 2005 the option was considered to be neither deeply in the money nor deeply out of the money. However, the asset was readily marketable and freely transferable by the transferor and was accordingly derecognised because the entity, while neither transferring nor retaining substantially all the risks and rewards of the asset, no longer controls it (see C above).

At 31 December 2008 the financial asset that was the subject of the transfer ceases to be listed and is therefore not readily marketable. Had this been the case at the time of the original transfer, the entity would have been regarded as retaining control of the asset, which would not have been derecognised (see C II above). What is the accounting consequence of this change?

Again, matters are not entirely clear. The rule in paragraph AG41 of IAS 39 that a previously derecognised asset should not be re-recognised (other than on reacquisition of the asset) applies, as drafted, only where derecognition results from a transfer of substantially all the risks and rewards associated with the asset. In this case, derecognition has resulted from a loss of control over, not a transfer of substantially all the risks and rewards associated with, the asset. There is therefore some ambiguity as to whether AG41 is to be read:

- *generally* as prohibiting any re-recognition of a derecognised asset, or
- *specifically* as referring only to circumstances where derecognition results from transfer of substantially all the risks and rewards (i.e. it applies only to 'Box 6, Yes' transactions, and not to 'Box 8, No' transactions).

Again, however, we take the view that the original decision to derecognise the asset should not be revisited, unless (in exceptional circumstances) the original assessment was an accounting error within the scope of IAS 8. The fact that the asset was transferred on terms that the transferee could freely dispose of it means that the transferor did indeed lose control. This is proved by the fact that, if the transferee had exercised its right to dispose of the asset, and the transferor exercised then its call option, transferee would find it difficult, if not impossible, to deliver the actual asset (because it is not longer readily obtainable following its de-listing) and would probably be obliged to settle the option in cash. Conversely, if the asset had originally been transferred subject to conditions restricting its onward transfer by the transferee, derecognition would not have been achieved since the transferee would not have had the practical ability to dispose of the asset (see 4.6.1 above), indicating that control had been retained by the transferee.

4.7.3 Subordinated retained interests and credit guarantees

Where a financial asset is transferred, an entity may provide the transferee with credit enhancement by subordinating some or all of its interest retained in the transferred asset. Alternatively, an entity may provide the transferee with credit enhancement in the form of a credit guarantee that could be unlimited or limited to a specified amount.[86] Such techniques are commonly used in securitisation transactions (see 4.4.3 above).

IAS 39 notes that, if the entity retains substantially all the risks and rewards of ownership of the transferred asset, the asset continues to be recognised in its entirety. If the entity retains some, but not substantially all, of the risks and rewards of ownership and has retained control, derecognition is precluded to the extent of the amount of cash or other assets that the entity could be required to pay.[87] This 'guidance' is really no more than a repetition of the basic principles of the standard, adding no clarification specific to this type of transaction.

4.7.4   Total return swaps

An entity may sell a financial asset to a transferee and enter into a total return swap with the transferee, whereby the transferor pays an amount equivalent to fixed or floating rate interest on the consideration for the transfer and receives an amount equivalent to the cash flows from, together with any increases or decreases in the fair value of, the underlying asset. In such a case, derecognition of all of the asset is prohibited,[88] since the transaction has the effect that substantially all the risks and rewards associated with the asset are retained by the transferor.

4.7.5   Interest rate swaps

An entity may transfer a fixed rate financial asset and enter into an interest rate swap with the transferee to receive a fixed interest rate and pay a variable interest rate based on a notional amount equal to the principal amount of the transferred financial asset. IAS 39 states that the interest rate swap does not preclude derecognition of the transferred asset, provided that the payments on the swap are not conditional on payments being made on the transferred asset.[89]

If, however, the transferor and the transferee were to enter into an amortising interest rate swap (i.e. one whose the notional amount amortises so that it equals the principal amount of the transferred financial asset outstanding at any point in time), the transferor would generally retain substantial prepayment risk through the swap. In this case, the transferor would (depending on the other facts of the transaction, such as the transfer or retention of credit risk) continue to recognise the transferred asset either in its entirety (Figure 1, Box 7, Yes) or to the extent of the transferor's continuing involvement (Figure 1, Box 9).[90]

Conversely, if the transferor and the transferee were to enter into an amortising interest rate swap, the amortisation of the notional amount of which is not linked to the principal amount outstanding on the transferred asset, the transferor would no longer retain prepayment risk. Therefore such a swap would not preclude derecognition of the transferred asset, provided the payments on the swap were not conditional on interest payments being made on the transferred asset and the swap did not result in the entity retaining any other significant risks and rewards of ownership on the transferred asset.[91]

4.7.6   Factoring of trade receivables

IAS 39 does not specifically address one of the more common forms of 'off-balance sheet finance' – the factoring of trade receivables. The common aim of all factoring structures is to provide cash flow from trade receivables quicker than would arise from normal cash collections, which is generally achieved by a 'sale' of all, or certain selected, receivables to a financial institution. However, the conditions of such 'sales' are extremely varied (which may well explain the lack of any 'generic' guidance in the standard), ranging from true outright sales and 'pass-through arrangements' (resulting in full derecognition), to transactions with continuing involvement through guarantee or subordination arrangements.

It will therefore be necessary for an entity to consider the terms of its particular debt-factoring arrangement(s) carefully in order to determine the appropriate application of the derecognition provisions of IAS 39. Depending on circumstances, Examples 16.8 (see 4.8.1 below) 16.10 (see 4.8.1 B below), 16.13 (see 4.8.4 A below) and 16.18 (see 4.8.4 D below) may be of particular relevance.

4.8   Accounting treatment

This part of the Chapter deals with the accounting consequences of the derecognition criteria for financial assets – in other words how the principles discussed in 4.1 to 4.7 above translate into accounting entries.

In order to provide a link with the flowchart at 4.1.2 above we have used the following convention:

'Box 6, Yes'   the transaction would result in the answer 'Yes' at Box 6 in the flowchart

'Box 7, No'   the transaction would result in the answer 'No' at Box 7 in the flowchart

4.8.1   *Transfers that qualify for derecognition*

It is important to remember throughout this section that references to an asset being derecognised in its entirety include situations where a part of an asset to which the derecognition criteria are applied separately is derecognised in its entirety (see 4.2 above). In this context, IAS 39 uses the phrase 'in its entirety' in contrast to the accounting treatment applied to assets where there is continuing involvement (see 4.8.3 below) where some, but not all, of a financial asset, or part of an asset, is derecognised.

If, as a result of a transfer, a financial asset is derecognised in its entirety but the transfer results in the transferor obtaining a new financial asset or servicing asset (see B below) or assuming a new financial liability, or a servicing liability (see B below), IAS 39 requires the entity to recognise the new financial asset, servicing asset, financial liability or servicing liability at fair value.[92]

On derecognition of a financial asset in its entirety, IAS 39 requires the difference between:

(a)   the carrying amount of the asset; and

(b)   the sum of

(i)   the consideration received (including any new asset obtained less any new liability assumed), and

(ii)   any cumulative gain or loss that had been recognised directly in equity

to be recognised in profit or loss.[93]

The requirement in (b)(ii) above for 'recycling' of any cumulative gain or loss previously recognised directly in equity applies to assets accounted for as available-for-sale, and is discussed further in Chapter 18 at 3.2.

Example 16.8 illustrates these requirements.

Example 16.8   Derecognition of whole of financial asset in its entirety

At 1 October 2005 an entity has an available-for-sale financial asset carried at €1,400 in respect of which a cumulative loss of €200 has been recognised in equity. At that date, the asset is unconditionally sold to a third party in exchange for cash of €2,500 and a loan note issued to the third party. The loan note bears fixed rate interest below current market rates and is repayable at €1,150 but is considered to have a fair value of €1,100. The following accounting entries are made by the entity to record the disposal:

	€	€
Cash	2,500	
Loss on disposal	200	
Asset		1,400
Loan note		1,100
Equity ('recycling' of cumulative loss on asset)		200

Thereafter the loan note would be accreted up to its repayable amount of €1,150 over its expected life using the effective interest method (see Chapter 18 at 5).

If the asset had been of a type eligible for accounting using the amortised cost method, and had been so accounted for, and had a carrying amount of (say) €1,500 at the date of the transfer, the accounting entry would have been:

	€	€
Cash	2,500	
Loss on disposal	100	
Asset		1,500
Loan note		1,100

A   Transferred asset part of larger asset

If the transferred asset is part of a larger financial asset, for example when an entity transfers interest cash flows that are part of a debt instrument (see 4.2 above), and the part transferred qualifies for derecognition in its entirety, IAS 39 requires the previous carrying amount of the larger financial asset to be allocated between the part that continues to be recognised and the part that is derecognised. The allocation is based on the relative fair values of those parts on the date of the transfer. For this purpose, a retained servicing asset (see B below) is to be treated as a part that continues to be recognised.

IAS 39 requires the difference between:

(a)   the carrying amount allocated to the part derecognised; and

(b)   the sum of

    (i)   the consideration received for the part derecognised (including any new asset obtained less any new liability assumed), and

    (ii)   any cumulative gain or loss allocated to it previously recognised directly in equity to be recognised in profit or loss. Any cumulative gain or loss that had been recognised in equity is allocated between the part that continues to be recognised and the part that is derecognised, based on the relative fair values of those parts.[94] The requirement in (b)(ii) above for 'recycling' of any cumulative gain or loss previously recognised directly in equity applies to assets accounted for as available-for-sale, and is discussed further in Chapter 18 at 3.2.

IAS 39 notes that the accounting treatment prescribed for the derecognition of a part (or parts) of a financial asset requires an entity to determine the fair value of the part(s) that continue to be recognised. Where the entity has a history of selling parts similar to the part that continues to be recognised, or other market transactions exist for such parts, IAS 39 requires recent prices of actual transactions to be used to provide the best estimate of its fair value. When there are no price quotations or recent market transactions to support the fair value of the part that continues to be recognised, the best estimate of the fair value is the difference between:

- the fair value of the larger financial asset as a whole, and
- the consideration received from the transferee for the part that is derecognised.[95]

The application guidance to IAS 39 requires the fair value of the part derecognised and the part retained to be determined using paragraphs AG69 to AG82 of the application guidance in IAS 39 (which deal with the determination of fair value[96] – see Chapter 18 at 4).

Example 16.9 illustrates the requirements for full derecognition of a part of an asset.

Example 16.9   Derecognition of part of financial asset in its entirety

On 1 January 2001 an entity invested €1 million in a corporate bond with a par value of €1 million. The bond pays interest of €75,000 on 31 December annually in arrears and is to be redeemed at par on 31 December 2010. The entity accounts for the bond as a held-to-maturity asset at amortised cost.

On 1 January 2006 it unconditionally sells the right to receive the remaining five interest payments to a bank. The derecognition provisions of IAS 39 are applied to the interest payments as an identifiable part of the asset, leading to the conclusion that they are required to be derecognised.

The consideration received for, and the fair value of, the future interest payments (based on the net present value, as at 1 January 2006, of the payments at the current market interest rate that would be available to the bond issuer of 5%)[97] is €324,711 (€75,000 × [$1/1.05 + 1/1.05^2 \ldots + 1/1.05^5$]). By the same methodology the fair value of the principal repayment can be calculated as €783,526 (€1,000,000 × $1/1.05^5$), giving a total fair value for the bond of €1,108,237.

In order to calculate the gain or loss on disposal, the total carrying value of the bond of €1,000,000 is allocated between the part disposed of and the part retained, based on the fair values of those parts. This allocates €292,998 (€1,000,000 × 324,711/1,108,237) to the interest payments disposed of and €707,002 (€1,000,000 × 783,526/1,108,237) to the retained right to the repayment of principal. This generates the accounting entry:

	€	€
Cash	324,711	
Bond (portion of carrying amount allocated to interest payments)		292,998
Gain on disposal		31,713

If the bond had been accounted for as available-for-sale, it would have already have been carried at €1,108,237, so that the basic disposal journal would simply be:

	€	€
Cash	324,711	
Bond (portion of carrying amount allocated to interest payments)		324,711

However, if the bond had been accounted for as available-for-sale, it would also be necessary to recycle that portion of the cumulative revaluation gain of €108,237 that relates to the interest 'component' of the total carrying value from equity to the income statement. IAS 39 requires a pro-rata allocation of the cumulative gain or loss in equity based on the total fair value of the interest and principal – this would deem €31,713 (€108,237 × €324,711/1,108,237) of the cumulative revaluation gain to relate to interest. This would give rise to the further journal, resulting in the same gain on disposal as above:

	€	€
Equity	31,713	
Gain on disposal (income statement)		31,713

Whilst the treatment in Example 16.9 above is what IAS 39 clearly requires, it could be argued that it does not correctly identify the true historic cost of the part of the asset being disposed of. At the original effective interest rate of 7.5% implicit in the bond at the date of issue, the current carrying value of the bond of €1,000,000 represents future interest payments of €303,441 (i.e. €75,000 × [$1/1.075 + 1/1.075^2 \ldots + 1/1.075^5$]) and principal of €696,559 (€1,000,000 × $1/1.075^5$). This suggests that the true profit on disposal is only €21,270, representing the difference between net present value of the interest cash flows at the current discount rate of 5% (€324,711) and at the original discount rate of 7.5% (€303,441).

B   Servicing assets and liabilities

It is common for an entity to transfer a financial asset (or part of a financial asset) in its entirety, but to retain the right or obligation to service the asset (i.e. to collect payments as they fall due and undertake other administrative tasks) in return for a fee.

Where an entity transfers a financial asset in a transfer that qualifies for derecognition in its entirety and retains the right to service the financial asset for a fee, IAS 39 requires the entity to recognise either a servicing asset or a servicing liability for that servicing contract, as follows:

- If the fee to be received is not expected to compensate the entity adequately for performing the servicing, the entity should recognise a servicing liability for the servicing obligation at its fair value.

- If the fee to be received is expected to be more than adequate compensation for the servicing, the entity should recognise a servicing asset for the servicing right. This should be recognised at an amount determined on the basis of an allocation of the carrying amount of the larger financial asset (as described in A above).[98]

It is not immediately clear what is meant by this requirement. The application guidance expands on the point, as follows.

An entity may retain the right to a part of the interest payments on transferred assets as compensation for servicing those assets. The part of the interest payments that the entity would give up upon termination or transfer of the servicing contract is allocated to the servicing asset or servicing liability. The part of the interest payments that the entity would not give up is an interest-only strip receivable.

For example, if the entity would not give up any interest upon termination or transfer of the servicing contract, the entire interest spread is an interest-only strip receivable. Presumably, as the entity will still have a liability to service the portfolio, it will have to account for this if it allocates none of the interest spread to a servicing asset. For the purposes of applying requirements for disposals of part of an asset discussed in A above, the fair values of the servicing asset and interest-only strip receivable are used to allocate the carrying amount of the receivable between the part of the asset that is derecognised and the part that continues to be recognised. If there is no servicing fee specified, or the fee to be received is not expected to compensate the entity adequately for performing the servicing, a liability for the servicing obligation is recognised at fair value.[99]

Unfortunately, IAS 39 does not provide an example of what exactly is meant here, but we believe that something along the lines of Example 16.10 below was intended.

Example 16.10   Servicing assets and liabilities

An entity has a portfolio of originated domestic mortgages which are accounted for at amortised cost and have a carrying amount of £10 million. The mortgages bear interest at a fixed rate of 7.5%. The average life of the mortgages in the portfolio (taking account of prepayment risk) is 12 years and the fair value of the portfolio is £11 million, representing £4.5 million in respect of future interest payments and £6.5 million in respect of the principal amounts. The entity assesses the amount that would compensate it for servicing the asset to be £0.5 million.

The entity sells the entire portfolio to a bank (on terms such that it qualifies for derecognition under IAS 39) but continues to service the portfolio. If the entity does not retain any part of the interest payments, the selling price would be the fair value of the assets of £11 million (or very close to it). It would then assume a servicing liability of £0.5 million, giving rise to the accounting entry:

	£m	£m
Cash	11.0	
Mortgage portfolio		10.0
Servicing liability		0.5
Profit on disposal		0.5

Alternatively, it retains interest payments of 1% and the right to service the portfolio. The entity estimates that the fair value of the right to receive interest payments of 1% is £0.6 million. In this case, the bank would be expected to pay fair value of £10.4 million (or very close to it).

The standard states – see above – that, if (as is the case here) the entity would not give up any interest on termination or transfer of the contract, then the whole of the interest spread is an interest-only strip receivable. In order to calculate the amount of the portfolio to be derecognised, the carrying value of £10 million is pro-rated (as in Example 16.9 above) as to £9.45 million disposed of (£10m × 10.4/11) and the part retained of £0.55 million (£10m × 0.6/11). However, as it has allocated the full amount of the interest spread to an interest-only strip receivable, it would need to recognise a servicing liability of £0.5 million in respect of its obligations under the contract. This gives rise to the following accounting entry:

	£m	£m
Cash	10.40	
Interest-only strip receivable	0.55	
Mortgage portfolio ((£9.45m disposed of plus £0.55m reclassified as interest-only strip receivable)		10.00
Servicing liability		0.50
Profit on disposal		0.45

If the entity were to retain only £0.1 million of the interest spread on termination or transfer of the servicing contract, then IAS 39 requires – see above:

- the part of the interest payments that the entity would not give up (i.e. £0.1 million) to be treated as an interest-only strip receivable, and

- the part of the interest payments that the entity would give up (i.e. £0.45 million – i.e. £0.55 million as above less £0.1 million in previous bullet) upon termination or transfer of the servicing contract to be allocated to the servicing asset or servicing liability.

This suggests that the following accounting entry would be made:

	£m	£m
Cash	10.40	
Interest-only strip receivable	0.10	
Mortgage portfolio (£9.45m disposed of plus £0.1m reclassified as interest-only strip receivable and £0.45m allocated to servicing liability)		10.00
Servicing liability (£0.5m gross cost less interest payments that would be lost on termination or transfer – £0.45m)		0.05
Profit on disposal		0.45

4.8.2 Transfers that do not qualify for derecognition through retention of risks and rewards

If a transfer does not result in derecognition because the entity has retained substantially all the risks and rewards of ownership of the transferred asset (see 4.5 above), IAS 39 requires the entity to continue to recognise the transferred asset in its entirety and recognise a financial liability for any consideration received. In subsequent periods, the entity recognises any income on the transferred asset and any expense incurred on the financial liability.[100] This treatment is illustrated by Examples 16.11 and 16.12 below.

It should be noted that these provisions apply only where derecognition does not occur as a result of retention by the transferor of substantially all the risks and rewards of ownership of the transferred asset (Figure 1, Box 7, Yes). They do not apply where derecognition does not occur as a result of continuing involvement in an asset of which substantially all the risks and rewards of ownership are neither retained nor transferred (Figure 1, Box 8, Yes). Such transactions are dealt with by the separate provisions discussed in 4.8.3 and 4.8.4 below.

Example 16.11   Asset not qualifying for derecognition (risks and rewards retained)

An entity holds a publicly quoted loan receivable of £1,000 issued on 1 January 2001, paying interest of £65 annually in arrears and redeemable at par on 31 December 2005, which it accounts for as a held-to-maturity investment at amortised cost (see Chapter 18 at 5).

On 1 January 2005 it enters into a transaction whereby the loan is sold to a bank for its then fair value of €985, but with full recourse to the entity for any default on the loan. The guarantee provided by the entity has the effect that it retains substantially all the risks and rewards of the loan, which is therefore not derecognised (Figure 1, Box 7, Yes – see 4.5.2 above).[101]

The entity therefore continues to recognise the loan, and interest on it, as if it still held the loan. It accounts for the £985 proceeds as a liability which must be accreted up using the effective interest method (see Chapter 18 at 5) so that it will be equal to the carrying amount of the asset on the date on which it is expected that the asset will be derecognised.

In this case, the asset will be derecognised at maturity on 31 December 2005, when a payment of £1,065 (the final instalment of interest of £65 and return of principal of £1,000) is due on 31 December 2005. Accordingly, the liability must be accreted from £985 to £1,065 during the year ended 31 December 2005. The following accounting entries are made by the entity.

	£	£
1 January 2005		
Cash	985	
Liability		985
Consideration received from bank		
1 January-31 December 2005		
Loan (£1,065 at 31.12.05 – £1,000 at 1.1.05)	65	
Interest on loan (income statement)		65
Interest on liability (income statement)	80	
Liability (£1,065 at 31.12.05 – £985 at 1.1.05)		80
Accretion of interest income loan and liability		

31 December 2005
Liability   1,065
Loan receivable   1,065

'Redemption' of loan and 'discharge' of liability

This accounting treatment recognises an overall loss of £15 in 2005, which would be expected, as representing the difference between the carrying value of the asset at the date of transfer (£1,000) and the consideration received (£985). However, IAS 39 requires the various elements of the transaction to shown separately – it would not have been acceptable for the income statement simply to show a net loss of £15.

If the transferred asset had been accounted for at fair value, then it would already have been carried at £985 at the date of transfer – i.e. the loss of £15 would already have been reflected in the financial statements. The accounting entries at 1 January and 31 December 2005 would be the same as above. However, the following accounting entries would then have been made during the year ended 31 December:

	£	£
1 January–31 December 2005		
Interest on liability (income statement)	80	
Liability (£1,065 at 31.12.05 – £985 at 1.1.05)		80
Loan (£1,065 at 31.12.05 – £985 at 1.1.05)	80	
Interest on loan (income statement)		65
Change in fair value of loan (income statement)		15

Recognition of interest on, and change in fair value of,
loan and accretion of interest on liability

Whilst the overall amounts recorded in the income statement are the same overall, they are arrived at by different methodologies. The £80 increase in the carrying value of the loan receivable is recognised as it occurs whereas the £80 interest on the liability is accrued at a constant effective rate. This means that, if the entity were to prepare financial statements at an interim date, it might well show a net gain or loss on the transaction at that date, notwithstanding that ultimately no gain or loss will be reflected.

It would presumably be possible for the entity to avoid this result by designating the liability as at fair value through profit or loss (see Chapter 15 at 7), such that changes in the fair value of the liability would be matched in line with those in the fair value of the asset.

Example 16.12   Asset not qualifying for derecognition ('repo' transaction)

An entity holds a government bond of £2,000 issued on 1 January 2001, paying interest of £50 semi-annually in arrears and redeemable at par on 31 December 2006, which it accounts for as a held-to-maturity investment at amortised cost (see Chapter 18 at 5).

A   Gross-settled transaction

On 1 January 2005 the entity enters into a transaction whereby the bond is sold to a bank for its then fair value of £1,800, and the entity agrees to repurchase it on 1 January 2006 for £1,844. As the legal owner of the loan at 30 June 2005 and 31 December 2005, the bank will receive the £100 interest payable on the bond for the calendar year 2005. This £100, together with the £44 difference between the sale and repurchase price gives the bank £144, representing a lender's return of 8% on the £1,800 sale proceeds. Accordingly, the effect of the transaction is that the entity has retained the substantially all risks and rewards of ownership of the bond (Figure 1, Box 7, Yes – see 4.7.1 above).

The entity therefore continues to recognise the bond, and interest on it, as if it still held the bond. It accounts for the £1,800 proceeds as a liability which must be accreted up to £1,844 (the repurchase price due on 31 December 2005) over the period to 31 December 2005 using the effective interest method (see Chapter 18 at 5). The following accounting entries are made by the entity.

	£	£
1 January 2005		
Cash	1,800	
Liability		1,800
Consideration received from bank		
1 January-31 December 2005		
Interest on liability (income statement)	144	
Liability (£1,944 at 31.12.05 – £1,800 at 1.1.05)		144
Bond (£2,100 at 31.12.05 – £2,000 at 1.1.05)	100	
Interest on bond (income statement)		100
Accretion of income on bond and finance cost of liability		
31 December 2005		
Liability	100	
Bond		100
'Receipt' of interest on bond and 'transfer' thereof to bank		
1 January 2006		
Liability	1,844	
Cash		1,844
Execution of repurchase contract		

The above is arguably the strict translation into accounting entries of the accounting analysis of IAS 39 that the entity still retains ownership of the bond throughout 2005. As a matter of practicality, however, the same overall result could have been obtained by the following 'short-cut' approach, which avoids recording the notional receipt and transfer to the bank of bond interest received on 31 December:

	£	£
1 January 2005		
Cash	1,800	
Liability		1,800
Consideration received from bank		
1 January-31 December 2005		
Interest on liability (income statement)	144	
Interest on bond (income statement)		100
Liability (balance sheet)		44
Accretion of income on bond and finance cost of liability		
1 January 2006		
Liability	1,844	
Cash		1,844
Execution of repurchase contract		

If (as would be likely, given the nature of the transferred asset) the bank has the right to sell or pledge the bond during the period of its legal ownership, it would be necessary to reclassify the bond as a repurchase receivable during the period of the bank's ownership (see 4.7.1 A I above). In other words, the following additional accounting entries would be required.

	£	£
1 January 2005		
Repurchase receivable	2,000	
Bond		2,000
1 January 2006		
Bond	2,000	
Repurchase receivable		2,000

B   Net-settled transaction

The entity might enter into the transaction above, but on terms that the repurchase contract was to be net-settled. In other words, on 1 January 2006, a payment would be made to or by the bank for the difference between £1,844 (the notional repurchase price) and the fair value of the bond at that date. Assuming that the fair value of the bond at 1 January 2006 is £1,860, the bank would be required to pay the entity £16 (£1,860 – £1,844).

In this case, matters are further complicated by the fact that the economic effect of the net-settled forward is the same as if the entity sold the bond on 1 January 2006. As this is before the maturity date of the bond, it is questionable whether the entity can any longer classify it as held-to-maturity. In such a case, IAS 39 requires it to be reclassified as available-for-sale (see Chapter 18). The following accounting entries would be made.

	£	£
1 January 2005		
Cash	1,800	
Liability		1,800
Consideration received from bank		
Equity	200	
Bond (£2,000 carrying amount less £1,800 fair value)		200
Restatement of bond to fair value		
Repurchase receivable	1,800	
Bond		1,800
Reclassification of bond as receivable		
(see 4.7.1 A I above)		
1 January-31 December 2005		
Interest on liability (income statement)	144	
Interest on bond (income statement)		100
Liability (balance sheet)		44
Repurchase receivable	60	
Equity		60

Accretion of income on bond and finance cost of liability and restatement of repurchase receivable (represented by fair value of underlying bond accounted for as available-for-sale – £1,860)

1 January 2006
Cash	16	
Liability	1,844	
Repurchase receivable		1,860
Loss on disposal	140	
Equity		140

Net settlement of repurchase contract and 'recycling' of cumulative losses in equity

The loss on disposal at 1 January 2006 of £140 arises because the net-settled contract is equivalent to the entity disposing of the bond for its then fair value of £1,860, which is £140 lower than its cost, at the date of reclassification from held-to-maturity to available-for-sale, of £2,000.

This illustrates the point that, where the terms of net-settled forward contract over a transferred asset are such that the original asset cannot be derecognised, the result will be that the entity's balance show a gross position – i.e. the original asset and a liability for the consideration for the transfer. This may seem a strange accounting reflection of a contract that is required to be settled net. However, the IASB is to some extent forced into this approach as an anti-avoidance measure.

It is clear from the analysis in 4.7.1 A to D above that an asset sold subject to the obligation to repurchase the same or similar asset at a fixed price should not be derecognised. If the accounting treatment were to vary merely because the contract was net-settled, it would be possible to avoid IAS 39's requirements for continued recognition of assets subject to certain forward repurchase agreements simply by altering the terms of the agreement to allow net settlement.

4.8.3 Transfers with continuing involvement – summary

If an entity neither transfers nor retains substantially all the risks and rewards of ownership of a transferred asset, but retains control of the transferred asset (see 4.6 above), IAS 39 requires the entity to continue to recognise the transferred asset to the extent of its 'continuing involvement' – i.e. the extent to which it is exposed to changes in the value of the transferred asset.[102] Such transactions fall within Box 9 of the flowchart at 4.1.2 above.

The concept of 'continuing involvement' was first introduced in the exposure draft of proposed amendments to IAS 32 and IAS 39 published in June 2002. The IASB's intention at that time was to move towards an accounting model for derecognition based entirely on continuing involvement. However, this approach (or at least the methodology for implementing it proposed in the exposure draft) received little support in the exposure period and the IASB decided to abandon it and revert largely to an accounting model for derecognition based on the transfer of risks and rewards.[103] However, the continuing involvement approach remains relevant for certain transactions – mainly transfers of assets which result in the sharing, rather than the substantial transfer, of the risks and rewards.

The accounting requirements in respect of assets in which the entity has continuing involvement are particularly complex, and are summarised at A to E below, with worked examples at 4.8.4 below. In particular, and in contrast to the treatment for transactions that do not qualify for derecognition through retention of risks and rewards (see 4.8.2 above), the associated liability is often calculated as a balancing figure that will not necessarily represent the proceeds received as the result of the transfer (see C below).

A   Guarantees

When the entity's continuing involvement takes the form of guaranteeing the transferred asset, the extent of the entity's continuing involvement is the lower of:

- the amount of the asset; and

- the maximum amount of the consideration received that the entity could be required to repay ('the guarantee amount').[104]

An example of this treatment is given at 4.8.4 A below.

B   Options

When the entity's continuing involvement takes the form of a written and/or purchased option (including a cash-settled option or similar provision) on the transferred asset, the extent of the entity's continuing involvement is the amount of the transferred asset that the entity may repurchase. However, in case of a written put option (including a cash-settled option or similar provision) on an asset measured at fair value, the extent of the entity's continuing involvement is limited to the lower of the fair value of the transferred asset and the option exercise price.[105]

Examples of this treatment are given at 4.8.4 B and C below.

C   Associated liability

When an entity continues to recognise an asset to the extent of its continuing involvement, IAS 39 requires the entity to recognise an associated liability.[106] IAS 39 provides that 'despite the other measurement requirements in IAS 39', the transferred asset and the associated liability are to be measured on a basis that reflects the rights and obligations that the entity has retained. The associated liability is measured in such a way that the net carrying amount of the transferred asset and the associated liability is equal to:

(a)   if the transferred asset is measured at amortised cost, the amortised cost of the rights and obligations retained by the entity; or

(b)   if the transferred asset is measured at fair value, the fair value of the rights and obligations retained by the entity when measured on a stand-alone basis.[107]

The effect of (a) and (b) above is that the 'liability' is often calculated as a balancing figure that will not necessarily represent the proceeds received as the result of the transfer (see Examples 16.13 to 16.16 at 4.8.4 below). This does not fit very comfortably with the normal rules in IAS 39 for the initial measurement of financial liabilities (see Chapter 18 at 2) – hence the comment that this treatment applies 'despite the other measurement requirements in IAS 39'.

D Subsequent measurement of assets and liabilities

IAS 39 requires an entity to continue to recognise any income arising on the transferred asset to the extent of its continuing involvement and to recognise any expense incurred on the associated liability.[108] This is comparable to the requirements in respect of assets not derecognised through retention of substantially all risks and rewards (see 4.8.2 above).

When the transferred asset and associated liability are subsequently measured, IAS 39 requires recognised changes in the fair value of the transferred asset and the associated liability to be accounted for consistently with each other in accordance with the general provisions of IAS 39 for measuring gains and losses (see Chapter 18 at 3) and not offset.[109] Moreover, if the transferred asset is measured at amortised cost, the option in IAS 39 to designate a financial liability as at fair value through profit or loss (see Chapter 15 at 7.1) is not applicable to the associated liability.[110]

E Continuing involvement in part only of a larger asset

An entity may have continuing involvement in a part only of a financial asset, for example where the entity retains an option to repurchase part of a transferred asset, or retains a residual interest in part of an asset, such that the entity does not retain substantially all the risks and rewards of ownership, but does retain control.

In such a case, IAS 39 requires the entity to allocate the previous carrying amount of the financial asset between the part that it continues to recognise under continuing involvement, and the part that it no longer recognises on the basis of the relative fair values of those parts on the date of the transfer. The allocation is to be made on the same basis as applies on derecognition of part only of a larger financial asset – see 4.8.1 A and B above.

The difference between:

(a)   the carrying amount allocated to the part that is no longer recognised; and

(b)   the sum of:

    (i)   the consideration received for the part no longer recognised, and

    (ii)   any cumulative gain or loss allocated to it that had been recognised directly in equity

is recognised in profit or loss. A cumulative gain or loss that had been recognised in equity is allocated between the part that continues to be recognised and the part that is no longer recognised on the basis of the relative fair values of those parts.[111] The requirement in (b)(ii) above for 'recycling' of any cumulative gain or loss previously recognised directly in equity applies to assets accounted for as available-for-sale, and is discussed further in Chapter 18 at 3.2.

This is discussed further at 4.8.4 D below.

4.8.4   Transfers with continuing involvement – accounting examples

The provisions summarised at 4.8.3 above, even judged by the standards of IAS 39, are unusually impenetrable. However, the application guidance provides a number of clarifications and examples, the substance of which is reproduced below.

A   Transfers with guarantees

If a guarantee provided by an entity to pay for default losses on a transferred asset prevents the transferred asset from being derecognised to the extent of the continuing involvement, IAS 39 requires:

(a)   the transferred asset at the date of the transfer to be measured at the lower of:

   (i)   the carrying amount of the asset; and

   (ii)   the maximum amount of the consideration received in the transfer that the entity could be required to repay ('the guarantee amount'); and

(b)   the associated liability to be initially measured at the guarantee amount plus the fair value of the guarantee (which is normally the consideration received for the guarantee).

Subsequently, the initial fair value of the guarantee is recognised in profit or loss on a time proportion basis in accordance with IAS 18 and the carrying value of the asset is reduced by any impairment losses.[112]

This is illustrated in Example 16.13 below (which is based on the circumstances in Example 16.18 below).

Example 16.13   Continuing involvement through guarantee

An entity has a loan portfolio carried at €10 million with a fair value of €10.5 million. It sells the rights to 100% of the cash flows to a third party for a payment of €10.55 million, which includes a payment of €50,000 in return for the entity agreeing to absorb the first €1 million of default losses on the portfolio. The loans are fixed rate loans with significant prepayment risk.

The guarantee has the effect that the entity has transferred substantially all the rewards, but not substantially all the risks, of the portfolio (Figure 1, Box 6, No). However, the prepayment risk has been transferred to the transferee, so that the entity does not retain all significant risks if the loans (Figure 1, Box 7, No). The portfolio is not a readily marketable asset, so that the entity retains control of the asset (Figure 1, Box 8, Yes – see also 4.6 above), and the continuing involvement provisions of IAS 39 apply (Figure 1, Box 9).

The entity turns to the requirements above. The continuing involvement in the transferred asset must be measured at the lower of:

(i)   the amount of the asset transferred – i.e. €10 million; and

(ii)   the maximum amount of the consideration received in the transfer that the entity could be required to repay – i.e. €1 million (the amount guaranteed).

Therefore, the entity will set up an asset that represents its continuing involvement in the transferred asset of €1 million.

The entity then considers the carrying amount of the liability. This is required to be measured at the guarantee amount (i.e. €1 million) plus the fair value of the guarantee (i.e. the €50,000 guarantee payment), a total of €1.05 million. Therefore, the entity's continuing involvement in the transaction will be reflected as follows:

	€m	€m
Cash	10.55	
Loan portfolio transferred		10.00
Continuing involvement in the transferred asset	1.00	
Liability		1.05
Profit on disposal*		0.50

* Cash received (€10.55m) less guarantee payment (€50,000) = consideration for portfolio (€10.5m) less carrying amount of portfolio (€10m).

Over the remaining life of the transaction, the €50,000 of the liability that represents the consideration received for the guarantee is amortised to the income statement on a time proportion basis. This has the effect that the income earned by the entity for entering into the guarantee arrangement is reported as revenue on a time proportion basis. This is exactly the same result as would have been obtained by simply recognising the €50,000 as a liability and amortising it (as would have been required by IAS 18 – *Revenue*).

If in a subsequent period credit losses of €0.2 million are suffered, requiring a payment under the guarantee, IAS 39 requires the following accounting entries to be made:[113]

	€m	€m
Profit or loss (loss under guarantee)	0.20	
Cash (paid to transferee)		0.20
Liability	0.20	
Continuing involvement in the transferred asset		0.20

This is problematic from several points of view. First, it results in the recognition of the liability that is actually greater than the entity's maximum potential exposure (i.e. €1 million). Second, it is recognising a contingent liability as a full liability.

In effect the accounting is something of a hybrid: the asset accounting is equivalent to a partial derecognition of 90% of the asset, but the gain on disposal is calculated on the basis of a 100% disposal. Had the rules for partial derecognition (see 4.8.1 A above) been applied, the following accounting entry would have arisen:

	€m	€m
Cash	10.55	
Loan portfolio transferred		9.00
Liability (balancing figure)		1.10
Profit on disposal*		0.45

* Cash received (€10.55m) less guarantee payment (€50,000) = consideration for whole portfolio (€10.5m). Therefore consideration for 90% of portfolio is €9.45m, less carrying amount of 90% of portfolio €9m = €0.45m

The resulting €1.1m liability represents the guarantee payment of €50,000 plus €1.05m deferred consideration for the 10% not yet derecognised (i.e. total €10.5m less €9.45 taken into account in profit on disposal above). The IASB might have been deterred from such approach on the basis that is difficult to see the €1.05m as anything other than that affront to the IASB's *Framework*, deferred income.

B   Transfers of assets measured at amortised cost

If a put or call option prevents derecognition (see 4.5.3 and 4.7 above) of a transferred asset measured at amortised cost, IAS 39 requires the associated liability to be measured at cost (i.e. the consideration received) and subsequently adjusted for the amortisation of any difference between that cost and the amortised cost of the transferred asset at the expiration date of the option, as illustrated by Example 16.14 below.[114]

Example 16.14   Asset measured at amortised cost

An entity has a financial asset, accounted for at amortised cost, carried at £98. It transfers the asset to a third party in return for consideration of £95. The asset is subject to a call option whereby the entity can compel the transferee to sell the asset back to the entity for £102. The amortised cost of the asset on the option exercise date will be £100. The option is considered to be neither deeply in the money nor deeply out of the money. IAS 39 therefore requires the entity to continue to recognise the asset to the extent of its continuing involvement (Figure 1, Box 9 – see also 4.7.2 C above).

The initial carrying amount of the associated liability is £95. This is then accreted to £100 (i.e. the amortised cost of the asset on exercise date – *not* the £102 exercise price) through profit or loss using the effective interest method. Because the transferred asset is measured at amortised cost, the associated liability must also be accounted for at amortised cost, and not at fair value through profit or loss (see D at 4.8.3 above). This will give rise to the accounting entries:

	£	£
Date of transfer		
Cash	95	
Liability		95
After date of transfer		
Interest on liability	5	
Liability (£100 – £95)		5
Asset (£100 – £98)	2	
Income on asset		2

If the option is exercised, any difference between the carrying amount of the associated liability and the exercise price is recognised in profit or loss. This last requirement has the possibly counter-intuitive effect that the question of whether the entity records a profit or loss on exercise of the option is essentially a function of the difference between the liability (representing the amortised cost of the transferred asset) and the cash paid, not of whether it has in fact (i.e. in economic terms) made a gain or loss.

Thus, if the entity were to exercise its option at £102 it would apparently record the accounting entry

	£	£
Liability	100	
Loss	2	
Cash		102

However, the entity would not have exercised the option unless the asset had not been worth at least £102 (i.e. £2 more than its carrying amount), suggesting that the more appropriate treatment would be to add the £2 to the cost of the asset.

Likewise, if instead of the entity having a call option, the transferee had a put option at £98 which it exercised, the entity would apparently record the accounting entry:

	£	£
Liability	100	
Profit		2
Cash		98

However, the transferee would not have exercised its option if the asset had not been worth less than £98 (i.e. £2 less than its carrying amount). In this case, however, the IASB's thinking may have been that the exercise of the transferee's put option suggests an impairment of the asset which is required to be recognised in the financial statements (see Chapter 18 at 6). However, this would not necessarily the case (e.g. where a fixed-interest asset has a fair value below cost because of movements in interest rates but is not intrinsically impaired).

If the option were to lapse unexercised, the entity would simply derecognise the transferred asset and the associated liability, i.e.

	£	£
Liability	100	
Asset		100

C   *Transfers of assets measured at fair value*

IAS 39 discusses this issue in terms of transferred assets subject to:

- a transferor's call option (see I below),
- a transferee's put option (see II below), and
- a 'collar' transferor's call option combined with a transferee's put option (see III below).

The way in which the rules are articulated in IAS 39 is somewhat confusing, but the overall effect can be summarised as follows:

(a)   the fair value of the option (to the transferor) is calculated;

(b)   the carrying value of the asset is determined as:

    (i)   in the case of an asset subject to a transferor call option, its fair value (on the basis that the call option gives the transferor access to any increase in the fair value of the asset),

    (ii)   in the case of an asset subject to a transferee put option, the lower of fair value and the option exercise price (on the basis that the put option denies the transferor access to any increase in the fair value of the asset above the option price), and

(c)   the associated liability is calculated as the difference between (a) and (b).

This has the effect that net of the carrying value of the asset and that of the associated liability will always equal the fair value of the option.

I   Transferor's call option

If a transferor's call option prevents derecognition (see 4.5.3 and 4.7 above) of a transferred asset measured at fair value, IAS 39 requires the asset to be continued to be measured at its fair value. The associated liability is measured:

- if the option is in or at the money, at the option exercise price less the time value of the option, or

- if the option is out of the money, at the fair value of the transferred asset less the time value of the option.

The adjustment to the measurement of the associated liability ensures that the net carrying amount of the asset and the associated liability is the fair value of the call option right, as illustrated by Example 16.15 below.[115]

Example 16.15:   Asset measured at fair value subject to transferor's call option

An entity has a financial asset, accounted for at fair value, carried at €80. It transfers the asset to a third party, subject to a call option whereby the entity can compel the transferee to sell the asset back to the entity for €95. At the date of transfer, the call option has a time value of €5.

The option is considered to be neither deeply in the money nor deeply out of the money. IAS 39 therefore requires the entity to continue to recognise the asset to the extent of its continuing involvement (Figure 1, Box 9 – see also 4.7.2 C above), and to continue recording it at fair value. At the date of transfer, the call option is out of the money. IAS 39 therefore requires the liability to be measured at the fair value of the transferred asset less the time value of the option, i.e. €80 – €5 = €75 (which is the amount that the transferee would rationally pay for the asset). This has the result that the net of the carrying value of the asset (€80) and the carrying value of the liability (€75) equals the time value of the option (€5), i.e.:

	€	€
Date of transfer		
Cash	75	
Liability		75

A   Transferred asset increases in value

Suppose that one year later the fair value of the asset is €100 and the time value of the option is now €3. The option is now in the money, so that the liability is measured at the option exercise price less the time value of the option, i.e. €95 – €3 = €92. This has the result that the net of the carrying value of the asset (€100) and the carrying value of the liability (€92) equals the fair value of the option (€8, representing €3 time value and €5 intrinsic value). The liability could have been more straightforwardly calculated as the fair value of the asset (€100) less the fair value of the option (€8) = €92. This gives rise to the following accounting entries:

	€	€
During year 1		
Asset (€100 – €80)	20	
Liability (€92 – €75)		17
Gain (Profit or loss)		3

The €3 gain recorded in profit or loss effectively represents the increase in the fair value of the option from €5 to €8 over the period. If the entity were able to exercise the option at this point, and did so, it would record the entry:

	€	€
Liability	92	
Loss (income statement)	3	
Cash		95

The particular transaction results in no overall gain or loss being reflected in profit or loss (i.e. €3 gain during the year less €3 loss on exercise of option). This represents the net of the €20 gain in the fair value of the asset (€100 at end of period less €80 at start) and the net cash outflow of €20 (€75 in on initial transfer, €95 out on exercise of option).

B   Asset decreases in value

Suppose instead that during the first year the fair value of the asset fell to €65 and the time value of the option at the end of the year was only €1. The liability would be measured at the fair value of the transferred asset less the time value of the option, i.e. €65 – €1 = €64. This would generate the accounting entries:

	€	€
During year 1		
Liability (€64 – €75)	11	
Loss (profit or loss)	4	
Asset (€65 – €80)		15

Again the overall loss shown in profit or loss represents the movement in the fair value of the option over the period from €5 to €1. Suppose that one year later there was no change in the fair value of the asset, and the option expired unexercised. The entity would then record the accounting entry:

	€	€
At end of year 2		
Liability	64	
Loss (profit or loss)	1	
Asset (balance sheet)		65

This results in an overall loss for the transaction as a whole of €5 (€4 in year 1 and €1 in year 2), which represents the difference between the carrying value of the asset at the date of original transfer (€80) and the proceeds received (€75).

The amount of any consideration received is in principle not relevant to the measurement of the liability. If, for example, the entity originally received consideration of €72, it would still record a liability of €75 and a 'day one' loss of €3. If it received consideration of €80, it would still record a liability of €75 and a 'day one' profit of €5. The IASB no doubt presumes that such transactions are likely to be undertaken only by sophisticated market participants such that the consideration received will always be equivalent to the fair value of the asset less the fair value of the option. However, there may well be instances where this is not the case, such as in transactions between members of the same group or other related parties.

II   Transferee's put option

If a transferee's put option prevents derecognition (see 4.5.3 and 4.7 above) of a transferred asset measured at fair value, IAS 39 requires the asset to be measured at the lower of fair value and the option exercise price. The basis for this is treatment is that the entity has no right to increases in the fair value of the transferred asset above the exercise price of the option. The associated liability is measured at the option exercise price plus the time value of the option. This ensures that the net carrying amount of the asset and the associated liability is the fair value of the put option obligation, as illustrated by Example 16.16 below.[116]

Example 16.16:   Asset measured at fair value subject to transferee's put option

An entity has a financial asset, accounted for at fair value. At 1 January 2005 it transfers the asset, then carried at €98, to a third party, subject to a put option whereby the transferee can compel the entity to reacquire the asset for €100. The option is considered to be neither deeply in the money nor deeply out of the money. IAS 39 therefore requires the entity to continue to recognise the asset to the extent of its continuing involvement (Figure 1, Box 9 – see also 4.7.2 C above), and to continue recording it at the lower of (a) fair value and (b) €100 (the exercise price of the option). Assuming that the transferor pays €106 for the asset, representing €98 fair value of the asset plus €8 time value of the option, the entity would record the accounting entry:

	€	€
Date of transfer		
Cash	106	
Liability		106

A   Transferred asset increases in value

Suppose that at 31 December 2005, the option has a time value of €5 and the fair value of the asset is €120. IAS 39 requires the carrying value of the asset to be restricted to €100 (the exercise price of the option). The liability is measured at the exercise price plus the time value of the option (i.e. to the transferee), i.e. €100 + €5 = €105. This has the result that the net of the carrying value of the asset (€100) and the carrying value of the liability (€105) equals the fair value of the option to the transferor (–€5). Again, the liability could have been more easily calculated as the carrying value of the asset (€100) less the fair value of the option to the transferor (–€5) = €105.

This gives the accounting entry:

	€	€
Year 1		
Asset (€100 – €98)	2	
Liability (€105 – €106)	1	
Gain (profit or loss)		3

The gain of €3 effectively represents the decrease in the time value of the option (an *gain* from the transferor's perspective) from €8 to €5.

If the option were then to lapse unexercised, with no further change in the fair value of the asset, the entity would record the accounting entry:

	€	€
On lapse of option		
Liability	105	
Asset		100
Gain (profit or loss)		5

The total gain on the transaction of €8 (€3 in Year 1 and €5 on lapse) represents the option premium of €8 (i.e. the difference between the total consideration of €106 and the carrying value of the asset of €98) received at the outset.

B   *Transferred asset decreases in value*

Suppose instead that at 31 December 2005, the option has a time value of €5 but the fair value of the asset is €90. IAS 39 requires the carrying value of the asset to be measured at its fair value of €90. The liability is measured at the exercise price plus the time value of the option (i.e. to the transferee), i.e. €100 + €5 = €105.

This gives the accounting entry:

	€	€
Year 1		
Liability (€105 – €106)	1	
Loss (profit or loss)	7	
Asset (€90 – €98)		8

This has the result that the net of the carrying value of the asset (€90) and the liability (€105), i.e. €(-15) represents the fair value of the option to the transferor (i.e. intrinsic value €(–10) [€100 exercise price versus €90 value of asset] + time value €(–5)). The €7 loss represents the increase in the fair value of the option (a loss to the transferor) from €8 at the outset to €15 at 31 December 2005.

If the transferee were able to, and did, exercise its option at that point, the entity would record the accounting entry:

	€	€
On exercise of option		
Liability	105	
Cash		100
Gain (profit or loss)		5

The overall €2 loss (i.e. €5 gain above and €7 loss during Year 1) represents the net cash of €8 received from the transferee (€108 in at inception less €100 out on exercise) less the €10 fall in fair value of the transferred asset (€100 at inception less €90 at exercise).

III   'Collar' put and call options

Assets may be transferred in a way designed to ensure that the transferee is shielded from excessive losses on the transferred asset but has to pass significant gains on the asset back to the transferor. Such an arrangement is known as a 'collar', on the basis that it allocates a range of potential value movements in the asset to the transferee, with movements outside that range accruing to the transferor. A simple form of 'collar' would be to transfer an asset subject to a purchased call option (allowing the transferor to reacquire the asset if it increases in value beyond a certain level) and a written put option (allowing the transferee to compel the transferor to reacquire the asset if it falls in value beyond a certain level).

If a collar, in the form of a purchased call and written put option, prevents derecognition (see 4.5.3 and 4.7 above) of a transferred asset measured at fair value, IAS 39 requires the entity to continue to measure the asset at fair value. The associated liability is measured at:

- if the call option is in or at the money, the sum of the call exercise price and fair value of the put option less the time value of the call option, or

- if the call option is out of the money, the sum of the fair value of the asset and the fair value of the put option less the time value of the call option.

The adjustment to the associated liability ensures that the net carrying amount of the asset and the associated liability is the fair value of the options held and written by the entity, as illustrated by Example 16.17 below.[117]

Example 16.17:   Asset measured at fair value subject to collar put and call options

An entity has a financial asset, accounted for at fair value, carried at €100. It transfers the asset to a third party, subject to:

- a call option whereby the entity can compel the transferee to sell the asset back to the entity for €120, and

- a put option whereby the transferee can compel the entity to reacquire the asset for €80.

The options are considered to be neither deeply in the money nor deeply out of the money. IAS 39 therefore requires the entity to continue to recognise the asset to the extent of its continuing involvement (Figure 1, Box 9 – see also 4.7.2 C above), and to continue recording it at fair value.

At the date of transfer, the time value of the put and call are €1 and €5 respectively. At the date of transfer, the call option is out of the money, so that the associated liability is calculated as the sum of the fair value of the asset and the fair value of the put option less the time value of the call option, i.e. (€100+€1) – €5 = €96. The net of this and the fair value of the asset (€100) is €4 which is the net fair value of the two options (call €5 less put €1). Again the liability could have been calculated as the fair value of the asset (€100) less the fair value (to the transferor) of the put option (–€1) and the call option (€5), i.e. €100 – (–€1) – €5 = €96. Assuming that the transaction is undertaken at arm's length, the transferee would pay €96 for the asset and the entity would record the accounting entry:

	€	€
Date of transfer		
Cash	96	
Liability		96

A   *Transferred asset increases in value*

Suppose that, at 31 December 2005, the fair value of the asset is €140, and the time value of the put and call are €0.5 and €2 respectively. The call option is now in the money, so that IAS 39 requires the entity to recognise a liability equal to the sum of the call exercise price and fair value of the put option less the time value of the call option, i.e. (€120+€0.5) – €2 = €118.5. The net of this and the carrying value of the asset (€140) is €21.5 which is the net fair value of the two options (call €22 [time value €2 plus intrinsic value €20] less put €0.5 = €21.5). Again the liability could have been calculated as the fair value of the asset (€100) less the fair value (to the transferor) of the put option (–€0.5) and the call option (€22), i.e. €140 – (–€0.5) – €22 = €118.5. This gives the accounting entry:

	€	€
Year 1		
Asset (€140 – €100)	40.0	
Gain (profit or loss)		17.5
Liability (€118.5 – €96)		22.5

The gain represents the increase in fair value of the call option of €17 (€5 at outset and €22 at 31 December 2005) plus the €0.5 decrease (an gain from the transferor's perspective) in the fair value of the put option (€1 at outset and €0.5 at 31 December 2005).

If the entity were able to, and did, exercise its call option, it would record the entry:

	€	€
Exercise of call option		
Liability	118.5	
Loss (profit or loss)	1.5	
Cash		120.0

The overall gain of €16 on the transaction (€1.5 loss above and €17.5 profit recorded in Year 1) represents the increase in fair value of the asset of €40 (€100 at outset, €140 at 31 December 2005) less the net €24 paid to the transferee (€120 paid on exercise of call less €96 received on initial transfer).

B   *Transferred asset decreases in value*

Suppose instead that, at 31 December 2005, the fair value of the asset is €78, and the time value of the put and call are €0.5 and €2 respectively. The call option is now out of the money, so that IAS 39 requires the entity to recognise a liability equal to the sum of the fair value of the asset and the fair value of the put option (i.e. €2.5 – time value €0.5 plus intrinsic value €2 [€80 exercise price versus €78 fair value of asset]) less the time value of the call option, i.e. (€78+€2.5) – €2 = €78.5.

The net of this and the carrying value of the asset (€78) is €(–0.5) which is the net fair value of the two options (call €2 less put €2.5 = €(–0.5)). Again the liability could have been calculated as the fair value of the asset (€78) less the fair value (to the transferor) of the put option (–€2.5) and the call option (€2), i.e. €78 – (–€2.5) – €2 = €78.5. This gives the accounting entry:

	€	€
Year 1		
Liability (€78.5 – €96)	17.5	
Loss (profit or loss)	4.5	
Asset (€78 – €100)		22.0

The loss represents the decrease in the fair value of the call option of €3 (€5 at outset and €2 at 31 December 2005) plus the €1.5 increase (a decrease from the transferor's perspective) in the fair value of the put option (€1 at outset and €2.5 at 31 December 2005).

If the transferee were able to, and did, exercise its put option, the entity would record the entry:

	€	€
Exercise of put option		
Liability	78.5	
Loss (profit or loss)	1.5	
Cash		80.0

The overall loss of €6 on the transaction (€1.5 loss above and €4.5 loss recorded in Year 1) represents the decrease in fair value of the asset of €22 (€100 at outset, €78 at 31 December 2005) offset by the net €16 received from the transferee (€96 received on initial transfer less €80 paid on exercise of put).

D   Continuing involvement in part only of a financial asset

IAS 39 gives the following example of the application of the continuing involvement approach to continuing involvement with part only of a financial asset.[118]

Example 16.18: Continuing involvement in part only of a financial asset

An entity has a portfolio of prepayable loans whose coupon and effective interest rate is 10% and whose principal amount and amortised cost is €10 million. It enters into a transaction in which, in return for a payment of €9.115 million, the transferee obtains the right to €9 million of any collections of principal plus 9.5% interest.

The entity retains rights to €1 million of any collections of principal plus interest at 10%, plus the remaining 0.5% ('excess spread') on the remaining €9 million of principal. Collections from prepayments are allocated between the entity and the transferee proportionately in the ratio of 1:9, but any defaults are deducted from the entity's interest of €1 million until that interest is exhausted.

The fair value of the loans at the date of the transaction is €10.1 million and the estimated fair value of the excess spread of 0.5 per cent is €40,000.

The entity determines that it has transferred some significant risks and rewards of ownership (for example, significant prepayment risk) but has also retained some significant risks and rewards of ownership because of its subordinated retained interest (Figure 1, Box 7, No) and has retained control (Figure 1, Box 8, Yes). It therefore applies the continuing involvement approach (Figure 1, Box 9).

The entity analyses the transaction as:

*   a retention of a fully proportionate retained interest of €1 million, plus
*   the subordination of that retained interest to provide credit enhancement to the transferee for credit losses.

The entity calculates that €9.09 million (90% of €10.1 million) of the consideration received of €9.115 million represents the consideration for a fully proportionate 90% share. The remainder of the consideration (€25,000) received represents consideration received by the entity for subordinating its retained interest to provide credit enhancement to the transferee for credit losses. In addition, the excess spread of 0.5% represents consideration received for the credit enhancement. Accordingly, the total consideration received for the credit enhancement is €65,000 (€25,000 received from transferee plus €40,000 fair value of excess spread).

The entity first calculates the gain or loss on the sale of the 90% share of cash flows. Assuming that separate fair values of the 10% part transferred and the 90% part retained are not available at the date of the transfer, the entity allocates the carrying amount of the asset pro-rata to the fair values of those parts (see 4.8.1 A and B and 4.8.3 E above). The total fair value of the portfolio is considered to be €10.1 million (see above), and the fair value of the consideration for the part disposed of €9.09 million. The carrying amount of the whole portfolio is €10 million. This implies a carrying amount for the part disposed of €10m × 9.09/10.1 = €9 million, and for the part retained €1 million. The gain on the sale of the 90% is therefore €90,000 (€9.09 million – €9 million).

In addition, IAS 39 requires the entity to recognise the continuing involvement that results from the subordination of its retained interest for credit losses. Accordingly, it recognises an asset of €1 million (the maximum amount of the cash flows it would not receive under the subordination), and an associated liability of €1.065 million (the maximum amount of the cash flows it would not receive under the subordination, i.e. €1 million, plus the consideration for the subordination of €65,000). It also recognises an asset for the fair value of the excess spread which forms part of the consideration for the subordination.

This gives rise to the accounting entry:

	€000	€000
Cash	9,115	
Asset for the subordination of the residual interest	1,000	
Excess spread received for subordination	40	
Loan portfolio		9,000
Liability for subordination		1,065
Gain on disposal		90

It is crucial to an understanding of this example that, as a result of the transaction, the original asset (the portfolio of prepayable loans) is being accounted for as two separate assets. Because the cash flows from the portfolio are split in fully proportionate (pro-rata) shares (see 4.2 above), each of these assets must be considered separately.

The first of these assets, the right to cash flows of €9 million, continues to be recognised only to the extent of the entity's continuing involvement, which in this case is via the credit enhancement. The approach is very similar to continuing involvement through guarantee (see Example 16.13 at A above), except that the liability for subordination includes the maximum cash flow that the entity might not receive from its retained share (i.e. €1 million) rather than, as in Example 16.13, a potential cash outflow (the guarantee amount, which is the maximum amount that the entity could be required to repay). This is aggregated with the fair value of the amount received in respect of the credit enhancement, in order to calculate the full liability for subordination. This parallels the way that the fair value of the guarantee is added to the guarantee amount in order to calculate the associated liability.[119]

The second asset is the entity's proportionate retained share of €1 million. It is, seemingly, irrelevant to the accounting analysis in IAS 39 that this has already been taken into account in calculating the entity's continuing involvement in the remaining €9 million of the portfolio.

The effect is to gross up the balance sheet with a subordination asset and liability. As IAS 39 notes, immediately following the transaction, the carrying amount of the asset is €2.04 million (i.e. €1 million part retained plus €1 million subordination asset plus €40,000 excess spread) – in respect of an asset whose fair value is only €1.01 million!

We have some reservations concerning the example above. First, we challenge whether, as a point of principle, it is appropriate to apply the derecognition criteria to part of an asset where the part that is retained provides credit enhancement for the transferee. As discussed more fully at 4.2.1 above, IAS 39 is implicitly drawing a distinction between:

- a guarantee that could result in an outflow of the total resources of the transferor, or a return of consideration for the transfer already received (which would not allow partial derecognition), and

- a guarantee that could result in the transferor losing the right to receive a specific future cash inflow, but not being obliged to make any other payment should that specific future cash inflow not materialise.

Moreover, even in the context of the analysis presented by IAS 39, we do not understand the basis of the treatment of the excess spread. The example simply asserts that this forms part of the consideration for providing the subordination, although it is not clear that it forms any more or any less of the consideration for the subordination than the interest and principal on the 10% of the portfolio retained.

In our view, a more logical analysis would have been that:

- the entity has disposed of not 90% of the whole portfolio, but 90% of the principal balances and 9.5% interest on that 90%, and

- the consideration for the subordination is still €65,000, on the basis that if:

  (a)   the fair value of the consideration for a fully proportionate share of 90% (i.e. including 10% interest) is €9,090,000, and

  (b)   the fair value of the excess spread of 0.5% interest is €40,000, then

  the fair value of consideration for a fully proportionate share less the excess spread is €9,050,000 (i.e. €9,090,000 less €40,000). This in turn means that the balance of the total consideration of €9,115,000 (i.e. €65,000) relates to the subordination.

In addition, of course, Example 16.18 ignores the possibility that the excess spread is retained by the transferor because it continues to service the portfolio, although this may be an attempt to avoid overcomplicating matters even further.

4.8.5   *Miscellaneous provisions*

IAS 39 contains a number of accounting provisions generally applicable to transfers of assets, as follows.

A   *Offset*

IAS 39 provides that, if a transferred asset continues to be recognised, the entity must not offset:

- the asset with the associated liability, or

- any income arising from the transferred with any expense incurred on the associated liability.[120]

Whilst IAS 39 does not say so specifically, this is clearly intended to apply both to assets that continue to be recognised in full and to those that continue to recognised to the extent of their continuing involvement.

This requirement apparently over-rides the offset criteria in IAS 32[121] (see 6 below), as illustrated, for example, by the various situations highlighted in the discussion at 4.7 and 4.8.1 to 4.8.4 above where a transaction required to be net-settled (which would normally be required to be accounted for as such under IAS 32) is accounted for as if it were to be gross-settled.

B   Collateral

If a transferor provides non-cash collateral (such as debt or equity instruments) to the transferee, the accounting treatment for the collateral by both the transferor and the transferee depends on:

- whether the transferee has the right to sell or repledge the collateral, and
- whether the transferor has defaulted.

If the transferee has the right by contract or custom to sell or repledge a collateral asset, the transferor should reclassify that asset in its balance sheet (e.g. as a loaned asset, pledged equity instruments or repurchase receivable) separately from other assets.

If the transferee sells collateral pledged to it, it recognises the proceeds from the sale and a liability measured at fair value for its obligation to return the collateral.

If the transferor defaults under the terms of the contract and is no longer entitled to redeem the collateral, it derecognises the collateral, and the transferee either:

- recognises the collateral as its asset initially measured at fair value or,
- if it has already sold the collateral, derecognises its obligation to return the collateral.

In no other circumstances should the transferor derecognise, or the transferee recognise, the collateral as an asset.[122]

C   *Rights or obligations over transferred assets that continue to be recognised*

Where a transfer of a financial asset does not qualify for derecognition, the transferor may well have contractual rights or obligations related to the transfer, such as options or forward repurchase contracts, that are derivatives of a type that would normally be required to be recognised under IAS 39.

IAS 39 prohibits separate recognition of such derivatives, if recognition of the derivative together with either the transferred asset or the liability arising from the transfer would result in recognising the same rights or obligations twice.

For example, IAS 39 notes that a call option retained by the transferor may prevent a transfer of financial assets from being accounted for as a sale (see 4.7 above). In that case, the call option must not be separately recognised as a derivative asset.[123]

5 DERECOGNITION – FINANCIAL LIABILITIES

The provisions of IAS 39 with respect to the derecognition of financial liabilities are generally more straightforward and less subjective than those for the derecognition of financial assets. However, they are also very different from the rules for derecognition of assets which focus primarily on the economic substance of the transaction. By contrast, the rules for derecognition of liabilities, like the provisions of IAS 32 for the identification of instruments as financial liabilities (see Chapter 17), focus more on legal obligations than on economic substance – or, as the IASB would doubtless argue, they are based on the view that the economic substance of whether an entity has a liability to a third party is ultimately dictated by the legal rights and obligations that exist between them.

IAS 39 contains provisions relating to:

- the extinguishment of debt (see 5.1 below);

- the substitution or modification of debt by the original lender (see 5.2 below); and

- the calculation of any profit or loss arising on the derecognition of debt (see 5.3 below).

5.1 Extinguishment of debt

IAS 39 requires an entity to derecognise (i.e. remove from its balance sheet) a financial liability (or a part of a financial liability – see 5.1.1 below) when, and only when, it is 'extinguished', that is, when the obligation specified in the contract is discharged, cancelled, or expires.[124] This will be achieved when the debtor either:

- discharges the liability (or part of it) by paying the creditor, normally with cash, other financial assets, goods or services; or

- is legally released from primary responsibility for the liability (or part of it) either by process of law or by the creditor.[125] Extinguishment of liabilities by legal release is discussed further at 5.1.2 below.

If the issuer of a debt instrument repurchases the instrument, the debt is extinguished even if the issuer is a market maker in that instrument, or otherwise intends to resell or reissue it in the near term.[126] IAS 39 focuses only on whether the entity has a legal obligation to reissue the debt, not on whether it is a commercial imperative for it to do so.

5.1.1 *What constitutes 'part' of a liability?*

As noted above, the requirements of IAS 39 for the derecognition of liabilities apply to all or 'part' of a financial liability. It is not entirely clear what is meant by 'part' of a liability in this context. The rules, and the examples, in IAS 39 seem to be drafted in the context of transactions that settle all remaining cash flows (i.e. interest and principal) of a portion of a liability, such as the repayment of £25 million of a £100 million loan.

However, these provisions are presumably also intended to apply in situations where an entity prepays the interest only (or a portion of future interest payments) or the principal only (or a portion of future principal payments) on a loan.

5.1.2   *Legal release by creditor*

As noted above, a liability can be derecognised by a debtor if the creditor legally releases the debtor from the liability. It is clear that IAS 39 regards legal release as crucial, with the effect that very similar (if not identical) situations may lead to different results purely because of the legal form.

For example, IAS 39 provides that:

(a)   where a debtor is legally released from a liability, derecognition is not precluded by the fact that the debtor has given a guarantee in respect of the liability;[127] but

(b)   if a debtor pays a third party to assume an obligation and notifies its creditor that the third party has assumed the debt obligation, the debtor derecognises the debt obligation if, and only if, the creditor legally releases the debtor from its obligations.[128]

The effect of these requirements can be shown by Example 16.19.

Example 16.19:   Transfer of debt obligations with and without legal release

Scenario 1

Entity A issues bonds that have a carrying amount and fair value of $1,000,000. A pays $1,000,000 to Entity B for B to assume responsibility for paying interest and principal on the bonds to the bondholders. The bondholders are informed that B has assumed responsibility for the debt. However, A is not legally released from the obligation to pay interest and principal by the bondholders. Accordingly, if B does not make payments when due, the bondholders may seek payment from A.

Scenario 2

Entity A issues bonds that have a carrying amount and fair value of $1,000,000. A pays $1,000,000 to Entity B for B to assume responsibility for paying interest and principal on the bonds to the bondholders. The bondholders are informed that B has assumed responsibility for the debt and legally release A from any further obligation under the debt. However, A enters into a guarantee arrangement whereby, if B does not make payments when due, the bondholders may seek payment from A.

It is clear, in our view, that in either scenario above the bondholders are in the same economic and legal position – they will receive payments from B and, if B defaults, they will have recourse to A.

However, IAS 39 gives rise to the, in our view, anomalous result that:

* Scenario 1 is accounted for by the continuing recognition of the debt because no legal release has been obtained; but

* Scenario 2 is accounted for by derecognition of the debt, and recognition of the guarantee, notwithstanding that the effect of the guarantee is to put A back in the same position as if it had not been released from its obligations under the original bond.

IAS 39 also clarifies that, if a debtor:

- transfers its obligations under a debt to a third party and obtains legal release from its obligations by the creditor, but

- undertakes to make payments to the third party so as to enable it to meet its obligations to the creditor,

it should derecognise the original debt, but recognise a new debt obligation to the third party.[129]

5.1.3 'In-substance defeasance' arrangements

Entities sometimes enter into so-called 'in-substance defeasance' arrangements in respect of financial liabilities. These typically involve a lump sum payment to a third party (other than the creditor) such as a trust, which then invests the funds in (typically) very low-risk assets to which the entity has no, or very limited, rights of access. These assets are then applied to discharge all the remaining interest and principal payments on the original financial liabilities. It is sometimes argued that the risk-free nature of the assets, and the entity's lack of access to them, means that the entity is in substance in no different position than if it had actually repaid the original financial liability.

IAS 39 regards such arrangements as not giving rise to derecognition of the original liability in the absence of legal release by the creditor.[130]

5.1.4 Extinguishment in exchange for transfer of assets not meeting the derecognition criteria

IAS 39 notes that in some cases legal release may be achieved by transferring assets to the creditor which do not meet the criteria for derecognition (see 4 above). In such a case, the debtor will derecognise the liability from which it has been released, but recognise a new liability relating to the transferred assets that may be equal to the derecognised liability.[131] It is not entirely clear what is envisaged here, but it may be some such scenario as the following.

Example 16.20: Extinguishment of debt in exchange for transfer of assets not meeting derecognition criteria.

An entity has a bank loan of €1 million. The bank agrees to accept in full payment of the loan the transfer to it by the entity of a portfolio of corporate bonds with a market value of €1 million. The entity and the bank then enter into a put and call option over the bonds, the effect of which will be that the entity will repurchase the bonds in three years' time at a price that gives the bank a lender's return on €1 million. As discussed further at 4 above, this would have the effect that the entity is unable to derecognise the bonds.

Under the provisions of in IAS 39, the entity would be able to derecognise the original bank loan, as it has been legally released from it. However, the provisions under discussion here have the overall result that a loan effectively continues to be recognised. Strictly, however, the analysis is that the original loan has been derecognised and a new one recognised. In effect the accounting is representing that the entity has repaid the original loan and replaced it with a new one secured on a bond portfolio.

5.2   Exchange and modification of debt by original lender

It is common for an entity, particularly but not necessarily when in financial difficulties, to approach its major creditors for a restructuring of its debt commitments – for example, an agreement to postpone the repayment of principal in exchange for higher interest payments in the meantime, or to roll up interest into a single 'bullet' payment of interest and principal at the end of the term. Such changes to the terms of debt can be effected through a number of ways, in particular:

- a notional repayment of the original loan followed by an immediate re-lending of all or part of the proceeds of the notional repayment as a new loan ('exchange'), or

- legal amendment of the original loan agreement ('modification').

The accounting issue raised by such transactions is essentially whether there is, in fact, anything to account for. For example, if an entity owes £100 million at floating rate interest and negotiates with its bankers to change the interest to a fixed coupon of 7%, should the accounting treatment reflect that fact that:

(a)   the entity still owes £100 million to the same lender, and so is in the same position as before; or

(b)   the modification of the interest profile has altered the net present value of the total obligations under the loan?

IAS 39 requires an exchange between an existing borrower and lender of debt instruments with 'substantially different' terms to be accounted for as an extinguishment of the original financial liability and the recognition of a new financial liability. Similarly, a substantial modification of the terms of an existing financial liability, or a part of it, (whether or not due to the financial difficulty of the debtor) should be accounted for as an extinguishment of the original financial liability and the recognition of a new financial liability.[132]

IAS 39 regards the terms of exchanged or modified debt as 'substantially different' if the net present value of the cash flows under the new terms (including any fees paid net of any fees received) discounted at the original effective interest rate is at least 10% different from the discounted present value of the remaining cash flows of the original debt instrument.[133] Whilst IAS 39 does not say so explicitly, it seems clear that the discounted present value of the remaining cash flows of the original debt instrument must also be determined using the original effective interest rate, so that there is a 'like for like' comparison.

It should be noted that IAS 39 does not prohibit an entity from accounting for an exchange or modification of a liability where the net present value of the cash flows under the new terms is less than 10% different from the discounted present value of the remaining cash flows of the original debt instrument. There may be situations in which the modification of the debt is so fundamental (e.g. where it is changed from Euro debt to US dollar debt) that immediate recognition of smaller changes in fair value may be appropriate.

5.2.1   Costs and fees

An entity will almost always be required to pay fees to the lender and incur costs (such as legal expenses) on an exchange or modification of a financial liability.

If an exchange of debt instruments or modification of terms is accounted for as an extinguishment of the original debt, IAS 39 requires any costs or fees incurred to be recognised as part of the gain or loss on the extinguishment (see 5.3 below). However, if the exchange or modification is not accounted for as an extinguishment, any costs or fees incurred are an adjustment to the carrying amount of the liability and are amortised over the remaining term of the modified liability.[134]

5.2.2   Illustrative examples

The requirements of IAS 39 for exchanges and modifications of debt are reasonably straightforward in principle but give rise to a number of practical issues, as illustrated by Examples 16.21 and 16.22 below.

Example 16.21:   Modification of debt not treated as extinguishment

On 1 January 2001 an entity borrowed £100 million on, at that time, arm's length market terms that interest of 7% was to be paid annually in arrears and the loan repaid in full on 31 December 2010. Transaction costs of £5 million were incurred. Assuming that the loan had run to term, the entity would have recorded the following amounts using the effective interest rate method. The loan is originally recorded at the issue proceeds of £100 million less transaction costs of £5 million, and the effective interest rate of 7.69% is derived by computer program or trial and error (for more detailed discussion of the effective interest rate method, see Chapter 18 at 5).

Year	Liability b/f £m	Interest at 7.69% £m	Cash paid £m	Liability c/f £m
1.1.2001	95.00	7.30	(7.00)	95.30
2001	95.30	7.33	(7.00)	95.63
2002	95.63	7.36	(7.00)	95.99
2003	95.99	7.38	(7.00)	96.37
2004	96.37	7.41	(7.00)	96.78
2005	96.78	7.44	(7.00)	97.22
2006	97.22	7.48	(7.00)	97.70
2007	97.70	7.51	(7.00)	98.21
2008	98.21	7.56	(7.00)	98.77
2009	98.77	7.59	(7.00)	99.36
2010	99.36	7.64	(107.00)	–

During 2005 the entity is in financial difficulties and approaches the bondholders for a modification of the terms of the bond. These are agreed on 1 January 2006 as follows. No cash interest will be paid in 2006 or 2007. From 2008 onwards interest of 9% will be paid annually in arrears, and the term of the loan will be extended for two years until 31 December 2012. Legal fees of £2 million are incurred, and paid on 1 January 2006.

The entity is required to compute the present value of the new arrangement using the original effective interest rate of 7.69%. This gives a net present value for the modified debt of £92.77 million calculated as follows.

Year	Cash flow	£m	Discount factor	£m
1.1.2006	Legal fees	2.00	1	2.00
2008	Interest	9.00	$1/1.0769^3$	7.21
2009	Interest	9.00	$1/1.0769^4$	6.69
2010	Interest	9.00	$1/1.0769^5$	6.21
2011	Interest	9.00	$1/1.0769^6$	5.77
2012	Interest and principal	109.00	$1/1.0769^7$	64.89
			Total	92.77

This represents 95.4% of the current carrying value of the debt as at the end of 2005 of £97.22 million, so that the net present value of the modified bond (discounted at the effective interest rate of the original bond) is 4.6% different from that of the original bond. This is less than 10%, so that the modification is not automatically required to be treated as an extinguishment under IAS 39.

However, the difference between the net present values of the original and the modified bonds presents a problem. Clearly, if the entity were to continue to apply the original effective interest rate to the existing carrying value of the bond a significant unamortised amount would emerge as a result of the change to the timing and quantum of the new future cash flows. In order for the numbers to 'work', either the carrying amount of the liability, or the effective interest rate, must be changed.

Here there is a conflict between the specific rules of IAS 39 relating to exchanges and modification of liabilities and the general requirements for application of the effective interest method. The specific rule relating to exchanges and modifications of debt not regarded as an extinguishment is clear that:

(a)   there should be no derecognition of the original debt, and

(b)   any transaction costs associated with the modified debt should be amortised over the remaining term of the modified liability.

In other words, the current carrying value of £97.22 million must stand and the effective interest rate must be changed.

On the other hand, the general rules for the application of the effective interest method (see Chapter 18 at 5) are equally clear:

'If an entity revises its estimates of payments or receipts the entity shall adjust the carrying amount of the financial asset or financial liability (or group of financial instruments) to reflect actual and revised estimated cash flows. The entity recalculates the carrying amount by computing the present value of estimated future cash flows at the financial instrument's original effective interest rate. The adjustment is recognised as income or expense in profit or loss.'[135]

Applied in this situation, this would result in the carrying amount of the loan being restated to the £92.77 million calculated above with the recognition of a gain of £4.45 million (£97.22m current carrying value less £92.77m recalculated net present value). The £92.77 million would then be amortised at the original effective interest rate.

In our view, the specific rules dealing with derecognition of financial liabilities must take precedence. If they do not, then the exemption in IAS 39 from treating exchanges and modifications within the 10% 'band' as extinguishments would have no practical effect. The only way that the numbers can then be processed mechanically is to derive a new effective interest rate for the exchanged or modified borrowing, treating the carrying amount of the original borrowing as the issue proceeds. This was effectively the method prescribed in the guidance (in Q&A 62-1) to the original version of IAS 39 (whose requirements for derecognition of liabilities have been carried forward without major change into the current version).

Under this approach the carrying value of the of bond at the end of 2005 of £97.22 million, net of the transaction costs of £2 million, is treated as a new borrowing of £95.22 million, accounted for as follows, using the newly derived effective interest rate of 6.872%.

Year	Liability b/f £m	Interest at 6.872% £m	Cash paid £m	Liability c/f £m
2006	95.22	6.54		101.76
2007	101.76	6.99		108.75
2008	108.75	7.48	(9.00)	107.23
2009	107.23	7.37	(9.00)	105.60
2010	105.60	7.26	(9.00)	103.86
2011	103.86	7.13	(9.00)	101.99
2012	101.99	7.01	(109.00)	–

Example 16.22: Modification of debt treated as extinguishment

Assume the same facts as in Example 16.21 above, except that on 1 January 2006 the entity comes to an arrangement with the bondholders to modify the terms of the bonds as follows.

No cash interest will be paid in 2006 or 2007. From 2008 onwards interest of 12.5% will be paid annually in arrears, and the term of the loan will be extended for three years until 31 December 2013. Legal fees of £2 million are incurred, and paid on 1 January 2006.

As in Example 16.21 above, the entity is required to compute the net present value of the new arrangement using the original effective interest rate of 7.69%. This gives a net present value for the modified debt of £107.3 million calculated as follows.

Year	Cash flow	£m	Discount factor	£m
1.1.2006	Legal fees	2.00	1	2.00
2008	Interest	12.50	$1/1.0769^3$	10.01
2009	Interest	12.50	$1/1.0769^4$	9.29
2010	Interest	12.50	$1/1.0769^5$	8.63
2011	Interest	12.50	$1/1.0769^6$	8.02
2012	Interest	12.50	$1/1.0769^7$	7.44
2013	Interest and principal	112.50	$1/1.0769^8$	62.19
			Total	107.58

This represents 110.6% of the current carrying value of the debt as at the end of 2005 of £97.22 million, so that the net present value of the modified bond (discounted at the effective interest rate of the original bond) is 10.6% different from that of the original bond. This is greater than 10%, so that the modification is required to be treated as an extinguishment under IAS 39.

This will involve derecognising the existing liability and recognising a new liability. The issue is then at what amount the new liability should be recognised. It is not the £107.58 million above, since this includes the transaction costs of £2 million, which are required to be treated as integral to the cash flows of the modified bond for the purposes of comparing it with the original bond, but are then required to be expensed immediately if the test identifies an extinguishment.

Moreover, as the accounting treatment is intended to represent the derecognition of an existing liability and the recognition of a new one, the modified bond must – in accordance with the general measurement provisions of IAS 39 (see Chapter 18) – be recognised at fair value and amortised using its own effective interest rate, not that applicable to the original bond.

The difficulty is obviously in determining the fair value of the modified bonds. If the bonds were quoted, a market value might be available. Another possible approach might be to discount the cash flows of the modified bond at the interest rate at which the entity could have issued a new bond on similar terms to the modified bond.

If the view were taken that the fair value of the modified bond was £98 million, the accounting treatment for the modification would be (see also 5.3 below):

	£m	£m
Original bond	97.22	
Loss on extinguishment of debt (income statement)	2.78	
Modified bond		98.00
Cash (transaction costs)		2.00

In this particular case, this has the result that the actual gain or loss recognised is actually somewhat smaller than the difference calculated between the net present value of the original and modified bonds that led to the requirement to recognise the gain or loss in the first place.

5.2.3 Settlement of financial liability with issue of new equity instrument

A related area not specifically covered in either IAS 32 or IAS 39 is the accounting treatment to be adopted where an entity issues non-convertible debt, but subsequently enters into an agreement with the debt-holder to discharge the liability under the debt in full or in part for an issue of equity instruments. This most often occurs when the entity is in financial difficulties.

This is discussed in Chapter 17 at 4.4.5.

5.3 Gains and losses on extinguishment of debt

When a financial liability (or part of a liability) is extinguished or transferred to another party, IAS 39 requires the difference between the carrying amount of the transferred financial liability (or part of a liability) and the consideration paid, including any non-cash assets transferred or liabilities assumed, to be recognised in profit or loss.[136]

If an entity repurchases only a part of a financial liability, it calculates the carrying value of the part disposed of (and hence the gain or loss on disposal) by allocating the previous carrying amount of the financial liability between the part that continues to be recognised and the part that is derecognised based on the relative fair values of those parts on the date of the repurchase.[137] In other words, the carrying amount of the liability is not simply reduced by consideration received.

This is illustrated in Example 16.23 below.

Example 16.23: Partial derecognition of debt

On 1 January 2005 an entity issues 500 million €1 10-year bonds which are traded in the capital markets. Issue costs of €15 million were incurred and the carrying value of the bonds at 31 December 2008 is €490 million. On 31 December 2008 the entity makes a market purchase of 120 million bonds at their then current market price of €0.97. The entity records the following accounting entry:

	£m	£m
Bonds (120/500 × €490m)	117.6	
Cash (120m × €0.97)		116.4
Gain on repurchase of debt		1.2

In some cases, as discussed in 5.2 above, a creditor may release a debtor from its present obligation to make payments, but the debtor assumes an obligation to pay if the party assuming primary responsibility defaults. In such a case, IAS 39 requires the debtor to recognise:

(a)   a new liability based on the fair value for the obligation for the guarantee; and

(b)   a gain or loss based on the difference between

(i)   any proceeds, and

(ii)   the carrying amount of the original liability (including any related unamortised costs) less the fair value of the new liability.[138]

5.4   Derivatives that can be financial assets or financial liabilities

A potential difficulty not addressed by IAS 39 is the required treatment for the transfer of a non-optional derivative, such as a swap or forward contract, that by its nature can be either a financial asset or a financial liability at various times during its life. A literal reading of IAS 39 could suggest that the rules for derecognition of financial assets should be applied when the derivative has a positive fair value to the entity and the rules for derecognition of financial liabilities should be applied when the derivative has a negative fair value to the entity. This could lead to very different results, given the significantly different approaches underlying each set of rules (see 5 above).

In practice, however, any transfer of such derivatives is likely to require the consent of the counterparty to the entity's legal release from its obligations under the contract, and the possible payment of a fee to compensate the counterparty for the difference between the creditworthiness of the entity and that of the transferee. Such procedures are much closer to those envisaged in the derecognition rules for financial liabilities than those implicit in the derecognition rules for financial assets. Accordingly, we believe that IAS 39's provisions for the derecognition of financial liabilities should be applied to all transfers of non-optional derivatives, irrespective of whether they have a positive or negative fair value at the date of transfer.

6 OFFSET

IAS 1 sets out a general principle that assets and liabilities should not be offset except where such offset is permitted or required by another accounting standard (see Chapter 3 at 4.1.5). IAS 32 provides some exceptions to this general rule applicable to financial assets and liabilities. As noted at 1.1 above, however, it is arguable that, conceptually speaking, the rules in IAS 32 are less exceptions to the general prohibition on offset than the identification of situations where an entity has separate assets and liabilities in form, but a single net asset or liability in substance.

IAS 32 requires a financial asset and a financial liability to be offset and the net amount reported in the balance sheet when, and only when, an entity:

(a)   has a legally enforceable right to set off the recognised amounts; and

(b)   intends either to settle on a net basis, or to realise the asset and settle the liability simultaneously.

However, in accounting for the transfer of an asset that does not qualify for derecognition, the transferred asset and any associated liability must not be offset,[139] even if they otherwise satisfy the offset criteria (see 4.8.4 above).

IAS 32 argues that offset is appropriate in the circumstances set out in (a) and (b) above, because the entity has in effect only a single cash flow and, hence, a single financial asset or financial liability. In other circumstances, financial assets and financial liabilities are presented separately from each other, consistently with their characteristics as resources or obligations of the entity.[140] Offset is not equivalent to derecognition, since no gain or loss can ever arise on offset, but may arise on derecognition.[141]

IAS 32 elaborates further on the detail of the conditions as follows.

6.1 Legal framework

IAS 32 describes a right of set-off as 'a debtor's legal right, by contract or otherwise, to settle or otherwise eliminate all or a portion of an amount due to a creditor by applying against that amount an amount due from the creditor.' The effectiveness of the right of set-off is thus essentially a legal matter, so that the specific conditions supporting the right may vary from one legal jurisdiction to another. Care must therefore be taken to establish which laws apply to the relationships between the parties.[142]

In unusual circumstances, a debtor (A) may have a legal right to apply an amount due from a third party (B) against an amount due to a creditor (C), provided that there is an agreement among A, B and C that clearly establishes A's right to set off amounts due from B against those due to C.[143]

6.2   Right and intention to settle net

IAS 32 emphasises that, in order to achieve offset of a financial asset and financial liability, it is necessary not only that the reporting entity is legally able to settle them net but also that it actually intends to do so. It is not sufficient to have the right (but not the intention) or the intention (but not the right) to settle net.

IAS 32 acknowledges that an enforceable right to set off a financial asset and a financial liability affects the rights and obligations associated with that asset and liability and may affect an entity's exposure to credit and liquidity risk. However, such a right is not, in itself, a sufficient basis for offsetting, since, in the absence of an intention to exercise the right or to settle simultaneously, the amount and timing of an entity's future cash flows are not affected. Similarly, an intention by one or both parties to settle on a net basis without the legal right to do so is not sufficient to justify offsetting because the rights and obligations associated with the individual financial asset and financial liability remain unaltered.[144]

IAS 32 notes that an entity's intentions with respect to settlement of particular assets and liabilities may be influenced by its normal business practices, the requirements of the financial markets and other circumstances that may limit the ability to settle net or simultaneously. When an entity has a right of set-off, but does not intend to settle net or to realise the asset and settle the liability simultaneously, the effect of the right on the entity's credit risk exposure is disclosed by giving the general credit risk disclosures required by IAS 32[145] (see Chapter 20 at 4.2).

6.3   Simultaneous settlement

IAS 32 also clarifies that the reference to 'simultaneous' settlement in the conditions for offset above is to be interpreted literally, as applying only to the realisation of a financial asset and settlement of a financial liability at the same moment. The standard gives as an example the type of overall market settlement that occurs in a clearing house or in a face-to-face exchange. In other circumstances, an entity may settle two instruments by receiving and paying separate amounts, becoming exposed to credit risk for the full amount of the asset or liquidity risk for the full amount of the liability. Such risk exposures, though relatively brief, may be significant, so that offset is not therefore appropriate. Accordingly, IAS 32 treats the realisation of a financial asset and settlement of a financial liability as simultaneous only when the transactions occur at the same moment.[146]

6.4   Situations where offset is not normally be appropriate

IAS 32 comments that its offset criteria are not normally satisfied in the following circumstances.

6.4.1   *Synthetic instruments*

An entity may enter into a number of different financial instruments designed to replicate the features of a single financial instrument (referred to as a 'synthetic instrument'). For example, if an entity issues floating rate debt and then enters into a pay fixed/receive floating interest rate swap, the combined economic effect is that the entity has issued fixed rate debt.

IAS 32 argues that each of the individual financial instruments that together constitute a 'synthetic instrument':

- represents a contractual right or obligation with its own terms and conditions,
- may be transferred or settled separately, and
- is exposed to risks that may differ from those to which the other financial instruments in the 'synthetic instrument' are exposed.

Accordingly, when one financial instrument in a 'synthetic instrument' is an asset and another is a liability, they are not offset and presented on an entity's balance sheet on a net basis unless they meet the criteria above.

While disclosures are provided about the significant terms and conditions of each financial instrument, an entity may indicate in addition the nature of the relationship between the individual instruments (see Chapter 20 at 3.4).[147]

6.4.2   *Other*

Offset is also usually inappropriate where:

(a)   financial assets and financial liabilities arise from financial instruments having the same primary risk exposure (e.g. assets and liabilities within a portfolio of forward contracts or other derivative instruments) but involving different counterparties;

(b)   financial or other assets are pledged as collateral for non-recourse financial liabilities;

(c)   financial assets are set aside in trust by a debtor for the purpose of discharging an obligation without those assets having been accepted by the creditor in settlement of the obligation (e.g. a sinking fund arrangement) – see also 5.1.3 above; or

(d)   obligations incurred as a result of events giving rise to losses are expected to be recovered from a third party by virtue of a claim made under an insurance policy.[148]

6.5   Master netting agreements

It is common practice for an entity that undertakes a number of financial instrument transactions with a single counterparty to enter into a 'master netting arrangement' with that counterparty. These arrangements are typically used by financial institutions to restrict their exposure to loss in the event of bankruptcy or other events that result in a counterparty being unable to meet its obligations. Such an agreement commonly creates a right of set-off that becomes enforceable, and affects the realisation or settlement of individual financial assets and financial liabilities, only following a specified event of default or in other circumstances not expected to arise in the normal course of business.

Where an entity has entered into such an agreement, the agreement does not provide the basis for the offset of assets and liabilities unless the criteria summarised above are satisfied.[149] This will typically be the case only if the default (or other event specified in the contract) has actually occurred. When financial assets and financial liabilities subject to a master netting arrangement are not offset, the effect of the arrangement falls within the scope of the disclosure requirements of IAS 32 relating to credit risk[150] (see Chapter 20 at 4.2).

7   TRANSITIONAL AND FIRST-TIME ADOPTION ISSUES

As noted at 2 above, the new versions of IAS 32 and IAS 39 must be applied for annual periods beginning on or after 1 January 2005. Entities are 'permitted' (rather than 'encouraged', as in the case of other recently issued standards) to adopt both standards in earlier periods, but must disclose that they have done so. They must also adopt IAS 39 as amended in March 2004, not as originally issued, and must adopt both IAS 32 and IAS 39 (as amended) at the same time.[151]

Except as specifically noted below, the requirements of IAS 32 and IAS 39 discussed in this chapter must be applied retrospectively, with full restatement of comparative amounts.[152] However, in the case of items subject to the requirements of IAS 39 (but not IAS 32), comparative amounts need not be restated if restatement would be impracticable, in which case the entity must disclose that fact and indicate the extent to which the information was restated.[153]

7.1   Transitional issues – derecognition of assets

The basic rule in IAS 39 is that an entity should apply the derecognition provisions for assets (discussed at 4 above) prospectively. Accordingly, if an entity derecognised financial assets under the previous IAS 39 (revised 2000) as a result of a transaction that occurred before 1 January 2004, it must not recognise those assets, even if they would not have been derecognised under the new version of IAS 39.[154]

However, notwithstanding this basic provision, an entity may apply the derecognition requirements discussed at 4 above retrospectively from any date of the entity's choosing, provided that the information needed to apply the new version of IAS 39 to assets and liabilities derecognised as a result of past transactions was obtained at the time of initially accounting for those transactions.[155]

7.2   First-time adoption issues

7.2.1   *Comparative information*

IFRS 1 – *First-time adoption of International Financial Reporting Standards* – exempts an entity that adopts IFRS for the first time before 1 January 2006 from complying with IAS 32 and IAS 39 in any comparative period presented in its first IFRS financial statements. An entity taking advantage of this exemption is required to:

(a)   apply its previous GAAP in the comparative information to financial instruments within the scope of IAS 32 and IAS 39;

(b)   disclose this fact, together with the basis used to prepare this information; and

(c)   disclose the nature of the main adjustments that would make the information comply with IAS 32 and IAS 39.

The entity need not quantify those adjustments. However, it must treat any adjustment between the balance sheet:

- at the comparative period's reporting date (i.e. the balance sheet that includes comparative information under previous GAAP), and

- at the start of the first IFRS reporting period (i.e. the first period that includes information that complies with IAS 32 and IAS 39 and IFRS 4)

as arising from a change in accounting policy and give the disclosures required by paragraph 28(a)-(e) and (f)(i) of IAS 8. Paragraph 28(f)(i) (i.e. the requirement to disclose the effect of a change of accounting policy on each line item in the financial statements) applies only to amounts presented in the balance sheet at the comparative period's reporting date.[156]

This exemption is addressed in more detail in Chapter 15 at 8.

7.2.2   *Recognition and derecognition*

The basic rule in IFRS 1 is that a first-time adopter should recognise all financial assets and financial liabilities that qualify for recognition, and have not yet qualified for derecognition, under IAS 39.[157]

However, an entity should not recognise non-derivative financial assets and liabilities derecognised under its previous GAAP as a result of a transaction that occurred before 1 January 2004, unless:

(a)   they qualify for recognition as the result of a later transaction or event;[158] or

(b)   derecognition occurred as the result of a transfer to an entity treated as an SPE under SIC–12 (see B below).

Notwithstanding this provision, however, an entity may apply the derecognition requirements discussed at 4 and 5 above retrospectively from any date of the entity's choosing, provided that the information needed to apply the new version of IAS 39 to assets and liabilities derecognised as a result of past transactions was obtained at the time of initially accounting for those transactions.[159]

A Multiple transfers under same arrangement

IFRS 1 acknowledges that some arrangements for the transfer of assets, particularly securitisations, may last for some time, with the result that transfers might be made both before and on or after 1 January 2004 under the same arrangement. IFRS 1 clarifies that transfers made under such arrangements fall within the first-time adoption provisions only if they occurred before 1 January 2004. Transfers on or after 1 January 2004 are subject to the full requirements of IAS 39.[160]

B Transfers to SPEs

The provisions of SIC–12 with regard to the consolidation of SPEs are fully retrospective for first-time adopters. Thus if, under its previous GAAP, an entity derecognised non-derivative financial assets and liabilities as the result of a transfer to an entity treated as an SPE by SIC–12, those assets and liabilities will be re-recognised on transition to IFRS, but as the result of consolidation of the SPE rather than through application of IAS 39. Of course, if the SPE itself then subsequently achieved derecognition of the items concerned under the entity's previous GAAP (other than by transfer to a second SPE or member of the entity's group), then the items remain derecognised on transition.

References

1　IAS 39, *Financial Instruments: Recognition and Measurement*, IASB, December 2003 (amended March 2004).

2　IAS 32, *Financial Instruments: Presentation and Disclosure*, IASB, December 2003 (amended March 2004).

3　SIC-12, Consolidation – *Special Purpose Entities*, SIC, November 1998 (amended December 2003).

4　IAS 32, para. 96. IAS 39, para. 103.

5　IAS 32, Application Guidance, para. before para. AG1.

6　IAS 32, Illustrative Examples, para. after main heading.

7　IAS 39, Application Guidance, para. before para. AG1.

8　IAS 39, Guidance on Implementing, para. before main heading Section A; Illustrative Example, para. after main heading.

9　IAS 39, para. BC43.

10　IAS 39, paras. IN9-IN15.

11　IAS 32, para. 11

12　IAS 32, para. 11

13　IAS 32, para. 11

14　IAS 32, para. 11

15　IAS 32, para. 12 and IAS 39, para. 9.

16　IAS 32, para. 11

17　IAS 39, para. 14.

18　IAS 39, para. AG35(a).

19　IAS 39, para. AG35(b).

20　IAS 39, para. AG35(b).

21　IAS 39, paras. BC149-BC154.

22　IAS 39, para. 35(c).

23　IAS 39, para. AG40(d)

24　IAS 39, para. AG39(c)

25　IAS 39, para. F.3.7

26　IAS 39, para. 35(d).

27　IAS 39, para. 3.

28　IAS 39, para. 9.

29　IAS 39, para. AG54.

30　IAS 39, paras. AG55-AG56.

31　IAS 39, paras. AG55-AG56.

32　IAS 39, paras. 38 and AG53.

33　IAS 39, para. AG55.

34　IAS 39, paras. 57 and AG56.

35　IAS 39, para. D.2.2.

36　IAS 39, paras. D.2.1 and D.2.2.

37　IAS 39, para. D.2.3.

38　IAS 39, paras. AG34 and AG50.

39　IAS 39, para. AG50.

40　IAS 39, para. AG36.

41　SIC-12, para. 8.

42　IAS 39, para. 16.

43　IAS 39, para. 16.

44　IAS 39, para. 17

45　IAS 39, para. 18.

46　IAS 39, para. AG37.

47　IAS 39, para. 19.

48　IAS 39, para. AG38.

49　IAS 39, para. 20.

50　IAS 39, para. 20(a).

51　IAS 39, para. AG41.

52　IAS 39, para. 20(b).

53　IAS 39, para. 20(c).

54　IAS 39, para. 21.

55　IAS 39, para. 22.

56　IAS 39, paras. 21 and AG39.

57　IAS 39, paras. 21 and AG40.

58　IAS 39, para. AG51(g)-(h).

59　IAS 39, para. AG52.

60　IAS 39, para. 20(c).

61　IAS 39, para. 23.

62　IAS 39, para. AG42.

63　IAS 39, para. AG43.

64　IAS 39, para. AG43.

65　IAS 39, para. AG44.

66　IAS 39, para. AG44.

67　IAS 39, para. AG51(a).

68　IAS 39, para. AG51(a).

69　IAS 39, para. AG51(b).

70　IAS 39, para. AG51(c).

71　IAS 39, para. AG51(k).

72　IAS 39, para. AG51(j).

73　IAS 39, para. AG51(d).

74　IAS 39, para. AG51(e).

75　IAS 39, para. AG51(f).

76　IAS 39, para. AG51(g).

77　IAS 39, paras. AG51(h)-(i).

78　IAS 39, para. AG51(h).

79　IAS 39, para. AG51(h).

80　IAS 39, para. AG51(i).

81　IAS 39, para. AG51(i).

82　IAS 39, para. AG51(j).

83　IAS 39, para. AG51(k).

84　IAS 39, para. AG51(l).

85　IAS 39, para. AG51(m).

86　IAS 39, para. AG51(n).

87　IAS 39, para. AG51(n).

88　IAS 39, para. AG51(o).

89　IAS 39, para. AG51(p).

90　IAS 39, para. AG51(q).

91　IAS 39, para. AG51(q).

92　IAS 39, paras. 24-25.

93　IAS 39, para. 26.

94　IAS 39, para. 27

95　IAS 39, para. 28.

96　IAS 39, para. AG46.

97 In practice, other factors might be relevant to the valuation.
98 IAS 39, para. 24.
99 IAS 39, para. AG45.
100 IAS 39, para. 29.
101 IAS 39, para. AG47.
102 IAS 39, para. 30.
103 IAS 39, paras. BC44-BC52.
104 IAS 39, para. 30(a).
105 IAS 39, para. 30(b)-(c).
106 IAS 39, para. 31.
107 IAS 39, para. 31.
108 IAS 39, para. 32.
109 IAS 39, para. 33.
110 IAS 39, para. 35.
111 IAS 39, para. 27.
112 IAS 39, para. AG48(a).
113 IAS 39, para. AG52.
114 IAS 39, para. AG48(b).
115 IAS 39, para. AG48(c).
116 IAS 39, para. AG48(d).
117 IAS 39, para. AG48(e).
118 IAS 39, para. AG52.
119 IAS 39, para. AG48(a).
120 IAS 39, para. 36.
121 IAS 32, para. 42.
122 IAS 39, para. 37.
123 IAS 39, para. AG49.
124 IAS 39, para. 39.
125 IAS 39, para. AG57.
126 IAS 39, para. AG58.
127 IAS 39, para. AG57(b).
128 IAS 39, para. AG60.
129 IAS 39, para. AG60.
130 IAS 39, para. AG59.
131 IAS 39, para. AG61.
132 IAS 39, para. 40.
133 IAS 39, para. AG62.
134 IAS 39, para. AG62.
135 IAS 39, para. AG8.
136 IAS 39, para. 41.
137 IAS 39, para. 42.
138 IAS 39, para. AG63
139 IAS 32, para. 42.
140 IAS 32, para. 43.
141 IAS 32, para. 44.
142 IAS 32, para. 45.
143 IAS 32, para. 45
144 IAS 32, para. 46.
145 IAS 32 para. 47.
146 IAS 32, para. 48.
147 IAS 32, paras. 49(a) and AG39.
148 IAS 32, para. 49(b)-(e).
149 IAS 32, paras. 50 and AG39.
150 IAS 32, para. 50.
151 IAS 32, para. 96 and IAS 39, para. 103.
152 IAS 32, para. 96 and IAS 39, para. 103.
153 IAS 39, para. 104.
154 IAS 39, para. 106.
155 IAS 39, para. 107.
156 IFRS 1, *First-time Adoption of International Financial Reporting Standards*, IASB, June 2003 (amended March 2004), para. 36A.
157 IFRS 1, paras. 27 and IG53.
158 IFRS 1, paras. 27 and IG53.
159 IFRS 1, para. 27A.
160 IFRS 1, para. IG53.

Chapter 17 Financial instruments: Financial liabilities and equity

1 INTRODUCTION

1.1 Background

The accounting treatment of liabilities (such as loans or bonds) and equity instruments (such as shares, stock or warrants) by their issuer was not historically regarded as presenting significant problems. Essentially the accounting was dictated by the legal form of the instrument, since the traditional distinction between equity and liabilities is clear. The issue of equity creates an ownership interest in a company, remunerated by dividends, which are accounted for as a distribution of retained profit, not a charge made in arriving at the result for a particular period. Liabilities, such as loan finance, on the other hand, are remunerated by interest, which is charged in the income statement as an expense. In general, lenders rank before shareholders in priority of claims over the assets of the company, although in practice there may also be differential rights between different categories of lenders and classes of shareholders. The two forms of finance often have different tax implications, both for the investor and the investee.

In economic terms, however, the distinction between share and loan capital can be far less clear-cut than the legal categorisation would suggest. For example, a redeemable preference share could be considered to be, in substance, much more like a liability than equity. Conversely, many would argue that a bond which can never be repaid but which will be mandatorily converted into ordinary shares deserves to be thought of as being more in the nature of equity than of debt, even before conversion has occurred.

The ambiguous economic nature of such instruments, has, particularly since 1980 or so, encouraged the development of a number of complex forms of finance which exhibit characteristics of both equity and debt. The 'holy grail' is generally to devise an instrument regarded as a liability by the tax authorities (such that the costs of servicing it are tax-deductible) but treated as equity for accounting and/or regulatory purposes (so that the instrument is not considered as a component of net borrowings).

The accounting profession has not always found it easy to decide how to balance competing considerations of substance and form in accounting for these instruments, especially since the fundamental distinction between debt and equity is rooted in form to begin with.

In general, the approach both of national standards setters and of the IASB has tended towards a presumption that an instrument is a liability until proven otherwise. This stance was doubtless coloured in part by the memory of various corporate bonds issued in the 1980s which were accounted for as quasi-equity by their issuers on the basis that repayment could occur only in very remote circumstances. In reality, however, those 'very remote' circumstances (typically a fall or a lower than expected rise in the issuer's share price) did in fact occur, with the result that the entities concerned had to make significant payments to discharge liabilities that, according to their previously published financial statements, did not exist.

The accounting classification of an instrument as a liability or equity is much more than a matter of allocation – i.e. where particular amounts are shown in the financial statements. The increasing requirement of IFRS for certain liabilities, in particular derivatives, to be carried at fair value means that the classification of an item as a liability can introduce significant volatility into reported results that would not arise if the item were classified as an equity instrument (it being a fundamental principle of the IASB's *Framework* that changes in the fair value of equity are not reflected in financial statements – see Chapter 2)

1.2   Development of IFRS on classification of liabilities and equity

Under IFRS, the classification of items as liabilities or equity is dealt with mainly in IAS 32 – *Financial Instruments: Disclosure and Presentation*, with some cross-reference to IAS 39 – *Financial Instruments: Recognition and Measurement.*

IAS 32 was originally issued in March 1995 and subsequently amended in 1998 and 2000 as the result of the issue of, and subsequent changes to, IAS 39. However, in December 2003, the previous version of IAS 32 was withdrawn and superseded by a new version, which has itself been amended by new standards issued since December 2003. The new version of IAS 32 must be applied for accounting periods beginning on or after 1 January 2005. Entities are 'permitted' (rather than 'encouraged', as in the case of other recently issued standards) to adopt it for earlier periods, but must disclose that they have done so. Moreover, they must also adopt IAS 39 (as reissued in December 2003 and amended in March 2004) at the same time.[1]

The main text of IAS 32 is supplemented by application guidance (which is an integral part of the standard)[2] and by illustrative examples (which accompany, but are not part of, the standard).[3]

The main changes acknowledged by the IASB to have been made by the current version of IAS 32 to previous IFRS with regard to the classification of debt and equity (other than the incorporation into IAS 32 of requirements previously contained in other pronouncements) were to:[4]

- revise the definitions of 'financial asset' and 'financial liability', and the description of an equity instrument, such that certain transactions involving the delivery or receipt of the entity's equity instruments that might previously have been classified as equity are now classified as financial assets or financial liabilities;

- require an entity's obligation to purchase its own shares to be shown as a liability;

- eliminate the options in the previous version of IAS 32 for measuring the liability and equity components of a compound financial instrument. An entity must now measure the liability component based on its fair value with the equity component as a residual.

In addition to the changes acknowledged in the introduction to revised IAS 32, there have also been important changes to the application guidance, so as to:

- require an entity, in its consolidated financial statements, to consider the obligations of the group as whole in respect of a financial instrument, and not just those of the issuing entity. Thus a share issued by a subsidiary may be treated as a liability, and not minority interest, on consolidation if another member of the group guarantees payment of dividends on, or redemption of, the shares; and

- require an entity, when assessing whether a non-redeemable share is a liability or equity, to ignore certain factors that were treated, in the previous version of IAS 32, as indicators that the shares might be a liability. Thus, certain non-redeemable shares previously classified as liabilities may now be classified as equity.

2   OBJECTIVE, SCOPE AND DEFINITIONS

2.1   Objective

The objective of IAS 32 is 'to enhance financial statement users' understanding of the significance of financial instruments to an entity's financial position, performance and cash flows.'[5]

It is the presentation, rather than the disclosure, requirements of IAS 32 that are of specific relevance to the issues discussed in this Chapter. The presentation requirements apply to:[6]

- the classification of financial instruments, from the perspective of the issuer, into financial assets, financial liabilities and equity instruments (see 3 and 4 below);

- the classification of related interest, dividends, losses and gains (see 5 below); and

- the circumstances in which financial assets and financial liabilities should be offset (see Chapter 16 at 6).

IAS 32 also contains guidance on accounting for:

- treasury shares – i.e. an entity's own equity instruments held by the entity (see 6 below); and

- forward contracts or options for the receipt or delivery of the entity's own equity instruments (see 7 below).

2.2   Scope

The scope of IAS 32 is discussed in detail in Chapter 15 at 3.

2.3   Definitions

The following definitions in IAS 32 are relevant to the issues discussed in this Chapter. Further general discussion on the meaning and implications of the definitions may be found in Chapter 15 at 2.

A *financial instrument* is any contract that gives rise to a financial asset of one entity and a financial liability or equity instrument of another entity.[7]

A *financial asset* is any asset that is:

(a)   cash;

(b)   an equity instrument of another entity;

(c)   a contractual right:

    (i)   to receive cash or another financial asset from another entity; or

    (ii)   to exchange financial assets or financial liabilities with another entity under conditions that are potentially favourable to the entity; or

(d) a contract that will or may be settled in the entity's own equity instruments and is:

    (i) a non-derivative for which the entity is or may be obliged to receive a variable number of the entity's own equity instruments; or

    (ii) a derivative that will or may be settled other than by the exchange of a fixed amount of cash or another financial asset for a fixed number of the entity's own equity instruments. For this purpose the entity's own equity instruments do not include instruments that are themselves contracts for the future receipt or delivery of the entity's own equity instruments.[8]

A *financial liability* is any liability that is:

(a) a contractual obligation:

    (i) to deliver cash or another financial asset to another entity; or

    (ii) to exchange financial assets or financial liabilities with another entity under conditions that are potentially unfavourable to the entity; or

(b) a contract that will or may be settled in the entity's own equity instruments and is:

    (i) a non-derivative for which the entity is or may be obliged to deliver a variable number of the entity's own equity instruments; or

    (ii) a derivative that will or may be settled other than by the exchange of a fixed amount of cash or another financial asset for a fixed number of the entity's own equity instruments. For this purpose the entity's own equity instruments do not include instruments that are themselves contracts for the future receipt or delivery of the entity's own equity instruments.[9]

An *equity instrument* is any contract that evidences a residual interest in the assets of an entity after deducting all of its liabilities.[10]

A *derivative* is a financial instrument or other contract within the scope of IAS 39 (see Chapter 15 at 3) with all three of the following characteristics:

- its value changes in response to the change in a specified interest rate, financial instrument price, commodity price, foreign exchange rate, index of prices or rates, credit rating or credit index, or other variable (sometimes called the 'underlying');

- it requires no initial net investment or an initial net investment that is smaller than would be required for other types of contracts that would be expected to have a similar response to changes in market factors; and

- it is settled at a future date.[11]

Fair value is the amount for which an asset could be exchanged, or a liability settled, between knowledgeable, willing parties in an arm's length transaction.[12]

In these definitions (and throughout IAS 32 and the discussion in this Chapter):

- *Contract* and *contractual* refer to an agreement between two or more parties that has clear economic consequences that the parties have little, if any, discretion to avoid, usually because the agreement is enforceable by law. Contracts, and thus financial instruments, may take a variety of forms and need not be in writing.[13]

- *Entity* includes individuals, partnerships, incorporated bodies, trusts and government agencies.[14]

3   LIABILITIES AND EQUITY

The most important presentation issue dealt with by IAS 32 is the classification of financial instruments (or their components) by their issuer as financial liabilities, financial assets or equity instruments (including minority interests). The extent to which an entity funds its operations through debt or equity is regarded as highly significant not only by investors, but also by other users of financial statements such as regulators (particularly in the financial services industry) and tax authorities. This means that the question of whether a particular instrument is a liability or equity raises issues of much greater and wider sensitivity than the mere matter of financial statement classification.

Moreover, the increasing requirement of IFRS for certain liabilities, in particular derivatives, to be carried at fair value means that the classification of an item as a liability can introduce significant (and, from the perspective of many preparers, undesirable) volatility into reported results that would not arise if the item were classified as an equity instrument. As a consequence of this, the whole area remains a live battleground between the IASB (and national standard setters) and those seeking ever more ingenious loopholes in the rules.

3.1   General provisions of IAS 32

The rule in IAS 32 for classification of items as financial liabilities or equity is essentially simple. An issuer of a financial instrument must classify the instrument (or its component parts) on initial recognition as a financial liability, a financial asset or an equity instrument in accordance with the substance of the contractual arrangement and the definitions of a financial liability, a financial asset and an equity instrument (see 2.3 above).[15] The application of this principle in practice, however, is not always straightforward.

Application of the basic definitions in IAS 32 means that an instrument is an equity instrument if and only if both the following conditions are met:

- The instrument includes no contractual obligation either:
  - (i)   to deliver cash or another financial asset to another entity; or
  - (ii)   to exchange financial assets or financial liabilities with another entity under conditions that are potentially unfavourable to the issuer.

- If the instrument will or may be settled in the issuer's own equity instruments, it is either:

  (i) a non-derivative that includes no contractual obligation for the issuer to deliver a variable number of its own equity instruments; or

  (ii) a derivative that will be settled only by the issuer exchanging a fixed amount of cash or another financial asset for a fixed number of its own equity instruments. For this purpose the issuer's own equity instruments do not include instruments that are themselves contracts for the future receipt or delivery of the issuer's own equity instruments.[16]

IAS 32 emphasises that a contractual obligation, including one arising from a derivative financial instrument, that will or may result in the future receipt or delivery of the issuer's own equity instruments, but does not meet the conditions above, is not an equity instrument.[17] This is discussed further at 3.3 below.

3.1.1 Examples of equity instruments

On the criteria above, equity instruments under IAS 32 will include non-puttable ordinary shares and some types of preference share (see 3.2 below).[18]

They also include warrants or written call options that allow the holder to subscribe for or purchase a *fixed* number of non-puttable ordinary shares in the issuing entity in exchange for a *fixed* amount of cash or another financial asset, or the *fixed* stated principal of a bond.[19] The meaning of a 'fixed amount of cash' is not as self-evident as it might appear and is discussed further at 3.3.1 A below. The meaning of the 'fixed stated principal' of a bond is discussed further at 4.4.2 below.

Conversely, an instrument would be a financial liability (or financial asset) of the issuer if it gave the holder the right to obtain:

- a *variable* number of non-puttable ordinary shares in the issuing entity in exchange for a fixed amount of cash or another financial asset;[20] or

- a *fixed* number of non-puttable ordinary shares in the issuing entity in exchange for a *variable* amount of cash or another financial asset.[21]

An obligation for the entity to issue or purchase a fixed number of its own equity instruments in exchange for a fixed amount of cash or another financial asset is an equity instrument of the entity. However, if such a contract contains an obligation – or even a potential obligation – for the entity to pay cash or another financial asset, it gives rise to a liability for the present value of the redemption amount (which results in a reduction of equity, not an expense – see 3.3.3 below).[22]

Whilst non-puttable shares are typically equity, an issuer of non-puttable ordinary shares nevertheless assumes a liability when it formally acts to make a distribution and becomes legally obliged to the shareholders to do so. This may be the case following the declaration of a dividend, or when, on a winding up, any assets remaining after discharging the entity's liabilities become distributable to shareholders.[23]

A purchased call option or other similar contract acquired by an entity that gives it the right to reacquire a fixed number of its own equity instruments in exchange for delivering a fixed amount of cash or another financial asset is not a financial asset of the entity. Moreover, any consideration paid for such a contract is deducted from equity[24] (see 7.2.1 below).

3.1.2 Comparison with IFRS 2 – Share-based Payment

As the discussion above illustrates, in order for an instrument to be classified as an equity instrument under IAS 32, it is not sufficient that it involves the reporting entity delivering or receiving its own equity (as opposed to cash or another financial asset). The number of equity instruments delivered, and the consideration for them, must be fixed (see 3.3 below). The IASB considered that to treat any transaction settled in the entity's own shares as an equity instrument would not deal adequately with transactions in which an entity is using its own shares as 'currency' – for example, where it has an obligation to pay a fixed or determinable amount that is settled in a variable number of its own shares.[25] In such transactions the counterparty bears no share price risk, and is therefore not in the same position as a 'true' equity shareholder.

However, IAS 32's approach is different from that in IFRS 2 – *Share-based Payment.* IFRS 2 essentially treats any transaction that falls within its scope and can be settled only in shares (or other equity instruments) as an equity instrument, regardless of whether the number of shares to be delivered is fixed or variable (see Chapter 29 at 2.3). There are also significant differences between the treatment of financial instruments that can be settled in either equity instruments or cash (or other financial assets) in IAS 32 (see 3.5 below) and in IFRS 2 (see Chapter 29 at 7.2.1).

The IASB offers some (pragmatic rather than conceptual) explanation for these differences in the Basis for Conclusions to IFRS 2. First, it is argued that to apply IAS 32 to share option plans would mean that a variable share option plan (i.e. one where the number of shares varied according to performance) would give rise to more volatile (and typically greater) cost than a fixed plan (i.e. one where the number of shares to be awarded is fixed from the start), even if the same number of shares was ultimately delivered under each plan, which would have 'undesirable consequences'.[26] This serves only to beg the question of why it is not equally 'undesirable' for the same result to arise in accounting for share-settled contracts within the scope of IAS 32 rather than IFRS 2. Second, it is argued that this is just one of several inconsistencies between IAS 32 which will be addressed in the round as part of the IASB's review of accounting for debt and equity.[27]

3.2   Contractual obligation to deliver cash or other financial assets

It is apparent from the discussion in 3.1 above that a critical feature in differentiating a financial liability from an equity instrument is the existence of a contractual obligation of one party to the financial instrument (the issuer) either:

- to deliver cash or another financial asset to the other party (the holder), or
- to exchange financial assets or financial liabilities with the holder under conditions that are potentially unfavourable to the issuer.[28]

The holder of an equity instrument (e.g. a non-puttable share) is entitled to receive a pro rata share of such dividends or other distributions of equity as are made. However, since the issuer does not have a contractual obligation to make such distributions (because it cannot be required to deliver cash or another financial asset to another party), the instrument is not a financial liability of the issuer.[29]

IAS 32 requires the issuer of a financial instrument to classify a financial instrument by reference to its substance rather than its legal form, although it is conceded that substance and form are 'commonly', but not always, the same. Typical examples of instruments that are equity in legal form but liabilities in substance are certain types of preference share (see 3.2.1 below) and units in open-ended funds, unit trusts and similar entities (see 3.2.2 below).[30]

IAS 32 further clarifies that a financial instrument is an equity instrument, and not a financial liability, not merely if the issuer has no legal obligation to deliver cash or other financial assets to the holder at the reporting date, but only if it also has an unconditional right to avoid doing so in all future circumstances other than liquidation. Thus, a financial instrument is classified as a financial liability even if:

- the issuer's ability to discharge its obligations under the instrument is restricted (e.g. by a lack of funds, the need to obtain regulatory approval to make payments on the instrument, or a shortfall of distributable profits, or other statutory restriction);[31] or

- the holder has to perform some action (e.g. formally exercise a redemption right) in order for the issuer to become obliged to transfer cash or other financial assets.[32]

Moreover, a financial instrument that does not explicitly establish a contractual obligation to deliver cash or another financial asset may nevertheless establish an obligation indirectly through its terms and conditions,[33] as illustrated by Example 17.1.

Example 17.1:   *Financial instrument with non-financial obligation that must be settled if, and only if, the entity fails to redeem the instrument*

The reporting entity borrows €1 million from its bank for five years on terms that, at the end of five years, the entity must deliver its head office building to the bank but may instead repay the loan at €1 million plus rolled-up interest at market rates.

IAS 32 states a that financial instrument, such as that in Example 17.1 above, containing a non-financial obligation that can be avoided only by making a transfer of cash or another financial asset is a financial liability.[34]

Whilst this position seems entirely sensible, it is inconsistent with the definition of 'financial liability' at 2.3 above, which refers merely to an obligation to deliver cash or another financial asset or to exchange financial instruments on potentially unfavourable terms – there is no reference to an obligation that can be avoided only by a transfer of other non-financial assets.

The application guidance asserts that 'the definition of a financial instrument also encompasses a contract that gives rise to a non-financial asset or non-financial liability in addition to a financial asset or financial liability.'[35] The context of this comment is a discussion of a bond where the holder has the option of requiring settlement in a fixed amount of cash or a fixed quantity of oil. Whilst it is true that an instrument that allows the *holder* to choose settlement in cash or a non-financial asset is a financial liability of the issuer (since the issuer can always be compelled to pay cash), it is, in our view, not the case where the option to choose settlement in cash or a non-financial asset rests with the *issuer*. The definition of financial liability refers to a 'contractual obligation' to deliver cash or other financial assets. In Example 17.1 above the issuer clearly has no contractual obligation to pay cash, however economically irrational it might be not to do so.

In our view, it would have been preferable if the IASB had dealt with this significant point in the definition of 'financial liability' rather than as something of an afterthought. In effect, the (in our view, entirely appropriate) conclusion of Example 17.1 relies on the concept of economic compulsion, rather than contractual obligation.

A financial instrument is also a financial liability if it provides that on settlement the entity will deliver either:

(a)   cash or another financial asset; or

(b)   a number of its own shares whose value is determined to exceed substantially the value of the cash or other financial asset.

IAS 32 explains that, although the entity does not have an explicit contractual obligation to deliver cash or another financial asset, the value of the share settlement alternative is such that the entity will settle in cash. In any event, the holder has in substance been guaranteed receipt of an amount that is at least equal to the cash settlement option.[36]

IAS 32's reasoning seems slightly confused here, since any instrument that involves delivery of an amount of equity of a given value is so clearly a financial liability (see 2.3 above) that no further clarification should be necessary. Perhaps the IASB meant to refer in (b) above to a *fixed* number of the entity's own shares – the point being that an instrument which allows for repayment in a number of shares that is fixed (and therefore *prima facie* not a financial liability according to the definition), but so large as to be punitive (therefore effectively forcing the entity to choose to repay in cash) is a financial liability. However, if this was the IASB's intention, it sits rather uneasily with the reference to a 'guaranteed' amount at least equal to the cash settlement option. The right to receive a fixed number of shares, however large, can never 'guarantee' delivery of a minimum value (since the share price could collapse so much that the fixed number of shares is in fact worth less than the cash alternative).

3.2.1 Preference shares

Whilst the discussion below (and the guidance in IAS 32) is framed in terms of 'preference shares', it should, in our view, be applied equally to any financial instrument, however described, with similar characteristics.

Preference shares may be issued with various rights. In determining whether a preference share is a financial liability or an equity instrument, IAS 32 requires an issuer to assess the particular rights attaching to the share to determine whether it exhibits the fundamental characteristic of a financial liability.[37]

IAS 32 does this by drawing a distinction between:

- preference shares mandatorily redeemable or redeemable at the holder's option (see A below);

- other preference shares – i.e. those redeemable at the issuer's option or not redeemable (see B below).

A   Preference shares redeemable mandatorily or at holder's option

A preference share that:

- provides for mandatory redemption by the issuer for a fixed or determinable amount at a fixed or determinable future date; or

- gives the holder the right to require the issuer to redeem the instrument at or after a particular date for a fixed or determinable amount,

contains a financial liability, since the issuer has an obligation, or potential obligation, to transfer cash or other financial assets to the holder. This obligation is not negated by the potential inability of an issuer to redeem a preference share when contractually required to do so, whether because of a lack of funds, a statutory restriction or insufficient profits or reserves.[38]

It is more correct to say that a redeemable preference share 'contains' rather than 'is' a financial liability. For example, if a redeemable preference share is issued on terms that any dividends paid on the share are entirely at the issuer's discretion, it is only the amount payable on redemption that is a liability. This would probably lead to a 'split accounting' treatment (see 4 below), whereby the share would, at issue, be classified as a liability to the extent of the net present value of the amount payable on redemption and as equity as to the balance of the issue proceeds.[39]

B   Other preference shares

A preference share redeemable in cash at the option of the issuer does not satisfy the definition of a financial liability in IAS 32, because the issuer does not have a present obligation to transfer financial assets to the shareholders. In this case, redemption of the shares is solely at the discretion of the issuer. An obligation may arise, however, when the issuer of the shares exercises its option, usually by formally notifying the shareholders of an intention to redeem the shares.[40]

Likewise, where preference shares are non-redeemable, there is clearly no financial liability in respect of the 'principal' amount of the shares. In reality there may be little distinction between shares redeemable at the issuer's option and non-redeemable shares, given that in many jurisdictions an entity can 'repurchase' its 'irredeemable' shares subject to no greater restrictions than would apply to a 'redemption' of 'redeemable' shares.

Ultimately, the classification of preference shares redeemable only at the holder's option or not redeemable according to their terms must be determined by the other rights that attach to them. IAS 32 requires the classification to be based on an assessment of the substance of the contractual arrangements and the definitions of a financial liability and an equity instrument.[41] If the share establishes a contractual right to a dividend, subject only to restrictions on payment of dividends in the relevant jurisdiction, it contains a financial liability in respect of the dividends. This would lead to a 'split accounting' treatment (see 4 below), whereby the net present value of the right to receive dividends would be shown as a liability and the balance of the issue proceeds as equity. In such a case, it is quite likely that the issue proceeds would be equivalent to the fair value (at the date of issue) of dividends payable in perpetuity, such that the entire proceeds would be classified as a financial liability.

However, when distributions to holders of the preference shares, whether cumulative or non-cumulative, are at the discretion of the issuer, the shares are equity instruments. The classification of a preference share as an equity instrument or a financial liability is not affected by, for example:

- a history of making distributions;

- an intention to make distributions in the future;

- a possible negative impact on the price of ordinary shares of the issuer if distributions are not made (because of restrictions on paying dividends on the ordinary shares if dividends are not paid on the preference shares);

- the amount of the issuer's reserves;

- an issuer's expectation of a profit or loss for a period; or

- an ability or inability of the issuer to influence the amount of its profit or loss for the period.[42]

The treatment of non-redeemable preference shares, or other instruments with preferred rights, under IAS 32 is a particularly difficult issue, since such shares often inhabit the border territory between financial liabilities and equity instruments. A non-redeemable preference share whose dividend rights are simply that a dividend (whether of a fixed, capped or discretionary amount) will be paid at the issuing entity's sole discretion is clearly equivalent to an ordinary equity share, and therefore appropriately characterised as equity.

However, a number of entities have issued non-redeemable preference shares (or preference shares redeemable only at the issuer's option) with the following broad terms:

- a discretionary annual dividend will be paid up to a capped maximum amount; and

- unless a full discretionary dividend is paid to non-redeemable preference shareholders, no dividend can be paid to ordinary shareholders.

The economic reality is that many entities that issue such instruments are able to do so at a cost not significantly higher than that of callable perpetual debt. This indicates that investors regard themselves as having reasonable security of receiving their 'discretionary' dividend in the form of the adverse economic consequences for the entity of not paying it (if sufficiently solvent to do so), namely:

- the disaffection of ordinary shareholders who would not be able to receive any dividends; and

- the fact that the entity would find it very difficult to raise any similar finance again.

These factors could admit an argument that such instruments are equivalent to perpetual debt (see 3.2.3 below) in all respects except that the holder has no right to sue for non-payment of the discretionary dividend. However, the analysis in IAS 32 is based on the implicit counter-argument that the position of a holder of non-redeemable preference shares is equivalent to that of an ordinary shareholder. Ordinary shares do not cease to be equity instruments simply because an entity that failed to pay dividends to its ordinary shareholders when manifestly able to do so would be subject to adverse economic pressures from those shareholders, and might find it very difficult to raise additional share capital.

The treatment of non-redeemable preference shares with discretionary dividends illustrates that, while IAS 32 requires the issuer of a financial instrument to classify a financial instrument by reference to its substance rather than its legal form, in reality the substance is determined, if not by the legal *form*, then certainly by the legal *rights* of the holder of the financial instrument concerned. Ultimately, it appears that what tips the balance between a preference share being treated as a financial liability or an equity instrument is whether the terms of the instrument give the holder a contractual right to receive cash or other financial assets which can be sued for at law, subject only to restrictions outside the terms of the instrument (e.g. statutory dividend controls).

This emphasis on legal and contractual rights also helps to clarify the apparent inconsistency with the requirement to take account of 'economic compulsion' in categorising financial instruments such as that in Example 17.1 above but to ignore the 'economic compulsion' to pay a discretionary dividend. The difference is that, in Example 17.1, if the issuer fails to deliver cash, it suffers an adverse consequence (i.e. the obligation to deliver another, probably more valuable, asset) under the terms of the instrument. By contrast, if an issuer of a discretionary preference share fails to pay any discretionary dividends, it suffers an adverse consequence (i.e. damage to its financial reputation) arising from external economic factors rather than from the holder's rights under the terms of the share. This analysis is reinforced by the fact that the matters which IAS 32 specifically requires to be ignored in assessing whether or not a non-redeemable share is equity are all external economic factors and pressures and do not arise from any legal rights or obligations inherent in the share itself.

C   Hedging of shares classified as equity

A consequence of the requirement, discussed in B above, to treat discretionary shares with certain debt-like characteristics as equity is that the issuer will not be able to adopt hedge accounting in respect of any instrument taken out as a hedge of the shares (e.g. a receive fixed, pay floating interest rate swap taken out to hedge a fixed rate discretionary dividend on non-redeemable shares). This is because IAS 39 does not recognise a hedge of own equity as a valid hedging relationship (see Chapter 19). Accordingly, if an issuer of non-redeemable shares bearing a fixed rate discretionary dividend did enter into an interest rate swap to hedge the dividend flows, the swap would be accounted for under the normal rules for derivatives not forming part of a hedging relationship – i.e. at fair value with all value changes recognised in profit or loss (see Chapter 18). Although, economically speaking, any such gains and losses are offset by equal gains and losses (due to interest rate movements) on the shares, the latter, like all movements in the fair value of own equity, are ignored for financial reporting purposes under IFRS.

3.2.2   Puttable instruments

A 'puttable instrument' is a financial instrument that gives the holder the right to put the instrument back to the issuer for cash or another financial asset.[43]

IAS 32 classifies any puttable instrument as a financial liability. This is so even when the amount of cash or other financial assets is determined on the basis of an index or other item that has the potential to increase or decrease, or when the legal form of the puttable instrument gives the holder a right to a residual interest in the assets of the issuer. The effect of the holder's option to put the instrument back to the issuer for cash or another financial asset is that the puttable instrument meets the definition of a financial liability[44] (see 2.3 above).

This analysis has what some regard as a rather startling effect on the financial statements of entities such as open-ended mutual funds, unit trusts, partnerships and some co-operative entities. Such entities often provide their unitholders or members with a right to redeem their interests in the issuer at any time for cash equal to their proportionate share of the asset value of the issuer. Any entity whose holders have this right could have net assets of nil under IAS 32 since what would, in normal usage, be regarded as the 'equity' of (say) a unit trust or a professional partnership (i.e. its assets less external borrowings) is classified as a financial liability under IAS 32.

The IASB takes the view that the accounting treatment required by IAS 32 is appropriate, but points out that the classification of members' interests in such entities as a financial liability does not preclude:

- the use of captions such as 'net asset value attributable to unitholders' and 'change in net asset value attributable to unitholders' on the face of the financial statements of an entity that has no equity capital (such as some mutual funds and unit trusts); or

- the use of additional disclosure to show that total members' interests comprise items such as reserves that meet the definition of equity and puttable instruments that do not.[45]

The illustrative examples appended to IAS 32 give specimen disclosures to be used in such cases – see Chapter 20 at 6.1.5 and 6.3.3.

A   Possible future developments

The requirements of IAS 32 were implicitly drafted in the context of entities (such as investment funds) the full fair value of whose assets will typically be reflected in its financial statements. This has the end result that such entities will show net assets of zero.

However, there are entities (such as some co-operative and professional partnerships) whose owners are entitled to have their ownership interests purchased at their share of the fair value of the net assets of the entity, where the fair value of the net assets is not reflected in the financial statements. This is because a significant part of the fair value of such entities may be represented by property accounted for at cost rather than fair value or by internally generated goodwill which cannot be recognised in financial statements under IFRS.

Clearly, if such an entity were to recognise a liability for the right of its owners to be bought out at fair value, it would show net liabilities, which will increase the more the fair value of the entity increases, which is a difficult result to justify other than on rather technical grounds.

Accordingly, the IASB has tentatively agreed to amend IAS 32 so as to allow certain tightly specified categories of instruments puttable at fair value to be classified as equity.[46]

IFRIC has also issued a draft interpretation D8 – *Members' Shares in Co-operative Entities*,[47] which deals with the specific issues raised by such entities, where members may have a right to request redemption of their interests.

D8 proposes that such a member's right to request redemption of his interest does not of itself require an interest that would, absent such a right, be classified as equity to be reclassified as a financial liability. Specifically members' interests should be treated as equity to the extent that:

(a)   the entity has an unconditional right to refuse redemption; or

(b)   the entity is precluded by local legal requirements from making redemptions.[48]

The proposal in (b) above could be read as conflicting with the requirements of IAS 32 in respect of the classification of shares, which explicitly state that an issuer's liability under a share is not negated by the potential inability of the issuer to redeem a preference share when contractually required to do so, whether because of a lack of funds, a statutory restriction or insufficient profits or reserves (see 3.2.1 above).

However, the illustrative examples in D8 indicate that IFRIC's intention was to restrict the recognition of liabilities only in cases where the entity is required by local law, regulation or its governing charter to have a minimum number of equity instruments in issue (as opposed to a requirement to maintain a minimum level of equity or liquidity, expressed as a particular monetary amount).

3.2.3 Perpetual debt

'Perpetual debt' instruments are those that provide the holder with the contractual right to receive payments on account of interest at fixed dates extending into the indefinite future, either with no right to receive a return of principal or a right to a return of principal under terms that make it very unlikely or very far in the future. However, this does not mean that 'perpetual debt' is to be classified as equity, since the issue proceeds will typically represent the net present value of the liability for interest payments.

For example, an entity may issue a financial instrument requiring it to make annual payments in perpetuity equal to a stated interest rate of 8% applied to a stated par or principal amount of €1 million. Assuming 8% to be the market rate of interest for the instrument when issued, the issuer assumes a contractual obligation to make a stream of future interest payments having a fair value (present value) of €1 million. Thus perpetual debt gives rise to a financial liability of the issuer.[49]

3.3 Contracts settled by delivery of the entity's own equity instruments

In the following discussion, 'delivery' includes delivery to or from the reporting entity – in other words it does not matter (except where specifically indicated) whether the reporting entity is the 'buyer' or 'seller' of its own equity instruments.

As noted in 3.1 above, a contract is not an equity instrument solely because it may result in the receipt or delivery of the entity's own equity instruments. Where such a contract is not classified as an equity instrument by IAS 32, it will be accounted for in accordance with the general provisions of IAS 39 for derivatives – i.e. it will be measured at fair value with all changes in fair value reflected in profit or loss. In other words, entities will recognise gains and losses based on the movement of their own share price.

Broadly speaking:

- a non-derivative contract involving the delivery of a fixed number of own equity instruments is an equity instrument (see 3.3.1 below);

- a non-derivative contract involving the delivery of a variable number of own equity instruments is a financial liability (see 3.3.2 below);

- a derivative contract involving the delivery of fixed number of own equity instruments for a fixed amount of cash or other financial assets is an equity instrument (see 3.3.1 below);

- a derivative contract involving the delivery of:

  - a fixed number of own equity instruments for a variable amount of cash or other financial assets;

  - a variable number of own equity instruments for a variable amount of cash or other financial assets; or

  - an amount of cash or own equity instruments with a fair value equivalent to the difference between a fixed number of own equity instruments and a fixed amount of cash or other financial assets is a financial asset or financial liability (see 3.3.2 below); and

- a derivative contract for the purchase by an entity of its own equity instruments, even if for a fixed amount of cash or other financial assets (and therefore an equity instrument) may give rise to a financial liability in respect of the cash or other financial assets to be paid. However, the liability results in a reduction in equity and not in an expense (see 3.3.3 below).

There are also some difficulties of interpretation surrounding the treatment of certain contracts to issue equity (see 3.3.4 below) and the meaning of a 'fixed amount' of cash or other financial assets (see 3.3.1 A below).

3.3.1   *Contracts accounted for as equity instruments*

As noted above, a contract that will be settled by the entity delivering or receiving a fixed number of its own equity instruments in exchange for a fixed amount of cash (see A below) or another financial asset is an equity instrument. An example would be an issued share option that gives the counterparty a right to buy a fixed number of the entity's shares for a fixed price or for a fixed stated principal amount of a bond (see 4.4.2 below).[50]

The fair value of such a contract may change due to variations in market interest rates and the share price. However, provided that such changes in fair value do not affect the amount of cash or other financial assets to be paid or received, or the number of equity instruments to be received or delivered, on settlement of the contract, the contract is an equity instrument.[51]

Any consideration received (such as the premium received for a written option or warrant on the entity's own shares) is added directly to equity. Any consideration paid (such as the premium paid for a purchased option) is deducted directly from equity. Changes in the fair value of an equity instrument are not recognised in financial statements.[52] This is consistent with the treatment of equity under the *Framework* (and as defined in IAS 32 – see 2.3 above) as a residual after deducting total liabilities from total assets rather than an item 'in its own right'.

A   'Fixed amount' of cash (or other financial assets)

It is not beyond doubt what is meant by a 'fixed amount' of cash or other financial assets. The problem is illustrated by the example in paragraph 24 of IAS 32 (referred to in 3.3.2 B below) of a contract being a financial asset or financial liability where the reporting entity is required 'to deliver 100 of its own equity instruments in return for an amount of cash calculated to equal the value of 100 ounces of gold'.

This seems straightforward enough. If, however, one substitutes '100 US dollars' for '100 ounces of gold', the latent problem becomes apparent. Suppose a UK entity (with the pound sterling as its functional currency) issues a 100 US dollar bond convertible into a fixed number of shares of that UK entity. The conversion feature effectively gives the bondholder the right to acquire a fixed number of shares for $100 – is this a 'fixed amount' of cash, or is it to be regarded as being just as variable, in terms of its conversion into the functional currency of the pound sterling, as 100 ounces of gold?

The answer to this question is highly significant. If the conclusion is that the $100 is a fixed amount of cash, then the conversion right is accounted for as an equity component of the bond – in other words a value is assigned to it on initial recognition and it is not subsequently remeasured (see 4.3.1 below). If, on the other hand, the conclusion is that the $100 is not a fixed amount of cash, then the conversion right (as an embedded derivative not regarded by IAS 39 as closely related to the host contract – see Chapter 15 at 5) is accounted for as a separate derivative financial asset or financial liability, introducing potentially significant volatility into the financial statements.

There is no obvious answer to this. A contention that the $100 is a fixed amount of cash is hard to reconcile with the fact that a contract to issue shares for 'as many pounds sterling as are worth $100' involves the issue of a fixed number of shares for a variable amount of cash and would therefore not be an equity instrument. Conversely, a contention that the $100 is not a fixed amount of cash leads to the rather strange result that the classification of the instrument varies depending on the functional currency of the issuing entity. For example, if the UK entity's US subsidiary (with a functional currency of US dollars) were to issue a bond convertible into its own equity convertible in turn into the UK parent's equity, the conversion right would (from the perspective of the US subsidiary) clearly involve the issue of a fixed number of shares for a fixed amount of cash and thus be an equity instrument. Moreover, this classification would not change on consolidation since IFRS has no concept of a group functional currency (see Chapter 9).

In our view, a fixed amount of cash other than the functional currency of the reporting entity should be regarded as a 'fixed amount of cash' for the purposes of classifying a financial instrument under IAS 32.

3.3.2 Contracts accounted for as financial assets or financial liabilities

A   Variable number of equity instruments

An entity may have a contractual right or obligation to receive or deliver a number of its own shares or other equity instruments that varies so that the fair value of the entity's own equity instruments to be received or delivered equals the amount of the contractual right or obligation.

The right or obligation may be for:

- a fixed amount – e.g. as many shares as are worth £100;
- an amount that fluctuates in part or in full in response to changes in a variable other than the market price of the entity's own equity instruments, such as movements in interest rates, commodity prices, or the price of a financial instrument – e.g. as many shares as are worth:
  - 100 ounces of gold;
  - £100 plus interest at LIBOR plus 200 basis points;
  - 100 government bonds; or
  - 100 shares in a particular entity

Such a contract is a financial asset or liability. Even though the contract must, or may, be settled through receipt or delivery of the entity's own equity instruments, the number of own equity instruments required to settle the contract will vary. Accordingly, the contract does not evidence a residual interest in the entity's assets after deducting all of its liabilities,[53] and is therefore a financial asset or financial liability.

I   Contracts based on the price of the entity's equity instruments

There is some confusion in IAS 32 as to the treatment of contracts settled in a variable number of equity instruments where the number of equity instruments to be delivered varies with the price of the entity's own equity instruments. Paragraph 21 of the standard (summarised above) refers to a contract being a financial asset or liability where the value of shares to be delivered fluctuates in response to changes in a variable '*other than* the market price of the entity's own equity instruments'. This could lead to the inference that a contract where the value of shares to be delivered does fluctuate in response to changes in the market price of the entity's own equity instruments is not a financial asset or liability.

However, paragraph AG27(d) of the application guidance clarifies that a contract settled in a variable number of the entity's own shares is a financial asset or liability 'even if the underlying variable is the entity's own share price'.

B   Fixed number of equity instruments for variable consideration

A contract that will be settled by the entity delivering or receiving a fixed number of its own equity instruments in exchange for a variable amount of cash or another financial asset is a financial asset or financial liability. An example is a contract for the entity to deliver 100 of its own equity instruments in return for an amount of cash calculated to equal the value of 100 ounces of gold,[54] or 100 government bonds.

C   *Fixed number of equity instruments with variable value*

A contract is a financial asset or financial liability if it is to be settled in a fixed number of shares the value of which will be varied (e.g. by modification of the rights attaching to them) so as to be equal to a fixed amount or an amount based on changes in an underlying variable.[55] This would include, for example, contracts to deliver as many shares as are worth €1,000.

D   *Net-settled contracts over own equity*

A contract over an entity's own equity instruments may be valued at the date of settlement as the difference between the fixed number of equity instruments to be delivered by one party and the fixed amount of cash (or other financial assets) to be delivered by the other party. Such a contract can then be settled, either by a net payment in cash (or other financial assets), or by a transfer of the entity's own equity, of a fair value equal to this difference. It is inherent in the general definition of an equity instrument in IAS 32 (see 3.1 above) that a contract settled by a single net payment (generally referred to as net cash-settled or net equity-settled as the case may be) is a financial asset or financial liability and not an equity instrument, notwithstanding that an economically equivalent contract settled gross (i.e. by physical delivery of the equity instruments in exchange for cash or other financial assets) would be treated as an equity instrument (see 3.3.3 and 7 below).

3.3.3   *Gross-settled contracts for the purchase of the entity's own equity instruments*

The discussion that follows relates only to contracts which must be settled by the counterparty delivering shares and the entity paying cash (gross-settled contracts). Contracts which can be settled net (i.e. by payment of the difference between the fair value, at the time of settlement, of the shares and that of the consideration given) are accounted as financial assets or financial liabilities[56] (see 3.5 and 7 below).

Entering into a gross-settled contract for the purchase of own shares gives rise to a financial liability in respect of the obligation to pay the purchase or redemption price[57] (but resulting in a reduction of equity rather than an expense). This treatment may be intended to reflect the idea that a forward contract or written option to repurchase an equity share gives rise to a liability similar to that contained within a redeemable share (see 3.2.1 above).

This is the case even if:

- the contract is an equity instrument;
- the contract is a written put option (i.e. a contract that gives the counterparty the right to require the entity to buy its own shares) rather than a forward contract (i.e. a firm commitment by the entity to purchase its own shares); or
- the number of shares subject to the contract is not fixed.[58]

The reference in the final bullet point above to the number of shares not being fixed gives rise to some confusion. Surely if the number of shares is not fixed, the contract is a financial asset or financial liability, and therefore not relevant to the discussion in this section?

We assume that what was intended might be a contract whereby the reporting entity writes a put option with a counterparty whereby the counterparty can require the entity to purchase between 1,000 and 5,000 of its own equity shares at €2 per share. The fact that it is a fixed price contract means that it is an equity instrument. However, it is not known in advance exactly how many shares the entity will be required to repurchase, so that (in terms of the final bullet above) the number of shares is not fixed. In other words, IAS 32 appears to be clarifying that the entity cannot avoid recognising a liability for the contract on the argument that it does not know exactly how many of its own shares it will be compelled to purchase.

When such a liability first arises it must be recognised, in accordance with IAS 39, at its fair value, i.e. the net present value of the redemption amount. Subsequently, the financial liability is measured in accordance with IAS 39 (see Chapter 18 at 3.1 and 3.2).[59] IAS 32 offers no guidance as to how this is to be calculated when, as might be the case with respect to a written put option such as that described in the previous paragraph, the number of shares to be purchased and/or the date of purchase is not known.

In our view, it would be consistent with the requirement of IAS 39 that liabilities with a demand feature such as a demand bank deposit should be measured at the amount payable on demand[60] (see Chapter 18 at 4.5) to adopt a 'worst case' approach. In other words, it should be assumed that the purchase will take place on the earliest possible date for the maximum number of shares. This is also consistent with IAS 32's emphasis, in the general discussion of the differences between liabilities and equity instruments, on a liability arising except to the extent that an entity has an 'unconditional' right to avoid delivering cash or other financial assets (see 3.2 above).

The treatment proposed in the previous paragraph would lead to a different accounting treatment for written 'American' put options (i.e. those that can be exercised at any time during a period ending on a future date) and written 'European' put options (i.e. those that can be exercised only at a given future date). In the case of an American option, a liability would be recorded immediately for the full potential liability. In the case of a European option, a liability would be recorded for the net present value of the full potential liability and interest accrued on that liability until the date of potential exercise. If this interpretation is correct, it has the effect that:

- a gross-settled written American put option has no impact on profit or loss (because the full amount payable on settlement would be charged to equity on inception of the contract), but

- a gross-settled European put option does impact on profit or loss (because the net present value of the amount payable on settlement would be charged to equity on inception of the contract and accrued to the full settlement amount through profit or loss).

If the contract expires without delivery of the shares, the carrying amount of the financial liability is reclassified to equity. This has the rather curious effect that a share purchase contract that expires unexercised (and therefore has no impact on the entity's net assets, other than the receipt or payment of the option premium) can nevertheless give rise to a loss to the extent that interest has been recognised on the liability between initial recognition and its transfer to equity (see Example 17.16 at 7.3.2 below).

3.3.4   Gross-settled contracts for the sale or issue of the entity's own equity instruments

The discussion that follows relates only to contracts which must be settled by the counterparty delivering shares and the entity paying cash (gross-settled contracts). Contracts which can be settled net (i.e. by payment of the difference between the fair value, at the time of purchase, of the shares and that of the consideration given) are accounted as financial assets or financial liabilities[61] (see 3.5 and 7 below).

If an entity enters into a gross-settled contract to sell its own shares, the contract is economically the 'mirror image' of a contract for the purchase of own equity. However, there is there no provision in IAS 32 that the contract gives rise to a financial asset, as compared to the specific provision that a contract to purchase own equity gives rise to a financial liability (see 3.3.3 above). Consequently, it appears that such contracts give rise to no accounting entries until settlement. This analysis is confirmed by an illustrative example in the appendix to IAS 32 (see Example 17.11 at 7.1.2 below).

The Basis for Conclusions in IAS 32 offers no explanation for the inconsistency between the treatment of a contract to purchase, and a contract to sell or issue, equity instruments. Some clarification would have been welcome. If a contract to purchase equity giving rise to an unavoidable obligation (however contingent) of the entity to deliver cash or another financial asset to a third party creates a financial liability, a contract to sell or issue equity giving rise to an unavoidable obligation of a third party to deliver cash or another financial asset to the entity must logically create a financial asset.

Contracts for the sale or issue of own equity arise in situations such as those in Examples 17.2 and 17.3 below.

Example 17.2:   Share issue payable in fixed instalments

A government intends to privatise a nationalised industry through an initial public offering (IPO) at €5 per share. In order to encourage widespread share ownership, the terms of the issue are that shares are issued on 1 January 2005, but subscribers to the IPO are required to pay only €3 per share on 1 January 2005 followed by two further instalments of €1 per share on 1 January 2006 and 1 January 2007.

Example 17.3:   Right to call for additional equity capital

A start-up technology entity is unsure of its working capital requirements for the first few years of its operations. It therefore enters into an agreement with its major shareholders whereby it can require those shareholders to contribute an additional £2 per share at any time during the next seven years.

One view might be that the situation in Example 17.2 is not a contract for the future issue of equity – the share has already been issued, and so it would be quite appropriate to record a receivable for the deferred subscription payments. On the other hand, it is clear from IAS 32 that no receivable should be recognised if the arrangement provided for the entity actually to issue further shares (pro-rata to the shares initially issued) for €1 on 1 January 2006 and 1 January 2007, which is equivalent to the position in Example 17.3. Given that there is no clear economic difference between the transactions, it is strange that the accounting treatment for them varies simply depending on the form, but this appears to be the case.

One potentially relevant fact not mentioned in either of Examples 17.2 and 17.3 is the consequence for the shareholder of not paying the additional amounts. If failure to pay the further amounts led to forfeiture of the shares already held, this might support an argument that the circumstances were sufficiently different from a straightforward forward sale of shares to justify recognition of a receivable.

3.4   Contingent settlement provisions

Some financial instruments (e.g. certain convertible bonds, in respect of the principal amount of the bond) may require the entity to deliver cash or another financial asset, or otherwise to settle it in such a way that it would be a financial liability, in the event of the occurrence or non-occurrence of uncertain future events (or on the outcome of uncertain circumstances) that are beyond the control of both the issuer and the holder of the instrument. These might include:

- a change in a stock market index or a consumer price index;
- changes in interest rates;
- changes in tax law; or
- the issuer's future revenues, net income or debt-to-equity ratio.[62]

IAS 32 provides that, since the issuer of such an instrument does not have the unconditional right to avoid delivering cash or another financial asset (or otherwise to settle it in such a way that it would be a financial liability), the instrument is a financial liability of the issuer unless:

(a)   the part of the contingent settlement provision that could require settlement in cash or another financial asset (or otherwise in such a way that it would be a financial liability) is not genuine (see below); or

(b)   the issuer can be required to settle the obligation in cash or another financial asset (or otherwise to settle it in such a way that it would be a financial liability) only in the event of liquidation of the issuer.[63]

The application guidance goes on to clarify that a requirement to settle an instrument in cash or another financial asset (or otherwise in such a way that it would be a financial liability) is not genuine (see (a) above) if the requirement would arise 'only on the occurrence of an event that is extremely rare, highly abnormal and very unlikely to occur'.[64]

Similarly, if the terms of an instrument provide for its settlement in a fixed number of the entity's equity instruments, but there are circumstances, beyond the entity's control, in which such settlement may be contractually precluded, those circumstances can be ignored if there is 'no genuine possibility' that they will occur. In other words, the instrument continues to be regarded as an equity instrument and not as a financial liability.[65]

3.4.1 Terms that are 'not genuine'

The promise in the Basis for Conclusions of IAS 32 of guidance as to what is meant by redemption terms that are 'not genuine'[66] is unfortunately fulfilled in the standard only by the litany of synonyms noted above. It may, however, be helpful to consider the changes made by the revised version of IAS 32 to SIC–5 – *Classification of Financial Instruments – Contingent Settlement Provisions*[67] (which is now withdrawn, and its essential substance incorporated in these provisions of IAS 32). SIC–5 previously required redemption terms to be ignored if they were 'remote'. Examples given by SIC–5 were where the issue of shares is contingent merely on formal approval by the authorities, or where cash settlement is triggered by an index reaching an 'extreme' level relative to its level at the time of initial recognition of the instrument.[68]

However, the Basis for Conclusions to IAS 32 makes clear the IASB's belief that it is not appropriate to disregard events that are merely 'remote'. Accordingly, IAS 32 deliberately does not reproduce the reference to, or the examples of, 'remote' events in SIC–5.[69] Thus it is clear that, under the revised version of IAS 32, it is not appropriate to disregard a redemption term that is triggered only when an index reaches an extreme level. This suggests that it is not open to an entity to argue (for example) that a bond that is redeemed in cash only if the entity's share price falls below, or fails to reach, a certain level can be treated as an equity instrument on the grounds that there is no genuine possibility that the share price will perform in that way.

The wording in IAS 32 is presumably intended to deal with clauses inserted into financial instruments for some arcane legal or tax reason (e.g. so as to make conversion 'conditional' rather than mandatory) but having no real economic purpose or consequence.

3.4.2 Liabilities that arise only on liquidation

As noted above, IAS 32 provides that a redemption term that comes into play only on liquidation of the issuer may be ignored in determining whether or not a financial instrument is a financial liability. It should be noted that IAS 32 refers specifically to 'liquidation'. In other words, if an instrument provides for redemption on the occurrence of events that are a likely precursor of liquidation (e.g. extreme insolvency, the financial statements not being prepared on a going concern basis, a shareholders' resolution for orderly winding-up) but falling short of formal liquidation, the instrument must be treated as a financial liability.

3.5   Derivative financial instruments with settlement options

A derivative financial instrument may have settlement options – in other words, it gives one party a choice over how it is settled (e.g. the issuer or the holder can choose settlement net in cash, net in shares, or by exchanging shares for cash). Where a derivative has settlement options, IAS 32 requires it to be treated as a financial asset or a financial liability unless all possible settlement alternatives would result in it being an equity instrument.[70] An example of a derivative financial instrument with a settlement option that is a financial liability is a share option that the issuer can decide to settle net in cash or by exchanging its own shares for cash.[71]

These provisions will apply mostly to contracts involving the sale or purchase by an entity of its own equity instruments. However, they will also be relevant to those contracts to buy or sell a non-financial item in exchange for the entity's own equity instruments that are within the scope of IAS 32 (rather than IFRS 2) because they can be settled either by delivery of the non-financial item or net in cash or another financial instrument (see Chapter 15 at 3). Such contracts are financial assets or financial liabilities and not equity instruments.[72]

3.6   Consolidated financial statements

In consolidated financial statements, IAS 32 requires an entity to present minority interests – i.e. the interests of other parties in the equity and income of its subsidiaries – in accordance with IAS 1 – *Presentation of Financial Statements* (see Chapter 3 at 3.1.5) and IAS 27 – *Consolidated and Separate Financial Statements* (see Chapter 5 at 6.7).[73]

However, when classifying a financial instrument (or a component of it) in consolidated financial statements, an entity must consider all terms and conditions agreed between all members of the group and the holders of the instrument in determining whether the group as a whole has an obligation to deliver cash or another financial asset in respect of the instrument or to settle it in a manner that results in its classification as a financial liability.[74]

For example, a subsidiary in a group may issue a financial instrument and a parent or other group entity may then agree additional terms directly with the holders of the instrument so as to guarantee some or all of the payments to be made under the instrument. The effect of this is that the subsidiary may have discretion over distributions or redemption, but the group as a whole does not.[75]

Accordingly, the subsidiary may appropriately classify the instrument without regard to these additional terms in its individual financial statements. For the purposes of the consolidated financial statements, however, the effect of the other agreements between members of the group and the holders of the instrument is to create an obligation or settlement provision, so that the instrument (or the component of it that is subject to the obligation) is classified as a financial liability.[76]

Thus it is quite possible for a financial instrument to be classified as an equity instrument in the financial statements of the issuing subsidiary but as a financial liability in the financial statements of the group.

4   COMPOUND FINANCIAL INSTRUMENTS

4.1   Background

A compound financial instrument is a non-derivative financial instrument that, from the issuer's perspective, contains both a liability and an equity component.[77] Examples include:

- A bond convertible into a fixed number of equity instruments, which effectively comprises:

    - a financial liability (the issuer's obligation to pay interest and, potentially, to redeem the bond in cash); and

    - an equity instrument (the holder's right to call for shares of the issuer).

    IAS 32 states that the economic effect of issuing such an instrument is substantially the same as issuing simultaneously a debt instrument with an early settlement provision and warrants to purchase ordinary shares, or issuing a debt instrument with detachable share purchase warrants.[78] However, this analysis is questionable in the sense that if a company did issue such instruments separately, it is extremely unlikely that one would lapse as the result of the exercise of the other (as happens on the conversion or redemption of a convertible bond).

- A mandatorily redeemable preference share with dividends paid at the issuer's discretion, which effectively comprises:

    - a financial liability (the issuer's obligation to redeem the shares in cash); and

    - an equity instrument (the holder's right to receive dividends if declared).[79]

IAS 32 requires the issuer of a non-derivative financial instrument to evaluate the terms of the financial instrument to determine whether it contains both a liability and an equity component. If such components are identified, they must be accounted for separately as financial liabilities, financial assets or equity,[80] and the liability and equity components shown separately on the balance sheet.[81]

This treatment, commonly referred to as 'split accounting', is discussed in more detail in 4.2 to 4.5 below. For simplicity, the discussion below (like that in IAS 32 itself) is framed in terms of convertible bonds, by far the most common form of compound financial instrument, but is equally applicable to other types of compound instrument.

4.1.1 Treatment by holder and issuer contrasted

'Split accounting' is to be applied only by the issuer of a compound financial instrument. The accounting treatment by the holder is dealt with in IAS 39[82] (see Chapter 15 at 5.1.5 Chapter 18 at 3) and is significantly different. In particular:

- In the issuer's financial statements, under IAS 32:

    - the fair value of the liability component is calculated first and the equity component is treated as a residual; and

    - the equity component is never remeasured after initial recognition

- In the holder's financial statements, under IAS 39 (see Chapter 15 at 5 and Chapter 18 at 2.5):

    - the equity component (from the issuer's perspective) is a derivative financial asset of the holder, the fair value of which is calculated first with the liability component (from the issuer's perspective) treated as a residual amount; and

    - the derivative financial asset of the holder is likely to be constantly remeasured at fair value.

4.2 The components of a compound instrument

4.2.1 Determining the components of a financial instrument

Arguably the most difficult aspect of 'split accounting' is the initial determination of what the various components of the instrument actually are. In the examples in 4.1 above, it is fairly clear what these are. However, in some instruments the analysis is far from clear, as illustrated by Example 17.4 below.

Example 17.4   Decomposition of compound financial instrument into components

An entity issues a bond for €100, paying an annual cash coupon of 5% on the issue price and mandatorily convertible after five years on the following terms. If, at the date of conversion, the entity's share price is €1.25 or higher, the holder will receive 80 shares. If the entity's share price is €1.00 or lower, the holder will receive 100 shares. If the entity's share price is in the range €1.00 to €1.25, the holder will receive such number of shares (between 80 and 100) as have a fair value of €100.

Any analysis must begin by determining whether the bond as whole is a non-derivative instrument. This is the case, since the issuing entity receives full consideration for its issue. The next step is to break the instrument down into its components so as to identify any equity components in the whole. At least four possible analyses suggest themselves.

I   Analysis 1

The bond is a non-derivative for which the entity is obliged to deliver a variable number of equity instruments (since the number may vary between 80 and 125 shares), and therefore is in its entirety a financial liability as defined in IAS 32 (see 2.3 and 3.1 above). There is then a discussion to be had as to whether the share-price link is an embedded derivative requiring separation under IAS 39 (see Chapter 15 at 5).

II   Analysis 2

The bond comprises three components:

(a)   an obligation to pay interest – a financial liability;

(b)   a non-derivative requiring the issuer to deliver a fixed number of shares (the 80 shares that the entity will be required to issue in any event) – an equity instrument; and

(c)   an obligation to deliver up to 20 more shares depending on the ultimate share price – a derivative financial liability.

III   Analysis 3

The bond comprises four components:

(a)   an obligation to pay interest – a financial liability;

(b)   an obligation to deliver as many shares as are worth €100 – a financial liability;

(c)   a written call option, whereby the holder can require the issuer to exchange 80 shares for €100 (i.e. the fixed stated principal of the bond – see 4.4.2 below) – an equity instrument; and

(d)   a purchased put option, whereby the issuer can require the holder to exchange 100 shares for €100 (i.e. the fixed stated principal of the bond – see 4.4.2 below) – an equity instrument.

However, some might argue that the reference in IAS 32 to the 'fixed stated principal' of a bond (see 4.4.2 below) is relevant only where it is a proxy for a fixed amount of 'real' cash, such as the cash that is foregone on conversion of a bond where there is no obligation to convert. In this case, it could be argued that no cash is foregone (since the bond is mandatorily convertible) and that the true consideration for the put and call options in (c) and (d) above is not €100 cash but the €100 worth of shares delivered under (b) above. This suggests Analysis 4 below.

IV   Analysis 4

The bond comprises four components:

(a)   an obligation to pay interest – a financial liability;

(b)   an obligation to deliver as many shares as are worth €100 – a financial liability

(c)   a written call option, whereby the holder can require the issuer to exchange 80 shares for as many shares as are worth €100 (i.e. effectively exchanging the number of shares notionally delivered under (b) above, if less than 80 shares, for 80 shares) – a derivative financial liability; and

(d)   a purchased put option, whereby the issuer can require the holder to exchange 100 shares for as many shares as are worth €100 (i.e. effectively exchanging the number of shares notionally delivered under (b) above, if greater than 100 shares, for 100 shares) – a derivative financial liability.

V   Summary

Whichever analysis is chosen will have a significant impact on the accounting treatment. Under Analyses 1 and 4, the bond would not fall within IAS 32's provisions for compound financial instruments at all, as there is no identified equity component. Under Analyses 2 and 3 by contrast, there is at least one identified equity component, so that the bond would fall within IAS 32's provisions for compound financial instruments.

We question whether Analysis 1 properly addresses the requirement of IAS 32 to separate a compound financial instrument into its component parts. To take an extreme case, suppose that the bond converted into one billion shares in some cases and one billion and one shares in others. Would it really be appropriate to classify the whole instrument as a liability on the basis of a variability of one share in a billion?

Analysis 1 could be valid if it could be shown that neither the floor of 80 shares nor the ceiling of 125 shares would ever be reached in any foreseeable scenario. However, it would be difficult to sustain such an argument in most cases. It can generally be assumed that conditions such as these are included in the terms of financial instruments because there is considered to be a real, if remote, possibility that the relevant events will occur.

Ultimately, however, we believe that Analysis 1 is flawed because it fails to identify any equity component in an instrument that clearly contains some equity features. The same objection can be made against Analysis 4.

We believe that a case can be made for either Analysis 2 or Analysis 3. However, Analysis 2 could be said not to follow the underlying principle of IAS 32 (and the IAS *Framework* in general) that equity is a residual amount, since it effectively identifies the equity component first rather than the underlying liability to deliver €100 worth of own shares. Also, Analysis 2, by identifying the majority of the instrument as equity, would deny the issuer the ability to achieve (to any significant degree) hedge accounting for any hedge of the instrument (since an entity may not apply hedge accounting to a hedge of its own equity instruments – see Chapter 19).

In our view, the main conclusion to be drawn from examples such as this is that the provisions of IAS 32, which were originally drafted in the mid 1990s to deal with 'traditional' convertible instruments, are not adequate for dealing with the increasingly complex range of instruments with a link to the issuer's share price currently available in the financial markets.

4.2.2   Separated (i.e. not closely-related) embedded derivatives

As noted above, in order to qualify for split accounting, a financial instrument, when considered as whole, must be a non-derivative instrument. However, one or more of its identified components may well be embedded derivatives. Indeed, the conversion right in any convertible bond represents a holder's call option whereby the entity can be required to issue a fixed number of shares for a fixed consideration (the 'fixed stated principal' of the bond – see 4.4.2 below), which is accordingly identified as an equity component.

A bond may well contain other non-equity derivatives, such as options for either the issuer or the holder to require early repayment or conversion or to extend the period until conversion. On the face of things, they are subject to the normal requirement of IAS 39 for embedded derivatives to be accounted for separately if they are not considered to be closely related to the host contract (see Chapter 15 at 5)

There is, however, a certain ambiguity in the drafting of IAS 32 as to how any non-equity derivatives should be treated. The detailed guidance in IAS 32 on initial recognition of compound instruments (see 4.3 below) requires 'the fair value of any embedded non-equity derivative features [to be] determined and included in the liability component'[83] – suggesting that they are always accounted for as part of the liability component and never separated. However, this is inconsistent with the overall (bold paragraph) requirement of IAS 32 to classify the components of a compound instrument 'separately as financial liabilities, financial assets or equity' (see 4.1 above). Clearly, if all non-equity embedded derivatives were accounted for as part of the liability component, there would never be any recognition of financial assets.

In our view, the requirements of IAS 39 for separate accounting for certain embedded derivatives are intended to be applied to any non-equity derivatives identified in the decomposition of a compound financial instrument.

4.3   Initial recognition

On initial recognition of a compound instrument such as a convertible bond, IAS 32 requires the issuer to:

(a)   identify the various components of the instrument;

(b)   determine the fair value of the liability component (see below); and

(c)   determine the equity component as a residual amount, essentially the issue proceeds of the instrument less the liability component determined in (b) above.

Thereafter the liability component (and any identified financial asset component) is accounted for in accordance with the rules for measurement of financial liabilities (and, if relevant, financial assets) in IAS 39 (see Chapter 18 at 3.1 and 3.2).[84]

The liability component of a convertible bond should be measured first, at the fair value of a similar liability, including any embedded non-equity derivative features (e.g. an issuer's or holder's right to require early redemption of the bond), of a similar liability that does not have an associated equity conversion feature.

In practical terms, this will be done by determining the net present value of all potential contractually determined future cash flows under the instrument, discounted at the rate of interest applied by the market at the time of issue to instruments of comparable credit status and providing substantially the same cash flows, on the same terms, but without the conversion option. The fair value of any embedded non-equity derivative features is then determined and 'included in the liability component'[85] – see, however, the further discussion of this point at 4.2.1 above.

IAS 32 notes that:

- the equity component of a convertible bond is an embedded option to convert the liability into equity of the issuer;

- the fair value of the option comprises its time value and its intrinsic value, if any; and;

- this option has value on initial recognition even when it is out of the money.[86]

Whilst this is all true, it is actually irrelevant to the accounting, since the equity component is not (other than by coincidence) recorded at its fair value. Instead, in accordance with the general definition of equity as a residual, the equity component of the bond is simply the difference between the total issue proceeds of the bond and the liability component as determined above. Because of this 'residual' treatment, IAS 32 does not address the issue of how, or whether, the issue proceeds are to be allocated where more than one equity component is identified (as in Analysis 3 at 4.2.1 above).

This has the effect that the sum of the carrying amounts assigned to the liability and equity components on initial recognition is always equal to the fair value that would be ascribed to the instrument as a whole. No gain or loss arises from initially recognising the components of the instrument separately.[87]

This treatment is illustrated in Examples 17.5 and 17.6 below.

Example 17.5: Convertible bond – basic 'split accounting'[88]

An entity issues 2,000 convertible bonds. The bonds have a three-year term, and are issued at par with a face value of €1,000 per bond, giving total proceeds of €2,000,000. Interest is payable annually in arrears at a nominal annual interest rate of 6% (i.e. €120,000 per annum). Each bond is convertible at any time up to maturity into 250 ordinary shares. When the bonds are issued, the prevailing market interest rate for similar debt without conversion options is 9% per annum. The entity incurs issue costs of €100,000.

The economic components of this instrument are:

- a liability component, being a discounted fixed rate debt, perhaps with an imputed holder's put option (due to the holder's right to convert at any time), and

- an equity component, representing the holder's right to convert at any time before maturity. In effect this is a written call option (from the issuer's perspective) on American terms (i.e. it can be exercised at any time until maturity of the bond).

The practical problem with this analysis is that it is not clear what is the strike price of the holder's options to put the debt and call for shares, specifically whether it is the €2,000,000 face value of the bond or the discounted amount at which it is recorded until maturity – see the further discussion of this issue at 3.3.1 A and 4.2.1 above. Perhaps for this reason, IAS 32 does not require the true fair values of these components to be calculated.

Instead the liability component is measured first at the net present value of the maximum potential cash payments that the issuer could be required to make, and the difference between the proceeds of the bond issue and this calculated fair value of the liability is assigned to the equity component. The net present value (NPV) of the liability component is calculated as €1,848,122, using a discount rate of 9%, the market interest rate for similar bonds having no conversion rights, as shown.

Year	Cash flow	€	Discount factor (at 9%)	NPV of cash flow €
1	Interest	120,000	1/1.09	110,092
2	Interest	120,000	$1/1.09^2$	101,001
3	Interest and principal	2,120,000	$1/1.09^3$	1,637,029
		Total liability component		1,848,122
		Total equity component (balance)		151,878
		Total proceeds		2,000,000

It is next necessary to deal with the issue costs of €100,000. In accordance with the requirements of IAS 32 for such costs (see 5.1 below), these would be allocated to the liability and equity components on a pro-rata basis. This would give the following allocation of the net issue proceeds.

	Liability component €	Equity component €	Total €
Gross proceeds (allocated as above)	1,848,122	151,878	2,000,000
Issue costs (allocated pro-rata to gross proceeds)	(92,406)	(7,594)	(100,000)
Net proceeds	1,755,716	144,284	1,900,000

The €144,284 credited to equity is not subsequently remeasured (see 4.2.1 above). On the assumption that the liability is not classified as at fair value through profit and loss (see Chapter 15 at 7.1), the €1,755,716 liability component would be accounted for under the effective interest rate method (see Chapter 18 at 3.1, 3.2 and 5). It should be borne in mind that, after taking account of the issue costs, the effective interest rate is not the 9% used to determine the gross value of the liability component, but 10.998%, as shown below.

Year	Liability b/f €	Interest at 10.998% €	Cash paid €	Liability c/f €
1	1,755,716	193,094	(120,000)	1,828,810
2	1,828,810	201,134	(120,000)	1,909,944
3	1,909,943	210,056	(2,120,000)	–
	Total finance cost	604,284		

The total finance cost can be proved as follows.

	€
Cash interest	360,000
Gross issue proceeds originally allocated to equity component	151,878
Issue costs allocated to liability component	92,406
	604,284

In many jurisdictions only the cash interest paid and the issue costs are deductible for tax purposes, and may well be deductible in periods different from those in which they are recognised in the financial statements. These factors will give rise to temporary differences between the carrying value of the liability component of the bond and its tax base, giving rise to deferred tax required to be accounted for under IAS 12 – *Income Taxes* (see Chapter 24, particularly at 3.2.1 B and 4.2.1 D).

Example 17.6:   *Convertible bond – split accounting with multiple embedded derivative features[89]*

The proceeds received on the issue of a callable convertible bond are £60 million. The value of a similar bond without a call or equity conversion option is £57 million. Based on an option-pricing model, it is determined that the value to the entity of the embedded call feature in a similar bond without an equity conversion option is £2 million. In this case, the value is allocated so as to reduce the liability component to £55 million (£57m – £2m) and the value allocated to the equity component is £5 million (£60m – £55m).

Unfortunately, IAS 32 does not specifically clarify on what basis the embedded call feature has been treated as a reduction of the liability component rather than as a separate asset (see 4.2.1 above), and in particular whether:

- the requirements of IAS 39 for the treatment of embedded derivatives were considered at all, or

- they were considered, and it was concluded that the call option did not require separation on the assumption that the option exercise price (which is not addressed in the assumed facts in Example 17.6) was, at each potential exercise date approximately equal to the amortised cost of the host liability[90] – see Chapter 15 at 5.1.3.

4.3.1 Accounting for the equity component

On initial recognition of a compound financial instrument, the equity component (e.g. the €144,284 identified in Example 17.5 above) is credited direct to equity. IAS 32 does not prescribe:

- whether the credit should be to a separate component of equity (although IFRS 1 – *First-time Adoption of International Financial Reporting Standards* – suggests that there is such a requirement – see 8.1 below); or

- if the entity chooses to treat it as such, how it should be described.

We imagine that the IASB deliberately allowed complete freedom in this respect so as to ensure that there was no conflict between, on the one hand, the basic requirement of IAS 32 that there should be a credit in equity and, on the other, the legal requirements of various jurisdictions as to exactly how that credit should be allocated within equity.

After initial recognition, the classification of the liability and equity components of a convertible instrument is not revised, for example as a result of a change in the likelihood that a conversion option will be exercised, even when exercise of the option may appear to have become economically advantageous to some holders. IAS 32 points out that holders may not always act in the way that might be expected because, for example, the tax consequences resulting from conversion may differ among holders. Furthermore, the likelihood of conversion will change from time to time. The entity's contractual obligation to make future payments remains outstanding until it is extinguished through conversion, maturity of the instrument or some other transaction.[91]

The amount originally credited to equity is not subsequently recycled to the income statement. Thus, as illustrated by Example 17.5 above, the effective interest rate shown in the income statement for a simple convertible bond will be equivalent to the rate that would have been paid for non-convertible debt. In effect, the dilution of shareholder value represented by the embedded conversion right is shown as an interest expense. Similarly, the dilution of shareholder value inherent in employee share options is shown as an expense under IFRS 2 (see Chapter 29), albeit using a methodology very different to that in IAS 32.

However, on conversion of a convertible instrument, it may be appropriate to transfer the equity component within equity (see 4.4.1 below).

4.4 Conversion, early repurchase and modification

4.4.1 Conversion at maturity

On conversion of a convertible instrument at maturity, IAS 32 requires the entity to derecognises the liability component and recognise it as equity. There is no gain or loss on conversion at maturity.[92]

Thus, for example, if the bond in Example 17.4 above were converted at maturity, the accounting entry required by IAS 32 is:

	€	€
Liability	2,000,000	
Equity		2,000,000

The precise allocation of the credit to equity (e.g. as between share capital, additional paid-in capital, share premium, other reserves and so on) would be a matter of local legislation. In addition, IAS 32 permits the €144,284 originally allocated to the equity component in Example 17.4 above to be reallocated within equity.[93]

A   Embedded derivatives

IAS 32 does not specifically address the treatment of any non-equity embedded derivatives outstanding at the time of conversion. The issue of principle is that when a holder exercises its right to convert, it is effectively requiring the issuer to issue equity in consideration for the bondholder ceding its rights. These may include any right to receive future payments of principal and/or interest or to require early repayment of the bond. It seems entirely appropriate that any amounts carried in respect of such rights should be transferred to equity on conversion.

Where, however, conversion has the effect of removing an issuer's right (for example, to compel early redemption or conversion), this could be seen as a loss to the issuer rather than as consideration given by the holder for an issue of equity. In our view, the loss of such a right by the issuer on conversion by the holder simply represents a reduction in the proceeds received for the issue of equity, and should therefore by accounted for as a charge to equity (see also 5.1 below).

4.4.2 Conversion before maturity

A 'Fixed stated principal' of a bond

The consideration given for the issue of equity instruments on conversion of a bond is the discharge by the holder of the issuer from the liability to pay any further interest or principal payments on the bond. If conversion can take place only at maturity, the amount of the liability transferred to equity on conversion will always (in Example 17.5 above) be €2,000,000. Hence, the conversion right involves the delivery of a fixed number of shares for the waiver of the right to receive a fixed amount of cash and so is clearly an equity instrument.

However, the bond in Example 17.5 allows conversion at some point before the full term. Therefore, conversion might occur at the end of year 2, when the carrying value of the bond had been accreted to only €1,909,944. Hence, the carrying amount of the liability that is forgiven on conversion can vary depending on whether conversion occurs. This begs the question as to whether the conversion right now involves the delivery of a fixed number of shares for the waiver of the right to receive a *variable* amount of cash, suggesting that it is no longer an equity instrument.

It is for this reason, in our view, that IAS 32 defines as an equity instrument one that involves the exchange of a fixed number of shares for the 'fixed stated principal' rather than the 'carrying amount' of a bond. In other words, IAS 32 regards the 'fixed stated principal' of the bond in Example 17.5 as a constant €2,000,000. The intention is to clarify that the variation in the bond's carrying amount during its term does not preclude the conversion right from being classified as an equity instrument.

B Accounting treatment

IAS 32 refers to treatment summarised in 4.4.1 above being applied on conversion 'at maturity', leaving open the question of the treatment to be adopted if a holder converts prior to maturity (as would have been possible under the terms of the bond in Example 17.5).

A simple approach would be simply to transfer to equity the carrying value of the liability at the date of conversion – as calculated after accrual of finance costs on a continuous basis, rather than at the amount shown in the most recently published financial statements. In such a case, the consideration for the issue of equity instruments is the release, by the bondholder, of the issuer from its liability to make future contractual payments under the bond, measured at the net present value of those payments.

Whilst we support such an approach as a matter of practicality, it does jar with the premise that the equity component of the bond is an equity instrument on the grounds that it represents the holder's right to call for a fixed number of shares for fixed consideration, in the form of the 'fixed stated principal' of the bond – see A above.

It could be argued that the logical implication of this is that, on a holder's early conversion of the bond in Example 17.5 above, the issuer should immediately recognise a finance cost for the difference between the then carrying amount of the liability component of the bond and the fixed stated principal of €2,000,000. This would create a liability of €2,000,000 immediately before conversion, so as to acknowledge that the strike price under the holder's call option is the waiver of the right to receive a fixed stated principal of €2,000,000, rather than whatever the carrying value of the bond happens to be at the time.

Issues such as this, and those discussed at 4.2.2 above, suggest to us that the IASB needs to consider further:

- exactly what components are being accounted for in 'split accounting', and
- whether, and why, the accounting treatment should differ from that applicable to separate instruments equivalent to those components.

4.4.3   Early repurchase

It is not uncommon for the issuer of a convertible bond to repurchase it before the end of its full term, either through exercise of rights inherent in the bond or through subsequent negotiation with bondholders. When an entity extinguishes a convertible instrument before maturity through an early redemption or repurchase in which the original conversion privileges are unchanged, IAS 32 requires the entity to allocate the consideration paid and any transaction costs for the repurchase or redemption to the liability and equity components of the instrument at the date of the transaction.[94]

It is not entirely clear what is meant by a 'redemption or repurchase in which the original conversion privileges are unchanged'. However, we assume that it is intended to imply that the repurchase must either be according to the original terms of the compound instrument, or must be at a price representing a fair value for the instrument on its original terms. A repurchase at a value implying a substantial modification of the original terms of the instrument should presumably be dealt with according to the provisions of IAS 32 for the modification of a compound instrument (see 4.4.4 below) or those in IAS 39 for the exchange and modification of debt (see Chapter 16 at 5.2).

The method used for allocating the consideration paid and transaction costs to the separate components should be consistent with that used in the original allocation to the separate components of the proceeds received by the entity when the convertible instrument was issued (see 4.2 above).[95]

Once this allocation of the consideration has been made:

- the difference between the consideration allocated to the liability component and the carrying amount of the liability is recognised in profit or loss; and
- the amount of consideration relating to the equity component is recognised in equity.[96]

The treatment of a negotiated repurchase at fair value of a convertible instrument at fair value is illustrated by Example 17.7 below.[97]

Example 17.7:   *Early repurchase of convertible instrument*

For simplicity this example:

- assumes that at inception the face amount of the instrument was equal to the carrying amount of its liability and equity components in the financial statements – i.e. there was no premium or discount on issue; and

- ignores transaction costs and tax.

On 1 January 2000, an entity issued a convertible bond with a face value of €100 million maturing on 31 December 2009, at which point the holder may opt for repayment of €100 million or conversion into 4 million shares. Interest is paid half-yearly in arrears at a nominal annual interest rate of 10% (i.e. €5m per half year). At the date of issue, the entity could have issued non-convertible debt with a ten-year term bearing interest at 11%. On issue, the carrying amount of the bond was allocated as follows:

	€m
Present value of the principal – €100m payable at the end of ten years[1]	34.3
Present value of the interest – 20 6-monthly payments of €5m[2]	59.7
Total liability component	94.0
Equity component (balance)	6.0
Proceeds of the bond issue	100.0

The amounts above are discounted using a semi-annual rate of 5.5% (11%/2 as follows)

1) $€100m/1.055^{20}$

2) $€5m \times (1/1.055 + 1/1.055^2 + 1/1.055^3 + \ldots 1/1.055^{20})$

On 1 January 2005, the entity makes a tender offer to the holder of the bond to repurchase the bond at its then fair value of €170 million, which the holder accepts. At the date of repurchase, the entity could have issued non-convertible debt with a five-year term with interest payable half-yearly in arrears at an annual coupon interest rate of 8%.

At the time of repurchase, the carrying amount of the liability component of the bond, discounted at the original semi-annual rate of 5.5% is as follows.

	€m
Present value of the principal – €100m payable at the end of five years[1]	58.5
Present value of the interest – 10 6-monthly payments of €5m[2]	37.7
Carrying value of liability component	96.2

1) $€100m/1.055^{10}$

2) $€5m \times (1/1.055 + 1/1.055^2 + 1/1.055^3 + \ldots 1/1.055^{10})$

The fair value of the liability element of the bond, discounted at the current semi-annual rate of 4% 8%/2) is as follows.

	€m
Present value of the principal – €100m payable at the end of five years[1]	67.6
Present value of the interest – 10 6-monthly payments of €5m[2]	40.5
Carrying value of liability component	108.1

1) €100m/1.04^{10}
2) €5m × $(1/1.04 + 1/1.04^2 + 1/1.04^3 + ...1/1.04^{10})$

The fair value calculation indicates that, of the repurchase price of €170 million, €108.1 million is to be treated as redeeming the liability component of the bond, and €61.9 million as redeeming the equity component. This gives rise to the accounting entry:

	€m	€m
Liability component of bond	96.2	
Equity	61.9	
Debt settlement expense (income statement)	11.9	
Cash		170.0

The debt settlement expense represents the difference between the carrying value of the debt component (€96.2m) and its fair value (€108.1m).

Any costs of the repurchase would have been allocated between the income statement and equity in proportion to the fair value of the liability and equity components at the time of redemption.

4.4.4 Modification

An entity may amend the terms of a convertible instrument to induce early conversion, for example by offering a more favourable conversion ratio or paying other additional consideration in the event of conversion before a specified date. The difference, at the date the terms are amended, between:

- the fair value of the consideration the holder receives on conversion of the instrument under the revised terms and,

- the fair value of the consideration the holder would have received under the original terms

is recognised as a loss in profit or loss.[98] IAS 32 illustrates this treatment, as shown in Example 17.8 below.[99]

Example 17.8: Modification of terms of bond to induce early conversion

Suppose that the entity in Example 17.7 above wished, on 1 January 2001, to induce the bondholder to convert the bond early. The original terms of the bond allowed for conversion into 4 million shares. The entity offers the bondholder the right to convert into 5 million shares during the period 1 January-28 February 2001. The market value of the entity's shares is €40 per share.

The enhanced conversion terms offer the bondholder the right to receive an additional 1 million shares. Accordingly, the entity recognises a cost of €40m (1m shares × share price €40/share).

We are far from convinced by the approach taken in Example 17.8. It appears to be based on the premise that the only additional benefit being given is the right to

1 million additional shares. However, in our view, this misses the point that there is a significant difference between the right to call for 4 million shares in nine years' time embedded in the original bond and the right to call for those shares within the next two months embedded in the proposed early conversion terms.

In our view, an approach more consistent with that in Example 17.7 above would have been to say that the entity is proposing to purchase, in exchange for 5 million shares the holder's right to receive:

(a) interest for the next nine years and, and

(b) in nine years' time, either:

(i) a repayment of principal; or

(ii) the right to convert the principal into 4 million shares.

The entity would then (as in Example 17.7 above) determine the fair value of the liability component by reference to current market rates and allocate the fair value of the consideration given of €200 million (i.e. 5 million shares at €40 per share) between the liability and equity component. The carrying value of the liability component at the end of 2001 would be €94.34 million.

	€m
Liability component at 1.1.00 (see above)	94.00
Finance charge (94 × 11%)	10.34
Interest paid – 2 6-monthly payments of €5m	(10.00)
Liability component at 1.1.01	94.34

Suppose that the current fair value of the liability component at 1 January 2001 was determined to be €105 million; the implication must be that €95 million of the total €200 million consideration must relate to the equity component. That would suggest the accounting entry:

	€m	€m
Liability component of bond	94.3	
Debt settlement expense (income statement) – note 1	10.7	
Equity – note 2		105.0

1   Fair value of consideration given for liability component (€105m) less carrying value of liability component (€94.3m).

2   Fair value of equity issued (€200m) less cost of settling existing conversion right (€95m).

However, this raises two questions not specifically addressed by IAS 32:

• the accounting treatment to be applied when a financial liability is settled with a new equity instrument (i.e. not pursuant to the original terms of the liability) – see 4.4.5 below), and

• the accounting treatment to be applied when an equity instrument is settled at an amount different from its fair value, as might well be occurring in Example 17.8 above (see 6.1 below).

4.4.5   Settlement of financial liability with new equity instrument

An issue not specifically covered in IAS 32, or IAS 39, is the accounting treatment to be adopted where an entity issues non-convertible debt, but subsequently enters into an agreement with the debt-holder to discharge the liability under the debt in full or in part for an issue of equity. This most often occurs when the entity is in financial difficulties, as shown in Example 17.9 below.

Example 17.9:   Discharge of liability for fresh issue of equity

During 2000 an entity issued £100 million bonds due to be repaid in 2010. By 2005 the entity is in some financial difficulty and reaches an agreement with the holders of the bonds whereby they will accept equity shares in the entity with a fair value of £60 million in full and final settlement of all amounts due under the bonds. How should this transaction be accounted for?

The basic rules in IAS 39 for derecognition of financial liabilities (see Chapter 16 at 5) provide that, where a liability is settled in exchange for a transfer of cash or other assets (or the assumption of a new or modified liability) with a value different to that of the liability being settled, a gain or loss should be recognised. This could support the argument that, although there is no specific guidance on the treatment of a liability settled for the issue of an equity instrument, the transaction above is equivalent to:

- the entity redeeming the original liability at £60 million (thereby giving rise to a gain of £40 million – see Chapter 16 at 5); and

- the former bond holders using that £60 million to subscribe for new shares in the entity at market value.

Another argument for recognition of a gain might be that IAS 39 requires a gain or loss to be recognised on any significant modification of the terms of a debt (see Chapter 16 at 5.2), and the conversion of previously repayable debt into equity is a significant modification.

However, a counter-argument might be that the rules in IAS 32 governing the conversion of convertible debt simply require the carrying value of the liability component at the time of conversion to be transferred into equity (see 4.4.2 above), irrespective of the fact that this may not be equivalent to the fair value of the debt at that time. On this analogy, the £100 million carrying amount of the debt should be transferred to equity.

In our view, absent further guidance from IFRIC or the IASB, either approach can be argued to be acceptable, provide that it is applied consistently. This lack of clarity arises from a more general problem – the absence in IFRS of any general accounting rules for the recording of an issue of equity instruments. The IASB would no doubt respond that to have such rules would be inconsistent with the general principle of IFRS that equity is a residual and should therefore be measured by reference to the movements in assets and liabilities that give rise to it rather than 'in its own right'.

4.5   Issuer cash settlement options

As discussed as 3.5 above, IAS 32 requires a derivative with two or more settlement options to be treated as a financial asset or a financial liability unless all possible settlement alternatives would result in it being an equity instrument. Many convertible bonds currently in issue contain a provision whereby, if the holder exercises its conversion option, the issuer may instead pay cash equal to the fair value of the shares that it would otherwise have been required to deliver. This is to allow for unforeseen circumstances, such as an inability to issue the necessary number of shares to effect conversion at the appropriate time.

Where a bond has such a term, the conversion right is a derivative (in effect, a written call option over the issuer's own shares) which may potentially be settled in cash, such that there is a settlement alternative that does not result in it being an equity instrument. This means that the 'equity component' of a bond with an issuer cash settlement option is not in fact an equity instrument, but a financial liability. The financial reporting implication of this is that the conversion right must be accounted for as a derivative at fair value, with changes in value included in profit or loss – in other words the financial statements will reflect gains and losses based on the movement of the reporting entity's own share price.

Entities may be well advised to review the terms of any outstanding bonds for such issuer cash-settlement options and consider removing them. In many jurisdictions this may be done unilaterally, since the removal of the right does not prejudice the holder's rights in any way.

5 INTEREST, DIVIDENDS, GAINS AND LOSSES

The basic principle of IAS 32 is that inflows and outflows of cash (and other assets) associated with equity instruments are recognised in equity and the net impact of inflows and outflows of cash (and other assets) associated with financial liabilities is ultimately recognised in the income statement. Accordingly IAS 32 requires:

- interest, dividends, losses and gains relating to a financial instrument or a component that is a financial liability to be recognised as income or expense in profit or loss;

- distributions to holders of an equity instrument (net of any related income tax benefit) to be debited directly to equity;

- the transaction costs of an equity transaction (net of any related income tax benefit) to be accounted for as a deduction from equity, other than the costs of issuing an equity instrument that are directly attributable to the acquisition of a business (which are accounted for under IFRS 3 – see Chapter 6 at 2.3.2 D).[100]

The treatment of the costs and gains associated with instruments is determined by their classification in the financial statements under IAS 32, and not by their legal form. Thus dividends paid on shares classified as financial liabilities (see 3.2.1 above) will be recognised as an expense in profit or loss, not as an appropriation of equity. Gains and losses associated with redemptions or refinancings of financial liabilities are recognised in profit or loss, whereas redemptions or refinancings of equity instruments are recognised as changes in equity.[101]

Similarly, gains and losses related to changes in the carrying amount of a financial liability are recognised as income or expense in profit or loss, even when they relate to an instrument that includes a right to the residual interest in the assets of the entity in exchange for cash or another financial asset (see 3.2.2 above). However, IAS 32 notes that IAS 1 requires any gain or loss arising from the remeasurement of such an instrument to be shown separately on the face of the income statement where it is relevant in explaining the entity's performance.[102]

Changes in the fair value of an equity instrument are not recognised in the financial statements.[103]

IAS 32 permits dividends classified as an expense to be presented in the income statement either with interest on other liabilities or as a separate item. The standard notes that, in some circumstances, separate disclosure is desirable, because of the differences between interest and dividends with respect to matters such as tax deductibility. Disclosure of interest and dividends is required by IAS 1 (see Chapter 3 at 3.2.1), IAS 32 (see Chapter 20 at 6.1.1 and 6.1.2), and IAS 30 – *Disclosures in the Financial Statements of Banks and Similar Financial Institutions* (not covered in detail in this book). Disclosures of the tax effects are made in accordance with IAS 12 – *Income Taxes* (see Chapter 24 at 8).[104]

5.1   Transaction costs of equity transactions

An entity typically incurs various costs in issuing or acquiring its own equity instruments, such as registration and other regulatory fees, amounts paid to legal, accounting and other professional advisers, printing costs and stamp duties. The transaction costs of an equity transaction are accounted for as a deduction from equity (net of any related income tax benefit), but only to the extent they are incremental costs directly attributable to the equity transaction that otherwise would have been avoided. The costs of an equity transaction that is abandoned are recognised as an expense.[105]

Transaction costs that relate to the issue of a compound financial instrument are allocated to the liability and equity components of the instrument in proportion to the allocation of proceeds (see Example 17.5 at 4.3 above). Transaction costs that relate jointly to more than one transaction (for example, costs of a concurrent offering of some shares and a stock exchange listing of other shares) are allocated to those transactions using a basis of allocation that is rational and consistent with similar transactions.[106]

The amount of transaction costs accounted for as a deduction from equity in the period is required to be disclosed separately under IAS 1 (see Chapter 3 at 3.3 and Chapter 20 at 6.2). Any related tax relief recognised directly in equity is included in the aggregate amount of current and deferred income tax credited or charged to equity disclosed under IAS 12 (see Chapter 24 at 8).[107]

6   TREASURY SHARES

Treasury shares are shares issued by an entity that are held by the entity itself, or by a subsidiary of the entity, or by another entity controlled by the entity[108] (see 6.1 below).

Holdings of treasury shares may arise in a number of ways. For example:

- The entity holds the shares as the result of a direct transaction, such as a market purchase, or a buy-back of shares from shareholders as a whole, or a particular group of shareholders.

- The entity is in the financial services sector with a market-making operation that buys and sells its own shares along with those of other listed entities in the normal course of business, or holds them in order to 'hedge' issued derivatives.

- In consolidated financial statements:

    - the shares were purchased by another entity which subsequently became a subsidiary of the reporting entity, either through acquisition or changes in financial reporting requirements;

    - the shares have been purchased by an entity that is a consolidated SPE of the reporting entity.

The circumstances in which an entity is permitted to hold treasury shares are a matter for legislation in the jurisdiction concerned.

Treasury shares do not include own shares held by an entity on behalf of others, such as when a financial institution holds its own equity on behalf of a client. In such cases, there is an agency relationship and as a result those holdings are not included in the entity's balance sheet, either as assets or as a deduction from equity.[109]

If an entity reacquires its own equity instruments, IAS 32 requires those instruments to be deducted from equity. They are not recognised as financial assets, regardless of the reason for which they are reacquired. No gain or loss is recognised in profit or loss on the purchase, sale, issue or cancellation of an entity's own equity instruments. Accordingly, any consideration paid or received in connection with treasury share must be recognised directly in equity.[110]

IAS 1 requires the amount of treasury shares to be disclosed separately either on the face of the balance sheet or in the notes (see Chapter 3 at 3.1.6 and Chapter 20 at 6.3.2). In addition IAS 24 – *Related Party Disclosures* – requires an entity to make disclosures where it reacquires its own equity instruments from related parties (see Chapter 33 at 2.5.5 and Chapter 20 at 6.2).[111]

As in the case of the requirements for the treatment of the equity component of a compound financial instrument (see 4 above), IAS 32 does not prescribe precisely what components of equity should be adjusted as the result of a treasury share transaction. This may have been to ensure that there was no conflict between, on the one hand, the basic requirement of IAS 32 that there should be an adjustment to equity and, on the other hand, the legal requirements of various jurisdictions as to exactly how that adjustment should be allocated within shareholders' funds.

As literally drafted, IAS 32 appears to require not only that the cost of purchasing treasury shares be charged to equity, but also that the treasury shares themselves be deducted from equity. However, this would yield a 'three-legged' accounting entry which cannot have been the IASB's intention. It is clear from the illustrative examples in the Appendix to IAS 32 (see 7 below) that the true intention of the standard is simply that the cost of purchasing treasury shares should be charged, and the proceeds of reissuing them credited, directly to equity.

6.1   Entities 'controlled' by the entity

IAS 32 does not include specific guidance on what constitutes an entity controlled by the reporting entity (such that any shares in the reporting entity by that other entity are treated as treasury shares).

In practical terms, a controlled entity will include any entity consolidated as a subsidiary or special purpose entity under IAS 27 and SIC–12 – *Consolidation – Special Purpose Entities*. It will not therefore generally include shares held by:

- any associates,
- the entity's pension fund, or
- currently, employee benefit trusts. However, this will change if the proposed amendments to SIC–12 are made (see Chapter 5 at 3.2.1 A).

However, IAS 1 requires disclosure of own shares held by associates,[112] and IAS 19 – *Employee Benefits* – requires disclosure of own shares held by defined benefit plans.[113]

6.2   Comparison with IFRS 2 – *Share-based payment*

The apparently unequivocal of requirement of IAS 32 that no profits or losses should ever be recognised on transactions in own equity instruments is inconsistent with IFRS 2. If an employee share award is characterised as an equity instrument under IFRS 2 (a 'share-settled' award) and settled in cash (or other assets) at more than its fair value, the excess of the consideration over the fair value is recognised as an expense (see Chapter 29 at 4.10, 5.3.2 and 7.2.2).

It is not clear whether or not the IASB specifically considered transactions in own equity other than at fair value in the context of IAS 32, particularly since the relevant provisions of IAS 32 essentially reproduce requirements previously contained in SIC–16 – *Share Capital – Reacquired Own Equity Instruments (Treasury Shares)*, which was implicitly addressing market purchases and sales at fair value. In other words, the provision can be seen merely as clarifying that, if an entity buys one of its own shares in the market for £10 which it later reissues in the market at £12 or £7, it has not made, respectively, a profit of £2 or a loss of £3. This is slightly different to the situation where an entity purchases an equity instrument for more than its fair value – i.e. if the original purchase had been for £11 when the market price was £10.

Such a transaction could occur, for example:

- where the entity wishes to rid itself of a troublesome shareholder or group of shareholders, or

- where the entity has issued an equity instrument with a high fixed annual coupon which it no longer wishes to pay to a holder that would rather have a low-cost, high-yield asset than an asset giving a current market yield.

In either case, the entity might have to offer a premium specific to the holder over and above the 'true' fair value of the equity instruments concerned.

There could be an argument that such a transaction does not fall within the type of transaction envisaged by the rules for treasury shares, such that the holder-specific premium should be accounted for in profit or loss, not equity. However, if this position is accepted, it would suggest that if an entity were to pay a dividend in excess of the dividend yield implicit in the fair value of its shares, that excess should also be recognised in profit or loss – a highly controversial proposition, to put it mildly.

In our view, this is an area which the IASB may wish to consider further, but without rushing to judgement.

7   CONTRACTS OVER OWN EQUITY INSTRUMENTS

A significant change made to IAS 32 as a result of its revision in December 2003 was the addition of a number of detailed examples of the accounting treatment required, under the provisions of revised IAS 32 and IAS 39, to be adopted by an entity for contracts in its own equity instruments. Examples are given of each of the main possible permutations, namely:

- a forward purchase (see 7.1.1 below);
- a forward sale (see 7.1.2 below);
- a purchased call option (see 7.2.1 below);
- a written call option (see 7.2.2 below);
- a purchased put option (see 7.3.1 below); and
- a written put option (see 7.3.2 below).

All such contracts can be either:

(a)   net cash-settled (i.e. the contract provides that the parties will compare the fair value of the shares to be delivered by the seller to the amount of cash payable by the buyer and make a cash payment between themselves for the difference);

(b)   net share-settled (i.e. the contract provides that the parties will compare the fair value of the shares to be delivered by the seller to the amount of cash payable by the buyer and make a transfer between themselves of as many of the entity's shares as have a fair value equal to the difference);

(c)   gross settled (i.e. the contract provides that the seller will deliver shares to the buyer in exchange for cash); or

(d)   subject to various settlement options, whereby the manner of settlement is not predetermined, and instead one or other party can choose the manner of settlement (i.e. gross, net cash or net shares).

Each example considers the options above in turn.

7.1   Forward contracts

7.1.1   Forward purchase

In a forward purchase transaction, the entity and a counterparty agree that on a given future date the counterparty will sell a given number of the entity's shares to the entity. Such a contract is illustrated in Example 17.10 below.[114]

Example 17.10:   Forward purchase of shares

The reporting entity (A), which has a year end of 31 December, and another party (B) enter into a forward contract for the purchase of A's shares by A, for which the following are the major assumptions.

Contract date	1 February 2005
Maturity date	31 January 2006
Market price per share on 1 February 2005	€100
Market price per share on 31 December 2005	€110
Market price per share on 31 January 2006	€106
Fixed forward price to be paid on 31 January 2006	€104
Present value of forward price on 1 February 2005	€100
Number of shares under contract	1,000
Fair value of forward to A on 1 February 2005	€0
Fair value of forward to A on 31 December 2005	€6,300
Fair value of forward to A on 31 January 2006	€2,000

For simplicity, it is assumed that no dividends are paid on the underlying shares (i.e. the 'carry return' is zero) so that the present value of the forward price equals the spot price when the fair value of the forward contract is zero. The fair value of the forward has been computed as the difference between the market share price and the present value of the fixed forward price. At settlement date this is €2,000 representing 1000 shares at €2, being the difference between the market price of €106 and the contract price of €104

A   Net cash settlement

If the contract is entered into as cash-settled, on 1 February 2005, A enters into a contract with B to pay, or receive as the case may be, on 31 January 2006 a cash payment for the difference between the fair value, at 31 January 2006, of 1,000 of A's own shares and €104,000 (i.e. 1000 shares at the forward price of €104 per share). IAS 32 classifies this derivative contract as a financial asset or liability (see 3.3.2 D and 3.5 above), which IAS 39 requires to be accounted for at fair value (see Chapter 18 at 3.1, 3.2 and 4). A records the following accounting entries.

	€	€

1 February 2005

*No entry is required because the fair value of the contract
is zero at inception and no cash is paid or received*

31 December 2005

	€	€
Forward contract (balance sheet)	6,300	
Gain on forward (income statement)		6,300

To record increase in fair value of forward

31 January 2006

	€	€
Loss on forward (income statement)	4,300	
Forward contract (balance sheet)		4,300

To record decrease in fair value of forward

	€	€
Cash	2,000	
Forward contract (balance sheet)		2,000

To record settlement of forward

B   *Net share settlement*

If the contract is entered into as net share-settled, on 1 February 2005, A enters into a contract with B to pay, or receive as the case may be, on 31 January 2006 a payment of as many of A's shares as have a fair value equal to the difference between the fair value, at 31 January 2006, of 1,000 of A's own shares and €104,000 (i.e. 1000 shares at the forward price of €104 per share). IAS 32 classifies this derivative contract as a financial asset or liability (see 3.3.2 D and 3.5 above), which IAS 39 requires to be accounted for at fair value (see Chapter 18 at 3.1, 3.2 and 4). A records the following accounting entries.

	€	€

1 February 2005

*No entry is required because the fair value of the contract
is zero at inception and no cash is paid or received*

31 December 2005

	€	€
Forward contract (balance sheet)	6,300	
Gain on forward (income statement)		6,300

To record increase in fair value of forward

31 January 2006

	€	€
Loss on forward (income statement)	4,300	
Forward contract (balance sheet)		4,300

To record decrease in fair value of forward

	€	€
Equity	2,000	
Forward contract (balance sheet)		2,000

*To record net settlement of forward by transfer of €2,000
worth of A's shares by B to A. This is shown as a deduction
from equity in accordance with IAS 32's requirements for
treasury shares (see 6 above).*

C   Gross settlement

If the contract is entered into as gross-settled, on 1 February 2005, A enters into a contract with B to pay B, on 31 January 2006, €104,000 in exchange for 1,000 of A's own shares. IAS 32 classifies this derivative contract as an equity instrument giving rise to a financial liability for the purchase price (see 3.3.3 above). On the assumption that A accounts for this liability under the effective interest method in IAS 39 (see Chapter 18 at 3.1, 3.2 and 5), A records the following accounting entries.

	€	€
1 February 2005		
Equity	100,000	
Forward contract (balance sheet)		100,000
To record net present value of liability on forward contract		
31 December 2005		
Interest expense	3,660	
Forward contract (balance sheet)		3,660
To record accrual of interest on liability to settle forward contract		
31 January 2006		
Interest expense	340	
Forward contract (balance sheet)		340
To record further accrual of interest on liability		
Forward contract (balance sheet)	104,000	
Cash		104,000
To record settlement of liability		

D   Settlement options

If there are settlement options (such as net in cash, net in shares or by an exchange of cash and shares), the forward contract is a financial asset or a financial liability – see 3.3.4 and 3.5 above. If one of the settlement alternatives is to exchange cash for shares, A recognises a liability for the obligation to deliver cash.

7.1.2   Forward sale

In a forward sale transaction, the entity and a counterparty agree that on a given future date the entity will sell (or issue) a given number of the entity's shares to the counterparty. Such a contract is illustrated in Example 17.11 below.[115]

Example 17.11:   Forward sale of shares

The reporting entity (A), which has a year end of 31 December, and another party (B) enter into a forward contract for the purchase of A's shares by B, for which the following are the major assumptions.

Contract date	1 February 2005
Maturity date	31 January 2006
Market price per share on 1 February 2005	€100
Market price per share on 31 December 2005	€110
Market price per share on 31 January 2006	€106

Fixed forward price to be paid on 31 January 2006	€104
Present value of forward price on 1 February 2005	€100
Number of shares under contract	1,000
Fair value of forward to A on 1 February 2005	€0
Fair value of forward to A on 31 December 2005	€(6,300)
Fair value of forward to A on 31 January 2006	€(2,000)

For simplicity, it is assumed that no dividends are paid on the underlying shares (i.e. the 'carry return' is zero) so that the present value of the forward price equals the spot price when the fair value of the forward contract is zero. The fair value of the forward has been computed as the difference between the market share price and the present value of the fixed forward price. At settlement date this is negative €2,000 representing 1000 shares at €2, being the difference between the market price of €106 and the contract price of €104.

A   *Net cash settlement*

If the contract is entered into as cash-settled, on 1 February 2005, A enters into a contract with B to pay, or receive as the case may be, on 31 January 2006 a cash payment for the difference between the fair value, at 31 January 2006, of 1,000 of A's own shares and €104,000 (i.e. 1000 shares at the forward price of €104 per share). IAS 32 classifies this derivative contract as a financial asset or liability (see 3.3.2 D and 3.5 above), which IAS 39 requires to be accounted for at fair value (see Chapter 18 at 3.1, 3.2 and 4). A records the following accounting entries.

	€	€
1 February 2005		
No entry is required because the fair value of the contract is zero at inception and no cash is paid or received.		
31 December 2005		
Loss on forward (income statement)	6,300	
Forward contract (balance sheet)		6,300
To record decrease in fair value of forward		
31 January 2006		
Forward contract (balance sheet)	4,300	
Gain on forward (income statement)		4,300
To record increase in fair value of forward		
Forward contract (balance sheet)	2,000	
Cash		2,000
To record net settlement of forward by payment of €2,000 cash by A to B		

B   Net share settlement

If the contract is entered into as net share-settled, on 1 February 2005, A enters into a contract with B to pay, or receive as the case may be, on 31 January 2006 a payment of as many of A's shares as are equal to the difference between the fair value, at 31 January 2006, of 1,000 of A's own shares and €104,000 (i.e. 1000 shares at the forward price of €104 per share). IAS 32 classifies this derivative contract as a financial asset or liability (see 3.3.2 D and 3.5 above), which IAS 39 requires to be accounted for at fair value (see Chapter 18 at 3.1, 3.2 and 4). A records the following accounting entries.

	€	€
1 February 2005		
No entry is required because the fair value of the contract is zero at inception		
31 December 2005		
Loss on forward (income statement)	6,300	
Forward contract (balance sheet)		6,300
To record decrease in fair value of forward		
31 January 2006		
Forward contract (balance sheet)	4,300	
Gain on forward (income statement)		4,300
To record increase in fair value of forward		
Forward contract (balance sheet)	2,000	
Equity		2,000
To record net settlement of forward by issue of €2,000 worth of A's shares to B		

C   Gross settlement

If the contract is entered into as gross-settled, on 1 February 2005, A enters into a contract with B whereby B will pay A, on 31 January 2006, €104,000 in exchange for 1,000 A's own shares. IAS 32 classifies this contract as an equity instrument (see 3.3.4 above); therefore no entries are recorded, other than on settlement of the contract:

	€	€
31 January 2006		
Cash	104,000	
Equity		104,000
To record settlement of forward contract		

D   Settlement options

If there are settlement options (such as net in cash, net in shares or by an exchange of cash and shares), the forward contract is a financial asset or a financial liability – see 3.3.4 and 3.5 above. A accounts for the forward contract as a derivative (as in A and B above), with the accounting entry made on settlement determined by the manner of settlement (i.e. equity or cash).

7.1.3 'Back-to-back' forward contracts

The accounting treatment in 7.1.1 and 7.1.2 produces rather strange results when applied to 'back-to-back' forward contracts, such as might be entered into by a financial institution with two different clients. Example 17.12 below illustrates the point.

Example 17.12: 'Back-to-back' forward contracts

Suppose that a bank entered into the forward purchase contract in Example 17.10 above with a client and laid off its risk by entering into the reciprocal forward sale contract in Example 17.11 above with a second client. If both contracts are required to be settled gross, the overall effect of the accounting entries required to be made by the bank (assuming that the bank was the reporting entity in Examples 17.10 and 17.11) can be summarised as set out below. Note that these are not the actual entries that would be made, but the arithmetical sum of all the entries:

	€	€
Income statement (interest expense on liability for purchase contract)	4,000	
Equity (€104,000 on sale less €100,000 on purchase)		4,000

If the purchase contract is required to be settled gross, but the sale contract net in cash, the required accounting entries (again, not the actual entries, but the arithmetical sum of all the entries) can be summarised as:

	€	€
Income statement (loss on sale contract €2,000 plus interest on liability for purchase contract €4,000)	6,000	
Equity (purchase contract)	100,000	
Cash (€104,000 on purchase, €2,000 on sale)		106,000

If the purchase contract is required to be settled net in cash, but the sale contract gross, the required accounting entries (again, not the actual entries, but the arithmetical sum of all the entries) can be summarised as:

	€	€
Cash (€104,000 in on sale, €2,000 in on purchase)	106,000	
Income statement (gain on purchase contract)		2,000
Equity (sale contract)		104,000

If both contracts are net settled, no net gain or loss arises.

Some might argue that this exposes a flaw in the requirements of IAS 32. Self-evidently, these contracts are matched and should therefore, if both run to term, give rise to no economic profit or loss, irrespective of how they are settled. However, IAS 32 requires three different results to be shown depending on whether both contracts are settled gross, or one gross and the other net. This is less understandable in the case where both contracts are settled gross. However, in cases where one contract is settled net and that contract gives rise to an initial receipt or payment of cash, then some difference is bound to occur due to interest effects.

7.2   Call options

7.2.1   *Purchased call option*

In a purchased call option, the entity pays a counterparty for the right, but not the obligation, to purchase a given number of its own equity instruments from the counterparty for a fixed price at a future date. The accounting for such a contract is illustrated in Example 17.13 below.[116]

Example 17.13:   Purchased call option on shares

The reporting entity (A), which has a year end of 31 December, purchases a call option over its own shares from another party (B), for which the following are the major assumptions.

Contract date	1 February 2005
Exercise date (European terms – i.e. can be exercised only on maturity)	31 January 2006
Market price per share on 1 February 2005	€100
Market price per share on 31 December 2005	€104
Market price per share on 31 January 2006	€104
Fixed exercise price to be paid on 31 January 2006	€102
Number of shares under contract	1,000
Fair value of option to A on 1 February 2005	€5,000
Fair value of option to A on 31 December 2005	€3,000
Fair value of option to A on 31 January 2006	€2,000

The fair value of the option would be computed using an option pricing model and would be a function of a number of factors, principally the market value of the shares, the exercise price, and the time value of money.

A   *Net cash settlement*

If the contract is entered into as cash-settled, on 1 February 2005 A enters into a contract with B whereby A can require B, on 31 January 2006, to make a cash payment to A of any excess of the fair value, at 31 January 2006, of 1,000 of A's own shares over €102,000 (i.e. 1000 shares at the option price of €102 per share). IAS 32 classifies this derivative contract as a financial asset or liability (see 3.3.2 D and 3.5 above), which IAS 39 requires to be accounted for at fair value (see Chapter 18 at 3.1, 3.2 and 5). A records the following accounting entries.

	€	€
1 February 2005		
Call option asset	5,000	
Cash		5,000
Payment of option premium (equal to fair value of option) to B		
31 December 2005		
Loss on option (income statement)	2,000	
Call option asset		2,000
To record decrease in fair value of option		

31 January 2006

	€	€
Loss on option (income statement)	1,000	
Call option asset		1,000

To record decrease in fair value of option

Cash	2,000	
Call option asset		2,000

To record net settlement of option by payment of €2,000 cash by B to A

B Net share settlement

If the contract is entered into as net share-settled, on 1 February 2005, A enters into a contract with B, whereby A can require B, on 31 January 2006, to deliver to A as many of A's own shares as have a fair value equal to any excess of the fair value, at 31 January 2006, of 1,000 of A's own shares over €102,000 (i.e. 1000 shares at the option price of €102 per share). IAS 32 classifies this derivative contract as a financial asset or liability (see 3.3.2 D and 3.5 above), which IAS 39 requires to be accounted for at fair value (see Chapter 18 at 3.1, 3.2 and 4). A records the following accounting entries.

	€	€

1 February 2005

	€	€
Call option asset	5,000	
Cash		5,000

Payment of option premium (equal to fair value of option) to B

31 December 2005

Loss on option (income statement)	2,000	
Call option asset		2,000

To record decrease in fair value of option

31 January 2006

Loss on option (income statement)	1,000	
Call option asset		1,000

To record decrease in fair value of option

Equity	2,000	
Call option asset		2,000

To record net settlement of option by transfer of €2,000 worth of A's shares by B to A. This is shown as a deduction from equity in accordance with IAS 32's requirements for treasury shares (see 6 above).

C Gross settlement

If the contract is entered into as gross-settled, on 1 February 2005, A enters into a contract with B whereby A can require B, on 31 January 2006, to deliver 1,000 of A's shares in return for a payment by A of €102,000. IAS 32 classifies this derivative contract as an equity instrument (see 3.3.3 above); therefore no entries are recorded, other than to record the cash flows arising under the contract:

	€	€
1 February 2005		
Equity	5,000	
Cash		5,000

Payment of option premium (equal to fair value of option) to B

	€	€
31 January 2006		
Equity	102,000	
Cash		102,000

To record gross settlement of option by payment of €102,000 cash to B in exchange for 1,000 own shares.

If the option had lapsed unexercised, because the market price of A's shares had fallen below €102 as at 31 January 2006, the £5,000 premium would remain in equity, even though it is, from an economic perspective, clearly a loss rather than an amount paid to repurchase A's own shares. This is because IFRS regards any holder of an instrument classified as equity under IAS 32 as an 'owner'.

It should be noted that, in contrast to the treatment of a gross-settled forward purchase (see 7.1.1 above) and a gross-settled written put option (see 7.3.2 below), which also require a gross outflow of cash on settlement, there is no requirement to record a liability at the outset of the contract on which interest is accrued during the period of the contract. This is because:

- in a gross-settled forward purchase or written put option, the entity can be required to make a payment of cash, but
- in a purchased call option, there is no liability, since the entity has no obligation to exercise its right to call for the shares even if the option is 'in the money' and it is in the entity's interest to do so.

D Settlement options

If there are settlement options (such as net in cash, net in shares or by an exchange of cash and shares), the option is a financial asset. A accounts for the forward contract as a derivative (as in A and B above), with the accounting entry made on settlement determined by the manner of settlement (i.e. equity or cash).

7.2.2 Written call option

In a written call option, the entity receives a payment from a counterparty for granting to the counterparty the right, but not the obligation, to purchase a given number of the entity's own equity instruments from the entity for a fixed price at a future date. The accounting for such a contract is illustrated in Example 17.14 below.[117]

Example 17.14: Written call option on shares

The reporting entity (A), which has a year end of 31 December, writes a call option over its own shares with another party (B), for which the following are the major assumptions.

Contract date	1 February 2005
Exercise date (European terms – i.e. can be exercised only on maturity)	31 January 2006
Market price per share on 1 February 2005	€100
Market price per share on 31 December 2005	€104
Market price per share on 31 January 2006	€104
Fixed exercise price to be paid on 31 January 2006	€102
Number of shares under contract	1,000
Fair value of option to A on 1 February 2005	€(5,000)
Fair value of option to A on 31 December 2005	€(3,000)
Fair value of option to A on 31 January 2006	€(2,000)

The fair value of the option would be computed using an option pricing model and would be a function of a number of factors, principally the market value of the shares, the exercise price, and the time value of money.

A   *Net cash settlement*

If the contract is entered into as cash-settled, on 1 February 2005, A enters into a contract with B whereby B can require A, on 31 January 2006, to make a cash payment to B of any excess of the fair value, at 31 January 2006, of 1,000 of A's own shares over €102,000 (i.e. 1000 shares at the option price of €102 per share). IAS 32 classifies this derivative contract as a financial liability (see 3.3.2 D and 3.5 above), which IAS 39 requires to be accounted for at fair value (see Chapter 18 at 3.1, 3.2 and 4). A records the following accounting entries:

	€	€
1 February 2005		
Cash	5,000	
Call option liability		5,000
Receipt of option premium (equal to fair value of option) from B		
31 December 2005		
Call option liability	2,000	
Gain on option (income statement)		2,000
To record decrease in fair value of option		
31 January 2006		
Call option liability	1,000	
Gain on option (income statement)		1,000
To record decrease in fair value of option		
Call option liability	2,000	
Cash		2,000
To record net settlement of option by payment of €2,000 cash to B		

B   Net share settlement

If the contract is entered into as net share-settled, on 1 February 2005, A enters into a contract with B, whereby B can require A, on 31 January 2006, to deliver to B as many of A's own shares as have a fair value equal to any excess of the fair value, at 31 January 2006, of 1,000 of A's own shares over €102,000 (i.e. 1000 shares at the option price of €102 per share). IAS 32 classifies this derivative contract as a financial liability (see 3.3.2 D and 3.5 above), which IAS 39 requires to be accounted for at fair value (see Chapter 18 at 3.1, 3.2 and 4). A records the following accounting entries.

	€	€
1 February 2005		
Cash	5,000	
Call option liability		5,000
Receipt of option premium (equal to fair value of option) from B		
31 December 2005		
Call option liability	2,000	
Gain on option (income statement)		2,000
To record decrease in fair value of option		
31 January 2006	1,000	
Call option liability		1,000
Gain on option (income statement)		
To record decrease in fair value of option		
Call option liability	2,000	
Equity		2,000
To record net settlement of option by issue of €2,000 worth of A's shares to B		

C   Gross settlement

If the contract is entered into as gross-settled, on 1 February 2005, A enters into a contract with B whereby B can require A, on 31 January 2006, to deliver 1,000 of A's shares in return for a payment by B of €102,000. IAS 32 classifies this derivative contract as an equity instrument (see 3.3.3 above); therefore no entries are recorded, other than to record the cash flows arising under the contract:

	€	€
1 February 2005		
Cash	5,000	
Equity		5,000
Receipt of option premium (equal to fair value of option) to B		
31 January 2006		
Cash	102,000	
Equity		102,000
To record gross settlement of option by receipt of €102,000 cash to B in exchange for 1,000 own shares.		

If the option had lapsed unexercised, because the market price of A's shares had fallen below €102 as at 31 January 2006, the £5,000 premium would remain in equity, even though it is, from an economic perspective, clearly a gain rather than an amount received from an owner. This is because IFRS regards any holder of an instrument classified as equity under IAS 32 as an 'owner'.

D   Settlement options

If there are settlement options (such as net in cash, net in shares or by an exchange of cash and shares), the option is a financial liability. A accounts for the forward contract as a derivative (as in A and B above), with the accounting entry made on settlement determined by the manner of settlement (i.e. equity or cash).

7.3   Put options

7.3.1   Purchased put option

In a purchased put option, the entity makes a payment to a counterparty for the right, but not the obligation, to require the counterparty to purchase a given number of the entity's own equity instruments from the entity for a fixed price at a future date. The accounting for such a contract is illustrated in Example 17.15 below.[118]

Example 17.15:   Purchased put option on shares

The reporting entity (A), which has a year end of 31 December, purchases a put option over its own shares from another party (B), for which the following are the major assumptions.

Contract date	1 February 2005
Exercise date (European terms – i.e. can be exercised only on maturity)	31 January 2006
Market price per share on 1 February 2005	€100
Market price per share on 31 December 2005	€95
Market price per share on 31 January 2006	€95
Fixed exercise price to be paid on 31 January 2006	€98
Number of shares under contract	1,000
Fair value of option to A on 1 February 2005	€5,000
Fair value of option to A on 31 December 2005	€4,000
Fair value of option to A on 31 January 2006	€3,000

The fair value of the option would be computed using an option pricing model and would be a function of number of factors, principally the market value of the shares, the exercise price, and the time value of money.

A   Net cash settlement

If the contract is entered into as cash-settled, on 1 February 2005, A enters into a contract with B whereby A can require B, on 31 January 2006, to make a cash payment to A of any excess, at 31 January 2006, of €98,000 (i.e. 1000 shares at the option price of €98 per share) over the fair value of 1,000 of A's own shares. IAS 32 classifies this derivative contract as a financial asset or liability (see 3.3.2 D and 3.5 above), which IAS 39 requires to be accounted for at fair value (see Chapter 18 at 3.1, 3.2 and 4). A records the following accounting entries.

	€	€
1 February 2005		
Put option asset	5,000	
Cash		5,000
Payment of option premium (equal to fair value of option) to B		
31 December 2005		
Loss on option (income statement)	1,000	
Put option asset		1,000
To record decrease in fair value of option		
31 January 2006		
Loss on option (income statement)	1,000	
Put option asset		1,000
To record decrease in fair value of option		
Cash	3,000	
Put option asset		3,000
To record net settlement of option by receipt of €3,000 cash from B		

B   Net share settlement

If the contract is entered into as share-settled, on 1 February 2005, A enters into a contract with B, whereby A can require B, on 31 January 2006, to deliver to A as many of A's own shares as have a fair value equal to any excess of €98,000 (i.e. 1000 shares at the option price of €98 per share) over the fair value, at 31 January 2006, of 1,000 of A's own shares. IAS 32 classifies this derivative contract as a financial asset or liability (see 3.3.2 D and 3.5 above), which IAS 39 requires to be accounted for at fair value (see Chapter 18 at 3.1, 3.2 and 5). A records the following accounting entries.

	€	€
1 February 2005		
Put option asset	5,000	
Cash		5,000
Payment of option premium (equal to fair value of option) to B		
31 December 2005		
Loss on option (income statement)	1,000	
Put option asset		1,000
To record decrease in fair value of option		

31 January 2006

Loss on option (income statement)	1,000	
Put option asset		1,000

To record decrease in fair value of option

Equity	3,000	
Put option asset		3,000

To record net settlement of option by receipt of €3,000 worth of A's shares from B. This is shown as a deduction from equity in accordance with IAS 32's requirements for treasury shares (see 6 above).

C   Gross settlement

If the contract is entered into as gross-settled, on 1 February 2005, A enters into a contract with B whereby A can require B, on 31 January 2006, to take delivery 1,000 of A's shares in return for a payment by B of €98,000. IAS 32 classifies this derivative contract as an equity instrument (see 3.3.4 above); therefore no entries are recorded, other than to record the cash flows arising under the contract:

	€	€

1 February 2005

Equity	5,000	
Cash		5,000

Payment of option premium (equal to fair value of option) to B

31 January 2006

Cash	98,000	
Equity		98,000

To record gross settlement of option by delivery of 1,000 own shares to B in exchange for €98,000.

If the option had lapsed unexercised, because the market price of A's shares had risen above €98 as at 31 January 2006, the £5,000 premium would remain in equity, even though it is, from an economic perspective, clearly a loss rather than an amount paid to repurchase A's own shares.

D   Settlement options

If there are settlement options (such as net in cash, net in shares or by an exchange of cash and shares), the option is a financial asset. A accounts for the forward contract as a derivative (as in A and B above), with the accounting entry made on settlement determined by the manner of settlement (i.e. equity or cash).

7.3.2   Written put option

In a written put option, the entity receives a payment from a counterparty for granting to the counterparty the right, but not the obligation, to sell a given number of the entity's own equity instruments to the entity for a fixed price at a future date. The accounting for such a contract is illustrated in Example 17.16 below.[119]

Example 17.16:   Written put option on own shares

The reporting entity (A), which has a year end of 31 December, writes a put option over its own shares with another party (B), for which the following are the major assumptions.

Contract date	1 February 2005
Exercise date (European terms – i.e. can be exercised only on maturity)	31 January 2006
Market price per share on 1 February 2005	€100
Market price per share on 31 December 2005	€95
Market price per share on 31 January 2006	€95
Fixed exercise price to be paid on 31 January 2006	€98
Number of shares under contract	1,000
Fair value of option to A on 1 February 2005	€(5,000)
Fair value of option to A on 31 December 2005	€(4,000)
Fair value of option to A on 31 January 2006	€(3,000)

The fair value of the option would be computed using an option pricing model and would be a function of a number of factors, principally the market value of the shares, the exercise price, and the time value of money.

A   Net cash settlement

If the contract is entered into as cash-settled, on 1 February 2005, A enters into a contract with B whereby B can require A, on 31 January 2006, to make a cash payment to B of any excess of €98,000 (i.e. 1000 shares at the option price of €98 per share) over the fair value, at 31 January 2006, of 1,000 of A's own shares. IAS 32 classifies this derivative contract as a financial asset or liability (see 3.3.2 D and 3.5 above), which IAS 39 requires to be accounted for at fair value (see Chapter 18 at 3.1, 3.2 and 4). A records the following accounting entries.

	€	€
1 February 2005		
Cash	5,000	
Put option liability		5,000
Receipt of option premium (equal to fair value of option) from B		
31 December 2005		
Put option liability	1,000	
Gain on option (income statement)		1,000
To record increase in fair value of option		

31 January 2006

Put option liability	1,000	
Gain on option (income statement)		1,000

To record increase in fair value of option

Put option liability	3,000	
Cash		3,000

To record net settlement of option by payment of €3,000 cash to B

B   Net share settlement

If the contract is entered into as net share-settled, on 1 February 2005, A enters into a contract with B, whereby B can require A, on 31 January 2006, to deliver to B as many of A's own shares as have a fair value equal to any excess of €98,000 (i.e. 1000 shares at the option price of €98 per share) over the fair value, at 31 January 2006, of 1,000 of A's own shares. IAS 32 classifies this derivative contract as a financial asset or liability (see 3.3.2 D and 3.5. above), which IAS 39 requires to be accounted for at fair value (see Chapter 18 at 3.1, 3.2 and 5). A records the following accounting entries.

	€	€

1 February 2005

Cash	5,000	
Put option liability		5,000

Receipt of option premium (equal to fair value of option) from B

31 December 2005

Put option liability	1,000	
Gain on option (income statement)		1,000

To record increase in fair value of option

31 January 2006

Put option liability	1,000	
Gain on option (income statement)		1,000

To record increase in fair value of option

Put option liability	3,000	
Equity		3,000

To record net settlement of option by issue of €3,000 worth of own shares to B

C   Gross settlement

If the contract is entered into as gross-settled, on 1 February 2005, A enters into a contract with B whereby B can require A, on 31 January 2006, to take delivery of 1,000 of A's shares in return for a payment by A of €98,000. IAS 32 classifies this derivative contract as an equity instrument giving rise to a financial liability for the purchase price (see 3.3.3 and 3.5 above). On the assumption that A accounts for this liability under the effective interest method in IAS 39 (see Chapter 18 at 3.1, 3.2 and 5), A records the following accounting entries.

	€	€

1 February 2005

Cash	5,000	
Equity	90,000	
Liability (net present value of €98,000 potentially payable under option)		95,000

Receipt of option premium (equal to fair value of option) from B and recording of potential liability to settle option

31 December 2005

| Interest (income statement) | 2,750 | |
| Liability | | 2,750 |

To accrue interest on the liability

31 January 2006

| Interest expense (income statement) | 250 | |
| Liability | | 250 |

To accrue interest on the liability

| Liability | 98,000 | |
| Cash | | 98,000 |

To record gross settlement of option by delivery of 1,000 own shares to B in exchange for €98,000

If the option had lapsed unexercised, because the market price of A's shares had risen above €98 as at 31 January 2006, the economic consequence is clearly that A has made a profit of €5,000 – the premium that it received from B, for which it has ultimately had to give nothing in return. However the overall effect of the treatment that would be required by IAS 32 can be summarised as follows:

	€	€
Cash	5,000	
Income statement (interest on potential liability to pay cash)	3,000	
Equity (€98,000 carrying amount of liability transferred at date of lapse less €90,000 debited on 1.2.05)		8,000

To some, to record a loss on a transaction that makes a profit (on any natural meaning of the word) might seem a distortion of economic reality; to the IASB, it is merely an inexorable consequence of the *Framework*.

D   Settlement options

If there are settlement options (such as net in cash, net in shares or by an exchange of cash and shares), the option is a financial asset. A accounts for the forward contract as a derivative (as in A and B above), with the accounting entry made on settlement determined by the manner of settlement (i.e. equity or cash).

8   TRANSITIONAL AND FIRST-TIME ADOPTION PROVISIONS

As noted at 1.2 above, the new version of IAS 32 must be applied for accounting periods beginning on or after 1 January 2005. Entities are permitted to adopt it for earlier periods, but must disclose that they have done so. Moreover, an entity adopting the revised version of IAS 32 in an earlier period must also adopt the revised version of IAS 39 at the same time.[120] The standards must be applied with full retrospective effect,[121] subject to some provisions relating to first-time adopters (see 8.1 below).

8.1   First-time adopters

8.1.1   *Comparative information*

IFRS 1 exempts an entity that adopts IFRS for the first time before 1 January 2006 from complying with IAS 32 and IAS 39 in any comparative period presented in its first IFRS financial statements. An entity taking advantage of this exemption is required to:

(a)   apply its previous GAAP in the comparative information to financial instruments within the scope of IAS 32 and IAS 39;

(b)   disclose this fact, together with the basis used to prepare this information; and

(c)   disclose the nature of the main adjustments that would make the information comply with IAS 32 and IAS 39.

The entity need not quantify those adjustments. However, it must treat any adjustment between:

- the balance sheet at the comparative period's reporting date (i.e. the balance sheet that includes comparative information under previous GAAP), and

- the balance sheet at the start of the first IFRS reporting period (i.e. the first period that includes information that complies with IAS 32 and IAS 39 and IFRS 4)

as arising from a change in accounting policy and give the disclosures required by paragraph 28(a)-(e) and (f)(i) of IAS 8 – *Accounting Policies, Changes in Accounting Estimates and Errors*. Paragraph 28(f)(i) (i.e. the requirement to disclose the effect of a change of accounting policy on each line item in the financial statements) applies only to amounts presented in the balance sheet at the comparative period's reporting date.[122]

8.1.2   Other matters

IFRS 1 also contains two more general provisions in respect of the classification of financial instruments on first-time adoption of IFRS.

IFRS 1 requires the entity to apply the criteria in IAS 32 to classify financial instruments issued (or components of compound instruments issued) as either financial liabilities or equity instruments in accordance with the substance of the contractual arrangement when the instrument first satisfied the recognition criteria in IAS 32, without considering events after that date (other than changes to the terms of the instruments). IFRS 1 draws particular attention to the requirement of IAS 32 that, following initial recognition, the classification of the liability and equity components of a compound financial instrument is not revised (for example to reflect an increased or decreased probability of conversion) – see 4.3.1 above.[123]

In other words, if an entity has issued a compound financial instrument, for which IAS 32 requires 'split accounting' (see 4 above), and some or all of the liability component of which is outstanding at the date of transition to IFRS, the entity must determine the carrying amount of the liability and equity components at transition at the amounts at which they would have been carried if 'split accounting' had been adopted from the date of issue of the bond. The fair value of the liability component of the bond should therefore be determined by reference to the interest rate which would have been applicable to a non-convertible bond issued by the entity at the original issue date and not the (potentially significantly different) rate at the date of transition.[124]

IFRS 1 also contains the following transitional provision in respect of compound financial instruments, where none of the liability component is outstanding at the date of transition:

> 'IAS 32 *Financial Instruments: Disclosure and Presentation* requires an entity to split a compound financial instrument at inception into separate liability and equity components. If the liability component is no longer outstanding, retrospective application of IAS 32 involves separating two portions of equity. The first portion is in retained earnings and represents the cumulative interest accreted on the liability component. The other portion represents the original equity component. However, under this IFRS, a first-time adopter need not separate these two portions if the liability component is no longer outstanding at the date of transition to IFRSs.'[125]

This is slightly curious in that it refers to a 'requirement' in IAS 32 to credit the equity component arising on initial recognition of a compound instrument to a separate component of equity. We are unable to identify such a requirement – IAS 32 requires merely that the amount be credited to equity (see 4.3.1 above). Moreover, the concession granted by IFRS 1 implies a further requirement that the amount originally credited to the equity component must remain in that separate component permanently. However, this is arguably contradicted by the application guidance to IAS 32 which, on conversion of a convertible bond, allows a transfer within equity of the amount originally credited there in respect of the equity component (see 4.4.1 above). Thus, even if, on initial recognition of a compound instrument, the entity had been required to credit the equity component to a separate component of equity, on final conversion or settlement it could, on subsequent conversion of the instrument, notionally have transferred the separately recognised component of equity to another component of equity (e.g. retained earnings), so that no further adjustment would be required on transition to IFRS.

References

1 IAS 32, *Financial Instruments: Disclosure and Presentation*, IASB, December 2003 (amended March 2004), para. 96.
2 IAS 32, Application Guidance, para. before para. AG1.
3 IAS 32, Illustrative Examples, para. after main heading.
4 IAS 32, paras. IN5-IN15.
5 IAS 32, para. 1.
6 IAS 32, para. 2.
7 IAS 32, para. 11
8 IAS 32, para. 11
9 IAS 32, para. 11
10 IAS 32, para. 11
11 IAS 32, para. 12 and IAS 39, *Financial Instruments: Recognition and Measurement*, IASB, December 2003 (amended March 2004), para. 9.
12 IAS 32, para. 11
13 IAS 32, para. 13.
14 IAS 32, para. 14.
15 IAS 32, para. 15.
16 IAS 32, para. 16.
17 IAS 32, para. 16.
18 IAS 32, para. AG13.
19 IAS 32, paras. 22 and AG13.
20 IAS 32, para. 21.
21 IAS 32, para. 24.
22 IAS 32, para. AG13.
23 IAS 32, para. AG13.
24 IAS 32, para. AG14.
25 IAS 32, para. BC21.
26 IFRS 2, *Share-based Payment*, IASB, February 2004, para. BC109.
27 IFRS 2, para. BC110.
28 IAS 32, para. 17.
29 IAS 32, para. 17.
30 IAS 32, para. 18.
31 IAS 32, paras. 19 and AG25.
32 IAS 32, para. 19.
33 IAS 32, para. 20
34 IAS 32, para. 20.
35 IAS 32, para. AG23.
36 IAS 32, para. 20.
37 IAS 32, para. AG25.
38 IAS 32, paras. 18(a) and AG25.
39 IAS 32, para. AG37.
40 IAS 32, para. AG25.
41 IAS 32, para. AG26.
42 IAS 32, para. AG26.
43 IAS 32, para. 18(b).
44 IAS 32, para. 18(b).
45 IAS 32, paras. 18(b) and BC7-BC8.
46 *IASB Update*, IASB, July 2004.
47 Draft Interpretation D8, *Members' Shares in Co-operative Entities*, IFRIC, June 2004.
48 IFRIC D8, paras. 5-8.
49 IAS 32, para. AG6.
50 IAS 22, *Business Combinations*, IASC, September 1998, (superseded March 2004), para. 22.
51 IAS 22, para. 22.
52 IAS 32, paras. 22 and AG27(a).
53 IAS 32, paras. 21 and AG27(d).
54 IAS 32, para. 24.
55 IAS 32, para. AG27(d).
56 IAS 32, para. AG27(c).
57 IAS 32, paras. 23 and AG27(a)-(b).
58 IAS 32, paras. 23 and AG27(a)-(b).
59 IAS 32, paras. 23 and AG27(b).
60 IAS 39, para. 49.
61 IAS 32, para. AG27(c).
62 IAS 32, para. 25
63 IAS 32, para. 25
64 IAS 32, para. AG28.
65 IAS 32, para. AG28.
66 IAS 32, para. BC19.
67 SIC-5, *Classification of Financial Instruments – Contingent Settlement Provisions*, SIC, May 1998 (superseded December 2003).
68 SIC-5, para. 9.
69 IAS 32, paras. BC16-BC17.
70 IAS 32, para. 26.
71 IAS 32, para. 27.

72 IAS 32, para. 27.
73 IAS 32, para. AG29.
74 IAS 32, para. AG29.
75 IAS 32, para. AG29.
76 IAS 32, para. AG29.
77 IAS 32, paras. 28 and AG30.
78 IAS 32, para. 29.
79 IAS 32, para. AG37.
80 IAS 32, para. 28.
81 IAS 32, para. 29.
82 IAS 32, para. AG30.
83 IAS 32, paras. 32 and AG31(a).
84 IAS 32, paras. 31-32.
85 IAS 32, paras. 32 and AG31(a).
86 IAS 32, AG31(b).
87 IAS 31, *Interests in Joint Ventures*, IASB,
    December 2003, (amended March 2004), para. 31.
88 Based on Example 9 in IAS 32, paras. IE34-IE36.
89 Based on Example 10 in IAS 32, paras. IE37-
    IE38.
90 IAS 39, para. AG30(g).
91 IAS 32, para. 30.
92 IAS 32, para. AG32.
93 IAS 32, para. AG32.
94 IAS 32, para. AG33.
95 IAS 32, para. AG33.
96 IAS 32, para. AG34.
97 Based on example in IAS 32, paras. IE39-IE46.
98 IAS 32, para. AG35.
99 IAS 32, paras. IE47-IE50.
100 IAS 32, para. 35.
101 IAS 32, para. 36.
102 IAS 32, para. 41.
103 IAS 32, para. 36.
104 IAS 32, para. 40.
105 IAS 32, para. 37.
106 IAS 32, para. 38.
107 IAS 32, para. 39.
108 IAS 32, para. 33.
109 IAS 32, para. AG36.
110 IAS 32, paras. 33 and AG36.
111 IAS 32, para. 34.
112 IAS 1, *Presentation of Financial Statements*,
     IASB, December 2003 (amended March 2004),
     para. 76(a)(vi).
113 IAS 19, *Employee Benefits*, IASB, February 1998
     (amended March 2004), para. 120(d)(i).
114 IAS 32, paras. IE2-IE6.
115 IAS 32, paras. IE7-IE11.
116 IAS 32, paras. IE12-IE16.
117 IAS 32, paras. IE17-IE21.
118 IAS 32, paras. IE22-IE26.
119 IAS 32, paras. IE27-IE31.
120 IAS 32, para. 96.
121 IAS 32, para. 97.
122 IFRS 1, *First-time Adoption of International
     Financial Reporting Standards*, IASB, June 2003
     (amended March 2004), para. 36A.

123 IFRS 1, para. IG35.
124 IFRS 1, para. IG36
125 IFRS 1, para. 23.

Chapter 18   Financial instruments: Measurement

1   INTRODUCTION

The Introduction to Chapter 15 provides a general background to the development of accounting for financial instruments. It explains that the long-term goal of most standard setters, particularly the IASB, remains a 'full fair value' accounting model for financial instruments. Under such a model all financial instruments would be recognised in the balance sheet at their fair value with changes in value recorded in the income statement.

Notwithstanding the IASB's desires, the current accounting requirements for financial instruments (which are largely set out in IAS 39 – *Financial Instruments: Recognition and Measurement*) are more accurately described as a 'mixed attribute' model. In other words, financial instruments are generally accounted for using either historical cost or fair value measures. However, even this is something of a simplification. Depending upon its nature and the decisions of management, an instrument will rarely be accounted for on a pure historical cost, or a pure fair value, basis, e.g. as a result of one or more of the following:

*   all financial instruments are subject to the general requirements of IAS 21 – *The Effects of Changes in Foreign Exchange Rates* – so that monetary financial instruments denominated in foreign currencies are normally retranslated at closing rates with gains and losses recognised in the income statement;

*   similarly, financial instruments held by foreign entities are retranslated at closing rates, along with the entities' other assets and liabilities, but associated gains and losses are recognised in equity;

*   financial assets that are measured at cost or amortised cost are subject to review for impairment and impaired assets are written down, normally to an amount derived using net present value techniques;

- some financial assets that are measured at fair value in the balance sheet are, effectively, accounted for at cost or amortised cost in profit or loss – the residual gains and losses are temporarily recognised in equity pending their subsequent recognition in profit or loss by way of 'recycling' adjustments; and

- the prescribed methods of hedge accounting involve the over-ride of other general accounting requirements, including those applicable to financial instruments.

It is this mixture of historical cost and fair value accounting bases that causes much of the complexity within IAS 39. This is particularly true in the case of hedge accounting, which depends to a large extent on management intent (although the IASB generally believes management intent should not, in principle, influence accounting).

However, it has been conceded by the IASB that the basic principles of IAS 39 already established will be in place for a considerable period.[1] Therefore, in the improvements project, the scope of the overhaul of IAS 39 was restricted to improving the existing requirements, rather than making any fundamental change to the underlying approach. Notwithstanding this, some important changes have been made to the main building blocks of measurement, specifically the requirements surrounding the estimation of fair values, recognition of impairment losses and, to a lesser extent, calculation of amortised cost using the effective interest method.

In what was described as a further attempt to simplify the accounting requirements under the mixed attribute model, the IASB also decided to allow any financial instrument to be designated as 'at fair value through profit or loss'. Such instruments are effectively accounted for as if in a 'full fair value' model. In spite of the official explanation, this move was probably inspired as much by a desire to allow entities to experiment with such a model to assist the standard setters in their project research. However, even if the 'fair value option' (as the IASB refers to it) survives in its current form – the European Central Bank has used its political influence to try and restrict the scope of this experiment and in April 2004 the IASB bowed to pressure and issued an exposure draft proposing limitations on its use (see Chapter 15 at 9) – outside of the financial services industry we suspect it will be used only in very limited circumstances.

This chapter deals only with the basic measurement requirements of IAS 39. The special form of accounting that is allowed for instruments within designated effective hedging relationships is dealt with in Chapter 19.

2   INITIAL MEASUREMENT

2.1   General requirements

At a conceptual level, the revised version of IAS 39 introduced a significant change to the initial measurement basis for financial assets and liabilities. Previously all financial instruments recognised under IAS 39 were measured by reference to their cost; under the new standard they are now measured by reference to their fair value. More precisely, on initial recognition, financial assets and liabilities at fair value through profit or loss are normally measured at their fair value on the date they are initially recognised. The initial measurement of other financial instruments is also based on their fair value, but adjusted in respect of any transaction costs that are directly attributable to the acquisition or issue of the instrument.[2]

For most entities this will make little, if any, practical difference – not least because the previous implementation guidance explained that if the apparent cost differed from the instrument's fair value then part of the cost was deemed to relate to something other than the instrument itself.[3] It does, however, represent an important shift of emphasis and is a further demonstration of the increasing use of fair value measures in accounting for financial instruments. It can also have important implications for those entities that actively trade in financial instruments as discussed at 4.7 below.

2.2 Initial fair value

IAS 39 contains a formal definition of the term 'fair value' and requirements for determining the fair value of financial instruments, which are considered in detail at 4 below. This subsection deals with those aspects of fair value measurement that are particularly applicable on initial recognition.

The initial fair value of a financial instrument will normally be the transaction price, i.e. the fair value of the consideration given or received. However, this will not always be the case. The standard explains that if part of the consideration given or received is for something other than the financial instrument, the fair value of the instrument should be estimated using a valuation technique (see 4.2 below). For example, the fair value of a long-term loan or receivable that carries no interest can be estimated as the present value of all future cash receipts discounted using the prevailing market rate(s) of interest for instruments that are similar as to currency, term, type of interest rate, credit risk and other factors. Any additional amount advanced is an expense or a reduction of income unless it qualifies for recognition as some other type of asset.[4]

Example 18.1:   Interest-free loan to supplier

Company A lends €1,000 to Company B for five years and classifies the resulting asset within loans and receivables. The loan carries no interest and, instead, A expects (or possibly contracts) to receive other future economic benefits, such as a right to receive goods or services at favourable prices or an implicit right to exert influence over the activities of B.

On initial recognition, the market rate of interest for a similar five-year loan with payment of interest at maturity is 10% per year. The initial fair value of the loan is the present value of the future payment of €1,000, discounted using the market rate of interest for a similar loan of 10% for five years. This equates to €621.

Rationally, A would also expect to obtain other future economic benefits that have a fair value of €379 (the difference between the total consideration given of €1,000 and the loan's initial fair value of €621). The difference is not a financial asset, since it is paid to obtain expected (or possibly contracted) future economic benefits other than the right to receive payment on the loan asset. A recognises that amount as an expense unless it qualifies for recognition as an asset, for example under IAS 38 – *Intangible Assets* (see Chapter 11).[5]

What this approach is trying to do is isolate a 'pure' financial instrument from the remainder of an arrangement. In practice, however, identifying the financial instrument component of an arrangement like this is not always so simple. Often the financial and non-financial elements of an arrangement are interlinked, making separation more difficult. This problem is illustrated in the following example.

Example 18.2:   Interest-free loan to employee

As part of their remuneration package, employees of Company F may borrow up to €1,000 from F on interest free terms. These loans are repayable only in the event that employment ceases (which may be at the option either of the employee or of F, subject to relatively short contractual notice periods and perhaps certain statutory requirements). F determines that the average service life of an employee is five years and the market rate of interest for a five-year loan with payment of interest at maturity is 10% per year. Accordingly, when an employee joins and borrows €1,000, as in Example 18.1 above, F may calculate that the initial fair value of the loan is €621.

However, if this approach is adopted, the question arises as to what the 'spare' €379 represents. There is often a high degree of scepticism expressed at the recognition of prepaid employment costs as it is often questionable whether such costs can ever be recovered. However, in this case, it is clear that the €379 will be recovered in the event that the employee leaves, so this is clearly one alternative.

The €379 may also be seen as representing the value of a contract whereby F has the choice of receiving cash (repayment of the loan, say in the event that F was to terminate the employee's service contract) or employment services. In a similar way to the oil-linked bond considered in Chapter 15 at 2.2.5 this element might also be considered a financial instrument. Because it is also a financial instrument, there appears to be no reason why this part of the contract should be accounted for separately from the remainder of the financial instrument (unless it is considered an embedded derivative).

One could also view F's ability to terminate the employment contract and force settlement of the loan at face value as an embedded call option that is not closely related to the host instrument because the strike price, €1,000, is significantly different from the loan's amortised cost, initially €621 (see Chapter 15 at 5.1.3). This would be another form of financial instrument, in this case a derivative, although it is again hard to see why this should be accounted for separately.

Finally, notwithstanding its expected life based on average service lives, there is an argument to be made that the fair value of the loan is approximately €1,000 if F can demand payment of €1,000 within a short space of time (albeit by terminating the employment contract), suggesting there is no (significant) spare debit.

In practice, a number of approaches might be considered acceptable in situations such as this but it is hard to say which is the more appropriate under the standard.

If a financial instrument is recognised where the terms are 'off-market' (i.e. the consideration given or received does not equal the instrument's fair value) but instead a fee is paid or received in compensation, the instrument should still be recognised at its fair value, i.e. net of the fee received or paid.[6]

Example 18.3:   Off-market loan with origination fee

Bank J lends $1,000 to Company K. The loan carries interest at 5% and is repayable in full in five years' time, even though the market rate for similar loans is 8%. To compensate J for the below market rate of interest, K pays J an origination fee of $120. There are no other directly related payments by either party.

The loan is recorded at its fair value of $880 (net present value of $50 interest payable annually for five years and $1,000 principal repaid after five years, all discounted at 8%). This equals the net amount of cash exchanged ($1,000 loan less $120 origination fee) and hence no gain or loss is recognised on initial recognition of the loan.[7]

Again, applying the requirements of IAS 39 to the simple fact pattern provided by the IASB is a relatively straightforward exercise. In practice, however, it may be more difficult to identify those fees that are required by IAS 39 to be treated as part of the financial instrument and those that should be dealt with in another way, for example under IAS 18 – *Revenue*. Particularly, it may be difficult to determine the extent to which fees associated with a financial instrument that is not quoted in an active market represents compensation for off-market terms or for the genuine provision of services.

A degree of pragmatism is introduced when accounting for short-term receivables and payables with no stated interest rate. The standard explains that these may be measured at the original invoice amount if the effect of discounting is immaterial. The alternative would be to discount the invoice amount for the time value of money over the expected or contractual settlement period and accrue interest on this amount.[8]

In connection with this, IFRIC has considered the accounting for extended payment terms, such as six-month's interest-free credit and concluded that the accounting treatment under IAS 39 was clear. In such circumstances, the effect of the time value of money should be reflected when this is material. It was noted that a different conclusion might be drawn from reading IAS 18 in isolation, but considered the wording in IAS 18 lacked clarity and needed to be improved.[9]

Aside from the situations discussed above (i.e. where part of the consideration given or received is for something other than the financial instrument) it is theoretically possible to make a profit or loss on initial recognition in other circumstances. This will only be the case if there is sufficient evidence to demonstrate that the amount paid or received is different to the fair value of the instrument and the circumstances in which this can arise will be rare for most entities. This issue is considered in further detail at 4.7 below.

2.3   Transaction costs

Transaction costs are defined as incremental costs that are directly attributable to the acquisition, issue or disposal of a financial asset or liability. An incremental cost is one that would not have been incurred had the financial instrument not been acquired, issued or disposed of.[10] Expenses that would be incurred on the subsequent transfer or disposal of a financial instrument are not transaction costs.[11]

Example 18.4:   Transaction costs – initial measurement

Company A acquires an equity security that will be classified as available-for-sale. The security has a fair value of £100 and this is the amount A is required to pay. In addition, A also pays a purchase commission of £2. If the asset was to be sold, a sales commission of £3 would be payable.

The initial measurement of the asset is £102, i.e. the sum of its initial fair value and the purchase commission. The commission payable on sale is not considered for this purpose.[12]

Transaction costs include fees and commissions paid to agents (including employees acting as selling agents), advisers, brokers, and dealers. They also include levies by regulatory agencies and securities exchanges, transfer taxes and duties. Debt premiums or discounts, financing costs and allocations of internal administrative or holding costs are not transaction costs.[13]

Payments to sales staff, and employees acting as such, are common in the insurance industry and many bodies of GAAP require these payments to be deferred and recognised in profit or loss over the life of the related contracts. Following the publication of IFRS 4 – *Insurance Contracts* – many instruments that might previously have been considered insurance contracts now fall within the scope of IAS 39. In order for this legacy accounting treatment to be preserved under the revised version of the standard, an amendment was made so that these payments are now considered transaction costs.

Treating internal costs as transaction costs could open up a number of possibilities for abuse by allowing entities to inappropriately defer expenses. However, it is made clear that internal costs should be treated as transaction costs only if they are incremental and directly attributable to the acquisition, issue or disposal of a financial asset or financial liability.[14] Therefore, it will be rare for internal costs (other than, say, commissions paid to sales staff in respect of an instrument sold) to be treated as transaction costs.

In connection with the creation or acquisition of a financial asset that is not classified at fair value through profit or loss, the appendix to IAS 18 acknowledges that an entity may incur 'related direct costs' that are accounted for in a similar way to transaction costs.[15] IAS 18 does not contain a definition of such costs; particularly it does not refer to the need for them to be 'incremental'. However, it would appear inappropriate to apply a wider definition of transaction costs than is contained in IAS 39 to determine whether such an expense should be accounted for in this way.

2.4   Bid-ask spreads

In some markets, dealers or market makers charge minimal or no explicit transaction costs, but instead quote differential prices for purchases and sales. Such prices are often referred to as 'bid' and 'ask' prices (see 4.1 below). The standard states that the term bid-ask spread (normally interpreted as the difference between quoted bid and ask prices) is used to include only transaction costs and not other adjustments to arrive at fair value such as for counterparty credit risk.[16] Nevertheless, the guidance in IAS 39 seems to imply that in practice the entire bid-ask spread is deemed to be a transaction cost as illustrated in the following example.

Example 18.5:   Bid-ask spread – initial measurement

As in Example 18.4 above, Company A acquires an equity security which will be classified as available-for-sale. In this case A purchases the asset in an active market where no explicit transaction costs are charged, but separate bid and offer prices are quoted. On acquisition the security has an asking price of £102, which is the amount A is required to pay, and a bid price of £97, which is what A would receive were it to sell the asset.

The fair value of a quoted asset is deemed to be its bid price (see 4.1 below) and this suggests that A should initially measure the asset at £97. This would result in an immediate loss of £5, the difference between the initial fair value of the asset and the cash paid. What is more, this loss would be recognised in the income statement as it does not arise on remeasurement of the asset (see 3.2 below).

However, what the standard appears to be saying is that the £5 'loss' (i.e. the bid-ask spread) is deemed to be a transaction cost and, therefore, should be included in the initial measurement of the asset. The asset would then be initially measured at £102 (which happens to be what was paid for it) with no immediate loss recognised in the income statement.

If, instead, the security had been classified at fair value through profit or loss, the accounting treatment on initial recognition would have been significantly different. For such assets, transaction costs are recognised in profit or loss and A *would* have recorded a £5 loss.

Consequently, under this interpretation, the initial measurement requirements do not appear to depend on how a particular market operates, i.e. whether transaction costs are charged explicitly by dealers or market makers or are included within a bid-ask spread. Although this is what might be expected, it is interesting to contrast this with the subsequent measurement requirements shown in Examples 18.10 and 18.11 at 4.1 below.

2.5   Embedded derivatives and financial instrument hosts

In Chapter 15 at 5.2, it was explained that the initial carrying amounts of an embedded derivative that is required to be separated and the associated host should be determined so that the derivative is initially recorded at its fair value and the host as the residual (at least for an optional derivative – a non-option embedded derivative will have a fair value and initial carrying amount of zero).[17] Originally, this was to prevent entities recording an immediate profit or loss on the derivative's subsequent remeasurement to fair value.[18] However, as noted at 4.7 below, the IASB now appears to accept that profits can sometimes be made on initial recognition.

The standard does not clarify what it is that entities are meant to be determining the residual of. In two separate instances, the implementation guidance suggests that a host financial instrument should be recognised as the residual of the *purchase price* after adjusting for the fair value of the embedded derivative.[19] This does not correctly reflect the revisions to IAS 39 (which require measurement to be based on the instrument's fair value, not its purchase price – see 2.1 above) but we see this as no more than an oversight on the part of the IASB. We suspect the IASB's most likely intention was that the host should initially be measured based on the residual of the *fair value* of the hybrid instrument (adjusted for any transaction costs) and also after adjusting for the fair value of the embedded derivative.

2.6   Regular way transactions

When settlement date accounting is used for regular way transactions (see Chapter 16 at 3.1) and those transactions result in the recognition of assets that are subsequently measured at amortised cost or (very rarely) cost, there is an exception to the general requirement at 2.1 above.

The standard explains that, in such circumstances, rather than being initially measured by reference to their fair value on the date they are first recognised, i.e. settlement date, these financial instruments are initially measured by reference to their fair value on the trade date.[20] Or, as some would say, those assets that are to be subsequently measured at cost or amortised cost should initially be measured at their cost!

In practice, the difference will rarely be significant because of the short time scale involved between trade date and settlement date, the main reason the IASB tolerates this special accounting treatment for these 'derivatives'.[21]

2.7   Assets and liabilities arising from loan commitments

Loan commitments are a form of derivative financial instrument, although for pragmatic reasons the IASB decided that certain loan commitments could be excluded from the requirements of the revised version of IAS 39 (see Chapter 15 at 3.4). This exclusion creates a degree of confusion over how assets and liabilities arising from such arrangements should be measured on initial recognition, as illustrated in the following example.

Example 18.6:   Drawdown under a committed borrowing facility

Company H obtains from Bank Q a committed facility allowing it to borrow up to €10,000 at any time over the following five years, provided certain covenants specified in the facility agreement are not breached. Interest on any drawdowns is payable at LIBOR plus a fixed margin, representing Q's initial assessment of H's credit risk. Any such borrowings can be repaid at any time at the option of H, but must be repaid at the end of five years unless the facility is renegotiated and extended. They also become repayable immediately in the event that H breaches the covenants. For the purposes of this illustration, any other amounts payable by H to Q (such as non-utilisation fees) have been ignored.

Both H and Q choose to exclude the commitment from the requirements of IAS 39 and any asset or liability arising from drawdowns under the facility will be classified within loans and receivables by Q and within other liabilities by H. Q applies IAS 37 – *Provisions, Contingent Liabilities and Contingent Assets* – and assesses whether the facility is an onerous contract (effectively by assessing the probability of H's default following a future drawdown). If it were, Q would recognise a provision.

After one year, no drawdowns have been made and H's credit risk has increased (although it has not breached any of the covenants and there is no expectation of default, i.e. it is not an onerous contract as defined in IAS 37). As a result of this change in credit risk, the fair value of the facility is, say, €200 (positive value to H, negative value to Q). Because the commitment is not accounted for under IAS 39 and because it is not onerous, nothing is recognised in the accounts of either Q or H in respect of the facility.

Shortly afterwards H draws down the maximum €10,000 available under the facility. Because of the change in credit risk the drawdown results in the recognition of an asset (liability) by Q (H) that has a fair value at that date of, say, €9,800.

The €200 difference between the €9,800 fair value of the financial instrument created and the €10,000 cash transferred effectively represents the change in fair value of the commitment arising from the change in H's credit risk.

Should Q (H) initially measure the resulting asset (liability) at its €9,800 fair value or at €10,000, being the amount of cash actually exchanged? If it is recognised at €9,800, how is the 'spare' €200 accounted for, particularly does Q (H) recognise it as a loss (profit)?

The general requirement noted at 2.1 above would imply that the asset (liability) should initially be measured at €9,800. Consequently a loss (profit) of €200 would be recognised – this is because the spare €200 does not represent any other asset or liability arising form the transaction.

However, in the Basis for Conclusions to IAS 39, it is explained that the effect of the loan commitment exception is that, consistent with the likely measurement basis of the resulting loan, the fair value of these commitments from changes in market interest rates or credit spreads will not be recognised or measured.[22] This is exactly what the 'spare' €200 represents so, in accordance with the underlying rationale and objective of allowing loan commitments to be excluded from the scope of IAS 39, it seems entirely appropriate to initially measure the asset or liability arising in this case at €10,000.

Such treatment is also consistent with that for similar assets arising from regular way transactions recognised using settlement date accounting (see 2.6 above). This is relevant because the IASB introduced the loan commitment exception as a result of issues identified by the IGC and the only solution the IGC could identify at the time involved treating loan commitments as regular way transactions and using settlement date accounting.[23]

If, in the above example, Q (H) accounted for the loan commitment at fair value through profit or loss this issue would not arise. At the time the loan was drawn down the commitment would be recognised as a €200 liability (asset) and an equivalent loss (profit) would have been recorded in the income statement. The loan would be recognised at its fair value of €9,800 and the €200 balance of the cash movement over this amount would be treated as the settlement of the loan commitment liability (asset). Therefore, no further gain or loss would need to be recognised at this point.

3 SUBSEQUENT MEASUREMENT AND RECOGNITION OF GAINS AND LOSSES

As set out in Chapter 15 at 7, IAS 39 classifies most financial assets and liabilities into one of the following five categories:

- at fair value through profit or loss;
- held-to-maturity investments;
- loans and receivables;
- available-for-sale assets; and
- other financial liabilities.

Following the initial recognition of financial assets and liabilities, their subsequent accounting treatment depends principally on the classification of the instrument, although there are a small number of exceptions.[24] These requirements are summarised in the following table and are considered in more detail in the remainder of this section.

Classification	Instrument type	Balance sheet	Fair value gains and losses	Interest and dividends	Impairment	Foreign exchange
At fair value through profit or loss (including all derivatives that are not designated in effective hedges)	Debt, Equity or Derivative	Fair value	Profit or loss*	Profit or loss*	Profit or loss* (assets)	Profit or loss*
	Equity or equity derivative: not reliably measurable	Cost	–	Profit or loss: dividends receivable	Profit or loss (assets)	–
Held-to-maturity investments	Debt	Amortised cost	–	Profit or loss: effective interest rate	Profit or loss	Profit or loss
Loans and receivables	Debt	Amortised cost	–	Profit or loss: effective interest rate	Profit or loss	Profit or loss
Available-for-sale assets	Debt	Fair value	Equity †	Profit or loss: effective interest rate	Profit or loss	Profit or loss
	Equity	Fair value	Equity †	Profit or loss: dividends receivable	Profit or loss	Equity †
	Equity: not reliably measurable	Cost	–	Profit or loss: dividends receivable	Profit or loss	–
Other financial liabilities	Debt	Amortised cost	–	Profit or loss: effective interest rate	–	Profit or loss

* no guidance is given on how gains and losses should be disaggregated – see Chapter 20 at 6.1.1.
† recycled to profit or loss on disposal or impairment.

3.1   Balance sheet measurement

After initial recognition, financial assets (including derivatives that are assets) should, in general, be measured at fair value, with no deduction for sale or disposal costs, except for:

- held-to-maturity investments;
- loans and receivables; and
- investments in equity instruments that do not have a quoted market price in an active market and whose fair value cannot be reliably measured and derivative assets that are linked to and must be settled by delivery of such unquoted equity instruments.[25]

In addition, financial liabilities that are classified as at fair value through profit or loss (including derivatives that are liabilities) should be measured at fair value except for derivative liabilities that are linked to and must be settled by delivery of an unquoted equity instrument whose fair value cannot be reliably measured.[26]

Section 4 below deals with the requirements of IAS 39 relating to the determination of fair values for those instruments required to be measured on this basis. Investments in equity instruments whose fair value cannot be reliably measured and derivatives that are linked to, and must be settled by delivery of, such instruments (see 4.4 below) are generally measured at cost.[27]

The basic requirement for held-to-maturity investments, loans and receivables and other liabilities (as that term is used in Chapter 15 at 7) is that they are measured at amortised cost using the effective interest method.[28] For loans and receivables as defined, this method of accounting is applied whether they are intended to be held-to-maturity or not.[29] Absent such intent, other assets cannot be measured at amortised cost (see Chapter 15 at 7.2.3). This method of accounting is dealt with in Section 5 below.

Except for those that are *measured* at fair value through profit or loss, all financial assets are subject to review for impairment.[30] Therefore, those assets that are *classified* as at fair value through profit or loss but for which it is not possible to reliably measure fair value are subject to review for impairment. Section 6 below deals with the impairment requirements of IAS 39.

Financial assets and liabilities that are designated as hedged items are subject to measurement under the hedge accounting requirements of IAS 39[31] and these can over-ride the general accounting requirements noted above. Hedge accounting is covered in Chapter 19.

There are special requirements for financial liabilities that arise when transfers of financial assets do not qualify for derecognition, or are accounted for using the continuing involvement approach,[32] and these are dealt with in Chapter 16 at 4.8.3.

3.2 Gains and losses

All gains and losses arising from recognised changes in the fair value of financial assets and liabilities that are classified at fair value through profit or loss are, not surprisingly, recognised in the income statement.[33]

For financial instruments carried at amortised cost (held-to-maturity investments, loans and receivables and other liabilities), gains and losses are recognised in the income statement when the instrument is derecognised or (for assets) impaired, as well as through the amortisation process.[34]

Accounting for available-for-sale assets is slightly more complex. Gains and losses arising from changes in fair value (after adjusting for interest accruals and certain foreign exchange gains and losses) are initially recognised directly in equity and reported in the statement of changes in equity (see Chapter 3 at 3.3). When an asset is derecognised, often by way of sale, or is impaired, the cumulative gain or loss previously recognised in equity is recycled and recognised in profit or loss.[35] For example, consider an equity security that is purchased for its fair value of €100, has a fair value of €120 at the end of the year and is sold subsequent to the year-end for €130. In the first year a gain of €20 is recognised in equity as a result of remeasuring the security at its fair value. In the second year a profit of €30 is recognised in the income statement – this effectively represents the €10 difference between the proceeds received (€130) and the previous carrying amount of the asset (€120) and the recycling of the €20 gain previously recognised in equity.

Where appropriate, interest receivable on available-for-sale assets is recognised in the income statement using the effective interest method (see 5 below), and dividends receivable are recognised in profit or loss when a right to receive payment is established (see Chapter 26). Impairment and foreign currency retranslation are covered in more detail at 6 and 7 respectively.[36]

The accounting requirements for available-for-sale assets are further illustrated in the examples below.

Example 18.7:　Gain or loss on available-for-sale shares in takeover target

Company S holds a small number of shares in Company T. The shares are classified as available-for-sale. On 20 December 2005, the fair value of the shares is $120 and the cumulative gain recognised in equity is $20. On the same day, Company U, a large public company, acquires T. As a result, S receives shares in U in exchange for those it had in T of equal fair value.

The transaction qualifies for derecognition (see Chapter 16 at 4), therefore the cumulative gain of $20 that has been recognised in equity should now be recognised in the income statement[37] even though the gain has not been realised in any traditional sense.

Example 18.8:　Available-for-sale asset – determination of interest

A company acquires a zero coupon bond at the end of 2005 for £760, its fair value, which matures at the beginning of 2009 at £1,000. It is classified as available-for-sale asset and, accordingly, associated fair value gains and losses are reported in equity. Its fair value at the end of 2006, 2007 and 2008 is £850, £950 and £1,000 respectively and it can be determined that the effective interest rate is 9.6% (the effective interest method is discussed in more detail at 5 below).

The financial statements would therefore include the accounting entries set out in the following table (amortised cost is memorandum information used to determine interest).

Year	Amortised cost at start of year £		Interest – income statement £		Gains and losses – equity £		Cash flow £	Fair value B/S £
2005	–		–		–		–	760
2006	760		73	*[=760 × 9.6%]*	17	*[=850 – {760 + 73}]*	–	850
2007	833	*[=760 + 73]*	80	*[=833 × 9.6%]*	20	*[=950 – {850 + 80}]*	–	950
2008	913	*[=833 + 80]*	87	*[=913 × 9.6%]*	(37)	*[=1,000 – {950+87}]*	–	1,000
2009	1,000	*[=913 + 87]*	–		–		1,000	–

The standard does not specify the cost basis to be used for fungible available-for-sale assets (or, indeed, for any other fungible financial instrument). This is in contrast to, say, IAS 2 – *Inventories* – which specifies the use of a weighted average cost or FIFO (first in first out) basis in most circumstances.[38] On a theoretical level, an asset-by-asset approach is arguably the most technically pure. This would, for example, prevent the offsetting of an impairment arising on one asset against an unrealised gain on another. However, it could also allow entities to manipulate their earnings. For example, when selling an asset an entity could choose to sell one with a low (or high) cost base in order to maximise (minimise) the profit on disposal. In practice, average cost bases are typically used (perhaps applied to individual portfolios within the entity), although others may be acceptable. The financial statements of UBS disclose that it uses an average cost method.

Extract 18.1: UBS AG (2003)

Note 1   Summary of Significant Accounting Policies [extract]

n)   Financial investments [extract]

Available-for-sale financial investments are carried at fair value. Unrealized gains or losses on available-for-sale investments are reported in Shareholders' equity, net of applicable income taxes, until such investments are sold, collected or otherwise disposed of, or until such investment is determined to be impaired. On disposal of an available-for-sale investment, the accumulated unrealized gain or loss included in Shareholders' equity is transferred to net profit or loss for the period and reported in Other income. Gains and losses on disposal are determined using the average cost method.

The standard does not address the situation when there is a change in the relationship between the reporting entity and the entity holding the assets. For example, consider the disposal of a subsidiary. Should the gains and losses recorded in equity in respect of the assets held by that subsidiary be recycled at the date of disposal? This issue is covered in more detail in Chapter 5 at 6.6.

Financial assets and liabilities that are designated as hedged items are subject to measurement under the hedge accounting requirements of IAS 39. These can override the general requirements noted above.[39] Monetary financial instruments may also be designated as hedging instruments, which can affect whether foreign currency gains and losses are recognised in the income statement or initially in equity.[40] Hedge accounting is covered in Chapter 19.

Where settlement date accounting is used for regular way transactions, any change in the fair value of the asset to be received arising between trade date and settlement date is not recognised for those assets that will be measured at cost or amortised cost (see also 2.6 above). For assets that will be recorded at fair value, such changes in value are recognised:

- in the income statement for assets to be classified as at fair value through profit or loss; and

- initially in equity (except for impairments and certain foreign exchange gains and losses as above) for available-for-sale assets.[41]

On disposal, changes in value of such assets between trade date and settlement date are not recognised because the right to changes in fair value ceases on the trade date.[42] This illustrated in Chapter 16 at 3.1.2.

3.3   Reclassifications and changes in measurement basis

As set out in Chapter 15 at 7.5, the revised standard has restricted the scope for reclassifying instruments between the main categories, although reclassifications between available-for-sale assets and held-to-maturity investments are still possible.

Where a held-to-maturity investment is reclassified as available-for-sale, the asset should be remeasured to fair value and any associated gain or loss recognised in equity.[43]

If an available-for-sale asset is reclassified as held-to-maturity, the fair value carrying amount of the financial asset on that date becomes its new amortised cost. Any previous gain or loss on that asset that has been recognised in equity should be amortised over the remaining life of the investment using the effective interest method. Any difference between the new amortised cost and maturity amount should be similarly amortised, akin to the amortisation of a premium or discount.[44]

Example 18.9:   Debt instrument reclassified as held-to-maturity

Company Y acquires a debt instrument that it classifies as available-for-sale. The purchase price equals the fair value of the instrument, £110. Its terms are such that it pays a fixed coupon for ten years and a principal payment of £100. Subsequently, when the fair value of the instrument is £120, a gain of £12 has been recognised in equity, and £2 of the initial cost has been amortised to profit or loss, Y reclassifies the debt instrument as held-to-maturity.

The £120 fair value carrying amount becomes the new amortised cost of the instrument thereby giving rise to an effective premium of £20 that is amortised over the remaining term to maturity using the effective interest method. In addition, the £12 gain in equity is also amortised to profit or loss over the remaining period to maturity.

In effect, the income statement should be broadly the same as if the instrument had not been reclassified (or had always been classified as held-to-maturity).

If the asset subsequently becomes impaired, any gain or loss remaining in equity should be recognised in profit or loss.[45]

As noted at 3.1 above, there are occasionally situations where the fair value of a trading instrument or available-for-sale asset cannot be reliably measured. In such cases the instrument is measured at cost. If a reliable measure of fair value subsequently becomes available, the asset should be remeasured at that fair value, and the gain or loss reported in the income statement or equity as appropriate.[46] If a reliable measure ceases to be available, it should thereafter be measured at 'cost', which is deemed to be the fair value carrying amount on that date. Any gain or loss previously recognised in equity should be left there until the asset has been sold, otherwise disposed of or impaired, at which time it should be recycled into income.[47]

4   FAIR VALUE MEASUREMENT CONSIDERATIONS

Consistent with the previous version of IAS 39, and various other standards, fair value is defined as 'the amount for which an asset could be exchanged, or a liability settled, between knowledgeable, willing parties in an arm's length transaction.'[48] However, the guidance supporting the application of that definition to financial instruments has been amended significantly in the revised standard. These amendments will be of limited relevance to many entities but will be extremely important to banks and similar institutions that actively trade in financial instruments.

Underlying the definition is a presumption that an entity is a going concern without any intention or need to liquidate, curtail materially the scale of operations, or undertake a transaction on adverse terms. Fair value is not, therefore, the amount that would be received or paid in a forced transaction, involuntary liquidation, or distress sale. It does, however, reflect an instrument's credit quality.[49] This may be obvious for a financial asset but, more controversially, it applies equally to financial liabilities. The IASB's reasons for adopting this requirement are considered further at 4.8 below.

For the purpose of determining an instrument's fair value, the application guidance distinguishes between two main types of instrument – those for which there exist quoted prices in an active market and all others. As ever, there is no clear bright line between the two and judgment will be necessary at the margins. This distinction takes on a particular significance in the classification of instruments. As explained in Chapter 15 at 7.3, a financial asset cannot be classified within loans and receivables if it is quoted in an active market. It can also make a difference as to whether an immediate gain or loss can be recognised on the initial recognition of a financial instrument (see 4.7 below).

The requirements to be followed in determining the fair value of financial instruments for which no quoted market price is available has been significantly expanded (see 4.2 to 4.4). This is because IASB decided it was desirable to provide clear and reasonably detailed guidance about the objective and use of valuation techniques to achieve reliable and comparable fair value estimates when financial instruments are measured at fair value.[50]

4.1 Quoted prices in an active market

The standard now explains that the existence of published price quotations in an active market *is* the best evidence of fair value.[51] Previously such prices would *normally* be considered the best evidence of fair value[52] although only one exception to this was countenanced (other than for certain regular way sales recognised using settlement date accounting – see 3.2 above). Therefore, such prices are to be used even if the entity believes valuation techniques are more appropriate for measuring fair value, even if valuation models are consistent with industry best practice (e.g. for pricing contracts) and even where they are accepted for regulatory capital purposes.[53]

This requirement received a good deal of attention during the improvements project, but the IASB reaffirmed (and strengthened slightly) the position in the previous standard that quoted prices are the best indicator of fair value because:

- in an active market, the best evidence of fair value is the quoted price, given that fair value is defined in terms of a price agreed by a knowledgeable, willing buyer and a knowledgeable, willing seller;

- it results in consistent measurement across entities; and

- fair value as defined does not depend on entity-specific factors.[54]

Additional guidance is now included explaining what the term 'quoted in an active market' means: quoted prices should be readily and regularly available from an exchange, dealer, broker, industry group, pricing service or regulatory agency, and those prices should represent actual and regularly occurring market transactions on an arm's length basis.[55] In practice, this will encompass instruments traded on most regulated exchanges, although a quoted price does not necessarily mean there is an active market in a particular instrument. For example, some debt securities may have a 'technical' listing on an exchange, often for credit rating purposes, even though the instrument is rarely traded. Conversely, the existence of a formal exchange is not always necessary to satisfy this term. Prices reflecting an active market may be quoted in many different ways, e.g. in trade journals or on websites.

As noted at 3.1 above, fair value should be measured without any deduction for transaction costs that may be incurred on sale or disposal. This is illustrated in the following example.

Example 18.10:   Transaction costs – subsequent measurement

In Example 18.4 at 2.3 above, Company A acquired an available-for-sale equity security that was initially measured at £102 – fair value of £100 plus £2 purchase commission; no account was taken of £3 sales commission that would be paid in the event of disposal.

If Company A had a balance sheet date immediately after purchase, assuming the fair value had not changed, A would measure the security at £100 (again ignoring potential transaction costs) and recognise a loss of £2 in equity.[56]

The standard uses the terms 'bid price' and 'asking price' ('current offer price' or 'offer price') in the context of quoted market prices.[57] In the context of an asset an entity would receive the bid price if it sold the asset; it would have to pay the asking price to acquire the asset.

The appropriate quoted market price for an asset held, or liability to be issued, is usually the current bid price; for an asset to be acquired or liability held, the current asking (or offer) price. Using bid rather than, say, mid-market price (average of bid and ask prices) is a controversial requirement that has been retained largely unchanged in the revised standard. The one concession granted was to extend, slightly, the situations when mid-market prices may be used to those when assets and liabilities with offsetting market risks are held (e.g. within a portfolio of interest rate swaps).[58] Previously, mid-market prices could be used only when asset and liability positions (rather than risk components) matched.[59]

As noted at 2.4 above, the term 'bid-ask spread' is used to include only transaction costs.[60] Whilst this appears to eliminate accounting anomalies on initial recognition, it still leaves inconsistencies in the subsequent measurement of instruments. Consider the following extension of Example 18.5 at 2.4 above.

Example 18.11: Bid-ask spread – subsequent measurement

Company A has acquired an available-for-sale equity security that was initially measured at £102 – fair value (bid price) of £97 plus £5 bid-ask spread deemed to be a transaction cost.

If A had a balance sheet date immediately after purchase, assuming the quoted prices had not changed, A would measure the security at £97 (bid price) and recognise a loss of £5 in equity.

Comparing this outcome to that in Example 18.10 above, it becomes apparent that instruments may be measured differently in the balance sheet depending on whether dealers and market makers charge transaction costs explicitly or include them within a bid-ask spread. For many companies the amounts involved are unlikely to be significant (and will normally be recognised outside of income for available-for-sale assets). However, at a conceptual level, the IASB does not appear to have fully resolved this issue.

Rules applicable to some investment funds require net asset values to be reported to investors based on mid-market prices. However, the existence of such regulations does not justify a departure from the general requirement to use the current bid price in the absence of a matching liability position. Therefore, in its financial statements, an investment fund should normally measure its assets at current bid prices and, in reporting its net asset value to investors, it may wish to provide a reconciliation between the fair values reported on its balance sheet and the prices used for the net asset value calculation.[61] Zero Dividend Recovery Fund has included just such a note, actually in its financial statements, as shown in the following extract.

Extract 18.2: Zero Dividend Recovery Fund Limited (2004)

12. Net Asset Value per Share

The net asset value per Ordinary Share is based on the net assets attributable to equity shareholders of £5,454,148 (2003: £3,202,093) and on 12,000,000 (2003: 12,000,000) Ordinary Shares in issue at the end of the period.

The accounts have been prepared in accordance with the provisions of International Accounting Standard No. 39 ("IAS 39"), "Financial Instruments: Recognition and Measurement". The effect of this is to bring into the Statement of Net Assets the concept of "fair value", with the Company's investment portfolio being valued at market bid prices. This is in contrast to a United Kingdom domiciled investment trust that, under United Kingdom Accounting Standards and the principles set out in the Statement of Recommended Practice for Financial Statements of Investment Trust Companies, values the investment portfolio at mid-market prices in its Statement of Net Assets. The monetary effects of IAS 39 have resulted in a reduction in the net asset value per Ordinary Share of 0.82p (2003: 1.18p) as at 31 March 2004.

Reconciliation of net asset value to published net asset value:

	2004 £'000	2004 per share	2003 £'000	2003 per share
Published net asset value	5,552	46.27p	3,343	27.86p
Valuation of investments at bid prices *(note)*	(98)	(0.82)p	(141)	(1.18)p
Net asset value per IAS	5,454	45.45p	3,202	26.68p

note   In accordance with IAS 39, investments have been valued at Stock Exchange quoted market bid prices at the close of business on the balance sheet date. However, in accordance with the SORP for ITC's, the net asset value reported each month to the London Stock Exchange and The Channel Islands Stock Exchange reflects these investments valued at Stock Exchange quoted market mid prices.

The IASB has now acknowledged that some entities operate in different markets and that the prices in those markets may be different. For example, a trader may originate derivatives with its corporate clients in an active 'retail' market and offset these by taking out derivatives in an active dealers' wholesale market where prices may be more favourable. Accordingly, the standard now clarifies that the objective of determining fair value is to arrive at the price at which a transaction in a particular instrument would occur in the *most advantageous* active market to which the entity has immediate access. However, the price in the more advantageous market should be adjusted to reflect any differences in counterparty credit risk between instruments actually traded in that market and those being valued.[62]

The fair value of a portfolio of financial instruments is always the product of the number of units of the instrument held and its quoted market price.[63] Often quoted prices only reflect the price a dealer or market maker is prepared to pay for a maximum deal size. In transactions involving large holdings, a buyer may be prepared to pay a higher price, or a seller may need to accept a lower price, than the one quoted. However, no adjustment is made in these circumstances as illustrated in the following example based on the implementation guidance to IAS 39.

Example 18.12: Valuing publicly quoted shares at other than market price

Company X holds 15% of the share capital in Company Y. The shares are publicly traded in an active market, the currently quoted price is €100, and daily trading volume is 0.1% of outstanding shares. Because X believes that the fair value of the shares it owns, if sold as a block, is greater than the quoted market price, it obtains several independent estimates of the price it would obtain if it were to sell its holding. These estimates indicate that it would be able to obtain a price of €105, a 5% premium above the quoted price.

The published price quotation in an active market is the best estimate of fair value. Therefore, the published price quotation (€100) should be used. X cannot depart from the quoted market price solely because independent estimates indicate that it would obtain a higher (or lower) price by selling the holding as a block.[64]

The use of the words 'solely because' suggest there is some scope for not using the quoted price. However, this is not the case as these words are simply a hangover from the previous version of the implementation guidance. Under the previous version of the standard it was acknowledged that the quoted price could be adjusted to reflect the existence of objective reliable evidence, such as a contract to sell the asset to a third party for an amount different to the quoted price.[65] Nevertheless, entities are no longer permitted to take account of such evidence.

We share the IASB's concern with applying a *premium* to the quoted price, such as in the situation described in Example 18.12 above, or where a portfolio of equities is said to command a 'control premium'. In the absence of an actual transaction, it is hard to verify the value of such premiums. However, in the case of a large holding of debt instruments, disposals are commonly made at a discount to the prevailing quoted price. It therefore seems imprudent to defer the inherent loss until the disposal actually takes place.

If quoted prices do not exist for an instrument in its entirety, but active markets exist for its component parts, fair value should be determined on the basis of the prices for the component parts.[66] An example might be a debt instrument containing an embedded forward based on a stock market index where active markets exist for similar debt instruments and similar forward contracts, but not for the combined instrument itself.

If a rate (rather than a price) is quoted in an active market, that market-quoted rate should be used as an input into a valuation technique to determine fair value. If the market-quoted rate does not include credit risk or other factors that market participants would include in valuing the instrument, adjustments should be made for those factors.[67] Valuation techniques are discussed in more detail at 4.2 and 4.3 below.

When current prices are unavailable, the most recent transaction price should be used in determining the current fair value, provided there has been no subsequent change in economic circumstances. If circumstances have changed, the fair value should reflect the change in conditions by reference to current prices (or rates) for similar instruments as appropriate. For example, a change in the risk-free interest rate following the most recent price quote for a corporate bond should be reflected in determining the fair value of that bond. Similarly, if it can be demonstrated that the last quoted transaction did not take place at fair value, e.g. because it reflected the amount paid or received in a forced transaction, involuntary liquidation or distress sale, that price should also be adjusted.[68]

4.2 Valuation techniques where there is no active market

The June 2002 exposure draft proposed a rigid measurement hierarchy under which the fair value of instruments not quoted in an active market would normally be determined by reference to recent market transactions. Only if there were no recent market transactions would valuation techniques be used. However, in the revised standard, this hierarchy was simplified. The fair value of all instruments that are not quoted in active markets is to be determined on the basis of valuation techniques. It is acknowledged that such techniques include, where available, the use of recent market transactions between knowledgeable, willing parties in arm's length transactions.[69]

There are many other valuation techniques available – including discounted cash flow analyses and option pricing models, as well as making reference to the current fair value of other instruments that are substantially the same. However, if there is a valuation technique that is commonly used by market participants to price an instrument, and that technique has been demonstrated to provide reliable estimates of prices obtained in actual market transactions, that technique should be used.[70]

It is explained that the objective of using a valuation technique is to establish what the transaction price would have been, on the measurement date, in an arm's length exchange motivated by normal business considerations. A valuation technique that makes maximum use of market inputs, and relies as little as possible on entity-specific inputs, is considered more likely to meet this objective. Also, the technique should reasonably reflect how the market could be expected to price a particular instrument. Accordingly, the inputs should represent, so far as possible, market expectations and measures of the risk-return factors inherent in the instrument.[71]

In other words, valuation techniques should incorporate all factors that market participants would consider in setting a particular price and be consistent with accepted economic methodologies for pricing financial instruments. They should also be calibrated and tested for validity using prices from any observable current market transactions in the same instrument (without modification or repackaging) or based on any available observable market data. Market data should be obtained from the same market in which the instrument was originated or purchased.[72]

The best evidence of fair value at initial recognition is taken to be the transaction price (i.e. the fair value of the consideration given or received) unless fair value is evidenced by comparison with other observable current market transactions in the same instrument (without modification or repackaging) or based on a valuation technique whose variables include only data from observable markets.[73] This single sentence is very important to those entities that trade in financial instruments. Its effect is to prevent the immediate recognition of a profit on initial recognition of most financial instruments that are not quoted in active markets – see 4.7 below.

The transaction price arising from a market transaction is said to provide a 'foundation' for estimating fair value. For example, the fair value of a loan can be determined by reference to the transaction price at acquisition or origination as well as current market conditions or interest rates currently charged (by the originator or by others) for instruments that are similar as to remaining maturity, cash flow pattern, currency, credit risk, collateral and interest basis. Alternatively, provided there has been no change in the debtor's credit risk and applicable credit spreads, an estimate of the current market interest rate may be derived by using a benchmark interest rate reflecting a better credit quality than the underlying instrument, holding the credit spread constant and adjusting for the change in the benchmark interest rate. However, if conditions have changed since the most recent market transaction, corresponding changes in fair value are determined by reference to current prices or rates for similar instruments, adjusted as appropriate for any differences from the one being valued.[74]

The same information may not be available each time an instrument is measured. For example, at the date a loan is made (or debt instrument acquired) there is a transaction price that is also a market price. At the next measurement date, although updated general market interest rates are likely be available, there may be no information from new or recent transactions to determine the level of, say, credit risk that market participants would now consider in pricing the instrument. In the absence of evidence to the contrary, it would be reasonable to assume that no changes have taken place from the original spread, although reasonable efforts should be made to determine whether there is any such evidence. When evidence of a change exists, the effects of the change should be considered in determining an instrument's fair value.[75]

In applying discounted cash flow analyses, the discount rate(s) used should equal the prevailing rates of return for instruments with substantially the same terms and characteristics, including currency, credit quality and the remaining term(s) for interest rate resets and principal repayments. As for initial measurement, short-term receivables and payables with no stated interest rate may be measured at the original invoice amount if the effect of discounting is immaterial (see 2.2 above).[76]

4.3 Inputs to valuation techniques

Appropriate techniques for estimating fair value should incorporate observable market data about the market conditions and other factors that are likely to affect the fair value of an instrument. The revised standard explains that one or more of the following factors (and perhaps others) will need to be incorporated into the valuation technique.

(a) *The time value of money (i.e. interest at the basic or risk-free rate)*. Basic interest rates can usually be derived from observable government bond prices and are often quoted in financial publications. These rates typically vary with the expected dates of the projected cash flows. For example, the annual interest rate applicable to a cash flow occurring in five years will be different to that applicable to one occurring in ten years. These interest rates can be plotted against different time horizons to form what is often known as a 'yield curve'.

For practical reasons, a well-accepted and readily observable general rate, such as LIBOR or a swap rate, may be used as the benchmark rate. However, because such rates are not the risk-free interest rate, any credit risk adjustment is determined in relation to the credit risk in this benchmark rate rather than the risk-free rate.

In some countries, central government bonds may carry a significant credit risk and may not provide a stable benchmark basic interest rate for instruments denominated in that currency. In fact, some entities in these countries may have a better credit standing and a lower borrowing rate than the central government. In such cases, basic interest rates may be more appropriately determined by reference to the highest rated corporate bonds issued in the currency of that jurisdiction.

(b) *Credit risk*. The effect on fair value of credit risk (i.e. the premium over the basic interest rate for credit risk) may be derived from observable market prices for traded instruments of different credit quality or from observable interest rates charged by lenders for loans of various credit ratings.

(c) *Foreign currency exchange prices*. Active currency exchange markets exist for most major currencies, and prices are quoted daily in financial publications.

(d) *Commodity prices*. There are observable market prices for many commodities.

(e) *Equity prices*. Prices (and price indices) of traded equity instruments are readily observable in some markets. Present value based techniques may be used to estimate the current market price of equity instruments for which there are no observable prices.

(f) *Volatility (i.e. the magnitude of future changes in price of the financial instrument or other item).* Measures of the volatility of actively traded items can normally be reasonably estimated on the basis of historical market data or by using volatilities implied in current market prices.

(g) *Prepayment risk and surrender risk.* This is the risk that an option to settle a debt instrument before its maturity will be exercised – rationally, such an option may be expected to be exercised by a borrower paying a fixed rate of interest if interest rates fall. Expected prepayment patterns for financial assets and expected surrender patterns for financial liabilities can be estimated on the basis of historical data. However, the fair value of a financial liability that can be surrendered by the counterparty cannot be less than the present value of the surrender amount – see 4.5 below.

(h) *Servicing costs for a financial asset or a financial liability.* Costs of servicing can be estimated using comparisons with current fees charged by other market participants. If the costs of servicing a financial asset or liability are significant and other market participants would face comparable costs, the issuer would consider them in determining the fair value of that financial asset or financial liability. It is likely that the fair value at inception of a contractual right to future fees equals the origination costs paid for them, unless future fees and related costs are out of line with market comparables.[77]

4.4 Unquoted equity instruments and related derivatives

There are special accounting requirements for certain equity instruments that do not have a quoted market price in an active market and derivatives that are linked to, and must be settled by delivery of, such unquoted equity instruments. Specifically, they should be measured at cost, less impairment, if their fair value cannot be reliably measured (see 3.1 above).

The fair value of these instruments is deemed to be reliably measurable if:

- the variability in the range of reasonable fair value estimates is not significant for that instrument; or

- the probabilities of the various estimates within the range can be reasonably assessed and used in estimating fair value.[78]

It is explained that there are many situations in which the variability in the range of reasonable fair value estimates of such investments is likely not to be significant and that, normally, it is possible to estimate the fair value of a financial asset that has been acquired from a third party. However, if the range of reasonable fair value estimates is significant and the probabilities of the various estimates cannot be reasonably assessed, such instruments are precluded from fair value measurement.[79]

This relaxation can apply only to instruments with a link to unquoted equities. The fair value of any other type of instrument is deemed to be reliably measurable as illustrated in the following example.

Example 18.13:   Complex stand-alone derivative – no unquoted equity underlying

Company Z acquires a complex stand-alone derivative that is based on several underlying variables, including commodity prices, interest rates, and credit indices. There is no active market or other price quotation for the derivative and no active markets for some of its underlying variables.

The presumption that the derivative's fair value can be reliably determined cannot be overcome because it is not linked to, or required to be settled by delivery of, an unquoted equity instrument. It cannot, therefore, be carried at cost.[80]

The presumption that the fair value of all such instruments can be reliably measured is a controversial one. In fact, in our experience, even professional valuation specialists can be reluctant to provide valuation services in respect of some complex instruments, explaining that any estimate is likely to be purely speculative. Nevertheless, the standard contains no relaxation from its requirement to determine an estimate of fair value in these circumstances.

Where a financial instrument contains an embedded derivative whose fair value cannot be reliably measured (see Chapter 15 at 5) the relaxation may apply to the hybrid (or combined) contract if it contains a link to an unquoted equity instrument.

Example 18.14:   Embedded derivative cannot be reliably measured

A company enters into a contract containing an embedded derivative that requires separation. However, the derivative cannot be reliably measured because it will be settled by delivery of an unquoted equity instrument whose fair value cannot be reliably measured. An example of such an instrument might be a convertible bond issued by a company whose shares are unquoted.

The entire combined contract is treated as a financial instrument held for trading (see Chapter 15 at 5). If the fair value of the combined instrument can be reliably measured, it is measured at fair value. However, the equity component of the combined instrument may be sufficiently significant to preclude the reliable estimation of its fair value. In this case, the combined contract is measured at cost less impairment.[81]

4.5   Demand deposits and similar liabilities

Financial institutions often manage risk on the assumption that demand liabilities paying no interest (such as many current accounts) or lower than market interest rates (some deposit accounts) will remain outstanding for long periods of time. Such assumptions are normally borne out by empirical evidence, including the historical behaviour of similar instruments. Accordingly, it might be argued that the fair value of such instruments is less than the demand amount (discounted if it cannot be called immediately). The price at which portfolios of such instruments are transferred in genuine third party transactions normally supports this assertion.

The IASB disagreed with this argument. Although reasonably predictable, at least at a point in time for a particular portfolio, the value to the financial institution of a customer choosing not to demand repayment at the earliest opportunity, thereby continuing to receive a low rate of interest, is not considered part of the contract that gives rise to the financial liability. Rather, it is value reflecting the 'economically irrational' behaviour of the customer. This value may be recognised as an intangible asset in certain circumstances[82] but should not be taken into account in measuring the financial liability. Recognition criteria for intangible assets (such as core deposit intangibles, i.e. the difference between the value of a portfolio of deposits measured under IAS 39 and the amount that would actually be transferred to acquire or assume the portfolio) are covered in Chapter 6 and Chapter 11.

It is explained that, in many cases, the market price observed for such financial liabilities is the price at which they are originated between the customer and the deposit-taker, i.e. the demand amount, and recognising such a liability at less than the demand amount would give rise to an immediate gain on origination, which the IASB believed inappropriate (see 4.7 below).[83] Accordingly, the standard states that the fair value of a financial liability with a demand feature is not less than the amount payable on demand, discounted from the first date that the amount could be required to be paid.[84]

It is not the direct effect of this decision that worries most banks – it is unlikely that any such institution would ever consider recognising an immediate profit on acceptance of a deposit – but it has serious implications for those wishing to use the provisions of the March 2004 macro-hedging amendments to IAS 39 (see Chapter 15 at 1.5 and Chapter 19 at 6).

4.6   Negative assets and liabilities

The standard helpfully points out that if the fair value of a financial asset falls below zero it becomes a financial liability (assuming it is measured at fair value).[85] The only real alternative would be treatment as a negative asset which would not be sensible. It does not go on to explain what happens if the fair value of a financial liability become positive, but it is safe to assume that it becomes a financial asset not a negative liability.

4.7   'Day 1' profits

Historically, dealers in financial instruments have recognised an amount of profit on (or just after) origination of an instrument – this is often referred to as recognising a 'day 1' profit. The profit effectively represents the margin that has been 'locked in' as a result of the differential between the price charged to a customer and prices available to the dealer in wholesale markets.

The practice of recognising day 1 profits continued under the previous version of IAS 39. Although instruments were initially recognised at cost, the guidance on determining fair value allowed remeasurement to a different fair value very shortly after origination (provided there was adequate supporting evidence), thereby resulting in the immediate recognition of profit. However, the revised standard has restricted the scope for recognising day 1 profits somewhat.

As noted at 4.1 above, if an instrument is quoted in an active market and the dealer has access to another, more favourable, active market in (virtually) the same instrument, the instrument's initial fair value is determined by reference to the more advantageous market (appropriately adjusted for any differences between the instruments, e.g. in credit risk). The use of the more advantageous price may give rise to a day 1 profit.

For instruments that are not quoted in an active market, the initial fair value should be determined by reference to a valuation technique, the starting point for which is the transaction price. Only if supported by prices of other transactions in the same instrument, or the use of a valuation technique in which all inputs include data from observable markets (see 4.2 above), can an immediate profit be recognised. The IASB concluded that these conditions were necessary and sufficient to provide reasonable assurance that fair value was actually different to the transaction price for the purpose of recognising day 1 profits or losses. In other cases, the transaction price is deemed to give the best evidence of fair value, an approach that achieves convergence with US GAAP.[86]

A disingenuous reading of the requirements in the standard might suggest that, although recognition of a day 1 profit in these circumstances is prohibited, there is nothing to prevent the recognition of a profit on 'day 2'. This was obviously not the intention of the IASB and they have moved quickly to clear this up. In July 2004, an exposure draft was issued proposing amendments to IAS 39 to make this clear (see 9.1 below). Consequently, locked in profits will emerge over the life of the instrument, although precisely how they should emerge is not at all clear.

Given the emphasis that the standard now puts on active market quotes, comparing the following two situations can give rise to a slightly counter-intuitive outcome.

- Where an instrument is quoted in an active market, it may be measured by reference to a similar (but not identical) instrument that is quoted in a different active market.

- However, where the instrument is not quoted in an active market, it is the inactive market in which it is originated that is deemed to provide the most reliable information as to the instrument's fair value. This is the case even if a similar (but not identical) instrument *is* quoted in an active market.

In voting against publication of the revised standard, one of the IASB members disagreed with the principle of using a market in which an instrument has not been traded, noting that there were many related issues that needed addressing.[87] We tend to agree.

Another situation in which day 1 profits (or losses) appear to arise is on the acquisition of a large holding of instruments that are quoted in an active market. Consider the following extension of Example 18.12 at 4.1 above.

Example 18.15: Valuing publicly quoted shares at other than market price

Company Z acquires from Company X its 15% holding in the share capital of Company Y for €105 when the quoted price in an active market is €100. It intends to hold the shares as a strategic investment and they are classified as available-for-sale.

It appears that there is no scope for overcoming the presumption that a published price quotation in an active market is the best estimate of fair value. Therefore, the shares should be recorded at €100 resulting in a loss on initial recognition of €5 per share. Moreover, because the loss arises on initial recognition, not remeasurement, of an available-for-sale asset, it appears that the loss should be recognised in the income statement.

We are not entirely convinced that this was the IASB's intention in these circumstances and, in practice, price volatility and the market's reaction to such a transaction may make it difficult to isolate and measure such a loss accurately. However, the above treatment appears to flow from the requirements of the standard, at least in theory.

4.8   Own credit risk

One of the more controversial aspects of the fair value option is that in determining the fair value of a financial liability, the credit risk associated with the instrument should be taken into account. This can result in the rather counter-intuitive result of a financially distressed entity reporting significant gains as the fair value of its debt deteriorates (and vice versa). For example, in its 2003 financial statements, Marconi disclosed the following information on the book and fair value of its financial liabilities.

Extract 18.3: *Marconi Corporation plc (2003)*

28   Financial instruments [extracts]

d   Fair value of financial assets and liabilities [extracts]

The book values and fair values of the Group's financial assets and liabilities at 31 March 2003 and 31 March 2002 were:

	Book value		Fair value	
	2003 **£million**	2002 £ million	**2003** **£ million**	2002 £ million
Short-term financial liabilities and current portion of long-term borrowings	**(4,745)**	(2,436)	**(1,068)**	(2,436)
Long-term borrowings and long-term financial liabilities	**(30)**	(2,208)	**(30)**	(707)

The fair values of the traded outstanding long-term borrowings ... have been determined by references available from the markets on which the instruments are traded. ... [O]ther fair values have been calculated by discounting cash flows at prevailing interest rates.

Had Marconi been accounting for its debt instruments under the fair value option, it would have measured these financial liabilities at approximately £1.1 billion at 31 March 2003, rather than £4.8 billion, and recorded a cumulative additional profit in its income statement of £3.7 billion. Based on the book and fair values disclosed above, approximately £2.2 billion of this additional profit would have been recorded in the year to 31 March 2003 alone.[88] This is, of course, an extreme example, but it illustrates the issue very well.

In the Basis for Conclusions to IAS 39, the IASB states that it considered responses to the exposure draft that suggested, in effect, that fair value should exclude the effects of changes in own credit risk.[89] However, the IASB decided that because financial statements are prepared on a going concern basis, credit risk affects the value at which liabilities could be repurchased or settled. Accordingly, the fair value of a financial liability does, in fact, reflect the credit risk relating to that liability. Therefore, it was decided to include credit risk relating to a financial liability in the fair value measurement of that liability for the following reasons:

- entities realise changes in fair value, including fair value attributable to own credit risk, for example, by renegotiating or repurchasing liabilities or by using derivatives;

- changes in credit risk affect the observed market price of a financial liability and hence its fair value;

- it is difficult from a practical standpoint to exclude changes in credit risk from an observed market price; and

- the fair value of a financial liability (i.e. the price of that liability in an exchange between a knowledgeable, willing buyer and a knowledgeable, willing seller) on initial recognition reflects the credit risk relating to that liability and the IASB believes that it is inappropriate to include credit risk in the initial fair value measurement of financial liabilities, but not subsequently.[90]

The IASB also considered whether the portion of the fair value of a financial liability attributable to changes in credit quality should be specifically disclosed, separately presented in the income statement, or separately presented in equity. It was decided that separately presenting or disclosing such changes would often not be practicable because it might not be possible to separate and measure reliably that part of the change in fair value. However, it was noted that disclosure of such information would be useful to users of financial statements and would help alleviate the concerns expressed. Therefore, it was decided to require disclosure of the changes in fair value of a financial liability that is not attributable to changes in a benchmark interest rate. The IASB believes this is a reasonable proxy for the change in fair value that is attributable to changes in the liability's credit risk, in particular when such changes are large, and will provide users with information with which to understand the profit or loss effect of such a change in credit risk.[91] In addition, entities are also required to disclose the difference between the carrying amount of such a liability and the amount it would be contractually required to pay at maturity to the holder of the obligation.[92] These disclosures are considered further in Chapter 20 at 5.4.

Finally, the IASB decided, in the revised standard, to clarify that this issue relates only to the credit risk of the financial liability, rather than the creditworthiness of the entity, because this was considered to describe more appropriately the objective of what is included in the fair value measurement of financial liabilities.[93] Of course the two are very closely related, but the deterioration of an issuer's creditworthiness may not, of itself, result in a corresponding deterioration in the credit risk of all of its liabilities. For example, the fair value of liabilities secured by valuable collateral, guaranteed by third parties or ranking ahead of virtually all other liabilities is generally unaffected by changes in the entity's creditworthiness.[94]

5   AMORTISED COST AND THE EFFECTIVE INTEREST METHOD

IAS 39 contains three key definitions relating to this method of accounting, which are set out below. They are broadly consistent with the previous version of IAS 39, although some changes have been made.

The *amortised cost* of a financial instrument is defined as the amount at which it was measured at initial recognition minus principal repayments, plus or minus the cumulative amortisation using the 'effective interest method' of any difference between that initial amount and the maturity amount, and minus any write-down (directly or through the use of an allowance account) for impairment or uncollectibility. The *effective interest method* is a method of calculating the amortised cost of a financial instrument (or group of instruments) and of allocating the interest income or expense over the relevant period.

The *effective interest rate* is the rate that exactly discounts estimated future cash payments or receipts over the expected life of the instrument or, when appropriate, a shorter period, to the instrument's net carrying amount. The calculation of the effective interest rate should include all fees and points paid or received between the contracting parties to the extent they are an integral part of the effective interest rate. The definition refers to IAS 18 for further guidance on what should and should not be considered integral (see Chapter 26). The calculation should also include transaction costs, and all other premiums or discounts, but not the effect of future credit losses.[95]

There is a presumption that the cash flows and the expected life of a group of similar financial instruments can be estimated reliably. However, in those rare cases when it is not possible to estimate reliably the cash flows or the expected life of a financial instrument (or group of instruments), the contractual cash flows over the full contractual term of the financial instrument (or group of instruments) should be used.[96]

During the improvements project, the IASB considered whether the effective interest rate for all financial instruments should be calculated on the basis of *estimated* cash flows, or whether *contractual* cash flows should be used for individual financial instruments with the use of estimated cash flows being restricted to groups of financial instruments. The position adopted was chosen because the IASB believes it achieves consistent application of the effective interest method throughout the standard. In the Basis for Conclusions, this treatment is stated to be consistent with the original IAS 39,[97] although, in our view, the position for individual instruments was never that clear.

The application guidance explains that, in some cases, financial assets are acquired at a deep discount that reflects incurred (as opposed to expected or future) credit losses. Therefore, in accordance with the definition above, *incurred* credit losses should be included in the estimated cash flows when computing the effective interest rate[98] (otherwise higher interest income than that inherent in the price paid for the instrument would be recognised). However, expected future defaults should not be included in estimates of cash flows because this would be a departure from the incurred loss model for impairment recognition.[99] Unfortunately, as set out at 6 below, the distinction between incurred, expected and future losses is not entirely clear.

The IASB acknowledged that it was not always clear how to interpret the previous requirement that the effective interest rate must be based on discounting cash flows through maturity or the next market-based repricing date. In particular, it was not always clear whether fees, transaction costs and other premiums or discounts should be amortised over the period until maturity or the period to the next market-based repricing date.[100] For consistency with the estimated cash flows approach, it was decided to clarify that the effective interest rate is calculated over the expected life of the instrument or, when applicable, a shorter period. A shorter period is used when the variable (e.g. interest rates) to which the fee, transaction costs, discount or premium relates is repriced to market rates before the expected maturity of the instrument. In such a case, the appropriate amortisation period is the period to the next such repricing date.[101] The application of this requirement is considered in more detail at 5.3 below.

5.1 Fixed interest, fixed term instruments

The effective interest method is most easily applied to instruments that have fixed payments and a fixed term. The following examples (as well as Example 18.8 at 3.2 above) illustrate this.

Example 18.16: Effective interest method –
amortisation of premium or discount on acquisition

At the end of 2005 a company purchases a debt instrument with five years remaining to maturity for its fair value of US$1,000 (including transaction costs). The instrument has a principal amount of US$1,250 and carries fixed interest of 4.7% payable annually (US$1,250 × 4.7% = US$59 per year). In order to allocate interest receipts and the initial discount over the term of the instrument at a constant rate on the carrying amount, it can be shown that interest needs to be accrued at the rate of 10% annually. The table below provides information about the amortised cost, interest income, and cash flows of the debt instrument in each reporting period.[102]

Year	(a) Amortised cost at start of year (US$)	(b = a × 10%) Interest income (US$)	(c) Cash flows (US$)	(d = a + b − c) Amortised cost at end of year (US$)
2006	1,000	100	59	1,041
2007	1,041	104	59	1,086
2008	1,086	109	59	1,136
2009	1,136	113	59	1,190
2010	1,190	119	1,250 + 59	–

Example 18.17:   Effective interest method – stepped interest rates

On 1 January 2005, Company A acquires a debt instrument for its fair value of £1,250 (including transaction costs). The principal amount is £1,250 which is repayable on 31 December 2010. The rate of interest is specified in the debt agreement as a percentage of the principal amount as follows: 6% in 2005 (£75), 8% in 2006 (£100), 10% in 2007 (£125), 12% in 2008 (£150) and 16.4% in 2009 (£205). It can be shown that the interest rate that exactly discounts the stream of future cash payments to maturity is 10%. In each period, the amortised cost at the beginning of the period is multiplied by the effective interest rate of 10% and added to the amortised cost. Any cash payments in the period are deducted from the resulting balance. Accordingly, the amortised cost, interest income and cash flows of the debt instrument in each period is as follows:

Year	(a) Amortised cost at start of year (£)	(b = a × 10%) Interest income (£)	(c) Cash flows (£)	(d = a + b − c) Amortised cost at end of year (£)
2005	1,250	125	75	1,300
2006	1,300	130	100	1,330
2007	1,330	133	125	1,338
2008	1,338	134	150	1,322
2009	1,322	133	1,250 + 205	–

It can be seen that, although the instrument is issued for £1,250 and has a maturity amount of £1,250, its amortised cost does not equal £1,250 at each balance sheet date.[103]

Methods for determining the effective interest rate for a given set of cash flows (as in the examples above) include simple trial and error techniques as well as more methodical iterative algorithms. Alternatively, many spreadsheet applications contain 'goal-seek' or similar functions that can also be used to derive effective interest rates.

5.2   Prepayment, call and similar options

The standard explains that when calculating the effective interest rate, all contractual terms of the financial instrument, for example prepayment, call and similar options, should be considered.[104] The following simple example illustrates how this principle is applied.

Example 18.18:   Effective interest rate – embedded prepayment options

Bank ABC originates 1,000 ten-year loans of £10,000 with 10% stated interest. Prepayments are probable and it is possible to reasonably estimate their timing and amount. ABC determines that the effective interest rate including loan origination fees received by ABC is 10.2% based on the *contractual* payment terms of the loans as the fees received reduce the initial carrying amount.

However, if the *expected* prepayments were considered, the effective interest rate would be 10.4% since the difference between the initial amount and maturity amount is amortised over a shorter period.

The effective interest rate that should be used by ABC for this portfolio is 10.4%.[105]

In the revised standard, the IASB added an explanation of how changes to estimates of payments or receipts (e.g. because of a reassessment of the extent to which prepayments will occur) should be dealt with. Previously it was unclear how to deal with these situations.

Where estimates change, the carrying amount of the financial instrument (or group of instruments) should be adjusted to reflect actual and revised estimated cash flows. More precisely, the carrying amount should be calculated by computing the present value of estimated future cash flows at the instrument's original effective interest rate. Any consequent adjustment should be recognised immediately in profit or loss.[106]

It was noted that this approach has the practical advantage that it does not require recalculation of the effective interest rate, i.e. an entity simply recognises the remaining cash flows at the original rate. Consequently, a possible conflict with the requirement to discount estimated cash flows using the original effective interest rate when assessing impairment is avoided.[107]

This requirement is illustrated in the following example taken from the implementation guidance to IAS 39.

Example 18.19: Effective interest method – revision of estimates

At the end of 2005 a company purchases a debt instrument with the same terms as the instrument in Example 18.16 at 5.1 above, except that the contract also specifies that the borrower has an option to prepay the instrument and that no penalty will be charged for prepayment (i.e. any prepayment will be made at the principal amount of US$1,250 or a proportion thereof).

At inception, there is an expectation that the borrower will not prepay and so the information about the instrument's effective interest rate, amortised cost, interest income and cash flows in each reporting period would be the same as that in Example 18.16.

On the first day of 2008 the investor revises its estimate of cash flows. It now expects that 50% of the principal will be prepaid at the end of 2008 and the remaining 50% at the end of 2010. Therefore, the opening balance of the debt instrument in 2008 is adjusted to an amount calculated by discounting the amounts expected to be received in 2008 and subsequent years using the original effective interest rate (10%). This results in the new opening balance in 2008 of US$1,138. The adjustment of US$52 (US$1,138 – US$1,086) is recorded in profit or loss in 2008.

The table below provides information about the amortised cost, interest income and cash flows as they would be adjusted taking into account this change in estimate.

Year	(a) Amortised cost at start of year (US$)	(b = a × 10%) Interest and similar income (US$)	(c) Cash flows (US$)	(d = a + b − c) Amortised cost at end of year (US$)
2006	1,000	100	59	1,041
2007	1,041	104	59	1,086
2008	1,086 + 52	114 + 52	625 + 59	568
2009	568	57	59	595
2010	595	60	625 + 59	–

This amortised cost calculation would be applicable whether the instruments were classified as held-to-maturity or available-for-sale.[108]

The application of these requirements to instruments with unusual embedded derivatives that are deemed closely related to the host (for example, an interest-only strip with an embedded prepayment option discussed in Chapter 15 at 5.1.3) can produce some surprising results. In some cases, applying the effective interest method to instruments such as these can give rise to a more volatile income statement than designating the instrument at fair value through profit or loss.

Although not explained in the standard, for hybrid instruments containing terms such as prepayment and similar options that are accounted for separately as embedded derivatives (see Chapter 15 at 5.1.3) those terms should not be taken into account in applying the effective interest method. It is only the host (not the hybrid) instrument that is being accounted for at amortised cost and the deemed terms of the host will not normally contain those terms. If a prepayment option, say, were accounted for as an embedded derivative at fair value, it would effectively be accounted for twice if it was also taken into account in determining the effective interest rate of the host.

In Example 18.19, which is based on the implementation guidance to IAS 39, it is not clear why the prepayment option has *not* been separately accounted for as an embedded derivative. The exercise price is US$1,250 and the option may be exercised at any time, yet the amortised cost is initially only US$1,000. Therefore, unless these two figures were considered approximately equal, the option would not be regarded as closely related to the host (see Chapter 15 at 5.1.3). We find it hard to believe that the IASB considers two numbers, one of which is 25% larger than the other, to be approximately equal. More likely, the requirements regarding embedded derivatives were overlooked when developing the above example as it is intended, primarily, to illustrate the new accounting requirements for estimate revisions.

This actually raises other questions with regards to the issue of whether prepayment and similar options should be regarded as closely related to the host instrument. In assessing whether the exercise price is approximately equal to the amortised cost at each exercise date, should one consider the amortised cost of the hybrid on the assumption the option is regarded as closely related, or the amortised cost of the host on the assumption that it is not? This conundrum is illustrated in the following simple example (which also provides further illustrations of the application of the effective interest method to instruments containing prepayment options).

Example 18.20: Embedded prepayment option

Company P borrows €1,000 on terms that require it to pay annual fixed rate coupons of €80 and €1,000 principal at the end of ten years. The terms of the instrument also allow P to redeem the debt after seven years by paying the principal of €1,000 and a penalty of €100.

The debt instrument can be considered to comprise the following two components:

- a host debt instrument requiring ten annual payments of €80 followed be a €1,000 payment of principal; and
- an embedded prepayment option, exercisable only at the end of seven years with an exercise price of €1,100.

If, at inception, the prepayment option was expected *not* to be exercised, the effective interest rate of the *hybrid* would be 8%. This is the rate that would discount the expected cash flows of €80 per year for ten years plus €1,000 at the end of ten years to the initial carrying amount of €1,000. The table below provides information about the amortised cost, interest income and cash flows using this assumption.

Year	(a) Amortised cost at start of year (€)	(b = a × 8%) Interest and similar income (€)	(c) Cash flows (€)	(d = a + b − c) Amortised cost at end of year (€)
1	1,000	80	80	1,000
2	1,000	80	80	1,000
3	1,000	80	80	1,000
4	1,000	80	80	1,000
5	1,000	80	80	1,000
6	1,000	80	80	1,000
7	1,000	80	80	1,000
8	1,000	80	80	1,000
9	1,000	80	80	1,000
10	1,000	80	80 + 1,000	−

However if, at the outset, the option *was* expected to be exercised, the effective interest rate of the *hybrid* would be 9.08% as this is the rate that discounts the expected cash flows of €80 per year for seven years, plus €1,100 at the end of seven years, to the initial carrying amount of €1,000. The table below provides information about the amortised cost, interest income and cash flows using this alternative assumption.

Year	(a) Amortised cost at start of year (€)	(b = a × 9.08%) Interest and similar income (€)	(c) Cash flows (€)	(d = a + b − c) Amortised cost at end of year (€)
1	1,000	91	80	1,011
2	1,011	92	80	1,023
3	1,023	93	80	1,036
4	1,036	94	80	1,050
5	1,050	95	80	1,065
6	1,065	97	80	1,082
7	1,082	98	80 + 1,100	−

On the face of it, therefore, comparing the amortised cost of the hybrid with the exercise price of the option at the date it could be exercised suggests the prepayment option might be considered closely related if it was likely to be exercised but not if exercise was unlikely.

However, even this is not the whole story. If the option (on inception) was not expected to be exercised, but at a later date exercise became likely, the amortised cost carrying amount would be revised so that it represented the expected future cash flows discounted at the original effective interest rate. For example, if at the end of Year 5, it became likely that the option would be exercised, the carrying amount would be revised so that it represented €80 discounted for one year at 8% plus €1,180 discounted for two years at 8% – in other words, €1,086 rather than €1,065. The difference of €21 would be recognised in profit or loss immediately and the amortised cost carrying amount would subsequently accrete so that it represented the final cash outflow (option exercise price of €1,100 plus coupon of €80) at the end of Year 7. So even in this situation there is an argument to suggest that the prepayment option should not be separated as the exercise price will always equal the amortised cost (at least to the extent that the option is exercised).

If the assessment was performed based on the amortised cost of the *host*, the initial fair value of the prepayment option is needed. From P's perspective it will have a positive fair value and for the purpose of this example this is assumed to be €50. Therefore, the initial value of the host will be €1,050 (€1,000 + €50). The effective interest rate of the host can be demonstrated to be 7.28% and the amortised cost each year would be as follows:

Year	(a) Amortised cost at start of year (€)	(b = a × 7.28%) Interest and similar income (€)	(c) Cash flows (€)	(d = a + b − c) Amortised cost at end of year (€)
1	1,050	76	80	1,046
2	1,046	76	80	1,042
3	1,042	76	80	1,038
4	1,038	76	80	1,034
5	1,034	75	80	1,029
6	1,029	75	80	1,024
7	1,024	75	80	1,019
8	1,019	74	80	1,013
9	1,013	74	80	1,007
10	1,007	73	80 + 1,000	–

In this case, the amortised cost at the date the option can be exercised is €1,019. Comparing this with the exercise price of €1,100 suggests the option may not be considered closely related in this case.

In fact if this analysis were applied to prepayment options for which there was no associated penalty (i.e. the instrument would always be redeemed at its principal amount), separating the embedded derivative in this way would artificially create a difference between the amortised cost of the *host* and the exercise price. However, we are entirely unconvinced it would be appropriate to separate an embedded derivative from such a simple instrument.

Unfortunately, the standard is silent on these issues and preparers of accounts will be required to exercise judgment as to the most appropriate method to use in their individual circumstances.

5.3   Floating rate instruments

Applying the general requirements for the effective interest method to a floating rate instrument could produce some surprising results, as shown in the following example.

Example 18.21:   Effective interest method – variable rate loan

At the start of July 2005, Company G originates a floating rate debt instrument. Its fair value is equal to its principal amount of $1,000 and no transaction costs are incurred. The instrument pays, in arrears at the end of June, a variable rate coupon, determined by reference to 12 month LIBOR at the start of each previous July. It has a term of five years and is repayable at its principal amount at the end of June 2010.

On origination, 12 month LIBOR is 5% and this establishes the first payment, to be made in June 2006, at $50. Based on a market-derived yield curve, G estimates that the subsequent floating rate payments will be $60, $70, $80 and $90 (yield curve rises steeply). It can be demonstrated that the interest rate that exactly discounts these estimated coupon payments and the $1,000 principal at maturity to the current carrying amount of $1,000 is 6.87% (the definition does not acknowledge the possibility of more than one effective interest rate that would be reflective of a yield curve that is not flat).

In this situation, recognising interest at 6.87% in the first year would seem entirely counter-intuitive and is inconsistent with traditional notions of interest recognition for floating rate instruments, something even the IASB agrees with. Therefore the standard contains additional guidance for applying the effective interest method to floating rate instruments.

Normally, the effective interest rate remains constant over the life of an instrument. However, for floating rate instruments, it is stated that periodic re-estimation of cash flows to reflect movements in market interest rates *does* alter the effective interest rate. The standard goes on to explain that where such an instrument is initially recognised at an amount equal to the principal repayable on maturity, re-estimating the future interest payments normally has no significant effect on the carrying amount of the instrument.[109]

Further, whilst payments, receipts, discounts and premiums included in the effective interest method calculation are normally amortised over the expected life of the instrument, there may be situations when they are amortised over a shorter period (see 5 above). This will be the case when the variable to which they relate reprices to market rates before the instrument's expected maturity. In such cases, the appropriate amortisation period is to the next repricing date.[110]

For example, if a premium or discount on a floating rate instrument reflects interest that has accrued since interest was last paid, or changes in market rates since the floating interest rate was reset to market rates, it will be amortised to the next date when the interest rate is reset to market rates. If, however, it results from a change in the credit spread over the floating rate specified in the instrument, or other variables that are not reset to market rates, it is amortised over the expected life of the instrument.[111]

The following examples illustrate the requirements of applying a discount resulting from a credit downgrade and accrued interest.

Example 18.22: Effective interest method –
amortisation of discount arising from credit downgrade

A twenty-year bond is issued at £100, has a principal amount of £100, and requires quarterly interest payments equal to current three-month LIBOR plus 1% over the life of the instrument. The interest rate reflects the market-based required rate of return associated with the bond issue at issuance. Subsequent to issuance, the credit quality of the bond deteriorates resulting in a rating downgrade. It therefore trades at a discount, although there is no objective evidence of impairment. Company A purchases the bond for £95 and classifies it as held-to-maturity.

The discount of £5 is amortised to income over the period to the maturity of the bond and not to the next date interest rate payments are reset as it results from a change in credit spreads.[112]

Example 18.23:   Effective interest method –
amortisation of discount arising from accrued interest

At the start of November 2005, Company P acquires the bond issued by Company G in Example 18.21 above – current interest rates have not changed since the end of July 2005 and G's credit risk has not changed since origination so P pays $1,016.

The premium of $16 paid by P relates to interest accrued since the last reset date and so is amortised to income over the period to the next repricing date, June 2006; further, the $50 cash flow received at the end of June 2006 is also 'amortised' over this period.

Consequently, for the eight months ended June 2006, P will record interest of $34 ($50 – $16), which is also the approximate equivalent of eight months interest at current rates (5%) earned on P's initial investment.

This treatment is consistent with the requirements of IAS 18 that apply when unpaid interest has accrued before the acquisition of an interest-bearing investment. In such cases, it is explained (in more traditional terms) that the subsequent receipt of interest should be allocated between pre-acquisition and post-acquisition periods and only the post-acquisition portion should be recognised as revenue.[113] In fact for most floating rate instruments, it will often be appropriate to apply a simplistic method of accounting – for example, by amortising transaction costs on a straight line basis over the life of the instrument combined with a simple time apportionment approach to the floating rate coupons.

5.4   Perpetual debt instruments

Where perpetual debt instruments are originated and interest is paid either at a fixed or variable rate, the amortised cost (the present value of the stream of future cash payments discounted at the effective interest rate) equals the principal amount in each period and the difference between the initial consideration and zero ('the maturity amount') is not amortised.[114]

However, where the stated rate of interest on perpetual debt decreases over time, some or all of the interest payments are, from an economic perspective, repayments of the principal amount as illustrated in the following example.[115]

Example 18.24:   Amortised cost – perpetual debt with decreasing interest rate

On 1 January 2005 Company A subscribes £1,000 for a debt instrument which yields 25% interest for the first five years and 0% in subsequent periods. The funds are transferred directly to the issuer and it is classified as an originated loan. It can be determined that the effective yield is 7.9% and the amortised cost is shown in the table below.[116]

Year	(a) Amortised cost at start of year (£)	(b = a × 7.9%) Interest income (£)	(c) Cash flows (£)	(d = a + b − c) Amortised cost at end of year (£)
2005	1,000	79	250	829
2006	829	66	250	645
2007	645	51	250	446
2008	446	36	250	232
2009	232	18	250	–
2010	–	–	–	–

6 IMPAIRMENT

The impairment requirements of IAS 39 might appear somewhat over-engineered for what is a relative simple subject for many entities, i.e. making appropriate provisions for bad and doubtful debts. The reason for this complexity is that IAS 39 is designed for use by all entities, including financial institutions for which impairment losses are often highly material. Accordingly, the IASB has tried to lay down clear guidelines as to when impairment losses should (and should not) be recognised in order to ensure that a consistent approach is taken both from period to period for individual entities and from entity to entity.

The topic is one in which different, and hard to reconcile, views are held by many, especially those setting the standards. This manifested itself under the original standard when the IGC attempted to issue guidance interpreting the original impairment requirements. A number of draft Q&A were issued but never finalised and it became apparent that the IASB would need to address the topic as part of its improvements project. The revised approach set out in the June 2002 exposure draft did not convince all IASB members and one even felt the need to formally dissent on the subject of impairment.[117] The proposals in the exposure draft were amended somewhat before the revised standard was published, but this time three IASB members, citing impairment as an area of disagreement, voted against publication.[118]

The two most controversial issues related to impairment are (a) whether an individual asset that has been reviewed for impairment and found not to be impaired can then be included in a portfolio of assets that are subject to a collective impairment assessment and (b) how to deal with losses arising on available-for-sale equity instruments. These are covered in the remainder of this section.

Further, in the revised standard, the IASB explains that the accounting model proposed is based on 'incurred losses' (rather than, say, expected losses and certainly not on future losses). It believes that such a model, which does not take account of future events or transactions, is more consistent with an amortised cost basis of accounting.[119] Accordingly, lengthy guidance explaining what is meant by 'incurred' is included in the revised standard. Whether this achieves what was intended remains to be seen as the detailed requirements may potentially be subject to somewhat different interpretations.

6.1 Impairment reviews

All financial assets, except for those measured at fair value through profit or loss, are subject to review for impairment.[120] Assessments should be made at each balance sheet date as to whether there is any objective evidence that a financial asset or group of assets is impaired. If such evidence exists, the requirements set out at 6.2 to 6.4 below should be followed to determine the amount of any impairment loss.[121]

A financial asset or a group of assets is impaired (and impairment losses are incurred) if, and only if, there is objective evidence of impairment as a result of one or more events that occurred after initial recognition (a 'loss event') and that loss event (or events) has an impact on the estimated future cash flows of the financial asset or group of assets that can be reliably estimated.[122]

It may not be possible to identify a single, discrete event that caused the impairment; rather, the combined effect of several events may have caused the impairment. However, losses expected as a result of future events, no matter how likely, are not recognised.[123] Similarly, an impairment loss may not be recognised at the time an asset is originated (i.e. before a loss event can have occurred) as illustrated in the following example.[124]

Example 18.25: Immediate recognition of impairment

Bank B lends $1,000 to Customer M. Based on historical experience, B expects that 1% of the principal amount of loans given will not be collected, but an immediate impairment loss of $10 cannot be recognised.[125]

Objective evidence that a financial asset or group of assets is impaired includes observable data that comes to the attention of the holder about the following loss events:

- significant financial difficulty of the issuer or obligor;
- breach of contract, such as a default or delinquency in interest or principal payments;
- the lender, for economic or legal reasons relating to the borrower's financial difficulty, granting to the borrower a concession that would not otherwise be considered;
- it becoming probable that the borrower will enter bankruptcy or other financial reorganisation;
- the disappearance of an active market for that asset because of financial difficulties (but not simply because the asset is no longer publicly traded[126]); or
- observable data indicating that there is a measurable decrease in the estimated future cash flows from a group of financial assets since initial recognition, although the decrease cannot yet be identified with the individual assets in the group, including:
  - adverse changes in the payment status of borrowers in the group (e.g. an increased number of delayed payments or an increased number of credit card borrowers who have reached their credit limit and are paying the minimum monthly amount); or
  - national or local economic conditions that correlate with defaults on the assets in the group (e.g. an increase in the unemployment rate in the geographical area of the borrowers, a decrease in property prices for mortgages in the relevant area, a decrease in oil prices for loan assets to oil producers, or adverse changes in industry conditions that affect the borrowers in the group).[127]

A downgrade of an entity's credit rating is not, of itself, evidence of impairment, although it may be when considered with other available information.[128] Other factors that would be considered in determining whether an impairment has been incurred include information about the debtors' or issuers' liquidity, solvency and business and financial risk exposures, levels of and trends in delinquencies for similar financial assets, national and local economic trends and conditions, and the fair value of collateral and guarantees.[129] A decline in the fair value of a financial asset below its cost or amortised cost is not necessarily evidence of impairment – for example, the fair value of a debt instrument may decline only from an increase in the risk-free interest rate.[130] Therefore, it is possible that an 'available-for-sale reserve' in equity can be negative.

The previous version of the standard did not include guidance about impairment indicators that are specific to investments in equity instruments and consequently questions had been raised about when, in practice, such investments become impaired.[131] The IASB acknowledged that, for marketable equity investments, any impairment trigger other than a decline in fair value below cost is likely to be arbitrary to some extent. If markets are reasonably efficient, today's market price is the best estimate of the discounted value of the future market price. However, it was considered important to provide guidance to address the questions raised in practice.[132]

Accordingly, the revised standard explains that the following are objective evidence of impairment of an equity investment:

- information about significant changes with an adverse effect that have taken place in the technological, market, economic or legal environment in which the issuer operates, and indicates that the cost of the investment in the equity instrument may not be recovered; and

- a significant or prolonged decline in the fair value of an investment in such an instrument below its cost.[133]

  The meaning of the terms 'significant' and 'prolonged' are not defined or explained further. For example, if the price of Company A's shares is significantly more volatile than that of shares in Company B, can a decline of, say, 10% be significant for the purposes of investments in B but not in A? Clearly judgment will be necessary in applying this part of the standard, but any revaluation below cost is likely to be viewed with some suspicion.

These triggers apply in addition to those specified above, which focus on the assessment of impairment in debt instruments.[134]

Sometimes, the observable data required to estimate an impairment loss may be limited, or no longer fully relevant to current circumstances, for example when a borrower is in financial difficulties and there are few available historical data relating to similar borrowers. In such cases, judgement and experience should be used to estimate the amount of any impairment loss and to adjust observable data for a group of financial assets to reflect current circumstances. The fact that an impairment loss is difficult to measure is not a reason for not recognising a loss that has been incurred. The use of reasonable estimates is an essential part of the preparation of financial statements and does not undermine their reliability.[135]

6.2   Financial assets carried at amortised cost

6.2.1   *Individual and collective assessments*

The standard requires that impairment assessments should be carried out as follows:

- for assets that are individually significant, assessment should be made on an individual basis;

- other assets may also be assessed individually, although such an assessment is not necessarily required;

- assets that have been individually assessed, but for which there is no objective evidence of impairment, should be included within a group of assets with similar credit risk characteristics and collectively assessed for impairment;

- assets that are individually assessed for impairment and for which an impairment loss is (or continues to be) recognised cannot be subject to a collective impairment assessment; and

- any other assets, i.e. those that have not been individually assessed, should also be the subject of a collective assessment.[136]

The above requirements might be read as allowing an asset that is not individually significant, but known to be impaired, to be included in a collective assessment thereby avoiding the recognition of a loss if, say, the fair value of other assets in the group exceed their amortised cost. However, the implementation guidance clearly states that in such a case the impairment loss should be recognised.[137]

As noted at 6 above, the ability to include individual assets that have been reviewed for impairment in a collective assessment is a controversial one and two IASB members cited this as a reason for them voting against publication of the revised standard.[138] The Basis for Conclusions to the revised standard contains an extensive discussion of the arguments for and against the proposal[139] but it essentially boils down to whether or not one believes a loan can actually be impaired even if a review has not identified it as such.

If, in performing an individual review, the lender had access to all relevant information about the loan and the borrower, it might seem quite reasonable to conclude that there is no need to perform an additional collective review. However, in practice, not all information is going to be readily available on a timely basis, and any individual assessment is likely to be incomplete. Therefore, in our view, it is entirely appropriate to require an additional collective review.

6.2.2   *Measurement – general requirements*

If there is objective evidence that an impairment loss has been incurred on loans and receivables or held-to-maturity investments, that loss should be measured as the difference between the asset's carrying amount and the present value of estimated future cash flows. Those cash flows, which should exclude future credit losses that have not been incurred, should be discounted at the original effective interest rate of the financial asset, i.e. the effective interest rate computed at initial recognition.[140] The original effective interest rate is used because discounting at the current market interest rate would, in effect, impose fair-value measurement on assets that would otherwise be measured at amortised cost.[141]

The standard allows the carrying amount of an impaired asset to be reduced, either directly or through use of an allowance account, but emphasises that the loss should always be recognised in profit or loss.[142]

If the terms of an instrument are renegotiated or otherwise modified because of the borrower's financial difficulties, impairment should be measured using the original effective interest rate before the modification of terms. For variable rate assets, the discount rate for measuring the recoverable amount is the current effective interest rate(s) determined under the contract. As a practical expedient, impairment may be measured based on an instrument's fair value using an observable market price.[143] Previously, this concession was only allowed for floating rate assets,[144] but under the revised standard it may be used for fixed rate assets too. There is little conceptual merit in this, but it aligns IAS 39 more closely with US GAAP.[145]

The implementation guidance makes it clear that recognition of impairment losses in excess of those that are determined based on objective evidence (either at an individual asset or collective group level) is not permitted.[146]

These basic principles are illustrated in the following example.

Example 18.26: Impairment – changes in amount or timing of payments

A bank is concerned that, because of financial difficulties, five customers, Companies A to E, will not be able to make all principal and interest payments due on originated loans in a timely manner. It negotiates a restructuring of the loans and expects the customers will meet their restructured obligations. The restructured terms are as follows:

- A will pay the full principal amount of the original loan five years after the original due date, but none of the interest due under the original terms.

- B will pay the full principal amount of the original loan on the original due date, but none of the interest due under the original terms.

- C will pay the full principal amount of the original loan on the original due date but with interest at a lower interest rate than the interest rate inherent in the original loan.

- D will pay the full principal amount of the original loan five years after the original due date and all interest accrued during the original loan term, but no interest for the extended term.

- E will pay the full principal amount of the original loan five years after the original due date and all interest, including interest on all outstanding amounts for both the original term of the loan and the extended term.

An impairment loss has been incurred if there is objective evidence of impairment – this is assumed to be the case here because of the customers' financial difficulties. The amount of the impairment loss for a loan measured at amortised cost is the difference between the loan's carrying amount and the present value of future principal and interest payments, discounted at the loan's original effective interest rate.

For A to D, the present value of the future principal and interest payments discounted at the loan's original effective interest rate will be lower than the carrying amount of the loan. Therefore an impairment loss is recognised in those cases. For E, even though the timing of payments has changed, the bank will receive interest on interest, so that the present value of the future principal and interest payments, discounted at the loan's original effective interest rate, will equal the carrying amount of the loan. Therefore, there is no impairment loss. However, this fact pattern is unlikely given Company E's financial difficulties.[147]

Consistent with the initial measurement requirements (see 2.2 above), cash flows relating to short-term receivables are not discounted if the effect of discounting is immaterial.[148] This does not mean that such instruments are not, as a matter of principle, discounted, as illustrated in the following example.

Example 18.27:   Impairment of short-term receivable

A construction company, K, agrees to build a new stadium for a professional football club, L. The project takes approximately six months and payment of €10 million is due six weeks after completion. On completion, K has recognised revenue and a corresponding receivable of €10 million because the effect of discounting at the current annualised rate of 5% is immaterial.

Shortly after completion, it becomes apparent that L is in financial difficulties and is unlikely to be able to settle the €10 million debt. In order to avoid formal insolvency proceedings, L attempts to restructure its financial obligations and offers to pay K €1 million per year for the next 10 years. Because it believes this arrangement appears to offer the best prospects for the recovery of its debt, K accepts.

On the face of it (and assuming no defaults on the rescheduled debt are expected), it might be argued that K need not recognise an impairment loss because it will receive all of the money owed and the debt's original effective interest rate was 0%. However, the original receivable was, in principle, discounted – it is just that the effects of discounting were not reflected in the financial statements as they were not material. Therefore, the effect of discounting the rescheduled payments at 5% per annum (approximately €2.28 million) should be recognised as an impairment loss.

It is common practice for companies to determine bad debt provisions using a provisioning matrix or similar formula based on the number of days a loan or debt is overdue, e.g. 0% if less than 90 days, 20% if 90 to 180 days, 50% if 180 to 365 days and 100% if more than 365 days overdue. This will be acceptable only if the formula can be demonstrated to produce an estimate sufficiently close to one determined under the methodology specified in IAS 39.[149]

In measuring the impairment of a collateralised or secured loan, the cash flows used should reflect those that may result from foreclosure less costs for obtaining and selling the collateral, whether or not foreclosure is probable.[150] Previously, such cash flows would only be taken into account if foreclosure was probable.[151] However, even if foreclosure is probable, collateral does not generally meet the recognition criteria until it is transferred to the lender. Therefore, it should not normally be recognised as a separate asset.[152]

To a lender, guarantees provided by a third (sometimes related) party such as a parent, other shareholder or fellow subsidiary, are little different to collateral – they provide a source of funds in the event that the debtor defaults. In the previous implementation guidance it was made clear that guarantees should be taken into account in determining the amount of an impairment loss.[153] Unfortunately, this guidance has been removed from the revised standard and, on a pure technical level, it is not clear that the accounting treatment should remain the same.

The guarantee is clearly a financial instrument (see Chapter 15 at 2.2.3). Based on the analysis in Chapter 15 at 6, it will normally be considered a separate financial instrument, even if it cannot be transferred independently from the loan. This is because there will almost certainly be a substantive business purpose for structuring the arrangement in this way, i.e. to reduce the lender's exposure to default. The guarantee is likely to satisfy the definition of an insurance contract in IFRS 4[154] but will be excluded from the scope of that standard because it is a direct insurance contract not held by a cedant.[155] (A cedant is an insurer that is the policyholder under a reinsurance contract.[156]) If the guarantee satisfies the definition of an insurance contract in IFRS 4 it is outside the scope of IAS 39[157] irrespective of whether it is within the scope of IFRS 4 (see Chapter 15 at 3.3). Therefore it is hard to avoid the conclusion that the guarantee is a contingent asset within the scope of IAS 37 because it is not 'covered' by another standard[158] (see Chapter 25 at 2.2.1 B).

What this means is that the guarantee can only be recognised as an asset when it is 'virtually certain' that a recovery will be made. In conceptual terms this seems a more onerous test than that for recognising an impairment loss on the associated loan asset. Therefore, it might seem necessary to recognise an impairment loss on the asset (that would be fully recovered under the guarantee) but without being able to recognise an offsetting recovery from the guarantee. This seems entirely wrong.

There is more than one counter-argument to this analysis. For example, it might be considered that the guarantee and the loan should be accounted for as a single 'synthetic' instrument, irrespective of what is said in Chapter 15 at 6, especially where the two parties are related. A degree of support for this treatment can be found in the Basis for Conclusions to IAS 39 where it is stated that 'the fair value of liabilities ... guaranteed by third parties ... is generally unaffected by changes in the entity's creditworthiness'.[159] This suggests that the IASB considers a third party guarantee of a borrowing to be an integral part of the borrowing arrangement rather than a separate instrument. Further, where the guarantor is a member of the same group as the borrower, IAS 32 requires both elements of the transaction to be considered together when determining the appropriate classification of the instrument from the point of view of the group's consolidated financial statements (see Chapter 17 at 3.6).

Even if it is considered that IAS 37 should apply to the guarantee, some might argue that it is more appropriate to characterise it as a 'reimbursement' in respect of the impairment loss, rather than as a standalone contingent asset. As set out in Chapter 25 at 4.4, a reimbursement is recognised as an asset when it is virtually certain that the reimbursement will be received if the obligation for which a provision has been established is settled. By analogy, therefore, the guarantee would be recognised as an asset to the extent it is virtually certain a recovery could be made if the lender suffered the impairment loss on the loan.

Unless this issue is resolved as part of the IASB's project on financial guarantees (which seems unlikely, as that is focused on the accounting treatment of the guarantor), in practice entities are likely to continue using their current accounting policies and treat guarantees as part of a single (synthetic) asset.

6.2.3   Measurement – detailed requirements

The revised standard contains a significant amount of detailed application guidance on the processes to be used for the assessment and calculation of impairment losses within groups of financial assets carried at amortised cost. In practice, this will be of limited relevance to entities that are determining a bad debt provision in respect of a portfolio of short-term trade receivables. However, for banks and other financial institutions with significant portfolios of loans and receivables, these detailed requirements will be highly relevant and could have a major impact on the way that loan impairments are assessed. This guidance might also be more relevant for entities providing goods or services on deferred settlement terms, such as retailers operating their own store-cards.

Although the substance of the application guidance is reproduced below, its application in practice is proving problematic. We are aware, for example, of some industry bodies that are attempting to produce further interpretative guidance to explain how their members should apply the application guidance.

The guidance explains that the process for estimating impairment should consider all credit exposures, not only those of low credit quality. For example, if an internal credit grading system is used, all credit grades should be considered, not only those reflecting a severe credit deterioration.[160] In other words, the possibility of an impairment existing in a portfolio of high quality assets that contain a low risk of default should not be ignored.

Whatever process is used to estimate an impairment loss, it may produce either a single amount or a range of possible amounts. In the latter case, the best estimate within the range should be recognised as the impairment loss. This estimate should take into account all relevant information about known conditions that existed at the balance sheet date. The standard cross-refers to IAS 37 for guidance on selecting the best estimate in a range of possible outcomes (see Chapter 25 at 4.1).[161]

When performing a collective evaluation of impairment, assets should be grouped on the basis of similar credit risk characteristics that are indicative of the debtors' ability to settle according to the contractual terms of the instruments concerned. For example, this may be done on the basis of a credit risk evaluation or grading process that considers some or all of the following characteristics depending on their relevance: asset type, industry, geographical location, collateral type, past-due status as well as other factors.[162]

It is stated that loss probabilities and other loss statistics differ at a group level between (a) assets that have been individually evaluated for impairment and found not to be impaired, and (b) assets that have not been individually evaluated for impairment, with the result that a different amount of impairment may be required.[163] In practice, the extent of the difference in approach to these groups will depend on the quality of the individual assessments – i.e. the less detailed or accurate they are, the less the loss probabilities should differ from those not individually assessed.

Further, it is explained that if an entity does not have a group of assets with similar risk characteristics, it should not make any additional assessment over and above that performed at an individual level.[164] It is this situation that the two dissenting IASB members found hard to accept. If one entity owned 50% of a loan asset for which there was no evidence of impairment when assessed on an individual basis, but it owned no similar assets, then it would recognise no impairment loss. However, if another entity owned the other 50% of the loan asset and also owned a number of similar assets, that entity may end up recognising an impairment loss in respect of its identical asset.[165]

This anomaly may be rationalised in a number of ways. For example, if a company owned only one significant asset, rather than a group of similar assets, it is quite likely to assess impairment of that asset in a more detailed manner than a company with a group of similar assets. Also, this situation is not dissimilar to the treatment of warranty claims under IAS 37. If there was a small probability, say 1%, of a warranty claim arising on each sale made, a company that had sold one unit would not normally recognise a provision. However, a company that had sold thousands of identical units would almost certainly recognise a provision.

It is explained that impairment losses recognised on a group basis represent an interim step pending the identification of impairment losses on individual assets in the group. Accordingly, as soon as information is available that specifically identifies losses on individually impaired assets, those assets should be removed from the group.[166]

Estimates of future cash flows for a group of financial assets should be based on historical loss experience for assets with credit risk characteristics similar to those in the group. Entities that have no, or insufficient, entity-specific loss experience, should use peer group experience for comparable groups of assets. Historical loss experience should be adjusted on the basis of current observable data to reflect the effects of current conditions that did not affect the period on which the historical loss experience is based, and to remove the effects of conditions in the historical period that do not exist currently. Estimates of changes in future cash flows should reflect, and be directionally consistent with, changes in related observable data from period to period (such as changes in unemployment rates, property prices, commodity prices, payment status or other factors that are indicative of incurred losses in the group and their magnitude). The methodology and assumptions used for estimating future cash flows should be reviewed regularly to reduce any differences between loss estimates and actual loss experience.[167]

As an example of this approach, historical experience may demonstrate that one of the main causes of default on credit card loans is the death of the borrower. Although the death rate may be unchanged since the previous year, some of the group of borrowers could have died in the year. This would indicate that an impairment loss has occurred, even if it was not possible to identify which specific borrowers had died at the year-end, and it would be appropriate for an impairment loss to be recognised for these 'incurred but not reported' losses. However, it would not be appropriate to recognise an impairment loss for deaths that are expected to occur in a future period. In that case the necessary loss event (the death of the borrower) has not yet occurred.[168]

When using historical loss rates in estimating future cash flows, it is important that information about historical loss rates is applied to groups that are defined in a manner consistent with the groups for which the historical loss rates were observed. Therefore, the method used should enable each group to be associated with information about past loss experience in groups of assets with similar credit risk characteristics and relevant observable data that reflect current conditions.[169]

Formula-based approaches or statistical methods may be used to determine impairment losses in a group of financial assets (e.g. for smaller balance loans) as long as they are consistent with the general requirements of the standard. Therefore any model used should incorporate the effect of the time value of money, consider the cash flows for all of the remaining life of an asset (not only the next year), consider the age of the loans within the portfolio and not give rise to an impairment loss on initial recognition.[170]

6.2.4   Impairment of assets subject to hedges

Where an asset with fixed interest rate payments is hedged against the exposure to interest rate risk by a receive-variable, pay-fixed interest rate swap, the carrying amount of the asset will include an adjustment for fair value changes attributable to movements in interest rates (see Chapter 19 at 4.1.1). As a result, in accounting for the asset, the original effective interest rate and amortised cost of the loan are adjusted to take into account these recognised fair value changes and the adjusted effective interest rate is calculated using the adjusted carrying amount of the loan.[171]

In order to take account of the hedge effects on the carrying amount of the asset, any impairment loss on the hedged loan should be calculated as the difference between its carrying amount *after* adjustment for fair value changes attributable to the risk being hedged and the expected future cash flows of the loan discounted at the *adjusted* effective interest rate.[172]

When a loan is included in a portfolio hedge of interest rate risk (see Chapter 19 at 6) the change in the fair value of the hedged portfolio should be allocated to the loans (or groups of similar loans) being assessed for impairment on a systematic and rational basis.[173]

6.2.5   Reversal of impairment losses

If, in a subsequent period, the amount of the impairment or bad debt loss decreases and the decrease can be objectively related to an event occurring after the write-down (such as an improvement in the debtor's credit rating), the previously recognised impairment loss should be reversed, either directly or by adjusting an allowance account. The reversal should not result in a carrying amount of the asset that exceeds what its amortised cost would have been at the date of reversal, had the impairment not been recognised. The amount of the reversal should be recognised in the income statement.[174]

6.3 Available-for-sale assets

When a decline in the fair value of an available-for-sale asset has been recognised directly in equity and there is objective evidence that the asset is impaired (see 6.1 above), the cumulative loss in equity should be recycled into profit or loss even though the asset has not been derecognised.[175] The amount of the loss that should be recycled is the difference between its acquisition cost (net of any principal repayment and amortisation for assets measured using the effective interest method) and current fair value, less any impairment loss on that asset previously recognised in profit or loss.[176]

For non-monetary assets, such as equity instruments, the cumulative net loss included in equity will include any portion attributable to foreign currency changes. It follows that this element of the loss should also be recognised in the income statement.[177]

If, in a subsequent period, the fair value of an available-for-sale *debt* instrument increases, and the increase can be objectively related to an event occurring after the loss was recognised in the income statement, the impairment loss should be reversed and recognised in profit or loss.[178] However, in the case of *equity* instruments, impairments cannot be reversed through the income statement.[179] This restriction on the reversal of impairments of available-for-sale equity instruments represents a significant change from the previous version of the standard.

The Basis for Conclusions includes an explanation for the difference in treatment. In particular, in the context of the reversal of impairments on available-for-sale debt securities, it is noted that:

- the reversal of impairment losses of non-financial assets (e.g. inventories, property, plant and equipment and intangible assets) is required if circumstances change;

- the treatment provides consistency with the requirement to reverse impairment losses on loans and receivables and on assets classified as held-to-maturity; and

- determining an increase in fair value attributable to an improvement in credit standing is more objectively determinable than for equity instruments.[180]

The IASB, however, could not find an acceptable way to distinguish reversals of impairment losses from other increases in fair value of available-for-sale equity instruments. Therefore, it decided that precluding such reversals was the only appropriate solution, even though a number of other approaches were considered.[181] In the end this approach probably seemed most expedient as it is comparable to US GAAP.[182] One IASB member formally disagreed with the approach adopted and would have preferred all losses below original cost to be recognised as impairments,[183] i.e. in profit or loss.

This raises a related question, especially for those entities that prepare interim financial statements on a quarterly and/or half-yearly basis, i.e. how frequently should available-for-sale equity instruments be assessed for impairment? It might seem sensible to perform such reviews at each balance sheet date, be that the end of an interim or annual period. However, this could give rise to what some see as anomalous results.

Consider, for example, an entity that purchases an equity share for €100 at the start of its reporting period. If the fair value of the share had fallen to €60 at the end of the half-year, it is very likely to conclude that the share had become impaired. Consequently, a €40 loss would be recognised in profit or loss. However, if the share price had recovered to €100 by the end of the full financial year, should this loss be reversed? The introduction to IAS 34 – *Interim Financial Reporting* – states that 'The frequency of an enterprise's reporting – annual, half-yearly, or quarterly – should not affect the measurement of its annual results.'[184] This might suggest that the impairment loss at the half-year could be reversed. However, the accounting requirements of IAS 39 are generally applied on a continuous basis and it could equally be argued that ignoring losses between balance sheet dates (whatever their frequency) fails to apply properly the requirements of the standard. Nevertheless, in practice it is unlikely that material impairments will be overlooked by examining instruments only at the balance sheet date.

6.4 Financial assets carried at cost

As set out at 3.1 above, unquoted equity instruments and derivative assets that are linked to and must be settled by delivery of such instruments whose fair value cannot be reliably measured, are measured at cost.

If there is objective evidence that an impairment loss has been incurred on such an asset, the amount of the impairment loss is measured as the difference between the carrying amount of the financial asset and the present value of estimated future cash flows, discounted at the current market rate of return for a similar financial asset (see 4.3 above).[185] There is something a little inconsistent in the requirement to determine and include in the financial statements such a net present value when, supposedly, the fair value of the instrument cannot be reliably measured. However, this is not explicitly addressed or even acknowledged.

Consistent with the treatment for other available-for-sale equity securities, any such impairment losses may not be reversed.[186]

6.5 Interest income after impairment recognition

Once a financial asset, or group of similar assets, has been written down as a result of an impairment loss, interest income is thereafter recognised based on the rate of interest that was used to discount the future cash flows for the purpose of measuring the impairment loss.[187]

It is not clear how this requirement should be applied to a fixed interest rate debt instrument that has been written down to its fair value (rather than its net present value using the original effective interest rate of the instrument – see 6.2.2 above). Using an appropriate long-term interest rate at the date of the impairment would seem consistent with the measurement basis adopted, although this is not strictly in accordance with the standard.

7 FOREIGN CURRENCIES

7.1 Foreign currency instruments

The provisions of IAS 21 apply to transactions involving financial instruments in just the same way as they do for other transactions, although the manner in which certain hedges are accounted for can over-ride its general requirements.

Consequently, the balance sheet measurement of a foreign currency financial instrument is determined as follows:

- firstly, it is recorded and measured in the foreign currency in which it is denominated, whether it is carried at fair value, cost, or amortised cost;

- secondly, that amount is retranslated to the entity's functional currency using:

  - closing rate, for all monetary items (e.g. a debt security) and for non-monetary items (e.g. an equity share) carried at fair value; or

  - an historical rate, for non-monetary items carried at cost because their fair value cannot be reliably measured.

Therefore, for a foreign currency denominated monetary asset carried at amortised cost under IAS 39, amortised cost is calculated in the currency in which it is denominated. That foreign currency amount is then retranslated into the entity's functional currency at the closing rate.

As an exception, if the financial instrument is designated as a hedged item in a fair value hedge of foreign currency exposure, it is remeasured for changes in foreign currency rates even if it would otherwise have been reported using a historical rate (see Chapter 19 at 4.1).

The reporting of changes in the carrying amount of a financial instrument in the income statement or in equity depends on a number of factors, including whether it is an exchange difference or other change in carrying amount, whether the instrument is a monetary or non-monetary item and whether it is designated as part of a foreign currency cash flow hedge or hedge of a net investment.

Profit and loss items associated with financial instruments, e.g. dividends receivable, interest payable or receivable and impairments, are recorded at the spot rate ruling when they arise (although average rates may be used when they represent an appropriate approximation to spot rates throughout the period). Exchange differences arising on retranslating monetary items are generally reported in profit or loss, although they may be recognised in equity for instruments designated as hedges of future foreign currency transactions or net investments in foreign entities (see Chapter 19 at 4.2 and 4.3). All other fair value changes (e.g. the change in value of a debt instrument as a result of interest rate movements) are reported in profit or loss if the instrument is classified at fair value through profit or loss, or equity if it is available-for-sale.

In cases where some portion of the change in carrying amount is reported in profit or loss and some in equity, e.g. if the fair value of a bond has increased in foreign currency and decreased in the measurement currency, those two components cannot be offset for the purposes of determining gains or losses that should be recognised in profit or loss and equity.[188]

These principles are illustrated in the following example.

Example 18.28: Available-for-sale foreign currency debt security

On 31 December 2005 Company A, whose measurement currency is the euro, acquires a dollar bond for its fair value of $1,000. The bond is the same as the one in Example 18.16 at 5.1 above, i.e. it has five years to maturity and a $1,250 principal, carries fixed interest of 4.7% paid annually ($1,250 × 4.7% = $59 per year), and has an effective interest rate of 10%.

A classifies the bond as available-for-sale. The exchange rate is $1 to €1.50 and the carrying amount of the bond is €1,500 ($1,000 × 1.50).

	€	€
Bond	1,500	
Cash		1,500

On 31 December 2006, the dollar has appreciated and the exchange rate is $1 to €2.00. The fair value of the bond is $1,060 and therefore its carrying amount is €2,120 ($1,060 × 2.00). Its amortised cost is $1,041 (or €2,082 = $1,041 × 2.00) and the cumulative gain or loss to be included in equity is the difference between its fair value and amortised cost, i.e. a gain of €38 (€2,120 – €2,082; or, alternatively, [$1,060 – $1,041] × 2.00).

Interest received on the bond on 31 December 2006 is $59 (or €118 = $59 × 2.00). Interest income determined in accordance with the effective interest method is $100 ($1,000 × 10%) of which $41 ($100 – $59) is the accretion of the initial discount.

It is assumed that the average exchange rate during the year is $1 to €1.75 and that the use of an average exchange rate provides a reliable approximation of the spot rates applicable to the accrual of interest during the year. Therefore, reported interest income is €175 ($100 × 1.75) including accretion of the initial discount of €72 ($41 × 1.75).

The exchange difference reported in profit or loss is €525, which comprises three elements: a €500 gain from the retranslation of the initial amortised cost ($1,000 × [2.00 – 1.50]); a €15 gain from the retranslation of interest income received ($59 × [2.00 – 1.75]) and a €10 gain on the retranslation of the interest income accreted ($41 × [2.00 – 1.75]).

	€	€
Bond	620	
Cash	118	
Interest income (P&L)		175
Exchange gain (P&L)		525
Fair value change (equity)		38

On 31 December 2007, the dollar has appreciated further and the exchange rate is $1 to €2.50. The fair value of the bond is $1,070 and therefore its carrying amount is €2,675 ($1,070 × 2.50). Its amortised cost is $1,086 (or €2,715 = $1,086 × 2.50) and the cumulative gain or loss to be included in equity is the difference between its fair value and the amortised cost, i.e. a loss of €40 (€2,675 – €2,715; or, alternatively, [$1,070 – $1,086] × 2.50). Therefore, there is a debit to equity equal to the change in the difference during 2007 of €78 (€40 + €38).

Interest received on the bond on 31 December 2007 is $59 (or €148 = $59 × 2.50). Interest income determined in accordance with the effective interest method is $104 ($1,041 × 10%), of which $45 ($104 – $59) is the accretion of the initial discount.

Using the same assumptions as in the previous year, interest income is €234 ($104 × 2.25) including accretion of the initial discount of €101 ($45 × 2.25).

The exchange difference reported in profit or loss is €547, which again comprises three elements: a €521 gain from the retranslation of the opening amortised cost ($1,041 × [2.50 – 2.00]); a €15 gain from the retranslation of interest income received ($59 × [2.50 – 2.25]) and an €11 gain on the retranslation of the interest income accreted ($45 × [2.50 – 2.25]).[189]

	€	€
Bond	555	
Cash	148	
Fair value change (equity)	78	
Interest income (P&L)		234
Exchange gain (P&L)		547

It is worth repeating that the treatment would be different for available-for-sale equity instruments. Under IAS 21, these are not considered monetary items and exchange differences would form part of the change in the fair value of the instrument, which would be reported in equity.

7.2   Foreign entities

IAS 39 does not amend application of the net investment method of accounting for foreign entities set out in IAS 21 (see Chapter 9 at 2.7). Therefore, for the purpose of preparing its own accounts for inclusion in consolidated accounts, a foreign entity that is part of a group applies the principles at 7.1 above by reference to its own functional currency. Consequently, the treatment of gains and losses on, say, trading assets held by a foreign entity should follow the treatment in the example below.

Example 18.29:   Interaction of IAS 21 and IAS 39 – foreign currency debt investment

Company A is domiciled in the US and its functional currency and presentation currency is the US dollar. A has a UK domiciled subsidiary, B, whose functional currency is sterling. B is the owner of a debt instrument which is held for trading and is therefore carried at fair value.

In B's financial statements for 2005, the fair value and carrying amount of the debt instrument is £100. In A's consolidated financial statements, the asset is translated into US dollars at the spot exchange rate applicable at the balance sheet date, say 2.0, and the carrying amount is US$200 (£100 × 2.0).

At the end of 2006, the fair value of the debt instrument has increased to £110. B reports the trading asset at £110 in its balance sheet and recognises a fair value gain of £10 in profit or loss. During the year, the spot exchange rate has increased from 2.0 to 3.0 resulting in an increase in the fair value of the instrument from US$200 to US$330 (£110 × 3.0). Therefore, A reports the trading asset at US$330 in its consolidated financial statements.

Since B is classified as a foreign entity, A translates B's income statement 'at the exchange rates at the dates of the transactions'. Since the fair value gain has accrued through the year, A uses the average rate of 2.5 (= [3.0 + 2.0] ÷ 2) as a practical approximation. Therefore, while the fair value of the trading asset has increased by US$130 (US$330 – US$200), A recognises only US$25 (£10 × 2.5) of this increase in profit or loss. The resulting exchange difference, i.e. the remaining increase in the fair value of the debt instrument of US$105 (US$130 – US$25), is classified as equity until the disposal of the net investment in the foreign entity.[190]

8 EFFECTIVE DATE, TRANSITIONAL PROVISIONS AND FIRST-TIME ADOPTION

8.1 Effective date

The revised version of IAS 39 must be applied for annual periods beginning on or after 1 January 2005. Entities are 'permitted' (rather than 'encouraged', as in the case of other recently issued standards) to adopt the standard in earlier periods, but must disclose that they have done so. They must also adopt both IAS 32 – *Financial Instruments: Presentation and Disclosure* – and IAS 39 at the same time and must adopt IAS 39 as amended in March 2004, not as originally issued.[191]

8.2 Transitional provisions

In general, IAS 39 should be applied retrospectively and the opening balance of retained earnings for the earliest period presented and all other comparative amounts should be adjusted as if it had always been in use.[192]

As set out in Chapter 15 at 8.2, when the revised version of IAS 39 is first applied, previously recognised financial assets or financial liabilities may be designated at fair value through profit or loss, or as available-for-sale, in spite of the general requirement to make such designation upon initial recognition. For instruments redesignated under this concession:

- the instrument should be restated using the new designation in the comparative financial statements; and

- the fair value of the instruments designated into each category, together with the classification and carrying amount in the previous financial statements, should be disclosed.

In addition, for financial assets designated as available-for-sale, cumulative changes in fair value should be recognised in a separate component of equity (until subsequent derecognition or impairment, at which point that cumulative gain or loss will be recognised in profit or loss).[193]

It does not take much creativity to realise that this concession provides many opportunities for entities to manage their results in a favourable manner, as illustrated in the following example.

Example 18.30: Transitional provisions

At the end of 2004, Company X held an investment in an equity investment which, under the previous version of IAS 39, was classified as available-for-sale. The original cost of the investment was €100 but towards the end of 2004 its market value fell to €90, although it was not considered impaired. Therefore, a loss of €10 was recognised in equity in 2004. In 2005, the year in which X adopted the revised version of IAS 39, the investment was subsequently sold for its then market value of €85.

If X retained its original classification of this instrument, it would report a loss of €15 in its 2005 income statement (including €10 recycled from equity). However, if advantage was taken of the concession to designate this instrument at fair value through profit or loss, it would report a loss of only €5 in its 2005 income statement and its 2004 income statement would be restated to include an additional loss of €10.

We are not suggesting that entities should attempt to use the transitional provisions to redesignate instruments in this manner. Even if such 'cherry picking' was considered appropriate, the disclosure requirements above are likely to make it quite transparent to readers of the accounts. Further, stakeholders may well expect companies to explain their rationale for any redesignation, even though it is not an explicit requirement of IAS 39, and it might well be seen as best practice.

One transitional issue has already been considered by IFRIC, i.e. whether there are circumstances in which the revised version of IAS 39 would require recognition of an impairment loss that the previous version would not; and if so, whether the loss should be recognised as a transitional adjustment to opening retained earnings.

IFRIC were of the view that the words 'a significant or prolonged decline in fair value of an investment in an equity instrument below its cost is also objective evidence of impairment' referred to at 6.1 above was an unequivocal trigger for the impairment requirements and could therefore give rise to an impairment where there was none under the previous standard. In addition, because the revised standard should generally be applied retrospectively and the issue did not fall within one of the concessions, IFRIC decided that it was clear that retrospective application of the standard was required. This would mean that if a significant or prolonged decline occurred prior to the start of the period in which the revised IAS 39 was adopted, comparatives should be amended. However, it is quite possible for the impairment to have occurred in the current period, in which case there would be no restatement.[194]

In July 2004, the IASB published an exposure draft of an amendment to IAS 39 that proposed allowing (but not requiring) entities to adopt certain aspects of the fair value measurement guidance prospectively from 25 October 2002, rather than retrospectively. This exposure draft is considered further at 9.1 below.

8.3 First-time adoption

IFRS 1 – *First-time Adoption of International Financial Reporting Standards* – is dealt with comprehensively in Chapter 4 and the particular aspects of that standard applying to financial instruments are principally covered at 2.6 of that chapter. The aspects related to the topics covered in this chapter are summarised below. Further similar sections are included in Chapters 15 to 17, 19 and 20.

8.3.1 Exemption from the requirement to restate comparatives

The IASB issued the revised versions of IAS 32 and IAS 39 in December 2003; and the amendment to IAS 39 – *Fair Value Hedge Accounting for a Portfolio Hedge of Interest Rate Risk* – in March 2004. To allow entities adopting IFRS for the first time before 1 January 2006 sufficient time to comply with the requirements of those standards, the IASB decided not to require them to prepare comparative information under IAS 32 and IAS 39.[195] Instead, a first-time adopter that chooses to present comparative information that does not comply with IAS 32 and IAS 39 in its first year of transition should:

- apply its previous GAAP in the comparative information to financial instruments that are within the scope of IAS 32 and IAS 39. In other words, this exemption also affects the application of certain aspects of other standards. For example, it overrides the requirements of IAS 1 on the balance sheet presentation of financial instruments and IAS 18 – *Revenue* – on the application of the effective interest method; and

- make certain additional disclosures (see below).[196]

(A similar exemption applies to insurance contracts within the scope of IFRS 4.)

A first-time adopter that does not present comparative information under IAS 32 and IAS 39 should use *the beginning of the first IFRS reporting period* (e.g. 1 January 2005 for an entity reporting at 31 December 2005) as the relevant date for the application of the first-time adoption rules in IFRS 1, and not the *date of transition to IFRS*, for the purpose of these standards only.[197]

In applying this exemption, a first-time adopter should be aware of the following:

- the wording of the standard does not explicitly require the exemption to be applied to IAS 32 and IAS 39 as a package. However, even though the transitional provisions in both IAS 32 and IAS 39 that require the standards to be adopted simultaneously do not apply to first-time adopters, the IASB clearly intended both standards to be adopted simultaneously. In any case, the many cross-references between the two standards make it virtually impossible to adopt one of the standards without the other. Therefore, we believe that the exemption applies to IAS 32 and IAS 39 as a package;

- a first-time adopter that presents two comparative periods under IFRS will not be permitted to restate the most recent comparative financial period because the exemption must be applied as of the beginning of the first IFRS reporting period (e.g. an entity reporting at 31 December 2005 would not be allowed to restate 2004 unless it also restated 2003); and

- the exemption only covers items that are within the scope of IAS 32 and IAS 39 (and IFRS 4). The comparative information relating to all other items must be restated under IFRS.

Where an entity makes this election, it needs to:[198]

- disclose that the comparative information does not comply with IAS 32 and IAS 39, but that it has been prepared on the basis of its previous GAAP;

- disclose the nature, but not the amount, of the main adjustments that would make the information comply with IAS 32 and IAS 39; and

- treat any adjustment between the balance sheet at the comparative period's reporting date and the start of the first IFRS reporting period as arising from a change in accounting policy. This difference is accounted for as an adjustment to the opening balance of each affected component of equity at the start of the first IFRS reporting period.[199] The entity is required to make the disclosures prescribed by paragraphs 28(a)-(e) and (f)(i) of IAS 8 (see Chapter 3 at 6.1.2 A).[200]

Originally, IFRS 1 also required first-time adopters to prepare comparative information that complied with IAS 32 and IAS 39 because this improved 'comparability within the first IFRS financial statements' and because the IASB believed that this should not be a problem for entities that planned the adoption of IFRS in a timely manner.[201] Unfortunately, the less-than-timely publication of the revised versions of IAS 32 and IAS 39 obliged the IASB to exempt entities adopting IFRS before 1 January 2006 from applying these standards in preparing comparative information.

8.3.2   *Measurement of financial instruments*

In preparing its opening IFRS balance sheet (or the balance sheet at the beginning of its first IFRS reporting period, if comparatives are not restated) an entity should apply the criteria in IAS 39 to identify those financial instruments that are measured at fair value and those that are measured at amortised cost (see Chapter 15 at 8.3.2).[202]

A   *Assets and liabilities measured at amortised cost*

For those financial instruments measured at amortised cost in the opening IFRS balance sheet (or the balance sheet at the beginning of its first IFRS reporting period, if comparatives are not restated) their cost should be determined on the basis of circumstances existing when they first satisfied the recognition criteria in IAS 39. However, if they were acquired in a past business combination, their carrying amount under the entity's previous GAAP immediately following the business combination should be taken as their deemed cost under IFRS at that date.[203]

To determine amortised cost using the effective interest method, it is necessary to determine the transaction costs incurred when the instrument was originated. During the development of IFRS 1, some argued that determining these transaction costs could involve undue cost or effort for financial instruments originated long before the date of transition to IFRS and argued for concessions to be made, e.g. by allowing transaction costs to be ignored.[204] However, the IASB believes that the unamortised portion of transaction costs at the date of transition to IFRS (or at the beginning of the first IFRS reporting period, if comparatives are not restated) is unlikely to be material for most financial instruments. Further, even where the unamortised portion may be material, reasonable estimates are believed possible. Therefore, no exemption was created in this area.[205]

B   *Loan impairments*

It is explained that estimates of loan impairments at the date of transition to IFRS (or the beginning of the first IFRS reporting period, if comparatives are not restated) should be consistent with estimates made for the same date under previous GAAP (after adjustments to reflect any difference in accounting policies), unless there is objective evidence that those assumptions were in error. Consequently, the impact of any later revisions to those estimates should be treated as impairment losses (or, if the criteria in IAS 39 are met, reversals of impairment losses) of the period in which revisions are made.[206]

In the context of the detailed requirements for loan impairments within the revised version of IAS 39, it is very unclear where the dividing line between estimates and accounting policies lies. Therefore, for entities where loan impairment provisions are highly material, such as banks and similar financial institutions, this requirement overlooks a very important point of detail and, consequently, appears to include a rather glib statement.

C   Derivatives and other trading instruments

It almost goes without saying that all derivative financial instruments should be measured at fair value at the date of transition (or the beginning of the first IFRS reporting period, if comparatives are not restated) but the implementation guidance does make this clear.[207]

However, in July 2004, the IASB published an exposure draft of an amendment to IAS 39 that proposed allowing (but not requiring) entities to adopt certain aspects of the fair value measurement guidance prospectively from 25 October 2002 rather than retrospectively. This exposure draft is considered further at 9.1 below.

D   Embedded derivatives

Under IAS 39, some embedded derivatives are accounted for separately at fair value. Some argued that retrospective application of this requirement would be costly and suggested either an exemption from retrospective application of this requirement, or a requirement or option to use the fair value of the host instrument at the date of transition to IFRS (or the beginning of the first IFRS reporting period, if comparatives are not restated) as the deemed cost of the instrument at that date should be introduced.[208]

Although the IASB recognised that an option not to account separately for some pre-existing embedded derivatives was provided when the equivalent US GAAP requirements became mandatory, it concluded that the failure to measure embedded derivatives at fair value would diminish the relevance and reliability of an entity's first IFRS financial statements. It also observed that IAS 39 addresses an inability to measure an embedded derivative and the host contract separately (in such cases, the entire combined contract is measured at fair value).[209] Accordingly, no exception was created in this area.

E   Transition adjustments: available-for-sale assets

Retrospective application of IAS 39 to available-for-sale financial assets requires a first-time adopter to recognise the cumulative fair value changes in a separate component of equity in the opening IFRS balance sheet (or the balance sheet at the beginning of the first IFRS reporting period, if comparatives are not restated) and transfer those fair value changes to the income statement on subsequent disposal or impairment of the asset.[210]

During the development of IFRS 1, some suggested that the cost of determining the amount to be included in a separate component of equity would exceed the benefits. However, the IASB noted that these costs would be minimal if a first-time adopter carried the available-for-sale financial assets under previous GAAP at cost or the lower of cost and market value. They acknowledged that these costs might be more significant if they were carried at fair value, but in that case those assets might well be classified as held for trading. Therefore, the requirement that a first-time adopter should apply IAS 39 retrospectively to available-for-sale financial assets was retained in the standard.[211]

Given the requirements in respect of impairments of available-for-sale equity instruments (see 6.3 above) full retrospective application in this area may not be as straightforward as the IASB thinks. However, this does not change the fact that no exceptions have been made in this respect.

F   *Transition adjustments: other instruments*

With the exception of hedges (which are dealt with in Chapter 19) other adjustments to the carrying amount of financial assets or liabilities that arise from the adoption of IAS 39 should be recognised in the opening balance of retained earnings (or the balance at the beginning of the first IFRS reporting period, if comparatives are not restated).[212]

9   FUTURE DEVELOPMENTS

As set out in the Introduction and Future Developments sections of Chapter 15, the IASB has acknowledged that it is willing to revise IAS 39 in the short term. To date it has published two exposure drafts of proposed amendments to IAS 39 that deal with the measurement of financial instruments and these are summarised below.

9.1   'Day 1' profits

As noted at 8.2 and 8.3 above, the IASB published in July 2004 an exposure draft proposing relief for entities adopting the revised measurement requirements of IAS 39 (including those applying IFRS for the first time). The proposals would allow (but not require) adoption of those parts of the fair value measurement requirements that prohibit entities from recognising 'day 1' profits prospectively to transactions entered into from 25 October 2002 rather than fully retrospectively.[213]

There is no underlying conceptual basis for these proposals. Rather, they are entirely pragmatic in that they aim to align the transitional requirements of IAS 39 with those of similar requirements in US GAAP, and thereby ease transition for those entities that might already be reporting under US GAAP.[214] Somewhat embarrassingly, however, it now appears that most people interpreted the relevant date under US GAAP to be 21 November, not 25 October, 2002!

In addition, the IASB believed that confusion had arisen over how any gain or loss not recognised on 'day 1' should be recognised subsequently. In particular, some suggested that the entire gain or loss might be recognised on 'day 2', something that had not been intended. Therefore, in the exposure draft it is 'clarified' that subsequent measurement of the financial asset or liability, and the subsequent recognition of gains and losses, should be consistent with the requirements in IAS 39. Accordingly, a gain or loss should be recognised after initial recognition only to the extent that it arises from a change in a factor (including time) that market participants would consider in setting a price.[215]

The exposure draft does not explain *how* any 'locked-in' profits (see 4.7 above) should emerge. The reference to 'time' may be seen as implicit acknowledgement that a straight-line basis is appropriate but we doubt this is what the IASB intended. It is certainly hard to reconcile such an approach to a fair value method of accounting.

The IASB plans to implement these proposals so that they are effective for periods commencing on or after 1 January 2005, i.e. they will have the same implementation date as the revised version of IAS 39.[216]

9.2 Financial guarantees

Also in July 2004, the IASB issued an exposure draft proposing amendments to IAS 39 and IFRS 4 that would specify the accounting requirements for many financial guarantee contracts that are currently within the scope of IFRS 4 (see Chapter 15 at 3.3.1).[217]

The proposals would require the issuer of such a financial guarantee contract to measure the contract:

- initially at fair value. If the financial guarantee contract was issued in a stand-alone arm's length transaction to an unrelated party, its fair value at inception is likely to equal the premium received, unless there is evidence to the contrary; and

- subsequently at the higher of:

  - the amount determined in accordance with IAS 37; and

  - the amount initially recognised less, when appropriate, cumulative amortisation recognised in accordance with IAS 18.[218]

These requirements would be mandatory for accounting periods commencing 1 January 2006, although earlier adoption would be encouraged.[219]

References

1 IAS 39, *Financial Instruments: Recognition and Measurement*, IASB, December 2003 (amended March 2004), para. BC14.
2 IAS 39, para. 43.
3 IAS 39, Implementation Guidance, Questions and Answers, IAS 39 Implementation Guidance Committee, July 2001, Q&A 66-3.
4 IAS 39, para. AG64.
5 IGC, Q&A 66-3.
6 IAS 39, para. AG65.
7 Extrapolated from example in IAS 39, para. AG65.
8 IAS 39, para. AG79.
9 *IFRIC Update*, IASB, July 2004.
10 IAS 39, para. 9.
11 IAS 39, para. E.1.1.
12 IAS 39, para. AG67.
13 IAS 39, para. AG13.
14 IAS 39, para. BC222(d).
15 IAS 18, *Revenue*, IASB, December 1993, (amended March 2004), Appendix, para. 14(a)(i).
16 IAS 39, para. AG67.
17 IAS 39, para. AG28.
18 IGC Q&A 23-3.
19 IAS 39, paras. C.3 and C.5.

20 IAS 39, para. 44.
21 IAS 39, para. AG12.
22 IAS 39, para. BC16.
23 IGC Q&A 30-1.
24 IAS 39, paras. 45 and 47.
25 IAS 39, para. 46.
26 IAS 39, para. 47.
27 IAS 39, paras. 46(c)-47(a).
28 IAS 39, paras. 46(a)-(b) and 47.
29 IAS 39, para. AG68.
30 IAS 39, para. 46.
31 IAS 39, paras. 46-47.
32 IAS 39, para. 47(b).
33 IAS 39, para. 55(a).
34 IAS 39, para. 56.
35 IAS 39, para. 55(b).
36 IAS 39, para. 55(b).
37 IAS 39, para. E.3.1.
38 IAS 2, *Inventories*, IASB, December 2003, para. 25.
39 IAS 39, para. 56.
40 IAS 39, paras. 72, 95 and 102.
41 IAS 39, paras. 55 and 57.
42 IAS 39, para. D.2.2.
43 IAS 39, paras. 51-52.
44 IAS 39, para. 54(a).
45 IAS 39, para. 54(a).
46 IAS 39, para. 53.
47 IAS 39, para. 54(b).
48 IAS 39, para. 9.
49 IAS 39, para. AG69.
50 IAS 39, para. BC95.
51 IAS 39, para. AG71.
52 IAS 39 (2000), *Financial Instruments: Recognition and Measurement*, IASB, December 1998 to October 2000, para. 99.
53 IAS 39, paras. BC96-BC97.
54 IAS 39, paras. BC96-BC97.
55 IAS 39, para. AG71.
56 IAS 39, para. AG67.
57 IAS 39, para. AG70.
58 IAS 39, para. AG72.
59 IAS 39 (2000), para. 99.
60 IAS 39, para. AG70.
61 IAS 39, para. E.2.1.
62 IAS 39, paras. AG71 and BC98.
63 IAS 39, para. AG72.
64 IAS 39, para. E.2.2.
65 IAS 39 (2000), para. 98 and IGC Q&A 100-1.
66 IAS 39, para. AG72.
67 IAS 39, para. AG73.
68 IAS 39, para. AG72.
69 IAS 39, paras. AG74 and BC102-BC103.
70 IAS 39, para. AG74.
71 IAS 39, para. AG75.
72 IAS 39, para. AG76.
73 IAS 39, para. AG76.
74 IAS 39, para. AG77.
75 IAS 39, para. AG78.
76 IAS 39, para. AG79.
77 IAS 39, para. AG82.
78 IAS 39, para. AG80.
79 IAS 39, para. AG81.
80 IGC Q&A 70-1.
81 IAS 39, para. C.11.
82 IAS 39, para. F.2.3.
83 IAS 39, paras. BC93-BC94.
84 IAS 39, para. 49.
85 IAS 39, para. AG66.
86 IAS 39, para. BC104.
87 IAS 39, para. DO6.
88 These financial statements were not prepared under IFRS, but the accounting principles for simple borrowing arrangements, and the requirements to disclose fair values, under Marconi's local GAAP are very similar to the requirements in IAS 32 and IAS 39.
89 IAS 39, para. BC88.
90 IAS 39, para. BC89.
91 IAS 39, para. BC90.
92 IAS 32, *Financial Instruments: Disclosure and Presentation*, IASB, December 2003 (amended March 2004), para. 94(f)(ii).
93 IAS 39, para. BC91.
94 IAS 39, para. BC92.
95 IAS 39, para. 9.
96 IAS 39, para. 9.
97 IAS 39, para. BC30.
98 IAS 39, para. AG5.
99 IAS 39, para. BC32.
100 IAS 39, para. BC34.
101 IAS 39, para. BC35.
102 IGC Q&A 73-1.
103 IAS 39, para. B.27.
104 IAS 39, para. 9.
105 IGC Q&A 10-19.
106 IAS 39, para. AG8.
107 IAS 39, para. BC36.
108 IAS 39, para. B.2.
109 IAS 39, para. AG7.
110 IAS 39, para. AG6.
111 IAS 39, para. AG6.
112 IGC Q&A 76-1.
113 IAS 18, para. 32.
114 IAS 39, para. B.24.
115 IAS 39, para. B.25.
116 Based on the example in IAS 39, para. B.25.
117 Exposure Draft, *Amendments to IAS 32, Financial Instruments: Disclosure and Presentation, and IAS 39, Financial Instruments: Recognition and Measurement*, IASB, June 2002, para. D6.
118 IAS 39, paras. DO2, DO4, DO7 and DO12-DO14.
119 IAS 39, paras. BC108-BC110.
120 IAS 39, para. 46.

121 IAS 39, para. 58.
122 IAS 39, para. 59.
123 IAS 39, para. 59.
124 IAS 39, para. E.4.2.
125 IAS 39, para. E.4.2.
126 IAS 39, para. 60.
127 IAS 39, para. 59.
128 IAS 39, para. 60.
129 IAS 39, para. E.4.1.
130 IAS 39, paras. 60 and E.4.10.
131 IAS 39, para. BC105.
132 IAS 39, para. BC106.
133 IAS 39, para. 61.
134 IAS 39, para. BC107.
135 IAS 39, para. 62.
136 IAS 39, para. 64.
137 IAS 39, para. E.4.7.
138 IAS 39, paras. DO2, DO4 and DO7.
139 IAS 39, paras. BC108-BC121.
140 IAS 39, para. 63.
141 IAS 39, para. AG84.
142 IAS 39, para. 63.
143 IAS 39, para. AG84.
144 IGC Q&A 113-3.
145 IAS 39, para. BC221(f).
146 IAS 39, para. E.4.6.
147 IAS 39, para. E.4.3.
148 IAS 39, para. AG84.
149 IAS 39, para. E.4.5.
150 IAS 39, para. AG84.
151 IAS 39 (2000), para. 113.
152 IAS 39, para. E.4.8.
153 IGC Q&A 113-1.
154 IFRS 4, *Insurance Contracts*, IASB, March 2004, Appendix A (Defined terms).
155 IFRS 4, para. 4(f).
156 IFRS 4, Appendix A (Defined terms).
157 IAS 39, para. 2(e).
158 IAS 37, *Provisions, Contingent Liabilities and Contingent Assets*, IASB, September 1998 (amended March 2004), paras. 1(c) and 5(e).
159 IAS 39, para. BC92.
160 IAS 39, para. AG85.
161 IAS 39, para. AG86.
162 IAS 39, para. AG87.
163 IAS 39, para. AG87.
164 IAS 39, para. AG87.
165 IAS 39, para. DO4.
166 IAS 39, para. AG88.
167 IAS 39, para. AG89.
168 IAS 39, para. AG90.
169 IAS 39, para. AG91.
170 IAS 39, para. AG92.
171 IAS 39, para. E.4.4
172 IAS 39, para. E.4.4
173 IAS 39, para. E.4.4
174 IAS 39, para. 65.
175 IAS 39, para. 67.
176 IAS 39, para. 68.
177 IAS 39, para. E.4.9.
178 IAS 39, para. 70.
179 IAS 39, para. 69.
180 IAS 39, para. BC128.
181 IAS 39, para. BC130.
182 IAS 39, para. BC221(g).
183 IAS 39, para. DO13.
184 IAS 39, para. 66.
185 IAS 39, para. 66.
186 IAS 39, para. 66.
187 IAS 39, para. AG93.
188 IAS 39, paras. AG83 and E.3.4.
189 IAS 39, para. E.3.2.
190 IAS 39, para. E.3.3.
191 IAS 39, para. 103.
192 IAS 32, para. 97 and IAS 39, para. 104.
193 IAS 39, para. 105.
194 *IFRIC Update*, IASB, March 2004.
195 IFRS 1, *First-time Adoption of International Financial Reporting Standards*, IASB, June 2003 (amended March 2004), para. BC89A.
196 IFRS 1, para. 36A.
197 IFRS 1, para. 36A.
198 IFRS 1, para. 36A.
199 IAS 8, *Accounting Policies, Changes in Accounting Estimates and Errors*, IASB, December 2003, (amended March 2004), para. 24.
200 IAS 8, para. 28.
201 IFRS 1, para. BC89.
202 IFRS 1, para. IG56.
203 IFRS 1, paras. B2(e) and IG57.
204 IFRS 1, para. BC72.
205 IFRS 1, para. BC73.
206 IFRS 1, paras. 31 and IG58.
207 IFRS 1, para. IG56(c).
208 IFRS 1, para. BC65.
209 IFRS 1, para. BC65.
210 IFRS 1, paras. IG59 and BC81.
211 IFRS 1, para. BC83.
212 IFRS 1, para. IG58A.
213 Exposure Draft, Amendments to IAS 39, Financial Instruments: Recognition and Measurement, *Transition and Initial Recognition of Financial Assets and Financial Liabilities*, IASB, July 2004, Background, para. 6.
214 ED, Background, para. 5.
215 ED, Background, para. 7.
216 ED, Background, para. 6.
217 Exposure Draft, *Amendments to IAS 39, Financial Instruments: Recognition and Measurement and IFRS 4 Insurance Contracts – Financial Guarantee Contracts and Credit Insurance*, IASB, July 2004.
218 ED, para. IN3.
219 ED, para. IN10.

Chapter 19   Financial instruments: Hedge accounting

1   INTRODUCTION

1.1   Background

The Introduction to Chapter 15 provides a general background to the development of accounting for financial instruments and notes the fundamental changes that have been experienced in international financial markets. The markets for derivatives, especially, have seen remarkable and continued growth over the past two or three decades. This reflects the increasing use of such instruments by businesses, commonly to 'hedge' their financial risks. Accordingly, the accounting treatment for derivatives and hedging activities has taken on a high degree of importance. Historically, however, the accounting guidance has struggled to keep up with business practices and, at best, issues were dealt with very much on a piecemeal basis. Therefore, until recently, entities were left largely to their own devices in developing accounting policies for hedges so that their financial statements reflected the objectives for entering into such transactions.

'Hedging' itself is a much wider topic than hedge accounting and is *not* the primary subject of this chapter. It is an imprecise term although standard setters frequently describe hedging in terms of designating a hedging instrument that has a value that is expected, wholly or partly, to offset changes in the value or cash flows of a 'hedged position'.[1] In this context, hedged positions normally include recognised assets and liabilities, contractual commitments and expected, but uncontracted, future transactions. Whilst this may be an appropriate description for many hedges, it does not necessarily capture the essence of all risk management activities involving financial instruments. Nevertheless, it forms the basis for the hedge accounting requirements under IFRS.

1.2   What is hedge accounting?

Hedge accounting is often seen as 'correcting' deficiencies in the accounting requirements that would otherwise apply to each leg of the hedge relationship. Typically, it involves recognising gains and losses on a hedging instrument in the same period(s) and/or in the same place in the financial statements as gains or losses on the hedged position. It may be used in a number of situations, for example to correct for:[2]

- *Measurement differences*

  These might arise where the hedge is of a recognised asset or liability that is measured on a different basis to the hedging instrument. An example is an investment in shares that is recorded in the financial statements at cost, but whose value is hedged by a put option that enables shares of the same class to be sold at a predetermined price. In this case, both the hedging instrument and the hedged position exist and are recognised in the financial statements, but they are likely to be measured on different bases.

  In this situation hedge accounting could be achieved in a number of ways. Unrealised gains and losses on the put option might simply not be recognised and realised gains and losses could be deferred (e.g. separately as assets or liabilities or by including them within the carrying amount of the investment) until the investment is sold. Alternatively, if unrealised gains and losses on the put option were recognised in profit or loss, the measurement basis of the investment could be changed to reflect changes in its fair value in profit or loss.

- *Performance reporting differences*

  Even if the measurement bases of the hedging instrument and hedged item are the same, performance reporting differences might arise if gains and losses are reported in a different place in the financial statements. In the example above, the investment and the put option may both be measured at fair value. However, if gains and losses on the investment were recognised in equity (or its equivalent) whilst those on the put option were recognised in profit or loss, there would be a mismatch in the income statement. Similarly, gains and losses on retranslating the net assets of a foreign operation are normally recorded in equity (or its equivalent) whilst retranslation gains and losses on a borrowing used to hedge that net investment would generally be recorded in profit or loss.

  In the case of the investment and the put option, hedge accounting might involve reporting gains and losses on the investment in profit or loss, or gains and losses on the put option in equity. For the foreign operation, hedge accounting normally involves reporting the retranslation gains and losses on the borrowing in equity.

- *Recognition differences*

  These might arise where the hedge is of contractual rights or obligations that are not recognised in the financial statements. An example is a foreign currency denominated operating lease where the unrecognised contractual commitment to pay lease rentals in another currency is hedged by a series of forward currency contracts (i.e. each payment is effectively 'fixed' in functional currency terms).

In this case, hedge accounting might involve treating the lease as a 'synthetic' functional currency denominated lease. A similar outcome would be obtained if unrealised gains and losses on each forward contract remained unrecognised until the accrual of the lease payment it was hedging.

- *Existence differences*

  These might arise where the hedge is of cash flows arising from an uncontracted future transaction, i.e. a transaction that does not yet exist. An example is a foreign currency denominated sale expected next year that is hedged by a forward currency contract.

  Again, hedge accounting might involve treating the future sale as a 'synthetic' functional currency sale or it might involve deferring the gain or loss on the forward contract until the sale is recognised in profit or loss.

1.3 Development of hedge accounting standards

Hedge accounting does not sit well with the standard setters' desired goal for financial instrument accounting, i.e. a full fair value model (see Chapter 15 at 1.3). Only in the case of measurement differences, and some performance reporting differences, would the accounting treatment under the full fair value model reflect a degree of offset within the income statement (and then only if the hedge was of a financial instrument rather than, say, an item of inventory).

Further, hedge accounting relies on management intent to link (for accounting purposes) what the standard setters see as two or more separate transactions. It also overrides accounting requirements that would otherwise apply to those transactions when viewed separately. Although accounting for such transactions separately is likely to result in mismatches in the income statement, many standard setters do not see this as an accounting recognition or measurement problem. In their view, separate accounting is the best way to 'tell it as it is' and, instead, might prefer a more comprehensive analysis of an entity's gains and losses combined with a detailed explanation from management of what those gains and losses mean in the context of their overall risk management strategy.

In spite of the standard setters' long term ambitions, it became clear that the wider financial reporting community could not be persuaded to accept the abolition of hedge accounting (at least for the time being). Therefore, to address some of their more fundamental concerns about hedge accounting, the standard setters needed another approach. Eventually, the FASB published SFAS 133 – *Accounting for Derivative Instruments and Hedging Activities* – in June 1998, the first accounting standard to deal comprehensively with hedge accounting. To a large extent, SFAS 133 was used as the basis for most of the hedge accounting requirements of IAS 39 – *Financial Instruments: Recognition and Measurement* – which was approved for publication in December of the same year.

These standards have established requirements that mean hedge accounting is available only for certain hedge relationships. Particularly, formal documentation of the hedge is required and it must be demonstrated (both at inception and on an ongoing basis) that the hedge is 'highly effective'. An important corollary of these requirements is that hedge accounting may not be available for every arrangement an entity considers a hedge. In fact, because hedge accounting requires additional action by management, it is essentially voluntary.

The methods of hedge accounting were also defined by these standards, although they had to fit within a new accounting model for derivatives. Whilst a full fair value model was some way off, the standard setters had concluded that the only relevant balance sheet measure for derivatives was fair value. Further, because gains and losses from remeasuring derivatives to fair value do not meet the standard setters' definition of assets or liabilities they should not be recorded in the balance sheet as if they do. As a result, hedge accounting mostly involves:

- where the hedge reduces the risk of variability in cash flows associated with a future transaction (a cash flow hedge), the gain or loss arising on the hedging instrument is initially reported in equity and subsequently recycled to profit or loss as the hedged transaction affects profit or loss;

- where the hedge offsets the risk of volatility in the fair value of a recognised asset or liability (a fair value hedge), the gain or loss on the hedging instrument is recognised in profit or loss, together with a broadly offsetting gain or loss as a result of adjusting the hedged item to reflect certain changes in its fair value; or

- where the hedge is of a net investment in a foreign operation (a net investment hedge), the gain or loss arising on the hedging instrument is initially reported in equity and subsequently recycled to profit or loss on disposal of that foreign operation.

Further, to the extent that a *highly* effective hedge is not *perfectly* effective, the degree of ineffectiveness should be identified and recognised in profit or loss. For a fair value hedge this will automatically follow from the accounting treatment noted above. For a cash flow hedge, the amount of the gain or loss recognised in equity must be adjusted.

Although this topic accounts for some of the most complex and controversial aspects of IAS 39, few changes were proposed as a result of the improvements project (see Chapter 15 at 1.5). However, commentators raised several concerns in this area and before publishing the revised standard (and subsequently) the IASB revisited a number of the detailed aspects of the hedge accounting requirements, but not the overall approach. Most notably, as discussed at 6 below, amendments were made to make it easier for banks and similar financial institutions to obtain hedge accounting for portfolio (or macro) hedges of interest rate risk. Even so, as explained in Chapter 15 at 1.6, the future of IAS 39 and its hedge accounting requirements is somewhat uncertain, particularly in Europe.

2   HEDGING INSTRUMENTS AND HEDGED ITEMS

In the terminology of IAS 39, the two main ingredients of a hedge are the hedging instrument and the hedged item. The definition of these and related terms are as follows:

- *Hedging instrument:* a designated derivative or (for a hedge of the risk of changes in foreign currency exchange rates only) a designated non-derivative financial asset or non-derivative financial liability whose fair value or cash flows are expected to offset changes in the fair value or cash flows of a designated hedged item;

- *Hedged item:* an asset, liability, firm commitment, highly probable forecast transaction or net investment in a foreign operation that (a) exposes the entity to risk of changes in fair value or future cash flows and (b) is designated as being hedged;

- *Firm commitment:* a binding agreement for the exchange of a specified quantity of resources at a specified price on a specified future date or dates; and

- *Forecast transaction:* an uncommitted but anticipated future transaction.[3]

The standard contains one other definition related to hedge accounting, i.e. of 'hedge effectiveness' and this is covered at 5.3 below.

2.1   Hedging instruments

There are a number of restrictions on what type of item may be used as the hedging instrument in a 'valid' hedge, i.e. one that can qualify for hedge accounting, and these operate on many levels as set out below. One of these restrictions stems from the definition of a hedging instrument and requires an entity to have an expectation that its fair value or cash flows will offset changes in the fair value or cash flows of the hedged item attributable to the hedged risk. This requirement principally manifests itself in the provisions on hedge effectiveness, which are dealt with at 5.3 below.

2.1.1   Derivative financial instruments

The distinction between derivative and non-derivative financial instruments is covered in Chapter 15 at 4. With the exception of certain written options (see below), the circumstances in which a derivative may be designated as a hedging instrument are not restricted, provided the conditions for hedge accounting set out at 5 below are met.[4] Those conditions mean that a derivative that is not carried at fair value because it is linked to and must be settled by delivery of an unquoted equity instrument whose fair value cannot be reliably measured (see Chapter 18 at 4.4) cannot be designated as a hedging instrument.[5]

In order to be able to qualify as a hedging instrument, the derivative must be accounted for as such under IAS 39. Therefore, an embedded derivative that is accounted for separately from its host contract (see Chapter 15 at 5) can be used as a hedging instrument. However, a contract that is considered a normal sale or purchase, and is therefore accounted for as an executory contract (see Chapter 15 at 3.8), could not.[6]

Example 19.1:   Hedging with a sales commitment

Company J has the Japanese yen as its functional currency. J has issued a fixed rate debt instrument with semi-annual interest payments that matures in two years with principal due at maturity of US$5 million. It has also entered into a fixed price sales commitment for US$5 million that matures in two years and is not accounted for as a derivative because it qualifies for the normal sales exemption.

Because the sales commitment is accounted for as a firm commitment rather than a derivative instrument it cannot be a hedging instrument in a hedge of the foreign currency risk associated with the debt instrument. However, if the foreign currency component of the sales commitment was required to be separated as an embedded derivative (essentially a forward contract to buy US dollars for yen) that component could be designated as the hedging instrument in such a hedge.[7]

Similarly, a forecast transaction or planned future transaction cannot be the hedging instrument as it is not a recognised financial instrument,[8] and is therefore not be a derivative.

A   Options and collars

It is explained that an option an entity writes is not effective in reducing the profit or loss exposure of a hedged item. In other words, the potential loss on a written option could be significantly greater than the potential gain in value of a related hedged item. Therefore, a written option is prohibited from qualifying as a hedging instrument unless it is designated as an offset to a purchased option, including one that is embedded in another financial instrument. An example of this might be a written call option that is used to hedge a callable liability. In contrast, a purchased option has potential gains equal to or greater than losses and therefore has the potential to reduce profit or loss exposure from changes in fair values or cash flows. Accordingly, a purchased option can qualify as a hedging instrument.[9]

It follows that a derivative such as an interest rate collar that includes a written option cannot be designated as a hedging instrument if it is a net written option. However, a derivative instrument that includes a written option may be designated as a hedging instrument if it is a net purchased option or zero cost collar[10] (i.e. it is neither a net written nor net purchased option).

The following factors, taken together, indicate that an instrument is not a net written option:

- no net premium is received, either at inception or over the life of the instrument – the distinguishing feature of a written option is the receipt of a premium to compensate for the risk incurred;

- except for the strike prices, the critical terms and conditions of the written and purchased option components are the same, including underlying variable(s), currency denomination and maturity date; and

- the notional amount of the written option component is not greater than that of the purchased option component.[11]

The application of these requirements is illustrated in the following two examples.

Example 19.2: Foreign currency collar (or 'cylinder option')

Company E, which has sterling as its functional currency, has forecast that it is highly probable it will receive €1,000 in six months time in respect of an expected sale to a customer in France.

E is concerned that sterling might have appreciated by the time the payment is received and wishes to protect the profit margin on the sale without paying the premium that would be required with an ordinary currency option. E also wishes to benefit from some of the upside in the event that sterling depreciates, so would prefer not to use a forward contract.

Accordingly, E enters into an instrument under which it effectively:

- purchases an option that allows it to buy sterling for €1,000 euro from the counterparty at €1.53:£1.00; and

- sells an option that allows the counterparty to sell sterling to E for €1,000 euro at €1.47:£1.00.

In the foreign currency markets, such an instrument is often called a 'cylinder option' rather than a 'collar' and it operates as follows. If, in six months time, the spot exchange rate exceeds €1.53:£1.00, E will exercise its option to sell €1,000 at €1.53:£1.00, effectively fixing its minimum proceeds on the sale (in sterling terms) at £654. Similarly, if the rate is below €1.47:£1.00, the counterparty will exercise its option to buy €1,000 at €1.47:£1.00, effectively capping E's maximum proceeds on the sale at £680. If the rate is between €1.47:£1.00 and €1.53:£1.00, both options will lapse unexercised and E will be able to sell its €1,000 for sterling at the spot rate, generating between £654 and £680.

The premium that E would pay to acquire the purchased option equals the premium it would receive to sell the written option and therefore no premium is paid or received on inception. The critical terms and conditions, including the notional amounts, of the written and purchased option components are the same except for the strike price. Therefore, E concludes that the instrument is not a net written option and, consequently, it may be used as the hedging instrument in a hedge of the foreign currency risk associated with the future sale.

It is possible that the counterparty might, instead, have offered E a variation on the instrument described above. If the notional amount on E's purchased option component was reduced, say to €500, the counterparty could have offered a better rate on that component, say €1.51. However, in this case, the notional amount on the written option component is twice that of the purchased option component and the instrument would be seen as a net written option. Accordingly, even if E had very good business reasons for using such an instrument to manage its foreign exchange risk, it could not qualify as a hedging instrument under IAS 39. Therefore, hedge accounting would be precluded.

Example 19.3: 'Knock-out' swap

Company Y has a significant amount of long-dated floating rate borrowings. In order to hedge the cash flow interest rate risk arising from these borrowings, Y has entered into a number of matching pay-fixed, receive-floating interest rate swaps that effectively convert the interest rates on the borrowings to fixed rate.

Under the terms of one of these swaps, on each fifth anniversary of its inception until maturity the swap counterparty may choose to simply terminate the swap at no cost. This is often referred to as a knock-out feature. In return for agreeing to this, Y benefits by paying a lower interest rate on the swap's fixed leg than it would on a conventional swap. In other words, Y receives a premium for taking on the risk of the counterparty cancelling the swap.

This instrument contains a net written option, i.e. the knock-out feature, and therefore cannot be used as a hedging instrument unless it is used in a hedge of an equivalent purchased option. (In practice, it is somewhat unlikely that the hedged borrowings will contain such an option feature.)

B   Credit break clauses

It is not uncommon for certain derivatives (e.g. interest rate swaps) to contain terms that allow the counterparties to settle the instrument at 'fair value' in certain circumstances. Such terms, often called 'credit break clauses', enable the counterparties to manage their credit risk in markets where collateral or margin accounts and master netting agreements are not used. They are particularly common where a long-duration derivative is transacted between a financial and non-financial institution. For example, the terms of a twenty-year interest rate swap may allow either party to settle the instrument at fair value on the fifth, tenth and fifteenth anniversary of its inception.

These terms can be seen as options on counterparty credit risk. However, provided the two parties have equivalent rights to settle the instrument at fair value, the credit break clause will generally not prevent the derivative from qualifying as a hedging instrument. Particularly, in assessing whether a premium is received for agreeing to the incorporation of such terms into an instrument, care needs to be exercised. For example, marginally better underlying terms offered by one potential counterparty (as a result of market imperfections) should not be mistaken for a very small option premium.

2.1.2   Cash instruments

In contrast to the position for derivatives, there are significant restrictions over the use as hedging instruments of non-derivative financial assets and liabilities, or 'cash instruments' as the IASB sometimes refer to them.[12] Essentially, a cash instrument may be designated as a hedging instrument only for a hedge of foreign currency risk.[13]

This would allow, say, a held-to-maturity investment carried at amortised cost to be designated as a hedging instrument in a hedge of foreign currency risk[14] as well as other instruments such as loans and receivables, available for sale debt instruments and borrowings. However, an investment in an unquoted equity instrument that is not carried at fair value because its fair value cannot be reliably measured (see Chapter 18 at 4.4), cannot be designated as a hedging instrument.[15]

The following two examples illustrate the types of permitted hedge relationships where the hedging instrument is a non-derivative.

Example 19.4:   Hedging with a non-derivative liability

In Example 19.1 above, Company J had issued a fixed rate debt instrument with principal due at maturity in two years of US$5 million. J had also entered into a fixed price sales commitment, accounted for as an executory contract, for US$5 million that matured in two years as well.

J could not designate the debt instrument as a hedge of the exposure to *all* fair value changes of the fixed price sales commitment because the hedging instrument is a non-derivative. However, J could designate it as a hedge of the foreign currency exposure associated with the future receipt of US dollars on the fixed price sales commitment.[16]

Example 19.5:   Hedge of foreign currency bond

Company J has also issued US$5 million five year fixed rate debt and owns a US$5 million five year fixed rate bond, which is classified as available for sale.

J's bond has exposure to changes in both foreign currency and interest rates, as does the liability. However, the liability can only be designated as a hedge of the bond's foreign currency, not interest rate, risk because it is a non-derivative instrument.

In fact in this case, hedge accounting is unnecessary because the amortised cost of the hedging instrument and the hedged item are both remeasured using closing rates with differences reported in profit or loss as required by IAS 21 – *The Effects of Changes in Foreign Exchange Rates.*[17]

In revising IAS 39, the IASB considered whether to allow cash instruments to qualify as hedging instruments in less restrictive circumstances. However, although it was acknowledged that some entities did actually use non-derivatives to manage risks other than foreign currency risk, for various reasons it was concluded that the existing prohibition should be retained.[18]

2.1.3   Combinations of instruments

Two or more derivatives, or proportions of them (see 2.1.4 below) may be viewed in combination and jointly designated as a hedging instrument. This is the case even when the risk(s) arising from some derivatives offset(s) those arising from others. However, an interest rate collar or other derivative instrument that combines a written option and a purchased option cannot qualify as a hedging instrument if it is, in effect, a net written option (for which a net premium is received).[19]

Similarly, two or more instruments (or proportions of them) may be designated as a hedging instrument only if *none of them* is a written option or a net written option.[20] Under the previous version of the standard, two or more derivatives, or proportions thereof could be viewed in combination and jointly designated as the hedging instrument, provided the *combination* was not a net written option.[21]

In practice, many zero cost collars are transacted as legally separate written and purchased options. On the face of it, therefore, such transactions can no longer be treated as a combined hedging instrument. However, we are not at all convinced the IASB intended such a prohibition to take effect in practice. This is especially the case if the reason the collar takes the legal form of two options is for the seller's administrative ease, which would in many cases be irrelevant to the entity purchasing the collar. In fact, if it can be demonstrated that the only substantive business purpose for entering into such an arrangement is to purchase a zero cost collar to hedge an underlying exposure, the logic in some of the implementation guidance would *require* these contracts to be treated as a single instrument for this purpose (see 2.3.3 below and Chapter 15 at 4.5 and 6).

In the case of a hedge of foreign currency risk, the revised standard also allows two or more non-derivatives, or proportions of them, to be viewed in combination and designated as a hedging instrument. Further, in what seems like a significant change (or at least a major clarification), a combination of derivatives and non-derivatives, or proportions of them, may now be similarly combined.[22]

Unlike for combinations of derivatives, the standard does not clarify whether it is acceptable for these combinations to contain offsetting terms although in the absence of an indication to the contrary we believe it is. For example, an entity with the euro as its functional currency may have issued a yen denominated floating rate borrowing and entered into a matching receive-yen floating (plus principal at maturity), pay-US dollar floating (plus principal at maturity) cross-currency interest rate swap. These instruments, which effectively synthesise a US dollar floating rate borrowing, contain offsetting terms, i.e. the whole of the borrowing and the yen leg of the swap. The entity could designate the combination of these two instruments in a hedge of the entity's foreign currency risk arising from, say, an asset with an identifiable exposure to yen/US dollar exchange rates.

2.1.4 Portions and proportions of hedging instruments

A Time and interest elements of options and forwards

In contrast to the position for hedged financial items (see 2.2.1 below), there are significant restrictions on what components of an individual financial instrument can be carved out and designated as a hedging instrument. It is explained that there is normally a single fair value measure for a hedging instrument in its entirety and the factors that cause changes in its fair value are co-dependent. Normally, therefore, a financial instrument (or proportion thereof – see B below) can only be designated as a hedging instrument in its entirety.[23]

Example 19.6: Combination of written and purchased options

Company Y transacts a combination of a written option and purchased option (such as an interest rate collar) as a single instrument with one counterparty. Y cannot split the derivative instrument into its written and purchased option components and designate the purchased option component as a hedging instrument.[24]

Similarly, the 'knock-out swap' in Example 19.3 above could not be split into a conventional interest rate swap, to be used as a hedging instrument, and the knock-out feature (a written swaption, i.e. an option for the counterparty to enter into an offsetting interest rate swap with the same terms as the conventional swap).

However, the following are two of the principal exceptions to this general rule:

- separating the intrinsic value and time value of an option contract and designating as the hedging instrument only the change in intrinsic value of the option and excluding changes in its time value; and
- separating the interest element and spot price of a forward contract.

These are permitted because the intrinsic value of the option and the premium on the forward can generally be measured separately.[25]

There are a number of reasons an entity may wish to take advantage of these exceptions. For example, excluding these portions may be consistent with the entity's overall hedging strategy, such as where the interest element of forward contracts are managed with the rest of the entity's interest rate exposures rather than in conjunction with the associated spot rate exposures. Excluding these components may also make it administratively easier to process the hedges and it can certainly improve a hedge's effectiveness (especially when using an option – see 5.3.10 below).

However, the use of these exceptions is not mandatory. For example, a dynamic hedging strategy that assesses both the intrinsic value and time value of an option contract can qualify for hedge accounting (see 5.1 below).[26]

B   *Proportions of instruments*

In addition to the above exceptions, a proportion of the entire hedging instrument, such as 50% of the notional amount, may also be designated in a hedging relationship. However, a hedging relationship may not be designated for only a portion of the time period in which the hedging instrument is outstanding.[27]

C   *Cash instruments*

There is one further situation where a portion of an instrument may be designated as a hedging instrument (in fact, is required to be). In the case of a cash instrument used as a hedge of foreign currency risk, it is essentially only the spot rate retranslation risk of, say, a borrowing that is used as the hedging instrument and not the other components, such as its changes in fair value arising from interest rate risk.

D   *Notional decomposition*

We also believe it is acceptable to split a derivative (or allowable portion thereof) into component parts provided:

(a)   all of those components are designated and qualify for hedge accounting; and

(b)   any separate part is clearly identifiable from the original terms of the contract.

Without restriction (b), a derivative could be split in a potentially infinite number of ways that could include risks that were clearly not present in the original contract.

The implementation guidance contains an example of just such an approach – see Example 19.7 at 2.1.6 below.

E   *Restructuring of derivatives*

An entity may exchange a derivative that does not qualify as a hedging instrument (say, the knock-out swap in Example 19.3 above) for two separate derivatives that, together, have the same fair value as the original instrument (say, a conventional interest rate swap and a written swaption). Such an exchange is likely to be motivated by a desire to obtain hedge accounting for one of these new instruments, perhaps in preparation for transition to IFRS.

In order to determine whether the new arrangement can be treated as two separate derivatives, rather than a continuation of the original derivative, we believe it is necessary to determine whether the exchange transaction has any substance, which is clearly a matter of judgement.

For example, in the case of the knock-out swap, if the two new contracts had the same counterparty and, in aggregate, the same terms as the original contract this would not necessarily lead to the conclusion that the exchange lacked substance. However if, in addition, the swaption would be settled by delivery of the conventional interest rate swap in the event that it was exercised, this is a strong indicator that the exchange does lack substance.

2.1.5   Reduction of risk

The implementation guidance explains that risk exposures should be assessed on a transaction basis and, therefore, a hedging instrument need not reduce risk at an entity-wide level. For example, if an entity has a fixed rate asset and a fixed rate liability, each with the same principal terms, it may enter into a pay-fixed, receive-variable interest rate swap to hedge the fair value of the asset even though the effect of the swap is to create an interest rate exposure for the entity that previously did not exist.[28]

However, a hedging instrument does need to reduce risk at the transaction level. Consider a 'basis swap' that effectively converts one variable interest rate index (say a central bank base rate) to another (say LIBOR). Instruments of this nature would not normally qualify as a hedging instrument because they do not reduce or eliminate risk in any meaningful way. Unless they are used in a hedge of offsetting asset and liability positions (see 2.1.6 below) they simply convert one risk to another similar risk.

A basis swap or similar instrument may also qualify as a hedging instrument when considered in combination with another instrument (see 2.1.3 above). For example, the basis swap described above and a pay-fixed, receive-LIBOR interest rate swap may qualify as a hedging instrument in a hedge of a borrowing that pays interest based on a central bank rate.

2.1.6   Hedging different risks with one instrument

A single hedging instrument may be designated as a hedge of more than one type of risk, provided that:

- the risks hedged can be identified clearly;
- the effectiveness of the hedge can be demonstrated (see 5.3 below); and
- it is possible to ensure that there is specific designation of the hedging instrument and different risk positions.[29]

The implementation guidance provides the following example to illustrate this point.

Example 19.7:   Foreign currency forward hedging positions in two foreign currencies

Company J, which has Japanese yen as its functional currency, issues five year floating rate US dollar debt and acquires a ten year fixed rate sterling bond. The principal amounts of the asset and liability, when converted into Japanese yen, are the same. J enters into a single foreign currency forward contract to hedge its foreign currency exposure on both instruments under which it receives US dollars and pays sterling at the end of five years.

Designating a single hedging instrument as a hedge of multiple types of risk is permitted if three conditions are met:

- the hedged risks can be clearly identified.

    In this case the risks are exposures to changes in the US dollar/yen and yen/sterling exchange rates respectively;

- the effectiveness of the hedge can be demonstrated.

    For the sterling bond, effectiveness can be measured as the degree of offset between the fair value of the principal repayment in sterling and the fair value of the sterling payment on the forward exchange contract.

    For the US dollar liability, effectiveness can be measured as the degree of offset between the fair value of the principal repayment in US dollars and the US dollar receipt on the forward exchange contract.

    Even though the bond has a ten year life and the forward only protects it for the first five years, hedge accounting is permitted for only a portion of the exposure (see 2.2.1 below); and

- it is possible to ensure that there is a specific designation of the hedging instrument and the different risk positions.

    The hedged exposures are identified as the principal amounts of the liability and the bond in their respective currency of denomination.

The hedging instrument satisfies all of these conditions and J can designate the forward as a hedging instrument in a cash flow hedge against the foreign currency exposure on the principal repayments of both instruments and qualify for hedge accounting.[30]

In this example, the hedging instrument is effectively decomposed and viewed as two forward contracts, each with an offsetting position in yen, i.e. J's functional currency.

By analogy with Example 19.7 above, we believe it would be acceptable to use a basis swap as a hedge of relevant asset and liability positions. For example, an entity may have made a $1m loan that earns LIBOR based interest and a $1m liability that pays interest based on the central bank rate. In this case it may use as a hedging instrument an interest rate swap under which it pays LIBOR based interest and receives interest based on the central bank rate on a notional amount of $1m.

The implementation guidance also explains that a single hedging instrument may be designated in both a cash flow hedge and a fair value hedge, provided the above conditions are met (section 3 covers the three different types of hedge recognised by IAS 39). For example, entities may use a combined interest rate and currency swap to convert a variable rate position in a foreign currency to a fixed rate position in the functional currency. Such a swap could be designated separately as a fair value hedge of the currency risk and a cash flow hedge of the interest rate risk.[31]

The implementation guidance takes the concept of hedging different risks a little further, as set out in the following example.

Example 19.8:   *Cross-currency interest rate swap hedging two foreign currency*
                    exchange rate exposures and fair value interest rate exposure

Company J now issues five-year floating rate US dollar debt and acquires a ten-year fixed rate sterling bond and wishes to hedge the foreign currency exposure on both the bond and the debt as well as the fair value interest rate exposure on the bond. To do this it enters into a matching cross-currency interest rate swap to receive floating rate US dollars, pay fixed rate sterling and exchange the US dollars for sterling at the end of five years.

Hedge accounting is permitted for components of risk, provided effectiveness can be measured (see 2.2.1 below) and a single hedging instrument may be designated as a hedge of more than one type of risk if the risks can be identified clearly, effectiveness can be demonstrated, and specific designation of the hedging instrument and the risk positions can be ensured.

Therefore, the swap may be designated as a hedging instrument in a fair value hedge of the sterling bond against exposure to changes in its fair value associated with the interest rate payments on the bond until year five and the change in value of the principal payment due at maturity to the extent affected by changes in the yield curve relating to the five years of the swap (see Example 19.9 at 2.2.1 below) as well as the exchange rate between sterling and US dollars.

The mechanics of hedge accounting for fair value hedges is discussed at 4.1 below. In summary, the swap would be measured at fair value with changes in fair value reported in profit or loss. The carrying amount of the receivable would be adjusted for changes in its fair value caused by changes in UK interest rates for the first five-year portion of the yield curve. Both the receivable and payable are remeasured using spot exchange rates under IAS 21 and the changes to their carrying amounts recorded in profit or loss.[32]

Taken literally, the designation set out above takes no account of the existence of the US dollar liability and thereby suggests that the exchange rate between sterling and US dollars (the hedged risk) is seen as a component of the risk associated with the sterling bond (the hedged item). Mathematically this is clearly true from the point of view of a yen functional entity – together, the sterling/US dollar rate and the US dollar/yen rate give the sterling/yen exchange rate, i.e. the true foreign currency risk arising on the sterling bond. However, without considering the US dollar liability (which does not appear to be part of the designated hedge relationship) the hedge provides no real offset against the currency risk of the sterling liability. Instead it simply converts one foreign currency risk (exposure to sterling) to another (exposure to US dollars) and, as set out at 2.1.5 above, this would not normally be considered an acceptable hedging relationship. The IASB obviously sees the existence of the US dollar liability as important (otherwise it would not have been introduced into the example) but the point it is trying to articulate is not perfectly clear. In all likelihood, their failure to refer to the US dollar liability in the description of the hedge designation was simply an oversight.

The guidance above discussed combinations of (a) different cash flow hedges, (b) different fair value hedges and (c) a cash flow hedge and a fair value hedge. However, there appears to be no reason why a single instrument could not, in theory, be designated in other combinations of hedges, for example a cash flow hedge and a hedge of a net investment.

2.1.7 Own equity instruments

An entity's own equity instruments are not financial assets or liabilities of the entity and, therefore, cannot be hedging instruments.[33] This prohibition would also apply to instruments that give rise to minority interests in consolidated financial statements – under IFRS it is now clear that minority interests are part of an entity's equity.

2.2 Hedged items

The basic requirement for a hedged item is for it to be one of the following:

- a recognised asset or liability;
- an unrecognised firm commitment;
- a highly probably forecast transaction; or
- a net investment in a foreign operation,

and it should expose the entity to the risk of changes in fair value or future cash flows.[34]

Recognised assets and liabilities can include, in addition to financial items, non-financial items such as inventory. They can also include recognised firm commitments that are not routinely recognised as assets or liabilities absent the effects of hedge accounting for such items (see 3.4 below). Most internally generated intangibles (e.g. for a bank, a core deposit intangible – see 2.2.8 below) are not recognised assets and therefore cannot be hedged items.[35]

2.2.1 Financial items: portions and proportions

If the hedged item is a financial asset or liability, it may be a hedged item with respect to the risks associated with only a portion of its cash flows or fair value, such as one or more selected contractual cash flows or portions of them or a percentage of the fair value (i.e. a proportion of the asset or liability). For example, an identifiable and separately measurable portion of the interest rate exposure of an interest-bearing asset or liability may be designated as the hedged risk. Such a portion might be a risk-free interest rate or benchmark interest rate component of the total interest rate exposure of a hedged financial instrument. This is always subject to the proviso that effectiveness can be measured (see 5.3 below).[36]

This has the effect that a hedge can be designated for part of the term that a hedged item remains outstanding as illustrated in the following example.

Example 19.9: Partial term hedging

Company A acquires a 10% fixed rate government bond with a remaining term to maturity of ten years and classifies it as available-for-sale. To hedge against the fair value exposure on the bond associated with the first five years' interest payments, it acquires a five year pay-fixed receive-floating swap.

The swap may be designated as hedging the fair value exposure of the interest rate payments on the government bond until year five and the change in value of the principal payment due at maturity to the extent affected by changes in the yield curve relating to the five years of the swap.[37]

In finalising the 'portfolio hedge' amendments to IAS 39, the IASB received comments that demonstrated the meaning of a 'portion' was unclear. Accordingly, the following guidance on what may, or may not, be designated as a hedged portion, was added to the standard to explain this concept further.[38]

In general, if a portion of the cash flows of a financial asset or liability is designated as the hedged item, that designated portion must be less than its total cash flows. For example, in the case of a liability whose effective interest rate is below LIBOR, designating the following components is not permitted:

- a portion of the liability equal to the principal amount plus interest at LIBOR; and

- a negative residual portion.[39]

This is unlikely to be of major concern to many companies outside of the financial services sector. In contrast to banks and similar financial institutions that take deposits from customers (who often accept a return that is lower than prevailing market rates) many such entities cannot access variable-rate funding at below LIBOR rates. However, those entities with a particularly strong credit rating are sometimes able to borrow at sub-LIBOR rates, even in the capital markets.

In these cases, all of the cash flows of the entire financial asset or liability may be designated as the hedged item in a hedge of only one particular risk (e.g. only for changes that are attributable to changes in LIBOR). For example, an entire financial liability whose effective interest rate is 100 basis points (1%) below LIBOR (i.e. the principal plus interest at LIBOR minus 100 basis points) can be designated as the hedged item in a hedge of the change in the fair value or cash flows of that entire liability that is attributable to changes in LIBOR. Nevertheless, some ineffectiveness will occur and, in order to improve the effectiveness of the hedge, a hedge ratio of other than one-to-one may be chosen (see 2.2.2 below).[40]

The guidance goes on to explain that if a fixed rate financial instrument is hedged some time after its origination and interest rates have changed in the meantime, a portion equal to a benchmark rate that is actually higher than the contractual rate paid on the item *can* be designated as the hedged item. This is provided that the benchmark rate is less than the effective interest rate calculated on the assumption that the instrument had been purchased on the day it was first designated as the hedged item.[41] This is illustrated below.

Example 19.10:   Hedge of a portion of an existing fixed rate financial asset following a rise in interest rates

Company B originates a fixed rate financial asset of €100 that has an effective interest rate of 6% at a time when LIBOR is 4%. B begins to hedge that asset some time later when LIBOR has increased to 8% and the fair value of the asset has decreased to €90.

B calculates that if it had purchased the asset on the date it first designated it as the hedged item for its then fair value of €90, the effective yield would have been 9.5%. Because LIBOR is less than this effective yield, the entity can designate a LIBOR portion of 8% that consists partly of the contractual interest cash flows and partly of the difference between the current fair value (€90) and the amount repayable on maturity (€100).[42]

It is not uncommon for entities to have borrowed money when prevailing rates were low and decide, at a later date after rates have increased, to 'convert' that low fixed rate borrowing into a floating rate borrowing. The guidance illustrated in Example 19.10 above will assist such entities in designating these hedges in a way that significantly reduces ineffectiveness. In fact, as noted at 5.3.8 below, the ability to designate a portion of a financial instrument as the hedged item can enable many hedges to be designated in a way that minimises or even eliminates ineffectiveness.

The implementation guidance explains that the foreign currency risk associated with a holding of publicly traded shares may be hedged if they give rise to a clear and identifiable exposure to changes in foreign exchange rates. It is asserted that this will be the case if:

- the shares are not traded on an exchange, or other established market, in which trades are denominated in the same currency as the holder's functional currency; and

- dividends on the shares are not denominated in that currency.

Consequently, if the share trades in multiple currencies, one of which is the holder's functional currency, hedge accounting would not be permitted.[43] However, this does not stand up to close scrutiny, as illustrated in the following example.

Example 19.11: Foreign currency risk associated with equity shareholding

ABC plc, a UK company whose functional currency is sterling, acquires a small shareholding in IJK Limited. IJK is a South African company whose operations are based solely in that country and whose income, expenditure and dividends are all denominated in South African rand. IJK's shares are listed on the Johannesburg Stock Exchange where trades are denominated in rand.

The implementation guidance suggests that, potentially, ABC could hedge the foreign currency risk arising from the sterling/rand exchange rate on its IJK holding, which appears quite sensible. If, on day 1, the shares trade at R50 and the exchange rate is R10 to £1, the shares would have a sterling value of £5.00 (= R50 ÷ 10). If, on day 2, the exchange rate moves to R8 to £1, all other things being equal, the rand value of IJK should not change, but its sterling value would be £6.25 (= R50 ÷ 8), exactly mirroring the exchange rate movement.

If IJK subsequently obtained a secondary listing on the London Stock Exchange where trades were denominated in sterling, but its business fundamentals were unchanged, in the scenario outlined above ABC's foreign exchange exposure would be exactly the same. In fact, the operation of the markets should ensure that share price in London on days 1 and 2 is £5.00 and £6.25 respectively. However, the guidance suggests that because of the secondary listing, ABC no longer has a clear and identifiable exposure to changes in foreign exchange rates on the IJK shares.

2.2.2 Non-financial items: portions and proportions

It is explained that changes in the price of an ingredient or component of a non-financial asset or liability generally do not have a predictable, separately measurable effect on the price of the item that is comparable to the effect of, say, a change in market interest rates on the price of a bond. Therefore, because of the difficulty of isolating and measuring the appropriate portion of cash flows or fair value changes attributable to specific risks (other than foreign currency risks) a non-financial asset or liability can be designated as a hedged item only:

- in its entirety for all risks; or
- for foreign exchange risks.[44]

A number of commentators disagree with this assertion, at least in certain situations, and some urged the IASB in revising IAS 39 to reconsider this restriction. For example, Swiss International Air Lines, in responding to the June 2002 exposure draft, wrote the following:

'Like any airline SWISS is short of jet fuel. The Company is exposed to the daily price fluctuations of crude oil and the prices of inter product spreads (cracks, differentials) that convert crude oil into gas oil and finally into jet fuel.

There is more liquidity in crude oil for positions beyond two years. Therefore, it is part of SWISS' fuel risk management strategy to do long-term hedges with crude oil. These positions are then rolled into gas oil and jet fuel as they move closer to the settlement dates.

Paragraphs 129-130 [of the Exposure Draft] state that non-financial assets and liabilities can only be hedged in their entirety or separately with respect to foreign exchange risk.

Crude oil hedges therefore must be designated as hedging the risk of price movements of jet fuel in its entirety. The critical terms of the hedging instrument and the hedged item therefore do not perfectly match – frequently a certain ineffectiveness will result. Even if the hedge can be expected to be highly effective due to a high historical correlation of the price movements of crude and jet fuel, actual effectiveness might fall outside the 80-125% range in some periods and the hedge will have to be dedesignated.

We believe that due to the special properties of jet fuel prices, it should be allowed to designate the price changes of a jet fuel component such as crude oil as the hedged risk.

The reason given in paragraphs 129 and 130 is that risk components of non-financial instruments generally do not have a predictable, separately measurable effect on the price of the entire item. This is a generalization that does not account for the special properties of jet fuel pricing.

Jet fuel is a derivative of crude oil. Crude oil is then converted into gas oil. The difference of the crude and the gas oil price is called gas oil crack. Gas oil is finally converted into jet fuel, the price difference being called jet differential.

It is not difficult to isolate and measure the portion of the changes of jet fuel prices attributable to the price risk of these components. Crude, gas oil crack, and jet differential are separately traded and market prices are available through market information systems such as Platt's as for jet fuel itself. The price of jet fuel actually is calculated from the prices of its components.

Changes in the price of the components of jet fuel do have a predictable, separately measurable effect on the price of jet fuel. This effect can be compared to the effect of a change in the market interest rates on the price of a bond.'[45]

However, in spite of protestations such as this, the IASB noted that in many cases, changes in the cash flows or fair value of a portion of a non-financial hedged item *are* difficult to isolate and measure and therefore the restriction was retained largely unchanged.[46] This was much to the disappointment of various airlines and entities with similar fuel requirements who would have preferred the standard to adopt a different approach, e.g. to establish a 'rebuttable presumption' that components could not be identified and separately hedged.

The IASB also considered whether the interest rate risk portion of loan servicing rights could be designated as the hedged item on the grounds that this portion can be separately identified and measured, and that changes in market interest rates have a predictable and separately measurable effect on the value of such rights. In fact the possibility of treating loan servicing rights as financial assets rather than non-financial assets, perhaps on an elective basis, was also considered. However, it was concluded that no exceptions should be permitted for this matter either.[47]

It is clear from the logic of the above restriction that an entity may hedge a non-financial exposure for all risks *except* foreign currency risk (even if it is not clear from the standard itself), as illustrated in the following example.

Example 19.12: Hedge of foreign currency denominated commodity risk

Company P has the FC as its functional currency. It has forecast, with a high probability, the need to purchase a fixed quantity of crude oil in twelve months time. To hedge part of its exposure to the price risk inherent in this purchase it enters into an exchange traded twelve-month cash-settled crude oil forward contract. The strike price of the forward is denominated in US dollars (there is no active market in FC denominated crude oil futures) and P chooses not to hedge the risk associated with FC to US dollar exchange rates. This might be because of illiquidity in the foreign currency markets for FCs or, perhaps, because P has forecast US dollar inflows that provide a natural hedge of the foreign exchange risk.

P may designate the forward contract as the hedging instrument in a hedge of the exposure to the US dollar denominated price risk associated with its forecast purchase of crude oil.

In many cases it appears it will be difficult to identify a separately measurable effect on non-financial assets, even for foreign currency risk, as illustrated in the following example from the implementation guidance.

Example 19.13: Foreign currency borrowings hedging a ship

A Danish shipping company, D, has a US subsidiary that has the same functional currency as the parent, the Danish krone. Accordingly in D's consolidated financial statements, ships owned by the subsidiary, which are carried at depreciated historical cost, are reported in Danish krone using historical exchange rates. To hedge the potential currency risk on the disposal of the ships in US dollars, purchases of ships are normally financed with loans denominated in US dollars.

US dollar borrowings cannot be classified as fair value hedges of a ship because ships do not contain any separately measurable foreign currency risk even if their purchase was, and sale is likely to be, denominated in US dollars.

The proceeds from the anticipated sale of the ship may, however, be designated in a cash flow hedge, provided all the hedging criteria are met (see 5 below). Those conditions require that the sale is highly probable, which is only likely if the sale is expected to occur in the immediate future.[48]

Unfortunately, the statement that a ship does not contain any separately measurable foreign currency risk is not explained any further, which makes it difficult to apply this guidance in other situations. For example, it is hard to argue that a commodity such as crude oil, which is traded throughout the world in US dollars, does not contain a measurable exposure to US dollars. If another commodity was regularly traded and quoted both in US dollars and in euro (the implementation guidance suggests this might be the case for natural gas – see Chapter 15 at 5.1.9) it might seem sensible to treat that commodity as containing both US dollar and euro exposures. However, by analogy with the guidance on quoted shares (see 2.2.1 above), a commodity that is traded and quoted in more than one currency would probably be deemed to have no measurable currency exposure from the perspective of an entity whose functional currency is one of those currencies.

Inevitably, for many hedges of non-financial items there will be a difference between the terms of the hedging instrument and the hedged item (as well as the restriction on hedging portions of the non-financial item, there may simply be no perfectly matching hedging instruments). For example, a forward contract to purchase Colombian coffee might be used as a hedge of the forecast purchase of Brazilian coffee on otherwise similar terms. Such a hedge may, nonetheless, qualify as a hedge relationship, provided all the conditions at 5 are met.[49]

To meet these conditions, it must be expected that the hedge will be highly effective. For this purpose, the amount of the hedging instrument may be greater or less than that of the hedged item if this improves the effectiveness of the hedging relationship. For example, a regression analysis could be performed to establish a statistical relationship between the hedged item (e.g. a transaction in Brazilian coffee) and the hedging instrument (e.g. a transaction in Columbian coffee). If there is a valid statistical relationship between the two variables (i.e. between the unit prices of Brazilian coffee and Columbian coffee), the slope of the regression line can be used to establish the hedge ratio that will maximise expected effectiveness. For example, if the slope of the regression line is 1.02, a hedge ratio based on 0.98 quantities of hedged items to 1.00 quantities of the hedging instrument maximises expected effectiveness. However, the hedging relationship may result in ineffectiveness that is recognised in profit or loss during the term of the hedging relationship.[50] This idea is a recurring theme in the standard and is referred to a number of times.

2.2.3   Groups of items as hedged items

The standard explains that a hedged item can be a single item or a group of such items with similar risk characteristics.[51] To aggregate and hedge similar assets or liabilities as a group, the individual items need to share the risk exposure for which they are hedged. Further, the standard requires that fair value changes attributable to the hedged risk for each individual item should be approximately proportional to the equivalent fair value change of the entire group.[52] For example, the risk characteristics of the individual shares in a portfolio designed to replicate a share index will be different from each other and from the portfolio as a whole. Therefore, the portfolio could not be hedged with respect to movements in the index[53] even though, in economic terms, the portfolio of shares may well be perfectly (or near perfectly) hedged. In situations like this, an entity may choose to designate the assets within the portfolio at fair value through profit or loss. In this way, gains and losses from the hedging instrument and hedged items should offset in the income statement.

As discussed at 5.3 below, hedge effectiveness is assessed by comparing the change in value or cash flow of hedging instruments and of hedged items. Therefore, comparing a hedging instrument to an overall net position, e.g. the net of all fixed rate assets and fixed rate liabilities with similar maturities, rather than to a specific hedged item, cannot qualify for hedge accounting.[54] Similarly, the net cash flows arising from a portfolio of floating rate assets and liabilities cannot be designated as the hedged item.[55]

However, approximately the same effect on profit or loss can be achieved by designating part of the underlying items as the hedged position. For example, a European company with firm commitments to make purchases and sales of US$100 and US$90 respectively could hedge the net exposure by acquiring a derivative and designating it as a hedging instrument associated with purchases of US$10. Similarly, a bank with €100 of assets and €90 of liabilities with risks and terms of a similar nature could hedge the net exposure by designating €10 of those assets as the hedged item.[56]

2.2.4 Hedges of general business risk

To qualify for hedge accounting, the hedge must relate to a specific identified and designated risk, and not merely to the entity's general business risks; also, it must ultimately affect profit or loss. Therefore, a hedge of the risk of obsolescence of a physical asset or the risk of expropriation of property by a government is not eligible for hedge accounting (effectiveness cannot be measured because those risks are not measurable reliably).[57] Similarly, the risk that a transaction will not occur is an overall business risk that is not eligible as a hedged item.[58]

A firm commitment to acquire a business in a business combination cannot be a hedged item, except for foreign exchange risk, because the other risks being hedged cannot be specifically identified and measured. These other risks are also said to be general business risks.[59]

2.2.5 Held-to-maturity investments

Unlike loans and receivables, a held-to-maturity investment (whether it pays fixed or floating interest rates) cannot be a hedged item with respect to interest rate risk or prepayment risk. This is because designating an investment as held-to-maturity requires an intention to hold the investment until maturity without regard to changes in the fair value or cash flows of such an instrument attributable to changes in interest rates (see Chapter 15 at 7.2).[60]

However, a held-to-maturity investment (or related cash flows) can be a hedged item in the following circumstances:

- the investment may be a hedged item with respect to risks from changes in foreign currency exchange rates and credit risk;[61]

- the forecast purchase of such an investment may be a hedged item, say to lock in current interest rates – this is because an investment is not given an IAS 39 classification until it is actually recognised;[62] and

- the forecast reinvestment of fixed or variable interest receipts can be hedged items with respect to the risk of interest rate changes.[63]

    It should be noted that this hedge relationship is significantly different from a hedge of the interest rate risk on the held-to-maturity investment itself. This is most commonly used as a building block in the cash flow macro-hedging model (see 6) below.

2.2.6 *Derivatives*

Unless they are designated and effective hedging instruments, derivative financial instruments are always deemed held for trading and measured at fair value with gains and losses recognised in profit or loss. Therefore, a derivative cannot normally be a hedged item. However, as noted at 2.1.1 above, there is an exception where a written option is used to hedge a purchased option.[64]

2.2.7 *Own equity instruments*

Transactions in an entity's own equity instruments (including distributions to holders of such instruments) are generally recognised directly in equity by the issuer (see Chapter 17) and do not affect profit or loss. Therefore, such instruments cannot be designated as a hedged item. However, a declared dividend that qualifies for recognition as a financial liability, e.g. because the entity has become legally obliged to make the payment, may qualify as a hedged item. For example, a recognised liability to pay a dividend in a foreign currency would give risk to foreign exchange risk. Similarly, a forecast transaction in an entity's own equity instruments or forecast dividend payment cannot qualify as a hedged item.[65]

2.2.8 *Recognised core deposit intangibles*

The term 'core deposit intangible' is used to represent the difference between:

(a)   the fair value of a portfolio of core deposits (e.g. current or deposit accounts); and

(b)   the aggregate of the individual fair values of the liabilities within the portfolio.

It was noted at 2.2 above that an internally generated core deposit intangible cannot be a hedged item because it is not a recognised asset. If a core deposit intangible is acquired together with a related portfolio of deposits, it is required to be recognised separately as an intangible asset (or as part of the related acquired portfolio of deposits) if it meets the recognition criteria in IAS 38 – *Intangible Assets.*[66]

Theoretically, therefore, a recognised core deposit intangible asset could be designated as a hedged item. However this will only be the case if it meets the conditions for hedge accounting, including the requirement that the effectiveness of the hedge can be measured reliably (see 5.3 below). Because it is often difficult to measure reliably the fair value of a core deposit intangible asset other than on initial recognition, it is unlikely that this requirement will be met.[67]

2.3 Internal hedges and other group accounting issues

One of the most pervasive impacts that IAS 39 can have on groups, especially those operating centralised treasury functions, is the need to reassess hedging strategies that involve intra-group transactions. To a layman this might come as something of a surprise because the standard does little more than reinforce the general principle (established many years ago in accounting standards such as IAS 27 – *Consolidated and Separate Financial Statements*) that transactions between different entities within a group should be eliminated in the consolidated financial statements of that group. Nevertheless, a significant amount of the standard and related implementation guidance is devoted to this subject.

2.3.1 Internal hedging instruments

The starting point for this guidance is the principle of preparing consolidated financial statements in IAS 27 that requires that 'intragroup balances, transactions, income and expenses shall be eliminated in full'.[68]

Although individual entities within a consolidated group (or divisions within a single legal entity) may enter into hedging transactions with other entities within the group (or divisions within the entity), such as internal derivative contracts to transfer risk exposures between different companies (or divisions), any such intra-group (or intra-entity) transactions are eliminated on consolidation. Therefore, such hedging transactions do not qualify for hedge accounting in the consolidated financial statements of the group[69] (or in the individual or separate financial statements of an entity for hedging transactions between divisions of the entity). Effectively, this is because they do not exist in an accounting sense.

As a consequence, IAS 39 makes it very clear that for hedge accounting purposes only instruments that involve a party external to the reporting entity (i.e. external to the group, segment or individual entity that is being reported on) can be designated as hedging instruments.[70]

The implementation guidance explains that IAS 39 does not specify how an entity should *manage* its risk. Accordingly, where an internal contract is offset with an external party, the external contract may be regarded as the hedging instrument. In such cases, the hedging relationship (which is between the external transaction and the item that is the subject of the internal hedge) may qualify for hedge accounting.[71] The following example illustrates this.

Example 19.14:   Internal derivatives

The banking division of Bank A enters into an internal interest rate swap with A's trading division. The purpose is to hedge the interest rate risk exposure of a loan (or group of similar loans) in the loan portfolio. Under the swap, the banking division pays fixed interest payments to the trading division and receives variable interest rate payments in return.

Assuming a hedging instrument is not acquired from an external party, hedge accounting treatment for the hedging transaction undertaken by the banking and trading divisions is not allowed, because only derivatives that involve a party external to the entity can be designated as hedging instruments. Further, any gains or losses on intragroup or intra-entity transactions should be eliminated on consolidation. Therefore, transactions between different divisions within A cannot qualify for hedge accounting treatment in Bank A's financial statements. Similarly, transactions between different entities within a group cannot qualify for hedge accounting treatment in A's consolidated financial statements.

However, if, in addition to the internal swap in the above example, the trading division entered into an interest rate swap or other contract with an external party that offset the exposure hedged in the internal swap, hedge accounting would be permitted. For the purposes of IAS 39, the hedged item is the loan (or group of similar loans) in the banking division and the hedging instrument is the external interest rate swap or other contract.

The trading division may aggregate several internal swaps or portions of them that are not offsetting each other (see 2.3.2 below) and enter into a single third party derivative contract that offsets the aggregate exposure. Such external hedging transactions may qualify for hedge accounting treatment provided that the hedged items in the banking division are identified and the other conditions for hedge accounting are met. It should be noted, however, that hedge accounting is not permitted where the hedged items are held-to-maturity investments and the hedged risk is the exposure to interest rate changes.[72]

It follows that internal hedges may qualify for hedge accounting in the individual or separate financial statements of individual entities within the group, as well as in segment reporting, provided they are external to the individual entity or segment that is being reported on.[73]

The implementation guidance contains the following summary of the application of IAS 39 to internal hedging transactions:

- IAS 39 does not preclude an entity from using internal derivative contracts for risk management purposes and it does not preclude internal derivatives from being accumulated at the treasury level or some other central location so that risk can be managed on an entity-wide basis or at some higher level than the separate legal entity or division.

- Internal derivative contracts between two separate entities within a consolidated group can qualify for hedge accounting by those entities in their individual or separate financial statements, even though the internal contracts are not offset by derivative contracts with a party external to the consolidated group.

- Internal derivative contracts between two separate divisions within the same legal entity can qualify for hedge accounting in the individual or separate financial statements of that legal entity only if those contracts are offset by derivative contracts with a party external to the legal entity.

- Internal derivative contracts between separate divisions within the same legal entity and between separate entities within the consolidated group can qualify for hedge accounting in the consolidated financial statements only if the internal contracts are offset by derivative contracts with a party external to the consolidated group.

- If the internal derivative contracts are not offset by derivative contracts with external parties, the use of hedge accounting by group entities and divisions using internal contracts must be reversed on consolidation.[74]

The premise on which the restriction on internal hedging instruments is based is not completely true. As noted at 2.3.4 below, foreign currency intra-group balances may well give rise to gains and losses in profit or loss that are not eliminated on consolidation. However, this does not change the fact that no internal transactions can be used as a hedging instrument in consolidated financial statements.

Although the June 2002 exposure draft did not explicitly address this topic (essentially, it retained the existing requirements unchanged) the IASB received a great deal of comment on it. Particularly, many constituents argued that internal hedges should be allowed to qualify for hedge accounting. They even pointed to US GAAP, which allows internal derivative contracts to be designated as hedging instruments in hedges of some forecast foreign currency transactions. However, the only changes made were to clarify that intra-group transactions could qualify for hedge accounting in segment reporting or in the individual financial statements of entities or segments, provided they were external to the segment or entity.[75]

2.3.2 Offsetting internal hedging instruments

As noted at 2.3.1 above, if an internal contract used in a hedging relationship is offset with an external party, the external contract may be regarded as a hedging instrument and the hedge may qualify for hedge accounting.[76] The implementation guidance elaborates on this further in the context of both interest rate and foreign currency risk management, particularly in the situation where the internal derivatives are offset before being laid off with a third party.

A Interest rate risk

As set out in Example 19.14 above, central treasury functions sometimes enter into internal derivative contracts with subsidiaries and, perhaps, divisions within the consolidated group to manage interest rate risk on a centralised basis. If, before laying off the risk, the internal contracts are first netted against each other and only the net exposure is offset in the marketplace with external derivative contracts, the internal contracts cannot qualify for hedge accounting in the consolidated financial statements.[77]

An internal contract designated at the subsidiary level, or by a division, as a hedge results in the recognition of changes in the fair value of the item being hedged in profit or loss (for a fair value hedge – see 4.1.1 below) or in the recognition of the changes in the fair value of the internal derivative in equity (for a cash flow hedge – see 4.2.1 below). On consolidation, there is no basis for changing the measurement attribute of the item being hedged in a fair value hedge unless the exposure is offset with an external derivative. Similarly, on consolidation, there is no basis for including the gain or loss on the internal derivative in equity for one entity and recognising it in profit or loss by the other entity unless it is offset with an external derivative.[78]

Where two or more internal derivatives used to manage interest rate risk on assets or liabilities at the subsidiary or division level are offset at the treasury level, the effect of designating the internal derivatives as hedging instruments is that the hedged non-derivative exposures at the subsidiary or division levels would be used to offset each other on consolidation. Accordingly, since IAS 39 does not permit designating non-derivatives as hedging instruments (except for foreign currency exposures) the results of hedge accounting from the use of internal derivatives at the subsidiary or division level that are not laid off with external parties must be reversed on consolidation.[79]

It should be noted, however, that there will be no effect on profit or loss and equity of reversing the effect of hedge accounting in consolidation for internal derivatives that offset each other at the consolidation level if they are used in the same type of hedging relationship at the subsidiary or division level and, in the case of cash flow hedges, where the hedged items affect profit or loss in the same period. Just as the internal derivatives offset at the treasury level, their use as fair value hedges by two separate entities or divisions within the consolidated group will also result in the offset of the fair value amounts recognised in profit or loss. Similarly, their use as cash flow hedges by two separate entities or divisions within the consolidated group will also result in the fair value amounts being offset against each other in equity.[80]

However, there may be an effect on individual line items in both the consolidated income statement and the consolidated balance sheet, for example when internal derivatives that hedge assets (or liabilities) in a fair value hedge are offset by internal derivatives that are used as a fair value hedge of other assets (or liabilities) that are recognised in a different balance sheet or income statement line item. In addition, to the extent that one of the internal contracts is used as a cash flow hedge and the other is used in a fair value hedge, the effect on profit or loss and equity would not offset since the gain (or loss) on the internal derivative used as a fair value hedge would be recognised in profit or loss and the corresponding loss (or gain) on the internal derivative used as a cash flow hedge would be recognised in equity.[81]

Notwithstanding this, under the principles set out at 2.2.3 above, it may be possible to designate the external derivative as a hedge of *some* of the underlying exposures as illustrated in the following example.

Example 19.15: Internal contracts offset on a net basis

Company A uses what it describes as internal derivative contracts to document the transfer of responsibility for interest rate risk exposures from individual divisions to a central treasury function. The central treasury function aggregates the internal derivative contracts and enters into a single external derivative contract that offsets the internal derivative contracts on a net basis.

On one particular day the central treasury function enters into three internal receive-fixed, pay-variable interest rate swaps that lay off the exposure to variable interest cash flows on variable rate liabilities in other divisions and one internal receive-variable, pay-fixed interest rate swap that lays off the exposure to variable interest cash flows on variable rate assets in another division. It enters into an interest rate swap with an external counterparty that exactly offsets the four internal swaps.

A hedge of an overall net position does not qualify for hedge accounting. However, designating a part of the underlying items as the hedged position on a gross basis is permitted (see 2.2.3 above). Therefore, even though the purpose of entering into the external derivative was to offset internal derivative contracts on a net basis, hedge accounting is permitted if the hedging relationship is defined and documented as a hedge of a part of the underlying cash inflows or cash outflows on a gross basis and assuming that the hedge accounting criteria are met.[82]

B   Foreign exchange risk

Although much of the discussion at A above applies equally to hedges of foreign currency risk, there is one important distinction between the two situations. As set out at 2.1.2 above, IAS 39 does allow non-derivative financial instruments to be used as the hedging instrument in the hedge of foreign currency risk. Therefore, in this case, internal derivatives may be used as a basis for *identifying* external transactions that qualify for hedge accounting provided that the internal derivatives represent the transfer of foreign currency risk on underlying non-derivative financial assets or liabilities. However, for consolidated financial statements, it is necessary to *designate* the hedging relationship so that it involves only external transactions.[83]

Furthermore, as set out at 2.1.1 above, forecast transactions and unrecognised firm commitments cannot qualify as hedging instruments under IAS 39. Accordingly, to the extent that two or more offsetting internal derivatives represent the transfer of foreign currency risk on such items, hedge accounting cannot be applied. As a result, if any cumulative net gain or loss on an internal derivative has been included in the initial carrying amount of an asset or liability (a 'basis adjustment') or deferred in equity (see 4.2.1 and 4.2.2 below), it would have to be reversed on consolidation if it cannot be demonstrated that the offsetting internal derivative represented the transfer of a foreign currency risk on a financial asset or liability to an external hedging instrument.[84]

The following example illustrates this principle – it also illustrates the mechanics of accounting for cash flow hedges and fair value hedges, which are discussed in more detail at 4.1 and 4.2 below.

Example 19.16:   Using internal derivatives to hedge foreign currency risk[85]

In each of the following cases, 'FC' represents a foreign currency, 'LC' represents the local currency (which is the entity's functional currency) and 'TC' the group's treasury centre.

Case 1: Offset of fair value hedges

Subsidiary A has trade receivables of FC100, due in 60 days, which it hedges using a forward contract with TC. Subsidiary B has payables of FC50, also due in 60 days, which it hedges using a forward contact with TC.

TC nets the two internal derivatives and enters into a net external forward contract to pay FC50 and receive LC in 60 days.

At the end of month 1, FC weakens against LC. A incurs a foreign exchange loss of LC10 on its receivables, offset by a gain of LC10 on its forward contract with TC. B makes a foreign exchange gain of LC5 on its payables, offset by a loss of LC5 on its forward contract with TC. TC makes a loss of LC10 on its internal forward contract with A, a gain of LC5 on its internal forward contract with B and a gain of LC5 on its external forward contract.

Accordingly, the following entries are made in the individual or separate financial statements of A, B and TC at the end of month 1. Entries reflecting intra-group transactions or events are shown in italics.

A's entries

	LC	LC
Foreign exchange loss	10	
Receivables		10
Internal contract (TC)	*10*	
Internal gain (TC)		*10*

B's entries

	LC	LC
Payables	5	
Foreign exchange gain		5
Internal loss (TC)	*5*	
Internal contract (TC)		*5*

TC's entries

	LC	LC
Internal loss (A)	*10*	
Internal contract (A)		*10*
Internal contract (B)	*5*	
Internal gain (B)		*5*
External forward contract	5	
Foreign exchange gain		5

Both A and B could apply hedge accounting in their individual financial statements provided all necessary conditions were met. However, because gains and losses on the internal derivatives and the offsetting losses and gains on the hedged receivables and payables are recognised immediately in profit or loss without hedge accounting, hedge accounting is unnecessary (see 3.3 for further information on hedges of foreign currency denominated monetary items).

In the consolidated financial statements, the internal derivative transactions are eliminated. In economic terms, B's payable hedges FC50 of A's receivables. The external forward in TC hedges the remaining FC50 of A's receivable. In the consolidated financial statements, hedge accounting is again unnecessary because monetary items are measured at spot foreign exchange rates under IAS 21 irrespective of whether hedge accounting is applied.

The net balances, before and after elimination of the accounting entries relating to the internal derivatives, are the same, as set out below. Accordingly, there is no need to make any further accounting entries to meet the requirements of IAS 39.

	LC	LC
Receivables	–	10
Payables	5	–
External forward contract	5	–
Gains and losses	–	–
Internal contracts	–	–

Case 2: Offset of cash flow hedges

To extend the example, A also has highly probable future revenues of FC200 on which it expects to receive cash in 90 days. B has highly probable future expenses of FC500 (advertising cost), also to be paid for in 90 days. A and B enter into separate forward contracts with TC to hedge these exposures and TC enters into an external forward contract to receive FC300 in 90 days.

As before, FC weakens at the end of month 1. A incurs a 'loss' of LC20 on its anticipated revenues because the LC value of these revenues decreases and this is offset by a gain of LC20 on its forward contract with TC. Similarly, B incurs a 'gain' of LC50 on its anticipated advertising cost because the LC value of the expense decreases and this is offset by a loss of LC50 on its transaction with TC.

TC incurs a gain of LC50 on its internal transaction with B, a loss of LC20 on its internal transaction with A and a loss of LC30 on its external forward contract.

Both A and B complete the necessary documentation, the hedges are effective and both A and B qualify for hedge accounting in their individual financial statements. A defers the gain of LC20 on its internal derivative transaction in a hedging reserve in equity and B does the same with its loss of LC50. TC does not claim hedge accounting, but measures both its internal and external derivative positions at fair value, which net to zero.

Accordingly, the following entries are made in the individual or separate financial statements of A, B and TC at the end of month 1. Entries reflecting intra-group transactions or events are shown in italics.

A's entries

	LC	LC
Internal contract (TC)	*20*	
Equity		*20*

B's entries

	LC	LC
Equity	*50*	
Internal contract (TC)		*50*

TC's entries

	LC	LC
Internal loss (A)	*20*	
Internal contract (A)		*20*
Internal contract (B)	*50*	
Internal gain (B)		*50*
Foreign exchange loss	30	
External forward contract		30

IAS 39 requires that, in the consolidated financial statements, the accounting effects of the internal derivative transactions must be eliminated.

If there were no hedge designation for the consolidated financial statements, the gains and losses recognised in equity and profit or loss on the internal derivatives would be reversed. Consequently, a loss of LC30 would be recognised in profit or loss in respect of the external forward contract held by TC.

However, for the consolidated financial statements, TC's external forward contract on FC300 *is* designated, at the beginning of month 1, as a hedging instrument of the first FC300 of B's highly probable future expenses. Therefore, LC30 of the gain recognised in equity by B may remain in equity on consolidation, because it involves an external derivative. Accordingly, the net balances, before and after elimination of the accounting entries relating to the internal derivatives, are as set out below and there is no need to make any further accounting entries in order for the requirements of IAS 39 to be met.

	LC	LC
External forward contract	–	30
Equity	30	–
Gains and losses	–	–
Internal contracts	–	–

Case 3: Offset of fair value and cash flow hedges

The example is extended further and it is assumed that the exposures and the internal derivative transactions are the same as in Cases 1 and 2. In other words, Subsidiary A has trade receivables of FC100, due in 60 days, and highly probable future revenues of FC200 on which it expects to receive cash in 90 days. Subsidiary B has payables of FC50, due in 60 days, and highly probable future expenses of FC500 to be paid for in 90 days. Each of these exposures is hedged using forward contacts with TC. However, in this case, instead of entering into two external derivatives to hedge separately the fair value and cash flow exposures, TC enters into a single net external derivative to receive FC250 in exchange for LC in 90 days.

Consequently, TC has four internal derivatives, two maturing in 60 days and two maturing in 90 days. These are offset by a net external derivative maturing in 90 days. The interest rate differential between FC and LC is minimal, and therefore the ineffectiveness resulting from the mismatch in maturities is expected to have a minimal effect on profit or loss in TC.

As in Cases 1 and 2, A and B apply hedge accounting for their cash flow hedges and TC measures its derivatives at fair value. A defers a gain of LC20 on its internal derivative transaction in equity and B does the same with its loss of LC50.

Accordingly, the following entries are made in the individual or separate financial statements of A, B and TC at the end of month 1. Entries reflecting intra-group transactions or events are shown in italics.

A's entries

	LC	LC
Foreign exchange loss	10	
Receivables		10
Internal contract (TC)	*10*	
Internal gain (TC)		*10*
Internal contract (TC)	*20*	
Equity		*20*

B's entries

	LC	LC
Payables	5	
Foreign exchange gain		5
Internal loss (TC)	*5*	
Internal contract (TC)		*5*
Equity	*50*	
Internal contract (TC)		*50*

TC's entries

	LC	LC
Internal loss (A)	*10*	
Internal contract (A)		*10*
Internal loss (A)	*20*	
Internal contract (A)		*20*
Internal contract (B)	*5*	
Internal gain (B)		*5*
Internal contract (B)	*50*	
Internal gain (B)		*50*
Foreign exchange loss	25	
External forward contract		25

The gains and losses recognised on the internal contracts in A and B can be summarised as follows:

	A LC	B LC	Total LC
Income (fair value hedges)	10	(5)	5
Equity (cash flow hedges)	20	(50)	(30)
Total	30	(55)	(25)

In the consolidated financial statements, IAS 39 requires the accounting effects of the internal derivative transactions to be eliminated.

If there were no hedge designation for the consolidated financial statements, the gains and losses recognised in equity and profit or loss on the internal derivatives would be reversed. Consequently, a loss of LC30 would be recognised in profit or loss in respect of the external receivable and payable held by A and B respectively and the external forward contract held by TC.

However, for the consolidated financial statements, the following designations *are* made at the beginning of month 1:

- the payable of FC50 in B is designated as a hedge of the first FC50 of the highly probable future revenues in A.

  Therefore, at the end of month 1, the following entries are made in the consolidated financial statements: Dr Payable LC5; Cr Equity LC5;

- the receivable of FC100 in A is designated as a hedge of the first FC100 of the highly probable future expenses in B.

    Therefore, at the end of month 1, the following entries are made in the consolidated financial statements: Dr Equity LC10, Cr Receivable LC10; and

- the external forward contract on FC250 in TC is designated as a hedge of the next FC250 of highly probable future expenses in B.

    Therefore, at the end of month 1, the following entries are made in the consolidated financial statements: Dr Equity LC25; Cr External forward contract LC25.

Combining these entries produces the total net balances as follows:

	LC	LC
Receivables	–	10
Payables	5	–
External forward contract	–	25
Equity	30	–
Gains and losses	–	–
Internal contracts	–	–

Case 4: Offset of fair value hedges with adjustment to carrying amount of inventory

Similar transactions to those in Case 3 are assumed except that the anticipated cash outflow of FC500 in B relates to the purchase of inventory that is delivered after 60 days. It is also assumed that the entity has a policy of basis-adjusting hedged forecast non-financial items (see 4.2.2 below).

To recap, Subsidiary A has trade receivables of FC100, due in 60 days, and highly probable future revenues of FC200 on which it expects to receive cash in 90 days. Subsidiary B has payables of FC50, due in 60 days, and a highly probable future purchase of inventory for FC500, to be delivered in 60 days and paid for in 90 days. Each of these exposures is hedged using forward contacts with TC, and TC enters into a single net external derivative to receive FC250 in exchange for LC in 90 days.

At the end of month 2, there are no further changes in exchange rates or fair values. At that date, the inventory is delivered and the loss of LC50 on B's internal derivative, deferred in equity in month 1, is adjusted against the carrying amount of inventory in B. The gain of LC20 on A's internal derivative is deferred in equity as before.

In the consolidated financial statements, there is now a mismatch compared with the result that would have been achieved by unwinding and redesignating the hedges. The external derivative (FC250) and the receivable (FC50) offset FC300 of the anticipated inventory purchase. There is a natural hedge between the remaining FC200 of anticipated cash outflow in B and the anticipated cash inflow of FC200 in A. This relationship does not qualify for hedge accounting under IAS 39 and this time there is only a partial offset between gains and losses on the internal derivatives that hedge these amounts.

Accordingly, the following entries are made in the individual or separate financial statements of A, B and TC at the end of month 1. Entries reflecting intra-group transactions or events are shown in italics.

A's entries (all at the end of month 1)

	LC	LC
Foreign exchange loss	10	
Receivables		10
Internal contract (TC)	*10*	
Internal gain (TC)		*10*
Internal contract (TC)	*20*	
Equity		*20*

B's entries (at the end of month 1)

	LC	LC
Payables	5	
Foreign exchange gain		5
Internal loss (TC)	*5*	
Internal contract (TC)		*5*
Equity	*50*	
Internal contract (TC)		*50*

B's entries (at the end of month 2)

	LC	LC
Inventory	50	
Equity		50

TC's entries (all at the end of month 1)

	LC	LC
Internal loss (A)	*10*	
Internal contract (A)		*10*
Internal loss (A)	*20*	
Internal contract (A)		*20*
Internal contract (B)	*5*	
Internal gain (B)		*5*
Internal contract (B)	*50*	
Internal gain (B)		*50*
Foreign exchange loss	25	
External forward contract		25

The gains and losses recognised on the internal contracts in A and B can be summarised as follows:

	A LC	B LC	Total LC
Income (fair value hedges)	10	(5)	5
Equity (cash flow hedges)	20	–	20
Basis adjustment (inventory)	–	(50)	(50)
Total	30	(55)	(25)

Combining these amounts with the external transactions (i.e. those not marked in italics above) produces the total net balances before elimination of the internal derivatives as follows:

	LC	LC
Receivables	–	10
Payables	5	–
External forward contract	–	25
Equity	–	20
Basis adjustment (inventory)	50	–
Gains and losses	–	–
Internal contracts	–	–

For the consolidated financial statements, the following designations are made at the beginning of month 1:

- the payable of FC50 in B is designated as a hedge of the first FC50 of the highly probable future revenues in A.

  Therefore, at the end of month 1, the following entry is made in the consolidated financial statements: Dr Payables LC5; Cr Equity LC5.

- the receivable of FC100 in A is designated as a hedge of the first FC100 of the highly probable future inventory purchase in B.

  Therefore, at the end of month 1, the following entries are made in the consolidated financial statements: Dr Equity LC10; Cr Receivable LC10; and at the end of month 2, Dr Inventory LC10; Cr Equity LC10.

- the external forward contract on FC250 in TC is designated as a hedge of the next FC250 of highly probable future inventory purchase in B.

  Therefore, at the end of month 1, the following entry is made in the consolidated financial statements: Dr Equity LC25; Cr External forward contract LC25; and at the end of month 2, Dr Inventory LC25; Cr Equity LC25.

The total net balances after elimination of the accounting entries relating to the internal derivatives are as follows:

	LC	LC
Receivables	–	10
Payables	5	–
External forward contract	–	25
Equity	–	5
Basis adjustment (inventory)	35	–
Gains and losses	–	–
Internal contracts	–	–

These total net balances are different from those that would be recognised if the internal derivatives were not eliminated, and it is these net balances that IAS 39 requires to be included in the consolidated financial statements. The accounting entries required to adjust the total net balances before elimination of the internal derivatives are as follows:

- to reclassify LC15 of the loss on B's internal derivative that is included in inventory to reflect that FC150 of the forecast purchase of inventory is not hedged by an external instrument (neither the external forward contract of FC250 in TC nor the external payable of FC100 in A); and

- to reclassify the gain of LC15 on A's internal derivative to reflect that the forecast revenues of FC150 to which it relates is not hedged by an external instrument.

The net effect of these two adjustments is as follows:

	LC	LC
Equity	15	
Inventory		15

It is apparent that extending the principles set out in this relatively simple example to the more complex, and higher volume, situations that are likely to be encountered in practice is not going to be straightforward.

2.3.3 *Offsetting external hedging instruments*

The implementation guidance explains that where two offsetting derivatives are transacted at the same time, it is generally not permitted to designate one of them as a hedging instrument in a (fair value) hedge unless:

- the second swap was not entered into in contemplation of the first; or

- there is a 'substantive business purpose' for structuring the transactions separately.

It is emphasised that judgement should be applied in determining what is a substantive business purpose. For example, a centralised treasury company may enter into third party derivative contracts on behalf of other subsidiaries to hedge their interest rate exposures and, to track those exposures within the group, enter into internal derivative transactions with those subsidiaries. It may also enter into a derivative contract with the same counterparty during the same business day with substantially the same terms as a contract entered into as a hedging instrument on behalf of another subsidiary as part of its trading operations, or because it wishes to rebalance its overall portfolio risk. In this case, there is a valid business purpose for entering into each contract. However, a desire to achieve fair value accounting for the hedged item is deemed not to be a substantive business purpose.[86]

The following example, based on the implementation guidance, explores this issue a little further.

Example 19.17: External derivative contracts settled net

A company uses internal derivative contracts to transfer interest rate risk exposures from individual divisions to a central treasury function. For each internal derivative contract, the central treasury function enters into a derivative contract with a single external counterparty that offsets the internal derivative contract. For example, if the central treasury function has entered into a receive-5% fixed, pay-LIBOR interest rate swap with another division that has entered into the internal contract with central treasury to hedge the exposure to variability in interest cash flows on a pay-LIBOR borrowing, central treasury would enter into a pay-5% fixed, receive-LIBOR interest rate swap on the same principal terms with the external counterparty.

Although each external derivative contract is formally documented as a separate contract, only the net of the payments on all of the external derivative contracts is settled since there is a netting agreement with the external counterparty.

Even though the external derivatives are settled on a net basis the individual external derivative contracts, such as the pay-5% fixed, receive-LIBOR interest rate swap above, can generally be designated as hedging instruments of underlying gross exposures, such as the exposure to changes in variable interest payments on the pay-LIBOR borrowing above.

External derivative contracts that are legally separate contracts and serve a valid business purpose, such as laying off risk exposures on a gross basis, qualify as hedging instruments even if those external contracts are settled on a net basis with the same external counterparty, provided the hedge accounting criteria in IAS 39 are met.[87]

In the context of interest rate instruments, the facts in this example appear a little unlikely. This is because most master netting agreements have a practical effect only in the event of default by, or insolvency of, one of the counterparties – otherwise payments tend to be made gross. The above situation seems possible only where the instruments are settled through a clearing house (or where the clearing house is the counterparty).

For foreign currency instruments, a number of financial institutions provide services that are broadly analogous to the one described in Example 19.17. Under these arrangements a treasury function will transact, say, legally separate forward exchange contracts with the financial institution to offset each individual intra-group derivative it has entered into with a subsidiary or division. These contracts will be administered under a centralised facility with settlements being made on a net basis. Further, the financial institution will often price these contracts to reflect the reduced credit risk and administrative burden associated with the arrangements so that the cost of transacting individual contracts is significantly reduced.

Some may express surprise that the guidance explains that arrangements such as those illustrated in Example 19.17 above may qualify for hedge accounting. In substance, they are little different from the entity offsetting its internal contracts before entering into an offsetting external transaction, which as explained at 2.3.2 above, would not permit hedge accounting to be applied for each item hedged using an internal contract. However, this is nothing compared to what follows. The implementation guidance considers an extension to the arrangement set out above:

> 'Treasury observes that by entering into the external offsetting contracts and including them in the centralised portfolio, it is no longer able to evaluate the exposures on a net basis. Treasury wishes to manage the portfolio of offsetting external derivatives separately from other exposures of the entity. Therefore, it enters into an additional, single derivative to offset the risk of the portfolio.'[88]

The guidance explains that the purpose of structuring the external derivatives like this is consistent with the entity's risk management policies and strategies and, generally, hedge accounting may still be used. Even if this final external derivative is effected with the same counterparty under the same netting arrangement, and notwithstanding the fact that all exposures with that counterparty will, as a result, net to zero, it is implied that this constitutes a substantive business purpose as described at the start of this sub-section.[89]

In essence, the guidance appears to suggest that the use of internal derivatives for hedge accounting is allowed, provided that an agreement is reached with a third party to give the appearance of laying off the exposure even though the risk is immediately taken back again. This seems a long way from what the standard requires and, in fact, begs the question of why an entity should even go to the trouble of creating such an artificial external agreement that appears to lacks any commercial substance. We have serious reservations over this part of the guidance, particularly we question whether it really would be possible to demonstrate the existence of a valid business purpose for such an arrangement. It remains to be seen to what extent this becomes accepted practice.

2.3.4 Internal hedged items

Only assets, liabilities, firm commitments or highly probable forecast transactions that involve a party external to the entity can be designated as hedged items. It follows that hedge accounting can be applied to transactions between entities or segments in the same group only in the individual or separate financial statements of those entities or segments and not in the consolidated financial statements of the group.[90]

As an exception, IAS 39 allows the foreign currency risk of an intra-group monetary item (e.g. a payable or receivable between two subsidiaries) to qualify as a hedged item in the consolidated financial statements if it results in an exposure to foreign exchange rate gains or losses that are not fully eliminated on consolidation under IAS 21. Under IAS 21, foreign exchange gains and losses on such items are not fully eliminated on consolidation when they are transacted between two group entities that have different functional currencies (see Chapter 9 at 2.7.2 A)[91] as illustrated in the following example.

Example 19.18: Intra-group monetary items that will affect consolidated profit or loss

Company A has two subsidiaries, Company B and Company C. A and B have the euro as their functional currencies, while C has the US dollar as its functional currency. On 31 March, C purchases goods from B for US$110, payable on 30 June.

In this case, the intra-group monetary item of US$110 may be designated as a hedged item in a hedge of foreign currency risk both by B in its separate financial statements and by A in its consolidated financial statements.

While B's foreign currency receivable is eliminated against C's foreign currency payable on consolidation, the exchange differences that arise for B cannot be eliminated since C has no corresponding exchange differences.

Thus, the intra-group monetary item results in an exposure to variability in the foreign currency amount of the intra-group monetary item that will affect profit or loss in the consolidated financial statements. Therefore, the intra-group monetary item may be designated as a hedged item in a foreign currency hedge.[92]

Under the previous version of IAS 39, a *forecast* intra-group transaction could also be designated as a hedged item if, on occurrence, it would give rise to an intra-group monetary item that itself could qualify as a hedged item.[93] The revised standard, however, prohibits such a hedge relationship, although the IASB has subsequently published an exposure draft[94] that would allow such arrangements to qualify for hedge accounting in certain circumstances. This exposure draft is covered in more detail at 8.1 below.

2.3.5 Hedged item and hedging instrument held by different group entities

The implementation guidance explains that, in a group, it is not necessary for the hedging instrument to be held by the same entity as the one that has the exposure being hedged in order to qualify for hedge accounting in the consolidated financial statements.[95] This is illustrated in the following example.

Example 19.19:   Subsidiary's foreign exchange exposure hedged by parent

Company S is based in Switzerland and prepares consolidated financial statements in Swiss francs. It has an Australian subsidiary, Company A, whose functional currency is the Australian dollar and is included in the consolidated financial statements of S. A has forecast purchases in Japanese yen that are highly probable and S enters into a forward contract to hedge the change in yen relative to the Australian dollar.

Because A did not hedge the foreign currency exchange risk associated with the forecast purchases in yen, the effects of exchange rate changes between the Australian dollar and the yen will affect A's profit or loss and, therefore, would also affect consolidated profit or loss. Therefore that hedge may qualify for hedge accounting in S's consolidated financial statements provided the other hedge accounting criteria in IAS 39 are met.[96]

3   TYPES OF HEDGING RELATIONSHIPS

There are three types of hedging relationship defined in IAS 39:

- *fair value hedge:* a hedge of the exposure to changes in the fair value of a recognised asset or liability or an unrecognised firm commitment, or an identified portion of such an asset, liability or firm commitment, that is attributable to a particular risk and could affect profit or loss;
- *cash flow hedge:* a hedge of the exposure to variability in cash flows that:
  - (i)   is attributable to a particular risk associated with a recognised asset or liability (such as all or some future interest payments on variable rate debt) or a highly probable forecast transaction; and
  - (ii)   could affect profit or loss; and
- *hedge of a net investment in a foreign operation:* as defined in IAS 21 (see Chapter 9 at 2.5 and 3.4.1).[97]

These definitions are considered further in the remainder of this section.

3.1   Fair value hedges

An example of a fair value hedge is a hedge of the exposure to changes in the fair value of a fixed rate debt instrument as a result of changes in interest rates – if interest rates increase, the fair value of the debt decreases and vice versa. Such a hedge could be entered into either by the issuer or by the holder[98] (provided it was not classified as held-to-maturity – see 2.2.5 above).

On the face of it, if a fixed rate loan that is classified within loans and receivables is held until it matures (as is the case for many such loans), changes in the fair value of the loan would not affect profit or loss. However, the implementation guidance explains that such assets may be hedged items in a fair value hedge because the loan *could* be sold, in which case fair value changes *would* affect profit or loss.[99] The same would be true of a fixed rate borrowing for which settlement before maturity is very unlikely.

A variable rate debt may be the hedged item in a fair value hedge in certain circumstances. For example, the fair value of such an instrument will change if the issuer's credit risk changes. There may also be changes in its fair value relating to movements in the market rate in the periods between which the variable rate is reset. For example, if a debt instrument provides for annual interest payments reset to the market rate each year, a portion of the debt instrument has an exposure to changes in fair value during the year.[100]

The exposure to changes in the price of inventories that are carried at the lower of cost and net realisable value may also be the subject of a fair value hedge because their fair value will affect profit or loss when they are sold or written down. For example, a copper forward may be used as the hedging instrument in a hedge of the copper price associated with copper inventory.[101]

An equity method investment cannot be a hedged item in a fair value hedge because the equity method recognises in profit or loss the investor's share of the associate's profit or loss, rather than changes in the investment's fair value. For a similar reason, an investment in a consolidated subsidiary cannot be a hedged item in a fair value hedge because consolidation recognises in profit or loss the subsidiary's profit or loss, rather than changes in the investment's fair value.[102]

3.2   Cash flow hedges

An example of a cash flow hedge is the use of an interest rate swap to change floating rate debt to fixed rate debt, i.e. a hedge of a future transaction where the future cash flows being hedged are the future interest payments.[103]

As noted at 3.1 above, a hedge of the exposure to changes in the fair value of a fixed rate debt instrument as a result of changes in interest rates could be treated as a fair value hedge. This could not be a cash flow hedge because changes in interest rates will not affect the cash flows on the hedged item, only its fair value.[104]

It was also noted at 3.1 above that a copper forward, say, may be used in a fair value hedge of copper inventory. Alternatively, the same hedging instrument may qualify as a cash flow hedge of the future sale of the inventory.[105]

The following example from the implementation guidance explains how a company might lock in current interest rates by way of a cash flow hedge of the anticipated issuance of fixed rate debt.

Example 19.20:   Hedge of anticipated issuance of fixed rate debt

Company R periodically issues new bonds to refinance maturing bonds, provide working capital, and for various other purposes. When R decides it will be issuing bonds, it sometimes hedges the risk of changes in long-term interest rates to the date the bonds are issued. If long-term interest rates go up (down), the bond will be issued either at a higher (lower) rate, with a higher (smaller) discount or with a smaller (higher) premium than was originally expected. The higher (lower) rate being paid or decrease (increase) in proceeds is normally offset by the gain (loss) on the hedge.

In August 2005 R decides it will issue £2m seven-year bonds in January 2006. Historical correlation studies suggest that a seven-year treasury bond adequately correlates to the bonds R expects to issue, assuming a hedge ratio of 0.93 futures contracts to one debt unit (adjusting the hedge ratio to maximising expected effectiveness is discussed further at 2.2.2 above). Therefore, it hedges the anticipated issuance of the bonds by selling ('shorting') £1.86m worth of futures on seven-year treasury bonds.

From August 2005 to January 2006 interest rates increase and the short futures positions are closed on the date the bonds are issued. This results in a £120,000 gain, which offsets the increased interest payments on the bonds and, therefore, will affect profit or loss over the life of the bonds. The hedge may qualify as a cash flow hedge of the interest rate risk on the forecast debt issuance (assuming all other conditions for hedge accounting are met).[106]

Similarly, the forecast reinvestment of interest cash flows from a fixed rate asset can be the subject of a cash flow hedge using, say, a forward rate agreement to lock in the interest rate that will be received on that reinvestment.[107]

3.3   Hedges of foreign currency monetary items

A foreign currency monetary asset or liability that is hedged using a forward exchange contract may be treated as a fair value hedge because its fair value will change as foreign exchange rates change. Alternatively, it may be treated as a cash flow hedge because changes in exchange rates will affect the amount of cash required to settle the item (as measured by reference to the entity's functional currency).[108]

3.4   Hedges of firm commitments

A hedge of a firm commitment (e.g. a hedge of the change in fuel price relating to an unrecognised contractual commitment by an electric utility to purchase fuel at a fixed price) is considered a hedge of an exposure to a change in fair value. Accordingly, such a hedge is a fair value hedge.[109] This is a change from the previous version of IAS 39 under which hedges of firm commitments were treated as cash flow hedges.[110]

There was widespread support for the original requirement and this change has proved to be controversial. The differences in opinion can be seen to arise as a result of different philosophical views as to the basis of financial reporting. The standard setters see a firm commitment as an asset or liability (as defined) that is accounted for at historical cost (which, for the most part, just happens to be zero). The more traditional view of a firm commitment is that it is something that simply doesn't belong in the financial statements until performance has taken place; and that applies whether or not the transaction that arises from the commitment is the subject of a hedge. However, in spite of these objections, the IASB saw this change as an opportunity to reduce the differences between IAS and US GAAP and, ultimately, this is likely to have been a key factor in their decision.[111]

Nevertheless, even under the revised standard, a hedge of the foreign currency risk of a firm commitment may be accounted for as a cash flow hedge.[112] This is because foreign currency risk affects both the cash flows and the fair value of the hedged item. Accordingly, a foreign currency cash flow hedge of a forecast transaction need not be redesignated as a fair value hedge when the forecast transaction becomes a firm commitment.[113]

3.5 All-in-one hedges

There are situations where an instrument that is accounted for as a derivative under IAS 39 is expected to be settled gross by delivery of the underlying asset in exchange for the payment of a fixed price. The implementation guidance states that such an instrument can be designated as the hedging instrument in a cash flow hedge of the variability of the consideration to be paid or received in the future transaction that will occur on gross settlement of the derivative contract itself. It is explained that this is acceptable because there *would* be an exposure to variability in the purchase or sale price without the derivative.[114]

For example, consider an entity that enters into a fixed price contract to sell a commodity and that contract is accounted for as a derivative under IAS 39. This might be because the entity has a practice of settling such contracts net in cash or of taking delivery of the underlying and selling it within a short period after delivery for the purpose of generating a profit from short-term fluctuations in price or dealer's margin. In this case, the fixed price contract may be designated as a cash flow hedge of the variability of the consideration to be received on the sale of the asset (a future transaction) even though the fixed price contract is the contract under which the asset will be sold.[115]

Similarly, an entity may enter into a forward contract to purchase a debt instrument that will be settled by delivery, but the forward contract is a derivative. This will be the case if its term exceeds the regular way delivery period in the marketplace (see Chapter 16 at 3.1). In this case the forward may be designated as a cash flow hedge of the variability of the consideration to be paid to acquire the debt instrument (a future transaction), even though the derivative is the contract under which the debt instrument will be acquired.[116]

It might come as a surprise to many entities that such contracts are, in fact, derivatives as defined. Therefore, the use of an 'all-in-one hedge' strategy for such instruments could prove useful in keeping fair value gains and losses, on what might be considered little more than purchase or sale orders, from being recognised immediately in profit or loss.

However, it seems best to accept the all-in-one hedge for what it is, i.e. a pragmatic concession, rather than trying to determine how it is derived from the principles of the standard. For example, the hedged item in each of the above two paragraphs, i.e. the spot price payment on the future purchase or sale of the asset, appears to be a cash flow that will never to happen because the asset will be purchased or sold for the fixed price specified in the contract. Further, the hedged item also appears to be accounted for as a derivative, which is generally prohibited (see 2.2.6 above).

3.6   Hedges of net investments in foreign operations

As noted at 3.1 above, equity method investments and consolidated subsidiaries cannot be hedged items in a fair value hedge. A hedge of a net investment in a foreign operation is said to be different because it is a hedge of the foreign currency exposure, not a fair value hedge of the change in the value of the investment.[117]

In fact a hedge of a net investment is something of an anomaly, especially in the context of IAS 39. As noted at 2.2 above, the hedged item should expose the entity to the risk of changes in fair value or future cash flows. Similarly, there needs to be an expectation that changes in the fair values or cash flows of the hedging instrument will offset the changes in fair values or cash flows of the hedged item (see 2 above).[118]

These requirements apply equally to a hedge of a net investment in a foreign operation as they do to a cash flow hedge and a fair value hedge, yet the only thing that is really being hedged in these terms is an accounting entry, i.e. the associated retranslation gains and losses that are recognised in equity. Accordingly, as discussed in further detail at 5.3.11 below, it is quite difficult to determine what instruments can legitimately be used in such a hedge.

4   ACCOUNTING FOR EFFECTIVE HEDGES

If there is a designated hedging relationship between a hedging instrument and a hedged item as described at 3 above and it meets the conditions set out at 5 below, the accounting for the gain or loss on the hedging instrument and the hedged item will be as set out in the remainder of this section.[119] This is referred to as 'hedge accounting' and is said to recognise the offsetting effects on profit or loss of changes in the fair values of the hedging instrument and the hedged item.[120]

4.1   Fair value hedges

4.1.1   Ongoing fair value hedge accounting

If a fair value hedge meets the conditions set out at 5 below during the period, it should be accounted for as follows:

- the gain or loss from remeasuring the hedging instrument at fair value (for a derivative hedging instrument) or the foreign currency component of its carrying amount measured in accordance with IAS 21 (for a non-derivative hedging instrument) should be recognised in profit or loss; and

- the gain or loss on the hedged item attributable to the hedged risk adjusts the carrying amount of the hedged item and is recognised in profit or loss. This applies if the hedged item is an available-for-sale financial asset (and that gain or loss would otherwise be recognised in equity) or if it is otherwise measured at cost.[121]

It will be rare for the change in fair value of the hedging instrument (or, for non-derivative hedging instruments, foreign exchange gains or losses) to be exactly the same as the change in fair value of the hedged item attributable to the hedged risk, even for highly effective hedges. To the extent these amounts differ, a net profit or loss will be recognised in the income statement. The recognition of this difference is commonly referred to as the measurement of hedge ineffectiveness.

The following simple example illustrates how the treatment above might apply to a hedge of fair value interest rate risk on an investment in fixed rate debt.

Example 19.21: Fair value hedge

During Year 1 an investor purchases a fixed rate debt security for £100 and classifies it as available-for-sale. At the end of Year 1, the fair value of the asset is £110. To protect this value, the investor enters into a hedge by acquiring a derivative with a nil fair value. By the end of Year 2, the derivative has a fair value of £5 and the debt security has a corresponding decline in fair value (its fair value does not change as a result of any factors other than interest rates).

The investor would record the following accounting entries:

Year 1

	£	£
Debt security	100	
Cash		100

To reflect the acquisition of the security.

	£	£
Debt security	10	
Equity		10

To reflect the increase in the security's fair value.

Year 2

	£	£
Derivative	–	
Cash		–

To record the acquisition of the derivative at its fair value of nil.

	£	£
Derivative	5	
Profit or loss		5

To record the increase in the derivative's fair value.

	£	£
Profit or loss	5	
Debt security		5

To record the decrease in the security's fair value.[122]

The example is taken from the previous version of the standard and was not carried forward into the revised standard, although it is not entirely clear why not. Even if it was considered too simplistic to be a useful practical example (it does not deal, for example, with net cash settlements on the derivative, coupon payments on the debt or the subsequent impact on the recognition of interest under the effective interest method) it does illustrate the basic mechanics of fair value hedge accounting quite well.

The standard explains that if only particular risks attributable to a hedged financial instrument are hedged, recognised changes in the fair value of the hedged item that are unrelated to the hedged risk should be recognised as set out in Chapter 18 at 3.2.[123] Therefore, for instruments measured at amortised cost, these other gains and losses would generally not be recognised; for available-for-sale assets those gains and losses would generally be recognised in equity. Exceptions to this would include foreign currency retranslation gains or losses on monetary items and impairment losses, which would be recognised in profit or loss in any event. The following example illustrates this.

Example 19.22:   Hedging foreign currency risk of publicly traded shares

Company C, whose functional currency is sterling, acquires 100,000 shares in a listed US corporation for US$1m, which it classifies as available-for-sale. It is assumed the shares gives rise to a clear and identifiable exposure to changes in the US dollar/sterling exchange rate and to protect itself from changes in this exchange rate, C enters into a forward contract to sell US$0.75m which it intends to roll over for as long as the shares are held.

A portion of an exposure may be designated as a hedged item, and so the forward contract may be designated as a hedge of part of the shareholding. It could be a fair value hedge of the foreign exchange exposure of US$0.75m associated with the shares (alternatively it could be a cash flow hedge of a forecast sale of the shares but only if the timing of the sale is identified with sufficient certainty). Any variability in the fair value of the shares in US dollars would not affect the assessment of hedge effectiveness unless their fair value fell below US$0.75m.[124]

Gains and losses on the forward contract would be reported in profit or loss. Gains and losses arising from remeasuring the dollar value of the hedged proportion of the shares to sterling would also be reported in profit or loss and the remainder would be reported in equity (as would all of the foreign currency amount were it not for the hedge relationship).

The basic hedge accounting treatment above applies equally to fair value hedges of unrecognised firm commitments. Therefore, where an unrecognised firm commitment is designated as a hedged item in a fair value hedge, the subsequent cumulative change in its fair value attributable to the hedged risk should be recognised as an asset or liability with a corresponding gain or loss recognised in profit or loss. Thereafter, the firm commitment would be a *recognised* asset or liability (albeit that its carrying amount will not represent either its cost or, necessarily, its fair value). The changes in the fair value of the hedging instrument would also be recognised in profit or loss.[125]

4.1.2 Dealing with adjustments to the hedged item

In general, adjustments to the hedged asset or liability arising from the application of hedge accounting as described at 4.1.1 above are dealt with in accordance with the normal accounting treatment for that item. For example, copper inventory might be the hedged item in a fair value hedge of the exposure to changes in the copper price. In this case, the adjusted carrying amount of the copper inventory becomes the cost basis for the purpose of applying the lower of cost and net realisable value test under IAS 2 – *Inventories* (see Chapter 21).[126]

Where the hedged item is a financial instrument for which the effective interest method of accounting is used, the adjustment should be amortised to profit or loss. Amortisation may begin as soon as the adjustment exists and should begin no later than when the hedged item ceases to be adjusted for changes in its fair value attributable to the hedged risk. The adjustment should be based on a recalculated effective interest rate at the date amortisation begins and should be fully amortised by maturity.[127]

When an entity enters into a firm commitment to acquire an asset or assume a liability that is a hedged item in a fair value hedge, the initial carrying amount of the asset or liability that results from the entity meeting the firm commitment is adjusted to include the cumulative change in the fair value of the firm commitment attributable to the hedged risk that was recognised in the balance sheet.[128]

Example 19.23: Hedge of a firm commitment to acquire equipment

Company X has the euro as its functional currency. It has chosen to treat all hedges of foreign currency risk associated with firm commitments as fair value hedges. In January 2005 it contracts with a US supplier (with the US dollar as its functional currency) to purchase an item of machinery it intends to use in its business. The machine will be delivered at the start of July 2005 and the contracted price, payable on delivery, is US$1,000.

X has no appetite to take on foreign currency exchange risk in relation to euro/US dollar exchange rates and so contracts with a bank to purchase US$1,000 at the start of July in exchange for €900 (six month forward exchange rate is US$1:€0.90). In other words, X has effectively fixed the price it will pay for the machine (in euro terms) at €900.

If the fair value of the forward contract at the end of March 2005 (X's year end) is €30 positive to X, on delivery is €50 positive to X (spot exchange rate is US$1:€0.95) and assuming the hedge is perfectly effective (this might be the case if the hedged risk is identified as the forward exchange rate rather than the spot rate – see 5.3.3 and 5.3.8 below) and meets all the requirements for hedge accounting, the journal entries to record this hedging relationship would be as follows:

January 2005

No entries are required as the firm commitment is unrecognised, the forward contract is recognised but has a zero fair value and no cash is paid or received.

March 2005

	€	€
Forward contract	30	
Profit or loss		30

To record the change in fair value of the forward contract.

	€	€
Profit or loss	30	
Firm commitment		30

To record the change in fair value of the (previously) unrecognised firm commitment in respect of changes in forward exchange rates.

July 2005

	€	€
Forward contract	20	
Profit or loss		20

To record the change in fair value of the forward contract.

	€	€
Profit or loss	20	
Firm commitment		20

To record the change in fair value of the (now recognised) firm commitment in respect of changes in forward exchange rates.

	€	€
Cash	50	
Forward contract		50

To record the settlement of the forward contract at its fair value.

	€	€
Machine	950	
Cash		950

To record the settlement of the firm commitment at the contracted price of US$1,000 at the spot rate of US$1:€0.95.

	€	€
Firm commitment	50	
Machine		50

To remove the carrying amount of the firm commitment from the balance sheet and adjust the initial carrying amount of the machine that results from the firm commitment.

In summary, the result of these accounting entries is as follows:

	€	€
Machine	900	
Cash		900

which is somewhat reassuring given the starting presumption, i.e. that X had effectively fixed the purchase price of its machine at €900.

However, to some, the route to get to this position may seem slightly convoluted. This is especially so when one considers that, in addition to the above net entry in the balance sheet, both a profit and a loss of €50 have been recognised in the income statement and, as the balance sheet at the end of March 2005 illustrates, an asset or liability representing part of the fair value (or change in fair value) of X's commitment to purchase the item of machinery is also recognised temporarily.

4.1.3   Discontinuing fair value hedge accounting

The ongoing fair value hedge accounting set out at 4.1.1 above should be discontinued prospectively if any one of the following occurs:

- the hedging instrument expires or is sold, terminated, or exercised.

  For this purpose, the replacement or a rollover of a hedging instrument into another is not an expiration or termination if that is part of the documented hedging strategy;

- the hedge no longer meets the criteria for hedge accounting in 5 below; or

- the designation is revoked.[129]

If the reason the hedge no longer meets the criteria for qualification for hedge accounting is that it does not meet the hedge effectiveness criteria, hedge accounting should be discontinued from the last date on which compliance with hedge effectiveness was demonstrated. However, if the event or change in circumstances that caused the hedging relationship to fail the effectiveness criteria can be identified, and it can be demonstrated that the hedge was effective before the event or change in circumstances occurred, the hedge accounting should be discontinued from the date of the event or change in circumstances.[130]

Example 19.24:   Hedge of foreign exchange risk from currency pegged to the US dollar

Company U has the euro as its functional currency and prepares annual financial statements for the year ended 31 December. It also prepares interim financial statements for the six months ended 30 June and, in general, assesses the effectiveness of hedges at these dates.

In January 2005, U acquires an equity instrument issued by a company whose functional currency is the FC. It is assumed the investment has a clear and identifiable exposure to changes in the FC/euro exchange rate and is classified as available-for-sale. For many years the value of the FC has been has pegged to the US dollar and historical studies show that during this time the FC/US dollar exchange rate has never moved outside of a corridor representing 2.5% of the mean rate. Furthermore, there is no evidence to suggest that the peg will not continue for the foreseeable future.

Accordingly, in January 2005, U is able to designate a US dollar denominated borrowing as a highly effective hedge of the foreign currency risk associated with part of the equity instrument.

At the end of June 2005, U performs an effectiveness assessment and determines that the hedge has been highly effective and, therefore, changes in the value of the equity instrument attributable to changes in the FC/euro exchange rate are recognised in profit or loss rather than equity, together with the exchange differences on the US dollar borrowing.

At the beginning of October 2005, there is an unexpected financial crisis, the peg ceases and the FC is devalued by 25% relative to the US dollar.

When U assesses the effectiveness of the hedge in December 2005 it concludes that, because of the cessation of the peg and consequent devaluation, the hedge can no longer be regarded as highly effective and that hedge accounting should cease.

However, U is able to determine that the failure of the hedge arose because of the cessation of the FC/US dollar peg and subsequent devaluation at the beginning of October 2005. Therefore, it is able to apply hedge accounting for the first three months of its second interim period. Thus, changes in the value of the equity instrument attributable to changes in the FC/euro exchange rate for that period will be recognised in profit or loss, but thereafter will be reflected in equity when accounting for the available-for-sale asset at fair value.

In other cases, hedge accounting should be discontinued from the date the hedging instrument expires or is sold, terminated or exercised, or the hedge designation is revoked. For example, if the forward contract in Example 19.23 above were settled (or the hedge designation was revoked) at the end of March 2005, no further adjustments to the carrying value of the firm commitment (€30) would be made after that date.

4.2   Cash flow hedges

4.2.1   *Ongoing cash flow hedge accounting*

If a cash flow hedge meets the conditions in 5 below, it should be accounted for as follows:

- the portion of the gain or loss on the hedging instrument that is determined to be an effective hedge should be recognised directly in equity; and
- the ineffective portion should be reported immediately in profit or loss.[131]

More specifically, the accounting should be as follows:

- the separate component of equity associated with the hedged item is adjusted to the lesser of the following (in absolute amounts):
    - (i)   the cumulative gain or loss on the hedging instrument from inception of the hedge; and
    - (ii)   the cumulative change in fair value (present value) of the expected future cash flows on the hedged item from inception of the hedge;
- any remaining gain or loss on the hedging instrument or designated component of it (that is not an effective hedge) is recognised in profit or loss; and
- if the documented risk management strategy for a particular hedging relationship excludes from the assessment of hedge effectiveness a specific component of the gain or loss or related cash flows on the hedging instrument, that excluded component of gain or loss is recognised as set out in Chapter 18 at 3.2 (effectively in profit or loss for a derivative hedging instrument).

    Those excluded components can include the time value of an option, the interest element of a forward contract or a proportion of an instrument (see 2.1.4 above).[132]

This is illustrated in the following examples.

Example 19.25: *Cash flow hedge of anticipated commodity sale*

On 30 September 2005, Company A hedges the anticipated sale of 24 tonnes of pulp on 1 March 2006 by entering into a short forward contract. The contract requires net settlement in cash, determined as the difference between the future spot price of 24 tonnes of pulp on a specified commodity exchange and £1m. A expects to sell the pulp in a different, local market.

A determines that the forward contract is an effective hedge of the anticipated sale and that the other conditions for hedge accounting are met. It assesses hedge effectiveness by comparing the entire change in the fair value of the forward contract with the change in the fair value of the expected cash inflows. On 31 December 2005, the spot price of pulp has increased both in the local market and on the exchange, although the increase in the local market exceeds the increase on the exchange. As a result, the present value of the expected cash inflow from the sale on the local market is £1.1m and the fair value of the forward is £85,000 negative. The hedge is determined to be still highly effective.

The cumulative change in the fair value of the forward contract is £85,000, while the fair value of the cumulative change in expected future cash flows on the hedged item is £0.1m. Ineffectiveness is not recognised in the financial statements because the cumulative change in the fair value of the hedged cash flows exceeds the cumulative change in the value of the hedging instrument. The whole of the fair value change in the forward contract would be recognised in equity.

However if A concluded that the hedge was no longer highly effective, it would discontinue hedge accounting prospectively as from the date the hedge ceased to be highly effective (see 4.2.3 below).[133]

Example 19.26: *Cash flow hedge of a floating rate liability*

Company A has a floating rate liability of £1m with five years remaining to maturity. It enters into a five year pay-fixed, receive-floating interest rate swap with the same principal terms to hedge the exposure to variable cash flow payments on the floating rate liability attributable to interest rate risk.

At inception, the swap's fair value is £nil. Subsequently, there is an increase of £49,000 which consists of a change of £50,000 resulting from an increase in market interest rates and a change of minus £1,000 resulting from an increase in the credit risk of the swap counterparty. There is no change in the fair value of the floating rate liability, but the fair value (present value) of the future cash flows needed to offset the exposure to variable interest cash flows on the liability increases by £50,000.

Even if A determines that the hedge of interest rate risk is 'highly effective' (simplistically, the offset ratio is 49,000/50,000 or 98%, so this is quite likely) it is not fully effective if part of the change in the fair value of the derivative is due to the counterparty's credit risk (see 5.3.8 below). However, because the hedge relationship is still 'highly effective', A credits the effective portion of the swap's fair value change, £49,000, to equity. There is no debit to profit or loss for the change in fair value of the swap attributable to the deterioration in the credit quality of the swap counterparty because the cumulative change in the present value of the future cash flows needed to offset the exposure to variable interest cash flows on the hedged item, £50,000, exceeds the cumulative change in value of the hedging instrument, £49,000. If A concluded that the hedge was no longer highly effective, it would discontinue hedge accounting prospectively as from the date the hedge ceased to be highly effective (see 4.2.3 below).

Alternatively, if the fair value of the swap increased to £51,000 of which £50,000 results from the increase in market interest rates and £1,000 from a decrease in the counterparty's credit risk, there would be a credit to profit or loss of £1,000 for the change in the swap's fair value attributable to the improvement in the counterparty's credit quality. This is because the cumulative change in the value of the hedging instrument, £51,000, exceeds the cumulative change in the present value of the future cash flows needed to offset the exposure to variable interest cash flows on the hedged item, £50,000. The difference of £1,000 represents the excess ineffectiveness attributable to the swap, and is reported in profit or loss.[134]

It can be seen that the measurement of hedge ineffectiveness differs for a cash flow hedge when compared to a fair value hedge. In a cash flow hedge, if the fair value of the derivative increases by €10 and the present value of the hedged expected cash flows change by only €8, the €2 difference is reflected in profit or loss (as would be the case for a fair value hedge). However, if the present value of the hedged expected cash flows changes by €10, but the fair value of the derivative changes by only €8, this €2 of hedge ineffectiveness is *not* reflected in profit or loss (which would not be the case for a fair value hedge).

Because of this, an entity might consider deliberately under-hedging an exposure in a cash flow hedge. It might do this by targeting an offset of, say, 85% to 90%, which would keep it within the prescribed 80% to 125% range (see 5.3.1 below) but avoid the need to recognise ineffectiveness in profit or loss. However, as discussed at 5.3.6 below, this is not permitted.

As an exception to the general accounting requirements set out at the start of this sub-section, if there is a hedging relationship between a non-derivative monetary asset and a non-derivative monetary liability, changes in the foreign currency component of both those financial instruments should be recognised in profit or loss.[135] This might be the case if a foreign currency denominated receivable is designated as the hedging instrument in a cash flow hedge of the repayment of the principal of a foreign currency denominated borrowing[136] (although hedge accounting would be unnecessary for this relationship).

4.2.2   Recycling gains and losses from equity

If a hedged forecast transaction subsequently results in the recognition of a *financial* asset or liability, the associated gains or losses that were recognised directly in equity should be recycled into profit or loss in the same period(s) during which the asset acquired or liability assumed affects profit or loss, e.g. in the periods that interest income or interest expense is recognised. However, if it is expected that all or a portion of a loss recognised directly in equity will not be recovered in one or more future periods, the amount that is not expected to be recovered should be recycled into profit or loss immediately.[137]

If a hedged forecast transaction subsequently results in the recognition of a *non-financial* asset or liability (or a forecast transaction for a *non-financial* asset or liability becomes a firm commitment for which fair value hedge accounting is applied) then a choice of accounting policies is available. In these circumstances, an entity should either:

- recycle the associated gains and losses that were recognised directly in equity into the income statement in the same period(s) during which the asset acquired or liability assumed affects profit or loss, e.g. in the periods that depreciation expense or cost of sales is recognised. However, if it is expected that all or a portion of a loss recognised directly in equity will not be recovered in one or more future periods, the amount that is not expected to be recovered should be recycled into profit or loss. Essentially this is the same treatment as for hedges of financial items; or

- remove the associated gains and losses that were recognised directly in equity and include them in the initial cost or other carrying amount of the asset or liability[138] as a 'basis adjustment'.

An entity should adopt one of these as its accounting policy and apply it consistently to all relevant hedges.[139] These treatments are illustrated in the following example.

Example 19.27: Hedge of a firm commitment to acquire equipment

Consider a variation of the situation in Example 19.23 at 4.1.2 above whereby Company X has chosen to treat all hedges of foreign currency risk associated with firm commitments as cash flow hedges, rather than as fair value hedges, as permitted by the standard (see 3.4 above). In the first case, X's accounting policy is to apply a basis adjustment to cash flow hedges that result in the recognition of non-financial assets or liabilities; in the second case it does not. Otherwise, the underlying facts and assumptions are the same. The accounting entries made at the end of March 2005 in have not been shown separately (as they were in Example 19.23) because they are not relevant to the issue being illustrated.

Case 1: Basis adjustment

The journal entries to record this hedging relationship would be as follows:

January 2005

No entries are required as the firm commitment is unrecognised, the forward contract is recognised but has a zero fair value and no cash is paid or received.

July 2005

	€	€
Forward contract	50	
Equity		50

To record the change in fair value of the forward contract and, because no ineffectiveness arises, the whole of this change is recognised in equity.

	€	€
Cash	50	
Forward contract		50

To record the settlement of the forward contract at its fair value.

	€	€
Machine	950	
Cash		950

To record the settlement of the firm commitment at the contracted price of US$1,000 at the spot rate of US$1:€0.95.

	€	€
Equity	50	
Machine		50

To recycle the gain recognised in equity and adjust the carrying amount of the machine that results from the hedged transaction by this amount.

In summary, the result of these accounting entries is as follows:

	€	€
Machine	900	
Cash		900

which again reflects the starting presumption, i.e. that X had effectively fixed the purchase price of its machine at €900. However, the route to get to this position may also seem slightly convoluted.

Case 2: No basis adjustment

The journal entries to record this hedging relationship would be as follows:

January 2005

No entries are required as the firm commitment is unrecognised, the forward contract is recognised but has a zero fair value and no cash is paid or received.

July 2005

	€	€
Forward contract	50	
Equity		50

To record the change in fair value of the forward contract and, because no ineffectiveness arises, the whole of this change is recognised in equity.

	€	€
Cash	50	
Forward contract		50

To record the settlement of the forward contract at its fair value.

	€	€
Machine	950	
Cash		950

To record the settlement of the firm commitment at the contracted price of US$1,000 at the spot rate of US$1:€0.95.

In summary, the result of these accounting entries is as follows:

	€	€
Machine	950	
Cash		900
Equity		50

The gain deferred in equity would be recycled into profit or loss as the machine affects profit or loss, e.g. as it is depreciated, impaired or derecognised. If the machine has a very long useful economic life, this might involve tracking this adjustment for many years. The result might be considered less intuitive than before.

Under the previous version of the standard, the 'basis adjustment' accounting treatment was required for all cash flow hedges where the hedged transaction resulted in the recognition of an asset or liability.[140] This was irrespective of whether the asset or liability was financial or non-financial. This was another controversial amendment to the standard, with many commentators supporting the retention of the original approach and most of the IASB wanting a prohibition on basis adjustments.

The IASB sees basis adjustments as 'contaminating' the carrying amount of a hedged asset or liability with gains and losses arising on a completely separate transaction (i.e. the hedging instrument), which results in a lack of comparability. For example, it believes that two identical assets that are purchased at the same time and in the same way (except for the fact that one was hedged) should be recognised at the same amounts. Commentators expressed pragmatic as well as conceptual concerns about the removal of basis adjustments. For example, without a basis adjustment, tracking the effects of cash flow hedges after the asset or liability is acquired could be complicated and could require systems changes[141] and, as demonstrated in Example 19.27 above, gains and losses in equity could take many years to recycle.

What we are left with is a political fudge that allows preparers to move a little closer to US GAAP (under which all basis adjustments are prohibited) but the element of choice allows them not to. Three IASB members formally objected to this change, essentially because they disagree with basis adjustments, but also because they see the introduction of this choice into IAS 39 as a retrograde step.[142]

For all other cash flow hedges (i.e. those that do not result in the recognition of an asset or a liability), amounts that had been recognised directly in equity should be recycled into the income statement in the same period or periods during which the hedged forecast transaction affects profit or loss, e.g. when a forecast sale occurs[143] or when variable rate interest income or expense is recognised. In fact, when instruments such as conventional interest rate swaps are used as a hedging instrument in a cash flow hedge, it is common for entities to simply recognise, on an accruals basis, each periodic cash settlement in profit or loss. Strictly, however, each cash settlement simply represents a realisation of the fair value of the swap, i.e. in a fair value model using continuous (or real-time) accounting, they simply represent balance sheet movements between cash and the carrying value of the swap. In principle, therefore, the amount that is recycled into profit or loss should be completely independent of the swap accruals. Nevertheless, for most simple hedges of interest rate risk, this treatment is likely to result in income statement entries that are sufficiently precise.

It was stated at 3.3 above that using a forward exchange contract to hedge a foreign currency payable or receivable could be treated either as a fair value hedge, or a cash flow hedge, under IAS 39. In a fair value hedge, the gain or loss on remeasurement of the forward contract and the hedged item are recognised immediately in profit or loss. However, in a cash flow hedge, the gain or loss on remeasuring the forward contract is initially recognised in equity and recycled into profit or loss when the payable or receivable affects profit or loss. Because the payable or receivable is remeasured continuously in respect of for changes in foreign exchange rates, the gain or loss on the forward contract will recycled to profit or loss as the payable or receivable is remeasured, not when the payment occurs.[144] This should be very similar, if not identical, to the fair value hedge treatment. Indeed, it is similar to the accounting required if hedge accounting was not adopted for such transactions.

Where a forward exchange contract is used as a hedging instrument in a cash flow hedge, the discount or premium in the contract (i.e. the difference between the spot and forward rates, which is normally referred to in IAS 39 as the interest element) cannot be amortised to profit or loss over the contract term (which may have been an entity's accounting policy prior to the adoption of IAS 39). This is because derivatives are always measured at fair value. Where cash flow hedge accounting is applied, the effective portion of the gain or loss on the forward contract should initially be included in equity pending recycling into profit or loss. The interest element of the fair value of a forward may be excluded from the designated hedge relationship (see 2.1.4 A above) although in this case changes in the fair value of the interest element would be recognised immediately in profit or loss.[145] This could produce very different results to amortising the net premium or discount as illustrated in Example 19.31 at 5.3.3 below.

4.2.3   Discontinuing cash flow hedge accounting

Cash flow hedge accounting should be discontinued prospectively in any of the following circumstances:

(a)   the hedging instrument expires or is sold, terminated, or exercised.

For this purpose, the replacement or a rollover of a hedging instrument into another hedging instrument is not an expiration or termination if such replacement or rollover is part of the documented hedging strategy.

In this case the cumulative gain or loss that remains recognised directly in equity from the period when the hedge was effective should remain in equity until the forecast transaction occurs. Thereafter, it is required to be dealt with as set out at 4.2.2 above.

The standard doesn't entertain the possibility that, subsequently, the hedged forecast transaction might not occur. However, it would seem appropriate to deal with this situation in the same way as for hedges where the hedged instrument has not been terminated, i.e. as in (c) below;

(b)   the hedge no longer meets the criteria for hedge accounting at 5 below.

In this case, the cumulative gain or loss that remains in equity is dealt with in same way as in (a) above;

(c)   the forecast transaction is no longer expected to occur.

In this case, the cumulative gain or loss on the hedging instrument that remains in equity should be recognised in profit or loss. However, a forecast transaction that is no longer highly probable (and therefore the hedge no longer meets the criteria for hedge accounting at 5 below) may still be expected to occur, in which case (b) above will apply;

(d)   the designation as a hedge is revoked.

In this case, the cumulative gain or loss that remains in equity is dealt with in same way as in (a) above. However, if the transaction is no longer expected to occur, (c) applies.[146]

As for fair value hedges, if the reason the hedge no longer meets the criteria for qualification for hedge accounting is that it does not meet the hedge effectiveness criteria, hedge accounting should normally be discontinued from the last date on which compliance with hedge effectiveness was demonstrated. However, if the event or change in circumstances that caused the hedging relationship to fail the effectiveness criteria can be identified, and it can be demonstrated that the hedge was effective before the event or change in circumstances occurred, the hedge accounting should be discontinued from the date of the event or change in circumstances.[147]

The standard does not address the situation when the hedge relationship ceases because there is a change in the relationship between the reporting entity and the entity that is holding the hedging instrument and/or is exposed to the hedged transaction, for example when a subsidiary is disposed of. This issue is covered in more detail in Chapter 5 at 6.6.

4.3   Accounting for hedges of a net investment in a foreign operation

Hedges of a net investment in a foreign operation, including a hedge of a monetary item that is accounted for as part of the net investment (see Chapter 9 at 3.4.1), should be accounted for in a similar way to cash flow hedges:

- the portion of the gain or loss on the hedging instrument that is determined to be an effective hedge should be recognised directly in equity through the statement of changes in equity; and
- the ineffective portion should be recognised in profit or loss.[148]

The gain or loss on the hedging instrument relating to the effective portion of the hedge that has been recognised directly in equity should be recognised in profit or loss on disposal of the foreign operation (see Chapter 9 at 2.7.3).[149]

Unfortunately, this is pretty much all of the guidance there is on accounting for net investment hedges. Even the meaning of 'similarly to cash flow hedges' is unclear. For example, is it simply a reference to the fact that gains and losses are recognised initially in equity (as they are for cash flow hedges)? Or does it mean that ineffectiveness should be measured in the same way, i.e. no ineffectiveness is recognised in profit or loss if the gain or loss on the hedging instrument is less, in absolute terms, than the gain or loss on the hedged item (see 4.2.1 above)?

Although it is clear that ineffectiveness should be recorded for under-hedges as well as over-hedges under US GAAP,[150] this does not necessarily define the accounting treatment under IFRS. Therefore, whilst there is a case to be made for the US GAAP treatment (and we can see that companies with secondary reporting requirements will use this argument), an equally strong case can be made for the alternative interpretation.

5   QUALIFYING CONDITIONS FOR HEDGE ACCOUNTING

A hedging relationship qualifies for hedge accounting as set out at 4 above if, and only if, all of the following conditions are met:

(a)   at the inception of the hedge there is formal designation and documentation both of the hedging relationship and the entity's risk management objective and strategy for undertaking the hedge;

(b)   the hedge is expected to be highly effective in achieving offsetting changes in fair value or cash flows attributable to the hedged risk, consistently with the originally documented risk management strategy for that particular hedging relationship;

(c)   a forecast transaction that is the subject of a cash flow hedge must be highly probable and must present an exposure to variations in cash flows that could ultimately affect net profit or loss;

(d)   the effectiveness of the hedge can be reliably measured, i.e. the fair value or cash flows of the hedged item that are attributable to the hedged risk and the fair value of the hedging instrument can be reliably measured (see Chapter 18 at 4 for guidance on determining fair value); and

(e)   the hedge is assessed on an ongoing basis and determined actually to have been highly effective throughout the financial reporting periods for which the hedge was designated.[151]

These conditions are considered in further detail in the remainder of this section.

5.1   Documentation and designation

The documentation supporting the hedge should include identification of:

- the hedging instrument;

- the hedged item or transaction;

- the nature of the risk being hedged; and

- how the entity will assess the hedging instrument's effectiveness in offsetting the exposure to changes in the hedged item's fair value or cash flows attributable to the hedged risk.[152]

Designation of a hedge relationship takes effect prospectively from the date all of the criteria at 5 are met. In particular, hedge accounting can be applied only from the date all of the necessary documentation is completed. Therefore, hedge relationships cannot be designated retrospectively.[153]

As noted at 2.1.4 A above, the standard explains that a dynamic hedging strategy that assesses both the intrinsic value and time value of an option contract can qualify for hedge accounting.[154] The implementation guidance explains that this allows the use of a delta-neutral hedging strategy as well as other dynamic hedging strategies under which the quantity of the hedging instrument is constantly adjusted in order to maintain a desired hedge ratio (e.g. to achieve a delta-neutral position, insensitive to changes in the fair value of the hedged item), to qualify for hedge accounting. For example, a portfolio insurance strategy that seeks to ensure that the fair value of the hedged item does not drop below a certain level, while allowing the fair value to increase, may qualify for hedge accounting.[155]

For a dynamic hedging strategy to qualify for hedge accounting, the documentation must specify how the hedge will be monitored and updated and how effectiveness will be measured. In addition, the entity must be able to track properly all terminations and redesignations of the hedging instrument, in addition to demonstrating that all other criteria for hedge accounting are met. Also, it must be demonstrated that the hedge is expected to be highly effective for a specified short period of time during which adjustment of the hedge is not expected.[156]

Hedge designation need not take place at the time a hedging instrument is entered into. For example, a derivative contract may be designated and formally documented as a hedging instrument any time after entering into the derivative contract. Hedge accounting will apply prospectively from designation, provided all other conditions are met.[157] However, there is often a hidden danger when designating a derivative as a hedging instrument subsequent to its inception. For non-option derivatives, such as forwards or interest rate swaps, any fair value is likely to create 'noise' in a hedge effectiveness assessment that may not be fully offset by changes in the hedged item, especially in the case of a cash flow hedge. Consequently, there is likely to be more ineffectiveness recognised and, in extremis, could cause the hedge not be regarded as highly effective. Only by coincidence will a derivative still have a fair value that is zero, or close to zero, which would minimise this problem.

5.2   Forecast transactions

In the case of a hedge of a forecast transaction, the documentation should identify the date on, or time period in which, the forecast transaction is expected to occur. This is because to qualify for hedge accounting:

- the hedge must relate to a specific identified and designated risk;
- it must be possible to measure its effectiveness reliably; and
- the hedged forecast transaction must be highly probable.

To meet these criteria, entities are not required to predict and document the exact date a forecast transaction is expected to occur. However, the time period in which the forecast transaction is expected to occur should be identified and documented within a reasonably specific and generally narrow range of time from a most probable date, as a basis for assessing hedge effectiveness. To determine that the hedge will be highly effective, it is necessary to ensure that changes in the fair value of the expected cash flows are offset by changes in the fair value of the hedging instrument and this test may be met only if the timing of the cash flows occur within close proximity to each other.[158]

If a forecast transaction such as a commodity sale is properly designated in a hedge and, subsequently, its expected timing changes to an earlier period, this does not affect the validity of the original designation. The entity can conclude that this transaction is the same as the one designated as being hedged. However, this may well affect the assessment of the hedge's effectiveness, especially as the hedging instrument will be designated for the remaining period of its existence, which will exceed the period to the forecast sale.[159]

Further, hedged forecast transactions must be identified and documented with sufficient specificity so that when the transaction occurs, it is clear whether the transaction is, or is not, the hedged transaction. Therefore, a forecast transaction may be identified as the sale of the first 15,000 units of a specific product during a specified three-month period, but it could not be identified as the last 15,000 units of that product sold because they cannot be identified when they occur. For the same reason, a forecast transaction cannot be specified solely as a percentage of sales or purchases during a period.[160]

Finally, the standard requires a forecast transaction that is the subject of a cash flow hedge to be 'highly probable'. The implementation guidance explains that this term indicates a *much* greater likelihood of happening than the term 'more likely than not' (a term used throughout the IASB's work to describe, or define, 'probable').[161] The implementation guidance to the previous version of the standard referred to a '*significantly* greater likelihood'[162] although it is very difficult to know whether or not to read anything into this subtle change of words, even for someone whose first language is English. In fact, we can claim no originality in pointing out that there is a serious risk that non-native English speakers will be unable to distinguish the important nuances of meaning within phrases such as these that are used extensively by the IASB.[163]

Before returning to the matter in hand, it is interesting to note that 'highly probable' is defined in IFRS 5 – *Non-current Assets Held for Sale and Discontinued Operations* – a standard published only a few weeks after the revised version of IAS 39. It may come as a surprise, therefore, that the relevant test when applying IFRS 5 is the seemingly outdated term '*significantly* more likely'.[164] Furthermore, in the basis for conclusions to IFRS 5, it is explained that in the equivalent US GAAP requirements, the phrase 'likely to occur' describes the term 'probable' and that the IASB regards 'highly probable' as implying the same probability as 'likely to occur'.[165] Taking this wordplay to its logical conclusion, one might be tempted to deduce that the IASB regards probable as meaning 'significantly (or much) more likely than probable'!

Concerns about the precise meaning of words aside, the guidance does add some slightly more practical pointers. It states that probability should be supported by observable facts and attendant circumstance and should not be based solely on management intent, because intentions are not verifiable. In making this assessment, consideration should be given to the following circumstances:

- the frequency of similar past transactions;
- the financial and operational ability to carry out the transaction;
- substantial commitments of resources to a particular activity, e.g. a manufacturing facility that can be used in the short run only to process a particular type of commodity;

- the extent of loss or disruption of operations that could result if the transaction does not occur;

- the likelihood that transactions with substantially different characteristics might be used to achieve the same business purpose, e.g. there are several ways of raising cash ranging from a short-term bank loan to a public share offering; and

- the entity's business plan.[166]

The length of time until a forecast transaction is projected to occur is also a consideration in determining probability. Other factors being equal, the more distant a forecast transaction is, the less likely it is to be considered highly probable and the stronger the evidence that would be needed to support an assertion that it is highly probable. For example, a transaction forecast to occur in five years may be less likely to occur than a transaction forecast to occur in one year. However, forecast interest payments for the next 20 years on variable-rate debt would typically be highly probable if supported by an existing contractual obligation.[167]

In addition, other factors being equal, the greater the physical quantity or future value of a forecast transaction in proportion to transactions of the same nature, the less likely it is that the transaction would be considered highly probable and the stronger the evidence that would be required to support such an assertion. For example, less evidence would generally be needed to support forecast sales of 100,000 units in the next month than 950,000 units when recent sales have averaged 950,000 units for each of the past three months.[168]

The implementation guidance uses the following example to elaborate on this:

Example 19.28: Hedge of foreign currency revenues

An airline operator uses sophisticated models based on past experience and economic data to project its revenues in various currencies. If it can demonstrate that forecast revenues for a period of time into the future in a particular currency are 'highly probable', it may designate a currency borrowing as a cash flow hedge of the future revenue stream.

However it is unlikely that 100% of revenues for a future year could be reliably predicted. On the other hand, it is possible that a portion of predicted revenues, normally those expected in the short-term, will meet the 'highly probable' criterion.[169]

It is also explained that cash flows arising after the prepayment date on an instrument that is prepayable at the issuer's option may be highly probable for a group or pool of similar assets for which prepayments can be estimated with a high degree of accuracy, e.g. mortgage loans, or if the prepayment option is significantly out of the money. In addition, the cash flows after the prepayment date may be designated as the hedged item if a comparable option exists in the hedging instrument.[170]

The implementation guidance states that a history of having designated hedges of forecast transactions and then determining that the forecast transactions are no longer expected to occur, calls into question both the ability to accurately predict forecast transactions and the propriety of using hedge accounting in the future for similar forecast transactions.[171] This is clearly common sense, however the standard contains no prescriptive 'tainting' provisions in this area akin to those applied to held-to-maturity investments (see Chapter 15 at 7.2.3). Therefore, entities are not automatically prohibited from using cash flow hedge accounting if a forecast transaction fails to occur. Instead, whenever such a situation arises the particular facts, circumstances and evidence should be assessed to determine whether doubt has, in fact, been cast on an entity's ongoing hedging strategies.

5.3   Assessing hedge effectiveness

One of the fundamental requirements of IAS 39 is that to use hedge accounting, the hedge must be an effective one. To this end, hedge effectiveness is defined as:

> 'the degree to which changes in the fair value or cash flows of the hedged item that are attributable to a hedged risk are offset by changes in the fair value or cash flows of the hedging instrument.'[172]

There is little doubt that demonstrating the effectiveness of a hedge can be one of the most challenging aspects of IAS 39. The assessment of a hedge's effectiveness has the potential to be an extremely difficult exercise, involving the use of complex statistical techniques and valuation models of which many accountants have, at best, only limited experience. All of this is not helped by the fact that the IASB has provided very limited practical guidance on how to go about testing effectiveness.

One important point to note at the outset is that the method used in the *assessment* of hedge *effectiveness* need not be the same as that used in the *measurement* (i.e. recognition in profit or loss) of hedge *ineffectiveness*. The measurement requirements are dealt with at 4.1.1 and 4.2.1 above for fair value and cash flow hedges respectively. However, the calculations used to measure ineffectiveness may be used to assess effectiveness (see 5.3.2 below).

5.3.1   Basic requirements

As noted at 5 above, three of the qualifying conditions for hedge accounting involve hedge effectiveness as follows:

- the entity should expect the hedge to be highly effective in achieving offsetting changes in fair value or cash flows attributable to the hedged risk, consistently with the originally documented risk management strategy for that particular hedging relationship;

- the effectiveness of the hedge can be reliably measured, i.e. the fair value or cash flows of the hedged item that are attributable to the hedged risk and the fair value of the hedging instrument can be reliably measured; and

- the hedge should be assessed on an ongoing basis and determined actually to have been highly effective throughout the financial reporting periods for which the hedge was designated.[173]

Qualification for hedge accounting is based on an expectation of future (prospective) effectiveness, the objective of which is to ensure there is firm evidence to support an expectation of high effectiveness, and an evaluation of actual (retrospective) effectiveness.[174] The application guidance explains that a hedge is regarded as highly effective only if both of the following conditions are met:

(a)   at the inception of the hedge, and in subsequent periods, the hedge is expected to be highly effective in achieving offsetting changes in fair value or cash flows attributable to the hedged risk during the period for which the hedge is designated.

Such an expectation can be demonstrated in various ways, including a comparison of past changes in the fair value or cash flows of the hedged item that are attributable to the hedged risk with past changes in the fair value or cash flows of the hedging instrument, or by demonstrating a high statistical correlation between the fair value or cash flows of the hedged item and those of the hedging instrument. A hedge ratio of other than one to one may be chosen in order to improve the effectiveness of the hedge (see 2.2.2 above); and

(b)   the actual results of the hedge are within a range of 80% to 125%.

For example, if actual results are such that the loss on the hedging instrument is €120 and the gain on the cash instrument is €100, offset can be measured by 120/100, which is 120%, or by 100/120, which is 83%. In this example, assuming the hedge meets the condition in (a), it would be concluded that the hedge has been highly effective.[175]

Effectiveness should be assessed, at a minimum, at the time annual or interim financial reports are prepared.[176] However, there is nothing to prevent effectiveness assessments being performed more frequently. In fact this might be desirable if there is a risk of the hedge ceasing to be considered highly effective (although the prospective test should ensure such a risk is actually very low). The sooner an ineffective hedge is identified, the sooner the accounting volatility that results from a failure to obtain hedge accounting can be managed. For example, following a failure, it might be possible to redesignate the hedge (perhaps with some adjustment to the hedging instrument) but hedge accounting for that new hedge relationship will be available only prospectively.

No single method for assessing hedge effectiveness is specified by IAS 39 – the method used will depend on the entity's risk management strategy adopted. For example, if the risk management strategy is to adjust the amount of the hedging instrument periodically to reflect changes in the hedged position, it needs to be demonstrated that the hedge is expected to be highly effective only for the period until the amount of the hedging instrument is next adjusted.[177]

Hedge effectiveness may also be assessed on a pre-tax or after-tax basis. If effectiveness is to be assessed on an after-tax basis, this should be designated at inception as part of the formal documentation of the hedging strategy.[178]

In some cases, an entity will adopt different methods for different types of hedges. The documentation of its hedging strategy should include its procedures for assessing effectiveness and those procedures should state whether the assessment will include all of the gain or loss on a hedging instrument or whether the time value of the instrument is excluded (see 2.1.4 above).[179]

The appropriateness of a given method will depend on the nature of the risk being hedged and the type of hedging instrument used. The method must be reasonable and consistent with other similar hedges unless different methods are explicitly justified. An entity is required to document, at the inception of the hedge, how effectiveness will be assessed and then to apply that effectiveness test on a consistent basis for the duration of the hedge. Several mathematical techniques can be used including ratio analysis, i.e. a comparison of hedging gains and losses to the corresponding gains and losses on the hedged item at a point in time, and statistical measurement techniques such as regression analysis. If regression analysis is used, the entity's documented policies for assessing hedge effectiveness must specify how the results of the regression will be assessed.[180]

Expected hedge effectiveness may be assessed on a cumulative basis if that is how the hedge is designated and that condition is reflected in the hedging documentation. Therefore, even if a hedge is not expected to be highly effective in a particular period, hedge accounting is not precluded if effectiveness is expected to remain sufficiently high over the life of the hedging relationship.[181]

Example 19.29: Cumulative hedge effectiveness

A company designates an interest rate swap linked to LIBOR as a hedge of a borrowing whose interest is a UK base rate plus a margin. The UK base rate changes, perhaps, once each quarter or less, in increments of 25 to 50 basis points, while LIBOR changes daily. Over a one to two year period, the hedge is expected to be almost perfect. However, there will be quarters when the UK base rate does not change at all while LIBOR has changed significantly. This would not necessarily preclude hedge accounting.[182]

The time value of money will generally need to be considered in assessing the effectiveness of a hedge. The fair value of an interest rate swap derives from its net settlements and the fixed and variable rates on a swap can be changed without affecting the net settlement if both are changed by the same amount. In other words, a pay-7% fixed, receive-LIBOR swap should have the same fair value as a pay-6% fixed, receive-LIBOR minus 1% swap with otherwise identical terms. Consequently, the fixed rate on a hedged item need not exactly match the fixed rate on a swap designated as a fair value hedge. Nor does the variable rate on an interest-bearing asset or liability need to be the same as the variable rate on a swap designated as a cash flow hedge.[183]

In the case of interest rate risk, it is suggested that hedge effectiveness may be assessed by preparing a maturity schedule for financial assets and liabilities that shows the net interest rate exposure for each time period, provided that the net exposure is associated with a specific asset or liability (or a specific group of assets or liabilities or a specific portion of them) giving rise to the net exposure, and hedge effectiveness is assessed against that asset or liability.[184] The macro-hedging models (see 6 below) have their origins in just such an approach.

5.3.2　The 'dollar-offset' method

As noted at 5.3.1 above, one method that may be used to assess hedge effectiveness is a comparison of hedging gains and losses to the corresponding gains and losses on the hedged item at a point in time.[185]

This method essentially uses the mechanics of *measuring* hedge ineffectiveness set out at 4.1.1 and 4.2.1 above as a basis for *assessing* effectiveness. In other words, it compares the monetary amounts of the change in fair value of the hedging instrument with the monetary amount of the change in fair value or cash flows of the hedged item or transactions attributable to the hedged risk over the assessment period. To the extent that dividing these monetary amounts results in a fraction between 0.80 and 1.25, the hedge will be seen as highly effective on a retrospective basis. Largely because of the terminology used under US GAAP, this has become known as the 'dollar-offset' method.

The dollar-offset method is commonly used as a basis for assessing hedge effectiveness on an ongoing basis because it uses the calculations that have to be performed for determining the hedge accounting bookkeeping entries, and therefore requires limited additional effort.

Example 19.30 below contains a very comprehensive illustration of the dollar offset method for a cash flow hedge that is based on the implementation guidance to IAS 39. Although it is somewhat esoteric, and many accountants will find the calculations difficult to follow, it is an important example. Particularly, it establishes two relatively practical methods of measuring ineffectiveness, and assessing effectiveness, for cash flow hedges. They are normally referred to as the 'hypothetical derivative method' and the 'change in fair value method' (which is what they are called under US GAAP).

As its name suggests, the hypothetical derivative method involves establishing a notional derivative that would be the ideal hedging instrument for the hedged exposure (normally an interest rate swap or forward contract with no unusual terms and a zero fair value at inception of the hedge relationship). The fair value of hypothetical derivative is then used as a proxy for the net present value of the hedged future cash flows against which changes in value of the actual hedging instrument are compared to assess ineffectiveness and measure ineffectiveness.

Example 19.30:　Measuring effectiveness for a hedge of a forecast transaction in a debt instrument

A forecast investment in an interest-earning asset or forecast issue of an interest-bearing liability creates a cash flow exposure to interest rate changes because the related interest payments will be based on the market rate that exists when the forecast transaction occurs. The objective of a cash flow hedge of the exposure to interest rate changes is to offset the effects of future changes in interest rates so as to obtain a single fixed rate, usually the rate that existed at the inception of the hedge that corresponds with the term and timing of the forecast transaction. However, during the period of the hedge, it is not possible to determine what the market interest rate for the forecast transaction will be at the time the hedge is terminated or when the forecast transaction occurs.

During this period, effectiveness can be measured on the basis of changes in interest rates between the designation date and the interim effectiveness measurement date. The interest rates used to make this measurement are the interest rates that correspond with the term and occurrence of the forecast transaction that existed at the inception of the hedge and that exist at the measurement date as evidenced by the term structure of interest rates.

Generally it will not be sufficient simply to compare cash flows of the hedged item with cash flows generated by the derivative hedging instrument as they are paid or received, since such an approach ignores the entity's expectations of whether the cash flows will offset in subsequent periods and whether there will be any resulting ineffectiveness.

It is assumed that Company X expects to issue a €100,000 one-year debt instrument in three months. The instrument will pay interest quarterly with principal due at maturity. X is exposed to interest rate increases and establishes a hedge of the interest cash flows of the debt by entering into a forward starting interest rate swap. The swap has a term of one year and will start in three months to correspond with the terms of the forecast debt issue. X will pay a fixed rate and receive a variable rate, and it designates the risk being hedged as the LIBOR-based interest component in the forecast issue of the debt.

Yield curve

The yield curve provides the foundation for computing future cash flows and the fair value of such cash flows both at the inception of, and during, the hedging relationship. It is based on current market yields on applicable reference bonds that are traded in the marketplace. Market yields are converted to spot interest rates ('spot rates' or 'zero coupon rates') by eliminating the effect of coupon payments on the market yield. Spot rates are used to discount future cash flows, such as principal and interest rate payments, to arrive at their fair value. Spot rates also are used to compute forward interest rates that are used to compute variable and estimated future cash flows. The relationship between spot rates and one-period forward rates is shown by the following formula:

Spot-forward relationship

$$F = \frac{(1 + SR_t)^t}{(1 + SR_{t-1})^{t-1}} - 1$$

where   F = forward rate (%)

SR = spot rate (%)

t = period in time (e.g. 1, 2, 3, 4, 5)

It is assumed that the following quarterly-period term structure of interest rates using quarterly compounding exists at the inception of the hedge.

Yield curve at inception (beginning of period 1)

Forward periods	1	2	3	4	5
Spot rates	3.75%	4.50%	5.50%	6.00%	6.25%
Forward rates	3.75%	5.25%	7.51%	7.50%	7.25%

The one-period forward rates are computed on the basis of spot rates for the applicable maturities. For example, the current forward rate for Period 2 calculated using the formula above is equal to $[1.0450^2 / 1.0375] - 1 = 5.25\%$. The current one-period forward rate for Period 2 is different from the current spot rate for Period 2, since the spot rate is an interest rate from the beginning of Period 1 (spot) to the end of Period 2, while the forward rate is an interest rate from the beginning of Period 2 to the end of Period 2.

Hedged item

In this example, X expects to issue a €100,000 one-year debt instrument in three months with quarterly interest payments. X is exposed to interest rate increases and would like to eliminate the effect on cash flows of interest rate changes that may happen before the forecast transaction takes place. If that risk is eliminated, X would obtain an interest rate on its debt issue that is equal to the one-year forward coupon rate currently available in the marketplace in three months. That forward coupon rate, which is different from the forward (spot) rate, is 6.86%, computed from the term structure of interest rates shown above. It is the market rate of interest that exists at the inception of the hedge, given the terms of the forecast debt instrument. It results in the fair value of the debt being equal to par at its issue.

At the inception of the hedging relationship, the expected cash flows of the debt instrument can be calculated on the basis of the existing term structure of interest rates. For this purpose, it is assumed that interest rates do not change and that the debt would be issued at 6.86% at the beginning of Period 2. In this case, the cash flows and fair value of the debt instrument would be as follows at the beginning of Period 2.

Issue of fixed rate debt (beginning of period 2) – no rate changes (spot based on forward rates)

	Total	1	2	3	4	5
Original forward periods		1	2	3	4	5
Remaining periods			1	2	3	4
Spot rates			5.25%	6.38%	6.75%	6.88%
Forward rates			5.25%	7.51%	7.50%	7.25%
	€		€	€	€	€
Cash flows:						
Fixed interest at 6.86%			1,716	1,716	1,716	1,716
Principal						100,000
Fair value:						
Interest*	6,592		1,694	1,663	1,632	1,603
Principal*	93,408					93,408
	100,000					

* cash flow discounted at the spot rate for the relevant period, e.g. fair value of principal is calculated as $€100,000/(1 + [0.0688/4])^4 = €93,408$

Since it is assumed that interest rates do not change, the fair value of the interest and principal amounts equals the par amount of the forecast transaction. The fair value amounts are computed on the basis of the spot rates that exist at the inception of the hedge for the applicable periods in which the cash flows would occur had the debt been issued at the date of the forecast transaction. They reflect the effect of discounting those cash flows on the basis of the periods that will remain after the debt instrument is issued. For example, the spot rate of 6.38% is used to discount the interest cash flow that is expected to be paid in Period 3, but it is discounted for only two periods because it will occur two periods after the forecast transaction.

The forward interest rates are the same as shown previously, since it is assumed that interest rates do not change. The spot rates are different but they have not actually changed. They represent the spot rates one period forward and are based on the applicable forward rates.

Hedging instrument

The objective of the hedge is to obtain an overall interest rate on the forecast transaction and the hedging instrument that is equal to 6.86%, which is the market rate at the inception of the hedge for the period from Period 2 to Period 5. This objective is accomplished by entering into a forward starting interest rate swap that has a fixed rate of 6.86%. Based on the term structure of interest rates that exist at the inception of the hedge, the interest rate swap will have such a rate. At the inception of the hedge, the fair value of the fixed rate payments on the interest rate swap will equal the fair value of the variable rate payments, resulting in the interest rate swap having a fair value of zero. The expected cash flows of the interest rate swap and the related fair value amounts are shown as follows.

Interest rate swap

	Total	1	2	3	4	5
Original forward periods		1	2	3	4	5
Remaining periods			1	2	3	4
	€		€	€	€	€
Cash flows:						
Fixed interest at 6.86%			1,716	1,716	1,716	1,716
Forecast variable interest*			1,313	1,877	1,876	1,813
Forecast based on forward rate			5.25%	7.51%	7.50%	7.25%
Net interest			(403)	161	160	97
Fair value						
Discount rate (spot)			5.25%	6.38%	6.75%	6.88%
Fixed interest	6,592		1,694	1,663	1,632	1,603
Forecast variable interest	6,592		1,296	1,819	1,784	1,693
Fair value of interest rate swap	0		(398)	156	152	90

* forecast variable rate cash flow based on forward rate, e.g. €1,313 = €100,000 x (0.0525/4)

At the inception of the hedge, the fixed rate on the forward swap is equal to the fixed rate X would receive if it could issue the debt in three months under terms that exist today.

Measuring hedge effectiveness

If interest rates change during the period the hedge is outstanding, the effectiveness of the hedge can be measured in various ways.

Assume that interest rates change as follows immediately before the debt is issued at the beginning of Period 2 (this effectively uses the yield curve existing at Period 1 with a 200 basis point (2%) shift).

Yield curve assumption

	1	2	3	4	5
Forward periods	1	2	3	4	5
Remaining periods		1	2	3	4
Spot rates		5.75%	6.50%	7.50%	8.00%
Forward rates		5.75%	7.25%	9.51%	9.50%

Under the new interest rate environment, the fair value of the pay-fixed at 6.86%, receive-variable interest rate swap that was designated as the hedging instrument would be as follows.

Fair value of interest rate swap

	Total		1	2	3	4	5
Original forward periods			1	2	3	4	5
Remaining periods				1	2	3	4
	€			€	€	€	€
Cash flows:							
Fixed interest at 6.86%				1,716	1,716	1,716	1,716
Forecast variable interest				1,438	1,813	2,377	2,376
Forecast based on new forward rate				5.75%	7.25%	9.51%	9.50%
Net interest				(279)	97	661	660
Fair value							
New discount rate (spot)				5.75%	6.50%	7.50%	8.00%
Fixed interest	6,562			1,692	1,662	1,623	1,585
Forecast variable interest	7,615			1,417	1,755	2,248	2,195
Fair value of interest rate swap	1,053			(275)	93	625	610

In order to compute the effectiveness of the hedge, it is necessary to measure the change in the present value of the cash flows or the value of the hedged forecast transaction. There are at least two methods of accomplishing this measurement.

Method A – Compute change in fair value of debt

	Total		1	2	3	4	5
Original forward periods			1	2	3	4	5
Remaining periods				1	2	3	4
	€			€	€	€	€
Cash flows:							
Fixed interest at 6.86%				1,716	1,716	1,716	1,716
Principal							100,000
Fair value:							
New discount rate (spot)				5.75%	6.50%	7.50%	8.00%
Interest	6,562			1,692	1,662	1,623	1,585
Principal	92,385						92,385*
Total	98,947						
Fair value at inception	100,000						
Difference	(1,053)						

* €100,000/(1 + [0.08/4])^4

Under Method A, a computation is made of the fair value in the new interest rate environment of debt that carries interest that is equal to the coupon interest rate that existed at the inception of the hedging relationship (6.86%). This fair value is compared with the expected fair value as of the beginning of Period 2 that was calculated on the basis of the term structure of interest rates that existed at the inception of the hedging relationship, as illustrated above, to determine the change in the fair value. Note that the difference between the change in the fair value of the swap and the change in the expected fair value of the debt (€1,053) exactly offset in this example, since the terms of the swap and the forecast transaction match each other.

Method B – Compute change in fair value of cash flows

	Total	1	2	3	4	5
Original forward periods		*1*	*2*	*3*	*4*	*5*
Remaining periods			*1*	*2*	*3*	*4*
Market rate at inception			6.86%	6.86%	6.86%	6.86%
Current forward rate			5.75%	7.25%	9.51%	9.50%
Rate difference			1.11%	(0.39%)	(2.64%)	(2.64%)
Cash flow difference (principal × rate)			€279	(€97)	(€661)	(€660)
Discount rate (spot)			*5.75%*	*6.50%*	*7.50%*	*8.00%*
Fair value of difference	(€1,053)		€275	(€93)	(€625)	(€610)

Under Method B, the present value of the change in cash flows is computed on the basis of the difference between the forward interest rates for the applicable periods at the effectiveness measurement date and the interest rate that would have been obtained if the debt had been issued at the market rate that existed at the inception of the hedge. The market rate that existed at the inception of the hedge is the one-year forward coupon rate in three months. The present value of the change in cash flows is computed on the basis of the current spot rates that exist at the effectiveness measurement date for the applicable periods in which the cash flows are expected to occur. This method also could be referred to as the 'theoretical swap' method (or 'hypothetical derivative' method) because the comparison is between the hedged fixed rate on the debt and the current variable rate, which is the same as comparing cash flows on the fixed and variable rate legs of an interest rate swap.

As before, the difference between the change in the fair value of the swap and the change in the present value of the cash flows exactly offset in this example, since the terms match.

Other considerations

There is an additional computation that should be performed to compute ineffectiveness before the expected date of the forecast transaction that has not been considered for the purpose of this illustration. The fair value difference has been determined in each of the illustrations as of the expected date of the forecast transaction immediately before the forecast transaction, i.e. at the beginning of Period 2. If the assessment of hedge effectiveness is performed before the forecast transaction occurs, the difference should be discounted to the current date to arrive at the actual amount of ineffectiveness. For example, if the measurement date were one month after the hedging relationship was established and the forecast transaction is now expected to occur in two months, the amount would have to be discounted for the remaining two months before the forecast transaction is expected to occur to arrive at the actual fair value. This step would not be necessary in the examples provided above because there was no ineffectiveness. Therefore, additional discounting of the amounts, which net to zero, would not have changed the result.

Under Method B, ineffectiveness is computed on the basis of the difference between the forward coupon interest rates for the applicable periods at the effectiveness measurement date and the interest rate that would have been obtained if the debt had been issued at the market rate that existed at the inception of the hedge. Computing the change in cash flows based on the difference between the forward interest rates that existed at the inception of the hedge and the forward rates that exist at the effectiveness measurement date is inappropriate if the objective of the hedge is to establish a single fixed rate for a series of forecast interest payments. This objective is met by hedging the exposures with an interest rate swap as illustrated in the above example. The fixed interest rate on the swap is a blended interest rate composed of the forward rates over the life of the swap. Unless the yield curve is flat, the comparison between the forward interest rate exposures over the life of the swap and the fixed rate on the swap will produce different cash flows whose fair values are equal only at the inception of the hedging relationship. This difference is shown in the table below.

	Total	1	2	3	4	5
Original forward periods		1	2	3	4	5
Remaining periods			1	2	3	4
Forward rate at inception			5.25%	7.51%	7.50%	7.25%
Current forward rate			5.75%	7.25%	9.51%	9.50%
Rate difference			(0.50%)	0.26%	(2.00%)	(2.25%)
Cash flow difference (principal × rate)			(€125)	€64	(€501)	(€563)
Discount rate (spot)			*5.75%*	*6.50%*	*7.50%*	*8.00%*
Fair value of difference	€1,055		(€123)	€62	(€474)	(€520)
Fair value of interest rate swap	€1,053					
Ineffectiveness	(€2)					

If the objective of the hedge is to obtain the forward rates that existed at the inception of the hedge, the interest rate swap is ineffective because the swap has a single blended fixed coupon rate that does not offset a series of different forward interest rates. However, if the objective of the hedge is to obtain the forward coupon rate that existed at the inception of the hedge, the swap is effective, and the comparison based on differences in forward interest rates suggests ineffectiveness when none may exist. Computing ineffectiveness based on the difference between the forward interest rates that existed at the inception of the hedge and the forward rates that exist at the effectiveness measurement date would be an appropriate measurement of ineffectiveness if the hedging objective is to lock in those forward interest rates. In that case, the appropriate hedging instrument would be a series of forward contracts each of which matures on a repricing date that corresponds with the date of the forecast transactions.

It also should be noted that it would be inappropriate to compare only the variable cash flows on the interest rate swap with the interest cash flows in the debt that would be generated by the forward interest rates. That methodology has the effect of measuring ineffectiveness only on a portion of the derivative, and IAS 39 does not permit the bifurcation of a derivative for the purposes of assessing effectiveness in this situation (see 2.1.4 above). It is recognised, however, that if the fixed interest rate on the interest rate swap is equal to the fixed rate that would have been obtained on the debt at inception, there will be no ineffectiveness assuming that there are no differences in terms and no change in credit risk or it is not designated in the hedging relationship.[186]

5.3.3 Dollar-offset: comparison of spot rate and forward rate methods

It was explained at 2.1.4 above that the spot and interest elements of a forward contract could be treated separately for the purposes of hedge designation. The next example, based on the implementation guidance, contrasts two variations of the dollar-offset method. Case 1 can be used when the whole of a forward contract is treated as the hedging instrument and the hedged risk is identified by reference to changes attributable to the forward rate (forward rate method). Case 2 can be used when the interest component is excluded and the hedged risk is identified by reference to changes attributable to the spot rate (spot rate method).

To demonstrate these methods, the implementation guidance uses a type of hedge that is very common in practice, the hedging of foreign currency risk associated with future purchases using a forward exchange contract. The example also illustrates the difference in the accounting for such hedges depending on whether the spot and interest elements of a forward contract are treated separately for the purposes of hedge designation.

*Example 19.31:   Cash flow hedge of firm commitment to purchase inventory in a
                   foreign currency*

Company A has the Local Currency (LC) as its functional and presentation currency.
A's accounting policy is to apply basis adjustments to non-financial assets that result from hedged
forecast transactions and it chooses to treat hedges of the foreign currency risk of a firm
commitment as cash flow hedges.

On 30 June 2005, A enters into a forward exchange contract to receive Foreign Currency (FC)
100,000 and deliver LC109,600 on 30 June 2006 at an initial cost and fair value of zero. On
inception, it designates the forward exchange contract as a hedging instrument in a cash flow hedge
of a firm commitment to purchase a certain quantity of paper for FC100,000 on 31 March 2006
and, thereafter, as a fair value hedge of the resulting payable of FC100,000, which is to be paid on
30 June 2006. It is assumed that all hedge accounting conditions in IAS 39 are met.

On 30 June 2005, the spot exchange rate is LC1.072 to FC1, while the twelve-month forward
exchange rate is LC1.096 to FC1. On 31 December 2005, the spot exchange rate is LC1.080 to
FC1, while the six-month forward exchange rate is LC1.092 to FC1. On 31 March 2006, the spot
exchange rate is LC1.074 to FC1, while the three-month forward rate is LC1.076 to FC1. On
30 June 2006, the spot exchange rate is LC1.072 to FC1. The applicable yield curve in the local
currency is flat at 6% per annum throughout the period. The fair value of the forward exchange
contract is negative LC388 on 31 December 2005 ($\{[1.092 \times 100{,}000] - 109{,}600\} \div 1.06^{(6/12)}$),
negative LC1,971 on 31 March 2006 ($\{[1.076 \times 100{,}000] - 109{,}600\} \div 1.06^{(3/12)}$), and negative
LC2,400 on 30 June 2006 ($1.072 \times 100{,}000 - 109{,}600$).

This is summarised in the following table:

Date	Spot rate	Forward rate to 30 June 2006	Fair value of forward contract
30 June 2005	1.072	1.096	–
31 December 2005	1.080	1.092	(388)
31 March 2006	1.074	1.076	(1,971)
30 June 2006	1.072	–	(2,400)

Case 1: Changes in the fair value of the forward contract are designated in the hedge

The hedge is expected to be fully effective because the critical terms of the forward exchange
contract and the purchase contract and the assessments of hedge effectiveness are based on the
forward price.

The accounting entries are as follows.

30 June 2005

	LC	LC
Forward	–	
Cash		–

To record the forward exchange contract at its initial fair value, i.e. zero.

31 December 2005

	LC	LC
Equity	388	
Forward – liability		388

To record the change in the fair value of the forward contract between 30 June 2005 and 31 December
2005, i.e. 388 – 0 = LC388, in equity. The hedge is fully effective because the loss on the forward

exchange contract, LC388, exactly offsets the change in cash flows associated with the purchase contract based on the forward price $\{([1.092 \times 100,000] - 109,600) \div 1.06^{(6/12)}\} - \{([1.096 \times 100,000] - 109,600) \div 1.06\} = -LC388$. The negative figure denotes a reduction in the net present value of cash outflows and, therefore, effectively represents a 'gain' to offset the loss on the forward in equity.

31 March 2006

	LC	LC
Equity	1,583	
Forward – liability		1,583

To record the change in the fair value of the forward contract between 1 January 2006 and 31 March 2006, i.e. $1,971 - 388 = LC1,583$, in equity. The hedge is fully effective because the loss on the forward exchange contract, LC1,583, exactly offsets the change in cash flows associated with the purchase contract based on the forward price $\{([1.076 \times 100,000] - 109,600) \div 1.06^{(3/12)}\} - \{([1.092 \times 100,000] - 109,600) \div 1.06^{(6/12)}\} = -LC1,583$. The negative figure denotes a reduction in the net present value of cash outflows and, therefore, effectively represents a 'gain' to offset the loss on the forward in equity.

	LC	LC
Paper (purchase price)	107,400	
Paper (hedging loss)	1,971	
Equity		1,971
Payable		107,400

To record the purchase of the paper at the spot rate (1.074 × 100,000) and remove the cumulative loss on the forward reported in equity, LC1,971, and include it in the initial measurement of the purchased paper. Accordingly, the initial measurement of the purchased paper is LC 109,371 consisting of a purchase consideration of LC 107,400 and a hedging loss of LC 1,971.

30 June 2006

	LC	LC
Payable	107,400	
Cash		107,200
Profit or loss		200

To record the settlement of the payable at the spot rate (100,000 × 1.072 = LC107,200) and the associated exchange gain of $LC200 = 107,400 - 107,200$.

	LC	LC
Profit or loss	429	
Forward – liability		429

To record the loss on the forward exchange contract between 1 April 2006 and 30 June 2006, i.e. $2,400 - 1,971 = LC429)$ in profit or loss. The hedge is considered to be fully effective because the loss on the forward exchange contract, LC429, exactly offsets the change in the fair value of the payable based on the forward price $[1.072 \times 100,000] - 109,600 - \{([1.076 \times 100,000] - 109,600) \div 1.06^{(3/12)}\} = -LC429$. The negative figure denotes a reduction in the net present value of the payable and, therefore represents a gain to offset the loss on the forward contract.

	LC	LC
Forward – liability	2,400	
Cash		2,400

To record the net settlement of the forward exchange contract.

Although this arrangement has been set up to be a 'perfect hedge', the loss on the forward in the last three months is significantly different from the gain recorded on retranslating the hedged payable. The principal reason for this is that the change in the fair value of the forward contract includes changes in its interest element, as well as its currency element. The interest element of the payable is generally not accounted for (even on an amortised cost basis) because it is immaterial (see Chapter 18 at 2.2).

Case 2: Changes in the spot element of the forward contract only are designated in the hedge

The hedge is expected to be fully effective because the critical terms of the forward exchange contract and the purchase contract are the same and the change in the premium or discount on the forward contract is excluded from the assessment of effectiveness.

30 June 2005

	LC	LC
Forward	–	
Cash		–

To record the forward exchange contract at its initial fair value, i.e. zero.

31 December 2005

	LC	LC
Profit or loss (interest element of forward)	1,165	
Equity (spot element)		777
Forward – liability		388

To record the change in the fair value of the forward contract between 30 June 2005 and 31 December 2005, i.e. $388 - 0 = LC388$. The change in the present value of spot settlement of the forward exchange contract is a gain of $LC777 = \{([1.080 \times 100{,}000] - 107{,}200) \div 1.06^{(6/12)}\} - \{([1.072 \times 100{,}000] - 107{,}200) \div 1.06\})$, which is recognised directly in equity. The change in the interest element of the forward exchange contract (the residual change in fair value) is a loss of $LC1{,}165 = 388 + 777$, which is recognised in profit or loss. The hedge is fully effective because the gain in the spot element of the forward contract, LC777, exactly offsets the change in the purchase price at spot rates $\{([1.080 \times 100{,}000] - 107{,}200) \div 1.06^{(6/12)}\} - \{([1.072 \times 100{,}000] - 107{,}200) \div 1.06\} = LC777$. The positive figure denotes an increase in the net present value of cash outflows and, therefore, effectively represents a 'loss' to offset the gain on the forward in equity.

31 March 2006

	LC	LC
Equity (spot element)	580	
Profit or loss (interest element)	1,003	
Forward – liability		1,583

To record the change in the fair value of the forward contract between 1 January 2006 and 31 March 2006, i.e. $1{,}971 - 388 = LC1{,}583$. The change in the present value of spot settlement of the forward exchange contract is a loss of $LC580 = \{([1.074 \times 100{,}000] - 107{,}200) \div 1.06^{(3/12)}\} - \{([1.080 \times 100{,}000] - 107{,}200) \div 1.06^{(6/12)}\}$, which is recognised in equity. The change in the interest element of the forward contract (the residual change in fair value) is a loss of $LC1{,}003 = 1{,}583 - 580$), which is recognised in profit or loss. The hedge is fully effective because the loss in the spot element of the forward contract, LC580, exactly offsets the change in the purchase price at spot rates $\{([1.074 \times 100{,}000] - 107{,}200) \div 1.06^{(3/12)}\} - \{([1.080 \times 100{,}000] - 107{,}200) \div 1.06^{(6/12)}\} = -LC580$. The negative figure denotes a reduction in the net present value of cash outflows and, therefore, effectively represents a 'gain' to offset the loss on the forward in equity.

	LC	LC
Paper (purchase price)	107,400	
Equity	197	
Paper (hedging gain)		197
Payable		107,400

To recognise the purchase of the paper at the spot rate (= 1.074 × 100,000) and remove the cumulative gain on the spot element of the forward contract that has been recognised in equity (777 − 580 = LC197) and include it in the initial measurement of the purchased paper. Accordingly, the initial measurement of the purchased paper is LC107,203 consisting of a purchase consideration of LC107,400 and a hedging gain of LC197.

30 June 2006

	LC	LC
Payable	107,400	
Cash		107,200
Profit or loss		200

To record the settlement of the payable at the spot rate (100,000 × 1.072 = LC107,200) and the associated exchange gain of LC200 (= − [1.072 − 1.074] × 100,000).

	LC	LC
Profit or loss (spot element)	197	
Profit or loss (interest element)	232	
Forward – liability		429

To record the change in the fair value of the forward between 1 April 2006 and 30 June 2006, i.e. 2,400 − 1,971 = LC429). The change in the present value of spot settlement of the forward exchange contract is a loss of LC197 = {[1.072 × 100,000] − 107,200 − {([1.074 × 100,000] − 107,200) ÷ $1.06^{(3/12)}$}, which is recognised in profit or loss. The change in the interest element of the forward contract (the residual change in fair value) is a loss of LC232 = 429 −197, which is recognised in profit or loss. The hedge is fully effective because the loss in the spot element of the forward contract, LC197, exactly offsets the gain on the payable reported using spot rates = {[1.072 × 100,000] − 107,200 − {([1.074 × 100,000] − 107,200) ÷ $1.06^{(3/12)}$} = −LC197. The negative figure denotes a reduction in the net present value of the payable and, therefore represents a gain to offset the loss on the forward contract.

	LC	LC
Forward – liability	2,400	
Cash		2,400

To record the net settlement of the forward exchange contract.

The following table provides an overview of the components of the change in fair value of the hedging instrument over the term of the hedging relationship. It illustrates that the way in which a hedging relationship is designated affects the subsequent accounting for that hedging relationship, including the assessment of hedge effectiveness and the recognition of gains and losses.[187]

Period ending	Change in spot settlement LC	Far value of change in spot settlement LC	Change in forward settlement LC	Fair value of change in forward settlement LC	Fair value of change in interest element LC
30 June 2005	–	–	–	–	–
31 December 2005	800	777	(400)	(388)	(1,165)
31 March 2006	(600)	(580)	(1,600)	(1,583)	(1,003)
30 June 2006	(200)	(197)	(400)	(429)	(232)
Total	–	–	(2,400)	(2,400)	(2,400)

In each case, the hedge is perfectly effective because of the way effectiveness is measured, but there is a significant difference on profit or loss. In part (a) all gains and losses on the forward are initially deferred in equity whereas in part (b) changes in the fair value of the interest element of the forward are immediately recognised in profit or loss. The example also sets out how a single hedge can initially be a cash flow hedge of the future sale and then become a fair value hedge of the associated payable, provided it is documented as such.

5.3.4   Law of small numbers

As set out at 5.3.2 above, the dollar-offset method of assessing effectiveness is commonly used because it requires limited additional effort over and above that required to determine the amount of ineffectiveness to be recorded in profit or loss. However, there can be significant problems in achieving high correlation, particularly when the actual movements in fair value or cash flows of the hedging instrument and hedged item are small.

Consider a fair value hedge where the change in fair value of the hedging instrument for the period was €1,000 and the corresponding change in fair value of the hedged item was €2,000. This would indicate that the hedging relationship was only 50% effective and it would therefore not qualify for hedge accounting. However, if the changes in fair value in relation to the fair value of the contract being hedged were examined, the fair value of the hedged item in this case might have changed from €1,000,000 to €1,002,000. Further, if the change in value of the hedged item was €50,000, the change in value in the hedging instrument might have been €49,000 and the strategy may actually have been highly effective. This scenario is often described as 'the law of small numbers' problem. Although well documented, the standard does not address this phenomenon and certainly offers no insight as to how an entity might deal with it.

A common approach is, for the purposes of *assessing* hedge effectiveness, to simply ignore changes in fair value that are below a given fixed limit (strictly, for the purpose of *measuring* ineffectiveness, these amounts should be recorded but they will not be material). This limit should be established at the inception of the hedge and should be included in the hedge documentation. Care should be taken in setting this limit – too high and the entity could be accused of not establishing an appropriate method of assessing effectiveness; too low and the risk of failing the assessment is increased.

5.3.5 *Regression analysis and other statistical methods*

The use of regression analysis is referred to in the standard in the context of optimising the ratio of hedging instrument quantities to hedged item quantities in order to improve the effectiveness of a hedge.[188] The implementation guidance also explains (as noted at 5.3.1 above) that statistical measurement techniques such as regression analysis may also be used for assessing hedge effectiveness.[189]

Implementing methodologies that use statistical techniques is clearly going to require more effort than, say, a dollar-offset based analysis, simply because they are so much more complex. It is also beyond the scope of a publication such as this to cover these techniques in any detail. It is worth noting, however, that they do tend to be more forgiving than dollar-offset based methods. Therefore, it is often worth investing the necessary time and effort in order to improve the chances of obtaining hedge accounting, especially where a qualitative assessment of effectiveness (see 5.3.8 below) is not appropriate.

Whilst it is untrue that *anything* can be proved with statistics, care does need to be taken when applying regression analysis or other statistical approaches to assessing effectiveness. These methodologies require appropriate interpretation and an understanding of statistical inferences. For example, statistical techniques may be able to demonstrate a correlation between two variables, but that statistical technique is only relevant to the extent that it is actually predictive of the hedge relationship under assessment.

5.3.6 *'Almost fully offset' and under-hedging*

In the previous version of the standard, the prospective test was expressed as 'almost fully offset', whereas the retrospective test was 'within a range of 80% to 125%'.[190] This requirement appeared to be significantly more onerous than the equivalent test under US GAAP, which is described in terms of 'highly effective' expectations. Consequently, during the improvements project, many commentators suggested that the IASB amend IAS 39 to be more consistent with US GAAP in this respect.

However, the IASB was concerned that, without this requirement, entities might wish to purposely hedge, say, 85% of the total exposure and designate this as a hedge of 100% of the exposure. For a cash flow hedge, this could reduce the amount of ineffectiveness recognised (see 4.2.1 above) and the previous implementation guidance explained that under-hedging in this way was not permitted because such a hedge would fail the 'almost fully offset' aspect of the prospective test.[191] Therefore, the original wording was initially retained in order to prevent entities from under-hedging, but this was not the end of the issue.[192]

When finalising the requirements for portfolio hedges of interest rate risk (see 6 below), the IASB received further representations that many hedges would fail the 'almost fully offset' test in IAS 39, including some that would qualify for the short-cut method in US GAAP (see 5.3.7 below) and thus be assumed to be 100% effective. This time, the IASB was persuaded and decided to remove the words 'almost fully offset' from the prospective test requirements (see 5.3.1 above).[193]

In order to address their concerns about under-hedging, the standard now states that if an entity hedges less than 100% of the exposure on an item, such as 85%, it should designate the hedged item as being 85% of the exposure and measure ineffectiveness based on the change in that designated 85%. However, when hedging the designated 85% exposure, a hedge ratio of other than one to one may be used if that improves the expected effectiveness of the hedge, as explained at 2.2.2 above.[194]

5.3.7 'Short-cut method'

Under US GAAP, an entity is allowed to assume that there will be no ineffectiveness in a hedge of interest rate risk using an interest rate swap as the hedging instrument, provided specified criteria are met. This is known as the 'shortcut method' for assessing hedge effectiveness.[195] The previous version of IAS 39 precluded such an approach and during the improvements project many commentators urged the IASB to permit the use of the shortcut method under IAS 39.[196] However, one of the general principles of IAS 39 is that ineffectiveness in a hedging relationship is measured and recognised in profit or loss and the IASB did not want to make an exception to this principle. Therefore, IAS 39 was not amended to permit the shortcut method.[197] Nevertheless, as set out at 5.3.8 below, an approach to assessing effectiveness may be adopted in some situations that requires only a little more effort than the short-cut method.

5.3.8 Perfect effectiveness and qualitative assessments

The application guidance explains that if the principal terms of the hedging instrument and of the hedged asset, liability, firm commitment or highly probable forecast transaction are the same, the changes in fair value and cash flows attributable to the risk being hedged may be likely to offset each other fully, both when the hedge is entered into and afterwards. For example, an interest rate swap is likely to be an effective hedge if the notional and principal amounts, term, repricing dates, dates of interest and principal receipts and payments, and basis for measuring interest rates are the same for the hedging instrument and the hedged item.[198]

Similarly, a hedge of a highly probable forecast purchase of a commodity with a forward contract is likely to be highly effective if:

- the forward contract is for the purchase of the same quantity of the same commodity at the same time and location as the hedged forecast purchase;

- the fair value of the forward contract at inception is zero; and

- either the change in the discount or premium on the forward contract is excluded from the assessment of effectiveness and included directly in profit or loss or the change in expected cash flows on the forecast transaction is based on the forward price for the commodity (see 5.3.3 above).[199]

Sometimes, however, the hedging instrument offsets only part of the hedged risk. For example, if the hedging instrument and hedged item are denominated in different currencies that do not move in tandem, the hedge would not be fully effective. Also, a hedge of interest rate risk using a derivative would not be fully effective if part of the change in the fair value of the derivative is attributable to the counterparty's credit risk.[200] Therefore, when assessing effectiveness, both at inception and thereafter, the risk of counterparty default should be considered. In a cash flow hedge, if default becomes probable the hedging relationship is unlikely to achieve offsetting cash flows and hedge accounting would be discontinued. In a fair value hedge, if there is a change in the counterparty's creditworthiness, the hedging instrument's fair value will change which affects its effectiveness and hence whether it qualifies for continued hedge accounting.[201]

In deciding not to permit the short-cut method, the IASB noted that IAS 39 permits the hedging of portions of financial assets and liabilities in cases where US GAAP does not. Therefore, an entity may hedge a portion of a financial instrument (e.g. interest rate risk or credit risk – see 2.2.2 above) and if the critical terms of the hedging instrument and the hedged item were the same, the entity would, in many cases, recognise no ineffectiveness.[202] The implementation guidance continues with this theme and explains that, to improve hedge effectiveness, an entity may designate only certain risks in an overall exposure as being hedged. For example, if an interest rate swap issued by a counterparty with a AA credit rating is used to hedge the fair value of a fixed interest rate debt instrument, designating only the exposure in the debt related to AA rated interest rate movements will reduce the impact on effectiveness of market changes in credit spreads.[203]

Therefore it can be seen, at least for hedges of financial items, that the designation of the hedge can be tailored to significantly reduce the ineffectiveness that can feasibly occur. However, because ineffectiveness may still arise because of other attributes (e.g. liquidity of the hedging instrument or its credit risk), hedge, effectiveness cannot be assumed throughout the life of the hedge even if the principal terms of the hedging instrument and hedged item are the same.[204] Consideration should also be given to the issues covered at 5.3.9 below, particularly the frequency with which variable interest rates are reset on an instrument such as an interest rate swap.

This does not mean that a mathematical analysis need be performed each time the effectiveness of such a hedge is assessed. If the hedge has been designated in such a way that it is 'perfect' (in the terms described above), a qualitative method for assessing hedge effectiveness may suffice. For example, it may be possible to demonstrate that, feasibly, ineffectiveness can arise in a particular hedge only if the credit risk of the hedging instrument changes. In such a case, the qualitative assessment might involve a periodic examination that the hedge is still 'perfect' (e.g. the critical terms still match), combined with a review of the credit rating of the counterparty. Assuming this assessment highlights no anomalies, no further assessment need be performed.

Sometimes, a hedging relationship might be close to 'perfect' but not quite. In these cases, a presumption of no ineffectiveness may be inappropriate. However, measurement of ineffectiveness does not necessarily have to be a complex process after the initial assessment. For example, a company may believe that its interest rate risk hedge design is marginally ineffective, perhaps because the repricing dates of the swap and the hedged item do not exactly match. However, the company may be able to approximate the maximum amount of ineffectiveness that could arise so long as market interest rates remain within a reasonable range, say between 4% and 8%. If this 'worst case' ineffectiveness is clearly immaterial, it would be acceptable not to perform further detailed effectiveness assessments so long as market conditions remained within that reasonable range. However, hedge ineffectiveness should always be measured and recognised in profit or loss.

5.3.9 Interest accruals and 'clean' vs. 'dirty' values

Another problem that entities can face when assessing the effectiveness of hedging instruments such as interest rate swaps, is the fair value 'noise' that is generated between interest rate reset dates. The payments on an interest rate swap are typically established at the beginning of a reset period and paid at the end of that period. Between these two dates the swap is no longer a pure pay-fixed receive-variable (or vice versa) instrument because both the next payment and the next receipt are fixed. Accordingly, the corresponding changes in the fair value of the hedged item (e.g. fixed rate debt) will not strictly mirror that of the swap. This problem becomes more acute the less frequent it is that variable interest rates reset to market rates.

The IASB does not seem to see this as a potential source of ineffectiveness. For example, it is stated in IAS 39 that 'an interest rate swap is likely to be an effective hedge if the notional and principal amounts, term, repricing dates, dates of interest and principal receipts and payments, and basis for measuring interest rates are the same for the hedging instrument and the hedged item'.[205] Further, given the IASB's statements (see 5.3.8 above) regarding the decision not to permit the short-cut method, which is only available for hedge relationships involving interest rate swaps, it seems safe to assume that they do not normally expect ineffectiveness from interest rate repricings to arise on such relationships where the hedge is 'perfect'. In fact, it is interesting to note that the one comprehensive example showing the measurement of effectiveness of an interest rate swap (see Example 19.30 at 5.3.2 above) completely avoids this issue.

Entities are therefore left with little practical guidance in dealing with the apparent ineffectiveness that can result even from hedges that seem perfectly effective. A common approach to avoid much of this noise is to use 'clean' fair values (which effectively ignore the effects of the next net settlement or interest payment) rather than 'dirty' fair values (which includes them). The mathematics of an effectiveness assessment using this approach should mean there is a much lower likelihood of the hedge failing the test. This approach is likely to prove acceptable in many situations, especially where the interval between repricings is frequent enough, e.g. quarterly rather than yearly, so as to minimise the changes in fair value from the fixed net settlement or next interest payment. However, in principle, ineffectiveness should always be measured and recognised in profit or loss.

5.3.10 *Effectiveness of options*

It was explained at 2.1.4 A above that the time value of an option may be excluded from the hedge relationship and, in many cases, this may make it easier to demonstrate the effectiveness of a hedge. In such cases, if the documented hedged risk is appropriately customised there will, in many cases, be no ineffectiveness to record, as set out in the following example.

Example 19.32: Out of the money put option used to hedge an equity share

Company A has an investment in one hundred shares of Company Z. The share is classified as available-for-sale, therefore associated fair value gains and losses are recognised initially in equity. The shares have a quoted price of £100 each and to partially protect itself against decreases in the share price, A acquires a put option, which gives it the right to sell one hundred shares in Z for £90 each.

A is permitted to designate changes in the option's intrinsic value as the hedging instrument. The changes in the intrinsic value of the option provide protection against the risk of variability in Z's share price below or equal to the strike price of the put of £90. For prices above £90, the option is out of the money and has no intrinsic value. Accordingly, gains and losses on the shares in Z for prices above £90 are not attributable to the hedged risk for the purposes of assessing hedge effectiveness and recognising gains and losses on the hedged item.

Therefore, changes in the fair value of the shares in Z are recognised in equity if associated with variations in share price above £90. Changes in the fair value of the shares in Z associated with price declines below £90 form part of the designated fair value hedge and are recognised in profit or loss. Assuming the hedge is effective, those changes are offset by changes in the intrinsic value of the put, which are also recognised in profit or loss (see 4.1.1 above).

Changes in the time value of the put are excluded from the designated hedging relationship and recognised in profit or loss as they arise.[206]

Hedges such as this are likely to be suitable for the type of qualitative hedge effectiveness assessments set out at 5.3.8 above and, consequently, can be quite easy to administer. The downside associated with designating the hedge in this way is that changes in the time value of the option are recognised in profit or loss, resulting in some inescapable volatility.

Under US GAAP, subsequent to the publication of SFAS 133, an interpretation was issued that set out a method of assessing effectiveness and measuring ineffectiveness of an entire option (i.e. including its time value) in certain cash flow hedges, which normally resulted in the measurement of no ineffectiveness.[207] This allows entities to defer all changes in the fair value of an option (including the time value) in equity until the hedged transaction affects profit or loss. Prior to this, the conventional wisdom was that the only way to assess effectiveness of a purchased option (or zero-cost collar) designated in a cash flow hedge was to focus on changes in the intrinsic value of the option.

From the perspective of IAS 39, this interpretation is problematic. The current consensus opinion appears to be that it simply creates an exception to the general principles of hedge accounting under US GAAP, rather than providing an interpretation of them. Consequently, the use of this method has, to date, been seen as incompatible with IAS 39.

5.3.11 Net investment hedges

From the perspective of an investor (e.g. a parent) it is clear that an investment in a foreign operation is likely to give rise to a degree of foreign currency exchange rate risk. It is also clear that on an economic level this risk exists irrespective of the accounting treatment adopted in the investor's consolidated financial statements. However, in consolidated financial statements, a foreign operation is not normally accounted for as if it is a separate investment of the parent, but as an integral part of the reporting entity itself. In other words, it is the assets and liabilities of the foreign operation (rather than the foreign operation itself) that are accounted for in the consolidated financial statements. Therefore, only part of this risk (albeit potentially a large part) manifests itself in the accounting treatment for such investments, i.e. the gain or loss recognised in equity that arises from retranslating the net assets of the foreign operation at the closing exchange rate.

Although, in economic terms, an investing entity might believe it is hedging the foreign currency risk associated with the whole of its investment (e.g. the entire fair value or, perhaps, all the expected future cash flows such as dividends) this is not how it is seen for accounting purposes. In fact, a hedge of a net investment in a foreign operation is, in many ways, a hedge of the accounting entry referred to in the previous paragraph, i.e. the retranslation gain or loss recognised in equity. It is certainly not a fair value hedge (see 3.6 above) and any future dividends are internal transactions, so these cannot be hedged items in a cash flow hedge (see 2.3.4 above).

Perhaps because this accounting entry has little economic meaning (it is a function of the carrying amount of the foreign operation's assets and liabilities, many of which can be measured on an historical cost basis or not recognised at all) there are some that argue it is simply not a legitimate hedging relationship and hedge accounting should not be allowed. Another view, with a similar conclusion, is that in an ideal world, all recognised gains and losses should be reported in the income statement (even those arising from the retranslation of net investments). Consequently, correcting this aspect of current accounting practice would remove the need for this hedge accounting anomaly.

A more traditional perspective might see the net investment hedge as an attempt to reflect the offsetting effects of genuine economic hedges within the current accounting framework in so far as it is possible (i.e. to the extent that the underlying hedged assets and liabilities have been recognised in the financial statements). However, it is not uncommon to see entities deliberately hedging the (outdated) book values of net investments, rather than any economic value they may have, and the objective of such hedges is often to improve the net finance cost shown in the income statement (with little regard to the real foreign currency gains and losses that are reported, out of harm's way, in equity). Faced with these situations it is difficult, even for those holding the traditional view, not to share some sympathy with those that would prohibit the practice. Nevertheless, IAS 39 does permit it and the remainder of this section deals with some of the practical aspects of such hedges.

A   Non-derivative liabilities used as the hedging instrument

It seems quite clear that a foreign currency denominated non-derivative financial liability, such as a borrowing, can be used as the hedging instrument in a hedge of a net investment in a foreign operation. This can be seen as a pure 'accounting' hedge, i.e. the retranslation gain or loss on the borrowing (an accounting entry representing a part of its change in fair value that is accounted for on a continuous basis) can offset the retranslation gain or loss on the net investment (another accounting entry). In fact, if the liability is:

- denominated in the same currency as the functional currency of the hedged net investment;

- has an amortised cost that is lower than the net investment in the foreign operation; and

- is designated appropriately,

the hedge is likely to be perfectly effective in terms of the offsetting retranslation gains and losses on the liability and the hedged proportion of the net investment. Accordingly, a qualitative assessment of effectiveness should identify any potential ineffectiveness (see 5.3.8 above).

If a borrowing or similar liability is denominated in a different currency to the functional currency of the net investment, it may still be possible to designate it as the hedging instrument. However, it will need to be demonstrated that the two currencies are sufficiently correlated so that the hedging instrument is expected to result in offsetting gains and losses over the period that the hedge is designated. This might be the case if the two currencies are formally pegged or otherwise linked to one another or if the relevant exchange rates move in tandem because of, say, similarities in the underlying economies.

Even if such a hedge is highly effective, it is likely to result in some ineffectiveness (unless the link between the two currencies is near-perfect). Accordingly, a qualitative assessment is unlikely to be appropriate in these cases. Under US GAAP it is suggested that the retranslation gains and losses on the actual instrument should be compared to those on a hypothetical non-derivative (e.g. a borrowing in the correct currency) with any difference reported in profit or loss.[208] This approach should normally be acceptable under IAS 39.

B   Derivatives used as the hedging instrument

It is harder to determine what types of derivative may be used in a hedge of a net investment. The same definition of effectiveness applies to such hedges (see 5.3 above), but what are the changes in the fair value or cash flows of the hedged item that are attributable to the hedged risk that are to be offset by changes in the fair value or cash flows of the hedging instrument? Again it is only an accounting entry that it being hedged but, unlike in A above, the hedging instrument will be accounted for at fair value. Even for the simplest derivative that fair value is likely to reflect factors other than changes in the spot exchange rate.

Under US GAAP a number of interpretations to SFAS 133 have been issued setting out what types of derivative may be designated in a net investment hedge and how changes in the value of those derivatives should be accounted for. This guidance is summarised in the following table:[209]

Type of derivative	Method of assessing effectiveness*	
	Spot rate method	**Forward rate method**
Forward contract	Changes in value attributable to spot rate changes recorded in equity Changes in value of interest element recorded in profit or loss	All changes in value (including interest element) recorded in equity
Purchased option	Changes in intrinsic value recorded in equity Changes in time value recorded in profit or loss	All changes in value (including time value) recorded in equity
Cross-currency interest rate swap: both legs floating rate	Interest settlements accrued in profit or loss All other changes in value recognised in equity	All changes in value (including interest settlements) recorded in equity
Cross-currency interest rate swap: both legs fixed rate	Changes in value from retranslating notional at spot exchange rates recorded in equity Interest settlements accrued in profit or loss Other changes in value (e.g. from changes in interest rates) recorded in profit or loss	All changes in value (including interest settlements) recorded in equity
Cross-currency interest rate swap: one floating rate leg, one fixed	Hedge accounting not available	Hedge accounting not available

* one method to be applied consistently for all derivatives designated as hedges of a net investment.

This table assumes the contracts are denominated in the same currency as the functional currency of the hedged net investment and that there are no other sources of ineffectiveness. The applicability of this guidance to IAS 39 is considered below.

I   Forward currency contracts

It is very common for forward currency contracts to be used as the hedging instrument in a hedge of a net investment – in fact this is the one example that is acknowledged in the implementation guidance. Therefore, applying the US GAAP guidance under IAS 39 seems relatively uncontroversial. However, as noted at 4.2.2 above, where the spot rate method is used (i.e. the interest element of the forward is excluded from the hedge relationship) the premium or discount cannot be amortised to profit or loss.[210] Inevitably, therefore, some income statement volatility will arise and the longer the term of the forward, the greater is the potential volatility.

Some may wonder why entities might choose the spot rate method over the forward rate method. Prior to the development of standards such as IAS 39, the interest element of a forward contract (and similar instruments) was commonly recognised as interest on an accruals basis. Depending on the relative interest rates of the two currencies in the forward, accounting for the interest element in this way could potentially result in a credit to the income statement, which is clearly desirable from the perspective of preparers of the financial statements. Where an entity is prepared to accept the volatility associated with this method, a similar effect on the income statement (over time) may be achieved by using the spot rate method.

In many cases where the forward contract is denominated in the 'right' currency, a qualitative effectiveness assessment will be acceptable. However, if it is denominated in a different currency to the functional currency of the net investment it is likely that, at best, some ineffectiveness will arise (unless the link between the two currencies is near-perfect). Under US GAAP a comparison of the forward contract with a hypothetical derivative (a forward contract in the right currency) would be made to measure the amount of ineffectiveness[211] and this approach would normally be acceptable under IAS 39.

II   Purchased options

The spot rate method involves designating the intrinsic value of a purchased option as the hedging instrument (i.e. its time value is excluded from the hedge relationship). This is clearly acceptable under IAS 39 (see 2.1.4 A and 5.3.10 above), although this will always result in an expense being recorded in profit or loss as the time value decays.

Under the forward rate method, the whole option would be designated as the hedging instrument. However, as discussed at 5.3.10 above, there are currently believed to be conceptual problems in designating the entire value of a purchased option as the hedging instrument under IAS 39 and recording all changes in value in equity.

III   Cross-currency interest rate swaps

Like forward contracts, these instruments are commonly used as hedging instruments in net investment hedges. At a conceptual level, it is easy to see that the changes in value of a cross-currency swap with two floating-rate legs are likely to offset the retranslation gains and losses of a net investment, provided the floating rate resets sufficiently frequently. It is also reasonably easy to see that a swap with one floating-rate leg and one fixed-rate leg is unlikely to provide the necessary offset because the fixed rate leg will give rise to changes in the swap's value that are unrelated to changes in exchange rates.

It is less easy to see that a swap with two fixed-rate legs will provide a good hedge against the retranslation gains and losses (again the fixed-rate legs will give rise to changes in the swap's value that are unrelated to changes in exchange rates). However, such an instrument may be viewed as a combination of forward contracts, each of which could be designated in a hedge of a net investment (see I above). Using the forward rate method, this interpretation makes a good deal of sense. The 'spot rate' treatment under US GAAP, however, is generally considered to have limited technical merit. Nevertheless, there is a school of thought (that may be gaining acceptance) that this treatment can be applied under IAS 39.[212]

C   *Combinations of derivative and non-derivative instruments used as the hedging instrument*

It is not uncommon for entities to hedge their net investments using synthetic foreign currency debt instruments. For example, consider a parent with the euro as its functional currency that has a net investment in a Japanese subsidiary with yen as its functional currency. Such an entity might borrow in US dollars and enter into a pay-Japanese yen, receive-US dollar cross-currency interest rate swap. In this way the two instruments might be considered a synthetic Japanese yen borrowing (although under IAS 39 they will be accounted for separately – see Chapter 15 at 6).

As noted at 2.1.3 above, a combination of derivatives and non-derivatives may now be viewed in combination and jointly designated as a hedging instrument under IAS 39.[213] This would appear to permit the synthetic Japanese yen borrowing described above to be designated as a hedge of the net investment in the Japanese subsidiary (assuming all other conditions for applying hedge accounting are met).

D   *Unrecognised assets*

In many cases the full economic value of a net investment will not be recognised in the financial statements. The most common reason will be the existence of assets such as goodwill that are either not recognised or measured at an amount below their current value. In these situations, if an investor hedges the entire economic value of its net investment (or, more commonly, the original purchase price) it will not be able to obtain hedge accounting for the proportion of the hedging instrument that exceeds the recognised net assets.

E   *Individual or separate financial statements*

It is common for an entity with an investment in a subsidiary, associate or joint venture to be party to a financial instrument (a borrowing, say) that in the entity's consolidated financial statements is designated as the hedging instrument in a hedge of its net investment in the subsidiary, associate or joint venture. However, in the entity's individual or separate financial statements, the investment will generally be accounted for as an asset measured at cost or as a financial asset in accordance with IAS 39.[214] In other words, it will not be accounted for by way of consolidation, the equity method or proportional consolidation.

Accordingly, from the perspective of the individual or separate financial statements, the reporting entity will not have a net investment in a foreign operation. Therefore, the borrowing could not be designated as the hedging instrument in a net investment hedge for the purposes of the separate financial statements. However, if hedge accounting is desirable, it may be possible to designate the borrowing as the hedging instrument in another type of hedge. Typically, this would be a fair value hedge of the foreign currency risk arising from the investment. This will be an independent hedge relationship, separate from the net investment hedge in the consolidated financial statements. Therefore, all of the other hedge accounting criteria (including the documentation requirements) will need to be met for this hedge too.

6 PORTFOLIO (OR MACRO) HEDGING

At a detailed level, the topic of portfolio (or macro) hedging for banks and similar financial institutions is beyond the scope of a general financial reporting publication such as this. However, no discussion of hedge accounting would be complete without an overview of the high level issues involved and an explanation of how the standard setters have tried to accommodate these entities.

The underlying philosophy of IAS 39's approach to hedge accounting is that individual hedging instruments are designated as hedging individual assets, liabilities or other risk exposures. However, banks and similar financial institutions typically manage their interest rate risk exposures on a portfolio (or macro) level. Accordingly, there is a fundamental difference between the hedging activities of the financial institution and the hedge accounting requirements of the standard. This can serve as a significant impediment to obtaining hedge accounting treatment for such entities.

Following the publication of the original version of IAS 39, a number of financial institutions worked with the Implementation Guidance Committee to develop a model under which cash flow hedge accounting could be achieved where interest rate risk is managed over a whole portfolio on a net basis. As a result of this effort, some of the most complex implementation guidance to the standard was published.[215] This was a significant achievement, although it did not necessarily provide a low cost solution. In fact, it was sometimes easier for entities to develop a parallel system, completely separate from their primary risk management systems, solely to manage their IAS 39 hedge accounting requirements.

Further, the cash flow hedge accounting model was not sufficient to satisfy many of the banks that would be required to adopt IAS 39 in 2005, particularly those in Europe. One of the problems is that banks are not just concerned with minimising volatility in their earnings, the primary focus for many entities preparing to adopt IAS 39. Because cash flow hedge accounting can give rise to significant volatility in an entity's equity, this could potentially give rise to genuine problems for some banks because of the capital adequacy requirements imposed by prudential regulators. Unfortunately, to some regulators, a recognised liability is considered a liability even if it is an effective hedge of a future transaction. Therefore, because derivatives are always recognised on the balance sheet at their fair value under IAS 39, an effective hedge that has not been recognised in profit or loss could still reduce an entity's capital (as measured using the prudential regulator's rules).

Notwithstanding this growing opposition from an important part of the IASB's constituency, in developing the revised version of IAS 39, the basic principles of hedge accounting were not immediately readdressed and no attempt was made to address the banks' concerns. In fact, when the revised standard was finally published in December 2003, the original guidance for macro cash flow hedges was simply incorporated as guidance to the standard and was largely unchanged.[216]

However, as set out in Chapter 15 at 1.5, this is not the whole story. In August 2003, the IASB published an exposure draft of proposed amendments to the revised version of IAS 39 (which was, at the time, unpublished) dealing with macro-hedging issues for banks.[217] The exposure draft proposed a number of limited amendments to IAS 39 that would make it easier for banks to apply fair value hedge accounting to portfolios of fixed interest assets and liabilities, particularly those assets that were subject to prepayment risk. The key advantage of such an accounting model is that it could reduce the volatility in a bank's equity: although derivative hedging instruments would be recorded on the balance sheet at fair value, equivalent changes in the fair value of the hedged assets and liabilities would also be recognised on the balance sheet within assets or liabilities.

IAS 39 was eventually amended in March 2004 along the lines set out in the exposure draft.[218] Unfortunately, not all of the banks' concerns were addressed. In particular, as set out in Chapter 18 at 4.5, there is a significant restriction on the fair value measurement requirements for liabilities with a demand feature and this effectively prevents banks from applying fair value hedge accounting to the majority of their current and deposit accounts. Accordingly, in Europe at least, the future developments surrounding IAS 39 remain uncertain (for example, see Chapter 15 at 1.5 and 8.2 below).

7   EFFECTIVE DATE, TRANSITIONAL PROVISIONS AND FIRST-TIME ADOPTION

7.1   Effective date

The revised version of IAS 39 must be applied for annual periods beginning on or after 1 January 2005. Entities are 'permitted' (rather than 'encouraged', as in the case of other recently issued standards) to adopt the standard in earlier periods, but must disclose that they have done so. They must also adopt both IAS 32 – *Financial Instruments: Presentation and Disclosure* – and IAS 39 at the same time and must adopt IAS 39 as amended in March 2004, not as originally issued.[219]

7.2   Transitional provisions

With few exceptions, the revised version of IAS 39 should be applied retrospectively and the opening balance of retained earnings for the earliest period presented, and all other comparative amounts should be adjusted, as if it had always been in use. If restatement is impracticable, that fact should be disclosed and the extent to which the information was restated should be indicated.[220]

This has the effect that if a hedge relationship could not qualify for hedge accounting under the revised standard (e.g. because it was a hedge of a forecast intra-group sale or purchase – see 2.3.4 above), the previous hedge accounting treatment in the comparative period would need to be unwound.

As a concession, the carrying amount of non-financial assets and non-financial liabilities should not be adjusted to exclude gains and losses related to cash flow hedges that were included in the carrying amount before the beginning of the financial year in which the revised version of IAS 39 is first applied.[221] This will only be relevant to those entities that choose to stop using basis adjustments for cash flow hedges that result in the recognition of non-financial assets or liabilities (see 4.2.2 above). It should also be noted that there is no equivalent concession for basis adjustments applied to financial items.

Also, at the beginning of the financial period in which the revised standard is first applied, any amount recognised directly in equity for a hedge of a firm commitment that is accounted for as a fair value hedge under the new standard should be reclassified as an asset or liability, except for a hedge of foreign currency risk that continues to be treated as a cash flow hedge.[222]

7.3   First-time adoption

IFRS 1 – *First-time Adoption of International Financial Reporting Standards* – is dealt with comprehensively in Chapter 4 and the particular aspects of that standard applying to financial instruments are principally covered at 2.6 of that chapter. The aspects related to hedge accounting are summarised below. Further similar sections are included in Chapters 15 to 18 and 20.

7.3.1   Exemption from the requirement to restate comparatives

The IASB issued the revised versions of IAS 32 and IAS 39 in December 2003; and the amendment to IAS 39 – *Fair Value Hedge Accounting for a Portfolio Hedge of Interest Rate Risk* – in March 2004. To allow entities adopting IFRS for the first time before 1 January 2006 sufficient time to comply with the requirements of those standards, the IASB decided not to require them to prepare comparative information under IAS 32 and IAS 39.[223] Instead, a first-time adopter that chooses to present comparative information that does not comply with IAS 32 and IAS 39 in its first year of transition should:

- apply its previous GAAP in the comparative information to financial instruments that are within the scope of IAS 32 and IAS 39. In other words, this exemption also affects the application of certain aspects of other standards. For example, it overrides the requirements of IAS 1 – *Presentation of Financial Statements* – on the balance sheet presentation of financial instruments, IAS 18 – *Revenue* – on the application of the effective interest method and IAS 21 on the effects of foreign exchange rates; and

- make certain additional disclosures (see below).[224]

(A similar exemption applies to insurance contracts within the scope of IFRS 4.)

A first-time adopter that does not present comparative information under IAS 32 and IAS 39 should use *the beginning of the first IFRS reporting period* (e.g. 1 January 2005 for an entity reporting at 31 December 2005) as the relevant date for the application of the first-time adoption rules in IFRS 1, and not the *date of transition to IFRS*, for the purpose of these standards only.[225]

In applying this exemption, a first-time adopter should be aware of the following:

- the wording of the standard does not explicitly require the exemption to be applied to IAS 32 and IAS 39 as a package. However, even though the transitional provisions in both IAS 32 and IAS 39 that require the standards to be adopted simultaneously do not apply to first-time adopters, the IASB clearly intended both standards to be adopted simultaneously. In any case, the many cross-references between the two standards make it virtually impossible to adopt one of the standards without the other. Therefore, we believe that the exemption applies to IAS 32 and IAS 39 as a package;

- a first-time adopter that presents two comparative periods under IFRS will not be permitted to restate the most recent comparative financial period because the exemption must be applied as of the beginning of the first IFRS reporting period (e.g. an entity reporting at 31 December 2005 would not be allowed to restate 2004 unless it also restated 2003);

- the exemption only covers items that are within the scope of IAS 32 and IAS 39 (and IFRS 4). The comparative information relating to all other items must be restated under IFRS; and

- a first-time adopter not applying IAS 39 would need to apply its previous GAAP in accounting for hedges.

Where an entity makes this election, it needs to:[226]

- disclose that the comparative information does not comply with IAS 32 and IAS 39, but that it has been prepared on the basis of its previous GAAP;

- disclose the nature, but not the amount, of the main adjustments that would make the information comply with IAS 32 and IAS 39; and

- treat any adjustment between the balance sheet at the comparative period's reporting date and the start of the first IFRS reporting period as arising from a change in accounting policy. This difference is accounted for as an adjustment to the opening balance of each affected component of equity at the start of the first IFRS reporting period.[227] The entity is required to make the disclosures prescribed by paragraphs 28(a)-(e) and (f)(i) of IAS 8 – *Accounting Policies, Changes in Accounting Estimates and Errors* (see Chapter 3 at 6.1.2 A).[228]

Originally, IFRS 1 also required first-time adopters to prepare comparative information that complied with IAS 32 and IAS 39 because this improved 'comparability within the first IFRS financial statements' and because the IASB believed that this should not be a problem for entities that planned the adoption of IFRS in a timely manner.[229] Unfortunately, the less-than-timely publication of the revised versions of IAS 32 and IAS 39 obliged the IASB to exempt entities adopting IFRS before 1 January 2006 from applying these standards in preparing comparative information.

7.3.2   Cumulative translation differences and related hedges

As set out in Chapter 4 at 2.7.2, IFRS 1 contains a concession for the treatment of cumulative translation differences arsing on net investments in foreign operations accounted for under IAS 21. Accordingly, an entity is not required to identify such differences prior to the date of transition to IFRS and classify them in a separate component of equity. Instead, it may 'reset' this separate component of equity to zero at this date.

Unfortunately, IFRS 1 is not entirely clear whether this concession extends to similar gains and losses arising on related hedges. Paragraph 22, which contains the concession, explains that a first-time adopter need not comply with 'these requirements'.[230] The requirements referred to are those summarised in paragraph 21 which explain that IAS 21 requires an entity

(a)   to classify some translation differences as a separate component of equity; and

(b)   on disposal of a foreign operation, to transfer the cumulative translation difference for that foreign operation (*including, if applicable, gains and losses on related hedges*) to the income statement as part of the gain or loss on disposal.[231]

The problem arises because paragraph 21 does not refer to the initial recognition of hedging gains or losses in a separate component of equity (only the subsequent recycling thereof). Accordingly, a very literal reading of the standard might suggest that an entity *is* required to identify historical gains and losses on such hedges. However, even if this position is accepted, on what basis this might be done is not at all clear. For example, it is quite likely that such hedges would not have met the conditions for hedge accounting in IAS 39 and, other than in paragraph 21, IFRS 1 does not specifically address net investment hedges at all.

It is clear that the reasons cited by the IASB for including this concession apply as much to related hedges as they do to the underlying exchange differences. The fact that IFRS 1 can be read otherwise might be seen as little more than poor drafting. In fact there is already clear evidence that paragraph 21 was not subject to the most rigorous scrutiny before publication – it is IAS 39, not IAS 21, that deals with the recycling of gains and losses taken to equity in a net investment hedge. Accordingly, we believe it is entirely appropriate for this concession to be applied to net investment hedges as well as the underlying gains and losses.

Where an entity chooses to prepare comparatives that do not comply with IAS 39 (see 7.3.1 above), some might question whether the cumulative gains and losses on net investment hedges should be reset to zero at the entity's date of transition or the beginning of its first IFRS reporting period. We consider it to be most appropriate to follow paragraph 21 and use the date of transition.

7.3.3   *Hedge accounting: prohibition on retrospective application*

IFRS 1 explains that entities are prohibited from applying retrospectively some of the hedge accounting provisions of IAS 39.[232] In the basis for conclusions, it is explained that:

> '... it is unlikely that most entities would have adopted IAS 39's criteria for (a) documenting hedges at their inception and (b) testing the hedges for effectiveness, even if they intended to continue the same hedging strategies after adopting IAS 39. Furthermore, retrospective designation of hedges (or retrospective reversal of their designation) could lead to selective designation of some hedges to report a particular result.[233]

> 'To overcome these problems, the transitional requirements in [the previous version of] IAS 39 require an entity already applying IFRS to apply the hedging requirements prospectively when it adopts IAS 39. As the same problems arise for a first-time adopter, the IFRS requires prospective application by a first-time adopter.'[234]

Unfortunately, there is only a limited amount of guidance in IFRS 1 regarding hedge accounting and therefore it is not entirely clear what applying these requirements of IAS 39 'prospectively' actually involves, especially insofar as the opening IFRS balance sheet is concerned. However, the basis for conclusions continues:

> 'ED 1 included a redrafted version of the transitional provisions in IAS 39 and related Questions and Answers (Q&As) developed by the IAS 39 Implementation Guidance Committee. The Board confirmed in the Basis for Conclusions published with ED 1 that it did not intend the redrafting to create substantive changes. However, in the light of responses to ED 1, the Board decided in finalising IFRS 1 that the redrafting would not make it easier for first-time adopters and others to understand and apply the transition provisions and Q&As. However, the project to improve IAS 32 and IAS 39 resulted in certain amendments to the transition requirements. In addition, this project incorporated selected other Q&As (i.e. not on transition) into IAS 39. The Board therefore took this opportunity to consolidate all the guidance for first-time adopters in one place, by incorporating the Q&As on transition into IFRS 1.'[235]

This indicates that the transitional provisions set out in the previous version of IAS 39 and IGC Q&As, ED 1 – *First-time Application of International Financial Reporting Standards* – and IFRS 1 are intended to be broadly consistent. Consequently, the fact that all three sources are expressed in different ways can be useful in interpreting this aspect of IFRS 1. These documents are referred to at 7.3.4 below where they assist in understanding the requirements set out in IFRS 1.

7.3.4   Hedge accounting: opening IFRS balance sheet

A   Measurement of derivatives and elimination of deferred gains and losses

Under its previous GAAP an entity's accounting policies might have included a number of accounting treatments for derivatives that formed part of a hedge relationship. For example, accounting policies might have included those where the derivative was:

- not explicitly recognised as an asset or liability (e.g. in the case of a forward contract used to hedge an expected but uncontracted future transaction);

- recognised as an asset or liability but at an amount different from its fair value (e.g. a purchased option recognised at its original cost, perhaps less amortisation; or an interest rate swap accounted for by accruing the periodic interest payments and receipts); or

- subsumed within the accounting for another asset or liability (e.g. a foreign currency denominated monetary item and a matching forward contract or swap accounted for as a 'synthetic' functional currency denominated monetary item).

Whatever the previous accounting treatment, a first-time adopter should isolate and separately account for all derivatives in its opening IFRS balance sheet as assets or liabilities measured at fair value.[236]

The implementation guidance explains that all derivatives, other than those that are designated and effective hedging instruments, are classified as held for trading. Accordingly, the difference between the previous carrying amount of a derivative (which may have been zero) and its fair value should be recognised as an adjustment of the balance of retained earnings at the beginning of the financial year in which IFRS 1 is initially applied (other than for a derivative that is a designated and effective hedging instrument).[237]

Hedge accounting policies under an entity's previous GAAP might also have included one or both of the following accounting treatments:

- derivatives were measured at fair value but, to the extent they were regarded as hedging future transactions, the gain (or loss) arising was reported as a liability (or asset) such as deferred (or accrued) income;

- realised gains or losses arising on the termination of a previously unrecognised derivative used in a hedge relationship (such as an interest rate swap hedging a borrowing) were included in the balance sheet as deferred or accrued income and amortised over the remaining term of the hedged exposure.

In all cases, an entity is required to eliminate deferred gains and losses arising on derivatives 'that were reported under previous GAAP as if they were assets or liabilities.'[238] Essentially, this is because deferred gains and losses do not meet the definition of assets or liabilities under the IASB's *Framework*. In contrast to adjustments made to restate derivatives at fair value, the implementation guidance does not specify in general terms how to deal with adjustments to eliminate deferred gains or losses, i.e. whether they should be taken to retained earnings or a separate component of equity.

The requirement to eliminate deferred gains and losses does not appear to extend to those that have been included in the carrying amount of other assets or liabilities that will continue to be recognised under IFRS. For example, under an entity's previous GAAP, the carrying amount of non-financial assets such as inventories or property, plant and equipment might have included the equivalent of a basis adjustment (i.e. hedging gains or losses were considered an integral part of the asset's cost). In fact, carrying forward this treatment into an entity's first set of IFRS financial statements would be consistent with the transitional provisions of the revised IAS 39 (see 7.2 above). Of course, entities should also consider any other provisions of IFRS 1 that apply to those hedged items.

The way in which an entity accounts for these adjustments will, to a large extent, dictate how its existing hedge relationships will be reflected in its ongoing IFRS financial statements. Particularly, an entity's future results will be different depending on whether the adjustments are taken to retained earnings or to a separate component of equity – in the latter case they would be recycled to profit or loss at a later date but would not in the former. Similarly, its future results would be affected if the carrying amount of related assets or liabilities are changed to reflect these adjustments (as opposed to the adjustments being made to retained earnings).

For short-term hedges (e.g. of sales and inventory purchases) these effects are likely to work their way out of the IFRS financial statements relatively quickly. However, for other hedges (e.g. of long term borrowings) an entity's results may be affected for many years. The question of which hedge relationships should be reflected in an entity's opening IFRS balance sheet is dealt with at B to D below.

B   *Hedge relationships reflected in the opening IFRS balance sheet*

The standard states that a first-time adopter *should not* reflect a hedging relationship in its opening IFRS balance sheet (or the balance sheet at the beginning of its first IFRS reporting period, if comparatives are not restated) if that hedging relationship is of a type that *does not* qualify for hedge accounting under IAS 39. As examples of this it cites many hedging relationships where the hedging instrument is a cash instrument or written option; where the hedged item is a net position; or where the hedge covers interest risk in a held-to-maturity investment.[239]

However, if an entity had designated a net position as a hedged item under its previous GAAP, the IASB decided that an individual item within that net position *may* be designated as a hedged item under IFRS, provided that it does so no later than the date of transition to IFRS (or the beginning of the first IFRS reporting period, if comparatives are not restated).[240] In other words, such designation could allow the hedge relationship to be reflected in the opening IFRS balance sheet (or the balance sheet at the beginning of its first IFRS reporting period, if comparatives are not restated).

Further, a first-time adopter is not permitted to designate hedges retrospectively in relation to transactions entered into before the date of transition to IFRS (or the beginning of the first IFRS reporting period, if comparatives are not restated).[241] This would appear to prevent an entity from reflecting hedge relationships in its opening balance sheet that it did not identify as such under its previous GAAP.

It might seem to follow that a hedge relationship designated under an entity's previous GAAP *should* be reflected in its opening IFRS balance sheet (or the balance sheet at the beginning of its first IFRS reporting period, if comparatives are not restated) if that hedging relationship *is* of a type that *does* qualify for hedge accounting under IAS 39. In fact, if an entity was allowed not to reflect such a hedge in its opening IFRS balance sheet (or the balance sheet at the beginning of its first IFRS reporting period, if comparatives are not restated) this would effectively allow the retrospective reversal of the hedge designation. As noted at A above, this is something the IASB has sought to avoid.[242] However, while such a 'principle' seems to be implied by the implementation guidance (see C and D below), the IASB has not actually articulated it in these terms.

There are, perhaps, a number of reasons for the IASB's reticence. For example, under an entity's previous GAAP, it might not have been clear whether a derivative instrument was actually designated as a hedge. Further, even if it were clear that a derivative had previously been designated as a hedge, the hedged item might not have been identified with sufficiently specificity to allow the effects of the hedge to be reflected in the opening IFRS balance sheet and/or, thereafter, to be 'unwound' at the appropriate time.

C Reflecting cash flow hedges in the opening IFRS balance sheet

The implementation guidance to IFRS 1 explains that a first-time adopter may, under its previous GAAP, have deferred gains and losses on a cash flow hedge of a forecast transaction. If, at the date of transition to IFRS (or the beginning of the first IFRS reporting period, if comparatives are not restated) the hedged forecast transaction is not highly probable, but is expected to occur, the entire deferred gain or loss should be recognised in equity.[243] To be consistent, this would be included in the same component of equity an entity would use to record future gains and losses on cash flow hedges.

This raises the question of how to deal with such a hedge if, at the date of transition to IFRS (or the beginning of the first IFRS reporting period, if comparatives are not restated), the forecast transaction *was* highly probable. It would make no sense if the former was required to be reflected in the opening IFRS balance sheet, but the latter (which is clearly a 'better' hedge) was not. Therefore, it must follow that a cash flow hedge should be reflected in the opening IFRS balance sheet in the way set out above if the hedged item is a forecast transaction that is highly probable. Similarly, it follows that a cash flow hedge of the variability in cash flows attributable to a particular risk associated with a recognised asset or liability (such as all or some future interest payments on variable rate debt) should also be reflected in the opening balance sheet.

If, at the date of transition to IFRS (or the beginning of the first IFRS reporting period, if comparatives are not restated), the forecast transaction was *not* expected to occur, this would be a relationship of a type that does not qualify for hedge accounting under IAS 39. Therefore, the hedging relationship should not be reflected in the opening IFRS balance sheet. In fact ED 1 was explicit on this point.[244]

There are various ways in which gains or losses might have been deferred under an entity's previous GAAP. ED 1 explained that, in this context, deferral included:

- treating deferred gains as if they were liabilities and deferred losses as if they were assets; and

- not recognising changes in the fair value of the hedging instrument.[245]

Even though this explanation was not incorporated into IFRS 1, at a conceptual level there is scarce reason why it should not apply under the standard. However, it is possible to read parts of the implementation guidance as preventing this treatment if the hedge has not been designated in an effective hedge under IAS 39 by the date of transition (or the beginning of the first IFRS reporting period, if comparatives are not restated). The following example highlights this issue.

Example 19.33   Unrecognised gains and losses on existing cash flow hedge

Company T has the euro as its functional currency. In September 2003 it entered into a forward currency contract to sell dollars for euros in twelve months to hedge dollar denominated sales it forecasts are highly probable to occur in September 2004. T will apply IAS 39 from 1 January 2004, its date of transition to IFRS. The historical cost of the forward contract is €nil and at the date of transition it had a positive fair value of €100.

Case 1: Gains and losses deferred

Under T's previous GAAP, until the sales occurred the forward contract was recognised in the balance sheet at its fair value and the resulting gain or loss was deferred in the balance sheet as a liability or asset. When the sale occurred, any deferred gain or loss was recognised in profit or loss as an offset to the revenue recognised on the hedged sales.

Case 2: Gains and losses unrecognised

Under T's previous GAAP, the contract was not recognised in the balance sheet. When the sale occurred, any unrecognised gain or loss was recognised in profit or loss as an offset to the revenue recognised on the hedged sales.

In Case 1 the relationship can clearly be reflected in T's opening IFRS balance sheet whether or not it is designated as an effective hedge in accordance with IAS 39 at the date of transition: there is no restriction on transferring the deferred gain to a separate component of equity and there is no adjustment to the carrying amount of the forward contract.

Case 2 is slightly more problematical. As noted at A above, the implementation guidance explains that the difference between the previous carrying amount of a derivative and its fair value should be recognised as an adjustment of the balance of retained earnings (other than for a derivative that is a designated and effective hedging instrument).[246] Read literally, if T had not designated the relationship as an effective hedge in accordance with IAS 39 at the date of transition, this implementation guidance could prevent the relationship from being reflected in T's opening IFRS balance sheet. This is because the adjustment to the carrying amount of the forward would be recorded in retained earnings rather than a separate component of equity.

Such an interpretation would allow T to choose not to designate (in accordance with IAS 39) certain cash flow hedges, say those that are in a loss position, until one day after its date of transition, thereby allowing associated hedging losses to bypass profit or loss completely. Notwithstanding this, at least one other commentator has suggested the literal interpretation is appropriate.[247] However, this would effectively result in the retrospective de-designation of hedges to achieve a desired result, thereby breaching this general principle of IFRS 1. Arguably, this general principle of the standard should take precedence over the implementation guidance.

D   Reflecting fair value hedges in the opening IFRS balance sheet

The implementation guidance to IFRS 1 explains that a first-time adopter may, under its previous GAAP, have deferred or not recognised gains and losses on a fair value hedge of a hedged item that is not measured at fair value. For such a fair value hedge, the entity should adjust the carrying amount of the hedged item at the date of transition to IFRS (or the beginning of the first IFRS reporting period, if comparatives are not restated). The adjustment, which is essentially the effective part of the hedge that was not recognised in the carrying amount of the hedged item under the previous GAAP, should be calculated as the lower of:

(a)   that portion of the cumulative change in the fair value of the hedged item that reflects the designated hedged risk and was not recognised under previous GAAP; and

(b)   that portion of the cumulative change in the fair value of the hedging instrument that reflects the designated hedged risk and, under previous GAAP, was either (i) not recognised or (ii) deferred in the balance sheet as an asset or liability.[248]

This requirement is consistent with the requirement in the previous version of IAS 39 (and the proposals in ED 1) under which any balance sheet positions in fair value hedges of existing assets and liabilities would be accounted for in the opening balance sheet in (broadly) the same manner as above.[249]

Available-for-sale assets are measured at fair value so the guidance above would not appear to apply to fair value hedges of such instruments. However, it would be logical to apply an equivalent adjustment to the cost or amortised cost of such assets.

7.3.5   Hedge accounting: subsequent treatment

The implementation guidance explains that hedge accounting can be applied prospectively only from the date the hedge relationship is fully designated and documented. Therefore, if the hedging instrument is still held at the date of transition to IFRS (or the beginning of the first IFRS reporting period, if comparatives are not restated), the designation and documentation of a hedge relationship must be completed on or before that date if the hedge relationship is to qualify for hedge accounting on an ongoing basis from that date.[250]

An entity may, before the date of transition to IFRS (or the beginning of the first IFRS reporting period, if comparatives are not restated), have designated a transaction as a hedge that does not meet the conditions for hedge accounting in IAS 39. In these cases it should following the general requirements in IAS 39 for discontinuing hedge accounting – these are dealt with at 4.1.3 for fair value hedges and at 4.2.3 for cash flow hedges.[251]

For cash flow hedges, any net cumulative gain or loss that was reclassified to equity on initial application of IAS 39 (see 7.3.4 C above) should remain in equity until:

(a) the forecast transaction subsequently results in the recognition of a non-financial asset or non-financial liability;

(b) the forecast transaction affects profit or loss; or

(c) subsequently circumstances change and the forecast transaction is no longer expected to occur, in which case any related net cumulative gain or loss that had been recognised directly in equity is recognised in profit or loss.[252]

The requirements above do little more than reiterate the general requirements of IAS 39, i.e. that hedge accounting can only be applied prospectively if the qualifying conditions are met, and entities should experience few interpretative problems in dealing with this aspect of the hedge accounting requirements.

7.3.6 Hedge accounting: examples

The following examples illustrate the guidance considered at 7.3.3 to 7.3.5 above.

Example 19.34   Existing cash flow hedges

Case 1: All hedge accounting conditions met from date of transition and thereafter

In 1997 Company Q borrowed €10m from a bank. The terms of the loan provide that a coupon of 3 month LIBOR plus 2% is payable quarterly in arrears and the principal is repayable in 2012. In 2000, Q decided to 'fix' its coupon payments for the remainder of the term of the loan by entering into a twelve-year pay-fixed, receive-floating interest rate swap. The swap has a notional amount of €10m and the floating leg resets quarterly based on 3 month LIBOR.

In Q's final financial statements prepared under its previous GAAP, the swap was clearly identified as a hedging instrument in a hedge of the loan and was accounted for as such. The fair value of the swap was not recognised in Q's balance sheet and the periodic interest settlements were accrued and recognised as an adjustment to the loan interest expense. On 1 January 2004, Q's date of transition to IFRS, the loan and the swap were still in place and the swap had a positive fair value of €1m and a €nil carrying amount. In addition, Q met all the conditions in IAS 39 to permit the use of hedge accounting for this arrangement throughout 2004 and 2005.

Q should in its opening IFRS balance sheet:

• recognise the interest rate swap as an asset at its fair value of €1m; and

• credit €1m to a separate component of equity, to be recycled as the hedged transactions (future interest payments on the loan) affect profit or loss.

In addition, hedge accounting would be applied throughout 2004 and 2005.

Case 2: Hedge terminated prior to date of transition

The facts are as in Case 1 except that in April 2003 Q decided to terminate the hedge and the interest rate swap was settled for its then fair value of €1.5m. Under its previous GAAP, Q's stated accounting policy in respect of terminated hedges was to defer any realised gain or loss on terminated hedging instruments where the hedged exposure remained. These gains or losses would be recognised in profit or loss at the same time as gains or losses on the hedged exposure. At the end of December 2003, Q's balance sheet included a liability (unamortised gain) of €1.4m.

IFRS 1 does not explicitly address hedges terminated prior to the date of transition but we see no reason why these relationships should not be reflected in an entity's opening IFRS balance sheet in the same way as other cash flow hedges that are reflected in an entity's closing balance sheet under its previous GAAP. Accordingly, Q should in its opening IFRS balance sheet:

- remove the deferred gain of €1.4m from the balance sheet; and
- credit €1.4m to a separate component of equity, to be recycled as the hedged transactions (future interest payments on the loan) affect profit or loss.

Example 19.35: Existing fair value hedges

Case 1: All hedge accounting conditions met from date of transition and thereafter (1)

On 15 November 2003, Company Y entered into a forward contract to sell 50,000 barrels of crude oil to hedge all changes in the fair value of certain inventory. Y will apply IAS 39 from 1 January 2004, its date of transition to IFRS. The historical cost of the forward contract is $nil and at the date of transition the forward had a negative fair value of $50.

In Y's final financial statements prepared under its previous GAAP, the forward was clearly identified as a hedging instrument in a hedge of the inventory and was accounted for as such. The contract was recognised in the balance sheet as a liability at its fair value and the resulting loss was deferred in the balance sheet as an asset. In the period between 15 November 2003 and 1 January 2004 the fair value of the inventory increased by $47. In addition, Y met all the conditions in IAS 39 to permit the use of hedge accounting for this arrangement throughout 2004 until the forward expired.

Y should in its opening IFRS balance sheet:

- continue to recognise the forward contract as a liability at its fair value of $50;
- derecognise the $50 deferred loss on the forward contract;
- recognise the crude oil inventory at its historical cost plus $47 (the lower of the change in fair value of the crude oil inventory, $47, and that of the forward contract, $50); and
- record the net adjustment of $3 in retained earnings.

In addition, hedge accounting would be applied throughout 2004 until the forward expired.

Case 2: All hedge accounting conditions met from date of transition and thereafter (2)

In 1997 Company Z borrowed €10m from a bank. The terms of the loan provide that a coupon of 8% is payable quarterly in arrears and the principal is repayable in 2012. In 2000, P decided to alter its coupon payments for the remainder of the term of the loan by entering into a twelve-year pay-floating, receive-fixed interest rate swap. The swap has a notional amount of €10m and the floating leg resets quarterly based on 3 month LIBOR.

In Z's final financial statements prepared under its previous GAAP, the swap was clearly identified as a hedging instrument in a hedge of the loan and accounted for as such. The fair value of the swap was not recognised in Z's balance sheet and the periodic interest settlements on the swap were accrued and recognised as an adjustment to the loan interest expense.

On 1 January 2004, Z's date of transition to IFRS, the loan and the swap were still in place and the swap had a negative fair value of €1m and a €nil carrying amount. The cumulative change in the fair value of the loan attributable to changes in 3 month LIBOR was €1.1m, although this change was not recognised in Z's balance sheet because the loan was accounted for at cost. In addition, Z met all the conditions in IAS 39 to permit the use of hedge accounting for this arrangement throughout 2004 and 2005.

Z should in its opening IFRS balance sheet:

- recognise the interest rate swap as a liability at its fair value of €1m; and

- reduce the carrying amount of the loan by €1m (the lower of the change in its fair value attributable to the hedged risk, €1.1m, and that of the interest rate swap, $1m).

In addition, hedge accounting would be applied throughout 2004 and 2005.

Case 3: Hedge terminated prior to date of transition

The facts are as in Case 2 above except that in April 2003 Z decided to terminate the hedge and the interest rate swap was settled for its then negative fair value of €1.5m. Under its previous GAAP, Z's stated accounting policy in respect of terminated hedges was to defer any gain or loss on the hedging instrument as a liability or an asset where the hedged exposure remained and this gain or loss was recognised in profit or loss at the same time as the hedged exposure. At the end of December 2003 the unamortised loss recognised as an asset in Z's balance sheet was €1.4m. In 2003 the cumulative change in the fair value of the loan attributable to changes in 3 month LIBOR that had not been recognised was €1.6m.

Z should in its opening IFRS balance sheet:

- remove the deferred loss of €1.4m from the balance sheet; and

- reduce the carrying amount of the loan by €1.4m (the lower of the change in its fair value attributable to the hedged risk, €1.6m, and the change in value of the interest rate swap that was deferred in the balance sheet, €1.4m).

The €1.4m adjustment to the loan would be amortised to profit or loss over its remaining term (see 4.1.2 above).

Case 4: Documentation completed after the date of transition

The facts are as in Case 2 above except that, at the date of transition, Z had not prepared documentation that would allow it to apply hedge accounting under IAS 39. Hedge documentation was subsequently prepared as a result of which the hedge qualified for hedge accounting with effect from the beginning of July 2004 and throughout 2005.

As in Case 2, Z should in its opening IFRS balance sheet:

- recognise the interest rate swap as a liability at its fair value of €1m; and

- reduce the carrying amount of the loan by €1m (the lower of the change in its fair value attributable to the hedged risk, €1.1m, and that of the interest rate swap, €1m).

For the period from January 2004 to June 2004, hedge accounting would not be available. Accordingly, the interest rate swap would be remeasured to its fair value and any gain or loss would be reported in profit or loss with no offset from remeasuring the loan. With effect from July 2004 hedge accounting would be applied prospectively.

8 FUTURE DEVELOPMENTS

In Chapter 15 at 1.5, it was explained that the IASB is continuing to make and consider further revisions to IAS 39 in the short term, whilst looking for its replacement in the long term. The principle developments that may affect the hedge accounting provisions of the standard are set out below.

8.1 Cash flow hedges of forecast intra-group transactions

As noted at 2.3.4 above, under the previous version of IAS 39, a forecast intra-group transaction that would result in a foreign currency intra-group balance, gains and losses on which would not eliminate fully on consolidation, could be designated as the hedged item in a cash flow hedge. The IASB considered that this concession had little conceptual merit and. in the revised standard, it was removed. Essentially, until the forecast transaction has occurred, there is no real exposure to the group.[253] However, following the publication of the revised standard, constituents raised the following concerns:

- it is common practice for entities to designate a forecast intra-group transaction as the hedged item;

- some entities using IFRS and entities that are planning to adopt IFRS in 2005 have established a practice of designating forecast intragroup transactions as hedged items and have entered into derivative instruments to hedge the resulting exposures; and

- the revised standard creates a difference from US GAAP, which permits hedge accounting for foreign currency risk on forecast intra-group transactions.[254]

After considering the issue further the IASB published an exposure draft of proposed amendments to IAS 39. This states that the revised standard permits entities that had designated a forecast intra-group transaction as the hedged item to obtain hedge accounting by designating as the hedged item a highly probable forecast *external* transaction (normally the on-sale of the asset transferred in the intra-group transaction). If the hedge is designated in this way, the forecast intra-group transaction can be used as part of the tracking mechanism (or 'audit trail') for associating the hedging instrument with an external transaction.[255]

However, the IASB noted that there is confusion about whether the designation outlined above is actually permitted. Accordingly, it decided to clarify that in consolidated financial statements a group *can* designate as the hedged item, in a foreign currency cash flow hedge, a highly probable forecast external transaction denominated in the functional currency of the entity (e.g. subsidiary) entering into the transaction. This is provided the transaction gives rise to an exposure that will have an effect on consolidated profit or loss (i.e. it is denominated in a currency other than the group's presentation currency).[256] It is proposed that the effective date of the amendment would be accounting periods beginning on or after 1 January 2006, with earlier application permitted.[257]

This proposal is not as uncontroversial as it might seem. There is a widely held view that a transaction by a subsidiary in its own functional currency does not give rise to anything other than an accounting exposure and, therefore, hedge accounting should not be available for such a transaction. Some would say that accepting the existence of a genuine exposure between the presentation currency of a group and the currency of a transaction entered into by one of its subsidiaries would be contrary to the fundamental principles of IAS 21.[258]

The proposed changes would also seem to allow hedging strategies that might otherwise have been considered inappropriate. Consider, for example, a group with the following characteristics:

- the parent has the euro as its functional currency;

- the parent's consolidated financial statements are prepared using the euro as the presentation currency;

- a US based subsidiary has the US dollar as its functional currency; and

- the US subsidiary is largely self-contained, i.e. it does not have significant transactions with the rest of the group.

These changes would allow, in the group's consolidated financial statements, the US dollar denominated transactions of the US subsidiary, say its sales, to be designated as the hedged item in a hedge of the foreign currency risk against changes in the US dollar/euro exchange rate.

If, however, the parent decided to change the group's presentation currency to the US dollar (something that IAS 21 allows to be done at will, effectively because it has no economic consequence) this would seem to prevent hedge accounting being used for these arrangements. Perhaps more surprisingly, if the parent simultaneously prepared additional consolidated financial statements with US dollars as the presentation currency (say for the benefit of its US investors), the hedge accounting in its euro financial statements would have to be reversed in its US dollar financial statements.

In fact, the proposed changes would allow groups that hedge the translation risk of the profits of subsidiaries, the functional currency of which is not the group's presentation currency, to obtain hedge accounting for these arrangements provided the hedge is properly designated on a gross basis (e.g. as a hedge of the subsidiary's sales – see 2.2.3 above).

Notwithstanding these conceptual problems, with the exception of one member of the IASB who voted against publication of the exposure draft, the IASB does not appear to see these as major concerns.[259]

We agree that there is little conceptual merit in allowing a forecast intra-group transaction to be treated as a hedged item, although we accept there are many pragmatic reasons to allow hedge accounting for forecast intra-group transactions (thereby converging with US GAAP). Therefore, in our view, it would be more appropriate, and consistent with the principles of IAS 21, to simply to create an isolated and restricted exception within IAS 39. In our opinion, the IASB should also consider introducing transitional relief for those entities using a hedging strategy allowed under the previous version of the standard (see 7.2 above).

8.2 Interest margin hedges

There have been continuing discussions between representatives of the IASB and Fédération Bancaire de l'Union Européenne ('FBE') in order to try and resolve some of the more contentious aspects of the hedge accounting requirements, particular as they apply to portfolio (or macro) hedging of interest rate risk (see 6 above).[260]

The main focus of these discussions is FBE's proposal that a new type of hedge accounting should be developed for hedges of interest rate margin. The IASB has acknowledged that the goal was for FBE to develop, as soon as possible, its proposal to the point that it would be appropriate for presentation to the IASB. The IASB would then consider whether an exposure draft, based on this proposal, should be issued.[261]

It is not entirely clear how quickly these proposals will be developed and make their way onto the IASB's agenda. Even if they are progressed in the near term, the possibility of their being incorporated into IAS 39 is extremely difficult to assess. In spite of the IASB being seen to embrace FBE's work, there is little doubt the IASB retains a good degree of scepticism about the proposals.[262]

References

1 For example, see IAS 39 (2000), *Financial Instruments: Recognition and Measurement*, IASC, December 1998 to October 2000, para. 10.

2 Based, in part, on Discussion Paper, *Derivatives and Other Financial Instruments*, ASB, June 1996, Summary of issues and the Board's initial conclusions, paras. 34-38.

3 IAS 39, *Financial Instruments: Recognition and Measurement*, IASB, December 2003 (amended March 2004), para. 9.

4 IAS 39, para. 72.

5 IAS 39, para. AG96.

6 IAS 39, para. F.1.2.

7 IAS 39, para. F.1.2.

8 IAS 39, paras. AG35(e) and F.1.6.

9 IAS 39, para. AG94.

10 IAS 39, para. F.1.3.

11 IAS 39, para. F.1.3.

12 IAS 39, para. BC144.

13 IAS 39, para. 72.

14 IAS 39, para. AG95.

15 IAS 39, para. AG96.

16 IAS 39, para. F.1.2.

17 IAS 39, para. F.1.1.

18 IAS 39, paras. BC144-BC145.

19 IAS 39, para. 77.

20 IAS 39, para. 77.

21 IAS 39 Implementation Guidance, *Questions and Answers*, IAS 39 Implementation Guidance Committee, July 2001, Q&A 122-1.

22 IAS 39, para. 77.

23 IAS 39, para. 74.

24 IAS 39, para. F.1.8.

25 IAS 39, para. 74.

26 IAS 39, para. 74.

27 IAS 39, para. 75.

28 IAS 39, para. F.2.6

29 IAS 39, para. 76.

30 IAS 39, para. F.1.13.

31 IAS 39, para. F.1.12.

32 IAS 39, para. F.2.18.

33 IAS 39, para. AG97.

34 IAS 39, para. 9.

35 IAS 39, para. F.2.3.

36 IAS 39, para. 81.

37 IAS 39, para. F.2.17.

38 IAS 39, para. BC135A.

39 IAS 39, para. AG99A.

40 IAS 39, para. AG99A.

41 IAS 39, para. AG99B.

42 IAS 39, para. AG99B.

43 IAS 39, para. F.2.19.

44 IAS 39, paras. 82 and AG100.

45 *Comments of Swiss International Air Lines Ltd. on Paragraphs 129 and 130 of the "Exposure*

Draft of Proposed Amendments to IAS 39
Financial Instruments: Recognition and
Measurement", Swiss International Air
Lines Ltd, October 2002.
46 IAS 39, paras. BC137-BC138.
47 IAS 39, paras. BC140-BC143.
48 IAS 39, para. F.6.5.
49 IAS 39, para. AG100.
50 IAS 39, para. AG100.
51 IAS 39, para. 78.
52 IAS 39, para. 83.
53 IAS 39, para. F.2.20.
54 IAS 39, para. 84.
55 IAS 39, para. F.2.21.
56 IAS 39, para. AG101.
57 IAS 39, para. AG110.
58 IAS 39, para. F.2.8.
59 IAS 39, para. AG98.
60 IAS 39, paras. 79 and F.2.9.
61 IAS 39, para. 79.
62 IAS 39, para. F.2.10.
63 IAS 39, para. F.2.11.
64 IAS 39, para. F.2.1.
65 IAS 39, para. F.2.7.
66 IAS 39, para. F.2.3.
67 IAS 39, para. F.2.3.
68 IAS 27, Consolidated and Separate Financial
    Statements, IASB, December 2003 (amended
    March 2004), para. 24 and IAS 39, para. F.1.4.
69 IAS 39, paras. 73 and F.1.4.
70 IAS 39, para. 73.
71 IAS 39, para. F.1.4
72 IAS 39, para. F.1.4.
73 IAS 39, para. 73.
74 IAS 39, para. F.1.4.
75 IAS 39, paras. BC165-BC172.
76 IAS 39, para. F.1.4.
77 IAS 39, para. F.1.5.
78 IAS 39, para. F.1.5.
79 IAS 39, para. F.1.5.
80 IAS 39, para. F.1.5.
81 IAS 39, para. F.1.5.
82 IAS 39, para. F.2.15.
83 IAS 39, para. F.1.6.
84 IAS 39, para. F.1.6.
85 IAS 39, para. F.1.7.
86 IAS 39, para. F.1.14.
87 IAS 39, para. F.2.16.
88 IAS 39, para. F.2.16.
89 IAS 39, para. F.2.16.
90 IAS 39, para. 80.
91 IAS 39, para. 80.
92 IGC Q&A 137-13.
93 IGC Q&A 137-14.
94 Exposure Draft, Amendments to IAS 39,
    Financial Instruments: Recognition and
    Measurement, Cash flow Hedge Accounting of

Forecast Intragroup Transactions, IASB, July
    2004.
95 IAS 39, para. F.2.14.
96 IAS 39, para. F.2.14.
97 IAS 39, para. 86.
98 IAS 39, para. AG102.
99 IAS 39, para. F.2.13.
100 IAS 39, para. F.3.5.
101 IAS 39, para. F.3.6.
102 IAS 39, para. AG99.
103 IAS 39, para. AG103.
104 IAS 39, para. F.3.1.
105 IAS 39, para. F.3.6.
106 IAS 39, para. F.2.2.
107 IAS 39, para. F.3.2.
108 IAS 39, paras. F.3.3 and F.3.4.
109 IAS 39, para. AG104.
110 IAS 39 (2000), para. 140.
111 See IAS 39, paras. BC149-BC154 and BC221(h).
112 IAS 39, paras. 87 and AG104.
113 IAS 39, para. BC154.
114 IAS 39, para. F.2.5.
115 IAS 39, para. F.2.5.
116 IAS 39, para. F.2.5.
117 IAS 39, para. AG99.
118 IAS 39, para. 9.
119 IAS 39, para. 71.
120 IAS 39, para. 85.
121 IAS 39, para. 89.
122 IAS 39 (2000), para. 154.
123 IAS 39, para. 90.
124 IAS 39, para. F.2.19.
125 IAS 39, para. 93.
126 IAS 39, para. F.3.6.
127 IAS 39, para. 92.
128 IAS 39, para. 94.
129 IAS 39, para. 91.
130 IAS 39, para. AG113.
131 IAS 39, paras. 95 and F.4.5.
132 IAS 39, para. 96.
133 IAS 39, para. F.5.3.
134 IAS 39, para. F.5.2.
135 IAS 39, para. AG83.
136 IAS 39, para. F.5.1.
137 IAS 39, para. 97.
138 IAS 39, para. 98.
139 IAS 39, para. 99.
140 IAS 39 (2000), para. 160.
141 See IAS 39, paras. BC155-BC164.
142 See IAS 39, paras. BC164, BC221(i)-(j), DO2,
     DO5 and DO8-DO11.
143 IAS 39, para. 100.
144 IAS 39, paras. F.3.3 and F.3.4.
145 IAS 39, para. F.6.4.
146 IAS 39, para. 101.
147 IAS 39, para. AG113.
148 IAS 39, para. 102.
149 IAS 39, para. 102.

150 Statement 133 Implementation Issue H8, *Foreign Currency Hedges: Measuring the Amount of Ineffectiveness in a Net Investment Hedge*, FASB (Derivatives Implementation Group), February 2001.
151 IAS 39, para. 88.
152 IAS 39, para. 88(a).
153 IAS 39, para. F.3.8.
154 IAS 39, para. 74.
155 IAS 39, para. F.1.9.
156 IAS 39, para. F.1.9.
157 IAS 39, para. F.3.9.
158 IAS 39, para. F.3.11.
159 IAS 39, para. F.5.4.
160 IAS 39, para. F.3.10.
161 IAS 39, para. F.3.7.
162 IGC Q&A 142-1.
163 For example, see *Uncertain terms*, Ron Paterson, Accountancy Magazine, September 2003.
164 IFRS 5, *Non-current Assets Held for Sale and Discontinued Operations*, IASB, March 2004, para. BC81.
165 IFRS 5, Appendix A (Defined terms).
166 IAS 39, para. F.3.7.
167 IAS 39, para. F.3.7.
168 IAS 39, para. F.3.7.
169 IAS 39, para. F.2.4.
170 IAS 39, para. F.2.12.
171 IAS 39, para. F.3.7.
172 IAS 39, para. 9.
173 IAS 39, para. 88.
174 IAS 39, paras. BC136 and BC136B.
175 IAS 39, para. AG105.
176 IAS 39, para. AG106.
177 IAS 39, para. AG107.
178 IAS 39, para. F.4.1
179 IAS 39, para. AG107.
180 IAS 39, para. F.4.4.
181 IAS 39, para. F.4.2.
182 IAS 39, para. F.4.2.
183 IAS 39, para. AG112.
184 IAS 39, para. AG111.
185 IAS 39, para. F.4.4.
186 IAS 39, para. F.5.5.
187 IAS 39, para. F.5.6.
188 IAS 39, para. AG100.
189 IAS 39, para. F.4.4.
190 IAS 39 (2000), para. 146.
191 IGC Q&A 146-3 and IAS 39, para. F.4.6 (deleted, March 2004).
192 IAS 39, paras. BC136 and BC136A.
193 IAS 39, para. BC136A.
194 IAS 39, para. AG107A.
195 IAS 39, para. BC132.
196 IAS 39, para. BC133.
197 IAS 39, para. BC134.
198 IAS 39, para. AG108.
199 IAS 39, para. AG108.
200 IAS 39, para. AG109.
201 IAS 39, para. F.4.3.
202 IAS 39, para. BC135.
203 IAS 39, para. F.4.7.
204 IAS 39, para. F.4.7.
205 IAS 39, para. AG108.
206 IAS 39, para. F.1.10.
207 Statement 133 Implementation Issue G20, *Cash Flow Hedges: Assessing and Measuring the Effectiveness of a Purchased Option Used in a Cash Flow Hedge*, FASB (Derivatives Implementation Group), August 2001.
208 Statement 133 Implementation Issue H8, *Foreign Currency Hedges: Measuring the Amount of Ineffectiveness in a Net Investment Hedge*, FASB (Derivatives Implementation Group), February 2001, Question 2.
209 Statement 133 Implementation Issue H8, Question 1 and Statement 133 Implementation Issue H9, *Foreign Currency Hedges: Hedging a Net Investment with a Compound Derivative That Incorporates Exposure to Multiple Risks*, FASB (Derivatives Implementation Group), December 2000.
210 IAS 39, para. F.6.4.
211 Statement 133 Implementation Issue H8, Question 2.
212 For example, see *Financial Instruments: Applying IAS 32 and IAS 39*, Deloitte Touche Tohmatsu, October 2001, p. 205-206.
213 IAS 39, para. 77.
214 IAS 27, para. 37.
215 IGC Q&As 121-1 and 121-2 and Appendix to Q&A 121-2.
216 IAS 39, paras. F.6.1, F.6.2 and F.6.3.
217 Exposure Draft, *Amendments to IAS 39, Financial Instruments: Recognition and Measurement, Fair Value Hedge Accounting for a Portfolio Hedge of Interest Rate Risk*, IASB, August 2003.
218 See particularly, IAS 39, paras. 78, 81A, 89A, 92, AG114-AG132, IE1-IE31, DO1 and DO2.
219 IAS 39, para. 103.
220 IAS 39, para. 104.
221 IAS 39, para. 108.
222 IAS 39, para. 108.
223 IFRS 1, *First-time Adoption of International Financial Reporting Standards*, IASB, June 2003 (amended March 2004), para. BC89A.
224 IFRS 1, para. 36A.
225 IFRS 1, para. 36A.
226 IFRS 1, para. 36A.
227 IAS 8, *Accounting Policies, Changes in Accounting Estimates and Errors*, IASB, December 2003 (amended March 2004), para. 24.
228 IAS 8, para. 28.
229 IFRS 1, para. BC89.

230 IFRS 1, para. 22.

231 IFRS 1, para. 21.

232 IFRS 1, para. 26(b).

233 IFRS 1, para. BC75.

234 IFRS 1, para. BC76.

235 IFRS 1, para. BC77.

236 IFRS 1, para. 28.

237 IFRS 1, para. IG58A.

238 IFRS 1, para. 28.

239 IFRS 1, para. 29.

240 IFRS 1, para. 29.

241 IFRS 1, para. 30.

242 IFRS 1, para. BC75.

243 IFRS 1, para. IG60B.

244 ED 1, *First-time Application of International Financial Reporting Standards*, IASB, July 2002, para. C3(c)(i).

245 ED 1, para. C4.

246 IFRS 1, para. IG58A.

247 *A guide to IFRS 1: First-time adoption*, Deloitte Touche Tohmatsu, August 2004, Part IV, Question E2: Hedge of a forecasted transaction.

248 IFRS 1, para. IG60A.

249 IAS 39 (2000), para. 172(e) and ED 1, para. C3(b).

250 IFRS 1, paras. IG60 and IG60B.

251 IFRS 1, para. 30.

252 IFRS 1, para. IG60B.

253 Exposure Draft (ED), *Amendments to IAS 39, Financial Instruments: Recognition and Measurement – Cash flow Hedge Accounting of Forecast Intragroup Transactions*, IASB, July 2004, para. BC7.

254 ED, Background, para. 3.

255 ED, Background, para. 4.

256 ED, Background, para. 5.

257 ED, Background, para. 6.

258 ED, paras. BC12, AV1 and AV2.

259 ED, paras. AV1 and AV2.

260 *IASB Update*, IASB, May 2004.

261 *IASB Update*, IASB, May 2004.

262 For example, see *Written Statement of Sir David Tweedie, Chairman, International Accounting Standards Board, to the Committee on Economic and Monetary Affairs of the European Parliament*, IASB, September 2004.

Chapter 20   Financial instruments: Disclosures

1   INTRODUCTION

The Introduction to Chapter 15 provides a general background to the development of accounting for, and disclosure of, financial instruments. It explains that, currently, disclosure of financial instruments is largely dealt with in IAS 32 – *Financial Instruments: Disclosure and Presentation*. The original version of IAS 32 was published in March 1995 and was subject to subsequent minor revisions, particularly to make it more consistent with IAS 39 – *Financial Instruments: Recognition and Measurement* – following approval of that standard in December 1998. A more fundamental review took place as part of the IASB's 'improvements' project, which resulted in the publication of a revised standard in December 2003. There have been a number of consequential amendments since then, notably as IFRS 4 – *Insurance Contracts* – and other new standards have been published. As a result of the December 2003 revisions, all disclosures relating to financial instruments in IAS 39 were moved to IAS 32.

In IAS 32 it is explained that the objective of the standard is to enhance financial statement users' understanding of the significance of financial instruments to an entity's financial position, performance and cash flows.[1] The standard identifies the information that should be disclosed about financial instruments and requires disclosure of information about factors that affect the amount, timing and certainty of an entity's future cash flows relating to financial instruments as well as the accounting policies applied to those instruments. Disclosure of information about the nature and extent of an entity's use of financial instruments, the business purposes they serve, the risks associated with them, and management's policies for controlling those risks are also required.[2] The principles in IAS 32 are designed to complement the recognition and measurement principles in IAS 39 which are covered in Chapters 15 to 19.[3]

The basic disclosure requirements in IAS 32 are no different for banks or other financial institutions, although a flexible approach is allowed to suit an entity's particular circumstances. In addition, IAS 30 – *Disclosures in the Financial Statements of Banks and Similar Financial Institutions* – contains further disclosure requirements which complement, and sometime overlap with, those in IAS 32, although a standard as specialised as IAS 30 is beyond the scope of this publication.

IAS 32 also contains requirements regarding the presentation of financial instruments. These requirements apply to the classification of financial instruments, from the perspective of the issuer, into financial assets, financial liabilities and equity instruments; the classification of related interest, dividends, losses and gains; and the circumstances in which financial assets and financial liabilities should be offset.[4] These requirements are principally covered in Chapters 16 and 17.

2   GENERAL MATTERS

2.1   Scope

Section 3 of Chapter 15 contains a detailed explanation both of the scope of IAS 32 and of IAS 39. It is important to recognise that the scope of IAS 32 is somewhat wider than that of IAS 39. Therefore IAS 32 can apply to instruments that are not subject to the recognition and measurement provisions of IAS 39, for example finance leases, certain loan commitments, and an entity's issued equity instruments.

Although IAS 32 was not developed to apply to commodity or other contracts that do not satisfy the definition of a financial instrument or are otherwise within the scope of the standard (see Chapter 15 at 3.8), it may be regarded as appropriate to apply the relevant disclosure requirements to such contracts.[5]

2.2   Risks arising from financial instruments

The standard explains that transactions in financial instruments may result in the assumption or transfer of one or more of the following types of financial risk:

(a)   *Market risk*, of which there are three types:

    (i)   *Currency risk*, the risk that the value of a financial instrument will fluctuate because of changes in foreign exchange rates.

    (ii)   *Fair value interest rate risk*, the risk that the value of a financial instrument will fluctuate because of changes in market interest rates.

    (iii)   *Price risk*, the risk that the value of a financial instrument will fluctuate as a result of changes in market prices whether those changes are caused by factors specific to the individual instrument or its issuer or factors affecting all instruments traded in the market.

    The term 'market risk' embodies not only the potential for loss but also the potential for gain.

(b)   *Credit risk* is the risk that one party to a financial instrument will fail to discharge an obligation and cause the other party to incur a financial loss.

(c) *Liquidity risk,* also referred to as funding risk, is the risk of encountering difficulty in raising funds to meet commitments associated with financial instruments. Liquidity risk may result from an inability to sell a financial asset quickly at close to its fair value.

(d) *Cash flow interest rate risk* is the risk that future cash flows of a financial instrument will fluctuate because of changes in market interest rates. In the case of a floating rate debt instrument, for example, such fluctuations result in a change in the effective interest rate of the financial instrument, usually without a corresponding change in its fair value.

The required disclosures are intended to provide information that assists users in assessing the extent of risk related to an entity's financial instruments, particularly those risks noted above.[6]

2.3 Format, location and degree of aggregation

Neither the format of the disclosures, nor their location within the financial statements, is prescribed by the standard. Therefore, management will need to consider the most appropriate method of presenting the information required by the standard. This information will include a combination of narrative descriptions and specific quantified data, as appropriate to the nature of the instruments and their relative significance to the entity.[7]

The standard emphasises that judgment should be exercised in determining the level of detail to be disclosed, taking into account the relative significance of the particular instruments concerned. A balance should be maintained between providing excessive detail and obscuring important information in aggregated disclosures. Summarised information by reference to particular classes of instrument will be appropriate when dealing with large homogenous groups whilst specific information about an individual instrument may be important when, for example, that instrument represents a material component in an entity's capital structure.[8]

Financial instruments should therefore be grouped into classes that are appropriate to the nature of the information disclosed, taking into account matters such as the characteristics of the instruments and the measurement basis applied. In general, classes should distinguish items carried at cost or amortised cost from items carried at fair value and there should be sufficient information to permit a reconciliation to relevant balance sheet line items,[9] although information presented on the face of the financial statements need not be repeated in the notes.[10]

Financial instruments that are not within the scope of IAS 32 (see Chapter 15 at 3) constitute a class or classes of financial assets or liabilities separate from those within the scope of the standard. Disclosures about these instruments are also dealt with by other standards.[11]

3   NARRATIVE DISCLOSURES

3.1   Risk management policies

Entities are required to describe their financial risk management objectives and policies, including their policies for hedging each major type of forecasted transaction for which hedge accounting is used.[12]

Not only should this description provide specific information about particular balances and transactions related to financial instruments but it should also include a discussion of:

- the extent to which financial instruments are used;
- the business purposes served by those instruments; and
- the associated risks.

It should also include a discussion of management's policies for controlling those risks including policies on matters such as:

- hedging risk exposures;
- avoidance of undue concentrations of risk; and
- requirements for collateral to mitigate credit risk.

The standard explains that such a discussion should provide a valuable additional perspective that is independent of the specific instruments held or outstanding at a particular time.[13]

The following extracts from the financial statements of Nokia and Novartis show how risk management policies have been disclosed in practice – Nokia's disclosures are particularly comprehensive.

Extract 20.1: Nokia Corporation (2003)

Notes to the consolidated financial statements [extract]

34.   Risk management [extract]

General risk management principles

Nokia's overall risk management concept is based on visibility of the key risks preventing Nokia from reaching its business objectives. This covers all risk areas; strategic, operational, financial and hazard risks. Risk management at Nokia is a systematic and proactive way to analyze, review and manage all opportunities, threats and risks related to Nokia's objectives rather than to solely eliminate risks.

The principles documented in Nokia's Risk Policy and accepted by the Audit Committee of the Board of Directors require risk management and its elements to be integrated into business processes. One of the main principles is that the business or function owner is also the risk owner, however, it is everyone's responsibility at Nokia to identify risks preventing us from reaching our objectives.

Key risks are reported to the business and Group level management to create assurance on business risks and to enable prioritization of risk management implementation at Nokia. In addition to general principles there are specific risk management policies covering, for example, treasury and customer finance risks.

Financial risks

The key financial targets for Nokia are growth, profitability, operational efficiency and a strong balance sheet. The objective for the Treasury function is twofold: to guarantee cost-efficient funding for the Group at all times, and to identify, evaluate and hedge financial risks in close co-operation with the business groups. There is a strong focus in Nokia on creating shareholder value. The Treasury function

---

supports this aim by minimizing the adverse effects caused by fluctuations in the financial markets on the profitability of the underlying businesses and by managing the balance sheet structure of the Group.

Nokia has Treasury Centers in Geneva, Singapore/Beijing and Dallas/Sao Paolo, and a Corporate Treasury unit in Espoo. This international organization enables Nokia to provide the Group companies with financial services according to local needs and requirements.

The Treasury function is governed by policies approved by top management. Treasury Policy provides principles for overall financial risk management and determines the allocation of responsibilities for financial risk management in Nokia. Operating Policies cover specific areas such as foreign exchange risk, interest rate risk, use of derivative financial instruments, as well as liquidity and credit risk. Nokia is risk averse in its Treasury activities. Business Groups have detailed Standard Operating Procedures supplementing the Treasury Policy in financial risk management related issues.

Market risk
Foreign exchange risk

Nokia operates globally and is thus exposed to foreign exchange risk arising from various currency combinations. Foreign currency denominated assets and liabilities together with expected cash flows from highly probable purchases and sales give rise to foreign exchange exposures. These transaction exposures are managed against various local currencies because of Nokia's substantial production and sales outside the Euro zone.

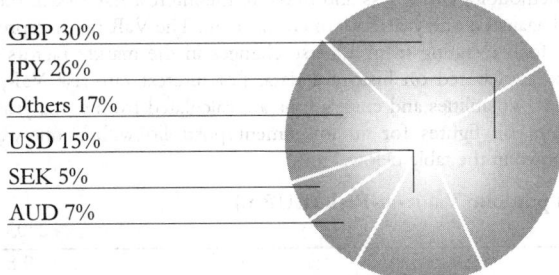

GBP 30%
JPY 26%
Others 17%
USD 15%
SEK 5%
AUD 7%

Due to the changes in the business environment, currency combinations may also change within the financial year. The most significant non-euro sales currencies during the year were US dollar (USD), UK pound sterling (GBP) and Australian dollar (AUD). In general, depreciation of another currency relative to the euro has an adverse effect on Nokia's sales and operating profit, while appreciation of another currency has a positive effect, with the exception of Japanese yen, being the only significant foreign currency in which Nokia has more purchase than sales.

The chart above shows the breakdown by currency of the underlying net foreign exchange transaction exposure as of December 31, 2003 (in some of the currencies, especially the US dollar, Nokia has both substantial sales as well as cost, which have been netted in the chart).

According to the foreign exchange policy guidelines of the Group, material transaction foreign exchange exposures are hedged. Exposures are mainly hedged with derivative financial instruments such as forward foreign exchange contracts and foreign exchange options. The majority of financial instruments hedging foreign exchange risk have a duration of less than a year. The Group does not hedge forecasted foreign currency cash flows beyond two years.

Nokia uses the Value-at-Risk ("VaR") methodology to assess the foreign exchange risk related to the Treasury management of the Group exposures. The VaR figure represents the potential fair value losses for a portfolio resulting from adverse changes in market factors using a specified time period and confidence level based on historical data. To correctly take into account the non-linear price function of certain derivative instruments, Nokia uses Monte Carlo simulation. Volatilities and correlations are calculated from a one-year set of daily data. The VaR figures assume that the forecasted cash flows materialize as expected. The VaR figures for the Group transaction foreign exchange exposure, including hedging transactions and Treasury exposures for netting and risk management purposes, with a one-week horizon and 95% confidence level, are shown in the table below.

Transaction foreign exchange position Value-at-Risk (EURm)

VaR	2003	2002
At December 31	16.7	5.9
Average for the year	9.3	14.3
Range for the year	5.8–16.7	4.9-27.6

Since Nokia has subsidiaries outside the Euro zone, the euro-denominated value of the shareholders' equity of Nokia is also exposed to fluctuations in exchange rates. Equity changes caused by movements in foreign exchange rates are shown as a translation difference in the Group consolidation. Nokia uses, from time to time, foreign exchange contracts and foreign currency denominated loans to hedge its equity exposure arising from foreign net investments.

Interest rate risk

The Group is exposed to interest rate risk either through market value fluctuations of balance sheet items (i.e. price risk) and through changes in interest income or expenses (i.e. re-investment risk). Interest rate risk mainly arises through interest-bearing liabilities and assets. Estimated future changes in cash flows and balance sheet structure also expose the Group to interest rate risk.

Treasury is responsible for monitoring and managing the interest rate exposure of the Group. Due to the current balance sheet structure of Nokia, emphasis is placed on managing the interest rate risk of investments.

Nokia uses the VaR methodology to assess and measure the interest rate risk in the investment portfolio, which is benchmarked against a one-year investment horizon. The VaR figure represents the potential fair value losses for a portfolio resulting from adverse changes in the market factors using a specified time period and confidence level based on historical data. For interest rate risk VaR, Nokia uses variance-covariance methodology. Volatilities and correlations are calculated from a one-year set of daily data. The VaR-based interest rate risk figures for an investment portfolio with a one-week horizon and 95% confidence level are shown in the table below.

Treasury investment portfolio Value-at-Risk (EURm)

VaR	2003	2002
At December 31	9.8	5.4
Average for the year	6.7	5.1
Range for the year	4.7-11.9	3.1-8.7

Equity price risk

Nokia has certain strategic minority investments in publicly traded companies. These investments are classified as available-for-sale. The fair value of the equity investment s at December 31, 2003 was EUR 8 million (EUR 137 million in 2002).

There are currently no outstanding derivative financial instruments designated as hedges of these equity investments. The VaR figures for equity investments, shown in the table below, have been calculated using the same principles as for interest rate risk.

Equity investments Value-at-Risk (EURm)

VaR	2003	2002
At December 31	0.2	6.5
Average for the year	3.5	8.8
Range for the year	0.2-9.4	5.5-19.0

In addition to the listed equity holdings, Nokia invests in private equity through Nokia Venture Funds. The fair value of these available-for-sale equity investments at December 31, 2003 was USD 85 million (USD 54 million in 2002). Nokia is exposed to equity price risk on social security costs relating to stock compensation plans. Nokia hedges this risk by entering into cash settled equity swap and option contracts.

Credit risk

Customer Finance Credit Risk

Network operators in some markets sometimes require their suppliers to arrange or provide term financing in relation to infrastructure projects. Nokia has maintained a financing policy aimed at close cooperation with banks, financial institutions and Export Credit Agencies to support selected customers in their financing of infrastructure investments. Nokia actively mitigates, market conditions permitting, this exposure by arrangements with these institutions and investors.

Credit risks related to customer financing are systematically analyzed, monitored and managed by Nokia's Customer Finance organization, reporting to the Chief Financial Officer. Credit risks are approved and monitored by Nokia's Credit Committee along principles defined in the Company's credit policy and according to the credit approval process. The Credit Committee consists of the CFO, Group Controller, Head of Group Treasury and Head of Nokia Customer Finance.

At the end of December 31, 2003 our long-term loans to customers, net of allowances and write-offs, totalled EUR 354 million (EUR 1,056 million in 2002), while financial guarantees given on behalf of third parties totalled EUR 33 million (EUR 91 million in 2002). In addition, we had financing commitments totalling EUR 490 million (EUR 857 million in 2002). Total customer financing (outstanding and committed) stood at EUR 877 million (EUR 2,004 million in 2002).

The term customer financing portfolio at December 31, 2003 was:

	Outstanding	Financing Commitments	Totals
Total Portfolio EURm	387	490	877

The term customer financing portfolio at December 31, 2003 mainly consists of outstanding and committed customer financing to wireless operators Hutchison 3G UK Ltd in the United Kingdom and to TNL PCS S.A. (Telemar) in Brazil. Total committed customer financing to Hutchison 3G UK Ltd amounted to EUR 653 million, of which outstanding financing was EUR 354 million, while total committed customer financing to Telemar amounted to EUR 191 million, of which none was outstanding.

Financial credit risk

Financial instruments contain an element of risk of the counterparties being unable to meet their obligations. This risk is measured and monitored by the Treasury function. The Group minimizes financial credit risk by limiting its counterparties to a sufficient number of major banks and financial institutions, as well as through entering into netting arrangements, which gives the Company the right to offset in the case that the counterparty would not be able to fulfil the obligations.

Direct credit risk represents the risk of loss resulting from counterparty default in relation to on-balance sheet products. The fixed income and money market investment decisions are based on strict creditworthiness criteria. The outstanding investments are also constantly monitored by the Treasury. Nokia does not expect the counterparties to default given their high credit quality.

Liquidity risk

Nokia guarantees a sufficient liquidity at all times by efficient cash management and by investing in liquid interest being securities. Due to the dynamic nature of the underlying business Treasury also aims at maintaining flexibility in funding by keeping committed and uncommitted credit lines available. During the year Nokia refinanced all its Revolving Credit Facilities. At the end of December 31, 2003 the new committed facility totalled USD 2.0 billion. The committed credit facility is intended to be used for US and Euro Commercial Paper Programs back up purposes. The commitment fee on the facility is 0.10% per annum.

The most significant existing funding programs include:

> Revolving Credit Facility of USD 2,000 million, maturing in 2008
> Local commercial paper program in Finland, totalling EUR 750 million
> Euro Commercial Paper (ECP) program, totalling USD 500 million
> US Commercial Paper (USCP) program, totalling USD 500 million

None of the above programs have been used to a significant degree in 2003.

Nokia's international creditworthiness facilitates the efficient use of international capital and loan markets. The ratings of Nokia from credit rating agencies have not changed during the year. The ratings as at December 31, 2003 were:

Short-term	Standard & Poor's	A-1
	Moody's	P-1
Long-term	Standard & Poor's	A
	Moody's	A1

Extract 20.2: Novartis AG (2003)

Notes to the Novartis Group Consolidated Financial Statement [extract]

16   Marketable securities and derivative financial instruments [extract]

Market risk

The Group is exposed to market risk, primarily related to foreign exchange, interest rates and market value of the investment of liquid funds. Management actively monitors these exposures. To manage the volatility relating to these exposures the Group enters into a variety of derivative financial instruments. The Group's objective is to reduce, where it is deemed appropriate to do so, fluctuations in earnings and cash flows associated with changes in interest rates, foreign currency rates and market rates of investment of liquid funds and of the currency exposure of certain net investments in foreign subsidiaries. It is the Group's policy and practice to use derivative financial instruments to manage exposures and to enhance the yield on the investment of liquid funds. The Group does not enter any financial transaction containing a risk that cannot be quantified at the time the transaction is concluded; i.e. it does not sell short assets it does not have, or does not know it will have, in the future. The Group only sells existing assets or hedges transactions and future transactions (in the case of anticipatory hedges) it know it will have in the future based on past experience. In the case of liquid funds it write options on assets it has, or on positions it wants to acquire, and for which it has the required liquidity. The Group therefore expects that any loss in value for these instruments generally would be offset by increases in the value of the hedged transactions.

a)   Foreign exchange rates

The Group uses the US dollar as its reporting currency and is therefore exposed to foreign exchange movements, primarily in European, Japanese, other Asian and Latin American currencies. Consequently, it enters into various contracts which change in value as foreign exchange rates change, to preserve the value of assets, commitments and anticipated transactions. The Group uses forward contracts and foreign currency option contracts to hedge certain anticipated foreign currency revenues and the net investment in certain foreign subsidiaries.

b)   Commodities

The Group has only a very limited exposure to price risk related to anticipated purchases of certain commodities used as raw materials by the Group's businesses. A change in those prices may alter the gross margin of a specific business, but generally by not more than 10% of that margin and is thus within the Group's risk management tolerance level. Accordingly, the Group does not enter into commodity future, forward and option contracts to manage fluctuations in prices of anticipated purchases.

c)   Interest rates

The Group manages its exposure to interest rate risk by changing the proportion of fixed rate debt and variable rate debt in its total debt portfolio. To manage this mix the Group may enter into interest rate swap agreements, in which it exchanges the periodic payments, based on a notional amount and agreed upon fixed and variable interest rates.

Use of the above-mentioned derivative financial instruments has not had a material impact on the Group's financial position at December 31, 2003 and 2002 or the Group's results of operations for the years ended December 31, 2003, 2002 and 2001.

> **Counterparty risk**
>
> Counterparty risk encompasses issuer risk on marketable securities, settlement risk on derivative and money market contracts and credit risk on cash and time deposits. Issuer risk is minimized by only buying securities which are at least AA rated. Settlement and credit risk is reduced by the policy of entering into transactions with counterparties that are usually at least AA rated banks or financial institutions. Exposure to these risks is closely monitored and kept within predetermined parameters.
>
> The Group does not expect any losses from non-performance by these counterparties and does not have any significant grouping of exposures to financial sector or country risk.

3.2 Hedging Activities

The following should be disclosed separately for designated fair value hedges, cash flow hedges and hedges of a net investment in a foreign operation (see Chapter 19):

- a description of the hedge;
- a description of the financial instruments designated as hedging instruments and their fair values at the balance sheet date;
- the nature of the risks being hedged; and
- for cash flow hedges:
  - the periods in which the cash flows are expected to occur;
  - when the cash flows are expected to enter into the determination of profit or loss; and
  - a description of any forecast transaction for which hedge accounting had previously been used but which is no longer expected to occur.[14]

Such disclosures may be integrated with the narrative disclosures covered at 3.1 above and, perhaps, with the numerical disclosures covered at 4.3.1 below.

3.3 Accounting policies

For each class of financial asset, financial liability and equity instrument, disclosure should be made of all significant accounting policies, including the general principles adopted and the method of applying those principles to transactions, other events and conditions arising in the business. These should include:

- the criteria applied in determining when to recognise and derecognise financial assets and liabilities;
- the measurement basis applied on initial recognition and subsequently; and
- the basis on which associated income and expenses are recognised and measured.[15]

They should also include, for each of the four categories of financial assets (see Chapter 15 at 7), an explanation of whether regular way purchases and sales are accounted for at trade date or settlement date (see Chapter 16 at 3.1).[16]

The following extract from the financial statements of Novartis includes many of the more common accounting policies adopted under IAS 39 (although it should be noted that these financial statements were prepared under the previous version of that standard).

Extract 20.3: Novartis AG (2003)

Notes to the Novartis Group Consolidated Financial Statements [extracts]

1.   Accounting policies [extracts]

Derivative financial instruments and hedging

Derivative financial instruments are initially recognized in the balance sheet at cost and subsequently re-measured to their fair value. The method of recognizing the resulting gain or loss is dependent on whether the derivative contract is designed to hedge a specific risk and qualifies for hedge accounting. On the date a derivative contract is entered into, the Group designates derivatives which qualify as hedges for accounting purposes as either a) a hedge of the fair value of a recognized asset or liability (fair value hedge), or b) a hedge of a forecasted transaction or firm commitment (cash flow hedge) or c) a hedge of a net investment in a foreign entity.

Changes in the fair value of derivatives which are fair value hedges and that are highly effective are recognized in the income statement, along with any changes in the fair value of the hedged asset or liability that is attributable to the hedged risk. Changes in the fair value of derivatives in cash flow hedges are recognized in equity. Where the forecasted transaction or firm commitment results in the recognition of an asset or liability, the gains and losses previously included in equity are included in the initial measurement of the asset or liability. Otherwise, amounts recorded in equity are transferred to the income statement and classified as revenue or expense in the same period in which the forecasted transaction affects the income statement.

Hedges of net investments in foreign entities are accounted for similarly to cash flow hedges. The Group hedges certain net investments in foreign entities with foreign currency borrowings. All foreign exchange gains or losses arising on translation are recognised in equity and included in cumulative translation differences.

Certain derivative instruments, while providing effective economic hedges under the Group's policies, do not qualify for hedge accounting. Changes in the fair value of any derivative instruments that do not qualify for cash flow hedge accounting are recognized immediately in the income statement.

When a hedging instrument expires or is sold, or when a hedge no longer meets the criteria for hedge accounting, any cumulative gain or loss existing in equity at that time remains in equity and is recognized in the income statement, when the committed or forecasted transaction is ultimately recognized in the income statement. However, if a forecasted or committed transaction is no longer expected to occur, the cumulative gain or loss that was recognized in equity is immediately transferred to the income statement.

The purpose of hedge accounting is to match the impact of the hedged item and the hedging instrument in the income statement. To qualify for hedge accounting, the hedging relationship must meet several strict conditions with respect to documentation, probability of occurrence, hedge effectiveness and reliability of measurement. At the inception of the transaction the Group documents the relationship between hedging instruments and hedged items, as well as its risk management objective and strategy for undertaking various hedge transactions. This process includes linking all derivatives designated as hedges to specific assets and liabilities or to specific firm commitments or forecasted transactions. The Group also documents its assessment, both at the hedge inception and on an ongoing basis, as to whether the derivatives that are used in hedging transactions are highly effective in offsetting changes in fair values or cash flows of hedged items.

Trade accounts receivable

The reported values represent the invoiced amounts, less adjustments for doubtful receivables.

> **Marketable securities**
>
> Marketable securities consist of equity and debt securities which are traded in liquid markets. The Group has classified all its marketable securities as available-for-sale, as they are not acquired to generate profit from short-term fluctuations in price. All purchases and sales of marketable securities are recognized on the trade date, which is the date that the Group commits to purchase or sell the asset. Marketable securities are initially recorded at cost and subsequently carried at fair value. Exchange rate gains and losses on bonds are recorded in the income statement. All other changes in the fair value of unhedged securities are deferred as a fair value adjustment in equity and recycled to the income statement when the asset is sold or impaired. The change in fair value of effectively hedged securities is recorded in the income statement where it offsets the gains or losses of the hedging derivative.
>
> Unrealised losses on marketable securities are included in Financial income, net in the income statement when there is objective evidence that the marketable securities are impaired.
>
> **Repurchase agreements**
>
> The underlying securities are included within marketable securities. The repurchase agreements for the securities sold and agreed to be repurchased under the agreement are recognised gross and included in short-term financial debts. Income and expenses are recorded in interest income and expense, respectively.

For some items entities will have a choice of accounting policies (or bases of applying a policy) and such policies (or bases) should be disclosed where they have a material effect on the financial statements. For example, Extract 18.1 in Chapter 18 at 3.2 illustrates UBS' disclosure of the costing formula applied to its available-for-sale assets.

3.4 Terms and conditions

The contractual terms and conditions of an instrument affect the amount, timing and certainty of associated cash receipts and payments. Therefore, when financial instruments are significant to the financial position or future operating results, either individually or as a class, their terms and conditions should be disclosed.[17] Unlike many other disclosure requirements of IAS 32, this information is also required for each class of equity instrument (which will include minority interests) issued by an entity.[18] This is in addition to the information about share capital, required by IAS 1 – *Presentation of Financial Statements* (see 6.3.2 below).

More specifically, for each class of financial asset, financial liability and equity instrument, information should be disclosed about the extent and nature of those instruments, including significant terms and conditions that may affect the amount, timing and certainty of future cash flows.[19] If no single instrument is individually significant, the essential characteristics of the instruments should be described by reference to appropriate groupings of like instruments.[20]

When financial instruments held or issued, either individually or as a class, create a potentially significant exposure to the risks described at 2.2 above, terms and conditions that warrant disclosure include:

(a) the principal, stated, face or other similar amount, which for some derivatives might be the notional amount;

(b) the date of maturity, expiry or execution;

(c)   early settlement options held by either party to the instrument, including the period in which, or date at which, the options can be exercised and the exercise price or range of prices;

(d)   options held by either party to convert the instrument into, or exchange it for, another financial instrument or some other asset or liability, including the period in which, or date at which, the options can be exercised and the conversion or exchange ratio(s);

(e)   the amount and timing of principal repayments, including instalment repayments and any sinking fund or similar requirements;

(f)   the stated rate or amount of interest, dividend or other periodic return on principal and the timing of payments;

(g)   any collateral held or pledged;

(h)   the currency in which cash flows are denominated, where this is not the entity's functional currency;

(i)   in the case of an instrument that provides for an exchange, information described in (a) to (h) for the instrument to be acquired in the exchange; and

(j)   any condition or associated covenant that, if contravened, would significantly alter any of the other terms (for example, a maximum debt-to-equity ratio in a bond covenant that, if contravened, would make the full principal amount of the bond due and payable immediately).[21]

When the balance sheet presentation of a financial instrument differs from its legal form, the standard indicates that it is desirable for the nature of the instrument to be explained.[22] This could be the case for preference shares that are classified as liabilities as illustrated in Extract 20.13 at 6.1.2 below.

The standard states that the usefulness of this information is enhanced when it highlights any relationship between individual instruments that can significantly affect the amount, timing or certainty of the future cash flows. For example, it may be important to disclose hedging relationships such as might exist when an investment in shares is held for which a put option has been purchased. The extent to which a risk exposure is altered by the relationship among the assets and liabilities may be apparent to financial statement users from information of the type described in (a) to (j) above but in some circumstances further disclosure will be necessary.[23]

In practice, some of the most comprehensive disclosures can be found in respect of an entity's capital. This is illustrated in the following extracts from the financial statements of Jardine Matheson and Roche (showing information about their borrowings) and Zurich Financial Services (showing information about its minority interests). These financial statements were all prepared under the previous version of IAS 32 and it is possible that the treatment of some of the instruments illustrated may change when they adopt the revised standard.

Extract 20.4: Jardine Matheson Holdings Limited (2003)

Notes to the Financial Statements [extract]

22.   Borrowings

	2003		2002	
	Carrying amount US$m	Fair value US$m	Carrying amount US$m	Fair value US$m
Current				
— bank overdrafts	15	15	28	28
— other bank advances	240	240	138	138
— other borrowings	9	9	6	6
	264	264	172	172
Current portion of long-term borrow				
— Bank	98	98	213	213
— Other	–	–	195	195
	98	98	408	408
	362	362	580	580
Long-term borrowings				
— Bank	1,579	1,580	1,444	1,445
— 4.75% Guaranteed Bonds due 2007	502	571	490	540
— 6.375% Guaranteed Bonds due 2011	295	341	295	304
— 6.75% Convertible Bonds due 2005	14	16	14	16
— Other	18	18	39	39
	2,408	2,526	2,282	2,344
	2,770	2,888	2,862	2,924

	2003 US$m	2002 US$m
Secured	1,058	1,039
Unsecured	1,712	1,823
	2,770	2,862

Due dates of repayment:		
Within one year	362	580
Between one and two years	146	137
Between two and five years	1,616	1,703
Beyond five years	646	442
	2,770	2,862

Currency:	Fixed rate borrowings				
	Weighted average interest rates %	Weighted average period outstanding Years	US$m	Floating rate borrowings US$m	Total US$m
2003					
Euro	5.8	4.7	16	–	16
Hong Kong Dollar	2.7	2.7	327	322	649
Malaysian Ringgit	5.0	2.9	26	82	108
New Taiwan Dollar	2.2	1.6	20	21	41
New Zealand Dollar	5.7	–	–	12	12
Singapore Dollar	1.7	1.1	83	439	522
Swiss Franc	3.2	8.0	15	26	41
United Kingdom Sterling	4.7	2.3	31	204	235
United States Dollar	6.0	6.0	813	321	1,134
Other	5.3	–	–	12	12
			1,331	**1,439**	**2,770**
2002					
Australian Dollar	6.0	2.1	28	50	78
Euro	5.8	5.7	14	–	14
Hong Kong Dollar	4.0	1.8	308	320	628
Malaysian Ringgit	4.7	2.2	13	30	43
New Taiwan Dollar	3.1	0.2	6	21	27
New Zealand Dollar	6.4	–	–	14	14
Singapore Dollar	2.8	1.0	260	274	534
Swiss Franc	4.2	5.8	12	–	12
United Kingdom Sterling	5.1	3.2	29	228	257
United States Dollar	5.5	7.0	801	445	1,246
Other	6.2	–	–	9	9
			1,471	**1,391**	**2,862**

All borrowings were within subsidiary undertakings

The 4.75% Guaranteed Bonds with nominal value of US$550 million due 2007 were issued by a wholly-owned subsidiary undertaking and are guaranteed by the Company. The bonds are exchangeable, at the option of the holders, into shares of common stock of J.P. Morgan Chase on the basis of 15.83 shares for each US$1,000 principal amount of the bonds from 6th September 2001 until 30th August 2007. The bonds will mature on 6th September 2007.

The 6.375% Guaranteed Bonds with nominal value of US$300 million due 2011 were issued by a wholly-owned subsidiary undertaking of Jardine Strategic and are guaranteed by Jardine Strategic. The bonds will mature on 8th November 2011.

The 6.75% Convertible Bonds with nominal value of US$76 million due 2005 were issued by Mandarin Oriental. The bonds are convertible up to and including 23rd February 2005 into fully paid ordinary shares of Mandarin Oriental at a conversion price of US$0.671 per ordinary share. At 31st December 2003, US$61 million *(2002: US$61 million)* of the bonds were held by Jardine Strategic and the carrying amount of US$60 million *(2002: US$59 million)* was netted-off the carrying amount of the bonds.

Secured borrowings at 31st December 2003 included US$468 million *(2002: US$371 million)* which were secured against Mandarin Oriental's tangible fixed assets and US$98 million *(2002: US$157 million)* which were secured against Jardine Cycle & Carriage's assets.

The weighted average interest rates and period of fixed rate borrowings are stated after taking into account hedging transactions.

Extract 20.5: Roche Holding Ltd (2003)

Notes to Roche Group Consolidated Financial Statements [extract]

31.   Debt in millions of CHF [extract]

	2003	2002
Debt instruments	**10,579**	11,586
Amounts due to banks and other financial institutions	**3,666**	7,238
Capitalised lease obligations	**890**	1,049
Obligation to repurchase own equity instruments	**–**	2,413
Other borrowings	**152**	64
Total debt	**15,287**	22,350
Reported as:		
- Long-term debt	**10,246**	14,167
- Short-term debt	**5,041**	8,183
Total debt	**15,287**	22,350

Repayment terms of debt

	2003	2002
Within one year	**5,041**	8,183
Between one and two years	**2,327**	4,477
Between two and three years	**493**	4,173
Between three and four years	**2,223**	792
Between four and five years	**3,010**	1,655
Thereafter	**2,193**	3,070
Total debt	**15,287**	22,350

The 'LYONs' zero coupon US dollar exchangeable notes (see below) are reflected as due the first year that the holders of the notes can request the Group to purchase the notes.

The fair value of the debt instruments is 11.6 billion Swiss francs (2002: 12.6 billion Swiss francs) and the fair value of total debt is 16.3 billion Swiss francs (2002: 23.3 billion Swiss francs). This is calculated based upon the present value of the future cash flows on the instrument, discounted at a market rate of interest for instruments with similar credit status, cash flows and maturity periods.

There are no pledges on the Group's assets in connection with debt, except as noted below. The obligation arising from leases at Genentech is supported by restricted cash of 57 million US dollars (70 million Swiss francs). In addition, this obligation is secured on property, plant and equipment which has a net book value of 723 million Swiss francs as at 31 December 2003.

Amounts due to banks and other financial institutions

Interest rates on these amounts, which are primarily denominated in US dollars and euros, average approximately 3.4% (2002: 2.8%). Repayment dates vary between 1 and 24 years. 1,571 million Swiss francs (2002: 4,631 million Swiss francs) are due within one year.

Debt instruments

The carrying value of the Group's debt instruments is given in the table below.

	Effective interest rate	2003	2002
European Medium Term Note programme			
4% bonds due 9 October 2008, principal 750 million euros	4.16%	**1,159**	–
5.375% bonds due 29 August 2023, principal 250 million pounds sterling	5.46%	**541**	–
3.25% bonds due 2 October 2007, principal 750 million US dollars	3.28%	**926**	–
Swiss franc bonds			
'Bullet' 2% due 21 March 2003, principal 1.25 billion Swiss francs	–	**–**	1,249
'Rodeo' 1.75% due 20 March 2008, principal 1 billion Swiss francs	3.00%	**956**	945
US dollar bonds			
'Chameleon' 6.75% due 6 July 2009, principal 1 billion US dollars	6.77%	**1,229**	1,377
Swiss franc convertible bonds			
'Helveticus' dividend-linked convertible bonds, due 31 July 2003, principal 1 billion Swiss francs	–	**–**	207
Zero coupon US dollar exchangeable notes			
'LYONs II' due 20 April 2010, principal 2.15 billion US dollars	–	**–**	1,757
'LYONs III' due 6 May 2012, principal 3 billion US dollars	6.91%	**2,136**	2,240
'LYONs IV' due 19 January 2015, principal 1.506 billion US dollars	4.26%	**1,171**	1,259
'LYONs V' due 25 July 2021, principal 2.051 billion US dollars	4.14%	**1,233**	1,329
Japanese yen exchangeable bonds			
'Sumo' 0.25% due 25 March 2005, principal 104.6 billion Japanese yen	1.89%	**1,186**	1,179
Limited conversion preferred stock			
due 11 November 2004	3.00%	**2**	3
Japanese yen convertible bonds issued by Chugai			
'Series 6 Chugai Pharmaceutical Unsecured Convertible Bonds' 1.05% due 30 September 2008, principal amount of 3.5 billion Japanese yen	1.05%	**40**	41
Total debt instruments		**10,579**	11,586

Issues of new debt instruments, with their net proceeds, are shown in the table below:

	2003	2002
European Medium Term Note programme:		
4% euro-denominated bonds issued 9 April 2003	**1,104**	–
5.375% sterling-denominated bonds issued 29 August 2003	**547**	–
3.25% US dollar-denominated bonds issued 2 October 2003	**984**	–
Total issues during the year	**2,635**	–

Repayments, redemptions and conversations of debt instruments, with their net cash outflows, are shown in the table below:

	2003	2002
'Bullet' Swiss franc bonds: repayment of the principal on the due date of 21 March 2003.	**(1,250)**	–
'LYONs II' US dollar exchangeable notes: exercise by the Group of its option to redeem the principal plus accrued original issue discount (OID) on 20 April 2003.	**(1,830)**	–
'Helveticus' Swiss franc convertible bonds: additional cash payment of CHF 200 per bond upon the conversion of all of the remaining principal by the due date of 31 July 2003.	**(5)**	–
'Samurai' Japanese yen bonds: repayment of the principal on the due date of 15 May 2002.	**–**	(1,258)
Total repayments and retirements during the year	**(3,085)**	(1,258)

Conversion of 'Helveticus' Swiss franc convertible bonds: By the due date of 31 July 2003 all of the remaining Swiss franc convertible bonds originally issued in 1995 were converted into non-voting equity securities *(Genussscheine)*. A total of 2,167,600 non-voting equity securities were used to meet the conversion obligations of the 'Helveticus' bonds in 2003. In accordance with the terms of the bonds, an additional cash payment of CHF 200 per bond was made upon the conversion of the remaining principal. The conversion reduced debt by 207 million Swiss francs, of which 202 million Swiss francs was in the form of non-voting equity securities and 5 million Swiss francs in the form of cash.

Terms of outstanding convertible debt instruments

'LYONs III': The notes are exchangeable for American Depositary Shares (ADSs) at an exchange ratio of 3.62514 exchange ADSs per USD 1,000 principal amount at maturity of the notes. The Group will purchase any note for cash, at the option of the holder, on 6 May 2004 and 6 May 2008 for a purchase price per USD 1,000 principal amount of the notes of USD 605.29 and USD 778.01, respectively. In addition, the notes will be redeemable at the option of the Group in whole or in part at any time after 6 May 2004 at the issue price plus accrued original issue discount (OID). If the notes outstanding at 31 December 2003 were all exchanged it would require 10,875,420 non-voting equity securities to meet the obligation.

'LYONs IV': The notes are exchangeable for Genentech shares at an exchange ratio of 8.65316 Genentech shares per USD 1,000 principal amount at any time up to the maturity of the notes. The Group has the right to pay cash equal to the market value of the Genentech shares in lieu of delivering Genentech shares. The Group will purchase any note for cash, at the option of the holder, on 19 January 2004 and 19 January 2010 for a purchase price per USD 1,000 principal amount of the notes of USD 740.49 and USD 872.35, respectively. In addition, the notes will be redeemable at the option of the Group in whole or in part at any time after 19 January 2004 at the issue price plus accrued original issue discount (OID). If the notes outstanding at 31 December 2003 were all exchanged it would require 13,034,531 Genentech shares to meet the obligation. If all of the notes wee converted the Group's percentage ownership in Genentech would decrease by approximately 2.5%.

'LYONs V': The notes are exchangeable for ADSs at an exchange ratio of 5.33901 exchange ADSs per USD 1,000 principal amount at maturity of the notes. The Group will purchase any note for cash, at the option of the holder, on 25 January 2005, 25 July 2007 and 25 July 2011 for a purchase price per USD 1,000 principal amount of the notes of USD 552.79, USD 604.74 and USD 698.20, respectively. In addition, the notes will be redeemable at the option of the Group in whole or in part at any time after 25 July 2007 at the issue price plus accrued original issue discount (OID). If the notes outstanding at 31 December 2003 were all exchanged it would require 10,952,268 non-voting equity securities to meet the obligation.

'Sumo': Each bond of JPY 1,410,000 par value is exchangeable for 103.292 non-voting equity securities of Roche Holding Ltd. The bonds will be redeemable at maturity at the issue price (96.4%) plus accrued original issue discount (OID) at 100%. If the bonds outstanding at 31 December 2003 were all exchanged it would require 7,664,266 non-voting equity securities to meet the obligation.

'Limited Conversion Preferred Stock': The limited conversion preferred stock is in substance a financial liability rather than an equity instrument, and therefore it is classified as long-term debt in the balance sheet and the related dividend payments are treated as interest expense. The par value of each share is USD 1,000. The shares are subject to mandatory redemption on 11 November 2004 at par plus 3% accrued annual interest. Each share is exchangeable at the option of the holder for 14.29 non-voting equity securities or redeemable at the option of the holder for par plus 3% accrued annual interest at 11 November each year. If the shares outstanding at 31 December 2003 were all converted it would require 32,569 non-voting equity securities to meet the obligation.

'Series 6 Chugai Pharmaceutical Unsecured Convertible Bonds': Each bond of JPY 1,000,000 par value is convertible for 1,311 shares of Chugai. Conversion is at the option of the bondholder and may be made at any time up to the due date of 30 September 2008. The bonds will be redeemable at maturity at the issue price. If the bonds outstanding at 31 December 2003 were all converted it would require 4,508,852 Chugai shares to exactly meet the obligation. The Group's percentage ownership in Chugai would not be affected by any conversion, as the Group has bonds convertible into Chugai shares that mirror those that Chugai has outstanding with third parties (see also Note 6).

Unamortised discount
Included within the carrying value of debt instruments are the following unamortized discounts:

	2003	2002
Swiss franc bonds	44	57
US dollar bonds	8	10
Euro bonds	11	–
Sterling bonds	11	–
Zero coupon US dollar exchangeable notes	3,564	5,493
Japanese yen exchangeable bonds	23	44
Total unamortized discount	3,661	5,604

Extract 20.6: Zurich Financial Services Group (2003)

Notes to the consolidated financial statements [extract]

22.   Minority interests [extract]

Minority interests

In USD millions, as at December 31	2003	2002
Preferred securities	390	969
Other	579	238
Total	969	1,207

Minority interests include third-party equity interests, preferred securities and similar instruments issued by consolidated subsidiaries of the Group in connection with providing structured financial solutions to its customers.

In December 1999, Zurich Financial Services (Jersey) Limited, a subsidiary of Zurich Group Holding (formerly Zurich Financial Services), issued 12,000,000 perpetual non-voting, non-cumulative Series A Preference Shares on the Euromarket with a par value of EUR 25 (EUR 300,000,000). The securities benefit from a subordinated support agreement of Zurich Group Holding and carry a fixed coupon of 7.125% payable quarterly. The securities are, subject to certain conditions, redeemable at the option of the issuer in whole, but not in part, from time to time on or after five years from the issue date. Proceeds from the issue were used to refinance existing intercompany debt and for general corporate purposes. With this issue, the Group was able to reinforce its capital base while raising equity-like but non-dilutive long-term funds.

As at December 31, 2003 and 2002, minority interests in Zurich Capital Markets ("ZCM") totalled USD 212 million and USD 680 million, respectively. Minority interests as at December 31, 2002 primarily represented third-party interests in preferred securities issued by consolidated subsidiaries. During 2003, approximately USD 655 million of preferred securities were redeemed and as at December 31, 2003, only USD 12 million represented third-party interest in preferred securities of subsidiaries. In 2003, other third-party equity interest increased by approximately USD 187 million to USD 200 million primarily due to consolidation of alternative investment vehicles arising from ZCM's managed asset business.

Novartis provides the following information in respect of derivative instruments it is party to.

Extract 20.7: Novartis AG (2003)

Notes to the Novartis Group Consolidated Financial Statements [extract]

16   Marketable securities and derivative financial instruments [extract]

Derivative financial instruments

The following tables show the contract or underlying principal amounts and fair values of derivative financial instruments analyzed by type of contract at December 31, 2003 and 2002. Contract or underlying principal amounts indicate the volume of business outstanding at the balance sheet date and do not represent amounts at risk. The fair values are determined by the markets or standard pricing models at December 31, 2003 and 2002.

Derivative financial instruments

	Contract or underlying principal amount		Positive fair values		Negative fair values	
	2003 USD millions	2002 USD millions	**2003 USD millions**	2002 USD millions	**2003 USD millions**	2002 USD millions
Currency related instruments						
Forward foreign exchange rate contracts	5,470	6,184	360	217	-398	-171
Over the counter currency options	4,016	6,561	34	28	-29	-130
Cross currency swaps	1,123	1,973	223	30		
Total of currency related instruments	**10,609**	**14,718**	**617**	**275**	**-427**	**-301**
Interest rate related instruments						
Interest rate swaps	3,826	2,986	12	50	-10	-1
Forward rate agreements	6,194	2,743	2		-3	-7
Interest rate options	520	677		1	-1	-5
Total of interest rate related instruments	**10,540**	**6,406**	**14**	**51**	**-14**	**-13**
Options on equity securities	**1,242**	**2,084**	**68**	**106**	**-58**	**-96**
Total derivative financial instruments included in marketable securities and in short-term financial debt	**22,391**	**23,208**	**699**	**432**	**-499**	**-410**
Currency related instruments included in other current assets and liabilities						
Forward foreign exchange rate contracts	1,946	2,399	23	141	-34	
Over the counter currency options	2	1,192		7		-1
Total currency related instruments includes in other current assets and liabilities	**1,948**	**3,591**	**23**	**148**	**-34**	**-1**
Total derivative financial instruments	**24,339**	**26,799**	**722**	**580**	**-533**	**-411**

The contract or underlying principal amount of derivative financial instruments at December 31, 2003 and 2002 are set forth by currency in the table below.

	CHF	EUR	USD	JPY	Other	Total 2003	Total 2002
	USD millions	USD millions	USD millions	USD millions	USD millions	USD millions	USD millions
Currency related instruments							
Forward foreign exchange rate contracts	41	3,207	2,885	930	353	7,416	8,583
Over the counter currency options		1,871	1,335	280	532	4,018	7,753
Cross currency swaps		1,123				1,123	1,973
Currency related derivatives	**41**	**6,201**	**4,220**	**1,210**	**885**	**12,557**	**18,309**
Interest rate related instruments							
Interest rate swaps	1,080	1,746	1,000			3,826	2,986
Forward rate agreements		2,994	3,200			6,194	2,743
Interest rate options	120		400			520	677
Interest rate related derivatives	**1,200**	**4,740**	**4,600**			**10,540**	**6,406**
Options on equity securities		**411**	**639**	**144**	**48**	**1,242**	**2,084**
Total derivative financial instruments	**1,241**	**11,352**	**9,459**	**1,354**	**933**	**24,339**	**26.799**

AMVESCAP (which is not yet required to prepare its financial statements under IFRS) provides detailed information regarding its banking covenants.

Extract 20.8: AMVESCAP Plc (2003)

NOTES TO THE FINANCIAL STATEMENTS [extract]

Note 16.   Long-Term Debt [extract]

The credit facility provides for borrowings of various maturities and contains certain conditions including a restriction to declare and pay cash dividends in excess of 60% of cumulative consolidated net profit before goodwill amortization arising after December 31, 2000. The Company also has an unused 364-day revolving $200 million credit facility available. Interest is payable on both facilities based upon LIBOR, Prime, or Federal Funds rates in existence at the time of each borrowing. The financial covenants under the credit agreement include the quarterly maintenance of a debt/EBITDA ratio of not greater than 3.00:1.00 and a coverage ratio of not less than 4.00:1.00 (EBITDA/interest payable for the four consecutive fiscal quarters ended before the date of determination).

---

4 PRINCIPAL NUMERICAL DISCLOSURES

4.1 Interest rate risk disclosures

Changes in interest rates can have a direct effect on the cash flows associated with some financial instruments and on the fair value of others. Therefore IAS 32 requires disclosure of information concerning interest rate exposure.[24] This information should include, for each class of financial asset and financial liability:

- contractual repricing or maturity dates, whichever dates are earlier; and
- effective interest rates, when applicable.[25]

Maturity dates, or repricing dates when earlier, indicate for how long interest rates are fixed; effective interest rates indicate the levels at which they are fixed. This provides a basis for evaluating the exposure to interest rate fair value risk and the associated potential for gain or loss. For instruments that reprice to a market rate before maturity, the period until the next repricing is more important for this purpose than the period to maturity.[26]

To supplement this, information about *expected* repricing or maturity dates may be given when those dates differ significantly from the contractual dates. Such information may be particularly relevant when, for example, it is possible to predict with reasonable reliability the amount of fixed rate mortgage loans that will be repaid before maturity and this information is used as the basis for managing interest rate risk exposure. Such information should explain that it is based on management's expectations and include an explanation of the assumptions used and how they differ from the contractual dates.[27]

An indication should be given of which instruments are:

- exposed to fair value interest rate risk, such as fixed rate instruments;
- exposed to cash flow interest rate risk, such as floating rate instruments that reset as market rates change; and
- not directly exposed to interest rate risk, such as some investments in equity instruments.[28]

Effective interest rates should be disclosed for bonds, notes, loans and similar instruments that create a return and a cost reflecting the time value of money. This requirement does not apply to those instruments that do not bear a determinable effective interest rate such as investments in equity instruments and derivatives – whilst interest rate swaps, forward rate agreements and options are exposed to fair value or cash flow risk from changes in interest rates, disclosure of an effective interest rate is not required. However, when providing such information, the effect of hedging transactions such as interest rate swaps should be disclosed.[29]

Where an instrument has been issued that contains both a liability and an equity component and the instrument has multiple embedded derivative features whose values are interdependent, such as a callable convertible debt instrument (see Chapter 17 at 4.3) the effective interest rate on the liability component (excluding any embedded derivatives that are accounted for separately) should be disclosed.

Together with the disclosure of the existence of these features, this information means their impact on the amounts reported as liabilities, equity and interest expense will be highlighted. The IASB sees this as important given what they recognise is an arbitrary allocation of the joint value attributable to this interdependence under the revised version of IAS 32. Hence they have added these new disclosure requirements.[30]

Interest rate risk can arise from transactions in which no financial instrument is recognised and information should be provided to explain the nature and extent of these exposures. In the case of a commitment to lend funds, this information will normally include the stated principal, interest rate and term to maturity of the amount to be lent and any other significant terms of the transaction.[31]

The nature of an entity's business and the extent of its activity in financial instruments will determine whether interest rate risk information is presented in narrative form, in tables, or by using a combination of the two. The standard suggests that one or more of the following approaches may be used:

- Tables showing the carrying amounts of instruments exposed to interest rate risk, grouped by those that will mature or be repriced in the following periods after the balance sheet date:
    - in one year or less;
    - in more than one year but not more than two years;
    - in more than two years but not more than three years;
    - in more than three years but not more than four years;
    - in more than four years but not more than five years; and
    - in more than five years.[32]

    The previous version of the standard suggested the use of only one band for instruments maturing in more than one year but not more than five years, rather than the four above.[33]

- When performance is significantly affected by interest rate exposure, more detailed information is desirable, for example banks may use the following additional groupings:
    - in one month or less after the balance sheet date;
    - in more than one month but not more than three months after the balance sheet date; and
    - more than three months but not more than twelve months after the balance sheet date.

- Similarly, tables aggregating the carrying amount of floating rate instruments maturing within various future time periods give an indication of cash flow interest rate risk.

- Information may be disclosed for individual instruments; alternatively weighted average rates or a range of rates may be presented for each class. Instruments denominated in different currencies or having substantially different credit risks may be grouped into separate classes when these factors result in substantially different effective interest rates.[34]

Examples of interest rate risk disclosures given in practice can be seen in Extracts 20.4 and 20.5 at 3.4 above.

The standard suggests that indicating the effect of a hypothetical change in market rates on the fair value of financial instruments and future earnings and cash flows may provide useful information. Such information may be based on an assumed one percentage point (100 basis points) change in rates occurring at the balance sheet date. The effects should include changes in interest income and expense relating to floating rate financial instruments and gains or losses resulting from changes in the fair value of fixed rate instruments, but may be restricted to the direct effects on interest-bearing instruments recognised at the reporting date because the indirect effects of a rate change on financial markets and individual entities cannot normally be predicted reliably. When disclosing interest rate sensitivity information, the basis on which the information has been prepared should be indicated, including any significant assumptions.[35] For example, the disclosures would normally include an explanation of how hedging contracts had been dealt with.

4.2 Credit risk

A failure by counterparties to discharge their obligations could reduce the amount of future cash inflows from financial assets recognised at the balance sheet date or require a cash outflow from other credit exposures (such as a credit derivative or an issued guarantee of the obligations of a third party) thereby giving rise to a recognised loss. Consequently, to allow an assessment of the extent of such failures, IAS 32 requires disclosure of information relating to credit risk.[36]

For each class of financial assets and other credit exposures, information about credit risk exposure should be disclosed, including:

- the amount that best represents the maximum credit risk exposure at the balance sheet date in the event of other parties failing to perform their obligations, without taking account of the fair value of any collateral; and
- significant concentrations of credit risk.[37]

This information need not include an assessment of the probability of losses arising in the future.[38]

The reasons given for ignoring potential recoveries from the realisation of collateral are to provide a consistent measure of credit risk exposure for financial assets and other credit exposures and to take into account the possibility that the maximum exposure may differ from the carrying amount of financial assets recognised at the balance sheet date.[39]

The carrying amount of a financial asset, net of any applicable provisions, usually represents the credit risk exposure at a particular point in time. For example, the maximum exposure to loss for an interest rate swap carried at fair value is normally its carrying amount as this represents its current replacement cost in the event of default. In these circumstances, no additional disclosure beyond that provided on the balance sheet is necessary.[40] Consequently, the required disclosures in respect of credit risk for many entities could be minimal.

Depending on an entity's particular circumstances, however, the maximum potential loss from some financial instruments may differ significantly from their carrying amount and from other disclosed amounts such as their fair value or principal amount. In such circumstances, additional disclosure is necessary.[41]

For example, financial assets subject to legally enforceable rights of set-off against financial liabilities are not presented net unless settlement is intended to take place net or simultaneously (see Chapter 16 at 6). However, where a legal right of set-off exists, a loss can be avoided in the event of default if the receivable is due before a payable of equal or greater amount. When a liability is due to be settled before an asset, credit risk exposure may also be mitigated if default is known about before the liability is settled. On the other hand, if the likely response to default is the extension of the asset's term, an exposure would exist if collection is deferred beyond the date the liability is due. Therefore the existence of legal rights of set-off should normally be disclosed to explain the maximum potential loss, but only when the relevant asset is expected to be collected in accordance with its terms.[42]

Master netting arrangements can mitigate credit risk but do not always meet the offset criteria. When such arrangements significantly reduce credit risk, additional information about the arrangement should be provided, indicating that:

- credit risk is eliminated only to the extent that amounts due to the same counterparty will be settled after the assets are realised; and

- the extent to which overall credit risk is reduced may change substantially within a short period because the exposure is affected by each transaction subject to the arrangement.

The standard states it is also desirable to disclose the terms of master netting arrangements that determine the extent of the reduction in credit risk.[43]

An entity may be exposed to credit risk as a result of a transaction in which no financial asset is recognised on its balance sheet, such as a financial guarantee or credit derivative contract (see Chapter 15 at 3.3). Guaranteeing an obligation of another party creates a liability and exposes the guarantor to credit risk that shold be taken into account in making the credit risk disclosures.[44] An entity is likely to conclude that credit risk information in respect of guarantees should be disclosed separately from similar information regarding recognised financial assets (see 2.3 above).

Significant credit risk concentrations should be disclosed when they are not otherwise apparent. These concentrations may represent exposures to a single debtor or to groups of debtors whose ability to meet their obligations is expected to be affected by similar changes in economic or other conditions.[45] The information disclosed should include a description of the shared characteristic that identifies each concentration and the amount of the maximum credit risk exposure associated with all financial assets sharing that characteristic.[46]

Characteristics that may give rise to a concentration of risk include the nature of the debtors' activities, such as the industry in which they operate, the geographical area in which activities are undertaken and the level of creditworthiness of groups of borrowers. For example, a manufacturer of equipment for oil and gas producers will normally have debtors for which the risk of non-payment is affected by economic changes in the energy industry. A bank that lends internationally may have many loans outstanding to less developed nations, which may be adversely affected by local economic conditions.[47]

The standard acknowledges that identification of significant concentrations is a matter of judgement and suggests using the guidance in IAS 14 – *Segment Reporting* – to identify industry and geographical segments within which concentrations may arise (see Chapter 28).[48]

Bayer includes in its financial statements the following information on credit risk.

Extract 20.9: Bayer AG (2003)

Notes to the Balance Sheets [extract]

38.   Financial instruments [extract]

Primary financial instruments [extract]

Credit risk

Credit risk arises from the possibility of asset impairment occurring because counterparties cannot meet their obligations in transactions involving financial instruments.

Since we do not conclude master netting arrangements with our customers, the total of the amounts recognized in assets represents the maximum exposure to credit risk.

Derivative financial instruments [extract]

Credit risk

Credit risk exposure is €733 million (2002: €578 million), this amount being the total of the positive fair values of derivatives that give rise to claims against the other parties to the instruments. It represents the losses that could result from non-performance of contractual obligations by these parties. We minimize this risk by imposing a limit on the volume of business in derivative financial instruments transacted with individual parties.

The financial statements of Munich Re, which has a much more significant exposure to credit risk, contains more comprehensive disclosures about credit risk including the following analysis of its available-for-sale fixed interest securities.

Extract 20.10: Münchener Rückversicherungs-Gesellschaft AG (2003)

Notes to the Consolidated Financial Statements [extract]

(7)   Other securities, available for sale [extract]

Rating of fixed-interest securities on fair-value basis

All figures in €m	31.12.2003	Prev. year
AAA	**58,767**	54,279
AA	**24,364**	20,362
A	**10,043**	7,023
BBB	**3,847**	3,183
Lower	**274**	254
No rating	**1,538**	1,575
Total	**98,833**	86,676

4.3   Fair values

Given the long-term goal of the standard setters to record all financial instruments in the balance sheet using measures based on fair value rather than historical cost, it is not surprising that, in the interim, the IASB sees the disclosure of information about their fair value as being an important requirement. It is explained in the following terms:

'Fair value information is widely used for business purposes in determining an entity's overall financial position and in making decisions about individual financial instruments. It is also relevant to many decisions made by users of financial statements because, in many circumstances, it reflects the judgement of the financial markets about the present value of expected future cash flows relating to an instrument. Fair value information permits comparisons of financial instruments having substantially the same economic characteristics, regardless of why they are held and when and by whom they were issued or acquired. Fair values provide a neutral basis for assessing management's stewardship by indicating the effects of its decisions to buy, sell or hold financial assets and to incur, maintain or discharge financial liabilities.'[49]

Therefore, when financial assets or liabilities are not measured on a fair value basis, information on fair values should be given by way of supplementary disclosures.[50] The detailed disclosure requirements have changed a little in the revised standard, mainly to align them with the accounting requirements in the revised version of IAS 39, and the principal amendments are highlighted below.

4.3.1   General disclosure requirements

Except as set out at 4.3.2 below, the fair value of each class of financial assets and liabilities should be disclosed in a way that permits comparison with the corresponding carrying amounts in the balance sheet. All guidance on determining fair values has been removed from IAS 32 and is now included in IAS 39 – this is covered in Chapter 18 at 4.[51] In providing this disclosure, instruments should be offset only to the extent that their related carrying amounts are also offset in the balance sheet.[52]

In addition, the following information should be disclosed:

(a)   the methods and significant assumptions applied in determining fair values, separately for significant classes of financial assets and liabilities.[53]

For example, this might include information about the assumptions relating to prepayment rates, rates of estimated credit losses and interest or discount rates if they are significant;[54]

(b)   whether those fair values are determined directly, in full or in part, by reference to published price quotations in an active market or are estimated using a valuation technique;

(c)   whether financial instruments are measured at fair values determined in full or in part using a valuation technique based on assumptions that are not supported by observable market prices or rates.

If changing any such assumption to a reasonably possible alternative would result in a significantly different fair value, this fact should be stated and the effect on the fair value of a range of reasonably possible alternative assumptions should be disclosed. For this purpose, significance shall be judged with respect to profit or loss and total assets or total liabilities;

(d)   the total amount of the change in fair value estimated using a valuation technique that was recognised in profit or loss during the period.[55]

These disclosures are applicable equally to all classes of financial instruments with the exception of (d) which is clearly not applicable to financial instruments that are not measured at fair value through profit or loss. The extent to which these disclosures are presented separately for those instruments that are measured at fair value, and those for which fair values are only disclosed, will depend on an entity's specific circumstances.

In concluding on the disclosures to be required by the revised standard, the IASB decided that, to provide a sense of the potential variability of fair value estimates, information about the use of valuation techniques should be disclosed, for example the sensitivities of fair value estimates to the main valuation assumptions. The IASB considered the view that disclosure of sensitivities could be difficult, in particular when there are many valuation assumptions to which the disclosure would apply and these assumptions are interdependent. However, it noted that a detailed quantitative disclosure of sensitivity to all valuation assumptions was not required, only those that could result in a significantly different estimate of fair value. Also, the standard does not require all interdependencies between assumptions to be reflected when making the disclosure.[56] Rather, the sensitivity disclosure is required only if:

• the fair value is sensitive to a particular assumption;

• reasonably possible alternatives for that assumption would result in a significantly different result; and

• that assumption is not supported by observable market prices or rates.[57]

The IASB also considered view that such disclosure might imply that a fair value established by a valuation technique is less valid than one established by other means. However, it was noted that fair values that are estimated by valuation techniques are more subjective than those established from an observable market price, and concluded that users should be given information to help them in assessing this subjectivity.[58] Entities may find it challenging to provide meaningful sensitivity disclosures and it remains to be seen how this requirement will be dealt with in practice.

As set out at 3.2 above, the fair values of financial instruments designated as hedging instruments should be disclosed separately for designated fair value hedges, cash flow hedges and hedges of a net investment in a foreign operation.[59] It will often be possible to combine those disclosures within the general fair value disclosures. However, a single hedging instrument may be simultaneously designated in a cash flow and a fair value hedge (see Chapter 19 at 2.1.6), in which case the instrument in question would need to be included in the disclosures for both cash flow hedges and fair value hedges.[60]

Previously, financial assets carried at an amount in excess of fair value were subject to additional disclosure requirements, including the reasons for not reducing the carrying amount.[61] However, these disclosures were seen as redundant, especially given the measurement provisions of IAS 39 and the requirement in IAS 32 to disclose fair values in a manner that allows them to be compared to carrying amounts. Accordingly these requirements have now been removed.[62]

Examples of fair value disclosures given in practice can be seen in Extracts 20.4, 20.5 and 20.7 at 3.4 above. In addition, Zurich Financial Services provides the following information about the fair value of its financial instruments (as well as certain other items) including an explanation of how those fair values are derived.

Extract 20.11: Zurich Financial Services Group (2003)

Notes to the consolidated financial statements [extract]

9.   Fair value of financial instruments

The methods and assumptions used by the Group in estimating the fair value of the financial instruments are:

- Debt securities: Fair values are generally based upon quoted market prices. Where market prices are not readily available, fair values are estimated using either values obtained from independent pricing services or quoted market prices of comparable investments.

- Equity securities: Fair values are based on quoted market prices.

- Investments in associates are accounted for using the equity method. Accordingly, these participations are carried at the Group's proportional interest of the investee's shareholder's equity. The fair value of these entities, particularly for publicly traded entities, may differ from the carrying value.

- Investments held by investment companies: Estimated fair values are determined by the investment managers.

- Real estate: Fair value is determined on a regular basis with reference to current market conditions.

- Mortgage loans: Fair values of loans on real estate are estimated using discounted cash flow calculations based upon the Group's current incremental lending rates for similar types of loans.

- Policyholders' collateral and other loans: Fair values of policyholders' collateral loans are estimated using discounted cash flow calculations based upon the Group's current incremental lending rates for similar types of loans. The fair values of other loans are not calculated and are not significant to the Group.

- Short-term investments: Carrying amounts approximate fair values.

- Other: Quoted market prices are not readily available for these assets. They are not fair valued and are not significant to the Group.

- Cash and cash equivalents: Carrying amounts approximate fair values.

- Derivative trading assets and liabilities are estimated based on quoted market prices, prices provided by independent brokers or accepted valuation models.

- Universal life and other investment contracts: Fair values are estimated using discounted cash flow calculations based on interest rates currently being offered for similar contracts with maturities consistent with those remaining for the contracts being valued.

- Debt: Fair values are estimated using discounted cash flow calculations based upon the Group's current incremental borrowing rates for similar types of borrowings with maturities consistent with those remaining for the debt being valued.

- Obligations to repurchase securities are recorded at cost which approximates fair value.

Table 9

Fair value of financial instruments	Total fair value		Total carrying value	
In USD millions, as at December 31	**2003**	2002	**2003**	2002
Debt securities	**113,393**	102,543	**113,002**	102,498
Equity securities (incl. Trading equity portfolios in capital markets and banking activities)	**19,491**	25,888	**19,491**	25,888
Investments in associates	**991**	860	**991**	908
Other investments:				
Investments held by investment companies	**1,576**	1,328	**1,576**	1,328
Real estate	**7,462**	7,378	**7,462**	7,378
Mortgage loans	**11,387**	9,011	**11,283**	8,811
Policyholders' collateral and other loans	**7,484**	7,145	**7,479**	7,159
Short-term investments	**998**	1,098	**998**	1,098
Other	**149**	276	**149**	276
Total other investments	**29,056**	26,236	**28,947**	26,050
Cash and cash equivalents	**13,536**	8,444	**13,536**	8,444
Derivative trading assets	**2,579**	1,475	**2,579**	1,475
Total of financial instruments (assets)	**179,046**	165,446	**178,546**	165,263
Universal life and other investment contracts	**(12,343)**	(13,456)	**(12,345)**	(13,770)
Debt	**(11,037)**	(12,065)	**(10,736)**	(11,808)
Obligations to repurchase securities	**(3,742)**	(3,416)	**(3,742)**	(3,416)
Derivative trading liabilities	**(2,442)**	(3,953)	**(2,442)**	(3,953)
Total of financial instruments (liabilities)	**(29,564)**	(32,890)	**(29,265)**	(32,947)

4.3.2 Exceptions

Pragmatically, disclosure of fair values is not required for instruments such as short-term trade receivables and payables when their carrying amount reasonably approximates fair value.[63]

To align with the measurement provisions of IAS 39, fair values need not be given for investments in unquoted equity instruments, or derivatives linked to such instruments, that are measured at cost because their fair value cannot be measured reliably (see Chapter 18 at 4.4). However, these instruments are singled out for additional disclosure. This is to assist users of the financial statements in making their own judgements about the extent of possible differences between the carrying amount of such financial assets and liabilities and their fair value.[64] Particularly, disclosure should be made of the fact that they are measured at cost because their fair value cannot be reliably measured together with:

- a description of the instruments;
- their carrying amount;
- an explanation of why fair value cannot be measured reliably; and
- if possible, the range of estimates within which fair value is highly likely to lie.[65]

  Where such a range is provided, there is no explicit requirement to disclose the methods and significant assumptions information applied in determining those fair values, or other information equivalent to that set out at 4.3.1 above. However, such information is likely to be useful and relevant.

This information should include an explanation of the principal characteristics of the instruments that are pertinent to their value as well as information about the market for the instruments. The standard acknowledges that, in some cases, the disclosed terms and conditions (see 3.4 above) may provide sufficient information.[66]

Also, when it has a reasonable basis for doing so, management may indicate its opinion on the relationship between the instruments' fair value and carrying amount.[67] For example, management might have a reasonable basis for stating that the fair value of an investment or portfolio of investments is 'likely to be in excess' or 'significantly in excess' of cost.

If financial assets whose fair value previously could not be reliably measured are sold, that fact should be disclosed as well as:

- the carrying amount of such financial assets at the time of sale; and
- the amount of gain or loss recognised.[68]

As set out in Chapter 15 at 3.3 some instruments (normally life insurance policies) contain a discretionary participation feature. If the fair value of that feature cannot be reliably measured, that fact should be disclosed together with a description of the contract, its carrying amount, an explanation of why fair value cannot be measured reliably and, if possible, the range of estimates within which fair value is highly likely to lie.[69]

For all other financial instruments, the IASB believes it is reasonable to expect that fair value can be determined with sufficient reliability within constraints of timeliness and cost. It therefore concluded that there should be no exception from the requirement to disclose fair value information for these instruments.[70]

5 OTHER DISCLOSURES

5.1 Derecognition

Where certain arrangements in respect of financial assets have been entered into that do not qualify as a transfer of those assets and they continue to be recognised, or are recognised to the extent of the entity's continuing involvement, the following should be disclosed for each class of financial asset:

- the nature of the assets;
- the nature of the risks and rewards of ownership to which the entity remains exposed;
- when the entity continues to recognise all of the asset, the carrying amounts of the asset and of the associated liability; and
- when the entity continues to recognise the asset to the extent of its continuing involvement, the total amount of the asset, the amount of the asset that the entity continues to recognise and the carrying amount of the associated liability.[71]

This is a new disclosure requirement. It has been included in response to the revised derecognition provisions of IAS 39 because the IASB considers it will help users to evaluate the significance of such transactions. The types of arrangement for which such disclosures are required are discussed in Chapter 16 at 4. This disclosure may be required, for example, if an entity sells a portfolio of receivables and provides a limited guarantee of only one risk – the amount of the transferred receivables the transferor continues to recognise may be much riskier than the amount it derecognises.[72]

5.2   Defaults and breaches

With respect to defaults of principal, interest, sinking fund or redemption provisions during the period on loans payable recognised as at the balance sheet date, and any other breaches during the period of loan agreements when those breaches can permit the lender to demand repayment, the following information should be disclosed:

*   details of those breaches;

*   the amount recognised as at the balance sheet date in respect of the loans payable on which the breaches occurred; and

*   with respect to these amounts, whether the default has been remedied or the terms of the loans payable renegotiated before the date the financial statements were authorised for issue.[73]

However, disclosure is not required for breaches that are remedied, or in response to which the terms of the loan are renegotiated, on or before the balance sheet date.[74]

For these purposes, loans payable include issued debt instruments and financial liabilities other than short-term trade payables on normal credit terms.[75]

When such a breach has occurred during the period, and the breach was not remedied or the terms of the loan payable were not renegotiated by the balance sheet date, the standard includes a reminder that the effect of the breach on the classification of the liability as current or non-current is determined under IAS 1 (see Chapter 3 at 3.1.4).[76]

These are new requirements introduced into the revised standard to provide relevant information about an entity's creditworthiness and its prospects of obtaining future loans.[77] They also complement changes made to IAS 1 in this respect.

5.3   Reclassifications

Where a financial asset has been reclassified as one measured at cost or amortised cost rather than at fair value (see Chapter 15 at 7.5) the reason for that reclassification should be disclosed.[78]

5.4   Financial instruments at fair value through profit or loss

The decision by the IASB to allow any financial instrument to be designated at fair value through profit or loss was not an uncontroversial one, particularly insofar as it relates to non-derivative liabilities. In fact, the most common concern is not that such liabilities may be designated at fair value through profit or loss, it is the fact that the IASB's definition of fair value takes into account the instrument's credit risk which, depending on the terms of the instrument, will be based to a greater or lesser degree on the creditworthiness of the issuing entity.

Some commentators argued that recognising a gain or loss when there is a change in an entity's own creditworthiness results in potentially misleading information and that users may misinterpret the profit or loss effects of changes in credit risk, especially in the absence of disclosures.[79]

The IASB was not persuaded by any arguments to exclude changes in credit risk from the measurement of liabilities, but agreed that disclosure of the change in fair value of the financial liability that is caused by changes in its credit risk would help alleviate the concerns expressed. However, it noted that this would often not be practicable because it may not be possible to identify and measure reliably that part of the change in fair value separately. Consequently, IAS 32 calls for a 'reasonable proxy' of this information to be disclosed to provide users with information with which to understand the profit or loss effect of such a change in credit risk.[80]

Therefore, where a (non-derivative) financial *liability* has been *designated* at fair value through profit or loss, i.e. it is not classified as trading, the amount of change in its fair value that is not attributable to changes in a benchmark interest rate, e.g. LIBOR, should be disclosed.[81] For a liability whose fair value is determined on the basis of an observed market price, this amount can be estimated as follows:

(a)   first, the liability's internal rate of return at the start of the period is computed using the observed market price and contractual cash flows at that time and from this is deducted the benchmark interest rate at the start of the period, to arrive at an instrument specific component of the internal rate of return;

(b)   next, the present value of the liability is calculated using the liability's contractual cash flows at the start of the period and a discount rate equal to the sum of the benchmark interest rate at the end of the period and the instrument-specific component of the internal rate of return at the start of the period as determined in (a);

(c)   the amount determined in (b) is then decreased for any cash paid on the liability during the period and increased to reflect the increase in fair value that arises because the contractual cash flows are one period closer to their due date; and

(d)   the difference between the observed market price of the liability at the end of the period and the amount determined in (c) is the change in fair value that is not attributable to changes in the benchmark interest rate and this is the amount to be disclosed.[82]

In addition, the IASB concluded that the difference between the carrying amount of such a liability and the amount the entity would be contractually required to pay at maturity to the holder of the obligation should also be disclosed.[83] The fair value may differ significantly from the settlement amount, particularly for liabilities with a long duration when the entity has experienced a significant deterioration in creditworthiness subsequent to issuance.[84]

Finally, separate disclosure should be made of the carrying amounts of financial assets and liabilities that:

- are classified as held for trading; and
- were, upon initial recognition, designated as financial instruments at fair value through profit or loss (i.e. those that are not classified as held for trading).[85]

Although there is no difference in the accounting treatment for such instruments, this disclosure is intended to provide an indication of the extent to which financial assets and liabilities are *designated* at fair value through profit or loss and is considered useful because there are no restrictions on the items that can be so designated and because they do not meet the definition of held for trading.[86]

5.5 Collateral

The carrying amount of financial assets pledged as collateral for liabilities and for contingent liabilities should be separately disclosed, along with any material terms and conditions relating to those assets.[87] There is no explicit requirement to disclose the fair value of such assets, although entities may conclude that pledged assets constitute a separate class (see 2.3 above) in which case information about the fair value of such assets could be derived from the disclosures at 4.3 above.

It is very common to see information about non-financial, as well as financial, collateral where this is a principal term or condition of a borrowing. Examples of disclosure about collateral can be seen in Extracts 20.4 and 20.5 at 3.4 above, as well as in the following extract from the financial statements of TeliaSonera.

Extract 20.12: TeliaSonera AB (2003)

Notes to Consolidated Financial Statements IFRS/IAS [extract]

31.   Contingent Assets, Collateral Pledged and Contingent Liabilities [extract]

		December 31,	
SEK in millions	2003	2002	2001
Collateral pledged			
For derivative instruments:			
Blocked funds in bank accounts	–	–	5
For guarantee provisions:			
Blocked funds in bank accounts	1,168	–	–
For deposits from customers:			
Blocked funds in bank accounts	91	96	4
For off-balance sheet items:			
Blocked funds in bank accounts	–	6	–
For long-term liabilities to credit institutions:			
Real estate mortgages	20	20	–
Chattel mortgages	262	–	–
Current receivables	36	42	–
Shares in Turun Puhelin Oy	570	–	–
Shares in Suntel Ltd.	–	90	82
Shares in Svenska UMTS-nät AB	489	–	–
Shares in OAO MegaFon	153	119	–
Total	**2,789**	**373**	**91**

Some loan covenants agreed limit the scope for divesting or pledging certain assets.

When collateral has been accepted by an entity that it is permitted to sell or repledge in the absence of default by the owner, the following should be disclosed:

- the fair value of the collateral accepted (both financial and non-financial assets);

- the fair value of any such collateral sold or repledged and whether there is an obligation to return it; and

- any material terms and conditions associated with the use of this collateral.[88]

6   PRESENTATION ON THE FACE OF THE FINANCIAL STATEMENTS AND RELATED DISCLOSURES

Although it requires certain minimum disclosures, IAS 32 provides little guidance as to where financial instruments and related gains and losses should be presented on the face of the financial statements nor how such items should be disaggregated. Further, the disclosures required by IAS 32 need not always reflect how items are presented on the face of the statements. Therefore, for the time being at least, management must use its judgment in deciding how best to present much of the information relating to financial instruments, taking account of the minimum requirements of IAS 32 (and other related standards) as well as the provisions of IAS 1 (see Chapter 3 at 3) and, for relevant entities, IAS 30.

6.1 Income statement

6.1.1 Presentation on the face of the income statement

The effects of an entity's various activities, transactions and other events (including those relating to financial instruments) differ in frequency, potential for gain or loss and predictability. Accordingly, IAS 1 explains, disclosing the components of financial performance assists in providing an understanding of the financial performance achieved and in making projections of future results.[89]

IAS 1 prescribes minimum requirements for inclusion on the face of the income statement but only one caption, 'finance costs', clearly relates to financial instruments.[90]

Additional line items, headings and subtotals should be presented on the face of the income statement when such presentation is relevant to an understanding of the elements of an entity's financial performance. Factors that should be considered include materiality and the nature and function of the components of income and expenses. For example, a bank should amend the descriptions to apply the more specific requirements in IAS 30.[91]

The following items should also be disclosed on the face of the income statement as allocations of profit or loss for the period:

- profit or loss attributable to minority interest; and
- profit or loss attributable to equity holders of the parent.[92]

The amount of dividends recognised as distributions to equity holders during the period, and the related amount per share, may be disclosed on the face of the income statement. Alternatively, this information can be disclosed on the face of the statement of changes in equity or in the notes.[93]

6.1.2 Further analysis of gains and losses recognised in the income statement

IAS 32 requires disclosure of material items of income and expense and gains and losses resulting from financial assets and liabilities that are included in the income statement. It goes on to state that these items should include at least the following:

- total interest income, calculated using the effective interest method, for financial assets that are not at fair value through profit or loss;
- total interest expense on financial liabilities on the same basis;
- the amount of any gain or loss that was removed from equity in respect of available-for-sale financial assets and recognised in the income statement for the period; and
- the amount of interest income accrued on impaired financial assets.[94]

Whilst finance leases are included within the scope of IAS 32, strictly they are not accounted for using the effective interest method (although for most leases the method prescribed in IAS 17 – *Leases* – results in a very similar treatment). Accordingly, where material, finance income (charges) arising on finance leases should be shown separately from the interest income (expense) shown above.

IAS 18 – *Revenue* – also requires separate disclosure of interest income arising on assets that do not arise from leases.[95] In fact, it will often be appropriate to include such items within the same caption on the face of the income statement and include a sub-analysis in the notes.

Dividends classified as an expense (for example those payable to holders of redeemable preference shares) may be presented either with interest on other liabilities or as a separate item. Such items are subject to the requirements of IAS 1 (and, for relevant entities, IAS 30). In some circumstances, because of the differences between interest and dividends with respect to matters such as tax deductibility, it is desirable to disclose them separately in the income statement.[96]

The following extract shows one entity that discloses separately on the face of its income statement the accretion of a redemption premium on its subsidiary's zero dividend preference shares that are classified as liabilities in its consolidated financial statements.

Extract 20.13: Exeter Smaller Companies Income Fund Limited (2003)

Consolidated statement of operations

for the year ended 30 September 2003 [extract]	Note	1 October 2002 to 30 September 2003 £'000	1 October 2001 to 30 September 2002 £'000
Expenses [extract]	1		
Interest payable	4	**(348)**	(2,554)
Interest rate swap breakage costs	23	**(1,375)**	(1,147)
Amortisation on zero dividend preference shares	13	**(943)**	(865)
Notes to the financial statements [extract]			
13. Zero dividend preference shares		**2003** £'000	2002 £'000
Brought forward		**10,475**	9,610
Finance costs on zero dividend preference shares		**943**	865
At 30 September		**11,418**	10,475

In accordance with the articles of association of ESCIF Securities Limited, the holders of the 8,798,000 zero dividend preference shares, are entitled on a winding up to an amount equal to 100p per ZDP share as increased daily at the compound rate as would give a final capital entitlement of 183.24p on the ZDP repayment date, the first such increase occurring on 22 September 2000 and the last on the date of actual payment. At 30 September 2003 the accrued value was £11,418,013. Due to the fall in value of the portfolio the net assets available for the ZDP shareholders amounted to £5,563,831. This is the accrued value of £11,418,013 less the net liabilities of £5,563,182. At 30 September 2003, the fair value of the ZDP shares is £3,343,240 (2003: £1,055,760) based on a market offer price of 38 pence per share (2002: 12 pence per share).

The following gains and losses reported in the income statement should also be disclosed:

*   the amount of revenue arising from dividends;[97]

*   changes in fair value that relate to instruments at fair value through profit or loss.

The implementation guidance to IAS 39 explains that IAS 32 neither requires nor prohibits disclosure of components of the change in fair value by the way items are classified for internal purposes. For example, the change in fair value of those derivatives that IAS 39 classifies as held for trading but the entity classifies as part of risk management activities outside of the trading portfolio may be disclosed separately.[98]

Little guidance is given on other aspects of disaggregating gains and losses from instruments classified as at fair value through profit or loss. For example, the components of the change in fair value of a debt instrument can include:

- interest accruals;

- foreign currency retranslation;

- movements arising from changes in the issuer's credit risk; and

- changes in market interest rates.

An entity is neither required to disaggregate, nor prohibited from disaggregating, these components on the face of the income statement provided the minimum disclosure requirements are met (e.g. see 5.4 above). Accordingly, the interest accrual component, say, may be included separately within an interest receivable caption or it may be included within the same caption as other components of the gain or loss such as dealing profit;

- changes in fair value that relate to hedging instruments.[99]

Taken at face value, this particular disclosure will include, in aggregate, gains and losses on derivative hedging instruments that are part of a fair value hedge relationship and ineffectiveness recognised in the income statement in respect of hedging instruments that are part of either a cash flow hedge or a hedge of a net investment. In practice such an analysis will mean little and entities can be expected to disaggregate these amounts in a more appropriate manner.

Further, there is no explicit requirement to disclose changes in the fair value of assets or liabilities that are a hedged item in a fair value hedge. However, entities may choose to disclose such gains and losses in order to assist users to understand the effect of these hedges on their financial statements;

- the amount of exchange differences recognised in the income statement under IAS 21 – *The Effects of Changes in Foreign Exchange Rates* – except for those arising on financial instruments measured at fair value through profit or loss;[100] and

- the amount of any impairment loss recognised in the income statement in respect of financial assets – these should be disclosed separately for each significant class of financial asset, together with an indication of the nature of the loss.[101]

In IAS 1 it is explained that when items of income and expense are material, their nature and amount are required to be disclosed separately.[102] Circumstances that can give rise to separate disclosure include the disposal of investments[103] (e.g. available-for-sale assets) and the early settlement of liabilities. However, gains and losses should not be reported as extraordinary items, either on the face of the income statement or in the notes.[104]

6.1.3 Offsetting and hedges

IAS 1 explains that income and expenses should not be offset unless required or permitted by another standard. This is because offsetting detracts from the ability of users to understand fully the transactions, other events and conditions that have occurred and to assess the entity's future cash flows (except where it reflects the substance of the transaction or other event).[105] It goes on to explain that gains and losses on the disposal of non-current investments (such as many available-for-sale assets) are reported by deducting the carrying amount of the asset and related selling expenses from the proceeds on disposal rather than showing gross proceeds as revenue[106] – in the case of available-for-sale assets the profit or loss on disposal will also include any gains and losses that are recycled from equity. It also explains that gains and losses arising from groups of similar transactions should be reported on a net basis, for example gains and losses arising on financial instruments held for trading or foreign exchange differences. The individual transactions should, however, be reported separately if they are material.[107]

Whilst IAS 32 prescribes when financial assets and liabilities should be offset in the balance sheet (see Chapter 16 at 6) it contains no guidance on when related income and expenses should be offset. IAS 39 is largely silent on the subject too, but it does state that hedge accounting 'recognises the offsetting effects on profit or loss of changes in the fair values of the hedging instrument and the hedged item'.[108] This is a little short of an explicit requirement or permission for showing income or expenses net of related hedging gains and losses. However, it is entirely consistent with the objective of hedge accounting to include within an income statement caption related hedging gains and losses even if that results in a degree of offset. Further support for this position is found within IAS 30, which explains that income and expense items 'shall not be offset except for those relating to hedges and to assets and liabilities that have been offset…'.[109]

Example 20.1:   Hedge of a forecast sale

Company K has the euro as its functional currency. On 1 January 2005 it forecasts the sale of certain goods in dollars in six months and, to hedge that exposure, enters into a forward foreign exchange contract maturing on 1 July 2005. The hedge is designated as a cash flow hedge and meets the conditions for hedge accounting throughout the term of the hedge.

On 1 July 2005 the forecast sale occurs and is recorded using the prevailing spot rate resulting in, say, €1,000 being recognised in revenue. The forward contract is settled on this date at which point a related loss of, say, €100 has been recognised in equity.

The mechanics of cash flow hedge accounting require the €100 loss to be recycled out of equity and into the income statement on 1 July 2005. Using the analysis above, K presents the €100 loss as a deduction from revenue resulting in the hedged sale being recognised at a net amount of €900.

Although the €100 loss recycled out of equity is being offset in the income statement it will, however, be disclosed in the statement of changes in equity (see 6.2 below).

6.1.4 Embedded derivatives

IAS 39 states that it does not address whether embedded derivatives should be presented separately on the face of the financial statements.[110] In practice, it will depend on the nature both of the hybrid and the host whether related profits and losses are included in the same or separate income statement captions.

For example, an investment in a credit linked note that is accounted for as a debt instrument host and an embedded credit derivative might give rise to interest income and credit losses respectively that could well be reported in separate income statement captions. Alternatively, changes in the fair value of an embedded prepayment option in a host debt instrument that is accounted for separately may be included in the same income statement caption as interest on the debt instrument if the value of the option varies largely as a result of change in interest rates.

6.1.5 Entities whose share capital is not equity

Gains and losses related to changes in the carrying amount of a financial liability are recognised as income or expense in profit or loss even when they relate to an instrument that includes a right to the residual interest in the assets of the entity in exchange for cash or another financial asset, such as shares in mutual funds and co-operatives (see Chapter 17 at 3.2.2). Any gain or loss arising from the remeasurement of such an instrument should be presented separately on the face of the income statement when it is relevant in explaining the entity's performance.[111]

The following example illustrates an income statement format that may be used by entities such as mutual funds that do not have equity as defined in IAS 32, although other formats may be acceptable.

Example 20.2:   Income statement format for a mutual fund

Income statement for the year ended 31 December 2005[112]

	2005 €	2004 €
Revenue	2,956	1,718
Expenses (classified by nature or function)	(644)	(614)
Profit from operating activities	2,312	1,104
Finance costs		
– other finance costs	(47)	(47)
– distributions to members	(50)	(50)
Change in net assets attributable to unit holders	2,215	1,007

Although it may not be immediately clear, the final line item in this format is an expense. Therefore the entity's 'profit or loss' (as that term is used in IAS 1) for 2005 is €2,312 – €47 – €50 – €2,215 = €nil.

The next example illustrates an income statement format that may be used by entities whose share capital is not equity as defined in IAS 32 because the entity has an obligation to repay the share capital on demand, for example co-operatives, but which do have some equity. Again, other formats may be acceptable.

Example 20.3:   Income statement format for a co-operative

Income statement for the year ended 31 December 2005[113]

	2005	2004
	€	€
Revenue	472	498
Expenses (classified by nature or function)	(367)	(396)
Profit from operating activities	105	102
Finance costs		
– other finance costs	(4)	(4)
– distributions to members	(50)	(50)
Change in net assets attributable to members	51	48

In this example, the line item 'Finance costs – distributions to members' is an expense and the final line item is equivalent to 'profit or loss'.

Corresponding balance sheet formats for both of these examples are shown at 6.3.3 below.

6.2   Statement of changes in equity

IAS 1 requires the presentation of a statement of changes in equity that includes the profit or loss for the period as well as other items of income and expense not recognised within profit or loss.[114] Material items of income and expense and gains and losses that result from financial assets and liabilities and are included in equity are required to be disclosed separately and should include at least the following:

- changes in fair value of available-for-sale financial assets,[115] including:
  - the amount of any gain or loss recognised directly in equity during the period; and
  - the amount that was removed from equity and recognised in the income statement for the period; and[116]
- for cash flow hedges:
  - the amount of gains or losses on designated hedging instruments recognised in equity during the period;
  - the amount removed from equity during the period and reported in the income statement; and
  - the amount removed from equity during the period and included in the initial measurement of the acquisition cost of hedged non-financial assets or liabilities.[117]

The implementation guidance to IAS 39 states that disclosure should be provided of changes in the fair value of hedging instruments that are recognised in equity.[118] This will include, in aggregate, gains and losses on hedging instruments in both cash flow hedges and hedges of net investments. However, this may often be dealt with by presenting for hedges of net investments similar information to that noted above for cash flow hedges.

The following information in respect of transactions in equity instruments should be shown either on the face of the statement of changes in equity or in the notes:

- the amounts of transactions with equity holders acting in their capacity as equity holders, showing distributions separately; and

- a reconciliation between the carrying amount of each class of contributed equity and each reserve at the beginning and the end of the period, separately disclosing each change.[119]

In addition, IAS 32 notes that the amount of transaction costs accounted for as a deduction from equity in the period should disclosed separately.[120]

If an entity reacquires its own equity instruments from related parties disclosure should be provided in accordance with IAS 24 – *Related Party Disclosures* (see Chapter 33).[121]

If an entity such as a mutual fund or a co-operative has no issued equity instruments, it may still need to present a statement of changes in equity. For example, such an entity may have gains or losses arising on available-for-sale assets that are recognised in equity.

6.3   Balance sheet

6.3.1   Assets and liabilities

IAS 1 does not prescribe the order or format in which items are to be presented on the face of the balance sheet, but states that the following items relating to financial instruments, are sufficiently different in nature or function to warrant separate presentation:

- trade and other receivables;
- cash and cash equivalents;
- other financial assets;
- trade and other payables;
- provisions; and
- other financial liabilities.[122]

However, additional line items, headings and subtotals should be presented on the face of the balance sheet when the size, nature or function of an item or aggregation of similar items is such that separate presentation is relevant to an understanding of the entity's financial position.[123] The judgement on whether additional items are presented separately should be based on an assessment of:

- the nature and liquidity of assets;
- the function of assets within the entity; and
- the amounts, nature and timing of liabilities.[124]

The descriptions used and the ordering of items or aggregation of similar items may be amended according to the nature of the entity and its transactions, to provide information that is relevant to an understanding of the entity's financial position. For example, banks should amend the captions and apply the more specific requirements in IAS 30.[125]

Although, for measurement purposes, IAS 39 classifies financial assets into four categories (see Chapter 15 at 7), other descriptors for these categories or other categorisations may be used when presenting information on the face of the financial statements.[126]

However, the use of different measurement bases for different classes of assets suggests that their nature or function differs and, therefore, that they should be presented as separate line items.[127] For example, loans and receivables measured at amortised cost would often be presented separately from available-for-sale assets measured at fair value.

As noted at 6.1.3 above, IAS 39 states that it does not address whether embedded derivatives should be presented separately on the face of the financial statements[128] and this applies to the balance sheet as much as to the income statement. However, the guidance in the previous paragraph suggests that embedded derivatives will often be presented separately on the face of the balance sheet.

Further sub-classifications of the line items presented should be disclosed, either on the face of the balance sheet or in the notes, classified in a manner appropriate to the entity's operations.[129] The detail provided in sub-classifications will depend on the size, nature and function of the amounts involved and will vary for each item. For example, receivables should be disaggregated into amounts receivable from trade customers, receivables from related parties and other amounts. Assets included within receivables that are not financial instruments, such as many prepayments, should also be shown separately.[130]

6.3.2 *Equity*

IAS 1 explains that, as a minimum, the face of the balance sheet should include line items that present the following amounts within equity:

- minority interest, presented within equity; and
- issued capital and reserves attributable to equity holders of the parent.[131]

As for assets and liabilities, additional line items, headings and subtotals should be presented on the face of the balance sheet when such presentation is relevant to an understanding of the entity's financial position[132] and further sub-classifications of the line items presented should be disclosed, either on the face of the balance sheet or in the notes, classified in a manner appropriate to the entity's operations.[133] The detail provided in the sub-classifications will depend on the size, nature and function of the amounts involved and will vary for each item. For example, equity capital and reserves should be disaggregated into various classes, such as paid-in capital, share premium and reserves.[134] A description of the nature and purpose of each reserve within equity should also be provided.[135]

For each class of share capital, the following information should be disclosed, either on the face of the balance sheet or in the notes:

- the number of shares authorised;

- the number of shares issued and fully paid, and issued but not fully paid;

- par value per share, or that the shares have no par value;

- a reconciliation of the number of shares outstanding at the beginning and at the end of the period;

- the rights, preferences and restrictions attaching to that class including restrictions on the distribution of dividends and the repayment of capital;

- shares in the entity held by the entity or by its subsidiaries (treasury shares[136]) or associates; and

- shares reserved for issue under options and contracts for the sale of shares, including the terms and amounts.[137]

An entity without share capital, such as a partnership or trust, should disclose equivalent information, showing changes during the period in each category of equity interest, and the rights, preferences and restrictions attaching to each category of equity interest[138] (assuming of course it has actually issued instruments that meet the definition of equity).

6.3.3 Entities whose share capital is not equity

Continuing Examples 20.2 and 20.3 at 6.1.5 above, the following examples illustrate corresponding balance sheet formats that may be used by entities such as mutual funds that do not have equity as defined in IAS 32, or entities such as co-operatives whose share capital is not equity as defined in IAS 32 because the entity has an obligation to repay the share capital on demand.

Example 20.4: Balance sheet format for a mutual fund

Balance sheet at 31 December 2005[139]

	2005 €	2005 €	2004 €	2004 €
ASSETS				
Non-current assets (classified in accordance with IAS 1)	91,374		78,484	
Total non-current assets		91,374		78,484
Current assets (classified in accordance with IAS 1)	1,422		1,769	
Total current assets		1,422		1,769
Total assets		92,796		80,253
LIABILITIES				
Current liabilities (classified in accordance with IAS 1)	647		66	
Total current liabilities		(647)		(66)
Non-current liabilities excluding net assets attributable to unit holders (classified in accordance with IAS 1)	280		136	
		(280)		(136)
Net assets attributable to unit holders		91,869		80,051

As for the equivalent income statement format, it may not be immediately clear what the final line item in this format represents. It is, in fact, a liability and therefore the entity's 'equity' (as that term is used in IAS 1) at the end of 2005 is €92,796 – €647 – €280 – €91,869 = €nil.

Example 20.5:   Balance sheet format for a co-operative

Balance sheet at 31 December 2005[140]

	2005		2004	
	€	€	€	€
ASSETS				
Non-current assets (classified in accordance with IAS 1)	908		830	
Total non-current assets		908		830
Current assets (classified in accordance with IAS 1)	383		350	
Total current assets		383		350
Total assets		1,291		1,180
LIABILITIES				
Current liabilities (classified in accordance with IAS 1)	372		338	
Share capital repayable on demand	202		161	
Total current liabilities		(574)		(499)
Total assets less current liabilities		717		681
Non-current liabilities (classified in accordance with IAS 1)	187		196	
		187		196
RESERVES*				
Reserves, e.g. revaluation reserve, retained earnings	530		485	
		530		485
		717		681
MEMORANDUM NOTE TOTAL MEMBERS' INTERESTS				
Share capital repayable on demand		202		161
Reserves		530		485
		732		646

*In this example, the entity has no obligation to deliver a share of its reserves to its members.

The line item 'Share capital repayable on demand' is part of the entity's liabilities and the items within 'Reserves' represent its equity.

Although not required by IAS 1, an entity adopting this type of balance sheet format may choose to present an analysis of movements in (or reconciliation of) total members' interests if this is considered to provide useful information; this would not remove the need to present a statement of changes in equity.

6.4 Cash flow statement

The implementation guidance to IAS 39 acknowledges that the terminology in IAS 7 – *Cash Flow Statements* – was not updated to reflect the publication of IAS 39 (neither the original nor revised version) but does explain that the classification of cash flows arising from hedging instruments within the cash flow statement should be consistent with the classification of these instruments as hedging instruments. In other words, such cash flows should be classified as operating, investing or financing activities, on the basis of the classification of the cash flows arising from the hedged item.[141]

7 EFFECTIVE DATE, TRANSITIONAL PROVISIONS AND FIRST-TIME ADOPTION

7.1 Effective date

The revised version of IAS 32 must be applied for annual periods beginning on or after 1 January 2005. Entities are 'permitted' (rather than 'encouraged', as in the case of other recently issued standards) to adopt the standard in earlier periods, but must disclose that they have done so. They must also adopt both IAS 32 and IAS 39 at the same time and must adopt IAS 39 as amended in March 2004, not as originally issued.[142]

7.2 Transitional provisions

IAS 32 should be applied retrospectively[143] and no transitional concessions are granted. Therefore disclosures under the revised standard should be given in full for all corresponding periods.

7.3 First-time adoption

IFRS 1 – *First-time Adoption of International Financial Reporting Standards* – is dealt with comprehensively in Chapter 4 and the particular aspects of that standard applying to financial instruments are principally covered at 2.6 of that chapter. The aspects related to the topics covered in this chapter are summarised below. Further similar sections are included in Chapters 15 to 19.

7.3.1 Exemption from the requirement to restate comparatives

The IASB issued the revised versions of IAS 32 and IAS 39 in December 2003; and the amendment to IAS 39– *Fair Value Hedge Accounting for a Portfolio Hedge of Interest Rate Risk* – in March 2004. To allow entities adopting IFRS for the first time before 1 January 2006 sufficient time to comply with the requirements of those standards, the IASB decided not to require them to prepare comparative information under IAS 32 and IAS 39.[144] Instead, a first-time adopter that chooses to present comparative information that does not comply with IAS 32 and IAS 39 in its first year of transition should:

- apply its previous GAAP in the comparative information to financial instruments that are within the scope of IAS 32 and IAS 39. In other words, this exemption also affects the application of certain aspects of other standards. For example, it overrides the requirements of IAS 1 on the balance sheet presentation of financial instruments; and

- make certain additional disclosures (see below).[145]

(A similar exemption applies to insurance contracts within the scope of IFRS 4.)

In applying this exemption a first-time adopter should be aware of the following:

- the wording of the standard does not explicitly require the exemption to be applied to IAS 32 and IAS 39 as a package. Even though the transitional provisions in both IAS 32 and IAS 39 that require the standards to be adopted simultaneously do not apply to first-time adopters, the IASB clearly intended both standards to be adopted simultaneously. In any case, the many cross-references between the two standards make it virtually impossible to adopt one of the standards without the other. Therefore, we believe that the exemption applies to IAS 32 and IAS 39 as a package; and

- the exemption only covers items that are within the scope of IAS 32 and IAS 39 (and IFRS 4). The comparative information relating to all other items must be restated under IFRS.

Where an entity makes this election, it needs to:[146]

- disclose that the comparative information does not comply with IAS 32 and IAS 39, but that it has been prepared on the basis of its previous GAAP;

- disclose the nature, but not the amount, of the main adjustments that would make the information comply with IAS 32 and IAS 39; and

- treat any adjustment between the balance sheet at the comparative period's reporting date and the start of the first IFRS reporting period as arising from a change in accounting policy. This difference is accounted for as an adjustment to the opening balance of each affected component of equity at the start of the first IFRS reporting period.[147] The entity is required to make the disclosures prescribed by paragraphs 28(a)-(e) and (f)(i) of IAS 8 – *Accounting Policies, Changes in Accounting Estimates and Errors* (see Chapter 3 at 6.1.2 A).[148]

Originally, IFRS 1 also required first-time adopters to prepare comparative information that complied with IAS 32 and IAS 39 because this improved 'comparability within the first IFRS financial statements' and because the IASB believed that this should not be a problem for entities that planned the adoption of IFRS in a timely manner.[149] Unfortunately, the less-than-timely publication of the revised versions of IAS 32 and IAS 39 obliged the IASB to exempt entities adopting IFRS before 1 January 2006 from applying these standards in preparing comparative information.

7.3.2 Designation of financial instruments

As set out in Chapter 15 at 8.3.2 B and E, first time adopters may designate previously recognised financial assets or liabilities at fair value through profit or loss or financial assets as available-for-sale. Where this is done the following should be disclosed for each of those categories:

- the fair value of any financial assets or financial liabilities designated into it; and
- the classification and carrying amount in the previous financial statements.[150]

7.3.3 Other disclosures

IFRS 1 contains many other disclosure requirements that apply to financial instruments as well as other items in the financial statements, such as reconciliations designed to assist a user of the financial statements understand how the transition to IFRS has been effected. These requirements are covered in Chapter 4.

8   FUTURE DEVELOPMENTS

In 2001 the IASB inherited from the IASC a project principally focused on revising IAS 30. This project was taken onto the IASB's initial technical agenda, but has now evolved into a comprehensive review of all disclosure requirements related to financial instruments, not just for banks and similar financial institutions.

The project has progressed and an exposure draft of a new standard[151] was published in July 2004, which the IASB plans to convert into a standard in 2005. This is not part of the IASB's 'stable platform' for mandatory adoption in 2005 and it is likely that adoption of the new standard will only be required for periods commencing on or after 1 January 2007.

The new standard would apply to all risks arising from virtually all financial instruments. Also, it would apply to all entities, including those with few financial instruments (e.g. a manufacturer whose only financial instruments are accounts receivable and accounts payable) as well as those that have many financial instruments (e.g. a financial institution most of whose assets and liabilities are financial instruments).[152]

The proposals would require disclosure of the significance of financial instruments to an entity's financial position and performance and incorporate many of the requirements previously in IAS 32.[153] Consequently, all disclosure requirements currently included within IAS 32 would be withdrawn, leaving that as a standard dealing with only the presentation of financial instruments; IAS 30 would be withdrawn completely.

In addition to the requirements currently included in IAS 32, the proposals would require:

(a)   enhanced balance sheet and income statement disclosures; and

(b)   disclosures about an allowance account when one is used to reduce the carrying amount of impaired financial assets.[154]

Qualitative and quantitative disclosures about exposure to risks arising from financial instruments would be required. The qualitative disclosures would describe management's objectives, policies and processes for managing those risks. The quantitative disclosures would provide information about the extent to which the entity is exposed to risk, based on information provided internally to the entity's key management personnel. Together, these proposed disclosures are intended to provide an overview of the entity's use of financial instruments and the exposures to risks they create.[155] Specified minimum disclosures about credit risk, liquidity risk and market risk (including interest rate risk) are proposed.[156]

The proposals would also require disclosure of qualitative information about an entity's objectives, policies and processes for managing capital, quantitative data about the instruments the entity regards as capital and any capital targets set by management. More controversially, disclosure would also be required of the nature of externally imposed capital requirements and how they are managed by the entity. Of particular concern is a proposal to require disclosure of information regarding breaches of those capital requirements.[157]

The exposure draft is accompanied by implementation guidance that describes how the proposed disclosures might be provided and illustrative examples that illustrative the application of the capital disclosure requirements.[158]

References

1 IAS 32, *Financial Instruments: Disclosure and Presentation*, IASB, December 2003 (amended March 2004), para. 1.
2 IAS 32, para. 2.
3 IAS 32, para. 3.
4 IAS 32, para. 2.
5 IAS 32, para. AG24.
6 IAS 32, para. 52.
7 IAS 32, para. 53.
8 IAS 32, para. 54.
9 IAS 32, para. 55.
10 IAS 32, para. 53.
11 IAS 32, para. 55.
12 IAS 32, para. 56.
13 IAS 32, para. 57.
14 IAS 32, para. 58.

15 IAS 32, paras. 60 and 66.
16 IAS 32, para. 61.
17 IAS 32, para. 62.
18 IAS 32, para. 60.
19 IAS 32, para. 60.
20 IAS 32, para. 62.
21 IAS 32, para. 63.
22 IAS 32, para. 64.
23 IAS 32, para. 65.
24 IAS 32, para. 68.
25 IAS 32, para. 67.
26 IAS 32, para. 69.
27 IAS 32, para. 70.
28 IAS 32, para. 71.
29 IAS 32, para. 72.
30 IAS 32, paras. 94(d) and BC42.
31 IAS 32, para. 73.
32 IAS 32, para. 74.
33 IAS 32 (revised 2000), *Financial Instruments: Disclosure and Presentation*, October 2000, para. 64.
34 IAS 32, para. 74.
35 IAS 32, para. 75.
36 IAS 32, para. 77.
37 IAS 32, para. 76.
38 IAS 32, para. 77.
39 IAS 32, para. 78.
40 IAS 32, para. 79.
41 IAS 32, para. 79.
42 IAS 32, para. 80.
43 IAS 32, para. 81.
44 IAS 32, para. 82.
45 IAS 32, paras. 83-84.
46 IAS 32, para. 85.
47 IAS 32, para. 84.
48 IAS 32, para. 83.
49 IAS 32, para. 87.
50 IAS 32, para. 87.
51 IAS 32, para. 86.
52 IAS 32, para. 89.
53 IAS 32, para. 92.
54 IAS 32, para. 93.
55 IAS 32, para. 92.
56 IAS 32, para. BC36.
57 IAS 32, para. BC49(i).
58 IAS 32, para. BC36.
59 IAS 32, para. 58(b).
60 IAS 39, *Financial Instruments: Recognition and Measurement*, IASB, December 2003 (amended March 2004), para. F.1.12.
61 IAS 32 (2000), paras. 88-90.
62 IAS 32, para. BC37.
63 IAS 32, para. 88.
64 IAS 32, para. 91.
65 IAS 32, para. 90.
66 IAS 32, para. 91.
67 IAS 32, para. 91.
68 IAS 32, para. 90.
69 IAS 32, para. 91A.
70 IAS 32, para. BC35.
71 IAS 32, para. 94(a).
72 IAS 32, para. BC38.
73 IAS 32, para. 94(j).
74 IAS 32, para. 94(j).
75 IAS 32, para. 95.
76 IAS 32, para. 95.
77 IAS 32, para. BC48.
78 IAS 32, para. 94(g).
79 IAS 32, para. BC45.
80 IAS 32, paras. BC44 and BC46.
81 IAS 32, para. 94(f)(i).
82 IAS 32, para. AG40.
83 IAS 32, para. 94(f)(ii).
84 IAS 32, para. BC47.
85 IAS 32, para. 94(e).
86 IAS 32, para. BC43.
87 IAS 32, para. 94(b).
88 IAS 32, para. 94(c).
89 IAS 1, *Presentation of Financial Statements*, IASB, December 2003 (amended March 2004), para. 84.
90 IAS 1, para. 81(b).
91 IAS 1, paras. 83-84.
92 IAS 1, para. 82.
93 IAS 1, para. 95.
94 IAS 32, para. 94(h).
95 IAS 18, *Revenue*, IASB, December 1993 (amended March 2004), paras. 6(a) and 35(b)(iii).
96 IAS 32, para. 40.
97 IAS 18, para. 35(b)(iv).
98 IAS 39, para. G.1.
99 IAS 39, para. G.1.
100 IAS 21, *The Effects of Changes in Foreign Exchange Rates*, IASB, December 2003, para. 52(a).
101 IAS 32, para. 94(i).
102 IAS 1, para. 86.
103 IAS 1, para. 87.
104 IAS 1, para. 85.
105 IAS 1, paras. 32-33.
106 IAS 1, para. 34.
107 IAS 1, para. 35.
108 IAS 39, para. 85.
109 IAS 30, *Disclosures in the Financial Statements of Banks and Similar Financial Institutions*, IASB, August 1990 (amended December 2003), para. 13.
110 IAS 39, para. 11.
111 IAS 32, para. 41.
112 IAS 32, para. IE32.
113 IAS 32, para. IE33.
114 IAS 1, paras. 8 and 96.
115 IAS 39, para. G.1.
116 IAS 32, para. 94(h).
117 IAS 32, para. 59.

118 IAS 39, para. G.1.
119 IAS 1, para. 97.
120 IAS 32, para. 39.
121 IAS 32, para. 34.
122 IAS 1, paras. 68 and 71.
123 IAS 1, paras. 69 and 71(a).
124 IAS 1, para. 72.
125 IAS 1, para. 71(b).
126 IAS 39, para. 45.
127 IAS 1, para. 73.
128 IAS 39, para. 11.
129 IAS 1, para. 74.
130 IAS 1, para. 75(b).
131 IAS 1, paras. 68(o)-(p).
132 IAS 1, para. 69.
133 IAS 1, para. 74.
134 IAS 1, para. 75(e).
135 IAS 1, para. 76(b).
136 IAS 32, para. 34.
137 IAS 1, para. 76(a).
138 IAS 1, para. 77.
139 IAS 32, para. IE32.
140 IAS 32, para. IE33.
141 IAS 39, para. G.2.
142 IAS 32, para. 96 and IAS 39, para. 103.
143 IAS 32, para. 97.
144 IFRS 1, *First-time Adoption of International Financial Reporting Standards*, IASB, June 2003 (amended March 2004), para. BC89A.
145 IFRS 1, para. 36A.
146 IFRS 1, para. 36A.
147 IAS 8, *Accounting Policies, Changes in Accounting Estimates and Errors*, IASB, December 2003, (amended March 2004), para. 24.
148 IAS 8, para. 28.
149 IFRS 1, para. BC89.
150 IFRS 1, para. 43A.
151 Exposure Draft ED 7, *Financial Instruments: Disclosures*, IASB, July 2004.
152 ED 7, para. IN4.
153 ED 7, para. IN5.
154 ED 7, para. IN6.
155 ED 7, para. IN7.
156 ED 7, para. IN8.
157 ED 7, paras. IN9 and 46.
158 ED 7, para. IN10.

Chapter 21   Inventories

1   INTRODUCTION

Under IAS the relevant standard for inventories (called 'stock' in some jurisdictions) is IAS 2 – *Inventories*. Long-term contracts and the associated work in progress are the subject of a separate standard, IAS 11 – *Construction contracts* – which is dealt with in Chapter 22. The term 'inventories' includes raw materials, work-in-progress, finished goods and goods for resale, although the standard does not include all instances of these categories; some are covered by other standards. This chapter deals only with the inventories within the scope of IAS 2.

1.1   Objectives of inventory measurement

Historically, the principal objective of inventory measurement within the historical cost accounting system has been the proper determination of income through the process of matching costs with related revenues. Costs of inventories comprise expenditure which has been incurred in the normal course of business in bringing the product or service to its present location and condition. All costs incurred in respect of inventories are charged as period costs, except for those which relate to those unconsumed inventories which are expected to be of future benefit to the entity. These are carried forward, to be matched with the revenues that they will generate in the future. Therefore, in measuring income under the historical cost system, inventories in the balance sheet have characteristics similar to those of prepaid expenses or property, plant and equipment – they are effectively deferred costs.

The IASB is clearly moving in the direction of stating all assets and liabilities at fair value. In line with this policy the revised version of IAS 2, published in late 2003 as a result of the IASB's Improvements project, has had all references to matching and to the historical cost system deleted. However, the second objective of inventory measurement – which is to define the basis on which inventory is presented in the balance sheet – has become increasingly important in the light of the current conceptual framework debate set out in Chapter 2.

1.2   Cost flow assumptions

In many industries, particularly those dealing in fast moving consumer goods or non-deteriorating raw material inventories, inventory movements are not tracked individually by the accounting system. Rather some sort of aggregation takes place and the cost of inventory sold, used, or transferred to work-in-progress, is calculated based on the number or quantity used up, multiplied by the price paid for that item. However, as buying prices for inventories often change, it has been necessary to develop systematic bases for the recognition of the cost of sales, founded on certain cost flow assumptions. The principal methods used are outlined below.

1.2.1   Specific identification/actual cost

Where it is both possible and practicable to attach a specific cost to each item of inventory, the costs of goods sold are specifically identified and matched with the goods physically sold. In practice this is a relatively unusual method of valuation, as the clerical effort required does not make it feasible unless there are relatively few high value items being bought or produced. Consequently, it would normally be used where the inventory comprised items such as antiques, jewellery and cars in the hands of dealers.

1.2.2   FIFO (first-in, first-out)

In the vast majority of businesses it will not be practicable to keep track of the cost of identical items of inventory on an individual unit basis; nevertheless, it is desirable to approximate to the actual physical flows as far as possible. The FIFO method probably gives the closest approximation to actual cost flows, since it is assumed that when inventories are sold or used in a production process, the oldest are sold or used first. Consequently the balance of inventory on hand at any point represents the most recent purchases or production.[1] This can best be illustrated in the context of a business which deals in perishable goods (e.g. food retailers) since clearly such a business will use the first goods received earliest. The FIFO method, by allocating the earliest costs incurred against revenue, matches actual cost flows with the physical flow of goods reasonably accurately. In any event, even in the case of businesses which do not deal in perishable goods, this would reflect what would probably be a sound management policy. Therefore, in practice where it is not possible to value inventory on an actual cost basis, the FIFO method is generally used since it is most likely to approximate the physical flow of goods sold, resulting in the most accurate measurement of cost flows.

1.2.3   Weighted average

This method, which like FIFO is suitable where inventory units are identical or near identical, involves the computation of an average unit cost by dividing the total cost of units by the number of units. The average unit cost then has to be revised with every receipt of inventory, or alternatively at the end of predetermined periods.[2] In practice, weighted average systems are widely used in packaged inventory systems that are computer controlled, although its results are not very different from FIFO in times of relatively low inflation, or where inventory turnover is relatively quick.

Nevertheless, there are certain businesses which hold large quantities of relatively homogeneous inventory for which the weighted average method of inventory valuation is the most appropriate.

1.2.4   LIFO (last-in, first-out)

This method is, as its name suggests, the opposite to FIFO and assumes that the most recent purchases or production are used first. In certain cases this could represent the physical flow of inventory (e.g. if a store is filled and emptied from the top). LIFO is an attempt to match current costs with current revenues so that the profit and loss account excludes the effects of holding gains. Essentially, therefore, LIFO is an attempt to achieve something closer to replacement cost accounting for the profit and loss account, whilst disregarding the balance sheet. Consequently, the period-end balance of inventory on hand represents the earliest purchases of the item, resulting in inventories being stated in the balance sheet at amounts which may bear little relationship to recent cost levels. Since the revised version of IAS 2 was issued, with effect from periods beginning on 1 January 2005, the use of LIFO is not permitted by IAS 2. This would include comparative figures.

2   THE REQUIREMENTS OF IAS 2

2.1   Scope and definitions

IAS 2 applies to inventories in all financial statements except work-in-progress arising under construction contracts including directly related service contracts (both of which are dealt with by IAS 11, see Chapter 22), financial instruments, biological assets related to agricultural activity and agricultural produce at the point of harvest.[3]

The provisions of the standard do not apply to the measurement of inventories held by:

(a)   producers of agricultural and forest products, agricultural produce after harvest, and minerals and mineral products, to the extent that they are measured at net realisable value in accordance with well-established practices in those industries.[4] Agricultural products after harvest and minerals that have been extracted may be the subject of government price support or a forward contract.[5] When such inventories are measured at net realisable value, changes are recognised in profit or loss in the period of the change.

(b)   commodity broker-traders who measure their inventories at fair value less costs to sell. If these inventories are measured at fair value less costs to sell, the changes are recognised in profit or loss in the period of the change.[6] The broker traders' inventories are those that have been bought with the intention of trading and generating a profit from fluctuations in price or broker-traders' margin.[7]

In either case, the standard stresses that these inventories are scoped out only from the measurement requirements of IAS 2, i.e. not from the standard's other requirements.

Inventories are defined by IAS 2 as:

(a)   assets held for sale in the ordinary course of business;

(b)   assets in the process of production for such sale; or

(c)   materials or supplies to be consumed in the production process or in the rendering of services.[8]

The standard's basic rule is that inventories should be measured at the lower of cost and net realisable value.[9] Net realisable value is 'the estimated selling price in the ordinary course of business less the estimated costs of completion and the estimated costs necessary to make the sale.'[10] Fair value is 'the amount for which an asset could be exchanged, or a liability settled, between knowledgeable, willing parties in an arm's length transaction.'[11] The standard points out that net realisable value is an entity-specific value – the amount that the entity actually expects to make from selling that particular inventory – while fair value is not. Therefore, net realisable value may not be the same as fair value less costs to sell.[12]

Inventories can include all types of goods purchased and held for resale including, for example, merchandise purchased by a retailer and other tangible assets such as land and other property held for resale, though investment property accounted for under IAS 40 is not treated as an inventory item. The term also encompasses finished goods produced, or work in progress being produced by the entity, and includes materials and supplies awaiting use in the production process. If the entity is a service provider, its inventories may be intangible (e.g. the costs of the service for which the entity has not yet recognised the related revenue).[13] The inventory of service providers will probably consist mainly of the labour costs of the people providing the service.

2.2   Measurement

As stated above, inventories must be measured at the lower of cost and net realisable value.[14] This inevitably raises the question of what may be included in an inventory's cost.

2.2.1   *What may be included in cost*

The costs attributed to inventories under IAS 2 comprise all costs of purchase, costs of conversion and other costs incurred in bringing the inventories to their present location and condition.[15] These costs include import duties and other unrecoverable taxes, transport and other costs directly attributable to the inventories; but trade discounts and similar rebates should be deducted from the costs attributed to inventories.[16]

Costs of conversion include direct costs such as direct labour, and also overheads. Overhead costs must be apportioned using a 'systematic allocation of fixed and variable production overheads that are incurred in converting materials into finished goods'.[17] The standard also suggests that there may be indirect materials and labour that vary with the volume of production.[18] Fixed production overheads are indirect costs that remain relatively constant over a wide range of production, such as building and equipment maintenance and depreciation, and factory management and administration expenses. The allocation of fixed production overheads is to be based on the normal capacity of the facilities. Normal capacity is defined as 'the production expected to be achieved on average over a number of periods or seasons under normal circumstances, taking into account the loss of capacity resulting from planned maintenance.'[19] While actual capacity may be used if it approximates to normal capacity, increased overheads may not be allocated to production as a result of low output or idle capacity. In these cases the unrecovered overheads must be expensed. The contrary situation is also considered; in periods of abnormally high production, the fixed overhead absorption must be reduced as otherwise inventories would be recorded at an amount in excess of cost.[20]

Extract 21.1 below shows how Voestalpine AG describe the inclusion of overheads in its inventory valuations.

Extract 21.1: Voestalpine AG (2004)

Notes to the Consolidated Financial Statements using IFRS [extract]
D.   Accounting and Valuation Principles [extract]
Current assets

Inventories comprise raw materials, supplies and consumables as well as merchandise valued at acquisition cost and products valued at manufacturing cost. Should the net realisable be lower on the balance sheet date, due to a decrease in prices on the stock exchange or the market, those lower values are presented.

Manufacturing costs comprise exclusively directly associated cost (manufacturing material, manufacturing wages) and pro-rated general materials and manufacturing costs based on capacity utilization. General administrative expenses and expenses for voluntary social contributions and contributions to the company's retirement provisions and interest on borrowed capital are not recognized as manufacturing costs.

Acquisition and manufacturing costs are determined for similar assets based on the method of weighted average prices or similar methods. For risks to the inventory, appropriate discounts due to storage time or reduced usability are calculated.

IAS 2 mentions the treatment to be adopted when a production process results in the output of more than one product, for example a main product and a by-product. If the costs of converting each product are not separately identifiable, they should be allocated between the products on a rational and consistent basis, for example this might be the relative sales value of each of the products. If the value of the by-product is immaterial, it may be measured at net realisable value and this value deducted from the cost of the main product.[21]

Other costs are to be included in inventories only to the extent that they bring them into their present location and condition. An example is given in IAS 2 of design costs for a special order for a particular customer as being allowable,[22] and as a result other non-production overheads may possibly be appropriately included. However a number of examples are given of costs that are specifically disallowed. These include:

(a)   abnormal amounts of wasted materials, labour, or other production costs;

(b)   storage costs, unless those costs are necessary in the production process prior to a further production stage;

(c)   administrative overheads that do not contribute to bringing inventories to their present location and condition; and

(d)   selling costs.[23]

IAS 2 states that, in limited circumstances, borrowing costs may be included in the costs of inventories.[24] These circumstances are identified in IAS 23 – *Borrowing Costs* – discussed in Chapter 14. However, these circumstances would appear to be extremely limited. The standard states that on some occasions, an entity might purchase inventories on deferred settlement terms, accompanied by a price increase that effectively makes the arrangement a combined purchase and financing. Under these circumstances the price difference is to be recognised as an interest expense over the period of the financing.[25]

IAS 2 deals specifically with the inventories of service providers – effectively their work-in-progress. For this type of business, IAS allows the labour and other costs of personnel directly engaged in providing the service, including supervisory personnel and attributable overheads, to be included in the cost of inventories. However, labour and other costs relating to sales and general administrative personnel must be expensed as incurred and inventories should not include profit margins or non-attributable overheads.[26]

Agricultural produce that has been harvested by the entity from its biological assets, is initially recognised at its fair value, less estimated point of sale costs at the point of harvest, as set out in IAS 41 – *Agriculture* (see Chapter 36). This figure becomes the cost of inventories at that date for the purposes of IAS 2.[27]

2.2.2 Cost measurement methods

IAS 2 specifically allows the use of standard costing methods, or of the retail method (see 3.3 below) provided that the method gives a result which approximates to cost. Standard costs should take into account normal levels of materials and supplies, labour, efficiency and capacity utilisation. They must be regularly reviewed and revised where necessary.[28] Where the retail method is used, an appropriate gross margin may be applied, though adjustments must be made to take into account any inventory marked down for sale below its cost, if material amounts are involved.[29]

Items that are not interchangeable and goods or services produced for specific projects should have their costs specifically identified.[30] However, this method is inappropriate where there are large numbers of items that are interchangeable; as specific identification of costs could distort the profit or loss arising from these inventories.[31]

Where it is necessary to use a cost-flow assumption (i.e. when there are large numbers of ordinarily interchangeable items) IAS 2 allows either a FIFO or a weighted average cost formula to be used (see 1.2.2 and 1.2.4 above).[32] The standard makes it clear that the same cost formula should be used for all inventories having a similar nature and use to the entity, although items with a different nature and use may justify the use of a different cost formula.[33] For example the standard allows that inventories used in one business segment may have a use to the entity different from the same type of inventories used in another business segment. However, a difference in geographical location of inventories (or in their respective tax rules) is not sufficient, by itself, to justify the use of different cost formulas.[34]

2.2.3 *Net realisable value*

IAS 2 in paragraphs 28 to 33 carries substantial guidance on the identification of net realisable value, where this is below cost and therefore requires inventory to be written down.

The cost of inventory may have to be reduced to its net realisable value if it has become damaged, is wholly or partly obsolete or if its selling price has declined. Additionally, the costs to complete or the estimated selling costs may have increased to levels such that the costs of inventory may not be recovered from sale.[35]

Writing inventory down to net realisable value should normally be done on an item-by-item basis, but it may be necessary to write down an entire product line or group of inventories in a given geographical area that cannot be practicably evaluated separately. IAS 2 specifically states that it is not appropriate to write down an entire class of inventory, such as finished goods, or all the inventory of a particular industry. Service contracts usually accumulate costs on a contract-by-contract basis and net realisable value must be considered on this basis.[36]

Estimates of net realisable value must be based on the most reliable evidence available and take into account fluctuations of price or cost after the end of the period if this is evidence of conditions at the end of the period.[37] They must also take into account the purpose for which the inventory is held. Therefore inventory held for a particular contract has its net realisable value based on the contract price, and only any excess inventory held would be based on general selling prices. If there is a firm contract to sell and this is in excess of inventory quantities that the entity holds or is able to obtain under a firm purchase contract, this may give rise to a provision that should be recognised in accordance with IAS 37 – *Provisions, Contingent Liabilities and Contingent Assets* (see Chapter 25).[38]

Specifically concerning materials for use in the production of inventories, IAS 2 states that:

> 'Materials and other supplies held for use in the production of inventories are not written down below cost if the finished products in which they will be incorporated are expected to be sold at or above cost. However, when a decline in the price of materials indicates that the cost of the finished products will exceed net realisable value, the materials are written down to net realisable value. In such circumstances, the replacement cost of the materials may be the best available measure of their net realisable value.'[39]

When the circumstances that previously caused inventories to be written down below cost no longer exist, or when there is clear evidence of an increase in net realisable value because of changed economic circumstances, the amount of the write-down is reversed. The reversal cannot be greater than the amount of the original write-down, so that the new carrying amount will always be the lower of the cost and the revised net realisable value.[40]

2.3   Recognition in the income statement

IAS 2 specifies that when inventory is sold, the carrying amount of the inventory must be recognised as an expense in the period in which the revenue is recognised.[41] It is also clear that a failure to recognise revenue would not justify the non-recognition as an expense of inventory over which the entity no longer had control. Any writes-down or losses of inventory must be recognised as an expense when the write-down or loss occurs. Reversals of previous writes-down should be recognised as a reduction in the inventory expense recognised in the period in which the reversal occurs.[42]

Inventory that goes into the creation of another asset, for instance into a self constructed item of property, plant or equipment, is expensed through the depreciation of that item during its useful life.[43]

2.4   Disclosure requirements of IAS 2

The financial statements should disclose:

(a)   the accounting policies adopted in measuring inventories, including the cost formula used;

(b)   the total carrying amount of inventories and the carrying amount in classifications appropriate to the entity;

(c)   the carrying amount of inventories carried at fair value less costs to sell;

(d)   the amount of inventories recognised as an expense during the period;

(e)   the amount of any write-down of inventories recognised as an expense in the period;

(f)   the amount of any reversal of any write-down that is recognised as a reduction in the amount of inventories recognised as expense in the period;

(g)   the circumstances or events that led to the reversal of a write-down of inventories; and

(h)   the carrying amount of inventories pledged as security for liabilities.[44]

IAS 2 does not specify the precise classifications that must be used to comply with (b) above. However it states that 'information about the carrying amounts held in different classifications of inventories and the extent of the changes in these assets is useful to financial statement users', and suggests suitable examples of common classifications such as merchandise, production supplies, materials, work-in-progress, and finished goods.[45]

Extract 21.2 below shows how TUI AG disclosed the amounts of inventories pledged as collateral in the period and also the amounts of inventory written back in the period.

Extract 21.2: TUI AG (2003)

Notes on the Consolidated Balance Sheet [extract]

19. Inventories

€ million	31 Dec 2003	31 Dec 2002
Raw materials and supplies	75.9	113.3
Work in progress	43.3	65.1
Finished goods and merchandise	194.7	301.4
Payments on account	221.6	161.7
	535.5	**641.5**
./. Advanced payments received	3.1	3.2
Total	**532.4**	**638.3**

Of the total of inventories, €11.8 million (previous year: €16.8 million) were carried at net realisable value. Write-backs of inventories of €2.3 million (previous year: none) were effected in the Group.

Inventories primarily related to the US steel service companies and companies operating as tour operators in the tourism division. The decline of €105.9 million was mainly due to the disposal of the companies of the AMC Group, sold in October 2003, which held corresponding inventories since they were trading companies.

The payments on account made mainly comprised advance payments for future tourism services, in particular hotel services, customary in the sector. Where these payments on account were made for a period of more than one season, they were carried under non-current assets in the balance sheet.

Inventories totalling €72.9 million (previous year: none) were pledged as collateral by the US steel service companies in taking up a loan.

Extract 21.3 below from Holcim Ltd shows a typical inventory classification, and also disclosure of the amount of inventory write-down in the period.

Extract 21.3: Holcim Ltd (2003)

Notes to the Consolidated Financial Statements [extract]

17. Inventories

Millions CHF	2003	2002
Raw materials and additives	149	163
Semi-finished and finished products	512	590
Fuels	113	119
Parts and supplies	391	380
Unbilled services	10	13
Total	1,175	1,265
Of which pledged/restricted	0	25

In 2003, the Group recognized inventory write-downs to net realizable value of CHF 21 million (2002: 29).

The amount of inventories recognised as an expense in the period is normally included in cost of sales; this category includes unallocated production overheads and abnormal costs as well as the costs of inventory that has been sold. However, the circumstances of the entity may warrant the inclusion of distribution costs into cost of sales.[46]

Extract 21.4 below shows how Agfa-Gevaert disclosed the inventory recognised as an expense in the period.

Extract 21.4: Agfa-Gevaert N.V. (2003)

Notes to the Consolidated Financial Statements [extract]

14.   Inventories

Million Euros	**2003**	2002
Raw materials and supplies	**118**	145
Work in process, finished goods and goods purchased for resale	**692**	794
Advance payments	**3**	9
Total	**813**	**948**

Accumulated write-downs on inventories decreased by 13 million Euros during 2003 (2002: decrease 23 million Euros).

The cost of inventories recognised as an expense in the income statement was as follows:

Million Euros	**2003**	2002
Cost of raw materials, supplies and goods purchased for resale	**1,366**	1,485
Cost of services purchased	**80**	68
Total	**1,446**	**1,553**

Finally the disclosure requirements note that some entities adopt a format for profit or loss that results in amounts other than the cost of inventories being disclosed as an expense during the period. This will happen if an entity presents an analysis of expenses using a classification based on the nature of expenses. The entity then discloses the costs recognised as an expense for raw materials and consumables, labour costs and other costs together with the amount of the net change in inventories for the period.[47]

Formats for the income statement are discussed in Chapter 3.

3   PRACTICAL ISSUES

3.1   Constituents of cost

For the most part there are few problems over the inclusion of direct costs in inventories. However, problems may arise over the inclusion of certain types of overheads, and over the allocation of overheads into the inventory valuation.

The costs of inventories include the cost of bringing them to their 'present location and condition'.[48] While the standard gives examples of costs that are excluded, there is little guidance regarding the identification of costs that should be included and it is therefore a matter of interpretation and judgement depending on the particular facts and circumstances surrounding the business in question. It must always be borne in mind that the inclusion of overheads is not voluntary. However, consistency must also mean that overheads should be allocated to the cost of inventory on a consistent basis from year to year, and should not be omitted in anticipation of a net realisable value difficulty. These points are discussed below.

3.1.1   Distribution and storage costs

Although distribution costs are obviously a cost of bringing an item to its present location, the question arises whether costs of transporting inventory from one location to another are always allowable. If the condition of the inventory is not changed at either location, none of the warehousing costs may be included in inventory costs. Therefore it is not clear on what sensible basis transportation costs between two such locations could be included in inventory costs.

Storage costs are not allowed unless they are necessary in the production process. This appears to prohibit including the costs of the warehouse and the overheads of the retail outlet as part of inventory as neither of these is a prelude to a further production stage. Costs of distribution to the customer are not allowed; they are selling costs and the standard prohibits their inclusion in the carrying value of inventory. It therefore seems probable that distribution costs of inventory whose production process is complete should not be included in its carrying value.

Where it is necessary to store raw materials or work in progress prior to a further processing or manufacturing stage, the costs of such storage should be included in production overheads. In addition, it would appear reasonable to allow the costs of storing maturing stocks, such as cheese, wine or whisky, in the cost of production.

3.1.2   General and administrative overheads

IAS 2 specifically disallows administrative overheads that do not contribute to bringing inventories to their present location and condition.[49] Other costs, and overheads, that do contribute, are allowable as costs of production. There is a judgement to be made about such matters, as on a very wide interpretation any department could be considered to make a contribution. For example, the accounts department will normally support the following functions:

(a)   production – by paying direct and indirect production wages and salaries, by controlling purchases and related payments, and by preparing periodic financial statements for the production units;

(b)   marketing and distribution – by analysing sales and by controlling the sales ledger; and

(c)   general administration – by preparing management accounts and annual financial statements and budgets, by controlling cash resources and by planning investments.

Only those costs of the accounts department that can be allocated to the production function fall to be included in the cost of conversion. Part of the management and overhead costs of a large retailer's logistical department may be included in cost if it can be related to bringing the inventory to its present location and condition. However, these types of cost are unlikely to be material in the context of the inventory total held by organisations. Nevertheless in our view, an entity wishing to include a material amount of overhead of a borderline nature must ensure it can sensibly justify its inclusion under the provisions of IAS 2 by presenting an analysis of the function and its contribution to the production process similar to the above example.

3.1.3   *Allocation of overheads*

IAS 2 states that the allocation of fixed production overheads is based on the normal capacity of the production facilities, although the actual production level can be used if it approximates to normal circumstances.[50]

Although it is important to bear in mind that normal levels of activity relate to all costs including direct costs, in computing the costs to be allocated via the overhead recovery rate, costs such as distribution and selling must be excluded, together with cost of storing raw materials and work in progress, unless it is necessary (which it would normally be) that these latter costs be incurred prior to further processing.

Although the normal level of activity when allocation of overheads is a judgemental area, it is relatively straightforward when dealing with manufacturing and processing of physical inventory. It is far harder to establish what this can mean in the context of service industries where the 'inventory' is intangible and based on work performed for customers that has not yet been recognised as income. There really is no equivalent to the normal capacity of production facilities in these cases. However, the standard still requires the inclusion of attributable overheads and entities must take care to establish an appropriate benchmark to avoid the distortions that could occur if overheads were attributed on the basis of actual 'output'.

3.2   Net realisable value

As already discussed, the basic rule of accounting for inventories under IAS 2 is that they are stated at the lower of their cost and net realisable value. The comparison of cost and net realisable value of finished goods is normally straightforward as long as there are established selling prices for the finished goods. Net realisable value of the raw materials themselves, it is made clear in IAS 2, depends on the ultimate selling price of a completed product, rather than the current price of the raw materials involved.[51] Thus, a whisky distiller would not write down an inventory of grain because of a fall in the grain price, so long as it expected still to sell the whisky at a profit. Conversely though, where a write down is required in respect of finished goods, the carrying value of any related raw materials must also be reviewed to see if they too need to be written down.

Often raw materials are used to make a number of different products. In these cases it is normally not possible to arrive at a particular net realisable value for each item of raw material based on the selling price of any one type of finished item. If current replacement cost is less than historical cost, however, a provision is only required to be made if the finished goods into which they will be made are expected to be sold at a loss. No provision should be made just because the anticipated profit will be less than normal.

3.3   The valuation of high volumes of similar items of inventory

Practical problems in the valuation of inventory arise in the case of businesses with high volumes of various line items of inventory. This situation occurs extensively in the retail trade where similar mark-ups are applied to ranges of inventory items or groups of items, and the selling price is marked on each individual item of inventory (e.g. in the case of a supermarket). In such a situation, it may be time-consuming to determine the cost of the period-end inventory on a conventional basis. Consequently, the most practical method of determining period-end inventory may be to record inventory on hand at selling prices and then convert it to cost by removing the normal mark-up. Not surprisingly, this method of inventory valuation is known as the 'retail method'.

Example 21.5 below shows how Gucci Group N.V. discloses its accounting policy concerning its use of the retail method to value inventory.

Extract 21.5: Gucci Group N.V. (2004)

Notes to the consolidated financial statements [extract]

Summary of significant accounting policies [extract]

Inventories

Inventories are stated at the lower of purchase or production cost or market value. Purchase or production cost is determined under the retail method for retail inventories and average cost method for production and wholesale inventories.

Under the retail inventory method, the valuation of inventories at cost and the resulting gross margins are determined by applying a calculated cost-to-retail ratio, for various groupings of similar items, to the retail value of inventories. Consequently, the cost of the inventory reflected on the consolidated balance sheet is decreased by charges to cost of sales during the period that it is first determined that the merchandise will be sold at mark-down value.

However, a complication in applying the retail method is in determining the margin to be applied to the inventory at selling price to convert it back to cost. The percentage has to take account of circumstances in which inventories have been marked down to below original selling price. Adjustments have to be made to eliminate the effect of these markdowns so as to prevent any item of inventory being valued at less than both its cost and its net realisable value. In practice, however, entities that use the retail method apply a gross profit margin computed on an average basis appropriate for departments and/or ranges, rather than applying specific mark-up percentages. This practice is, in fact, acknowledged by IAS 2 that states: 'an average percentage for each retail department is often used'.[52]

4   CONCLUSION

This is one area of financial reporting that remains fairly uncontroversial. One question that will inevitably be asked sooner or later is whether the gradual move towards a system of accounting that recognises an ever-broadening range of assets and liabilities in the balance sheet at their fair values, will ultimately see the measurement of inventories at fair value as well? The valuation of inventories at selling prices is part of a full fair value system, therefore given the fair value agenda of the IASB it could be a possibility, however unbelievable to any experienced accountant or businessperson this may seem.

It is our earnest hope that valuing inventory at selling prices is not on the agenda of the IASB. Making the sale is the most difficult and unpredictable part of being in business, as anyone with commercial experience knows, and whether or not the sale is made represents the fundamental essence of business risk. If it is part of the agenda of the standard setters to value inventories at selling prices rather than cost (which is usually the effect of valuing inventories at fair value), it is our view that both the relevance and the reliability of financial statements would be noticeably diminished. We consider that to assume sales will occur and consequently to recognise a profit, just because inventory is available, would be a serious departure from the business and commercial reality that, fundamentally, financial reporting exists to describe.

References

1 IAS 2, *Inventories*, December 2003, IASB, para. 27.
2 IAS 2, para. 27.
3 IAS 2, para. 2.
4 IAS 2, para. 3.
5 IAS 2, para. 4.
6 IAS 2, para. 3.
7 IAS 2, para. 5.
8 IAS 2, para. 6.
9 IAS 2, para. 9.
10 IAS 2, para. 6.
11 IAS 2, para. 6.
12 IAS 2, para. 7.
13 IAS 2, para. 8.
14 IAS 2, para. 9.
15 IAS 2, para. 10.
16 IAS 2, para. 11.
17 IAS 2, para. 12.
18 IAS 2, para. 12.
19 IAS 2, para. 13.
20 IAS 2, para. 13.
21 IAS 2, para. 14.
22 IAS 2, para. 15.
23 IAS 2, para. 16.
24 IAS 2, para. 17.
25 IAS 2, para. 18.
26 IAS 2, para. 19.
27 IAS 2, para. 20.
28 IAS 2, para. 21.
29 IAS 2, para. 22.
30 IAS 2, para. 23.
31 IAS 2, para. 24.
32 IAS 2, para. 25.
33 IAS 2, para. 25.
34 IAS 2, para. 26.
35 IAS 2, para. 28.
36 IAS 2, para. 29.
37 IAS 2, para. 30.
38 IAS 2, para. 31.
39 IAS 2, para. 32.
40 IAS 2, para. 33.
41 IAS 2, para. 34.
42 IAS 2, para. 34.
43 IAS 2, para. 35.
44 IAS 2, para. 36.
45 IAS 2, para. 37.
46 IAS 2, para. 38.
47 IAS 2, para. 39.
48 IAS 2, paras. 10-11.
49 IAS 2, para. 16.
50 IAS 2, para. 13.
51 IAS 2, para. 32.
52 IAS 2, para. 22.

Chapter 22   Construction contracts

1   INTRODUCTION

IAS 11 – *Construction contracts* – is a standard designed to deal under the historical cost system with the accounting issues raised by its subject. Like a number of other older standards that have not yet been significantly revised by the IASB (IAS 11 was originally approved in 1978 and last revised in 1993), the focus is on the income statement and the basis on which income and expenditure should be recognised. IAS 11 identifies its principle purpose as the allocation of contract revenue and contract costs to the accounting periods in which contract work is performed, not on the identification of assets and liabilities as defined by the IASB Framework.

In the short term, the IFRIC is considering, as part of the IASB's convergence project with the FASB, whether the detailed guidance for combining and segmenting contracts in AICPA Statement of Position 81-1 – *Accounting for Performance of Construction-Type and Certain Production-Type Contracts* – should be incorporated into the standard. This is discussed further in 4.1 below.

In the longer term, the IASB is developing an approach to revenue recognition that is based on changes in assets and liabilities rather than on an approach that applies the concept of an earnings process, which is discussed in Chapter 26. This may well lead to fundamental changes in the way in which construction contracts are accounted for because revenue will be defined by changes in assets and liabilities.

1.1   Scope and definitions

IAS 11 applies to accounting for construction contracts in the financial statements of the contractor.[1]

A construction contract is defined as follows:

> 'a contract specifically negotiated for the construction of an asset or a combination of assets that are closely interrelated or interdependent in terms of their design, technology and function or their ultimate purpose or use.'[2]

Therefore, something that will be accounted for as a single construction contract may comprise a number of different elements. Single constructions could include a bridge, a building, a dam, a pipeline, a road, a ship or a tunnel. Other single contracts include groups of inter-related assets such as an oil refinery or complex pieces of plant and equipment.[3] Whether a contract is, in fact a single construction contract or one that should be separated into components, each of which is dealt with individually, is one of the more difficult and subjective areas of contract accounting and one that is currently being considered by the IFRIC (see 4.1 below).

Contracts for services directly related to contracts are covered by IAS 11 and not by IAS 18 – *Revenue*. These include contracts for the services of project managers and architects. Contracts for demolition and restoration of assets and restoration of the environment after an asset is demolished are also construction contracts.[4]

The standard identifies two specific types of construction contract:

> 'A *fixed price contract* is a construction contract in which the contractor agrees to a fixed contract price, or a fixed rate per unit of output, which in some cases is subject to cost escalation clauses.
>
> A *cost plus contract* is a construction contract in which the contractor is reimbursed for allowable or otherwise defined costs, plus a percentage of these costs or a fixed fee'.[5]

These types determine the basis on which income is recognised, as is discussed in 2.3 below.

Contracts that contain elements of both types, e.g. a cost plus contract that has an agreed maximum price, will have to be analysed in order to determine when to recognise contract revenue and expenses.[6]

1.2   Combination and segmentation of contracts

IAS 11 should be applied separately to each construction contract.[7] However, in order to reflect the substance of the transaction it may be necessary for a contract to be sub-divided and the standard to be applied individually to each component, or for a group of contracts to be treated as one.

IAS 11 provides guidance in three separate cases. The first is where a single contract covers the construction of a number of separate assets, each of which is in substance a separate contract, i.e.

(a)   separate proposals have been submitted for each asset;

(b)   the contractor and customer have negotiated separately for each asset and can accept or reject that part of the contract relating to each asset; and

(c)   the costs and revenues relating to each asset can be identified.[8]

The second case is effectively the reverse of the first and deals with situations where in substance there is only a single contract with a customer, or a group of customers. This group of contracts should be treated as a single contract where:

(a)   the group of contracts is negotiated as a single package;

(b)   the contracts are so closely interrelated that they are, in effect, part of a single project with an overall profit margin; and

(c)   the contracts are performed concurrently or in a continuous sequence.[9]

Finally it is possible that a contract may envisage the construction of a further asset at the customer's discretion. IAS 11 identifies two criteria, each of which would indicate that it should be accounted for as a separate contract:

(a)   the asset differs significantly in design, technology or function from the asset or assets covered by the original contract; or

(b)   the price of the asset is negotiated without regard to the original contract price.[10]

The issues in connection with combining and segmenting contracts are considered further in 4.1 below, while options to construct additional assets are discussed at 4.2 below.

2   CONTRACT REVENUE, COSTS AND EXPENSES

2.1   Contract revenue

Contract revenue comprises the amount of revenue initially agreed by the parties together with any variations, claims and incentive payments as long as it is probable that they will result in revenue and can be measured reliably.[11] The standard states that such revenue is to be measured at the fair value of the consideration received and receivable. In this context, 'fair value' appears to refer solely to the process whereby the consideration is to be revised as events occur and uncertainties are resolved; any estimates must be regularly reviewed and adjustments made as the uncertainties are resolved. These may include contractual matters such as increases in revenue in a fixed price contract as a result of cost escalation clauses or, when a contract involves a fixed price per unit of output, contract revenue may increase as the number of units is increased. Penalties for delays may reduce revenue. In addition, variations and claims must be taken into account.[12]

Variations are instructions by the customer to change the scope of the work to be performed under the contract, including changes to the specification or design of the asset or of the duration of the contract. Variations may only be included in contract revenue when it is probable that the customer will approve the variation and the amount to be charged for it, and the amount can be reliably measured.[13]

Given the extended periods over which contracts are carried out and changes in circumstances prevailing whilst the work is in progress, it is quite normal for a contractor to submit claims for additional sums to a customer. Claims may be made for costs not included in the original contract or arising as an indirect consequence of approved variations, such as customer caused delays, errors in specifications or design and disputed variations. Because their settlement is by negotiation (which can in practice be very protracted), they are subject to a high level of uncertainty;

consequently, no credit should be taken for them unless negotiations have reached an advanced stage such that:

- it is probable that the customer will accept the claim; and

- the amount that it is probable will be accepted by the customer can be measured reliably.[14]

This means that, as a minimum, the claims have been agreed in principle and, in the absence of an agreed sum, the amount to be accrued should be prudently assessed.

Contracts may provide for incentive payments, for example, for early completion or superior performance. They may only be included in contract revenue when the contract is at such a stage that it is probable the required performance will be achieved and the amount can be measured reliably.[15]

2.2   Contract costs

Contract costs are those that relate directly to the specific contract and to those that are attributable to contract activity in general that can be allocated to the contract. In addition, they include costs that are specifically chargeable to the customer under the terms of the contract.[16]

Directly related costs include:

(a)   direct labour costs, including site supervision;

(b)   costs of materials used in construction;

(c)   depreciation of plant and equipment used on the contract;

(d)   costs of moving plant, equipment and materials to and from the contract site;

(e)   costs of hiring plant and equipment;

(f)   costs of design and technical assistance that is directly related to the contract;

(g)   the estimated costs of rectification and guarantee work, including expected warranty costs; and

(h)   claims from third parties.[17]

If the contractor generates incidental income from any directly related cost, e.g. by selling surplus materials and disposing of equipment at the end of the contract, this is treated as a reduction in contract costs.[18]

The second category of costs comprises those attributable to contract activity in general that can be allocated to a particular contract. These include design and technical assistance not directly related to an individual contract, insurance, and construction overheads such as the costs of preparing and processing the payroll for the personnel actually working on the contract. These must be allocated using a systematic and rational method, consistently applied to all costs having similar characteristics. Allocation must be based on the normal level of construction activity.[19] The allocation of overheads is considered further in 4.3 below.

Borrowing costs may also be attributable to contract activity in general and can be allocated to specific contracts when the contractor adopts the IAS 23 allowed alternative treatment of capitalising interest costs.[20] See Chapter 15 for a detailed discussion of capitalisation of interest.

There are various costs that, in most circumstances, are specifically precluded by IAS 11 from being attributed to contract activity or allocated to a contract. These include general administration costs, selling costs, research and development costs and the depreciation of idle plant and equipment that is not used on a particular contract.[21] However, the entity is allowed to classify general administration costs and research and development as contract costs if they are specifically reimbursable under the terms of the contract.[22]

Costs may be attributed to a contract from the date on which it is secured until its final completion. Additionally, costs relating directly to the contract, which have been incurred in gaining the business, may be included in contract costs if they have been incurred once it is probable the contract will be obtained. These costs must be separately identified and measured reliably.[23] This is not dissimilar to the general rules for recognition of an asset. An asset is defined in the IASB Framework as 'a resource controlled by the enterprise as a result of past events and from which future economic benefits are expected to flow to the enterprise'.[24] Therefore, we believe that this should be read restrictively and that these costs should not be recognised until they can themselves be seen as an asset of the entity through its control of the future economic benefits from the contract.

Costs that have been written off cannot be reinstated if the contract is obtained in a subsequent period.[25]

Costs incurred in securing a contract mean such things as the building of models (including computer modelling exercises) for tender purposes, travelling costs of technicians to survey sites, technical tendering costs, and similar expenses relating specifically to a given contract.

2.3 The recognition of contract revenue and expenses

If the basic rule of accounting for inventories were applied to contracts, it would result in an annual income statement that reflected only the outcome of contracts completed during the year. In a contracting company this might bear no relation to the company's actual level of activity for that year. IAS 11 therefore requires revenue and expenses to be recognised on uncompleted contracts in order to present a consistent view of the results of the company's activities during the period and from one period to the next. The underlying principle in IAS 11 is that, once the outcome of a construction contract can be reliably estimated, revenue and expenses associated with the construction contract should be recognised by reference to the stage of completion of the contract activity at the balance sheet date.[26] The standard does not define the attributable profit in a contract, which will therefore be the balancing figure once revenue and expenses are known.

If it is anticipated that the contract will be loss-making, the expected loss must be recognised immediately. This is described further in 2.3.6 below.

2.3.1   Types of construction contract

IAS 11 identifies two types of construction contract, fixed price and cost plus contracts.

A   Fixed price contracts

In the case of a fixed price contract, the standard states that the outcome of a construction contract can be estimated reliably when all the conditions discussed below are satisfied.

Firstly, it must be probable that the economic benefits associated with the contract will flow to the entity, which must be able to measure total contract revenue reliably. As discussed further below, these conditions will usually be satisfied when there are adequate contractual arrangements between the parties.

Secondly, both the contract costs to complete the contract and the stage of contract completion at the balance sheet date must be able to be measured reliably.

Thirdly, the entity must be able to identify and measure reliably the contract costs attributable to the contract so that actual contract costs incurred can be compared with prior estimates.[27] This means that it must have adequate reporting and budgeting systems.

B   Cost plus contracts

Cost plus contracts are not subject to all of the same uncertainties as fixed price contracts. As with any transaction, it must be probable that the economic benefits associated with the contract will flow to the entity in order to recognise income at all. In most contracts this will be evidenced by the contract documentation. The fundamental criterion for a cost plus contract is the proper measurement of contract costs. Therefore, the contract costs attributable to the contract, whether or not specifically reimbursable, must be clearly identified and measured reliably.[28]

2.3.2   The stage of completion method

There are certain general principles that apply whether the contract is classified as fixed cost or as cost plus. Recognition of revenue and expense is by reference to the stage of completion, also known as the 'percentage of completion method'. Contract revenue and costs are recognised as revenue and expensed in the income statement in the period in which the work is performed. An excess of contract costs over contract income (i.e. a loss on the contract) is recognised as soon as it is anticipated.[29]

This does not mean that contract activity is based on the total costs that have been incurred by the entity. Contract costs that relate to future contract activity may be deferred and recognised as an asset as long as it is probable that they will be recovered. These costs are usually called contract work in progress.[30]

An entity does not adjust the cumulative revenue it has recognised if it transpires in a subsequent period that there are doubts about the recoverability of an amount it has recognised as revenue and it therefore has to make provision against its debtor.

Instead the amount that is no longer considered recoverable is written off as an expense.[31]

In order to be able to recognise revenue, the construction entity must be able to make reliable estimates of its income and costs. It is usually possible to do so once the parties have agreed to a contract that establishes both parties' enforceable rights, the contract consideration and the manner and terms of settlement. However, the entity must also be able to review and, where necessary, revise the estimates of contract revenue and contract costs as the contract progresses. This means that the entity must have an effective system of internal financial budgets and reporting systems.[32]

The standard allows the stage of completion of a contract to be determined in a number of ways, including:

- the proportion that contract costs incurred for work performed to date bear to the estimated total contract costs;
- surveys of work performed; or
- completion of a physical proportion of the contract work.[33]

These could, of course, give different answers regarding the stage of completion of a contract as demonstrated in the following example.

Example 22.1: Determination of revenue

A company is engaged in a construction contract with an expected sales value of £10,000. It is the end of the accounting period during which the company commenced work on this contract and it needs to compute the amount of revenue to be reflected in the profit and loss account for this contract.

Scenario (i)   **Stage of completion is measured by the proportion that contract costs incurred for work performed to date bear to the estimated total contract costs**

The company has incurred and applied costs of £4,000. £3,000 is the best estimate of costs to complete. The company should therefore recognise revenue of £5,714, being the appropriate proportion of total contract value, and computed thus:

$$\frac{4,000}{7,000} \times 10,000 = 5,714$$

Scenario (ii)   **Surveys of work performed**

An independent surveyor has certified that at the period-end the contract is 55% complete and that the company is entitled to apply for cumulative progress payments of £5,225 (after a 5% retention). In this case the company would record revenue of £5,500 being the sales value of the work done. (If it is anticipated that rectification work will have to be carried out to secure the release of the retention money then this should be taken into account in computing the attributable contract costs – it should have no bearing on the amount of revenue to be recorded.)

Scenario (iii)   **Completion of a physical proportion of the contract work**

The company's best estimate of the physical proportion of the work it has completed is that it is 60% complete. The value of the work done and, therefore, the revenue to be recognised is £6,000.

Note that in each of the above scenarios the computation of the amount of revenue is quite independent of the question of how much (if any) profit should be taken. This is as it should be, because even if a contract is loss-making the sales price will be earned and this should be reflected by recording revenue as the contract progresses. In the final analysis, any loss arises because costs are greater than revenue, and costs should be reflected through cost of sales. Different methods of determining revenue will, as disclosed above, produce different results, which highlights the importance of disclosing the method adopted by the entity.

There are, of course, ways other than cost of measuring work done, e.g. labour hours, which depending upon the exact circumstances might lead to a more appropriate basis for computing revenue.

The above example applies only to fixed-price contracts. Where a contract is on a cost-plus basis, it is necessary to examine the costs incurred to ensure they are of the type and size envisaged in the terms of the contract. Only once this is done and the recoverable costs identified can the figure be grossed up to arrive at the appropriate revenue figure.

If the stage of completion is determined by reference to the contract costs incurred to date, it is fundamental that this figure includes only those contract costs that reflect work actually performed so far. Any contract costs that relate to future activity on the contract must be excluded. This includes the costs of materials that have been delivered to a contract site or set aside for use in a contract but not yet installed, used or applied during contract performance, unless the materials have been made especially for the contract. Payments made to subcontractors in advance of work performed under the subcontract would similarly not relate to work performed to date and have to be excluded.[34]

Example 22.2:   Determination of revenue – exclusion of unapplied costs

The circumstances are as in Scenario (i) of Example 22.1 above. The entity has incurred and applied costs of £4,000. £3,000 is the best estimate of costs to complete. If the costs incurred to date included, say, £500 in respect of unapplied raw materials, then the revenue to be recognised falls to £5,000 being:

$$\frac{\text{costs incurred and applied}}{\text{total costs}} = \frac{(4,000 - 500)}{7,000} \times 10,000 = 5,000$$

2.3.3   Changes in estimates

The percentage of completion method is applied on a cumulative basis in each accounting period to the current estimates of contract revenues and costs. The effect of any changes in estimates of revenue and costs, or the effect of any change in the estimate of the outcome of a contract, must be treated as a change in accounting estimate, in accordance with IAS 8. The revised estimates must be used in determining the amount of revenue and expenses recognised in the income statement in the period in which the change is made, and in subsequent periods.[35]

2.3.4 The determination of contract revenue and expenses

It is now possible to see how these features of accounting for construction contracts are put together to calculate the timing and measurement of contract revenue and expenses throughout the term of a construction contract, as in the following example, based on that in the Appendix to IAS 11:

Example 22.3: *Cumulative example –*
the determination of contract revenue and expenses

The following example illustrates the determination of the stage of completion of a contract and the timing of the recognition of contract revenue and expenses, measured by the proportion that contract costs incurred for work performed to date bear to the estimated total contract costs.

A construction contractor has a fixed price contract for €9,000 to build a bridge. The initial amount of revenue agreed in the contract is €9,000. The contractor's initial estimate of contract costs is €8,000. It will take 3 years to build the bridge.

By the end of year 1, the contractor's estimate of contract costs has increased to €8,050.

In year 2, the customer approves a variation resulting in an increase in contract revenue of €200 and estimated additional contract costs of €150. At the end of year 2, costs incurred include €100 for standard materials stored at the site to be used in year 3 to complete the project.

The contractor determines the stage of completion of the contract by calculating the proportion that contract costs incurred for work performed to date bear to the latest estimated total contract costs. A summary of the financial data during the construction period is as follows:

	Year 1 €	Year 2 €	Year 3 €
Initial amount of revenue agreed in contract	9,000	9,000	9,000
Variation	–	200	200
Total contract revenue	9,000	9,200	9,200
Contract costs incurred to date	2,093	6,168	8,200
Contract costs to complete	5,957	2,023	–
Total estimated contract costs	8,050	8,200	8,200
Estimated profit	950	1,000	1,000
Stage of completion	26%	74%	100%

The constructor uses the percentages calculated as above to calculate the revenue, contract costs and profits over the term of the contract. The stage of completion for year 2 (74%) is determined by excluding from contract costs incurred for work performed to date the €100 of standard materials stored at the site for use in year 3.

The amounts of revenue, expenses and profit recognised in the income statement in the three years are as follows:

	To Date	Recognised in prior years	Recognised in current years
Year 1			
Revenue (9,000 × 26%)	2,340	–	2,340
Expenses (8,050 × 26%)	2,093	–	2,093
Profit	247	–	247
Year 2			
Revenue (9,200 × 74%)	6,808	2,340	4,468
Expenses (8,200 × 74%)	6,068	2,093	3,975
Profit	740	247	493
Year 3			
Revenue (9,200 × 100%)	9,200	6,808	2,392
Expenses	8,200	6,068	2,132
Profit	1,000	740	260

2.3.5 Inability to estimate the outcome of a contract reliably

When the outcome of a construction contract cannot be estimated reliably, an entity will first of all have to determine whether it has incurred costs that it is probable will be recovered under the contract. It can then recognise revenue to the extent of these costs. Contract costs should be recognised as an expense in the period in which they are incurred,[36] which means, of course, that they have been calculated according to the method that the entity uses to establish the stage of completion of a contract.

It is often difficult to estimate the outcome of a contract reliably during its early stages. This means that it is not possible to recognise contract profit. However, the entity may be satisfied that some, at least, of the contract costs it has incurred will be recovered; it will be able to recognise revenue to this extent. If it is probable that total costs will exceed total revenues, even if the outcome of the contract cannot be estimated reliably, any expected excess of contract costs must be expensed immediately.[37] This means that the entity will record the revenue equal to contract costs attributable to its estimated contract activity in the period, assuming that it is not expecting to make an overall loss on the contract.

If it is probable that contract costs cannot be recovered they must be recognised as expenses immediately. The standard identifies a number of situations that may give rise to irrecoverable contract costs. There may be deficiencies in the contract, which means that it is not fully enforceable. Other problems may be caused by the operation of law, such as the outcome of pending litigation or legislation or the expropriation of property. The customer or the contractor may no longer be able to meet their obligations or the contractor may be unable for some reason to complete the contract.[38]

Once uncertainties that prevent the outcome of the contract being estimated reliably no longer exist, revenue and expenses are recognised by the stage of completion method.[39]

2.3.6   Loss-making contracts

As soon as the entity considers that it is probable that the contract costs will exceed contract revenue it must recognise the expected loss as an expense immediately. It is irrelevant whether or not work has commenced on the contract or the stage of completion of contract activity. In addition, the entity may not take into account any anticipated profits on other contracts with the same customer unless all of these contracts are treated as a single construction contract.[40]

3   DISCLOSURE REQUIREMENTS OF IAS 11

IAS 11 has detailed and onerous disclosure requirements. The following disclosures must be given by entities in respect of construction contracts:

(a)   the amount of contract revenue recognised as revenue in the period;

(b)   the methods used to determine the contract revenue recognised in the period; and

(c)   the methods used to determine the stage of completion of contracts in progress.[41]

The standard includes in its Appendix examples of accounting policy disclosures:

Example 22.4:   Disclosure of accounting policies

Revenue from fixed price construction contracts is recognised on the percentage of completion method, measured by reference to the percentage of labour hours incurred to date to estimated total labour hours for each contract.

Revenue from cost plus contracts is recognised by reference to the recoverable costs incurred during the period plus the fee earned, measured by the proportion that costs incurred to date bear to the estimated total costs of the contract.

In the case of contracts in progress at the balance sheet date, an enterprise should disclose each of the following:

(a)   the aggregate amount of costs incurred and recognised profits (less recognised losses) to date;

(b)   the amount of advances received; and

(c)   the amount of retentions.[42]

Retentions, progress billings and advances are defined as follows:

'Retentions are amounts of progress billings which are not paid until the satisfaction of conditions specified in the contract for the payment of such amounts or until defects have been rectified. Progress billings are amounts billed for work performed on a contract whether or not they have been paid by the customer. Advances are amounts received by the contractor before the related work is performed.'[43]

In addition, an enterprise should present:

(a) the gross amount due from customers for contract work as an asset for all contracts in progress for which costs incurred plus recognised profits (less recognised losses) exceed progress billings (i.e. the net amount of costs incurred plus recognised profits, less the sum of recognised losses and progress billings); and

(b) the gross amount due to customers for contract work as a liability for all contracts in progress for which progress billings exceed costs incurred plus recognised profits (i.e. the net amount of costs incurred plus recognised profits, less the sum of recognised losses and progress billings).[44]

The following example is based on the Appendix to IAS 11, and serves to illustrate the financial statement disclosure requirements of the standard as they apply to the various circumstances that might arise concerning construction contracts.

Example 22.5:   Disclosure of numerical information regarding construction contracts

A contractor has reached the end of its first year of operations. All its contract costs incurred have been paid for in cash and all its progress billings and advances have been received in cash. Contract costs incurred for contracts B, C and E include the cost of materials that have been purchased for the contract but which have not been used in contract performance to date.

For contracts B, C and E, the customers have made advances to the contractor for work not yet performed.

The status of the entity's five contracts in progress at the end of year 1 is as follows:

Contract	A	B	C	D	E	Total
Contract Revenue recognised in accordance with paragraph 22 (see 2.3 above)	145	520	380	200	55	1,300
Contract Expenses recognised in accordance with paragraph 22 (see 2.3 above)	110	450	350	250	55	1,215
Expected Losses recognised in accordance with paragraph 36 (see 2.6 above)	–	–	–	40	30	70
Recognised profits less recognised losses	35	70	30	(90)	(30)	15
Contract Costs incurred in the period	110	510	450	250	100	1,420
Contract Costs incurred recognised as contract expenses in the period in accordance with paragraph 22	110	450	350	250	55	1,215
Contact Costs that relate to future activity recognised as an asset in accordance with paragraph 27	–	60	100	–	45	205
Contact Revenue	145	520	380	200	55	1,300
Progress Billings (paragraph 41: see above)	100	520	380	180	55	1,235
Unbilled Contract Revenue	45	–	–	20	–	65
Advances (paragraph 41: see above)	–	80	20	–	25	125

The amounts to be disclosed in accordance with the Standard are as follows:

Contract revenue recognised as revenue in the period	1,300
Contract costs incurred and recognised profits (less recognised losses) to date	1,435
Advances received	125
Gross amount due from customers for contract work (presented as an asset)	220
Gross amount due to customers for contract work (presented as a liability)	(20)

These amounts are calculated as follows:

Contract	A	B	C	D	E	Total
Contract Costs incurred	110	510	450	250	100	1,420
Recognised profits less recognised losses	35	70	30	(90)	(30)	15
	145	580	480	160	70	1,435
Progress billings	100	520	380	180	55	1,235
Due from customers	45	60	100	-	15	220
Due to customers	–	–	–	(20)	–	(20)

The amount disclosed in accordance with paragraph 40(a) (the aggregate amount of costs incurred and recognised profits (less recognised losses) to date) is the same as the amount for the current period because the disclosures relate to the first year of operation.

4   PRACTICAL ISSUES

4.1   Combining and segmenting of contracts: future developments and the convergence project

Contractors may provide different goods or services to its customers as part of a single contract or group of contracts. IAS 11 contains little guidance on the combining and segmenting of contracts. It really only considers the combining or otherwise of contracts in very clear-cut circumstances, i.e. where a number of contracts that purport to be separate have been negotiated as a single package or where a series of separate contracts have been subsumed within a single contract document but where the individual contracts should be dealt with separately (see 1.2 above). However, there is no further guidance in the standard on whether or how individual contracts or groups of contracts should be segmented or combined and contract revenue and costs recognised on the basis of the individual segments. These treatments can have a major effect on the recognition of income. Segmenting a contract can affect the profile of income recognition, perhaps allowing earlier recognition of revenue. If a series of contracts is negotiated as a package with the objective of achieving an overall profit margin, this will not be reflected if the individual contracts are accounted for separately, while inappropriate combining of the segments of a contract could mean that losses are not recognised on the basis required by the standard.

As part of its convergence project, the IASB has discussed whether some of the detailed guidance for combining and segmenting contracts in AICPA Statement of Position 81-1 – *Accounting for Performance of Construction-Type and Certain Production-Type Contracts* – should be incorporated into IAS 11.[45] Segmentation and combination of contracts has been taken onto the IFRIC agenda but no draft Interpretation has yet been issued.

We are not in agreement with applying SOP 81-1's criteria for combining contracts *verbatim*. SOP 81-1 is more restrictive than IAS 11 in allowing the combination of contracts and would allow contracts with more than one party to be combined only in very unusual circumstances.[46] We consider that these circumstances are actually relatively common. For example, a developer may be building a block of apartments, each of which is being sold to a different party. It is clear to us that this should be treated as a single construction contract.

In the mean time and until the IFRIC issues an interpretation, segmentation and combination of construction contracts should be assessed in accordance with paragraphs 8 and 9 of IAS 11, as described above.

The IFRIC has begun to consider other aspects of accounting for construction contracts. These include:

- The interaction with IAS 23 – *Borrowing costs*.[47] Borrowing costs are discussed in Chapter 14; and

- Whether revenue should be allocated to phases of a project based on different project margins or on the profit margin for the project as a whole. (This could have the same effect as segmenting the contract.)

As a result of the work on service concession agreements (see Chapter 27) the IFRIC is concerned about the impact of any guidance it might issue on service revenue recognition. IAS 18 – *Revenue* – states that the requirements of IAS 11 are generally applicable to the recognition of revenue and associated expenses if the transaction involves the rendering of services (revenue recognition for service contracts is discussed in Chapter 26).[48] The IFRIC has now concluded that the scope of the project should be extended and it is working on developing an Interpretation that will apply to both IAS 11 and IAS 18.[49]

4.2   Options for the construction of an additional asset

Another area where it is necessary to consider whether contracts should be combined is in contract options and additions. Once again, combining of contracts is important because of its potential impact on the recognition of revenue and profits on transactions. If the optional asset is treated as part of the original contract, contract revenue will be recognised using the percentage of completion method over the combined contract.

As described in 1.2 above, IAS 11 considers the circumstances in which a contract gives a customer an option for an additional asset (or is amended in this manner) and concludes that this should be treated as a new contract if:

a)   the asset differs significantly in design, technology or function from the asset or assets covered by the original contract; or

(b)   the price of the asset is negotiated without regard to the original contract price.[50]

This would mean, for example, that the contract for an additional, identical asset would be treated as a separate contract if its price were negotiated separately from the original contract price. Costs almost always decline with additional production, not only because of the effects of initial costs but also of the 'learning curve' (the time taken by the workforce to perform activities decreases with practice and repetition). This could result in a much higher profit margin on the additional contract. If, for example, a Government department takes up its option with a defence contractor for five more aircraft, in addition to the original twenty-five that had been contracted for, but the option was unpriced and the new contract is priced afresh, then it cannot be combined with the original contract regardless of the difference in profit margins. Note that this conclusion appears consistent with SOP 81-1, which would only allow contracts not executed at the same time to be combined if they were negotiated as a package in the same economic environment. This means that the time period must be reasonably short.[51] Although 'short' is not defined, it is unlikely to cover a period of several years, as could happen in defence contracting.

Combining of contracts may also have unexpected results. If, for example, an entity has a contract with a government to build two satellites and a priced option to build a third, it may be obliged to combine the contracts as at the point at which the option is exercised. This could well be in a different accounting period to the commencement of the contract. Using the rules outlined in 2.3.3 above, there will be a cumulative catch-up of revenue, and probably also of profits. In subsequent periods results will be based on the combined contracts.

Guidance on the effect of options is to be included by the IFRIC in the draft Interpretation that it is preparing primarily on segmentation and combination of contracts (see 4.2 above).[52]

4.3   Service concession agreements

Service concession agreements commonly include the construction of an asset followed by a period in which the constructor maintains and services that asset; this secondary period may include asset replacement and refurbishment as well as service elements. Alternatively the contract might provide for the refurbishment of an existing infrastructure asset together with related services. These agreements provide particular accounting difficulties because they combine contract accounting issues and issues arising from a number of other accounting standards including IAS 17 – *Leases* – and IAS 18. The accounting issue raised by service concessions are discussed further in Chapter 27 at 6.

5   FIRST-TIME ADOPTION

IFRS 1 – *First-time Adoption of International Financial Reporting Standards*[53] – contains no specific requirements or exemptions with regard to IAS 11. There are no exemptions from the application of IAS 11's measurement rules as at the date of transition, so there are no equivalents of the 'deemed costs' permitted in respect of property, plant and equipment or investment property (these are described in Chapter 12 at 4.1). Therefore, the standard has to be applied with full retrospective application as at the entity's first reporting date under IFRS.

Many jurisdictions entities permit the use of the completed contract method for some or all construction contracts. Under this method, revenue is only recognised when the contract is complete or substantially complete and until this point costs and amounts billed to the customer are recorded in the balance sheet. Although IAS 11 is primarily concerned with recording contract activity it also affects the balances carried forward to the extent that profits and losses have been recognised on individual contracts in previous periods. Therefore, entities will be required to review all such contracts as at transition and to ensure that their carrying amounts have been recorded in a manner that is appropriate for IAS 11.

References

1 IAS 11, *Construction contracts*, IASC, December 1993, para. 1.
2 IAS 11, para. 3.
3 IAS 11, para. 4.
4 IAS 11, para. 5.
5 IAS 11, para. 3.
6 IAS 11, para. 6.
7 IAS 11, para. 7.
8 IAS 11, para. 8.
9 IAS 11, para. 9.
10 IAS 11, para. 10.
11 IAS 11, para. 11.
12 IAS 11, para. 12.
13 IAS 11, para. 13.
14 IAS 11, para. 14.
15 IAS 11, para. 15.
16 IAS 11, para. 16.
17 IAS 11, para. 17.
18 IAS 11, para. 17.
19 IAS 11, para. 18.
20 IAS 11, para. 18.
21 IAS 11, para. 20.
22 IAS 11, paras. 19-20.
23 IAS 11, para. 21.
24 IASB Framework, IASC April 1989, adopted by the IASB April 2001, para. 49(a).
25 IAS 11, para. 21.
26 IAS 11, para. 22.
27 IAS 11, para. 23.
28 IAS 11, para. 24.
29 IAS 11, paras. 25-26.
30 IAS 11, para. 27.
31 IAS 11, para. 28.
32 IAS 11, para. 29.
33 IAS 11, para. 30.
34 IAS 11, para. 31.
35 IAS 11, para. 38.
36 IAS 11, para. 32.
37 IAS 11, para. 33.
38 IAS 11, para. 34.
39 IAS 11, para. 35.
40 IAS 11, paras. 36-37.
41 IAS 11, para. 39.
42 IAS 11, para. 40.
43 IAS 11, para. 41.
44 IAS 11, paras. 42-44.
45 *IFRIC Update*, March 2004, p.1.
46 SOP 81-1, *Accounting for Performance of Construction-Type and Certain Production-Type Contracts*, AICPA, July 1981, para. 37.
47 IAS 23, *Borrowing costs*, IASC, December 1993 (amended December 2003).
48 IAS 18, *Revenue*, IASB, December 1993 (amended March 2004), para. 21.
49 *IFRIC Update*, June 2004, p.1.
50 IAS 11, para. 10.
51 SOP 81-1, para. 37.
52 *IFRIC Update*, June 2004, p.2.
53 IFRS 1, *First-time Adoption of International Financial Reporting Standards*, IASB, June 2003 (amended March 2004).

Chapter 23   Leases

1   INTRODUCTION

IAS 17 – together with the FASB's SFAS 13 in the US, SSAP 21 in the UK and its other equivalent standards around the world – has been in place for many years.[1] These standards, are all dealing with accounting for leases, were the first to apply the concept of substance over form and the first to incorporate the present value basis of measurement into the historical cost model. In prescribed circumstances they required companies to capitalise assets in their balance sheets (together with the corresponding obligations) irrespective of the fact that legal title to those assets vested in another party.

The substance over form approach is based on the view that a lease that transfers substantially all of the risks and benefits of ownership to the lessee should be accounted for as (i) the acquisition of the asset and the assumption of an obligation by the lessee, and (ii) as a sale or financing by the lessor. Such leases are termed 'finance leases' and are equivalent to what are known as 'capital leases' in the US. The lease accounting standards required relatively few changes for leases, now known as 'operating leases', that did not transfer substantially all the risks and rewards of ownership of an asset to the lessee. Operating leases do not require capitalisation in the lessee's balance sheet. Instead, operating lease rentals are charged to the profit and loss account of the lessee over the lease term, usually on a straight-line basis.

The IASB's requirements for lease accounting have remained essentially unchanged for about two decades. Consequently the accounting requirements are generally well understood and the distinction between finance and operating leases, and the related accounting consequences, are widely accepted internationally and applied in practice. At the same time, though, conventional accounting in this area has been challenged. The IASB is now developing proposals under which the finance/operating distinction will be removed and all rights and obligations arising under lease contracts will be recognised at fair value in the balance sheets of lessees. This proposed new approach is discussed at 1.2 below.

1.1   Background: the development of IAS 17

IAS 17 – *Accounting for Leases* – was issued in September 1982 for accounting periods beginning on or after 1 January 1984.[2] The standard was clearly based on the pre-existing UK standard, SSAP 21. It defined a finance lease as one that 'transfers substantially all the risks and rewards incident to ownership of an asset' to the lessee.[3] All leases not meeting the finance lease definition were, by default, operating leases. The standard came under review during the late 1980s as part of a more general review by the (then) IASC, but detailed consideration was deferred. At the time, the (then) IASC stated that further study was required 'on the recognition of finance income on those leases on which the lessor's net investment outstanding is materially affected by income tax factors.'[4] This comment was made in the context of the fact that the standard allowed lessors accounting for finance leases to recognise finance income so as to reflect a constant periodic rate of return on either the net investment or net cash investment in the lease.

The IASC eventually gave the subject its attention in 1997, when it published Exposure Draft E56 – *Leases*. E56 proposed a very limited review of IAS 17, focusing only on those issues that the International Organization of Securities Commissions (IOSCO) considered essential for the purpose of fulfilling the IASC/IOSCO plan to complete a comprehensive set of core accounting standards that would be acceptable to all major stock exchanges for cross-border listings.

In December 1997, E56 was converted to IAS 17 (revised 1997) – *Leases*, which superseded the original IAS 17 with effect from 1 January 1999. IAS 17 was revised again in November 2003 as part of the IASB's project *Improvements to International Accounting Standards*, with an effective date of 1 January 2005. This limited revision dealt primarily with the classification of leases and buildings, as the unamended standard might have caused some specific accounting problems in a number of jurisdictions. The classification of land and buildings is dealt with in 2.3.4 below.

1.2   The G4+1's proposed new approach to lease accounting

The fair value based conceptual frameworks being adopted by the IASB and the FASB, as discussed in Chapter 2, could fundamentally change the way in which financial contracts such as leases are accounted for. In the case of lease accounting, assets and liabilities are the most relevant elements, and the IASB's *Framework for the Preparation and Presentation of Financial Statements* defines these particular elements as follows: an asset is 'a resource controlled by the enterprise as a result of past events and from which future economic benefits are expected to flow to the enterprise'; whilst a liability is 'a present obligation of the enterprise arising from past events, the settlement of which is expected to result in an outflow from the enterprise of resources embodying economic benefits'.[5]

An inescapable consequence of these two definitions is that most leases, including non-cancellable operating leases, will qualify for recognition as assets and liabilities. This is because, irrespective of whether the lease is finance or operating in nature, the lessee is likely to both control and enjoy the future economic benefits embodied in the leased asset, and will have an unavoidable legal obligation to transfer economic benefits to the lessor. Therefore the distinction between operating and finance leases is not supported at the conceptual level.

1.2.1 The G4+1's 1996 Discussion Paper

This is the conclusion that was reached by a Working Group consisting of staff members of the standard-setting bodies of Australia, Canada, New Zealand, UK, the USA and the (then) IASC (known as the G4+1 group of accounting standard-setters). In 1996 the Working Group published a discussion paper entitled *Accounting for leases: a new approach*, which discussed the limitations of current lease accounting standards and set out a new approach to lease accounting.[6] Although the paper was not officially approved by the boards of the various standard-setters involved in its preparation, it was seen to be influential.

The Working Group claimed that 'current lease accounting standards are now agreed by many observers to be unsatisfactory, at least with respect to accounting by lessees'.[7] It asserted that the 'most frequently noted concern relates to the fact that the standards do not require rights and obligations arising under operating leases to be recognised as assets and liabilities in the lessee's financial statements'.[8] According to the paper, the result has been that the standards have inadvertently promoted the structuring of financial arrangements so as to meet the conditions for classification as an operating lease, thereby avoiding recognition in lessees' balance sheets of material assets and liabilities arising from operating lease contracts. Consequently, the paper advocated a new approach to accounting for lease contracts that was aimed at overcoming these perceived concerns about the effectiveness of existing lease accounting practice.

The Working Group's proposed new approach to accounting for lease contracts was based on the definitions of assets and liabilities contained in the various conceptual frameworks. According to the Working Group, the clear implication of applying the (then) IASC's *Framework for the Preparation and Presentation of Financial Statements* to accounting for lease contracts 'is that it can be reasoned that all finance leases and most, if not all, operating leases qualify for recognition as assets and liabilities'.[9]

The Working Group's reasoning seems to have been based on the belief that the rights and obligations established by operating leases are no different in nature to those established by finance leases. This conclusion was reached through the application of the asset and liability definitions of *Framework*: under both finance and operating leases, the lessee acquires a contractual right to enjoy the future economic benefits embodied in the leased property and incurs a contractual obligation to compensate the lessor for the use of the leased property over the lease term.[10] However, the question that should be asked is whether the conclusion reached reflects a shortcoming in existing lease accounting or whether it exposes a flaw in the *Framework*.

Overall, the Working Group's paper was well written and thought provoking. On the other hand, though, whilst it raised a number of legitimate issues, it did not provide many solutions. For example, the paper was critical of the existing criteria laid down in accounting standards to distinguish between finance and operating leases (describing them as being 'arbitrary') and suggested a distinction based on cancellable and non-cancellable leases in its place. However, it did not resolve the problem of how to distinguish between cancellable and non-cancellable leases. Furthermore, the paper did not distinguish between non-cancellable leases and other commitments or executory contracts, such as electricity supply agreements, service contracts and contracted capital commitments. This was a major shortcoming of the paper that was later addressed by the G4+1.

In any event, the G4+1 continued its discussions of these and other technical issues that emerged from the 1996 discussion paper, and in December 1999 issued a new Position Paper on the same subject.

1.2.2 The G4+1's 1999 Position Paper

This Position Paper, entitled *Leases: Implementation of a new approach*, explored further the principles that should determine the extent of the assets and liabilities that lessees and lessors would recognise under leases, and how they might be applied to account for many of the features that are found in lease contracts.

Following the criticism received on the 1996 paper's failure to deal with executory contracts, the Position Paper addressed this issue. It concluded that leases can be distinguished from executory contracts by the fact that leases cease to be executory when the lessor has provided the lessee with access to the leased property for the lease term. Based on this distinction, the G4+1 was able to assert that the proposals set out in the new Position Paper would, therefore, not apply to executory contracts, including take-or-pay contracts or service contracts (an assertion that has now, somewhat ironically, been contradicted by the IFRIC – see 2.2 below).

In dealing with accounting by lessees, the paper proposed that the objective should be to record, at the beginning of the lease term, the fair value of the rights and obligations that are conveyed by the lease. It defined fair value as the consideration given by the lessee, including the liabilities incurred, except where the fair value of the asset received is more clearly evident.[11] This means that where a renewal or purchase option has a significant value that can be ascertained with sufficient reliability, the option should be accounted for separately from the rights to use the property for the non-cancellable period of the lease. Additionally a portion of the minimum lease payments would be deemed to relate to the purchase of the option.

Although leases normally specify minimum rentals that must be paid over the lease term, some leases require the lessee to pay additional amounts that are not fixed in advance. Instead, the actual amounts that the lessee will be required to pay are contingent on the outcome of uncertain future events. Such rentals are commonly referred to as contingent rentals. Common examples are motor vehicle leases containing clauses where rentals are increased to reflect the actual mileage driven above an initially agreed mileage; property leases in the retail industry where rentals are related to the turnover in the lessee's business; and property leases where rents are periodically reset to current market values to take account of inflation. Arrangements involving leases of intangible assets, such as licences of trade marks, patents or other intellectual property, also commonly require payments that are linked to the licensee's exploitation of the rights acquired (such as royalties on sales derived from the use of the property). Under IAS 17 contingent rentals are not included in the minimum lease payments for the purpose of determining whether a lease is a finance lease or an operating lease. Nor are they included in the minimum lease payments that are recognised as assets and liabilities in the event that the lease is treated as a finance lease. Nevertheless, the treatment of contingent rentals is important under the approach advocated by the G4+1 because it directly affects the amount of assets and liabilities that would be recognised for many leases.

The paper asserts that leases that contain renewal and purchase options give rise to similar issues to leases that contain contingent rentals, especially those that vary with usage. The similarity is that both kinds of lease give the lessee the option to 'purchase more' of the asset; the difference is simply whether the lessee purchases more time or more usage. In view of this similarity, the paper suggests that the same principles ought to apply to both circumstances. From this follows the suggestion that if the minimum payments required by the lease (such as the minimum payments specified in leases with contingent rentals) are clearly unrepresentative of the value of the property rights conveyed by the lease, an amount reflecting the fair value of such rights should be recognised instead. Thus the fair value of the property rights conveyed by a lease might be determined by reference to the payments required by a similar lease that had no provision for contingent rentals.

Where a lease conveys the right to use the leased item for part of its economic life only and the lessee provides a guarantee of its residual value at the end of the lease, the paper suggests that an asset and liability should be recognised at the beginning of the lease term measured at the present value of the payments the lessee is required to make during the lease term and the fair value of the guarantee (if it is practical to quantify it). The asset initially recognised represents the fair value of the right to use the item for the lease term.

The paper therefore recommends that after initial recognition the carrying value of the residual value guarantee obligation should be remeasured to reflect changes in the current estimate of the expenditure expected to be required to settle the obligation. The G4+1's preferred view was that the carrying amount of both the lease liability and the lease asset should be increased or decreased (subject to the carrying amount of the asset not being increased above a value that would cause an impairment loss), and the asset's revised carrying amount should be depreciated over the remainder of the lease term.

The following table provides an overview of the items that would be included in the liabilities of a lessee (and reported as such, with an asset at the beginning of the lease of a corresponding amount) and those that would not.

Items included in initial assets and liabilities	Items excluded from initial assets and liabilities
Minimum payments required by lease	
Amounts payable in respect of obtaining renewal options	Rentals relating to optional renewal periods
Contingent rentals that represent consideration for the fair value of rights conveyed to the lessee	Contingent rentals relating to optional additional usage
Fair value of residual value guarantees	Residual values guaranteed where transfer of economic benefits in settlement is not probable

Leases that are at present characterised as operating leases (and therefore not included on the balance sheet) would give rise to assets and liabilities – but only to the extent of the fair values of the rights and obligations that are conveyed by the lease.

The general effect of the approach proposed by the G4+1 is that the amounts recognised as an asset and a liability by a lessee in respect of a lease of a given item would vary in amount depending on the nature of the lease. The financial statements would thus reflect the extent to which different leasing arrangements result in financial obligations and provide financial flexibility.

The Paper also proposed significant changes to lessor accounting practices.[12] Lessors would report financial assets (representing amounts receivable from the lessee) and residual interests as separate assets. In the G4+1's view, this would be a marked improvement in lessor accounting, on the basis that a lessor's investment in a leased asset has two distinct elements, receivables and residual interests, which are subject to quite different risks. The amounts reported as financial assets by lessors would, in general, be the converse of the amounts reported by lessees as liabilities.

1.2.3   Comment on the G4+1 Position Paper

It has long been inevitable that lease accounting would be brought into line with more recent standards and the fair value agenda of the IASB, because IAS 17 clearly has a different underlying basis. However, whatever theoretical underpinnings are used to support the accounting treatment, we believe that it is fundamental that a revised leasing standard should be based on a theoretical approach that is consistent with that taken in the IASB's other standards, for example, those dealing with provisions such as IAS 37 – *Provisions, Contingent Liabilities and Contingent Assets* – and IFRS 3 – *Business Combinations* – and investment property, IAS 40 – *Investment Property*.

It is a matter of some debate how the changes in the balance sheet structure of reporting entities that would result from the proposals would be viewed by the markets. Logic dictates that, because the proposed accounting has no impact on the prediction of future cash flows, users of accounts should not be unduly concerned by changes in the way in which leases are accounted for. Nevertheless, although changes in accounting in themselves do not change cash flows, they may focus attention on existing ancillary problems by making the resulting inconsistencies more obvious.

We believe that the Paper is confused in its approach to the initial measurement of assets and liabilities of lessees. This confusion lies in the manner in which the Paper rationalises its accounting for rights and obligations under lease contracts as being the simple application of 'the normal principle of recognising assets and liabilities'. The Paper states quite correctly that 'assuming arm's length parties, the cost of an acquired asset is normally measured by the fair value of the consideration given'.[13] This is the principle that is followed throughout IAS, including for the initial recognition under IAS 38 – *Intangible Assets* – and IAS 40.[14] However, what follows in the Discussion Paper is, in our view, a distortion of this principle. The distortion comes through in the Paper's ensuing discussion of the precise nature of the recognised asset.

The issue is that the Paper focuses in conceptual terms on the recognition of the acquired asset (right) 'obtained by the lease', whilst the mechanics of the accounting are driven entirely by the recognition of the corresponding liability. The Paper focuses on the lessee recognising at 'fair value' a tangible asset and corresponding liability, whilst the economic substance is that the lessee has incurred a liability (equal to the present value of the expected payments under the lease contract), and acquired an *intangible* asset in the form of the right to use the asset. The fair value of the liability represents the cost of an intangible asset, not the fair value of a tangible asset. We believe that this is a distinction that is important to the disclosure of the asset in the accounts as well as to its initial and subsequent measurement. It would be misleading to describe, for example, a short-term non-assignable property lease in the balance sheet as tangible fixed asset land and buildings; in our view, both in terms of economic substance and legal form, this is an intangible right to use an asset for a specified period and we believe that it should be described and presented as such in the accounts.

The problem is then exacerbated in the discussion of subsequent remeasurement,[15] where in our view the Paper misuses the symmetry argument. The only time there is symmetry between the asset and liability is on initial recognition when the liability is recognised at present value of the expected payments under the contract, and the asset is measured at its corresponding cost. Subsequent accounting of the liability and asset should thereafter be governed by principles equivalent to those set out in IAS 37 and IAS 38, respectively.[16]

1.2.4 *The next step*

It has long been the announced intention of the IASB and other major standard setters to remove the distinction between operating and finance leases and responses to the G4+1 Position Paper showed significant support for the idea of a single accounting approach to all leases. However respondents raised concerns about how such an approach might be implemented, and whether the proposals as presented would secure similar accounting for economically similar transactions.

The IASB discussed a draft plan for the leasing project in May 2003 and tentatively agreed that the objective of the project is to develop a single method of accounting based on a conceptual model for leases that is consistent with the IASB's *Framework*.[17] At their November 2003 meeting the Board tentatively agreed that the proposed approach of analysing the contractual rights and obligations arising from lease contracts should be developed further. It was noted that consideration would have to be given to the decisions being made in other projects, such as revenue recognition, to ensure consistency.[18]

As part of the IASB's partnership strategy of involving national standard setters, the UK's ASB is undertaking the research project on behalf of the IASB. It reports that the leasing research project will examine initially leases of property, plant and equipment; how to distinguish between such leases and contracts for services; lessee recognition of time components of assets and obligations to pay for them; contingent rentals and optional features; the treatment of lessee guarantees and accounting for sale and leasebacks. Lessor issues to be addressed include accounting for investment property, short-term leases and revenue recognition. Financial reporting by lessors is to be addressed in order to ensure transparent reporting of financial and non-financial assets and liabilities. The project will subsequently consider how the principles derived for tangible assets may be applied to intangible assets.[19]

The IASB has tentatively agreed that the assets and liabilities to be recognised should reflect the conveyance of the right of use and control of associated future economic benefits for the period of the contract, rather than the conveyance of the whole of the physical property. That is, the IASB intends to follow the general approach in the G4+1 Position Paper regarding the nature of the 'lease asset'. However, several of the IASB's other ongoing projects will interact with the leasing project and in some cases other developments mean that some of the fundamental elements of the approach in the G4+1 Position Paper are having to be reconsidered. For example, delivery of the physical asset was proposed in the Position Paper as the point at which the asset and liability are recognised. What will probably be numbered as IFRIC Interpretation 3 – *Determining whether an arrangement contains a lease*[20] (approved by the IFRIC at their October 2004 meeting and discussed at 2.2.1 below) would result in some supply arrangements (such as take-or-pay contracts) being classified as leases, even though the underlying physical property is never delivered to the purchaser. As a result, further consideration is being given to the nature of the rights being conveyed, the point at which the entity obtains control over these rights, and therefore when recognition is appropriate.[21]

2 SCOPE AND CLASSIFICATION OF LEASES

2.1 Scope of IAS 17

The standard applies in accounting for all leases other than:

- lease agreements to explore for or use minerals, oil, natural gas and similar non-regenerative resources; and
- licensing agreements for such items as motion picture films, video recordings, plays, manuscripts, patents and copyrights.

Furthermore, the standard should not be applied to the measurement by:

- lessees of investment property held under finance leases; or
- lessors of investment property leased out under operating leases,

as in these cases IAS 40 applies; (see Chapter 12); or

- lessees of biological assets held under finance leases; or
- lessors of biological assets leased out under operating leases,

as in these cases IAS 41 – *Agriculture* – applies (see Chapter 36).[22]

2.2 What are leases?

IAS 17 defines a lease as 'an agreement whereby the lessor conveys to the lessee in return for a payment or series of payments the right to use an asset for an agreed period of time.'[23] The standard applies to agreements that transfer the right to use assets even though substantial services by the lessor may be called for in connection with the operation or maintenance of such assets. On the other hand, it does not apply to agreements that are contracts for services that do not transfer the right to use assets from one contracting party to the other. The definition of a lease includes contracts for the hire of an asset that contain a provision giving the hirer an option to acquire title to the asset when agreed conditions have been agreed (sometimes known as hire purchase contacts).[24] However, in recent years new types of arrangements have arisen in practice that do not take the legal form of leases. They take many forms but essentially combine rights to use assets and the provision of services or outputs for agreed periods of time in return for a payment or series of payments. As it was uncertain whether IAS 17 applied to such arrangements, the issues have been considered by the IFRIC, which at its October 2004 meeting approved (what will probably be numbered as) IFRIC Interpretation 3 – *Determining whether an arrangement contains a lease* – that is considered further in 2.2.1 below.[25] Some of the arrangements under service concession arrangements give rise to further accounting issues that have been separately addressed by the IFRIC; these are discussed in 3.7 below. The SIC had previously considered whether all transactions in the legal form of a lease should be considered under IAS 17 at all. The results of these deliberations, SIC-27 – *Evaluating the Substance of Transactions Involving the Legal Form of a Lease*,[26] are covered in 2.2.2 below.

2.2.1   Determining whether an arrangement contains a lease

The IFRIC issued Draft Interpretation D3 – *Determining whether an Arrangement contains a Lease* – in January 2004,[27] that was subsequently approved at its October 2004 meeting. Although the IFRIC considered that it was similar to the equivalent US guidance and indeed had the same title (EITF 01-8 – *Determining whether an arrangement contains a lease*),[28] it was the case that the same arrangement could be assessed differently under D3 and EITF 01-8. As a result of comments received and further consideration of the issues, the IFRIC concluded that 'there was no compelling reason' for different assessments under IFRSs and US GAAP. The IFRIC therefore decided that it would seek to eliminate the differences by adopting the approach, and as far as possible the actual wording, in EITF 01-8 for determining whether an arrangement contains a lease.[29]

What will probably be numbered as IFRIC Interpretation 3 notes that arrangements have developed in recent years that do not take the legal form of a lease but that convey rights to use items for agreed periods of time in return for a payment or series of payments.[30] However, the interpretation not only addresses this type of arrangement but also the more traditional forms of arrangement that are also within its scope.

The Interpretation focuses on the accounting implications of the following, in all of which an entity (the supplier) conveys a right to use an asset to another entity (the purchaser), together with related services or outputs:

- outsourcing arrangements, including outsourcing of the data processing functions of an entity;

- arrangements in the telecommunications industry, where suppliers of network capacity enter into contracts to provide purchasers with rights to capacity; and

- take-or-pay and similar contracts, in which purchasers must make specified payments regardless of whether they take delivery of the contracted products or services (e.g. where purchasers are committed to acquiring substantially all of the output of a supplier's power generator).[31]

Service concession arrangements, which were specifically referred to in the interpretation, are the subject of a separate IFRIC project on Service Concession Arrangements described in Chapter 27. This project also deals with the decision as to whether a specific arrangement may fall within the scope of the IFRIC Interpretation – *Determining whether an arrangement contains a lease.*

The IFRIC concluded that an arrangement of one of these types could be within the scope of IAS 17 if it met the definition of a lease, e.g. if it conveyed to the lessee in return for a payment or series of payments the right to use an asset for an agreed period of time.[32] IAS 17 applies to the lease element of the arrangement notwithstanding the related services or outputs because IAS 17 applies to 'agreements that transfer the right to use assets even though substantial services by the lessor may be called for in connection with the operation or maintenance of such assets.'[33] This is regardless of the fact that the arrangement is not described as a lease and is likely to grant rights that are significantly different from those in a formal lease agreement. The IFRIC therefore concluded that it should provide guidance to assist in determining whether an arrangement is, or contains, a lease.[34]

The IFRIC Interpretation – *Determining whether an arrangement contains a lease*[35] – approved by the IFRIC at their October 2004 meeting, has the objective only of dealing with the practical issues that arise when applying IAS 17 to arrangements that are not leases in form: how to identify an arrangement that is in substance a lease, when to make the assessment and how to measure the lease element.[36] The Interpretation does not provide any guidance for determining how such a lease should be classified under IAS 17[37] (in other words, it could be a finance lease or an operating lease under IAS 17), nor does it expect the guidance to extend the scope of that standard. If an arrangement turns out to contain a lease or licence of a type excluded from the scope of IAS 17 (see 2.1 above), the Interpretation does not apply.[38]

A   How to determine whether an arrangement is, or contains, a lease

The IFRIC Interpretation – *Determining whether an arrangement contains a lease* – defines two criteria that must be met in order to determine whether an arrangement is, or contains a lease, as follows:[39]

(a)   fulfilment of the arrangement depends on a specific asset or assets; and

(b)   the arrangement conveys a right to use the asset

These are discussed in B and C below.

B   Identification of an asset

IAS 17 only applies to an arrangement in which there is a 'right to use an asset', so an arrangement will not contain a lease unless it depends on a specific asset or assets. The Interpretation notes that some arrangements transfer the right to use an asset that is a component of a larger asset but the issue of whether and when such rights should be accounted for as leases is not dealt with in the Interpretation – *Determining whether an Arrangement contains a Lease.*[40]

There are many such arrangements in practice. For example, a plant that consists of more than one production unit or line might be regarded as a single 'component' or alternatively each of its units or lines might be regarded as a separate 'component'. Similar examples from the telecommunications industry include communication satellites that contain dozens of identical transponders and fibre optical cables that contain more than 100 pairs of fibre. The Interpretation does not attempt to address whether there is any conceptual difference between, say, using a quarter of the capacity of a whole pipeline and all of the capacity of a pipeline a quarter of the size.

Nevertheless, it is fundamental to the Interpretation that an arrangement only contains a lease if it contains the rights to use an asset. It provides the following additional guidance.

A specific asset that is explicitly identified by the arrangement will not be the subject of a lease if the arrangement is not dependent on the asset. If the seller is required under the arrangement to deliver a specified quantity of goods or services and has the right or ability to provide those goods using other assets not specified in the agreement, the arrangement will not contain a lease.[41]

To take a relatively simple example, an arrangement in which an entity outsources its product delivery department will not contain a lease if the seller is obliged to make available a certain number of delivery vehicles of a certain standard specification and the seller is a delivery organisation with many other vehicles available. However, if the seller has to supply and maintain a specified number of specialist vehicles in the purchaser's livery, then this arrangement is more likely to contain a lease. The latter arrangement may be commercially more akin to outsourcing the entity's delivery vehicle purchasing functions rather than its delivery functions. Similar issues would have to be taken into account if the data processing functions are outsourced as these may require substantial investment by the seller in computer hardware and terminals dedicated to the use of a single customer.

On the other hand, an arrangement may still contain a lease if a specific item is not explicitly identified but it would not be economically feasible or practical for the supplier to provide the use of alternative items. For example, the supplier may only own one suitable asset.[42]

Some arrangements may require the supplier to replace the underlying item with a similar item if the original item is unavailable (e.g. because it is unexpectedly inoperable). The IFRIC takes the view as that such a requirement is in effect a warranty obligation and does not preclude lease treatment.[43]

C   *The arrangement conveys a right to use the item*

An arrangement does not convey the right to use an asset unless the purchaser has the right to control the use of the underlying item, which depends on any one of the following conditions being met:[44]

(a)   The purchaser has the ability or right to operate the asset or direct others to operate the asset in a manner it determines while obtaining or controlling more than an insignificant amount of the output or other utility of the asset,

(b)   The purchaser has the ability or right to control physical access to the underlying asset while obtaining or controlling more than an insignificant amount of the output or other utility of the asset, or

(c)   Facts and circumstances indicate that it is remote that one or more parties other than the purchaser will take more than an insignificant amount of the output or other utility that will be produced or generated by the asset during the term of the arrangement, and the price that the purchaser will pay for the output is neither contractually fixed per unit of output nor equal to the current market price per unit of output as of the time of delivery of the output.

Therefore, control of the asset may be obtained in circumstances in which an entity obtains 'more than an insignificant amount of the output' but *only* if it has the ability or right to operate (or direct others to operate) in a manner that it determines or can control physical access to the asset.

On the other hand, a purchaser that pays market price at the date of transfer will not control the asset just because it takes almost all of the output. It would also have to be demonstrated that it controlled the asset by virtue of (a) or (b) above. The same applies if the price is contractually fixed, which is typically the case in take-or-pay contracts. Just because the price is fixed it does not necessarily follow that the arrangement contains a lease. Control of the underlying asset must be demonstrated under (a) or (b).

The effects of this are demonstrated by the following examples.

D   Analysing the arrangements

The following examples of arrangements that may or may not contain a lease explain the identification of an asset and the application of the control criteria described above. Example 23.1 is based on an illustrative example in what will probably be numbered as IFRIC Interpretation 3 – *Determining whether an arrangement contains a lease* – approved by the IFRIC at their October 2004 meeting:[45]

Example 23.1:   An arrangement that contains a lease

A production company (the purchaser) enters into an arrangement with a third party (the supplier) to supply a minimum quantity of gas needed in its production process for a specified period of time. The supplier designs and builds a facility neat to the purchaser's plant to produce the needed gas and maintains ownership and control over all significant aspects of operating the facility. The agreement provides for the following:

- The facility is explicitly identified in the arrangement, and the supplier has the contractual right to supply gas from other sources. However, supplying gas from other sources is not economically feasible or practicable.

- The supplier has the right to provide gas to other customers and to remove and replace the facility's equipment and modify or expand the facility to enable the supplier to do so. However, at inception of the arrangement, the supplier has no plans to modify or expand the facility. The facility is designed to meet only the purchaser's needs.

- The supplier is responsible for repairs, maintenance and capital expenditures.

- The supplier must stand ready to deliver a minimum quantity of gas each month.

- On a monthly basis, the purchaser will pay a fixed capacity charge and a variable charge based on actual production taken. The purchaser must pay the fixed capacity charge irrespective of whether it takes any of the facility's production. The variable charge includes the facility's actual energy costs, which comprise approximately 90 per cent of the facility's total variable costs. The supplier is subject to increased costs resulting from the facility's inefficient operations.

- If the facility does not produce the stated minimum quantity, the supplier must return all or a portion of the fixed capacity charge.

The arrangement contains a lease within the scope of IAS 17. An asset (the facility) is explicitly identified in the arrangement and fulfilment of the arrangement is dependent on the facility. While the supplier has the right to supply gas from other sources, its ability to do so is not substantive. The purchaser has obtained the right to use the facility because, on the facts presented-in particular, that the facility is designed to meet only the purchaser's needs and the supplier has no plans to expand or modify the facility-it is remote that one or more parties other than the purchaser will take more than an insignificant amount of the facility's output and the price the purchaser will pay is neither contractually fixed per unit of output nor equal to the current market price per unit of output as of the time of delivery of the output.

Having concluded that the arrangement contains a lease, it is then necessary to classify it as an operating or a finance lease. Identifying the relevant lease payments is dealt with in F below.

The following example indicates circumstances in which an arrangement does not contain a lease because no specific asset has been identified:

Example 23.2:   An arrangement that does not contain a lease

A purchaser enters into a take-or-pay contract to buy industrial gases from a supplier. The supplier is a large company operating similar plants at various locations. The amount of gas that the purchaser is committed to buy is roughly equivalent to the total output of one of the plants. Because a good distribution network is available, the supplier is able to provide gas from various locations to fulfil its supply obligation.

In this example, the arrangement does not depend upon a specific asset. This is because it is economically feasible and practical for the supplier to fulfil the arrangement by providing use of more than one plant. A specific asset has therefore not been identified either explicitly or implicitly.

Payments under the contract may be unavoidable (because it is a take-or-pay arrangement) and the purchaser may in fact take all of the output of a single plant but the arrangement does not convey a right to use the asset. The purchaser does not have the right to control the use of the underlying asset. It does not have the ability or right to operate the asset in a manner it determines (or to direct others to do so on its behalf), and it does not control physical access. The arrangement does not contain a lease.

The significance of the control concept is clearly illustrated in the following example based on the second illustrative example in (what will probably be numbered as) IFRIC Interpretation 3 – *Determining whether an arrangement contains a lease.*[46]

Example 23.3:   An arrangement in which the purchaser does not control the asset

A manufacturing company (the purchaser) enters into an arrangement with a third party (the supplier)to supply a specific component part of its manufactured product for a specified period of time. The supplier designs and constructs a plant next to the purchaser's factory to produce the component part. The designed capacity of the plant exceeds the purchaser's current needs, and the supplier maintains ownership and control over all significant aspects of operating the plant.

The supplier's plant is explicitly identified in the arrangement, but the supplier has the right to fulfil the arrangement by shipping the component parts from another plant owned by the supplier. However, to do so for any extended period of time would be uneconomical. The supplier must stand ready to deliver a minimum quantity. The purchaser is required to pay a fixed price per unit for the actual quantity taken. Even if the purchaser's needs are such that they do not need the stated minimum quantity, they still pay only for the actual quantity taken.

The supplier has the right to sell the component parts to other customers and has a history of doing so (by selling in the replacement parts market) so it is expected that parties other than the purchaser will take more than an insignificant amount of the component parts produced at the supplier's plant.

The supplier is responsible for repairs, maintenance, and capital expenditures of the plant.

This arrangement does not contain a lease. An asset (the plant) is explicitly identified in the arrangement and fulfilment of the arrangement is dependent on the facility. While the supplier has the right to supply component parts from other sources, the supplier would not have the ability to do so because it would be uneconomical. However, the purchaser has not obtained the right to use the plant because it does not control it, for the following reasons:

(a)   the purchaser does not have the ability or right to operate or direct others to operate the plant or control physical access to the plant, and

(b)   the likelihood that parties other than the purchaser will take more than an insignificant amount of the component parts produced at the plant is more than remote, based on the facts presented.

E   *When to assess the arrangements*

The IFRIC Interpretation – *Determining whether an arrangement contains a lease* –approved by the IFRIC at their October 2004 meeting, states that the assessment described at A above, i.e. whether an arrangement contains a lease, should be made at the inception of the arrangement, being the earlier of the date of the arrangement and the date of commitment by the parties to the principle terms of the arrangement, and on the basis of all the facts and circumstances. A reassessment of whether the arrangement contains a lease should be made only if:[47]

(a)   there is a change in the terms of the contract, except for a renewal or extension of the arrangement;

(b)   a renewal option is exercised or an extension is agreed, unless these had been taken into account in the original assessment of the lease term in accordance with IAS 17;[48]

(c)   a change in whether or not the arrangement depends on specified item; or

(d)   a substantial physical change to the specified assets.

Changes to estimates, for example of the amount of output that would be taken by the purchaser, would not trigger a reassessment.[49]

If the arrangement is reassessed and found to contain a lease or vice versa then lease accounting will be applied or discontinued as from the time that the arrangement is reassessed.[50]

F   *Separation of leases from other payments within the arrangement*

If an arrangement contains a lease, both parties to the arrangement are to apply IAS 17 to the lease element of the arrangement unless it is an arrangement that is not within IAS 17's scope. It must be stressed that this means that the lease element of the arrangement may be classified as an operating or finance lease. Other elements of the arrangement must be accounted for in accordance with the appropriate standards.[51]

Therefore, having identified the lease payments, the entity may still classify the arrangement as an operating lease if it does not transfer substantially all the risks and rewards incident to ownership of an asset[52] (see 2.3 below).

In order to apply IAS 17, the payments and other consideration under the arrangement must be separated at inception or on reassessment between those for the lease of the asset and those for other services and outputs. What will probably be numbered as IFRIC Interpretation 3 – *Determining whether an arrangement contains a lease* – requires this to be done on the basis of their relative fair values.[53] This may require the purchaser to use estimation techniques – this appears to be somewhat of an understatement as, unless the price to be paid for both elements is clear and they have both been negotiated at market value, it will always be necessary to use some form of estimation. The Interpretation suggests that it may be possible to estimate either the lease payments (by comparison with similar leases that do not contain other elements) or the other elements (using comparable arrangements) and then deduct the estimated amount from the total under the arrangement.[54]

This is not a straightforward exercise and the Interpretation does not go into any further detail as to how it would be carried out. There may be no market-based evidence of fair value of the underlying assets because of their specialised nature or because they are rarely sold, in which case it will be necessary to use valuation techniques. Discounted cash flow projections based on estimated future cash flows that will be generated by specialised assets may be difficult to obtain, although it should be possible to make some form of estimate, if need be with the assistance of valuation experts. The service elements within these agreements are by no means standardised and it may not be easy to identify comparable arrangements. The exercise will be complicated by the fact that the fair value of a bundle of services is not necessarily the same as the aggregation of their individual fair values and making such an assumption could lead to an overstatement of the service element and consequent understatement of the fair value of the lease element. The discount rates should reflect current market assessments of the uncertainty and timing of the cash flows, i.e. the risk inherent in the separate elements of the transaction. There are usually very different risk profiles for the provision of services and for leasing assets. If, as suggested by the Interpretation, the entity estimates one of the elements under the arrangement and derives the other by deduction, it will always be necessary to carry out a 'sense check' on the derived payments.

The IFRIC Interpretation – *Determining whether an arrangement contains a lease* – also suggests that only in rare cases will a purchaser conclude that it is impracticable to separate the payments reliably. In the case of a finance lease, the entity should recognise an asset at an amount equal to the fair value of the underlying asset that it has identified as the subject of the lease, as described in B above. A liability should be set up at the same amount as the asset. The entity would impute a finance charge based on the purchaser's incremental borrowing rate of interest and, from this, compute the reduction in the liability as payments are made.[55] Presumably the IFRIC considers that the entity's incremental borrowing rate would have to be used because, if it were possible to determine the interest rate implicit in the lease, the arrangement would not be one in which it was impracticable to separate the payments reliably.

What this means, of course, is that an entity may be required to account for an asset held under a finance lease when it is, in fact, unable to identify the lease payments. It is to be hoped that the application of the control model means that this will not often happen in practice; control is more likely to result in an entity being able to identify the underlying payment streams.

If the lease is assessed as an operating lease, applying the Interpretation might affect the recognition of revenue over the term of the arrangement. IAS 17 requires lessors and lessees to recognise operating lease payments on a straight-line basis over the lease term (unless another systematic basis is more representative) and this may not be in line with the payments for the lease element so some adjustments might be required.[56]

There are disclosure implications if the arrangement is deemed to contain an operating lease and the purchaser concludes that it is impracticable to separate the payments reliably. These are discussed further below.

G   *Disclosure requirements*

IAS 17 required a general description of the lessee's material leasing arrangements,[57] which will require disclosure of the details of major transactions that have fallen within (what will probably be numbered as) IFRIC Interpretation 3 – *Determining whether an arrangement contains a lease.*

There are no specific disclosure requirements if the arrangements are assessed as containing finance leases as these arrangements are deemed to be within the scope of IAS 17 and therefore within its disclosure requirements.

However, if it were considered to be an operating lease, the Interpretation may result in additional disclosures, because IAS 17 specifies that the lessor and lessee should disclose the future minimum lease payments. Although the arrangements discussed in the Interpretation typically represent significant future commitments, purchasers are not required to disclose them in the financial statements unless they fall within IAS 17. The IFRIC argues that bringing such arrangements within the scope of IAS 17 will provide users of financial statements with relevant information that is useful for assessing the purchaser's solvency, liquidity and adaptability.[58]

As long as the entity is able to distinguish the lease payments from other element of the lease, then the disclosed information will relate only to the lease element of the arrangement. There appears to be no intention to require entities to disclose the service (executory) element of arrangements; the IFRIC agreed that it would consider addressing disclosure of executory contracts more generally in a separate project.[59] However, if the arrangement is one of those in which it is impracticable to separate the payments reliably, the Interpretation – *Determining whether an arrangement contains a lease* – requires disclosure of all payments under the arrangement separately from other minimum lease payments, together with a statement that that the disclosed payments also include payments for non-lease elements in the arrangement.[60]

H   *Effective date and transitional arrangements*

What will probably be numbered as IFRIC Interpretation 3 – *Determining whether an arrangement contains a lease* – approved by the IFRIC at their October 2004 meeting, applies to annual periods beginning on or after 1 January 2006. Early adoption is encouraged but entities complying early must disclose this fact.[61]

The Interpretation is to be applied with retrospective effect in accordance with IAS 8 – *Accounting policies, changes in accounting estimates and errors* – see Chapter 3. However, if a transaction has been entered into prior to the start of the earliest period for which comparative information is presented, it need only assess whether the arrangement contains a lease on the basis of the facts and circumstances existing at the start of that earliest period.[62] It need not go back to the inception of the arrangement.

2.2.2   Transactions that are not, in substance, leases

While there are some arrangements that contain leases that are not formally lease contracts, the reverse is also true: there are some 'lease agreements' that are not, in substance leases. These issues are addressed by SIC-27.[63] The Interpretation became effective on 31 December 2001, with retrospective effect as a change in accounting policy in accordance with IAS 8.

Essentially, the SIC-27 deals with the issue of how to evaluate the substance of transactions, or a series of linked transactions, in the legal form of a lease. The main purpose of the Interpretation is to reinforce the principle of substance over form, and to ensure that, where appropriate, a series of linked transactions should be accounted for as one transaction. If the transaction does not meet the definition of a lease under IAS 17, SIC-27 deals with the extent to which the arrangement gives rise to other assets and liabilities of the reporting entity, the reporting of any other obligations and the recognition of fee income.[64]

An entity may enter into a transaction or a series of structured transactions (an arrangement) with an unrelated party or parties (an investor) that involves the legal form of a lease. Although the details may vary considerably, a typical example involves an entity leasing or selling assets to an investor and leasing the same assets back. The lease and leaseback transactions are often entered into so that the investor may achieve a tax advantage.[65] The following example, from SIC–27 illustrates an arrangement that does not, in substance, involve a lease under IAS 17:

Example 23.4:   Substance of an arrangement

An entity (Company A) leases a specialised asset that it requires to conduct its business to an Investor and leases the same asset back for a shorter period of time under a sublease. At the end of the sublease period, Company A has the right to buy back the rights of the Investor under a purchase option. If Company A does not exercise its purchase option, the Investor has options available to it under each of which it receives a minimum return on its investment in the headlease – the Investor may put the underlying asset back to Company A, or require it to provide a return on the Investor's investment in the headlease.

The arrangement achieves a tax advantage for the Investor who pays a fee to Company A and prepays the lease payment obligations under the headlease. The agreement requires the amount prepaid to be invested in risk-free assets and, as a requirement of finalising the execution of the legally binding arrangement, placed into a separate investment account held by a Trustee outside of the control of the entity.

Over the term of the sublease, the sublease payment obligations are satisfied with funds of an equal amount withdrawn from the separate investment account. Company A guarantees the sublease payment obligations, and will be required to satisfy the guarantee should the separate investment account have insufficient funds. Company A, but not the Investor, has the right to terminate the sublease early under certain circumstances (e.g., a change in local or international tax law causes the Investor to lose part or all of the tax benefits, or Company A decides to dispose of (e.g., replace, sell or deplete) the underlying asset) and upon payment of a termination value to the Investor. If Company A chooses early termination, then it would pay the termination value from funds withdrawn from the separate investment account, and if the amount remaining in the separate investment account is insufficient, the difference would be paid by Company A.[66]

SIC-27 argues that a series of transactions that involve the legal form of a lease should be accounted for as one transaction when the overall economic effect cannot be understood without reference to the series of transactions as a whole. All aspects and implications of an arrangement should be evaluated to determine the substance of the arrangement, with greater weight given to those aspects and implications that will have an economic effect in practice. The accounting should reflect the substance of the arrangement.[67]

First, it must be part of a single 'arrangement'. The series of transactions must be closely interrelated, negotiated as a single transaction, and take place concurrently or in a continuous sequence.[68]

Second, there must be indicators that individually demonstrate that an arrangement may not, in substance, involve a lease under IAS 17. SIC-27 states that in the example above, these indicators are as follows:

(a)   the entity retains all the risks and rewards of ownership and there is no significant change in its rights to use the asset;

(b)   the primary reason for the arrangement is to achieve a particular tax result, and not to convey the right to use an asset; and

(c)   the options on which the arrangement depends are included on terms that make their exercise almost certain (e.g., a put option that is exercisable at a price sufficiently higher than the expected fair value when it becomes exercisable).[69]

In other words, the entity retains more rights than it would in a straightforward sale and finance leaseback. In the example, for instance, it retains all of the residual interests in the asset. The investor has no interest at all in the underlying asset while a lessor under a finance lease will often retain title and some residual value in the asset. The investor has only entered into the transaction to obtain a tax benefit.[70]

Third, the balances arising under the arrangement (in the example these comprise the separate investment account and the lease payment obligations under the sublease) must be assessed to see whether they represent assets and liabilities of the entity. SIC-27 refers to definitions of assets and liabilities and guidance in paragraphs 49-64 of the Framework. It argues that:

(a)   the investment account is not an asset of the entity because it cannot control it;

(b)   there is only a remote risk that the entity will have to pay out under the guarantee or reimburse the entire amount of any fee received; and

(c)   once the arrangement has been set up and the initial payments have been made, no further cash flows will be made by Company A.

Company A cannot use the cash in the investment account for its own benefit, nor can it prevent it being used to make lease payments to the investor. The lease payments will be satisfied solely from funds withdrawn from the separate investment account established with the initial cash flows. In the example, the terms of the arrangement require that a prepaid amount is invested in risk-free assets that are expected to generate sufficient cash flows to satisfy the lease payment obligations.[71] This also demonstrates, *inter alia,* that Company A is not, in substance, entering into a financing arrangement, as it has no need of the funds.

However, other obligations of the entity, including any guarantees provided and obligations incurred upon early termination, should be accounted for under IAS 37 or IAS 39, depending on the terms of the arrangement.[72] Therefore, if Company A were to elect to terminate the arrangement, it would have to provide for its exposure in excess of the available funds in the investment account.

Fourth, SIC-27 addresses the recognition of fee income. There are many factors that could affect the economic substance and nature of the fee and it may not be appropriate to recognise it in its entirety at the inception of the agreement if the entity has significant future performance obligations, retained risks or a significant risk of repayment. Factors to be taken into account include:

(a)   obligations that are conditions of earning the fee so that entering into the agreement is not the most significant act required by the arrangement;

(b)   limitations are put on the use of the underlying asset that lead to significant changes in the entity's rights to use the asset, e.g. the entity's right to deplete or sell it or pledge it as collateral;

(c)   the possibility of reimbursing any amount of the fee and possibly paying some additional amount is not remote. This occurs when, for example,

    (i)   the underlying asset is essential for the entity's business, in which case there is a possibility that the entity may be prepared to pay to terminate the arrangement early (and thereby be required to repay all or part of the fee); or

    (ii)   the possibility that there are insufficient assets in the investment account to meet the lease payment obligations is not remote, and therefore it is possible that the entity may be required to pay some additional amount. This may occur if the entity is required, or has some or total discretion, to invest in assets carrying more than an insignificant amount of risk (e.g., currency, interest rate or credit risk).[73]

Finally there are some specific presentation and disclosure requirements. The fee must be presented in the income statement based on its economic substance and nature.[74] The entity must disclose the following in each period that an arrangement exists:

An entity has to make the disclosures that are necessary to understand the arrangement and the accounting treatment adopted, including the following:

(a)   a description of the arrangement including:

    (i)   the underlying asset and any restrictions on its use;

    (ii)   the life and other significant terms of the arrangement;

    (iii) the transactions that are linked together, including any options; and

(b)   the accounting treatment of any fee received, the amount that has been recognised as income in the period, and the line item of the income statement in which it is included.

These disclosures should be provided individually for each arrangement or in aggregate for each class of arrangement. A class is a grouping of arrangements with underlying assets of a similar nature.[75]

2.3 Lease classification

2.3.1 Finance and operating leases

A finance lease is a 'lease that transfers substantially all the risks and rewards incident to ownership of an asset', and an operating lease is 'a lease other than a finance lease',[76] i.e. a lease that does not transfer substantially all the risks and rewards incidental to ownership.

However, the individual circumstances of a lessor and lessee may differ in respect of a single lease contract. As a result, it is perfectly possible that the application of the definitions to the different circumstances of the lessor and lessee may result in the same lease being classified differently by them. For example, a lease may be classified as an operating lease by the lessee and as a finance lease receivable by the lessor if it includes a residual value guarantee provided by a third party.[77] These are discussed further under 4.1.1 below.

2.3.2 Determining the substance of transactions

The classification of leases adopted in the standard is based on the extent to which the risks and rewards incident to ownership of a leased asset lie with the lessor or the lessee. Risks include the possibilities of losses from idle capacity or technological obsolescence and of variations in return due to changing economic conditions. Rewards may be represented by the expectation of profitable operation over the asset's economic life and of gain from appreciation in value or realisation of a residual value.[78] However, unlike some national standards (which include the rebuttable presumption that the transfer of substantially all of the risks and rewards occurs if, at the inception of the lease, the present value of the minimum lease payments amounts to substantially all (normally 90% or more) of the fair value of the leased asset) IAS 17 provides no numerical guidelines to be applied in classifying a lease as either finance or operating. It seems that it was a conscious decision of the (then) IASC Board not to refer to a percentage such as 90% in the standard, as it wanted to avoid the possibility of lease classification being reduced to a single pass or fail test.

Instead, the standard takes a more principles-based substance over form approach. It makes the statement that the classification of a lease depends on the substance of the transaction rather than the form of the contract, and lists a number of examples of situations that individually or in combination would normally lead to a lease being classified as a finance lease:[79]

(a)   the lease transfers ownership of the asset to the lessee by the end of the lease term;

(b)   the lessee has the option to purchase the asset at a price which is expected to be sufficiently lower than the fair value at the date the option becomes exercisable such that, at the inception of the lease, it is reasonably certain that the option will be exercised (frequently called a 'bargain purchase' option);

(c)   the lease term is for the major part of the economic life of the asset even if title is not transferred;

(d)   at the inception of the lease the present value of the minimum lease payments amounts to at least substantially all of the fair value of the leased asset; and

(e)   the leased assets are of a specialised nature such that only the lessee can use them without major modifications being made.

All of these are indicators that the lessor will look to no-one other than the lessee from whom to obtain a return from the leasing transaction, so it can be presumed that the lessee will, in fact, pay for the asset.

Although the first criterion refers to title being transferred, it is clear from the standard that title does not have to be transferred to the lessee for a lease to be classified as a finance lease.[80] The point is that, if title does transfer, then the lease will almost certainly be classified as a finance lease. 'Fair value' is defined as the amount for which an asset could be exchanged or a liability settled, between knowledgeable, willing parties in an arm's length transaction (see 3.1.2 below).[81] Options such as those referred to under (b) are common in lease agreements. The bargain purchase option is designed to give the lessor its expected lender's return but no more (comprising interest on its investment perhaps together with a relatively small fee), over the life of the agreement.

Criteria (c) and (d) above also include the unquantified expressions 'major part of' and 'substantially all'. By contrast, in US GAAP the equivalent to (c) above in SFAS 13 does quantify when a lease will be a capital lease, (the equivalent of a finance lease). In SFAS 13, if the lease term is equal to 75% or more of the estimated economic life of the leased asset, the lease will normally be a capital lease (there is an exception if the beginning of the lease term falls within the last 25% of the total estimated economic life of the leased property, including earlier years of use, where this criterion is not used for purposes of classifying the lease).[82] However in practice, if the lease is for the major part of the economic life of the asset then it is unlikely that the lessor will look to any party other than the lessee to obtain its return from the lease.

Similarly, whilst (d) above refers to the present value of the minimum lease payments being at least 'substantially all of the fair value of the asset', it does so without putting a percentage to it. We have already speculated as to why this may be; nevertheless, we see no harm in practice in at least applying the '90% test' described above as a rule of thumb benchmark as part of the overall process in reaching a judgement as to the classification of a lease. Clearly, though, it cannot be applied as a hard and fast rule.

For an example of the 90% test, see Example 23.6 at 3.1.9 below. In the example, the present value of the minimum lease payments is calculated to be 92.74% of the asset's fair value; as this exceeds 90%, this would indicate that the lease is a finance lease.

However, we would stress that the 90% test is not an explicit requirement of the standard and should not be applied as a rule or in isolation but it may be a useful tool to use in practice in attempting to determine the economic substance of a lease arrangement.

The standard then goes on to list the following indicators of situations that, individually or in combination, could also lead to a lease being classified as a finance lease:[83]

(a)   if the lessee can cancel the lease, the lessor's losses associated with the cancellation are borne by the lessee;

(b)   gains or losses from the fluctuation in the fair value of the residual fall to the lessee (for example, in the form of a rent rebate equalling most of the sales proceeds at the end of the lease); and

(c)   the lessee has the ability to continue the lease for a secondary period at a rent which is substantially lower than market rent.

In our view, other considerations that could be made in determining the economic substance of the lease arrangement include the following:

• are the lease rentals based on a market rate for use of the asset (which would indicate an operating lease) or a financing rate for use of the funds, which would be indicative of a finance lease?

• is the existence of put and call options a feature of the lease? If so, are they exercisable at a predetermined price or formula (indicating a finance lease) or are they exercisable at the market price at the time the option is exercised (indicating an operating lease)?

And finally, we have found the following to be a useful 'acid test' question to consider:

• does the lessor intend to earn his total return on this transaction alone or does he intend to rely on subsequent sales or lease revenue?[84] Clearly, if the lessor is looking to a return from a single lessee, then this would indicate that it is a finance lease.

2.3.3   *Changes to lease provisions*

Lease classification is made at the inception of the lease,[85] which is the earlier of the date of the lease agreement or of a commitment by the parties to the principal provisions of the lease.[86] Lease classification is only changed if, at any time during the lease, the lessee and the lessor agree to change the provisions of the lease (without renewing it) in such a way that it would have been classified differently at inception had the changed terms been in effect at that time. The revised agreement is considered as a new agreement and accounted for appropriately prospectively over the remaining term of the lease. On the other hand, changes in estimates (for example, changes in estimates of the economic life or of the residual value of the leased item) or changes in circumstances (for example, default by the lessee) do not result in the lease being reclassified for accounting purposes.[87] This is of particular relevance given the requirement in IAS 16 that the residual value and useful life of an asset must be reviewed at least at each financial year-end.[88]

2.3.4   Leases of land and buildings

Leases of land and buildings are classified as operating or finance leases in the same way as leases of other assets. However, land normally has an indefinite economic life and, unless title is expected to pass to the lessee by the end of the lease term, the lessee does not receive substantially all of the risks and rewards incident to ownership. A premium paid for a leasehold interest in land represents pre-paid lease payments that are amortised over the lease term in accordance with the pattern of benefits provided.[89] This means that they are not tangible fixed assets but should be disclosed as non-current assets, as appropriate, in the entity's balance sheet.

The following is an example of disclosure in the balance sheet, together with the supporting note.

Extract 23.1: Mandarin Oriental International Limited (2003)

Consolidated Balance Sheet [extract]

	Note	2003 US$m	Restated 2002 US$m
Net Assets			
Goodwill	7	18.0	22.0
Tangible assets	8	687.1	512.3
Leasehold land payments	9	193.4	187.6
Associates and joint ventures	10	240.2	271.2
Other investments	11	18.2	26.3
Pension assets	12	13.3	14.0
Deferred tax assets	13	6.4	4.1
Non-current assets		1,176.6	1,037.5

9   Leasehold land payments

	2003 US$m	2002 US$m
At 1st January	187.6	187.7
Acquisition of subsidiary (refer note 25c)	6.2	–
Additions	–	0.3
Amortization (refer note 2)	(0.4)	(0.4)
At 31st December	193.4	187.6

The above represent the upfront payments to acquire long-term interests in property owned by the principal subsidiaries listed on pages 68 and 69.

A characteristic of property leases in some jurisdictions (such as the UK) is that it is not possible to lease a building without leasing the land on which it stands – under UK property law all such leases are leases of land. There is no separate fair value for the land and buildings elements as they cannot be disposed of separately. However, in substance such leases may differ little from buying a property.[90] Under IAS 17 (revised 1997), there was some uncertainty as to how to account for this type of property lease; the standard gave no guidance on whether the elements were to be separately dealt with or how an apportionment was to be made. The 2004 revised standard now states explicitly that the land and buildings elements of leases are considered separately for the purposes of lease classification.[91]

The initial classification is based on whether or not title passes:

- if title to both elements passes, both land and buildings will be classified as finance leases and it is irrelevant whether it is classified as one lease or two (unless it is clear from other features that the lease does not transfer substantially all of the risks and rewards incidental to ownership of one or both elements); and

- where title to the land does not pass and it has an indefinite economic life, the land will be classified as an operating lease while the buildings element will be an operating lease or finance lease according to the classification in the standard.[92]

If either or both parts of the lease comprise a finance lease, the minimum lease payments are to be allocated between the land and buildings elements in proportion to the respective fair values of the leasehold interest in the land and buildings elements at the inception of the lease. The minimum lease payments must, of course, include any up-front payments, such as the payment for a lease premium.[93]

The allocation of the minimum lease payments should be weighted to reflect the fair value of the land and buildings components to the extent they are the subject of the lease. This means that the amount that is being allocated is the lessee's leasehold interest in the land and buildings and the compensation received by the lessor, not the relative fair values of the land and buildings. The amount for which the land could be purchased at the inception of the lease is not the same as the value of that interest to the lessee. As land has an indefinite life, the value to the lessor may not be significantly affected by the grant of the lease.[94]

The standard addresses the fact that it may not be possible to determine the fair values of the elements at inception and allows the following:

- if it is difficult or impossible to allocate the payments between the two elements, then the entire lease may be classified as a finance lease unless it is obvious that both the land and buildings elements are operating leases.[95]

- if the land element is immaterial, the lease may be treated as a single unit and classified as a finance or operating lease. The economic life of the entire leased asset will be the economic life of the buildings.[96]

Some examples of the ways in which these exemptions may operate in practice are as follows:

Example 23.5:   Leases of land and buildings

Company A leases a building (and the underlying land) for 10 years. The remaining economic life of the building when the lease is entered into is 30 years. The lease is for considerably less than the economic life of the building so it is obvious that both land and buildings elements are operating leases and no separation is necessary.

Company B takes on a 30-year lease of a new building and the underlying land. Although the building has a fabric life of 60 years, its economic life is estimated to be 30 years, after which it is expected to be technologically obsolete. The lease is for most of the economic life of the buildings and the present value of the minimum lease payments amounts to substantially all of the fair value of the building. It is not legally possible to lease the building without leasing the underlying land or, therefore, to estimate the relative fair values reliably. In any event, the lessor retains the residual value in the land and the lessee's interest in the land must be insignificant. The lease is accounted for as a finance lease of the building with an economic life of 30 years.

Company C acquires for an up-front premium a 75-year head lease of retail outlets on a retail park with an estimated economic life of 15 years, together with the underlying land and some car parking space. In this case, the lease would not be eligible for the exemptions noted above and the land and buildings elements of the lease must be considered separately for the purposes of lease classification, based on the relative fair values of the leasehold interests. It is clear that the building element is a finance lease, to be depreciated over 15 years. The land element is an operating lease but in this case the leasehold interest in the land will have a value to the lessee; its length is sufficient, for example, to allow Company C to redevelop the site. It will be separated from the interest in the building However, Company C may be a property developer or property investment company. If it is the former then the purchase of the leasehold interest may be part of the cost of constructing an asset for sale.). If it is a property investment company that uses the fair value model, it will account for the premium it has paid in accordance with 2.3.5 below.

2.3.5 *Leases and investment properties*

Until both IAS 17 and IAS 40 were amended in 2003, it was not possible under IFRS for an interest in property held under an operating lease to be classified as an investment property. This was of great significance to the property industry in places such as the UK, where long leasehold interests in property are common, and to other jurisdictions such as Hong Kong where there are no freehold interests. Such interests in the UK are normally acquired for an up-front premium that, if not recognised as an investment property asset would have to be treated as a prepayment and gradually amortised. The amortisation of the prepayment would have effectively forced these entities to depreciate assets that had not previously been depreciated. Now, entities are to be allowed to treat interests under operating leases as investment properties as long as they apply the fair value model (see Chapter 12). This change is clearly of major significance to entities that invest in property.

IAS 17 requires leases to be separated into land and building components, subject to this being possible or the land element being material (see 2.3.4 above). If the interest is to be an investment property carried at fair value in accordance with IAS 40, there is no requirement to separate the land and buildings elements of the lease.[97]

Once the lessee has chosen to account for an operating lease property interest as if it were held under a finance lease, it must continue to do so even if subsequent changes in circumstances mean that the property interest is no longer an investment property to the lessee. IAS 17 gives two examples:

(a)   the lessee occupies the property, in which case it is transferred to owner-occupied property at fair value at the date of change of use; or

(b)   the lessee grants a sublease over substantially all of its property interest to an unrelated third party. It will treat the sublease as a finance lease to the third party even though the interest may well be accounted for as an operating lease by that party.[98]

3 ACCOUNTING FOR FINANCE AND OPERATING LEASES

3.1 Finance leases – summary of accounting by lessees and lessors

Lessees recognise finance leases as assets and liabilities in their balance sheets at the commencement of the lease term at amounts equal at the inception of the lease to the fair value of the leased item or, if lower, at the present value of the minimum lease payments. In calculating the present value of the minimum lease payments the discount factor is the interest rate implicit in the lease, if this is practicable to determine; if not, the lessee's incremental borrowing rate should be used. Any initial direct costs of the lessee are added to the asset.[99] 'Fair value' and 'minimum lease payments' are defined in 3.1.2 and 3.1.3 below.

The fair value and the present value of the lease payments are both determined as at the inception of the lease. At commencement, the asset and liability for the future lease payments are recognised in the balance sheet at the same amount, with initial direct costs of the lessee then being added to the asset.[100] The terms and calculations of initial recognition by lessees are discussed further in 3.1.1 to 3.1.7 below.

Lease payments made by the lessee are apportioned between the finance charge and the reduction of the outstanding liability. The finance charge should be allocated to periods during the lease term so as to produce a constant periodic rate of interest on the remaining balance of the liability for each period.[101] This is covered in 3.2 below.

Lessors recognise assets held under a finance lease as receivables in their balance sheets and present them as a receivable at an amount equal to the net investment in the lease.[102] Lessors who are not manufacturers or dealers include costs that they have incurred in connection with arranging and negotiating a lease as part of the initial measurement of the finance lease receivable. Initial recognition by lessors, which is in many respects a mirror image of lessee recognition, follows at 3.3 below. The recognition of finance income and other issues in connection with subsequent measurement of the lessor's assets arising from finance leases is dealt with in 3.3.1 to 3.3.3 below.

Manufacturer or dealer lessors have specific issues with regard to recognition of selling profit and finance income. These are dealt with under 3.3.5 below.

3.1.1 Inception and commencement of the lease

The standard now distinguishes between the inception of the lease (when leases are classified) and the commencement of the lease term (when recognition takes place). The *inception* of the lease is the earlier of the date of the lease agreement and the date of commitment of the parties to the principal terms of the lease. This is the date on which a lease is classified as a finance or operating lease and, for finance leases, the date at which the amounts to be recognised at commencement are recognised.[103] The *commencement* of the lease term is the date on which the lessee is entitled to exercise its right to use the leased asset and is the date of initial recognition of the assets, liabilities, income and expenses of the lease in the accounts.[104] This means that the entity makes an initial calculation of the assets and liabilities under a finance lease at inception of the lease but does not recognise these in the accounts until the commencement date, if this is later. These amounts may in some circumstances be revised; this is discussed below.

IAS 17 (revised 1997) also required lease classification and the measurement of the initial asset and liability at inception but it did not define the commencement date, assuming that both would be the same. However, it is not uncommon for these two dates to be different, especially if the asset is under construction. Lease payments may be adjusted for changes in the lessor's costs during the period between inception and commencement. The lease may allow for changes in respect of costs of construction, acquisition costs, changes in the lessor's financing costs or any other factor, such as changes in general price levels, during the construction period. Changes to the lease payments as a result of such events are deemed to take place at inception of the lease.[105] In other words, if the final cost of the asset, and hence its fair value, is not known until after the date of inception, hindsight is used to establish that fair value. The lessee may also make lease payments during the construction period, although IAS 17 does not address this. The lessee will treat these payments as prepayments until the commencement date.

The standard also considers what will happen if the lease terms are changed so radically (but without entering into a new lease agreement) that it would have been classified in a different way, e.g. it would have been a finance lease instead of an operating lease. Such changes could happen at any stage during the lease (see 2.3.3 above) but if they happen in the period between inception and commencement, the lease will be classified at inception in accordance with the revised terms as if they had existed as at that date.

3.1.2   *Fair value*

Fair value is defined, as elsewhere in IAS, as the amount for which an asset could be exchanged or a liability settled, between knowledgeable, willing parties in an arm's length transaction.[106] In practice, the transaction price, i.e. the purchase price or construction cost of the asset that is the subject of the lease, will be its fair value, unless there is evidence to the contrary.

3.1.3   *Minimum lease payments*

The minimum lease payments are the payments over the lease term that the lessee is or can be required to make, excluding contingent rent, costs for services and taxes to be paid by and reimbursed to the lessor, together with:

(a)   for a lessee, any amounts guaranteed by the lessee or by a party related to the lessee;

(b)   for a lessor, any residual guaranteed to the lessor by:

   (i)   the lessee or by a party related to the lessee; or

   (ii)   a third party unrelated to the lessor who is financially capable of discharging the obligations under the guarantee.

The lessee may have an option to purchase the asset at a price which is expected to be sufficiently lower than the fair value at the date the option becomes exercisable so that, at the inception of the lease, it is reasonably certain to be exercised. In this case the minimum lease payments comprise the minimum payments payable over the lease term to the expected date of exercise of this purchase option and the payment required to exercise it.[107]

3.1.4 *Lease term and non-cancellable period*

The lease term is the non-cancellable period for which the lessee has contracted to lease the asset, together with any further terms for which the lessee has the option to continue to lease the asset, with or without further payment, if it is reasonably certain at the inception of the lease that the lessee will exercise the option.[108] A non-cancellable lease is either a lease that has no cancellation terms or one that has terms that effectively force the lessee to continue to use the asset for the period of the agreement. Therefore, a lease is considered to be non-cancellable if it can be cancelled only:

(a)   on the occurrence of a remote contingency; or

(b)   with the permission of the lessor; or

(c)   if the lessee enters into a new lease with the same lessor for the same or an equivalent asset; or

(d)   if the lessee is required to pay additional amounts that make it reasonably certain at inception that the lessee will continue the lease.[109]

An example of (d) is a requirement that the lessee pay a termination payment equivalent to the present value of the remaining lease payments.

3.1.5 *Interest rate implicit in the lease*

The interest rate implicit in the lease is the discount rate that, at the inception of the lease, causes the aggregate present value of

(a)   the minimum lease payments; and

(b)   the unguaranteed residual value

to be equal to the sum of the fair value of the leased asset and any initial direct costs of the lessor.

The lessee's incremental borrowing rate of interest is the rate of interest the lessee would have to pay on a similar lease or, if that is not determinable, the rate that, at the inception of the lease, the lessee would have to pay to borrow over a similar term, and with a similar security, the funds necessary to purchase the asset.[110]

3.1.6   *Residual value*

The guaranteed residual value is:

(a)   for a lessee, the part of the residual value that is guaranteed by itself or by one of its related parties. The amount of the guarantee is the maximum amount that could, in any event, become payable; and

(b)   for a lessor, it is the part of the residual value that is guaranteed by the lessee or by a third party unrelated to the lessor who is financially capable of discharging the obligations under the guarantee.

The lessor's unguaranteed residual value is any part of the residual value of the leased asset, the realisation of which is not assured or is guaranteed solely by a party related to it.[111]

3.1.7   *Contingent rents*

Contingent rents (which are excluded from minimum lease payments) are defined in the standard as that portion of the lease payments that are not fixed in amount, but are based on a factor other than just the passage of time (for example, percentage of sales, amount of usage, price indices, market rates of interest).[112]

Lessees expense contingent rents in the period in which they are incurred.[113]

Contingent rents are embedded derivatives, as defined by IAS 39. This has not affected the accounting for the specific examples of contingent rents referred to above. The issues are considered in 3.6 below.

3.1.8   *Initial direct costs*

Initial direct costs are incremental costs that are directly attributable to negotiating and arranging a lease, except for such costs incurred by manufacturer or dealer lessors.[114]

If the lessee incurs costs that are directly attributable to activities it has performed to obtain a finance lease, these are added to the amount recognised as an asset.[115]

One of the principal changes introduced when IAS 17 was revised in 2003 was in respect of the initial direct costs of lessors. Initial direct costs of lessors include amounts such as commissions, legal fees and internal costs that are incremental and directly attributable to negotiating and arranging a lease. Internal costs must exclude general overheads such as those incurred by a sales or marketing team.[116] Lessors must add internal direct costs to the carrying value of leased assets under both finance and operating leases – see 3.3 and 3.4.4 below – unless they are manufacturer and dealer lessors, in which case they must be expensed – see 3.3.5 below. This change was to ensure that there was consistency of definition and treatment by all lessors; prior to the revision, lessors were also permitted to expense the costs immediately. The revised standard also clarifies the different treatment now required for the initial direct costs of manufacturer and dealer lessors.

3.1.9 Calculation of the implicit interest rate and present value of minimum lease payments

The following example illustrates the calculation of the implicit interest rate and present value of minimum lease payments:

Example 23.6: *Calculation of the implicit interest rate and present value of minimum lease payments*

Details of a non-cancellable lease are as follows:

(i)   Fair value = €10,000

(ii) Five annual rentals payable in advance of €2,100

(iii) Lessor's unguaranteed estimated residual value at end of five years = €1,000

The implicit interest rate in the lease is that which gives a present value of €10,000 for the five rentals plus the total estimated residual value at the end of year 5. This rate can be calculated as 6.62%, as follows:

Year	Capital sum at start of period €	Rental paid €	Capital sum during period €	Finance charge (6.62% per annum) €	Capital sum at end of period €
2005	10,000	2,100	7,900	523	8,423
2006	8,423	2,100	6,323	419	6,742
2007	6,742	2,100	4,642	307	4,949
2008	4,949	2,100	2,849	189	3,038
2009	3,038	2,100	938	62	1,000
		10,500		1,500	

In other words, 6.62% is the implicit interest rate that, at the inception of the lease, causes the aggregate present value of the minimum lease payments (€10,500) and the unguaranteed residual value (€1000) to be equal to the fair value of the leased asset. Lessor's initial direct costs have been excluded for simplicity.

This implicit interest rate is then used to calculate the present value of the minimum lease payments, i.e. €10,500 discounted at 6.62%. This can be calculated at €9,274, which is 92.74% of the asset's fair value, indicating that the present value of the minimum lease payments is substantially all of the fair value of the leased asset and a finance lease is therefore indicated.

It would be appropriate for the lessee to record the asset at €9,274 as the present value of the minimum lease payments is lower than the fair value and this would take account of the lessor's residual interest in the asset.

The lessor will know all of the information in the above example, as it will have been used in the pricing decision for the lease. However, the lessee may not know either the fair value or the unguaranteed residual value and, therefore, not know the implicit interest rate. In such circumstances the lessee will substitute a rate from a similar lease or its incremental borrowing rate. The lessee is also unlikely to know the lessor's initial direct costs even if the other information is known, but this is unlikely to have more than a marginal effect on the implicit interest rate.

3.2   Accounting by lessees – finance leases

3.2.1   Initial recognition

At commencement of the lease, the asset and liability for the future lease payments are recorded in the balance sheet at the same amount, which is an amount equal to the fair value of the leased asset or the present value of the minimum lease payments, if lower, with initial direct costs of the lessee being added to the asset.[117] An example of the calculation is given in Example 23.6 above.

3.2.2   Allocation of finance costs

The standard requires that lease payments should be apportioned between the finance charge and the reduction of the outstanding liability. The finance charge should be allocated to periods during the lease term so as to produce a constant periodic rate of interest on the remaining balance of the liability for each period.[118]

Example 23.7:   Allocation of finance costs

In Example 23.6 above, the present value of the lessee's minimum lease payments was calculated at €9,274 by using the implicit interest rate of 6.62%. The total finance charges of €1,226 (total rentals paid of €10,500 less their present value of €9,274) are allocated over the lease term as follows:

Year	Liability at start of period €	Rental paid €	Liability during period €	Finance charge (6.62% per annum) €	Liability at end of period €
2005	9,274	2,100	7,174	475	7,649
2006	7,649	2,100	5,549	367	5,917
2007	5,917	2,100	3,817	253	4,070
2008	4,070	2,100	1,970	130	2,100
2009	2,100	2,100	–	–	–
		10,500		1,226	

The standard notes that, in practice, when allocating the finance charge to periods during the lease term some form of approximation may be used to simplify the calculation.[119] However, it provides no guidance as to the methodology that should be applied in allocating finance charges to accounting periods.

Two methods that are used in practice as approximations to this method are 'sum of the digits' ('rule of 78') or straight-line.[120] These are progressively easier to apply but also give progressively less accurate answers. There is, therefore, a trade-off to be made between the costs versus benefits of achieving complete accuracy, but in making this trade-off, the question of materiality is important. If differences between allocated finance charges under each method are immaterial, the simplest method may be used for convenience. The converse also applies and, of course, a number of individually immaterial differences may in aggregate be material. The following example illustrates the implicit interest rate and sum of the digits methods of allocating finance charges to accounting periods

Example 23.8: Sum-of-digits allocation as compared to implicit interest rate

Continuing the lease example from Example 23.6 above, the sum of the digits method calculation is as follows:

Year	Number of rentals not yet due	×	total finance charge / sum of number of rentals =	Finance charge per annum €
2005	4	×	€2,000 ÷ 10 =	490
2006	3	×	€2,000 ÷ 10 =	368
2007	2	×	€2,000 ÷ 10 =	245
2008	1	×	€2,000 ÷ 10 =	123
2009	–	×	€2,000 ÷ 10 =	
	10			1,226

We can now compare the finance charges in each of the five years under the implicit interest rate (IRR) as calculated in Example 23.6 and sum of the digits methods:

Year	Annual finance charge as % of total rentals — IRR €	Annual finance charge as % of total rentals — Sum of the digits €	Annual finance charge as % of total rentals — IRR %	Annual finance charge as % of total rentals — Sum of the digits %
2005	475	490	39	40
2006	367	368	30	30
2007	253	245	20	20
2008	130	123	11	10
2009	–	–	–	–
	1,226	1,226	100	100

As can be seen above, in situations where the lease term is not very long (typically not more than seven years) and interest rates are not very high, the sum of the digits method gives an allocation of finance charges that is close enough to that under the implicit interest rate method to allow the simpler approach to be used.

3.2.3 Recording the liability

The carrying amount of the liability will always be calculated in the same way, by adding the finance charge (however calculated) to the outstanding balance and deducting cash paid. The finance charge depends on the method used to apportion the finance costs; if the IRR method is used, the liability in each of the years, as apportioned between the current and non-current liability, is as follows:

Example 23.9:   Lessee's liabilities and interest expense

The entity entering into the lease in Example 23.6 will record the following liabilities and interest expense in its balance sheet:

Year	Liability at end of period €	Current liability at end of period €	Non-current liability at end of period €	Interest expense (at 6.62%) for the period €
2005	7,649	1,732	5,917	475
2006	5,917	1,847	4,070	367
2007	4,070	1,970	2,100	253
2008	2,100	2,100	–	130
2009	–	–	–	–
				1,226

3.2.4 Accounting for the leased asset

At commencement of the lease, the asset and liability for the future lease payments are recorded in the balance sheet at the same amount, with initial direct costs of the lessee being added to the asset.[121] These are costs that are directly attributable to the lease in question and are added to the carrying value[122] in an analogous way to the treatment of the acquisition costs of tangible assets.

Accounting for the leased asset follows the general rules for accounting for tangible or intangible fixed assets. A finance lease gives rise to a depreciation expense for depreciable assets as well as a finance expense for each accounting period. The depreciation policy for depreciable leased assets should be consistent with that for depreciable assets that are owned, and the depreciation recognised should be calculated in accordance with IAS 16 – *Property, Plant and Equipment*, and IAS 38. If there is reasonable certainty that the lessee will obtain ownership by the end of the lease term, the period of expected use is the useful life of the asset. If there is no reasonable certainty that the lessee will obtain ownership by the end of the lease term, the asset shall be fully depreciated over the shorter of the lease term or its useful life.[123] The useful life is the estimated remaining period, from the commencement of the lease term, over which the entity expects to consume the economic benefits embodied in the asset.[124]

Because the lease expense and depreciation must be calculated separately, the asset and liability are unlikely to be the same after the commencement of the lease term. Therefore, it is not appropriate simply to treat the lease payments as expenses for the period.[125] This is demonstrated in the following example.

Example 23.10: Lessee's depreciation and interest expense

The entity that has entered into the lease agreement described in Example 23.6 will depreciate the asset (whose initial carrying value, disregarding initial direct costs, is €9,274) on a straight-line basis over five years in accordance with its depreciation policy for owned assets, i.e. an amount of €1855 per annum. The balances for asset and liability in the accounts in each of the years 2005 – 2009 will be as follows:

Year	Carrying value of asset at end of period €	Total liability at end of period €	Total charged to income statement* €	Lease payments €
2005	7,419	7,649	2,330	2,100
2006	5,564	5,917	2,222	2,100
2007	3,709	4,070	2,108	2,100
2008	1,854	2,100	1,985	2,100
2009	–	–	1,855	2,100
			10,500	10,500

* The total charge combines the annual depreciation of €1,855 and the interest calculated according to the IRR method in Example 23.7, which is in aggregate the initial carrying value of the asset of €9,472 and the total finance charge of €1,226, i.e. the total rent paid of €10,500. Note that this example assumes that the asset is being depreciated to a residual value of zero over the lease term, which is shorter than its useful life, so IAS 16's requirement to reconsider the residual value and useful life at least at each financial year end is unlikely to have an effect.[126]

An entity applies IAS 36 – *Impairment of Assets* – to determine whether the leased asset has become impaired in value (see Chapter 13).[127]

3.3   Accounting by lessors – finance leases

Under a finance lease, a lessor retains legal title to an asset but passes substantially all the risks and rewards of ownership to the lessee in return for a stream of rentals. In substance, therefore, the lessor provides finance and expects a return thereon.

The standard requires lessors to recognise assets held under a finance lease in their balance sheets as a receivable at an amount equal to the net investment in the lease.[128] The lease payments received from the lessee are treated as repayments of principal and finance income.[129] Initial direct costs, which may include commissions, legal fees and internal costs that are incremental and directly attributable to negotiating and arranging the lease, are included in the measurement of the net investment in the lease at inception and reflected in the calculation of the implicit interest rate.[130]

The recognition of finance income should be based on a pattern reflecting a constant periodic rate of return on the lessor's net investment outstanding in respect of the finance lease.[131]

3.3.1 The lessor's net investment in the lease

The lessor's gross investment in the lease is the aggregate of the minimum lease payments receivable by the lessor under a finance lease and any unguaranteed residual value to which the lessor is entitled. The net investment in the lease is the gross investment discounted at the interest rate implicit in the lease,[132] i.e. at any point in time it comprises the gross investment after deducting gross earnings allocated to future periods.

The lessor's gross investment is, therefore, the same as the aggregate figures used to calculate the implicit interest rate and the net investment is the present value of those same figures – see 3.1.9 and Example 23.6 above.

Therefore, at inception, the lessor's net investment in the lease is the cost of the asset as increased by its initial direct costs. The difference between the net and gross investments is the gross finance income to be allocated over the lease term. Example 23.11 below illustrates this point.

3.3.2 Allocation of finance income

As noted above the lessor recognises finance income based on a pattern reflecting a constant periodic rate of return on the lessor's net investment outstanding in respect of the finance lease.[133] Lease payments, excluding costs for services, are applied against the gross investment in the lease to reduce both the principal and the unearned finance income.[134] The standard does not refer to the use of approximations by lessors and, accordingly, these methods should not be used unless the differences are clearly immaterial.

Example 23.6 at 3.1.9 can be examined from the lessor's perspective:

Example 23.11: The lessor's gross and net investment in the lease

The lease has the same facts as described in Example 23.6, i.e. the asset has a fair value of €10,000, the lessee is making five annual rentals payable in advance of €2,100 and the total unguaranteed estimated residual value at the end of five years is estimated to be €1,000. The lessor's direct costs have been excluded for simplicity.

The lessor's gross investment in the lease is the total rents receivable of €10,500 and the unguaranteed residual value of €1,000. The gross earnings are therefore €1,500. The initial carrying value of the receivable is its fair value of €10,000, which is also the present value of the gross investment discounted at the interest rate implicit in the lease of 6.62%.

Year	Receivable at start of period €	Rental received €	Finance income (6.62% per annum) €	Gross investment at end of period €	Gross earnings allocated to future periods €	Receivable at end of period €
2005	10,000	2,100	523	9,400	977	8,423
2006	8,423	2,100	419	7,300	558	6,742
2007	6,742	2,100	307	5,200	251	4,949
2008	4,949	2,100	189	3,100	62	3,038
2009	3,038	2,100	62	1,000	–	1,000
		10,500	1,500			

The gross investment in the lease at any point in time comprises the aggregate of the rentals receivable in future periods and the unguaranteed residual value, e.g. at the end of 2006, the gross investment of €7,300 is three years' rental of €2,100 plus the unguaranteed residual of €1,000. The net investment, which is the amount at which the debtor will be recorded in the balance sheet, is €7,300 less the earnings allocated to future periods of €558 = €6,742.

3.3.3   Residual values

Income recognition by lessors can be extremely sensitive to the amount recognised as the asset's residual value. This is because the amount of the residual directly affects the computation of the amount of finance income earned over the lease term – this is illustrated in Example 23.12 below. The standard gives no guidance regarding the estimation of unguaranteed residual values but it does require them to be reviewed regularly. If there has been a reduction in the estimated value, the income allocation over the lease term is revised and any reduction in respect of amounts accrued is recognised immediately.[135]

Example 23.12:   Reduction in residual value

Taking the same facts as used in Example 23.11 above, the lessor concludes at the end of 2006 that the residual value of the asset is only €500 and revises the income allocation over the lease term accordingly. It continues to apply the same implicit interest rate, 6.62%, as before.

Year	Receivable at start of period €	Rental received €	Finance income (6.62% per annum) €	Gross investment at end of period* €	Gross earnings allocated to future periods €	Receivable at end of period €
2006	8,423	2,100	419	6,800	471	6,329
2007	6,329	2,100	280	4,700	191	4,509
2008	4,509	2,100	160	2,600	31	2,569
2009	2,569	2,100	31	500	–	500
		10,500				

*   The gross investment in the lease now takes account of the unguaranteed residual of €500, not €1,000.

The lessor will have to write off €413, being the difference between the carrying amount of the receivable as previously calculated and the revised balance above (€6,742-€6,329). This is the present value as at the end of 2006 of the part of the unguaranteed residual written off.

Impairment of lease receivables is within the scope of IAS 39 – *Financial Instruments: Recognition and Measurement*,[136] and this methodology is required by IAS 39 paragraph 63, described in 3.6.2 below.

3.3.4   Disposals by lessors of assets held under finance leases

If a lessor is to dispose of an asset under a finance lease (i.e. its net investment in the finance lease) that is classified as held for sale, or is included in a disposal group that is so classified, it is to apply the requirements of IFRS 5 to the disposal.[137] IFRS 5 applies to annual periods beginning on or after 1 January 2005, with earlier implementation being encouraged. Its requirements are dealt with in Chapter 3.

3.3.5   *Manufacturer or dealer lessors*

Manufacturers or dealers often offer customers the choice of either buying or leasing an asset. A finance lease of an asset by a manufacturer or dealer lessor gives rise to two types of income:

(a)   the profit or loss equivalent to the profit or loss resulting from an outright sale of the asset being leased, at normal selling prices, reflecting any applicable volume or trade discounts; and

(b)   the finance income over the lease term.[138]

In those situations where the customer is offered the choice of paying the cash price for the asset immediately or paying for it on deferred credit terms then, as long as the credit terms are the manufacturer or dealer's normal terms, the cash price (after taking account of applicable or volume discounts) can be used for determining the selling profit.[139] However, in many cases such an approach should not be followed as the manufacturer or dealer's marketing considerations often influence the terms of the lease. For example, a car dealer may offer 0% finance deals instead of reducing the normal selling price of his cars. It would be wrong in this instance for the dealer to record a profit on the sale of the car and no finance income under the lease.

The standard, therefore, requires sales revenue to be based on the fair value of the asset (i.e. the cash price) or, if lower, the present value of the minimum lease payments computed at a market rate of interest. As a result, if artificially low rates of interest are quoted, selling profit is restricted to that which would apply if a commercial rate of interest were charged.[140] The cost of sales is reduced to the extent that the lessor retains an unguaranteed residual interest in the asset.[141]

Initial direct costs should be recognised as an expense in the income statement at the inception of the lease. This is not the same as the treatment when a lessor arranges a finance lease, where the costs are added to the finance lease receivable; the standard argues that this is because the costs are mainly related to earning the selling profit.[142] If the manufacturer or dealer is in the (relatively unlikely) position of incurring an overall loss because the total rentals receivable under the finance lease are less than the cost to it of the asset then this loss should be taken to the profit and loss account at the inception of the lease. IAS 17 assumes that the manufacturer or dealer will have a normal implicit interest rate based on its other leasing activity. However, in other situations where the manufacturer or dealer does not conduct other leasing business, an estimate will have to be made of the implicit rate for such leasing activity. A manufacturer or dealer lessor does not recognise any selling profit on entering into an operating lease because it is not the equivalent of a sale.[143]

3.3.6   *Lessor accounting – net investment or net cash investment?*

The original IAS 17 provided a free choice of method in the allocation of finance income by a lessor, namely the recognition of income basing on a pattern reflecting a constant periodic rate of return based on either:

•   the lessor's net investment outstanding in respect of the finance lease; or

•   the lessor's net cash investment outstanding in respect of the finance lease.

The net cash investment in a lease at a point in time is the amount of funds invested in a lease by a lessor. It therefore takes account of a number of other cash flows, primarily taxation payments and receipts (including the effect of capital allowances), the effect of interest and government grants, in allocating the lessor's earnings over the lease term.

It is less than clear why it was that, in revising IAS 17 in 1997, the (then) IASC eliminated as an option the net cash investment method of recognising finance lease income. It is understood that IOSCO had asked the (then) IASC to clarify the position as to when each of the two methods was appropriate – however this does not necessarily mean the elimination of one of them. What is clear is that in certain circumstances the net investment method is not appropriate (for example, when there are significant tax cash flows which affect the lessor) and therefore it does not make sense to require the net investment method to be applied in all circumstances. US GAAP requires the net investment method to be applied except in the case of leveraged leases as defined in SFAS 13, for which the net cash investment method is required. However, the (then) IASC chose not to adopt a similar approach. Where interest rates are low and tax allowances less important, there may be insufficient difference between the two methods to warrant the extra complexity of the net cash investment approach.

In its revision of IAS 17 in 2003, the IASB continued to require the use of the net investment method.

3.4 Operating leases

3.4.1 Operating leases in the accounts of lessees

IAS 17 requires that lease payments under an operating lease (excluding costs for services such as insurance and maintenance) should be recognised as an expense on a straight-line basis over the lease term unless another systematic basis is representative of the time pattern of the user's benefit, even if the payments are not on that basis.[144]

3.4.2 Lease incentives – accounting by lessees

On the matter of operating lease incentives, the SIC was asked to consider the accounting implications of a lessor providing incentives for a lessee to enter into a new or renewed operating lease agreement. Examples of such incentives are an up-front cash payment to the lessee or the reimbursement or assumption by the lessor of costs of the lessee (such as relocation costs, leasehold improvements and costs associated with a pre-existing lease commitment of the lessee). Alternatively, the lessor may grant the lessee rent-free or reduced rent initial periods to the lease term.[145]

The consensus reached by the SIC in Interpretation SIC-15 – *Operating Leases – Incentives* – was that all incentives for the agreement of a new or renewed operating lease should be recognised as an integral part of the net consideration agreed for the use of the leased asset, irrespective of the incentive's nature or form or the timing of payments.[146] It was agreed further the lessee should recognise the aggregate benefit of incentives as a reduction of rental expense over the lease term, on a straight-line basis unless another systematic basis is representative of the time pattern of the lessee's benefit from the use of the leased asset.[147] Finally, SIC-15 requires that costs incurred by the lessee, including costs in connection with a pre-existing lease (for example, costs for termination, relocation or leasehold improvements), should be accounted for by the lessee in accordance with the IAS applicable to those costs, including costs which are effectively reimbursed through an incentive arrangement.[148]

In an Appendix to SIC-15, the SIC has set out the following two examples that illustrate the application of the Interpretation:[149]

Example 23.13: Application of SIC-15

Example 1

An entity agrees to enter into a new lease arrangement with a new lessor. The lessor agrees to pay the lessee's relocation costs as an incentive to the lessee for entering into the new lease. The lessee's moving costs are 1,000. The new lease has a term of 10 years, at a fixed rate of 2,000 per year.

The accounting is:

The lessee recognises relocation costs of 1,000 as an expense in Year 1. Net consideration of 19,000 consists of 2,000 for each of the 10 years in the lease term, less a 1,000 incentive for relocation costs. Both the lessor and lessee would recognise the net rental consideration of 19,000 over the 10 year lease term using a single amortisation method in accordance with paragraphs 4 and 5 of SIC–15.

Example 2

An entity agrees to enter into a new lease arrangement with a new lessor. The lessor agrees to a rent-free period for the first three years as incentive to the lessee for entering into the new lease. The new lease has a term of 20 years, at a fixed rate of 5,000 per annum for years 4 through 20.

The accounting is:

Net consideration of 85,000 consists of 5,000 for each of 17 years in the lease term. Both the lessor and lessee would recognise the net consideration of 85,000 over the 20-year lease term using a single amortisation method in accordance with paragraphs 4 and 5 of this Interpretation.

3.4.3 Onerous contracts

Although IAS 37 prohibits the recognition of provisions for future operating losses,[150] the standard does specifically address the issue of onerous contracts. It requires that if an entity has a contract that is onerous, the present obligation under the contract should be recognised and measured as a provision.[151]

The standard defines an onerous contract as 'a contract in which the unavoidable costs of meeting the obligations under it exceed the economic benefits expected to be received under it'.[152] This is taken to mean that the contract itself is onerous to the point of being directly loss-making, not simply uneconomic by reference to current prices. A common example of an onerous contract seen in practice relates to operating leases for the rent of property, and the standard includes the following example in Appendix C:

Example 23.14: An onerous contract

An entity operates profitably from a factory that it has leased under an operating lease. During December 2000 the entity relocates its operations to a new factory. The lease on the old factory continues for the next four years, it cannot be cancelled and the factory cannot be re-let to another user.

Present obligation as a result of a past obligating event	The obligating event is the signing of the lease contract, which gives rise to a legal obligation.
Transfer of economic benefits in settlement	When the lease becomes onerous, a transfer of economic benefits is probable. (Until the lease becomes onerous, the entity accounts for the lease by applying IAS 17, Leases.)
Conclusion	A provision is recognised for the best estimate of the unavoidable lease payments (see IAS 37, paragraphs 5(c), 14 and 66).

Care must be taken to ensure that the lease itself is onerous. If an entity has a number of retail outlets and one of these is loss-making, this is not sufficient to make the lease onerous. However, if the entity vacates the premises and sub-lets them at an amount less than the rent it is paying, then the lease becomes onerous and the entity should provide for its best estimate of the unavoidable lease payments. This will include the difference between the lease and sub-lease payments, together with provision as appropriate for any period where there is no sub-tenant.

The accounting for onerous contracts is discussed in more detail in Chapter 25.

3.4.4 Operating leases in the accounts of lessors

Lessors should present assets subject to operating leases in their balance sheets according to the nature of the asset. Lease income from operating leases should be recognised in income on a straight-line basis over the lease term, unless another systematic basis is more representative of the time pattern in which, the standard states, 'use benefit derived from the leased asset is diminished'.[153] Generally, the only other basis that is encountered is based on unit-of-production or service.

Lease income excludes receipts for services provided such as insurance and maintenance. Costs, including depreciation, incurred in earning the lease income are recognised as an expense.[154] Initial direct costs incurred specifically to earn revenues from an operating lease are added to the carrying amount of the leased asset and allocated to income over the lease term in proportion to the recognition of lease income.[155] This means that the costs will be depreciated on a straight-line basis if this is the method of recognising the lease income, regardless of the depreciation basis of the asset.

The depreciation policy for depreciable leased assets is to be consistent with the entity's policy for similar assets that are not subject to leasing arrangements and calculated in accordance with IAS 16 or IAS 38, as appropriate.[156] If the lessor does not use similar assets in its business then the depreciation policy must be set solely by reference to IASs 16 and 38. This also means that the lessor is obliged in accordance with IAS 16 to consider the residual value and economic life of the assets at least at each financial year-end.[157] There are similar requirements in the case of intangible assets, although IAS 38 notes that they rarely have a residual value.[158] These matters are discussed in Chapters 11 and 12. These assets are also tested for impairment in a manner consistent with other tangible and intangible fixed assets; IAS 17 refers to IAS 36 in providing guidance on the need to assess the possibility of an impairment of assets.[159]

3.4.5 Lease incentives – accounting by lessors

In negotiating a new or renewed operating lease, a lessor may provide incentives for the lessee to enter into the arrangement. For example, in the case of a property lease, the tenant may be given a rent-free period but other types of incentive may include up-front cash payments to the lessee or the reimbursement or assumption by the lessor of lessee costs such as relocation costs, leasehold improvements and costs associated with a pre-existing lease commitment of the lessee. This issue was addressed by the SIC in Interpretation SIC-15, which states that the lessor should recognise the aggregate cost of incentives as a reduction of rental income over the lease term, on a straight-line basis unless another systematic basis is representative of the time pattern over which the benefit of the leased asset is diminished.[160] The SIC rejected the argument that lease incentives for lessors are part of the initial direct costs of negotiating or arranging the contract; instead concluding that they are in substance, related to the amount of consideration received by the lessor for the use of the asset. This view was confirmed in the IASB's 2003 revision of IAS 17 which requires initial direct costs to be capitalised as part of the carrying value of the asset – see 3.4.4 above). Lessor accounting is, therefore, the mirror image of lessee accounting for the incentives, as described in 3.4.2 above.

3.5 Sale and leaseback transactions

These transactions involve the original owner of an asset selling it to a provider of finance and immediately leasing it back. These parties will be termed the seller/lessee (the original owner) and buyer/lessor (the finance provider) respectively. Sometimes, instead of selling the asset outright, the original owner will lease the asset to the other party under a finance lease and then lease it back. Such a transaction is known as a 'lease and leaseback' and has similar effects. The term 'sale and leaseback' is taken to include such a transaction.

Sale and leaseback transactions are a fairly common feature of a number of industries (such as the retail and hotel industries), where it is as accepted a form of financing as taking out a mortgage or a bank overdraft. Many parties are involved as buyer/lessors, not only finance houses and banks but also pension funds and property groups. From a commercial point of view, the important point of difference lies between an entity that decides that it is cheaper to rent than to own – and is willing to pass on the property risk to the landlord – and an entity which decides to use the property as a means of raising finance – and will therefore retain the property risk. However from the accounting point of view, a major consideration is whether a profit can be reported on such transactions.

The buyer/lessor will treat the lease in the same way as it would any other lease that was not part of a sale and leaseback transaction. The accounting treatment of the transaction by the seller/lessee depends on the type of lease involved, i.e. whether the leaseback is under a finance or an operating leaseback.[161]

3.5.1 Sale and finance leaseback

In order to assess whether the leaseback is under a finance lease, the seller/lessee will apply the qualitative tests in IAS 17 that are described at 2.3.2 above. If a sale and leaseback transaction results in a finance lease, any excess of sales proceeds over the carrying amount should not be recognised immediately as income by a seller-lessee. Instead, the excess is deferred and amortised over the lease term.[162] It is inappropriate to show a profit on disposal of an asset which has then, in substance been reacquired by the entity under a finance lease as the lessor is providing finance to the lessee with the asset as security.[163]

The wording is extremely ambiguous. The reference to the 'excess of sales proceeds being deferred and amortised over the lease term implies that the asset must be restated to its fair value (or the present value of the minimum lease payments, if lower) in exactly the same way as any other asset acquired under a finance lease. On the other hand, the standard describes the transaction as 'a means whereby the lessor provides finance to the lessee, with the asset as security',[164] for which the most appropriate treatment is to leave the previous carrying value unchanged, with the sales proceeds being shown as a creditor that represents the finance lease liability under the leaseback. Because of the lack of clarity in IAS 17 itself, we have considered the impact of IAS 18 – *Revenue* - on these transactions. Restating the asset to fair value could be seen as a two-stage process, disposal of the original asset and recognition of a new asset, an interest under a finance lease. However, IAS 18 states that a transaction is not a sale and revenue is not recognised if the enterprise retains significant risks of ownership.[165] By definition the entity will have retained the significant risks and rewards, because it now holds the asset under a finance lease. Therefore, we consider that the leased asset has to be recorded at its previous carrying amount (if any) and continue to be accounted for as before, while the proceeds will be recorded as a liability to be accounted for in accordance with IAS 39 (this is discussed in 3.6 below).

If the sales value is less than the carrying with reference to value then the apparent 'loss' need not be taken to income unless there has been an impairment under IAS 36.[166] There may be an obvious reason why the sales proceeds are less than the carrying value; for example, the fair value of a second-hand vehicle or item of plant and machinery is frequently lower than its book value, especially soon after the asset has been acquired by the entity. This fall in fair value after sale has no effect on the asset's value in use.

3.5.2 *Operating leaseback*

If a sale and leaseback transaction results in an operating lease, and it is clear that the transaction is established at fair value, any profit or loss should be recognised immediately.

If the sale price is below fair value, any profit or loss should be recognised immediately unless the loss is compensated by future lease payments at below market price, in which case it should be deferred and amortised in proportion to the lease payments over the period for which the asset is expected to be used. If the sale price is above fair value, the excess over fair value should be deferred and amortised over the period for which the asset is expected to be used.[167]

The rationale behind the above treatments is that if the sales value is not based on fair values then it is likely that the normal market rents will have been adjusted to compensate. For example, a sale at above fair value followed by above-market rentals, is similar to a loan of the excess proceeds by the lessor that is being repaid out of the rentals. Accordingly, the transaction should be recorded as if it had been based on fair value.

However, this will not always be the case. Where the sales value is less than fair value there may be legitimate reasons for this to be so, for example where the seller has had to raise cash quickly. In such situations, as the rentals under the lease have not been reduced to compensate, the profit or loss should be based on the sales value.

The standard includes an Appendix, which comprises the following tabulation of the standard's requirements concerning sale and leaseback transactions, and is aimed at providing guidance in interpreting the various permutations of facts and circumstances that are set out in the requirements.

Sale price established at fair value (paragraph 61)	Carrying amount equal to fair value	Carrying amount less than fair value	Carrying amount above fair value
Profit	no profit	recognise profit immediately	not applicable
Loss	no loss	not applicable	recognise loss immediately

Sale price below fair value (paragraph 61)			
Profit	no profit	recognise profit immediately	no profit (note 1)
Loss not compensated by future lease payments at below market price	recognise loss immediately	recognise loss immediately	(note 1)
Loss compensated by future lease payments at below market price	defer and amortise loss	defer and amortise loss	(note 1)

Sale price above fair value (paragraph 61)			
Profit	defer and amortise profit	defer and amortise profit	defer and amortise profit (note 2)
Loss	no loss	no loss	(note 1)

Note 1   These parts of the table represent circumstances that would have been dealt with under paragraph 63 of the Standard. Paragraph 63 requires the carrying amount of an asset to be written down to fair value where it is subject to a sale and leaseback.

Note 2   The profit would be the difference between fair value and sale price as the carrying amount would have been written down to fair value in accordance with paragraph 63.

IAS 17's disclosure requirements for lessees and lessors apply equally to sale and leaseback transactions. The requirement in paragraph 35(d) of the standard for lessees to give a general description of their significant leasing arrangements will lead to the disclosure of unique or unusual provisions of the agreement or terms of the sale and leaseback transactions.[168] Furthermore, sale and leaseback transactions may meet the separate disclosure criteria for 'exceptional items' set out in IAS 1 (see Chapter 3).[169]

Sale and leaseback arrangements may also include features such as repurchase options. These are not addressed by IAS 17 and are discussed at 4.4 below.

3.6   Leases as financial instruments

In accordance with the accounting model in IAS 17, a finance lease is essentially regarded as an entitlement to receive, and an obligation to make, a stream of payments that are substantially the same as blended payments of principal and interest under a loan agreement. Consequently the lessor accounts for its investment in the amount receivable under the lease contract rather than for the leased asset itself. An operating lease, on the other hand, is regarded primarily as an uncompleted contract committing the lessor to provide the use of an asset in future periods in exchange for consideration similar to a fee for a service. The lessor continues to account for the leased asset itself rather than any amount receivable in the future under the contract.

Accordingly, a finance lease is regarded as a financial instrument and an operating lease is not regarded as a financial instrument (except as regards individual payments currently due and payable).[170]

In general the lease rights and obligations that come about as a result of IAS 17's recognition and measurement rules are not included within the scope of IAS 39. However, the following aspects of accounting for leases are within its scope:

(a)   lease receivables recognised by a lessor, which are subject to the derecognition and impairment provisions of IAS 39;

(b)   finance lease payables recognised by a lessee are subject to the derecognition provisions; and

(c)   derivatives that are embedded in leases are subject to IAS 39's embedded derivatives provisions.[171]

These matters are discussed further in 3.6.1 to 3.6.4 below.

IAS 39 will have little impact on traditional, straightforward leases. However, its requirements will have to be considered in many more complex situations.

3.6.1   Derecognition of lease receivables by lessors

A financial asset is derecognised when the contractual rights to the cash flows from that asset have expired.[172] This will apply to most leases at the end of the term when the lessor has no more right to cash flows from the lessee.

If the cash flows from the financial asset have not expired, it is derecognised when, and only when, the entity 'transfers' the asset within the specified meaning of the term in IAS 39, and the transfer has the effect that the entity has either:

(a)   transferred substantially all the risks and rewards of the asset or

(b)   neither transferred nor retained substantially all the risks and rewards of the asset and has not retained control of the asset.[173]If the rights to the cash are retained then there are other tests that must be met.[174]

An entity is regarded by IAS 39 as 'transferring' a financial asset if, and only if, it either:

(a)   transfers the contractual rights to receive the cash flows of the financial asset; or

(b)   retains the contractual rights to receive the cash flows of the financial asset, but assumes a contractual obligation to pay the cash flows to one or more recipients in an arrangement that meets the following conditions specified in the standard.[175]

   (i)   the entity has no obligation to pay amounts to the eventual recipients unless it collects equivalent amounts from the original asset. Short-term advances by the entity with the right of full recovery of the amount lent plus accrued interest at market rates do not violate this condition;

   (ii)   the entity is prohibited by the terms of the transfer contract from selling or pledging the original asset other than as security to the eventual recipients for the obligation to pay them cash flows; and

   (iii) the entity has an obligation to remit any cash flows it collects on behalf of the eventual recipients without material delay. In addition, the entity is not entitled to reinvest such cash flows, except in cash or cash equivalents as defined in IAS 7 – *Cash Flow Statements* (see Chapter 32 at 2.2.1) during the short settlement period from the collection date to the date of required remittance to the eventual recipients, with any interest earned on such investments being passed to the eventual recipients.[176]

These requirements are relevant to common lease situations such as sub-leases and back-to-back leases, dealt with at 4.3 below.

Derecognition of financial assets is a complex area discussed in particular in section 4 of Chapter 16.

3.6.2   Impairment of lease receivables

If a lease receivable is impaired, for example, because the lessee is in default of lease payments, the amount of the impairment is measured as the difference between the carrying value of the receivable and the present value of the estimated future cash flows, discounted at the implicit interest rate used on initial recognition. Therefore, if the lessor makes an arrangement with the lessee and reschedules and/or reduces amounts due under the lease, the loss is by reference to the new carrying amount of the receivable, calculated by discounting the estimated future cash flows at the original implicit interest rate.[177] This methodology has been used in Example 23.12 at 3.3.3 above.

3.6.3   Derecognition of lease payables

IAS 39 requires an entity to derecognise (i.e. remove from its balance sheet) a financial liability (or a part of a financial liability) when, and only when, it is 'extinguished', that is, when the obligation specified in the contract is discharged, cancelled, or expires.[178] This will be achieved when the debtor either:

- discharges the liability (or part of it) by paying the creditor, normally with cash, other financial assets, goods or services; or
- is legally released from primary responsibility for the liability (or part of it) either by process of law or by the creditor.[179]

The difference between the carrying amount of a financial liability (or part of a financial liability) extinguished or transferred to another party and the consideration paid, including any non-cash assets transferred or liabilities assumed, is to be recognised in profit or loss.

In order to identify the part of a liability derecognised, it allocates the previous carrying amount of the financial liability between the part that continues to be recognised and the part that is derecognised based on the relative fair values of those parts on the date of the repurchase.[180]

The derecognition of financial liabilities is dealt with in Chapter 16 at 5.

3.6.4   Embedded derivatives and contingent rentals

It is a basic principle in IAS 39 that derivative instruments be recognised at fair value in the accounts of entities (see Chapter 18). The same holds true of an embedded derivative, which is a component of a hybrid or combined instrument that also includes a non-derivative host contract; it has the effect that some of the cash flows of the combined instrument vary in a similar way to a stand-alone derivative. In other words it causes some or all of the cash flows that otherwise would be required by the contract to be modified according to a specified underlying.[181] IAS 39 does not require separation of the host contract and the derivative and separate recognition of the derivative in the accounts of the entity if it is closely related to the economic characteristics and risks of the host contract.[182]

Common terms within leases that are embedded derivatives as defined by IAS 39 are:

- rental increases in line with a consumer price index;
- contingent rentals based on turnover or sales; or
- contingent rentals based on variable interest rates.

IAS 17 describes these lease terms as contingent rentals (see 3.1.5 above).

The Application Guidance to IAS 39 states that these embedded derivatives are closely related to the host lease contract; accordingly, they do not have to be separated from the lease contract as a whole, unless, for example, the lease is leveraged and the index relates to inflation in another economic environment.[183] This means that lessees continue to expense such contingent payments are they arise. In the case of more complex lease terms, reference should be made to IAS 39 paragraphs 10 to 13 and Section 5 of Chapter 15.

3.7   Service concessions and similar arrangements

'Service concession arrangements' have been developed as a new mechanism for procuring public services that give the public access to major economic and social facilities provided using private capital, although they are not necessarily arrangements solely between the public sector and private sector bodies.

The accounting challenge is to reflect the substance of these payments fairly in the accounts of both of the contracting parties. It would be possible simply to take the contracts at fair value and account for the amounts paid and received as service payments; however, closer analysis may sometimes reveal that this is in reality a composite transaction whereby the public sector body is buying assets as well as services. In addition, there is the issue of how to account for the executory element of the contract, which may also include asset replacement and refurbishment as well as more obvious services.

The complex accounting issues raised by service concessions have been subject to prolonged and as yet unresolved debate by the IFRIC. Some service concessions will be deemed to be leases in substance under the terms of the IFRIC Interpretation – *Determining whether an arrangement contains a lease* – described at 2.2.1 above. However, as these issues range across a number of other accounting standards, including IAS 11 – *Construction contracts*, IAS 18 – *Revenue* – and IAS 38, accounting for service concessions is discussed in detail in Chapter 27.

3.8   Disclosures required by IAS 17

This section deals only with the disclosure requirements of IAS 17 and those of other accounting standards to which it specifically refers. Disclosures required by SIC-27 are dealt with in 2.2.2 above.

3.8.1   *Disclosures relating to financial assets and liabilities*

Because finance lease assets and obligations (and individual payments currently due and payable under operating leases) are financial assets and liabilities, lessees and lessors are required to meet the requirements of IAS 32 – *Financial Instruments: Disclosure and Presentation*. This principally applies to the general requirements regarding classification and disclosure of financial assets and obligations in the balance sheet and disclosure of interest income and expense, together with other gains and losses arising from financial instruments, whether reflected in the income statement or equity.[184] However, if the lease arrangements contain more complex terms then there may be additional disclosure requirements, which are summarised in Chapter 20.

3.8.2   *Disclosure by lessees: finance leases*

IAS 17 requires lessees to make the following disclosures for finance leases:

(a)   for each class of asset, the net carrying amount at the balance sheet date.

(b)   a reconciliation between the total of future minimum lease payments at the balance sheet date, and their present value. In addition, an entity shall disclose the total of future minimum lease payments at the balance sheet date, and their present value, for each of the following periods:

　　(i)   not later than one year;

　　(ii)   later than one year and not later than five years;

　　(iii)   later than five years.

(c)   contingent rents recognised as an expense in the period.

(d)   the total of future minimum sublease payments expected to be received under non-cancellable subleases at the balance sheet date.

(e)   a general description of the lessee's material leasing arrangements including, but not limited to, the following:

　　(i)   the basis on which contingent rent payable is determined;

　　(ii)   the existence and terms of renewal or purchase options and escalation clauses; and

　　(iii)   restrictions imposed by lease arrangements, such as those concerning dividends, additional debt, and further leasing.[185]

The following is an example of disclosures made in practice:

Extract 23.2: TeliaSonera (2003)

28   Leasing Agreements and Contractual Obligations [extract]

TeliaSonera as a Lessee

As a lessee, TeliaSonera has entered into financial and operating leases and rental contracts. For a financial leasing agreement, the consolidated accounts include the leased asset as a tangible fixed asset and the future obligation to the lessor as a liability in the balance sheet. Other agreements are operating leases, with the leasing costs amortized evenly throughout the period of the agreement.

Financial leases

The Group's financial leasing concerns computers and other IT equipment, production vehicles, company cars to employees, and other vehicles. There is no subleasing .

The book value of the leased assts as of the balance sheet date was as follows.

	December 31,		
SEK in millions	**2003**	**2002**	**2001**
Acquisition value	1,834	385	367
Less accumulated depreciation	-1,302	-88	-59
Net value of financial leasing agreements	**532**	**297**	**308**

Depreciation and write-downs totalled SEK 274 million, SEK 56 million and SEK 134 million for the years 2003, 2002 and 2001, respectively. Leasing fees paid during these years totalled SEK 301 million, SEK 72 million and SEK 147 million, respectively.

As of December 31, 2003, future minimum leasing fees and their present value as per financial agreements that could not be cancelled in advance and were longer than one year in duration were as follows.

SEK in millions Maturity	Future leasing fees	Present value of future minimum leasing fees
2004	236	225
2005	164	149
2006	56	49
2007	48	40
2008	50	43
Later years	29	20
Total	**583**	**526**

As of the balance sheet date, the present value of future minimum leasing fees under noncancelable financial leasing agreements was as follows.

SEK in millions	December 31, 2003	2002	2001
Total future minimum leasing fees	583	342	362
Less interest charges	-57	-43	-48
Present value of future minimum leasing fees	**526**	**299**	**314**

In addition, the leased asset is accounted for as a fixed asset of the reporting entity and the requirements for disclosure in accordance with IAS 16 (Chapter 12), IAS 36 (Chapter 13), IAS 38 (Chapter 11), IAS 40 (Chapter 12) and IAS 41 (Chapter 36) are applicable as appropriate.[186]

3.8.3   *Disclosure by lessees: operating leases*

Lessees shall, in addition to meeting the requirements of IAS 32, make the following disclosures for operating leases:

(a)   the total of future minimum lease payments under noncancellable operating leases for each of the following periods:

    (i)   not later than one year;

    (ii)   later than one year and not later than five years;

    (iii) later than five years.

(b)   the total of future minimum sublease payments expected to be received under non-cancellable subleases at the balance sheet date.

(c)   lease and sublease payments recognised as an expense in the period, with separate amounts for minimum lease payments, contingent rents, and sublease payments.

(d)   a general description of the lessee's significant leasing arrangements including, but not limited to, the following:

    (i)   the basis on which contingent rent payable is determined;

    (ii)   the existence and terms of renewal or purchase options and escalation clauses; and

    (iii) restrictions imposed by lease arrangements, such as those concerning dividends, additional debt and further leasing.

An example of the disclosures made by a lessee in respect of their obligations under operating leases is as follows.

Extract 23.3: TeliaSonera (2003)

28   Leasing Agreements and Contractual Obligations [extract]

TeliaSonera as a Lessee

As a lessee, TeliaSonera has entered into financial and operating leases and rental contracts. For a financial leasing agreement, the consolidated accounts include the leased asset as a tangible fixed asset and the future obligation to the lessor as a liability in the balance sheet. Other agreements are operating leases, with the leasing costs amortized evenly throughout the period of the agreement.

Financial leases

The Group's financial leasing concerns computers and other IT equipment, production vehicles, company cars to employees, and other vehicles. There is no subleasing .

The book value of the leased assts as of the balance sheet date was as follows.

SEK in millions	December 31,		
	2003	**2002**	**2001**
Acquisition value	1,834	385	367
Less accumulated depreciation	-1,302	-88	-59
Net value of financial leasing agreements	**532**	**297**	**308**

Depreciation and write-downs totalled SEK 274 million, SEK 56 million and SEK 134 million for the years 2003, 2002 and 2001, respectively. Leasing fees paid during these years totalled SEK 301 million, SEK 72 million and SEK 147 million, respectively.

As of December 31, 2003, future minimum leasing fees and their present value as per financial agreements that could not be cancelled in advance and were longer than one year in duration were as follows.

SEK in millions Maturity	Future leasing fees	Present value of future minimum leasing fees
2004	236	225
2005	164	149
2006	56	49
2007	48	40
2008	50	43
Later years	29	20
Total	**583**	**526**

As of the balance sheet date, the present value of future minimum leasing fees under noncancelable financial leasing agreements was as follows.

SEK in millions	December 31,		
	2003	**2002**	**2001**
Total future minimum leasing fees	583	342	362
Less interest charges	-57	-43	-48
Present value of future minimum leasing fees	**526**	**299**	**314**

Rezidor SAS Hospitality A/S makes the following disclosures with regard to its contingent rentals, first in respect of the amounts recognised as an expense in the period and second its commitments under such leases:

Extract 23.4: Rezidor SAS Hospitality A/S (2003)

Notes to the Accounts [extract]

5. Rental expense, insurance of properties & property tax

	2003	2002
Minimum lease payments	**68,408**	58,830
Contingent lease payments	**19,714**	19,804
Other	**15,348**	15,213
Total rent, insurance and tax	**103,470**	93,847

18. Management contract commitments

The management agreements can have commitments by Rezidor SAS with respect to financial liabilities. Rezidor SAS has in some cases guaranteed to the hotel owners a minimum annual cash flow. In most of the agreements the guarantee is limited to a maximum amount over the term of the agreement as well as a maximum annual amount. The maximum amount over the term of the agreement is usually equal to 2-3 times the annual guaranteed amount.

As at the end of 2003, Rezidor SAS had granted some kind of financial commitment in 36 Management contracts.

The management contracts containing such financial risk for the Group will expire as presented in the table below:

Year	Number of Management contracts expiring
2004-2008	0
2009-2013	2
2014-2018	8
2019-2023	11
2024-2028	15

The total guaranteed annual cash flow according to these management contracts is the following:

Year	Total guaranteed annual cash flow
2004	56,000
2005	58,000
2006	49,000
2007	26,000
2008	16,000

3.8.4 Disclosure by lessors: finance leases

In addition to meeting the requirements in IAS 32 (see 3.8.1 above), lessors shall disclose the following for finance leases:

(a) a reconciliation between the gross investment in the lease at the balance sheet date, and the present value of minimum lease payments receivable at the balance sheet date. In addition, an entity shall disclose the gross investment in the lease and the present value of minimum lease payments receivable at the balance sheet date, for each of the following periods:

    (i) not later than one year;

    (ii) later than one year and not later than five years;

    (iii) later than five years.

(b) unearned finance income.

(c) the unguaranteed residual values accruing to the benefit of the lessor.

(d)   the accumulated allowance for uncollectible minimum lease payments receivable.

(e)   contingent rents recognised as income in the period.

(f)   a general description of the lessor's material leasing arrangements.[187]

IAS 17 also recommends but does not require disclosure of the gross investment less unearned income in new business added during the period, after deducting the relevant amounts for cancelled leases as a useful indicator of growth.[188]

TeliaSonera discloses its activities as a finance lessor as follows.

Extract 23.5: TeliaSonera (2003)

TeliaSonera as financial lessor [extract]

TeliaSonera owns assets that it leases to customers under financial leasing agreements. These assets are recorded at the gross investment cost in the lease, less un-earned financial revenues. Some of the leasing receivables have been securitized. Based on the terms of the securitization contracts, the leasing receivables have been included in the Group balance sheet.

As of the balance sheet date, the present value of future minimum lease payment receivables under noncancelable financial leasing agreements was as follows.

	December 31,		
SEK in millions	**2003**	**2002**	**2001**
Gross investment in financial lease contracts	7,129	8,457	7,750
Less unearned financial revenues	-674	-876	-803
Net investment in financial lease contracts	**6,455**	**7,581**	**6,947**
Less: Unguaranteed residual values of leased properties for the benefit of the lessor	-33	-15	-19
Present value of future minimum lease payment receivables	**6,422**	**7,566**	**6,928**

As of December 31, 2003, the gross investment and present value of receivables relating to future minimum lease payments under non-cancellable financial leasing agreements were distributed as follows.

SEK in millions Maturity	**Gross investment**	**Present value of future minimum lease payments**
2004	3,325	3,123
2005	2,126	1,911
2006	1,043	889
2007	401	323
2008	166	127
Later years	68	49
Total	**7,129**	**6,422**

Reserve for doubtful receivables regarding minimum lease payments totalled SEK 41 million as of December 31, 2003.

The leasing portfolio comprises financing of products and services related to TeliaSonera's product and service offerings in Sweden and Denmark. At the end of 2003, the Danish part of the total portfolio was 14 per cent.

The term of the contract stock is approximately 15 quarters. The term of new contracts signed in 2003 is 14 quarters. Of all contracts, 75 per cent carry a floating interest rate and 25 per cent a fixed rate. Most contracts are renewable.

3.8.5 *Disclosure by lessors: operating leases*

Lessors shall, in addition to meeting the requirements of IAS 32, disclose the following for operating leases:

(a)   the future minimum lease payments under non-cancellable operating leases in the aggregate and for each of the following periods:

    (i)   not later than one year;

    (ii)   later than one year and not later than five years;

    (iii) later than five years.

(b)   total contingent rents recognised as income in the period.

(c)   a general description of the lessor's leasing arrangements.[189]

TeliaSonera's lessor's interests in operating leases are disclosed as follows.

Extract 23.6: *TeliaSonera (2003)*

TeliaSonera as operating lessor [extract]

Fiber and duct are sole as part of the operations of TeliaSonera's international carrier business. TeliaSonera has decided to view these as integral equipment. Under the agreements, title was not transferred to the lessee. The transactions are therefore recorded as operating lease agreements. Direct expenditures incurred in connection with agreements are capitalised and written off over the term of the agreement. The contracted sales price is chiefly paid in advance and is recognised as revenue during the period of the agreement. Sales not recognised in income are recorded as long-term liabilities and prepaid revenues.

The book value of the leased assets as of the balance sheet date was as follows:

	December 31,		
SEK in millions	**2003**	**2002**	**2001**
Acquisition value	3,260	2,535	1,750
Less accumulated depreciation	-1,259	-595	-150
Gross book value	**2,001**	**1,940**	**1,600**
Plus prepaid sales costs	2	7	9
Less prepaid lease payments	-1,030	-1,837	-2,286
Net value of operating leasing agreements	**973**	**110**	**-677**

Depreciation and write-downs totalled SEK 548 million, SEK 336 million and SEK 141 million for the years 2003, 2002 and 2001.

Future minimum lease payment receivables under operating agreements in effect as of December 31, 2003 that could not be cancelled in advance and were in excess of one year were as follows.

SEK in millions **Maturity**	**Future lease payment**
2004	615
2005	357
2006	208
2007	124
2008	107
Later years	7
Total	**1,418**

The leasing portfolio includes some twenty agreements with other international operators and over 100 other contracts. Contract periods range between 10 and 25 years, with an average term of 20 years.

In addition, the leased asset is accounted for as a fixed asset of the reporting entity and the requirements for disclosure in accordance with IAS 16 (Chapter 12), IAS 36 (Chapter 13), IAS 38 (Chapter 11), IAS 40 (Chapter 12) and IAS 41 (Chapter 36) as appropriate.[190]

4 PRACTICAL ISSUES

4.1 Lease classification

It goes without saying that lessees and lessors often have different and incompatible goals when entering into leases. Many lessors have little desire to take the residual risk in an asset, as they are banks or other financial institutions and their prime business is providing finance. Many lessees prefer not to capitalise leased assets because capitalisation adversely affects their gearing and return on assets ratios. These differences underlie many of the problems with lease classification.

4.1.1 *The residual value of an asset*

If the residual value of an asset is significant and is not guaranteed by the lessee or a party related to it, then the lease is likely to be classified as an operating lease. This is explained by the fact that the risks of recovering the significant residual value will be the lessor's, consequently it is unlikely that the risks and rewards of ownership will have passed to the lessee. There are frequently problems of interpretation regarding the significance of residual values in lease classification. Lessees may, for example, find it difficult to obtain information about the unguaranteed residual values or verify information that they have been given by the lessor. In addition, lessees may guarantee all or part of the residual value of the asset and this has to be taken into account in the lease classification.

A *Residual value guarantees by the lessee*

Although a lessee may give a residual value guarantee in a lease, the lease itself may be structured so that the most likely outcome of events relating to the residual value indicates that no significant risk will attach to the lessee.

Example 23.16:   *A lease structured such that the most likely outcome is that the lessee has no significant residual risk*

Brief details of a motor vehicle lease are:

Fair value   –   €10,000
Rentals   –   20 monthly payments @ €275, followed by a final rental of €2,000

At the end of the lease, the lessee sells vehicle as agent for the lessor and if sold for:

(i)   more than €3,000, 99% of the excess is repaid to the lessee; or

(ii) less than €3,000, lessee pays the deficit to the lessor up to a maximum of 0.4 pence per mile above 25,000 miles p.a. on average that the leased vehicle has done.

This lease involves a guarantee by the lessee of the residual value of the leased vehicle of €3,000, as a result of (ii) above. However, the guarantee will only be called upon if both:

(a)   the vehicle's actual residual value is less than €3,000; and

(b)   the vehicle has travelled more than 25,000 miles per year on average over the lease term.

Further, the lessee is only liable to pay a certain level of the residual; namely, €100 for each 2,500 miles above 25,000 miles that the vehicle has done.

One could argue that the guarantee should be assumed to apply only to the extent that experience or expectations of the sales price and/or the mileage that vehicles have done (and the inter-relationship between these) indicate that a residual payment by the lessee will be made and if this best estimate is that a zero or minimal payment will be made, this should be used for the purposes of lease classification. This would apply the principles in IAS 37, for example, to the calculation of the liability. However, IAS 17 states that the amount of the guarantee is 'the maximum amount that could, in any event, become payable'. Therefore, the standard appears to require the maximum guarantee of €3,000 to be taken into account.

B   *Residual value guarantors*

A lessee and lessor may legitimately classify the same lease differently because, for example, the lessor has received a residual value guarantee provided by a third party.[191] Residual value guarantors undertake to acquire the assets from the lessor at an agreed amount at the end of the lease term because they can dispose of the assets on a ready and reliable market. As a result, the lease is an operating lease for the lessee and a finance lease for the lessor. This is particularly common with vehicle leases where there is an efficient second-hand market, including price guides, many car dealers and car auctions. However, residual value guarantors may be prepared to take the residual risk with many types of assets as long as there is a second-hand market.

In some instances the residual value guarantor agrees to purchase the asset from the lessee at the end of a lease, rather than from the lessor. This may mean that the lease can be classified by the lessee as an operating lease.

4.1.2   *Rental rebates*

IAS 17 suggests that an indicator that the lease is a finance lease is that 'the gains or losses from the fluctuation in the fair value of the residual fall to the lessee (for example, in the form of a rent rebate equalling most of the sales proceeds at the end of the lease)'.[192] This is because a lessee that obtains most of the sales proceeds has received all of the risks and rewards of the residual value in the asset. This would indicate that the lessor has already been compensated for the transaction and hence that it is a finance lease.

Other leases require the asset to be sold at the end of the lease but the lessor receives the first tranche of proceeds and only those proceeds above a certain level are remitted to the lessee. These arrangements may have a different significance as the lessor may be taking the proceeds to meet its unguaranteed residual value. Lessors are prepared to take risks on residual values of such assets if there is an established and reliable market in which to sell them. This could mean that the gains or losses from the fluctuation in the fair value of the residual do not fall predominantly to the lessee and, in the absence of other factors, could indicate that it is an operating lease.

Example 23.17: Rental rebates

The lease arrangements are as in Example 23.16, except that at end of the lease, the lessee sells the vehicle as agent for the lessor, and if it is sold for

(i)   up to £3,000, all of the proceeds are received by the lessor; or

(ii)   more than £3,000, 99% of excess is repaid to the lessee. The lessee does not have to make good any deficit, should one arise.

In this example, it appears that the lessor is using the sale proceeds to meet its unguaranteed residual value but it is also taking the first loss provision. Only thereafter does the lessee gain or lose from the fluctuations in the fair value. This makes it much more likely that the arrangements is an operating lease.

4.2   Derecognition of leases and termination payments

4.2.1   Lease classification

The expectations of lessors and lessees regarding the timing of termination of a lease may affect the classification of a lease as either operating or finance. This is because it will affect the expected lease term, level of payments under the lease and expected residual value of the lease assets.

Termination during the primary lease term will generally not be anticipated at the lease inception because the lessee can be assumed to be using the asset for at least that period. In addition, such an early termination will be unlikely because most leases are non-cancellable. A termination payment is usually required which will give the lessor an amount equivalent to most or all of the rental receipts which would have been received if no such termination had taken place, which means that it is reasonably certain at inception that the lease will continue to expiry.

4.2.2   Operating leases

If a lease has been classified as an operating lease at its inception, then no major difficulty arises on a termination. Any termination payment due under the lease agreement will be accounted for as income when receivable by the lessor and as an expense when due by the lessee.

4.2.3   Finance leases – lessee

Early termination of a finance lease results in derecognition of the capitalised asset by the lessee, with any remaining balance of the capitalised asset being written off as a loss on disposal. Any payment made by the lessee will reduce the lease obligation that is being carried in the balance sheet. If either a part of this obligation is not eliminated or the termination payment exceeds the previously existing obligation, then the remainder or excess will be included as a gain or loss (respectively) on derecognition of a financial liability.

A similar accounting treatment is required where the lease terminates at the expected date and there is a residual at least partly guaranteed by the lessee. For the lessee, a payment made under such a guarantee will reduce the obligation to the lessor as the guaranteed residual would obviously be included in the lessee's finance lease obligation. If any part of the guaranteed residual is not called upon, then the lessee would treat this as a gain/loss on derecognition of a financial liability.

The effect on the derecognition of the capitalised asset will depend on the extent to which the lessee expected to make the residual payment as this will have affected the level to which the capitalised asset has been depreciated. For example, if the total guaranteed residual was not expected to become payable by the lessee, then the depreciation charge may have been calculated to give a net book value at the end of the lease term equal to the residual element not expected to become payable. If this estimate was correct then the remaining obligation will equal the net book value of the relevant asset, so that the gain on derecognition of the liability will be equal to the loss on derecognition of the asset.

Example 23.18:   Early termination of finance leases by lessees

We can consider this in the context of Example 23.17 in 4.1.2 above, where there is effectively a guarantee of a residual of €3,000 dependent on the mileage done by the leased vehicle. Assuming that the lease is capitalised as a finance lease, if the lessee considers at the lease inception that the guarantee will not be called upon, then he will depreciate the vehicle to an estimated residual value of €3,000 over the lease term. In the event that his estimate is found to be correct, then the loss on disposal of the asset at its written down value will be equal and opposite to the gain on derecognition of the lease obligation of €3,000. However, if, for example, €1,000 of the guarantee was called upon, whereas the lessee had estimated that it would not be, then the net book value of €3,000 and the unused guarantee of €2,000 will both be derecognised and a loss of €1,000 will be shown on disposal of the vehicle.

4.2.4   Finance leases – lessor

Any termination payment received by a lessor upon an early termination will reduce the lessor's net investment in the lease shown as a receivable. If the termination payment is greater than the previously shown net investment, then a gain on derecognition of the lease will be shown by the lessor. On the other hand, if the termination payment is smaller than the net investment, a loss will be shown. Such a loss is usually deducted from finance lease income unless it is exceptionally large, in which case it is separately disclosed.

Any loss on termination is unlikely to arise in most situations because a finance lease is likely to have termination terms such that the lessor is compensated fully for early termination and the lessor has legal title to the asset. Because it has title, the lessor can continue to include the asset in current assets as a receivable to the extent that sales proceeds or new finance lease receivables are expected to arise. If the asset is then re-leased under an operating lease, the asset may be transferred to fixed assets and depreciated over its remaining useful life.

To some extent, these two reasons (full compensation and legal title remaining with the lessor) that explain why losses on termination of a finance lease are unlikely to arise, are complementary. If the termination payment is intended to give full compensation, then the asset may be retained by the lessee and sold with any proceeds going to him. On the other hand, if the termination payment is not structured in this way then the lessor will repossess the asset and sell or re-lease it.

4.3   Sub-leases and back-to-back leases

4.3.1   *Introduction*

Situations arise where there are more parties to a lease arrangement than simply one lessor and one lessee. The discussion below relates to situations involving an original lessor, an intermediate party and an ultimate lessee. The intermediate party may be acting either as both a lessee and lessor of the asset concerned or, alternatively, as an agent of the lessor in the transaction.

Both sub-leases and back-to-back leases involve the intermediate party acting as both lessor and lessee of the asset. The difference between the two arrangements is that, for a back-to-back lease, the terms of the two lease agreements match to a greater extent than would be the case for a sub-lease arrangement. This difference is really only one of degree, and the important decision to be made concerns whether the intermediate party is acting as both lessee and lessor in two related but independent transactions or whether the nature of the interest is such that it need not recognise the rights and obligations under the leases in its financial statements.

4.3.2   *The original lessor and the ultimate lessee*

The accounting treatment adopted by these parties will not be affected by the existence of sub-leases or back-to-back leases. The original lessor has an agreement with the intermediate party, which is not affected by any further leasing of the assets by the intermediate party unless the original lease agreement is thereby replaced.

Similarly, the ultimate lessee has a lease agreement with the intermediate party. The lessee will have use of the asset under that agreement and must make a decision, in the usual way, as to whether the lease is of a finance or operating type under the requirements of IAS 17.

4.3.3 The intermediate party

It is common for entities whose business is the leasing of assets to third parties to finance these assets themselves through leasing arrangements. There are also arrangements in which a party on-leases assets as an intermediary between a lessor and a lessee while taking a variable degree of risk in the transaction. The appropriate accounting treatment by the intermediate party depends on the substance of the series of transactions. Either the intermediate party will act as lessee to the original lessor and lessor to the ultimate lessee or, if in substance it has transferred the risks and rewards of ownership, it may be able to derecognise the assets and liabilities under its two lease arrangements and recognise only its own commission or fee income.

In order to analyse the issues that may arise, it is worth considering the various combinations of leases between lessor/intermediate and intermediate/lessee, which are summarised in the following table:

	Lessor	Intermediate party		Lessee
	Lease to Intermediate	*Lease from Lessor*	*Lease to Lessee*	*Lease from Intermediate*
(1)	Operating lease	Operating lease	Operating lease	Operating lease
(2)	Finance lease	Finance lease	Operating lease	Operating lease
(3)	Finance lease	Finance lease	Finance lease	Finance lease

Only in unusual circumstances could there be an operating lease from the lessor to the intermediate and a finance lease from the intermediate to the lessee. The intermediate would have to acquire an additional interest in the asset from a party other than the lessor in order to be in a position to transfer substantially all of the risks and rewards incidental to ownership of that asset to the lessee.

There are no significant accounting difficulties for the intermediate party regarding (1), an operating lease from the lessor to the intermediate and from the intermediate to the lessee. The intermediate may be liable to the lessor if the lessee defaults, in which case it would have to make an appropriate provision, but otherwise both contracts are executory and will be accounted for on an accruals basis according to the contract terms.

In situation (2), the intermediate will record at inception an asset acquired under a finance lease and an obligation to the lessor of an equal and opposite amount. As it has granted an operating lease to the lessee, its risks and rewards incidental to ownership of the asset exceed those assumed by the lessee under the lease. It is appropriate for the intermediate party to record a fixed asset, which it will have to depreciate as set out in 3.2.4 above.

However, under scenario (3), the intermediate is the lessee under a finance lease with the lessor and lessor under a finance lease with the lessee. Its balance sheet, *prima facie*, records a finance lease receivable from the lessee and a finance lease obligation to the lessor. Both of these are financial instruments.

The intermediate may be in a position to derecognise its financial asset and liability if it transfers to the lessor the contractual right to receive the cash flows of the lessee and thereby extinguishes its liability under the lease.[193] However, it is more likely that it retains the contractual right to receive the cash flow under the lease and a contractual obligation to pay the cash flows to the lessor. In accordance with the derecognition rules in IAS 39 it can derecognise its asset and liability if, and only if, it meets certain criteria, which are summarised in 3.6.1 above and described in detail in Chapter 16 at 4.4. In the context of leases, the most important is that the intermediate has no obligation to pay amounts to the lessor unless in collects equivalent amounts from the lessee.[194] If the ultimate lessee defaults on its lease obligations (for whatever reason), the original lessor must have no recourse against the intermediate party for the outstanding payments under the lease if derecognition is to be appropriate. Another important factor is what happens if the original lessor defaults, for example through insolvency. The analysis will also have to take account of the following conditions for derecognition of a financial asset in IAS 39:

(a)   the entity is prohibited by the terms of the transfer contract from selling or pledging the original asset; and

(b)   the entity has an obligation to remit any cash flows it collects without material delay. Investment in cash or cash equivalents is permitted, but interest earned must be passed to the eventual recipients.[195]

If these factors indicate that the intermediate party has derecognised its interest in the two leases, i.e. commercially it is acting merely as a broker or agent for the original lessor, it should not include any asset or obligation relating to the leased asset in its balance sheet. The income received by such an intermediary should be taken to profit and loss account on a systematic and rational basis – the discussion of the recognition of fee income in SIC-27, as discussed in 2.2.2 above, may be helpful. If, on the other hand, the intermediate party is taken to be acting as both lessee and lessor in two independent although related transactions, the assets and obligations under finance leases should be recognised in the normal way.

It should not be inferred from the above discussion that all situations encountered can be relatively easily analysed. In practice this is unlikely to be the case, as the risks and rewards will probably be spread between the parties involved. This is especially likely where more than the three parties discussed above are involved. Therefore, even if the arrangements meet the definition of a 'transfer' under IAS 39, the intermediate may have retained some of the risks and rewards of ownership or control of the asset and it may be necessary to recognise other assets and liabilities in this respect. This complex area is dealt with in Chapter 16 in Section 4 regarding the derecognition of financial assets.

4.4 Sale and leaseback arrangements including options

IAS 17 identifies a particular condition that may result in a lease being classified as a finance lease: where the lessee has a 'bargain purchase' option to acquire the asset. However, the standard does not deal explicitly with the function of options in the context of sale and leaseback arrangements, where circumstances are more complex and there may be a variety of options that may affect the overall assessment of the lease.

If a lease arrangement includes an option that can only be exercised by the seller/lessee at the then fair value of the asset in question, the risks and rewards inherent in the residual value of the asset have passed to the buyer/lessor. The option amounts to a right of first refusal to the seller/lessee.

Where there is both a put and a call option in force on equivalent terms at a determinable amount other than the fair value, it is clear that the asset will revert to the seller/lessee. It must be in the interests of one or other of the parties to exercise the option so as to secure a profit or avoid a loss, and therefore the likelihood of the asset remaining the property of the buyer/lessor rather than reverting to the seller must be remote. In such a case, this is a bargain purchase option and the seller/lessee has entered into a finance leaseback.

However, the position is less clear where there is only a put option or only a call option in force, rather than a combination of the two. Where there is only a put option, the effect will be (in the absence of other factors) that the seller/lessee has disposed of the rewards of ownership to the buyer/lessor but retained the risks. This is because the buyer/lessor will only exercise his option to put the asset back to the seller/lessee if its value at the time is less than the repurchase price payable under the option. This means that if the asset continues to rise in value the buyer/lessor will keep it and reap the benefits of that enhanced value; conversely if the value of the asset falls, the option will be exercised and the downside on the asset will be borne by the seller/lessee.

This analysis does not of itself answer the question whether the deal should be treated as an operating or financing leaseback. The overall commercial effect will still have to be evaluated, taking account of all the terms of the arrangement and by considering the motivations of both of the parties in agreeing to the various terms of the deal; in particular it will need to be considered why they have each agreed to have this one-sided option.

Where there is only a call option, the position will be reversed. In this case, the seller/lessor has disposed of the risks, but retained the rewards to be attained if the value of the asset exceeds the repurchase price specified in the option. Once again, though, the overall commercial effect of the arrangement has to be evaluated in deciding how to account for the deal. Emphasis has to be given to what is likely to happen in practice, and it is instructive to look at the arrangement from the point of view of both parties to see what their expectations are and what has induced them to accept the deal on the terms that have been agreed. It may be obvious from the overall terms of the arrangement that the call option will be exercised, in which case the deal will again be a financing arrangement and should be accounted for as such. For example, the exercise price of the call option may be set at a significant discount to expected market value, the seller may need the asset to use on an ongoing basis in its business, or the asset may provide in effect the only source of the seller's future income. Equally, the financial effects of *not* exercising the option, such as continued exposure to escalating costs, may make it obvious that the option will have to be exercised (so-called 'economic compulsion').

The following is an example of a sale and leaseback deal where the seller has a call option to repurchase the asset but has no commitment to do so:

Example 23.19:   Sale and leaseback transaction involving escalating rentals and call options

Company S sells a property to Company B for £100,000,000 and leases it back on the following terms:

Rental for years 1 to 5	£3,900,000 per annum
Rental for years 6 to 10	£5,875,000 per annum
Rental for years 11 to 15	£8,830,000 per annum
Rental for years 16 to 20	£13,280,000 per annum
Rental for years 21 to 25	£19,970,000 per annum
Rental for years 26 to 30	£30,025,000 per annum
Rental for years 31 to 35	£45,150,000 per annum
Rental thereafter	open market rent

Rentals are payable annually in advance.

Company S has a call option to buy back the property at the following dates and prices:

At the end of year 5	£125,000,000
At the end of year 10	£150,000,000
At the end of year 15	£168,000,000
At the end of year 20	£160,000,000
At the end of year 25	£100,000,000

Company B has no right to put the property back to Company S.

An analysis of the economics of this deal suggests that whilst Company S has no legal obligation to repurchase the property, there is no genuine commercial possibility that the option will not be exercised. This is because the rentals and option prices are structured in such a way as to give the buyer of the property a lender's return whilst, at the same time, there is no commercial logic for the seller not to exercise the option at year 25, if not earlier. Exercising the option at the end of year 25 will mean that Company S will regain ownership of the property and will have had the use of the £100,000,000 at an effective rate of approximately 8.2% per annum; failure to exercise the option will mean additional lease obligations of £375,875,000 over the ten years from years 25 to 35, followed by the obligation to pay market rents thereafter.

5 EFFECTIVE DATE, TRANSITIONAL PROVISIONS AND FIRST-TIME ADOPTION

5.1 Effective date

The revised standard applies to annual periods beginning on or after 1 January 2005. Earlier application is encouraged. If an entity applies this Standard for a period beginning before 1 January 2005 it shall disclose that fact.[196]

5.2 Transitional provisions

There are two significant revisions to IAS 17 (revised 1997): the clarification of the classification of leases of land and buildings and the elimination of accounting alternatives for initial direct costs in the accounts of lessors (see 2.3.4 and 3.1.6 above).

Entities are encouraged to apply the revised requirements of the standard retrospectively, but this is not required. If the standard is not applied retrospectively, the balance of any pre-existing finance lease is deemed to have been properly determined by the lessor and will be accounted for prospectively in accordance with the provisions of this Standard.[197]

There is an exception to this requirement if the entity took advantage of the transitional rules in IAS 17 (revised 1997). This did not require retrospective application and similarly deemed the balance of any pre-existing finance lease to have been properly determined by the lessor. As a result, entities could still be including in their financial statements assets and liabilities relating to finance leases that were not restated when IAS 17 (revised 1997) came into force (for accounting periods beginning on or after 1 January 1999). IAS 17 does not require such assets to be adjusted retrospectively. All leases entered into since the entity applied IAS 17 (revised 1997) must be adjusted, as appropriate.[198]

5.3 First-time adoption

As required by IFRS 1, IAS 17 must be applied with full retrospective effect in the transition date balance sheet with all adjustments to assets and liabilities taken to retained earnings. This means, in particular, that leases must be classified as operating or finance leases in accordance with IAS 17 and assets and liabilities arising be measured in accordance with its requirements. IFRS 1 contains no exception to this general rule in respect of lease accounting. First-time adoption and the requirements of IFRS 1 are covered in Chapter 4.

6 CONCLUSION

IAS 17 has been in force for a long time and practice under it is well established. In any event, though, it should be regarded as a standard with a relatively short remaining life. It is clear that the initiatives started by the G4+1 to change fundamentally the approach to lease accounting will be pursued further by the IASB, in conjunction with one or more of the national standard setters. Now that the IASB's main preoccupation with improving IFRSs in the run up to 2005 is in the past, this is likely to become more of a priority.

It is therefore likely that in due course, the distinction between finance and operating leases will most likely be removed, and the rights and obligations of all leases will be recorded in the balance sheet at their fair values.

References

1 IAS 17 (1982), *Accounting for Leases*, IASC, September 1982, Revised 1997 and 2003; SFAS 13, *Accounting for Leases*, FASB, November 1976 and SSAP 21, *Accounting for leases and hire purchase contracts*, ASC, August 1984.

2 IAS 17 (1982).

3 IAS 17 (1982), para. 3.

4 Statement of Intent, *Comparability of Financial Statements*, Appendix 3.

5 *Framework for the Preparation and Presentation of Financial Statements*, IASB, September 1989, para. 49(a)-(b)

6 Warren McGregor, *Accounting for leases: a new approach: Recognition by Lessees of Assets and Liabilities Arising under Lease Contracts*, FASB, 1996.

7 Warren McGregor, *Accounting for leases: a new approach: Recognition by Lessees of Assets and Liabilities Arising under Lease Contracts*, p. 3.

8 Warren McGregor, *Accounting for leases: a new approach: Recognition by Lessees of Assets and Liabilities Arising under Lease Contracts*, p. 3.

9 Warren McGregor, *Accounting for leases: a new approach: Recognition by Lessees of Assets and Liabilities Arising under Lease Contracts*, p. 16.

10 Warren McGregor, *Accounting for leases: a new approach: Recognition by Lessees of Assets and Liabilities Arising under Lease Contracts*, p. 17.

11 G4+1 Group of Accounting Standard Setters, Position Paper, *Leases: Implementation of a new approach*, December 1999, Part II, *passim.*

12 G4+1 *Leases: Implementation of a new approach*, Part II, Part III, *passim.*

13 G4+1 *Leases: Implementation of a new approach*, Part II, para. 3.13.

14 IAS 38, *Intangible assets*, IASB, March 2004; IAS 40, *Investment property*, IASB, December 2003 (amended March 2004).

15 G4+1 *Leases: Implementation of a new approach*, Part II, para. 4.86 *et seq.*

16 IAS 37, *Provisions, Contingent Liabilities and Contingent Assets*, IASB, September 1998 (amended March 2004).

17 *IASB Update*, May 2003.

18 *IASB Update*, November 2003.

19 *ASB Inside Track 38*, January 2004.

20 IFRIC Interpretation, *Determining whether an Arrangement contains a Lease*, (IFRIC Draft Interpretation D3 approved by IFRIC in October 2004) IASB, October 2004.

21 *IASB Update*, November 2003.

22 IAS 17, *Leases*, IASB, December 2003, (amended March 2004), para. 2.

23 IAS 17, para. 4.

24 IAS 17, para. 6.

25 IFRIC D3.

26 SIC-27, *Evaluating the Substance of Transactions Involving the Legal Form of a Lease*, SIC, December 2001 (amended March 2004).

27 IFRIC D3.

28 EITF 01-8, *Determining Whether an Arrangement Contains a Lease*, FASB, May 2003.

29 IFRIC D3, paras. BC20-BC21.

30 IFRIC D3, para. 1

31 IFRIC D3, para. 1
32 IFRIC D3, para. BC2.
33 IAS 17, para. 3
34 IFRIC D3, para. BC2.
35 IFRIC D3.
36 IFRIC D3, para. 5.
37 IFRIC D3, para. 2.
38 IFRIC D3, para. 4.
39 IFRIC D3, para. 6.
40 IFRIC D3, para. 3.
41 IFRIC D3, para. 7.
42 IFRIC D3, para. 8.
43 IFRIC D3, para. 7.
44 IFRIC D3, para. 9.
45 IFRIC D3, paras. IE 1-IE2.
46 IFRIC D3, paras. IE 3-IE4.
47 IFRIC D3, para. 10.
48 IAS 17, para. 4.
49 IFRIC D3, para. 11.
50 IFRIC D3, para. 11.
51 IFRIC D3, para. 12.
52 IAS 17, paras. 4 and 8.
53 IFRIC D3, para. 13.
54 IFRIC D3, para. 14.
55 IFRIC D3, para. 15.
56 IFRIC D3, para. BC38.
57 IAS 17, para. 31(e).
58 IFRIC D3, para. BC38.
59 IFRIC D3, para. BC38.
60 IFRIC D3, para. 15.
61 IFRIC D3, para. 16.
62 IFRIC D3, para. 17.
63 SIC-27.
64 SIC-27, para. 2.
65 SIC-27, para. 1.
66 SIC-27, Appendix A.
67 SIC-27, paras. 3-4.
68 SIC-27, para. 3.
69 SIC-27, para. 5.
70 SIC-27, para. 5.
71 SIC-27, para. 6.
72 SIC-27, para. 7.
73 SIC-27, para. 8.
74 SIC-27, para. 9.
75 SIC-27, para. 10.
76 IAS 17, paras. 4 and 8.
77 IAS 17, para. 9.
78 IAS 17, para. 7.
79 IAS 17, para. 10.
80 IAS 17, para. 4.
81 IAS 17, para. 4.
82 SFAS 13, para. 7(c).
83 IAS 17, para. 11.
84 For further discussion on determining the substance of a lease, see ICAEW Technical Release 664, *Implementation of SSAP 21* 'Accounting for leases and hire purchase contracts', July 1987.

85 IAS 17, para. 13.
86 IAS 17, para. 4.
87 IAS 17, para. 13.
88 IAS 16, *Property, Plant and Equipment,* IASB, December 2003, (amended March 2004), para. 51.
89 IAS 17, para. 14.
90 IAS 17, para. BC5.
91 IAS 17, para. 15.
92 IAS 17, para. 15.
93 IAS 17, para. 16.
94 IAS 17, paras. BC9-BC11.
95 IAS 17, para. 16.
96 IAS 17, para. 17.
97 IAS 17, para. 18.
98 IAS 17, para. 19.
99 IAS 17, para. 20.
100 IAS 17, para. 22.
101 IAS 17, para. 25.
102 IAS 17, para. 36.
103 IAS 17, para. 4.
104 IAS 17, para. 4.
105 IAS 17, para. 5.
106 IAS 17, para. 4.
107 IAS 17, para. 4.
108 IAS 17, para. 4.
109 IAS 17, para. 4.
110 IAS 17, para. 4.
111 IAS 17, para. 4.
112 IAS 17, para. 4.
113 IAS 17, para. 25.
114 IAS 17, para. 4.
115 IAS 17, para. 24.
116 IAS 17, para. 38.
117 IAS 17, para. 22
118 IAS 17, para. 25.
119 IAS 17, para. 26.
120 These methods are described in the Guidance Notes on SSAP 21, para. 20.
121 IAS 17, para. 22.
122 IAS 17, para. 24.
123 IAS 17, paras. 27-28.
124 IAS 17, para. 4.
125 IAS 17, para. 29.
126 IAS 16, para. 51.
127 IAS 17, para. 30.
128 IAS 17, para. 36.
129 IAS 17, para. 37.
130 IAS 17, para. 38.
131 IAS 17, para. 39.
132 IAS 17, para. 4.
133 IAS 17, para. 39.
134 IAS 17, para. 40.
135 IAS 17, para. 41.
136 IAS 39, *Financial Instruments: Recognition and Measurement,* IASB, December 2003 (amended March 2004), para. 2(b).
137 IAS 17, para. 41A.
138 IAS 17, para. 43.

139 IAS 17, para. 42.
140 IAS 17, paras. 44-45.
141 IAS 17, para. 44.
142 IAS 17, para. 46.
143 IAS 17, para. 55.
144 IAS 17, paras. 33-34.
145 SIC-15, *Operating Leases – Incentives*, SIC, July 1998 (amended December 2003), para. 1
146 SIC-15, para. 3.
147 SIC-15, para. 5.
148 SIC-15, para. 6.
149 SIC-15, Appendix, Examples 1-2.
150 IAS 37, para. 63.
151 IAS 37, para. 66.
152 IAS 37, para. 10.
153 IAS 17, paras. 49-50.
154 IAS 17, para. 51.
155 IAS 17, para. 52.
156 IAS 17, para. 53.
157 IAS 16, para. 51.
158 IAS 38, paras. 100 and 104.
159 IAS 17, para. 54.
160 SIC-15, para. 4.
161 IAS 17, para. 58.
162 IAS 17, para. 59.
163 IAS 17, para. 60
164 IAS 17, para. 60
165 IAS 18, *Revenue*, IASB, December 1993 (amended March 2004), para. 16. Note that IAS 18's scope exemption in para. 6(a) applies only to revenue under lease agreements so it does not affect this analysis
166 IAS 17, para. 64.
167 IAS 17, paras. 61-62.
168 IAS 17, para. 65.
169 IAS 17, para. 66.
170 IAS 32, *Financial Instruments: Disclosure and Presentation*, IASB, December 2003, (amended March 2004), para. AG9.
171 IAS 39, para. 2(b).
172 IAS 39, para. 17.
173 IAS 39, para. 17.
174 IAS 39, paras. 19-20.
175 IAS 39, para. 18.
176 IAS 39, para. 19.
177 IAS 39, para. 63.
178 IAS 39, para. 39.
179 IAS 39, para. AG57.
180 IAS 39, paras. 41-42.
181 IAS 39, para. 10.
182 IAS 39, para. 11.
183 IAS 39, para. AG33(f).
184 IAS 32, paras. 15 and 94.
185 IAS 17, para. 31.
186 IAS 17, para. 32.
187 IAS 17, para. 47.
188 IAS 17, para. 48.
189 IAS 17, para. 56.
190 IAS 17, para. 57.
191 IAS 17, para. 9.
192 IAS 17, para. 11.
193 IAS 39, para. 18.
194 IAS 39, paras. 18-19.
195 IAS 39, para. 19.
196 IAS 17, para. 69.
197 IAS 17, para. 67.
198 IAS 17, para. 68.

Chapter 24   Income taxes

1   INTRODUCTION

1.1   The nature of taxation

A discussion of how to deal with taxation in financial statements must begin with some consideration of what it is that is to be accounted for. Although it might be supposed that this is a simple question, taxation has certain characteristics which set it apart from other business expenses and which might justify a different treatment, in particular:

- tax payments are not made in exchange for goods or services specific to the business (as opposed to access to generally available national infrastructure assets); and
- the business has no say in whether or not the payments are to be made.

It is held by some that these characteristics mean that taxation is more in the nature of a distribution than an expense – in essence that the government is a stakeholder in the success of the business and participates in its results (generally in priority to other stakeholders).

Adoption of a 'distribution' view of taxation would render irrelevant most of the accounting questions which follow, since these are essentially concerned with the allocation of taxation expense to accounting periods. If taxation were regarded as a distribution, however, the question of allocation would not arise, since distributions are generally not allocated to accounting periods in the same way as items of expense.

A 'distribution' view of taxation is not adopted in practice, although some of the accounting approaches that are sometimes proposed to deal with certain issues have their roots within it. For all practical purposes, taxation is dealt with as an expense of the business, and the accounting standards which have been developed both by the IASB and by national standard setters are based on that premise.

1.2   Allocation between periods

The most significant accounting question which arises in relation to taxation is how to allocate the tax expense between accounting periods. The recognition of trading transactions in the financial statements in a particular period is governed by the application of IFRS. However, the timing of the recognition of transactions for the purposes of measuring the taxable profit is governed by the application of tax law, which sometimes prescribes an accounting treatment different from that used in the financial statements. The generally accepted view is that it is necessary to seek some reconciliation between these different treatments. The mechanism for this reconciliation, referred to as deferred taxation, is broadly to recognise the tax effects of transactions in financial statements in the same period as the transactions themselves.

Over the last seventy years or so, there have evolved two methods (or, more correctly, groups of methods) for accounting for deferred tax. The earlier methods, known as 'timing difference' approaches, focused on the differences that arise between the timing of the recognition of income and expenditure for financial reporting and tax purposes. More detail of the history and methodology of the various 'timing difference' approaches can be found in the seventh (final) edition of Ernst & Young' s *UK and International GAAP*, pages 1648 to 1660.

However, these income statement based approaches sit uneasily with a conceptual framework, such as the IASB's own *Framework*, that is focused on the balance sheet. Accordingly in the late 1980s and early 1990s the US FASB developed a method of accounting for tax based on all differences, whether arising from the performance statements or not, between the carrying amount of assets and liabilities and the amount attributed to them for tax purposes. This new US methodology, known as the 'temporary difference' approach, was adopted, with relatively minor modification, in IAS 12 – *Income Taxes*.[1]

1.3   Timing and temporary differences contrasted

1.3.1   Timing differences

Although the timing difference approach is not used in IFRS, in our view IAS 12 cannot be fully understood without some knowledge of it. This is because there are a number of circumstances where IAS 12 abandons a strict temporary difference approach so as to adopt what is, in reality, a timing difference approach.

Timing differences represent items of income or expenditure which are taxable or tax-deductible, but in periods different from those in which they are dealt with in the financial statements. They therefore arise when items of income and expenditure enter into the measurement of profit for both accounting and taxation purposes, but in different accounting periods. They are said to 'originate' in the first of these periods and 'reverse' in one or more subsequent periods. Under the timing difference approaches, deferred taxation is the taxation which relates to timing differences.

A common form of timing difference is that created by differences between accounting depreciation and tax depreciation[2] of property, plant and equipment

(PPE). Tax depreciation is the amount by which PPE may be written down to arrive at taxable profit, and is therefore the tax equivalent of the charge for depreciation in the financial statements. Tax depreciation is often intended to provide some economic incentive for businesses to invest, and is therefore given at a faster rate than the rate at which depreciation is charged in the financial statements, as illustrated in Example 24.1.

Example 24.1: Deferred tax on timing differences

An item of equipment is purchased on 1 January 2005 for £48,000 and is estimated to have a seven year useful life, at the end of which it is estimated that it will be sold for £6,000. There is no change to this estimated residual amount over the life of the equipment. The depreciation charge will therefore be £6,000 per year. (£48,000 – £6,000 = £42,000/7).

The entity pays tax at 30% and the tax depreciation for the equipment is as shown below. Timing differences will arise in each of the seven years ended 31 December 2005 to 2011 as follows (all figures in £s):

Table 1	2005	2006	2007	2008	2009	2010	2011
Financial statements							
Net book value b/f	48,000	42,000	36,000	30,000	24,000	18,000	12,000
Depreciation	6,000	6,000	6,000	6,000	6,000	6,000	6,000
Net book value c/f	42,000	36,000	30,000	24,000	18,000	12,000	6,000
Tax computation							
Tax base b/f	48,000	36,000	27,000	20,000	15,000	11,000	8,000
Tax depreciation	12,000	9,000	7,000	5,000	4,000	3,000	2,000
Tax base c/f	36,000	27,000	20,000	15,000	11,000	8,000	6,000
Timing difference arising							
Book depreciation	6,000	6,000	6,000	6,000	6,000	6,000	6,000
Tax depreciation	12,000	9,000	7,000	5,000	4,000	3,000	2,000
Originating/(reversing)	6,000	3,000	1,000	(1,000)	(2,000)	(3,000)	(4,000)
Cumulative timing difference	6,000	9,000	10,000	9,000	7,000	4,000	0

The entity's tax computations for each year would show the following (all figures in £s):

Table 2	2005	2006	2007	2008	2009	2010	2011
Accounting profit	80,000	80,000	80,000	80,000	80,000	80,000	80,000
Accounting depreciation	6,000	6,000	6,000	6,000	6,000	6,000	6,000
Tax depreciation	(12,000)	(9,000)	(7,000)	(5,000)	(4,000)	(3,000)	(2,000)
Taxable profit	74,000	77,000	79,000	81,000	82,000	83,000	84,000
Tax payable @ 30%	22,200	23,100	23,700	24,300	24,600	24,900	25,200

Table 1 shows that there is a cumulative originating difference of £10,000 over the first three years, but this progressively diminishes, and eventually reverses completely, in subsequent years. For each of the first three years of the asset's life, the tax currently assessed (and hence the amount provided in the financial statements as the current year tax charge for those years) is lower than the tax that will eventually fall to be paid on the profit reported in the financial statements. The difference reverses from 2008 onwards, when the tax allowances have fallen below the level of the depreciation charge. The tax assessed (and hence the amount provided in the financial statements as the current year tax charge for those years) will be higher than the sum due on the profit reported in the financial statements.

This entity in this example would calculate deferred tax on the timing differences above as follows, assuming that:

- it adopted the liability method with full provision for deferred tax, whereby deferred tax is provided for on net cumulative timing differences at the tax rate at which they are expected to reverse. A fuller discussion can be found in the seventh (final) edition of Ernst & Young' s *UK and International GAAP*, pages 1651 to 1653; and

- it had no timing differences apart from those in Table 1 above.

Its income statements will show the following (all figures in £s):

Table 3	2005	2006	2007	2008	2009	2010	2011
Profit before tax	80,000	80,000	80,000	80,000	80,000	80,000	80,000
Current tax @ 30%[1]	22,200	23,100	23,700	24,300	24,600	24,900	25,200
Deferred tax[2]	1,800	900	300	(300)	(600)	(900)	(1,200)
Profit after tax	56,000	56,000	56,000	56,000	56,000	56,000	56,000

1   See Table 2 above.

2   Timing differences in Table 1 above @ 30%.

The amount shown for deferred tax in the balance sheet (representing the cumulative charges and credits for deferred tax recognised in the income statement) will be (all figures in £s):

Table 4	2005	2006	2007	2008	2009	2010	2011
	1,800	2,700	3,000	2,700	2,100	1,200	0

1.3.2   Temporary differences

A   The 'temporary difference' approach

As noted above the essential difference between the 'timing' and 'temporary' difference approaches is that the timing difference approach focuses on the (comprehensive) income statement and the temporary difference approach on the balance sheet. The temporary difference approach, broadly speaking, calculates the tax that would be paid if the net assets of the reporting entity were realised at book value. A temporary difference is the difference between the carrying amount of an asset or liability and its 'tax base' (essentially, the amount at which the item concerned is recognised for tax purposes). Under the temporary difference approach, deferred taxation is the taxation which relates to temporary differences.

Example 24.2 illustrates how the temporary difference approach would be applied to the entity in Example 24.1 above.

Example 24.2: Deferred tax on temporary differences

An item of equipment is purchased in 2005 for £48,000 and is estimated to have a seven year useful life, at the end of which it is estimated that it will be sold for £6,000. There is no change to this estimated residual amount over the life of the equipment. The depreciation charge will therefore be £6,000 per year. (£48,000 – £6,000 = £42,000/7).

Again, the tax depreciation for the equipment is assumed to be as in Example 24.1 above.

The entity's current tax computations would be the same as in Example 24.1 above (all figures in £s):

Table 1	2005	2006	2007	2008	2009	2010	2011
Accounting profit	80,000	80,000	80,000	80,000	80,000	80,000	80,000
Accounting depreciation	6,000	6,000	6,000	6,000	6,000	6,000	6,000
Tax depreciation	(12,000)	(9,000)	(7,000)	(5,000)	(4,000)	(3,000)	(2,000)
Taxable profit	74,000	77,000	79,000	81,000	82,000	83,000	84,000
Tax payable @ 30%	22,200	23,100	23,700	24,300	24,600	24,900	25,200

The entity would determine its deferred tax by first calculating temporary differences as follows (all figures in £s):

Table 2	2005	2006	2007	2008	2009	2010	2011
Financial statements							
Net book value b/f	48,000	42,000	36,000	30,000	24,000	18,000	12,000
Depreciation	6,000	6,000	6,000	6,000	6,000	6,000	6,000
Net book value c/f	42,000	36,000	30,000	24,000	18,000	12,000	6,000
Tax computation							
Tax base b/f	48,000	36,000	27,000	20,000	15,000	11,000	8,000
Tax depreciation	12,000	9,000	7,000	5,000	4,000	3,000	2,000
Tax base c/f	36,000	27,000	20,000	15,000	11,000	8,000	6,000
Temporary difference arising							
Net book value	42,000	36,000	30,000	24,000	18,000	12,000	6,000
Tax base	36,000	27,000	20,000	15,000	11,000	8,000	6,000
Temporary difference	6,000	3,000	10,000	9,000	7,000	4,000	0
Deferred tax provision							
Temporary difference above @ 30%	1,800	2,700	3,000	2,700	2,100	1,200	0

Its accounts will show the following:

Table 3	2005	2006	2007	2008	2009	2010	2011
Profit before tax	80,000	80,000	80,000	80,000	80,000	80,000	80,000
Current tax @ 30%	22,200	23,100	23,700	24,300	24,600	24,900	25,200
Deferred tax[1]	1,800	900	300	(300)	(600)	(900)	(1,200)
Profit after tax	56,000	56,000	56,000	56,000	56,000	56,000	56,000

1   Movement in balance sheet provision for deferred tax (see Table 2 above).

Simple examples like this result in no arithmetical difference between the approaches, which can lead to the incorrect conclusion that they are basically the same. There are in fact a number of instances of temporary differences that are not timing differences, and in more complex situations (such as in the financial statements of a multinational group) the two methods can produce radically different results.

In particular, the 'timing difference' approach uses the concept of 'permanent differences'. As their name implies, these are differences between the tax computation and the income statement that arise as a result of items that are recognised for financial reporting purposes but not for tax purposes (e.g. a fine not deductible in computing tax), or items that are recognised for tax purposes but not financial reporting purposes (e.g. tax depreciation of PPE based on an amount in excess of the actual cost of the PPE). Under the timing difference approach, permanent differences are ignored when computing deferred tax.

Under the temporary difference approach, however, there is no concept of a permanent difference. Any difference between the carrying value of an asset or liability or its tax base is a temporary difference. It is particularly important that first-time adopters of IFRS, the majority of which may well be accounting for deferred tax under some form of timing difference method under their current national GAAP, fully appreciate these differences.

Examples 24.3 to 24.6 below give examples of temporary differences that are not timing differences.

Example 24.3:   'Timing' versus 'temporary' differences (1)

An entity buys inventory for €120, of which only €90 is deductible for tax purposes when the inventory is sold.

Under the timing difference approach, the purchase of the inventory creates no taxable or accounting income, and therefore no timing difference. The non-deductible €30 would be reflected in the financial statements by an effective tax rate (i.e. tax charge in the financial statements divided by profit or loss before tax) higher than the statutory tax rate when the inventory is sold.

Under the temporary difference approach, however, a temporary difference of €30 arises on purchase of the inventory, being the difference between its carrying amount and the amount deductible for tax. However, IAS 12 would not necessarily require a deferred tax liability to be recognised on this temporary difference (see 4.2.1 below). It is possible that IAS 12 may be amended to change the treatment of such differences – see 4.2.6 and 9 below.

Example 24.4:   'Timing' versus 'temporary' differences (2)

An entity acquires PPE for €1,000,000, but is entitled to claim deductions of €1,300,000 in respect of the PPE for tax purposes.

Under the timing difference approach, the purchase of the PPE creates no taxable or accounting income, and therefore no timing difference. The additional deductions of €300,000 would be reflected in the financial statements by an effective tax rate lower than the statutory tax rate when the PPE is depreciated.

Under the temporary difference approach, however, a temporary difference of €300,000 arises on purchase of the PPE, being the difference between its carrying amount and the amount deductible for tax. However, IAS 12 would not necessarily require a deferred tax asset to be recognised on this temporary difference (see 4.2.2 below). It is possible that IAS 12 may be amended to change the treatment of such differences – see 4.2.6 and 9 below.

Example 24.5:   *'Timing' versus 'temporary' differences (3)*

On 1 January 2005 an entity purchases land in a jurisdiction where the tax base of land is raised annually in line with inflation so that purely inflationary gains on sale of the land are not subject to tax. The land cost €2,000,000 and is not depreciated in the financial statements. During 2005 the annual inflation rate is 2.5% so that at 31 December 2005 the tax base of the land has increased to €2,050,000.

Under the timing difference approach, this increase creates no taxable or accounting income, and therefore no timing difference. The extra €50,000 potential deduction would be reflected in the financial statements by an effective tax rate lower than the statutory tax rate if the land is sold for an amount greater than its carrying amount at the time of sale.

Under the temporary difference approach, however, at 31 December 2005 a temporary difference of €50,000 arises on the increase in the value of the land for tax purposes. In principle this gives rise to a deferred tax asset, but whether or not this asset could actually be recognised under IAS 12 is subject to further restrictions (see 4.2.2 and following below).

Example 24.6:   *'Timing' versus 'temporary' differences (4)*

On 1 January 2005 an entity which, under IAS 21 – *The Effect of Changes in Foreign Exchange Rates*,[3] has determined its functional currency as US dollars (see Chapter 9), purchases plant for $1 million, which will be depreciated to its estimated residual value of zero over 10 years. The entity is taxed in the local currency LC, and is entitled to receive tax deductions for the depreciation charged in the financial statements. The exchange rate is $1=LC2 at 1 January 2005 (so that the cost of the asset for local tax purposes is LC2,000,000) and $1=LC2.5 at 31 December 2005.

Under the timing difference approach, no timing difference arises since tax allowances claimed always equal depreciation charged, expressed in LC.

Under the temporary difference approach, however, at 31 December 2005 a temporary difference of $180,000 arises being the difference between the net book value of the plant of $900,000 (cost $1,000,000 less depreciation $100,000) and its tax base of $720,000 (cost LC2,000,000 less depreciation LC200,000 = LC1,800,000 translated at year end rate of $1=LC2.5). In this situation IAS 12 would require a deferred tax liability to be recognised. In the converse situation, where the net book value of the asset is lower than its tax base, a deferred tax asset would be recognised subject to the general restrictions in IAS 12 on recognition of tax assets (see 4.2.2 and following below).

It is also important to be aware that, whilst IAS 12 draws heavily on US GAAP and FAS 109 – *Income Taxes*,[4] there are some differences between them. For example, FAS 109 would prohibit the recognition of deferred tax on the temporary difference in Example 24.6 above.[5] These differences can appear rather esoteric, but are likely to be a real issue in an entity of any size and can in fact have a significant impact on the reported numbers. Accordingly, entities that currently report under US GAAP should not simply assume that deferred tax will be the same under IFRS as under US GAAP.

The main differences between IAS 12 and FAS 109 are highlighted in the discussion at 9 below on the issues raised in respect of accounting for income taxes by the short-term convergence project currently being undertaken by the IASB and FASB with a view to eliminating differences between US GAAP and IFRS.

B   *Conceptual basis of the temporary difference approach*

The examples above demonstrate that the temporary difference approach provides a reasonably workable methodology for calculating deferred tax. However, it does raise the question of what the resulting deferred tax assets and liabilities represent. Under IFRS an asset or liability can be recognised in the balance sheet only if it meets the definition of asset or liability in the IASB's *Framework* – i.e. if it represents a right to receive, or an obligation to transfer, economic benefits as the result of a past event.

Deferred tax is an accounting model based on the premise that, for financial reporting purposes, the tax effects of transactions should be recognised in the same period as the transactions themselves. In reality, however, tax is paid or refunded in accordance with the rules determined by the tax authorities. The tax authorities cannot demand payment of an entity's deferred tax liability until it forms part of the legal tax liability for a future period; equally, an entity cannot recover its deferred tax assets from the tax authorities until they form a deduction in arriving at the legal tax liability for a future period. Does that then imply that deferred tax is not an asset or liability at all? Supporters of the temporary difference approach believe that there is an asset or liability[6] on the following argument.

If an asset is currently carried in the balance sheet at, say, €1,000 there is an implicit assumption in the financial statements that the asset will ultimately be recovered or realised by a cash inflow of at least €1,000. If that inflow will enter into the determination of future taxable income, the tax (if any) on realisation of the €1,000 carrying amount of the asset should be provided for. For example, if the entity pays tax at 40% and will be able to deduct only €600 in respect of the asset for tax purposes, it will pay tax of €160 (40% of €[1,000-600]) as the asset is realised. This deferred tax of €160 is as much a liability as the €1,000 asset is an asset. It would be internally inconsistent for the financial statements simultaneously to represent that the asset can recovered at €1,000 while ignoring the tax consequences of doing so.

Conversely, if a liability is currently carried in the balance sheet at, say, €1,000 there is an implicit assumption in the financial statements that the liability will ultimately be settled by a cash outflow of at least €1,000. If that outflow will enter into the determination of future taxable income, the tax deduction (if any) on realisation of the €1,000 carrying amount of the asset should in principle be recognised as an asset. Again, it would be internally inconsistent for the financial statements simultaneously to represent that the liability will be settled at €1,000 while ignoring the tax consequences of doing so.[7]

This argument does not convince everybody, including the UK's Accounting Standards Board.[8] One perceived flaw in the argument is that it seeks to provide for only one of the additional liabilities (i.e. tax) that will be incurred in realising an asset. No-one would suggest that other future costs and overheads that will be incurred in realising the asset (e.g. wages, power, raw materials etc.) are a present liability, so why – some argue – is the future tax?[9] Some go further and question whether the argument above would have occurred to anyone, if deferred tax had not already been a generally accepted accounting practice in the early 1990s, suggesting that it is really an attempt to rationalise existing practice rather than a natural interpretation of the *Framework*, which could be argued to support the flow-through approach (see 1.4 below).

1.4 The flow-through method

The flow-through method is not really a method of accounting for deferred tax at all, but rather a justification for not accounting for it. Under the flow-through method, the tax charge is simply the amount payable based on the taxable profits of that year, with no attempt to reallocate it between periods. The method therefore deals with tax as if it were either a period cost or a distribution (see 1.1 above).

Flow-through is not presently generally regarded as an acceptable approach. Those who support flow-through do so for one of two reasons. One argument is that tax is assessed annually on profits as determined for tax purposes, not on accounting profits. The tax authorities impose a single tax assessment on the entity and that is its only liability to tax for that period. Any tax assessed in future years will depend on future events and hence is not a present liability as defined in the IASB's *Framework*.

Others argue that even if, in principle, temporary differences do give rise to tax liabilities, in practice such liabilities cannot always be measured reliably. The future tax consequences of current transactions depend upon a complex interaction of future events, such as the profitability, investment and financing transactions of the entity, and changes in tax rates and laws. Only those that could be measured reliably (typically very short-term discrete differences) should be provided for.

The main conceptual argument against the flow-through method is that it is essentially cash accounting at odds with the accruals basis on which financial statements are normally prepared. Also the army of tax planners and advisers employed by any major company suggests a general belief in the underlying stability of the tax system, which lies uneasily with the assumptions of unpredictability underlying the flow-through approach.

1.5 The development of IAS 12

The original version of IAS 12 – *Accounting for Taxes on Income* – was published in 1979. This was so accommodating as to hardly merit the name 'standard', since it allowed virtually every variant of the timing difference approach used in the world at the time. This was inevitable given the divergence of treatment in the countries that constituted the main members of the IASC at the time.

In January 1989, the IASC published an exposure draft E33 – *Accounting for Taxes on Income*, which proposed some standardisation, although still requiring a timing difference approach. This exposure draft was not taken further, largely because it was overtaken by the development of temporary difference approach in the United States, and the issue of the US standard SFAS 109.

A new exposure draft E49 – *Income Taxes* – was issued in 1994, proposing an approach to deferred tax that drew heavily on SFAS 109. This was subsequently converted into a revised version of IAS 12 in October 1996, which came into force for accounting periods beginning on or after 1 January 1998. Some relatively minor changes were made to IAS 12 in 2000, followed by some slightly more substantial amendments as a result of the improved and new standards issued in 2003-4. In addition, the SIC has issued two interpretations of IAS 12:

- SIC–21 – *Income Taxes – Recovery of Revalued Non-Depreciable Assets;*[10] and

- SIC–25 – *Income Taxes – Changes in the Tax Status of an Entity or its Shareholders.*[11]

2   OBJECTIVE AND SCOPE OF IAS 12

2.1   Objective

The stated objective of IAS 12 is 'to prescribe the accounting treatment for income taxes. The principal issue in accounting for income taxes is how to account for the current and future tax consequences of:

(a)   the future recovery (settlement) of the carrying amount of assets (liabilities) that are recognised in an entity's balance sheet; and

(b)   transactions and other events of the current period that are recognised in an entity's financial statements.'[12]

IAS 12 requires the temporary difference approach to be adopted, which it explains by saying that it is inherent in the recognition of an asset or liability that the reporting entity expects to recover or settle the carrying amount of that asset or liability. IAS 12 requires an entity to consider whether it is probable that recovery or settlement of that carrying amount will result in future tax payments larger (or smaller) than they would be if such recovery or settlement had no tax consequences.[13] If it is probable that such larger or smaller tax payment will arise, in most cases IAS 12 requires an entity to recognise a deferred tax liability (or deferred tax asset). This is discussed further at 3 to 5 below.

IAS 12 also requires an entity to account for the tax consequences of transactions and other events in the same way that it accounts for the transactions and other events themselves. In other words:

- tax effects of transactions recognised in the income statement are also recognised in the income statement;

- tax effects of transactions and other events recognised directly in equity are also recognised directly in equity; and

- deferred tax assets and liabilities recognised in a business combination affect:

  - the amount of goodwill arising in that business combination; or

  - the amount of any excess of the acquirer's interest in the net fair value of the acquiree's identifiable assets, liabilities and contingent liabilities over the cost of the combination.[14]

This is discussed in more detail at 6 below.

Finally the standard deals with:

- recognition of deferred tax assets arising for unused tax losses or unused tax credits (see 4.2.3 below);

- the presentation of income taxes in financial statements (see 7 below); and

- the disclosure of information relating to income taxes (see 8 below).

2.2 Scope

IAS 12 should be applied in accounting for income taxes, defined as including:

(a) all domestic and foreign taxes which are based on taxable profits; and

(b) taxes, such as withholding taxes, which are payable by a subsidiary, associate or joint venture on distributions to the reporting entity. [15]

IAS 12 does not apply to accounting for government grants, which fall within the scope of IAS 20 – *Accounting for Government Grants and Disclosure of Government Assistance*, or investment tax credits. However, it does deal with the accounting for temporary differences that may arise from grants or investment tax credits. [16]

2.2.1 What is an 'income tax'?

This is not as clear as might at first sight appear, since the definition is circular. As noted above, income tax is a tax based on 'taxable profits', which are in turn defined (see 3 below) as profits 'upon which income taxes are payable'!

It is clear that those taxes that take as their starting profit the net profit or loss before appropriations are income taxes. However, several jurisdictions raise 'taxes' on sub-components of net profit. These include:

(a) sales taxes;

(b) goods and services taxes;

(c) value added taxes;

(d) levies on the sale or extraction of minerals and other natural resources;

(e) taxes on certain goods as they reach a given state of production or are moved from one location to another; or

(f) taxes on gross production margins.

Where taxes are simply collected by the entity on behalf of a third party (generally local or national government) they are, in our view, clearly not 'income taxes' for the purposes of IAS 12. This view is supported by the requirement of IAS 18 – *Revenue* – that taxes which are collected from customers by the entity on behalf of third parties do not form part of the entity's revenue [17] (and therefore, by implication, are not an expense of the entity either).

In cases where such taxes are a liability of the entity, they may often have some characteristics both of production or sales taxes (in that they are payable at a particular stage in the production or extraction process and may well be allowed as an expense in arriving at the tax on net profits) and of income taxes (in that they may be determined after deduction of certain allowable expenditure). This makes such taxes difficult to classify.

In practice, it is difficult to formulate a single view as to the treatment of such taxes, such that there treatment will need to be addressed on a case-by-case basis depending on the particular terms of the 'taxes' concerned and the entity's own circumstances.

Even where such taxes are not income taxes, if they are deductible against current or future income taxes, they may nevertheless give rise to tax assets which do fall within the scope of IAS 12 (see 4.2.3 below).

2.3 Discontinued operations – interaction with IFRS 5

IFRS 5 – *Non-current Assets Held for Sale and Discontinued Operations* – requires the post-tax results of discontinued operations to be shown separately on the face of the income statement. This may be done by giving the results of discontinued operations after those of continuing operations. This is discussed further in Chapter 3.

The definitions of income tax, tax expense and taxable profit in IAS 12 (see 3 below) do not distinguish between the results of continuing and discontinued operations, or the tax on those results. Thus, IAS 12 applies not only to the tax income or expense on continuing operations (i.e. the amount shown in the 'tax line' in the income statement) but also to any tax income or expense relating to the results of discontinued operations separately disclosed after those of continuing operations.

3   DEFINITIONS

3.1   General definitions

IAS 12 uses the following general definitions.

Accounting profit is profit or loss for a period before deducting tax expense.

Taxable profit (tax loss) is the profit (loss) for a period, determined in accordance with the rules established by the taxation authorities, upon which income taxes are payable (recoverable).

Tax expense (tax income) is the aggregate amount included in the determination of net profit or loss for the period in respect of current tax and deferred tax.

Current tax is the amount of income taxes payable (recoverable) in respect of the taxable profit (tax loss) or a period.

Deferred tax liabilities are the amounts of income taxes payable in future periods in respect of *taxable temporary differences* (see 3.2 below).

Deferred tax assets are the amounts of income taxes recoverable in future periods in respect of *deductible temporary differences* (see 3.2 below), together with the carryforward of unused tax losses and tax credits.[18]

Tax expense (tax income) is the aggregate amount included in the determination of profit or loss for the period in respect of current tax and deferred tax.[19]

3.2 Definitions of 'temporary difference' and 'tax base'

Temporary differences are differences between the carrying amount of an asset or liability in the balance sheet and its *tax base*. Temporary differences may be either:

(a) *taxable temporary differences*, which are temporary differences that will result in taxable amounts in determining taxable profit (tax loss) of future periods when the carrying amount of the asset or liability is recovered or settled; or

(b) *deductible temporary differences*, which are temporary differences that will result in amounts that are deductible in determining taxable profit (tax loss) of future periods when the carrying amount of the asset or liability is recovered or settled.

The *tax base* of an asset or liability is 'the amount attributed to that asset or liability for tax purposes'.[20]

As the definition of tax base in the one on which all the others relating to deferred tax ultimately depend, understanding it is key to a proper interpretation of IAS 12. A more detailed discussion follows below. However, the overall effect of IAS 12 can be summarised as follows:

A taxable temporary difference will arise when:

(a) The carrying amount of an asset is higher than its tax base.

For example, an item of PPE is recorded in the financial statements at €8,000, but has a tax base of only €7,000. In future periods tax will be paid on €1,000 more profit than is recognised in the financial statements (since €1,000 of the remaining accounting depreciation is not tax-deductible).

(b) The carrying amount of a liability is lower than its tax base.

For example, a loan payable of €100,000 is recorded in the financial statements at €99,000, net of issue costs of €1,000 which have already been allowed for tax purposes (so that the loan is regarded as having a tax base of €100,000 – see 3.2.1 B below). In future periods tax will be paid on €1,000 more profit than is recognised in the financial statements (since the €1,000 issue costs will be charged to the income statement but not be eligible for further tax deductions).

Conversely, a deductible temporary difference will arise when:

(a) The carrying amount of an asset is lower than its tax base.

For example, an item of PPE is recorded in the financial statements at €7,000, but has a tax base of €8,000. In future periods tax will be paid on €1,000 less profit than is recognised in the financial statements (since tax deductions will be claimed in respect of €1,000 more depreciation than is charged to the income statement in those future periods).

(b)   The carrying amount of a liability is higher than its tax base.

For example, the financial statements record a liability for unfunded pension costs of €2 million. A tax deduction is available only as cash is paid to settle the liability (so that the liability is regarded as having a tax base of nil – see 3.2.1 B below). In future periods tax will be paid on €2 million less profit than is recognised in the financial statements (since tax deductions will be claimed in respect of €2 million more expense than is charged to the income statement in those future periods).

3.2.1   Tax base

IAS 12 elaborates on the definition of tax base as discussed below.

A   Tax base of assets

The tax base of an asset is the amount that will be deductible for tax purposes against any taxable economic benefits that will flow to an entity when it recovers the carrying amount of the asset. If those economic benefits will not be taxable, the tax base of the asset is equal to its carrying amount.[21]

In some cases the 'tax base' of an asset is relatively obvious. In the case of a tax-deductible item of PPE, it is the tax-deductible amount of the asset at acquisition less tax depreciation already claimed (see Example 24.2 at 1.3.2 A above). Other items, however, require more careful analysis.

For example, an entity may have accrued interest receivable of €1,000 that will be taxed only on receipt. The tax base is nil, even though it will eventually be subject to tax. This is because the interest is, as yet, a 'nothing' from the point of view of the tax authorities. In other words, if the tax authorities were to draw up a balance sheet of the entity from their perspective, the interest, and hence this debtor, would not yet be included.

Conversely, an entity may have a receivable of €1,000 that will attract no tax payment when it is realised. In this case, the tax base is €1,000 on the rule above that where realisation of an asset will not be taxable, the tax base of the asset is equal to its carrying amount. This applies irrespective of whether the asset concerned arises from:

- a transaction already recognised in the income statement and subject to tax on initial recognition (e.g. in most jurisdictions, a sale);

- a transaction already recognised in the income statement and exempt from tax (e.g. tax-free dividend income); or

- a transaction not affecting the income statement at all (e.g. the principal of a loan receivable).[22]

The effect of deeming the tax base of the €1,000 receivable to be equal to its cost will be that the temporary difference associated with it is nil, and that no deferred tax is recognised in respect of it (see 4 below). This is appropriate given that, in the first case, the debtor represents a sale that has already been taxed and, in the second and third cases, the debtors represent items that are outside the scope of tax.

B   *Tax base of liabilities*

The tax base of a liability is its carrying amount, less any amount that will be deductible for tax purposes in respect of that liability in future periods. In the case of revenue which is received in advance, the tax base of the resulting liability is its carrying amount, less any amount of the revenue that will not be taxable in future periods.[23]

As in the case of assets, the tax base of some items is relatively obvious. For example, an entity may have recognised a provision for environmental damage of CHF 5 million, which will be deductible for tax purposes only on payment. The liability has a tax base of nil. This is because the provision is, as yet, a 'nothing' from the point of view of the tax authorities. If the tax authorities were to draw up a balance sheet of the entity from their perspective, the expense, and hence this provision, would not yet be included.

Likewise if the entity records as a liability revenue received in advance that was taxed on receipt, its tax base is nil. Again, the logic is that, if the tax authorities were to draw up a balance sheet of the entity from their perspective, this liability would not be included in the balance sheet, since the relevant amount would, in the notional tax financial statements, have already been taken to income.

An entity may have a liability of (say) €1,000 that will attract no tax deduction when it is settled. In this case, the tax base is €1,000 (on the analogy with the rule in A above that where realisation of an asset will not be taxable, the tax base of the asset is equal to its carrying amount). This applies irrespective of whether the liability concerned arises from:

- a transaction already recognised in the income statement and already subject to a tax deduction on initial recognition (e.g. in most jurisdictions, the cost of goods sold or accrued expenses);

- a transaction already recognised in the income statement and outside the scope of tax (e.g. non tax-deductible fines and penalties); or

- a transaction not affecting the income statement at all (e.g. a the principal of a loan payable).[24]

This is appropriate given that, in the first case, the liability represents a cost that has already been deducted for tax purposes and, in the second and third cases, the liabilities represent items that are outside the scope of tax.

However, there are some instances where a liability may have a tax base even though, on the literal wording of the standard, its settlement will not have any tax consequences – see also the discussion at D below of items whose tax base is not immediately apparent. For example, if an entity borrows €100,000 and incurs issue costs of €1,000, under IAS 39 – *Financial Instruments: Recognition and Measurement* – it would record the liability at €99,000 and expense the €1,000 over the term of the loan, with a corresponding increase in the carrying amount of the liability to the full €100,000 actually repayable (see Chapter 18 at 5). However, if this cost had been deductible for tax purposes immediately, a notional balance sheet prepared by the tax authorities would show a liability for the full €100,000 (since the amortisation of the issue costs that has yet to occur in the financial statements has already occurred in the notional tax authority financial statements). Therefore there is a taxable temporary difference of €1,000 associated with the loan (tax base €100,000 less carrying amount €99,000).

Rather counter-intuitively perhaps, the same temporary difference arises if the issue costs are never tax deductible. This is because the notional tax authority financial statements would not have recorded the issue costs as an expense at all, so that they would again show a liability for the full €100,000 – see 3.3.1 B and 4.2.1 D below.

C   *Tax base of items not recognised as assets or liabilities in financial statements*

Certain items are not recognised as assets or liabilities in financial statements, but nevertheless have a tax base. Examples may include:

- research costs (which are required to be expensed immediately by IAS 38 – *Intangible Assets* – see Chapter 11);

- the cost of equity-settled share-based payment transactions (which under IFRS 2 – *Share-based Payment* – give rise to an increase in equity and not a liability – see Chapter 29); and

- goodwill written off direct to equity under previous IFRS or national GAAP.

Where such items are tax-deductible, their tax base is the difference between their carrying amount (i.e. nil) and the amount deductible in future periods.[25] This may seem somewhat contrary to the definition of tax base, in which it is inherent that, in order for an item to have a tax base, that item must be an asset or liability, whereas none of the items above was ever recognised as an asset.[26] The implicit argument may be that all these items were initially recognised as assets before being immediately written off in full.

D   *Items whose tax base is not immediately apparent*

Paragraph 10 of IAS 12 indicates that where the tax base of an asset or liability is not immediately apparent, it is helpful to consider the fundamental principle on which the standard is based: that an entity should, with certain limited exceptions, recognise a deferred tax liability (asset) wherever recovery or settlement of the carrying amount of an asset or liability would make future tax payments larger (smaller) than they would be if such recovery or settlement were to have no tax consequences. In other words: provide for the tax that would be payable if the balance sheet were to be liquidated at book value.

If this is indeed the underlying principle of IAS 12, it would be more correct to say that the tax base of an item is whatever it needs to be to generate the right deferred tax number in accordance with that principle. In other words in the basic 'equation' of IAS 12, i.e.

carrying amount – tax base = temporary difference,

the true unknown is not in fact the temporary difference (as implied by the definitions of tax base and temporary difference) but the tax base (as implied by paragraph 10).

E   Items with more than one tax base

Some assets and liabilities have more than one tax base, depending on the manner in which they are realised or settled. These are discussed further at 5.2.2 below.

F   Temporary differences in consolidated financial statements

In consolidated financial statements, temporary differences are determined by comparing the carrying amounts of assets and liabilities in the consolidated financial statements with the appropriate tax base. The appropriate tax base is determined:

- in those jurisdictions in which a consolidated tax return is filed, by reference to that return; and

- in other jurisdictions, by reference to the tax returns of each entity in the group.[27]

3.3   Examples of temporary differences

The following are examples of taxable temporary differences, deductible temporary differences and items where the tax base and carrying value are the same so that there is no temporary difference. They are mostly based on those given in IAS 12,[28] but include others that are encountered in practice. It will be seen that a number of assets and liabilities may result in either a taxable or a deductible temporary difference.

Not all of these items will result in deferred tax being recorded under IAS 12, as they may be subject to other provisions of the standard restricting the recognition of deferred tax assets and liabilities, which are discussed at section 4 below.

3.3.1   Taxable temporary differences

A   Transactions that affect the income statement

IAS 12 gives the following examples of taxable temporary differences arising from transactions that affect the income statement.

- Interest revenue is received in arrears and is included in accounting profit on a time apportionment basis but is included in taxable profit on a cash basis.

- Revenue from the sale of goods is included in accounting profit when goods are delivered but is included in taxable profit when cash is collected. (As explained in 3.3.2 A below, there is also a deductible temporary difference associated with any related inventory).

- Depreciation of an asset is accelerated for tax purposes.

- Development costs have been capitalised and will be amortised to the income statement but were deducted in determining taxable profit in the period in which they were incurred.

- Prepaid expenses have already been deducted on a cash basis in determining the taxable profit of the current or previous periods.

B   *Transactions that affect the balance sheet*

IAS 12 gives the following examples of taxable temporary differences arising from transactions that affect the balance sheet.

- Depreciation of an asset is not deductible for tax purposes and no deduction will be available for tax purposes when the asset is sold or scrapped.

- A borrower records a loan at the proceeds received (which equal the amount due at maturity), less transaction costs. Subsequently, the carrying amount of the loan is increased by amortisation of the transaction costs to accounting profit. The transaction costs were deducted for tax purposes in the period when the loan was first recognised.

- A loan payable was measured on initial recognition at the amount of the net proceeds, net of transaction costs. The transaction costs are amortised to accounting profit over the life of the loan. Those transaction costs are not deductible in determining the taxable profit of future, current or prior periods.

- The liability component of a compound financial instrument (for example a convertible bond) is measured at a discount to the amount repayable on maturity (see 4.2.1 D below). The discount is not deductible in determining taxable profit (tax loss).

C   *Revaluations*

IAS 12 gives the following examples of taxable temporary differences arising from revaluations.

- Financial assets or investment property are carried at fair value which exceeds cost but no equivalent adjustment is made for tax purposes.

- An entity revalues property, plant and equipment (under the allowed alternative treatment in IAS 16 – *Property, Plant and Equipment*) but no equivalent adjustment is made for tax purposes.

D   *Business combinations and consolidation*

IAS 12 gives the following examples of taxable temporary differences arising from business combinations and consolidation.

- The carrying amount of an asset is increased to fair value in a business combination and no equivalent adjustment is made for tax purposes.

- Reductions in the carrying amount of goodwill are not deductible in determining taxable profit and the cost of the goodwill would not be deductible on disposal of the business.

- Unrealised losses resulting from intragroup transactions are eliminated by inclusion in the carrying amount of the assets or liabilities that are the subject of the transaction.

- Retained earnings of subsidiaries, branches, associates and joint ventures are included in consolidated retained earnings, but income taxes will be payable if the profits are distributed to the reporting parent.

- Investments in foreign subsidiaries, branches or associates or interests in foreign joint ventures are affected by changes in foreign exchange rates.

- An entity accounts in its own currency for the cost of the non-monetary assets of a foreign operation that is integral to the reporting entity's operations but the taxable profit or tax loss of the foreign operation is determined in the foreign currency (see Example 24.6 at 1.3.2 A above).

E　　Hyperinflation

IAS 12 gives the following example of a taxable temporary difference arising from hyperinflation.

- Non-monetary assets are restated in terms of the measuring unit current at the balance sheet date under IAS 29 – *Financial Reporting in Hyperinflationary Economies* – and no equivalent adjustment is made for tax purposes.

3.3.2　Deductible temporary differences

A　　Transactions that affect the income statement

IAS 12 gives the following examples of deductible temporary differences arising from transactions that affect the income statement.

- Retirement benefit costs are deducted in determining accounting profit as service is provided by the employee, but are not deducted in determining taxable profit until the entity pays either retirement benefits or contributions to a fund.

- Similar deductible temporary differences arise where other expenses, such as product warranty costs or interest, are deductible on a cash basis in determining taxable profit.

- Accumulated depreciation of an asset in the financial statements is greater than the cumulative depreciation allowed up to the balance sheet date for tax purposes.

- The cost of inventories sold before the balance sheet date is deducted in determining accounting profit when goods or services are delivered but is deducted in determining taxable profit when cash is collected. (As explained in 3.3.1 A above, there is also a taxable temporary difference associated with the related trade receivable).

- The net realisable value of an item of inventory, or the recoverable amount of an item of property, plant or equipment, is less than the previous carrying amount and an entity therefore reduces the carrying amount of the asset, but that reduction is ignored for tax purposes until the asset is sold.

- Research costs (or organisation or other start up costs) or the cost of a share-based payment transaction are recognised as an expense in determining accounting profit but are not permitted as a deduction in determining taxable profit until a later period.

- Income is deferred in the balance sheet but has already been included in taxable profit in current or prior periods.

- A government grant which is included in the balance sheet as deferred income will not be taxable in future periods.

B   *Fair value adjustments and revaluations*

IAS 12 gives the following examples of deductible temporary differences arising from transactions that affect the balance sheet.

- Financial assets or investment property are carried at fair value which is less than cost, but no equivalent adjustment is made for tax purposes.

- Assets are rebased for tax purposes, but no equivalent adjustment is made for financial reporting purposes.

C   *Business combinations and consolidation*

IAS 12 gives the following examples of deductible temporary differences arising from business combinations and consolidation.

- A liability is recognised at its fair value in a business combination, but none of the related expense is deducted in determining taxable profit until a later period.

- Unrealised profits resulting from intragroup transactions are eliminated from the carrying amount of assets or liabilities that are the subject of the transactions, but no equivalent adjustment is made for tax purposes.

- Investments in foreign subsidiaries, branches or associates or interests in foreign joint ventures are affected by changes in foreign exchange rates.

- An entity accounts in its own currency for the cost of the non-monetary assets of a foreign operation that is integral to the reporting entity's operations but the taxable profit or tax loss of the foreign operation is determined in the foreign currency (see Example 24.5 at 1.3.2 A above).

3.3.3   Assets and liabilities with no temporary difference (because tax base equals carrying amount)

IAS 12 gives the following examples of assets and no liabilities giving rise to no temporary difference because their tax base is (or is treated as) being equal to their carrying amount.

- Accrued expenses have already been deducted in determining an entity's current tax liability for the current or earlier periods.

- A loan payable is measured at the amount originally received and this amount is the same as the amount repayable on final maturity of the loan.

- Accrued expenses will never be deductible for tax purposes.

- Accrued income will never be taxable.

3.4   Possible future developments

At its June 2004 meeting the IASB discussed the definition of tax base and related matters at some length. It tentatively agreed to amend the definition of a temporary difference to bring it more in line with that in FAS 109. In particular:

- IAS 12 regards any difference between the carrying amount of an asset and its tax base as giving rise to a temporary difference. This means that it is sometimes necessary to deem certain assets and liabilities that in reality have a tax base of zero to have a tax base equal to their carrying amount in order to avoid the recognition of spurious deferred tax balances (see 3.2.1 A and B above).

- Under FAS 109 a difference between the tax base and the carrying amount of an asset or liability that gives rise to no taxable or tax-deductible amounts when the carrying amount of the asset or liability is recovered or settled is not regarded as a temporary difference.

The end result is the same in both cases – no temporary difference, and thus no deferred tax.[29]

The IASB also 'decided that the tax base is a function of the tax law in a particular jurisdiction and that management's intentions on how an asset will be recovered or settled do not affect the determination of the tax base. However, assuming there is a temporary difference, management's intentions may affect the measurement of a deferred tax asset or liability'.[30] The IASB has therefore tentatively agreed to delete the current requirement of IAS 12 to have regard to management's intentions in determining the tax base of an asset or liability (see 5.2.2. below).

This is somewhat puzzling, since an assertion that management's intentions do not affect the determination of the tax base is simply incorrect. As noted by IAS 12 itself – see 5.2 below – in many tax jurisdictions there are circumstances where management's intention to recover an asset through either use or sale affects not only the rate of tax paid but also the amount on which tax is paid (because this is calculated by reference to more than one tax base).

4   RECOGNITION OF TAX ASSETS AND LIABILITIES

4.1   Current tax

Current tax for current and prior periods should, to the extent unpaid, be recognised as a liability. If the amount already paid in respect of current and prior periods exceeds the amount due for those periods, the excess should be recognised as an asset.[31]

The benefit relating to a tax loss that can be carried back to recover current tax of a previous period should be recognised as an asset. When a tax loss is used to recover current tax of a previous period, an entity recognises the benefit as an asset in the period in which the tax loss occurs because it is probable that the benefit will flow to the entity and the benefit can be reliably measured.[32]

4.2   Deferred Tax

4.2.1   *Taxable temporary differences*

IAS 12 requires a deferred tax liability to be recognised in respect of all taxable temporary differences except those arising from:

(a)   the initial recognition of goodwill; or

(b)   the initial recognition of an asset or liability in a transaction which:

    (i)   is not a business combination; and

    (ii)   at the time of the transaction, affects neither accounting profit nor taxable profit (tax loss).

Taxable temporary differences associated with investments in subsidiaries, branches and associates, and interests in joint ventures, are subject to further detailed provisions of IAS 12 (see 4.2.5 below). [33]

Examples of taxable temporary differences are given in 3.3.1 above.

The, at first sight somewhat arbitrary, exceptions in (a) and (b) above are difficult to understand without some explanation as to the reason for them, and are discussed in A and B below.

A   *Initial recognition of goodwill*

In many jurisdictions goodwill is not tax-deductible either as it is impaired or on ultimate disposal, such that it gives rise to a temporary difference equal to its carrying amount (representing its carrying amount less its tax base of zero).

The recognition exemption for deferred tax relating to goodwill is primarily necessary so as to avoid the 'vicious circle' that would otherwise be set off where goodwill is not tax deductible. (Where goodwill is tax-deductible, the temporary difference on recognition would be zero anyway.)

Goodwill is a function of all the net assets of the acquired business, including deferred tax. It follows that, if deferred tax is provided for on goodwill, the goodwill itself is increased, which means that the deferred tax on the goodwill is increased further, which means that the goodwill increases again, and so on. IAS 12 takes the view that this would not be appropriate, since goodwill is intended to be a residual arising after fair values have been determined for the assets and liabilities acquired in a business combination. [34]

I   *Non tax-deductible goodwill*

Subsequent reductions in a deferred tax liability that is not recognised because it arises on initial recognition of goodwill are also regarded as arising from the initial recognition of goodwill. Where goodwill is not tax-deductible, no deferred tax arises if its carrying value (and therefore the temporary difference arising from the goodwill) is reduced at a later date as the result of an impairment loss. The new lower temporary difference is still regarded as part of that arising on the initial recognition of the goodwill. [35]

II   Tax-deductible goodwill

Where goodwill is tax deductible, however, new temporary differences will arise after its initial recognition as a result of the interaction between tax deductions claimed and impairments (if any) of the goodwill in the financial statements. These temporary differences do not relate to the initial recognition of goodwill, and therefore deferred tax should be recognised on them, as illustrated by Example 24.7.[36]

Example 24.7:   Tax-deductible goodwill

On 1 January 2005 an entity with a tax rate of 35% acquires goodwill in a business combination with a cost of €1 million, which is deductible for tax purposes at a rate of 20% per year, starting in the year of acquisition.

During 2005 the entity claims the full 20% tax deduction and writes off €120,000 of the goodwill as the result of an impairment exercise. Thus at the end of 2005 the goodwill has a carrying amount of €880,000 and a tax base of €800,000. This gives rise to a taxable temporary difference of €80,000 that does not relate to the initial recognition of goodwill, and accordingly the entity recognises a deferred tax liability at 35% of €28,000.

B   Initial recognition of assets and liabilities

The discussion below, like that in the paragraphs of IAS 12 on which it is based, is in fact broadly applicable not only to deferred tax liabilities and but also to deferred tax assets which are subject to similar restrictions on initial recognition (see 4.2.2 below).

Where a temporary difference arises on initial recognition of an asset or liability, its treatment depends on the circumstances which give rise to the recognition of the asset or liability.

If the temporary difference arises as the result of a business combination, deferred tax is recognised on the temporary difference with a corresponding adjustment to goodwill or to the amount of any excess over the cost of the combination of the acquirer's interest in the net fair value of the acquiree's identifiable assets, liabilities and contingent liabilities.

If the temporary difference arises in a transaction that gives rise to an accounting or taxable profit or loss, deferred tax is recognised on the temporary difference.

If the temporary difference arises in any other circumstances (i.e. not in a business combination or in a transaction that gives rise to an accounting or taxable profit or loss) no deferred tax is recognised.[37]

A typical example of such a transaction will be the purchase of an asset that is either:

(a)   not deductible for tax purposes (see Example 24.8 below); or

(b)   eligible for tax deductions for an amount greater or less than its cost (see 4.2.6 below).

Example 24.8:   No deferred tax recognised on initial recognition of non-deductible asset

An entity intends to use an asset which cost €1,000 throughout its useful life of five years and then dispose of it for a residual value of nil. The tax rate is 40%. Depreciation of the asset is not deductible for tax purposes. On disposal, any capital gain would not be taxable and any capital loss would not be deductible.

As it recovers the carrying amount of the asset, the entity will earn taxable income of €1,000 and pay tax of €400 (€1,000 @ 40%). The entity does not recognise the resulting deferred tax liability of €400 because it results from the initial recognition of the asset.[38]

Essentially, IAS 12's prohibition on the recognition of deferred tax on initial recognition of such assets and liabilities is a pragmatic 'fix' to deal with the fact that, if deferred tax were recognised, the result would be either:

(a)   recognition of tax income or expense on acquisition of the asset. For example, if the entity in Example 24.8 above were to provide for deferred tax of €400 on initial recognition of the asset, there would be an immediate tax expense of €400 before the asset has even begun to be depreciated. This result is not merely undesirable but also meaningless, since the entity has clearly not suffered any loss simply by purchasing a non-deductible asset.

The IASC's thinking here was probably influenced by the fact that such a temporary difference arising on initial recognition would, under a timing difference approach, have been regarded as a permanent difference outside the scope of deferred tax accounting altogether (see 1.3.2 A above); or

(b)   adjustment of the real cost of the asset to the notional cost that would have been paid for an equivalent, but fully tax-deductible asset (as is effectively required by US GAAP – see 4.2.6 A below). IAS 12 currently states that to make such adjustments to the carrying value of the asset would make the financial statements 'less transparent'.[39] However, the IASB has in principle agreed to adopt this treatment (see 4.2.6 A below).

I   *Subsequent changes to temporary differences arising on initial recognition*

Subsequent changes to an initially unrecognised deferred tax asset or liability relating to such an asset (e.g. as a result of depreciation or impairment of the asset) are also regarded as arising on initial recognition of the asset and are therefore not recognised. This is consistent with the treatment of changes to the temporary differences associated with non tax-deductible goodwill (see .A I above), and is illustrated by Example 24.9 below.

Example 24.9:   No deferred tax recognised on movements in temporary difference arising on initial recognition of non-deductible asset

The facts are as in Example 24.8 above, except that it is now the end of the first accounting period following initial recognition of the asset.

The entity's accounting policy is to charge a full year's depreciation in the year of purchase, so that the carrying amount of the asset is now €800. In earning taxable income of €800, the entity will pay tax of €320 (€800 @ 40%). The entity does not recognise the deferred tax liability of €320 because it results from the initial recognition of the asset.[40]

II   New temporary differences emerging after initial recognition

If *after* initial recognition of an asset or liability a temporary difference arises in respect of that asset or liability in circumstances that do not give rise to an accounting or taxable profit or loss, the restrictions that apply *on* initial recognition do not apply and deferred tax should be recognised (subject to any restrictions on recognition of deferred tax assets – see 4.2.2 below). An example of such a situation would be a rebasing of assets or liabilities for tax purposes by the tax authorities either as part of the ongoing operation of the tax system (as illustrated by Example 24.5 at 1.3.2 A above), or as a 'one-off' exercise (as has recently been the case for certain entities in Australia).

C   Assets carried at fair value

IAS 12 notes that certain IFRSs permit or require assets to be carried at fair value or to be revalued. These include:

- IAS 16 – *Plant, Property and Equipment*
- IAS 38 – *Intangible Assets*
- IAS 39 – *Financial Instruments: Recognition and Measurement*, and
- IAS 40 – *Investment Property.*

In some jurisdictions, the revaluation or other restatement of an asset to fair value affects taxable profit (tax loss) for the current period. In such cases, the tax base of the asset is adjusted and no temporary difference arises. In other jurisdictions, the revaluation or restatement of an asset does not affect taxable profit in the period of the revaluation or restatement and, consequently, the tax base of the asset is not adjusted. Nevertheless, the future recovery of the carrying amount will result in a taxable flow of economic benefits to the entity and the amount that will be deductible for tax purposes (i.e. the original tax base) will differ from the amount of those economic benefits.

The difference between the carrying amount of a revalued asset and its tax base is a temporary difference and gives rise to a deferred tax liability or asset. This is true even if:

(a)   the entity does not intend to dispose of the asset. In such cases, the revalued carrying amount of the asset will be recovered through use and this will generate taxable income which exceeds the depreciation that will be allowable for tax purposes in future periods; or

(b)   tax on capital gains is deferred if the proceeds of the disposal of the asset are invested in similar assets. In such cases, the tax will ultimately become payable on sale or use of the similar assets.[41]

I   Revaluations of non-deductible assets

As discussed in B above a temporary difference arises when a non tax-deductible asset is acquired. However, where the asset is acquired separately (i.e. not as part of a larger business combination) in circumstances giving rise to neither an accounting nor a taxable profit or loss, no deferred tax liability is recognised for that temporary difference.

If such an asset is subsequently revalued, however, deferred tax would be recognised on the new temporary difference arising as a result of the revaluation since this does not arise on initial recognition of the asset (and moreover gives rise to an accounting profit, albeit not one necessarily recorded in the income statement), as illustrated in Example 24.10.

Example 24.10:   Revaluation of non-deductible asset

On 1 January 2005 an entity paying tax at 30% acquires a non tax-deductible office building for €1,000,000 in circumstances in which IAS 12 prohibits recognition of the deferred tax liability associated with the temporary difference of €1,000,000.

Application of IAS 16 results in no depreciation being charged on the building.

On 1 January 2008 the entity revalues the building to €1,200,000. The temporary difference associated with the building is now €1,200,000, only €1,000,000 of which arose on initial recognition. Accordingly, the entity recognises a deferred tax liability based on a temporary difference of €200,000 giving deferred tax expense at 30% of €60,000. In this case the tax expense would be charged direct to equity (see 6 below).

D   Initial recognition of compound financial instruments

IAS 32 – *Financial Instruments: Disclosure and Presentation* – requires 'compound' financial instruments (those with both a liability feature and an equity feature, such as convertible bonds), to be accounted for using so-called split accounting. This is discussed in more detail in Chapter 17 at 4, but in essence an entity is required to split the proceeds of issue of such an instrument (say €1 million) into a liability component, measured at its fair value (say €750,000), with the balance being treated an equity component (in this case €250,000).

Over the life of the instrument, the €750,000 carrying value of the liability element will be accreted back up to €1,000,000 (or such lower or higher amount as might be potentially repayable), so that the income statement interest charge will comprise:

(a)   any actual cash interest payments made (which are tax-deductible in most jurisdictions); and

(b)   the €250,000 accretion of the liability from €750,000 to €1,000,000 (which is not tax-deductible in most jurisdictions).

Where such an instrument is issued, IAS 12 requires the treatment in Example 24.11 to be adopted.[42]

Example 24.11: Compound financial instrument

An entity issues a zero-coupon convertible loan of €1,000,000 on 1 January 2005 repayable at par on 1 January 2008. In accordance with IAS 32, the entity classifies the instrument's liability component as a liability and the equity component as equity. The entity assigns an initial carrying amount of €750,000 to the liability component of the convertible loan and €250,000 to the equity component. Subsequently, the entity recognises the imputed discount of €250,000 as interest expense at the effective annual rate of 10% on the carrying amount of the liability component at the beginning of the year. The tax authorities do not allow the entity to claim any deduction for the imputed discount on the liability component of the convertible loan. The tax rate is 40%.

Temporary differences arise on the liability element as follows (all figures in €000).

	1.1.05	*31.12.05*	*31.12.06*	*31.12.07*
Carrying value of liability component	750	825[1]	908[1]	1,000[1]
Tax base	1,000	1,000	1,000	1,000
Taxable temporary difference	250	175	92	–
Deferred tax liability @ 40%	100	70	37	–

1   Balance carried forward at end of previous period plus 10% accretion of notional interest.

The deferred tax arising at 1 January 2005 is charged to equity. IAS 12 does not explain why, but it may be on the argument that transactions accounted for in equity should also be accounted for in equity – see 6.1 below. However, this is questionable – see the discussion below.

Subsequent reductions in the deferred tax balance are recognised in the income statement, resulting in an effective tax rate of 40%. For example, in 2005, the entity will accrete notional interest of €75,000 (closing loan liability €825,000 less opening balance €750,000) with deferred tax income of €30,000 (closing deferred tax liability €70,000 less opening liability €100,000).

Whilst this is the treatment required by IAS 12, it appears to have little conceptual basis. In the first instance, it contravenes the prohibition on recognition of deferred tax on temporary differences arising on the initial recognition of assets and liabilities (other than in a business combination) that do not give rise to accounting or taxable profit or loss. IAS 12 argues that this temporary difference does not arise on initial recognition of a liability but as a result of the initial recognition of the equity component as a result of split accounting.[43]

Even if this rather sophistic argument is accepted, it remains unclear why the deferred tax should be recognised in equity, since it relates to a transaction has been recognised not in equity, but in the balance sheet. The analysis in IAS 12 is that this deferred tax relates to the €250 temporary difference on the *liability* component, not to the (coincidentally equal) €250 temporary difference on the *equity* component. The 'other half' of the accounting entry giving rise to the liability component is an increase in cash, not a decrease in equity.

The accounting treatment required by Example 24.11 above could be seen as no more than 'tax equalisation' accounting – i.e. the recognition of such an amount of deferred tax that, when released to profit or loss, will yield an effective tax rate equivalent to the statutory rate. Some would question whether it is appropriate to represent a charge to the income statement that in reality attracts no tax deduction as being deductible for tax. This issue is discussed further at 4.2.6 A below.

4.2.2 Deductible temporary differences

IAS 12 requires a deferred tax asset to be recognised in respect of all deductible temporary differences to the extent that it is probable that taxable profit will be available against which the deductible temporary difference will be utilised except those arising from the initial recognition of an asset or liability in a transaction which:

(a)   is not a business combination; and

(b)   at the time of the transaction, affects neither accounting profit nor taxable profit (tax loss). [44]

IAS 12 does not currently define the meaning of 'probable' in this context. However, we consider that, as in other IFRS, it should be taken to mean 'more likely than not'. Moreover, the IASB has indicated that it intends to amend IAS 12 so as to clarify that this is the intended meaning (see 9.3 below). [45]

Deductible temporary differences associated with investments in subsidiaries, branches and associates, and interests in joint ventures, are subject to further detailed provisions of IAS 12 (see 4.2.5 below).

Examples of deductible temporary differences are given in 3.3.2 above.

The background to, and issues raised by, the restrictions on recognition in (a) and (b) above are essentially the same as those relating to the equivalent restrictions discussed at 4.2.1 B above relating to certain deferred tax liabilities arising on initial recognition of the assets and liabilities giving rise to them.

A   Assets subject to tax-free government grants

IAS 12 specifically emphasises that the restriction in (a) and (b) applies on initial recognition of an asset subject to a tax-free government grant. This will give rise to a deductible temporary difference because under IAS 20 (see Chapter 27) the grant will be either:

*   deducted from the cost of the asset (so that the tax base of the asset is higher than its carrying amount); or

*   set up as deferred income (which will have a tax base of nil). [46]

B   Restrictions on recognition of deferred tax assets

An essential difference between deferred tax liabilities and deferred tax assets is that, whilst in principle an entity has only to recover its existing net assets at their carrying value in order to crystallise net deferred tax liabilities, in order to realise net deferred tax assets in full it must earn profits over and above those represented by its net assets in order to generate sufficient taxable profits against which the deductions represented by deferred tax assets can be offset. Accordingly IAS 12 imposes restrictions on the full recognition of deferred tax assets, by requiring that they be recognised only to the extent that it is probable that taxable profit will be available against which the deductible temporary differences can be utilised. [47]

It is 'probable' that there will be sufficient taxable profit if a deferred tax asset can be offset against a deferred tax liability relating to the same tax authority which will reverse in the same period as the asset, or in a period into which a loss arising from the asset may be carried back or forwards. [48]

Where there are insufficient deferred tax liabilities relating to the same tax authority to offset a deferred tax asset, the asset should be recognised to the extent that:

(a)   it is probable that in future periods there will be sufficient taxable profits:

   (i)   relating to the same tax authority;

   (ii)   relating to the same taxable entity; and

   (iii) arising in the same period as the reversal of the deductible temporary difference or in a period into which a loss arising from the deferred tax asset may be carried back or forward – see also I below; or

(b)   tax planning opportunities are available that will create taxable profit in appropriate periods – see II below.[49]

Where an entity has a history of recent losses it should also consider the guidance in IAS 12 for recognition of such losses (see 4.2.3 below).[50]

I   *Assessment of future profits to ignore future deductible temporary differences*

In assessing future profits for the purposes of (a) above, an entity must ignore taxable profits that arise from the emergence of new deductible temporary differences in future periods. This is because those new deductible differences will themselves require future taxable profit in order to be utilised.[51]

II   *Tax planning opportunities*

'Tax planning opportunities' are actions that the entity would take in order to create or increase taxable income in a particular period before the expiry of a tax loss or tax credit carryforward. IAS 12 notes that, in some jurisdictions, taxable profit may be created or increased by:

(a)   electing to have interest income taxed on either a received or receivable basis;

(b)   deferring the claim for certain deductions from taxable profit;

(c)   selling, and perhaps leasing back, assets that have appreciated but for which the tax base has not been adjusted to reflect such appreciation; and

(d)   selling an asset that generates non-taxable income (such as, in some jurisdictions, a government bond) in order to purchase another investment that generates taxable income.

Where tax planning opportunities advance taxable profit from a later period to an earlier period, the utilisation of a tax loss or tax credit carryforward still depends on the existence of future taxable profit from sources other than future originating temporary differences.[52]

It should be noted that the requirement to have regard to future tax planning opportunities applies only to the measurement of deferred tax assets. It does not apply to the measurement of deferred tax liabilities. Thus, for example, it would not be open to an entity subject to tax at 30% to argue that it should provide for deferred tax liabilities at some lower rate on the grounds that it intends to invest in 'super-deductible' assets attracting investment tax credits (see 4.2.6 below).

C   *Deductible temporary differences arising on initial recognition of goodwill*

IAS 12 does not specifically address the recognition of deferred tax assets arising from the initial recognition of goodwill (i.e. whether a deferred tax asset arising from an excess of the tax base of goodwill over the carrying amount of goodwill should be recognised as part of the accounting for a business combination). Consequently, the general requirements of IAS 12 (summarised above) apply, requiring the deferred tax asset to be recognised to the extent it is probable that taxable profit will be available against which the deductible temporary difference could be utilised.

The IASB has tentatively decided to amend IAS 12 so as to explicitly require recognition of a deferred tax asset arising from excess tax goodwill as part of the business combination accounting.[53]

4.2.3   Unused tax losses and unused tax credits

A deferred tax asset should be recognised for the carryforward of unused tax losses and unused tax credits to the extent that it is probable that future taxable profit will be available against which the unused tax losses and unused tax credits can be utilised.[54]

The criteria for recognition are the same as those for deductible temporary differences, as set out in 4.2.2 B above. However, IAS 12 emphasises that the existence of unused tax losses is strong evidence that taxable profits (other than those represented by deferred tax liabilities) may not be available. Therefore, an entity with a history of recent losses recognises a deferred tax asset arising from unused tax losses or tax credits only to the extent that:

(a)   it has sufficient taxable temporary differences; or

(b)   there is other convincing evidence that sufficient taxable profit will be available against which the unused tax losses or unused tax credits can be utilised by the entity.

IAS 12 requires disclosure in respect of losses recognised in the circumstances in (b) above (see 8.3 below).[55]

Additionally, the entity should consider whether:

(a)   the entity has sufficient taxable temporary differences relating to the same taxation authority and the same taxable entity, which will result in taxable amounts against which the unused tax losses or unused tax credits can be utilised before they expire;

(b)   the entity will have taxable profits before the unused tax losses or unused tax credits expire;

(c)   whether the unused tax losses result from identifiable causes which are unlikely to recur; and

(d)   whether tax planning opportunities (see 4.2.2 B above) are available to the entity that will create taxable profit in the period in which the unused tax losses or unused tax credits can be utilised.

To the extent that it is not probable that taxable profit will be available against which the unused tax losses or unused tax credits can be utilised, a deferred tax asset is not recognised.[56]

IAS 12 does not provide more specific guidance on the assessment of the availability of future taxable profits. However, it would clearly be appropriate to give more weight to (say) revenues from existing orders and contracts than to those from merely anticipated future trading.

4.2.4   *Re-assessment of deferred tax assets*

An entity must review its deferred tax assets, both recognised and unrecognised, at each balance sheet date.

A   Previously unrecognised assets

An entity recognises a previously unrecognised deferred tax asset to the extent that it has become probable that sufficient taxable profit will be available to enable the asset to be recovered. For example, an improvement in trading conditions may make it more probable that the entity will be able to generate sufficient taxable profit in the future for the deferred tax asset to meet the recognition criteria discussed in 4.2.2. B and 4.2.3 above. Special considerations apply when an entity re-appraises deferred tax assets of an acquired business at the date of the business combination or subsequently (see 6.2.2 below).[57]

B   Previously recognised assets

An entity should reduce the carrying amount of a deferred tax asset to the extent that it is no longer probable that sufficient taxable profit will be available to enable the asset to be recovered. Any such reduction should be reversed if it subsequently becomes probable that sufficient taxable profit will be available.[58]

4.2.5   *Subsidiaries, branches, associates and joint ventures*

Temporary differences arise between the carrying amount of investments in subsidiaries, branches and associates or interests in joint ventures and the tax base of the investment or interest. For this purpose 'carrying amount' means the parent's or investor's share of the net assets of the investment or interest concerned including the carrying amount of goodwill.

The most common cause of such temporary differences will be the undistributed profits of such entities, where distribution to the investor would trigger a tax liability. Temporary differences also arise from exchange movements affecting, provisions against, or revaluations of, the carrying value of investments.

Such temporary differences arise in both consolidated and separate financial statements and may well be different, due to the different bases used to account for subsidiaries, branches and associates or interests in joint ventures in consolidated and separate financial statements,[59] as illustrated by Example 24.12 below. This also illustrates that, other than by coincidence, the temporary difference associated with subsidiaries, branches and associates or interests in joint ventures is not equivalent to the retained earnings of such investees.

Example 24.12: Temporary differences associated with subsidiaries, branches, associates and joint ventures

On 1 January 2005 entity H acquired 100% of the shares of entity S, whose functional currency is different from that of H, for €600m. The tax rate in H's tax jurisdiction is 30% and the tax rate in S's tax jurisdiction is 40%.

The fair value of the identifiable assets and liabilities (excluding deferred tax assets and liabilities) of S acquired by H is set out in the following table, together with their tax base in S's tax jurisdiction and the resulting temporary differences (all figures in € million).

	Fair value	Tax base	*(Taxable)/* deductible temporary difference
PPE	270	155	(115)
Accounts receivable	210	210	–
Inventory	174	124	(50)
Retirement benefit obligations	(30)	–	30
Accounts payable	(120)	(120)	–
Fair value of net assets acquired excluding deferred tax	504	369	(135)
Deferred tax (135 @ 40%)	(54)		
Fair value of identifiable net assets acquired	450		
Goodwill (balancing figure)	150		
Total cost of combination	600		

No deferred tax is recognised on the goodwill, in accordance with the requirements of IAS 12 as discussed at 4.2.1 above.

At the date of combination, the tax base, in H's tax jurisdiction, of H's investment in S is €600 million. Therefore, in H's jurisdiction no temporary difference is associated with the investment, either in the consolidated financial statements of H (where the investment is represented by net assets and goodwill of €600 million), or in its separate financial statements, if prepared (where the investment is shown as an investment at cost of €600 million).

During 2005:

• S makes a profit after tax, as reported in H's consolidated financial statements, of €150 million, of which €80 million is declared as a dividend before 31 December 2005, leaving a net retained profit of €70 million. H would provide for any withholding tax payable on the dividend.

• In accordance with IAS 21 – *The Effects of Changes in Foreign Exchange Rates*, H's consolidated financial statements record a loss of €15 million on retranslation to the closing exchange rate of S's opening net assets and profit for the period.

• In accordance with IAS 36 – *Impairment of Assets*, H's consolidated financial statements record an impairment loss of €10 million in respect of goodwill.

Thus in H's consolidated financial statements the carrying value of its investment in S is €645 million, comprising:

	€m
Net assets and goodwill at 1.1.05	600
Retained profit	70
Exchange loss	(15)
Impairment of goodwill	(10)
Net assets and goodwill at 31.12.05	645

Assuming that the tax base in H's jurisdiction remains €600 million, there is therefore a taxable temporary difference of €45 million (carrying amount €645m less tax base €600m) associated with S in H's consolidated financial statements. Whether or not any deferred tax is required to be provided for on this difference is determined in accordance with the principles discussed in A below. Irrespective of whether provision is made for deferred tax, H would be required to make disclosures in respect of this difference (see 8.2 below).

The amount of any temporary difference in H's separate financial statements would depend on the accounting policy adopted in those statements. IAS 27 – *Consolidated and Separate Financial Statements* allows entities the choice of accounting for investments in group companies at either cost (less impairment) or at fair value – see Chapter 5 at 7. Suppose that, notwithstanding the impairment of goodwill required to be recognised in the consolidated financial statements, the investment in S taken as a whole is not impaired, and indeed its fair value at 31 December 2005 is €660 million.

If, in its separate financial statements, H accounts for its investment at cost of €600 million, there would be no temporary difference associated with S in H's separate financial statements, since the carrying amount and tax base of S would both be €600 million.

If, in its separate financial statements, H accounts for its investment at its fair value of €660 million, there would be a taxable temporary difference of €60 million (carrying amount €660m less tax base €600m) associated with S in H's separate financial statements. Whether or not any deferred tax is required to be provided for on this difference is determined in accordance with the principles discussed in A below. Irrespective of whether provision is made for deferred tax, H would be required to make disclosures in respect of this difference (see 8.2 below).

A   Taxable temporary differences

IAS 12 requires a deferred tax liability to be recognised for all taxable temporary differences associated with investments in subsidiaries, branches and associates or interests in joint ventures differences, unless:

(a)   the parent, investor or venturer is able to control the timing of the reversal of the temporary difference; and

(b)   it is probable that the temporary difference will not reverse in the foreseeable future.[60]

Any such tax liability would be measured and presented as discussed in C below.

What this means in practice is best illustrated by reference to its application to the retained earnings of subsidiaries, branches and joint ventures on the one hand, and those of associates on the other.

In the case of a subsidiary or a branch, the parent is able to control when and whether the retained earnings are distributed. Therefore, no provision need be made for the tax consequences of distribution of profits that the parent has determined will not be distributed in the foreseeable future.[61] In the case of a joint venture, provided that the investor can control the distribution policy, similar considerations apply.[62]

In the case of an associate, however, the investor cannot control distribution policy. Therefore provision should be made for the tax consequences of the distribution of the retained earnings of an associate, except to the extent that there is a shareholders' agreement that those earnings will not be distributed.

Some might consider this an almost perverse result. In reality, it is extremely unusual for any entity (other than one set up for a specific project) to pursue a policy of full distribution. To the extent that it occurs at all, it is much more likely in a wholly-owned subsidiary than in an associate; and yet IAS 12 effectively treats full distribution by associates as the norm and that by subsidiaries as the exception. Moreover, it seems to ignore the fact that the development of equity accounting in the 1960s had its origins in the perceived ability of investors in associates to exert some degree of control over the amount and timing of dividends from them. This is discussed further in the introduction to Chapter 7.

I   Possible future developments

In July 2003 the IASB agreed in principle to amend IAS 12 so as to require full provision for deferred tax liabilities arising from taxable temporary differences arising from investments in subsidiaries, branches and associates or interests in joint ventures. The grounds for such a change are essentially that the current exemption depends on the intentions of management, which are not generally taken into account by IAS 12 in the recognition of deferred tax, although they are relevant to measurement (see 5.2 below).[63]

No concrete proposals for change have yet been published. A real difficulty with such a requirement for full provision would be how the provision should be measured. Broadly speaking, investors can realise their share of the unremitted earnings of an investment in one of two ways – directly (by remittance of the earnings) or indirectly (through sale of the investment) – which in many jurisdictions have very different tax consequences. This begs the question as to what assumptions should be made by an entity in calculating the deferred tax associated with unremitted earnings.

As discussed in C below, IAS 12 in fact requires an entity simply to follow the general rule in IAS 12 (see 5.2 below) that, where an asset could be realised or a liability settled in more than one way, each with different potential tax consequences, the entity should measure deferred tax on the basis of the manner of expected realisation or settlement. However, it is one thing to apply such an approach to a real transaction, but quite another to apply it to a hypothetical one which the entity has no intention of undertaking (i.e. in the case of a multi-national group, its wholesale liquidation or sale).

Interestingly, in June 2004 the IASB conceded that 'there may be practical considerations with respect to [calculating deferred tax on the temporary differences associated with] foreign subsidiaries and joint ventures'[64] and has agreed that the IASB staff will work with that of the FASB to analyse these difficulties, as part of the short-term convergence project to eliminate differences between IFRS and US GAAP (see 9 below).

B   Deductible temporary differences

IAS 12 requires a deferred tax asset to be recognised for all deductible temporary differences associated with investments in subsidiaries, branches and associates or interests in joint ventures differences (i.e. deferred tax liabilities), only to the extent that it is probable that:

(a)   the temporary difference will reverse in the foreseeable future; and

(b)   taxable profit will be available against which the temporary difference can be utilised.[65]

The guidance discussed in 4.2.2 and 4.2.3 above is used to determine whether or not a deferred tax asset can be recognised for such deductible temporary differences.[66]

Any such tax asset would be measured and presented as discussed in C below.

C Measurement and presentation

If application of the principles in A and B leads to the conclusion that a deferred tax asset or liability is required to be recognised, the question arises as to how it should be measured. As noted in A 1 above, the difficulty is that, broadly speaking, investors can realise their share of the unremitted earnings of an investment in one of two ways – either directly (by remittance of the earnings) or indirectly (through sale of the investment), which in many jurisdictions have very different tax consequences.

IAS 12 indicates that the entity must apply the general rule (discussed in more detail at 5.2 below) that, where there is more than one method of settling a tax liability (or recovering a tax asset), the entity should measure the liability or asset by reference to the expected manner of settlement or recovery.[67] In other words, if the temporary difference is expected to be realised through sale, the deferred tax is measured according to the tax rules applicable on sale, but if the temporary difference is expected to be realised through distribution of retained earnings, the deferred tax is measured according to the tax rules applicable on distribution.

It is also necessary to have regard to the rule that the tax effects of a transaction should be recognised in the same manner as the transaction itself (see 6 below).[68] Suppose, for example, that the entity H in Example 24.12 above had determined that it was necessary in its consolidated financial statements to provide in full for deferred tax of €13.5 million (30% of the taxable temporary difference of €45 million arising). It can be seen by reference to Example to 24.12 that the temporary difference can be analysed as having been accounted for as follows.

	€m	
Retained profit	70	Income statement
Exchange loss	(15)	Equity
Impairment of goodwill	(10)	Income statement
Taxable temporary difference at 31.12.05	45	

This indicates that the total deferred tax expense should be allocated as follows.

	€m	€m
Income statement[1]	18.0	
Equity[2]		4.5
Deferred tax (balance sheet)		13.5

Note 1 30% of €60m (retained profit €70m less goodwill impairment €10m)

Note 2 30% of €15m (exchange loss)

I   Temporary differences arising on non-controlled entities

IAS 12 acknowledges that, where an investing entity is required by IAS 12 to recognise deferred tax on a temporary difference relating to a non-controlled entity such as an associate, the investing entity will not necessarily be able to quantify the deferred tax, since it cannot control the means by which its underlying investment will be realised. In such cases, the investing entity should account for the minimum amount of tax that could arise.[69]

D   *Anticipated intragroup dividends in future periods*

IAS 10 – *Events after the Balance Sheet Date* – and IAS 18 have the effect that dividends may be recognised in both the paying and receiving company only when they have been declared by the paying company.

This raises the question of whether an entity should provide in its consolidated financial statements for the likely tax consequences of a dividend expected to be paid up the group in a future period out of the retained profits of subsidiaries as at the reporting date. For example, is there an argument that no such provision should be made on the grounds that such future dividends will not, as at the reporting date, have qualified for recognition as assets and liabilities in the separate financial statements of the relevant members of the group?

In our view, IAS 12 requires the group to make provision for the taxes payable on the retained profits of the group as at each reporting date based on the best evidence available to it at the reporting date. In other words, if in preparing its accounts for 31 December 2005, a group believes that, in order to meet the dividend expectations of its shareholders in 2006 and 2007, it will have to cause the retained earnings of certain overseas subsidiaries (as included in the group accounts at 31 December 2005) to be distributed, the group should provide for any tax consequences of such distributions in its consolidated financial statements for the period ended 31 December 2005.

We consider that it is irrelevant that such dividends have not yet been recognised in the separate financial statements of the relevant members of the group, particularly since such dividends will never be recognised in the group financial statements, as they will be eliminated on consolidation. What IAS 12 requires is a best estimate of the taxes ultimately payable on the net assets of the group as at 31 December 2005. However, for this reason it would not, in our view, be appropriate to recognise any liability for the tax anticipated to be paid out of an intragroup dividend in a future period that is likely to be covered by profits made in *future* periods, since such profits do not form part of the net assets of the group as at 31 December 2005.

E   *Temporary differences arising from differences between functional currency and tax currency*

Temporary differences arising because an entity's functional currency is different from the currency in which it is assessed to tax are accounted for according to the normal rules for recognition of deferred tax assets and liabilities discussed in 4.2.1 and 4.2.2 above, rather than under the special rules for temporary differences relating to investments discussed in A and B above.[70] An instance of such a difference is given in Example 24.6 at 1.3.2 A above.

4.2.6   *Partially deductible and 'super-deductible' assets*

IAS 12 provides no specific guidance on the particular issues raised by partially deductible and 'super-deductible' assets (i.e. assets which are eligible for tax deductions for an amount, respectively, less or greater than their cost, as opposed to being entirely non-deductible or deductible for an amount equal to their cost). The issues raised by such assets are illustrated in Examples 24.13 and 24.14 below.

Example 24.13:   Partially deductible asset

An entity acquires an asset with a cost of €100,000 and a tax base of €60,000 in circumstances where IAS 12 prohibits recognition of deferred tax on the taxable temporary difference of €40,000 arising on initial recognition of the asset. The asset is depreciated to a residual value of zero over 10 years, and qualifies for tax deductions of 20% per year. The temporary differences associated with the asset over its life will therefore be as follows.

Year	Carrying amount €	Tax base €	Temporary difference €
0	100,000	60,000	40,000
1	90,000	48,000	42,000
2	80,000	36,000	44,000
3	70,000	24,000	46,000
4	60,000	12,000	48,000
5	50,000	–	50,000
6	40,000	–	40,000
7	30,000	–	30,000
8	20,000	–	20,000
9	10,000	–	10,000
10	–	–	–

These differences are clearly a function both of:

- the €40,000 temporary difference arising on initial recognition relating to the non-deductible element of the asset, and

- the emergence of temporary differences arising from the claiming of tax deductions for the €60,000 deductible element in advance of its depreciation.

Whilst IAS 12 does not mandate the treatment to be followed here, in our view a sensible approach would be to pro-rate the total carrying amount of the asset into a 60% deductible element and a 40% non-deductible element, and provide for deferred tax on the temporary difference between the 60% deductible element and its tax base. Under this approach, the temporary differences would be calculated as follows:

Year	Book value a	40% non-deductible element b (40% of a)	60% deductible element c (60% of a)	Tax base d	Temporary difference c − d
0	100,000	40,000	60,000	60,000	–
1	90,000	36,000	54,000	48,000	6,000
2	80,000	32,000	48,000	36,000	12,000
3	70,000	28,000	42,000	24,000	18,000
4	60,000	24,000	36,000	12,000	24,000
5	50,000	20,000	30,000	–	30,000
6	40,000	16,000	24,000	–	24,000
7	30,000	12,000	18,000	–	18,000
8	20,000	8,000	12,000	–	12,000
9	10,000	4,000	6,000	–	6,000
10	–	–	–	–	–

If the entity pays tax at 30%, the amounts recorded for this transaction during year 1 (assuming that there are sufficient other taxable profits to absorb the tax loss created) would be as follows:

	€
Depreciation of asset	(10,000)
Current tax income[1]	(3,600)
Deferred tax charge[2]	1,800
Net tax credit	1,800
Post tax depreciation	(8,200)

1   €100,000 [cost of asset] × 60% [deductible element] × 20% [tax depreciation rate] × 30% [tax rate]

2   €6,000 [temporary difference] × 30% [tax rate] – brought forward balance [nil]

If this calculation is repeated for all 10 years, the following would be reported in the financial statements.

Year	Depreciation a	Current tax credit b	Deferred tax (charge)/ credit c	Total tax credit d (=b+c)	Effective tax rate e (=d/a)
1	(10,000)	3,600	(1,800)	1,800	18%
2	(10,000)	3,600	(1,800)	1,800	18%
3	(10,000)	3,600	(1,800)	1,800	18%
4	(10,000)	3,600	(1,800)	1,800	18%
5	(10,000)	3,600	(1,800)	1,800	18%
6	(10,000)		1,800	1,800	18%
7	(10,000)		1,800	1,800	18%
8	(10,000)		1,800	1,800	18%
9	(10,000)		1,800	1,800	18%
10	(10,000)		1,800	1,800	18%

This methodology has the result that the reported effective tax rate in each period corresponds to the effective tax rate for the transaction as a whole – i.e. cost of €100,000 attracting total tax deductions of €18,000 (€60,000 at 30%), an overall rate of 18%.

However, this approach cannot be said to be required by IAS 12 and other methodologies could well be appropriate, provided that they are applied consistently in similar circumstances. For example, an entity might deem that the first or the last €40,000 of depreciation charged on the asset, rather than a portion of each year's charge, represented the non-deductible element. If this approach were adopted, clearly the effective tax rate would fluctuate from year to year.

Example 24.14: 'Super-deductible' asset (investment tax credits)

The converse situation to that in Example 24.14 exists in some jurisdictions which seek to encourage certain types of investment by giving tax allowances for expenditure in excess of that actually incurred (sometimes referred to as investment tax credits). Suppose for example that an entity invests $1,000,000 in PPE with a tax base of $1,200,000 in circumstances where IAS 12 prohibits recognition of deferred tax on the deductible temporary difference of $200,000 arising on initial recognition of the asset. The asset is depreciated to a residual value of zero over 10 years, and qualifies for annual tax deductions of 20% of its deemed tax cost of $1,200,000.

The methodology we propose in Example 24.13 could be applied 'in reverse' – i.e. with the tax base, rather than the carrying amount, of the asset being apportioned in the ratio 10:2 into a 'cost' element and a 'super deduction' element, and the temporary difference calculated by reference to the 'cost' element as follows.

Year	Book value	Tax base	'Super deduction' element	Cost element	Temporary difference
	a	b	c (=2/12 of b)	d (=10/12 of b)	a – d
0	1,000,000	1,200,000	200,000	1,000,000	–
1	900,000	960,000	160,000	800,000	100,000
2	800,000	720,000	120,000	600,000	200,000
3	700,000	480,000	80,000	400,000	300,000
4	600,000	240,000	40,000	200,000	400,000
5	500,000	–	–	–	500,000
6	400,000	–	–	–	400,000
7	300,000	–	–	–	300,000
8	200,000	–	–	–	200,000
9	100,000	–	–	–	100,000
10	–	–	–	–	–

If the entity pays tax at 30%, the amounts recorded for this transaction during year 1 (assuming that there are sufficient other taxable profits to absorb the tax loss created) would be as follows:

	$
Depreciation of asset	(100,000)
Current tax income[1]	72,000
Deferred tax[2]	(30,000)
Net tax credit	42,000
Profit after tax	(58,000)

1 $1,200,000 [deemed tax cost of asset] × 20% [tax depreciation rate] × 30% [tax rate]
2 $100,000 [temporary difference] × 30% [tax rate] – brought forward balance [nil]

If this calculation is repeated for all 10 years, the following would be reported in the financial statements.

Year	Depreciation	Current tax credit	Deferred tax (charge)/ credit	Total tax credit	Effective tax rate
		a	b	c	d (=b+c)	e (=d/a)
1	(100,000)	72,000	(30,000)	42,000	42%
2	(100,000)	72,000	(30,000)	42,000	42%
3	(100,000)	72,000	(30,000)	42,000	42%
4	(100,000)	72,000	(30,000)	42,000	42%
5	(100,000)	72,000	(30,000)	42,000	42%
6	(100,000)		30,000	30,000	30%
7	(100,000)		30,000	30,000	30%
8	(100,000)		30,000	30,000	30%
9	(100,000)		30,000	30,000	30%
10	(100,000)		30,000	30,000	30%

This results in an effective 42% tax rate for this transaction being reported in years 1 to 5, and a rate of 30% in years 6 to 10, in contrast to the true effective rate of 36% for the transaction as a whole – i.e. cost of $1,000,000 attracting total tax deductions of $360,000 ($1,200,000 at 30%). This is because, whilst in the case of a partially deductible asset as in Example 24.13 above there is an accounting mechanism (i.e. depreciation) for allocating the non-deductible cost on a straight-line basis, in the present case of a 'super deductible' asset there is no ready mechanism for spreading the additional $60,000 tax deductions on a straight-line basis.

In individual cases it might be possible to argue that the additional tax deductions had sufficient of the characteristics of a government grant (e.g. if it were subject to conditions more onerous that those normally associated with tax deductions in the jurisdiction concerned) to allow application of the principles of IAS 20 *Government Grants* so as to allocate the additional tax deductions over the life of the asset. However, it would be difficult to sustain such an approach as a matter of routine. IAS 12 is fundamentally a balance sheet approach, and a volatile tax rate must sometimes be accepted as an inevitable consequence of that approach.

Again, as in Example 24.13 above, no one approach can be said to be required by IAS 12 and other methodologies could well be appropriate, provided that they are applied consistently in similar circumstances. For example, might the entity deem that the first $60,000 of the tax deductions received effectively represented the 'super deduction'? If this approach were adopted, clearly the effective tax rate would fluctuate even more from year to year.

A   Possible future developments

As discussed at 4.2.1 B above, IAS 12's restriction on the recognition of deferred tax on some temporary differences arising on initial recognition of the assets and liabilities to which they relate avoids results that many find instinctively unattractive. However, a view that these results are 'undesirable' could be said to be held by reference to the timing difference approaches to accounting for deferred tax, where such 'day one' differences would be ignored because they arise neither from an accounting performance statement nor from the tax computation. Such considerations should not, conceptually speaking, influence the accounting treatment under the temporary difference approach, which purports to take the balance sheet and not the income statement as its reference point.

The EITF in the United States has considered this issue and issued guidance that, under the temporary difference approach in SFAS 109, deferred tax should be provided for on such 'day one' differences, but by adjusting the carrying amount of the asset concerned, so as not to create a 'day one' gain or loss.[71] The methodology prescribed by the EITF, set out in Examples 24.15 and 24.16 below, is sometimes referred to as the 'simultaneous equations method' although the equations required for an algebraic solution are not true simultaneous equations (i.e. two equations each with two unknowns).

Example 24.15: 'Simultaneous equations' method – partially deductible asset

An entity that pays tax at 40% buys inventory for €120, of which only €90 is deductible for tax purposes when the inventory is sold. The simultaneous equations method is essentially founded on the premise that the transaction implies that the entity expects recover the asset through pre-tax income of €140, representing:

(a) €90 as regards the tax-deductible element of the asset; and

(b) €50 [€30/(1 - 0.4)] as regards the non-deductible element of the asset (being the amount of pre-tax income that must be earned for the entity to earn €30 after tax).

Accordingly deferred tax is recognised by grossing up the carrying value of the asset as €140 and recording deferred tax of €20, the overall journal being:

	€	€
Inventory	140	
Deferred tax		20
Cash		120

This could have been derived algebraically by calling the desired carrying value of the inventory 'x' and the deferred tax liability 'y' and solving for the equations:

$$x - 0.4 (x - 90) = 120$$
$$x - y = 120$$

As noted above, these are not simultaneous equations since the first has only one unknown and once that is solved, the second has only one unknown as well.

The overall effect of this approach will be that the income statement will portray inventory of €140 being sold with tax deductions of €56 (€36 actual tax deductions [€90 @ 40%] plus the release of the deferred tax liability €20). This creates an effective tax rate of 40% in the income statement (€140 @ 40% = €56).

Example 24.16: 'Simultaneous equations' method – 'super deductible' asset

Conversely, if the entity had acquired inventory for €90 which was eligible for tax deductions of €120, the argument is that the entity expects to earn an after-tax return of €42 (€90 cost less tax deductions of €48 [€120 @ 40%]). This is equivalent to the post-tax return that would have been earned from normally (i.e. 100%) deductible inventory of €70 (€42/[1 - 0.4]). Accordingly the €90 purchase price is taken to represent €70 of 'true' inventory and a €20 deferred tax asset, the overall journal being:

	€	€
Inventory	70	
Deferred tax	20	
Cash		90

Again this could have been derived algebraically by calling the desired carrying value of the inventory 'x' and the deferred tax asset 'y' and solving for the equations:

$$x - 0.4 (x - 120) = 90$$
$$x + y = 90$$

The overall effect of this approach will be that the income statement will portray inventory of €70 being sold with tax deductions of €28 (€48 actual tax deductions as above less the write-off of the deferred tax asset €20). This creates an effective tax rate of 40% in the income statement (€70 @ 40% = €28).

In April 2004, the IASB (in a joint meeting with the FASB) made a tentative decision to adopt a modified 'simultaneous equations method' whereby:

- the asset is recognised at fair value (which would typically assume full deductibility for tax);

- deferred tax is recognised on the difference between the fair value of the asset and its tax base;

- any difference between the sum of the fair value of the asset and the recognised tax amount and the consideration paid for the asset would be recognised as a 'purchase discount allowance' on the deferred tax amount. This discount allowance would be recognised in profit or loss as the related tax benefits are realised.[72]

Until an amendment to IAS 12 is made, however, the 'simultaneous equations method' is prohibited under IFRS.

Some would question whether such an amendment is desirable, arguing that the 'simultaneous equations method' is no more than tax equalisation – i.e. creating an effective tax rate equivalent to the statutory rate. The economic reality is that the inventories in Examples 24.15 and 24.16 above are not in fact 100% tax-deductible, and it could be said that the 'simultaneous equations method' results in a carrying amount for the inventories representing neither their cost nor their net realisable value, and therefore not in compliance with IAS 2 – *Inventories*.

Supporters of the 'simultaneous equations' method argue that, whatever its drawbacks, it is preferable to the two alternatives, i.e.

- 'day one' gains or losses, or

- the rather clumsy initial recognition exemptions in IAS 12 (see 4.2.1 and 4.2.2 above).

However, those who have concerns as to the validity of the temporary difference approach could counter this argument by pointing out that, if those outcomes are seen as a problem, it is a problem caused by using an accounting model based on book-tax differences arising from the balance sheet rather than from the income statement – the differences arising on the initial recognition of the inventories in Examples 24.13 to 24.16 above would not be timing differences in an income statement model. On this view, the 'simultaneous equations method' is merely covering the cracks in the model rather than addressing their underlying cause.

5   MEASUREMENT

5.1   Legislation at the balance sheet date

Current tax should be measured by reference to tax rates and laws that have been enacted or substantively enacted by the balance sheet date.[73] Deferred tax should be measured by reference to the tax rates and laws, as enacted or substantively enacted by the balance sheet date, that are expected to apply in the periods in which the assets and liabilities to which the deferred tax relates are realised or settled.[74]

IAS 12 comments that in some jurisdictions, announcements of tax rates (and tax laws) by the government have the substantive effect of actual enactment, which may follow the announcement by a period of several months. In these circumstances, tax assets and liabilities are measured using the announced tax rate (and tax laws).[75]

When different tax rates apply to different levels of taxable income, deferred tax assets and liabilities are measured using the average rates that are expected to apply to the taxable profit (tax loss) of the periods in which the temporary differences are expected to reverse.[76]

Where changes in tax rates or tax laws are announced after the balance sheet date, an entity is required to disclose any significant effect of those changes on its current and deferred tax assets and liabilities in accordance with IAS 10 (see Chapter 34 at 2.1.2).[77]

5.2   Expected manner of settlement

Deferred tax should be measured by reference to the tax consequences that would follow from the manner in which the entity expects, at the balance sheet date, to recover or settle the asset or liability to which it relates.[78]

IAS 12 notes that, in some jurisdictions, the manner in which an entity recovers (settles) the carrying amount of an asset (liability) may affect either or both of:

(a)   the tax rate applicable when the entity recovers (settles) the carrying amount of the asset (or liability); and

(b)   the tax base of the asset (or liability).

In such cases, an entity should measure deferred tax assets and liabilities using the tax rate and the tax base that are consistent with the expected manner of recovery or settlement.[79]

This is best illustrated with a simple example.

Example 24.17: Calculation of deferred tax depending on method of realisation of asset

A building, which is fully tax-deductible, originally cost €1 million. At the balance sheet date it is carried at €1,750,000, but tax allowances of €400,000 have been claimed in respect of it. If the building were sold the tax base of the building would be €1.5 million due to increases in its tax base due to inflation.

Any gain on sale (calculated as sale proceeds less tax base of €1.5 million) would be taxed at 40%. If the asset is consumed in the business, its depreciation will be charged to profits that are taxed at 30%. What deferred tax liability is required to be established under IAS 12?

If the intention is to retain the asset in the business, it will be recovered out of future income of €1.75 million, on which tax of €345,000 will be paid, calculated as:

	€000
Gross income	1,750
Future tax allowances for asset	
(£1m less £400,000 claimed to date)	600
	1,150
Tax at 30%	345

If, however, the intention is to sell the asset, the required deferred tax liability is only €100,000, calculated as:

	€000
Sales proceeds	1,750
Tax base	(1,500)
	250
Tax at 40%	100

IAS 12 provides further examples illustrating this requirement.[80]

5.2.1 Revalued non-depreciable assets

IAS 16 allows plant, property and equipment (PPE) to be accounted for using a revaluation model under which PPE is continuously revalued to fair value and not depreciated (see Chapter 12). SIC-21 clarifies that where a non-depreciable asset is revalued, any deferred tax on the revaluation should be calculated by reference to the tax consequences that would arise if the asset were sold at book value irrespective of the basis on which it is valued (e.g. value in use), or the manner in which economic benefits of the asset are expected to be realised. The rationale for this treatment is that, in accounting terms, the asset is never recovered through use, as it is not depreciated.[81]

5.2.2 Determination of tax base

It will be noted from the summary of the measurement rules in IAS 12 above that the expected manner of settlement of an asset or realisation of a liability is also relevant to measuring its tax base. In practice it can be difficult to apply this rule, as illustrated by Example 24.18.

Example 24.18: Calculation of tax base on method of realisation of asset

An entity purchases a quarry for €10 million. The tax system of the jurisdiction where the quarry is located provides that, if the site is sold (with or without the minerals *in situ*), the €10 million will be allowed as a deduction in calculating the taxable profit on sale. If the quarry is exploited through excavation and sale of the minerals, no tax deduction is available.

The entity intends fully to exploit the quarry and then to make good the area and sell the land for retail development. However, any sales proceeds will be relatively small, such that the entity will create a substantial capital loss (i.e. relatively low sales proceeds less €10m) for tax purposes, which it is extremely unlikely that the entity will be able to recover.

It is not clear what exactly IAS 12 requires.

One view (Option A) would be to regard the tax base of the quarry as €10m (on the grounds that, when the asset is sold, a deduction of €10m will appear in the tax return) but not recognise the deferred tax asset that emerges as the quarry is mined on the basis that the asset will never be recovered.

An alterative view (Option B) would be to regard the tax base of the quarry as nil on the basis that:

(i) the €10m deduction notionally available on sale is, for the reasons set out above, worthless to the point of being effectively non-existent; and

(ii) the €10m trading profit required to recover the carrying value of the quarry will be fully taxable.

If the quarry were acquired separately, it would make no difference what view was taken, since any temporary difference arising as a result of choosing Option B above would not be recognised as it arises on initial recognition of an asset in a transaction that is not a business combination and affects neither accounting nor taxable profit or loss (see 4.2.1 above).

If, however, the quarry were acquired in a business combination, there would be a significant difference in the accounting consequences.

If Option A were followed, no deferred tax would be recognised. If Option B were followed, however, a deferred tax liability would be recognised in accounting for the combination with a consequent increase in goodwill or decrease in the excess of the acquirer's interest in the net fair value of the acquiree's identifiable assets, liabilities and contingent liabilities over the cost of the combination (see 6.2 below). Entities which regard their effective tax rate as a key performance indicator might well prefer Option B, since it has the effect of reducing the effective tax rate by the release, as the quarry is exploited, of the deferred tax liability set up at the time of the original combination.

A   *Possible future developments*

As discussed further at 3.4 above, the IASB has tentatively agreed to remove the requirement of IAS 12 to have regard to management's intention in determining the tax base of an asset or liability.

5.2.3   *Dividends*

In some jurisdictions, the rate at which is tax is paid depends on whether profits are distributed or retained. In other jurisdictions, distribution may lead to an additional liability to tax, or a refund of tax already paid. IAS 12 requires current and deferred taxes to be measured using the rate applicable to undistributed profits until a liability to pay a dividend is recognised, at which point the tax consequences of that dividend should also be recognised, as illustrated in Example 24.19 below.[82]

Example 24.19:   Different tax rates applicable to retained and distributed profits

An entity operates in a jurisdiction where income taxes are payable at a higher rate on undistributed profits (50%) with an amount being refundable when profits are distributed. The tax rate on distributed profits is 35%. At the balance sheet date, 31 December 2005, the entity does not recognise a liability for dividends proposed or declared after the balance sheet date. As a result, no dividends are recognised in the year 2005. Taxable income for 2005 is €100,000. Net taxable temporary differences have increased during the year ended 31 December 2005 by €40,000.

The entity recognises a current tax liability and a current income tax expense of €50,000 (€100,000 taxable profit @ 50%). No asset is recognised for the amount potentially recoverable as a result of future dividends. The entity also recognises a deferred tax liability and deferred tax expense of €20,000 (€40,000 @ 50%) representing the income taxes that the entity will pay when it recovers or settles the carrying amounts of its assets and liabilities based on the tax rate applicable to undistributed profits.

Subsequently, on 15 March 2006 the entity declares, and recognises as a liability, dividends of €10,000 from previous operating profits. At that point, the entity recognises the recovery of income taxes of €1,500 (€10,000 @ [50% − 35%]), representing the refund of tax due in respect of the dividends recognised as a liability, as a current tax asset and as a reduction of current income tax expense for the year ended 31 December 2006.

5.3   Discounting

IAS 12 prohibits discounting of deferred tax, on the basis that:

(a)   it would be unreasonable to require discounting, given that it requires scheduling of the reversal of temporary differences, which can be impracticable or at least highly complex; and

(b)   it would be inappropriate to permit discounting because of the lack of comparability between financial statements in which discounting was adopted and those in which it was not. [83]

However, it is noted that when deferred tax is recognised in relation to an item that is itself discounted (such as a liability for post-employment benefits or a finance lease liability), the deferred tax, being based on the carrying amount of that item, is also effectively discounted, [84] albeit by reference to the expected cash flows of the item to which it relates.

5.4   Unrealised intragroup profits and losses in consolidated financial statements

As noted in 3.3.1 and 3.3.2 an unrealised intragroup profit or loss eliminated on consolidation will give rise a to temporary difference where the profit or loss arises on a transaction that alters the tax base of the item(s) subject to the transaction. Such an alteration in the tax base creates a temporary difference because there is no corresponding change in the carrying amount of the assets or liabilities in the consolidated financial statements, due to the intragroup eliminations.

IAS 12 does not specifically address the measurement of such items. However, IAS 12 generally requires an entity, in measuring deferred tax, to have regard to the expected manner of recovery or settlement of the tax. It would generally be consistent with this requirement to measure deferred tax on temporary differences arising from intragroup transfers at the tax rates and laws applicable to the 'transferee' company rather than those applicable to the 'transferor' company, since the 'transferee' company will be taxed when the asset or liability subject to the transfer is realised or sold.

This interpretation is reinforced by the fact that in US GAAP deferred tax on such intragroup temporary differences is measured using the 'transferor' company's tax rate and law as an explicit exception to the general application of the temporary difference approach, [85] implying that, absent such an exception, the 'transferee' company's tax rate and laws would apply.

There are some jurisdictions where the tax history of an asset or liability subject to an intragroup transfer remains with the 'transferor' company. In such cases, the general principles of IAS 12 should be used to determine whether any deferred tax should be measured at the tax rate of the 'transferor' or the 'transferee' company.

The effect of the treatment required by IAS 12 is that tax income or expense may be recognised on transactions eliminated on consolidation, as illustrated by Example 24.20.

Example 24.20: Elimination of intragroup profit

ABC, an entity taxed at 30%, has a subsidiary DEF, which is taxed at 34%. On 15 December 2005 DEF sells inventory with a cost of €100,000 to ABC for €120,000, giving rise to a taxable profit of €20,000 and tax at 34% of €6,800. On 31 January 2006, ABC sells the inventory on to a third party for €150,000, giving rise to a taxable profit (at the entity level) of €30,000 and tax of €9,000. If ABC were preparing consolidated financial statements for the year ended 31 December 2005, the profit made by DEF on the sale to ABC would be eliminated.

Under IAS 12, a deferred tax asset would be recognised on the unrealised profit of €20,000, based on ABC's 30% tax rate, i.e. €6,000. The additional €800 tax actually paid by DEF would be recognised in the profit and loss account for the period ended 31 December 2005, the accounting entry being:

	DR €	CR €
Current tax (income statement)	6,800	
Current Tax (balance sheet)		6,800
Deferred tax (balance sheet)	6,000	
Deferred tax (income statement)		6,000

The net €800 tax charge to the income statement (current tax charge €6,800 less deferred tax credit €6,000) reflects the fact that, by transferring the inventory from one tax jurisdiction to another with a lower tax rate, the group has effectively denied itself tax deductions of €800 (i.e. €20,000 at the tax rate differential of 4%) for the cost of the inventory that would have been available had the inventory been sold by DEF to the third party and not by ABC.

6   ALLOCATION OF TAX CHARGE OR CREDIT

Current and deferred tax is normally recognised as income or an expense in the profit or loss for the period, except to the extent that it arises from:

(a)   an item that has been recognised directly in equity, whether in the same period or in a different period (see 6.1 below); or

(b)   a business combination (see 6.2 below).[86]

There are also special rules applicable to the tax deductions arising on share-based payment transactions (see 6.3 below).

Where a deferred tax asset or liability is remeasured subsequent to its initial recognition, the change should be accounted for in the income statement, unless it relates to an item originally recognised in equity, in which case the change should also be accounted for in equity. Such remeasurement might result from:

•   a change in tax law;

•   a re-assessment of the recoverability of deferred tax assets (see 4.2.4 above); or

•   a change in the expected manner of recovery of an asset or settlement of a liability (see 5.2 above).[87]

Whilst IAS 12 as drafted refers only to remeasurement of 'deferred' tax, it seems clear that these principles should also be applied to any remeasurement of current tax.

6.1   Items credited or charged directly to equity

Any current tax or deferred tax on items recognised directly in equity is also recognised directly in equity. Such items include:

(a)   revaluations of property, plant and equipment under IAS 16 (see 6.1.1 below);

(b)   retrospective restatements or retrospective applications arising from corrections of errors and changes in accounting policy under IAS 8 – *Accounting Policies, Changes in Accounting Estimates and Errors* (see 6.1.2 below);

(c)   exchange differences arising on translation of the financial statements of a foreign operation under IAS 21 – *The Effects of Changes in Foreign Exchange Rates*; and

(d)   amounts taken to equity on initial recognition of a compound financial instrument (so called 'split accounting') under IAS 32 (see 4.2.1 D above).[88]

IAS 12 acknowledges that, in exceptional circumstances, it may be difficult to determine the amount of tax that relates to items recognised in equity. In these cases a reasonable pro-rata method, or another method that achieves a more appropriate allocation in the circumstances, may be used. IAS 12 gives the following examples of situations where such an approach may be appropriate:

(a)   there are graduated rates of income tax and it is impossible to determine the rate at which a specific component of taxable profit (tax loss) has been taxed;

(b)   a change in the tax rate or other tax rules affects a deferred tax asset or liability relating (in whole or in part) to an item that was previously charged or credited to equity; or

(c)   an entity determines that a deferred tax asset should be recognised, or should no longer be recognised in full, and the deferred tax asset relates (in whole or in part) to an item that was previously charged or credited to equity.[89]

6.1.1   Revalued assets

Where an entity depreciates a revalued item of PPE, it may choose to transfer the depreciation in excess of the amount that would have arisen on a historical cost basis from revaluation surplus to retained earnings. In such cases, the relevant portion of any deferred tax liability recognised on the revaluation should also be transferred to retained earnings. A similar treatment should be adopted by an entity which has a policy of transferring revaluation gains to retained earnings on disposal of a previously revalued asset.[90]

When an asset is revalued for tax purposes and that revaluation is related to an accounting revaluation of an earlier period, or to one that is expected to be carried out in a future period, the tax effects of both the asset revaluation and the adjustment of the tax base are credited or charged to equity in the periods in which they occur.

However, if the revaluation for tax purposes is not related to an accounting revaluation of an earlier period, or to one that is expected to be carried out in a future period, the tax effects of the adjustment of the tax base are recognised in the income statement.[91]

In broad terms this means that, where an asset that is carried at cost is subject to a rebasing or revaluation for tax purposes (as in Example 24.4 at 1.3.2 A above), the effect will be recognised in the income statement – subject, in the case of a deferred tax asset, to its qualifying for recognition at all under the criteria discussed in 4.2.3 and 4.2.4 above.

6.1.2   Retrospective restatements or applications

IAS 8 requires retrospective restatements or retrospective applications arising from corrections of errors and changes in accounting policy to be accounted for as an adjustment to equity in the period in which the retrospective restatement or application occurs.

Therefore, as noted above, IAS 12 quite appropriately requires the tax effect of a retrospective restatement or application to be dealt with as an adjustment to equity also. However, as drafted IAS 12 can also be read as requiring any remeasurement of such tax effects to be accounted for in equity also. This would give rise to a rather surprising result, as illustrated by Example 24.21 below.

Example 24.21:   Remeasurement of deferred tax liability recognised as the result of retrospective application

An entity's date of transition to IFRS is 1 January 2004. As a result of the adoption of IAS 37 – *Provisions, Contingent Liabilities and Contingent Assets*, its first IFRS financial statements (prepared for the year ended 31 December 2005) show an additional liability for environmental rectification costs of €5 million as an adjustment to opening reserves, together with an associated deferred tax asset at 40% of €2 million.

The environmental liability does not change substantially over the next few accounting periods, but during the year ended 31 December 2008 the tax rate falls to 30%. This requires the deferred tax asset to be remeasured to €1.5 million giving rise to tax expense of €500,000. Should this expense be recognised in profit or loss for the period or in equity?

If read literally, IAS 12 can be construed as requiring this expense to be accounted for in equity, as being a remeasurement of an amount originally recognised in equity. However, we question whether this was really the intention of IAS 12. There is a fundamental difference between an item that by its nature would always be recognised *directly* in equity (e.g. certain foreign exchange differences or revaluations of plant, property and equipment) and an item which in the normal course of events would be accounted for in the income statement, but when recognised for the first time as the result of a change in accounting policy (such as in Example 24.21 above) is dealt with as a 'catch up' adjustment to opening equity.

Such a 'catch up' adjustment is necessary only because the entity is not presenting comparative information for all periods since it first commenced business. If it had done so, all the charge for environmental costs (and all the related deferred tax) would have been reflected in previous income statements. In our view, once such items have been recognised as a 'catch up' adjustment, any subsequent changes should in principle be accounted for in the income statement as if the new accounting policy had always been in force.

6.1.3 Dividends

Where taxes are remeasured as a result of the recognition of a liability to pay a dividend (see 5.2.3 above), the difference should normally be recognised in the income statement rather than in equity, even though the dividend itself is recognised in equity under IFRS. IAS 12 takes the view that the additional (or lower) tax liability is more directly linked to the original profit that is now being distributed than to the distribution itself. Where, however, the dividend is paid out of profit arising from a transaction that was originally recognised in equity, the adjustment to the tax liability should also be recognised in equity.[92]

Where dividends are paid by the reporting entity subject to withholding tax, the withholding tax should be included as part of the dividend charged to equity.[93] Where, however, withholding tax is suffered on intragroup transactions (e.g. dividends eliminated on consolidation), the withholding tax does not relate to an item recognised in equity in the consolidated financial statements (since it has been eliminated in those financial statements), and should therefore be accounted for in the profit or loss for the period. Thus, when a subsidiary pays a dividend to its parent subject to withholding tax, the tax will be charged to equity in the separate financial statements of the subsidiary, but to the income statement in the consolidated financial statements of the parent.

IAS 12 does not directly address the treatment of incoming dividends on which tax has been suffered (i.e. whether they should be shown at the amount received, or gross of withholding tax together with a corresponding tax charge).

6.1.4 'Recycled' gains and losses

Several IFRSs[94] require gains and losses that have been accounted for in equity to be 'recycled' in the income statement at a later date when the assets or liabilities to which they relate are realised or settled. Whilst IAS 12 requires any tax consequences of the original recognition of the gains or losses in equity also to be accounted for in equity, it is silent on the treatment to be adopted when the gains or losses are recycled. In our view, any tax consequences of 'recycled' gains or losses originally recognised in equity should also be 'recycled' through the income statement in the same period as the gains or losses to which they relate. Indeed, such 'recycling' is often an automatic consequence of the reversal of previously recognised deferred tax income or expense and its 're-recognition' as current tax income or expense, as illustrated in Example 24.22.

Example 24.22: Tax on 'recycled' items

During the period ended 31 December 2005 an entity purchases for €2,000 an equity security that it classifies as available-for-sale ('AFS') – see Chapter 15. At 31 December 2005 it restates the security to its fair value of €2,400. On 1 July 2006 it disposes of the investment for €2,100.

The entity's tax rate for 2005 is 40% and for 2006 35%. The change of rate was made in legislation enacted on 1 May 2006. The entity is subject to tax on disposal of the investment (based on disposal proceeds less cost) in the period of disposal.

The accounting entries for this transaction would be as follows.

	€	€
1 January 2005		
AFS asset	2,000	
Cash		2,000
31 December 2005		
AFS asset [€2,400 – €2,000]	400	
Deferred tax (balance sheet) [€400 @ 40%]		160
Equity		240
Recognition of increase in value of asset, and related deferred tax		
1 May 2006		
Deferred tax (balance sheet) [€400 @ (35% – 40%)]	20	
Equity		20
Remeasurement of deferred tax (assuming that there has been no change in the fair value of the AFS asset)		
1 July 2006		
Cash	2,100	
Equity ('recycling' of €400 (before tax) credited 31.12.05)	400	
AFS asset		2,400
Profit on disposal of AFS asset [cash €2,100 less original cost €2,000]		100
Deferred tax (balance sheet)	140	
Deferred tax income (equity)		140
Current tax (income statement)	35	
Current tax (balance sheet) [35% of €100 pre-tax profit]		35

6.2 Business combinations

Additional deferred tax arises on business combinations as a result of items such as:

- the application of IAS 12 to the assets and liabilities of the acquired business in the consolidated financial statements when it has not been applied in the separate financial statements of that business;

- fair value adjustments made to the assets and liabilities of the acquired business, with consequential changes in the temporary differences associated with those assets and liabilities; or

- where the acquired entity already applies IAS 12 in its own financial statements, the recognition in the fair value exercise of deferred tax in respect of assets and liabilities of the acquired entity where no deferred tax is provided in those financial statements (e.g. because it relates to a temporary difference arising on initial recognition of an asset or liability in the acquired entity's own financial statements. Deferred tax would be then recognised in the acquiror's consolidated financial statements, because, in those statements, the difference arises on initial recognition in a business combination.)

Any deferred tax assets or liabilities on temporary differences that arise on a business combination affect the amount of goodwill or the amount of any excess of the acquirer's interest in the net fair value of the acquiree's identifiable assets, liabilities and contingent liabilities over the cost of the combination.[95] Example 24.12 at 4.2.5 above illustrates the application of this principle.

6.2.1   *First-time adoption of IFRS*

IFRS 1 – *First-time Adoption of International Financial Reporting Standards* – has the effect that where, on first-time adoption of IFRS, an entity recognises or remeasures deferred tax assets acquired or liabilities assumed in a business combination in accordance with IFRS (and does not retrospectively apply IFRS 3 – *Business Combinations* – to the combination), any adjustment is made against retained earnings, rather than to goodwill or the amount of any excess of the acquirer's interest in the net fair value of the acquiree's identifiable assets, liabilities and contingent liabilities over the cost of the combination.[96] This is discussed in more detail in Chapter 4 at 2.4.3.

6.2.2   *Deferred tax assets*

A   *Assets of the acquirer*

If, as a result of a business combination, the acquiring entity is able to recognise a previously unrecognised tax asset of its own (e.g. unused tax losses), the recognition of the asset should be accounted for as income, and not as goodwill or as excess of the acquirer's interest in the net fair value of the acquiree's identifiable assets, liabilities and contingent liabilities over the cost of the combination.[97]

B   *Assets of the acquiree*

If a deferred tax asset of the acquiree which was not recognised at the time of the business combination is subsequently recognised, the resulting credit is taken to the profit or loss for the period. At the same time, the carrying amount of goodwill is reduced to the amount at which it would have been carried if the deferred tax asset had been recognised as an identifiable asset at the time of the combination, and the resulting write-off is charged to profit in the same period. However, no adjustment is made to goodwill to the extent that it would either:

- create an excess of the acquirer's interest in the net fair value of the acquiree's identifiable assets, liabilities and contingent liabilities over the cost of the combination, or

- add to an excess previously recognised.[98]

In effect, IAS 12 requires a credit to the tax line of the income statement and a reduction to pre-tax profit in respect of the goodwill. However, these amounts may not necessarily be equal if there has been a change in tax rates since the combination, as illustrated by Example 24.23 below.

Example 24.23:   Deferred tax asset of acquired entity recognised after combination

In the year ended 31 December 2005, an entity acquired a subsidiary which had deductible temporary differences of £300,000. The tax rate at the time of the combination was 30%, and has remained so since. The resulting deferred tax asset of £90,000 was not recognised as an identifiable asset in determining the goodwill of £500,000 resulting from the combination. During the year ended 31 December 2007, the entity assesses that it is probable that there will be future taxable profit sufficient for the benefit of all the deductible temporary differences to be recovered.

The entity recognises a deferred tax asset of £90,000 (£90,000 at 30%) and, in the income statement, deferred tax income of £90,000. It also reduces the cost of the goodwill by £90,000 and an expense of £90,000 in the income statement. Consequently, the cost of the goodwill is reduced to £410,000 – the amount that would have been recorded if a deferred tax asset of £90,000 had been recognised as an identifiable asset at the date of the business combination.

If the tax rate in 2007 had increased to 40%, the entity would have recognised a deferred tax asset of £120,000 (£300,000 at 40%) and, in the income statement, deferred tax income of £120,000. However, the adjustment to goodwill remains as before, since the requirement of IAS 12 is to adjust the goodwill to what it would have been if the deferred tax asset had been recognised at the date of combination, which would have been determined by reference to the then tax rate of 30%.

This treatment results in a net credit of £30,000 to the income statement (£90,000 written off goodwill, £120,000 deferred tax income). In net terms this is that same result as would have been obtained if a deferred tax asset of £90,000 had been recognised at the date of combination and subsequently remeasured to £120,000 on the change in tax rate. However, in that case that would have been accounted for as a single credit of £30,000 to deferred tax income. Overall, it is hard to discern the underlying rationale of the treatment required by IAS 12 which appears to be an attempt to reconcile two conceptually different approaches – i.e. treating the additional tax asset as, on the one hand, an adjustment to the accounting for the business combination and, on the other hand, as post-combination income.

IAS 12 does not specifically address the converse situation – where a deferred tax asset recognised on a business combination is subsequently derecognised. In the absence of such guidance, general application of the principles of IAS 12 points to the appropriate accounting being simply to recognise tax expense (i.e. with no adjustment to the business combination accounting). This would also be the analysis under US GAAP, on which IAS 12 is based.

C   Treatment of 'grandfathered' business combinations

The treatment required by IAS 12 is not entirely clear when a deferred tax asset is recognised by a first-time adopter of IFRS in respect of a business combination that took place before the date of transition, where advantage has been taken of the exemption in IFRS 1 not to apply IFRS 3 retrospectively to pre-transition combinations (see Chapter 4 at 2.4). Example 24.24 illustrates the point.

Example 24.24:   Deferred tax asset of acquired entity recognised by first-time adopter of IFRS following a pre-transition combination

In the year ended 31 December 2002, an entity acquired a subsidiary which had deductible temporary differences of £300,000. The tax rate at the time of the combination was 30%, and has remained so since. The resulting deferred tax asset of £90,000 was not recognised as an identifiable asset in determining the goodwill of £500,000 resulting from the combination. Under its previous national GAAP, the entity amortised the goodwill over 20 years, i.e. at £25,000 a year. Accordingly, at 1 January 2004 (the date of the entity's transition to IFRS), the goodwill was stated net of two years' amortisation at £450,000.

No adjustment was required to the carrying amount of goodwill on transition to IFRS.

As in Example 24.23 above, during the year ended 31 December 2007, the entity assesses that it is probable that there will be future taxable profit sufficient for the benefit of all the deductible temporary differences to be recovered.

As in Example 24.23 the entity recognises a deferred tax asset of £90,000 (£300,000 at 30%) and, in the income statement, deferred tax income of £90,000. The issue is how to deal with the goodwill. IAS 12 paragraph 68 requires the goodwill to be reduced 'to the amount that would have been recognised if the deferred tax asset had been recognised as an identifiable asset from the acquisition date'.

If the deferred tax asset had been recognised at the original combination date in 2002, the goodwill originally arising would have been £410,000 (£500,000 less £90,000), which would have been amortised to £369,000 as at the date of transition (£410,000 less two years' amortisation at £20,500 a year). This suggests that goodwill should be reduced by only £81,000 (carrying amount £450,000 less £369,000).

On the other hand, the general implication of Appendix B in IFRS 1 (see Chapter 4 at 2.4) is that the carrying amount of goodwill at transition (however determined under predecessor GAAP) is not to be adjusted, except for some specific exemptions in IFRS 1 dealing with certain classes of intangible asset. On this view, the £450,000 carrying amount on transition could be regarded as a 'deemed cost', so that the adjustment made under IAS 12 is to reduce this by the full £90,000 to £360,000.

In our view, the second treatment (i.e. reduction of goodwill by £90,000) is more consistent with the overall approach of IFRS 1, but not explicitly required by IAS 12 and IFRS 1.

Similar issues may arise for entities already preparing financial statements under IFRS that have taken advantage of the 'grandfathering' provisions in IFRS 3 and, previously, IAS 22.

However, the IASB may well be proposing a change to the accounting treatment of deferred tax assets of acquired entities recognised after the original business combination, whereby there would be no adjustment to goodwill, unless the deferred tax asset is recognised within one year of the combination (see D below). This would resolve issues such as that in Example 24.24 above.

Another transition issue might be that under its previous GAAP an entity wrote all goodwill off against reserves. In such cases, we believe that the effect of IFRS 1 is that such goodwill effectively ceases to exist on transition (for example, it is never recycled through the income statement on subsequent disposal of the business or investment to which it relates). Accordingly, if a deferred tax asset is recognised in respect of a combination where the goodwill was written off at the time of the combination, in our view the only accounting entry required by IAS 12 in the income statement is to credit tax income.

D   Possible future developments

The IASB has tentatively decided to propose a significant change to the current requirements of IAS 12 and IFRS 3 with regard to the recognition of deferred tax assets of acquired entities subsequent to the date of the combination. The effect of the proposed change would be that the realisation of a previously unrecognised deferred tax asset of the acquiree would generally be treated as tax income with no adjustment to goodwill. However, if the realisation occurs within one year of the business combination, there would be a rebuttable presumption that realisation of the asset indicates conditions at the date of the combination, and would be dealt with as an adjustment to the initial accounting for the business combination.[99]

6.2.3   Deferred tax liabilities of acquired entities

IAS 12 contains no specific provisions regarding the recognition of a deferred tax liability of an acquired entity after the date of the original combination. The recognition of such liabilities should therefore be accounted for in accordance with the normal rules of IAS 12, unless the failure to recognise the liability at the time of the combination was an error, in which case the provisions of IAS 8 should be applied – see Chapter 3 at 4.6.

6.3 Share-based Payment Transactions

The accounting treatment of share-based payment transactions, some knowledge of which is required to understand the discussion below, is dealt with in Chapter 29.

In some tax jurisdictions, an entity receives a tax deduction in respect of remuneration paid in shares, share options or other equity instruments of the entity. The amount of any tax deduction may differ from the related cumulative remuneration expense, and may arise in a later accounting period. For example, in some jurisdictions, an entity may recognise an expense for employee services in accordance with IFRS 2 (based on the fair value of the award at the date of grant), but not receive a tax deduction until the share options are exercised (based on the intrinsic value of the award at the date of exercise). As noted in 3.2.1 C above, IAS 12 effectively considers the cumulative expense associated with share-based payment transactions as an asset that has been fully expensed in the financial statements in advance of being recognised for tax purposes, thus giving rise to a deductible temporary difference.[100]

If the tax deduction available in future periods is not known at the end of the period, it should be estimated based on information available at the end of the period. For example, if the tax deduction will be dependent upon the entity's share price at a future date, the measurement of the deductible temporary difference should be based on the entity's share price at the end of the period.[101] Where the amount of any tax deduction (or estimated future tax deduction) exceeds the amount of the related cumulative remuneration expense, the current or deferred tax associated with the excess should be recognised directly in equity.[102] This treatment is illustrated by Example 24.25 below.

Example 24.25: Tax deductions on share based payment transactions

An entity with a tax rate of 40% grants options at the start of year 1, which vest at the end of year 3 and are exercised at the end of year 5. Tax deductions are received at the date of exercise of the options, based on their intrinsic value at the date of exercise. Details of the expense recognised for employee services received and consumed in each accounting period, the number of options expected to vest by the entity at each year-end during the vesting period and outstanding after the end of the vesting period, and the intrinsic value of the options at each year-end, are as follows:

Year	IFRS 2 expense for period £	Cumulative IFRS 2 expense £	Number of options	Intrinsic value per option £	Total intrinsic value £
1	188,000	188,000	50,000	5	250,000
2	185,000	373,000	45,000	8	360,000
3	190,000	563,000	40,000	13	520,000
4		563,000	40,000	17	680,000
5		563,000	40,000	20	800,000

The tax base of, and the temporary difference and deferred tax asset associated with, the employee services is calculated as follows. Since the book value of the employee services is all cases zero, the temporary difference associated with the services is at all times equal to their tax base as set out below.

Year	Intrinsic value (see table above) £ a	Expired portion of vesting period[1] b	Tax base (and temporary difference) £ c = a × b	Tax asset[2] £ 40% of c	Tax income[3] £
1	250,000	1/3	83,333	33,333	33,333
2	360,000	2/3	240,000	96,000	62,667
3	520,000	3/3	520,000	208,000	112,000
4	680,000	3/3	680,000	272,000	64,000
5	800,000	3/3	800,000	320,000	48,000

1 The expired portion of the vesting period is consistent with that used to calculate the cumulative charge employee costs under IFRS 2 (see Chapter 29).

2 Deferred tax asset in years 1 to 4 and current tax asset in year 5.

3 Year-on-year increase in asset

By comparing the 'Cumulative IFRS 2 expense' column in the first table with the 'Tax base (and temporary difference)' column in the second table it can be seen that in years 1 to 3 the expected tax deduction is lower than the cumulative expense charged, and is therefore dealt with entirely in the income statement. However in years 4 and 5 the expected (and in year 5 actual) tax deduction is higher than the cumulative expense charged. The tax relating to the cumulative expense charged is dealt with in the income statement, and the tax relating to the excess of the tax-deductible amount over the amount charged in the income statement is dealt with in equity as follows.

	DR	CR
Year 1		
Deferred tax (balance sheet)	33,333	
Deferred tax (income statement)		33,333
Year 2		
Deferred tax (balance sheet)	62,667	
Deferred tax (income statement)		62,667
Year 3		
Deferred Tax (balance sheet)	112,000	
Deferred Tax (income statement)		112,000
Year 4		
Deferred Tax (balance sheet)	64,000	
Deferred Tax (income statement)[1]		17,200
Equity		46,800
Year 5		
Deferred tax (income statement)	225,200	
Deferred tax (equity)	46,800	
Deferred tax (balance sheet)		272,000
Current Tax (balance sheet)	320,000	
Current tax (income statement)[2]		225,200
Current tax (equity)		94,800

1 Cumulative tax credit to income statement restricted to 40% of cumulative expense of £563,000 = £225,200. Amount credited in years 1 to 3 is £(33,333 + 62,667 + 112,000) = £212,000. Therefore amount recognised in income is £(225,200 – 212,000) = £17,200.

2 Current tax credit in the income statement is restricted to £225,000 as explained in note 1 above. The £48,000 net increase in total cumulative tax income since year 4 (£320,000-£272,000) is dealt with entirely in equity (current tax income €94,800 less deferred tax charge €46,800).

Example 24.25 above is based on Example 5 in Appendix B to IAS 12 (as inserted by IFRS 2). However, the example included in IAS 12 states that the cumulative tax income is based on the number of options 'outstanding' at each period end. This is inconsistent with the methodology in IFRS 2 (see Chapter 29), which would require the share-based payment expense during the vesting period to be based on the number of options expected to vest, not the total number of options outstanding at the period end. It would only be once the vesting period is complete that the number of options outstanding becomes relevant. We assume that this is no more than a drafting slip by the IASB.

IAS 12 asserts that the treatment in Example 24.25 is appropriate on the basis that the fact that the tax deduction (or estimated future tax deduction) exceeds the amount of the related cumulative remuneration expense 'indicates that the tax deduction relates not only to remuneration expense but also to an equity item.'[103]

However, some (including the IASB itself in ED 2!) take the view that any tax deductions in excess of the amount charged to the income statement relates to an increase in the fair value of the award from the date of grant to the date of exercise, which, under the 'grant date measurement' model in IFRS 2, is not recognised in equity, or indeed anywhere in the financial statements. It therefore does not fall within the criteria for recognition in equity in IAS 12, and should therefore by default be accounted for in the income statement.

In fact, it appears the IASB is itself less than wholly enthusiastic for treatment required by IFRS 2. It seems to have been adopted in part for consistency with US GAAP, although, as the IASB acknowledges, while the allocation of tax between the income statement and equity is broadly consistent with US GAAP, the basis on which it is measured at reporting dates before exercise date is not.[104]

6.4 Change in tax status of entity or shareholders

Sometimes there is a change in an entity's tax assets and liabilities as a result of a change in the tax status of the entity itself or that of its shareholders. SIC-25 clarifies that the effect of such a change should be recognised in the income statement, except to the extent that it involves a remeasurement of tax originally accounted for in equity, in which case the change should also be dealt with in equity.[105]

7 PRESENTATION

7.1 Balance sheet

Tax assets and liabilities should be shown separately from other assets and liabilities and current tax should be shown separately from deferred tax on the face of the balance sheet. Deferred tax should not be shown as part of current assets or liabilities.[106]

7.1.1   Offset

A   Current Tax

Current tax assets and liabilities should be offset if, and only if, the entity:

(a)   has a legally enforceable right to set off the recognised amounts; and

(b)   intends either to settle them net or simultaneously.[107]

These restrictions are based on the offset criteria in IAS 32 (see Chapter 16 at 6). It should be noted that, while entities in many jurisdictions have a right to offset current tax assets and liabilities, and the tax authority permits the entity to make or receive a single net payment, IAS 12 permits offset in financial statements only where there is a positive intention for simultaneous net settlement.[108]

The offset restrictions also have the effect that, in consolidated financial statements, a current tax asset of one member of the group may be offset against a current tax liability of another only if the two group members have a legally enforceable right to make or receive a single net payment and a positive intention to recover the asset or settle the liability simultaneously.[109]

B   Deferred Tax

Deferred tax assets and liabilities should be offset if, and only if:

(a)   the entity has a legally enforceable right to set off current tax assets and liabilities; and

(b)   the deferred tax assets and liabilities concerned relate to income taxes raised by the same taxation authority on either:

    (i)   the same taxable entity; or

    (ii)   different taxable entities which intend, in each future period in which significant amounts of deferred tax are expected to be settled or recovered, to settle their current tax assets and liabilities either on a net basis or simultaneously.[110]

The offset criteria for deferred tax are less clear than those for current tax. The position is broadly that, where in a particular jurisdiction current tax assets and liabilities relating to future periods will be offset, deferred tax assets and liabilities relating to that jurisdiction and those periods must be offset (even if the deferred tax balances actually recognised in the balance sheet would not satisfy the criteria for the offset of current tax).

IAS 12 suggests that this slightly more pragmatic approach was adopted in order to avoid the detailed scheduling of the reversal of temporary differences that would be necessary to apply the same criteria as for current tax.[111]

However, IAS 12 notes that, in rare circumstances, an entity may have a legally enforceable right of set-off, and an intention to settle net, for some periods but not for others. In such circumstances, detailed scheduling may be required to establish reliably whether the deferred tax liability of one taxable entity in the group will result in increased tax payments in the same period in which a deferred tax asset of a second taxable entity in the group will result in decreased payments by that second taxable entity.[112]

7.2   Income statement

The tax expense (or income) related to profit or loss from ordinary activities should be presented on the face of the income statement. [113]

IAS 12 notes that, whilst IAS 21 requires certain exchange differences to be recognised within the income statement, it does not specify where exactly in the income statement they should be presented. Accordingly, exchange differences relating to deferred tax assets and liabilities may be classified as deferred tax expense (or income), if that presentation is considered to be the most useful to users of the financial statements.[114] IAS 12 makes no reference to the treatment of exchange differences on current tax assets and liabilities but, presumably, the same considerations apply.

8   DISCLOSURE

IAS 12 imposes quite extensive disclosure requirements as follows.

8.1   Components of tax expense

The major components of tax expense (or income) should be disclosed separately. These may include:

(a)   current tax expense (or income);

(b)   any adjustments recognised in the period for current tax of prior periods;

(c)   the amount of deferred tax expense (or income) relating to the origination and reversal of temporary differences;

(d)   the amount of deferred tax expense (or income) relating to changes in tax rates or the imposition of new taxes;

(e)   the amount of the benefit arising from a previously unrecognised tax loss, tax credit or temporary difference of a prior period that is used to reduce current tax expense;

(f)   the amount of the benefit from a previously unrecognised tax loss, tax credit or temporary difference of a prior period that is used to reduce deferred tax expense;

(g)   deferred tax expense arising from the write-down, or reversal of a previous write-down, of a deferred tax asset; and

(h)   the amount of tax expense (or income) relating to those changes in accounting policies and errors which are included in the profit or loss in accordance with IAS 8 because they cannot be accounted for retrospectively (see Chapter 3 at 4.6).[115]

8.2   Other disclosures

The following should also be disclosed separately:

(a)   the aggregate current and deferred tax relating to items that are charged or credited to equity;

(b)   an explanation of the relationship between tax expense (or income) and accounting profit in either or both of the following forms:

    (i)   a numerical reconciliation between tax expense (or income) and the product of accounting profit multiplied by the applicable tax rate(s), disclosing also the basis on which the applicable tax rate(s) is (are) computed; or

    (ii)   a numerical reconciliation between the average effective tax rate (i.e. tax expense (or income) divided by accounting profit)[116] and the applicable tax rate, disclosing also the basis on which the applicable tax rate is computed;

    This requirement is discussed further at 8.2.1 below.

(c)   an explanation of changes in the applicable tax rate(s) compared to the previous accounting period;

(d)   the amount (and expiry date, if any) of deductible temporary differences, unused tax losses, and unused tax credits for which no deferred tax asset is recognised in the balance sheet;

(e)   the aggregate amount of temporary differences associated with investments in subsidiaries, branches and associates and interests in joint ventures, for which deferred tax liabilities have not been recognised;

    This is discussed further at 8.2.2 below.

(f)   in respect of each type of temporary difference, and in respect of each type of unused tax losses and unused tax credits:

    (i)   the amount of the deferred tax assets and liabilities recognised in the balance sheet for each period presented;

    (ii)   the amount of the deferred tax income or expense recognised in the income statement, if this is not apparent from the changes in the amounts recognised in the balance sheet; and

(g)   in respect of discontinued operations, the tax expense relating to:

    (i)   the gain or loss on discontinuance; and

    (ii)   the profit or loss from the ordinary activities of the discontinued operation for the period, together with the corresponding amounts for each prior period presented; and

(h)   the amount of income tax consequences of dividends to shareholders of the entity that were proposed or declared before the financial statements were authorised for issue, but are not recognised as a liability in the financial statements.[117]

    Further disclosures are required in respect of the tax consequences of distributing retained earnings, which are discussed at 8.4 below.

8.2.1   Tax (or tax rate) reconciliation

IAS 12 explains that the purpose of the tax reconciliation required by (b) above is to enable users of financial statements to understand whether the relationship between tax expense (or income) and accounting profit is unusual and to understand the significant factors that could affect that relationship in the future. The relationship may be affected by the effects of such factors as:

- revenue and expenses that are outside the scope of taxation;
- tax losses; and
- foreign tax rates.[118]

Accordingly, in explaining the relationship between tax expense (or income) and accounting profit, an entity should use an applicable tax rate that provides the most meaningful information to the users of its financial statements.

Often, the most meaningful rate is the domestic rate of tax in the country in which the entity is domiciled. In this case the tax rate applied for national taxes should be aggregated with the rates applied for any local taxes which are computed on a substantially similar level of taxable profit (tax loss). However, for an entity operating in several jurisdictions, it may be more meaningful to aggregate separate reconciliations prepared using the domestic rate in each individual jurisdiction.[119] Where this latter approach is adopted, the entity may need to discuss the effect of significant changes in either tax rates, or the mix of profits earned in different jurisdictions, in order to meet requirement (c) at 8.2 above.

Example 24.26 illustrates how the selection of the applicable tax rate affects the presentation of the numerical reconciliation.

Example 24.26:   Alternative presentations of tax reconciliation

In 2005 an entity has accounting profit of €3,000m (2004: €2,500m) comprising €1,500m (2004: €2,000m) in its own jurisdiction (country A) and €1,500m (2004: €500m) in country B. The tax rate is 30% in country A and 20% in country B. In country B, expenses of €200m (2004: €100m) are not deductible for tax purposes. There are no other differences between accounting profit and profit that is subject to current tax or on which deferred tax has been provided for under IAS 12.

Thus the accounting tax charge in the financial statements for each period will be as follows

	2005 €m	2004 €m
Country A €1,500/€2,000 @ 30%	450	600
Country B €[1,500 + 200]/€[500 + 100] @ 20%	340	120
Total tax charge	790	720

Reconciliation based on A's domestic tax rate

If the entity presents a tax reconciliation based on its own (i.e. country A's) domestic tax rate, the following presentation would be adopted.

	2005 €m	2004 €m
Accounting profit	3,000	2,500
Tax at domestic rate of 30%	900	750
Effect of:		
Expenses not deductible for tax purposes[1]	60	30
Overseas tax rates[2]	(170)	(60)
Tax expense	790	720

1   €200/€100 @ 30%

2   B's taxable profit €1,700/€600 @ (20% – 30%)

Reconciliation based on each jurisdiction's tax rate

If the entity presents a tax reconciliation based on each jurisdiction's domestic tax rate, the following presentation would be adopted.

	2005 €m	2004 €m
Accounting profit	3,000	2,500
Tax at domestic rates applicable to individual group entities[1]	750	700
Effect of:		
Expenses not deductible for tax purposes[2]	40	20
Tax expense	790	720

1   2005: A = €450 [€1,500 @ 30%], B = €300 [€1,500 @ 20%], total €750

      2004: A = €600 [€2,000 @ 30%], B = €100 [€500 @ 20%], total €700

2   €200/€100 @ 20%

In the extracts at 8.6 below, Nokia (Extract 24.1) calculates 'notional' tax by reference to the domestic Finnish tax rate, with the effect of overseas tax rates shown as a reconciling item, whereas Nestlé (Extract 24.2) calculates 'notional' tax by reference to the tax rates of the underlying subsidiaries.

As noted at 2.3 above, IAS 12 must be applied to tax income and expense of both continuing operations and those accounted for as discontinuing operations under IFRS 5. Therefore the tax reconciliation required by IAS 12 must cover both continuing and discontinuing operations.

8.2.2   Temporary differences relating to subsidiaries, associates, branches and joint ventures

It will be noted that IAS 12 requires an entity to disclose the temporary differences associated with subsidiaries, associates, branches and joint ventures, as opposed to the unrecognised deferred tax on those temporary differences – see (c) under 8.2 above.

IAS 12 clarifies that this approach is adopted because it would often be impracticable to compute the amount of unrecognised deferred tax. Nevertheless, where practicable, entities are encouraged to disclose the amounts of the unrecognised deferred tax liabilities because financial statement users may find such information useful.[120]

An example of this disclosure can be found in the financial statements of Nestlé (see Extract 24.2 at 8.6 below).

8.3 Reason for recognition of certain tax assets

Separate disclosure is required of the amount of any deferred tax asset that is recognised, and the nature of the evidence supporting its recognition, when:

(a) utilisation of the deferred tax asset is dependent on future profits in excess of those arising from the reversal of deferred tax liabilities; and

(b) the entity has suffered a loss in the current or preceding period in the tax jurisdiction to which the asset relates.[121]

In effect these disclosures are required when the entity has rebutted the presumption inherent in the recognition rules of IAS 12 that tax assets should not normally be recognised in these circumstances (see 4.2.3 above).

8.4 Dividends

As discussed at 5.2.3 above, where there are different tax consequences for an entity depending on whether profits are retained or distributed, tax should be measured on the rates applicable to retained profits except to the extent that there is a liability to pay dividends at the balance sheet date, where the rate applicable to distributed profits should be used.

Where such differential tax rates apply, the entity should disclose the nature of the potential income tax consequences that would arise from a payment of dividends to shareholders. It should quantify the amount of potential income tax consequences that is practicably determinable and disclose whether there are any potential income tax consequences that are not practicably determinable.[122] This will include disclosure of the important features of the income tax systems and the factors that will affect the amount of the potential income tax consequences of dividends.[123]

The reason for this rather complicated requirement is that, as IAS 12 acknowledges, it can often be very difficult to quantify the tax consequences of a full distribution of profits (e.g. where there are a large number of overseas subsidiaries). Moreover, IAS 12 concedes that there is a tension between, on the one hand, the exemption from disclosing the deferred tax associated with temporary differences associated with subsidiaries and other investments (see 8.2.2 above) and, on the other hand, this requirement to disclose the tax effect of distributing undistributed profits – in some cases they could effectively be the same number.

However, to the extent that any liability can be quantified, it should be disclosed. This may mean that consolidated financial statements will disclose the potential tax effect of distributing the earnings of some, but not all, subsidiaries, associates, branches and joint ventures.

IAS 12 emphasises that, in an entity's separate financial statements, this requirement applies only to the undistributed earnings of the entity itself and not those of any subsidiaries, associates, branches and joint ventures.[124]

8.5   IAS 37 – *Provisions, Contingent Liabilities and Contingent Assets*

IAS 12 clarifies that, while IAS 37 – *Provisions, Contingent Liabilities and Contingent Assets* generally excludes income taxes from its scope, its provisions may nevertheless be relevant to tax-related contingent assets and contingent liabilities, such as unresolved disputes with the taxation authorities.[125]

In our view, this is not intended to imply that such items fall within the scope of IAS 37, because ultimately such assets and liabilities are a measurement of current tax. IAS 12 is simply indicating that the principles in IAS 37 (see Chapter 25) should be applied in determining whether or not a contingent tax asset or liability should be recognised. However, any asset or liability that is recognised should be accounted for in accordance with IAS 12.

8.6   Example of disclosures

Examples of some of the disclosures required under IAS 12 are given by Nokia and Nestlé.

Extract 24.1: Nokia Corporation (2003)

Notes to the Consolidated Financial Statements [extract]
11.   Income taxes

	2003 EURm	2002 EURm	2001 EURm
Current tax	**-1 686**	-1 423	-1 542
Deferred tax	**-13**	-61	350
Total	**-1 699**	**-1 484**	**-1 192**
Finland	**-1 118**	-1 102	-877
Other countries	**-581**	-382	-315
Total	**-1 699**	-1 484	-1 192

The differences between income tax expense computed at statutory rates (29% in Finland in 2003, 2002 and 2001) and income tax expense provided on earnings are as follows at December 31:

	2003 EURm	2002 EURm	2001 EURm
Income tax expense at statutory rate	**1 555**	1 431	1 011
Deduction for write-down of investments in subsidiaries	**–**	–	-37
Amortization of goodwill	**46**	59	87
Impairment of goodwill	**58**	70	197
Provisions without income tax benefit/expense	**–**	-10	5
Tax for prior years	**56**	8	23
Taxes on foreign subsidiaries' net income in excess of income taxes at statutory rates	**-77**	-59	-106
Operating losses with no current tax benefit	**8**	6	16
Other	**53**	-21	-4
Income tax expense	**1 699**	1 484	1 192

At December 31, 2003 the Group had loss carry forwards, primarily attributable to foreign subsidiaries of EUR 186 million (EUR 425 million in 2002 and EUR 75 million in 2001), most of which will expire between 2005 and 2023.

Certain of the Group companies' income tax returns for periods ranging from 1998 through 2002 are under examination by tax authorities. The Group does not believe that any significant additional taxes in excess of those already provided for will arise as a result of the examinations.

24. Deferred taxes

	2003 EURm	2002 EURm
Deferred tax assets:		
Intercompany profit in inventory	40	48
Tax losses carried forward	36	109
Warranty provision	157	118
Other provisions	179	183
Other temporary differences	233	168
Untaxed reserves	98	105
Total deferred tax assets	743	731
Deferred tax liabilities:		
Untaxed reserves	-33	-33
Fair value gains/losses	-22	–25
Other	-186	-149
Total deferred tax liabilities	-241	-207
Net deferred tax asset	502	524
The tax (charged)/credited to shareholders' equity is as follows:		
Fair value and other reserves, fair value gains/losses	22	-25

Deferred income tax liabilities have not been established for withholding tax and other taxes that would be payable on the unremitted earnings of certain subsidiaries, as such earnings are permanently reinvested. At December 31, 2003 the Group had loss carry forwards of EUR 75 million (EUR 91 million in 2002) for which no deferred tax asset was recognized due to uncertainty of utilization of these loss carry forwards. These loss carry forwards will expire in years 2005 through 2010.

Extract 24.2: Nestlé S.A. (2003)

Notes [extract]
5. Taxes

In millions of CHF	2003	2002
Reconciliation of tax expense		
Tax at the theoretical domestic rates applicable to profits of taxable entities in the countries concerned	2,247	1,624
Tax effect of non-deductible amortisation and impairment of goodwill	466	696
Tax effect of non-deductible or non-taxable items	(410)	(429)
Transfers (from)/to unrecognised tax assets	5	56
Difference in tax rates	9	(25)
Other tax [a]	(10)	373
	2,307	2,295

(a) Includes withholding tax levied on transfer of income.

23.   Deferred taxes

In millions of CHF	2003	2002
Tax assets by types of temporary differences		
Property, plant and equipment	**269**	200
Intangible assets	**65**	109
Employee benefits	**1,216**	844
Inventories, receivables, payables and provisions	**930**	1,013
Unused tax losses and unused tax credits	**139**	110
Other	**491**	533
	3,110	2,809
Tax liabilities by types of temporary differences		
Property, plant and equipment	**1,113**	790
Intangible assets	**438**	533
Employee benefits	**376**	90
Inventories, receivables, payables and provisions	**14**	96
Other	**347**	273
	2,288	1,782
Net assets	**822**	1,027
Reflected in the balance sheet as follows:		
Deferred tax assets	**1,398**	1,519
Deferred tax liabilities	**(576)**	(492)
Net assets	**822**	1,027
Temporary differences for which no deferred tax is recognised:		
on investments in affiliated companies (taxable temporary difference)	**10,882**	10,000
on unused tax losses, tax credits and other items	**1,442**	1,548

Unused tax losses expire mainly after 5 years.

9   SHORT-TERM CONVERGENCE PROJECT

Accounting for income taxes is one of the areas being discussed as part of the short-term convergence project being undertaken by the IASB and the FASB with a view to eliminating differences between US GAAP and IFRS. The following issues have been identified.[126]

9.1   Exceptions to the temporary difference approach

While both IAS 12 and FAS 109 make some exceptions to the temporary difference approach, the exceptions made are somewhat different. The main differences, and the IASB's proposals for dealing with them are as follows.

9.1.1   Goodwill and 'initial recognition exemption'

Both IAS 12 and FAS 109 prohibit recognition of deferred tax on goodwill and there are no plans to change this treatment. However, IAS 12 also contains an 'initial recognition exemption' – in other words, it prohibits the recognition of deferred tax on temporary differences arising on the initial recognition of an asset or liability in a transaction that is not a business combination and, at the time of the transaction, affects neither accounting nor taxable profit. There is no 'initial recognition exemption' in FAS 109. The IASB has tentatively agreed to remove the exemption and move towards an approach based on modified US GAAP (see 4.2.1 B and 4.2.6 above).

9.1.2 Investments in subsidiaries, branches and associates

Currently, IAS 12 provides an exception from the recognition of a deferred tax liability for taxable temporary differences relating to investments in subsidiaries, branches, and associates, and interests in joint ventures if the parent can control the timing of the reversal and it is probable the temporary difference will not reverse in the foreseeable future. FAS 109 prohibits a deferred tax liability from being recognised for the excess for financial reporting purposes over the tax base of an investment in a foreign subsidiary or a foreign corporate joint venture that is essentially permanent in duration. The IASB has tentatively decided that an entity should recognise the income tax consequences of all temporary differences arising in the consolidated financial statements (see 4.2.5 above). In addition, the IASB has tentatively decided to eliminate from IAS 12 the notion of 'branches'.

9.1.3 Intragroup transactions

As noted in 5.4 above, IAS 12 requires deferred tax on intragroup transfers of assets that remain within the group to be provided for using the transferee company's tax rate. FAS 109 requires any tax paid by the transferor company to be deferred, and prohibits the recognition of any deferred tax asset arising from tax base differences between the jurisdictions of the transferor and transferee companies. The IASB does not propose to change IAS 12 and has suggested that the FASB should explore the possibility of changing IAS 109 so as to conform it to IAS 12.

9.1.4 Foreign non-monetary assets and liabilities

IAS 12 requires deferred tax to be recognised on temporary differences arising from differences between the functional currency in which an asset or liability is reported in the financial statements and its tax base denominated in local currency (see 4.2.5 E above). FAS 109 prohibits recognition of deferred tax on such temporary differences relating to non-monetary assets translated at historical rates to the extent that they arise from exchange differences or indexing for tax purposes. The IASB does not propose to change IAS 12 and has suggested that the FASB should explore the possibility of changing IAS 109 so as to conform it to IAS 12.

9.2 Measurement

As noted at 5.1 above, IAS 12 requires deferred tax to be measured using and enacted or substantially enacted tax rates and laws. FAS 109 requires only enacted legislation to be used. The IASB has tentatively agreed not to change IAS 12, but to add clarification that substantially enacted legislation may be used only where enactment is virtually certain.

9.3   Deferred tax assets

Under IAS 12 deferred tax assets are recognised only where it 'probable' that it will be realised (see 4.2.2 to 4.2.4 above). Under FAS 109, all deferred tax assets are recognised and a valuation allowance is recognised to the extent that it is 'more likely than not' that the deferred tax assets will not be realised. This results in a difference in presentation and disclosure requirements, if not in the overall net impact on the financial statements. The IASB has tentatively decided not to amend IAS 12.

However, the IASB has agreed that IAS 12 should be amended to clarify that, consistent with FAS 109 and other IFRSs, 'probable' means 'more likely than not'. There is a concern that in some jurisdictions 'probable' is interpreted as implying a higher degree of certainty than 'more likely than not'.

9.4   Allocation of tax charges and credits to equity

Under IAS 12 tax that relates to an item accounted for in equity, whether in the current or a previous period, is also accounted for in equity (see 6.1 above). Under FAS 109, tax that relates to an item accounted for in equity in the current period is accounted for in equity, but is otherwise dealt with in the income statement. This avoids the need to track the 'history' of where previous transactions were recorded. The IASB notes, a little enigmatically, that it has 'discussed the complexity of the requirement and directed the staff to work with the FASB to develop the analysis further'.

9.5   Balance sheet classification of assets and liabilities

IAS 12 requires classification of all deferred tax assets and liabilities as non-current (see 7.1 above). FAS 109 requires classification of deferred tax assets and liabilities as either current or non-current based on the classification of the related non-tax asset or liability for financial reporting. The IASB has tentatively decided to amend IAS 12 to converge with FAS 109.

9.6   Disclosure

Since most of the disclosure differences between IAS 12 and FAS 109 are the result of other differences between the two standards, disclosure will be addressed once the other differences have been resolved.

10.   TRANSITIONAL ARRANGEMENTS AND FIRST-TIME ADOPTION ISSUES

The transitional arrangements in IAS 12 are no longer of any practical relevance as they applied to periods beginning in 1998 and 2001.[127]

There are no particular provisions in IFRS 1 with regard to the first-time adoption of IAS 12, although the implementation guidance notes that IAS 12 requires entities to provide for deferred tax on temporary differences measured by reference to enacted or substantively enacted legislation.[128]

Therefore IAS 12 must be applied by a first-time adopter as if it had always been in force, with the exception in relation to deferred tax arising on pre-transition business combinations noted at 6.2.1 above, whereby any additional deferred tax recognised on transition is treated as an adjustment to equity, rather than to the original accounting for the business combination. This means that entities must be aware of the 'history' of various items in the accounts. For example any temporary differences that arose on initial recognition of an asset or liability in circumstances where IAS 12 prohibits recognition of deferred tax (essentially, where the asset or liability did not arise as the result of a business combination – see 4.2.1 above) must be identified to ensure that no deferred tax is provided on such differences at transition.

The main issue for many first-time adopters of IFRS will be that their predecessor national standards either required no provision for deferred tax, or required provision under a timing difference approach. They also need to be aware that many of the other adjustments made to the transition balance sheet will also have a deferred tax effect that must be accounted for. Entities that currently report under US GAAP must also bear in mind that IAS 12, though derived from FAS 109, is different from it in a number of important respects.

References

1 IAS 12, *Income Taxes*, IASB, October 1996 (amended March 2004).

2 'Tax depreciation' is used in this Chapter to mean any tax deduction given for the cost of PPE, however described in the local tax legislation.

3 IAS 21, *The Effect of Changes in Foreign Exchange Rates*, IASB, December 2003.

4 SFAS 109, *Accounting For Income Taxes*, FASB, February 1992.

5 SFAS 109, para. 9.

6 In this Chapter, references to liabilities or assets only should generally be understood referring to both assets and liabilities, unless the context makes it clear that only one or the other is being referred to.

7 IAS 12, Objective and paras. 16 and 25.

8 FRS 19, *Deferred Tax*, UK Accounting Standards Board (ASB), December 2000, Appendix V, paras. 28-37.

9 Discussion Paper, *Accounting for Tax*, ASB, March 1995, Appendix A.

10 SIC-21, *Income Taxes – Recovery of Revalued Non-Depreciable Assets*, SIC, July 2000.

11 SIC-25, *Income Taxes – Changes in the Tax Status of an Entity or its Shareholders*, SIC, July 2000.

12 IAS 12, Objective.

13 IAS 12, paras. 16 and 25.

14 IAS 12, Objective.

15 IAS 12, paras. 1-2.

16 IAS 12, para. 4.

17 IAS 18, *Revenue*, IASB, December 1993 (amended March 2004), para. 8.

18 IAS 12, para. 5

19 IAS 12, paras. 5-6.

20 IAS 12, para. 5.

21 IAS 12, para. 7

22 IAS 12, para. 7.

23 IAS 12, para. 8.

24 IAS 12, para. 8.

25 IAS 12, para. 9.

26 In some cases research and share-based payment costs may be included as part of the cost of other assets, such as inventories or PPE.

27 IAS 12, para. 11

28 IAS 12, paras. 17-20 and 26, Appendix A (as amended by IFRS 3, *Business Combinations*)

29 *IASB Update*, IASB, June 2004.

30 *IASB Update*, IASB, June 2004.

31 IAS 12, para. 12.

32 IAS 12, paras. 13-14.

33 IAS 12, para. 15.

34 IAS 12, para. 21.

35 IAS 12, para. 21A.

36 IAS 12, para. 21B.
37 IAS 12, para. 22.
38 IAS 12, Example illustrating para. 22(c).
39 IAS 12, para. 22(c).
40 IAS 12, Example illustrating para. 22(c).
41 IAS 12, para. 20.
42 IAS 12, para. 23, Appendix B, Example 4.
43 IAS 12, para. 23.
44 IAS 12, para. 24.
45 *IASB Update*, IASB, April 2004.
46 IAS 12, para. 33.
47 IAS 12, para. 27.
48 IAS 12, para. 28.
49 IAS 12, para. 29.
50 IAS 12, para. 31.
51 IAS 12, para. 29.
52 IAS 12, para. 30.
53 *IASB Update*, IASB, May 2004.
54 IAS 12, para. 34.
55 IAS 12, para. 35.
56 IAS 12, para. 36.
57 IAS 12, para. 37.
58 IAS 12, para. 56.
59 IAS 12, para. 38.
60 IAS 12, para. 39.
61 IAS 12, para. 40.
62 IAS 12, para. 43.
63 *IASB Update*, April 2003 and June 2003, Short-term convergence project summary.
64 *IASB Update*, IASB, June 2004.
65 IAS 12, para. 44.
66 IAS 12, para. 45.
67 IAS 12, Appendix B, Example 3.
68 IAS 12, Appendix B, Example 3.
69 IAS 12, para. 42.
70 IAS 12, para. 41.
71 EITF 98-11, *Accounting for Acquired Temporary Differences in Certain Purchase Transactions That Are Not Accounted for as Business Combinations*, EITF, September 1998.
72 *IASB Update*, IASB, April 2004.
73 IAS 12, para. 46.
74 IAS 12, para. 47.
75 IAS 12, para. 48.
76 IAS 12, para. 49.
77 IAS 12, para. 88.
78 IAS 12, para. 51.
79 IAS 12, para. 52
80 IAS 12, para. 52 and Appendix A, Examples A-C.
81 SIC-21, paras. 6-7.
82 IAS 12, paras. 52A-52B.
83 IAS 12, para. 54.
84 IAS 12, paras. 55.

85 FAS 109, para. 9e.
86 IAS 12, para. 58.
87 IAS 12, para. 60.
88 IAS 12, paras. 61-62.
89 IAS 12, para. 63.
90 IAS 12, para. 64.
91 IAS 12, para. 65.
92 IAS 12, para. 52B.
93 IAS 12, para. 65A.
94 Notably IAS 21 and IAS 39 – *Financial Instruments: Recognition and Measurement*, IASB, December 2003 (amended March 2004).
95 IAS 12, para. 66.
96 IFRS 1, *First-time Adoption of International Financial Reporting Standards*, IASB, June 2003 (amended March 2004), para. B2.
97 IAS 12, para. 67.
98 IAS 12, para. 68.
99 *IASB Update*, IASB, June 2004.
100 IAS 12, paras. 68A-68B.
101 IAS 12, para. 68B.
102 IAS 12, para. 68C.
103 IAS 12, para. 68C.
104 IFRS 2, *Share-based payment*, IASB, February 2004, paras. BC311-BC329.
105 SIC-25, para. 4.
106 IAS 1, *Presentation of Financial Statements*, IASB, December 2003 (amended March 2004), paras. 69-70.
107 IAS 12, para. 71.
108 IAS 12, para. 72.
109 IAS 12, para. 73.
110 IAS 12, para. 74.
111 IAS 12, para. 75.
112 IAS 12, para. 76.
113 IAS 12, para. 77.
114 IAS 12, para. 78.
115 IAS 12, paras. 79-80.
116 IAS 12, para. 86.
117 IAS 12, para. 81.
118 IAS 12, para. 84.
119 IAS 12, para. 85.
120 IAS 12, para. 87.
121 IAS 12, para. 82.
122 IAS 12, para. 82A.
123 IAS 12, para. 87A.
124 IAS 12, paras. 87A-87C.
125 IAS 12, para. 88.
126 *Project summary: Short-term Convergence*, IASB, June 2004; *IASB Update*, IASB, June 2004.
127 IAS 12, paras. 89-91.
128 IFRS 1, Implementation Guidance, paras. IG5-6.

Chapter 25   Provisions, contingent liabilities and contingent assets

1   INTRODUCTION

1.1   Background

This chapter focuses only on those provisions that are the subject of IAS 37 – *Provisions, Contingent Liabilities and Contingent Assets*. Thus it only deals with provisions that are shown as liabilities in a balance sheet since the definition of a provision in IAS 37 is 'a liability of uncertain timing or amount'.[1] Like IAS 37, the chapter does not deal with items termed 'provisions' that reduce the carrying amount of assets.

Prior to the issue of IAS 37 in 1998, the accounting for provisions had traditionally been based on an approach that losses and expenses should be provided for on a prudent basis, both in terms of when provision was made and in terms of the amount. However, consistent with its *Framework*, the IASC was anxious to ensure that only those amounts that meet its definition of liabilities are reported as such in the balance sheet. A liability is defined as 'a present obligation of the entity arising from past events, the settlement of which is expected to result in an outflow from the entity of resources embodying economic benefits'.[2]

IAS 37 was developed in parallel with the equivalent UK standard, FRS 12, under a joint project between the IASC and the ASB. As a result, the two standards were published on the same day and, indeed, the text was mostly identical.

There is obviously an area of overlap between provisions and contingent liabilities; although contingent liabilities are clearly not certain to give rise to outflows, provision may nonetheless be required for them if they are sufficiently likely to do so. Accordingly, the IASC addressed provisions and contingent liabilities in the same standard, and threw in contingent assets for good measure. Previously, contingent assets and liabilities were governed by IAS 10.[3]

A further demarcation line has to be drawn between provisions and other liabilities, such as trade payables and accruals. The standard differentiates provisions on the basis that the uncertainty about the timing or amount of the future expenditure required in settlement is greater than that relating to trade payables and accruals.[4]

This is true, but by concentrating on trade payables and their associated accruals only the most straightforward case has been cited. In practice the difference between provisions and other liabilities is often far from clear-cut, and reclassification from one category to the other is not uncommon. (This is discussed further at 2.2.2 below.)

One reason why this distinction matters is that provisions are subject to disclosure requirements that do not apply to other payables, as discussed at 6.1 below. In fact, although questions of recognition and measurement are important, transparency of disclosure is also a very significant issue in relation to accounting for provisions. The problem is that, once a provision has been established, expenditure that is charged to it bypasses the income statement and to some extent therefore disappears from view. The original charge may well have been dealt with as an exceptional item (or as an extraordinary item before such items were outlawed) and glossed over by management in any discussion of their performance, and the subsequent application of the provision has no further impact on earnings – giving rise to a kind of 'off income statement' treatment. Also, in the early 1990s, prior to the issue of IAS 37 and its UK equivalent, FRS 12, some of the provisions that had been set up had been extremely large and wide-ranging. An example is to be found in the 1993 financial statements of what was then British Gas:

Extract 25.1: British Gas plc (1993)

Review of operating results [extract]

Operating costs [extract]

The results for 1993 include an exceptional charge of £1,650 million for the major restructuring of the UK Gas Business. This restructuring into five separate business streams will ensure that the Company's UK Gas Business will be leaner, more competitive and more commercially focused at a time when the gas market in Great Britain is undergoing radical change. The exceptional charge comprises severance and pension costs associated with the reduction in approximately 25,000 people and the related costs of restructuring the integrated UK Gas Business. The cash effect of this restructuring will be borne largely over the next three years.

The corresponding note to the profit and loss account (income statement) contained substantially the same information but added that the amount also included 'other incremental costs that will be required to implement the restructuring, such as training, property related costs and information technology costs'. The effect of this charge was to convert a pre-tax profit of approximately £1 billion into a loss of £613 million.

The need to restrict the creation of such 'big bath' provisions provided much of the impetus for the IASC's (and the ASB's) projects on provisions, although some other important issues have been addressed as well, most notably how provisions should be measured.

1.2   Development of an international standard

1.2.1   IAS 10

The first international standard in this field was IAS 10 – *Contingencies and Events Occurring After the Balance Sheet Date*. The requirements of IAS 10 in respect of contingencies were very similar in effect to those now in IAS 37, even though the approach and the definitions used by IAS 37 are rather different. In particular, IAS 37 approaches the subject from a balance sheet perspective, setting rules for the recognition of assets and liabilities (which of course give rise to gains and losses), whereas IAS 10 focused on the recognition of gains and losses.

1.2.2   IAS 37

In November 1996, the IASC issued a Draft Statement of Principles – *Provisions and Contingencies*, proposing to take contingencies out of IAS 10 and to deal with them in the same standard as provisions, using the same recognition and measurement rules.[5] In July 1997, the IASC published an exposure draft on this basis, which was converted into a standard – IAS 37 – in September 1998. This standard applied to accounting periods beginning on or after 1 July 1999.[6]

As indicated at 1.1 above, IAS 37 was developed in parallel with the UK standard, FRS 12, under a joint project between the IASC and the ASB and the two standards were published on the same day. There were no differences of substance between the requirements of the two standards – indeed the text is still mostly identical despite the amendments to IAS 37 noted below – but FRS 12 touches on two additional areas:

- recognition of an asset when a provision is recognised (see 3.3 below), and
- slightly more guidance on the discount rate to be used in the net present value calculation (see 4.2 below).

In December 2003, a number of minor consequential amendments were made to IAS 37 (principally relating to the scope of the standard) following the publication of some of the IASB's revised standards under its improvements project (IAS 8 – *Accounting Policies, Changes in Accounting Estimates and Errors*, IAS 10 – *Events after the Balance Sheet Date*, and IAS 16 – *Property, Plant and Equipment*) and the revised IAS 39 – *Financial Instruments: Recognition and Measurement*. Further consequential amendments were made in March 2004 following the publication of IFRS 3 – *Business Combinations*, IFRS 4 – *Insurance Contracts* and IFRS 5 – *Non-current Assets Held for Sale and Discontinued Operations*. This amended standard should be applied for annual periods beginning on or after 1 January 2005. If an entity applies any of these amending standards for an earlier period, the amendments made by that standard to IAS 37 should also be applied for that earlier period.

The requirements of IAS 37 are dealt with at 2 to 6 below.

1.2.3   IFRIC 1

In May 2004, the IASB issued IFRIC 1 – *Changes in Existing Decommissioning, Restoration and Similar Liabilities.* This interpretation now provides guidance on how to account for the effect of changes in the measurement of existing provisions for obligations to dismantle, remove or restore items of property, plant and equipment, referred to as 'decommissioning, restoration and similar liabilities'. This is discussed at 4.2 and 5.4.2 A below.

1.2.4   Future developments

In September 2002, the IASB agreed to add a short-term convergence project to its active agenda, the object being to reduce differences between IFRS and US GAAP. As a result of this project and Phase II of its business combinations project (see Chapter 6 at 5.2), the IASB expects to issue an exposure draft in the final quarter of 2004 proposing a number of amendments to IAS 37. This is discussed at 8.1 below.

In May 2003, the IFRIC issued IFRIC D1 – *Emission Rights*, which, *inter alia*, proposes that where an entity is a participant in an emission rights scheme, then a liability has to recognised for the obligation to deliver allowances equal to the emissions that have been made by the entity, and that such liability falls within the scope of IAS 37. This is discussed at 8.2 below.

Another issue that is being considered by the IFRIC is the accounting by an entity when it participates in a decommissioning fund, the purpose of which is to segregate assets to fund some or all of the costs of its decommissioning or environmental liabilities for which it has to make a provision under IAS 37 (see 5.4.1 and 5.4.2 below). In January 2004, it issued a draft interpretation D4 – *Decommissioning, Restoration and Environmental Rehabilitation Funds* – to deal with this issue. This is discussed at 8.3 below.

More recently, the IFRIC has been considering the interpretation of an 'obligating event' under IAS 37 (see 3.1.1 below) in the context of the EU Directives on *Waste Electrical and Electronic Equipment.* This is discussed at 8.4 below.

2   OBJECTIVE AND SCOPE OF IAS 37

2.1   Objective

The objective of IAS 37 'is to ensure that appropriate recognition criteria and measurement bases are applied to provisions, contingent liabilities and contingent assets and that sufficient information is disclosed in the notes to enable users to understand their nature, timing and amount'.[7]

2.2   Scope

As indicated at 1.1 above, IAS 37 only deals with provisions that are liabilities. 'Provisions' for depreciation, impairment of assets and doubtful debts are not addressed in the standard, since these are adjustments to the carrying amounts of assets.[8] In addition, certain specific provisions, contingent liabilities and contingent assets are exempt.[9]

2.2.1   Exemptions

A   Executory contracts, except where the contract is onerous

The standard uses the term executory contracts to mean 'contracts under which neither party has performed any of its obligations or both parties have partially performed their obligations to an equal extent'.[10] This means that contracts such as supplier purchase contracts and capital commitments, which would otherwise fall within the scope of the standard, are exempt.

This exemption prevents the balance sheet from being grossed up by all sorts of commitments that an entity has entered into, and is to be welcomed as a pragmatic measure. However, there is little theoretical justification for the exemption, in that such items meet the definition of liabilities used by the standard, and of course give rise to corresponding assets. The need for this exemption arises because the liability framework on which this standard is based would otherwise give rise to unwelcome effects.

An executory contract will still require provision if the contract becomes onerous. Onerous contracts are dealt with in 5.3 below.

B   Provisions, contingent liabilities or contingent assets covered by another standard

Where there is a more specific standard, it should be applied to the provision, contingent liability or contingent asset it addresses instead of IAS 37. Examples given in the standard are:[11]

- contingent liabilities assumed in a business combination (dealt with in IFRS 3 – *Business Combinations*);
- construction contracts (dealt with in IAS 11 – *Construction Contracts*);
- income taxes (dealt with in IAS 12 – *Income Taxes*);
- leases (dealt with in IAS 17 – *Leases*). However, the standard argues that if operating leases become onerous, there are no specific requirements within IAS 17 to address the issue and thus IAS 37 applies to such leases;
- employee benefits (dealt with in IAS 19 – *Employee Benefits*); and
- insurance contracts (dealt with in IFRS 4 – *Insurance Contracts*). However, IAS 37 requires an insurer to apply the standard to provisions, contingent liabilities and contingent assets, other than those arising from its contractual obligations and rights under insurance contracts within the scope of IFRS 4.

The standard does not apply to financial instruments (including guarantees) that are within the scope of IAS 39 (see Chapter 15).[12] Prior to its amendment in December 2003, the standard only made an exemption for provisions, contingent liabilities and contingent assets resulting from such financial instruments carried at fair value, and it emphasised, on the other hand, that it did apply to financial instruments (including guarantees) that are *not* carried at fair value.[13]

The combination of the exemptions for insurance contracts and financial instruments now mean that, once the amended standard is applicable (see 1.2.2 above), guarantees of third party borrowings (including those of subsidiaries, associates and joint ventures) are no longer covered by IAS 37 (see 3.2.1 below).

IAS 37 also notes that some amounts treated as provisions may relate to the recognition of revenue, for example where an entity gives guarantees in exchange for a fee, and states that the standard does not address the recognition of revenue. This is dealt with by IAS 18 – *Revenue* (see Chapter 26), and IAS 37 does not change the requirements of that standard.[14]

2.2.2   *Provisions and other liabilities*

As noted at 1.1 above, IAS 37 draws a demarcation line between provisions and other liabilities, such as trade payables and accruals. The standard differentiates provisions on the basis that 'there is uncertainty about the timing or amount of the future expenditure required in settlement. By contrast:

(a)   trade payables are liabilities to pay for goods or services that have been received or supplied and have been invoiced or formally agreed with the supplier; and

(b)   accruals are liabilities to pay for goods or services that have been received or supplied but have not been paid, invoiced or formally agreed with the supplier, including amounts due to employees (for example, amounts relating to accrued vacation pay). Although it is sometimes necessary to estimate the amount or timing of accruals, the uncertainty is generally much less than is the case for provisions.

Accruals are often reported as part of trade and other payables whereas provisions are reported separately.'[15]

This is true, but by concentrating on trade payables and their associated accruals the IASC has cited only the most straightforward case. In practice the difference between provisions and other liabilities is often far from clear-cut, and reclassification from one category to the other is not uncommon.

An example of a company reclassifying provisions as other liabilities, presumably as a result of implementing IAS 37, is Nestlé as shown below.

Extract 25.2: Nestlé S.A. (2000)

22. Provisions
In millions of CHF

	Restruc- turing	Environ ment	Litigation	Other	**2000** Total	1999 Total
At 1st January					**2,289**	2,415
Introduction of IAS 37					**(132)**	
Restated figures at 1st January	322	74	1,633	128	**2,157**	
Currency retranslation	(11)	2	3	5	**(1)**	
Provisions made in the period	166	2	211	66	**445**	
Modification of the scope of consolidation	–	–	135	33	**168**	
Amounts used	(277)	(2)	(121)	(56)	**(456)**	
Unused amounts reversed	(6)	(6)	(64)	(33)	**(109)**	
At 31st December	194	70	1,797	143	**2,204**	2,289

At 1st January 1999, this caption included provisions for impairment of assets as well as certain other liabilities for a total of CHF 491 million. In 1999, this amount has been reclassified as a reduction of the carrying value of the related assets or shown as accrued liabilities.

TI Group provides an example of a company making a reclassification to provisions from creditors (payables) on implementation of the equivalent UK standard, FRS 12:

Extract 25.3: TI Group plc (1998)

22   PROVISIONS FOR LIABILITIES AND CHARGES [extract]

	Pensions and Other Post- Retirement Obligations £m	Product Warranty And Onerous Contracts £m	Deferred Taxation £m	Other Liabilities £m	Group Total £m
At 31st December 1997	112.2	–	30.4	–	142.6
Exchange rate adjustments	1.0	0.3	0.1	–	1.4
Transferred from creditors	6.7	11.6	–	0.9	19.2
Transferred to debtors falling due within one year	–	–	21.9	–	21.9
New subsidiaries	27.7	14.6	(6.7)	15.7	51.3
Utilised	(6.9)	(3.5)		(7.9)	(18.3)
Profit and loss account	9.6	3.5	(3.3)	5.5	15.3
At 31st December 1998	**150.3**	**26.5**	**42.4**	**14.2**	**233.4**

Provisions for liabilities and charges include provisions for

- Unfunded post-retirement medical and welfare benefit schemes, unfunded pension arrangements, principally overseas, and the actuarially estimated deficit in the EIS Group UK pension schemes (see note 32);

- Future product warranty costs arising in the normal course of business from prior period sales, and onerous contract liabilities;

- Deferred taxation;

- Other liabilities, which include actual and potential legal claims where resolution is anticipated during 1999 and committed reorganisation expenditure.

Following the adoption of FRS 12 'Provisions, Contingent Liabilities and Contingent Assets', certain balances relating to the above items, previously reported within Creditors, have been reclassified as Provisions with effect from 1st January 1998. 1997 comparatives have not been restated.

One reason why this distinction matters is that provisions are subject to disclosure requirements that do not apply to other payables, as discussed at 6.1 below.

2.2.3 Provisions and contingent liabilities

As noted at 1.1 above, there is clearly an overlap between provisions and contingent liabilities and IAS 37 deals with both of them.

The standard notes that in a general sense, all provisions are contingent because they are uncertain in timing or amount. However, in IAS 37 the term 'contingent' is used for liabilities and assets that are not recognised because their existence will be confirmed only by the occurrence of one or more uncertain future events not wholly within the entity's control. In addition, the term 'contingent liability' is used for liabilities that do not meet the recognition criteria.[16]

Accordingly, the standard distinguishes between:

(a) provisions – which are recognised as liabilities (assuming that a reliable estimate can be made) because they are present obligations and it is probable that an outflow of resources embodying economic benefits will be required to settle the obligations; and

(b) contingent liabilities – which are not recognised as liabilities because they are either:

(i) possible obligations, as it has yet to be confirmed whether the entity has an obligation that could lead to an outflow of resources embodying economic benefits; or

(ii) present obligations that do not meet the recognition criteria in the standard because either it is not probable that an outflow of resources embodying economic benefits will be required to settle the obligation, or a sufficiently reliable estimate of the amount of the obligation cannot be made.[17]

The recognition criteria are dealt with below.

3   RECOGNITION

3.1   Provisions

IAS 37 requires that a provision should be recognised when:

(a) an entity has a present obligation (legal or constructive) as a result of a past event;

(b) it is probable that an outflow of resources embodying economic benefits will be required to settle the obligation; and

(c) a reliable estimate can be made of the amount of the obligation.

If these conditions are not met, no provision should be recognised.[18]

Each of these three conditions is discussed separately below.

3.1.1   *'An entity has a present obligation (legal or constructive) as a result of a past event'*

The standard defines both legal and constructive obligations. The definition of a legal obligation is fairly straightforward and uncontroversial; it refers to an obligation that derives from a contract (through its explicit or implicit terms), legislation or other operation of law.[19]

Constructive obligations, on the other hand, may give rise to more problems of interpretation. A constructive obligation is defined as 'an obligation that derives from an entity's actions where:

(a)   by an established pattern of past practice, published policies or a sufficiently specific current statement, the entity has indicated to other parties that it will accept certain responsibilities; and

(b)   as a result, the entity has created a valid expectation on the part of those other parties that it will discharge those responsibilities'.[20]

The essence of the idea is that the entity may be committed to certain expenditure because any alternative would be too unattractive to contemplate. The standard cites habitual refunds made to customers, and contamination clean-ups as examples of this.[21]

The standard states that in almost all cases it will be clear whether a past event has given rise to a present obligation. However, it notes that there will be some rare cases, such as a lawsuit against an entity, where this will not be so. In these cases, a past event is deemed to give rise to a present obligation if, taking account of all available evidence (including, for example, the opinion of experts), it is more likely than not that a present obligation exists at the balance sheet date. The evidence to be considered includes any additional evidence provided by events after the balance sheet date. Accordingly, if on the basis of the evidence it is concluded that a present obligation is more likely than not to exist, a provision will be required (assuming that the other recognition criteria are met).[22] Unfortunately, this is a direct contradiction of the standard's condition (a) for the recognition of a provision as set out at 3.1 above, which requires there to be a definite obligation, not just a probable one!

The second half of this condition uses the phrase 'as a result of a past event'. This is based on the concept of an obligating event, which the standard defines as 'an event that creates a legal or constructive obligation and that results in an entity having no realistic alternative to settling that obligation'.[23] The standard says that this will be the case only:

(a)   where the settlement of the obligation can be enforced by law; or

(b)   in the case of a constructive obligation, where the event (which may be an action of the entity) creates valid expectations in other parties that the entity will discharge the obligation.[24]

This concept of obligating event is used in the standard when discussing specific examples of recognition, which we discuss further in 5 below. However, it is worth mentioning here that this concept, like that of a constructive obligation, is open to interpretation, as the obligating event is not always easy to identify.

The standard notes that the financial statements deal with the financial position of an entity at the end of its reporting period, not of its possible position in the future. Accordingly, no provision is to be recognised for costs that need to be incurred to operate in the future. The only liabilities to be recognised are those that exist at the balance sheet date.[25]

IAS 37 disallows certain provisions that might otherwise qualify to be recognised by stating that it 'is only those obligations arising from past events existing independently of an entity's future actions (i.e. the future conduct of its business) that are recognised as provisions'.[26] It illustrates this restriction with an example of an entity required, because of commercial pressures or legal requirements, to fit smoke filters in a factory. It argues that the entity can avoid the expenditure by its future actions, for example by changing its method of operation, so there is no present obligation for the future expenditure.[27] Other kinds of provisions disallowed because the entity can avoid the future expenditure are refurbishment costs, and future staff training, both of which are illustrated in the examples.[28]

There is no requirement for an entity to know to whom an obligation is owed. The obligation may be to the public at large. It follows that the obligation could be to one party, but the amount ultimately payable will be to another party. For example, in the case of a constructive obligation for an environmental clean-up, the obligation is to the public, but the liability will be settled by making payment to the contractors engaged to carry out the clean-up. However, the principle is that there must be another party for the obligation to exist. It follows from this that a management or board decision will not give rise to a constructive obligation unless it is communicated in sufficient detail to those affected by it before the balance sheet date.[29] The most significant application of this requirement relates to restructuring provisions, which is discussed further in 5.1 below.

The standard discusses the possibility that an event that does not give rise to an obligation immediately may do so at a later date, because of changes in the law or an act by the entity which gives rise to a constructive obligation.[30] Changes in the law will be relatively straightforward to identify. The only issue that arises will be exactly when that change in the law should be recognised. IAS 37 states that an obligation arises only when the legislation is virtually certain to be enacted as drafted, and suggests that in many cases, this will not be until it is enacted.[31]

The more subjective area is the possibility that an act by the entity will give rise to a constructive obligation. The example given is of an entity publicly accepting responsibility for rectification of previous environmental damage in a way that creates a constructive obligation.[32] This seems to introduce a certain amount of flexibility to management in reporting results. By bringing forward or delaying a public announcement of a commitment that management had always intended to honour, it can affect the period in which a provision is charged.

As the FASB in the US has also commented,[33] the critical event that creates a constructive obligation tends to be elusive, and this is demonstrated by the discussion of some of the examples in 5 below. That is not to say that we believe that only legal obligations should be recognised in the balance sheet, but we doubt if this particular approach is the best way of determining which additional items ought to be recognised. As with other aspects of the IASB's framework and its recognition criteria in particular, we think that the question is in reality one of expense recognition – in what period should the cost be charged to the income statement – not liability recognition at all.

3.1.2   'It is probable that an outflow of resources embodying economic benefits will be required to settle the obligation'

This requirement has been included as a result of the standard's attempt to incorporate contingent liabilities within the definition of provisions. This is discussed in detail in 3.2 below.

The interpretation of *probable* in these circumstances is that the outflow of resources is more likely than not to occur; that is, it has a probability greater than 50%. The standard also makes it clear that where there are a number of similar obligations, the probability that an outflow will occur is based on the class of obligations as a whole. This is because in the case of certain obligations such as warranties, the possibility of an outflow for an individual item may be small (likely to be much less than 50%) whereas the possibility of at least some outflow of resources for the population as a whole will be much greater (almost certainly greater than 50%).[34]

3.1.3   'A reliable estimate can be made of the amount of the obligation'

The standard takes the view that a sufficiently reliable estimate can always be made for a provision where an entity can determine a range of possible outcomes. Hence, it will only be in extremely rare cases that a range of outcomes cannot be determined and so no provision is recognised. In these circumstances, the liability should be disclosed as a contingent liability (see disclosure requirements in 6.2 below).[35]

3.2   Contingencies

IAS 37 says that contingent liabilities and contingent assets should not be recognised, but only disclosed.[36]

As indicated at 2.2.1 B above, contingent liabilities that are recognised separately as part of allocating the cost of a business combination are covered by the requirements of IFRS 3. These are discussed in Chapter 6 at 2.3.3 C.

As outlined at 8.1.1 below, the IASB has decided to make changes to the requirements of IAS 37 in respect of contingent assets and liabilities as part of an exposure draft that is expected to be issued in the final quarter of 2004.

3.2.1   Contingent liabilities

At least for contingent liabilities, this treatment in IAS 37 may seem a surprising position to take and one which is different from the previous regime under IAS 10. However, the explanation lies in the peculiar way in which a contingent liability has been defined. It is:

(a)   a possible obligation that arises from past events and whose existence will be confirmed only by the occurrence or non-occurrence of one or more uncertain future events not wholly within the control of the entity; or

(b)   a present obligation that arises from past events but is not recognised because:

    (i)   it is not probable that an outflow of resources embodying economic benefits will be required to settle the obligation; or

    (ii)   the amount of the obligation cannot be measured with sufficient reliability.[37]

This approach is very different from that used in IAS 10. What the IASC did was to define the category in a back to front way that depends on the recognition rule that it wanted to apply. Contingent liabilities as defined are now meant to be those that the IASC does not think should be recognised.

Even with that explanation, the above definition is not easy to understand. One problem with (a) is that the term 'possible' is not defined. Literally, it could mean any probability greater than 0% and less than 100%. However, in the context of the standard, a more sensible assumption is that since 'probable' is used within the standard as meaning 'more likely than not to occur' (see 3.1.2 above), i.e. a probability of greater than 50%, then 'possible' means a probability of 50% or less. Appendix A to IAS 37 in summarising the main requirements of the standard uses the phrase 'a possible obligation ... that may, but probably will not, ...' which seems to support this argument. Assuming that this is what is meant, the definition restricts contingent liabilities to those where either the existence of the liability or the transfer of economic benefits arising is less than 50+% probable (or where the obligation cannot be measured at all, but as noted in 3.1.3 above, this would be relatively rare).

The standard's definition of a contingent liability is therefore tortuous and counter-intuitive. To say that a contingent liability is no longer contingent if it becomes more than 50% probable is likely to cause a great deal of confusion. It is contrary to the natural meaning of the words, whereby a contingent liability is a liability that is contingent on a future event.

If the meaning of contingent liabilities is restricted in this way, the question obviously arises as to what happens to those items where the existence of the liability and the resulting transfer of economic benefits are greater than 50% probable. The answer is that the standard has attempted to catch these within provisions. As noted in 3.1 above, the recognition criteria for provisions include the requirement that it is probable that a transfer of economic benefits will be required to settle the obligation. Hence an item that would previously have been regarded as a contingent liability under IAS 10, for which an outflow of resources is probable, is classified as a provision under IAS 37.

However, the uncertainty surrounding a liability is not always related only to whether an outflow of resources will arise, but may also relate to whether the liability exists at all. For example, take the case of litigation against an entity. The facts may suggest that the entity will probably be found negligent and required to pay appropriate damages, but it is still contesting the action and may win the case. In these circumstances, as well as uncertainty over any level of damages, there is currently uncertainty over whether the entity has a liability at all.

Nevertheless, as discussed at 3.1.1 above, the standard has attempted to deal with these circumstances by stating that there will be some rare cases, such as a lawsuit against an entity, where it will not be clear that there is a 'present obligation'. In these cases, a past event is deemed to give rise to a present obligation if, taking account of all available evidence (including, for example, the opinion of experts), 'it is more likely than not that a present obligation exists at the balance sheet date'. The evidence to be considered includes any additional evidence provided by events after the balance sheet date. Accordingly, if on the basis of the evidence it is concluded that a present obligation is more likely than not to exist, a provision will be required (assuming that the other recognition criteria are met). If it is considered that it is more likely that no present obligation exists, then the entity discloses a contingent liability (unless the possibility of a transfer of economic resources is remote).[38] The disclosure requirements are detailed at 6.2 below.

The standard requires that contingent liabilities are assessed continually to determine whether an outflow of resources embodying economic benefits has become probable. Where this becomes the case, then provision should be made in the period in which the change in probability occurs (except in the rare circumstances where no reliable estimate can be made).[39] To illustrate this, the Appendix to IAS 37 included an example of an entity guaranteeing the borrowings of another entity, the financial condition of which deteriorates from one year to the next such that provision then needs to be made for the obligation, rather than continuing to just disclose the contingent liability.[40] Following the issue of IFRS 4, the example has been amended to reflect the fact that such a guarantee is an insurance contract under IFRS 4. The permitted accounting policy illustrated in the example indicates that there is no disclosure of a contingent liability in the first year, the guarantee being recognised at its fair value, and that the guarantee is subsequently remeasured at the best estimate of the obligation under IAS 37 if this is higher then the amount initially recognised less, when appropriate, cumulative amortisation in accordance with IAS 18.[41]

3.2.2 Contingent assets

A contingent asset is defined in a more normal way. It is 'a possible asset that arises from past events and whose existence will be confirmed only by the occurrence or non-occurrence of one or more uncertain future events not wholly within the control of the entity'.[42] In this case, the word 'possible' is *not* confined to a level of probability of 50% or less, which may further increase the confusion over the different meaning of the word in the definition of contingent liabilities.

Contingent assets usually arise from unplanned or other unexpected events that give rise to the possibility of an inflow of economic benefits to the entity. An example is a claim that an entity is pursuing through legal process, where the outcome is uncertain.[43]

The standard states that a contingent asset should not be recognised, as this could give rise to recognition of income that may never be realised. However, when the realisation of income is virtually certain, then the related asset is no longer regarded as contingent and recognition is appropriate.[44] IAS 10 had a similar criterion, but used the phrase 'reasonably certain' rather than 'virtually certain'. It is not clear whether the IASC intended there to be a different level of certainty required by using the phrase 'virtually certain', but in practice the level of certainty required was already high (a suggested interpretation being between 95% and 100% probable).

The standard requires disclosure of the contingent asset when the inflow of economic benefits is probable.[45] As noted earlier, 'probable' is used within the standard as meaning 'more likely than not to occur' (see 3.1.2 above). The disclosure requirements are detailed in 6.3 below.

As with contingent liabilities, any contingent assets should be assessed continually. If it has become virtually certain that an inflow of economic benefits will arise, the asset and the related income should be recognised in the period in which the change occurs. If an inflow becomes probable, then the contingent asset should then be disclosed.[46]

3.2.3   Summary

Despite the changes in terminology that IAS 37 introduced, in practice contingent liabilities and contingent assets continue to be dealt with on a similar basis to the regime established by IAS 10.

The following matrix summarises the treatment of contingencies under IAS 37:

Likelihood of outcome	Accounting treatment: contingent liability	Accounting treatment: contingent asset
Virtually certain (say, >95% probable)	Not a contingent liability, therefore provide	Not a contingent asset, therefore accrue
Probable (say, 50+ – 95% probable)	Not a contingent liability, therefore provide	Disclose
Possible but not probable (say, 5 – 50% probable)	Disclose	No disclosure permitted
Remote (say, <5% probable)	No disclosure required	No disclosure permitted

The standard does not put a numerical measure of probability on either 'virtually certain' or 'remote', which lie at the outer ends of the range, but we think it reasonable to regard them as falling above the 95th percentile and below the fifth percentile respectively. However, these are not definitive guides and each case must be decided on its merits. In any event, it is usually possible to assess the probability of the outcome of a particular event only very approximately.

3.3 Recognising an asset when recognising a provision

In most cases, the recognition of a provision results in an immediate charge to the income statement. Nevertheless, in some cases it may be appropriate to recognise an asset. As indicated at 1.2.2 above, this is not discussed in IAS 37, although it was dealt with explicitly in FRS 12, the UK equivalent standard. The reason for the requirements in FRS 12 is to deal with provisions which are set up under the standard for decommissioning costs. Since an obligation for such costs is incurred by commissioning, say, an oil rig, the standard therefore requires recognition of the liability at that time. However, since the oil rig provides access to oil reserves over the years of its operations, an asset is recognised at the same time.[47] IAS 37 only says 'Other International Accounting Standards specify whether expenditures are treated as assets or as expenses. These issues are not addressed in this Standard. Accordingly, this Standard neither prohibits nor requires capitalisation of the costs recognised when a provision is made.'[48]

However, IAS 16 requires the cost of an item of property, plant and equipment to include the initial estimate of the costs of dismantling and removing an asset and restoring the site on which it is located, the obligation for which an entity incurs either when the item is acquired or as a consequence of having used the item during a particular period for purposes other than to produce inventories during that period.[49] IAS 37 does allude to such costs being included as part of the cost of an oil rig in an example in the Appendix to the standard.[50] This issue is discussed further at 5.4.2 below.

Extract 25.13 at 5.4.2 below illustrates an example of a company capitalising costs in respect of its provision for decommissioning costs.

4 MEASUREMENT

4.1 Best estimate of provision

A provision is to be measured before tax, as the tax consequences of the provision, and changes to it, are dealt with under IAS 12 (see Chapter 24).[51]

IAS 37 says that the amount provided should be the best estimate of the expenditure required to settle the present obligation at the balance sheet date.[52] The standard equates this estimate with 'the amount that an entity would rationally pay to settle the obligation at the balance sheet date or to transfer it to a third party at that time'.[53] It is interesting that a hypothetical transaction of this kind should be proposed as the conceptual basis of the measurement required, rather than putting the main emphasis upon the actual expenditure that is expected to be incurred in the future.

The standard does acknowledge that it would often be impossible or prohibitively expensive to settle or transfer the obligation at the balance sheet date. However, it goes on to state that 'the estimate of the amount that an entity would rationally pay to settle or transfer the obligation gives the best estimate of the expenditure required to settle the present obligation at the balance sheet date'.[54]

The estimates of outcome and financial effect are determined by the judgement of the entity's management, supplemented by experience of similar transactions and, in some cases, reports from independent experts. The evidence considered will include any additional evidence provided by events after the balance sheet date.[55]

Different methods of dealing with the uncertainties surrounding the amount to be recognised as a provision are detailed in the standard. Where a large population of items is being measured, such as warranty costs, the standard advances the use of 'expected values'. This is a statistical computation which weights the cost of all the various possible outcomes according to their probabilities, as illustrated in the following example taken from IAS 37.[56]

Example 25.1:   Calculation of expected value

An entity sells goods with a warranty under which customers are covered for the cost of repairs of any manufacturing defects that become apparent within the first six months after purchase. If minor defects were detected in all products sold, repair costs of £1 million would result. If major defects were detected in all products sold, repair costs of £4 million would result. The entity's past experience and future expectations indicate that, for the coming year, 75 per cent of the goods sold will have no defects, 20 per cent of the goods sold will have minor defects and 5 per cent of the goods sold will have major defects. In accordance with paragraph 24 of IAS 37 (see 3.1.2 above) an entity assesses the probability of a transfer for the warranty obligations as a whole.

The expected value of the cost of repairs is:

(75% of nil) + (20% of £1m) + (5% of £4m) = £400,000.

Another measurement approach described in the standard covers the situation where there is a continuous range of possible outcomes and each point in that range is as likely as any other. IAS 37 requires that, in this case, the mid-point of the range should be used.[57] This is not a particularly helpful example. It does not make it clear what the principle is meant to be, since the mid-point in this case represents the median as well as the expected value. The latter may have been what the IASC had in mind, but the median could be equally well justified on the basis that it is 50% probable that at least this amount will be payable, while anything in excess of that constitutes a possible but not a probable liability, that should be disclosed rather than accrued. Interestingly, US GAAP has a different approach to this issue in relation to contingencies. FASB Interpretation No. 14 states that where a contingent loss could fall within a range of amounts then, if there is a best estimate within the range, it should be accrued, with the remainder noted as a contingent liability. However, if there is no best estimate then the *lowest* figure within the range should be accrued, with the remainder up to the maximum potential loss noted as a contingent liability.[58]

Where the obligation being measured relates to a single item, the standard suggests that the best estimate of the liability may be the individual most likely outcome.[59] However, it notes that regard should be had to other possible outcomes. It gives an example of an entity that has to rectify a fault in a major plant that it has constructed for a customer. The most likely outcome is that the repair will succeed at the first attempt. However, a provision should be made for a larger amount if there is a significant chance that further attempts will be necessary.[60] This again sounds like a vague leaning towards an expected value approach.

This example illustrates an inconsistency between these measurement rules and the recognition rules for contingent liabilities. Compare the above example with a case where the most likely outcome is that no repair will be required at all, but there is still a significant chance that a repair will be needed. In this scenario, there is a less than 50% probability that a cash outflow will arise, and so the item will fall within the definition of a contingent liability and no provision will be required. No account will have been taken of any other possible outcomes, unlike the first scenario.

It is also interesting to consider how the measurement rules detailed above should reflect prudence. The standard does not refer to prudence as such, however it does discuss the concept of risk. It refers to risk as being variability of outcome, and states that 'the risks and uncertainties that inevitably surround many events and circumstances should be taken into account in reaching the best estimate of a provision'. It suggests that a risk adjustment may increase the amount at which a liability is measured, but gives no indication of how this may be done. It indicates that caution is needed in making judgements under conditions of uncertainty, so that expenses or liabilities are not understated. However, it says that uncertainty does not justify the creation of excessive provisions or a deliberate overstatement of liabilities. The paragraph goes on to warn against duplicating adjustments for risk, for example by estimating costs of an adverse outcome on a prudent basis and then overestimating its probability.[61] Any uncertainties surrounding the amount of the expenditure are to be disclosed (see 6.1 below).[62]

The overall result of all this is somewhat confusing. The measurement rules do not appear to take account of prudence. Certainly, using a best estimate based on the expected value concept or the mid-point of a range cannot be building in prudence to the estimate. However, the discussion on risk gives the impression that some sort of adjustment should be made which builds prudence into the estimate, but quite how this might be done is unclear. This rather vague drafting leaves a certain amount of scope in the estimation of provisions.

4.2　Discounting to present value

The standard requires that where the effect of the time value of money is material, the amount of a provision should be the present value of the expenditures expected to be required to settle the obligation.[63] The discount rate (or rates) to be used in arriving at the present value should be 'a pre-tax rate (or rates) that reflect(s) current market assessments of the time value of money and the risks specific to the liability. The discount rate(s) should not reflect risks for which the future cash flow estimates have been adjusted.'[64] However, it is worth noting that for many provisions, no discounting will be required as the cash flows will not be sufficiently far into the future for discounting to have a material impact.[65]

IAS 37 gives no guidance as to how these requirements are to be applied. On the other hand, FRS 12 in the UK gives some guidance on the discount rate to be used in the net present value calculation. The main types of provision where the impact of discounting will be significant are those relating to decommissioning and other environmental restoration liabilities. IFRIC 1 now addresses some of the issues relating to the use of discounting (in the context of provisions for obligations to dismantle, remove or restore items of property, plant and equipment, referred to as 'decommissioning, restoration and similar liabilities') which are discussed at 5.4.2 A below.

4.2.1 Real v. nominal rate

IAS 37 does not indicate whether the discount rate should be a real discount rate or a nominal discount rate (although the example disclosure for decommissioning costs illustrates the use of a real discount rate).[66] FRS 12 in the UK notes that the discount rate used depends on whether:

(a)   the future cash flows are expressed in current prices, in which case a real discount rate (which excludes the effects of general inflation) should be used; or

(b)   the future cash flows are expressed in expected future prices, in which case a nominal discount rate (which includes a return to cover expected inflation) should be used.[67]

FRS 12 then allows either method to be used, and both these methods may produce the same figure for the initial present value of the provision. However, the effect of the unwinding of the discount will be different in each case (see 4.2.4 below).

4.2.2 Adjusting for risk

As noted at 4.1 above, IAS 37 also requires that risk is taken into account in the calculation of a provision, but gives little guidance as to how this should be done. Within the discounting section, it merely says that the discount rate should not reflect risks for which the future cash flow estimates have been adjusted.[68] FRS 12 in the UK suggests that using a discount rate that reflects the risk associated with the liability (a risk-adjusted rate) may be the easiest method of reflecting risk.[69] It gives no indication of how to calculate such a risk adjusted rate, but a little more information can be obtained from the ASB's earlier Working Paper – *Discounting in Financial Reporting*,[70] which included this example.

Example 25.2:   Calculation of a risk-adjusted rate

A company has a provision for which the expected value of the cash outflow in three years' time is £150, and the risk-free rate is 5%. The company is risk averse and would settle instead for a certain payment of £160 in three years' time. The effect of risk in calculating the present value is that either:

(a) the 'certainty equivalent' of £160 is discounted at the risk-free rate of 5%, giving a present value of £138; or

(b) the expected cash flow of £150 is discounted at a risk-adjusted rate that will give the present value of £138, i.e. a rate of 2.8%.

As can be seen from this example, the risk-adjusted rate is a *lower* rate than the risk-free rate. The problem with this approach is that this risk-adjusted rate is a theoretical rate (which may even be negative) and has no obvious meaning in real life. It is also difficult to see how a risk-adjusted rate could be obtained in practice. In this example, it was obtained only by working backwards; it was already known that the net present value that we wanted to obtain was £138, so the risk-adjusted rate was just the discount rate applied to £150 to give that result.

FRS 12 does offer an alternative approach – instead of using a risk-adjusted discount rate, the cash flows themselves can be adjusted for risk and then discounted using a risk-free rate.[71] This does of course give the problem of how to adjust the cash flows for risk. However, this may be easier than attempting to risk-adjust the discount rate.

FRS 12 suggests that an example of a risk-free rate would be a government bond rate.[72] Presumably, this government bond rate should strictly have a similar remaining term to the liability, although this is not specified in the standard.

For the purposes of discounting post-employment benefit obligations, IAS 19 requires the discount rate to be determined by reference to market yields at the balance sheet date on high quality corporate bonds (although in countries where there is no deep market in such bonds, the market yields on government bonds should be used).[73] Although IAS 19 indicates that this discount rate reflects the time value of money (but not the actuarial or investment risk), we do not believe it is appropriate to use the yield on a high quality corporate bond for determining a risk-free rate to be used in discounting provisions under IAS 37.

Whichever method of reflecting risk is adopted, IAS 37 emphasises that care must be taken that the effect of risk is not double-counted by inclusion in both the cash flows and the discount rate.[74]

4.2.3   Pre-tax discount rate

Since IAS 37 requires provisions to be measured before tax, it follows that cash flows should be discounted at a pre-tax discount rate. No further explanation of this is given in the standard. On the other hand, FRS 12 in the UK does have some discussion about pre- and post-tax rates in an appendix.[75]

However, it is unlikely that entities will need to compute a pre-tax rate from post-tax information. This is because, in reality, the discount rate will be calculated directly as a pre-tax discount rate. Supposing, for example, that the risk-free rate of return is being used, then the discount rate used will be a government bond rate. This rate will be obtained gross. Thus, the idea of obtaining a required post-tax rate of return and adjusting it for the tax consequences of different cash flows will seldom be relevant.

The calculation is illustrated in the following example.

Example 25.3:   Use of discounting and tax effect

It is estimated that the settlement of an environmental provision will give rise to a gross cash outflow of £500,000 in three years time. The gross interest rate on a government bond maturing in three years time is 6%. The tax rate is 30%.

The net present value of the provision is £419,810 (£500,000 × 1/(1.06)³). Hence, a provision of £419,810 should be booked in the balance sheet. A corresponding deferred tax asset of £125,943 (30% of £419,810) would be set up if it met the criteria for recognition in IAS 12. (See Chapter 24 at 4.2.2.)

4.2.4 Unwinding of the discount

As discussed at 4.6 below, IAS 37 indicates that where discounting is used, the carrying amount of a provision increases in each period to reflect the passage of time, and that this increase is recognised as a borrowing cost. This is the only guidance that the standard gives on the unwinding of the discount. IFRIC 1 in relation to provisions for decommissioning, restoration and similar liabilities requires that the periodic unwinding of the discount is recognised in profit or loss as a finance cost as it occurs.[76] The IFRIC concluded that the unwinding of the discount is not a borrowing cost as defined in IAS 23 – *Borrowing Costs*, and thus cannot be capitalised under the allowed alternative treatment of capitalisation under that standard (see Chapter 14).[77]

However, there is no discussion of the impact that the original selection of discount rate can have on its unwinding, that is the selection of real versus nominal rates, and risk-free versus risk-adjusted rates. The IASB (and the ASB) appear to have overlooked the fact that these different discount rates will unwind differently. This is best illustrated by way of an example.

Example 25.4:   Effect of different bases of interest

A provision is required to be set up for an expected cash outflow of €100,000 (estimated at current prices), payable in three years' time. The appropriate nominal discount rate is 7.5%, and inflation is estimated at 5%. If the provision is discounted using the nominal rate, the expected cash outflow has to reflect future prices. Accordingly, if prices increase at the rate of inflation, the cash outflow will be €115,762 (€100,000 × 1.05³). The net present value of €115,762, discounted at 7.5%, is €93,184 (€115,762 × 1/(1.075)³). If all assumptions remain valid throughout the three-year period, the movement in the provision would be as follows:

	Undiscounted cash flows	Provision
	€	€
Year 0	115,762	93,184
Unwinding of discount (€93,184 × 0.075)		6,989
Revision to estimate		–
Year 1	115,762	100,173
Unwinding of discount (€100,173 × 0.075)		7,513
Revision to estimate		–
Year 2	115,762	107,686
Unwinding of discount (€107,686 × 0.075)		8,076
Revision to estimate		–
Year 3	115,762	115,762

If the provision is calculated based on the expected cash outflow of €100,000 (estimated at current prices), then it needs to be discounted using a real discount rate. This may be thought to be 2.5%, being the difference between the nominal rate of 7.5% and the inflation rate of 5%. However, it is more accurately calculated using the Fisher relation or formula as 2.381%, being (1.075/1.05) – 1. Accordingly, the net present value of €100,000, discounted at 2.381%, is €93,184 (€100,000 × 1/(1.02381)³), the same as the calculation using future prices discounted at the nominal rate. If all assumptions remain valid throughout the three-year period, the movement in the provision would be as follows:

	Undiscounted cash flows	Provision
	€	€
Year 0	100,000	93,184
Unwinding of discount (€93,184 × 0.02381)		2,219
Revision to estimate (€100,000 × 0.05)	5,000	4,770
Year 1	105,000	100,173
Unwinding of discount (€100,173 × 0.02381)		2,385
Revision to estimate (€105,000 × 0.05)	5,250	5,128
Year 2	110,250	107,686
Unwinding of discount (€107,686 × 0.02381)		2,564
Revision to estimate (€110,250 × 0.05)	5,512	5,512
Year 3	115,762	115,762

It can be seen from the second table in the above example that using the real discount rate will give rise to a much lower finance charge each year. However, this doesn't lead to a lower provision in the balance sheet at the end of each year. Provisions have to be revised annually to reflect the current best estimate of the obligation (see 4.6 below). Thus, the provision in the above example at the end of each year needs to be adjusted to reflect current prices at that time (and any other adjustments that arise from changes in estimate of the provision), as well as being adjusted for the unwinding of the discount. For example, the revised provision at the end of Year 1 is €100,173, being €105,000 discounted for two years at 2.381%. After allowing for the unwinding of the discount, this required an additional provision of €4,770. Although the total expense in each year is the same under either method, what will be different under the two methods is the allocation of the change in provision between operating costs (assuming the original provision was treated as an operating expense) and finance charges. If the real discount rate is used, the finance charge each year will be lower and the operating costs higher than if the nominal rate is used.

A more significant difference will arise where the recognition of the original provision is included as part of the cost of property, plant or equipment, rather than an expense, such as when a decommissioning provision is recognised. In that case, using a real discount rate will result initially in a lower charge to the income statement, since under IFRIC 1 any revision to the estimate of the provision is not taken to the income statement but is treated as an adjustment of the related asset, which is then depreciated prospectively over the remaining life of the asset (see 5.4.2 below).

A similar issue arises with the option of using the risk-free or the risk-adjusted discount rate. However, this is a more complex problem, because it is not clear what to do with the risk-adjustment built into the provision. This is illustrated in the following example, using the same facts as in Example 25.2 at 4.2.2 above:

Example 25.5:   Use of risk-free and risk-adjusted figures

As before, a company is required to make a provision for which the expected value of the cash outflow in three years' time is £150, when the risk-free rate is 5%. The reporting entity is risk averse and would settle instead for a certain payment of £160 in three years' time. The discounting options are:

(a) the 'certainty equivalent' of £160 is discounted at the risk-free rate of 5%, giving a present value of £138; or

(b) the expected cash flow of £150 is discounted at a risk-adjusted rate that will give the present value of £138, i.e. a rate of 2.8%.

Assuming that there are no changes in estimate required to be made to the provision during the three-year period, alternative (a) will unwind to give an overall finance charge of £22 and a final provision of £160. Alternative (b) will unwind to give an overall finance charge of £12 and a final provision of £150.

In this example, the unwinding of different discount rates gives rise to different provisions. The difference of £10 relates to the risk adjustment that has been made to the provision. The standard gives no guidance as to how to treat this £10 if the provision is unwound at the risk-free rate. Given that the expected cash outflow is only £150, this additional £10 is likely to have to be released at some point, but it is unclear how to do this. Two alternatives are that it could be done gradually over the period in which the provision is unwound (perhaps as a reassessment of the required provision as it becomes less risky), or it could be taken in total once the provision has been settled. The lack of explicit guidance in the standard appears to give entities flexibility on this point.

4.2.5   Change in interest rates

The standard requires the discount rate to reflect current market assessments of the time value of money.[78] This appears to mean that where interest rates change, the provision should be recalculated on the basis of revised interest rates. This interpretation is reinforced by the disclosure requirement in the standard that entities should disclose the effect of any change in discount rate.[79]

This will give rise to an adjustment, but the standard does not explicitly say how this should be treated. Arguably, it could be treated in the same way as the unwinding of the discount and therefore included as a borrowing or finance cost in the year of change, which may be either a debit or a credit depending on which way interest rates move. However, we believe that the adjustment to the provision is a change in accounting estimate, as discussed in IAS 8 (see Chapter 3 at 4.5). Accordingly, it should be reflected in the financial statement classification in which the provision was originally recorded. Indeed, this latter approach is the one required by IFRIC 1 in relation to provisions for decommissioning, restoration and similar liabilities (see 5.4.2 A below). However, in that case the adjustment is not taken to the income statement but added to or deducted from the cost of the asset to which it relates; the adjusted depreciable amount of the asset is then depreciated prospectively over its remaining useful life. For other provisions, the adjustment would have to be taken to the appropriate expense category in the income statement.

Calculating this adjustment is not straightforward either, because the standard gives no guidance on how it should be done. For example, it is unclear whether the new discount rate should be applied during the year or just at the year-end, and whether the rate should be applied to the new estimate of the provision or the old estimate. Although IFRIC 1 requires that changes in the provision resulting from a change in the discount rate is added to, or deducted from, the cost of the related asset in the current period, it does not deal specifically with these points and none of the illustrative examples to IFRIC 1 include a change in discount rate. However, since other changes affecting the estimate of a provision for decommissioning, restoration and similar liabilities are reflected as a change in the liability at the time the revised estimate is made, then it would appear that a change in the discount rate would also only be applied at that time, and thus the revised discount rate would be applied to the new estimate of the provision from that point on.

4.3 Future events

The standard states that 'future events that may affect the amount required to settle an obligation should be reflected in the amount of a provision where there is sufficient objective evidence that they will occur'.[80] The types of future events that the standard has in mind are advances in technology and changes in legislation.

This is intended to mean that a provision cannot be reduced simply on the basis that new technology may be developed in the intervening period before the liability is settled. There will need to be sufficient objective evidence of this new technology. For example, an entity may believe that the cost of cleaning up a site at the end of its life will be reduced by future changes in technology. The amount recognised has to reflect a reasonable expectation of technically qualified, objective observers, taking account of all available evidence as to the technology that will be available at the time of the clean-up. Thus it is appropriate to include, for example, expected cost reductions associated with increased experience in applying existing technology or the expected cost of applying existing technology to a larger or more complex clean-up operation than has previously been carried out. However, an entity does not anticipate the development of a completely new technology for cleaning up unless it is supported by sufficient objective evidence.[81]

Similarly, if new legislation is to be anticipated, there will need to be evidence of what the legislation will demand, and whether it is virtually certain to be enacted and implemented in due course. In many cases sufficient objective evidence will not exist until the new legislation is enacted.[82]

These requirements are most likely to impact provisions for liabilities that will be settled some distance in the future, such as decommissioning costs (see 5.4.2 below).

4.4   Recoveries from third parties

In some circumstances an entity is able to look to a third party to reimburse part of the costs required to settle a provision or to pay the amounts directly. Examples are insurance contracts, indemnity clauses and suppliers' warranties.[83]

In the majority of cases where a recovery is expected, the entity would remain liable for the whole costs if the third party failed to pay for any reason, for example as a result of the third party's insolvency. In such situations, the provision should be made gross and any reimbursement should be treated as a separate asset (provided it is virtually certain that the reimbursement will be received if the entity settles the obligation). The amount recognised for the reimbursement should not exceed the amount of the provision.[84]

Although the provision and the reimbursement are shown as separate items in the balance sheet, in the income statement, the expense relating to the provision may be presented net of the amount recognised for the reimbursement.[85]

The above requirements will apply in most such cases. However, where the entity will not be liable for the costs in question if the third party fails to pay, then in such a case the entity has no liability for those costs and they are not included in the provision.[86]

Extract 25.10 at 5.4.1 below illustrates an example of a company treating amounts recoverable from third parties as separate assets.

One area where it might be thought appropriate to gross up for an expected recovery is a vacant leasehold property provision, where the calculation of the provision reflects cash flows that may arise from sub-letting the property. However, as discussed further at 5.3 below we believe that the most appropriate treatment for provisions for such onerous contracts is that they are shown at the net amount.

The main area of concern with these requirements is whether the strict criteria that need to be applied to the corresponding asset might mean that some reimbursements will not be able to be recognised at all. For items such as insurance contracts, this may not be an issue, as entities will probably be able to argue that a recovery on an insurance contract is virtually certain if the entity is required to settle the obligation (although it may be more difficult for complex situations). For other types of reimbursement, however, recovery may be less certain.

It is interesting to contrast this approach with the case where an entity is jointly and severally liable for an obligation. In that case, the entity provides only for its own share and the remainder that is expected to be met by other parties is treated only as a contingent liability.[87] This means that a similar economic position is not always portrayed in the same way. If it were, then a liability would have to be set up for the whole amount for which the entity is jointly and severally liable, with a corresponding asset being recognised for the amount expected to be met by other parties.

4.5   Gains on disposals of related assets

IAS 37 states that gains from the expected disposal of assets should not be taken into account in measuring a provision, even if the expected disposal is closely linked to the event giving rise to the provision. Such gains should be recognised at the time specified by the IAS dealing with the assets concerned.[88] This is likely to be of particular relevance in relation to restructuring provisions (see 5.1.3 below). However, it may also apply in other situations. Extract 25.13 at 5.4.2 below illustrates an example of a company excluding gains from the expected disposal of assets in determining its provision for decommissioning costs.

The introduction of the equivalent requirement in FRS 12 in the UK led British Aerospace to write off the sum of £267 million, as shown in this extract:

Extract 25.4: British Aerospace Public Limited Company (1998)

24 Reserves [extract]

FRS 12 – Provisions, contingent liabilities and contingent assets

In previous years, expenditure on rationalisation schemes initiated before 1991 was included within development properties to the extent that it was recoverable from the estimated disposal proceeds. FRS 12 does not permit such expected gains to be taken into account when assessing the level of provision relating to such schemes. These rationalisation costs which amounted to £267 million at 31 December 1997 are now no longer included.

4.6   Changes and uses of provisions

IAS 37 requires that provisions should be reviewed at each balance sheet date and adjusted to reflect the current best estimate. If it is no longer probable that an outflow of resources embodying economic benefits will be required to settle the obligation, the provision should be reversed.[89] Where discounting is used, the carrying amount of a provision increases in each period to reflect the passage of time. This increase is recognised as a borrowing cost.[90] This seems uncontroversial, other than in relation to changes in provisions for decommissioning, restoration and similar liabilities, including those arising from changes in discount rates, which are discussed at 4.2.5 above and 5.4.2 A below. As discussed at 4.2.4 above, IFRIC 1 in relation to provisions for decommissioning, restoration and similar liabilities requires that the periodic unwinding of the discount is recognised as a finance cost, and that it is not a borrowing cost capable of being capitalised under IAS 23.[91]

The standard emphasises that a provision should be used only for expenditures for which the provision was originally recognised, as to do otherwise would conceal the impact of two different events.[92] This means that the questionable practice of charging costs against a provision that was set up for a different purpose is specifically prohibited and the income statement will have to charge the new expenses separately from any release of an unused provision.

5   APPLICATION OF THE RECOGNITION AND MEASUREMENT RULES

IAS 37 expands on the general recognition and measurement rules outlined at 3 and 4 above, by also including more specific requirements for particular situations, i.e. restructuring, future operating losses and onerous contracts. These are discussed at 5.1 to 5.3 below. In addition, IAS 37 contains a number of examples in an appendix which illustrate how the general recognition and measurement rules apply to other types of items where entities may or may not have made provision in the past. These are dealt with at 5.4 below.

5.1   Restructuring provisions

The requirements of IAS 37 in respect of restructuring provisions are discussed below. As outlined at 8.1.5 below, the IASB has decided to withdraw these requirements as part of an exposure draft that is expected to be issued in the final quarter of 2004.

5.1.1   *Definition*

IAS 37 defines a restructuring as 'a programme that is planned and controlled by management, and materially changes either:

(a)   the scope of a business undertaken by an entity; or

(b)   the manner in which that business is conducted'.[93]

This is said to include:

(a)   the sale or termination of a line of business;

(b)   the closure of business locations in a country or region or the relocation of business activities from one country or region to another;

(c)   changes in management structure, for example, eliminating a layer of management; and

(d)   fundamental reorganisations that have a material effect on the nature and focus of the entity's operations.[94]

This definition is very wide, and could encourage entities to classify all kinds of operating costs as restructuring costs, and thereby invite the reader to perceive them in a different light from the 'normal' costs of operating in a dynamic business environment. Even though IAS 37 prevents such costs being expensed too early (see recognition rules below), their separate disclosure as restructuring costs may nonetheless cause users of financial statements to misinterpret the business's performance. 'Restructuring' is a term of art which can be, and is, used to cover a multitude of sins, and there is a risk that the standard will perpetuate this. The reality is that change, and its consequent costs, has become a perennial feature of business and it is potentially misleading to afford it any special status in accounting terms.

IAS 37 emphasises that when a restructuring meets the definition of a discontinued operation under IFRS 5, additional disclosures may be required under that standard (see Chapter 3 at 3.2.3).[95]

5.1.2   *Recognition*

IAS 37 requires that restructuring costs are recognised only when the general recognition criteria in the standard are met (discussed at 3.1 above).[96] The interpretation of these criteria give rise to further specific requirements that a constructive obligation to restructure arises only when an entity:

(a)   has a detailed formal plan for the restructuring identifying at least:

    (i)   the business or part of a business concerned;

    (ii)   the principal locations affected;

    (iii)   the location, function, and approximate number of employees who will be compensated for terminating their services;

    (iv)   the expenditures that will be undertaken; and

    (v)   when the plan will be implemented; and

(b)   has raised a valid expectation in those affected that it will carry out the restructuring by starting to implement that plan or announcing its main features to those affected by it'.[97]

The standard gives examples of the entity's actions that may provide evidence that the entity has started to implement a plan, quoting the dismantling of plant or selling of assets, or the public announcement of the main features of the plan. However, it also emphasises that the public announcement of a detailed plan to restructure will not automatically create an obligation; the important principle is that the entity's actions give rise to valid expectations in other parties such as customers, suppliers and employees.[98]

The standard also suggests that for a plan to give rise to a constructive obligation, its implementation needs to be planned to begin as soon as possible and to be completed in a timeframe that makes significant changes to the plan unlikely. Any extended period before commencement of implementation, or if the restructuring will take an unreasonably long time, will mean that recognition of a provision is premature, because the entity is still likely to have a chance of changing the plan.[99]

In summary, these conditions require the plan to be detailed and specific, to have gone beyond the directors' powers of recall and to be put into operation without delay or significant alteration.

The criteria set out above for the recognition of provisions mean that a board decision, if it is the only relevant event arising before the balance sheet date, is no longer sufficient. This message is reinforced specifically in the standard, the argument being made that a constructive obligation is not created by a management decision. There will only be a constructive obligation where the entity has, before the balance sheet date:

(a)   started to implement the restructuring plan; or

(b)   announced the main features of the restructuring plan to those affected by it in a sufficiently specific manner to raise a valid expectation in them that the entity will carry out the restructuring.[100]

Examples are given in an appendix to IAS 37 illustrating the impact of these conditions.[101]

The standard acknowledges that there will be examples where a board decision does trigger recognition, but this would only be if earlier events such as negotiations with employee representatives for termination payments, or with purchasers for the sale of an operation, have been concluded subject only to board approval. In such circumstances, it is reasoned that when board approval has been obtained and communicated to the other parties, the entity is committed to restructure, assuming all other conditions are met.[102]

There is also discussion in the standard of the situation that may arise in some countries where, for example, employee representatives may sit on the board, so that a board decision effectively communicates the decision to them, which may result in a constructive obligation to restructure.[103]

When the ASB in the UK was developing its proposed FRS 12, a large number of commentators suggested that board decisions should act as a trigger for recognition of provisions, particularly if supported by subsequent events between the year end and approval of the financial statements which indicate that the board decision was a meaningful one. However, the ASB made no concessions to this view, and IAS 37 takes a similar approach. Under the standard, if an entity starts to implement a restructuring plan, or announces its main features to those affected, only after the balance sheet date, a provision cannot be made. However, disclosure may be required as a non-adjusting event after the balance sheet date under IAS 10 (see Chapter 34 at 2.1.2).[104]

We are not convinced that the change in recognition of reorganisation costs that IAS 37 has brought about is a beneficial one. We believe that it is misguided to ignore the effect of management intentions in portraying the financial performance and position of an entity, as this can often be highly relevant to an understanding of the entity's affairs. Although board decisions are capable of being reversed, this does not happen as a general rule.

Furthermore, the exclusion of the effect of management decisions is not a principle that has been applied consistently by the IASB. Take the example of a restructuring that is announced shortly after the balance sheet date involving the closure of plants and large scale redundancies. The reporting entity will be precluded from recognising the direct costs of the restructuring, as it does not have a constructive obligation at the balance sheet date. However, the entity will be required to make provision for impairment in the carrying value of plant and other assets at the affected sites under IAS 36 (see Chapter 13). Hence, board decisions would appear to be relevant when assessing impairment of assets but not when determining the reporting entity's liabilities, with the result that only some of the costs that result from the closure decision are recognised.

It is also the case that the apparently robust tests of a constructive obligation set out in the standard are weaker than they seem. The interpretation of the concept of actions that 'raise a valid expectation in third parties' is extremely difficult and subjective. Even if a trigger point is easily identifiable, such as when an entity makes a detailed public announcement that meets all the specified criteria, it does not necessarily commit management to the 'restructuring' as such, but only to specific items of expenditure such as redundancy costs. Nevertheless, in practice, once a trigger point has been identified, an entity will presumably provide for all the costs of the reorganisation, assuming that they meet the measurement criteria set out in 5.1.3 below.

Furthermore, the test is at least as manipulable as board decisions. Entities anxious to accelerate or postpone recognition of a liability could do so by advancing or deferring an event that signals such a commitment, such as a public announcement, without any change to the substance of their position.

IAS 37 has some further specific rules governing when to recognise the loss arising on the sale of an operation. It is unclear why this should have been the case, since such provisions are really adjustments to the carrying amounts of the assets concerned, not provisions as defined by the standard. Indeed, if the operation is a 'disposal group' classified as held for sale under IFRS 5, then there will be no need for a separate provision for the loss on sale since under that standard the disposal group is measured at the lower of its carrying amount and the fair value less costs to sell (see Chapter 3 at 5).

IAS 37 states that no obligation arises for the sale of an operation until the entity is committed to the sale, i.e. there is a binding sale agreement.[105] Thus a provision cannot be made for a loss on sale unless there is a binding sale agreement by the year-end. The standard says that this applies even when an entity has taken a decision to sell an operation and announced that decision publicly, it cannot be committed to the sale until a purchaser has been identified and there is a binding sale agreement. Until there is such an agreement, the entity will be able to change its mind and indeed will have to take another course of action if a purchaser cannot be found on acceptable terms.

Where it is considered that a provision for the loss on disposal cannot be recognised, then the standard emphasises that where the sale of the operation is envisaged as part of a larger restructuring, the standard notes that the assets of the operation must be reviewed for impairment under IAS 36. This may therefore mean that the income statement reflects effectively the same loss; it is just that the provision is presented as a reduction of the carrying amount of assets rather than as a liability. The standard also recognises that where a sale is part of a larger restructuring, the entity could be committed to the other parts of restructuring before the binding sale agreement is in place.[106] Hence, the costs of the restructuring will be spread over different accounting periods.

5.1.3 *Costs that can be recognised within a restructuring provision*

The recognition tests for reorganisation costs that are set out above are designed to establish whether or not there is a liability at the balance sheet date, which is consistent with the conceptual approach of the standard and indeed with the IASB's *Framework*. It is therefore rather surprising to find an additional paragraph in the standard that further limits the costs that can be provided for and which is founded on quite a different conceptual approach. It states that 'a restructuring provision should include only the direct expenditures arising from the restructuring, which are those that are both:

(a)   necessarily entailed by a restructuring; and

(b)   not associated with the ongoing activities of the entity'.[107]

While (a) is perhaps a further elaboration of the rules for defining the extent of the entity's obligations, the rationale for (b) is not so straightforward. The justification given for it ties in with the more general requirement in the standard that 'it is only those obligations arising from past events existing independently of an entity's future actions that should be recognised'.[108] Hence, these costs are recognised on the same basis as if they arose independently of the restructuring.[109]

In reality, this is an approach based on expense recognition, in that the costs associated with ongoing activities will produce future benefits, and thus should not be anticipated, whether or not a liability for them exists. Expense recognition is a concept not adequately acknowledged by the IASB's *Framework*, but one which the Board seems unable to do without.

The standard gives specific examples of those costs that may not be included within the provision. Such costs include:

(a)   retraining or relocating continuing staff;

(b)   marketing; or

(c)   investment in new systems and distribution networks.[110]

No examples of allowable costs are given within the standard. However, the exposure draft that preceded FRS 12 in the UK gave certain examples. These were the costs of:

(a)   making employees redundant;

(b)   terminating leases and other contracts whose termination results directly from the reorganisation; and

(c)   expenditures to be made in the course of the reorganisation, such as employees' remuneration while they are engaged in such tasks as dismantling plant, disposing of surplus stocks and fulfilling contractual obligations.[111]

Examples (a) and (b) would certainly be permitted under the rules in IAS 37. Example (c) is slightly more contentious in relation to employee remuneration, in that unless an employee is being retained solely for the purpose of dismantling plant, etc, before being made redundant, it is questionable whether the remuneration costs meet the definition of being 'necessarily entailed by a restructuring'.

A further rule in IAS 37 is that the provision should not include identifiable future operating losses up to the date of the restructuring, unless they relate to an onerous contract.[112] This is consistent with the more general requirement in the standard that provision should not be made for future operating losses, discussed in 5.2 below.

The general rule noted in 4.5 above that gains on the expected disposal of assets cannot be taken into account in the measurement of provisions is also particularly relevant to the measurement of restructuring provisions.[113] This has meant that larger restructuring provisions than before have been required as any corresponding expected gains on assets are no longer available for set off, as was the case with British Aerospace in the UK as shown in Extract 25.4 at 4.5 above. However, sometimes the impact of this rule will be mitigated by the fact that fewer costs will also be recognised within a provision, as some will not meet the criteria set out above.

One company which makes provision for restructuring costs on the basis of IAS 37 is Syngenta as shown in its accounting policies in Extract 25.10 at 5.4.1 below. The following extract from its financial statements gives further information about its provision for such costs.

Extract 25.5: Syngenta AG (2003)

22.   Restructuring provisions

(US$ million)	Employee termination costs	Other third party costs	Total
January 1, 2001	**178**	**172**	**350**
Cash payments	(111)	(241)	(352)
Additions charged to income	91	178	269
Releases credited to income	(7)	1	(6)
Other movements	(2)	5	3
Translation (gains)/losses net	(2)	(5)	(7)
December 31, 2001	**147**	**110**	**257**
Cash payments	(84)	(162)	(246)
Additions charged to income	119	157	276
Releases credited to income	(14)	–	(14)
Reclassifications	(11)	(11)	(22)
Translation (gains)/losses net	13	9	22
December 31, 2002	**170**	**103**	**273**
Cash payments	(110)	(100)	(210)
Additions charged to income	72	117	189
Releases credited to income	(5)	(9)	(14)
Reclassifications	6	(1)	5
Translation (gains)/losses net	12	7	19
December 31, 2003	**145**	**117**	**262**

Restructuring provisions and costs relate to business changes which, in the opinion of management, will have a material effect on the nature and focus of Syngenta's operations. For the periods presented they relate mainly to Syngenta's business integration restructuring plans, embarked upon following the formation of Syngenta in November 2000. Such plans involve termination of employees, integration of systems and the closure of duplicate head office, research and development and manufacturing facilities. The merger restructuring plans are due to complete by the end of 2005.

Approximately 3,950 jobs that existed at the formation of Syngenta will be eliminated in respect of plans announced by December 31, 2003, and 3,600 employees had already left the group by that date. Provisions for employee termination costs include severance, pension and other costs directly related to these employees.

Provisions for other third party costs principally include payments for early termination of contracts with third parties related to redundant activities.

The charge to income of US$189 million in 2003 mainly represents:

- The plans announced in June 2003 to restructure Syngenta's HQ functions. These involve a reduction of 140 jobs by the end of 2005. The total cost expected to be incurred is US$52 million, which was recognized in 2003. This largely represents employee termination costs.

- Further restructuring of Syngenta's Crop Protection operations in France, involving a reduction of 80 jobs by the end of 2004. The total cost of the restructuring is US$33 million, of which US$29 million was recognized in 2003 and represents employee termination costs.

- Further restructuring of Crop Protection manufacturing facilities. The cost incurred in 2003 was US$43 million.

- Costs of implementing common business processes and systems. Costs incurred in 2003 were US$28 million.

- Restructuring of research and development, and the transfer to Diversa Corporation of biotechnology research activities, announced by December 2002. Provision for contract termination costs of US$10 million was recognized in 2003.

- Approximately 1,000 employees left Syngenta during 2003 as a result of restructuring initiatives.

The charge to income of US$276 million in 2002 largely represents costs related to further progress in the synergy plans, including plans to close a further four manufacturing sites, and the announced plan to refocus the activities of each of Syngenta's main research and development sites on specific activities and out license certain activities linked to the alliance with Diversa Corporation announced in Quarter 4. Of the total charge to income in 2002, US$49 million of employee termination costs and US$21 million of other third party costs relate to the manufacturing integration plans, and US$53 million of employee termination costs and US$35 million of other third party costs relate to the research and development integration plans. The charge also included employee termination costs of US$4 million relating to restructuring the Seeds business in South Korea.

The charge to income of US$269 million in 2001 arising from the integration of the combined Syngenta businesses represents principally the creation of new organizational structures to replace the previous separate legacy organisations and the plans announced in August 2001 to close certain manufacturing sites and refocus other continuing manufacturing sites.

Although the note refers to 'integration of systems' as being part of the plans, it may appear that such costs have been included in the provision. However, the company's accounting policy included in Extract 25.10 at 5.4.1 below, states that 'Costs relating to the ongoing activities of Syngenta are not recognized until they have been incurred.'

5.2   Operating losses

IAS 37 explicitly states that 'provisions should not be recognised for future operating losses'.[114] This is because such losses do not meet the definition of a liability and the general recognition criteria of the standard (see 3.1 above).[115] Such costs should be left to be reported in the future in the same way as future profits are.

However, it would be wrong to assume that this requirement has effectively prevented any future operating losses from being anticipated, because they are sometimes recognised as a result of requirements in another standard. For example:

- under IAS 2, inventories are written down to the extent that they will not be recovered from future revenues, rather than leaving the non-recovery to show up as future operating losses (see Chapter 21 at 2.2.3);

- under IAS 11 provision is made for losses expected on construction contracts (see Chapter 22 at 2.3.6); and

- under IAS 36, impairment of assets is measured on the basis of the present value of future operating cash flows, meaning that provision will be made not simply for future operating losses but for sub-standard operating profits as well (see Chapter 13 at 3.3.3 B). IAS 37 specifically makes reference to the fact that an expectation of future operating losses may be an indication that certain assets are impaired.[116]

This is therefore a rather more complex issue than IAS 37 acknowledges.

5.3 Onerous contracts

Although future operating losses in general cannot be provided for, IAS 37 requires that 'if an entity has a contract that is onerous, the present obligation under the contract should be recognised and measured as a provision'.[117]

The standard notes that many contracts (for example, some routine purchase orders) can be cancelled without paying compensation to the other party, and therefore there is no obligation. However, other contracts establish both rights and obligations for each of the contracting parties. Where events make such a contract onerous, the contract falls within the scope of the standard and a liability exists which is recognised. As noted at 2.2.1 above, executory contracts that are not onerous fall outside the scope of the standard.[118]

IAS 37 defines an onerous contract as 'a contract in which the unavoidable costs of meeting the obligations under the contract exceed the economic benefits expected to be received under it'.[119] This seems to require that the contract is onerous to the point of being directly loss-making, not simply uneconomic by reference to current prices.

IAS 37 considers that 'the unavoidable costs under a contract reflect the least net cost of exiting from the contract i.e. the lower of the cost of fulfilling it and any compensation or penalties arising from failure to fulfil it'.[120] An example of such a provision was BG's gas contract loss provisions, which stood at £215 million at 31 December 2000, and are described in this extract.

Extract 25.6: BG plc (2000)

22 PROVISIONS FOR LIABILITIES AND CHARGES [extract]

Long-term gas contract loss provisions

These represent forecast future losses under certain gas purchase and supply sales contracts assigned to BG on the demerger of Centrica plc in 1997. Some of the contracts terminated this year, with others due to terminate in 2009. The estimated net losses have been discounted at around 10% and are dependent upon factors such as prices, which vary with a basket of indices, and supply and demand volumes, BG also uses its own gas to supply these contracts. To account for BG's own gas sales and transportation of all gas at the contract prices, the difference between market and contract prices is included within Other activities.

The most common example of an onerous contract in practice probably relates to leasehold property. From time to time entities may hold vacant leasehold property (or property which is only partly occupied) which they have substantially ceased to use for the purpose of their business and where sub-letting is either unlikely, or would be at a significantly reduced rental from that being paid by the entity. This is reinforced by the inclusion of a specific example of a provision for a vacant leasehold property in an appendix to the standard.[121]

Entities have to make systematic provision when such properties become vacant, and on a discounted basis where the effect is sufficiently material. Indeed, it could be argued that it is not just when the properties become vacant that provision would be required, but that provision should be made at the time the expected economic benefits of using the property fall short of the unavoidable costs under the lease. As outlined at 8.1.6 below, the IASB as part of its convergence project with the FASB has tentatively agreed that when a contract becomes onerous as a result of an entity's own actions, the resulting provision should not be recognised until that action has occurred, and has said that in the case of an operating lease on a property that will become vacant as a result of a restructuring, the provision for the unavoidable lease commitment should be recognised only when the entity vacates the property. However, the Board's discussion did not address the situation of an ongoing lease contract that might become onerous, before the entity has taken any specific action in respect of the lease. The IFRIC Agenda Committee recommended that the IFRIC take up this issue, because it was not clear when a provision for an onerous contract should be recognised or how it should be measured. Although the IFRIC had a preliminary discussion about the issue in December 2003, including whether it should be expanded to cover other types of executory contracts such as a take or pay contract, it agreed that the issue should not be taken onto its agenda at that time.[122]

Nevertheless, where a provision is to be recognised a number of difficulties remain. The first is how the provision should be calculated. It is unlikely that the provision will simply be the net present value of the future rental obligation, because if a substantial period of the lease remains, the entity will probably be able either to agree a negotiated sum with the landlord to terminate the lease early, or to sub-lease the building at some point in the future. Hence, the entity will have to make a best estimate of its future cash flows taking all these factors into account.

Another issue that arises from this is whether the provision should be shown net of any cash flows that may arise from sub-leasing the property, or whether the provision must be shown gross, with a corresponding asset set up for expected cash flows from sub-leasing only if they meet the recognition criteria of being 'virtually certain' to be received. The strict offset criteria in the standard (see 4.4 above) would suggest the latter to be required, as the entity would normally retain liability for the full lease payments if the sub-lessor defaulted. However, the standard makes no explicit reference to this issue. One company which on adopting FRS 12 in the UK recognised such provision on a gross basis, with any expected recovery from sub-letting as a corresponding debtor was Thorntons as illustrated below.

Extract 25.7: Thorntons PLC (1999)

8 Prior period adjustment – onerous leases

FRS 12 'Provisions, Contingent Assets and Contingent Liabilities' was adopted with effect from 28 June 1998, and as a result, the comparatives for the period ended 27 June 1998 and the opening balances have been restated to reflect the new guidelines with respect to the recognition of onerous lease obligations.

The effects of adopting this new accounting standard are summarised below:

	1999 £'000	1999 £'000	1998 £'000	1998 £'000
Consolidated profit and loss account:				
Provision created for onerous lease obligations	**(982)**		(3,561)	
Asset created for onerous lease sublet receivables	**180**		105	
		(802)		(3,456)
Provision released on exit from onerous leases		**1,374**		887
Net onerous lease obligations credited/(charged) in the period		**572**		(2,569)
Release of UK restructuring provision		**–**		211
Increase/(decrease) to profit before tax in the financial period		**572**		(2,358)
Taxation		**(172)**		731
Increase/(decrease) to retained profit in the financial period		**400**		(1,627)
Consolidated balance sheet:				
Onerous lease sublet receivables debtor due after more than one year		**1,651**		1,677
Onerous lease sublet receivables debtor due within one year		**190**		140
Corporation tax recoverable on amounts provided		**1,071**		1,243
Onerous lease provision carried forward		**(4,955)**		(5,827)
Decrease to net assets in the financial period		**(2,043)**		(2,767)

24 Provisions for liabilities and charges [extract]

The provision for onerous leases is in respect of closed leasehold properties, from which the Group no longer trades, but is liable to fulfil rent and other property commitments up to the lease expiry date. If a property is sub-let below the head rent, a separate asset has been established and disclosed within debtors. Obligations are payable within a range of one to 18 years, the average being ten years. Amounts have been provided on current rentals which, following a rent review, could require additional provision.

However, the company had a change of heart the following year, adopting a net approach since this was 'best practice' in the UK and restating the comparative information for 1999 in its 2000 financial statements as shown below.

Extract 25.8: Thorntons PLC (2000)

Changes in financial information [extract]

FRS 12 'Provisions, Contingent Assets and Contingent Liabilities' was adopted with effect from 28 June 1998, and reflected in the 1999 Annual Report as a prior period adjustment. Subsequent to those financial statements, in line with best practice we have disclosed the effect of onerous lease provisions as the net impact of the full provision and any sublet receivables provided. We have therefore restated the sublet receivables debtor within provisions as at 26 June 1999.

24 Provisions for liabilities and charges [extract]

	Group and Company Deferred tax £'000	Group and Company Onerous leases £'000	Group and Company UK restructure £'000	Group and Company Total £'000
Summary of provisions				
At 26 June 1999 – as reported	–	4,955	1,480	6,435
Re-disclose onerous lease sublet receivables	–	(1,841)	–	(1,841)
At 26 June 1999 – as restated	–	3,114	1,480	4,594
Accelerated write-down of fixed assets (see note 15)	–	–	(639)	(639)
Expenditure in the period	–	(245)	(841)	(1,086)
Released to the consolidated profit and loss account	–	(1,428)	–	(1,428)
At 24 June 2000	**–**	**1,441**	**–**	**1,441**

The provision for onerous leases is in respect of closed leasehold properties, from which the Group no longer trades, but is liable to fulfil rent and other property commitments up to the lease expiry date. If a property is sublet below the head rent, or for a period shorter than the remaining lease term, an asset has been established for the total sublet receivables. Obligations are payable within a range of one to 17 years (1999: one to 18 years), the average being nine years (1999: ten years). Amounts have been provided on current rentals which, following a rent review, could require additional provision.

We believe that such a net approach is the most appropriate treatment for such onerous contracts under IAS 37. Indeed, it could be argued that the provision is only in respect of the onerous element of the contract and therefore there is no corresponding asset to be recognised. In any event, as indicated at 8.1.6 below, the IASB has decided to specify that if an onerous contract is an operating lease, the provision should be reduced by the sublease rentals that could reasonably be obtained for the property.

In the past, some entities may have maintained that no provision is required for vacant properties, because if the property leases are looked at on a portfolio basis, the overall economic benefits from properties exceed the overall costs. However, this argument does not appear to be sustainable under IAS 37, as the definition of an onerous contract refers specifically to costs and economic benefits *under the contract*.

It is more difficult to apply the definition of onerous contracts to the lease on a head office which is not generating revenue specifically. If the definition were applied too literally, one might end up concluding that all head office leases should be provided against because no specific economic benefits are expected under them. It would be more sensible to conclude that the entity as a whole obtains economic benefits from its head office, which was presumably the reason for entering in to the lease to start with. However, this does not alter the fact that if circumstances change and the head office becomes vacant, a provision should then be made against the lease.

IAS 37 requires that any impairment loss that has occurred in respect of assets dedicated to an onerous contract is recognised before establishing a provision for the onerous contract.[123] For example, any leasehold improvements that have been capitalised should be written off before provision is made for excess future rental costs.

One company which has provided for onerous leases under IAS 37 is Jardine Matheson as indicated by the following extract.

Extract 25.9: Jardine Matheson Holdings Limited (2003)

Principal Accounting Policies [extract]

Provisions

Provisions are recognized when the Group has present legal or constructive obligations as a result of past events, it is probable that an outflow of resources embodying economic benefits will be required to settle the obligations, and a reliable estimate of the amount of the obligations can be made.

23   Provisions

	Motor vehicle warranties US$m	Closure cost provisions US$m	Obligations under onerous leases US$m	Others US$m	Total US$m
At 1st January 2003	33	9	20	7	69
Exchange differences	4	1	2	–	7
Additional provisions	13	9	1	21	44
Disposals	(13)	–	–	–	(13)
Unused amounts reversed	(7)	(3)	(1)	–	(11)
Utilized	(10)	(4)	(1)	(4)	(19)
At 31st December 2003	**20**	**12**	**21**	**24**	**77**
Current	14	12	15	24	65
Non-current	6	–	6	–	12
	20	**12**	**21**	**24**	**77**

Motor vehicle warranties are estimated liabilities that fall due under the warranty terms offered on sale of new and used vehicles beyond that which is reimbursed by the manufacturers.

Closure cost provisions are established when legal or constructive obligations arise on closure or disposal of business.

Provisions are made for obligations under onerous operating leases when the properties are not used by the Group and the net costs of exiting from the leases exceed the economic benefits expected to be received.

Other provisions comprise provisions in respect of indemnities on disposal of businesses, lease dilapidations and legal claims.

5.4   Other types of provisions

IAS 37 also deals with other types of situations where provisions may or may not have been made in the past. Although the standard does not include particular requirements about such items, it has either included an example in an appendix dealing with such situations or has mentioned them in passing while discussing the general recognition requirements of the standard. These, together with other situations discussed in FRS 12 in the UK, are dealt with below.

5.4.1   *Environmental provisions*

The standard illustrates two examples of circumstances where environmental provisions would be required. The first deals with the situation where it is virtually certain that legislation will be enacted which will require the clean up of land already contaminated.[124] In these circumstances, a provision would obviously be required. However, in its discussion about what constitutes an obligating event, the standard notes that 'differences in circumstances surrounding enactment make it impossible to specify a single event that would make the enactment of a law virtually certain. In many cases, it will be impossible to be virtually certain of the enactment of a law until it is enacted.'[125] The second example deals with the situation where an entity has contaminated land, but is not legally required to clean it up.[126] In these circumstances, a provision is required if the entity has a constructive obligation to clean up the land. In the example given, a constructive obligation is said to exist because the entity has a widely publicised environmental policy undertaking to clean up all contamination that it causes, and has a record of honouring this policy.

These requirements are not particularly controversial, apart from the general difficulty in knowing exactly when a constructive obligation comes into existence.

One company which makes provision for environmental costs is Syngenta as shown below.

Extract 25.10: Syngenta AG (2003)

2.   Accounting policies [extract]

Provisions

A provision is recognized in the balance sheet when Syngenta has a legal or constructive obligation as a result of a past event and it is probable that an outflow of economic benefits will be required to settle the obligation. If the effect of discounting is material, provisions are determined by discounting the expected value of future cash flows at a pre-tax rate that reflects current market assessments of the time value of money and, where appropriate, the risks specific to the liability. Where some or all of the expenditure required to settle a provision is expected to be reimbursed by another party, the reimbursement is recognized only when reimbursement is virtually certain. The amount to be reimbursed is recognized as a separate asset. Where Syngenta has a joint and several liability with one or more other parties, no provision is recognized to the extent that those other parties are expected to settle part or all of the obligation.

Environmental provisions

Syngenta is exposed to environmental liabilities relating to its past operations, principally in respect of remediation costs. Provisions for non-recurring remediation costs are made when there is a present obligation, it is probable that expense on remediation work will be required within ten years (or a longer period if specified by a legal obligation) and the cost can be estimated within a reasonable range of possible outcomes. The costs are based on currently available facts; technology expected to be available at the time of the clean-up, laws and regulations presently or virtually certain to be enacted and prior experience in remediation of contaminated sites. Environmental liabilities are recorded at the estimated amount at which the liability could be settled at the balance sheet date.

Restructuring provisions

A provision for restructuring is recognized when Syngenta has approved a detailed and formal restructuring plan and the restructuring has either commenced or been announced publicly. Costs relating to the ongoing activities of Syngenta are not recognized until they have been incurred.

21. Provisions

(US$ million)	2003	2002	2001
Environmental provisions (Note 29)	381	381	355

The following table analyzes the movement in provisions during 2003:

(US$ million)	Balance at January 1, 2003	Charged to income	Release of provisions credited to income	Payments	Reclass-ifications	Translation effects	Balance at December 31, 2003
Environmental provisions (Note 29)	381	35	(1)	(55)	(1)	22	381

29. Commitments and contingencies [extract]
Environmental Matters

Syngenta has environment liabilities at some currently or formerly owned, leased and third party sites throughout the world.

In the USA, Syngenta, or its indemnities, has been named under federal legislation (the Comprehensive Environmental Response, Compensation and Liability Act of 1980, as amended) as a potentially responsible party ("PRP") in respect of several sites. Syngenta expects to be indemnified against a proportion of the liabilities associated with a number of these sites by the seller of the businesses associated with such sites and, where appropriate, actively participates in or monitors the clean-up activities at the sites in respect of which it is a PRP.

Syngenta has provisions in respect of environmental remediation costs in accordance with the accounting policy described in Note 2 and as shown in Note 21, Provisions. The environmental provision is principally related to potential liabilities at various locations. The estimated provision takes into consideration the number of other PRPs at each site and the identity and financial positions of such parties in light of the joint and several nature of the liability.

The requirement in the future for Syngenta ultimately to take action to correct the effects on the environment of prior disposal or release of chemical substances by Syngenta or other parties, and its costs, pursuant to environment laws and regulations, is inherently difficult to estimate. The material components of the environmental provisions consist of a risk assessment based on investigation of the various sites. Syngenta's future remediation expenses are affected by a number of uncertainties which include, but are not limited to, the method and extent of remediation, the percentage of material attributable to Syngenta at the remediation sites relative to that attributable to other parties, and the financial capabilities of the other potentially responsible parties. It is not possible to estimate the amounts expected to be recovered via reimbursement, indemnification or insurance due to the uncertainty inherent in this area.

Syngenta believes that its provisions are adequate based upon currently available information. However, given the inherent difficulties in estimating liabilities in this area, it cannot be guaranteed that additional costs will not be incurred beyond the amounts accrued. The effect of resolution of environmental matters on results of operations cannot be predicted due to uncertainty concerning both the amount and the timing of future expenditures and the results of future operations. Management believes that such additional amounts, if any, would not be material to Syngenta's financial condition but could be material to Syngenta's results of operations in a given period.

Potentially, the more significant effect of the standard is its requirement that provisions should be discounted, which will have a material impact if the expenditure is not expected to be incurred for some time. As a result of implementing FRS 12 in the UK, BP (then BP Amoco) changed its policy to reflect this, which had the effect of reducing its environmental provision by £350 million because of the discount factor, and its current policy is as shown in the following extract.

Extract 25.11: BP plc (2003)

Accounting policies [extract]

Environment liabilities

Environmental expenditures that relate to current or future revenues are expensed or capitalized as appropriate. Expenditures that relate to an existing condition caused by past operations and that do not contribute to current or future earnings are expensed.

Liabilities for environmental costs are recognized when environmental assessments or clean-ups are probable and the associated costs can be reasonably estimated. Generally, the timing of these provisions coincides with the commitment to a formal plan of action or, if earlier, on divestment or on closure of inactive sites. The amount recognized is the best estimate of the expenditure required. Where the liability will not be settled for a number of years the amount recognized is the present value of the estimated future expenditure.

29 Other provisions [extract]		$ million
	Decommissioning	**Environmental**
At 1 January 2003	4,168	2,122
Exchange adjustments	257	28
New provisions	1,159	515
Unwinding of discount	107	46
Utilized/deleted	(971)	(413)
At 31 December 2003	**4,720**	**2,298**

The group makes full provision for the future cost of decommissioning oil and natural gas production facilities and related pipelines on a discounted basis on the installation of those facilities. At 31 December 2003, the provision for the costs of decommissioning these production facilities and pipelines at the end of their economic lives was $4,720 million ($4,168 million). The provision has been estimated using existing technology, at current prices and discounted using a real discount rate of 2.5% (2.5%). These costs are expected to be incurred over the next 30 years. While the provision is based on the best estimate of future costs and the economic lives of the facilities and pipelines, there is uncertainty regarding both the amount and timing of incurring these costs.

Provisions for environmental remediation are made when a clean-up is probable and the amount reasonably determinable. Generally, this coincides with commitment to a formal plan of action or, if earlier, on divestment or closure of inactive sites. The provision for environment liabilities at 31 December 2003 was $2,298 million ($2,122 million). The provision has been estimated using existing technology, at current prices and discounted using a real discount rate of 2.5% (2.5%). These costs are expected to be incurred over the next 10 years. The extent and cost of future remediation programmes are inherently difficult to estimate. They depend on the scale of any possible contamination, the timing and extent of corrective actions, and also the group's share of liability.

5.4.2 Decommissioning provisions

Decommissioning costs are those that arise, for example, when an oil rig or nuclear power station has to be dismantled at the end of its life.[127] The impact of the standard on such costs is profound.

Prior to the issue of IAS 37, previous practice was to build up the required provision over the life of the facility by appropriate charges against revenues. IAS 37, on the other hand, requires that the liability is recognised as soon as the obligation exists, which will normally be at commencement of operations.

The accounting for decommissioning costs is dealt with in IAS 37 by way of an example in an appendix. The example discusses the situation where ninety per cent of the damage is done by building the rig, and ten per cent through the extraction of oil.[128] In these circumstances, a provision for ninety per cent of the total costs will be set up when the rig has been constructed, with the balance being recognised as the oil is extracted. This example requires that an entity should recognise a liability as soon as the decommissioning obligation is created, which is normally when the facility is constructed and the damage that needs to be restored is done. The total decommissioning cost is estimated, discounted to its present value and it is this amount which forms the initial provision and is added to the corresponding asset's cost. Thereafter, the asset is depreciated over its useful life, while the discounted provision is progressively unwound, with the unwinding charge showing as a borrowing cost.

Although we understand why the IASB's *Framework* pushes it towards recognition of the full liability, it seems that this can only be achieved by including a spurious asset on the other side of the balance sheet. In any case, if the principle that a liability should be recognised once costs have become unavoidable were really to be applied on a consistent basis, various other commitments (for example, expenditure commitments under licence agreements) would also be caught and there would be considerable grossing up of balance sheets. We therefore question whether this change introduced by IAS 37 has much merit.

The more significant change for most entities, however, involved the use of discounting for the measurement of the liability. Although it had been used for some time in the nuclear industry, discounting was not consistent with previous accounting practice for oil companies. The effect of discounting on the income statement is to split the cost of the eventual decommissioning into two components: an operating cost based on the discounted amount of the provision; and a finance element representing the unwinding of the discount. The overall effect is to produce a rising pattern of cost over the life of the facility, often with much of the total cost of the decommissioning recognised as a finance cost. In contrast, previous practice for oil companies was to show the whole amount in arriving at their operating results, and to aim to charge a level amount for each barrel of oil extracted, although the effects of changing estimates of costs, particularly inflation (which was not factored into the original estimates made), meant that this was not precisely achieved.

One company affected by these requirements was AngloGold, which explained the restatement of its prior year figures as a result of implementing IAS 37 in its 1999 financial statements as follows:

Extract 25.12: AngloGold Limited (1999)

Restatement of prior year

The group has adopted International Accounting Standard No. 37 (IAS 37) "Provisions, contingent liabilities and contingent assets" with effect from 1 January 1998, prior to the effective date of this statement. In accordance with IAS 37, full provision has been made for the group's estimated future decommissioning costs. Previously the provision for environmental rehabilitation had been built up on a units of production basis over the life of a mine.

A decommissioning asset has now been recognised in respect of the net present value of future decommissioning costs and is amortised using the units of production method over the life of a mine.

The decommissioning obligation is unwound over the life of the mine and included in the income statement.

Estimated restoration costs are accrued and expensed over the operating life of a mine using the units-of-production method.

The implementation of IAS 37 had no unfavourable effect on the current year's income statement, when compared to the rehabilitation provision raised in accordance with the previous policy and the prior year adjustment is disclosed below:

SA Rands	Decom-missioning assets	Accumulated amortisation	Decom-missioning obligation	Restoration obligation	Environ-mental Rehabilitation	Retained earnings
As at 31 December 1997 as previously reported inclusive of merger adjustment	–	–	–	–	551.4	1,279.6
Adjustment in respect of adoption of IAS 37	196.9	130.7	196.9	354.5	(551.4)	66.2
As restated at 31 December 1997	196.9	130.7	196.9	354.5	–	1,345.8

AngloGold's accounting policies and provisions note in respect of decommissioning obligations and restoration obligations are shown in the following extract from its 2003 financial statements:

Extract 25.13: AngloGold Limited (2003)

1.   Accounting policies [extract]

Provisions

Provisions are recognised when the group has a present obligation, whether legal or constructive, as a result of a past event for which it is probable that an outflow of resources embodying economic benefits will be required to settle the obligation and a reliable estimate can be made of the amount of the obligation.

Environmental expenditure

Long-term environmental obligations comprising decommissioning and restoration are based on the group's environmental management plans, in compliance with the current environmental and regulatory requirements.

Decommissioning costs

The provision for decommissioning represents the cost that will arise from rectifying damage caused before production commenced.

Decommissioning costs are provided at the present value of the expenditures expected to settle the obligation, using estimated cash flows based on current prices. When this provision gives access to future economic benefits, an asset is recognised and included within mining infrastructure. The unwinding of the decommissioning obligation is included in the income statement. The estimated future costs of decommissioning obligations are regularly reviewed and adjusted as appropriate for new circumstances or changes in law or technology. The estimates are discounted at a pre-tax rate that reflects current market assessments of the time value of money.

Gains from the expected disposal of assets are not taken into account when determining the provision.

Restoration costs

The provision for restoration represents the cost of restoring site damage after the commencement of production. Increases in the provision are charged to the income statement as a cost of production.

Gross restoration costs are estimated at the present value of the expenditures expected to settle the obligation, using estimated cash flows based on current prices. The estimates are discounted at a pre-tax rate that reflects current market assessments of the time value of money.

Restoration costs are accrued and expensed over the operating life of each mine using the units-of-production method based on estimated proved and probable mineral reserves. Expenditure on ongoing restoration costs is brought to account when incurred.

Environmental Rehabilitation Trust

Annual contributions are made to the AngloGold Environmental Rehabilitation Trust, created in accordance with South African statutory requirements, to fund the estimated cost of rehabilitation during and at the end of the life of a mine. The funds that have been paid into the trust fund plus the growth in the trust fund are shown as an asset on the balance sheet.

The environmental rehabilitation obligations in respect of the non-South African operations are not funded through an established trust fund. Bank guarantees and reclamation bonds are provided for some of these liabilities.

Figures in million	2003	2002
	US Dollars	
29. Provisions [extract]		
Environmental rehabilitation obligations		
Provision for decommissioning		
Balance at beginning of year	47	44
Acquisition and disposals (note 34)	(4)	(10)
Change in estimates	–	1
Unwinding of decommissioning obligation (note 7)	4	4
Reversal of over-provision (note 9)	(7)	–
Translation	9	8
Balance at end of year	49	47
Provision for restoration		
Balance at beginning of year	93	90
Acquisition and disposals (note 34)	(21)	(16)
Reversal of over-provision (note 9)	(7)	–
Charge to income statement	12	15
Change in estimates	1	1
Less: Utilised during the year	(5)	(4)
Translation	11	7
Balance at end of year	84	93

It can be seen from the above extract that AngloGold has made a distinction between decommissioning costs and restoration costs. The former are provided in full at the point of creating the damage and a corresponding asset created, whereas the latter costs are being provided over the life of the mine using a unit-of-production method (which is the method that had been used for all of the environmental costs prior to IAS 37 as shown in Extract 25.12 above). This is presumably because the costs of restoring the damage caused by extracting the minerals from the mine at any balance sheet date is proportional to the overall restoration costs once the mine is at the end of its life.

As noted at 4.6 above, the standard requires provisions to be revised annually to reflect the current best estimate of the provision. However, the standard gives no guidance on accounting for changes in the decommissioning provision. Similarly, IAS 16 is unclear about the extent to which an item's carrying amount should be affected by changes in the estimated amount of dismantling and site restoration costs that occur *after* the estimate made upon initial measurement. This has now been addressed by the IASB with the publication of IFRIC 1 in May 2004.

A   IFRIC 1 – Changes in existing decommissioning, restoration and similar liabilities

IFRIC 1 applies to any decommissioning or similar liability that has been both included as part of an asset measured in accordance with IAS 16 and measured as a liability in accordance with IAS 37.[129] It deals with how the effect of the following events that change the measurement of an existing decommissioning, restoration or similar liability should be accounted for:[130]

(a)   a change in the estimated outflow of resources embodying economic benefits (e.g. cash flows) required to settle the obligation;

(b)   a change in the current market-based discount rate (this includes changes in the time value of money and the risks specific to the liability); and

(c)   an increase that reflects the passage of time (also referred to as the unwinding of the discount).

IFRIC 1 requires that (c) above, the periodic unwinding of the discount, is recognised in profit or loss as a finance cost as it occurs.[131] IFRIC concluded that the unwinding of the discount is not a borrowing cost as defined in IAS 23, and thus cannot be capitalised under the allowed alternative treatment of capitalisation under that standard (see Chapter 14).[132]

For a change caused by (a) or (b) above, however, the adjustment is not taken to the income statement as it occurs, but added to or deducted from the cost of the asset to which it relates; the adjusted depreciable amount of the asset is then depreciated prospectively over its remaining useful life. The specific requirements differentiate between the treatment of the related assets depending on whether they are accounted for under the cost or valuation model under IAS 16,[133] and are discussed further in Chapter 12 at 2.3.1 A.

As indicated at 4.2.5 above, IAS 37 is unclear whether a new discount rate should be applied during the year or just at the year-end, and whether the rate should be applied to the new estimate of the provision or the old estimate. Although IFRIC 1 requires that changes in the provision resulting from a change in the discount rate is added to, or deducted from, the cost of the related asset in the current period, it does not deal specifically with these points and none of the illustrative examples to IFRIC 1 include a change in discount rate. However, since other changes affecting the estimate of a provision for decommissioning, restoration and similar liabilities are reflected as a change in the liability at the time the revised estimate is made, then it would appear that a change in the discount rate would also only be applied at that time, and thus the revised discount rate would be applied to the new estimate of the provision from that point on.

IFRIC 1 applies to annual periods beginning on or after 1 September 2004. Earlier application is encouraged. If an entity applies the interpretation for a period beginning before 1 September 2004, it must disclose that it has done so.[134]

Any changes in measurement as a result of implementing the interpretation are changes in accounting policies to be accounted for in accordance with IAS 8. If an entity applies IFRIC 1 for a period beginning before 1 January 2005, it must follow the requirements of the previous version of IAS 8, which was entitled *Net Profit or Loss for the Period, Fundamental Errors and Changes in Accounting Policies*, unless the entity is applying the revised version of IAS 8 as at that earlier period.[135]

B   Decommissioning funds

Some entities (for example, see Extract 25.13 above) may participate in a decommissioning fund, the purpose of which is to segregate assets to fund some or all of the costs of its decommissioning or environmental liabilities for which the entity has to make a provision under IAS 37. The issues that this gives rise to are:

(a)   How should a contributor account for its interest in a fund?

(b)   When a contributor has an obligation to make additional contributions, for example, in the event of the bankruptcy of another contributor, how should that obligation be accounted for?

These are being addressed by the IFRIC, and in January 2004, it issued a draft interpretation D4 to deal with this issue. This is discussed further at 8.3 below.

5.4.3   Cyclical repairs

This is another area which is dealt with by way of examples in an appendix, both dealing with cyclical refurbishment costs. The examples it gives are of a furnace that has a lining that needs replacing every five years, and an aircraft that needs overhauling every three years.[136] Neither of these provisions is allowed to be set up on the basis that there is no obligation to carry out the expenditure independently of the entity's future actions. This argument is used even in the circumstances where there is a legal requirement for the asset in question to be repaired, since it is asserted that, even then, the entity could avoid the expenditure by, for example, selling the asset. (It is unclear why a similar argument has not been used in respect of decommissioning costs, where presumably an entity could avoid such costs by selling its oil and gas assets!)

The effect of this prohibition on setting up provisions for repairs obviously impacts on balance sheet presentation. It may not always, however, have as much impact on the income statement. This is because it is suggested that depreciation might be adjusted to take account of the repairs. For example, in the case of the furnace lining, the lining should be depreciated over five years in advance of its expected repair. Similarly, in the case of the aircraft overhaul, the example in the standard suggests that an amount equivalent to the expected maintenance costs is depreciated over three years. The result of this is that the overall charge to the income statement that will now arise from depreciation may be equivalent to that which would previously have arisen from the combination of depreciation and provision for repair.

One company which had to change its policy as a result of this requirement is Kemira as shown by the following extract from its 1999 financial statements when it implemented IAS 37.

Extract 25.14: Kemira Oyj (1999)

SUMMARY OF SIGNIFICANT ACCOUNTING POLICIES [extract]

Large, seldom performed maintenance works

Large, seldom performed maintenance works are treated as a capital expenditure as from 1999 and acquisition costs are depreciated over their useful lifetimes (IAS 37). Previously, provisions for expenses were booked for them in advance. The effect of the change on net income and shareholders' equity is stated in Note 16.

16. SHAREHOLDERS' EQUITY [extract]

The change in accounting principles includes a charge of EUR 9.2 million for the deferred tax liability on revaluations (IAS 12) in 1998, and an increase in equity of EUR 18.6 million after taxes for the change in accounting policy for major maintenance works (IAS 37). The change in accounting policy for maintenance works, after tax, was a charge of EUR 0.1 million in the income statement in 1999.

5.4.4   Dilapidation and other provisions relating to leased assets

The requirements discussed above relate to repairs and maintenance of owned assets (including assets held under finance leases). Operating leases often contain clauses which specify that the tenant should incur periodic charges for maintenance or make good dilapidations or other damage occurring during the rental period. Hence, some entities in the past have built up a provision over the life of the lease for costs of repair and renovation of the property.

The question arises as to whether such a provision meets the recognition criteria in the standard. The issue, whilst not addressed in IAS 37 itself, is mentioned briefly in the appendix to FRS 12 in the UK in discussing the development of that standard. This notes that 'the principle illustrated in [the example on repairs] does not preclude the recognition of such liabilities once the event giving rise to the obligation under the lease has occurred'.[137] Since the repair examples in IAS 37 are the same as those in FRS 12, then we believe that the same comment should also apply to IAS 37.

This means that a provision for specific damage done to the property would meet the criteria, as the event giving rise to the obligation under the lease has certainly occurred. For example, if an entity has erected partitioning or internal walls and under the lease these have to be removed at the end of the lease, then provision should be made for this cost (on a discounted basis, if material) at the time of putting up the partitioning or the walls. In this case, an equivalent asset would be created and depreciated over the term of the lease. This is similar to a decommissioning provision discussed at 5.4.2 above.

What is less clear is whether a more general provision can be built up over time for maintenance charges and dilapidation costs. It could be argued that in this case, the event giving rise to the obligation under the lease is simply the passage of time, and so a provision can be built up over time. However, a stricter interpretation of the phrase 'the event giving rise to the obligation under the lease' may lead one to conclude that a more specific event has to occur; there has to be specific evidence of dilapidation etc before any provision can be made.

The fact that provision for repairs can be made at all in these circumstances might appear inconsistent with the circumstances where the asset is owned by the entity. In these circumstances, as discussed in 5.4.3 above, no provision for repairs could be made. There is, however, a difference between the two cases. Where the entity owns the asset, it has the choice of selling it rather than repairing it, and so the obligation is not independent of the entity's future actions. However, in the case of an entity leasing the asset, it has a legal obligation to repair any damage from which it cannot walk away.

Extract 25.9 at 5.3 above, shows an example of a company that has provided for dilapidation costs.

5.4.5 Warranty provisions

Warranty provisions are specifically addressed in one of the examples appended to IAS 37, which concludes that such provisions are appropriate.[138] The example deals with a manufacturer that gives warranties at the time of sale of its product. Under the terms of contract for sale the manufacturer undertakes to make good, by repair or replacement, manufacturing defects that become apparent within 3 years from the date of sale. On past experience, it is probable (i.e. more likely than not) that there will be some claims under the warranties. The obligating event giving rise to the legal obligation is the sale of the product on which the warranty is given. We concur with this view, although in practice considerations of materiality may sometimes permit it to be treated on a pay-as-you-go basis.

As noted in 4.1 above, the standard makes it clear that where there are a number of similar obligations, the probability that an economic outflow will occur is based on the class of obligations as a whole. Hence, the probability of an economic outflow occurring for warranties as a whole will need to be evaluated. If this probability exceeds 50% (which seems very likely), then the expected value of the estimated warranty costs should be calculated and provided for. IAS 37 discusses this method of 'expected value' and illustrates how it is calculated in an example of a warranty provision.[139]

An example of a company that makes a warranty provision is Nokia as shown below.

Extract 25.15: Nokia Corporation (2003)

1.   Accounting principles [extract]

Provisions [extract]

Provisions are recognized when the Group has a present legal or constructive obligation as a result of past events, it is probable that an out-flow of resources will be required to settle the obligation and a reliable estimate of the amount can be made. Where the Group expects a provision to be reimbursed, the reimbursement would be recognized as an asset but only when the reimbursement is virtually certain.

The Group recognizes the estimated liability to repair or replace products still under warranty at the balance sheet date. The provision is calculated based on historical experience of the level of repairs and replacements.

5.4.6   Litigation and other legal claims

IAS 37 includes an example of a court case in its appendix to illustrate how its principles for recognising a provision should be applied in such situations.[140] However, the assessment of the particular case is clear-cut. In most situations, assessing the need to provide for legal claims is one of the most difficult tasks in the field of provisioning. This is due mainly to the inherent uncertainty in the judicial process itself, which may be very long and drawn out. Furthermore, this is an area where either provision or disclosure might risk prejudicing the outcome of the case, because they give an insight into the entity's own view on the strength of its defence that can assist the claimant. Similar considerations apply in other related areas, such as tax disputes.

In principle, whether a provision should be made will depend on whether the 3 conditions for recognising a provision are met, i.e.

(a)   there is a present obligation as a result of a past event;

(b)   it is probable that an outflow of resources embodying economic benefits will be required to settle the obligation; and

(c)   a reliable estimate can be made of the amount of the obligation.[141]

As noted at 3.1.1 above, in situations such as these, a past event is deemed to give rise to a present obligation if, taking account of all available evidence (including, for example, the opinion of experts), it is more likely than not that a present obligation exists at the balance sheet date. The evidence to be considered includes any additional evidence occurring after the balance sheet date. Accordingly, if on the basis of the evidence it is concluded that a present obligation is more likely than not to exist, a provision will be required, assuming the other conditions are met.

Condition (b) will be met if the transfer of economic benefits is more likely than not to occur, that is, it has a probability greater than 50%. In making this assessment, it is likely that account should be taken of any expert advice.

As far as condition (c) is concerned, as noted at 3.1.3 above, the standard takes the view that a reasonable estimate can generally be made and it is only in extremely rare cases that this will not be the case.

Clearly, whether an entity should make provision for the costs of settling a case or to meet any award given by a court will depend on a reasoned assessment of the particular circumstances, based on appropriate legal advice.

5.4.7   Refunds policy

An example is given in the appendix of IAS 37 of a retail store that has a policy of refunding goods returned by dissatisfied customers. There is no legal obligation to do so, but the company's policy of making refunds is generally known.[142]

The example argues that the conduct of the store has created a valid expectation on the part of its customers that the store will refund purchases. The obligating event is the original sale of the item, and the probability of some economic outflow is greater than 50%, as there will nearly always be some customers demanding refunds. Hence, a provision should be made, presumably calculated again on the 'expected value' basis (see 4.1 above).

This example is straightforward when the store has a very specific and highly publicised policy on refunds. However, some stores' policies on refunds might not be so clear cut. A store may offer refunds under certain circumstances, but not widely publicise its policy. In these circumstances, it is likely to be open to interpretation as to whether the store has created a valid expectation on the part of its customers that the store will refund purchases.

5.4.8   Staff training costs

IAS 37 gives an example of the government introducing changes to the income tax system, such that an entity in the financial services sector needs to retrain a large proportion of its administrative and sales workforce in order to ensure continued compliance with financial services regulation. At the balance sheet date no retraining has taken place.[143]

The standard argues that the obligating event is the staff retraining, and since at the year end no training has taken place, there is no obligating event, and so no provision should be made. We agree with this outcome, but the reasoning behind it seems fragile. This example again seems to illustrate the subjectivity of the concepts of 'constructive obligations' and 'obligating events'. Another interpretation of the position could be that the entity has a constructive obligation to retrain its sales force, as it has built up a valid expectation in its employees and customers that the sales force will be up to date on changes to the income tax system which affect the products it sells, to enable it to adequately meet the needs of its customers. If this approach were taken, a provision would be required. The argument could be strengthened if the entity had published some sort of policy statement reassuring employees and customers that the sales force would receive adequate training on the income tax changes.

A counter argument might be that the standard states that an entity can only provide for obligations which are independent of the entity's future actions. Hence, in this case, the entity can avoid the costs of staff training by changing its method of operation and no longer selling certain products to customers. However, this argument does not help in distinguishing staff training costs from provisions for refunds, which are required to be made. After all, the customer in the example on refunds has no legal right to a refund. The entity could refuse, but presumably would not because of the bad publicity and loss of goodwill that would be suffered. Similarly, in this example, the sales force could cease selling certain financial products, but would not do so because it would lose customers.

In reality, the distinction between the two examples comes down to when the benefits are obtained in each case, not whether the entity has a liability at the year-end. In the case of the refund policy, the revenue from the sale has already been booked, so any reversal of it should be recognised. However, in the case of staff training, the benefits of the training will be the impact on future sales, so it is not appropriate to provide for the costs of training in advance. This dimension of revenue and expense recognition is not acknowledged in the standard, but it does seem to underlie a number of the conclusions that are reached.

5.4.9   Self insurance

Another situation where entities have sometimes made provisions is self insurance which arises when an entity decides not to take out external insurance in respect of a certain category of risk because it would be uneconomic to do so. The same position may arise when a group insures its risks with a captive insurance subsidiary, the effects of which have to be eliminated on consolidation. This is the only situation illustrated in the examples in FRS 12 in the UK where there is no equivalent example in IAS 37.

The example in FRS 12 considers the question of whether provision can be made for the amount expected to arise in a normal year. The conclusion reached is that no such provision can be made, as the entity does not have a present obligation for this amount.[144] Instead, it should recognise the reality of the situation – that it is uninsured – and report losses based on their actual incidence, rather than smoothing them from period to period by reference to a simulated insurance premium that it has not in fact paid. As a result, any provisions that appear in the balance sheet should reflect only the amounts expected to be paid in respect of those losses that have occurred by the balance sheet date.

In fact, however, the example is somewhat misleading, since it deals with a very basic case where it is known with certainty at the time of preparing the financial statements that no losses have arisen in the period. In real life, a provision will often be needed not simply for known incidents, but also for those which insurance companies call IBNR – Incurred But Not Reported – representing an estimate of the latent liabilities at the year end that experience shows will come to the surface only gradually. We believe that it is entirely appropriate that provision for such expected claims is made.

6 DISCLOSURE REQUIREMENTS

6.1 Provisions

For each class of provision an entity should disclose a reconciliation of the carrying amount of the provision at the beginning and end of the period showing:

(a)   additional provisions made in the period, including increases to existing provisions;

(b)   amounts used, i.e. incurred and charged against the provision, during the period;

(c)   unused amounts reversed during the period; and

(d)   the increase during the period in the discounted amount arising from the passage of time and the effect of any change in the discount rate.

Comparative information is not required.[145]

Disclosure (d) effectively requires the charge for discounting that is recognised in the income statement to be split between the element that relates to the straightforward unwinding of the discount, and any further charge or credit that arises if discount rates have changed during the period. It is interesting that there is no specific requirement to disclose the discount rate used.

One of the important disclosures which is reinforced here is the requirement to disclose the release of provisions found to be unnecessary. This disclosure, along with the requirement in the standard that provisions should be used only for the purpose for which the provision was originally recognised, is designed to prevent entities from concealing expenditure by charging it against a provision that was set up for another purpose.

In addition, for each class of provision an entity should disclose the following:

(a)   a brief description of the nature of the obligation and the expected timing of any resulting outflows of economic benefits;

(b)   an indication of the uncertainties about the amount or timing of those outflows. Where necessary to provide adequate information, an entity should disclose the major assumptions made concerning future events, as addressed in paragraph 48 of the standard (discussed at 4.3 above). This refers to future developments in technology and legislation and is of particular relevance to environmental liabilities; and

(c)   the amount of any expected reimbursement, stating the amount of any asset that has been recognised for that expected reimbursement.[146]

Appendix D to the standard provides examples of suitable disclosures in relation to warranties and decommissioning costs.

Most of the above disclosures are illustrated in the extract below.

Extract 25.16: Roche Holding Ltd (2003)

29.   Provisions and contingent liabilities (in millions of CHF)

	Environmental and legal provisions	Restructuring provisions	Other provisions	2003 Total	2002 Total
At beginning of year	2,110	523	227	**2,860**	3,967
Chugai	–	–	–	**–**	12
Other changes in Group organisation	(3)	(12)	15	**–**	–
Vitamin case					
- additional provision created	–	–	–	**–**	1,770
- utilised during the year	(638)	–	–	**(638)**	(3,266)
Major legal cases					
- additional provisions created	–	–	–	**–**	778
- unused amounts reversed	(108)	–	–	**(108)**	–
- utilised during the year	(25)	–	–	**(25)**	–
Other provisions					
- additional provisions created	84	125	96	**305**	398
- unused amounts reversed	(37)	(41)	(21)	**(99)**	(92)
- unutilised during the year	(17)	(159)	(50)	**(226)**	(475)
Increase in discounted amount due to passage of time or change in discount rate	89	7	–	**96**	152
Currency translation effects and other	(143)	–	(10)	**(153)**	(384)
At end of year	1,312	443	257	**2,012**	2,860
Of which					
- Current portion of provisions	256	187	99	**542**	1,158
- Non-current portions of provisions	1,056	256	158	**1,470**	1,702
Total provisions	1,312	443	257	**2,012**	2,860
Expected outflow of resources					
Within one year	256	187	99	**542**	1,158
Between one to two years	943	134	90	**1,167**	556
Between two to three years	17	56	15	**88**	944
Over three years	96	66	53	**215**	202
Total provisions	1,312	443	257	**2,012**	2,860

Environmental and legal provisions

These provisions include 208 million Swiss francs (2002: 179 million Swiss francs) for environmental matters and 1,104 million Swiss francs (2002: 1,931 million Swiss francs) for litigation, including major legal cases and the vitamin case.

Provisions for environmental matters cover various separate environmental issues in a number of countries. Approximately half of these were pre-existing in companies acquired by the Group. The Group has recorded additional environmental provisions in respect of certain indemnities given to DSM in respect of any remedial actions at the sites of the VFC business (see Note 7). By their nature the amounts and timing of any outflows are difficult to predict. The Group estimates that approximately half of the amount provided for may result in cash outflows over the next five years. Significant provisions are discounted by between 4% and 7%.

Restructuring provisions

These arise from planned programmes that materially change the scope of business undertaken by the Group or the manner in which business is conducted. Such provisions include only the costs necessarily entailed by the restructuring which are not associated with the on-going activities of the Group. Expected outflows in 2004 include the remaining 28 million Swiss francs relating to the restructuring of Disetronic and 231 million Swiss francs relating to closure costs that are part of the Pharmaceuticals Division restructuring announced in 2001. The remaining amounts are mostly in respect of obligations towards former employees arising from the Pharmaceuticals Division restructuring and other previous restructuring plans. The timings of these cash outflows are reasonably certain on a global basis and are shown in the above table. Significant provisions are discounted by 4%.

Other provisions

Other provision consist mostly of claims arising from trade and various other provisions from Group companies that do not fit into the above categories. The timings of cash outflows are by their nature uncertain and the best estimates are shown in the above table. These provisions are not discounted as the time value of money is not considered material in this case.

Contingent liabilities

The operations and earnings of the Group continue, from time to time and in varying degrees, to be affected by political, legislative, fiscal and regulatory developments, including those relating to environmental protection, in the countries in which it operates. The industries in which the Group is engaged are also subject to physical risks of various kinds. The nature and frequency of these developments and events, not all of which are covered by insurance, as well as their effect on future operations and earnings are not predictable. See also Note 7 in respect of the vitamin case and Note 8 in respect of major legal cases.

The Group has entered into strategic alliances with various companies in order to gain access to potential new products or to utilise other companies to help develop the Group's own potential new products. Potential future payments may become due to certain collaboration partners achieving certain milestones as defined in the collaboration agreements. The Group's best estimate of future commitments for such payments is 119 million Swiss francs in 2004, 171 million Swiss francs in 2005 and 133 million Swiss francs in 2006.

The standard states that in determining which provisions may be aggregated to form a class, it is necessary to consider whether the nature of the items is sufficiently similar for a single statement about them to fulfil the requirements of (a) and (b) above. An example is given of warranties: it is suggested that, while it may be appropriate to treat warranties of different products as a single class of provision, it would not be appropriate to aggregate normal warranties with amounts that are subject to legal proceedings.[147] This requirement could be interpreted to mean that in disclosing restructuring costs, the different components of the costs, such as redundancies, termination of leases, etc, should be disclosed separately. However, materiality will be an important consideration in judging how much analysis is required.

As indicated at 5.1.1 above, IAS 37 emphasises that when a restructuring meets the definition of a discontinued operation under IFRS 5, additional disclosures may be required under that standard (see Chapter 3 at 3.2.3).[148]

6.2   Contingent liabilities

IAS 37 requires the following disclosure for each class of contingent liability at the balance sheet date unless the possibility of any outflow in settlement is remote:

(a)   a brief description of the nature of the contingent liability, and where practicable:

   (i)   an estimate of its financial effect, measured in accordance with paragraphs 36–52 of IAS 37 (discussed at 4 above);

   (ii)   an indication of the uncertainties relating to the amount or timing of any outflow; and

   (iii)   the possibility of any reimbursement.[149]

Where any of the information above is not disclosed because it is not practicable to do so, that fact should be stated.[150]

The guidance given in the standard on determining which provisions may be aggregated to form a class referred to in 6.1 above also applies to contingent liabilities.

A further point noted in the standard is that where a provision and a contingent liability arise from the same circumstances, an entity should ensure that the link between the provision and the contingent liability is clear.[151] This may arise, for instance, where there is a range of possible losses under a claim, for which part of the potential maximum has been provided. A further example of when this may arise would be where an entity is jointly and severally liable for an obligation. As noted in 4.4 above, in these circumstances the part that is expected to be met by other parties is treated as a contingent liability.

It is not absolutely clear what is meant by 'financial effect' in (i) above. Is it the *potential* amount of the loss or is it the *expected* amount of the loss? The explicit cross-reference to the measurement principles in paragraphs 36–52 might imply the latter, but in our view the former would be preferable.

6.3   Contingent assets

IAS 37 requires disclosure of contingent assets where an inflow of economic benefits is probable. The disclosures required are:

(a)   a brief description of the nature of the contingent assets at the balance sheet date; and

(b)   where practicable, an estimate of their financial effect, measured using the principles set out for provisions in paragraphs 36–52 of IAS 37.[152]

Where any of the information above is not disclosed because it is not practicable to do so, that fact should be stated.[153] The standard goes on to emphasise that the disclosure must avoid giving misleading indications of the likelihood of a profit arising.[154]

One problem that arises with IAS 37 is that it requires the disclosure of an estimate of the potential financial effect for contingent assets to be measured in accordance with the measurement principles in the standard. Unfortunately, the measurement principles in the standard are all set out in terms of the measurement of provisions, and these principles cannot readily be applied to the measurement of contingent assets. Hence, judgement will have to be used as to how rigorously these principles should be applied.

6.4   Exemption from disclosure when seriously prejudicial

IAS 37 contains an exemption from disclosure of information in the following circumstances. It says that, 'in extremely rare cases, disclosure of some or all of the information required by [the disclosure requirements in 6.1 to 6.3 above] can be expected to prejudice seriously the position of the entity in a dispute with other parties on the subject matter of the provision, contingent liability or contingent asset'.[155]

In such circumstances, the information need not be disclosed. However, disclosure will still need to be made of the general nature of the dispute, together with the fact that, and the reason why, the required information has not been disclosed.[156]

7   TRANSITIONAL ARRANGEMENTS AND FIRST-TIME ADOPTION ISSUES

7.1   Transitional arrangements for entities already reporting under IFRS

As indicated at 1.2.2 above, when IAS 37 was issued in September 1998, it was to be applied to accounting periods beginning on or after 1 July 1999, although earlier application was encouraged.[157] Transitional arrangements within IAS 37 are no longer relevant for entities already reporting under IFRS, since they required the effect of adopting the standard on its effective date (or earlier) to be reported as an adjustment to the opening balance of retained earnings for the period in which the standard was first adopted. Entities were encouraged, but not required, to adjust the opening balance of retained earnings for the earliest period presented and to restate comparative information, and if that was not done, that fact was to be disclosed.[158]

There are no transitional arrangements when applying the amended standard resulting from the consequential amendments made in December 2003 or March 2004 (see 1.2.2. above). The amended standard should be applied for annual periods beginning on or after 1 January 2005. If an entity applies any of the amending standards for an earlier period, the amendments made by that standard to IAS 37 should also be applied for that earlier period.

As indicated at 5.4.2 A above, any changes in measurement as a result of implementing IFRIC 1 are changes in accounting policies to be accounted for in accordance with IAS 8. There are no transitional arrangements.

7.2   First-time adoption issues

For first-time adopters, there are no specific transitional arrangements in relation to IAS 37 in IFRS 1 and it is emphasised that an entity does not apply the transitional arrangements in IAS 37 described above in preparing its opening IFRS balance sheet.[159]

The main issue for a first-time adopter is that IFRS 1 prohibits retrospective application of some aspects of IFRS relating to estimates (see Chapter 4 at 2.8.1). IFRS 1 notes that the estimates used to determine whether an entity recognises a provision under IAS 37 (and to measure any such provision) at the date of transition to IFRS are to be consistent with estimates made for the same date under previous GAAP (after adjustments to reflect any difference in accounting policies), unless there is objective evidence that those estimates were in error. The entity has to report the impact of any later revisions to those estimates as an event of the period in which it makes the revisions.[160]

Also, in assessing whether it needs to recognise a provision under IAS 37 (and in measuring any such provision) at the date of transition to IFRS, an entity may need to make estimates for that date that were not necessary under its previous GAAP. Such estimates and assumptions do not reflect conditions that arose after the date of transition to IFRS.[161]

These requirements also apply to provisions at the end of the comparative period presented in an entity's first IFRS financial statements.[162] Accordingly, an entity cannot use hindsight in determining the provisions under IAS 37 to be included within its IFRS balance sheet at the date of transition (and at the end of the comparative period).

Example 25.6:   Application of IFRS 1 to estimates relating to provisions[163]

Entity A's first IFRS financial statements have a reporting date of 31 December 2005 and include comparative information for one year. In its previous GAAP financial statements for 31 December 2003, Entity A accounted for a provision of $150,000 in connection with a court case. Entity A's accounting policy was consistent with the requirements of IAS 37, except for the fact that Entity A did not discount the provision for the time value of money. The discounted value of the provision at 31 December 2003 would have been $135,000. The case was settled for $190,000 during 2004.

In its opening IFRS balance sheet Entity A will measure the provision at $135,000. IFRS 1 does not permit an entity to adjust the estimate itself, unless it was in error, but does require an adjustment to reflect the difference in accounting policies. The unwinding of the discount and the adjustment due to the under-provision will be included in the comparative income statement for 2004.

Entity B's first IFRS financial statements have a reporting date of 31 December 2005 and include comparative information for one year. In its previous GAAP financial statements for 31 December 2004, Entity B did not recognise a provision for a court case arising from events that occurred in September 2004. When the court case was concluded on 30 June 2005, Entity B was required to pay €1,000,000 and paid this on 10 July 2005.

In preparing its comparative balance sheet at 31 December 2004, the treatment of the court case at that date depends on the reason why Entity B did not recognise a provision under its previous GAAP at that date.

Scenario 1 – Previous GAAP was consistent with IAS 37. At the date of preparing its 2004 financial statements, Entity B concluded that the recognition criteria were not met. In this case, Entity B's assumptions under IFRS are to be consistent with its assumptions under previous GAAP. Therefore, Entity A does not recognise a provision at 31 December 2004 and the effect of settling the court case is reflected in the 2005 income statement.

Scenario 2 – Previous GAAP was not consistent with IAS 37. Therefore, Entity B develops estimates under IAS 37. Under IAS 37, an entity determines whether an obligation exists at the balance sheet date by taking account of all available evidence, including any additional evidence provided by events after the balance sheet date (see 3.1.1 above). Similarly, under IAS 10, the resolution of a court case after the balance sheet date is an adjusting event after the balance sheet date if it confirms that the entity had a present obligation at that date. In this instance, the resolution of the court case confirms that Entity B had a liability in September 2004 (when the events occurred that gave rise to the court case). Therefore, Entity B recognises a provision at 31 December 2004. Entity B measures that provision by discounting the €1,000,000 paid on 10 July 2005 to its present value, using a discount rate that complies with IAS 37 and reflects market conditions at 31 December 2004.

A first-time adopter can opt not to apply IFRIC 1 retrospectively to changes in its decommissioning, restoration or similar liabilities that occurred before its date of transition to IFRS. However, a first-time adopter that uses this exemption still has to measure such liabilities as at its date of transition to IFRS in accordance with IAS 37. The exemption allowed under IFRS 1 relates to the accounting for the related asset. This is discussed further in Chapter 4 at 2.7.5.

8 FUTURE DEVELOPMENTS

As indicated at 1.2.4 above, the IASB and the IFRIC are working on a number of projects that may result in amendments to IAS 37 or have implications for accounting for particular items under IAS 37.

8.1 Exposure draft to amend IAS 37

In September 2002, the IASB agreed to add a short-term convergence project to its active agenda, the object being to reduce differences between IFRS and US GAAP. As a result of this project and Phase II of its business combinations project (see Chapter 6 at 5.2), the IASB expects to issue an exposure draft in the final quarter of 2004 proposing a number of amendments to IAS 37. These are summarised below.

8.1.1 Contingent assets and liabilities

A   Definitions

The IASB has decided that the definitions of contingent assets and contingent liabilities in IAS 37 (see 3.2 above) should be replaced with the following definitions:

'A contingent asset is a conditional right that arises from past events from which future economic benefits may flow based on the occurrence or non-occurrence of one or more uncertain future events not wholly within the control of the entity.'

'A contingent liability is a conditional obligation that arises from past events that may require an outflow of resources embodying economic benefits based on the occurrence or non-occurrence of one or more uncertain future events not wholly within the control of the entity.'[164]

B   Recognition and measurement

The Board has observed that contingent assets (or liabilities) are sometimes accompanied by associated unconditional rights (or obligations) that satisfy the definition of an asset (or liability). For a contingent asset that is within the scope of IAS 37, any accompanying unconditional right would be a non-monetary asset without physical substance and, if it satisfied the 'identifiability' criterion in IAS 38, would meet the definition of an intangible asset. The Board therefore decided that such an unconditional right that accompanies a contingent asset should be accounted for in accordance with IAS 38.

For a contingent liability that is within the scope of IAS 37, any accompanying unconditional obligation would meet the definition of a provision (liability). The Board therefore decided that an unconditional obligation that accompanies a contingent liability (that is within the scope of IAS 37) should be accounted for under IAS 37.

The IASB has also decided that, in the absence of accompanying unconditional rights (or obligations), contingent assets (or liabilities) are themselves not assets (or liabilities) and are not considered for recognition separately as assets (or liabilities) in or outside of a business combination.[165]

8.1.2 Constructive obligations

The IASB has decided to amend the definition of a constructive obligation in IAS 37 (see 3.1.1 above) to be 'an obligation that derives from an entity's actions where:

(a)   by an established pattern of past practice, published policies or a sufficiently specific current statement, the entity has indicated to other parties that it will accept certain particular responsibilities; and

(b)   as a result, the entity has created a valid expectation on the part of in those other parties that it will discharge they can reasonably rely on it to discharge those responsibilities'.

Additional explanatory material will be given to assist entities in determining whether they have met the definition of a constructive obligation.[166]

8.1.3   Recognition

The IASB has decided to add to the existing recognition guidance in IAS 37 to explain that the outflow of economic resources required to settle an obligation can be the provision of services. For example, an entity that has issued a product warranty has an unconditional obligation to provide a service for the duration of the warranty. The entity is therefore considered to have satisfied the probable outflow criterion (see 3.1 above) regardless of the likelihood of the product developing a fault.[167]

8.1.4   Measurement

The IASB has decided to make the following limited amendments to the existing measurement requirements of IAS 37 (see 4 above) for clarification and to remove inconsistencies:

(a)   provisions should be measured at the amount that an entity would rationally pay to settle the obligation at the balance sheet date or to transfer it to a third party at that time;

(b)   the amount that an entity would rationally pay to settle the obligation at the balance should reflect the risks and uncertainties surrounding the obligation;

(c)   using an expected value estimation technique would generally be consistent with principle (a) above, whilst measuring a provision at a single point estimate of the most likely outcome would not;

(d)   provisions should be remeasured at each reporting date using a current discount rate.[168]

8.1.5   Restructuring costs

The IASB has decided to withdraw the existing guidance on provisions for restructuring costs in IAS 37 (see 5.1 above) and to specify that the existence and announcement of a restructuring plan does not by itself create an obligation. The standard will explain that costs associated with a restructuring are to be recognised as a provision on the same basis as if those costs arose independently of a restructuring.

The Board has also decided that it will specify the treatment of costs that are often incurred in a restructuring as follows:

(a)   the cost of employee termination benefits are to be recognised in accordance with a revised IAS 19 (see 8.1.7 below);

(b)   the cost of terminating a contract before the end of its term are to be recognised in accordance with the requirements for onerous contracts (see 8.1.6 below); and

(c)   the liability for costs that will continue to be incurred under a contract for its remaining term without economic benefit to the entity are to be recognised in accordance with the requirements for onerous contracts (see 8.1.6 below).[169]

8.1.6 *Onerous contracts*

The IASB has tentatively agreed that when a contract becomes onerous as a result of an entity's own actions, the resulting provision should not be recognised until that action has occurred, and has said that in the case of an operating lease on a property that will become vacant as a result of a restructuring, the provision for the unavoidable lease commitment should be recognised only when the entity vacates the property.

It has also decided to specify that if an onerous contract is an operating lease, the provision should be reduced by the sublease rentals that could reasonably be obtained for the property.[170]

8.1.7 *Termination benefits*

The IASB has decided that the requirements in IAS 19 (see Chapter 30 at 6.3) will be amended such that:

(a)   the recognition of termination benefits depends on whether those benefits relate to employees' past service or are paid in exchange for employees' future services (i.e. are a 'stay bonus');

(b)   termination benefits are to be regarded as paid in exchange for employees' future services if they:

   (i)   are not provided under the terms of an established benefit arrangement (i.e. employment contract, legislation, union agreement, prior business practice);

   (ii)   do not vest until the employment is terminated; and

   (iii)   are provided to employees who will be retained beyond the minimum retention period (i.e. the period of notice that an entity is required to provide to employees in advance of terminating their employment).

(c)   no liability for termination benefits is to be recognised until the entity has communicated its plan of termination to the affected employees. More specifically:

   (i)   termination benefits that relate to employees' past services are to be recognised when the entity has a present obligation to provide termination benefits. In the case of involuntary termination benefits, this is when the entity has a formal plan of termination that it has communicated to the affected employees. In the case of voluntary termination benefits, this is when the employees accept the entity's offer of voluntary redundancy.

   (ii)   termination benefits that are payable in exchange for employees' future services are recognised over that period of future service.[171]

8.2 IFRIC Draft Interpretation D1 Emission Rights

Several governments either have, or are in the process of developing, schemes to encourage reduced emissions of pollutants, in particular of greenhouse gases. Some schemes are based on a cap and trade model whereby participants are allocated emission rights or allowances equal to a cap (i.e. target level of emissions) and are permitted to trade those allowances.

Because there is presently no guidance on the accounting for such schemes and because no consensus has emerged among market participants on what the accounting treatment should be, the IFRIC concluded that an interpretation should be issued to explain how IFRS should be applied to such schemes.

Accordingly, in May 2003 the IFRIC issued IFRIC D1 – *IFRIC Draft Interpretation D1 Emission Rights*, which addresses accounting for emission rights that arise from a 'cap and trade' scheme.

The draft interpretation (which is discussed further in Chapter 11 at 2.2.3 A) provides guidance on accounting for the following elements that an emission rights scheme gives rise to:[172]

(a) *an asset for emission rights held (allowances)* – 'Allowances, whether allocated by government or purchased, are intangible assets that shall be accounted for under IAS 38 *Intangible Assets*. Allowances that are allocated for less than fair value shall be measured initially at their fair value. Allowances shall not be amortised but may be impaired';[173]

(b) *a government grant* – The difference between the amount paid and fair value is a government grant that should be accounted for under IAS 20. The grant is initially recognised as deferred income in the balance sheet and subsequently recognised as income on a systematic basis over the compliance period for which the allowances were allocated;[174]

(c) *a liability for the obligation to deliver allowances equal to emissions that have been made* – This liability is a provision that falls within the scope of IAS 37. The liability is settled by delivering allowances, incurring a penalty or a combination of both. The liability should be measured at the best estimate of the expenditure required to settle the present obligation at the balance sheet date:

- this will normally be the present market price of the number of allowances required to cover emissions made up to the balance sheet date; or

- if the participant's best estimate is that some or all of the obligation will be settled by incurring a cash penalty, it shall measure that part of its obligation at the cost of the penalty rather than at the market price of the relevant number of allowances.[175]

Items (a) to (c) above should not be presented as a net asset or liability.[176]

In March 2004, the IFRIC decided to suspend work on IFRIC D1 in the light of the Board's plans to amend IAS 20 by adopting the accounting model for government grants contained in IAS 41 – *Agriculture*.[177] However, in September 2004, the IFRIC noted it was unlikely that the Board would issue a final amended IAS 20 for at least another year and hence that the IFRIC would be unable to finalise IFRIC D1 until that time. Given that the EU Emissions Trading Scheme starts at the beginning of 2005, and given the potential for diversity of accounting for that scheme, the IFRIC reconsidered whether it should finalise its original proposals. The view of the majority of IFRIC members present was that IFRIC D1 should be finalised in substantially its present form and issued in the final quarter of 2004.[178]

8.3   IFRIC Draft Interpretation D4 Decommissioning, Restoration and Environmental Rehabilitation Funds

Another issue that is being considered by the IFRIC is the accounting by an entity when it participates in a decommissioning fund, the purpose of which is to segregate assets to fund some or all of the costs of its decommissioning or environmental liabilities for which it has to make a provision under IAS 37 (see 5.4.1 and 5.4.2 above). In January 2004, the IASB issued IFRIC D4 – *IFRIC Draft Interpretation D4 Decommissioning, Restoration and Environmental Rehabilitation Funds* – to deal with this issue.

Such funds generally have the following features:[179]

- the fund is separately administered by independent trustees;

- entities (contributors) make contributions to the fund, which are invested in a range of assets that may include both debt and equity investments, and are available to help pay the contributors' decommissioning costs. The trustees determine how contributions are invested, within the constraints set by the fund's governing documents and any applicable legislation or other regulations;

- the contributors retain the obligation to pay decommissioning costs. However, contributors are able to obtain reimbursement of decommissioning costs from the fund up to the lower of the decommissioning costs incurred and the entity's share of assets of the fund; and

- the contributors may have restricted or no access to any surplus of assets of the fund over those used to meet eligible decommissioning costs.

Funds within the scope of IFRIC D4 may have one of the following common structures:[180]

- the fund is established by a single contributor to fund its own decommissioning obligations, whether for a particular site, or for a number of geographically dispersed sites; or

- the fund is established with multiple contributors to fund their individual or joint decommissioning obligations, and the contributors are entitled to reimbursement for decommissioning expenses to the extent of their fund contributions plus any actual earnings on those contributions less their share of the costs of administering the fund. In addition, contributors may have an obligation to make potential additional contributions, for example, in the event of the bankruptcy of another contributor; or

- the fund is established with multiple contributors to fund their individual or joint decommissioning obligations, and the required level of contributions is based on the current activity of a contributor, but the benefit obtained by that contributor is based on its past activity. Thus, there is a potential mismatch in the amount of contributions made by a contributor (based on current activity) and the value realisable from the fund (based on past activity).

As indicated at 5.4.2 B above, the issues addressed by IFRIC D4 are:[181]

(a) How should a contributor account for its interest in a fund?

(b) When a contributor has an obligation to make additional contributions, for example, in the event of the bankruptcy of another contributor, how should that obligation be accounted for?

As far as issue (a) is concerned, IFRIC D4 proposes that the contributor determines whether it has control, joint control or significant influence over the fund by reference to IAS 27 – *Consolidated and Separate Financial Statements*, IAS 31 – *Interests in Joint Ventures*, IAS 28 – *Investments in Associates* and SIC-12 – *Consolidation – Special Purpose Entities*. If the contributor determines that it has such control, joint control or significant influence, it should account for its interest in the fund in accordance with the relevant standards (see Chapters 5, 8 and 7 respectively).[182] Otherwise, the contributor should account for its interest in the fund as follows:

- when the fund does not relieve the contributor of its obligation to pay decommissioning costs, an asset and a liability shall be recognised by the contributor;[183]

- the contributor should recognise the right to receive reimbursement from the fund as a reimbursement in accordance with IAS 37 (see 4.4 above). This reimbursement should be measured at the lower of:

  - the amount of the decommissioning obligation recognised; and

  - the entity's share of the fair value of the net assets of the fund adjusted for actual or expected factors that affect the entity's ability to access these assets;[184] and

- changes in the carrying value of the right to receive reimbursement other than contributions to and payments from the fund should be recognised in profit or loss in the period in which these changes occur.[185]

As far as the second issue is concerned, IFRIC D4 proposes that when a contributor has an obligation to make potential additional contributions, for example, in the event of the bankruptcy of another contributor, this obligation is a contingent liability that is within the scope of IAS 37. The contributor shall recognise a liability only if it is probable that additional contributions will be made.[186]

In September 2004, the IFRIC agreed:

- to confirm the approach exposed in IFRIC D4 namely:

  - rights to reimbursement in services are economically similar to rights to reimbursement in cash;

  - both of these rights should be accounted for in accordance with IAS 37 and an amendment to IAS 39 should be made to achieve this; and

  - in the absence of guidance on measurement in IAS 37, the IFRIC should give guidance that both types of reimbursement rights are measured at fair value through profit and loss;

- to provide clarification that a residual interest in a fund, such as a contractual right to distributions once all the decommissioning has been completed or on winding up of the fund, may be a financial instrument within the scope of IAS 39;

- to provide discussion in the Basis for Conclusions that the IFRIC had explored constituents views on the 'asset cap' in paragraph 53 of IAS 37 (i.e. that the amount recognised for the reimbursement should not exceed the amount of the provision) and concluded that in the case of an asset for the reimbursement right the asset cap should apply; and

- that it was not necessary to re-expose its conclusions for public comment.

The principles of the final Interpretation were voted on and agreed. Subject to a review of the drafting by IFRIC members and the Board's approval, the Interpretation will be published without further discussion at a meeting.[187]

8.4   EU Directives on 'Waste Electrical and Electronic Equipment'

In June 2004, the IFRIC gave preliminary consideration to an issue raised on the interpretation of an 'obligating event' under IAS 37 (see 3.1.1 above) in the context of the EU Directives on *Waste Electrical and Electronic Equipment* (WE&EE).[188]

The IFRIC noted that the unusual financing features in the Directives define that the cost of waste management for certain equipment will fall to producers of that type of equipment who are in the market when disposal occurs and not necessarily to the actual producers of that equipment. Thus, future market share (i.e. market share at the time disposal occurs) will be the basis to determine the obligation. The critical issue with regard to the application of IAS 37, therefore is whether:

- putting those types of equipment onto the market is the obligating event and future market share is just a measurement issue, or

- future market share at the date when the WE&EE costs occur is the obligating event.

The IFRIC tentatively concluded that having market share at the time disposal occurs constitutes the obligating event. The IFRIC asked the Accounting Interpretation Committee of the German Accounting Standards Board (AIC) which raised this issue in the Agenda Committee, to draft an interpretation on that issue. In particular the IFRIC came to the following decisions:

- the scope of the draft interpretation should be all types of obligations that are dependent upon future market share including (but not limited to) WE&EE costs;

- the draft interpretation should incorporate the WE&EE financing feature concerning historical equipment sold to private households as an example to demonstrate the rationale of the decision; and

- the IFRIC tentatively agreed to include in the draft interpretation measurement issues (e.g. uncertainties in determining the market share) that may arise.

The IFRIC also commented that how disposals physically occurring throughout the year and how market share are defined and measured have yet to be determined by EU Member States.[189]

The issue has been discussed further by the IFRIC in July and September 2004, and at its September meeting unanimously voted in favour of publishing an exposure draft. The IFRIC agreed that the scope of the draft should not be widened to include waste management cost of commercial users, since the existing requirements in IAS 16, IAS 37 and IFRIC 1 were considered to be adequate. The IFRIC noted that commercial users normally had an obligation arising from the passing of legislation requiring them to recycle historical waste electrical and electronic equipment.[190]

9   CONCLUSION

The subject of provisions and contingencies is a wide ranging one, but at its heart lie fundamental questions concerning the recognition and measurement of items in the financial statements. The IASB (and the ASB in the UK) see these issues straightforwardly in terms of balance sheet recognition, and have sought to apply their respective conceptual frameworks as a means of resolving them, but in many cases we think this does not work well and that it is more fruitful to address the question from the point of view of expense recognition. In particular, we think the concepts of 'obligating events' and 'constructive obligations' are rather more nebulous than they are represented to be, and not always useful in identifying reliably when to include certain items in the financial statements. We would not be as dismissive as the standard setters about the relevance of management intent, since financial statements necessarily represent the report of management and it is futile to try to divorce them from that context. We are also concerned that the approach of IAS 37 means that the balance sheet will be inappropriately grossed up in some cases so as to include dubious assets.

The measurement requirements also have their difficulties. We are concerned that they seem to be seeking to derive some form of theoretical market value for the obligations reported whereas we would prefer to focus more directly on the actual expenditure that the entity is likely to make. We also think that the rules on discounting should have been given much deeper consideration. The use of discounting also means that the operating results of an entity are often heavily flattered at the expense of finance costs.

As a result, we do not think that IAS 37 is a very satisfactory standard. While the answers it gives rise to are usually acceptable, the reasoning that lies behind them is frequently suspect and is more likely to puzzle readers than enlighten them.

References

1 IAS 37, *Provisions, Contingent Liabilities and Contingent Assets*, IASB, September 1998 (amended March 2004), para. 10.
2 IAS 37, para. 10.
3 IAS 10 (1978), *Contingencies and Events Occurring After the Balance Sheet Date*, IASC, October 1978.
4 IAS 37, para. 11.
5 Draft Statement of Principles, *Provisions and Contingencies*, IASC, November 1996, paras. 89-95.
6 IAS 37, para. 95.
7 IAS 37, Objective.
8 IAS 37, para. 7.
9 IAS 37, para. 1.
10 IAS 37, para. 3.
11 IAS 37, para. 5.
12 IAS 37, para. 2.
13 IAS 37 (1998), paras. 1-2.
14 IAS 37, para. 6.
15 IAS 37, para. 11.
16 IAS 37, para. 12.
17 IAS 37, para. 13.
18 IAS 37, para. 14.
19 IAS 37, para. 10.
20 IAS 37, para. 10.
21 IAS 37, Appendix C, Examples 4 and 2B.
22 IAS 37, paras. 15-16.
23 IAS 37, para. 10.
24 IAS 37, para. 17.
25 IAS 37, para. 18.
26 IAS 37, para. 19.
27 IAS 37, para. 19 and Appendix C, Example 6.
28 IAS 37, Appendix C, Examples 11A and 7.
29 IAS 37, para. 20.
30 IAS 37, para. 21.
31 IAS 37, para. 22.
32 IAS 37, para. 21.
33 *FASB Newsletter*, No. 310, 25 February 1999, p. 5.
34 IAS 37, paras. 23-24.
35 IAS 37, paras. 25-26.
36 IAS 37, paras. 27-28, 31 and 34.
37 IAS 37, para. 10.
38 IAS 37, paras. 15-16.
39 IAS 37, para. 30.
40 IAS 37 (1998), Appendix C, Example 9.
41 IAS 37, Appendix C, Example 9.
42 IAS 37, para. 10.
43 IAS 37, para. 32.
44 IAS 37, para. 33.
45 IAS 37, paras. 34 and 89.
46 IAS 37, para. 35.
47 FRS 12, *Provisions, Contingent Liabilities and Contingent Assets*, ASB, September 1998, paras. 66-67.
48 IAS 37, para. 8.
49 IAS 16, *Property, Plant and Equipment*, IASB, December 2003 (amended March 2004), para. 16.
50 IAS 37, Appendix C, Example 3.
51 IAS 37, para. 41.
52 IAS 37, para. 36.
53 IAS 37, para. 37.
54 IAS 37, para. 37.
55 IAS 37, para. 38.
56 IAS 37, para. 39.
57 IAS 37, para. 39.
58 FASB Interpretation No. 14, *Reasonable Estimation of the Amount of a Loss*, FASB, September 1976, para. 3.
59 IAS 37, para. 40.
60 IAS 37, para. 40.

61 IAS 37, paras. 42-43.
62 IAS 37, para. 44.
63 IAS 37, para. 45.
64 IAS 37, para. 47.
65 IAS 37, para. 46.
66 IAS 37, Appendix D, Example 2.
67 FRS 12, para. 50.
68 IAS 37, para. 47.
69 FRS 12, para. 49.
70 *Discounting in Financial Reporting*, ASB, April 1997.
71 FRS 12, para. 49.
72 FRS 12, para. 49.
73 IAS 19, *Employee benefits*, IASB, February 1998 (amended March 2004), para. 78
74 IAS 37, para. 47.
75 Paragraph 27 in Appendix VII to FRS 12 on the *Development of the FRS* states that 'the discount rate should be the rate of return that will, after tax has been deducted, give the required post-tax rate of return'. The paragraph goes on to explain that because the tax consequence of different cash flows may be different, the pre-tax rate of return is not always the post-tax rate of return grossed up by the standard rate of tax.
76 IFRIC 1, *Changes in Existing Decommissioning, Restoration and Similar Liabilities*, IFRIC, May 2004, para. 8
77 IFRIC 1, paras. 8 and BC26-BC27.
78 IAS 37, para. 47.
79 IAS 37, para. 84(e).
80 IAS 37, para. 48.
81 IAS 37, para. 49.
82 IAS 37, para. 50.
83 IAS 37, para. 55.
84 IAS 37, paras. 53 and 56.
85 IAS 37, para. 54.
86 IAS 37, para. 57.
87 IAS 37, paras. 29 and 58.
88 IAS 37, paras. 51-52.
89 IAS 37, para. 59.
90 IAS 37, para. 60.
91 IFRIC 1, paras. 8 and BC26-BC27.
92 IAS 37, paras. 61-62.
93 IAS 37, para. 10.
94 IAS 37, para. 70.
95 IAS 37, para. 9.
96 IAS 37, para. 71.
97 IAS 37, para. 72.
98 IAS 37, para. 73.
99 IAS 37, para. 74.
100 IAS 37, para. 75.
101 IAS 37, Appendix C, Examples 5A-5B.
102 IAS 37, para. 76.
103 IAS 37, para. 77.
104 IAS 37, para. 75.
105 IAS 37, para. 78.
106 IAS 37, para. 79.
107 IAS 37, para. 80.
108 IAS 37, para. 19.
109 IAS 37, para. 81.
110 IAS 37, para. 81.
111 FRED 14, *Provisions and Contingencies*, ASB, June 1997, para. 61.
112 IAS 37, para. 82.
113 IAS 37, para. 83.
114 IAS 37, para. 63.
115 IAS 37, para. 64.
116 IAS 37, para. 65.
117 IAS 37, para. 66.
118 IAS 37, para. 67.
119 IAS 37, para. 10.
120 IAS 37, para. 68.
121 IAS 37, Appendix C, Example 8.
122 *IFRIC Update*, IASB, December 2003, pp. 4-5
123 IAS 37, para. 69.
124 IAS 37, Appendix C, Example 2A.
125 IAS 37, para. 22
126 IAS 37, Appendix C, Example 2B.
127 IAS 37, para. 19.
128 IAS 37, Appendix C, Example 3.
129 IFRIC 1, para. 2.
130 IFRIC 1, para. 3.
131 IFRIC 1, para. 8
132 IFRIC 1, paras. 8 and BC26-BC27.
133 IFRIC 1, paras. 4-7.
134 IFRIC 1, para. 9.
135 IFRIC 1, para. 10.
136 IAS 37, Appendix C, Examples 11A-11B.
137 FRS 12, Appendix VII, para. 39.
138 IAS 37, Appendix C, Example 1.
139 IAS 37, para. 39.
140 IAS 37, Appendix C, Example 10.
141 IAS 37, para. 14.
142 IAS 37, Appendix C, Example 4.
143 IAS 37, Appendix C, Example 7.
144 FRS 12, Appendix III, Example 12.
145 IAS 37, para. 84.
146 IAS 37, para. 85.
147 IAS 37, para. 87.
148 IAS 37, para. 9.
149 IAS 37, para. 86.
150 IAS 37, para. 91.
151 IAS 37, para. 88.
152 IAS 37, para. 89.
153 IAS 37, para. 91.
154 IAS 37, para. 90.
155 IAS 37, para. 92.
156 IAS 37, para. 92.
157 IAS 37, para. 95.
158 IAS 37, para. 93.
159 IFRS 1, *First-time Adoption of International Financial Reporting Standards*, IASB, June 2003 (amended March 2004), paras. 9 and IG42.
160 IFRS 1, para. IG40.
161 IFRS 1, para. IG41.

162 IFRS 1, paras. 31-34.

163 IFRS 1, para. IG3 and IG Example 1.

164 Project summary, *Short-term Convergence*, IASB, 18 June 2004, p. 3.

165 Project summary, *Short-term Convergence*, p. 3.

166 Project summary, *Short-term Convergence*, p. 4.

167 Project summary, *Short-term Convergence*, p. 4.

168 Project summary, *Short-term Convergence*, p. 4.

169 Project summary, *Short-term Convergence*, p. 5.

170 Project summary, *Short-term Convergence*, p. 5.

171 Project summary, *Short-term Convergence*, pp. 5-6.

172 IFRIC D1, *Emission Rights*, IFRIC, May 2003, para. 5.

173 IFRIC D1, para. 6.

174 IFRIC D1, para. 7.

175 IFRIC D1, para. 8.

176 IFRIC D1, para. 5.

177 *IFRIC Update*, IASB, March 2004, p.1.

178 *IFRIC Update*, IASB, September 2004, p.1.

179 IFRIC D4, *Decommissioning, Restoration and Environmental Rehabilitation Funds*, IFRIC, March 2004, para. 2.

180 IFRIC D4, para. 3.

181 IFRIC D4, para. 4.

182 IFRIC D4, para. 5.

183 IFRIC D4, paras. 6 and BC5-BC6.

184 IFRIC D4, para. 7.

185 IFRIC D4, para. 8.

186 IFRIC D4, para. 9.

187 *IFRIC Update*, IASB, September 2004, p.2.

188 Directive 2002/96/EC of the European Parliament and of the Council of 27 January 2003 on waste electrical and electronic equipment and Directive 2003/108/EC of the European Parliament and of the Council of 8 December 2003 amending Directive 2002/96/EC on waste electrical and electronic equipment.

189 *IFRIC Update*, IASB, June 2004, pp. 2-3.

190 *IFRIC Update*, IASB, September 2004, p. 4.

Chapter 26   Revenue

1   THE NATURE OF REVENUE

Revenue is generally discussed in accounting literature in terms of inflows of assets to an entity that occur as a result of outflows of goods and services from the entity. For this reason, the concept of revenue has normally been associated with specific accounting procedures that were primarily directed towards determining the timing and measurement of revenue and, until very recently, the debate has taken place in the context of the historical cost double-entry system. For example, this can be traced back as far as APB Statement No. 4, which defined revenue as the 'gross increases in assets or gross decreases in liabilities recognized and measured in conformity with generally accepted accounting principles that result from those types of profit-directed activities of an entity that can change owners' equity'.[1] Similarly, the original version of IAS 18 – *Revenue Recognition* – was issued in 1982 and defined revenue as the 'gross inflow of cash, receivables or other consideration arising in the course of the ordinary activities of an entity from the sale of goods, from the rendering of services, and from the use by others of entity resources yielding interest, royalties and dividends'.[2] The accounting principles that evolved focused on determining when transactions should be recognised in the financial statements, what amounts were involved in each transaction, how these amounts should be classified and how they should be allocated between accounting periods.

Historical cost accounting in its pure form avoids having to take a valuation approach to financial reporting by virtue of the fact that it is transactions-based; in other words, it relies on transactions to determine the recognition and measurement of assets, liabilities, revenues and expenses. Over the life of an entity, its total income will be represented by net cash flows generated; however, because of the requirement to prepare periodic financial statements, it is necessary to break up the entity's operating cycle into artificial periods. The effect of this is that at each reporting date the entity will have entered into a number of transactions that are incomplete; for example, it might have delivered a product or service to a customer for which payment has not been received, or it might have received payment in respect of a product or service yet to be delivered. Alternatively, it might have expended cash on costs that relate to future sales transactions, or it might have received goods and services that it has not yet paid for in cash.

Consequently, the most important accounting questions that have to be answered revolve around how to allocate the effects of these incomplete transactions between periods for reporting purposes, as opposed to simply letting them fall into the periods in which cash is either received or paid. Under historical cost accounting this allocation process is based on two, sometimes conflicting, fundamental accounting concepts: accruals (or matching), which attempts to move the costs associated with earning revenues to the periods in which the related revenues will be reported; and prudence (or conservatism), under which revenue and profits are not anticipated, whilst anticipated losses are provided for as soon as they are foreseen, with the result that costs are not deferred to the future if there is doubt as to their recoverability.

As a result, the pure historical cost balance sheet contains items of two types: cash (and similar monetary items), and debits and credits that arise as a result of shifting the effects of transactions between reporting periods by applying the accruals and prudence concepts; in other words, the balance sheet simply reflects the balances that result from the entity preparing an accruals-based profit and loss account rather than a receipts and payments account. A non-monetary asset under the historical cost system is purely a deferred cost that has been incurred before the balance sheet date and, by applying the accruals concept, is expected (provided it passes the prudence test) to benefit periods beyond the balance sheet date, so as to justify its being carried forward. Similarly, the balance sheet incorporates non-monetary credit balances that are awaiting recognition in the profit and loss account but, as a result of the application of the prudence concept, have been deferred to future reporting periods.

However, financial reporting under IFRS is not a pure historical cost system; it incorporates a mixed model that embraces both historical costs and fair values. Moreover, the IASB clearly intends to promulgate an accounting model based on fair values, meaning that gains and losses are determined by reference to the change in fair value that has occurred over the financial reporting period. This approach is plainly evident in a number of standards, including IAS 39 – *Financial Instruments: Recognition and Measurement*, IAS 40 – *Investment Property*, IAS 41 – *Agriculture* and IFRS 2 – *Share-based payment*. Other standards, such as IAS 16 – *Property, Plant and Equipment*, IAS 38 – *Intangible Assets*, IAS 37 – *Provisions, Contingent Liabilities and Contingent Assets* and IFRS 5 – *Non-current Assets Held for Sale and Discontinued Operations* contain elements of fair value measurement. It is clear also that as new standards are developed, greater emphasis will be placed on the balance sheet, with fair value as the relevant measurement attribute.

Interestingly, this view is supported by remarks made in August 2004 at the 2004 Annual Meeting of the American Accounting Association by Mr Donald Nicolaisen, Chief Accountant of the SEC, who said the following: 'I should also mention here that I still hear some accountants focusing on conservatism [prudence] and the matching principle. While one or both of those ideas underlie certain accounting standards that are still in place today, those ideas should not be the focal point or end point of discussion. Much of the focus of standard setters is on assets and liabilities.'[3]

The focus of both the IASB and FASB is, indeed, on assets and liabilities. The two Boards have embarked on a joint project to develop a new balance sheet approach to revenue recognition based on asset/liability recognition and measurement. However, the Board has yet to publish any formal proposals and it will be some time before a new standard is issued.

At the same time, though, the international standard that deals with revenue recognition, IAS 18 – *Revenue* – was issued in its original form in 1982 and received its last major revision in 1993. Consequently, it is a standard that is based on historical cost principles, not fair value. Thus, it is a standard that focuses on the income statement, not assets and liabilities and – despite Mr Nicolaisen's comments – relies heavily on the concepts of prudence and matching.

This means that the traditional historical cost approach to revenue recognition remains in place for most practical purposes. For companies adopting IFRS in 2005 this is problematic: IAS 18 does not cope very well with a mixed model approach and does not address many of the complex transactions undertaken by modern business. In particular, transactions involving multiple deliverables – such as those found in the telecommunications sector – present difficulties that simply are not dealt with in the literature.

Consequently, it is the aim of this chapter to suggest broad principles under the existing mixed model accounting system for the recognition of revenues earned from operations. The chapter discusses the subject drawing on both IASB and US pronouncements. For companies reporting under IFRS, IAS 18 – *Revenue* – is the main source of authoritative guidance on revenue recognition, but several other standards also address revenue recognition issues. These include IAS 11 – *Construction Contracts*, IAS 17 – *Leases*, IFRS 4 – *Insurance Contracts*, SIC–13 – *Jointly Controlled Entities–Non-Monetary Contributions by Venturers*, and SIC–31 – *Revenue–Barter Transactions Involving Advertising Services*. In most cases, this revenue recognition guidance was developed in order to deal with specific issues on a piecemeal basis, rather than to follow any form of conceptual approach to revenue recognition. However, the US in particular has a substantial body of literature on revenue recognition that can prove useful when there is no IFRS guidance available.

2 THE TIMING OF REVENUE RECOGNITION

Under the historical cost system revenues are the inflows of assets to an entity as a result of the transfer of products and services by the entity to its customers during a period of time, and are recorded at the cash amount received or expected to be received (or, in the case of non-monetary exchanges, at their cash equivalent) as the result of these exchange transactions. However, because of the system of periodic financial reporting, it is necessary to determine the point (or points) in time when revenue should be measured and reported. This has traditionally been governed by what is known as the 'realisation principle', which acknowledges the fact that for revenue to be recognised it is not sufficient merely for a sale to have been made – there has to be a certain degree of performance by the vendor as well. In the US, this principle was formally codified in 1970 in APB Statement No. 4 as follows: 'revenue is generally recognised when both of the following conditions are met: (1) the earning process is complete or virtually complete, and (2) an exchange has taken place'.[4]

The accounting practice that had developed under this principle was essentially as follows:

(a)   revenue from the sale of goods was recognised at the date of delivery to customers;

(b)   revenue from services was recognised when the services had been performed and were billable;

(c)   revenue derived from permitting others to use entity resources (e.g. rental, interest and royalty income) was recognised either on a time basis or as the resources were used; and

(d)   revenue from the sale of assets other than products of the entity was recognised at the date of sale.[5]

As stated above, revenue is recognised at the amount received or expected to be received as a consequence of the exchange transaction.

Although APB Statement No. 4 did acknowledge that there were certain exceptions to the sales basis of revenue recognition established under the realisation principle (for example, in the case of long-term construction contracts),[6] many more exceptions have developed in recent years. Nevertheless, the realisation principle still underpins revenue recognition practice under US GAAP. This is evidenced, for example, by the statement by the SEC staff in SAB 104 that 'revenue generally is realized or realizable and earned when all of the following criteria are met:

•   Persuasive evidence of an arrangement exists;

•   Delivery has occurred or services have been rendered;

•   The seller's price to the buyer is fixed or determinable; and

•   Collectibility is reasonably assured.'[7]

As a result, no common basis of revenue recognition exists in contemporary financial accounting for all types of exchange transaction; different (and sometimes inconsistent) rules exist for different circumstances. Nevertheless, these rules have been derived from three broad approaches to the recognition of revenue: the critical event, accretion and revenue allocation approaches, each of which is appropriate under particular circumstances. Each of the three approaches is discussed in turn below.

2.1   The critical event approach

In general terms, the operating cycle of an entity involves the acquisition of merchandise or raw materials, the production of goods, the sale of goods or services to customers, the delivery of the goods or performance of the services and the ultimate collection of cash; in some cases it might even extend beyond the cash collection stage, for example, if there are on-going after-sales service obligations. The critical event approach is based on the belief that revenue is earned at the point in the operating cycle when the most critical decision is made or the most critical act is performed.[8] It is therefore necessary to identify the event that is considered to be critical to the revenue earning process. In theory, the critical event could occur at various stages during the operating cycle; for example, at the completion of production, at the time of sale, at the time of delivery or at the time of cash collection.

Revenue recognition is subject to a number of uncertainties; these include the estimation of the production cost of the asset, the selling price, the additional selling costs and the ultimate cash collection. However, since these uncertainties fall away at various stages throughout the operating cycle, it is necessary to identify a point in the cycle at which the remaining uncertainties can be estimated with sufficient accuracy to enable revenue to be recognised. In other words, the critical event should not be judged to occur at a point when the prudence concept would preclude recognition by virtue of the uncertainties that still remain.

2.1.1 The recognition of revenue at the completion of production

Clearly, the uncertainty surrounding the cost of production is removed when the product is completed; it is therefore necessary to evaluate the remaining uncertainties in order to determine whether or not the completion of production can be used as the critical event for revenue recognition. Where the entity has entered into a firm contract for the production and delivery of a product, the sales price will have been determined and the selling costs will have already been incurred. Consequently, provided that both the delivery expenses and the bad debt risk can satisfactorily be assessed, it may be appropriate to report revenue on this basis. An application of this practice is the completed contract method of recognising revenue on construction contracts, in terms of which revenue is recognised only when the contract is completed or substantially completed.

It has also become accepted practice in a limited number of industries to recognise revenue at the completion of production, even though a sales contract may not have been entered into. This practice would be adopted, for example, in the case of the production of certain minerals and mineral products, provided that the following criteria are met:[9]

(a)   the minerals have been extracted;

(b)   sale is assured under a forward contract or a government guarantee or an active market exists and there is a negligible risk of failure to sell; and

(c)   the market price should be determinable and stable.

The historical cost principles of IAS 2 – *Inventories* – do not apply mandatorily to 'producers of agricultural and forest products, agricultural produce after harvest, and minerals and mineral products, to the extent that they are measured at net realisable value in accordance with well-established practices in those industries.'[10] However, in order to be able to apply this scope exemption, changes in net realisable value must be recognised in profit or loss in the period of the change.[11] Net realisable value is defined in IAS 2 as 'the estimated selling price in the ordinary course of business less the estimated costs of completion and the estimated costs necessary to make the sale'.[12]

The Concepts Statement 5 – *Recognition and Measurement in Financial Statements of Business Enterprises* – refers to such assets as being 'readily realisable' (since they are saleable at readily determinable prices without significant effort), and acknowledges that revenue may be recognised on the completion of production of such assets, provided that they consist of interchangeable units and quoted prices are available in an active market that can rapidly absorb the quantity held by the entity without significantly affecting the price.[13] The accounting treatment for this basis would be to value closing stock of items such as minerals and mineral products at net realisable value (i.e. sales price less estimated selling costs), and write off the related production costs.

An extension of this approach is to be found in the generally accepted accounting practice adopted by many commodity broker-traders of including commodities in their financial statements at fair value less costs to sell. This practice is specifically recognised in IAS 2 – *Inventories* – provided that changes in fair value less costs to sell are recognised in profit or loss in the period of the change.[14] IAS 2 defines fair value as 'the amount for which an asset could be exchanged, or a liability settled, between knowledgeable, willing parties in an arm's length transaction'.[15]

2.1.2   *The recognition of revenue at the time of sale*

The time of sale is probably the most widely used basis of recognising revenue from transactions involving the sale of goods. The reason is that, in most cases, the sale is the critical point in the earning process when most of the significant uncertainties are eliminated; the only uncertainties which are likely to remain are those of possible return of the goods (where the customer has the right to do so, thereby cancelling the sale), the failure to collect the sales price (in the case of a credit sale), and any future liabilities in terms of any express or implied customer warranties. However, under normal circumstances, these uncertainties will be both minimal and estimable to a reasonable degree of accuracy, based, *inter alia*, on past experience.

Nevertheless, the time of sale basis of revenue recognition is not always straightforward. In a large number of cases, a contract for the sale of goods would be entered into after the goods have been acquired or produced by the seller, and delivery takes place either at the same time as the contract, or soon thereafter. However, should revenues be recognised at the time of sale if the sale takes place before production, or if delivery only takes place at some significantly distant time in the future? In practice, the time of sale is generally taken to be the point of delivery.

This, in fact, would appear to be the principle implicit in the conditions for recognition set out in Concepts Statement 5, which states that 'Revenues are not recognized until earned. An entity's revenue-earning activities involve delivering or producing goods, rendering services, or other activities that constitute its ongoing major or central operations, and revenues are considered to have been earned when the entity has substantially accomplished what it must do to be entitled to the benefits represented by the revenues. ... If sale or cash receipt (or both) precedes production and delivery (for example, magazine subscriptions), revenues may be recognised as earned by production and delivery.'[16] The use of the words 'substantially accomplished' in Concepts Statement 5 means that US GAAP and related SEC Staff

Accounting Bulletins require delivery in order to recognise revenue. However, the position under IFRS is more flexible in this regard – see 3.5 below for a discussion of the principles laid down by the IASB in IAS 18 – *Revenue* – for determining when to recognise revenue from a transaction involving the sale of goods.

2.1.3 The recognition of revenue subsequent to delivery

Under certain circumstances, the uncertainties that exist after delivery are of such significance that recognition should be delayed beyond the normal recognition point. Where the principal uncertainty concerns collectibility, a possible approach would be to record the sale and defer recognition of the profit until cash is received; alternatively, it might be appropriate to defer recognition of the whole sale (and not just the profit) until collection is reasonably assured – as is the requirement under US GAAP.

A further example of where it might be appropriate to defer the recognition of revenue beyond the date of delivery is where the entity sells its product but gives the customer the right to return the goods (for example, in the case of a mail order business where the customer is given an approval period of, say, 14 days). In such circumstances, revenue may be recognised on delivery if future returns can be reasonably predicted; if this is not possible, then revenue should be recognised on receipt of payment for the goods, or on customer acceptance of the goods and express or implied acknowledgement of the liability for payment, or after the 14 days have elapsed – whichever is considered to be the most appropriate under the circumstances.

In fact, this is an area where practice has been somewhat inconsistent. A transaction with a right of return is usually accounted for as a sale, whereas revenue from a transaction with a 14-day acceptance period is usually deferred – despite the fact that the transactions are virtually identical in terms of the legal rights and obligations of the parties.

This area of uncertainty is dealt with in the US under SFAS 48 – *Revenue Recognition When Right of Return Exists* – which states that if an entity sells its product but gives the buyer the right to return the product, revenue from the sales transaction is recognised at time of sale only if *all* of the following conditions are met:

(a) the seller's price to the buyer is substantially fixed or determinable at the date of sale;

(b) the buyer has paid the seller, or the buyer is obligated to pay the seller and the obligation is not contingent on resale of the product;

(c) the buyer's obligation to the seller would not be changed in the event of theft or physical destruction or damage of the product;

(d) the buyer acquiring the product for resale has economic substance apart from that provided by the seller (i.e. the buyer does not merely exist 'on paper' with little or no physical facilities, having been established by the seller primarily for the purpose of recognising revenue);

(e)   the seller does not have significant obligations for future performance to directly bring about resale of the product by the buyer; and

(f)   the amount of future returns can be reasonably estimated.[17]

Revenue that was not recognised at the time of sale because the above conditions were not met, should be recognised either when the return privilege has 'substantially expired', or when all the above conditions are met, whichever occurs first.[18]

The ability to make a reasonable estimate of future returns depends on many factors and will vary from one case to the next. Furthermore, SFAS 48 lists the following factors as being those that might impair a seller's ability to make such an estimate:

(a)   the susceptibility of the product to significant external factors, such as technological obsolescence or changes in demand;

(b)   relatively long periods in which a particular product may be returned;

(c)   absence of historical experience with similar types of sales of similar products, or inability to apply such experience because of changing circumstances; for example, changes in the selling entity's marketing policies or its relationships with its customers; and

(d)   absence of a large volume of relatively homogeneous transactions.[19]

The right of return is, therefore, viewed as a significant uncertainty that would preclude recognition under circumstances when the level of returns cannot be estimated. This means, for example, that a 14-day acceptance period would not require deferral of a sale – provided that the 14-day period is normal and routine. In such cases, the sale would be recognised, and either an accrual would be recognised under SFAS 48 or, if the acceptance related to a warranty issue, there would be an accrual of a warranty reserve.

2.2   The accretion approach

The accretion approach involves the recognition of revenue during the process of 'production', rather than at the end of a contract or when production is complete. There are three broad areas of entity activity where the application of the accretion approach might be appropriate.

2.2.1   *The use by others of entity resources*

The traditional accrual basis of accounting recognises revenue as entity resources are used by others; this approach is followed, for example, in the case of recognising rental, royalty or interest income. However, the question of uncertainty of collection should always be considered (for example, accrual of operating lease rentals receivable from a tenant that is in financial difficulty), in which case it might be appropriate to delay recognition until cash is received or where ultimate collection is assured beyond all reasonable doubt.

2.2.2 Long-term contracts

The second accepted application of the accretion approach to revenue reporting may be found in the accounting practice for long-term construction contracts. For example, under IAS 11 – *Construction contracts* – the amount of revenue to be recognised on construction contracts is determined according to the 'percentage-of-completion method', whereby contract revenue is matched with the contract costs incurred in reaching the stage of completion, resulting in the reporting of revenue, expenses and profit that can be attributed to the proportion of work completed at each balance sheet date.[20] Normally, the main uncertainties in the application of this approach are the estimation of the total costs and the degree of completion attained at the balance sheet date, particularly in the early stages of the contract. However, the selling price is sometimes uncertain as well, owing to contract modifications that give rise to revenue from 'extras'. (Accounting for construction contacts is dealt with in detail in Chapter 22.)

2.2.3 Natural growth and 'biological transformation'

Where an entity's activity involves production through natural growth or ageing, the accretion approach would suggest that revenue should be recognised at identifiable stages during this process. For example, in the case of livestock, there could be market prices available at the various stages of growth; revenue could, therefore, be recognised throughout the production process by making comparative stock valuations and reporting the accretions at each accounting date.

In fact, this is dealt with in IAS 41 – *Agriculture.* The standard requires application of fair value accounting to all 'biological assets' (which are defined as being living animals and plants) throughout their period of growth, which the Board refers to as 'biological transformation'. Biological transformation is defined as being 'the processes of growth, degeneration, production, and procreation that cause qualitative or quantitative changes in a biological asset'.[21]

The standard defines agricultural activity as 'the management by an entity of the biological transformation of biological assets for sale, into agricultural produce, or into additional biological assets',[22] and requires entities that undertake agricultural activity to measure all biological assets at fair value less estimated point-of-sale costs,[23] whilst all agricultural produce should be measured at fair value less estimated point-of-sale costs at the point of harvest, and thereafter inventory accounting (IAS 2) should be applied.[24] Fair value is defined as 'the amount for which an asset could be exchanged or a liability settled between knowledgeable, willing parties in an arm's length transaction'.[25] If an active market exists for a biological asset or agricultural produce, the quoted price in that market is the appropriate basis for determining the fair value of that asset. If an entity has access to different active markets, the entity uses the most relevant one. For example, if an entity has access to two active markets, it would use the price existing in the market expected to be used.[26]

The change in fair value of biological assets during a period is to be reported in net profit or loss for the period.[27] The standard acknowledges that the change in fair value of biological assets is part physical change (growth, etc.) and part unit price change. However, separate disclosure of the two components by group or otherwise is only encouraged but not required.[28] As stated above, fair value measurement stops at harvest, and IAS 2 – *Inventories* – or another applicable International Accounting Standard applies after harvest.[29] IAS 41 also draws a distinction between biological assets, agricultural land and intangible assets related to agricultural activity, requiring agricultural land to be accounted for under either IAS 16 – *Property, Plant and Equipment* or IAS 40 – *Investment Property*, and intangible assets to be accounted for under IAS 38 – *Intangible Assets*.[30]

In taking this approach in IAS 41, it seems that the IASB has formulated its ideas on a number of assumptions that do not appear necessarily to be true. These are that:

- it is assumed that efficient markets exist for all biological assets;
- it is assumed that there exist active and liquid markets for all biological assets, at all stages of growth;
- it is assumed that biological transformation can be measured with a degree of reliability which is sufficient for recognition in the accounts; and
- it is assumed that all sectors of agriculture are sufficiently similar as to be accounted for on the same basis.

We consider it unlikely that these assumptions are universally valid. For instance, it seems unlikely that there exist active and liquid markets for all intermediate agricultural products, particularly those that have long life-cycles and for which there are no liquid markets for immature products – such as forests. Practical difficulties also arise in situations where biological assets can only be sold together with the land that they grow on – for example, vineyards. This creates a significant problem of allocation, and leads ultimately to a mark-to-model approach to valuation.

The standard does, in fact, give some acknowledgement of the difficulties surrounding the reliability of measurement, providing preparers some relief in situations where reliability cannot be achieved. So whilst IAS 41 is built on the presumption that fair value can be measured reliably for a biological asset, the standard goes on to state that this presumption can be rebutted only on initial recognition for a biological asset for which market-determined prices or values are not available and for which alternative estimates of fair value are determined to be clearly unreliable. In such a case, the biological asset must be measured at its cost less any accumulated depreciation and any accumulated impairment losses until the fair value of such a biological asset becomes reliably measurable, at which time the entity reverts back to fair value less point of sale costs.[31]

In any event, IAS 41 does put a significant burden on the preparers of accounts to the extent that the costs of applying the standard (including audit costs) may outweigh the benefits. Users of financial statements should be aware that accounting for agricultural activities under IFRS is the most advanced outpost of fair value accounting to date whereby the chicks are literally counted before they are hatched. (IAS 41 is dealt with in detail in Chapter 36.)

2.3 The revenue allocation approach

The revenue allocation approach is essentially a combination of the critical event and accretion approaches. One of the difficulties in adopting, for example, the time of sale as the critical event for revenue recognition, is the existence of the uncertainty surrounding after-sale costs (such as customer support service and warranty costs). One way of dealing with these costs could be to make a provision for the future costs to be incurred on the basis of best estimate; alternatively, an approach could be followed whereby revenue is apportioned on the basis of two or more critical events. Consequently, part of the sale price could be treated as revenue at the point of sale, and the balance could either be recognised on an accretion basis over a warranty period or on the expiration of the warranty. The recognition of profit by manufacturer/dealer lessors is an example of such an application (see Chapter 23 at 3.3.5).

Under US GAAP, customer support services would always be treated as a separate element of revenue, not to be bundled but rather to be treated as a separate earnings event. In this regard, EITF 00-21 – *Revenue Arrangements with Multiple Deliverables* – deals with the difficult issue of separating elements of revenue.

3 THE REQUIREMENTS OF IAS 18

3.1 Scope

The original version of IAS 18 – *Revenue Recognition* – was issued in 1982 and defined revenue as the 'gross inflow of cash, receivables or other consideration arising in the course of the ordinary activities of an entity from the sale of goods, from the rendering of services, and from the use by others of entity resources yielding interest, royalties and dividends'.[32] In revising IAS 18 in 1993, the IASC attempted to retain the approach of the original standard, whilst at the same time create a link between the revised standard and the IASC's conceptual framework.

Consequently, the revised IAS 18 – *Revenue* – now includes the definition of income from the IASB's conceptual framework and states that 'revenue is income that arises in the course of ordinary activities of an entity and is referred to by a variety of different names including sales, fees, interest, dividends and royalties'.[33] It goes on to explain that the objective of the standard is to prescribe the accounting treatment of revenue arising from the following types of transactions and events:

(a) the sale of goods;

(b) the rendering of services; and

(c) the use by others of entity assets yielding interest, royalties and dividends.[34]

The term 'goods' includes goods produced by the entity for the purpose of sale and goods purchased for resale, such as merchandise purchased by a retailer or land and other property held for resale.[35]

The rendering of services typically involves the performance by the entity of a contractually agreed task over an agreed period of time. The services may be rendered within a single period or over more than one period. However, some contracts for the rendering of services are directly related to construction contracts, for example, those for the services of project managers and architects. Consequently, revenue arising from these contracts is not dealt with in IAS 18, but is dealt with in accordance with the requirements for construction contracts as specified in IAS 11 (see Chapter 22).[36]

The use by others of entity assets gives rise to revenue in the form of:

(a)   interest – charges for the use of cash or cash equivalents or amounts due to the entity;

(b)   royalties – charges for the use of long-term assets of the entity, for example, patents, trademarks, copyrights and computer software; and

(c)   dividends – distributions of profits to holders of equity investments in proportion to their holdings of a particular class of capital.[37]

It is important to note that there are a number of matters that the standard expressly states that it does not deal with. These are:[38]

(a)   lease agreements (see IAS 17 – *Leases*), although IAS 17 itself does not apply to licensing agreements for such items as motion picture films, video recordings, plays, manuscripts, patents and copyrights,[39] thus leaving a substantial gap in the revenue recognition literature;

(b)   dividends arising from investments that are accounted for under the equity method (see IAS 28 – *Investments in Associates*);

(c)   insurance contracts within the scope of IFRS 4 – *Insurance Contracts*;

(d)   the changes in the fair value of financial assets and financial liabilities or their disposal (see IAS 39 – *Financial Instruments: Recognition and Measurement*);

(e)   the changes in the value of other current assets;

(f)   revenue arising from the initial recognition and from changes in the fair value of biological assets related to agricultural activity (see IAS 41 – *Agriculture*);

(g)   the initial recognition of agricultural produce (see IAS 41 – *Agriculture*); and

(h)   the extraction of mineral ores.

3.2   The distinction between income, revenue and gains

The IASB's *Framework for the Preparation and Presentation of Financial Statements* defines income as 'increases in economic benefits during the accounting period in the form of inflows or enhancements of assets or decreases of liabilities that result in increases in equity, other than those relating to contributions from equity participants'.[40] The *Framework* explains that this definition of income encompasses both 'revenue' and 'gains'. Revenue arises in the course of the ordinary activities of an entity and is referred to by a variety of different names including sales, fees, interest, dividends, royalties and rent; gains represent other items that meet the definition of income and may, or may not, arise in the course of the ordinary activities of an entity. Gains include, for example, those arising on the disposal of non-current assets. The definition of income also includes unrealised gains; for example, those arising on the revaluation of marketable securities and those resulting from increases in the carrying amount of long-term assets.[41] Consequently, in distinguishing between 'gains' and 'revenue' in its definition of income, the IASB is able to exclude 'gains' from the scope of IAS 18, thereby avoiding the issue of the recognition of gains that are earned but unrealised.

The rules on offset set out in IAS 1 also distinguish between revenue and gains. The standard states that an entity undertakes, in the course of its ordinary activities, other transactions that do not generate revenue but are incidental to the main revenue-generating activities. The results of such transactions are presented, when this presentation reflects the substance of the transaction or other event, by netting any income with related expenses arising on the same transaction. For example, gains and losses on the disposal of non-current assets, including investments and operating assets, are reported by deducting from the proceeds on disposal the carrying amount of the asset and related selling expenses.[42] IAS 16 – *Property, Plant and Equipment* – also makes it clear that 'gains shall not be classified as revenue'.[43]

IAS 18 defines 'revenue' as the 'gross inflow of economic benefits during the period arising in the course of the ordinary activities of an entity when those inflows result in increases in equity, other than increases relating to contributions from equity participants',[44] thus making it clear that gains (not being part of the ordinary activities) fall outside its scope. IAS 18 makes it clear also that revenue includes only the gross inflows of economic benefits received and receivable by the entity on its own account. Amounts collected on behalf of third parties such as sales taxes, goods and services taxes and value added taxes are not economic benefits that flow to the entity and do not result in increases in equity. Therefore, they are excluded from revenue. Similarly, in an agency relationship, the gross inflows of economic benefits include amounts collected on behalf of the principal and which do not result in increases in equity for the entity. The amounts collected on behalf of the principal are not revenue; instead, revenue is the amount of commission.[45]

However, it is noteworthy that, having established the link between the *Framework* and IAS 18's definition of revenue, the IASB then abandons the *Framework's* implied asset/liability approach to revenue recognition, and reverts to the transactions-based critical event approach for the recognition of revenues derived from the sale of goods and the rendering of services, and an accretion approach in respect of revenues derived from the use by others of entity resources. It is this inconsistency that is driving the IASB's project to develop a new approach to revenue recognition that is more closely aligned to the *Framework* (see 5 below).

It should be noted that IAS 18 specifically and IFRSs generally do not address the issue of realisation. Whether or not revenue and gains recognised in accordance with IFRS are distributable to shareholders of an entity will depend entirely on the national laws and regulations with which the entity needs to comply. Thus, income reported in accordance with IFRS does not necessarily imply that such income gain would either be realised or distributable under a reporting entity's applicable national legislation.

3.3   Measurement of revenue

Revenue should be measured at the fair value of the consideration received or receivable.[46] IAS 18 states that the amount of revenue arising on a transaction is usually determined by agreement between the entity and the buyer or user of the asset. This means that it is measured at the fair value of the consideration received or receivable taking into account the amount of any trade discounts and volume rebates allowed by the entity.[47] The standard defines fair value as 'the amount for which an asset could be exchanged, or a liability settled, between knowledgeable, willing parties in an arm's length transaction'.[48]

Usually, this will present little difficulty as the consideration will normally be in the form of cash or cash equivalents and the amount of revenue will be the amount of cash or cash equivalents received or receivable. However, an issue does arise when the inflow is deferred, since the fair value of the consideration will then be less than the nominal amount of cash received or receivable. IAS 18 attempts to deal with this by introducing a discounting requirement under these circumstances. Consequently, when an arrangement effectively constitutes a financing transaction, the fair value of the consideration is determined by discounting all future receipts using an imputed rate of interest. The imputed rate of interest is the more clearly determinable of either:

(a)   the prevailing rate for a similar instrument of an issuer with a similar credit rating; or

(b)   a rate of interest that discounts the nominal amount of the instrument to the current cash sales price of the goods or services.

The difference between the fair value and the nominal amount of the consideration is recognised as interest revenue using the effective interest method as set out in IAS 39, paragraphs 9 and AG5 to AG8.[49] The application of the effective interest rate method is discussed in Chapter 18 at 5.

3.4   Identification of the transaction

IAS 18 states that the recognition criteria of the standard are usually applied separately to each transaction. However, it goes on to say that, in certain circumstances, it is necessary to apply the recognition criteria to the separately identifiable components of a single transaction in order to reflect the substance of the transaction.[50] This means quite simply that transactions have to be analysed in accordance with their economic substance in order to determine whether they should be combined or segmented for revenue recognition purposes. For example, when the selling price of a product includes an identifiable amount for subsequent servicing, that amount is deferred and recognised as revenue over the period during which the service is performed. Conversely, the recognition criteria are applied to two or more transactions together when they are linked in such a way that the commercial effect cannot be understood without reference to the series of transactions as a whole. For example, an entity may sell goods and, at the same time, enter into a separate agreement to repurchase the goods at a later date, thus negating the substantive effect of the transaction; in such a case, the two transactions are dealt with together.[51]

However, despite this requirement, IAS 18 does not establish criteria for segmenting and combining revenue transactions. On the other hand, IAS 11 – *Construction Contracts* – includes a requirement similar to that of IAS 18 in that it requires companies to apply the standard to separately identifiable components of a single construction contract or to a group of contracts together in order to reflect the substance of a contract or a group of contracts.[52] IAS 11 also sets down the following criteria to be used as guidance in determining whether construction contracts should be combined or segmented:[53]

When a contract covers a number of assets, the construction of each asset should be treated as a separate construction contract when:

(a)   separate proposals have been submitted for each asset;

(b)   each asset has been subject to separate negotiation and the contractor and customer have been able to accept or reject that part of the contract relating to each asset; and

(c)   the costs and revenues of each asset can be identified.

A group of contracts, whether with a single customer or with several customers, should be treated as a single construction contract when:

(a)   the group of contracts is negotiated as a single package;

(b)   the contracts are so closely interrelated that they are, in effect, part of a single project with an overall profit margin; and

(c)   the contracts are performed concurrently or in a continuous sequence.

A contract may provide for the construction of an additional asset at the option of the customer or may be amended to include the construction of an additional asset. The construction of the additional asset should be treated as a separate construction contract when:

(a)   the asset differs significantly in design, technology or function from the asset or assets covered by the original contract; or

(b)   the price of the asset is negotiated without regard to the original contract price.

In the absence of any equivalent guidance in IAS 18, we recommend that entities take the above criteria set out in IAS 11 into account in determining whether revenue transactions should be combined or segmented. The practical application of these criteria to construction contracts is dealt with in Chapter 22 at 1.2. In the case of certain arrangements with multiple deliverables, it may also be helpful, under the hierarchy in IAS 8,[54] to refer to EITF 00-21 – *Revenue Arrangements with Multiple Deliverables* – which deals with the difficult issue of separating elements of revenue (see 7.13.4 below).

3.5   The sale of goods

IAS 18 lays down the following five criteria that must be satisfied in order to recognise revenue from the sale of goods:[55]

(a)   the entity has transferred to the buyer the significant risks and rewards of ownership of the goods;

(b)   the entity retains neither continuing managerial involvement to the degree usually associated with ownership nor effective control over the goods sold;

(c)   the amount of revenue can be measured reliably;

(d)   it is probable that the economic benefits associated with the transaction will flow to the entity; and

(e)   the costs incurred or to be incurred in respect of the transaction can be measured reliably.

If the costs incurred cannot be measured reliably, the standard requires that 'any consideration already received for the sale of the goods is recognised as a liability.'[56]

It is clear that IAS 18 views the passing of risks and rewards as the most crucial of the five criteria, giving the following four examples of situations in which an entity may retain the significant risks and rewards of ownership:

(a)   when the entity retains an obligation for unsatisfactory performance not covered by normal warranty provisions;

(b)   when the receipt of the revenue from a particular sale is contingent on the derivation of revenue by the buyer from its sale of the goods;

(c)   when the goods are shipped subject to installation and the installation is a significant part of the contract which has not yet been completed by the entity; and

(d)   when the buyer has the right to rescind the purchase for a reason specified in the sales contract and the entity is uncertain about the probability of return.[57]

On closer examination of these examples, though, it is clear that the standard still advocates an earnings process-driven critical event approach to revenue recognition – despite its attempt to create a link with the asset/liability approach to income articulated in the IASB's *Framework.*

It is, therefore, necessary to establish at which point in the earnings process both the significant risks and rewards of ownership are transferred from the seller to the buyer and any significant uncertainties (which would otherwise delay recognition) are removed. For example, the responsibilities of each party during the period between sale and delivery should be established, possibly by examination of the customer agreements. If the goods have merely to be uplifted by the buyer, and the seller has performed all his associated responsibilities, then the sale may be recognised immediately. However, if the substance of the sale is merely that an order has been placed, and the goods have still to be acquired or manufactured by the seller, then the sale should not be recognised.

One issue that IAS 18 does not address is whether or not, in order to recognise revenue, it is necessary for the buyer of the goods to have economic substance beyond that provided by the seller. For example, this question arises when sales are made to 'exclusive' dealers or agents under an agency agreement. Paragraph 14(a) of IAS 18 requires transfer of the 'significant risks and rewards of ownership', and paragraph 14(b) requires that a selling entity retains neither continuing managerial involvement to the degree usually associated with ownership nor effective control in order for revenue to be recognised from the sale of goods. Further, paragraph 6 of the Appendix to IAS 18 states that 'revenue from [sales to intermediate parties, such as distributors, dealers or others for resale] is generally recognised when the risks and rewards of ownership have passed. However, when the buyer is acting, in substance, as an agent, the sale is treated as a consignment sale.' Accordingly, in the case of an agency agreement or other situation involving a sale to an intermediary, the risks and rewards of ownership generally have not passed, and the seller treats the transaction as a consignment sale.[58]

IAS 18 also recognises that, under certain circumstances, goods are sold subject to reservation of title in order to protect the collectibility of the amount due; in such circumstances, provided that the seller has transferred the significant risks and rewards of ownership, the transaction can be treated as a sale and revenue can be recognised.[59] The standard assumes that 'in most cases, the transfer of risks and rewards of ownership coincides with the transfer of legal title or the passing of possession to the buyer',[60] but acknowledges that this may not always be the case. Transfer of legal title is, therefore, not a condition for revenue recognition under IAS 18,[61] as the standard recognises that transactions occur where the transfer of risks and rewards of ownership occurs at a different time from the transfer of legal title or the passing of possession.[62]

This point is reinforced in the Appendix to IAS 18, which notes that the laws in different countries may mean that the recognition criteria in the standard are met at different times. In particular, the law may determine the point in time at which an entity transfers the significant risks and rewards of ownership. Therefore, the examples in the Appendix need to be read in the context of the laws relating to the sale of goods in the country in which the transaction takes place.[63]

Examples of accounting policies for the recognition of revenues from the sale of goods are illustrated below:

Extract 26.1: AngloGold Limited (2003)

Notes to Group Financial Statements [extract]

1.　Accounting policies [extract]

Revenue recognition [extract]

Revenue is recognised to the extent that it is probable that the economic benefits will flow to the group and the revenue can be reliably measured. The following criteria must also be present:

- the sale of mining products is recognised when the significant risks and rewards of ownership of the products are transferred to the buyer;

The following extract from the accounts of Roche provides a good illustration of both the measurement principles of IAS 18 and the application of the critical event approach in determining the timing of revenue recognition:

Extract 26.2: Roche Holding Ltd (2003)

Notes to Roche Group Financial Statements [extract]

1.   Summary of significant accounting policies [extract]

Revenues and cost of sales

Sales represent amounts received and receivable for goods supplied to customers after deducting trade discounts, cash discounts and volume rebates and excluding sales and value added taxes. Revenues from the sale of products are recognised upon transfer to the customer of significant risks and rewards, usually upon shipment. Other revenues are recorded as earned or as the services are performed. Cost of sales includes the corresponding direct production costs and related production overhead of goods manufactured and services rendered. Start-up costs between validation and the achievement of normal production capacity are expensed as incurred. Royalty income is recognised on an accrual basis in accordance with the economic substance of the agreement and is reported as part of other operating income.

As stated above, IAS 18 refers to the situation where the receipt of the revenue from a particular sale is contingent on the derivation of revenue by the buyer from its sale of the goods, and uses this as an example of where it might be concluded that an entity retains the significant risks and rewards of ownership.[64] Altana AG provides a good illustration of an accounting policy that deals with this situation in practice:

Extract 26.3: Altana AG (2003)

Notes [extract]

Significant accounting policies [extract]

Revenue recognition [extract]

The Company recognizes revenues from sales of products and services if the revenue can be reliably measured, it is probable that the economic benefits of the transaction will flow to the Company and all related costs can be reliably measured. As such, the Company records revenue from product sales when the goods are shipped and title has passed to the customer. With respect to licensing agreements where revenue in excess of a defined minimum price is contingent on the buyer's ultimate resale price, sales are recognized at the contractual minimum price with additional sales recognized when realized. Provisions for discounts and rebates to customers and returns are recorded in the same period in which the related sales are recorded. Such provisions are based on management's best estimate.

As already mentioned, neither IAS 18 nor IAS 17 deals with revenue recognition related to licensing agreements in respect of patents and similar items. Consequently, companies such as Roche and Altana have to develop accounting policies that deal with such arrangements, and both provide good examples of such policies:

Extract 26.4: Roche Holding Ltd (2003)

Notes to Roche Group Financial Statements [extract]

1. Summary of significant accounting policies [extract]

In-licensing, milestone and other up-front receipts and payments

Certain Group companies, notably Genentech, receive from third-parties up-front, milestone and other similar non-refundable payments relating to the sale or licensing of products or technology. Revenue associated with performance milestones is recognised based on achievement of the milestone, as defined in the respective agreements. Revenue from non-refundable up-front payments and licence fees is initially reported as deferred income and is recognised in income as earned over the period of the development collaboration or the manufacturing obligation. Payments made by Group companies to third parties and associated companies for such items are charged against income as research and development costs unless it is probable that future economic benefits will flow to the Group, which is normally evidenced by regulatory approval. In this case they are capitalised as development costs and amortised as described above. In practice this means that most in-licensing and milestone payments for pharmaceutical products are expensed as incurred, as in most cases they have not yet gained regulatory approval. Receipts and payments between consolidated subsidiaries, such as between Genentech, Chugai and other Roche Group subsidiaries, are eliminated on consolidation, except to the extent of any impacts on minority interests.

Extract 26.5: Altana AG (2003)

Notes [extract]

Significant accounting policies [extract]

Revenue recognition [extract]

Consistent with its research and development strategy, the Company enters into co-development and co-promotion agreements to enhance the scope and depth of our research portfolio. These agreements contain multiple elements and varying consideration terms, such as up-front, milestone and other related payments. The Company reviewed its arrangements to determine if the multiple elements can be divided into separate units of accounting and how the arrangement consideration should be recognized. When an arrangement can be divided into separate units, the arrangement consideration is recognized amongst those varying units and recognized over the respective performance period. When the arrangement cannot be divided into separate units, the total arrangement consideration is allocated on a straight-line basis over the estimated collaboration period. In regard to agreements the Company has entered into to date, up-front payments and other similar non-refundable payments received which relate to the sale or licensing of products or technology are reported as deferred income and recognized as other income over the related period of collaboration on a straight-line basis. In previous years, non-refundable up-front fees were deferred over the research and development period and non-refundable milestone payments were recognized as revenue when received. The revised method is appropriate for recognizing revenue under its existing agreements and has not resulted in a material impact on the Company's prior year consolidated balance sheets, income statements or cash flows.

3.6   The rendering of services

IAS 18 requires that when the outcome of a transaction involving the rendering of services can be estimated reliably, revenue is recognised 'by reference to the stage of completion of the transaction at the balance sheet date'[65] (in other words, using the percentage-of-completion method). In applying the percentage-of-completion method, the requirements of IAS 11 – *Construction Contracts* – are 'generally applicable to the recognition of revenue and the associated expenses for a transaction involving the rendering of services.'[66]

According to IAS 18, the outcome of a transaction can be estimated reliably when all the following conditions are satisfied:[67]

(a)   the amount of revenue can be measured reliably;

(b)   it is probable that the economic benefits associated with the transaction will flow to the entity;

(c)   the stage of completion of the transaction at the balance sheet date can be measured reliably; and

(d)   the costs incurred for the transaction and the costs to complete the transaction can be measured reliably.

When the outcome cannot be estimated reliably, revenue is recognised only to the extent of the expenses recognised that are recoverable.[68] During the early stages of a transaction, it is often the case that the outcome of the transaction cannot be estimated reliably. Nevertheless, it may be probable that the enterprise will recover the transaction costs incurred. Therefore, revenue is recognised only to the extent of costs incurred that are expected to be recoverable. As the outcome of the transaction cannot be estimated reliably, no profit is recognised.[69] When the outcome of a transaction cannot be estimated reliably and it is not probable that the costs incurred will be recovered, revenue is not recognised and the costs incurred are recognised as an expense. When the uncertainties that prevented the outcome of the contract being estimated reliably no longer exist, revenue is recognised by reference to the stage of completion of the transaction at the balance sheet date.[70]

The Appendix to IAS 18 provides several illustrative examples of transactions involving the rendering of services. All the examples are provided on the assumption that the amount of revenue can be measured reliably, it is probable that the economic benefits will flow to the entity and the costs incurred or to be incurred can be measured reliably. It is clear from these examples that, in the case of a transaction involving the rendering of services, the performance of the service is the critical event for revenue recognition.[71]

The standard claims that an entity is generally able to make reliable estimates after it has agreed to the following with the other parties to the transaction:[72]

(a)   each party's enforceable rights regarding the service to be provided and received by the parties;

(b)   the consideration to be exchanged; and

(c)   the manner and terms of settlement.

The standard suggests further that it is usually necessary for the entity to have an effective internal financial budgeting and reporting system. The entity reviews and, when necessary, revises the estimates of revenue as the service is performed. The need for such revisions does not necessarily indicate that the outcome of the transaction cannot be estimated reliably.[73]

When it comes to determining the stage of completion of a transaction, IAS 18 suggests three methods that may be used:[74]

(a)   surveys of work performed;

(b)   services performed to date as a percentage of total services to be performed; or

(c)   the proportion that costs incurred to date bear to the estimated total costs of the transaction. Only costs that reflect services performed to date are included in costs incurred to date. Only costs that reflect services performed or to be performed are included in the estimated total costs of the transaction.

For practical purposes, though, when services are performed by an indeterminate number of acts over a specified period, the standard permits revenue to be recognised on a straight-line basis over the specified period unless there is evidence that some other method better represents the stage of completion. However, when a specific act is much more significant than any other acts, the standard again reverts to critical event theory requiring that the recognition of revenue be postponed until the significant act is executed.[75]

Nokia provides a good illustration of an accounting policy whereby revenue from contracts involving solutions achieved through modification of equipment is recognised using the percentage-of-completion method:

Extract 26.6: Nokia Corporation (2003)

Notes to Consolidated Financial Statements [extract]

Revenue Recognition

Sales from the majority of the Group are recognized when persuasive evidence of an arrangement exists, delivery has occurred, the fee is fixed and determinable and collectibility is probable. The remainder of the sales is recorded under the percentage of completion method.

Sales and cost of sales from contracts involving solutions achieved through modification of telecommunications equipment are recognized on the percentage of completion method when the outcome of the contract can be estimated reliably. A contract's outcome can be estimated reliably when total contract revenue and the costs to complete the contract can be estimated reliably, it is probable that the economic benefits associated with the contract will flow to the company and the stage of contract completion can be measured reliably. When the Group is not able to meet those conditions, the policy is to recognize revenues only equal to costs incurred to date, to the extent that such costs are expected to be recovered.

Completion is measured by reference to cost incurred to date as a percentage of estimated total project costs, the cost-to-cost method.

The percentage of completion method relies on estimates of total expected contract revenue and costs, as well as dependable measurement of the progress made towards project completion. Recognized revenues and profits are subject to revisions during the project in the event that the assumptions regarding the overall project outcome are revised. The cumulative impact of a revision in estimates is recorded in the period such revisions become known and estimable. Losses on projects in progress are recognized immediately when known and estimable.

All the Group's material revenue streams are recorded according to the above policies.

3.7 Exchanges of goods and services

Under IAS 18, when goods or services are exchanged or swapped for goods or services that are of a similar nature and value, the exchange is not regarded as a transaction that generates revenue. This is often the case with commodities like oil or milk, where suppliers exchange or swap inventories in various locations to fulfil demand on a timely basis in a particular location. When goods are sold or services are rendered in exchange for dissimilar goods or services, the exchange is regarded as a transaction that generates revenue. The revenue is measured at the fair value of the goods or services received, adjusted by the amount of any cash or cash equivalents transferred. When the fair value of the goods or services received cannot be measured reliably, the revenue is measured at the fair value of the goods or services given up, adjusted by the amount of any cash or cash equivalents transferred.[76]

3.8 Exchanges of property plant and equipment

The accounting for exchanges of property, plant and equipment is dealt with in IAS 16, which takes a different approach from IAS 18 concerning exchanges of goods and services. Following IAS 16's amendment in 2003 under the IASB's improvements' project, the IASB removed the distinction between similar and dissimilar assets. Instead, IAS 16 now requires property, plant and equipment acquired in exchange for a non-monetary asset or assets, or a combination of monetary and non-monetary assets to be accounted for at fair value, 'unless (a) the exchange transaction lacks commercial substance or (b) the fair value of neither the asset received nor the asset given up is reliably measurable. The acquired item is measured in this way even if an entity cannot immediately derecognise the asset given up. If the acquired item is not measured at fair value, its cost is measured at the carrying amount of the asset given up.'[77] The application of these requirements is dealt with in detail in Chapter 12 at 2.3.2.

IAS 38 deals with exchanges of intangible assets, and includes the same requirements with respect to intangible assets as IAS 16 does for exchanges of property, plant and equipment.[78]

Paragraph 24 of IAS 16 is silent on whether the fair value of the monetary and non-monetary items received in an exchange must be presented as revenue or whether it is a gain. However, since paragraph 68 is clear that gains arising from derecognition shall not be classified as revenue, we believe that this applies equally to derecognition by way of an exchange, which means that an exchange of property, plant and equipment does not result in the recognition of revenue.

It should also be noted that IFRS 5 – *Non-current Assets Held for Sale and Discontinued Operations* – lays down additional requirements for assets held for disposal; these requirements include measurement rules, which clearly affect the measurement of the amount of the gain on disposal to be recognised. These are discussed in Chapter 3 at 5.2.

3.9 Barter transactions involving advertising services

This is an issue that arose during the dotcom boom of the late 1990s and early 2000s, and is addressed in a SIC Interpretation SIC-31 – *Revenue–Barter transactions involving advertising services*. The issue arises where an entity (the Seller) enters into a barter transaction to provide advertising services in exchange for receiving advertising services from its customer (the Customer). Advertisements may be displayed on the Internet or poster sites, broadcast on the television or radio, published in magazines or journals, or presented in another medium. In some cases, no cash or other consideration is exchanged between the entities. In some other cases, equal or approximately equal amounts of cash or other consideration are also exchanged.

It is clear that, under IAS 18, a Seller that provides advertising services in the course of its ordinary activities recognises revenue from a barter transaction involving advertising when, amongst other criteria, the services exchanged are dissimilar,[79] and the amount of revenue can be measured reliably.[80] An exchange of similar advertising services is not a transaction that generates revenue under IAS 18.

The issue that the Standing Interpretations Committee considered was under what circumstances can a Seller reliably measure revenue at the fair value of advertising services received or provided in a barter transaction involving dissimilar services?[81]

The SIC concluded that revenue from a barter transaction involving advertising cannot be measured reliably at the fair value of advertising services received. However, a Seller can reliably measure revenue at the fair value of the advertising services it provides in a barter transaction, by reference only to non-barter transactions that:

(a)   involve advertising similar to the advertising in the barter transaction;

(b)   occur frequently;

(c)   represent a predominant number of transactions and amount when compared to all transactions to provide advertising that is similar to the advertising in the barter transaction;

(d)   involve cash and/or another form of consideration (e.g. marketable securities, non-monetary assets, and other services) that has a reliably measurable fair value; and

(e)   do not involve the same counterparty as in the barter transaction.[82]

The conditions represent a relatively high hurdle for companies to overcome, and it would seem that in most instances they would find it difficult to be able to recognise any revenue. For example, a swap of cheques for equal or substantially equal amounts between the same entities that provide and receive advertising services does not provide reliable evidence of fair value. An exchange of advertising services that also includes only partial cash payment provides reliable evidence of the fair value of the transaction to the extent of the cash component (except when partial cash payments of equal or substantially equal amounts are swapped), but does not provide reliable evidence of the fair value of the entire transaction.[83]

In our view, SIC–31 was issued as a specific anti-abuse rule that does not have wider implications and should not be applied to other situations by analogy.

3.10   Interest, royalties and dividends

When it is probable that the economic benefits associated with the transaction will flow to the entity and that the amount of revenue can be measured reliably, IAS 18 requires that the revenue arising from the use by others of entity assets yielding interest, royalties and dividends should be recognised as follows:[84]

(a)   *interest:* using the effective interest method as set out in IAS 39, paragraphs 9 and AG5-AG8;

(b)   *royalties:* on an accrual basis in accordance with the substance of the relevant agreement; and

(c)   *dividends:* when the shareholder's right to receive payment is established.

AngloGold provides a straightforward example of accounting policies for dividends and interest:

Extract 26.7: AngloGold Limited (2003)

Notes to Group Financial Statements [extract]

1.   Accounting policies [extract]

Revenue recognition [extract]

Revenue is recognised to the extent that it is probable that the economic benefits will flow to the group and the revenue can be reliably measured. The following criteria must also be present:

●   ...

●   dividends are recognised when the right to receive payment is established; and

●   Interest is recognised on a time proportion basis, taking account of the principal outstanding and the effective rate over the period to maturity, when it is determined that such income will accrue to the group.

When unpaid interest has accrued before the acquisition of an interest-bearing investment, the subsequent receipt of interest is allocated between pre-acquisition and post-acquisition periods; only the post-acquisition portion is recognised as revenue. When dividends on equity securities are declared from pre-acquisition net income, those dividends are deducted from the cost of the securities. If it is difficult to make such an allocation except on an arbitrary basis, dividends are recognised as revenue unless they clearly represent a recovery of part of the cost of the equity securities.[85]

Royalties accrue in accordance with the terms of the relevant agreement and are usually recognised on that basis unless, having regard to the substance of the agreement, it is more appropriate to recognise revenue on some other systematic and rational basis.[86]

3.11   Uncollectible revenue

Revenue is recognised only when it is probable that the economic benefits associated with the transaction will flow to the entity. In some cases, this may not be probable until the consideration is received or until an uncertainty is removed. However, when an uncertainty arises about the collectibility of an amount already included in revenue, the uncollectible amount or the amount in respect of which recovery has ceased to be probable is recognised as an expense, rather than as an adjustment of the amount of revenue originally recognised.[87]

3.12 Disclosure

IAS 18's disclosure requirements relate to both revenue recognition policies and amounts included in the accounts under the different categories of revenue. They are set down in the standard as follows:[88]

(a) the accounting policies adopted for the recognition of revenue including the methods adopted to determine the stage of completion of transactions involving the rendering of services;

(b) the amount of each significant category of revenue recognised during the period including revenue arising from:

    (i) the sale of goods;

    (ii) the rendering of services;

    (iii) interest;

    (iv) royalties;

    (v) dividends; and

(c) the amount of revenue arising from exchanges of goods or services included in each significant category of revenue.

Clearly, the disclosures required under (b) and (c) above may be provided in the notes to the financial statements, rather than on the face of the income statement.

3.13 What should be shown in the income statement within revenue?

The requirements regarding what must be disclosed on the face of the income statement are set out in IAS 1, as follows:[89]

As a minimum, the face of the income statement shall include line items that present the following amounts for the period:

(a) revenue;

(b) finance costs;

(c) share of the profit or loss of associates and joint ventures accounted for using the equity method;

(d) tax expense;

(e) a single amount comprising the total of (i) the post-tax profit or loss of discontinued operations and (ii) the post-tax gain or loss recognised on the measurement to fair value less costs to sell or on the disposal of the assets or disposal group(s) constituting the discontinued operation; and

(f) profit or loss.

IAS 1 goes on to state that additional line items, headings and subtotals shall be presented on the face of the income statement when such presentation is relevant to an understanding of the entity's financial performance. Additional line items are included on the face of the income statement, and the descriptions used and the ordering of items are amended when this is necessary to explain the elements of financial performance. Factors to be considered include materiality and the nature and function of the components of income and expenses.[90]

These requirements provide a company with a substantial amount of flexibility with regard to the presentation of its income statement generally. However, they do also raise a number of practical questions with regard to the presentation of revenue, such as:

- can the amount relating to the line 'share of the profit or loss of associates and joint ventures accounted for using the equity method' be shown within revenue, or must it be shown separately outside revenue?

- can the amount for 'finance costs' be shown net of interest and other finance income?

- can gains on disposal of property, plant and equipment be shown within revenue?

3.13.1   *The disclosure of share of the profit or loss of associates and joint ventures accounted for using the equity method*

At first glance, IAS 1 appears unequivocal as to the minimum requirements regarding the basic structure of the income statement. However, the standard builds in a substantial amount of flexibility as to the introduction of additional line items and sub-totals, as well as to the order in which items appear on the face of the statement. Nevertheless, some may think that paragraph 81 of IAS 1 requires the line 'share of the profit or loss of associates and joint ventures accounted for using the equity method' to be shown separately from 'revenue'. However, we do not believe this to be the case.

This view is supported by paragraph 16 of IAS 14, which defines 'segment result' as 'segment revenue less segment expense'.[91] 'Segment expense' is then defined as the 'expense resulting from the operating activities of a segment that is directly attributable to the segment and the relevant portion of an expense that can be allocated on a reasonable basis to the segment, including expenses relating to sales to external customers and expenses relating to transactions with other segments of the same entity'[92] and specifically excludes 'an entity's share of losses of associates, joint ventures, or other investments accounted for under the equity method'.[93] However, 'segment revenue' is defined as 'revenue reported in the entity's income statement that is directly attributable to a segment and the relevant portion of entity revenue that can be allocated on a reasonable basis to a segment, whether from sales to external customers or from transactions with other segments of the same entity'.[94] Significantly, the definition then goes on to state that 'segment revenue includes an entity's share of profits or losses of associates, joint ventures, or other investments accounted for under the equity method only if those items are included in consolidated or total entity revenue'.[95]

This clearly indicates that IAS 14 acknowledges specifically the possibility of a company including in the revenue line of its income statement its share of equity-accounted profits or losses of associates and joint ventures.

3.13.2 *Interest and other finance income*

It used to be fairly widespread practice under a number of national GAAPs for companies to show finance costs net of interest and other finance income. However, IAS 1 is unequivocal that this is not permitted under IFRS. The offset rules in IAS 1 state that 'assets and liabilities, and income and expenses, shall not be offset unless required or permitted by a Standard or an Interpretation.'[96] It goes on to state that 'it is important that assets and liabilities, and income and expenses, are reported separately. Offsetting in the income statement or the balance sheet, except when offsetting reflects the substance of the transaction or other event, detracts from the ability of users both to understand the transactions, other events and conditions that have occurred and to assess the entity's future cash flows'.[97] Nevertheless, IAS 1 does permit gains and losses arising from a group of similar transactions to be reported on a net basis, for example, foreign exchange gains and losses or gains and losses arising on financial instruments held for trading. Such gains and losses are, however, reported separately if they are material.[98]

Even so, there is no Standard or Interpretation that permits interest income to be offset against interest expense; in any event, IAS 18 requires interest income to be included and disclosed within revenue.[99] Of course, there is nothing to prevent an entity presenting gross interest income and gross interest expense on the face of the income statement, and then striking a sub-total that shows net interest.

More importantly, though, we believe that net presentation is appropriate in the case of trading activities; in our view, the interest income on financial instruments (e.g. bonds) that are held as trading assets (e.g. by a financial institution) could be included within net trading income. UBS provides a good example of such an approach:

Extract 26.8: UBS AG (2003)

Financial Statements [extract]
UBS Income Statement

CHF million, except per share data For the year ended	Note	31.12.03	31.12.02	31.12.01	% change from 31.12.02
Operating income					
Interest income	3	40,159	39,963	52,277	0
Interest expense	3	(27,860)	(29,417)	(44,236)	(5)
Net interest income		12,299	10,546	8,041	17
Credit loss (expense)/recovery		(116)	(206)	(498)	(44)
Net interest income after credit loss expense		12,183	10,340	7,543	18
Net fee and commission income	4	17,345	18,221	20,211	(5)
Net trading income	3	3,883	5,572	8,802	(30)
Other income	5	561	(12)	558	
Total operating income		33,972	34,121	37,114	0

Operating expenses					
Personnel expenses	6	17,231	18,524	19,828	(7)
General and administrative expenses	7	6,086	7,072	7,631	(14)
Depreciation of property and equipment	14	1,364	1,521	1,614	(10)
Amortization of goodwill and other intangible assets	15	943	2,460	1,323	(62)
Total operating expenses		25,624	29,577	30,396	(13)
Operating profit before tax and minority interests		8,348	4,544	6,718	84
Tax expense	21	1,618	678	1,401	139
Net profit before minority interests		6,730	3,866	5,317	74
Minority interests	22	(345)	(331)	(344)	4
Net profit		6,385	3,535	4,973	81
Basis earnings per share (CHF)	8	5.72	2.92	3.93	96
Diluted earnings per share (CHF)	8	5.61	2.87	3.78	95

UBS then clearly explains their approach to presenting the components of net interest and trading income, together with a detailed analysis thereof:

Extract 26.9: UBS AG (2003)

Notes to the Financial Statements [extract]

Note 3   Net Interest and Trading Income

Accounting standards require separate disclosure of net interest income and net trading income (see the tables on the following page). This required disclosure, however, does not take into account that net interest and trading income are generated by a range of different business activities. In many cases, a particular business activity can generate both net interest and trading income. Fixed income trading activity, for example, generates both trading profits and coupon income. UBS management therefore analyzes net interest and trading income according to the business activity generating it. The table below provides information that corresponds to this management view. For example, net income from trading activities is further broken down into the four sub-components of Equities, Fixed income, Foreign exchange and Other. These activities generate both types of income (interest and trading revenue) and therefore this analysis is not comparable to the breakdown provided in the third table on the next page (Net trading income only).

Net Interest and Trading Income

CHF million For the year ended	31.12.03	31.12.02	31.12.01	% change from 31.12.02
Net interest income	12,299	10,546	8,041	17
Net trading income	3,883	5,572	8,802	(30)
Total net interest and trading income	16,182	16,118	16,843	0

Breakdown by business activity

CHF million For the year ended	31.12.03	31.12.02	31.12.01	% change from 31.12.02
Net income from interest margin products	5,077	5,275	5,694	(4)
Equities	2,464	2,794	3,661	(12)
Fixed Income	6,530	6,041	6,294	8
Foreign Exchange	1,501	1,500	1,490	0
Other	315	270	84	17
Net income from trading activities	10,810	10,605	11,529	2
Net income from treasury activities	1,415	1,667	1,424	(15)
Other[1]	(1,120)	(1,429)	(1,804)	22
Total net interest and trading income	16,182	16,118	16,843	0

1 Principally external funding costs of the Paine Webber Group, Inc. acquisition.

Net interest Income[1]

CHF million For the year ended	31.12.03	31.12.02	31.12.01	% change from 31.12.02
Interest income				
Interest earned on loans and advances	10,542	11,600	16,955	(9)
Interest earned on securities borrowed and reverse repurchase agreements	11,148	11,184	18,337	0
Interest and dividend income from financial investments	75	165	453	(55)
Interest and dividend income from trading portfolio	18,394	17,014	16,532	8
Total	40,159	39,963	52,277	0
Interest expense				
Interest on amounts due to banks and customers	5,093	6,383	14,088	(20)
Interest on securities lent and repurchase agreements	9,623	10,081	14,517	(5)
Interest and dividend expense from trading portfolio	10,101	8,366	7,815	21
Interest on debt issued	3,043	4,587	7,816	(34)
Total	27,860	29,417	44,236	(5)
Net interest income	12,299	10,546	8,041	17

Net trading income[1]

CHF million For the year ended	31.12.03	31.12.02	31.12.01	% change from 31.12.02
Equities	1,679	2,638	4,026	(36)
Fixed income[2]	452	1,061	2,731	(57)
Foreign exchange and other	1,752	1,873	2,045	(6)
Net trading income	3,883	5,572	8,802	(30)

1 Please refer to the table "Net Interest and Trading Income" on the previous page for the Equities, Fixed Income, Foreign exchange and Other business results (for an explanation, read the corresponding introductory comment).
2 Includes commodities trading income.

3.13.3 *Gains on disposal of property, plant and equipment*

As already discussed above, the IASB's *Framework* explains that income encompasses both 'revenue' and 'gains'. Revenue arises in the course of the ordinary activities of an entity and is referred to by a variety of different names including sales, fees, interest, dividends, royalties and rent; gains represent other items that meet the definition of income and may, or may not, arise in the course of the ordinary activities of an entity. Gains include, for example, those arising on the disposal of non-current assets. IAS 16 also makes it clear that 'gains shall not be classified as revenue'.[100]

This means that gains arising on the disposal of property, plant and equipment do not form part of revenue. However, in our view, it is acceptable to show such gains net of any losses on disposal as part of income, whilst net losses on disposal should be shown within expenses.

3.13.4 *Example of income statement presentation of revenue*

Set out below is an example of one way that a company might present its revenue on the face of its income statement, taking into account the requirements of both IAS 1 and IAS 18. Of course, the detailed analysis of revenue could be presented in the notes to the financial statements instead of on the face of the income statement.

Income Statement

Revenue

Sales and other operating revenues

Earnings from associates – after interest and tax

Earnings from jointly controlled entities – after interest and tax

Interest income

Total revenue

    Net gain on sale of property, plant and equipment

    Total revenue and other income

---

4 REVENUE RECOGNITION UNDER US GAAP

4.1 Applicability of US literature

Although IAS 18 does lay down general principles of revenue recognition, there is a lack of specific guidance in relation to matters such as multiple-element revenue arrangements and industry-specific issues, such as those relating to the software and telecommunications industries. Consequently, whilst the US literature can never override the specific requirements of IFRS, it may well be that companies might choose to avail themselves of the hierarchy set out in paragraph 11 of IAS 8 in order to use US GAAP to formulate appropriate accounting policies with respect to specific transactions. At the same time, though, it is crucial to bear in mind that

that not all industry practices under US GAAP are permissible under IFRS – for example, utility companies should not adopt a revenue recognition policy that gives rise to regulatory assets/liabilities.

The important point to note is that the approach to revenue recognition under US GAAP is closely aligned with that of IAS 18, in that it is based clearly on the earnings process and realisation principle. In other words, it adopts the same critical event approach as IAS 18, and it is therefore often the case that US revenue recognition guidance is compatible with IAS 18.

4.2 The general approach to revenue recognition under US GAAP

The accounting literature on revenue recognition includes both broad conceptual discussions as well as certain industry-specific guidance. If a transaction is within the scope of specific authoritative literature that provides revenue recognition guidance, that literature should be applied. However, in the absence of authoritative literature addressing a specific arrangement or a specific industry, the SEC staff will consider the existing authoritative accounting standards as well as the broad revenue recognition criteria specified in the FASB's conceptual framework that contain basic guidelines for revenue recognition.[101]

The FASB's Concepts Statement No. 5 – *Recognition and Measurement in Financial Statements of Business Enterprises* – has dealt primarily with recognition issues from the angle of providing reliability of measurement. However, the broad principle for revenue recognition laid down by Concepts Statement 5 is that revenues are not recognised until they are (a) realised or realisable and (b) earned.[102] Concepts Statement 5 states that 'an entity's revenue-earning activities involve delivering or producing goods, rendering services, or other activities that constitute its ongoing major or central operations, and revenues are considered to have been earned when the entity has substantially accomplished what it must do to be entitled to the benefits represented by the revenues'.[103] It goes on to state that 'the two conditions (being realized or realizable and being earned) are usually met by the time product or merchandise is delivered or services are rendered to customers, and revenues from manufacturing and selling activities and gains and losses from sales of other assets are commonly recognized at time of sale (usually meaning delivery)'[104]. In addition, it states that 'if services are rendered or rights to use assets extend continuously over time (for example, interest or rent), reliable measures based on contractual prices established in advance are commonly available, and revenues may be recognized as earned as time passes.'[105]

The SEC staff believes that revenue generally is realised or realisable and earned when all of the following criteria are met:

- Persuasive evidence of an arrangement exists;
- Delivery has occurred or services have been rendered;
- The seller's price to the buyer is fixed or determinable; and
- Collectibility is reasonably assured.

Generally, the SEC staff believes that a sales price is not fixed or determinable when a customer has the unilateral right to terminate or cancel the contract and receive a cash refund. A sales price or fee that is variable until the occurrence of future events (other than product returns that are within the scope of SFAS 48) generally is not fixed or determinable until the future event occurs. The revenue from such transactions should not be recognised in earnings until the sales price or fee becomes fixed or determinable.[106]

4.3   US literature

There exist a number of FASB Statements and AICPA Statements of Position that deal with either the recognition of certain forms of revenue, or the recognition of revenue in certain specific industries. Set out below is a list of just some of the existing literature on revenue recognition:

- SFAS 13:   Accounting for Leases
- SFAS 45:   Accounting for Franchise Fee Revenue
- SFAS 48:   Revenue Recognition When Right of Return Exists
- SFAS 49:   Accounting for Product Financing Arrangements
- SFAS 66:   Accounting for Sales of Real Estate
- SFAS 91:   Accounting for Nonrefundable Fees and Costs Associated with Originating or Acquiring Loans and Initial Direct Costs of Leases
- SOP 81-1:   Accounting for Performance of Construction-Type and Certain Production-Type Contracts
- SOP 97-2:   Software Revenue Recognition
- SOP 98-9:   Modification of SOP 97-2, Software Revenue Recognition, With Respect to Certain Transactions
- EITF 99-19:   Reporting Revenue Gross as a Principal versus Net as an Agent
- EITF 00-21:   Revenue Arrangements with Multiple Deliverables
- EITF 00-22:   Accounting for 'Points' and Certain Other Time-Based or Volume-Based Sales Incentive Offers, and Offers for Free Products or Services to Be Delivered in the Future
- SAB 104:   SEC Staff Accounting Bulletins, Topic 13: Revenue Recognition

The most relevant, useful and up-to-date guidance can be found in Staff Accounting Bulletin No. 104 (SAB 104), issued in December 2003.[107] SAB 104 supersedes SAB 101, but has not resulted in any notable new developments in revenue recognition literature in the US; instead, it serves to codify the existing concepts in one place.

5 THE IASB/FASB JOINT REVENUE RECOGNITION PROJECT[108]

5.1 Project background

In June 2002 the IASB decided to undertake a project on revenue recognition jointly with the FASB. Its decision was taken on the basis of the following considerations:

- questions of revenue definition and recognition are among the most difficult and contentious in practice;

- the definition and recognition criteria for revenue in the IASB's *Framework* and IAS 18 do not accord with the *Framework's* definitions of assets and liabilities;

- IAS 18 does not deal well with transactions involving components (multiple-element revenue arrangements); and

- the importance of pursuing international convergence of conceptual frameworks and accounting standards in respect of revenue definition and recognition. The FASB had decided to undertake a high priority project on revenue recognition.

The FASB is taking the lead in this project, and its primary objective is to develop a comprehensive set of principles for revenue recognition that will eliminate the inconsistencies in the existing authoritative literature and accepted practices under US GAAP. For its part, the IASB's plan is to develop a discussion paper for public comment that will include the Board's preliminary views on its proposed principles for revenue recognition. This is expected to occur late 2005. Thereafter, the Board will issue exposure drafts aimed at revising the Framework and IAS 18. Other standards with requirements relating to revenue recognition (such as IAS 11) are expected also to be amended as a result of the revenue project.

5.2 The general approach

By the end of July 2004, the IASB had discussed revenue recognition at about twenty meetings, including meetings of the National Standard Setters, the Standards Advisory Council and several joint meetings with the FASB. The IASB is exploring an approach that is based on the following main decisions:

- the Board should move away from the risks and reward approach and the concept of an earnings process or the principle of realisation. This is illustrated by the following assertion made by the Board: 'Recognising revenues for settling each obligation makes revenue recognition a direct consequence of how each obligation is measured rather than a process of allocating the customer consideration to various earnings processes';

- instead, the Board should follow an asset and liability approach to revenue;

- revenue should be based on changes in assets and liabilities;

- revenue is the net of contractual rights and obligations at inception;

- contractual obligations arise when the customer pays for the deliverables; and

- these contractual performance obligations, should be measured from a reporting entity perspective at fair value, which is referred to as the 'legal layoff amount'. Legal layoff amount is the price that would have to be paid to a third party of comparable credit standing to assume legal responsibility for performing all of the entity's remaining obligations.

This approach has been referred to by the Board as the 'Conceptual Model'. Set out below are the main features of the proposed 'conceptual model' as it applies to contractual rights and obligations:[109]

The Board has tentatively decided that:

- A 'contract' should be defined as a set of promises that a court will enforce.
- Contracts need to be enforceable for assets and liabilities to arise from them. A reporting entity's contractual rights and obligations are not enforceable if the counterparty, or the reporting entity, respectively, can cancel the contract without incurring a penalty.

The Board has considered the following types of contractual rights and obligations:

- *Conditional*—performance is subject to the occurrence of an event that is not certain to occur (such as performance by the counterparty to the contract).
- *Unconditional*—nothing other than the passage of time is required to make its performance due.
- *Mature*—performance is not subject to any event, not even the passage of time. It is due immediately.

The Board has tentatively decided that:

- Conditional rights and obligations do not meet the definitions of an asset and a liability.
- To meet the definitions of an asset and a liability, respectively, contractual rights and obligations must be unconditional or mature and require future transfers of economic benefits.
- The assets and liabilities that exist before contractual promises are performed should be recognised on a net basis for the contract as a whole unless the legal remedy of specific performance is available *and* necessary to compensate the contracting parties for a breach of contract. In other cases the subject of the contract is said to be 'fungible'.

The Board has tentatively decided that unconditional rights and obligations that exist until either party to a contract performs its stated conditional obligation should be described as 'pre-performance assets and liabilities'. For sale-purchase contracts, pre-performance assets and liabilities (such as price guarantees) are similar to call options and put options.

The Board has also tentatively decided that unconditional rights and obligations that exist after either party to a contract performs its stated conditional obligation should be described as 'post-performance assets and liabilities'. Post-performance assets and liabilities include familiar assets and liabilities such as accounts receivable and accounts payable.

Finally, the Board has tentatively decided that pre-performance and post-performance assets and liabilities should be measured at their fair values at initial recognition (as a working principle).

5.3 An example of the application of the 'conceptual model'

During its discussions, the IASB has made frequent reference to a series of case studies and worked examples. Set out below is one of the more straightforward examples that contrasts the practical application of the 'conceptual model' with IAS 18.[110]

Example 26.1 *Illustration of the application of the 'conceptual model' to a service contract*

On 31 December 2003, MobileCo, a wireless communications service provider, activates a new subscriber. The parties sign a one-year contract in which:

MobileCo undertakes to provide unlimited-minutes wireless services to the customer.

The customer has a choice of either paying €95 per month (i.e. €1,140 over a 12-month period) or prepaying the entire contract fee in a lump-sum payment of €1,050.

MobileCo may terminate the contract on 30-day's notice. If MobileCo terminates the contract, the customer is entitled to a pro-rata refund of the prepayment for the services not rendered.

If the customer terminates the contract, MobileCo is entitled to liquidated damages equal to the full price of the contract (i.e. the provider is not required to refund prepayments, if any, and is entitled to all remaining amounts due under the contract).

MobileCo has the right to assign the contract (i.e. a third party of MobileCo's choice may assume its legal rights and obligations under the contract).

The customer chooses the prepayment option and remits €1,050 at the time of activation on 31 December 2003.

MobileCo can outsource its performance obligations for phone services and customer care activities (i.e. processing of customer inquiries and complaints) for a monthly fee of €75 per customer. However, MobileCo decides to provide the service itself. The financial year-end of MobileCo is 31 December.

Revenue recognition under current practice (IAS 18)

Current practice would be to recognise monthly service revenue of €87.50 (i.e. one twelfth of €1,050) and no other revenue.

Revenue recognition under the 'conceptual model'

The fair value of the services to be provided (i.e. excluding retail access and other selling services already provided by MobileCo) is the amount that MobileCo would have to pay in order to outsource its performance under the contract (€75 per month or €900 for a year).* Accordingly, MobileCo would recognise selling revenue of €150 (i.e. €1,050 minus €900) on 31 December 2003 and monthly service revenue of €75 (i.e. €900 divided by 12 months).

* For simplicity, the time value of money is ignored. It is also assumed that the legal layoff price for a year's services is 12 times the month-by-month price (thus ignoring the risk premium that would be received by marketplace participants for bearing the uncertainty in the €75 month-by-month price).

This is obviously a simplified example; in practice, contracts for mobile services include multiple elements, such as free or subsidised handsets, different combinations of free calls and call rates, depending on the level of monthly fees etc. Nevertheless this example illustrates clearly the difference between the earnings and contractual liability approaches to revenue recognition; in particular, it shows the extent to which there might be upfront revenue recognition, whilst glossing over the practical difficulties that would be encountered in determining the fair value of the performance obligation.

5.4   The way forward

It is now clear that both the IASB and FASB are intent on pursuing an approach to revenue recognition that focuses on changes in assets and liabilities and is not overridden by tests based on principles of realisation and completion of an earnings process. It is clear also that this approach is consistent with both the definition of income in the IASB's *Framework* and the definition of revenues in the FASB Concepts Statement 6.

This approach is justified by the two Boards by arguing that the realisation and earnings approach involves the recognition of deferred debits and deferred credits on the balance sheet that do not meet the definitions of assets and liabilities under their respective conceptual frameworks. Consequently, because the definitions of assets and liabilities are the cornerstones of the elements' definitions in the conceptual frameworks, the Boards believe that their asset/liability approach is both conceptually pure and appropriate. In other words, because the application of the prudence and matching concepts inevitably results in the recognition of deferred income and expenses, the two Boards consider that the concept of an earnings process or the principle of realisation have no place in GAAP.

On the other hand, some – including regulators and prudential supervisors – might argue that an approach that abandons prudence and opens the door to greater front-end recognition of revenue is not in the best interests of improving financial reporting governance. Others argue that the notion of fair value of contractual performance obligations raises questions about the realism of the Boards' proposed approach. Where there is no active market in contractual performance obligations, but they are nevertheless to be carried at fair value, it is necessary to hypothesise what a market price would be in the event that there were a market. This involves a number of hypotheses and assumptions, including, for example, that there is a counter-party willing and able to stand ready to assume legal responsibility for performing all of the entity's remaining obligations. In the event that the legal layoff amount is to be derived by modelling a hypothetical market, there is a risk that the carrying amounts of performance obligations might be used to report speculative future income.

In any event, the two Boards clearly have substantial work to do before their current proposals are ready for public consultation. We therefore await the Boards' discussion paper that is due for publication in 2005, and look forward to observing the market reaction thereto.

6 SUMMARY OF BROAD APPROACHES TO REVENUE RECOGNITION

Although, the IASB is attempting to move towards a balance sheet approach to revenue recognition, to date we see no evidence that this has had any significant effect on the general principles of revenue recognition which are currently enshrined in IFRS: namely that the buyer must assume from the seller the significant risks and rewards of ownership of the assets sold and that the amount of revenue must be reliably measurable and certain. It is clear that the IASB's revenue recognition project has fundamental implications for revenue recognition and it remains to be seen how this develops and whether the balance sheet approach gains acceptance.

However, in the meantime, the following table summarises the broad approaches to revenue reporting that would appear to have achieved general acceptance through existing reporting practice. The table indicates the circumstances under which it might be appropriate to apply each of the approaches; nevertheless, it is essential that each situation is considered on its individual merits, with particular attention being paid to the risks and uncertainties that remain at each stage of the earning process and the extent to which the amount of revenue can be measured reliably.

The timing of recognition	Criteria	Examples of practical application
During production (accretion)	Revenues accrue over time, and no significant uncertainty exists as to measurability or collectibility. A contract of sale has been entered into and future costs can be estimated with reasonable accuracy.	The accrual of interest, royalty and dividend income. Accounting for construction contracts using the percentage-of-completion method.
At the completion of production	There should exist a ready market for the commodity that could rapidly absorb the quantity held by the entity; the commodity should comprise interchangeable units; the market price should be determinable and stable; there should be insignificant marketing costs involved.	Certain precious metals and commodities. Agriculture.
At the time of sale (but before delivery)	Goods must have already been acquired or manufactured; goods must be capable of immediate delivery to the customer; selling price has been established; all material related expenses (including delivery) have been ascertained; no significant uncertainties remain (e.g. ultimate cash collection, returns).	Certain sales of goods (e.g. 'bill and hold' sales). Property sales where there is an irrevocable contract.
On delivery	Criteria for recognition before delivery were not satisfied and no significant uncertainties remain.	Most sales of goods and services. Property sales where there is doubt that the sale will be completed.
Subsequent to delivery	Significant uncertainty regarding collectibility existed at the time of delivery; at the time of sale it was not possible to value the consideration with sufficient accuracy.	Certain sales of goods and services (e.g. where the right of return exists). Goods shipped subject to conditions (e.g. installation and inspection/performance).
On an apportionment basis (the revenue allocation approach)	Where revenue represents the supply of initial and subsequent goods/services.	Franchise fees. Sale of goods with after sales service.

7   PRACTICAL ISSUES

Because of the lack of comprehensive generally accepted principles for revenue recognition, coupled with the fact that minimal specific guidance is given in IFRS as to the timing of revenue reporting, it is necessary to examine specific areas in practice which might be open to inconsistent, controversial or varied accounting practices. Many of the issues discussed below relate to specific industries that pose their own particular revenue recognition problems; in fact, much of the accounting literature on the subject has been developed (predominantly in the US) in the context of these industries.

7.1   'Bill and hold' sales

The term 'bill and hold' sales is used to describe a transaction where delivery is delayed at the buyer's request, but the buyer takes title and accepts billing.

Under the guidance provided in the Appendix to IAS 18, revenue is recognised when the buyer takes title, provided:

(a)   it is probable that delivery will be made;

(b)   the item is on hand, identified and ready for delivery to the buyer at the time the sale is recognised;

(c)   the buyer specifically acknowledges the deferred delivery instructions; and

(d)   the usual payment terms apply.

Revenue is not recognised when there is simply an intention to acquire or manufacture the goods in time for delivery.[111]

7.2   Goods shipped subject to conditions

The Appendix to IAS 18 identifies four scenarios where goods are shipped subject to various conditions:[112]

(a)   *installation and inspection*

Revenue is normally recognised when the buyer accepts delivery, and installation and inspection are complete. However, revenue is recognised immediately upon the buyer's acceptance of delivery when:

(i)   the installation process is simple in nature, for example the installation of a factory tested television receiver which only requires unpacking and connection of power and antennae; or

(ii)   the inspection is performed only for purposes of final determination of contract prices, for example, shipments of iron ore, sugar or soya beans.

(b)   *on approval when the buyer has negotiated a limited right of return*

If there is uncertainty about the possibility of return, revenue is recognised when the shipment has been formally accepted by the buyer or the goods have been delivered and the time period for rejection has elapsed.

(c)   *consignment sales under which the recipient (buyer) undertakes to sell the goods on behalf of the shipper (seller)*

Revenue is recognised by the shipper when the goods are sold by the recipient to a third party.

(d)   *cash on delivery sales*

Revenue is recognised when delivery is made and cash is received by the seller or its agent.

7.3   Layaway sales

The term 'lay away sales' applies to transactions where the goods are delivered only when the buyer makes the final payment in a series of instalments. This is fairly common in the retail sector – for example, clothing and household goods. Revenue from such sales is recognised when the goods are delivered. However, when experience indicates that most such sales are consummated, revenue may be recognised when a significant deposit is received provided the goods are on hand, identified and ready for delivery to the buyer.[113]

7.4   Payments in advance for goods not held in inventory

In certain sectors (such as furniture and kitchen retail) payment (or partial payment) is received from the customer when he places his order for the goods. This is often well in advance of delivery of the goods, which are either not presently held in inventory, or are still to be manufactured or will be delivered directly to the customer by a third party. In such cases, revenue is recognised when the goods are delivered to the buyer.[114] Leica Geosystems provides a good illustration of the adoption of such an approach:

Extract 26.10: Leica Geosystems Holdings AG (2003)

Summary of risk management objectives and significant accounting policies [extract]

O.   Revenue Recognition

Revenue is recognized when significant risks and rewards of ownership of goods have been transferred to a third party. This would normally occur following delivery of the products or services and acceptance by the customers. Revenues from maintenance contracts paid by customers in advance are recognized over the period of the contract in accordance with the terms specified therein.

Advance payments received from customers are deferred, and recorded as income when the related product has been delivered or services performed.

7.5   Sale and repurchase agreements

Sale and repurchase agreements take many forms: the seller concurrently agrees to repurchase the same goods at a later date, or the seller has a call option to repurchase, or the buyer has a put option to require the repurchase, by the seller, of the goods.

For a sale and repurchase agreement on an asset other than a financial asset, the terms of the agreement need to be analysed to ascertain whether, in substance, the seller has transferred the risks and rewards of ownership to the buyer and hence revenue is recognised. When the seller has retained the risks and rewards of ownership, even though legal title has been transferred, the transaction is a financing arrangement and does not give rise to revenue. For a sale and repurchase agreement on a financial asset, IAS 39 applies.[115]

7.6 Instalment sales

The term 'instalment sales' refers to sales where the goods are delivered to the customer, but payment is made by a number of instalments, which include a financing charge. In such cases, revenue attributable to the sale price, exclusive of interest, is recognised at the date of sale. The sale price is the present value of the consideration, determined by discounting the instalments receivable at the imputed rate of interest. The interest element is recognised as revenue as it is earned, using the effective interest method set out in IAS 39, paragraphs 9 and AG5 to AG8.[116]

7.7 Receipt of initial fees

The practice that has developed in certain industries of charging an initial fee at the inception of a service, followed by subsequent service fees, can present revenue allocation problems. The reason for this is that it is not always altogether clear what the initial fee represents; consequently, it is necessary to determine what proportion (if any) of the initial fee has been earned on receipt, and how much relates to the provision of future services. In some cases, large initial fees are paid for the provision of a service, whilst continuing fees are relatively small in relation to future services to be provided; if it is probable that the continuing fees will not cover the cost of the continuing services to be provided, then a portion of the initial fee should be deferred over the period of the service contract such that a reasonable profit is earned throughout the service period.

7.7.1 Franchise fees

The franchise agreements that form the basis of the relationships between franchisors and franchisees can vary widely both in their complexity and in the extent to which various rights, duties and obligations are dealt with in the agreements. For this reason, no standard form franchise agreement exists which would dictate standard accounting practice for the recognition of all franchise fee revenue. Consequently, only a full understanding of the franchise agreement will reveal the substance of a particular arrangement so that the most appropriate accounting treatment can be determined; nevertheless, the following are the more common areas which are likely to be addressed in any franchise agreement and which would be relevant to franchise fee revenue reporting:[117]

(a) *rights transferred by the franchisor:* the agreement would give the franchisee the right to use the trade name, processes, know-how of the franchisor for a specified period of time or in perpetuity.

(b) *the amount and terms of payment of initial fees:* payment of initial fees (where applicable) may be fully or partially due in cash, and may be payable immediately, over a specified period or on the fulfilment of certain obligations by the franchisor.

(c)   *amount and terms of payment of continuing franchise fees:* the franchisee will normally be required to pay a continuing fee to the franchisor – usually on the basis of a percentage of gross revenues.

(d)   *services to be provided by the franchisor initially and on a continuing basis:* the franchisor will usually agree to provide a variety of services and advice to the franchisee, such as:

  • site selection;

  • the procurement of fixed assets and equipment – these may be either purchased by the franchisee, leased from the franchisor or leased from a third party (possibly with the franchisor guaranteeing the lease payments);

  • advertising;

  • training of franchisee's personnel;

  • inspecting, testing and other quality control programmes; and

  • bookkeeping services.

(e)   *acquisition of equipment, stock and supplies:* the franchisee may be required to purchase these items either from the franchisor or from designated suppliers. Some franchisors manufacture products for sale to their franchisees, whilst others act as wholesalers.

The Appendix to IAS 18 includes a broad discussion of the receipt of franchise fees, where it is stated that they 'are recognised as revenue on a basis that reflects the purpose for which the fees were charged'.[118] The standard states that the following methods of franchise fee recognition are appropriate:[119]

A   Supplies of equipment and other tangible assets

The amount, based on the fair value of the assets sold, is recognised as revenue when the items are delivered or title passes.

B   Supplies of initial and subsequent services

Fees for the provision of continuing services, whether part of the initial fee or a separate fee are recognised as revenue as the services are rendered. When the separate fee does not cover the cost of continuing services together with a reasonable profit, part of the initial fee, sufficient to cover the costs of continuing services and to provide a reasonable profit on those services, is deferred and recognised as revenue as the services are rendered.

The franchise agreement may provide for the franchisor to supply equipment, inventories, or other tangible assets, at a price lower than that charged to others or a price that does not provide a reasonable profit on those sales. In these circumstances, part of the initial fee, sufficient to cover estimated costs in excess of that price and to provide a reasonable profit on those sales, is deferred and recognised over the period the goods are likely to be sold to the franchisee. The balance of an initial fee is recognised as revenue when performance of all the initial services and other obligations required of the franchisor (such as assistance with site selection, staff training, financing and advertising) has been substantially accomplished.

The initial services and other obligations under an area franchise agreement may depend on the number of individual outlets established in the area. In this case, the fees attributable to the initial services are recognised as revenue in proportion to the number of outlets for which the initial services have been substantially completed.

If the initial fee is collectable over an extended period and there is a significant uncertainty that it will be collected in full, the fee is recognised as cash instalments are received.

C   Continuing Franchise Fees

Fees charged for the use of continuing rights granted by the agreement, or for other services provided during the period of the agreement, are recognised as revenue as the services are provided or the rights used.

D   Agency Transactions

Transactions may take place between the franchisor and the franchisee which, in substance, involve the franchisor acting as agent for the franchisee. For example, the franchisor may order supplies and arrange for their delivery to the franchisee at no profit. Such transactions do not give rise to revenue.

E   Summary

In summary, therefore, we suggest that the following basic principles may be applied for the recognition of initial franchise fees:

(a)   first, it is necessary to break down the fee into its various components; for example, fee for franchise rights, fee for initial services to be performed by the franchisor, fair value of tangible assets sold etc. The reason for this is that the individual components may be recognised at different stages; the portion that relates to the franchise rights may be recognised in full immediately, or part of it may have to be deferred (see (b) below); the fee for initial services to be performed should only be recognised when the services have been 'substantially performed' (it is unlikely that substantial performance will have been completed before the franchisee opens for business); and the portion of the fee which relates to tangible assets may be recognised when title passes;

(b)   next, it should be considered whether or not the continuing fee will cover the cost of continuing services to be provided by the franchisor. If not, then a portion of the initial fee should be deferred and amortised over the life of the franchise;

(c)   if the collection period for the initial fees is extended and there is doubt as to the ultimate collectibility, revenue should be recognised on a cash received basis; and

(d)   in the event of the franchisor having the option to buy out the franchisee, and there is considered to be a significant probability that he will do so, initial franchise fee revenue should be deferred in full and credited against the cost of the investment when the buy-out occurs.

7.7.2   Advance royalty/licence receipts

The general guidance relating to licence fees and royalties is found in the Appendix to IAS 18, which states that 'fees and royalties paid for the use of an entity's assets (such as trademarks, patents, software, music copyright, record masters and motion picture films) are normally recognised in accordance with the substance of the agreement. As a practical matter, this may be on a straight line basis over the life of the agreement, for example, when a licensee has the right to use certain technology for a specified period of time.'[120]

Therefore, under normal circumstances, the accounting treatment of advance royalty/licence receipts is straightforward; under the accruals concept the advance should be treated as deferred income when received, and released to the profit and loss account when earned under the royalty/licence agreement. However, there are certain industries where the forms of agreement entered into are such that advance receipts comprise a number of components, each requiring different accounting treatments.

For example, in the record and music industry, a record company will normally enter into a contractual arrangement with either a recording artist or a production company to deliver finished recording masters over a specified period of time. The albums are then manufactured and shipped to retailers for ultimate sale to the customer. The recording artist will normally be compensated through participating in the record company's sales and licence fee income (i.e. a royalty), although he may receive a non-refundable fixed fee on delivery of the master to the record company.

Example 26.2   Revenue recognition for licensors in the record and music industry

For each recording master delivered by a pop group, THRAG, the group (which operates through a service company) receives a payment of €1,000,000. This amount comprises a non-returnable, non-recoupable payment of €200,000, a non-returnable but recoupable advance of €600,000 and a returnable, recoupable advance of €200,000. The recoupable advances can be recouped against royalties on net sales earned both on the album concerned and on earlier and subsequent albums. This is achieved by computing the total royalties on net sales on all albums delivered under THRAG's service company's agreement with its recording company, and applying against this total the advances and royalties previously paid on those albums.

It is clear that the non-recoupable advance should be recognised in income when received, since it is not related to any future performance; at the other end of the spectrum, recognition of the refundable advance should be deferred and recognised only when recouped. However, the question arises as to whether the non-refundable but recoupable advance on royalties should be recognised immediately or deferred. If one accepts that revenue may be recognised when it is absolutely assured, there is an argument to justify the immediate recognition of the recoupable advance, since it is non-refundable; furthermore, it might be argued that, as far as THRAG is concerned, the earning process is complete, since the group does not have any further performance obligations. Conversely, some might argue that although the advance is non-refundable, it is not earned until it is recouped; furthermore, immediate recognition of royalty advances is likely to lead to a significant distortion of reported income, resulting in there being little correlation between reported income and album sales.

Clearly, therefore, there is no clear-cut answer, and it is our view that either approach is acceptable – i.e. the non-refundable but recoupable advance may be recognised in full as soon as the master is delivered to the recording company or, alternatively, it may be treated as deferred income when received and matched to subsequent album sales, being released to the profit and loss account in the period in which the sales are made. The most important point is that, whichever method is adopted, it is applied consistently.

Similar recognition principles should be applied in the case of advance fees paid on the sale of film/TV rights. Receipts that are non-refundable and non-recoupable should be recognised immediately, whilst any non-refundable but recoupable royalty advances may either be recognised immediately, or be deferred and recognised as earned; again, the accounting policy selected should be applied consistently.

7.7.3 Financial service fees

The Appendix to IAS 18 includes a series of illustrative examples which relate to financial service fees, pointing out that the recognition of revenue for financial service fees depends on the purposes for which the fees are assessed and the basis of accounting for any associated financial instrument.[121] The description of fees for financial services may not be indicative of the nature and substance of the services provided. Therefore, it is necessary to distinguish between fees that are an integral part of the effective interest rate of a financial instrument, fees that are earned as services are provided, and fees that are earned on the execution of a significant act. The Appendix to IAS 18 makes this distinction as follows:[122]

A   *Fees that are an integral part of the effective interest rate of a financial instrument*

Such fees are generally treated as an adjustment to the effective interest rate. However, when the financial instrument is measured at fair value with the change in fair value recognised in profit or loss the fees are recognised as revenue when the instrument is initially recognised.

(i)   Origination fees received by the entity relating to the creation or acquisition of a financial asset other than one that under IAS 39 is classified as a financial asset 'at fair value through profit or loss'

Such fees may include compensation for activities such as evaluating the borrower's financial condition, evaluating and recording guarantees, collateral and other security arrangements, negotiating the terms of the instrument, preparing and processing documents and closing the transaction. These fees are an integral part of generating an involvement with the resulting financial instrument and, together with the related direct costs, are deferred and recognised as an adjustment to the effective interest rate.

(ii)   Commitment fees received by the entity to originate a loan when the loan commitment is outside the scope of IAS 39

If it is probable that the entity will enter into a specific lending arrangement and the loan commitment is not within the scope of IAS 39, the commitment fee received is regarded as compensation for an ongoing involvement with the acquisition of a financial instrument and, together with the related direct costs, is deferred and recognised as an adjustment to the effective interest rate. If the commitment expires without the entity making the loan, the fee is recognised as revenue on expiry. Loan commitments that are within the scope of IAS 39 are accounted for as derivatives and measured at fair value.

(iii)   Origination fees received on issuing financial liabilities measured at amortised cost

These fees are an integral part of generating an involvement with a financial liability. When a financial liability is not classified as 'at fair value through profit or loss', the origination fees received are included, with the related transaction costs incurred, in the initial carrying amount of the financial liability and recognised as an adjustment to the effective yield. An entity distinguishes fees and costs that are an integral part of the effective interest rate for the financial liability from origination fees and transaction costs relating to the right to provide services, such as investment management services.

B   *Fees earned as services are provided*

(i)   Fees charged for servicing a loan

Fees charged by an entity for servicing a loan are recognised as revenue as the services are provided.

(ii)   Commitment fees to originate a loan when the loan commitment is outside the scope of IAS 39

If it is unlikely that a specific lending arrangement will be entered into and the loan commitment is outside the scope of IAS 39, the commitment fee is recognised as revenue on a time proportion basis over the commitment period. Loan commitments that are within the scope of IAS 39 are accounted for as derivatives and measured at fair value.

(iii) Investment management fees

Fees charged for managing investments are recognised as revenue as the services are provided.

Incremental costs that are directly attributable to securing an investment management contract are recognised as an asset if they can be identified separately and measured reliably and if it is probable that they will be recovered. As in IAS 39, an incremental cost is one that would not have been incurred if the entity had not secured the investment management contract. The asset represents the entity's contractual right to benefit from providing investment management services, and is amortised as the entity recognises the related revenue. If the entity has a portfolio of investment management contracts, it may assess their recoverability on a portfolio basis.

Some financial services contracts involve both the origination of one or more financial instruments and the provision of investment management services. An example is a long-term monthly saving contract linked to the management of a pool of equity securities. The provider of the contract distinguishes the transaction costs relating to the origination of the financial instrument from the costs of securing the right to provide investment management services.

C   *Fees that are earned on the execution of a significant act.*

The fees are recognised as revenue when the significant act has been completed, as in the examples below.

(i)   Commission on the allotment of shares to a client.

The commission is recognised as revenue when the shares have been allotted.

(ii)   Placement fees for arranging a loan between a borrower and an investor.

The fee is recognised as revenue when the loan has been arranged.

(iii)   Loan syndication fees.

A syndication fee received by an entity that arranges a loan and retains no part of the loan package for itself (or retains a part at the same effective interest rate for comparable risk as other participants) is compensation for the service of syndication. Such a fee is recognised as revenue when the syndication has been completed.

7.7.4   Credit card fees

It is common practice in some countries for credit card companies to levy a charge, payable in advance, on its cardholders. Although such charges may be seen as commitment fees for the credit facilities offered by the card, they clearly cover the many other services available to cardholders as well. Accordingly, we would suggest that the fees which are periodically charged to cardholders should be deferred and recognised on a straight-line basis over the period the fee entitles the cardholder to use the card.[123]

7.7.5   Entrance and membership fees

The issue of entrance and membership fees is dealt with briefly in the Appendix to IAS 18, which states that revenue recognition depends on the nature of the services provided. If the fee permits only membership, and all other services or products are paid for separately, or if there is a separate annual subscription, the fee is recognised as revenue when no significant uncertainty as to its collectibility exists. If the fee entitles the member to services or publications to be provided during the membership period, or to purchase goods or services at prices lower than those charged to non-members, it is recognised on a basis that reflects the timing, nature and value of the benefits provided.[124]

7.8   Subscriptions to publications

Publication subscriptions are generally paid in advance and are non-refundable. Nevertheless, since the publications will still have to be produced and delivered to the subscriber, the subscription revenue cannot be regarded as having been earned until production and delivery takes place. This is the approach adopted by IAS 18, which requires that when the items involved are of similar value in each time period, revenue is recognised on a straight-line basis over the period in which the items are despatched. When the items vary in value from period to period, revenue is recognised on the basis of the sales value of the item despatched in relation to the total estimated sales value of all items covered by the subscription.[125]

7.9   Installation fees

Installation fees are recognised as revenue by reference to the stage of completion of the installation, unless they are incidental to the sale of a product in which case they are recognised when the goods are sold.[126]

7.10   Advertising revenue

The Appendix to IAS 18 adopts the performance of the service as the critical event for the recognition of revenue derived from the rendering of advertising services. Consequently, media commissions are recognised when the related advertisement or commercial appears before the public. Production commissions are recognised by reference to the stage of completion of the project.[127]

7.11   Insurance agency commissions

The critical event for the recognition of insurance agency commissions is the commencement of the policy. Hence, the Appendix to IAS 18 states that insurance agency commissions received or receivable which do not require the agent to render further service are recognised as revenue by the agent on the effective commencement or renewal dates of the related policies. However, when it is probable that the agent will be required to render further services during the life of the policy, the commission, or part thereof, is deferred and recognised as revenue over the period during which the policy is in force.[128]

7.12   Software revenue recognition

There are a number of issues relating to the timing of revenue recognition in the software services industry. The basic issues that arise surround the question of when to recognise revenue from contracts to develop software, software licensing fees, customer support services and data services. However, these issues have not been addressed in the IFRS literature and, because of the nature of the products and services involved, applying the general revenue recognition principles to software transactions can sometimes be difficult. The result of this has been that in practice software companies have used a variety of methods to recognise revenue, often producing significantly different financial results for similar transactions. IAS 18 provides only one sentence of guidance: fees from the development of customised software are recognised as revenue by reference to the stage of completion of the development, including completion of services provided for post delivery service support.[129] Clearly, this is of no help in addressing the complex revenue recognition issues that characterise the software services industry.

This problem was recognised in the US by the FASB and SEC who encouraged the AICPA to provide guidance on software revenue recognition methods. This culminated in AICPA Statement of Position (SOP) 91–1, which was issued in December 1991. The SOP applied to all entities that earned revenue from licensing, selling, leasing or otherwise marketing computer software, although it did not apply to revenue from the sale or licensing of a product containing software that is incidental to the product as a whole, such as software sold as part of a motor car.

However, it was found that certain provisions of SOP 91–1 were being applied inconsistently, thereby leading to diversity in practice. As a result, in October 1997 the AICPA issued SOP 97–2,[130] entitled Software Revenue Recognition, which superseded SOP 91–1. In 1998 two further SOPs were issued amending SOP 97–2: SOP 98–4 (which merely deferred the effective date of a provision of SOP 97–2), and SOP 98–9[131] (which modified SOP 97-2 with respect to certain transactions, allowing the use of the 'residual method' that in situations where vendor-specific objective evidence exists for all undelivered elements but does not exist for one or more of the delivered elements. Under the residual method, the undiscounted vendor-specific objective evidence of fair value of the undelivered elements is deferred, and the difference (residual) between the total fee and the amount deferred for the undelivered elements is recognised as revenue related to the delivered elements).

Whilst SOP 97–2 has no direct bearing on companies reporting under IFRS, many such companies could well use the hierarchy in IAS 8 to adopt the US requirements in the absence of a comparable IFRS pronouncement, particularly if they either have a US listing or have ambitions of a US listing. We encourage companies to at least consider the provisions of the SOP in all appropriate circumstances, as we believe that at present it represents best practice. Set out below is a broad overview of SOP 97-2, an extremely detailed and complex statement.

7.12.1   The basic principles of SOP 97–2

Software arrangements range from those that simply provide a licence for a single software product, to those that require significant production, modification or customisation of the software. Arrangements also may include multiple products or services. SOP 97–2 states that if the arrangement does not require significant production, modification or customisation of existing software (i.e. contract accounting does not apply – see below), revenue should be recognised when all of the following criteria are met:[132]

- persuasive evidence of an arrangement exists (e.g. signed contract, purchase authorisation, on-line authorisation);

- delivery has occurred (and no future elements to be delivered are essential to the functionality of the delivered element);

- the vendor's fee is fixed or determinable (the 'determinable' criterion relates to the issue as to whether the fee is subject to factors such as acceptance and refund); and

- collectibility is probable (i.e. whether the customer has the ability to pay).

Under SOP 97–2, it is neither necessary nor appropriate to differentiate between significant and insignificant vendor obligations. The licence fee under an arrangement with multiple elements should be allocated to the elements according to the 'vendor-specific objective evidence of fair value'.

In addition, SOP 97–2 requires a company to allocate a portion of the licence fee from a software arrangement to elements that are deliverable on a when-and-if-available basis, whereby a vendor agrees to deliver software only when or if it becomes deliverable while the agreement is in effect. Furthermore, SOP 97–2 requires that if a vendor has a customary practice of obtaining written contracts, revenues should not be recognised until the contract is signed by both parties. Therefore, in the absence of a signed contract, revenue should not be recognised even if the software has been delivered and payment made.

7.12.2 Accounting for arrangements which require significant production, modification or customisation of software

Where companies are running well-established computer installations with systems and configurations that they do not wish to change, off-the-shelf software packages are generally not suitable for their purposes. For this reason, some software companies will enter into a customer contract whereby they agree to customise a generalised software product to meet the customer's specific processing needs. A simple form of customisation would be to modify the system's output reports so that they integrate with the customer's existing management reporting system. However, customisation will often entail more involved obligations; for example, having to translate the software so that it is able to run on the customer's specific hardware configuration, data conversion, system integration, installation and testing.

The question that arises, therefore, is on what basis should a software company be recognising revenue where it enters into this type of contract that involves significant contractual obligations? It is our view that the principles laid down in IAS 11 – *Construction contracts* – should be applied in this situation.[133] This is supported by IAS 18, which states that the requirements of IAS 11 are generally applicable to the recognition of revenue and the associated expenses for a transaction involving the rendering of services.[134]

IAS 11 defines a construction contract as 'a contract specifically negotiated for the construction of an asset or a combination of assets that are closely interrelated or interdependent in terms of their design, technology and function or their ultimate purpose or use'.[135] The standard requires that 'when the outcome of a construction contract can be estimated reliably, contract revenue and contract costs associated with the construction contract should be recognised as revenue and expenses respectively by reference to the stage of completion of the contract activity at the balance sheet date. An expected loss on the construction contract should be recognised as an expense immediately'.[136]

Consequently, where the software company is able to make reliable estimates as to the extent of progress toward completion of a contract, related revenues and related costs, and where the outcome of the contract can be assessed with reasonable certainty, the percentage-of-completion method of profit recognition should be applied. Under IAS 11, the stage of completion of a contract may be determined in a variety of ways, and entities should use the method that measures reliably the work performed. Depending on the nature of the contract, the methods may include:[137]

(a)   the proportion that contract costs incurred for work performed to date bear to the estimated total contract costs;

(b)   surveys of work performed; or

(c)   completion of a physical proportion of the contract work.

One company that follows this approach is Deutsche Börse AG, which provides software development services to its customers:

Extract 26.11: Deutsche Börse AG (2003)

Notes [extract]

4.   Accounting policies [extract]

Revenue Recognition

Trading and settlement fees on cash and derivatives markets are recognized immediately at the trade date and billed on a monthly basis. Custodian and settlement fees, and fees from the sale of information services and systems operation services, are generally billed and recognized ratably on a monthly basis. Revenue of the entory subgroup relating to fixed-price software development contracts is recognized using the percentage of completion method. In accordance with IAS 11.30, revenue is recognized in the proportion of the contract costs incurred for work performed to the estimated total contract costs. Interest income is accrued when it arises.

On the other hand, under IAS 11, when the outcome of a construction contract cannot be estimated reliably:

(a)   revenue should be recognised only to the extent of contract costs incurred that it is probable will be recoverable; and

(b)   contract costs should be recognised as an expense in the period in which they are incurred.[138]

Under SOP 97-2, if an arrangement to deliver software or a software system, either alone or together with other products or services, requires significant production, modification or customisation of software, the entire arrangement should be accounted for in accordance with Accounting Research Bulletin (ARB) No. 45 – *Long-Term Construction-Type Contracts* – and SOP 81–1 – *Accounting for Performance of Construction-Type and Certain Production-Type Contracts.*[139]

7.12.3 Accounting for arrangements with multiple elements

Software arrangements may provide licences for multiple software products or for multiple software products and services (referred to in SOP 97–2 as 'multiple elements') such as: additional software products, upgrades/enhancements, rights to exchange or return software, post-contract customer support (PCS) or other services including elements deliverable only on a when-and-if-available basis. SOP 97-2 requires deferral of all revenue from multiple-element arrangements that are not accounted for using long-term contract accounting if sufficient vendor-specific objective evidence does not exist for the allocation of revenue to the various elements of the arrangement. However, there may be instances in which there is vendor-specific objective evidence of the fair values of all undelivered elements in an arrangement, but vendor-specific objective evidence of fair value does not exist for one or more of the delivered elements in the arrangement. In such instances, the fee should be recognised using the residual method, provided that:

(a) all other applicable revenue recognition criteria in SOP 97-2 are met; and

(b) the fair value of all of the undelivered elements is less than the arrangement fee.

Under the residual method, the arrangement fee is recognised as follows:

(a) the total fair value of the undelivered elements, as indicated by vendor-specific objective evidence, is deferred; and

(b) the difference between the total arrangement fee and the amount deferred for the undelivered elements is recognised as revenue related to the delivered elements.[140]

If a discount is offered in a multiple-element arrangement, a proportionate amount of that discount should be applied to each element included in the arrangement based on each element's fair value without regard to the discount. However, no portion of the discount should be allocated to any upgrade rights. Moreover, to the extent that a discount exists, the residual method attributes that discount entirely to the delivered elements.[141]

7.12.4 Determining fair value based on vendor-specific objective evidence

SOP 97–2 states that if an arrangement includes multiple elements, the fee should be allocated to the various elements based on vendor-specific objective evidence of fair value, regardless of any separate prices stated within the contract for each element.[142] Under the SOP, vendor-specific objective evidence of fair value is limited to the following:

• the price charged when the same element is sold separately; and

• for an element not yet being sold separately, the price established by management having the relevant authority; it must be probable that the price, once established, will not change before the separate introduction of the element into the marketplace.[143]

With the exception of changes in the estimated percentage of customers not expected to exercise an upgrade right, the amount allocated to undelivered elements is not subject to later adjustment.[144] However, if it becomes probable that the amount allocated to an undelivered element will result in a loss on that element of the arrangement, the loss should be recognised.[145]

If a multiple-element arrangement includes an upgrade right, the fee should be allocated between the elements based on vendor-specific objective evidence of fair value. The fee allocated to the upgrade right is the price for the upgrade/enhancement that would be charged to existing users of the software product being updated. If the upgrade right is included in a multiple-element arrangement on which a discount has been offered, no portion of the discount should be allocated to the upgrade right, because it is undelivered. If sufficient vendor-specific evidence exists to reasonably estimate the percentage of customers that are not expected to exercise the upgrade right, the fee allocated to the upgrade right should be reduced to reflect that percentage. SOP 97–2 goes on to state that this estimated percentage should be reviewed periodically, and that the effect of any change in that percentage should be accounted for as a change in accounting estimate.[146]

As stated above, if sufficient vendor-specific objective evidence does not exist for the allocation of revenue to the various elements of the arrangement, the SOP provides that all revenue from the arrangement should be deferred until the earlier of the dates at which:

(a)   such sufficient vendor-specific objective evidence does exist; or

(b)   all elements of the arrangement have been delivered.[147]

However, the SOP provides for the following exceptions to this principle:

*   if the only undelivered element is post-contract customer support (PCS), the entire fee is recognised on a pro-rata basis over the PCS period;[148]

*   if the only undelivered element is services that do not involve significant production, modification or customisation of software, the entire fee should be recognised over the period during which the services are expected to be performed;[149]

*   if the arrangement is in substance a subscription, the entire fee should be recognised on a pro-rata basis;[150] and

*   if the fee is based on the number of copies, the revenue should be accounted for on an allocation basis, as specified in the SOP.[151] For example, some fixed fee licence arrangements provide customers with the right to reproduce or obtain copies at a specified price per copy of two or more software products up to the total amount of the fixed fee. A number of the products covered by the arrangement may not be deliverable or specified at the inception of the arrangement. In such cases, the revenue allocated to the delivered products should be recognised when the product master or first copy is delivered. If during the term of the arrangement, the customer reproduces or receives enough copies of these delivered products so that revenue allocable to the delivered products exceeds the revenue previously recognised, such additional revenue should be recognised as the copies are reproduced or delivered. The revenue allocated to the undeliverable product(s) should be reduced by a corresponding amount.[152]

Again, there may be instances in which there is vendor-specific objective evidence of the fair values of all undelivered elements in an arrangement, but vendor-specific objective evidence of fair value does not exist for one or more of the delivered elements in the arrangement. In such instances, the fee should be recognised using the residual method, provided that:

(a)   all other applicable revenue recognition criteria in SOP 97-2 are met; and

(b)   the fair value of all of the undelivered elements is less than the arrangement fee.[153]

7.12.5 *Upgrades, enhancements and post-contract customer support (PCS)*

As part of a multiple-element arrangement, a vendor may agree to deliver software currently and to deliver additional software in the future. The additional deliverables may include upgrades/enhancements or additional software products. Additionally, a vendor may provide the customer with the right to exchange or return software, including the right to transfer software from one hardware platform or operating system to one or more other platforms or operating systems ('a platform-transfer right').[154]

Under SOP 97–2, the right to receive specified upgrades or enhancements is considered a separate element of a licensing arrangement. However, rights to receive unspecified upgrades/enhancements on a 'when-and-if-available' basis are PCS services and generally should be recognised as revenue on a pro rata basis over the term of the PCS arrangement. SOP 97–2 defines PCS to exclude rights to specific upgrades/enhancements.[155] For a specific upgrade, a portion of the total licensing fee should be allocated to the elements using the 'vendor-specific objective evidence of fair value' criteria. The fee allocated to the upgrade right is the price for the upgrade/enhancement that would be charged to existing users of the software product being updated.[156]

If a multiple-element software arrangement includes explicit or implicit rights to PCS, the total fees from the arrangement should be allocated among the elements based on vendor-specific objective evidence of fair value. The fair value of the PCS should be determined by reference to the price the customer will be required to pay when it is sold separately (that is, the renewal rate). The portion of the fee allocated to PCS should be recognised as revenue on a pro rata basis over the term of the PCS arrangement, because PCS services are assumed to be provided on a pro rata basis. However, revenue should be recognised over the period of the PCS arrangement in proportion to the amounts expected to be charged to expense for the PCS services rendered during the period if:

- sufficient vendor-specific historical evidence exists demonstrating that costs to provide PCS are incurred on other than a straight-line basis; and

- the vendor believes that it is probable that the costs incurred in performing under the current arrangement will follow a similar pattern.[157]

If the PCS term is implicit as opposed to be being explicit, a period needs to be determined based on an estimated life of the software or the customer relationship.

In addition, because the timing, frequency, and significance of unspecified upgrades/enhancements can vary considerably, the point at which unspecified upgrades/enhancements are expected to be delivered should not be used to support income recognition on other than a straight-line basis.[158]

This approach is consistent with the small amount of guidance found in the Appendix to IAS 18, which states that when the selling price of a product includes an identifiable amount for subsequent servicing (for example, after sales support and product enhancement on the sale of software), that amount is deferred and recognised as revenue over the period during which the service is performed. The amount deferred is that which will cover the expected costs of the services under the agreement, together with a reasonable profit on those services.[159]

7.12.6 Evaluation of whether a fee is fixed or determinable and arrangements that include extended payment terms

One of the SOP's basic criteria for software revenue recognition is determining whether the fee under the arrangement is fixed or determinable. The SOP states that any extended payment terms in a software licensing arrangement may indicate that the fee is not fixed or determinable.[160] Furthermore, it goes on to state that a software licensing fee should be presumed not to be fixed if payment of a significant portion of the fee is not due until after expiration of the licence or more than twelve months after delivery of the software. However, this presumption may be overcome by evidence that the vendor has a standard business practice of using long-term or instalment contracts and a history of successfully collecting under the original payment terms without making concessions.[161]

If it cannot be concluded that the fee is fixed or determinable at the outset of the arrangement, revenue should be recognised as payments from customers become due (assuming, of course, that the other revenue recognition criteria have been met).[162]

7.12.7 Rights to return or exchange software

As part of a software licensing arrangement, a software vendor may provide a customer with the right to return or exchange software. Depending on the circumstances, the customer might exchange software for a product with minimal or more than minimal differences in price, functionality and features. Consistent with SFAS 48 – *Revenue Recognition When Right of Return Exists*, SOP 97–2 requires a software vendor to establish a reserve for estimated returns; however, no amounts should be reserved for the right to exchange because exchange rights do not affect revenue recognition, although any estimated costs for such exchanges should be accrued. SOP 97–2 also provides that exchanges of software products for different software products or for similar software products with more than minimal differences in price, functionality or features are considered returns and are accounted for in conformity with SFAS 48.[163]

However, it should be noted that exchange accounting is not available to re-sellers of software. Although a re-seller may meet all of the criteria for a return to qualify as an exchange, the re-seller must account for that exchange as a return.

7.12.8 Services

Many software arrangements include both software and service elements (services). Services may include training, installation or consulting (but do not include PCS-related services). Consulting services often include implementation support, software design or development or the customisation or modification of the licensed software.[164]

According to the SOP, if an arrangement includes such services, a determination must be made as to whether the service element can be accounted for separately as the services are performed.[165] The SOP lays down the following criteria that must be met in order to account separately for the service element of an arrangement that includes both software and services:

- sufficient vendor-specific objective evidence of fair value must exist to permit allocation of the revenue to the various elements of the arrangement;
- the services must not be essential to the functionality of any other element of the transaction; and
- the services must be described in the contract such that the total price of the arrangement would be expected to vary as the result of the inclusion or exclusion of the services.[166]

If these criteria are met, revenue should be allocated between the service and software elements of the contract. This allocation should be based on vendor-specific objective evidence of fair value. Revenue from the service element should be recognised as the services are performed or on a straight-line basis over the service period if no pattern of performance is discernible.[167]

7.13   Revenue recognition issues in the telecommunications sector

There are significant revenue recognition issues that affect the telecommunications sector, and about which IFRS is effectively silent. The issues differ depending upon the type of telecommunications services being considered. For example fixed line (i.e. telephone and similar) services have recognition issues that differ from wireless (i.e. mobile 'phone) services. It is the latter wireless services that provide many of the accounting challenges: wireless is a relatively new sector that is rapidly developing; there is a wide range of offerings that encompass international as well as national operations; and there are considerable differences in the regulatory framework in different jurisdictions. The wireless revenue recognition problems fall into two broad groupings:

- recording of revenue in respect of multiple service elements; and
- whether revenue should be recorded gross or net.

7.13.1   Recording revenue for multiple service elements

In certain circumstances, it is necessary to apply the recognition criteria to the separately identifiable components of a single transaction in order to reflect the substance of that transaction. IAS 18 refers specifically to situations where the selling price of a product includes an identifiable amount for subsequent servicing, in which case that amount is deferred and recognised as revenue over the period during which the service is performed.[168] This is directly relevant to some aspects of multiple service offerings, where customers are offered a 'bundle' of assets and services.

Usually, when a consumer enters into a mobile 'phone contract with a provider, he is provided with a package that may include a handset, free minutes of talktime (either voice or video) and other services such as data downloads, SMS, MMS etc. It is also possible that the 'bundle' will include talktime and data (content, MMS, SMS etc), while the wireless provider's systems may not be able to track the usage of such bundled services. Moreover, consumers may pay for their bundle in a number of different ways. For example, there may be many variations on the following possibilities: a payment for the handset (which may be heavily discounted); connection charges related to the costs of connection (or market-based initial fees that are not directly related to connection costs); contracts that provide for monthly payments by subscribers; non-binding contracts that provide for prepayments by credit card or by voucher, and which may or may not be discounted at the point of sale. None of these payments may correspond directly to the cost of the services being provided by the operator, and operators also may be involved in loyalty programs that entail the provision of future free services.

7.13.2 *Whether to record revenue gross or net*

The difficulty of deciding whether to record revenue gross or net is endemic to the telecommunications sector. The problem occurs because of the difficulty of deciding whether the parties involved in any particular agreement are acting as principal or agent. IAS 18 states that 'in an agency relationship, the gross inflows of economic benefits include amounts collected on behalf of the principal and which do not result in increases in equity for the entity. The amounts collected on behalf of the principal are not revenue. Instead, revenue is the amount of commission.'[169] This guidance does not necessarily help decide the matter in the following scenarios, all of which are commercially common in the wireless sector:

- operators may sell handsets either directly to customers or via distribution channels;

- it can be difficult to identify the separate elements of the commission earned by a distribution channel. This is because part may relate to a possible discount on the handset, while part may relate to the commission earned on the payments the customer makes for the services provided by the distributor;

- often there is data content provided by third parties that is subject to a separate provider agreement; and

- there are issues of 'number portability', where the same customer telephone number is retained but the provider changes (this is also becoming an issue in the fixed line sector).

A number of general factors underlie the accounting issues, for example: local regulatory laws may dictate the way business is done by the operators; there may be restrictions on the discounting of handsets; handsets may be branded in some countries but not in others; both branded and unbranded handsets may co-exist in the same country; and, in addition, there may be varying degrees of price protection.

These revenue recognition difficulties are discussed more fully below. The problems relating to connection and up-front fees and number portability are also common to the fixed line operations. It is also possible that in the future, as discounted modems are used to attract broadband customers and as services such as voice, data and media are increasingly bundled, the problems discussed below will become increasing applicable to fixed line operators.

7.13.3 *Connection and up-front fees*

When the mobile telecoms industry was in its infancy, upfront costs such as connection fees, contract handling fees, registration fees, fees for changing plans etc., were commonly charged by operators to cover their administrative costs. Such costs have been phased out over the years and are no longer a prevalent feature in a number of markets.

Any amounts prepaid upfront should be capitalised as deferred income and amortised on a straight-line basis over the life of the subscription. In our view, the life of the subscription may not necessarily be the contract period, but may be the estimated average life of the customer relationship, provided that this can be estimated reliably.

7.13.4 *Multiple deliverables ('bundled offers')*

There is no guidance within IFRS on this topic; therefore as suggested by the hierarchy contained within IAS 8, suitable guidance from other standard setting bodies may be used. This discussion is based upon the US GAAP guidance offered by EITF 00-21 – *Revenue Arrangements with Multiple Deliverables.*

A *Handsets*

Handsets are often used as an incentive to encourage subscribers to sign up for fixed contract periods, thereby providing mobile operators with a more predictable revenue stream. The problem faced by operators is whether the distribution channels they employ to distribute these handsets are acting as agents on their behalf, or as principals in their own right.

If distributors are considered agents, then handsets and services are a single bundled offering with multiple deliverables, and the handset revenue should only be recognised in the profit and loss account when the handset is connected to the network via a new subscription. On the other hand, if distributors are considered principals, then handsets and services are separate offerings, and the handset revenue can be recognised immediately in the profit and loss account as handsets are sold to the distributor, without waiting to be connected to the network by a new subscriber.

If treated in this latter manner, problems may arise if handsets that were initially sold to a distribution channel and recognised as revenue in the profit and loss account, are subsequently at the request or on the authority of the operator, supplied as free upgrades to consumers. In this case the handset costs become subscriber retention costs (SRCs), and an adjustment would be required to reverse the equipment revenue that was initially recognised.

B *'Free' services*

'Free' services are often included in the monthly fee for contract subscribers as an additional incentive to encourage subscribers to sign up for a fixed contract period, typically twelve months.

'Free' services can either be provided up front as inclusive services for a fixed monthly fee, or as an incentive after a specific threshold has been exceeded to encourage subscribers to spend more than a specified amount .

These 'free' services may be provided to subscribers either in the form of 'free' talktime (e.g. 300 free minutes each month) or free credit (e.g. €50 to spend on any of the services offered each month). The matter is further complicated as increasing competition has led to the bundling of 'free' services, including talktime (voice and video), MMS, SMS and content downloads (wallpapers, ringtones, games etc.).

As a result, one of the problems that mobile operators increasingly face will be the allocation of the monthly fee between each element within the bundle. This analysis is a key requirement of investment analysts and may also be necessary for segmental disclosure purposes, and will probably have to be based on the fair value of each element of the free services provided. A significant degree of estimation is involved, as the usage profile for an operator's subscribers has to be determined before the monthly revenue can be allocated.

7.13.5 *The distribution channel*

As mentioned earlier, distribution channels are often used by mobile operators to provide handsets to new or existing subscribers, either free or at a heavily discounted price. This practice is common in the US and Europe, but is less common in Asia where handsets are usually sold separately by third party vendors and the mobile operators deal mainly with the provision of services.

The mechanism whereby handsets are provided either without charge or heavily discounted, is by way of a commission payable by the mobile operators to their distributors. Commissions can be based on the type of handset sold, the price plan the consumer is signed up to, the length of the contract and various other factors such as seasonal promotions.

The difficulty faced by mobile operators is how to analyse the nature of each transaction – for example, whether the sale of a handset constitutes a separate transaction from the connection of a new subscriber, or whether the handset and the subscription are constituent elements of a single multiple deliverable transaction.

An argument for considering the sale of handsets as a separate transaction is that they are commonly despatched to the distributors with no right of return, the distributors usually bear the physical inventory risk and cost of insurance, the sales are not contingent on the distributors being able to connect the handsets to new subscribers, and the amounts due are payable to the mobile operators within standard terms of trade.

On the other hand, the sale of handsets could be considered an element within a multiple deliverable transaction because of the nature of the mobile operator's business, i.e. its main business activity is the provision of services rather than the sale of handsets.

If the two elements are considered separate transactions, then revenue can be recognised separately on each transaction independently of each other. If the sale of handsets and the provision of services are considered multiple deliverables within a single transaction, then a final point of sale has to be determined to enable appropriate revenue recognition. If the final point of sale for the transaction is determined to be when a new subscriber is connected to the operator's network, then the handsets sold to distributors are effectively stocks held on consignment and should be recorded in the balance sheet of the mobile operator until they are connected to the network. The revenue received from the sale of handsets should then be recorded as deferred revenue until connection occurs.

7.13.6 *Other 'gross versus net' issues*

A   *Third party content providers*

Content, such as ringtones, wallpapers, games and traffic updates, is increasingly used to differentiate a mobile operator from its competitors. These products/services can either be included in the monthly price plan, or purchased separately on an *ad hoc* basis. Operators can either develop the content themselves in-house, or use third party providers to offer a range of services to their subscribers, with charges based either on duration (news, traffic updates etc.) or on quantity (number of ringtones, games etc.).

In the absence of specific guidance in IFRS, it seems reasonable to consider the US GAAP guidance contained within EITF 99-19 – *Reporting Revenue Gross as a Principal versus Net as an Agent*. This lays down the following criteria that need to be identified in order for the appropriate revenue recognition of content provided to be determined:[170]

- The operator is the primary obligor under the terms of the contracts;
- The operator bears any general and physical inventory risks;
- The operator is able to determine the price of the content;
- The operator is able to change the product;
- The operator has discretion in selecting the suppliers for the products and/or services;
- The operator is involved in the determination of the product or service specifications; and
- The operator bears any credit risks.

Analysis of the fact patterns of the agreement against the above criteria is critical to determine whether the mobile operator is the primary obligor in the arrangement and how the transaction should be accounted for. If the content is deemed to be an own-brand product/service provided by the mobile operator, then the revenue receivable from subscribers should be recorded as revenue by the operator, and the amounts payable to the third party content providers should be recorded as costs.

On the other hand, if the content is deemed to be a non-branded product/service that is merely using the mobile operator's network as a medium to access its subscriber base, then the income receivable from subscribers should not be recorded as revenue. Instead, only the commissions receivable from the content providers for the use of the operator's network should be recognised as revenue.

B   Number portability

Number portability refers to the service that will allow a subscriber, who was previously with another operator, to keep his existing phone number when transferring to a new operator. Operators are obliged to provide number portability in certain jurisdictions.

When a consumer switches from operator A to operator B and keeps his number; in most jurisdictions the phone number remains an operator A phone number and will be recognised as such by the other network operators. When this number is called, the call will first be routed to operator A, who then hands over the call to Operator B, who sends the call to the final destination – i.e. causes the consumer's phone to ring. Operator A is acting as a pass through and therefore should account for the transaction on a net basis.

Example 26.3

When a subscriber (S) makes a phone call, the mobile operator (A) incurs a cost in terms of network traffic, but charges S for the phone call. In cases where S's number has been transferred via number portability to another operator (B), there are no apparent changes to S when a phone call is made, as S still gets billed for the call (by B instead of A). However, the additional operations behind the scenes are as follows. The call still goes through A's network, as it still owns the number. A then transfers the call to B's network and charges B a 'termination' (pass-through) fee. B then connects the call to the intended recipient with no discernible time lag to S.

In our view, the termination fee received by A from B should not be recognised as revenue by A, and should be netted off against cost of sales in A's accounts. This is because the pass-through of the call by A to B's network is not a value-added or revenue generating activity. The fee received by A is merely a contribution by B to A for reimbursement of A's costs in passing the call on.

This feature is mainly used as an incentive to attract those subscribers who want to switch networks, but who do not want to change their numbers due to the inconvenience involved.

7.14   Film exhibition rights

Revenue received from the licensing of films for exhibition at cinemas and on television should be recognised in accordance with the general recognition principles discussed in this chapter. Contracts for the television broadcast rights of films normally allow for multiple showings within a specific period; these contracts usually expire either on the date of the last authorised telecast, or on a specified date, whichever occurs first. It is our view that the revenue from the sale of broadcast or exhibition rights may be recognised in full (irrespective of when the licence period begins), provided the following conditions are met:

(a)   a contract has been entered into;

(b)   the film is complete and available for delivery;

(c)   there are no outstanding performance obligations, other than having to make a copy of the film and deliver it to the licensee; and

(d)   collectibility is reasonably assured.

Rights for the exhibition of films at cinemas are generally sold either on the basis of a percentage of the box office receipts or for a flat fee. In the case of the percentage basis, revenue should be recognised as it accrues through the showing of the film. Where a non-refundable flat fee is received, we suggest that revenue be recognised on the same basis as described above for television broadcast rights.

The Appendix to IAS 18 states that 'An assignment of rights for a fixed fee or non refundable guarantee under a non cancellable contract which permits the licensee to exploit those rights freely and the licensor has no remaining obligations to perform is, in substance, a sale.'[171] When a licensor grants rights to exhibit a motion picture film in markets where it has no control over the distributor and expects to receive no further revenues from the box office receipts, revenue is recognised at the time of sale.[172]

7.15   The disposal of property, plant and equipment

IAS 16 requires that the gain or loss arising from the derecognition of an item of property, plant and equipment shall be included in profit or loss when the item is derecognised (unless IAS 17 requires otherwise on a sale and leaseback). Gains shall not be classified as revenue.[173] In determining the date of disposal of an item, an entity should apply the criteria in IAS 18 for recognising revenue from the sale of goods (see 3.5 above). IAS 17 applies to disposal by a sale and leaseback.[174]

IAS 18's criteria for the recognition of revenue from the sale of goods are essentially built around the transfer of significant risks and rewards of ownership.[175] Although IAS 18 states that in most cases the transfer of the risks and rewards of ownership coincide with the transfer of legal title, it acknowledges that legal title sometimes passes at a different time.[176]

Consequently, the general principles of revenue recognition should be applied in order to determine the point in time at which property sales should be recognised in the income statement. There are two significant points in the earning process that could, depending on the circumstances of the sale, be considered to be the critical event for recognition. The first point is on exchange of contracts, at which time the vendor and purchaser are both bound by a legally enforceable contract of sale; whilst the second possible point of recognition is on completion of the contract.

Although legal title and beneficial ownership do not pass until the contract is completed and the transfer is registered, it is likely that the earnings process is sufficiently complete to permit recognition to take place on exchange of contracts. The reason for this is that the selling price would have been established, all material related expenses would have been ascertained and, usually, no significant uncertainties would remain. If, however, on exchange of contracts there exists doubt that the sale will ultimately be completed, recognition should take place on the receipt of sales proceeds at legal completion.

In our view, both approaches should be regarded as being acceptable accounting practice. This view is supported by the discussion in the Appendix to IAS 18, which states that, in the case of real estate sales, revenue is normally recognised when legal title passes to the buyer; however, at the same time, it acknowledges that recognition might take place before legal title passes, provided that the seller has no further substantial acts to complete under the contract.[177] Nevertheless, we believe that care should be taken before adopting this latter approach, and it may be that in many cases involving the sale of real estate, legal completion is the more appropriate point at which to recognise revenue.

The gain or loss arising from the derecognition of an item of property, plant and equipment shall be determined as the difference between the net disposal proceeds, if any, and the carrying amount of the item.[178] This means that any revaluation surplus relating to the asset disposed of is transferred within equity when the asset is derecognised and not reflected in profit or loss.

The consideration receivable on disposal of an item of property, plant and equipment is recognised initially at its fair value. If payment for the item is deferred, the consideration received is recognised initially at the cash price equivalent. The difference between the nominal amount of the consideration and the cash price equivalent is recognised as interest revenue in accordance with IAS 18 reflecting the effective yield on the receivable (see 3.3 above).[179]

It should also be noted that IFRS 5 – *Non-current Assets Held for Sale and Discontinued Operations* – lays down additional requirements for assets held for disposal; these requirements include measurement rules, which clearly affect the measurement of the amount of the gain on disposal to be recognised. These are discussed in Chapter 3 at 5.2.

7.16 Sale and leaseback transactions

A sale and leaseback transaction takes place when an owner sells an asset and immediately reacquires the right to use the asset by entering into a lease with the purchaser. The accounting treatment of any apparent profit arising on the sale of the asset will depend on whether the leaseback is an operating or finance lease. In general terms, if the leaseback is an operating lease, the seller-lessee has disposed of substantially all the risks and rewards of ownership of the asset, and so has realised a profit on disposal. Conversely, if the leaseback is a finance lease, the seller-lessee is, in effect, reacquiring substantially all the risks and rewards of ownership of the asset; consequently, it would be inappropriate to recognise a profit on an asset that, in substance, was never disposed of.

This view is confirmed in the discussion in the Appendix to IAS 18 regarding continuing involvement. The discussion observes that, in some cases, real estate may be sold with a degree of continuing involvement by the seller, such that the risks and rewards of ownership have not been transferred. The examples mentioned are sale and repurchase agreements that include put and call options, and agreements whereby the seller guarantees occupancy of the property for a specified period, or guarantees a return on the buyer's investment for a specified period. In such cases, the nature and extent of the seller's continuing involvement determines how the transaction is accounted for. It may be accounted for as a sale, or as a financing, leasing or some other profit sharing arrangement. If it is accounted for as a sale, the continuing involvement of the seller may delay the recognition of revenue.[180]

The accounting treatment of the profit arising on sale and leaseback transactions is discussed in Chapter 23 at 3.5.1.

8   CONCLUSION

The growing complexity and diversity of business activity have given birth to a variety of forms of revenue-earning transactions which were never contemplated when the point of sale was established several decades ago as the general rule for revenue recognition. Added to this, the gradual move away from strict adherence to the realisation concept has resulted in contemporary generally accepted practice for the recognition of revenue becoming haphazard. Whilst there appears to be a growing practice of recognising revenue during the course of productive activity, it is generally done on the basis of exception, rather than in terms of an established principle.

At the current time, the IASB and FASB are pushing forward a balance sheet based fair-value approach to revenue recognition. This approach, if implemented, would replace the long-established accounting process in use throughout the world, whereby transactions are allocated to accounting periods by reference to the matching and prudence concepts. Nevertheless, the IASB/FASB joint project on revenue recognition contrasts two approaches that provide vastly different outcomes:

- the current approach, which is based on the principles of the earnings process and realisation and the belief that no profit should be recognised until the risks in the operating cycle have substantially been eliminated; and

- the new fair value balance sheet ('conceptual') approach that focus on the recognition, measurement, re-measurement and derecognition of unconditional rights and obligations.

It is clearly the second approach that the two Boards favour, as it sits more comfortably with their wider fair value-based balance sheet view of financial reporting. These developments and uncertainties are further brought into prominence by the plans of the IASB for a single statement of financial performance, which in our view, if adopted, will confuse two very different aspects of commercial activity. The operating performance of a business, resulting from its success or otherwise in selling its products, is at the heart of the current income statement. In our view, users need to have this aspect of company performance – real commercial success at the operating level – clearly distinguished from holding gains. We are concerned that the current revenue recognition and performance statement proposals of the IASB do not sufficiently reflect this important distinction.

References

1 APB Statement No. 4, *Basic Concepts and Accounting Principles Underlying Financial Statements of Business Enterprises*, AICPA, October 1970, para. 134.

2 IAS 18 (Original), *Revenue Recognition*, IASC, December 1982, para. 4.

3 Donald T. Nicolaisen, Chief Accountant US Securities and Exchange Commission, Speech by SEC Staff: American Accounting Association: 2004 Annual Meeting: The future of Standards Setting for Public Companies.

4 APB Statement No. 4, para. 150.

5 APB Statement No. 4, para. 151.

6 APB Statement No. 4, para. 152.

7 SEC, Staff Accounting Bulletins, Topic 13: Revenue Recognition, *1. Revenue Recognition – general.*

8 John H. Myers, 'The Critical Event and Recognition of Net Profit', Accounting Review 34, October 1959, pp. 528-532.

9 IAS 2, *Inventories*, IASB, December 2003, paras. 3(a) and 4.

10 IAS 2, para. 3(a).

11 IAS 2, para. 3(a).

12 IAS 2, para. 6.

13 SFAC No. 5, *Recognition and Measurement in Financial Statements of Business Enterprises*, FASB, December 1984, paras. 83-84.

14 IAS 2, paras. 3(b) and 5.

15 IAS 2, para. 6.

16 SFAC No. 5, paras. 83-84.

17 SFAS 48, *Revenue Recognition When Right of Return Exists*, FASB, June 1981, para. 6.

18 SFAS 48, para. 6.

19 SFAS 48, para. 8.

20 IAS 11, *Construction Contracts*, IASC, December 1993, para. 25.
21 IAS 41, *Agriculture*, IASB, January 2001 (amended March 2004), para. 5.
22 IAS 41, para. 5.
23 IAS 41, para. 12.
24 IAS 41, para. 13.
25 IAS 41, para. 8.
26 IAS 41, para. 17.
27 IAS 41, para. 26.
28 IAS 41, para. 51.
29 IAS 41, para. 13.
30 IAS 41, para. 2.
31 IAS 41, para. 30.
32 IAS 18 (Original), para. 4.
33 IAS 18, *Revenue*, IASB, December 1993 (amended March 2004), Objective.
34 IAS 18, para. 1.
35 IAS 18, para. 3.
36 IAS 18, para. 4.
37 IAS 18, para. 5.
38 IAS 18, para. 6.
39 IAS 17, *Leases*, IASB, December 2003 (amended March 2004), para. 2.
40 *Framework for the Preparation and Presentation of Financial Statements*, IASB, September 1989, para. 70(a).
41 Framework, paras. 74-76.
42 IAS 1, *Presentation of Financial Statements*, IASB, December 2003 (amended March 2004), para. 34.
43 IAS 16, *Property, Plant and Equipment*, IASB, December 2003 (amended March 2004), para. 68.
44 IAS 18, para. 7.
45 IAS 18, para. 8.
46 IAS 18, para. 9.
47 IAS 18, para. 10.
48 IAS 18, para. 7.
49 IAS 18, paras. 11 and 30(a).
50 IAS 18, para. 13.
51 IAS 18, para. 13.
52 IAS 11, para. 7.
53 IAS 11, paras. 8-10.
54 IAS 8, *Accounting Policies, Changes in Accounting Estimates and Errors*, IASB, December 2003 (amended March 2004), para. 12.
55 IAS 18, para. 14.
56 IAS 18, para. 19.
57 IAS 18, para. 16.
58 IAS 18, Appendix, para. 6.
59 IAS 18, para. 17.
60 IAS 18, para. 15.
61 IAS 18, para. 14.
62 IAS 18, para. 15.
63 IAS 18, Appendix, Sale of Goods.
64 IAS 18, para. 16(b).
65 IAS 18, para. 20.
66 IAS 18, para. 21.
67 IAS 18, para. 20.
68 IAS 18, para. 26.
69 IAS 18, para. 27.
70 IAS 18, para. 28.
71 IAS 18, Appendix, paras. 10-19.
72 IAS 18, para. 23.
73 IAS 18, para. 23.
74 IAS 18, para. 24.
75 IAS 18, para. 25.
76 IAS 18, para. 12.
77 IAS 16, para. 24.
78 IAS 38, *Intangible Assets*, IASB, March 2004, paras. 45-47.
79 IAS 18, para. 12.
80 IAS 18, para. 20(a)
81 SIC-31, *Revenue – Barter Transactions Involving Advertising Services*, SIC, December 2001, para. 4.
82 SIC-31, para. 5.
83 SIC-31, para. 9.
84 IAS 18, paras. 29-30.
85 IAS 18, para. 32.
86 IAS 18, para. 33.
87 IAS 18, paras. 18, 22 and 34.
88 IAS 18, para. 35.
89 IAS 1, para. 81.
90 IAS 1, paras. 83-84.
91 IAS 14, *Segment Reporting*, IASB, August 1997 (amended March 2004), para. 16.
92 IAS 14, para. 16.
93 IAS 14, para. 16.
94 IAS 14, para. 16.
95 IAS 14, para. 16.
96 IAS 1, para. 32.
97 IAS 1, para. 33.
98 IAS 1, para. 35.
99 IAS 18, para. 35(b).
100 IAS 16, para. 68.
101 SEC, Staff Accounting Bulletins, Topic 13: Revenue Recognition, *1. Revenue Recognition – general.*
102 SFAC No. 5, para. 83.
103 SFAC No. 5, para. 83(b).
104 SFAC No. 5, para. 84(a).
105 SFAC No. 5, para. 84(d).
106 SEC, Staff Accounting Bulletins, Topic 13: Revenue Recognition, *4. Fixed or determinable sales price.*
107 SEC, Staff Accounting Bulletins, Topic 13: Revenue Recognition.
108 The information on this joint IASB/FASB project has been summarised from the project summaries posted on the respective Boards' websites and the Observer Notes made available at IASB Board meetings.
109 Extracted from Information for observers, IASB Board meeting, 20 July 2004.

110 Extracted from Information for observers, IASB Board meeting, 20 July 2004.

111 IAS 18, Appendix, para. 1.

112 IAS 18, Appendix, para. 2.

113 IAS 18, Appendix, para. 3.

114 IAS 18, Appendix, para. 4.

115 IAS 18, Appendix, para. 5.

116 IAS 18, Appendix, para. 8.

117 Based on the AICPA Industry Accounting Guide, *Accounting for Franchise Fee Revenue*, AICPA, 1973.

118 IAS 18, Appendix, para. 18.

119 IAS 18, Appendix, para. 18.

120 IAS 18, Appendix, para. 20.

121 IAS 18, Appendix, para. 14.

122 IAS 18, Appendix, para. 14.

123 This is also the view taken in the US; see SFAS 91 at para. 10.

124 IAS 18, Appendix, para. 17.

125 IAS 18, Appendix, para. 7.

126 IAS 18, Appendix, para. 10.

127 IAS 18, Appendix, para. 12.

128 IAS 18, Appendix, para. 13.

129 IAS 18, Appendix, para. 19.

130 Statement of Position 97-2, *Software Revenue Recognition*, Accounting Standards Executive Committee, AICPA, October 27, 1997.

131 Statement of Position 98-9, *Modification of SOP 97-2, Software Revenue Recognition, With Respect to Certain Transactions*, Accounting Standards Executive Committee, AICPA, December 22, 1998.

132 SOP 97-2, para. 8.

133 Companies reporting under US GAAP would apply Accounting Research Bulletin (ARB) No. 45, *Long-Term Construction-Type Contracts*, and SOP 81-1, *Accounting for Performance of Construction-Type and Certain Production-Type Contracts*.

134 IAS 18, para. 21.

135 IAS 11, para. 3.

136 IAS 11, para. 22.

137 IAS 11, para. 30.

138 IAS 11, para. 32.

139 SOP 97-2, para. 7.

140 SOP 97-2, para. 12, as amended by SOP 98-9, para. 6(b).

141 SOP 97-2, para. 11, as amended by SOP 98-9, para. 6(a).

142 SOP 97-2, para. 10.

143 SOP 97-2, para. 10.

144 SOP 97-2, para. 10.

145 SOP 97-2, para. 10. Companies reporting under IFRS would recognise the loss in accordance with IAS 37, *Provisions, Contingent Liabilities and Contingent Assets*, IASB, September 1998 (amended March 2004) whilst companies reporting under US GAAP would apply SFAS 5, *Accounting for Contingencies*, FASB, March 1975.

146 SOP 97-2, para. 37.

147 SOP 97-2, para. 12.

148 SOP 97-2, paras. 56-62.

149 SOP 97-2, paras. 63-71.

150 SOP 97-2, paras. 48 and 49.

151 SOP 97-2, paras. 43-47.

152 SOP 97-2, paras. 43 and 47.

153 SOP 97-2, para. 12, as amended by SOP 98-9, para. 6(b).

154 SOP 97-2, para. 35.

155 SOP 97-2, para. 36.

156 SOP 97-2, para. 37.

157 SOP 97-2, para. 57.

158 SOP 97-2, para. 57.

159 IAS 18, Appendix, para. 11.

160 SOP 97-2, para. 28.

161 SOP 97-2, para. 28.

162 SOP 97-2, para. 29.

163 SOP 97-2, para. 51.

164 SOP 97-2, para. 63.

165 SOP 97-2, para. 64.

166 SOP 97-2, para. 65.

167 SOP 97-2, para. 66.

168 IAS 18, para. 13.

169 IAS 18, para. 8.

170 EITF 99-19, *Reporting Revenue Gross as a Principal versus Net as an Agent*, EITF, July 2000, paras. 7-14.

171 IAS 18, Appendix, para. 20.

172 IAS 18, Appendix, para. 20.

173 IAS 16, para. 68.

174 IAS 16, para. 69.

175 IAS 18, paras. 14-16.

176 IAS 18, para. 15.

177 IAS 18, Appendix, para. 9.

178 IAS 16, para. 71.

179 IAS 16, para. 72.

180 IAS 18, Appendix, para. 9.

Chapter 27 — Transactions with governments: grants and service concession arrangements

1 INTRODUCTION

This chapter deals with two very different aspects of transactions that most commonly (but not exclusively) take place between governments and private sector bodies. The first of these is the treatment and disclosures in relation to government grants, where the accounting standard, IAS 20 – *Accounting for Government Grants and Disclosure of Government Assistance* – became applicable for the first time more than twenty years ago.[1] After such a period of time it is perhaps not surprising that the standard is showing its age: it is arguably no longer consistent with more recent accounting models and may well undergo radical revision in the near future. The discussion of government grants and other forms of assistance begins at 2 below.

The second aspect is service concession arrangements, which have a much shorter history and, as yet, no settled accounting treatment. These are arrangements of great complexity, often devised to meet political as well as purely commercial ends. The issues cross the boundaries of a number of accounting standards and this has made it extremely difficult to devise an adequate accounting model. Service concession arrangements are discussed at 6 below.

2 GOVERNMENT GRANTS

Government grants are defined in IAS 20 as assistance by government in the form of transfers of resources to an entity in return for past or future compliance with certain conditions relating to the operating activities of the entity.[2] Such assistance has been available to commercial businesses for many years, although its form and extent will often have undergone various changes according to the shifting economic philosophies of the government of the day. The purpose of government grants (or subsidies, subventions or premiums as they are sometimes called)[3] and other forms of government assistance is often to encourage an entity to take a course of action that it would not normally have taken if the assistance had not been provided.[4] As the standard notes, the receipt of government assistance by an entity may be significant for the preparation of the financial statements for two reasons:[5]

- if resources have been transferred, an appropriate method of accounting for the transfer must be found; and

- it is desirable to give an indication of the extent to which an entity has benefited from such assistance during the reporting period, because this facilitates comparison of its financial statements with those of prior periods and with those of other entities.

The main accounting issue that arises from government grants is how to deal with the income which the grant represents. IAS 20 adopts a matching approach as its guiding principle, whereby grants of a capital nature, which are intended to subsidise the purchase of fixed assets, are credited to revenue over the life of the assets involved. The standard in fact predates the IASB's Framework. Therefore, its matching approach may at times be at odds with the IASB's Framework, which does not allow the recognition of items in the balance sheet that do not meet the definition of assets or liabilities.[6]

The standard recognises that an entity may receive other forms of government assistance, such as advice, subsidised loans or guarantees. However, rather than prescribe how these should be accounted for, it requires disclosure about such assistance.

In December 1999 the G4+1 issued a Discussion Paper – *Accounting by Recipients for Non-Reciprocal Transfers, Excluding Contributions by Owners: Their Definition, Recognition and Measurement.*[7] Since February 2003 the IASB has been discussing IAS 20 and at the time of writing it appears likely that it will issue an exposure draft proposing a significantly amended standard effectively based on the approach recommended by the G4+1. These future developments are discussed further at 5 below.

2.1 Requirements of IAS 20

The principal international standard that deals with government grants is IAS 20 – *Accounting for Government Grants and Disclosure of Government Assistance.* This was issued in 1983, and reformatted in 1994 without substantive amendment. IAS 8 – *Accounting Policies, Changes in Accounting Estimates and Errors,* which removed references to extraordinary items, amended the standard in December 2003. In January 1998, the SIC issued an interpretation dealing with certain forms of government assistance, SIC-10, *Government Assistance – No Specific Relation to Operating Activities* (see 2.2 below). Government grants related to biological assets are excluded from the scope of IAS 20 and are dealt with in IAS 41 – *Agriculture* (see 2.7 below and Chapter 36 at 2.4).

2.1.1   Nature of government grants and government assistance

IAS 20 should be applied in 'accounting for, and in the disclosure of, government grants and in the disclosure of other forms of government assistance'.[8] Under the standard, *government grants* represent assistance by government in the form of transfers of resources to an entity in return for past or future compliance with certain conditions relating to the operating activities of the entity.[9] The standard identifies the following types of government grants:[10]

- *grants related to assets* are government grants whose primary condition is that an entity qualifying for them should purchase, construct or otherwise acquire long-term assets. Subsidiary conditions may also be attached restricting the type or location of the assets or the periods during which they are to be acquired or held; and

- *grants related to income* are government grants other than those related to assets.

The standard regards the term 'government' to include governmental agencies and similar bodies whether local, national or international.[11] Government grants exclude:

(a)   assistance to which no value can reasonably be assigned, e.g. free technical or marketing advice, provisions of guarantees or the receipt of loans at below market interest rates;[12] and

(b)   transactions with government which cannot be distinguished from the normal trading transactions of the entity, e.g. where the entity is being favoured by a government's procurement policy.[13]

Such excluded items are to be treated as falling within the standard's disclosure requirements for *government assistance*, which is defined as 'action by government designed to provide an economic benefit to an enterprise or range of enterprises qualifying under certain criteria' (see 2.6 below).[14] Government assistance takes many forms 'varying both in the nature of the assistance given and in the conditions which are usually attached to it'.[15] However, such assistance does not include benefits provided only indirectly through action affecting general trading conditions, such as the provision of infrastructure in development areas or the imposition of trading constraints on competitors.[16]

The distinction between government grants and other forms of government assistance is important because the standard's accounting requirements only apply to the former.

2.2   Scope

As noted above, IAS 20 should be 'applied in accounting for, and in the disclosure of, government grants and in the disclosure of other forms of government assistance',[17] but the standard does not deal with:

'(a)   the special problems arising in accounting for government grants in financial statements reflecting the effects of changing prices or in supplementary information of a similar nature;

(b)   government assistance that is provided for an enterprise in the form of benefits that are available in determining taxable income or are determined or limited on the basis of income tax liability (such as income tax holidays, investment tax credits, accelerated depreciation allowances and reduced income tax rates);

(c)   government participation in the ownership of the enterprise, and

(d)   government grants covered by IAS 41, *Agriculture*.'[18]

The reason for exclusion (d) above is that the (then) IASC considered that the presentation permitted by IAS 20 of deducting government grants from the carrying amount of the asset (see 2.4.1 below), was inconsistent with a fair value model in which an asset is measured at its fair value.[19] The requirements of IAS 41 in relation to government grants are dealt with in Chapter 36 at 2.4.

Interestingly, in issuing IAS 40, which adopts a similar fair value model for investment properties (see Chapter 12 at 3.3.2), the IASC did not introduce any requirements for government grants in that standard, nor did it revise IAS 20 to deal with the matter.

However, one issue which has been considered by the SIC is the situation in some countries where government assistance is aimed at entities in certain regions or industry sectors, but without there being any conditions specifically relating to the operating activities of the entity concerned. In January 1998, the SIC determined that such forms of government assistance are to be treated as government grants.[20] This ruling was to avoid any implication that such forms of assistance were not governed by the standard and could be credited directly to equity.

2.3   Accounting for government grants

2.3.1   *Recognition*

IAS 20 requires that government grants should be recognised only when there is reasonable assurance that:

(a)   the entity will comply with the conditions attaching to them; and

(b)   the grants will be received.[21]

The standard notes that just because a grant has been received does not of itself provide conclusive evidence that the conditions attaching to the grant have been or will be fulfilled.[22] After an entity has recognised a government grant, any related contingent liability or contingent asset should be accounted for under IAS 37 – *Provisions, Contingent Liabilities and Contingent Assets.*[23]

The accounting for government grants is not affected by the manner in which they are received, i.e. grants received in cash, as a non-monetary amount, or forgiveness of a government loan, are all accounted for in the same manner.[24] A forgivable loan – the repayment of which will be waived under certain prescribed conditions[25] – from government is to be treated as a government grant when there is reasonable assurance that the entity will meet the terms for forgiveness of the loan.[26]

A government grant in the form of a transfer of a non-monetary asset, such as land or other resources, which is intended for use of the entity, is usually recognised at the fair value of that asset. Fair value is 'the amount for which an asset could be exchanged between a knowledgeable, willing buyer and a knowledgeable willing seller in an arm's length transactions'.[27] However, the alternative of recognising such assets, and the related grant, at a nominal amount is not prohibited.[28]

2.3.2 Matching grants against related costs

A   Income approach and capital approach

The 'capital approach', under which a grant is credited directly to equity,[29] was rejected by the (then) IASC despite the following arguments in its favour:

'(a)   government grants are a financing device and should be dealt with as such in the balance sheet rather than be passed through the income statement to offset the items of expense which they finance. Since no repayment is expected, they should be credited directly to shareholders' interests; and

(b)   it is inappropriate to recognise government grants in the income statement, since they are not earned but represent an incentive provided by government without related costs.'[30]

Instead the Board adopted the 'income approach', under which grants are taken to income over one or more periods,[31] because:[32]

(a)   government grants are receipts from a source other than shareholders, they should not be credited directly to shareholders' interests but should be recognised as income in appropriate periods;

(b)   government grants are rarely gratuitous. An entity earns them through compliance with their conditions and meeting the envisaged obligations. They should therefore be recognised as income and matched with the associated costs which the grant is intended to compensate; and

(c)   as income and other taxes are charges against income, it is logical to deal also with government grants, which are an extension of fiscal policies, in the income statement.

B   Application of the income approach

Grants should be recognised in income on a systematic basis that matches them with the related costs that they are intended to compensate. They should not be credited directly to shareholders' funds.[33] Income recognition on a receipts basis, which is not in accordance with the accruals accounting assumption, is only acceptable if no basis existed for allocating a grant to periods other than the one in which it was received.[34]

IAS 20 envisages that in most cases, the periods over which an entity recognises the costs or expenses related to the government grant are readily ascertainable and thus grants in recognition of specific expenses are recognised as income in the same period as the relevant expense.[35]

Grants related to depreciable assets are usually recognised as income over the periods, and in the proportions, in which depreciation on those assets is charged.[36] Grants related to non-depreciable assets may also require the fulfilment of certain obligations, in which case they would be recognised as income over the periods in which the costs of meeting the obligations are incurred. For example, a grant of land may be conditional upon the erection of a building on the site and it may be appropriate to recognise it as income over the life of the building.[37]

IAS 20 acknowledges that grants may be received as part of a package of financial or fiscal aids to which a number of conditions are attached. In such cases, the standard indicates that care is needed in identifying the conditions giving rise to the costs and expenses, which determine the periods over which the grant will be earned. It may also be appropriate to allocate part of the grant on one basis and part on another.[38]

Where a grant relates to expenses or losses already incurred, or for the purpose of giving immediate financial support to the entity with no future related costs, the grant should be recognised in income when it becomes receivable.[39] If such a grant is recognised as income of the period in which it becomes receivable, the entity should disclose its effects to ensure that these are clearly understood.[40]

Many of the problems in accounting for government grants relate to that of interpreting the requirement to match the grant with the related costs, particularly because of the international context in which IAS 20 is written, since it does not address specific questions which relate to particular types of grant that are available in individual countries.

2.4 Presentation of grants

2.4.1 Presentation of grants related to assets

Grants that are related to assets (i.e. those whose primary condition is that an entity qualifying for them should purchase, construct or otherwise acquire long-term assets) should be presented in the balance sheet either:[41]

(a) by setting up the grant as deferred income, which is recognised as income on a systematic and rational basis over the useful life of the asset;[42] or

(b) by deducting the grant in arriving at the carrying amount of the asset, in which case the grant is recognised in income as a reduction of depreciation.[43]

IAS 20 regards both these methods of presenting grants in financial statements as acceptable alternatives.[44]

An example of a company adopting the former treatment is Serono as shown below.

Extract 27.1: Serono International S.A. (2003)

1. Basis of preparation [extract]

1.5 Government grants

Government grants received are deferred and recognized in the income statement over the period necessary to match them with the costs they are intended to compensate, except for those amounts received for the purchase of property, plant and equipment, which are recorded as deferred income in the balance sheet, in other current liabilities and other long-term liabilities as appropriate, and amortized over the useful life of the asset. Government grants become non-refundable upon the achievement of designated milestones.

4. Research and development, net

	Year ended December 31		
	2003	2002	2001
	US$000	US$000	US$000
Research and development expense, gross	**467,875**	358,267	308,720
Less government grants	**(96)**	(168)	(159)
Research and development expense, net	**467,779**	358,099	308,561

An example of a company adopting a policy of deducting grants related to assets from the cost of the assets is GN Store Nord as illustrated below.

Extract 27.2: GN Store Nord A/S (2003)

Accounting Policies [extract]

Government grants

Government grants relate to grants and funding for R&D activities, investment grants, etc.

Grants for R&D activities, which are recognized directly in the income statement, are recognized as development costs, thereby matching the costs for which they compensate. Grants for the acquisition of assets and development activities that are recognized as assets are set off against the cost of the assets for which grants are awarded.

The purchase of assets and the receipt of related grants can cause major movements in the cash flow of an entity. Therefore, such movements are often disclosed as separate items in the cash flow statement regardless of whether or not the grant is deducted from the related asset for the purpose of balance sheet presentation.[45]

2.4.2 Presentation of grants related to income

Grant related to income should be presented either as:[46]

(a) a credit in the income statement, either separately or under a general heading such as 'other income'; or

(b) a deduction in reporting the related expense.

The standard points out that supporters of method (a) consider it inappropriate to present income and expense items on a net basis and that 'separation of the grant from the expense facilitates comparison with other expenses not affected by a grant'. Furthermore, method (a) is consistent with the general prohibition of offsetting in IAS 1 – *Presentation of Financial Statements*.[47] However, supporters of method (b) would argue that 'the expenses might well not have been incurred by the entity if the grant had not been available and presentation of the expense without offsetting the grant may therefore be misleading'.[48] Despite the fact that the arguments in favour of method (b) are not that convincing (it compares the accounting for the actual facts with that for a scenario that did not take place), the standard regards both methods as acceptable for the presentation of grants related to income.[49] In any case, the standard considers that disclosure of the 'grant may be necessary for a proper understanding of the financial statements'. Furthermore, disclosure of the effect of grants on any item of income or expense, which should be disclosed separately, is usually appropriate.[50]

An example of a company adopting a policy of presenting grants as a separate credit in the income statement is Danisco as illustrated below.

Extract 27.3: Danisco A/S (2003)

Accounting Policies [extract]

Government grants

Government grants include grants for R&D as well as investment grants, etc. R&D grants are recognised in the profit and loss account on a systematic basis to match the related costs. Investment grants are set off against the cost of the subsidised assets.

Other operating income

Other operating income comprises income of a secondary nature in relation to the activities of the Group, including government grants for research and development, profits on the sale of intangible and tangible fixed assets and rental income.

32 Government grants

During the year ended, the Group received government grants for research and development of DKK 2 million (2001/02 DKK 4 million), for investments of DKK 0 (2001/02 DKK 1 million), and of DKK 4 million (2001/02 DKK 4 million) for other purposes.

Serono is an example of a company presenting the grant as a reduction from the related expense as illustrated in Extract 27.1 above.

2.5   Repayment of government grants

A government grant that becomes repayable should be accounted for as a revision to an accounting estimate. Repayment of a grant related to income should be charged against the related unamortised deferred credit and any excess should be recognised as an expense immediately.[51]

Repayment of a grant related to an asset should be recognised by increasing the carrying amount of the related asset or reducing the related unamortised deferred credit. The cumulative additional depreciation that would have been recognised to date as an expense in the absence of the grant should be charged immediately to income.[52] It appears that the impact of a repayment differs depending on the balance sheet treatment of the grant. If an entity has an existing deferred credit balance of £50,000 and has to repay £40,000 of grants then all of the repayment can be charged against the deferred credit; no charge to the income account is necessary. However, if the entity had netted the original grant against the asset, then the repayment would be added to the asset. If the asset were halfway through its useful life, then £20,000 additional depreciation would need to be charged.

IAS 20 emphasises that the circumstances giving rise to the repayment of a grant related to an asset may require consideration to be given to the possible impairment of the asset.[53]

2.6 Government assistance

As indicated above, IAS 20 excludes 'from the definition of government grants ... certain forms of government assistance which cannot reasonably have a value placed upon them and transactions with government which cannot be distinguished from the normal trading transactions of the enterprise'.[54] In many cases the 'existence of the benefit might be unquestioned but any attempt to segregate the trading activities from government assistance could well be arbitrary'.[55] The standard therefore requires disclosure of significant government assistance (see 2.7.2 below).

It should be noted that under IAS 20, 'government assistance does not include the provision of infrastructure by improvement to the general transport and communication network and the supply of improved facilities such as irrigation or water reticulation that is available on an ongoing indeterminate basis for the benefit of an entire local community'.[56]

2.7 Disclosures

2.7.1 General

IAS 20 requires that entities should disclose the following information regarding government grants:[57]

(a)   the accounting policy, including the method of presentation adopted in the financial statements;

(b)   a description of the nature and extent of the grants recognised and an indication of other forms of government assistance from which the entity has directly benefited; and

(c)   unfulfilled conditions or contingencies attaching to government assistance that has been recognised.

An example of a brief accounting policy is given by Novartis as shown below.

Extract 27.4: Novartis AG (2003)

Notes to the Novartis Group consolidated financial statements [extract]

1. Accounting policies [extract]

Government grants

Government grants are deferred and recognized in the income statement over the period necessary to match them with the related costs which they are intended to compensate for.

A fuller accounting policy is provided by Melexis as illustrated in the following extract.

Extract 27.5: Melexis NV (2003)

7.2. Notes to the consolidated financial statements [extract]

Government grants

Government grants are deferred and amortized into income over the period necessary to match them with the related costs that they are intended to compensate. Grants received are treated as deferred income in the accompanying consolidated financial statements. Income relating to government grants is recognized as a deduction from the appropriate expense.

The company recognizes government grants if they have reasonable assurance that the grants will be received. They are recognized as income on a systematic and rational basis over the periods necessary to match them with the related costs. The grant related revenue is recorded net of the related expense in the income statement and as deferred income on the balance sheet.

O Government grants

The revenue from government grants recognized in 2003, 2002 and 2001 comprises:

| | 31st December | | |
	2003 EUR	2002 EUR	2001 EUR
Investment grants in building, machinery and employment grants	871.384	1.516.332	955.126
Grants for research and development	1.554.490	975.289	–
	2.425.874	2.491.621	955.126

2.7.2 Government assistance

In addition to the disclosures noted above, for those forms of government assistance that are excluded from the definition of government grants, the significance of such benefits may be such that the disclosure of the nature, extent and duration of the assistance is necessary to prevent the financial statements from being misleading.[58]

3   PRACTICAL ISSUES

3.1   Achieving the most appropriate matching

Most problems of accounting for grants fall into a single category: that of interpreting the requirement to match the grant against the costs towards which it is intended to compensate. This apparently simple principle can be extremely difficult to apply, because it is sometimes far from clear what the essence of the grant was, and in practice grants are sometimes given for a particular kind of expenditure which forms an element of a larger project, making the allocation a highly subjective matter. For example, government assistance which is in the form of a training grant might be:

(a)   matched against direct training costs; or

(b)   taken over a period of time against the salary costs of the employees being trained, for example over the estimated duration of the project; or

(c)   taken over the estimated period for which the company or the employees are expected to benefit from the training; or

(d)   not distinguished from other project grants received and therefore matched against total project costs; or

(e)   taken to income systematically over the life of the project, for example the total grant receivable may be allocated to revenue on a straight-line basis; or

(f)   as in (d) or (e) above, but using, instead of project life, the period over which the grant is paid; or

(g)   taken to income when received in cash.

Depending on the circumstances, any of these approaches might produce an acceptable result. However, we would comment on them individually as follows:

Under method (a), the grant could be recognised as income considerably in advance of its receipt, since often the major part of the direct training costs will be incurred at the beginning of a project and payment is usually made retrospectively. As the total grant receivable may be subject to adjustment, this may not be prudent or may lead to mismatching.

Methods (b) to (e) all rely on different interpretations of the expenditure to which the grant is expected to contribute, and could all represent an appropriate form of matching.

Method (f) has less to commend it, but the period of payment of the grant might in fact give an indication (in the absence of better evidence) of the duration of the project for which the expenditure is to be subsidised.

Similarly, method (g) is unlikely to be the most appropriate method per se, but may approximate to one of the other methods, or may, in the absence of any conclusive indication as to the expenditure intended to be subsidised by the grant, be the only practicable method which can be adopted.

In some jurisdictions grants are taxed as income on receipt; consequently, this is often the argument advanced for taking grants to income when received in cash. However, it is clear that the treatment of an item for tax purposes does not necessarily determine its treatment for accounting purposes, and immediate recognition in the income statement may result in an unacceptable departure from the principle that government grants should be matched with the costs towards which they are intended to compensate. Consequently, the recognition of a grant in the income statement in a different period from that in which it is taxed, gives rise to a temporary difference, and should be accounted for in accordance with IAS 12 – *Income Taxes* (see Chapter 24).

In the face of the problems (described above) of attributing a grant to related costs, it is difficult to offer definitive guidance; entities will have to make their own judgements as to how the matching principle is to be applied. The only overriding considerations are that the method should be systematically and consistently applied, and that the policy adopted (in respect of both capital and revenue grants, if material) should be adequately disclosed. However, it is possible to offer the following points for consideration.

3.1.1   Should the grant be split into its elements?

The grant received may be part of a package, the elements of which have different costs/conditions. In such cases, it will often be appropriate to treat these different elements on different bases rather than accounting for the entire grant in one way. However, IAS 20 does caution that care is needed in identifying the conditions giving rise to the costs and expenses, which determine the periods over which the grant will be earned.[59]

3.1.2   What was the purpose of the grant?

The method by which the amount of grant receivable is calculated does not conclusively determine its accounting treatment. For example, the amount of the grant may be based on the creation of jobs but it may be intended to contribute towards the costs of acquiring long-term assets or other costs as well. It will be necessary to examine the full circumstances of the grant in order to determine its purpose.

3.1.3   What is the period to be benefited by the grant?

The qualifying conditions that have to be satisfied are not necessarily conclusive evidence of the period to be benefited by the grant. For example, certain grants may become repayable if assets cease to be used for a qualifying purpose within a certain period; notwithstanding this condition, the grant should be recognised over the whole life of the asset, not over the qualifying period.

3.1.4   Is a grant related to long-term assets or income?

In general, we recommend that grants should be regarded as linked to long-term assets where this is a possible interpretation and there is no clear indication to the contrary, particularly where the payment of the grant is based on the cost of acquisition of long-term assets. However, we believe that the most important consideration where there are significant questions over how the grant is to be recognised, and where the effect is material, is that the financial statements should explicitly state what treatment has been chosen and disclose the financial effect of adopting that treatment.

4   TRANSITION AND FIRST-TIME ADOPTION

IAS 20 became operative for financial statements covering periods beginning on or after 1 January 1984.[60] The transitional provisions in IAS 20 required an entity adopting the standard to comply with all disclosure requirements, but gave it the option to either:

(a)   adjust its financial statements for the change in accounting policy in accordance with IAS 8; or

(b)   apply the accounting provisions of the standard only to grants or portions of grants becoming receivable or repayable after the effective date of the standard.[61]

However, under IFRS 1 a first-time adopter cannot make use of this transitional regime. Instead, it should apply IAS 20 fully retrospectively.[62]

5   POSSIBLE FUTURE DEVELOPMENTS

5.1   G4+1 Discussion Paper on government grants

As indicated at 1 above, in December 1999 the G4+1 group issued a Discussion Paper – *Accounting by Recipients for Non-Reciprocal Transfers, Excluding Contributions by Owners: Their Definition, Recognition and Measurement.*[63] This examines how items such as government grants and charitable donations should be accounted for by those who receive them. The paper reviews the appropriate accounting treatment in the light of the IASB's conceptual framework (see Chapter 2).

The paper's principal conclusion is that such items should be recognised as assets (or reductions in liabilities) and credited to income when the Framework's definitions and criteria are met, rather than being based on the matching of related revenues and expenses as is done presently by IAS 20; an approach that is essentially the same as the one taken by IAS 41 in respect of government grants of biological assets.

As far as government grants are concerned, the main impact of these proposals will clearly be on grants related to long-term assets as indicated in the following extract from the ASB's press notice when it published the discussion paper in the UK:

'Under the paper's proposals, a grant of £10,000 received for the purchase of a fixed asset of £15,000 (without further conditions) should not be accounted for as a reduction in the cost of the asset (with a corresponding reduction in the depreciation charged over the asset's life) or treated as deferred income. Instead the grant should be recognised as income in the period it is made and the carrying amount of the asset (and subsequent depreciation) should be based on the asset's cost of £15,000.'[64]

5.2   Amendment of IAS 20

The IASB started discussing IAS 20 in February 2003 as the standard posed specific problems in connection with IFRIC D1 – *IFRIC Draft Interpretation D1 Emission Rights* (see Chapter 11 at 2.2.3 A). The Board considered various options for replacing IAS 20, including withdrawal of the standard and adopting accounting models at present prescribed by pronouncements of other standard-setting bodies. However, ultimately the Board agreed that withdrawing IAS 20 would leave constituents with insufficient guidance and decided to amend IAS 20 by adopting the accounting model for government grants contained in IAS 41 (see Chapter 36 at 2.4).[65] At the time of writing it appears likely that the IASB will issue an Exposure Draft of the significantly amended IAS 20 before the end of the year.

6   SERVICE CONCESSIONS ARRANGEMENTS

6.1   Introduction

'Service concession arrangements' have been developed as a new mechanism for procuring public services. Under a service concession arrangement, private capital is used to provide major economic and social facilities for public use, although they are not necessarily arrangements solely between the public sector and private sector bodies. The initial idea was that, rather than having bodies in the public sector taking on the entire responsibility for funding and building roads, bridges, railways, hospitals, prisons and other infrastructure assets, some of these should be contracted out to private sector entities from which the public sector bodies would buy services. As time has passed, the types of services covered by such arrangements have changed and they no longer necessarily include the construction of a major asset. Many service concessions now require the private sector to bring an existing facility or service up to an agreed standard and continue to maintain it for a contracted period; these have covered a range of projects from the refurbishment of social housing and street lighting to major civil engineering projects to restore a city's underground rail system. In addition, there has been a development of similar arrangements between private sector bodies where there is a very indistinct boundary between service concession-type and outsourcing arrangements.

The accounting challenge is to reflect the substance of these arrangements fairly in the accounts of both of the contracting parties. It would be possible simply to take the contracts at fair value and account for the amounts paid and received as service payments; however, closer analysis may sometimes reveal that this is in reality a composite transaction whereby the public sector body is buying assets as well as services. In addition, there is the issue of how to account for the executory element of the contract, which may also include asset replacement and refurbishment as well as more obvious services.

The issues raised by service concessions range across a number of accounting standards, including (at least) IAS 11 – *Construction contracts,*[66] IAS 16 – *Property, plant and equipment,*[67] IAS 17 – *Leases,*[68] (what will probably be numbered as) IFRIC Interpretation 3 – *Determining whether an arrangement contains a lease,*[69] IAS 18 – *Revenue,*[70] IAS 32 – *Financial Instruments: Disclosure and Presentation,*[71] IAS 37 – *Provisions contingent liabilities and contingent assets,* IAS 38 – *Intangible assets,*[72] and IAS 39 – *Financial Instruments: Recognition and Measurement,*[73] which makes it extremely difficult to develop a coherent accounting model that deals with all of the features of service concessions simultaneously, and from the position of both the private (i.e. the 'operator') and public sector bodies (i.e. the 'grantor'). Moreover, entrenched national positions have developed and differing accounting treatments have been widely adopted in various jurisdictions, with or without a basis in specific local accounting standards. For example:

- under arrangements often used in France, many operators are of the view that an intangible asset for the 'right to operate' is created by the concession arrangement;

- in Spain, financial statement users are concerned primarily with revenue recognition rather than the recognition of assets in the balance sheet of the concession operators;[74] and

- in the UK, where there is formal accounting guidance, operators are required to analyse assets constructed for the concession as tangible fixed assets or as financial assets (receivables due from the public sector body).[75]

Indeed, some jurisdictions accept more than one treatment of broadly similar arrangements, some of which are associated with a taxation basis that has been agreed with the jurisdictional revenue authorities. Such varied approaches are further complicated by the fact that at least one government (the UK) has developed its own interpretation of the application of the local accounting guidance.

In May 2001, SIC-29 – *Disclosure – Service Concession Arrangements* – was issued.[76] This did not attempt to address the accounting issues but considered the information that should be disclosed in the notes to the financial statements of a Concession Operator and a Concession Provider. Its requirements are described further at 7 below.

Since then, the complex accounting issues raised by service concessions have been subject to prolonged and as yet unresolved debate. The IFRIC has been considering the problems since the autumn of 2003 without yet reaching a conclusion although it has developed a proposed approach, described below, and a an exposure draft is expected to be published in late 2004 or early 2005.

6.2   The IFRIC's proposed approach to accounting for service concessions

The IFRIC has had as an objective the need to clarify, before 2005, how certain aspects of the IASB's standards are to be applied in accounting for service concessions and similar projects. As of November 2004, the IFRIC has prepared and discussed three draft Interpretations, none of which has yet been published. These are:

- D10A – *Service Concession Arrangements – Determining The Accounting Model*

- D10B – *Service Concession Arrangements – The Financial Asset Model*

- D10C – *Service Concession Arrangements – The Intangible Asset Model*[77]

The discussion that follows is, therefore, based solely on the IFRIC *Updates* and *Information for Observers* issued by the IASB.

Briefly, the IFRIC sees the primary decision as being between:

- infrastructure assets where the grantor cedes control to the operator, or assets (whether constructed for the concession or otherwise) that remain within the operator's control; and

- infrastructure assets constructed for the concession that become those of the grantor because it controls them, or existing assets that remain under its control.

The IFRIC suggests that the first category (where the asset is either derecognised by the grantor or is an asset constructed for the concession that the grantor never controls) can be dealt with adequately by other accounting standards or interpretations. The operator will need to consider whether there is a straightforward lease arrangement with the grantor or whether it is an arrangement that contains a lease that should be assessed under (what will probably be numbered as) IFRIC Interpretation 3 – *Determining whether an arrangement contains a lease.* (see Chapter 23).

The second category (infrastructure assets constructed for the concession that become those of the grantor because it controls them, or existing assets that remain under its control) is to be the subject of the draft Interpretations relating to service concessions.

The IFRIC's proposed accounting framework for determining the accounting model can be summarised in the following diagram, discussed at the October 2004 IFRIC meeting in London:

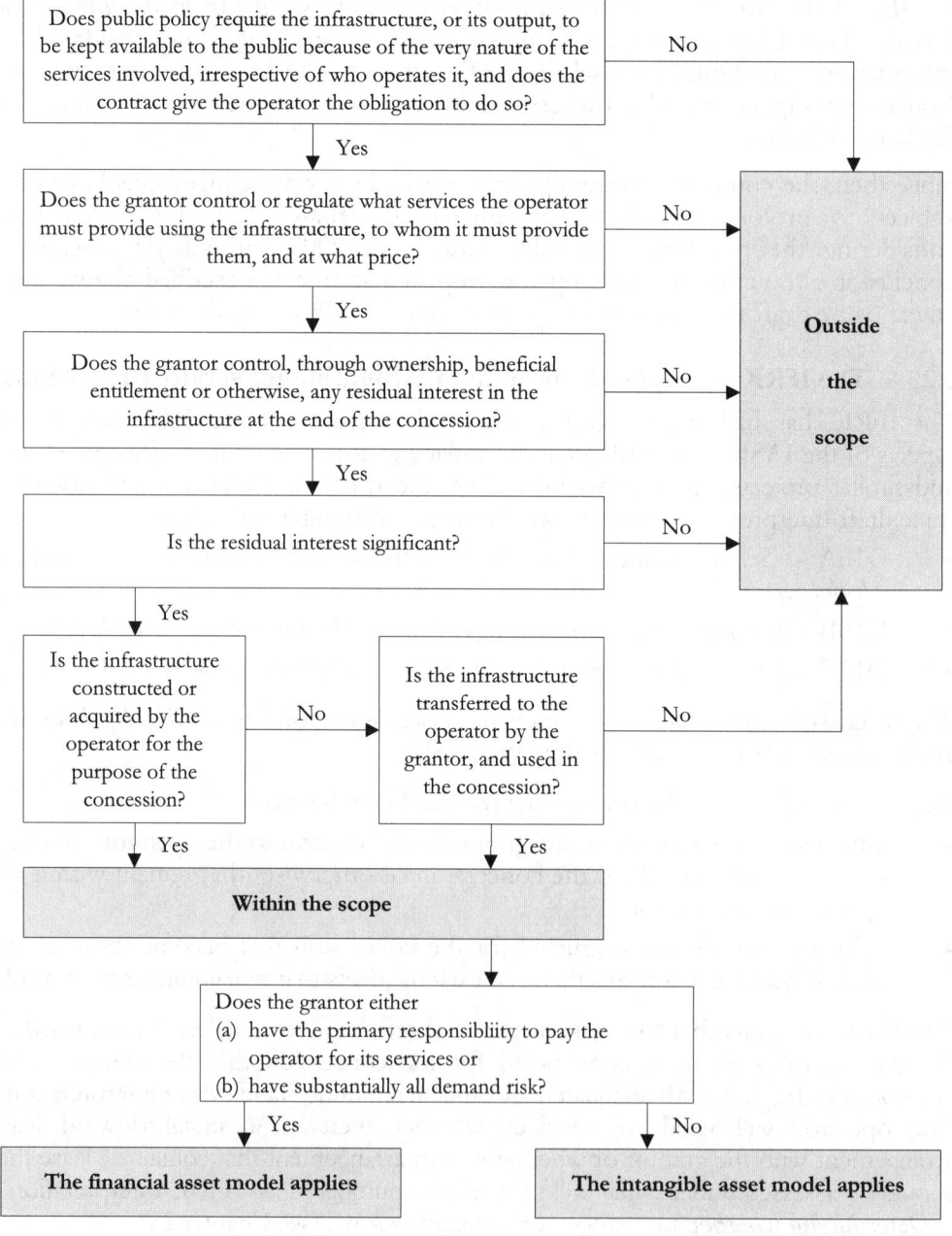

As distributed at the public meeting of EFRAG held on 6 October 2004, and amended following discussion at a public meeting of IFRIC held on 8 October 2004.

Thus any infrastructure that remains under the control of the grantor will have one of the two service concession models applied to it – the 'financial asset' model or the 'intangible asset' model. These are considered further in 6.2.2 below.

'Control' is a central concept under the IFRIC approach and its definition and consequences are discussed further below.

6.2.1 Scope of the project and the control model

One of the first problems faced by IFRIC has been defining the scope of any Interpretation. In the process, it has changed the terminology from that applied in SIC-29; the party that grants the concession is now called the grantor (formerly the concession provider), and the party that operates the concession is called the operator (formerly the concession operator)[78].

By its September 2004 meeting, the IFRIC had concluded that the scope should be limited to the accounting by the operator in a service concession:

(a)   for arrangements having the characteristics of infrastructure service concessions – the most significant characteristic being that the grantor is obliged to keep the infrastructure, or its output, available to the public because of the nature of the services involved, regardless of who operates it; and

(b)   where the grantor controls the property

The IFRIC may be intending to link 'arrangements having the characteristics of infrastructure service concessions' to the description of service concessions in SIC-29 that are described below at 6.4.

The grantor (including parties related to it) will be considered to control the property if it:

(a)   controls or regulates the services that the operator must provide using the property, to whom it must provide them, and at what price; and

(b)   controls, through ownership, beneficial entitlement or otherwise, the residual interest in the property at the end of the concession, and the residual interest is significant. Control through an option to acquire the residual interest (which is not certain to be exercised) meets this condition.

The grantor may exercise control even if the operator owns the property.

There are no significant accounting issues with respect to previously existing infrastructure assets of either the operator or the grantor. These should continue to be recognised by that party unless derecognition is appropriate under IAS 16.

The IFRIC concluded that accounting for infrastructure assets constructed or acquired for the purpose of the concession should be based on who controls the right to use the infrastructure. Crucially, control may be separated from ownership. Therefore, if the grantor controls the infrastructure assets, it should be accounted for according to one of the service concession models. If it is not controlled by the grantor, then the accounting will follow (what will probably be numbered) IFRIC Interpretation 3 – *Determining whether an arrangement contains a lease* – or IAS 17 (See Chapter 23).[79]

6.2.2   Accounting for the infrastructure asset: choosing between the financial asset and intangible asset models

Before discussing further the two models and the choice that must be made between them, it is worth considering in more detail the nature of the operator's asset under the financial asset model. The IFRIC is arguing that the operator's receivable in respect of contract services is a financial asset under IAS 32 – *Financial Instruments: Disclosure and Presentation* – because it is a contractual right to receive cash or another financial asset from another entity.[80] The fact that the right may be contingent does not prevent the asset meeting this definition.

Following from this, it is argued that the receivable will often meet the definition of loans and receivables in IAS 39, i.e. they are financial assets with fixed or determinable payments that are not quoted in an active market, do not qualify as 'trading' assets and have not been designated as 'at fair value through profit or loss' or 'available for sale'.[81]

This 'financial asset' appears to be the entity's construction revenue (i.e. costs and a profit margin) recognised under IAS 11 as from the point of initial recognition of the service concession. We have considered whether the IFRIC is in fact only considering the asset in the entity's balance sheet after the construction is complete, by which point the IAS 11 asset has been replaced by a debtor that is an amount receivable from the client. However, we are satisfied that this is not the case and that the IFRIC has interpreted all asset balances under IAS 11 as being financial assets.[82]

6.2.3   The financial asset model

The IFRIC tentatively agreed at its September 2004 meeting that the financial asset model should apply whenever:

(a)   the grantor has the primary responsibility to pay the operator for its services. This would apply even if payments by the grantor depended on usage; or

(b)   although the operator is entitled to be paid by users, the effect of the contractual arrangements is that the grantor retains substantially all of the demand risk (both upwards and downwards) associated with the service concession.

In any other case, the intangible asset model would apply.

As outlined above, it is argued that this is a financial asset. The IFRIC acknowledges that there is an issue with the analysis of the arrangements in (b) above. If the grantor (rather than users) has the primary responsibility to pay the operator for its services, but those payments depend upon usage that was outside the grantor's control, the asset would not appear to meet the definition of a receivable under IAS 39 (the payments would not be 'determinable', for example). In addition, the operator's asset has many of the characteristics of an intangible asset such as a licence, blurring the distinction between IFRIC's two models. However, a majority of the IFRIC tentatively agreed that the asset would still meet the definition of a financial asset under IAS 32 and should be accounted for as such. Under IAS 39, however, this asset would not be a receivable qualifying for amortised cost treatment, but would be accounted for as an available-for-sale asset (i.e. at fair value with changes in value taken to equity), unless it were designated as 'at fair value through profit or loss'. These definitions are further described in Chapter 15 at 6.

The financial asset would therefore fall into one of the following three categories:

- a loan or receivable;
- an available-for-sale financial asset; or
- at fair value through profit or loss, if so designated on initial recognition and if the fair value can be recognised reliably.

In the first two cases, interest income would be recognised, calculated using the effective interest method.[83]

The IFRIC was not yet satisfied that this analysis still applied if the contract were segmented so that the provision of construction services was treated as a separate contract from the provision of other services. However, it seemed clear from the discussion at their October 2004 meeting that they consider that service concession contracts should generally not be segmented but recognition of different profit margins on different 'phases' of the contract is acceptable and that this does not affect the financial asset model. Given cumulative revenue recognition in IAS 11, the recognition of different margins should have the same result in terms of revenue recognition. Extensive discussion at the October meeting surrounded the more detailed points of drafting, rather then overall principles, that appeared to be accepted largely unchanged from the previous discussions. There was, however, some considerable unease displayed by individual IFRIC members about the underlying consequences of their two-model analysis, namely that two economically virtually identical service concession arrangements could receive two different accounting treatments.

6.2.4 The intangible model

If the financial asset model does not apply, it is proposed that the operator's asset be an intangible asset. This model will apply if, for instance, the operator is paid directly by users, unless, of course, the grantor retains demand risk through specified returns and clawbacks or similar arrangements. It is argued that, because the physical infrastructure is an asset of the grantor, the operator must have an intangible asset, for example the right to collect tolls from a road or a bridge.

Furthermore, it is proposed that an inevitable consequence of applying the intangible model is that there must be an exchange transaction in which the operator receives the intangible right in exchange for its 'receivable in respect of contract services'. As this is an asset exchange of dissimilar assets IAS 18 would require the recognition of revenue based on the fair value of the assets received (unless the fair value of the assets given up can be measured more reliably).

The intangible asset would be subsequently accounted for in accordance with IAS 38 (see Chapter 11).[84]

6.2.5   Implications of the two models

The IFRIC considers that the consequences of its two models can be demonstrated by the following simple example:

Example 27.1:   Financial asset and intangible models

An operator builds a road at a cost of 100. The construction profit is 10 and total cash inflows over the life of the concession are 200.

Under the financial asset model, the operator would recognise construction revenue of 110 and a receivable of 110. Of the future cash inflows of 200, 110 would be treated as repaying the receivable, with the remaining 90 being recognised as revenue over the life of the concession. Total revenue would be 200.

Under the intangible asset model, the operator would recognise construction revenue of 110, an intangible of 110, and a construction profit of 10. Over the life of the concession, the intangible asset of 110 would be amortised against revenues (which in this case would be from users) of 200. The net position is the same as in the financial asset case, but total revenues would be 310 rather than 200.

It is fair to say that the IFRIC is not satisfied by this. In fact, the September 2004 *Update* stated that 'the majority of the IFRIC strongly disliked this outcome'. However, the IFRIC decided that the draft Interpretations should be prepared on this basis, but asked that their concerns should be brought to the attention of the IASB.[85]

6.2.6   The construction period

IAS 11 and IAS 18 will apply to the operator's activities during the construction period. Contract obligations and related rights will be recognised and measured in accordance with these standards. No obligation or related right will be recognised to the extent that contracts are executory.

Once the construction is complete, for those service concession arrangements that fall within the proposed draft interpretations, the primary decision is whether the operator's asset is a financial asset or an intangible asset.

6.2.7   Expenditure during the concession agreement

A significant issue in practice is that service concession arrangements are composite transactions. They usually have a long duration (twenty five to thirty years is not uncommon) during which time the operator has a variety of obligations. These may be in connection with the infrastructure asset itself and include:

- infrastructure components that must be replaced in their entirety;
- infrastructure subject to major cyclical repairs; and
- regular repairs and maintenance.

In addition, many service concession arrangements involve the provision of services. In the case of a hospital, for example, this could include utilities (such as water and electricity) and a wide range of 'soft' services such as cleaning, laundry, meals, portering, security and grounds maintenance, amongst others. All of these might be paid for as a single unitary charge that would probably be adjusted according to performance. An adequate model for service concessions must be able to deal with all of these issues.

The IFRIC has discussed, without reaching a consensus, replacement assets in the context of its control model. It has debated whether the grantor controls the whole of the infrastructure asset, including these replacement parts or whether they should be separately identified under IAS 16 and control considered separately. Newly constructed items might then have to be treated as assets of the operator if they were to be replaced over the life of the concession, although (under what will probably be numbered) IFRIC Interpretation 3 there might be a finance lease of those items from the operator to the grantor.[86] This debate did not help clarify how subsequent expenditure should be accounted for. We consider these issues further at 6.3 below.

The IFRIC has concluded that it is appropriate to segment the construction and services components of a service concession contract where they have substantially different margins and that, in so doing, it was not necessary to satisfy the criteria in IAS 11 for segmenting a contract (see Chapter 22 at 1.2).[87] Therefore, it is appropriate to separate the service element of the concession and account for this separately under IAS 18 – although this may well become circular, as IAS 18 suggests that revenue under contracts that involve the rendering of services should be accounted for using the percentage-of-completion method under IAS 11.

6.2.8 Application of IFRIC Interpretation – Determining whether an arrangement contains a lease

At their October 2004 meeting IFRIC voted in favour of issuing an interpretation based on its exposure draft D3. What will probably be numbered as IFRIC Interpretation 3 – *Determining whether an arrangement contains a lease* – would only apply if the grantor did not recognise the infrastructure asset, in which case it would be recognised as an asset of the operator. Under the IFRIC approach, this would depend on who controlled the assets and it is therefore only likely to occur if the grantor did not retain the residual interest in the asset (see 6.2.1). It would then be necessary to consider whether the arrangement contained a lease in accordance with Interpretation 3 and, if so, whether it is a finance or operating lease. This is described in Chapter 23 at 2.2.1.

6.2.9 Comment on the IFRIC approach to choosing the accounting model

The above is of necessity a very brief outline of the results of a prolonged series of discussions by the IFRIC. In addition, it focuses on the choice of the accounting model because there is, as yet, very little detail in the public domain regarding other details of the IFRIC approach.

However, we remain to be convinced by the IFRIC approach and see considerable difficulties if it continues to pursue its financial asset and intangible asset models. The IFRIC has focused on a control model that we do not consider to be a fundamental principle underlying IFRS, rather than on the risks and rewards of ownership. It has interpreted one standard using concepts from another in a manner that we believe is unsustainable and this is the underlying reason why IFRIC has reached conclusions that it finds unsatisfactory.

The scope of the proposals: we consider that there are a number of causes for concern in the scope of the proposed draft interpretations. It is clear that the scope is being pulled in two directions, between a broad interpretation based on principles under which any transaction meeting the control definition would be within the scope (which would cause many existing outsourcing and similar arrangements to be considered under any Interpretation) and a narrow interpretation, restricted to service concession arrangements with the public sector. The most recent discussions suggest that the latter approach is the one that will be adopted. It appears that, at most, there will be some flexibility that will allow entities to apply the interpretation to arrangements between two private sector bodies. As a consequence, similar arrangements entered into by an operator with similar underlying substances could legitimately be accounted for differently if one is with a private sector body and the other with the public sector, which does not objectively seem to be a satisfactory solution.

It is not altogether clear whether proposals in which no asset is constructed for the purpose will fall within the scope, although this may be a matter of making it clear that arrangements will be covered even when the infrastructure asset remains that of the grantor and is not derecognised by that body. More to the point, we have not yet seen anything in the proposals that deals with the problems of accounting for expenditure on an infrastructure asset over the term of the contract as distinct from the beginning.

We have serious concerns about the analysis of service concession arrangements into the financial asset and the intangible asset models.

The financial asset model: we consider that the 'financial asset' model is founded on a misguided attempt to reconcile IAS 11, an older standard whose stated objective is the allocation of contract revenue and contract costs to the accounting periods in which construction work is performed,[88] and IAS 39. IAS 11 defers costs and recognises assets in the balance sheet under the matching principle, while the principles underlying the IASB's *Framework* and such standards as IAS 39, are based on the recognition of assets and liabilities at fair value.

The *Information for Observers* for the IFRIC's September meeting states that, 'IASs 11, 18 and 39 are consistent. All require the receivable to be measured at fair value'. In fact, IAS 11 refers only once to fair value and that is in the context of contract revenue, where it states, 'contract revenue is measured at the fair value of the consideration received or receivable';[89] even here there is no suggestion, for example that contract income and costs should be discounted on a comparable basis to take account of the timing of progress payments. At no point does it state that the asset recognised in the balance sheet is at fair value. IAS 11 describes the balance sheet asset in respect of contracts in progress as 'the gross amount due from customers for contract work', being the net amount of costs incurred plus recognised profits less the sum of recognised losses and progress billings; this figure will be a liability if progress billings exceed costs incurred plus recognised profits (less recognised losses).[90] This seems to be clearly contrary to the assertion that the balance sheet figure is carried at fair value and hence a receivable as defined by IAS 39.

Even if the IFRIC's analysis is accepted, it is obvious that if the IAS 11 asset is a financial asset for the purposes of this analysis, then surely it must be a financial asset in all contexts. The consequences of this conclusion have not been considered.

At this point it is worth noting that the IFRIC was concerned whether the financial asset model analysis still applied if the contract were segmented into the provision of construction services and the provision of other services. It seems to us that if the contract were segmented in this way there is a much more plausible analysis, which is that, on completion of the construction, the entity has received a financial asset (a receivable) in exchange for a non-monetary asset. In other words, it has built an asset under a contract for the public sector, sold it to the body and recognised a receivable in respect of the proceeds it expects to receive. The IFRIC model would then have symmetry between the financial asset and intangible models as both would contain an exchange transaction.

The intangible model: if the transaction is not one that is recognised in accordance with the financial asset model, the IFRIC suggests that its intangible model would apply. It is argued that, because the physical infrastructure is an asset of the grantor, the operator must have an intangible asset, for example the right to collect tolls from a road or a bridge. This appears to be based on both a rigorous application of definitions of tangible and intangible assets and a concern that pervades IFRSs that more than one party cannot satisfy the criteria for recognition of the same asset at the same time.[91] In fact, the grantor and operator both have different interests in the same underlying asset. The IFRIC has chosen to define one of these interests as the physical asset and, therefore, must by its own rules define the other as a different sort of asset, in this case an intangible asset, with all of the accounting consequences that this distinction must bring.

Furthermore, if the operator does hold an intangible asset, then we believe that it is more consistent with the position taken by the IFRIC that the intangible asset is granted at inception of the contract. In this case the entity would have to recognise a liability in respect of the obligation to construct the asset (an alternative, the recognition of deferred income, is unlikely to be acceptable under the current framework).

While we can understand the argument that under the control model there must be an exchange transaction, we fail completely to see why revenue recognised during the course of construction in accordance with IAS 11 should not be taken into account when calculating the revenue on exchange.

The result of the IFRIC model is that there could be major differences in the way in which the arrangements are recorded, but only fine distinctions between the arrangements themselves. Moreover, it may be possible for entities to manipulate the arrangements depending on their preferred accounting result.

6.3   Accounting for service concessions: an alternative view

We had always feared that the problems in accounting for service concession arrangements were so great that they could not be a matter for the IFRIC. As that body has now been considering the problems for a year, at the end of which time its deliberations appear to have reached a position that it finds unpalatable and from which there is no obvious escape, we have not changed our minds. These issues are too complex to be within the IFRIC's remit and should be addressed by the IASB itself.

In our view, a crucial feature of accounting for service concession arrangements is that the model must be capable of addressing all of their aspects. It must provide the tools and the analysis to enable operators to deal with the construction of an asset and its subsequent recognition and measurement (if the contract involves construction of such an asset). It must also be able adequately to deal with expenditure during the contract term which includes infrastructure components, major cyclical repairs and regular repairs and maintenance (whether or not the entity has constructed an asset) and with the treatment of the service element of the contract.

It is fundamental that it addresses expenditure during the concession term, which is actually the feature common to all service concessions, albeit to a greater or lesser degree. It is not the case that significant replacement of assets only takes place in the early stages of a contract or are only a major issue in the case of contracts in which the operator is required to refurbish an existing infrastructure asset (although they are an extremely important feature of the latter type of contract). There are many contracts that require parts or components to be replaced at intervals during the contract term and most have another peak of anticipated expenditure towards the end of the contract because entities are required to restore the asset to an agreed state when it is returned to the public sector (e.g. a road must be returned to the public sector with a remaining useful life of twenty years).

Property plant and equipment models cope poorly with such expenditure. For example, if an entity undertakes a major refurbishment of an underground rail system, it may agree that it will maintain all escalators to a specified standard. This will probably involve a major programme of replacement at the beginning of the contract but other escalators that were initially of an acceptable standard will fall due for replacement throughout the twenty-five years of the concession. Further let us assume that all assets remain those of the grantor and there is no amount payable on termination (a common concession term, especially in arrangements that do not involve construction of an infrastructure asset). If the same type of escalator is constructed at year 2, year 16 and year 23 of the concession and the operator treats them as items of property, plant and equipment under IAS 16, then it will presumably have to depreciate them over 23, 9 and 2 years respectively. The entity will not be able to take account of the future replacement through depreciation of the existing asset or derecognition of its carrying amount, as it does not hold the existing asset. There will be a considerable amount of expenditure in year 23 because of the hand over conditions in the concession, and this would probably mean that the concession is heavily loss making in its last few years. This could, of course, be affected by the terminal arrangements, the price (if any) to be paid by the grantor and the basis on which such a price were to be calculated.

If the expenditure on the escalators were seen as part of the expenditure on an intangible asset, it would appear that it would have to be expensed as incurred. IAS 38 presumes that only rarely will subsequent expenditure (expenditure incurred after the initial recognition of an acquired intangible asset or after completion of an internally generated intangible asset) be recognised in the carrying amount of an asset. The standard argues that 'the nature of intangible assets is such that, in many cases, there are no additions to such an asset or replacements of part of it. Accordingly, most subsequent expenditures are likely to maintain the expected future economic benefits embodied in an existing intangible asset rather than meet the definition of an intangible asset and the recognition criteria in this Standard. In addition, it is often difficult to attribute subsequent expenditure directly to a particular intangible asset rather than to the business as a whole.'[92]

Financial asset models do not deal any better with the problem of expenditure during the contract term. If the operator's asset is a receivable or an available-for-sale asset, are all of these components additions to the original financial asset or further financial assets in their own right? Either would require interest income to be recalculated throughout the concession (technically an extremely difficult task) and cause similar problems in the last years of a concession as the IAS 16 model described above.

We believe that accounting for service concession arrangements can only be assessed realistically once it is acknowledged that they are contracts with another party, whether this party is in the private or public sector. Applying IAS 11 to expenditure and attributable income arising during the concession term creates none of the anomalies and practical problems described above. Recognition of revenue and expense would be by reference to the percentage-of-completion method. Contract revenue and costs would be recognised as revenue and expenses in the income statement in the period in which the work was performed.[93] Of course, there would still be difficulties in determining the stage of completion, but these would be much more straightforward than the problems of applying any of the other models.

We turn now to the issue of the infrastructure assets constructed by operators for the purposes of the concession.

On completion of the construction of the infrastructure asset, we consider that the operator will record this as either a receivable or a fixed asset.

Under the IFRIC's proposed model, any infrastructure asset would be an asset of the grantor if it:

(a)   controls or regulates the services that the operator must provide using the property, to whom it must provide them, and at what price; and

(b)   controls, through ownership, beneficial entitlement or otherwise, the residual interest in the property at the end of the concession, and the residual interest is significant. Control through an option to acquire the residual interest (which is not certain to be exercised) meets this condition.

As already noted, we are not convinced by the control model and consider that IFRSs generally apply a risks and rewards model. However, control could be defined as being control over activities so as to obtain benefits from those activities as, for example, in IAS 27's definition of control.[94] Under this definition, we would be concerned principally with the impact of two features, demand risk (including price risk) and residual risk.

This impact is particularly clear when considering the financial asset model. The two criteria identified by the IFRIC as identifying a transaction to be accounted for under the financial asset model are as follows:

(a)   the grantor has the primary responsibility to pay the operator for its services. This would apply even if payments by the grantor depended on usage; or

(b)   although the operator is entitled to be paid by users, the effect of the contractual arrangements is that the grantor retains substantially all of the demand risk (both upwards and downwards) associated with the service concession.

A risks and rewards model would come to the same conclusion regarding condition (b) where demand risk is in substance retained by the grantor but would deal differently with condition (a). Only those arrangements in which the grantor retained the demand risk could be treated as receivables by the operator.

In addition, a risks and rewards model would change the stress on residual risk in a concession agreement. If the asset transferred to the grantor at market value at the end of the concession, then residual risk would remain with the operator. In the far more common arrangement under which it reverts for nil consideration or for a nominal amount, then the risks and rewards of ownership would rest with the grantor.

It is our view that the operator should not recognise a receivable in respect of an infrastructure asset in circumstances in which it bears the risks and rewards of ownership.

If the risks and rewards of ownership are borne by the grantor then the operator will record a financial asset (a receivable) on completion of the construction contract. There will be an exchange transaction in which the entity derecognises the carrying amount under IAS 11 and recognises a receivable in respect of the fair value of infrastructure asset. In other words, the accounting will reflect the fact that the operator has in substance built an asset for the public sector under a contract, sold it to that body and recognised a receivable in respect of the proceeds it expects to receive. The only amount that will be recognised in revenue is the excess of the fair value of the asset/present value of the future cash flows over the carrying value of the amount recorded as receivable under the contract because, in accordance with IAS 11, revenue will have been recognised on a cumulative basis throughout the contract (see Chapter 22 at 2.3).

If the operator itself bears the risks and rewards of ownership (most commonly because it bears demand risk) then it will recognise the costs of an internally generated intangible asset. We consider that it would be inappropriate under a risk and reward model for the operator to record a profit during the construction phase of the contract. This means that there would be a difference between the carrying value of the receivable and the intangible asset on their initial recognition (the construction profit), no difference in total revenue recorded over the term of the concession but differences in the timing of its recognition.

Finally:

- If the operator's asset is a receivable, interest income will be recognised using the effective interest method. Income receivable under the concession must be separated into payments for services and payments allocated to the receivable. This may not always be straightforward and the issues are discussed in Chapter 23 at 2.2.1 in connection with a similar exercise that may have to be performed in accordance with (what will probably be numbered as) IFRIC Interpretation 3.[95]

- Payments for services should be identified as a separate segment and accounted for in accordance with IAS 18.

- Borrowing costs may only be capitalised in accordance with IAS 23, which is dealt with in Chapter 14.[96] The effect is that under both models borrowing costs may be capitalised on borrowings attributable to the construction of an infrastructure asset. Borrowing costs would only be capitalised during the part of the contract relating to the concession term if there were borrowings directly attributable to that segment and the borrowings relate to a 'qualifying asset',[97] which may well not be the case. Capitalisation of borrowing costs is discussed in 6.4.2 below.

- We have also considered the depreciation method to be applied if the operator has an intangible asset. We accept that IAS 38 states that there will rarely, if ever, be persuasive evidence to support an amortisation method for intangible assets that results in a lower amount of accumulated amortisation than under the straight-line method[98] and note that IFRIC has stated that interest methods of depreciation are not appropriate.[99] However, there is a particular issue with service concession arrangements. The effect of amortising an asset on a straight-line basis means that there is a considerable difference in the profit or loss reported under the receivable method. We are uncertain why interest-based depreciation has been considered unsuitable in the case of service concession arrangements. It would remove the principal source of differences in reported results under the two methods and we would encourage the IFRIC and the IASB to reconsider its use.

6.4   Accounting for service concessions: practical issues

Having outlined the IFRIC approach and suggested an alternative, it is appropriate to see how these might work in practice, as well as highlighting problems with the IFRIC's models in the context of specific types of arrangement. In addition, we consider another practical problem, the capitalisation of borrowing costs, at 6.4.2 below.

6.4.1   Accounting for different service concession arrangements

For the purposes of the discussion we have outlined a number of commonly encountered service concession arrangements, as follows:

Example 27.2:   Examples of common service concession arrangements

1   A hospital

A local public sector health authority in Country X contracts with a consortium of private sector companies (the operator) to build a new hospital. It is granted a lease over the land for 75 years (the legal form of the right may be a licences to occupy rather than a lease but it is assessed that this makes no substantial difference to the rights of the operator). Under the agreement it will take three years to build the hospital and this will be followed by a twenty-five year concession period in which the operator will maintain the building (both its interior and exterior) and provide services. Under the concession it will be responsible for utilities (including water, electricity and sewerage) and will provide services such as cleaning, laundry, meals, porters, security and grounds maintenance – in fact, everything except for clinical services. At the end of the concession the building and the remaining period outstanding on the lease/licence will be transferred back to the public sector for an agreed notional sum; the building will have an assessed remaining life of 30 years.

Payment starts after the building is complete and formally accepted by the health authority. There is a unitary charge made up of an availability payment and an amount for services (both of these increase in line with a prices index with minimum and maximum levels of increase), less deductions for unavailability or service performance of less than an agreed standard. The services element will be reassessed periodically throughout the contract, being 'benchmarked' to ensure that the amounts being charged correspond to current market rates.

2   A toll bridge

The government in Country Y contracts with an operator to build and maintain a toll bridge, giving the operator the right to collect the tolls for a period of twenty years. Tolls are agreed between the operator and the government and the operator has only limited powers to change these beyond an inflation-linked annual increase. The operator's toll revenues are capped so as to give it an agreed rate of return on the capital cost of the asset, after which all rights under the concession revert to the government.

3   A new road with a shadow toll structure

An operator is contracted to build a new ring road and maintain it for twenty-five years, after which it will be returned to the public sector for nil consideration and with a remaining useful life of at least ten years (with regard to the road structure) and twenty-five years for any bridges, underpasses or similar structures. Payment is by way of a banded shadow toll, i.e. the government pays based on usage of the road but the banding has the effect of limiting, but not removing, the concessionaire's upside and downside risk. Payment commences when the new road is completed.

4   A road upgrade with a shadow toll structure

An existing road is to be upgraded and partially replaced. It is currently predominantly dual carriageway (but some sections are single lane only) and there are many intersections that are either traffic-light controlled or use roundabouts. As part of the concession agreement, the operator has to ensure that the route remains accessible to traffic during construction. The payment is to be by way of a banded shadow toll commencing when the new road is completed but the operator also receives a payment, calculated at a percentage of the shadow toll, during the construction period in respect of the volume of traffic then being carried.

5   An upgrade of an underground rail network

The refurbishment and maintenance of part of an underground system is granted to an operator for a period of twenty-five years. At the end of the concession the network must be in an agreed state and all assets will become those of the grantor for nil consideration. The infrastructure assets are not formally transferred, and no form of lease or licence over the assets is granted to the operator. Although there is a considerable amount of replacement and refurbishment at inception, the operator agrees to maintain parts of the network to an agreed specification. These parts include tunnels, rails, rail beds, signalling and transmission equipment and also those parts of the system to which the public have access, such as platforms, escalators, indicator boards, etc. There will be a regular programme of replacement of assets throughout the contract; this will include assets whose service potential was acceptable at inception of the contract as well as shorter-lived assets that have to be replaced in their entirety at least once during the concession term. Other assets will undergo regular cyclical repairs.

A   *The IFRIC approach*

Under the approach being proposed by the IFRIC, our interpretation is that Cases (1) to (4), all of which include the construction of an infrastructure asset would be dealt with under the financial asset model, as follows:

(a)   *Case (1): the hospital concession* would be accounted for under the financial asset model, in this case as a receivable.

(b)   *Case (2): the toll bridge* would also be a receivable under the financial asset model although because the cash flows are not initially wholly determinable, an estimation process would have to be used to apply the effective interest method.

(c)   *Case (3): the new road with the shadow toll structure* would be accounted for under the financial asset model. Whether it was classified as a receivable or alternatively as available-for-sale or at fair value through profit or loss will depend on the degree to which the grantor has retained demand risk through the banding structure.

(d)   *Case (4): a road upgrade with a shadow toll structure* would be assessed in the same way as case (3) above.

In all cases the service costs would be separated and accounted for under IAS 18.

We assume that in cases (1) to (3) the construction contract would comprise two (or more) phases, of which the first would comprise the construction of the infrastructure asset. Revenue would be recognised on the contract in accordance with IAS 11. When the infrastructure asset was complete the operator's asset would comprise the construction cost together with the appropriate construction profit. Although it is not clear when the operator would have to start attributing interest to the carrying amount, we presume that it is at the point at which the asset is complete, accepted by the grantor and the operator starts to receive cash flows in respect of the use of the asset. The second phase of the contract would comprise the regular repairs and maintenance, the replacement of infrastructure components and cyclical repairs. Revenue would continue to be attributed to the construction contract in accordance with IAS 11, based on the phase of the contract. We are unsure whether this secondary 'contract asset' is also a financial asset and, if so, how the effective interest method would apply.

The problem with Case (4), a road upgrade with a shadow toll structure, is that the construction of an asset and a maintenance contract take place simultaneously, together with a payment structure that starts at inception but has no obvious basis in the services being performed. We are unsure as to how this contract would be assessed; it is possible that a 'holistic' approach would be taken and the initial phase would be taken as the construction of a 'concession asset', notwithstanding that it has two such distinct elements. However, the operator is receiving cash flows from the grantor from inception of the contract. Therefore, the 'construction asset' may become a financial asset at inception, with all of the practical problems that this might entail.

This issue is even more acute in Case (5), the upgrade of an underground rail network, because there is no physical asset being constructed by the concession. It effectively comprises only the 'phase' subsequent to construction of the above examples. As yet, we do not understand whether the financial asset model ought to apply or how it would be applied in practice.

B   The alternative approach

If we consider accounting for service concessions under the alternative approach outlined above at 6.3, then the infrastructure asset in Cases (1) to (4) would be accounted for as follows:

(a)   *Case (1): the hospital concession* would be accounted for as a receivable. As the operator has in substance sold a hospital to the public sector, it is able to recognise construction profit to the extent that it has not already done so under the construction period under IAS 11.

(b)   *Case (2): the toll bridge* would also be a receivable and the same considerations would apply regarding construction profit.

In both of these cases, it would be necessary to identify the fair value of the asset being constructed and the estimated cash flows attributable to the receivable. These issues are discussed in Chapter 23 at 2.2.1.

(c)   *Case (3): the new road with the shadow toll structure* would be either an intangible asset or a receivable, depending on the amount of demand risk being borne by the operator. On the basis that the demand risk is genuine and that the operator is exposed to most of the upside and downside risk in the arrangement, the road would be an intangible asset of the operator.

(d)   *Case (4): a road upgrade with a shadow toll structure* would be assessed in the same way as case (3) above as far as the road is concerned. The accounting problem is the extent to which it is possible to distinguish the maintenance contract elements of the contract from the new road. It may not be possible in practice, in which case it would be appropriate to treat all costs as those of the construction of the new road. Similar issues arise with the shadow toll received on the basis of the number of drivers that access the route during construction. If the element that relates directly to driver access can be identified, then it should be recognised on an accruals basis. Otherwise, it is more appropriate to deal with it as a series of advance payments for the construction of the new road.

In all cases the service costs would be separated and accounted for under IAS 18.

6.4.2   *Capitalisation of borrowing costs*

We noted at 6.3 above that borrowing costs would be capitalised in accordance with IAS 23 if the entity adopts a policy of capitalisation. It is therefore fundamental that only those borrowing costs that are directly attributable to the acquisition, construction or production of a qualifying asset should be capitalised as part of the cost of that asset.[100] A qualifying asset is an asset that necessarily takes a substantial period of time to get ready for its intended use or sale.[101] Although IAS 23 is not explicit on this matter, we take it to mean that borrowing costs may only be capitalised if the contract is to construct a physical asset. We believe this to be a matter of fact so that the model followed by the operator is not relevant. Therefore, borrowing costs may be capitalised during the concession period during which an infrastructure asset is being constructed regardless of whether it is subsequently accounted for as a financial asset or an intangible asset. However, borrowing costs may only be capitalised during any subsequent period if the borrowings are directly attributable to a qualifying asset. We cannot state categorically that this could not apply during the remainder of the concession term but the operator would have to be able to identify such assets, their costs and the attributable borrowings before additional borrowing costs could be capitalised.

This means that if an entity borrowed €100 million at 6% per annum to construct a road, the construction period took three years and the construction cost was €100 million then the maximum borrowing costs that could be capitalised would be €18 million – less, if any part of the borrowing were repaid before the completion of the asset. This is regardless of the manner in which interest is charged by the lenders. All borrowing costs in excess of this would have to be expensed (barring the identification of subsequent qualifying assets).

6.5   Accounting for service concessions: conclusion

In summary, we consider that operators ought to account for service concession arrangements using a risks and rewards model. This means that they will recognise either an internally generated intangible asset or account for the construction in accordance with IAS 11. That standard must be applied separately to the post-construction segments of the service concession, or the entirety of a contract in which no infrastructure asset is constructed, as appropriate.

These are complex, composite transactions that give rise to ambiguous assets. We do not believe that it is appropriate that minor differences between arrangements, and minor emphases in interpretation, should lead to widely different reported results.

7   CURRENT DISCLOSURE REQUIREMENTS: SIC-29

It is important to note that the scope of SIC-29 – *Disclosure of service concession arrangements* – is much broader than the proposed Draft Interpretations relating to service concession arrangements described above. It applies to a type of transaction that is described although not really defined and which does not depend on the control criteria described in 6.2.1 above. It also applies to both sides of the transaction, whereas the proposed draft interpretations apply only to the operator under the concession agreement.

SIC-29 describes service concessions as arrangements in which an entity (the Concession Operator) provides services on behalf of another entity (the Concession Provider, which may be a public or private sector entity, including a governmental body) that give the public access to major economic and social facilities. The examples of service concession arrangements given by SIC-29 include water treatment and supply facilities, motorways, car parks, tunnels, bridges, airports and telecommunication networks.[102]

SIC-29 states that the common characteristic of all service concession arrangements is that the Concession Operator both receives a right and incurs an obligation to provide public services.[103] It excludes from its scope an entity outsourcing the operation of its internal services (e.g. employee cafeteria, building maintenance, and accounting or information technology functions).[104] This means that some of the arrangements that do not include the construction of a major capital asset, as discussed above, may not be caught by the requirements of the SIC, although there is no hard-and-fast dividing line between service concessions and outsourcing arrangements. For example, if a major information technology project provides computer services for a Government office that issues passports to the public, and that Government office previously had little or nothing in the way of such support, it would appear to be more in the nature of a service concession and therefore fall to be included with SIC-29's requirements. On the other hand, a contract between a Government department and an Operator to maintain the existing computer system, including replacement of hardware and software as appropriate, may be outside the scope of SIC-29.

SIC-29 summarises the rights and obligations as follows:

For the period of the concession, the Concession Operator has received from the Concession Provider:

(a)   the right to provide services that give the public access to major economic and social facilities, and

(b)   in some cases, the right to use specified tangible assets, intangible assets, and/or financial assets,

in exchange for the Concession Operator:

(a)   committing to provide the services according to certain terms and conditions during the concession period, and

(b)   when applicable, committing to return at the end of the concession period the rights received at the beginning of the concession period and/or acquired during the concession period. [105]

The disclosure requirements in respect of such projects are as follows:

SIC-29 requires disclosure in addition to that required by other standards that may cover part of the transaction, such as IAS 16 Property, plant and equipment (see Chapter 12), IAS 17 (see Chapter 23) and IAS 38 (see Chapter 11). [106] All aspects of a service concession arrangement should be considered in determining the appropriate disclosures in the notes to the financial statements. [107]

A Concession Operator and a Concession Provider should disclose the following in each period:

(a)   a description of the arrangement;

(b)   significant terms of the arrangement that may affect the amount, timing and certainty of future cash flows (e.g. the period of the concession, re-pricing dates and the basis upon which re-pricing or re-negotiation is determined);

(c)   the nature and extent (e.g. quantity, time period or amount as appropriate) of:

(i)   rights to use specified assets;

(ii)   obligations to provide or rights to expect provision of services;

(iii) obligations to acquire or build items of property, plant and equipment;

(iv)   obligations to deliver or rights to receive specified assets at the end of the concession period;

(v)   renewal and termination options; and

(vi)   other rights and obligations (e.g. major overhauls); and

(d)   changes in the arrangement occurring during the period.

These disclosures should be provided individually for each service concession arrangement or in aggregate for each class of service concession arrangements. A class is a grouping of service concession arrangements involving services of a similar nature (e.g. toll collections, telecommunications and water treatment services). [108]

8   CONCLUSION

This chapter deals with two distinct forms of government/private entity transactions. The need for an up to date standard on government grants is important because – whether companies like to admit to it or not – many industries receive significant government support. Equally, the growth and complexity of service concession arrangements provides an entirely new set of accounting problems that the IASB needs to address.

It is clear that IAS 20 is an old standard that needs to be modernised to bring it more in line with the IASB's other standards. Fortunately, the IASB is currently preparing an Exposure Draft of an amended IAS 20. Hopefully, the Board will take this as an opportunity to provide practical guidance on how preparers should account for the grants they receive.

It is our view that accounting is a dynamic social construct that needs to be able to respond to the changing needs of business and to changing economic developments. The appearance of service concession arrangements is an example of the business dynamics that accounting must be capable of responding to. Service concessions arrangements have appeared as a direct result of Governments' wishing to attract private capital to finance what has (at least in European countries since 1950) been regarded as the reserve of public expenditure. It may be that the balance sheet approach of the IASB's Framework (based as it is on FASB work dating from the 1970s) is not entirely adequate for the task. The challenge for the IASB is therefore to put forward suitable, understandable and practically workable solutions to the problems service concession arrangements pose.

References

1 IAS 20, *Accounting for Government Grants and Disclosure of Government Assistance*, IASB, April 1983 (amended December 2003), para. 41.
2 IAS 20, para. 3.
3 IAS 20, para. 6.
4 IAS 20, para. 4.
5 IAS 20, para. 5.
6 *Framework for the Preparation and Presentation of Financial Statements*, IASB, September 1989, para. 95.
7 *Accounting by Recipients for Non-Reciprocal Transfers, Excluding Contributions by Owners: Their Definition, Recognition and Measurement*, Westwood and Mackenzie, December 1999.
8 IAS 20, para. 1.
9 IAS 20, para. 3.
10 IAS 20, para. 3.
11 IAS 20, para. 3.
12 IAS 20, paras. 3, 35 and 37.
13 IAS 20, paras. 3 and 35.
14 IAS 20, para. 3.
15 IAS 20, para. 4.
16 IAS 20, para. 3.
17 IAS 20, para. 1.
18 IAS 20, para. 2.
19 IAS 41, *Agriculture*, IASB, January 2001, (amended March 2004), para. B66.
20 SIC-10, *Government Assistance – No Specific Relation to Operating Activities*, SIC, July 1998, para. 3.
21 IAS 20, para. 7.
22 IAS 20, para. 8.
23 IAS 20, para. 11.
24 IAS 20, para. 9.
25 IAS 20, para. 3.
26 IAS 20, para. 10.
27 IAS 20, para. 3.
28 IAS 20, para. 23.
29 IAS 20, para. 13.
30 IAS 20, para. 14.
31 IAS 20, para. 13.
32 IAS 20, para. 15.
33 IAS 20, para. 12.
34 IAS 20, para. 16.
35 IAS 20, para. 17.
36 IAS 20, para. 17.
37 IAS 20, para. 18.
38 IAS 20, para. 19.
39 IAS 20, paras. 20-22.
40 IAS 20, paras. 21-22.
41 IAS 20, para. 24.
42 IAS 20, para. 26.
43 IAS 20, para. 27.
44 IAS 20, para. 25.
45 IAS 20, para. 28.
46 IAS 20, para. 29.
47 IAS 1, *Presentation of Financial Statements*, IASB, December 2003 (amended March 2004), paras. 32-33.
48 IAS 20, para. 30.
49 IAS 20, para. 31.
50 IAS 20, para. 31.
51 IAS 20, para. 32.
52 IAS 20, para. 32.
53 IAS 20, para. 33.
54 IAS 20, para. 34.
55 IAS 20, para. 35.
56 IAS 20, para. 38.
57 IAS 20, para. 39.
58 IAS 20, para. 36.
59 IAS 20, para. 19.
60 IAS 20, para. 41.
61 IAS 20, para. 40.
62 IFRS 1, *First-time Adoption of International Financial Reporting Standards*, IASB, June 2003 (amended March 2004), paras. 7 and 9.
63 *Accounting by Recipients for Non-Reciprocal Transfers, Excluding Contributions by Owners: Their Definition, Recognition and Measurement*, Westwood and Mackenzie, December 1999.
64 ASB PN 155, 13 January 2000.
65 Project Summary, *Short-term Convergence*, IASB, 18 June 2004, p. 7.
66 IAS 11, *Construction contracts*, IASC, December 1993.
67 IAS 16, *Property, plant and equipment*, IASB, December 2003, (amended March 2004).
68 IAS 17, *Leases*, IASB, December 2003, (amended March 2004).
69 IFRIC D3 *Determining Whether an Arrangement Contains a Lease*, IFRIC, January 2004.
70 IAS 18, *Revenue*, IASB, December 1993, (amended March 2004).
71 IAS 32, *Financial Instruments: Disclosure and Presentation*, IASB, December 2003, (amended March 2004).
72 IAS 38, *Intangible assets*, IASB, March 2004.
73 IAS 39, *Financial Instruments: Recognition and Measurement*, IASB, December 2003, (amended March 2004).
74 IFRIC website, *Service Concession Arrangements*, 18th May 2004.
75 FRS 5, *Reporting the substance of transactions*, ASB, April 1994 (with subsequent amendments), Application Note F, *Private finance initiative and similar contracts*.

76 SIC-29, *Disclosure – Service Concession Arrangements*, SIC, December 2001 (amended December 2003).

77 *IFRIC Update*, IFRIC, July 2004, page. 2.

78 SIC-29, para. 1.

79 *IFRIC Update*, September 2004, pages. 2 and 3.

80 IAS 32, para. 11.

81 IAS 39, para. 9.

82 The arguments have most recently been presented in the *Information for Observers* for the IFRIC meeting in September 2004.

83 *IFRIC Update*, IFRIC, September 2004, p. 2-3, *Information for Observers*, September 2004.

84 *IFRIC Update*, September 2004, p. 2-3, *Information for Observers*, September 2004.

85 *IFRIC Update*, September 2004, p. 2-3.

86 *IFRIC Update*, September 2004, p. 2-3.

87 *IFRIC Update*, IFRIC, May 2004, p. 4.

88 IAS 11, Objective.

89 IAS 11, para. 12.

90 IAS 11, para. 43.

91 See, for example, the treatment by transferees of transfers of financial assets not qualifying for derecognition by the transferor in IAS 39, paras. AG34, AG50, described in Chapter 16 at 3.2.

92 IAS 38, para. 20.

93 IAS 11, paras. 25-26.

94 IAS 27, *Consolidated and Separate Financial Statements*, IASB, December 2003, (amended March 2004), para. 4.

95 IFRIC D3.

96 IAS 23, *Borrowing Costs*, IASC, December 1993, (amended December 2003).

97 IAS 23, paras. 4 and 11.

98 IAS 38, para. 89.

99 IFRIC website, *Service Concession Arrangements*, 18th May 2004

100 IAS 23, para. 11.

101 IAS 23, para. 4.

102 SIC-29, para. 1.

103 SIC-29, para. 3.

104 SIC-29, para. 1.

105 SIC-29, para. 3.

106 SIC-29, para. 3.

107 SIC-29, para. 3.

108 SIC-29, paras. 6-7.

Chapter 28   Segment reporting

1   INTRODUCTION

Segmental reporting has been debated since the emergence and growth of the multinational conglomerate in the early 1960s. As entities became involved in an increasing number of distinct products and markets, even industries, the readers of their financial statements found it increasingly difficult to understand the effect of different segments' results on past performance and the likely effect on future prospects. Clearly, there could be a variety of rates of profitability, opportunities for growth and risk factors concealed within the consolidated financial statements of a diversified multinational business entity. Pressures grew, mainly from the investment analyst community, for disclosure of the results and resources of the different segments which comprised the whole business.

The international accounting standard on the issue, IAS 14 – *Segment Reporting*, was originally published by the IASC in August 1981[1] and reformatted in 1994. It was revised again in 1997. Further amendments have been made as a consequence of the December 2003 revisions to IAS 2 – *Inventories*, IAS 8 – *Accounting Policies, Changes in Accounting Estimates and Errors*, and IAS 16 – *Property, Plant and Equipment*, and the publication in 2004 of IFRS 3 – *Business Combinations* – and IFRS 5 – *Non-current Assets Held for Sale and Discontinued Operations*.

The amended version of IAS 14 is mandatory for financial periods beginning on or after 1 January 2005. However, if an entity applies any of these standards for an earlier period, the entity is required also to apply the amended version of IAS 14 for that earlier period.

2   THE REQUIREMENTS OF IAS 14

2.1   Objective and scope

2.1.1   *Objective*

IAS 14 aims to help users of financial statements better understand past performance, better assess the entity's risks and returns and make more informed judgements about the entity as a whole, by establishing principles for reporting financial information about the different types of products and services an entity produces and the different geographical areas in which it operates.[2]

2.1.2   *Scope*

The requirements of IAS 14 should be applied in complete sets of published financial statements that comply with IFRS,[3] with 'complete' meaning that a balance sheet, income statement, cash flow statement, a statement showing changes in equity, and notes are included, as provided in IAS 1 – *Presentation of Financial Statements.*[4] The standard is mandatory for all entities whose equity or debt securities are publicly traded, or are about to be.[5] The latter reference would include companies preparing a prospectus for the issuance of equity or debt securities in the public securities markets. Entities whose securities are not publicly traded are encouraged to disclose segment information voluntarily in financial statements prepared in accordance with IFRS.[6] The standard is clear that if segment information is presented on a voluntary basis it must be prepared in full compliance with the requirements of IAS 14.[7]

Where both parent entity and consolidated financial statements are presented, segment information only needs to be reported on the basis of the consolidated financial statements.[8] Similarly, if the financial statements of an entity's equity method associates or joint ventures are attached to its financial statements, segment information only needs to be reported on the basis of the entity's own financial statements.[9] If the securities of a subsidiary are publicly traded, segment information will have to be presented in the subsidiary's own financial statements.[10] By the same token, an entity whose securities are publicly traded is not exempt from the requirement to give segment information in its own financial statements because it is an associate or joint venture of another entity.[11]

There are no exemptions in IAS 14 from the requirement to disclose segment information, or components of such information, for example on the grounds of commercial sensitivity or confidentiality.

2.1.3   *First-time adoption*

There are no specific exemptions or concessions available to first-time adopters in respect of the requirements to report segment information. Accordingly, entities will have to ensure that internal reporting systems allow management to meet the measurement and disclosure requirements of IAS 14 for all periods following its date of transition.

2.1.4   General approach

IAS 14 requires information to be disclosed for both business segments and geographical segments, with one of these being designated as the primary basis and the other as the secondary basis (less information is required to be disclosed in relation to the secondary basis), depending on which is regarded as providing the more meaningful analysis of the predominant source and nature of risks and returns.[12] The principle underlying the approach in IAS 14 is that an entity's organisational and management structure develops along lines related to the predominant sources of its risks and returns. Accordingly, the process of identifying segments for external reporting purposes begins with the information used by the board of directors and the chief executive officer to evaluate past performance and to make decisions about future allocations of resources. This is sometimes called the 'management approach'.[13]

The standard defines the elements of segment reporting and sets out how, based on an understanding of the dominant sources of the entity's risks and returns, the information reported to the board should be refined and if necessary restated for external reporting purposes.

2.2   Definitions

2.2.1   Definitions from other standards

In defining the elements of segment reporting, IAS 14 uses the following terms with the meanings specified in IAS 7 – *Cash Flow Statements*, IAS 8 – *Accounting Policies, Changes in Accounting Estimates and Errors*, and IAS 18 – *Revenue*.[14]

Operating activities are the principal revenue-producing activities of the entity and other activities that are not investing or financing activities.[15]

Accounting policies are the specific principles, bases, conventions, rules and practices applied by an entity in preparing and presenting financial statements.[16]

Revenue is the gross inflow of economic benefits during the period arising in the course of the ordinary activities of an entity when those inflows result in increases in equity, other than increases relating to contributions from equity participants.[17]

2.2.2   Business, geographical and reportable segments

A   Business segment

A business segment is defined as 'a distinguishable component of an entity that is engaged in providing an individual product or service or a group of related products or services and that is subject to risks and returns that are different from those of other business segments'. The standard suggests that in order to determine whether products and services are related, management should take into account the following:[18]

(a)   the nature of the products or services;

(b)   the nature of the production processes;

(c)   the type or class of customer for the products or services;

(d)   the methods used to distribute the products or provide the services; and

(e)   if applicable, the nature of the regulatory environment.

No particular priority is given to any single factor.[19] However, IAS 14 clearly prohibits the inclusion of products and services subject to significantly differing risks and returns within the same business segment and requires that products and services included in a single business segment are similar with respect to at least a majority of the above factors.[20]

B   *Geographical segment*

A geographical segment is defined as 'a distinguishable component of an entity that is engaged in providing products or services within a particular economic environment and that is subject to risks and returns that are different from those of components operating in other economic environments'. In identifying geographical segments management should consider the following:[21]

(a)   similarity of economic and political conditions;

(b)   relationships between operations in different geographical areas;

(c)   proximity of operations;

(d)   special risks associated with operations in a particular area;

(e)   exchange control regulations; and

(f)   the underlying currency risks.

As in the identification of business segments, no particular priority is given to any single factor.[22] Whilst a geographical segment can be a single country, a group of two or more countries, or a region within a country, operations in economic environments with significantly differing risks and returns cannot be included in the same geographical segment.[23]

Geographical segments can be based either on the location of the entity's operations or on the location of its markets and customers, depending on which represents the dominant source of geographical risks.[24] The choice of basis should be supported by evidence provided from the entity's organisational and internal reporting structure.[25] For example, the internal reporting of an international consumer products business might well be dominated by analysis of its markets and customers, despite also having production facilities all over the world. Alternatively an international oil and gas entity might well concentrate on the location of its production facilities, despite supplying global markets. Of course, it is possible for the location of operations and markets to be the same.

C   *Determining the composition of a business or geographical segment*

IAS 14 does not prescribe how many business or geographical segments an entity should have, nor what activities each segment should contain. These decisions involve the exercise of judgement. In making that judgement management is required to take into account the reporting objective of IAS 14 and the qualitative characteristics of financial statements as identified in the IASB Framework (which include the relevance, reliability and comparability over time of reported segment information and the usefulness of that information in assessing the risks and returns of the entity as a whole).[26]

In practice this requires management to recognise that whilst an entity would not combine elements that are subject to differing rates of profitability, opportunities for growth, future prospects and risks,[27] a level of segmentation can be reached where its value to users is diminished. For example this would be the case where disclosed information is not material to users' decision-making needs or where the allocation of revenue, expense, assets and liabilities between segments becomes too subjective.

D   *Reportable segment*

A reportable segment is a business segment or geographical segment for which segment information is required to be disclosed by the standard.[28] The process for determining which segments are reportable is discussed in 2.3 below.

2.2.3   *Segment revenue, expense, result, assets, liabilities and accounting policies*

IAS 14 contains the following detailed definitions of terms that affect the measurement and presentation of segment information:

A   *Segment revenue*

Segment revenue is that part of revenue reported in the income statement that is directly attributable to a segment together with the relevant portion of revenue that can be allocated to it on a reasonable basis, whether from sales to external customers or from transactions with other segments. Segment revenue includes the entity's share of revenue from jointly controlled entities accounted for by proportionate consolidation in accordance with IAS 31 – *Interests in Joint Ventures*.[29] Whilst the standard is silent in this respect, it would follow that revenue from jointly controlled assets and jointly controlled operations are included in segment revenue.

Unless the segment's operations are primarily of a financial nature, segment revenue excludes interest or dividend income, gains on sales of investments or gains on extinguishment of debt.[30] IAS 14 states that segment revenue includes an entity's share of profits or losses of associates, joint ventures, or other investments accounted for under the equity method only if those items are included in consolidated or total entity revenue.[31]

B   Segment expense

Segment expense comprises directly attributable expenses resulting from the operating activities of a segment together with the relevant portion of an expense that can be allocated to a segment on a reasonable basis, including those relating to sales to external customers and relating to transactions with other segments. Segment expense includes the entity's share of the expenses of jointly controlled entities accounted for by proportionate consolidation in accordance with IAS 31,[32] and on the same basis as noted above, would include the entity's share of the expenses relating to jointly controlled assets and jointly controlled operations. Segment expense also includes any impairment losses recognised for goodwill.[33]

Segment expense does not include income tax expense. Neither does it include general administrative expenses or head-office and other expenses that arise at the entity level and cannot be directly attributed or allocated to the segment on a reasonable basis. The entity's share of losses of associates, joint ventures, or other investments accounted for under the equity method are also excluded from segment expense. Unless the segment's operations are primarily of a financial nature, segment expense also excludes interest (including that incurred on advances or loans from other segments), losses on sales of investments or losses on extinguishment of debt. For a segment's operations that are primarily of a financial nature, the standard allows a single net amount to be presented in the segment disclosures for interest income and interest expense. However, this is only permitted if the entity presented a single net amount in the consolidated or entity financial statements.[34]

C   Segment result

Segment result is segment revenue less segment expense and is determined before any adjustments for minority interest.[35] For segments whose operations are not primarily of a financial nature, the definitions of segment revenue and segment expense mean that interest is excluded. In such cases segment result represents an operating, rather than a net-of-financing, profit or loss.[36]

D   Segment assets

Segment assets are those operating assets that are employed by a segment in its operating activities and that either are directly attributable to the segment or can be allocated to it on a reasonable basis. Where segment result includes interest or dividend income, the segment assets include the related receivables, loans, investments or other income-producing assets. Segment assets include the entity's share of the operating assets of jointly controlled entities accounted for by proportionate consolidation in accordance with IAS 31,[37] and the entity's share of jointly controlled assets and the operating assets of jointly controlled operations.

Segment assets do not include income tax assets and would include investments accounted for under the equity method only if the profit or loss from such investments were included in segment revenue. The carrying value of segment assets is stated after deducting related allowances that are reported as direct offsets in the entity's balance sheet.[38] Such allowances would include, for example, provisions against the recoverable value of inventories and receivables.

Segment assets include current assets used in the operating activities of the segment, property, plant and equipment, assets held under finance leases and intangible assets (including goodwill). If a particular item of expense is included in segment expenses, then the related asset is included in segment assets. Segment assets do not include assets used for general entity or head office purposes.[39]

E   Segment liabilities

Segment liabilities are those operating liabilities that result from the operating activities of a segment and that either are directly attributable to the segment or can be allocated to it on a reasonable basis, and excludes income tax liabilities. Where segment result includes interest expense, the segment liabilities include the related interest-bearing liabilities. Segment liabilities include the entity's share of the liabilities of jointly controlled entities accounted for by proportionate consolidation in accordance with IAS 31,[40] and the entity's share of liabilities resulting from operating activities relating to jointly controlled assets and jointly controlled operations.

Segment liabilities include trade and other payables, accruals, customer advances, warranty provisions and other claims relating to the provision of goods and services. Segment liabilities do not include borrowings, liabilities under finance leases and other liabilities incurred for financing purposes. Only segments whose operations are primarily of a financial nature would include interest expense in segment result and related interest-bearing liabilities in segment liabilities. Also, because debt is often issued at the head office level or on an entity-wide basis, it is often not possible to regard such interest-bearing liabilities as directly attributable or reasonably allocable to segments whose operations are not primarily of a financial nature.[41] An entity should refer to the guidance in IAS 7 to determine whether bank overdrafts should be included as a component of cash or should be reported as borrowings.[42] See Chapter 32 at 2.2.2.

F   What is meant by 'directly attributable to a segment'?

IAS 14 requires an entity to look at its internally reported financial information to determine, at least initially, which items of revenue, expense, assets and liabilities are directly attributable to a segment or can be so allocated on a reasonable basis. This means that there is a presumption that amounts identified for internal reporting purposes as segment revenue, expense, assets and liabilities satisfy the requirement in the standard of being directly attributable or reasonably allocable to a reportable segment.[43] Adjustments may be required either to reverse allocations that, whilst understood by management, could be regarded as subjective, arbitrary or difficult to understand by users of the financial statements; or to attribute items to segments that, whilst meeting the definitions of segment revenue, expense, assets or liabilities, are not so allocated for internal reporting purposes.[44] Guidance in other standards might be useful in determining what is a 'reasonable basis' for allocating costs to segments, such as IAS 2 (see Chapter 21 at 2.2.1) and IAS 11 – *Construction Contracts* (see Chapter 22 at 2.2).[45]

G   Segment accounting policies

Segment accounting policies are the accounting policies adopted for preparing and presenting the financial statements of the consolidated group or entity as well as those accounting policies that relate specifically to segment reporting.[46] The application and disclosure of segment accounting policies are discussed in 2.4.1 below.

2.3   Identifying externally reportable segments

As indicated in 2.1.4 above, IAS 14 requires a 'management approach' to identifying externally reportable segments. This demands a direct link between the segment disclosures in the financial statements and the entity's organisational structure and internal financial reporting system, primarily in respect of information reported to the board of directors and the chief executive officer.[47] However, this does not mean that the standard requires the reporting format in the financial statements to be a simple copy of the information given to the board. Internally reported operating segments may be separately disclosed, combined with others, or left unallocated, depending on their significance. Appendix A to IAS 14 summarises this process in a 'Segment Definition Decision Tree'.

Accordingly, the process of identifying externally reportable segments involves understanding which operating segments are reported internally, confirming that they meet the definitions of business segments and geographical segments discussed at 2.2.2 above and then making the following judgements:

- whether the primary segment reporting format will be business segments or geographical segments;

- whether internally reported operating segments can be combined;

- whether an operating segment is also a reportable segment; and

- whether to include an internally reported operating segment as an unallocated reconciling item.

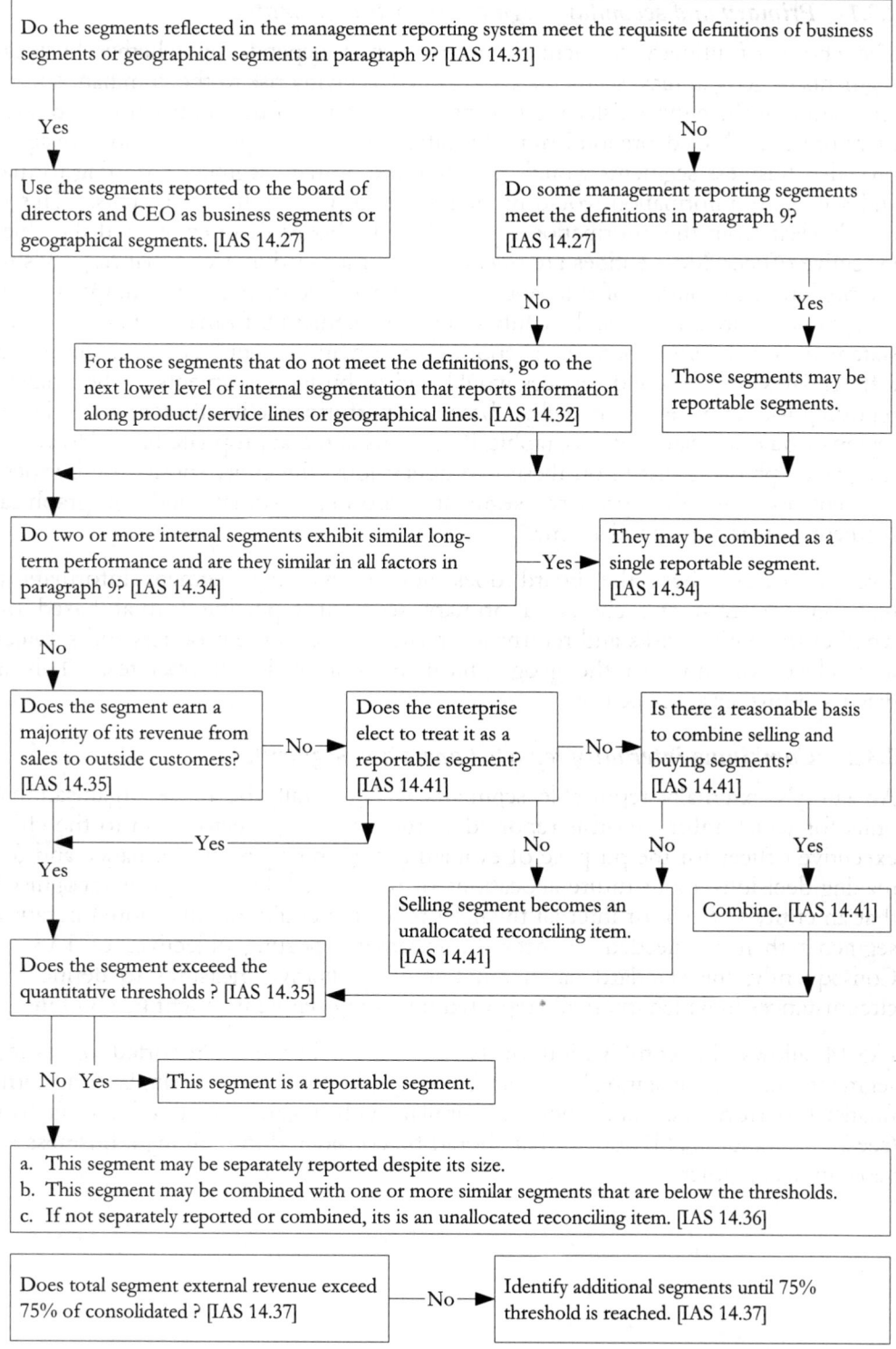

2.3.1 Primary and secondary segment reporting formats

The choice of primary segment reporting format depends on whether business segments or geographical segments are regarded as giving rise to the dominant source and nature of the entity's risks and returns. For example, if the entity's risks and rates of return are affected predominantly by differences in the products and services it provides, business segments would constitute the primary segment reporting format and secondary information would be presented for geographical segments.[48] This is usually clear from the information reported to the board of directors and the chief executive officer. Most entities are organised and managed in a way that responds to the predominant sources of risks and returns. Therefore there is a presumption that, except in rare circumstances, the entity will report segment information in its financial statements on the same basis as it reports to top management.[49] A presentation that differentiates products and services would lead to business segments as the primary reporting format, whereas an analysis based on performance in different countries or regions would indicate that geographical segments is the appropriate basis. However, if equal emphasis is placed on these two dimensions, the entity should use business segmentation as the primary segment reporting format and geographical segmentation as the secondary one.[50]

Even in cases where the board does not receive any segment information, management must still choose a primary segment reporting format based on whether the entity's risks and returns are related more to the products and services it produces or more to the geographical areas in which it operates.[51] This is discussed further at 3.2 below.

2.3.2 Combining internally reported operating segments

An entity's externally reportable segments will generally be those organisational units for which information is reported to the board of directors and to the chief executive officer for the purpose of evaluating the unit's past performance and for making decisions about future allocations of resources.[52] However, it is recognised that an entity's system of internal financial reporting could identify more operating segments than are needed to meet the external reporting objectives of IAS 14. Consequently, the standard has a number of qualitative measures to define the circumstances in which internally reported operating segments might be combined.

IAS 14 allows the combination of two or more internally reported operating segments that are substantially similar, but only when they exhibit similar long-term financial performance and they are similar with regard to all of the factors (see 2.2.2.A and 2.2.2.B above) that should be considered in defining a business or geographical segment.[53]

Example 28.1:   Combining internally reported operating segments

In the information presented to the board of directors, a single-product company has six internally reported operating segments, Australia, France, Germany, Italy, UK and USA. The company dominates its markets in Australia and Germany and consequently enjoys superior operating profits. Its other markets are fragmented, competition is greater and therefore margins are lower. Can any segments be combined for external reporting purposes?

Operating segments can be combined if they are 'substantially similar'. Looking at the factors listed in 2.2.2.B above, it would not be possible to combine geographical segments with different underlying currency risks. That would leave only France, Germany and Italy as candidates for combination, since they all operate within the Euro zone. However, Germany could not be included because, whilst similar in all other ways, its long-term financial performance is not comparable to France and Italy. On this basis the company could only combine its operations in France and Italy for external segment reporting purposes.

2.3.3   Reportable segments

The standard then has a number of quantitative measures for determining whether the identified business and geographical segments are reportable segments for external reporting purposes. Reportable segments are defined initially on the basis of their size. A business segment or geographical segment should be identified as a reportable segment when it derives a majority of its revenue from sales to external customers and:

(a)   its internal and external revenue is 10% or more of the total revenue (internal and external) of all segments; or

(b)   its segment result – whether profit or loss – is, in absolute terms, 10% or more of the greater of (1) the combined results of all profitable segments or (2) the combined results of all segments in loss; or

(c)   its assets are 10% or more of the total assets of all segments.[54]

(The standard emphasises that these 10% thresholds are not intended to be a guide for determining materiality for any aspect of financial reporting, other than identifying reportable segments.)[55]

Example 28.2:   *Identifying reportable segments*

An entity divides its business into 9 operating units for internal reporting purposes, as follows:

	Unit 1 £000	Unit 2 £000	Unit 3 £000	Unit 4 £000	Unit 5 £000	Unit 6 £000	Unit 7 £000	Unit 8 £000	Unit 9 £000	Total £000
Revenue:										
External	34,000	3,000	15,000	30,000	35,000	35,000	83,000	55,500	25,000	315,500
Internal	35,000	34,000	12,500	2,200	0	1,500	2,300	2,300	0	89,800
Total	69,000	37,000	27,500	32,200	35,000	36,500	85,300	57,800	25,000	405,300
Result	14,500	24,500	(4,500)	2,300	10,000	14,500	3,500	35,000	(21,250)	78,550
Assets	12,250	77,800	25,000	24,000	40,000	7,730	145,000	55,000	4,300	391,080

Assuming that these operating units meet the definitions for a business segment in IAS 14, which units are required to be reported as business segments in the entity's financial statements?

Applying the above criteria, Units 5, 6, 7, 8 and 9 should be identified as reportable segments, as follows:

- The quantitative measures should be applied to each segment that derives a majority of its revenue from sales to external customers. This means that Unit 1 and Unit 2 are not required to be treated as reportable segments. (Different criteria apply to segments which are part of a vertically integrated operation as discussed in 2.3.4 below).

- A Unit whose internal and external revenue is 10% or more of the total revenue of all segments is a reportable segment. On this criterion Unit 7 (21%) and Unit 8 (14%) are reportable segments.

- A Unit is a reportable segment if its segment result, in absolute terms, is 10% or more of the greater of the combined results of all profitable segments or the combined results of all segments in loss. The combined result of all profitable segments is £104.3m, which is greater than the total of £25.75m for segments in loss. On this basis, Unit 6 (14%), Unit 8 (34%) and the loss-making Unit 9 (20%) are reportable segments.

- A Unit is also a reportable segment if its assets are 10% or more of the total assets of all segments. On this test, Unit 5 (10%) joins the list of reportable segments, with Unit 7 (37%) and Unit 8 (14%) having been already identified under other criteria.

Internally reported operating segments that fall below all of the above thresholds may be designated as reportable segments despite their size or may be combined with other similar internally reported segments that fall below all of the above thresholds. The criteria under which such smaller operating segments can be combined are more relaxed than the 'substantially similar' test in 2.3.2 above. In this case only a majority of the factors listed in 2.2.2.A and 2.2.2.B above need to be the same.[56] However, a proposed combination can create neither a business segment that includes products or services with significantly different risks and returns[57] nor a geographical segment that includes operations in economic environments with significantly different risks and returns.[58]

If any segment in a proposed combination exceeds any of the above size thresholds, the entity must revert to the 'substantially similar' test. The standard states that segments that are not separately reported or combined should be included as an unallocated reconciling item.[59] However, that may not be the end of the matter as a result of further provisions within the standard discussed below.

2.3.4 *Vertically integrated activities*

Because a reportable segment is defined as having derived a majority of its revenue from sales to external customers, there is no requirement in IAS 14 for the different stages of vertically integrated operations to be disclosed as separate business segments. However, the standard notes that current practice in some industries is to report certain vertically integrated activities as separate business segments, for example in the way that many international oil companies separately report their upstream (exploration and production) and downstream (refining and marketing) activities, even if most or all of the upstream product (crude petroleum) is transferred internally to the entity's refining operation.[60]

Therefore the standard encourages entities to report vertically integrated activities as separate segments on a voluntary basis, with appropriate description including disclosure of the basis of pricing inter-segment transfers (see 2.4.2 below).[61]

However, where the internal reporting system treats vertically integrated activities as separate selling and buying segments and the entity does not regard them as separate reportable segments, IAS 14 requires the selling and buying segments to be combined. The only exception to this requirement is where there is no reasonable basis for doing so, in which case the selling segment must be included as an unallocated reconciling item.[62]

Example 28.3:   Vertically integrated activities

Suppose in Example 28.2 above, Unit 2 is an iron foundry producing castings which are used primarily as components for the products of Unit 7. In this case the entity would have the option of either disclosing Unit 2 as a separate reportable business segment, or combining it with Unit 7. Only if there were no reasonable basis for a combination with Unit 7 would Unit 2 be included as an unallocated reconciling item.

2.3.5 *Unallocated internally reported operating segments*

As indicated at 2.3.3 above, the standard states that segments that are not separately reported or combined are included as an unallocated reconciling item. However, IAS 14 then contains provisions preventing the unreconciled category from being too large. If total external revenue attributable to segments already identified as reportable is less than 75% of total consolidated revenue, the entity should identify additional segments for external reporting until the 75% target is reached. In this situation segments will have to be reported separately even if they fall below the size thresholds described at 2.3.3 above.[63]

However, there is no requirement to identify as a reportable segment the next largest internally reported operating unit. The choice of additional reporting segments is aimed simply to reach the 75% threshold, as illustrated below:

Example 28.4:   Reaching the threshold of 75% of external revenue

In Example 28.2 above, Units 5, 6, 7, 8 and 9 were identified as reporting segments. Assuming that in Example 28.3 above the external revenue of Unit 2 is combined with Unit 7 as a vertically integrated activity, the total external revenue attributable to these reportable segments is £236.5m. This is less than the required 75% of total consolidated revenue of £315.5m.

The entity is therefore required to identify additional segments as reportable segments, even if they do not meet the size thresholds in 2.3.3 above. Unit 3, with external revenue of £15m (4.8%) and Unit 4, with external revenue of £30m (9.5%) would each take the total above the required 75%. The entity can choose to present either of these as a reportable segment, leaving the other to be combined with Unit 1 to form the unallocated reconciling item.

2.3.6   Restatement of segments reported in comparative periods

When a segment is identified as a reportable segment for the first time, the prior period segment data that is presented for comparative purposes should be restated to reflect the newly reportable segment regardless of whether it would have satisfied the size thresholds in the prior period, unless it is impracticable to do so.[64]

A previously identified reportable segment usually continues to be reported separately until it no longer satisfies the size thresholds or is sold or combined with other segments. An explanation should be given when a previously reported segment is no longer disclosed.[65] However, an entity should continue to disclose such segments in the current period, if management judges that the segment is of sufficient continuing significance.[66] It follows that an entity would continue to disclose a previously reported segment after its sale, but would describe the segment as being attributable to discontinued operations.

The notes on segment reporting in the financial statements of Bayer provide an insight as to how the process of disaggregating and combining internally reported management information might operate in practice.

Extract 28.1: Bayer AG (2003)

Notes on Segment Reporting [extract]

In accordance with IAS 14 (Segment Reporting), a breakdown of certain data in the financial statements is given by segments and geographical region. The segments and regions are the same as those used for internal reporting, allowing a reliable assessment of risks and returns. The aim is to provide users of the financial statements with information regarding the profitability and future prospects of the Group's various activities.

As of December 31, 2003 the Bayer Group comprised four subgroups whose operations are subdivided into divisions (HealthCare), business groups (CropScience), business units (Chemicals) or strategic business entities (Polymers). Their activities are aggregated into the seven reporting segments listed below according to economic characteristics, products, production processes, customer relationships and methods of distribution.

The subgroups' activities are as follows:

Subgroup	Activities
Healthcare	
Pharmaceuticals, Biological Products	Development and marketing of prescription pharmaceuticals and biological products
Consumer Care, Diagnostics	Development and marketing of over-the-counter medications, nutritional supplements and diagnostic products for laboratory testing, near-patient testing and self-testing applications
Animal Health	Development and marketing of veterinary medicines, nutritionals and grooming products for companion animals and livestock
CropScience	
CropScience	Development and marketing of a comprehensive portfolio of fungicides, herbicides, insecticides, seed treatment products, non-agricultural applications, plant biotechnology and conventional seeds to meet a wide range of regional requirements
Polymers	
Plastics, Rubber	Manufacturing and marketing of engineering plastics with a variety of raw materials for the rubber and tire industries
Polyurethanes, Coatings, Fibers	Development, manufacturing and marketing of a range of polyurethane raw materials for a wide variety of applications as well as coating and adhesive raw materials
Chemicals	
Chemicals	Manufacture and marketing of bulk and specialty chemicals, metal and ceramic powders and cellulosics

As part of the reorganization of the Polymers operations in 2003, responsibility for the organic and inorganic pigments businesses was transferred to the Chemicals segment. At the same time, the industrial basic chemicals business (mainly chlorine electrolysis) was transferred to the Polyurethanes, Coatings, Fibers segment. The prior-year figures have been restated to reflect these organizational changes.

2.4 Measurement

2.4.1 Segment accounting policies

Those accounting policies applied in preparing and presenting the financial statements should also be applied in preparing segment information.[67] This requirement is derived from the presumption that, in preparing the consolidated or entity-wide financial statements, an entity's directors and management select those accounting policies that they believe to be the most appropriate for external reporting purposes. It therefore follows that these policies should be used in preparing segment information, the purpose of which is to help users of financial statements better understand and make more informed judgements about the entity as a whole. However, this does not mean that segment information should be prepared as if it were for stand-alone reporting entities and in particular the application of entity-wide accounting policies should not prevent the allocation of revenues, expenses, assets or liabilities between segments if there is a reasonable basis for doing so.[68] Similarly IAS 14 permits disclosure of additional segment information that is prepared on a different basis to the consolidated financial statements, provided that the additional information is already reported internally to the entity's key decision-makers and the alternative basis of measurement is clearly described.[69] This additional segment information might include measures of performance such as return on sales, gross cash flow or return on capital employed as shown in Extract 28.5 at 2.5.1.D below.

An entity's disclosure of accounting policies under IAS 1 may therefore have to include those specific to segment reporting, such as identification of segments, method of pricing inter-segment transfers and the basis of allocating revenues and expenses to segments.[70] Changes in such segment specific accounting policies fall within the scope of IAS 8. As a result, any changes in segment accounting policies that have a material effect on segment information should be disclosed and prior periods restated, even though there will have been no effect on the aggregate financial information reported for the entity as a whole. Narrative disclosures would also be required to describe the nature of the change, the reasons for it, the fact that prior periods have been restated and the financial effect. If an entity redefines its reporting segments and prior period adjustment cannot be made because it is impracticable to do so, it must present for the current period segment information for both the new and the old bases of segmentation.[71]

An example of the additional accounting policy disclosures for segment reporting is set out below:

Extract 28.2: Roche Holding Ltd (2003)

Notes to Roche Group consolidated financial statements[extract]

1. Summary of significant accounting policies [extract]

Segment reporting

The Group's primary format for segment reporting is business segments and the secondary format is geographical segments. The risks and returns of the Group's operations are primarily determined by the different products that the Group produces rather than the geographical location of the Group's operations. This is reflected by the Group's divisional management and organisational structure and the Group's internal financial reporting systems.

The Group has two divisions, Pharmaceuticals and Diagnostics. Until its disposal on 30 September 2003 the Group had a third division, Vitamins and Fine Chemicals. Within the Pharmaceuticals Division there are four sub-divisions, Roche Prescription, Genentech Prescription, Chugai Prescription and Consumer Health (OTC). The four sub-divisions have separate management and reporting structures within the Pharmaceuticals Division and are considered separately reportable segments. Certain corporate activities that cannot be reasonably allocated to the other reportable segments, such as the costs of Corporate Headquarters, are reported as 'Others'. The Group's geographical segments are determined by geographical location and similarity of economic environments.

Transfer prices between business segments are set on an arm's length basis. Divisional assets and liabilities consist of property, plant and equipment, goodwill and intangible assets, trade receivables/payables and inventories. Other segment assets and liabilities consist of other assets and liabilities which can be reasonably attributed to the reported business segments. These include pension assets/liabilities and provisions. Non-segment assets and liabilities mainly include current and deferred income tax balances, and financial assets and liabilities. These are principally cash, marketable securities, other investments and debt. Capital expenditure comprises additions to goodwill, intangible assets and additions to property, plant and equipment, including those arising from acquisitions.

2.4.2 Consolidation adjustments and inter-segment revenue

Measurements of segment assets and liabilities include adjustments made for business combinations, even if they are reflected only in the consolidated financial statements. Similarly, revaluations of property, plant and equipment in accordance with the revaluation model in IAS 16 are also included.[72] Segment assets, liabilities, revenue and expense are determined before elimination of intra-group balances and transactions outside that segment.[73]

Inter-segment revenue should be measured and reported on the basis that was actually used by the entity to price those transfers. The basis of pricing inter-segment transfers and any change therein should be disclosed in the financial statements.[74] A change in pricing method is not a change in accounting policy.[75]

2.4.3 Shared assets

Assets that are used by more than one segment should be allocated to segments only if their related revenues and expenses are also allocated to those segments.[76] IAS 14 does not prescribe a single basis for allocating assets, liabilities, revenues and expenses between segments, nor does it demand allocation of items that relate jointly to two or more segments. Determining the appropriate allocation method will depend upon the nature of the specific items being considered, the activities conducted by the segment and the segment's relative autonomy. Nevertheless the standard does recognise that the definitions of segment revenue, expense, assets and liabilities (see 2.2.3 above) are interrelated and demands that they are applied consistently. For example, an asset is included in segment assets only if the related depreciation or amortisation is deducted in measuring segment result.[77]

2.5 Information to be disclosed about reportable segments

The level of disclosure required for a reportable segment depends on whether that segment appears in the primary or secondary reporting format. Whilst entities are encouraged to provide the full disclosures for both primary and secondary reporting formats, less detailed disclosure is mandatory on the secondary basis.[78] The application of these disclosure requirements are illustrated in Appendix B to the standard.[79]

2.5.1 Primary segment information

A Mandatory primary segment disclosures

For each reportable segment in the primary segment format, IAS 14 requires the following to be disclosed:[80]

(a) segment revenue (separately reporting external sales and revenue from intra-segment transactions);[81]

(b) segment result (separately reporting the result from continuing operations and the result from discontinued operations);[82]

(c) total carrying amount of segment assets;[83]

(d) segment liabilities;[84]

(e)   total cost incurred during the period (on an accruals basis) to acquire assets that are expected to be used in more than one period (property, plant, equipment, and intangible assets);[85]

(f)   total amount included in segment result for depreciation and amortisation of segment assets;[86] and

(g)   other significant non-cash expenses deducted in measuring segment result.[87]

The comparative disclosures for item (b) above should be restated to ensure that they reflect discontinued operations as defined at the current balance sheet date.[88] Items (f) and (g) above need not be disclosed if any entity provides the segment cash flow disclosures that are encouraged by paragraphs 50(d) and 52 of IAS 7.[89] See Chapter 32 at 2.6.2.

Nokia Corporation provides primary segment disclosures by business segment.

Extract 28.3: Nokia Corporation (2003)

Notes to the consolidated financial statements [extract]

2. Segment information [extract]

2003, EURm	Nokia Mobile Phones	Nokia Networks	Nokia Ventures Organization	Common Group Functions	Total reportable segments	Elimina- tions	Group
Profit and loss information							
Net sales to external customers	23 475	5 620	349	11	29 455		29 455
Net sales to other segments	143	–	17	-11	149	-149	–
Depreciation and amortization	441	520	8	169	1 138		1 138
Impairment and customer finance charges	–	200	40	–	240		240
Operating profit	5 483	-219	-161	-92	5 011		5 011
Share of results of associated companies	–	–	–	-18	-18		-18
Balance sheet information							
Capital expenditures	331	44	3	54	432		432
Segment assets of which:	4 832	4 108	106	1 071	10 117	-22	10 095
Investments in associated companies	–	–	–	76	76		76
Unallocated assets							13 825
Total assets							23 920
Segment liabilities	5 273	1 628	147	159	7 207	-22	7 185
Unallocated liabilities							1 423
Total liabilities							8 608

2002, EURm	Nokia Mobile Phones	Nokia Networks	Nokia Ventures Organization	Common Group Functions	Total reportable segments	Elimina-tions	Group
Profit and loss information							
Net sales to external customers	22 997	6 538	441	40	30 016		30 016
Net sales to other segments	214	1	18	-40	193	-193	–
Depreciation and amortization	546	542	33	190	1 311		1 311
Impairment and customer finance charges	–	400	83	55	538		538
Operating profit	5 201	-49	-141	-231	4 780		4 780
Share of results of associated companies	–	–	–	-19	-19		-19
Balance sheet information							
Capital expenditures	224	93	8	107	432		432
Segment assets	4 888	6 163	114	965	12 130	-26	12 104
of which: Investment in associated companies	–	–	–	49	49		49
Unallocated assets							11 223
Total assets							23 327
Segment liabilities	5 080	1 861	188	225	7 354	-24	7 330
Unallocated liabilities							1 543
Total liabilities							8 873

B   Equity accounted investments

If substantially all of the operations of an associate, joint venture or other investment accounted for under the equity method fall within a single primary format segment, the entity should report, as a single line item, its share of the profit or loss of that associate or joint venture within the disclosures for that reportable segment. If more than one equity accounted investment falls within a primary format segment, only aggregate disclosure is required.[90]

If the entity's share of the profit or loss of equity accounted investments is disclosed by reportable segment, the aggregate investments in those associates and joint ventures should also be disclosed by reportable segment.[91]

For equity accounted investments whose operations are not substantially all within a single reportable segment, it follows that the share of profit or loss and aggregate investment in those associates and joint ventures would be included in the unallocated reconciling item. Given that allocation to segments is required only for equity accounted entities with 'substantially all' of their operations falling within a single business segment, we do not believe it would be appropriate to apply any apportionment between reported segments.

Extract 28.5 below includes the disclosures by geographical segment of the equity accounted investments of Bayer.

C   Reconciliation to the financial statements

An entity should present a reconciliation between the information disclosed for reportable segments and the aggregated information in the entity's financial statements in the following manner:[92]

(a)   segment revenue should be reconciled to revenue from external customers. Revenue from external customers not included in any reportable segment should be disclosed separately;

(b)   segment result from continuing operations should be reconciled to a comparable measure of entity operating profit or loss from continuing operations as well as to entity profit or loss from continuing operations;

(c)   segment result from discontinued operations should be reconciled to entity profit or loss from discontinued operations;

(d)   segment assets and liabilities should be reconciled to the entity's assets and liabilities, respectively.

Many entities integrate the reconciliation to the consolidated financial statements into their primary segment format, as in Extract 28.3 above. Lufthansa provides a reconciliation separately from its primary segment disclosures.

Extract 28.4: Deutsche Lufthansa AG (2003)

Other disclosures [extract]

Reconciliation of segment information with consolidated figures in €m:

	Segment total		Reconciliation		Group	
	2003	2002	**2003**	2002	**2003**	2002
External revenue	15,957	16,971	–	–	15,957	16,971
- of which traffic revenue	11,662	12,032	–	–	11,662	12,032
Inter-segment revenue	2,572	2,437	-2,572	-2,437	–	–
Total revenue	18,529	19,408	-2,572	-2,437	15,957	16,971
Other revenue	1,920	2,516	-163	-398	1,757	2,118
- of which from investments accounted for using the equity method	-176	-91	176	91	–	–
Cost of materials	9,472	9,345	-2,267	-2,149	7,205	7,196
Staff costs	4,615	4,684	-3	-24	4,612	4,660
Amortisation and depreciation	1,981	1,275	-51	-32	1,930	1,243
- of which impairments	818	66	-35	-33	783	33
Other operating expenses	4,806	5,154	-692	-756	4,114	4,398
Results	**-425**	**1,466**	**278**	**126**	**-147**	**1,592**
- of which from investments accounted for using the equity method	-176	-91	176	91	–	–
Assets	14,261	14,704	2,471	4,433	16,732	19,137
-of which from investments accounting for using the equity method	720	914	–	–	720	914
Liabilities	10,299	10,576	3,737	4,389	14,036	14,965
- of which from investments accounted for using the equity method	–	–	–	–	–	–
Average number of employees	94,798	94,135	–	–	94,798	94,135

The reconciliation column includes both the effects resulting from consolidation procedures and the amounts resulting from the different interpretation of segment item contents in comparison with the corresponding Group items.

The eliminated revenue of the business segments generated with other consolidated business segments may be gathered from the reconciliation column. As regards the other segment revenue, income originating from relationships with the other business segments has been eliminated as well ("other revenue" reconciliation column). In financial year 2003, this concerned especially exchange gains from intra-group loans in foreign currency in the amount of €105m (prior year: €274m) as well as income from intra-group services of €48m (prior year: €48m). In so far as the eliminated revenue and other income is compared with segment expenses with regard to the companies which took up the services, such expenses have been eliminated, too ("expenses" reconciliation column). Certain components of the Group's financial result have also been allocated to the business segment's income, in particular results from the equity accounting of investments of the business segment. Since, in the Group's view, such results are not allocated to the operating result but the financial result, they have to be eliminated upon reconciliation with regard to the Group's operating result.

The amounts included in the "results" reconciliation column originate mainly from the reallocation of the negative results from accounting at equity, which results are part of the segment results of the business segments, however not of the Group's operating result.

The reconciliation column for segment assets and segment liabilities contains eliminated receivables and payables among the business segments, the difference between market values and carrying amounts of financial instruments as well as, on the assets side, the carrying amounts of equity investments eliminated within the scope of capital consolidation.

D   *Voluntary primary segment disclosures*

As well as reporting segment result, entities are encouraged to disclose additional measures of segment profitability, provided that their computation does not involve making arbitrary allocations and that such additional measures are appropriately described. Clear disclosure is required of any basis used in preparing such additional measures of segment performance that differs from the accounting policies adopted by the entity in preparing the financial statements.[93] Examples of additional measures to consider include gross margin on sales, profit or loss from ordinary activities (either before or after income taxes) and profit or loss.[94]

An entity is also encouraged, but not required, to disclose separately the nature and amount of any segment revenue or expense items of such size, nature or incidence, that their disclosure is relevant to explain segment performance for the period.[95] Such items might include write-downs of inventories and property, plant and equipment, provisions for restructurings, disposals of property, plant and equipment and long-term investments, discontinuing operations, litigation settlements and reversals of provisions. The standard is clear that whilst this encouraged disclosure changes the level at which the significance of such items is evaluated for disclosure purposes (that is, at the segment rather than entity level), there should be no change in how these items are classified or measured.[96]

IAS 14 repeats the encouragement given in IAS 7 to disclose the amount of the cash flows arising from the operating, investing and financing activities of each reported industry and geographical segment (See Chapter 32 at 2.6.2.). It also suggests entities consider disclosing significant non-cash revenues that are included in segment revenue.[97]

Bayer provides additional measures in its geographical segment disclosures, including return on sales, gross cash flow, return on capital employed ("CFROI") and number of employees, as shown below in its analysis of performance by region.

Extract 28.5: Bayer AG (2003)

Notes [extract]

Key Data by Region

Regions

€ million	Europe		North America		Asia/Pacific	
	2002	2003	2002	2003	2002	2003
Net sales (external) – by market	12,266	12,162	9,005	8,636	4,901	4,529
Net sales (external) – by point of origin	13,894	13,518	9,135	8,763	4,010	3,913
of which discontinuing operations	*4,147*	*3,717*	*2,322*	*1,848*	*727*	*564*
- Change in €	+ 0.4%	-2.7%	-9.3%	-4.1%	+ 2.0%	-2.4%
- Change in local currencies	+ 0.5%	-2.7%	-3.9%	+ 11.4%	+ 7.6%	+ 10.2%
Interregional sales	3,181	3,833	1,961	1,876	227	266
Other operating income	2,447	812	90	64	86	84
Operating result [EBIT]	1,891	(277)	(676)	(1,247)	207	65
of which discontinuing operations	*1.050*	*(839)*	*(388)*	*(772)*	*34*	*(53)*
Return on sales	13.6%	(2.0)%	(7.4)%	(14.2)%	5.2%	1.7%
Gross cash flow	1,843	1,639	740	899	360	342
Capital invested	21,338	20,000	11,594	9,325	2,460	2,258
CFROI	8.6%	7.9%	5.9%	8.6%	12.6%	14.5%
Equity-method income (loss)	5	(166)	0	0	0	0
Equity-method investments	572	452	505	412	2	2
Total assets	23,694	22,400	11,565	9,045	3,225	2,731
Capital expenditures	1,422	1,047	676	496	188	138
Amortization and depreciation	1,746	2,351	1,344	1,963	153	333
Liabilities	14,370	15,898	6,390	5,253	1,613	1,189
Research and development expenses	1,801	1,674	708	650	51	74
Number of employees (as of Dec.31)	70,600	66,700	24,600	23,300	15,400	13,900

Regions

€ million	Latin America/Africa/ Middle East		Reconciliation		Bayer Group	
	2002	2003	2002	2003	2002	2003
Net sales (external) – by market	3,452	3,240			29,624	28,567
Net sales (external) – by point of origin	2,585	2,373			29,624	28,567
of which discontinuing operations	*390*	*260*			*7,586*	*6,389*
- Change in €	+ 5.9%	-8.2%			-2.2%	-3.6%
- Change in local currencies	+ 33.3%	+ 11.1%			+ 2.6%	+ 5.0%
Interregional sales	139	151	(5,508)	(6,126)		
Other operating income	83	198	0	0	2,706	1,158
Operating result [EBIT]	410	433	(222)	(177)	1,610	(1,203)
of which discontinuing operations	*64*	*12*			*760*	*(1,652)*
Return of sales	15.9%	18.2%			5.4%	(4.2)%
Gross cash flow	363	398	(221)	(34)	3,085	3,244
Capital invested	1,322	1,197	(2)	1,617	36,712	34,397
CFROI	25.4%	31.6%			8.3%	9.2%
Equity-method income (loss)	0	1	0	0	5	(165)
Equity-method investments	16	4	0	0	1,095	870
Total assets	1,734	1,627	1,474	1,642	41,692	37,445
Capital expenditures	97	58			2,383	1,739
Amortization and depreciation	64	69	5	19	3,312	4,735
Liabilities	945	675	2,919	2,094	26,237	25,109
Research and development expenses	17	16			2,577	2,414
Number of employees (as of Dec.31)	12,000	11,500			122,600	115,400

Notes on Segment Reporting [extract]

The segment data are calculated as follows:

- The intersegment and interregional sales reflect intragroup transactions effected at transfer prices fixed on an arm's-length basis.

- The return on sales is the ratio of the operating result (EBIT) to external net sales.

- The gross cash flow comprises the operating result (EBIT) plus depreciation, amortization and write-downs, less gains on the sale of assets, less income taxes, adjusted for the change in long-term provisions.

- The net cash flow is the cash flow from operating activities as defined in IAS 7.

- The capital invested comprises all assets serving the respective segment that are required to yield a return on their costs of acquisition. Noncurrent assets are included at cost of acquisition or construction throughout their useful lives because the calculation of CFROI requires that depreciation and amortization be excluded. Interest-free liabilities are deducted. The capital invested in stated as of December 31.

- The CFROI is the ratio of the gross cash flow to the average capital invested for the year and is thus a measure of the return on capital employed.

- The equity items are those reflected in the balance sheet and income statement. They are allocated to the segments where possible. The reconciliation of the balance of equity-method income and expense to the income statement line "Income (expense) from investments in affiliated companies – net" is apparent from Note [8].

- Capital expenditures, amortization and depreciation relate to intangible assets, property, plant and equipment.

- Employees by segment: the reconciliation line comprises the employees of the service companies who were employees of the subgroups before the service companies became separate legal entities. The prior-year figures have been restated accordingly.

Bayer also provided similar additional information by business segment.

2.5.2 *Secondary segment information*

The nature of the detailed disclosures required for secondary segment reporting depends on whether the primary segment format is based on business segments or geographical segments and, if based on geographical segments, whether the location of the entity's assets and operations is different from the location of its customers and markets.[98]

A   *Where the primary format is business segments*

If an entity's primary reporting format is based on business segments, it should also disclose the following segment information:[99]

(a)   segment revenue from external customers by geographical area – based on customer location – for each geographical segment whose external sales revenue is 10% or more of the entity's total revenue from sales to all external customers;

(b)   the total carrying amount of segment assets by geographical area – based on location of assets – for each geographical segment whose segment assets are 10% or more of the total assets of all geographical segments; and

(c)   the total cost incurred to acquire segment assets that are expected to be used during more than one period (property, plant, equipment and intangible assets) by geographical location of assets, for each geographical segment whose segment assets are 10% or more of the total assets of all geographical segments.

Danisco provides additional information in its secondary segment reporting format, sub-dividing its segment assets between fixed assets and current assets and analysing its investment in assets between ongoing investment and business acquisitions.

Extract 28.6: Danisco A/S (2003)

GEOGRAPHIC SEGMENTS

SECONDARY SEGMENTS

DKK million	Net sales		Segment fixed assets		Segment current assets	
	01/02	02/03	01/02	02/03	01/02	02/03
Denmark	2,213	1,986	3,721	3,132	1,655	1,589
Other Nordic countries	4,616	4,654	4,287	4,180	2,102	2,285
Rest of Western Europe	3,864	3,253	4,259	4,418	1,486	1,563
Eastern Europe	1,345	1,353	317	299	446	504
North America	2,421	2,242	1,326	1,566	1,060	876
Latin America	794	730	666	483	404	383
Asia-Pacific	1,620	1,652	689	591	688	634
Rest of the world	793	681	67	71	88	95
Total	**17,666**	**16,551**	**15,332**	**14,740**	**7,929**	**7,929**

DKK million	Segment assets total		Investments, tangible fixed assets		Investments, acquisitions	
	01/02	02/03	01/02	02/03	01/02	02/03
Denmark	5,376	4,721	308	241	1	–
Other Nordic countries	6,389	6,465	261	242	–	–
Rest of Western Europe	5,745	5,981	90	105	5	473
Eastern Europe	763	803	26	20	–	–
North America	2,386	2,442	93	178	402	–
Latin America	1,070	866	27	27	97	–
Asia-Pacific	1,377	1,225	30	28	358	(3)
Rest of the world	155	166	3	3	–	–
Total	**23,261**	**22,669**	**838**	**844**	**863**	**470**

The above information has been specified by location of customers and assets.

Geographic segments	Countries outside Denmark where Danisco has production or sales units
Other Nordic countries	Finland, Iceland, Norway, Sweden.
Rest of Western Europe	Austria, Belgium, France, Germany, Italy, Netherlands, Spain, Switzerland, United Kingdom.
Eastern Europe	Croatia, Czech Republic, Estonia, Lithuania, Poland, Romania, Russia, Slovakia, Yugoslavia.
North America	Canada, USA.
Latin America	Argentina, Brazil, Chile, Colombia, Mexico.
Asia-Pacific	Australia, China, Japan, Korea, Malaysia, New Zealand, Singapore, Thailand.
Rest of the world	India, South Africa.

B   *Where the primary format is geographical segments*

If an entity's primary reporting format is based on geographical segments, it should also disclose the following segment information for each business segment whose revenue from sales to external customers is 10% or more of the entity's total external sales or whose segment assets are 10% or more of the total assets of all business segments:[100]

(a)   segment revenue from external customers;

(b)   the total carrying amount of segment assets; and

(c)   the total cost incurred during the period to acquire segment assets that are expected to be used during more than one period (property, plant, equipment and intangible assets).

Nestlé shows business segment data in its secondary reporting format, disclosing in addition to the information required above an analysis of earnings before interest tax and amortisation (EBITA), impairment of assets and restructuring costs by product group.

Extract 28.7: Nestlé S.A. (2003)

Notes [extract]

1. Segmental information [extract]

By product group

In millions of CHF	2003	2002	2003	2002
	Sales		EBITA	
Beverages	23 520	23 325	4 038	4 075
Milk products, nutrition and ice cream	23 283	23 376	2 796	2 756
Prepared dishes and cooking aids	16 068	15 834	1 884	1 712
Petcare	9 816	10 719	1 444	1 418
Chocolate, confectionery and biscuits	10 240	10 774	1 047	1 180
Pharmaceutical products	5 052	5 132	1 329	1 267
	87 979	89 160	12 538	12 408
Unallocated items (a)			(1 532)	(1 468)
EBITA			11 006	10 940

(a) Mainly corporate expenses as well as research and development costs.

In millions of CHF	2003	2002
	Assets	
Beverages	11 237	11 283
Milk products, nutrition and ice cream	10 303	10 972
Prepared dishes and cooking aids	5 787	6 291
Petcare	3 481	3 790
Chocolate, confectionery and biscuits	5 208	5 403
Pharmaceutical products	2 708	2 847
	38 724	40 586

In millions of CHF	2003	2002
	Capital expenditure	
Beverages	936	1 004
Milk products, nutrition and ice cream	421	495
Prepared dishes and cooking aids	251	304
Petcare	254	284
Chocolate, confectionery and biscuits	208	285
Pharmaceutical products	86	101
	2 156	2 473
Administration, distribution, research and development	1 181	1 104
	3 337	3 577

In millions of CHF	2003	2002	2003	2002
	Impairment of assets		Restructuring costs	
Beverages	121	350	248	117
Milk products, nutrition and ice cream	63	612	128	388
Prepared dishes and cooking aids	14	275	60	104
Petcare	19	740	26	313
Chocolate, confectionery and biscuits	5	209	133	134
Pharmaceutical products	–	–	4	1
	222	2 186	599	1 057
Administration, distribution, research and development	–	10	4	73
	222	2 196	603	1 130

Where the entity's assets are located in different geographical areas from its customers, additional geographical segment disclosures are required in the secondary format, as follows:

(a) If the entity's primary reporting format is based on the location of assets, the entity should disclose sales to external customers for each customer-based geographical segment whose external sales is 10% or more of the entity's total revenue from sales to all external customers.[101]

(b) If the entity's primary reporting format is based on location of customers, it should disclose the following segment information for each asset-based geographical segment whose revenue from sales to external customers is 10% or more of total external sales or whose assets are 10% or more of total assets:[102]

(i) the total carrying amount of segment assets by location; and

(ii) the total cost incurred during the period to acquire segment assets that are expected to be used during more than one period (property, plant, equipment and intangible assets) by location.

2.5.3 Other disclosure matters

An entity should describe which types of products and services are included in each reported business segment and indicate the composition of each reported geographical segment.[103] Without knowing what activities are included in a business segment, a user of the financial statements cannot assess the impact of such matters as shifts in demand, changes in input prices or other factors of production, and the development of alternative products and processes on a business segment. Similarly, it is important to know the composition of a geographical segment to understand the impact of changes in the economic and political environment on its risks and rates of return.[104]

Gucci Group provides the following description of its business segments:

Extract 28.8: Gucci Group N.V. (2003)

Notes to the consolidated financial statements [extract]

(4)   Segment information [extract]

The Group has five operating segments: Gucci Division (excluding Gucci Timepieces), Gucci Group Watches, Yves Saint Laurent, YSL Beauté and Other Operations. Gucci Division (excluding Gucci Timepieces) includes all revenues from the sale and licensing of Gucci branded products other than those from the wholesale distribution activities of the Gucci brand watches. Gucci Group Watches includes the production and wholesale distribution of Gucci and other Gucci Group brand watches. Yves Saint Laurent includes all revenues from the sale and licensing of Yves Saint Laurent branded products other than those from the wholesale distribution of Yves Saint Laurent perfumes, cosmetics and watches. YSL Beauté includes revenues from the sale of perfume, make-up and skincare products other than Gucci brand perfume. Other Operations includes revenues from operations, which are not individually material. The non-operating segment Corporate includes the parent company and certain subsidiaries which are involved principally in financial transactions and which do not generally sell to third parties as well as the expenses related to certain employees and members of management, who perform Group corporate functions, which are not allocated to the individual operating business segments. Inter-segment transactions are priced on an arm's length basis in a manner similar to transactions with third parties.

If a business or geographical segment that is reported to the entity's board of directors is not a reportable segment – on the basis that a majority of its revenue is derived from sales to other segments – but its sales to external customers is 10% or more of the entity's total revenue from sales to all external customers, the entity should disclose:[105]

(a)   the aforementioned fact;

(b)   the value of sales to external customers; and

(c)   internal sales to other segments.

The effect of this requirement in Example 28.2 at 2.3.3 above would be as follows:

Example 28.5:   Internal segments which are not reportable

Unit 1 is not a reportable segment because it derives a majority of its revenue from internal sales. However its external revenue (£34m) is greater than 10% of the entity's total external sales (£315.5m). Accordingly the segment reporting disclosures should include a statement that the unallocated reconciling item includes Unit 1, a segment reported to the board that accounts for more than 10% of external revenues but which is not a reportable segment under IAS 14 because it derives most of its revenue from other business segments. The entity should also disclose the value of external and internal revenues, at £34m and £35m respectively, with comparative values for the preceding period.

3   PROBLEM AREAS

3.1   Disclosure of commercially sensitive information

The criteria for determining the externally reportable segments, as discussed in 2.3 above, attempt to define which internally reported operating units can be combined, those which must be reported separately and those which are included in an unallocated reconciling item. The interaction between these criteria, in particular with the requirement that segments cannot be combined if they exhibit different long-term financial performance, leaves entities open to the risk of having to disclose information that management would be concerned about sharing with competitors, customers, suppliers or employees.

However, IAS 14 does not permit the omission of segment information when management believe that its disclosure is commercially sensitive or potentially detrimental to the entity's competitive position. Indeed, IAS 1 requires an entity not only to present information in a manner that provides relevant, reliable, comparable and understandable information, but also to provide *additional* disclosures if compliance with an individual standard is insufficient to enable users to understand the entity's financial position and financial performance.[106] The only justification for failing to meet these requirements is if disclosure would be so misleading that it would conflict with the objective of financial statements set out in the IASB Framework.[107]

Given that the objective of IAS 14 is to help users of financial statements better understand past performance, better assess the entity's risks and returns and make more informed judgements about the entity as a whole, this possibility would seem to be remote. Therefore in our opinion it is not acceptable to omit certain or all required segment disclosures on the basis that the information is commercially sensitive or potentially detrimental to the entity.

3.2   Identifying the primary segment format

As discussed in 2.3.1 above, because most entities are organised and managed in a way that responds to the predominant sources of risks and returns, there is a presumption in IAS 14 that, except in rare circumstances, an entity will report segment information in its financial statements on the same basis as it reports internally to top management.[108] However, there are cases where the choice of primary segment reporting format is not always clear from the information reported to the board of directors and the chief executive officer. This might be because internal reporting places equal emphasis on product and service lines and geographical areas, because it emphasises neither by reporting, for example, solely by legal entity within the group, or because reporting to the board favours one class of segment and ignores the other. These cases are discussed below.

3.2.1 Equal emphasis and the matrix presentation

If equal emphasis is placed on products and markets, as evidenced by a 'matrix approach' to internal reporting, the entity should use business segmentation as the primary segment reporting format and geographical segmentation as the secondary one.[109] Entities might find this requirement restrictive.

IAS 14 does not require, but nor does it prohibit, a matrix presentation in the segment reporting disclosures.[110] Entities can therefore choose to give full primary segment disclosures for both its business segments and its geographical segments.

3.2.2 Neither business nor geographical segments are reported internally

In cases where the board does not receive any business or geographical segment information, the process of identifying externally reportable segments (as described in 2.3 above) breaks down because there are operating segments reported to top management which do not meet the definition of a business or geographical segment. Nevertheless, this does not exempt an entity from the requirements of IAS 14 and management must still choose a primary segment reporting format based on either business or geographical segments.[111]

For example, where internal reporting is organised solely by legal entity and comprises groups of unrelated products and services, IAS 14 requires the directors and management to determine whether the entity's risks and returns are ultimately driven by products and services or by geography and to choose a primary segment reporting format on that basis. In doing so, management might consider how it would achieve a reasonable degree of comparability with other entities, enhance understandability of the resulting information and meet the expressed needs of users.[112] In practice, management might make this determination based on their understanding and knowledge of the entity's activities, without significant additional analysis. Alternatively, a more formal approach might be adopted to document the activities of the entity and determine whether the balance of risks and returns relates more to products and services or geography.

The process does not end at this point. Once management has decided whether the primary segment format will be business or geographical segments, it must determine what segment information to report. To achieve this, management will have to look beyond the information presented to the board and identify operating units of the entity that meet the definitions of a business or geographical segment for external reporting purposes.[113] This is discussed at 3.3 below.

3.2.3 Only business or geographical segments are reported internally

Except for the cases noted in 3.2.1 and 3.2.2, IAS 14 requires the selection of primary and secondary reporting format to be determined by the system of internal financial reporting to top management.[114]

However, a literal interpretation of this requirement could lead an entity to present only limited segment information if management reporting contains only business or geographical segments, as illustrated in the following example:

Example 28.6:   Only one business segment is reported to the board

An entity operates in a single business segment and reports to the board of directors and the chief executive officer only on that basis, in spite of the fact that this one product group is sold in a number of geographical markets. With only business segment information being considered by the board, this is chosen as the primary segment reporting format. However, the result of this choice is that the primary format analyses only one business segment and the information given on the different geographical segments is limited. Does this meet the objectives of IAS 14?

These circumstances are not addressed explicitly in IAS 14, but until the issue is resolved by the IASB in our opinion entities that operate in a single business segment and in a number of geographical segments should be encouraged to identify the geographical segments as the primary segment reporting format.

3.3   Identifying reportable segments when information is not provided to top management

As discussed at 3.2.2 above, even when information is not made available to top management on product and service or geographical lines, an entity must still provide segment disclosures within the primary and secondary formats and based on business and geographical segments.[115] In these circumstances, IAS 14 requires the following process to be applied:

3.3.1   Looking beyond the information reported to top management

Where operating units reported to top management do not meet the definitions of a business or geographical segment as set out in 2.2.2 above, management should look to the next lower level of internal reporting that presents information along either product and service lines or on geographical lines (in a way that does meet the definitions of business or geographical segment).[116]

In adopting this approach, the information already presented to the board should not be ignored. In particular, there should be no further segmentation of an operating unit reported internally to the board that already meets the definition of a business or geographical segment.[117] This is illustrated in the following example:

Example 28.7:   Internal reporting by legal entity

Entity A is the parent of a multinational group with 10 direct subsidiaries and reporting to the board and chief executive officer is segmented between these legal entities. Some of these legal entities had been established to operate in certain geographic areas for regulatory reasons, others had been established on product and service lines, but there are some that comprise groups of unrelated products and services and operate in different areas. Therefore, management cannot rely solely on the information presented to the board for the purpose of identifying the entity's business and geographical segments.

The first step is to confirm whether any of the information reported to top management meets the definition of business or geographical segment, as set out in 2.2.2 above. The table below summarises the activities of the 10 direct subsidiaries reported to top management.

Subsidiary	Products and services	Markets
1	Various	UK only
2	Transport only	Various
3	Electronics only	Various
4	Electronics only	USA only
5	Engineering only	USA only
6	Engineering only	Various
7	Equipment Leasing only	USA only
8	Engineering only	Various
9	Various	France only
10	Various	Germany only

The table above shows that top management receive some information that already meets the definitions of business or geographical segment. Seven subsidiaries operate wholly within a single business segment, with one operating in Transport (No. 2), two entities operating only in Electronics (Nos. 3 and 4), three in Engineering (Nos. 5, 6 and 8) and one in Equipment Leasing (No. 7). In addition, information on six subsidiaries already falls within the definition of a geographical segment, whereby No. 1 operates solely in the UK, No. 9 trades only in France, No. 10 in Germany and three entities operate solely in the USA (Nos. 4, 5 and 7). No further investigation or segmentation is required for this information presented to top management.

The second step is to consider the information reported to the board which contains elements that do not fall within the definitions of business and geographical segment in IAS 14. For these elements, management has to look at the next level of internal reporting.

To complete the business segment analysis, this means looking at the next level of internal reporting for subsidiaries 1, 9 and 10. If the information reported to the management of subsidiaries 1, 9 and 10 is segmented on the basis of products and service lines (say, Electronics, Engineering and Equipment Leasing), this internally reported information is combined with that presented to the board to give a business segment analysis as follows:

Business segment	Information presented to top management	Information presented to subsidiary management
Transport	Subsidiary 2	–
Electronics	Subsidiaries 3 and 4	Subsidiaries 1, 9 and 10
Engineering	Subsidiaries 5, 6 and 8	Subsidiaries 1, 9 and 10
Equipment leasing	Subsidiary 7	Subsidiaries 1, 9 and 10

Subsidiaries 2, 3, 6 and 8 are then considered so that the analysis of geographical segments can be completed.

Suppose that the information presented to the boards of subsidiaries 3, 6 and 8 is segmented on geographical lines and that subsidiary 2 is itself a parent company (and its management receives information on a number of transport entities operating in different countries). In this case, the geographical segments presented to the management of subsidiaries 3, 6 and 8 will be combined with that presented to top management for subsidiaries 1, 4, 5, 7, 9 and 10, but the task is not complete in respect of subsidiary 2.

If the management of subsidiary 2 receives information that meets the IAS 14 definition of a geographical segment, this is used and combined as above. However, if there is information that still fails to meet the definition (for example where a transport subsidiary itself operates across a number of areas), then the next level of internal reporting will have to be explored in the manner described above until an IAS 14 compliant geographical segment has been identified.

Supposing that each subsidiary of the transport company (denoted below as 'T1', 'T2' etc.) operates in a single country, the final geographical analysis might be developed as follows:

Geographical segment	Information presented to top management	Information presented to subsidiary management
China	–	Subsidiaries 3 and 8
Czech Republic	–	Subsidiaries 6 and 8
France	Subsidiary 9	Subsidiaries 6 and T1
Germany	Subsidiary 10	Subsidiaries 3 and T2
India	–	Subsidiaries 3, 6 and 8
Italy	–	Subsidiaries 3, 6 and T3
Korea	–	Subsidiaries 6 and 8
Poland	–	Subsidiaries 3 and 6
United Kingdom	Subsidiary 1	Subsidiary T4
USA	Subsidiaries 4, 5 and 7	–

3.3.2 Identifying externally reportable segments

Once the activities of the entity's internally reported operating units have been divided into segments that meet the definitions in IAS 14, they may be reconstituted or combined on business or geographical lines to form reportable segments in the way described in 2.3 above.[118]

Example 28.8:   Internal reporting by legal entity

The entity in Example 28.7 has reached the stage where management has identified all of its business and geographical segments. Management now has to determine the external reporting segments for the entity.

Management might then reduce the number of reportable segments by applying the 'substantially similar' test, set out in 2.3.2 above. From this exercise, management determines that the entity has four business segments (Electronics, Engineering, Equipment Leasing and Transport) and that it operates in five geographical areas, being Asia (combining China, India and Korea), Eastern Europe (Czech Republic and Poland), Western Europe (France, Germany and Italy), United Kingdom and USA.

At this stage, the difficulties associated with reporting non-segment information to top management are resolved. Management would then apply the quantitative criteria in IAS 14 to determine the entity's externally reportable segments in the way described in 2.3.3 above.[119]

3.4   Measuring the segment assets and liabilities of a subsidiary

In preparing financial information for the board of directors and the chief operating officer, an entity might combine the financial reports of its subsidiaries, and leave consolidation adjustments to revenue, expense, assets and liabilities as a reconciling item. Accordingly, the financial position and performance of an entity's business or geographical segments might be monitored at board level using the carrying amounts in the subsidiaries separate financial statements and decisions on future investment made on that basis. Management might therefore believe that they are justified in adopting the same approach to the measurement of assets and liabilities in the entity's external segment reporting disclosures.

However, whilst segment assets, liabilities, revenue and expense are determined before elimination of intra-group balances and transactions outside that segment,[120] measurements of segment assets and liabilities include adjustments made for business combinations and for revaluations of property, plant and equipment, even if they are reflected only in the consolidated financial statements.[121]

Therefore, for the purposes of segment reporting in the consolidated financial statements, adjustments will have to be made to internally reported information to restate all assets and liabilities at the value attributed to them at group entity level. Similarly, certain assets that are recognised in the consolidated financial statements, but not in the subsidiary to which they relate (such as identifiable intangible assets recognised at the date of the subsidiary's acquisition), need to be allocated to the reportable segment to which they relate for external reporting purposes.

4   CONCLUSION

Whilst IAS 14 demands a direct link between the segment disclosures in the financial statements and the information reported to the board of directors and the chief executive officer, this does not mean that the format of reporting in the financial statements will be a simple copy of the information given to the board. A certain amount of judgment is required in determining whether financial information should be restated and assessing the extent to which internally reported operating segments are separately disclosed, combined with others, or left unallocated in the financial statements.

Being a standard devoted to disclosure rather than measurement, the concepts underlying IAS 14 are reasonably clear to preparers and users of financial statements alike. Large entities typically devote a substantial amount of space in their annual reports to the description and analysis of their activities by business and geographical segments. What is more challenging for preparers of financial statements is its implications on the volume and detail of financial information that enters the public domain.

References

1 IAS 14 (1981), *Reporting Financial Information by Segment*, IASC, 1981.
2 IAS 14, *Segment Reporting*, IASB, August 1997 (amended March 2004), Objective.
3 IAS 14, para. 1.
4 IAS 14, para. 2.
5 IAS 14, para. 3.
6 IAS 14, para. 4.
7 IAS 14, para. 5.
8 IAS 14, para. 6.
9 IAS 14, para. 7.
10 IAS 14, para. 6.
11 IAS 14, para. 7.
12 IAS 14, para. 26.
13 IAS 14, para. 33.
14 IAS 14, para. 8.
15 IAS 7, *Cash Flow Statements*, IASB, December 1992 (amended March 2004), para. 6.

16 IAS 8, *Accounting Policies, Changes in Accounting Estimates and Errors*, IASB, December 2003 (amended March 2004), para. 5.
17 IAS 18, *Revenue*, IASB, December 1993 (amended March 2004), para. 7.
18 IAS 14, para. 9.
19 IAS 14, para. 10.
20 IAS 14, para. 11.
21 IAS 14, para. 9.
22 IAS 14, para. 10.
23 IAS 14, para. 12.
24 IAS 14, paras. 13-14.
25 IAS 14, para. 14.
26 IAS 14, para. 15.
27 IAS 14, Objective.
28 IAS 14, para. 9.
29 IAS 14, para. 16.
30 IAS 14, para. 16.
31 IAS 14, para. 16.
32 IAS 14, para. 16.
33 IAS 14, para. 19.
34 IAS 14, para. 16.
35 IAS 14, para. 16.
36 IAS 14, para. 20.
37 IAS 14, para. 16.
38 IAS 14, para. 16.
39 IAS 14, para. 19.
40 IAS 14, para. 16.
41 IAS 14, para. 20.
42 IAS 14, para. 23.
43 IAS 14, para. 17.
44 IAS 14, para. 18.
45 IAS 14, para. 22.
46 IAS 14, para. 16.
47 IAS 14, para. 33.
48 IAS 14, para. 26.
49 IAS 14, para. 28.
50 IAS 14, para. 27.
51 IAS 14, para. 27.
52 IAS 14, para. 31.
53 IAS 14, para. 34.
54 IAS 14, para. 35.
55 IAS 14, para. 38.
56 IAS 14, para. 36.
57 IAS 14, para. 11.
58 IAS 14, para. 12.
59 IAS 14, para. 36.
60 IAS 14, para. 39.
61 IAS 14, para. 40.
62 IAS 14, para. 41.
63 IAS 14, para. 37.
64 IAS 14, para. 43.
65 IAS 14, para. 83.
66 IAS 14, para. 42.
67 IAS 14, para. 44.
68 IAS 14, para. 45.
69 IAS 14, para. 46.
70 IAS 14, para. 25.
71 IAS 14, paras. 76-79.
72 IAS 14, para. 21.
73 IAS 14, para. 24.
74 IAS 14, para. 75.
75 IAS 14, para. 80.
76 IAS 14, para. 47.
77 IAS 14, para. 48.
78 IAS 14, para. 49.
79 IAS 14, paras. 49 and 73.
80 IAS 14, para. 50.
81 IAS 14, para. 51.
82 IAS 14, para. 52.
83 IAS 14, para. 55.
84 IAS 14, para. 56.
85 IAS 14, para. 57.
86 IAS 14, para. 58.
87 IAS 14, para. 61.
88 IAS 14, para. 52A.
89 IAS 14, para. 63.
90 IAS 14, paras. 64-65.
91 IAS 14, para. 66.
92 IAS 14, para. 67.
93 IAS 14, para. 53.
94 IAS 14, para. 54.
95 IAS 14, para. 59.
96 IAS 14, para. 60.
97 IAS 14, para. 62.
98 IAS 14, para. 68.
99 IAS 14, para. 69.
100 IAS 14, para. 70.
101 IAS 14, para. 71.
102 IAS 14, para. 72.
103 IAS 14, para. 81.
104 IAS 14, para. 82.
105 IAS 14, para. 74.
106 IAS 1, *Presentation of Financial Statements*, IASB, December 2003 (amended March 2004), para. 15.
107 IAS 1, para. 17.
108 IAS 14, para. 28.
109 IAS 14, para. 27.
110 IAS 14, para. 29.
111 IAS 14, para. 27(b).
112 IAS 14, para. 30.
113 IAS 14, para. 32.
114 IAS 14, para. 27.
115 IAS 14, para. 27(b).
116 IAS 14, para. 32(b).
117 IAS 14, para. 32(a).
118 IAS 14, para. 32(c).
119 IAS 14, para. 32(c).
120 IAS 14, para. 24.
121 IAS 14, para. 21.

Chapter 29   Share-based payment

1   INTRODUCTION

1.1   Background

Share-based payment has a strong claim to being the most controversial project recently tackled by the IASB, arousing as it does strong passions not only among the IASB's normal constituency but also at the highest political levels. The reason for this is that most share-based payment transactions undertaken by companies are awards of shares and options as remuneration to employees, in particular senior management and directors. In several countries, shares and options now comprise the greatest element of the total remuneration package of senior personnel, a trend encouraged by the current consensus that it is a matter of good corporate governance to promote significant long-term shareholdings by senior management, so as to align their economic interests with those of shareholders.

The advantage of shares and options as remuneration is that they need not entail any cash cost to the entity. If an executive is entitled under a bonus scheme to a free share, the entity can satisfy this award simply by printing another share certificate, which the executive can sell, so that the cash cost of the award is effectively borne by shareholders rather than by the entity itself. However, it is this very advantage which has been the source of the controversy surrounding share-based remuneration.

Over the past twenty years or so investors became increasingly concerned that share-based remuneration was resulting in a significant cost to them, through dilution of their existing shareholdings. Shareholders protested that they might well not have agreed to such awards in the first place had their dilutive cost been more transparent at the time that they were originally approved. As result, there emerged an increasing consensus among investors that share options should be recognised as a cost in the financial statements.

The opposing view, held by most companies, was that the financial statements were simply reflecting the economic reality that share options are ultimately a cost to other shareholders and not to the entity. Moreover, the information that shareholders were alleging had been withheld from them had been available all the time, in the disclosure of diluted earnings per share. Another powerful argument for those opposed to expensing options was to point out that some patently successful companies, particularly in the new technology sector, would never have shown a profit if they had been required to book an accounting expense for options. Some US critics argue that a key factor in US economic success has been the much greater 'social mobility' of wealth in the US than in Europe, and point to the important role played by stock options in achieving this.

To complicate matters, there is an unlikely alliance between opponents of expensing share-based awards and those who support expensing in principle but feel that there is as yet no option valuation model robust enough to generate a reliable accounting measure.

The strength of feeling amongst opponents of expensing share-based remuneration was graphically illustrated in the early 1990s when the FASB in the US attempted to issue an accounting standard requiring options to be expensed, only to be forced into a partial climb-down by an unprecedented political campaign, at one stage involving a lobby of the FASB by US companies with bands and cheer-leaders. As a result the current US standard FAS 123 – *Accounting for stock based compensation* – is a compromise which requires the fair value of shares or options issued to employees to be disclosed, but merely recommends,[1] without requiring, those fair values to be expensed in the financial statements. Even so, this represents a significant achievement compared to that of most other national standard setters.

1.2   Development of IFRS 2

IOSCO's Assessment Report on international accounting standards issued in 2000 (see Chapter 1 at 2.4) identified the lack of a standard on accounting for share-based payment as a deficiency in IAS as it stood at that time,[2] and concluded that the IASC should consider the issue. In July 2000 the 'G4+1' group (see Chapter 1 at 2.8) issued a discussion paper,[3] proposing that an expense be recognised for share-based payment transactions. The scope of this paper, like that of the subsequent IASB project, extended to all share-based payment transactions for goods or services, not just share-based employee remuneration. The paper proposed that an expense should be recognised for transactions that vest (i.e. become an unconditional entitlement of the counterparty) based on the fair value at vesting date.

The IASB added share-based payment to its projects in July 2001, and began by seeking additional comments on the G4+1 paper. In November 2002 the IASB issued its own exposure draft ED 2 – *Share-based Payment* – proposing that share-based payments for goods and services should be expensed, but using a methodology rather different from that proposed in the G4+1 paper. Essentially, the proposal was that an expense should be recognised for all awards to employees for which service is rendered (whether ultimately vesting or not) measured at the fair value at grant date.

Perhaps sensing that the tide was turning in favour of those advocating that share-based remuneration should be expensed, the IASB's chairman Sir David Tweedie felt sufficiently confident of the outcome as to stake the credibility of the then newly-structured Board on achieving a workable standard. However, the exposure draft proved highly controversial. Those who supported it in principle nevertheless had concerns on nearly every detail of the accounting treatment proposed, in particular the fact that it did not permit 'truing up', i.e. reversing any expense previously charged for an award that never actually crystallises. More fundamentally, many questioned whether there yet existed a methodology sufficiently robust for valuing shares and share options subject to the restrictions and performance conditions typically associated with employee share awards. There also remained a significant minority who still questioned the whole principle of expensing options and other share awards.

Despite these comments, the IASB finalised its proposals with the publication of IFRS 2 – *Share-based Payment* – in February 2004, although some significant changes had been necessary – in particular, IFRS 2 is now much closer than ED 2 to FAS 123, by requiring an expense to be recognised only for awards that vest. Nevertheless, IFRS 2 remains contentious: for example, there is still only limited provision for 'truing up', with the result that significant costs can potentially be recognised for awards that ultimately have no value to their recipients, and give rise to no dilution of the interests of other shareholders. Some commentators continue to question whether existing option valuation models can produce a reliable valuation of employee share awards. Moreover, the consensus in favour of the principle of expensing remains fragile. For example, at the time of writing a bill is before the US Congress seeking to restrict the FASB from issuing any more onerous requirements on share-based payment transactions.

2 THE OBJECTIVE AND SCOPE OF IFRS 2

2.1 Objective

IFRS 2 was published on 19 February 2004. Its stated objective is 'to specify the financial reporting by an entity when it undertakes a share-based payment transaction. In particular, it requires an entity to reflect in its profit or loss and financial position the effects of share-based payment transactions, including expenses associated with transactions in which share options are granted to employees'.[4]

2.2 Scope

2.2.1 Definitions

The following definitions are relevant to the scope of IFRS 2.

A *share-based payment transaction* is 'a transaction in which the entity receives goods or services as consideration for equity instruments of the entity (including shares or share options), or acquires goods or services by incurring liabilities to the supplier of those goods or services for amounts that are based on the price of the entity's shares or other equity instruments of the entity'.[5]

An *equity instrument* is 'a contract that evidences a residual interest in the assets of an entity after deducting all of its liabilities'.[6]

A *share option* is 'a contract that gives the holder the right, but not the obligation, to subscribe for the entity's shares at a fixed or determinable price for a specified period of time'.[7]

An *equity-settled share-based payment transaction* is 'a share-based payment transaction in which the entity receives goods or services as consideration for equity instruments of the entity (including shares or share options)'.[8]

A *cash-settled share-based payment transaction* is 'a share-based payment transaction in which the entity receives goods or services by incurring a liability to transfer cash or other assets to the supplier of those goods or services for amounts that are based on the price (or value) of the entity's shares or other equity instruments of the entity'.[9]

It will be seen from these definitions that IFRS 2 applies not only to awards of shares and share options but also to awards of cash (or other assets) of a value equivalent to that of a particular number of shares. These may arise in a number of situations. For example:

- a parent company may wish to extend its share scheme to the employees of overseas subsidiaries in jurisdictions where it may be difficult, or even illegal, to trade in the parent's shares, or where delivering shares would not give the same tax benefits to employees as would apply in the parent's own jurisdiction; or

- the entity may not wish to dilute existing shareholdings by significant share awards to employees.

In such cases, the employees may instead be offered cash equivalent to the value of the shares that they would otherwise have obtained.

IFRS 2 is supplemented by Implementation Guidance which 'accompanies, but is not part of, IFRS 2'.[10]

2.2.2   Transactions within the scope of IFRS 2

Subject to the exceptions noted in 2.2.3 below, IFRS 2 must be applied to all share-based payment transactions, including:

(a)   equity-settled share-based payment transactions (discussed at 4 and 5 below);

(b)   cash-settled share-based payment transactions (discussed at 6 below); and

(c)   transactions where either the entity or the supplier of goods or services can choose whether the transaction is to be equity-settled or cash-settled (discussed at 7 below).[11]

Whilst the boundaries between these types of scheme are reasonably self-explanatory, there may be cases, discussed in more detail at 6 and 7 below, where employee share schemes that an entity may intuitively regard as equity-settled are in fact required to be treated as cash-settled under IFRS 2.

Although IFRS 2 was primarily a response to concerns over share-based remuneration, its scope is not restricted to transactions with employees. For example, if an external supplier of goods or services is paid in shares or share options, or cash of equivalent value, IFRS 2 must be applied. Goods include:

- inventories;
- consumables;
- property plant and equipment;

- intangibles; and
- other non-financial assets.[12]

The enthusiasm in the late 1990s among suppliers to internet start-up companies for receiving payment in shares proved, for obvious reasons, rather short-lived. Such transactions are not at present very common in practice (except perhaps as intragroup transactions), with suppliers generally preferring more traditional modes of payment.

It will be seen that 'goods' do not include financial assets, which raises some further issues (see 2.2.3 E below).

A   Transactions by shareholders and other group entities

The scope of IFRS 2 is not restricted to share-based payment transactions undertaken by a reporting entity itself using its own equity instruments. It also applies to transfers of:

- equity instruments of the reporting entity by a shareholder of the reporting entity, or
- equity instruments of a parent of the reporting entity (or another entity within the same group as the reporting entity)

to parties than have supplied goods or services to the reporting entity.[13]

For example, if the employees of a subsidiary are granted options by the parent company over its shares in exchange for services to the subsidiary, the subsidiary must record a cost for that award within its own financial statements, even though it may not legally be a party to it. In effect, the accounting treatment is representing that the subsidiary has received a capital contribution from the parent, which the subsidiary has then spent on employee remuneration.

Conversely, if employees of a parent company in a group are granted an award based on the shares of a subsidiary, IFRS 2 requires a share-based payment expense to be recognised in both the consolidated and the separate financial statements of that parent company.

Unfortunately, there are a number of points of detail on which IFRS 2 is not as clear as it might be as to its intentions in the context of group share schemes. These are discussed in more detail at 10.3 below.

B   Transactions with employee benefit trusts and similar vehicles

In some jurisdictions, it is common for an entity to establish a trust to hold shares in the entity for the purpose of satisfying, or 'hedging' the cost of, share-based awards to employees. In such cases, it is often the trust, rather than any entity within the legal group, that actually makes share-based awards to employees. Such awards will be within the scope of IFRS 2, irrespective of whether or not the trust is consolidated under IAS 27 – *Consolidated and Separate Financial Statements,*[14] because the trust is a shareholder of the reporting entity.

Many such trusts would, but for their exemption from the scope of SIC–12 – *Special Purposes Entities,* be treated as subsidiaries under IAS 27. In July 2004 IFRIC published a draft interpretation IFRIC D7 – *Scope of SIC-12 Consolidation – Special Purpose Entities* – proposing the removal of this exemption (see Chapter 5 at 3.2.1).

2.2.3   Transactions not within the scope of IFRS 2

The following transactions are exempt from IFRS 2:

(a)   transfers of equity instruments by the entity's shareholders that are 'clearly not' payments for goods and services (see A below);[15]

(b)   transactions with shareholders as a whole (see B below);[16]

(c)   business combinations (see C below);[17] and

(d)   transactions in the scope of IAS 32 and IAS 39 (see D below).[18] The scope exemptions in IFRS 2 combined with those in IAS 32 and IAS 39 appear to have the effect that there is no specific guidance in IFRS for accounting for certain types of investments when acquired for shares (see E below).

There is no exemption from IFRS 2 for all-employee share schemes (see F below).

A   Transactions that are clearly not payments for goods and services

IFRS 2 does not elaborate on what is meant here. An example might be that a shareholder of an entity owes an employee of the entity a debt of €1,000 arising from a private transaction between them. If the debt is settled by the transfer of shares worth €1,000 from the shareholder to the employee, this transaction would 'clearly not' be a payment for goods or services supplied to the entity, and would therefore be outside the scope of IFRS 2.[19]

B   Transactions with shareholders as a whole

IFRS 2 does not apply to transactions with employees (and others) purely in their capacity as shareholders. For example, an employee may already hold shares in the entity as a result of previous share-based payment transactions. If the entity then raises funds through a rights issue, whereby all shareholders (including the employee) can acquire additional shares at less than the current fair value of the shares, such a transaction is not a 'share-based payment transaction' for the purposes of IFRS 2.

C   Business combinations

IFRS 2 does not apply to share-based payments to acquire goods (such as inventories or property, plant and equipment) in the context of a business combination to which IFRS 3 – *Business Combinations* – applies. However, equity instruments granted to the employees of the acquiree in their capacity as employees (e.g. in return for continued service) are within the scope of IFRS 2, as are the cancellation, replacement or modification of a share-based payment transaction as the result of a business combination or other equity restructuring.[20]

Thus, if the vendor of an acquired entity receives a share-based payment for transferring control of the entity and for remaining in continuing employment, it is necessary to determine how much of the share-based payment relates to the acquisition of control (which forms part of the cost of the combination, accounted for under IFRS 3) and how much relates to the provision of future services (which is a post-combination operating expense accounted for under IFRS 2). Neither IFRS 2 nor IFRS 3 provides detailed guidance on this often difficult and contentious area of accounting. However, in determining such a split, it would obviously be helpful to compare any payment made to persons who are both vendors and employees to payments made to vendors who are not employees or to employees who are not vendors.

Existing GAAP in the United States and the United Kingdom (to which entities might refer under the 'GAAP hierarchy' set out in IAS 8 – *Accounting Policies, Changes in Accounting Estimates and Errors* – see Chapter 3 at 4.3) effectively create a presumption that amounts contingent on post-combination service conditions represent post-combination compensation expense rather than forming part of the cost of the combination and therefore included in the measurement of goodwill. See also the discussion at 10.1 below on the treatment of options issued by an acquiror to replace those issued by the acquired entity prior to the business combination.

D   Transactions in the scope of IAS 32 and IAS 39

IFRS 2 does not apply to transactions within the scope of IAS 32 – *Financial Instruments: Disclosure and Presentation* or IAS 39 – *Financial Instruments: Recognition and Measurement*. Therefore, if an entity enters into a share-based payment transaction to purchase a commodity surplus to its production requirements or with a view to short-term profit taking, the contract is treated as a financial instrument under IAS 32 and IAS 39 rather than a share-based payment contract under IFRS 2.

E   Transactions in financial assets not in the scope of IAS 32 and IAS 39

As noted in 2.2.2 above IFRS 2 applies to share-based payment transactions involving goods or services, with 'goods' defined so as to exclude financial assets, presumably on the basis that these fall within IAS 32 and IAS 39. However, investments in subsidiaries, associates and corporate joint ventures in the separate financial statements of the investing entity are financial assets as defined in IAS 32 (and hence outside the scope of IFRS 2), but are outside the scope of IAS 39 where the entity chooses to account for them at cost (see Chapter 5 at 7.2.1 and Chapter 15 at 3.1).

Moreover, IFRS has no general requirements for accounting for the issue of equity instruments. Rather, consistent with the position taken by the *Framework* that equity is a residual rather than an item 'in its own right', the amount of an equity instrument is normally measured by reference to the item (expense or asset) in consideration for which the equity is issued, as determined in accordance with IFRS applicable to that other item.

This means that when (as is commonly the case) an entity acquires an investment in a subsidiary, associate or joint venture for the issue of an equity instrument, there is no explicit guidance in IFRS as to the required accounting in the separate financial statements of the investor, and in particular as to how the 'cost' of such an item is to be determined. This is discussed further in Chapter 5 at 7.2.1 A.

F   *'All employee' share plans*

Many countries encourage wider share-ownership by allowing companies to award a limited number of free or discounted shares to employees without either the employee or the employer incurring tax liabilities which would apply where other benefits in kind were given to employees.

Some existing national standards (for example those in the United States and the United Kingdom) exempt some such plans from their scope, to some extent as the result of local political pressures. During the exposure period of ED 2, the IASB received some strong representations that IFRS should give a similar exemption, on the grounds that not to do so would discourage companies from continuing with such schemes, with obvious deleterious economic effects.

The IASB concluded that such an exemption would be wrong in principle and difficult to draft in practice. By way of concession, the Basis for Conclusions hints that if the IFRS 2 charge for such schemes is (as asserted by some of the proponents of an exemption) *de minimis*, then there would be no charge under IFRS 2 anyway, since, like all IFRS, it applies only to material items.[21] However, our experience so far is that, in many cases, a contention that the charge is not material will not be sustainable.

2.3   Overall approach of IFRS 2

IFRS 2 is a complex standard, in part because its overall accounting approach is something of a hybrid. Essentially the total cost (i.e. measurement) of an award is calculated by determining whether it is a liability or an equity instrument, and then applying the measurement principles generally applicable to liabilities or equity instruments under IAS 32 and IAS 39. However the periodic allocation (i.e. recognition) of the cost[22] is determined using something more akin to a straightforward accruals methodology, which would not generally be used for financial instruments.

This inevitably has the result that, depending on its legal form, a transaction of equal value to the recipient can result in several different potential charges in the income statement, causing some to call into question the comparability of the information provided. Moreover, IFRS 2 is in some respects a rules-based 'anti-avoidance' standard, an impression reinforced rather than allayed by its unusually long Basis for Conclusions. At 87 pages, this is slightly longer than the standard itself and its implementation guidance, leaving the reader to wonder whether a standard resting on clear conceptual foundations would have required such copious explanation.

A   *Classification differences between IFRS 2 and IAS 32/IAS 39*

It should be noted that not merely are there differences between the accounting treatment of liabilities or equity under IFRS 2 as compared with that under IAS 32 and IAS 39, but the classification of a transaction as a liability or equity transaction under IFRS 2 may differ from that under IAS 32, as illustrated by Example 29.1 below.

Example 29.1: Classification of transaction as equity-settled or cash-settled

An entity offers a bonus scheme to an executive whereby, subject to the executive's meeting certain performance targets, he will receive as many of the entity's shares as are worth £1 million at the date that the award is payable. Neither the employee nor the entity can require settlement in cash.

Under IAS 32, this transaction would be classified as a liability (and accounted for as such under IAS 39), since the entity may be obliged to deliver a variable number of its own equity instruments (see Chapter 17 at 3.3).[23]

Under IFRS 2, however, this transaction is treated as an equity instrument since it is an equity-settled share-based payment transaction – i.e. one 'in which in which the entity receives goods or services as consideration for equity instruments of the entity (including shares or share options)' – see 2.2.1 above. This is reinforced by the fact that the definition of a cash-settled transaction in IFRS 2 is one which gives rise to 'a liability to transfer *cash or other assets*' (see 2.2.1 above) – in other words, unlike the definition of liability in IAS 32, it does not include an obligation to deliver a variable number of equity instruments.[24]

The significance of this, as will become clear from the analysis in the remainder of the Chapter, is that the total expense recognised for the transaction in Example 29.1 above would be less than £1 million (since it would reflect the time value of £1 million at the date on which the award was granted), whereas if the executive were simply paid £1 million in cash, the expense recognised would be the £1 million paid.

In practice, however, an entity (and the executive) would be unlikely to enter into such a transaction exactly the same as that in Example 29.1 (i.e. with no cash alternative) because of the risk that the entity would be legally or commercially unable to deliver the requisite number of shares – for example, if the share price fell to a level where the effect of satisfying the award would be to give the executive a substantial shareholding in the entity.

Once a cash alternative is introduced, it is quite possible that IFRS 2 would require the award to be accounted for, in whole or in part, as a liability (see 7 below).

The IASB offers some (pragmatic rather than conceptual) explanation for these differences in the Basis for Conclusions to IFRS 2. First, it is argued that to apply IAS 32 to share option plans would mean that a variable share option plan (i.e. one where the number of shares varied according to performance) would give rise to a more volatile (and typically greater) cost than a fixed plan (i.e. one where the number of shares to be awarded is fixed from the start), even if the same number of shares was ultimately delivered under each plan, which would have 'undesirable consequences'.[25] Second, it is argued that this is just one of several inconsistencies between IAS 32 which will be addressed in the round as part of the IASB's review of accounting for debt and equity.[26]

3 GENERAL RECOGNITION PRINCIPLES

The recognition rules in IFRS 2 are based on a so-called 'service date model'. In other words, IFRS 2 requires the goods or services received or acquired in a share-based payment transaction to be recognised when the goods are acquired or the services rendered. This contrasts with the measurement rules, which sometimes require a share-based payment transaction to be measured as at the date on which the transaction was entered into, which may be some time before or after the related services are received – see 4 below.

A share-based payment transaction results in the recognition of a cost. Where the goods or services received or acquired do not qualify for recognition as assets they should be expensed.[27] The standard notes that typically services will not qualify as assets and should therefore be expensed immediately, whereas goods will generally be initially recognised as assets and expensed later as they are consumed.[28] However, some payments for services may be capitalised (e.g. as part of the cost of PPE or inventories) and some payments for goods may be expensed immediately (e.g. where they are for items included within development costs written off as incurred).

The corresponding credit entry is, in the case of an equity-settled transaction, an increase in equity and, in the case of a cash-settled transaction, a liability[29] (or decrease in cash or other assets).

The application of these rules to transactions with persons other than employees is unlikely to cause significant difficulty in practice. Their application to transactions with employees is considerably more complex, and is dealt with in the discussion in the remainder of this Chapter.

3.1   'Vest' and related terms

Under IFRS 2, the point at which services are treated as having been received depends on the concept of 'vesting'.

A share-based payment to a counterparty is said to *vest* when it becomes an entitlement of the counterparty. Under IFRS 2, a share-based payment arrangement vests upon satisfaction of any specified 'vesting conditions'.[30]

Vesting conditions are conditions that must be satisfied in order for the counterparty to a share-based payment transaction to become entitled to receive cash, other assets or equity instruments of the entity.[31] Vesting conditions include service conditions and performance conditions.

A service condition is one which merely requires the counterparty to complete a specified period of service. For example, if an employee is granted a share option with a service condition of remaining in employment for three years, the award vests three years after the date of grant if the employee is still employed at that date. Some schemes may provide for the forfeiture of awards in the event of serious misconduct by the employee, but falling short of gross misconduct leading to termination of employment.

A performance condition is one that either requires the counterparty to achieve a personal goal, or (more typically) requires that the entity itself has attained a particular goal to which the counterparty has contributed.

Examples of performance conditions might include achievement of:

- a target profit or earnings per share;
- a target share price;
- total shareholder return (TSR), a target return on the share price, often judged against a comparator group of companies, when it is referred to as 'relative TSR'; or
- a non-financial goal such as the opening of a target number of new retail outlets.

The *vesting period* is the period over which vesting conditions are to be satisfied.[32] It is important to realise that this is not the same as the exercise period or the life of the option, as illustrated by Example 29.2 below.

Example 29.2: Meaning of 'vesting period' (1)

An employee is awarded options that can be exercised, if the employee remains in service for at least three years from the date of the award, at any time between three and ten years from the date of the award. For this award, the vesting period is three years; the exercise period is seven years; and the life of the option is ten years. However, as discussed further in 5 below, for the purposes of calculating the cost of the award under IFRS 2, the life of the award is taken as the period ending with the date on which the counterparty is most likely actually to exercise the option, which may be some time before the full ten-year life expires.

It is also important to distinguish between vesting conditions and other restrictions on the exercise of options and/or trading in shares, as illustrated by Example 29.3 below.

Example 29.3: Meaning of 'vesting period' (2)

An employee is awarded options that can be exercised, if the employee remains in service for at least three years from the date of the award, at any time between five and ten years from the date of the award. In this case, the vesting period remains three years as in Example 29.2 above, provided that the employee's entitlement to the award becomes absolute at the end of three years – in other words, the employee has to provide no services to the entity in years 4 and 5. The restriction on exercise of the award in the period after vesting would be reflected in the original valuation of the award at the date of grant.

In some cases the dividing line between service conditions and restrictions on exercise or trading may be more blurred. Suppose for example that the employee would not lose the right to exercise the option if he merely left the employment of the entity in years 4 or 5, but would do so if he joined a competitor in that period. In the particular economic and employment circumstances of the individual concerned (e.g. that he has to work and with his skills could work only for the entity or a competitor), such a condition might well effectively require that he remain in employment during years 4 and 5 and thus in substance be equivalent to a vesting condition.

It may well be necessary to consider the substance of such restrictions on a case-by-case basis.

The implications of vesting conditions and vesting periods for equity-settled transactions are discussed in 4 below and for cash-settled transactions in 5 below.

4 EQUITY-SETTLED TRANSACTIONS

This part of the chapter deals with all aspects of the measurement of equity-settled transactions other than detailed aspects of the valuation of such transactions, which are discussed in 5 below.

The detailed provisions of IFRS 2, which are discussed in 4.1 to 4.10 below, are complex, but their key points can be summarised as follows.

- All equity-settled transactions are measured at fair value. However, transactions with employees are normally measured using a 'grant date model' (i.e. the transaction is recorded at the fair value of the equity instrument at the date when it is originally granted), whereas transactions with non-employees are normally measured using a 'service date model' (i.e. the transaction is recorded at the fair value of the goods or services received at the date they are received). As noted in 3 above, all transactions, however *measured*, are *recognised* using a 'service date model'.

- Where an award is made subject to future fulfilment of conditions, the effect of those conditions is generally ignored in determining the fair value of the award. However, a 'market condition' (i.e. one related to the entity's share price) is taken into account in determining the fair value of the award.

- Where an award is made subject to future fulfilment of conditions, its cost is recognised over the period during which the conditions are fulfilled. The corresponding credit entry is recorded within equity.

- Until an equity instrument has vested (i.e. the entitlement to it has become unconditional) any amounts recorded are in effect contingent and will be adjusted if more or fewer awards vest that were originally anticipated to do so. However, no adjustments are made, either before or after vesting, to reflect the fact that an award has no value to the person entitled to it (e.g. in the case of a share option, because the option exercise price is above the current market price of the share). This means that it is quite possible for the financial statements to record a cost for options that are never exercised.

- An equity instrument awarded subject to a 'market condition' is considered to vest irrespective of whether or not that market condition is fulfilled, provided that all other conditions (if any) are satisfied, on the grounds that the effect of the condition has already been taken into account in determining the fair value of the award at the date of grant.

- If an equity instrument is cancelled before vesting, any amount remaining to be expensed is charged in full at that point. If an equity instrument is modified before vesting (e.g. in the case of a share option, by changing the performance conditions or the exercise price), the financial statements must continue to show a cost for at least the fair value of the original instrument, together with any excess of the fair value of the modified instrument over that of the original instrument, as measured at the date of modification.

- In determining the cost of an equity-settled transaction under IFRS 2, whether the entity satisfies its obligations under the transaction with a fresh issue of shares or by purchasing own shares in the financial markets is completely irrelevant to the income statement charge, although there is clearly a difference in the cash flows. Where own shares are purchased, they are accounted for as treasury shares under IAS 32[33] (see Chapter 17 at 6).

4.1 Overview

The general measurement rule in IFRS 2 is that an entity must measure the goods or services received, and the corresponding increase in equity, directly, at the fair value of the goods or services received, unless that fair value cannot be estimated reliably. If the fair value of the goods or services received cannot be estimated reliably, the entity must measure their value, and the corresponding increase in equity, indirectly, by reference to the fair value of the equity instruments granted.[34] 'Fair value' is the amount for which an asset could be exchanged, a liability settled, or an equity instrument granted could be exchanged, between knowledgeable, willing parties in an arm's length transaction.[35]

Thus, on their own, the general measurement principles of IFRS 2 would suggest that the reporting entity must determine in each case whether the fair value of the equity instruments granted or that of the goods or services received is more reliably determinable. However, IFRS 2 goes on to clarify that:

- in the case of transactions with employees, the fair value of the equity instruments must be used (see 4.2 below), except in those extremely rare cases where it is not possible to measure this fair value reliably, when the intrinsic value of the equity instruments may be used instead (see 5.3 below); but

- in the case of transactions with non-employees, there is a rebuttable presumption that the fair value of the goods or services provided is more reliably determinable (see 4.3 below).

Moreover, transactions with employees are measured at the date of grant (see 4.2 below), whereas those with non-employees are measured at the date when goods or services are received (see 4.3 below).

The overall position can be summarised by the following matrix.

Counterparty	Measurement basis	Measurement date	Recognition date
Employee	Fair value of equity instruments awarded	Grant date	Service date
Non-employee	Fair value of goods or services received	Service date	Service date

The Basis for Conclusions addresses the issue of why the accounting treatment for apparently identical transactions should, in effect, depend on the identity of the counterparty.

The main argument put forward to justify the approach adopted for transactions with employees is essentially that, once an award has been agreed, the value of the services provided pursuant to the transaction does not change significantly with the value of the award.[36] However, some might question this proposition, on the grounds that employees are more likely to work harder when the value of their options is rising than when it has sunk irretrievably.

As regards transactions with non-employees, the IASB offers two main arguments for the use of measurement at service date.

The first is that, if the counterparty is not firmly committed to delivering the goods or services, the counterparty would consider whether the fair value of the equity instruments at the delivery date is sufficient payment for the goods or services when deciding whether to deliver the goods or services. This suggests that there is a high correlation between the fair value of the equity instruments at the date the goods or services are received and the fair value of those goods or services.[37] This argument is clearly vulnerable to the challenge that it has no relevance where (as would more likely be the case) the counterparty is firmly committed to delivering the goods or services.

The second is that non-employees generally provide services over a short period commencing some time after grant date, whereas employees generally provide services over an extended period beginning on the grant date. This leads to a concern that transactions with non-employees could be entered into well in advance of the due date for delivery of goods or services. If an entity were able to measure the expense of such a transaction at the grant date fair value, the result, assuming that the entity's share price rises, would be to understate the cost of goods and services delivered.[38]

The true reason for the IASB's approach may have been political as much as theoretical. One effect of a grant date measurement model is that, applied to a grant of share options that is eventually exercised, it 'freezes' the accounting cost at the (typically) lower fair value at the date of grant. This excludes from the post-grant financial statements the increased cost and volatility that would be associated with a model that constantly remeasured the award to fair value until exercise date. The IASB might well have perceived it as a marginally easier task to persuade the corporate sector of the merits of a 'lower cost, zero volatility' approach as opposed to a 'fair value at exercise date' model (such as is used for cash-settled awards – see 6 below).

The price to be paid in accounting terms for the grant date model is that, when an award falls in value after grant date, it continues to be recognised at its higher grant date value. It is therefore quite possible that, during a period of general economic downturn, financial statements will show significant costs for options granted in previous years, but which are currently worthless. This could well lead to (in fact, sometimes groundless) accusations of rewarding management for failure.

4.1.1 The 'credit entry'

As noted in the summary above, the basic accounting entry for an equity-settled share-based payment transaction is:

> DR   Profit or loss for the period (Employee costs)
>
>   CR   Equity.

IFRS 2 does not prescribe whether the credit should be to a separate component of equity, or, if the entity chooses to treat it as such, how it should be described.

We imagine that the IASB deliberately allowed complete freedom in this respect so as to ensure there was no conflict between, on the one hand, the basic requirement of IFRS 2 that there should be a credit in equity and, on the other, the legal requirements of various jurisdictions as to exactly how that credit should be allocated within equity.

Occasionally there will be a credit to profit or loss (see for instance Example 29.8 at 4.6.4 below) and a corresponding reduction in equity.

4.2   Transactions with employees

These will comprise the great majority of transactions accounted for under IFRS 2, and include all remuneration in the form of shares, share options, share appreciation rights and any other form of reward linked to the entity's share price.

4.2.1 Who is an 'employee'?

Given the important difference between the accounting treatment of equity-settled transactions with employees and that of those with non-employees, it is obviously important for IFRS 2 to define what is meant by employees. In fact IFRS 2 strictly refers to 'employees and other providing similar services',[39] who are defined as individuals who render personal services to the entity and either:

(a) the individuals are regarded as employees for legal or tax purposes;

(b) the individuals work for the entity under its direction in the same way as individuals who are regarded as employees for legal or tax purposes; or

(c) the services rendered are similar to those rendered by employees.

The term encompasses all management personnel, i.e. those persons having authority and responsibility for planning, directing and controlling the activities of the entity, including non-executive directors.[40]

The implication of (b) and (c) in the definition above is that, where a third party provides services pursuant to a share-based payment transaction that could be provided by an employee (e.g. where an external IT consultant works alongside an in-house IT team), that third party is treated as an employee rather than a non-employee for the purposes of IFRS 2.

4.2.2 Basis of measurement

As noted above, IFRS 2 requires equity-settled transactions with employees to be measured by reference to the fair value of the equity instruments granted at 'grant date' (see A below).[41] IFRS 2 asserts that this approach is necessary because shares, share options and other equity instruments are typically only part of a larger remuneration package, such that it would not be practicable to determine the value of the work performed in consideration for the cash element of the total package, the benefit-in-kind element, the share option element and so on.[42]

In essence, this is really an anti-avoidance provision. The underlying concern is that, if an entity were able to value options by reference to the services provided for them, it might assert that the value of those services was zero, on the argument that its personnel are already so handsomely rewarded by the non-equity elements of their remuneration package (such as cash and health benefits), that no additional services are (or indeed could be) obtained by granting options.

A   Grant date

As noted above, IFRS 2 requires equity-settled transactions with employees to be accounted for at fair value at grant date, defined as 'the date at which the entity and another party (including an employee) agree to a share-based payment arrangement, being when the entity and the counterparty have a shared understanding of the terms and conditions of the arrangement.'[43]

IFRS 2 and the accompanying implementation guidance emphasise that this occurs only when all the conditions are known and agreed. Thus, for example, if an entity makes an award 'in principle' to an employee of options whose terms are subject to review or approval by a remuneration committee or the shareholders, 'grant date' is the later date when the necessary formalities have been completed.[44]

The implementation guidance to IFRS 2 notes that employees may begin rendering services in consideration for an award before it has been formally ratified. For example, a new employee might join the entity on 1 January 2005 and be granted options relating to performance for a period beginning on that date, but subject to formal approval by the remuneration committee at its quarterly meeting on 15 March 2005. In that case, the entity would begin expensing the award from 1 January 2005 based on a best estimate of its fair value, but would subsequently adjust that estimate so that the ultimate cost of the award was its actual fair value at 15 March 2005.[45]

4.3   Transactions with non-employees

In accounting for equity-settled transactions with non-employees, the entity must adopt a rebuttable presumption that the value of the goods or services received provides the more reliable indication of the fair value of the transaction. The fair value to be used is that at the date on which the goods are obtained or the services rendered.[46] This implies that, where the goods or services are received on a number of dates over a period, the fair value at each date should be used, although in most cases there may no great fluctuation in fair value.

If 'in rare cases' the presumption is rebutted, the entity may use as a surrogate measure the fair value of the equity instruments granted, but as at the date when the goods or services are received, not the original grant date. However, where the goods or services are received over a relatively short period where the share price does not change significantly, an average share price can be used in calculating the fair value of equity instruments granted.[47]

4.4   Determining the fair value of equity instruments

As discussed in 4.2 and 4.3 above, IFRS 2 requires the following equity-settled transactions to be measured by reference to the fair value of the equity instruments issued rather than that of the goods or services received:

*   all transactions with employees (except where is impossible to determine fair value – see below); and

*   transactions with non-employees where, exceptionally, the presumption that the fair value of goods or services provided is more reliably measurable is rebutted.

For all transactions measured by reference to the fair value of the equity instruments granted, IFRS 2 requires fair value to be measured at the 'measurement date' – i.e. grant date in the case of transactions with employees and service date in the case of transactions with non-employees.[48] Fair value should be based on market prices if available.[49] In the absence of market prices, a valuation technique should be used to estimate what the market price would have been on the measurement date in an arm's-length transaction between informed and willing parties. The technique used should be a recognised technique and incorporate all factors that would be taken into account by knowledgeable and willing market participants.[50]

Appendix B to IFRS 2 contains more detailed guidance on valuation, which is discussed at 5.1 and 5.2 below. IFRS 2 also deals with those 'rare' cases where it is not possible to value equity instruments reliably. This is more likely to apply in the case of awards of options rather than those of shares, and is discussed further at 5.3 below.

Paragraph 16 of IFRS 2 rather confusingly states that the fair value of equity instruments granted must take into account the terms and conditions on which they were granted, but this requirement is said to be 'subject to paragraphs 19-22'.[51] When those paragraphs are consulted, however, a somewhat different picture emerges, since they draw a distinction between vesting conditions which are market conditions (i.e. those related to the entity's share price) and other vesting conditions. These are discussed in more detail at 4.6, 4.7 and 5 below, but the essential difference is that, while market conditions must be factored into any valuation, other conditions must be ignored.[52] Moreover, where an option with a reload feature (see 4.8 below) is awarded, the reload feature is ignored in determining the fair value of the options.[53]

4.5 Transactions in which services are received – allocation of expense

Such transactions, particularly those with employees, raise particular accounting problems since they are often subject to vesting conditions (see 3.1 above) that can be satisfied only over an extended vesting period. This raises the issue of whether a share-based payment transaction should be recognised:

(a)   when the relevant equity instrument is first granted;

(b)   when it vests;

(c)   during the vesting period; or

(d)   during the life of the option.

Where an award of equity instruments vests immediately, IFRS 2 creates a presumption that, in the absence of evidence to the contrary, the award is in respect of services that have already been rendered, and should therefore be expensed in full at grant date.[54]

Where equity instruments are granted subject to vesting conditions (as in many cases they will be, particularly where payments to employees are concerned), IFRS 2 creates a presumption that they are a payment for services to be received in the future, during the 'vesting period', with the transaction being recognised during that period, as illustrated in Example 29.4.[55]

Example 29.4:   Award with service condition only

An entity grants a director share options (the fair value of which at the date of grant is determined to be €300,000) on condition that the director remain in employment for 3 years. The entity will record a cost of €100,000 a year in the income statement for three years, with a corresponding increase in equity.

In practice, the calculations required by IFRS 2 are unlikely to be as simple as that in Example 29.4. In particular:

• The final number of awards that vest cannot be known until the vesting date (because employees may leave or be dismissed before the vesting date, or because relevant performance conditions may not be met).

- The length of the vesting period may not be known in advance (since vesting may depend on satisfaction of a performance condition with no, or a variable, time-limit on its attainment).

IFRS 2's approach to such issues is discussed in 4.6 and 4.7 below, which address in turn the treatment of vesting conditions other than market conditions and the treatment of market conditions.

4.6   Vesting conditions other than market conditions

An award of equity instruments to employees is often subject to one or more vesting conditions (see 3.1 above). Where one of the conditions is a 'market condition' (i.e. one linked to the entity's share price) the special provisions discussed in 4.7 below apply. Where none of the conditions is a market condition, the accounting treatment can be summarised as follows.

4.6.1   *Summary of accounting treatment*

The overall objective is that, at the end of the vesting period, the cumulative charge to the income statement should represent the number of equity instruments that have actually vested multiplied by their fair value, excluding the effect of the vesting conditions, at the date of grant. This result is arrived at via a continuous re-estimation process as follows:

(a)   at grant date, the fair value of the award (excluding the effect of vesting conditions) is determined;

(b)   at each subsequent reporting date until vesting, the entity calculates a best estimate of the cumulative charge to the income statement at that date, being the product of:

    (i)   the grant date fair value of the award determined in (a) above;

    (ii)   the current best estimate of the number of awards that will vest (taking into account such factors as the likelihood of employee turnover during the vesting period, or of certain performance hurdles being met); and

    (iii)   the expired portion of the vesting period;

(c)   the charge to the income statement for the period is the cumulative amount calculated in (b) above less the amounts already charged in previous periods. There is a corresponding credit to equity;[56]

(d)   once the awards have vested, no further accounting adjustments are made to the cost of the award, except in respect of certain modifications to the award – see 4.10 below; and

(e)   if a vested award is not exercised, an entity may (but need not) make a transfer between components of equity – see 4.9 below.

This is illustrated by Examples 29.5 and 29.6 below.[57]

Example 29.5: *Award with no re-estimation of number of awards vesting*

An entity grants 100 share options to each of its 500 employees. Vesting is conditional upon the employees working for the entity over the next three years. The entity estimates that the fair value of each share option is €15. The entity estimates that 20% of employees will leave during the three-year period and therefore forfeit their rights to the share options.

If everything turns out exactly as expected, the entity will recognise the following amounts during the vesting period for services received as consideration for the share options.

Year	Calculation of cumulative expense	Cumulative expense (€)	Expense for period[3] (€)
1	50,000 options × 80%[1] × €15 × 1/3[2]	200,000	200,000
2	50,000 options × 80% × €15 × 2/3	400,000	200,000
3	50,000 options × 80% × €15 × 3/3	600,000	200,000

1   The entity expects 20% of employees to leave and therefore only 80% of the options to vest.

2   The vesting period is 3 years, and 1 year of it has expired.

3   In each case the period expense is the difference between the calculated cumulative expense at the beginning and end of the period.

Example 29.6: *Award with re-estimation of number of awards vesting due to staff turnover*

As in Example 29.5 above, an entity grants 100 share options to each of its 500 employees. Vesting is conditional upon the employee working for the entity over the next three years. The entity estimates that the fair value of each share option is €15.

In this case, however, 20 employees leave during the first year, and the entity's best estimate at the end of year 1 is that 15% of employees will have left before the end of the vesting period. During the second year, a further 22 employees leave, and the entity revises its estimate of total employee departures over the vesting period from 15% to 12%. During the third year, a further 15 employees leave. Hence, a total of 57 employees (20+22+15) forfeit their rights to the share options during the three year period, and a total of 44,300 share options (443 employees × 100 options per employee) finally vest.

The entity will recognise the following amounts during the vesting period for services received as consideration for the share options.

Year	Calculation of cumulative expense	Cumulative expense (€)	Expense for period (€)
1	50,000 options × 85% × €15 × 1/3	212,500	212,500
2	50,000 options × 88% × €15 × 2/3	440,000	227,500
3	44,300 options × €15 × 3/3	664,500	224,500

Note that in Example 29.6 above, the number of employees that leave during year 1 and year 2 is not directly relevant to the calculation of cumulative expense in those years, but would naturally be a factor taken into account by the entity in estimating the likely number of awards finally vesting.

The effect of this treatment is that, while services were received from the employees who left before vesting, no cost is ultimately recognised for those services. In general, IFRS 2 requires no cost to be recognised for awards that do not vest for failure to satisfy a vesting condition,[58] unless the vesting condition is a market condition, in which case it is irrelevant whether that condition is satisfied or not (see 4.7 below).

4.6.2   Equity instruments vesting in instalments

Sometimes an entity may make share-based payments that vest in instalments. For example, an entity might grant an employee 300 options, 100 of which vest if the employee remains in service for one year, a further 100 after two years and the final 100 after three years. IFRS 2 requires such an award to be treated as three separate awards of 100 options, on the grounds that the different vesting periods will mean that the three tranches of the award have different fair values.[59]

4.6.3   Transactions with variable vesting periods

An award may be made whose vesting period is subject to variation. For example, an award might be made contingent upon achievement of a particular target (such as the opening of a given number of new outlets) within a given period, but vesting immediately the target has been reached. Alternatively, an award might be contingent on levels of earnings growth over a period, but with vesting occurring more quickly if growth is achieved more quickly. Also some plans provide for 'retesting', whereby an original target is set for achievement within a given vesting period, but if that target is not met, a new target and/or a different vesting period are substituted.

In such cases, the entity needs to estimate the length of the vesting period at grant date, based on the most likely outcome of the performance condition. Subsequently, it is necessary continuously to re-estimate not only the number of awards that will finally vest, but also the date of vesting, as shown by Example 29.7.[60] This contrasts with the treatment of awards with market conditions and variable vesting periods, where the initial estimate of the vesting period is not revised (see 4.7.4 below).

Example 29.7:   Award with non-market condition and variable vesting period

At the beginning of year 1, the entity grants 100 shares each to 500 employees, conditional upon the employees remaining in the entity's employment during the vesting period. The shares will vest:

* at the end of year 1 if the entity's earnings increase by more than 18%
* at the end of year 2 if the entity's earnings increase by more than an average of 13% per year over the two-year period
* at the end of year 3 if the entity's earnings increase by more than an average of 10% per year over the three-year period.

The award is estimated to have a fair value of $30 per share at grant date. It is expected that no dividends will be paid during the whole three-year period.

By the end of the first year, the entity's earnings have increased by 14%, and 30 employees have left. The entity expects that earnings will continue to increase at a similar rate in year 2, and therefore expects that the shares will vest at the end of year 2. The entity expects, on the basis of a weighted average probability, that a further 30 employees will leave during year 2, and therefore expects that an award of 100 shares each will vest for 440 (500-30-30) employees at the end of year 2.

By the end of the second year, the entity's earnings have increased by only 10% and therefore the shares do not vest at the end of that year. 28 employees have left during the year. The entity expects that a further 25 employees will leave during year 3, and that the entity's earnings will increase by at least 6%, thereby achieving the average growth of 10% per year necessary for an award after 3 years, so that an award of 100 shares each will vest for 417 (500-30-28-25) employees at the end of year 3.

By the end of the third year, 23 employees have left and the entity's earnings have increased by 8%, resulting in an average increase of 10.67% per year. Therefore, 419 (500-30-28-23) employees receive 100 shares at the end of year 3.

The entity will recognise the following amounts during the vesting period for services received as consideration for the shares.

Year	Calculation of cumulative expense	Cumulative expense ($)	Expense for period ($)
1	440 employees × 100 shares × $30 × 1/2[1]	660,000	660,000
2	417 employees × 100 shares × $30 × 2/3[1]	834,000	174,000
3	419 employees × 100 shares × $30	1,257,000	423,000

1   The entity's best estimate at the end of year 1 is that it is one year through a two-year vesting period and at the end of year 2 that it is two years through a three-year vesting period.

It will be noted that in Example 29.7, which is based on IG Example 2 in the Implementation Guidance to IFRS 2, it is assumed that no dividends will be paid on the shares throughout the maximum possible three-year vesting period. This has the effect that the fair value of the shares to be awarded is (some might say, rather too conveniently) equivalent to their market value at the date of grant.

If dividends were expected to be paid during the vesting period, this would no longer be the case. Employees would be better off if they received shares after two years rather than three, since they would have right to receive dividends from the end of year two. In practice, an entity is unlikely to suspend dividend payments in order to simplify the calculation of its IFRS 2 expense, and it is unfortunate that no guidance is given for dealing a more realistic situation than that in Example 29.7.

One solution might be to use the approach in IG Example 4 in the implementation guidance to IFRS 2 (the substance of which is reproduced as Example 29.9 at 4.6.5 below). That example deals with an award whose exercise price is either CHF12 or CHF16, dependent upon various performance conditions. Because vesting conditions must be ignored in determining the value of an award, the approach is in effect to treat the award as the simultaneous grant of two awards, whose value, in that case, varies by reference to the different exercise prices.

The same principle could be applied to an award of shares that vests at different times according to the performance conditions, by determining different fair values for the shares (in this case depending on whether they vest after one two or three years). The charge during the vesting period would be based on a best estimate of which outcome will occur, and the final cumulative charge would be based on the actual outcome.

A difficulty with such an approach is that it appears to be taking account of vesting conditions in determining the fair value of an award, contrary to the basic principle of paragraph 19 of IFRS 2 (see 4.6.1 above). The argument has to be that it is not the vesting conditions that are being taken into account *per se*, but the fact that the varying vesting periods will give rise to different lives for the award (which are required to be taken into account – see 4.10.2 A and 5.2.1 below).

Economically speaking, the entity in Example 29.7 has made a single award, the fair value of which must be a function of the weighted probabilities of the various outcomes occurring. However, under the accounting model for share-settled awards in IFRS 2, the probability of achieving non-market performance conditions is not taken into account in valuing an award. If this is required to be ignored, the only approach open is to proceed as above.

Some might object that this is not relevant to the award in Example 29.7 above, since it is an award of shares rather than, in the case of Example 29.9 below, an award of options. However, a counter to this would be that an award of shares is no more than an award of options with an exercise price of zero. Moreover, the treatment in the previous paragraph is broadly consistent with the rationale given by IFRS 2 for the treatment of an award vesting in instalments (see 4.6.2 above).

4.6.4   *Transactions with variable number of equity instruments awarded*

More common than awards with a variable vesting period are those where the number of equity instruments awarded varies, typically increasing to reflect the margin by which a particular target is exceeded. In accounting for such awards, the entity must continuously revise its estimate of the number of shares to be awarded, as illustrated in Example 29.8 below (which is based on Example 3 in the implementation guidance to IFRS 2).

Example 29.8:   Award with non-market condition and variable number of equity instruments

At the beginning of year 1, an entity grants an option over a variable number of shares (see below), estimated to have a fair value at grant date of £20 per share under option, to each of its 100 employees working in the sales department on the following terms. The share options will vest at the end of year 3, provided that the employees remain in the entity's employment, and provided that the volume of sales of a particular product increases by at least an average of 5% per year. If the volume of sales of the product increases by an average of between 5% and 10% per year, each employee will be entitled to exercise 100 share options. If the volume of sales increases by an average of between 10% and 15% each year, each employee will be entitled to exercise 200 share options. If the volume of sales increases by an average of 15% or more, each employee will be entitled to exercise 300 share options.

By the end of the first year, seven employees have left and the entity expects that a total of 20 employees will leave by the end of year 3. Product sales have increased by 12% and the entity expects this rate of increase to continue over the next two years, so that 80 employees will be entitled to exercise 200 options each.

By the end of the second year, a further five employees have left. The entity now expects only three more employees to leave during year 3, and therefore expects a total of 15 employees to have left during the three-year period. Product sales have increased by 18%, resulting in an average of 15% over the two years to date. The entity now expects that sales will average 15% or more over the three-year period, so that 85 employees will be entitled to exercise 300 options each.

By the end of year 3, a further seven employees have left. Hence, 19 employees have left during the three-year period, and 81 employees remain. However, due to trading conditions significantly poorer than expected, sales have increased by a 3-year average of only 12%, so that the 81 remaining employees are entitled to exercise only 200 share options.

The entity will recognise the following amounts during the vesting period for services received as consideration for the options.

Year	Calculation of cumulative expense	Cumulative expense (£)	Expense for period (£)
1	80 employees × 200 options × £20 × 1/3	106,667	106,667
2	85 employees × 300 options × £20 × 2/3	340,000	233,333
3	81 employees × 200 options × £20	324,000	(16,000)

The above example reinforces the point that, under the methodology in IFRS 2, it is quite possible to get a credit to the income statement for an equity-settled transaction during the period to vesting.

4.6.5 Transactions with variable exercise price

Another mechanism for delivering higher value to the recipient of a share award so as to reflect the margin by which a particular target is exceeded might be to vary the exercise price depending on performance. Accordingly, the mechanism required by IFRS 2 for dealing with such a situation is to treat the award as two awards, determine the fair value of each, and to base the cost during the vesting period on the best estimate of which outcome will occur, with the final cumulative charge being based on the actual outcome.[61]

This is illustrated in Example 29.9 below.

Example 29.9: Award with non-market condition and variable exercise price

An entity grants to a senior executive 10,000 share options, conditional upon the executive's remaining in the entity's employment for three years. The exercise price is CHF40. However, the exercise price drops to CHF30 if the entity's earnings increase by at least an average of 10% per year over the three-year period.

On grant date, the entity estimates that the fair value of the share options, with an exercise price of CHF30, is CHF16 per option. If the exercise price is CHF40, the entity estimates that the share options have a fair value of CHF12 per option. During year 1, the entity's earnings increased by 12%, and the entity expects that earnings will continue to increase at this rate over the next two years. The entity therefore expects that the earnings target will be achieved, and hence the share options will have an exercise price of CHF30.

During year 2, the entity's earnings increased by 13%, and the entity continues to expect that the earnings target will be achieved. During year 3, the entity's earnings increased by only 3%, and therefore the earnings target was not achieved. The executive completes three years' service, and therefore satisfies the service condition. Because the earnings target was not achieved, the 10,000 vested share options have an exercise price of CHF40.

The entity will recognise the following amounts during the vesting period for services received as consideration for the options.

Year	Calculation of cumulative expense	Cumulative expense (CHF)	Expense for period (CHF)
1	10,000 options × CHF16 × 1/3	53,333	53,333
2	10,000 options × CHF16 × 2/3	106,667	53,334
3	10,000 options × CHF12	120,000	13,333

At first sight this may seem a rather surprising approach. In reality, has not the entity in Example 29.9 made a single award, the fair value of which must lie between CHF12 and CHF16, as a function of the weighted probabilities of either outcome occurring? Economically speaking, this is the case. However, under the accounting model for share-settled awards in IFRS 2, the probability of achieving non-market performance conditions is not taken into account in valuing an award. If this is required to be ignored, the only approach open is to proceed as above.

4.7 Market conditions

4.7.1 What is a 'market condition'?

IFRS 2 defines a market condition as 'a condition upon which the exercise price, vesting or exercisability of an equity instrument depends that is related to the market price of the entity's equity instruments, such as attaining a specified share price or a specified amount of intrinsic value of a share option, or achieving a specified target that is based on the market price of the entity's equity instruments relative to an index of market prices of equity instruments of other entities.'[62]

The 'intrinsic value' of a share option means 'the difference between the fair value of the shares to which the counterparty has the (conditional or unconditional) right to subscribe or which it has the right to receive, and the price (if any) the counterparty is (or will be) required to pay for those shares.'[63] In other words, an option to acquire for $8 a share with a fair value of $10 has an intrinsic value of $2. A performance condition based on the share price and one based on the intrinsic value of the option are effectively the same, since the value of each will obviously move in parallel.

Examples of market conditions might be:

- any condition based on total shareholder return ('TSR'). TSR is a measure of the increase or decrease in a given sum invested in an entity over a period on the assumption that all dividends received in the period had been used to purchase further shares in the entity. The market price of the entity's shares is an input to the calculation; or

- a condition based upon a general stock market index in which the entity's shares are included, which again has as an input the market price of the entity's shares.

However, a condition linked to a purely internal financial performance measure such as profit or earnings per share is not a market condition. Such measures will affect the share price, but are not directly linked to it, and hence are not market conditions.

Moreover, a condition linked to a market index to which the reporting entity's share price is not an input is not necessarily a market condition. For example, suppose that an entity engaged in investment management and listed only in London grants options to an employee responsible for the Far East equities portfolio. The options have a performance condition linked to movements in a general index of shares of entities listed in Hong Kong, so as to compare the performance of the portfolio of investments for which the employee is responsible with that of the overall market in which they are traded. That condition would not be regarded as a market condition under IFRS 2, because even though it relates to the performance of a market, the reporting entity's own share price is not relevant to the satisfaction of the condition.

However, if the performance condition were that the entity's own share price had to outperform a general index of shares of entities listed in Hong Kong, that condition would be a market condition, because the reporting entity's own share price is then relevant to the satisfaction of the condition. The fact that the entity's own shares are not listed in Hong Kong, and are therefore not included in the Hong Kong index, is not relevant.

4.7.2 Summary of accounting treatment

As noted at various points above, the key feature of the accounting treatment of an equity-settled transaction subject to a market condition is that the market condition is taken into account in valuing the award at the date of grant, but then subsequently ignored, so that an award is treated as vesting irrespective of whether the market condition is satisfied, provided that all other vesting conditions are satisfied,[64] as explained in Example 29.10.

Example 29.10: Award with market condition

An entity grants an employee an option to buy a share on condition of remaining in employment for three years and the share price at the end of that period being at least €7. The share price condition is factored into the initial valuation of the option, and the option is considered to vest provided that the employee remains for 3 years, irrespective of whether the share price does in fact reach €7. Thus, IFRS 2 treats as vesting (and recognises a cost for) awards that do not actually vest in any natural sense of the word (or indeed in its defined sense in IFRS 2!).

This treatment is clearly significantly different from that for transactions not involving a market condition, where no cost would be recognised where the conditions were not met. The Basis for Conclusions indicates that the IASB accepted this difference for two main reasons:

(a) it is consistent with the approach in the US standard FAS 123; and

(b) in principle, the same approach should have been adopted for all performance conditions. However, whereas market conditions can be readily incorporated into the valuation of options, other conditions cannot.[65]

In our view, the over-riding reason for the IASB's approach was almost certainly harmonisation with US GAAP, since the second reason given does not really stand up to scrutiny. As discussed in 4.6 above, the methodology prescribed by IFRS 2 for transactions with a condition other than a market condition is to determine the fair value of the option ignoring the condition and then essentially to multiply that fair value by the estimated (and ultimately the actual) probability of that condition occurring, which in broad terms is no different from incorporating those probabilities in the valuation in the first place.

One of the reasons for adoption of this approach under US GAAP (not referred to in the Basis for Conclusions in IFRS 2) was as an 'anti-avoidance' measure. The concern was that the introduction of certain market conditions could effectively allow for the reversal of the expense for 'underwater' options (i.e. those whose exercise price is higher than the share price such that it is not in the holder's interest to exercise the option) for which all significant vesting conditions had been satisfied, contrary to the general principle of FAS 123 (and IFRS 2) that no revisions should be made to the expense for an already vested option.

For example, an entity could grant an employee an option, when the share price is £10, exercisable at £10, provided that a certain sales target had been met within one year. If the target were achieved, IFRS 2 would require an expense to be recognised even if the share price at the end of the year were only £8, so that the employee would not rationally exercise the option. If, however, the performance conditions were that (a) the sales target was achieved and (b) the share price was at least £10.01, the effect would be (absent specific provision for market conditions) that the entity could reverse any expense for 'underwater' options.

Whilst this concern is easily understood, some might question whether an accounting methodology designed to thwart the use of artificial market conditions necessarily produces appropriate results when applied to meaningful market conditions. However, it appears that it may be possible to soften the impact of the rules for market-based conditions relatively easily by introducing a non-market related condition closely correlated to the market condition. For instance, the option in Example 29.10 above could be modified so that exercise was dependent not only upon the €7 target share price and continuous employment, but also on a target growth in earnings per share. Whilst there would not be a perfect correlation between earnings per share and the share price, it would be expected that they would move roughly in parallel, particularly if the entity has historically had a fairly consistent price/earnings ratio. Thus, if the share price target was not met, it would be highly likely that the earnings per share target would not be met either. This would allow the entity to show no cumulative cost for the option, since only one (i.e. not *all*) of the non-market related vesting conditions would have been met.

Similarly, entities in sectors where the share price is closely related to net asset value (e.g. property companies and investment trusts) could incorporate a net asset value target as a non-market performance condition that would be highly likely not to be satisfied if a given market condition was not satisfied.

The matrices below illustrate the interaction of market and non-market conditions. Matrix 1 summarises the possible outcomes for an award with the following two vesting conditions:

- the employee remaining in service for three years ('service condition'); and
- the entity's TSR relative to that of a peer group being in the top 10% of its peer group at the end of the period ('TSR target').

Matrix 1

	Service condition met?	TSR target met?	IFRS 2 expense?
1	Yes	Yes	Yes
2	Yes	No	Yes
3	No	Yes	No
4	No	No	No

It will be seen that, to all intents and purposes, the 'TSR target met?' column is redundant, as this is not relevant to whether or not the award is treated as vesting by IFRS 2. The effect of this is that the entity would recognise an expense for outcome 3, even though no awards truly vest.

Matrix 2 summarises the possible outcomes for an award with the same conditions as in Matrix 1, plus a requirement for earnings per share to grow by a general inflation index plus 10% over the period ('EPS target').

Matrix 2

	Service condition met?	TSR target met?	EPS target met?	IFRS 2 expense?
1	Yes	Yes	Yes	Yes
2	Yes	No	Yes	Yes
3	Yes	Yes	No	No
4	Yes	No	No	No
5	No	Yes	Yes	No
6	No	No	Yes	No
7	No	Yes	No	No
8	No	No	No	No

Again it will be seen that, to all intents and purposes, the 'TSR target met?' column is redundant, as this is not relevant to whether or not the award is treated as vesting by IFRS 2. The effect of this is that the entity would recognise an expense for outcome 2, even though no awards truly vest. However, no expense would be recognised for outcome 4, which is, except for the introduction of the EPS target, equivalent to outcome 3 in Matrix 1, for which an expense is recognised. This illustrates that the introduction of a non-market condition closely related to a market condition may mitigate the impact of IFRS 2.

Examples of the application of the accounting treatment for transactions involving market conditions are given in 4.7.3 and 4.7.4 below.

4.7.3　*Transactions with market conditions and known vesting periods*

The accounting for these is essentially the same as that for transactions with no market conditions and a known vesting period, except that adjustments are made to reflect the changing probability of the achievement of the non-market conditions only, as illustrated by Example 29.11 below.[66]

Example 29.11:　Award with market condition and fixed vesting period

At the beginning of year 1, an entity grants to 100 employees 1,000 share options each, conditional upon the employees remaining in the entity's employment until the end of year 3. However, the share options cannot be exercised unless the share price has increased from €50 at the beginning of year 1 to more than €65 at the end of year 3.

If the share price is above €65 at the end of year 3, the share options can be exercised at any time during the next seven years, i.e. by the end of year 10. The entity applies a binomial option pricing model (see 5 below), which takes into account the possibility that the share price will exceed €65 at the end of year 3 (and hence the share options become exercisable) and the possibility that the share price will not exceed €65 at the end of year 3 (and hence the options will be forfeited). It estimates the fair value of the share options with this market condition to be €24 per option.

IFRS 2 requires the entity to recognise the services received from a counterparty who satisfies all other vesting conditions (e.g. services received from an employee who remains in service for the specified service period), irrespective of whether that market condition is satisfied. It makes no difference whether the share price target is achieved, since the possibility that the share price target might not be achieved has already been taken into account when estimating the fair value of the share options at grant date. However, the options are subject to another condition (i.e. continuous employment) and the cost recognised should be adjusted to reflect the ongoing best estimate of employee retention.

By the end of the first year, seven employees have left and the entity expects that a total of 20 employees will leave by the end of year 3, so that 80 employees will have satisfied all conditions other than the market condition (i.e. continuous employment).

By the end of the second year, a further five employees have left. The entity now expects only three more employees will leave during year 3, and therefore expects a total of 15 employees will have left during the three-year period, so that 85 employees will have satisfied all conditions other than the market condition.

By the end of year 3, a further seven employees have left. Hence, 19 employees have left during the three-year period, and 81 employees remain. However, the share price is only €60, so that the options cannot be exercised. Nevertheless, as all conditions other than the market condition have been satisfied, a cumulative cost is recorded as if the options had fully vested in 81 employees.

The entity will recognise the following amounts during the vesting period for services received as consideration for the options (which in economic reality do not vest).

Year	Calculation of cumulative expense	Cumulative expense (€)	Expense for period (€)
1	80 employees × 1,000 options × €24 × 1/3	640,000	640,000
2	85 employees × 1,000 options × €24 × 2/3	1,360,000	720,000
3	81 employees × 1,000 options × €24	1,944,000	584,000

4.7.4 Transactions with variable vesting periods due to market conditions

Where a transaction has a variable vesting period due to a market condition, a best estimate of the most likely vesting period will have been used in determining the fair value of the transaction at the date of grant. IFRS 2 requires the expense for that transaction to be recognised over a vesting period consistent with the assumptions used in the valuation, without any subsequent revision. [67]

This may mean, for example, that, if the actual vesting period for an employee share option award turns out to be longer than that anticipated for the purposes of the initial valuation, a cost is nevertheless recorded in respect of all employees who reach the end of the *anticipated* vesting period, even if they do not reach the end of the *actual* vesting period, as shown by Example 29.12, which is based on Example 6 in the implementation guidance in IFRS 2.

Example 29.12: Award with market condition and variable vesting period

At the beginning of year 1, an entity grants 10,000 share options with a ten-year life to each of ten senior executives. The share options will vest and become exercisable immediately if and when the entity's share price increases from £50 to £70, provided that the executive remains in service until the share price target is achieved.

The entity applies a binomial option pricing model, which takes into account the possibility that the share price target will be achieved during the ten-year life of the options, and the possibility that the target will not be achieved. The entity estimates that the fair value of the share options at grant date is £25 per option. From the option pricing model, the entity determines that the most likely vesting period is five years. The entity also estimates that two executives will have left by the end of year 5, and therefore expects that 80,000 share options (10,000 share options × 8 executives) will vest at the end of year 5.

Throughout years 1 to 4, the entity continues to estimate that a total of two executives will leave by the end of year 5. However, in total three executives leave, one in each of years 3, 4 and 5. The share price target is achieved at the end of year 6. Another executive leaves during year 6, before the share price target is achieved.

Paragraph 15 of IFRS 2 requires the entity to recognise the services received over the expected vesting period, as estimated at grant date, and also requires the entity not to revise that estimate. Therefore, the entity recognises the services received from the executives over years 1–5. Hence, the transaction amount is ultimately based on 70,000 share options (10,000 share options × 7 executives who remain in service at the end of year 5). Although another executive left during year 6, no adjustment is made, because the executive had already completed the expected vesting period of 5 years.

The entity will recognise the following amounts during the initial expected 5-year vesting period for services received as consideration for the options.

Year	Calculation of cumulative expense	Cumulative expense (£)	Expense for period (£)
1	8 employees × 10,000 options × £25 × 1/5	400,000	400,000
2	8 employees × 10,000 options × £25 × 2/5	800,000	400,000
3	8 employees × 10,000 options × £25 × 3/5	1,200,000	400,000
4	8 employees × 10,000 options × £25 × 4/5	1,600,000	400,000
5	7 employees × 10,000 options × £25	1,750,000	150,000

4.8   Reload features

A 'reload feature' is a feature in a share option that provides for an automatic grant of additional share options (reload options) whenever the option holder exercises previously granted options using the entity's shares, rather than cash, to satisfy the exercise price.[68]

IFRS 2 requires reload features to be ignored in the initial valuation of options that contain them. Instead any reload option should be treated as if it were a newly granted option at the time that it is granted.[69]

4.9   Accounting after vesting

Once a share-settled transaction has vested (or, in the case of a transaction subject to one or more market conditions, has been treated as vested under IFRS 2 – see 4.7 above), no further accounting entries are made to reverse the cost already charged, even if the instruments that are the subject of the transaction are subsequently forfeited or, in the case of options, are not exercised. However, the entity may make a transfer between different components of equity.[70] For example, an entity's accounting policy might be to credit all amounts recorded for share-based transactions to a separate reserve such as 'Shares to be issued'. Where an award lapses after vesting, it would then be appropriate to transfer an amount equivalent to the cumulative cost for the lapsed award from 'Shares to be issued' to another component of equity.

This prohibition against 'truing up' (i.e. reversing the cost of vested awards that lapse) is controversial, since it has the effect that a cost is still recognised for options that are never exercised, typically because they are 'underwater' (i.e. the current share price is lower than the option exercise price), so that it is not in the holder's interest to exercise the option. Some commentators have observed that an accounting standard that can result in an accounting cost for non-dilutive options does not meet the needs of those shareholders whose concerns about dilution were the catalyst for the share-based payment project in the first place (see 1 above).

The IASB counters such objections by pointing out that the treatment in IFRS 2 is perfectly consistent with that for other 'contingent' equity instruments, such as warrants, that ultimately result in no share ownership. Where an entity issues warrants that lapse unexercised, the entity recognises no gain under IFRS. The IASB notes that a gain could only be recognised under the *Framework* if the warrants were originally recognised as liabilities, and not as equity, under the *Framework*.[71]

However, some would contend that the *Framework* is not as clear on this matter as the IASB suggests. It would be common ground that, under the *Framework*, the proceeds of an issue of warrants gives rise to an asset (cash) and equity rather than a liability. Warrants would be classified as a liability only if (unusually) they are refundable or require the entity to issue a variable rather than a fixed number of shares. On the other hand, the *Framework* essentially defines income as increases in equity, other than those relating to contributions from equity participants.[72] Some argue that this definition does not exclude from income all transactions initially accounted for in equity, but only those arising from 'contributions from equity participants'. On this view, there is a debate to be had as to whether the proceeds of lapsed warrants should be:

- considered to be 'contributions from equity participants' simply by virtue of the fact that they do not constitute a financial liability and were therefore originally accounted for (by default) as equity, or

- considered not to be 'contributions from equity participants', since as a matter of law and economic substance the holders of warrants have no right to participate in equity until and unless the warrants are exercised.

4.10   Modification, cancellation and settlement

4.10.1   *Background*

It is quite common for equity instruments to be modified or cancelled before or after vesting. Typically this is done where the conditions for an award have become so onerous as to be virtually unachievable, or (in the case of an option) where the share price has fallen so far below the exercise price of an option that it is unlikely that the option will ever be 'in the money' to the holder during its life. In such cases, an entity may take the view that such equity awards are so unattainable as to have little or no motivational effect, and accordingly replace them with less onerous alternatives. Conversely, and more rarely, an entity may make the terms of a share award more onerous (possibly because of shareholder concern that targets are insufficiently demanding). In addition an entity may 'settle' an award, i.e. cancel it in return for cash or other consideration.

IFRS 2 contains detailed provisions for modification, cancellation and settlement. Whilst these provisions (like the summary of them below) are framed in terms of share-based-payment transactions with employees they apply to transactions with parties other than employees that are measured by reference to the fair value of the equity instruments granted (see 4.3 above). In that case, however, all references to 'grant date' should be taken as references to that date on which the third party supplied goods or rendered service.[73]

The basic principles of the rules for modification, cancellation and settlement, which are discussed in more detail at 4.10.3 and 4.10.4 below, can be summarised as follows.

- As a minimum, the entity must recognise the amount that would have been recognised for the award if it remained in place on its original terms (i.e. subject to adjustments for vesting conditions other than market conditions, as summarised in 4.6 above).

- If the value of an award to an employee is reduced (e.g. by reducing the number of equity instruments subject to the award or, in the case of an option, by increasing the exercise price), there is no reduction in the cost recognised in the income statement.[74]

- However, where the effect of the modification, cancellation or settlement is to increase the value of the award to an employee (e.g. by increasing the number of equity instruments subject to the award or, in the case of an option, by reducing the exercise price), the incremental fair value must be recognised as a cost. The incremental fair value is the difference between the fair value of the original award and that of the modified award, both measured at the date of modification.[75]

4.10.2 Valuation requirements

These provisions have the important practical consequence that, when an entity modifies, cancels or settles an award, it must obtain a fair value not only for the modified award, but also for the original award, updated to the date of modification. If the award had not been modified, there would have been no need to obtain a valuation for the original award after the date of grant.

Some argue that, when an award has been modified, and certainly when it has been cancelled altogether, it no longer exists and that it is therefore not appropriate to recognise any cost for it. However, such a view is consistent with a vesting date measurement model rather than with the grant/service date measurement model of IFRS 2. The value of an award at grant date or service date cannot be changed by subsequent events.

Another reason given for the approach in IFRS 2 is that if entities were able not to recognise the cost of modified or cancelled options they would in effect be able to apply a selective form of 'truing up', whereby options that increased in value after grant would remain 'frozen' at their grant date valuation under the general principles of IFRS 2, whilst options that decreased in value could be modified or cancelled after grant date and credit taken for the fall in value.[76]

A   Impact of modifications of performance conditions

Whilst any modification of a performance condition clearly has an impact on the value of an award, it may have no direct effect on the value of the award for the purposes of IFRS 2. This is because, as discussed at 4.6 and 4.7 above, whilst a market-related performance condition is taken into account in valuing an award, a non market-related condition is not. Accordingly, by implication, a change to a non market-related performance condition will not necessarily affect the expense recognised for the award under IFRS 2.

For example, if an award is contingent upon sales of a given number of units and the number of units required to be sold is decreased, the value of the award is clearly increased. However, as the performance condition was never relevant to the original determination of the value of the award, it is not an incremental fair value required to be accounted for by IFRS 2.

If an award is modified by changing the service period, the situation is somewhat more complex. Whilst a service condition does not of itself change the fair value of the award for the purposes of IFRS 2, a change in service period may well indirectly change the life of the award, which is relevant to its value (see 5.2.2. below). For example, if an award was previously subject to a three-year service period (and exercisable during a two week period immediately thereafter) and its terms are changed such that it now has a two-year vesting period (and again exercisable during a two week period thereafter), the value of the award will change, because its life has been reduced by one year. Similar consideration apply where performance conditions are modified in such as way as to alter the anticipated vesting date.

4.10.3 *Modification*

When an award is modified, the entity must as a minimum recognise the cost of the original award as if it had not been modified (i.e. at the original grant date fair value, spread over the original vesting period, and subject to the original vesting conditions).[77]

In addition, a further cost must be recognised for any modifications that increase the fair value of the award. This additional cost is spread over the period from the date of modification until the vesting date of the modified options, which might not be the same as that of the original award. Where a modification is made after the original vesting period has expired, and is subject to no further vesting conditions, any incremental fair value should be recognised immediately.[78]

Whether a modification increases or decreases the fair value of an award is determined as at the date of modification, as illustrated by Example 29.13.[79]

Example 29.13: Does a modification increase or decrease the value of an award?

On 1 January 2005 an entity grants two executives, A and B, a number of options worth $100 each.

On 1 January 2006, A's options are modified such that they have a fair value of $85, their current fair value being $80. This is treated as an increase in fair value of $5 (even though the modified award is worth less than the original award when first granted). Therefore an additional $5 of expense would be recognised in respect of A's options.

On 1 January 2007, B's options are modified such that they have a fair value of $120, their current fair value being $125. This is treated as reduction in fair value of $5 (even though the modified award is worth more than the original award when first granted). There is no change to the expense recognised for B's options.

This treatment ensures that movements in the fair value of the original award are not reflected in the entity's income statement, consistent with the treatment of other equity instruments under IFRS.

IFRS 2 provides further detailed guidance on this requirement as follows.

A   Modifications that increase the value of an award

I   Increase in fair value of equity instruments granted

If the modification increases the fair value of the equity instruments granted, (e.g. by reducing the exercise price or changing the exercise period), the incremental fair value, measured at the date of modification, must be recognised over the period from the date of modification to the date of vesting for the modified instruments, as illustrated in Example 29.14 below.[80]

Example 29.14:   Award modified by repricing

At the beginning of year 1, an entity grants 100 share options to each of its 500 employees. Each grant is conditional upon the employee remaining in service over the next three years. The entity estimates that the fair value of each option is €15.

By the end of year 1, the entity's share price has dropped, and the entity reprices its share options, and the repriced share options vest at the end of year 3. The entity estimates that, at the date of repricing, the fair value of each of the original share options granted (i.e. before taking into account the repricing) is €5 and that the fair value of each repriced share option is €8.

40 employees leave during year 1. The entity estimates that a further 70 employees will leave during years 2 and 3, so that there will be 390 employees at the end of year 3 (500-40-70).

During year 2, a further 35 employees leave, and the entity estimates that a further 30 employees will leave during year 3, so that there will be 395 employees at the end of year 3 (500-40-35-30).

During year 3, a total of 28 employees leave, and hence a total of 103 employees ceased employment during the original 3-year vesting period, so that, for the remaining 397 employees, the original share options vest at the end of year 3.

IFRS 2 requires the entity to recognise

- the cost of the original award at grant date (€15 per option) over a three year vesting period beginning at the start of year 1, plus

- the incremental fair value of the repriced options at repricing date (€3 per option, being the €8 fair value of each repriced option less the €5 fair value of the original option) over a two-year vesting period beginning at the date of repricing (end of year one).

This would be calculated as follows.

Year	Calculation of cumulative expense Original award (a)	Modified award (b)	Cumulative expense (€) (a+b)	Expense for period (€)
1	390 employees × 100 options × €15 × 1/3		195,000	195,000
2	395 employees × 100 options × €15 × 2/3	395 employees × 100 options × €3 × 1/2	454,250	259,250
3	397 employees × 100 options × €15	397 employees × 100 options × €3	714,600	260,350

In effect, IFRS 2 treats the original award and the incremental value of the modified award as if they were two separate awards. It should be noted that if the same economic result were delivered by cancelling the original award altogether and granting a new award on terms identical to those of the modified award in Example 29.14, there would be a different IFRS 2 charge because of the different rules for cancellation of awards (see Example 29.20 at 4.10.4 D II below).

A similar treatment to that in Example 29.14 above is adopted where the fair value of an award subject to a market condition has its value increased by the removal or mitigation of the condition.[81] Where a condition other than a market condition is changed, the treatment set out in III below is adopted.

II   *Increase in number of equity instruments granted*

If the modification increases the number of equity instruments granted, the fair value of the additional instruments, measured at the date of modification, must be recognised over the period from the date of modification to the date of vesting for the modified instruments. If there is no further vesting period for the modified options, the incremental cost should be recognised immediately.[82]

III   *Removal or mitigation of non-market related vesting conditions*

Where a vesting condition, other than a market condition, is modified, the modified vesting condition should be taken into account when applying the general requirements of IFRS 2 as discussed in 4.5 to 4.7 above[83] – in other words, the entity would continuously estimate the number of awards likely to vest and/or the vesting period. This is consistent with the general principle of IFRS 2 that vesting conditions, other than market conditions, are not factored into the valuation of awards, but are reflected by recognising a cost for those instruments that ultimately vest pursuant to those conditions. See also the discussion at 4.10.2 A above.

IFRS 2 does not provide an example that addresses this point specifically, but we assume that something along the lines of Example 29.15 below is intended.

Example 29.15:   Modification of non-market performance condition in employee's favour

At the beginning of year 1, the entity grants 1,000 share options to each member of its sales team, with exercise conditional upon the employee's remaining in the entity's employment for three years, and the team selling more than 50,000 units of a particular product over the three-year period. The fair value of the share options is £15 per option at the date of grant.

At the end of year 1, the entity estimates that a total of 48,000 units will be sold, and accordingly records no cost for the award in year one.

During year 2, there is so severe a downturn in trading conditions that the entity believes that the sales target is too demanding to have any motivational effect, and reduces the target to 30,000 units, which it believes is achievable. It also expects 14 members of the sales team to remain in employment throughout the three-year performance period. It therefore records an expense in year 2 of £140,000 (£15 × 14 employees × 1,000 options × 2/3). This cost is based on the originally assessed value of the award (i.e. £15) since the performance condition was never factored into the original valuation, such that any change in performance condition likewise has no effect on the valuation.

By the end of year 3, the entity has sold 35,000 units, and the share options vest. Twelve members of the sales team have remained in service for the three-year period. The entity would therefore recognise a total cost of £180,000 (12 employees × 1,000 options × £15), giving an additional cost in year 3 of £40,000 (total charge £180,000, less £40,000 charged in year 2).

The difference between the accounting consequences for different methods of enhancing an award could cause confusion in some cases. For example, it may sometimes not be clear whether an award has been modified by increasing the number of equity instruments or by lowering the performance hurdles, as illustrated in Example 29.16.

Example 29.16:   Increase in number of equity instruments or modification of vesting conditions?

An entity grants a performance-related award which provides for different numbers of options to vest after 3 years, depending on different performance hurdles as follows.

Profit growth	Number of options
5%-10%	100
over 10%-15%	200
over 15%	300

During the vesting period, the entity concludes that the criteria are too demanding and modifies them as follows.

Profit growth	Number of options
5%-10%	200
over 10%	300

This raises the issue of whether the entity has changed:

(a)   the performance conditions for the vesting of 200 or 300 options; or

(b)   the number of equity instruments awarded for achieving 5%-10% or over 10% growth.

In our view, the reality is that the change is to the performance conditions for the vesting of 200 or 300 options, and should therefore be dealt with as in III, rather than II, above. Suppose, however, that the conditions had been modified as follows.

Profit growth	Number of options
5%-10%	200
over 10%-15%	300
over 15%	400

In that case, there has clearly been an increase in the number of equity instruments subject to an award for in increase of over 15% growth, which would have to be accounted for as such (i.e. under II, rather than III, above). In such a case, it might seem more appropriate to deal with the changes to the lower bands as changes to the number of shares awarded rather than changes to the performance conditions.

B   Modifications that decrease the value of an award

I   Decrease in fair value of equity instruments granted

If the modification decreases the fair value of the equity instruments (e.g. by increasing the exercise price or reducing the exercise period), the decrease in value is effectively ignored and the entity continues to recognise a cost for services as if the awards had not been modified.[84] Reductions in the fair value of an award by the addition of a market condition or by making an existing market condition more onerous are similarly ignored.[85]

II   Decrease in number of equity instruments granted

If the modification reduces the number of equity instruments granted, IFRS 2 requires the reduction to be treated as a cancellation (see 4.10.4 below).[86] Essentially this has the effect that any previously unrecognised cost of the cancelled shares is immediately recognised in full, whereas the cost of an award whose value is reduced by other means continues to be spread in full over the remaining vesting period.

III *Additional or more onerous non-market related vesting conditions*

Where a vesting condition, other than a market condition, is modified in a manner not beneficial to the employee, again it is ignored and a cost recognised as if the original award had not been modified, as shown by Example 29.17.[87]

Example 29.17: Award modified by changing performance conditions

At the beginning of year 1, the entity grants 1,000 share options to each member of its sales team, conditional upon the employee remaining in the entity's employment for three years, and the team selling more than 50,000 units of a particular product over the three-year period. The fair value of the share options is £15 per option at the date of grant. During year 2, the entity believes that the sales target is insufficiently demanding and increases it to 100,000 units. By the end of year 3, the entity has sold 55,000 units, and the share options are forfeited. Twelve members of the sales team have remained in service for the three-year period.

On the basis that the original target would have been met, and twelve employees would have been eligible for awards, the entity would recognise a total cost of £180,000 (12 employees × 1,000 options × £15). The cumulative cost in years 1 and 2 would, as in the examples above, reflect the entity's best estimate of the *original* 50,000 unit sales target being achieved at the end of year 3. If, conversely, sales of only 49,000 units had been achieved, any cost booked for the award in years 1 and 2 would have been reversed in year 3, since the original target of 50,000 units would not have been met.

C *Modifications with altered vesting period*

As noted above, where an award is modified so that its value increases, IFRS 2 requires the grant date fair value of the unmodified award to continue to be recognised over the original vesting period, even where the vesting period of the modified award is different. This appears to have the effect that an expense may be recognised for awards that do not actually vest, as illustrated by Example 29.18 (which is based on Example 29.14 above).

Example 29.18: Award modified by repricing and extension of vesting period

At the beginning of year 1, an entity grants 100 share options to each of its 500 employees, with vesting conditional upon the employee remaining in service over the next three years. The entity estimates that the fair value of each option is €15.

By the end of year 1, the entity's share price has dropped, and the entity reprices its share options. The repriced share options vest at the end of year 4. The entity estimates that, at the date of repricing, the fair value of each of the original share options granted (i.e. before taking into account the repricing) is €5 and that the fair value of each repriced share option is €7.

40 employees leave during year 1. The entity estimates that a further 70 employees will leave during years 2 and 3, and a further 25 employees during year 4, such that there will be 390 employees at the end of year 3 (500-40-70) and 365 (500-40-70-25) at the end of year 4.

During year 2, a further 35 employees leave, and the entity estimates that a further 30 employees will leave during year 3 and 30 more in year 4, such that there will be 395 employees at the end of year 3 (500-40-35-30) and 365 (500-40-35-30-30) at the end of year 4.

During year 3, a total of 28 employees leave, and hence a total of 103 employees ceased employment during the original 3-year vesting period, so that, for the remaining 397 employees, the original share options would have vested at the end of year 3. The entity now estimates that only a further 20 employees will leave during year 4, leaving 377 at the end of year 4. In fact 25 employees leave, so that 372 satisfy the criteria for the modified options at the end of year 4.

In our view IFRS 2 requires the entity to recognise:

- the cost of the original award at grant date (€15 per option) over a three year vesting period beginning at the start of year 1, based on the ongoing best estimate of, and ultimately the actual, number of employees at the end of the *original 3-year* vesting period;

- the incremental fair value of the repriced options at repricing date (€2 per option, being the €7 fair value of each repriced option less the €5 fair value of the original option) over a three-year vesting period beginning at the date of repricing (*end* of year one), but based on the ongoing best estimate of, and ultimately the actual, number of employees at the end of the *modified 4-year* vesting period.

This would be calculated as follows.

Year	Calculation of cumulative expense		Cumulative expense (£)	Expense for period (£)
	Original award	Modified award		
1	390 employees × 100 options × €15 × 1/3		195,000	195,000
2	395 employees × 100 options × €15 × 2/3	365 employees × 100 options × €2 × 1/3	419,333	224,333
3	397 employees × 100 options × €15	377 employees × 100 options × €2 × 2/3	645,767	226,434
4	397 employees × 100 options × €15	372 employees × 100 options × €2	669,900	24,133

It may seem strange that a cost is being recognised for the original award in respect of the 25 employees who leave during year 4, who are never entitled to anything. However, in our view, this is consistent with:

- the overall requirement of IFRS 2 that the minimum cost of a modified award should be the cost that would have recognised if the award had not been modified; and

- IG Example 8 in IFRS 2 (the substance of which is reproduced in Example 29.17 above) where an expense is clearly required to be recognised to the extent that the original performance conditions would have been met if the award had not been modified.

Moreover, as Examples 29.17 and 29.18 illustrate, the rule in IFRS 2 requiring recognition of a minimum expense for a modified award (i.e. as if the original award had remained in place) applies irrespective of whether the modification results in an award becomes less valuable to the employee (as in Example 29.17) or more valuable to the employee (as in Example 29.18).

4.10.4 Cancellation and settlement

Where an award is cancelled or settled (i.e. cancelled with some form of compensation), other than by forfeiture for failure to satisfy the vesting conditions:

(a) if the cancellation or settlement occurs during the vesting period, it is treated as an acceleration of vesting, and the entity recognises immediately the amount that would otherwise have been recognised for services over the vesting period;

(b) any compensation paid up to the fair value of the award at cancellation or settlement date (whether before or after vesting) is accounted for as a deduction from equity, as being equivalent to the redemption of an equity instrument;

(c)   any compensation paid in excess of the fair value of the award at cancellation or settlement date (whether before or after vesting) is accounted for as an expense in the income statement; and

(d)   if the entity grants new equity instruments during the vesting period and, on the date that they are granted, identifies them as replacing the cancelled or settled instruments, the entity is required to account for the new equity instruments as if they were a modification of the cancelled or settled award. Otherwise it accounts for the new instruments as an entirely new award.[88]

The treatment of the cancelled or settled award in (a) above is similar, in terms of the income statement, to the result that would have occurred if:

- the fair value of the equity instruments issued had been recorded in full at grant date with a corresponding debit to a prepayment for 'services to be rendered';

- the prepayment were written off on a periodic basis until cancellation or settlement; and

- any remaining prepayment at the date of cancellation or settlement were written off in full.

It should be noted that the calculation of any additional expense in (b) above depends on the fair value of the award at the date of cancellation or settlement, not on the cumulative expense already charged. This has the important practical consequence that, when an entity pays compensation on cancellation or settlement of an award, it must obtain a fair value for the original award, updated to the date of cancellation or settlement. If the award had not been cancelled or settled, there would have been no need to obtain a valuation for the original award after the date of grant.

These requirements raise some further detailed issues of interpretation on a number of areas, as follows:

- the distinction between 'cancellation' and 'forfeiture' (see A below);

- the distinction between 'cancellation' and 'modification' (see B below);

- some detailed aspects of the accounting treatment of a cancellation (see C below); and

- replacement options (see D below).

A   Distinction between cancellation and forfeiture

The above provisions of IFRS 2 apply when a grant of equity instruments award is cancelled or settled 'other than a grant cancelled by forfeiture when the vesting conditions are not satisfied'.[89] The significance of this is that the terms of many share-based awards provide that they are, or can be, cancelled on forfeiture. In such cases, should the entity apply the rules in IFRS 2 for forfeiture (i.e. reversing any cost already recognised, subject to the exceptions for market conditions) or the very different rules for cancellation (i.e. immediately recognising any cost not yet booked)? By referring to a cancellation 'other than ... by forfeiture when the vesting conditions are not satisfied', IFRS 2 is clarifying that in such circumstances the entity should apply the rules for forfeiture.

In other cases, there may be more room for debate as to whether cancellation or forfeiture has occurred. For example, if an entity cancels an employee's options for gross misconduct, and the scheme rules explicitly provide for such cancellation, then the forfeiture rules would apply (because the employee has failed to satisfy the implied vesting condition of refraining from such gross misconduct). If there were no such express provision in the scheme, it might be argued that the employee has in fact done nothing to merit forfeiture of the options, such that the rules for cancellation apply. On the other hand, it could be equally (and, in our view, more realistically) argued that refraining from gross misconduct is an implied term of any employment contract, such that the forfeiture provisions should be applied in this case also.

In some jurisdictions, employee share option schemes are linked to a savings contract. For example, the employee may be required to contribute, during the vesting period of the options, a certain percentage of pay to a fund, which is then used to exercise the option. Often the employee is entitled to withdraw from the savings contract before vesting, but at the price of losing the entitlement to exercise the options, which are then cancelled. Again, in our view, IFRS 2 requires this to be accounted for as a forfeiture, not a cancellation, since the employee has failed to fulfil the implied vesting condition of continuing to make savings during the vesting period.

B   Distinction between cancellation and modification

One general issue raised by IFRS 2 is where the boundary lies between 'modification' of an award in the entity's favour and outright cancellation of the award. As a matter of legal form, the difference is obvious. However, if an entity were to modify an award in such a way that there was no realistic change of it ever vesting (for example, by introducing a requirement that the share price increase 1,000,000 times by vesting date), some might argue that this amounts to a *de facto* cancellation of the award. The significance of the distinction is that, whereas the cost of a 'modified' award continues to be recognised on a periodic basis (see 4.10.3 above), the remaining cost of a cancelled award is recognised immediately (see above).

C   The required accounting treatment

The basic accounting treatment for a cancellation and settlement is illustrated in Example 29.19 below.

Example 29.19: Cancellation and settlement of an option

At the start of year 1 an entity grants 300 options each to a group of 500 employees on condition that they remain in employment for three years. Each option is determined to have a fair value of $10.

At the end of year 1, the entity believes that 470 employees will still be in employment at the end of year 3, and accordingly recognises a cost for the award in year 1 of $470,000 (470 employees × 300 options × $10 × 1/3).

At the end of year 2, the entity's share price has suffered a decline which the entity does not expect to have reversed by the end of year 3, such that the options, while still 'in the money' now have a fair value of only $6. Moreover, the entity is under pressure from major shareholders to end option schemes with no performance criteria other than continuing employment.

Accordingly, the entity cancels the options and in compensation pays the 482 employees remaining at the end of year 2 $6.50 per option cancelled, a total payment of $939,900 (482 employees × 300 options × $6.50).

IFRS 2 first requires the entity to record a cost as if the options had vested immediately. The total cumulative cost for the award must be $1,446,000 (482 employees × 300 options × $10). $470,000 was recognised in year 1, so that an additional cost of $976,000 is recognised.

As regards the compensation payment, the fair value of the awards cancelled is $867,600 (482 employees × 300 options × $6.00). Accordingly, $867,600 of the payment is accounted for as a deduction from equity, with the remaining payment in excess of fair value, $72,300, charged to the income statement.

The net effect of this is that an award that ultimately results in a cash payment to employees of $939,900 (i.e. $6.50 per option) has resulted in a total charge to the income statement of $1,518,300 (i.e. $10.50 per option, representing grant date fair value $10 + $6.50 compensation payment – $6.00 cancellation date fair value).

Whilst we believe that Example 29.19 illustrates the treatment for cancellation required by IFRS 2, there is an ambiguity in the drafting of paragraph 28(a) of the standard, which reads as follows:

> 'the entity shall account for the cancellation or settlement as an acceleration of vesting, and shall therefore recognise immediately the amount that would otherwise have been recognised for services received over the remainder of the vesting period.'

The words 'account for the cancellation or settlement as an acceleration of vesting' imply the accounting treatment in Example 29.19 above – in other words the accounting must assume that the award vested in the 482 employees remaining at the end of year 2. However, the words 'the amount that would otherwise have been recognised for services received over the remainder of the vesting period' might suggest that either:

(a)   a further adjustment is needed so as to take account of expected leavers in year 3; or even

(b)   in addition, the accounting should in fact be revisited at the end of year 3 and an adjustment made so that that the final cumulative expense reflects the actual number of awards that would have vested at the end of year 3 but for the cancellation.

In our view, this is no more than an unfortunate drafting slip, and it would be contrary to the overall principle of the cancellation rules in IFRS 2 either to calculate the charge at cancellation by reference to future anticipated leavers or to revisit the charge at the end of year 3.

It should also be noted that IFRS 2 creates an accounting arbitrage between an award that is 'out of the money' but not cancelled (which continues to be spread over the remaining period to vesting) and one which is formally cancelled (the cost of which is recognised immediately). Entities might well prefer to opt for cancellation so as to create a 'one off' charge to earnings rather than continue to show, particularly during difficult trading periods, significant periodic costs for options that no longer have any real value.

D   Replacement options

The required accounting treatment of replacement options, whilst generally clear, nevertheless raises some issues of interpretation.

I   Designation of option as replacement option

Whether or not an option is a 'replacement' option (and therefore recognised at only its incremental, not its full, fair value) is determined by whether or not the entity designates it as such on the date that it is granted. In other words, the accounting treatment effectively hinges on management intent, notwithstanding the IASB's systematic exclusion of management intent from many other areas of financial reporting. The Basis for Conclusions does not really explain the reason for this approach, which is hard to reconcile with the fact that the value of an option is clearly unaffected by whether, or when, the entity declares it to be a 'replacement' option for the purposes of IFRS 2.

Entities need to ensure that designation occurs on grant date as defined by IFRS 2 (see 4.2.2 A above). For example, if an entity writes to an employee on 15 March 2005 notifying the employee of its intention to procure that the remuneration committee will grant replacement options at its meeting on 15 May 2005, such notification (although formal and in writing) may not meet IFRS 2's requirement for designation at grant date (i.e. 15 May 2005).

II   Incremental fair value of replacement option

Where an option is designated as a replacement option, it must be recognised, over its vesting period, at its incremental fair value. This is the difference between the fair value of the replacement option and the 'net fair value' of the cancelled or settled option, both measured at the date on which the replacement options are granted. The net fair value of the cancelled or settled option is the fair value of the option, immediately before cancellation, less any compensation payment that is accounted for as a deduction from equity.[90] Thus the 'net fair value' of the original option can never be less than zero (since any compensation payment in excess of the fair value of the cancelled option would be accounted for in the income statement, not in equity – see Example 29.19 above).

There is a curious accounting arbitrage between the treatment of replacement options and that of modified options, as shown by Example 29.20 below.

Example 29.20:   Accounting arbitrage between modification and cancellation of award

At the beginning of year 1, an entity grants 100 share options to each of its 500 employees. Each grant is conditional upon the employee remaining in service over the next three years. The entity estimates that the fair value of each option is €15.

By the end of year 1, 40 employees have left and the entity's share price has dropped. The entity cancels the existing options and issues options which it identifies as replacement options, which also vest at the end of year 3. The entity estimates that, at the date of cancellation, the fair value of each of the original share options granted is €5 and that the fair value of each replacement share option is €8.

During year 2, a further 35 employees leave, and the entity estimates that a further 30 employees will leave during year 3, so that there will be 395 employees at the end of year 3 (500-40-35-30).

During year 3, a total of 28 employees leave, and hence a total of 103 employees ceased employment during the original 3-year vesting period, so that, for the remaining 397 employees, the replacement share options vest at the end of year 3.

IFRS 2 requires the entity to recognise:

- the entire cost of the original options at the end of year 1 (since cancellation has the effect that they are treated as vesting at that date), based on the 460 employees at that date,

- the incremental fair value of the replacement options at repricing date (€3 per option, being the €8 fair value of each replacement option less the €5 fair value of the cancelled option) over a two-year vesting period beginning at the date of cancellation (end of year one), based on the (at first estimated and then actual) number of employees at the end of year 3.

This would be calculated as follows.

Year	Calculation of cumulative expense Original award	Replacement award	Cumulative expense (£)	Expense for period (£)
1	460 employees × 100 options × €15	–	690,000	690,000
2	460 employees × 100 options × €15	395 employees × 100 options × €3 × 1/2	749,250	59,250
3	460 employees × 100 options × €15	397 employees × 100 options × €3	809,100	59,850

The facts in this example are identical with those in Example 29.14 at 4.10.3 above, except that whereas in Example 29.20 the original options are cancelled and replaced with new ones with a fair value of €8, in Example 29.14 the original options are modified so that they have a fair value of €8. From the point of view of the holder, these positions are clearly economically equivalent. However, under IFRS 2, they result in a significant difference in both the total cost and its periodic recognition.

This is because the modified option in Example 29.14 continues to be expensed over the original vesting period, so that the cumulative cost is based on the number of employees at the original vesting date, whereas in Example 29.20 the hitherto unrecognised cost of the cancelled option is expensed in full at cancellation, based on the number of employees at the cancellation date. Under either scenario, however, the total, and the periodic allocation, of the incremental cost arising on modification/replacement remains the same.

This inconsistency suggests to us that the provisions in IFRS 2 for replacement options were probably thought of by the IASB as a concession from the basic principle that cancellation should trigger a full recognition of previously unrecognised cost.

III   *Replacement options issued after original options vested*

The rules for replacement options summarised at 4.10.4 (d) above apply 'if the entity cancels or settles a grant of equity instruments during the vesting period ...'.[91] This begs the question of the required treatment for a replacement option granted after the original option has vested. There is of course no question of accelerating the cost of the cancelled award in such cases, as it has already been recognised during the vesting period. The issue is rather the treatment of the new award itself. Whilst IFRS 2 does not explicitly address this point, it appears that such a replacement option should be treated as if it were a completely new award. In other words, its full fair value should be recognised immediately or, if there are any vesting conditions for the replacement option, over its vesting period.

By contrast the rules for modification of awards discussed in 4.10.3 above apply whether the award has vested or not. Paragraphs 26 and 27 of IFRS 2 (modifications) are not restricted to events 'during the vesting period' in contrast to paragraph 28 (cancellation and settlement, including replacement awards) which is restricted to events 'during the vesting period'.

This has the effect that the accounting cost of modifying an already vested award (i.e. the incremental fair value of the modified award) is lower that that of cancelling and replacing it, which requires the full fair value of the new award to be expensed.

5   DETERMINING THE FAIR VALUE OF EQUITY INSTRUMENTS

This is a key issue for the implementation of IFRS 2, on which the IASB provides some guidance in Appendix B to the standard, which is summarised below. Whilst the guidance is framed in terms of awards to employees which are valued at grant date, many of the general principles would apply equally to awards valued at service date.[92]

The discussion below does not discuss option valuation techniques such as the Black-Scholes-Merton formula or a binomial model, for which readers should refer to specialist finance publications.

5.1   Shares

Shares granted to employees should be valued at their market price (where one exists) or an estimated market value (where the shares are not publicly traded), in either case adjusted to take account of the terms and conditions on which the shares were granted, other than vesting conditions that IFRS 2 requires to be excluded in determining the grant date fair value (see 4.6 above).[93]

For example, the valuation should take account of restrictions on the employee's right:

- to receive dividends in the vesting period (see 5.1.1 below); or
- to transfer shares after vesting, but only to the extent that such restrictions would affect the price that a knowledgeable and willing market participant would pay for the shares. Where the shares are traded in a deep and liquid market, the effect may be negligible.

The valuation should not, however, take account of restrictions that arise directly from the existence of the vesting conditions (such as the right to transfer shares during the vesting period).[94]

5.1.1 Impact of expected dividends

Whether dividends should be taken into account in measuring the fair value of shares depends on whether the counterparty is entitled to dividends or dividend equivalents (which might be paid in cash) during the vesting period. When the grant date fair value of shares granted to employees is estimated, no adjustment is required if the employees are entitled to receive dividends during the vesting period (as they are in no different position in this respect than if they already held shares). However, the valuation should be reduced by the present value of dividends expected to be paid during the vesting period.[95] The basis on which expected dividends during the vesting period might be determined is discussed in the context of the impact of expected dividends on the fair value of share options at 5.2.4 below.

5.2 Share options

Where, as will almost invariably be the case, there are no traded options over the entity's equity instruments that mirror the terms of share options granted to employees, the fair value of options granted should be estimated using an option pricing model. The entity must consider all factors that would be considered by knowledgeable and willing market participants in selecting a model.[96]

IFRS 2 states that the Black-Scholes-Merton formula may not be appropriate for long-lived options which can be exercised before the end of their life and which are subject to variation in the various inputs to the model, such as volatility, over the life of the option. However, IFRS 2 suggests that the Black-Scholes-Merton formula may give materially correct results for shorter lived options with a relatively short exercise period.[97]

5.2.1 Inputs to pricing models

Option pricing models take into account, as a minimum:

(a)   the exercise price of the option;

(b)   the life of the option (see 5.2.2 below);

(c)   the current price of the underlying shares;

(d)   the expected volatility of the share price (see 5.2.3 below);

(e)   the dividends expected on the shares (if appropriate – see 5.2.4 below); and

(f)   the risk-free interest rate for the life of the option (see 5.2.5 below).[98]

Other factors that knowledgeable, willing market participants would consider in setting the price should also be taken into account, except for vesting conditions and reload features that are excluded from the measurement of fair value – see 4.6 to 4.8 above. Such factors include:

- restrictions on exercise during the vesting period or during periods where trading by those with inside knowledge is prohibited by securities regulators (unless the model used is consistent with such restrictions); or

- the possibility of early exercise of options (see 5.2.2 below).[99]

However, the entity should not consider factors that are relevant only to an individual employee and not to the market as a whole (such as the effect of an award of options on the personal motivation of an individual).[100]

The objective of estimating the expected volatility of, and dividends on, the underlying shares is to approximate the expectations that would be reflected in a current market or negotiated exchange price for the option. Similarly, when estimating the effects of early exercise of employee share options, the objective is to approximate the expectations about employees' exercise behaviour that would be developed by an outside party with access to detailed information at grant date. Where (as is likely) there is a range of reasonable expectations about future volatility, dividends and exercise behaviour, an expected value should be calculated, by weighting each amount within the range by its associated probability of occurrence.[101]

Such expectations are often based on past data. In some cases, however, such historical information may not be relevant (e.g. where the business of the entity has changed significantly) or even available (e.g. where the entity is unlisted or newly listed). An entity should not base estimates of future volatility, dividends or exercise behaviour on historical data without considering the extent to which they are likely to be reasonably predictive of future experience.[102]

5.2.2 Expected early exercise

Employees often exercise options early for a number of reasons, most typically:

- restrictions on transferability mean that this is the only way of realising the value of the option in cash;

- aversion to the risk of not exercising 'in the money' options in the hope that they increase in value; or

- in the case of leavers, a requirement to exercise, or forfeit, all vested options on or shortly after leaving.

The effect of early exercise can be reflected:

- in a pricing model such as the Black-Scholes-Merton formula, by treating the expected, rather than the contractual, life of the option as an input to the model; or

- by using a binomial or similar model.[103]

Factors to consider in estimating early exercise include:

(a) the length of the vesting period, because the share option typically cannot be exercised until the end of the vesting period. Hence, determining the valuation implications of expected early exercise is based on the assumption that the options will vest;

(b) the average length of time similar options have remained outstanding in the past;

(c) the price of the underlying shares. Experience may indicate that employees tend to exercise options when the share price reaches a specified level above the exercise price;

(d)   the employee's level within the organisation. For example, experience might indicate that higher-level employees tend to exercise options later than lower-level employees (see also A below); and

(e)   the expected volatility of the underlying shares. On average, employees might tend to exercise options on highly volatile shares earlier than on shares with low volatility.[104]

A   Grouping employees with homogeneous exercise behaviour

IFRS 2 emphasises that the estimated life of an option is critical to its valuation. Therefore, where options are granted to a group of employees, it will generally be necessary to ensure that either:

(a)   all the employees are expected to exercise their options within a relatively narrow time-frame; or

(b)   if not, that the group is divided into sub-groups of employees who are expected to exercise their options within a similar relatively narrow time-frame.

IFRS 2 suggests that it may become apparent that middle and senior management tend to exercise options later than lower-level employees, either because they choose to do so, or because they are encouraged or compelled to do so as a result of required minimum levels of share ownership among more senior employees.[105]

5.2.3   Expected volatility

Expected volatility is a measure of the amount by which a price is expected to fluctuate during a period. The measure of volatility used in option pricing models is the annualised standard deviation of the continuously compounded rates of return on the share over a period of time. The rate of return (which may be positive or negative) on a share for a period measures how much a shareholder has benefited from dividends and appreciation (or depreciation) of the share price. Volatility is typically expressed in annualised terms that are comparable regardless of the time period used in the calculation (for example, daily, weekly or monthly price observations). The expected annualised volatility of a share is the range within which the continuously compounded annual rate of return is expected to fall approximately two-thirds of the time.[106]

Factors to consider in estimating expected volatility include:

(a)   implied volatility from traded share options (i.e. the volatility derived by using an option pricing model with the traded option price as an input and solving for the volatility as the unknown) on the entity's shares, or other traded instruments of the entity that include option features (such as convertible debt), if any;

(b)   the historical volatility of the share price over the most recent period that is generally commensurate with the expected term of the option (taking into account the remaining contractual life of the option and the effects of expected early exercise);

(c) the length of time an entity's shares have been publicly traded. A newly listed entity might have a high historical volatility, compared with similar entities that have been listed longer. Further guidance for newly listed entities is given in A below;

(d) the tendency of volatility to revert to its long-term average level, and other factors indicating that expected future volatility might differ from past volatility. For example, if an entity's share price was extraordinarily volatile for some identifiable period of time because of a failed takeover bid or a major restructuring, that period could be disregarded in computing historical average annual volatility; and

(e) appropriate and regular intervals for price observations. The price observations should be consistent from period to period. For example, an entity might use the closing price for each week or the highest price for the week, but it should not use the closing price for some weeks and the highest price for other weeks. Also, the price observations should be expressed in the same currency as the exercise price.[107]

A   Newly listed entities

As noted in (d) above, an entity should consider historical volatility of the share price over the most recent period that is generally commensurate with the expected option term. If a newly listed entity does not have sufficient information on historical volatility, it should compute historical volatility for the longest period for which trading activity is available. It could also consider the historical volatility of similar entities. For example, an entity that has been listed for only one year and grants options with an average expected life of five years might consider the historical volatility of entities in the same industry for the first six years in which the shares of those entities were publicly traded.[108]

B   Unlisted entities

An unlisted entity will have neither historical nor current market information to consider when estimating expected volatility. IFRS 2 suggests that in some cases, an unlisted entity that regularly issues options or shares might have set up an internal market for its shares. The volatility of those share prices could be considered when estimating expected volatility. Alternatively, if the entity has based the value of its shares on the share prices of similar listed entities, the entity could consider the historical or implied volatility of the shares of those similar listed entities.[109]

If the entity has not used a valuation methodology based on the share prices of similar listed entities, the entity could derive an estimate of expected volatility consistent with the valuation methodology used. For example, the entity might value its shares on a net asset or earnings basis, in which case it could consider the expected volatility of those net asset values or earnings.[110]

C   *Listed entities that have undergone significant restructuring*

An issue not specifically addressed by IFRS 2 is the approach required in the case of an entity that has been listed for some time but which has recently undergone significant restructuring or refocusing of the business (e.g. as a result of acquisitions, disposals or refinancing). In such cases, it may well be that the approach advocated for newly listed entities in A above is the most appropriate one to adopt.

5.2.4   *Expected dividends*

The valuation of an award of options depends whether or not the holder is entitled to dividends or dividend equivalents (whether in the form of cash payments or reductions in the exercise price) before the award is ultimately exercised. Where employees are entitled to dividends or dividend equivalents, the options granted should be valued as if no dividends will be paid on the underlying shares, so that the input for expected dividends (which would otherwise reduce the valuation of an option) is zero. Conversely, where employees are not entitled to dividends or dividend equivalents, the expected dividends should be included in the application of the pricing model.[111]

While option pricing models generally call for an expected dividend yield, they may be modified to use an expected dividend amount rather than a yield. Where an entity uses expected payments rather than expected yields, it should consider its historical pattern of increases in dividends. For example, if an entity's policy has generally been to increase dividends, its estimated option value should not assume a fixed dividend amount throughout the option's life unless there is evidence to support that assumption.[112]

Generally assumptions about expected dividends should be based on publicly available information. Thus, an entity that does not pay dividends and has no plans to do so should assume an expected dividend yield of zero. However, an emerging entity with no history of paying dividends might expect to begin paying dividends during the expected lives of its employee share options. Such entities could use an average of their past dividend yield (zero) and the mean dividend yield of an comparable peer group of entities.[113]

5.2.5   *Risk-free interest rate*

Typically, the risk-free interest rate is the implied yield currently available on zero-coupon government issues of the country in whose currency the exercise price is expressed, with a remaining term equal to the expected term of the option being valued (based on the option's remaining contractual life and taking into account the effects of expected early exercise). It may be necessary to use an appropriate substitute, if no such government issues exist, or where the implied yield on zero-coupon government issues may not be representative of the risk-free interest rate (for example, in high inflation economies). An appropriate substitute should also be used if market participants would typically determine the risk-free interest rate by using that substitute.[114]

5.2.6   Capital structure effects

Typically, traded share options are written by third parties, not the entity. When these share options are exercised, the writer delivers to the option holder shares acquired from existing shareholders. Hence the exercise of traded share options has no dilutive effect. In contrast, when share options written by the entity are exercised, new shares may be issued (either in form or in substance, if shares previously repurchased and held in treasury are used), giving rise to dilution. This actual or potential dilution might reduce the share price, so that the option holder does not make as large a gain on exercise as on exercising an otherwise similar traded option that does not dilute the share price.[115]

Whether or not this has a significant effect on the value of the share options granted depends on various factors, such as the number of new shares that will be issued on exercise of the options compared with the number of shares already issued. Also, if the market already expects that the option grant will take place, the market may have already factored the potential dilution into the share price at the date of grant. However, the entity should consider whether the possible dilutive effect of the future exercise of the share options granted might have an impact on their estimated fair value at grant date. Option pricing models can be adapted to take into account this potential dilutive effect.[116]

5.3   Awards whose fair value cannot be measured reliably

IFRS 2 acknowledges that there may be rare cases where it is not possible to determine the fair value of equity instruments granted. In such cases, the entity is required to adopt a method of accounting based on the intrinsic value of the award (i.e. the price of the underlying share less the exercise price, if any, for the award). This is slightly puzzling in the sense that, for unlisted entities, a significant obstacle to determining a reliable fair value for equity instruments is the absence of a market share price, which is also a key input in determining intrinsic value. In fact, the intrinsic value model is arguably more onerous than the fair value model since, as discussed further in 5.3.1 and 5.3.2 below, it requires intrinsic value to be determined not just once, but at service date and each subsequent reporting date until exercise.

5.3.1   Intrinsic value method – the basic accounting treatment

Under the intrinsic value method:

(a) the entity measures the intrinsic value of the award at each reporting date between grant date and settlement (whether through exercise, forfeit or lapse);

(b) at each reporting date during the vesting period the cumulative expense should be determined as the intrinsic value of the award at that date multiplied by the expired portion of the vesting period, with all changes in the cumulative expense recognised in profit or loss; and

(c) once options have vested, all changes in their intrinsic value until settlement should be recognised in profit or loss.[117]

The cumulative expense during the vesting period, like that for awards measured at fair value, should always be based on the best estimate of the number of awards that will actually vest (see 4.5 and 4.6 above). However, the distinction between market conditions and other conditions that would apply to awards measured at fair value (see 4.5 to 4.7 above) does not apply in the case of awards measured at intrinsic value.[118] In other words, where an award measured at intrinsic value is subject to a market condition that is not met, there is ultimately no accounting expense for that award. This is consistent with a model requiring constant remeasurement.

The cost of awards measured at intrinsic value is ultimately revised to reflect the number of awards that are actually exercised. However, during the vesting period the cost should be based on the number of awards estimated to vest and thereafter on the number of awards that have vested. In other words, any post-vesting forfeiture or lapse should not be anticipated, but should be accounted for as it occurs.[119]

Example 29.21 illustrates the intrinsic value method.

Example 29.21: Intrinsic value method

At the beginning of year 1, an entity grants 1,000 share options to 50 employees.

The share options will vest at the end of year 3, provided the employees remain in service until then and can be exercised at the end of year 4, and then at the end of each subsequent year up to and including year 10. The exercise price, and the entity's grant date share price, is €60. At the date of grant, the entity concludes that it cannot estimate reliably the fair value of the share options granted.

At the end of year 1, the entity estimates that 80% of the share options will vest. At the end of year 2, the entity revises its estimate of the number of share options that it expects will vest to 86%.

During the vesting period, a total of seven employees leave, so that 43,000 share options vest.

The intrinsic value of the options, and the number of share options exercised during years 4-10, are as follows.

Year	Intrinsic value €	Number exercised
1	3	
2	5	
3	15	
4	28	6,000
5	40	8,000
6	30	5,000
7	36	9,000
8	45	8,000
9	48	5,000
10	55	2,000

The expense recognised under IFRS 2 will be as follows. In the period up to vesting the 'cumulative expense' methodology used in the Examples in sections 4.5 to 4.7 above can be adopted to derive the expense for each period:

Year	Calculation of cumulative expense	Cumulative expense (€)	Expense for period (€)
1	50,000 options × €3 × 80% × 1/3	40,000	40,000
2	50,000 options × €5 × 86% × 2/3	143,333	103,333
3	43,000 options × €15	645,000	501,677

In years 4 to 10 it is more straightforward to calculate the expense directly. Since all options exercised during each year are exercised at the end of that year, the annual expense can be calculated as the change in intrinsic value during each year of the options outstanding at the *start* of the year.

Year		Expense for period (€)
4	43,000 options × €(28-15)	559,000
5	43,000 – 6,000 = 37,000 options × €(40-28)	444,000
6	37,000 – 8,000 = 29,000 options × €(30-40)	(290,000)
7	29,000 – 5,000 = 24,000 options × €(36-30)	144,000
8	24,000 – 9,000 = 15,000 options × €(45-36)	135,000
9	15,000 – 8,000 = 7,000 options × €(48-45)	21,000
10	7,000 – 5,000 = 2,000 options × €(55-48)	14,000

If more realistically, the options had been exercisable, and were exercised, at other dates, it would have been necessary to record as an expense for those options the movement in intrinsic value from the start of the year until exercise date. For example, if the 6,000 options in year 4 had been exercised during the year when the intrinsic value was €20, the expense for that period would have been €511,000 comprising €481,000 change in value for the options outstanding at the end of year [37,000 options × €(28-15)] and €30,000 change in value of options exercised during the period [6,000 options × €(20-15)].

5.3.2 Modification, cancellation and settlement

The methodology of the intrinsic value method has the effect that modification or cancellation is dealt with automatically, and the rules for modification and cancellation of awards measured at fair value (see 4.10 above) therefore do not apply.[120]

Where an award accounted for at intrinsic value is settled in cash, the following provisions apply, which are broadly similar to the rules for settlement of awards accounted for at fair value.

If settlement occurs before vesting, the entity 'must recognise immediately the amount that would have been recognised for services over the remainder of the vesting period'.[121] The wording here is the same as that applicable to settlement of awards accounted for at fair value, which we discuss in more detail at 4.10.4 B above.

Any payment made on settlement must be deducted from equity, except to the extent that it is greater than the intrinsic value of the award at settlement date. Any such excess is accounted for as an expense.[122]

6   CASH-SETTLED TRANSACTIONS

6.1   Scope of requirements

Cash-settled share-based payment transactions are usually easy to identify, and include such things as:

- share appreciation rights (SARs), where employees are entitled to a cash payment equivalent to the gain that would have arisen from a holding of a particular number of shares from the date of grant to the date of exercise; or

- phantom options, where employees are entitled to a cash payment equivalent to the gain that would have been made by exercising options at a notional price over a notional number of shares and then selling the shares at the date of exercise.[123]

However, IFRS 2 looks beyond the simple issue of whether an award entitles an employee to receive instruments that are in form shares or options to the terms of those instruments. For example, an award of shares or options over shares whose terms provide for their redemption either mandatorily according to their terms (e.g. on cessation of employment) or at the employee's option would be treated as a cash-settled, not an equity-settled, award under IFRS 2.[124] This is consistent with the fact that IAS 32 would regard a share with these terms as a financial liability rather than an equity instrument of the issuer (see Chapter 17 at 3).

6.2   Required accounting

6.2.1   Basic accounting treatment

It is clear that that the ultimate cost of a cash-settled transaction must be the actual cash paid to the counterparty, which will be the fair value at settlement date. Moreover, the cumulative cost recognised until settlement is clearly a liability, not a component of equity.

The periodic determination of this liability is as follows:

(a)   at each reporting date between grant and settlement the fair value of the award is determined;

(b)   during the vesting period, the liability recognised at each reporting date is the fair value of the award at that date multiplied by the expired portion of the vesting period;

(c)   from the end of the vesting period until settlement, the liability recognised is the full fair value of the liability at the reporting date; and

(d)   all changes in the liability are recognised in the profit or loss for the period.[125]

The fair value of the liability should be determined, initially and at each reporting date until it is settled, by applying an option pricing model, taking into account the terms and conditions on which the share appreciation rights were granted, and the extent to which the employees have rendered service to date.[126]

This has the effect that, although the liability will ultimately be settled at its then intrinsic value, its measurement at reporting dates before settlement is based on its fair value. During the exposure period of ED 2, a number of respondents suggested that, for reasons of consistency and simplicity of calculation, cash-settled transactions should be measured at intrinsic value throughout their entire life. The IASB, while accepting these merits of the intrinsic value approach (together with the fact that it is also required under US GAAP), rejected it on the basis that, since it does not include a time value, it is not an adequate measure of either the liability or the cost of services consumed.[127]

6.2.2 Application of the accounting treatment

This treatment required by IFRS 2 for cash-settled transactions is illustrated by Example 29.22.

Example 29.22: Cash-settled transaction

An entity grants 100 cash share appreciation rights (SARs) to each of its 500 employees, on condition that the employees remain in its employment for the next three years. The SARs can be exercised on the third, fourth and fifth anniversary of the grant date.

During year 1, 35 employees leave. The entity estimates that a further 60 will leave during years 2 and 3 (i.e. the award will vest in 405 employees).

During year 2, 40 employees leave and the entity estimates that a further 25 will leave during year 3 (i.e. the award will vest in 400 employees).

During year 3, 22 employees leave, so that the award vests in 403 employees. At the end of year 3, 150 employees exercise their SARs (leaving 253 employees still to exercise).

Another 140 employees exercise their SARs at the end of year 4, leaving 113 employees still to exercise, who do so at the end of year 5.

The entity estimates the fair value of the SARs at the end of each year in which a liability exists as shown below. The intrinsic values of the SARs at the date of exercise (which equal the cash paid out) at the end of years 3, 4 and 5 are also shown below.

Year	Fair value	Intrinsic value
	£	£
1	14.40	
2	15.50	
3	18.20	15.00
4	21.40	20.00
5		25.00

The entity will recognise the cost of this award as follows.

Year	Calculation of liability	Calculation of cash paid	Liability (£)	Cash paid (£)	Expense for period (£)[1]
1	405 employees × 100 SARs × £14.40 × 1/3		194,400	–	194,400
2	400 employees × 100 SARs × £15.50 × 2/3		413,333	–	218,933
3	253 employees × 100 SARs × £18.20	150 employees × 100 SARs × £15.00	460,460	225,000	272,127
4	113 employees × 100 SARs × £21.40	140 employees × 100 SARs × £20.00	241,820	280,000	61,360
5	–	113 employees × 100 SARs × £25.00	–	282,500	40,680

1   Liability at end of period + cash paid in period – liability at start of period

The accounting treatment for cash-settled transactions is therefore (despite some similarities in the methodology) significantly different from that for equity-settled transactions. An important practical issue is that, for a cash-settled transaction, the entity must determine the fair value at each reporting date and not merely at grant date (and at the date of any subsequent modification or settlement) as would be the case for equity-settled transactions. However, as Example 29.22 shows, it is not actually necessary, although required by IFRS 2, to determine the fair value of a cash-settled transaction at grant date, at least to determine the expense under IFRS 2. However, for entities subject to IAS 33 – *Earnings per Share*, the grant date fair value is required in order to make the disclosures required by that standard – see Chapter 31 at 6.4.2 A.

IFRS 2 raises some issues of interpretation on detailed aspects of the methodology such as:

- determining the vesting period (see A below);
- periodic allocation of cost (see B below);
- treatment of vesting conditions (see C below);
- treatment of market conditions (see D below); and
- treatment of modification, cancellation and settlement (see E below).

A   Determining the vesting period

The rules for determining vesting periods are the same as those applicable to equity-settled transactions (see 4.5 to 4.7 above). Where an award of instruments vests immediately, IFRS 2 creates a presumption that, in the absence of evidence to the contrary, the award is in respect of services that have already been rendered, and should therefore be expensed in full at grant date. [128]

Where cash-settled awards are made subject to vesting conditions (as in many cases they will be, particularly where payments to employees are concerned), IFRS 2 creates a presumption that they are a payment for services to be received in the future, during the 'vesting period', with the transaction being recognised during that period, as illustrated in Example 29.22 above. [129]

B   Periodic allocation of cost

Paragraph 30 of IFRS 2 states that the required treatment for cash-settled transactions is simply to measure the fair value of the liability at each reporting date, which might suggest that the *full* fair value, and not just a time-apportioned part of it, should be recognised at each reporting date – as would be the case for any liability that is a financial instrument and measured at fair value under IAS 39.

However, paragraphs 32 and 33 clarify that the liability is to be measured at an amount that reflects 'the extent to which employees have rendered service to date', and the cost is to be recognised 'as the employees render service'. This, together with IG Example 12 in IFRS 2 (the substance of which is reproduced as Example 29.22 above), indicates that a spreading approach is to be adopted.

C   Vesting conditions

As drafted, IFRS 2 does not specifically address the impact of vesting conditions in the context of cash-settled transactions – the provisions of IFRS 2 relating to vesting conditions are to be found in paragraphs 19-21 of IFRS 2, all of which fall under the main heading 'Equity-settled share-based payment transactions' immediately before paragraph 10.

Where a vesting condition is a minimum service period, IG Example 12 in IFRS 2 (broadly reproduced as Example 29.22 above) clearly indicates that, during the period to vesting, the liability should be estimated on the basis of the current best estimate of the number of awards that will vest, exactly as for a share-settled transaction.

As regards other performance conditions (other than market conditions), based on the analogy of the treatment of service periods in IG Example 12, we believe that the liability until vesting date should be based on the current best estimate of the outcome of those conditions.

However, as in the case of equity-settled transactions, the impact of performance and service conditions should not be factored into the valuation of cash-settled awards.

D   Market conditions

There is no specific guidance in IFRS 2 as to whether, in the case of a cash-settled transaction, a distinction is to be drawn between a vesting condition that is a market condition and other vesting conditions as would be the case for an equity-settled transaction (see 4.6 and 4.7 above). However, it seems clear that no such distinction should be drawn since a cash-settled transaction must ultimately reflect the amount of cash paid. A cash-settled award is required to be valued at each balance reporting date, so that there will be no cost for an subject to a market condition that is not satisfied. This is different from the accounting model for equity-settled transactions with market conditions, which can result in a cost being recognised for awards subject to a market condition that is not satisfied (see 4.7 above).

E   Modification, cancellation and settlement

IFRS 2 provides no specific guidance on modification, cancellation and settlement of cash-settled awards. However, as cash-settled awards are accounted for using a full fair value model no such guidance is needed. It is clear that:

- where an award is modified, the liability recognised at and after the point of modification will be based on its new fair value, with the effect of any movement in the liability recognised immediately;
- where an award is cancelled the liability will be derecognised, with a credit immediately recognised in profit or loss; and
- where an award is settled, the liability will be derecognised, and any gain or loss on settlement immediately recognised in profit or loss.

7 TRANSACTIONS WITH CASH ALTERNATIVES

It is common for share-based payment transactions (particularly those with employees) to provide either the entity or the counterparty with the choice of settling the transaction in either shares (or other equity instruments) or cash (or other assets). The general principle of IFRS 2 is that a transaction with a cash[130] alternative, or the components of that transaction, should be accounted for:

(a) as a cash-settled transaction if, and to the extent that, the entity has incurred a liability to settle in cash; or

(b) as an equity-settled transaction if, and to the extent that, no such liability has been incurred.[131]

More detailed guidance is provided as to how that general principle should be applied to transactions:

- where the counterparty has choice of settlement (see 7.1 below); and
- where the entity has choice of settlement (see 7.2 below).

7.1 Transactions where the counterparty has choice of settlement

Where the counterparty has the right to elect for settlement in either shares or cash, IFRS 2 regards the transaction as a compound transaction to which split accounting must be applied. The general principle is that the transaction must be analysed into a liability component (the counterparty's right to demand settlement in cash) and an equity component (the counterparty's right to demand settlement in shares).[132] Once split, the two components are accounted for separately. Somewhat confusingly, the methodology of split accounting required by IFRS 2 is somewhat different from that required by IAS 32 for issuers of other compound instruments (see Chapter 17 at 4).

A practical issue is that, where a transaction gives the counterparty a choice of settlement, it will be necessary to establish a fair value for the liability component both at grant date and at each subsequent reporting date until settlement. By contrast, in the case of transactions that can be settled in cash only, no fair value is required at grant date, but is required at each subsequent reporting date until settlement (see 6 above). However, for entities subject to IAS 33 – *Earnings per Share*, the grant date fair value is required in order to make the disclosures required by that standard – see Chapter 31 at 6.4.2 A.

7.1.1 *Transactions in which the fair value is measured directly*

Transactions with non-employees are normally measured by reference to the fair value of goods and services supplied at service date (i.e. the date at which the goods or services are supplied) – see 4.1 to 4.3 above.

Accordingly where an entity enters into such a transaction where the counterparty has choice of settlement, it determines the fair value of the liability component at service date. The equity component is the difference between the fair value (at service date) of the goods or services received and the fair value of the liability component.[133]

7.1.2   Other transactions

All other transactions, including those with employees, are measured by reference to the fair value of the instruments issued at 'measurement date', being grant date in the case of transactions with employees and service date in the case of transactions with non-employees[134] – see 4.1 to 4.3 above.

The fair value should take into account the terms and conditions on which the rights to the equity instruments were issued.[135] IFRS 2 does not elaborate further on this, but we assume that the IASB intends a reporting entity to apply:

- as regards the equity component of the transaction, the provisions of IFRS 2 relating to the impact of terms and conditions on the valuation of equity-settled transactions (see 4.4 to 4.8 above); and

- as regards the liability component of the transaction, the provisions of IFRS 2 relating to the impact of terms and conditions on the valuation of cash-settled transactions (see 6.2 above).

The entity should first measure the fair value of the liability component and then that of the equity component. The fair value of the equity component must be reduced to take into account the fact that the counterparty must forfeit the right to receive cash in order to receive shares. In practice, IG Example 13 in IFRS 2 (the substance of which is reproduced as Example 29.23 below) suggests that this will be done by establishing the fair value of the equity alternative and subtracting from it the fair value of the liability component. The sum of the two components is the fair value of the whole compound instrument.[136] This treats the fair value of the transaction as a whole as the balancing residual, in contrast to the methodology in 7.1.1 above (and IAS 32) which determines the fair value of the whole transaction and that of the liability component, and treats the equity component as the residual.

In many share-based payment transactions with a choice of settlement, the value of the share and cash alternatives is equal. The counterparty will have the choice between (say) 1,000 shares or the cash value of 1,000 shares. This will mean that the fair value of the liability component is equal to that of the transaction as a whole, so that the fair value of the equity component is zero. In other words, the transaction is accounted for as if it were a cash-settled transaction.

However, in some jurisdictions it is not uncommon, particularly in transactions with employees, for the equity-settlement alternative to have more value. For example, an employee might be able to choose at vesting between the cash value of 1,000 shares immediately or 2,000 shares (often subject to further conditions such as a minimum holding period, or a further service period). In such cases the equity component will have an independent value.[137]

7.1.3   Accounting treatment

A   During vesting period

Having established a fair value for the liability and equity components as set out in 7.1.1. and 7.1.2 above, the entity accounts for the liability component according to the rules for cash-settled transactions (see 6 above) and the equity component according to the rules for equity-settled transactions (see 4 and 5 above).[138]

Example 29.23 below illustrates the accounting treatment for a transaction with an employee (i.e. as summarised in 7.1.2 above) where the equity component has a fair value independent of the liability component.

Example 29.23:   Award with employee choice of settlement with different fair values for cash-settlement and equity-settlement

An entity grants to an employee an award with the right to choose settlement in either:

- 1,000 phantom shares, i.e. a right to a cash payment equal to the value of 1,000 shares, or
- 1,200 shares.

Vesting is conditional upon the completion of three years' service. If the employee chooses the share alternative, the shares must be held for three years after vesting date.

At grant date, the entity estimates that the fair value of the share alternative, after taking into account the effects of the post-vesting transfer restrictions, is €48 per share. The fair value of the cash alternative is estimated as:

	€
Grant date	50
Year 1	52
Year 2	55
Year 3	60

The grant date fair value of the equity alternative is €57,600 (1,200 shares × €48). The grant date fair value of the cash alternative is €50,000 (1,000 phantom shares × €50). Therefore the fair value of the equity component excluding the right to receive cash is €7,600 (€57,600 − €50,000). The entity recognises a cost based on the following amounts.

	Equity component			Liability component		
Year	Calculation of cumulative expense	Cumulative expense (€)	Expense for year (€)	Calculation of cumulative expense	Cumulative expense (€)	Expense for year (€)
1	€7,600 × 1/3	2,533	2,533	1,000 phantoms × €52 × 1/3	17,333	17,333
2	€7,600 × 2/3	5,066	2,533	1,000 phantoms × €55 × 2/3	36,667	19,334
3	€7,600	7,600	2,534	1,000 phantoms × €60	60,000	23,333

This generates the following accounting entries.

	€	€
Year 1		
Income statement (employment costs)	19,866	
Liability		17,333
Equity		2,533
Year 2		
Income statement (employment costs)	21,867	
Liability		19,334
Equity		2,533
Year 3		
Income statement (employment costs)	25,867	
Liability		23,333
Equity		2,534

The above example is based on IG Example 13 in IFRS 2, in which the fair value of the cash-alternative is treated as being the share price at each reporting date. This is clearly an error of principle in the example in IFRS 2, since as discussed more fully at 6 above, the fair value of a cash award is not the same as the share price, a point reinforced by IG Example 12 in IFRS 2 (the basis for Example 29.22 at 6.2.2 above). Accordingly, in adapting IG Example 13 as Example 29.23 above, we have deliberately described the numbers used in respect of the liability component as 'fair value' and not as the 'share price'.

Example 29.23 also ignores the fact that transactions of this type often have different vesting periods for the two settlement alternatives. For instance, the employee might have been offered:

(a)   the cash equivalent of 1,000 shares in three years' time subject to performance conditions; or

(b)   subject to the performance criteria in (a) above being met over three years, 3,000 shares after a further two years' service.

IFRS 2 offers no guidance as to how such transactions are to be accounted for. Presumably, however, the equity component would be recognised over a five-year period and the liability component over a three-year period.

B   Settlement

At the date of settlement, the liability component is restated to fair value. If the counterparty elects for settlement in equity, the liability is transferred to equity. If the liability is settled in cash, the cash is obviously applied to reduce the liability.[139] In other words, if the transaction in Example 29.23 above had been settled in shares the accounting entry would have been:

	€	€
Liability[1]	60,000	
Equity[2]		60,000

1   There is no need to remeasure the liability in this case as it has already been stated at fair value at vesting date, which is the same as settlement date.

2   The precise allocation of this amount within equity, and its impact on distributable reserves, will depend on a number of factors, including jurisdictional legal requirements, which are not discussed here.

If the transaction had been settled in cash the entry would simply have been:

	€	€
Liability	60,000	
Cash		60,000

If the transaction is settled in cash, any amount taken to equity during the vesting period (€7,600 in Example 29.23 above) is not adjusted. However, the entity may transfer it from one component of equity to another (see 4.1.1 above).[140]

7.1.4 Transactions with cash-settlement alternative for employee introduced after grant date

Such transactions are not specifically addressed in the main body of IFRS 2. However, IG Example 9 in the implementation guidance does address this issue, in the context of the rules for the modification of awards discussed in 4.10 above. The substance of this example is reproduced as Example 29.24 below.

Example 29.24: Award with employee cash-settlement alternative introduced after grant

At the beginning of year 1, the entity grants 10,000 shares with a fair value of $33 per share to a senior executive, conditional upon the completion of three years' service. By the end of year 2, the fair value of the award has dropped to $25 per share. At that date, the entity adds a cash alternative to the grant, whereby the executive can choose whether to receive 10,000 shares or cash equal to the value of 10,000 shares on vesting date. The share price is $20 on vesting. The implementation guidance to IFRS 2 proposes the following approach.

For the first two years, the entity would recognise an expense of $110,000 per year, (representing 10,000 shares × $33 × 1/3), giving rise to the cumulative accounting entry by the end of year 2:

	$	$
Income statement (employee costs)	220,000	
Equity		220,000

The addition of a cash alternative at the end of year 2 constitutes a modification of the award, but does not increase the fair value of the award at the date of modification, which under either settlement alternative is $250,000 (10,000 shares × $25), excluding the effect of the non-market vesting condition as required by IFRS 2.

The fact that the employee now has the right to be paid in cash requires the 'split accounting' treatment set out in 7.1 above. Because of the requirement, under the rules for modification of awards (see 4.10.3 above), to recognise at least the fair value of the original award, the total fair value of the equity alternative of the award is deemed to remain $330,000. This is then reduced (in accordance with the rules in 7.1 above) to reflect the fact that the equity-settlement option would entail the sacrifice of the cash-settled option (modification date fair value $250,000), giving an implied value for the equity-settlement option of $80,000 ($330,000-$250,000).

The award is now 2/3 through its vesting period, implying that the cumulative amount accounted for in equity should be only $53,333 ($80,000 × 2/3), as opposed to the $220,000 that has actually been accounted for in equity. Accordingly, the difference of $166,667 is transferred from equity to liabilities, the entry being:

	$	$
Equity	166,667	
Liability		166,667

The $166,667 carrying amount of the liability can be seen as representing 2/3 of the $250,000 fair value of the liability component at modification date.

From now on, the accounting for the equity component will be based on this implied value of $80,000. This results in the following accounting entry for the expense in year 3.

	$	$
Profit and loss account	60,000[1]	
Liability		33,333[2]
Equity		26,667[3]

1   Balancing figure.

2   Carried forward liability $200,000 (10,000 shares × year 3 fair value $20) less the brought forward liability $166,667.

3   $80,000 equity component (as determined above) × 1/3.

This results in a total cumulative expense for the award of $280,000 ($220,000 for years 1 and 2 and $60,000 for year 3), which represents the actual cash liability at the end of year 3 of $200,000 plus the $80,000 deemed excess of the fair value of the equity component over the liability component at the end of year 2.

The $280,000 expense could also be analysed (as is done by the implementation guidance IFRS 2 itself), as representing the grant date fair value of the award ($330,000) less the movement in the fair value of the liability alternative ($50,000, representing the fair value of $250,000 at the end of year 2 less the fair value of $200,000 at vesting). The implementation guidance may have adopted this approach to support an argument that, despite all appearances to the contrary, this methodology does not breach the fundamental principle of the modification rules for equity-settled transactions that the minimum expense recognised for a modified award should be the expense that would have been recognised had the award not been modified (see 4.10.3 above).

7.2   Transactions where the entity has choice of settlement

The accounting treatment for transactions where the entity has a choice of settlement is quite different from transactions where the counterparty has choice of settlement, in that:

- where the counterparty has choice of settlement, a liability component and an equity component are identified (see 7.1 above), whereas

- where the entity has a choice of settlement, the accounting treatment is binary – in other words the whole transaction is treated either as cash-settled or as equity-settled, depending on whether or not the entity has a present obligation to settle in cash,[141] determined according to the criteria discussed in 7.2.1 below.

7.2.1   *Transactions treated as cash-settled*

IFRS 2 requires a transaction to be treated as a liability (and accounted for using the rules for cash-settled transactions discussed in 6 above) if:

(a)   the choice of settlement has no commercial substance (for example, because the entity is legally prohibited from issuing shares);

(b)   the entity has a past practice or stated policy of settling in cash; or

(c)   the entity generally settles in cash whenever the counterparty asks for cash settlement.[142]

These criteria are fundamentally different for those in IAS 32 for derivatives over own shares (which is what cash-settled share-based payment transactions are) not within the scope of IFRS 2. IAS 32 rejects an approach based on past practice or intention and broadly requires all derivatives over own equity that could result in cash settlement to be treated as giving rise to a financial liability (see Chapter 17 at 3).

An important practical effect of these criteria is that some schemes that may appear at first sight to be equity-settled may in fact have to be treated as cash-settled. For example, if an entity has consistently adopted a policy of granting ex gratia cash compensation to all 'good'[143] leavers (or all 'good' leavers of certain seniority) in respect of partially vested options, such a scheme may well be treated as cash-settled for the purposes of IFRS 2.

Another common example is that an entity may have a global share scheme with an entity option for cash settlement which it always exercises in respect of awards to employees in jurisdictions where it is difficult or illegal to hold shares in the parent. Such a scheme should be treated as a cash-settled scheme in respect of those jurisdictions. It would, however, in our view, be appropriate to account for the scheme in other jurisdictions as equity-settled (provided of course that none of the criteria in (a) to (c) above were met for those jurisdictions).

IFRS 2 gives no specific guidance as to the accounting treatment on settlement, but it is clear from other provisions of IFRS 2 that the liability should be remeasured to fair value at settlement date and:

- if cash settlement occurs, the cash paid is applied to reduce the liability; and
- if equity-settlement occurs, the liability is transferred into equity (see 7.1.3 B above).

A   Change in classification after grant date

IFRS 2 is not specific as to whether the assessment of whether a transaction should be accounted for as equity-settled or cash-settled is to be made only at the inception of the transaction or also at each reporting date until it is settled.

However, in describing the accounting treatment IFRS 2 states several times that the accounting depends on whether the entity '*has a present obligation* to settle in cash'. In our view, this suggests that IFRS 2 intends the position to be reviewed at each reporting date and not just considered at the inception of the transaction.

7.2.2   Transactions treated as equity-settled

A transaction not meeting the criteria in 7.2.1 above should be accounted for as an equity-settled transaction using the rules for such transactions discussed in 4 and 5 above.[144]

However, when the transaction is settled the following approach is adopted:[145]

(a)   subject to (b) below:

    (i)   if the transaction is cash-settled, the cash is accounted for as a deduction of equity; or

    (ii)   if the transaction is equity-settled, there is a transfer from one component of equity to another (if necessary); and

(b)   if the two methods of settlement are of different fair value at the date of settlement, and the entity chooses the method with the higher fair value, the entity recognises an additional expense for the excess fair value of the chosen method.

This is illustrated in Examples 29.25 and 29.26 below.

Example 29.25:   *Settlement of transaction treated as equity-settled where fair value of cash settlement exceeds fair value of equity settlement*

An entity has accounted for a share-based payment transaction where it has the choice of settlement as an equity-settled transaction, and has recognised a cumulative expense of £1,000 based on the fair value at grant date.

At settlement date the fair value of the equity-settlement option is £1,700 and that of the cash-settlement option £2,000. If the entity settles in equity, no further accounting entry is required by IFRS 2. However, either at the entity's discretion or in compliance with local legal requirements, there may be a transfer within equity of the £1,000 credited to equity during the vesting period.

If the entity settles in cash, the entity must recognise an additional expense of £300, being the difference between fair value of the equity-settlement option (£1,700) and that of the cash-settlement option (£2,000). The accounting entry is:

	£	£
Profit or loss (employee costs)	300	
Equity	1,700	
Cash		2,000

Example 29.26:   *Settlement of transaction treated as equity-settled where fair value of equity settlement exceeds fair value of cash settlement*

As in Example 29.25, an entity has accounted for a share-based payment transaction where it has the choice of settlement as an equity-settled transaction, and has recognised a cumulative expense of £1,000 based on the fair value at grant date.

In this case, however, at settlement date the fair value of the equity-settlement option is £2,000 and that of the cash-settlement option £1,700. If the entity chooses to settle in equity, it must recognise an additional expense of £300, being the difference between fair value of the equity-settlement option (£1,700) and that of the cash-settlement option (£2,000). The accounting entry is:

	£	£
Income statement (employee costs)	300	
Equity		300

No further accounting entry is required by IFRS 2. However, either at the entity's discretion or in compliance with local legal requirements, there may be a transfer within equity of the £1,300 credited during the vesting period and on settlement.

If the entity settles in cash, no extra expense is recognised, and the accounting entry is:

	£	£
Equity	1,700	
Cash		1,700

It can be seen in this case that, if the transaction is settled in equity, an additional expense is recognised. If, however, the transaction had simply been an equity-settled transaction (i.e. with no cash alternative), there would have been no additional expense on settlement and the cumulative expense would have been only £1,000 based on the fair value at grant date.

8   DISCLOSURES

IFRS 2 requires three main groups of disclosures, explaining:

- the nature and extent of share-based payment arrangements (see 8.1 below);
- the valuation of share-based payment arrangements (see 8.2 below); and
- the impact on the financial statements of share-based payment arrangements (see 8.3 below).

8.1   Nature and extent of share-based payment arrangements

IFRS 2 requires an entity to 'disclose information that enables users of the financial statements to understand the nature and extent of share-based payment arrangements that existed during the period'.[146]

In order to satisfy this general principle, the entity must disclose at least:[147]

(a)   a description of each type of share-based payment arrangement that existed at any time during the period, including the general terms and conditions of each arrangement, such as vesting requirements, the maximum term of options granted, and the method of settlement (e.g. whether in cash or equity). An entity with substantially similar types of share-based payment arrangements may aggregate this information, unless separate disclosure of each arrangement is necessary to satisfy the general principle above;

(b)   the number and weighted average exercise prices of share options for each of the following groups of options:

  (i)   outstanding at the beginning of the period;

  (ii)   granted during the period;

  (iii) forfeited during the period;

  (iv)   exercised during the period;

  (v)   expired during the period;

  (vi)   outstanding at the end of the period; and

  (vii) exercisable at the end of the period;

(c)   for share options exercised during the period, the weighted average share price at the date of exercise. If options were exercised on a regular basis throughout the period, the entity may instead disclose the weighted average share price during the period; and

(d)   for share options outstanding at the end of the period, the range of exercise prices and weighted average remaining contractual life. If the range of exercise prices is wide, the outstanding options must be divided into ranges that are meaningful for assessing the number and timing of additional shares that may be issued and the cash that may be received upon exercise of those options.

8.2   Valuation of share-based payment arrangements

IFRS 2 requires an entity to 'disclose information that enables users of the financial statements to understand how the fair value of the goods or services received, or the fair value of the equity instruments granted, during the period was determined'.[148]

As drafted, this requirement, and some of the detailed disclosures below, appear to apply only to equity-settled transactions. However, it would be clearly anomalous if detailed disclosures were required about the valuation of an award to be settled in shares, but not when it was to be settled in cash. In our view, therefore, the disclosures apply both to equity-settled and to cash-settled transactions.

If the entity has measured the fair value of goods or services received as consideration for equity instruments of the entity indirectly, by reference to the fair value of the equity instruments granted (i.e. transactions with employees and, in exceptional cases only, with non-employees), the entity must disclose at least the following:[149]

(a) for share options granted during the period, the weighted average fair value of those options at the measurement date and information on how that fair value was measured, including:

   (i) the option pricing model used and the inputs to that model, including the weighted average share price, exercise price, expected volatility, option life, expected dividends, the risk-free interest rate and any other inputs to the model, including the method used and the assumptions made to incorporate the effects of expected early exercise;

   (ii) how expected volatility was determined, including an explanation of the extent to which expected volatility was based on historical volatility; and

   (iii) whether and how any other features of the option grant were incorporated into the measurement of fair value, such as a market condition;

(b) for other equity instruments granted during the period (i.e. other than share options), the number and weighted average fair value of those equity instruments at the measurement date, and information on how that fair value was measured, including:

   (i) if fair value was not measured on the basis of an observable market price, how it was determined;

   (ii) whether and how expected dividends were incorporated into the measurement of fair value; and

   (iii) whether and how any other features of the equity instruments granted were incorporated into the measurement of fair value;

(c) for share-based payment arrangements that were modified during the period:

   (i) an explanation of those modifications;

   (ii) the incremental fair value granted (as a result of those modifications); and

   (iii) information on how the incremental fair value granted was measured, consistently with the requirements set out in (a) and (b) above, where applicable.

These requirements can be seen to some extent as an anti-avoidance measure. It would not be surprising if the IASB had concerns that entities might seek to minimise the impact of IFRS 2 by using assumptions that result in a low fair value for share-based payment transactions. The disclosures above seem designed to deter entities from using unsustainable assumptions. However, these disclosures give information about other commercially sensitive matters. For example, (a)(i) above requires disclosure of future dividend policy for a longer period than is generally covered by such forecasts. Entities may need to consider the impact on investors and analysts of dividend yield assumptions disclosed under IFRS 2.

In making these disclosures, it is important that companies ensure that any assumptions disclosed, particularly those relating to future performance, are consistent with used in other areas of financial reporting that rely on estimates of future events, such as the impairment of fixed assets and goodwill, income taxes (recovery of losses out of future profits) and pensions and other post-retirement benefits.

If the entity has measured a share-based payment transaction directly by reference to the fair value of goods or services received during the period, the entity must disclose how that fair value was determined (e.g. whether fair value was measured at a market price for those goods or services).[150]

As discussed in 4.3 above, IFRS 2 creates a rebuttable presumption in respect of an equity-settled transaction with a counterparty other than an employee that the fair value of goods and services received provides the more reliable basis for assessing the fair value of the transaction. Where the entity has rebutted this presumption, and has valued the transaction by reference to the fair value of equity instruments issued, it must disclose this fact, and give an explanation of why the presumption was rebutted.[151]

8.3   Impact of share-based transactions on financial statements

IFRS 2 requires an entity to 'disclose information that enables users of the financial statements to understand the effect of share-based payment transactions on the entity's profit or loss for the period and on its financial position.'[152]

In order to do this, it must disclose at least:[153]

(a)   the total expense recognised for the period arising from share-based payment transactions in which the goods or services received did not qualify for recognition as assets and hence were recognised immediately as an expense, including separate disclosure of that portion of the total expense that arises from transactions accounted for as equity-settled share-based payment transactions;

(b)   for liabilities arising from share-based payment transactions:

(i)   the total carrying amount at the end of the period; and

(ii)   the total intrinsic value at the end of the period of liabilities for which the counterparty's right to cash or other assets had vested by the end of the period (e.g. vested share appreciation rights).

The requirement in (b)(ii) above is slightly curious, in the sense that the IASB specifically rejected the suggestion of many respondents to ED 2 that cash-settled transactions should be accounted for using an intrinsic value methodology, rather than the fair value methodology required by IFRS 2, stating that the intrinsic value method 'is not an adequate measure of either the ... liability or the cost of services consumed'.[154] This rather begs the question of why the IASB requires disclosure of what is, in its eyes, a defective measure.

8.4 Specimen disclosure

The Implementation Guidance to IFRS 2 gives the following specimen disclosures illustrating the requirements summarised in 8.1 to 8.3 above. Whilst this provides some indication of the IASB's intentions, for an entity of any size a somewhat greater level of disclosure will almost certainly be required. In particular, it does not give examples of the disclosures relating to:

- modification of share awards (see (c) at 8.2 above),

- details of transactions measured directly by reference to the fair value of goods or services provided (see 8.2 above), or

- details of equity-settled transactions with non-employees measured by reference to the fair value of the equity instruments issued (see 8.2 above).[155]

Example 29.27: Illustrative disclosure

Share-based Payment

During the period ended 31 December 2005, the Company had four share-based payment arrangements, which are described below.

Type of arrangement	Senior management share option plan	General employee share option plan	Executive share plan	Senior management share appreciation cash plan
Date of grant	1 January 2004	1 January 2005	1 January 2005	1 July 2005
Number granted	50,000	75,000	50,000	25,000
Contractual life	10 years	10 years	N/A	
Vesting conditions	1.5 years' service and achievement of a share price target, which was achieved.	Three years' service	Three years' service and achievement of a target growth in earnings per share.	Three years' service and achievement of a target increase in market share.

The estimated fair value of each share option granted in the general employee share option plan is €23.60. This was calculated by applying a binomial option pricing model. The model inputs were the share price at grant date of €50.00, exercise price of €50.00, expected volatility of 30%, no expected dividends, contractual life of ten years, and a risk-free interest rate of 5%. To allow for the effects of early exercise, it was assumed that the employees would exercise the options after vesting date when the share price was twice the exercise price. Historical volatility was 40%, which includes the early years of the Company's life; the Company expects the volatility of its share price to reduce as it matures.

The estimated fair value of each share granted in the executive share plan is €50.00, which is equal to the share price at the date of grant.

Further details of the two share option plans are as follows:

	2004		2005	
	Number of options	**Weighted average exercise price**	**Number of options**	**Weighted average exercise price**
Outstanding at start of year	0	–	45,000	€40
Granted	50,000	€40	75,000	€50
Forfeited	(5,000)	€40	(8,000)	€46
Exercised	0	–	(4,000)	€40
Outstanding at end of year	45,000	€40	108,000	€46
Exercisable at end of year	0	€40	38,000	€40

The weighted average share price at the date of exercise for share options exercised during the period was €52.00. The options outstanding at 31 December 2005 had an exercise price of €40.00 or €50.00, and a weighted average remaining contractual life of 8.64 years.

	2004 €	2005 €
Expense arising from share-based payment transactions	495,000	1,105,867
Expense arising from share and share option plans	495,000	1,107,000
Closing balance of liability for cash share appreciation plan	–	98,867
Expense arising from increase in fair value of cash share appreciation plan		9,200

9   TAX DEDUCTIONS

In many jurisdictions entities may receive tax deductions for share-based payment transactions. In many, if not most, cases the tax deduction is given for a cost different to that recorded under IFRS 2. For example, some jurisdictions give a tax deduction for the fair or intrinsic value of the award at the date of exercise; others may give a tax deduction for amounts charged to a subsidiary by its parent or a trust controlled by the parent in respect of the cost of group awards to the employees of that subsidiary. In either case, both the amount and timing of the expense for tax purposes will be different to the amount and timing of the expense required by IFRS 2.

IFRS 2 amends IAS 12 – *Income Taxes* – so as to address particular issues raised by share-based payment transactions. These are discussed further in Chapter 24 at 6.3.

10   SOME PRACTICAL ISSUES

We discuss below the following aspects of the practical application of IFRS 2 that do not fit easily into any of the sections above:

- replacement options issued in a business combination (see 10.1 below);
- 'hedging' share-based payments (see 10.2 below); and
- group share schemes (see 10.3 below).

10.1   Replacement options issued in a business combination

It frequently occurs that an entity (A) acquires another (B) which at the time of the business combination has outstanding employee share options or other share-based awards. If no action were taken by A, employees of B would be entitled, once any vesting conditions had been satisfied, to shares in B. This is not a very satisfactory outcome for either party: A now has minority shareholders in its hitherto wholly-owned subsidiary B, and the employees of B are the proud owners of unmarketable shares in an effectively wholly-owned subsidiary.

The obvious solution, adopted in the majority of cases, is for some mechanism to be put in place such that the employees of B end up holding shares in the new parent A. This can be achieved, for example, by:

- A granting the employees of B options over the shares of A in exchange for the surrender of their options over the shares of B; or

- changing the terms of the options so that they are over a special class of shares in B which are mandatorily convertible into shares of A.

This raises the question of how such a substitution transaction should be accounted for in the consolidated financial statements of A (the treatment in the single entity financial statements of B would fall under the general provisions of IFRS 2 for modification, cancellation and settlement discussed in 4.10 above).

Where vested options in B are surrendered for equivalent vested options in A, or other compensation, we consider that the exchange should be accounted for as a transaction with the owners of B and that the fair value of the consideration given by A should be treated as part of the purchase cost of B.

However, where the surrendered options in B have not yet vested, matters are less clear. In our view, at least two analyses are possible, most easily illustrated by means of an example.

Example 29.28:   Replacement options granted by acquiror in a business combination

A (acquiring entity) acquires B (target entity) in a business combination for which the date of the combination is 1 July 2007.

An employee of B holds 5,000 options granted on 1 July 2005 which will vest on 1 July 2008 if the employee is in service at that date. At the date of acquisition (i.e. 1 July 2007), A cancels the employee's options and in exchange grants 1,000 options over A shares with identical terms (i.e. they will vest on 1 July 2008 if the employee is still in service at that date). The fair value of the Entity A options at 1 July 2007 is €300,000.

One view would be that, as the vesting period is 2/3 expired, the A options have been given 2/3 in consideration for services already rendered (and €200,000 should therefore be accounted for immediately as part of the purchase cost of B) and 1/3 for services to be rendered (and €100,000 should therefore be accounted for as post-combination compensation expense, with the reversal of any expense recognised for awards forfeited before vesting). This is broadly the approach required by current US GAAP[156] and commonly adopted, although not mandatory, under UK GAAP.[157]

Another view would be that in reality A has granted an option with a one year vesting period, all of which should be accounted for as post-acquisition compensation expense. This argument would be strengthened where the unvested option gave no ownership rights (e.g. rights to dividends). Moreover, any amount recorded for the option in the equity of B's own financial statements under IFRS 2 as at the date of acquisition could potentially be reversed in full if the employee left.

This supports an argument that the employee has a contingent rather than an actual ownership interest, such that it is not appropriate to deal with any part of the replacement A option as a transaction with an owner.

In our view, either approach appears possible under IFRS 2. However, whichever approach is adopted, should, in accordance with the basic principles of IAS 1 and IAS 8, be followed consistently. Entities should also have regard to the possible change to IFRS discussed at 10.1.1 below.

10.1.1 Possible future developments

The IASB discussed this issue in June 2004 in the context of its Business Combinations (Phase II) project, and reached the following tentative conclusions:

- a replacement share-based payment award should be regarded as relating to a business combination if the acquirer had an obligation to replace the acquiree's award;

- the fair value guidance in IFRS 2 (see 5 above) should be applied when measuring the fair value of the acquiree award and the fair value of the replacement acquirer award at the acquisition date;

- if, at the acquisition date, the fair value of the replacement acquirer award exceeds the fair value of the acquiree award, that incremental fair value should be accounted for as post-combination compensation expense of the acquirer;

- any remaining fair value of the acquirer replacement award (i.e. the total fair value of that award less any incremental fair value) should be allocated between the purchase price and post-combination compensation expense; and

- no subsequent adjustments should be made to the purchase price. Hence, the effects of subsequent events should be accounted for in the post-combination period.[158]

10.2 'Hedging' share-based payment transactions

Entities often seek to hedge the cost of share-based payment transactions, most commonly by buying their own equity instruments in the market. For example, an entity could grant an employee options over 10,000 shares and buy 10,000 own shares into treasury at the date that the award is made. If the award is share-settled, the entity will deliver the shares to the counterparty. If it is cash-settled, it can sell the shares to raise the cash it is required to deliver to the counterparty. In either case, the cash cost of the award is capped at the market price of the shares at the date the award is made, less any amount paid by the employee on exercise. It could of course be argued that such an arrangement is not a true hedge at all. If the share price goes down so that the option is never exercised, the entity is encumbered by holding 10,000 own shares that cost more than they are now worth.

Whilst these strategies may provide a hedge of the cash cost of share-based payment transactions that are eventually exercised, they will not have any effect in hedging the income statement charge required by IFRS 2 for such transactions. This is because purchases and sales of own shares are accounted for movements in equity and are therefore never included in the income statement (see introduction to 4 above). In any event, IAS 39 does not recognise a hedge of own equity as a valid hedging relationship (see Chapter 19).

10.3 Group share schemes

The analysis of IFRS 2 above has been written in the context of a single legal or reporting entity. In the great majority of cases, however, IFRS 2 will have to be applied to employee share and share option schemes operated by groups of companies, raising further accounting questions not directly addressed by IFRS 2

Suppose, for instance, that P is a parent and S is one of its operating subsidiaries. Employees of S are granted options over the shares of P. S may be required to make a payment (either direct to P or to a trust that administers the option scheme) to cover the cost of the award.

It is clear from the scope of IFRS 2 (see 2.2.2 above) that both P and S are required to account for this transaction. This raises the question of how the transaction should be dealt with in the financial statements of:

(a)   the parent (consolidated financial statements) – see 10.3.1 below;

(b)   the subsidiary – see 10.3.2 below; and

(c)   the parent (separate financial statements) – see 10.3.3. below.

10.3.1 Consolidated financial statements

P's consolidated financial statements will simply adopt the accounting treatment as discussed in 2 to 9 above. The transaction will be determined as being either equity-settled or cash-settled and give rise to, respectively, either an increase in equity or a liability together, in each case, with an expense.

10.3.2 Subsidiary's financial statements

A   Equity-settled transactions

Where the transaction is equity-settled, and S is not required to make any payment in respect of it, S should record an increase in equity and an expense according to the general principles of IFRS 2. The increase in equity represents a capital contribution from P, which has provided S, free of charge, with resources (i.e. shares in P) with which S can pay its employees.

Where S is required to make a payment to P or to a trust, the position is less clear. At least the following four possible analyses suggest themselves:

(a)   The scheme is, from the perspective of S, a cash-settled scheme which should be accounted for as such, with the cost eventually adjusted to reflect the actual amount of cash paid.

(b)   The transaction should continue to be accounted for as an equity-settled transaction, with the cash payments to P or a trust accounted for according to the rules for cash settlement of equity-settled transactions (see 4.10.4 above), whereby payments up to the fair value of the award at the date of settlement are charged to equity, and those in excess of the fair value of the award are charged to the income statement.

(c)   The transaction should continue to be accounted for as an equity-settled transaction. Any payments made to P or a trust are a separate transaction should be accounted for in full as a deduction from equity, on the grounds that they are not payments to settle the transaction with the counterparty (i.e. the employees), but in effect a distribution to P or the trust (i.e. the shareholder that granted the award to the employee).

(d)   As in (c), there are two separate transactions, but characterised as: an equity-settled share-based transaction and an intragroup management charge, both of which should be accounted for separately, giving rise to a double charge to the income statement.

In our view, (c) is the most appropriate treatment, and most likely what the IASB intended.

In our view option (a) is unsatisfactory since the expense that IFRS 2 requires the subsidiary to record is in respect of a transaction with a counterparty (i.e. its employees). In our view, the question of whether or not S has an equity-settled or cash-settled transaction should be determined by whether it has a (direct or indirect) obligation to pay cash to those employees. In a situation where the payments are made purely as matter of intra-group funding or tax policies, and are not effectively passed directly to its employees, there is in our view no liability to the employees, and accordingly the transaction should be treated as equity-settled.

Similar objections apply to the treatment in (b). The provisions of IFRS 2 with regard to cash settlement of equity-settled transactions are clearly addressing settlement with the counterparty to the transaction. If option (a) is rejected because no cash is paid to the employees, then option (b) must similarly be rejected because there is no settlement with the employees. If the transaction were cash-settled by S direct to the employee, S would account for it according to the relevant provisions of IFRS 2 discussed above.

We consider (d) objectionable on the basis that it clearly overstates the cost of the award.

B   Cash-settled transactions

Where a cash-settled transaction is settled by S directly with its employees, the general provisions of IFRS 2 for cash-settled transactions apply (see 6 above).

If (rather unusually) a cash-settled transaction were settled on behalf of S by P, then it would seem appropriate for S to:

- recognise an expense for the transaction under general provisions of IFRS 2 for cash-settled transactions; and

- to transfer the liability, when settled by P, to equity, on the grounds that it represents a capital contribution to S by its owner P.

10.3.3 Parent's separate financial statements

The position here is slightly more complex.

A Equity-settled transactions

In the case of an equity-settled transaction, P will need to record an increase (or movement) in equity since, in order to satisfy the award, it will either be issuing new shares or reissuing treasury shares to the employees of S. This raises three issues:

- what the corresponding debit entry should be;
- the amount at which it should be measured; and
- when it should be recognised.

A simple solution might be to mirror the accounting in S's separate financial statements – i.e. to increase equity and the cost of P's investment in S by an amount equivalent to the IFRS 2 charge in S's financial statements. However, such an approach raises a number of issues.

First, the transaction is not within the scope of IFRS 2 as far as the *separate* financial statements of P are concerned, since it is not a share-based payment by P in consideration for the provision of employee services to P (the single entity) but to S and the P group. It might be argued that any provision of services to S is indirectly a provision of services to P, so that P's separate financial statements are within the scope of IFRS 2. However, such an argument would also lead to the conclusion that not only P, but also each and every and every intermediate parent of S between P and S, is in the scope of IFRS 2 for the purposes of this transaction. In our view, this would not be a sensible result – it could potentially result in an IFRS 2 charge throughout a 'chain' of practically dormant intermediate holding companies, which we doubt was the IASB's intention.

Another objection to the 'mirror image' approach is that it is open to question whether P has increased its investment in S, since it has not contributed cash or any other asset with any value to the subsidiary. On the other hand, it could be argued that it has transferred value to S just as if P had issued the shares subject to option in the market, and contributed the cash to S, and S had used the cash to pay its employees. If the investment in S were increased in this way, the provisions of IFRS relating to impairment would need to be carefully considered (see Chapters 13 and 18). In particular, the 'mirror image' approach would be difficult to apply where it is P's accounting policy to account for investments in subsidiaries in its separate financial statements at fair value under IAS 39 rather than at cost (see Chapter 5 at 7.2), since it is hard to see how the fair value of S can have increased merely as the result of S granting its employees options over P's equity.

An alternative approach (and possibly the only available treatment where it is P's accounting policy to account for investments in subsidiaries in its separate financial statements under IAS 39 rather than at cost – see Chapter 5 at 7.2) would be for P's separate financial statements simply to show the issue of fresh shares, or reissue of treasury shares, when it occurs. Such an approach has the merit of simplicity, but, from the perspective of a proponent of the 'mirror-image' approach discussed above, fails to reflect the transfer of value from P to S.

In cases where S is required to make a payment to P (or to a trust or similar vehicle whose assets and liabilities are accounted for as those of P),[159] the question arises of how such a treatment should be treated. If, as we argue above, such a payment is treated as a distribution by S, it would be logical to treat it as such in the hands of P. The accounting treatment of distributions received by parent entities from subsidiaries is dealt with in IAS 27 and discussed in Chapter 5 at 7.2.

B   Cash-settled transactions

In the case of a cash-settled transaction, it would be expected that the liability actually rested with S and not with P.

If (rather unusually) a cash-settled transaction were settled on behalf of S by P, then it would seem appropriate for P to reflect the payment as an increase in its investment in S, subject to the provisions of IFRS relating to impairment (see Chapters 13 and 18).

11   TRANSITIONAL AND FIRST-TIME ADOPTION ISSUES

IFRS 2 is to be applied for annual periods beginning on or after 1 January 2005. Earlier adoption is encouraged. If an entity applies the IFRS for a period beginning before 1 January 2005, it must disclose that it has done so.[160]

The transitional and first-time adoption provisions are quite complex, particularly as regards the application of the accounting provisions for equity-settled transactions

11.1   Accounting requirements

11.1.1 Equity-settled transactions

A   Existing IFRS reporters

The transitional provisions for entities already reporting under IFRS distinguish between:

(a)   transactions settled in equity instruments granted:

    (i)   or before 7 November 2002;[161] or

    (ii)   after 7 November 2002 but vested before the effective date of IFRS 2 (see IV below); and

(b)   all other transactions, i.e. those granted after 7 November 2002 that have not vested before the effective date of IFRS 2 (see IV below).[162]

I   Mandatory application of IFRS 2

The accounting requirements of IFRS 2 must be applied in full to all transactions falling within (b) above.

The accounting requirements of IFRS 2 need not be applied to transactions falling within (a) above, except that, where such an award is modified, cancelled or settled, the rules regarding modification, cancellation and settlement (see 4.10 above) apply in full, unless the modification, cancellation or settlement occurs before the effective date of IFRS 2 (see IV below).[163]

There is slight ambiguity on this point in the wording of IFRS 2, paragraph 57 of which refers only to the *modification* of awards falling within (a) above. This could allow a literalistic argument that IFRS 2 does not prescribe any specific treatment when an entity cancels or settles (as opposed to modifying) an award within (a) above. However, paragraph 57 also requires an entity to apply 'paragraphs 26-29' of IFRS 2 to 'modified' awards. Paragraphs 26-29 deal not only with modification but also with cancellation and settlement, and indeed paragraphs 28 and 29 are not relevant to modification. This makes it clear, in our view, that the IASB intended IFRS 2 to be applied not only to the modification, but also to any cancellation or settlement of an award falling within (a) above, unless the modification, cancellation or settlement occurs before the effective date of IFRS 2 (see IV below). [164]

II   Voluntary application of IFRS 2

An entity is encouraged to apply the accounting requirements of IFRS 2 to transactions falling within (a) above where it has previously disclosed publicly the fair value of the equity instruments concerned at the relevant measurement date (i.e. grant date for transactions with employees or service date for most other transactions).[165] Whereas it appears that an existing IFRS reporter may voluntarily apply the accounting provisions of IFRS 2 to transactions falling within (a) above whether or not it has published fair value information, a first time adopter may do so only if it has previously published such fair value information (see B II below).[166]

III   Comparative information

For grants of equity instruments to which IFRS 2 is applied, whether mandatorily or voluntarily, the entity must restate comparative information and, where applicable, adjust the opening balance of retained earnings for the earliest period presented.[167]

IV   'Effective date' of IFRS 2

IFRS 2 does not define precisely what it means by 'the effective date'. However, paragraph 60 of IFRS 2 reads as follows:

'EFFECTIVE DATE

60   An entity shall apply this IFRS for annual periods beginning on or after 1 January 2005. Earlier application is encouraged. If an entity applies the IFRS for a period beginning before 1 January 2005, it shall disclose that fact.'

This clearly implies that the effective date is the first date of the first accounting period in which IFRS 2 is applied.

This creates a curious difference between the transitional rules for existing IFRS reporters and those for first-time adopters (see B below). IFRS 1 requires that for a first-time adopter, the 'effective date' of IFRS 2, for the purposes of equity-settled transactions, is the later of 1 January 2005 and the date of transition to IFRS. Thus for those EU entities adopting IFRS in 2005, the effective date is 1 January 2005 irrespective of their year end (since the date of transition will in all cases be earlier).

Suppose that an existing IFRS reporter in Switzerland and a competitor twenty kilometres across the border in France both have a year end of 31 March. Both companies are required to adopt IFRS 2 in the year ended 31 March 2006. The French first-time adopter need not apply IFRS 2 to any awards granted after 7 November 2002 that have vested before 1 January 2005. However, the Swiss existing IFRS reporter need not apply IFRS 2 to any awards granted after 7 November 2002 that have vested before 1 April 2005 (i.e. three months later than for the first-time adopter). It is not clear that why IASB chose to treat the first-time adopter less generously than the existing IFRS user.

B   *Equity-settled transactions – first-time adopters of IFRS*

The transitional provisions for first-time adopters of IFRS distinguish between:

(a)   transactions settled in equity instruments granted:

    (i)   on or before 7 November 2002;[168] or

    (ii)   after 7 November 2002 but vested before the later of:

- 1 January 2005; and

- the date of transition to IFRS; and

(b)   all other transactions, i.e. those granted after 7 November 2002 that have not vested before the later of:

- 1 January 2005; and

- the date of transition to IFRS.[169]

The 'date of transition to IFRS' is the first day of the earliest comparative period presented in a first-time adopter's first set of IFRS financial statements – see Chapter 4.

I   *Mandatory application of IFRS 2*

The accounting requirements of IFRS 2 must be applied in full to all transactions falling within (b) above.

The accounting requirements of IFRS 2 need not be applied to transactions falling within (a) above, except that, where such an award is modified, cancelled or settled, the rules regarding modification, cancellation and settlement (see 4.10 above) apply in full, unless the modification, cancellation or settlement occurs before the later of:

- 1 January 2005; and

- the date of transition to IFRS.[170]

There is slight ambiguity on this point in the wording of IFRS 2 and IFRS 1. Paragraph 57 of IFRS 2 and paragraph 25B of IFRS 1 refer only to the *modification* of awards falling within (a) above. This could allow a literalistic argument that IFRS 2 and IFRS 1 do not prescribe any specific treatment when an entity cancels or settles (as opposed to modifying) an award within (a) above. However, these paragraphs also require an entity to apply 'paragraphs 26-29' of IFRS 2 to 'modified' awards. Paragraphs 26-29 deal not only with modification but also with cancellation and settlement, and indeed paragraphs 28 and 29 are not relevant to modification. This makes it clear, in our view, that the IASB intended

IFRS 2 to be applied not only to modification, but also to any cancellation or settlement of an award falling within (a) above, unless the modification, cancellation or settlement occurs before the later of:

- 1 January 2005; and
- the date of transition to IFRS. [171]

II *Voluntary application of IFRS 2*

A first-time adopter is encouraged to apply the accounting requirements of IFRS 2 to transactions falling within (a) above where it has previously disclosed publicly the fair value of the equity instruments concerned at the relevant measurement date (i.e. grant date for transactions with employees or service date for most other transactions),[172] but only if it has previously published such fair value information.[173]

There is no explicit requirement in IFRS 1 or IFRS 2 that any voluntary retrospective application of IFRS 2 must be based on the fair value previously disclosed. This would appear to allow a first time adopter the flexibility of using a different valuation for IFRS 2 purposes than that previously used for disclosure purposes. However, the requirements of IFRS 1 in relation to estimates under previous GAAP (see Chapter 4 at 2.8.1) mean that the assumptions used in any different accounting model must be consistent with those used in the original disclosed valuation.

III *Comparative information*

For grants of equity instruments to which IFRS 2 is applied, whether mandatorily or voluntarily, the entity must restate comparative information and, where applicable, adjust the opening balance of retained earnings for the earliest period presented.[174]

IV *Costs recorded by first-time adopters under pre-transition GAAP*

It may be that a first-time adopter has at the date of transition a number of equity-settled transactions falling within (a) above for which it is recognising a cost in accordance with its pre-transition GAAP. Some have raised the issue of whether it would be appropriate for such a first-time adopter to take advantage of the transitional provisions in IFRS 2 not to apply IFRS 2 to such transactions, but to continue to recognise a cost based on pre-transition GAAP, so that such awards do not fall out of account altogether. In our view, this would not be acceptable. To us the clear implication of IFRS 2 is that a first-time adopter must either apply IFRS 2 in full to all transactions, or take advantage of the transitional arrangements, with the result that transactions subject to those arrangements effectively cease to exist for recognition and measurement purposes, although some disclosures may be required (see 11.2 below).

11.1.2 Cash-settled transactions

A *Existing IFRS users*

The accounting provisions of IFRS 2 must be applied to all liabilities arising from cash-settled transactions existing at the 'effective date' of IFRS 2 (see 11.1.1 A IV above). The entity must restate comparative information and, where applicable, adjust the opening balance of retained earnings for the earliest period presented, except that there is no requirement for restatement of information where it relates to a period or date earlier than 7 November 2002.[175]

Entities are encouraged, but not required, to apply the accounting provisions of IFRS 2 to other cash-settled transactions, for example liabilities settled during a period for which comparative information is presented.[176]

B   First-time adopters

The accounting provisions of IFRS 2 must be applied to all liabilities arising from cash-settled transactions existing at the 'effective date' of IFRS 2. This is the first date of the first accounting period in which IFRS 2 is adopted (see 11.1.1 A IV above), not 1 January 2005 as an absolute date, as in the case of the first-time adoption provisions for equity-settled transactions (see 11.1.1 B above). The entity must restate comparative information and, where applicable, adjust the opening balance of retained earnings for the earliest period presented, except that there is no requirement for restatement of information where it relates to a period or date earlier than 7 November 2002.[177]

First-time adopters are encouraged, but not required, to apply the accounting provisions of IFRS 2 to cash-settled transactions settled before 1 January 2005.[178]

Additionally, a first-time adopter 'is encouraged, but not required, to apply the accounting provisions of IFRS 2 to cash-settled transactions settled before the date of transition to IFRS'.[179] It is not entirely clear what lies behind this exemption, since a first-time adopter would never be required to report a share-based payment transaction (or indeed any transaction!) settled pre-transition.

11.1.3   Transactions where the counterparty has a choice of settlement method – all preparers

These are not specifically addressed in the transitional rules. It therefore appears that, where such transactions give rise to recognition of both an equity component and a liability component, the equity component is subject to the transitional rules for equity-settled transactions and the liability component to those for cash-settled transactions. This could well mean that the liability component of such a transaction is recognised in the financial statements, whilst the equity component is not.

11.2   Disclosure

The disclosure requirements of IFRS 2 discussed in 8.1 above apply in full to all share-based payment transactions, whether or not the accounting requirements of the standard have been applied to them.[180] The disclosure requirements discussed in 8.2 and 8.3 above naturally apply only to transactions to which the accounting provisions of IFRS 2 have been applied.

References

1 In 2004, the FASB issued an exposure draft of proposals to amend FAS 123 so as to require the expensing of stock options.

2 The then current version of IAS 19 – *Employee Benefits* required extensive disclosures in respect of share-based awards to employees.

3 Discussion paper, *Share-based payment*, G4+1 group, July 2000.

4 IFRS 2, *Share-based Payment*, IASB, February 2004, para. 1.

5 IFRS 2, Appendix A.

6 IFRS 2, Appendix A.

7 IFRS 2, Appendix A.

8 IFRS 2, Appendix A.

9 IFRS 2, Appendix A.

10 IFRS 2, note before heading to para. IG1

11 IFRS 2, para. 2.

12 IFRS 2, para. 5.

13 IFRS 2, para. 3.

14 IAS 27, *Consolidated and Separate Financial Statements*, IASB, December 2003 (amended March 2004).

15 IFRS 2, para. 3.

16 IFRS 2, para. 4.

17 IFRS 2, para. 5.

18 IFRS 2, para. 6.

19 IFRS 2, para. 3.

20 IFRS 2, para. 5.

21 IFRS 2, paras. BC8-BC17.

22 For convenience throughout this Chapter we refer to the recognition of a cost for share-based payments. In some cases, however, a share-based payment transaction may initially give rise to an asset (e.g. where employee costs are capitalised as part of the cost of PPE or inventories).

23 IAS 32, *Financial Instruments: Disclosure and Presentation*, IASB, Decemer 2003 (amended March 2004), para. 11.

24 IFRS 2, paras. BC106-BC110.

25 IFRS 2, para. BC109.

26 IFRS 2, para. BC110.

27 IFRS 2, para. 8.

28 IFRS 2, para. 9.

29 IFRS 2, para. 7.

30 IFRS 2, Appendix A.

31 IFRS 2, Appendix A.

32 IFRS 2, Appendix A.

33 IFRS 2, paras. BC330-BC333.

34 IFRS 2, para. 10.

35 IFRS 2, Appendix A.

36 IFRS 2, paras. BC88-96.

37 IFRS 2, para. BC126.

38 IFRS 2, paras. BC126-BC127.

39 IFRS 2, para. 10.

40 IFRS 2, Appendix A.

41 IFRS 2, para. 11.

42 IFRS 2, para. 12.

43 IFRS 2, Appendix A.

44 IFRS 2, Appendix A and paras. IG1-IG3.

45 IFRS 2, IG4.

46 IFRS 2, para. 13.

47 IFRS 2, paras. 13 and IG5-IG7.

48 IFRS 2, Appendix A.

49 IFRS 2, para. 16.

50 IFRS 2, para. 17.

51 IFRS 2, para. 16.

52 IFRS 2, paras. 19-21

53 IFRS 2, para. 22.

54 IFRS 2, para. 14.

55 IFRS 2, para. 15.

56 IFRS 2, paras. 19-20.

57 IFRS 2, para. IG11.

58 IFRS 2, para. 19.

59 IFRS 2, para. IG11.

60 IFRS 2, paras. 15(b) and IG12.

61 IFRS 2, para. IG12 (Example 4).

62 IFRS 2, Appendix A.

63 IFRS 2, Appendix A.

64 IFRS 2, paras. 21 and IG13

65 IFRS 2, paras. BC183-184.

66 IFRS 2, paras. 19-21 and IG13 (Example 5).

67 IFRS 2, paras. 15(b) and IG14.

68 IFRS 2, Appendix A.

69 IFRS 2, para. 22.

70 IFRS 2, para. 23.

71 IFRS 2, paras. BC218-221.

72 *Framework for the Preparation and Presentation of Financial Statements*, IASB, September 1989, para. 70(a).

73 IFRS 2, para. 26.

74 IFRS 2, paras. 27, B42 and B44.

75 IFRS 2, paras. 27 and B43.

76 IFRS 2, paras. BC222-BC237.

77 IFRS 2, paras. 27, B42-B43

78 IFRS 2, paras. 27 and B42-B43

79 IFRS 2, paras. 27 and B42-B44.

80 IFRS 2, para. B43(a) and IG15 (Example 7).

81 IFRS 2, para. B43(c).

82 IFRS 2, para. B43(b).

83 IFRS 2, para. B43(c).

84 IFRS 2, para. B44(a).

85 IFRS 2, para. B44(c)

86 IFRS 2, para. B44(b).

87 IFRS 2, para. B44(c) and IG15 (Example 8).

88 IFRS 2, paras. 28-29.

89 IFRS 2, para. 28.

90 IFRS 2, para. 28(c).

91 IFRS 2, para. 28 (opening).

92 IFRS 2, para. B1.
93 IFRS 2, para. B2.
94 IFRS 2, para. B3.
95 IFRS 2, paras. B31 and B33-B34.
96 IFRS 2, paras. B4-B5.
97 IFRS 2, para. B5
98 IFRS 2, para. B6.
99 IFRS 2, paras. B7-B9.
100 IFRS 2, para. B10.
101 IFRS 2, paras. B11-B12.
102 IFRS 2, paras. B13-B15.
103 IFRS 2, paras. B16-B17.
104 IFRS 2, para. B18.
105 IFRS 2, paras. B19-B21.
106 IFRS 2, paras. B22-B24.
107 IFRS 2, para. B25.
108 IFRS 2, para. B26.
109 IFRS 2, paras. B27-B29.
110 IFRS 2, para. B30.
111 IFRS 2, paras. B31-B32 and B34.
112 IFRS 2, para. B35.
113 IFRS 2, para. B36.
114 IFRS 2, para. B37.
115 IFRS 2, paras. B38-B39.
116 IFRS 2, paras. B40-B41.
117 IFRS 2, para. 24(a).
118 IFRS 2, para. 24(b).
119 IFRS 2, para. 24(b).
120 IFRS 2, para. 25.
121 IFRS 2, para. 25(a).
122 IFRS 2, para. 25(b).
123 IFRS 2, para. 31.
124 IFRS 2, para. 31.
125 IFRS 2, paras. 30-33, IG Example 12.
126 IFRS 2, para. 33.
127 IFRS 2, paras. BC246-BC251.
128 IFRS 2, para. 32.
129 IFRS 2, para. 32.
130 Throughout the discussion in section 7, 'cash' is
     to be read as including other assets, and 'shares'
     as including other equity instruments.
131 IFRS 2, para. 34.
132 IFRS 2, para. 35.
133 IFRS 2, para. 35.
134 IFRS 2, Appendix A.
135 IFRS 2, para. 36.
136 IFRS 2, para. 37.
137 IFRS 2, para. 37.
138 IFRS 2, para. 38.
139 IFRS 2, paras. 39-40.
140 IFRS 2, para. 40.
141 IFRS 2, para. 41.
142 IFRS 2, paras. 41-42.
143 A 'good' leaver generally refers to one who has
     not been dismissed and does not leave in the
     early part of the vesting period.
144 IFRS 2, para. 43.
145 IFRS 2, para. 43.

146 IFRS 2, para. 44.
147 IFRS 2, para. 45.
148 IFRS 2, para. 46.
149 IFRS 2, para. 47.
150 IFRS 2, para. 48.
151 IFRS 2, para. 49.
152 IFRS 2, para. 50.
153 IFRS 2, para. 51.
154 IFRS 2, para. BC250.
155 IFRS 2, para. IG23.
156 FIN44, *Accounting for Certain Transactions
     involving Stock Compensation, an interpretation
     of APB Opinion No. 25*, FASB, March 2000.
157 Ernst & Young's *UK and International GAAP*,
     Seventh Edition, Ernst & Young, 2001,
     page 1478.
158 *IASB Update*, IASB, June 2004.
159 There is no generic guidance on this issue in
     IFRS.
160 IFRS 2, para. 60.
161 The publication date of ED 2.
162 IFRS 2, paras. 53 and 60; IFRS 1, *First-time
     Adoption of International Financial Reporting
     Standards*, IASB, June 2003 (amended March
     2004), paras. 25B and IG64-IG65 (as inserted by
     IFRS 2 para. C8).
163 IFRS 2, paras. 57 and 60.
164 IFRS 2, paras. 57 and 60.
165 IFRS 2, para. 54, Appendix 1.
166 IFRS 1, para. 25B.
167 IFRS 2, para. 55.
168 The publication date of ED 2.
169 IFRS 2, paras. 53 and 60; IFRS 1, paras. 25B
     and IG64-65.
170 IFRS 2, paras. 57 and 60; IFRS 1, para. 25B.
171 IFRS 2, paras. 57 and 60; IFRS 1, para. 25B.
172 IFRS 2, para. 54, Appendix 1.
173 IFRS 1, para. 25B.
174 IFRS 2, para. 55.
175 IFRS 2, para. 58.
176 IFRS 2, para. 59.
177 IFRS 2, para. 58; IFRS 1, para. 25C.
178 IFRS 2, para. 59; IFRS 1, para. 25C.
179 IFRS 1, para. 25C.
180 IFRS 2, para. 56; IFRS 1, para. 25B.

Chapter 30   Employee benefits

1   INTRODUCTION

Employee benefits typically form a very significant part of any entity's costs, and can take many and varied forms. Accordingly, international accounting standards devote considerable attention to them in two separate standards. IFRS 2 – *Share-based Payments* – which was issued primarily in response to concerns over share-based remuneration deals with the controversial topic of share-based payments and is discussed in Chapter 29. All other employee benefits are dealt with in IAS 19 – *Employee Benefits*, discussed in this Chapter.

Many issued raised in accounting for employee benefits can be straight forward, such as the allocation of wages paid to an accounting period, and are generally dealt with by IAS 19 accordingly. In contrast, accounting for the costs of retirement benefits in the financial statements of employer companies presents one of the most difficult challenges in the whole field of financial reporting. The amounts involved are large, the timescale is long, the estimation process is complex and involves many areas of uncertainty which have to be made the subject of assumptions; in addition the actuarial mechanisms used for allocating the costs to years of employment are complicated and their selection open to debate. Furthermore, the complexities for an International Standard are multiplied by the wide variety of arrangements found in different jurisdictions. In light of this it is perhaps not surprising that the requirements of IAS in this area are complex and have changed frequently, sometimes radically, over the years.

In January 1983, the IASC issued IAS 19 – *Accounting for Retirement Benefits in the Financial Statements of Employers* – which was revised ten years later in November 1993 with the shortened title of *Retirement Benefit Costs*. Put simply, the original IAS 19 was an 'income statement standard' which sought to charge to income systematically the long-term cost of providing retirement benefits.

In October 1996, however, the IASC published an exposure draft proposing to make fundamental changes to IAS 19.[1] In particular, the whole focus of the standard was to be shifted from the income statement to the balance sheet. This led to the issue of a further revised version of IAS 19 in February 1998, to take effect for accounting periods beginning on or after 1 January 1999. The title of the standard was also changed to 'Employee Benefits' reflecting a broadening of its scope to cover pre-retirement and post-retirement benefits as well as disclosure requirements for employee equity compensation benefits (these latter requirements being superseded in 2003 by the publication of IFRS 2). In 1999, IAS 10 – *Events After the Balance Sheet Date* – made some minor consequential amendments to IAS 19, effective for periods beginning on or after 1 January 2000. In October 2000 some further adjustments were made to IAS 19 relating to the treatment of assets in the form of insurance policies and reimbursement rights. These refinements came into force for periods beginning on or after 1 January 2001. The standard was revised again in 2002 to correct a perceived anomaly that in some circumstances the interaction of the standard's complex (indeed, conceptually conflicting) requirements could lead to the recognition of profits purely as a result of actuarial *losses* in a pension fund (and vice versa). These changes took effect for periods ending on or after 31 May 2002.

In April 2004, the IASB published an exposure draft of some further revisions to IAS 19.[2] Even these changes are not the final chapter in the evolution of IAS 19, as the Board acknowledges that further development may be necessary as it progresses its project on comprehensive income.[3] The possible future development of the standard is discussed at 10 below.

2   OBJECTIVE AND SCOPE OF IAS 19

2.1   Objective

IAS 19 sets out its objective as follows:

'The objective of this Standard is to prescribe the accounting and disclosure for employee benefits. The Standard requires an enterprise to recognise:

(a)   a liability when an employee has provided service in exchange for employee benefits to be paid in the future; and

(b)   an expense when the enterprise consumes the economic benefit arising from service provided by an employee in exchange for employee benefits.'[4]

It is fair to say the above is more of a summary than an objective (the objective of *all* accounting standards is to 'prescribe ... accounting and disclosure...' for some aspect of financial reporting) or at best an objective that is by definition self fulfilling. However, it provides the first glimpse of the new direction taken by the revised standard. Driven by the balance sheet approach in the IASB's *Framework*[5] it approaches the issues from a balance sheet perspective although as we shall discuss later it currently stops short of a full fair value balance sheet treatment.

2.2   Scope

As mentioned above, the 1998 version of IAS 19 became entitled 'Employee Benefits', and as this name suggests it is not confined to pensions and other post-retirement benefits, but rather addresses all forms of consideration (aside of share based payments which are dealt with by IFRS 2 and discussed in Chapter 29) given by an employer in exchange for service rendered by employees.[6] In particular, in addition to post-retirement benefits employee benefits include:[7]

(a) short-term benefits, including wages and salaries, paid annual leave, bonuses, benefits in kind, etc. The accounting treatment of these is discussed at 6.1;

(b) long-term benefits, such as long-service leave, long-term disability benefits, long-term bonuses, etc. These are to be accounted for in a similar way to post-retirement benefits by using actuarial techniques and are discussed at 6.2 below;

(c) termination benefits. These are to be provided for and expensed when the employer becomes committed to the redundancy plan, on a similar basis to that required by IAS 37 – *Provisions, Contingent Liabilities and Contingent Assets* – for provisions generally, and are discussed at 6.3 below.

The standard addresses only the accounting by employers, and excludes from its scope reporting by employee benefit plans themselves. These are dealt with in IAS 26 – *Accounting and Reporting by Retirement Benefit Plans*.[8] The specialist nature of these requirements puts them beyond the scope of this book.

Until the requirements were superseded by IFRS 2 in 2003, IAS 19 also dealt with equity compensation benefits, such as share option schemes, share purchase schemes at a discount, phantom share schemes etc. IAS 19 ducked the difficult (not to mention highly controversial) recognition and measurement issues that have continued to trouble other standard setters and only prescribed a set of disclosures about such arrangements. IFRS 2 finally grasped the nettle by requiring (from 2005) the expensing of share-based remuneration in the income statement based on an estimate of fair value. This is discussed in Chapter 29.

Aside of the above two scope exclusions the standard makes clear it applies widely, and in particular to benefits:

(a) provided to all employees (whether full-time, part-time, permanent, temporary or casual staff and specifically including directors and other management personnel);[9]

(b) however settled – including payments in cash or goods or services, whether paid directly to employees, their dependents (spouses, children or others) or any other party (such as insurance companies);[10] and

(c) however provided, including:

(i) under formal plans or other formal agreements between an entity and individual employees, groups of employees or their representatives;

(ii) under legislative requirements, or through industry arrangements, whereby entities are required to contribute to national, state, industry or other multi-employer plans; or

(iii) by those informal practices that give rise to a constructive obligation, that is where the entity has no realistic alternative but to pay employee benefits. An example of a constructive obligation is where a change in the entity's informal practices would cause unacceptable damage to its relationship with employees.[11]

The following extract illustrates some of the variety of employee benefits addressed by the standard.

Extract 30.1: Telekom SA Limited (2003)

Notes to the consolidated annual financial statements [extract]

2.   Significant accounting policies [extract]

Employee benefits [extract]

Post-employment benefits

The Group provides defined benefit and defined contribution plans for the benefit of employees. These plans are funded by the employees and the Group, taking into account recommendations of the independent actuaries. The post retirement medical and telephone rebate liabilities are unfunded.

Defined contribution plans

The Group's funding of the defined contribution plans is charged to the income statement in the same period as the related service is provided.

Defined benefit plans

The Group provides defined benefit pans for pension, medical aid costs, and telephone rebates to qualifying employees. The Group's net obligation in respect of defined benefits is calculated separately for each plan by estimating the amount of future benefits earned in return for services rendered.

The amount recognised in the balance sheet represents the present value of the defined benefit obligations, calculated using the project unit credit method, as adjusted for unrecognised actuarial gains and losses, unrecognised past service costs and reduced by the fair value of plan assets. The amount of any surplus recognised is limited to unrecognised actuarial losses and past service costs plus the present value of available refunds and reductions in future contributions to the plan. To the extent that there is uncertainty as to the entitlement to the surplus, no asset is recognised.

Actuarial gains and losses are recognised as income or expense when the cumulative unrecognised gains and losses for each individual plan exceed 10% of the greater of the present value of the Group's obligation or the fair value of plan assets. These gains or losses are amortised on a straight-line basis over ten years.

Past service costs are recognised immediately to the extent that the benefits are vested, otherwise they are recognised on a straight-line basis over the average period the benefits become vested.

Short-term employee benefits

The cost of all short-term employee benefits is recognised during the period employees render services.

Leave benefits

Holiday leave is provided for over the period that the leave accrues and is subject to a cap. Sick leave is provided for on days accrued and is also subject to a cap.

3   PENSIONS AND OTHER POST-EMPLOYMENT BENEFITS – DEFINED CONTRIBUTION AND DEFINED BENEFIT PLANS

3.1   The distinction between defined contribution plans and defined benefit plans

In common with other accounting standards around the world, IAS 19 draws the natural, but important, distinction between defined contribution plans and defined benefit plans. The approach it takes is to define the former, with the latter being the default category. The relevant terms defined by the standard are as follows:

'*Post-employment benefits* are employee benefits (other than termination benefits) which are payable after the completion of employment.'

'*Post-employment benefit plans* are formal or informal arrangements under which an enterprise provides post-employment benefits for one or more employees.'

'*Defined contribution plans* are post-employment benefit plans under which an enterprise pays fixed contributions into a separate entity (a fund) and will have no legal or constructive obligation to pay further contributions if the fund does not hold sufficient assets to pay all employee benefits relating to employee service in the current and prior periods.'

'*Defined benefit plans* are post-employment benefit plans other than defined contribution plans'[12]

IAS 19 applies to all post-employment benefits (whether or not they involve the establishment of a separate entity to receive contributions and pay benefits) which include, for example, retirement benefits such as pensions; and post-employment life assurance or medical care.[13] A less common benefit is the provision of services. Extract 30.1 at 2.2 above provides an example of a company providing telephone rebates to former employees. Under defined benefit plans the employer's obligation is not limited to the amount that it agrees to contribute to the fund. Rather, the employer is obliged (legally or constructively) to provide the agreed benefits to current and former employees. Examples of defined benefit schemes given by IAS 19 are:

(a)   plans where the benefit formula is not linked solely to the amount of contributions;

(b)   guarantees, either directly or indirectly through a plan, of a specified return on contributions; and

(c)   those informal practices that give rise to a constructive obligation. For example, a history of increasing benefits for former employees to keep pace with inflation even where there is no legal obligation to do so.[14]

The most significant difference between defined contribution and defined benefit plans is that, under defined benefit plans, both actuarial risk and investment risk fall on the employer. This means that if actuarial or investment experience is worse than expected, the employer's obligation may be increased.[15] Consequently, because the employer is underwriting the actuarial and investment risks associated with the plan, the expense recognised for a defined benefit plan is not necessarily the amount of the contribution due for the period.[16] Conversely, under defined contribution plans the benefits received by the employee are determined by the amount of contributions paid (either by the employer, or both the employer and the employee) together with investment returns, and hence actuarial and investment risk a borne by the employee.[17]

3.2   Insured benefits

One factor that can complicate making the distinction between defined benefit and defined contribution plans is the use of external insurers. IAS 19 recognises that some employers may fund their post-employment benefit plans by paying insurance premiums and observes that the benefits insured need not have a direct or automatic relationship with the entity's obligation for employee benefits. However it makes clear that post-employment benefit plans involving insurance contracts are subject to the same distinction between accounting and funding as other funded plans.[18]

Where insurance premiums are paid to fund post employment benefits, the employer should treat the plan as a defined contribution plan unless it has a legal or constructive obligation to:

(a)   pay the employee benefits directly when they fall due; or

(b)   pay further amounts if the insurer does not pay all future employee benefits relating to employee service in the current and prior periods.

If the employer has retained such a legal or constructive obligation it should treat the plan as a defined benefit plan.[19] In that case, the employer recognises its rights under a 'qualifying insurance policy' as a plan asset and recognises other insurance policies as reimbursement rights.[20] Plan assets are discussed at 5.2.1 below.

By way of final clarification, the standard notes that where an insurance policy is in the name of a specified plan participant or a group of plan participants and the employer does not have any legal or constructive obligation to cover any loss on the policy, the employer has no obligation to pay benefits to the employees and the insurer has sole responsibility for paying the benefits. In that case, the payment of fixed premiums under such contracts is, in substance, the settlement of the employee benefit obligation, rather than an investment to meet the obligation. Consequently, the employer no longer has an asset or a liability. Accordingly, it should treat the payments as contributions to a defined contribution plan.[21] The important point here is that employee entitlements will be of a defined benefit nature unless the employer has no obligation whatsoever to pay them should the insurance fail or otherwise be insufficient.

The standard's analysis of insured plans described above, along with the definition of defined benefit and defined contribution plans seems comprehensive at first glance. However, there will be circumstances where careful consideration will be required and which reveal that the distinction may not be that cut and dried after all. For example, it is possible that an employer buys insurance on a regular basis (say annually), retaining no further obligation in respect of the benefits insured, but has an obligation (legal or constructive) to keep doing so in the future. In such a scenario the employer may be exposed to future actuarial variances reflected in a variable cost of purchasing the required insurance in future years (for example, due to changing mortality estimates by the insurer). An example would be where each year the employee earns an entitlement to a pension of (say) 2% of that year's (i.e. current as opposed to final) salary and that the employer purchases each year an annuity contract to commence on the date of retirement.

In our view the standard is not entirely clear as to the nature of such an arrangement. On the one hand, it could be argued that it is a defined contribution plan because the definition of defined contribution plans is met when:

- 'fixed' payments are paid to a separate fund; and

- the employer is not obliged to pay further amounts if the fund has insufficient assets to pay the benefits relating to employee service in the *current and prior periods*.

Further, as noted above the standard considers the payment of 'fixed' premiums to purchase insurance specific to an employee (or group thereof) with no retention of risk in respect of the insured benefits to be a defined contribution arrangement.

On the other hand, it could be argued that this is a defined benefit plan on the grounds that:

- the premiums of future years are not 'fixed' in any meaningful sense (certainly not in the same way as an intention simply to pay a one-off contribution of a given % of salary);

- the standard acknowledges that one factor that can mean insured arrangements are defined benefit in nature is when the employer retains an obligation indirectly through the mechanism for setting future premiums; and

- the standard observes that under defined benefit plans '...actuarial risk (that benefits will cost more than expected) and investment risk fall, in substance, on the enterprise. If actuarial or investment experience are worse than expected, the enterprise's obligation may be increased.'[22]

Much would seem to depend on just what 'fixed' means in such circumstances. Although not expressly addressed by the standard, in our view such arrangements will very likely be defined benefit in nature, albeit with regular (and perhaps only partial) settlement and, if so, should be accounted for as such. This is because the employer has retained actuarial risks by committing to pay whatever it takes in future years to secure the requisite insurance. Naturally, for any schemes that are determined to be defined benefit plans, the next step would be to see whether the frequent settlement renders the output of the two accounting models materially the same. That would depend, inter alia, on the attribution of the benefit to years of service and the impact of an unwinding discount. The wide variety of possible arrangements in practice mean that careful consideration of individual circumstances will be required to determine the true substance of such arrangements.

3.3   Multi-employer plans

Multi-employer plans, other than state plans (see 3.4 below), under IAS 19 are defined contribution plans or defined benefit plans that:

(a)   pool assets contributed by various entities that are not under common control; and

(b)   use those assets to provide benefits to employees of more than one entity, on the basis that contribution and benefit levels are determined without regard to the identity of the entity that employs the employees concerned.[23]

Accordingly, they exclude group administration plans, which simply pool the assets of more than one employer, for investment purposes and the reduction of administrative and investment costs, but keep the claims of different employers segregated for the sole benefit of their own employees. The standard observes that group administration plans pose no particular accounting problems because information is readily available to treat them in the same way as any other single employer plan and because they do not expose the participating employers to actuarial risks associated with the current and former employees of other entities. Accordingly, the standard requires group administration plans to be classified as defined contribution plans or defined benefit plans in accordance with the terms of the plan (including any constructive obligation that goes beyond the formal terms).[24]

The standard gives a description of one example of a multi-employer scheme as follows:

(a)   the plan is financed on a pay-as-you-go basis such that: contributions are set at a level that is expected to be sufficient to pay the benefits falling due in the same period; and future benefits earned during the current period will be paid out of future contributions; and

(b)   employees' benefits are determined by the length of their service and the participating entities have no realistic means of withdrawing from the plan without paying a contribution for the benefits earned by employees up to the date of withdrawal. Such a plan creates actuarial risk for the entity: if the ultimate cost of benefits already earned at the balance sheet date is more than expected, the entity will have to either increase its contributions or persuade employees to accept a reduction in benefits. Therefore, such a plan is a defined benefit plan.[25]

A multi-employer plan should be classified as either a defined contribution plan or a defined benefit plan in accordance with its terms in the normal way (see 3.1 above). If a multi-employer plan is classified as a defined benefit plan, IAS 19 requires that the employer should account for its proportionate share of the defined benefit obligation, plan assets and costs associated with the plan in the same way as for any other defined benefit plan (see 5 below). The employer should also disclose the same information as is required for any other defined benefit plan.[26]

The standard does, however, contain a practical exemption if insufficient information is available to use defined benefit accounting. This could be the case, for example, where:

(a) the entity does not have access to information about the plan that satisfies the requirements of the standard; or

(b) the plan exposes the participating entities to actuarial risks associated with the current and former employees of other entities, with the result that there is no consistent and reliable basis for allocating the obligation, plan assets and cost to individual entities participating in the plan.[27]

In such circumstances, an entity should:[28]

(a) account for the plan as if it were a defined contribution plan;

(b) disclose that the plan is a defined benefit plan and the reason why insufficient information is available to account for the plan as a defined benefit plan; and

(c) to the extent that a surplus or deficit in the plan may affect future contributions, disclose:

   (i)   any available information about that surplus or deficit;

   (ii) the basis used to determine the surplus or deficit; and

   (iii) any implications for the entity.

As noted above, IAS 19 provides that defined benefit plans that pool the assets contributed by various entities under common control, for example a parent and its subsidiaries, are not multi-employer plans and that, therefore, an entity treats all such plans as defined benefit plans.[29] The test for allowing a defined benefit multi-employer plan to be accounted for as a defined contribution plan is, as described earlier, that insufficient information is available. By completely excluding entities that are under common control from the definition of multi-employer plans the standard is essentially saying that for these employers sufficient information is deemed always to be available. In April 2004 the IASB published proposals to relax (at least partially) this strict stance. This is discussed at 10.2 below.

IAS 19 also contains a reminder that IAS 37 requires an entity to recognise, or disclose information in relation to, certain contingent liabilities, and notes that such contingencies may arise (in the context of a multi-employer plan) from:

(a) actuarial losses relating to the other participating entities because each entity that participates in a multi-employer plan shares in the actuarial risks of every other participating employer; or

(b) any responsibility under the terms of a plan to finance any shortfall in the plan if other entities cease to participate.[30] IAS 37 is discussed in Chapter 25.

3.4   State plans

IAS 19 observes that state plans are established by legislation to cover all entities (or all entities in a particular category, for example a specific industry) and are operated by national or local government or by another body (for example an autonomous agency created specifically for this purpose) which is not subject to control or influence by the reporting entity.[31] The standard requires that state plans be accounted for in the same way as for a multi-employer plan (see 3.3 above).[32] It goes on to note that although many state plans are:

- funded on a pay-as-you-go basis;

- with contributions set at a level that is expected to be sufficient to pay the required benefits falling due in the same period; and

- future benefits earned during the current period will be paid out of future contributions.

nevertheless, in most state plans, the entity has no legal or constructive obligation to pay those future benefits: its only obligation is to pay the contributions as they fall due and if the entity ceases to employ members of the state plan, it will have no obligation to pay the benefits earned by its own employees in previous years. For this reason, the standard considers that state plans are normally defined contribution plans. However, in the rare cases when a state plan is a defined benefit plan, IAS 19 requires it to be treated as such as a multi-employer plan.[33]

Some plans established by an entity provide both compulsory benefits which substitute for benefits that would otherwise be covered under a state plan and additional voluntary benefits. IAS 19 clarifies that such plans are not state plans.[34]

3.5   Plans that would be defined contribution plans but for the existence of a minimum return guarantee

It is common in some jurisdictions for the employer to make contributions to a defined contribution post retirement benefit plan and to guarantee a minimum level of return on the assets in which the contributions are invested. In other words the employee enjoys upside risk on the investments but has some level of protection from downside risk.

The existence of such a guarantee means the arrangement fails to meet the definition of a defined contribution plan (see 3.1 above) and accordingly is a defined benefit plan. Indeed, the standard is explicit as it uses plans which guarantee a specified return on contributions as an example a defined benefit arrangement.[35] The somewhat thornier issue is how exactly to apply defined benefit accounting to such an arrangement, as this would require projecting forward future salary increases and investment returns, and discounting these amounts at corporate bond rates. Although clearly required by the standard, some would consider this approach inappropriate in such circumstances. At the time of writing the issue is being debated by IFRIC, which published a draft interpretation on 8 July 2004 entitled D9 – *Employee Benefit Plans with a Promised Return on Contributions or Notional Contributions*. The approach taken in D9 is to distinguish two different types of benefits:

(a)   a benefit of contributions or notional contributions plus a guarantee of a fixed return (in other words, benefits which can be estimated without having to make an estimate of future asset returns); and

(b)   a benefit that depends on future asset returns.

For benefits under (a) above, IAS 19's defined benefit methodology is applied as normal. In summary, that means:

- calculating the benefit to be paid in the future by projecting forward the contributions or notional contributions at the guaranteed fixed rate of return;

- allocating the benefit to periods of service;

- discounting the benefits allocated to the current and prior periods at the rate specified in IAS 19 to arrive at the plan liability, current service cost and interest cost; and

- recognising any actuarial gains and losses in accordance with the entity's accounting policy.

For benefits covered by (b) above, the plan liability should be measured at the fair value at the balance sheet date of the assets upon which the benefit is specified (whether plan assets or notional assets). No projection forward of the benefits should be made, and discounting of the benefit is not therefore required.

Plans with a combination of a guaranteed fixed return and a benefit that depends on future asset returns should be accounted for by analysing the benefits into a fixed component and a variable component. The defined benefit asset or liability that would arise from the fixed component alone should be measured and recognised as described above. The defined benefit asset (or liability) that would arise from the variable component alone should then be calculated as described above and compared to the fixed component. An additional plan liability should be recognised to the extent that the asset (or liability) calculated for the variable component is smaller (or greater) than the asset (or liability) recognised in respect of the fixed component.

3.6 Death-in-service benefits

The provision of death-in-service benefits is a common part of employment packages (either as part of a defined benefit plan or on a stand alone basis). We think it is regrettable that IAS 19 provides no guidance on how to account for such benefits, particularly as E54 devoted considerable attention to the issue.[36] IAS 19 explains the removal of the guidance as follows. 'E54 gave guidance on cases where death-in-service benefits are not insured externally and are not provided through a post-employment benefit plan. The Board concluded that such cases will be rare. Accordingly, the Board agreed to delete the guidance on death-in-service benefits.'[37]

In our view this misses the point – E54 also gave guidance on cases where the benefits *are* externally insured and where they are provided through a post-employment benefit plan. In our view the proposals in E54 were quite sensible ones, and it is worth reproducing them here.

> 'An enterprise should recognise the cost of death-in-service benefits ... as follows:
>
> (a) in the case of benefits insured or re-insured with third parties, in the period in respect of which the related insurance premiums are payable; and

(b)   in the case of benefits not insured or re-insured with third parties, to the extent that deaths have occurred before the balance sheet date.

However, in the case of death-in-service benefits provided through a post-employment benefit plan, an enterprise should recognise the cost of those benefits by including their present value in the post-employment benefit obligation.

If an enterprise re-insures a commitment to provide death-in-service benefits, it acquires a right (to receive payments if an employee dies in service) in exchange for an obligation to pay the premiums.

Where an enterprise provides death-in-service benefits directly, rather than through a post-employment benefit plan, the enterprise has a future commitment to provide death-in-service coverage in exchange for employee service in those same future periods (in the same way that the enterprise has a future commitment to pay salaries if the employee renders service in those periods). That future commitment is not a present obligation as does not justify recognition of a liability. Therefore, an obligation arises only to the extent that a death has already occurred by the balance sheet date.

If death-in-service benefits are provided through a pension plan (or other post-employment plan) which also provides post-employment benefits to the same employee(s), the measurement of the obligation reflects both the probability of a reduction in future pension payments through death in service and the present value of the death-in-service benefits (see [E 54's discussion of mutual compatibility of actuarial assumptions]).

Death-in-service benefits differ from post-employment life insurance because post-employment life insurance creates an obligation as the employee renders services in exchange for that benefit; an enterprise accounts for that obligation in accordance with [the requirements for defined benefit plans]. Life insurance benefits that are payable regardless of whether the employee remains in service comprise two components: a death-in-service benefit and a post-employment benefit. An enterprise accounts for the two components separately.'

We would suggest that the above continues to represent valid guidance to the extent it doesn't conflict with extant IAS. In particular, we would recommend:

- death-in-service benefits provided as part of a defined benefit post-employment plan are factored into the actuarial valuation. In which case any insurance cover should be accounted for in accordance with IAS 19's normal rules (see 5.2.1 below);

- other death-in-service benefits which are externally insured are accounted for by expensing the premiums as they become payable;

- other death-in-service benefits which are not externally insured are provided for as deaths in service occur.

4 DEFINED CONTRIBUTION PLANS

4.1 Accounting requirements

Accounting for defined contribution plans is straightforward under IAS 19 because, as the standard observes, the reporting entity's obligation for each period is determined by the amounts to be contributed for that period. Consequently, no actuarial assumptions are required to measure the obligation or the expense and there is no possibility of any actuarial gain or loss to the reporting entity. Moreover, the obligations are measured on an undiscounted basis, except where they do not fall due wholly within twelve months after the end of the period in which the employees render the related service.[38] Where discounting is required, the discount rate should be determined in the same way as for defined benefit plans, which is discussed at 5.2.2 E below.[39] In general, though, it would seem unlikely for a defined contribution scheme to be structured with such a long delay between the employee service and the employer contribution.

IAS 19 requires that, when an employee has rendered services during a period, the employer should recognise the contribution payable to a defined contribution plan in exchange for that service:

(a) as a liability, after deducting any contribution already paid. If the contribution already paid exceeds the contribution due for service before the balance sheet date, the excess should be recognised as an asset when such prepayment will lead to a reduction in future payments or a cash refund; and

(b) as an expense, unless another International Accounting Standard requires or permits capitalisation of such expense.[40]

5 DEFINED BENEFIT PLANS

5.1 General

The standard notes that accounting for defined benefit plans is complex because actuarial assumptions are required to measure both the obligation and the expense, and there is a possibility of actuarial gains and losses. Moreover, the obligations are measured on a discounted basis because they may be settled many years after the employees render the related service.[41] Also, IAS 19 makes clear that it applies not just to unfunded obligations of employers but also to funded plans. The details of pension scheme arrangements vary widely form jurisdiction to jurisdiction and, indeed, within them. Frequently though, they involve some entity or fund, separate from the employer, to which contributions are made by the employer (and sometimes employees) and from which benefits are paid. Typically, the employer (through either legal or constructive obligations) essentially underwrites the fund in the event that the assets in the fund are insufficient to pay the required benefits. This is the key feature which means such an arrangement is a defined benefit plan.[42]

In addition to specifying accounting and disclosure requirements, IAS 19 provides what amounts to a work programme of the steps necessary to apply its rules, as follows:

(a)   using actuarial techniques, make a reliable estimate of the amount of benefit that employees have earned in return for their service in the current and prior periods. This requires an entity to determine how much benefit is attributable to the current and prior periods and to make estimates (actuarial assumptions) about demographic variables (such as employee turnover and mortality) and financial variables (such as future increases in salaries and medical costs) that will influence the cost of the benefit;

(b)   discount that benefit using the projected unit credit method in order to determine the present value of the defined benefit obligation and the current service cost;

(c)   determine the fair value of any plan assets;

(d)   determine the total amount of actuarial gains and losses and the amount of those actuarial gains and losses that should be recognised;

(e)   where a plan has been introduced or changed, determine the resulting past service cost; and

(f)   where a plan has been curtailed or settled, determine the resulting gain or loss.[43]

Retirement benefits will often be very significant in the context of an employer's financial statements. However, the standard acknowledges that in some circumstances estimates, averages and computational shortcuts may provide a reliable approximation.[44]

Where an employer has more than one defined benefit plan, it should apply the steps above for each material plan separately.[45]

The standard contains a detailed worked example illustrating how the various accounting entries are arrived at from the underlying data.[46]

5.2   Valuation of the plan surplus or deficit

5.2.1   Plan assets

A   Definition of plan assets

IAS 19 provides a definition of plan assets (which exclude unpaid contributions due from the employer to the fund, and any non-transferable financial instruments issued by the employer and are to be reduced by any liabilities of the fund not related to employee benefits – such as trade and other payables and derivative financial instruments[47]) as follows:

'*Plan assets* comprise:

(a)   assets held by a long-term employee benefit fund; and

(b)   qualifying insurance policies.

Assets held by a long-term employee benefit fund are assets (other than non-transferable financial instruments issued by the reporting enterprise) that:

(a) are held by an entity (a fund) that is legally separate from the reporting enterprise and exists solely to pay or fund employee benefits; and

(b) are available to be used only to pay or fund employee benefits, are not available to the reporting enterprise's own creditors (even in bankruptcy), and cannot be returned to the reporting enterprise, unless either:

    (i) the remaining assets of the fund are sufficient to meet all the related employee benefit obligations of the plan or the reporting enterprise; or

    (ii) the assets are returned to the reporting enterprise to reimburse it for employee benefits already paid.

A qualifying insurance policy is an insurance policy issued by an insurer that is not a related party (as defined in IAS 24 – *Related Party Disclosures*) of the reporting enterprise, if the proceeds of the policy:

(a) can be used only to pay or fund employee benefits under a defined benefit plan;

(b) are not available to the reporting enterprise's own creditors (even in bankruptcy) and cannot be paid to the reporting enterprise, unless either:

    (i) the proceeds represent surplus assets that are not needed for the policy to meet all the related employee benefit obligations; or

    (ii) the proceeds are returned to the reporting enterprise to reimburse it for employee benefits already paid.'[48]

In 2004 IFRS 4 – *Insurance Contracts* – introduced a footnote to this definition to clarify that a qualifying insurance policy is not necessarily an insurance contract as defined in IFRS 4.

Whilst non-transferable financial instruments issued by the employer are excluded from the definition of plan assets, it is not uncommon for plans to own shares in the employer. Such shareholdings can sometimes be very substantial as illustrated in the following extract.

Extract 30.2: Novartis AG (2003)

Notes to the Novartis Group Consolidated Financial Statements [extract]

25   **Employee benefits** [extract]

The number of Novartis AG shares held by pension and similar benefit funds at December 31, 2003 was 31.5 million shares with a market value of USD 1.3 billion (2002: 31.5 million shares with a market value of USD 1.1 billion). These funds did not dispose of any Novartis AG shares during the year ended December 31, 2003 (2002: 2.5 million shares). The amount of dividends received on Novartis AG shares held as plan assets by these funds were USD 22 million for the year ended December 31, 2003 (2002: USD 22 million).

B   *Measurement of plan assets*

IAS 19 requires plan assets to be measured at their fair value,[49] which is defined as the amount for which an asset could be exchanged between knowledgeable, willing parties in an arm's length transaction.[50] There is no further explanation in IAS 19 as to the meaning of fair value. However, it is defined in exactly the same way as in IAS 39 – *Financial Instruments: Recognition and Measurement.* That standard does contain further elaboration, and in particular makes clear that for quoted securities held, fair value usually means bid price with no deduction for transaction costs which may be incurred on disposal.[51] When no market price is available, IAS 19 notes that the fair value needs to be estimated, for example by discounting expected future cash flows at a discount rate reflecting both the risk and maturity date (or expected disposal date) of the asset.[52] Where plan assets include qualifying insurance policies that exactly match the amount and timing of some or all of the benefits payable under the plan, the fair value of those insurance policies is deemed to be the present value of the related obligations, subject to any reductions required if the amounts receivable under the insurance policies are not recoverable in full.[53]

Some employers may have in place arrangements to fund defined benefit obligations which do not meet the definition of qualifying insurance policies above but which do provide for another party to reimburse some or all of the expenditure required to settle a defined benefit obligation. In such a case, the expected receipts under the arrangement are not *classified* as plan assets under IAS 19 (and hence they are not presented as part of a net pension asset/liability – see 5.3.1 below). Instead, the employer should recognise its right to reimbursement as a separate asset, but only when it is virtually certain that another party will reimburse some or all of the expenditure required to settle a defined benefit obligation. The asset should be measured at fair value. In all other respects it should be treated in the same way as plan assets. In the income statement, the expense relating to a defined benefit plan may be presented net of the amount recognised for a reimbursement.[54]

The requirement that such rights are to be treated, aside of balance sheet presentation, in the same way as if they were plan assets extends to the use of the corridor mechanism discussed at 5.3.1 A below. What this means is that whilst the reimbursement right is shown separately at its fair value, any cumulative unrecognised actuarial gains and losses in respect of it are included along with any other unrecognised gains and losses as part of the net pension asset or liability in the balance sheet.[55]

As is the case for qualifying insurance policies, for reimbursement rights that exactly match the amount and timing of some or all of the benefits payable fair value is determined as the present value of the related obligation.[56]

The standard illustrates the requirements regarding such rights as follows:

Example 30.1:   Reimbursement rights

	€
Present value of obligation	1,241
Unrecognised actuarial gains	17
Liability recognised in balance sheet	1,258
Rights under insurance policies that exactly match the amount and timing of some of the benefits payable under the plan. Those benefits have a present value of 1,092.	1,092

The unrecognised actuarial gains of 17 are the net cumulative actuarial gains on the obligation and on the reimbursement rights.

C   Contributions to defined benefit funds

Contributions to defined benefit plans under IAS 19 are a balance sheet movement – the reduction in cash for the employer being reflected by an increase in the plan assets. Perhaps because of this straightforward accounting, the standard provides no guidance on contributions, which it implicitly deals with as always being in the form of cash.

Although contributions are very commonly in cash, there is no reason why an employer could not contribute any other assets to a defined benefit plan and that raises the question of how to account for the disposal – particularly as from the point of transfer the assets will be measured at fair value under IAS 19. In our view, such transfers of non-cash assets should be treated as disposals, with proceeds equal to the assets' fair values. That would give rise to gains and losses in the income statement (unless the asset in question was already carried at fair value) and, for certain assets (such as available for sale securities), the recycling into income of amounts previously recognised directly in equity.

5.2.2   Plan liabilities

A   Legal and constructive obligations

IAS 19 refers to the liabilities of defined benefit plans as the present value of defined benefit obligations, which it defines as '... the present value, without deducting any plan assets, of expected future payments required to settle the obligation resulting from employee service in the current and prior periods'.[57]

The obligations should include not only the benefits set out in the plan, but also any constructive obligations that arise from the employer's informal practices which go beyond the formal plan terms, and should where relevant include an estimate of expected future salary increases (taking into account inflation, seniority, promotion and other relevant factors, such as supply and demand in the employment market).[58]

A constructive obligation exists where a change in the employer's informal practices would cause unacceptable damage to its relationship with employees and which therefore leaves the employer with no realistic alternative but to pay those employee benefits.[59] The term constructive obligation is not defined by IAS 19, however as can be seen from the above it is very similar to the meaning of the term as used in IAS 37 where it is defined as follows:

'A constructive obligation is an obligation that derives from an enterprise's actions where:

(a)   by an established pattern of past practice, published policies or a sufficiently specific current statement, the enterprise has indicated to other parties that it will accept certain responsibilities; and

(b)   as a result, the enterprise has created a valid expectation on the part of those other parties that it will discharge those responsibilities.'[60]

However, IAS 19 goes on to add a subtly different nuance. The standard observes that it is usually difficult to cancel a retirement benefit plan whilst still retaining staff, and in light of this it requires that reporting entities assume (in the absence of evidence to the contrary) any currently promised benefits will continue for the remaining working lives of employees.[61] In our view this is a somewhat lower hurdle, and could bring into the scope of defined benefit accounting promises which are (strictly) legally unenforceable and which would not necessarily be considered constructive obligations under IAS 37.

An employer's obligations (legal or constructive) may also extend to making changes to benefits in the future. The standard requires all such effects to be built into the computation of the obligation and gives the following examples of what they might comprise:

(a)   a past history of increasing benefits, for example, to mitigate the effects of inflation, and no indication that this practice will change in the future; or

(b)   actuarial gains have already been recognised in the financial statements and the employer is obliged (legally – under the terms of the plan or legislation – or constructively) to use any surplus in the plan for the benefit of plan participants. In this case, the increase in the obligation is an actuarial loss (and not a past service cost, discussed at 5.4.6 below.[62]

By contrast, any other future changes in the obligation (i.e. where no legal or constructive obligation previously existed) will be reflected in future current service costs, future past service costs or both (discussed at 5.4.1 and 5.4.6 respectively).[63]

IAS 19 also deals with the situation where the level of defined benefits payable by a scheme vary with the level of state benefits. When this is the case any changes in state benefit may only be factored into the actuarial computations if they are enacted by the balance sheet date or are predictable based on past history or other evidence.[64]

B   Actuarial methodology

Plan obligations are to be measured using the projected unit credit method,[65] (sometimes known as the accrued benefit method pro-rated on service or as the benefit/years of service method). This method sees each period of service as giving rise to an additional unit of benefit entitlement and measures each unit separately to build up the final obligation.[66] IAS 19 provides a simple example of what this entails as follows:[67]

Example 30.2: The projected unit credit method

A lump sum benefit is payable on termination of service and equal to 1% of final salary for each year of service. The salary in year 1 is 10,000 and is assumed to increase at 7% (compound) each year. The discount rate used is 10% per annum. The following table shows how the obligation builds up for an employee who is expected to leave at the end of year 5, assuming that there are no changes in actuarial assumptions. For simplicity, this example ignores the additional adjustment needed to reflect the probability that the employee may leave the entity at an earlier or later date.

Year	1	2	3	4	5
Benefit attributed to:					
– prior years	0	131	262	393	524
– current year (1% of final salary)	131	131	131	131	131
– current and prior years	131	262	393	524	655
Opening Obligation	–	89	196	324	476
Interest at 10%	–	9	20	33	48
Current Service Cost	89	98	108	119	131
Closing Obligation	89	196	324	476	655

Note:

– The Opening Obligation is the present value of benefit attributed to prior years.

– The Current Service Cost is the present value of benefit attributed to the current year.

– The Closing Obligation is the present value of benefit attributed to current and prior years.

As can be seen in this simple example, the projected unit credit method also produces a figure for current service cost and interest cost (and, although not illustrated here, would where appropriate produce a figure for past service cost). These cost components are discussed at 5.4 below.

This example from the standard contains no underlying workings or proofs. The most useful would be as follows:

Final salary at year 5 (10,000 compounded at 7%) $10,000 \times (1 + 0.07)^4 = 13,100$

1% of final salary attributed to each year   131

Expected final benefit   5 years $\times$ 1% $\times$ 131,000 = 655

Current service cost, being present value of 131 discounted at 10%: e.g.

Year 1 $131 \times (1 + 0.1)^{-4} = 89$

Year 2 $131 \times (1 + 0.1)^{-3} = 98$

Closing obligation, being years served multiplied by present value of 131: e.g.

Year 3   3 years $\times$ 131 $\times$ $(1 + 0.1)^{-2} = 324$

C   *Attributing benefit to years of service*

The projected unit credit method requires benefits to be attributed to the current period (in order to determine current service cost) and the current and prior periods (in order to determine the present value of defined benefit obligations). IAS 19 requires benefits to be attributed to the periods in which the obligation to provide post-employment benefits arises. That is taken to be when employees render services in return for post-employment benefits which an entity expects to pay in future reporting periods. In the standard's view, actuarial techniques allow an entity to measure that obligation with sufficient reliability to justify recognition of a liability.[68]

In applying the projected unit credit method, IAS 19 normally requires benefits to be attributed to periods of service under the plan's benefit formula (as is the case in Example 30.2 above). If, however, an employee's service in later years will lead to a materially higher level of benefit, the benefit should be attributed on a straight-line basis from:

(a)   the date when service by the employee first leads to benefits under the plan; until

(b)   the date when further service by the employee will lead to no material amount of further benefits under the plan, other than from further salary increases.[69]

The standard considers that this requirement is necessary because the employee's service throughout the entire period will ultimately lead to benefit at that higher level.[70]

The standard explains that employee service gives rise to an obligation under a defined benefit plan even if the benefits are conditional on future employment (in other words they are not vested). Employee service before the vesting date is considered to give rise to a constructive obligation because, at each successive balance sheet date, the amount of future service that an employee will have to render before becoming entitled to the benefit is reduced. In measuring its defined benefit obligation, an entity should consider the probability that some employees may not satisfy any vesting requirements. Similarly, although certain post-employment benefits, for example, post-employment medical benefits, become payable only if a specified event occurs when an employee is no longer employed, an obligation is considered to be created when the employee renders service that will provide entitlement to the benefit if the specified event occurs. The probability that the specified event will occur affects the measurement of the obligation, but does not determine whether for accounting purposes the obligation exists.[71]

The obligation is considered to increase until the date when further service by the employee will lead to no material amount of further benefits, and accordingly all benefit should be attributed to periods ending on or before that date.[72]

IAS 19 illustrates the attribution of benefits to service periods with a number of worked examples as follows.[73]

Example 30.3:   *Attributing benefits to years of service*

1. A defined benefit plan provides a lump-sum benefit of 100 payable on retirement for each year of service.

   A benefit of 100 is attributed to each year. The current service cost is the present value of 100. The present value of the defined benefit obligation is the present value of 100, multiplied by the number of years of service up to the balance sheet date.

   If the benefit is payable immediately when the employee leaves the entity, the current service cost and the present value of the defined benefit obligation reflect the date at which the employee is expected to leave. Thus, because of the effect of discounting, they are less than the amounts that would be determined if the employee left at the balance sheet date.

2. A plan provides a monthly pension of 0.2% of final salary for each year of service. The pension is payable from the age of 65.

   Benefit equal to the present value, at the expected retirement date, of a monthly pension of 0.2% of the estimated final salary payable from the expected retirement date until the expected date of death is attributed to each year of service. The current service cost is the present value of that benefit. The present value of the defined benefit obligation is the present value of monthly pension payments of 0.2% of final salary, multiplied by the number of years of service up to the balance sheet date. The current service cost and the present value of the defined benefit obligation are discounted because pension payments begin at the age of 65.

3. A plan pays a benefit of 100 for each year of service. The benefits vest after ten years of service.

   A benefit of 100 is attributed to each year. In each of the first ten years, the current service cost and the present value of the obligation reflect the probability that the employee may not complete ten years of service.

4. A plan pays a benefit of 100 for each year of service, excluding service before the age of 25. The benefits vest immediately.

   No benefit is attributed to service before the age of 25 because service before that date does not lead to benefits (conditional or unconditional). A benefit of 100 is attributed to each subsequent year.

5. A plan pays a lump-sum benefit of 1,000 that vests after ten years of service. The plan provides no further benefit for subsequent service.

   A benefit of 100 (1,000 divided by ten) is attributed to each of the first ten years. The current service cost in each of the first ten years reflects the probability that the employee may not complete ten years of service. No benefit is attributed to subsequent years.

6. A plan pays a lump-sum retirement benefit of 2,000 to all employees who are still employed at the age of 55 after twenty years of service, or who are still employed at the age of 65, regardless of their length of service.

   For employees who join before the age of 35, service first leads to benefits under the plan at the age of 35 (an employee could leave at the age of 30 and return at the age of 33, with no effect on the amount or timing of benefits). Those benefits are conditional on further service. Also, service beyond the age of 55 will lead to no material amount of further benefits. For these employees, the entity attributes benefit of 100 (2,000 divided by 20) to each year from the age of 35 to the age of 55.

   For employees who join between the ages of 35 and 45, service beyond twenty years will lead to no material amount of further benefits. For these employees, the entity attributes benefit of 100 (2,000 divided by 20) to each of the first twenty years.

   For an employee who joins at the age of 55, service beyond ten years will lead to no material amount of further benefits. For this employee, the entity attributes benefit of 200 (2,000 divided by 10) to each of the first ten years.

For all employees, the current service cost and the present value of the obligation reflect the probability that the employee may not complete the necessary period of service.

7.   A post-employment medical plan reimburses 40% of an employee's post-employment medical costs if the employee leaves after more than ten and less than twenty years of service and 50% of those costs if the employee leaves after twenty or more years of service.

Under the plan's benefit formula, the entity attributes 4% of the present value of the expected medical costs (40% divided by ten) to each of the first ten years and 1% (10% divided by ten) to each of the second ten years. The current service cost in each year reflects the probability that the employee may not complete the necessary period of service to earn part or all of the benefits. For employees expected to leave within ten years, no benefit is attributed.

8.   A post-employment medical plan reimburses 10% of an employee's post-employment medical costs if the employee leaves after more than ten and less than twenty years of service and 50% of those costs if the employee leaves after twenty or more years of service.

Service in later years will lead to a materially higher level of benefit than in earlier years. Therefore, for employees expected to leave after twenty or more years, the entity attributes benefit on a straight-line basis under paragraph 68 of the standard. Service beyond twenty years will lead to no material amount of further benefits. Therefore, the benefit attributed to each of the first twenty years is 2.5% of the present value of the expected medical costs (50% divided by twenty).

For employees expected to leave between ten and twenty years, the benefit attributed to each of the first ten years is 1% of the present value of the expected medical costs. For these employees, no benefit is attributed to service between the end of the tenth year and the estimated date of leaving.

For employees expected to leave within ten years, no benefit is attributed.

9.   Employees are entitled to a benefit of 3% of final salary for each year of service before the age of 55.

Benefit of 3% of estimated final salary is attributed to each year up to the age of 55. This is the date when further service by the employee will lead to no material amount of further benefits under the plan. No benefit is attributed to service after that age.

None of the above illustrations are controversial. The following points of note are brought out in the above:

*   the scenarios in 3 and 5 are economically identical, and are attributed to years of service accordingly. In each case benefits only vest after ten years, however an obligation is to be built up over that period rather than at the end; and

*   example 8 illustrates that accruing a 10% benefit over a period of 20 years of service which jumps to 50% once 20 years has been completed is an example of service in later years leading to a materially higher level of benefit. Accordingly the obligation is to be built-up on a straight-line basis over 20 years.

As regards example 9, the standard explains that where the amount of a benefit is a constant proportion of final salary for each year of service, future salary increases will affect the amount required to settle the obligation that exists for service before the balance sheet date, but do not create an additional obligation. Therefore:

(a)   for the purpose of allocating benefits to years of service, salary increases are not considered to lead to further benefits, even though the amount of the benefits is dependent on final salary; and

(b)   the amount of benefit attributed to each period should be a constant proportion of the salary to which the benefit is linked.[74]

D　　Actuarial assumptions

The long timescales and numerous uncertainties involved in estimating obligations for post-employment benefits require many assumptions to be made when applying the projected unit credit method. These are termed actuarial assumptions and comprise:

(a)　demographic assumptions about the future characteristics of current and former employees (and their dependants) who are eligible for benefits and deal with matters such as:

　　(i)　mortality, both during and after employment;

　　(ii)　rates of employee turnover, disability and early retirement;

　　(iii)　the proportion of plan members with dependants who will be eligible for benefits; and

　　(iv)　claim rates under medical plans; and

(b)　financial assumptions, dealing with items such as:

　　(i)　the discount rate;

　　(ii)　future salary and benefit levels;

　　(iii)　in the case of medical benefits, future medical costs, including, where material, the cost of administering claims and benefit payments; and

　　(iv)　the expected rate of return on plan assets.[75]

IAS 19's requirements in this regard are set out below, with the exception of the discount rate which is discussed at E below.

The standard requires that actuarial assumptions be unbiased (that is, neither imprudent nor excessively conservative[76]), mutually compatible and represent the employer's best estimates of the variables that will determine the ultimate cost of providing post-employment benefits.

The financial assumptions must be based on market expectations at the balance sheet date, for the period over which the obligations are to be settled.[77] Actuarial assumptions are mutually compatible if they reflect the economic relationships between factors such as inflation, rates of salary increase, the return on plan assets and discount rates. For example, all assumptions which depend on a particular inflation level (such as assumptions about interest rates and salary and benefit increases) in any given future period should assume the same inflation level in that period.[78]

Assumptions about medical costs should take account of inflation as well as specific changes in medical costs (including technological advances, changes in health care utilisation or delivery patterns, and changes in the health status of plan participants).[79] The standard provides a quite detailed discussion of the factors that should be taken into account in making actuarial assumptions about medical costs, in particular it notes:

(a)　measuring post-employment medical benefits requires assumptions about the level and frequency of future claims, and the cost of meeting them. An employer should make such estimates based on its own experience, supplemented where necessary by historical data from other sources (such as other entities, insurance companies and medical providers);[80]

(b)   the level and frequency of claims is particularly sensitive to the age, health status and sex of the claimants, and may also be sensitive to their geographical location. This means that any historical data used for estimating future claims needs to be adjusted to the extent that the demographic mix of the plan participants differs from that of the population used as the basis for the historical data. Historical data should also be adjusted if there is reliable evidence that historical trends will not continue;[81] and

(c)   estimates of future medical costs should take account of any contributions that claimants are required to make based on the terms (whether formal or constructive) of the plan at the balance sheet date. Changes in such terms will constitute past service costs or, where applicable, curtailments (discussed at 5.4.6 and 5.4.5 respectively).[82]

The following extract shows a discussion of health care cost trend rates.

Extract 30.3: UBS AG (2003)

Notes to the financial statements [extract]

Note 31   Pension and Other Post-Retirement Benefit Plans [extract]

b)   Post-retirement medical and life plans

The assumed average health care cost trend rates used in determining post-retirement benefit expense is assumed to be 10.3% for 2003 and to decrease to an ultimate trend rate of 5% in 2010. Assumed health care cost trend rates have a significant effect on the amounts reported for the health care plan. A one-percentage-point change in the assumed health care cost trend rates would change the US post-retirement benefit obligation and the service and interest cost components of the net periodic post-retirement benefit costs as follows:

CHF million	1% increase	1% decrease
Effect on total service and interest cost	5	(4)
Effect on the post-retirement benefit obligation	25	(19)

Clearly, the application of actuarial techniques to compute plan obligations is a complex task, and it seems likely that few entities would seek to prepare valuations without the advice of qualified actuaries. However, IAS 19 only encourages, but does not require that an entity takes actuarial advice.[83]

However sophisticated actuarial projections may be, reality will (aside of the most simple scenarios) always diverge from assumptions. This means that when a surplus or deficit is estimated, it will almost certainly be different from the predicted value based on the last valuation. These differences are termed actuarial gains and losses. The standard observes that actuarial gains and losses may result from increases or decreases in either the present value of a defined benefit obligation or the fair value of any related plan assets. Causes of actuarial gains and losses could include, for example:

(a)   unexpectedly high or low rates of employee turnover, early retirement or mortality or of increases in salaries, benefits (if the formal or constructive terms of a plan provide for inflationary benefit increases) or medical costs;

(b) the effect of changes in estimates of future employee turnover, early retirement or mortality or of increases in salaries, benefits (if the formal or constructive terms of a plan provide for inflationary benefit increases) or medical costs;

(c) the effect of changes in the discount rate; and

(d) differences between the actual return on plan assets and the expected return on plan assets.

Accounting for actuarial gains and losses is discussed at 5.3.1 A below.

E   *Discount rate*

Due to the long timescales involved, post-employment benefit obligations are discounted. Also, the whole obligation should be discounted, even if some falls due within a year.[84] The standard requires that the discount rate reflect the time value of money but not the actuarial or investment risk. Furthermore, the discount rate should not reflect the entity-specific credit risk borne by the entity's creditors, nor should it reflect the risk that future experience may differ from actuarial assumptions.[85] The discount rate should reflect the estimated timing of benefit payments. For example, an appropriate rate may be quite different for a payment due in, say, ten years as opposed to one due in twenty. The standard observes that in practice, an acceptable answer can be obtained by applying a single weighted average discount rate that reflects the estimated timing and amount of benefit payments and the currency in which the benefits are to be paid.[86]

The rate used should be determined 'by reference to' the yield (at the balance sheet date) on high quality corporate bonds of currency and term consistent with the liabilities. In countries where there is no deep market in such bonds, the yields on government bonds should be used instead.[87]

In our view, the requirement that the rate be determined 'by reference to' high quality bond rates adds an important nuance – in particular, it is very different from requiring the rate to *be* that of an observable instrument. It means that observed current market yields may need to form the starting point for this determination.

The standard gives an example of this in the context of the availability of bonds with sufficiently long maturities. It observes that in some cases, there may be no deep market in bonds with a sufficiently long maturity to match the estimated maturity of all the benefit payments. In such cases, the standard requires the use of current market rates of the appropriate term to discount shorter-term payments, and estimation of the rate for longer maturities by extrapolating current market rates along the yield curve. It goes on to observe that the total present value of a defined benefit obligation is unlikely to be particularly sensitive to the discount rate applied to the portion of benefits that is payable beyond the final maturity of the available corporate or government bonds.[88] To us this last observation seems to belong more in the basis of conclusions rather that the standard itself as it appears to try and justify the rule rather than simply set it out. Furthermore, we remain to be convinced that it is in fact true, as the standard sets out no evidence supporting the assertion.

Of the three characteristics of corporate bonds stipulated by the standard (quality, currency and term) the above example is making an adjustment to observed yields with respect to term. In our view, it would be equally acceptable for adjustments to observable market data to be made in respect of the other characteristics if that would produce a reliable and appropriate rate still 'determined by reference to' corporate bonds. Whilst it would be wrong to understate the liabilities of the plan by using an inappropriately high rate (say, because the only relevant bonds in issue are not 'high quality') it would be equally wrong, in our view, to overstate them by using the default rate of government debt when a reliable rate could be estimated by reference to market yields. Indeed, the standard suggests this in its discussion of actuarial assumptions in general, requiring that they be unbiased, that is neither imprudent nor excessively conservative.[89]

Another important strand in determining the required rate is that it be determined by reference to the yield on 'high quality' corporate bonds. High quality is a term of art in IAS 19, and reporting entities need to develop policies for determining what it means and applying them consistently. The phrase 'high quality' is not further defined nor elaborated upon in the standard. It is sometimes suggested that this should mean bonds granted a certain grade by credit rating agencies – such as AA. In our view, if the IASC had intended that level of prescription, they would have put the requirement in the standard (as the UK's ASB did,[90] and the SEC staff require for US GAAP[91]) and that it would not be appropriate to impute such a requirement into the standard. At the other end of the spectrum, it is sometimes suggested that high quality should mean the highest quality issuer in the relevant jurisdiction, irrespective of the quality of the bond. Again, we believe that if the IASC had meant that it would have said so. In particular, such an approach could lead to an unjustifiably high discount rate and an inappropriate understatement of the liabilities. On balance, we believe that bonds rated AA (or its equivalent) would generally be held to be of high quality and that if the only available corporate bonds are of a lesser quality it will become increasingly likely that reference to government bonds would be appropriate.

IAS 19 also stipulates that the discount rate (and other financial assumptions) should be determined in nominal (stated) terms, unless estimates in real (inflation-adjusted) terms are more reliable, for example, in a hyper-inflationary economy (see Chapter 10 for a discussion of IAS 29 – *Financial Reporting in Hyperinflationary Economies*), or where the benefit is index-linked and there is a deep market in index-linked bonds of the same currency and term.[92]

The basic part of this requirement – that a nominal rate be used – is consistent with the definition of the present value of a defined benefit obligation in that it should be '... the present value ... of expected future payments required to settle the obligation ...' (see 5.2.2 A above). In other words, as the future cash flows are stated at the actual amounts expected to be paid, the rate used to discount them should reflect that and not be adjusted to remove the effects of expected inflation. In contrast, the reference to the use of index-linked bonds seems to allow taking account of inflation through the discount rate (which would require expressing cash flows in current prices). This approach seems to be in conflict with the definition of the obligation, although in practice few index-linked corporate bonds exist (so it may be quite rare to have a deep market in them) so a more reliable approach may often be to take account of inflation via the projected cash flows.

F   *Frequency of valuations*

When it addresses the frequency of valuations, IAS 19 does not give particularly prescriptive guidance. Rather, its starting point is simply to require that the present value of defined benefit obligations, and the fair value of plan assets, should be determined frequently enough to ensure that the amounts recognised in the financial statements do not differ materially from the amounts that would be determined at the balance sheet date.[93] A reasonable argument could be launched that without a full valuation as at the balance sheet date to compare with, it cannot be possible to know whether any less precise approach is materially different. However, it is reasonably clear that the intention of the standard is not necessarily to require full actuarial updates as at the year-end. This is because the standard goes onto observe that for practical reasons a valuation may be carried out before the balance sheet date and that if such amounts determined before the balance sheet date are used, they should be updated to take account of any material transactions or changes in circumstances up to the balance sheet date.[94] Much may turn on what is considered to be a 'material change', however it is expressly to include changes in market prices (hence requiring asset values to be those at the balance sheet date) and interest rates, as well as financial actuarial assumptions.[95] In this regard, it is also worth noting the observation in the standard that 'In some cases, estimates, averages and computational shortcuts may provide a reliable approximation of the detailed computations illustrated in this Standard.'[96] It is worth remembering, though, that it is the amounts in the financial statements which must not differ materially from what they would be based on a balance sheet valuation. For funded schemes, the net balance sheet amount (before taking account of the corridor mechanism – see 5.3.1 below) is usually the difference between two very large figures – plan assets and plan liabilities. Such a net item is inevitably highly sensitive, in percentage terms, to a given percentage change in the gross amounts.

In summary, these rules will require a detailed valuation on a frequent on an annual basis, but not necessarily as at the balance sheet date. If not as at the balance sheet date, the valuation will then need to be updated at the balance sheet date to reflect *at least* changes in financial assumptions, asset values and discount rates. The need for updates in respect of other elements of the valuation will depend on individual circumstances.

5.3   Balance sheet treatment of defined benefit plans

5.3.1   *Measurement of the plan surplus or deficit*

A   The corridor mechanism

The starting point under IAS 19 is that (subject to the special transitional provisions available to ongoing IAS reporters when the standard was introduced in 1999 – see 8.2 below) a plan surplus or deficit is reflected directly in the employer's balance sheet. However, not all of the movements in the fair value of a surplus or deficit need be reflected in the balance sheet.

The IASC encountered the same fundamental problem in developing its standard on pension accounting as some other standard setters around the world (notably the US and the UK which each have a conceptual framework similar to that in IAS[97]). The zeal for balance sheet fair values which these respective conceptual frameworks demand leads inevitably to volatility considered by many to be unacceptable. For example, the investment portfolios of the pension funds of many companies exceed the market capitalisation of the company itself. Although asset allocations vary, many have a high equity weighting. Mark-to-market accounting for portfolios of that size and nature yields very large and volatile results, which will not be hedged by the liabilities determined under the projected unit method. The approach taken by the UK's ASB (then chaired by Sir David Tweedie, currently IASB chairman) to overcome earnings volatility was, in essence, to account for budgeted figures in the profit or loss for the period with variances consigned (permanently) to equity as actuarial gains and losses. As discussed at 10.2.1 below the IASB has proposed allowing this treatment for entities which recognise all actuarial gains and losses in full – a decision prompted largely as a result of the UK standard. Currently, IAS 19 adopts an approach very similar to US GAAP.

The IASC decided to adopt a 'corridor' mechanism. In what at first glance appears to be a balance sheet approach, IAS 19 does not require immediate recognition of actuarial gains and losses. Instead an employer need only recognise a portion of the actuarial gains and losses to the extent that the net cumulative unrecognised actuarial gains and losses at the end of the previous reporting period exceeded the greater of:

(a)   10% of the present value of the defined benefit obligation; and

(b)   10% of the fair value of any plan assets.

The above 'corridor test' needs to be applied separately for each defined benefit plan. As a minimum, an amount of cumulative gains/losses must be recognised each period equal to the excess outside the 'corridor' divided by the expected average remaining working lives of employees participating in the plan. A simple example of the mechanics of this is included in Example 30.6 at 5.4.3 below. An entity may recognise actuarial gains and losses more quickly using any systematic method– as long as the same basis is applied to both gains and losses – even if they fall within the limits of the corridor.[98]

It is entirely possible that 10% of gross assets or liabilities will exceed the net balance sheet figure. This means that the balance sheet figure under IAS 19 could easily be 'wrong' by 100% or more, and even those actuarial movements that are recognised may be spread forward over a number of years. IAS 19 explains its corridor mechanism by observing that actuarial gains and losses may, in the long term, offset each other and that estimates of the obligation are best viewed as a range around a best estimate. Whilst permitting recognition of movements in the balance within this range, the standard stops short of requiring it.[99]

It remains to be seen whether the current work of the IASB on performance reporting will result in the mandatory immediate recognition of actuarial gains and losses – this is discussed at 10.1 below.

As a result of the above, IAS 19 requires the balance sheet figure relating to a defined benefit plan to be the net total of:

(a) the present value of the defined benefit obligation at the balance sheet date, before deducting the fair value of any plan assets (see 5.2.2 above);

(b) plus actuarial gains and less actuarial losses not yet recognised (discussed below);

(c) less past service cost not yet recognised (see 5.4.6 below); and

(d) less the fair value of plan assets, at balance sheet date, out of which the obligations are to be settled directly (see 5.2.1 above).[100]

B Restriction of assets to their recoverable amounts

The resulting balance sheet figure may be an asset. An asset may arise where a defined benefit plan has been overfunded or in certain cases where actuarial gains are recognised. The standard justifies the recognition of an asset in such cases because:

(a) the entity controls a resource, which is the ability to use the surplus to generate future benefits;

(b) that control is a result of past events (contributions paid by the entity and service rendered by the employee); and

(c) future economic benefits are available to the entity in the form of a reduction in future contributions or a cash refund, either directly to the entity or indirectly to another plan in deficit.[101]

When the mechanics above result in a balance sheet asset it is then subject to a ceiling test, and is restricted so as not to exceed the net total of:

(a) any unrecognised actuarial losses and past service cost (see 5.4.6 below); and

(b) the present value of any economic benefit available in the form of refunds from the plan or reductions in future contributions to the plan (determined by using the same discount rate as used for the plan liabilities).[102]

The ceiling test is illustrated by the standard with the following example.[103]

Example 30.4:   Restriction of assets to their recoverable amounts

A defined benefit plan has the following characteristics:

	€ million
Present value of the obligation	1,100
Fair value of plan assets	(1,190)
	(90)
Unrecognised actuarial losses	(110)
Unrecognised past service cost	(70)
Unrecognised increase in the liability on initial adoption of the Standard	(50)
Negative amount before any restriction	(320)
Present value of available future refunds and reductions in future contributions	90

The limit of the asset to be recognised is computed as follows:

Unrecognised actuarial losses	110
Unrecognised past service cost	70
Present value of available future refunds and reductions in future contributions	90
Limit	270

€270m is less than €320m. Therefore, the entity recognises an asset of €270m and discloses that the limit reduced the carrying amount of the asset by €50.

This ceiling test overrides the original transitional option to recognise any reduction in net assets over a period of up to five years (see 8.2 below). It does not, however, override the delayed recognition of certain actuarial losses under the corridor approach described above. IAS 19 provides a worked example illustrating the interaction between this ceiling test and the 'normal' delayed recognition allowed by the corridor approach.[104]

This limitation is in fact quite problematic. First of all, it seems to limit the recognition of the benefit of any surplus to its cash flow benefit. This would appear to mean that if the employer intends to use a surplus to improve the benefits under the plan without further contributions having to be paid, it may not recognise the surplus as an asset. That seems the natural reading of 'reductions in future contributions' – i.e. a reduction from their current level. On the other hand, it could have been intended to mean a reduction from what the contributions would have been in the absence of a surplus. Whilst it is regrettable that the standard is unclear in this regard, the IASB do seem aware of the issue and have debated in Board meetings the introduction of further guidance, which may be forthcoming in due course. At the time of writing, though, nothing has been published by the Board. Second, it is not clear whether 'reductions in future contributions' refers to actual or hypothetical future cash flow benefits. If the former (which is the natural meaning of the words), the standard would only allow a surplus to be recognised to the extent that the employer intended to run it off, and this may seldom apply. Furthermore, any refunds or reductions in contributions would usually be based on a different actuarial valuation, producing a different surplus, than the one being used for accounting purposes. It is quite possible that the valuation for funding purposes is more conservative than that used for accounting purposes, so any limitation that is founded on actual or putative funding adjustments may be quite a severe one. It will therefore be interesting to see how practice develops in the interpretation of this restriction, particularly with the enlargement of the IASB's constituency by the mandatory adoption of IAS by all listed European companies in 2005.

C   *Restriction of the recognition of profits (losses) solely as a result of actuarial losses (gains)*

Only a few years after its publication an anomaly in the standard came to light. It was that in some circumstances the interaction of the standard's complex (indeed, conceptually conflicting) requirements could lead to the recognition of profits purely as a result of actuarial *losses* in a pension fund (and vice versa). Accordingly the standard was revised, with the changes taking effect for periods ending on or after 31 May 2002.

The anomaly is best explained with a numerical example (based on Appendix C to IAS 19) as follows.

Example 30.5:   *Restriction of the recognition of a profit solely as a result of an actuarial loss*

	A	B	C	D = A + C	E = B + C	F = lower of D and E	G
Year	Surplus in plan	Economic benefits available	Losses unrecognised due to the corridor	Unrestricted asset	Present value of future economic benefits	Asset ceiling, i.e. recognised asset	Gain recognised in year 2
1	100	0	0	100	0	0	
2	70	0	30	100	30	30	30

At the end of year 1, there is a surplus of 100 in the plan (column A in the table above), but no economic benefits are available to the entity either from refunds or reductions in future contributions (column B). There are no unrecognised gains and losses (column C). So, if there were no asset ceiling, an asset of 100 would be recognised, being the amount determined by the 'normal' output of the surplus in the scheme and the corridor mechanism (column D). The asset ceiling (see B above) restricts the asset to nil (column F).

In year 2 there is an actuarial loss in the plan of 30 that reduces the surplus from 100 to 70 (column A) the recognition of which is deferred under the corridor mechanism (column C). So, if there were no asset ceiling, an asset of 100 (column D) would be recognised. The asset ceiling before the standard was amended in this regard would be 30 (column E). An asset of 30 would be recognised (column F), giving rise to a gain in income (column G) even though all that has happened is that a surplus from which the entity cannot benefit has decreased.

A similarly counter-intuitive effect could arise with actuarial gains (to the extent that they reduce cumulative unrecognised actuarial losses).

The reason for this 'anomaly' is a direct consequence of the allowed deferral of actuarial gains and losses. Any resulting asset in the balance sheet is best characterised as a prepayment and to apply a recoverability test based on asset valuation principles to such an item is meaningless. Indeed, one member of the IASB observed the following when dissenting from the 2002 amendment 'Ms O'Malley dissents from this amendment of IAS 19. In her view, the perceived problem being addressed is an inevitable result of the interaction of two fundamentally inconsistent notions in IAS 19. The corridor approach allowed by IAS 19 permits the recognition of amounts on the balance sheet that do not meet the Framework's definition of assets. The asset ceiling then imposes a limitation on the recognition of some of those assets based on a recoverability notion. A far preferable limited amendment would be to delete the asset ceiling in paragraph 58. This would resolve the identified problem and at least remove the internal inconsistency in IAS 19. It is asserted that the amendment to the standard will result in a more representationally faithful portrayal of economic events. Ms O'Malley believes that it is impossible to improve the representational faithfulness of a standard that permits recording an asset relating to a pension plan that actually has a deficiency, or a liability in respect of a plan that actually has a surplus.'[105]

When the plan has a surplus, and the balance sheet asset is restricted (because the surplus cannot be fully recovered by refunds or reduced contributions) any actuarial loss or past service which arises but is deferred by the corridor mechanism *increases* the amount to which the asset is restricted. The credit entry is to income.[106]

To fix this problem, further overlaying requirements were added to the standard requiring that the application of the asset ceiling should not result in:

- a gain being recognised solely as a result of an actuarial loss or past service cost in the current period; or

- in a loss being recognised solely as a result of an actuarial gain in the current period.

Accordingly, whenever the asset is restricted (see B above) the following should be recognised immediately:

(a) net actuarial losses of the current period and past service cost of the current period to the extent that they exceed any reduction in the present value of the economic benefits determined under the ceiling test. If there is no change or an increase in the present value of the economic benefits, the entire net actuarial losses of the current period and past service cost of the current period should be recognised immediately;

(b) net actuarial gains of the current period after the deduction of past service cost of the current period to the extent that they exceed any increase in the present value of the economic benefits available. If there is no change or a decrease in the present value of the economic benefits, the entire net actuarial gains of the current period after the deduction of past service cost of the current period should be recognised immediately.[107]

What that means for the scenario in the above example is that, because there is no change in the economic benefits available, the entire actuarial loss of 30 is recognised immediately in year 2. Hence, the asset ceiling remains at nil and no net gain is recognised.

D   Business combinations

In a business combination, an entity recognises assets and liabilities arising from post-employment benefits at the present value of the obligation less the fair value of any plan assets (see IFRS 3 – *Business Combinations* – discussed in Chapter 6). The present value of the obligation includes all of the following, even if the acquiree had not yet recognised them at the date of the acquisition:

(a)   actuarial gains and losses that arose before the date of the acquisition (whether or not they fell inside the 10% corridor);

(b)   past service cost that arose from benefit changes, or the introduction of a plan, before the date of the acquisition; and

(c)   amounts that, under the transitional provisions see 8.2 below the acquiree had not recognised.[108]

5.3.2   Presentation of balance sheet amounts

Neither IAS 19 nor IAS 1 specifies where in the balance sheet an asset or liability in respect of a defined benefit plan should be presented, nor whether such balances should be shown separately on the face of the balance sheet or only in the notes – this is left to the discretion of the reporting entity subject to the general requirements of IAS 1 discussed in Chapter 3. If the format of the balance sheet distinguishes current assets and liabilities from non-current ones, the question arises as to whether this split needs also to be made for pension balances. IAS 19 does not specify whether such a split should be made, on the grounds that it may sometimes be arbitrary.[109]

Employers with more than one plan may find that some are in surplus while others are in deficit. IAS 19 contains offset criteria closely modelled on those in IAS 32.[110] An asset relating to one plan may only be offset against a liability relating to another plan when there is a legally enforceable right to use a surplus in one plan to settle obligations under the other plan, and the employer intends to settle the obligations on a net basis or realise the surplus and settle the obligation simultaneously.[111] In our view these offset criteria are unlikely to be met in practice.

The following extract shows a company presenting a non-current asset and a non-current liability relating to pensions on the face of the balance sheet.

Extract 30.4: Jardine Matheson Holdings Limited (2003)

Consolidated Balance Sheet

at 31st December 2003

	Note	2003 US$m	Restated 2002 US$m
Net operating assets			
Goodwill	8	151	54
Tangible assets	9	1,521	1,375
Investment properties	10	359	411
Leasehold land payments	11	484	467
Associates and joint ventures	12	2,793	2,752
Other investments	13	696	509
Deferred tax assets	14	37	31
Pension assets	15	79	89
Other non-current assets	16	16	13
Non-current assets		6,136	5,701
Properties for sale	17	340	285
Stocks and work in progress	18	832	894
Debtors and prepayments	19	603	784
Current tax assets		11	12
Bank balances and other liquid funds	20	955	1,273
Current assets		2,741	3,248
Creditors and accruals	21	(1,687)	(1,721)
Borrowings	22	(362)	(580)
Current tax liabilities		(57)	(52)
Current provisions		(65)	(45)
Current liabilities		(2,171)	(2,398)
Net current assets		570	850
Long-term borrowings	22	(2,408)	(2,282)
Deferred tax liabilities	14	(158)	(145)
Pension liabilities	15	(16)	(13)
Non-current provisions	23	(12)	(24)
Other non-current liabilities	24	(27)	(31)
		4,085	4,056
Total equity			
Shares capital	26	151	153
Share premium	28	2	–
Revenue and other reserves	29	3,199	3,110
Own shares held	31	(670)	(670)
Shareholders' funds		2,682	2,593
Outside interests	32	1,403	1,463
		4,085	4,056

An alternative approach is to include assets and liabilities relating to post-employments benefits within a suitable balance sheet caption and provide an analysis in the note, as illustrated by the following extract.

Extract 30.5: Novartis AG (2003)

Notes to the Novartis Group Consolidated Financial Statements [extract]

25   Employee benefits [extract]

The net asset in the balance sheet consists of:

	2003 **USD** **millions**	2002 USD millions
Prepaid pension expense included in financial and other assets	3,976	3,527
Accrued pensions costs included in other long-term liabilities	-930	-741
Total net asset	**3,046**	2,786

5.4   Income statement treatment of defined benefit plans

IAS 19 identifies six components of annual pension cost as follows:

(a)   current service cost;

(b)   interest cost;

(c)   the expected return on any plan assets (and any reimbursement rights);

(d)   actuarial gains and losses (to the extent they are recognised);

(e)   past service cost (to the extent they are recognised); and

(f)   the effect of any curtailments or settlements.[112]

The standard requires the net total of the above to be recognised as expense or income, unless another standard requires or permits its inclusion in the cost of an asset – for example IAS 2 – *Inventories* – and IAS 16 – *Property, Plant and Equipment.* Where the post-employment benefit costs are included in the cost of an asset the appropriate proportion of *all* the above items must be included.[113] There is no guidance in the standard as to what an 'appropriate' proportion of these items might be, although both IAS 2 and IAS 16 are clear that only those costs which are directly attributable to the asset qualify for capitalisation. In our view, it is not necessarily the case that the appropriate proportion will be the same for all of the components and judgement will be required in deciding how much of each item can meaningfully be said to relate to the production of an asset.

In terms of income statement 'geography' the standard is far from clear. What is says is this. 'This Standard does not specify whether an enterprise should present current service cost, interest cost and the expected return on plan assets as components of a single item of income or expense on the face of the income statement'.[114] This sentence doesn't make clear whether it is the prominence of disclosure on the face of the income statement (as opposed to just in the notes) or the inclusion of all the elements in one caption of the income statement that the standard is not specifying. The standard does, however, seem to contemplate the inclusion of pension items in more than one income statement caption because it specifically requires disclosure of which captions the items are in (disclosure is discussed at 7.2 below). Also, the requirement in the final standard is a change from E54 which explicitly required all components of the income statement charge/credit to be included in the same line item.[115] We believe that a number of approaches (within the general confines of IAS 1) would be acceptable. In particular, some entities may wish to locate the expected return on assets and the interest cost with other financial items.

Each of the components listed above is discussed below.

5.4.1 Current service cost

The current service cost, which should be determined using the projected unit credit method, is the increase in the present value of the defined benefit obligation resulting from employee service in the current period.[116] The basic computation is illustrated in Example 30.2 at 5.2.2 B above.

5.4.2 Interest cost

Interest cost is the increase during a period in the present value of a defined benefit obligation which arises because the benefits are one period closer to settlement.[117] Interest cost is calculated by multiplying the discount rate at the beginning of the period by the present value of the defined benefit obligation (i.e. the gross obligation, not the net balance sheet amount) throughout that period, taking account of any material changes in the obligation.[118] The standard gives no further explanation of what is meant by the requirement to multiply the discount rate not by the opening obligation but by the obligation 'throughout that period taking into account any material changes in the obligation'. The comprehensive worked example contained in Appendix A to the standard sheds no further light on this because it notes that 'To keep interest computations simple, all transactions are assumed to occur at the year end.'

At the extreme, it could be read to require a re-computation on, say, a monthly or weekly basis and to take account of all changes in scheme obligations (such as payments of benefits by the fund, accrual of further benefits by members, adjustments for leavers and joiners, changes in demographic assumptions etc). However, it seems unlikely that such an onerous requirement was intended by the IASC – particularly in light of the reference to 'material' changes and the fairly vague requirements in respect of the frequency of valuations (see 5.2.2 F above). It seems fairly likely this may be one of the areas where the ' ... estimates, averages and computational shortcuts [which] may provide a reliable approximation of the detailed computations ...' envisaged by the standard come into play.[119] For example, entities might take the view that adjustments need to be made only for significant one-off changes in the scheme, such as settlements and curtailments, benefit improvements and updated actuarial valuations. Furthermore, those entities which update actuarial valuations for the purposes of interim reporting would be able to take account of those valuations when computing the interest cost. Similar issues arise in relation to expected asset returns, discussed at 5.4.3 below.

5.4.3 *Expected return on plan assets (and any reimbursement rights)*

IAS 19 gives a definition of return on plan assets as follows:[120]

'The return on plan assets is interest, dividends and other revenue derived from the plan assets, together with realised and unrealised gains or losses on the plan assets, less any costs of administering the plan and less any tax payable by the plan itself.'

The *expected* return on plan assets is just that – a forward-looking expectation or estimate. It is based on market expectations at the beginning of the period for returns over the entire life of the related obligation, and should reflect changes in the fair value of plan assets during the period arising from contributions to and benefits paid out of the fund.[121] Clearly this is a very subjective assumption – an increase in which directly creates income at the expense of (quite likely unrecognised) actuarial losses. This potential for accounting arbitrage has received some debate and criticism of late. The IASB is proposing to respond to the issue by requiring the disclosure of the basis used to determine the rate.[122] Both the expected and actual returns on plan assets are determined after deducting administration costs other than those included in the actuarial assumptions to measure the plan obligations.[123] The difference between the expected return and actual return on plan assets is an actuarial gain or loss.[124] IAS 19 illustrates the computation of the expected and actual return on plan assets with a simple worked example upon which the following is based:[125]

Example 30.6:   Expected return on plan assets

At 1 January 2005, the fair value of plan assets was €10,000 and net cumulative unrecognised actuarial gains were €760. On 30 June 2005, the plan paid benefits of €1,900 and received contributions of €4,900. At 31 December 2005, the fair value of plan assets was €15,000 and the present value of the defined benefit obligation was €14,792. Actuarial losses on the obligation for 2005 were 60.

At 1 January 2005, the reporting entity made the following estimates, based on market prices at that date:

	%
Interest and dividend income, after tax payable by the fund	9.25
Realised and unrealised gains on plan assets (after tax)	2.00
Administration costs	(1.00)
Expected rate of return	10.25

For 2005, the expected and actual return on plan assets are as follows:	€
Return on €10,000 held for 12 months at 10.25%	1,025
Return on €3,000 held for six months at 5% (equivalent to 10.25% annually, compounded every six months)	150
Expected return on plan assets for 2005	1,175

Fair value of plan assets at 31 December 2005	15,000
Less fair value of plan assets at 1 January 2005	(10,000)
Less contributions received	(4,900)
Add benefits paid	1,900
Actual return on plan assets	2,000

The difference between the expected return on plan assets (€1,175) and the actual return on plan assets (€2,000) is an actuarial gain of €825. Therefore, the cumulative net unrecognised actuarial gains are €1,525 (€760 plus €825 less €60). The limits of the corridor (see 5.3.1 A above) are set at €1,500 (greater of: (i) 10% of €15,000 and (ii) 10% of €14,792). In the following year (2006), the entity recognises in the income statement an actuarial gain of €25 (€1,525 less €1,500) divided by the expected average remaining working life of the employees concerned.

The expected return on plan assets for 2006 will be based on market expectations at 1 January 2006 for returns over the entire life of the obligation.

The requirement to compute the expected return not just by reference to the assets at the beginning of the year but to adjust for changes in them throughout the year, raises similar questions as to the required precision as noted in relation to interest costs (see 5.4.2 above). The example above conveniently assumes only one benefit payment and one contribution in the year, both on the same day, which is clearly for the purpose of providing a simple example rather than a reflection of likely reality. In our view, the 'estimates, averages and computational shortcuts' anticipated by the standard (see 5.4.2 above) may well be relevant here, with some employers experiencing fairly stable inflows and outflows of funds only considering it necessary to adjust for significant events (such as special contributions or major portfolio reallocations).

5.4.4   Actuarial gains and losses

Actuarial gains and losses comprise experience adjustments (the effects of differences between the previous actuarial assumptions and what has actually occurred) and the effects of changes in actuarial assumptions. These can result, for example, from:

(a)   unexpectedly high or low rates of: employee turnover, early retirement, mortality, increases in salaries or benefits, or medical costs;

(b)   the effect of changes in estimates of: future employee turnover, early retirement, mortality, increases in salaries or benefits, or medical costs;

(c)   the effect of changes in the discount rate; and

(d)   differences between the actual return on plan assets and the expected return on plan assets.[126]

Under IAS 19 actuarial gains and losses need not be recognised in full as they occur. This is discussed at 5.3.1 above.

5.4.5   Settlements and curtailments

A settlement occurs when an employer enters into a transaction that eliminates all further legal or constructive obligations for part or all of the benefits provided under a defined benefit plan, for example, when a lump-sum cash payment is made to, or on behalf of, plan participants in exchange for their rights to receive specified post-employment benefits.[127] IAS 19 observes that an employer may acquire an insurance policy to fund some or all of the employee benefits relating to employee service in the current and prior periods. The acquisition of such a policy is not a settlement if the employer retains a legal or constructive obligation to pay further amounts if the insurer does not pay the employee benefits specified in the insurance policy.[128]

A curtailment occurs when an employer (1) is demonstrably committed to make a material reduction in the number of employees covered by a plan or (2) amends the terms of a defined benefit plan such that a material element of future service by current employees will no longer qualify for benefits or will qualify only for reduced benefits. The standard makes the somewhat circular observation that an event is material enough to qualify as a curtailment if the recognition of a curtailment gain or loss would have a material effect on the financial statements.[129] A curtailment may arise from an isolated event, such as the closing of a plant, discontinuance of an operation or termination or suspension of a plan. IAS 19 notes that curtailments are often linked to a restructuring, in which case the curtailment gain or loss should be accounted for at the same time as the related restructuring.[130]

Gains or losses on the settlement or curtailment of a defined benefit plan should be recognised when the settlement or curtailment occurs. The gain or loss should comprise:

(a)   any resulting change in the present value of the defined benefit obligation;

(b)   any resulting change in the fair value of the plan assets; and

(c)   any related actuarial gains and losses and past service cost that had not previously been recognised.[131]

Before determining the effect of a settlement or curtailment, the standard requires that the obligation and any related plan assets be remeasured using current actuarial assumptions including current market interest rates and other current market prices.[132] These should be taken account of in the normal way for the period preceding the settlement or curtailment (which, as shown in example 30.7 below, includes the corridor mechanism).

Where a curtailment relates to only some employees covered by a plan or only part of an obligation is settled, the gain or loss should include a proportionate share of the previously unrecognised past service costs and actuarial gains and losses.

The proportionate share is determined on the basis of the present value of the obligations before and after the curtailment or settlement, unless another basis is more rational in the circumstances. For example, it may be appropriate to apply any gain arising on a curtailment or settlement of the same plan to first eliminate any unrecognised past service cost relating to the same plan.[133]

The standard illustrates this as follows:[134]

Example 30.7:   Curtailment gains

An entity discontinues a business segment and employees of the discontinued segment will earn no further benefits. This is a curtailment without a settlement. Using current actuarial assumptions (including current market interest rates and other current market prices) immediately before the curtailment, the entity has a defined benefit obligation with a net present value of 1,000, plan assets with a fair value of 820 and net cumulative unrecognised actuarial gains of 50. The entity had first adopted the Standard one year before. This increased the net liability by 100, which the entity chose to recognise over five years. The curtailment reduces the net present value of the obligation by 100 to 900.

Of the previously unrecognised actuarial gains and transitional amounts, 10% (=100/1,000) relates to the part of the obligation that was eliminated through the curtailment. Therefore, the effect of the curtailment is as follows:

	Before curtailment	Curtailment gain	After curtailment
Net present value of obligation	*1,000*	*(100)*	*900*
Fair value of plan assets	*(820)*	*–*	*(820)*
	180	*(100)*	*80*
Unrecognised actuarial gains	*50*	*(5)*	*45*
Unrecognised transitional amount (100 × 4/5)	*(80)*	*8*	*(72)*
Net liability recognised in balance sheet	*150*	*(97)*	*53*

This example illustrates determining the proportionate share of previously unrecognised amounts on the basis of the percentage change in the obligation resulting from the curtailment. As noted above, this is the default method but others should be used if more rational in the circumstances.

IAS 19 notes that a settlement occurs together with a curtailment when a plan is terminated such that the obligation is settled and the plan ceases to exist. However, if the plan is replaced by a new plan offering benefits that are, in substance, identical to the old one, the event is not a settlement or a curtailment.[135]

This is the only mention in the standard of the closure of a defined benefit plan. Over recent years, the closure of plans to future accrual has become increasingly common in some jurisdictions. However, such closure is not always accompanied by full settlement – very often the plan will be left in place to 'run-off' the liability over time. Closure to future accrual is a curtailment, and accordingly all previously unrecognised actuarial gains and losses would be recognised (assuming the closure is for all employees).

Closure to future accrual raises two particular accounting questions, which are not dealt with by the standard:

(a)   having recognised all previously unrecognised actuarial gains and losses, is it still acceptable to defer the recognition of those arising subsequently using the corridor mechanism?

(b)   is it still acceptable to spread forward these gains and losses over the remaining service lives of employees?

These deferral mechanisms are discussed at 5.3.1 A above.

In our view, the most convincing justification for the corridor mechanism presented by the IASC was one of precision. In particular, the IASC considered that '... the purpose of the 'corridor' is to deal with the inevitable imprecision in the measurement of defined benefit obligations.'[136] Also, the standard observes that 'In the long term, actuarial gains and losses may offset one another. Therefore, estimates of post-employment benefit obligations are best viewed as a range (or 'corridor') around the best estimate.'[137] On that basis, it could be argued that the corridor remains appropriate for closed schemes. One quite powerful counter view is that the 'imprecision argument' is much less convincing for a closed scheme because for many schemes two significant uncertainties may have been resolved (future salary progression, if that is the case, and the impact of future staff retention rates on the computation of the liability in any event).

As for the smoothing of actuarial variances over service lives, the standard offers no explanation. Whether one believes that the result of the accounting should be to 'get the balance sheet right' or to achieve matching in the income statement (by charging employee costs in the period the employees earn entitlement to benefits) it seems to us that there conceptual consistency in not deferring recognition of gains and losses under a balance sheet model once future service no longer changes the employee's entitlement and the employer's obligations. However, there is also a school of thought that says that retirement benefits are a long-term liability that should be accounted for on a long-term basis.

Given the lack of guidance in the standard it is likely that practice in this area will be mixed. However, the IASB has already proposed to do away with both of these smoothing mechanisms, so the question may become an academic one if the IASB's plans come to fruition (see 10.1 below).

5.4.6   Past service costs

Past service cost is the increase in the present value of the defined benefit obligation for employee service in prior periods, which occurs in the current period from the introduction of, or changes to, post-employment benefits or other long-term employee benefits.[138] It excludes:

(a)   the effect of differences between actual and previously assumed salary increases on the obligation to pay benefits for service in prior years (there is no past service cost because actuarial assumptions allow for projected salaries, accordingly the effect of any such difference is an actuarial gain or loss, see 5.2.2 above);

(b)   under and over estimates of discretionary pension increases where an entity has a constructive obligation to grant such increases (there is no past service cost because actuarial assumptions allow for such increases, accordingly the effect of any such under or overestimate is an actuarial gain or loss, see 5.2.2 above);

(c)   estimates of benefit improvements that result from actuarial gains that have already been recognised in the financial statements if the entity is obliged, by either the formal terms of a plan (or a constructive obligation that goes beyond those terms) or legislation, to use any surplus in the plan for the benefit of plan participants, even if the benefit increase has not yet been formally awarded (the resulting increase in the obligation is an actuarial loss and not past service cost, see 5.2.2 above);

(d)   the increase in vested benefits when, in the absence of new or improved benefits, employees complete vesting requirements (there is no past service cost because the estimated cost of benefits was recognised as current service cost as the service was rendered, accordingly the effect of any such increase is an actuarial gain or loss, see 5.2.2 above); and

(e)   the effect of plan amendments that reduce benefits for future service (a curtailment, see 5.4.5 above).[139]

Where an entity reduces certain benefits payable under an existing defined benefit plan and, at the same time, increases other benefits payable under the plan for the same employees, the entity treats the change as a single net change.[140]

Past service cost may be either positive (where benefits are introduced or improved) or negative (where existing benefits are reduced).[141] IAS 19 requires that in measuring its defined benefit liability, an employer should recognise past service cost as an expense (income) on a straight-line basis over the average period until the benefits become vested (although this is subject to the particular provisions relating to the restriction of assets discussed at 5.3.1 B above).[142] This is on the grounds that past service awards are granted in return for employee service over the vesting period, and is regardless of the fact that the cost refers to employee service in previous periods.[143] If benefits are vested immediately following the changes to a defined benefit plan, the past service cost should be recognised immediately.[144] The standard illustrates these requirements with a worked example as follows:[145]

Example 30.8:   Past service costs

An entity operates a pension plan that provides a pension of 2% of final salary for each year of service. The benefits become vested after five years of service. On 1 January 2005 the entity improves the pension to 2.5% of final salary for each year of service starting from 1 January 2001. At the date of the improvement, the present value of the additional benefits for service from 1 January 2001 to 1 January 2005 is as follows:

Employees with more than five years' service at 1/1/05	150
Employees with less than five years' service at 1/1/05	
(average period until vesting: three years)	120
	270

The entity recognises 150 immediately because those benefits are already vested. The entity recognises 120 on a straight-line basis over three years from 1 January 2005.

Not requiring the full recognition of the rise in the defined benefit obligation represents a third departure from the 'balance sheet purity' of a full fair value balance sheet model (the other two being the corridor and spreading mechanisms discussed at 5.3.1 above).

If done rigorously, the mechanics of this approach could impose a burdensome extra layer of record keeping on employers. This is because the obligation computed under the projected unit method at and after the past service award would include an increase due to the benefit improvement (making assumptions about how many staff will remain until vesting). The deferral of a reducing portion of the unvested benefit is, in accounting terms, an asset which adjusts the amount recorded in the balance sheet. To achieve accounting accuracy any subsequent adjustment to the obligation due to experience adjustments or changes in assumptions relating to the level of benefit to vest would require an equivalent adjustment to the deferred past service cost. For example, if the number of staff for whom the benefit is expected to vest:

- falls, the resulting actuarial gain should be compensated for by an accelerated release of an appropriate portion of the deferred past service cost. Otherwise the accrual of the cost would be recorded as an asset and its reversal taken to income;

- rises, the actuarial loss is taken account of in full in the obligation (subject to the corridor etc) whereas if that level of vesting had been correctly predicted at the date of the past service award the cost would have qualified for deferral.

The IASC took the view that it would be impractical to track the impact of these complexities. Accordingly it provides that an amortisation schedule for past service cost should be established when the benefits are introduced or changed. Noting that it would be impracticable to maintain the detailed records needed to identify and implement subsequent changes in that amortisation schedule. Moreover, the standard argues that the effect is likely to be material only where there is a curtailment or settlement. For this reason an amendment to the amortisation schedule for past service cost is required only if there is a curtailment or settlement.[146]

6 OTHER EMPLOYEE BENEFITS

6.1 Short-term employee benefits

Short-term employee benefits are employee benefits (other than termination benefits) which fall due wholly within twelve months after the end of the period in which the employees render the related service.[147] They include:

- wages, salaries and social security contributions;

- short-term compensated absences (such as paid annual leave and paid sick leave) where the absences are expected to occur within twelve months after the end of the period in which the employees render the related service;

- profit sharing and bonuses payable within twelve months after the end of the period in which the employees render the related service; and

- non-monetary benefits (such as medical care, housing, cars and free or subsidised goods or services) for current employees.[148]

IAS 19 observes that accounting for short-term employee benefits is generally straightforward because no actuarial assumptions are required to measure the obligation or the cost and there is no possibility of any actuarial gain or loss.

Moreover, short-term employee benefit obligations are measured on an undiscounted basis.[149]

6.1.1   General recognition criteria for short-term employee benefits

An entity should recognise the undiscounted amount of short-term benefits attributable to services that have been rendered in the period as an expense, unless another IAS requires or permits the benefits to be included in the cost of an asset. This may particularly be the case under IAS 2 (see Chapter 21 at 2.2.1) and IAS 16 (see Chapter 12 at 2.3.1). Any difference between the amount of cost recognised and cash payments made should be treated as a liability or prepayment as appropriate.[150] There are further requirements in respect of short-term compensated absences and profit sharing and bonus plans.

6.1.2   Short-term compensated absences

These include absences for vacation (holiday), sickness and short-term disability, maternity or paternity leave, jury service and military service. These can either be accumulating and non-accumulating absences. Accumulating absences are those that can be carried forward and used in future periods if the entitlement in the current period is not used in full. They can be either vesting entitlements (which entitle employees to a cash payment in lieu of absences not taken on leaving the entity) or non-vesting entitlement (where no cash compensation is payable). Non-accumulating absences are those where there is no entitlement to carry forward unused days.[151]

A   Accumulating absences

The cost of accumulating absences should be recognised when employees render the service that increases their entitlement to future compensated absences. No distinction should be made between vesting and non-vesting entitlements (see above), on the basis that the liability arises as services are rendered in both cases. However, in measuring non-vesting entitlements, the possibility of employees leaving before receiving them should be taken into account.[152]

The cost of accumulating absences should be measured as the additional amount that the entity expects to pay as a result of the unused entitlement that has accumulated at the balance sheet date. In the case of unused paid sick leave, provision should be made only to the extent that it is expected that employees will use the sick leave in subsequent periods. The standard observes that in many cases, it may not be necessary to make detailed computations to estimate that there is no material obligation for unused compensated absences. For example, IAS 19 considers it unlikely that a sick leave obligation will be material unless if there is a formal or informal understanding that unused paid sick leave may be taken as paid vacation.[153]

The standard provides an example to illustrate the requirements for accumulating absences upon which the following is based:[154]

Example 30.9:   Accumulating absences

An entity has 100 employees, who are each entitled to five working days of paid sick leave for each year. Unused sick leave may be carried forward for one calendar year. Sick leave is taken first out of the current year's entitlement and then out of any balance brought forward from the previous year (a LIFO basis). At 31 December 2004, the average unused entitlement is two days per employee. The entity expects, based on past experience which is expected to continue, that 92 employees will take no more than five days of paid sick leave in 2005 and that the remaining eight employees will take an average of six and a half days each.

The entity expects that it will pay an additional 12 days of sick pay as a result of the unused entitlement that has accumulated at 31 December 2004 (one and a half days each, for eight employees). Therefore, the entity recognises a liability equal to 12 days of sick pay.

B   Non-accumulating absences

The cost of non-accumulating absences should be recognised as and when they arise, on the basis that the entitlement is not directly linked to the service rendered by employees in the period. This is commonly the case for sick pay (to the extent that unused past entitlement cannot be carried forward), maternity or paternity leave and compensated absences for jury service or military service.[155]

6.1.3   *Profit sharing and bonus plans*

An entity should recognise the expected cost of profit sharing and bonus payments when, and only when:

- the entity has a present legal or constructive obligation to make such payments as a result of past events; and
- a reliable estimate of the obligation can be made.[156]

A   *Present legal or constructive obligation*

A present obligation exists when, and only when, the entity has no realistic alternative but to make the payments.[157] IAS 19 clarifies that where a profit-sharing plan is subject to a loyalty period (i.e. a period during which employees must remain with the entity in order to receive their share), a constructive obligation is created during the period in which the relevant profit is earned. However, the possibility of employees leaving during the loyalty period should be taken into account in measuring the cost of the plan.[158] The standard attempts to illustrate the approach as follows:

Example 30.10:   Profit sharing and bonus plans

A profit-sharing plan requires an entity to pay a specified proportion of its net profit for the year to employees who serve throughout the year. If no employees leave during the year, the total profit-sharing payments for the year will be 3% of net profit. The entity estimates that staff turnover will reduce the payments to 2.5% of net profit.

The entity recognises a liability and an expense of 2.5% of net profit.

It is a little hard to know what to make of this example. Whilst claiming to illustrate accruing a bonus over a period *excluding* the loyalty period, it selects a fact pattern where the 'earning period' and the loyalty period both end at the balance sheet date! Moreover, when preparing accounts for the year it will no longer be uncertain whether all eligible employees become entitled to the bonus, as that is determined at the year-end. That means the reduction in the accrual from 3% to 2.5% should be an observable fact not an estimate. The requirement to account for short-term bonuses over the period during which employees render service that increases the amount to be paid if they remain in service for a further period (in other words, excluding the loyalty period) is in marked contrast to the requirements for long-term bonuses. If the loyalty period exceeds one year from the balance sheet date the bonus becomes an 'other long-term employee benefit' to which the projected unit method is applied. This is discussed at 6.2 below.

The standard also states that where an entity has a practice of paying bonuses, it has a constructive obligation to pay a bonus, even though there may be no legal obligation for it to do so. Again, however, in measuring the cost, the possibility of employees leaving before receiving a bonus should be taken into account.[159]

B   Reliable estimate of provision

A reliable estimate of a legal or constructive obligation under a profit sharing or bonus plan can be made when, and only when:

- the formal terms of the plan contain a formula for determining the amount of the benefit;

- the entity determines the amounts to be paid before the financial statements are approved for issue; or

- past practice gives clear evidence of the amount of the entity's constructive obligation.[160]

IAS 19 states that an obligation under a profit sharing or bonus plan must be accounted for as expense and not a distribution of profit, since it results from employee service and not from a transaction with owners.[161] Where profit sharing and bonus payments are not due wholly within twelve months of the end of the period in which the employees render the relevant service, they should be accounted for as other long-term employee benefits (see 6.2 below).[162]

6.2   Long-term employee benefits other than post-employment benefits

6.2.1   Meaning of other long-term employee benefits

These are employee benefits (other than post-employment benefits and termination benefits) which do not fall due wholly within twelve months after the end of the period in which the employees render the related service.[163] They include:

- long-term compensated absences such as long-service or sabbatical leave;

- jubilee or other long-service benefits;

- long-term disability benefits;

- profit sharing and bonuses payable twelve months or more after the end of the period in which the employees render the related service; and

- deferred compensation paid twelve months or more after the end of the period in which it is earned.[164]

6.2.2 Recognition and measurement

For such benefits IAS 19 requires a simplified version of the accounting treatment required in respect of defined benefit plans (which is discussed in detail at 5 above). The amount recognised as a liability for other long-term employee benefits should be the net total, at the balance sheet date, of the present value of the defined benefit obligation and the fair value of plan assets (if any) out of which the obligations are to be settled directly. The net total of the following amounts should be recognised as expense or income, except to the extent that another IAS requires or permits their inclusion in the cost of an asset:

(a) current service cost;

(b) interest cost;

(c) the expected return on any plan assets and on any reimbursement right recognised as an asset;

(d) actuarial gains and losses, which should all be recognised immediately;

(e) past service cost, which should all be recognised immediately; and

(f) the effect of any curtailments or settlements.

All assets, liabilities, income and expenditure relating to such benefits should be accounted for in the same way, and subject to the same restrictions on the recognition of assets and income, as those relating to a defined benefit pension plan (see 5.3.1 B and C above), except that:

- actuarial gains and losses are recognised immediately (i.e. they are not limited to a 'corridor' – see 5.3.1 A above); and

- all past service costs are recognised immediately (i.e. they not spread over the period to vesting – see 5.4.6 above).[165]

A Annually determined bonuses with a loyalty period greater than one year

It is quite common practice for certain employees (particularly more senior ones) to receive bonuses whereby the amount to be received is determined some time in advance of payment (the 'earning' period) with entitlement to it then only subject to the requirement for continued employment for a further period (the 'loyalty' period). Often the amount payable will be determined by reference to performance in the earning period – such as corporate financial performance – but that need not be the case. As discussed at 6.1.3 A above, when the arrangement meets the definition of a short-term benefit (i.e. all amounts fall due within a year after the end of the earning period), the standard considers that an obligation is created as 'employees render service that increases the amount to be paid *if they remain in service until the end of the specified period.*' [emphasis added]. In other words, for a typical 'annual' scheme (with payments based on, say, profits for the year) if the loyalty period ends within a year of the balance sheet date then all the payments are accrued in the year (the earnings period) and not spread forward over the loyalty period.

Should the loyalty period be any longer than this (say, a year and a day), however, a very different model is used by IAS 19. In these circumstances, the arrangement is an 'other long-term employee benefit' to which the projected unit credit method should be applied. As discussed at 5.2.2 above this involves attributing benefits to years of service from:

- the date when service by the employee first leads to benefits under the plan (whether or not the benefits are conditional on further service); until

- the date when further service by the employee will lead to no material amount of further benefits under the plan, other than from further salary increases.

This is because the benefit does not vest until the end of the loyalty period. Accordingly, attributing benefits to periods of service under the plan's formula would lead to all benefits being attributed to the very last period. In these circumstances, IAS 19 requires the benefits to be attributed on a straight-line basis over the vesting period. This requirement is illustrated in items 5 to 8 in Example 30.3 at 5.2.2 C above. Crucially, there is no allowance to recognise the liability any earlier than this – in particular there is no reference to a shorter period during which 'the amount to be paid [increases] if they remain in service until the end of the specified period.'

That this is genuinely the intention of the standard seems to be confirmed by the fact that IFRS 2 makes the same requirement to allocate the cost of share-based payments over the full vesting period, including any loyalty period.[166]

In light of this, choosing to allow 'special' simplified accruals accounting for such amounts when they are payable soon after the year-end seems to be just a pragmatic simplification in the standard. Inevitably that will produce slightly curious results when the vesting period ends just before as opposed to just after the period chosen (a year in IAS 19). In particular, the flip between short term accruals accounting and the long-term projected unit method will mean that a bonus determined within a year and payable one year later will all be charged in the first year, whereas if the recipient must remain employed one day longer for the benefit to vest it will be spread over two years and the cost will comprise part current service cost and part interest cost.

B   Long-term disability benefit

Where long-term disability benefit depends on the length of service of the employee, an obligation arises as the employee renders service, which is to be measured according to the probability that payment will be required and the length of time for which payment is expected to be made. If, however, the level of benefit is the same for all employees regardless of years of service, the cost is recognised only when an event causing disability occurs.[167]

It is not clear why the IASC made this distinction, since in principle both types of benefit are equally susceptible to actuarial measurement. If anything the cost of benefits applicable to all employees regardless of service is probably easier to quantify actuarially. It may be that the reason is another departure from the balance sheet purity of the standard because of unpalatable income statement results. Given that an exposure to disability benefits which grows with years of service is fully provided for (actuarially) as it grows over time, it would seem logical for full provision to be made immediately for an exposure which comes into being (in full) on the day the employee commences employment. The problem with such an approach would be what to do with the debit entry. It wouldn't represent an asset as envisaged in the conceptual framework, which would tend to imply an instant charge to the income statement. These issues are similar to those surrounding death-in-service benefits discussed at 3.6 above.

6.3   Termination benefits

Termination benefits are employee benefits payable as a result of either:

- an entity's decision to terminate an employee's employment before the normal retirement date; or

- an employee's decision to accept voluntary redundancy in exchange for those benefits.[168]

They are accounted for differently from other employee benefits because the event that gives rise an obligation for them is the termination rather than the rendering of service by the employee.[169]

6.3.1   *Recognition*

An entity should recognise termination benefits as a liability and an expense when, and only when, the entity is demonstrably committed (see below) to either:

- terminate the employment of an employee or group of employees before the normal retirement date; or

- provide termination benefits as a result of an offer made in order to encourage voluntary redundancy.[170]

An entity is demonstrably committed to a termination when, and only when, the entity has a detailed formal plan for the termination and is without realistic possibility of withdrawal. The detailed plan should include, as a minimum:

- the location, function, and approximate number of employees whose services are to be terminated;

- the termination benefits for each job classification or function; and

- the time at which the plan will be implemented. Implementation should begin as soon as possible and the period of time to complete implementation should be such that material changes to the plan are not likely.[171]

IAS 19 distinguishes between those benefits that are payable as a result of the termination of employment by the entity and those payable to employees on leaving, regardless of the reason for their departure.

Benefits resulting from a termination by the entity are 'termination benefits' as defined by the standard, whether the obligation is imposed by law, contractual agreement with employees or their representatives, custom, or a desire to act equitably. They are generally given as lump-sum payments, but may include enhancement of retirement benefits or of other post-employment benefits (either indirectly through an employee benefit plan or directly) and salary until the end of a specified notice period if the employee renders no further service that provides economic benefits to the entity.[172] The restriction that salary over a notice period may only be considered a termination benefit if the employee renders no further service that provides economic benefits to the entity is an important one. In a corporate restructuring it may frequently be the case that some employees are paid (perhaps at enhanced rates) to stay on and achieve an orderly wind-down of the operations rather than leave once the termination is announced. Such payments would not fall to be treated as termination benefits.

By contrast benefits payable to employees on leaving (subject possibly to minimum service or vesting requirements) in all circumstances are not 'termination benefits' as defined in IAS 19, notwithstanding that they may be referred to as such in some jurisdictions. Benefits of this nature should be accounted for as post-employment benefits (see 5 above). It may also be that a type of hybrid arrangement operates, whereby employees receive a lower benefit for a voluntary termination at their request than for an involuntary one, and a higher benefit for an involuntary termination at the request of the entity. In such cases, only the difference between the lower and higher levels of benefit should be treated as a termination benefit.[173]

The cost of termination benefits should be recognised immediately on the grounds that they do not provide an entity with future economic benefits.[174] IAS 19 also points out that the recognition of termination benefits will often give rise to the need to account for a curtailment of retirement benefits or other employee benefits (see 5.4.5 above).[175]

The treatment of termination benefits is a topic currently under review by the IASB as part of their 'convergence' project. At the time of writing, no exposure draft of amendments has been produced, however at their meeting in December 2002, the Board agreed to amend the requirements for termination benefits in IAS 19 to specify that:

(a)   the recognition of involuntary termination benefits requires the communication of those benefits to the employees;

(b)   where employees are required to render service to be entitled to involuntary termination benefits, those benefits are recognised over the future service period; and

(c)   voluntary termination benefits are recognised when employees accept the offer of voluntary termination.[176]

6.3.2   Measurement

Where termination benefits fall due more than twelve months after the balance sheet date, they should be discounted. The rate used should be determined in the same way as for defined benefit post-employment benefits discussed at 5.2.2 E above.[177]

Where an offer has been made to encourage voluntary redundancy, the termination benefits should be measured by reference to the number of employee expected to accept the offer.[178]

7 DISCLOSURE REQUIREMENTS

7.1 Defined contribution plans

IAS 19 requires the disclosure of the expense recognised for defined contribution plans.[179]

Where a multi-employer defined benefit plan is treated as a defined contribution plan (see 3.3 above) the following additional disclosures are required:

(a) the fact that the plan is a defined benefit plan; and

(b) the reason why sufficient information is not available to enable the entity to account for the plan as a defined benefit plan; and

(c) to the extent that a surplus or deficit in the plan may affect the amount of future contributions:

    (i) any available information about that surplus or deficit;

    (ii) the basis used to determine that surplus or deficit; and

    (iii) the implications, if any, for the entity.[180]

The standard provides an illustration of what the above disclosures might look like in Appendix B.

Where required by IAS 24, information should also be disclosed about contributions to defined contribution plans for key management personnel.[181] IAS 24 is discussed in Chapter 33.

7.2 Defined benefit plans

IAS 19 requires extensive disclosure in relation to defined benefit plans, as follows:[182]

(a) the accounting policy for recognising actuarial gains and losses;

(b) a general description of the type of plan (to distinguish, for example, flat salary pension plans from final salary pension plans and from post-employment medical plans but with no further detail required[183]);

(c) a reconciliation of the assets and liabilities recognised in the balance sheet, showing at least:

    (i) the present value at the balance sheet date of defined benefit obligations that are wholly unfunded;

    (ii) the present value (before deducting the fair value of plan assets) at the balance sheet date of defined benefit obligations that are wholly or partly funded;

    (iii) the fair value of any plan assets at the balance sheet date;

    (iv) the net actuarial gains or losses not recognised in the balance sheet;

    (v) the past service cost not yet recognised in the balance sheet;

    (vi) any amount not recognised as an asset because of the limit (to recoverable amount) set by IAS 19;

     (vii)   the fair value at the balance sheet date of any reimbursement right recognised as a separate asset – together with a brief description of the link between the reimbursement right and the related obligation; and

     (viii) the other amounts recognised in the balance sheet;

(d)   the amounts included in the fair value of plan assets for:

     (i)   each category of the reporting entity's own financial instruments; and

     (ii)   any property occupied by, or other assets used by, the reporting entity;

(e)   a reconciliation showing the movements during the period in the net liability (or asset) recognised in the balance sheet;

(f)   the total expense recognised in the income statement for each of the following, and the line items of the income statement in which they are included:

     (i)   current service cost;

     (ii)   interest cost;

     (iii)   expected return on plan assets;

     (iv)   expected return on any reimbursement right recognised as a separate asset;

     (v)   actuarial gains and losses;

     (vi)   past service cost; and

     (vii)   the effect of any curtailment or settlement;

(g)   the actual return on plan assets and the actual return on any reimbursement right recognised as an asset; and

(h)   the principal actuarial assumptions used as at the balance sheet date, including, where applicable:

     (i)   the discount rates;

     (ii)   the expected rates of return on any plan assets for the periods presented in the financial statements;

     (iii)   the expected rates of return for the periods presented in the financial statements on any reimbursement right recognised as an asset;

     (iv)   the expected rates of salary increases and of changes in an index or other variable specified in the formal or constructive terms of a plan as the basis for future benefit increase;

     (v)   medical cost trend rates; and

     (vi)   any other material actuarial assumptions used;

The actuarial assumptions should be disclosed in absolute terms and not just as a margin between different percentages or other variables.[184]

There is some flexibility allowed in aggregating disclosure where an employer has more than one plan. In these circumstances, the required disclosures may be made separately for each plan, in total or in such groupings as are considered most useful. Examples of possible groupings which may be considered useful include: geographical location (e.g. distinguishing between domestic and foreign plans) and plans which are subject to materially different risks (e.g. distinguishing flat salary pension plans from final salary pension plans and from post-retirement medical plans). When disclosures are given in total for a grouping of plans, they should be provided in the form of weighted averages or of relatively narrow ranges.[185] The standard provides a detailed illustration of what its required disclosures might look like in Appendix B.

The standard also contains a reminder that:

(i)   Where required by IAS 24 (see Chapter 33) information about:

    (i)   related party transactions with post-employment benefit plans; and

    (ii)   post-employment benefits for key management personnel;[186] and

(j)   Where required by IAS 37 (see Chapter 25), information about contingent liabilities arising from post-employment benefit obligations.[187]

7.3   Short-term employee benefits

IAS 19 has no specific disclosure requirements in respect of short-term employee benefits, but contains reminders that:

- IAS 24 requires disclosure of employee benefits for key management personnel (see Chapter 33 at 2.3.6); and
- IAS 1 requires disclosure of employee benefits expense.[188]

7.4   Long-term employee benefits

IAS 19 requires no specific disclosures in respect of other long-term benefits but notes that other IAS may require disclosure, for example where:

- the expense resulting from such benefits is material (as required by IAS 1 – see Chapter 3 at 3.2.4); or
- the expense relates to key management personnel (as required by IAS 24 (see Chapter 33 at 2.3.6).[189]

7.5   Termination benefits

IAS 19 contains no specific disclosure requirements for termination benefits, but notes that the following requirements of other IAS will be relevant:

- where an offer of termination benefits is made to employees and the number of employees who will accept it is uncertain, a contingent liability exists, details of which must be disclosed under IAS 37 (see Chapter 25 at 3.2.1), unless the possibility of an outflow in settlement is remote;
- termination benefits may be material, therefore the nature and amount of the expense will be disclosed as required by IAS 1 (see Chapter 3 at 3.2.4); and
- termination benefits payable to key management personnel will be disclosed under IAS 24 (see Chapter 33 at 2.3.6)[190]

8   TRANSITIONAL ARRANGEMENTS AND FIRST-TIME ADOPTION ISSUES

8.1   General

As mentioned at 1 above, IAS 19 has been evolving steadily since it was first published in 1998 with its broadened scope of 'employee benefits'. The original version contained some (optional) transitional provisions which could continue to affect financial statements for five years from adoption, and each of the subsequent amendments had its own effective date. These issues are discussed at 8.2 below. Different provisions apply, under IFRS 1 – *First-time adoption of International Financial Reporting Standards*, to first time adopters and these are discussed at 8.3 below.

8.2   Transitional arrangements for entities already reporting under IFRS

The 1998 revised version of IAS 19 applied to financial statements covering periods beginning on or after 1 January 1999, though early adoption was encouraged.[191] For reporting periods beginning after 1 January 2001 further revisions were made relating to the treatment of qualifying insurance policies, any other insurance policies and reimbursements rights (see 5.2.1 above).[192] The standard was revised again in 2002 to correct the anomaly that in some circumstances the interaction of the standard's complex requirements could lead to the recognition of profits purely as a result of actuarial *losses* in a pension fund (and vice versa). These changes took effect for periods ending on or after 31 May 2002 and are discussed at 5.3.1 C above.[193]

On first adopting IAS 19 it was necessary for an entity to determine the 'transitional liability' for defined benefit plans as:

(a)   the present value of the obligation at the date of adoption;

(b)   minus the fair value of plan assets at the date of adoption;

(c)   minus any past service cost that should be recognised in later periods.[194]

If the transitional liability exceeded the liability under the employer's previous accounting policy, then it was required to make an irrevocable choice to recognise that increase:

(a)   immediately in accordance with the provisions of IAS 8 (discussed in Chapter 3 at 4.4); or

(b)   as an expense on a straight-line basis over a maximum of five years from the date of adoption. In this case the entity should:

    (i)   apply the limit set by IAS 19 (see 5.3.1 B above) in measuring any asset recognised in the balance sheet;

    (ii)   disclose at each balance sheet date the amount of the increase that remains unrecognised and the amount recognised in the current period;

(iii) limit the recognition of subsequent actuarial gains to unrecognised actuarial gains in excess of the unrecognised transitional obligation liability; and

(iv) include the related part of the unrecognised transitional liability in determining any subsequent gain or loss on settlement or curtailment.

If the transitional liability was less that the liability under the previous accounting policy, the employer was required to recognise that decrease immediately under IAS 8.[195] Whichever route is taken, the effect of the change in accounting policy included all actuarial gains and losses that arose in earlier periods even if they fell inside the 10% corridor.[196]

IAS 19 illustrates the computation of this transitional liability by way of a numerical worked example.[197] Given this transitional effect could last for up to five years, at the time of writing its effects will still be evident for some entities.

8.3 First-time adoption issues

IFRS 1 is discussed in detail in Chapter 4. In brief, it allows a choice for first time adopters to either:

(a) apply the extant version of IAS 19 fully retrospectively (including the corridor mechanism); or

(b) recognise all cumulative actuarial gains and losses in the balance sheet at the date of transition.

The same choice must be applied to all defined benefit plans.[198] It is worth stressing that that option (a) would require applying current IAS 19 from the inception of the plan – in other words the original effective date (1999) and the original transitional provisions (see above) are not available to first time adopters. For very many entities option (a) would, therefore, require the retrospective application to go back many decades which seems unlikely to be possible. Accordingly, we believe most first time adopters will be essentially forced into option (b).

9 IAS 19 IN PRACTICE

The disclosures required by IAS 19 can often be quite lengthy. Set out below are extracts from the accounts of two companies which illustrate a number of different requirements under the standard.

Extract 30.6: Jardine Matheson Holdings Limited (2003)

Notes to the Financial Statements [extract]

15   Pension Plans

The Group has a large number of defined benefit pension plans, covering all the main territories in which it operates with the major plans relating to employees in Hong Kong and the United Kingdom. Most of the pension plans are final salary defined benefit plans and are either fund or unfunded. The assets of the funded plans are held independently of the Group's assets in separate trustee administered funds. The Group's major plans are valued by independent actuaries annually using the projected unit credit method.

The amounts recognized in the consolidated balance sheet are as follows:

	2003 US$m	2002 US$m
Fair value of plan assets	592	477
Present value of funded obligations	(619)	(587)
	(27)	(110)
Present value of unfunded obligations	(15)	(14)
Unrecognized actuarial losses	105	199
Unrecognized past service cost	–	1
Net pension assets	63	76

Analysis of net pension assets:

Pension assets	79	89
Pension liabilities	(16)	(13)
	63	76

Movements for the year:

At 1st January	76	76
Expenses recognized in the consolidated profit and loss account	(40)	(27)
Subsidiary undertakings disposed of	(2)	–
Contributions paid	29	27
At 31st December	63	76

The principal actuarial assumptions used for accounting purposes at 31st December are as follows:

	2003 Weighted Average %	2002 Weighted Average %
Discount rate applied to pension obligations	5.5	5.7
Expected return on plan assets	6.5	7.1
Future salary increases	4.1	4.8

The amounts recognized in the consolidated profit and loss account are as follows:

	2003 US$m	2002 US$m
Current service cost	26	27
Interest cost	33	34
Expected return on plan assets	(32)	(38)
Net actuarial losses recognized	12	3
Past service cost	–	1
Loss on curtailment and settlement	1	–
	40	27
Actual surplus/(deficit) on plan assets in the year	92	(48)

The above amounts are all recognized in arriving at operating profit and are included in cost of sales, selling and distribution costs and administration expenses.

Extract 30.7: Roche Holding Ltd(2003)

Notes to the Roche Group Consolidated Financial Statements [extract]

1.　　Summary of significant accounting policies [extract]

Employee benefits

Wages, salaries, social security contributions, paid annual leave and sick leave, bonuses, and non-monetary benefits are accrued in the year in which the associated services are rendered by employees of the Group. Where the Group provides long-term employee benefits, the cost is accrued to match the rendering of the services by the employees concerned.

The Group operates a number of defined benefit and defined contribution plans throughout the world. The cost for the year for defined benefit plans is determined using the projected unit credit method. This reflects service rendered by employees to the dates of valuation and incorporates actuarial assumptions primarily regarding discount rates used in determining the present value of benefits, projected rates of remuneration growth, and long-term expected rates of return for plan assets. Discount rates are based on the market yields of high-quality corporate bonds in the country concerned. Differences between assumptions and actual experiences and effects of changes in actuarial assumptions are allocated over the estimated average remaining working lives of employees, where these differences exceed a defined corridor. Past service costs are allocated over the average period until the benefits become vested. Pension assets and liabilities in different defined benefit schemes are not offset unless the Group has a legally enforceable right to use the surplus in one plan to settle obligations in the other plan. Pension assets are only recognised to the extent that the Group is able to derive future economic benefits in the way of refunds from the plan or reductions of future contributions. The Group's contributions to the defined contribution plans are charged to the income statement in the year to which they relate.

The Group operates several equity compensation plans, including separate plans at Genentech and Chugai. For fixed plans, such as the Roche Option Plan and the equivalent plans at Genentech and Chugai, no expense is recognised at the date of issue as the exercise price is greater or equal to the fair value of the underlying equity instrument at the date of issue. Subsequent cash flows from any exercises of vested grants are recorded to equity or, in the case of Genentech and Chugai plans, to balance sheet minority interests. For performance related variable plans, such as the Roche Performance Share Plan or the Stock Appreciation Rights, an expense is accrued over the vesting period for the difference between the exercise price and the fair value of the underlying equity instrument. The Group discloses the values of issued options using the Black-Scholes option valuation model. The Black-Scholes model was developed for traded options with no vesting or transfer restrictions, and since the various plans used by the Group include such restrictions, the fair value of any options issued would be lower than an unadjusted value implied by the Black-Scholes methodology.

9.　　Employees benefits in million of CHF

	2003	2002
Wages and salaries	**6,494**	6,055
Social security costs	**777**	717
Post-employment benefits: defined benefit plans	**469**	279
Post-employment benefits: defined contribution plans	**117**	146
Other employee benefits	**397**	331
Total employees' remuneration	**8,254**	7,528

The charges for employee benefits are included in the relevant expenditure line by function. The number of employees at the year-end was 65,357 (2002: 69,659). Other employee benefits consist mainly of life insurance schemes and certain other insurance schemes providing medical and dental cover.

10. Pensions and other post-employment benefits (in millions of CHF)

Most employees are covered by retirement benefit plans sponsored by Group companies. The nature of such plans varies according to legal regulations, fiscal requirements and economic conditions of the countries in which the employees are employed. The majority of such plans are defined benefit plans, the largest of which are located in Switzerland, the United States, Germany, the United Kingdom and Japan. Other post-employment benefits consist mostly of post-retirement healthcare and life insurance schemes, principally in the United States. Plans are usually funded by payments from the Group and by employees to trusts independent of the Group's finances. Where a plan is unfunded, notably for the major defined benefit plans in Germany, a liability for the whole obligation is recorded in the Group's balance sheet.

The amounts recognised in arriving at operating profit for post-employment defined benefit plans are as follows:

	2003	2002
Current service cost	351	314
Interest cost	584	627
Expected return on plan assets	(602)	(688)
Net actuarial (gains) losses recognised	109	22
Past service cost	4	4
(Gains) losses on curtailment	23	–
Total included in employees' remuneration	469	279

The actual return on plan assets was 1,050 million Swiss francs (2002: negative return of 1,022 million Swiss francs).

In September 2002 the Group paid an additional contribution of 340 million US dollars (530 million Swiss francs) into a post-employment defined benefit plan of one of its US subsidiaries, due to falls in the market value of this plan's assets during 2002. This payment is included in 'contributions paid' in the table below and is accounted for as part of the recognised surplus on funded pensions plans (see also Note 22) in the Group's consolidated financial statements in 2002. Thereafter it has been included in the actuarial calculation of the Group's pension expenses and balances.

The movements in the net asset (liability) recognised in the balance sheet for post-employment defined benefit plans are as follows:

	2003	2002
At beginning of year	(1,165)	(1,279)
Disetronic [3]	(7)	–
Chugai [6]	–	(351)
Vitamins and Fine Chemicals business [7]	242	–
Total expenses included in employees' remuneration (as above)	(469)	(279)
Contributions paid	340	679
Benefits paid (unfunded plans)	94	100
Currency translation effects and other	(241)	(35)
At end of year (as below)	(1,206)	(1,165)

Amounts recognised in the balance sheet for post-employment defined benefit plans are as follows:

	2003	2002
Funded plans		
Actuarial present value of funded obligations due to past and present employees	(9,785)	(9,337)
Plan assets held in trusts at fair value	9,490	8,751
Plan assets in excess (deficit) of actuarial present value of funded obligations	(295)	(586)
Unrecognised actuarial (gains) losses	1,459	1,807
Unrecognised past service costs	27	33
Net recognised asset (liability) for funded obligations due to past and present employees	1,191	1,254

Unfunded plans

Recognised (liability) for actuarial present value of unfunded obligations due to past and present employees	**(2,397)**	(2,419)
Total recognised asset (liability) for funded and unfunded obligations due to past and present employees	**(1,206)**	(1,165)
Reported as		
– Surplus recognised as part of other long-term assets [22]	**1,549**	1,761
Deficit recognised as part of liabilities for post-employment		
– benefits	**(2,755)**	(2,926)
Total net asset (liability) recognised	**(1,206)**	(1,165)

The above amounts included non-pension post-employment benefit schemes, principally medical plans as follows:

	2003	2002
Actuarial present value of obligations due to past and present employees	**(886)**	(806)
Plan assets held in trusts at fair value	**369**	387
Plan assets in excess (deficit) of actuarial present value of funded obligations	**(517)**	(419)
– less unrecognised actuarial (gains) losses	**395**	206
Net recognised asset (liability)	**(122)**	(213)

Amounts recognised in the balance sheet for post-employment defined benefit plans are predominantly non-current and are reported as long-term assets and non-current liabilities.

Plan assets of the funded plans do not include any of the Group's own equity instruments (2002: 900,000 non-voting equity securities with a fair value of 87 million Swiss francs).

The Group operates defined benefit schemes in many countries and the actuarial assumptions vary based upon local economic and social conditions. The range of assumptions used in the actuarial valuations of the most significant defined benefit plans, which are in countries with stable currencies and interest rates, is as follows:

	2003		2002	
	Weighted average	**Range**	Weighted average	Range
Discount rates	**4.90%**	**3%–7%**	5.02%	2%–7%
Projected rates of remuneration growth	**3.37%**	**1%–9%**	3.10%	2%–9%
Expected rates of return on plan assets	**6.41%**	**2%–9%**	6.42%	2%–9%
Healthcare cost trend rate	**8.30%**	**4%–12%**	8.46%	4%–12%

10   POSSIBLE FUTURE DEVELOPMENTS

10.1   The long-term intentions of the IASB

The IASC when writing IAS 19 observed the following: 'The Board found the immediate recognition approach attractive. However, the Board believes that it is not feasible to use this approach for actuarial gains and losses until the Board resolves substantial issues about performance reporting.'[199]

In fact, in our view the most reasoned explanation for the corridor mechanism in IAS 19 is also contained in the basis for conclusions of the standard, which says '… the purpose of the 'corridor' is to deal with the inevitable imprecision in the measurement of defined benefit obligations.'[200] Whilst that may well have been the IASC's view, it does not explain why variations outside the corridor should be deferred over the working lives of employees, nor the resultant inclusion in the balance sheet of items which fail to meet the definition of assets or liabilities in the conceptual framework. In reality, the corridor is a practical damping mechanism to limit the impact on the financial statements of large and volatile fluctuations in value. With the steady expansion of the use of 'fair values' in the balance sheet the credibility of IAS 19's argument of imprecision begins to wane. For example, financial statements are now required to include estimates of fair values for share options under IFRS 2 (although typically the timescales involved are not as long) and very long-tail uncertain liabilities such as nuclear decommissioning (under IAS 37). A credible case can be made that these estimates, which are recognised in full, are no less imprecise than the projected unit credit method. Indeed, the IASB has now expressly stated that in its view a defined benefit asset or liability can be measured with sufficient reliability to justify its recognition.[201] However, the corridor was introduced after much debate as a practical damping measure, reflecting a view that in the absence of any intention or necessity to liquidate a plan the combination of very long timescales and inherent imprecision renders balance sheet date estimates of fair values less relevant than a reasonably stable income statement charge. We can see no reason why that widely held view will have changed, and suspect that the IASB's intentions (discussed below) may meet with substantial opposition.

Nevertheless, the stance of the IASB comes as no surprise. In its published record of its July 2002 meeting, it states 'A majority of the Board agreed that actuarial gains and losses should be recognised immediately. However, the Board noted that it would not be possible to proceed with a standard based on this conclusion until the project on reporting performance had finalised its proposals on the presentation of the actuarial gains and losses.'[202]

In November 2003 the IASB took the decision to postpone its performance reporting project, and with it any progression of the move to mandatory immediate recognition of actuarial gains and losses. Instead, the Board intends to develop a proposal for a comprehensive project on post-employment benefits for consideration by the joint agenda working party with the FASB. Time will tell how and when these issues progress.

10.2   Short-term project

10.2.1 The IASB's proposals

In light of the delay to the Board's desired move to full recognition of actuarial gains and losses, it agreed in December 2003 to develop in the short term a more limited revision to IAS 19. In April 2004 it published proposals to amend IAS 19 (with effect from 2006 but with earlier adoption encouraged) to:

(a)   allow an entity choosing to recognise actuarial gains and losses in full in the period in which they occur to recognise them outside profit or loss in a statement of recognised income and expenses (without subsequent recycling into profit);

(b)   allow certain individual entities in a consolidated group that participate in a defined benefit plan that covers the group to treat the plan as a multi-employer plan (and hence, in some circumstances, apply defined contribution accounting) in their separate or individual financial statements. This is considered to be justified on cost/benefit grounds, and is intended only to apply to entities meeting criteria similar to those for the exemption in IAS 27 from the requirement to prepare consolidated financial statements. Accordingly the proposed exemption is only available if:

(i)   the entity is:

     (i)   a parent that produces consolidated financial statements that are available for public use and comply with IFRS; or

     (ii)   a wholly-owned subsidiary of an ultimate or any intermediate parent that produces consolidated financial statements that are available for public use and comply with IFRS; and

(ii)   the entity's debt or equity instruments are not traded in a public market (a domestic or foreign stock exchange or an over-the-counter market, including local and regional markets); and

(iii)   the entity did not file, nor is in the process of filing, its financial statements with a securities commission or other regulatory organisation for the purpose of issuing any class of instruments in a public market;

(c)   require disclosure in percentage terms of the major classes of assets held by a defined benefit plan and the expected rate of return for each class of asset;

(d)   require separate reconciliations of opening and closing balances for each of:

     (i)   the present value of plan obligations; and

     (ii)   the fair value of plan assets;

(e)   require a narrative description of the basis of used to determine the expected rate of return on assets;

(f)   require disclosure of the sensitivity of current service cost, interest cost and plan obligations to changes in the assumed medical cost trend rate;

(g)   require the disclosure of five-year histories of:

     (i)   the present value of the plan liabilities, the fair value of the plan assets and the surplus/deficit in the plan and

     (ii)   the experience adjustments arising on the plan liabilities and the plan assets expressed as (1) an amount and (2) as a percentage of the plan liabilities/assets at the balance sheet date; and

(h)   require disclosure of the employer's best estimate, as soon as it can reasonably be determined, of the contributions expected to be paid to the plan during the next year.[203]

At the time of writing we anticipate that the output of this project will be available, for early adoption in 2005.

The proposals in (c) to (g) above are not controversial, and draw on current requirements of other jurisdictions. The proposal in (a) is acknowledged by the Board to be a temporary measure and may prove attractive to some entities because, whilst balance sheet volatility will be introduced the income statement charge for post-employment benefits will be much more stable. The proposal in (b) strikes us as somewhat peculiar, and seemingly only justifiable on pragmatic grounds. When developing IAS 19 the IASC was very clear that any entity faced with defined benefit obligations should account for them as such – with the only exception being when insufficient information is available. In justification of this, the IASC noted the (at the time) recent issues faced by the French banking sector as follows. 'Also, the Board believes that it is misleading to use defined contribution accounting for multi-employer plans that are defined benefit plans. This is illustrated by the case of French banks that used defined contribution accounting for defined benefit pension plans operated under industry-wide collective agreements on a pay-as-you-go basis. Demographic trends made these plans unsustainable and a major reform in 1993 replaced these by defined contribution arrangements for future service. At this point, the banks were compelled to quantify their obligations. Those obligations had previously existed, but had not been recognised as liabilities.'[204] Furthermore, it explicitly considered and rejected an exemption for subsidiaries proposed by respondents to the project.[205] Whilst it is fair to say that the primary focus of the IASB is group financial statements it strikes us as hard to justify conceptually the step that an exemption for subsidiaries would represent, particularly when other subsidiaries in the group might not qualify for the exemption. In our view, such an exemption would be a pragmatic one, to be made on cost-benefit grounds.

Some of the proposed additional disclosure requirements are already seen in practice, as shown in the following two extracts.

Extract 30.8: TeliaSonera AB (2003)

Notes to Consolidated Financial Statements – IFRS/IAS [extract]

22   Provisions for Pensions and Employment Contracts [extract]

Strategic asset allocation

As of the balance sheet date, plan assets market values were as follows.

	December 31,					
	2003		**2002**		**2001**	
Asset category	SEK in millions	%	SEK in millions	%	SEK in millions	%
Fixed income instruments	8,838	61.8	8,754	62.6	5,825	43.3
Shares and other equity instruments	5,457	38.2	5,233	37.4	7,639	56.7
Total	14,295	100.0	13,987	100.0	13,464	100.0

Plan assets include shares in TeliaSonera AB with a market value of SEK 81 million, SEK 78 million and SEK 114 million as of December 31, 2003, 2002 and 2001, respectively.

As of December 31, 2003, the strategic asset allocation for the Swedish pension fund, representing approximately 85 percent of total plan assets, was 60 percent fixed income, 30 percent equities and 10 per cent alternative investments. The alternative investments include hedge funds, private equity, emerging market debt and high yield bonds. Out of the total assets 35 per cent are domestic index (inflation) linked government bonds and 25 percent refers to other domestic fixed income assets with low credit risk. Out of the equity holdings one third is domestic and the rest is global equities.

The actual allocation may fluctuate from the strategic allocation in a range of +/- 10 per cent between equities and fixed income.

Extract 30.9: Syngenta AG (2003)

Notes to the Syngenta Group Consolidated Financial Statements [extract]

26.   Employee benefits [extract]

The expected long-term rates of return on the assets and the fair values of the assets and liabilities of the major defined benefit pension schemes, together with aggregated data for other defined benefit schemes in the Group, are as follows:

At December 31, 2003	Switzerland		UK	
	Expected rate of return %	Fair value US$m	Expected rate of return %	Fair value US$m
Equities	7.0	279	7.5	471
Property	4.5	114	–	–
Bonds	4.5	436	4.9	670
Other assets	1.5	88	4.9	114
Fair value of assets	5.0	917	6.0	1,255
Benefit obligation		(949)		(1,473)
Funded status		**(32)**		**(218)**

At December 31, 2002	Switzerland		UK	
	Expected rate of return %	Fair value US$m	Expected rate of return %	Fair value US$m
Equities	7.0	208	7.5	475
Property	4.5	92	–	–
Bonds	4.5	382	4.9	381
Other assets	1.5	47	4.9	133
Fair value of assets	5.0	729	6.0	989
Benefit obligation		(782)		(1,277)
Funded status		**(53)**		**(238)**

At December 31, 2001	Switzerland (1)		UK	
	Expected rate of return %	Fair value US$m	Expected rate of return %	Fair value US$m
Equities		244	7.2	527
Property		77	–	–
Bonds		239	5.3	335
Other assets		79	5.3	83
Fair value of assets	5.0	639	6.4	945
Benefit obligation		(556)		(1,070)
Funded status		**83**		**(125)**

At December 31, 2003	USA Expected rate of return %	USA Fair value US$m	Other plans Fair value US$m	Group Fair value US$m
Equities	8.5	134	82	966
Property	8.0	–	–	114
Bonds	6.0	195	131	1,432
Other assets	8.5	25	101	328
Fair value of assets	7.5	354	314	2,840
Benefit obligation		(494)	(448)	(3,364)
Funded status		**(140)**	**(134)**	**(524)**

At December 31, 2002	USA Expected rate of return %	USA Fair value US$m	Other plans (1)Fair value US$m	Group (1)Fair value US$m
Equities	9.5	189		
Property	9.5	5		
Bonds	6.1	68		
Other assets	6.1	53		
Fair value of assets	7.5	315	254	2,287
Benefit obligation		(460)	(380)	(2,849)
Funded status		**(145)**	**(126)**	**(562)**

At December 31, 2001	USA Expected rate of return %	USA Fair value US$m	Other plans (1) Fair value US$m	Group (1) Fair value US$m
Equities		182		
Property		16		
Bonds		103		
Other assets		15		
Fair value of assets	9.0	316	232	2,132
Benefit obligation		(396)	(291)	(2,313)
Funded status		**(80)**	**(59)**	**(181)**

A legally separate trust was established for Syngenta's US post retirement healthcare plans in 2003. Previously, these plans were unfunded. There are no significant post retirement healthcare plans in countries other than the USA. The plan assets for the US trust at December 31, 2003 were held as cash and cash equivalents.

(1) Comparative data for these plans is available at total plan asset level only.

10.2.2 *The IFRIC's work programme*

At the time of writing, the IFRIC is deliberating two issues relating to IAS 19.

A Multi-employer schemes

In May 2004 IFRIC Draft Interpretation D6 – *Multi-employer plans* was published. The issues addressed in D6 are:

(a) when do plans meet the definition of a multi-employer plan?

(b) how should a participant in a multi-employer plan apply the requirements in IAS 19 relating to defined benefit plans?

(c) when might the information necessary for defined benefit accounting not be available? and

(d) how should state plans be treated?

The overall thrust of these proposals is to increase the use of defined benefit accounting, and stems from a concern that the paragraphs in IAS 19 on multi-employer plans have been interpreted to allow all participating entities in multi-employer plans an automatic exemption from defined benefit accounting.

It may strike some observers as a little confusing, given that as noted above the IASB is proposing to revise the standard's provisions in this area, that the IFRIC should be simultaneously considering the same issue. More curious still, is the fact that an appendix to D6 is a proposal by the IASB to *amend* IAS 19, not interpret it.

B Defined contribution schemes guaranteeing a minimum investment return

As discussed at 3.5 above, the issue is being debated by IFRIC and, at the time of writing, a draft interpretation (D9) has been issued.

11 CONCLUSION

Accounting for post-employment benefits is clearly a very challenging area for the IASB. There is a tension in the standard produced by what is, in the words of one Board member, 'the interaction of two fundamentally inconsistent notions in IAS 19. The corridor approach allowed by IAS 19 permits the recognition of amounts on the balance sheet that do not meet the Framework's definition of assets. The asset ceiling then imposes a limitation on the recognition of some of those assets based on a recoverability notion.' This, in our view, lies at the heart of the complexity of the standard and also of the seemingly unending need to revise it or have the IFRIC interpret it. Other issues remaining contentious include the nature (or even existence) of constructive obligations and the selection of a discount rate for liabilities.

The IASB has indicated that in due course it will undertake a more extensive review of IAS 19. In our view this is a necessary step which should re-challenge all of the underlying principles of the standard.

References

1 E54, *Exposure Draft E54 Proposed International Accounting Standard: Employee Benefits*, IASC, October 1996.

2 Exposure Draft, *Amendments to IAS 19 Employee Benefits – Actuarial Gains and Losses, Group Plans and Disclosures*, IASB, April 2004.

3 Exposure Draft, *Amendments to IAS 19 Employee Benefits – Actuarial Gains and Losses, Group Plans and Disclosures*, para. BC10.

4 IAS 19, *Employee benefits*, IASB, February 2004 (amended March 2004), Objective.

5 *Framework for the Preparation and presentation of Financial Statements*, IASB, September 1989.

6 IAS 19, paras. 1 and 7.

7 IAS 19, para. 4.

8 IAS 19, paras. 1-2

9 IAS 19, para. 6.

10 IAS 19, para. 5.

11 IAS 19, para. 3.

12 IAS 19, para. 7.

13 IAS 19, para. 24.

14 IAS 19, paras. 26-27.

15 IAS 19, para. 27.

16 IAS 19, para. 49.

17 IAS 19, para. 25.

18 IAS 19, para. 40.

19 IAS 19, para. 39.

20 IAS 19, para. 41.

21 IAS 19, para. 42.

22 IAS 19, para. 27.

23 IAS 19, para. 7.

24 IAS 19, para. 33.

25 IAS 19, para. 31.

26 IAS 19, para. 29.

27 IAS 19, para. 32.

28 IAS 19, paras. 30 and 32.

29 IAS 19, para. 34.

30 IAS 19, para. 35.

31 IAS 19, para. 37.

32 IAS 19, para. 36.

33 IAS 19, para. 38.

34 IAS 19, para. 37.

35 IAS 19, para. 26(b).

36 E54, paras. 17-21.

37 IAS 19, Basis for Conclusions, para. 89.

38 IAS 19, para. 43.

39 IAS 19, para. 45.

40 IAS 19, para. 44.

41 IAS 19, para. 48.

42 IAS 19, para. 49.

43 IAS 19, para. 50.

44 IAS 19, para. 51.

45 IAS 19, para. 50.

46 IAS 19, Appendix A.

47 IAS 19, para. 103.

48 IAS 19, para. 7.

49 IAS 19, para. 54.

50 IAS 19, para. 7.

51 IAS 39, *Financial Instruments: Recognition and Measurement*, IASB, December 2004 (amended March 2004), para. 46 and AG72.

52 IAS 19, para. 102.

53 IAS 19, para. 104.

54 IAS 19, paras. 104A-104B.

55 IAS 19, para. 104C.

56 IAS 19, para. 104D.

57 IAS 19, paras. 7 and 55.

58 IAS 19, paras. 52 and 83-84.

59 IAS 19, para. 52.

60 IAS 37, *Provisions, Contingent Liabilities and Contingent Assets*, IASB, September 1998 (amended March 2004), para. 10.

61 IAS 19, para. 53.

62 IAS 19, paras. 85 and 98.

63 IAS 19, para. 86.

64 IAS 19, paras. 83 and 87.

65 IAS 19, para. 64.

66 IAS 19, para. 65.

67 IAS 19, Example illustrating para. 65.

68 IAS 19, para. 68.

69 IAS 19, para. 67.

70 IAS 19, para. 70.

71 IAS 19, para. 69.

72 IAS 19, para. 70.

73 IAS 19, paras. 68-71.

74 IAS 19, para. 71.

75 IAS 19, para. 73.

76 IAS 19, para. 74.

77 IAS 19, paras. 72-73 and 77.

78 IAS 19, para. 76.

79 IAS 19, paras. 88-89.

80 IAS 19, para. 89.

81 IAS 19, para. 90.

82 IAS 19, para. 91.

83 IAS 19, para. 57.

84 IAS 19, para. 66.

85 IAS 19, para. 79.

86 IAS 19, para. 80.

87 IAS 19, para. 78.

88 IAS 19, para. 81.

89 IAS 19, paras. 72 and 74.

90 FRS 17, *Retirement Benefits*, ASB, November 2000, para. 33.

91 Letter from the Chief Accountant of the SEC to the September 1993 meeting of the EITF discussing the SEC staff's expectations regarding discount rates.

92 IAS 19, para. 76.

93 IAS 19, para. 56.
94 IAS 19, para. 57.
95 IAS 19, paras. 57 and 77.
96 IAS 19, para. 51.
97 In the UK, *Statement of Principles for Financial Reporting*, ASB, December 1999. In the US, seven *Statements of Financial Accounting Concepts*, FASB, 1978-2000.
98 IAS 19, paras. 92-93.
99 IAS 19, para. 95.
100 IAS 19, paras. 54-55.
101 IAS 19, para. 59.
102 IAS 19, para. 58.
103 IAS 19, Example illustrating para. 60.
104 IAS 19, para. 60.
105 IAS 19, Appendix E.
106 IAS 19, para. 58B.
107 IAS 19, para. 58A.
108 IAS 19, para. 108.
109 IAS 19, para. 118 and Basis for Conclusions, para 81.
110 IAS 19, para. 117.
111 IAS 19, para. 116.
112 IAS 19, para. 61.
113 IAS 19, para. 62.
114 IAS 19, para. 119.
115 E54, paras. 109-110.
116 IAS 19, paras. 7 and 64.
117 IAS 19, para. 7.
118 IAS 19, para. 82.
119 IAS 19, para. 51.
120 IAS 19, para. 7.
121 IAS 19, para. 106.
122 Exposure Draft, *Amendments to IAS 19 Employee Benefits – Actuarial Gains and Losses, Group Plans and Disclosures*, para. 120(k).
123 IAS 19, para. 107.
124 IAS 19, paras. 105.
125 IAS 19, Example illustrating para. 106.
126 IAS 19, paras. 7 and 94.
127 IAS 19, para. 112.
128 IAS 19, para. 113.
129 IAS 19, para. 111.
130 IAS 19, para. 111.
131 IAS 19, para. 109.
132 IAS 19, para. 110.
133 IAS 19, para. 115.
134 IAS 19, Example illustrating para. 115.
135 IAS 19, para. 114.
136 IAS 19, Basis for Conclusions, para. 54.
137 IAS 19, para. 95.
138 IAS 19, para. 7.
139 IAS 19, para. 98.
140 IAS 19, para. 101.
141 IAS 19, para. 7.
142 IAS 19, paras. 96 and 100.
143 IAS 19, para. 97.
144 IAS 19, para. 96.
145 IAS 19, Example illustrating para. 97.
146 IAS 19, para. 99.
147 IAS 19, para. 7.
148 IAS 19, para. 8.
149 IAS 19, para. 9.
150 IAS 19, para. 10.
151 IAS 19, paras. 12-13.
152 IAS 19, paras. 11(a) and 13.
153 IAS 19, paras. 14-15.
154 IAS 19, Example illustrating paras. 14-15.
155 IAS 19, paras. 11(b) and 16.
156 IAS 19, para. 17.
157 IAS 19, para. 17.
158 IAS 19, para. 18.
159 IAS 19, para. 19.
160 IAS 19, para. 20.
161 IAS 19, para. 21.
162 IAS 19, para. 22.
163 IAS 19, para. 7.
164 IAS 19, para. 126.
165 IAS 19, paras. 127-129.
166 IFRS 2, *Share-based Payment*, IASB, February 2004, para. 15.
167 IAS 19, para. 130.
168 IAS 19, para. 7.
169 IAS 19, para. 132.
170 IAS 19, para. 133.
171 IAS 19, para. 134.
172 IAS 19, para. 135.
173 IAS 19, para. 136.
174 IAS 19, para. 137.
175 IAS 19, para. 138.
176 *IASB Update*, IASB, December 2002, p. 4.
177 IAS 19, paras. 78 and 139.
178 IAS 19, para. 140.
179 IAS 19, para. 46.
180 IAS 19, paras. 30 and 123.
181 IAS 19, para. 47.
182 IAS 19, para. 120.
183 IAS 19, para. 121.
184 IAS 19, para. 120.
185 IAS 19, para. 122.
186 IAS 19, para. 124.
187 IAS 19, para. 125.
188 IAS 19, para. 23.
189 IAS 19, para. 131.
190 IAS 19, paras. 141-143.
191 IAS 19, para. 157.
192 IAS 19, para. 159.
193 IAS 19, para. 159A.
194 IAS 19, para. 154.
195 IAS 19, para. 155.
196 IAS 19, para. 156.
197 IAS 19, para. 156.
198 IFRS 1, *First-time adoption of International Financial Reporting Standards*, IASB, June 2003 (amended March 2004) , para. 20.
199 IAS 19, Basis for Conclusions, para. 41.

200 IAS 19, Basis for Conclusions, para. 54.
201 Exposure Draft, *Amendments to IAS 19 Employee Benefits – Actuarial Gains and Losses, Group Plans and Disclosures*, para. BC7.
202 *IASB Update*, IASB, July 2002, p. 4.
203 Exposure Draft, *Amendments to IAS 19 Employee Benefits – Actuarial Gains and Losses, Group Plans and Disclosures*.
204 IAS 19, Basis for Conclusions, para. 8.
205 IAS 19, Basis for Conclusions, para. 10.

Chapter 31   Earnings per share

1   INTRODUCTION

Earnings per share (EPS) is one of the most widely quoted statistics in financial analysis. It came into great prominence in the US during the late 1950s and early 1960s due to the widespread use of the price earnings ratio (PE) as a yardstick for investment decisions. As a result, standard setters in some jurisdictions (notably the USA and the UK) have had rules on EPS for many years. However, it was not until 1997 that an international accounting standard on the subject was published.

IAS 33 – *Earnings per Share*, was introduced for accounting periods beginning on or after 1 January 1998.[1] In February 2000 the SIC issued SIC-24 to clarify that, for diluted EPS purposes, any instrument that may result in the issue of shares (i.e. those involving a choice by either the issuer or the holder) are potential ordinary shares.[2] In December 2003, as part of the improvements project, the IASB updated IAS 33. The objective of this project was a limited revision to provide additional guidance and illustrative examples on selected complex matters, such as the effects of contingently issuable shares; potential ordinary shares of subsidiaries, joint ventures or associates; participating equity instruments; written put options; purchased put and call options; and mandatorily convertible instruments.[3] Subsequent to this, some further amendments were made to the standard by IFRS 2 – *Share-based Payment* – and IFRS 3 – *Business Combinations*.[4]

The revised version of IAS 33 applies to periods beginning on or after 1 January 2005 with earlier adoption encouraged. If it is applied early that fact should be disclosed.[5] There are no special transitional arrangements in the standard which means comparative figures may need amending. Furthermore, IFRS 1 – *First-time Adoption of International Financial Reporting Standards* – contains no special arrangements for first time adopters of IFRS.

The requirements of IAS 33 are discussed at 2 to 7 below, and the standard's illustrative examples of particular issues are included in the text of the chapter, whilst its comprehensive worked example is included as an Appendix.

2   OBJECTIVE AND SCOPE OF IAS 33

2.1   Objective

IAS 33 sets out its objective as follows: 'to prescribe principles for the determination and presentation of earnings per share, so as to improve performance comparisons between different entities in the same reporting period and between different reporting periods for the same entity. Even though earnings per share data have limitations because of the different accounting policies that may be used for determining 'earnings', a consistently determined denominator enhances financial reporting. The focus of this Standard is on the denominator of the earnings per share calculation.'[6]

The standard requires the computation of both basic and diluted EPS, explaining the objective of each as follows:

- the objective of basic earnings per share information is to provide a measure of the interests of each ordinary share of a parent entity in the performance of the entity over the reporting period;[7] and

- the objective of diluted earnings per share is consistent with that of basic earnings per share – to provide a measure of the interest of each ordinary share in the performance of an entity – while giving effect to all dilutive potential ordinary shares outstanding during the period.[8]

The underlying logic here is that EPS, including diluted EPS, should be an historical performance measure. This impacts particularly on the reporting of diluted EPS, in steering it away from an alternative purpose: to warn of potential future dilution. Indeed the tension between these differing objectives is evident in the standard. As discussed more fully at 6.4.6 below, IAS 33 sets out a very restrictive regime for including certain potentially dilutive shares in the diluted EPS calculation. Yet diluted EPS is only to take account of those potential shares that would dilute earnings from *continuing* operations which seems to have more of a forward looking 'warning signal' flavour.

Also noteworthy is that although the emphasis in the objective is on the denominator of the calculation, effectively making it a 'per share' standard, the standard actually also contains provisions relating to the numerator.

2.2   Scope

IAS 33 applies to all entities whose ordinary shares (or potential ordinary shares) are publicly traded and to entities that are in the process of issuing ordinary shares (or potential ordinary shares) in public markets.[9] IAS 33 also applies to any other entity that discloses earnings per share.[10] Where both the parent's and consolidated financial statements are presented, the standard only requires consolidated earnings per share to be given. If the parent chooses to present EPS data based on its separate financial statements the standard requires that the disclosures be restricted to the face of the parent-only income statement and not be included in the consolidated financial statements.[11]

3   THE BASIC EPS

IAS 33 requires the computation of basic EPS for the profit or loss (and, if presented, the profit or loss from continuing operations) attributable to ordinary equity holders.[12] It defines, or rather describes, basic earnings per share in the following manner: 'Basic earnings per share shall be calculated by dividing profit or loss attributable to ordinary equity holders of the parent entity (the numerator) by the weighted average number of ordinary shares outstanding (the denominator) during the period.'[13]

The components of the calculation are illustrated in the following extract.

Extract 31.1: Leica Geosystems Holdings AG (2004)

Notes to the Consolidated Financial Statements [extract]
6.   Earnings per share

Basic earnings per share are calculated by dividing the net profit available for shareholders by the weighted average number of ordinary shares outstanding and issued during the year, excluding the number of shares purchased by the Company and held as treasury shares.

	Year ended March 31		
	2004	**2003**	**2002**
	CHF	CHF	CHF
Net income/(loss) attributable to shareholders	5,633	21,915	(55,250)
Weighted average number of ordinary shares in issue	2,220	2,237	2,240
Basic earnings per share (single Swiss francs per individual share)	2.54	9.80	(24.67)

For the share options, a calculation is performed to determine the number of shares that could have been acquired at market price. This serves to calculate the extent of the dilutive effect. No adjustments are made to net profit for this options calculation.

	Year ended March 31		
	2004	**2003**	**2002**
	CHF	CHF	CHF
Net income/(loss) attributable to shareholders	5,633	21,915	(55,250)
Weighted average number of ordinary shares in issue	2,220	2,237	2,240
Adjustment for share options	47	5	–
Weighted average number of ordinary shares for diluted earnings per share	2,267	2,242	2,240
Diluted earnings per share	2.48	9.78	(24.67)

For the diluted earnings per share the weighted average number of ordinary shares in issue is adjusted to assume conversion of all potentially dilutive ordinary shares (see Note 21). The Company has share options granted to management and employees that qualify as potentially dilutive ordinary shares.

Leica Geosystems Holdings AG paid no dividends in Fiscal Years 2004, 2003 or 2002.

3.1   Earnings

The starting point for determining the earnings figure to be used in the basic EPS calculation (both for total earnings and, if appropriate, earnings from continuing operations) is the net profit or loss for the period attributable to ordinary equity holders.[14] This will, in accordance with IAS 1 – *Presentation of Financial Statements* – include all items of income and expense, including, dividends on preference shares classified as liabilities and tax and is stated after the deduction of minority interests.[15] This is then adjusted for the after-tax amounts of preference dividends, differences arising on the settlement of preference shares, and other similar effects of preference shares classified as equity.[16] These adjustments are discussed at 5.2 below.

3.2   Number of shares

An ordinary share is defined as 'an equity instrument that is subordinate to all other classes of equity instruments'.[17] 'Equity instrument' has the same meaning as in IAS 32 – *Financial Instruments: Disclosure and Presentation*, that is 'any contract that evidences a residual interest in the assets of an enterprise after deducting all of its liabilities'.[18] IAS 33 goes on to observe that ordinary shares participate in profit for the period only after other types of share such as preference shares have participated.[19] The standard also clarifies that there may be more than one class of ordinary share and requires the computation and presentation of EPS for each class that has a different right to share in profit for the period.[20] In practice, it is usually straightforward to determine which instruments are ordinary shares for EPS purposes. The treatment of different classes of shares is discussed at 5.4 below.

The basic rule in IAS 33 is that all outstanding ordinary shares are brought into the basic EPS computation – time-weighted for changes in the period (changes in ordinary shares is discussed at 4 below).[21] There are three exceptions to this:

- ordinary shares that are issued as partly paid are included in the weighted average as a fraction of a share based on their dividend participation relative to fully paid shares (so, if although only partly paid they ranked equally for dividends they would be included in full);[22]

- treasury shares, which are presented in the financial statements as a deduction from equity are not considered outstanding for EPS purposes for the period they are held in treasury. Although not stated explicitly in the standard itself, this requirement is clearly logical (as although the shares are still in issue, they are accounted for as if redeemed) and is illustrated in one of the examples appended to the standard (see Example 31.1 at 4.1 below)[23] Extract 31.9 at 6.4.2 A below shows a company presenting the deduction of treasury shares in the EPS calculation; and

- shares that are contingently returnable (that is, subject to recall) are not treated as outstanding until they cease to be subject to recall, and hence are excluded from basic EPS until that time.[24]

The standard contains some specific guidance on when newly issued ordinary shares should be considered outstanding. In general shares are to be included from the date consideration is receivable (considered by the standard to generally be the date of their issue), for example:[25]

- shares issued in exchange for cash are included when cash is receivable;

- shares issued on the voluntary reinvestment of dividends on ordinary or preference shares are included when the dividends are reinvested;

- shares issued as a result of the conversion of a debt instrument to ordinary shares are included as of the date interest ceases accruing;

- shares issued in place of interest or principal on other financial instruments are included as of the date interest ceases accruing;

- shares issued in exchange for the settlement of a liability of the entity are included as of the settlement date;

- shares issued as consideration for the acquisition of an asset other than cash are included as of the date on which the acquisition is recognised;

- shares issued in exchange for the rendering of services to the entity are included as the services are rendered; and

- shares that will be issued upon the conversion of a mandatorily convertible instrument are included in the calculation of basic earnings per share from the date the contract is entered into.[26]

Most of these provisions are straightforward, however some are worthy of note.

Shares issued in exchange for services will be accounted for in accordance with IFRS 2, with a charge in the income statement matched by a credit to equity. IAS 33 has some guidance on the inclusion of such potential shares in *diluted* EPS (see 6.4.5 below), however there is no further elaboration of the meaning of 'included as the services are rendered'. What this would seem to require, for example when shares are issued at the beginning of an extended period of service delivery, is that the number of ordinary shares used in an EPS calculation part way through the period is lower that the number actually in issue, to take account of the fact that some shares have not yet been 'earned' by the service provider.

The final bullet point represents a change from the previous version of IAS 33, but the standard does not define what a mandatorily convertible instrument is, and the Basis for Conclusions makes no reference to this change. However, in our view the requirement to account for the shares in EPS from inception must mean it refers to instruments where the proceeds also are received at inception. Accordingly, it would exclude a forward contract for the issue of shares which (as required by the first bullet above) would increase the denominator of basic EPS only from the time the cash is receivable.

More generally, the standard goes on to say the timing of inclusion is determined by the attaching terms and conditions, and also that due consideration should be given to the substance of any contract associated with the issue.[27] No illustrations are given of such associated contracts, but one example could be convertible unsecured loan stock (CULS). Although less fashionable in recent years, these were a not uncommon mechanism allowing companies to finance potential acquisitions by the issue of shares, while retaining the flexibility to return funds not subsequently needed.

Tomkins PLC (a UK company), for example, issued CULS to finance an acquisition and converted it into shares a short time later. The loan stock carried no interest and was simply an intermediate step in the share issue. The practical impact was that 60% of the consideration for the shares was received over a month before they were actually issued.

Extract 31.2: Tomkins PLC (1993)

18 SHARE CAPITAL [extract]

The Company financed the purchase of RHM by way of a rights issue which took the form of 5p nominal non-interest bearing convertible unsecured loan stock (loan stock) which was payable in two instalments of 120p and 80p on 30 November 1992 and 4 January 1993 respectively. ... The 335,784,658 units of loan stock, which were issued under the rights issue at 200p per unit, were converted into fully paid ordinary shares of 5p each, on a one for one basis, on 5 January 1993.

One question that arises is when should the new shares be brought into the calculation of the weighted average in such circumstances? Given the examples in the standard which focus on the date consideration is received, and the requirement to consider the substance of associated contracts, it seems such shares should be deemed to be issued in partly paid form on 30 November.

Ordinary shares that are issuable on the satisfaction of certain conditions (contingently issuable shares) are to be included in the calculation of basic EPS only from the date when all necessary conditions have been satisfied; in effect when they are no longer contingent.[28] This provision is interpreted strictly, as illustrated in Example 7 appended to the standard (see Example 31.14 at 6.4.6 A below). In that example earnings in a year, by meeting certain thresholds, would trigger the issue of shares. Because it is not certain that the condition is met until the last day of the year (when earnings become known with certainty) the new shares are excluded from basic EPS until the following year. Where shares will be issued at some future date (that is, solely after the passage of time) they are not considered contingently issuable by IAS 33, as the passage of time is a certainty.[29] In principle, this would seem to mean that they should be included in basic EPS from the agreement date. However, careful consideration of the individual facts and circumstances would be necessary.

The calculation of the basic EPS is often simple but a number of complications can arise; these may be considered under the following two headings:

(a)   changes in ordinary shares outstanding; and

(b)   matters affecting the numerator.

These are discussed in the next two sections.

4 CHANGES IN OUTSTANDING ORDINARY SHARES

Changes in ordinary share outstanding can occur under a variety of circumstances, the most common of which are dealt with below. Whenever such a change occurs during the accounting period, an adjustment is required to the number of shares in the EPS calculation for that period; furthermore, in certain situations the EPS for previous periods will also have to be recalculated.

4.1 Weighted average number of shares

Implicit in the methodology of IAS 33 is a correlation between the capital of an entity (or rather the income generating assets it reflects) and earnings. Accordingly, to compute EPS as a performance measure requires adjusting the number of shares in the denominator to reflect any variations in the period to the capital available to generate that period's earnings. The standard observes that using the weighted average number of ordinary shares outstanding during the period reflects the possibility that the amount of shareholders' capital varied during the period as a result of a larger or smaller number of shares being outstanding at any time. The weighted average number of ordinary shares outstanding during the period is the number of ordinary shares outstanding at the beginning of the period, adjusted by the number of ordinary shares bought back or issued during the period multiplied by a time-weighting factor. The time-weighting factor is the number of days that the shares are outstanding as a proportion of the total number of days in the period; IAS 33 notes that a reasonable approximation of the weighted average is adequate in many circumstances.[30] Computation of a weighted average number of shares is illustrated in the following example:

Example 31.1:   Weighted average calculation[31]

		Shares issued	Treasury shares*	Shares outstanding
1 January 2005	Balance at beginning of year	2,000	300	1,700
31 May 2005	Issue of new shares for cash	800	–	2,500
1 December 2005	Purchase of treasury shares for cash	–	250	2,250
31 December 2005	Balance at year end	2,800	550	2,250

Calculation of weighted average:
$(1,700 \times 5/12) + (2,500 \times 6/12) + (2,250 \times 1/12)$ $= 2,146$ shares *or*
$(1,700 \times 12/12) + (800 \times 7/12) - (250 \times 1/12)$ $= 2,146$ shares

* Treasury shares are equity instruments reacquired and held by the issuing entity itself or by its subsidiaries.

The use of a weighted average number of shares is necessary because the increase in the share capital would have affected earnings only for that portion of the year during which the issue proceeds were available to management for use in the business.

The following extract illustrates the approach taken by Interbrew SA to quantify the impact on the weighted average number of shares of shares issued during the period.

Extract 31.3: Interbew SA (2003)

NOTES TO THE CONSOLIDATED FINANCIAL STATEMENTS [extract]
20.   EARNINGS PER SHARE

BASIC EARNINGS PER SHARE

The calculation of basic earnings per share is based on the net profit attributable to ordinary shareholders of 505m euro (2002: net profit of 467m euro) and a weighted average number of ordinary shares outstanding during the year, calculated as follows:

WEIGHTED AVERAGE NUMBER OF ORDINARY SHARES

Million shares	2003	2002
Issued ordinary shares at 1 January	431.6	431.1
Effect of shares issued	0.1	0.3
Weighted average number of ordinary shares at 31 December	431.7	431.4

DILUTED EARNINGS PER SHARE

The calculation of diluted earnings per share is based on net profit attributable to ordinary shareholders of 505m euro (2002: 467m euro) and a weighted average number of ordinary shares (diluted) outstanding during the year, calculated as follows:

WEIGHTED AVERAGE NUMBER OF ORDINARY SHARES (DILUTED)

Million shares	2003	2002
Weighted average number of ordinary shares at 31 December	431.7	431.4
Effect of share option on issue	2.1	3.1
Weighted average number of ordinary shares (diluted) at 31 December	433.8	434.5

4.2   Purchase and redemption of own shares

An entity may, if it is authorised to do so by its constitution and it complies with any relevant legislation, purchase or otherwise redeem its own shares (see Chapter 17 at 6). Assuming this is done at fair value, then the earnings should be apportioned over the weighted average share capital in issue for the year. This was illustrated in Example 31.1 above in relation to the purchase of treasury shares. If, on the other hand, the repurchase is at significantly more than market value then IAS 33 requires adjustments to be made to EPS for periods before buy-back. This is discussed at 4.3.5 below.

4.3   Changes in ordinary shares without corresponding changes in resources

IAS 33 requires the number of shares used in the calculation to be adjusted (for all periods presented) for any transaction (other than the conversion of potential ordinary shares) that changes the number of shares outstanding without a corresponding change in resources.[32] This is also to apply where some, but curiously not all, such changes have happened after the year-end but before the approval of the financial statements.

The standard gives the following as examples of changes in the number of ordinary shares without a corresponding change in resources:

(a)   a capitalisation or bonus issue (sometimes referred to as a stock dividend);

(b)   a bonus element in any other issue, for example a bonus element in a rights issue to existing shareholders;

(c)   a share split; and

(d)   a reverse share split (share consolidation).[33]

Another example not mentioned by the standard would be any bonus element in a buy-back, such as a put warrant involving the repurchase of shares at significantly more than their fair value.[34] The adjustments required to EPS for each of these is discussed below.

As noted above, IAS 33 requires retrospective adjustment for all such events that happen in the reporting period. However, it only requires restatement for those in (a), (c) and (d) if they happen after the year-end but before the financial statements are authorised for issue.[35] We are not convinced that this was the intention of the board, and suspect that it may be the result of less than precise drafting (particularly as the paragraph requiring restatement for these post-balance sheet changes also applies to events that have happened during the reporting period, but refers only to the same items) – however it is what the standard literally requires.

Although the standard is silent on the matter, we believe that any other per share disclosures for earlier periods, for example dividends per share, should similarly be adjusted for such changes.

4.3.1   Capitalisation, bonus issue, share split and share consolidation

A   Capitalisation, bonus issues and share splits

A capitalisation or bonus issue or share split has the effect of increasing the number of shares in issue without any inflow of resources, as further ordinary shares are issued to existing shareholders for no consideration. Consequently, no additional earnings will be expected to accrue as a result of the issue. The additional shares should be treated as having been in issue for the whole period and also included in the EPS calculation of all earlier periods presented so as to give a comparable result. For example, on a two-for-one bonus issue, the number of ordinary shares outstanding before the issue is multiplied by three to obtain the new total number of ordinary shares, or by two to obtain the number of additional ordinary shares.[36]

The EPS calculation involving a bonus issue is illustrated in the following example.

Example 31.2:   A bonus issue[37]

Profit attributable to ordinary equity holders of the parent entity 2004	€180
Profit attributable to ordinary equity holders of the parent entity 2005	€600
Ordinary shares outstanding until 30 September 2005	200

Bonus issue 1 October 2005	2 ordinary shares for each ordinary share outstanding at 30 September 2005 $200 \times 2 = 400$

Basic earnings per share 2005
$$\frac{€\,600}{\left(200 + 400\right)} = €1.00$$

Basic earnings per share 2004
$$\frac{€180}{\left(200 + 400\right)} = €0.30$$

Because the bonus issue was without consideration, it is treated as if it had occurred before the beginning of 2004, the earliest period presented.

Again, although the standard is silent on the matter, we believe that any financial ratios disclosed for earlier periods, which are based on the number of equity shares at a year-end (e.g. dividend per share) should also be adjusted by in a similar manner.

B   Stock dividends

Stock or scrip dividends refer to the case where an entity offers its shareholders the choice of receiving further fully paid up shares in the company as an alternative to receiving a cash dividend. It could be argued that the dividend foregone represents payment for the shares, usually at fair value, and hence no restatement is appropriate. Alternatively, the shares could be viewed as being, in substance, bonus issues which require the EPS for the earlier period to be adjusted. IAS 33 seems to suggest the latter view, as it notes that capitalisation or bonus issues are sometimes referred to as stock dividends. However, entities often refer to these arrangements as dividend reinvestment plans which suggests the acquisition of new shares for valuable consideration.

In our view, this distinction should be a factual one. If an entity (say, through proposal and subsequent approval by shareholders) has a legal obligation to pay a dividend in cash or, at the shareholder's option, shares then the cash payment avoided if the scrip dividend is taken up is consideration for the shares. This may be equivalent to an issue at fair value or it may contain some bonus element requiring retrospective adjustment of EPS. In practice the fair value of shares received as a scrip alternative may exceed the cash alternative; this is often referred to as an enhanced scrip dividend. In these cases IAS 33 will require a bonus element to be identified, and prior EPS figures restated accordingly. This is essentially the same as adjustments for the bonus element in a rights issue, discussed at 4.3.3 below. Furthermore, in this scenario, during the period between the obligation coming into existence and its settlement (in cash or shares) it would strictly speaking represent a written call option and hence potentially affect diluted EPS (see 6.4.2 B below). Given that the standard is silent on this aspect of some stock dividends we doubt that such an approach was intended. In any event it strikes us as unlikely in most cases that the effect would be significant. Conversely, if the entity issues fresh shares *instead of* a dividend it is a bonus issue requiring full retrospective adjustment to EPS.

C   Share consolidations

Occasionally, entities will consolidate their equity share capital into a smaller number of shares. Such a consolidation generally reduces the number of shares outstanding without a corresponding outflow of resources, and this would require an adjustment to the denominator for periods before the consolidation.[38]

4.3.2   Share consolidation with a special dividend

Share consolidations as discussed above normally do not involve any outflow of funds from the entity. However, a number of entities have been returning surplus cash to their shareholders by paying special dividends accompanied by a share consolidation, the purpose of which is to maintain the value of each share following the payment of the dividend. This issue is specifically addressed by IAS 33 as revised in 2003 (the original standard being silent on the issue), perhaps because such schemes had been quite common when it was being revised. The normal rule of restating the outstanding number of shares for all periods for a share consolidation is not applied when the overall effect is a share repurchase at fair value because in such cases the reduction of shares *is* the result of a corresponding reduction in resources. In such cases the weighted average number of shares is adjusted for the consolidation from the date the special dividend is recognised.[39]

One IAS reporter in this situation was Dairy Farm. These financial statements pre-date the revision to IAS 33 which expressly requires this treatment, but illustrate the 'in substance buy back' approach.

Extract 31.4: Dairy Farm International Holdings Limited (1999)

6. EARNINGS PER SHARE [extract]

Basic earnings per share are calculated on the profit attributable to ordinary shareholders of US$37.3 million (1998: US$157.3 million) and on the weighted average number of 1,795.7 million ordinary shares issued during the year (1998: 1,833.0 million). The weighted average number excludes the shares held by the Trustee under the Senior Executive Share Incentive Schemes (note 19).

18. SHARE CAPITAL [extract]

In October 1999, every ten ordinary shares of US¢5 each were consolidated into nine new ordinary shares of US¢5 5/9 each.

CORPORATE GOVERNANCE [extract]

Special Dividend and Share Capital Consolidation

At a Special General Meeting held on 30th September 1999, shareholders approved the payment of a special dividend of US¢9.65 per ordinary share and the consolidation of every ten ordinary shares of US¢5 each into nine new ordinary shares of US¢5 5/9 each. As a result, an aggregate of 1,886,481,512 were consolidated into 1,691,418,772 new ordinary shares of US¢5 5/9 each.

Although not expressly discussed by Dairy Farm, it seems the consolidation and special dividend have been treated, for EPS purposes, as a re-purchase of shares at fair value. This is because the quantity of shares disclosed in the 1999 financial statements as used in the computation for the prior period (1,833 million shares) is the same as that used in the 1998 financial statements. This indicates that the comparative EPS figure has not been adjusted to take account of the share consolidation.

There is undoubtedly a conceptual attraction in trying to standardise adjustments made to prior years' EPS figures. However, in our view the approach taken by the standard is rather piecemeal, in that restatement is only ever triggered by a change in the number of shares, and it will not necessarily achieve the objective of standardising the restatement of EPS. Capital may be returned to shareholders in various different ways, including demergers and group reconstructions, as well as share buybacks and special dividends. In many such cases the number of shares in issue is only reduced if the entity opts to consolidate its shares. The natural consequence of returning capital is that earnings will fall, so it is debatable whether a fall in EPS in these circumstances should be regarded as a distortion that needs to be corrected at all. Of course, if an entity buys back its shares, the number of shares will automatically be reduced and therefore affect the EPS calculation in a way that other returns of capital do not, but this does not necessarily mean that a special dividend should be treated as if it were a share buyback. However, the standard is now clear, so entities must apply these provisions so that this specific type of return of capital will fall to be treated as a share repurchase, but only when the entity also chooses to consolidate its shares.

4.3.3 Rights issue

A rights issue is a popular method through which entities are able to access the capital markets for further capital. Under the terms of such an issue, existing shareholders are given the opportunity to acquire further shares in the entity on a pro-rata basis to their existing shareholdings.

The 'rights' shares will usually be offered either at the current market price or at a price below that. In the former case, the treatment of the issue for EPS purposes is as discussed in 4.1 above. However, where the rights price is at a discount to market it is not quite as straightforward, since the issue is equivalent to a bonus issue (see 4.3.1 above) combined with an issue at full market price. In such cases, IAS 33 requires an adjustment to the number of shares outstanding before the rights issue to reflect the bonus element inherent in it.[40]

The bonus element of the rights issue available to all existing shareholders is given by the following adjustment factor, sometimes referred to as the bonus fraction:[41]

$$\frac{\text{Fair value per share immediately before the exercise of rights}}{\text{Theoretical ex - rights fair value per share}}$$

The fair value per share immediately before the exercise of rights is the *actual* price at which the shares are quoted inclusive of the right to take up the future shares under the rights issue. Where the rights are to be traded separately from the shares the fair value used is the closing price on the last day on which the shares are traded inclusive of the right.[42]

The 'ex-rights fair value' is the *theoretical* price at which the shares would be expected to be quoted, other stock market factors apart, after the rights issue shares have been issued. It is calculated by adding the aggregate market value of the shares immediately before the exercise of the rights to the proceeds from the exercise, and dividing by the number of shares outstanding after the exercise.[43] The EPS calculation involving a rights issue is illustrated in the following example.

Example 31.3:   *Illustration of calculation of EPS following a rights issue at less than full market price*[44]

		2003	2004	2005
Profit attributable to ordinary equity holders of the parent entity		€1,100	€1,500	€1,800

Shares outstanding before rights issue	500 shares
Rights issue	One new share for each five outstanding shares (100 new shares total) Exercise price: €5.00 Date of rights issue: 1 January 2004 Last date to exercise rights: 1 March 2004
Market price of one ordinary share immediately before exercise on 1 March 2004	€11.00
Reporting date	31 December

Calculation of theoretical ex-rights value per share

$$\frac{\text{Fair value of all outstanding shares before the exercise of rights} + \text{Total amount received from exercise of rights}}{\text{Number of shares outstanding before exercise} + \text{Number of shares issued in the exercise}} =$$

$$\frac{(€11.00 \times 500 \text{ shares}) + (€5.00 \times 100 \text{ shares})}{500 \text{ shares} + 100 \text{ shares}}$$

Theoretical ex-rights value per share = €10.00

Calculation of adjustment factor

$$\frac{\text{Fair value per share before exercise of rights}}{\text{Theoretical ex - rights value per share}} = \frac{€11.00}{€10.00} = 1.10$$

Calculation of basic earnings per share

	2003	*2004*	*2005*

2003 basic EPS as originally reported:

€1,100/500 shares = €2.20

2003 basic EPS restated for rights issue:

$€1,100/(500 \text{ shares} \times 1.1) =$ €2.00

2004 basic EPS including effects of rights issue:

$$\frac{€1,500}{(500 \times 1.1 \times 2/12) + (600 \times 10/12)} = €2.54$$

2005 basic EPS:

€1,800/600 shares = €3.00

Rather than multiplying the denominator by 11/10ths, the previous year's EPS (and any EPS disclosures in a historical summary) could alternatively be arrived at by multiplying the original EPS by 10/11ths.

Whilst the rights are outstanding they represent, strictly speaking, a written call option over the entity's shares which could have implications for diluted EPS (see 6.4.2 below). However, as is the case for some stock dividends (discussed above) we doubt that such complexity was intended by the IASB.

It is possible that shares could be issued as a result of open offers, placings and other offerings of equity shares not made to existing shareholders, at a discount to the market price. In such cases it would be necessary to consider whether the issue contained a bonus element, or rather simply reflected differing views on the fair value of the shares. In our opinion the latter seems a far more realistic alternative. Accordingly the shares should be dealt with on a weighted average basis without calculating any bonus element when computing the EPS.

4.3.4 B share schemes

One method by which some entities have returned capital to shareholders is the so-called 'B share scheme'. These schemes involve issuing 'B shares' (usually undated preference shares with low or zero coupons) to existing shareholders, either as a bonus issue or via a share split. These are then repurchased for cash and cancelled, following which the ordinary shares are consolidated. The overall effect is intended to be the same as a repurchase of ordinary shares at fair value, and accordingly no retrospective adjustment to EPS is necessary.[45] A typical example is Severn Trent. Although this pre-dates the revised IAS 33 (and, indeed, the financial statements are not in accordance with IAS) it illustrates the issue.

Extract 31.5: Severn Trent Plc (1998)

Directors' report [extract]

Capital reorganisation

On 8 August 1997 the company effected a capital reorganisation under which each Ordinary Share of £1 was divided into one ordinary share of 62p and one B share of 38p. Following this sub-division every 20 ordinary shares of 62p each were consolidated into 19 Ordinary Shares of 65 5/19p each. Schroders acting as agents for the company offered to purchase from shareholders all their B Shares at their nominal value on 11 August 1997. A second repurchase offer was made in September 1997. ...

8 Earnings per share [extract]

Earnings per share is calculated on the net basis on earnings of £14.7 million being profit for the financial year of £14.9 million (1997: £316.7 million), less £0.2 million B share dividend (1997: nil), divided by 343.6 million shares, being the weighted average number of Ordinary Shares in issue during the year (1997: 363.3 million), excluding those held in the Severn Trent Employee Share Ownership Trust on which dividends have been waived. ...

18 Called up share capital [extract]

b) Capital reorganisation

As a result of the 19 for 20 consolidation and issue of B shares on 8 August 1997, 356,623,364 ordinary shares of £1 became 338,792,195 ordinary shares of 65 5/19p and 356,623,364 B Shares of 38p. ...

c) Shares purchased during the year

In August 1997 and September 1997, the company purchased for cancellation 297,054,463 and 35,723,317 B Shares of 38p ...

The number of shares used in the EPS calculation for the comparative year of 363.3 million is unchanged from the 1997 annual financial statements. This indicates that the prior periods' EPS figures have not been restated for the share consolidation. Instead Severn Trent, in common with other companies who had returned capital in this way, took the view that the substance of the combined transaction is a buy-back at fair value, and hence no restatement is needed. In our view this would be the appropriate treatment under IAS 33.

One further subtlety relates to how closely the ratio of share consolidation succeeds in mirroring the commercial effect of a fair value repurchase. In the Severn Trent example above, of the potential repurchase of 356,623,364 B shares only 332,777,780 were in fact bought back. It seems likely that the consolidation of 19 for 20 would have been calculated so as to reproduce the effects of a fair value repurchase assuming *all* the B shares were redeemed. If so then the share consolidation is *more* than adjusting for the resources that have left the group. IAS 33 would strictly require that some element of the consolidation should be viewed as happening without a corresponding change in resource, and hence prior periods' EPS adjusted accordingly.

4.3.5   *Put warrants priced above market value*

As noted at 4.3 above, an example of a change in the number of shares outstanding without a corresponding change in resources not mentioned by the standard would be any bonus element in a buy-back, such as a put warrant involving the repurchase of shares at significantly more than their fair value.

A company in this situation was GEC, and although not an IAS reporter its financial statements reflect the treatment that would be required by IAS 33.[46] GEC's 1998 financial statements outlined the proposed scheme as follows:

Extract 31.6: The General Electric Company plc (1998)

Finance Director's review [extract]

To manage the balance sheet structure of the Group and ensure all shareholders participate equitably, the Board also proposes to make a bonus issue of Put Warrants to shareholders, pro rata to their shareholdings. The Put Warrants will entitle each shareholder to sell to the Company one share for every 50 shares they hold, at a price that is 150 pence higher than the market price, subject to a maximum of 650 pence per share. This enables shareholders either to maintain their percentage shareholding and receive a distribution of cash of up to 13 pence per share held on 4th September, 1998 which will provide a total cash distribution (including the dividend) of 24.43 pence per share; or shareholders can retain all their shares and will still benefit from these proposals by increasing their percentage ownership and selling the warrants for up to 150 pence each (3 pence per share).

If shareholders wish to sell their entitlement to Put Warrants they need take no action and will bear no expense; the Company will automatically organise the sale.

The scheme was effected the following year, and the 1999 financial statements disclosed adjustments to prior period EPS as follows:

Extract 31.7: The General Electric Company plc (1999)

8 Earnings per share [extract]

Earnings per share are calculated by reference to a weighted average of 2,711.6 million ordinary shares (1998 restated 2,793.4 million ordinary shares) in issue during the year, which have been adjusted following the exercise of the put warrants on 6th October, 1998, as required by FRS 14.

Unfortunately IAS 33 does not give an illustrative calculation for a put warrant at significantly more than fair value, but it does for the familiar rights issue (rights issues are discussed at 4.3.3 above). In a rights issue new shares are issued at a discount to market value, whereas with put warrants shares are bought back at a premium to market value. In both cases the remaining shares are viewed as being devalued for the purposes of comparing EPS over time. Applying the logic of adjusting EPS when there is a change in the number of shares without a corresponding change in resources seems to require that put warrants are treated as a reverse rights issue. This would mean calculating a similar 'adjustment factor', and applying it to the number of shares outstanding before the transaction. The difference in the calculation would be that the number of shares issued and the consideration received for them would be replaced by negative amounts representing the number of shares put back to the entity and the amount paid for them.

An illustration of what this might entail is as follows:

Example 31.4:   Put warrants priced above market value

The following example takes the same scenario as Example 31.3 above (a rights issue), altered to illustrate a put warrant scheme. In that example the shares are issued at a discount of €6.00 to the €11.00 market price on a one for five basis 2 months into the year. Reversing this would give a put warrant to sell shares back to the company at a €6 premium, again on a one for five basis. All other details have been left the same for comparability, although in reality the rising earnings following a rights issue may well become falling earnings after a buy-back. The calculation would then become:

Calculation of theoretical ex-warrant value per share

$$\frac{\text{fair value of all outstanding shares} - \text{total amount paid on}}{\text{before the exercise of warrants}} = \frac{\text{exercise of warrants}}{\text{shares outstanding before exercise} - \text{shares cancelled in the exercise}}$$

$$\frac{(€11 \times 500) - (€17 \times 100)}{500 - 100} = €9.50$$

Calculation of adjustment factor

$$\frac{\text{Fair value per share before exercise of warrants}}{\text{Theoretical ex - warrant value per share}} = \frac{€11}{€9.5} = 1.16$$

Calculation of basic earnings per share

	2003 €	2004 €	2005 €
2003 EPS as originally reported: €1,100 / 500 shares =	2.20		
2003 EPS restated for warrants: €1,100 / (500 shares × 1.16) =	1.90		
2004 EPS including effects of warrants: $\frac{€1,500}{(500 \times 1.16 \times 2/12) + (600 \times 8/12)} =$		3.02	
2005 basic EPS: €1,800/600 shares =			3.00

Whilst the above seems a sensible interpretation of the requirements, as the procedure is not specified there may be scope for other interpretations.

4.4   Options exercised during the year

Shares issued as a result of options being exercised should be dealt with on a weighted average basis in the basic EPS.[47] Furthermore, options that have been exercised during the year will also affect diluted EPS calculations. If the options in question would have had a diluting effect on the basic EPS had they been exercised at the beginning of the year, then they should be considered in the diluted EPS calculation as explained in 6.4.2 below, but on a weighted average basis for the period up to the date of exercise. The exercise of options is a 'conversion of potential ordinary shares'. The standard excludes such conversions from the general requirement (see 4.3 above) to adjust prior periods' EPS when a change in the number of shares happens without a corresponding change in resources.[48]

4.5 Post balance sheet changes in capital

The EPS shown in the income statement should not reflect any changes in the capital structure occurring after the accounting date, but before the financial statements are approved, which was effected for fair value. This is because any proceeds received from the issue were not available for use during the period. However, EPS for all periods presented should be adjusted for any bonus element in certain post year-end changes in the number of shares, as discussed at 4.3 above. When this is done that fact should be stated.[49]

4.6 Issue to acquire another business

4.6.1 *Acquisitions*

As a result of a share issue to acquire another business, funds or other assets will flow into the business and extra profits will be expected to be generated. When calculating EPS, it should be assumed that the shares were issued on the acquisition date (even if the actual date of issue is later), since this will be the date from which the results of the newly acquired business are recognised in the income statement.[50]

4.6.2 *Reverse acquisitions*

Reverse acquisition is the term used to describe a business combination whereby the legal parent entity after the combination is in substance the acquired and not the acquiring entity (discussed in Chapter 6 at 2.3.8). IAS 33 is silent on the subject, however, an appendix to IFRS 3 contains a discussion of the implications for EPS of such transactions. Following a reverse acquisition the equity structure appearing in the consolidated financial statements will reflect the equity of the legal parent, including the equity instruments issued by it to effect the business combination.[51]

For the purposes of calculating the weighted average number of ordinary shares outstanding during the period in which the reverse acquisition occurs:

(a) the number of ordinary shares outstanding from the beginning of that period to the acquisition date is taken to be the number of ordinary shares issued by the legal parent to the owners of the legal subsidiary; and

(b) the number of ordinary shares outstanding from the acquisition date to the end of that period is taken be the actual number of ordinary shares of the legal parent outstanding during that period.[52]

The basic EPS disclosed for each comparative period before the acquisition date is calculated by dividing the profit or loss of the legal subsidiary attributable to ordinary shareholders in each of those periods by the number of ordinary shares issued by the legal parent to the owners of the legal subsidiary in the reverse acquisition.[53]

The calculations outlined above assume that there were no changes in the number of the legal subsidiary's shares during the comparative periods and during the period from the beginning of the period in which the reverse acquisition occurred to the acquisition date. The calculation of EPS should be appropriately adjusted to take into account the effect of a change in the number of the legal subsidiary's issued ordinary shares during those periods.[54]

IFRS 3 presents an illustrative example of a reverse acquisition, including the EPS calculation, see Example 6.12 at 2.3.8 D in Chapter 6.

4.6.3 Establishment of a new parent undertaking

Prior to IFRS 3, IAS 22 allowed (in exceptional circumstances) for business combinations to be accounted for not as acquisitions but as 'unitings of interests' (sometimes called poolings of interests or mergers. For ease we will refer to such transactions as mergers in the following discussion). Under IAS 22 mergers were accounted for using the pooling of interests method, which portrayed the combined entity as if the entities coming together had always been combined. Accordingly, no fair value exercise was needed to restate the net assets of an acquired entity, and no goodwill was recognised. Whilst IFRS 3 has abolished this approach, it (like IAS 22) excludes from its scope business combinations involving entities under common control. Very common examples of such transactions are group reorganisations, such as the introduction of a new holding company to a group. As indicated in Chapter 6 at 2.2.2, IFRS 3 does not address at all the methods of accounting that may be appropriate when a business combination involves entities under common control, and we consider that the pooling of interest method is still available for such combinations until the IASB publishes its conclusions for such transactions as part of phase II of its business combinations project.

In the case where a new parent entity is established by means of a share for share exchange and the pooling of interest method has been adopted, the number of shares taken as being in issue for both the current and preceding periods would be the number of shares issued by the new parent entity. However, EPS calculations for previous periods in the new parent entity's financial statements would have to reflect any changes in the number of outstanding ordinary shares of the former parent entity that may have occurred in those periods, as illustrated in the example below:

Example 31.5:   Calculation of EPS where a new holding company is established

Entity A has been established as the newly formed parent entity of Entity B in a one for one share exchange on 30 June 2005. At that date, Entity B has 1,000,000 €1 ordinary shares in issue. Previously, on 30 June 2004 Entity B had issued 200,000 €1 ordinary shares for cash at full market price. Both entities have a 31 December year-end and the trading results of Entity B are as follows:

	2005 €	2004 €
Profit for equity shareholders after taxation	500,000	300,000

The earnings per share calculation of Entity A is shown below:

	2005		2004
Number of equity shares		$800,000 \times \dfrac{6}{12} =$	400,000
		$1,000,000 \times \dfrac{6}{12} =$	500,000
	1,000,000		900,000
EPS	$\dfrac{500,000}{1,000,000} = €0.50$		$\dfrac{300,000}{900,000} = €0.33$

If, in the above example, the share exchange did not take place on a one for one basis, but Entity A issued three shares for every one share held in Entity B, then the number of shares issued by Entity B in 2004 would have to be apportioned accordingly before carrying out the weighted average calculation. The earnings per share calculation would, therefore, have been as follows:

	2005		2004
Number of equity shares		$2,400,000 \times \dfrac{6}{12} =$	1,200,000
		$3,000,000 \times \dfrac{6}{12} =$	1,500,000
	3,000,000		2,700,000
EPS	$\dfrac{500,000}{3,000,000} = €0.17$		$\dfrac{300,000}{2,700,000} = €0.11$

4.7   Adjustments to EPS in historical summaries

In order to ensure comparability of EPS figures, the previously published EPS figures for all periods presented in IFRS financial statements should be adjusted for subsequent changes in capital not involving full consideration at fair value (apart from the conversion of potential ordinary shares) in the manner described in 4.3 above; they should also be adjusted, in our view, for certain group reconstructions. Often entities will include EPS figures in historical summaries (typically five years) in the analyses and discussions accompanying (but not part of) the financial statements. We suggest that all such analyses need similar adjustments in order not to be misleading. We would also suggest that the resultant figures should be described as restated.

5 MATTERS AFFECTING THE NUMERATOR

5.1 Earnings

The earnings figure on which the basic EPS calculation is based should be the consolidated net profit or loss for the year after tax, minority interests and after adjusting for returns to preference shareholders that are not already included in net profit (as will be the case for preference shares classified as liabilities under IAS 32).

5.2 Preference dividends

The adjustments to net profit attributable to ordinary shareholders in relation to returns to preference shareholders should include:

- the after-tax amount of any preference dividends on non-cumulative preference shares declared in respect of the period;[55]

- the after-tax amount of the preference dividends for cumulative preference shares required for the period, whether or not the dividends have been declared. This does not include the amount of any preference dividends for cumulative preference shares paid or declared during the current period in respect of previous periods;[56]

- any original issue discount or premium on increasing rate preference shares which is amortised to retained earnings using the effective interest method. Increasing rate preference shares are those that provide: a low initial dividend to compensate an entity for selling them at a discount; or an above-market dividend in later periods to compensate investors for purchasing them at a premium (see Example 31.6 below);[57]

- the excess of the fair value of the consideration paid to shareholders over the carrying amount of the preference shares when the shares are repurchased under an entity's tender offer to the holders. As this represents a return to the holders of the shares (and a charge to retained earnings for the entity) it is deducted in calculating profit or loss attributable to ordinary equity holders of the parent entity;[58]

- the excess of the fair value of the ordinary shares or other consideration paid over the fair value of the ordinary shares issuable under the original conversion terms when early conversion of convertible preference shares is induced through favourable changes to the original conversion terms or the payment of additional consideration. This is a return to the preference shareholders, and accordingly is deducted in calculating profit or loss attributable to ordinary equity holders of the parent entity;[59] and

- any excess of the carrying amount of preference shares over the fair value of the consideration paid to settle them. This reflects a gain to the entity and is added in calculating profit or loss attributable to ordinary equity holders.[60]

The computation of EPS involving increasing rate preference shares is illustrated in the following example.

Example 31.6:   Increasing rate preference shares[61]

Entity D issued non-convertible, non-redeemable class A cumulative preference shares of €100 par value on 1 January 2005. The class A preference shares are entitled to a cumulative annual dividend of €7 per share starting in 2008.

At the time of issue, the market rate dividend yield on the class A preference shares was 7 per cent a year. Thus, Entity D could have expected to receive proceeds of approximately €100 per class A preference share if the dividend rate of €7 per share had been in effect at the date of issue.

In consideration of the dividend payment terms, however, the class A preference shares were issued at €81.63 per share, i.e. at a discount of €18.37 per share. The issue price can be calculated by taking the present value of €100, discounted at 7 per cent over a three-year period.

Because the shares are classified as equity, the original issue discount is amortised to retained earnings using the effective interest method and treated as a preference dividend for earnings per share purposes. To calculate basic earnings per share, the following imputed dividend per class A preference share is deducted to determine the profit or loss attributable to ordinary equity holders of the parent entity:

Year paid	Carrying amount of class A preference shares 1 January €	Imputed dividend (at 7%) €	Carrying amount of class A preference shares 31 December[1] €	Dividend €
2005	81.63	5.71	87.34	–
2006	87.34	6.12	93.46	–
2007	93.46	6.54	100.00	–
Thereafter :	100.00	7.00	107.00	(7.00)

[1] This is before dividend payment.

5.3   Retrospective adjustments

Where comparative figures have been restated (for example, to correct a material error or as a result of a change in accounting policy), earnings per share for all periods presented should also be restated.[62]

5.4   Participating equity instruments and two class shares

As noted at 3.2 above, IAS 33 envisages entities having more than one class of ordinary shares and requires the calculation and presentation of EPS for each such class.[63] Although perhaps not exactly obvious from the definition, some instruments that have a right to participate in profits are viewed by the standard as ordinary shares. The standard observes that the equity of some entities includes:

(a)   instruments that participate in dividends with ordinary shares according to a predetermined formula (for example, two for one) with, at times, an upper limit on the extent of participation (for example, up to, but not beyond, a specified amount per share); and

(b)   a class of ordinary shares with a different dividend rate from that of another class of ordinary shares but without prior or senior rights.[64]

In our view whilst category (a) could encompass some participating preference shares (as illustrated in Example 31.7 below), not all participating preference shares would necessarily fall to be treated as ordinary shares for EPS purposes. This is because the participation features of some instruments could mean that they are not subordinate to all other classes of equity instrument. The meaning of ordinary shares for EPS purposes is discussed at 3.2 above.

To calculate basic (and diluted) earnings per share:

(a)   profit or loss attributable to ordinary equity holders of the parent entity is adjusted (a profit reduced and a loss increased) by the amount of dividends declared in the period for each class of shares and by the contractual amount of dividends (or interest on participating bonds) that must be paid for the period (for example, unpaid cumulative dividends);

(b)   the remaining profit or loss is allocated to ordinary shares and participating equity instruments to the extent that each instrument shares in earnings as if all of the profit or loss for the period had been distributed. The total profit or loss allocated to each class of equity instrument is determined by adding together the amount allocated for dividends and the amount allocated for a participation feature; and

(c)   the total amount of profit or loss allocated to each class of equity instrument is divided by the number of outstanding instruments to which the earnings are allocated to determine the earnings per share for the instrument.

For the calculation of diluted earnings per share, all potential ordinary shares assumed to have been issued are included in outstanding ordinary shares.[65] This is discussed at 6.4.1 below.

Participating equity instruments and two-class ordinary shares are illustrated with the following example.

Example 31.7:   Participating equity instruments and two-class ordinary shares[66]

Profit attributable to equity holders of the parent entity	€100,000
Ordinary shares outstanding	10,000
Non-convertible preference shares	6,000
Non-cumulative annual dividend on preference shares (before any dividend is paid on ordinary shares)	€5.50 per share

After ordinary shares have been paid a dividend of €2.10 per share, the preference shares participate in any additional dividends on a 20:80 ratio with ordinary shares (i.e. after preference and ordinary shares have been paid dividends of €5.50 and €2.10 per share, respectively, preference shares participate in any additional dividends at a rate of one-fourth of the amount paid to ordinary shares on a per-share basis).

Dividends on preference shares paid	€33,000	(€5.50 per share)
Dividends on ordinary shares paid	€21,000	(€2.10 per share)

Basic earnings per share is calculated as follows:

	€	€
Profit attributable to equity holders of the parent entity		100,000
Less dividends paid:		
Preference	33,000	
Ordinary	21,000	
		(54,000)
Undistributed earnings		46,000

Allocation of undistributed earnings:
Allocation per ordinary share = A
Allocation per preference share = B; B = 1/4 A

$$(A\ 10,000) + (1/4\ A\ 6,000) = CU\ 46,000$$
$$A = CU\ 46,000 \div (10,000 + 1,500)$$
$$A = CU\ 4.00$$
$$B = 1/4\ A$$
$$B = CU\ 1.00$$

Basic per share amounts:

	Preference shares	*Ordinary shares*
Distributed earnings	€5.50	€2.10
Undistributed earnings	€1.00	€4.00
Totals	€6.50	€6.10

NB. This example does not illustrate the classification of the components of convertible financial instruments as liabilities and equity or the classification of related interest and dividends as expenses and equity as required by IAS 32.

It is worth noting that this calculation provided by the standard doesn't actually follow the procedure specified by IAS 33. As noted above, the method outlined by the standard is to allocate dividends and then all remaining profits to the different classes of share then divide this by the number of shares in each class. The above example computes dividends and then remaining profit on a per-share basis and then combines them.

5.5   Other bases

It is very common for entities to supplement the EPS figures required by IAS 33 by voluntarily presenting additional amounts per share. For additional *earnings* per share amounts, the standard requires that:

(a)   the denominator used should be that required by IAS 33;

(b)   basic and diluted amounts be disclosed with equal prominence and presented in the notes;

(c)   an indication of the basis on which the numerator is determined, including whether amounts per share are before or after tax; and

(d)   if the numerator is not reported as a line item in the income statement, a reconciliation between it and a line item that is reported in the income statement.[67]

The requirement in (b) is a curious one – or at least curiously phrased. The wording of the standard requires that additional EPS figures be 'presented in the notes'. Some commentators have asserted that this amounts to banning the presentation of such figures on the face of the income statement. In our view a requirement to put a disclosure in the notes cannot amount to a prohibition on also presenting it elsewhere as well. We also struggle to believe that the IASB intended such a prohibition. Many companies routinely present additional EPS figures on the face of the income statement. If the Board had intended to outlaw such a common practice we believe that would have been mentioned in the development of the revised standard, which it was not.

The requirements above apply to voluntarily presented *earnings* per share figures. The standard doesn't mention the presentation of other 'per share' figures. We believe that if the per share disclosure is of some measure of performance over time (say, cash flow per share) then it would be necessary to use the same denominator as required by the standard for EPS. Other measures may relate to a point in time (say, net assets per share). In such cases the quantity of shares as at the measurement date would be a more appropriate denominator.

6 DILUTED EARNINGS PER SHARE

6.1 The need for diluted EPS

The presentation of basic EPS seeks to show a performance measure, by computing how much profit an entity has earned for each of the shares in issue for the period. Entities often enter into commitments to issue shares in the future which would result in a change in basic EPS. IAS 33 refers to such commitments as potential ordinary shares, which it defines as 'a financial instrument or other contract that may entitle its holder to ordinary shares'.[68]

Examples of potential ordinary shares given by IAS 33 are:

(a) financial liabilities or equity instruments, including preference shares, that are convertible into ordinary shares;

(b) options and warrants (whether accounted for under IAS 32 or IFRS 2);

(c) shares that would be issued upon the satisfaction of conditions resulting from contractual arrangements, such as the purchase of a business or other assets.[69]

When potential shares are actually issued, the impact on basic EPS will be two-fold. First, the number of shares in issue will change; second, profits could be affected, for example by lower interest charges or the return made on cash inflows. Scenarios whereby such an adjustment to basic EPS is unfavourable are described by the standard as dilution, defined as 'a reduction in earnings per share or an increase in loss per share resulting from the assumption that convertible instruments are converted, that options or warrants are exercised, or that ordinary shares are issued upon the satisfaction of specified conditions'.[70] This potential fall in EPS is quantified by computing diluted EPS, and as a result:

(a)   profit or loss attributable to equity holders is increased by the after-tax amount of dividends and interest recognised in the period in respect of the dilutive potential ordinary shares and is adjusted for any other changes in income or expense that would result from the conversion of the dilutive potential ordinary shares; and

(b)   the weighted average number of ordinary shares outstanding is increased by the weighted average number of additional ordinary shares that would have been outstanding assuming the conversion of all dilutive potential ordinary shares.[71]

6.2   Calculation of diluted EPS

IAS 33 requires a diluted EPS figure to be calculated for the profit or loss attributable to ordinary equity holders of the parent and, if presented, profit or loss from continuing operations attributable to them.[72] For these purposes, the profit or loss attributable to ordinary equity holders and the weighted average number of shares outstanding should be adjusted for the effects of all potential ordinary shares.[73] In calculating diluted EPS, the number of shares should be that used in calculating basic EPS, plus the weighted average number of shares that would be issued on the conversion of all the dilutive potential ordinary shares into ordinary shares. As is the case for outstanding shares in the basic EPS calculation, potential ordinary shares should be weighted for the period they are outstanding.[74] Accordingly, potential ordinary shares:

• should be deemed to have been converted into ordinary shares at the beginning of the period or, if not in existence at the beginning of the period, the date of their issue;[75]

• which are cancelled or allowed to lapse should be included only for the period they are outstanding; and

• which convert into ordinary shares during the period are included up until the date of conversion (from which point they will be included in the basic EPS).[76]

The number of dilutive potential ordinary shares should be determined independently for each period presented, and not subsequently revisited. In particular, prior periods' EPS are not restated for changes in assumptions about the conversion of potential shares into shares. IAS 33 also stresses, unnecessarily in our view, that the number of dilutive potential ordinary shares included in the year-to-date period is not a weighted average of the dilutive potential ordinary shares included in each interim computation.[77] The reason the standard stresses this point is probably that it represents a change from the proposal in the draft 'improved' standard.[78]

6.2.1   Earnings

The earnings figure should be that used for basic EPS adjusted to reflect any changes that would arise if the potential shares outstanding in the period were actually issued. Adjustment is to be made for the post-tax effects of:

(a)   any dividends or other items related to dilutive potential ordinary shares deducted in arriving at the earnings figure used for basic EPS;

(b) any interest recognised in the period related to dilutive potential ordinary shares; and

(c) any other changes in income or expense that would result from the conversion of the dilutive potential ordinary shares.[79]

These adjustments will also include any amounts charged in the income statement in accordance with the effective interest method prescribed by IAS 39 as a result of allocating transaction costs, premiums or discounts over the term of the instrument.[80] Instruments with a choice of settlement method may also require adjustments to the numerator as discussed at 6.2.2 below.

An example of an adjustment covered by (b) above is as follows:

Extract 31.8: Novartis AG (2003)

Notes to the Novartis Group Consolidated Financial Statements [extract]
7.   Earnings per share (EPS) [extract]

The diluted EPS calculation takes into account all potential dilutions to the earnings per share arising from the convertible debt and options on Novartis shares. Net income is adjusted to eliminate the applicable convertible debt interest expense less the tax effect. Share equivalents of 16.4 million (2002: 16.2 million) were excluded from the calculation of diluted earnings per share as they were anti-dilutive.

	2003	2002
Net income		
(USD million)	5,016	4,725
Elimination of interest expense on convertible debt (net of tax effect)		2
Net income used to determine diluted earnings per share	5,016	4,727
Weighted average number of shares outstanding	2,473,522,565	2,515,311,685
Call options on Novartis shares	27,446,092	54,891,036
Adjustment for dilutive share options	4,346,940	2,264,236
Weighted average number of shares for diluted earnings per share	2,505,315,597	2,572,466,957
Diluted earnings per share (USD)	**2.00**	**1.84**

The standard notes that certain earnings adjustments directly attributable to the instrument could have a knock-on impact on other income statement items which will need to be accounted for. For example, the lower interest charge following conversion of convertible debt could lead to higher charges under profit sharing schemes.[81]

No imputed earnings are taken into account in respect of the proceeds to be received on exercise of share options or warrants. The effect of such potential ordinary shares on the diluted EPS is reflected in the computation of the denominator. This is discussed at 6.4.2 below.

6.2.2   Number of shares

IAS 33 discusses a number of specific types of potential ordinary shares, and how they should be brought into the calculation, which are discussed at 6.4 below.

More generally, the standard also discusses scenarios where the method of conversion or settlement of potential ordinary shares is at the discretion of one of the parties, as follows:

(a)   The number of shares that would be issued on conversion should be determined from the terms of the potential ordinary shares. When more than one basis of conversion exists, the calculation should assume the most advantageous conversion rate or exercise price from the standpoint of the holder of the potential ordinary shares;[82]

(b)   When an entity has issued a contract that may be settled in shares or cash at its option, it should presume that the contract will be settled in shares. The resulting potential ordinary shares would be included in diluted earnings per share if the effect is dilutive.[83] When such a contract is presented for accounting purposes as an asset or a liability, or has an equity component and a liability component, the numerator should be adjusted for any changes in profit or loss that would have resulted during the period if the contract had been classified wholly as an equity instrument. That adjustment is similar to the adjustments discussed at 6.2.1 above;[84] and

(c)   For contracts that may be settled in ordinary shares or cash at the holder's option, the more dilutive of cash settlement and share settlement should be used in calculating diluted earnings per share.[85]

An example of an instrument covered by (b) above is a debt instrument that, on maturity, gives the issuer the unrestricted right to settle the principal amount in cash or in its own ordinary shares (see Example 31.10 at 6.4.1 A below). An example of an instrument covered by (c) is a written put option that gives the holder a choice of settling in ordinary shares or cash.[86]

In our view, the standard's requirements in (b) and (c) above relating to settlement options are somewhat confused. In particular they seem to envisage a binary accounting model based on the strict legal form of settlement (cash or shares). However, IAS 32 sets out rules for *three* different settlement methods – net cash, net shares and gross physical settlement (discussed in Chapter 17 at 7). One consequence of the above is that, if taken literally, the numerator is only required to be adjusted to remove income statement items arising from a liability when there is a choice of settlement method. However, mandatory net share settlement also gives rise to a liability and income/expense under IAS 32. In our view any such income statement items should be removed for diluted EPS purposes.

6.3 Dilutive potential ordinary shares

Only those potential shares whose issue would have a dilutive effect on EPS are brought into the calculation. Potential ordinary shares are 'antidilutive' when their conversion to ordinary shares would increase earnings per share or decrease loss per share.[87] The calculation of diluted earnings per share should not assume conversion, exercise, or other issue of potential ordinary shares that would have an antidilutive effect on earnings per share.[88] The standard gives detailed guidance for determining which potential shares are deemed to be dilutive, and hence brought into the diluted EPS calculation. This guidance covers: the element of profit which needs to be diluted to trigger inclusion, and the sequence in which potential shares are tested to establish cumulative dilution. Each is discussed below.

6.3.1 Dilution judged by effect on profits from continuing operations

Potential ordinary shares are only to be treated as dilutive if their conversion to ordinary shares would decrease earnings per share or increase loss per share from *continuing* operations.[89] The 'control number' that this focuses on is therefore the net result from continuing operations, which is the net profit or loss attributable to the parent entity, after deducting items relating to preference shares (see 5.2 above) and after excluding items relating to discontinuing operations.[90] The same denominator is required to be used to compute diluted EPS from continuing operations and total diluted EPS. By determining which potential shares are to be included by reference to their impact on continuing EPS can produce some slightly curious results for total EPS. For example, it is possible to exclude instruments which would dilute basic EPS (but not continuing EPS), and include items which are anti-dilutive as regards total profit. This latter point is acknowledged by the standard as follows.

> 'To illustrate the application of the control number notion ... assume that an entity has profit from continuing operations attributable to the parent entity of CU 4,800, a loss from discontinuing operations attributable to the parent entity of (CU 7,200), a loss attributable to the parent entity of (CU 2,400), and 2,000 ordinary shares and 400 potential ordinary shares outstanding. The entity's basic earnings per share is CU 2.40 for continuing operations, (CU 3.60) for discontinuing operations and (CU 1.20) for the loss. The 400 potential ordinary shares are included in the diluted earnings per share calculation because the resulting CU 2.00 earnings per share for continuing operations is dilutive, assuming no profit or loss impact of those 400 potential ordinary shares. Because profit from continuing operations attributable to the parent entity is the control number, the entity also includes those 400 potential ordinary shares in the calculation of the other earnings per share amounts, even though the resulting earnings per share amounts are antidilutive to their comparable basic earnings per share amounts, i.e. the loss per share is less [(CU 3.00) per share for the loss from discontinuing operations and (CU 1.00) per share for the loss].'[91]

6.3.2   *Dilution judged by the cumulative impact of potential shares*

Where a entity has a number of different potential ordinary shares, in deciding whether they are dilutive (and hence reflected in the calculation), each issue or series of potential ordinary shares is to be considered in sequence from the most to the least dilutive. Only those potential shares which produce a cumulative dilution are to be included. This means that some potential shares which would dilute basic EPS if viewed on their own may need to be excluded. This results in a diluted EPS showing the maximum overall dilution of basic EPS. The standard observes that options and warrants should generally be included first as they do not affect the numerator in the diluted EPS calculation (but see the discussion at 6.4.2 below).[92] The way this is to be done is illustrated in the following example.

Example 31.8:   *Calculation of weighted average number of shares: determining the order in which to include dilutive instruments*[93]

Earnings	€
Profit from continuing operations attributable to the parent entity	16,400,000
Less dividends on preference shares	(6,400,000)
Profit from continuing operations attributable to ordinary equity holders of the parent entity	10,000,000
Loss from discontinuing operations attributable to the parent entity	(4,000,000)
Profit attributable to ordinary equity holders of the parent entity	6,000,000
Ordinary shares outstanding	2,000,000
Average market price of one ordinary share during year	€75.00

Potential Ordinary Shares

Options	100,000 with exercise price of €60
Convertible preference shares	800,000 shares with a par value of €100 entitled to a cumulative dividend of €8 per share. Each preference share is convertible to two ordinary shares.
5% convertible bonds	Nominal amount €100,000,000. Each €1,000 bond is convertible to 20 ordinary shares. There is no amortisation of premium or discount affecting the determination of interest expense.
Tax rate	40%

Increase in Earnings Attributable to Ordinary Equity Holders on Conversion of Potential Ordinary Shares

	Increase in earnings	Increase in number of ordinary shares	Earnings per incremental share
	€		€
Options			
Increase in earnings	Nil		
Incremental shares issued for no consideration			
$100,000 \times (€75 - €60)/€75 =$		20,000	Nil
Convertible preference shares			
Increase in earnings			
$€800,000 \times 100 \times 0.08 =$	6,400,000		
Incremental shares			
$2 \times 800,000 =$		1,600,000	4.00
5% convertible bonds			
Increase in earnings			
$€100,000,000 \times 0.05 \times (1 - 0.40) =$	3,000,000		
Incremental shares			
$100,000 \times 20 =$		2,000,000	1.50

The order in which to include the dilutive instruments is therefore:

(1) Options
(2) 5% convertible bonds
(3) Convertible preference shares

Calculation of Diluted Earnings per Share

	Profit from continuing operations attributable to ordinary equity holders of the parent entity (control number)	Ordinary shares	Per share	
	€		€	
As reported	10,000,000	2,000,000	5.00	
Options	–	20,000		
	10,000,000	2,020,000	4.95	Dilutive
5% convertible bonds	3,000,000	2,000,000		
	13,000,000	4,020,000	3.23	Dilutive
Convertible preference shares	6,400,000	1,600,000		
	19,400,000	5,620,000	3.45	Antidilutive

Because diluted earnings per share is increased when taking the convertible preference shares into account (from €3.23 to €3.45), the convertible preference shares are antidilutive and are ignored in the calculation of diluted earnings per share. Therefore, diluted earnings per share for profit from continuing operations is €3.23:

	Basic EPS	Diluted EPS
	€	€
Profit from continuing operations attributable to ordinary equity holders of the parent entity	5.00	3.23
Loss from discontinuing operations attributable to ordinary equity holders of the parent entity	(2.00) (a)	(0.99) (b)
Profit attributable to ordinary equity holders of the parent entity	3.00 (c)	2.24 (d)

(a)   (€4,000,000) ÷ 2,000,000 = (€2.00)
(b)   (€4,000,000) ÷ 4,020,000 = (€0.99)
(c)   €6,000,000 ÷ 2,000,000 = €3.00
(d)   (€6,000,000 + €3,000,000) ÷ 4,020,000 = €2.24

This example does not illustrate the classification of the components of convertible financial instruments as liabilities and equity or the classification of related interest and dividends as expenses and equity as required by IAS 32.

6.4   Particular types of dilutive instruments

6.4.1   Convertible instruments

In order to secure a lower rate of interest, entities sometimes attach benefits to loan stock, debentures or preference shares in the form of conversion rights. These permit the holder to convert his holding in whole or part into equity capital. The right is normally exercisable between specified dates. The ultimate conversion of the instrument will have the following effects:

(a)   there will be an increase in earnings by the amount of the interest (or items relating to preference shares) no longer payable. As interest is normally allowable for tax purposes, the effect on earnings may be net of a tax deduction relating to some or all of the items; and

(b)   the number of ordinary shares in issue will increase. The diluted EPS should be calculated assuming that the instrument is converted into the maximum possible number of shares.[94]

Convertible preference shares will be antidilutive whenever the amount of the dividend on such shares declared in or accumulated for the current period per ordinary share obtainable on conversion exceeds basic earnings per share. Similarly, convertible debt will be antidilutive whenever its interest (net of tax and other changes in income or expense) per ordinary share obtainable on conversion exceeds basic earnings per share.[95]

A   Convertible debt

The EPS calculation for convertible bonds is illustrated in the following example:

Example 31.9:   Treatment of convertible bonds in diluted EPS calculations[96]

Profit attributable to ordinary equity holders of the parent entity	€1,004
Ordinary shares outstanding	1,000
Basic earnings per share	€1.00
Convertible bonds	100

Each block of 10 bonds is convertible into three ordinary shares

Interest expense for the current year relating to the liability component of the convertible bonds	€10
Current and deferred tax relating to that interest expense	€4

Note: the interest expense includes amortisation of the discount arising on initial recognition of the liability component (see IAS 32 – *Financial Instruments: Disclosure and Presentation*).

Adjusted profit attributable to ordinary equity holders of the parent entity	€1,004 + €10 – €4 = €1,010
Number of ordinary shares resulting from conversion of bonds	30
Number of ordinary shares used to calculate diluted earnings per share	1,000 + 30 = 1,030
Diluted earnings per share	€1,010 / 1,030 = €0.98

This example does not illustrate the classification of the components of convertible financial instruments as liabilities and equity or the classification of related interest and dividends as expenses and equity as required by IAS 32.

As discussed at 6.2.2 above, the standard also discusses the impact on diluted EPS of different settlement options. As discussed earlier, we believe this should be taken to mean that for diluted EPS purposes earnings should be adjusted to remove any items that arose from an instrument being classified as an asset or liability rather than equity. The standard claims to illustrate settlement options with the following example.

Example 31.10:   Convertible bonds settled in shares or cash at the issuer's option.[97]

An entity issues 2,000 convertible bonds at the beginning of Year 1. The bonds have a three-year term, and are issued at par with a face value of CU 1,000 per bond, giving total proceeds of CU 2,000,000. Interest is payable annually in arrears at a nominal annual interest rate of 6 per cent. Each bond is convertible at any time up to maturity into 250 common shares. The entity has an option to settle the principal amount of the convertible bonds in ordinary shares or in cash.

When the bonds are issued, the prevailing market interest rate for similar debt without a conversion option is 9 per cent. At the issue date, the market price of one common share is CU 3. Income tax is ignored.

Profit attributable to ordinary equity holders of the parent entity Year 1	CU 1,000,000
Ordinary shares outstanding	1,200,000
Convertible bonds outstanding	2,000
Allocation of proceeds of the bond issue:	
Liability component	* CU 1,848,122
Equity component	CU 151,878
	CU 2,000,000

The liability and equity components would be determined in accordance with IAS 32 – *Financial Instruments: Disclosure and Presentation.* These amounts are recognised as the initial carrying amounts of the liability and equity components. The amount assigned to the issuer conversion option equity element is an addition to equity and is not adjusted.

*   This represents the present value of the principal and interest discounted at 9% – CU 2,000,000 payable at the end of three years; CU 120,000 payable annually in arrears for three years.

Basic earnings per share Year 1:

$$\frac{CU\,1,000,000}{1,200,000} = CU0.83 \text{ per ordinary share}$$

Diluted earnings per share Year 1:

It is presumed that the issuer will settle the contract by the issue of ordinary shares. The dilutive effect is therefore calculated in accordance with paragraph 59 of the Standard.

$$\frac{CU\,1,000,000 + CU\,166,331^{(a)}}{1,200,000 + 500,000^{(b)}} = CU\,0.69 \text{ per ordinary share}$$

(a)   Profit is adjusted for the accretion of CU 166,331 (CU 1,848,122 × 9%) of the liability because of the passage of time.

(b)   500,000 ordinary shares = 250 ordinary shares × 2,000 convertible bonds

It is a little hard to know what to make of this example, which seems to raise more questions than it answers without actually illustrating any impact on the calculation. As regards settlement options, it really adds nothing to the text of the standard and the basic approach to convertibles shown in Example 31.9 above – aside of saying that, because the issuer can choose to settle in shares or cash, share settlement is assumed and a diluted EPS calculated at all. Furthermore, the description of the terms that the entity 'has an option to settle the principal is shares or cash' is far from precise, and its meaning far from clear. Given that a component of the instrument is classified as a liability, we presume that the settlement option means that if the holder does not convert the issuer could choose to deliver a *variable* quantity of shares having a value equal to the principal (CU 2,000,000). This is because all of the instrument would be equity if the quantity of shares was fixed (discussed at 3.3 in Chapter 17). That would then mean that the number of shares to be issued would either be:

- 500,000 assuming the holder converts; or

- such a quantity that has a value at the repayment date of CU 2,000,000.

Regrettably, neither the text of the standard nor the example appended to it gives any indication of which of these should be used, or how the latter should be calculated. One possible approach would be to compare the principal of the convertible debt at the balance sheet with the market value of the entity's shares at that date. This would then enable the more dilutive of the two options to be used.

B   *Convertible preference shares*

The rules for convertible preference shares are very similar to those detailed above in the case of convertible debt, i.e. dividends and other returns to preference shareholders are added back to earnings used for basic EPS and the maximum number of ordinary shares that could be issued on conversion should be used in the calculation.

As discussed at 5.2 above, one possible return to preference shareholders is a premium payable on redemption or induced early conversion in excess of the original terms. IAS 33 notes that the redemption or induced conversion of convertible preference shares may affect only a portion of the previously outstanding convertible preference shares. In such cases, the standard makes clear that any excess consideration is attributed to those shares that are redeemed or converted for the purpose of determining whether the remaining outstanding preference shares are dilutive. In other words, the shares redeemed or converted are considered separately from those shares that are not redeemed or converted.[98]

C   *Participating equity instruments and two class shares with conversion rights*

The treatment for basic EPS of participating equity instruments and two class shares is discussed at 5.4 above. When discussing these instruments the standard observes that when calculating diluted EPS;

- conversion is assumed for those instruments that are convertible into ordinary shares if the effect is dilutive;

- for those that are not convertible into a class of ordinary shares, profit or loss for the period is allocated to the different classes of shares and participating equity instruments in accordance with their dividend rights or other rights to participate in undistributed earnings.[99]

What the standard seems to be hinting at here, without directly addressing, is how to present EPS for two or more classes of ordinary shares (say, class A and class B) when one class can convert into another (say, class B can convert into class A). It this scenario, in our view the basic EPS for each class should be calculated based on profit entitlement (see 5.4 above). For diluted EPS it would be necessary to attribute to class A the profits attributed to class B in the basic EPS – if the overall effect were dilutive to class A, conversion should be assumed.

6.4.2   Options, warrants and their equivalents

A   The numerator

IAS 33 contains a fair quantity of detailed guidance on the treatment for diluted EPS purposes of options, warrants and their equivalents which it defines as 'financial instruments that give the holder the right to purchase ordinary shares'.[100] However, it was largely written before the significant recent developments in accounting for such instruments (IFRS 2 and IAS 32). Although the standard was updated as part of the 'improvements' project in 2003 and further amended as a consequence of IFRS 2, in our view the result is a somewhat unclear patchwork.

IAS 33 clearly states that 'Options and warrants ... do not affect the numerator of the calculation'[101] and this text was added in 2003 as part of the improvements project, so clearly drafted against the back drop of the impending move to expensing share-based payments and also the recent changes to IAS 32 regarding accounting for derivatives over an entity's own shares. As regards employee share options in particular, neither IAS 33 (as updated by IFRS 2) nor the worked example appended to it (see Example 31.13 at 6.4.5 below) make reference to removing either some or all the income statement charge when computing diluted EPS. However, this seems to sit somewhat awkwardly (particularly for options outwith the scope of IFRS 2) with the general requirement for calculating diluted EPS that earnings be adjusted for the effects of 'any other changes in income or expense that would result from the conversion of the dilutive potential ordinary shares.'[102] Furthermore, IAS 33 explicitly requires an adjustment to the numerator in some circumstances:

(a)   as discussed at 6.2.2 above, adjustment to the numerator may be required for a contract (which could include options and warrants) that may be settled in ordinary shares or cash at the entity's option when such a contract is presented for accounting purposes as an asset or a liability, or has an equity component and a liability component. In such a case, the standard requires that 'the entity shall adjust the numerator for any changes in profit or loss that would have resulted during the period if the contract had been classified wholly as an equity instrument'. For contracts that may be settled in ordinary shares or cash at the holder's option, 'the more dilutive of cash settlement and share settlement shall be used in calculating diluted earnings per share';[103]

(b)   where an option agreement requires or permits the tendering of debt in payment of the exercise price (and, if the holder could choose to pay cash, that tendering debt is more advantageous to him) the numerator should be adjusted for the after tax amount of any such debt assumed to be tendered (see E below); and[104]

(c)   where option proceeds are required to be applied to redeem debt or other instruments of the entity (see F below).[105]

For situations covered by (b) and (c) above the standard's specific requirements for adjusting the numerator should be followed. In other circumstances, the interaction of these complex and conflicting requirements with each other and with IFRS 2 and IAS 32 seem to lead to the following requirements when computing the numerator for diluted EPS:

(a)   for instruments accounted for under IAS 32:

   (i)   for a contract classified wholly as an equity instrument, no adjustment to the numerator will be necessary; and

   (ii)   for a contract not classified wholly as an equity instrument, the numerator should be adjusted for any changes in profit or loss that would have resulted if it had been classified wholly as an equity instrument; and

(b)   for instruments accounted for under IFRS 2:

   (i)   for those treated as equity settled, the IFRS 2 charge should *not* be adjusted for; and

   (ii)   for those treated as cash settled, the numerator should be adjusted for any changes in profit or loss that would have resulted if the instrument had been classified wholly as an equity instrument.

In respect of (b), part (i) is supported by the IASB's view regarding share-based payments as follows. 'Some argue that any cost arising from share-based payment transactions is already recognised in the dilution of earnings per share (EPS). If an expense were recognised in the income statement, EPS would be 'hit twice'. However, the Board noted that this result is appropriate. For example, if the entity paid the employees in cash for their services and the cash was then returned to the entity, as consideration for the issue of share options, the effect on EPS would be the same as issuing those options direct to the employees. The dual effect on EPS simply reflects the two economic events that have occurred: the entity has issued shares or share options, thereby increasing the number of shares included in the EPS calculation – although, in the case of options, only to the extent that the options are regarded as dilutive – and it has also consumed the resources it received for those options, thereby decreasing earnings. ... In summary, the Board concluded that the dual effect on diluted EPS is not double-counting the effects of a share or share option grant – the same effect is not counted twice. Rather, two different effects are each counted once.'[106]

As for part (ii) of (b) above, this is the explicit requirement of IAS 33 when the entity can choose cash or share settlement. It is, in our view, also implicit in the requirement of the standard that for contracts that may be settled in ordinary shares or cash at the holder's option, the more dilutive of cash settlement and share settlement should be used in calculating diluted earnings per share.

One company which adjusts the numerator of the calculation for the effects of own equity derivatives is UBS as shown in the following extract.

Extract 31.9: UBS AG (2003)

Notes to the Financial Statements [extract]
Note 8   Earnings per share (EPS) and Shares Outstanding

For the year ended	31.12.03	31.12.02	31.12.01	% change from 31.12.02
Basic Earnings (CHF million)				
Net profit	6,385	3,535	4,973	81
Diluted Earnings (CHF million)				
Net profit	6,385	3,535	4,973	81
Less: profit on own equity derivative contracts deemed dilutive	1	(20)	(99)	
Net profit for diluted EPS	6,386	3,515	4,874	82
Weighted average shares outstanding				
Weighted average shares outstanding	1,116,953,623	1,208,586,678	1,266,038,193	(8)
Potentially dilutive ordinary shares resulting from options and warrants outstanding [1]	21,847,002	14,796,264	22,539,745	48
Weighted average shares outstanding for diluted EPS	1,138,800,625	1,223,382,942	1,288,577,938	(7)
Earnings per share (CHF)				
Basic EPS	5.72	2.92	3.93	96
Diluted EPS	5.61	2.87	3.78	95

1   Total equivalent shares outstanding on options that were not dilutive for the respective periods but could potentially dilute earnings per share in the future were 37,234,538, 75,385,368 and 28,741,886 for the years ended 31 December 2003, 31 December 2002 and 31 December 2001, respectively.

Shares outstanding As at	31.12.03	31.12.02	31.12.01	% change from 31.12.02
Total ordinary shares issued	1,183,046,764	1,256,297,678	1,281,717,499	(6)
Second trading line treasury shares				
2001 program			23,064,356	
2002 first program		67,700,000		
2002 second program		6,335,080		
2003 program	56,707,000			
Other treasury shares	54,653,692	23,146,014	18,190,595	136
Total treasury shares	111,360,692	97,181,094	41,254,951	15
Shares outstanding	1,071,686,072	1,159,116,584	1,240,462,548	(8)

B   *Written call options*

Entities may issue options or warrants which give holders the right to subscribe for shares at fixed prices on specified future dates. If the options or warrants are exercised then:

(a)   the number of shares in issue will be increased; and

(b)   funds will flow into the company and these will produce income.

For calculating diluted EPS, IAS 33 requires the exercise of all dilutive options and warrants to be assumed.[107] Options and warrants are considered dilutive when they would result in the issue of ordinary shares for less than the average market price of ordinary shares during the period. The amount of the dilution is taken to be the average market price of ordinary shares during the period minus the issue price.[108]

Under IAS 33 the effects of such potential ordinary shares on the diluted EPS are reflected in the computation of the denominator using a method sometimes called the 'treasury stock method'.

For this purpose, the weighted average number of shares used in calculating the basic EPS is increased, but not by the full number of shares that would be issued on exercise of the instruments. To work out how many additional shares to include in the denominator, the assumed proceeds from these issues are to be treated as having been received in exchange for:

•   a certain number of shares at their average market price for the period (i.e. no EPS impact); and

•   the remainder for no consideration (i.e. full dilution with no earnings enhancement).[109]

This means that the excess of the total number of potential shares over the number that could be issued at their average market price for the period out of the issue proceeds is included within the denominator; the calculation is illustrated as follows:

Example 31.11:   Effects of share options on diluted earnings per share[110]

Profit attributable to ordinary equity holders of the parent entity for year	€1,200,000
Weighted average number of ordinary shares outstanding during year	500,000 shares
Average market price of one ordinary share during year	€20.00
Weighted average number of shares under option during year	100,000 shares
Exercise price for shares under option during year	€15.00

Calculation of earnings per share

	Earnings	Shares	Per share
Profit attributable to ordinary equity holders of the parent entity for year	€1,200,000		
Weighted average shares outstanding during year		500,000	
Basic earnings per share			€2.40
Weighted average number of shares under option		100,000	
Weighted average number of shares that would have been issued at average market price: (100,000 × €15.00) ÷ €20.00	*	(75,000)	
Diluted earnings per share	€1,200,000	525,000	€2.29

*   Earnings have not increased because the total number of shares has increased only by the number of shares (25,000) deemed to have been issued for no consideration.

The number of shares viewed as fairly priced (and hence neither dilutive nor antidilutive) for this purpose is calculated on the basis of the average price of the ordinary shares during the reporting period.[111] The standard observes that, in theory, calculating an average share price for the period could include every market transaction in the shares. However, it notes that as a practical matter an average (weekly or monthly) will usually be adequate.[112] The individual prices used should generally be the closing market price unless prices fluctuate widely, in which case the average of high and low prices may be more representative. Whatever method is adopted, it should be used consistently unless it ceases to yield a representative price. For example, closing prices may have been used consistently in a series of relatively stable periods then a change to high/low average could be appropriate when prices begin to fluctuate more widely.[113]

The shares would be deemed to have been issued at the beginning of the period or, if later, the date of issue of the warrants or options. Options which are exercised or lapse in the period are included for the portion of the period during which they were outstanding.[114]

The following extract provides an example of an entity's description of the diluted EPS effects of options.

Extract 31.10: Del Monte Pacific Limited (2003)

Notes to the Financial Statements [extract]
25.   Earnings per share

Basic earnings per share is calculated by dividing the net profit attributable to shareholders by the weighted average number of ordinary shares in issue during the year.

	2003	2002
Net profit attributable to shareholders ($'000)	30,197	35,168
Weighted average number of ordinary shares in issue ('000)	1,071,838	1,071,629
Basic earnings per share (in cents)	2.82	3.28

For the diluted earnings per share, the weighted average number of ordinary shares in issue is adjusted to assume conversion of all dilutive potential ordinary shares which are the share options granted to employees.

For the diluted earnings per share in relation to the share options, a calculation is done to determine the number of shares that could have been acquired at market price (determined as the average share price of the Company's shares for the financial year) based on the monetary value of the subscription rights attached to outstanding share options. This calculation serves to determine the 'unpurchased' shares to be added to the ordinary shares outstanding for the purpose of computing the dilution. For the share options calculation, no adjustment is made to net profit attributable to shareholders.

	2003	2002
Net profit attributable to shareholders, representing amount used to determine diluted earnings per share ($'000)	30,197	35,198
Weighted average number of ordinary shares in issue ('000)	1,071,838	1,071,629
Adjustments for share options ('000)	930	–
Weighted average number of ordinary shares for diluted earnings per share ('000)	1,072,768	1,071,629
Diluted earnings per share (in cents)	2.81	3.28

Although the standard seems to require that the fair value used should be the average for the reporting period for all outstanding options or warrants, in our view, for instruments issued, lapsed or exercised during the period a credible case could be made for using an average price for that part of the reporting period that the instrument was outstanding. Indeed, this view is supported by the comprehensive example included in the standard (see the appendix to this chapter), where in computing the number of warrants to be included in calculating the diluted EPS for the full year, the average price used was not that for the full year, but only for the period that the warrants were outstanding.

One practical problem with this requirement is that the average market price of ordinary shares for the reporting period may not be available. Examples would include an entity only listed for part of the period, or an unlisted entity giving voluntary disclosures. In such cases estimates of the market price would need to be made.

C   *Written put options and forward purchase agreements*

Contracts that require the entity to repurchase its own shares, such as written put options and forward purchase contracts, should be reflected in the calculation of diluted earnings per share if the effect is dilutive. If these contracts are 'in the money' during the period (i.e. the exercise or settlement price is above the average market price for that period), IAS 33 requires the potential dilutive effect on EPS to be calculated as follows:

- it should be assumed that at the beginning of the period sufficient ordinary shares are issued (at the average market price during the period) to raise proceeds to satisfy the contract;

- the proceeds from the issue are then assumed to be used to satisfy the contract (i.e. to buy back ordinary shares); and

- the incremental ordinary shares (the difference between the number of ordinary shares assumed issued and the number of ordinary shares received from satisfying the contract) should be included in the calculation of diluted earnings per share.[115]

The standard illustrates this methodology as follows: '... assume that an entity has outstanding 120 written put options on its ordinary shares with an exercise price of CU 35. The average market price of its ordinary shares for the period is CU 28. In calculating diluted earnings per share, the entity assumes that it issued 150 shares at CU 28 per share at the beginning of the period to satisfy its put obligation of CU 4,200. The difference between the 150 ordinary shares issued and the 120 ordinary shares received from satisfying the put option (30 incremental ordinary shares) is added to the denominator in calculating diluted earnings per share.'[116]

D   *Options over convertible instruments*

Although not common, it is possible that an entity grants options or warrants to acquire not ordinary shares directly but other instruments convertible into them (such as convertible preference shares or debt). In this scenario, IAS 33 sets a dual test:

- exercise is assumed whenever the average prices of both the convertible instrument and the ordinary shares obtainable upon conversion are above the exercise price of the options or warrants; but

- exercise is not assumed unless conversion of similar outstanding convertible instruments, if any, is also assumed.[117]

E   *Settlement of option exercise price with debt or other instruments of the entity*

The standard notes that options or warrants may permit or require the tendering of debt or other instruments of the entity (or its parent or a subsidiary) in payment of all or a portion of the exercise price. In the calculation of diluted earnings per share, those options or warrants have a dilutive effect if (a) the average market price of the related ordinary shares for the period exceeds the exercise price or (b) the selling price of the instrument to be tendered is below that at which the instrument may be tendered under the option or warrant agreement and the resulting discount establishes an effective exercise price below the market price of the ordinary shares obtainable upon exercise. In the calculation of diluted EPS, those options or warrants should be assumed to be exercised and the debt or other instruments assumed to be tendered. If tendering cash is more advantageous to the option or warrant holder and the contract permits it, tendering of cash should be assumed. Interest (net of tax) on any debt assumed to be tendered is added back as an adjustment to the numerator.[118]

Similar treatment is given to preference shares that have similar provisions or to other instruments that have conversion options that permit the investor to pay cash for a more favourable conversion rate.[119]

F   *Specified application of option proceeds*

IAS 33 observes that the underlying terms of certain options or warrants may require the proceeds received from the exercise of those instruments to be applied to redeem debt or other instruments of the entity (or its parent or a subsidiary). In which case it requires that in 'the calculation of diluted earnings per share, those options or warrants are assumed to be exercised and the proceeds applied to purchase the debt at its average market price rather than to purchase ordinary shares. However, the excess proceeds received from the assumed exercise over the amount used for the assumed purchase of debt are considered (i.e. assumed to be used to buy back ordinary shares) in the diluted earnings per share calculation. Interest (net of tax) on any debt assumed to be purchased is added back as an adjustment to the numerator.'[120]

In our view this drafting is far from clear, and with it the intentions of the IASB. However, it seems to have in mind what one might call an 'in substance convertible bond' made up of a straight option and a requirement that the proceeds be used to redeem debt. On that basis, the phrase 'rather than purchase ordinary shares' presumably means that the 'normal' treasury stock rules for options are not applied, but rather more shares are brought into the denominator and interest is added back to the numerator. Put another way, we believe this provision is trying to achieve consistency with the requirements for convertible debt.

6.4.3   *Purchased options and warrants*

IAS 33 states that a holding by an entity of options over its own shares will always be antidilutive because:

- put options would only be exercised if the exercise price were higher than the market price; and

- call options would only be exercised if the exercise price were lower than the market price.

Accordingly, the standard requires that such instruments are not included in the calculation of diluted EPS.[121]

This ostensibly rather neat dismissal of the issue strikes us as another example of IAS 33 failing to recognise the new accounting requirements of IAS 32. It is true that the application of the treasury stock method to an option which is in-the-money from the entity's perspective (by reference to the average share price for the period) would *reduce* the number of shares in the denominator, and hence be anti-dilutive. However, dependent upon the settlement mechanism and the share price at the beginning and end of the period, the option could have resulted in a gain reported in the income statement (see Chapter 17 at 7.2 and 7.3). It is possible that the removal of the gain from the numerator could have a greater dilutive effect than the reduction in the denominator and hence render the option dilutive. If that is the case, we believe the option should be included in the diluted EPS calculation.

6.4.4 Partly paid shares

As noted at 3 above, shares issued in partly paid form are to be included in the basic EPS as a fraction of a share, based on dividend participation. As regards diluted EPS they are to be treated, to the extent that they are not entitled to participate in dividends, as the equivalent of options or warrants. The unpaid balance is assumed to represent proceeds used to purchase ordinary shares. The number of shares included in diluted earnings per share is the difference between the number of shares subscribed and the number of shares assumed to be purchased.[122] The mechanics of this treatment are not further spelt out in the standard, but curiously the phrase 'treated as a fraction of an ordinary share' is not repeated. Instead, it is 'the number of shares subscribed' which the standard says should be compared to the number assumed purchased to measure dilution. Unfortunately 'the number of shares subscribed' is not defined. Whilst this could be read to mean that the remaining unpaid consideration is to be treated as the exercise price for options over *all* of the shares issued in partly paid form, the results would make little sense. In our view, the more sensible interpretation is that the unpaid capital should be viewed as the exercise price for options over the proportion of the shares not reflected in the basic EPS. This would mean that if the average share price for the period were the same as the total issue price, then no dilution would be reported. Furthermore, an issue of partly paid shares, say 50% paid with 50% dividend entitlement is, economically identical to an issue of half the quantity as fully paid (with full dividend entitlement) and a forward contract for the remaining half. In that scenario, the issued shares would be incorporated into the basic and diluted EPS in full from the date of issue. The forward contract would be included in diluted EPS calculation by comparing the contracted number of shares with the number of shares that could be bought out of proceeds based on the average share price for the period. In our view, these economically identical transactions should produce the same diluted EPS – that would be achieved by interpreting 'the number of shares subscribed' as the number *economically* subscribed, i.e. the proportion of part-paid shares not already included in basic EPS.

An illustration of what the calculation would look like is as follows:

Example 31.12: Partly paid shares

Capital structure
Issued share capital as at 31 December 2004:
2,000,000 ordinary shares of 10c each

Issued on 1 January 2005:
500,000 part paid ordinary shares of 10c each. Full consideration of 50c per share (being fair value at 1 January 2005) paid up 50% on issue. Dividend participation 50% until fully paid. New shares remain part paid at 31 December 2005.

Average fair value of one ordinary share for the period 60c.

Trading results
Net profit attributable to ordinary shareholders for the year ended 31 December 2005: €100,000.

Computation of basic and diluted EPS

	Net profit attributable to ordinary shareholders €	Ordinary shares No.	Per share
Fully paid shares	100,000	2,000,000	
Partly paid shares (1)		250,000	
Basic EPS	100,000	2,250,000	4.44c
Dilutive effect of partly paid shares (2)		41,667	
Diluted EPS	100,000	2,291,667	4.36c

(1) 50% dividend rights for 500,000 shares.

(2) Outstanding consideration of €125,000 (500,000 × 25c), using fair value of 60c this equates to 208,333 shares, hence the number of dilutive shares deemed issued for free is 41,667 (250,000-208,333).

The example assumes the fair value of the shares over the year is higher than the issue price, which explains why some extra shares fall to be included in the diluted EPS. If the average fair value remained at the issue price of 50p then no additional shares would be included for diluted EPS.

6.4.5 Share based payments

Share options and other incentive schemes are an increasingly common feature of employee remuneration, and can come in many forms. For diluted EPS purposes, IAS 33 identifies two categories and specifies the diluted EPS treatment for each. The categories are:

(a) performance-based employee share options; and

(b) employee share options with fixed or determinable terms and non-vested ordinary shares.[123]

Before moving on to the diluted EPS treatment, it is worth noting an issue that arises from the way IAS 33 phrases this categorisation and subsequent guidance. The drafting doesn't make clear whether the two categories cover all possible schemes. In our view all schemes should fall to be treated as either category (a) or category (b). Any arrangements where entitlement is subject to future performance would fall into category (a) with category (b) being the default for all other arrangements.

Schemes in the first category are to be treated as contingently issuable shares (see 6.4.6 below) because their issue is contingent upon satisfying specified conditions in addition to the passage of time.[124] This gives rise to an apparent paradox relating to shares held in treasury (and shown as a deduction from equity). Frequently employee share schemes will be arranged in this way, with shares released from treasury to satisfy the exercise of options. The rules for, and indeed the title, 'contingently issuable shares' seems to refer to shares which do not exist at the balance sheet date, but may be issued subsequently. Shares held in treasury to satisfy employee options are obviously already 'in issue', so a literal reading of the standard would seem to imply that these have no dilutive impact. In our view this makes little sense, and does not seem to be what the standard setters intended. A sensible interpretation would be to consider the vesting of treasury shares, and hence ceasing to be treated as cancelled for EPS purposes (see 3.2 above), as an issue for calculating diluted EPS.

Those in the second category are to be treated as options (see 6.4.2 above). They should be regarded as outstanding from the grant date, even if they vest, and hence can be realised by the employees, at some later date.[125] An example would be an unexpired loyalty period. This means that some shares may be included in diluted EPS which never, in fact, get issued to employees because they fail to remain with the company for this period. Whilst this requirement is clear, it sits rather awkwardly with the rules for contingently issuable shares which, as discussed at 6.4.6 below, tend to restrict the number of potential shares accounted for. Furthermore, for share options and other share-based payment arrangements to which IFRS 2 applies, the proceeds figure to be used in calculating the dilution under such schemes should include the fair value of any goods or services to be supplied to the entity in the future under the arrangement.[126] An example illustrating the this latter point is as follows:

Example 31.13: Determining the exercise price of employee share options[127]

Weighted average number of unvested share options per employee	1,000
Weighted average amount per employee to be recognised over the remainder of the vesting period for employee services to be rendered as consideration for the share options, determined in accordance with IFRS 2 – *Share-based Payment*	€1,200
Cash exercise price of unvested share options	€15
Calculation of adjusted exercise price	
Fair value of services yet to be rendered per employee:	€1,200
Fair value of services yet to be rendered per option: (€1,200 / 1,000)	€1.20
Total exercise price of share options: (€15.00 + €1.20)	€16.20

Whilst the standard requires that the additional deemed proceeds is the *fair value* of goods or services yet to be received (which could, in theory, vary over time), the example seems to clarify that it is the IFRS 2 expense yet to be charged to income.

What this requirement seeks to reflect is that for such options the issuer will receive not just the cash proceeds (if any) under the option when it is exercised but also valuable goods and services over its life. This will result in the dilutive effect of the options increasing over time as the deemed proceeds on exercise of the options reduces.

6.4.6   *Contingently issuable shares*

As part of the improvements project, IAS 33 was updated to contain considerable detailed guidance, including a numerical worked example, on contingently issuable shares. Contingently issuable ordinary shares are defined as 'ordinary shares issuable for little or no cash or other consideration upon satisfaction of specified conditions in a contingent share agreement.' A contingent share agreement is, perhaps unnecessarily, also defined by the standard as 'an agreement to issue shares that is dependent on the satisfaction of specified conditions.'[128] The basic rule is that the number of contingently issuable shares to be included in the diluted EPS calculation is 'based on the number of shares that would be issuable if the end of the period were the end of the contingency period'.[129] This requirement to look at the status of the contingency at the balance sheet date, rather than to consider the most likely outcome, seems to have the overall result of *reducing* the amount of dilution disclosed. Furthermore, these detailed rules on contingently issuable shares are arguably at odds with the more general requirement of 'giving effect to *all* dilutive potential ordinary shares outstanding during the period'.[130] (Emphasis added).

The standard's discussions cover three broad categories: earnings-based contingencies, share-price-based contingencies, and other contingencies. These are discussed in turn below.

The number of shares contingently issuable may depend on future earnings and future prices of the ordinary shares. In such cases, the standard makes clear that the number of shares included in the diluted EPS calculation is based on both conditions (i.e. earnings to date and the current market price at the end of the reporting period). In other words, contingently issuable shares are not included in the diluted EPS calculation unless both conditions are met.[131]

A   *Earnings-based contingencies*

The standard discusses the scenario where shares would be issued contingent upon the attainment or maintenance of a specified amount of earnings for a period. In such a case the standard requires that 'if that amount has been attained at the end of the reporting period but must be maintained beyond the end of the reporting period for an additional period, then the additional ordinary shares are treated as outstanding, if the effect is dilutive, when calculating diluted earnings per share. In that case, the calculation of diluted earnings per share is based on the number of ordinary shares that would be issued if the amount of earnings at the end of the reporting period were the amount of earnings at the end of the contingency period'.[132] Although perhaps not the clearest of drafting, this seems to be saying that earnings-based contingencies need to be viewed as an absolute cumulative hurdle which either is met or not met at the reporting date. Often, such contingencies may be contractually expressed in terms of *annual* performance over a number of years, say an average of €1million profit per year for three years. In our view, 'the attainment or maintenance of a specified amount of earnings for a period' in this scenario would mean generating a total of €3million of profits. If that is achieved by the end of a reporting period, the shares are outstanding for diluted EPS purposes and included in the computation if the effect is dilutive. It could, perhaps, be argued that the potential shares should be considered outstanding if profits of €1million were generated at the end of the first year. However, the requirement that the calculation be 'based on the number of ordinary shares that would be issued if the amount of earnings at the end of the reporting period were the amount of earnings at the end of the contingency period' means that the test must be: would shares be issued if the current earnings of €1million were all the profits earned by the end of the three year contingency period? In this example the answer is no, as that amount of earnings would fall short of averaging €1million per year. The standard then notes that, because earnings may change in a future period, the calculation of basic EPS does not include such contingently issuable shares until the end of the contingency period because not all necessary conditions have been satisfied.[133]

An earnings-based contingency is illustrated in the following example:

Example 31.14:   Contingently issuable shares[134]

Ordinary shares outstanding during 2005	1,000,000 (there were no options, warrants or convertible instruments outstanding during the period)

An agreement related to a recent business combination provides for the issue of additional ordinary shares based on the following conditions:

> 5,000 additional ordinary shares for each new retail site opened during 2005
> 1,000 additional ordinary shares for each €1,000 of consolidated profit in excess of €2,000,000 for the year ended 31 December 2005

Retail sites opened during the year:

> one on 1 May 2005
> one on 1 September 2005

Consolidated year-to-date profit attributable to ordinary equity holders of the parent entity:

> €1,100,000 as of 31 March 2005
> €2,300,000 as of 30 June 2005
> €1,900,000 as of 30 September 2005 (including a €450,000 loss from a discontinuing operation)
> €2,900,000 as of 31 December 2005

Basic earnings per share

	First quarter	Second quarter	Third quarter	Fourth quarter	Full year
Numerator (€)	1,100,000	1,200,000	(400,000)	1,000,000	2,900,000
Denominator:					
Ordinary shares outstanding	1,000,000	1,000,000	1,000,000	1,000,000	1,000,000
Retail site contingency	–	3,333 (a)	6,667 (b)	10,000	5,000 (c)
Earnings contingency (d)	–	–	–	–	–
Total shares	1,000,000	1,003,333	1,006,667	1,010,000	1,005,000
Basic earnings per share (€)	1.10	1.20	(0.40)	0.99	2.89

(a) 5,000 shares × 2/3
(b) 5,000 shares + (5,000 shares × 1/3)
(c) (5,000 shares × 8/12) + (5,000 shares × 4/12)
(d) The earnings contingency has no effect on basic earnings per share because it is not certain that the condition is satisfied until the end of the contingency period. The effect is negligible for the fourth-quarter and full-year calculations because it is not certain that the condition is met until the last day of the period.

Diluted earnings per share

	First quarter	Second quarter	Third quarter	Fourth quarter	Full year
Numerator (€)	1,100,000	1,200,000	(400,000)	1,000,000	2,900,000
Denominator:					
Ordinary shares outstanding	1,000,000	1,000,000	1,000,000	1,000,000	1,000,000
Retail site contingency	–	5,000	10,000	10,000	10,000
Earnings contingency	– (e)	300,000 (f)	(g)	900,000 (h)	900,000 (h)
Total shares	1,000,000	1,305,000	1,010,000	1,910,000	1,910,000
Diluted earnings per share (€)	1.10	0.92	(0.40) (i)	0.52	1.52

(e) Year-to-date profits do not exceed €2,000,000 at 31 March 2005. The Standard does not permit projecting future earnings levels and including the related contingent shares.
(f) [(€2,300,000 – €2,000,000) / 1,000] × 1,000 shares = 300,000 shares.
(g) Year-to-date profit is less than €2,000,000.
(h) [(€2,900,000 – €2,000,000) / 1,000] × 1,000 shares = 900,000 shares.
(i) Because the loss during the third quarter is attributable to a loss from a discontinuing operation, the antidilution rules do not apply. The control number (i.e. profit or loss from continuing operations attributable to the equity holders of the parent entity) is positive. Accordingly, the effect of potential ordinary shares is included in the calculation of diluted earnings per share.

Curiously, this example illustrates *quarterly* financial reporting. However, the principles are the same whether the reporting period is illustrated as three months or one year. The example does illustrate that the earnings target is a cumulative hurdle over the entire contingency period (four reporting periods in the example) rather than including potential shares based on the assumption that the level of quarterly profit would be maintained for the four quarters.

We do not agree that such a methodology necessarily gives the most meaningful diluted EPS figure. A better approach, in our view, would have been to base the dilution on a reasonable assessment of the outcome of the contingency; this would also be more consistent with the treatment of other contingent forms of finance. For example if contingent consideration under an earn-out clause in a business combination is payable in cash, IFRS 3 requires the best estimate of the amount payable to be provided at its present value (assuming the payment is probable and can be measured reliably), with the result that EPS will bear interest on this amount as the discount unwinds.[135] It would seem appropriate for diluted EPS similarly to reflect the likely dilution when the consideration is in the form of shares. Indeed, IFRS 3 asserts that 'It is usually possible to estimate the amount of any such adjustment at the time of initially accounting for the combination without impairing the reliability of the information, even though some uncertainty exists.'[136] It seems to us that if such estimates are satisfactory for accounting purposes, there is no good reason not to consider them adequate for financial analysis like EPS. Notwithstanding this, the rule for contingencies determined solely by an entity's earnings is now clear. However, the treatment of contingencies which are partly determined by earnings and partly by other criteria is less clear.

The standard only discusses earnings criteria based on *absolute* measures; in the example above a cumulative profit of in excess of CU 2,000,000. In our experience such criteria are rare. In practice criteria are often phrased in terms of *relative* performance against an external benchmark. Examples would be earnings growth targets of inflation plus 2% or EPS growth being in the top quartile of a group of competitors. For contingencies such as these it is impossible to establish an absolute target in order to ask whether it is met at the period end. For example, consider the earnings contingency in IAS 33, discussed above, to achieve profits in excess of €2,000,000 over four quarters. If this instead required the profits to be €2,000,000 adjusted in line with inflation, it would be impossible to know how many shares would be issued if the cumulative profit at the end of the second quarter of €2,300,000 were the amount of earnings at the end of the contingency period. Until the end of the year the absolute level of profit required would be unknown; it would be more or less than €2,000,000 depending on the level of inflation or deflation over the period.

There would seem to be (at least) two different ways of interpreting the requirements of IAS 33 in such a scenario, each resulting in a different diluted EPS figure. One approach would be to consider such criteria as being based on 'a condition other than earnings or market price'. That would mean (as discussed under C below) that the number of shares brought into diluted EPS would be based on the status of the condition at the balance sheet date.[137] So, if the target was earnings for the year in excess of €2,000,000 adjusted in line with inflation and at the end of the second quarter inflation had been 4%, then the target would become €2,080,000 and hence 220,000 shares would be included for diluted EPS for the second quarter. An alternative approach would be to regard it as an earnings-based contingency and make an assumption as to future inflation over the contingency period. This would allow a cumulative hurdle to be calculated and compared with actual earnings to date. So if at the end of the second quarter it was estimated that the annual inflation for the year was 5%, then the target would become €2,100,000 and hence 200,000 shares would be included for diluted EPS for the second quarter. Given the lack of clarity in the standard, it seems likely that either of the above approaches may be selected in practice.

B   *Share-price-based contingencies*

The provisions here are more straightforward. In these cases, if the effect is dilutive, the calculation of diluted EPS is based on the number of shares that would be issued if the market price at the end of the reporting period were the market price at the end of the contingency period. If the condition is based on an average of market prices over a period of time that extends beyond the end of the reporting period, the average for the period of time that has lapsed should be used. Again the standard explains that, because the market price may change in a future period, the calculation of basic earnings per share does not include such contingently issuable ordinary shares until the end of the contingency period because not all necessary conditions have been satisfied.[138]

C   *Other contingencies*

The requirement regarding contingencies not driven by earnings or share price is as follows: 'assuming that the present status of the condition remains unchanged until the end of the contingency period, the contingently issuable ordinary shares are included in the calculation of diluted earnings per share according to the status at the end of the reporting period.'[139]

The standard illustrates the 'other contingency' rules by the example of shares being issued depending upon the opening of a specified number of retail sites, and such a contingency is included in the standard's numerical example (see Example 31.14 above). As is the case for earnings-based contingencies discussed above, it would seem that such conditions are always deemed to be expressed as a cumulative hurdle which may or may not be met by the balance sheet date. Accordingly, the required treatment would be the same if the condition had been expressed in terms of achieving a certain average annual level of shop openings. It seems illogical to us that management plans for a shop opening programme should be disregarded for EPS purposes when such estimates would be essential in other accounting areas, for example to determine the estimates required by IFRS 3 of adjustments to the cost of a business combination contingent on future events.[140] However, this is what the standard requires.

6.4.7   *Potential ordinary shares of investees*

A subsidiary, joint venture or associate may issue to parties other than the parent, venturer or investor potential ordinary shares that are convertible into either ordinary shares of the subsidiary, joint venture or associate, or ordinary shares of the parent, venturer or investor (the reporting entity). If these potential ordinary shares of the subsidiary, joint venture or associate have a dilutive effect on the basic EPS of the reporting entity, they should be included in the calculation of diluted earnings per share.[141]

The standard requires that such potential ordinary shares should be included in the calculation of diluted EPS as follows:

(a)   instruments issued by a subsidiary, joint venture or associate that enable their holders to obtain ordinary shares of the subsidiary, joint venture or associate should be included in calculating the diluted EPS data of the subsidiary, joint venture or associate. Those EPS are then included in the reporting entity's EPS calculations based on the reporting entity's holding of the instruments of the subsidiary, joint venture or associate; and

(b)   instruments of a subsidiary, joint venture or associate that are convertible into the reporting entity's ordinary shares should be considered among the potential ordinary shares of the reporting entity for the purpose of calculating diluted EPS. Similarly, options or warrants issued by a subsidiary, joint venture or associate to purchase ordinary shares of the reporting entity should be considered among the potential ordinary shares of the reporting entity in the calculation of consolidated diluted EPS.[142]

For the purpose of determining the EPS effect of instruments issued by a reporting entity that are convertible into ordinary shares of a subsidiary, joint venture or associate, the standard requires that the instruments are assumed to be converted and the numerator (profit or loss attributable to ordinary equity holders of the parent entity) adjusted as necessary in accordance with the normal rules (see 6.2.1 above). In addition to those adjustments, the numerator is adjusted for any change in the profit or loss recorded by the reporting entity (such as dividend income or equity method income) that is attributable to the increase in the number of ordinary shares of the subsidiary, joint venture or associate outstanding as a result of the assumed conversion. The denominator of the diluted EPS calculation is not affected because the number of ordinary shares of the reporting entity outstanding would not change upon assumed conversion.[143]

The computation under (a) above is illustrated in the following example.

Example 31.15: Warrants issued by a subsidiary[144]

Parent:

Profit attributable to ordinary equity holders of the parent entity	€12,000 (excluding any earnings of, or dividends paid by, the subsidiary)
Ordinary shares outstanding	10,000
Instruments of subsidiary owned by the parent	800 ordinary shares
	30 warrants exercisable to purchase ordinary shares of subsidiary
	300 convertible preference shares

Subsidiary:

Profit	€5,400
Ordinary shares outstanding	1,000
Warrants	150, exercisable to purchase ordinary shares of the subsidiary
Exercise price	€10
Average market price of one ordinary share	€20
Convertible preference shares	400, each convertible into one ordinary share
Dividends on preference shares	€1 per share

No inter-company eliminations or adjustments were necessary except for dividends. For the purposes of this illustration, income taxes have been ignored.

Subsidiary's earnings per share

Basic EPS   €5.00   calculated:

$$\frac{€5,400^{(a)} - €400^{(b)}}{1,000^{(c)}}$$

Diluted EPS   €3.66   calculated:

$$\frac{€5,400^{(d)}}{1,000 + 75^{(e)} + 400^{(f)}}$$

(a)   Subsidiary's profit.

(b)   Dividends paid by subsidiary on convertible preference shares.

(c)   Subsidiary's ordinary shares outstanding.

(d)   Subsidiary's profit attributable to ordinary equity holders (€5,000) increased by €400 preference dividends for the purpose of calculating diluted earnings per share.

(e)   Incremental shares from warrants, calculated: $[(€20 - €10) / €20] \times 150$.

(f)   Subsidiary's ordinary shares assumed outstanding from conversion of convertible preference shares, calculated: 400 convertible preference shares × conversion factor of 1.

Consolidated earnings per share

Basic EPS   €1.63   calculated: $\dfrac{€12,000^{(g)} + €4,300^{(h)}}{10,000^{(i)}}$

Diluted EPS   €1.61   calculated: $\dfrac{€12,000 + €2,928^{(j)} + €55^{(k)} + €1,098^{(l)}}{10,000}$

(g)   Parent's profit attributable to ordinary equity holders of the parent entity.

(h)   Portion of subsidiary's profit to be included in consolidated basic earnings per share, calculated: (800 × CU 5.00) + (300 × €1.00)

(i)   Parent's ordinary shares outstanding.

(j)   Parent's proportionate interest in subsidiary's earnings attributable to ordinary shares, calculated: (800 / 1,000) × (1,000 shares × €3.66 per share)

(k)   Parent's proportionate interest in subsidiary's earnings attributable to warrants, calculated: (30 / 150) × (75 incremental shares × €3.66 per share)

(l)   Parent's proportionate interest in subsidiary's earnings attributable to convertible preference shares, calculated: (300 / 400) × (400 shares from conversion × €3.66 per share)

This example does not illustrate the classification of the components of convertible financial instruments as liabilities and equity or the classification of related interest and dividends as expenses and equity as required by IAS 32.

6.4.8   *Contingently issuable potential ordinary shares*

The standard requires that contingently issuable potential ordinary shares (other than those covered by a contingent share agreement, such as contingently issuable convertible instruments) to be included in the diluted EPS calculation as follows:

(a)   determine whether the potential ordinary shares may be assumed to be issuable on the basis of the conditions specified for their issue in accordance with the standard's contingent ordinary share provisions (see 6.4.6) above; and

(b)   if those potential ordinary shares should be reflected in diluted EPS, determine their impact on the calculation of diluted earnings per share by following the provisions of the standard for that type of potential ordinary share.

However, exercise or conversion is not to be assumed for the purpose of calculating diluted earnings per share unless exercise or conversion of similar outstanding potential ordinary shares that are not contingently issuable is assumed.[145]

This two-stage test (essentially, are the contingencies met and are the resulting potential shares dilutive?) is a perfectly logical stance for the standard to take. However, we are mystified by the somewhat cryptic scope of these provisions in that they apply to 'contingently issuable potential ordinary shares (other than those covered by a contingent share agreement, such as contingently issuable convertible instruments)'. A contingent share agreement is defined as 'an agreement to issue shares that is dependent on the satisfaction of specified conditions'.[146] We fail to see how a contingent agreement to issue *potential* ordinary shares could be 'covered' by an agreement 'to issue shares'. In our view the methodology described above seems appropriate for a contingently issuable convertible bond.

7   PRESENTATION, RESTATEMENT AND DISCLOSURE

7.1   Presentation

IAS 33 requires the presentation of basic and diluted EPS (with equal prominence and even if the amounts are negative – i.e. a loss per share) for each period for which an income statement is presented.[147] This is required for the profit or loss attributable to ordinary equity holders for:

(a)   overall profit;

(b)   profit or loss from continuing operations; and

(c)   profit or loss from discontinuing operations, if any.[148]

In the case of (a) and (b), separate figures are required for each class of ordinary shares with a different right to share in profits for the period. The figures for (a) and (b) must be displayed on the face of the income statement.[149] Those for (c) may be either on the face or in the notes.[150] The standard (somewhat unnecessarily given the requirement to show basic and diluted EPS for all periods) states that if diluted EPS is given for at least one period it must be given for all periods presented. In what some might view as a further statement of the obvious, IAS 33 notes that if basic and diluted EPS are equal, dual presentation can be accomplished in one line on the income statement.[151] It stops short, however, of explaining that this is only true if the caption is amended to address both.

Regarding (c), the wording of the standard isn't very clear. In particular, if an entity has more than one discontinued operation it doesn't clarify whether separate EPS disclosures are required for each or whether one aggregate figure is needed. The wording leans to the former, as it uses the singular – 'An entity that reports a discontinuing operation shall disclose the basic and diluted amounts per share for the discontinuing[152] operation …'. However, IFRS 5 only requires the income statement to identify the total result from all discontinued operations.[153] In light of this, we believe aggregate figures are acceptable.

7.2   Restatement

IAS 33 contains requirements to restate prior periods' EPS for events that change the number of shares outstanding without a corresponding change in resources. Additionally it specifies circumstances when EPS should not be restated.

Basic and diluted EPS for all periods presented should be adjusted for:

- events (other than the conversion of potential ordinary shares) which change the number of ordinary shares without a corresponding change in resources (discussed at 4.3 above);[154]

- the effects of errors and adjustments resulting from changes in accounting policies accounted for retrospectively (see 5.3 above);[155] and

- in our opinion, the effects of business combinations that are accounted for as a uniting of interests (discussed at 4.6 above).

No adjustment should be made:

- to basic or diluted EPS when a share consolidation is combined with a special dividend where the overall commercial effect is that of a share repurchase at fair value (discussed at 4.3.2 above);[156]

- to previously reported diluted EPS due to changes in the prices of ordinary shares which would have given a different dilutive effect for options and warrants;[157]

- to prior period diluted EPS as a result of a contingency period coming to an end without the conditions attaching to contingently issuable shares being met;[158] or

- to prior period diluted EPS for changes in the assumptions used in the calculations or for the conversion of potential ordinary shares into ordinary shares.[159]

7.3 Disclosure

IAS 33 requires disclosure of the following:

(a) the amounts used as the numerators in calculating basic and diluted EPS, and a reconciliation of those amounts to profit or loss attributable to the parent entity for the period. The reconciliation should include the individual effect of each class of instruments that affects EPS;

(b) the weighted average number of ordinary shares used as the denominator in calculating basic and diluted earnings per share, and a reconciliation of these denominators to each other. The reconciliation should include the individual effect of each class of instruments that affects EPS;

(c) instruments (including contingently issuable shares) that could potentially dilute basic EPS in the future, but were not included in the calculation because they were antidilutive for the period(s) presented; and

(d) a description of ordinary share transactions or potential ordinary share transactions (other than those accounted for in EPS for the year – see 4.3 above – in which case that fact should be stated), that occur after the balance sheet date and that would have changed significantly the number of ordinary shares or potential ordinary shares outstanding at the end of the period if those transactions had occurred before the end of the reporting period.[160]

Examples of transactions in (d) include:

(a) an issue of shares for cash;

(b) an issue of shares when the proceeds are used to repay debt or preference shares outstanding at the balance sheet date;

(c) the redemption of ordinary shares outstanding;

(d) the conversion or exercise of potential ordinary shares outstanding at the balance sheet date into ordinary shares;

(e)　　an issue of options, warrants, or convertible instruments; and

(f)　　the achievement of conditions that would result in the issue of contingently issuable shares.

The standard observes that EPS amounts are not adjusted for such transactions occurring after the balance sheet date because such transactions do not affect the amount of capital used to produce profit or loss for the period.[161] Changes in ordinary shares are discussed at 4 above.

The standard observes that financial instruments and other contracts generating potential ordinary shares may incorporate terms and conditions that affect the measurement of basic and diluted earnings per share. These terms and conditions may determine whether any potential ordinary shares are dilutive and, if so, the effect on the weighted average number of shares outstanding and any consequent adjustments to profit or loss attributable to ordinary equity holders. The disclosure of the terms and conditions of such financial instruments and other contracts is encouraged by IAS 33, if not otherwise required by IAS 32 (discussed in Chapter 20).[162]

8　CONCLUSION

In our view ratios for financial analysis, like EPS, do not properly fall within the remit of accounting standard setters. Entities use their annual report and financial statements to communicate with shareholders on a variety of issues, many of which are supplementary to giving a fair presentation of financial performance and cash flows for the period and the financial position at the balance sheet date. A widespread practice of giving information is not, of itself, sufficient grounds for regulators to start specifying computational methods. Many entities frequently disclose other financial analysis statistics, such as return on capital and gearing, yet (thankfully) there seems no impetus for accounting standards on these.

As regards the content of IAS 33, most of its provisions are not unreasonable and should prove workable for most entities. However, as described earlier the standard is both unclear and contradictory in places. In our view the developments in accounting for share based payments and derivatives over an entity's shares (where the use of estimates of fair values attempts to capture dilution with a charge to income) should be a catalyst to reassess the purpose and meaning of a diluted EPS figure.

APPENDIX

CALCULATION OF BASIC AND DILUTED EARNINGS PER SHARE AND INCOME STATEMENT PRESENTATION (COMPREHENSIVE EXAMPLE)

Reproduced below is IAS 33's comprehensive worked example of the computation and presentation of EPS.[163] It illustrates four quarters and then the full year, but the principles and calculations would be the same whatever the length of the periods considered.

This example illustrates the quarterly and annual calculations of basic and diluted earnings per share in the year 20X1 for Company A, which has a complex capital structure. The control number is profit or loss from continuing operations attributable to the parent entity. Other facts assumed are as follows:

Average market price of ordinary shares: The average market prices of ordinary shares for the calendar year 20X1 were as follows:

First quarter	CU 49
Second quarter	CU 60
Third quarter	CU 67
Fourth quarter	CU 67

The average market price of ordinary shares from 1 July to 1 September 20X1 was CU 65.

Ordinary shares: The number of ordinary shares outstanding at the beginning of 20X1 was 5,000,000. On 1 March 20X1, 200,000 ordinary shares were issued for cash.

Convertible bonds: In the last quarter of 20X0, 5 per cent convertible bonds with a principal amount of CU 12,000,000 due in 20 years were sold for cash at CU 1,000 (par). Interest is payable twice a year, on 1 November and 1 May. Each CU 1,000 bond is convertible into 40 ordinary shares. No bonds were converted in 20X0. The entire issue was converted on 1 April 20X1 because the issue was called by Company A.

Convertible preference shares: In the second quarter of 20X0, 800,000 convertible preference shares were issued for assets in a purchase transaction. The quarterly dividend on each convertible preference share is CU 0.05, payable at the end of the quarter for shares outstanding at that date. Each share is convertible into one ordinary share. Holders of 600,000 convertible preference shares converted their preference shares into ordinary shares on 1 June 20X1.

Warrants: Warrants to buy 600,000 ordinary shares at CU 55 per share for a period of five years were issued on 1 January 20X1. All outstanding warrants were exercised on 1 September 20X1.

Options: Options to buy 1,500,000 ordinary shares at CU 75 per share for a period of 10 years were issued on 1 July 20X1. No options were exercised during 20X1 because the exercise price of the options exceeded the market price of the ordinary shares.

Tax rate: The tax rate was 40 per cent for 20X1.

20X1	*Profit (loss) from continuing operations attributable to the parent entity (a)* CU	*Profit (loss) attributable to the parent entity* CU	
First quarter	5,000,000	5,000,000	
Second quarter	6,500,000	6,500,000	
Third quarter	1,000,000	(1,000,000)	(b)
Fourth quarter	(700,000)	(700,000)	
Full year	11,800,000	9,800,000	

(a) This is the control number (before adjusting for preference dividends).

(b) Company A had a CU 2,000,000 loss (net of tax) from discontinuing operations in the third quarter.

First Quarter 20X1

Basic EPS calculation			*CU*
Profit from continuing operations attributable to the parent entity			5,000,000
Less: preference shares dividends			(40,000) (c)
Profit attributable to ordinary equity holders of the parent entity			4,960,000

Dates	*Shares Outstanding*	*Fraction of period*	*Weighted-average shares*
1 January 28 February	5,000,000	2/3	3,333,333
Issue of ordinary shares on 1 March	200,000		
1 March 31 March	5,200,000	1/3	1,733,333
Weighted-average shares			5,066,666

Basic EPS	**CU 0.98**

(c)   800,000 shares × CU 0.05

Diluted EPS calculation			
Profit attributable to ordinary equity holders of the parent entity			CU 4,960,000
Plus: profit impact of assumed conversions			
Preference share dividends	CU 40,000	(d)	
Interest on 5% convertible bonds	CU 90,000	(e)	
Effect of assumed conversions			CU 130,000
Profit attributable to ordinary equity holders of the parent entity including assumed conversions			CU 5,090,000
Weighted-average shares			5,066,666
Plus: incremental shares from assumed conversions			
Warrants		0 (f)	
Convertible preference shares		800,000	
5% convertible bonds		480,000	
Dilutive potential ordinary shares			1,280,000
Adjusted weighted-average shares			6,346,666

Diluted EPS	**CU 0.80**

(d)   800,000 shares × CU 0.05

(e)   (CU 12,000,000 × 5%) ÷ 4; less taxes at 40%

(f)   The warrants were not assumed to be exercised because they were antidilutive in the period (CU 55 [exercise price] > CU 49 [average price]).

Second Quarter 20X1

Basic EPS calculation	*CU*
Profit from continuing operations attributable to the parent entity	6,500,000
Less: preference shares dividends	(10,000) (g)
Profit attributable to ordinary equity holders of the parent entity	6,490,000

Dates	*Shares outstanding*	*Fraction of period*	*Weighted-average shares*
1 April	5,200,000		
Conversion of 5% bonds on 1April	480,000		
1 April – 31 May	5,680,000	2/3	3,786,666
Conversion of preference shares on 1June	600,000		
1 June – 30 June	6,280,000	1/3	2,093,333
Weighted-average shares			5,880,000
Basic EPS			**CU 1.10**

(g)   200,000 shares × CU 0.05

Diluted EPS calculation		
Profit attributable to ordinary equity holders of the parent entity		CU 6,490,000
Plus: profit impact of assumed conversions		
Preference share dividends	CU 10,000 (h)	
Effect of assumed conversions		CU 10,000
Profit attributable to ordinary equity holders of the parent entity including assumed conversions		CU 6,500,000
Weighted-average shares		5,880,000
Plus: incremental shares from assumed conversions		
Warrants	50,000 (i)	
Convertible preference shares	600,000 (j)	
Dilutive potential ordinary shares		650,000
Adjusted weighted-average shares		6,530,000
Diluted EPS		**CU 1.00**

(h)   200,000 shares × CU 0.05

(i)   CU 55 × 600,000 = CU 33,000,000; CU 33,000,000 ÷ CU 60 = 550,000;
       600,000 – 550,000 = 50,000 shares OR [(CU 60 – CU 55) ÷ CU 60] × 600,000 shares
       = 50,000 shares

(j)   (800,000 shares × 2/3) + (200,000 shares × 1/3)

Third Quarter 20X1

Basic EPS calculation	*CU*
Profit from continuing operations attributable to the parent entity	1,000,000
Less: preference shares dividends	(10,000)
Profit from continuing operations attributable to ordinary equity holders of the parent entity	990,000
Loss from discontinuing operations attributable to the parent entity	(2,000,000)
Loss attributable to ordinary equity holders of the parent entity	(1,010,000)

Dates	*Shares outstanding*	*Fraction of period*	*Weighted-average shares*
1 July -31 August	6,280,000	2/3	4,186,666
Exercise of warrants on 1 September	600,000		
1 September-30 September	6,880,000	1/3	2,293,333
Weighted-average shares			6,480,000

Basic EPS

Profit from continuing operations	**CU 0.15**
Loss from discontinuing operations	**(CU 0.31)**
Loss	**(CU 0.16)**

Diluted EPS calculation

Profit from continuing operations attributable to ordinary equity holders of the parent entity		CU 990,000
Plus: profit impact of assumed conversions		
Preference shares dividends	CU 10,000	
Effect of assumed conversions		CU 10,000
Profit from continuing operations attributable to ordinary equity holders of the parent entity including assumed conversions		CU 1,000,000
Loss from discontinuing operations attributable to the parent entity		(CU 2,000,000)
Loss attributable to ordinary equity holders of the parent entity including assumed conversions		(CU 1,000,000)

Weighted-average shares			6,480,000
Plus: incremental shares from assumed conversions			
Warrants	61,538	(k)	
Convertible preference shares	200,000		
Dilutive potential ordinary shares			261,538
Adjusted weighted-average shares			6,741,538

Diluted EPS

Profit from continuing operations	**CU 0.15**
Loss from discontinuing operations	**(CU 0.30)**
Loss	**(CU 0.15)**

(k)   [(CU 65 – CU 55) ÷ CU 65] × 600,000 = 92,308 shares; 92,308 × 2/3 = 61,538 shares
Note: The incremental shares from assumed conversions are included in calculating the diluted per-share amounts for the loss from discontinuing operations and loss even though they are antidilutive. This is because the control number (profit from continuing operations attributable to ordinary equity holders of the parent entity, adjusted for preference dividends) was positive (i.e. profit, rather than loss).

Fourth Quarter 20X1

Basic and diluted EPS calculation	*CU*
Loss from continuing operations attributable to the parent entity	(700,000)
Add: preference shares dividends	(10,000)
Loss attributable to ordinary equity holders of the parent entity	(710,000)

Dates	*Shares outstanding*	*Fraction of period*	*Weighted-average shares*
1October-31 December	6,880,000	3/3	6,880,000
Weighted-average shares			6,880,000

Basic and diluted EPS

Loss attributable to ordinary equity holders of the parent entity	**(CU 0.10)**

Note: The incremental shares from assumed conversions are not included in calculating the diluted per-share amounts because the control number (loss from continuing operations attributable to ordinary equity holders of the parent entity adjusted for preference dividends) was negative (i.e. a loss, rather than profit).

Full Year 20X1

Basic EPS calculation	*CU*
Profit from continuing operations attributable to the parent entity	11,800,000
Less: preference shares dividends	(70,000)
Profit from continuing operations attributable to ordinary equity holders of the parent entity	11,730,000
Loss from discontinuing operations attributable to the parent entity	(2,000,000)
Profit attributable to ordinary equity holders of the parent entity	9,730,000

Dates	*Shares Outstanding*	*Fraction of period*	*Weighted-average shares*
1 January-28 February	5,000,000	2/12	833,333
Issue of ordinary shares on 1March	200,000		
1 March-31 March	5,200,000	1/12	433,333
Conversion of 5% bonds on 1April	480,000		
1 April-31 May	5,680,000	2/12	946,667
Conversion of preference shares on 1June	600,000		
1 June-31 August	6,280,000	3/12	1,570,000
Exercise of warrants on 1September	600,000		
1 September-31 December	6,880,000	4/12	2,293,333
Weighted-average shares			6,076,667

Basic EPS

Profit from continuing operations	**CU 1.93**
Loss from discontinuing operations	**(CU 0.33)**
Profit	**CU 1.60**

Diluted EPS calculation

Profit from continuing operations attributable to ordinary equity holders of the parent entity		CU 11,730,000
Plus: profit impact of assumed conversions		
Preference share dividends	CU 70,000	
Interest on 5% convertible bonds	CU 90,000 (l)	
Effect of assumed conversions		CU 160,000
Profit from continuing operations attributable to ordinary equity holders of the parent entity including assumed conversions		CU 11,890,000
Loss from discontinuing operations attributable to the parent entity		(CU 2,000,000)
Profit attributable to ordinary equity holders of the parent entity including assumed conversions		CU 9,890,000
Weighted-average shares		6,076,667
Plus: incremental shares from assumed conversions		
Warrants	14,880 (m)	
Convertible preference shares	450,000 (n)	
5% convertible bonds	120,000 (o)	
Dilutive potential ordinary shares		584,880
Adjusted weighted-average shares		6,661,547
Diluted EPS		
Profit from continuing operations		**CU 1.78**
Loss from discontinuing operations		**(CU 0.30)**
Profit		**CU 1.48**

(l) (CU 12,000,000 × 5%) ÷ 4; less taxes at 40%

(m) [(CU 57.125* − CU 55) ÷ CU 57.125] × 600,000 = 22,320 shares; 22,320 × 8/12 = 14,880 shares

   * The average market price from 1 January 20X1 to 1 September 20X1

(n) (800,000 shares × 5/12) + (200,000 shares × 7/12)

(o) 480,000 shares × 3/12

The following illustrates how Company A might present its earnings per share data on its income statement. Note that the amounts per share for the loss from discontinuing operations are not required to be presented on the face of the income statement.

	For the year ended 20X1 *CU*
Earnings per ordinary share	
Profit from continuing operations	1.93
Loss from discontinuing operations	(0.33)
Profit	1.60
Diluted earnings per ordinary share	
Profit from continuing operations	1.78
Loss from discontinuing operations	(0.30)
Profit	1.48

The following table includes the quarterly and annual earnings per share data for Company A. The purpose of this table is to illustrate that the sum of the four quarters' earnings per share data will not necessarily equal the annual earnings per share data. The Standard does not require disclosure of this information.

	First quarter CU	Second quarter CU	Third quarter CU	Fourth quarter CU	Full year CU
Basic EPS					
Profit (loss) from continuing operations	0.98	1.10	0.15	(0.10)	1.93
Loss from discontinuing operations	–	–	(0.31)	–	(0.33)
Profit (loss)	0.98	1.10	(0.16)	(0.10)	1.60
Diluted EPS					
Profit (loss) from continuing operations	0.80	1.00	0.15	(0.10)	1.78
Loss from discontinuing operations	–	–	(0.30)	–	(0.30)
Profit (loss)	0.80	1.00	(0.15)	(0.10)	1.48

This example does not illustrate the classification of the components of convertible financial instruments as liabilities and equity or the classification of related interest and dividends as expenses and equity as required by IAS 32.

References

1 IAS 33 (1997), *Earnings per Share*, IASC, February 1997.
2 SIC-24, *Earnings Per Share – Financial Instruments and Other Contracts that May Be Settled in Shares*, SIC, November 2000 (superseded December 2003).
3 IAS 33, *Earnings per Share*, IASB, December 2003 (amended March 2004), para. IN3.
4 IFRS 2, *Share-based Payment*, IASB, February 2004 and IFRS 3, *Business Combinations*, IASB, March 2004.
5 IAS 33, para. 74.
6 IAS 33, para. 1.
7 IAS 33, para. 11.
8 IAS 33, para. 32.
9 IAS 33, para. 2.
10 IAS 33, para. 3.
11 IAS 33, para. 4.
12 IAS 33, para. 9.
13 IAS 33, para. 10.
14 IAS 33, para. 12.
15 IAS 33, paras. 13 and A1; IAS 1, *Presentation of Financial Statements*, IASB, December 2003 (amended March 2004), paras. 78 and 82.
16 IAS 33, para. 12.
17 IAS 33, para. 5.
18 IAS 33, para. 8 and IAS 32, *Financial Instruments: Disclosure and Presentation*, IASB, December 2003 (amended March 2004), para. 11.
19 IAS 33, para. 6.
20 IAS 33, paras. 6 and 66.
21 IAS 33, para. 19.
22 IAS 33, para. A15.
23 IAS 33, Illustrative Examples, Example 2.
24 IAS 33, para. 25.
25 IAS 33, para. 21.
26 IAS 33, para. 23.
27 IAS 33, para. 21.
28 IAS 33, para. 24.
29 IAS 33, para. 24.
30 IAS 33, para. 20.
31 IAS 33, Illustrative Examples, Example 2.
32 IAS 33, para. 26.
33 IAS 33, para. 27.
34 A put warrant, involving the repurchase of shares at significantly more than their fair value is included as an example in the equivalent standard in the UK which was developed at the same time as, and is very similar to, IAS 33.
35 IAS 33, para. 64.
36 IAS 33, para. 28.
37 IAS 33, Illustrative Examples, Example 3.
38 IAS 33, para. 29.
39 IAS 33, para. 29.

40 IAS 33, paras. 26-27.
41 IAS 33, para. A2.
42 IAS 33, para. A2.
43 IAS 33, para. A2.
44 IAS 33, Illustrative Examples, Example 4.
45 IAS 33, para. 29.
46 The relevant UK standard is FRS 14 – *Earnings per share*. It was developed at the same time as IAS 33 and the US standard FAS 128 in conjunction with the IASC and the FASB. All three standards contain very similar requirements.
47 IAS 33, para. 38.
48 IAS 33, para. 26.
49 IAS 33, para. 64.
50 IAS 33, paras. 21(f) and 22.
51 IFRS 3, para. B12.
52 IFRS 3, para. B13.
53 IFRS 3, para. B14.
54 IFRS 3, para. B15.
55 IAS 33, para. 14(a).
56 IAS 33, para. 14(b).
57 IAS 33, para. 15.
58 IAS 33, para. 16.
59 IAS 33, para. 17.
60 IAS 33, para. 18.
61 IAS 33, Illustrative Examples, Example 1.
62 IAS 33, para. 64.
63 IAS 33, para. 66.
64 IAS 33, para. A13.
65 IAS 33, para. A14.
66 IAS 33, Illustrative Examples, Example 11.
67 IAS 33, para. 73.
68 IAS 33, para. 5.
69 IAS 33, para. 7.
70 IAS 33, para. 5.
71 IAS 33, para. 32.
72 IAS 33, para. 30.
73 IAS 33, para. 31.
74 IAS 33, paras. 36 and 38.
75 IAS 33, para. 36.
76 IAS 33, para. 38.
77 IAS 33, paras. 37 and 65.
78 Proposed Improvements to International Accounting Standard IAS 33, IASB, December 2003, Invitation to Comment Question 2 and Appendix B, examples 7 and 12.
79 IAS 33, para. 33.
80 IAS 33, para. 34.
81 IAS 33, para. 35.
82 IAS 33, para. 39.
83 IAS 33, para. 58.
84 IAS 33, para. 59.
85 IAS 33, para. 60.
86 IAS 33, para. 61.
87 IAS 33, paras. 5 and 43.
88 IAS 33, para. 43.
89 IAS 33, para. 41; The consequential amendments made by IFRS 5, *Non-current Assets Held for*

Sale and Discontinued Operations, IASB, March 2004, to other standards failed to replace references in IAS 33 to discontinuing operations with references to discontinued operations. In our view this is just a drafting oversight.
90 IAS 33, para. 42.
91 IAS 33, para. A3.
92 IAS 33, para. 44.
93 IAS 33, Illustrative Examples, Example 9.
94 IAS 33, para. 49.
95 IAS 33, para. 50.
96 IAS 33, Illustrative Examples, Example 6.
97 IAS 33, Illustrative Examples, Example 8.
98 IAS 33, para. 51.
99 IAS 33, para. A14.
100 IAS 33, para. 5.
101 IAS 33, para. 44.
102 IAS 33, para. 33.
103 IAS 33, paras. 59-60.
104 IAS 33, para. A7.
105 IAS 33, para. A9.
106 IFRS 2, paras. BC54-BC57.
107 IAS 33, para. 45.
108 IAS 33, para. 46.
109 IAS 33, paras. 45-46.
110 IAS 33, Illustrative Examples, Example 5.
111 IAS 33, para. 46.
112 IAS 33, para. A4.
113 IAS 33, para. A5.
114 IAS 33, paras. 36 and 38.
115 IAS 33, para. 63.
116 IAS 33, para. A10.
117 IAS 33, para. A6.
118 IAS 33, para. A7.
119 IAS 33, para. A8.
120 IAS 33, para. A9.
121 IAS 33, para. 62.
122 IAS 33, para. A16.
123 IAS 33, para. 48.
124 IAS 33, para. 48.
125 IAS 33, para. 48.
126 IAS 33, para. 47A.
127 IAS 33, Illustrative Examples, Example 5A.
128 IAS 33, para. 5.
129 IAS 33, para. 52.
130 IAS 33, para. 32.
131 IAS 33, para. 55.
132 IAS 33, para. 53.
133 IAS 33, para. 53.
134 IAS 33, Illustrative Examples, Example 7.
135 IFRS 3, para. 32.
136 IFRS 3, para. 33.
137 IAS 33, para. 56.
138 IAS 33, para. 54.
139 IAS 33, para. 56.
140 IFRS 3, paras. 32-33.
141 IAS 33, para. 40.
142 IAS 33, para. A11.

143 IAS 33, para. A12.
144 IAS 33, Illustrative Examples, Example 10.
145 IAS 33, para. 57.
146 IAS 33, para. 5.
147 IAS 33, paras. 66 and 69.
148 IAS 33, paras. 66 and 68.
149 IAS 33, para. 66.
150 IAS 33, para. 68.
151 IAS 33, para. 67.
152 The consequential amendments made by IFRS 5 to other standards failed to replace references in IAS 33 to discontinuing operations with references to discontinued operations. In our view this is just a drafting oversight.
153 IFRS 5, para. 33.
154 IAS 33, paras. 26 and 64.
155 IAS 33, para. 64.
156 IAS 33, para. 29.
157 IAS 33, para. 47.
158 IAS 33, para. 52.
159 IAS 33, para. 65.
160 IAS 33, para. 70.
161 IAS 33, para. 71.
162 IAS 33, para. 72.
163 IAS 33, Illustrative Examples, Example 12.

Chapter 32   Cash flow statements

1   INTRODUCTION

The importance of providing cash flow information was originally recognised in the US by the FASB through its concepts statements. SFAC No. 1 states that 'financial reporting should provide information to help present and potential investors and creditors and other users in assessing the amounts, timing, and uncertainty of prospective cash receipts from dividends or interest and the proceeds from the sale, redemption, or maturity of securities or loans. The prospects for those cash receipts are affected by an enterprise's ability to generate enough cash to meet its obligations when due and its other cash operating needs, to reinvest in operations, and to pay cash dividends ... Thus, financial reporting should provide information to help investors, creditors, and others assess the amounts, timing, and uncertainty of prospective net inflows to the related enterprise.'[1]

Further recognition of the need to provide cash flow information was given by SFAC No. 5, which states that 'a full set of financial statements for a period should show: ... cash flows during the period.'[2] It adds that 'a statement of cash flows directly or indirectly reflects an entity's cash receipts classified by major sources and its cash payments classified by major uses during a period. It provides useful information about an entity's activities in generating cash through operations to repay debt, distribute dividends, or reinvest to maintain or expand operating capacity; about its financing activities, both debt and equity; and about its investing or spending of cash. Important uses of information about an entity's current cash receipts and payments include helping to assess factors such as the entity's liquidity, financial flexibility, profitability, and risk.'[3]

As a result of the increasing recognition of the significance of cash flow information, the FASB issued SFAS 95 – *Statement of Cash Flows* – in November 1987. The US requirement to present a statement of cash flows started a worldwide trend in financial reporting.

The IASC had originally approved IAS 7 – *Statement of Changes in Financial Position* – in July 1977. This had required the presentation of a statement of sources and uses of funds. A project on cash flow statements was started in April 1989 and this culminated in the publication in 1992 of a revised version of IAS 7 – *Cash Flow Statements* – which, as the title suggests, required entities to prepare a cash flow statement.[4] Further amendments have been made as a consequence of the revisions to IAS 21 – *The Effects of Changes in Foreign Exchange Rates* – and IAS 8 – *Accounting Policies, Changes in Accounting Estimates and Errors,* – published in December 2003. Additional cash flow disclosures have been introduced in IFRS 4 – *Insurance Contracts* – and IFRS 5 – *Non-current Assets Held for Sale and Discontinued Operations.*

The amended version of IAS 7 is mandatory for financial periods beginning on or after 1 January 2005. If an entity applies any of the above standards for an earlier period, the entity is required also to apply the amended version of IAS 7.

2   THE REQUIREMENTS OF IAS 7

2.1   Objective and scope

2.1.1   Objective

The stated objective of IAS 7 is 'to require the provision of information about the historical changes in cash and cash equivalents of an entity by means of a cash flow statement which classifies cash flows during the period from operating, investing and financing activities'. In this way the standard aims to give users of financial statements a basis with which to evaluate the entity's ability to generate cash and cash equivalents and its needs to utilise those cash flows.[5]

The standard puts forward a number of benefits of cash flow information, stating that a cash flow statement can be used with the rest of the financial statements to provide information that helps users evaluate among other things the ability of the entity to influence its cash flows to adapt in the face of changing circumstances and opportunities. The cash flow statement also plays an important role in allowing the operating performance of different entities to be compared, as it eliminates the effects of using different accounting treatments for the same transactions and events.[6] The standard also suggests that historical cash flow information is often used as an indicator of the amount, timing and certainty of future cash flows and that it is useful in checking the accuracy of past assessments of future cash flows and in examining the relationship between profitability and net cash flow and the impact of changing prices.[7]

It is questionable whether all these properties can really be attributed to a statement that shows the historical changes in an entity's cash and cash equivalents. Generally it is useful in highlighting both similarities and differences between the elements of profitability and net cash flow. It is also the case that cash flow information is influenced less by the effect of different accounting treatments, although arguably the efforts of standard setters to limit the availability of alternative treatments, harmonise standards across jurisdictions and reduce ambiguity in their application have a greater role to play in this regard. However, even in conjunction with the other disclosures in the financial statements, a user would find it difficult to assess an entity's financial adaptability, the timing and certainty of future cash flows and the impact of changing prices without a meaningful management commentary accompanying the financial statements.

2.1.2 Scope

IAS 7 applies to all entities, regardless of size, ownership structure or industry, and therefore includes wholly owned subsidiaries and banks, insurance entities and other financial institutions. The reason for this is explained as follows: 'Users of an entity's financial statements are interested in how the entity generates and uses cash and cash equivalents. This is the case regardless of the nature of the entity's activities and irrespective of whether cash can be viewed as the product of the entity, as may be the case with a financial institution. Entities need cash for essentially the same reasons however different their principal revenue-producing activities might be. They need cash to conduct their operations, to pay their obligations, and to provide returns to their investors. Accordingly, this Standard requires all entities to present a cash flow statement.'[8]

2.1.3 First-time adoption

Just as there are no exemptions or concessions available to entities that already apply IAS 7, all entities making the transition to IFRS are required to present cash flow information in accordance with the standard for all periods following the date of transition.

In addition, if an entity presented a cash flow statement under its previous GAAP, it is required to explain the material adjustments to the cash flow statement.[9] Such disclosures would include an explanation of material cash flows that have been reclassified in the cash flow statement prepared under IFRS[10] and would have to identify material differences in the measurement of cash flows, for example in relation to foreign currencies (see 2.5.2 below).

2.2 Cash and cash equivalents

2.2.1 Definitions

Since the objective of a cash flow statement is to provide an analysis of changes in cash and cash equivalents, the definitions of cash and cash equivalents are essential to its presentation. However, as will be seen below, the definition of cash equivalents can cause some difficulty in practice.

Cash and cash equivalents are defined in IAS 7 as follows:

Cash – 'Cash on hand and demand deposits'.[11]

Cash equivalents – 'Short-term, highly liquid investments that are readily convertible to known amounts of cash and which are subject to an insignificant risk of changes in value'.[12]

2.2.2   *Components of cash and cash equivalents*

Cash equivalents are held for the purpose of meeting short-term cash commitments rather than for investment or other purposes. For an investment to qualify as a cash equivalent it must be readily convertible to a known amount of cash and be subject to an insignificant risk of changes in value. Normally only an investment with a short maturity of, say, three months or less from the date of acquisition qualifies under the above definition. Equity investments are excluded unless they are cash equivalents in substance, an example being redeemable preference shares acquired within a short period of their maturity and with a specified redemption date.[13]

Although bank borrowings are generally considered to be financing activities, bank overdrafts repayable on demand are included as a component of cash and cash equivalents. This is because such arrangements can form an integral part of an entity's cash management processes and typically the bank balance often fluctuates from being positive to overdrawn.[14]

IAS 7 defines cash flows as 'inflows and outflows of cash and cash equivalents'.[15] This definition aims to reflect the reality of the cash management policies employed by an entity. Cash management includes the investment of cash in excess of immediate needs into cash equivalents,[16] such as short-term investments. Provided these investments are highly liquid, are readily convertible into known amounts of cash and are subject to insignificant risk of changes in value, they are in substance equivalent to cash.[17] As such, cash flows under IAS 7 exclude movements between cash in hand and highly liquid investments because these are components of an entity's cash management, rather than part of its operating, investing and financing activities.[18]

An investment that is quoted in an active market would be readily convertible to known amounts of cash and, as such, could be regarded as highly liquid. However, this is not enough to meet the definition of a cash equivalent, which requires the risk of changes in value to be insignificant.[19] The longer the term of the investment, the greater the risk that a change in market conditions (such as interest rates) can have an effect on its value that is other than insignificant. For this reason IAS 7 restricts the definition of cash equivalents to short-term investments, and suggests that normally this would include only investments with a short maturity of, say, three months or less from the date of acquisition.[20] After its acquisition an investment with a longer term is not reclassified as a cash equivalent, for example from the date on which there is less than three months remaining to its maturity. If such reclassifications were permitted, the cash flow statement would have to reflect movements between investments and cash equivalents. This would be misleading because no actual cash flows would have occurred.

VTech Holdings includes short-term investments and bank overdrafts as components of cash equivalents.

Extract 32.1: VTech Holdings Limited (2003)

Principal Accounting Policies [extract]

P   CASH AND CASH EQUIVALENTS [extract]

For the purpose of the cash flow statement, cash and cash equivalents comprise cash on hand, demand deposits with banks and other financial institutions, short-term highly liquid investments that are readily convertible into known amounts of cash and which are subject to an insignificant risk of changes in value and which have a maturity of three months or less at acquisition. Bank overdrafts that are repayable on demand and form an integral part of the Group's cash management are also included as a component of cash and cash equivalents.

Lufthansa reconciles the requirement to report cash and cash equivalents (as defined in IAS 7) with the wish to include all the assets used by the entity to manage its liquidity, by adding lines of analysis to the foot of the cash flow statement. The cash flow statement is shown in Extract 32.8 at 2.3.4 below and management adds the following note to the financial statements.

Extract 32.2: Deutsche Lufthansa AG (2003)

Note to the Consolidated Cash Flow Statement

The cash flow statement shows the change in cash and cash equivalents of the Lufthansa Group in the year under review. As required by IAS 7, cash flows have been divided into operating cash flow (corresponding to the cash inflow from operating activities) as well as investing and financing activities. Cash and cash equivalents disclosed in the cash flow statement comprise bank balances (without time deposit credit balances) and cash in hand. The balance of liquid funds in a wider sense can be determined by including securities held as current assets and long-term time deposit credit balances.

The amount shown alongside the caption in the balance sheet for 'cash and cash equivalents' will not always be a reliable guide for IAS 7 purposes.[21] Apart from the need to include overdrafts for cash flow purposes, many entities present the constituents of cash and cash equivalents separately on the face of the balance sheet, such as 'cash and bank balances' and 'bank deposits'. However, the standard requires an entity to disclose the components of cash and cash equivalents and to present a reconciliation to the balance sheet,[22] which means that any difference between 'cash and cash equivalents' for IAS 7 purposes and in the balance sheet presentation will be evident in the notes to the financial statements.

Entities are also required to disclose the policy adopted in determining the composition of cash and cash equivalents.[23] Changes in that policy, such as a reclassification of financial instruments previously considered as being part of an entity's investment portfolio, should be reported under IAS 8.[24]

Mandarin Oriental International provides a reconciliation of the components of cash and cash equivalents, which includes overdrafts.

Extract 32.3: Mandarin Oriental International Limited (2003)

25 Notes to the consolidated cash flow statement [extract]

e) Analysis of cash and cash equivalents

	2003 US$m	2002 US$m
Cash at bank	66.1	65.9
Bank overdrafts	(0.1)	(0.1)
	66.0	65.8

Principal accounting policies [extract]

J Cash and cash equivalents

Cash and cash equivalents are carried in the balance sheet at cost. For the purposes of the cash flow statement, cash and cash equivalents comprise deposits with banks and financial institutions and bank and cash balances, net of bank overdrafts. In the balance sheet, bank overdrafts are included within borrowings in current liabilities.

2.2.3   Restrictions on the use of cash and cash equivalents

The amount of significant cash and cash equivalent balances that are not available for use by the group should be disclosed, together with a commentary by management to explain the circumstances of the restriction.[25] It would seem that this requirement is referring to the balance sheet amounts, not the cash flows during the period.

Examples include cash and cash equivalents held by a subsidiary operating under exchange controls or other legal restrictions that prevent their general use by the parent or other subsidiaries.[26]

Extract 32.4: Netia S.A. (2003)

6   Restricted Investments, Cash and Cash Equivalents [extract]

	December 31, 2002 (PLN)	December 31, 2003 (PLN)
Current portion		
2000 Notes – Investment Account	54,866	–
2002 Notes – Restricted Accounts	199,345	–
	254,211	–

On December 20, 2002 the Company established a restricted account as a temporary security for the 2002 Notes. As at December 31, 2002 cash deposited into this account amounted to PLN 63,256. On December 23, 2002, the Company entered into agreements on security assignment of rights to investment accounts as a temporary security for obligations of NH BV arising from the issue of the 2002 Notes. The value of these accounts amounted to PLN 136,089 as at December 31, 2002. On January 3, 2003 securities of PLN 80,265 were transferred to an escrow account securing the 2002 Notes. On March 24, 2003, the Company redeemed the outstanding 2002 Notes amounting to EUR 51,096 (PLN 221,482 at the exchange rate in effect on that date) including interest accrued until that date. Restricted cash and cash equivalents established as temporary security for 2002 Notes, were released in connection with the redemption.

2.3   Presentation of the cash flow statement

The cash flow statement reports inflows and outflows of cash and cash equivalents during the period classified under:[27]

- operating activities;
- investing activities; and
- financing activities.

This classification is intended to allow users to assess the impact of these three types of activity on the financial position of the entity and the amount of its cash and cash equivalents. Components fall under operating, investing or financing cash flows in a manner which is most appropriate to the business of the entity.[28] The standard notes that a single transaction may comprise differently classified cash flows. For example, when repayments on a loan include both interest and capital, the interest element may be included in operating activities whereas the capital repayment is a financing cash flow.[29] Whilst not stated explicitly in the standard, the presentation usually follows this sequence and a total net cash flow for each standard heading should be shown. Comparative figures are required for all items in the cash flow statement and the related notes.[30]

The format of the cash flow statement is illustrated in Extract 32.5. As permitted by the standard (and as discussed further at 2.3.4), Nestlé has included interest received and paid under operating activities, dividends received from associates under investing activities and dividends paid under financing activities. However, it is not clear why the cash flows related to marketable securities and other liquid assets as well as short term investments are included as part of financing rather than investing activities. Possibly, this is because the entity regards investing in these assets as part of its normal treasury management.

Extract 32.5: Nestlé S.A. (2003)

Consolidated cash flow statement for the year ended 31st December 2003 [extract]

In millions of CHF	**2003**	2002
Operating activities		
Net profit of consolidated companies	**6,000**	7,389
Depreciation of property, plant and equipment	**2,408**	2,542
Impairment of property, plant and equipment	**148**	1,316
Amortisation of goodwill	**1,571**	1,438
Impairment of goodwill	**–**	839
Depreciation of intangible assets	**255**	189
Impairment of intangible assets	**74**	41
Increase/(decrease) in provision and deferred taxes	**312**	343
Decrease/(increase) in working capital	**(688)**	787
Other movements	**45**	(4,636)
Operating cash flow[(a)]	**10,125**	10,248

Investing activities		
Capital expenditure	**(3,337)**	(3,577)
Expenditure on intangible assets	**(682)**	(690)
Sale of property, plant and equipment	**244**	338
Acquisitions	**(1,950)**	(5,395)
Disposals	**725**	4,684
Income from associates	**208**	154
Other movements[(b)]	**64**	(268)
Cash flow from investing activities	**(4,728)**	(4,754)
Financing activities		
Dividend for the previous year	**(2,705)**	(2,484)
Purchase of treasury shares	**(318)**	(605)
Sale of treasury shares and options	**660**	395
Movements with minority interests	**(197)**	(195)
Bonds issued	**2,305**	3,926
Bonds repaid	**(693)**	(1,639)
Increase/(decrease) in other medium/long term financial liabilities	**(134)**	(47)
Increase/(decrease) in short term financial liabilities	**(2,930)**	(3,805)
Decrease/(increase) in marketable securities and other liquid assets	**(736)**	1,309
Decrease/(increase) in short term investments	**734**	(1,251)
Other movements[(c)]	**–**	(364)
Cash flow from financing activities	**(4,014)**	(4,760)
Translation differences on flows	**(457)**	(1,648)
Increase/(decrease) in cash and cash equivalents	**926**	(914)
Cash and cash equivalents at beginning of year	**6,338**	7,617
Effects of exchange rate changes on opening balance	**(190)**	(365)
Cash and cash equivalents retranslated at beginning of year	**6,148**	7,252
Cash and cash equivalents at end of year	**7,074**	6,338

(a)	Taxes paid amount to CHF 2267 million (2002: CHF 2824 million). Net interest paid amounts to CHF 532 million (2002: CHF 661 million).
(b)	Tax payments related to investing activities amounted to CHF 660 million in 2002.
(c)	Tax payments related to financing activities amounted to CHF 406 million in 2002.

2.3.1 *Reporting cash flows from operating activities*

Operating activities are defined as 'the principal revenue-producing activities of the entity and other activities that are not investing or financing activities'.[31] This means that operating is the 'default category', with all cash flows which do not fall within either the investing or financing classifications being automatically deemed to be of an operating nature. The standard states that the value of information on operating cash flows is twofold. It provides a key indicator of extent to which the entity has generated sufficient cash flows from its operations to repay debt, pay dividends and make investments to maintain and increase its operating capability without recourse to external sources of financing. Also, information about the components of historical operating cash flows may assist in the process of forecasting future operating cash flows,[32] but on its own the predictive value of this information would be limited.

Cash flows from operating activities generally result from transactions and other events that enter into the determination of profit or loss. Examples include:[33]

(a)   cash receipts from the sale of goods and the rendering of services;

(b)   cash receipts from royalties, fees, commissions and other revenue;

(c)   cash payments to suppliers for goods and services;

(d)   cash payments to and on behalf of employees;

(e)   cash receipts and cash payments of an insurance entity for premiums and claims, annuities and other policy benefits;

(f)   cash payments or refunds of income taxes unless they can be specifically identified with financing and investing activities; and

(g)   cash receipts and payments from contracts held for dealing or trading purposes.

When an entity holds securities and loans for dealing or trading purposes they are similar to inventory acquired specifically for resale. Therefore any related cash flows are classified as operating activities. Similarly, cash advances and loans made by financial institutions are usually classified as operating activities since they relate to the main revenue-generating activity of that entity.[34]

An example of an item that enters into the determination of profit or loss that is *not* an operating cash flow arises from the sale of property, plant and equipment, which is included in cash flows from investing activities.[35]

Cash flows from operating activities may be reported on a gross or net basis, also known as the direct and indirect methods.[36]

A   The direct method

Under the direct method, major classes of gross cash receipts and gross cash payments are disclosed.[37] IAS 7 encourages entities to use the direct method, on the grounds that it provides information which may be useful in estimating future cash flows and which is not available under the indirect method.[38]

Under the direct method, information about major classes of gross cash receipts and payments may be obtained either:[39]

(a)   from the accounting records of the entity (essentially based on an analysis of the cash book); or

(b)   by adjusting sales, cost of sales (interest and similar income and interest expenses and similar charges for a financial institution) and other items in the income statement for:

(i)   changes during the period in inventories and operating receivables and payables;

(ii)   other non-cash items; and

(iii)   other items for which the cash effects are investing or financing cash flows.

The financial statements should include the same disclosures of gross cash receipts and gross cash payments irrespective of which approach has been used to determine their value. In particular, there is no requirement for entities using the approach described in (b) above to present a reconciliation showing the adjustments made between, for example, revenue in the income statement and cash receipts from customers.

The IASB is contemplating whether reporting under the direct method should be mandatory, as it considers its project on reporting comprehensive income (see Chapter 3 at section 7).[40] This is somewhat surprising since most entities preparing consolidated financial statements choose to avoid using the direct method, probably because of the additional clerical burden arising from the need to collect and analyse cash transactions across a whole group.

However, AngloGold is an example of an entity using the direct method for presenting its cash flows from operating activities.

Extract 32.6: AngloGold Limited (2003)

Group cash flow statement for the year ended 31 December 2003 [extract]

2002	2003	Figures in millions	2003	2002
SA Rands			**US Dollars**	
		Cash flows from operating activities		
19,020	**15,712**	Cash receipts from customers	**2,075**	1,808
(10,765)	**(11,185)**	Cash paid to suppliers and employees	**(1,483)**	(1,050)
8,255	**4,527**	Cash generated from operations	**592**	758
331	**245**	Interest received	**33**	32
(169)	**(232)**	Environmental contributions and expenditure	**(31)**	(16)
19	**9**	Dividends received from associates	**1**	2
(410)	**(291)**	Finance costs	**(40)**	(40)
–	**681**	Recoupments tax received: Free State assets	**91**	–
–	**(681)**	Recoupments tax paid: Free State assets	**(91)**	–
(1,376)	**(780)**	Taxation paid	**(102)**	(131)
6,650	**3,478**	Net cash inflow from operating activities	**453**	605

B   The indirect method

The indirect method arrives at the same value for net cash flow from operating activities, but does so by working back from reported profit or loss in the form of a reconciliation, adjusting for the effects of:[41]

(a)   changes during the period in inventories and operating receivables and payables);

(b)   non-cash items such as depreciation, provisions, deferred taxes, unrealised foreign currency gains and losses, undistributed profits of associates and minority interests; and

(c)   all other items for which the cash effects are investing or financing cash flows.

Extract 32.7: VTech Holdings Limited (2003)

CONSOLIDATED CASH FLOW STATEMENT [extract]

For the year ended 31st March 2003

	2003 **US$ million**	2002 US$ million
Operating activities		
Operating profit	**59.5**	23.0
Depreciation charges	**24.1**	33.8
Amortization of leasehold land payments	**0.1**	0.1
Impairment of leasehold land payments	**0.2**	–
Impairment of tangible assets	–	3.6
Impairment of investment properties	–	0.5
Loss on disposal of tangible assets and leasehold land	**1.4**	2.0
Gain on settlement of a lawsuit	**(34.0)**	–
Write down of discontinued stocks	–	1.7
Decrease in stocks	**10.4**	91.4
Decrease in debtors and prepayments	**25.4**	90.8
Decrease in creditors and accruals	**(7.7)**	(63.4)
Increase/(decrease) in provisions	**1.2**	(27.2)
Cash generated from operations	**80.6**	156.3
Net proceeds on settlement of a lawsuit	**34.0**	–
Interest received	**1.2**	3.0
Interest paid	**(2.2)**	(11.6)
Taxes Paid	**(3.0)**	(0.9)
Net cash generated from operating activities	**110.6**	146.8

Alternatively, the presentation under the indirect method can show the revenues and expenses disclosed in the income statement and the changes during the period in inventories and operating receivables and payables.[42]

To obtain the cash flow information for the indirect method, the balance sheet figures have to be analysed according to the three standard headings in the cash flow statement. Thus the reconciliation of profit or loss to cash flow from operating activities will include, not the increase or decrease in all debtors or creditors, but only those elements which relate to operating activities. For example, accrued interest or amounts payable in respect of the acquisition of property, plant and equipment, intangibles or investments will be excluded from the movement in creditors included in this reconciliation. Although this may not present practical difficulties in the preparation of single entity cash flow statements, it is necessary to ensure that sufficient information is collected from subsidiaries for purposes of preparing the group cash flow statement. Where a group has made an acquisition of a subsidiary during the year, the change in working capital items will have to be split between the increase due to the acquisition (to the extent that the purchase consideration was settled in cash this will effectively be shown under investing activities) and the element related to operating activities which will be shown in the reconciliation.

2.3.2   Cash flows from investing activities

Investing activities are defined as 'the acquisition and disposal of long-term assets and other investments not included in cash equivalents'.[43] This classification allows users of the financial statements to understand the extent to which expenditures have been made for resources intended to generate future income and cash flows. Cash flows arising from investing activities include:[44]

(a)   payments to acquire, and receipts from the sale of, property, plant and equipment, intangibles and other long-term assets (including payments and receipts relating to capitalised development costs and self-constructed property, plant and equipment);

(b)   payments to acquire, and receipts from the sale of, equity or debt instruments of other entities and interests in jointly controlled entities (other than payments and receipts for those instruments considered to be cash equivalents or those held for dealing or trading purposes);

(c)   advances and loans made to, and repaid by, other parties (other than advances and loans made by a financial institution); and

(d)   cash payments for, and receipts from, futures contracts, forward contracts, option contracts and swap contracts except when the contracts are held for dealing or trading purposes, or the cash flows are classified as financing activities.

When a contract is accounted for as a hedge of an identifiable position, the cash flows of the contract are classified under the same heading as the cash flows of the position being hedged.[45]

An example is an interest rate swap. An entity wishing to convert an existing fixed rate borrowing into a floating rate equivalent could enter into an interest rate swap under which it receives fixed rates and pays floating rates. All the cash flows under the swap should be reported under the same cash flow heading (this would be either as financing activities or operating activities, in accordance with the entity's determined policy (see 2.3.4 below) because they are equivalent to interest or are hedges of interest payments.

Major classes of gross receipts and gross payments arising from investing activities should be reported separately, except for those items that can be reported on a net basis, as discussed in 2.5.1 below.[46]

2.3.3 Cash flows from financing activities

Financing activities are defined as those 'activities that result in changes in the size and composition of the contributed equity and borrowings of the entity'.[47] The standard states that this information is useful in predicting claims on future cash flows by providers of capital to the entity.[48] However it would seem more likely that information on financing cash flows would indicate the extent to which the entity has had recourse to external financing to meet its operating and investing needs in the period. The disclosure of the value and maturity of the entity's financial liabilities would contribute more to predicting future claims on cash flows.

Cash flows arising from financing activities include:[49]

(a) proceeds from issuing shares or other equity instruments;

(b) payments to owners to acquire or redeem the entity's shares;

(c) proceeds from issuing, and outflows to repay, debentures, loans, notes, bonds, mortgages and other short or long-term borrowings; and

(d) payments by a lessee for the reduction of the outstanding liability relating to a finance lease.

Major classes of gross receipts and gross payments arising from financing activities should be reported separately, except for those items that can be reported on a net basis, as discussed in 2.5.1 below.[50]

2.3.4 Allocating items to operating, investing and financing activities

Sometimes it is not clear how cash flows should be classified between operating, investing and financing activities. IAS 7 provides additional guidance on the classification of interest, dividends and income taxes. However, this guidance does little to impose consistency and comparability between entities.

A   Interest and dividends

An entity can choose to classify cash flows from interest and dividends received and paid as either operating, investing or financing activities, provided that a consistent approach is adopted from period to period and that each class of cash flow is disclosed separately.[51] For a financial institution, interest paid and interest and dividends received are usually classified as operating cash flows. However IAS 7 notes that there is no consensus on the classification of these cash flows for other entities and suggests that interest paid can be classified under either operating or financing activities, and interest and dividends received can be included in either operating or investing cash flows.[52] The standard allows dividends paid to be classified as a financing cash flow (because they are a cost of obtaining financial resources) or as a component of cash flows from operating activities.[53]

In Extract 32.5 in 2.3 above, Nestlé has included interest received and paid under operating activities, dividends received from associates under investing activities and dividends paid under financing activities, as permitted by the standard.

Nevertheless, it could be argued that entities which do not include interest or dividends received within revenue should not include interest or dividends in operating cash flows, because cash flows from operating activities are primarily derived from the principal revenue-producing activities of the entity,[54] and the amount of cash flows arising from operating activities is intended to be a key indicator of the extent to which the operations of the entity has generated sufficient cash flows to repay loans, pay dividends and make new investments without recourse to external sources of financing.[55] On this basis, interest paid would be a financing cash flow and interest and dividends received classified as investing cash flows.[56] Such entities would also treat dividends paid as a financing cash flow because they are a cost of obtaining financial resources.[57]

This approach is taken by Lufthansa.

Extract 32.8: Deutsche Lufthansa AG (2003)

Consolidated Cash Flow Statement [extract]

	2003 €m	2002 €m
Purchase of tangible assts and intangible assets	- 839	-364
Purchase of financial assets	-138	- 90
Additions to repairable aircraft spare parts	-68	-79
Proceeds from sale of non-consolidated equity investments	13	808
Acquisition of non-consolidated equity investments	-45	-126
Acquisition of consolidated equity investments	-133	-10
Proceeds from disposals of intangible assets, tangible assets and other financial assets	416	176
Interest received	182	136
Dividends received	55	50
Net cash used in investing activities	**- 557**	**501**
Securities/fixed-term deposits	-137	- 578
Net cash used in investing activities and cash investments	**-694**	**-77**
Premium from bond floatation	–	128
Long-term borrowings	291	1,020
Repayments of long-term borrowings	-1,135	- 531
Other borrowings	13	- 489
Dividends paid	-229	–
Interest paid	-277	-289
Net cash used in financing activities	**- 1,337**	**- 161**
Net decrease/increase in cash and cash equivalents	**- 450**	**2,074**
Effects of exchange rate changes	- 2	1
Cash and cash equivalents on 31 December	**2,001**	**2,453**
Securities	720	584
Term deposits	–	601
Total liquid funds	**2,721**	**3,638**

In our opinion both treatments are equally acceptable. In addition the standard requires the total amount of interest paid during the period to be disclosed in the cash flow statement whether it has been recognised as an expense or capitalised as part of the cost of an asset in accordance with the allowed alternative under IAS 23 – *Borrowing Costs*.[58] Whilst a literal reading of this requirement might suggest that interest paid should be disclosed as a single figure under one of the three headings, it would seem appropriate to follow the US approach of classifying the element of interest that has been capitalised as an investing activity,[59] provided that where this is done the total amount of interest paid is also disclosed, either on the face of the cash flow statement or in the notes.

B   Taxes on income

Cash flows arising from taxes on income should be separately disclosed within operating cash flows unless they can be specifically identified with investing or financing activities.[60]

Taxes paid are usually classified as cash flows from operating activities because it is often impracticable to match tax cash flows with specific investing and financing activities and the cash flows may arise in a different period to the underlying transaction.[61] This is the presentation adopted by VTech Holdings in Extract 32.7 at 2.3.1 above. However, when it is practicable to make this determination, the tax cash flow is identified as an investing or financing activity in accordance with the individual transaction that gives rise to such cash flows. In cases where tax cash flows are allocated outside operating activities, the entity should disclose the total amount for taxes paid.[62] Nestlé has identified tax cash flows within investing and financing activities in Extract 32.5 at 2.3 above and disclosed the amounts included within each classification by way of footnote. However, it is not clear whether footnote (a) discloses the tax cash flows included in operating activities or, as required by IAS 7, the total amount for taxes paid.

2.3.5   *Exceptional and extraordinary items*

The December 2003 revisions to IAS 1 and IAS 8 eliminate the concept of extraordinary items and IAS 1 goes on to prohibit the presentation of extraordinary items either on the face of the income statement or in the notes.[63] Consequently, IAS 7 no longer refers to extraordinary items, which previously had to be classified according to their nature as either operating, investing or financing flows and disclosed separately.[64]

IAS 1 still requires the nature and amount of material items of income and expense to be disclosed separately[65] and requires additional line items, headings and sub-totals to be presented on the face of the balance sheet when this is relevant to an understanding of the entity's financial position.[66] Therefore, whilst IAS 7 is now silent on the matter, it is not unreasonable for material cash flows or cash flows relating to material items in the income statement to be presented as separate line items on the face of the cash flow statement, provided that they remain classified according to their nature as either operating, investing or financing cash flows.

2.4   Groups

IAS 7 does not distinguish between single entities and groups and there are no specific requirements as to how an entity should prepare a consolidated cash flow statement. In the absence of specific requirements, cash inflows and outflows would be treated in the same way as income and expenses under IAS 27 – *Consolidated and*

Separate Financial Statements. Applying these principles, the cash flow statement presented in consolidated financial statements should reflect only the flows of cash and cash equivalents into and out of the group, i.e. consolidated cash flows are presented as those of a single economic entity.[67] Cash flows that are internal to the group (such as payments and receipts for intra-group sales, management charges, dividends, interest and financing arrangements) should be eliminated.[68] However, dividends paid to minority shareholders in subsidiaries represent an outflow of cash from the perspective of the shareholders in the parent entity. They should accordingly be included under cash flows from financing activities or operating activities, in accordance with the entity's determined policy (see 2.3.4 above).

2.4.1 *Preparation of the group cash flow statement*

In principle, the group cash flow statement should be built up from the cash flow statements prepared by individual subsidiaries with intra-group cash flows being eliminated as part of the aggregation process. This would generally be the case for entities presenting operating cash flows under the direct method, where information on gross cash receipts and payments has been obtained from each group entity's accounting records.

In practice, however, it may be possible to prepare a cash flow statement at a more consolidated level, by starting with the disclosures in the consolidated income statement and balance sheet and then applying the adjustments reflected as part of the financial statements consolidation process together with information provided on external cash flows by individual subsidiaries. Thus, an entity adopting the direct method could use this information to derive the value of the major classes of gross cash receipts and gross cash payments.[69] An entity presenting operating cash flows under the indirect method would use this information to calculate the values for movements in inventories, operating receivables and payables and other non-cash items that appear in the reconciliation of consolidated profit or loss to the group's cash flow from operating activities.[70]

Cash flows from investing and financing activities could similarly be derived from a reconciliation of the relevant headings in the consolidated income statement to balance sheet movements. However, for this to be possible subsidiaries would have to provide supplementary information (as part of internal group reporting) to prevent gross cash flows from being netted off and to ensure that the cash flows are shown under the correct classifications. In particular, detailed information about receivables and payables would be essential to ensure that the movements in operating, investing and financing receivables and payables are identified.

2.4.2 *Acquisitions and disposals*

When a subsidiary joins or leaves the group, it should be included in the consolidated cash flow statement for the same period as its results are reported in the consolidated income statement.

An entity should present separately within investing activities the aggregate cash flows arising from acquisitions and from disposals of subsidiaries or other business units.[71]

For both acquisitions and disposals of subsidiaries or other business units during the period, disclosure is also required, in aggregate, of each of the following:[72]

(a)   the total purchase or disposal consideration;

(b)   the portion of the purchase or disposal consideration discharged by means of cash and cash equivalents;

(c)   the amount of cash and cash equivalents in the subsidiary or business unit acquired or disposed of; and

(d)   the amount of the assets and liabilities other than cash or cash equivalents in the subsidiary or business unit acquired or disposed of, summarised by each major category.

The aggregate amount of cash paid or received as purchase or sale consideration is reported in the cash flow statement net of cash and cash equivalents acquired or disposed of.[73] The cash flow effects of disposals are not deducted from those of acquisitions.[74] This implies that entities should present one analysis for all acquisitions and another for all disposals, such as that presented by Danisco.

Extract 32.9: Danisco A/S (2003)

NOTES TO THE CASH FLOW STATEMENT

24 Purchase and sale of undertakings and activities DKK million	**GROUP** 2001/02	**2002/03**
Purchase of undertakings and activities: During the financial year 2002/03, the Group purchased the ingredients company Perlarom. The figures for 2002/03 also include adjustments relating to the acquisition of Germantown in 2001/02.		
Intangible fixed assets	–	(103)
Tangible fixed assets	(147)	(90)
Financial fixed assets	–	–
Stocks	(83)	(74)
Debtors and prepayments	(87)	(247)
Cash and cash equivalents	(34)	(24)
Other provisions	75	25
Provisions for deferred tax	(71)	62
Financial liabilities	–	148
Non-interest-bearing debt	84	222
Corporation tax	11	(22)
Net assets	**(252)**	**(103)**
Goodwill on purchase of undertakings and activities	(645)	(391)
Adjustment of cash and cash equivalents	34	24
Cash purchase amount	**(863)**	**(470)**
Financial liabilities	–	(148)
Purchase amount total	**(863)**	**(618)**

Sale of undertakings and activities:		
Intangible fixed assets	352	–
Tangible fixed assets	2,047	–
Financial fixed assets	(637)	–
Stocks	896	–
Debtors and prepayments	1,431	–
Cash and cash equivalents	47	–
Other provisions	(137)	–
Provisions for deferred tax	10	–
Financial liabilities	(655)	–
Non-interest-bearing debt	(1,222)	–
Corporation tax	(21)	–
Net assets	**2,111**	–
Gain on divestments	–	–
Adjustment of cash and cash equivalents	(47)	–
Cash sale amount	**2,064**	–
Financial liabilities	655	–
Sales amount total	**2,719**	–

A question that sometimes arises is how to treat a payment made to the vendor of a new subsidiary to take over a loan that is owed to the vendor by that subsidiary. Payments made to acquire debt instruments of other entities are normally included under investing activities.[75] This presentation can be contrasted with the repayment of external debt in the new subsidiary, using funds provided by the parent, which falls to be included as a cash outflow from financing activities.[76]

A similarly fine distinction might apply on the demerger of subsidiaries. These sometimes involve the repayment of intra-group indebtedness out of external finance raised by the demerged subsidiary. If the money is raised immediately prior to the subsidiary leaving the group, it is strictly a financing inflow in the consolidated cash flow statement, being cash proceeds from issuing short or long-term borrowings.[77] If the subsidiary both raises the external funding and repays the intra-group debt after the demerger, the inflow is shown in the consolidated cash flow statement under investing activities, being a cash receipt from the repayment of advances and loans made to other parties.[78]

2.4.3   Cash flows in subsidiaries, associates and joint ventures

Changes in cash and cash equivalents relating to entities accounted for under the equity or cost method will impact on the entity's cash flow statement only to the extent of the cash flows between the group and the investee. Examples include cash dividends received and loans advanced or repaid.[79] This is also the case for jointly controlled entities accounted for under the equity method.[80]

Where an interest in a jointly controlled entity is accounted for using proportionate consolidation, the consolidated cash flow statement will reflect the group's proportionate share of the jointly controlled entity's cash flows on a line-by-line basis.[81] Whilst IAS 7 is not explicit in this regard, the same treatment must apply for cash flows arising from an entity's interest in both a jointly controlled operation and jointly controlled assets (see Chapter 8 at 3.1 and 3.2).

This means that the presentation of the cash flow statement can be materially changed depending on whether a jointly controlled entity is accounted for using the equity method or proportionate consolidation. This is certainly an exception to the assertion in the standard that cash flow information eliminates the effects of using different accounting treatments for the same transactions and events.[82] If this leads management to question the suitability of the resulting cash flow presentation, it may mean that the decision to adopt either the equity method or proportionate consolidation should be revisited.

2.5 Measurement of movements presented in the cash flow statement

2.5.1 Gross or net presentation of cash flows

In general, major classes of gross receipts and gross payments should be reported separately.[83] Operating, investing or financing cash flows can be reported on a net basis if they arise from:[84]

(a)   cash flows that reflect the activities of customers rather than those of the entity; or

(b)   cash flows that relate to items in which the turnover is quick, the amounts are large, and the maturities are short.

Examples of cash receipts and payments that reflect the activities of customers rather than those of the entity include the acceptance and repayment of demand deposits by a bank, funds held for customers by an investment entity and rents collected on behalf of, and paid over to, the owners of properties.[85] Other transactions where the entity is acting as an agent or collector for another party would be included in this category, such as the treatment of cash receipts and payments relating to concession sales.

Examples of cash receipts and payments in which turnover is quick, the amounts are large and the maturities are short include advances made for and the repayment of:

(a)   principal amounts relating to credit card customers;

(b)   the purchase and sale of investments; and

(c)   other short-term borrowings, such as those with a maturity on draw down of three months or less.[86]

2.5.2 Foreign currency cash flows

IAS 21 excludes from its scope the translation of cash flows of a foreign operation and the presentation of foreign currency cash flows in a cash flow statement.[87] Nevertheless, IAS 7 requires foreign currency cash flows to be reported in a manner consistent with IAS 21.[88]

Accordingly, cash flows arising from transactions in a foreign currency should be reported in an entity's functional currency in the cash flow statement by applying the exchange rate ruling on the date of the cash flow.[89] Similarly, the cash flows of a foreign subsidiary should be translated using the exchange rates prevailing at the dates of the cash flows.[90]

For practical reasons, an entity can apply a rate that approximates the actual rate on the date of the cash flow (such as a weighted average for a period), but like IAS 21, translation using the exchange rate as at the balance sheet date is not permitted.[91]

Although the effect of unrealised exchange rate movements on foreign currency cash and cash equivalents is not a cash flow, it is necessary to include these exchange differences in the cash flow statement in order to reconcile the movement in cash and cash equivalents to the equivalent amounts shown in the balance sheet at the beginning and end of the period. This amount is presented at the foot of the cash flow statement, separately from operating, investing and financing cash flows and includes the differences, if any, had those cash flows been reported at end of period exchange rates.[92] In its cash flow statement, Lufthansa includes the caption 'Effects of exchange rate changes' after the total for Net decrease/increase in cash and cash equivalents, as shown in Extract 32.8 at 2.3.4 above. In Extract 32.5 at 2.3 above, Nestlé has split the effect of changing exchange rates into two items, one being the translation difference on the cash flows for the period ('Translation difference on flows') and the other being the exchange rate changes on the opening balance.

A   Entities applying the direct method

When an entity enters into a transaction denominated in a foreign currency, there are no consequences for the cash flow statement until payments are received or made. The receipts and payments will be recorded in the entity's accounting records at the exchange rate ruling at the date of payment and these amounts should be reflected in the cash flow statement.[93]

The consolidated cash flow statement uses the foreign currency financial statements of each foreign subsidiary as the starting point.

B   Entities applying the indirect method

Under the indirect method, profit or loss is adjusted for the effects of transactions of a non-cash nature, any deferrals of operating cash receipts or payments and income or expenses associated with investing or financing cash flows.[94] Exchange differences will appear in the income statement when the settled amount differs from the amount recorded at the date of the transaction. Alternatively, if the transaction remains unsettled at the balance sheet date, exchange differences will also be taken to the income statement on the retranslation of the unsettled monetary items at closing rates. Entities must determine what adjustments should be made to ensure that foreign currency items are shown at the value as translated on the date of settlement.

I   Foreign currency operating transactions settled in the period

Where the exchange differences relate to operating items such as sales or purchases of inventory by an entity, no further adjustments need be made when the indirect method of calculating the cash flow from operating activities is used. For example, if a sale transaction and cash settlement take place in the same period, the operating profit will include both the amount recorded at the date of sale and the amount of the exchange difference on settlement, the combination of which gives the amount of the actual cash flow.

II   Unsettled foreign currency operating transactions

Similarly, where an exchange difference has been recognised on an unsettled balance no reconciling item is needed. This is because the movement in the related receivable or payable included in the reconciliation to operating profit will incorporate the exchange gain or loss. Adjusting profit for the movement on the receivable or payable will eliminate the effect of movements in exchange rates since the date of the transaction.

III   Determining the value of non-operating cash flows

Any exchange difference arising on a settled transaction relating to non-operating cash flows will give rise to an adjustment between profit and the cash flow from operating activities.

For example, the foreign currency purchase of property, plant and equipment would be recorded initially at the rate ruling on the date of the transaction. The difference on payment of the foreign currency payable would be taken to the income statement as an exchange gain or loss. If left unadjusted in the cash flow statement, the investing cash flow for the asset purchase would be recorded at the historical rate, rather than at the exchange rate ruling at the date of settlement. This difference needs to be taken into account in calculating the cash flow to be shown under the relevant classification, in this case investing cash flows, which would otherwise be recorded at the amount shown in the note of the movements in the balance sheet value of property, plant and equipment.

IV   The indirect method and foreign subsidiaries

Entities should take care when applying the indirect method at the 'more consolidated level' as described in 2.4.1 above when there are foreign subsidiaries. If the translated financial statements are used, exchange differences will be included in the movements between the opening and closing group balance sheets. For example, an increase in inventories held by a US subsidiary from $240 to $270 during the year will be reported as an unchanged amount of £150 if the opening exchange rate of £1=$1.60 becomes £1=$1.80 by the year-end. In these circumstances an entity should take the functional currency financial statements of the foreign subsidiary as the starting point. The $30 increase in inventories can then be translated at the average exchange rate.

C   Hedging transactions

Cash flows arising from futures contracts, forward contracts, option contracts and swap contracts which are accounted for as hedges of an identifiable position should be classified in the same manner as the cash flows of the position being hedged.[95] The terminology used in IAS 7 has not been updated to reflect IAS 39 – *Financial Instruments: Recognition and Measurement* – but this should not change the treatment of these contracts in the cash flow statement when they are accounted for as fair value hedges or cash flow hedges under IAS 39.[96]

For example if an entity enters into a forward currency contract as a cash flow hedge against the future cost of property, plant and equipment to be paid for in a foreign currency, the cash flows under the forward contract should be reported under the same cash flow heading as the asset cost, which in this case would be within cash flows from investing activities.

2.5.3 Non-cash transactions

Investing and financing transactions that do not involve cash or cash equivalents are excluded from the cash flow statement. Disclosure is required elsewhere in the financial statements in order to provide all relevant information about these investing and financing activities.[97] Examples of such non-cash transactions include the conversion of debt to equity; acquiring assets by assuming directly related liabilities or by means of a finance lease; and issuing equity as consideration for the acquisition of another entity.[98]

Extract 32.10: TeliaSonera AB (2003)

33 Cash Flow Information [extract]

Non-cash transactions

Sonera
The completion of the merger with Sonera Oyj was mainly effected through an exchange of shares (see note "Merger with Sonera Oyj").

Vehicles
TeliaSonera leases vehicles through financial leasing, primarily from GE Capital. New acquisitions during the year entailed non-cash investments of SEK 47 million.

Infrastructure/capacity swaps
Within the international carrier operations, swap contracts for infrastructure and capacity are signed with other carriers. Until both parties have fulfilled all deliveries as agreed, the value provided may differ from the value received. As of December 31, 2003, no such unbalance was recognized.

AUCS
Claims of SEK 157 million on the Dutch associated company AUCS Communications Services v.o.f. were converted to equity in the company during the year.

The purchase of assets on deferred terms can be a complicated area because it may not be clear whether the associated cash flows should be classified under investing activities, as capital expenditure, or within financing activities, as the repayment of borrowings. In the US, SFAS 95 takes the line that only advance payments, the down payment or other amounts paid at or near to the time of purchase of fixed assets are investing cash flows.[99] This treatment also appears to be implicit in IAS 7. Where an entity acquires an asset under a finance lease, the acquisition of the asset is clearly a non-cash transaction,[100] and the payments to reduce the outstanding liability relating to a finance lease are clearly financing cash flows.[101] In our opinion this distinction should be adopted in all cases where financing is provided by the seller of the asset. Nevertheless, short-term differences between the timing of acquisition and payment should not be interpreted as changing the nature of the cash flow from capital expenditure to financing. Therefore the payment of a short-term payable for the purchase of an asset is an investing cash flow, whereas payments to reduce the liability relating to a finance lease or other finance provided for the purchase of an asset should be included in financing cash flows.

2.6   Voluntary disclosures

IAS 7 encourages the disclosure of additional cash flow related information that may help users better understand the financial position of the entity, including a commentary by management, as follows.[102]

(a)   the amount of undrawn borrowing facilities that may be available for future operating activities and to settle capital commitments, indicating any restrictions on the use of these facilities;

(b)   the aggregate amounts of the cash flows from each of operating, investing and financing activities related to interests in joint ventures reported using proportionate consolidation;

(c)   the aggregate amount of cash flows that represent increases in operating capacity separately from those cash flows that are required to maintain operating capacity; and

(d)   the amount of the cash flows arising from the operating, investing and financing activities of each reported industry and geographical segment under IAS 14.

2.6.1   Cash flows to increase and maintain operating capacity

IAS 7 does not contain any guidance as to how to distinguish cash flows for expansion from cash flows for maintenance in relation to the voluntary disclosure referred to under (c) above. The standard merely states that this information is useful in helping the user to determine whether the entity is investing adequately in the maintenance of its operating capacity or whether it may be sacrificing future profitability for the sake of current liquidity and distributions to owners.[103]

Hongkong Land Holdings distinguishes renovations expenditure from developments capital expenditure in its analysis of investing cash flows.

Extract 32.11: Hongkong Land Holdings Ltd (2003)

Consolidated Cash Flow Statement [extract]

		Restated
For the year ended 31st December 2003	**2003**	2002
	US$m	US$m
Cash flows from investing activities		
Major renovations expenditure	**(25.0)**	(21.5)
Developments capital expenditure	**(47.0)**	(102.7)
Investments in and loans to joint ventures	**(59.3)**	(20.3)
Purchase of other investments	**–**	(1.3)
Disposal of associates, joint ventures and other investments	**118.1**	4.0
	(13.2)	(141.8)

2.6.2   Segment cash flow disclosures

Disclosure is encouraged of segmental cash flows because it reveals the availability and variability of cash flows in each segment and allows users to better understand the relationship between the cash flows of business segments and those of the entity as a whole.[104]

IAS 7 contains an example of the segmental disclosure advocated under (d) above.[105] However, this example reports cash flows of either the entity's geographical or its business segments (rather than both as implied above) and in practice it might be difficult to allocate financing cash flows across the segments, given that this is not how treasury functions tend to operate.

GN Store Nord provides an analysis of operating and investing cash flows by its primary segment reporting format, business segments. Cash flows from acquisitions and disposals are included within investing activities on the face of the cash flow statement, but shown separately below. The entity does not disclose financing cash flows by business segment.

Extract 32.12: GN Store Nord A/S (2003)

PRIMARY SEGMENT 2003 – BUSINESS AREAS AND ACTIVITIES [extract]
Cash flow statement 2003

(DKK millions)	GN Netcom	GN ReSound	Other/ elimin- ations	Core- business areas	Dis- continuing operations	Con- solidated total
Cash flows from operating activities	72	377	378	827	–	827
Cash flows from investing activities	(57)	(280)	68	(269)	(89)	(358)
Cash flows from operating and investing activities	15	97	446	558	(89)	469
Cash flows from company acquisitions/company disposals	–	–	–	–	–	–
Total cash flows	**15**	**97**	**446**	**558**	**(89)**	**469**

PRIMARY SEGMENT 2002 – BUSINESS AREAS AND ACTIVITIES [extract]
Cash flow statement 2002

(DKK millions)	GN Netcom	GN ReSound	Other/ elimin- ations	Core- business areas	Dis- continuing operations	Con- solidated total
Cash flows from operating activities	167	183	207	557	(316)	241
Cash flows from investing activities	(104)	(257)	113	(248)	(204)	(452)
Cash flows from operating and investing activities	63	(74)	320	309	(520)	(211)
Cash flows from company acquisitions/company disposals	(21)	–	–	(21)	(231)	(252)
Total cash flows	**42**	**(74)**	**320**	**288**	**(751)**	**(463)**

3 REQUIREMENTS OF OTHER STANDARDS

3.1 Cash flows of discontinued operations

IFRS 5 requires an entity to disclose the net cash flows attributable to the operating, investing and financing activities of discontinued operations. These disclosures can be presented either on the face of the cash flow statement or in the notes. Disclosure is not required for disposal groups that are newly acquired subsidiaries which are classified as held for sale in accordance with IFRS 5.[106] The general requirements of IFRS 5 are dealt with in Chapter 3 at 3.2.3.

Bayer provides this information for discontinuing operations under the equivalent requirements of IAS 35 – *Discontinuing Operations,* the standard that preceded IFRS 5, not only as a memorandum item on the face of the cash flow statement, but also by business segment, as shown below.

Extract 32.13: Bayer AG (2003)

Bayer Group Consolidated Statements of Cash Flows [extract]
€ million

	Note	2002	2003
Gross cash provided by operating activities		3,085	3,244
Of which discontinuing operations	[42]	416	228
Net cash provided by operating activities		4,458	3,293
Of which discontinuing operations	[42]	461	33
Net cash provided by (used in) investing activities		(6,570)	460
Of which discontinuing operations	[42]	973	(186)
Net cash provided by (used in) financing activities		2,171	(1,761)
Of which discontinuing operations	[42]	(60)	153
Change in cash and cash equivalents due to business activities		59	1,992

Notes to the Statements of Cash Flows
[42]   Discontinuing operations
Discontinuing operations affected the Group cash flow statements as follows:

€ million	Polyurethanes, Coatings, Fibers		Plastics, Rubber		Chemicals	
	2002	2003	2002	2003	2002	2003
Net cash provided by (used in) operating activities	9	16	139	(3)	355	118
Net cash provided by (used in) investing activities	–	–	–	–	–	–
Net cash provided by (used in) financing activities	–	–	–	–	–	–
Change in cash and cash equivalents	–	–	–	–	–	–

€ million	Reconciliation		Total Lanxess		Plasma business	
	2002	2003	2002	2003	2002	2003
Net cash provide by (used in) operating activities	–	–	503	131	(129)	(98)
Net cash provided by (used in) investing activities	(285)	(163)	(285)	(163)	(28)	(23)
Net cash provided by (used in) financing activities	(218)	32	(218)	32	157	121
Change in cash and cash equivalents	–	–	**0**	**0**	**0**	**0**

€ million	Haarmann & Reimer		Total discontinuing operations	
	2002	2003	2002	2003
Net cash provided by (used in) operating activities	87	–	461	33
Net cash provided by (used in) investing activities	1,286	–	973	(186)
Net cash provided by (used in) financing activities	1	–	(60)	153
Change in cash and cash equivalents	**1,374**	**–**	**1,374**	**0**

3.2   Cash flows arising from insurance contracts

IFRS 4 requires that where an insurance entity presents its operating cash flows using the direct method, it should separately disclose cash flows arising from insurance contracts.[107] Comparative information is required.[108]

4   FINANCIAL INSTITUTIONS

As noted in 2.1.2 above, IAS 7 applies to banks, insurance entities and other financial institutions. Nevertheless there are some differences in application as compared to non-financial entities. For example, in considering the components of cash and cash equivalents, banks would not usually have borrowings with the characteristics of an overdraft and cash for their purposes should normally include cash and balances at central banks, together with loans and advances to other banks repayable on demand.

Extract 32.14: Allianz AG (2003)

10   Cash and cash equivalent

	12/31/2003 € mn	12/31/2002 € mn
Balances with banks payable on demand	19,021	14,979
Balances with central banks	4,053	3,139
Checks and cash on hand	1,520	1,763
Treasury bills, discounted treasury notes and similar treasury securities	799	850
Bills of exchange	135	277
Total	25,528	21,008

Compulsory deposits on accounts with the national central banks under restrictions due to required reserves from the European Central Bank totalled €3,357 mn for the credit institutions.

Balances with central banks include balances held with the Deutsche Bundesbank of €3,321 (2002: 1,205) mn, which also have the function of meeting minimum reserve requirements.

IAS 7 contains a number of additional provisions affecting the preparation of cash flow statements by financial institutions. These are covered in broad outline below.

4.1   Presentation of the cash flow statement

4.1.1   *Reporting cash flows from operating activities*

Cash advances and loans made by financial institutions are usually classified as operating activities (and not as investing activities as for other entities) since they relate to a financial institution's main revenue-producing activity.[109] Similarly, receipts from the repayment of loans and advances would be included in operating cash flows.[110]

Interest paid and interest and dividends received are usually classified as operating cash flows for a financial institution.[111]

For an insurance entity, cash receipts and cash payments for premiums and claims, annuities and other policy benefits would be included in its operating cash flows.[112]

Under the direct method of reporting operating cash flows, a financial institution that does not obtain information from its accounting records can derive the disclosures for major classes of gross cash receipts and payments by adjusting interest and similar income and interest expenses and similar charges and other items in the income statement for:[113]

(a)   changes during the period in inventories and operating receivables and payables;

(b)   other non-cash items; and

(c)   other items for which the cash effects are investing or financing cash flows.

Where an insurance entity presents its operating cash flows using the direct method, it should separately disclose cash flows arising from insurance contracts.[114] Comparative information is required.[115]

4.1.2   Reporting cash flows on a net basis

Cash flows from each of the following activities of a financial institution may be reported on a net basis:[116]

(a)   cash receipts and payments for the acceptance and repayment of deposits with a fixed maturity date;

(b)   the placement of deposits with and withdrawal of deposits from other financial institutions; and

(c)   cash advances and loans made to customers and the repayment of those advances and loans.

An example of a cash flow statement of a financial institution is that of UBS AG.

Extract 32.15: UBS AG (2003)

UBS Statement of Cash Flows
CHF Million

For the year ended	31.12.03	31.12.02	31.12.01
Cash flow from/(used in) operating activities			
Net profit	6,385	3,535	4,973
Adjustments to reconcile net profit to cash flow from/(used in) operating activities			
Non-cash items included in net profit and other adjustments:			
Depreciation of property and equipment	1,364	1,521	1,614
Amortization of goodwill and other intangible assets	943	2,460	1,323
Credit loss expense/(recovery)	116	206	498
Equity in income of associates	(123)	(7)	(72)
Deferred tax expense/(benefit)	514	(509)	292
Net loss/(gain) from investing activities	(63)	986	513
Net (increase)/decrease in operating assets:			
Net due from/to banks	42,921	(22,382)	27,306
Reverse repurchase agreements and cash collateral on securities borrowed	(101,381)	(944)	(60,536)
Trading portfolio and net replacement values	(52,264)	21,967	(78,456)
Loans/due to customers	38,594	(11,537)	42,813
Accrued income, prepaid expenses and other assets	(16,100)	2,875	(424)
Net increase/(decreased) in operating liabilities:			
Repurchase agreements and cash collateral on securities lent	65,413	4,791	80,006
Accrued expenses and other liabilities	18,188	(4,754)	(5,235)
Income taxes paid	(1,104)	(572)	(1,742)
Net cash flow from/(used in) operating activities	3,403	(2,364)	12,873

Cash flow from/(used in) investing activities			
Investments in subsidiaries and associates	(428)	(60)	(467)
Disposal of subsidiaries and associates	834	984	95
Purchase of property and equipment	(1,376)	(1,763)	(2,021)
Disposal of property and equipment	123	67	380
Net (investment in)/divestment of financial investments	2,317	2,153	(5,770)
Net cash flow from/(used in) investing activities	1,470	1,381	(7,783)
Cash flow from/(used in) financing activities			
Net money market paper issued/(repaid)	(14,737)	(26,206)	24,226
Net movements in treasury shares and treasury share contract activity	(6,810)	(5,605)	(6,038)
Capital issuance	2	6	12
Capital repayment by par value reduction	0	(2,509)	(683)
Dividends paid	(2,298)		
Issuance of long-term debt	23,644	17,132	18,233
Repayment of long-term debt	(13,165)	(14,911)	(18,477)
Increase in minority interests [1]	755	0	1,291
Dividend payments to/and purchase from minority interests	(278)	(377)	(461)
Net cash flow from/(used in) financial activities	(13,337)	(32,470)	18,103
Effects of exchange rate differences	(524)	(462)	(304)
Net increase/(decrease) in cash and cash equivalents	(8,988)	(33,915)	22,889
Cash and cash equivalents, beginning of the year	82,344	116,259	93,370
Cash and cash equivalents, end of the year	73,356	82,344	116,259
Cash and cash equivalents comprise:			
Cash and balances with central banks	3,584	4,271	20,990
Money market paper [2]	40,599	46,183	69,938
Due from banks maturing in less than three months	29,173	31,890	25,331
Total	73,356	82,344	116,259

1 Includes issuance of trust preferred securities of CHF 372 million for the year ended 31 December and CHF 1,291 million for the year ended 31 December 2001.

2 Money market paper is included in the Balance sheet under Trading portfolio assets and Financial investments. CHF 6,430 million, CHF 10,475 million and CHF 29,895 million were pledged at 31 December 2003, 31 December 2002 and 31 December 2001, respectively.

5   CONCLUSION

IAS 7 is generally well understood by both preparers and users of financial statements. This is due to its relative simplicity and flexibility. The objective of the standard is clear, to require disclosures about the historical changes in cash and cash equivalents, and its application is relatively straightforward, requiring cash flows to be classified under only three headings (operating, investing and financing). Its inherent flexibility can be seen, for example, in the way entities can determine their own policy for the classification of interest and dividend cash flows, provided they are separately disclosed and this is applied consistently from period to period.

This simplicity of objective and flexibility in approach is what allows the standard to be applied by all entities, including financial institutions. The standard can accommodate the need of entities to provide additional information specific to their circumstances and indeed encourages additional disclosures, for example relating to segmental cash flows and undrawn borrowing facilities. However, IAS 7 is not without anomalies, for example the treatment of cash flows in jointly controlled entities is significantly different depending on whether the reporting entity adopts proportionate consolidation or the equity method in its financial statements. The standard aims to report cash flows independently of the effects of using different accounting treatments for the same transactions and events and unfortunately fails in this respect.

The future of IAS 7 is closely linked to the IASB's project on reporting comprehensive income. This might provide an opportunity for the IASB to further improve IAS 7. However, we would not welcome amendments that add unnecessary complexity, for example by making the rarely-used direct method mandatory and introducing as a reporting objective the assessment of an entity's liquidity and financial adaptability.

References

1 SFAC No. 1, *Objectives of Financial Reporting by Business Enterprises*, FASB, November 1978, para. 37.
2 SFAC No. 5, *Recognition and Measurement in Financial Statements of Business Enterprises*, FASB, December 1984, para. 13.
3 SFAC No.5, para. 52.
4 IAS 7, *Cash Flow Statements*, IASB, December 1992 (amended March 2004), paras. 1-2.
5 IAS 7, Objective.
6 IAS 7, para. 4.
7 IAS 7, para. 5.
8 IAS 7, para. 3.
9 IFRS 1, *First-time Adoption of International Financial Reporting Standards*, IASB, June 2003 (amended March 2004), para. 40.
10 IFRS 1, para. IG63 and IG Example 11.
11 IAS 7, para. 6.
12 IAS 7, para. 6.
13 IAS 7, para. 7.
14 IAS 7, para. 8.
15 IAS 7, para. 6.
16 IAS 7, para. 9.
17 IAS 7, para. 6.
18 IAS 7, para. 9.
19 IAS 7, para. 6.
20 IAS 7, para. 7.
21 IAS 1, *Presentation of Financial Statements*, IASB, December 2003 (amended March 2004), para. 68.
22 IAS 7, para. 45.
23 IAS 7, para. 46.
24 IAS 7, para. 47.
25 IAS 7, para. 48.
26 IAS 7, para. 49.
27 IAS 7, para. 10.
28 IAS 7, para. 11.
29 IAS 7, para. 12.
30 IAS 1, para. 36.
31 IAS 7, para. 6.
32 IAS 7, para. 13.
33 IAS 7, para. 14.
34 IAS 7, para. 15.
35 IAS 7, para. 14.
36 IAS 7, para. 18.
37 IAS 7, para. 18.
38 IAS 7, para. 19.
39 IAS 7, para. 19.
40 *IASB Update*, IASB, April 2004, p.5.
41 IAS 7, paras. 18 and 20.
42 IAS 7, para. 20.
43 IAS 7, para. 6.
44 IAS 7, para. 16.
45 IAS 7, para. 16.
46 IAS 7, para. 21.
47 IAS 7, para. 6.
48 IAS 7, para. 17.
49 IAS 7, para. 17.
50 IAS 7, para. 21.
51 IAS 7, para. 31.
52 IAS 7, para. 33.
53 IAS 7, para. 34.
54 IAS 7, para. 14.
55 IAS 7, para. 13.
56 IAS 7, para. 33.
57 IAS 7, para. 34.
58 IAS 7, para. 32.
59 SFAS 95, *Statement of Cash Flows*, FASB, November 1987, para. 17, footnote.
60 IAS 7, para. 35.
61 IAS 7, para. 36.
62 IAS 7, para. 36.
63 IAS 1, para. 85.
64 IAS 7, para. 29.
65 IAS 1, para. 86.
66 IAS 1, para. 69.
67 IAS 27, *Consolidated and Separate Financial Statements*, IASB, December 2003 (amended March 2004), para. 4
68 IAS 27, para. 24.
69 IAS 7, para. 19(a).
70 IAS 7, para. 19(b).
71 IAS 7, para. 39.
72 IAS 7, para. 40.
73 IAS 7, para. 42.
74 IAS 7, para. 41.
75 IAS 7, para. 16.
76 IAS 7, para. 17.
77 IAS 7, para. 17.
78 IAS 7, para. 16.
79 IAS 7, para. 37.
80 IAS 7, para. 38.
81 IAS 7, para. 38.
82 IAS 7, para. 4.
83 IAS 7, para. 21.
84 IAS 7, para. 22.
85 IAS 7, para. 23.
86 IAS 7, para. 23.
87 IAS 21, *The Effects of Changes in Foreign Exchange Rates,* IASB, December 2003, para. 7.
88 IAS 7, para. 27.
89 IAS 7, para. 25.
90 IAS 7, para. 26.
91 IAS 7, para. 27.
92 IAS 7, para. 28.
93 IAS 7, para. 25.

94 IAS 7, para. 18.
95 IAS 7, para. 16.
96 IAS 39, *Financial Instruments: Recognition and Measurement*, IASB, December 2003 (amended March 2004), para. G.2.
97 IAS 7, para. 43.
98 IAS 7, para. 44.
99 SFAS 95, para. 17.
100 IAS 7, para. 44.
101 IAS 7, para. 17.
102 IAS 7, para. 50.
103 IAS 7, para. 51.
104 IAS 7, para. 52.
105 IAS 7, Appendix A.
106 IFRS 5, *Non-current Assets Held for Sale and Discontinued Operations*, IASB, March 2004, para. 33(c).
107 IFRS 4, *Insurance Contracts*, IASB, March 2004, para. 37(b).
108 IFRS 4, para. 42.
109 IAS 7, paras. 15 and 16(e).
110 IAS 7, para. 16(f).
111 IAS 7, para. 33.
112 IAS 7, para. 14(e).
113 IAS 7, para. 19.
114 IFRS 4, para. 37(b).
115 IFRS 4, para. 42.
116 IAS 7, para. 24.

Chapter 33

Related party disclosures

1 INTRODUCTION

Related party relationships and transactions between related parties are a normal feature of business. Many entities carry on their business activities through subsidiaries, joint ventures and associates and there will inevitably be transactions between the parties comprising the group. It is also common for entities under common control, but not comprising a group for financial reporting purposes, to transact with each other. However, experience shows that the existence of related party relationships brings with it the scope for abuse.

1.1 The related party issue

The problem with related party relationships and transactions is expressed in IAS 24 as follows:

'A related party relationship could have an effect on the profit or loss and financial position of an entity. Related parties may enter into transactions that unrelated parties would not. For example, an entity that sells goods to its parent at cost might not sell on those terms to another customer. Also, transactions between related parties may not be made at the same amounts as between unrelated parties.

'The profit or loss and financial position of an entity may be affected by a related party relationship even if related party transactions do not occur. The mere existence of the relationship may be sufficient to affect the transactions of the entity with other parties. For example, a subsidiary may terminate relations with a trading partner on acquisition by the parent of a fellow subsidiary engaged in the same activity as the former trading partner. Alternatively, one party may refrain from acting because of the significant influence of another—for example, a subsidiary may be instructed by its parent not to engage in research and development.'[1]

1.2 Possible solutions

1.2.1 Remeasurement of transactions at fair values

One solution would be to try to adjust the financial statements to reflect the transaction as if it had occurred with an independent third party and record the transaction at the corresponding arm's length price. However, as a study by the Accountants International Study Group stated, it often is impossible to establish what would have been the terms of any non-arm's length transaction had it been bargained on an arm's length basis, because no comparable transactions may have taken place and, in any event, the transaction might never have taken place at all if it had been bargained using different values.[2]

1.2.2 Disclosure of transactions

As a result of the above difficulty, accounting standards internationally have required disclosure of related party transactions and relationships, rather than adjustment of the financial statements. This is the approach adopted by the IASB in IAS 24. The purpose of the disclosures is to give users of the financial statements knowledge of related party transactions, outstanding balances and relationships that may affect their assessment of an entity's operations, including assessments of the risks and opportunities facing the entity.[3]

The main issues which have to be considered in determining the disclosures to be made are as follows:

- identification of related parties;
- types of transactions and arrangements; and
- information to be disclosed.

1.3 Development of IAS 24

The relevant international standard which deals with the disclosure of related parties and transactions between a reporting entity and its related parties is IAS 24 – *Related Party Disclosures*. This was originally issued by the IASC in July 1984 and subsequently issued in a revised format by the IASC in 1994.

However, in December 2003, the IASB issued a revised version of the standard which is applicable for annual periods beginning on or after 1 January 2005, although earlier application is encouraged.[4]

1.3.1 Reasons for revising IAS 24

The IASB developed this revised IAS 24 as part of its project on Improvements to International Accounting Standards. The project was undertaken in the light of queries and criticisms raised in relation to the standards by securities regulators, professional accountants and other interested parties. The objectives of the project were to reduce or eliminate alternatives, redundancies and conflicts within the standards, to deal with some convergence issues and to make other improvements.[5]

For IAS 24 the Board's main objective was to provide additional guidance and clarity in the scope of the standard, the definitions and the disclosures for related parties. The Board did not reconsider the fundamental approach to related party disclosures contained in IAS 24.[6]

1.3.2 The main changes from the IASC's version of IAS 24

The main changes from the previous version of IAS 24 are described in the introduction to the standard as follows:

A   Scope

The standard requires disclosure of the compensation of key management personnel.[7] Whether this is a change is debatable, since the previous version of the standard had no exemption for the disclosure of key management personnel compensation. However, it is fair to say that many financial statements purporting to comply with international standards did not give any disclosures about emoluments of key management personnel. It does, however, represent a change from the IASB's exposure draft that preceded the revised standard where it had been proposed that disclosure of management compensation, expense allowances and similar items paid on the ordinary course of the entity's operations would not be required.[8]

State-controlled entities are within the scope of International Financial Reporting Standards, i.e. those that are profit-oriented are no longer exempted from disclosing transactions with other state-controlled entities.[9]

Surprisingly, the summary of the main changes in IAS 24 does not highlight what is in fact the most significant change in the scope of the standard which is that there is now no longer any exemption about related party disclosures in:

(a)   parent financial statements when they are made available or published with the consolidated statements; and

(b)   financial statements of a wholly-owned subsidiary if its parent is incorporated in the same country and provides consolidated financial statements in that country.[10]

The IASB had proposed to continue these exemptions in specified circumstances, although six board members disagreed with the proposal.[11] Most respondents to the exposure draft objected to the exemption, so the IASB decided to remove the exemptions and require disclosures in the financial statements of such entities.[12]

B   Purpose of related party disclosures

Discussions on the pricing of transactions and related disclosures between related parties have been removed because the standard does not apply to the measurement of related party transactions.[13]

C   Definitions

The definition of 'related party' has been expanded by adding:[14]

- parties with joint control over the entity;
- joint ventures in which the entity is a venturer; and
- post-employment benefit plans for the benefit of employees of an entity, or of any entity that is a related party to that entity.

The standard adds a definition of 'close members of the family of an individual' and clarifies that non-executive directors are key management personnel.[15]

The standard clarifies that two venturers are not related parties simply because they share joint control over a joint venture.[16]

D   Disclosure

The standard further clarifies the disclosure requirements about:[17]

- outstanding balances with related parties together with their terms and conditions including whether they are secured, and the nature of the consideration to be provided in settlement;
- details of any guarantees given or received;
- provisions for doubtful debts; and
- the settlement of liabilities on behalf of the entity or by the entity on behalf of another party.

The standard clarifies that an entity discloses that the terms of related party transactions are equivalent to those that prevail in arm's length transactions only if such terms can be substantiated.[18]

Other new disclosures required include the following:[19]

- the amounts of transactions and outstanding balances with respect to related parties. Disclosure of proportions of transactions and outstanding balances is no longer sufficient;
- the expense recognised during the period in respect of bad or doubtful debts due from related parties;
- classification of amounts payable to, and receivable from, related parties into different categories of related parties; and
- the name of the entity's parent and, if different, the ultimate controlling party. If neither of these two parties produces financial statements available for public use, the name of the next most senior parent that does so is required.

Although the introduction to the standard refers to the standard requiring disclosure of the compensation of key management personnel under the discussion of the scope of the standard, it should be noted that the standard has specific disclosure requirements about such compensation (see 2.5.4 below) that go further than the general requirements of the previous version of the standard.

2 REQUIREMENTS OF IAS 24

IAS 24 is mandatory for annual periods beginning on or after 1 January 2005, although earlier application is encouraged. If an entity applies it for an earlier period, it shall disclose that fact.[20]

There are no transitional arrangements under the standard for entities already reporting under IFRS. Consequently, in view of the changes discussed at 1.3.2 above, related party disclosures may now need to be given in relation to comparative periods that were not given before in the previously reported financial statements. For first time adopters, there are no specific arrangements in relation to IAS 24 under IFRS 1.

2.1 Objective of the standard

IAS 24 states that its objective 'is to ensure that an entity's financial statements contain the disclosures necessary to draw attention to the possibility that its financial position and profit or loss may have been affected by the existence of related parties and by transactions and outstanding balances with such parties'.[21]

Accordingly, IAS 24 requires disclosure of all related party transactions and outstanding balances, together with the names of any parties who can control the reporting entity.

2.2 Scope

IAS 24 states that it shall be applied in:[22]

(a) identifying related party relationships and transactions;

(b) identifying outstanding balances between an entity and its related parties;

(c) identifying the circumstances in which disclosure of the items in (a) and (b) is required; and

(d) determining the disclosures to be made about those items.

As indicated at 1.3.2 above, the standard no longer has any exemptions for parent financial statements when they are made available or published with the consolidated statements. The standard explicitly requires disclosure of related party transactions and outstanding balances in the separate financial statements of a parent, venturer or investor presented in accordance with IAS 27 – *Consolidated and Separate Financial Statements.*[23]

As also indicated at 1.3.2 above, there is now longer any exemption for wholly-owned subsidiaries. Accordingly, all entities within a group that prepare their financial statements under IFRS will have to disclose related party transactions and outstanding balances with other entities in the group in their financial statements.[24]

The standard states that 'intragroup related party transactions and outstanding balances are eliminated in the preparation of consolidated financial statements of the group'.[25] This is presumably intended to mean that disclosure of such transactions and balances are therefore not required in the consolidated financial statements since, so far as those financial statements are concerned, such items do not exist, rather than just being a statement about a consolidation procedure.

2.3   Identification of related parties

Rather than having a broad definition of 'related party' as in the previous version of IAS 24 with an indication of the types of related party that met that definition, the standard now contains a detailed definition of 'related party' which is discussed below. In considering each possible related party relationship, the standard emphasises that attention is directed to the substance of the relationship and not merely the legal form.[26]

Under the definition of 'related party' within IAS 24, the following parties are related parties of a reporting entity.

2.3.1   *Parties that control, are controlled by, or are under common control with, the entity*

'A party is related to an entity if:

(a)   directly, or indirectly through one or more intermediaries, the party:

    (i)   controls, is controlled by, or is under common control with, the entity (this includes parents, subsidiaries and fellow subsidiaries)'[27]

For this purpose, 'control' is defined as 'the power to govern the financial and operating policies of an entity so as to obtain benefits from its activities'.[28] This is the same as the definition of 'control' used in IAS 27 for the purposes of determining what is a subsidiary of an entity (see Chapter 5 at 3.1). Since (i) above already refers explicitly to parents, subsidiaries and fellow subsidiaries, this additional definition is really only of relevance when a reporting entity is considering whether individuals or other entities have control over it, or whether another party is under common control from the same source as the reporting entity, such that it would make them related parties as far as the reporting entity is concerned.

The reference to 'common control' means that members of so-called 'horizontal' groups (i.e. entities controlled by the same non-corporate shareholders such as individuals, partnerships or trusts) are related parties of each other, even though they may not be members of the same group for financial reporting purposes.

This definition of related party based on 'control' appears to focus on a 'controlling shareholder' role, rather than on, say, control by a director or a board of directors, particularly as directors come within another part of the definition of related party, that of 'key management personnel' (see 2.3.6 below). Accordingly, it would seem that where two entities are subject to control from boards having a 'controlling nucleus' of directors or key management personnel in common, but are not under common control from the same shareholders, they are not related parties under IAS 24.

2.3.2 *Parties that have significant influence over the entity*

'A party is related to an entity if:

(a)   directly, or indirectly through one or more intermediaries, the party:

    ...

    (ii)   has an interest in the entity that gives it significant influence over the entity'[29]

For this purpose, 'significant influence' is defined as 'the power to participate in the financial and operating policy decisions of an entity, but is not control over those policies'.[30] This is almost identical to that used in IAS 28 – *Investments in Associates* – for the purposes of determining what is an associate of an entity (see Chapter 7 at 2.2.1). Thus, the main type of related party that is covered by this category is an investor in the entity that regards the reporting entity as an associate, or would do if it were reporting under IFRS. It will also include an investor that is a venture capital organisation or a mutual fund, unit trust or similar entity, even where that investor is not accounting for its investment in the entity under the equity method under IAS 28 (see Chapter 7 at 2.1.1). IAS 24 goes on to say that significant influence 'may be gained by share ownership, statute or agreement'.[31] It appears that IAS 24 envisages that there could be circumstances in which an entity could be a related party due to significant influence, but in such a way that it was not an associate under IAS 28. In practice, however, we see the effect of the two standards as essentially the same.

Although it might be thought that this definition of related party based on 'significant influence' is the corollary of 2.3.4 below, it should be noted that it does not lead to reciprocal disclosures in the financial statements of the reporting entities as illustrated in the example below:

Example 33.1

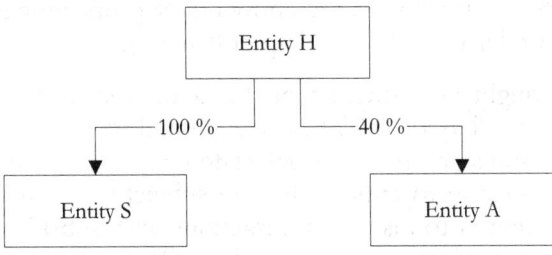

If H is the reporting entity, A is a related party of both H and the H group (because it is an associate of both – see 2.3.4 below). Thus any transactions between A and either H or S will automatically be disclosed in H's consolidated financial statements. If, however, A is the reporting entity, H is a related party of A (because it is the investor of which A is an associate), but S is not (because it does not have an interest in A that gives it significant influence over A). This has the effect that, if A transacts directly with H, those transactions will be disclosed in A's financial statements, but, if it undertakes identical transactions with S, disclosure is not required.

The above example illustrates that, although entities that are under common control of the same shareholder are related parties under part (a) (i) of the definition (see 2.3.1 above), entities whereby only one of them is under control and the other is only subject to significant influence from the same shareholder, are not. Similarly, if in the above example Entity S had only been a 30% associate of Entity H, then any transactions between the two associates would not be disclosable in either of their financial statements. This is despite the fact that Entity H is in a position to engineer transactions not only between its subsidiaries and associates, but possibly also between different associates (or joint ventures).

2.3.3   Parties that have joint control over the entity

'A party is related to an entity if:

(a)   directly, or indirectly through one or more intermediaries, the party:

       ...

       (iii)   has joint control over the entity'[32]

For this purpose, 'joint control' is defined as 'the contractually agreed sharing of control over an economic activity'.[33] This was the same as the definition of 'joint control' used in IAS 31 – *Interests in Joint Ventures* – for the purposes of determining what is a joint venture of an entity. However, IFRS 3 – *Business Combinations* – has made a consequential amendment to the definition within IAS 31 such that it goes on to say that 'it exists only when the strategic financial and operating decisions relating to the activity require the unanimous consent of the parties sharing control (the venturers)' (see Chapter 8 at 2.2). Thus, the main type of related party that is covered by this category is a venturer in the entity that regards the reporting entity as a jointly controlled entity, or would do if it were reporting under IFRS. It will also include a venturer that is a venture capital organisation or a mutual fund, unit trust or similar entity, even where that venturer is not accounting for its interest in the entity under proportionate consolidation or the equity method under IAS 31 (see Chapter 8 at 2.1).

Again, although it might be thought that this definition of related party based on joint control is the corollary of 2.3.5 below, it should be noted that it does not lead to reciprocal disclosures in the financial statements of the reporting entities as discussed above in relation to entities that are subject to significant influence. The entity will not be required to disclose transactions with subsidiaries of its venturer, or with other joint venture entities or associates of the venturer.

2.3.4 Associates

'A party is related to an entity if:

...

(b) the party is an associate (as defined in IAS 28 – *Investments in Associates*) of the entity'[34]

This is relatively straightforward. Any entity that the reporting entity has determined is an associate under IAS 28 will be a related party. As noted at 2.3.2 above, this applies to investments made by a venture capital organisation or a mutual fund, unit trust or similar entity, even where that investor is not accounting for its investment in the entity under the equity method under IAS 28 (see Chapter 7 at 2.1.1).

2.3.5 Joint ventures

'A party is related to an entity if:

...

(c) the party is a joint venture in which the entity is a venturer (see IAS 31 – *Interests in Joint Ventures*)'[35]

Again, this is relatively straightforward. Any interest that the reporting entity has determined is a joint venture under IAS 31 will be a related party. As noted at 2.3.3 above, this applies to investments made by a venture capital organisation or a mutual fund, unit trust or similar entity, even where that venturer is not accounting for its interest in the entity under proportionate consolidation or the equity method under IAS 31 (see Chapter 8 at 2.1).

2.3.6 Key management personnel

'A party is related to an entity if:

...

(d) the party is a member of the key management personnel of the entity or its parent'[36]

For this purpose, 'key management personnel' are those persons having authority and responsibility for planning, directing and controlling the activities of the entity, directly or indirectly, including any director (whether executive or otherwise) of that entity.[37]

It can be seen that this will include all directors, including non-executive directors, of the entity and of its parent. Although the wording suggests that an entity only has one parent, we believe that that it includes all directors of all parents of the entity, i.e. its immediate parent, any intermediate parent and the ultimate parent.

However, it is clear from the wording that it is intended to encompass other individuals that are not directors of the entity or any of its parents. The main intention of the definition is presumably to ensure that transactions with persons with responsibilities similar to those of directors, and their compensation, do not escape disclosure simply because they are not directors. This would otherwise have provided an obvious loophole in the standard. However, it is not clear whether many individuals will fall within this heading.

In the first place, the individual concerned must apparently have the 'authority and responsibility for planning, directing and controlling the activities of the entity' – i.e. all of them, not just one or some of the activities. It is doubtful whether most board directors would have such power, let alone other employees. We therefore believe that the IASB's intention is that it relates to a major activity of the entity. Even then, it is still doubtful whether many persons (other than directors) will fall into this category. For example, a purchasing manager may have wide discretion to choose suppliers and negotiate prices, but he will generally be subject to various constraints imposed by the board, so that his authority falls short of an ability to 'direct and control' the purchasing function.

In our view, the type of person most likely to be a 'key manager' (apart from directors of the entity) is a director of a subsidiary of the entity, but not of the entity itself, who nevertheless participates in the management of the reporting entity, or a divisional chief executive. Entities may argue that, if the individual concerned was truly part of the 'key management' of the group, he would be on the parent entity's board. However, this would be inconsistent with the view taken by the IASB that 'key management' may be found outside the boardroom.

While such additional members of 'key management personnel' would normally be employees of the reporting entity (or of another entity in the same group), seconded staff and persons engaged under management or outsourcing contracts may well have a level of authority or responsibility such that they should be regarded as 'key management personnel'. Similarly, although the wording of the definition of 'key management personnel' appears to restrict its application to natural persons, it may be that corporate entities could also be included. For example, corporate entities providing investment management services to an investment fund relating to all of the fund's investments.

2.3.7   Close family members

'A party is related to an entity if:

...

(e)   the party is a close member of the family of any individual referred to in (a) or (d) above'[38]

The individuals referred to above are those who have control, joint control or have significant influence over the entity (see 2.3.1, 2.3.2 and 2.3.3 above) or those who are members of key management personnel of the entity or any parent of the entity (see 2.3.6 above).

This is presumably intended to prevent entities (or the individuals) from circumventing the requirements of the standard by transacting with these family members rather than with the individuals.

For this purpose, 'close members of the family of an individual' are defined as 'those family members who may be expected to influence, or be influenced by, that individual in their dealings with the entity'. The standard goes on to state that they may include:[39]

- the individual's domestic partner and children;

- children of the individual's domestic partner; and

- dependants of the individual or the individual's domestic partner.

We do not believe that these should necessarily be the only family members that fall within the definition. Other family members such as parents, brothers, sisters could also be included, particularly where they have been influenced by or had influence over the individual in their dealings with the entity.

2.3.8   Entities controlled, jointly controlled or significantly influenced by certain individuals

'A party is related to an entity if:

...

(f)   the party is an entity that is controlled, jointly controlled or significantly influenced by, or for which significant voting power in such entity resides with, directly or indirectly, any individual referred to in (d) or (e)'[40]

The individuals referred to above are those that those who are members of key management personnel of the entity or any parent of the entity (see 2.3.6 above) or those close family members that are related parties (see 2.3.7 above).

Like part (e) of the definition (see 2.3.7 above), this is presumably intended to prevent entities (or the individuals) from circumventing the requirements of the standard by transacting with entities rather than with the individuals themselves.

Examples of such related parties are illustrated below:

Example 33.2

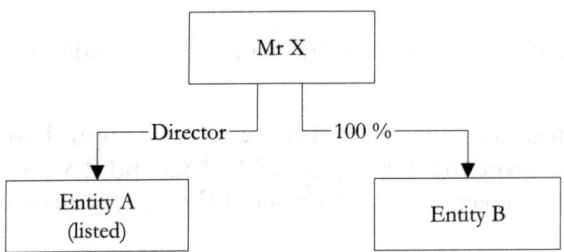

Since Mr X is a director of Entity A then he is a member of the key management personnel of Entity A, and as he controls Entity B, that entity is a related party of Entity A. If Mr X only had a 25% interest in Entity B, but this gave him significant influence over Entity B, it would still be a related party of Entity A. It would only be if Mr X's interest in Entity B was such that it did not give him significant influence over that entity, or could not be said to have significant voting power in that entity, that Entity B would not be a related party of Entity A.

This is another example of where related party relationships are not reciprocal. As far as Entity B is concerned, Entity A is not a related party if Mr X is only a director of that entity. This seems slightly counter-intuitive, since, if Entity A (a listed entity) and Entity B (a small private entity) are transacting, the chances are that those transactions are in fact more significant to Entity B than to Entity A.

Example 33.3

Assume the same facts as Example 33.2 above, except that Mrs X, the wife of Mr X, owns Entity B.

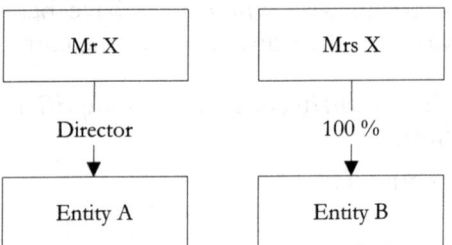

Since Mrs X controls Entity B, and she is a close family member of Mr X, a member of the key management personnel of Entity A, then Entity B is a related party of Entity A. If Mrs X only had a 25% interest in Entity B, but this gave her significant influence over Entity B, it would still be a related party of Entity A. It would only be if Mrs X's interest in Entity B was such that it did not give her significant influence over that entity, or could not be said to have significant voting power in that entity, that Entity B would not be a related party of Entity A. Again, however, Entity A is not a related party of Entity B if Mr X is only a director of Entity A.

Example 33.4

Assume the same facts as Example 33.3 above, except that Mr X is not a director or otherwise a member of the key management personnel of Entity A, but has a 25% interest in Entity A, such that he has significant influence over it.

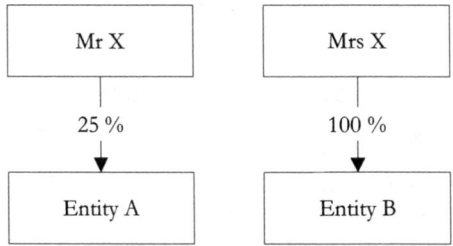

Since Mrs X controls Entity B, and she is a close family member of Mr X, an individual who has an interest that gives him significant influence over Entity A, then Entity B is a related party of Entity A. If Mrs X only had a 25% interest in Entity B, but this gave her significant influence over Entity B, it would still be a related party of Entity A. It would only be if Mrs X's interest in Entity B was such that it did not give her significant influence over that entity, or could not be said to have significant voting power in that entity, that Entity B would not be a related party of Entity A. In this instance, however, Entity A *is* a related party of Entity B, since Entity A is an entity that is significantly influenced by Mr X, a close family member of Mrs X, the controlling shareholder of Entity B.

Example 33.5

Assume the same facts as Example 33.4 above, except that Mrs X does not control Entity B, but only has a 30% interest that gives her significant influence over it and she is not a member of the key management personnel of Entity B.

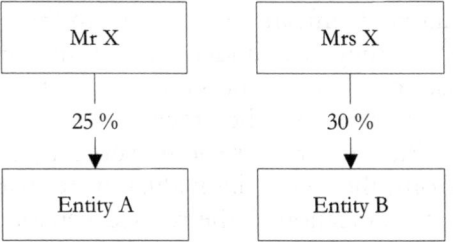

As in Example 33.4 above, since Mr X has an interest that gives him significant influence over Entity A, and he is a close family member of Mrs X, an individual who has an interest that gives her significant influence over Entity B, then Entity A is a related party of Entity B.

It can be seen from the above examples that the 'tentacles' of this particular definition of a related party are quite far-reaching. However, the last example exposes a flaw in the definition of a related party in IAS 24. Suppose the situation in the last example had been as follows:

Example 33.6

Assume the same facts as Example 33.5 above, except that rather than Mrs X having the 30% interest that gives her significant influence over Entity B, it is Mr X that has the interest.

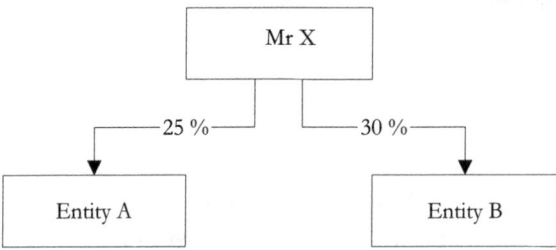

As far as Entity A is concerned, Entity B is not an entity that is significantly influenced by a member of the key management personnel of Entity A. Neither is Entity B significantly influenced by a close family member of such an individual and nor is it significantly influenced by a close family member of an individual that has an interest that gives that individual significant influence over Entity B. Accordingly, Entity B is not a related party of Entity A under this part of the definition. For the same reason, Entity A is not a related party of Entity B.

The situation in the above example is not caught by any of the other elements of the definition, in particular part (a) of the definition. As discussed at 2.3.2 above, although entities that are under common control of the same shareholder are related parties, entities whereby only one of them is under control and the other is only subject to significant influence from the same shareholder, or where both of them are only subject to significant influence from the shareholder, are not.

It seems incongruous that Entities A and B in the above example are not related parties when they are under significant influence from the same individual, yet they are related parties when they are under significant influence from different individuals that are close members of the same family. It would appear that this is an unintentional consequence of the revision to the standard under the improvement project, since in the previous version entities that were under significant influence from the same individual were within the scope of the standard,[41] and there is no indication in the revised version of the standard, or the Basis for Conclusions, that any change was intended.

2.3.9   Post-employment benefit plans

'A party is related to an entity if:

...

(g)   the party is a post-employment benefit plan for the benefit of employees of the entity, or of any entity that is a related party of the entity'[42]

The standard gives no indication as to why such a post-employment benefit plan should be a related party of the entity, although it is likely that it is recognising that an entity sponsoring a post-employment benefit plan will at least have significant influence over the plan. This is another example of the possible non-reciprocal nature of the related party relationships in the standard, since where the plan is the reporting entity, the sponsoring employing entities are not specifically identified as being related parties of the plan, although they may be caught by 2.3.2 above.

2.3.10　Parties presumed not to be related parties

Having included such a detailed definition of related party, the standard states that the following are not necessarily related parties:[43]

- two entities 'simply' because they have a director or other member of key management personnel in common, notwithstanding parts (d) and (f) in the definition of 'related party';

- two venturers simply because they share control over a joint venture;

- providers of finance, trade unions, public utilities, and government departments and agencies, simply by virtue of their normal dealings with an entity (even though they may affect the freedom of action of an entity or participate in its decision-making process);

- a customer, supplier, franchisor, distributor or general agent with whom the entity transacts a significant volume of business, merely by virtue of the resulting economic dependence.

The reason for these exclusions is that, without them, many entities that would not normally be regarded as related parties could potentially fall within the detailed definition of related party. For example, a small clothing manufacturer selling 90% of its output to a high street chain could be said to be under the effective control of that customer.

An exclusion is effective only where these parties would be considered as related to the reporting entity 'simply' as a result of the relationship noted above. If there are other reasons why a party would be considered a related party, the exclusion does not apply. For example, the water company that supplies the reporting entity is not considered a related party if the only link between the two is the supply of water. If, however, the water company is also an associate of the reporting entity, the exclusion does not apply and the two are considered related parties, in which case transactions relating to the supply of water must be disclosed if material.

2.4　Disclosure of controlling relationships

IAS 24 asserts that to enable users of financial statements to form a view about the effects of related party relationships on an entity, it is appropriate to disclose the related party relationship when control exists, irrespective of whether there have been transactions between the related parties.[44]

Accordingly, the standard requires that relationships between parents and subsidiaries shall be disclosed irrespective of whether there have been transactions between those related parties.[45] This suggests that a parent entity has to disclose information about its relationships with its subsidiaries, but the standard gives no indication of what information is required. All that is stated is that 'the identification of related party relationships between parents and subsidiaries is in addition to the disclosure requirements in IAS 27, IAS 28 and IAS 31, which require an appropriate listing and description of significant investments in subsidiaries, associates and jointly controlled entities'.[46] The references to IAS 28 and IAS 31, and to associates and jointly controlled entities, are redundant in this context. The requirements of IAS 27 are discussed in Chapter 5 at 8.

The main focus of the disclosure requirement is on the controlled entity, i.e. the subsidiary. The standard therefore requires that 'an entity shall disclose the name of the entity's parent and, if different, the ultimate controlling party. If neither the entity's parent nor the ultimate controlling party produces financial statements available for public use, the name of the next most senior parent that does so shall also be disclosed.'[47] The next most senior parent is the first parent in the group above the immediate parent that produces consolidated financial statements available for public use.[48]

2.5   Disclosure of related party transactions

A related party transaction is defined as 'a transfer of resources, services or obligations between related parties, regardless of whether a price is charged'.[49] Read literally, this definition requires many transactions to be disclosed more than once. For example, if a entity buys goods on credit from a related party and pays for them 30 days later, both the original purchase and the final payment represent a 'transfer of resources ... between related parties' and should therefore on the face of it be separately disclosed. However, we doubt that this was the IASB's intention, and the nature of the disclosures required by IAS 24 seems to support this view.

2.5.1   *Disclosable transactions*

IAS 24 requires disclosures in respect of key management personnel compensation and other transactions with related parties.

A   *Key management personnel compensation*

'Compensation' for this purpose includes all employee benefits (as defined in IAS 19 – *Employee Benefits*, see Chapter 30 at 2.2) including employee benefits to which IFRS 2 – *Share-based Payment* – applies (see Chapter 29 at 2.2). Employee benefits are all forms of consideration paid, payable or provided by the entity, or on behalf of the entity, in exchange for services rendered to the entity. It also includes such consideration paid on behalf of a parent of the entity in respect of the entity.[50] It can be seen that the compensation to be disclosed by an entity in its financial statements is that which is in respect of services to that entity, irrespective of whether the entity has paid the consideration or not.

IAS 24 goes on to say that compensation includes:[51]

(a)   short-term employee benefits, such as wages, salaries and social security contributions, paid annual leave and paid sick leave, profit-sharing and bonuses (if payable within twelve months of the end of the period) and non-monetary benefits (such as medical care, housing, cars and free or subsidised goods or services) for current employees;

(b) post-employment benefits such as pensions, other retirement benefits, post-employment life insurance and post-employment medical care;

(c) other long-term employee benefits, including long-service leave or sabbatical leave, jubilee or other long-service benefits, long-term disability benefits and, if they are not payable wholly within twelve months after the end of the period, profit-sharing, bonuses and deferred compensation;

(d) termination benefits; and

(e) share-based payment.

B   *Other transactions*

IAS 24 provides a list, not intended to be exhaustive, of the types of transaction which should be disclosed:[52]

(a) purchases or sales of goods (finished or unfinished);

(b) purchases or sales of property and other assets;

(c) rendering or receiving of services;

(d) leases;

(e) transfers of research and development;

(f) transfers under licence agreements;

(g) transfers under finance arrangements (including loans and equity contributions in cash or in kind);

(h) provisions of guarantees or collateral; and

(i) settlement of liabilities on behalf of the entity or by the entity on behalf of another party.

The standard does not contain any exemptions on the basis of the nature of the transaction. Consequently, it embraces transactions such as dividends payments and the issue of shares under rights issues to major shareholders (i.e. those that fall within the definition of related parties), despite the fact that their participation may be no different from that of other shareholders. It also includes transactions with those individuals identified as related parties where their dealings with the entity are undertaken in a private capacity, rather than in a business capacity.

As indicated at 2.5 above, disclosure is required irrespective of whether or not a price is charged. This means that the standard applies to gifts of assets or services and to asset swaps. Common examples of such transactions include:

•   administration by an entity of another entity within a group (or of its post-employment benefit plan) free of charge;

•   transfer of tax assets from one member of a group to another without payment;

•   guarantees by directors of bank loans to the entity.

2.5.2   *Materiality*

In determining whether related party transactions need to be disclosed in financial statements, the general concept of 'materiality' should be applied. No specific reference to this is made within IAS 24, since this is dealt with in IAS 1, which states that 'applying the concept of materiality means that a specific disclosure requirement in a Standard or an Interpretation need not be satisfied if the information is not material'.[53] Omissions or misstatements of items are defined as material within IAS 1 'if they could, individually or collectively, influence the economic decisions of users taken on the basis of the financial statements. Materiality depends on the size and nature of the omission or misstatement judged in the surrounding circumstances. The size or nature of the item, or a combination of both, could be the determining factor.'[54]

This has the effect that virtually any related party transaction whose disclosure is sensitive (for tax reasons perhaps) is by definition material, because it is expected by the reporting entity to influence a user of the financial statements. It is therefore not possible to avoid disclosing such items on the grounds that they are financially immaterial. Also, the fact that IAS 24 requires disclosure of related party transactions, irrespective of whether or not a price is charged, means that disclosure cannot be avoided by arguing that if the amount charged is nil it therefore must be immaterial.

2.5.3   *Aggregation of items of a similar nature*

Presumably, because of the potentially voluminous disclosures that could result if each related party transaction were shown separately, IAS 24 permits aggregation of items of a similar nature, except when separate disclosure is necessary for an understanding of the effects of the related party transactions in the financial statements of the entity.[55] The standard does not expand on this particular requirement, but it would seem that, for example, purchases or sales of goods with other subsidiaries within a group could be aggregated, but any purchases or sales of property, plant and equipment or of intangible assets with such entities should be shown as a separate category.

The amount of aggregation that is permissible will also be limited by the fact that the standard requires separate disclosure of transactions with particular categories of related parties (see 2.5.5 below).

2.5.4   *Disclosures required in respect of key management personnel compensation*

As discussed at 2.5.1 A above, IAS 24 requires disclosures in respect of key management personnel compensation. The standard requires that an entity shall disclose key management personnel compensation in total and for each of the following categories:[56]

(a)   short-term employee benefits;

(b)   post-employment benefits;

(c)   other long-term benefits;

(d) termination benefits; and

(e) share-based payment.

As noted at 1.3.2 above, the IASB had originally planned that there should be no disclosures required in respect of management compensation. However, the Board was persuaded by the respondents' views on the exposure draft and decided that the standard should require disclosure of key management personnel compensation because:

- the principle underpinning the requirements in IAS 24 is that transactions with related parties should be disclosed, and key management personnel are related parties of an entity;

- key management personnel compensation is relevant to decisions made by users of financial statements when it represents a material amount. The structure and amount of compensation are major drivers in the implementation of the business strategy; and

- the benefit of this information to users of financial statements largely outweighs the potential lack of comparability arising from the absence of recognition and measurement requirements for all forms of compensation.[57]

Although the disclosure requirement sounds straightforward, it is unclear from the standard the basis on which the amount for each of the categories is to be determined, so that a meaningful total is disclosed. For example, is it the amount paid or payable by the entity (or on its behalf) during the period, the amount paid or payable by the entity (or on its behalf) for services rendered during the period, the expense recognised by the entity (or by another entity on its behalf) during the period under the relevant standard, or some other basis (such as the value attributed to the benefit for tax purposes)? In the Basis for Conclusions accompanying the standard, the Board noted that the guidance on compensation in IAS 19 is sufficient to enable entities to disclose the relevant information,[58] which might suggest that it is expecting the amounts to based on the charge based under the relevant standards. However, that statement has not been revised following the issue of IFRS 2.

In determining the amounts to be included, it should be remembered that the definition of compensation refers to 'employee benefits ... paid, payable or provided ... in exchange for services rendered'.

Issues relating to each of the categories are discussed below.

A   Short-term employee benefits

As indicated at 2.5.1 A above, these will include wages, salaries and social security contributions, paid annual leave and paid sick leave, profit-sharing and bonuses (if payable within twelve months of the end of the period) and non-monetary benefits (such as medical care, housing, cars and free or subsidised goods or services). Most of these should not cause particular difficulty since the charge for such items under IAS 19 (see Chapter 30 at 6.1) is generally equivalent to the amount payable for the period, although a value may have to be attributed to non-monetary benefits. Where the overall charge under IAS 19 reflects a reduction for staff turnover (for example, the charge in respect of a profit-sharing plan) this should be ignored in determining the amount to be included in respect of the members of key management personnel.

B   Post-employment benefits

As indicated at 2.5.1 A above, these will include pensions, other retirement benefits, post-employment life insurance and post-employment medical care. The inclusion of such a category suggests that amounts are included while the members of key management are providing the services. If amounts were only to be included when the final benefits were payable, then in many cases there would be no disclosure since the individuals would no longer be members of key management. For defined contribution plans, it would seem appropriate that the amount to be included should be based on the charge under IAS 19 which is the equivalent of the contributions payable to the plan in respect of service rendered for the period (see Chapter 30 at 4).

The main issue will be in respect of defined benefit plans where the charge under IAS 19 is not the equivalent of the contributions payable to the plan (see Chapter 30 at 5.4). It is unlikely that the contributions payable will be an appropriate basis, particularly where the entity is benefiting form a contribution holiday, since this does not reflect the benefits provided by the entity in exchange for the services rendered. One approach would be to include an amount based on the IAS 19 charge in the income statement. However, this would require an appropriate apportionment of the overall charge to be made, for example based on the proportion of the pensionable salaries of key management to that of all employees within the plan. As discussed in Chapter 30 at 5.4, this overall charge includes items such as interest, recognised actuarial gains and losses and the effects of curtailments and settlements. It could be argued that these should be taken into account to the extent that they relate to the individuals concerned. Alternatively, since these relate more to the overall plan, such items should not be taken into account in determining the benefits provided in exchange for the services rendered by the members of key management, and that the amount to be included should be the current service cost and, where applicable, past service cost related to those individuals. This could be done by obtaining an actuarial valuation of such amounts or by making an appropriate apportionment of these elements of the charge.

C   Other long-term benefits

As indicated at 2.5.1 A above, these will include long-service leave or sabbatical leave, jubilee or other long-service benefits, long-term disability benefits and, if they are not payable wholly within twelve months after the end of the period, profit-sharing, bonuses and deferred compensation. Since the accounting for such items under IAS 19 is on a similar basis to that for post-employment benefits (see Chapter 30 at 6.2), similar issues to those discussed at (b) above are applicable.

D Termination benefits

These should not cause particular difficulty since the charge for such items, particularly in respect of key management personnel, under IAS 19 (see Chapter 30 at 6.3) will generally be made only when the entity has an obligation to make the termination payment to individual concerned.

E Share-based payment

This will include share options, share awards or cash-settled share-based payments given in return for service by the members of key management. The accounting for such transactions is discussed in Chapter 29. For equity-settled transactions, such as share options or share awards, IFRS 2 requires a charge to be reflected on the basis of their fair value at grant date over the period that services are rendered by employees (see Chapter 29 at 4). For cash-settled share-based payment transactions, IFRS 2 requires a charge based on the cash ultimately paid (see Chapter 29 at 6). One approach would be to include an amount based on the IFRS 2 charge in the income statement. This will not cause any particular additional difficulty to those already encountered in arriving at the IFRS 2 charge. An alternative approach would be to disclose amounts based on the ultimate value that the individual has received (based on the value of the shares at date of vesting or at date of exercise of share options or the cash that is ultimately payable) at those later dates, rather than reflecting amounts over the period of the service.

Whichever method is adopted in determining the amounts to be included within the above categories of compensation we believe that it should be applied on a consistent basis.

F Groups

One additional practical difficulty for entities within a group is that the disclosure of its key management personnel compensation is in respect of the services rendered to that entity. Accordingly, where any individuals within the key management personnel of that entity also provide services to other entities within the group, an apportionment of the compensation will be necessary. In situations where directors or employees of a parent entity effectively serve as non-executive directors of subsidiaries within the group, and that does not involve a significant amount of time, it may be appropriate to conclude that no compensation requires to be included for those individuals in the financial statement of the subsidiaries concerned. However, where they serve in an executive capacity, then an appropriate apportionment of their compensation would be necessary.

2.5.5 *Other disclosures required in respect of related party transactions*

IAS 24 requires that if there have been transactions between related parties, an entity shall disclose the nature of the related party relationship as well as information about the transactions and outstanding balances necessary for an understanding of the potential effect of the relationship on the financial statements. These disclosure requirements are in addition to the requirements in respect of key management personnel compensation discussed above at 2.5.4.[59]

The standard states that, at a minimum, the disclosures shall include:[60]

(a) the amount of the transactions;

(b) the amount of outstanding balances and:

  (i) their terms and conditions, including whether they are secured, and the nature of the consideration to be provided in settlement; and

  (ii) details of any guarantees given or received;

(c) provisions for doubtful debts related to the amount of outstanding balances; and

(d) the expense recognised during the period in respect of bad or doubtful debts due from related parties.

The standard gives no exemption from disclosure on the grounds of sensitivity or confidentiality. However, given that there is no requirement for the name of the related party to be given, this is unlikely to be an issue.

These disclosures shall be made separately for each of the following categories:[61]

(a) the parent;

(b) entities with joint control or significant influence over the entity;

(c) subsidiaries;

(d) associates;

(e) joint ventures in which the entity is a venturer;

(f) key management personnel of the entity or its parent; and

(g) other related parties.

Although (a) above suggests that an entity only has one parent, we believe that the category should include all parents of the entity, i.e. its immediate parent, any intermediate parent and the ultimate parent.

It should be noted that, in the context of the financial statements of an entity within a group, it would appear to be insufficient to have a category of, say, 'group companies', but separate categories would be required for parent(s), subsidiaries and, at least within 'other related parties', fellow subsidiaries.

Although the standard implies that there will one final category of 'other related parties', it may be that this will need to be further analysed in order for the 'nature of the related party relationship' to be disclosed.

The standard notes that the classification of amounts payable to, and receivable from, related parties in the different categories is an extension of the disclosure requirement in IAS 1 for information to be presented either on the balance sheet or in the notes. The categories are extended to provide a more comprehensive analysis of related party balances and apply to related party transactions.[62]

IAS 24 discourages entities from making 'boiler plate' disclosures to the effect that transactions have been undertaken on normal commercial terms or on an arm's length basis, by stating that 'disclosures that related party transactions were made on terms equivalent to those that prevail in arm's length transactions are made only if such terms can be substantiated'.[63]

3 CONCLUSION

We broadly welcome the changes introduced by the IASB in its revised version of IAS 24, because the previous version had not been updated significantly since it was first issued in 1984 and was due for an overhaul. In particular, we agree with the decision for the standard to ensure a minimum level of disclosure of key management personnel compensation.

We consider that the revised standard now provides a workable framework for the disclosure of related party transactions. However, we still have some concerns about its requirements, particularly the lack of clear guidance within the standard as to how some of the categories of compensation should be measured for the purpose of the disclosures about key management personnel compensation.

References

1 IAS 24, *Related Party Disclosures*, IASB, December 2003, paras 6-7.
2 Accountants International Study Group, *Related Party Transactions*, para. 15.
3 IAS 24, para. 8.
4 IAS 24, para. 23.
5 IAS 24, para. IN2.
6 IAS 24, para. IN3.
7 IAS 24, para. IN5.
8 Exposure Draft of Revised IAS 24, IASB, May 2002, para. 2.
9 IAS 24, para. IN6.
10 IAS 24 (1994), *Related Party Disclosures*, IASC, July 1984 (reformatted 1994), para. 4.
11 Exposure Draft of Revised IAS 24, Appendix B.
12 IAS 24, paras. BC8-BC14.
13 IAS 24, para. IN7.
14 IAS 24, para. IN8.
15 IAS 24, para. IN9.
16 IAS 24, para. IN10.
17 IAS 24, para. IN11.
18 IAS 24, para. IN12.
19 IAS 24, para. IN13.
20 IAS 24, para. 23.
21 IAS 24, para. 1.
22 IAS 24, para. 2.
23 IAS 24, para. 3.
24 IAS 24, para. 4.
25 IAS 24, para. 4.
26 IAS 24, para. 10.
27 IAS 24, para. 9.
28 IAS 24, para. 9.
29 IAS 24, para. 9.
30 IAS 24, para. 9.
31 IAS 24, para. 9.
32 IAS 24, para. 9.
33 IAS 24, para. 9.
34 IAS 24, para. 9.

35 IAS 24, para. 9.
36 IAS 24, para. 9.
37 IAS 24, para. 9.
38 IAS 24, para. 9.
39 IAS 24, para. 9.
40 IAS 24, para. 9.
41 IAS 24 (1994), paras. 3(c) and (e).
42 IAS 24, para. 9.
43 IAS 24, para. 11.
44 IAS 24, para. 13.
45 IAS 24, para. 12.
46 IAS 24, para. 14.
47 IAS 24, para. 12.
48 IAS 24, para. 15.
49 IAS 24, para. 9.
50 IAS 24, para. 9.
51 IAS 24, para. 9.
52 IAS 24, para. 20.
53 IAS 1, *Presentation of Financial Statements*, IASB, December 2003 (amended March 2004), para. 31.
54 IAS 1, para. 11.
55 IAS 24, para. 22.
56 IAS 24, para. 16.
57 IAS 24, para. BC6.
58 IAS 24, para. BC7.
59 IAS 24, para. 17.
60 IAS 24, para. 17.
61 IAS 24, para. 18.
62 IAS 24, para. 19.
63 IAS 24, para. 21.

Chapter 34

Events after the balance sheet date

1 INTRODUCTION

IAS 10 – *Contingencies and Events Occurring After the Balance Sheet Date*, was issued by the IASC in October 1978. In 1998 the portion of that standard dealing with contingencies was replaced by IAS 37 – *Provisions, Contingent Liabilities and Contingent Assets*[1] – and IAS 10 was revised in May 1999 so as to deal only with events after the balance sheet date. However, this revision only made a number of limited changes to the standard. Minor changes were made in December 2003 as part of the IASB's improvements project. The main change comprised a limited clarification of the wording of the standard regarding dividends declared after the balance sheet date.[2] The improvements project also made one significant change to the treatment of refinancing arrangements executed after the balance sheet date. Although not dealt with in IAS 10, IAS 1 – *Presentation of Financial Statements* – previously required that (subject to certain conditions) long-term interest-bearing liabilities should continue to be classified as non-current, even when they were due to be settled within twelve months of the balance sheet date if an agreement to refinance, or to reschedule payments, had been completed before the financial statements were authorised for issue.[3] The improvements project changed this to base the criteria for classifying liabilities as current or non-current solely on the conditions existing at the balance sheet date (discussed in Chapter 3 at 3.1.4). Finally, in March 2004 IFRS 3 and IFRS 5 introduced limited consequential amendments to IAS 10. This latest version applies to periods beginning on or after 1 January 2005, with earlier application encouraged. If the standard is applied early, that fact should be stated in the financial statements.[4]

'Events after the balance sheet date' are defined by IAS 10 as 'those events, favourable and unfavourable, that occur between the balance sheet date and the date when the financial statements are authorised for issue'.[5] The definition, therefore, incorporates all events occurring between those dates – irrespective of whether or not they relate to conditions which existed at the balance sheet date. Consequently, the principal issue to be resolved is which events after the balance sheet date should be reflected in the financial statements?

Since the financial statements of an entity purport to present, inter alia, its financial position at the balance sheet date, it is clear that the statements should be adjusted for all events which offer greater clarity of conditions that existed at the balance sheet date. The standard therefore requires that entities should adjust the amounts recognised in the financial statements for those 'adjusting events' that provide evidence of conditions that existed at the balance sheet date. Those events after the balance sheet date which concern conditions that only arose after that date should not be recognised in the financial statements. However, where such non-adjusting events are significant the standard calls for certain disclosures to be made.

Whether adjustments should be made will depend on the particular circumstances and also on the requirements of more specific accounting standards; in particular, IAS 36 – *Impairment of Assets*,[6] IAS 37 – *Provisions, Contingent Liabilities and Contingent Assets*[7] and IFRS 5 – *Non-current Assets Held for Sale and Discontinued Operations*[8]). These standards are discussed in Chapters 13, 25 and 3 respectively.

One exception to the standard's general rule of not making adjustments for non-adjusting events is where the going concern basis is no longer appropriate, see 2.2.2 below and Chapter 3 at 4.1.2.

The requirements of IAS 10 and practical issues resulting therefrom are dealt with at 2 and 3 below.

2   REQUIREMENTS OF IAS 10

2.1   Objective, scope and definitions

The objective of IAS 10 is to prescribe:

*   when an entity should adjust its financial statements for events after the balance sheet date; and

*   the disclosures that an entity should give about the date when the financial statements were authorised for issue and about events after the balance sheet date.

The standard also requires that an entity should not prepare its financial statements on a going concern basis if events after the balance sheet date indicate that the going concern assumption is not appropriate.[9] The going concern basis is discussed in Chapter 3 at 4.1.2.

IAS 10 specifies the accounting and disclosure requirements for events after the balance sheet date.[10] As noted above, IAS 10 defines events after the balance sheet date as 'those events, favourable and unfavourable, that occur between the balance sheet date and the date when the financial statements are authorised for issue'. This therefore includes events that provide additional evidence as to conditions which existed at the balance sheet date and those that do not. The former are adjusting events, the latter are non-adjusting events.[11] Adjusting and non-adjusting events are discussed further at 2.1.1 and 2.1.2 below.

Given the definition above, the meaning of the date on which financial statements are authorised for issue is clearly important. The standard observes that the process involved in authorising financial statements for issue will vary depending upon the management structure, statutory requirements and procedures followed in preparing and finalising the financial statements.[12]

The standard identifies two particular scenarios, as follows:

(a)   an entity may be required to submit its financial statements to its shareholders for approval (as is the case in France, for example) after the financial statements have been issued. In such cases, the financial statements are considered authorised for issue by IAS 10 on the date of issue, not the date when shareholders approve the financial statements;[13] and

(b)   the management of an entity may be required to issue its financial statements to a supervisory board (made up solely of non-executives) for approval. In such cases, the financial statements are considered authorised for issue by IAS 10 when the management authorises them for issue to the supervisory board.[14]

IAS 10 illustrates these scenarios with two examples, as follows.

Example 34.1:   Financial statements to be approved by shareholders[15]

The management of an entity completes draft financial statements for the year to 31 December 2005 on 28 February 2006. On 18 March 2006, the board of directors reviews the financial statements and authorises them for issue. The entity announces its profit and selected other financial information on 19 March 2006. The financial statements are made available to shareholders and others on 1 April 2006. The shareholders approve the financial statements at their annual meeting on 15 May 2006 and the approved financial statements are then filed with a regulatory body on 17 May 2006.

The financial statements are authorised for issue on 18 March 2006 (date of board authorisation for issue).

Example 34.2:   Financial statements to be approved by supervisory board[16]

On 18 March 2006, the management of an entity authorises financial statements for issue to its supervisory board. The supervisory board is made up solely of non-executives and may include representatives of employees and other outside interests. The supervisory board approves the financial statements on 26 March 2006. The financial statements are made available to shareholders and others on 1 April 2006. The shareholders approve the financial statements at their annual meeting on 15 May 2006 and the financial statements are then filed with a regulatory body on 17 May 2006.

The financial statements are authorised for issue on 18 March 2006 (date of management authorisation for issue to the supervisory board).

In Example 34.1 above, selected information was announced before the distribution of the full financial statements to shareholders and their subsequent approval by them. However, the announcement was *after* the date of authorisation for issue. In some jurisdictions, an entity may be allowed to release preliminary information to the market based of substantially complete draft financial statements, before the date of authorisation for issue. In these cases, events after the balance sheet date will include those that arose between the date of the preliminary announcement and the date on which the financial statements are authorised for issue.[17] Accordingly it is possible (although perhaps unlikely) that the information in the financial statements may differ from the equivalent information in the initial public announcement.

Naturally, such governance structures vary from jurisdiction to jurisdiction – and even within one jurisdiction entities may have scope to organise their procedures in different ways.

An example of a company covered by (a) above is Holcim as illustrated in the following extract:

Extract 34.1: Holcim Ltd (2003)

39   Authorisation of the Financial Statements for Issuance

The financial statements were authorised for issuance by the Board of Directors of Holcim Ltd on 5 March, 2004 and are subject to shareholder approval at the Annual General Meeting of Shareholders scheduled for May, 2004.

Regarding (b) above, the phrase 'made up solely of non-executives' is not defined by the standard, although, as indicated in Example 34.2 above, the standard contemplates a supervisory board including representatives of employees and other outside interests. However, it seems to be seeking to draw a distinction between those responsible for the executive management of an entity (and the preparation of its financial statements) from those in a position of high level oversight (including reviewing and approving the financial statements). This seems to be describing the typical two-tier board system seen in some jurisdictions (for example Germany). An example of a company with this structure is Bayer, as illustrated in the following extract.

Extract 34.2: Bayer AG (2003)

Corporate Governance [extract]

Two-tier governance system: constant dialogue between Management and Supervisory Boards

As a company headquartered in Germany, Bayer AG is subject to German law, on which the Corporate Governance Code is founded. A basic principle of German corporate law is the two-tier governance system, comprising a Board of Management and a Supervisory Board that have separate responsibilities but engage in constant dialogue. The task of Bayer AG's 20-member Supervisory Board is to oversee the work of the Board of Management and provide advice. Under the German Codetermination Act, half the members of the Supervisory Board are elected by the stockholders, and half by the workforce. It is directly involved in decisions on matters of fundamental importance to the company and confers with the Board of Management regarding the company's strategic alignment. It also holds regular discussions with the Board of Management on the business strategy and the status of its implementation.

This two-tier governance structure contrasts with the Anglo-American system, where corporate management and oversight are the tasks of a single governing body, the board of directors.

2.1.1 Adjusting events

Adjusting events are 'those that provide evidence of conditions that existed at the balance sheet date.'[18]

Examples given of events classified as adjusting are as follows:[19]

(a) the settlement after the balance sheet date of a court case that confirms that the entity had a present obligation at the balance sheet date. In which situation an entity would adjust any previously recognised provision related to this court case in accordance with IAS 37 or recognise a new provision. The standard explains that mere disclosure of a contingent liability would not be sufficient because the settlement provides additional evidence that would be considered in accordance with IAS 37 (see Chapter 25 at 3.1.1 and 3.2.1);

(b) the receipt of information after the balance sheet date indicating that an asset was impaired at the balance sheet date, or that the amount of a previously recognised impairment loss for that asset needs to be adjusted. For example:

    (i) the bankruptcy of a customer that occurs after the balance sheet date usually confirms that a loss existed at the balance sheet date on a trade receivable and that the entity needs to adjust the carrying amount of the trade receivable; and

    (ii) the sale of inventories after the balance sheet date may give evidence about their net realisable value at the balance sheet date;

(c) the determination after the balance sheet date of the cost of assets purchased, or the proceeds from assets sold, before the balance sheet date;

(d) the determination after the balance sheet date of the amount of profit-sharing or bonus payments, if the entity had a present legal or constructive obligation at the balance sheet date to make such payments as a result of events before that date (see Chapter 30 at 6.1.3);

(e) the discovery of fraud or errors that show that the financial statements are incorrect.

In addition, IAS 33 requires an adjustment to earnings per share for certain share transactions after the balance sheet date (such as bonus issues, share splits or share consolidations discussed in Chapter 31 at 4.3), even though the transactions themselves are not adjusting events and would only be non-adjusting events (see 2.1.2 below).[20]

2.1.2 Non-adjusting events

The standard states that non-adjusting events are 'those that are indicative of conditions that arose after the balance sheet date'.[21]

The standard gives examples of non-adjusting events, as follows:[22]

(a) a major business combination after the balance sheet date (IFRS 3 – *Business Combinations* – requires specific disclosures in such cases, see Chapter 6 at 2.3.9 B) or disposing of a major subsidiary;

(b) announcing a plan to discontinue an operation;

(c)   major purchases of assets, classification of assets as held for sale in accordance with IFRS 5, other disposals of assets, or expropriation of major assets by government (see Chapter 3 at 6.4);

(d)   the destruction of a major production plant by a fire after the balance sheet date;

(e)   announcing, or commencing the implementation of, a major restructuring (discussed in Chapter 25 at 5.1);

(f)   major ordinary share transactions and potential ordinary share transactions after the balance sheet date (although as noted at 2.2.1 above, some transactions in ordinary shares will be adjusting events for the purposes of disclosing earnings per share);

(g)   abnormally large changes after the balance sheet date in asset prices or foreign exchange rates;

(h)   changes in tax rates or tax laws enacted or announced after the balance sheet date that have a significant effect on current and deferred tax assets and liabilities (discussed in Chapter 24 at 5.1);

(i)   entering into significant commitments or contingent liabilities, for example, by issuing significant guarantees;

(j)   commencing major litigation arising solely out of events that occurred after the balance sheet date;

(k)   a decline in market value of investments between the balance sheet date and the date when the financial statements are authorised for issue; and

(l)   the declaration of dividends to holders of equity instruments (as defined in IAS 32, discussed in Chapter 17 at 3) after the balance sheet date.

The reference in (a) and (c) above to asset disposals is not quite the whole story, as it is quite possible that an impairment charge would be required. In addition, (b) and (e) above may also lead to an impairment charge in respect of assets (see Chapter 13 at 3).

Regarding (k) above, the standard notes that the decline in market value does not normally relate to the condition of the investments at the balance sheet date, but reflects circumstances that have arisen subsequently. Therefore, the amounts recognised in financial statements for the investments should not be adjusted. Similarly, the standard states that an entity should not update the amounts disclosed for the investments as at the balance sheet date, although it may need to give additional disclosure as discussed at 2.3 below.[23]

In respect of (l) above, IAS 10 takes a strict balance sheet approach. If dividends are declared (that is, they are appropriately authorised and no longer at the discretion of the entity) after the balance sheet date but before the financial statements are authorised for issue, they should not recognised as a liability because they do not meet the criteria of a present obligation in IAS 37. IAS 10 contains a reminder that such dividends should be disclosed in the notes to the financial statements in accordance with IAS 1 (see Chapter 3 at 6.5.1).[24] In some jurisdictions the common practice is for an entity to propose a dividend in respect of the period (typically communicated as part of the issue of the financial statements), which is subject to the approval of the entity's shareholders. Such dividends will not become a liability of the entity (the meaning of 'declared' above) until shareholder approval is received, i.e. after the financial statements are authorised for issue. IAS 1 requires the disclosure of dividends proposed as well as those declared after the balance sheet date.[25]

An example of a company having to change its treatment as a result of adopting IAS 10 is AngloGold as shown in Extract 34.3 below.

Extract 34.3: AngloGold Limited (2000)

37 Comparative figures

Where appropriate, comparative figures have been restated to facilitate improved disclosure.

Dividends to shareholders are now accounted for on the date of declaration as a result of the adoption of IAS10. As a result, the retained earnings have been restated as disclosed in the statement of changes in shareholders' equity.

Similar issues arise regarding the declaration of dividends by subsidiaries and associates. Although IAS 10 does not specifically address such items, IAS 18 – *Revenue* – requires that dividends be recognised by the shareholder when its right to receive payment is established.[26] Accordingly, such dividends would be recognised when the dividend is declared and therefore are non-adjusting events.

2.2 The treatment of adjusting events

2.2.1 *Events requiring adjustment to the amounts recognised, or disclosures made, in the financial statements*

IAS 10 requires that the amounts recognised in the financial statements be adjusted to take account of an adjusting event.[27]

The standard also notes that an entity may receive information after the balance sheet date about conditions existing at that date relating to disclosures made in the financial statements but not affecting the amounts recognised in them.[28] When this happens, the standard requires that the disclosures that relate to those conditions be updated in the light of the new information.[29]

An example of the need to update disclosures given by the standard is when evidence becomes available after the balance sheet date about a contingent liability that existed at the balance sheet date. In addition to considering whether it should recognise or change a provision under IAS 37, IAS 10 requires an entity to update its disclosures about the contingent liability in the light of that evidence.[30]

2.2.2 *Events indicating that the going concern basis is not appropriate*

IAS 10 requires that if it is determined by management after the balance sheet date either that it intends to liquidate the entity or to cease trading, or that it has no realistic alternative but to do so, the financial statements should not be prepared on the going concern basis.[31]

The standard observes that a deterioration in operating results and financial position after the balance sheet date may indicate a need to consider whether the going concern assumption is still appropriate. If the going concern assumption is no longer appropriate, the standard considers that the effect is so pervasive that it requires a fundamental change in the basis of accounting, rather than an adjustment to the amounts recognised within the original basis of accounting.[32] As noted in Chapter 3 at 4.1.2, IFRS contains no further guidance on just what this 'fundamental change in the basis of accounting' may entail. Accordingly, entities will need to consider carefully their individual circumstances to arrive at an appropriate basis.

The standard also contains a reminder that IAS 1 requires the following disclosures in relation to the going concern basis:

(a)   that the financial statements are not prepared on a going concern basis, if that is the case; or

(b)   if management is aware of material uncertainties related to events or conditions that may cast significant doubt upon the entity's ability to continue as a going concern.

Regarding (b), the events or conditions requiring disclosure may arise after the balance sheet date.[33]

2.3   The treatment of non-adjusting events

IAS 10 prohibits the adjustment of amounts recognised in financial statements to reflect non-adjusting events after the balance sheet date.[34] The standard states that if non-adjusting events after the balance sheet date are material, non-disclosure could influence the economic decisions of users taken on the basis of the financial statements. Accordingly, an entity should disclose the following for each material category of non-adjusting event after the balance sheet date:

(a)   the nature of the event; and

(b)   an estimate of its financial effect, or a statement that such an estimate cannot be made.[35]

The non-adjusting events which appear most regularly in financial statements are possibly the acquisition/disposal of a non-current asset, normally an investment in a subsidiary or a business, subsequent to the balance sheet date.

Examples of disclosure of non-adjusting events are shown in the following extracts:

Extract 34.4: AngloGold Limited (2003)

Notes to the group financial statements [extract]

38. Events after balance sheet date

Disposal of Union Reefs Gold Mine

AngloGold Australia Limited announced on 14 November 2003 that it had entered into an agreement with Greater Pacific Gold Limited to sell its 100% owned Northern Territory gold mining assets. These comprise the Union Reefs gold mine at Pine Creek and associated assets and tenements. The sale is dependent upon Greater Pacific Gold Limited meeting the staged payments schedule and various other AngloGold Australia Limited related performance criteria. The transaction is conditional upon a satisfactory due diligence outcome, the attainment of all regulatory approvals, shareholder approval and securing requisite financing arrangements. The agreed staged purchase consideration for these assets is A$6m ($5m, R31m). The potential profit on the disposal of Union Reefs is A$5m ($3m, R25m). Additional profit may arise if the rehabilitation provision is not fully depleted prior to sale or if interest is payable on payments not paid by the due date.

Sale of Western Tanami Project

AngloGold Australia Limited announced on 24 November 2003 that it had agreed to sell its Western Tanami Project to Tanami Gold NL. The Western Tanami project comprises an established exploration camp and associated equipment, a number of Exploration Licences in northern Western Australia and includes the Coyote gold project. The sale agreement was concluded on 20 January 2004. In addition to the deposit made on 24 November 2003 of A$0.3m ($0,2m, R1m), Tanami Gold has made a further A$4m ($3m, R19m) cash payment and issued 25 million fully paid ordinary shares to AngloGold. A further payment of A$5m ($3m,R25m) will be made by 16 May 2004 and future royalty payments will be made on gold produced about 300,000oz up to 1 Moz. The potential profit on the disposal of the Western Tanami project is A$3m ($2m, R15m) excluding the potential royalty payments. Including the royalty payments, the potential profit would be dependent on the final gold production.

Proposed Merger between AngloGold and Ashanti

AngloGold and Ashanti Goldfields Company Limited issued a joint announcement on 4 August 2003, which detailed the proposed merger of the two companies. The Transaction Agreement which was signed by both parties outlined the terms and structure of the merger. On 15 October 2003, it was announced that Lonmin Plc, which holds 27.6% of Ashanti's issued share capital, had undertaken to vote its shares in favour of the merger. The merger is conditional on the support of the government of Ghana as shareholder and regulator of Ashanti, the approval of the scheme of arrangement and its confirmation by the High Court of Ghana and certain other regulatory approvals and third party consents, as detailed in the 4 August 2003 announcement.

AngloGold announced on 12 December 2003, the terms and conditions of the Support Deed entered with the Government of Ghana, whereby the Government agreed to vote its shares in Ashanti in favour of the merger, as well as the definitive terms of a Stability Agreement to be entered into with the government concerning certain fiscal and regulatory undertakings in its role as regulator of Ashanti.

On 26 January 2004, AngloGold announced that confirmation had been received from the United States Securities and Exchange Commission (SEC) of the availability of an exemption under Section 3(a)(10) of the US Securities Act of 1933 that will enable AngloGold to issue its shares in the scheme relating to the merger of AngloGold and Ashanti, without registration in the United States. Once the required approvals of the parliament and government of Ghana have been received, the scheme documents will be finalised and distributed to Ashanti shareholders.

AngloGold anticipates that the transaction will be completed during April 2004.

Launch of Convertible Bonds Offer

On 19 February 2004 AngloGold announced the final terms of an offering of $900m (subject to increase by up to $100m pursuant to an option) Convertible Bonds which are due 2009, by its wholly owned subsidiary, AngloGold Holdings plc. The bonds are guaranteed by AngloGold.

On 20 February 2004, AngloGold announced it had placed all $900m of the convertible bonds at a semi-annual coupon of 2.375%.

On 25 February 2004, the above-mentioned option was exercised, increasing the total bonds issued by AngloGold to $1,000m.

The bonds are convertible into American Depositary Shares (ADS) of AngloGold, at a strike price of $65 per ADS, at the option of the holder. Each ADS represents one order share of AngloGold. The conversion premium to the reference volume weighted average price of the ADSs on the New York Stock Exchange of $40.625 on the launch day, was 60%. If all bond holders exercise their conversion options, 15,384,615 new ADSs would be created. If the bonds have not been converted by 20 February 2009, they will be redeemed at par on 27 February 2009. Other terms include an issuer call at 130% after 3 years and a conversion ratio adjustment to cater for events such as share splits and capital distributions, etc.

The proceeds of the offering of the Bonds will be used to repay outstanding indebtedness, to pay transaction costs relating to the proposed merger with Ashanti Goldfields Company Limited and for general corporate purposes.

Application has been made to, and approval received from, the UK listing Authority for the bonds to be admitted to the Official List, and the London Stock Exchange plc for the Bonds to be admitted to trading on the London Stock Exchange plc's market for listed securities.

Extract 34.5: Clariant Ltd (2003)

Notes to the consolidated financial statements [extract]

29. Events subsequent to the balance sheet date

In 2003 Clariant started a large-scale project to critically review all structures of the Group and find ways to make them more efficient, with the goal to improve operational performance substantially. Leading members of Clariant Management were assigned to this project and elaborated new solutions with the help of external consultants.

The review demonstrated that many functional processes can be handled in a more efficient manner by reassigning them from the divisions, where they have been managed up to now, to either regional responsibility centers or headquarters directly. As a result of these findings, deep-going measures of reorganization to reassign these functional responsibilities will be introduced in the course of 2004. Furthermore Clariant will thoroughly reorganize its manufacturing and supply chain structure in order to optimize the internal streams of goods and revenues.

Altogether, these measures will entail a reduction of the workforce by about 4,000 employees, which will take place in the years 2004 and 2005. It is estimated that 40% of this reduction will occur in manufacturing, while 60% will concern administration, supply chain and infrastructure.

Clariant expects the costs of these measures to amount to about CHF 500-600 million mainly spread over the next three years, whereby most of this will be cash out expenses. Savings from the program are expected to reach CHF 100 million in 2004. They will increase continuously over the next years and reach their full impact by 2007. In line with the announcement made in August 2003, Clariant expects to implement measures with an EBIT impact of CHF 700-900 million. After accounting for business risks and price erosion, Clariant expects to reach a sustainable EBIT improvement of at least CHF 400 million by the end of 2007.

On February 19, 2004, the Board of Directors decided to propose to the shareholders at the upcoming General Meeting to deliberate the increase of the current share capital of CHF 767,200,000 by way of an ordinary capital increase by a maximum par amount of CHF 460,320,000 to up to a maximum par amount of CHF 1,227,520,000. The preemptive rights of existing shareholders shall be granted. The rights issue is announced as a fully underwritten transaction at standard market conditions on February 24, 2004. As a result, Clariant will see a total net increase in equity of approximately CHF 880 million if the shareholders approve the Board's proposal for a capital increase.

Extract 34.6: Nestlé S.A. (2003)

Notes [extract]

35. Events after the balance sheet date

Garoto

The Administrative Council of Economic Defence of Brazil (CADE) issued a ruling in February 2004 requesting Nestlé to sell the assets it acquired from Chocolates Garoto S.A. in 2002. CADE said the combined operations of Nestlé and Garoto were a threat to fair competition. Nestlé is considering various options to resolve this matter with CADE; the final outcome is expected in 2004.

L'Oréal

On 3rd February 2004 Nestlé and the Bettencourt family who own respectively 49% and 51% of Gesparal Holding Company, which in turn owns 53.8% of L'Oréal, reached an agreement proposing a merger of Gesparal into L'Oréal. This merger will be proposed at the next annual shareholders' meeting of L'Oréal on 29th April 2004. After the merger, Nestlé will own 26.4% of L'Oréal. They have also agreed not to modify their respective shareholdings for an agreed period and to grant mutual pre-emption rights on their respective shareholdings for a ten-year period.

Other subsequent events

At 25th February 2004, date of approval of the accounts by the Board of Directors, the Group had no subsequent adjusting events that warrant a modification of the value of assets and liabilities.

Extract 34.7: Netia S.A. (2003)

Notes to Consolidated Financial Statements [extract]

25. Subsequent events

Resignations of the Management Board members

On January 5, 2004 Ms Elizabeth McElroy, the Chief Commercial Officer informed the Company of her resignation from the position in the Management Board with the effect as of the end of February 2004.

On February 25, 2004 Mr Zbigniew Lapinski resigned from the position as the member of the Management Board with immediate effect. Duties of the financial director of Netia will be temporarily performed by Mr Dariusz Sokolowski, who was appointed a proxy of the Company. Previously, Mr. Sokolowski was the Management Board member and the financial director of RST El-Net SA.

Acquisitions of shares of the Company

On January 23, 2004 the Company received a notification from Powszechny Zaklad Ubezpieczen SA ("PZU SA") stating that a 5% threshold of the total number of votes at the Company's General Meeting of Shareholders has been exceeded. According to the notification, PZU SA and its subsidiary PZU Zycie SA jointly held 17,543,387 of Netia's shares, which constituted 5.09% of the Netia's share capital, and entitled the holders thereof to exercise 17,543,387 votes at the Company's General meting of Shareholders, constituting 5.09% of the total number of votes at Netia's General Meeting of Shareholders at the date of notification.

On February 25, 2004 the Company received a notification stating that following the purchase of the Company's shares, the following subsidiaries of J.P. Morgan Chase & Co.: J.P. Morgan Securities Ltd. and J.P. Morgan Fleming Asset Management (UK) Limited jointly held 28,917,766 Netia's shares, which represented 8.38% of Netia's outstanding share capital an 8.38% of the total voting power at Netia's General Meeting of Shareholders, as of that date.

Resignation of the Supervisory Board member

On January 23, 2004 the Company was informed about Mr Andrzej Wiercinski's resignation from his position as a member of Netia's Supervisory Board. His resignation will be effective on the day immediately following the Supervisory Board's approval of Netia's 2003 financial statements, but not later than March 5, 2004.

Acquisition of alternative telecommunications operator El-Net (not in thousands)

On January 29, 2004 the Company acquired Regionalne Sieci Telekomunikacyjne El-Net S.A. ("El-Net"), marking an important step in the Company plans related to consolidation of the Polish telecommunications market. El-Net is one of the largest alternative fixed-line telecommunications operators in Poland, providing services to over 61 thousand customers, including 17 thousand business customers, located in the cities of Warsaw and Bydgoszcz. El-Net's product portfolio includes fixed-line telephony, ISDN, Internet access, leased lines and cable TV services. In 2003 El-Net expects to report approximately PLN 115 million in revenues and PLN 24 million in EBITDA. Approximately 59% of El-Net's voice service revenues are from business customers.

The purchase consideration included cash of PLN 3.1 million paid for 100% of voting shares acquired and PLN 93.3 million paid to BRE Bank S.A. for certain receivables from El-Net under certain loans granted by El-Net's previous shareholder and affiliates amounting to PLN 672.8 million including due interests, secured by registered pledges on El-Net's property in Warsaw and receivables from El-Net under a syndicated bank loan for a principal amount of PLN 206.3 million including due interests, secured by registered pledges on El-Net's property in Warsaw and Bydgoszcz (the "Loan Receivables"). The Management of the Company considers that it is impracticable to disclose information about the fair value of net assets acquired since the full valuation of El-Net's assets has not been completed yet.

The Company is going to account for the purchase of El-Net shares using acquisition method and start to consolidate the results of El-Net from January 31, 2004.

Exercise of warrants (not in thousands)

As at March 1, 2004 8,737,944 of warrants have been exercised and the Company's share capital was accordingly increased by 8,737,944 series J shares. As a result at March 1, 2004 the Company's share capital consisted of 352,782,156 ordinary shares and of 1,000 of series A1 shares.

Extract 34.8: Wella AG (2003)

Notes to the Consolidated Financial Statements [extract]

[42]   Post-closing events

On 29 January 2004, Wella signed an agreement initially valid until the end of 2008 with Procter & Gamble International Operations S.A., based in Petit Lancy, Switzerland, covering global licensing of Wella's Consumer business division. Proctor & Gamble is thereby entitled to market and sell Wella consumer brand products. An extraordinary general meeting was held on 3 February 2004 upon the request of a group of minority shareholders. The proposal of the minority shareholders to hold a vote of no-confidence in chief executive officer Dr. Gürtler was rejected by the general meeting, as was the demand pursuant to § 83, para. 1 of the Stock Corporation Act to the Management Board to prepare a domination agreement and to apply for the appointment of auditors to carry out a special audit pursuant to § 142 of the Stock Corporation Act. The general meeting decided to postpone the end of the financial year to 30 June and to form an abridged financial year for the period from 1 January 2004 to 30 June 2004.

The general meeting furthermore appointed new members to the Supervisory Board, concerning which we point to the details in the notes under "Corporate Boards in detail".

These extracts all pre-date IFRS 3 which, as noted at 2.1.2 above, requires specific disclosures relating to major business combination or divestments after the balance sheet date.

2.4   Other disclosure requirements

The disclosers required in respect of non-adjusting events after the balance sheet date are discussed at 2.3 above. As IAS 10 only requires consideration to be given to events which occur up to the date on which the financial statements are authorised for issue, it is important for users to know what that date was, since the financial statements will not reflect events after that date.[36] Accordingly, the standard requires that date to be disclosed.[37] Furthermore, IAS 10 requires disclosure of who gave the authorisation for the issue of the financial statements and, if the owners of the entity or others have the power to amend them after issue, disclosure of that fact.[38] In practice, this could be presented in a number of ways:

(a) the information could be presented on the face of a primary statement. For example, entities that are required to have the balance sheet signed could include the information at that point;

(b) the information could be presented in the note dealing with other IAS 10 disclosures, or another note, such as the summary of significant accounting policies; or

(c) the information could be presented a separate statement, such as a statement of directors' responsibilities in respect of the financial statements.

Strictly speaking, this information must be presented within the financial statements. So, if (c) were chosen, either the whole report would need to be part of the financial statements or the information could be incorporated into them by way of a cross-reference.

Option (b) above is perhaps the most common, and is the method used Nestlé as illustrated in Extract 34.6 above.

3 PRACTICAL ISSUES

3.1 The valuation of inventory realised after the balance sheet date

The sale of inventories after the balance sheet date is normally a good indicator of the net realisable value (NRV) at that date, and this is acknowledged by IAS 10 which states that such sales 'may give evidence about ... net realisable value at the balance sheet date'.[39] However, there will be circumstances where there is evidence which suggests that a fall in NRV has taken place because of conditions which did not exist at the balance sheet date.

The problem, therefore, is determining when the fall in realisable value occurred; did the fall in value occur as a result of circumstances which existed at the balance sheet date, or did it occur as a result of circumstances which arose subsequently? A decrease in price is merely a response to changing conditions, and so it is important that the reasons behind these changes are fully assessed.

This can be seen by reviewing some examples of changing conditions:

(a) Price reductions due to a sudden increase in cheap imports

Whilst it could be argued that the 'dumping' of cheap imports after the balance sheet date is a condition that has arisen subsequent to that date, it is more likely to be the case that this will be a reaction to a condition which already existed, such as overproduction in other parts of the world. Thus, it might be more appropriate in such a situation to adjust the value of inventories to its subsequent NRV.

(b)   Price reductions due to increased competition

It is common for entities to adjust the valuation of inventories when their fall in value is due to price reductions of competitors. This is because the reasons for price reductions will not have arisen overnight, but will normally have occurred over a period of time. For example, a competitor may have built up a comparative advantage because of investment in more efficient machinery in the past. Thus, it is usually appropriate for an entity to adjust its valuation in inventories, as its past investment in technology will have been inferior to its competitors, and will not have arisen subsequent to the balance sheet date.

(c)   Price reductions due to the introduction of an improved competitive product

As an improved product introduced by competitors is unlikely to have been developed overnight it is correct to adjust the valuation of inventories to its net realisable value following that introduction. This is because it reflects the entity's failure to maintain its position in relation to technological improvements.

It can be seen in these cases that when an entity is forced to reduce its prices after the balance sheet date, the fall provides additional evidence of conditions which existed at the balance sheet date. The reason for this is that, in general, the post balance sheet reduction in the NRV of inventories represents the culmination of conditions which existed over a relatively long period of time, with the result that their effects would normally require adjustment in the financial statements. However, there will be certain types of inventory for which there is clear evidence of a higher price available at the year-end, when it would be inappropriate to write down the inventory to reflect a subsequent decline. An example of this would be inventories for which there was a price on an appropriate commodities market. Finally, inventory could be physically damaged or destroyed after the balance sheet date (say, by fire, flood or other disaster). In this case no adjustment would be appropriate in the financial statements.

3.2   Construction contracts

It is not uncommon for events to take place after the balance sheet date which provide further evidence as to the profitability of construction contracts that were in progress at the balance sheet date. It is our view that *all* further evidence of eventual profit or loss should be taken into account in determining the amounts of contract revenues and contract costs to be recognised as revenue and expenses under the percentage of completion method under IAS 11 – *Construction Contracts* (see Chapter 22).

3.3   Insolvency of a debtor

The insolvency of a debtor and his inability to pay his debts usually builds up over a period of time which would commence long before the balance sheet date. Consequently, if a debtor has an amount outstanding at the year-end, and this amount has to be written off due to information received subsequent to the period end, it is normal to classify the event as adjusting. The standard acknowledges this by noting that 'the bankruptcy of a customer that occurs after the balance sheet date usually confirms that a loss existed at the balance sheet date'.[40] If, however, there is evidence to suggest that the insolvency of the debtor has been determined solely by an event occurring after the balance sheet date, then the event would fall to be treated as non-adjusting.

4   FIRST-TIME ADOPTION ISSUES

In its first set of IFRS financial statements, a first time adopter should apply IAS 10 as normal to the treatment of events subsequent to the balance sheet date for the current period.

IFRS 1 – *First-time adoption of International Financial Reporting Standards* – requires some modification to the requirements of IAS 10 as regards estimates which are required under IFRS in the preparation of financial statements covering earlier periods: that is, the balance sheet at the date of transition to IFRS and financial statements for the comparative period (and for each of them if more than one is presented). IFRS 1 is discussed in Chapter 4.

When an entity prepares its first set of financial statements under IFRS it may have more up to date information relating to conditions that existed at earlier balance sheet dates than it had when earlier financial statements were prepared under its previous GAAP. When such information relates to estimates needed under IFRS at those dates, IFRS 1 draws a distinction between two types of estimates:

(a)   estimates that an entity had made under previous GAAP; and

(b)   estimates that an entity had not had to make under previous GAAP.

IFRS 1 requires that estimates under IFRSs at the date of transition to IFRS (and at the date of the comparative balance sheet) be consistent with estimates made for the same date under previous GAAP (after adjustments to reflect any difference in accounting policies), unless there is objective evidence that those estimates were in error.[41]

IFRS 1 provides an example of this requirement as follows.[42]

Example 34.3:   Fresh information about estimates required under previous GAAP

Assume that an entity's date of transition to IFRSs is 1 January 2004 and new information on 15 July 2004 requires the revision of an estimate made under previous GAAP at 31 December 2003. The entity shall not reflect that new information in its opening IFRS balance sheet (unless the estimates need adjustment for any differences in accounting policies or there is objective evidence that the estimates were in error). Instead, the entity shall reflect that new information in its income statement (or, if appropriate, other changes in equity) for the year ended 31 December 2004.

Regarding (b) above, IFRS 1 states that to 'achieve consistency with IAS 10', those estimates under IFRS should reflect conditions that existed at the relevant date and in particular, estimates of market prices, interest rates or foreign exchange rates should reflect market conditions at the relevant date.[43] This would mean taking account of any information received after that date but before the first set of IFRS financial statements are authorised for issue. The three examples given by the standard (market prices, interest rates and foreign exchange rates) will quite possibly be *observed* in active markets rather than estimated, so the question of whether an estimate should reflect events after the balance sheet date does not arise. It may be that some estimates use such observed data as inputs into the estimation process. In which case, those inputs should reflect market conditions at the relevant date.

The implementation guidance accompanying IFRS 1 provides some further guidance relating to the use of hindsight, which is discussed further in Chapter 4 at 2.8.1.

The requirements outlined above seem to seek to balance the prevention of the 're-writing of history' based on hindsight over an extended period with the requirement to apply IFRS to earlier periods as if it had always applied. So, it is only when a particular estimate was not required under previous GAAP that it may be informed by events occurring subsequent to the authorisation for issue of the previous GAAP financial statements. Even then, the normal requirements of IAS 10 apply in that adjustment should only be made for events that provide evidence of conditions that existed at the balance sheet date. As the period between a balance sheet date and the date of new information becoming available grows, it will probably become less likely that the new information reflects conditions at that earlier date.

References

1 IAS 37 (1998), *Provisions, Contingent Liabilities and Contingent Assets*, IASC, September 1998.
2 IAS 10, *Events After the Balance Sheet Date*, IASB, December 2003, paras. IN2-IN4.
3 IAS 1 (1997), *Presentation of Financial Statements*, IASB, Revised 1997, para. 63.
4 IAS 10, para. 23.
5 IAS 10, para. 3.
6 IAS 36, *Impairment of Assets*, IASB, March 2004.
7 IAS 37, *Provisions, Contingent Liabilities and Contingent Assets*, IASB, September 1998 (amended March 2004).
8 IFRS 5, *Non-current Assets Held for Sale and Discontinued Operations*, IASB, March 2004.
9 IAS 10, para. 1.
10 IAS 10, para. 2.
11 IAS 10, para. 3.
12 IAS 10, para. 4.
13 IAS 10, para. 5.
14 IAS 10, para. 6.
15 IAS 10, para. 5.
16 IAS 10, para. 7.
17 IAS 10, para. 6.
18 IAS 10, para. 3.
19 IAS 10, para. 9.
20 IAS 10, para. 22.
21 IAS 10, para. 3.
22 IAS 10, paras. 11-12 and 22.
23 IAS 10, para. 11.
24 IAS 10, para. 13.
25 IAS 1, para. 125.
26 IAS 18, *Revenue*, IASB, December 1993 (amended March 2004), para. 30.
27 IAS 10, para. 8.
28 IAS 10, para. 20.
29 IAS 10, para. 19.
30 IAS 10, para. 20.
31 IAS 10, para. 14.
32 IAS 10, para. 15.
33 IAS 10, para. 16.
34 IAS 10, para. 10.
35 IAS 10, para. 21.
36 IAS 10, para. 18.
37 IAS 10, para. 17.
38 IAS 10, para. 17.
39 IAS 10, para. 9.
40 IAS 10, para. 9.
41 IFRS 1, *First-time adoption of International Financial Reporting Standards*, IASB, June 2003 (amended March 2004), paras. 31 and 34.
42 IFRS 1, para. 32.
43 IFRS 1, paras. 33-34.

Chapter 35   Interim reporting

1   INTRODUCTION

1.1   Background

The most frequently debated issue relating to interim financial reporting is whether the interim period should be regarded as a discrete period in its own right, or whether it should be seen primarily as a mere instalment of the financial year. Under the first perspective, it would be appropriate to apply the same accounting policies and principles as are used for the annual financial statements, treating the interim period in just the same way as the full financial year. Under the second, some modifications to these policies and principles are made to allow the interim report to give a better guide to the outcome of the year as a whole. The former approach is generally referred to as the 'discrete' approach, and the latter as the 'integral' approach. In practice, however, these categories are less clear-cut than the above description might suggest, and in the past entities generally followed an approach that was a hybrid of these two theoretical extremes. IAS 34 – *Interim Financial Reporting* – is largely based on the 'discrete' approach, with only minor exceptions where it follows an 'integral' approach.

The integral approach has no clear definition. It implies some pragmatic modification of the inter-period allocation of transactions, so as to match costs more evenly with revenues in the different halves (or quarters) of the year. Critics would say that this is not matching, but smoothing, and that it obscures the results of the interim period rather than presents them more fairly. On the other hand, supporters would say that such modifications are necessary to prevent meaningless distortions arising; an interim period is an even more artificial interval than a financial year, and that to report transactions without trying to relate them to the annual cycle of activity for which they have been incurred would not make sense.

The extent of disclosure in interim reports raises similar issues. If interim reporting is no different in concept from annual reporting, but is simply a more frequent version of the same thing, then one might suppose that the form and content of the report should also be the same. If, however, it is seen as a subsidiary form of reporting which only deals with an instalment of a longer period, then it is easier to justify a different reporting package. Present practice under IFRS undoubtedly reflects the latter view, although probably more as an expedient compromise than as the result of an attempt to meet a carefully researched need.

1.2   EU Transparency Directive

In Europe, the normal frequency of reporting is biannual. Relatively few European companies follow the North American practice of reporting every quarter. The European Union's Council of Economics and Finance Ministers (ECOFIN) is expected to approve and issue the *Proposal for a Directive of the European Parliament and of the Council on the harmonisation of transparency requirements with regard to information about issuers whose securities are admitted to trading on a regulated market and amending Directive 2001/34/EC* (draft Transparency Directive) in its final form in the autumn of 2004. Article 5.3 of that Directive will require in respect of half-yearly financial reports that 'where the issuer is required to prepare consolidated accounts, the condensed set of financial statements shall be prepared in accordance with the international accounting standard applicable to the interim financial reporting as adopted pursuant to the procedure provided for under Article 6 of Regulation (EC) No. 1606/2002.'[1] This means that half-yearly reports are expected to comply with IAS 34 once the draft Transparency Directive has been approved. However, quarterly reports will be exempt from this requirement.

2   REQUIREMENTS OF IAS 34

2.1   Objective

The (then) IASC issued in February 1998 a standard on interim reporting, IAS 34, which applies to entities presenting their interim financial statements in accordance with IFRS for accounting periods beginning on or after 1 January 1999.[2] The stated objective of the standard is 'to prescribe the minimum content of an interim financial report and to prescribe the principles for recognition and measurement in complete or condensed financial statements for an interim period. Timely and reliable interim financial reporting improves the ability of investors, creditors, and others to understand an entity's capacity to generate earnings and cash flows and its financial condition and liquidity.'[3]

2.2   Scope

IAS 34 does not 'mandate which entities should be required to publish interim financial reports, how frequently, or how soon after the end of an interim period. However, governments, securities regulators, stock exchanges, and accountancy bodies often require entities whose debt or equity securities are publicly traded to publish interim financial reports'. Instead, IAS 34 only applies if an entity either elects to publish an interim financial report under IFRS or if another party requires the entity to do so.[4] The standard is not mandatory; hence entities may still prepare annual IFRS financial statements even if their interim financial statements do not comply with IAS 34.[5] Nevertheless, the IASB encourages publicly traded entities to provide interim financial reports that conform to the recognition, measurement and disclosure principles set out in IAS 34. Those entities are specifically encouraged:

'(a)   to provide interim financial reports at least as of the end of the first half of their financial year; and

(b)   to make their interim financial reports available not later than 60 days after the end of the interim period.'[6]

An entity is only permitted to describe an interim financial report as complying with IFRS if it complies with all of the requirements of IAS 34.[7] Therefore, an entity that applies all IFRS recognition and measurement requirements in its interim financial report, but that does not meet all disclosure requirements in IAS 34 should not describe the interim financial report as complying with IFRS.

2.3   Content of an interim financial report

The standard defines an interim period as 'a financial reporting period shorter than a full financial year'.[8] An interim financial report may contain either a complete set of financial statements (as described in IAS 1 – *Presentation of Financial Statements*) or a set of condensed financial statements as described in IAS 34 for an interim period.[9] The standard does not prohibit or discourage an entity from:[10]

- publishing a complete set of financial statements in its interim financial report, rather than condensed financial statements and selected explanatory notes; or

- including in condensed interim financial statements more than the minimum line items or selected explanatory notes as set out in IAS 34.

The recognition and measurement guidance in the standard, together with the specific note disclosures applicable to interim periods, required by the standard apply to both complete and condensed financial statements.[11]

2.3.1   Components, form and content of an interim financial report

A   Complete set of financial statements

An entity that publishes a complete set of financial statements in its interim financial report should include the following components:

'(a)   a balance sheet;

(b)   an income statement;

(c)   a statement of changes in equity showing either:

   (i)   all changes in equity, or

   (ii)   changes in equity other than those arising from transactions with equity holders acting in their capacity as equity holders;

(d)   a cash flow statement; and

(e)   notes, comprising a summary of significant accounting policies and other explanatory notes.'[12]

If an entity publishes a 'complete set of financial statements in its interim financial report, the form and content of those statements should conform to the requirements of IAS 1'.[13] In addition, the entity should disclose the information specifically required by IAS 34 in respect of interim financial reports (particularly those discussed at 2.3.2 below).[14]

B   Condensed financial statements

In the interest of timeliness and cost considerations and to avoid repetition of information previously reported, an entity may be required to or may elect to provide less information at interim dates as compared with its annual financial statements.[15] The standard defines the minimum content of an interim report as follows:

'(a)   condensed balance sheet;

(b)   condensed income statement;

(c)   condensed statement showing either (i) all changes in equity or (ii) changes in equity other than those arising from capital transactions with owners and distributions to owners;

(d)   condensed cash flow statement; and

(e)   selected explanatory notes.'[16]

The purpose of an interim financial report is to provide an update on the latest complete set of annual financial statements. Therefore, it should avoid duplication of information previously reported and focus on new activities, events and circumstances.[17]

The format of the condensed statements should include at least all of the headings and subtotals that were included in the equivalent primary statements in the entity's last annual financial statements and the selected explanatory notes required by the standard. Additional line items or notes should be included where their omission would be misleading.[18]

Other standards specify 'disclosures that should be made in financial statements. In that context, financial statements means complete sets of financial statements of the type normally included in an annual financial report and sometimes included in other reports.' If an entity's interim financial report includes only condensed financial statements and selected explanatory notes then the disclosures required by those other standards are not required.[19]

C   Complete and condensed financial information

The following requirements apply irrespective of whether an entity provides complete and condensed financial statements:

- basic and diluted earnings per share should be presented on the face of the condensed income statement for an interim period. However, IAS 34 does not specifically require disclosure of earnings per share information in respect of discontinued operations;[20]

- the presentation of changes in equity should follow the same format as in the annual financial statements;[21] and

- if the last annual financial statements were consolidated financial statements, the interim financial report is also prepared on a consolidated basis, with no requirement to give the parent's separate financial statements.[22]

2.3.2 Selected explanatory notes

IAS 34 presumes that 'a user of an entity's interim financial report will also have access to the most recent annual financial report of that enterprise'. Therefore, it is unnecessary for the notes to an interim financial report to provide relatively insignificant updates to the information that was already reported in the notes in the most recent annual report, because such disclosures are not significant to an understanding of the changes in financial position and performance of the entity since the last annual reporting date.[23] Conversely this means that when information has changed significantly, for example when assets and liabilities are marked to market, an entity will need to disclose information similar to that in its annual financial report.

An entity should include the following information, as a minimum, in the notes to its interim financial statements if it is not disclosed elsewhere in the interim financial report:

'(a) a statement that the same accounting policies and methods of computation are followed in the interim financial statements as compared with the most recent annual financial statements or, if those policies or methods have been changed, a description of the nature and effect of the change;

(b) explanatory comments about the seasonality or cyclicality of interim operations;

(c) the nature and amount of items affecting assets, liabilities, equity, net income, or cash flows that are unusual because of their nature, size, or incidence;

(d) the nature and amount of changes in estimates of amounts reported in prior interim periods of the current financial year or changes in estimates of amounts reported in prior financial years, if those changes have a material effect in the current interim period;

(e) issuances, repurchases, and repayments of debt and equity securities;

(f) dividends paid (aggregate or per share) separately for ordinary shares and other shares;

(g) segment revenue and segment result for business segments or geographical segments, whichever is the entity's primary basis of segment reporting (disclosure of segment data is required in an entity's interim financial report only if IAS 14 – *Segment Reporting* – requires that entity to disclose segment data in its annual financial statements);

(h) material events subsequent to the end of the interim period that have not been reflected in the financial statements for the interim period;

(i) the effect of changes in the composition of the entity during the interim period, including business combinations, acquisition or disposal of subsidiaries and long-term investments, restructurings, and discontinued operations. In the case of business combinations, the entity shall disclose the information required to be disclosed under paragraphs 66-73 of IFRS 3 –

Business Combinations. IFRS 3 requires such information to be 'disclosed in aggregate for business combinations effected during the reporting period that are individually immaterial'.[24] However, materiality needs to be assessed in relation to the interim period, which implies that IFRS 3 may require more detailed disclosures on business combinations in an interim period than in the annual financial statements; and

(j)   changes in contingent liabilities or contingent assets since the last annual balance sheet date.[25]

This information should normally be reported on a financial year-to-date basis, but the entity should also disclose any events or transactions that are material to an understanding of the current interim period.[26]

IAS 34 gives the following examples of disclosures required in interim financial reports:[27]

- the write-down of inventories to net realisable value and the reversal of such a write-down;

- recognition of a loss from the impairment of property, plant, and equipment, intangible assets, or other assets, and the reversal of such an impairment loss;

- the reversal of any provisions for the costs of restructuring;

- acquisitions and disposals of items of property, plant, and equipment;

- commitments for the purchase of property, plant, and equipment;

- litigation settlements;

- corrections of prior period errors;

- any loan default or breach of a loan agreement that has not been remedied on or before the balance sheet date; and

- related party transactions.

Furthermore, individual standards and interpretations also provide guidance regarding disclosures for many of these items.

The extract below illustrates how Bertelsmann complies with the disclosure requirements under (a) and (b) above.

Extract 35.1: Bertelsmann AG (Q2, 2003)

General Principles [extract]

This interim financial report for Bertelsmann AG was prepared in accordance with IAS 34 *"Interim Financial Reporting"*. The same accounting policies were used as those applied in the annual financial statements for the year ended December 31, 2002, in which the accounting policies are described in detail. The interim report was reviewed by our auditors.

Outlook for 2003 [extract]

Due to the seasonal nature of much of Bertelsmann's business, higher revenues and operating profits can be expected in the second half of the year than in the first six months. Bertelsmann holds to its forecast of attaining a higher Operating EBITA for the whole of 2003 than for 2002.

The explanatory comments about the seasonality or cyclicality of interim operations may need to be much more extensive when the business is particularly seasonal in nature.

Extract 35.2: TUI AG (Q1, 2004)

Financial position [extract]

Financing

At the end of the first quarter of 2004, the net financial debt totalled €3.7 billion (31 Dec 2003: €3.8 billion). The variations resulted from the seasonal nature of the tourism business and proceeds from divestments.

Destinations [extract]

Hotel companies

In the first quarter of 2004, for seasonal reasons only some of the hotels grouped under TUI Hotels & Resorts were open. Their total occupancy rate stood at around 73% and was thus up on the previous year. RIU hotels recorded an above-average occupancy rate for its long-haul destinations; hotels on the Balearic Islands also reported good booking levels. In contrast, Grupotel hotels in this area, which reopened in February, saw their occupancy rates drop year-on-year. Robinson only operated two thirds of its clubs all the year round. Its occupancy rates rose slightly compared to the last year. Magic Life only operated six of its clubs throughout the year. Like Iberotel, it recorded particularly good booking levels for its complexes in Egypt. In Greece, Grecotels closed down for the winter.

Shipping

The business trend in container shipping was characterised by persistently strong demand for transport volume – which, however, was below the level for the previous quarter for seasonal reasons – as well as persistently high freight rates on high-volume routes in the major shipping areas. Transport in the Far East, Trans-Pacific and North Atlantic shipping areas rose substantially year-on-year, while the South America shipping area only reported moderate growth due to weak economic activity in this region.

Notes on the consolidated profit and loss statement [extract]

Overall, the earnings situation is characterised by the seasonal nature of the tourism business. As a result, the profit contributions of the tourism division are mainly made in the second and third quarter of any one year.

The extract below shows a typical disclosure of changes in the composition of an entity during the interim period.

Extract 35.3: BMW AG (Q1, 2004)

Notes to the Interim Group Financial Statements for the 1st quarter 2004
Accounting Principles and Policies [extract]

[2] Consolidated companies

The BMW Group financial statements for the first quarter 2004 include, besides BMW AG, 39 German and 128 foreign subsidiaries. This includes 18 special securities funds and 16 special purpose entities (almost all used for asset backed financing transactions). BMW Financial Services Korea Co., Ltd., Seoul, and BMW Leasing de Mexico S. A. de C.V., Mexico City, were consolidated for the first time in the first quarter 2004. Both of these subsidiaries are part of financial operations.

Compared to the first quarter 2003, a total of nine foreign subsidiaries, including eight special purpose entities, are no longer consolidated and nine foreign subsidiaries, including seven special purpose entities, are consolidated for the first time. Of the entities for which the equity method is applied, one is no longer consolidated and one has been consolidated for the first time. The changes in the composition of the Group do not have a material impact on the earnings performance, financial position and net assets of the Group.

2.3.3 Disclosure of compliance with IFRS

If an interim financial report complies with the requirements of IAS 34, this fact should be disclosed. Furthermore, an interim financial report should not be described as complying with IFRS unless it complies with all the requirements of International Financial Reporting Standards,[28] a requirement similar to the one found in IAS 1.[29]

Extract 35.4: BMW AG (Q1, 2004)

Notes to the Interim Group Financial Statements for the 1st quarter 2004
Accounting Principles and Policies [extract]

[1] Basis of preparation [extract]

The consolidated financial statements of BMW AG at 31 December 2003 were drawn up in accordance with International Financial Reporting Standards (IFRSs) issued by the International Accounting Standards Board (IASB), London, and valid at the balance sheet date. The interim Group financial statements at 31 March 2004, which have been prepared in accordance with International Accounting Standard (IAS) 34 (*Interim Financial Reporting*), have been drawn up using the same accounting methods as in the 2003 Group financial statements. All interpretations of the International Financial Reporting Interpretations Committee (IFRIC), formerly the Standing Interpretations Committee (SIC), which are mandatory at 31 March 2004, were also applied.

2.3.4 Periods for which interim financial statements are required to be presented

Irrespective of whether an entity presents condensed or complete interim financial statements, its interim reports should include the following:

'(a) balance sheet as of the end of the current interim period and a comparative balance sheet as of the end of the immediately preceding financial year;

(b) income statements for the current interim period and cumulatively for the current financial year to date, with comparative income statements for the comparable interim periods (current and year-to-date) of the immediately preceding financial year;

(c) statement showing changes in equity cumulatively for the current financial year to date, with a comparative statement for the comparable year-to-date period of the immediately preceding financial year; and

(d) cash flow statement cumulatively for the current financial year to date, with a comparative statement for the comparable year-to-date period of the immediately preceding financial year.'[30]

Furthermore, if an entity's business is highly seasonal, the standard encourages it to disclose additional financial information for 'the twelve months ending on the interim reporting date and comparative information for the prior twelve-month period'.[31]

The standard does not require an entity to present a balance sheet for the comparable interim period. However, in practice many entities reporting under IFRS disclose this information on a voluntary basis.

The examples below illustrate the periods that an entity is required and encouraged to disclose under IAS 34.[32]

Example 35.1:   Entity publishes interim financial reports half-yearly

If an entity's financial year ends 31 December (calendar year). It should present the following financial statements (condensed or complete) in its half-yearly interim financial report as of 30 June 2005:

Half-yearly interim report	*End of the comparative interim period*	*Immediately preceding year-end*	*End of the current interim period*
	30/6/2004	31/12/2004	30/6/2005
Balance sheet		●	●
Income statement			
– 6 months ending	●		●
– 12 months ending	○		○
Statement of changes in equity			
– 6 months ending	●		●
– 12 months ending	○		○
Cash flow statement			
– 6 months ending	●		●
– 12 months ending	○		○

● Required   ○ Disclosure encouraged if the entity's business is highly seasonal

If an entity were to publish a separate interim financial report for the final interim period (i.e. second half of its financial year), it should present the following financial statements (condensed or complete) in its second half-yearly interim financial report as of 31 December 2005:

Second half-yearly interim report	*End of the comparative interim period*	*End of the current interim period*
	31/12/2004	31/12/2005
Balance sheet	●	●
Income statement		
– 6 months ending	●	●
– 12 months ending	●	●
Statement of changes in equity		
– 12 months ending	●	●
Cash flow statement		
– 12 months ending	●	●

● Required

Example 35.2:　Entity publishes interim financial reports quarterly

If an entity's financial year ends 31 December (calendar year). It should present the following financial statements (condensed or complete) in its quarterly interim financial reports for 2005:

First quarter interim report	*End of the comparative interim period*	*Immediately preceding year-end*	*End of the current interim period*
	31/3/2004	31/12/2004	31/3/2005
Balance sheet		●	●
Income statement			
– 3 months ending	●		●
– 12 months ending	○		○
Statement of changes in equity			
– 3 months ending	●		●
– 12 months ending	○		○
Cash flow statement			
– 3 months ending	●		●
– 12 months ending	○		○

● Required　○ Disclosure encouraged if the entity's business is highly seasonal

Second quarter interim report	*End of the comparative interim period*	*Immediately preceding year-end*	*End of the current interim period*
	30/6/2004	31/12/2004	30/6/2005
Balance sheet		●	●
Income statement			
– 3 months ending	●		●
– 6 months ending	●		●
– 12 months ending	○		○
Statement of changes in equity			
– 6 months ending	●		●
– 12 months ending	○		○
Cash flow statement			
– 6 months ending	●		●
– 12 months ending	○		○

● Required　○ Disclosure encouraged if the entity's business is highly seasonal

Third quarter interim report	End of the comparative interim period 30/9/2004	Immediately preceding year-end 31/12/2004	End of the current interim period 30/9/2005
Balance sheet		•	•
Income statement			
– 3 months ending	•		•
– 9 months ending	•		•
– 12 months ending	○		○
Statement of changes in equity			
– 9 months ending	•		•
– 12 months ending	○		○
Cash flow statement			
– 9 months ending	•		•
– 12 months ending	○		○

• Required   ○ Disclosure encouraged if the entity's business is highly seasonal

If an entity were to publish a separate interim financial report for the final interim period (i.e. fourth quarter of its financial year), it should present the following financial statements (condensed or complete) in its fourth quarter interim financial report as of 31 December 2005:

Fourth quarter interim report	End of the comparative interim period 31/12/2004	End of the current interim period 31/12/2005
Balance sheet	•	•
Income statement		
– 3 months ending	•	•
– 12 months ending	•	•
Statement of changes in equity		
– 12 months ending	•	•
Cash flow statement		
– 12 months ending	•	•

• Required

First-time adopters of IFRS need to disclose certain reconciliations between their equity and income under IFRS and under their previous GAAP. Details on the required disclosures can be found at 3.1 below and in Chapter 4 at 2.10.3.

A   Length of interim reporting period

Although it is often taken as a given, IAS 34 does not actually require an entity to present either quarterly or half-year reports, as the extract below illustrates it is also possible to present an interim report for, for example, a 4-month interim period.

Extract 35.5: Bossard Holding AG (January 1 – April 30, 2003)

1. Basis of preparation [extract]

The unaudited consolidated first four months interim financial statements are prepared in accordance with the International Financial Reporting Standards (IFRS) IAS 34 *"Interim Financial Reporting"*. The accounting policies used in the preparation and presentation of the interim financial statements are consistent with those used in the consolidated financial statements for the year ended December 31, 2002

2.3.5   Materiality

IAS 1 and IAS 8 – *Accounting Policies, Changes in Accounting Estimates and Errors* – define an item as material if its omission or misstatement could influence the economic decisions of users of the financial statements, but these standards do not contain quantitative guidance on materiality.[33] The same definition of 'material' also applies to the preparation of interim financial statements. An entity should – for the purpose of deciding how to recognise, measure, classify, or disclose an item in its interim financial report – assess materiality in relation to the interim period financial data.[34]

Under IAS 34, 'the overriding goal is to ensure that an interim financial report includes all information that is relevant to understanding an entity's financial position and performance during the interim period.' Therefore, the standard bases the 'recognition and disclosure decision on data for the interim period by itself for reasons of understandability of the interim figures', this is to avoid misleading inferences that might result from non-disclosure of, for example, unusual items, changes in accounting policies or estimates, and errors.[35]

Finally, the standard specifically states that in making assessments of materiality, it should be recognised that interim measurements may rely on estimates to a greater extent than measurements of annual financial data.[36]

2.3.6   Disclosure in annual financial statements

An estimate of an amount reported in an interim period can change significantly during the final interim period of the financial year. An entity that does not present a separate interim financial report for its final interim period should disclose the nature and amount of such a change in estimate in a note to the annual financial statements for that financial year.[37] This disclosure requirement is 'intended to be narrow in scope – relating only to the change in estimate. An entity is not required to include additional interim period financial information in its annual financial statements.'[38]

The requirement to disclose the above information is based on IAS 8 and paragraph 16(d) of IAS 34, which require disclosure of the nature and the amount of a change in estimate that either has a material effect in the current period or is expected to have a material effect in subsequent periods in annual financial statements and interim financial reports. The standard mentions 'changes in estimate in the final interim period relating to inventory write-downs, restructurings, or impairment losses that were reported in an earlier interim period of the financial year' as examples of items that should be disclosed.[39]

2.4 Recognition and measurement

2.4.1 Same accounting policies as in annual financial statements

Like other standard-setters, the IASB's approach reflects something of a hybrid between the discrete and the integral methods. The principles for recognising assets, liabilities, income and expenses for interim periods are the same as in the annual financial statements (except for accounting policy changes made after the date of the most recent annual financial statements that are to be reflected in the next annual financial statements). However, there is an additional principle in IAS 34 to say that 'the frequency of an enterprise's reporting (annual, half-yearly or quarterly) should not affect the measurement of its annual results. To achieve that objective, measurements for interim reporting purposes should be made on a year-to-date basis.'[40]

The effect of this is that certain measurement adjustments which would be regarded as irreversible if made at the year-end can be revisited if they were made in the first interim period and circumstances justify a different answer by the end of the year (or by the end of a subsequent interim period). In other words, requiring that an entity 'apply the same accounting policies in its interim financial statements as in its annual statements may seem to suggest that interim period measurements are made as if each interim period stands alone as an independent reporting period. However, by providing that the frequency of an entity's reporting should not affect the measurement of its annual results, [the standard] acknowledges that an interim period is a part of a larger financial year.'[41]

Still, principles for recognising assets, liabilities, income, and expenses for interim periods are the same as in annual financial statements.[42] Therefore, a liability at an interim reporting date must represent an existing obligation at that date, just as it must at an annual reporting date.[43] Similarly, 'costs that, by their nature, would not qualify as assets at the financial year-end would not qualify at interim dates either.[44] Under IAS 34, as under the IASB's *Framework*, 'an essential characteristic of income (revenue) and expenses is that the related inflows and outflows of assets and liabilities have already taken place. If those inflows or outflows have taken place, the related revenue and expense are recognised; otherwise they are not recognised.'[45]

The standard provides a number of examples to illustrate these points:

- Inventory write-downs, impairments or provisions for restructurings should be recognised and measured in the same way as if the interim period end was a financial year-end. If the estimate changes in a subsequent interim period in the financial year, the original estimate may need to be changed, either by recognising additional accruals or reversals of the previously recognised amount in the subsequent interim period;[46]

- IAS 34 states that 'a cost that does not meet a definition of an asset at the end of an interim period is not deferred on the balance sheet either to await future information as to whether it has met the definition of an asset or to smooth earnings over interim periods within a financial year'.[47] For example, in accordance with IAS 38 – *Intangible Assets* – costs incurred before the recognition criteria are met should be expensed. Only those costs incurred after the recognition criteria are met can be capitalised; there is no reinstatement as an asset in a later period of costs previously expensed because the recognition criteria were not met at that time; and

- Income tax expense should be 'recognised in each interim period based on the best estimate of the weighted average annual income tax rate expected for the full financial year. Amounts accrued for income tax expense in one interim period may have to be adjusted in a subsequent interim period of that financial year if the estimate of the annual income tax rate changes.'[48]

This is therefore a rather more subtle approach than the discrete method, because each quarter (say) is evaluated not as an isolated period but as part of a cumulative period that builds up to a full year whose results are not to be influenced by the operation of interim reporting practices. Amounts reported for previous interim periods are not retrospectively adjusted, and therefore year-to-date measurements may involve changes in estimates of amounts reported in previous interim periods of the current financial year. As discussed at 2.3.2 and 2.3.6 above, IAS 34 requires disclosure of the nature and amount of material changes in estimate, both in the interim financial statements and in the full year financial statements, if there are material changes in estimate since the latest interim financial statements.[49]

2.4.2 *Seasonal businesses*

A   Revenues received seasonally, cyclically, or occasionally

Some entities operate in businesses that are heavily seasonal, for example, agricultural businesses with seasonal crops, holiday companies, domestic fuel suppliers or retailers who depend on Christmas or holiday sales.[50] Their financial year is often chosen to fit their annual operating cycle, but this may equally mean that an individual interim period gives little indication of their likely annual results. In some cases, they may even have negligible sales in some interim periods.

An extreme application of the integral approach in theory might suggest that they should, for example, try to predict their annual results and contrive to report half of that in the half-year interim financial statements. However, this would be a pointless exercise – bearing little relation to the reality of their business in individual interim periods – and is not permitted under IAS 34. The standard states that 'revenues that are received seasonally, cyclically, or occasionally within a financial year should not be anticipated or deferred as of an interim date if anticipation or deferral would not be appropriate at the end of the enterprise's financial year.'[51] Seasonal entities, therefore, need to report their actual sales (if any) for individual interim periods under IFRS.

IAS 34 also requires an entity to give explanatory comments about the seasonality or cyclicality of interim operations (see 2.3.2 above).[52] Where businesses are highly seasonal, IAS 34 encourages reporting of additional information for the twelve months ending on the interim period date and comparatives for the prior twelve-month period (see 2.3.4 above).[53]

B   *Costs incurred unevenly during the financial year*

IAS 34 prohibits the anticipation or deferral of costs incurred unevenly throughout the financial year at the interim date if anticipation or deferral would be inappropriate at the year-end.[54] This harks back to the principle that assets and liabilities must be recognised and measured using the same criteria that would apply if the interim period were the financial year-end.[55] This principle would seem to prevent flexing of costs in seasonal businesses when this would result in assets or liabilities that would not have been appropriate were the interim period to be the year-end.

So far as direct costs are concerned this approach is entirely appropriate. The more controversial area concerns indirect costs that would normally be accounted for on a time basis. Recognising these indirect costs in the normal way could easily result in a loss being reported in an individual interim period because there are insufficient revenues to cover them. Nevertheless, IAS 34 does not permit an entity to anticipate or defer such costs in an interim period if such a policy would not be appropriate at year-end.

This application of the discrete approach would reflect the reality of that period's performance, but also emphasises the limited usefulness of the interim report, because it would show that the results of that period really have little meaning in isolation. On the other hand attempting to allocate costs in proportion to the expected activity levels in individual interim periods would be an attempt to show the results in their proper context, but it involves a higher degree of uncertainty and it becomes at least partly an exercise in forecasting rather than a report on the results of an expired period.

2.5   Examples of application of recognition and measurement principles

The standard provides in Appendix B numerous examples that illustrate the application of the general recognition and measurement principles to interim financial reports.[56]

As will be discussed below, for some items – taxation, staff bonuses or profit sharing, sales commissions, volume discounts on both purchases and sales, contingent lease payments – IAS 34 states that an entity should predict the outcome for the whole year in order to determine the effective rate to apply in measuring the results for the interim period. While this appears to apply an integral approach, in reality it is no different from the estimates that have to be made in annual financial statements whenever the base period for measuring a variable amount of this kind is different from the financial year.

2.5.1 Property, plant and equipment and intangible assets

A   Depreciation and amortisation

Depreciation and amortisation for an interim period is based only on assets owned during that interim period and does not take into account asset acquisitions or disposals planned for later in the financial year.[57]

An entity applying a straight-line method of depreciation (amortisation) should not allocate the depreciation (amortisation) charge between interim periods based on the level of activity. However, an entity is permitted under IAS 16 – *Property, Plant and Equipment* – to use a 'unit of production' method of depreciation, which results in a charge based on the expected use or output (see Chapter 12 at 2.4.2 E and 2.8.6 C). An entity can only apply this method if it 'most closely reflects the expected pattern of consumption of the future economic benefits embodied in the asset'. The chosen method should be 'applied consistently from period to period unless there is a change in the expected pattern of consumption of those future economic benefits'.[58] Therefore, an entity cannot apply a straight-line method of depreciation in its annual financial statements, while allocating the depreciation charge to interim periods using a 'unit of production' based approach.

B   Impairment of assets

IAS 36 – *Impairment of Assets* – requires an entity to recognise an impairment loss if the recoverable amount of an asset has declined below its carrying amount.[59] An entity should apply the same impairment testing, recognition, and reversal criteria at an interim date as it would at the end of its financial year.[60]

IAS 34 helpfully states that it 'does not mean, however, that an enterprise must necessarily make a detailed impairment calculation at the end of each interim period. Rather, an enterprise will review for indications of significant impairment since the end of the most recent financial year to determine whether such a calculation is needed.'[61] Nevertheless, the standard does not actually exempt an entity from performing impairment tests at the end of its interim periods. For example, an entity that recognised an impairment charge in the immediately preceding financial year, may find that it needs to update its impairment calculations at the end of subsequent interim periods because impairment indicators remain present.

C   Intangible assets

An entity should apply the IAS 38 definitions and recognition criteria for intangible assets in the same way in an interim period as in an annual period. Therefore, costs incurred before the recognition criteria are met should be recognised as an expense.[62] Expenditure on an intangible item that was initially recognised as an expense under IAS 38 cannot be reinstated and recognised as part of the cost of an intangible asset at a later date (e.g. in a later interim period).[63] Furthermore, 'deferring' costs as assets in an interim balance sheet in the hope that the recognition criteria will be met later in the financial year is not permitted. Only costs incurred after the specific point in time at which the criteria are met are recognised as part of the cost of an intangible asset.[64]

2.5.2   Employee benefits

A   Employer payroll taxes and insurance contributions

If employer payroll taxes, contributions to government-sponsored insurance funds or national insurance contributions are assessed on an annual basis, the employer's related expense should be recognised in interim periods using an estimated average annual effective rate, even if this does not reflect the timing of the payments made. 'A common example is an employer payroll tax or insurance contribution that is imposed up to a certain maximum level of earnings per employee. For higher income employees, the maximum income is reached before the end of the financial year, and the employer makes no further payments through the end of the year.'[65]

B   Year-end bonuses

The nature of year-end bonuses varies widely. Some bonus schemes only require continued employment whereas others require certain performance criteria to be attained on a monthly, quarterly or annual basis.[66] A bonus is anticipated for interim reporting purposes only if:[67]

(a)   the entity has a present legal or constructive obligation to make such payments as a result of past events; and

(b)   a reliable estimate of the obligation can be made.

A present obligation exists only when an entity has no realistic alternative but to make the payments.[68] IAS 19 – *Employee Benefits* – provides detailed guidance on accounting for profit sharing and bonus plans (see Chapter 30 at 6.1.3).[69]

C   Pensions

Pension costs for an interim period should be calculated on a year-to-date basis using the actuarially determined pension cost rate at the end of the prior year, adjusted for significant market fluctuations, curtailments, settlements, or other one-time events.[70]

D   Vacations, holidays, and other short-term compensated absences

IAS 19 distinguishes between accumulating and non-accumulating compensated absences.[71] Accumulating compensated absences are those that are carried forward and can be used in future periods if the current period's entitlement is not used in full. IAS 19 requires that an 'enterprise measure the expected cost of and obligation for accumulating compensated absences at the amount the enterprise expects to pay as a result of the unused entitlement that has accumulated at the balance sheet date' (see Chapter 30 at 6.1.2). The same principle applies to interim reporting. Conversely, an entity should not recognise an expense or liability for non-accumulating compensated absences at an interim reporting date, just as it recognises none at an annual reporting date.[72]

2.5.3   Inventories and cost of sales

A   Inventories

An entity should apply the recognition and measurement requirements of IAS 2 – *Inventories* – for interim financial reporting as it does for annual reporting purposes, despite the fact that 'inventories pose particular problems at any financial reporting date because of the need to determine inventory quantities, costs, and net realisable values.' However, IAS 34 does comment that 'to save cost and time, entities often use estimates to measure inventories at interim dates to a greater extent than at annual reporting dates.'[73]

Net realisable values should be determined using selling prices and costs to complete and dispose at the interim date. A write down should be reversed in a subsequent interim period only if it would be appropriate to do so at the end of the financial year.[74]

B   Contractual or anticipated purchase price changes

Both the payer and the recipient of volume rebates or discounts and other contractual changes in the prices of raw materials, labour, or other purchased goods and services should anticipate these items in their interim periods, if it is probable that they have been earned or will take effect. However, discretionary rebates and discounts should not be anticipated because the resulting asset or liability would not meet the recognition criteria in the IASB's Framework.[75]

C   Interim period manufacturing cost variances

Price, efficiency, spending, and volume variances of a manufacturing entity should only be 'recognised in income at interim reporting dates to the same extent that those variances are recognised in income at financial year-end'. However, deferral of variances 'that are expected to be absorbed by year-end is not appropriate because it could result in reporting inventory at the interim date at more or less than its portion of the actual cost of manufacture'.[76]

2.5.4   Taxation

A   Measuring interim income tax expense

IAS 34 states that income tax expense should be accrued by applying the estimated weighted average annual income tax rate to pre-tax income of the interim period.[77] IAS 34 states that 'this is consistent with the basic concept set out in paragraph 28 [of the standard] that the same accounting recognition and measurement principles should be applied in an interim financial report as are applied in annual financial statements.'[78]

The standard states that an entity should use an estimated weighted average annual income tax rate in order to 'reflect a blend of the progressive tax rate structure expected to be applicable to the full year's earnings including enacted or substantively enacted changes in the income tax rates scheduled to take effect later in the financial year'.[79] IAS 12 – *Income Taxes* – provides more detailed guidance on how an entity should determine when a change in tax rate is substantively enacted.[80] The entity should re-estimate the estimated average annual income tax rate on a year-to-date basis and disclose any significant change in estimate in accordance with IAS 34.[81]

The standard states that an entity should, to the extent practicable:

- estimate the average annual effective income tax rate for each taxing jurisdiction separately and apply it individually to the interim period pre-tax income of each jurisdiction; and

- apply different income tax rates to each individual category of interim period pre-tax income (such as capital gains or income earned in particular industries).

However, the standard recognises that 'while that degree of precision is desirable, it may not be achievable in all cases, and a weighted average of rates across jurisdictions or across categories of income is used if it is a reasonable approximation of the effect of using more specific rates.'[82]

Example 35.3:   Measuring interim income tax expense[83]

To illustrate the application of the foregoing principle, an entity reporting quarterly expects to earn 10,000 pre-tax each quarter and operates in a jurisdiction with a tax rate of 20 per cent on the first 20,000 of annual earnings and 30 per cent on all additional earnings. Actual earnings match expectations. The following table shows the amount of income tax expense that is reported in each quarter:

	Tax expense
First quarter	2,500
Second quarter	2,500
Third quarter	2,500
Fourth quarter	2,500
Annual	10,000

10,000 of tax is expected to be payable for the full year on 40,000 of pre-tax income.

Example 35.4:   Measuring interim income tax expense – quarterly losses[84]

An entity reports quarterly, earns 15,000 pre-tax profit in the first quarter but expects to incur losses of 5,000 in each of the three remaining quarters (thus having zero income for the year), and operates in a jurisdiction in which its estimated average annual income tax rate is expected to be 20 per cent. The following table shows the amount of income tax expense that is reported in each quarter:

	Tax expense
First quarter	3,000
Second quarter	(1,000)
Third quarter	(1,000)
Fourth quarter	(1,000)
Annual	0

As the interim tax charge is based on an estimate of the weighted average annual rate, the charge in a subsequent interim period may need to be adjusted if that estimate changes.[85] IAS 34 requires disclosure in interim financial statements of material changes in estimate of amounts reported in an earlier period, or in the annual financial statements, material changes in estimate of amounts reported in the latest interim financial statements.[86]

B   Difference in financial reporting year and tax year

If an entity's financial reporting year and the income tax year differ, the 'income tax expense for the interim periods of that financial reporting year is measured using separate weighted average estimated effective tax rates for each of the income tax years applied to the portion of pre-tax income earned in each of those income tax years'.[87] In other words, an entity needs to compute a weighted average estimated effective tax rate for each income tax year, but not for its financial year.

Example 35.5:   Difference in financial reporting year and tax year[88]

An entity's financial reporting year ends 30 June and it reports quarterly. Its taxable year ends 31 December. For the financial year that begins 1 July 2004 and ends 30 June 2005, the entity earns 10,000 pre-tax each quarter.

The estimated average annual income tax rate is 30 per cent in 2004 and 40 per cent in 2005.

Quarter ending	Tax expense
30 September 2004	3,000
31 December 2004	3,000
31 March 2005	4,000
30 June 2005	4,000
Annual	14,000

C   Tax loss and tax credit carrybacks and carryforwards

IAS 34 repeats the guidance in IAS 12 and states that for carryforward of unused tax losses and tax credits, a deferred tax asset should be recognised to the extent that it is probable that future taxable profit will be available against which the unused tax losses and unused tax credits can be utilised. In assessing whether future taxable profit is available, the criteria described in IAS 12 should be applied at the interim date. Where these criteria are met, 'the effect of the tax loss carryforward is reflected in the computation of the estimated average annual effective income tax rate.'[89]

Example 35.6: Tax loss carryforwards[90]

An entity that reports quarterly has an operating loss carryforward of 10,000 for income tax purposes at the start of the current financial year for which a deferred tax asset has not been recognised. The entity earns 10,000 in the first quarter of the current year and expects to earn 10,000 in each of the three remaining quarters. Excluding the carryforward, the estimated average annual income tax rate is expected to be 40 per cent. Including the carryforward, the estimated average annual income tax rate is expected to be 30 per cent. Accordingly, tax expense is as follows:

	Tax expense
First quarter	3,000
Second quarter	3,000
Third quarter	3,000
Fourth quarter	3,000
Annual	12,000

In contrast, 'the benefits of a tax loss carryback are reflected in the interim period in which the related tax loss occurs.'[91] IAS 12 provides that 'the benefit relating to a tax loss that can be carried back to recover current tax of a previous period should be recognised as an asset'.[92] Therefore, a corresponding reduction of tax expense or increase of tax income should be recognised.[93]

D Tax credits

IAS 34 also discusses in more detail the treatment of tax credits, which may for example be based on amounts of capital expenditures, exports, and research and development expenditures. Such anticipated benefits are usually granted and calculated on an annual basis and therefore should be reflected in computing the effective annual tax rate. Where they relate to a one-time event, however, they should be excluded from the annual rate and dealt with separately. Occasionally, such tax credits are more akin to a government grant and should be recognised in the interim period in which they arise.[94]

2.5.5 Foreign currency translation

A Foreign currency translation gains and losses

An entity measures foreign currency translation gains and losses for interim financial reporting using the same principles that IAS 21 – *The Effects of Changes in Foreign Exchange Rates* – requires it to apply at its financial year-end (see Chapter 9).[95] An entity should use the actual average and closing rates for the interim period, i.e. it is not permitted to anticipate some future changes in foreign exchange rates in the remainder of the current financial year in translating foreign operations at an interim date.[96] For example, an entity is not permitted to 'defer some foreign currency translation adjustments at an interim date if the adjustment is expected to reverse before the end of the financial year'.[97]

B Interim financial reporting in hyperinflationary economies

Interim financial reports in hyperinflationary economies are prepared by the same principles as at financial year-end.[98] IAS 29 – *Financial Reporting in Hyperinflationary Economies*, requires 'that the financial statements of an entity that reports in the currency of a hyperinflationary economy be stated in terms of the measuring unit current at balance sheet date, and the gain or loss on the net monetary position is included in net income. Also, comparative financial data reported for prior periods is restated to the current measuring unit' (see Chapter 10).[99]

In practice this means that interim reporting under IAS 34 can be quite onerous for an entity reporting in the currency of a hyperinflationary economy, because – as can be seen in Examples 35.2 and 35.3 above – IAS 34 requires an entity to disclose a significant amount of information in its primary financial statement that would need to be updated at every interim reporting date.

Finally, the standard does not permit an entity to annualise the recognition of gains or losses, nor is it permitted to use an 'estimated annual inflation rate in preparing an interim financial report in a hyperinflationary economy'.[100]

2.5.6 Other

A Provisions

IAS 34 requires an entity to apply the same criteria in recognising and measuring a provision at an interim date, as at the end of the financial year.[101] Hence an entity should recognise a provision when it 'has no realistic alternative but to make a transfer of economic benefits as a result of an event that has created a legal or constructive obligation'.[102] The standard emphasises that the existence or non-existence of an obligation to transfer benefits is a question of fact, and is not a function of the length of the reporting period.[103]

The standards states that 'the amount of the obligation is adjusted upward or downward, with a corresponding loss or gain recognised in the income statement, if the enterprise's best estimate of the amount of the obligation changes.'[104] However, it should be noted that after the adoption of IFRIC 1 – *Changes in Existing Decommissioning, Restoration and Similar Liabilities* – an entity might need to adjust the carrying amount of the corresponding asset rather than recognise a gain or loss in the income statement.

B Other planned but irregularly occurring costs

Many entities budget for costs that they incur irregularly during the financial year, such as advertising campaigns, employee training and charitable contributions. Even though these costs are planned and expected to recur from year to year, they tend to be discretionary in nature. Therefore, 'recognising an obligation at an interim financial reporting date for such costs that have not yet been incurred generally is not consistent with the definition of a liability.'[105]

As discussed at 2.4.2 B above, IAS 34 prohibits the anticipation or deferral of costs incurred unevenly throughout the financial year at the interim date if anticipation or deferral would be inappropriate at the year-end.[106]

Extract 35.6: Coca-Cola HBC (Q1, 2004)

Notes to the condensed consolidated financial statements (unaudited) [extract]
1. Accounting policies

The accounting policies used in the preparation of these financial statements are consistent with those used in the annual financial statements for the year ended 31 December 2003.

Costs that are incurred unevenly during the financial year are anticipated or deferred in the interim report only if it would also be appropriate to anticipate or defer such costs at the end of the financial year.

These consolidated condensed financial statements have been prepared in accordance with IAS 34, *'Interim Financial Reporting'* and should be read in conjunction with the 2003 annual financial statements, which include a full description of the Group's accounting policies.

C   Major planned periodic maintenance or overhaul

The cost of a planned major periodic maintenance or overhaul or other seasonal expenditure that is expected to occur late in the year is not anticipated for interim reporting purposes unless an event has caused the entity to have a legal or constructive obligation. The mere intention or necessity to incur expenditure related to the future is not sufficient to give rise to an obligation.[107] Similarly, an entity is not permitted to defer and amortise such costs if they are incurred early in the year, but do not satisfy the criteria for recognition as an asset.

D   Contingent lease payments

Contingent lease payments can result in a legal or constructive obligation that should be recognised as a liability. If a lease provides for contingent payments based on annual sales (or use of the asset), an obligation can arise in the interim periods of the financial year before the required level of annual sales (or usage) has been achieved. If the entity expects to achieve the required level of sales (or usage), it should recognise a liability because it has 'no realistic alternative but to make the future lease payment'.[108]

2.6   Use of estimates

IAS 34 also discusses the use of estimates and also illustrates this with specific examples in Appendix C.[109] The measurement procedures followed in an interim financial report should be designed to ensure that the resulting information is reliable and that all material financial information that is relevant to an understanding of the financial position or performance of the entity is appropriately disclosed. However, the standard recognises that interim financial statements will generally require greater use of estimation methods than at the year-end.[110] Consequently, in measuring assets and liabilities there may be less use of outside experts in determining amounts for items such as provisions, contingencies, pensions or non-current assets revalued at fair values. Reliable measurement of such amounts may simply involve updating the year-end position. Also the procedures may be less rigorous than those at the financial year-end. Appendix C to IAS 34 is reproduced in the Example below.[111]

Example 35.7:   Use of estimates

Inventories	Full stock-taking and valuation procedures may not be required for inventories at interim dates, although it may be done at financial year-end. It may be sufficient to make estimates at interim dates based on sales margins.
Classifications of current and non-current assets and liabilities	Entities may do a more thorough investigation for classifying assets and liabilities as current or non-current at annual reporting dates than at interim dates.
Provisions	Determination of the appropriate amount of a provision (such as a provision for warranties, environmental costs, and site restoration costs) may be complex and often costly and time-consuming. Entities sometimes engage outside experts to assist in the annual calculations. Making similar estimates at interim dates often entails updating of the prior annual provision rather than the engaging of outside experts to do a new calculation.
Pensions	IAS 19 requires that an entity determine the present value of defined benefit obligations and the market value of plan assets at each balance sheet date and encourages an entity to involve a professionally qualified actuary in measurement of the obligations. For interim reporting purposes, reliable measurement is often obtainable by extrapolation of the latest actuarial valuation.
Income taxes	Entities may calculate income tax expense and deferred income tax liability at annual dates by applying the tax rate for each individual jurisdiction to measures of income for each jurisdiction. Paragraph 14 of Appendix B (see 2.5.4 A above) acknowledges that while that degree of precision is desirable at interim reporting dates as well, it may not be achievable in all cases, and a weighted average of rates across jurisdictions or across categories of income is used if it is a reasonable approximation of the effect of using more specific rates.
Contingencies	The measurement of contingencies may involve the opinions of legal experts or other advisers. Formal reports from independent experts are sometimes obtained with respect to contingencies. Such opinions about litigation, claims, assessments, and other contingencies and uncertainties may or may not also be needed at interim dates.
Revaluations and fair value accounting	IAS 16 allows an entity to choose as its accounting policy the revaluation model whereby items of property, plant and equipment are revalued to fair value. Similarly, IAS 40 requires an entity to determine the fair value of investment property. For those measurements, an entity may rely on professionally qualified valuers at annual reporting dates though not at interim reporting dates.
Intercompany reconciliations	Some intercompany balances that are reconciled on a detailed level in preparing consolidated financial statements at financial year-end might be reconciled at a less detailed level in preparing consolidated financial statements at an interim date.
Specialised industries	Because of complexity, costliness, and time, interim period measurements in specialised industries might be less precise than at financial year-end. An example would be calculation of insurance reserves by insurance companies.

Entities should pay special attention to items that are valued at fair value and that are outside the scope of IAS 36. This to avoid that, by not using professionally qualified valuers at interim reporting dates and only updating the year-end position, potential impairments are not recognised in the proper interim period.

2.7   Restatement of previously reported interim periods

An entity should apply the same accounting policies as applied in the annual financial statements except for accounting policy changes that are to be reflected in the next annual financial statements.[112] The main objective of IAS 34's rules on the adoption of new accounting policies is to ensure that a single accounting policy is applied to a particular class of transactions throughout an entire financial year.[113] Under IAS 34, a change in accounting policy, for which no transitional arrangements are specified by a new IFRS or Interpretation, should be reflected:[114]

(a)   reflected by restating the financial statements of prior interim periods of the current financial year and the comparable interim periods of any prior financial years that will be restated in the annual financial statements in accordance with IAS 8; or

(b)   reflected – when it is impracticable to determine the cumulative effect at the beginning of the financial year of applying a new accounting policy to all prior periods – by:

    (i)   adjusting the financial statements of prior interim periods of the current financial year; and

    (ii)   applying the new accounting policy prospectively from the earliest date practicable in comparable interim periods of prior financial years.

The effect of this principle is to require that within the current financial year any change in accounting policy is applied either retrospectively or, if that is not practicable, prospectively, from no later than the beginning of the financial year. It is not permitted to apply 'two differing accounting policies … to a particular class of transactions within a single financial year', because this would result in 'interim allocation difficulties, obscured operating results, and complicated analysis and understandability of interim period information'.[115]

3   TRANSITIONAL RULES AND FIRST-TIME ADOPTION

IAS 34 has been in force since 1999 – it became operative for financial statements covering periods beginning on or after 1 January 1999 – and does not contain separate transitional rules.[116] Therefore, an existing IFRS reporting entity must apply the requirements of IAS 34 in full without any additional disclosures when it publishes its first interim financial reports under IFRS. However, additional requirements exist for first-time adopters of IFRS that present interim reports under IFRS, these requirements are discussed at 3.1 below (see also Chapter 4 at 2.10.3).

3.1   First-time adoption of IFRS

If a first-time adopter presents an interim financial report under IAS 34 for part of the period covered by its first IFRS financial statements, that report should:[117]

(a)   include reconciliations of:

- its equity under previous GAAP at the end of that comparable interim period to its equity under IFRS at that date; and

- its profit or loss under previous GAAP for that comparable interim period, both on a current and year-to-date basis, to its profit or loss under IFRS for that period; and

(b)   include the reconciliations described in Chapter 4 at 2.10.2 A above or a cross-reference to another published document that includes these reconciliations.

For an entity presenting annual financial statements under IFRS it is not compulsory to prepare interim financial reports under IAS 34. Therefore, the above requirements only apply to first-time adopters that prepare interim reports under IAS 34 on a voluntary basis or that are required to do so by a regulator or other party.[118]

Example 35.8:   Reconciliations to be presented in IFRS half-year reports

Entity A's date of transition to IFRS is 1 January 2004, its reporting date is 31 December 2005 and it publishes a half-year report as of 30 June under IAS 34. Which primary financial statements and reconciliations should A in its first IFRS half-year report?

	1 January 2004	30 June 2004	31 December 2004	30 June 2005
Balance sheet			●	●
Reconciliation of equity	● *)	●	● *)	
For the period ending				
Income statement		●		●
Cash flow statement		●		●
Statement of changes in equity		●		●
Reconciliation of profit or loss		●	● *)	
Explanation of material adjustments to cash flow statement			● *)	

*)   Additional reconciliations required under paragraph 39 of IFRS 1.

As can be seen from the table in Example 35.8, most of the additional reconciliations and explanations required under (b) above would be presented out of context, i.e. without the balance sheet, income statement and cash flow statement that they relate to. For this reason a first-time adopter may want either (1) to include the primary financial statements to which these reconciliations relate in its first IFRS half-year report or (2) to refer to another document that includes these reconciliations with the relevant primary financial statements.

Example 35.9: *Reconciliations to be presented in first IFRS financial statement and quarterly interim reports*[119]

Entity B's date of transition to IFRS is 1 January 2004, its reporting date is 31 December 2005 and it publishes quarterly reports under IAS 34. Which reconciliations should B present in its 2005 interim reports and in its first IFRS financial statements?

	Reconciliation of equity	Reconciliation of profit or loss	Explanation of material adjustments to cash flow statement
First quarter			
1 January 2004	o		
31 March 2004	●	●	
31 December 2004	o	o	o
Second quarter			
1 January 2004	o		
30 June 2004	●		
– Current period		●	
– Year-to-date		●	
31 December 2004	o	o	o
Third quarter			
1 January 2004	o		
30 September 2004	●		
– Current period		●	
– Year-to-date		●	
31 December 2004	o	o	o
First IFRS financial statements			
1 January 2004	●		
31 December 2004	●	●	●

● Mandatory disclosures required to be included in the interim report and the first IFRS financial statements.

o Instead of including these reconciliations in the interim report, the entity may include a cross-reference to another published document that includes these reconciliations (for the second and third quarter this other published document could be the first quarter interim report if the information was included in that interim report).

Interim financial reports under IAS 34 contain considerably less detail than annual financial statements because they 'are based on the assumption that users of the interim financial report also have access to the most recent annual financial statements'.[120] Therefore, a first-time adopter will have to ensure that its first interim financial report contains sufficient information about events or transactions that are material to an understanding of the current interim period. Hence it may be necessary for a first-time adopter to include in its first IFRS interim report significantly more information that it would normally include in an interim report; alternatively it could include a cross-reference to another published document that includes such information.[121]

4   CONCLUSION

The underlying issue that has been inadequately discussed concerns the essential purpose of interim reporting. The standard takes a *Framework*-based approach to recognition and measurement in interim reports. Using that as a starting point, it is no surprise that the discrete approach is favoured, particularly as this is such a tidy answer for a standard-setter to adopt. But is interim reporting *really* only a more frequent version of annual reporting, but with fewer disclosures? This is probably not how it is perceived by preparers and users, who see it much more as a signalling device as to the outcome of the real period they are interested in, the financial year.

What then is the role of interim reporting in the communication between a company and its shareholders? Present practice under IFRS undoubtedly reflects the view that interim reporting is a subsidiary form of reporting which only deals with an instalment of a longer period. However, this is probably more as an expedient compromise than as the result of an attempt to meet a carefully researched need. In fact, sometimes IAS 34 describes the purpose of an interim financial report as being 'to provide an update on the latest complete set of annual financial statements. Accordingly, it focuses on new activities, events, and circumstances and does not duplicate information previously reported.'[122] Whereas elsewhere it is claimed that 'the overriding goal is to ensure that an interim financial report includes all information that is relevant to understanding an entity's financial position and performance during the interim period',[123] which would require the financial information to be presented in their full context.

A review of even a modest selection of interim reports under IAS 34 shows that reporting entities themselves appear to hold wildly different opinions as to what information should be included in an interim report. On the one hand there are entities that present only the bare minimum disclosures required by IAS 34, while on the other hand there are those that try to contextualise the interim information that they present. There is a truly staggering diversity in practice in terms of content, depth of coverage and structure in today's interim financial reports.

Given these nagging uncertainties about the role of interim reporting it is perhaps no surprise that the standard 'does not mandate which enterprises should be required to publish interim financial reports, how frequently, or how soon after the end of an interim period'.[124] Moreover, IAS 34 is not even mandatory for those entities that apply IFRS in their annual financial statements, but that choose not to claim compliance with IFRS in their interim financial statements.[125]

Given the lack of an adequate analysis of the essential purpose of interim reporting, it would be fruitful to give deeper consideration to the essential purpose of the exercise before the next revision of the rules on interim reporting is undertaken.

References

1 *Proposal for a Directive of the European Parliament and of the Council on the harmonisation of transparency requirements with regard to information about issuers whose securities are admitted to trading on a regulated market and amending Directive 2001/34/EC*, Council of the European Union, Brussels, 22 April 2004, Article 5.

2 IAS 34, *Interim Financial Reporting*, IASB, February 1998 (amended March 2004), para. 46.

3 IAS 34, Objective.

4 IAS 34, para. 1.

5 IAS 34, para. 2.

6 IAS 34, para. 1.

7 IAS 34, para. 3.

8 IAS 34, para. 4.

9 IAS 34, para. 4.

10 IAS 34, para. 7.

11 IAS 34, para. 7.

12 IAS 34, para. 5.

13 IAS 34, paras. 9 and 12.

14 IAS 34, para. 7.

15 IAS 34, para. 6.

16 IAS 34, para. 8.

17 IAS 34, para. 6.

18 IAS 34, para. 10.

19 IAS 34, para. 18.

20 IAS 34, para. 11.

21 IAS 34, para. 13.

22 IAS 34, para. 14.

23 IAS 34, para. 15.

24 IFRS 3, *Business Combinations*, IASB, March 2004, para. 68.

25 IAS 34, para. 16.

26 IAS 34, para. 16.

27 IAS 34, para. 17.

28 IAS 34, para. 19.

29 IAS 1, *Presentation of Financial Statements*, IASB, December 2003 (amended March 2004), para. 14.

30 IAS 34, para. 20.

31 IAS 34, para. 21.

32 IAS 34, para. 22 and Appendix A.

33 IAS 34, para. 24.

34 IAS 34, para. 23.

35 IAS 34, para. 25.

36 IAS 34, para. 23.

37 IAS 34, para. 26.

38 IAS 34, para. 27.

39 IAS 34, para. 27.

40 IAS 34, para. 28.

41 IAS 34, para. 29.

42 IAS 34, paras. 29 and 31.

43 IAS 34, para. 32.

44 IAS 34, para. 32.

45 IAS 34, para. 33.

46 IAS 34, para. 30.

47 IAS 34, para. 30.

48 IAS 34, para. 30.

49 IAS 34, paras. 16, 26 and 34-36.

50 IAS 34, para. 38.

51 IAS 34, para. 37.

52 IAS 34, para. 16.

53 IAS 34, para. 21.

54 IAS 34, para. 39.

55 IAS 34, para. 29.

56 IAS 34, para. 40.

57 IAS 34, Appendix B, para. 24.

58 IAS 16, *Property, Plant and Equipment*, IASB, December 2003 (amended March 2004), para. 62.

59 IAS 34, Appendix B, para. 35.

60 IAS 34, Appendix B, para. 36.

61 IAS 34, Appendix B, para. 36.

62 IAS 34, Appendix B, para. 8.

63 IAS 38, *Intangible Assets*, IASB, March 2004, para. 71.

64 IAS 34, Appendix B, para. 8.

65 IAS 34, Appendix B, para. 1.

66 IAS 34, Appendix B, para. 5.

67 IAS 34, Appendix B, para. 6.

68 IAS 19, *Employee Benefits*, IASB, February 1998 (amended March 2004), para. 17.

69 IAS 19, paras. 17-22.

70 IAS 34, Appendix B, para. 9.

71 IAS 19, para. 12.

72 IAS 34, Appendix B, para. 10.

73 IAS 34, Appendix B, para. 25.

74 IAS 34, Appendix B, para. 26.

75 IAS 34, Appendix B, para. 23.

76 IAS 34, Appendix B, para. 28.

77 IAS 34, para. 30 and Appendix B, para. 12.

78 IAS 34, Appendix B, para. 13.

79 IAS 34, Appendix B, para. 13.

80 IAS 12, *Income Taxes*, IASB, October 1996 (amended March 2004), para. 48.

81 IAS 34, Appendix B, para. 13.

82 IAS 34, Appendix B, para. 14.

83 IAS 34, Appendix B, para. 15.

84 IAS 34, Appendix B, para. 16.

85 IAS 34, para. 30.

86 IAS 34, paras. 16 and 26.

87 IAS 34, Appendix B, para. 17.

88 IAS 34, Appendix B, para. 18.

89 IAS 34, Appendix B, para. 21.

90 IAS 34, Appendix B, para. 22.
91 IAS 34, Appendix B, para. 20.
92 IAS 12, para. 13.
93 IAS 34, Appendix B, para. 20.
94 IAS 34, Appendix B, para. 19.
95 IAS 34, Appendix B, para. 29.
96 IAS 34, Appendix B, para. 30.
97 IAS 34, Appendix B, para. 31.
98 IAS 34, Appendix B, para. 32.
99 IAS 34, Appendix B, para. 33.
100 IAS 34, Appendix B, para. 34.
101 IAS 34, Appendix B, para. 4.
102 IAS 34, Appendix B, para. 3.
103 IAS 34, Appendix B, para. 4.
104 IAS 34, Appendix B, para. 3.
105 IAS 34, Appendix B, para. 11.
106 IAS 34, para. 39.
107 IAS 34, Appendix B, para. 2.
108 IAS 34, Appendix B, para. 7.
109 IAS 34, Appendix C.
110 IAS 34, para. 41.
111 IAS 34, para. 42 and Appendix C.
112 IAS 34, para. 28.
113 IAS 34, para. 44.
114 IAS 34, para. 43.
115 IAS 34, para. 45.
116 IAS 34, para. 46.
117 IFRS 1, *First-time Adoption of International
    Financial Reporting Standards*, IASB, June 2003
    (amended March 2004), para. 45.
118 IFRS 1, para. IG37.
119 IFRS 1, IG Example 10.
120 IFRS 1, para. 46.
121 IFRS 1, para. 46.
122 IAS 34, para. 6.
123 IAS 34, para. 25.
124 IAS 34, para. 1.
125 IAS 34, paras. 2-3.

Chapter 36   Agriculture

1   INTRODUCTION

1.1   Background and need for a standard

Traditionally agricultural activities have always been accounted for under the historical cost framework. In practice this meant that biological assets (e.g. cattle, trees, vines and other plants) and agricultural produce (e.g. fruit, cotton, wool and tea leaves) were accounted for at historical cost. In both cases gains could only arise upon sale to a customer, while losses could arise upon sale or impairment. The costs of supporting activities such as pest control, orchard maintenance, irrigation and other costs relating to growing crops were generally deferred and accounted for as inventory, work-in-progress or deferred cost.

In 1994, with the financial support of the World Bank, the (then) IASC decided 'to develop an International Accounting Standard on agriculture and appointed a Steering Committee to help define the issues and develop possible solutions'.[1] The project was somewhat unusual because it dealt with industry specific accounting issues and was not part of the work on the IASC's core set of standards.[2] The Draft Statement of Principles on agriculture, which was published by the Steering Committee in 1996, 'specifically asked for views on the feasibility of developing a comprehensive International Accounting Standard on agriculture'.[3] The IASC reaffirmed its conclusion that a standard was needed,[4] despite the apparent lack of enthusiasm for the project expressed by commentators. The IASC's decided to proceed with the project, as it wanted to reduce the diversity in accounting for agricultural activity that occurred because:

- agricultural activities were excluded from the scope of many International Accounting Standards;

- accounting guidelines for agricultural activity had been developed by national standard setters on a piecemeal basis; and

- 'the nature of agricultural activity creates uncertainty or conflicts when applying traditional accounting models, particularly because the critical events associated with biological transformation ... that alter the substance of biological assets are difficult to deal with in an accounting model based on historical cost and realisation'.[5]

Other reasons that convinced the IASC that there was a greater need for financial statements based on sound and generally accepted accounting principles include:[6]

- its belief that even small agricultural entities seeking outside capital and subsidies, particularly from banks or government agencies, are increasingly required to produce general purpose financial statements; and

- the fact that the international trend toward deregulation has resulted in increasing scale, scope, and commercialism of agricultural activity.

In July 1999, the IASC issued Exposure Draft E65 – *Agriculture*, which was, after considering the comments received, approved by the IASC at its final meeting in December 2000 as IAS 41 – *Agriculture*.[7] The standard was approved although many commentators strongly objected to the extensive reliance on fair values (see 1.2 below) and many of them failed to see the need for the standard in the first place. It was probably with a sense of relief that the IASC's Chairman and Secretary-General wrote in the *IASC Annual Review* that 'the meeting in London saw completion of IAS 41 on Agriculture. The Standard on Agriculture is an important one, even though it is dealing with specialised transactions and was not part of the core set of standards. Financial support for the work on this project was originally provided by The World Bank. IASC had been working on the project for some six years and this partly reflects the difficulty of the issues, particularly in deciding on the relative emphases to be given to fair-value-based measurements as opposed to cost-based measurements of agricultural assets. We were very pleased that the IASC Board was able to conclude its work on agriculture before handing matters over to a new Board.'[8]

1.2 The use of fair values

IAS 41 relies heavily on fair-value-based measurements of biological assets and agricultural produce (see 2.3.2 below), which is not uncontroversial and gave to rise to a significant number of comments during the development of the standard. The arguments in favour of the use of fair value measurement included the following:

- 'the effects of changes brought about by biological transformation are best reflected by reference to the fair value changes in biological assets';[9]

- 'no income might be reported until first harvest and sale (perhaps 30 years) in a plantation forestry enterprise using a transaction-based, historical cost accounting model. On the other hand, income is measured and reported throughout the period until initial harvest if an accounting model is used that recognises and measures biological growth using current fair values';[10]

- fair value has greater relevance, reliability, comparability, and understandability as a measurement of future economic benefits expected from biological assets than historical cost because:[11]

- the presence of active markets with observable market prices for many biological assets increases the reliability of market value as an indicator of fair value;

- historical-cost-based measures of biological assets are sometimes less reliable that fair-value-based measures because 'joint products and joint costs can create situations in which the relationship between inputs and outputs is ill-defined, leading to complex and arbitrary allocations of cost between the different outcomes of biological transformation';

- 'relatively long and continuous production cycles, with volatility in both the production and market environment, mean that the accounting period often does not depict a full cycle. Therefore, period-end measurement (as opposed to time of transaction) assumes greater significance in deriving a measure of current period financial performance or position'; and

- under the historical cost approach animals and plants acquired at over time are accounted for at different values, whereas fair-value-based measurement enhances comparability and understandability result because similar assets are measured and reported using the same basis.

Those who opposed measuring biological assets at fair value argued that:[12]

- 'there is superior reliability in cost measurement because historical cost is the result of arm's length transactions, and therefore provides evidence of an open-market value at that point in time, and is independently verifiable';

- 'fair value is sometimes not reliably measurable and that users of financial statements may be misled by presentation of numbers that are indicated as being fair value but are based on subjective and unverifiable assumptions';

- 'market prices are often volatile and cyclical and not appropriate as a basis of measurement';

- 'it may be onerous to require fair valuation at each balance sheet date, especially if interim reports are required';

- 'the historical cost convention is well established and commonly used. The use of any other basis should be accompanied by a change in the IASC Framework ... For consistency with other International Accounting Standards and other activities, biological assets should be measured at their cost';

- 'cost measurement provides more objective and consistent measurement';

- 'active markets may not exist for some biological assets in some countries';

- 'fair value measurement results in recognition of unrealised gains and losses and contradicts principles in International Accounting Standards on recognition of revenue'; and

- 'market prices at a balance sheet date may not bear a close relationship to the prices at which assets will be sold, and many biological assets are not held for sale.'

The IASC noted that the Framework 'is neutral with respect to the choice of measurement basis, identifying that a number of different bases are employed to different degrees and in varying combinations, though noting that historical cost is most commonly adopted'.[13] On balance the Board concluded that the standard 'should require a fair value model for biological assets related to agricultural activity because of the unique nature and characteristics of agricultural activity. However, the Board also concluded that, in some cases, fair value cannot be measured reliably.'[14] Instead of including a benchmark treatment and allowed alternative treatment in the standard,[15] the Board decided to 'include a reliability exception for cases where market-determined prices or values are not available and alternative estimates of fair value are determined to be clearly unreliable. In those cases, biological assets should be measured at their cost less any accumulated depreciation and any accumulated impairment losses.'[16]

2   REQUIREMENTS OF IAS 41

The stated objective of IAS 41 is to 'prescribe the accounting treatment, financial statement presentation, and disclosures related to agricultural activity'.[17]

2.1   Definitions

2.1.1   *Agriculture-related definitions*

IAS 41 defines an *agricultural activity* as 'the management by an entity of the biological transformation of biological assets for sale, into agricultural produce, or into additional biological assets'.[18] The standard clarifies that the term 'agricultural activity' covers a wide range of activities, such as 'raising livestock, forestry, annual or perennial cropping, cultivating orchards and plantations, floriculture, and aquaculture (including fish farming)'.[19] Nevertheless, these agricultural activities have certain common features:

'(a)   *Capability to change* – Living animals and plants are capable of biological transformation;

(b)   *Management of change* – Management facilitates biological transformation by enhancing, or at least stabilising, conditions necessary for the process to take place (for example, nutrient levels, moisture, temperature, fertility, and light). Such management distinguishes agricultural activity from other activities. For example, harvesting from unmanaged sources (such as ocean fishing and deforestation) is not agricultural activity; and

(c)   *Measurement of change* – The change in quality (for example, genetic merit, density, ripeness, fat cover, protein content, and fibre strength) or quantity (for example, progeny, weight, cubic metres, fibre length or diameter, and number of buds) brought about by biological transformation is measured and monitored as a routine management function.'[20]

Biological transformation under IAS 41 'comprises the processes of growth, degeneration, production, and procreation that cause qualitative or quantitative changes in a biological asset'.[21] The standard explains that biological transformation results in the following types of outcomes:

'(a)   asset changes through:

(i)   growth (an increase in quantity or improvement in quality of an animal or plant);

(ii)   degeneration (a decrease in the quantity or deterioration in quality of an animal or plant); or

(iii)   procreation (creation of additional living animals or plants); or

(b)   production of agricultural produce such as latex, tea leaf, wool, and milk.'[22]

IAS 41 defines the following additional terms that are used throughout the standard:[23]

A *biological asset* is a living animal or plant.

A *group of biological assets* is an aggregation of similar living animals or plants.

Agricultural produce is the harvested product of the entity's biological assets.

Harvest is the detachment of produce from a biological asset or the cessation of a biological asset's life processes.

The standard provides the following examples to illustrate the above definitions:[24]

Biological assets	Agricultural produce	Products that are the result of processing after harvest
Sheep	Wool	Yarn, carpet
Trees in a plantation forest	Logs	Lumber
Plants	Cotton	Thread, clothing
	Harvested cane	Sugar
Dairy cattle	Milk	Cheese
Pigs	Carcass	Sausages, cured hams
Bushes	Leaf	Tea, cured tobacco
Vines	Grapes	Wine
Fruit trees	Picked fruit	Processed fruit

The standard only deals with the items listed in the first two columns, while IAS 2 – *Inventories* – typically deals with items in the third column.

2.1.2   General definitions

IAS 41 defines the general terms it uses throughout the standard as follows:[25]

An *active market* is a market where all the following conditions exist:

(a)   the items traded within the market are homogeneous;

(b)   willing buyers and sellers can normally be found at any time; and

(c)   prices are available to the public.

Carrying amount is the amount at which an asset is recognised in the balance sheet.

Fair value is the amount for which an asset could be exchanged, or a liability settled, between knowledgeable, willing parties in an arm's length transaction.

The standard requires an entity to take the present location and condition of the biological asset into account in determining its fair value. Given the logistical problems and generally high costs of transporting living animals and plants, there will be many different fair values for the same biological assets depending on their location. For example, 'the fair value of cattle at a farm is the price for the cattle in the relevant market less the transport and other costs of getting the cattle to that market'.[26] It is possible for an active market to exist in one geographical area but not in another area. For example, transportation costs may limit the geographical size of the market for agricultural produce significantly, possibly to the point where a local cooperative or factory is the only buyer. In the latter case, the local market – with one buyer and many sellers – might not meet the definition of an active market.

Government grants are as defined in IAS 20 – *Accounting for Government Grants and Disclosure of Government Assistance* (see Chapter 27 at 2.1).

2.2   Scope

IAS 41 applies to accounting for biological assets, agricultural produce at the point of harvest and government grants involving biological assets when they relate to agricultural activity.[27] Consequently, biological assets may be outside the scope of IAS 41 when they are not used in an agricultural activity. For this reason the animals in a zoo (or game park) that does not have an active breeding programme and rarely sells any animals or animal products would be outside the scope of the standard. Biological assets outside the scope of IAS 41 will fall normally within the scope of either IAS 16 – *Property, Plant and Equipment* – or IAS 2.

In addition, IAS 41 explicitly excludes the following assets from its scope:[28]

- land related to agricultural activity, which should be accounted for under either IAS 16 or IAS 40 – *Investment Property*;[29]
- intangible assets related to agricultural activity, which should be accounted for under IAS 38 – *Intangible Assets*.[30]

IAS 41 should be applied to agricultural produce only at the point of harvest. Subsequently, agricultural produce is accounted for under IAS 2.[31] The standard does not deal with the processing of agricultural produce after harvest for practical reasons rather conceptual objections. The (then) IASC did not 'consider it appropriate to undertake a partial revision of IAS 2, *Inventories*, which deals with the accounting treatment for inventories under the historical cost system'[32] and because it had concerns about the difficulties in differentiating agricultural activity from other manufacturing processes.[33]

The standard does not deal with the processing of agricultural produce after harvest, even when such 'processing may be a logical and natural extension of agricultural activity, and the events taking place may bear some similarity to biological transformation, such processing is not included within the definition of agricultural activity in this Standard'. For example, the processing of grapes into wine – a process in which yeast (a fungus) converts sugars into alcohol – is not deemed to be included within the definition of agricultural activity in the standard.[34] Similarly, cheese production would fall outside the definition of agricultural activity.

It is important to note that IAS 41 only applies to agricultural produce at the point of harvest, which means that before harvest agricultural produce should not be accounted for separately. Instead the unharvested agricultural produce is considered to be part of the biological asset from which it will be harvested. This means that, for example, grapes on the vine should be accounted for as part of the vines themselves right up to the point of harvest.

2.3 Recognition and measurement

2.3.1 Recognition

An entity should recognise a biological asset or agricultural produce only when:[35]

(a)   it controls the asset as a result of past events;

(b)   it is probable that future economic benefits associated with the asset will flow to the entity; and

(c)   the fair value or cost of the asset can be measured reliably.

In agricultural activity, an entity may evidence control by, for example, 'legal ownership of cattle and the branding or otherwise marking of the cattle on acquisition, birth, or weaning'.[36]

2.3.2 Measurement

A   Biological assets

A biological asset should be measured on initial recognition and at each balance sheet date at its fair value less estimated point-of-sale costs, unless the fair value cannot be measured reliably.[37] In the latter case, the entity should measure the biological assets at historical costs (see 2.3.4 below). The IASC Board rejected the argument that less frequent measurement of fair value should be permitted because of the (1) continuous nature of biological transformation, (2) lack of direct relationships between financial transactions and the outcomes of biological transformation and (3) general availability of reliable measures of fair value at reasonable cost.[38]

B   Agricultural produce

Agricultural produce harvested from an entity's biological assets should initially 'be measured at its fair value less estimated point-of-sale costs at the point of harvest'.[39] The standard presumes that an entity can always determine this amount and hence does not permit valuation at historical cost on the grounds that the fair value cannot be determined reliably.[40] The value resulting from initial measurement is subsequently used as cost in applying IAS 2 (if the agricultural produce is to be sold), IAS 16 (if harvested logs are used for the construction of a building) or other applicable International Financial Reporting Standards.[41]

An important reason for requiring agricultural produce at the point of harvest to be measured at fair value was to ensure that the basis of measurement would be consistent with that of biological assets and to avoid inconsistent and distorted reporting of current period performance upon harvest of agricultural produce.[42]

C   Point-of-sale costs

The IASC concluded that 'fair value less estimated point-of-sale costs is a more relevant measurement of biological assets, acknowledging that, in particular, failure to deduct estimated point-of-sale costs could result in a loss being deferred'.[43] A carrying amount based on fair value less estimated point-of-sale costs better represents 'the markets' estimate of the economic benefits that are expected to flow to the enterprise from that asset at the balance sheet date'.[44]

Point-of-sale costs 'include commissions to brokers and dealers, levies by regulatory agencies and commodity exchanges, and transfer taxes and duties' but 'exclude transport and other costs necessary to get assets to a market'.[45] Instead, transport costs are taken into account in determining the fair value of the asset.[46] Therefore, in theory the actual sale of agricultural produce will only result in a gain or loss if the fair value has changed between the time of harvest and the time of the sale.

D   Determining fair value

The standard states that 'the determination of fair value for a biological asset or agricultural produce may be facilitated by grouping biological assets or agricultural produce according to significant attributes; for example, by age or quality. An entity selects the attributes corresponding to the attributes used in the market as a basis for pricing.'[47]

The IASC considered setting an explicit hierarchy in fair value measurement in cases where no active market exists (see (b) below).[48] The Board concluded that 'a detailed hierarchy would not provide sufficient flexibility to appropriately deal with all the circumstances that may arise and decided not to set a detailed hierarchy in cases where no active market exists. However, the Board decided to indicate that an enterprise uses all available market-determined prices or values since otherwise there is a possibility that enterprises may opt to use present value of expected net cash flows from the asset even when useful market-determined prices or values are available.'[49] In other words, an entity is only permitted to use a discounted cash flow model (see (b)(ii) below) or use cost as an approximation of fair value (see (b)(iii) below) if there is no market-based information available. Interestingly, in May 2004, IFRIC agreed to recommend to the IASB Board to establish a fair value hierarchy in IAS 41 that is consistent with other standards (see 4.2 below).

The standard provides the following rules on determining the fair value of a biological asset or agricultural produce:

(a) *active market* – if an active market exists for a biological asset or agricultural produce, the quoted price in that market is the appropriate basis for determining the fair value of that asset. If the entity has access to different active markets, it should use the quoted price in the most relevant market (i.e. the price in the market which is expected to be used).[50] The standard does not require an entity to use the most advantageous (highest) price in the accessible markets,[51] because there may well be sound commercial reasons for not selling in just one geographical market;

(b) *no active market* – if an active market does not exist an entity should use the following methods for arriving at an estimate of fair value:

(i) *market-determined prices or values* – the entity should use one or more of the following information sources, when available, in determining fair value:[52]

– the most recent market transaction price, provided that there has not been a significant change in economic circumstances between the date of that transaction and the balance sheet date;

– market prices for similar assets with adjustment to reflect differences; and

– sector benchmarks such as the value of an orchard expressed per export tray, bushel, or hectare, and the value of cattle expressed per kilogram of meat.

If these information sources suggest different conclusions as to the fair value of a biological asset or agricultural produce, the entity should consider 'the reasons for those differences, in order to arrive at the most reliable estimate of fair value within a relatively narrow range of reasonable estimates';[53]

(ii) *discounted cash flows* – if market-determined prices or values are not available for a biological asset in its present condition, an entity should use 'the present value of expected net cash flows from the asset discounted at a current market-determined pre-tax rate in determining fair value'.[54]

The objective of a calculation of the present value of expected net cash flows is to determine the fair value of a biological asset in its present location and condition. An entity should consider this in determining an appropriate discount rate and in estimating expected cash flows.[55] An entity 'incorporates expectations about possible variations in cash flows into either the expected cash flows, or the discount rate, or some combination of the two'. Furthermore, it should ensure that it uses assumptions for determining a discount rate that are consistent with those used in estimating the expected cash flows; this to avoid double-counting or overlooking of risks.[56] In any case, the entity should exclude the cash flows for financing the assets, taxation or re-establishing biological assets after harvest, for example, the cost of replanting trees in a plantation forest after harvest.[57]

Finally, the present condition of a biological asset excludes 'any increases in value from additional biological transformation and future activities of the entity, such as those related to enhancing the future biological transformation, harvesting, and selling'.[58] As discussed at 4.2 below, IFRIC is currently considering issuing additional guidance on this subject.

(iii) *cost as an approximation of fair value* – sometimes an entity can use cost as an approximation of fair value, particularly when 'little biological transformation has taken place since initial cost incurrence' or when 'the impact of the biological transformation on price is not expected to be material (for example, for the initial growth in a 30-year pine plantation production cycle)'.[59]

IAS 41 does not require an entity to use an external independent valuer to determine the value of biological assets. In fact, the (then) IASC rejected the proposal to require external independent valuations because they are 'not commonly used for certain agricultural activity and it would be burdensome to require an external independent valuation. The Board believes that it is for enterprises to decide how to determine fair value reliably, including the extent to which independent valuers need to be involved.'[60] Furthermore, the Board even noted that disclosure of the extent to which the carrying amount of biological assets reflects a valuation by an external independent valuer would not be appropriate.[61] In any case, a requirement to use external independent valuers would be problematic as generally accepted agricultural valuation principles and a well-developed agricultural valuation profession have yet to emerge.

E   Forward sales contracts

When an entity enters into a contract to sell its biological assets or agricultural produce at a future date, the standard does not permit it to measure those assets at the contracted price, unless that price is equal to the fair value at the balance sheet date. The assets and the forward contract should be accounted for separately, i.e. 'the fair value of a biological asset or agricultural produce is not adjusted because of the existence of a contract'.[62] If the contracted price is lower than the fair value of the assets, the contract for the sale of a biological asset or agricultural produce may be an onerous contract, as defined in IAS 37 – *Provisions, Contingent Liabilities and Contingent Assets*, and should be accounted for under that standard (see Chapter 25). The (then) IASC considered whether it should require sales contracts to be measured at fair value, but concluded that no solution would be practicable without a complete review of the accounting for commodity contracts that are not in the scope of IAS 39 – *Financial Instruments: Recognition and Measurement*.[63]

F   Biological assets attached to land

The standard observes that 'biological assets are often physically attached to land (for example, trees in a plantation forest).' In many cases there is no separate market for biological assets that are attached to the land, but 'an active market may exist for the combined assets, that is, for the biological assets, raw land, and land improvements, as a package'. An entity can use the information regarding the combined assets to determine the fair value of the biological assets.[64] Extracts 36.1 and 36.2, which are from financial statements prepared under the Australian standard that deals with the valuation of biological assets and agricultural produce AASB 1037 – *Self Generating and Regenerating Assets*, illustrate how such an approach would work in practice.

Extract 36.1: Southcorp Limited (2003)

Notes to the financial statements [extract]

1. Statement of significant accounting policies [extract]

(k) Inventories [extract]

Harvested grapes are recorded in inventories in the period of harvest at net market value.

(p) Grape vines

Grape vines are measured at net market value. The net market value of vines is determined by the directors as the difference between the net present value of cash flows expected to be generated by the produce harvested from the vines and the net market value of the other integral fixed assets associated with the vineyard. In determining the net market value, the directors have made certain assumptions including market prices, yields and quality of grapes and vineyard operating costs.

Extract 36.2: BRL Hardy Limited (2002)

Notes to the financial statements [extract]

Note 1. Statement of accounting policies [extract]

Grape vines

Grape vines are valued at net market value. The net market value of grape vines is determined as the difference between the vineyard values and the values of the land and other vineyard improvements thereon. In determining the net market values, the directors have made certain assumptions about the yields and market prices of grapes in current and future vintages, the costs of running the vineyards and the quantity and quality of grapes growing on the vines at each balance date. The values of vineyards are based on the discounted net present values of expected future cash flows.

The above approach to valuing vines is commonly used in the wine industry. Nonetheless, it should be noted that the method might be difficult to apply in practice as is illustrated below.

Example 36.1: Biological assets attached to land

Entity A acquired a 10-hectare vineyard on 1 January 2004 for €1,200. The purchase price of the vineyard was attributed as follows:

1 January 2004	€
Purchase price	1,200
Land	(780)
Vineyard improvements	(130)
Grape vines	290

At the end of its financial year Entity A needs to determine the fair value of the grape vines in accordance with IAS 41 and invites two equally skilled professional valuers to determine the value of the grape vines.

	Valuer 1	Valuer 2
31 December 2004	€	€
Fair value of an average 10-hectare vineyard	1,105	1,100
Adjustment for soil and climatic conditions	135	150
Estimated fair value of Entity A's vineyard	1,240	1,250
Fair value of the land	(830)	(825)
Fair value of vineyard improvements	(135)	(125)
Grape vines	275	300

Valuer 1 and Valuer 2 make a virtually identical assessment of the market values of the vineyard, the land and the vineyard improvements. Nevertheless, because the value of grape vines is calculated by subtracting all the other known elements from the total value of the vineyard, a noticeable difference arises in the valuation of the grape vines. In a similar vain, entities that use only one valuer need to be aware that even small changes in assumptions from period to period could have a significant impact on the valuation of biological assets.

G   Subsequent expenditure

IAS 41 does not explicitly prescribe how an entity should account for subsequent expenditure in relation to biological assets, because the (then) IASC believed this to be unnecessary with a fair-value-based measurement approach.[65] Although, originally Exposure Draft E65 had proposed that 'costs of producing and harvesting biological assets should be charged to expense when incurred and that costs that increase the number of units of biological assets owned or controlled by the enterprise should be added to the carrying amount of the asset'.[66]

It is true that the treatment of subsequent expenditure will ultimately have no effect whatsoever on an entity's equity or net profit or loss for the period. However, the treatment of subsequent expenditure does have an effect on:

- the reconciliation of changes in the carrying amount of biological assets;
- the classification of the expenditure in the income statement as either an expense or as a deduction from the net gain or loss on biological assets; and
- the presentation of investments in biological assets in the cash flow statement.

It is therefore recommended that an entity apply an accounting policy on subsequent expenditure that is broadly in line with the principles in other standards such as IAS 16 and IAS 38. For example, in the case of a vineyard an entity may want to expense maintenance costs such as pruning, while capitalising additions such as planting new vines.

2.3.3   Gains and losses

Recognition of gains on biological assets and agricultural produce that have not been sold to a third party is controversial, but 'those who support this treatment argue that biological transformation is a significant event that should be included in profit or loss because:

(a)   the event is fundamental to understanding an enterprise's performance; and

(b)   this is consistent with the accrual basis of accounting.'[67]

Therefore, the standard requires that gains and losses arising on the initial recognition of a biological asset at fair value less estimated point-of-sale costs and from changes in that carrying amount should be included in profit or loss for the period in which they arise.[68] The standard warns that 'a loss may arise on initial recognition of a biological asset, because estimated point-of-sale costs are deducted in determining fair value less estimated point-of-sale costs of a biological asset.' On the other hand, a gain may arise on the initial recognition of a biological asset (e.g. when a calf is born).[69]

The rules for agricultural produce are similar; the standard requires that 'a gain or loss arising on initial recognition of agricultural produce at fair value less estimated point-of-sale costs should be included in profit or loss for the period in which it arises.'[70] An entity may need to recognise a gain or loss on initial agricultural produce upon harvesting.[71]

2.3.4 *Inability to measure fair value reliably*

Under IAS 41, there is a presumption that the fair value of all biological assets can be measured reliably. This presumption can only be rebutted 'on initial recognition for a biological asset for which market-determined prices or values are not available and for which alternative estimates of fair value are determined to be clearly unreliable'.[72] Therefore, an entity that previously measured a biological asset at its fair value less estimated point-of-sale costs cannot revert to a cost-based measurement in a later period, even if a fair value can no longer be measured reliably.[73] The (then) IASC considered that reliable estimates of fair value would rarely, if ever, cease to be available.[74]

If on initial recognition the fair value cannot be measured reliably, the biological asset should be measured at cost less any accumulated depreciation and any accumulated impairment losses.[75] In determining cost, the entity needs to consider the requirements of IAS 2, IAS 16 and IAS 36 – *Impairment of Assets*.[76] An entity that uses the reliability exception should disclose certain additional information in its financial statements (see 2.5.2 below).[77]

If it becomes possible at a later date to measure the fair value of a biological asset reliably, the entity should measure it at it fair value less estimated point-of-sale costs.[78] The IASC noted in this respect that 'in agricultural activity, it is likely that fair value becomes measurable more reliably as biological transformation occurs and that fair value measurement is preferable to cost in those cases'. Therefore, the Board 'decided to require fair value measurement once fair value becomes reliably measurable'.[79]

IAS 41 presumes that the fair value of a non-current biological asset that 'meets the criteria to be classified as held for sale (or is included in a disposal group that is classified as held for sale) in accordance with IFRS 5 *Non-current Assets Held for Sale and Discontinued Operations*' can always be measured reliably.[80]

2.4 Government grants

Government grants involving biological assets should only be accounted for under IAS 20 if the biological asset is 'measured at its cost less any accumulated depreciation and any accumulated impairment losses' (see Chapter 27).[81] Government grants relating to biological assets accounted for at fair value less estimated point-of-sale costs should be accounted for as discussed below.

An unconditional government grant related to 'a biological asset measured at its fair value less estimated point-of-sale costs should be recognised as income when, and only when, the government grant becomes receivable'.[82] An entity is therefore not permitted under IAS 41 to deduct a government grant from the carrying of the related asset. This would be inconsistent with a 'fair value model in which an asset is measured and presented at its fair value' because the entity would recognise even conditional government grants in income immediately.[83]

Any conditional government grant related to a biological asset measured at its fair value less estimated point-of-sale costs – including government grants that require an entity not to engage in a specified agricultural activity – should be recognised only when the conditions attaching to the grant are met.[84] IAS 41 permits an entity to recognise a government grant as income only to the extent that it (1) has met the terms and conditions of the grant and (2) has no obligation to return the grant. This approach is more consistent with the requirements of the IASB's Framework on the recognition of a liability than it is with IAS 18 – *Revenue*, which requires that economic benefits should be probable rather than absolutely certain.[85] The following example, which is taken from IAS 41, illustrates how an entity should apply these requirements.

Example 36.2: Conditional government grants[86]

A government grant requires an entity to farm in a particular location for five years and requires the entity to return the entire government grant if it farms for less than five years. The government grant is not recognised as income until the five years have passed.

A government grant allows part of the government grant to be retained based on the passage of time. The entity recognises the government grant as income on a time proportion basis.

2.5 Disclosure

2.5.1 General

A Balance sheet

IAS 1 – *Presentation of Financial Statements* – requires biological assets to be presented separately on the face of an entity's balance sheet (see Chapter 3).[87] Agricultural produce after the point of harvest should be accounted for under IAS 2, which does not require it to be disclosed separately on the face of the balance sheet. The following example, which is taken from the Appendix to IAS 41, illustrates the requirement to disclose biological assets on the balance sheet.[88]

Example 36.3:   *Balance sheet presentation of biological assets*

The balance sheet below illustrates how a diary farming business might present biological assets in its balance sheet.

XYZ Dairy Ltd.
Balance Sheet

ASSETS	31 December 20X1	31 December 20X0
Non-current assets		
Dairy livestock – immature *)	52,060	47,730
Dairy livestock – mature *)	372,990	411,840
Subtotal – biological assets	425,050	459,570
Property, plant and equipment	1,462,650	1,409,800
Total non-current assets	**1,887,700**	**1,869,370**
Current assets		
Inventories	82,950	70,650
Trade and other receivables	88,000	65,000
Cash	10,000	10,000
Total current assets	**180,950**	**145,650**
Total assets	**2,068,650**	**2,015,020**
EQUITY AND LIABILITIES		
Equity		
Issued capital	1,000,000	1,000,000
Accumulated profits	902,828	865,000
Total equity	**1,902,828**	**1,865,000**
Current liabilities		
Trade and other payables	165,822	150,020
Total current liabilities	**165,822**	**150,020**
Total equity and liabilities	**2,068,650**	**2,015,020**

*)   An entity is encouraged, but not required, to provide a quantified description of each group of biological assets, distinguishing between consumable and bearer biological assets or between mature and immature biological assets, as appropriate. An entity discloses the basis for making any such distinctions.

B   Income statement

IAS 1 is silent on the presentation of gains and losses on biological assets and agricultural produce in the income statement. IAS 41 requires that an entity should disclose 'the aggregate gain or loss arising during the current period on initial recognition of biological assets and agricultural produce and from the change in fair value less estimated point-of-sale costs of biological assets'.[89] It is worthwhile noting that the standard only requires disclosure of the aggregate gain or loss, it does not require or encourage disaggregating the gain or loss.[90] The example in the Appendix to IAS 41 illustrates that gains on biological assets and agricultural produce should be presented near the top of the income statement, although it is not entirely clear from the example whether losses on biological assets should be presented in the same position or elsewhere in the income statement.[91]

The extracts below from the financial statements of Stora Enso Oyj and Precious Woods Holding Ltd. illustrate the presentation of changes in the fair value of biological assets in the income statements.

Extract 36.3: *Stora Enso Oyj (2003)*

Consolidated Financial Statements [extract]

Consolidated Income Statement [extract]

| | Year Ended 31 December | | |
EUR million	2001	2002	2003
Sales	**13 508.8**	**12 782.6**	**12 172.3**
Other operating income	63.2	176.1	29.6
Changes in inventories of finished goods and work in progress	38.4	30.3	63.5
Change in net value of biological assets	–	–	11.6
Materials and services	-6 547.8	-6 373.2	-6 192.8
Freight and sales commissions	-1 234.0	-1 240.9	-1 286.8
Personnel expenses	-2 234.4	-2 282.0	-2 285.3
Other operating expenses	-839.7	-802.6	-828.0
Depreciation, amortisation and impairment charges	-1 267.6	-2 441.9	-1 200.4
Operating Profit / (Loss)	**1 486.9**	**-151.6**	**483.7**

Extract 36.4: *Precious Woods Holding Ltd. (2003)*

Consolidated statements of income, years ended 31 December 2003 and 2002 (in USD) [extract]

	Notes	2003	2002
Gross trading sales	14, 16	12 417 896	9 757 156
Less: Sales deductions		-1 365 716	-669 857
Net sales		**11 052 180**	**9 087 299**
Personnel related expenses		-2 971 494	-1 520 829
Depreciation and amortization		-1 305 147	-1 310 255
General costs of production		-3 573 800	-3 572 275
Cost of sales		**-7 850 441**	**-6 403 359**
Gross margin		**3 201 739**	**2 683 940**
Change in fair value biological assets – Central America		2 666 904	2 512 416
Operating expenses			
General and administrative expenses		-2 402 786	-1 882 350
Selling expenses		-757 346	-659 166
Depreciation and amortization		-470 654	-582 343
Other operating income		224 556	134 795
Total operating expenses		**-3 406 230**	**-2 989 064**
Profit from operating activities		**2 462 413**	**2 207 292**

The above extracts do not clearly illustrate the presentation of revenue from the sale of biological assets and agricultural produce in the income statement. Unfortunately the standard itself is not much clearer. IAS 1 prohibits offsetting of income and expenses in the income statement.[92] Therefore, if the sale of biological assets or agricultural produce meets the definition of revenue under IAS 18, i.e. it results in a gross inflow of economic benefits during the period arising from the ordinary activities of the entity, it should be presented on a gross basis in the income statement. However, if sales of non-current biological assets are incidental to the main revenue-generating activities of the entity they should be presented on a net basis.[93] It is worthwhile noting that, in the case of agricultural produce sold shortly after harvest the gross margin on the sale will usually be negligible. Furthermore, fair value gains on biological assets and revenue from the sale of biological assets and agricultural produce should not be aggregated as this may result in double counting.

C   Groups of biological assets

The standard requires an entity to provide a narrative or quantitative description of each group of biological assets.[94] An entity is encouraged to provide 'a quantified description of each group of biological assets, distinguishing between consumable and bearer biological assets or between mature and immature biological assets, as appropriate'.[95] The standard suggests that an entity may separately disclose the carrying amounts of:[96]

- consumable biological assets (i.e. assets that are to be harvested as agricultural produce or sold as biological assets); and

- bearer biological assets (i.e. assets that are not consumable but rather are self-regenerating).

The standard continues by suggesting that an entity 'may further divide those carrying amounts between mature and immature assets. These distinctions provide information that may be helpful in assessing the timing of future cash flows'.[97] Mature biological assets are defined by the standard as those assets 'that have attained harvestable specifications (for consumable biological assets) or are able to sustain regular harvests (for bearer biological assets)'.[98] If an entity makes the above distinctions, it should disclose the basis for making the distinction.[99]

D   Other

If not disclosed elsewhere in information published with the financial statements, an entity should describe:

'(a)   the nature of its activities involving each group of biological assets; and

(b)   non-financial measures or estimates of the physical quantities of:

    (i)   each group of the enterprise's biological assets at the end of the period; and

    (ii)   output of agricultural produce during the period.'[100]

In addition, an entity should disclose the following information:

(a)   the methods and significant assumptions applied in determining the fair value of each group of agricultural produce at the point of harvest and each group of biological assets;[101]

(b)   the fair value less estimated point-of-sale costs of agricultural produce harvested during the period, determined at the point of harvest;[102]

(c)   the existence and carrying amounts of biological assets whose title is restricted, and the carrying amounts of biological assets pledged as security for liabilities;[103]

(d)   the amount of commitments for the development or acquisition of biological assets;[104]

(e)   financial risk management strategies related to agricultural activity;[105]

(f)   a reconciliation of changes in the carrying amount of biological assets between the beginning and the end of the current period, which includes:[106]

   (i)   the gain or loss arising from changes in fair value less estimated point-of-sale costs;

   (ii)   increases due to purchases;

   (iii)   decreases attributable to sales and biological assets classified as held for sale (or included in a disposal group that is classified as held for sale) in accordance with IFRS 5;

   (iv)   decreases due to harvest;

   (v)   increases resulting from business combinations;

   (vi)   net exchange differences arising on the translation of financial statements into a different presentation currency, and on the translation of a foreign operation into the presentation currency of the reporting entity; and

   (vii)   other changes.

The standard encourages an entity 'to disclose, by group or otherwise, the amount of change in fair value less estimated point-of-sale costs included in profit or loss due to physical changes and due to price changes', because this information is 'useful in appraising current period performance and future prospects, particularly when there is a production cycle of more than one year'.[107] IAS 41 notes that physical change itself can be broken down further into growth, degeneration, production and procreation, but the standard does not specifically encourage disclosure of this information.[108] The standard provides the following example that explains how an entity should go about separating the effect of physical changes from those of price changes.

Example 36.4: *Physical Change and Price Change[109]*

A herd of ten 2-year-old animals was held at 1 January 2005. One animal aged 2½ years was purchased on 1 July 2005 for €108, and one animal was born on 1 July 2005. No animals were sold or disposed of during the period. Per-unit fair values less estimated point-of-sale costs were as follows:

	1/1/2005	*1/7/2005*	*31/12/2005*
Newborn animal	–	€70	€72
½ year old animal	–	–	€80
2 year old animal	€100	–	€105
2½ year old animal	–	€108	€111
3 year old animal	–	–	€120

Fair value less estimated point-of-sale costs of herd at 1 January 2005

$$(10 \times €100) = \qquad €1,000$$

Purchase on 1 July 2005

$$(1 \times €108) = \qquad €108$$

Increase in fair value less estimated point-of-sale costs due to price change:

$$10 \times (€105 - €100) = \qquad €50$$
$$1 \times (€111 - €108) = \qquad €3$$
$$1 \times (€72 - €70) = \qquad €2$$
$$€55$$

Increase in fair value less estimated point-of-sale costs due to physical change:

$$10 \times (€120 - €105) = \qquad €150$$
$$1 \times (€120 - €111) = \qquad €9$$
$$1 \times (€80 - €72) = \qquad €8$$
$$1 \times €70 = \qquad €70$$
$$€237$$

Fair value less estimated point-of-sale costs of herd at 31 December 2005

$$11 \times €120 = \qquad €1,320$$
$$1 \times €80 = \qquad €80$$
$$€1,400$$

The standard notes that agricultural activity is 'often exposed to climatic, disease and other natural risks. If an event occurs that gives rise to a material item of income or expense, the nature and amount of that item are disclosed in accordance with IAS 1' (see Chapter 3). For example, an entity may need to disclose events such as 'an outbreak of a virulent disease, a flood, a severe drought or frost, and a plague of insects'.[110]

The extracts below from the financial statements of Stora Enso Oyj, Precious Woods Holding and Del Monte Pacific illustrate the detailed disclosures required by IAS 41.

Extract 36.5: Stora Enso Oyj (2003)

Development of Operations in 2003 [extract]

Biological Assets [extract]

The new accounting standard IAS 41, *Agriculture*, under which Stora Enso's biological assets in the form of standing trees are fair market valued, came into effect on 1 January 2003. At the adoption of IAS 41, the Group's forest assets were measured at fair value, which increased the book value of EUR 705.9 million to a fair value of EUR 1 561.7 million. The revaluation reserve amounted to EUR 855.8 million, which resulted in an increase in equity of EUR 615.5 million after the deduction of deferred tax; in accordance with IAS 8, this was credited directly to Retained Earnings.

Periodic future changes resulting from growth, price and other factors are recorded through the Income Statement so that operating profit for the year includes an adjustment for the change in the value of the standing forest during the period. The change in value comprises growth, harvesting and price fluctuations. The result for 2003 includes EUR 116.2 million in respect of change in fair value (growth and price effect), less EUR 104.6 million for harvesting, resulting in a net gain of EUR 11.6 million.

At 31 December 2003 Stora Enso's biological assets had a fair value of EUR 1 587.8 million and were located by value in Sweden (95.0%), Portugal (3.3%), Canada (0.1%), China (0.3%) and Indonesia (1.3%). In addition, the Group has two Associated Companies where IAS 41 is taken into account in computing their results:

- Tornator Timberland Oy, a 41% owned associate which acquired the Group's Finnish forest interests in 2002, had biological assets at a fair value of EUR 628.9 million.

- Veracel Celulose S.A., a 50% owned associate in Brazil, also has substantial forest plantations fair valued at EUR 67.4 million.

The fair value adjustment of these associated companies had a combined effect of EUR 44 million on the Group's equity at 1 January 2003.

The following table, Valuation Sensitivity, indicates that assumption changes may have a material effect on values; the discount rate used in the calculation is 6.25% before tax (the Swedish forest), which is lower than the Group WACC due to the lower risk of forest assets compared to other assets, but the table shows that for every 0.5% change in the discount rate, there will be an impact of EUR 152 million.

Valuation Sensitivity

	Year Ended 31 December 2003	
Millions	Change In Base %	Change in Value EUR (+/-)
Discount	0.5%	152
Real wood prices	0.5% p.a.	206
Real logging costs	0.5% p.a.	61

Notes to the Consolidated Financial Statements [extract]

Note 1 Accounting Principles [extract]

Biological Assets

The new accounting standard, IAS 41 *Agriculture*, requires that biological assets in the form of standing trees are shown on the Balance Sheet at market value. Group forests are thus accounted for at fair value less estimated point-of-sale costs at harvest, there being a presumption that fair values can be measured for these assets.

The valuation of Stora Enso's forest assets is based on discounted cash flow models whereby the fair value of the biological assets is calculated using cash flows from continuous operations, that is, based on sustainable forest management plans taking into account growth potential. The yearly harvest made from the forecasted tree growth is multiplied by actual wood prices and the cost of fertiliser and harvesting is then deducted. The fair value of the biological asset is measured as the present value of the harvest from one growth cycle based on the productive forestland, taking into consideration environmental restrictions and other reservations. Biological assets that are physically attached to land are recognised and measured at their fair value separately from the land.

Note 12 Biological Assets

The new accounting standard IAS 41, *Agriculture*, under which Stora Enso's biological assets in the form of standing trees are fair market valued, came into effect on 1 January 2003. The value of Group forests was thus increased from a previous book value of EUR 705.9 million to a fair value of EUR 1 561.3 million. The revaluation reserve amounted to EUR 855.8 million, which resulted in an increase in equity of EUR 615.4 million after the deduction of deferred tax; in accordance with IAS 8, this was credited directly to Retained Earnings as non-distributable equity.

Periodic future changes resulting from growth, price and other factors will be entered in the Income Statement so that operating profit includes an adjustment for the change in value of the standing forest during the year. This change in value is made up of growth, harvesting and price fluctuations. The result for 2003 includes EUR 116.2 million in respect of the change in fair value, being the growth and price effect, less EUR 104.6 million for harvesting, resulting in the net gain of EUR 11.6 million shown in the Income Statement.

At 31 December 2003 Stora Enso's biological assets had a fair value of EUR 1 587.8 million and were located by value in Sweden (95.0%), Portugal (3.3%), Canada (0.1%), China (0.3%) and Indonesia (1.3%). In addition, the Group has two Associated Companies where IAS 41 is taken into account in computing their results:

- Tornator Timberland Oy, a 41% owned associate which acquired the Group's Finnish forest interests in 2002, had biological assets at a fair value of EUR 628.9 million.

- Veracel, a 50% owned associate in Brazil, also has substantial forest plantations fair valued at EUR 67.4 million, though with a growing cycle of only seven years.

The initial IAS 41 fair value adjustment to Group equity on account of these associates amounted to EUR 44.0 million net of deferred tax.

Biological Assets

EUR million	As at 31 December 2003
Assets reclassified from Fixed Assets (see Note 11)	705.9
Fair valuation surplus	855.8
Carrying value at 1 January 2003	1 561.7
Translation difference	8.3
Additions	7.2
Disposals	-1.0
Change in fair value	116.2
Decrease due to harvest	-104.6
Total Biological Assets	1 587.8

The value of the Group's freestanding trees is EUR 1 587.8 million, whereas the total value of the Group's forest assets amounts to EUR 1 705.6 million. The difference of EUR 117.8 million is represented by the land under the trees, EUR 98.5 million, and the roads thereon, EUR 19.3 million; the forestland is shown under Fixed Assets in Land and the forest roads are in Fixed Assets under Other Tangible Assets.

Extract 36.6: Precious Woods Holding Ltd. (2003)

Notes to consolidated Financial Statements [extract]

1. BASIS OF PRESENTATION AND ACCOUNTING POLICIES [extract]

f. Biological Assets Central America

The acquisition of land for the forest projects is originally recorded at cost. Biological assets are stated at fair value less estimated point-of-sale cost. The fair value is determined using the present value of expected net cash flows from the asset discounted at a rate as described in note 5.

5. BIOLOGICAL ASSETS CENTRAL AMERICA [extract]

General Valuation Principles according to IAS 41

According to IAS 41, biological assets with a life cycle of many years – in the case of Precious Woods, tree plantations – are to be valued annually at fair value. The gain or loss in fair value of these biological assets is reported in net profit. The measurement of biological growth in the field is an important element of this valuation. Initially, at the start of the plantation cycle, the fair value is equal to the standard costs of preparing and maintaining a plantation including the appropriate cost of capital, assuming efficient operations. Towards the end of the plantation cycle the fair value depends solely on the discounted value of the expected harvest less estimated point-of-sale cost.

Precious Woods has divided its plantations by species into five well defined "growth classes". Every year hundreds of representatively distributed sample plots are measured as the basis of assigning all planted areas to one of these growth classes. With good growth, a plot may move up to a higher growth class or alternately be downgraded to a lower growth class if growth is poor. Precious Woods has defined a cash flow stream for each growth class and species ("profile") estimating expected cost and income for each species and growth class for each year of the total life cycle of the plantation. On the one hand these estimates are based on the experience of Precious Woods, on the other hand they are based on conservative outside estimates of future harvest volumes and prices. An internal rate of return ("IRR") is calculated for each profile, which is applied as the discount rate of expected future income.

The following table shows as an example the fair value of biological assets (trees) without land ranging from the lowest growth class at the low end to the highest growth class at the high end.

Range of fair value of plantations in USD per hectare

	Teak Minimum	Teak Maximum	Pochote Minimum	Pochote Maximum
1½-years	1 800	2 100	1 600	1 700
5-years	4 200	6 100	2 900	4 300
10-years	7 700	14 100	4 200	8 600

Revision of valuation assumptions in 2003

Precious Woods introduced the valuation according to IAS 41 in fiscal year 2000 based on knowledge available at the time. The standard was applied by the Company in its published financial reports in 2002 before it became mandatory in 2003. The valuation model and its assumptions are annually reviewed and if necessary adjusted. Since the fiscal year 2000 important new information has been gained, much of which has already been described and taken into account in the valuation for fiscal year 2002. The following refinements and revisions were additionally implemented in the valuation approach and assumptions for 2003:

A.   Revised definition of sample plots

The representative distribution of the sample plots was carefully reviewed in 2003. Where the frequency was above average, the number of sample plots was reduced. At the same time the quality of the sample plots was improved by verifying the marking, orthogonal shape as well as identification and location with the support of a global positioning system. This review indicated that both extremely poor and excellent areas had been slightly over-represented.

B. Adjustment of standard cost profiles to actual cost

A retrospective review of the actual cost incurred during several years demonstrated a high correlation between the standard cost and the actual historical cost. The international overhead expense represented the only exception and these were subsequently increased in the standard cost profiles. New standard cost profiles were created for Nicaragua taking the lower land prices and lower cost of labour into account.

C. Assumptions regarding growth of teak

Teak trees actually grow higher in Central America as compared to observations in Trinidad and Tobago previously underlying our volume calculations. In 2002 sufficient data was not yet available to quantify this difference mathematically. Meanwhile, in 2003 the assumptions on tree growth were revised and the volume calculations adjusted to the growth rate actually observed in Central America. This led to higher final harvest volumes for average to excellent growth classes. On the other hand, these higher final harvest volumes require a more demanding selection when assigning the trees to growth classes during the initial years of growth. Many such plots were consequentially downgraded to lower growth classes.

D. Improved volume calculation

Two measures are available to determine the volume of wood commercially available at harvest: Diameter at chest height (DAP) and total length of usable trunk. Certain trees narrow significantly immediately above DAP while others are more conical in shape for several meters without significant narrowing. This narrowing varies greatly between individual trees leading to different volumes even when DAP and height are the same. Age and class of diameter are further variables. Only comparing the results of the calculation against the actual volume of a high number of trees actually felled will confirm that the volume formula corresponds to the natural occurrence. Such a validation was completed in 2003 and demonstrated that the calculation overstated the volume of trees with small diameters. The volume formula was revised accordingly. The results of the revised formula now correspond well with the actual observations for all classes of diameters. This revised volume calculation has led to significantly lower harvest volumes for poor growth classes and trees harvested in commercial thinnings.

E. Lower number of trunks harvested from commercial thinnings

The assumption on the number of trunks harvested in commercial thinnings of teak (which reduce the number of trees per hectare from 450 to 300) was reduced by one third for the "low" to "excellent" growth classes and even by two thirds in the "marginal" growth class. This adjustment takes into account the fact that due to earlier preliminary thinnings, natural mortality and the poor shape of trunks of some trees felled, an appropriate distribution of 450 trees per hectare is not available to support the originally assumed commercial harvest volumes. As for pochote, initial thinnings commencing at more than 300 trees per hectare are assumed to only cover the direct cost of harvest and are thus not viewed as commercially viable in the valuation model. This is due to the fact that pochote heartwood only forms after an age of ten years yielding only a low price for young trees harvested in initial thinnings.

All of the above refinements and revisions result in a slightly lower valuation of the plantations amounting to USD 227 112 or 0,8% of the biological assets (without land). In addition the IRR falls by a few tenths of a percent for the various growth classes. In Nicaragua, the IRR is generally higher as the labour cost and cost of land are lower than assumed for Costa Rica.

The share of the teak plantations of the total value of biological assets increases from year to year as Precious Woods has predominantly planted teak since 1995. As such it is of primary importance that the valuation model for teak is especially well founded. Pochote lacks the reliable data available for teak. Overall one can assume that the harvest volumes applied by the Company for pochote are markedly too low. So far this has not been corrected, as reliable market price information is also not available for pochote timber. A revision of the valuation model for pochote will only be pursued once more reliable information on market prices has become available. The valuation of the various indigenous species is subject to certain insecurity as more than a dozen heterogeneous species are represented in this group. Reliable data is hardly available for growth rates or achievable market prices. The average volume growth of 7m3/ha/p.a. assumed by the Company is however well within reason.

The following tables show the distribution of the area planted (in hectares and percent) with teak and pochote and their categorisation in individual growth classes as well as the IRR applied for each growth class and species as well as the resulting total valuation. For teak, the IRR is shown for plantations in Costa Rica as well as for those in the area of Rio San Juan in Nicaragua. Concerning the various indigenous species (caoba, ronron, cocobolo, almendro, etc.), Precious Woods currently applies a valuation model which does not differentiate between species or growth class. The value per hectare depends only on the age of the respective plantation.

Distribution of the areas planted with teak in growth classes and their valuation

Growth class	excellent	high	average	low	marginal	Total
Hectares	414	393	1 325	366	1 010	3 508
In percent	11,8%	11,2%	37,8%	10,4%	28,8%	100%
IRR/ Costa Rica	14,9%	12,7%	11,3%	10,2%	8,1%	–
IRR/ Nicaragua	16,9%	14,3%	12,7%	11,5%	9,3%	–
Value in Mio. USD	3,68	2,71	4,09	2,28	5,43	18,19

Average value per hectare: USD 5 185. Average age of the teak plantations: 5,5 Years.

Distribution of the areas planted with pochote in growth classes and their valuation

Growth class	excellent	high	average	low	marginal	Total
Hectares	462	197	169	59	83	970
In percent	47,6%	20,3%	17,4%	6,1%	8,6%	100%
IRR	10,0%	7,1%	5,7%	4,1%	2,1%	–
Value in Mio. USD	4,56	1,44	0,99	0,28	0,37	7,64

Average value per hectare: USD 7 877. Average age of the pochote plantations: 11,8 years.

Areas planted with various indigenous species

Total value of 343 Hectares: USD 1,71 Mio. Average value per hectare: USD 4 993. Average age: 6,8 years.

The balance sheet values of the biological assets in Costa Rica have developed as follows:

in USD	2003	2002
Carrying amount beginning of year	29 020 233	25 086 364
Purchase of land	842 483	205 568
Carrying amount end of year	33 867 837	29 020 233
Change in fair value attributable to biological growth	4 005 121	3 728 301
Personnel costs incurred during the year	-350 417	-294 585
Depreciation expense	-89 446	-72 895
Other general costs incurred during the year	-898 354	-848 405
Net change in fair value of biological assets	**2 666 904**	**2 512 416**

Details of the change in fair value attributable to biological growth

The change of fair value attributable to biological growth is summarised as follows:

in USD	2003	2002
Growth of previously existing plantations	4 247 687	2 853 669
New plantations in reporting period	252 985	453 564
Change of valuation assumptions	-227 112	482 088
Write-off of poorly growing plots	-268 439	-61 020
Change in fair value attributable to biological growth	**4 005 121**	**3 728 301**

Harvest

The Company only considers the final harvest – which takes place after completion of the full 26–30 year growth cycle – as the relevant factor in valuing biological assets according to IAS 41. Interim thinnings represent necessary ongoing maintenance required to achieve the intended income from the biological assets at the end of the growth cycle. Growth of the biological assets is calculated to be lower in those years when timber is commercially harvested in the course of the regularly planned thinnings. In 2003, net sales of timber from commercial thinnings amounted to USD 81 263 associated with a harvest cost of USD 27 485.

Comparison with historical cost

The historical cost of the plantations is shown in the following table:

in USD	2003	2002
Cost		
Actual cost of planting and maintenance	15 505 381	14 167 164
Land	6 323 775	5 481 291
Total historical cost	21 829 156	19 648 455
Cumulative net gain from change in fair value	12 038 681	9 371 778
Total Biological Assets	33 867 837	29 020 233

Risk management regarding biological assets

Management assesses the valuation of the teak plantations to be well founded and conservative. The increase in volume, achievable market prices and inclusion of adjustments for inflation are decisive for the determination of future income.

a)   Increase in volume: Comprehensive comparative data is not available for growth periods spanning more than 20 years in Costa Rica. However, a few 30 year plantations and a number of 15–20 year plantations exist whose current growth may be observed. Along with 200 years of experience with the growth of plantation teak in Asia, the assumptions on volume increase may be regarded as well founded. Expressed in figures, Precious Woods assumes an increase in commercially marketable timber volume of between 7 m3/ha/p.a. for the "marginal" up to 17m3/ha/p.a. for the "excellent" growth class. Other teak investments promoted in Switzerland and internationally assume a volume increase of 20m3/ha/p.a. and more.

b)   Prices: Precious Woods assumes prices between USD 63 and 162 per m3 for teak from commercial thinnings depending on the age and diameter of the logs. These are net prices for logs loaded onto a container at the Finca. All prices known to Precious Woods are in this range or up to four times higher. For the final harvest after 20-30 years of growth, Precious Woods assumes prices between USD 270 and 405 per m3 depending on the diameter for the best (lower) logs and between USD 77 and 180 for the smaller (upper) logs. Current prices actually paid in Costa Rica range from USD 300 to 1300 per m3. Other teak investments currently promoted in Europe which disclose this information assume prices for teak logs between USD 525 and 1285 per m3 and additionally assume inflationary and even real price increases. For reasons of prudence, Precious Woods maintains prior price assumptions.

c)   Precious Woods does not take inflation or real price increases into account to determine the fair value of the biological assets although one could safely assume that both will come into effect. An assumed 2% rate of inflation would lead to an approximate 20% increase in the valuation of the plantations.

Assurance of Completion

Tree plantations only retain their value if the Company can provide the financial resources required to maintain the plantations through final harvest on an ongoing basis. Depending on the rate of growth, teak plantations become financially self sufficient after a growth period of approximately ten years from which point in time the revenue from commercial thinnings exceeds the cost of ongoing maintenance. If Precious Woods were to cease the creation of new plantations effective 2004, cumulative maintenance expense of USD 3,2 million would need to be covered to carry all existing plantations through the age of 10 years. On the other hand, cumulative net revenue from commercial thinnings of existing plantations is coincidentally also expected to reach USD 3,2 million plantations between 2004 and 2013. The cumulative cost of maintenance will exceed the cumulative net revenue from commercial thinnings in the initial years of such a scenario. Management is confident it will be able to raise the required bridge financing to sustain and carry through the plantations in the case of such a crisis scenario.

Management of biological risks (fire, flooding, lightning)

During the dry season, the risk of damage from fire is significant for young plantations. The Company reduces this risk in the best possible manner by implementing appropriate fire prevention measures such as clearing underbrush ahead of the dry season, construction of fire breaks and 24 hour surveillance. Beyond a height of 4 to 6 meters, teak trees are no longer damaged by fire. In 1997, 7 hectares of a young teak plantation in the Finca Garza were lost to fire. This represents 0,15% of the area of all plantations created between 1990 and 2003. Tropical hurricanes may cause windfall and significant flooding. Since 1990, hurricane Mitch represented the one such event which affected the North of Costa Rica and Nicaragua. Precious Woods did not suffer any material loss of trees from windfall or flooding during that event. The undulating terrain of the plantations would very likely prevent significant loss from flooding. However, significant damage from a tropical hurricane cannot be totally excluded. A limited number of trees are lost annually to local lightning strikes. These losses are included in the Company's expectations for the natural mortality of trees. The Company has not obtained insurance coverage for these risks as the premium would be excessive in relation to the expected losses.

Extract 36.7: Del Monte Pacific Limited (2003)

Notes to the financial statements [extract]

2. Summary of significant accounting policies [extract]

Adoption of new accounting policy: IAS 41, Agriculture [extract]

IAS 41 which took effect for financial years beginning on or after 1 January 2003, establishes accounting treatment, financial statement preparation, and disclosures related to agricultural activity. Agricultural activity is the management by an enterprise of the biological transformation of living animals or plants (biological assets) for sale, into agricultural produce, or into additional biological assets.

The standard requires biological assets and agricultural produce, at the point of harvest, to be measured on initial recognition and, at each balance sheet date, at its fair value less estimated point-of-sales costs. Gain and loss arising from these measurements should be included in the net profit or loss for the period in which it arises. However, where the fair value of the biological assets cannot be measured reliably, the biological assets should be stated at cost less accumulated depreciation and any accumulated impairment losses.

The adoption of IAS 41 has resulted in the Group stating its biological assets (livestock) and its agriculture produce (harvested pineapples) at its fair value less estimated point-of-sale costs, except for some of its biological assets (growing crops) where the fair value cannot be measured reliably. For such biological assets, they are measured at costs less any accumulated depreciation and any accumulated impairment losses.

Previously, all of the Group's biological assets (including livestock) and agricultural produce (harvested pineapples) were stated in the balance sheet of the Group at the lower of cost and net realisable value. The change has been applied retrospectively by adjusting the opening balance of revenue reserves as at 1 January 2002. The comparative figures have been restated accordingly.

The adoption of this new accounting policy has resulted in the Group increasing the carrying value of its inventories and biological assets, net of tax, by $632,000, as at 1 January 2003 with a corresponding increase in the revenue reserves as at 1 January 2003.

10. Biological assets

	Group	
	2003 **$'000**	**2002** **$'000**
Livestock		
– at fair value	2,623	3,691
– at cost	1,122	2,033
	3,745	5,724
Deferred growing crops – at cost	30,489	30,970
	34,234	36,694

The Group's livestock comprises live cattle, growing herd, beef herd, dairy and cattle for slaughter. The fair value was determined based on the actual selling prices approximating those at year end less estimated point-of-sale costs. Live cattle are valued at fair value less estimated point-of-sale costs. Growing herd, beef herd, dairy and cattle for slaughter are valued at cost.

Reconciliation of changes in the carrying amount:

	Group	
	2003 $'000	2002 $'000
Livestock		
At beginning of year/date of acquisition	5,724	4,921
Currency realignment	(250)	(143)
Increases due to purchases	14,082	18,744
Gain (loss) arising from changes in fair value less estimated point-of-sale costs attributable to price changes	369	(292)
Decreases due to sales	(16,180)	(17,506)
At end of year	3,745	5,724

	Group	
	2003 $'000	2002 $'000
Deferred growing crops		
At beginning of year	30,970	30,563
Currency realignment	(1,302)	(901)
Additions	24,468	24,324
Harvested	(23,647)	(23,016)
At end of year	30,489	30,970

2.5.2 *Additional disclosures if fair value cannot be measured reliably*

If an entity measures biological assets at their cost less any accumulated depreciation and any accumulated impairment losses it should disclose the following information:

(a)   if the entity holds such assets at the end of the period:[111]

    (i)   a description of the biological assets;

    (ii)   an explanation of why fair value cannot be measured reliably;

    (iii)   if possible, the range of estimates within which fair value is highly likely to lie;

    (iv)   the depreciation method used;

    (v)   the useful lives or the depreciation rates used; and

    (vi)   the gross carrying amount and the accumulated depreciation (aggregated with accumulated impairment losses) at the beginning and end of the period;

(b)   if the entity held such assets at any point during the current period:[112]

    (i)   any gain or loss recognised on disposal of such biological assets;

(ii)   the reconciliation required by paragraph 50 of the standard (see 2.5.1 D above) should disclose amounts related to such biological assets separately;

(iii) that reconciliation should include the following amounts included in profit or loss related to those biological assets:

- impairment losses;

- reversals of impairment losses; and

- depreciation;

(c)   if the entity held such assets and their fair value became reliably measurable during the current period:[113]

(i)   a description of the biological assets;

(ii)   an explanation of why fair value has become reliably measurable; and

(iii) the effect of the change.

Extract 36.8: Precious Woods Holding Ltd. (2003)

Notes to consolidated Financial Statements [extract]

1. BASIS OF PRESENTATION AND ACCOUNTING POLICIES [extract]

g. Forest and Forest Improvements Brazil

The acquisition of land and forest, construction of permanent roads and investments in silvicultural measures in Precious Woods Brazil are recorded at cost or market, whichever is lower. The investments made in the methods of sustainable management of tropical forest are amortised according to the units-of-production method. The Company does not apply the fair value less estimated point-of-sale cost as fair values cannot be reliably measured in sustainable management of existing tropical forest.

6. FOREST, FOREST IMPROVEMENT AND INTANGIBLE ASSETS – BRAZIL

The forests of Precious Woods in Brazil are managed in a sustainable manner, which means that only incremental growth will be harvested and the substance of the forest will be preserved. These forests and forest improvements are valued at the lower of cost or market as described below. Due to the lack of reliable measurement of biological growth in the field, the fair value approach as for Costa Rica cannot be applied.

Precious Woods Amazon

In May 1994 the Company acquired two companies that owned approximately 80 000 hectares of tropical forests located near Itacoatiara, State of Amazonas in Brazil, for the main purpose of establishing and operating a project to extract and industrialise wood in a sustainable manner. In 2001 the Company acquired a new area of tropical forest of approximately 42 000 hectares also located near Itacoatiara. An additional forest area of 189 000 ha was purchased in 2003. Additional expense was incurred to achieve the FSC certification. FSC certification demonstrates fulfilment of social and ecological criteria while increasing the prices achievable for timber. In 2002 USD 746 627 of preoperational expense was incurred for the set up of the veneer manufacturing and establishment of Precious Woods Industries.

Precious Woods Pará

In 2001, the Group acquired a participation in two companies that own an area of approximately 46 000 hectares of tropical forest in Portél, State of Pará. In 2003 an additional 30 000 hectares of land were acquired and the processing facilities expanded.

Balance Sheet Valuation

The detail of the cumulative costs plus revaluation included in the forest, forest improvement and intangible assets in Brazil is as follows:

Intangible Assets Brazil	Forest planning and development costs	Industrialization preoperational expenses	Total
in USD			
Cost			
At 1 January 2003	2 452 163	2 893 869	5 346 032
Additions	181 242	0	181 242
At 31 December 2003	**2 633 405**	**2 893 869**	**5 527 274**
Accumulated Amortisation			
At 01 January 2003	780 848	1 211 091	1 991 939
Charge for the Year	229 094	302 920	532 014
At 31 December 2003	**1 009 942**	**1 514 011**	**2 523 953**
Carrying Amount			
At 31 December 2003	**1 623 463**	**1 379 858**	**3 003 321**
At 31 December 2002	1 671 315	1 682 778	3 354 093

Forest and forest improvements Brazil		
in USD	**2003**	**2002**
At January 1	12 528 984	10 970 932
Additions	4 572 447	1 558 052
At 31 December	**17 101 431**	**12 528 984**

It is noted that permanent forest roads are continuously maintained and kept in a conditional comparable to their original construction. Therefore permanent forest roads are not depreciated. The maintenance cost of these roads is however fully expensed.

2.5.3 *Government grants*

An entity that has received government grants in relation to biological assets should disclose the following information:

'(a) the nature and extent of government grants recognised in the financial statements;

(b) unfulfilled conditions and other contingencies attaching to government grants; and

(c) significant decreases expected in the level of government grants.'[114]

3   TRANSITIONAL RULES AND FIRST-TIME ADOPTION

IAS 41 became operative for annual financial statements covering periods starting on or after 1 January 2003. The standard encouraged early adoption and required early adopter to disclose that fact.[115] The standard does not contain any specific transitional provisions; hence an entity adopting the standard should apply IAS 8 – *Accounting Policies, Changes in Accounting Estimates and Errors.*[116] Similarly, IFRS 1 – *First-time Adoption of International Financial Reporting Standards* – requires full retrospective application of IAS 41 without any exemptions.

4   FUTURE DEVELOPMENTS

IFRIC has been discussing the following two issues in relation to the interpretation of IAS 41 since September 2003 and in May 2004 considered a draft Exposure Draft of proposed amendments to the standard.

4.1   How should an entity account for a legal or constructive obligation to replant a biological asset after harvest?

IFRIC confirmed in May 2004 its previous decisions that if an entity has an obligation to re-establish a biological asset after harvest, that obligation is attached to the land and does not affect the fair value of the biological assets currently growing on the land.

Normally, an entity should only account for the obligation to replant after harvest, unless such an obligation is similar to a hand-back obligation included in leasing agreements. However, the entity should account for such items under the leasing standard and apply the general requirements for liabilities. IFRIC therefore agreed not to consider this issue as part of its agriculture project.[117]

4.2   How should an entity calculate the fair value of a biological asset using a discounting model?

The main issue is that IAS 41 requires the net cash flow calculation to be based on the biological asset in its present location and conditions, ignoring any additional biological transformation (see 2.3.2 D above). The IFRIC agreed to take the issue on to its agenda with the aim to 'issue an Interpretation clarifying the meaning of fair value; i.e. that the exclusion of 'additional biological transformation' does not exclude the expected value of potential future growth from the fair value of a biological asset in its present location and condition'.[118] In May 2004, IFRIC agreed to recommend that the IASB Board should:

- 'amend IAS 41 to clarify which value in which market would be relevant to establish fair value, emphasising that the asset held must be the focal point.

- establish a fair value hierarchy in IAS 41 that is consistent with other standards.

- clarify that when fair value is determined by using valuation techniques an entity should incorporate assumptions that market participants would use on the basis of facts or information known or knowable as of the measurement date unless impracticable.

- retain the requirement that the recognised value of a biological asset should reflect the asset's present condition and location, i.e. the asset should be measured at its fair value less transport and other costs of getting the asset to the market and less other costs to sell.

- conform the terminology in IAS 41 to other Standards.'[119]

At that meeting IFRIC requested that the IASB staff modify the proposed Exposure Draft and prepare a discussion paper for the IASB Board highlighting the issues that need to be considered in relation to the guidance for determining fair value.[120]

5   CONCLUSION

Agricultural activities have historically always been accounted for at cost. For many the adoption of IAS 41 – which embraces the fair value model unreservedly – came as a bit of a surprise, even shock perhaps. It is true, of course, that market prices exist for some biological assets and most agricultural produce. However, does that mean that such assets should be measured at fair value? In answering that question it is useful to look at the main qualitative characteristics of financial statements as outlined in the IASB's *Framework* such as understandability, relevance, reliability and comparability.

It is likely that users of financial statements readily understand market prices of biological assets. However, in the absence of market prices the standard requires an entity to use alternative methods (e.g. sector benchmarks and discounted cash flow models) to estimate what the market price would have been had it existed. Whether such valuations are more readily understood than, for example, historical cost is debatable. In much the same way the (then) IASC never quite convincingly made the case that fair-value-based financial reporting for agricultural activities is more relevant and reliable and improves comparability.

The most pressing issue for entities applying the standard is that the practical costs of application often seem to outweigh the theoretical benefits of improved understandability, relevance, reliability and comparability. It is a cause for concern that so many of the companies currently applying IAS 41 are using discounted cash flow models as a basis for their estimate of the fair value of biological assets, rather than there being readily available market values or prices. Model-driven valuations are not as objective as market values and implementation of agricultural valuation models may be particularly onerous for small agricultural entities that need to apply the standard. At the time of writing very few examples of public companies applying IAS 41 were available. This is not surprising because there are not that many large international groups that have material agricultural activities that warrant separate disclosure. However, from 2005 onwards many more companies will apply IFRS and there will be a commensurate increase in the number of companies applying IAS 41. Hopefully, this will provide the impetus needed to establish 'generally accepted agricultural valuation principles' and a well-developed agricultural valuation profession.

References

1 IAS 41, *Agriculture*, IASB, January 2001 (amended March 2004), para. B1.
2 IAS 41, para. B3.
3 IAS 41, para. B6.
4 IAS 41, para. B7.
5 IAS 41, para. B4.
6 IAS 41, para. B5.
7 IAS 41, para. B2.
8 *IASC Annual Review 2000 – Review by Chairman and Secretary-General*, IASC, 2001, p. 3.
9 IAS 41, para. B14.

10 IAS 41, para. B15.
11 IAS 41, para. B16.
12 IAS 41, para. B17.
13 IAS 41, para. B18.
14 IAS 41, para. B19.
15 IAS 41, para. B21.
16 IAS 41, para. B20.
17 IAS 41, Objective.
18 IAS 41, para. 5.
19 IAS 41, para. 6.
20 IAS 41, para. 6.
21 IAS 41, para. 5.
22 IAS 41, para. 7.
23 IAS 41, para. 5.
24 IAS 41, para. 4.
25 IAS 41, para. 8.
26 IAS 41, para. 9.
27 IAS 41, para. 1.
28 IAS 41, para. 2.
29 IAS 41, paras. B55-B57.
30 IAS 41, paras. B58-B60.
31 IAS 41, para. 3.
32 IAS 41, para. B8.
33 IAS 41, paras. B11 and B44-B46.
34 IAS 41, para. 3.
35 IAS 41, para. 10.
36 IAS 41, para. 11.
37 IAS 41, para. 12.
38 IAS 41, para. B32.
39 IAS 41, para. 13.
40 IAS 41, paras. 32 and B43.
41 IAS 41, paras. 13 and B8.
42 IAS 41, para. B42.
43 IAS 41, para. B26.
44 IAS 41, para. B25.
45 IAS 41, para. 14.
46 IAS 41, para. B22.
47 IAS 41, para. 15.
48 IAS 41, para. B29.
49 IAS 41, para. B30.
50 IAS 41, para. 17.
51 IAS 41, para. B31.
52 IAS 41, para. 18.
53 IAS 41, para. 19.
54 IAS 41, para. 20.
55 IAS 41, para. 21.
56 IAS 41, para. 23.
57 IAS 41, para. 22.
58 IAS 41, para. 21.
59 IAS 41, para. 24.
60 IAS 41, para. B33.
61 IAS 41, para. B81.
62 IAS 41, para. 16.
63 IAS 41, paras. B50-B54.
64 IAS 41, para. 25.
65 IAS 41, para. B62.
66 IAS 41, para. B61.
67 IAS 41, para. B38.

68 IAS 41, para. 26.
69 IAS 41, para. 27.
70 IAS 41, para. 28.
71 IAS 41, para. 29.
72 IAS 41, para. 30.
73 IAS 41, para. 31.
74 IAS 41, para. B36.
75 IAS 41, para. 30.
76 IAS 41, para. 33.
77 IAS 41, para. B37.
78 IAS 41, para. 30.
79 IAS 41, para. B35.
80 IAS 41, para. 30.
81 IAS 41, paras. 37-38.
82 IAS 41, para. 34.
83 IAS 41, para. B66.
84 IAS 41, para. 35.
85 IAS 41, paras. B70-B73.
86 IAS 41, para. 36.
87 IAS 1, *Presentation of Financial Statements*, IASB, December 2003 (amended March 2004), para. 68.
88 IAS 41, Example 1.
89 IAS 41, para. 40.
90 IAS 41, paras. B78-B79.
91 IAS 41, Example 1.
92 IAS 1, para. 33.
93 IAS 1, para. 34.
94 IAS 41, paras. 41-42.
95 IAS 41, para. 43.
96 IAS 41, paras. 43-44.
97 IAS 41, para. 43.
98 IAS 41, para. 45.
99 IAS 41, para. 43.
100 IAS 41, para. 46.
101 IAS 41, para. 47.
102 IAS 41, para. 48.
103 IAS 41, para. 49.
104 IAS 41, para. 49.
105 IAS 41, para. 49.
106 IAS 41, para. 50.
107 IAS 41, paras. 51 and B74-B77.
108 IAS 41, para. 52.
109 IAS 41, Example 2.
110 IAS 41, para. 53.
111 IAS 41, para. 54.
112 IAS 41, para. 55.
113 IAS 41, para. 56.
114 IAS 41, para. 57.
115 IAS 41, para. 58.
116 IAS 41, para. 59.
117 *IFRIC Update*, IASB, May 2004, p. 3.
118 *IFRIC Update*, IASB, October 2003, p. 3.
119 *IFRIC Update*, IASB, May 2004, p. 2.
120 *IFRIC Update*, IASB, May 2004, p. 3.

Index of extracts from financial statements

Index of standards

IFRS 2, Share-based Payment, IASB, February 2004

IFRS 3, Business Combinations, IASB, March 2004

IFRS 4, Insurance Contracts, IASB, March 2004

IFRS 5, Non-current Assets Held for Sale and Discontinued Operations, IASB, March 2004

IAS 1, Presentation of Financial Statements, IASB, December 2003, (amended March 2004)

IAS 8, Accounting Policies, Changes in Accounting Estimates and Errors, IASB, December 2003, (amended March 2004)

IAS 10, Events After the Balance Sheet Date, IASB, December 2003

IAS 11, Construction Contracts, IASC, December 1993

IAS 12, Income Taxes, IASB, October 1996, (amended March 2004)

IAS 14, Segment Reporting, IASB, August 1997, (amended March 2004)

IAS 16, Property, Plant and Equipment, IASB, December 2003, (amended March 2004)

IAS 17, Leases, IASB, December 2003, (amended March 2004)

**IAS 18, Revenue, IASB, December 1993,
(amended March 2004)**

**IAS 19, Employee Benefits, IASB, February
1998, (amended March 2004)**

IAS 22, Business Combinations, IASC, September 1998, (superseded March 2004)

IAS 28, Investments in Associates, IASB, December 2003, (amended March 2004)

IAS 29, Financial Reporting in Hyperinflationary Economies, IASB, July 1989, (amended December 2003)

IAS 30, Disclosures in the Financial Statements of Banks and Similar Financial Institutions, IASB, August 1990, (amended December 2003)

IAS 31, Interests in Joint Ventures, IASB, December 2003, (amended March 2004)

IAS 32, Financial Instruments: Disclosure and Presentation, IASB, December 2003, (amended March 2004)

IAS 33, Earnings per Share, IASB, December 2003, (amended March 2004)

IAS 34, Interim Financial Reporting, IASB, February 1998, (amended March 2004)

IAS 36, Impairment of Assets, IASB, March 2004

IAS 37, Provisions, Contingent Liabilities and Contingent Assets, IASB, September 1998, (amended March 2004)

IAS 38, Intangible Assets, IASB, March 2004

IAS 39, Financial Instruments: Recognition and Measurement, IASB, December 2003, (amended March 2004)

IAS 40, Investment Property, IASB, December 2003, (amended March 2004)

IAS 41, Agriculture, IASB, January 2001, (amended March 2004)

Index